Stanley Gibbons
Stamp Catalogue

PART 3

Balkans

5th edition 2009

Stanley Gibbons Ltd
London and Ringwood

By Appointment to Her Majesty The Queen
Stanley Gibbons Ltd, London
Philatelists

Published by **Stanley Gibbons Ltd**
Editorial, Publications Sales Offices
and Distribution Centre:
7 Parkside, Christchurch Road, Ringwood,
Hants BH24 3SH
Telephone 01425 472363
(24 hour answer phone service),
Fax 01425 470247.
E-mail: *info@stanleygibbons.co.uk*
Publications Mail Order: FREEPHONE 0800 611 622
Monday-Friday 8.30 a.m. to 5 p.m.
Stanley Gibbons Publications has overseas licensees
and distributors for Australia, Belgium, Canada,
Denmark, Finland, France, Hong Kong, Italy, Japan,
Luxembourg, Netherlands, New Zealand, Norway,
Saudi Arabia, Singapore, Sweden and U.S.A.
Please contact the Ringwood address for details.

Stanley Gibbons Holdings Plc.
Head Office, 399 Strand, London WC2R 0LX
Telephone 020 7836 8444 and Fax 020 7836 7342
Website: *www.stanleygibbons.com* for all departments.

Stanley Gibbons Ltd, Stanley Gibbons Auctions.
Auction Room and Specialist Stamp Departments:
Open Monday-Friday, 9.30 a.m. to 5 p.m.
Shop: Open Monday-Friday 9 a.m. to 5.30 p.m.
and Saturday 9.30 a.m. to 5.30 p.m.
E-mail: *enquiries@stanleygibbons.co.uk*

Fraser's. Autographs, photographs, letters, documents.
Open Monday-Friday 9 a.m. to 5.30 p.m.
and Saturday 10 a.m. to 4 p.m.
Website: *www.frasersautographs.com*
E-mail: *info@frasersautographs.co.uk*

First edition in this form – July 1980
2nd edition – November 1982
3rd edition – April 1987
4th edition – February 1998
5th edition – May 2009

British Library Cataloguing in Publication Data.
A catalogue record for this book is available from the British Library.

ISBN-13 978-0-85259-711-8
ISBN-10 0-85259-711-8

Item No. R2832-09

Printed by MPGi Limited

About this Edition

This edition, the first in colour and completely re-set, has allowed us the opportunity to update images and include all the new issues have been issued in the last 11 years.

The break-up of Yugoslavia has led to the creation of new postal authorities and the return of Bosnia and Herzegovina, Serbia, Croatia and Montenegro as active, stamp-issuing countries. The philatelic repercussions of the complex political changes that have taken place in the area in the past 11 years are all covered in this volume, with new issues for Serbia complete to June 2008 and Montenegro up to May 2006.

The stamps of Bosnia and Herzegovina are now complete from 1879 to the present day, with early issues, formerly listed in Part 2, Austria and Hungary, now also included in this volume.

The catalogue lists the issues of the three separate postal administrations within Bosnia Herzegovina; the Sarajevo Government, Croatian Posts and Republika Srpska.

New design indexes have been included for Croatia, Greece and Slovenia.

Pricing has been completely revised throughout with early issues showing significant increases.

Hugh Jefferies
Clare de la Feuillade
Barbara Hawkins

New issues

The first supplement to this catalogue appears in *Gibbons Stamp Monthly* for May 2009.

Stamps added

Items added to this catalogue, not previously published in *Gibbons Stamp Monthly* supplements.

Albania
691a, 692a, 693a

Bulgaria
346a, 712a, 927a, 1313a, 1947b

Romania
2742a

Austro-Hungarian Military Posts
10a, 10b

Yugoslavia
1588a, 1630a, 2927a, 2929a, 2932a

Specialist Societies

We are grateful to individual collectors, members of the philatelic trade and specialist societies and study circles for their assistance in improving and extending the Stanley Gibbons range of catalogues. The addresses of societies and study circles relevant to this volume are:

ALBANIA STUDY CIRCLE
Secretary: N. Ames
Ashton House, Ashton Keynes,
Swindon, SN6 6NX
Email: *ames@dircon.co.uk*

CROATIAN PHILATELIC SOCIETY:
P.O. Box 696,
Fritch, Texas, 79036-0696, USA
Website: *www.croatianstamps.com*

YUGOSLAVIA STUDY GROUP
President: A.J. Bosworth FRPSL
18 Raymer Road,
Maidstone, Kent, ME14 2JQ
Website: *www.yugoslaviastudygroup.co.uk*

Contents

General Philatelic Information and Guidelines to the Scope of Stanley Gibbons Foreign Catalogues

The notes which follow seek to reflect current practice in compiling the Foreign Catalogue.

It scarcely needs emphasising that the Stanley Gibbons Stamp *Catalogue* has a very long history and that the vast quantity of information it contains has been carefully built up by successive generations through the work of countless individuals. Philately itself is never static and the Catalogue has evolved and developed during this long time-span. Thus, while these notes are important for today's criteria, they may be less precise the farther back in the listings one travels. They are not intended to inaugurate some unwanted series of piecemeal alterations in a widely respected work, but it does seem to us useful that Catalogue users know as exactly as possible the policies currently in operation.

THE CATALOGUE IN GENERAL

Contents. The Catalogue is confined to adhesive postage stamps, including miniature sheets. For particular categories the rules are

(a) Revenue (fiscal) stamps or telegraph stamps are listed only where they have been expressly authorised for postal duty.
(b) Stamps issued only precancelled are included, but normally issued stamps available additionally with precancel have no separate precancel listing unless the face value is changed.
(c) Stamps prepared for use but not issued, hitherto accorded full listing, are nowadays footnoted with a price (where possible).
(d) Bisects (trisects, etc.) are only listed where such usage was officially authorised.
(e) Stamps issued only on first day covers and not available separately are not listed but priced (on the cover) in a footnote.
(f) New printings, as such, are not listed, though stamps from them may qualify under another category, e.g. when a prominent new shade results.
(g) Official and unofficial reprints are dealt with by footnote.
(h) Stamps from imperforate printings of modern issues which also occur perforated are covered by footnotes or general notes, but are listed where widely available for postal use.

Exclusions. The following are excluded:

(a) non-postal revenue or fiscal stamps;
(b) postage stamps used fiscally;
(c) local carriage labels and private local issues;
(d) telegraph stamps;
(e) bogus or phantom stamps;
(f) railway or airline letter fee stamps, bus or road transport company labels;
(g) cut-outs;
(h) all types of non-postal labels;
(i) documentary labels for the postal service, e.g. registration, recorded delivery, airmail etiquettes, etc.;
(j) privately applied embellishments to official issues and privately commissioned items generally;
(k) stamps for training postal officers;
(l) specimen stamps.

Full listing. "Full listing" confers our recognition and implies allotting a catalogue number and (wherever possible) a price quotation.

In judging status for inclusion in the catalogue broad considerations are applied to stamps. They must be issued by a legitimate postal authority, recognised by the government concerned, and must be adhesives valid for proper postal use in the class of service for which they are inscribed. Stamps, with the exception of such categories as postage dues and officials, must be available to the general public, at face value, in reasonable quantities without any artificial restrictions being imposed on their distribution.

We record as abbreviated Appendix entries, without catalogue numbers or prices, stamps from countries which either persist in having far more issues than can be justified by postal need or have failed to maintain control over their distribution so that they have not been available to the public in reasonable quantities at face value. Miniature sheets and imperforate stamps are not mentioned in these entries.

The publishers of this catalogue have observed, with concern, the proliferation of "artificial" stamp-issuing territories. On several occasions this has resulted in separately inscribed issues for various component parts of otherwise united states or territories.

Stanley Gibbons Publications have decided that where such circumstances occur, they will not, in the future, list these items in the SG catalogue without first satisfying themselves that the stamps represent a genuine political, historical or postal division within the country concerned. Any such issues which do not fulfil this stipulation will be recorded in the Catalogue Appendix only.

For errors and varieties the criterion is legitimate (albeit inadvertent) sale over a post office counter in the normal course of business. Details of provenance are always important; printers' waste and fraudulently manufactured material is excluded.

Certificates. In assessing unlisted items due weight is given to Certificates from recognised Expert Committees and, where appropriate, we will usually ask to see them.

New issues. New issues are listed regularly in the Catalogue Supplement in *Gibbons Stamp Monthly*, whence they are consolidated into the next available edition of the Catalogue.

Date of issue. Where local issue dates differ from dates of release by agencies, "date of issue" is the local date. Fortuitous stray usage before the officially intended date is disregarded in listing.

Catalogue numbers. Stamps of each country are catalogued chronologically by date of issue. Subsidiary classes (e.g. postage due stamps) are integrated into one list with postage and commemorative stamps and distinguished by a letter prefix to the catalogue number.

The catalogue number appears in the extreme left column. The boldface type numbers in the next column are merely cross-references to illustrations. Catalogue numbers in the *Gibbons Stamp Monthly* Supplement are provisional only and may need to be altered when the lists are consolidated. Miniature sheets only purchasable intact at a post office have a single MS number; sheetlets – individual stamps available – number each stamp separately. The catalogue no longer gives full listing to designs originally issued in normal sheets, which subsequently appear in sheetlets showing changes of colour, perforation, printing process or face value. Such stamps will be covered by footnotes.

Once published in the Catalogue, numbers are changed as little as possible; really serious renumbering is reserved for the occasions when a complete country or an entire issue is being rewritten. The edition first affected includes cross-reference tables of old and new numbers.

Our catalogue numbers are universally recognised in specifying stamps and as a hallmark of status.

Illustrations. Stamps are illustrated at three-quarters linear size. Stamps not illustrated are the same size and format as the value shown unless otherwise indicated. Stamps issued only as miniature sheets have the stamp alone illustrated but sheet size is also quoted. Overprints, surcharges, watermarks and postmarks are normally actual size. Illustrations of varieties are often enlarged to show the detail.

CONTACTING THE CATALOGUE EDITOR

The editor is always interested in hearing from people who have new information which will improve or correct the Catalogue. As a general rule he must see and examine the actual stamps before they can be considered for listing; photographs or photocopies are insufficient evidence. Neither he nor his staff give opinions as to the genuineness of stamps.

Submissions should be made in writing to the Catalogue Editor, Stanley Gibbons Publications, 7 Parkside, Christchurch Road, Ringwood, Hants BH24 3SH. The cost of return postage for items submitted is appreciated, and this should include the registration fee if required.

Where information is solicited purely for the benefit of the enquirer, the editor cannot undertake to reply if the answer is already contained in these published notes or if return postage is omitted. Written communications are greatly preferred to enquiries by telephone and the editor regrets that he or his staff cannot see personal callers without a prior appointment being made.

The editor welcomes close contact with study circles and is interested, too, in finding local correspondents who will verify and supplement official information in overseas countries where this is deficient.

We regret we do not give opinions as to the genuineness of stamps, nor do we identify stamps or number them by our Catalogue.

TECHNICAL MATTERS

The meanings of the technical terms used in the Catalogue will be found in *Philatelic Terms Illustrated*, published by Gibbons (Price £14.95 plus postage).

1. Printing

Printing errors. Errors in printing are of major interest to the Catalogue. Authenticated items meriting consideration would include background, centre or frame inverted or omitted; centre or subject transposed; error of colour; error or omission of value; double prints and impressions; printed both sides; and so on. Designs *tête-bêche*, whether intentionally or by accident, are listable. *Se-tenant* arrangements of stamps are recognised in the listings or footnotes. Gutter pairs (a pair of stamps separated by blank margin) are excluded unless they have some philatelic importance. Colours only partially omitted are not listed, neither are stamps printed on the gummed side.

Printing varieties. Listing is accorded to major changes in the printing base which lead to completely new types. In recess-printing this could be a design re-engraved, in photogravure or photolithography a screen altered in whole or in part. It can also encompass flat-bed and rotary printing if the results are readily distinguishable.

To be considered at all, varieties must be constant.

Early stamps, produced by primitive methods, were prone to numerous imperfections; the lists reflect this, recognising re-entries, retouches, broken frames, misshapen letters, and so on. Printing technology has, however, radically improved over the years, during which time photogravure and lithography have become predominant. Varieties nowadays are more in the nature of flaws and these, being too specialised for a general catalogue, are almost always outside the scope. We therefore do not list such items as dry prints, kiss prints, doctor-blade flaws, blanket set-offs, doubling through blanket stretch, plate cracks and scratches, registration flaws (leading to colour shifts), lithographic ring flaws, and so on. Neither do we recognise fortuitous happenings like paper creases or confetti flaws.

Overprints (and surcharges). Overprints of different types qualify for separate listing. These include overprints in different colours; overprints from different printing processes such as litho and typo; overprints in totally different typefaces, etc.

Overprint errors and varieties. Major errors in machine-printed overprints are important and listable. They include overprint inverted or omitted; overprint double (treble, etc.); overprint diagonal; overprint double, one inverted; pairs with one overprint omitted, e.g. from a radical shift to an adjoining stamp; error of colour; error of type fount; letters inverted or omitted, etc. If the overprint is handstamped, few of these would qualify and a distinction is drawn.

Varieties occurring in overprints will often take the form of broken letters, slight differences in spacing, rising spacers, etc. Only the most important would be considered for footnote mention.

Sheet positions. If space permits we quote sheet positions of listed varieties and authenticated data is solicited for this purpose.

2. Paper

All stamps listed are deemed to be on "ordinary" paper of the wove type and white in colour; only departures from this are mentioned.

Types. Where classification so requires we distinguish such other types of paper as, for example, vertically and horizontally laid; wove and laid bâtonné; card(board); carton; cartridge, enamelled; glazed; GC (Grande Consommation); granite; native; pelure; porous; quadrillé; ribbed; rice; and silk thread.

Our chalky (chalk-surfaced) paper is specifically one which shows a black mark when touched with a silver wire. This and other coatings are easily lost or damaged through immersion in water.

The various makeshifts for normal paper are listed as appropriate. They include printing on: unfinished banknotes, war maps, ruled paper, Post Office forms, and the unprinted side of glossy magazines. The varieties of double paper and joined paper are recognised.

Descriptive terms. The fact that a paper is hand-made (and thus probably of uneven thickness) is mentioned where necessary. Such descriptive terms as "hard" and "soft"; "smooth" and "rough"; "thick", "medium" and "thin" are applied where there is philatelic merit in classifying papers.

Coloured, very white and toned papers. A coloured paper is one that is coloured right through (front and back of the stamp). In the Catalogue the colour of the paper is given in italics, thus

black/*rose* = black design on rose paper.

Papers have been made specially white in recent years by, for example, a very heavy coating of chalk. We do not classify shades of whiteness of paper as distinct varieties. There does exist, however, a type of paper from early days called toned. This is off-white, often brownish or buffish, but it cannot be assigned a definite colour. A toning effect brought on by climate, incorrect storage or gum staining is disregarded here, as this was not the state of the paper when issued.

Safety devices. The Catalogue takes account of such safety devices as varnish lines, grills, burelage or imprinted patterns on the front or moiré on the back of stamps.

Modern developments. Two modern developments also affect the listings, printing on self-adhesive paper and the tendency, philatelic in origin, for conventional paper to be reinforced or replaced by different materials. Some examples are the use of foils in gold, silver, aluminium, palladium and steel; application of an imitation wood veneer; printing on plastic moulded in relief; and use of a plastic laminate to give a three-dimensional effect. Examples also occur of stamps impregnated with scent; printed on silk; and incorporating miniature gramophone records.

3. Perforation and Rouletting

Perforation gauge. The gauge of a perforation is the number of holes in a length of 2 cm. For correct classification the size of the holes (large or small) may need to be distinguished; in a few cases the actual number of holes on each edge of the stamp needs to be quoted.

Measurement. The Gibbons Instanta gauge is the standard for measuring perforations. The stamp is viewed against a dark background with the transparent gauge put on top of it. Though the gauge measures to decimal accuracy, perforations read from it are generally quoted in the Catalogue to the nearest half. For example:

Just over perf.
12¾ to just under perf. 13¼ = perf. 13
Perf. 13¼ exactly, rounded up = perf. 13½
Just over perf.
13¼ to just under perf. 13¾ = perf. 13½
Perf. 13¾ exactly, rounded up = perf. 14

However, where classification depends on it, actual quarter-perforations are quoted.

Notation. Where no perforation is quoted for an issue it is imperforate. Perforations are usually abbreviated (and spoken) as follows, though sometimes they may be spelled out for clarity. This notation for rectangular stamps (the majority) applies to diamond shapes if "top" is read as the edge to the top right.

P 14: perforated alike on all sides (read: "perf. 14").

P 14×15: the first figure refers to top and bottom, the second to left and right sides (read: "perf. 14 by 15"). This is a compound perforation. For an upright triangular stamp the first figure refers to the two sloping sides and the second to the base. In inverted triangulars the base is first and the second figure refers to the sloping sides.

P 14-15: perforation measuring anything between 14 and 15: the holes are irregularly spaced, thus the gauge may vary along a single line or even along a single edge of the stamp (read: "perf. 14 to 15").

P 14 irregular. perforated 14 from a worn perforator, giving badly aligned holes irregular spaced (read "irregular perf. 14").

P *comp(ound)* 14×15: two gauges in use but not necessarily on opposite sides of the stamp. It could be one side in one gauge and three in the other, or two adjacent sides with the same gauge (Read: "perf. compound of 14 and 15"). For three gauges or more, abbreviated as "P 14, 14½, 15 or compound" for example.

P 14, 14½: perforated approximately 14¼ (read: "perf. 14 or 14½"). It does not mean two stamps, one perf. 14 and the other perf. 14½. This obsolescent notation is gradually being replaced in the Catalogue.

Imperf: imperforate (not perforated).

Imperf × P 14: imperforate at top and bottom and perf 14 at sides.

P 14 × *imperf* = perf 14 at top and bottom and imperforate at sides.

Such headings as "P 13 × 14 (vert) and P 14 × 13 (horiz)" indicate which perforations apply to which stamp format – vertical or horizontal.

Some stamps are additionally perforated so that a label or tab is detachable; others have been perforated suitably for use as two halves. Listings are normally for whole stamps, unless stated otherwise.

Other terms. Perforation almost always gives circular holes; where other shapes have been used they are specified, e.g. square holes; lozenge perf. Interrupted perfs are brought about by the omission of pins at regular intervals. Perforations have occasionally been simulated by being printed as part of the design. With few exceptions, privately applied perforations are not listed.

Perforation errors and varieties. Authenticated errors, where a stamp normally perforated is accidentally issued imperforate, are listed provided no traces of perforation (blind holes or indentations) remain. They must be provided as pairs, both stamps wholly imperforate, and are only priced in that form.

Stamps merely imperforate between stamp and margin (fantails) are not listed.

Imperforate-between varieties are recognised, where one row of perfs has been missed. They are listed and priced in pairs:

Imperf between (horiz pair): a horizontal pair of stamps with perfs all around the edges but none between the stamps.

Imperf between (vert pair): a vertical pair of stamps with perfs all around the edges but none between the stamps.

Where several of the rows have escaped perforation the resulting varieties are listable. Thus:

Imperf vert (horiz pair): a horizontal pair of stamps perforated top and bottom; all three vertical directions are imperf – the two outer edges and between the stamps.

Imperf horiz (vert pair): a vertical pair perforated at left and right edges; all three horizontal directions are imperf – the top, bottom and between the stamps.

Straight edges. Large sheets cut up before issue to post offices can cause stamps with straight edges, i.e. imperf on one side or on two sides at right angles. They are not usually listable in this condition and are worth less than corresponding stamps properly perforated all round. This does not, however, apply to certain stamps, mainly from coils and booklets, where straight edges on various sides are the manufacturing norm affecting every stamp. The listings and notes make clear which sides are correctly imperf.

Malfunction. Varieties of double, misplaced or partial perforation caused by error or machine malfunction are not listable, neither are freaks, such as perforations placed diagonally from paper folds. Likewise disregarded are missing holes caused by broken pins, and perforations "fading out" down a sheet, the machinery progressively disengaging to leave blind perfs and indentations to the paper.

Centering. Well-centred stamps have designs surrounded by equal opposite margins. Where this condition affects the price the fact is stated.

Type of perforating. Where necessary for classification, perforation types are distinguished. These include:

Line perforation from one line of pins punching single rows of holes at a time.

Comb perforation from pins disposed across the sheet in comb formation, punching out holes at three sides of the stamp a row at a time.

Harrow perforation applied to a whole pane or sheet at one stroke.

Rotary perforation from the toothed wheels operating across a sheet, then crosswise.

Sewing-machine perforation. The resultant condition, clean-cut or rough, is distinguished where required.

Pin-perforation is the commonly applied term for pin-roulette in which, instead of being punched out, round holes are pricked by sharp-pointed pins and no paper is removed.

Punctured stamps. Perforation holes can be punched into the face of the stamp. Patterns of small holes, often in the shape of initial letters, are privately applied devices against pilferage. These "perfins" are outside the scope. Identification devices, when officially inspired, are listed or noted; they can be shapes, or letters or words formed from holes, sometimes converting one class of stamp into another.

Rouletting. In rouletting the paper is cut, for ease of separation, but none is removed. The gauge is measured, when needed, as for perforations. Traditional French terms descriptive of the type of cut are often used and types include:

Arc roulette (percé en arc). Cuts are minute, spaced arcs, each roughly a semicircle.

Cross roulette (percé en croix). Cuts are tiny diagonal crosses.

Line roulette (parcé en ligne or en ligne droite). Short straight cuts parallel to the frame of the stamp. The commonest basic roulette. Where not further described, "roulette" means this type.

Rouletted in colour or coloured roulette (percé en lignes colorees or en lignes de coleur). Cuts with coloured edges, arising from notched rule inked simultaneously with the printing plate.

Saw-tooth roulette (percé en scie). Cuts applied zigzag fashion to resemble the teeth of a saw.

Serpentine roulette (percé en serpentin). Cuts as sharply wavy lines.

Zigzag roulettes (percé en zigzags). Short straight cuts at angles in alternate directions, producing sharp points on separation. U.S. usage favours "serrate(d) roulette" for this type.

Pin-roulette (originally *percé en points* and now *perforés trous d'epingle*) is commonly called pin-perforation in English.

4. Gum

All stamps listed are assumed to have gum of some kind; if they were issued without gum this is stated. Original gum (o.g.) means that which was present on the stamp as issued to the public. Deleterious climates and the presence of certain chemicals can cause gum to crack and, with early stamps, even make the paper deteriorate. Unscrupulous fakers are adept in removing it and regumming the stamp to meet the unreasoning demand often made for "full o.g." in cases where such a thing is virtually impossible.

Until recent times the gum used for stamps has been gum arabic, but various synthetic adhesives – tinted or invisible-looking – have been in use since the 1960s. Stamps existing with more than one type of gum are not normally listed separately, though the fact is noted where it is of philatelic significance, e.g. in distinguishing reprints or new printings.

The distinct variety of grilled gum is, however, recognised. In this the paper is passed through a gum breaker prior to printing to prevent subsequent curling. As the patterned rollers were sufficient to impress a grill into the paper beneath the gum we can quote prices for both unused and used examples.

Self-adhesive stamps are issued on backing paper from which they are peeled before affixing to mail. Unused examples are priced as for backing paper intact. Used examples are best kept on cover or on piece.

5. Watermarks

Stamps are on unwatermarked paper except where the heading to the set says otherwise.

Detection. Watermarks are detected for Catalogue description by one of four methods:

(1) holding stamps to the light;
(2) laying stamps face down on a dark background;
(3) adding a few drops of petroleum ether 40/60 to the stamp laid face down in a watermark tray; or
(4) by use of the Stanley Gibbons Detectamark, or other equipment, which works by revealing the thinning of the paper at the watermark. (Note that petroleum ether is highly inflammable in use and can damage photogravure stamps.)

Listable types. Stamps occurring on both watermarked and unwatermarked papers are different types and both receive full listing.

Single watermarks (devices occurring once on every stamp) can be modified in size and shape as between different issues; the types are noted but not usually separately listed. Fortuitous absence of watermark from a single stamp or its gross displacement would not be listable.

To overcome registration difficulties the device may be repeated at close intervals (a multiple watermark), single stamps thus showing parts of several devices. Similarly a large sheet watermark (or all-over watermark) covering numerous stamps can be used. We give informative notes and illustrations for them. The designs may be such that numbers of stamps in the sheet automatically lack watermark; this is not a listable variety. Multiple and all-over watermarks sometimes undergo modifications, but if the various types are difficult to distinguish from single stamps notes are given but not separate listings.

Papermakers' watermarks are noted where known but not listed separately, since most stamps in the sheet will lack them. Sheet watermarks which are nothing more than officially adopted papermakers' watermarks are, however, given normal listing.

Marginal watermarks, falling outside the pane of stamps, are ignored except where misplacement causes the adjoining row to be affected, in which case they are footnoted.

Watermark errors and varieties. Watermark errors are recognised as of major importance. They comprise stamps intended to be on unwatermarked paper but issued watermarked by mistake, or stamps printed on paper with the wrong watermark. Watermark varieties, on the other hand, such as broken or deformed bits on the dandy roll, are not listable.

Watermark positions. Paper has a side intended for printing and watermarks are usually impressed so that they read normally when looked through from that printed side.

Illustrations in the Catalogue are of watermarks in normal positions (from the front of the stamps) and are actual size where possible.

Differences in watermark position are collectable as distinct varieties. In this Catalogue, however, only normal sideways watermarks are listed (and "sideways inverted" is treated as "sideways"). Inverted and reversed watermarks have always been outside its scope: in the early days of flat-bed printing, sheets of watermarked paper were fed indiscriminately through the press and the resulting watermark positions had no particular philatelic significance. Similarly, the special make-up of sheets for booklets can in some cases give equal quantities of normal and inverted watermarks.

6. Colours

Stamps in two or three colours have these named in order of appearance, from the centre moving outwards. Four colours or more are usually listed as multicoloured.

In compound colour names the second is the predominant one, thus:

orange-red = a red tending towards orange;
red-orange = an orange containing more red than usual.

Standard colours used. The 200 colours most used for stamp identification are given in the Stanley Gibbons Colour Key. The Catalogue has used the Key as a standard for describing new issues for some years. The names are also introduced as lists are rewritten, though exceptions are made for those early issues where traditional names have become universally established.

Determining colours. When comparing actual stamps with colour samples in the Key, view in a good north daylight (or its best substitute: fluorescent "colour-matching" light). Sunshine is not recommended. Choose a solid portion of the stamp design; if available, marginal markings such as solid bars of colour or colour check dots are helpful. Shading lines in the design can be misleading as they appear lighter than solid colour. Postmarked portions of a stamp appear darker than normal. If more than one colour is present, mask off the extraneous ones as the eye tends to mix them.

Errors of colour. Major colour errors in stamps or overprints which qualify for listing are: wrong colours; one colour inverted in relation to the rest; albinos (colourless impressions), where these have Expert Committee certificates; colours completely omitted, but only on unused stamps (if found on used stamps the information is footnoted).

Colours only partially omitted are not recognised.

Colour shifts, however spectacular, are not listed.

Shades. Shades in philately refer to variations in the intensity of a colour or the presence of differing amounts of other colours. They are particularly significant when they can be linked to specific printings. In general, shades need to be quite marked to fall within the scope of this Catalogue; it does not favour nowadays listing the often numerous shades of a stamp, but chooses a single applicable colour name which will indicate particular groups of outstanding shades. Furthermore, the listings refer to colours as issued: they may deteriorate into something different through the passage of time.

Modern colour printing by lithography is prone to marked differences of shade, even within a single run, and variations can occur within the same sheet. Such shades are not listed.

Aniline colours. An aniline colour meant originally one derived from coal-tar; it now refers more widely to colour of a particular brightness suffused on the surface of a stamp and showing through clearly on the back.

Colours of overprints and surcharges. All overprints and surcharges are in black unless otherwise in the heading or after the description of the stamp.

7. Luminescence

Machines which sort mail electronically have been introduced in recent years. In consequence some countries have issued stamps on fluorescent or phosphorescent papers, while others have marked their stamps with phosphor bands.

The various papers can only be distinguished by ultraviolet lamps emitting particular wavelengths. They are separately listed only when the stamps have some other means of distinguishing them, visible without the use of these lamps. Where this is not so, the papers are recorded in footnotes or headings. (Collectors using the lamps should exercise great care in their use as exposure to their light is extremely dangerous to the eyes.)

Phosphor bands are listable, since they are visible to the naked eye (by holding stamps at an angle to the light and looking along them, the bands appear dark). Stamps existing with and without phosphor bands or with differing numbers of bands are given separate listings. Varieties such as double bands, misplaced or omitted bands, bands printed on the wrong side, are not listed.

8. Coil Stamps

Stamps issued only in coil form are given full listing. If stamps are issued in both sheets and coils the coil stamps are listed separately only where there is some feature (e.g. perforation) by which singles can be distinguished. Coil strips containing different stamps se-tenant are also listed.

Coil join pairs are too random and too easily faked to permit of listing; similarly ignored are coil stamps which have accidentally suffered an extra row of perforations from the claw mechanism in a malfunctioning vending machine.

9. Booklet Stamps

Single stamps from booklets are listed if they are distinguishable in some way (such as watermark or perforation) from similar sheet stamps. Booklet panes, provided they are distinguishable from blocks of sheet stamps, are listed for most countries; booklet panes containing more than one value se-tenant are listed under the lowest of the values concerned.

Lists of stamp booklets are given for certain countries and it is intended to extend this generally.

10. Forgeries and Fakes

Forgeries. Where space permits, notes are considered if they can give a concise description that will permit unequivocal detection of a forgery. Generalised warnings, lacking detail, are not nowadays inserted since their value to the collector is problematic.

Fakes. Unwitting fakes are numerous, particularly "new shades" which are colour changelings brought about by exposure to sunlight, soaking in water contaminated with dyes from adherent paper, contact with oil and dirt from a pocketbook, and so on. Fraudulent operators, in addition, can offer to arrange: removal of hinge marks; repairs of thins on white or coloured papers; replacement of missing margins or perforations; reperforating in true or false gauges; removal of fiscal cancellations; rejoining of severed pairs, strips and blocks; and (a major hazard) regumming. Collectors can only be urged to purchase from reputable sources and to insist upon Expert Committee certification where there is any doubt.

The Catalogue can consider footnotes about fakes where these are specific enough to assist in detection.

PRICES

Prices quoted in this Catalogue are the selling prices of Stanley Gibbons Ltd at the time when the book went to press. They are for stamps in fine condition for the issue concerned; in issues where condition varies they may ask more for the superb and less for the sub-standard.

All prices are subject to change without prior notice and Stanley Gibbons Ltd may from time to time offer stamps at other than catalogue prices in consequence of special purchases or particular promotions.

No guarantee is given to supply all stamps priced, since it is not possible to keep every catalogued item in stock. Commemorative issues may, at times, only be available in complete sets and not as individual values.

Quotations of prices. The prices in the left-hand column are for unused stamps and those in the right-hand column are for used.

Prices are expressed in pounds and pence sterling. One pound comprises 100 pence (£1 = 100p).

The method of notation is as follows: pence in numerals (e.g. 10 denotes ten pence); pounds and pence up to £100, in numerals (e.g. 425 denotes four pounds and twenty-five pence); prices above £100 expressed in whole pounds with the "£" sign shown.

Unused stamps. Prices for stamps issued up to the end of the Second World War (1945) are for lightly hinged examples and more may be asked if they are in unmounted mint condition. Prices for all later unused stamps are for unmounted mint. Where not available in this condition, lightly hinged stamps are often available at a lower price.

Used stamps. The used prices are normally for stamps postally used but may be for stamps cancelled-to-order where this practice exists.

A pen-cancellation on early issues can sometimes correctly denote postal use. Instances are individually noted in the Catalogue in explanation of the used price given.

Prices quoted for bisects on cover or on large piece are for those dated during the period officially authorised.

Stamps not sold unused to the public but affixed by postal officials before use (e.g. some parcel post stamps) are priced used only.

Minimum price. The minimum catalogue price quoted is 10p. For individual stamps prices between 10p and 95p are provided as a guide for catalogue users. The lowest price charged for individual stamps purchased from Stanley Gibbons Ltd. is £1.

Set prices. Set prices are generally for one of each value, excluding shades and varieties, but including major coulour changes. Where there are alternative shades, etc, the cheapest is usually included. The number of stamps in the set is always stated for clarity.

Where prices are given for *se-tenant* blocks or strips, any mint set price quoted for such an issue is for the complete *se-tenant* strip plus any other stamps included in the set. Used set prices are always for a set of single stamps.

Repricing. Collectors will be aware that the market factors of supply and demand directly influence the prices quoted in this Catalogue. Whatever the scarcity of a particular stamp, if there is no one in the market who wishes to buy it it cannot be expected to achieve a high price. Conversely, the same item actively sought by numerous potential buyers may cause the price to rise.

All the prices in this Catalogue are examined during the preparation of each new edition by expert staff of Stanley Gibbons and repriced as necessary. They take many factors into account, including supply and demand, and are in close touch with the international stamp market and the auction world.

GUARANTEE

All stamps are guaranteed genuine originals in the following terms:

If not as described, and returned by the purchaser, we undertake to refund the price paid to us in the original transaction. If any stamp is certified as genuine by the Expert Committee of the Royal Philatelic Society, London, or by B.P.A. Expertising Ltd, the purchaser shall not be entitled to make claim against us for any error, omission or mistake in such certificate. Consumers' statutory rights are not affected by this guarantee.

The establishment Expert Committees in this country are those of the Royal Philatelic Society, 41 Devonshire Place, London W1N 1PE, and B.P.A. Expertising Ltd, P.O. Box 137, Leatherhead, Surrey KT22 0RG. They do not undertake valuations under any circumstances and fees are payable for their services.

Abbreviations

Printers

A.B.N. Co.	American Bank Note Co, New York.
A. & M.	Alden & Mowbray Ltd., Oxford.
Aspioti-Elka (Aspiotis)	Aspioti-Elka, Corfu, Greece
B.A.B.N.	British American Bank Note Co. Ottawa
B.D.T.	B.D.T. International Security Printing Ltd, Dublin, Ireland.
B.W.	Bradbury Wilkinson & Co, Ltd.
C.B.N.	Canadian Bank Note Co, Ottawa.
Cartor	Cartor S.A., La Loupe, France
Chalot -Deheneffe	Chalot-Deheneffe S.A. Brussels, Belgium.
Continental B.N. Co.	Continental Bank Note Co.
Courvoisier	Imprimerie Courvoisier S.A., La-Chaux-de-Fonds, Switzerland.
D.L.R.	De La Rue & Co, Ltd, London.
Edila	Editions de l'Aubetin S.A.
Enschedé	Joh. Enschedé en Zonen, Haarlem, Netherlands.
Harrison	Harrison & Sons, Ltd. London
Heraclio Fournier	Heraclio Fournier S.A. Vitoria, Spain.
J.W.	John Waddington of Kirkstall Ltd
P.B.	Perkins Bacon Ltd, London.
Questa	Questa Colour Security Printers Ltd
Walsall	Walsall Security Printers Ltd
Waterlow	Waterlow & Sons, Ltd, London.

General Abbreviations

Alph	Alphabet
Anniv	Anniversary
Comp	Compound (perforation)
Des	Designer; designed
Diag	Diagonal; diagonally
Eng	Engraver; engraved
F.C.	Fiscal Cancellation
H/S	Handstamped
Horiz	Horizontal; horizontally
Imp, Imperf	Imperforate
Inscr	Inscribed
L	Left
Litho	Lithographed
mm	Millimetres
MS	Miniature sheet
N.Y.	New York
Opt(d)	Overprint(ed)
P or P-c	Pen-cancelled
P, Pf or Perf	Perforated
Photo	Photogravure
Pl	Plate
Pr	Pair
Ptd	Printed
Ptg	Printing
R	Right
R.	Row
Recess	Recess-printed
Roto	Rotogravure
Roul	Rouletted
S	Specimen (overprint)
Surch	Surcharge(d)
T.C.	Telegraph Cancellation
T	Type
Typo	Typographed
Un	Unused
Us	Used
Vert	Vertical; vertically
W or wmk	Watermark
Wmk s	Watermark sideways

(†) = Does not exist

(–) (or blank price column) = Exists, or may exist, but no market price is known.

/ between colours means "on" and the colour following is that of the paper on which the stamp is printed.

Colours of Stamps

Bl (blue); blk (black); brn (brown); car, carm (carmine); choc (chocolate); clar (claret); emer (emerald); grn (green); ind (indigo); mag (magenta); mar (maroon); mult (multicoloured); mve (mauve); ol (olive); orge (orange); pk (pink); pur (purple); scar (scarlet); sep (sepia); turq (turquoise); ultram (ultramarine); verm (vermilion); vio (violet); yell (yellow).

Colour of Overprints and Surcharges

(B.) = blue, (Blk.) = black, (Br.) = brown, (C.) = carmine, (G.) = green, (Mag.) = magenta, (Mve.) = mauve, (Ol.) = olive, (O.) = orange, (P.) = purple, (Pk.) = pink, (R.) = red, (Sil.) = silver, (V.) = violet, (Vm.) or (Verm.) = vermilion, (W.) = white, (Y.) = yellow.

Arabic Numerals

As in the case of European figures, the details of the Arabic numerals vary in different stamp designs, but they should be readily recognised with the aid of this illustration.

٠	١	٢	٣	٤	٥	٦	٧	٨	٩
0	1	2	3	4	5	6	7	8	9

International Philatelic Glossary

English	*French*	*German*	*Spanish*	*Italian*
Agate	Agate	Achat	Agata	Agata
Air stamp	Timbre de la poste aérienne	Flugpostmarke	Sello de correo aéreo	Francobollo per posta aerea
Apple Green	Vert-pomme	Apfelgrün	Verde manzana	Verde mela
Barred	Annulé par barres	Balkenentwertung	Anulado con barras	Sbarrato
Bisected	Timbre coupé	Halbiert	Partido en dos	Frazionato
Bistre	Bistre	Bister	Bistre	Bistro
Bistre-brown	Brun-bistre	Bisterbraun	Castaño bistre	Bruno-bistro
Black	Noir	Schwarz	Negro	Nero
Blackish Brown	Brun-noir	Schwärzlichbraun	Castaño negruzco	Bruno nerastro
Blackish Green	Vert foncé	Schwärzlichgrün	Verde negruzco	Verde nerastro
Blackish Olive	Olive foncé	Schwärzlicholiv	Oliva negruzco	Oliva nerastro
Block of four	Bloc de quatre	Viererblock	Bloque de cuatro	Bloco di quattro
Blue	Bleu	Blau	Azul	Azzurro
Blue-green	Vert-bleu	Blaugrün	Verde azul	Verde azzuro
Bluish Violet	Violet bleuâtre	Bläulichviolett	Violeta azulado	Violtto azzurrastro
Booklet	Carnet	Heft	Cuadernillo	Libretto
Bright Blue	Bleu vif	Lebhaftblau	Azul vivo	Azzurro vivo
Bright Green	Vert vif	Lebhaftgrün	Verde vivo	Verde vivo
Bright Purple	Mauve vif	Lebhaftpurpur	Púrpura vivo	Porpora vivo
Bronze Green	Vert-bronze	Bronzegrün	Verde bronce	Verde bronzo
Brown	Brun	Braun	Castaño	Bruno
Brown-lake	Carmin-brun	Braunlack	Laca castaño	Lacca bruno
Brown-purple	Pourpre-brun	Braunpurpur	Púrpura castaño	Porpora bruno
Brown-red	Rouge-brun	Braunrot	Rojo castaño	Rosso bruno
Buff	Chamois	Sämisch	Anteado	Camoscio
Cancellation	Oblitération	Entwertung	Cancelación	Annullamento
Cancelled	Annulé	Gestempelt	Cancelado	Annullato
Carmine	Carmin	Karmin	Carmín	Carminio
Carmine-red	Rouge-carmin	Karminrot	Rojo carmín	Rosso carminio
Centred	Centré	Zentriert	Centrado	Centrato
Cerise	Rouge-cerise	Kirschrot	Color de ceresa	Color Ciliegia
Chalk-surfaced paper	Papier couché	Kreidepapier	Papel estucado	Carta gessata
Chalky Blue	Bleu terne	Kreideblau	Azul turbio	Azzurro smorto
Charity stamp	Timbre de bienfaisance	Wohltätigkeitsmarke	Sello de beneficenza	Francobollo di beneficenza
Chestnut	Marron	Kastanienbraun	Castaño rojo	Marrone
Chocolate	Chocolat	Schokolade	Chocolate	Cioccolato
Cinnamon	Cannelle	Zimtbraun	Canela	Cannella
Claret	Grenat	Weinrot	Rojo vinoso	Vinaccia
Cobalt	Cobalt	Kobalt	Cobalto	Cobalto
Colour	Couleur	Farbe	Color	Colore
Comb-perforation	Dentelure en peigne	Kammzähnung, Reihenzähnung	Dentado de peine	Dentellatura e pettine
Commemorative stamp	Timbre commémoratif	Gedenkmarke	Sello conmemorativo	Francobollo commemorativo
Crimson	Cramoisi	Karmesin	Carmesí	Cremisi
Deep Blue	Blue foncé	Dunkelblau	Azul oscuro	Azzurro scuro
Deep bluish Green	Vert-bleu foncé	Dunkelbläulichgrün	Verde azulado oscuro	Verde azzurro scuro
Design	Dessin	Markenbild	Diseño	Disegno
Die	Matrice	Urstempel. Type Platte,	Cuño	Conio, Matrice
Double	Double	Doppelt	Doble	Doppio
Drab	Olive terne	Trüboliv	Oliva turbio	Oliva smorto
Dull Green	Vert terne	Trübgrün	Verde turbio	Verde smorto
Dull purple	Mauve terne	Trübpurpur	Púrpura turbio	Porpora smorto
Embossing	Impression en relief	Prägedruck	Impresión en relieve	Impressione a relievo
Emerald	Vert-eméraude	Smaragdgrün	Esmeralda	Smeraldo
Engraved	Gravé	Graviert	Grabado	Inciso
Error	Erreur	Fehler, Fehldruck	Error	Errore
Essay	Essai	Probedruck	Ensayo	Saggio
Express letter stamp	Timbre pour lettres par exprès	Eilmarke	Sello de urgencia	Francobollo per espresso
Fiscal stamp	Timbre fiscal	Stempelmarke	Sello fiscal	Francobollo fiscale
Flesh	Chair	Fleischfarben	Carne	Carnicino
Forgery	Faux, Falsification	Fälschung	Falsificación	Falso, Falsificazione
Frame	Cadre	Rahmen	Marco	Cornice

English	*French*	*German*	*Spanish*	*Italian*
Granite paper	Papier avec fragments de fils de soie	Faserpapier	Papel con filamentos	Carto con fili di seta
Green	Vert	Grün	Verde	Verde
Greenish Blue	Bleu verdâtre	Grünlichblau	Azul verdoso	Azzurro verdastro
Greenish Yellow	Jaune-vert	Grünlichgelb	Amarillo verdoso	Giallo verdastro
Grey	Gris	Grau	Gris	Grigio
Grey-blue	Bleu-gris	Graublau	Azul gris	Azzurro grigio
Grey-green	Vert gris	Graugrün	Verde gris	Verde grigio
Gum	Gomme	Gummi	Goma	Gomma
Gutter	Interpanneau	Zwischensteg	Espacio blanco entre dos grupos	Ponte
Imperforate	Non-dentelé	Geschnitten	Sin dentar	Non dentellato
Indigo	Indigo	Indigo	Azul indigo	Indaco
Inscription	Inscription	Inschrift	Inscripción	Dicitura
Inverted	Renversé	Kopfstehend	Invertido	Capovolto
Issue	Émission	Ausgabe	Emisión	Emissione
Laid	Vergé	Gestreift	Listado	Vergato
Lake	Lie de vin	Lackfarbe	Laca	Lacca
Lake-brown	Brun-carmin	Lackbraun	Castaño laca	Bruno lacca
Lavender	Bleu-lavande	Lavendel	Color de alhucema	Lavanda
Lemon	Jaune-citron	Zitrongelb	Limón	Limone
Light Blue	Bleu clair	Hellblau	Azul claro	Azzurro chiaro
Lilac	Lilas	Lila	Lila	Lilla
Line perforation	Dentelure en lignes	Linienzähnung	Dentado en linea	Dentellatura lineare
Lithography	Lithographie	Steindruck	Litografía	Litografia
Local	Timbre de poste locale	Lokalpostmarke	Emisión local	Emissione locale
Lozenge roulette	Percé en losanges	Rautenförmiger Durchstich	Picadura en rombos	Perforazione a losanghe
Magenta	Magenta	Magentarot	Magenta	Magenta
Margin	Marge	Rand	Borde	Margine
Maroon	Marron pourpré	Dunkelrotpurpur	Púrpura rojo oscuro	Marrone rossastro
Mauve	Mauve	Malvenfarbe	Malva	Malva
Multicoloured	Polychrome	Mehrfarbig	Multicolores	Policromo
Myrtle Green	Vert myrte	Myrtengrün	Verde mirto	Verde mirto
New Blue	Bleu ciel vif	Neublau	Azul nuevo	Azzurro nuovo
Newspaper stamp	Timbre pour journaux	Zeitungsmarke	Sello para periódicos	Francobollo per giornali
Obliteration	Oblitération	Abstempelung	Matasello	Annullamento
Obsolete	Hors (de) cours	Ausser Kurs	Fuera de curso	Fuori corso
Ochre	Ocre	Ocker	Ocre	Ocra
Official stamp	Timbre de service	Dienstmarke	Sello de servicio	Francobollo di
Olive-brown	Brun-olive	Olivbraun	Castaño oliva	Bruno oliva
Olive-green	Vert-olive	Olivgrün	Verde oliva	Verde oliva
Olive-grey	Gris-olive	Olivgrau	Gris oliva	Grigio oliva
Olive-yellow	Jaune-olive	Olivgelb	Amarillo oliva	Giallo oliva
Orange	Orange	Orange	Naranja	Arancio
Orange-brown	Brun-orange	Orangebraun	Castaño naranja	Bruno arancio
Orange-red	Rouge-orange	Orangerot	Rojo naranja	Rosso arancio
Orange-yellow	Jaune-orange	Orangegelb	Amarillo naranja	Giallo arancio
Overprint	Surcharge	Aufdruck	Sobrecarga	Soprastampa
Pair	Paire	Paar	Pareja	Coppia
Pale	Pâle	Blass	Pálido	Pallido
Pane	Panneau	Gruppe	Grupo	Gruppo
Paper	Papier	Papier	Papel	Carta
Parcel post stamp	Timbre pour colis postaux	Paketmarke	Sello para paquete postal	Francobollo per pacchi postali
Pen-cancelled	Oblitéré à plume	Federzugentwertung	Cancelado a pluma	Annullato a penna
Percé en arc	Percé en arc	Bogenförmiger Durchstich	Picadura en forma de arco	Perforazione ad arco
Percé en scie	Percé en scie	Bogenförmiger Durchstich	Picado en sierra	Foratura a sega
Perforated	Dentelé	Gezähnt	Dentado	Dentellato
Perforation	Dentelure	Zähnung	Dentar	Dentellatura
Photogravure	Photogravure, Heliogravure	Rastertiefdruck	Fotograbado	Rotocalco
Pin perforation	Percé en points	In Punkten durchstochen	Horadado con alfileres	Perforato a punti
Plate	Planche	Platte	Plancha	Lastra, Tavola
Plum	Prune	Pflaumenfarbe	Color de ciruela	Prugna
Postage Due stamp	Timbre-taxe	Portomarke	Sello de tasa	Segnatasse
Postage stamp	Timbre-poste	Briefmarke, Freimarke, Postmarke	Sello de correos	Francobollo postale
Postal fiscal stamp	Timbre fiscal-postal	Stempelmarke als Postmarke verwendet	Sello fiscal-postal	Fiscale postale
Postmark	Oblitération postale	Poststempel	Matasello	Bollo
Printing	Impression, Tirage	Druck	Impresión	Stampa, Tiratura
Proof	Épreuve	Druckprobe	Prueba de impresión	Prova
Provisionals	Timbres provisoires	Provisorische Marken. Provisorien	Provisionales	Provvisori

English	*French*	*German*	*Spanish*	*Italian*
Prussian Blue	Bleu de Prusse	Preussischblau	Azul de Prusia	Azzurro di Prussia
Purple	Pourpre	Purpur	Púrpura	Porpora
Purple-brown	Brun-pourpre	Purpurbraun	Castaño púrpura	Bruno porpora
Recess-printing	Impression en taille douce	Tiefdruck	Grabado	Incisione
Red	Rouge	Rot	Rojo	Rosso
Red-brown	Brun-rouge	Rotbraun	Castaño rojizo	Bruno rosso
Reddish Lilac	Lilas rougeâtre	Rötlichlila	Lila rojizo	Lilla rossastro
Reddish Purple	Poupre-rouge	Rötlichpurpur	Púrpura rojizo	Porpora rossastro
Reddish Violet	Violet rougeâtre	Rötlichviolett	Violeta rojizo	Violetto rossastro
Red-orange	Orange rougeâtre	Rotorange	Naranja rojizo	Arancio rosso
Registration stamp	Timbre pour lettre chargée (recommandée)	Einschreibemarke	Sello de certificado lettere	Francobollo per raccomandate
Reprint	Réimpression	Neudruck	Reimpresión	Ristampa
Reversed	Retourné	Umgekehrt	Invertido	Rovesciato
Rose	Rose	Rosa	Rosa	Rosa
Rose-red	Rouge rosé	Rosarot	Rojo rosado	Rosso rosa
Rosine	Rose vif	Lebhaftrosa	Rosa vivo	Rosa vivo
Roulette	Percage	Durchstich	Picadura	Foratura
Rouletted	Percé	Durchstochen	Picado	Forato
Royal Blue	Bleu-roi	Königblau	Azul real	Azzurro reale
Sage green	Vert-sauge	Salbeigrün	Verde salvia	Verde salvia
Salmon	Saumon	Lachs	Salmón	Salmone
Scarlet	Écarlate	Scharlach	Escarlata	Scarlatto
Sepia	Sépia	Sepia	Sepia	Seppia
Serpentine roulette	Percé en serpentin	Schlangenliniger Durchstich	Picado a serpentina	Perforazione a serpentina
Shade	Nuance	Tönung	Tono	Gradazione de colore
Sheet	Feuille	Bogen	Hoja	Foglio
Slate	Ardoise	Schiefer	Pizarra	Ardesia
Slate-blue	Bleu-ardoise	Schieferblau	Azul pizarra	Azzurro ardesia
Slate-green	Vert-ardoise	Schiefergrün	Verde pizarra	Verde ardesia
Slate-lilac	Lilas-gris	Schierferlila	Lila pizarra	Lilla ardesia
Slate-purple	Mauve-gris	Schieferpurpur	Púrpura pizarra	Porpora ardesia
Slate-violet	Violet-gris	Schieferviolett	Violeta pizarra	Violetto ardesia
Special delivery stamp	Timbre pour exprès	Eilmarke	Sello de urgencia	Francobollo per espressi
Specimen	Spécimen	Muster	Muestra	Saggio
Steel Blue	Bleu acier	Stahlblau	Azul acero	Azzurro acciaio
Strip	Bande	Streifen	Tira	Striscia
Surcharge	Surcharge	Aufdruck	Sobrecarga	Soprastampa
Tête-bêche	Tête-bêche	Kehrdruck	Tête-bêche	Tête-bêche
Tinted paper	Papier teinté	Getöntes Papier	Papel coloreado	Carta tinta
Too-late stamp	Timbre pour lettres en retard	Verspätungsmarke	Sello para cartas retardadas	Francobollo per le lettere in ritardo
Turquoise-blue	Bleu-turquoise	Türkisblau	Azul turquesa	Azzurro turchese
Turquoise-green	Vert-turquoise	Türkisgrün	Verde turquesa	Verde turchese
Typography	Typographie	Buchdruck	Tipografia	Tipografia
Ultramarine	Outremer	Ultramarin	Ultramar	Oltremare
Unused	Neuf	Ungebraucht	Nuevo	Nuovo
Used	Oblitéré, Usé	Gebraucht	Usado	Usato
Venetian Red	Rouge-brun terne	Venezianischrot	Rojo veneciano	Rosso veneziano
Vermilion	Vermillon	Zinnober	Cinabrio	Vermiglione
Violet	Violet	Violett	Violeta	Violetto
Violet-blue	Bleu-violet	Violettblau	Azul violeta	Azzurro violetto
Watermark	Filigrane	Wasserzeichen	Filigrana	Filigrana
Watermark sideways	Filigrane couché	Wasserzeichen liegend	Filigrana acostado	Filigrana coricata
Wove paper	Papier ordinaire, Papier uni	Einfaches Papier	Papel avitelado	Carta unita
Yellow	Jaune	Gelb	Amarillo	Giallo
Yellow-brown	Brun-jaune	Gelbbraun	Castaño amarillo	Bruno giallo
Yellow-green	Vert-jaune	Gelbgrün	Verde amarillo	Verde giallo
Yellow-olive	Olive-jaunâtre	Gelboliv	Oliva amarillo	Oliva giallastro
Yellow-orange	Orange jaunâtre	Gelborange	Naranja amarillo	Arancio giallastro
Zig-zag roulette	Percé en zigzag	Sägezahnartiger Durchstich	Picado en zigzag	Perforazione a zigzag

Complete List of Parts

Edward Stanley Gibbons published his first catalogue of postage stamps from Plymouth in November 1865. Its unillustrated 20 pages listed stamps and postal stationery from Antigua to Württemberg with price columns provided for unused or used, either as singles or by the dozen.

Since 1865 the catalogue range has grown to over 50 current titles, all profusely illustrated and reflecting current research and price information.

The foreign listings, of which this volume forms a part, were published as Part 2 of the Stanley Gibbons catalogue from 1897 to 1945. Circumstances were difficult in the austerity period following the Second World War so the foreign listings were split into seven smaller catalogues. From 1951 to 1970 these were consolidated into Part 2 Europe and Colonies and Part 3 America, Asia and Africa.

Collecting patterns do change, however, so in 1970–71 an experimental series of Sectional catalogues appeared which were, in turn, replaced by a series of three alphabetical volumes covering Europe and four covering Overseas.

The present system of 21 catalogues, covering individual countries or collecting groups, was initiated in 1979. Full details of each volume and its contents are provided below. The scheme has the advantage of allowing flexibility in response to changing collecting habits, with the listings being continually improved, currently by notes covering certain aspects of postal history and by the addition of stamp booklet listings and design indexes.

1 ***Commonwealth & British Empire Stamps 1840–1970*** (111th edition, 2009)

Foreign Countries

2 ***Austria & Hungary*** (6th edition, 2002)
• Austria • U.N. (Vienna) • Hungary

3 ***Balkans*** (5th edition, 2009)
• Albania • Bosnia & Herzegovina • Bulgaria • Croatia
• Greece & Islands • Macedonia • Montenegro• Romania
• Serbia• Slovenia • Yugoslavia

4 ***Benelux*** (5th edition, 2003)
• Belgium & Colonies • Luxembourg
• Netherlands & Colonies

5 ***Czechoslovakia & Poland*** (6th edition, 2002)
• Czechoslovakia • Czech Republic • Slovakia • Poland

6 ***France*** (6th edition, 2006)
• France • Colonies • Post Offices • Andorra • Monaco

7 ***Germany*** (8th edition, 2007)
• Germany • States • Colonies • Post Offices

8 ***Italy & Switzerland*** (6th edition, 2003)
• Italy & Colonies • Liechtenstein • San Marino
• Switzerland • U.N. (Geneva) • Vatican City

9 ***Portugal & Spain*** (5th edition, 2004)
• Andorra • Portugal & Colonies • Spain & Colonies

10 ***Russia*** (6th edition, 2008)
• Russia • Armenia • Azerbaijan • Belarus
• Estonia • Georgia • Kazakhstan • Kyrgyzstan
• Latvia • Lithuania • Moldova • Tajikistan
• Turkmenistan • Ukraine • Uzbekistan
• Mongolia

11 ***Scandinavia*** (6th edition, 2008)
• Aland Islands • Denmark • Faroe Islands
• Finland • Greenland • Iceland • Norway • Sweden

12 ***Africa since Independence A-E*** (2nd edition, 1983)
• Algeria • Angola • Benin • Burundi • Cameroun
• Cape Verde • Central African Republic • Chad
• Comoro Islands • Congo • Djibouti • Equatorial Guinea
• Ethiopia

13 ***Africa since Independence F-M*** (1st edition, 1981)
• Gabon • Guinea • Guinea-Bissau • Ivory Coast • Liberia
• Libya • Malagasy Republic • Mali • Mauritania • Morocco
• Mozambique

14 ***Africa since Independence N-Z*** (1st edition, 1981)
• Niger Republic • Rwanda • St. Thomas & Prince
• Senegal • Somalia • Sudan • Togo • Tunisia
• Upper Volta • Zaire

15 ***Central America*** (3rd edition, 2007)
• Costa Rica • Cuba • Dominican Republic • El Salvador
• Guatemala • Haiti • Honduras • Mexico • Nicaragua
• Panama

16 ***Central Asia*** (4th edition, 2006)
• Afghanistan • Iran • Turkey

17 ***China*** (7th edition, 2006)
• China • Taiwan • Tibet • Foreign P.O.s • Hong Kong
• Macao

18 ***Japan & Korea*** (5th edition, 2008)
• Japan • Korean Empire • South Korea • North Korea

19 ***Middle East*** (6th edition, 2005)
• Aden • Bahrain • Egypt • Iraq • Israel • Jordan • Kuwait
• Lebanon • Oman • Qatar • Saudi Arabia • Syria • U.A.E.
• Yemen

20 ***South America*** (4th edition, 2008)
• Argentina • Bolivia • Brazil • Chile • Colombia • Ecuador
• Paraguay • Peru • Surinam • Uruguay • Venezuela

21 ***South-East Asia*** (4th edition, 2004)
• Bhutan • Cambodia • Indo-China • Indonesia • Laos
• Myanmar • Nepal • Philippines • Thailand • Timor
• Vietnam

22 ***United States*** (6th edition, 2005)
• U.S. & Possessions • Canal Zone • Marshall Islands
• Micronesia • Palau • U.N. (New York, Geneva, Vienna)

Thematic Catalogues

Stanley Gibbons Catalogues for use with ***Stamps of the World.***

Collect Aircraft on Stamps (2nd edition, 2009)
Collect Birds on Stamps (5th edition, 2003)
Collect Chess on Stamps (2nd edition, 1999)
Collect Fish on Stamps (1st edition, 1999)
Collect Fungi on Stamps (2nd edition, 1997)
Collect Motor Vehicles on Stamps (1st edition, 2004)
Collect Railways on Stamps (3rd edition, 1999)

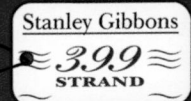

Albania

1913. 40 Paras = 1 Piastre or Grosh
1913. 100 Qint = 1 Franc
1947. Leks only
1965. 100 Qint = 1 New Lek

Qint is also expressed as Qintar, Qind or Qindar, the "ar" meaning gold.

The independence of Albania from Turkish rule was declared on 28 November 1912, during the first Balkan War, and was recognised by the Treaty of London, 30 May 1913.

Austrian Post Offices continued to function in Durrës, Sarandë, Shengjin, Shkodër and Vlórë until 1915 and Italian Post Offices in Ioannina until 1914 (and temporarily in 1917), Shkodër until 1915 and Durrës and Vlórë until 1923. Details of issues are listed under Post Offices in the Turkish Empire in Part 16 (*Central Asia*) of this catalogue and in Part 2 (*Austria and Hungary*) or Part 8 (*Italy and Switzerland*) respectively.

I. Provisional Government

1913–1914

Prior to the June overprinted issues, unoverprinted Turkish stamps were used. From May 1913 handstamped envelopes were made available. The first handstamp used consisted of two concentric circles with a double-eagle shield in the centre and "MINISTERIA E POST-TELEG E TELEFONEVET" between the circles. This was followed by a handstamp similar to Type **2** but without eagle or face value. Cut-outs of both handstamps are known used.

The second handstamp was produced in October 1913 in sheets with "sewing-machine" perforation.

Types of Turkey

25

(26)

28

Plate I

Plate II

(1)

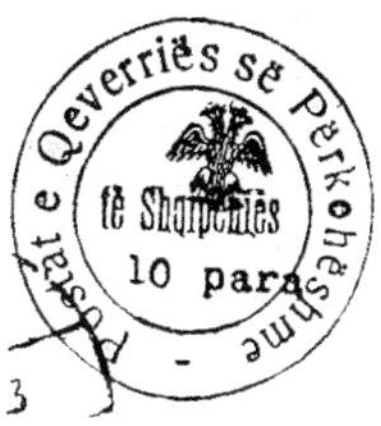

2

1913 (16 June). Stamps of Turkey handstamped with T **1**.

A. On issue of 1908 (T **25**). P 12

1	2½pi. brown	£750	£650
	a. Perf 13½	£750	£650

B. On issue of 1908, T **25** with opt T **26**. P 13½×12

2	10pa. green	£450	£350

C. On issue of 1909–11 (T **28**) (5, 10, 20pa., 1pi. Plate II). P 12

3	2pa. olive-green	£425	£425
4	5pa. yellow-buff	£425	£425
	a. Plate I		
5	10pa. green	£400	£250
	a. Perf 13½×12		
	b. Perf 12×13½		
6	20pa. rose-carmine	£375	£250
	a. Perf 13½×12		
	b. Perf 13½		
7	1pi. ultramarine	£325	£250
	a. Bright blue (Plate I) (*p* 12×13½)		
8	2pi. blue-black	£550	£475
9	5pi. slate-purple	£1400	£1200
	a. Perf 13½		
	b. Perf 12×13½ (handstamp inverted) .		
10	10pi. dull red	£5000	£4750

D. As last, but surch "10" in addition

11	10(pa.) on 20pa. rose-carmine	£1300	£1300

E. On T **28** (10, 20pa. Plate II) with opt T **26**. P 12×13½ (20pa.) or 12 (others)

12	10pa. green	£900	£850
13	20pa. rose-carmine	£800	£850
14	1pi. bright blue (Plate I)	£2000	£1800
	a. Ultramarine (Plate II)	£2000	£1800
14*b*	2pi. blue-black	£3500	£3250

F. On Postage Due stamp of 1908 (T **25**). P 12

15	1pi. black/*crimson*	£3250	£2750
	a. Perf 13½×12		

G. On Postage Due stamp of 1910 (T **28**, Plate II). P 12

15*b*	1pi. black/*crimson*	£3250	£2750

Stamps are known with handstamp T **1** in red, blue or violet.

2pa. on 5pa. (T **28**) and 25 and 50pi. (T **25** and T **28**) were not sold at the post office but were distributed to some officials.

Nos. 2/5, 7/9, 13 and 14*a* exist with handstamp inverted (*Prices*: No. 2, £1500 *used*; 4, £1500 *used*; 7, £950 *un or used*; 9, £3000 *un*, £2500 *used*; 14*a*, £3750 *un or used*) and No. 3 with handstamp sideways.

There are numerous forgeries of the handstamp.

1913. Handstamped as T **2**. Arms in second colour. Value typewritten in violet. Laid bâtonné paper. With or without gum (10pa.), no gum (others). Imperf.

16	10pa. violet and violet (25 Oct)	16·00	16·00
17	20pa. red and grey (25 Oct)	22·00	18·00
	a. Violet eagle		
18	1gr. grey and grey (25 Oct)	22·00	21·00
19	2gr. pale blue and violet (21 Nov)	27·00	21·00
20	5gr. violet and pale blue (21 Nov)	33·00	27·00
	a. Grey eagle		
21	10gr. blue and blue (25 Nov)	33·00	27·00

The eagle exists inverted, sideways or omitted.

Errors in typewritten value exist, including 1gr. for 10gr, "1 grodh" and "1 grosg".

Stamps can be found with part of papermaker's watermark, Atlas supporting the World.

Types **2** and **3** postmarked on the back are remainders.

3

4 Skanderbeg (after Heinz Kautsch)

1913 (28 Nov). Independence Anniversary. Issued at Vlórë (Valona). Handstamped from metal stamps. Arms and value in black. Horiz laid paper. P 11½.

22	**3**	10pa. green	5·50	4·25
		a. Vert laid paper	13·00	11·50
		b. Error. 10pa. red	20·00	20·00
		c. Error. 10pa. violet	20·00	20·00
23		20pa. red	8·25	6·25
		a. Vert laid paper	24·00	21·00
		b. Error. 20pa. green	38·00	26·00
24		30pa. violet	8·25	6·25
		a. Vert laid paper	24·00	21·00
		b. Error. 30pa. blue	27·00	26·00
		c. Error. 30pa. red	27·00	26·00
		d. Error. 30pa. black	27·00	26·00
25		1gr. blue	11·00	9·50
		a. Vert laid paper	31·00	28·00
		b. Error. 1gr. green	27·00	26·00
		c. Error. 1gr. violet	27·00	26·00
		d. Error. 1gr. black	27·00	26·00
26		2gr. black	16·00	10·50
		a. Vert laid paper	41·00	26·00
		b. Error. 2gr. violet	33·00	31·00
		c. Error. 2gr. blue	33·00	31·00

Type **3** was produced from separate handstamps for the frame, eagle and value.

All values exist with eagle or value, or both, inverted, and with eagle or value omitted, the 10pa. to 1gr. with frame double or eagle sideways and the 20pa. to 2gr. with value written in ink (*Prices* £50 *to* £120).

See final footnote below No. 21.

(Typo Government Printing Office, Turin)

1913 (1 Dec). P 14.

27	**4**	2q. chestnut and yellow	5·50	2·50
28		5q. green and yellow	5·50	2·50
29		10q. carmine and rose	5·50	2·50
30		25q. blue	5·50	2·50
31		50q. mauve and rose	13·00	5·25
32		1f. brown	30·00	16·00
27/32 *Set of* 6			60·00	28·00

II. Prince William of Wied

1914

Prince William was offered the Crown on 21 February 1914. He left Albania on 3 September.

(D 5)

(5)

1914 (23 Feb). POSTAGE DUE. Handstamped with Type D **5**.

D33	**4**	2q. chestnut and yellow (V., B. or Bk.)	13·00	5·25
D34		5q. green and yellow (R. or B.)	13·00	5·25
D35		10q. carmine and rose (V.)	18·00	5·25
D36		25q. blue (R.)	22·00	5·25
D37		50q. mauve and rose (Bk.)	33·00	17·00
D33/37 *Set of* 5			90·00	35·00

Separate handstamps were used for "T" and "TAKSË".

Values exist with one or both handstamps inverted or double, or with one handstamp omitted.

1914 (7 Mar). Arrival of Prince William of Wied. Handstamped with T **5**.

33	**4**	2q. chestnut and yellow	75·00	85·00
34		5q. green and yellow (V.)	75·00	85·00
35		10q. carmine and rose	75·00	85·00
36		25q. blue (V.)	75·00	85·00
37		50q. mauve and rose	75·00	85·00
38		1f. brown	75·00	85·00
33/38 *Set of* 6			£425	£450

Separate handstamps were used for "7. Mars" and rest of overprint.

Inverted and double handstamps exist.

5a (actual size 45×45 mm)

(**5b**)

1914 (19 Mar). Korçë (Koritza) Military Post Issue. Value handstamped in red as in T **5a**. Imperf.

38*a*	10pa. violet	£225	£200
38*b*	10pa. black	£325	£325
38*c*	25pa. violet	£225	£200
38*d*	25pa. black	£425	£425

Nos. 38*a*/*d* were produced by metal handstamps, the value being applied separately. At first the handstamps were used directly on covers and different kinds of paper are therefore found. Later examples were issued in sheets. Correctly franked covers have two copies of 10pa. or two copies of 25pa.

No. 38*a* is known with value inverted.

1914 (19 Mar)–**15**. Shkodër (Scutari) Provisional Issue. First Anniv of Hoisting of Albanian Flag on Fortress of Rozafat, Shkodër.

(a) POSTAGE. Nos. 40/45 further handstamped as T **5b**, in red

39	5pa. on 2q. chestnut and yellow	£110	£100
	a. Handstamped in violet	£130	£130
39*b*	10pa. on 5q. green and yellow	£110	£100
39*c*	20pa. on 10q. carmine and rose	£110	£100
39*d*	1gr. on 25q. blue	£110	£100
39*e*	2gr. on 50q. mauve and rose	£110	£100
39*f*	5gr. on 1f. brown	£800	£800

All values exist with handstamp inverted.

(b) POSTAGE DUE. T **4** handstamped with T **5b** in first colour given and further handstamped with large "T" in second colour given (1915)

D39*g*	10q. carmine and rose (Bk.+R.)	£425	£425
D39*h*	25q. blue (R.+Bk.)	£140	£140
D39*i*	50q. mauve and rose (R.+Bk.)	£130	£130

The Albanian Post Office in Shkodër (Scutari) was closed from May 1915 following occupation by Montenegro. The Austrians used their own Field Post Office there in 1916–18, and the Albanian Post Office was re-opened on 15 January 1919.

10
-PARA-
(6)

2
GROSH
(7)

1914 (2 Apr). Surch as T **6** or **7**.

40	**4**	5pa. on 2q. chestnut and yellow	3·25	3·25
		a. Surch inverted	£100	
		b. Pair, one with surch omitted, one with surch inverted	£150	
41		10pa. on 5q. green and yellow	3·25	3·25
		a. Surch inverted	£100	
		b. Pair, one with surch omitted	£150	
42		20pa. on 10q. carmine and rose	5·50	4·25
		a. Surch inverted	£100	
43		1gr. on 25q. blue	5·50	4·25
		a. Surch inverted	£100	
		b. Pair, one with surch omitted	£325	
44		2gr. on 50q. mauve and rose	5·50	5·25
		a. Surch inverted	£130	
45		5gr. on 1f. brown	22·00	16·00
		a. Surch inverted	£160	

1914 (16 Apr). POSTAGE DUE. Surch as T **6** and **7**, and handstamped with word "TAKSË" only, as in Type D **5**.

D46	**4**	10pa. on 5q. green and yellow	6·50	5·25
D47		20pa. on 10q. carmine and rose	6·50	5·25
D48		1gr. on 25q. blue	6·50	5·25
D49		2gr. on 50q. mauve and rose	6·50	5·25

The handstamp is known inverted, double, sideways, double inverted, etc.

1914 (15 Oct). Vlórë (Valona) Provisional Issue. Handstamped with Star within double-lined circle inscr "POSTE D'ALBANIE" at foot and in Turkish at top.

45*a*	**4**	2q. chestnut and yellow	£325	£325
45*b*		5q. green and yellow	£425	£425
45*c*		10q. carmine and rose	43·00	42·00
45*d*		25q. blue	43·00	42·00
45*e*		50q. mauve and rose	43·00	42·00
45*f*		1f. brown	£800	£800
45*g*		5pa. on 2q. chestnut and yellow	75·00	75·00
45*h*		10pa. on 5q. green and yellow	£110	£100
45*i*		20pa. on 10q. carmine and rose	55·00	50·00
45*j*		1gr. on 25q. blue	33·00	31·00
45*k*		2gr. on 50q. mauve and rose	38·00	37·00
45*l*		5gr. on 1f. brown	55·00	50·00

III. Provisional Government of Essad Pasha (Central Albania)

1914–16

From 13 September, 1914, Southern Albania was gradually occupied by Italian forces, and the north by Serbians and Montenegrins. After the defeat of Serbia at the end of 1915, northern Albania was occupied by Austrian troops till the end of 1918. Essad Pasha ruled in Central Albania from January 1914 to 24 February 1916 when the Austrians took control.

(8) 9 Shkodër (Scutari) 10 Tarabosh

1915 (9 Jan). Handstamped with T **8**, in violet, red, blue or black.

46	**4**	2q. chestnut and yellow	27·00	26·00
47		5q. green	60·00	60·00
48		10q. carmine and rose	38·00	37·00
48*a*		25q. blue	55·00	65·00
48*b*		50q. mauve and rose	55·00	65·00
49		5pa. on 2q. chestnut and yellow	38·00	37·00
50		10pa. on 5q. green	16·00	16·00
51		20pa. on 10q. carmine and rose	16·00	16·00
52		1gr. on 25q. blue	16·00	16·00
53		2gr. on 50q. mauve and rose	16·00	16·00
54		5gr. on 1f. brown	38·00	50·00

1915 (9 Jan). POSTAGE DUE. Nos. 46, etc, handstamped with large "T" in violet or blue-black.

D55	**4**	2q. chestnut and yellow	43·00	42·00
D56		10pa. on 5q. green	27·00	26·00
D57		20pa. on 10q. carmine and rose	27·00	26·00
D58		1gr. on 25q. blue	27·00	26·00
D59		2gr. on 50q. mauve and rose	27·00	26·00
D55/59 *Set of 5*			£140	£130

1915 (10 Feb). Unissued stamps handstamped with Crescent and Turkish inscr within circle, in violet or black.

55	**9**	2pa. orange	8·25	5·25
56		5pa. violet	8·25	7·75
57		10pa. green	8·25	8·25
58		20pa. red	8·25	5·25
59		40pa. blue	11·00	5·25
60		100pa. pink	27·00	10·50
61		5pi. black	80·00	31·00
55/61 *Set of 7*			£140	65·00

Handstamps in gold exist, produced for presentation purposes.

1915 (10 Feb). Same handstamp on fiscals of different type.

62	**10**	10pa. green	9·75	10·50
63		20pa. red	9·75	7·75
64		50pa. blue	6·50	5·25
65		3pi. pink	6·50	5·25
66		6pi. chocolate	16·00	12·50
62/66 *Set of 5*			44·00	37·00

IV. Autonomous Province of Korçë (Koritza)

1916–1918

French Currency

On 11 December 1916 the French Gen. Sarrail set up the area round Koritza in eastern Albania as an Autonomous Province, to counter Greek and Italian influences. In February 1918 the status of Autonomous Province was abolished and it became French-occupied territory. The area passed into Albanian control when French troops left in June 1920.

(10a)

11

1916 (25 Dec). Nos. 60, 77/8, 82 and 85 of Epirus handstamped as T **10a**.

66*a*	**36**	10c. on 2l. scarlet	£275	£200
66*b*	**30**	10c. on 2l. carmine	£1100	£500
66*c*	**29**	25c. on 3l. vermilion	£500	£250
66*d*	**30**	25c. on 25l. blue	£600	£375
66*e*	**31**	25c. on 50l. brown-purple	£6500	£4750

The eagle on the 25c. handstamp has four wings on each side.
The date given is earliest known cancellation.

(Typo, background litho A. A. Vangheli)

1917 (Jan). P 11½.

67	**11**	1c. brown and green	24·00	16·00
		a. Second "V" of "VETQEVERITARE" inverted	90·00	
		b. "S" of "SHQIPERIE" inverted	75·00	
68		2c. red-brown and green	24·00	16·00
		a. Second "V" of "VETQEVERITARE" inverted	90·00	
		b. "S" of "SHQIPERIE" inverted	80·00	
69		3c. grey and green	24·00	16·00
		a. Second "V" of "VETQEVERITARE" inverted	90·00	
		b. "S" of "SHQIPERIE" inverted	80·00	
70		5c. green and black	22·00	10·50
		a. Second "V" of "VETQEVERITARE" inverted	90·00	
		b. "S" of "SHQIPERIE" inverted	80·00	
71		10c. rose-carmine and black	22·00	10·50
		a. "S" of "SHQIPERIE" inverted	65·00	
72		25c. blue and black	22·00	10·50
		a. "S" of "SHQIPERIE" inverted	65·00	
73		50c. violet and black	22·00	13·50
		a. "S" of "SHQIPERIE" inverted	65·00	
74		1f. brown and black	22·00	13·50
		a. Second "V" of "VETQEVERITARE" inverted	£100	
		b. "S" of "SHQIPERIE" inverted	75·00	
67/74 *Set of 8*			£160	95·00

Inverted "S" occurs in position 5 of setting of 12. The inverted "V" was later corrected.

1917 (May). As last but inscr "REPUBLIKA SHQIPETARE" at sides. Typo. P 11½.

75		1c. brown and green	3·75	3·25
76		2c. red-brown and green	3·75	3·25
		a. "CTM" for "CTS"	£100	£160
77		3c. slate and green	3·75	3·25
		a. "CTM" for "CTS"	£110	£180
78		5c. green and black	5·50	5·25
		a. Inscriptions double		
79		10c. red and black	5·50	5·25
80		50c. purple and black	9·75	8·25
81		1f. red-brown and black	27·00	23·00
75/81 *Set of 7*			55·00	48·00

2 and 3c. were at first printed with "CTM" (76a, 77a) in all positions. The error was corrected in later printings.

1918 (2 Apr). No. 78 surch "QARKU I KORÇËS 25 CTS", in red.

81*a*		25 on 5c. green and black	£275	£325
		ab. Surch double		

The date given is earliest known cancellation.

1918 (5 Apr). As T **11**, but inscr "QARKU POSTES I KORÇËS".

82		25c. blue and black	£100	£130
		a. Inverted "U" in "QARKU"		
		b. Inverted "Q" in "QARKU"		
		c. "QRAKU"		
		d. "KORCËS" (no cedilla on "C")		
		e. Imperf between (horiz pair)		
		f. Imperf between (vert pair)		

Printed in sheets of 12. In first setting inverted "U" occurs in position 1, inverted "Q" in position 6, "QRAKU" in position 11 and "KORCËS" in positions 9 and 12. All errors were corrected in later settings.

Nos. 82e/f (which come from first two vert rows) also have various edges imperf. Completely imperforate pairs have been made from imperf between pairs by trimming perforated edges.

The date given is earliest known cancellation.

The inscription on Nos. 67/74 means "Koritza: Independent Albania"; that on Nos. 75/81, "Koritza: Albanian Republic"; and that on Nos. 81*a*/82, "Local Post of Koritza".

Type **11** (all inscriptions) overprinted "TAXE" are fiscal stamps.

From April 1918 until the end of the occupation French stamps were used; the canceller was inscribed "TRESOR ET POSTES".

V. Provisional Government

December 1918–February 1920

A Provisional Government under Turkhan Bey was set up in December 1918 with the aim of establishing complete independence and to free the country of Italian troops, who left on 2 September 1920.

Shkodër (Scutari) was governed by an Inter-Allied Commission, as a protection against Serbia, from the end of 1918 till 11 March 1920. Nos. 83/103, 111/3*d* and 114/22 were for use there.

12

13

13a

(Note different types of Eagle)

(Surcharged by Nikai, Shkodër)

1919 (15 Jan). Fiscal stamps used by the Austrians in Albania with value in heller, as T **12**, surch in black with new value and "POSTA e Shkodres SHQYPNIS" (Post of Scutari, Albania), and handstamped diagonally with T **13a** in blue (10q.) or red (others). Issued under the joint authority of the British, French and Italian commanders. P 12½.

83		(2)q. on 2h. brown	11·50	11·00
		a. Surch inverted		
84		05q. on 16h. green	11·50	11·00
		a. Surch inverted		
85		10q. on 8h. carmine	11·50	11·00
		a. Surch inverted		
86		25q. on 64h. blue	13·00	12·50
		a. Surch inverted		
		b. Type **13**	£550	£500
87		50q. on 32h. violet	11·50	11·00
		a. Surch inverted		
88		1f. on 1.28k. brown/*blue*	14·00	13·50
		a. "r" in "Frank" inverted	30·00	30·00
		b. "ë" for "e" in "Shkodres"	27·00	27·00
		c. Surch inverted		
83/88 *Set of 6*			65·00	65·00

The surcharge settings consisted of 40 positions (5×8) which were applied twice to the sheets of 80. For the 5 to 50q. values several different fonts were used for the numerals e.g. wide and narrow figure "0" and letter "O", "1" and "I", straight and curly-footed "2", serifed (two sizes) and sans-serif "5"; these occur in various combinations. The 1f. has the figure "1" on the left and the letter "I" on the right in all positions; Nos. 88a and 88b occur in positions 35 and 36 respectively of the setting.

The date (Type **13a**) was handstamped across the stamps to commemorate the re-opening of the Post Office. This is found double, inverted or omitted. It also exists in violet on 2, 5 and 25q. and in blue on 2q.

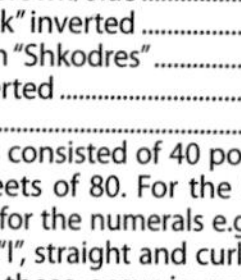

(D **14**)

1919 (15 Jan). POSTAGE DUE. Fiscal stamps with surch as in T **12** (but "qint" for "QINT"), without date, handstamped with Type D **14**, in violet. P 11½ (4q.) or 12½ (others).

D89		(4)q. on 4h. pink	16·00	12·50
		a. "qit" for "qint"		
D90		(10)q. on 10k. red/*green*	16·00	12·50
		a. "qit" for "qint"		
D91		20q. on 2k. orange/*lilac*	16·00	12·50
		a. "qit" for "qint"		
D92		50q. on 5k. brown/*yellow*	16·00	12·50
		a. "qit" for "qint"		
		b. "nt" of "qint" at right angle		
D89/92 *Set of 4*			60·00	45·00

Most stamps with "qit" error, which occurs in position 36 of the setting, also have the obliterating bars damaged on the left.

Type D **14** exists inverted on all values and sideways on Nos. D89/91. The handstamp is also found in red or blue; these are believed to be trials.

(14)

(15)

(16)

1919 (16 Jan). T **12** (without handstamped date) further handstamped with a "Comet", T **14** (from wooden die), in red or green (10q.).

89		(2)q. on 2h. brown	22·00	21·00
		a. Handstamped in blue	90·00	90·00
90		5q. on 16h. green	16·00	16·00
91		10q. on 8h. carmine	16·00	16·00
92		25q. on 64h. blue	£225	£200
		a. Type **13**	70·00	80·00
93		50q. on 32h. violet	22·00	21·00
94		1f. on 1.28k. brown/*blue*	22·00	21·00
		a. "r" in "Frank" inverted	75·00	75·00
		b. "ë" for "e" in "Shkodres"	75·00	75·00
		c. Surch double		
89/94 *Set of 6*			£150	£160

The handstamp exists in violet in 1f.

1919 (15 Feb). As Nos. 89/94 but comet with straight tail, T **15**, in violet (from a copper die).

96		(2)q. on 2h. brown	27·00	26·00
97		5q. on 16h. green	27·00	26·00
98		10q. on 8h. carmine	27·00	26·00
99		25q. on 64h. blue	27·00	26·00
		a. Type **13**	£225	£200
100		50q. on 32h. violet	27·00	26·00
		a. Surch double		
101		1f. on 1.28k. brown/*blue*	27·00	26·00
		a. "r" in "Frank" inverted	49·00	48·00
		b. "ë" for "e" in "Shkodres"	41·00	41·00
96/101 *Set of 6*			£150	£140

The handstamp exists in red or blue on 50q., and double on 5q. (both in violet or with one in red).

1919. No. 43 handstamped with T **16**, in violet.

103	**4**	1gr. on 25q. blue	26·00	17·00

No. 103 exists with handstamp inverted or double.

15 QIND 15 20QIND 20
POSTAT POSTAT

SHQIPTARE SHQIPTARE
(16a) (16b)

1919 (5 June). Fiscals as T **12**/**13**, surch at Durrës (Durazzo). P 12½.

(a) As T **16a**

104	**13**	10q. on 2h. brown	11·00	7·75
105	**12**	15q. on 8h. carmine	11·00	7·75
		a. Surch in violet		
		b. Error. 20q. on 8h.		
		c. Type **13**	£325	£325
106		20q. on 16h. green	11·00	7·75
		a. Perf 11½	11·00	7·75
		b. Error. 25q. on 16h.		
107	**13**	25q. on 64h. blue	11·00	7·75
108	**12**	50q. on 32h. violet	11·00	7·75
		a. Error. 25q. on 32h.		
109		1f. on 96h. orange (p 11½)	11·00	7·75
		a. Type **13** (p 12½)	£275	£250
110	**13**	2f. on 160h. violet	38·00	31·00
		a. Error. 1f. on 160h.		

(b) As T **16b**

111	**13**	10q. on 8h. carmine	11·00	7·75
		a. Type **12**	£350	£325
112		15q. on 8h. carmine (V.)	11·00	7·75
		a. Type **12**	£1100	£500
113	**12**	20q. on 16h. green	11·00	7·75
		a. Perf 11½		
113*b*		25q. on 32h. violet	11·00	7·75
113*c*		50q. on 64h. blue	30·00	21·00
113*d*		1f. on 96h. orange (p 11½)	13·00	10·50
113*e*	**13**	2f. on 160h. violet	22·00	16·00

VI. Regency

February 1920–21 January 1925

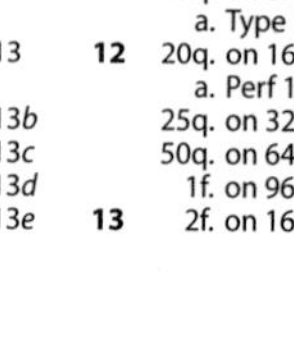

17 Prince William I

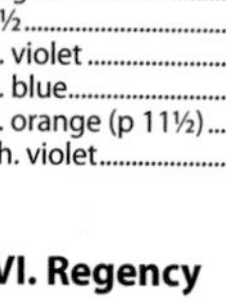

(18)

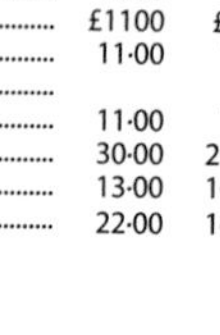

19 Skanderbeg

(Des Gurschner. Eng F. Schirnböck. Typo Austrian State Ptg Wks, Vienna)

1920 (16 Feb). Optd with T **18** or surch also. P 12½.

114 **17** 1q. grey. (B.) 80·00 £130
115 2q. on 10q. rose (Br.) 12·50 31·00
116 5q. on 10q. rose (G.) 12·50 26·00
117 10q. rose 12·50 26·00
118 20q. brown (B.) 35·00 50·00
119 25q. blue £425 £750
120 25q. on 10q. rose (B.) 12·50 21·00
121 50q. violet 47·00 95·00
122 50q. on 10q. rose (Br.) 12·50 42·00

Stamps of T **17** without the overprint were not issued and those offered came from looted stocks.

(Typo Govt Ptg Wks, Paris)

1920 (1 Apr). Optd at Shkodër (Scutari) with Posthorn to obliterate "SHKODER". P 14–13½.

123 **19** 2q. orange 9·50 12·50
124 5q. green 17·00 21·00
125 10q. red 28·00 47·00
126 25q. blue 50·00 44·00
127 50q. green 11·50 16·00
128 1f. mauve 11·50 16·00
123/128 *Set of* 6 £110 £140

D **20** Fortress of Shkodër

(**21**) ("BESA" =Oath of Peace)

D **22**

(Typo Govt Ptg Wks, Paris)

1920 (1 April). POSTAGE DUE. Optd with Posthorn. P 14×13½.

D129 D **20** 4q. olive-green 1·30 5·25
D130 10q. rose 2·50 7·75
D131 20q. bistre-brown 2·50 7·75
D132 50q. black 6·50 21·00
D129/132 *Set of* 4 11·50 38·00

Nos. 123/8 and D129/32 were not issued without the overprint.

1921. Handstamped with T **21** at foot.

135 **19** 2q. orange 6·25 10·50
136 5q. green 6·25 10·50
137 10q. red 12·50 18·00
138 25q. blue 23·00 31·00
139 50q. green 12·50 18·00
140 1f. mauves 12·50 18·00
a. Pair, one with handstamp omitted
135/140 *Set of* 6 65·00 95·00

The handstamp exists double.

The Oath of Peace was given to observe a truce in a blood feud. A general "Besa" was proclaimed throughout Albania in February 1920.

1922 (Mar). POSTAGE DUE. Typo. P 12½.

D141 D **22** 4q. black/*red* 1·80 5·25
a. Perf 11½
D142 10q. black/*red* 1·80 5·25
a. Perf 11½
D143 20q. black/*red* 1·80 5·25
a. Perf 11½
D144 50q. black/red 1·80 5·25
D141/144 *Set of* 4 4·50 19·00

BESA
(**22**)

Q 1
(**23**)

24

1922. Handstamped with T **22** at foot.

141 **19** 5q. green (Oct) 6·75 5·25
142 10q. red (Aug) 11·00 10·50

The handstamp exists double.

1922 (Oct). No. 135 handstamped with T **23**.

143 **19** 1q. on 2q. orange 11·00 10·50

No. 143 was issued for use on newspapers when the rate was lowered from 2q. to 1q.

(Typo Austrian State Ptg Wks, Vienna)

1923 (Jan). T **24** and similar horizontal views. P 12½.

144 2q. orange (Gjirokastër) 1·10 2·10
a. Perf 11½ 1·60 2·75
145 5q. yellowish green (Kanina) 1·10 1·60
a. Perf 11½ 2·20 3·25
146 10q. carmine (Berat) 1·10 1·60
a. Perf 11½
147 25q. blue (Veziri Bridge) 1·10 1·60
148 50q. deep bluish green (Rozafat Fortress, Shkodër) 1·10 1·60
149 1f. deep reddish lilac (Korçë) 1·10 1·60
150 2f. olive-green (Durrës) 6·50 8·25
144/150 *Set of* 7 12·00 17·00

Nos. 144/50 were released in the Spring of 1922 but were not put on sale at post offices before January 1923.

Mbledhje Kushtetuese

(**25**)

Mbledhje Kushtetuese
(**25a**)

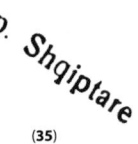

1924 (21 Jan). Opening of National Assembly. Nos. 144/8 optd in black with top line of T **25** (on 25q. with T **25a**) and handstamped in violet with rest of T **25**.

151 2q. orange 27·00 26·00
152 5q. yellowish green 27·00 26·00
153 10q. carmine 20·00 19·00
154 25q. blue 20·00 19·00
155 50q. deep bluish green 27·00 26·00
151/155 *Set of* 5 £110 £100

= 1 =
(**26**)

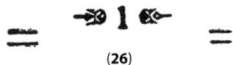

1924 (Apr). No. 144 surch with T **26**.

156 1 on 2q. orange 8·25 10·50
a. Perf 11½

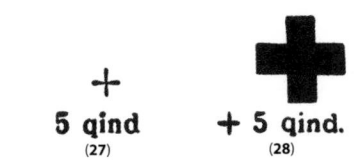

\+ 5 qind
(**27**)

\+ 5 qind.
(**28**)

1924. Red Cross.

(a) Nos. 145 etc surch with T **27** (Cross in red, value in black) (Nov)

157 5q. +5q. yellowish green 27·00 36·00
a. Perf 11½
b. Perf 12½×11½
158 10q. +5q. carmine 27·00 36·00
159 25q. +5q. blue 27·00 36·00
a. Surch inverted
160 50q. +5q. deep bluish green 26·00 36·00

(b) As last, surch with T **28** in addition (Cross in red, value in black) (Dec)

161 5q. +5q.+5q. yellowish green 27·00 31·00
a. Perf 11½
b. Perf 12½×11½
c. Large red cross of T **28** omitted
162 10q. +5q.+5q. carmine 27·00 31·00
a. "+ 5 qind." (T **28**) double
b. Large red cross of T **28** double
163 25q. +5q.+5 q. blue 27·00 31·00
164 50q. +5q.+5q. deep bluish green 27·00 31·00

VII. Republic

21 January 1925–1 September 1928

Triumf' i legalitetit
24 Dhetuer 1924
(**29**)

1925 (5 Mar). Return of Government to Capital in 1924. Nos. 156 and 144/9 optd with T **29**.

164*a* 1 on 2q. orange 8·25 9·50
165 2q. orange 8·25 9·50
166 5q. yellowish green 8·25 9·50
167 10q. carmine 8·25 9·50
168 25q. blue 8·25 9·50
a. Perf 11½
169 50q. deep bluish green 16·00 18·00
170 1f. deep reddish lilac 16·00 23·00
164*a*/170 *Set of* 7 65·00 80·00

In the setting of 50, 25 positions are as T **29**, one position (No. 26) has a thin second "e" in "Dhetuer" and the remaining 24 positions have some or all of the figures from a thinner fount; 11 of the latter also have a thin "D".

Republika Shqiptare
21 Kallnduer 1925
(**30**)

1925 (11 Apr). Proclamation of Republic. Nos. 156 and 144/9 optd with T **30**.

171 1 on 2q. orange 7·00 10·50
a. "1921" for "1925" 36·00 36·00
b. "Repubiika" 36·00 36·00
c. "Républika" 36·00 36·00
172 2q. orange 7·00 10·50
a. "1921" for "1925" 36·00 36·00
b. "Repubiika" 36·00 36·00
c. "Républika" 36·00 36·00
173 5q. yellowish green 7·00 10·50
a. "1921" for "1925" 36·00 36·00
b. "Repubiika" 36·00 36·00
c. "Républika" 36·00 36·00
174 10q. carmine 7·00 10·50
a. "1921" for "1925" 36·00 36·00
b. "Repubiika" 36·00 36·00
c. "Républika" 36·00 36·00
d. "Republika"
e. Opt inverted 65·00 65·00
175 25q. blue 7·00 10·50
a. "1921" for "1925" 36·00 36·00
b. "Repubiika" 36·00 36·00
c. "Républika" 36·00 36·00
176 50q. deep bluish green 7·00 10·50
a. "1921" for "1925" 36·00 36·00
b. "Repubiika" 36·00 36·00
c. "Républika" 36·00 36·00
d. Opt double, one inverted 65·00 65·00
177 1f. deep reddish lilac 7·00 10·50
a. "1921" for "1925" 36·00 36·00
b. "Repubiika" 36·00 36·00
c. "Républika" 36·00 36·00

The "Republika" error occurs on position 9, "Repubiika" on pos. 15, "Républika" on pos. 17 and "1921" on pos. 31.

Republika Shqiptare
(**31**)

Republika Shqiptare
(D **32**)

1925 (20 May). Nos. 156 and 144/50 optd with T **31**.

178 1q. on 2q. orange 2·20 2·10
a. Opt inverted 24·00 27·00
ab. Perf 11½. Opt inverted*
b. "Repubiiua" 16·00 21·00
c. "Shqiqtare" 16·00 21·00
d. "Repuqlika" 16·00 21·00
e. Opt double, both inverted
179 2q. orange 2·20 2·10
a. "Shqiqtare" 16·00 21·00
b. "Repubiiua" 16·00 21·00
c. "Repuqlika" 16·00 21·00
d. Opt inverted
e. Perf 11½
180 5q. yellowish green 2·20 2·10
a. "Repuqlika" 16·00 21·00
b. Opt inverted
c. Perf 11½
181 10q. carmine 2·20 2·10
a. "Repuqlika" 16·00 21·00
ab. Perf 11½*
b. Opt inverted
182 25q. blue 2·20 2·10
a. "Repuqlika" 16·00 21·00
b. Opt inverted
c. Perf 11½
183 50q. deep bluish green 2·20 2·10
a. "Repuqlika" 17·00 22·00
184 1f. deep reddish lilac 9·75 5·25
a. "Repuqlika" 33·00 42·00
185 2f. olive-green 15·00 5·25
a. "Repuqlika" 33·00 42·00
b. Opt inverted

T **31** exists with two types of "R", in same thickness as rest of overprint or thinner (as in illustration).

The "Repuqlika" error occurs on position 28.

*1q. perf 11½ has been seen with overprint inverted only, and 10q. perf 11½ with error "Repuqlika" only.

1925. POSTAGE DUE. Optd with Type D **32**, in white.

D186 D **22** 4q. black/*red* 5·50 5·25
D187 10q. black/*red* 5·50 5·25
D188 20q. black/*red* 5·50 5·25
a. Perf 11½
D189 50q. black/*red* 5·50 5·25
a. Opt inverted
D186/189 *Set of* 4 20·00 19·00

10q. exists with gold overprint, reading up or down. This is believed to be a trial printing.

32

33

34

Pres. Ahmed Zogu, later King Zog I

(Typo State Ptg Wks, Berlin)

1925 (30 May). AIR. Wmk Lozenges. P 14.

186 **32** 5q. green 4·25 4·25
187 10q. carmine 4·25 4·25
188 25q. blue 4·25 4·25
189 50q. deep green 7·50 7·25
190 1f. black and violet 13·00 12·50
191 2f. violet and olive-green 22·00 21·00
192 3f. deep green and chestnut 27·00 21·00
186/192 *Set of* 7 75·00 65·00

Nos. 186/92 exist imperf; these are proofs.

(Litho Aspiotis, Corfu)

1925 (24 Dec). P 13½×13 or 13½ (25q.).

193 **33** 1q. orange-yellow 45 30
194 2q. red-brown 50 90
195 5q. green 35 30
196 10q. rose-red 35 30
a. Perf 11½ 55·00 37·00
ab. Imperf between (horiz pair)
197 15q. deep brown 2·20 2·50
198 25q. deep blue 55 30
a. Perf 13½×11
199 50q. deep bluish green 2·20 1·90
200 **34** 1f. dull ultramarine and red 4·25 2·50
201 2f. yellow-orange and dull blue-green 5·50 2·50
202 3f. reddish violet and red-brown 11·00 6·25
203 5f. black and reddish violet 13·00 9·00
193/203 *Set of* 11 36·00 24·00

All values exist imperforate; these are proofs.

The 25q. exists perf 13½×13 in ultramarine, many examples having a double impression. The status of this variety is uncertain but there is no evidence of postal use.

A 1f. blue and brown and 2f. green and brown in a slightly different design were prepared but not issued.

D **35**

Rep. Shqiptare
(**35**)

Rep.
Upright "R"

1925 (24 Dec). POSTAGE DUE. Typo. P 13½×13.
D204 D **35** 10q. blue .... 2·20 4·25
D205 20q. green .... 2·20 4·25
D206 30q. red-brown .... 4·25 8·25
D207 50q. brown .... 7·50 16·00
D204/207 *Set of 4* .... 14·50 29·00
The above stamps are overprinted "QIND.AR" in red. Large stamps, with double-headed eagle, inscribed "SHTETI SHQYPTAR" and "TAKSE", are purely fiscals.

1927 (18 Jan). AIR. Optd diag downwards as T **35**.
204 **32** 5q. green .... 13·00 12·50
a. Opt double, one inverted .... 39·00 46·00
b. Upright "R" ....
205 10q. carmine .... 13·00 12·50
a. Opt inverted .... 35·00 42·00
b. Opt double, one inverted .... 39·00 46·00
c. Upright "R" ....
206 25q. blue .... 11·00 12·50
a. Upright "R" ....
207 50q. deep green .... 8·25 7·75
a. Opt inverted .... 35·00 42·00
b. Upright "R" ....
208 1f. black and violet .... 16·00 12·50
a. Opt inverted .... 35·00 42·00
b. Upright "R" ....
c. No full point after "Rep" (pos. 38)
209 2f. violet and olive-green .... 16·00 12·50
a. Upright "R" ....
210 3f. deep green and chestnut .... 22·00 18·00
a. Upright "R" ....
204/210 *Set of 7* .... 90·00 80·00
The upright "R" variety occurs four times in the sheet, in positions 36, 41, 46 and 47.

(**36**)

REP. SHQYPTARE
Fluturim' i I-ar
Vlonë–Brindisi
21. IV. 1928
(**37**)

1927 (1 Feb). Ahmed Zogu's Second Year as President. Optd with T **36**.
211 **33** 1q. orange-yellow (V.) .... 1·60 1·30
212 2q. red-brown (G.) 85 50
a. Opt double .... 43·00
213 5q. green (R.) .... 3·50 75
214 10q. rose-red (B.) 75 50
a. Perf 11½ .... 65·00 31·00
215 15q. deep brown (G.) .... 20·00 19·00
216 25q. deep blue (R.) .... 1·60 50
a. Opt double .... 43·00
217 50q. deep bluish green (B.) .... 1·60 50
218 **34** 1f. dull ultramarine and red .... 3·75 75
219 2f. yellow-orange and dull blue-green .... 3·75 1·00
220 3f. reddish violet and red-brown .... 6·50 2·10
221 5f. black and reddish violet .... 11·00 3·75
211/221 *Set of 11* .... 50·00 28·00
Overprints in different colours are trial printings.

1928 (21 April). AIR. Inauguration of Vlórë (Valona) Brindisi Air Service. Optd with T **37**, in violet.
222 **32** 5q. green .... 13·00 12·50
a. Opt inverted .... 16·00 13·50
b. Error. "SHQYRTARE" .... 21·00 24·00
c. Error. As b, opt inverted £110 £130
d. Comma for stop after "21" .... 21·00 27·00
223 10q. carmine .... 13·00 12·50
a. Error. "SHQYRTARE" .... 21·00 24·00
b. Comma for stop after "21" .... 21·00 24·00
224 25q. blue .... 13·00 12·50
a. Error. "SHQYRTARE" .... 21·00 26·00
b. Comma for stop after "21" .... 21·00 26·00
225 50q. deep green .... 27·00 26·00
a. Error. "SHQYRTARE" .... 43·00 31·00
b. Comma for stop after "21" .... 43·00 31·00
226 1f. black and violet £140 £140
a. Error. "SHQYRTARE" £180 £275
b. Comma for stop after "21" £180 £275
227 2f. violet and olive-green £140 £140
a. Error. "SHQYRTARE" £180 £275
b. Comma for stop after "21" £180 £170
228 3f. deep green and chestnut £140 £140
a. Error. "SHQYRTARE" £180 £225
b. Comma for stop after "21" £180 £225
222/228 *Set of 7* £425 £425
Sold at approximately 50 per cent above face value.
The "SHQYRTARE" error occurs on positions 23 and 48 and the "Comma" error on positions 13 and 38 in the sheet of 50, the overprint setting of 25 being applied twice.

= 1 =
(**38**)

1928. Nos. 214 and 216, surch as T **38**.
229 **33** 1 on 10q. rose-red .... 1·60 75
a. Surch inverted .... 4·25
b. Perf 11½ .... 33·00 21·00
230 5 on 25q. deep blue (R.) .... 1·60 75
a. Type **36** inverted .... 4·25

39 Pres. Ahmed Zogu, later King Zog I **40**

Mbledhjes Kushtetuese Kujtim i 25.8.28
(**41**)

Mbledhjes Kushtetuese Kujtim i 25. 8. 28.
(**42**)

"Dedicated to the memory of the Parliament of 25.8.28"

(Typo Govt Ptg Wks, Paris. Optd locally)

1928. National Assembly. Unissued stamps optd as T **41** or **42** (1f.). P 14×13½, or 13½×14 (1f.).
231 **39** 1q. red-brown .... 11·00 12·50
a. Opt inverted ....
232 2q. grey .... 11·00 12·50
a. Opt inverted ....
233 5q. green .... 11·00 16·00
a. Opt inverted ....
234 10q. red .... 11·00 16·00
235 15q. bistre .... 33·00 65·00
236 25q. blue .... 13·00 16·00
a. Opt inverted ....
237 50q. lilac-rose .... 22·00 21·00
238 **40** 1f. black and blue (C.) .... 13·00 16·00
231/238 *Set of 8* £110 £160
This set was sold at a premium of 25 per cent and was on sale for only two days.

VIII. Kingdom

King Zog I. 1 September 1928–7 April 1939

Mbretnia Shqiptare ZOG I 1.IX 1928
(**43**) "Kingdom of Albania. Zog I.I.IX.1928"

Mbretnia-Shqiptare. ·ZOG·I· 1.IX.1928.
(**44**)

1928 (1 Sept). Accession of King Zog I. Optd as T **43** or **44**. P 13½×14 (T **40**) or 14×13½ (others).
239 **39** 1q. red-brown .... 27·00 31·00
240 2q. grey (R.) .... 27·00 31·00
241 5q. green .... 22·00 26·00
242 10q. red .... 22·00 21·00
243 15q. bistre .... 33·00 37·00
244 25q. blue (R.) .... 22·00 21·00
245 50q. lilac-rose .... 22·00 21·00
246 **40** 1f. black and blue (R.) .... 27·00 26·00
247 2f. black and green (R.) .... 27·00 26·00
239/247 *Set of 9* £200 £225
Sold at double face value.

Mbretnia-Shqiptare
(**45**) "Kingdom of Albania"

1928. Optd as T **45**. P 13½×14 (T **40**) or 14×13½ (others).
248 **39** 1q. red-brown .... 1·10 1·60
249 2q. grey .... 1·10 1·60
250 5q. green .... 7·50 4·75
251 10q. red .... 1·10 1·60
252 15q. bistre .... 27·00 31·00
253 25q. blue .... 1·10 1·60
a. Pair, one with opt omitted ....
254 50q. lilac-rose .... 2·20 2·50
255 **40** 1f. black and blue .... 4·25 3·25
256 2f. black and green .... 4·25 5·25
257 3f. olive and carmine .... 15·00 16·00
258 5f. black and violet .... 16·00 21·00
248/258 *Set of 11* .... 75·00 80·00

Mbr. Shqiptare

RROFT-MBRETI

■ 15 ■
(**46**)

8 X 1929.
(**47**) "Long live the king"

1929. Optd with T **36** and surch as T **46**.
259 **33** 1 on 50q. dp bluish green (No. 217) .... 75 1·00
a. Surch double ....
b. Surch inverted ....
260 5 on 25q. deep blue (No. 216) .... 75 1·00
a. Surch inverted ....
b. Type **36** double ....
261 15 on 10q. rose-red (No. 214) .... 1·30 1·60
a. Perf 11½ .... 16·00
b. Surch inverted ....
c. Surch double ....
d. Type **36** inverted ....
259/261 *Set of 3* .... 2·50 3·25

1929 (6 Oct). King Zog's 34th Birthday. Optd with T **47**.
262 **33** 1q. orange-yellow .... 16·00 26·00
263 2q. red-brown .... 16·00 26·00
264 5q. green .... 16·00 26·00
265 10q. rose-red .... 16·00 26·00
266 25q. deep blue .... 16·00 26·00
267 50q. deep bluish green (R.) .... 22·00 31·00
268 **34** 1f. dull ultramarine and red .... 30·00 47·00
269 2f. yellow-orange and dull blue-green .... 30·00 47·00
262/269 *Set of 8* £150 £225

Mbr. Shqiptare
(**48**) "Kingdom of Albania"

1929 (3 Dec). AIR. Optd with T **48** in brown-red.
270 **32** 5q. green .... 11·00 16·00
271 10q. carmine .... 11·00 16·00
272 25q. blue .... 11·00 16·00
273 50q. deep green £225 £300
274 1f. black and violet £425 £500
275 2f. violet and olive-green £500 £550
276 3f. deep green and chestnut £600 £650
270/276 *Set of 7* £1600 £1800
Collectors are warned against forgeries of this overprint.

PRINTERS. The following issues to No. 388 were printed in photogravure by the Government Printing Works, Rome.

49 Lake of Butrinto

50 King Zog I

51 Ahmed Zogu Bridge, River Mati

51a Ruins of Zogu Castle

52

D **53** Arms of Albania

1930 (1 Sept). 2nd Anniv of Accession. W **52**. P 14×14½ or 14½×14.
277 **49** 1q. slate 55 30
278 2q. vermilion 55 30
279 **50** 5q. green 55 30
280 10q. scarlet 55 50
281 15q. sepia 55 50
282 25q. blue 55 50
283 **49** 50q. blue-green .... 1·10 75
284 **51** 1f. violet .... 2·20 1·30
285 2f. slate-blue .... 2·75 1·30
286 **51a** 3f. grey-green .... 8·25 2·10
287 5f. brown .... 11·00 5·25
277/287 *Set of 11* .... 26·00 12·00

1930 (1 Sept). POSTAGE DUE. W **52**. P 14×14½.
D288 D **53** 10q. blue .... 18·00 26·00
D289 20q. rose .... 6·50 16·00
D290 30q. violet .... 6·50 16·00
D291 50q. green .... 6·50 16·00
D288/291 *Set of 4* .... 34·00 65·00

53 Junkers F-13 over Tirana

TIRANË-ROME
6 KORRIK 1931
(**54**)

1930 (8 Oct). AIR. T **53** (qind values) and similar view. No wmk. P 14×14½.
288 5q. green .... 2·20 2·50
289 15q. scarlet .... 2·20 2·50
290 20q. steel-blue .... 2·20 2·50
291 50q. deep olive .... 5·50 5·25
292 1f. deep blue .... 8·25 7·75
293 2f. brown .... 27·00 26·00
294 3f. violet .... 33·00 31·00
288/294 *Set of 7* .... 70·00 70·00

1931 (6 July). AIR. Tirana–Rome Flight. Nos. 288/94 optd with T **54**.
295 5q. green .... 13·00 13·00
296 15q. scarlet .... 13·00 13·00
297 20q. steel-blue .... 13·00 13·00
298 50q. deep olive .... 13·00 13·00
299 1f. deep-blue .... 75·00 75·00
300 2f. brown .... 75·00 75·00
301 3f. violet .... 75·00 75·00
a. Opt inverted £300
295/301 *Set of 7* £250 £250

1 9 2 4–24 Dhetuer–4 1 9 3
(**55**)

Taksë
(D **56**)

1934 (24 Dec). Tenth Anniv of Revolution. Optd with T **55** (on horiz designs) or similar opt (vert designs).
302 **49** 1q. slate .... 13·00 16·00
303 2q. vermilion .... 13·00 16·00
304 **50** 5q. green .... 13·00 16·00
305 10q. scarlet .... 13·00 16·00

306		15q. sepia	13·00	16·00
307		25q. blue	16·00	17·00
308	49	50q. blue-green	22·00	21·00
309	51	1f. violet	22·00	26·00
310		2f. slate-blue	33·00	40·00
311	51a	3f. grey-green	49·00	50·00
302/311 *Set of* 10			£190	£200

1936. POSTAGE DUE. Optd with Type D **56**.

D312	50	10q. carmine	16·00	47·00
		a. Thin "T"	27·00	50·00
		b. "Takës"	£150	£200

The "Thin T" occurs 32 times in the sheet of 100.

Examples also exist overprinted "– Taksë –" but their status is uncertain.

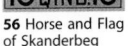

56 Horse and Flag of Skanderbeg

57 Albania in Chains

1937 (20 Nov). 25th Anniv of Independence. P 14.

312	56	1q. slate-violet	55	50
313	57	2q. sepia	80	75
314	–	5q. green	1·10	75
315	56	10q. olive-green	1·10	1·00
316	57	15q. scarlet	1·60	1·30
317	–	25q. pale blue	3·25	2·50
318	56	50q. deep blue-green	8·25	4·50
319	57	1f. bright violet	22·00	7·75
320	–	2f. chestnut	27·00	12·50
312/320 *Set of* 9			60·00	28·00
MS320*a* 140×140 mm. 20q. purple (T **56**), 30q. olive-brown (T **57**), 40q. scarlet (as 5q.)			33·00	£190

Design: Vert—5q., 25q., 2f. As T **57**, but eagle with opened wings (Liberated Albania).

58 Countess Geraldine Apponyi and King Zog

1938 (25 April). Royal Wedding. P 14.

321	58	1q. deep violet	55	50
322		2q. chestnut	55	50
323		5q. green	55	50
324		10q. olive-green	2·20	1·00
325		15q. scarlet	2·20	1·00
326		25q. bright blue	5·50	2·50
327		50q. deep blue-green	11·00	5·25
328		1f. bright violet	22·00	10·50
321/328 *Set of* 8			40·00	20·00
MS328*a* 110×140 mm: 2 each 20q. purple, 30q. olive-brown			65·00	£200

59 National Emblems

60 King Zog

1938 (30 Aug). Tenth Anniv of Accession. Inscr as in T **59**/**60**. P 14.

329	–	1q. deep purple	45	75
		a. Imperf between (vert pair)		
330	59	2q. vermilion	55	75
331	–	5q. myrtle green	1·10	80
332	60	10q. chestnut	1·10	1·30
333	–	15q. scarlet	2·20	1·60
334	60	25q. dull ultramarine	2·40	1·80
335	59	50q. black	20·00	7·75
336	60	1f. deep grey-green	27·00	11·50
329/336 *Set of* 8			50·00	24·00
MS336*a* 110×65 mm. 15q. scarlet (333), 20q. grey-green (**59**), 30q. violet (**60**)			49·00	£140

Design:—1q., 5q., 15q. As Type **60**, but Queen Geraldine's portrait.

IX. Italian Occupation

7 April 1939–September 1943

Mbledhja
Kushtetuëse
12-IV-1939
XVII
(**61**)

1939 (12 Apr).

(a) POSTAGE. Optd with T **61**, sideways (reading up) on vert designs

337	49	1q. slate	1·60	1·60
		a. "2" with straight foot		
338		2q. vermilion	1·60	1·60
339	50	5q. green	1·10	1·00
		a. "2" with straight foot		
340		10q. scarlet	1·10	1·00
341		15q. sepia	2·75	2·50
342		25q. blue	3·25	3·25
343	49	50q. blue-green	4·25	3·75
		a. "2" with straight foot		
		ab. Opt inverted		
344	51	1f. violet	6·50	4·75
345		2f. slate-blue	7·50	6·25
346	51a	3f. grey-green	16·00	14·50
347		5f. brown	22·00	25·00

(b) AIR. Optd horiz with T **61** or (No. 350) additionally surch "20 QIND"

348	53	5q. green	7·50	6·75
349		15q. scarlet	7·00	7·25
350		20q. on 50q. deep olive	12·00	11·50
337/350 *Set of* 14			85·00	80·00

62 Gheg

64 Broken Columns, Botrint

63 King Victor Emmanuel

65 King and Fiat G18V on Tirana–Rome Service

1939–40. P 14.

(a) POSTAGE

351	62	1q. slate-blue (1.1.40)	1·10	50
352	–	2q. olive-brown (1.1.40)	1·10	50
353	–	3q. red-brown (1.1.40)	1·10	50
354	–	5q. green (2.11.39)	1·60	20
355	63	10q. brown (8.39)	1·60	30
356		15q. scarlet (8.39)	1·70	30
357		25q. bright blue (8.39)	1·70	1·30
358		30q. bright violet (8.39)	2·75	2·10
359	–	50q. slate-violet (1.40)	4·25	1·80
360	–	65q. brown-lake (10.39)	12·00	8·25
361	–	1f. blue-green (24.12.39)	12·00	5·75
362	–	2f. lake (24.12.39)	27·00	18·00
363	64	3f. olive-black (24.12.39)	46·00	33·00
364	–	5f. slate-purple (24.12.39)	55·00	46·00

(b) AIR

365	65	20q. brown (4.8.39)	£110	18·00
351/365 *Set of* 15			£250	£120

Designs: As T **62**—2q. Tosk man; 3q. Gheg woman; 50q. Tosk woman. As T **63**—5q., 65q. Profile portrait of King Victor Emmanuel. As T **64**—1f. Krujë Fortress; 2f. Bridge over River Kiri at Mes; 5f. Amphitheatre ruins at Berat.

66 Sheep farming

D **67** Arms of Albania

1940 (20 Mar). AIR. As T **66** (various designs). P 14.

366		5q. green	2·50	1·60
367		15q. scarlet	2·75	2·10
368		20q. blue	5·50	3·25
369		50q. brown	7·75	7·75
370		1f. blue-green	8·25	9·50
371		2f. black	18·00	18·00
372		3f. purple	35·00	31·00
366/372 *Set of* 7			70·00	65·00

Designs (Savoia Marchetti S.M.75 airplane and): Horiz—20q. King of Italy and Durrës harbour; 1f. Bridge over River Kiri at Mes. Vert—15q. Aerial route map; 50q. Girl and valley; 2f. Archway and wall, Durrës; 3f. Women in North Epirus.

1940 (1 Mar). POSTAGE DUE. P 14.

D373	D 67	4q. vermilion	43·00	65·00
D374		10q. bright violet	43·00	65·00
D375		20q. brown	43·00	65·00
D376		30q. blue	43·00	65·00
D377		50q. carmine	43·00	65·00
D373/377 *Set of* 5			£200	£300

E **67** King Victor Emmanuel

67 King Victor Emmanuel

1940. EXPRESS LETTER. Type E **67** and similar type inscr "POSTAT EXPRES". P 14.

E373		25q. bright violet	9·75	10·50
E374		50q. vermilion	18·00	19·00

1942 (Apr). Third Anniv of Italian Occupation. P 14.

373	67	5q. green	2·40	2·50
374		10q. sepia	2·40	2·50
375		15q. scarlet	2·40	2·50
376		25q. blue	2·40	2·50
377		65q. red-brown	7·50	7·75
378		1f. slate-green	7·50	7·75
379		2f. dull purple	7·50	7·75
373/379 *Set of* 7			29·00	30·00

1 QIND.
(**68**)

69

1942 (Aug). No. 352 surch with T **68**.

380		1q. on 2q. olive-brown	4·25	5·25

1943 (1 Apr). Anti-Tuberculosis Fund. P 14.

381	69	5q. +5q. green	1·80	2·10
382		10q. +10q. olive-brown	1·80	2·10
383		15q. +10q. carmine	1·80	2·10
384		25q. +15q. blue	2·20	3·25
385		30q. +20q. violet	2·20	3·25
386		50q. +25q. orange	2·20	3·25
387		65q. +30q. grey-black	3·25	4·50
388		1f. +40q. brown	5·50	6·25
381/388 *Set of* 8			19·00	24·00

X. German Occupation

September 1943–29 November 1944

14
Shtator
1943
1 Qind.
(**70**)

71 War Refugees

1943. (a) Nos. 352/63 surch (or optd only as T **70**, in purple-brown (15q.) or red (others).

389	–	1q. on 3q. red-brown	1·60	5·00
		a. "1944" for "1943"	£250	£500
390	–	2q. olive-brown	1·60	5·00
		a. "1643" for "1943"	£250	£500
		b. "1948" for "1943"	£250	£500
391	–	3q. red-brown	1·60	5·00
		a. "1643" for "1943"	£250	£500
		b. "1948" for "1943"	£250	£500
		c. "1944" for "1943"	£250	£500
392	–	5q. green	1·60	5·00
		a. Opt inverted	£650	
		b. "1948" for "1943"	£250	£500
393	63	10q. brown	1·60	5·00
		a. Opt inverted	£650	
		b. "1948" for "1943"	£250	£500
394		15q. scarlet	1·60	5·00
		a. "1643" for "1943"	£250	£500
395		25q. bright blue	1·60	5·00
		a. "1643" for "1943"	£250	£500
		b. "1948" for "1943"	£250	£500
396		30q. bright violet	1·60	5·00
397	–	50q. on 65q. brown-lake	2·20	9·50
		a. "1944" for "1943"	£250	£500
398	–	65q. brown-lake	2·20	9·50
		a. "1944" for "1943"	£250	£500
399	–	1f. blue-green	11·00	22·00
		a. "1944" for "1943"	£250	£500
400	–	2f. lake	16·00	85·00
401	64	3f. olive-black	65·00	£200

(b) EXPRESS LETTER. No. E373 optd as in T **70**, in lake-brown

E402	E 67	25q. bright violet	27·00	33·00
389/E402 *Set of* 14			£120	£350

There were several settings of the overprint. One setting contained two errors, "1643" and "1948" on positions 29 and 51; the "1944" error on the qind values is on position 18 of a different setting.

The "1" in "14" and "1943", and also in the surcharge on No. 389, is found in two different fonts: with a horizontal serif at the top or with a shorter oblique serif. Different combinations are found throughout the settings, with the conjunction of two oblique-serifed figures being the least common.

(Photo State Ptg Wks, Vienna)

1944 (22 Sept). War Refugees Relief Fund. P 14.

402	71	5q. +5q. green	3·50	18·00
403		10q. +5q. brown	3·50	18·00
404		15q. +5q. lake	3·50	18·00
405		25q. +10q. blue	3·50	18·00
406		1f. +50q. olive	3·50	18·00
407		2f. +1f. violet	3·50	18·00
408		3f. +1f.50 orange	3·50	18·00
402/408 *Set of* 7			22·00	£110

XI. Independent State

22 October 1944–11 January 1946

QEVERIJA
DEMOKRAT.
E SHQIPERISE
22-X-1944
0 60
(**72**)

(**73**)

1945 (4 Jan). Nos. 353/8 and 360/2 surch as T **72** or with similar surch.

409	30q. on 3q. red-brown	8·25	16·00
410	40q. on 5q. green	8·25	16·00
411	50q. on 10q. brown	8·25	16·00
412	60q. on 15q. scarlet	8·25	16·00
413	80q. on 25q. bright blue (R.)	8·25	16·00
414	1f. on 30q. bright violet (R.)	8·25	16·00
415	2f. on 65q. brown-lake	8·25	16·00

416		3f. on 1f. blue-green	8·25	16·00
417		5f. on 2f. lake	8·25	16·00
409/417 *Set of 9*			65·00	£130

On Nos. 416/17 the second word is spelt in full: "DEMOKRATIKE".

1945 (10 July). 2nd Anniv of Formation of People's Army. Surch as T **73**. Star in red.

418	**49**	30q. on 1q. slate	5·50	7·75
419		60q. on 1q. slate	5·50	7·75
420		80q. on 1q. slate	5·50	7·75
421		1f. on 1q. slate	11·00	16·00
422		2f. on 2q. vermilion	13·00	18·00
423		3f. on 50q. blue-green	27·00	33·00
424	**51**	5f. on 2f. slate-blue	33·00	50·00
418/424 *Set of 7*			90·00	£130

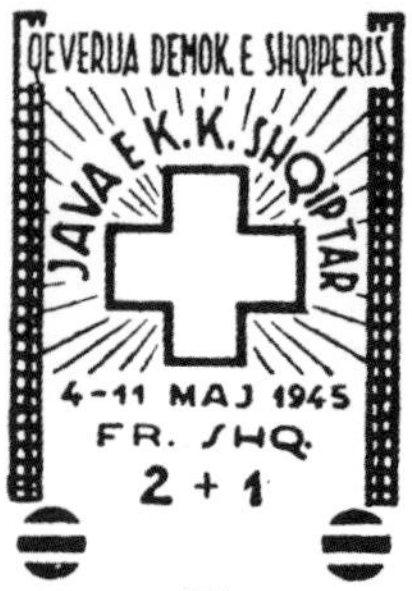

(**74**)

75 Labinot

1945 (4 May). Red Cross Week. Surch as T **74**, in carmine.

425	**69**	30q. +15q. on 5q.+5q. green	11·00	16·00
426		50q. +25q. on 10q.+10q. olive-brown	11·00	16·00
427		1f. +50q. on 15q.+10q. carmine	27·00	33·00
428		2f. +1f. on 25q.+15q. blue	38·00	47·00
425/428 *Set of 4*			80·00	£100

1945 (28 Nov). Horiz designs as T **75**. Typo. P 11½.

429	**75**	20q. blue-green	75	1·80
430		30q. orange	1·10	2·50
431	–	40q. brown	1·10	2·50
432	–	60q. claret	1·60	3·75
433	–	1f. rose-red	3·75	7·75
434	–	3f. blue	27·00	31·00
429/434 *Set of 6*			32·00	44·00

Designs:—40q. 60q. Bridge at Berat; 1f., 3f. Permet landscape.

Most stamps of this issue on the market are forgeries which can be recognised as they are lithographed and perf 11.

ASAMBLEJA
KUSHTETUESE

10 KALLNUER 1946

(**76**)

1946 (10 Jan). Constitutional Assembly. Nos. 429/34 optd with T **76**.

435	**75**	20q. blue-green	1·60	2·10
436		30q. orange	2·20	2·50
437	–	40q. brown	2·75	3·25
438	–	60q. claret	4·25	5·25
439	–	1f. rose-red	16·00	19·00
440	–	3f. blue	27·00	31·00
435/440 *Set of 6*			48·00	55·00

Lithographed forgeries exist of this and of Nos. 446/57.

XII. People's Republic

11 January 1946–29 April 1991

77 Globe, Dove and Olive branch

REPUBLIKA POPULLORE
E
SHQIPËRISË

(**77a**)

1946 (8 Mar). International Women's Congress. Typo.

A. P 11½

441A	**77**	20q. mauve and red	55	1·60
442A		40q. lilac and red	1·10	2·10
443A		50q. violet and red	2·20	3·25
444A		1f. blue and red	4·25	6·25
445A		2f. deep blue and red	5·50	10·50
441A/445 *Set of 5*			12·00	21·00

B. Imperf

441B	**77**	20q. mauve and red	55	1·60
442B		40q. lilac and red	1·10	2·10
443B		50q. violet and red	2·20	3·25
444B		1f. blue and red	4·25	6·25
445B		2f. deep blue and red	5·50	10·50
441B/445 *Set of 5*			12·00	21·00

1946 (1 July). Proclamation of Albanian People's Republic. Nos. 429/34 optd with T **77a**.

446	**75**	20q. blue-green	1·50	1·60
447		30q. orange	1·70	2·10
448	–	40q. brown	3·00	4·25
449	–	60q. claret	6·00	7·75
450	–	1f. rose-red	16·00	21·00
451	–	3f. blue	27·00	31·00
446/451 *Set of 6*			50·00	60·00

Nos. 446/57 were overprinted on a new printing of Nos. 429/34, with slightly different shades and ribbed gum.

KONGRESI
K.K.SH.
24-25-11-46
+0.15

(**78**)

79 Athletes

1946 (16 July). Albanian Red Cross Congress. Nos. 429/34 surch as T **78**. Cross in red.

452	**75**	20q. +10q. blue-green	24·00	37·00
453		30q. +15q. orange	24·00	37·00
454	–	40q. +20q. brown	24·00	37·00
455	–	60q. +30q. claret	24·00	37·00
456	–	1f. +50q. rose-red	24·00	37·00
457	–	3f. +1f.50 blue	24·00	37·00
452/457 *Set of 6*			£130	£200

1946 (6 Oct). Balkan Games, Tirana. Litho. P 11½.

458	**79**	1q. blackish green	16·00	12·50
459		2q. light green	16·00	12·50
460		5q. brown	16·00	12·50
461		10q. rose-red	16·00	12·50
462		20q. blue	16·00	12·50
463		40q. lilac	16·00	12·50
464		1f. orange	38·00	37·00
458/464 *Set of 7*			£120	£100

80 Qemal Stafa

81 Railway Construction

1947 (5 May). Fifth Death Anniv of Qemal Stafa (Communist activist). Litho. P 13×11½.

465	**80**	20q. brown and yellow-brown	13·00	16·00
466		28q. deep blue and blue	13·00	16·00
467		40q. deep brown and brown	13·00	16·00
465/467 *Set of 3*			35·00	43·00
MS467*a* 180×210 mm. Nos. 465/7. Imperf. No gum			£110	£130

1947 (16 May). Durrës–Elbasan Railway. Litho. P 11½×12.

468	**81**	1q. black and drab	5·50	1·80
469		4q. deep green and green	5·50	1·80
		a. Perf 13×12½		
470		10q. black-brown and light brown	5·75	2·10
471		15q. brown-lake and rose-red	5·75	2·10
472		20q. blue-black and slate-blue	13·00	2·50
		a. Perf 13×12½		
473		28q. deep blue and light blue	18·00	3·25
		a. Perf 13×12½		
474		40q. maroon and deep reddish purple	35·00	19·00
		a. Perf 13×12½		
475		68q. deep brown & red-brown (p 13×12½)	43·00	31·00
468/475 *Set of 8*			£120	55·00

The 1q. is inscribed "REPUBLIKA ROPULLORE" (instead of "POPULLORE"); the other values were similarly inscribed but the leg of the "R" has been erased, although still visible on some values, to form a "P".

82 Partisans

83 Enver Hoxha and Vasil Shanto

1947 (10 July). 4th Anniv of Formation of People's Army. Designs dated "1943–1947". Litho. P 11½.

476	**82**	16q. brown and orange-brown	9·75	10·50
477	**83**	20q. deep brown and brown	9·75	10·50
478	–	28q. deep blue and blue	9·75	10·50
479	–	40q. brown and mauve	9·75	10·50
476/479 *Set of 4*			35·00	38·00

Designs. Horiz—28q. Infantry column. Vert—40q. Portrait of Vojo Kushi.

New Currency

84 Ruined Conference Building

85 War Invalids

1947 (16 Sept). Fifth Anniv of Peza Conference. Litho. P 11½.

480	**84**	2l. purple and mauve	7·00	7·75
481		2l.50 deep blue and blue	7·00	7·75

1947 (17 Nov). 1st Congress of War Invalids. Photo. P 12½×11½.

482	**85**	1l. red	16·00	16·00

86 Peasants

87 Burning Village

1947 (17 Nov). Agrarian Reform. Various designs as T **86** inscr REFORMA AGRARE. Photo. P 11½×12½ (horiz) or 12½×11½ (vert).

483		1l.50 purple	9·75	10·50
484		2l. brown	9·75	10·50
485		2l.50 grey-blue	9·75	10·50
486		3l. rose-red	9·75	10·50
483/486 *Set of 4*			35·00	38·00

Designs: Horiz—2l. Banquet; 2l.50, Peasants rejoicing. Vert—3l. Soldier being chaired.

1947 (29 Nov). 3rd Anniv of the Liberation. Noriz designs as T **87**, inscr "29–XI–1944–1947". Photo. P 11½×12½.

487		1l.50 red	5·50	5·25
488		2l.50 maroon	5·50	5·25
489		5l. ultramarine and pale blue	11·00	8·25
490		8l. mauve	16·00	12·50
491		12l. brown	27·00	21·00
487/491 *Set of 5*			60·00	47·00

Designs:—2l.50, Riflemen; 5l. Machine-gunners; 8l. Mounted soldier; 12l. Infantry column.

Lek 0,50

(**87a**)

88 Railway Construction

1948 (22 Feb). Nos. 446/51 surch in "Lek", as T **87a**.

492		0l.50 on 30q. orange	55	75
		a. "Lck" for "Lek"		
493		1l. on 20q. blue-green	1·10	1·30
494		2l.50 on 60q. claret	2·75	3·75
495		3l. on 1f. rose-red	3·75	4·75
496		5l. on 3f. blue	8·25	7·75
497		12l. on 40q. brown	22·00	21·00
492/497 *Set of 6*			35·00	35·00

(Litho State Ptg Works, Belgrade)

1948 (1 June). Durrës–Tirana Railway. P 11½.

498	**88**	0l.50 claret and crimson	2·75	1·60
499		1l. green and greenish black	3·00	1·80
500		1l.50 rose and scarlet	4·50	2·50
501		2l.50 pale brown and brown	6·50	3·25
502		5l. light blue and blue	11·00	6·25
503		8l. orange-red and brown	18·00	10·50
504		12l. reddish purple and purple	22·00	12·50
505		20l. grey and black	43·00	26·00
498/505 *Set of 8*			£100	60·00

89 Parade of Infantrymen

90 Labourer, Globe and Flag

(Litho Belgrade)

1948 (10 July). Fifth Anniv of People's Army. T **89** and similar type inscr "10 KORRIK 1943–10 KORRIK 1948". P 11½.

506	**89**	2l.50 reddish brown	5·50	5·25
507		5l. blue	7·50	7·25
508	–	8l. slate (Troops in action)	14·00	10·50
506/508 *Set of 3*			24·00	21·00

(Photo State Ptg Wks, Budapest)

1949 (1 May). Labour Day. P 12½×12.

509	**90**	2l.50 sepia	1·60	2·50
510		5l. blue	3·25	4·25
511		8l. brown-purple	6·00	6·75
509/511 *Set of 3*			9·75	12·00

91 Soldier and Map

92 Albanian and Kremlin Tower

93 General Enver Hoxha

(T **91/2**, Photo Budapest)

1949 (10 July). Sixth Anniv of People's Army. P 12½×12.

512	**91**	2l.50 brown	1·60	2·50
513		5l. blue	3·25	4·25
514		8l. brown-orange	6·00	7·75
512/514 *Set of 3*			9·75	13·00

1949 (10 Sept). Albanian–Soviet Amity. P 12½×12.

515	**92**	2l.50 brown	1·60	2·50
516		5l. blue	3·75	5·25

(Eng J. Schmidt. Recess State Ptg Wks, Prague)

1949 (16 Oct). P 12½.

517		0l.50 reddish violet	35	10
518		1l. blue-green	40	10
519		1l.50 rose-carmine	55	10
520		2l.50 brown	1·10	15
521		5l. ultramarine	2·20	1·00
522		8l. brown-purple	4·25	3·25
523		12l. bright purple	11·50	5·75
524		20l. grey-blue	13·50	7·25
517/524 *Set of* 8			30·00	16·00

94 Soldier and Flag

95 Street Fighting

96 Joseph Stalin

(T **94/8**, Photo Prague)

1949 (29 Nov). Fifth Anniv of Liberation. P 12×12½ (horiz), 12½×12 (vert).

525	**94**	2l.50 brown	1·10	1·60
526	**95**	3l. brown-red	1·10	3·25
527	**94**	5l. violet	3·25	4·25
528	**95**	8l. black	6·50	7·75
525/528 *Set of* 4			11·00	15·00

1949 (21 Dec). 70th Birthday of Joseph Stalin. P 12½×12.

529	**96**	2l.50 yellow-brown	1·10	2·10
530		5l. blue	2·75	3·75
531		8l. lake	7·00	9·00
529/531 *Set of* 3			9·75	13·00

97

98 Sami Frasheri

1950 (1 July). 75th Anniv of Universal Postal Union. P 12×12½.

532	**97**	5l. blue	3·00	6·75
533		8l. purple	5·50	9·50
534		12l. black	11·00	18·00
532/534 *Set of* 3			18·00	31·00

1950 (5 Nov). Literary Jubilee. T **98** and portraits inscr "1950–JUBILEU I SHKRIMTAREVE TE RILINDJES". P 14.

535		2l. blue-green	1·60	1·60
536		2l.50 brown (A. Zako (Cajupi))	2·20	2·50
537		3l. brown-red (N. Frasheri)	4·25	5·25
538		5l. blue (K. Kristoforidhi)	5·50	6·25
535/538 *Set of* 4			12·00	14·00

99 Vuno-Himarë

100 Stafa and Shanto

(Eng B. Housa (0l.50, 5l.), J. Schmidt (2, 20l.), B. Roule (1, 10l.).Recess Prague)

1950 (15 Dec). AIR. Horiz designs as T **99**. P 12½.

539	**99**	0l.50 black	1·00	1·00
540	–	1l. brown-purple	1·00	1·00
541	–	2l. blue	1·70	2·10
542	**99**	5l. blue-green	6·00	5·75
543	–	10l. greenish blue	14·00	10·50
544	–	20l. violet	27·00	16·00
539/544 *Set of* 6			46·00	33·00

Designs: Douglas DC-3 airplane over—1l., 10l. Rozafat-Shkodër; 2l., 20l. Kështjellë-Butrinto.

(Des S. Toptani. Photo Budapest)

1950 (25 Dec). Albanian Patriots. Portraits as T **100** inscr "LAVDI HERONJVE TE POPULLIT". P 14.

545		2l. green	1·40	1·30
546		2l.50 violet	1·60	1·60
547		3l. scarlet	3·25	3·25
548		5l. blue	5·50	5·25
549		8l. brown	11·00	10·50
545/549 *Set of* 5			20·00	20·00

Portraits:—2l. Ahmet Haxhia, Hydajet Lezha, Naim Gjylbegu, Ndoc Mazi and Ndoc Deda; 2l.50, Asim Zeneli, Ali Demi, Kajo Karafili, Dervish Hekali and Asim Vokshi; 3l. Abaz Shehu, Bama Faja, Zoja Çure, Mustafa Matohiti and Gjok Doçi; 5l. Perlat Rexhepi, Koci Bako, Vojo Kushi, Reshit Çollaku and Misto Mame.

101 Arms and Flags

102 Skanderbeg

(Des and eng S. Toptani. Recess Budapest)

1951 (11 Jan). Fifth Anniv of Republic. P 14.

550	**101**	2l.50 carmine	2·20	3·25
551		5l. blue	4·25	6·25
552		8l. black	7·00	9·50
550/552 *Set of* 3			12·00	17·00

(Recess Budapest)

1951 (1 Mar). 483rd Anniv of Death of Skanderbeg (patriot). P 14.

553	**102**	2l.50 brown	2·20	2·50
554		5l. violet	4·25	5·25
555		8l. bistre	7·00	7·75
553/555 *Set of* 3			12·00	14·00

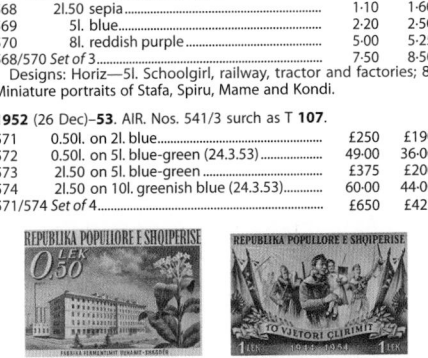

103 General Enver Hoxha and Assembly

(Photo Budapest)

1951 (24 May). Seventh Anniv of Permet Congress. P 12.

556	**103**	2l.50 brown	1·10	1·60
557		3l. carmine-lake	1·20	2·10
558		5l. blue	2·75	3·75
559		8l. mauve	5·00	6·25
556/559 *Set of* 4			9·00	12·50

104 Child and Globe

105 Enver Hoxha and Meeting-house

(Des S. Toptani. Photo Budapest)

1951 (1 June). International Children's Day. T **104** and horiz type inscr "DITA NDERKOMBETARE E FEMIJES". P 12.

560	**104**	2l. green	2·75	2·10
561	–	2l.50 brown	3·75	2·50
562	–	3l. scarlet	5·00	3·25
563	**104**	5l. blue	7·50	3·75
560/563 *Set of* 4			17·00	10·50

Design:—2l.50, 3l. Nurse weighing baby.

(T **105/6**, Photo Budapest)

1951 (8 Nov). Tenth Anniv of Foundation of Albanian Communist Party. P 14.

564	**105**	2l.50 yellow-brown	65	1·00
565		3l. brown-lake	75	1·40
566		5l. deep blue	1·70	2·10
567		8l. grey-black	3·25	3·50
564/567 *Set of* 4			5·75	7·25

106 Young Partisans

(107)

1951 (23 Nov). Tenth Anniv of Albanian Young Communists' Union. T **106** and similar types inscr "1941–1951". P 12.

568		2l.50 sepia	1·10	1·60
569		5l. blue	2·20	2·50
570		8l. reddish purple	5·00	5·25
568/570 *Set of* 3			7·50	8·50

Designs: Horiz—5l. Schoolgirl, railway, tractor and factories; 8l. Miniature portraits of Stafa, Spiru, Mame and Kondi.

1952 (26 Dec)–**53**. AIR. Nos. 541/3 surch as T **107**.

571		0.50l. on 2l. blue	£250	£190
572		0.50l. on 5l. blue-green (24.3.53)	49·00	36·00
573		2l.50 on 5l. blue-green	£375	£200
574		2l.50 on 10l. greenish blue (24.3.53)	60·00	44·00
571/574 *Set of* 4			£650	£425

108 Factory

109 Soldiers and Flags

(Photo Budapest)

1953 (1 Aug). Various designs as T **108**. P 12.

575		0l.50 Venetian red	80	10
576		1l. deep green	1·10	20
577		2l.50 sepia	1·50	50
578		3l. brown-carmine	1·90	75
579		5l. blue	3·25	1·30
580		8l. deep olive	3·75	1·60
581		12l. reddish purple	5·75	2·10
582		20l. indigo	11·00	4·75
575/582 *Set of* 8			26·00	10·00

Designs: Horiz—1l. Canal; 2l.50, Girl and cotton mill; 3l. Girl and sugar factory; 5l. Film studio; 8l. Textile worker and machinery; 20l. Hydro-electric dam. Vert—12l. Pylon and hydro-electric station.

1954 (29 Nov). Tenth Anniv of Liberation. Photo. P 12½×12.

583	**109**	0l.50 deep lilac	20	15
584		1l. yellow-green	70	50
585		2l.50 yellow-brown	1·10	1·00
586		3l. carmine	2·20	2·10
587		5l. indigo	3·25	3·25
588		8l. brown-purple	6·50	6·25
583/588 *Set of* 6			12·50	12·00

110 First Albanian School

111

(Photo Budapest)

1956 (23 Feb). 70th Anniv of Albanian Schools. T **110** and another horiz design inscr "1886 1956". P 12×12½.

589	**110**	2l. reddish purple	55	50
590	–	2l.50 dull green	90	1·00
591	–	5l. blue	2·00	2·10
592	**110**	10l. turquoise-blue	6·50	3·75
589/592 *Set of* 4			9·00	6·50

Design:—2l.50, 5l. Portraits of P. Sotiri, P. N. Luarasi and N. Naci.

(Recess Prague)

1957 (1 June). 15th Anniv of Albanian Workers' Party. T **111** and similar horiz designs inscr "VJETORI I THEME-LIMIT P. P SH. 1941 1956". P 11½.

593		2l.50 brown	80	50
594		5l. violet-blue	1·70	75
595		8l. reddish purple	3·00	3·00
593/595 *Set of* 3			5·00	3·75

Designs:—5l. Party headquarters, Tirana; 8l. Marx and Lenin.

112 Congress Emblem

113 Lenin and Cruiser *Aurora*

(Des S. I. Murati. Recess Prague)

1957 (4 Oct). Fourth World Trade Unions Congress, Leipzig. P 12×11½.

596	**112**	2l.50 dull slate-purple	60	20
597		3l. rose-red	65	50
598		5l. blue	75	75
599		8l. deep green	2·75	2·40
596/599 *Set of* 4			4·25	3·50

(Des S. Toptani. Photo State Ptg Wks, Tirana)

1957 (7 Nov). 40th Anniv of Russian Revolution. P 10½.

600	**113**	2l.50 chocolate	85	50
601		5l. deep violet-blue	1·60	1·60
602		8l. olive-black	2·10	1·80
600/602 *Set of* 3			4·00	3·50

PRINTERS. The following issues were printed at the State Printing Works, Tirana by lithography, *unless otherwise stated*.

114 Raising the Flag

115 N. Veqilharxhi

116 L. Gurakuqi

(T **114/16** des S. Toptani)

1957 (28 Nov). 45th Anniv of Proclamation of Independence. P 10½.

603	**114**	1l.50 reddish purple	80	30
604		2l.50 bistre-brown	1·40	50
605		5l. blue	1·80	1·60
606		8l. green	4·25	2·10
603/606 *Set of* 4			7·50	4·00

1958 (1 Feb). 160th Birth Anniv of Veqilharxhi (patriot). P 10½.

607	**115**	2l.50 deep brown	80	30
608		5l. deep violet-blue	1·60	50
609		8l. reddish purple	3·25	1·60
607/609 *Set of* 3			5·00	2·20

1958 (15 Apr). Removal of Ashes of Gurakuqi (patriot). P 10½.

610	**116**	1l.50 slate-green	35	20
611		2l.50 deep brown	55	40
612		5l. blue	70	50
613		8l. blackish brown	3·25	1·40
610/613 *Set of* 4			4·25	2·30

117 Freedom Fighters

118 Soldiers in Action

(T **117/18** des S. Toptani)

1958 (1 July). 50th Anniv of Battle of Mashkullore. T **117** and similar vert design. P 10½.

614	**117**	2l.50 brown-ochre	70	20
615	–	3l. green	70	80
616	**117**	5l. Prussian blue	1·60	1·20
617	–	8l. chestnut	2·75	1·60

614/617 *Set of* 4 5·25 2·50
Design:—3l., 8l. Tree and buildings.

1958 (10 July). 15th Anniv of Albanian People's Army. T **118** and similar horiz design. P 10½.
618 **118** 1l.50 blue-green 45 20
619 – 2l.50 chocolate 65 25
620 **118** 8l. rose-carmine 1·60 1·40
621 – 11l. pale blue 2·50 2·30
618/621 *Set of* 4 4·75 3·75
Design:—2l.50, 11l. Tank-driver, sailor, infantryman and tanks.

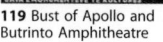

119 Bust of Apollo and Butrinto Amphitheatre

120 F. Joliot-Curie and Council Emblem

1959 (25 Jan). Cultural Monuments Week. P 10½.
622 **119** 2l.50 chocolate 80 30
623 6l.50 turquoise-green 3·25 1·30
624 11l. blue 4·25 2·10
622/624 *Set of* 3 7·50 3·25

1959 (1 July). Tenth Anniv of World Peace Council. P 10½.
625 **120** 1l.50 rose-carmine 2·20 50
626 2l.50 reddish violet 5·00 1·60
627 11l. blue 11·50 5·25
625/627 *Set of* 3 17·00 6·50

121 Basketball

122 Soldier

123 Mother and Child

1959 (20 Nov). First National Spartacist Games. T **121** and similar vert designs inscr "SPARTAKIADA 1959" etc. P 10½.
628 1l.50 reddish violet 1·10 25
629 2l.50 emerald 1·20 30
630 5l. carmine 2·20 1·00
631 11l. ultramarine 6·50 3·75
628/631 *Set of* 4 10·00 4·75
Designs:—2l.50, Football; 5l. Running; 11l. Runners with torches.

1959 (29 Nov). 15th Anniv of Liberation. T **122** and similar vert designs inscr "1944–1959". P 10½.
632 1l.50 rose-carmine 1·20 25
633 2l.50 red-brown 1·60 35
634 3l. blue-green 2·20 45
635 6l.50 red 4·75 4·00
632/635 *Set of* 4 8·75 4·50
MS635*a* 141×96 mm. Nos. 632/5 but in rose-carmine. Imperf 11·00 16·00
Designs:—2l.50, Security guard; 3l. Harvester; 6l.50, Laboratory workers.

1959 (5 Dec). Tenth Anniv of Declaration of Human Rights. P 10½.
636 **123** 5l. greenish blue 6·25 3·25
MS636*a* 72×65 mm. No. 636. Imperf 7·50 11·50

124

125 Congress Building

126 A. Moisiu

1960 (8 Mar). 50th Anniv of International Women's Day. P 10½.
637 **124** 2l.50 chocolate 1·10 50
638 11l. claret 4·25 1·60

1960 (25 Mar). 40th Anniv of Lushnjë Congress. P 10½.
639 **125** 2l.50 bistre-brown 55 30
640 7l.50 Prussian blue 1·60 1·00

1960 (20 Apr). 80th Birth Anniv of Moisiu (actor). P 10½.
641 **126** 3l. chocolate 70 50
642 11l. deep bluish green 2·40 1·00

127 Lenin

128 Vaso Pasha

129 Frontier Guard

1960 (22 Apr). 90th Birth Anniv of Lenin. P 10½.
643 **127** 4l. deep turquoise-blue 1·90 1·00
644 11l. crimson 6·00 5·25

1960 (5 May). 80th Anniv of Albanian Alphabet Study Association. T **128** and similar vert designs. P 10½.
645 1l. deep olive 55 20
646 1l.50 brown 1·00 25
647 6l.50 blue 2·10 85
648 11l. red 5·50 2·10
645/648 *Set of* 4 8·25 3·00
Designs:—1l.50, Jani Vreto; 6l.50, Sami Frasheri; 11l. Association statutes.

1960 (12 May). 15th Anniv of Frontier Force. P 10½.
649 **129** 1l.50 cerise 55 30
650 11l. greenish blue 3·25 1·50

130 Family with Policeman

131 Normal School, Elbasan

132 Soldier and Cannon

1960 (14 May). 15th Anniv of People's Police. P 10½.
651 **130** 1l.50 green 55 25
652 8l.50 brown 3·25 1·60

1960 (30 May). 50th Anniv of Normal School, Elbasan. P 10½.
653 **131** 5l. bluish green 2·75 1·60
654 6l.50 purple 2·75 1·60

1960 (2 Aug). 40th Anniv of Battle of Vlórë. P 10½.
655 **132** 1l.50 sepia 75 50
656 2l.50 brown-purple 1·20 75
657 5l. deep blue 2·75 1·00
655/657 *Set of* 3 4·25 2·00

133 Tirana Clock Tower, Kremlin and Tupolev Tu-104A Jetliner

134 Federation Emblem

135 Ali Kelmendi

1960 (18 Aug). 2nd Anniv of Tirana–Moscow Jet Air Service. P 10½.
658 **133** 1l. brown 1·10 80
659 7l.50 greenish blue 4·00 4·25
660 11l.50 deep grey 6·50 7·25
658/660 *Set of* 3 10·50 11·00

1960 (10 Nov). 15th Anniv of World Democratic Youth Federation. P 10½.
661 **134** 1l.50 ultramarine 65 30
662 8l.50 scarlet 2·20 1·00

1960 (5 Dec). 60th Birth Anniv of Ali Kelmendi (Communist). P 10½.
663 **135** 1l.50 olive 55 30
664 11l. maroon 2·20 1·00

136 Flags of Albania and Russia, and Clasped Hands

137 Marx and Lenin

138 Malsi e Madhe (Shkodër) Costume

1961 (10 Jan). 15th Anniv of Albanian–Soviet Friendship Society. P 10½.
665 **136** 2l. violet 55 30
666 8l. brown-purple 2·20 1·00

1961 (13 Feb). Fourth Albanian Workers' Party Congress. P 10½.
667 **137** 2l. rose-red 55 30
668 8l. ultramarine 2·20 1·00

1961 (28 Apr). Provincial Costumes. T **138** and similar vert designs. P 10½.
669 1l. black 1·10 50
670 1l.50 brown-purple 1·40 75
671 6l.50 bright blue 4·25 1·90
672 11l. scarlet 6·50 4·75
669/672 *Set of* 4 12·00 7·00
Costumes:—1l.50, Malsi e Madhe (Shkoder) (female); 6l.50, Lume; 11l. Mirdite.

139 European Otter

140 Dalmatian Pelicans

1961 (25 June). Albanian Fauna. T **139** and similar horiz designs. P 10½.
673 2l.50 grey-blue 4·00 1·00
674 6l.50 deep bluish green (Eurasian badger) 8·00 2·40
675 11l. chocolate (Brown bear) 16·00 8·25
673/675 *Set of* 3 25·00 10·50

1961 (30 Sept). Birds. T **140** and similar vert designs. P 14.
676 7l.50 carmine/*pink* 5·75 1·00
677 7l.50 violet/*blue* (Grey heron) 7·00 3·25
678 11l. red-brown/*pink* (Little egret) 9·75 3·75
676/678 *Set of* 3 20·00 7·25

141 Cyclamen

142 M. G. Nikolla

143 Lenin and Marx on Flag

1961 (27 Oct). Albanian Flowers. T **141** and similar vert designs. P 14.
679 1l.50 bright purple and greenish blue 2·20 50
680 8l. orange and bright reddish purple (Forsythia) 6·00 2·50
681 11l. carmine and blue-green (Lily) 7·50 3·25
679/681 *Set of* 3 14·00 5·75

1961 (30 Oct). 50th Birthday of Nikolla (poet). P 14.
682 **142** 0l.50 chocolate 65 30
683 8l.50 slate-green 2·20 1·60

1961 (8 Nov). 20th Anniv of Albanian Workers Party. P 14.
684 **143** 2l.50 red 65 30
685 7l.50 purple-brown 2·00 1·30

144

145 Yuri Gagarin and "Vostok 1"

POSTA AJRORE
(**146**)

1961 (23 Nov). 20th Anniv of Albanian Young Communists' Union. P 14.
686 **144** 2l.50 ultramarine 65 30
a. Perf 10½
687 7l.50 dull magenta 2·20 1·30

IMPERFORATE STAMPS. Many Albanian stamps and miniature sheets from No. 696 onwards exist imperforate and/or in different colours from limited printings.

1962 (15 Feb). World's First Manned Space Flight. P 14.

(a) POSTAGE
688 **145** 0l.50 blue 1·10 1·60
689 4l. bright purple 4·25 4·75
690 11l. deep grey-green 11·00 11·50

(b) AIR. Nos. 688/90 optd with T **146** in red and printed on toned paper
691 **145** 0l.50 blue/*cream* 38·00 50·00
a. Ovpt in black £110 £180
692 4l. bright purple/*cream* 38·00 50·00
a. Ovpt in black £110 £180
693 11l. deep grey-green/*cream* 38·00 50·00
a. Ovpt in black £110 £180
688/693 *Set of* 6 £120 £150

147 P. N. Luarasi

148 Campaign Emblem

149 Camomile

1962 (28 Feb). 50th Death Anniv of Petro N. Luarasi (patriot). P 14.
694 **147** 0l.50 greenish blue 55 30
695 8l.50 olive-brown 4·25 1·60

1962 (30 Apr). Malaria Eradication. P 14.
696 **148** 1l.50 blue-green 35 15
697 2l.50 brown-red 55 30
698 10l. bright purple 1·10 80
699 11l. greenish blue 1·40 1·00
696/699 *Set of* 4 3·00 2·00
MS699*a* 90×106 mm. Nos. 696/9 38·00 38·00

1962 (10 May). Medicinal Plants. T **149** and similar vert designs. P 14.
700 0l.50 yellow, green and blue 55 30
701 8l. green, yellow and grey 2·20 1·20
702 11l.50 violet, green and ochre 3·75 1·60
700/702 *Set of* 3 5·75 2·75
Designs:—8l. Silver linden; 11l.50, Sage.

150 Throwing the Javelin

151 "Sputnik 1" in orbit

1962 (31 May). Olympic Games, Tokyo (1964) (1st issue). T **150** and similar designs inscr "TOKIO 1964". P 14.
703 0l.50 black and light greenish blue 20 10
704 2l.50 sepia and light brown 40 15
705 3l. black and blue 55 20
706 9l. deep purple and reddish purple 2·20 1·00

707	10l. black and greyish olive	2·40	1·60
703/707 *Set of 5*		5·25	2·75
MS707*a* 81×63 mm. 15l. (as 3l.)		38·00	50·00

Designs: Vert—0l.50, Diving; 2l.50, Pole-vaulting; 10l. Putting the shot. Horiz—3l. Olympic flame.

See also Nos. 754/**MS**758*a*, 818/**MS**821*a* and 842/**MS**851*a*.

1962 (28 June). Cosmic Flights. T **151** and similar vert designs. P 14.

708	0l.50 yellow-orange and bluish violet	65	50
709	1l. brown and deep bluish green	1·10	85
710	1l.50 red and yellow	1·60	1·00
711	20l. blue and reddish purple	11·00	4·25
708/711 *Set of 4*		13·00	6·00
MS711*a* 101×76 mm. 14l. (+6l.) brown and blue (Rocket)		65·00	80·00

Designs:—1l. Dog "Laika" and "Sputnik 2"; 1l.50, Artificial satellite and Sun; 20l. "Lunik 3" photographing Moon.

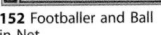

152 Footballer and Ball in Net

153 "Europa" and Albania Maps

1962 (3 July). World Football Championships, Chile. T **152** and similar horiz designs. P 14.

712	**152**	1l. violet and orange	55	30
713	–	2l.50 turquoise-blue and light green	1·60	85
714	**152**	6l.50 bright purple and yellow-brown	2·20	1·00
715	–	15l. brown-purple and turquoise-green	3·25	2·10
712/715 *Set of 4*			6·75	3·75
MS715*a* 82×66 mm. 20l. red-brown and green (as 713 but larger). P 14			50·00	80·00

Design:—2l.50, 15l. As T **152** but with Globe in place of ball in net.

1962 (Aug). Tourist Publicity. T **153** and similar vert design. P 14.

716	**153**	0l.50 red, yellow and blue-green	55	1·00
717	–	1l. red, deep purple and bright blue	1·10	2·50
718	–	2l.50 red, purple and light blue	8·75	14·50
719	**153**	11l. red, yellow and grey	16·00	18·00
716/719 *Set of 4*			24·00	32·00
MS719*a* 82×63 mm. 7l. red, yellow and violet-grey (**153**), 8l. carmine and violet-grey (as 717). P 14			50·00	80·00

Design:—1l., 2l.50, Statue and map.

154 Dardhë Woman

155 Chamois

156 Golden Eagle

1962 (Sept). Costumes of Albania's Southern Region. Vert designs as T **154**. P 14.

720	0l.50 carmine-red, deep purple and blue	45	20
721	1l. purple-brown and orange-buff	55	40
722	2l.50 black, bluish violet and yellow-green	1·60	1·30
723	14l. brown-red, red-brown and light green	7·00	3·75
720/723 *Set of 4*		8·75	5·00

Costumes of:—1l. Devoll man; 2l.50, Lunxheri woman; 14l. Gjirokastër man.

1962 (24 Oct). Albanian Animals. T **155** and similar designs. P 14.

724	0l.50 deep purple and grey-green	55	40
725	1l. black and orange-yellow	2·20	1·00
726	1l.50 black and red-brown	2·75	1·60
727	15l. brown-red and light yellow-green	22·00	5·25
724/727 *Set of 4*		25·00	7·50
MS727*a* 72×89 mm. 20l. red-brown and yellow-green (as 727 but larger). P 14		£140	£180

Animals: Horiz—1l. Lynx; 1l.50, Wild boar. Vert—15l. Roe deer.

1962 (28 Dec). 50th Anniv of Independence. T **156** and similar vert designs. P 14.

728	1l. red-brown and red	80	30
729	3l. black and light brown	3·75	1·00
730	16l. black and magenta	7·50	3·75
728/730 *Set of 3*		11·00	4·50

Designs:—3l. Ismail Qemali; 16l. Golden eagle over "RPSH" fortress.

157 Revolutionaries

158 Henri Dunant and Globe

1963 (15 Jan). 45th Anniv of October Revolution. T **157** and similar vert design. P 14.

731	5l. slate-violet and yellow	1·30	75
732	10l. black & orge-red (Statue of Lenin)	3·00	1·90

1963 (25 Jan). Centenary of Red Cross. Cross in red. P 14.

733	**158**	1l.50 black and claret	70	30
734		2l.50 black and light blue	1·10	50
735		6l. black and yellow-green	2·20	1·00
736		10l. black and ochre-yellow	3·75	2·50
733/736 *Set of 4*			7·00	3·75

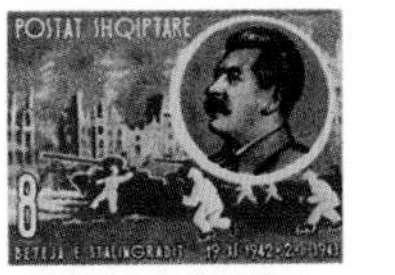

159 Stalin and Battle

160 Nikolaev and "Vostok 3"

1963 (2 Feb). 20th Anniv of Battle of Stalingrad. T **159** and similar horiz design. P 14.

(a) POSTAGE

737	8l. black and deep grey-green	11·00	4·25

(b) AIR. Inscr "AJRORE"

738	7l. crimson and deep green	11·00	4·25

Design:—7l. "Lenin" flag, map and tanks, etc.

1963 (28 Feb). First "Team" Manned Space Flights. T **160** and similar designs. P 14.

739	2l.50 purple-brown and ultramarine	65	40
740	7l.50 black and light blue	1·60	1·00
741	20l. purple-brown and violet	4·25	3·75
739/741 *Set of 3*		5·75	4·75
MS741*a* 88×73 mm. 25l. ultramarine and purple-brown (Popovich and Nikolaev)		45·00	45·00

Designs: Horiz—7l.50, "Vostoks 3 and 4" encircling Globe. Vert—20l. Popovich and "Vostok 4".

161 Crawling Cockchafer (*Polyphylla fullo*)

162 Policeman and Allegorical Figure

163 Great Crested Grebe (*Podiceps cristatus*)

1963 (20 Mar). Insects. T **161** and similar vert designs. P 14.

742	0l.50 brown and yellow-green	1·30	50
743	1l.50 red-brown and light blue	2·20	1·00
744	8l. blackish purple and red	9·25	2·50
745	10l. black and greenish yellow	12·00	3·75
742/745 *Set of 4*		22·00	7·00

Insects:—1l.50, Stag beetle (*Lucanus cervus*); 8l. *Procerus gigas* (ground beetle); 10l. *Cicindela albanica* (tiger beetle).

1963 (20 Mar). 20th Anniv of State Security Police. P 14.

746	**162**	2l.50 black, purple and carmine	1·10	80
747		7l.50 black, lake and vermilion	3·75	2·50

1963 (20 Apr). Birds. T **163** and similar vert designs. Multicoloured. P 14.

748	0l.50 Type **163**	1·60	40
749	3l. Golden eagle (*Aquila crysaetus*)	3·25	1·00
750	6l.50 Grey partridge (*Perdix perdix*)	8·25	1·70
751	11l. Capercaillie (*Tetrao urogallus*)	11·00	2·50
748/751 *Set of 4*		22·00	5·00

164 Official Insignia and Postmark of 1913

165 Boxing

1963 (5 May). 50th Anniv of First Albanian Stamps. T **164** and similar horiz design. P 14.

752	5l. brown, black, light blue and yellow	2·20	95
753	10l. green, black and carmine	3·75	2·10

Design:—10l. Albanian stamps of 1913, 1937 and 1962.

1963 (25 May). Olympic Games, Tokyo (1964) (2nd issue). T **165** and similar vert designs. P 12½×12.

754	2l. deep bluish green, red and yellow	70	1·00
755	3l. light brown, dp blue & orange-buff	90	2·10
756	5l. dull purple, lt brown & lt grey-blue	1·40	30
757	6l. black, grey and green	1·90	5·25
758	9l. blue and red-brown	3·75	8·25
754/758 *Set of 5*		7·75	15·00
MS758*a* 61×82 mm. 15l. multicoloured (Torch, rings and map). P 14		20·00	27·00

Designs:—3l. Basketball; 5l. Volleyball; 6l. Cycling; 9l. Gymnastics.

166 Gen. Enver Hoxha and Labinoti Council Building

167 Yuri Gagarin

1963 (10 July). 20th Anniv of Albanian People's Army. T **166** and similar horiz designs. P 12.

759	1l.50 yellow, black and red	55	30
760	2l.50 yellow-brown, chocolate and blue	1·10	65
761	5l. black, drab and blue-green	1·60	1·00
762	6l. blue, buff and red-brown	2·20	1·50
759/762 *Set of 4*		5·00	3·00

Designs:—2l.50, Soldier with weapons; 5l. Soldier attacking; 6l. Peacetime soldier.

1963 (30 July). Soviet Cosmonauts. T **167** and similar horiz designs. Portraits in yellow and brown. P 12.

763	3l. reddish violet	1·10	40
764	5l. dark blue (Titov)	1·30	50
765	7l. deep blue and grey (Nikolaev)	1·60	65
766	11l. deep blue and reddish-purple (Popovich)	3·25	1·00
767	14l. deep blue & blue-green (Bykovsky)	5·00	1·60
768	20l. blue (Tereshkova)	7·50	3·75
763/768 *Set of 6*		18·00	7·00

168 Volleyball (Rumania)

169 Celadon Swallowtail (*Papilio podulirius*)

1963 (31 Aug). European Sports Events, 1963 T **168** and similar horiz designs inscr "1963". P 12×12½.

769	2l. vermilion, black and yellow-olive	55	30
770	3l. bistre, black and carmine-red	85	50
771	5l. yellow-orange, black and green	1·10	85
772	7l. light green, black and rose-pink	1·60	1·30
773	8l. rose, black and blue	3·75	1·60
769/773 *Set of 5*		7·00	4·00

Designs:—3l. Weightlifting (Sweden); 5l. Football (European Cup); 7l. Boxing (Russia); 8l. Ladies' Rowing (Russia).

1963 (23 Sept). Butterflies and Moths. T **169** and similar vert designs. P 12×12½.

774	1l. black, pale greenish yellow and scarlet	65	25
775	2l. black, scarlet-vermilion and greenish blue	1·10	30
776	4l. black, greenish yellow and deep purple	2·20	1·00
777	5l. multicoloured	3·25	95
778	8l. black, scarlet and brown-ochre	5·50	2·10
779	10l. salmon, reddish brown and turquoise-blue	7·00	3·25
774/779 *Set of 6*		18·00	7·00

Designs:—2l. Jersey tiger moth (*Callimorpha hera*); 4l. Brimstone (*Gonepteryx rhamni*); 5l. Death's-head hawk moth (*Acherontia atropos*); 8l. Orange-tip (*Euchloe cardamines*); 10l. Peacock (*Vanessa io*).

170 Lunik 1

171 Food Processing Works

1963 (31 Oct). AIR. Cosmic Flights. T **170** and similar horiz designs. P 12.

780	2l. deep olive, yellow and orange	55	30
781	3l. vermilion, greenish yellow, mauve and deep bluish green	1·10	40
782	5l. dp olive, grnish yell, & reddish pur	1·60	65
783	8l. red, greenish yellow and slate-violet	2·75	1·20
784	12l. orange-red, orange and blue	5·50	3·75
780/784 *Set of 5*		10·50	5·75

Designs:—3l. Lunik 2; 5l. Lunik 3; 8l. Venus 1; 12l. Mars 1.

1963 (15 Nov). Industrial Buildings. T **171** and similar designs. P 14.

785	2l.50 rose-red/*pale pink*	1·10	50
786	20l. green/*pale green*	4·25	2·10
787	30l. reddish purple/*pale blue*	9·75	4·25
788	50l. yellow-brown/*pale cream*	11·00	5·25
785/788 *Set of 4*		23·00	11·00

Designs: Vert—20l. Naphtha refinery; 30l. Fruit-bottling plant. Horiz—50l. Copper-processing works.

172 Shield and Banner

173 Young Men of Three Races

1963 (24 Nov). First Army and Defence Aid Association Congress. P 12½×12.

789	**172**	2l. deep blue, red, ochre and turquoise-blue	75	30
790		8l. deep blue, red, ochre and light blue	2·20	1·60

1963 (10 Dec). 15th Anniv of Declaration of Human Rights. P 12.

791	**173**	3l. black and yellow-ochre	65	50
792		5l. blue and yellow-ochre	1·30	1·00
793		7l. violet and yellow-ochre	2·75	2·10
791/793 *Set of 3*			4·25	3·25

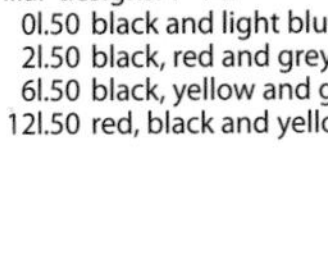

174 Bobsleighing

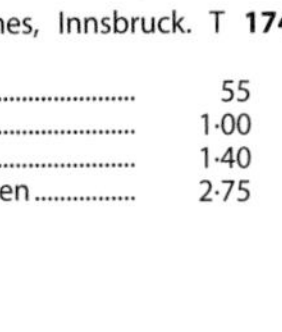

175 Lenin

1963 (25 Dec). Winter Olympic Games, Innsbruck. T **174** and similar designs. P 14.

794	0l.50 black and light blue	55	30
795	2l.50 black, red and grey	1·00	50
796	6l.50 black, yellow and grey	1·40	75
797	12l.50 red, black and yellow-green	2·75	2·10

794/797 *Set of 4* 5·25 3·25
MS797*a* 56×75 mm. 12l.50, black, grey-green and blue (Ski jumper) (49×31 mm) 35·00 50·00
Designs: Vert—2l.50, Skiing; 12l.50, Figure-skating. Horiz—6l.50, Ice-hockey.

1964 (21 Jan). 40th Death Anniv of Lenin. P 12½×12.
798 **175** 5l. deep olive and yellow-bistre 1·20 75
799 10l. deep olive and yellow-bistre 2·40 1·40

176 Hurdling

177 Sturgeon

1964 (21 Jan). GANEFO Games, Djakarta (1963). T **176** and similar designs. P 12½×12 (vert) or 12×12½ (horiz).
800 2l.50 ultramarine and lilac 55 30
801 3l. red-brown and green 1·10 50
802 6l.50 lake and blue 1·60 1·30
803 8l. ochre and light blue 2·75 2·10
800/803 *Set of 4* 5·50 3·75
Designs: Horiz—3l. Running; 6l.50, Rifleshooting. Vert—8l. Basketball.

1964 (26 Feb). Fishes. T **177** and similar horiz designs. Multicoloured. P 14.
804 0l.50 Type **177** 55 30
805 1l. Gilthead 1·10 40
806 1l.50 Striped mullet 1·60 50
807 2l.50 Carp 2·20 1·00
808 6l.50 Mackerel 3·25 2·10
809 10l. Salmon 5·50 3·25
804/809 *Set of 6* 13·00 6·75

178 Red Squirrel (*Sciurus vulgaris*)

179 Lighting Olympic Torch

1964 (28 Mar). Forest Animals. T **178** and similar horiz designs. Multicoloured. P 12½×12.
810 1l. Type **178** 55 25
811 1l.50 Beech marten (*Martes foina*) 85 30
812 2l. Red fox (*Canis vulpes*) 1·10 40
813 2l.50 East European hedgehog (*Erinaceus rumunicus*) 1·60 50
814 3l. Brown hare (*Lepus europaeus*) 2·20 75
815 5l. Golden jackal (*Canis aureus*) 2·75 85
816 7l. Wild cat (*Fells silvestris*) 4·25 95
817 8l. Wolf (*Canis lupus*) 5·50 1·30
810/817 *Set of 8* 17·00 4·75

1964 (18 May). Olympic Games, Tokyo (3rd issue). T **179** and similar vert designs. P 12×12½.
818 3l. greenish yellow, buff and yellow-green 55 75
819 5l. blue, violet and red 75 1·00
820 7l. light blue, blue and greenish yellow 1·10 1·60
821 10l. blue, violet, orange and black 1·60 2·50
818/821 *Set of 4* 3·50 5·25
MS821*a* 81×91 mm. 15l. buff, light blue and violet (as 820) (49×62 mm) 30·00 40·00
Designs:—5l. Torch and globes; 7l. Olympic Flag and Mt. Fuji; 10l. Olympic Stadium, Tokyo.

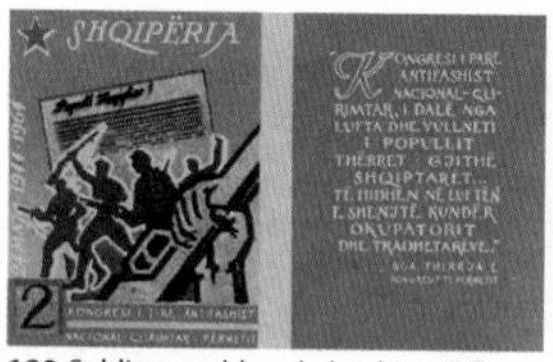

180 Soldiers and hand clutching Rifle, and Inscription

181 Revolutionaries with Flag

1964 (24 May). 20th Anniv of Permet Congress. T **180** and similar horiz designs. P 12½×12.
822 2l. sepia, red and orange-red 1·60 1·00
823 5l. black, red, yellow and light emerald 3·75 2·10
824 8l. black-purple, red and lake-red 8·25 6·25
822/824 *Set of 3* 12·00 8·50
Designs: (each with different inscription at right)—5l. Albanian Arms; 8l. Gen. Enver Hoxha.

1964 (10 June). 40th Anniv of Revolution. P 12½×12.
825 **181** 2l.50 black and red 55 30
826 7l.50 black and magenta 1·60 1·00

Rimini
25-VI-64
(182)

183 Full Moon

184 Winter Wren (*Troglodytes troglodytes*)

1964 (25 June). Verso Tokyo Stamp Exhibition, Rimini (Italy). No. 821 optd with T **182** in deep green.
827 10l. blue, violet, orange and black 8·75 8·75

1964 (27 June). Moon's Phases. T **183** and similar horiz designs. P 12×12½.
828 1l. yellow and reddish violet 55 20
829 5l. yellow and ultramarine 1·10 85
830 8l. yellow and blue 1·60 1·00
831 11l. yellow and deep bluish green 5·50 2·10
828/831 Set of 4 8·00 3·75
MS831*a* 67×78 mm. 15l. yellow and violet-blue (New Moon) (34×39 mm). P 12×imperf 27·00 35·00
Phases:—5l. Waxing Moon, 8l. Half-Moon, 11l. Waning Moon.

1964 (31 July). Albanian Birds. T **184** and similar vert designs. Multicoloured. P 12×12½.
832 0l.50 Type **184** 55 25
833 1l. Penduline tit (*Remiz pendulinus*) 1·10 30
834 2l.50 Green woodpecker (*Picus viridis*) 1·60 40
835 3l. Treecreeper (*Certhia familiaris*) 2·20 50
836 4l. European nuthatch (*Sitta europaea*). 2·75 1·00
837 5l. Great tit (*Parus major*) 3·25 1·30
838 6l. Goldfinch (*Carduelis garulus*) 3·75 1·60
839 18l. Golden oriole (*Oriolus oriolus*) 8·25 3·75
832/839 *Set of 8* 21·00 8·25

Riccione
23-8-1964
(185)

186 Running and Gymnastics

187 Chinese Republican Emblem

1964 (23 Aug). AIR. Riccione (Italy) Space Exhibition. Nos. 780, 783, optd with T **185** in violet.
840 2l. deep olive, yellow and orange 12·00 21·00
841 8l. red, greenish yellow and slate-violet 27·00 31·00

1964 (25 Sept). Olympic Games, Tokyo (4th issue). T **186** and similar vert designs. P 12×12½.
842 1l. red, light blue and light green 20 15
843 2l. yellow-brown, light blue and violet.. 25 20
844 3l. orange-brown, violet and yellow-olive 35 20
845 4l. yellow-olive, turquoise-green and ultramarine 55 30
846 5l. blue-green, reddish purple and carmine 85 50
847 6l. ultramarine, light blue and orange... 1·10 80
848 7l. yellow-green, orange and deep blue 1·30 85
849 8l. grey, light green and greenish yellow 1·40 95
850 9l. light blue, yellow and bright purple. 1·50 1·00
851 10l. yellow-brown, yellow-green and blue-green 1·70 1·60
842/851 *Set of 10* 8·25 6·00
MS851*a* 70×96 mm. 20l. violet and yellow- bistre (Winners on Dais) (40×67 mm) 25·00 30·00
Designs:—2l. Weightlifting and judo, 3l. Horse-jumping and cycling; 4l. Football and water-polo; 5l. Wrestling and boxing; 6l. Various sports and hockey; 7l. Swimming and yachting; 8l. Basketball and volleyball; 9l. Rowing and canoeing; 10l. Fencing and pistol-shooting.

1964 (1 Oct). 15th Anniv of Chinese People's Republic. T **187** and similar design. P 11½×12 (7l.) or 12×11½ (8l.).
852 7l. red, black and yellow 7·75 3·50
853 8l. black, red and yellow 7·75 4·75
Design: Horiz—8l. Mao Tse-tung.

188 Karl Marx

189 J. de Rada

1964 (5 Nov). Centenary of First International. T **188** and similar horiz designs. P 12.
854 2l. black, red and lavender 1·10 50
855 5l. greenish grey 2·75 1·60
856 8l. black, red and olive-yellow 5·50 2·10
854/856 *Set of 3* 8·50 3·75
Designs:—5l. St. Martin's Hall, London; 8l. F. Engels.

1964 (15 Nov). 150th Birth Anniv of Jeronim de Rada (poet). P 12½×12.
857 **189** 7l. green 1·60 1·00
858 8l. violet 2·75 1·60

190 Arms and Flag

191 Mercury

192 Chestnut

1964 (29 Nov). 20th Anniv of Liberation. T **190** and similar designs. P 12 (vert) or 12×11½ (horiz).
859 1l. black, orange-red, yellow and magenta 55 40
860 2l. ultramarine, red and yellow 1·10 85
861 3l. brown-purple, red and yellow 1·60 1·30
862 4l. deep bluish green, red and yellow.... 2·20 1·70
863 10l. black, red and blue 5·50 4·25
859/863 *Set of 5* 9·75 7·75
Designs: Horiz—2l. Industrial scene; 3l. Agricultural scene; 4l. Laboratory worker. Vert—10l. Hands holding Constitution, hammer and sickle.

1964 (15 Dec). Solar System Planets. T **191** and similar horiz designs. Multicoloured. P 12×12½.
864 1l. Type **191** 25 20
865 2l. Venus 55 30
866 3l. Earth 75 40
867 4l. Mars 80 45
868 5l. Jupiter 1·10 50
869 6l. Saturn 1·60 1·00
870 7l. Uranus 1·80 1·30
871 8l. Neptune 2·20 1·50
872 9l. Pluto 2·40 1·70
864/872 *Set of 9* 10·50 6·50
MS872*a* 88×72 mm. 15l. multicoloured (Solar system and rocket) (61×51 mm). P 12×imperf 35·00 47·00

1965 (25 Jan). Winter Fruits. T **192** and similar vert designs. Multicoloured. P 11½×12.
873 1l. Type **192** 35 20
874 2l. Medlars 55 30
875 3l. Persimmon 75 35
876 4l. Pomegranate 1·10 50
877 5l. Quince 2·20 75
878 10l. Orange 4·25 1·30
873/878 *Set of 6* 8·25 3·00

193 "Industry"

194 Buffalo grazing

1965 (20 Feb). 20th Anniv of Albanian Trade Unions. T **193** and similar vert designs inscr "B.P.SH. 1945–1965". P 11½×12.
879 2l. carmine, pink and black 7·50 7·25
880 5l. black, grey and yellow-ochre 11·50 11·00
881 8l. ultramarine, light blue and black 14·00 13·50
879/881 *Set of 3* 30·00 29·00
Designs: 5l. Set square, book and dividers ("Technocracy"), 8l. Hotel, trees and sunshade ("Tourism").

1965 (Mar). Water Buffalo. T **194** and similar horiz designs. P 12.
882 1l. multicoloured 1·10 50
883 2l. multicoloured 2·20 1·00
884 3l. multicoloured 3·25 1·60
885 7l. multicoloured 7·50 2·10
886 12l. multicoloured 13·00 2·50
882/886 *Set of 5* 24·00 7·00
Designs: 2l. to 12l. As T **194** showing different views of buffalo.

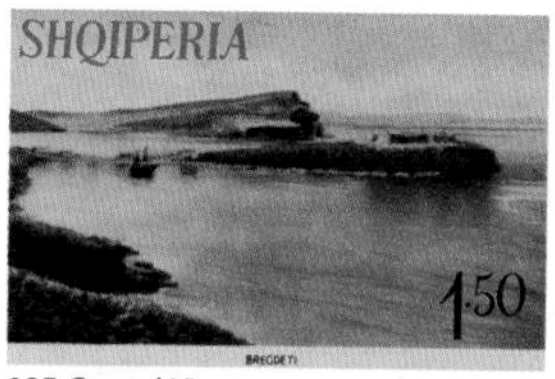

195 Coastal View

196 Frontier Guard

1965 (Apr). Scenery. T **195** and similar designs. Multicoloured. P 12½×12 (horiz) or 12×12½ (vert).
887 1l.50 Type **195** 1·60 50
888 2l.50 Mountain forest, Valbona 3·50 1·00
889 3l. Lugina Peak, Thethi Valley (vert) 3·75 1·30
890 4l. White River, Thethi (vert) 5·00 1·60
891 5l. Dry Mountain, Valbona 6·00 2·10
892 9l. Lake of Flowers, Lure 16·00 4·25
887/892 *Set of 6* 32·00 9·75

1965 (25 Apr). 20th Anniv of Frontier Force. P 12.
893 **196** 2l.50 multicoloured 1·60 1·00
894 12l.50 multicoloured 9·25 4·25

197 Rifleman

198 I.T.U. Emblem and Symbols

1965 (10 May). European Shooting Championships, Bucharest. T **197** and similar horiz designs. P 12×12½.
895 1l. brown-purple, cerise and reddish violet 35 20
896 2l. brown-purple, ultram & light blue 55 30
897 3l. red and pink 1·10 50
898 4l. brown-purple, black, grey and ochre 2·20 50
899 15l. brn-pur, blk, orge-brn & turq-grn 6·50 2·50
895/899 *Set of 5* 9·50 3·50
Designs: 2l., 15l. Rifle-shooting (different); 3l. "Target" map; 4l. Pistol-shooting.

1965 (17 May). Centenary of International Telecommunications Union. P 12½×12.

900	**198**	2l.50 magenta, black and blue-green	1·10	50
901		12l.50 blue, black and bright violet	6·50	1·80

199 Belyaev

200 Marx and Lenin

201 Mother and Child

1965 (15 June). Space Flight of "Voskhod 2". T **199** and similar vert designs. P 12½×12.

902	1l.50 brown and light blue	20	10
903	2l. blue, deep blue and lilac	35	20
904	6l.50 brown and reddish violet	1·10	50
905	20l. yellow, black and grey-blue	4·25	2·10
902/905 *Set of 4*		5·25	2·50
MS906	71×86 mm. 20l. yellow, black and light blue (as 905 but larger, 59×51 mm). P 12×imperf	20·00	31·00

Designs: 2l. "Voskhod 2"; 6l.50, Leonov; 20l. Leonov in space.

1965 (21 June). Postal Ministers' Congress, Peking. P 12½×12.

907	**200**	2l.50 sepia, red and greenish yellow	85	50
908		7l.50 bronze green, orange-red and greenish yellow	3·50	2·10

1965 (29 June). International Children's Day. T **201** and similar designs. Multicoloured. P 12×12½ (3l.) or 12½×12 (others).

909	1l. Type **201**	25	15
910	2l. Children planting tree	60	30
911	3l. Children and construction toy (horiz)	80	50
912	4l. Child on beach	1·10	85
913	15l. Child reading book	4·25	3·25
909/913 *Set of 5*		6·25	4·50

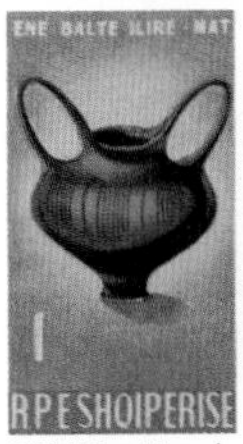
202 Wine Vessel

203 Fuchsia

0,80

(**204**)

1965 (20 July). Albanian Antiquities. T **202** and similar designs. Multicoloured. P 12.

914	1l. Type **202**	25	10
915	2l. Helmet and shield	55	30
916	3l. Mosaic of animal (horiz)	75	50
917	4l. Statuette of man	1·60	1·00
918	15l. Statuette of headless and limbless man	4·00	2·10
914/918 *Set of 5*		6·50	3·50

1965 (11 Aug). Albanian Flowers. T **203** and similar vert designs. Multicoloured. P 12½×12.

919	1l. Type **203**	25	15
920	2l. Cyclamen	75	30
921	3l. Lilies	1·30	50
922	3l.50 Iris	1·60	75
923	4l. Dahlia	1·80	85
924	4l.50 Hydrangea	2·20	95
925	5l. Rose	2·40	1·00
926	7l. Tulips	3·25	1·30
919/926 *Set of 8*		12·00	5·25

Currency revaluation. 100 Oint = 1 Lek.

1 New Lek = 10 Old Leks

1965 (16 Aug). Nos. 786/8 surch as T **204**.

927	5q. on 30l. reddish purple/*pale blue*	85	85
928	15q. on 30l. reddish purple/*pale blue*	1·10	1·00
929	25q. on 50l. yellow-brown/*pale cream*	1·60	1·60
930	80q. on 50l. yellow-brown/*pale cream*	3·75	3·75
931	1l.10 on 20l. green/*pale green*	5·50	5·25
932	2l. on 20l. green /*pale green*	8·75	8·25
927/932 *Set of 6*		19·00	19·00

205 White Stork (*Ciconia ciconia*)

206 "War Veterans" (after painting by B. Sejdini)

1965 (31 Aug). Migratory Birds. T **205** and similar vert designs. Multicoloured. P 12½×12.

933	10q. Type **205**	55	30
934	20q. European cuckoo (*Cuculus canorus*)	1·10	50
935	30q. Hoopoe (*Upupa epops*)	1·60	85
936	40q. European bee eater (*Merops apiaster*)	2·20	1·00
937	50q. European nightjar (*Caprimulgus europaeus*)	2·75	1·30
938	1l.50 Common quail (*Coturnix coturnix*)	8·25	3·75
933/938 *Set of 6*		15·00	7·00

1965 (26 Sept). War Veterans Conference. P 12×12½.

939	**206**	25q. deep olive-brown and black	3·25	85
940		65q. indigo and black	8·25	2·10
941		1l.10 black	11·00	4·25
939/941 *Set of 3*			20·00	6·50

207 Hunter stalking Capercaillie

208 *Nerium oleander*

1965 (6 Oct). Hunting. T **207** and similar horiz designs. P 12×12½.

942	10q. multicoloured	55	20
943	20q. lake-brown, sepia & yellow-green	1·10	20
944	30q. multicoloured	1·60	30
945	40q. reddish purple and emerald	2·20	50
946	50q. chestnut, grey-blue and black	2·75	1·00
947	1l. olive-brown, bistre and green	5·50	1·60
942/947 *Set of 6*		12·50	3·50

Designs:—20q. Shooting roe deer; 30q. Ring-necked pheasant; 40q. Shooting mallard; 50q. Dogs chasing wild boar; 1l. Hunter and brown hare.

1965 (26 Oct). Mountain Flowers. T **208** and similar vert designs. Multicoloured. P 12½×12.

948	10q. Type **208**	25	20
949	20q. *Myosotis alpestris*	55	25
950	30q. *Dianthus glacialis*	75	30
951	40q. *Nymphaea alba*	1·30	50
952	50q. *Lotus corniculatus*	1·60	75
953	1l. *Papaver rhoeas*	4·25	2·10
948/953 *Set of 6*		7·75	3·75

209 Tourist Hotel, Fier

210 Freighter *Teuta*

1965 (27 Oct). Public Buildings. T **209** and similar horiz designs. P 12×12½.

954	5q. black and light blue	10	10
955	10q. black and buff	15	10
956	15q. black and dull green	20	10
957	25q. black and violet	75	20
958	65q. black and light red-brown	1·60	40
959	80q. black and yellow-green	2·20	50
960	1l.10 black and reddish purple	2·75	75
961	1l.60 black and light violet-blue	4·25	1·60
962	2l. black and pink	5·50	2·10
963	3l. black and light grey	11·00	3·75
954/963 *Set of 10*		26·00	8·75

Buildings:—10q. Peshkopi Hotel; 15q. Sanatorium, Tirana; 25q. "House of Rest", Pogradec; 65q. Partisans Sports Palace, Tirana; 80q. "House of Rest", Dajti Mountain; 1l.10, Palace of Culture, Tirana; 1l.60, Adriatic Hotel, Durrës; 2l. Migjeni Theatre, Shkodër; 3l. "A. Moisiu" Cultural Palace, Durrës.

1965 (16 Nov). Evolution of Albanian Ships. T **210** and similar horiz designs. P 12×12½.

964	10q. olive-green and bright green	35	20
965	20q. bistre and olive-green	45	20
966	30q. ultramarine and new blue	55	30
967	40q. violet and light violet	75	50
968	50q. carmine-red and rose	1·60	75
969	1l. red-brown and yellow-ochre	3·75	1·30
964/969 *Set of 6*		6·75	3·00

Designs:—20q. Punt; 30q. 19th-century sailing ship; 40q. 18th-century brig; 50q. Freighter *Vlora*; 1l. Illyrian galliots.

211 Head of Brown Bear

212 Championships Emblem

1965 (7 Dec). Brown Bear. T **211** and similar designs each showing a bear. P 11½×12 (vert) or 12×11½ (horiz).

970	10q. brown and yellow-brown	45	15
971	20q. brown and yellow-brown	55	20
972	30q. brown, red and yellow-brown	1·10	35
973	35q. brown and yellow-brown	1·30	40
974	40q. brown and yellow-brown	1·60	45
975	50q. brown and yellow-brown	2·75	50
976	55q. brown and yellow-brown	3·25	75
977	60q. brown, red and yellow-brown	6·00	2·75
970/977 *Set of 8*		15·00	5·00

The 10q. to 40q. are vert, remainder horiz.

1965 (15 Dec). Seventh Balkan Basketball Championships, Tirana. T **212** and similar vert designs. Multicoloured. P 12½×12.

978	10q. Type **212**	35	10
979	20q. Competing players	45	15
980	30q. Clearing ball	75	20
981	50q. Attempted goal	1·60	50
982	1l.40 Medal and ribbon	3·25	1·30
978/982 *Set of 5*		5·75	2·00

213 Arms on Book

214 Cow

1966 (11 Jan). 20th Anniv of Albanian People's Republic. T **213** and similar vert designs. Arms in gold. P 12.

983	10q. rosine and brown	20	10
984	20q. light new blue and bright blue	35	20
985	30q. yellow and brown	75	50
986	60q. apple-green and blue-green	1·80	1·00
987	80q. rosine and brown	2·30	1·60
983/987 *Set of 5*		4·75	3·00

Designs:—Arms and: 20q. Chimney stacks; 30q. Ear of corn; 60q. Hammer, sickle and open book; 80q. Industrial plant.

1966 (25 Feb). Domestic Animals. T **214** and similar designs. Animals in natural colours; inscriptions in black; frame colours given. P 12½×12 (horiz) or 12×12½ (vert).

988	10q. turquoise-green	20	20
989	20q. apple-green (Pig)	55	30
990	30q. light violet-blue (Sheep)	1·30	40
991	35q. lavender (Goat)	1·60	50
992	40q. pink (Dog)	2·20	50
993	50q. light yellow (Cat) (vert)	2·75	65
994	55q. light blue (Horse) (vert)	3·00	75
995	60q. yellow (Ass) (vert)	5·50	1·00
988/995 *Set of 8*		15·00	3·75

215 Football

216 A. Z. Cajupi

217 Painted Lady (*Pyrameis cardui*)

1966 (20 Mar). World Cup Football Championship, England (1st series). T **215** and similar vert designs. P 12½×12.

996	5q. red-orange, greenish grey and pale buff	15	10
997	10q. deep reddish lilac, light blue, ochre and pale buff	20	10
998	15q. blue, grnish yellow & pale buff	25	15
999	20q. greenish blue, ultramarine, yellow-orange and pale buff	35	20
1000	25q. sepia, orange-red and pale buff	45	20
1001	30q. brown, yellow-green & pale buff	55	30
1002	35q. yellow-green, blue and pale buff	85	40
1003	40q. brown, rose and pale buff	90	50
1004	50q. red, bright purple, light green and pale buff	1·10	75
1005	70q. multicoloured	1·60	1·00
996/1005 *Set of 10*		5·75	3·25

Designs:—Footballer and map showing—10q. Montevideo (1930); 15q. Rome (1934); 20q. Paris (1938); 25q. Rio de Janeiro (1950); 30q. Berne (1954); 35q. Stockholm (1958); 40q. Santiago (1962); 50q. London (1966); 70q. World Cup and Football.

See also Nos. 1035/42.

1966 (27 Mar). Birth Centenary of Andon Cajupi (poet). P 12½×12.

1006	**216**	40q. indigo and slate-blue	1·10	60
1007		1l.10 bronze-green and grey-green	3·25	2·10

1966 (21 Apr). Butterflies and Dragonflies. T **217** and similar vert designs. Multicoloured. P 11½×12.

1008	10q. Type **217**	45	20
1009	20q. *Calopteryx virgo*	55	25
1010	30q. Pale clouded yellow (*Colias hyale*)	75	30
1011	35q. Banded agrion (*Calopteryx splendens*)	1·10	35
1012	40q. Banded agrion (different)	1·60	40
1013	50q. Swallowtail (*Papilio machaon*)	2·20	50
1014	55q. Danube clouded yellow (*Colias myrmidone*)	2·75	75
1015	60q. Hungarian glider (*Neptis lucilla*)	7·00	1·30
1008/1015 *Set of 8*		15·00	3·75

The 20, 35 and 40q. are dragonflies, remainder are butterflies.

218 W.H.O. Building

219 Leaf Star

1966 (3 May). Inauguration of W.H.O. Headquarters, Geneva. T **218** and similar designs. P 12×12½ (horiz) or 12½×12 (vert).

1016	25q. black and light blue	55	20
1017	35q. bright blue and red-orange	1·10	30
1018	60q. red, new blue and light green	1·60	75
1019	80q. new blue, yell-brn & grnish yell	2·20	1·30
1016/1019 *Set of 4*		5·00	2·30

Designs: Vert—35q. Ambulance and patient; 60q. Nurse and mother weighing baby. Horiz—80q. Medical equipment.

1966 (10 May). "Starfish". T **219** and similar vert designs. Multicoloured. P 12×12½.

1020	15q. Type **219**	45	30
1021	25q. Spiny Star	75	40
1022	35q. Brittle Star	1·30	50
1023	45q. Sea Star	1·60	65
1024	50q. Blood Star	1·80	75
1025	60q. Sea Cucumber	2·75	1·00
1026	70q. Sea Urchin	3·25	2·50
1020/1026 *Set of 7*		10·50	5·50

220 "Luna 10"

221 Water-level Map of Albania

1966 (10 June). Launching of "Luna 10". T **220** and similar horiz design. P 12×12½.

1027	**220**	20q. multicoloured	55	30
1028	–	30q. multicoloured	1·10	50
1029	**220**	70q. multicoloured	2·20	1·00
1030	–	80q. multicoloured	3·75	2·30
1027/1030 *Set of 4*			6·75	3·75

Design:—30q., 80q. Earth, Moon and trajectory of "Luna 10".

1966 (2 July). International Hydrological Decade. T **221** and similar vert designs. P 12.

1031	20q. black, orange and red	55	30
1032	30q. black, yellow-brown, chestnut and bright green	85	50
1033	70q. black and reddish violet	1·60	1·30
1034	80q. black, yellow, orange and blue	2·75	2·10
1031/1034 *Set of 4*		5·25	3·75

Designs:—30q. Water scale and fields; 70q. Turbine and electricity pylon; 80q. Hydrological decade emblem.

222 Footballers (Uruguay, 1930)

1966 (12 July). World Cup Football Championship (2nd series). T **222** and similar horiz designs. Inscriptions and values in black. P 12.

1035	10q. purple and yellow-orange	45	10
1036	20q. yellow-olive and light blue	55	15
1037	30q. greenish blue and orange-red	75	20
1038	35q. rose and blue	1·00	25
1039	40q. chestnut and yellow-green	1·10	30
1040	50q. yellow-green and chestnut	1·30	50
1041	55q. bright green and reddish purple	1·40	1·00
1042	60q. yellow-orange and claret	2·75	1·60
1035/1042 *Set of 8*		8·25	3·75

Designs:—Various footballers representing World Cup winners—20q. Italy, 1934; 30q. Italy, 1938; 35q. Uruguay, 1950; 40q. West Germany, 1954; 50q. Brazil, 1958; 55q. Brazil, 1962; 60q. Football and names of 16 finalists in 1966 Championship.

223 Tortoise

1966 (10 Aug). Reptiles. T **223** and similar horiz designs. Multicoloured. P 12½×12.

1043	10q. Type **223**	35	20
1044	15q. Grass-snake	45	25
1045	25q. Swamp tortoise	55	30
1046	30q. Lizard	65	40
1047	35q. Salamander	1·10	50
1048	45q. Green lizard	1·30	60
1049	50q. Slow-worm	1·40	75
1050	90q. Sand viper	2·75	1·60
1043/1050 *Set of 8*		7·75	4·25

224 Siamese Cat

225 P. Budi (writer)

1966 (20 Sept). Cats. T **224** and similar designs. Multicoloured. P 12×12½ (vert) or 12½×12 (horiz, 25q. to 30q.).

1051	10q. Type **224**	45	20
1052	15q. Tabby	55	25
1053	25q. Kitten	1·10	30
1054	45q. Persian	1·70	75
1055	60q. Persian	2·75	1·00
1056	65q. Persian	3·00	1·20
1057	80q. Persian	3·75	1·40
1051/1057 *Set of 7*		12·00	4·50

1966 (5 Oct). 400th Birth Anniv of P. Budi. P 12½×12.

1058	**225**	25q. bronze-green and flesh	1·10	50
1059		1l.75 maroon and light green	3·25	2·50

226 U.N.E.S.C.O. Emblem

228 Hand holding Book

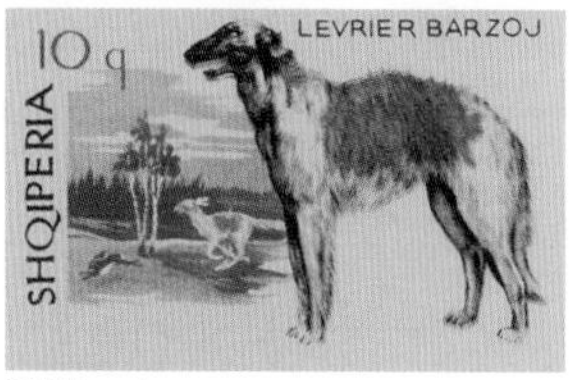

227 Borzoi

1966 (20 Oct). 20th Anniv of U.N.E.S.C.O. T **226** and similar designs. Multicoloured. P 12.

1060	5q. Type **226**	35	15
1061	15q. Tulip and open book	35	20
1062	25q. Albanian dancers	75	40
1063	1l.55 Jug and base of column	3·25	2·10
1060/1063 *Set of 4*		4·25	2·50

1966 (30 Oct). Dogs. T **227** and similar horiz designs. Multicoloured. P 12½×12.

1064	10q. Type **227**	55	20
1065	15q. Kuvasz	75	25
1066	25q. Setter	1·30	50
1067	45q. Cocker Spaniel	2·00	1·00
1068	60q. Bulldog	2·20	1·30
1069	65q. St. Bernard	3·00	1·60
1070	80q. Dachshund	4·25	2·10
1064/1070 *Set of 7*		12·50	6·25

1966 (1 Nov). Fifth Workers' Party Congress, Tirana. T **228** and similar vert designs. Multicoloured. P 12.

1071	15q. Type **228**	35	15
1072	25q. Emblems of agriculture and industry	60	15
1073	65q. Hammer and sickle, wheat and industrial skyline	1·60	85
1074	95q. Hands holding banner on bayonet and implements	2·20	1·30
1071/1074 *Set of 4*		4·25	2·20

229 Ndre Mjeda (poet)

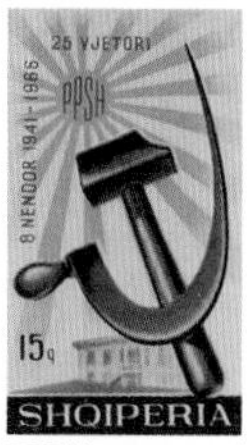

230 Hammer and Sickle

1966 (1 Nov). Birth Centenary of Ndre Mjeda. P 12½×12.

1075	**229**	25q. deep brown and bright new blue	65	50
1076		1l.75 deep brown and bright blue-green	3·75	1·80

1966 (8 Nov). 25th Anniv of Albanian Young Communists' Union. T **230** and similar vert designs. Multicoloured. P 12.

1077	15q. Type **230**	55	10
1078	25q. Soldier leading attack	75	20
1079	65q. Industrial worker	1·60	85
1080	95q. Agricultural and industrial vista	2·20	1·30
1077/1080 *Set of 4*		4·50	2·20

231 Young Communists and Banner

232 Golden Eagle (*Aquila chrysaëtos*)

1966 (8 Nov). 25th Anniv of Young Communists' Union. T **231** and similar designs. Multicoloured. P 12×11½ (10q.) or 11½×12 (others).

1081	5q. Manifesto (vert)	35	10
1082	10q. Type **231**	55	20
1083	1l.85 Partisans and banner (vert)	3·50	2·30
1081/1083 *Set of 3*		4·00	2·30

1966 (20 Dec). Birds of Prey. T **232** and similar vert designs. Multicoloured. P 11½×12.

1084	10q. Type **232**	55	20
1085	15q. White-tailed sea eagle (*Haliaëtus albicilla*)	75	30
1086	25q. Griffon vulture (*Gyps fulvus*)	1·10	50
1087	40q. European sparrow hawk (*Accipiter nisus*)	1·30	65
1088	50q. Osprey (*Pandion haliaëtus*)	1·80	75
1089	70q. Egyptian vulture (*Neophron percnopterus*)	2·75	1·30
1090	90q. Common kestrel (*Falco tinnunculus*)	3·75	1·60
1085/1090 *Set of 7*		11·00	4·75

233 Hake

234 Dalmatian Pelican

1967 (20 Jan). Fish. T **233** and similar horiz designs. Multicoloured. P 12.

1091	10q. Type **233**	45	20
1092	15q. Red Mullet	55	30
1093	25q. Opah	1·10	50
1094	40q. Wolf fish	1·30	65
1095	65q. Lumpsucker	1·60	75
1096	80q. Swordfish	2·75	1·30
1097	1l.15 Father Lasher	3·25	1·60
1091/1097 *Set of 7*		10·00	4·75

1967 (22 Feb). Dalmatian Pelicans. T **234** and similar designs. Multicoloured. P 12.

1098	10q. Type **234**	25	30
1099	15q. Three pelicans	55	40
1100	25q. Pelican and chicks at nest	1·60	50
1101	50q. Pelicans "taking off" and airborne	3·25	75
1102	2l. Pelican "yawning"	8·25	3·75
1098/1102 *Set of 5*		12·50	5·25

235 *Camellia williamsi*

236 Congress Emblem

1967 (10 Apr). Flowers. T **235** and similar designs. Multicoloured. P 12.

1103	5q. Type **235**	20	10
1104	10q. *Chrysanthemum indicum*	25	15
1105	15q. *Althaea rosea*	35	20
1106	25q. *Abutilon striatum*	1·10	30
1107	35q. *Paeonia chinensis*	1·30	50
1108	65q. *Gladiolus gandavensis*	2·20	1·00
1109	80q. *Freesia hybrida*	2·75	1·60
1110	1l.15 *Dianthus caryophyllus*	3·25	1·80
1103/1110 *Set of 8*		10·50	5·00

1967 (24 Apr). 6th Trade Unions Congress, Tirana. P 12.

1111	**236**	25q. red, sepia and light lilac	1·10	50
1112		1l.75 red, dp olive-green & grey	3·25	2·10

237 Rose

239 Fawn

238 Borsh Coast

1967 (15 May). Roses. T **237** and other vert designs showing different roses. P 12×12½.

1113	5q. multicoloured	45	20
1114	10q. multicoloured	55	30
1115	15q. multicoloured	65	40
1116	25q. multicoloured	75	50
1117	35q. multicoloured	1·10	65
1118	65q. multicoloured	1·40	75
1119	80q. multicoloured	1·60	1·00
1120	1l.65 multicoloured	3·25	1·60
1113/1120 *Set of 8*		8·75	4·75

1967 (10 June). Albanian Riviera. T **238** and similar designs showing resorts. Multicoloured. P 12×12½ (vert) or 12½×12 (horiz).

1121	15q. Butrinti (vert)	45	20
1122	20q. Type **238**	55	25
1123	25q. Piqeras Village	1·10	30
1124	45q. Coastal view	1·30	40

1125 50q. Himara coast ... 1·50 50
1126 65q. Saranda ... 2·20 75
1127 80q. Dhermi ... 2·40 1·00
1128 1l. Sunset at sea (vert) ... 3·25 1·60
1121/1128 *Set of 8* ... 11·50 4·50

1967 (20 July). Roe Deer. T **239** and similar designs. Multicoloured. P 12½×12 (horiz) or 12×12½ (vert).

1129 15q. Type **239** ... 55 20
1130 20q. Head of buck (vert) ... 55 30
1131 25q. Head of doe (vert) ... 1·10 50
1132 30q. Doe and fawn ... 1·10 50
1133 35q. Doe and new-born fawn ... 1·60 75
1134 40q. Young buck (vert) ... 1·60 75
1135 65q. Buck and doe (vert) ... 3·25 1·00
1136 70q. Running deer ... 4·25 1·60
1129/1136 *Set of 8* ... 12·50 5·00

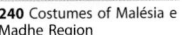

240 Costumes of Malésia e Madhe Region

241 Battle Scene and Newspaper

(Des P. Mele and S. Kristo)

1967 (20 Aug). National Costumes. T **240** and similar designs showing costumes. Multicoloured. P 12.

1137 15q. Type **240** ... 45 15
1138 20q. Zadrima ... 50 20
1139 25q. Kukësi ... 55 30
1140 45q. Dardhë ... 85 50
1141 50q. Myzeqë ... 1·00 75
1142 65q. Tirana ... 1·30 85
1143 80q. Dropulli ... 2·20 1·00
1144 1l. Labërisë ... 2·30 1·30
1137/1144 *Set of 8* ... 8·25 4·50

1967 (25 Aug). 25 Years of the Albanian Popular Press. T **241** and similar vert designs. Multicoloured. P 12½×12.

1145 25q. Type **241** ... 65 30
1146 75q. Newspapers and printery ... 1·70 75
1147 2l. Workers with newspaper ... 4·25 2·10
1145/1147 *Set of 3* ... 6·00 2·75

242 University, Torch and Open Book

243 Soldiers and Flag

1967 (15 Sept). Tenth Anniv of Tirana University. P 12½×12.

1148 **242** 25q. multicoloured ... 55 40
1149 1l.75 multicoloured ... 3·50 1·80

1967 (16 Sept). 25th Anniv of Albanian Democratic Front. T **243** and similar horiz designs. Multicoloured. P 12.

1150 15q. Type **243** ... 35 20
1151 65q. Pick, rifle and flag ... 1·10 50
1152 1l.20 Torch and open book ... 2·40 1·30
1150/1152 *Set of 3* ... 3·50 1·80

244 Grey Rabbits

245 "Shkodër Wedding" (detail, Kole Idromeno)

1967 (30 Sept). Rabbit-breeding. T **244** and similar multicoloured designs. P 12.

1153 15q. Type **244** ... 35 15
1154 20q. Black and white rabbit (vert) ... 45 20
1155 25q. Brown hare (*Lepus europaeus*) ... 65 30
1156 35q. Brown rabbits ... 1·10 40
1157 40q. Common rabbits (*Oryctolagus cuniculus*) ... 1·30 50
1158 50q. Grey rabbit (vert) ... 2·20 75
1159 65q. Head of white rabbit (vert) ... 2·40 85
1160 1l. White rabbit ... 3·50 1·60
1153/1160 *Set of 8* ... 11·00 4·25

1967 (25 Oct). Albanian Paintings. T **245** and similar designs. P 12½×12 (horiz) or 12×12½ (vert).

1161 15q. multicoloured ... 55 20
1162 20q. multicoloured ... 75 30
1163 25q. multicoloured ... 1·10 40
1164 45q. multicoloured ... 1·30 50
1165 50q. multicoloured ... 1·60 75
1166 65q. multicoloured ... 2·20 85
1167 80q. multicoloured ... 2·40 1·00
1168 1l. multicoloured ... 4·25 1·30
1161/1168 *Set of 8* ... 12·50 4·75

Designs: Vert—20q. "Head of the Prophet David" (detail, 16th-century fresco); 45q. Ancient mosaic head (from Durres); 50q. Detail, 16th-century icon; (30×51 mm.)—1l. "Our Sister (K. Idromeno). Horiz (51×30 mm.)—25q. "Commandos of the Hakmarrja Battalion" (S. Shijaku); 65q. "Co-operative (farm women, Z. Shoshi); 80q. Street in Korcë" (V. Mio).

246 Lenin and Stalin

247 Common Turkey

(Des Q. Prizreni)

1967 (7 Nov). 50th Anniv of October Revolution. T **246** and similar designs. Multicoloured. P 12.

1169 15q. Type **246** ... 35 20
1170 25q. Lenin with soldiers (vert) ... 75 50
1171 50q. Lenin addressing meeting (vert) ... 1·10 75
1172 1l.10 Revolutionaries ... 2·40 1·00
1169/1172 *Set of 4* ... 4·25 2·20

(Des N. Prizreni)

1967 (25 Nov). Domestic Fowl. T **247** and similar designs. Multicoloured. P 12×12½ (vert) or 12½×12 (horiz).

1173 15q. Type **247** ... 20 10
1174 20q. Goose ... 35 20
1175 25q. Hen ... 55 30
1176 45q. Cockerel ... 1·10 50
1177 50q. Helmet guineafowl ... 1·30 65
1178 65q. Greylag goose (horiz) ... 1·60 75
1179 80q. Mallard (horiz) ... 2·20 1·00
1180 1l. Chicks (horiz) ... 3·25 1·30
1173/1180 *Set of 8* ... 9·50 4·25

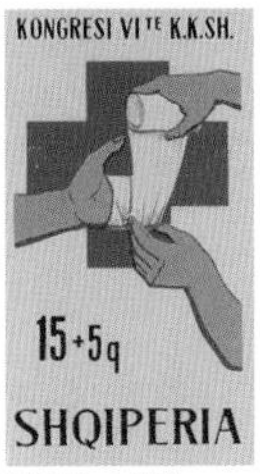

248 First Aid

249 Arms of Skanderbeg

(Des S. Bregu and J. Talo)

1967 (1 Dec). Sixth Red Cross Congress, Tirana. T **248** and similar vert designs. Multicoloured. P 12.

1181 15q. +5q. Type **248** ... 1·10 65
1182 25q. +5q. Stretcher-case ... 2·20 1·00
1183 65q. +25q. Heart patient ... 7·50 3·75
1184 80q. +40q. Nurse holding child ... 11·00 5·25
1181/1184 *Set of 4* ... 20·00 9·50

(Des N. Prizreni)

1967 (10 Dec). 500th Death Anniv of Castriota Skanderbeg (patriot) (First issue). T **249** and similar vert designs. Multicoloured. P 12×12½.

1185 10q. Type **249** ... 20 10
1186 15q. Skanderbeg ... 35 15
1187 25q. Helmet and sword ... 55 20
1188 30q. Kruja Castle ... 65 30
1189 35q. Petrela Castle ... 75 40
1190 65q. Berati Castle ... 1·10 50
1191 80q. Meeting of chiefs ... 2·20 75
1192 90q. Battle of Albulena ... 2·30 1·00
1185/1192 *Set of 8* ... 7·25 3·00

See also Nos. 1200/7.

250 Winter Olympics Emblem

251 Skanderbeg Memorial, Tirana

(Des S. Toptani)

1967 (29 Dec). Winter Olympic Games, Grenoble. T **250** and similar vert designs. Multicoloured. P 12×12½.

1193 15q. Type **250** ... 20 10
1194 25q. Ice hockey ... 25 15
1195 30q. Figure skating ... 35 20
1196 50q. Skiing (slalom) ... 55 30
1197 80q. Skiing (downhill) ... 1·10 50
1198 1l. Ski jumping ... 2·40 1·30
1193/1198 *Set of 6* ... 4·25 2·30

MS1199 58×67 mm. 2l. As Type **250** but larger. Imperf ... 9·25 10·50

(Des S. Toptani)

1968 (17 Jan). 500th Death Anniv of Castriota Skanderbeg (Second issue). T **251** and similar designs. Multicoloured. P 12×12½.

1200 10q. Type **251** ... 35 20
1201 15q. Skanderbeg portrait ... 55 30
1202 25q. Skanderbeg portrait (different) ... 1·00 40
1203 30q. Equestrian statue, Kruja ... 1·10 45
1204 35q. Skanderbeg and mountains (horiz) ... 1·30 50
1205 65q. Bust of Skanderbeg ... 2·20 75
1206 80q. Title page of biography ... 3·00 1·60
1207 90q. "Skanderbeg battling with the Turks" (painting) (horiz) ... 3·50 2·10
1200/1207 *Set of 8* ... 11·50 5·75

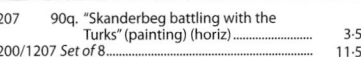

252 Alpine Dianthus

253 Ear of wheat and Electricity Pylon

(Des S. Qesku)

1968 (15 Feb). Flowers. T **252** and similar square designs. Multicoloured. P 12.

1208 15q. Type **252** ... 20 10
1209 20q. Chinese dianthus ... 25 15
1210 25q. Pink carnation ... 35 20
1211 50q. Red carnation and bud ... 1·10 30
1212 80q. Two red carnations ... 1·60 50
1213 1l.10 Yellow carnations ... 2·20 1·00
1208/1213 *Set of 6* ... 5·25 2·00

1968 (15 Mar). Fifth Agricultural Co-operative Congress. T **253** and similar designs. Multicoloured. P 12.

1214 25q. Type **253** ... 55 30
1215 65q. Tractor (horiz) ... 1·60 85
1216 1l.10 Cow ... 2·20 1·30
1214/1216 *Set of 3* ... 4·00 2·20

254 Long-horned Goat

255 Zef Jubani

(Des N. Prizreni)

1968 (25 Mar). Goats. T **254** and similar designs. Multicoloured. P 12×12½ (vert) or 12½×12 (horiz).

1217 15q. Zane female (vert) ... 20 10
1218 20q. Kid (vert) ... 35 15
1219 25q. Long-haired Capore (vert) ... 45 20
1220 30q. Black goat at rest ... 55 25
1221 40q. Kids dancing ... 65 30
1222 50q. Red and piebald goats ... 75 50
1223 80q. Long-haired Ankara ... 1·60 65
1224 1l.40 Type **254** ... 3·25 1·60
1217/1224 *Set of 8* ... 7·00 3·50

1968 (30 Mar). 150th Birth Anniv of Zef Jubani (patriot). P 12.

1225 **255** 25q. deep chocolate and yellow ... 55 30
1226 1l.75 indigo, black and lt violet ... 2·75 1·60

256 Doctor using Stethoscope

257 Servicewoman

1968 (7 Apr). 20th Anniv of World Health Organization. T **256** and similar designs. P 12×12½ (65q.) or 12½×12 (others).

1227 25q. claret and emerald ... 35 15
1228 65q. black, lt grnish blue & grnish yell ... 1·30 85
1229 1l.10 orange-brown and black ... 1·60 1·00
1227/1229 *Set of 3* ... 3·00 1·80

Designs: Horiz—65q. Hospital and microscope. Vert—1l.10, Mother feeding child.

1968 (14 Apr). 25th Anniv of Albanian Women's Union. T **257** and similar horiz designs. P 12.

1230 15q. brown-red and light salmon-red ... 45 20
1231 25q. bluish green and light green ... 55 30
1232 60q. yellow-brown and light ochre ... 1·60 75
1233 1l. bluish violet and light violet ... 2·75 1·30
1230/1233 *Set of 4* ... 4·75 2·30

Designs:—25q. Teacher; 60q. Farm-girl; 1l. Factory worker.

258 Karl Marx

259 Heliopsis

(Des S. Ballauri)

1968 (5 May). 150th Birth Anniv of Karl Marx. T **258** and similar square designs. Multicoloured. P 12.

1234 15q. Type **258** ... 1·10 50
1235 25q. Marx addressing students ... 1·60 75
1236 65q. "Das Kapital", "Communist Manifesto" and marchers ... 2·75 1·60

1237 95q. Portrait of Karl Marx 4·25 3·75
1234/1237 *Set of 4* 8·75 6·00

(Des S. Qesku)

1968 (10 May). Flowers. T **259** and similar vert designs. Multicoloured. P 12×12½.

1238 15q. Type **259** 20 10
1239 20q. Red flax 35 15
1240 25q. Orchid 45 20
1241 30q. Gloxinia 50 30
1242 40q. Orange lily 55 40
1243 80q. Hippeastrum 1·60 1·00
1244 1l.40 Purple magnolia 2·75 1·60
1238/1244 *Set of 7* 5·75 3·50

260 A. Frasheri and Torch

261 "Shepherd" (A. Kushi)

1968 (10 June). 90th Anniv of Prizren Defence League. T **260** and similar horiz designs. P 12.

1245 25q. black and bright green 55 20
1246 40q. multicoloured 1·10 50
1247 85q. multicoloured 1·60 1·00
1245/1247 *Set of 3* 3·00 1·50

Designs:—40q. League headquarters; 85q. Frasheri's manifesto and partisans.

1968 (20 June). Paintings in Tirana Gallery. T **261** and similar designs. Multicoloured. P 12½×12 (20q.) or 12×12½ (others).

1248 15q. Type **261** 15 10
1249 20q. "Tirana" (V. Mio) (horiz) 20 10
1250 25q. "Highlander" (G. Madhi) 20 10
1251 40q. "Refugees" (A. Buza) 55 20
1252 80q. "Partisans at Shahin Matrakut" (S. Xega) 1·10 30
1253 1l.50 "Old Man" (S. Papadhimitri) 2·75 85
1254 1l.70 "Shkodër Gate" (S. Rrota) 3·25 1·00
1248/1254 *Set of 7* 7·50 2·40
MS1255 90×114 mm. 2l.50, "Shkodër Costume" (Z. Colombi) (51×71 mm). P 12½×imperf 4·00 2·50

262 Soldier and Armoured Vehicles

1968 (10 July). 25th Anniv of People's Army. T **262** and similar designs. P 12½.

1256 15q. olive-green, black, buff and cerise 55 20
1257 25q. lightt sepia, black, greenish blue and yellow 65 25
1258 65q. brown-purple, black, greenish blue and ultramarine 2·20 1·00
1259 95q. orange, black, drab and yellow-green 3·25 1·60
1256/1259 *Set of 4* 6·00 2·75

Designs: Horiz—25q. Sailor and naval craft; 95q. Soldier and patriots. Vert—65q. Pilot and Mikoyan Gurevich MiG-17 jet fighter.

263 Common Squid (*Loligo vulgaris*)

(Des S. Qesku)

1968 (20 Aug). Marine Fauna. T **263** and similar horiz designs. Multicoloured. P 12.

1260 15q. Type **263** 35 20
1261 20q. Common lobster (*Homarus vulgaris*) 40 30
1262 25q. Common northern whelk (*Buccinum undatum*) 55 40
1263 50q. Edible crab (*Cancer pagurus*) 70 50
1264 70q. Spiny lobster (*Palinurus vulgaris*) 1·10 85
1265 80q. Common green crab (*Carcinus maenas*) 1·90 1·00
1266 90q. Norwegian lobster (*Nephrops norvegicus*) 2·20 1·60
1260/1266 *Set of 7* 6·50 4·25

264 Relay-racing

265 Enver Hoxha (Party Secretary)

(Des S. Toptani)

1968 (23 Sept). Olympic Games, Mexico. T **264** and similar diamond-shaped designs. Multicoloured. P 12.

1267 15q. Type **264** 15 10
1268 20q. Running 20 10
1269 25q. Throwing the discus 25 10
1270 30q. Horse-jumping 35 20
1271 40q. High-jumping 45 30
1272 50q. Hurdling 55 40
1273 80q. Football 1·10 50
1274 1l.40 High-diving 2·20 1·30
1267/1274 *Set of 8* 4·75 2·75
MS1275 90×81 mm. 2l. Olympic Stadium (64×54 mm). P 12½×imperf 4·00 2·50

(Des S. Toptani)

1968 (16 Oct). Enver Hoxha's 60th Birthday. P 12.

1276 **265** 25q. deep grey-blue 45 30
1277 35q. maroon 65 50
1278 80q. deep slate-violet 1·40 1·00
1279 1l.10 deep brown 1·70 1·30
1276/1279 *Set of 4* 3·75 2·75
MS1280 80½×91 mm. **265** 1l.50, deep slate- violet, red and gold. Imperf £160 £180

266 Alphabet Book

(Des S. Toptani)

1968 (14 Nov). 60th Anniv of Monastir Language Congress. P 12.

1281 **266** 15q. lake and slate-green 65 40
1282 85q. blackish brown and light bronze-green 3·25 2·10

267 Bohemian Waxwing (*Bombycila garrulus*)

(Des N. Prizreni)

1968 (15 Nov). Birds. Diamond-shaped designs as T **267**. Multicoloured. P 12.

1283 15q. Type **267** 35 10
1284 20q. Rose-coloured starling (*Pastor roseus*) 55 20
1285 25q. Common kingfishers (*Alcedo atthis ispida*) 75 30
1286 50q. Long-tailed tits (*Aegithalus caodatus*) 1·10 50
1287 80q. Wallcreeper (*Tichodroma muraria*) 2·20 1·00
1288 1l.10 Bearded reedling (*Panurus biarmicus*) 3·25 1·60
1283/1288 *Set of 6* 7·50 3·25

268 Mao Tse-tung

(Des I. Shehu)

1968 (26 Dec). Mao Tse-tung's 75th Birthday. P 12½×12.

1289 **268** 25q. black, rose-red and gold 1·10 50
1290 1l.75 black, rose-red and gold 7·00 4·75

269 Adem Reka (dock foreman)

(Des R. Ballauri)

1969 (10 Feb). Contemporary Heroes. T **269** and similar vert designs. Multicoloured. P 12×12½.

1291 5q. Type **269** 45 30
1292 10q. Pjeter Lleshi (telegraph linesman) 55 40
1293 15q. M. Shehu and M. Kepi (fire victims) 1·10 85
1294 25q. Shkurte Vata (railway worker) 1·60 1·30
1295 65q. Agron Elezi (earthquake victim) 1·90 1·40
1296 80q. Ismet Bruca (school teacher) 2·20 1·60
1297 1l.30 Fuat Cela (blind Co-op leader) 3·25 2·10
1291/1297 *Set of 7* 10·00 7·25

270 Meteorological Equipment

271 "Student Revolutionaries" (P. Mele)

(Des N. Prizreni)

1969 (25 Feb). 20th Anniv of Albanian Hydro-Meteorology. T **270** and similar square designs. Multicoloured. P 12.

1298 15q. Type **270** 55 30
1299 25q. "Arrow" indicator 85 50
1300 1l.60 Met balloon and isobar map 4·25 2·30
1298/1300 *Set of 3* 5·00 2·75

1969 (20 April). Albanian Paintings since 1944. T **271** and similar multicoloured designs. P 12×12½ (5q.) or 12½×12 (others).

1301 5q. Type **271** 20 10
1302 25q. "Partisans, 1944" (F. Haxhiu) 35 10
1303 65q. "Steel Mill" (C. Ceka) 55 20
1304 80q. "Reconstruction" (V. Kilica) 65 40
1305 1l.10 "Harvest" (N. Jonuzi) 1·30 75
1306 1l.15 "Seaside Terraces" (S. Kaceli) 1·60 1·30
1301/1306 *Set of 6* 4·25 2·50
MS1307 111×91 mm. 2l. "Partisans' Meeting" (N. Zajmi). Imperf 2·75 2·10

Nos. 1302/7 are all horiz, the 65q. as T **271**, 2l. size 77×56 mm and the others 50×30 mm.

272 Self-portrait

273 Congress Building

1969 (2 May). 450th Death Anniv of Leonardo da Vinci. T **272** and similar drawings and paintings. P 12½×12 (40q.) or 12×12½ (others).

1308 25q. agate, pale brown and gold 35 15
1309 35q. agate, pale brown and gold 65 20
1310 40q. agate, pale brown and gold 85 50
1311 1l. multicoloured 2·20 1·00
1312 2l. agate, pale brown and gold 4·25 1·80
1308/1312 *Set of 5* 7·50 3·25
MS1313 65×95 mm. 2l. multicoloured. Imperf 7·00 4·50

Designs: Vert—35q. "Lilies"; 1l. "Portrait of Beatrice"; 2l. (No. 1312), "Portrait of a Lady"; (47×75 mm) 2l. (**MS**1313), "Mona Lisa". Horiz—40q. Design for "Helicopter".

1969 (24 May). 25th Anniv of Permet Congress. T **273** and similar square designs. Multicoloured. P 12.

1314 25q. Type **273** 55 30
1315 2l.25 Two partisans 4·25 3·25
MS1316 95×101 mm. 1l. Albanian arms. Imperf 50·00 65·00

274 *Viola albanica*

275 Plum

(Des Q. Prizreni)

1969 (30 June). Flowers. Viola Family. Vert designs as T **274**. Multicoloured. P 12×12½.

1317 5q. Type **274** 15 10
1318 10q. *Viola hortensis* 20 10
1319 15q. *Viola heterophylla* 35 15
1320 20q. *Viola hortensis* (different) 45 20
1321 25q. *Viola odorata* 55 20
1322 80q. *Viola hortensis* (different) 1·60 85
1323 1l.95 *Viola hortensis* (different) 2·75 2·10
1317/1323 *Set of 7* 5·50 3·25

Nos. 1318, 1320 and 1322/3 show different versions of the same species.

(Des Q. Prizreni)

1969 (10 Aug). Fruit Trees. Vert designs as T **275** showing blossom and fruit. Multicoloured. P 12×12½.

1324 10q. Type **275** 20 10
1325 15q. Lemon 35 15
1326 25q. Pomegranate 55 20
1327 50q. Cherry 1·10 50
1328 80q. Apricot 1·80 1·00
1329 1l.20 Apple 2·75 1·60
1324/1329 *Set of 6* 6·00 3·25

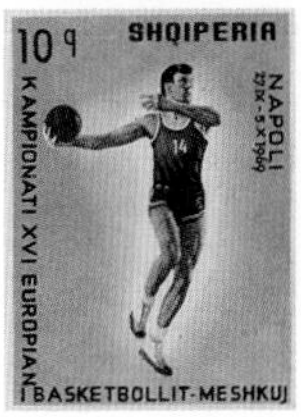

276 Throwing the Ball

277 Gymnastics

(Des S. Toptani)

1969 (15 Sept). 16th European Basketball Championships, Naples. T **276** and similar multicoloured designs. P 12.

1330 10q. Type **276** ... 35 10
1331 15q. Trying for goal ... 45 15
1332 25q. Ball and net (horiz) ... 55 20
1333 80q. Scoring a goal ... 1·60 30
1334 2l.20 Intercepting a pass ... 3·25 1·60
1330/1334 *Set of* 5 ... 5·50 2·10

(Des B. Dizdari)

1969 (30 Sept). National Spartakiad. Square designs as T **277**. Multicoloured. P 12.

1335 5q. Pickaxe, rifle, flag and stadium ... 15 10
1336 10q. Type **277** ... 20 10
1337 15q. Running ... 35 10
1338 20q. Pistol-shooting ... 45 15
1339 25q. Swimmer on starting block ... 55 20
1340 80q. Cycling ... 1·60 75
1341 95q. Football ... 2·20 1·30
1335/1341 *Set of* 7 ... 5·00 2·40

278 Mao Tse-tung

279 Enver Hoxha

(Des I. Shehu)

1969 (1 Oct). 20th Anniv of Chinese People's Republic. T **278** and similar multicoloured designs. P 12½×12 (85q.) or 12×12½ (others).

1342 25q. Type **278** ... 1·60 50
1343 85q. Steel ladle and control room (horiz). 5·50 2·10
1344 1l.40 Rejoicing crowd ... 9·25 3·75
1342/1344 *Set of* 3 ... 14·50 5·75

(Des R. Ballauri)

1969 (20 Oct). 25th Anniv of Second National Liberation Council Meeting, Berat. Vert designs as T **279**. Multicoloured. P 12×12½.

1345 25q. Type **279** ... 35 20
1346 80q. Star and Constitution ... 85 50
1347 1l.45 Freedom-fighters ... 2·20 1·30
1345/1347 *Set of* 3 ... 3·00 1·80

280 Entry of Provisional Government, Tirana

(Des I. Shehu)

1969 (29 Nov). 25th Anmv of Liberation. T **280** and similar horiz designs. Multicoloured. P 12½×12.

1348 25q. Type **280** ... 45 20
1349 30q. Oil Refinery ... 55 25
1350 35q. Combine-harvester ... 75 30
1351 45q. Hydro-electric power station ... 1·30 50
1352 55q. Soldier and partisans ... 1·80 75
1353 1l.10 People rejoicing ... 3·25 1·30
1348/1353 *Set of* 6 ... 7·25 3·00

281 Stalin

282 Head of Woman

(Des S. Toptani)

1969 (21 Dec). 90th Birth Anniv of Joseph Stalin. P 12.

1354 **281** 15q. reddish lilac ... 20 10
1355 25q. slate-blue ... 55 20
1356 1l. brown ... 1·80 75
1357 1l.10 chalky blue ... 2·20 1·00
1354/1357 *Set of* 4 ... 4·25 1·80

1969 (25 Dec). Mosaics (1st series). Multicoloured designs as T **282**. P 12×12½ (vert) or 12½×12 (horiz).

1358 15q. Type **282** ... 20 10
1359 25q. Floor pattern (horiz) ... 35 20
1360 80q. Bird and tree (horiz) ... 1·10 50
1361 1l.10 Diamond floor pattern (horiz) ... 1·60 65
1362 1l.20 Corn in oval pattern ... 2·20 75
1358/1362 *Set of* 5 ... 5·00 2·00

See also No. 1391/6, 1564/70 and 1657/62.

283 Manifesto and Congress Building

284 "25" and Workers

(Des R. Ballauri)

1970 (21 Jan). 50th Anniv of Lushnjë Congress. T **283** and similar vert design. P 12.

1363 25q. black, red and grey ... 55 30
1364 1l.25 black, greenish yellow and deep bluish green ... 3·25 2·10

Design:—1l.25, Lushnjë postmark of 1920.

(Des S. Prapaniku)

1970 (11 Feb). 25th Anniv of Albanian Trade Unions. P 12½×12.

1365 **284** 25q. black, red, brown and grey ... 55 30
1366 1l.75 black, red, sepia and lavender ... 3·25 2·10

285 *Lilium cernum*

286 Lenin

(Des N. Prizreni)

1970 (10 March). Lilies. Multicoloured designs as T **285**. P 12½×12 (vert) or 12×12½ (horiz).

1367 5q. Type **285** ... 25 15
1368 15q. *Lilium candidum* ... 35 20
1369 25q. *Lilium regale* ... 55 30
1370 80q. *Lilium martagon* (horiz) ... 1·60 1·00
1371 1l.10 *Lilium tigrinum* (horiz) ... 2·20 1·40
1372 1l.15 *Lilium albanicum* ... 2·75 1·80
1367/1372 *Set of* 6 ... 7·00 4·25

(Des N. Prizreni)

1970 (22 April). Birth Centenary of Lenin. Designs as T **286**, each black, silver and red. P 12.

1373 5q. Type **286** ... 20 10
1374 15q. Lenin making speech (horiz) ... 45 20
1375 25q. As worker (horiz) ... 55 30
1376 95q. As revolutionary (horiz) ... 1·30 75
1377 1l.10 Saluting ... 2·40 1·00
1373/1377 *Set of* 5 ... 4·50 2·10

287 Frontier Guard

(Des S. Prapaniku)

1970 (25 April). 25th Anniv of Frontier Force. P 12.

1378 **287** 25q. multicoloured ... 55 30
1379 1l.25 multicoloured ... 2·75 1·80

288 Jules Rimet Cup

(Des S. Toptani)

1970 (15 May). World Cup Football Championship, Mexico. T **288** and similar horiz designs. Multicoloured. P 12½×12.

1380 5q. Type **288** ... 10 10
1381 10q. Aztec Stadium ... 15 10
1382 15q. Three footballers ... 20 10
1383 25q. Heading goal ... 25 15
1384 65q. Two footballers ... 55 20
1385 80q. Two footballers ... 1·10 50
1386 2l. Two footballers ... 2·75 1·40
1380/1386 *Set of* 7 ... 4·50 2·30

MS1387 81×74 mm. 2l. Mexican horseman and Mt. Popocatepetl. P 12×imperf ... 4·00 3·00

Nos. 1384/6 show different incidents. The design of **MS**1387 is larger, 56×45 mm.

289 New UPU Headquarters Building

(Des S. Qesku)

1970 (30 May). New UPU Headquarters Building, Berne. P 12.

1388 **289** 25q. light blue, black and new blue ... 35 15
1389 1l.10 flesh, black and yellow-orange ... 1·60 65
1390 1l.15 light blue-green, black and light emerald ... 1·80 1·00
1388/1390 *Set of* 3 ... 3·50 1·60

290 Birds and Grapes

(Des S. Toptani)

1970 (10 July). Mosaics (2nd series). T **290** and similar multicoloured designs. P 12×12½ (2l.25) or 12½×12 (others).

1391 5q. Type **290** ... 20 10
1392 10q. Waterfowl ... 35 10
1393 20q. Pheasant and tree-stump ... 45 15
1394 25q. Bird and leaves ... 55 20
1395 65q. Fish ... 1·10 50
1396 2l.25 Peacock (vert) ... 3·75 2·10
1391/1396 *Set of* 6 ... 5·75 2·75

291 Harvester and Dancers

(Des Q. Prizreni)

1970 (28 Aug). 25th Anniv of Agrarian Reform. T **291** and similar horiz designs. P 12×11½.

1397 15q. slate-lilac and black ... 45 20
1398 25q. blue and black ... 55 30
1399 80q. brown and black ... 1·60 50
1400 1l.30 orange-brown and black ... 2·20 1·00
1397/1400 *Set of* 4 ... 4·25 1·80

Designs:—25q. Ploughed fields and open-air conference; 80q. Cattle and newspapers; 1l.30, Combine-harvester and official visit.

292 Partisans going into Battle

293 "The Harvesters" (I. Sulovari)

(Des Q. Prizreni)

1970 (3 Sept). 50th Anniv of Battle of Vlórë. Vert designs as T **292**. P 12.

1401 15q. orange-brown, light orange and black ... 35 20
1402 25q. bistre-brown, light yellow and black ... 75 30
1403 1l.60 myrtle-green, light green and black. ... 2·40 1·60
1401/1403 *Set of* 3 ... 3·25 1·90

Designs:—25q. Victory parade; 1l.60, Partisans.

1970 (25 Sept). 25th Anniv of Liberation. Prize-winning Paintings. Multicoloured designs as T **293**. P 12×12½ (vert) or 12½×12 (horiz).

1404 5q. Type **293** ... 10 10
1405 15q. "Return of the Partisan" (D. Trebicka) ... 20 10
1406 25q. "The Miners" (N. Zajmi) (horiz) ... 25 15
1407 65q. "Instructing the Partisans" (H. Nallbani) (horiz) ... 55 30
1408 95q. "Making Plans" (V. Kilica) (horiz) ... 1·10 75
1409 2l. "The Machinist" (Z. Shoshi) ... 3·25 2·10
1404/1409 *Set of* 6 ... 5·00 3·25

MS1410 67×96 mm. 2l. "The Guerrilla" (S. Shijaku) (54×75 mm.). Imperf ... 3·75 2·50

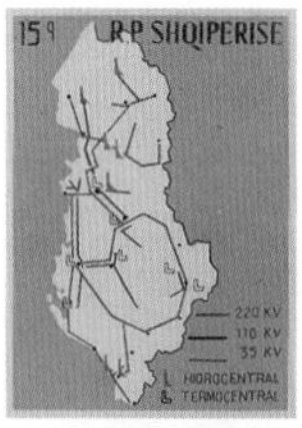

294 Electrification Map

295 Engels

(Des S. Toptani)

1970 (25 Oct). Completion of Rural Electrification. T **294** and similar vert designs. Multicoloured. P 12.

1411	15q. Type **294**	35	20
1412	25q. Lamp and graph	55	30
1413	80q. Erecting power lines	1·60	50
1414	1l.10 Uses of electricity	1·80	1·00
1411/1414 *Set of* 4		4·00	1·80

(Des N. Prizreni)

1970 (28 Nov). 150th Birth Anniv of Friedrich Engels. Vert designs as T **295**. P 12×12½.

1415	25q. deep blue and bistre	55	20
1416	1l.10 maroon and bistre	1·60	75
1417	1l.15 deep olive and bistre	1·80	85
1415/1417 *Set of* 3		3·50	1·60

Designs:—1l.10, Engels as young man, 1l.15, Engel, making speech.

295a Tractor Factory, Tirana.

1970 (4 Dec)–**71**. Industry. T **295a** and similar multicoloured designs. P 12.

1417*a*	10q. Type **295a** (20.1.71)	£275	£160
1417*b*	15q. Fertiliser factory, Fier	£275	£160
1417*c*	20q. Superphosphate factory, Laç (vert) (20.1.71)	£275	£160
1417*d*	25q. Cement factory, Elbasan (20.1.71)	£275	£160
1417*e*	80q. Factory, Qyteti Stalin	£275	£160
1415*a*/1417*e Set of* 5		£1200	£700

296 Beethoven's Birthplace

297 Republican Emblem

(Des S. Qesku)

1970 (16 Dec). Birth Bicent of Beethoven. Designs as T **296**. P 12.

1418	5q. reddish violet and gold	20	10
1419	15q. purple and silver	35	20
1420	25q. green and gold	55	30
1421	65q. bright purple and silver	1·30	85
1422	1l.10 deep blue and gold	2·40	1·00
1423	1l.80 black and silver	4·25	1·90
1418/1423 *Set of* 6		8·25	4·00

Designs: Vert—Beethoven: 15q. In silhouette; 25q. As young man; 65q. Full-face; 1l.10, Profile. Horiz—1l.80, Stage performance of "Fidelio".

(Des S. Qesku)

1971 (11 Jan). 25th Anniv of Republic. T **297** and similar horiz designs. P 12.

1424	15q. multicoloured	35	20
1425	25q. multicoloured	45	30
1426	80q. black, gold and bright green	1·30	1·00
1427	1l.30 black, gold & bright yell-brown	1·80	1·40
1424/1427 *Set of* 4		3·50	2·50

Designs:—25q. Proclamation; 80q. Enver Hoxha; 1l.30, Patriots.

298 Storming the Barricades

299 "Conflict of Race"

(Des S. Qesku)

1971 (18 Mar). Centenary of Paris Commune. Designs as T **298**. P 12.

1428	25q. blue and deep blue	55	20
1429	50q. deep yellow-green & slate-green	75	40
1430	65q. chestnut and blackish brown	1·10	50
1431	1l.10 slate-lilac and deep violet	2·20	1·00
1428/1431 *Set of* 4		4·25	1·90

Designs: Vert—25q. "La Marseillaise"; 50q. Women Communards. Horiz—1l.10, Firing squad.

(Des C. Ceka)

1971 (21 Mar). Racial Equality Year. T **299** and similar horiz designs. P 12×12½.

1432	25q. black and orange-brown	35	20
1433	1l.10 black and carmine	1·10	50
1434	1l.15 black and orange-red	1·30	65
1432/1434 *Set of* 3		2·50	1·20

Designs:—1l.10, Heads of three races; 1l.15, Freedom fighter.

300 Tulip

301 "Postrider"

(Des N. Prizreni)

1971 (25 Mar). Hybrid Tulips. T **300** and similar vert designs, showing different varieties of tulips. P 12×12½.

1435	5q. multicoloured	15	10
1436	10q. multicoloured	20	10
1437	15q. multicoloured	35	10
1438	20q. multicoloured	45	15
1439	25q. multicoloured	55	20
1440	80q. multicoloured	1·60	50
1441	1l. multicoloured	2·75	1·00
1442	1l.45 multicoloured	4·25	2·10
1435/1442 *Set of* 8		9·25	3·75

1971 (15 May). 500th Birth Anniv of Albrecht Dürer (painter and engraver). T **301** and similar designs showing Dürer's works. P 11½×12 (vert) or 12×11½ (horiz).

1443	10q. black and blackish olive	20	10
1444	15q. black and lavender	45	15
1445	25q. black and pale grey-blue	55	20
1446	45q. black and pale reddish purple	1·10	50
1447	65q. multicoloured	2·20	1·00
1448	2l.40 multicoloured	6·50	2·10
1443/1448 *Set of* 6		10·00	3·75
MS1449 93×90 mm. 2l.50, multicoloured. Imperf.		5·50	3·75

Designs: Vert—15q. "Three Peasants"; 25q. "Peasant Dancers"; 45q. "The Bagpiper". Horiz—65q. "View of Kalchreut"; 2l.40, "View of Trient". Larger—2l.50, Self-portrait.

302 Globe and Satellite (1970)

303 Mao Tse-tung

(Des N. Prizreni)

1971 (10 June). Chinese Space Achievements. T **302** and similar vert designs. Multicoloured. P 12.

1450	60q. Type **302**	1·10	50
1451	1l.20 Public Building, Tirana	2·20	1·60
1452	2l.20 Globe and satellite (1971)	4·25	3·25
1450/1452 *Set of* 3		6·75	4·75
MS1453 65×112 mm. 2l.50, Globe and arrow. Imperf		6·50	3·75

The date on No. 1451 refers to the passage of Chinese satellite over Tirana.

1971 (1 July). 50th Anniv of Chinese Communist Party. T **303** and similar multicoloured designs. P 12.

1454	25q. Type **303**	85	50
1455	1l.05 Party birthplace (horiz)	2·20	1·60
1456	1l.20 Chinese celebrations (horiz)	3·25	2·50
1454/1456 *Set of* 3		5·75	4·25

304 Crested Tit (*Parus cristatus mitratus*)

(Des N. Prizreni)

1971 (15 Aug). Birds. T **304** and similar horiz designs. Multicoloured. P 12.

1457	5q. Type **304**	35	10
	a. Block. Nos. 1457/63 plus label	17·00	
1458	10q. Serin (*Serinus canaria serinus*)	45	15
1459	15q. Linnet (*Acanthis canabina*)	65	15
1460	25q. Firecrest (wrongly inscr "*Regulus regulus*")	1·10	20
1461	45q. Rock thrush (*Monticola saxatilis*)	1·60	40
1462	60q. Blue tit (*Parus coeruleus*)	2·40	1·00
1463	2l.40 Chaffinch (*Fringilla coelebs*)	9·75	8·25
1457/1463 *Set of* 7		14·50	9·25

Nos. 1457/63 were issued together within the sheet in *se-tenant* blocks of seven stamps and one label showing a nest.

Blocks also exist cancelled to order with the design of the 2l.40 omitted. These were prepared for sale as c-t-o "short" sets.

305 Running

(Des S. Toptani)

1971 (15 Sept). Olympic Games, Munich (1972) (1st issue). T **305** and similar horiz designs (except **MS**1471). Multicoloured. P 12.

1464	5q. Type **305**	10	10
1465	10q. Hurdling	15	10
1466	15q. Canoeing	20	15
1467	25q. Gymnastics	55	20
1468	80q. Fencing	1·10	40
1469	1l.05 Football	1·30	50
1470	3l.60 Diving	4·50	1·60
1464/1470 *Set of* 7		7·00	2·75
MS1471 70×83 mm. 2l. Runner breasting tape (47×54 mm). Imperf.		4·00	3·00

See also Nos. 1522/**MS**1530.

306 Workers with Banner

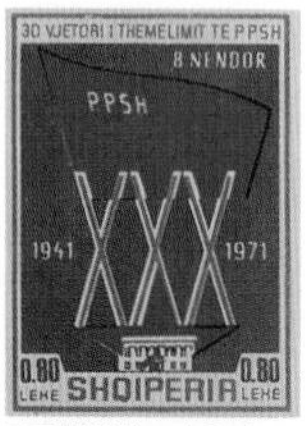

307 "XXX" and Red Flag

(Des N. Prizreni)

1971 (1 Nov). 6th Workers' Party Congress. T **306** and similar designs. P 12.

1472	25q. Type **306**	55	20
1473	1l.05 Congress Hall	1·60	1·40
1474	1l.20 "VI", flag, star and rifle (vert)	2·20	1·60
1472/1474 *Set of* 3		4·00	3·00

(Des. N. Prizreni)

1971 (8 Nov). 30th Anniv of Albanian Workers' Party. T **307** and similar multicoloured designs. P 12.

1475	15q. Workers and industry (horiz)	20	10
1476	80q. Type **307**	1·40	1·00
1477	1l.55 Enver Hoxha and flags (horiz)	2·75	1·90
1475/1477 *Set of* 3		4·00	2·75

308 "Young Man" (R. Kuci)

309 Emblems and Flags

1971 (20 Nov). Albanian Paintings. T **308** and similar multicoloured designs. P 12.

1478	5q. Type **308**	10	10
1479	15q. "Building Construction" (M. Fushekati) (horiz)	15	10
1480	25q. "Partisan" (D. Jukniu)	20	15
1481	80q. "Fighter Pilots" (S. Kristo) (horiz)	1·10	20
1482	1l.20 "Girl Messenger" (A. Sadikaj) (horiz)	1·40	85
1483	1l.55 "Medieval Warriors" (S. Kamberi) (horiz)	1·60	1·40
1478/1483 *Set of* 6		4·00	2·50
MS1484 89×70 mm. 2l. "Partisans in the Mountains" (I. Lulani). Imperf		4·00	3·00

(Des B. Dizdari)

1971 (23 Nov). 30th Anniv of Albanian Young Communists Union. P 12.

1485	**309**	15q. multicoloured	20	10
1486		1l.35 multicoloured	2·00	1·00

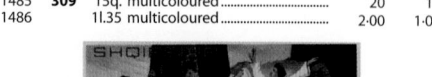

310 Village Girls

(Des T. Dajci)

1971 (27 Dec). Albanian Ballet "Halili and Hajria". T **310** and similar horiz designs showing ballet scenes. Multicoloured. P 12.

1487	5q. Type **310**	15	10
1488	10q. Parting of Halili and Hajria	20	10
1489	15q. Hajria before Sultan Suleiman	20	15
1490	50q. Hajria's marriage	75	50
1491	80q. Execution of Halili	1·30	75
1492	1l.40 Hajria killing her husband	2·20	1·30
1487/1492 *Set of* 6		4·25	2·50

311 Rifle-shooting (Biathlon)

(Des S. Toptani)

1972 (10 Feb). Winter Olympic Games, Sapporo, Japan. T **311** and similar horiz designs. Multicoloured. P 12.

1493	5q. Type **311**	10	10
1494	10q. Tobogganing	15	10
1495	15q. Ice hockey	15	10
1496	20q. Bobsleighing	20	10
1497	50q. Speed skating	85	50
1498	1l. Slalom skiing	1·30	85
1499	2l. Ski jumping	2·40	1·90
1493/1499	*Set of 7*	4·75	3·25
MS1500	71×91 mm. 2l.50, Figure skating. Imperf.	4·00	3·00

312 Wild Strawberries

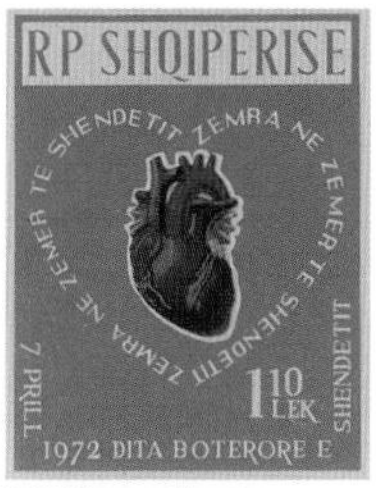

313 Human Heart

(Des N. Prizreni)

1972 (20 Mar). Wild Forest Fruits. T **312** and similar square designs. Multicoloured. P 12.

1501	5q. Type **312**	15	10
1502	10q. Blackberries	15	10
1503	15q. Hazelnuts	20	10
1504	20q. Walnuts	45	15
1505	25q. Strawberry-tree fruit	55	20
1506	30q. Dogwood berries	75	50
1507	2l.40 Rowanberries	4·25	1·60
1501/1507	*Set of 7*	5·75	2·50

(Des S. Toptani)

1972 (7 Apr). World Health Day. T **313** and similar vert design. Multicoloured. P 12.

1508	1l.10 Type **313**	1·80	1·30
1509	1l.20 Treatment of cardiac patient	2·00	1·40

314 Congress Delegates

315 Memorial Flame

(Des I. Shehu)

1972 (24 Apr). Seventh Albanian Trade Unions Congress. T **314** and similar vert design. Multicoloured. P 12×12½.

1510	25q. Type **314**	75	50
1511	2l.05 Congress Hall	3·00	1·80

(Des N. Prizreni)

1972 (5 May). 30th Anniv of Martyrs' Day and Death of Kemal Stafa. T **315** and similar designs. P 12×12½ (25q.) or 12½×12 (others).

1512	15q. multicoloured	20	10
1513	25q. pale grey, black and orange-red	55	20
1514	1l.90 black and yellow-ochre	2·75	1·30
1512/1514	*Set of 3*	3·25	1·40

Designs: Vert—25q. "Spirit of Defiance (statue). Horiz—1l.90, Kemal Stafa.

316 *Camellia japonica Kamelie*

(Des N. Prizreni)

1972 (10 May). Camellias. T **316** and similar vert designs, showing different varieties of flower. P 12.

1515	5q. multicoloured	15	10
1516	10q. multicoloured	20	10
1517	15q. multicoloured	25	15
1518	25q. multicoloured	55	20
1519	45q. multicoloured	75	30
1520	50q. multicoloured	1·30	50
1521	2l.50 multicoloured	5·00	2·50
1515/1521	*Set of 7*	7·50	3·50

317 High Jumping

(Des S. Toptani)

1972 (30 June). Olympic Games, Munich (2nd issue). T **317** and similar horiz designs. Multicoloured. P 12.

1522	5q. Type **317**	10	10
1523	10q. Running	15	10
1524	15q. Putting the shot	20	10
1525	20q. Cycling	35	15
1526	25q. Pole-vaulting	45	20
1527	50q. Hurdling	55	30
1528	75q. Hockey	1·10	50
1529	2l. Swimming	3·25	1·00
1522/1529	*Set of 8*	5·50	2·20
MS1530	59×76 mm. 2l.50, High-diving (vert). Imperf	4·00	3·00

Nos. 1522/9 were each issued in sheets of 8 stamps with a central stamp-size label showing Olympic rings.

318 Articulated Bus

319 "Trial of Strength"

(Des N. Prizreni)

1972 (25 July). Modern Transport. T **318** and similar horiz designs. Multicoloured. P 12×11½.

1531	15q. Type **318**	20	10
1532	25q. Diesel railway locomotive	55	15
1533	80q. Freighter *Tirana*	75	20
1534	1l.05 Motor-car	1·30	50
1535	1l.20 Container lorry	2·20	1·00
1531/1535	*Set of 5*	4·50	1·80

(Des I. Shehu)

1972 (18 Aug). First National Festival of Traditional Games. T **319** and similar square designs. Multicoloured. P 12.

1536	5q. Type **319**	10	10
1537	10q. Pick-a-back ball game	15	10
1538	15q. Leaping game	20	10
1539	25q. Rope game	55	20
1540	90q. Leap-frog	1·60	75
1541	2l. Women's throwing game	2·75	2·10
1536/1541	*Set of 6*	4·75	3·00

320 Newspaper "Mastheads"

(Des S. Toptani)

1972 (25 Aug). 30th Anniv of Press Day. T **320** and similar horiz designs. P 12.

1542	15q. black and light greenish blue	20	10
1543	25q. black, myrtle-green and scarlet	35	15
1544	1l.90 black and lavender	2·20	1·60
1542/1544	*Set of 3*	2·50	1·70

Designs:—25q. Printing press and partisan; 1l.90, Workers with newspaper.

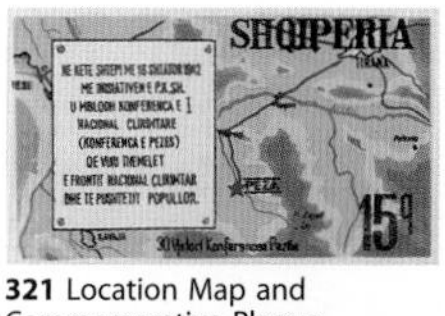

321 Location Map and Commemorative Plaque

323 Congress Emblem

322 "Partisan Conference" (S. Capo)

(Des T. Dajci)

1972 (16 Sept). 30th Anniv of Peza Conference. T **321** and similar horiz designs. Multicoloured. P 12×11½.

1545	15q. Type **321**	35	20
1546	25q. Partisans with flag	55	30
1547	1l.90 Conference Memorial	3·00	1·90
1545/1547	*Set of 3*	3·50	2·20

1972 (25 Sept). Albanian Paintings. T **322** and similar multicoloured designs. P 12.

1548	5q. Type **322**	10	10
1549	10q. "Head of a Woman" (I. Lulani) (vert)	15	10
1550	15q. "Communists" (L. Shkreli) (vert)	20	10
1551	20q. "Nendorit, 1941" (S. Shijaku) (vert)	35	15
1552	50q. "Farm Woman" (Z. Shoshi) (vert)	65	20
1553	1l. "Landscape" (D. Trebicka)	1·30	75
1554	2l. "Girls with Bicycles" (V. Kilica)	2·75	2·10
1548/1554	*Set of 7*	5·00	3·25
MS1555	55×83 mm. 2l.30, "Folk Dance" (A. Buza) (vert, 40×67 mm). Imperf	4·00	3·00

(Des B. Dizdari)

1972 (23 Oct). 6th Congress of Young Communists' Union. T **323** and similar vert design. P 12.

1556	25q. gold, red and silver	75	50
1557	2l.05 multicoloured	3·00	1·80

Design:—2l.05, Young worker and banner.

324 Lenin

325 Albanian Soldiers

(Des N. Prizreni)

1972 (7 Nov). 55th Anniv of Russian October Revolution. T **324** and similar vert design. P 11½×12.

1558	1l.10 multicoloured	1·60	1·00
1559	1l.20 black, vermilion and rose-red	3·25	1·30

Design:—1l.10, Hammer and sickle.

(Des B. Kaceli)

1972 (29 Nov). 60th Anniv of Independence. T **325** and similar designs. P 12×11½.

1560	15q. new blue, black and scarlet	15	15
1561	25q. black, carmine-red and lemon	35	20
1562	65q. multicoloured	85	50
1563	1l.25 black and red	2·75	1·30
1560/1563	*Set of 4*	3·75	1·90

Designs: Vert—25q. Ismail Qemali; 1l.25, Albanian double-headed eagle emblem. Horiz—65q. Proclamation of Independence, 1912.

326 Cockerel (mosaic)

327 Nicolas Copernicus

(Des F. Hasimja)

1972 (10 Dec). Ancient Mosaics from Apolloni and Butrint (3rd series). T **326** and similar multicoloured designs with silver borders. P 12½×12 (horiz) or 12×12½ (vert).

1564	5q. Type **326**	10	10
1565	10q. Bird (vert)	15	10
1566	15q. Partridges (vert)	20	10
1567	25q. Warrior's legs	45	30
1568	45q. Nude on dolphin (vert)	55	40
1569	50q. Fish (vert)	75	50
1570	2l.50 Warrior's head	3·75	2·50
1564/1570	*Set of 7*	5·25	3·50

(Des N. Prizreni)

1973 (19 Feb). 500th Birth Anniv of Copernicus. T **327** and similar vert designs. Multicoloured. P 12.

1571	5q. Type **327**	10	10
1572	10q. Copernicus and signature	15	10
1573	25q. Engraved portrait	20	15
1574	80q. Copernicus at desk	75	40
1575	1l.20 Copernicus and planets	2·20	1·00
1576	1l.60 Planetary diagram	3·25	1·60
1571/1576	*Set of 6*	6·00	3·00

328 Policeman and Industrial Scene

329/330 Cactus Flowers

(Des N. Prizreni)

1973 (20 Mar). 30th Anniv of State Security Police. T **328** and similar horiz design. P 12½×12.

1577	25q. black, new blue and pale blue	55	40
1578	1l.80 multicoloured	3·00	1·80

Design:— 1l.80, Prisoner under escort.

(Des S. Qesku)

1973 (25 Mar). Cacti. Various triangular designs showing different species, as in T **329/30**. P 12.

1579	10q. multicoloured	10	10
	a. Block of 8. Nos. 1579/86	9·75	
1580	15q. multicoloured	15	10
1581	20q. multicoloured	20	10
1582	25q. multicoloured	55	15
1583	30q. multicoloured	4·25	2·50
1584	65q. multicoloured	85	40
1585	80q. multicoloured	1·10	50
1586	2l. multicoloured	2·20	1·30
1579/1586 *Set of 8*		8·50	4·75

Nos. 1579/86 were issued together in *se-tenant* blocks of eight within the sheet, each block containing four pairs as T **329/30**.

Blocks also exist cancelled-to-order with the 30q. replaced by a label.

331 Common Tern (*Sterna hirundo*)

(Des N. Prizreni)

1973 (30 Apr). Sea Birds. T **331** and similar multicoloured designs. P 12½×12 (horiz) or 12×12½ (vert).

1587	5q. Type **331**	25	15
1588	15q. White-winged black tern (*Chlidonias leucoptera*) (vert)	45	20
1589	25q. Black-headed gull (*Larus ridibundus*)	55	30
1590	45q. Great black-headed gull (wrongly inscr "Larus argentatus")	1·10	75
1591	80q. Slender-billed gull (*Larus genei*) (vert)	2·20	1·60
1592	2l.40 Sandwich tern (*Sterna sandvicensis*)	4·25	3·25
1587/1592 *Set of 6*		8·00	5·75

332 Postmark of 1913, and Letters **333** Albanian Woman

(Des R. Ballauri)

1973 (5 May). 60th Anniv of First Albanian Stamps. T **332** and similar horiz design. Multicoloured. P 12×11½.

1593	25q. Type **332**	1·10	50
1594	1l.80 1913 postmark, and postman	4·25	2·10

(Des B. Dizdari)

1973 (4 June). 7th Congress of Albanian Women's Union. T **333** and similar design. P 12.

1595	25q. carmine-red and pink	55	30
1596	1l.80 black, red-orange and pale yellow	3·25	2·30

Design: Horiz—1l.80, Albanian female workers.

334 "Creation of the General Staff" (G. Madhi)

1973 (10 July). 30th Anniv of Albanian People's Army. T **334** and similar multicoloured designs, showing paintings or sculptures. P 12.

1597	25q. Type **334**	16·00	10·50
1598	40q. "August 1949" (statue, S. Haderi) (vert)	16·00	10·50
1599	60q. "Generation after Generation" (statue, H. Dule) (vert)	16·00	10·50
1600	80q. "Defend Revolutionary Victories" (M. Fushekati)	16·00	10·50
1597/1600 *Set of 4*		60·00	38·00

335 "Electrification" (S. Hysa)

1973 (10 Aug). Albanian Paintings. T **335** and similar multicoloured designs. P 12.

1601	5q. Type **335**	10	10
1602	10q. "Textile Worker" (N. Nallbani) (vert)	15	10
1603	15q. "Gymnastics Class" (M. Fushekati)	15	10
1604	50q. "Aviator" (F. Stamo) (vert)	65	40
1605	80q. "Downfall of Fascism" (A. Lakuriqi) (vert)	75	50
1606	1l.20 "Koci Bako" (demonstrators) (P. Mele) (vert)	1·10	85
1607	1l.30 "Peasant Girl" (Z. Shoshi) (vert)	2·20	1·60
1601/1607 *Set of 7*		4·50	3·25
MS1608 100×69 mm. 2l.05, "Battle of Tendes se Qypit" (F. Haxhiu) (88×47 mm). Imperf		4·00	3·00

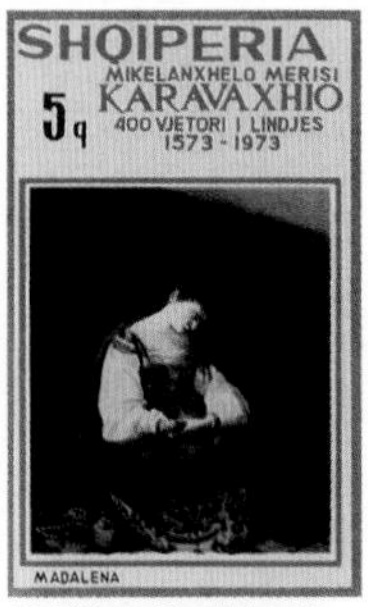

336 "Mary Magdalene"

1973 (28 Sept). 400th Birth Anniv of Caravaggio. T **336** and similar multicoloured designs, showing his paintings. P 12.

1609	5q. Type **336**	10	10
1610	10q. "Guitar Player" (horiz)	15	10
1611	15q. Self-portrait	20	10
1612	50q. "Boy with Fruit"	65	40
1613	80q. "Basket of Fruit" (horiz)	85	65
1614	1l.20 "Narcissus"	1·30	1·00
1615	1l.30 "Boy peeling Apple"	2·20	1·60
	a. Black (value and bottom inscr) omitted	£120	
1609/1615 *Set of 7*		5·00	3·50
MS1616 80×102 mm. 2l.05, "Man in Feathered Hat". Imperf		6·00	5·25

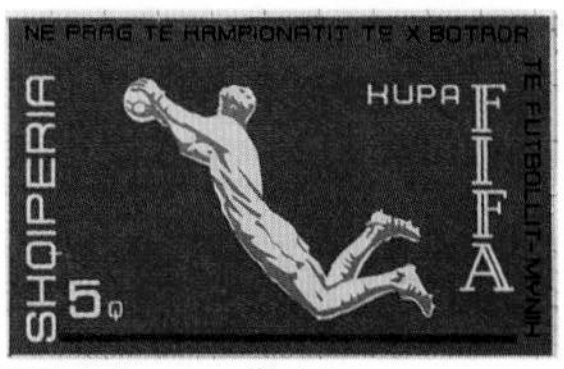

337 Goalkeeper with Ball

(Des S. Toptani)

1973 (15 Oct). World Cup Football Championship, Munich (1974) (1st issue). T **337** and similar horiz designs, showing goalkeepers in various poses. P 12.

1617	5q. multicoloured	10	10
1618	10q. multicoloured	15	10
1619	15q. multicoloured	15	10
1620	20q. multicoloured	20	15
1621	25q. multicoloured	25	15
1622	90q. multicoloured	1·30	40
1623	1l.20 multicoloured	1·50	75
1624	1l.25 multicoloured	2·20	1·00
1617/1624 *Set of 8*		5·25	2·50
MS1625 80×50 mm. 2l.05, multicoloured (Ball in net, and list of Championships). Imperf		4·50	3·25

See also Nos. 1663/**MS**1671.

338 Weightlifting **339** Ballet Scene

(Des N. Prizreni)

1973 (30 Oct). World Weightlifting Championships, Havana, Cuba. T **338** and similar designs showing various "lifts". P 12.

1626	5q. multicoloured	10	10
1627	10q. multicoloured	15	10
1628	25q. multicoloured	20	10
1629	90q. multicoloured	75	40
1630	1l.20 multicoloured (horiz)	1·10	75
1631	1l.80 multicoloured (horiz)	2·20	1·20
1626/1631 *Set of 6*		4·00	2·40

(Des Q. Prizreni)

1973 (5 Dec)–**74**. "Albanian Life and Work". T **339** and similar multicoloured designs. P 12½×12 (vert) or 12×12½ (horiz).

1632	5q. Cement works, Kavaje (20.3.74)	10	10
1633	10q. "Ali Kelmendi" lorry factory (horiz) (20.3.74)	20	10
1634	15q. Type **339**	55	10
1635	20q. Combine-harvester (horiz) (12.8.74)	25	10
1636	25q. "Telecommunications"	85	20
1637	35q. Skier and hotel, Dajt (horiz) (20.3.74)	65	20
1638	60q. Llogora holiday village (horiz) (20.3.74)	1·10	45
1639	80q. Lake scene	1·80	50
1640	1l. Textile Mill (horiz) (12.8.74)	45	20
1641	1l.20 Furnacemen (horiz) (12.8.74)	1·30	50
1642	2l.40 Welder and pipeline (horiz) (12.8.74)	2·75	1·60
1643	3l. Skanderbeg Statue, Tirana	4·25	2·50
1644	5l. Roman arches, Durrës (20.3.74)	5·00	3·25
1632/1644 *Set of 13*		17·00	8·75

340 Mao Tse-tung **341** "Horse's Head" (Géricault)

(Des S. Toptani)

1973 (26 Dec). 80th Birthday of Mao Tse-tung. T **340** and similar vert design. Multicoloured. P 12.

1645	85q. Type **340**	2·75	1·60
1646	1l.20 Mao Tse-tung at parade	3·75	2·50

1974 (18 Jan). 150th Death Anniv of Jean-Louis Géricault (French painter). T **341** and similar designs inscr "ZHERIKO". P 12.

1647	10q. multicoloured	15	10
1648	15q. multicoloured	15	10
1649	20q. blackish brown and gold	20	10
1650	25q. black, dull lavender and gold	55	30
1651	1l.20 multicoloured	2·20	75
1652	2l.20 multicoloured	3·75	2·10
1647/1652 *Set of 6*		6·25	3·00
MS1653 90×68 mm. 2l.05, multicoloured. Imperf		4·00	3·00

Designs: Vert—15q. "Male Model"; 20q. "Man and Dog"; 25q. "Head of a Negro"; 1l.20, Self-portrait. Horiz—2l.20, "Battle of the Giants". (Larger)—2l.05, "Raft of the Medusa".

342 "Lenin with Crew of the Aurora"

(D. Trebicka)

1974 (21 Jan). 50th Death Anniv of Lenin. T **342** and similar multicoloured paintings. P 12.

1654	25q. Type **342**	55	30
1655	60q. "Lenin" (P. Mele) (vert)	1·10	50
1656	1l.20 "Lenin" (seated) (V. Kilica) (vert)	3·25	2·10
1654/1656 *Set of 3*		4·50	2·50

343 Duck

1974 (20 Feb). Ancient Mosaics from Butrint, Pogradec and Apolloni (4th series). T **343** and similar horiz designs. Multicoloured. P 12.

1657	5q. Type **343**	10	10
1658	10q. Bird and flower	15	10
1659	15q. Ornamental basket and grapes	20	15
1660	25q. Duck (different)	35	20
1661	40q. Donkey and cockerel	45	30
1662	2l.50 Dragon	2·75	2·10
1657/1662 *Set of 6*		3·50	2·75

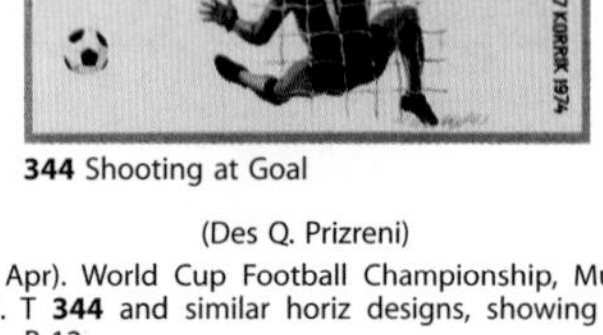

344 Shooting at Goal

(Des Q. Prizreni)

1974 (25 Apr). World Cup Football Championship, Munich (2nd issue). T **344** and similar horiz designs, showing players in action. P 12.

1663	10q. multicoloured	15	10
1664	15q. multicoloured	15	10
1665	20q. multicoloured	20	10
1666	25q. multicoloured	35	15
1667	40q. multicoloured	55	20
1668	80q. multicoloured	1·10	50
1669	1l. multicoloured	1·30	75
1670	1l.20 multicoloured	1·80	1·40
1663/1670 *Set of 8*		5·00	3·00
MS1671 72×75 mm. 2l.05, multicoloured (Trophy and names of competing countries). Imperf		4·00	3·00

345 Memorial and Arms

346 *Solanum dulcamara*

(Des Q. Prizreni)

1974 (24 May). 30th Anniv of Permet Congress. T **345** and similar vert design. Multicoloured. P 12.

1672	25q. Type **345**	55	30
1673	1l.80 Enver Hoxha and text	2·20	1·60

1974 (25 May). Useful Plants. T **346** and similar multicoloured designs. P 12×12½ (vert) or 12½×12 (horiz).

1674	10q. Type **346**	15	10
1675	15q. *Arbutus uva-ursi*	15	10
1676	20q. *Convallaria majalis*	20	10
1677	25q. *Colchicum autumnale*	55	10
1678	40q. *Borago officihalis* (horiz)	75	20
1679	80q. *Saponaria officinalis* (horiz)	1·30	50
1680	2l.20 *Gentiane lutea* (horiz)	3·75	2·10
1674/1680 *Set of 7*		6·25	3·00

347 Revolutionaries

(Des C. Ceka)

1974 (10 June). 50th Anniv of 1924 Revolution. T **347** and similar design. P 12½×12 (horiz) or 12×12½ (vert).

1681	25q. black, lilac and scarlet	55	30
1682	1l.80 multicoloured	2·20	1·60

Design: Vert—1l.80, Prominent revolutionaries.

348 Redwing (*Turdus musicus*)

(Des N. Prizreni)

1974 (15 July). Song Birds. T **348** and similar multicoloured designs. P 12½×12 (horiz) or 12×12½ (vert).

1683	10q. Type **348**	20	10
1684	15q. European robin (*Erithacus rubecula*)	25	15
1685	20q. Greenfinch (*Chloris chloris*)	35	15
1686	25q. Bullfinch (*Pyrrhula pyrrhula*) (vert)	55	20
1687	40q. Hawfinch (*Coccothraustes coccothraustes*) (vert)	85	25
1688	80q. Blackcap (*Sylvia atricapilla*) (vert)	2·40	75
1689	2l.20 Nightingale (*Luscina megarhyncha*) (vert)	4·25	2·10
1683/1689 *Set of 7*		8·00	3·25

349 Globe and Post Office Emblem

(Des S. Toptani)

1974 (25 Aug). Centenary of Universal Postal Union. T **349** and similar designs. P 12×12½.

1690	85q. multicoloured	1·80	85
1691	1l.20 dull green, lilac & dp reddish vio	2·75	1·30
MS1692	78×78 mm. 2l.05, multicoloured. Imperf	25·00	33·00

Designs: Vert—1l.20, U.P.U. emblem. Square (70×70 mm)—2l.05, Text on Globe.

350 "Widows" (Sali Shijaku)

1974 (25 Sept). Albanian Paintings. T **350** and similar multicoloured designs. P 12½×12 (horiz) or 12×12½ (vert).

1693	10q. Type **350**	10	10
1694	15q. "Road Construction" (Danish Jukniu) (vert)	20	10
1695	20q. "Fulfilling the Plans" (Clirim Ceka)	25	10
1696	25q. "Call to Action" (Spiro Kristo) (vert)	45	20
1697	40q. "Winter Battle" (Sabaudin Xhaferi)	55	20
1698	80q. "Three Comrades" (Clirim Ceka) (vert)	1·10	50
1699	1l. "Step By Step, Aid the Partisans" (Guri Madhi)	1·60	1·00
1700	1l.20 "At the War Memorial" (Kleo Nini)	2·20	1·30
1693/1700 *Set of 8*		5·75	3·25
MS1701	87×78 mm. 2l.05, "Comrades" (Guri Madhi). Imperf	4·00	3·00

351 Chinese Festivities

352 Volleyball

(Des I. Shehu)

1974 (1 Oct). 25th Anniv of Chinese People's Republic. T **351** and similar design. P 12.

1702	85q. multicoloured	3·50	2·10
1703	1l.20 black, rosine and gold	5·50	3·25

Design: Vert—1l.20, Mao Tse-tung.

(Des. Q. Prizreni)

1974 (9 Oct). National Spartakiad. T **352** and similar vert designs. Multicoloured. P 12×12½.

1704	10q. Type **352**	10	10
1705	15q. Hurdling	10	10
1706	20q. Hoop Exercises	15	10
1707	25q. Stadium parade	20	15
1708	40q. Weightlifting	55	20
1709	80q. Wrestling	75	40
1710	1l. Rifle drill	1·10	45
1711	1l.20 Football	1·60	50
1704/1711 *Set of 8*		4·00	1·80

353 Berat

354 Security Guards patrolling Industrial Plant

(Des M. Quarri)

1974 (20 Oct). 30th Anniv of 2nd Berat Liberation Council Meeting. T **353** and similar designs. P 12×12½ (vert) or 12½×12 (horiz).

1712	25q. carmine and black	55	30
1713	80q. greenish yellow, chocolate & blk	1·60	75
1714	1l. reddish purple and black	3·25	1·60
1712/1714 *Set of 3*		4·75	2·40

Designs: Horiz—80q. "Liberation" frieze. Vert—1l. Council members walking to meeting.

(Des. Q. Prizreni)

1974 (29 Nov). 30th Anniv of Liberation. T **354** and similar horiz designs. Multicoloured. P 12½×12.

1715	25q. Type **354**	15	10
1716	35q. Chemical Industry	20	10
1717	50q. Agriculture	35	15
1718	80q. Cultural Activities	45	25
1719	1l. Scientific Technology	85	50
1720	1l.20 Railway Construction	1·20	75
1715/1720 *Set of 6*		3·00	1·70
MS1721	81×70 mm. 2l.05, Albanians with Book (60×40 mm). Imperf	4·00	3·25

355 Head of Artemis

356 Clasped Hands

(Des S. Toptani and F. Sulo)

1974 (25 Dec). Archaeological Discoveries. T **355** and similar vert designs. P 12×12½.

1722	10q. black, mauve and greyish silver	10	10
1723	15q. black, turquoise-green and greyish silver	20	10
1724	20q. black, stone and greyish silver	35	20
1725	25q. black, brt mauve & greyish silver	55	40
1726	40q. multicoloured	1·10	85
1727	80q. black, pale blue and greyish silver	1·60	1·30
1728	1l. black, sage-grn & greyish silver	2·20	1·60
1729	1l.20 black, olive-sep & greyish silver	3·75	2·10
1722/1729 *Set of 8*		8·75	6·00
MS1730	96×96 mm. 2l.05, multicoloured. Imperf	4·00	3·25

Designs:—15q. Statue of Zeus; 20q. Statue of Poseidon; 25q. Illyrian helmet; 40q. Greek amphora; 80q. Bust of Agrippa, 1l. Bust of Demosthenes, 1l.20, Bust of Bilia. Square (84×84 mm)—2l.05, Head of Artemis and Greek vase.

(Des. B. Dizdari)

1975 (11 Feb). 30th Anniv of Albanian Trade Unions. T **356** and similar multicoloured designs. P 12.

1731	25q. Type **356**	55	20
1732	1l.80 Workers with arms raised (horiz)	2·20	1·40

357 *Cichorium intybus*

358 Head of Jesus (detail, Dom Tondo)

(Des N. Prizreni)

1975 (15 Feb). Albanian Flowers. T **357** and similar square designs. Multicoloured. P 12.

1733	5q. Type **357**	10	10
1734	10q. *Sempervivum montanum*	10	10
1735	15q. *Aquilegia alpina*	10	10
1736	20q. *Anemone hortensis*	15	10
1737	25q. *Hibiscus trionum*	15	10
1738	30q. *Gentiana kochiana*	20	10
1739	35q. *Lavatera arborea*	55	10
1740	2l.70 *Iris graminea*	3·00	1·90
1733/1740 *Set of 8*		4·00	2·30

(Des Q. Prizreni)

1975 (20 Mar). 500th Birth Anniv of Michelangelo. T **358** and similar vert designs. P 12×12½.

1741	5q. multicoloured	10	10
1742	10q. bistre-brown, bluish grey & gold	10	10
1743	15q. bistre-brown, bluish grey and gold	15	10
1744	20q. sepia, bluish grey and gold	20	10
1745	25q. multicoloured	20	10
1746	30q. purple-brown, bluish grey and gold	20	10
1747	1l.20 bistre, bluish grey and gold	1·10	65
1748	3l.90 multicoloured	2·75	1·90
1741/1748 *Set of 8*		4·25	2·75
MS1749	77×86 mm. 2l.05, multicoloured. Imperf	4·50	3·25

Designs: As T **358**—10q. "The Heroic Captive"; 15q. Head of "Dawn"; 20q. "Awakening Giant" (detail); 25q. Cumaean Sibyl (detail, Sistine chapel); 30q. Lorenzo di Medici; 1l.20, Head and shoulders of "David"; 3l.90, Delphic Sibyl (detail, Sistine chapel). 70×77 mm—2l.05, Head of Michelangelo.

Nos. 1742/4 and 1746/7 depict sculptures.

359 Horseman

(Des S. Toptani)

1975 (15 Apr). "Albanian Transport of the Past". T **359** and similar horiz designs. Multicoloured. P 12½×12.

1750	5q. Type **359**	10	10
1751	10q. Horse and cart	15	10
1752	15q. Ferry	25	10
1753	20q. Barque	25	15
1754	25q. Horse-drawn cab	35	15
1755	3l.35 Early motor car	3·75	1·60
1750/1755 *Set of 6*		4·25	2·00

360 Frontier Guard

(Des Q. Prizreni)

1975 (25 Apr). 30th Anniv of Frontier Force. T **360** and similar vert design. Multicoloured. P 12.

1756	25q. Type **360**	55	30
1757	1l.80 Guards patrolling Industrial Plant	2·20	1·60

361 Patriot affixing Anti-Fascist Placard

(Des B. Dizdari)

1975 (9 May). 30th Anniv of "Victory over Fascism". T **361** and similar horiz designs. Multicoloured. P 12½×12.

1758	25q. Type **361**	35	20
1759	60q. Partisans in Battle	75	50
1760	1l.20 Patriot defeating Nazi soldier	1·60	1·00
1758/1760	*Set of 3*	2·40	1·50

362 European wigeons (*Anas penelope*)

(Des N. Prizreni)

1975 (15 June). Albanian Waterfowl. T **362** and similar diamond-shaped designs. Multicoloured. P 12.

1761	5q. Type **362**	10	10
1762	10q. Red-crested pochards (*Netta rufina*)	15	10
1763	15q. White-fronted geese (*Anser albifrons*)	20	10
1764	20q. Pintails (*Anas acuta*)	20	10
1765	25q. Red-breasted mergansers (*Mergus serrator*)	35	15
1766	30q. Eiders (*Somateria mollissima*)	65	15
1767	35q. Whooper swan (*Cignus cignus*)	85	20
1768	2l.70 Shovelers (*Spatula clypeata*)	5·00	2·50
1761/1768	*Set of 8*	6·75	3·00

363 "Shygyri Kanapari" (Musa Qarri)

364 Farmer with Declaration of Reform

1975 (15 July). Albanian Paintings. People's Art Exhibition, Tirana. T **363** and similar multicoloured designs. P 12×12½ (vert) or 12½×12 (horiz).

1769	5q. Type **363**	10	10
1770	10q. "Sea rescue" (Agim Faja)	10	10
1771	15q. "28th November 1912" (Petrit Ceno) (horiz)	10	10
1772	20q. "Workers' Meeting" (Sali Shijaku)	15	10
1773	25q. "Shota Galica" (Ismail Lulani)	15	10
1774	30q. "Victorious Fighters" (Nestor Jonuzi)	20	15
1775	80q. "Partisan Comrades" (Vilson Halimi)	65	40
1776	2l.25 "Republic Day Celebration" (Fatmir Haxhiu) (horiz)	3·00	2·10
1769/1776	*Set of 8*	4·00	2·75
MS1777	68×98 mm. 2l.05, "Folk dance" (Abdurahim Buza). Imperf	3·75	3·25

Nos. 1769/76 were each printed in sheets of 32 stamps and 4 labels.

(Des M. Reci)

1975 (28 Aug). 30th Anniv of Agrarian Reform. T **364** and similar square design. Multicoloured. P 12.

1778	15q. Type **364**	55	30
1779	2l. Agricultural scene	2·75	1·80

365 *Alcyonium palmatum*

366 Cycling

(Des D. Theodori)

1975 (25 Sept). Marine Corals. T **365** and similar vert designs. Multicoloured. P 12×12½.

1780	5q. Type **365**	10	10
1781	10q. *Paramuricea chamaeleon*	15	10
1782	20q. *Coralium rubrum*	20	10
1783	25q. *Eunicella covalim*	35	15
1784	3l.70 *Cladocora cespitosa*	5·50	2·50
1780/1784	*Set of 5*	5·75	2·75

(Des Q. Prizreni)

1975 (20 Oct). Olympic Games, Montreal (1976). T **366** and similar vert designs. Multicoloured. P 12×12½.

1785	5q. Type **366**	10	10
1786	10q. Canoeing	10	10
1787	15q. Handball	20	10
1788	20q. Basketball	35	15
1789	25q. Waterpolo	45	15
1790	30q. Hockey	55	20
1791	1l.20 Pole vaulting	1·60	85
1792	2l.05 Fencing	2·75	1·60
1785/1792	*Set of 8*	5·50	3·00
MS1793	73×77 mm. 2l.15, Games emblem and sportsmen. Imperf	6·50	6·50

367 Power Lines leading to Village

368 Berat

(Des S. Toptani)

1975 (25 Oct). Fifth Anniv of Electrification of Albanian countryside. T **367** and similar vert designs. P 12×12½.

1794	15q. multicoloured	20	10
1795	25q. deep reddish violet, rose-lilac and bright lilac	35	20
1796	80q. grey-black, turquoise-green and deep grey-green	1·10	50
1797	85q. buff, bistre-brown and brown-ochre	2·20	1·80
1794/1797	*Set of 4*	3·50	2·30

Designs:—25q. High power insulators; 80q. Dam and power station; 85q. TV set, pylons and emblems of agriculture and industry.

(Des B. Dizdari)

1975 (25 Nov). AIR. Tourist Resorts. T **368** and similar horiz designs. Multicoloured. P 12.

1798	20q. Type **368**	35	20
1799	40q. Gjirokastër	55	20
1800	60q. Sarandé	85	30
1801	90q. Durrës	1·60	50
1802	1l.20 Krujaë	2·20	1·00
1803	2l.40 Boga	4·25	2·10
1804	4l.05 Tirana	6·50	3·75
1798/1804	*Set of 7*	14·50	7·25

369 Child, Rabbit and Bear planting Saplings

1975 (25 Dec). Children's Tales. T **369** and similar horiz designs. Multicoloured. P 12½×12.

1805	5q. Type **369**	10	10
1806	10q. Mother Fox and Cub	20	10
1807	15q. Ducks in School	25	10
1808	20q. Bears building	35	10
1809	25q. Animals watching television	45	10
1810	30q. Animals with log and electric light bulbs	50	10
1811	35q. Ants with spade and guitar	55	20
1812	2l.70 Boy and girl with sheep and dog	2·75	1·90
1805/1812	*Set of 8*	4·75	2·40

370 Arms and Rejoicing Crowd

371 Ice Hockey

(Des Q. Prizreni)

1976 (11 Jan). 30th Anniv of Albanian People's Republic. T **370** and similar horiz design. Multicoloured. P 12.

1813	25q. Type **370**	55	30
1814	1l.90 Folk-dancers	3·75	1·60

1976 (4 Feb). Winter Olympic Games, Innsbruck. T **371** and similar vert designs. Multicoloured. P 12×12½.

1815	5q. Type **371**	10	10
1816	10q. Speed skating	15	10
1817	15q. Rifle shooting (biathlon)	20	10
1818	50q. Ski jumping	35	15
1819	1l.20 Skiing (slalom)	1·10	40
1820	2l.30 Bobsleighing	2·00	1·00
1815/1820	*Set of 6*	3·50	1·70
MS1821	66×80 mm. 2l.15, Figure skating (pairs)	3·25	2·10

The miniature sheet includes two vertical rows of perforations within its design.

372 *Colchicum autumnale*

374 "Founding the Co-operatives" (Zef Shoshi)

373 Wooden Bowl and Spoon

(Des B. Marika)

1976 (10 Apr). Medicinal Plants. T **372** and similar vert designs. Multicoloured. P 12×12½.

1822	5q. Type **372**	10	10
1823	10q. *Atropa belladonna*	15	10
1824	15q. *Gentiana lutea*	20	10
1825	20q. *Aesculus hippocastanum*	20	10
1826	70q. *Polystichum filix*	75	20
1827	80q. *Althaea officinalis*	1·10	40
1828	2l.30 *Datura stramonium*	2·75	2·10
1822/1828	*Set of 7*	4·75	2·75

1976 (20 July). Ethnographic Studies Conference, Tirana. Albanian Artifacts. T **373** and similar multicoloured designs. P 12½×12 (horiz) or 12×12½ (vert).

1829	10q. Type **373**	10	10
1830	15q. Flask (vert)	15	10
1831	20q. Ornamental handles (vert)	20	10
1832	25q. Pistol and dagger	25	15
1833	80q. Hand-woven rug (vert)	75	30
1834	1l.20 Filigree buckle and earrings	1·10	50
1835	1l.40 Jugs with handles (vert)	2·20	1·40
1829/1835	*Set of 7*	4·25	2·40

1976 (8 Aug). Albanian Paintings. T **374** and similar multicoloured designs. P 12½×12 (horiz) or 12×12½ (vert).

1836	5q. Type **374**	10	10
1837	10q. "Going to Work" (Agim Zajmi) (vert)	15	10
1838	25q. "Listening to Broadcast" (Vilson Kilica)	20	10
1839	40q. "Female Welder" (Sabaudin Xhaferi) (vert)	45	20
1840	50q. "Steel Workers" (Isuf Sulovari) (vert)	85	30
1841	1l.20 "1942 Revolt" (Lec Shkreli) (vert)	1·10	85
1842	1l.60 "Returning from Work" (Agron Dine)	1·60	1·00
1836/1842	*Set of 7*	4·00	2·40
MS1843	93×79 mm. 2l.05, "The Young Pioneer" (Andon Lakuriqi)	3·25	2·10

The miniature sheet includes two horizontal rows of perforations within its design.

375 Demonstrators attacking Police

376 Party Flag, Industry and Agriculture

1976 (28 Oct). 35th Anniv of Anti-Fascist Demonstration led by Enver Hoxha. T **375** and similar vert design. Multicoloured. P 12×12½.

1844	25q. Type **375**	55	20
1845	1l.90 Crowd with flag	3·25	2·10

1976 (1 Nov). Seventh Workers' Party Congress. T **376** and similar vert design. Multicoloured. P 12.

1846	25q. Type **376**	55	20
1847	1l.20 Hand holding Party symbols, and flag	2·20	1·60

377 Communist Advance

378 Young Communists

1976 (8 Nov). 35th Anniv of Workers' Party. T **377** and similar vert designs. Multicoloured. P 12×12½.

1848	15q. Type **377**	20	10
1849	25q. Hands holding emblems, and revolutionary army	55	30
1850	80q. Soldiers, industrial scenes, pickaxe and rifle	1·10	50
1851	1l.20 Symbols of heavy industry and agriculture	1·60	1·00
1852	1l.70 Ballet scene and cultural symbols	2·20	1·60
1848/1852 *Set of* 5		5·00	3·25

1976 (23 Nov). 35th Anniv of Young Communists' Union. T **378** and similar horiz design. Multicoloured. P 12.

1853	80q. Type **378**	2·10	1·00
1854	1l.25 Young Communists in action	2·75	2·10

379 Ballet Dancers

380 Bashtoves Castle

1976 (15 Dec). Albanian Ballet Cuca e Maleve. T **379** and similar horiz designs showing ballet scenes. P 12.

1855	10q. multicoloured	10	30
1856	15q. multicoloured	20	50
1857	20q. multicoloured	35	1·00
1858	25q. multicoloured	55	2·10
1859	80q. multicoloured	1·30	3·25
1860	1l.20 multicoloured	1·80	3·75
1861	1l.40 multicoloured	2·20	4·25
1855/1861 *Set of* 7		5·75	13·50
MS1862 77×67 mm. 2l.05, multicoloured. P 12×imperf		5·00	5·25

(Des B. Zajmi)

1976 (25 Dec). Albanian Castles. T **380** and similar horiz designs. P 12.

1863	10q. black and cobalt	10	10
1864	15q. black and dull yellowish green	15	10
1865	20q. black and slate	20	15
1866	25q. black and light brown	35	20
1867	80q. black, rose-pink and brown-rose	1·10	50
1868	1l.20 black and dull violet-blue	1·60	95
1869	1l.40 black, brown-rose and rose-pink	1·70	1·00
1863/1869 *Set of* 7		4·75	2·75

Designs:—15q. Gjirokastër; 20q. Ali Pash Tepelenes; 25q. Petreles; 80q. Berat; 1l.20, Durrës, 1l.40, Krujes.

381 Skanderbeg's Shield and Spear

382 Ilia Oiqi

(Des Q. Prizreni)

1977 (28 Jan). Crest and Arms of Skanderbeg's Army. T **381** and similar vert designs. Multicoloured. P 12.

1870	15q. Type **381**	2·20	50
1871	80q. Helmet, sword and scabbard	7·50	3·75
1872	1l. Halberd, spear, bow and arrows	12·00	9·50
1870/1872 *Set of* 3		20·00	12·50

(Des Q. Prizreni)

1977 (28 Feb). Albanian Heroes. T **382** and similar horiz designs. Multicoloured. P 12×12½.

1873	5q. Type **382**	10	10
1874	10q. Ilia Dashi	20	20
1875	25q. Fran Ndue Ivanaj	55	30
1876	80q. Zeliha Allmetaj	1·60	50
1877	1l. Ylli Zaimi	1·80	75
1878	1l.90 Isuf Plloci	3·75	1·30
1873/1878 *Set of* 6		7·25	2·75

383 Polyvinyl-chloride Plant, Vlórë

384 Shote Galica

(Des B. Marika)

1977 (29 Mar). Sixth Five Year Plan. T **383** and similar vert designs. Multicoloured. P 12½×12.

1879	15q. Type **383**	35	30
1880	25q. Naphtha plant, Ballsh	55	40
1881	65q. Hydroelectric station, Fjerzes	1·60	85
1882	1l. Metallurgical complex, Elbasan	2·40	1·00
1879/1882 *Set of* 4		4·50	2·30

(Des B. Zajmi)

1977 (20 Apr). 50th Death Anniv of Shote Galica (Communist partisan). T **384** and similar vert design. P 12½×12.

1883	80q. deep rose-red and pink	1·60	85
1884	1q.25 grey-blue and pale grey-blue	2·40	1·50

Design:—1l.25, Shote Galica and father.

385 Crowd and Martyrs' Monument, Tirana

386 Doctor calling at Village House

(Des Z. Mati)

1977 (5 May). 35th Anniv of Martyrs' Day. T **385** and similar vert designs. Multicoloured. P 12.

1885	25q. Type **385**	55	30
1886	80q. Clenched fist and Albanian flag	1·80	75
1887	1l.20 Bust of Qemal Stafa	3·25	1·60
1885/1887 *Set of* 3		5·00	2·40

(Des B. Marika)

1977 (18 June). "Socialist Transformation of Villages". T **386** and similar horiz designs. Multicoloured. P 12×12½.

1888	5q. Type **386**	10	10
1889	10q. Cowherd with cattle	15	10
1890	20q. Harvesting	20	20
1891	80q. Modern village	1·60	75
1892	2l.95 Tractor and greenhouses	6·00	1·60
1888/1892 *Set of* 5		7·25	2·50

387 Workers outside Factory

388 Advancing Soldiers

(Des Q. Prizreni)

1977 (20 June). Eighth Trade Unions Congress. T **387** and similar horiz design. Multicoloured. P 12.

1893	25q. Type **387**	55	30
1894	1l.80 Three workers with flag	3·75	2·10

(Des Z. Mati)

1977 (10 July). "All the People are Soldiers". T **388** and similar horiz designs. Multicoloured. P 12.

1895	15q. Type **388**	40	20
1896	25q. Enver Hoxha and marching soldiers.	55	30
1897	80q. Soldiers and workers	1·60	1·00
1898	1l. The Armed Forces	2·75	2·10
1899	1l.90 Marching soldiers and workers	4·25	3·75
1895/1899 *Set of* 5		8·50	6·50

389 Two Girls with Handkerchiefs

390 Armed Worker with Book

(Des N. Bakalli)

1977 (20 Aug). National Costume Dances (1st issue). T **389** and similar vert designs. Multicoloured. P 12.

1900	5q. Type **389**	10	10
1901	10q. Two male dancers	15	10
1902	15q. Man and woman in kerchief dance	15	15
1903	25q. Two male dancers (different)	20	15
1904	80q. Two women dancers with kerchiefs.	75	40
1905	1l.20 "Elbow" dance	1·10	50
1906	1l.55 Two women with kerchiefs (different)	1·60	1·00
1900/1906 *Set of* 7		3·75	2·20
MS1907 56×74 mm. 2l.05, Sabre dance. P 12×imperf		4·00	3·25

See also Nos. 1932/6 and 1991/5.

1977 (Oct). New Constitution. T **390** and similar square design. P 12.

1908	25q. gold, scarlet and black	55	30
1909	1l.20 gold, scarlet and black	2·20	1·00

Design:—1l.20, Industrial and agricultural symbols and hand with book.

391 *Beni Ecen Vet*

392 Rejoicing Crowd and Independence Memorial, Tirana

1977 (25 Oct). Albanian Films. T **391** and similar horiz designs. P 12½×12.

1910	10q. deep bluish green and pale brownish grey	20	10
1911	15q. multicoloured	35	10
1912	25q. pale grey-green, black and pale brownish grey	55	30
1913	80q. multicoloured	2·20	1·60
1914	1l.20 pur-brn & pale brownish grey	3·25	2·50
1915	1l.60 multicoloured	3·75	3·25
1910/1915 *Set of* 6		9·25	7·00

Designs:—15q. *Rruge te Bardha*; 25q. *Rrugicat qe Kerkonin Diell*; 80q. *Ne Fillim te Veres*, 1l.20, *Lulekuqet Mbi Mure*, 1l.60, *Zonja nga Qyteti*.

(Des Q. Prizreni)

1977 (28 Nov). 65th Anniv of Independence. T **392** and similar horiz designs. Muhicoloured. P 12½×12 (15q.) or 12×12½ (others).

1916	15q. Type **392**	15	15
1917	25q. Independence leaders marching in Tirana	55	30
1918	1f.65 Albanians dancing under national flag	3·75	2·10
1916/1918 *Set of* 3		4·00	2·30

393 "Farm Workers"

394 Pan Flute

1977 (25 Dec). Paintings by V. Mio. T **393** and similar horiz designs. Multicoloured. P 12½×12.

1919	5q. Type **393**	10	10
1920	10q. "Landscape in the Snow"	10	10
1921	15q. "Sheep under a Walnut Tree, Springtime"	15	10
1922	25q. "Street in Korcë"	25	10
1923	80q. "Riders in the Mountains"	65	30
1924	1l. "Boats by the Seashore"	1·10	65
1925	1l.75 "Tractors Ploughing"	1·80	1·30
1919/1925 *Set of* 7		3·75	2·40
MS1926 67×102 mm. 2l.05, "Self-portrait"		4·00	3·25

The miniature sheet includes one horizontal row of perforations within its design.

(Des N. Bakalli)

1978 (20 Jan). Folk Music Instruments. T **394** and similar vert designs. P 12×12½.

1927	15q. dull rose, black & turquoise-grn	55	30
1928	25q. greenish yellow, black & lavender	1·10	50
1929	80q. salmon, black and light blue	2·75	1·60
1930	1l.20 yellow, black and pale grey-blue	5·50	3·25
1931	1l.70 pale reddish mauve, black and bright green	12·00	7·25
1927/1931 *Set of* 5		20·00	11·50

Designs:—25q. Single-string goat's head fiddle; 80q. Trumpet; 1l.20, Drum; 1l.70, Bagpipes.

(Des N. Bakalli)

1978 (15 Feb). National Costume Dances (2nd issue). Vert designs as T **389**. Multicoloured. P 12.

1932	5q. Girl dancers with scarves	20	10
1933	25q. Male dancers	35	20
1934	80q. Kneeling dancers	85	50
1935	1l. Female dancers	1·10	85
1936	2l.30 Male dancers with linked arms	2·75	2·10
1932/1936 *Set of* 5		4·75	3·50

395 "Tractor Drivers" (D. Trebicka)

396 Boy and Girl

(Des P. Sulo)

1978 (25 Mar). Paintings of the Working Class. T **395** and similar multicoloured designs. P 12.

1937	25q. Type **395**	20	10
1938	80q. "Steeplejack" (S. Kristo)	55	30
1939	85q. "A Point in the Discussion" (S. Milori)	65	40
1940	90q. "Oil Rig Crew" (A. Cini) (vert)	75	50
1941	1l.60 "Metal Workers" (R. Karanxha)	1·60	1·00
1937/1941 *Set of* 5		3·50	2·10
MS1942 73×99 mm. 2l.20, "The Political Discussion" (S. Sholla)		7·50	4·75

The miniature sheet includes two horizontal rows of perforations within its design.

(Des B. Zalmi)

1978 (1 June). International Children's Day. T **396** and similar vert designs. Multicoloured. P 12.

1943	5q. Type **396**	20	10
1944	10q. Boy and girl with pickaxe and rifle	35	20
1945	25q. Children dancing	75	50
1946	1l.80 Classroom scene	4·00	3·25
1943/1946 *Set of* 4		4·75	3·75

397 Woman with Pickaxe and Rifle

398 Battle of Mostar Bridge

(Des Q. Prizreni)

1978 (1 June). Eighth Women's Union Congress. T **397** and similar horiz design. P 12×11½.

1947 25q. scarlet and gold ... 55 30
1948 1l.95 carmine-red and gold ... 8·25 5·25

Design:—1l.95, Peasant and Militia Guard with industrial installation.

(Des Q. Prizreni)

1978 (10 June). Centenary of the League of Prizren. T **398** and similar vert designs. P 12.

1949 10q. multicoloured ... 20 10
1950 25q. multicoloured ... 35 20
1951 80q. multicoloured ... 1·60 1·00
1952 1l.20 pale blue, black and deep violet ... 2·20 1·60
1953 1l.65 multicoloured ... 3·25 2·50
1954 2l.60 apple green, black & bronze-grn ... 5·50 4·75
1949/1954 *Set of 6* ... 12·00 9·25
MS1955 75×69 mm. 2l.20, multicoloured. Imperf× p 12 ... 5·50 4·25

Designs:—25q. Spirit of Skanderbeg; 80q. Albanians marching under national flag; 1l.20, Riflemen; 1l.65, Abdyl Frasheri (founder); 2l.20, League building, crossed rifles, pen and paper; 2l.60, League Headquarters, Prizren.

399 Guerrillas with Flag

401 Man with Target Rifle

3.30L

26. 8. 1978

RICCIONE 78

(400)

(Des S. Prapanikú)

1978 (10 July). 35th Anniv of People's Army. T **399** and similar multicoloured designs. P 12½×12 (25q.) or 12×12½ (others).

1956 5q. Type **399** ... 55 30
1957 25q. Men of armed forces (horiz) ... 1·10 50
1958 1l.90 Men of armed forces, civil guards and Young Pioneers ... 7·00 6·25
1956/1958 *Set of 3* ... 7·75 6·25

1978 (26 Aug). International Fair, Riccione. No. 1832 surch with T **400**, in blue.

1959 3l.30 on 25q. multicoloured ... 17·00 15·00

(Des Z. Mati)

1978 (20 Sept). 32nd National Shooting Championship. T **401** and similar designs. P 12½×12 (horiz) or 12×12½ (vert).

1960 25q. black and lemon ... 35 20
1961 80q. black and bright orange ... 75 65
1962 95q. black and rosine ... 1·10 85
1963 2l.40 black and carmine ... 2·75 2·50
1960/1963 *Set of 4* ... 4·50 3·75

Designs: Horiz—95q. Shooting from prone position. Vert—80q. Woman with machine carbine; 2l.40, Pistol shooting.

402 Kerchief Dance

403 Enver Hoxha (after V. Kilica)

(Des N. Bakalli)

1978 (6 Oct). National Folklore Festival, Gjirokastër. T **402** and similar vert designs. Multicoloured. P 12.

1964 10q. Type **402** ... 10 10
1965 15q. Musicians ... 15 10
1966 25q. Fiddle player ... 20 15
1967 80q. Singers ... 55 30
1968 1l.20 Sabre dance ... 1·20 75
1969 1l.90 Girl dancers ... 2·40 1·80
1964/1969 *Set of 6* ... 4·25 3·00

1978 (16 Oct). Enver Hoxha's 70th Birthday. P 12×12½.

1970 **403** 80q. multicoloured ... 55 30
1971 1l.20 multicoloured ... 1·10 50
1972 2l.40 multicoloured ... 2·20 1·60
1970/1972 *Set of 3* ... 3·50 2·20
MS1973 68×88 mm. **403** 2l.20, multicoloured ... 4·25 3·25

The miniature sheet includes two horizontal rows of perforations within its design.

404 Woman with Wheatsheaf

405 Pupils entering School

(Des Q. Prizreni)

1978 (15 Dec). Agriculture and Stock Raising. T **404** and similar horiz designs. Multicoloured. P 12×12½.

1974 15q. Type **404** ... 55 30
1975 25q. Woman with boxes of fruit ... 75 50
1976 80q. Shepherd and flock ... 2·75 2·10
1977 2l.60 Dairymaid and cattle ... 9·75 7·25
1974/1977 *Set of 4* ... 12·50 9·25

1978. T **405** and simlilar horiz designs. P 12½×12.

1978 5q. deep brown, pale grey-brown and gold ... 15 10
1979 10q. blue, pale blue and gold ... 20 10
1980 15q. reddish vio, reddish lilac & gold ... 35 15
1981 20q. orange-brown, pale drab and gold ... 45 20
1982 25q. deep carmine, pink and gold ... 55 30
1983 60q. olive-green, pale grey-ol & gold ... 1·60 50
1984 80q. greenish blue, pale blue and gold ... 2·20 50
1985 1l.20 dp magenta, pale mauve & gold ... 3·25 1·00
1986 1l.60 deep turquoise-blue, pale turquoise-blue and gold ... 4·25 1·80
1987 2l.40 deep green, pale green and gold ... 6·50 3·25
1988 3l. dull ultramarine, pale blue and gold ... 7·50 5·25
1978/1988 *Set of 11* ... 24·00 12·00

Designs:—10q. Telephone, letters, telegraph wires and switchboard operators; 15q. Pouring molten iron; 20q. Dancers, musical instruments, book and artist's materials; 25q. Newspapers, radio, television and broadcasting tower; 60q. Assistant in clothes shop; 80q. Militiamen and women, tanks, ships, aircraft and radar equipment; 1l.20, Industrial complex and symbols of industry; 1l.60, Train and lorry; 2l.40, Workers hoeing fields, cattle and girl holding wheat sheaf; 3l. Microscope and nurse holding up baby.

406 Dora D'Istria

407 Stone-built Galleried House

(Des N. Bakalh)

1979 (22 Jan). 150th Birth Anniv of Dora D'Istria (pioneer of women's rights). T **406** and similar vert design. P 12.

1989 80q. deep olive and black ... 1·60 1·00
1990 1l.10 deep dull purple and black ... 2·75 2·10

Design:—1l.10, Full-face portrait.

(Des N. Bakalli)

1979 (25 Feb). National Costume Dances (3rd issue). Vert designs as T **389**. Multicoloured. P 12.

1991 15q. Girl dancers with scarves ... 35 20
1992 25q. Male dancers ... 55 30
1993 80q. Girl dancers with scarves (different) ... 2·20 1·00
1994 1l.20 Male dancers with pistols ... 2·75 1·60
1995 1l.40 Female dancers with linked arms ... 3·25 2·10
1991/1995 *Set of 5* ... 8·25 4·75

(Des B. Zajmi)

1979 (20 Mar). Traditional Albanian Houses (1st series). T **407** and similar designs. Multicoloured. P 12.

1996 15q. Type **407** ... 20 10
1997 25q. Tower house (vert) ... 35 15
1998 80q. House with wooden galleries ... 1·10 50
1999 1l.20 Galleried tower house (vert) ... 1·60 75
2000 1l.40 Three-storied fortified house (vert) ... 2·20 1·30
1996/2000 *Set of 5* ... 5·00 2·50
MS2001 62×75 mm. 1l.90, Fortified tower house. P 12ximperf ... 8·75 5·25

See also Nos. 2116/19.

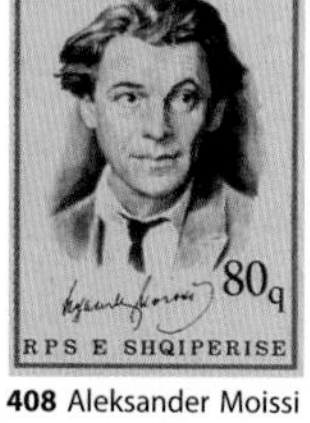

408 Aleksander Moissi

409 Vasil Shanto

1979 (2 Apr). Birth Centenary of Aleksander Moissi (actor). T **408** and similar vert design showing portrait. P 12.

2002 80q. deep green, black and gold ... 1·60 65
2003 1l.10 orange-brown, black and gold ... 2·20 1·60

1979 (5 May). Anti-fascist Heroes (1st series). T **409** and similar horiz designs. P 12.

2004 **409** 15q. multicoloured ... 25 10
2005 – 25q. multicoloured ... 55 30
2006 **409** 60q. multicoloured ... 2·20 1·00
2007 – 90q. multicoloured ... 3·25 2·10
2004/2007 *Set of 4* ... 5·75 3·2

Design:—25, 90q. Qemal Stafa.

See also Nos. 2052/5, 2090/3, 2126/9, 2167/70, 2221/4 and 2274/7.

410 Soldier, Crowd and Coat of Arms

411 Albanian Flag

(Des Q. Prizreni)

1979 (24 May). 35th Anniv of Permet Congress. T **410** and similar horiz design. Multicoloured. P 12.

2008 25q. Soldier, factories and wheat ... 1·10 50
2009 1l.65 Type **410** ... 5·00 2·50

(Des N. Prizreni)

1979 (4 June). 5th Congress of Albanian Democratic Front. P 12.

2010 **411** 25q. muilticoloured ... 1·10 50
2011 1l.65 multicoloured ... 5·00 3·25

412 "Ne Stervitje" (Arben Basha)

1979 (15 July). Painting from Gallery of Figurative Arts. T **412** and similar horiz designs. Multicoloured. P 12.

2012 15q. Type **412** ... 10 10
2013 25q. "Shtigje Lufte" (Ismail Lulani) ... 20 10
2014 80q. "Agim me Fitore" (Myrteza Fushekati) ... 1·10 50
2015 1l.20 "Gjithe Populli ushtare" (Muhamet Deliu) ... 1·80 75
2016 1l.40 "Zjarret Ndezur Mbajme" (Jorgji Gjikopulli) ... 2·20 1·00
2012/2016 *Set of 5* ... 4·75 2·20
MS2017 78×103 mm. 1l.90, "Cajme Rrethime" (Fatmir Haxhiu) ... 4·00 3·00

The miniature sheet includes two horizontal rows of perforation within its design.

413 Athletes round Party Flag

414 Founder-president

(Des Q. Prizreni)

1979 (1 Oct). 35th Anniv of Liberation Spartakiad. T **413** and similar vert designs. Multicoloured. P 12.

2018 15q. Type **413** ... 10 10
2019 25q. Rifle shooting demonstration ... 20 10
2020 80q. Girl gymnast ... 1·10 50
2021 1l.20 Footballers ... 1·60 1·00
2022 1l.40 High jump ... 1·80 1·30
2018/2022 *Set of 5* ... 4·25 2·75

(Des Q. Prizreni)

1979 (12 Oct). Centenary of Albanian Literary Society. T **414** and similar vert designs. P 12.

2023 25q. black, light orange-brown & gold ... 35 20
2024 80q. black, pale ochre and gold ... 1·10 65
2025 1l.20 black, blue and gold ... 1·60 1·00
2026 1l.55 black, bright reddish vio & gold ... 2·00 1·30
2023/2026 *Set of 4* ... 4·50 2·75
MS2027 78×66 mm. 1l.90, black, buff & gold. Imperf×12 ... 3·75 3·25

Designs:—25q. Foundation document and seal of 1880; 1l.20, Headquarters building, 1979; 1l.55, Headquarters building, 1879; 1l.90, Four founder members, book and quill.

415 Congress Building

416 Workers and Industrial Complex

(Des B. Erebara)

1979 (20 Oct). 35th Anniv of Berat Congress. T **415** and similar vert design. Multicoloured. P 12.

2028 25q. Arms and congress document ... 1·40 1·00
2029 1l.65 Type **415** ... 4·75 3·75

(Des H. Dhimo)

979 (29 Nov). 35th Anniv of Liberation. T **416** and similar horiz designs. Multicoloured. P 12.

030	25q. Type **416**	35	20
031	80q. Wheat and hand grasping hammer and pickaxe	1·10	65
032	1l.20 Open book, star and musical instrument	1·60	1·00
033	1l.55 Open book, compasses and gear wheel	2·20	1·30
030/2033 *Set of 4*		4·75	2·75

417 Stalin

418 Fireplace and Pottery, Korcë

(Des H. Dhimo)

979 (21 Dec). Birth Centenary of Joseph Stalin. T **417** and similar horiz design. P 12.

034	80q. indigo and scarlet	1·60	1·00
035	1l.10 indigo and bright scarlet	2·20	1·60

Design:—1l.10, Stalin and Enver Hoxha.

(Des Q. Prizreni)

980 (27 Feb). Interiors (1st series). T **418** and similar horiz designs. Multicoloured. P 12.

036	25q. Type **418**	35	20
037	80q. Carved bed alcove and weapons, Shkodër	75	50
038	1l.20 Cooking hearth and carved chair, Mirditë	1·60	1·00
039	1l.35 Turkish-style chimney, dagger and embroidered jacket, Gjirokastër	2·20	1·60
036/2039 *Set of 4*		4·50	3·00

See also Nos. 2075/8.

419 Lacework

420 Aleksander Xhuvani

(Des N. Majollari)

1980 (4 Mar). Handicrafts. T **419** and similar horiz designs. Multicoloured. P 12.

2040	25q. Pipe and flask	35	20
2041	80q. Leather handbags	75	50
2042	1l.20 Carved eagle and embroidered rug	1·60	1·00
2043	1l.35 Type **419**	2·20	1·60
2040/2043 *Set of 4*		4·50	3·00

(Des M. Fushekati)

1980 (14 Mar). Birth Centenary of Dr. Aleksander Xhuvani. P 12.

2044	**420**	80q. dull turquoise-blue, grey and black	2·20	1·60
2045		1l. yellow-brown, grey and black	2·75	2·10

421 Insurrectionists

(Des Z. Mati)

1980 (4 Apr). 70th Anniv of Kosovo Insurrection. T **421** and similar horiz design. P 12.

2046	80q. black and scarlet-vermilion	2·20	1·60
2047	1l. black and orange-vermilion	3·25	2·50

Design:—1l. Battle scene.

422 "Soldiers and Workers helping Stricken Population" (D. Jukniu and I. Lulani)

423 Lenin

1980 (15 Apr). 1979 Earthquake Relief. P 12½.

2048	**422**	80q. multicoloured	2·20	1·60
2049		1l. multicoloured	3·25	2·50

(Des M. Fushekati)

1980 (22 Apr). 110th Birth Anniv of Lenin. P 12.

2050	**423**	80q. grey, bright carmine and rose-pink	2·20	1·60
2051		1l. multicoloured	3·25	2·50

424 Misto Mame and Ali Demi

425 *Mirela*

(Des M. Fushekati)

1980 (5 May). Anti-fascist Heroes (2nd series). T **424** and similar horiz designs. Multicoloured. P 12.

2052	25q. Type **424**	35	20
2053	80q. Sadik Stavaleci, Vojo Kushi and Xhoxhi Martini	1·10	75
2054	1l.20 Bule Naipi and Persefoni Kokedhima	1·80	1·00
2055	1l.35 Ndoc Deda, Hydajet Lezha, Naim Gjylbegu, Ndoc Mazi and Ahmet Haxhia	2·20	1·60
2052/2055 *Set of 4*		5·00	3·25

(Des B. Kapexhiu)

1980 (7 June). Children's Tales. T **425** and similar horiz designs. Multicoloured. P 12.

2056	15q. Type **425**	10	10
2057	25q. *Shkarravina*	20	15
2058	80q. *Ariu Artist*	1·10	75
2059	2l.40 *Pika e Ujit*	4·00	3·25
2056/2059 *Set of 4*		4·75	3·75

426 "The Enver Hoxha Tractor Combine" (S. Shijaku and M. Fushekati)

427 Decorated Door (Pergamen miniature)

(Des P. Sulo)

1980 (22 July). Paintings from Gallery of Figurative Arts, Tirana. T **426** and similar horiz designs. Multicoloured. P 12½.

2060	25q. Type **426**	35	20
2061	80q. "The Welder" (Harilla Dhima)	1·10	75
2062	1l.20 "Steel Erector" (Petro Kokushta)	1·80	1·60
2063	1l.35 "Harvest Festival" (Pandeli Lena)	2·20	1·80
2060/2063 *Set of 4*		5·00	4·00
MS2064 65×82 mm. 1l.80, "Communists" (Vilson Kilica) (48×71 mm)		5·00	5·00

The miniature sheet includes two horizontal rows of perforations (p 12) within its design.

1980 (27 Sept). Art of the Middle Ages. T **427** and similar vert designs, each black and gold. P 12.

2065	25q. Type **427**	35	20
2066	80q. Bird (relief)	75	50
2067	1l.20 Crowned lion (relief)	1·40	1·00
2068	1l.35 Pheasant (relief)	1·60	1·30
2065/2068 *Set of 4*		3·75	2·75

428 Divjaka

429 Flag, Arms and Rejoicing Albanians

1980 (6 Nov). National Parks. T **428** and similar horiz designs. Multicoloured. P 12.

2069	80q. Type **428**	1·10	85
2070	1l.20 Lura	1·60	1·30
2071	1l.60 Thethi	2·75	2·30
2069/2071 *Set of 3*		5·00	4·00
MS2072 89×90 mm. 1l.80, Llogara (77×80 mm)		5·50	5·50

The miniature sheet includes two horizontal rows of perforations within its design.

(Des E. Hila)

1981 (11 Jan). 35th Anniv of Albanian People's Republic. T **429** and similar horiz design. Multicoloured. P 12.

2073	80q. Type **429**	1·60	85
2074	1l. Crowd and flags outside People's Party Headquarters	2·20	1·00

(Des Q. Prizreni)

1981 (25 Feb). Interiors (2nd series). Horiz designs as T **418**. Multicoloured. P 12.

2075	25q. Sleeping mats and spirit keg, Lábara	20	15
2076	80q. Tent and milk churn, Lábara	65	50
2077	1l.20 Fireplace and covered dish, Mat	1·30	75
2078	1l.35 Interior and embroidered jacket, Dibrës	1·80	1·40
2075/2078 *Set of 4*		3·50	2·50

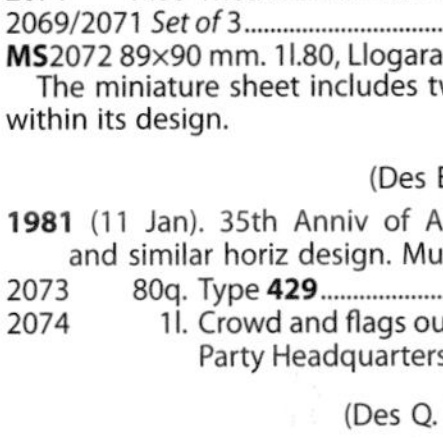

430 Wooden Cot

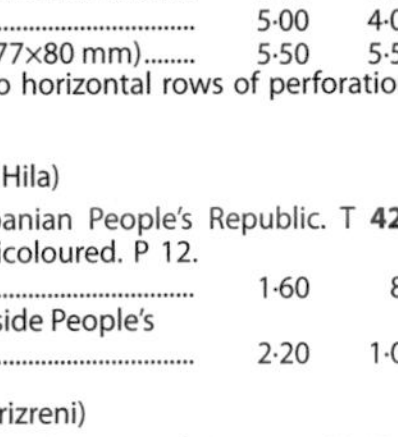

431 Footballers

(Des N. Marjoralli)

1981 (20 Mar). Folk Art. T **430** and similar horiz designs. Multicoloured. P 12.

2079	25q. Type **430**	35	20
2080	80q. Bucket and flask	85	75
2081	1l.20 Embroidered slippers	1·20	1·00
2082	1l.35 Jugs	1·50	1·40
2079/2082 *Set of 4*		3·50	3·00

1981 (31 Mar). World Cup Football Championship Eliminating Rounds. T **431** and similar horiz designs. Multicoloured. P 12.

2083	25q. Type **431**	1·30	60
2084	80q. Tackle	3·75	2·20
2085	1l.20 Player kicking ball	5·50	3·75
2086	1l.35 Goalkeeper saving goal	6·75	4·25
2083/2086 *Set of 4*		16·00	9·75

432 Rifleman

433 Acrobats

(Des N. Bakalli)

1981 (20 Apr). Centenary of Battle of Shtimje. T **432** and similar vert designs, each deep dull purple and Venetian red. P 12.

2087	80q. Type **432**	1·20	85
2088	1l. Albanian with sabre	1·50	1·00
MS2089 84×68 mm. 1l.80, Albanian with pistol. Imperf×P 12		5·00	5·00

(Des M. Fushekati)

1981 (5 May). Anti-fascist Heroes (3rd series). Horiz designs as T **424**. Multicoloured. P 12.

2090	25q. Perlat Rexhepi and Branko Kadia	35	20
2091	80q. Xheladin Beqiri and Hajdah Dushi	1·10	50
2092	1l.20 Koci Bako, Vasil Laci and Mujo Ulqinaku	1·30	1·00
2093	1l.35 Mine Peza and Zoja Cure	2·20	1·30
2090/2093 *Set of 4*		4·50	2·75

1981 (June). Children's Circus. T **433** and similar vert designs. P 12.

2094	15q. black, light green and stone	15	10
2095	25q. black, cobalt and brownish grey	20	15
2096	80q. black, bright mauve and flesh	65	50
2097	2l.40 black, yell-orge & greenish yell	2·20	2·00
2094/2097 *Set of 4*		3·00	2·50

Designs:—15q. Monocyclists; 25q. Human pyramid; 2l.40, Acrobats spinning from marquee pole.

434 "Rallying to the Flag, December 1911" (A. Zajmi)

435 Weightlifting

(Des P. Sulo)

1981 (10 July). Paintings. T **434** and similar multicoloured designs. P 12½.

2098	25q. "Allies" (Sh. Hysa) (horiz)	55	20
2099	80q. "Azem Galica breaking the Ring of Turks" (A. Buza) (horiz)	85	50
2100	1l.20 Type **434**	1·30	1·00
2101	1l.35 "My Flag is my Heart" (L. Çefa)	1·60	1·40
2098/2101 *Set of 4*		4·00	2·75
MS2102 81×109 mm. 1l.80, "Unite under the Flag" (N. Vasia) (55×79 mm)		5·00	5·00

The miniature sheet includes two horizontal rows of perforations (p 12) within its design.

(Des B. Zajmi)

1981 (30 Aug). Albanian Participation in International Sports. T **435** and similar horiz designs. Multicoloured. P 12.

2103	25q. Rifle shooting	35	20
2104	80q. Type **435**	75	50
2105	1l.20 Volleyball	1·10	85
2106	1l.35 Football	1·30	1·00
2103/2106 *Set of 4*		3·25	2·30

436 Flag and Hands holding Pickaxe and Rifle

437 Industrial and Agricultural Symbols

1981 (1 Nov). Eighth Workers' Party Congress. T **436** and similar horiz design. P 12.

2107	80q. brt scarlet, orange-brown & black	85	65
2108	1l. orange-vermilion and black	1·30	1·20

Design:—1l. Party flag, hammer and sickle.

1981 (8 Nov). 40th Anniv of Workers' Party. T **437** and similar vert designs. Multicoloured. P 12.
2109 80q. Type **437** ... 55 30
2110 2l.80 Albanian flag and hand holding pickaxe and rifle ... 2·75 2·10
MS2111 79×98 mm. 1l.80, Enver Hoxha and book (50×68 mm). P 12×imperf ... 5·50 5·50

438 Pickaxe, Rifle and Young Communists Flag

439 F. S. Noli

1981 (23 Nov). 40th Anniv of Young Communists' Union. T **438** and similar vert design. Multicoloured. P 12.
2112 80q. Type **438** ... 1·30 1·00
2113 1l. Workers' Party flag and Young Communists emblem ... 2·20 1·90

(Des B. Asllani)

1982 (6 Jan). Birth Centenary of F. S. Noli. P 12.
2114 **439** 80q. olive-green and gold ... 1·40 75
2115 1l.10 reddish brown and gold ... 1·80 1·00

1982 (Feb). Traditional Albanian Houses (2nd series). Vert designs as T **407**. Multicoloured. P 12.
2116 25q. House in Bulqizë ... 35 20
2117 80q. House in Kosovo ... 1·60 1·00
2118 1l.20 House in Bicaj ... 2·20 1·60
2119 1l.55 House in Mat ... 3·00 1·90
2116/2119 *Set of 4* ... 6·50 4·25

440 Map, Globe and Bacilli

441 "Prizren Castle" (G. Madhi)

1982 (24 Mar). Centenary of Discovery of Tuberculosis Bacilli. T **440** and similar horiz design. P 12.
2120 80q. multicoloured ... 5·50 2·10
2121 1l.10 pale grey-brown and deep brown ... 7·50 3·75
Design:—1l.10, Robert Koch (discoverer), microscope and bacilli.

1982 (25 Apr). Paintings of Kosovo. T **441** and similar multicoloured designs. P 12½.
2122 25q. Type **441** ... 55 30
2123 80q. "House of the Albanian League, Prizren" (K. Buza) (horiz) ... 1·60 1·30
2124 1l.20 "Mountain Gorge, Rugovë" (K. Buza) ... 2·75 1·60
2125 1l.55 "Street of the Haxhi, Zekë" (G. Madhi) ... 3·75 2·10
2122/2125 *Set of 4* ... 7·75 4·75

1982 (5 May). Anti-fascist Heroes (4th series). Horiz designs as T **424**. Multicoloured. P 12.
2126 25q. Hibe Palikuqi and Liri Gero ... 55 30
2127 80q. Mihal Duri and Kajo Karafili ... 1·30 85
2128 1l.20 Fato Dudumi, Margarita Tutulani and Shejnaze Juka ... 2·00 1·40
2129 1l.55 Memo Meto and Gjok Doçi ... 2·75 1·50
2126/2129 *Set of 4* ... 6·00 3·75

442 Factories and Workers

443 Ship in Harbour

1982 (6 June). Ninth Trade Unions Congress. T **442** and similar horiz design. Multicoloured. P 12.
2130 80q. Type **442** ... 3·75 2·20
2131 1l.10 Congress emblem ... 5·00 3·00

1982 (15 June). Children's Paintings. T **443** and similar horiz designs. Multicoloured. P 12½.
2132 15q. Type **443** ... 55 20
2133 80q. Forest camp ... 1·10 75
2134 1l.20 Houses ... 1·60 1·30
2135 1l.65 House and garden ... 3·25 2·00
2132/2135 *Set of 4* ... 5·75 3·75

444 "Village Festival" (Danish Jukniu)

445 *Voice of the People* (party newspaper)

1982 (30 July). Paintings from Gallery of Figurative Arts, Tirana. T **444** and similar horiz designs. Multicoloured. P 12½.
2136 25q. Type **444** ... 35 20
2137 80q. "Komanit Hydro-electric Station Builders" (Ali Miruku) ... 1·30 1·00
2138 1l.20 "Steel Workers" (Çlirim Ceka) ... 1·60 1·30
2139 1l.55 "Oil Drillers" (Pandeli Lena) ... 2·75 1·60
2136/2139 *Set of 4* ... 5·50 3·75
MS2140 75×90 mm. 1l.90, "First Tapping of the Furnace" (Jorgji Gjikopulli) ... 5·50 3·75
The miniature sheet includes two horizontal rows of perforations (p 12) in its design.

1982 (25 Aug). 40th Anniv of Popular Press. T **445** and similar vert design. Multicoloured. P 12.
2141 80q. Type **445** ... £120 £100
2142 1l.10 Hand duplicator producing first edition of Voice of the People ... £120 £100

446 Heroes of Peza Monument

447 Congress Emblem

1982 (16 Sept). 40th Anniv of Albanian Democratic Front. T **446** and similar horiz design. Multicoloured. P 12.
2143 80q. Type **446** ... 8·25 4·00
2144 1l.10 Peza Conference building and marchers with flag ... 12·00 5·50

1982 (4 Oct). Eighth Young Communists' Union Congress. P 12.
2145 **447** 80q. multicoloured ... 7·25 4·25
2146 1l.10 multicoloured ... 11·50 6·25

448 Tapestry

449 Freedom Fighters

1982 (30 Oct). Handicrafts. T **448** and similar multicoloured designs. P 12.
2147 25q. Type **448** ... 55 30
2148 80q. Bags (vert) ... 1·30 75
2149 1l.20 Butter churns ... 1·80 1·00
2150 1l.55 Jug (vert) ... 2·75 1·60
2147/2150 *Set of 4* ... 5·75 3·25

1982 (28 Nov). 70th Anniv of Independence. T **449** and similar horiz designs. P 12.
2151 20q. bright rose-red, vermilion and black ... 45 30
2152 1l.20 black, pale olive and carmine-red ... 2·20 1·30
2153 2l.40 reddish brn, buff & brt rose-red ... 4·00 2·50
2151/2153 *Set of 3* ... 6·00 3·75
MS2154 90×89 mm. 1l.90, multicoloured. P 12×imperf ... 6·50 4·25
Designs: As T **449**—20q. Ismail Qemali (patriot) and crowd around building; 2l.40, Six freedom fighters. 58×55 mm—1l.90, Independence Monument, Tirana.

450 Dhërmi

451 Male Dancers

(Des P. Sulo)

1982 (20 Dec). Coastal Views. T **450** and similar horiz designs. Multicoloured. P 12.
2155 25q. Type **450** ... 35 20
2156 80q. Sarandë ... 1·10 75
2157 1l.20 Ksamil ... 1·60 1·30
2158 1l.55 Lukovë ... 2·40 1·60
2155/2158 *Set of 4* ... 5·00 3·50

(Des H. Devolli)

1983 (20 Feb). Folk Dance Assemblies Abroad. T **451** and similar horiz designs. Multicoloured. P 12.
2159 25q. Type **451** ... 20 10
2160 80q. Male dancers and drummer ... 75 50
2161 1l.20 Musicians ... 1·30 1·00
2162 1l.55 Group of female dancers ... 1·60 1·50
2159/2162 *Set of 4* ... 3·50 2·75

452 Karl Marx

453 Electricity Generation

(Des M. Fushekati)

1983 (14 Mar). Death Centenary of Karl Marx. P 12.
2163 **452** 80q. multicoloured ... 2·20 1·00
2164 1l.10 multicoloured ... 2·75 1·60

(Des Q. Prizreni)

1983 (20 Apr). Energy Production. T **453** and similar vert design P 12.
2165 80q. dull ultramarine and orange ... 1·40 85
2166 1l.10 mauve and turquoise-green ... 1·80 1·30
Design:—1l.10, Gas and oil production.

(Des M. Fushekati)

1983 (5 May). Anti-fascist Heroes (5th series). Horiz designs as T **424**. Multicoloured. P 12.
2167 25q. Asim Zeneli and Nazmi Rushiti ... 35 20
2168 80q. Shyqyri Ishmi, Shyqyri Alimerko and Myzafer Asqeriu ... 1·10 50
2169 1l.20 Qybra Sokoli, Qeriba Derri and Ylbere Bilibashi ... 1·80 1·00
2170 1l.55 Themo Vasi and Abaz Shehu ... 2·75 1·60
2167/2170 *Set of 4* ... 5·50 3·00

454 Congress Emblem

455 Cycling

(Des Z. Mati)

1983 (1 June). Ninth Women's Union Congress. P 12½.
2171 **454** 80q. red, scarlet-vermilion and gold ... 1·50 1·00
2172 1l.10 greenish blue, vermilion and gold ... 2·00 1·60

(Des E. Hila)

1983 (20 June). Sport and Leisure. T **455** and similar horiz designs. Multicoloured. P 12.
2173 25q. Type **455** ... 35 20
2174 80q. Chess ... 1·10 50
2175 1l.20 Gymnastics ... 1·80 1·00
2176 1l.55 Wrestling ... 2·20 1·40
2173/2176 *Set of 4* ... 5·00 2·75

456 Soldier and Militia

457 "Sunny Day" (Myrteza Fushekati)

(Des P. Mele)

1983 (10 July). 40th Anniv of People's Army. T **456** and similar vert designs. P 12.
2177 20q. gold and Indian red ... 35 20
2178 1l.20 gold and carmine-red ... 1·80 1·00
2179 2l.40 gold and lake-brown ... 3·25 1·90
2177/2179 *Set of 3* ... 4·75 2·75
Designs:—1l.20, Soldier; 2l.40, Factory guard.

(Des P. Sulo)

1983 (28 Aug). Paintings from Gallery of Figurative Arts, Tirana. T **457** and similar horiz designs. Multicoloured. P 12½.
2180 25q. Type **457** ... 35 20
2181 80q. "Morning Gossip" (Niko Progri) ... 1·30 75
2182 1l.20 "29th November, 1944" (Harilla Dhimo) ... 1·60 1·00
2183 1l.55 "Demolition" (Pandi Male) ... 2·20 1·40
2180/2183 *Set of 4* ... 5·00 3·00
MS2184 111×74 mm. 1l.90, "Partisan Assault" (Sali Shijaku and Myrteza Fushekati) (99×59 mm). P 12×imperf ... 11·00 7·50

(Des N. Bakalli)

1983 (6 Oct). National Folklore Festival, Gjirokastër. Vert designs as T **402**. Multicoloured. P 12.
2185 25q. Sword dance ... 25 15
2186 80q. Kerchief dance ... 1·80 1·00
2187 1l.20 Musicians ... 2·40 1·60
2188 1l.55 Women dancers with garlands ... 3·75 2·50
2185/2188 *Set of 4* ... 7·50 4·75

458 Enver Hoxha

459 W.C.Y. Emblem and Globe

(Des V. Kilica)

1983 (16 Oct). 75th Birthday of Enver Hoxha. P 12½.
2189 **458** 80q. multicoloured ... 80 65
2190 1l.20 multicoloured ... 1·30 1·00
2191 1l.80 multicoloured ... 1·80 1·40
2189/2191 *Set of 3* ... 3·50 2·75
MS2192 77×98 mm. 1l.90, multicoloured (as T **458** but with inscriptions differently arranged) ... 4·25 4·25
The miniature sheet includes two horizontal lines of perforations (p 12) in its design.

(Des M. Fushekati)

1983 (10 Nov). World Communications Year. P 12.

2193 **459** 60q. multicoloured ... 75 50
2194 1l.20 blue, black & reddish orge ... 2·00 1·60

460 "Combine to Triumph" (J. Keraj)

1983 (10 Dec). Skanderbeg Epoch in Art. T **460** and similar horiz designs. Multicoloured. P 12½.

2195 25q. Type **460** ... 55 20
2196 80q. "The Heroic Resistance at Krujë" (N. Bakalli) ... 1·60 1·00
2197 1l.20 "United we are Unconquerable by our Enemies" (N. Progri) ... 2·20 1·30
2198 1l.55 "Assembly at Lezhë" (B. Ahmeti) ... 3·25 1·80
2195/2198 *Set of 4* ... 6·75 3·75
MS2199 77×90 mm. "Victory over the Tuks" (G. Madhi) ... 8·25 7·75

The miniature sheet includes two horizontal lines of perforations (p 12) in its design.

461 Amphitheatre, Butrint (Buthrotum)

462 Man's Head from Apoloni

(Des P. Sulo)

1983 (28 Dec). Graeco-Roman Remains in Illyria. T **461** and similar horiz designs. Multicoloured. P 12.

2200 80q. Type **461** ... 2·20 1·60
2201 1l.20 Colonnade, Apoloni-Çesma (Apollonium) ... 2·75 2·10
2202 1l.80 Vaulted gallery of amphitheatre, Dyrrah (Epidamnus) ... 3·25 2·50
2200/2202 *Set of 3* ... 7·50 5·50

(Des P. Sulo)

1984 (25 Feb). Archaeological Discoveries. T **462** and similar vert designs. Multicoloured. P 12×12½.

2203 15q. Type **462** ... 20 15
2204 25q. Tombstone from Korcë ... 35 20
2205 80q. Woman's head from Apoloni ... 1·30 85
2206 1l.10 Child's head from Tren ... 1·60 1·00
2207 1l.20 Man's head from Dyrrah ... 2·00 1·30
2208 2l.20 Bronze statuette of Eros from Dyrrah ... 3·25 1·60
2203/2208 *Set of 6* ... 7·75 4·50

463 Clock Tower, Gjirokastër

464 Student with Microscope

(Des Z. Mati)

1984 (30 Mar). Clock Towers. T **463** and similar vert designs. P 12.

2209 15q. slate-purple ... 20 15
2210 25q. deep grey-brown ... 35 20
2211 80q. slate-violet ... 1·10 75
2212 1l.10 scarlet ... 1·30 1·00
2213 1l.20 bronze-green ... 2·00 1·40
2214 2l.20 orange-brown ... 3·25 2·30
2209/2214 *Set of 6* ... 7·50 5·25

Designs:—25q. Kavajë; 80q. Elbasan; 1l.10, Tirana; 1l.20, Peqin; 2l.20, Krujë.

(Des P. Mele, Q. Prizreni and L. Kodheli)

1984 (20 Apr). 40th Anniv of Liberation (1st issue). T **464** and similar horiz designs. Multicoloured. P 12.

2215 15q. Type **464** ... 20 15
2216 25q. Soldier with flag ... 35 20
2217 80q. Schoolchildren ... 1·30 85
2218 1l.10 Soldier, ships, airplanes and weapons ... 1·60 1·00
2219 1l.20 Workers with flag ... 2·00 1·30
2220 2l.20 Armed guards on patrol ... 3·25 1·60
2215/2220 *Set of 6* ... 7·75 4·50

See also Nos. 2255/**MS**2257.

(Des M. Fushekati)

1984 (5 May). Anti-fascist Heroes (6th series). Horiz designs as T **424**. Multicoloured. P 12.

2221 15q. Manush Alimani, Mustafa Matohiti and Kastriot Muço ... 65 20
2222 25q. Zaho Koka, Reshit Çollaku and Maliq Muço ... 1·30 55
2223 1l.20 Lefter Talo, Tom Kola and Fuat Babani ... 2·40 1·40
2224 2l.20 Myslysm Shyri, Dervish Hekali and Skender Caci ... 4·25 2·75
2221/2224 *Set of 4* ... 7·75 4·50

465 Enver Hoxha

466 Children reading Comic

(Des Q. Prizreni)

1984 (24 May). 40th Anniv of Permet Congress. T **465** and similar vert design. P 12.

2225 80q. reddish brown, orange-vermilion and Venetian red ... 3·25 2·10
2226 1l.10 black, orange-yell & reddish lilac ... 4·00 2·50

Design:—1l.10, Resistance fighter (detail of monument).

(Des Z. Mati)

1984 (1 June). Children. T **466** and similar vert designs. Multicoloured. P 12.

2227 15q. Type **466** ... 55 20
2228 25q. Children with toys ... 1·10 50
2229 60q. Children gardening and rainbow ... 2·20 1·00
2230 2l.80 Children flying kite bearing Albanian arms ... 5·00 2·50
2227/2230 *Set of 4* ... 8·00 3·75

467 Football in Goal

468 "Freedom is Here" (Myrteza Fushekati)

(Des M. Fushekati)

1984 (12 June). European Football Championship Finals. T **467** and similar vert designs. Multicoloured. P 12.

2231 15q. Type **467** ... 1·10 30
2232 25q. Referee and football ... 1·60 50
2233 1l.20 Football and map of Europe ... 3·25 1·00
2234 2l.20 Football and pitch ... 3·75 2·10
2231/2234 *Set of 4* ... 8·75 3·50

1984 (12 July). Paintings from Gallery of Figurative Arts, Tirana. T **468** and similar multicoloured designs. P 12½.

2235 15q. Type **468** ... 55 20
2236 25q. "Morning" (Zamir Mati) (vert) ... 1·10 65
2237 80q. "My Darling" (Agim Zajmi) (vert) ... 2·75 1·60
2238 2l.60 "For the Partisans" (Arben Basha) ... 4·25 2·30
2235/2238 *Set of 4* ... 7·75 4·25
MS2239 80×93 mm. 1l.90, "Albania" (Zamir Mati) ... 11·00 9·00

The miniature sheet includes two horizontal rows of perforations (p 12) within its design.

469 Mulberry

1984 (20 Aug). Flowers. T **469** and similar vert designs. Multicoloured. P 12.

2240 15q. Type **469** ... 3·25 85
2241 25q. Plantain ... 4·25 1·30
2242 1l.20 Hypericum ... 12·00 4·75
2243 2l.20 Edelweiss (*Leontopodium alpinum*) ... 24·00 9·00
2240/2243 *Set of 4* ... 39·00 14·50

470 Sabre Dance

(Des N. Bakalli)

1984 (21 Sept). Ausipex 84 International Stamp Exhibition, Melbourne. Sheet 72×98 mm. P 12×imperf.

MS2244 **470** 1l.90, multicoloured ... 4·50 4·50

471 Truck driving through Forest

472 Gjirokastër

1984 (25 Sept). Forestry. T **471** and similar vert designs. Multicoloured. P 12.

2245 15q. Type **471** ... 1·10 65
2246 25q. Transporting logs on overhead cable ... 1·60 1·00
2247 1l.20 Sawmill in forest ... 5·50 3·25
2248 2l.20 Lumberjack sawing down tree ... 8·25 4·50
2245/2248 *Set of 4* ... 15·00 8·50

1984 (13 Oct). Eurphila '84 International Stamp Exhibition, Rome. P 12½.

2249 **472** 1l.20 multicoloured ... 2·75 2·50

473 Football

474 Agriculture and Industry

(Des E. Hila)

1984 (19 Oct). Fifth National Spartakiad. T **473** and similar vert designs. Multicoloured. P 12.

2250 15q. Type **473** ... 20 15
2251 25q. Running ... 55 20
2252 80q. Weightlifting ... 1·10 65
2253 2l.20 Pistol shooting ... 3·00 2·10
2250/2253 *Set of 4* ... 4·25 2·75
MS2254 70×90 mm. 1l.90, Opening ceremony ... 4·25 3·50

The miniature sheet includes two horizontal rows of perforations in its design.

(Des E. Laperi and S. Kristo)

1984 (29 Nov). 40th Anniv of Liberation (2nd issue). T **474** and similar multicoloured designs. P 12.

2255 80q. Type **474** ... 2·20 1·00
2256 1l.10 Soldiers and flag ... 2·75 1·60
MS2257 68×89 mm. 1l.90, Enver Hoxha making liberation speech. P 12×imperf ... 5·00 4·00

475 Pot

476 Kapo (bust)

(Des N. Baba)

1985 (25 Feb). Archaeological Discoveries in Illyria. T **475** and similar vert designs. Multicoloured. P 12×12½.

2258 15q. Type **475** ... 55 20
2259 80q. Terracotta head of woman ... 2·20 1·00
2260 1l.20 Terracotta bust of Aphrodite ... 2·75 1·40
2261 1l.70 Bronze statuette of Nike ... 4·25 2·10
2258/2261 *Set of 4* ... 8·75 4·25

(Des M. Fushekati)

1985 (4 Mar). 70th Birthday of Hysni Kapo (politician). P 12.

2262 **476** 90q. black and rose-red ... 2·20 1·60
2263 1l.10 black and cobalt ... 2·75 2·10

477 Running

478 Bach

(Des Q. Prizreni)

1985 (18 Mar). Olymphilex'85 Olympic Stamps Exhibition, Lausanne. T **477** and similar horiz designs. Multicoloured. P 12.

2264 25q. Type **477** ... 35 20
2265 60q. Weightlifting ... 85 65

2266 1l.20 Football .... 1·60 1·30
2267 1l.50 Pistol shooting .... 2·75 1·60
2264/2267 *Set of 4* .... 5·00 3·50

(Des Q. Prizreni)

1985 (31 Mar). 300th Birth Anniv of Johann Sebastian Bach (composer). T **478** and similar vert design. P 12.
2268 80q. dull orange, reddish brown and black .... 22·00 13·00
2269 1l.20 new blue, deep new blue and black 27·00 16·00
Design:—1l.20, Bach's birthplace, Eisenach.

479 Enver Hoxha

480 Frontier Guards

(Des V. Kilica)

1985 (11 Apr). Enver Hoxha Commemoration. P 12½.
2270 **479** 80q. multicoloured .... 2·75 2·10
MS2271 67×90 mm. **479** 1l.90, multicoloured. Imperf .... 4·25 4·25

(Des S. Spahiu and B. Marika)

1985 (25 Apr). 40th Anniv of Frontier Force. T **480** and similar horiz design. Multicoloured. P 12.
2272 25q. Type **480** .... 1·60 1·00
2273 80q. Frontier guard .... 3·75 3·25

(Des M. Fushekati)

1985 (5 May). Anti-fascist Heroes (7th series). Horiz designs as T **424**. Multicoloured. P 12.
2274 25q. Mitro Xhani, Nimete Progonati and Kozma Nushi 85 50
2275 40q. Ajet Xhindoli, Mustafa Kaçaçi and Estref Caka .... 1·30 1·00
2276 60q. Çelo Sinani, Llambro Andoni and Meleq Gosnishti .... 2·20 1·30
2277 1l.20 Thodhori Mastora, Fejzi Micoli and Hysen Cino .... 3·75 3·00
2274/2277 *Set of 4* .... 7·25 5·25

481 Scarf on Rifle Barrel

482 "Primary School" (Thoma Malo)

(Des H. Devolli and M. Fushekati)

1985 (9 May). 40th Anniv of V.E. (Victory in Europe) Day. T **481** and similar horiz design. Multicoloured. P 12.
2278 25q. Type **481** .... 33·00 50·00
2279 80q. Crumpled swastika and hand holding rifle butt .... 85·00 £130

(Des N. Baba)

1985 (25 June). Paintings from Gallery of Figurative Arts, Tirana. T **482** and similar multicoloured designs. P 12½.
2280 25q. Type **482** 35 20
2281 80q. "Heroes and Mother" (Hysen Devolli) (vert) .... 1·30 1·00
2282 90q. "Mother writing" (Angjelin Dodmasej) (vert) .... 1·60 1·30
2283 1l.20 "Women off to Work" (Ksenofon Dilo) .... 2·20 1·80
2280/2283 *Set of 4* .... 5·00 4·00
MS2284 74×88 mm. 1l.90, "Foundry Workers" (Mikel Gurashi) .... 5·00 3·75
The miniature sheet includes two horizontal rows of perforations (p 12) within its design.

483 Scoring a Goal

484 Oranges

(Des Z. Mati)

1985 (20 July). 10th World Basketball Championship, Spain. T **483** and similar vert designs. P 12.
2285 25q. blue and black 25 15
2286 80q. green and black .... 1·30 75
2287 1l.20 bluish violet and black .... 1·80 1·30
2288 1l.60 carmine-red and black .... 2·75 2·10
2285/2288 *Set of 4* .... 5·50 3·75
Designs:—80q. Player running with ball; 1l.20, Defending goal; 1l.60, Defender capturing ball.

(Des K. Dilo)

1985 (20 Aug). Fruit Trees. T **484** and similar vert designs. Multicoloured. P 12.
2289 25q. Type **484** 55 30
2290 80q. Plums .... 2·75 1·60
2291 1l.20 Apples .... 4·25 2·10
2292 1l.60 Cherries .... 5·50 3·25
2289/2292 *Set of 4* .... 11·50 6·50

485 Krujë

486 War Horse Dance

(Des K. Dilo)

1985 (20 Sept). Architecture. T **485** and similar horiz designs. P 12.
2293 25q. black and Indian red 55 30
2294 80q. black, grey and red-brown .... 2·75 1·60
2295 1l.20 black, light brown and new blue .... 3·25 2·10
2296 1l.60 black, brown and Indian red .... 4·25 2·50
2293/2296 *Set of 4* .... 9·75 5·75
Designs:—80q. Gjirokastër; 1l.20, Berat; 1l.60, Shkodër.

(Des N. Bakalli)

1985 (6 Oct). National Folklore Festival. Dances. T **486** and similar vert designs. P 12.
2297 25q. reddish brown, brown-red and black 55 30
2298 80q. reddish brown, brown-red and black 1·60 1·00
2299 1l.20 reddish brown, brown-red and black 2·20 1·30
2300 1l.60 reddish brown, brown-red and black 2·75 1·80
2297/2300 *Set of 4* .... 6·50 4·00
MS2301 56×82 mm. 1l.90, multicoloured. Imperf .... 4·25 3·75
Designs:—80q. Pillow dance; 1l.20, Ladies' kerchief dance; 1l.60, Men's one-legged pair dance; 1l.90, Fortress dance.

487 State Arms

488 Dam across River Drin

(Des H. Devolli)

1986 (11 Jan). 40th Anniv of Albanian People's Republic. T **487** and similar horiz design. P 12½.
2302 25q. gold, deep rose-red and black .... 1·60 1·00
2303 80q. multicoloured .... 3·25 2·10
Design:—80q. "Comrade Hoxha announcing the News to the People" (Vilson Kilica) and arms.

1986 (20 Feb). Enver Hoxha Hydro-electric Power Station. T **488** and similar vert design. Multicoloured. P 12.
2304 25q. Type **488** .... 5·50 2·10
2305 80q. Control building .... 12·00 7·25

489 *Gymnospermium shqipetarum*

490 Maksim Gorky (writer)

(Des H. Agolli)

1986 (20 Mar). Flowers. T **489** and similar vert design. Multicoloured. P 12.
2306 25q. Type **489** .... 2·20 1·00
a. Pair. Nos. 2306/7 .... 11·50 5·50
2307 1l.20 *Leucolum valentinum* .... 8·75 4·25
Nos. 2306/7 were issued together in *se-tenant* pairs in booklets. They also exist imperforate from a limited printing.

1986 (20 Apr). Anniversaries. T **490** and similar designs. P 12.
2308 25q. deep chestnut 55 30
a. Horiz strip. Nos. 2308/11 .... 14·50
2309 80q. dull violet .... 2·20 1·30
2310 1l.20 olive-green .... 3·75 2·10
2311 2l.40 reddish purple .... 7·50 4·75
2308/2311 Set of 4 .... 12·50 7·50
MS2312 88×72 mm. 1l.90, dull violet, ultramarine and orange-yellow .... 5·50 4·25
Designs: As T **490**—25q. Type **490** (50th death anniv); 80q. André Ampère (physicist and mathematician, 150th death anniv); 1l.20, James Watt (inventor, 250th birth anniv); 2l.40, Franz Liszt (composer, death centenary). 88×72 mm—1l.90, Heads of Gorky, Ampère, Watt and Liszt.
The miniature sheet includes two vertical rows of perforations (p 12½) in its design.
Nos. 2308/11 were issued in *se-tenant* strips of four in booklets.

(Des M. Fushekati)

1986 (5 May). Anti-fascist Heroes (8th series). Horiz designs as T **424**. Multicoloured. P 12.
2313 25q. Ramiz Aranitasi, Inajete Dumi and Laze Nuro Ferraj .... 2·20 1·60
2314 80q. Dine Kalenja. Kozma Naska, Met Hasa and Fahri Ramadani .... 5·50 2·50
2315 1l.20 Hiqmet Buzi, Bàjram Tusha, Mumin Selami and Hajredin Bylyshi .... 8·75 5·25
2313/2315 *Set of 3* .... 15·00 8·50

491 Trophy on Globe

492 Tyre within Ship's Wheel, Train and Traffic Lights

(Des M. Fushekati)

1986 (31 May). World Cup Football Championship, Mexico. T **491** and similar horiz designs. Multicoloured. P 12.
2316 25q. Type **491** 55 30
2317 1l.20 Goalkeeper's hands and ball .... 2·75 2·10
MS2318 97×63 mm. 1l.90, Globe-football (40×32 mm) .... 4·25 3·25
The miniature sheet includes horizontal and vertical rows of perforations (p 12½) enclosing the central motif, but the value of the sheet appears outside these perforations.

(Des M. Fushekati and H. Dhimo)

1986 (10 Aug). 40th Anniv of Transport Workers' Day. P 12.
2319 **492** 1l.20 multicoloured .... 14·00 7·75

493 Naim Frashëri (poet)

494 Congress Emblem

(Des H. Devolli)

1986 (20 Sept). Anniversaries. T **493** and similar horiz designs. Multicoloured. P 12.
2320 30q. Type **493** (140th birth anniv) 75 50
2321 60q. Ndre Mjeda (poet, 120th birth anniv) .... 1·30 1·00
2322 90q. Petro Nini Luarasi (journalist, 75th death anniv) .... 2·20 1·60
2323 1l. Andon Zako Qajupi (poet, 120th birth anniv) .... 2·75 1·90
2324 1l.20 Millosh Gjergj Nikolla (Migjeni) (revolutionary writer, 75th birth anniv) .... 3·25 2·30
2325 2l.60 Urani Rumbo (women's education pioneer, 50th death anniv) .... 8·75 4·25
2320/2325 *Set of 6* .... 17·00 10·50

(Des Z. Mati)

1986 (3 Nov). Ninth Workers' Party Congress, Tirana. P 12.
2326 **494** 30q. multicoloured .... 11·00 7·75

495 Party Stamp and Enver Hoxha's Signature

496 "Mother Albania"

(Des H. Devolli)

1986 (8 Nov). 45th Anniv of Workers' Party. T **495** and similar vert design. P 12.
2327 30q. rosine, gold and brownish grey .... 3·25 1·60
2328 1l.20 rosine, dull orange and gold .... 8·75 3·75
Design:—1l.20, Profiles of Marx, Engels, Lenin and Stalin and Tirana house where Party was founded.

(Des M. Fushekati)

1986 (29 Nov). P 12×12½.
2329 **496** 10q. deep turquoise-blue 10 10
2330 20q. Venetian red 10 10
2331 30q. scarlet-vermilion 10 10
2332 50q. bistre-brown 20 15
2333 60q. olive-green 35 20
2334 80q. carmine-red 55 30
2335 90q. ultramarine 75 50
2336 1l.20 deep blue-green .... 1·10 75
2337 1l.60 purple .... 1·60 10
2338 2l.20 slate-green .... 2·20 1·60
2339 3l. orange-brown .... 2·75 2·10
2340 6l. orange-yellow .... 5·50 3·75
2329/2340 *Set of 12* .... 14·00 8·75

497 Marble Head of Aesculapius

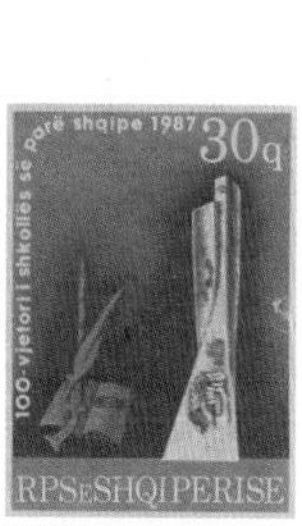

498 Monument and Centenary Emblem

1987 (20 Feb). Archaeological Discoveries. T **497** and similar vert designs. Multicoloured. P 12×12½.
2341 30q. Type **497** 1·10 65
2342 80q. Terracotta figure of Aphrodite 2·20 1·00
2343 1l. Bronze figure of Pan 3·25 1·50
2344 1l.20 Limestone head of Jupiter 4·25 2·75
2341/2344 *Set of 4* 9·75 5·25

(Des N. Prizreni)

1987 (7 Mar). Centenary of First Albanian School, Korcë. T **498** and similar designs. P 12.
2345 30q. yellow-brown, light brown and orange-yellow 55 30
2346 80q. multicoloured 1·60 75
2347 1l.20 multicoloured 2·20 1·60
2345/2347 *Set of 3* 4·00 2·40
Designs: Horiz—80q. First school building; 1l.20, Woman soldier running, girl reading book and boy doing woodwork.

499 Victor Hugo (writer)

500 *Forsythia europaea*

(Des H. Devolli)

1987 (20 Apr). Anniversaries. T **499** and similar vert designs. P 12.
2348 30q. bluish violet, lavender and black 55 30
2349 80q. chestnut, yellow-ochre and black 1·30 75
2350 90q. deep slate-blue, slate-blue and black 2·00 1·30
2351 1l.30 dp yellow-grn, dull yell-grn & blk 2·75 2·10
2348/2351 *Set of 4* 6·00 4·00
Designs:—30q. Type **499** (185th birth anniv); 80p. Galileo Galilei (astronomer, 345th death anniv); 90q. Charles Darwin (naturalist, 105th death anniv); 1l.30, Miguel de Cervantes (writer, 440th birth anniv).

(Des H. Agolli)

1987 (20 May). Flowers. T **500** and similar vert designs. Multicoloured. P 12.
2352 30q. Type **500** 75 40
2353 90q. *Moltkia doerfleri* 1·40 1·00
2354 2l.10 *Wulfenia baldacii* 3·25 2·75
2352/2354 *Set of 3* 4·75 3·75

501 Congress Emblem

502 "The Bread of Industry" (Myrteza Fushekati)

(Des Fatmir Biba)

1987 (25 June). Tenth Trade Unions Congress, Tirana. P 12.
2355 **501** 1l.20 deep carmine, vermilion & gold 5·50 4·25

1987 (20 July). Paintings from Gallery of Figurative Arts, Tirana. T **502** and similar multicoloured designs. P 12×12½ (vert) or 12½×12 (horiz).
2356 30q. Type **502** 55 30
2357 80q. "Partisan Gift" (Skender Kokobobo) 1·10 85
2358 1l. "Sowers" (Bujar Asllani) (horiz) 1·60 1·30
2359 1l.20 "At the Foundry" (Çlirim Ceka) (horiz) 2·20 1·90
2356/2359 *Set of 4* 5·00 4·00

503 Throwing the Hammer

1987 (29 Aug). World Light Athletics Championships, Rome. T **503** and similar horiz designs. Multicoloured. P 12½.
2360 30q. Type **503** 55 30
2361 90q. Running 1·50 1·00
2362 1l.10 Putting the shot 1·60 1·30
2360/2362 *Set of 3* 3·25 2·30
MS2363 85×59 mm. 1l.90, Runner, winners' podium and banner (64×24 mm). P 12½×12 4·25 4·25

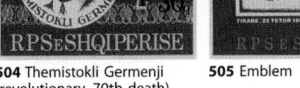

504 Themistokli Germenji (revolutionary, 70th death)

505 Emblem

(Des H. Devolli)

1987 (20 Sept). Anniversaries. T **504** and similar horiz designs. P 12.
2364 30q. deep yellow-brown, bright scarlet and black 35 25
2365 80q. carmine-lake, bright scarlet and black 1·30 65
2366 90q. dull violet, rosine and black 1·60 1·00
2367 1l.30 green, scarlet and black 2·75 1·90
2364/2367 *Set of 4* 5·50 3·50
Designs:—80q. Bajram Curri (organizer of Albanian League, 125th birth); 90q. Aleks Stavre Drenova (poet, 40th death); 1l.30, Gjerasim Qiriazi (educational pioneer, 126th birth).

(Des F. Biba)

1987 (22 Oct). Ninth Young Communists' Union Congress, Tirana. P 12.
2368 **505** 1l.20 multicoloured 7·00 5·25

506 National Flag

507 Post Office Emblem

(Des H. Devolli)

1987 (28 Nov). 75th Anniv of Independence. P 12.
2369 **506** 1l.20 multicoloured 7·00 5·25

(Des G. Hajdori)

1987 (5 Dec). 75th Anniv of Albanian Postal Administration. T **507** and similar vert design. Multicoloured. P 12.
2370 90q. Type **507** 7·50 5·25
2371 1l.20 National emblem on bronze medallion 11·00 10·50

508 Lord Byron (writer, bicentenary)

509 Oil Derrick, Tap, Houses and Wheat Ears

(Des H. Devolli)

1988 (10 Mar). Birth Anniversaries. T **508** and similar vert design. P 12.
2372 30q. grey-black and yellow-orange 5·50 4·25
2373 1l.20 black and mauve 22·00 17·00
Design:—1l.20, Eugène Delacroix (painter, 190th anniv).

(Des N. Kapulli)

1988 (7 Apr). 40th Anniv of World Health Organization. P 12.
2374 **509** 90q. multicoloured 30·00 25·00
2375 1l.20 multicoloured 41·00 33·00

510 *Sideritis raeseri*

511 Flag and Woman with Book

(Des A. Marika)

1988 (20 May). Flowers. T **510** and similar vert designs. Multicoloured. P 12.
2376 30q. Type **510** 11·00 6·25
a. Booklet pane. Nos. 2376/8 plus label 70·00
2377 90q. *Lunaria telekiana* 22·00 14·50
2378 2l.10 *Sanguisorba albanica* 33·00 21·00
2376/2378 *Set of 3* 60·00 38·00
Nos. 2376/8 were issued in horizontal *se-tenant* strips of three stamps and an inscribed label in booklets.

(Des N. Bakalli)

1988 (6 June). Tenth Women's Union Congress, Tirana. P 12.
2379 **511** 90q. black, bright rose-red and reddish orange 13·00 10·50

512 Footballers

513 Clasped Hands

(Des M. Fushekati)

1988 (10 June). Eighth European Football Championship, West Germany. T **512** and similar horiz designs. Multicoloured. P 12.
2380 30q. Type **512** 2·20 1·90
2381 80q. Players jumping for ball 3·25 3·00
2382 1l.20 Tackling 5·50 5·00
2380/2382 *Set of 3* 9·75 9·00
MS2383 78×67 mm. 1l.90, Goalkeeper saving ball. Imperf 13·00 13·00

(Des N. Prizreni)

1988 (10 June). 110th Anniv of League of Prizren. T **513** and similar vert design. Multicoloured. P 12.
2384 30q. Type **513** 45·00 45·00
2385 1l.20 League Headquarters, Prizren 75·00 75·00

514 Flag, Woman with Rifle and Soldier

515 Mihal Grameno (writer)

(Des Q. Prizreni)

1988 (10 July). 45th Anniv of People's Army. T **514** and similar vert design. Multicoloured. P 12.
2386 60q. Type **514** 45·00 45·00
2387 90q. Army monument, partisans and Labinot house 75·00 75·00

(Des H. Devolli)

1988 (15 Aug). T **515** and similar vert designs. Multicoloured. P 12.
2388 30q. Type **515** 16·00 16·00
2389 90q. Bajo Topulli (revolutionary) 27·00 27·00
2390 1l. Murat Toptani (sculptor and poet) 33·00 33·00
2391 1l.20 Jul Variboba (poet) 43·00 43·00
2388/2391 *Set of 4* £110 £110

516 Migjeni

517 *Dede Skurra*

(Des Z. Mati)

1988 (26 Aug). 50th Death Anniv of Millosh Nikolla (Migjeni) (writer). P 12.
2392 **516** 90q. silver and red-brown 13·00 12·50

(Des G. Leka)

1988 (5 Sept). Ballads. T **517** and similar square designs, each black and grey. P 12.
2393 30q. Type **517** 11·00 8·25
2394 90q. *Young Omer* 27·00 23·00
2395 1l.20 *Gjergj Elez Alia* 33·00 26·00
2393/2395 *Set of 3* 65·00 50·00

518 Bride wearing Fezzes, Mirdita

519 Hoxha

(Des N. Bakalli)

1988 (6 Oct). National Folklore Festival, Gjirokastër. Wedding Customs. T **518** and similar vert design. Multicoloured. P 12.
2396 30q. Type **518** 33·00 31·00
2397 1l.20 Pan Dance, Gjirokastër £120 95·00

(Des M. Fushekati and L. Kodheli)

1988 (16 Oct). 80th Birth Anniv of Enver Hoxha. T **519** and similar multicoloured design. P 12½.
2398 90q. Type **519** 5·50 5·25
2399 1l.20 Enver Hoxha Museum (horiz) 8·25 7·75

520 Detail of Congress Document

(Des Q. Prizreni)

1988 (14 Nov). 80th Anniv of Monastir Language Congress. T **520** and similar horiz design. Multicoloured. P 12.
2400 60q. Type **520** 27·00 23·00
2401 90q. Alphabet book and Congress building 43·00 37·00

521 Steam Locomotive and Map showing 1947 Railway line

(Des T. Pustina)

1989 (28 Feb). Railway Locomotives. T **521** and similar horiz designs. Multicoloured. P 12½×12.

2402	30q. Type **521**	45	10
2403	90q. Steam locomotive and map of 1949 network	1·30	50
2404	1l.20 Diesel locomotive and 1978 network	1·70	85
2405	1l.80 Diesel locomotive and 1985 network	2·50	1·00
2406	2l.40 Diesel locomotive and 1988 network	5·00	2·10
2402/2406 *Set of 5*		9·75	4·00

522 Entrance to Two-storey Tomb

523 Mother mourning Son

(Des T. Pustina)

1989 (10 Mar). Archaeological Discoveries in Illyria. T **522** and similar square designs. P 12.

2407	30q. black, deep brown and grey-brown	35	10
2408	90q. black and dull blue-green	1·30	1·00
2409	2l.10 multicoloured	2·20	1·90
2407/2409 *Set of 3*		3·50	2·75

Designs:—90q. Buckle showing battle scene; 2l.10, Earring depicting head.

(Des N. Bakalli)

1989 (5 Apr). Kostandini and Doruntina (folk tale). T **523** and similar vert designs. Multicoloured. P 12×12½.

2410	30q. Type **523**	55	30
2411	80q. Mother weeping over tomb and son rising from dead	1·10	75
2412	1l. Son and his sister on horseback	1·30	1·00
2413	1l.20 Mother and daughter reunited	1·60	1·30
2410/2413 *Set of 4*		4·00	3·00

524 *Aster albanicus*

525 Johann Strauss (composer, 90th death anniv)

1989 (10 May). Flowers. T **524** and similar vert designs. Multicoloured. P 12.

2414	30q. Type **524**	35	10
2415	90q. *Orchis paparisti*	1·30	1·00
2416	2l.10 *Orchis albanica*	2·20	1·90
2414/2416 *Set of 3*		3·50	2·75

(Des N. Bakalli)

1989 (3 June). Anniversaries. T **525** and similar vert designs, each deep brown and gold. P 12.

2417	30q. Type **525**	55	20
	a. Block of four. Nos. 2417/20	5·75	
2418	80q. Marie Curie (physicist, 55th death anniv)	1·10	75
2419	1l. Federico Garcia Lorca (writer, 53rd death anniv)	1·60	1·30
2420	1l.20 Albert Einstein (physicist, 110th birth anniv)	2·20	1·80
2417/2420 *Set of 4*		5·00	3·75

Nos. 3417/20 were issued together in *se-tenant* blocks of four within the sheet.

526 State Arms, Workers' Party Flag and Crowd

(Des P. Mele)

1989 (26 June). Sixth Albanian Democratic Front Congress, Tirana. P 12.

2421	**526**	1l.20 multicoloured	9·75	5·25

527 Storming of the Bastille

1989 (7 July). Bicentenary of French Revolution. T **527** and similar horiz design. Multicoloured. P 12½.

2422	90q. Type **527**	75	50
2423	1l.20 Monument	1·40	85

528 Galley

529 Pjeter Bogdani (writer)

1989 (25 July). Ships. T **528** and similar horiz designs. P 12.

2424	30q. dull blue-green and black	55	20
2425	80q. cobalt and black	1·00	75
2426	90q. violet-blue and black	1·10	95
2427	1l.30 bright lilac and black	1·60	1·40
2424/2427 *Set of 4*		3·75	3·00

Designs:—80q. Kogge; 90q. Schooner; 1l.30, Container ship.

1989 (30 Aug). Death Anniversaries. T **529** and similar vert designs. Multicoloured. P 12.

2428	30q. Type **529** (300th anniv)	20	15
2429	80q. Gavril Dara (writer, centenary)	75	50
2430	90q. Thimi Mitko (writer, centenary (1990))	1·40	85
2431	1l.30 Kole Idromeno (painter, 50th anniv)	2·00	1·00
2428/2431 *Set of 4*		4·00	2·30

530 Engels, Marx and Marchers

531 Gymnastics

1989 (28 Sept). 125th Anniv of "First International". T **530** and similar vert design. Multicoloured. P 12.

2432	90q. Type **530**	1·10	50
2433	1l.20 Factories, marchers and worker with pickaxe and rifle	1·60	75

(Des Z. Mati)

1989 (27 Oct). Sixth National Spartakiad. T **531** and similar vert designs. P 12½.

2434	30q. black, orange and bright scarlet	35	10
2435	80q. black, bright apple green and yellowish green	75	50
2436	1l. black, new blue and blue	85	65
2437	1l.20 black, bright purple and deep claret	1·30	1·00
2434/2437 *Set of 4*		3·00	2·00

Designs:—80q. Football; 1l. Cycling; 1l.20, Running.

532 Soldier

533 Chamois

(Des Z. Mati)

1989 (29 Nov). 45th Anniv of Liberation. T **532** and similar vert designs. Multicoloured. P 12½.

2438	30q. Type **532**	55	20
	a. Booklet pane. Nos. 2438/41	4·50	
2439	80q. Date	1·00	50
2440	1l. State arms	1·10	75
2441	1l.20 Young couple	1·60	1·30
2438/2441 *Set of 4*		3·75	2·50

Nos. 2438/41 were issued together in *se-tenant* strips of four in booklets.

(Des N. Prizreni)

1990 (15 Mar). Endangered Animals. The Chamois (*Rupicapra rupicapra*). T **533** and similar vert designs. Multicoloured. P 12.

2442	10q. Type **533**	35	10
	a. Block of four. Nos. 2442/5	5·75	
2443	30q. Mother and young	75	30
2444	80q. Chamois keeping lookout	2·10	1·00
2445	90q. Head of chamois	2·20	1·30
2442/2445 *Set of 4*		4·75	2·40

Nos. 2442/5 were issued together in *se-tenant* blocks of four within the sheet.

534 Eagle Mask

1990 (4 Apr). Masks. T **534** and similar vert designs. Multicoloured. P 12×12½.

2446	30q. Type **534**	35	10
2447	90q. Sheep	75	50
2448	1l.20 Goat	1·10	75
2449	1l.80 Stork	1·60	1·00
2446/2449 *Set of 4*		3·50	2·10

535 Caesar's Mushroom (*Amanita caesarea*)

536 Engraving Die

1990 (28 Apr). Fungi. T **535** and similar square designs. Multicoloured. P 12.

2450	30q. Type **535**	35	20
2451	90q. Parasol mushroom (*Lepiota procera*)	85	50
2452	1l.20 Cep (*Boletus edulis*)	1·40	1·20
2453	1l.80 *Clathrus cancelatus*	2·00	1·60
2450/2453 *Set of 4*		4·25	3·25

1990 (6 May). 150th Anniv of the Penny Black. T **536** and similar horiz designs. Multicoloured. P 12.

2454	90q. Type **536**	75	50
	a. Booklet pane. Nos. 2454/6 plus label	4·25	
2455	1l.20 Mounted postal messenger	1·10	85
2456	1l.80 Mail coach passengers reading letters	2·20	1·80
2454/2456 *Set of 3*		3·75	2·75

Nos. 2454/6 were issued in horizontal *se-tenant* strips of three stamps and a label, showing "London 90" International Stamp Exhibition emblem and letters, in booklets.

537 Mascot and Flags

538 Young Van Gogh and Paintings

(Des N. Bakalli)

1990 (8 June). World Cup Football Championship, Italy. T **537** and similar horiz designs. Multicoloured. P 12.

2457	30q. Type **537**	35	15
2458	90q. Mascot running	75	50
2459	1l.20 Mascot preparing to kick ball	1·30	1·00
2457/2459 *Set of 3*		2·20	1·50
MS2460	80×62 mm. 3l.30, Mascot as goalkeeper. Imperf	3·75	3·75

(Des N. Vasia)

1990 (27 July). Death Centenary of Vincent van Gogh (painter). T **538** and similar horiz designs. Multicoloured. P 12.

2461	30q. Type **538**	45	20
2462	90q. Van Gogh and woman in field	85	50
2463	2l.10 Van Gogh in asylum	2·00	1·60
2461/2463 *Set of 3*		3·00	2·10
MS2464	88×73 mm. 2l.40, Van Gogh and "Wheatfield with Crows". Imperf	3·25	3·25

539 Gjergj Elez Alia lying wounded

(Des N. Bakalli)

1990 (30 Aug). Gjergj Elez Alia (folk hero). T **539** and similar horiz designs. Multicoloured. P 12½×12.

2465	30q. Type **539**	35	20
2466	90q. Alia being helped onto horse	75	50
2467	1l.20 Alia fighting Bajloz	1·10	85
2468	1l.80 Alia on horseback and severed head of Bajloz	1·60	1·00
2465/2468 *Set of 4*		3·50	2·30

540 Mosque

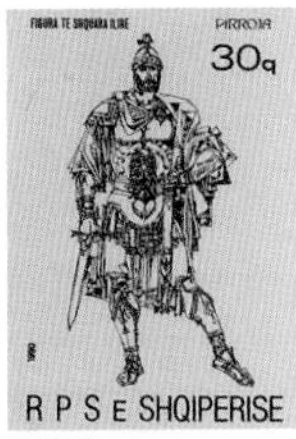

541 Pirroja

1990 (20 Sept). 2400th Anniv of Berat. T **540** and similar vert designs. Multicoloured. P 12½.

2469	30q. Type **540**	10	10
	a. Block. Nos. 2469/73 plus 4 labels	4·25	
2470	90q. St. Triadha's Church	60	40
2471	1l.20 River	70	50
2472	1l.80 Onufri (artist)	1·20	95
2473	2l.40 Nikolla	1·40	1·20
2469/2473	*Set of* 5	3·50	2·75

Nos. 2469/73 were issued together in *se-tenant* blocks of five stamps and four labels in a chessboard arrangement.

Commemorative folders containing a block were also sold.

1990 (20 Oct). Illyrian Heroes. T **541** and similar vert designs, each black. P 12.

2474	30q. Type **541**	20	10
2475	90q. Teuta	65	40
2476	1l.20 Bato	75	50
2477	1l.80 Bardhyli	1·10	85
2474/2477	*Set of* 4	2·40	1·70

542 School and "Globe" of Books

543 "Albanian Horsemen" (Eugène Delacroix)

1990 (30 Oct). International Literacy Year. P 12.

2478	**542**	90q. multicoloured	75	50
2479		1l.20 multicoloured	1·10	85

1990 (30 Nov). Albanians in Art. T **543** and similar vert designs. Multicoloured. P 12½.

2480	30q. Type **543**	35	10
2481	1l.20 "Albanian Woman" (Camille Corot)	1·00	75
2482	1l.80 "Skanderberg" (anon)	1·40	1·20
2480/2482	*Set of* 3	2·50	1·80

544 Boletini

545 Armorial Eagle

1991 (23 Jan). 75th Death Anniv of Isa Boletini (revolutionary). T **544** and similar vert design. Multicoloured. P 12×12½.

2483	90q. Type **544**	65	40
2484	1l.20 Boletini and flag	1·00	75

1991 (30 Jan). 800th Anniv (1990) of Founding of Arberi State. P 12.

2485	**545**	90q. multicoloured	65	50
2486		1l.20 multicoloured	1·00	75

546 "Woman reading"

547 *Cistus albanicus*

1991 (25 Feb). 150th Birth Anniv of Pierre Auguste Renoir (artist). T **546** and similar multicoloured designs. P 12½.

2487	30q. Type **546**	55	10
2488	90q. "The Swing"	85	75
2489	1l.20 "The Boat Club" (horiz)	1·30	1·00
2490	1l.80 Still life (detail) (horiz)	2·20	1·80
2487/2490	*Set of* 4	4·50	3·25
MS2491	94×75 mm. 3l. "Portrait of Artist with Beard". Imperf	4·25	4·25

(Des A. Marika)

1991 (30 Mar). Flowers. T **547** and similar vert designs. Multicoloured. P 12.

2492	30q. Type **547**	35	10
2493	90q. *Trifolium pilczii*	85	75
2494	1l.80 *Lilium albanicum*	1·60	1·30
2492/2494	*Set of* 3	2·50	1·90

XIII. Republic

29 April 1991

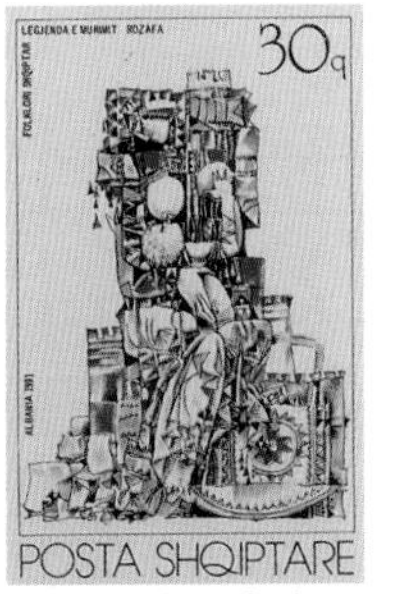

548 Rozafa breastfeeding Child

549 Mozart conducting

(Des N. Bakalli)

1991 (30 Sept). Imprisonment of Rozafa (folk tale). T **548** and similar vert designs. Multicoloured. P 12×12½.

2495	30q. Type **548**	20	10
2496	90q. The three brothers talking to old man	65	50
2497	1l.20 Building of walls around Rozafa	1·10	75
2498	1l.80 Figures symbolizing water flowing between stones	1·50	1·20
2495/2498	*Set of* 4	3·00	2·30

(Des H. Devolli)

1991 (5 Oct). Death Bicentenary of Wolfgang Amadeus Mozart (composer). T **549** and similar multicoloured designs. P 12.

2499	90q. Type **549**	75	50
2500	1l.20 Mozart and score	1·20	85
2501	1l.80 Mozart composing	2·10	1·50
2499/2501	*Set of* 3	3·75	2·50
MS2502	88×69 mm. 3l. Mozart medallion and score. Imperf	6·50	6·50

550 Vitus Bering

(Des A. Kapo)

1992 (10 Jan). Explorers. T **550** and similar horiz designs. Multicoloured. P 12½.

2503	30q. Type **550**	35	20
2504	90q. Christopher Columbus and his flagship *Santa Maria*	75	40
2505	1l.80 Ferdinand Magellan and his flagship *Vitoria*	1·60	95
2503/2505	*Set of* 3	2·40	1·40

551 Lilienthal Biplane Glider, 1896

552 Ski Jumping

(Des N. Prizreni)

1992 (27 Jan). Aircraft. T **551** and similar horiz designs. P 12½.

2506	30q. black, dull vermilion and pale blue	35	20
2507	80q. multicoloured	55	40
2508	90q. multicoloured	75	65
2509	1l.20 multicoloured	1·00	85
2510	1l.80 multicoloured	1·30	1·20
2511	2l.40 black, grey and magenta	1·60	1·50
2506/2511	*Set of* 6	5·00	4·25

Designs:—80q. Clément Ader's *Avion III*, 1897; 90q. Wright Brothers' Type A, 1903; 1l.20, Concorde supersonic jetliner; 1l.80, Tupolev Tu-144 jetliner (wrongly inscr "114"); 2l.40, Dornier Do-31E (wrongly inscr "Dernier").

(Des Z. Mati)

1992 (15 Feb). Winter Olympic Games, Albertville. T **552** and similar vert designs. Multicoloured. P 12½.

2512	30q. Type **552**	35	20
2513	90q. Skiing	75	65
2514	1l.20 Ice skating (pairs)	1·10	85
2515	1l.80 Luge	1·60	1·40
2512/2515	*Set of* 4	3·50	2·75

553 "Europe" and Doves

1992 (31 Mar). Admission of Albania to European Security and Co-operation Conference at Foreign Ministers' Meeting, Berlin. T **553** and similar horiz design. Multicoloured. P 12½.

2516	90q. Type **553**	1·20	1·00
2517	1l.20 Members' flags and map of Europe	1·50	1·30

554 Envelopes and Emblem

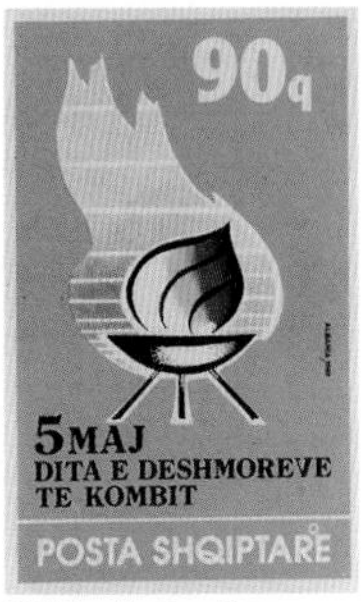

555 Everlasting Flame

1992 (25 Apr). Admission of Albania to European Posts and Telecommunications Conference. T **554** and similar horiz design. Multicoloured. P 12½.

2518	90q. Type **554**	1·30	1·20
	a. Pair. Nos. 2518/19	3·25	3·00
2519	1l.20 Emblem and tape reels	1·60	1·50

Nos. 2518/19 were issued together in *se-tenant* pairs in sheets of 10 stamps and two central labels either showing an ancient coin or inscribed "RODOS '91".

(Des Q. Prizreni and H. Dhimo)

1992 (5 May). National Martyrs' Day. T **555** and similar multicoloured design. P 12×12½.

2520	90q. Type **555**	70	65
2521	4l.10 Poppies (horiz)	3·25	2·75

556 Pictograms

557 Lawn Tennis

(Des B. Zajmi)

1992 (10 June). European Football Championship, Sweden. T **556** and similar horiz designs showing footballing pictograms. P 12.

2522	30q. pale yellowish green and dull yellowish green	60	30
2523	90q. Venetian red and chalky blue	1·20	75
2524	10l.80 ochre and brown-red	7·00	5·25
2522/2524	*Set of* 3	8·00	5·75
MS2525	90×69 mm. 5l. pink, brown-ochre and light turquoise-green. Imperf	4·00	4·00

(Des L. Sesferi)

1992 (14 June). Olympic Games, Barcelona. T **557** and similar horiz designs. Multicoloured. P 12.

2526	30q. Type **557**	45	20
2527	90q. Baseball	1·40	85
2528	1l.80 Table tennis	2·75	1·90
2526/2528	*Set of* 3	4·25	2·75
MS2529	89×69 mm. 5l. Torch bearer and running tracks. Imperf	4·75	4·75

558 Map and Doves

559 Arab

(Des H. Dhimo)

1992 (5 July). European Unity. P 12.

2530	**558**	1l.20 multicoloured	1·40	1·00

(Des N. Prizreni)

1992 (10 Aug). Horses. T **559** and similar multicoloured designs. P 12.

2531	30q. Native pony (horiz)	35	20
2532	90q. Hungarian nonius (horiz)	60	40
2533	1l.20 Type **559**	80	65
2534	10l.60 Haflinger	7·50	6·00
2531/2534	*Set of* 4	8·25	6·50

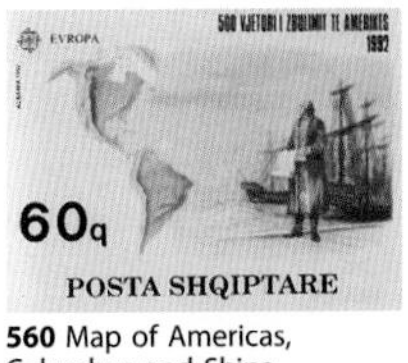

560 Map of Americas, Columbus and Ships

561 Mother Teresa and Child

1992 (20 Aug). Europa. 500th Anniv of Discovery of America by Columbus. T **560** and similar horiz designs. Multicoloured. P 12.

2535	60q. Type **560**	60	40
2536	3l.20 Map of Americas and Columbus meeting Amerindians	4·00	3·75
MS2537	90×70 mm. 5l. Map of Americas and Columbus. Imperf	85·00	85·00

1992 (4 Oct)–**95**. Mother Teresa (Agnes Gonxhe Bojaxhi) (founder of Missionaries of Charity). P 12×12½.

2538	**561**	40q. Venetian red	10	10

2539	60q. orange-brown	10	10
2540	1l. violet	10	10
2541	1l.80 slate	15	10
2542	2l. rose-carmine	35	20
2543	2l.40 light green	45	30
2544	3l.20 new blue	60	50
2545	5l. bluish violet (7.94)	70	65
2546	5l.60 purple	95	85
2547	7l.20 dull yellow-green	1·20	1·00
2548	10l. red-orange	1·40	1·30
2549	18l. orange (7.94)	1·50	1·40
2550	20l. bright purple (1994)	60	50
2551	25l. blue-green (7.94)	2·30	2·10
2552	60l. yellow-green (1995)	2·50	2·40
2538/2552	*Set of* 15	11·50	10·50

Numbers have been left for additions to this series.

562 Pope John Paul II

(**563**)

1993 (25 Apr). Papal Visit. P 12.

2555	**562**	16l. multicoloured	3·00	2·50

1993 (2 May). Nos. 2329/32 and 2335 surch as T **563**.

2556	**496**	3l. on 10q. deep turquoise-blue	25	20
2557		6l.50 on 20q. Venetian red	80	75
2558		13l. on 30q. scarlet-vermilion	2·30	2·10
2559		20l. on 90q. ultramarine	3·50	3·25
2560		30l. on 50q. bistre-brown	5·25	4·75
2556/2560		*Set of* 4	11·00	10·00

564 Lef Nosi (first Postal Minister)

565 "Life Weighs Heavily on Man" (A. Zajmi)

1993 (5 May). 80th Anniv of First Albanian Stamps. P 12.

2561	**564**	6l.50 bistre and olive-bistre	1·20	1·00

1993 (28 May). Europa. Contemporary Art. T **565** and similar multicoloured design. P 12.

2562	3l. Type **565**	1·20	1·00
2563	7l. "The Green Star" (E. Hila) (horiz)	4·75	4·25
MS2564	116×121 mm. 20l. "Gjirokastër" (B. Ahmeti). Imperf	8·25	8·25

Nos. 2562/3 were each issued in sheetlets of five stamps and one label showing an artist's palette.

566 Running

567 Frang Bardhi

1993 (20 June). Mediterranean Games, Agde and Roussillon (Languedoc), France. T **566** and similar horiz designs. Multicoloured. P 12.

2565	3l. Type **566**	25	20
2566	16l. Canoeing	2·30	2·10
2567	21l. Cycling	3·25	3·00
2565/2567	*Set of* 3	5·25	4·75
MS2568	117×84 mm. 20l. Map of Mediterranean. Imperf	4·00	4·00

1993 (20 Aug). 350th Death Anniv of Frang Bardhi (scholar). T **567** and similar design. P 12½.

2569	6l.50 reddish brown and stone	1·40	1·30
MS2570	94×107 mm. 20l. reddish brown and gold. Imperf	4·75	4·75

Design:—20l. Bardhi writing at desk.

568 Mascot and Flags around Stadium

569 Gjovalin Gjadri (construction engineer)

(Des L. Mema)

1994 (17 July). World Cup Football Championship, U.S.A. T **568** and similar vert design. Multicoloured. P 12.

2571	42l. Type **568**	1·40	1·30
2572	68l. Mascot kicking ball	2·10	1·90

(Des M. Temo. Litho Courvoisier)

1994 (31 Dec). Europa. Discoveries and Inventions. T **569** and similar vert design. P 14.

2573	50l. reddish brown, chestnut and brown	2·30	2·10
2574	100l. reddish brown, chestnut and brown	3·50	3·25
MS2575	60×80 mm. 150l. drab and reddish brown. Imperf	5·75	5·75

Designs:—100l. Karl Ritter von Ghega (railway engineer); 150l. Sketch of traffic project.

570 Emblem and Benz

(Des N. Luci. Litho Courvoisier)

1995 (21 Jan). 150th Birth Anniv (1994) of Karl Benz (engineer). T **570** and similar horiz designs. Multicoloured. P 14.

2576	5l. Type **570**	10	10
2577	10l. Modern Mercedes motor car	25	20
2578	60l. First four-wheel Benz motor car, 1886	1·40	1·30
2579	125l. Pre-war Mercedes touring car	4·00	3·75
2576/2579	*Set of* 4	5·25	4·75

571 Richard Wagner

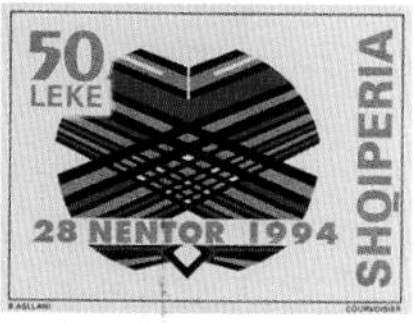

572 Intersections

1995 (26 Jan). Composers. T **571** and similar vert designs, each lake-brown and gold. P 12.

2580	3l. Type **571**	10	10
	a. Sheetlet of 4. Nos. 2580/3	1·60	
2581	6l.50 Edvard Grieg	25	20
2582	11l. Charles Gounod	35	30
2583	20l. Pyotr Tchaikovsky	80	75
2580/2583	*Set of* 4	1·40	1·20

Nos. 2580/3 were issued together in *se-tenant* sheetlets of four stamps.

(Des B. Asllani. Litho Courvoisier)

1995 (28 Jan). 50th Anniv (1994) of Liberation. P 14.

2584	**572**	50l. black and bright scarlet	1·70	1·60

573 Ali Pasha

574 Veskopoja, 1744 (left half)

(Des Q. Prizreni. Litho Courvoisier)

1995 (28 Jan). 250th Birth Anniv (1994) of Ali Pasha of Tepelenë (Pasha of Janina, 1788–1820). T **573** and similar horiz design. P 14.

2585 **573**	60l. black, yellow and chestnut	2·00	1·80
MS2586	80×60 mm. 100l. lake-brown and orange (Administration building, Tepelene). Imperf	3·50	3·50

(Des B. Asllani. Litho Courvoisier)

1995 (2 Feb). 250th Anniv (1994) of Veskopoja Academy. T **574** and similar vert design. Multicoloured. P 14.

2587	42l. Type **574**	1·20	1·00
	a. Horiz pair. Nos. 2587/8	3·25	2·75
2588	68l. Veskopoja, 1744 (right half)	1·70	1·60

Nos. 2587/8 were issued together in horizontal *se-tenant* pairs within the sheet, each pair forming a composite design.

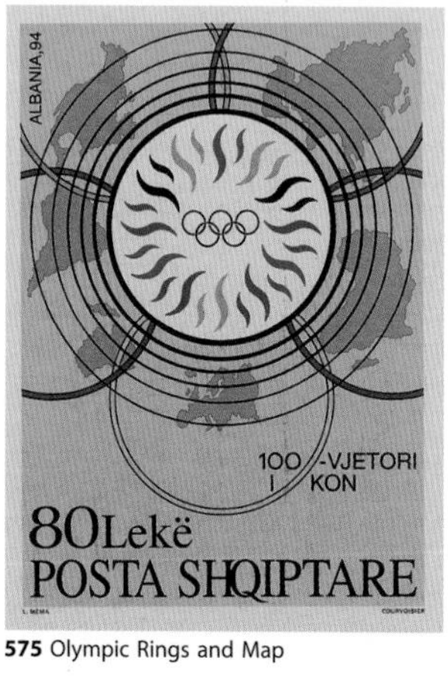

575 Olympic Rings and Map

(Des L. Mema. Litho Courvoisier)

1995 (2 Feb). Centenary of International Olympic Committee. Sheet 60×80 mm. Imperf.

MS2589	**575**	80l. multicoloured	2·50	2·50

576 Palace of Europe, Strasbourg

577 Hands holding Olive Branch

(Des R. Ballauri. Litho Alexandros Matsoukis, Athens, Greece)

1995 (29 June). Admission of Albania to Council of Europe. T **576** and similar horiz design. Multicoloured. P 14×13½.

2590	25l. Type **576**	95	85
2591	85l. State arms and map of Europe	3·75	3·25

(Des T. Pustina. Litho Alexandros Matsoukis, Athens, Greece)

1995 (10 Aug). Europa. Peace and Freedom. T **577** and similar vert designs. Multicoloured. P 13½×14.

2592	50l. Type **577**	2·30	2·10
2593	100l. Dove flying over hands	4·75	4·25
MS2594	80×60 mm. 150l. Figure stretching out hands. Imperf	7·00	7·00

578 Mice sitting around Table and Stork with Fox

579 Bee on Flower

(Des N. Vasia. Litho Alexandros Matsoukis, Athens, Greece)

1995 (20 Aug). 300th Death Anniv of Jean de La Fontaine (writer). T **578** and similar horiz designs. Multicoloured. P 14×13½.

2595	2l. Type **578**	15	10
2596	3l. Stork with foxes around table	25	10
2597	25l. Frogs under tree	95	85
2595/2597	*Set of* 3	1·20	95
MS2598	80×60 mm. 60l. La Fontaine and animals. Imperf	2·30	2·30

(Des Z. Shoshi. Litho)

1995 (20 Aug). The Honey Bee. T **579** and similar vert designs. Multicoloured. P 12.

2599	5l. Type **579**	25	10
2600	10l. Bee and honeycomb	35	20
2601	25l. Bee on comb	1·60	1·30
2599/2601	*Set of* 3	2·00	1·40

580 Fridtjof Nansen

581 Flags outside U.N. Building, New York

(Des N. Bakalli. Litho Alexandros Matsoukis, Athens, Greece)

1995 (14 Sept). Polar Explorers. T **580** and similar vert designs. Multicoloured. P 13½×14.

2602	25l. Type **580**	80	70
	a. Block of 4. Nos. 2602/5	3·50	
2603	25l. James Cook	80	70
2604	25l. Roald Amundsen	80	70
2605	25l. Robert Scott	80	70
2602/2605	*Set of* 4	3·00	2·50

Nos. 2602/5 were issued together in *se-tenant* blocks of four stamps within the sheet, each block forming a composite design.

(Des N. Vasia. Litho Alexandros Matsoukis, Athens, Greece)

1995 (14 Sept). 50th Anniv of United Nations Organization. T **581** and similar horiz design. Multicoloured. P 14×13½.

2606	2l. Type **581**	25	10
2607	100l. Flags flying to right outside U.N. building, New York	3·25	3·00

582 Male Chorus

583 "Poet"

(Des L. Merna. Litho Alexandros Matsoukis, Athens, Greece)

1995 (17 Oct). National Folklore Festival, Berat. T **582** and similar vert design. Multicoloured. P 13½×14.

2608 5l. Type **582** ... 35 20
2609 50l. Female participant ... 1·70 1·60

(Des N. Bakalli. Litho Alexandros Matsoukis, Athens, Greece)

1995 (17 Oct). Jan Kukuzeli (11th-century poet, musician and teacher). T **583** and similar multicoloured designs showing abstract representations of Kukuzeli. P 13½×14.

2610 18l. Type **583** ... 70 65
2611 20l. "Musician" ... 75 70
MS2612 80×80 mm. 100l. "Teacher". Imperf ... 3·50 3·50

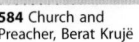

584 Church and Preacher, Berat Krujë

585 Paul Eluard

(Des I. Zabzuni. Litho Alexandros Matsoukis, Athens, Greece)

1995 (17 Oct). 20th Anniv of World Tourism Organization. T **584** and similar vert designs. Multicoloured. P 13½×14.

2613 18l. Type **584** ... 70 65
2614 20l. Street, Shkodër ... 80 75
2615 42l. Buildings, Gjirokastër ... 2·00 1·80
2613/2615 *Set of* 3 ... 3·25 3·00

(Des N. Bakalli. Litho Alexandros Matsoukis, Athens, Greece)

1995 (17 Oct). Poets' Birth Centenaries. T **585** and similar vert design. Multicoloured. P 13½×14.

2616 25l. Type **585** ... 80 75
a. Pair. Nos. 2616/17 ... 2·50 2·40
2617 50l. Sergei Yessenin ... 1·60 1·50

Nos. 2616/17 were issued together in *se-tenant* pairs within the sheet.

586 Louis, Film Reel and Projector

587 Elvis Presley

(Des L. Taçi. Litho Alexandros Matsoukis, Athens, Greece)

1995 (17 Nov). Centenary of Motion Pictures. Lumière Brothers (developers of cine camera). T **586** and similar vert design. Multicoloured. P 13½×14.

2618 10l. Type **586** ... 25 20
a. Horiz pair. Nos. 2618/19 ... 2·75 2·40
2619 85l. Auguste, film reel and cinema audience ... 2·30 2·10

Nos. 2618/19 were issued together in horizontal *se-tenant* pairs within the sheet.

(Des M. Temo. Litho Alexandros Matsoukis, Athens, Greece)

1995 (20 Nov). 60th Birth Anniv of Elvis Presley (entertainer). T **587** and similar horiz design. Multicoloured. P 14×13½.

2620 3l. Type **587** ... 25 20
2621 60l. Presley (different) ... 2·10 1·90

588 Banknotes of 1925

589 "5", crumbling Star, Open Book and Peace Dove

(Des M. Temo. Litho Alexandros Matsoukis, Athens, Greece)

1995 (25 Nov). 70th Anniv of Albanian National Bank. T **588** and similar vert design. Multicoloured. P 13½×14.

2622 10l. Type **588** ... 35 20
2623 25l. Modern banknotes ... 95 85

(Des E. Klefti. Litho Alexandros Matsoukis, Athens, Greece)

1995 (27 Nov). Fifth Anniv of Democratic Movement. T **589** and similar vert design. Multicoloured. P 13½×14.

2624 5l. Type **589** ... 25 10
2625 50l. Woman planting tree ... 1·90 1·70

590 Mother Teresa

591 Football, Union Jack, Map of Europe and Stadium

(Des L. Mema. Litho Alexandros Matsoukis, Athens, Greece)

1996 (5 May). Europa. Famous Women. Mother Teresa (founder of Missionaries of Charity). T **590** and similar vert design. P 13½×14.

2626 **590** 25l. multicoloured ... 1·20 1·00
2627 100l. multicoloured ... 4·00 3·75
MS2628 60×80 mm. 150l. Mother Teresa (different). Imperf ... 8·25 8·25

(Des E. Klefti. Litho Alexandros Matsoukis, Athens, Greece)

1996 (4 June). European Football Championship, England. T **591** and similar vert design. Multicoloured. P 14.

2629 25l. Type **591** ... 95 85
2630 100l. Map of Europe, ball and player ... 3·75 3·25

592 Satellite and Radio Mast

593 Running

(Des A. Baboçi. Litho Alexandros Matsoukis, Athens, Greece)

1996 (1 Aug). Inauguration of Cellular Telephone Network. T **592** and similar multicoloured design. P 13×13½ (10l.) or 13½×13 (60l.).

2631 10l. Type **592** ... 35 20
2632 60l. User, lorry, ship and mobile telephone (vert) ... 2·00 1·80

(Des L. Mema. Litho Alexandros Matsoukis, Athens, Greece)

1996 (3 Aug). Olympic Games, Atlanta. T **593** and similar vert designs. Multicoloured. P 13½×14.

2633 5l. Type **593** ... 25 10
2634 25l. Throwing the hammer ... 95 85
2635 60l. Long jumping ... 2·30 2·10
2633/2635 *Set of* 3 ... 3·25 2·75
MS2636 60×80 mm. 100l. Games emblem. Imperf ... 3·00 3·00

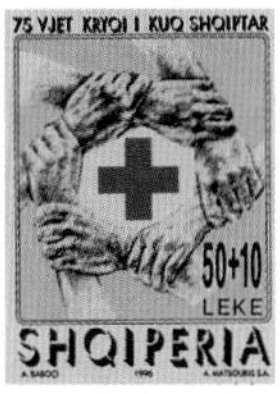

594 Linked Hands

595 Gottfried Wilhelm Leibniz (350th)

(Des A. Baboçi. Litho Alexandros Matsoukis, Athens, Greece)

1996 (5 Aug). 75th Anniv of Albanian Red Cross. P 13½×13.

2637 **594** 50l. +10l. multicoloured ... 2·10 1·90

(Des M. Temo. Litho Alexandros Matsoukis, Athens, Greece)

1996 (20 Sept). Philosopher-mathematicians' Birth Anniversaries. T **595** and similar horiz design. Multicoloured. P 14½×14.

2638 10l. Type **595** ... 60 40
2639 85l. René Descartes (400th) ... 3·00 2·50

596 "The Naked Maja"

597 Book Binding

(Des N. Bakalli. Litho Alexandros Matsoukis, Athens, Greece)

1996 (25 Sept). 250th Birth Anniv of Francisco de Goya (artist). T **596** and similar multicoloured designs. P 14×13½.

2640 10l. Type **596** ... 60 40
2641 60l. "Doña Isabel Cobos de Porcel" ... 2·10 1·90
MS2642 80×60 mm. 100l. "Self-portrait" (24×29 mm). P 12½×13 ... 3·00 3·00

(Des P. Sheqeri. Litho Alexandros Matsoukis, Athens, Greece)

1996 (5 Nov). Christian Art Exhibition. T **597** and similar vert designs. Multicoloured. P 13×14.

2643 5l. Type **597** ... 25 10
a. Block. Nos. 2643/5 plus label ... 4·50
2644 25l. Book clasp showing crucifixion ... 95 85
2645 85l. Book binding (different) ... 3·00 2·50
2643/2645 *Set of* 3 ... 3·75 3·00

Nos. 2643/5 were issued in *se-tenant* blocks of three stamps and one label showing a book clasp.

598 Princess

599 State Arms, Book and Fishta

(Des M. Temo. Litho Alexandros Matsoukis, Athens, Greece)

1996 (11 Nov). 50th Anniv of United Nations Children's Fund. Children's Paintings. T **598** and similar vert designs. P 13½×14.

2646 5l. Type **598** ... 25 10
2647 10l. Woman ... 35 20
2648 25l. Sea life ... 1·20 1·00
2649 50l. Harbour ... 1·70 1·60
2646/2649 *Set of* 4 ... 3·25 2·50

(Des L. Taçi. Litho Alexandros Matsoukis, Athens, Greece)

1996 (20 Dec). 125th Birth Anniv of Gjergj Fishta (writer and politician). T **599** and similar vert design. Multicoloured. P 13½×14.

2650 10l. Type **599** ... 35 20
2651 60l. Battle scene and Fishta ... 2·00 1·80

600 Omar Khayyam and Writing Materials

601 Gutenberg

(Des A. Baboçi. Litho Alexandros Matsoukis, Athens, Greece)

1997 (6 Mar). 950th Birth Anniv of Omar Khayyam (astronomer and poet). T **600** and similar vert design. Multicoloured. P 14.

2652 20l. Type **600** ... 60 40
2653 50l. Omar Khayyam and symbols of astronomy ... 1·40 1·30

Nos. 2652/3 are inscribed "850" in error.

(Des L. Taçi. Litho Alexandros Matsoukis, Athens, Greece)

1997 (20 Mar). 600th Birth Anniv of Johannes Gutenberg (printer). T **601** and similar vert designs. Multicoloured. P 14×14½.

2654 20l. Type **601** ... 60 40
a. Horiz pair. Nos. 2654/5 ... 2·40 2·10
2655 60l. Printing press ... 1·70 1·60

Nos. 2654/5 were issued together in horizontal *se-tenant* pairs within the sheet, each pair forming a composite design.

602 Pelicans

603 Dragon

(Des L. Mema. Litho Alexandros Matsoukis, Athens, Greece)

1997 (10 Apr). The Dalmatian Pelican (*Pelecanus crispus*). T **602** and similar vert design. Multicoloured. P 14×14½.

2656 10l. Type **602** ... 25 20
a. Horiz pair. Nos. 2656/7 ... 2·75 2·40
2657 80l. Pelicans on shore and in flight ... 2·30 2·10

Nos. 2656/7 were issued together in horizontal *se-tenant* pairs within the sheet, each pair forming a composite design.

(Des L. Taçi. Litho Alexandros Matsoukis, Athens, Greece)

1997 (5 May). Europa. Tales and Legends. "The Blue Pool". T **603** and similar vert design. Multicoloured. P 13×14.

2658 30l. Type **603** ... 1·20 1·00
2659 100l. Dragon drinking from pool ... 4·00 3·75

604 Faik Konica

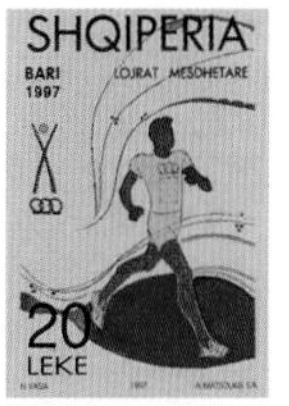

605 Male Athlete

(Des L. Boelen. Litho Alexandros Matsoukis, Athens, Greece)

1997 (25 June). 55th Death Anniv of Faik Konica (writer and politician). P 14×14½.

2660 **604** 10l. chocolate and black ... 35 20
2661 25l. indigo and black ... 1·00 95
MS2662 60×80 mm. **604** 80l. blackish brown ... 3·00 3·00

(Des N. Vasia. Litho Alexandros Matsoukis, Athens, Greece)

1997 (17 July). Mediterranean Games, Bari. T **605** and similar vert designs. Multicoloured. P 14×14½.

2663 20l. Type **605** ... 60 40
2664 30l. Female athlete and rowers ... 1·20 1·00
MS2665 60×80 mm. 100l. Discus-thrower, javelin-thrower and runner. Imperf ... 3·00 3·00

606 Skanderberg

(**607**)

(Des F. Kola. Litho Alexandros Matsoukis, Athens, Greece)

1997 (25 Aug). P 13.

2666 **606** 5l. scarlet and lake-brown ... 25 10
2667 10l. grey-olive and blackish olive ... 35 25
2668 20l. dull blue-green and bottle green ... 65 50
2669 25l. mauve and plum ... 75 65
2670 30l. bluish violet and deep lilac ... 95 80
2671 50l. grey and black ... 1·50 1·30
2672 60l. orange-brown and brown ... 1·80 1·60
2673 80l. light brown and brown ... 2·40 2·20
2674 100l. rose-carmine and brown-lake ... 3·00 2·75
2675 110l. blue and deep violet-blue ... 3·25 3·00
2666/2675 *Set of* 10 ... 13·50 12·00

1997 (13 Sept). Mother Teresa (founder of Missionaries of Charity) Commemoration. No. 2627 optd with T **607** in silver.

2676 **590** 100l. multicoloured ... 4·00 3·50

608 Codex Aureus (11th century)

609 Twin-headed Eagle (postal emblem)

(Des P. Sheqeri. Litho Alexandros Matsoukis, Athens, Greece)

1997 (15 Nov). Codices (1st series). T **608** and similar vert designs. Multicoloured. P 13×14.

2677 10l. Type **608** ... 25 10
a. Block. Nos. 2677/9 plus label ... 2·75
2678 25l. Codex Purpureus Beratinus (7th century) showing mountain and scribe ... 70 65
2679 60l. Codex Purpureus Beratinus showing church and scribe ... 1·60 1·50
2677/2679 *Set of* 3 ... 2·30 2·00

Nos. 2677/9 were issued together in *se-tenant* blocks of three stamps and one label depicting a church from the Codex Aureus.

See also Nos. 2712/14.

(Des N. Bakalli. Litho Alexandros Matsoukis, Athens, Greece)

1997 (4 Dec). 85th Anniv of Albanian Postal Service. T **609** and similar horiz design. P 14×13½.

2680 10l. multicoloured ... 25 10
2681 30l. multicoloured ... 95 85

The 30l. differs from Type **609** in minor parts of the design.

610 Nikete of Ramesiana

611 Man sitting at Table

(Des N. Bakalli. Litho Alexandros Matsoukis, Athens, Greece)

1998 (25 Mar). Nikete Dardani, Bishop of Ramesiana (philosopher and composer). P 14.

2682 **610** 30l. multicoloured ... 70 50
a. Horiz pair. Nos. 2682/3 ... 3·25 2·30
2683 100l. multicoloured ... 2·20 2·00

Nos. 2682/3 were issued together in horizontal *se-tenant* pairs within the sheet. There are minor differences of design between the two values.

(Des N. Bakalli. Litho Alexandros Matsoukis, Athens, Greece)

1998 (15 Apr). Legend of Pogradeci Lake. T **611** and similar vert designs. Multicoloured. P 14×14½.

2684 30l. Type **611** ... 70 50
a. Block of 4. Nos. 2684/7 ... 5·00
2685 50l. The Three Graces ... 1·00 85
2686 60l. Women drawing water ... 1·30 1·20
2687 80l. Man of ice ... 1·70 1·60
2684/2687 *Set of* 4 ... 4·25 3·75

Nos. 2684/7 were issued together in *se-tenant* blocks of four within the sheet.

612 Stylized Dancers

613 Abdyl Frasheri (founder)

(Des N. Bakalli. Litho Alexandros Matsoukis, Athens, Greece)

1998 (5 May). Europa. National Festivals. T **612** and similar vert designs. P 13×14.

2688 60l. multicoloured ... 2·30 2·10
2689 100l. multicoloured ... 3·00 2·50
MS2690 60×80 mm. 150l. multicoloured. Imperf ... 5·25 5·25

Designs:—100l. Female dancer; 150l. Two dancers.

(Des L. Taçi. Litho Alexandros Matsoukis, Athens, Greece)

1998 (10 June). 120th Anniv of League of Prizren. T **613** and similar vert designs. Multicoloured. P 13½×13.

2691 30l. Type **613** ... 70 50
a. Block of 4. Nos. 2691/4 ... 5·00
2692 50l. Sulejman Vokshi and partisan ... 1·00 85
2693 60l. Iljaz Pashe Dibra and crossed rifles ... 1·30 1·20
2694 80l. Ymer Prizreni and partisans ... 1·70 1·60
2691/2694 *Set of* 4 ... 4·25 3·75

Nos. 2691/4 were issued together in *se-tenant* blocks of four stamps within sheets of 8.

614 Player with Ball

615 Wrestlers in National Costume

(Des L. Mema. Litho Alexandros Matsoukis, Athens, Greece)

1998 (10 June). World Cup Football Championship, France. T **614** and similar vert designs. P 13½.

2695 60l. Type **614** ... 1·30 1·20
2696 100l. Player with ball (different) ... 2·20 2·00
MS2697 60×80 mm. 120l. Championship mascot. Imperf ... 3·00 3·00

(Des T. Pustina. Litho Alexandros Matsoukis, Athens, Greece)

1998 (5 July). European Junior Wrestling Championship. T **615** and similar horiz design. Multicoloured. P 13½.

2698 30l. Type **615** ... 60 40
a. Pair. Nos. 2698/9 ... 2·00 1·70
2699 60l. Ancient Greek wrestlers ... 1·30 1·20

Nos. 2698/9 were issued together in *se-tenant* pairs within the sheet.

616 Cabej

617 Diana, Princess of Wales

(Des M. Arapi. Litho Alexandros Matsoukis, Athens, Greece)

1998 (7 Aug). 90th Birth Anniv of Eqerem Cabej (linguist). T **616** and similar vert design. P 14.

2700 **616** 60l. black and orange-yellow ... 80 65
a. Pair. Nos. 2700/1 ... 2·10 1·80
2701 80l. orange-yellow, black and vermilion ... 1·20 1·00

Nos. 2700/1 were issued together in *se-tenant* pairs within the sheet.

(Litho Alexandros Matsoukis, Athens, Greece)

1998 (31 Aug). Diana, Princess of Wales Commemoration. T **617** and similar vert design. Multicoloured. P 13½.

2702 60l. Type **617** ... 1·70 1·60
2703 100l. With Mother Teresa ... 2·30 2·10

618 Mother Teresa holding Child

619 Detail of Painting

(Des Rita Morena (60l.), M. Temo (100l.). Photo Italian Govt Ptg Wks, Rome)

1998 (5 Sept). Mother Teresa (founder of Missionaries of Charity) Commemoration. T **618** and similar multicoloured design. P 14×13½ (60l.) or 13½×14 (100l.).

2704 60l. Type **618** ... 1·40 1·30
2705 100l. Mother Teresa (vert) ... 2·30 2·10

(Des G. Bakalli. Litho Alexandros Matsoukis, Athens, Greece)

1998 (10 Sept). 150th Birth Anniv of Paul Gauguin (artist). T **619** and similar multicoloured designs. P 13½.

2706 60l. Type **619** ... 1·20 1·00
a. Pair. Nos. 2706/7 ... 3·00 2·75
2707 80l. "Women of Tahiti" ... 1·60 1·50
MS2708 60×80 mm. 120l. Face. Imperf ... 3·00 3·00

Nos. 2706/7 were issued together in *se-tenant* pairs within the sheet.

620 Epitaph

621 Page

(Des M. Arapi. Litho Alexandros Matsoukis, Athens, Greece)

1998 (5 Oct). 625th Anniv of Epitaph of Gllavenica (embroidery of dead Christ). T **620** and similar horiz designs. Multicoloured. P 14.

2709 30l. Type **620** ... 60 40
2710 80l. Close-up of upper body ... 1·60 1·50
MS2711 80×60 mm. 100l. Detail of epitaph (24×29 mm). P 13 ... 2·00 2·00

(Des P. Sheqeri. Litho Alexandros Matsoukis, Athens, Greece)

1998 (15 Oct). Codices (2nd series). 11th-century Manuscripts. T **621** and similar vert designs. Multicoloured. P 13×14.

2712 30l. Type **621** ... 60 40
a. Block. Nos. 2712/14 plus label ... 3·50
2713 50l. Front cover of manuscript ... 95 75
2714 80l. Page showing mosque ... 1·60 1·50
2712/2714 *Set of* 3 ... 2·75 2·40

Nos. 2712/14 were issued together in *se-tenant* blocks of three stamps and one label showing the crucifixion.

(**622**)

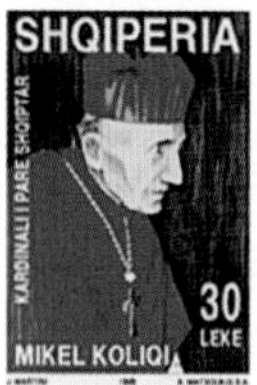

623 Koliqi

1998 (23 Oct). Italia '98 International Stamp Exhibition. No. **MS**2628 optd with T **622** in bright blue.

MS2715 60×80 mm. 150l. multicoloured ... 7·50 7·50

(Des J. Martini. Litho Alexandros Matsoukis, Athens, Greece)

1998 (28 Nov). First Death Anniv of Cardinal Mikel Koliqi (first Albanian Cardinal). T **623** and similar vert design. Multicoloured. P 14×14½.

2716 30l. Type **623** ... 60 40
a. Pair. Nos. 2716/17 ... 2·75 2·30
2717 100l. Koliqi (different) ... 2·00 1·80

Nos. 2716/17 were issued together in *se-tenant* pairs within the sheet.

624 George Washington (first President, 1789–97)

625 Monk Seals

(Des L. Taçi. Litho Alexandros Matsoukis, Athens, Greece)

1999 (15 Mar). American Anniversaries. T **624** and similar horiz designs. Multicoloured. P 14½×14.

2718 150l. Type **624** (death bicentenary) ... 3·50 3·25
a. Block. Nos. 2718/20 plus label ... 11·00
2719 150l. Abraham Lincoln (President 1861–65, 190th birth anniv) ... 3·50 3·25
2720 150l. Martin Luther King Jr. (civil rights campaigner, 70th birth anniv) ... 3·50 3·25
2718/2720 *Set of* 3 ... 8·50 8·75

Nos. 2718/20 were issued in blocks of three stamps and one label showing the carvings at Mount Rushmore.

(Des L. Mema. Litho Alexandros Matsoukis, Athens, Greece)

1999 (10 Apr). The Monk Seal (*Monachus albiventris*). T **625** and similar horiz designs. Multicoloured. P 14½×14.

2721 110l. Type **625** ... 2·50 2·30
a. Sheetlet of 4. Nos. 2721/4 ... 12·50
2722 110l. Two seals (both facing left) ... 2·50 2·30
2723 150l. As No. 2722 but both facing right ... 3·50 3·25
2724 150l. As Type **625** but seal at back facing left and seal at front facing right ... 3·50 3·25
2721/2724 *Set of* 4 ... 11·00 10·00

Nos. 2721/4 were issued together in *se-tenant* sheetlets of four stamps forming a composite design.

(626)

1999 (20 Apr). 50th Anniv of Council of Europe. No. 2590 surch with T **626**.
2725 **576** 150l. on 25l. multicoloured .... 4·00 3·50

(627)

628 Dove, Airplane and NATO Emblem

1999 (24 Apr). iBRA '99 International Stamp Exhibition, Nuremberg, Germany. No. 2496 surch with T **627** in black (new value) and multicoloured (emblem).
2726 150l. on 90q. multicoloured .... 3·75 3·25

(Des S. Taçi. Litho Alexandros Matsoukis, Athens, Greece)
1999 (25 Apr). 50th Anniv of North Atlantic Treaty Organization. T **628** and similar vert design. P 13½.
2727 **628** 10l. multicoloured 35 20
2728 100l. multicoloured .... 2·50 2·30
MS2729 69×85 mm. 250l. multicoloured. P 13 .... 5·75 5·75
Design: 28×49 mm—250l. As Type **628**, but with motifs differently arranged and without commemorative text.

629 Mickey Mouse

630 Thethi National Park, Shkodër

(Des S.Taçi. Litho Alexandros Matsoukis, Athens, Greece)
1999 (30 Apr). Mickey Mouse (cartoon film character). T **629** and similar vert designs. Multicoloured. P 13×14.
2730 60l. Type **629** .... 1·40 1·30
a. Strip of 4. Nos. 2730/3 .... 9·50
2731 80l. Mickey writing letter .... 2·10 1·90
2732 110l. Mickey thinking .... 2·30 2·10
2733 150l. Wearing black and red jumper .... 3·50 3·25
2730/2733 *Set of 4* .... 8·25 7·75
Nos. 2730/3 were issued together in *se-tenant* strips of four stamps within the sheet.

(Des S. Vllahu. Litho Alexandros Matsoukis, Athens, Greece)
1999 (1 May). Europa. Parks and Gardens. T **630** and similar horiz designs. Multicoloured. P 14×13.
2734 90l. Type **630** .... 3·00 2·50
2735 310l. Lura National Park, Dibra .... 7·50 6·75
MS2736 80×60 mm. 350l. Divjaka National Park, Lushnjë. Imperf .... 10·50 10·50

631 Coin

(Des M. Arapi. Litho Alexandros Matsoukis, Athens, Greece)
1999 (1 June). Illyrian Coins. T **631** and similar horiz designs. Multicoloured. P 13½.
2737 10l. Type **631** 25 10
a. Strip of 3. Nos. 2737/9 .... 6·00
2738 20l. Coins from Labeateve, Bylisi and Scutari 45 30
2739 200l. Coins of King Monuni .... 5·00 4·50
2737/2739 *Set of 3* .... 5·25 4·50
MS2740 80×60 mm. 310l. Coin of King Gent (29×49 mm). P 13 .... 7·50 7·50
Nos. 2737/9 were issued together in *se-tenant* strips of three stamps within the sheet.

(632)

633 Charlie Chaplin

1999 (2 June). Philexfrance '99 International Stamp Exhibition, Paris. No. 2512 surch with T **632** in black (new value), royal blue and scarlet-vermilion (emblem).
2741 **552** 150l. on 30q. multicoloured .... 3·75 3·25

(Des N. Bakalli. Litho Alexandros Matsoukis, Athens, Greece)
1999 (20 June). 110th Birth Anniv of Charlie Chaplin (film actor and director). T **633** and similar vert designs. Multicoloured. P 14×14½.
2742 30l. Type **633** 70 50
a. Imperf×p 14½. Booklets 70 50
ab. Booklet pane. Nos. 2742a/4a, each×2 .... 18·00
2743 50l. Raising hat .... 1·20 1·00
a. Imperf×p 14½. Booklets .... 1·20 1·00
2744 250l. Dancing .... 6·50 6·50
a. Imperf×p 14½. Booklets .... 6·50 5·75
2742/2744 *Set of 3* .... 7·50 7·25

634 Neil Armstrong on Moon

635 Prisoner behind Bars

(Des L. Mema. Litho Alexandros Matsoukis, Athens, Greece)
1999 (25 June). 30th Anniv of First Manned Moon Landing. T **634** and similar vert designs. Multicoloured. P 13½×14.
2745 30l. Type **634** 70 50
a. Horiz strip of 3. Nos. 2745/7 .... 12·50
2746 150l. Lunar module .... 3·75 3·25
2747 300l. Astronaut and American flag .... 7·50 6·75
2745/2747 *Set of 3* .... 11·00 9·50
MS2748 60×80 mm. 280l. Launch of "Apollo 11" (25×29 mm). P 13 .... 7·00 7·00
Nos. 2745/7 were issued together in horizontal *se-tenant* strips of three stamps within the sheet, each strip forming a composite design.

(Des G. Tafa. Litho Alexandros Matsoukis, Athens, Greece)
1999 (6 July). The Nazi Holocaust. P 14×14½.
2749 **635** 30l. multicolored 80 70
2750 150l. black and greenish yellow .... 4·00 3·75

636 Emblem

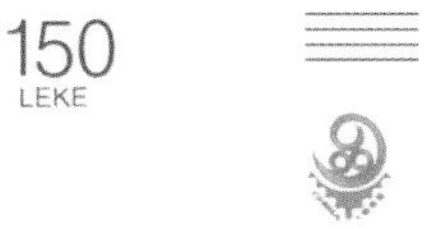

(637)

(Des L. Kakarriqi. Litho Alexandros Matsoukis, Athens, Greece)
1999 (1 Aug). 125th Anniv of Universal Postal Union. P 14×14½.
2751 **636** 20l. multicoloured 45 30
a. Pair. Nos. 2751/2 .... 2·10 1·80
2752 60l. multicoloured .... 1·50 1·40
Nos. 2751/2 were issued together in *se-tenant* pairs within the sheet.

1999 (20 Aug). China 1999 International Stamp Exhibition, Peking. No. 2497 surch with T **637** in brown (new value), vermilion and emerald (emblem).
2753 150l. on 1l.20 multicoloured .... 3·75 3·25

638 Javelin

639 Madonna and Child

(Des E. Klefti. Litho Alexandros Matsoukis, Athens, Greece)
1999 (2 Sept). 70th Anniv of National Athletic Championships. T **638** and similar vert designs. Multicoloured. P 14×14½.
2754 10l. Type **638** 25 10
a. Horiz strip of 3. Nos. 2754/6 .... 6·00
2755 20l. Discus 45 30
2756 200l. Running .... 5·00 4·50
2754/2756 *Set of 3* .... 5·25 4·50
Nos. 2754/6 were issued together in horizontal *se-tenant* strips of three stamps within the sheet.

(Litho Alexandros Matsoukis, Athens, Greece)
1999 (30 Oct). Icons by Onufri Shek (artist). T **639** and similar vert design. Multicoloured. P 14.
2757 30l. Type **639** 90 80
2758 300l. The Resurrection .... 7·00 6·25

640 Bilal Golemi (veterinary surgeon)

641 Carnival Mask

(Des L. Taçi. Litho Alexandros Matsoukis, Athens, Greece)
1999 (28 Nov). Birth Anniversaries. T **640** and similar horiz designs. Multicoloured. P 14½×14.
2759 10l. Type **640** (centenary) 25 10
a. Block of 4. Nos. 2759/62 .... 9·75
2760 20l. Azem Galica (revolutionary) (centenary) 45 30
2761 50l. Viktor Eftimiu (writer) (centenary) .... 1·30 1·20
2762 300l. Lasgush Poradeci (poet) (centenary, (2000)) .... 7·50 6·75
2759/2762 *Set of 4* .... 8·50 7·50
Nos. 2759/62 were issued together in *se-tenant* blocks of four stamps within the sheet.

(Des N. Bakalli. Litho Alexandros Matsoukis, Athens, Greece)
1999 (1 Dec). Carnivals. T **641** and similar vert design. Multicoloured. P 14.
2763 30l. Type **641** .... 1·10 95
2764 300l. Turkey mask .... 7·50 6·75

642 Bell and Flowers

643 Woman's Costume, Librazhdi

(Des T. Pustina and L. Kakarriqi. Litho Alexandros Matsoukis, Athens, Greece)
2000 (27 Mar). New Millennium. The Peace Bell. T **642** and similar vert design. Multicoloured. P 13½×14.
2765 40l. Type **642** .... 1·00 90
2766 90l. Bell and flowers (different) .... 2·30 2·00

(Des N. Bakalli. Litho Alexandros Matsoukis, Athens, Greece)
2000 (28 Mar). Regional Costumes (1st series). T **643** and similar vert designs. Multicoloured. P 13×14.
2767 5l. Type **643** 10 10
a. Sheetlet of 12. Nos. 2767/78 .... 11·50
2768 10l. Woman's costume, Malesia E Madhe 25 15
2769 15l. Man's costume, Malesia E Madhe 35 20
2770 20l. Man's costume, Tropoje 45 30
2771 30l. Man's costume, Dumrea 70 50
2772 35l. Man's costume, Tirane 80 65
2773 40l. Woman's costume, Tirane 95 75
2774 45l. Woman's costume, Arbereshe .... 1·00 85
2775 50l. Man's costume, Gjirokastra .... 1·20 1·00
2776 55l. Woman's costume, Lunxheri .... 1·30 1·20
2777 70l. Woman's costume, Çameria .... 1·60 1·50
2778 90l. Man's costume, Laberia .... 2·10 1·90
2767/2778 *Set of 12* .... 9·75 8·25
Nos. 2767/78 were issued together in *se-tenant* sheetlets of 12 stamps.
See also Nos. 2832/43, 2892/903, 2943/54, 3053/84, 3080/91 and 3171/82.

644 Gustav Majer

645 Donald Duck

(Litho Alexandros Matsoukis, Athens, Greece)

2000 (30 Mar). 150th Birth Anniv of Gustav Majer (etymologist). P 13½×14.

2779	**644**	50l. brown-olive	1·20	1·00
2780		130l. brown-lake	3·00	2·75

(Des S. Taçi. Litho Alexandros Matsoukis, Athens, Greece)

2000 (6 Apr). Donald and Daisy Duck (cartoon film characters). T **645** and similar vert designs. Multicoloured. P 13×14.

2781	10l. Type **645**	25	10
	a. Vert or horiz strip of 4. Nos. 2781/4	9·00	
2782	30l. Donald Duck	70	50
2783	90l. Daisy Duck	2·10	1·90
2784	250l. Donald Duck	5·75	5·25
2781/2784 *Set of* 4		8·00	7·00

Nos. 2781/4 were issued together in vertical or horizontal *se-tenant* strips of four stamps within the sheet.

646 Early Racing Car

(Des L. Kakarriqi. Litho Alexandros Matsoukis, Athens, Greece)

2000 (10 Apr). Motor Racing. T **646** and similar horiz designs. Multicoloured. P 14½×14.

2785	30l. Type **646**	1·00	90
	a. Sheetlet of 10. Nos. 2785/94, plus 2 labels	10·50	
2786	30l. Two-man racing car	1·00	90
2787	30l. Racing car with wire nose	1·00	90
2788	30l. Racing car with solid wheels	1·00	90
2789	30l. Car No. 1	1·00	90
2790	30l. Car No. 2	1·00	90
2791	30l. White Formula 1 racing car (facing left)	1·00	90
2792	30l. Blue Formula 1 racing car	1·00	90
2793	30l. Red Formula 1 racing car	1·00	90
2794	30l. White Formula 1 racing car (front view)	1·00	90
2785/2794 *Set of* 10		9·00	8·00

Nos. 2785/94 were issued together in *se-tenant* sheetlets of ten stamps and two labels showing the flags of participating nations in the Formula 1 racing competition.

647 Ristoz of Mborja Church, Korca

648 "Building Europe"

(Des S. Vllahu. Litho Alexandros Matsoukis, Athens, Greece)

2000 (22 Apr). Birth Bimillenary of Jesus Christ. T **647** and similar horiz designs. Multicoloured. P 14.

2795	15l. Type **647**	45	30
2796	40l. St. Kolli Church, Voskopoja	1·30	1·20
2797	90l. Church of Flori and Lauri, Kosovo	3·00	2·50
2795/2797 *Set of* 3		4·25	3·50
MS2798	80×60 mm. 250l. Fountain of Shengjin (mosaic), Tirana (37×37 mm). P 13½	5·25	5·25

(Des J.-P. Cousin. Litho Alexandros Matsoukis, Athens, Greece)

2000 (9 May). Europa. P 13×14.

2799	**648**	130l. multicoloured	4·00	3·75
MS2800		60×80 mm. 300l. Detail of design showing boy holding star (24×29 mm). P 13	10·50	10·50

649 Wolf (*Canis lupus*)

650 Gustav Mahler (composer) (40th death anniv)

(Des N. Bakalli. Litho Alexandros Matsoukis, Athens, Greece)

2000 (17 May). Animals. T **649** and similar horiz designs. Multicoloured. P 14½×14.

2801	10l. Type **649**	25	10
	a. Block of 4. Nos. 2801/4	8·50	
2802	40l. Brown bear (*Ursus arctos*)	95	75
2803	90l. Wild boar (*Sus scrofa*)	2·10	1·90
2804	220l. Red fox (*Vulpes vulpes*)	5·00	4·50
2801/2804 *Set of* 4		7·50	6·50

Nos. 2801/4 were issued together in *se-tenant* blocks of four stamps within the sheet.

(Des N. Bakalli. Litho Alexandros Matsoukis, Athens, Greece)

2000 (30 May). WIPA 2000 International Stamp Exhibition, Vienna. P 13½×14.

2805	**650**	130l. multicoloured	3·00	2·75

651 Footballer saving Ball

(Des T. Pustina. Litho Alexandros Matsoukis, Athens, Greece)

2000 (1 June). European Football Championship, Belgium and The Netherlands. T **651** and similar horiz design. Multicoloured. P 14×13½.

2806	10l. Type **651**	25	10
2807	120l. Footballer heading ball	3·00	2·50
MS2808	80×60 mm. 260l. Footballer kicking ball. Imperf	6·25	6·25

652 Musicans

653 Basketball

(Litho Alexandros Matsoukis, Athens, Greece)

2000 (7 June). Paintings by Picasso. T **652** and similar horiz designs. Multicoloured. P 14.

2809	30l. Type **652**	70	50
2810	40l. Abstract face	1·00	85
2811	250l. Two women running along beach	5·75	5·25
2809/2811 *Set of* 3		6·75	6·00
MS2812	60×80 mm. 400l. Painting of man (24×29 mm). P 13	9·25	9·25

(Des S. Taçi. Litho Alexandros Matsoukis, Athens, Greece)

2000 (1 July). Olympic Games, Sydney. T **653** and similar vert designs. Multicoloured. P 14×14½.

2813	10l. Type **653**	25	10
	a. Block of 4. Nos. 2813/16	9·25	
2814	40l. Football	95	75
2815	90l. Athletics	2·10	1·90
2816	250l. Cycling	5·75	5·25
2813/2816 *Set of* 4		8·25	7·25

Nos. 2813/16 were issued together in *se-tenant* blocks of four stamps within the sheet.

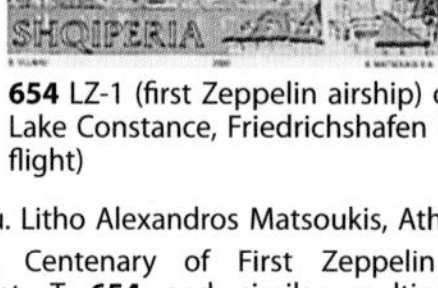

654 LZ-1 (first Zeppelin airship) over Lake Constance, Friedrichshafen (first flight)

(Des S. Vllhu. Litho Alexandros Matsoukis, Athens, Greece)

2000 (2 July). Centenary of First Zeppelin Flight. Airship Development. T **654** and similar multicoloured designs. P 14×13.

2817	15l. Type **654**	35	20
	a. Sheetlet of 3. Nos. 2817/19	7·75	
2818	30l. Santes-Dumont airship *Ballon No. 5* and Eiffel Tower (attempted round trip from St. Cloud via Eiffel tower, 1901)	70	50
2819	300l. Beardmore airship R-34 over New York (first double crossing of Atlantic)	6·50	5·75
2817/2819 *Set of* 3		6·75	5·75
MS2820	80×60 mm. 300l. Ferdinand von Zeppelin and airship (24×28 mm). P 13	6·50	6·50

Nos. 2817/19 were printed together in *se-tenant* sheetlets of three stamps.

655 "Self-portrait" (Picasso)

656 Yellow Gentian (*Gentiana lutea*)

(Litho Alexandros Matsoukis, Athens, Greece)

2000 (6 Oct). Espana 2000 World Stamp Exhibition, Madrid. P 14.

2821	**655**	130l. multicoloured	3·25	3·00

(Des L. Mema. Litho Alexandros Matsoukis, Athens, Greece)

2000 (10 Oct). Medicinal Plants. T **656** and similar vert design. Multicoloured. P 13½×14.

2822	50l. Type **656**	1·30	1·20
	a. Horiz pair. Nos. 2822/3	3·25	3·00
2823	70l. Cross-leaved gentian (*Gentiana crutiata*)	1·60	1·50

Nos. 2822/3 were issued together in horizontal *se-tenant* pairs within the sheet.

657 Naim Frashëri (poet) and Landscape

658 Mother holding Child

(Des L. Mema. Litho Alexandros Matsoukis, Athens, Greece)

2000 (28 Nov). Personalities. T **657** and similar horiz design. Multicoloured. P 14½×14.

2824	30l. Type **657**	70	50
	a. Horiz pair. Nos. 2824/5	2·10	1·80
2825	50l. Bajram Curri (revolutionary) and landscape	1·30	1·20

Nos. 2824/5 were issued together in horizontal *se-tenant* pairs within the sheet, each pair forming a composite design.

(Des S. Prapaniku. Litho Alexandros Matsoukis, Athens, Greece)

2000 (14 Dec). 50th Anniv of United Nations High Commission for Refugees. T **658** and similar vert design. Multicoloured. P 14×14½.

2826	50l. Type **658**	1·40	1·30
2827	90l. Mother breastfeeding child	2·10	1·90

659 Dede Ahmed Myftar Ahmataj

(660)

(Des I. Martini. Litho Alexandros Matsoukis, Athens, Greece)

2001 (22 Feb). Religious Leaders. T **659** and similar horiz design. Multicoloured. P 14½×14.

2828	90l. Type **659**	2·30	2·10
	a. Horiz pair. Nos. 2828/9	4·75	4·50
2829	90l. Dede Sali Njazi	2·30	2·10

Nos. 2828/9 were issued together in horizontal *se-tenant* pairs within sheets of four stamps.

2001 (12 Mar). "For Kosovo". Nos. 2592/3 surch as T **660** in black and red.

2830	80l.+10l. on 50l. multicoloured	5·25	4·75
2831	130l.+20l. on 100l. multicoloured	8·75	7·75

(Des N. Bakalli. Litho Alexandros Matsoukis, Athens, Greece)

2001 (15 Mar). Regional Costumes (2nd series). Vert designs as T **643**. Multicoloured. P 13×14.

2832	20l. Man's costume, Tropoje	60	50
	a. Sheetlet of 12. Nos. 2832/43	7·50	
2833	20l. Woman's costume, Lume	60	50
2834	20l. Woman's costume, Mirdite	60	50
2835	20l. Man's costume, Lume	60	50
2836	20l. Woman's costume, Zadrime	60	50
2837	20l. Woman's costume, Shpati	60	50
2838	20l. Man's costume, Kruje	60	50
2839	20l. Woman's costume, Macukulli	60	50
2840	20l. Woman's costume, Dardhe	60	50
2841	20l. Man's costume, Lushnje	60	50
2842	20l. Woman's costume, Dropulli	60	50
2843	20l. Woman's costume, Shmili	60	50
2832/2843 *Set of* 12		6·50	5·50

Nos. 2832/43 were issued together in *se-tenant* sheetlets of 12 stamps.

661 Southern Magnolia (*Magnolia gandiflora*)

662 Goofy in Shorts

(Des L. Kakarriqi. Litho Alexandros Matsoukis, Athens, Greece)

2001 (30 Mar). Scented Flowers. T **661** and similar vert designs. Multicoloured. P 14×14½.

2844	10l. Type **661**	35	20
	a. Block of 4. Nos. 2844/7	7·25	
2845	20l. Virginia rose (*Rosa virginiana*)	60	40
2846	90l. *Dianthus barbatus*	2·30	2·10
2847	140l. Lilac (*Syringa vulgaris*)	3·75	3·25
2844/2847 *Set of* 4		6·25	5·25

Nos. 2844/7 were issued together in *se-tenant* blocks of four within sheets of eight stamps.

(Des S. Taçi. Litho Alexandros Matsoukis, Athens, Greece)

2001 (6 Apr). Goofy (cartoon film character). T **662** and similar vert designs. Multicoloured. P 13×14.

2848	20l. Type **662**	45	30
	a. Horiz or vert strip of 4. Nos. 2848/51	7·25	
2849	50l. Goofy in blue hat	1·20	1·00

2850 90l. Goofy in red trousers 2·10 1·90
2851 140l. Goofy in purple waistcoat 3·25 3·00
2848/2851 *Set of 4* 6·25 5·50

Nos. 2848/51 were issued together in horizontal and vertical strips of four stamps within the sheet.

663 Vincenzo Bellini

(Des N. Bakalli. Litho Alexandros Matsoukis, Athens, Greece)

2001 (20 Apr). Composers' Anniversaries. T **663** and similar horiz design. Multicoloured. P 14×13.

2852 90l. Type **663** (birth centenary) 2·20 2·00
2853 90l. Guiseppe Verdi (death centenary) 2·20 2·00
MS2854 90×90 mm. 300l. Bellini and Verdi (75×38 mm). P 14 7·00 7·00

664 Cliffs and Stream

(Des L. Mema. Litho Alexandros Matsoukis, Athens, Greece)

2001 (29 Apr). Europa. Water Resources. T **664** and similar horiz designs. Multicoloured. P 14.

2855 40l. Type **664** 1·20 1·00
2856 110l. Waterfall 2·30 2·10
2857 200l. Lake 4·75 4·25
2855/2857 *Set of 3* 7·50 6·50
MS2858 60×80 mm. 350l. Ripples (24×78 mm). P 13 10·50 10·50

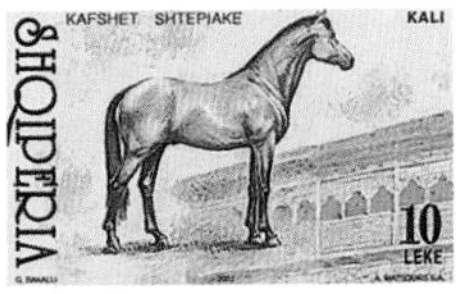

665 Horse

(Des G. Bakalli. Litho Alexandros Matsoukis, Athens, Greece)

2001 (17 May). Domestic Animals. T **665** and similar horiz designs. Multicoloured. P 14½×14.

2859 10l. Type **665** 25 10
a. Sheetlet of 4. Nos. 2859/62 5·00
2860 15l. Donkey 35 20
2861 80l. Siamese cat 1·90 1·70
2862 90l. Dog 2·20 2·00
2859/2862 *Set of 4* 4·25 3·50
MS2863 80×60 mm. 300l. Head of Siamese cat (49×29 mm). P 13 7·00 7·00

Nos. 2859/62 were issued together in *se-tenant* sheetlets of four stamps.

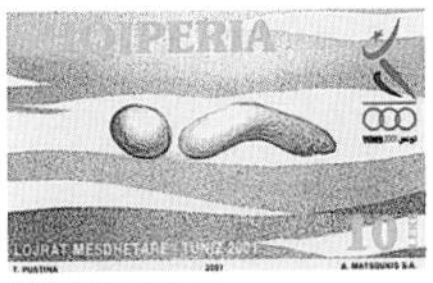

666 Swimming

(Des T. Pustina. Litho Alexandros Matsoukis, Athens, Greece)

2001 (1 June). Mediterranean Games, Tunis. T **666** and similar horiz designs. Multicoloured. P 14½×14.

2864 10l. Type **666** 35 20
a. Vert strip of 3. Nos. 2864/6 6·75
2865 90l. Athletics 2·30 2·10
2866 140l. Cycling 3·75 3·25
2864/2866 *Set of 3* 5·75 5·00
MS2867 60×80 mm. 260l. Discus (29×24 mm). P 13 6·50 6·50

Nos. 2864/6 were issued together in *se-tenant* vertical strips of three within sheets of six stamps.

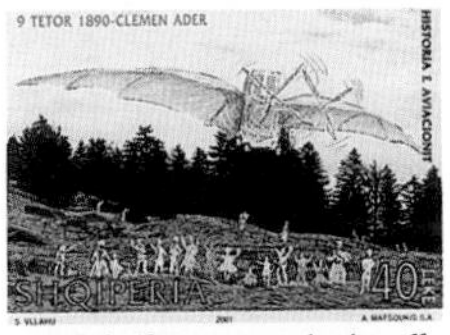

667 *Eole* (first powered take-off by Clément Ader, 1890)

(Des S. Vllahu. Litho Alexandros Matsoukis, Athens, Greece)

2001 (20 June). Aviation History. T **667** and similar horiz designs. Multicoloured. P 14×13.

2868 40l. Type **667** 1·20 1·00
a. Sheetlet of 8. Nos. 2868/75 9·75
2869 40l. *Blériot XI* (first powered crossing of English channel by Louis Blériot, 1909) 1·20 1·00
2870 40l. *Spirit of St. Louis* (first solo non-stop crossing of North Atlantic from Paris to New York by Charles Lindbergh, 1927) 1·20 1·00
2871 40l. First flight to Tirana, 1925 1·20 1·00
2872 40l. Antonov AH-10 (first flight, 1956) 1·20 1·00
2873 40l. Concorde (first flight, 1969) 1·20 1·00
2874 40l. Concorde (first commercial flight, 1970) 1·20 1·00
2875 40l. Space shuttle *Colombia* (first flight, 1981) 1·20 1·00
2868/2875 *Set of 8* 8·75 7·25

Nos. 2868/75 were issued together in *se-tenant* sheetlets of eight stamps.

668 Tabakeve

669 Dimitri of Arber

(Des S. Taçi. Litho Alexandros Matsoukis, Athens, Greece)

2001 (20 July). Old Bridges. T **668** and similar horiz designs. P 14×13½.

2876 10l. multicoloured 25 10
a. Sheetlet of 4. Nos. 2876/9 4·00
2877 20l. multicoloured 35 20
2878 40l. multicoloured 1·00 85
2879 90l. black 2·10 1·90
2876/2879 *Set of 4* 3·25 2·75
MS2880 80×60 mm. 2l.50 multicoloured 6·50 6·50

Designs: As Type **668**:—20l. Kamares; 40l. Golikut; 90l. Mesit. 49×22 mm—2l.50 Tabakeve.

Nos. 2876/9 were issued together in *se-tenant* sheetlets of four stamps.

(Des Gj. Varfi. Litho Alexandros Matsoukis, Athens, Greece)

2001 (12 Sept). Arms (1st series). T **669** and similar vert designs. P 13.

2881 20l. Type **669** 60 40
a. Booklet pane. No. 2881×4 2·75
2882 45l. Balsha principality 1·20 1·00
a. Booklet pane. No. 2882×4 5·00
2883 50l. Muzaka family 1·20 1·00
a. Booklet pane. No. 2883×4 5·00
2884 90l. George Castriot (Skanderbeg) 2·30 2·10
a. Booklet pane. No. 2884×4 9·50
2881/2884 *Set of 4* 4·75 4·00

See also Nos. 2918/21, 2965/8, 3018/21 and 3098/101.

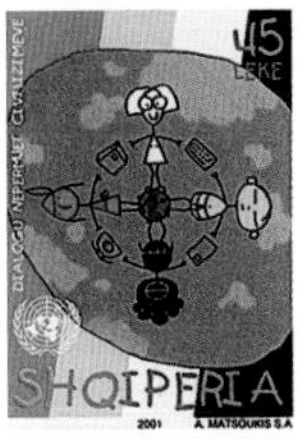

670 Children encircling Globe

671 Award Ceremony (Medicins sans Frontieres, 1999 Peace Prize) and Medal

(Des Urska Golob. Litho Alexandros Matsoukis, Athens, Greece)

2001 (6 Oct). United Nations Year of Dialogue among Civilizations. Multicoloured, background colours given. P 13½×14.

2885 **670** 45l. orange-red, yellow and black 1·20 1·00
2886 50l. orange and green 1·20 1·00
2887 120l. black and red 3·00 2·50
2885/2887 *Set of 3* 4·75 4·00

There are minor differences in Nos. 2886/7, with each colour forming a solid block above and below the central motif.

(Des M. Arapi. Litho Alexandros Matsoukis, Athens, Greece)

2001 (1 Dec). Centenary of Nobel Prizes. T **671** and similar horiz designs showing winners and Nobel medal. Multicoloured. P 14×13½.

2888 10l. Type **671** 25 10
2889 20l. Wilhelm Konrad Röntgen (1901 Physics prize) 45 30
2890 90l. Ferid Murad (1998 Medicine prize) 2·30 2·10
2891 200l. Mother Teresa (1979 Peace prize) 4·75 4·25
2888/2891 *Set of 4* 7·00 6·00

(Des N. Bakalli. Litho Alexandros Matsoukis, Athens, Greece)

2002 (20 Mar). Regional Costumes (3rd series). Vert designs as T **643**. Multicoloured. P 13×14.

2892 30l. Woman's costume, Gjakova 70 65
a. Sheetlet of 12. Nos. 2892/2903 8·75
2893 30l. Woman's costume, Prizreni 70 65
2894 30l. Man's costume, Shkodra 70 65
2895 30l. Woman's costume, Shkodra 70 65
2896 30l. Man's costume, Berati 70 65
2897 30l. Woman's costume, Berati 70 65
2898 30l. Woman's costume, Elbasani 70 65
2899 30l. Man's costume, Elbasani 70 65
2900 30l. Woman's costume, Vlora 70 65
2901 30l. Man's costume, Vlora 70 65
2902 30l. Woman's costume, Gjirokastra 70 65
2903 30l. Woman's costume, Delvina 70 65
2892/2903 *Set of 12* 7·50 7·00

Nos. 2892/903 were issued together in *se-tenant* sheetlets of 12 stamps.

672 Bambi and Thumper

673 Fireplace

(Des S. Taçi. Litho Alexandros Matsoukis, Athens, Greece)

2002 (6 Apr). Bambi (cartoon film character). T **672** and similar vert designs. Multicoloured. P 13×14.

2904 20l. Type **672** 45 30
a. Horiz or vert strip of 4. Nos. 2904/7 7·00
2905 50l. Bambi alone amongst flowers 1·20 1·00
2906 90l. Bambi and Thumper looking right 2·00 1·80
2907 140l. Bambi with open mouth 3·00 2·50
2904/2907 *Set of 4* 6·00 5·00

Nos. 2904/7 were issued together in horizontal and vertical strips of four stamps within the sheet.

(Des M. Arapi. Litho Alexandros Matsoukis, Athens, Greece)

2002 (15 Apr). Traditional Fireplaces. T **673** and similar vert designs showing fireplaces. Multicoloured. P 14.

MS2908 30l. Type **673**; 40l. With columns at each side; 50l. With foliage arch; 90l. With three medallions in arch 4·75 4·75

674 Acrobatic Jugglers

675 Heading the Ball

(Des T. Pustina. Litho Alexandros Matsoukis, Athens, Greece)

2002 (1 May). Europa. Circus. T **674** and similar vert designs. Multicoloured. P 13½×13 (**MS**2912) or 13×14 (others).

2909 40l. Type **674** 95 75
2910 90l. Female acrobat 2·00 1·80
2911 220l. Tightrope performers 5·75 5·25
2909/2911 *Set of 3* 7·75 7·00
MS2912 60×80 mm. 350l. Equestrienne performer (38×38 mm) 11·50 11·50

(Des M. Arapi. Litho Alexandros Matsoukis, Athens, Greece)

2002 (6 May). Football World Championship, Japan and South Korea. T **675** and similar horiz designs. Multicoloured. P 13½.

2913 20l. Type **675** 45 30
2914 30l. Catching the ball 70 50
2915 90l. Kicking the ball from horizontal position 2·10 1·90
2916 120l. Player and ball 2·50 2·30
2913/2916 *Set of 4* 5·25 4·50
MS2917 80×60 mm. 360l. Emblem (50×30 mm). P 13 8·25 8·25

(Des Gj. Varfi. Litho Alexandros Matsoukis, Athens, Greece)

2002 (12 May). Arms (2nd series). Vert designs as T **669**. Multicoloured. P 13.

2918 20l. Gropa family 45 30
a. Booklet pane. No. 2918×4 1·90
2919 45l. Skurra family 1·00 85
a. Booklet pane. No. 2919×4 4·25
2920 50l. Bua family 1·20 1·00
a. Booklet pane. No. 2920×4 5·00
2921 90l. Topia family 2·30 2·10
a. Booklet pane. No. 2921×4 9·50
2918/2921 *Set of 4* 4·50 3·75

676 *Opuntia catingiola*

677 Blood Group Symbols with Wings

(Des G. Bakalli. Litho Alexandros Matsoukis, Athens, Greece)

2002 (17 May). Cacti. T **676** and similar triangular designs. Multicoloured. P 14.

MS2922 50l. Type **676**; 50l. *Neoporteria pseudoreicheana*; 50l. *Lobivia shaferi*; 50l. *Hylocereus undatus*; 50l. *Borzicactus madisoniorum* 5·25 5·25

(Des S. Taçi. Litho Alexandros Matsoukis, Athens, Greece)

2002 (16 June). 50th Anniv of Blood Bank Service. T **677** and similar vert designs. Multicoloured. P 14×14½.

2923 90l. Type **677** 2·30 2·10
2924 90l. Blood group symbols containing figures 2·30 2·10

678 Naim Kryeziu (footballer)

679 Stamp, Torso and Emblem

(Des Ll. Taçi. Litho Alexandros Matsoukis, Athens, Greece)

2002 (3 July). Sports Personalities. T **678** and similar multicoloured designs. P 14.

2925 50l. Type **678** 1·20 1·00
a. Strip of 3. Nos. 2925/7 3·75
2926 50l. Riza Lushta (footballer) 1·20 1·00
2927 50l. Ymer Pampuri (weightlifter) 1·20 1·00
2925/2927 *Set of 3* 3·25 2·75
MS2928 61×81 mm. 300l. Loro Boriçi (footballer) (vert). Imperf 7·00 7·00

Nos. 2925/7 were issued in horizontal *se-tenant* strips of three stamps within the sheet.

(Des A. Mandija. Litho Alexandros Matsoukis, Athens, Greece)

2002 (1 Sept). 50th Anniv of International Federation of Stamp Dealers' Associations (IFSDA). T **679** and similar horiz design. Multicoloured. P 14×13½.

2929 50l. Type **679** ... 1·20 1·00
2930 100l. Part of stamp enlarged and emblem ... 2·40 2·20

680 Statue of Liberty

(Des T. Pustina. Litho Alexandros Matsoukis, Athens, Greece)

2002 (11 Sept). First Anniv of Attacks on World Trade Centre, New York. T **680** and similar multicoloured designs. P 14×13.

2931 100l. Type **680** ... 2·40 2·20
2932 150l. Burning towers and skyline ... 3·50 3·25
MS2933 61×81 mm. 350l. Statue of Liberty and World Trade Centre tower (vert) ... 8·50 8·50

681 Loggerhead Turtle (*Caretta caretta*)

(Des S. Vllahu. Litho Alexandros Matsoukis, Athens, Greece)

2002 (12 Sept). Fauna of Mediterranean Sea. Sheet 100×107 mm containing T **681** and similar horiz designs. Multicoloured. P 14½×14.

MS2934 50l. Type **681**; 50l. Common dolphin (*Delphinus delphis*); 50l. Blue shark (*Prionace glauca*); 50l. Fin whale (*Balenoptera physalus*); 50l. Ray (*Torpedo torpedo*); 50l. Octopus (*Octopus vulgaris*) ... 7·25 7·25

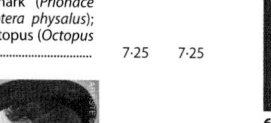

682 Tefta Tashko Koço

(Des H. Devolli. Litho Alexandros Matsoukis, Athens, Greece)

2002 (6 Oct). Personalities. The Stage. T **682** and similar horiz designs. Multicoloured. P 14.

2935 50l. Type **682** (singer) ... 1·20 1·10
a. Block of 4. Nos. 2935/8 ... 5·00
2936 50l. Naim Frasheri (actor) ... 1·20 1·10
2937 50l. Kristaq Antoniu (singer) ... 1·20 1·10
2938 50l. Panajot Kanaçi (choreographer) ... 1·20 1·10
2935/2938 *Set of 4* ... 4·25 4·00

Nos. 2935/8 were issued in *se-tenant* blocks of four stamps within the sheet.

683 Flags

684 Satellite Dish and Outline of Stamp

(Des N. Bakalli. Litho Alexandros Matsoukis, Athens, Greece)

2002 (28 Nov). 90th Anniv of Independence. T **683** and similar vert design. Multicoloured. P 13½×14.

2939 20l. Type **683** ... 55 50
2940 90l. People and Albanian flag ... 2·20 2·00

(Des M. Fushekati. Litho Alexandros Matsoukis, Athens, Greece)

2002 (4 Dec). 90th Anniv of Albanian Post and Telecommunications. T **684** and similar vert design. Multicoloured. P 13½×14.

2941 20l. Type **684** ... 55 50
2942 90l. Airmail envelope and telegraph machine ... 2·20 2·00

(Des N. Bakalli. Litho Alexandros Matsoukis, Athens, Greece)

2003 (1 Apr). Regional Costumes (4th series). Vert designs as T **643**. Multicoloured. P 13×14.

2943 30l. Woman's costume, Kelmendi ... 90 85
a. Sheetlet of 12. Nos. 2943/54 ... 11·50
2944 30l. Man's costume, Zadrime ... 90 85
2945 30l. Woman's costume, Zerqani ... 90 85
2946 30l. Man's costume, Peshkopi ... 90 85
2947 30l. Man's costume, Malesia Tiranes ... 90 85
2948 30l. Woman's costume, Malesia Tiranes ... 90 85
2949 30l. Woman's costume, Fushe Kruje ... 90 85
2950 30l. Man's costume, Shpati ... 90 85
2951 30l. Woman's costume, Myzeqe ... 90 85
2952 30l. Woman's costume, Labinoti ... 90 85
2953 30l. Man's costume, Korce ... 90 85
2954 30l. Woman's costume, Laberi ... 90 85
2943/2954 *Set of 12* ... 9·75 9·25

Nos. 2943/54 were issued together in *se-tenant* sheetlets of 12 stamps.

685 Popeye and Bluto

686 Port Palemo Castle

(Des S. Taçi. Litho Walsall)

2003 (6 Apr). Popeye (cartoon film character). T **685** and similar vert designs. Multicoloured. P 13½.

2955 40l. Type **685** ... 1·20 1·10
a. Horiz or vert strip of 4. Nos. 2955/8 ... 9·50
2956 50l. Popeye running ... 1·50 1·30
2957 80l. Popeye and Olive Oyl ... 2·40 2·20
2958 150l. Popeye ... 4·25 3·75
2955/2958 *Set of 4* ... 8·50 7·50

Nos. 2955/8 were issued in *se-tenant* strips of four stamps within the sheet.

(Des M. Arapi. Litho Walsall)

2003 (15 Apr). Castles. Sheet 118×98 mm. T **686** and similar horiz designs. P 13½.

MS2959 10l. grey and black; 20l. brown-olive and black; 50l. greenish grey and black; 120l. dull mauve and black ... 6·00 6·00

Designs:—10l. Type **686**; 20l. Petrela; 50l. Kruja; 120l. Preza.

687 Bearded Man

688 Envelopes

(Des T. Pustina and I. Martini. Litho Walsall)

2003 (30 Apr). Europa. Poster Art. T **687** and similar vert designs. Multicoloured. P 14.

2960 150l. Type **687** ... 4·50 4·25
2961 200l. Eye, apple and piano ... 6·00 5·50
MS2962 80×61 mm. 350l. Detail of No. 2960 ... 10·50 10·50

(Des N. Bakalli. Litho Walsall)

2003 (5 May). 90th Anniv of Albanian Post and Telecommunications (2nd series). T **688** and similar horiz design. Multicoloured. P 13½.

2963 50l. Type **688** ... 1·30 1·20
2964 1000l. Outline of stamps ... 29·00 26·00

(Des Gj. Varfi. Litho Walsall)

2003 (12 May). Arms (3rd series). Vert designs as T **669**. Multicoloured. P 13.

2965 10l. Ariantet family ... 25 10
a. Booklet pane. No. 2965×4 ... 1·10
2966 20l. Jonimajt family ... 65 60
a. Booklet pane. No. 2966×4 ... 2·75
2967 70l. Dukagjini family ... 2·00 1·80
a. Booklet pane. No. 2967×4 ... 8·50
2968 120l. Kopili family ... 3·50 3·00
a. Booklet pane. No. 2968×4 ... 15·00
2965/2968 *Set of 4* ... 5·75 5·00

689 Pomegranate (*Punica granatum*)

(Des G. Bakalli. Litho Walsall)

2003 (17 May). Fruit. T **689** and similar triangular designs. Multicoloured. Self-adhesive. Die-cut perf 6½.

MS2969 50l. Type **689**; 60l. Citron (*Citrus medica*); 70l. Cantaloupe (*Cucumis melo*); 80l. Fig (*Ficus*) (inscr "Fieus") ... 7·25 7·25

690 Diocletian

691 White Stork (*Cicona cicona*)

(Des M. Fushekati. Litho Walsall)

2003 (20 June). Roman Emperors. T **690** and similar horiz designs. Multicoloured. P 13½.

2970 70l. Type **690** ... 2·00 1·80
a. Block of 4. Nos. 2970/3 ... 8·25
2971 70l. Justinian ... 2·00 1·80
2972 70l. Claudius II ... 2·00 1·80
2973 70l. Constantine ... 2·00 1·80
2970/2973 *Set of 4* ... 7·25 6·50

Nos. 2970/3 were issued in *se-tenant* blocks of four stamps within the sheet.

(Des S. Vllahu. Litho Walsall)

2003 (20 Aug). Birds. Sheet 100×119 mm containing T **691** and similar vert designs. Multicoloured. P 14½.

MS2974 70l. Type **691**; 70l. Golden eagle (*Aquila chrysaetos*); 70l. Eagle owl (*Bubo bubo*); 70l. Capercaillie (*Tetrao urogallus*) ... 8·25 8·25

692 Players

693 "The Luncheon" (detail)

(Des N. Xharo. Litho Walsall)

2003 (2 Sept). 90th Anniv of Albanian Football. T **692** and similar vert design. Each olive-grey, black and red. P 14½.

2975 80l. Type **692** ... 2·20 2·00
a. Pair. Nos. 2975/6 ... 4·75 4·25
2976 80l. Group of players ... 2·20 2·00

Nos. 2975/6 were issued in horizontal *se-tenant* pairs within the sheet, each pair forming a composite design.

(Des S. Taci. Litho Walsall)

2003 (20 Sept). 120th Death Anniv of Edouard Manet (artist). T **693** and similar multicoloured designs. P 14½.

2977 40l. Type **693** ... 1·10 95
2978 100l. "The Fifer" ... 3·00 2·75
MS2979 80×60 mm. 250l. Edouard Manet (horiz) ... 7·00 7·00

694 Odhise Paskall

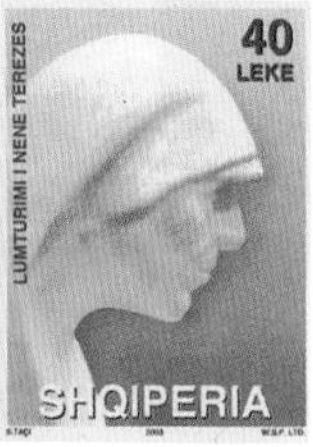

695 Profile of Mother Teresa

(Des L. Mema. Litho Walsall)

2003 (6 Oct). Albanian Sculptors. T **694** and similar horiz designs. Multicoloured. P 13½.

2980 50l. Type **694** ... 1·30 1·20
a. Block of 4. Nos. 2980/3 ... 5·50
2981 50l. Llazar Nikolla ... 1·30 1·20
2982 50l. Janaq Paco ... 1·30 1·20
2983 50l. Murat Toptani ... 1·30 1·20
2980/2983 *Set of 4* ... 4·75 4·25

Nos. 2980/3 were issued in *se-tenant* blocks of four stamps within the sheet.

(Des S. Taci. Litho)

2003 (19 Oct). Mother Teresa (humanitarian) Commemoration. T **695** and similar multicoloured designs. P 13½.

2984 40l. Type **695** ... 1·30 1·20
2985 250l. Mother Teresa facing front ... 6·50 6·00
MS2986 60×60 mm. 350l. Mother Teresa (statue) (40×40 mm) ... 9·25 9·25

696 Lake, Pelicans and Pine Trees (Divjaka forest)

(Des S. Vllahu. Litho Walsall)

2003 (20 Oct). Natural Heritage. T **696** and similar horiz designs. Multicoloured. P 13½.

2987 20l. Type **696** ... 55 50
2988 30l. House and fir trees (Hotova forest) ... 85 75
2989 200l. Snow-covered fir trees (Drenova forest) ... 6·25 5·75
2987/2989 *Set of 3* ... 7·00 6·25

697 Stylized Cyclist and Map of France

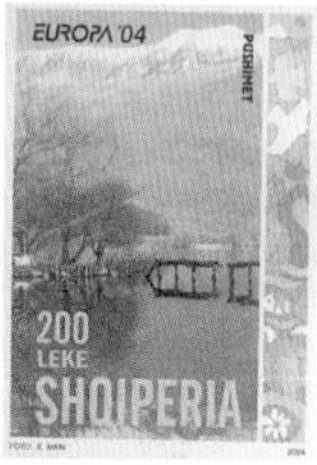

698 Trees, Lake and Mountain, Pushimet

(Des M. Arapi. Litho Walsall)

2003 (1 Nov). Centenary of Tour de France Cycle Race. T **697** and similar horiz design. P 14½.
2990 50l. new blue, bright scarlet and black 1·40 1·30
2991 100l. multicoloured 2·75 2·50
Designs:—50l. Type **697**; 100l. Two cyclists.

2004 (23 June). Europa. Holidays. T **698** and similar vert designs. Multicoloured. Litho. P 13½.
2992 200l. Type **698** 6·00 5·50
a. Booklet pane. Nos. 2992/3, each×4 50·00
2993 200l. Grassland, hills and mountains, Pushimet 6·00 5·50
MS2994 61×81 mm. 350l. Island, Pushimet 11·00 11·00

699 Goalkeeper

700 Discus Thrower (statue)

(Des I. Martini. Litho)

2004 (24 June). European Football Championship 2004, Portugal. T **699** and similar multicoloured designs. P 14.
2995 20l. Type **699** 75 70
2996 40l. Two players and goalkeeper catching ball 1·40 1·30
2997 50l. Two players 1·70 1·50
2998 200l. Players jumping for ball 7·00 6·50
2995/2998 *Set of 4* 9·75 9·00
MS2999 81×61 mm. 350l. Player with raised arms (38×38 mm) (circular) 11·00 11·00

(Des S. Taci. Litho)

2004 (12 Aug). Olympic Games, Athens. T **700** and similar vert designs. Multicoloured. P 14.
3000 10l. Type **700** 30 25
3001 200l. Face (statue) 6·25 5·75
MS3002 61×81 mm. 350l. Athlete carrying Olympic torch (39×55 mm) 11·00 11·00

701 Wilhelm von Wied

702 Bugs Bunny

(Des H. Devolli. Litho)

2004 (30 Aug). Wilhem von Wied (ruler, February 6th–September 5th, 1914) Commemoration. T **701** and similar vert designs. Multicoloured. P 13½.
3003 40l. Type **701** 1·30 1·20
3004 150l. Facing left 4·75 4·25

(Des S. Taci. Litho)

2004 (15 Sept). Bugs Bunny (cartoon character). T **702** and similar vert designs showing Bugs Bunny. Multicoloured. P 13½.
3005 40l. Type **702** 1·30 1·20
a. Strip of 4. Nos. 3005/8 10·50
3006 50l. With crossed arms 1·60 1·50
3007 80l. Wearing dinner jacket 2·75 2·40
3008 150l. Facing left 4·75 4·25
3005/3008 *Set of 4* 9·25 8·50
Nos. 3005/8 were issued in *se-tenant* horizontal and vertical strips of four stamps within the sheet.

703 Damaged Painting

(Des M. Arapi. Litho)

2004 (3 Oct). Mural Paintings by Nikolla Onufri, Church of Saint Mary Vllherna. T **703** and similar horiz designs. P 14.
3009 10l. Type **703** 45 40
3010 20l. Mary 75 70
3011 1000l. Saint 34·00 31·00
3009/3011 *Set of 3* 32·00 29·00
MS3012 80×65 mm. 400l. Crowned Christ. P 13½×14½ 12·50 12·50

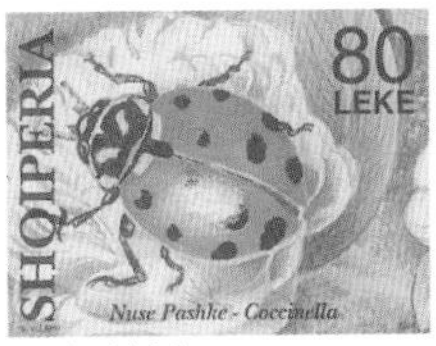

704 Ladybird

(Des B. Vllahu. Litho)

2004 (10 Oct). Ladybird (*Coccinella*). Sheet 120×95 mm containing T **704** and similar horiz designs showing ladybirds. Multicoloured. P 14.
MS3013 80l.×4, Type **704**; Six-spot; With open wings; 12-spot 10·00 10·00

705 Norek Luca

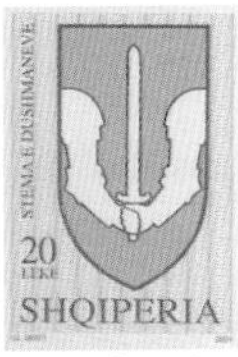

706 Dushmani Principality

(Des H. Devolli. Litho)

2004 (12 Oct). Personalities. T **705** and similar horiz designs. Multicoloured. P 14.
3014 50l. Type **705** (actor) (80th birth anniv) 1·50 1·40
a. Block of 4. Nos. 3014/17 6·25
3015 50l. Jorgjia Truja (singer) (10th death anniv) 1·50 1·40
3016 50l. Maria Kraja (singer) (5th death anniv) 1·50 1·40
3017 50l. Zina Andri (actor) (80th birth anniv) 1·50 1·40
3014/3017 *Set of 4* 5·50 5·00
Nos. 3014/17 were issued in *se-tenant* blocks of four stamps within the sheet.

(Des Gj. Varfi. Litho)

2004 (25 Oct). Arms (4th series). T **706** and similar vert designs. Multicoloured. P 14.
3018 20l. Type **706** 80 75
3019 40l. Gjuraj family 1·40 1·30
3020 80l. Zahariaj family 2·75 2·50
3021 150l. Spani principality 5·00 4·75
3018/3021 *Set of 4* 9·00 8·25

707 Cactus-type Dahlia

708 Madonna and Child (Anonim Shen Meria)

(Des G. Bakalli. Litho)

2004 (1 Nov). Dahlias. Sheet 164×77 mm containing T **707** and similar triangular designs showing dahlias. Multicoloured. P 14.
MS3022 80l.×4, Type **707**; Water lily type; Anemone type; Dahlia 10·00 10·00

(Des G. Panariti (3023/7 and 3043/7), A. Hasanau (3028/32 and 3038/42), A. Hado (3033/7). Litho)

2004 (20 Nov). 50th Anniv of National Art Gallery. T **708** and similar vert designs. Multicoloured. P 14.
3023 20l. Type **708** 60 55
a. Sheet of 25. Nos. 3023/47 16·00
3024 20l. Saint (Mihal Anagnosti) 60 55
3025 20l. Angel (Onufer Qiprioti) 60 55
3026 20l. Enthroned saint holding open book (Cetiret) 60 55
3027 20l. God and saints (Onuferi) 60 55
3028 20l. Woman wearing scarf (Kel Kodheli) 60 55
3029 20l. Crying woman (Vangjush Mio) 60 55
3030 20l. Woman wearing hat (Abdurahim Buza) 60 55
3031 20l. Semi-naked woman (Mustapha Arapi) 60 55
3032 20l. Man with moustache (Guri Madhi) 60 55
3033 20l. Soldier (sculpture) (Janaq Paco) 60 55
3034 20l. Still life with grapes (Zef Kolombi) 60 55
3035 20l. Flowers (Hasan Reci) 60 55
3036 20l. Still life with onions (Vladimir Jani) 60 55
3037 20l. Woman's head (sculpture) (Halim Beqiri) 60 55
3038 20l. Men seated (Edison Gjergo) 60 55
3039 20l. Men wearing traditional dress (Naxhi Bakalli) 60 55
3040 20l. Family (Agron Bregu) 60 55
3041 20l. Tree planting (Edi Hila) 60 55
3042 20l. Holding paintbrushes (Artur Muharremi) 60 55
3043 20l. Old man (Rembrandt) 60 55
3044 20l. Winged horseman (Gazmend Leka) 60 55
3045 20l. Multicoloured circle (Damien Hirst) 60 55
3046 20l. Corpse in cave (Edvin Rama) 60 55
3047 20l. Viking (Ibrahim Kodra) 60 55
3023/3047 *Set of 25* 13·50 12·50
Nos. 3023/47 were issued in *se-tenant* sheets of 25 stamps.

709 Bunting and NATO Emblem

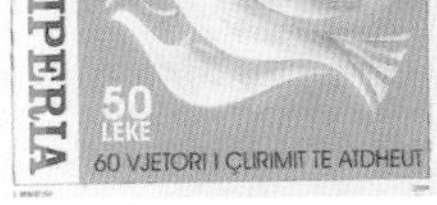

710 Two Doves

(Des X. Guga. Litho)

2004 (28 Nov). Fifth Anniv of NATO Peacekeeping in Kosovo. T **709** and similar vert designs. Multicoloured. P 14×13½.
3048 100l. Type **709** 3·00 2·75
3049 200l. Doves and United Nations flag 6·00 5·50
MS3050 80×60 mm. 350l. Houses flying Kosovo flag 11·00 11·00
The stamp and margin of No. **MS**3050 form a composite design.

(Des I. Martini. Litho)

2004 (29 Nov). 60th Anniv of Liberation. T **710** and similar horiz designs. Multicoloured. P 13½×14.
3051 50l. Type **710** 1·70 1·60
3052 200l. One dove 6·25 5·75

(Des N. Bakalli. Litho Alexandros Matsoukis, Athens, Greece)

2004 (4 Dec). Regional Costumes (5th series). Vert designs as T **643**. Multicoloured. P 13×14.
3053 30l. Back view of woman's costume, Gramshi 90 85
a. Sheetlet of 12. Nos. 3053/64 11·50
3054 30l. Front view of woman's costume, Gramshi 90 85
3055 30l. Woman's costume, Korca 90 85
3056 30l. Man's costume, Kolonja 90 85
3057 30l. Woman's costume, Korca (different) 90 85
3058 30l. Woman's costume, Librazhdi 90 85
3059 30l. Woman's costume, Permeti 90 85
3060 30l. Woman's costume, Pogradeci 90 85
3061 30l. Man's costume, Skrapari 90 85
3062 30l. Woman's costume, Skrapari 90 85
3063 30l. Woman's costume, Tepelena 90 85
3064 30l. Woman's costume, Vlora 90 85
3053/3064 *Set of 12* 9·75 9·25
Nos. 3053/64 were issued in *se-tenant* sheetlets of 12 stamps.

Nos. 3065/**MS**3067 and Type **711** have been left for "50th Anniv of Europa Stamps", not yet received.

712 Triangular Pies

713 Emblem

(Des X. Guga. Litho Alexandros Matsoukis, Athens)

2005 (5 Oct). Europa. Gastronomy. T **712** and similar vert design. Multicoloured. P 14.
3068 200l. Type **712** 7·00 6·50
a. Booklet pane. Nos. 3068/9, each×3 and **MS**3070 14·50
3069 200l. Stew 7·00 6·50

No. **MS**3070 has been left for miniature sheet not yet received.

(Des S. Taci. Litho Alexandros Matsoukis, Athens)

2005 (19 Oct). 50th Anniv of United Nations Membership. P 14.
3071 **713** 40l. multicoloured 1·90 1·70

714 Tom and Jerry

715 Mountain, City and Lake

(Des S. Taci. Litho Alexandros Matsoukis, Athens)

2005 (20 Oct). Tom and Jerry (cartoon characters). T **714** and similar vert designs. Multicoloured. P 13½.
3072 40l. Type **714** 1·00 90
a. Strip of 4. Nos. 3072/5 8·00
3073 50l. Heads of Tom and Jerry 1·30 1·20
3074 80l. Jerry 2·00 1·80
3075 150l. Tom 3·50 3·25
3072/3075 *Set of 4* 7·00 6·50
Nos. 3072/5 were issued in *se-tenant* horizontal and vertical strips of four stamps within the sheet.

(Des X. Guga. Litho Alexandros Matsoukis, Athens)

2005 (21 Oct). Art. Albanian Landscapes. T **715** and similar horiz designs. Multicoloured. P 13½.
3076 10l. Type **715** 30 30
a. Strip of 4. Nos. 3076/9 30·00
3077 20l. Aqueduct and castle 65 60
3078 30l. Crowd and minaret 95 90
3079 1000l. Lake and mountain fortress 27·00 25·00
3076/3079 *Set of 4* 26·00 24·00
Nos. 3076/9 were issued in *se-tenant* strips of four stamps within the sheet.

(Des N. Bakalli. Litho Alexandros Matsoukis, Athens, Greece)

2005 (24 Oct). Regional Costumes (6th series). Vert designs as T **643**. Multicoloured. P 13×14.
3080 30l. Man's costume, Tirane 1·10 1·00
a. Sheetlet of 12. Nos. 3080/91 13·50
3081 30l. Woman's costume, Bende Tirane 1·10 1·00
3082 30l. Back of woman's costume, Zall Dajt 1·10 1·00
3083 30l. Man's costume, Kavaje-Durres 1·10 1·00
3084 30l. Woman's costume, Has 1·10 1·00
3085 30l. Man's costume, Mat 1·10 1·00
3086 30l. Woman's costume, Liqenas 1·10 1·00
3087 30l. Woman's costume, Klenje 1·10 1·00
3088 30l. Woman's costume, Maleshove 1·10 1·00

3089 30l. Woman's costume, German 1·10 1·00
3090 30l. Woman's costume, Kruje 1·10 1·00
3091 30l. Man's costume, Reç 1·10 1·00
3080/3091 *Set of* 12 12·50 11·00

Nos. 3080/91 were issued in *se-tenant* sheetlets of 12 stamps.

716 Starting Blocks

(Des I. Martini. Litho Alexandros Matsoukis, Athens)

2005 (25 Oct). Mediterranean Games, Almera. T **716** and similar multicoloured designs. P 14½×14.

3092 20l. Type **716** 85 70
a. Strip of 3. Nos. 3092/4 7·50
3093 60l. Rings 2·10 1·80
3094 120l. Relay baton 4·25 3·50
3092/3094 *Set of* 3 6·50 5·50
MS3095 60×80 mm. 300l. Diver (30×50 mm). P 13 14·50 14·50

Nos. 3092/4 were issued in *se-tenant* strips of three stamps within the sheet.

The stamp of No. **MS**3095 is set at an angle.

717 Globe and Emblem

(Des N. Xharo. Litho Alexandros Matsoukis, Athens)

2005 (11 Nov). Centenary of Rotary International. T **717** and similar multicoloured design. P 14.

3096 30l. Type **717** 1·00 90
3097 150l. Emblem (vert) 5·25 4·50

(Des Gj. Varfi. Litho)

2005 (14 Nov). Arms (5th series). Vert designs as T **706**. Multicoloured. P 14.

3098 10l. Bua 40 35
a. Horiz strip of 4. Nos. 3098/101 10·50
b. Booklet pane. No. 3098×4 1·70
3099 20l. Karl Topia 1·00 90
a. Booklet pane. No. 3099×4 4·25
3100 70l. Dukagjini II 3·50 3·00
a. Booklet pane. No. 3100×4 15·00
3101 120l. Engjej 5·25 4·50
a. Booklet pane. No. 3101×4 22·00
3098/3101 *Set of* 4 9·25 8·00

Nos. 3098/101 were issued in horizontal *se-tenant* strips of four stamps within the sheet.

718 Yellow-flowered Portulaca

719 Cyclists

(Des G. Bakalli. Litho Alexandros Matsoukis, Athens)

2005 (17 Nov). Portulaca. Sheet 203×60 mm containing T **718** and similar triangular designs showing portulacas. Multicoloured. P 14.

MS3102 70l.×5, Type **718**; White flowers; Red and yellow flowers; Pale pink flowers; Double dark pink flower 12·50 12·50

(Des I. Martini. Litho Alexandros Matsoukis, Athens)

2005 (20 Nov). 80th Anniv of Cycle Race. P 13½×14.

3103 **719** 50l. multicoloured 1·70 1·60
a. Horiz strip. Nos. 3103/5 8·50
3104 60l. multicoloured 2·20 2·00
3105 120l. multicoloured 4·25 4·00
3103/3105 *Set of* 3 7·25 6·75

Nos. 3103/5 were issued in horizontal *se-tenant* strips of three stamps within the sheet.

720 Battle Scene

(Des G. Bakalli. Litho Alexandros Matsoukis, Athens)

2005 (28 Nov). 600th Birth Anniv of Gjergj Kastrioti (Skanderberg). Sheet 240×82 mm containing T **720** and similar multicoloured designs. P 14.

MS3106 40l. Type **720**; 50l. Chariot and fallen horse and rider; 60l. Archers, emblem and foot soldiers with spears; 70l. Shield bearer and archers; 80l. Soldier with raised sword and archers on rocks (30×30 mm) (circular); 90l. Archers firing from cliff ledge (30×30 mm) (circular) 14·00 14·00

The stamps and margins of No. **MS**3106 form a composite design of battle.

721 Roses growing through Helmet

722 Matia Kodheli-Marubi

(Des S. Vllahu. Litho Alexandros Matsoukis, Athens)

2005 (29 Nov). 60th Anniv of End of World War II. T **721** and similar vert design. Multicoloured. P 14.

3107 50l. Type **721** 1·70 1·50
a. Horiz pair. Nos. 3107/8 9·25 8·25
3108 200l. Allied flags and statues 7·25 6·50

Nos. 3107/8 were issued in horizontal *se-tenant* pairs within the sheet.

(Des H. Devolli. Litho Alexandros Matsoukis, Athens)

2005 (4 Dec). National Marubi Photograph Collection. T **722** and similar horiz designs. Multicoloured. P 14.

3109 10l. Type **722** 30 25
a. Horiz strip. Nos. 3109/12 11·00
3110 20l. Gege Marubi 70 65
3111 70l. Pjeter Marubi (Pietro Marubbi) (photographer, artist and architect) 2·50 2·30
3112 200l. Kel Marubi (Mikel Kodheli) 7·25 6·50
3109/3112 *Set of* 4 9·75 8·75

Nos. 3109/12 were issued in horizontal *se-tenant* strips of four stamps within the sheet.

[redacted] **40 lek**

(**723**)

724 Pres. George Bush

2006 (Nov–Dec). Various stamp numbers given in brackets surch in black as T **723**.

3113 40l. on 30q. multicoloured (2531) 1·40 1·30
3114 40l. on 18l. multicoloured (2549) 1·40 1·30
3115 40l. on 2l. multicoloured (2567) 1·40 1·30
3116 40l. on 2l. multicoloured (2595) 1·40 1·30
3117 40l. on 3l. multicoloured (2596) 1·40 1·30
3118 40l. on 25l. multicoloured (2597) 1·40 1·30
3119 40l. on 2l. multicoloured (2606) 1·40 1·30
3120 40l. on 18l. multicoloured (2610) 1·40 1·30
3121 40l. on 18l. multicoloured (2613) 1·40 1·30
3122 40l. on 25l. multicoloured (2620) 1·40 1·30
3123 40l. on 25l. multicoloured (2629) 1·40 1·30
3113/3123 *Set of* 11 14·00 13·00

The surcharges vary in detail, depending on the size and position of the old value obliterated.

2007 (10 June). President George Bush's visit to Albania. T **724** and similar designs. Multicoloured. P 13½.

3124 20l. Type **724** 75 70
a. Strip of 3. Nos. 3124/6 5·50
3125 40l. As Type **724** (suffused green) 1·50 1·40
3126 80l. As Type **724** (multicoloured) 3·00 2·75
3124/3126 *Set of* 3 4·75 4·25

Nos. 3124/6 were issued in horizontal *se-tenant* strips of three stamps within the sheet.

No. **MS**3127 has been left for miniature sheet not yet received.

725 Arms of Italy and Albania

727 Flags and Scouts

(Des B. Cami)

2007 (15 Sept). Tenth Anniv of Italians in Albania. Granite paper. P 13½.

3128 **725** 40l. multicoloured 1·80 1·60

Nos. 3129/41 and Type **726** have been left for 'Flags', issued 5 October 2007, not yet received.

Nos. 3142/52 have been left for 'Arms' (as Type **669**), issued 15–23 October 2007, not yet received.

(Des X. Guga)

2007 (24 Oct). Centenary of Scouting. T **727** and similar multicoloured designs. P 13½.

3153 100l. Type **727** 4·00 3·75
3154 150l. Flags and scouts (different) 6·00 5·75
MS3155 80×60 mm. 250l. Knot (30×25 mm) 10·00 10·00

728 Pink Panther

729 Roads (Arkida)

(Des S. Taci)

2007 (25 October). Pink Panther (cartoon character). T **728** and similar vert designs. Multicoloured. P 13×13½.

3156 40l. Type **728** 1·60 1·40
a. Strip of 4. Nos. 3156/9 13·50
3157 50l. With Inspector Clouseau 2·10 2·00
3158 80l. Leaning 3·00 2·75
3159 150l. Wearing tunic 6·50 6·00
3156/3159 *Set of* 4 12·00 11·00

Nos. 3156/9 were issued in horizontal *se-tenant* strips of four stamps within the sheet.

2007 (29 October). Children's Drawings. T **729** and similar multicoloured designs. P 13×13½.

3160 10l. Type **729** 40 35
a. Strip of 4. Nos. 3160/3 8·00
3161 40l. Boy and flowers (Amarilda Prifti) 1·70 1·60
3162 50l. Outline of houses and viaduct (Iliaz Kasa) 2·10 2·00
3163 80l. Buildings (K. Mezini) (horiz) 3·50 3·25
3160/3163 *Set of* 4 7·00 6·50

Nos. 3160/3 were issued in horizontal *se-tenant* strips of four stamps within the sheet, with No. 3163 laid at right angles to the other stamps, giving the appearence of a strip of four vertical stamps.

730 Galerio Maksimiliani

731 Sower (fresco by David Selenica)

(Des H. Dhiasa)

2007 (30 Oct). Rulers. T **730** and similar vert design. Multicoloured. P 13×13½.

3164 30l. Type **730** 1·40 1·20
a. Pair. Nos. 3164/5 6·75 6·25
3165 120l. Flavio Anastasi 5·00 4·75

Nos. 3164/5 were issued in vertical *se-tenant* pairs within the sheet.

(Des R. Tasho)

2007 (31 Oct). Art. T **731** and similar vert design. Multicoloured. P 13.

3166 70l. Type **731** 3·00 2·75
3167 110l. Flowers and garlands (wall painting) (Et'hem Bey Mosque, Tirana) 4·75 4·25

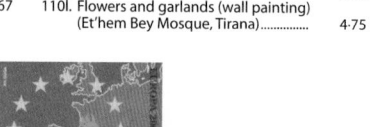

732 Young People, Map and Stars

733 Thethi National Park (Inscr 'Parku Kombetar I Thethit')

(Des X. Guga)

2007 (31 Oct). Europa. Integration. T **732** and similar multicoloured designs. P 13×13½ (vert) or 13½×13 (horiz).

3168 200l. Type **732** 6·75 6·25
3169 200l. Young people and double-headed eagle 6·75 6·25
MS3170 80×60 mm. 350l. Young people and flag (30×25 mm) 12·00 12·00

(Des N. Bakalli)

2007 (1 Nov). Regional Costumes (7th series). Vert designs as T **643**. Multicoloured. P 13×14.

3171 40l. Woman's costume (inscr 'German') 1·30 1·20
a. Sheetlet of 12. Nos. 3171/82 16·00
3172 40l. Man's costume, Kubrin 1·30 1·20
3173 40l. Woman's costume, Golloborde 1·30 1·20
3174 40l. Man's costume, Kerrabe Malesi 1·30 1·20
3175 40l. Woman's costume, Gur I Bardhe 1·30 1·20
3176 40l. Woman's costume, Martanesh 1·30 1·20
3177 40l. Woman's costume, Puke 1·30 1·20
3178 40l. Woman's costume, Serice Labinot 1·30 1·20
3179 40l. Woman's costume, Shen Gjergj 1·30 1·20
3180 40l. Woman's costume, Tirane Qytet 1·30 1·20
3181 40l. Man's costume, Zalle Dajt 1·30 1·20
3182 40l. Woman's costume, Zaranike Godolesh 1·30 1·20
3171/3182 *Set of* 12 14·00 13·00

Nos. 3171/82 were issued in *se-tenant* sheetlets of 12 stamps.

Nos. 3183/94 have been left for 'Regional Costumes (8th series), (vert designs as T **643**), issued on 2 November 2007, not yet received.

(Des L. Mema)

2007 (5 Nov). Tourism. T **733** and similar horiz designs. Multicoloured. P 13×13½.

3195 40l. Type **733** .... 1·60 1·40
a. Strip of 4. Nos. 3195/8 .... 9·00
3196 50l. Luras Lake (Inscr 'Liqenet e Lures') .... 2·00 1·80
3197 60l. Canine's Castle (Inscr 'Kalaja Kanines') .... 2·30 2·10
3198 70l. Laguna Karavastase .... 2·75 2·50
3195/3198 *Set of 4* .... 7·75 7·00

Nos. 3195/8 were issued in horizontal *se-tenant* strips of four stamps within the sheet.

734 Plane Tree

735 Pope Clement II

(Des X. Guga)

2007 (8 Nov). Natural Heritage. Elbasan Plane Trees. T **734** and similar horiz design. Multicoloured. P 13×13½.

3199 70l. Type **734** .... 3·00 2·75
3200 90l. Hollow tree .... 3·50 3·25

(Des L. Mema)

2007 (9 Nov). P 13×13½.

3201 **735** 30l. multicoloured .... 1·20 1·10
a. Pair. Nos. 3201/2 .... 6·25 5·50
3202 90l. multicoloured .... 4·75 4·25

Nos. 3201/2 were issued in vertical *se-tenant* pairs within the sheet.

736 Léopold Senghor

737 Team

(Des S. Taci)

2007 (10 Nov). Birth Centenary (2006) of Léopold Sédar Senghor (poet and first President of Senegal 1960–80). P 13×13½.

3203 **736** 40l. multicoloured .... 1·60 1·40
3204 80l. multicoloured .... 3·00 2·75

(Des A. Skenderi)

2007 (11 Nov). 60th Anniv of Albania as Balkan Football Champions. P 13×13½.

3205 **737** 10l. multicoloured 80 70
3206 80l. multicoloured .... 7·00 6·25

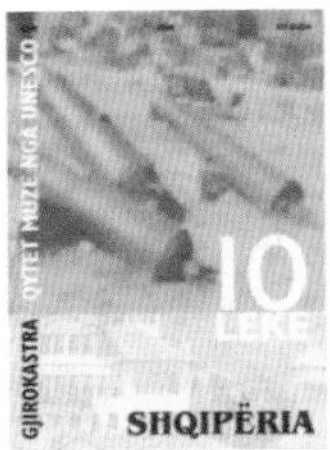

738 Cannon

739 Soldier wearing Gas Mask

(Des X. Guga)

2007 (12 Nov). World Heritage Site. Gjirokastra. Sheet 120×100 mm containing T **738** and similar vert designs. Multicoloured. P 13×13½.

MS3207 10l. Type **738**; 20l. Flowers in a roundel; 30l. 'Kule' (building with tall basement, a first floor for use in the cold season, and a second floor for the warm season); 60l. Bridge; 80l. Aerial view; 90l. Clock tower .... 12·00 12·00

(Des X. Guga)

2007 (13 Nov). Tenth Anniv of Albania's Participation in International Military Missions. T **739** and similar vert design. Multicoloured. P 13×13½.

3208 10l. Type **739** 45 40
3209 100l. Soldiers in inflatable boat .... 4·25 3·75

740 Mother Teresa

741 Gaia (statue)

(Des S. Taci)

2007 (15 Nov). Tenth Death Anniv of Agnes Ganzhou Bojaxhiu (Mother Teresa). T **740** and similar vert design. Multicoloured. P 13×13½.

3210 **740** 60l. multicoloured .... 3·00 2·75
3211 130l. multicoloured .... 5·50 5·00

No. **MS**3212 has been left for miniature sheet, not yet received.

(Des X. Guga)

2007 (16 Nov). Archaeology. Durres City. T **741** and similar multicoloured designs. P 13×13½.

3213 30l. Type **741** .... 1·20 1·10
a. Pair. Nos. 3213/14 .... 6·25 5·50
3214 120l. Gaia (close up) .... 4·75 4·25

Nos. 3213/14 were issued in vertical *se-tenant* pairs within the sheet.

No. **MS**3215 has been left for miniature sheet, not yet received.

742 Drawings

743 Osman Kazazi

(Des X. Guga)

2007 (19 Nov). Cultural History. Tren Cave System (first occupied during Eneolithic period c. 2500–2000 BC)). T **742** and similar multicoloured designs. P 13×13½ (vert) or 13½ (horiz).

3216 20l. Type **742** .... 1·10 1·00
3217 100l. Drawings (different) .... 4·25 3·75
MS3218 81×61 mm. 300l. Cave (horiz) .... 12·50 12·50

(Des L. Mema)

2007 (22 Nov). Personalities (1st issue). T **743** and similar horiz designs. Multicoloured. P 13×13½.

3219 10l. Type **743** (politician) 40 35
a. Strip of 4. Nos. 3219/22 .... 8·25
3220 20l. Pjeter Arbnori (politician) 80 75
3221 60l. Llazar Sotir Gusho (Lagush Poradeci) (poet) .... 2·50 2·40
3222 100l. Cesk Zadeja (composer) .... 4·25 4·00
3219/3222 *Set of 4* .... 7·25 6·75

Nos. 3219/22 were issued in horizontal *se-tenant* strips of four stamps within the sheet.

See also Nos. 3223/6.

744 Abdurrahim Buza

745 Spheres as Player

(Des L. Mema)

2007 (22 Nov). Personalities (2nd issue). T **744** and similar vert designs. Multicoloured. P 13×13½.

3223 50l. Type **744** (artist) .... 2·00 1·90
a. Strip of 4. Nos. 3223/6 .... 8·25
3224 50l. Aleks Buda (historian) .... 2·00 1·90
3225 50l. Thimi Mitko (folklorist and nationalist) .... 2·00 1·90
3226 50l. Martin Camaj (writer) .... 2·00 1·90
3223/3226 *Set of 4* .... 7·25 6·75

Nos. 3223/6 were issued in horizontal *se-tenant* strips of four stamps within the sheet.

(Des L. Mema)

2007 (26 Nov). World Cup Football Championship, Germany. T **745** and similar vert designs. Multicoloured. P 13×13½.

3227 30l. Type **745** .... 1·80 1·70
3228 60l. Triangles as player .... 3·00 2·75
3229 120l. Rectangles as player .... 5·25 4·75
3227/3229 *Set of 3* .... 9·00 8·25
MS3230 61×82 mm. 350l. Emblems .... 13·50 13·50

The stamp and margin of No. **MS**3230 form a composite design.

746 Ismail Kemal Bej Vlora (Ismail Qemali) (first head of state and government) and Arms

747 Garlic

(Des L. Mema)

2007 (28 Nov). 95th Anniv of Independence. T **746** and similar horiz design. Multicoloured. P 13×13½.

3231 50l. Type **746** .... 2·00 1·90
3232 110l. Ismail Qemali .... 4·50 4·00

(Des G. Bakalli)

2007 (3 Dec). Domestic Plants. T **747** and similar triangular designs. Multicoloured. P 14.

3233 80l. Type **747** .... 3·00 2·75
a. Strip of 4. Nos. 3233/6 .... 12·50
3234 80l. Onions .... 3·00 2·75
3235 80l. Peppers .... 3·00 2·75
3236 80l. Tomatoes .... 3·00 2·75
3233/3236 *Set of 4* .... 11·00 10·00

Nos. 3233/6 were issued in horizontal *se-tenant* strips of four stamps within the sheet.

748 Blooms and Leaves

749 Emblem

(Des A. Skenderi)

2007 (4 Dec). *Wulfenia baldacci*. T **748** and similar triangular design. Multicoloured. P 14.

3237 70l. Type **748** .... 3·00 2·75
a. Pair. Nos. 3237/8 .... 7·50 7·00
3238 100l. Flowers on single stem .... 4·25 4·00

Nos. 3237/8 were issued in *tête-bêche* pairs within the sheet.

(Des X. Guga)

2007 (5 Dec). 95th Anniv of National Post Office.

3239 **749** 80l. agate and vermilion .... 3·25 3·00
3240 90l. vermilion and black .... 3·75 3·25

750 New Road Surfacing

2007 (7 Dec). Infrastructure Improvements. Sheet 133×107 mm containing T **750** and similar horiz designs. Multicoloured. P 14.

MS3241 10l. Type **750**; 20l. Durres port; 30l. New building, Tirana; 40l. Mother Teresa airport; 50l. Shkodra street, Hani i Hotit; 60l. Tepelene road, Gjirokastra; 70l. Fier road, Lushnje; 80l. Kalimash road, Morine .... 13·50 13·50

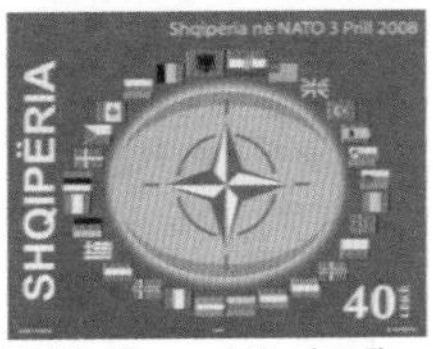

751 Emblem and Member Flags

(Des B. Kafexhiu)

2008 (12 Apr). Albania in NATO. T **751** and similar horiz design. Multicoloured. P 13×13½.

3242 40l. Type **751** .... 2·00 1·90
a. Pair. Nos. 3242/3 .... 4·75 4·50
3243 60l. Arms and emblem .... 2·50 2·40

Nos. 3242/3 were issued in horizontal *se-tenant* pairs within the sheet.

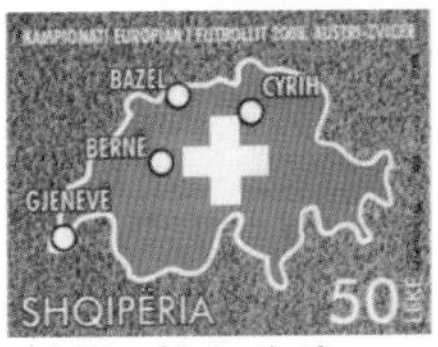

752 Map of Switzerland

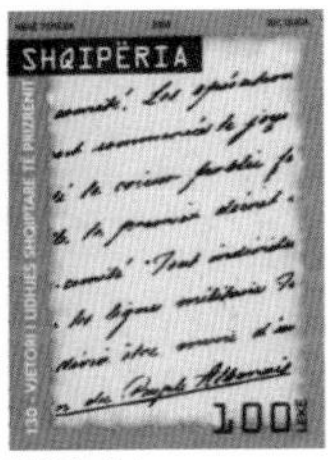

753 Script

(Des X. Guga)

2008 (16 June). EURO 2008 European Football Championship, Austria and Switzerland. T **752** and similar multicoloured designs. P 13×13½ (horiz) or 13½×13 (vert).

3244 50l. Type **752** .... 2·20 2·10
a. Pair. Nos. 3244/5 .... 13·00 12·50
3245 250l. Map of Austria .... 10·50 10·00
MS3246 60×80 mm. 200l. Mascots (vert) .... 9·50 9·50

Nos. 3244/5 were issued in horizontal *se-tenant* pairs within the sheet.

(Des X. Guga)

2008 (27 June). 130th Anniv of Albanian League of Prizren. T **753** and similar vert designs. P 13½×13.

3247 100l. Type **753** .... 4·25 4·00
a. Pair. Nos. 3247/8 .... 11·50 11·50
3248 150l. Building .... 7·00 6·75

Nos. 3247/8 were issued in vertical *se-tenant* pairs within the sheet.

754 Postmark

755 John Belushi (actor)

(Des Y. Beqiri)

2008 (30 June). 95th Anniv of Postal Service. P 13½×13.
3249 **754** 40l. multicoloured ... 2·00 1·90

(Des E. Faja)

2008 (9 July). Personalities of Albanian Descent. T **754** and similar horiz designs. Multicoloured. P 13×13½.
3250 5l. Type **755** ... 20 15
a. Horiz strip of 4. Nos. 3250/3 ... 10·50
3251 10l. Gjon Mili (photographer) ... 40 35
3252 20l. Koca Mi'mar Sinan Aga (Sinan) (Ottoman architect) ... 80 75
3253 200l. Ibrahim Kodra (artist) ... 8·75 8·50
3250/3253 *Set of 4* ... 9·25 8·75
Nos. 3250/3 were issued in horizontal *se-tenant* strips of four stamps within the sheet.

756 Hand holding Quill

757 Two Poppies

(Des B. Shijaku)

2008 (15 July). Europa. The Letter. T **756** and similar multicoloured designs. P 13½×13 (vert) or 13×13½ (horiz).
3254 100l. Type **756** ... 4·50 4·25
3255 150l. Hand holding quill writing Europa ... 7·00 6·75
MS3256 81×61 mm. 250l. 'Europa' (horiz) ... 11·50 11·50

(Des G. Varfi)

2008 (30 July). Poppy (*Papaver rhoeas*). T **757** and similar vert design. Multicoloured. P 13½×13.
3257 50l. Type **757** ... 2·20 2·10
a. Pair. Nos. 3257/8 ... 9·50 9·00
3258 150l. Poppy ... 7·00 6·75
Nos. 3257/8 were issued in vertical *se-tenant* pairs within the sheet.

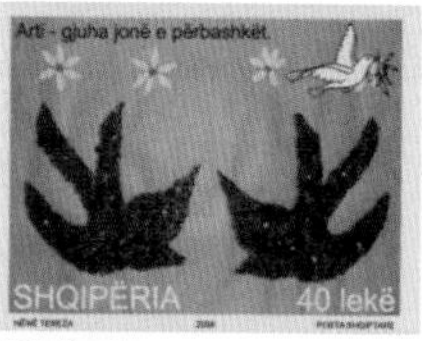

758 Swallows

2008 (1 Aug). Universal Language of Art. T **758** and similar horiz design. Multicoloured. P 13½.
3259 40l. Type **758** ... 2·00 1·90
a. Pair. Nos. 3259/60 ... 5·25 5·00
3260 70l. Parachutists ... 3·00 2·75
Nos. 3259/60 were issued in horizontal *se-tenant* pairs within the sheet.

759 Football

(Des B. Taci)

2008 (8 Aug). Olympic Games, Beijing. T **759** and similar vert designs. Multicoloured. P 13½.
3261 20l. Type **759** ... 80 75
a. Horiz strip. Nos. 3261/4 ... 6·75
3262 30l. Water polo ... 1·50 1·40
3263 40l. Athletics ... 2·00 1·90
3264 50l. Cycling ... 2·20 2·10
3261/3264 *Set of 4* ... 5·75 5·50
Nos. 3261/4 were issued in horizontal *se-tenant* strips of four stamps within the sheet.

760 Osumi Canyons

761 Ahmet Zogu

(Des S. Veseli)

2008 (25 Aug). Tourism. T **760** and similar vert design. Multicoloured. P 13×13½.
3265 60l. Type **760** ... 2·50 2·40
a. Pair. Nos. 3265/6 ... 13·50 13·00
3266 250l. Komani Lake ... 10·50 10·00
Nos. 3265/6 were issued in horizontal *se-tenant* pairs within the sheet.

(Des I. Martini)

2008 (1 Sept). 80th Anniv of Coronation of King Ahmet Zogu. P 13×13½.
3267 **761** 40l. multicoloured ... 2·00 1·90
a. Pair. Nos. 3267/8 ... 6·75 6·50
3268 100l. multicoloured ... 4·50 4·25
Nos. 3267/8 were issued in horizontal *se-tenant* pairs within the sheet.

762 Azem Hajdari (politician)

763 Ymer Prizreni

(Des Y. Beqiri)

2008 (12 Sept). Personalities. T **762** and similar vert design. Multicoloured. P 13×13½.
3269 40l. Type **762** ... 2·00 1·90
a. Pair. Nos. 3269/70 ... 11·50 11·00
3270 200l. Adem Jashari (Kosovo nationalist) ... 8·75 8·50
Nos. 3269/70 were issued in horizontal *se-tenant* pairs within the sheet.

2008 (20 Sept). Kosovo Nationalists. T **763** and similar vert designs. Multicoloured. P 13½.
3271 20l. Type **763** ... 80 75
a. Block. Nos. 3271/5 plus 4 labels ... 9·75
3272 30l. Isa Boletini ... 1·50 1·40
3273 40l. Ibrahim Rugova ... 2·00 1·90
3274 50l. Azem Galica ... 2·20 2·10
3275 70l. Adem Jashari ... 3·00 2·75
3271/3275 *Set of 5* ... 8·50 8·00
Nos. 3271/5 plus 4 labels were issued in *se-tenant* blocks of nine within the sheet, the stamps alternating with the labels giving a checkerboard effect.

764 Decius

765 Harry Potter (Daniel Radcliffe) and Professor Dumbledore (Michael Gambon)

(Des H. Dhimo)

2008 (3 Oct). Roman Emperors of Illyrian Ancestry. T **764** and similar vert design. Multicoloured. P 13×13½.
3276 30l. Type **764** ... 1·50 1·40

No. 3277 has been left for stamp not yet recieved.

(Des S. Taci)

2008 (15 Oct). Youth Stamps. Harry Potter (character created by J. K. Rowling). T **765** and similar horiz designs showing Harry Potter and other characters. Multicoloured. P 13½.
3278 20l. Type **765** ... 80 75
a. Block of 4. Nos. 3278/81 ... 9·25
b. Booklet pane. Nos. 3278/81 ... 9·50
3279 30l. With Dobby ... 1·50 1·40
3280 50l. With Hermione (Emma Watson) and friends ... 2·20 2·10
3281 100l. With Voldemort (Ralph Fiennes) ... 4·50 4·25
3278/3281 *Set of 4* ... 8·00 7·75
Nos. 3278/81 were issued in *se-tenant* blocks of four stamps within the sheet.

STAMP BOOKLETS

The following checklist covers, in simplified form, booklets issued by Albania. It is intended that it should be used in conjunction with the main listings and details of stamps and panes listed there are not repeated.

Prices are for complete booklets

Booklet No.	*Date*	*Contents and Cover Price*	*Price*
SB1	20.3.86	Flowers 1 pane, No. 2306a (1l.45)	12·00
SB2	20.4.86	Anniversaries 1 pane, No. 2308a (4l.65)	15·00
SB3	20.5.88	Flowers 1 pane, No. 2376a (3l.30)	75·00
SB4	29.11.89	45th Anniv of Liberation 1 pane, No. 2438a (3l.30)	4·75
SB5	6.5.90	150th Anniv of the Penny Black 1 pane, No. 2454a (3l.90)	4·50
SB6	20.6.99	Charlie Chaplin (T **633**) 1 pane, No. 2742ab (660l.)	19·00
SB7	12.9.01	Arms 4 panes, Nos. 2881a, 2882a, 2883a, 2884a (820l.)	23·00
SB8	12.5.02	Arms 4 panes, Nos. 2918a, 2919a, 2920a, 2921a	22·00
SB9	12.5.03	Arms 4 panes, Nos. 2965a, 2966a, 2967a, 2968a	28·00
SB10	5.10.05	Europa. Gastronomy 1 pane No. 3068a	15·00
SB11	14.11.05	Arms 4 panes, Nos. 3098b, 3099a, 3100a, 3101a	44·00
SB12	15.10.08	Youth Stamps 1 pane, No. 3278b	9·75

GREEK OCCUPATION

100 Lepta = 1 Drachma

Italian troops invaded Greece from Albania on 29 October 1940. The Greeks counter-attacked and occupied part of southern Albania, including Koritza, until the German invasion of Greece forced them to surrender on 21 April 1941. For stamps issued in this area in 1914–15, see under Epirus.

Stamps of Greece overprinted

ΕΛΛΗΝΙΚΗ
ΔΙΟΙΚΗCIC
(**1**)

1940 (10 Dec). Nos. 497, 499 to 512, 514 and 516 optd with T **1**.
1 **86** 5l. greenish blue and red-brown ... 15 30
a. Opt inverted ... £110
2 – 10l. red-brown and light blue ... 15 30
3 **87** 20l. blue-green and black ... 20 50
a. Opt inverted ... £110
4 **88** 40l. black and blue-green ... 20 50
5 – 50l. black and bistre-brown ... 20 50
6 – 80l. brown and dull violet ... 20 50
7 **89** 1d. green ... 30 1·30
a. Opt inverted ... £225
8 – 2d. ultramarine ... 35 1·30
9 **89** 3d. red-brown ... 45 1·30
10 – 5d. scarlet ... 65 2·00
11 – 6d. olive-brown ... 1·00 2·40
12 **90** 7d. chocolate ... 1·00 2·40
13 **89** 8d. deep blue ... 1·00 2·40
14 – 10d. red-brown ... 1·60 3·00
15 **91** 15d. blue-green ... 1·60 5·00
16 **92** 25d. deep blue ... 4·00 9·00
a. Opt inverted ... £160
17 **89a** 30d. brown-red ... 7·50 19·00
1/17 *Set of 17* ... 18·00 46·00

1940 (10 Dec). CHARITY TAX. Nos. C524/6 optd with T **1**.
18 C **96** 10l. carmine/*rose* ... 15 40
19 50l. green/*pale green* ... 25 85
a. Opt inverted ... 85·00
20 1d. blue/*pale blue* ... 65 1·90
18/20 *Set of 3* ... 95 2·75

1940 (10 Dec). POSTAGE DUE.

(a) Nos. D453 and D455/7 optd with T **1**
D21 D **20** 2d. vermilion ... 35 95
a. Opt inverted ... 85·00
D22 5d. grey-blue ... 80 1·90
D23 10d. green ... 50 1·60
D24 15d. red-brown ... 80 1·90

(b) No. D458 surch and similarly optd
D25 D **20** 50l. on 25d. scarlet ... 35 95
a. No accent (No. D458a) ... 85·00
D21/25 *Set of 5* ... 2·75 7·00

1941 (1 Mar). Greek Youth issue, Nos. 534/53, optd with T **1**, in red.

(a) POSTAGE
26 3d. blue, red and silver ... 55 1·00
27 5d. black and blue ... 2·75 2·10
28 10d. black and orange ... 3·75 5·25
29 15d. black and green ... 13·00 18·00
30 20d. black and lake ... 11·00 18·00
31 25d. black and blue ... 11·00 18·00
32 30d. black and purple ... 11·00 18·00
33 50d. black and lake ... 11·00 18·00
34 75d. gold, brown and blue ... 14·00 18·00
35 100d. blue, red and silver ... 15·00 24·00
a. Opt inverted ... £1200
26/35 *Set of 10* ... 85·00 £130

(b) AIR
36 2d. black and orange ... 55 1·00
a. Opt inverted ... £250
37 4d. black and green ... 2·75 4·25
a. Opt inverted ... £250
38 6d. black and lake ... 3·75 5·25
a. Opt inverted ... £250
39 8d. black and blue ... 5·50 8·25
40 16d. black and purple ... 11·00 16·00
41 32d. black and orange ... 12·00 19·00
42 45d. black and green ... 12·00 19·00
43 55d. black and carmine ... 12·00 19·00
44 65d. black and blue ... 12·00 19·00
45 100d. black and purple ... 22·00 16·00
36/45 *Set of 10* ... 85·00 £110
Nos. 36/45 were issued as postage and not air stamps.

SASENO

ITALIAN OCCUPATION

100 Centesimi = 1 Lira

Saseno (now Sazan), an Albanian island in the gulf of Valona, was occupied by Italian marines on 30 October 1914 and remained in Italian hands until 1943. Italy renounced her claims to the island by the Treaty of Paris, 10 February 1947.

1923 (April). Stamps of Italy, 1906–22, (various portraits of Victor Emmanuel III), optd "SASENO".
1 **38** 10c. rose ... 20·00 37·00
2 **37** 15c. slate ... 20·00 37·00
3 **41** 20c. orange (No. 105) ... 20·00 37·00
4 **39** 25c. blue ... 20·00 37·00
5 30c. orange-brown ... 20·00 37·00
6 **40** 50c. mauve ... 20·00 37·00
7 **39** 60c. lake ... 20·00 37·00
8 **34** 1l. brown and green ... 20·00 37·00
1/8 *Set of 8* ... £140 £250

Bosnia and Herzegovina

AUSTRO-HUNGARIAN MILITARY POST

1879. 100 Kreuzer = 1 Gulden
1900. 100 Heller = 1 Krone

AUSTRO-HUNGARIAN OCCUPATION, 1878–1908

Bosnia became part of the Turkish Empire in 1463 and Herzegovina in 1483. After the Russo-Turkish war, the Congress of Berlin, 1878, laid down that these two countries should remain under Turkish suzerainty but that Austria-Hungary could occupy them and maintain a garrison.

The occupation was achieved only by the use of force against large numbers of insurgents as well as Turks so that in 1878/79 the mail service was restricted to the military field post. On 9 January 1879 the service was partially opened to civilian use, employing Austrian and Hungarian stamps. When the first stamps for Bosnia and Herzegovina were issued on 1 July 1879 the use of Austrian and Hungarian stamps was discontinued.

PRINTERS. All the following were printed at the State Printing Works, Vienna.

1 Value at top

A B C D

I II III

The stamps of Type I were lithographed and were printed from reproductions from one original die. Types II and III (5k. value only) were typographed.

In Type I the three heraldic eaglets on the diagonal bar of the escutcheon are quite clean and white, and the eye of the lion is a fine dot, sometimes very faint.

In the 2k. the numerals have curved feet (A).

In the 15k. (Type C) the serif of the "I" is short and makes a wide angle with the vertical stroke, while in Type D the serif makes an acute angle.

There were numerous stones used for all values and these can be identified by slight but characteristic variations, and the flaws inseparable from the lithographic process.

The early stones were apparently laid down from single transfers, but later, strips of 4, of 10 and blocks of 10 were used to make the intermediate stones, giving rise to an equivalent number of sub-types. The figures on the 5k. varied considerably, both on the different printing stones and on the intermediate stones. There are several retouches on various values, some extensive.

In Type II the bottom eaglet has a coloured line across it, which sometimes extends to the middle one; the lion's eye is indicated by a thick spot of colour, which merges in the crown upon the lion's head, and the dots above the head have run together, instead of being separate and distinct.

In the 2k. the figures have straight feet (B).

Type III (5k. only) is similar to Type I, but the tail of the large eagle does not always touch the inner line of the oval, and it contains two distinct lines of shading only, whereas there are several in Type I.

1879 (1 July)–**1900**. Type **1**. Wmk "BRIEF-MARKEN" or (later) "ZEITUNGS-MARKEN" in double-lined capitals extending across two panes (100 each) of a sheet.

A. Type I. Litho (**1879–95**) Early perforations are irregular, at times very irregular, the pins not being set in a straight line or at regular intervals. One machine gauged 11½ to 12 and others from 12½ to 13, and all seem to have been overhauled more than once, as fairly regular perfs 12½ and 12¾ are found at certain dates.

About 1894-5 the Austrian machine giving 13–13½ was used, but can only be separated with certainty on dated copies, or stamps known to be from late stones.

The 1k. purple, in perfs (a) and (b) is an error of colour which was withdrawn and cancelled with blue pencil; the stamps are sometimes cleaned and forged postmarks added.

(a) P 12 irregular (1879–88)

1	1k. light grey	23·00	4·75
2	1k. deep grey	23·00	4·75
3	2k. orange	25·00	1·90
4	2k. orange-yellow	27·00	3·00
5	3k. emerald-green	35·00	4·25
6	3k. green	37·00	3·25
7	3k. deep green	43·00	4·75
8	5k. rose	75·00	1·20
9	5k. rose-red	70·00	85
10	10k. pale blue	£250	8·50
11	10k. blue	£190	2·75
12	10k. slate-blue	£225	3·75
13	15k. brown (C) (1879–81)	£450	55·00
14	15k. pale brown (D)	£190	10·00
15	15k. brown (D)	£190	10·00
16	15k. dark brown (D)	£190	10·00
17	25k. mauve	£200	16·00
18	25k. bright violet	£400	28·00
19	25k. aniline violet	£1200	30·00
20	25k. reddish mauve	£200	14·50

(b) P 12½–13, irregular

21	1k. grey-purple	21·00	£400
22	1k. light grey	21·00	2·30
23	1k. dark grey	21·00	2·30
24	1k. grey-black	21·00	2·30
25	2k. orange	30·00	1·80
26	2k. orange-yellow	30·00	1·80
	a. Bisected (1k.) (on wrapper)		
27	3k. emerald-green	37·00	3·75
28	3k. green	31·00	3·00
29	3k. yellow-green	31·00	3·00
30	3k. deep green	31·00	3·00
31	5k. rose	48·00	60
32	5k. rose-red	48·00	60
32*a*	5k. orange-red	£1900	£190
33	10k. pale blue	£190	1·90
	a. Bisected (5k.) on piece	†	—
34	10k. blue	£190	1·90
35	10k. slate-blue	£190	1·90
36	15k. brown (C) (1879–81)	£450	48·00
37	15k. grey-brown (C) (1879–81)	£450	48·00
38	15k. pale brown (D)	£180	10·00
39	15k. brown (D)	£180	9·25
40	15k. deep brown (D)	£180	9·25
41	25k. mauve	£200	14·50
42	25k. reddish mauve	£200	14·50
43	25k. dull purple	£200	14·50
43*a*	25k. bright violet	£1100	35·00

It was not intended to issue No. 21 to the public, most sheets being obliterated with blue crayon. Postally used examples are, however, known. The unused price quoted is for stamps showing the crayon mark, but the used price is for postally used examples.

(c) P 12×12½–13 (compound of (a) and (b))

44	1k. grey	47·00	17·00
45	2k. orange	47·00	13·00
46	2k. orange-yellow	47·00	13·00
47	3k. green	80·00	14·50
48	5k. rose	70·00	12·50
49	5k. rose-red	70·00	12·50
50	10k. blue	£250	14·50
51	10k. pale blue	£250	14·50
52	15k. pale brown (D)	£250	23·00
53	15k. brown (D)	£250	23·00
56	25k. dull purple		

(d) P 9–9½ (1890–93)

57	5k. red	£1600	£160
58	10k. blue	£275	£350

(e) P 11, regular; large holes (1890–94)

59	1k. dark grey	50·00	17·00
60	2k. orange-yellow	£100	18·00
61	3k. pale green	£130	19·00
62	3k. dark green	90·00	£160
63	5k. rose-red	£225	11·00
64	10k. blue	£275	19·00
65	15k. dark brown (D)	£600	43·00

(f) P 11×12½–13 or 12½–13×11 (compound of (b) and (e))

66	2k. orange-yellow (1890)	£190	39·00
66*a*	5k. rose-red	£160	39·00
66*b*	15k. brown	£900	£150

(g) P 11½, regular (1890–94 or 95)

67	1k. light grey	24·00	4·50
68	1k. dark grey	24·00	4·50
69	2k. orange	33·00	2·30
69*a*	2k. orange-brown	85·00	11·50
70	2k. orange-yellow	33·00	2·30
71	3k. green	35·00	4·00
72	3k. greyish green	38·00	4·50
73	5k. rose	70·00	95
74	5k. rose-red	70·00	95
75	10k. pale blue	£200	1·60
76	10k. blue	£200	1·60
77	10k. greyish blue	£250	3·00
78	15k. brown (D)	£190	11·50
79	15k. dark brown (D)	£225	14·50
80	20k. yellowish green (1893)	£850	15·00
81	20k. dull green	£850	15·00
82	25k. reddish mauve	£200	13·00
83	25k. dull purple	£200	13·00

(h) P 10½, regular (1891–94 or 95)

84	1k. light grey	25·00	4·50
85	1k. dark grey	25·00	4·50
86	2k. orange	29·00	2·20
87	2k. orange-yellow	29·00	2·20
88	3k. green	35·00	3·75
89	3k. greyish green	35·00	4·50
90	3k. yellow-green	35·00	4·50
91	5k. rose	55·00	95
92	5k. rose-red	70·00	1·30
93	10k. blue	£190	1·30
	a. Imperf between (horiz pair)	—	£1600
94	10k. greyish blue	£250	2·00
95	15k. light brown (D)	£190	9·75
96	15k. brown (D)	£190	11·50
97	15k. dark brown (D)	£190	11·50
98	20k. yellowish green	£750	13·00
99	20k. dull green	£850	14·50
100	25k. reddish mauve	£160	16·00
101	25k. dull purple	£160	16·00

(i) P 11½×10½ (compound of (g) and (h))

101*a*	2k. orange-yellow	£160	20·00
102	5k. rose-red	£325	10·00
103	10k. blue	£250	20·00

E F

½k. In Type F the fraction line of "½" in upper right corner is more nearly horizontal than in Type E.

B. Litho but showing line across bottom eaglet as Type II. Upper curled end of inner frame-line at bottom right corner joined to dot. Wmk "ZEITUNGS-MARKEN" as before (**1894**)

104	½k. black (E) (11.94)		
	a. Perf 11	£180	£140
	b. Perf 11½	25·00	39·00
	c. Perf 10½	25·00	39·00
	d. Compound b and c	45·00	55·00
	e. Imperf between (vert pair)	£1100	
105	3k. bottle-green		
	a. Perf 11½	£750	£150
	b. Perf 10½	95·00	£160

C. Type II. Typo (**1895–1900**)

(a) P 11½, regular (1895–99)

106	½k. black (F)	28·00	30·00
107	1k. grey	31·00	5·50
108	2k. orange-yellow	43·00	8·50
109	3k. yellow-green	43·00	8·50
110	3k. green	43·00	8·50
111	5k. rose	£750	8·50
112	10k. greyish blue	£120	6·25
113	15k. light brown	41·00	6·25
114	15k. chestnut-brown	41·00	6·25
115	20k. yellowish green	£1200	14·00
117	25k. reddish mauve	29·00	13·00

(b) P 10½, regular

119	½k. black (F)	20·00	22·00
120	1k. grey	16·00	1·90
121	1k. pearl-grey	16·00	1·90
122	2k. orange-yellow	16·00	90
123	3k. emerald-green	17·00	2·20
124	3k. yellow-green	17·00	2·20
125	5k. rose-red	£170	80
126	10k. greyish blue	22·00	1·60
127	10k. slate-blue	22·00	1·60
	a. Imperf between (vert pair)	£1300	
128	15k. brown	24·00	5·75
129	20k. yellow-green	21·00	7·00
130	20k. dull green	21·00	7·00
131	20k. bronze-green	21·00	7·00
132	25k. aniline mauve	33·00	10·00
133	25k. reddish purple	33·00	10·00

(c) P 12½, regular (1898–1900)

135	1k. pearl-grey	6·50	1·50
136	2k. orange-yellow	4·00	65
137	3k. blue-green	6·50	1·60
138	3k. yellow-green	6·50	1·60
139	10k. dull blue	9·25	1·20
140	15k. brown	8·25	4·50
141	20k. bronze-green	9·00	5·25
142	25k. reddish mauve	10·50	8·50

(d) P 13×12½ (comb-machine)

143	2k. orange-yellow	95·00	14·50

(e) P 10 (comb-machine)

143*a*	3k. green	£850	

D. Type III. Typo (**1898–1900**)

(a) P 11½, regular (1898)

144	5k. scarlet	95·00	3·00

(b) P 10½, regular

145	5k. scarlet	17·00	1·60
	a. Imperf between (horiz pair)	—	£1300

(c) P 12½, regular (1899–1900)

146	5k. dull red	6·50	80
146*a*	5k. scarlet	6·50	80

(d) P 12½×10½ (compound of (c) × (b))

147	5k. scarlet	£250	35·00

(e) P 10½×12½ (compound of (b) × (c))

147*a*	5k. scarlet	£130	£250

Reprints of Nos. 135/42 can be distinguished from original printings by their white paper, dull shades and pure white gum.

2 Value at bottom

3

1900 (1 Jan)–**01**. Currency changed. T **2** wmk "ZEITUNGS-MARKEN" as before, later no wmk; T **3** no wmk.

(a) P 12½

148	**2**	1h. grey-black (1.1.00)	45	15
		a. Ribbed paper	£100	47·00
149		2h. pearl-grey (1.4.00)	45	15
		a. Ribbed paper	£100	47·00
150		2h. pale drab	45	15
151		3h. orange-yellow (1.4.00)	45	15
152		5h. yellow-green (1.4.00)	40	10
		a. Ribbed paper	£130	24·00
153		5h. deep green	40	10
154		6h. bistre (1.4.00)	60	20
		a. Ribbed paper	95·00	35·00
155		10h. red (1.4.00)	40	10
		a. Ribbed paper	95·00	19·00
156		20h. pink (1.4.00)	£225	11·00
		a. Ribbed paper	£400	95·00

157		25h. blue (1.4.00)	1·70	40
		a. Ribbed paper	£600	£140
158		25h. deep blue	1·70	40
159		30h. pale bistre (1.4.00)	£250	12·50
		a. Ribbed paper	£400	90·00
160		40h. orange (10.00)	£325	16·00
		a. Ribbed paper	£475	90·00
161		50h. red-lilac (1.4.00)	1·20	80
		a. Ribbed paper	45·00	23·00
162	3	1k. carmine (10.00)	1·50	60
		a. Ribbed paper	31·00	17·00
163		2k. ultramarine (10.00)	2·40	1·90
		a. Ribbed paper	75·00	37·00
164		5k. deep blue-green (2.01)	5·00	5·75
		a. Ribbed paper	£100	85·00
		(b) P 10½		
165	2	1h. grey-black	£475	27·00
166		2h. pearl-grey	13·50	12·50
		a. Ribbed paper	£250	
167		3h. orange-yellow	£350	21·00
168		5h. yellow-green	£200	8·50
169		6h. bistre	9·75	6·50
		a. Ribbed paper	£300	£160
170		10h. red	£100	3·00
171		20h. pink	£300	9·25
172		25h. blue	£130	11·50
173		30h. pale bistre	£325	11·00
		(c) Perf compound of 12½ and 10½		
174	2	3h. orange-yellow	£650	£190
175		10h. red	£475	23·00
176		30h. pale bistre	—	£190

All the values of this issue are known in pairs or blocks in dual or triple compound perforations of imperf, and perf 6½, 9½ or 12½. These were experimental perforations which were not put into use. Some are also known imperf.

Reprints of the 20h. and 30h. perf 10½ and of the 40h. perf 12½, made in 1911, can be recognised by their duller colours, white paper and colourless gum. The strokes of the "4" on the 40h. are thinner in the reprint than in the original.

Stamps perforated 11 or 11½ are forgeries, which also exist imperforate.

1901 (Oct)–**06**. Numerals in black. P 12½.

177	2	20h. pink and black	75	55
		a. Ribbed paper	£170	80·00
178		30h. bistre and black	75	55
		a. Ribbed paper	£170	£250
179		35h. ultramarine and black	£325	8·50
		a. Ribbed paper	95·00	£275
180		35h. deep blue and black (1906)	1·20	85
181		40h. dull orange and black	85	85
		a. Ribbed paper	£250	£225
181*b*		40h. orange and black	85	85
182		45h. greenish blue and black (10.1.05)	95	85

Some of the above values are known imperf or with the varieties of perforation mentioned in note after No. 176.

D 4

1904 (1 Dec). POSTAGE DUE. Type D **4**. Typo. P 12½, 13.

D183	D **4**	1h. red, black and yellow	1·20	30
		b. Perf 10½	10·50	10·50
		c. Perf 9	4·25	
		d. Perf 12½, 13 and 10½ compound	11·00	
		e. Perf 12½, 13 and 9 compound	20·00	
		f. Imperf	4·00	
D184		2h. red, black and yellow	1·20	30
		b. Perf 10½	10·00	10·00
		c. Perf 9	4·25	
		d. Perf 12½, 13 and 10½ compound	11·00	
		e. Perf 12½, 13 and 9 compound	39·00	
		f. Imperf	4·00	
D185		3h. red, black and yellow	1·20	30
		b. Perf 10½		
		c. Perf 9	21·00	
		d. Perf 12½, 13 and 10½ compound		
		e. Perf 12½, 13 and 9 compound	5·50	
		f. Imperf	4·00	
D186		4h. red, black and yellow	1·20	30
		b. Perf 10½	10·00	10·00
		c. Perf 9	21·00	
		d. Perf 12½, 13 and 10½ compound	19·00	
		e. Perf 12½, 13 and 9 compound	13·00	
		f. Imperf	4·00	
D187		5h. red, black and yellow	5·75	30
		b. Perf 10½	14·50	14·50
		c. Perf 9	21·00	
		d. Perf 12½, 13 and 10½ compound	19·00	
		e. Perf 12½, 13 and 9 compound		
		f. Imperf	4·00	
D188		6h. red, black and yellow	1·20	30
		b. Perf 10½	18·00	18·00
		c. Perf 9	5·50	
		d. Perf 12½, 13 and 10½ compound	19·00	
		e. Perf 12½, 13 and 9 compound	9·75	
		f. Imperf	4·00	
D189		7h. red, black and yellow	8·25	4·00
		b. Perf 10½	14·00	14·00
		c. Perf 9	14·50	
		d. Perf 12½, 13 and 10½ compound	19·00	
		e. Perf 12½, 13 and 9 compound		
		f. Imperf	13·00	
D190		8h. red, black and yellow	8·25	1·90
		b. Perf 10½	41·00	41·00
		c. Perf 9	5·50	
		d. Perf 12½, 13 and 10½ compound		
		e. Perf 12½, 13 and 9 compound	11·50	
		f. Imperf	14·50	
D191		10h. red, black and yellow	1·60	30
		b. Perf 10½	16·00	16·00
		c. Perf 9	12·50	
		d. Perf 12½, 13 and 10½ compound	25·00	
		e. Perf 12½, 13 and 9 compound	22·00	
		f. Imperf	4·00	
D192		15h. red, black and yellow	1·60	30
		b. Perf 10½	43·00	43·00
		c. Perf 9	5·50	
		d. Perf 12½, 13 and 10½ compound	7·00	
		e. Perf 12½, 13 and 9 compound	16·00	
		f. Imperf	4·00	
D193		20h. red, black and yellow	11·00	40
		b. Perf 10½	43·00	43·00
		c. Perf 9	22·00	
		d. Perf 12½, 13 and 10½ compound	60·00	
		e. Perf 12½, 13 and 9 compound	19·00	
		f. Imperf	31·00	
D194		50h. red, black and yellow	5·50	80
		b. Perf 10½	43·00	43·00
		c. Perf 9	19·00	
		d. Perf 12½, 13 and 10½ compound	23·00	
		e. Perf 12½, 13 and 9 compound	25·00	
		f. Imperf	14·00	
D195		200h. red, black and green	27·00	2·75
		b. Perf 10½		
		c. Perf 9	23·00	
		d. Perf 12½, 13 and 10½ compound		
		e. Perf 12½, 13 and 9 compound	50·00	
		f. Imperf	47·00	

The used prices for Nos. D183/D195, b to f are for cancelled by favour.

4 View of Doboj

5 In the Carshija (business quarter), Sarajevo

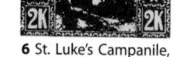

6 St. Luke's Campanile, at Jajce

7 Francis Joseph I

(Des K. Moser. Eng F. Schirnböck. Recess)

1906 (1 Nov). T **4** (various views and border designs) and **5/7**.

A. P 12½

186A	**4**	1h. black	15	15
187A		2h. violet	15	15
188A		3h. olive-yellow	15	15
189A		5h. deep green	40	10
190A		6h. brown	25	30
191A		10h. carmine	45	10
192A		20h. sepia	95	45
193A		25h. deep blue	2·30	1·60
194A		30h. green	2·30	80
195A		35h. deep green	2·30	80
196A		40h. orange	2·30	80
197A		45h. red	2·30	1·60
198A		50h. purple-brown	2·30	1·60
199A	**5**	1kr. lake	7·00	3·75
200A	**6**	2kr. myrtle-green	7·75	16·00
201A	**7**	5kr. grey-blue	6·25	9·75
186A/201A *Set of* 16			34·00	34·00

B. Perf 9½

186B	**4**	1h. black	80	85
187B		2h. violet	80	85
188B		3h. olive-yellow	80	85
189B		5h. deep green	85	85
190B		6h. brown	85	1·20
191B		10h. carmine	85	85
192B		20h. sepia	2·30	3·25
193B		25h. deep blue	6·25	9·25
194B		30h. green	6·25	6·50
195B		35h. deep green	6·25	6·50
196B		40h. orange	6·25	6·50
197B		45h. red	6·25	6·50
198B		50h. purple-brown	6·50	9·25
199B	**5**	1kr. lake	13·00	31·00
200B	**6**	2kr. myrtle-green	20·00	47·00
201B	**7**	5kr. grey-blue	19·00	45·00

C. Imperf

186C	**4**	1h. black	40	40
187C		2h. violet	45	40
188C		3h. olive-yellow	45	40
189C		5h. deep green	55	40
190C		6h. brown	85	70
191C		10h. carmine	55	40
192C		20h. sepia	2·20	1·20
193C		25h. deep blue	5·00	4·75
194C		30h. green	5·75	5·50
195C		35h. deep green	5·75	5·50
196C		40h. orange	5·75	5·50
197C		45h. red	6·50	6·25
198C		50h. purple-brown	6·50	6·25
199C	**5**	1kr. lake	11·50	13·00
200C	**6**	2kr. myrtle-green	17·00	21·00
201C	**7**	5kr. grey-blue	14·00	25·00

D. Perf 12½ and 9½ compound

186D	**4**	1h. black	4·00	5·00
187D		2h. violet	4·00	5·00
188D		3h. olive-yellow	4·00	5·00
189D		5h. deep green	4·00	5·00
190D		6h. brown	3·75	5·50
191D		10h. carmine	11·00	9·00
192D		20h. sepia	35·00	11·00
193D		25h. deep blue	16·00	30·00
194D		30h. green	37·00	30·00
195D		35h. deep green	37·00	30·00
196D		40h. orange	40·00	40·00
197D		45h. red	40·00	40·00
198D		50h. purple-brown	40·00	40·00
199D	**5**	1kr. lake	80·00	60·00
200D	**6**	2kr. myrtle-green	£130	£130
201D	**7**	5kr. grey-blue	£130	£130

E. Perf 12½, 9½ and 6½ compound

186E	**4**	1h. black	2·00	2·00
187E		2h. violet	3·00	2·00
188E		3h. olive-yellow	3·00	2·00
189E		5h. deep green	4·00	2·00
190E		6h. brown	3·00	3·00
191E		10h. carmine	4·00	4·00
192E		20h. sepia	12·00	12·00
193E		25h. deep blue	45·00	45·00
194E		30h. green	40·00	40·00
195E		35h. deep green	43·00	43·00
196E		40h. orange	43·00	43·00
197E		45h. red	43·00	43·00
198E		50h. purple-brown	45·00	45·00
199E	**5**	1kr. lake	80·00	80·00
200E	**6**	2kr. myrtle-green	£200	£200
201E	**7**	5kr. grey-blue	£130	£130

F. Perf 12½ and 6½ compound

186F	**4**	1h. black	3·25	3·25
187F		2h. violet	3·25	3·25
188F		3h. olive-yellow	3·25	3·25
189F		5h. deep green	3·25	3·25
190F		6h. brown	5·00	5·00
191F		10h. carmine	5·50	5·50
192F		20h. sepia	13·00	13·00
193F		25h. deep blue	18·00	18·00
194F		30h. green	19·00	19·00
195F		35h. deep green	23·00	23·00
196F		40h. orange	17·00	17·00
197F		45h. red	25·00	25·00
198F		50h. purple-brown	25·00	25·00
199F	**5**	1kr. lake	50·00	50·00
200F	**6**	2kr. myrtle-green	85·00	85·00
201F	**7**	5kr. grey-blue	80·00	80·00

G. Perf 9½ and 6½ compound

186G	**4**	1h. black	3·25	3·25
187G		2h. violet	3·25	3·25
188G		3h. olive-yellow	3·25	3·25
189G		5h. deep green	3·25	3·25
190G		6h. brown	5·00	5·00
191G		10h. carmine	5·50	5·50
192G		20h. sepia	13·00	13·00
193G		25h. deep blue	18·00	18·00
194G		30h. green	19·00	19·00
195G		35h. deep green	23·00	23·00
196G		40h. orange	17·00	17·00
197G		45h. red	25·00	25·00
198G		50h. purple-brown	25·00	25·00
199G	**5**	1kr. lake	50·00	50·00
200G	**6**	2kr. myrtle-green	85·00	85·00
201G	**7**	5kr. grey-blue	80·00	80·00

H. Perf 13½

190H	**4**	6h. brown	18·00	31·00
192H		20h. sepia	75·00	£140

I. Perf 6½

186I	**4**	1h. black	1·60	5·00
187I		2h. violet	1·60	5·00
188I		3h. olive-yellow	1·60	5·00
189I		5h. deep green	1·60	5·00
190I		6h. brown	9·50	6·50
191I		10h. carmine	12·50	5·00
192I		20h. sepia	15·00	9·50
193I		25h. deep blue	30·00	30·00
194I		30h. green	35·00	15·00
195I		35h. deep green	36·00	15·00
196I		40h. orange	43·00	15·00
197I		45h. red	43·00	29·00
198I		50h. purple-brown	43·00	23·00
199I	**5**	1kr. lake	80·00	£225
200I	**6**	2kr. myrtle-green	£130	£350
201I	**7**	5kr. grey-blue	£120	£400

J. Perf 10½

186J	**4**	1h. black	4·00	5·50
187J		2h. violet	4·00	6·75
188J		3h. olive-yellow	4·00	9·25
189J		5h. deep green	4·00	9·25
190J		6h. brown	9·50	9·75
191J		10h. carmine	5·00	6·75
192J		20h. sepia	19·00	29·00
193J		25h. deep blue	50·00	80·00
194J		30h. green	50·00	£110
195J		35h. deep green	50·00	£110
196J		40h. orange	70·00	£120
197J		45h. red	70·00	£120
198J		50h. purple-brown	70·00	£120
199J	**5**	1kr. lake	£150	£350
200J	**6**	2kr. myrtle-green	£225	£425
201J	**7**	5kr. grey-blue	£200	£400

K. Perf 10½ and 9½ compound

186K	**4**	1h. black	5·50	5·50
187K		2h. violet	9·50	9·50
188K		3h. olive-yellow	8·75	8·75
189K		5h. deep green	8·75	8·75
190K		6h. brown	9·50	9·50
191K		10h. carmine	10·50	10·50
192K		20h. sepia	15·00	15·00
193K		25h. deep blue	22·00	22·00
194K		30h. green	30·00	30·00
195K		35h. deep green	30·00	30·00
196K		40h. orange	21·00	21·00
197K		45h. red	33·00	33·00
198K		50h. purple-brown	45·00	45·00
199K	**5**	1kr. lake	50·00	50·00

200K	6	2kr. myrtle-green	£140	£140
201K	7	5kr. grey-blue	£110	£110
		L. Perf 10½ and 12½ compound		
186L	4	1h. black	6·00	6·00
187L		2h. violet	8·00	8·00
188L		3h. olive-yellow	6·00	6·00
189L		5h. deep green	6·00	6·00
190L		6h. brown	9·50	9·50
191L		10h. carmine	10·50	10·50
192L		20h. sepia	13·00	13·00
193L		25h. deep blue	26·00	26·00
194L		30h. green	30·00	30·00
195L		35h. deep green	21·00	21·00
196L		40h. orange	28·00	28·00
197L		45h. red	31·00	31·00
198L		50h. purple-brown	22·00	22·00
199L	5	1kr. lake	50·00	50·00
200L	6	2kr. myrtle-green	£130	£130
201L	7	5kr. grey-blue	£130	£130
		M. Perf 10½, 12½ and 9½ compound		
186M	4	1h. black	4·25	4·25
187M		2h. violet	6·00	6·00
188M		3h. olive-yellow	4·75	4·75
189M		5h. deep green	6·00	6·00
190M		6h. brown	9·75	9·75
191M		10h. carmine	11·00	11·00
192M		20h. sepia	13·00	13·00
193M		25h. deep blue	25·00	25·00
194M		30h. green	30·00	30·00
195M		35h. deep green	30·00	30·00
196M		40h. orange	30·00	30·00
197M		45h. red	32·00	32·00
198M		50h. purple-brown	31·00	31·00
199M	5	1kr. lake	48·00	48·00
200M	6	2kr. myrtle-green	£120	£120
201M	7	5kr. grey-blue	£120	£120

Designs: As Type **4**—1h. View of Doboj; 2h. Mostar; 3h. The old castle, Jajce; 5h. Naretva pass and Prenz Planina; 6h. Valley of the Rama; 10h. Valley of the Vrbas; 20h. Old Bridge, Mostar; 25h. The Begova Djamia (Bey's Mosque, Sarajevo; 30h. Post by beast of burden; 35h. Village and lake, Jezero; 40h. Mail wagon; 45h. Bazaar at Sarajevo; 50h. Postal motor-car.

ANNEXED TO AUSTRIA-HUNGARY, 1908–18

Bosnia and Herzegovina were annexed on 6 October 1908.

20

21

1910 (18 Aug). 80th Birthday of Francis Joseph I. As 1906–07 issue but with date-label at foot as in T **20**/**21**. P 12½.

343	1h. black	70	40
344	2h. violet	70	40
345	3h. olive-yellow	70	40
346	5h. deep green	75	40
347	6h. brown	1·00	40
348	10h. carmine	80	15
349	20h. sepia	2·50	2·30
350	25h. deep blue	4·25	3·75
351	30h. green	4·00	3·75
352	35h. deep green	4·00	3·75
353	40h. orange	4·00	4·50
354	45h. red	6·00	7·25
355	50h. purple-brown	7·50	7·25
356	1k. lake	7·50	7·75
357	2k. myrtle-green	31·00	29·00
358	5k. grey-blue	3·25	9·75
343/358 *Set of 16*		70·00	75·00

IMPERFORATE STAMPS. Most issues from No. 359 exist imperforate, made for presentation purposes.

1912 (1 June). As T **4** (new values and views). P 12½.

359	12h. ultramarine (Jajce)	5·50	6·50
360	60h. greenish slate (Konjica)	3·00	5·50
361	72h. carmine (Vishegrad)	14·50	27·00

25

26

N **27** Girl in Bosnian Costume

(Des K. Moser. Eng F. Schirnböck. Recess)

1912 (4 Oct)–**14**. Various frames. The kronen values are larger (27×25 mm). P 12½.

362	25	1h. olive-green	40	15
363		2h. turquoise-blue	40	15
364		3h. lake	40	15
365		5h. green	40	15
366		6h. black	40	15
367		10h. carmine	40	15
368		12h. sage green	55	35
369		20h. brown	5·00	20
370		25h. ultramarine	2·50	20
371		30h. vermilion	2·50	20
372	26	35h. blackish green	2·50	20
373		40h. deep violet	8·00	20
374		45h. olive-brown	5·00	35
		a. Imperf between (horiz pair)	£150	
375		50h. Prussian blue	3·50	20
376		60h. purple-brown	2·50	20
377		72h. deep blue	5·00	5·25
378	25	1k. lake-brown/*cream*	15·00	65
379		2k. indigo/*blue*	9·00	85
380	26	3k. carmine/*green*	12·00	11·50
381		5k. indigo-lilac/*greyish*	25·00	29·00
382	25	10k. blue/*grey* (5.10.14)	£100	£130
362/382 *Set of 21*			£180	£160

1913 (15 Oct). NEWSPAPER. Typo. Imperf.

N383	N **27**	2h. ultramarine	65	1·10
N384		6h. mauve	2·30	3·50
N385		10h. carmine	2·75	3·50
N386		20h. green	3·00	3·75
N383/386 *Set of 4*			5·00	4·25

These stamps perf 11½ were issued in Yugoslavia (Nos. 25/8).

❖ 1915. ❖

1914.
12 Heller
(**29**) (Type a, 1 mm spacing, normal "H")

12 Heller.
(**30**)

There are three types of the "4" in "1914": (a) narrow, closed at top; (b) wide, ditto; (c) wide, open at top. The setting included 42 Type a, 7 Type b (positions 1, 17, 22, 26, 27, 34, 36) and 1 Type c (position 29).

1914 (1 Nov). As T **4**, surch as T **29**. P 12½.

383	7h. on 5h. deep green (R.) (a)	60	75
	a. Low bar to "H" (a) (pos. 35)	23·00	23·00
	b. Type b	4·75	4·00
	c. Type c	25·00	35·00
384	12h. on 10h. carmine (R.) (a)	60	75
	a. Low bar to "H" (a) (pos. 35)	23·00	23·00
	b. 2½ mm between lines instead of 1 mm (a) (pos. 14)	4·75	4·00
	c. Type b	4·75	4·00
	d. Type c	25·00	35·00

The "H" with the low bar also shows damage to the top of the left-hand upward stroke.

1915 (10 July). Similar surch but date "1915". P 12½.

385	7h. on 5h. deep green (R.)	11·00	16·00
	a. Perf 9½	£425	
386	12h. on 10h. carmine (B.)	40	55

1915 (9 Oct). T **25** surch as T **30**.

387	7h. on 5h. green (R.)	85	1·20
	a. Date twice; value omitted	34·00	60·00
388	12h. on 10h. carmine (B.)	1·90	3·50
	a. Error. 7h. on 10h.	47·00	95·00

1916 (19 Jan). T **25** surch as T **30**, but date "1916".

389	7h. on 5h. green (R.)	80	80
	a. No stop after "Heller"	80	80
390	12h. on 10h. carmine (B.)	80	1·00

Sheets of No. 389 have 46 stamps with stop after "Heller", 54 without stop.

The postal value of Nos. 383 to 390 was only 5 or 10h., the premium being devoted to War Charities.

31

32

1916 (10 July). War Invalids' Fund. P 12½.

391	31	5h.(+2h.) green	1·10	1·80
392	32	10h.(+2h.) claret	1·70	2·40

See also Nos. 434/5.

33

34

1916 (1–30 Oct). P 12½.

393	33	3h. black	45	35
		a. Imperf horiz (vert pair)		
394		5h. olive-green	60	60
395		6h. violet	60	60
396		10h. bistre	2·50	3·00
397		12h. slate	75	95
398		15h. rose (1 Oct)	50	25
399		20h. brown	90	95
400		25h. blue	80	95
401		30h. deep green	80	95
402		40h. vermilion	80	95
403		50h. deep green	80	95
404		60h. claret	80	95
405		80h. orange-brown (1 Oct)	2·00	80
		a. Perf 11½	6·25	12·50
406		90h. deep purple (1 Oct)	2·00	1·40
		a. Perf 11½	£950	
407	34	2k. brown/*straw*	1·20	2·75
408		3k. green/*blue*	1·60	4·00
409		4k. carmine/*green* (1 Oct)	7·00	16·00
410		10k. violet/*grey*	28·00	38·00
393/410 *Set of 18*			47·00	65·00

It is believed that No. 406a only exists unused, examples being discovered among the remainders in 1918.

N **35** Mercury

D **35**

WITWEN- UND 1917 WAISENWOCHE
(**35**)

(Des A. Cossmann. Recess)

1916 (25 Oct). NEWSPAPER EXPRESS. P 12½.

N411	N **35**	2h. vermilion	55	65
		a. Perf 11½×12½	£400	£600
N412		5h. olive-green	80	1·00
		a. Perf 11½	18·00	43·00

1916 (30 Oct)–**18**. POSTAGE DUE. P 12½.

D411	D **35**	2h. red (10.7.18)	60	1·20
D412		4h. red (10.7.18)	75	1·20
D413		5h. red	1·20	1·20
D414		6h. red (10.7.18)	55	1·40
D415		10h. red	80	1·20
D416		15h. red	6·25	9·00
D417		20h. red	80	1·40
D418		25h. red	2·75	3·50
D419		30h. red	2·75	3·50
D420		40h. red	31·00	22·00
D421		50h. red	70·00	65·00
D422		1k. blue	4·00	11·50
D423		3k. blue	16·00	43·00
D411/423 *Set of 13*			48·00	85·00

1917 (9 May). War Widows' Fund. Optd with T **35**.

411	33	10h.(+2h.) bistre	25	35
412		15h.(+2h.) rose	25	35

36 Design for Memorial Church, Sarajevo

37 Archduke Francis Ferdinand

(Des A. Cossmann. Typo)

1917 (28 June). Assassination of Archduke Ferdinand. Fund for Memorial Church at Sarajevo. T **36**/**37** and similar horiz design. P 12½.

413	36	10h.(+2h.) violet-black	25	40
		b. Perf 11½	1·70	4·75
414	37	15h.(+2h.) lake	25	40
		b. Perf 11½	1·70	4·75
		ba. Imperf between (vert (pair)		
415	–	40h.(+2h.) blue	25	40
		b. Perf 11½	1·70	4·75

Design:—40h. Francis Ferdinand and Sophie.

39 Emperor Charles

(Des A. Cossmann. Typo)

1917 (1 July). P 12½.

416	39	3h. olive-grey	40	30
		a. Perf 11½	£130	£250
		b. Perf 12½×11½	23·00	60·00
417		5h. olive-green	25	25
418		6h. violet	1·00	90
419		10h. orange-brown	40	15
420		12h. blue	1·10	90
421		15h. bright rose	25	15
422		20h. red-brown	50	25
423		25h. ultramarine	1·60	80
424		30h. black-green	70	40
425		40h. olive-bistre	60	40
426		50h. deep green	1·60	80
427		60h. carmine	1·60	80
		a. Perf 11½	27·00	60·00
428		80h. steel-blue	90	55
429		90h. lilac	2·00	1·80
		Larger type (25×25 mm). Different border		
430		2k. carmine/*straw*	1·50	80
431		3k. green/*blue*	21·00	29·00
432		4k. carmine/*green*	8·00	20·00
433		10k. violet/*grey*	4·00	21·00
416/433 *Set of 18*			43·00	70·00

1918 (1 Mar). War Invalids' Fund. P 12½.

434	32	10h.(+2h.) blue-green	1·30	1·70
435	31	15h.(+2h.) red-brown	1·30	1·70

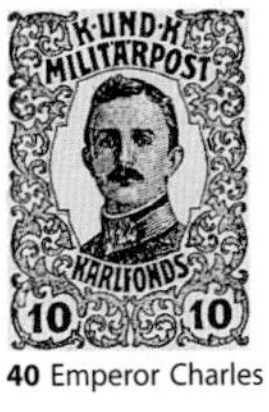

40 Emperor Charles

41 Empress Zita

1918
(**42**)

(Des A. Cossmann. Typo)

1918 (20 July). Emperor's Welfare Fund. P 12½×13.

436 **40** 10h.(+10h.) green........ 80 1·20
437 **41** 15h.(+10h.) chestnut........ 80 1·20
438 **40** 40h.(+10h.) purple........ 80 1·20

1918 (1 Sept). Nos. 344 and 363 optd with T **42**.

439 2h. violet (R.)........ 90 2·30
a. Opt inverted........ 75·00
440 2h. turquoise-blue (R.)........ 90 1·80
a. Opt inverted........ 75·00

In 1918, after the break-up of the Austro-Hungarian Empire, Bosnia and Herzegovina became part of the Kingdom of the Serbs, Croats and Slovenes, later renamed Yugoslavia. For overprinted stamps issued in 1918–19 before general issues for the Kingdom, see under Yugoslavia.

During the Second World War this region was incorporated into Croatia (q.v.). In 1945 Bosnia and Herzegovina became a constituent republic of the new federal Yugoslavia. Following the break-up of the Federation, Bosnia and Herzegovina declared itself independent on 5 April 1992 and achieved international recognition.

Hostilities subsequently broke out between the Croat, Moslem and Serbian inhabitants, which ultimately led to the establishment of three *de facto* administrations: the mainly Moslem Bosnian government, based in Sarajevo; the Croats in Mostar; and the Serbian Republic (Republika Srpska) in Pale.

Under the Dayton Agreement in November 1995 the Republic was split between a Moslem–Croat Federation and the Serbian Republic. This settlement was sponsored by N.A.T.O., whose military forces were deployed as peace-keepers.

I. SARAJEVO GOVERNMENT

The following issues were used for postal purposes in those areas controlled by the Sarajevo government.

1993. 100 Paras = 1 Dinar
1997. 100 Fennig = 1 Mark (= 100 (old) Dinars)

50 State Arms

51 Games Emblem

(Des Mulaomerović and Vasiljević. Litho Survey Dept, Sarajevo)

1993 (27 Oct). Imperf.

450 **50** 100d. ultramarine, lemon and greenish yellow........ 10 10
451 500d. ultramarine, lemon and salmon-pink........ 15 15
452 1000d. ultramarine, lemon and new blue........ 20 20
453 5000d. ultramarine, lemon and bright apple green........ 85 85
454 10000d. ultramarine, lemon and olive-yellow........ 1·70 1·70
455 20000d. ultramarine, lemon and olive-bistre........ 3·25 3·25
456 50000d. ultramarine, lemon and bluish grey........ 8·75 8·75
450/456 *Set of 7*........ 13·50 13·50

Nos. 450/6 were each supplied to post offices in booklets of 50.

(Des M. Kolobarić (457), F. Čatal, IMS/Studio 6 (**MS**458). Litho Survey Dept, Sarajevo)

1994 (8 Feb). Tenth Anniv of Winter Olympic Games, Sarajevo. T **51** and similar horiz designs. Multicoloured. Imperf.

457 **51** 50000d. black and yellow-orange........ 1·20 1·20
MS458 78×65 mm. 100000d. black, yellow-orange and deep lilac; 200000d. black, yellow-orange and deep lilac........ 9·75 9·75

Designs: 45×27 mm—100000d. Four-man bobsleigh; 200000d. Ice hockey.

No. 457 was issued in sheetlets of eight stamps and one label.

Currency Reform

10000 (old) Dinars = 1 (new) Diner

52 Koran Illustration

53 Façade

(Des M. Isanović. Litho Delo Ptg Wks, Ljubljana, Slovenia)

1995 (12 May). Bairam Festival. Sheet 105×50 mm containing T **52** and similar horiz design. Multicoloured. P 14.

MS459 400d. Type **52**; 600d. Koran illustration (different)........ 11·00 11·00

(Des Trio, Sarajevo. Litho Delo Ptg Wks, Ljubljana, Slovenia)

1995 (12 June). Sarajevo Head Post Office. T **53** and similar horiz designs. Multicoloured. P 14.

460 10d. Type **53**........ 10 10
a. Booklet pane. Nos. 460/6........ 5·25
461 20d. Interior........ 20 20
462 30d. As No. 461........ 25 25
463 35d. Before conflict........ 35 35
464 50d. As No. 463........ 55 55
465 100d. Present day........ 1·20 1·20
466 200d. As No. 465........ 2·40 2·40
460/466 *Set of 7*........ 4·50 4·50

54 Historical Map, 10th–15th Centuries

55 Postman and Globe

(Des E. Imamović and N. Čmajčanin. Litho Courvoisier)

1995 (12 Aug). Bosnian History. T **54** and similar multicoloured designs. P 11½.

467 35d. Type **54**........ 55 55
468 100d. 15th-century Bogomil tomb, Opličići (vert)........ 1·30 1·30
469 200d. Arms of Kotromanić Dynasty (14th–15th centuries) (vert)........ 2·40 2·40
470 300d. Charter by Ban Kulin of Bosnia, 1189........ 3·50 3·50
467/470 *Set of 4*........ 7·00 7·00

(Des S. Budalica and N. Meco. Litho Courvoisier)

1995 (25 Sept). World Post Day. P 11½.

471 **55** 100d. multicoloured........ 1·10 1·10

56 Dove with Olive Branch

57 Children and Buildings (A. Softić)

(Des S. Budalica and N. Meco. Litho Courvoisier)

1995 (25 Sept). Europa. Peace and Freedom. P 11½.

472 **56** 200d. multicoloured........ 3·50 3·50

(Litho Courvoisier)

1995 (12 Oct). Children's Week. P 11½.

473 **57** 100d. multicoloured........ 1·40 1·40

58 Tramcar, 1895

59 *Simphyandra hofmannii*

(Des M. Pepić. Litho Courvoisier)

1995 (12 Oct). Centenary of Sarajevo Electric Tram System. P 11½.

474 **58** 200d. multicoloured........ 2·75 2·75

(Des M. Pepić. Litho Courvoisier)

1995 (12 Oct). Flowers. T **59** and similar vert design. Multicoloured. P 11½.

475 100d. Type **59**........ 1·60 1·60
a. Pair. Nos. 475/6........ 4·50 4·50
476 200d. Turk's-head lily (*Lilium bosniacum*)........ 2·75 2·75

Nos. 475/6 were issued together in *se-tenant* pairs within the sheet.

60 *Aulopyge hügeli*

61 Kozija Bridge, Sarajevo

(Des M. Pepić. Litho Courvoisier)

1995 (12 Oct). Fish. T **60** and similar horiz design. Multicoloured. P 11½.

477 100d. Type **60**........ 1·60 1·60
a. Pair. Nos. 477/8........ 4·50 4·50
478 200d. *Paraphoxinus alepidotus*........ 2·75 2·75

Nos. 477/8 were issued together in *se-tenant* pairs within the sheet.

(Des B. Babić (20d.), Dž. Asad (30d.), F. Arifhodžić (35d.), S. Pezo (50d.), M. Mikulić (100d.). Litho Courvoisier)

1995 (15 Dec). Bridges. T **61** and similar horiz designs. Multicoloured. P 11½.

479 20d. Type **61**........ 20 20
480 30d. Arslanagića Bridge, Trebinje........ 35 35
481 35d. Latinska Bridge, Sarajevo........ 45 45
482 50d. Old bridge, Mostar........ 55 55
483 100d. Višegrad........ 1·10 1·10
479/483 *Set of 5*........ 2·40 2·40

62 Visiting Friends

63 Queen Jelena of Bosnia and Tomb (600th death anniv)

(Des E. Markičević and K. Mijić (100d.), K. Polić Pipal and G. Jurkić (200d.). Litho Courvoisier)

1995 (24 Dec). Christmas. T **62** and similar multicoloured design. P 11½.

484 100d. Type **62**........ 1·10 1·10
485 200d. Madonna and Child (vert)........ 2·20 2·20

(Des N. Čmajčanin and E. Imamović (30d.), M. Pepić (others). Litho Courvoisier)

1995 (31 Dec). T **63** and similar multicoloured designs. P 11½.

486 30d. Type **63**........ 35 35
487 35d. Husein Kapetan Gradaščević, "Dragon of Bosnia" (leader of 1831 uprising against Turkey)........ 45 45
488 100d. Mirza Safvet Bašagić (125th death anniv) (horiz)........ 1·10 1·10

64 Places of Worship and Graveyards

65 Stadium and Sports

(Des A. Nuhanović. Litho Courvoisier)

1995 (31 Dec). Religious Pluralism. P 11½.

489 **64** 35d. multicoloured........ 80 80

(Des M. Pepić. Litho Courvoisier)

1995 (31 Dec). Destruction of Olympic Stadium, Sarajevo. T **65** and similar multicoloured design. P 11½.

490 35d. Type **65**........ 45 45
491 100d. Stadium ablaze (vert)........ 1·60 1·60

66 Bahrija Hadžić (opera singer)

67 Child's Handprint

(Des N. Čmajčanin (80d.), M. Pepić (120d.). Litho Courvoisier)

1996 (15 Apr). Europa. Famous Women. T **66** and similar vert design. Multicoloured. P 15.

492 80d. Type **66**........ 1·30 1·30
493 120d. Nasiha Hadžić (children's writer and radio presenter)........ 2·00 2·00

(Des Group "MI" (150d.). Litho Courvoisier)

1996 (15 Apr). 50th Anniv of United Nations Children's Fund. T **67** and similar vert design. Multicoloured. P 11½.

494 50d. Child stepping on landmine (P. Mirna and K. Princes)........ 55 55
a. Pair. Nos. 494/5........ 2·30 2·30
495 150d. Type **67**........ 1·60 1·60

Nos. 494/5 were issued together in *se-tenant* pairs within the sheet.

68 Bobovac Castle

69 Roofed Fountain and Extract from Holy Koran

(Des N. Čmajčanin. Litho Courvoisier)

1996 (5 May). P 11½.

496 **68** 35d. black, blue and dull violet........ 60 60

(Des M. Pepić and O. Pavlović. Litho Delo Ptg Wks, Ljubljana, Slovenia)

1996 (5 May). Bairam Festival. P 14.

497 **69** 80d. multicoloured........ 1·10 1·10

No. 497 was issued in sheetlets of two stamps.

70 Town Hall

71 Hands on Computer Keyboard and Title Page of *Bosanki Prijatelj*

(Des N. Čmajčanin. Litho Courvoisier)

1996 (5 May). Centenary of Sarajevo Town Hall. P 11.
498 **70** 80d. multicoloured .... 1·10 1·10

(Des M. Pepić. Litho Courvoisier)

1996 (5 May). 150th Anniv of Journalists' Association. P 11½.
499 **71** 100d. multicoloured .... 1·30 1·30

72 Essen

73 Running

(Des M. Pepić. Litho Courvoisier)

1996 (25 May). Essen 96 International Stamp Fair, Essen. P 12.
500 **72** 200d. multicoloured .... 2·50 2·50

(Des O. Pavlović. Litho Courvoisier)

1996 (25 May). Centenary of Modern Olympic Games and Olympic Games, Atlanta. T **73** and similar vert designs. Multicoloured. P 11½.
501 30d. Type **73** 35 35
a. Block of 4. Nos. 501/4 .... 3·25
502 35d. Games emblem 40 40
503 80d. Torch and Olympic flag 85 85
504 120d. Pierre de Coubertin (founder) .... 1·30 1·30
501/504 *Set of 4* .... 2·50 2·50
Nos. 501/4 were issued together in *se-tenant* blocks of four stamps within the sheet, the backgrounds of which form a composite design of ancient Greek athletes.

74 *Campanula hercegovina*

75 Barak

(Des O. Pavlović. Litho Courvoisier)

1996 (10 July). Flowers. T **74** and similar vert design. Multicoloured. P 11½.
505 30d. Type **74** 40 40
a. Pair. Nos. 505/6 .... 90 90
506 35d. *Iris bosniaca* 45 45
Nos. 505/6 were issued together in *se-tenant* pairs within the sheet.

(Des O. Pavlović. Litho Courvoisier)

1996 (10 July). Dogs. T **75** and similar horiz design. Multicoloured. P 11½.
507 35d. Type **75** 45 45
a. Pair. Nos. 507/8 .... 1·40 1·40
508 80d. Tornjak 85 85
Nos. 507/8 were issued together in *se-tenant* pairs within the sheet.

76 Globe, Telephone and Alexander Bell

77 Charter with Seal

(Des O. Pavlović (80d.). Litho Courvoisier)

1996 (10 July). Anniversaries. T **76** and similar horiz design. Multicoloured. P 11½.
509 80d. Type **76** (120th anniv of Bell's invention of telephone) .... 1·00 1·00
510 120d. 1910 50h. stamp (centenary of post vans in Bosnia and Herzegovina) .... 1·40 1·40

(Des N. Čmajčanin. Litho Courvoisier)

1996 (10 July). Granting of Privileges to Dubrovnik by Ban Stepan II Kotromanić, 1333. P 11½.
511 **77** 100d. multicoloured .... 1·20 1·20

78 Hot-air Balloons

79 Moslem Costume of Bjelašnice

(Des F. Rapa. Litho Courvoisier)

1996 (1 Sept). SOS Children's Village, Sarajevo. P 11½.
512 **78** 100d. multicoloured .... 1·20 1·20

(Des N. Čmajčanin. Litho Courvoisier)

1996 (20 Sept). Traditional Costumes. T **79** and similar vert designs. Multicoloured. P 11½.
513 50d. Type **79** 55 55
a. Strip. Nos. 513/15 plus label .... 3·50
514 80d. Croatian .... 1·10 1·10
515 100d. Moslem Costume of Sarajevo .... 1·60 1·60
513/515 *Set of 3* .... 3·00 3·00
Nos. 513/15 were issued together in *se-tenant* strips of three stamps and one inscribed label within the sheet.

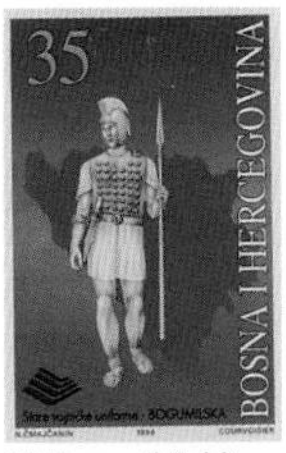

80 Bogomil Soldier

81 Mosque

(Des N. Čmajčanin and I. Hakžić (10d.), N. Čmajčanin (others). Litho Courvoisier)

1996 (20 Sept). Military Uniforms. T **80** and similar vert designs. Multicoloured. P 11½.
516 35d. Type **80** 45 45
a. Strip of 4. Nos. 516/19 .... 4·00
517 80d. Austro-Hungarian rifleman 85 85
518 100d. Turkish light cavalryman .... 1·10 1·10
519 120d. Medieval Bosnian king .... 1·40 1·40
516/519 *Set of 4* .... 3·50 3·50
Nos. 516/19 were issued together in *se-tenant* strips of four stamps within the sheet.

(Des M. Pepić. Litho Courvoisier)

1996 (25 Nov). Winter Festival, Sarajevo. P 11½.
520 **81** 100d. multicoloured .... 1·20 1·20

82 Map and State Arms

83 Crowd around Baby Jesus

(Des M. Pepić. Litho Courvoisier)

1996 (25 Nov). Bosnia Day. P 11½.
521 **82** 120d. multicoloured .... 1·40 1·40

(Des I. Lacković. Litho Courvoisier)

1996 (21 Dec). Christmas. P 11½.
522 **83** 100d. multicoloured .... 1·30 1·30

84 Pope John Paul II

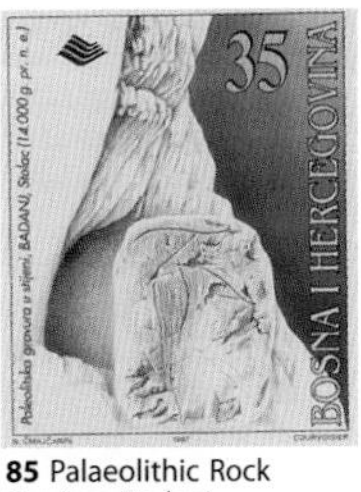

85 Palaeolithic Rock Carving, Badanj

(Des O. Pavlović. Litho Delo Ptg Wks, Ljubljana, Slovenia)

1996 (21 Dec). Papal Visit. P 14.
523 **84** 500d. multicoloured .... 7·25 7·25

(Des N. Čmajčanin. Litho Courvoisier)

1997 (31 Mar). Archaeological Finds. T **85** and similar vert designs. Multicoloured. P 15.
524 35d. Type **85** 45 45
525 50d. Neolithic ceramic head, Butmir 65 65
526 80d. Bronze Age "birds" wagon, Glasinac .... 1·10 1·10
524/526 *Set of 3* .... 2·00 2·00
MS527 100×72 mm. 100, 120d. Walls of Illyrian town of Daorson (composite design) .... 2·75 2·75

86 Ferhad Pasha Mosque, Banja Luka

87 "Clown" (Martina Nokto)

(Des N. Čmajčanin. Litho Courvoisier)

1997 (15 Apr). Bairam Festival. P 11½.
528 **86** 200d. multicoloured .... 2·50 2·50

(Litho Courvoisier)

1997 (15 Apr). Children's Week. P 11½.
529 **87** 100d. multicoloured .... 1·20 1·20

88 Komadina

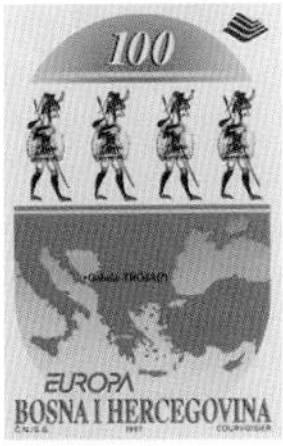

89 Trojan Warriors and Map

(Des M. Pepić. Litho Delo Ptg Wks, Ljubljana, Slovenia)

1997 (25 Apr). 72nd Death Anniv of Mujaga Komadina (developer and Mayor of Mostar). P 14.
530 **88** 100d. multicoloured .... 1·20 1·20

(Des N. Čmajčanin (100d.), Dž. Asad (120d.). Litho Courvoisier)

1997 (3 May). Europa. Tales and Legends. T **89** and similar vert design. Multicoloured. P 11½.
531 100d. Type **89** (theory of Roberto Prays) .... 1·60 1·60
532 120d. Man on prayer-mat and castle (The Miraculous Spring of Ajvatovica) .... 1·70 1·70

90 *Rainbow Warrior*

(Litho Courvoisier)

1997 (25 May). 26th Anniv of Greenpeace (environmental organization). T **90** and similar horiz designs showing the *Rainbow Warrior*. Multicoloured. P 11½.
533 35d. Type **90** 45 45
a. Block of 4. Nos. 533/6 .... 4·25
534 80d. Inscr "Dorreboom" 85 85
535 100d. Inscr "Beltra" .... 1·20 1·20
536 120d. Inscr "Morgan" .... 1·40 1·40
533/536 *Set of 4* .... 3·50 3·50
Nos. 533/6 were issued in *se-tenant* blocks of four within the sheet.

91 Open Air Cinema, Sarajevo

92 Games Emblem

(Des Obala. Litho Courvoisier)

1997 (15 June). Third International Film Festival, Sarajevo. P 11½.
537 **91** 110d. multicoloured .... 1·20 1·20

(Des N. Agdal. Litho Courvoisier)

1997 (15 June). Mediterranean Games, Bari. T **92** and similar vert design. Multicoloured. P 11½.
538 40d. Type **92** 45 45
539 130d. Boxing, basketball and kick boxing .... 1·40 1·40

93 Diagram of Electrons

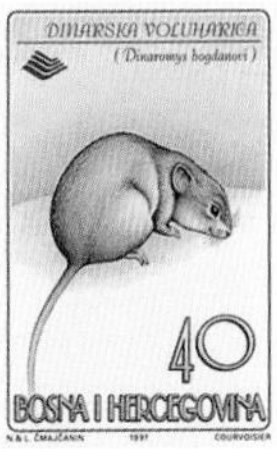

94 Vole (*Dinaromys bogdanovi*)

(Des M. Sarić (40d.), O. Pavlović (110d.), V. Raspudić (130d.), M. Pepić (150d). Litho Courvoisier)

1997 (25 June). Anniversaries and Event. T **93** and similar multicoloured designs. P 11½.

540 40d. Type **93** (centenary of discovery of electrons) 75 75
541 110d. Vasco da Gama (navigator) and map (500th anniv of science of navigation) (vert) .... 1·60 1·60
542 130d. Airmail envelope and airplane (Stamp Day) .... 1·80 1·80
543 150d. Steam locomotive Bosna (125th anniv of railway in Bosnia and Herzegovina) .... 2·00 2·00
540/543 *Set of* 4 .... 5·50 5·50

(Des N. and L. Čmajčanin (544, 546), N. Čmajčanin (others). Litho Courvoisier)

1997 (25 Aug). Flora and Fauna. T **94** and similar vert designs. Multicoloured. P 11½.

544 40d. Type **94** ....
a. Horiz pair. Nos. 544 and 546 .... 55 55
545 40d. *Oxytropis prenja* 55 55
a. Horiz pair. Nos. 545 and 547 .... 2·40 2·40
546 80d. Alpine newt (*Triturus alpestris*) .... 1·10 1·10
547 110d. *Dianthus freynii* .... 1·60 1·60
544/547 *Set of* 4 .... 3·50 3·50

Nos. 544 and 546 were issued together in horizontal se- tenant pairs within the sheet; Nos. 545 and 547 were similarly arranged.

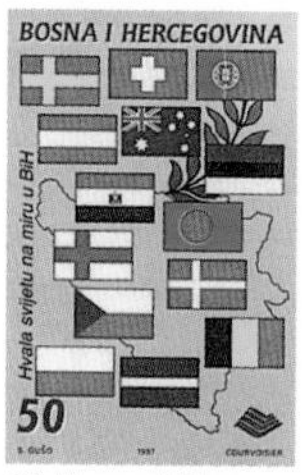

95 Map and Flags

96 House with Attic

(Des S. Gušo. Litho Courvoisier)

1997 (25 Aug). International Peace Day. T **95** and similar vert designs. Multicoloured. P 11½.

548 50d. Type **95** 55 55
a. Horiz strip of 4. Nos. 548/51 .... 3·50
549 60d. Flags and right half of globe showing Europe and Africa 65 65
550 70d. Flags and left half of globe showing the Americas 75 75
551 110d. Map and flags (including U.S.A. and U.K.) .... 1·20 1·20
548/551 *Set of* 4 .... 2·75 2·75

Nos. 548/51 were issued together in horizontal *se-tenant* strips of four stamps, Nos. 549/5 forming a composite design.

(Des N. Čmajčanin. Litho Courvoisier)

1997 (15 Sept). Architecture. T **96** and similar horiz designs. Multicoloured. P 11½.

552 40d. Type **96** 45 45
553 50d. Tiled stove and door 55 55
554 130d. Three-storey house .... 1·40 1·40
552/554 *Set of* 3 .... 2·20 2·20

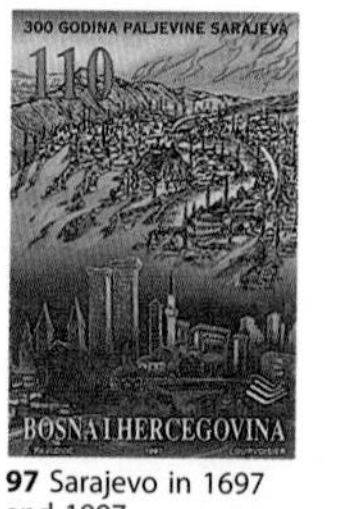

97 Sarajevo in 1697 and 1997

98 Augustin Tin Ujević

(Des O. Pavlović. Litho Courvoisier)

1997 (15 Sept). 300th Anniv of Great Fire of Sarajevo. P 11½.

555 **97** 110d. multicoloured .... 2·40 2·40

New Currency

100 Fennig = 1 Mark (= 100 (old) Dinars)

(Des M. Pepić (1d.30), M. Čmajčanin (2d.). Litho Courvoisier)

1997 (1 Nov). Personalities. T **98** and similar multicoloured design. P 11½.

556 1m.30 Type **98** (lyricist and essayist) .... 1·30 1·30
557 2m. Zaim Imamović (singer) (vert) .... 2·20 2·20

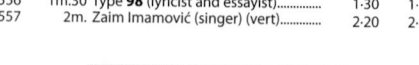

99 Sarajevo and Corps Emblem

(Des A. Adamo. Litho Delo Ptg Wks, Ljubljana, Slovenia)

1997 (1 Nov). Contribution of Italian Pioneer Corps in Reconstruction of Sarajevo. P 14.

558 **99** 1m.40 multicoloured .... 1·60 1·60

100 Diana, Princess of Wales, and Roses

(Des N. Čmajčanin. Litho German State Ptg Wks, Berlin)

1997 (3 Nov). Diana, Princess of Wales, Commemoration. P 14.

559 **100** 2m.50 multicoloured .... 5·50 5·50

101 "Gnijezdo" (Fikret Libovac)

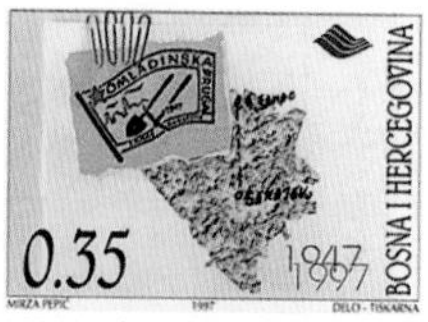

102 Youth Builders Emblem attached to Route Map

(Litho Courvoisier)

1997 (6 Nov). Art. T **101** and similar horiz design. Multicoloured. P 11½.

560 35f. Type **101** 35 35
561 80f. "Sarajevo Library" (sculpture, Nusret Pašić) 85 85

(Des M. Pepić. Litho Delo Ptg Wks, Ljubljana, Slovenia)

1997 (17 Nov). 50th Anniv of Šamac–Sarajevo Railway. P 14.

562 **102** 35f. multicoloured 45 45

103 Nativity (icon)

104 Slalom, Luge, Two-man Bobsleigh and Speed Skating

(Des S. Gušo (564). Litho Courvoisier)

1997 (22 Dec). Religious Events. T **103** and similar vert designs. Multicoloured. P 11½.

563 50f. Type **103** (Orthodox Christmas) 65 65
564 1m.10 Wreath on door (Christmas) .... 1·30 1·30
565 1m.10 Pupils before teacher (14th-century miniature) (Haggadah) .... 1·30 1·30
563/565 *Set of* 3 .... 3·00 3·00

(Des N. Agdal. Litho Delo Ptg Wks, Ljubljana, Slovenia)

1998 (15 Jan). Winter Olympic Games, Nagano, Japan. Sheet 78×60 mm containing T **104** and similar vert design. Multicoloured. P 14.

MS566 35f. Type **104**; 1m. Games emblem .... 1·60 1·60

105 Mosque Fountain

(Des M. Varupa and M. Sarić. Litho Delo Ptg Wks, Ljubljana, Slovenia)

1998 (28 Jan). Bairam Festival. P 14.

567 **105** 1m. multicoloured .... 1·10 1·10

106 Zvornik

(Des N. Čmajčanin. Litho Delo Ptg Wks, Ljubljana, Slovenia)

1998 (20 Mar). Old Fortified Towns. Booklet stamps. T **106** and similar horiz designs. Multicoloured. P 14.

568 35f. Type **106** 55 55
a. Booklet pane. Nos. 568/71 .... 5·00
569 70f. Bihać .... 1·10 1·10
570 1m. Počitelj .... 1·40 1·40
571 1m.20 Gradačac .... 1·60 1·60
568/571 *Set of* 4 .... 4·25 4·25

107 Muradbegović

108 Branislav Djurdjev

(Des S. Cěrkez and R. Vesna. Litho Delo Ptg Wks, Ljubljana, Slovenia)

1998 (20 Mar). Birth Centenary of Ahmed Muradbegović (dramatist and actor-director). P 14.

572 **107** 1m.50 multicoloured .... 1·60 1·60

(Des M. Ibrahimpašić. Litho Courvoisier)

1998 (5 May). Former Presidents of the University of Arts and Science. T **108** and similar vert designs. Multicoloured. P 11½.

573 40f. Type **108** 45 45
574 70f. Alojz Benac 75 75
575 1m.30 Edhem Čamo .... 1·40 1·40
573/575 *Set of* 3 .... 2·30 2·30

109 White Storks

110 International Theatre Festival, Sarajevo

(Des N. Čmajčanin and O. Pavlović. Litho Courvoisier)

1998 (5 May). Endangered Species. The White Stork (*Ciconia ciconia*). T **109** and similar vert designs. Multicoloured. P 11½.

576 70f. Type **109** .... 1·10 1·10
a. Block or strip of 4. Nos. 576/9 .... 5·75
577 90f. Two storks flying .... 1·40 1·40
578 1m.10 Two adult storks on nest .... 1·50 1·50
579 1m.30 Adult stork with young .... 1·60 1·60
576/579 *Set of* 4 .... 5·00 5·00

Nos. 576/9 were issued together in *se-tenant* blocks and strips of four stamps within the sheet.

(Des N. Amela. Litho Courvoisier)

1998 (5 May). Europa. National Festivals. P 11½.

580 **110** 1m.10 multicoloured .... 2·75 2·75

113 Common Morel (*Morchella esculenta*)

114 Tunnel

(Des T. Kuzmanović. Litho Courvoisier)

1998 (30 July). Fungi. T **113** and similar vert designs. Multicoloured. P 11½.

585 50f. Type **113** 55 55
586 80f. Chanterelle (*Cantharellus cibarius*) 85 85
587 1m.10 Edible mushroom (*Boletus edulis*) .... 1·20 1·20
588 1m.35 Caesar's mushroom (*Amanita caesarea*) .... 1·40 1·40
585/588 *Set of* 4 .... 3·50 3·50

(Des A. Mržljak. Litho Courvoisier)

1998 (30 July). Fifth Anniv of Sarajevo's Supply Tunnels. P 11½.

589 **114** 1m.10 multicoloured .... 1·10 1·10

115 Eiffel Tower and Underground Train

116 Henri Dunant (founder of Red Cross)

(Des D. Karkin. Litho Courvoisier)

1998 (30 Aug). Paris Metro. P 11½.

590 **115** 2m. multicoloured .... 2·20 2·20

(Des M. Žmukić. Litho Courvoisier)

1998 (14 Sept). Anti-tuberculosis Week. P 14.
591 **116** 50f. multicoloured 55 55

117 Vesna Mišanović **118** Travnik

(Des N. Stojanović and F. Strik (40f.), N. Stojanović (others). Litho Delo Ptg Wks, Ljubljana, Slovenia)

1998 (24 Sept). Bosnian and Herzegovina Chess Teams. Sheet 109×88 mm containing T **117** and similar horiz designs. Multicoloured. P 14.
MS592 20f. Type **117** (silver medal, tenth European Team Championship, Debrecen, 1992); 40f. Men's team (silver medal winners, 31st Chess Olympiad, Moscow, 1994); 60f. Women's team (32nd Chess Olympiad, Yerevan, 1996); 80f. National team (11th European Team championship, Pula, 1997) 2·20 2·20

(Des M. Gerstenhofer. Litho Delo Ptg Wks, Ljubljana, Slovenia)

1998 (24 Sept). Old Towns. T **118** and similar horiz design. P 14.
593 5f. black and pale green 10 10
597 38f. black and pale cinnamon 45 45
Design:—38f. Sarajevo. Numbers have been left for possible additions to this series.

119 Postal Workers in New Uniforms **120** Lutes

(Des E. Halilagić. Litho Courvoisier)

1998 (9 Oct). World Post Day. P 11½.
605 **119** 1m. multicoloured .... 1·10 1·10

(Des J. Vranić. Litho Courvoisier)

1998 (23 Oct). Musical Instruments. P 11½.
606 **120** 80f. multicoloured 85 85

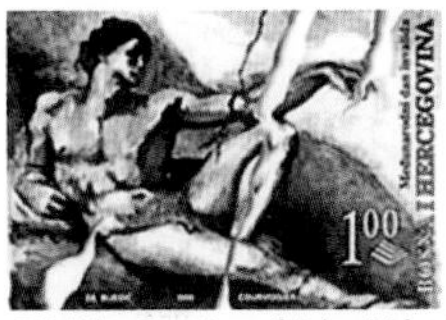

121 "The Creation of Adam" (detail of fresco on ceiling of Sistine Chapel, Michelangelo)

(Des Dž. Bijedić. Litho Courvoisier)

1998 (3 Dec). World Disabled Day. P 11½.
607 **121** 1m. multicoloured .... 1·60 1·60

122 Bjelašnica Mountain Range

(Des B. Sumenić-Bajić. Litho Courvoisier)

1998 (3 Dec). P 11½.
608 **122** 1m. multicoloured .... 1·10 1·10

123 People

(Des M. Pepić. Litho Courvoisier)

1998 (10 Dec). 50th Anniv of Universal Declaration of Human Rights. P 15.
609 **123** 1m.35 multicoloured .... 1·60 1·60

124 Christmas Tree (Lamija Pehilj) **125** Sarajevo University and "Proportion of Man" (Leonardo da Vinci)

(Des G. Jurkić and B. Sumenić-Bajić (1m. 50). Litho Courvoisier)

1998 (18 Dec). Christmas and New Year. T **124** and similar multicoloured design. P 11½.
610 1m. Type **124** .... 1·10 1·10
611 1m.50 Father Andeo Zvizdović .... 1·60 1·60

(Des M. Ibrahimpašić. Litho Courvoisier)

1999 (22 Apr). Anniversaries. T **125** and similar multicoloured design. P 11½.
612 40f. Type **125** (50th anniv) 45 45
613 40f. Sarajevo High School (120th anniv) (horiz) 45 45

126 Pigeons **127** Astronaut, Earth and Moon

(Des N. Čmajčanin (80l.), N and L. Čmajčanin (1m.10) . Litho Courvoisier)

1999 (22 Apr). Flora and Fauna. T **126** and similar horiz design. Multicoloured. P 11½.
614 80f. Type **126** .... 1·10 1·10
615 1m.10 Knautia sarajevensis .... 1·60 1·60

(Des O. Pavlović. Litho Courvoisier)

1999 (20 May). 30th Anniv of First Manned Moon Landing. P 11½.
616 **127** 2m. multicoloured .... 2·20 2·20

128 Slapovi Une

(Des M. Delić. Litho Courvoisier)

1999 (20 May). Europa. Parks and Gardens. P 11½.
617 **128** 2m. multicoloured .... 3·25 3·25

129 Gorazde **130** Children playing Football in Sun (Pranjković Nenad)

(Des M. Garibija. Litho Delo Ptg Wks, Ljubljana, Slovenia)

1999 (9 June). P 14.
618 **129** 40f. multicoloured 45 45

(Litho Courvoisier)

1999 (15 June). Children's Week. P 11½.
619 **130** 50f. multicoloured 55 55

131 House **132** Church, Mosque and Emblem

(Des S. Pezo. Litho Courvoisier)

1999 (15 June). World Environment Day. P 11½.
620 **131** 80f. multicoloured 85 85

(Des D. Karkin. Litho Courvoisier)

1999 (15 June). Philexfrance 99 International Stamp Exhibition, Paris, France. P 11½.
621 **132** 2m. multicoloured .... 2·20 2·20

133 Sarajevo on Stamp **134** Letters encircling Globe and Telephones

(Des Dž. Asad. Litho Courvoisier)

1999 (1 July). 120th Anniv of First Bosnia and Herzegovina Stamps. P 11½.
622 **133** 1m. multicoloured .... 1·10 1·10

(Des N. Agdal. Litho Courvoisier)

1999 (1 July). 125th Anniv of Universal Postal Union. P 11½.
623 **134** 1m.50 multicoloured .... 1·60 1·60

135 Tuzlait from Tušanj **136** Dove and Cathedral

(Des A. Suljević. Litho Courvoisier)

1999 (27 July). Minerals. T **135** and similar multicoloured designs. P 11½.
624 40f. Type **135** 45 45
625 60f. Siderit from Vitez 65 65
626 1m.20 Hijelofan from Busovača .... 1·30 1·30
627 1m.80 Quartz from Srebrenica (vert) .... 2·00 2·00
624/627 *Set of 4* .... 4·00 4·00

(Des N. Čmajčanin. Litho Delo Ptg Wks, Ljubljana, Slovenia)

1999 (29 July). Southern Europe Stability Pact, Sarajevo. P 14.
628 **136** 2m. multicoloured .... 2·20 2·20

137 Kursûm Medresa, Sarajevo, 1537 (site of library) **138** Koran, 1550

(Des M. Garibija (1m.). Litho Courvoisier)

1999 (23 Sept). Gazi-Husref Library. T **137** and similar vert design. Multicoloured. P 11½.
629 1m. Type **137** .... 1·10 1·10
630 1m.10 Miniature from Hval Codex, 1404 .... 1·20 1·20

1999 (23 Sept). Litho. P 12×11½.
631 **138** 1m.50 multicoloured .... 1·60 1·60

139 X-Ray and Thermal Image of Hands **140** Kreševljaković

1999 (7 Oct). Centenary of Radiology in Bosnia and Herzegovina. Litho. P 11½.
632 **139** 90f. multicoloured .... 1·00 1·00

(Des M. Garibija. Litho Courvoisier)

1999 (7 Oct). 40th Death Anniv of Hamdija Kreševljaković (historian). P 11½.
633 **140** 1m.30 multicoloured .... 1·40 1·40

141 Chess Emblems and Stars

(Des N. Stojanović and M. Ibrahimpašić. Litho Delo Ptg Wks, Ljubljana, Slovenia)

1999 (29 Oct). 15th European Chess Clubs Championship Final, Bugojno. P 14.
634 **141** 1m.10 multicoloured .... 1·20 1·20

142 Twipsy (exhibition mascot)

(Des F. Săbanović. Litho Courvoisier)

1999 (9 Nov). Expo 2000 World's Fair, Hanover, Germany. P 12×11½.

635	**142**	1m. multicoloured	1·10	1·10

143 Painting (Afan Ramić)

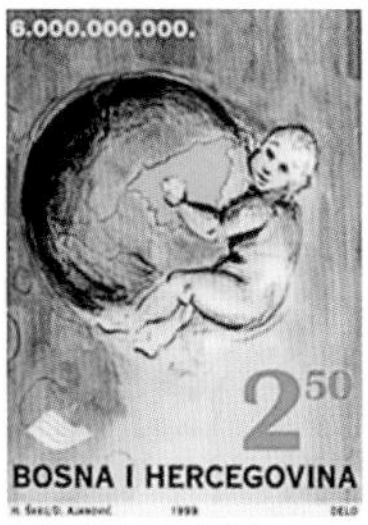

144 Globe and Baby

(Litho Courvoisier)

1999 (25 Nov). P 12×11½.

636	**143**	1m.20 multicoloured	1·30	1·30

(Des H. Škec and D. Ajanović. Litho Delo Ptg Wks, Ljubljana, Slovenia)

1999 (25 Nov). Birth of World's Six Billionth Inhabitant in Sarajevo. P 14.

637	**144**	2m.50 multicoloured	2·75	2·75

145 Bjelašnica Observatory

146 Philharmonic Orchestra Building, Sarajevo

(Des M. Garibija. Litho Delo Ptg Wks, Ljubljana, Slovenia)

1999 (15 Dec). 105th Anniv of Bjelašnica Meteorological Observatory. Sheet 100×60 mm. P 14.

MS638 **145** 1m.10 multicoloured		1·20	1·20

(Des A. Šehić. Litho Delo Ptg Wks, Ljubljana, Slovenia)

1999 (20 Dec). International Music Festival, Sarajevo. T **146** and similar vert design. P 14.

639	40f. black and orange-vermilion	45	45
640	1m.10 multicoloured	1·20	1·20

Design:—1m.10 Festival poster.

147 Woman

148 Map of Bosnia and Herzegovina and Emblem

(Des M. Berber. Litho Courvoisier)

2000 (15 Mar). Bairam Festival. P 11½×12.

641	**147**	1m.10 multicoloured	1·20	1·20

(Des S. Gušo. Litho Courvoisier)

2000 (10 Apr). Olympic Games, Sydney. Sheet 104×72 mm containing T **147** and similar horiz design. Multicoloured. P 15.

MS642 1m.30 Type **147**; 1m.70 Map of Australia and stylized sailing boats	3·25	3·25

149 Spaho

150 Morse Apparatus

(Des M. Ibrahimpašić. Litho Courvoisier)

2000 (15 Apr). 60th (1999) Death Anniv of Mehmed Spaho (politician). P 11½×12.

643	**149**	1m. multicoloured	1·10	1·10

(Des M. Pepić. Photo Courvoisier)

2000 (15 Apr). 50th Anniv of Amateur Radio in Bosnia and Herzegovina. P 11½×12.

644	**150**	1m.50 multicoloured	1·60	1·60

151 Illuminated Manuscript

152 Boračko River

(Des T. Jesenković. Litho Courvoisier)

2000 (15 Apr). 50th Anniv of Institute of Oriental Studies, Sarajevo University. P 11½×12.

645	**151**	2m. multicoloured	2·20	2·20

(Des M. Brdarić. Photo Courvoisier)

2000 (9 May). 15th Anniv of Emerald River Nature Protection Organization. T **152** and similar multicoloured design. P 12×11½ (40f.) or 11½ ×12 (1m.).

646	40f. Type **151**	65	65
647	1m. Figure of woman and river (vert)	1·70	1·70

153 Scorpionfish

(Litho Courvoisier)

2000 (9 May). Greenpeace (environmental organization). Sheet 100×72 mm containing T **153** and similar horiz designs. Multicoloured. P 12×11½.

MS648 50f. Type **153**; 60f. Crayfish; 90f. Crimson anemone; 1m.50 Wreck of *Rainbow Warrior* (campaign ship)	3·75	3·75

154 Griffon Vulture (*Gyps fulvus*)

(Des N. Čmajčanin. Photo Courvoisier)

2000 (9 May). Birds. T **154** and similar horiz design. Multicoloured. P 12×11½.

649	1m. Type **154**	1·10	1·10
650	1m.50 White spoonbill (*Platalea leucorodia*)	1·60	1·60

155 "Building Europe"

(Des J.-P. Cousin. Photo Courvoisier)

2000 (9 May). Europa. P 11½×12.

651	**155**	2m. multicoloured	3·00	3·00

156 Count Ferdinand von Zeppelin and LZ-1 (first airship)

(Des O. Resić. Photo Courvoisier)

2000 (10 June). Centenary of Zeppelin Airships. P 11½.

652	**156**	1m.50 multicoloured	1·60	1·60

157 Zenica

158 Millennium

(Des M. Gerstenhofer. Litho Delo Ptg Wks, Ljubljana, Slovenia)

2000 (9 June). Towns. T **157** and similar multicoloured designs. P 14.

653	50f. Type **157**	55	55
654	1m. Mostar	1·10	1·10
655	1m.10 Bihać	1·20	1·20
656	1m.50 Tuzla (vert)	1·60	1·60
653/656 *Set of 4*		4·00	4·00

(Des M. Zaimović. Litho Courvoisier)

2000 (20 Sept). New Millennium. Sheet 100×72 mm containing T **158** and similar multicoloured design. P 12.

MS657 80f. Type **158**; 1m.20 Millennium (57×57 mm)	2·20	2·20

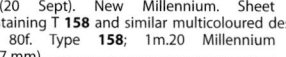

159 Vranduk

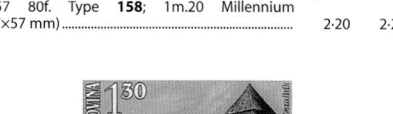

(Des S. Obralić (1m. 30), B. Sumenić-Bajić (1m. 50). Photo Courvoisier)

2000 (20 Sept). Towns. T **159** and similar horiz design. Multicoloured. P 12×11½.

658	1m.30 Type **159**	1·50	1·50
659	1m.50 Franciscan Abbey, Kraljeva Sutjeska.	1·70	1·70

160 Tom Sawyer, Hucklberry Finn (characters) and Mark Twain

(Des O. Pavlović. Litho Courvoisier)

2000 (20 Sept). *The Adventures of Tom Sawyer* (children's book by Mark Twain). P 12×11½.

660	**160**	1m.50 multicoloured	1·60	1·60

161 People walking (Ismet Mujezinović)

162 Children and Globe

(Litho Courvoisier)

2000 (5 Oct). Paintings. T **161** and similar horiz design. Multicoloured. P 12×11½.

661	60f. Type **161**	65	65
662	80f. Trees (Ivo Šeremet)	85	85

(Des I. Kojović. Litho Courvoisier)

2000 (5 Oct). International Children's Week. P 11½×12.

663	**162**	1m.60 multicoloured	1·70	1·70

163 Refugees

(Des M. Gerstenhofer. Litho Courvoisier)

2000 (14 Dec). 50th Anniv of United Nations Commissioner for Refugees. P 12×11½.

664	**163**	1m. multicoloured	1·10	1·10

164 Tušanj **165** Horse wearing Skirt

(Des M. Gerstenhofer. Litho Delo Ptg Wks, Ljubljana, Slovenia)

2001 (22 Mar). Towns. T **164** and similar multicoloured designs. P 14.

665	10f. Type **164**	10	10
666	20f. Bugojno (horiz)	20	20
667	30f. Konjic (horiz)	35	35
668	35f. Živinice (horiz)	45	45
669	2m. Cazin (horiz)	2·20	2·20
665/669	*Set of* 5	4·00	4·00

(Des Kurt & Plasto ID Nikšić. Litho Courvoisier)

2001 (22 Mar). Thelma (cartoon character). Sheet 125×170 mm containing T **165** and similar vert designs. Multicoloured. Fluorescent coated granite paper. P 12×11½.

MS670 30f. Type **165**; 30f. Bear chased by bees; 30f. Cat and boot; 30f. Thelma wet from watering can; 30f. Roast turkey ... 1·60 1·60

166 Kingfisher (*Alcedo athinis*) **167** Walt Disney

(Des S. Mujezinović (671/2) and A. Hafizović (673/4). Photo Courvoisier)

2001 (22 Mar). Fauna. T **166** and similar multicoloured designs. P 13.

671	90f. Type **166**	1·30	1·30
	a. Pair. Nos. 671/2	3·00	3·00
672	1m.10 Bohemian waxwing (*Bombycilla garrulus*)	1·40	1·40
673	1m.10 Serbian work horse (*Equus caballus*)	1·40	1·40
	a. Horiz pair. Nos. 673/4	4·00	4·00
674	1m.90 Head of Serbian horse	2·40	2·40
671/674	*Set of* 4	5·75	5·75

Nos. 671/2 and 673/4 were issued together in *se-tenant* pairs within the sheet.

(Des O. Pavlović. Photo Courvoisier)

2001 (22 Mar). Birth Centenary of Walt Disney (film maker). P 11½×12.

675 **167** 1m.10 multicoloured ... 1·20 1·20

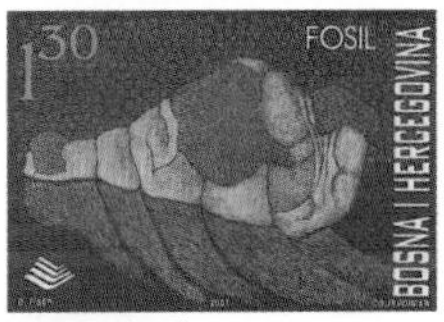

168 Sea Snail

(Des D. Fiser. Litho Courvoisier)

2001 (22 Mar). Fossils. T **168** and similar horiz design. Multicoloured. P 11½.

676	1m.30 Type **168**	1·40	1·40
	a. Pair. Nos. 676/7	3·50	3·50
677	1m.80 Ammonite	1·80	1·80

Nos. 676/7 were issued together in *se-tenant* pairs within the sheet.

169 Land and Sea Sports

(Des M. Garibija. Photo German State Ptg Wks, Berlin)

2001 (30 Mar). 14th Mediterranean Games, Tunis. P 14.

678 **169** 1m.30 multicoloured ... 1·40 1·40

170 Swans on Lake **171** Institute Buildings

(Des M. Dželatović. Litho Courvoisier)

2001 (10 Apr). Europa. Water Resources. Sheet 60×81 mm. P 11½.

MS679 **170** 2m. multicoloured ... 3·25 3·25

(Des H. Ć. I . A. K. Litho Delo Ptg Wks, Ljubljana, Slovenia)

2001 (24 May). Adil Zulfikarpasic Foundation Bosniak Institute (inter- denominational foundation). Sheet 81×50 mm. P 12.

MS680 **171** 1m.10 multicoloured ... 1·20 1·20

172 Emir Balic **173** Ferrari 625 F1 (1954)

(Des A. Hafizović. Litho Courvoisier)

2001 (30 May). Emir Balic (bridge diving competition winner). Sheet 66×47 mm. P 11½.

MS681 **172** 2m. multicoloured ... 2·20 2·20

2001 (20 June). Ferrari Racing Cars. T **173** and similar horiz designs. Multicoloured. Litho. P 14.

682	40f. Type **173**	45	45
	a. Block of 4. Nos. 682/5	4·50	
683	60f. Ferrari 312 B (1970)	65	65
684	1m.30 Ferrari 312 T3 (1978)	1·40	1·40
685	1m.70 Ferrari 126 C3 (1983)	1·80	1·80
682/685	*Set of* 4	3·75	3·75

Nos. 682/5 were issued in *se-tenant* blocks of four stamps within the sheet.

174 Željezničar, Sarajevo Football Team

(Photo German State Ptg Wks, Berlin)

2001 (18 July). National Football Champions, 2001. P 14.

68 **174** 1m. multicoloured ... 1·20 1·20

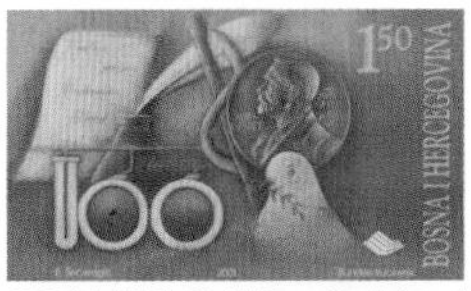

175 Ink Well, Quill Pen, Medal and Dove

(Des E. Šečeragić. Photo German State Ptg Wks, Berlin)

2001 (18 July). Centenary of First Nobel Prize. P 14.

687 **175** 1m.50 multicoloured ... 1·70 1·70

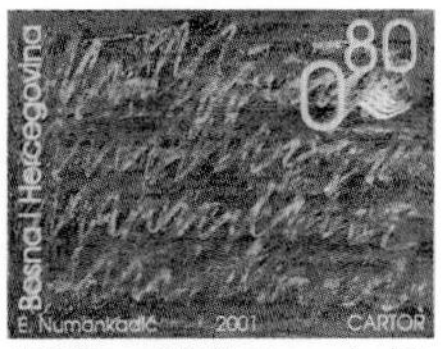

176 Charlie Chaplin **177** "Traces" (Edin Numankadić)

(Des Dz. Omerika. Photo German State Ptg Wks, Berlin)

2001 (18 July). Charlie Chaplin Commemoration. P 14.

688 **176** 1m.60 multicoloured ... 1·90 1·90

(Des F. Săbanović (2m.) Litho and thermography Cartor)

2001 (10 Sept). Art. T **177** and similar horiz design. Multicoloured. P 12½.

689	80f. Type **177**	1·20	1·20
690	2m. David (detail) (sculpture)	2·30	2·30

178 Feeding Bottle enclosed in Stop Sign and Baby at Breast

(Des D. Rehar. Litho German State Ptg Wks, Berlin)

2001 (1 Oct). International Breastfeeding Week. P 14.

691 **178** 1m.10 multicoloured ... 1·40 1·40

179 Acropolis, Castle and Pyramid **180** Horse-drawn Tram

(Des A. Bobrunaj. Photo German State Ptg Wks, Berlin)

2001 (9 Oct). United Nations Year of Dialogue Among Civilizations. P 14.

692 **179** 1m.30 multicoloured ... 1·60 1·60

(Des E. Šečeragić. Photo German State Ptg Wks, Berlin)

2001 (30 Oct). Posteurop Plenary, Sarajevo. P 14.

693 **180** 1m.10 multicoloured ... 1·40 1·40

181 Alija Bejtić and Monument **182** Albert Einstein and Formula

(Litho German State Ptg Wks, Berlin)

2001 (10 Nov). 20th Death Anniv of Alija Bejtić (cultural historian). P 14.

694 **181** 80f. multicoloured ... 95 95

(Des M. Garibija. Litho German State Ptg Wks, Berlin)

2001 (14 Dec). 80th Anniv of Albert Einstein's Nobel Prize for Physics (photoelectric effect). P 14.

695 **182** 1m.50 multicoloured ... 1·70 1·70

183 Davorin Popović

(Des E. Šečeragić. Photo Walsall Security Printers Ltd)

2002 (5 Apr). First Death Anniv of Davorin Popović (musician). P 14.

696 **183** 38f. multicoloured ... 60 60

184 Bridge, Figure and Books **185** Juraj Neidhardt

(Des M. Garibija. Litho German State Ptg Wks, Berlin)

2002 (15 Apr). 350th Birth Anniv of Mustafa Ejubović (Sejh Jujo) (writer). P 14.

697 **184** 1m. multicoloured ... 1·20 1·20

(Des Z. Ugljen. Photo German State Ptg Wks, Berlin)

2002 (15 Apr). Birth Centenary (2001) of Juraj Neidhardt (architect). P 14.

698 **185** 1m. multicoloured ... 1·20 1·20

186 Ševala Zidžić **187** Skier

(Des E. Šečeragić. Photo German State Ptg Wks, Berlin)

2002 (15 Apr). Birth Centenary (2003) of Ševala Zidžić (first female Bosnian doctor). P 14.

699	**186**	1m.30 multicoloured	1·70	1·70

(Des S. Drinovac. Photo German State Ptg Wks, Berlin)

2002 (15 Apr). Sarajevo's Candidacy for Winter Olympic Games, 2010. P 14.

700	**187**	1m.50 multicoloured	1·80	1·80

188 Trees

(Des I. L. Croata and O. Alić. Photo German State Ptg Wks, Berlin)

2002 (15 Apr). International Earth Day. P 14.

701	**188**	2m. multicoloured	2·40	2·40

189 Scout Camp

(Des Asad Nuhanović. Photo German State Ptg Wks, Berlin)

2002 (20 Apr). 80th Anniv of Bosnian Scouts. P 14.

702	**189**	1m. multicoloured	1·20	1·20

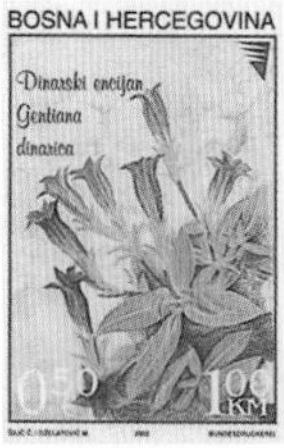

190 Gentian (*Gentiana dinarica*)

(Des C. Šilić and M. Dželatović. Photo German State Ptg Wks, Berlin)

2002 (20 Apr). Flora. T **190** and similar vert design. Multicoloured. P 14.

703	1m. Type **190**	1·40	1·40
704	1m.50 Aquilegia (*Aquilegia dinarica*)	2·20	2·20

191 "War and Peace" (Asad Nuhanović)

(Photo German State Ptg Wks, Berlin)

2002 (20 Apr). Tenth Anniv of Independence. P 14.

705	**191**	2m.50 multicoloured	3·50	3·50

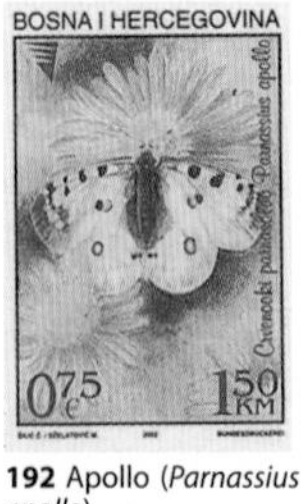

192 Apollo (*Parnassius apollo*)

193 Firemen fighting Fire

(Des C. Šilić and M. Dželatović. Photo German State Ptg Wks, Berlin)

2002 (20 Apr). Butterflies. T **192** and similar vert design. Multicoloured. P 14.

706	1m.50 Type **192**	1·80	1·80
707	2m.50 Scarce Swallowtail (*Iphiclides podalirius*)	3·50	3·50

(Des K. Polić. Photo German State Ptg Wks, Berlin)

2002 (20 Apr). 120th Anniv of Sarajevo Fire Brigades. Sheet 68×48 mm. P 14.

MS708	**193** 2m.20 multicoloured	3·00	3·00

194 Clown

195 Boy wearing Gag

(Des A. Kozić. Photo German State Ptg Wks, Berlin)

2002 (20 Apr). Europa. Circus. P 14.

709	**194**	2m.50 multicoloured	3·50	3·50

(Litho German State Ptg Wks, Berlin)

2002 (28 June). Letter Writing Campaign. Sheet 120×105 mm containing T **195** and similar vert designs showing scenes from "Young Philatelists" (animated film). Multicoloured. P 14.

MS710	40f. Type **195**; 40f. Boy with burnt face; 40f. Boy hit by frying pan; 40f. Boy hit by hammer; 40f. Boy hit with saucepan lids	3·25	3·25

196 Ćevpčići (traditional dish)

(Des O. Alić and L. Bešić. Litho German State Ptg Wks, Berlin)

2002 (28 June). P 14.

711	**196**	1m.10 multicoloured	1·70	1·70

197 Galley

(Des L. Bešić. Litho German State Ptg Wks, Berlin)

2002 (28 June). Roman Ships. Sheet 90×54 mm containing T **197** and similar horiz design. Multicoloured. P 14.

MS712	1m.20 Type **197**; 1m.80 Galleon	4·00	4·00

198 White Water Rafting

(Des I. Erdić. Litho German State Ptg Wks, Berlin)

2002 (28 June). 30th Anniv of Una International Regatta. P 14.

713	**198**	1m.30 multicoloured	1·90	1·90

199 Association Emblem

200 Mountaineer and Hut

(Des Katarina Polić-Pipal. Litho German State Ptg Wks, Berlin)

2002 (14 Sept). Centenary of Napredak (Croatian cultural association). P 14.

714	**199**	1m. multicoloured	1·50	1·50

(Des M. Garibija. Litho German State Ptg Wks, Berlin)

2002 (14 Sept). 110th Anniv of Mountaineering Association. P 14.

715	**200**	1m. multicoloured	1·50	1·50

201 Synagogue

(Des H. Polić. Litho German State Ptg Wks, Berlin)

2002 (14 Sept). Centenary of Ashkenazi Synagogue, Sarajevo. P 14.

716	**201**	2m. multicoloured	3·00	3·00

202 Metal Worker

(Des N. Šehić (80f., 1m.10) and M. Dželatović (1m.20, 1m.30). Litho German State Ptg Wks, Berlin)

2002 (10 Oct). Traditional Crafts. Sheet 110×75 mm containing T **202** and similar horiz designs. Multicoloured. P 14.

MS717	80f. Type **202**; 1m.10 Leather worker; 1m.20 Filigree jewellery; 1m.30 Lace work	6·50	6·50

203 Bosnia and Herzegovina Flag

(Des S. Duzel. Litho German State Ptg Wks, Berlin)

2002 (20 Nov). P 14.

718	**203**	1m. multicoloured	1·50	1·50

204 Coin and Map of Europe

205 Tvrtka I Coin (1376–1391)

(Des S. Duzel. Litho German State Ptg Wks, Berlin)

2002 (20 Nov). "The Euro" (European currency). P 14.

719	**204**	2m. multicoloured	3·00	3·00

(Des H. Šabanić. Litho German State Ptg Wks, Berlin)

2002 (10 Dec). Old Coins. T **205** and similar vert designs. P 14.

720	20f. grey, orange-vermilion and black	25	25
721	30f. emerald, orange-vermillion and black	40	40
722	50f. bright blue, orange-vermilion and black	65	65
720/722	*Set of* 3	1·20	1·20

Designs:—20f. Type **205**; 30f. Stepana Tomaša coin (1443–1461); 50f. Stepana Tomaševita coin (1461–1463).

206 Mother and Child Institute, Sarajevo

(Litho German State Ptg Wks, Berlin)

2002 (10 Dec). P 14.

723	**206**	38f. multicoloured	65	65

207 Horse's Head

208 Mak Dizdar

(Des Berber. Litho German State Ptg Wks, Berlin)

2002 (10 Dec). Art. T **207** and similar multicoloured designs. P 14.

724	40f. Type **207**	65	65
725	1m.10 Portrait of a woman (25×42 mm)	1·70	1·70
726	1m.50 Sculpture and Portrait of two women (42 × 25 mm)	2·30	2·30
724/726	*Set of* 3	4·25	4·25

(Des M. Ibrahimpašić. Litho German State Ptg Wks, Berlin)

2002 (10 Dec). 85th Birth Anniv of Mak Dizdar (poet). P 14.

727	**208**	1m. multicoloured	1·50	1·50

209 Emaciated Man

210 Josip Stadler

(Des N. Šehić. Litho German State Ptg Wks, Berlin)

2002 (10 Dec). Anti-Drugs Campaign. P 14.
728 **209** 1m. multicoloured 25 25

(Litho Grafotisak)

2003 (24 Jan). 160th Birth Anniv of Josip Stadler (first archbishop). P 13.
729 **210** 50f. multicoloured 65 65
A stamp of the same design was issued by Bosnia and Herzegovina Croatian Posts.

211 Musician

212 Stylized Skier

(Des J. Mujkic. Litho and thermography Cartor)

2003 (20 Feb). Centenary of Bosnian Cultural Union "Preporod". P 13.
730 **211** 1m. multicoloured ..... 1·30 1·30

(Des P. Mirić. Litho Cartor)

2003 (20 Feb). European Nordic Skiing Competition, Sarajevo (2006). P 13.
731 **212** 1m. multicoloured ..... 1·30 1·30

213 "Mother and Child"

214 Svetozar Zimonjic

(Litho Cartor)

2003 (31 Mar). Birth Centenary of Omer Mujadzic (artist). P 13.
732 **213** 70f. multicoloured ..... 1·10 1·00

(Des S. Fazlić. Litho Cartor)

2003 (31 Mar). 75th Birth Anniv of Svetozar Zimonjic (president of Sciences and Arts Academy). P 13½.
733 **214** 90f. multicoloured ..... 1·30 1·30

215 Edelweiss (*Leontopodium alpinium*)

(Des S. Redžić, M. Dželatović and O. Alić. Litho Cartor)

2003 (31 Mar). Flowers. T **215** and similar multicoloured design. P 13.
734 90f. Type **215** ..... 1·30 1·30
a. Pair. Nos. 725/6 ..... 2·75 2·75
735 90f. Yellow gentian (*Gentiana symphyandra*) ..... 1·30 1·30
No. 734 was perforated in a circle contained in an outer perforated square. Nos. 734/5 were issued in *se-tenant* pairs within the sheet.

216 Team Members

(Des S. Grabonjić. Litho Cartor)

2003 (31 Mar). National Volleyball Team—World Champions, 2002. P 13½×13.
736 **216** 1m. multicoloured ..... 1·70 1·50

217 Butterflies

(Des F. Säbanović. Litho Cartor)

2003 (9 May). Europa. Poster Art. P 13.
737 **217** 1m. multicoloured ..... 4·25 3·75
a. Booklet pane. No. 737×4 ..... 18·00

218 Pope John Paul II and Ivan Merz

(Des M. Ragu̇ž and R. Alilović. Litho Cartor)

2003 (22 June). Second Visit of Pope John Paul II. P 13½.
738 **218** 1m.50 multicoloured ..... 2·50 2·30
A stamp of the same design was issued by Bosnia and Herzegovina Croatian Posts.

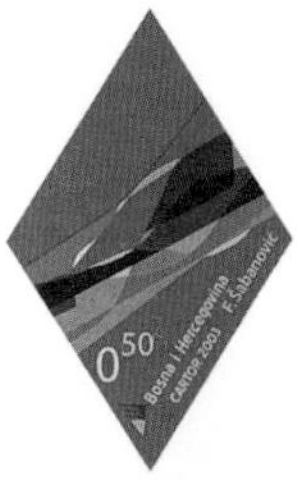

219 Stylized DNA

220 Man on Rooftop

(Des F. Säbanović. Litho Cartor)

2003 (30 June). 50th Anniv of the Discovery of DNA (genetic material). P 13½.
739 **219** 50f. multicoloured 75 65

(Litho Cartor)

2003 (30 June). Letter Writing Campaign. Sheet 116×73 mm containing T **220** and similar horiz designs showing scenes from "The Sleep of Monsters" (graphic novel by Enki Bilal). Multicoloured. P 14.
MS740 50f.×4, Type **220**; Flying taxi; Man and woman (37×25 mm); Faces (37×25 mm) ..... 3·00 2·75

221 Arches, Čekrelči Muslihudin Mosque

(Des S. Grabonjić and S. Fazlić. Litho Cartor)

2003 (30 Sept). Architecture. T **221** and similar multicoloured design. P 13½.
741 1m. Type **221** ..... 2·30 2·30
742 2m. Hajji Sinan Dervish Convent, Sarajevo (30×30 mm) ..... 4·75 4·75

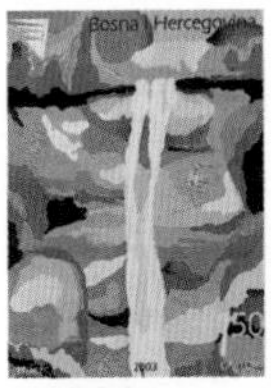

222 "Skakavac Waterfall" (Helena Škec)

223 Children

(Litho Cartor)

2003 (30 Sept). P 13½.
743 **222** 1m.50 multicoloured ..... 3·50 3·50

(Des Benazir Mahmutović. Litho Cartor)

2003 (3 Oct). Children's Week. T **223** and similar horiz design.
(a) Ordinary gum. P 13½.
744 **223** 50f. multicoloured ..... 1·00 1·00
(b) Self-adhesive gum. Die-cut perf 12½.
745 **223** 50f. multicoloured ..... 1·20 1·20

224 Alija Izetbegović

225 Lamps and Clock

(Des O. Pavlović. Litho Cartor)

2003 (27 Nov). Alija Izetbegović (first president) Commemoration. Sheet 68×52 mm. P 13½.
MS746 **224** 2m. multicoloured ..... 4·75 4·75

(Des S. Fazlić. Litho Cartor)

2003 (27 Nov). 90th Anniv of Post Building, Sarajevo. Sheet 80×65 mm. P 13.
MS747 **225** 3m. multicoloured ..... 7·00 7·00

226 Chamois (*Rupicapra rupicapra*)

227 "Plemenitas II" (Dzevad Hozo)

(Des S. Grabonjić and S. Fazlić. Litho Cartor)

2003 (9 Dec). Fauna. T **226** and similar multicoloured design. P 13½.
748 30f. Type **226** 80 80
749 50f. Grizzly bear (*Ursus arctos*) ..... 1·20 1·20

(Litho Cartor)

2003 (18 Dec). P 13½.
750 **227** 10f. multicoloured ..... 1·00 1·00

228 Sleigh and Hands holding Present

229 Orville and Wilbur Wright and Wright Flyer

(Des S. Fazlić. Litho Cartor)

2003 (19 Dec). Christmas. P 13½.
751 **228** 20f. multicoloured ..... 1·00 1·00

(Des O. Pavlović. Litho Cartor)

2003 (20 Dec). Centenary of Powered Flight. P 13½.
752 **229** 1m. multicoloured ..... 2·40 2·40

230 Allegorical Painting

231 Bird

(Litho Cartor)

2003 (20 Dec). 65th Birth Anniv of Ibrahim Ljubović (artist). P 12½.
753 **230** 1m.50 multicoloured ..... 3·75 3·75

(Des I and A. Mujkic. Litho Cartor)

2004 (19 Jan). Bayram Festival. P 13½.
754 **231** 50f. multicoloured ..... 1·30 1·30

232 Kulin on Horseback

233 Aries

(Litho Cartor)

2004 (26 Jan). 800th Anniv of Reign of Kulin Ban (king). P 13½.
755 **232** 50f. multicoloured ..... 1·20 1·20

(Des B. Stapic. Litho Cartor)

2004 (26 Jan). Western Zodiac. T **233** and similar square designs. Multicoloured.

(a) Self-adhesive booklet stamps. Die-cut perf

756	50f. Type **233**	95	95
757	50f. Taurus	95	95
758	50f. Gemini	95	95
759	50f. Cancer	95	95
760	50f. Leo	95	95
761	50f. Virgo	95	95
762	50f. Libra	95	95
763	50f. Scorpio	95	95
764	50f. Sagittarius	95	95
765	50f. Capricorn	95	95
766	50f. Aquarius	95	95
767	50f. Pisces	95	95
756/767 *Set of* 12		10·50	10·50

(b) Miniature sheets. P 13½

MS768 200×130 mm. 50f.×12, Nos. 756/67 ..... 14·00 14·00

Nos. 756/67 were issued in self-adhesive booklets of 12 stamps.

234 Hearts

235 Gloved Hand holding Torch

(Des F. Sababovic. Litho)

2004 (2 Feb). St. Valentine's Day. P 13½.

769 **234** 2m. multicoloured ..... 4·75 4·75

No. 769 was perforated in a heart shape enclosed in an outer perforated square.

2004 (7 Feb). 20th Anniv of Winter Olympics, Sarajevo. P 13½.

770 **235** 1m.50 multicoloured ..... 3·50 3·50

No. 770 was issued with two *se-tenant* labels, at left showing the games mascot and at right showing the games emblem.

236 Jajce

237 *Cattleya intermedia*

(Des D. Fejzic. Litho)

2004 (23 Feb–31 Dec). Towns. T **236** and similar multicoloured designs. P 13½.

770	10f. Breko (horiz)		
771	20f. Type **236** (5.4)	60	60
771*a*	20f. Livno (horiz) (31.12)	60	60
771*b*	30f. Vissoko (31.12)	80	80
771*c*	1m. Sanski Most (31.12)	2·30	2·30
772	50f. Jablanica (horiz) (5.4)	1·20	1·20
773	2m. Stolac (horiz) (15.3)	4·75	4·75
774	4m. Gradačac	9·25	9·25
775	5m. Fojinca (horiz)	11·50	11·50
771/775 *Set of* 9		29·00	29·00

Numbers have been left for possible additions to this series.

(Des A. Ajanović. Litho)

2004 (31 Mar). Orchids. T **237** and similar vert designs. Multicoloured. P 13½.

780	1m.50 Type **237**	4·00	4·00
	a. Pair. Nos. 780/1	9·25	9·25
	b. Booklet pane. Nos. 780/1, each×5	46·00	
781	2m. *Brassavola*	5·00	5·00

Nos. 780/1 were issued in *se-tenant* pairs within the sheet and were impregnated with the scent of orchid. Nos. 780/1, each×5, were issued in booklets of ten stamps, with a white border all round.

238 *Aloe barbardensis*

239 Centenary Emblem

(Des A. Ajanović. Litho)

2004 (31 Mar). Succulents. T **238** and similar vert designs. Multicoloured. P 13½.

782	1m.50 Type **238**	4·00	4·00
	a. Pair. Nos. 782/3	9·25	9·25
783	2m. *Carnegiea gigantean*	5·00	5·00

Nos. 782/3 were issued in *se-tenant* pairs within the sheet.

(Des S. Fazlić. Litho)

2004 (31 Mar). Centenary of FIFA (Fédération Internationale de Football Association). P 13½.

784 **239** 2m. multicoloured ..... 4·75 4·75

240 Alarm Clock on Skies

241 Speech Bubbles

(Des B. Stapic. Litho)

2004 (26 Apr). Europa. Holidays. T **240** and similar vert design. Multicoloured. P 13½ (on 2 or 3 sides) (booklets) or 13½ (others).

785	1m. Type **240**	2·30	2·30
	a. Pair. Nos. 785/6	6·00	6·00
	b. Booklet pane. Nos. 785/6, each×3	18·00	
786	1m.50 Alarm clocks on beach	3·50	3·50

Nos. 785/6 were issued in *se-tenant* pairs within the sheet. Nos. 785/6, each×3, were issued in booklets of six stamps. The stamps were perforated on two or three sides depending on position.

(Des S. Drinovac. Litho)

2004 (7 May). European Youth Peace Conference, Sarajevo. P 13½.

787 **241** 1m.50 multicoloured ..... 3·75 3·75

242 Clown holding Balloons

(Des B. Stapic. Litho)

2004 (15 May). Greetings Stamps. T **242** and similar horiz design. Multicoloured. P 13½.

788	50f. Type **242** (birthday)	95	95
	a. Horiz strip. Nos. 788/9 plus 2 labels	4·50	4·50
789	1m. Bride and bridegroom (wedding)	3·25	3·25

Nos. 788/9 were issued in horizontal *se-tenant* strips of two stamps, each with a ½-stamp size label attached at right within the sheet.

243 Bee on Flower

(Des O. Paviovic. Litho)

2004 (15 May). Bees. Sheet 100×50 mm containing T **243** and similar horiz design. Multicoloured. P 13½.

MS790 2m.×2, Type **243**; Flying bee ..... 8·75 8·75

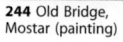

244 Old Bridge, Mostar (painting)

245 Athlete and Horses' Heads

(Des H. Ibrulj. Litho)

2004 (23 June). Reconstruction of Mostar Bridge. T **244** and similar multicoloured design. P 13 (**MS**793) or 13½ (others).

791	50f. Type **244**	1·20	1·20
791	100f. Bridge (different)		
MS793 287×110 mm. Nos. 791/2		3·50	3·50

No. **MS**793 was divided into five parts by four lines of rouletting, the inner parts containing a description of the reconstruction. The upper edges were curved so that the four outer parts fold over to form a painting of the bridge.

(Des S. Fazlić. Litho)

2004 (5 July). Olympic Games, Athens. Sheet 101×71 mm. P 13.

MS794 **245** 2m. multicoloured ..... 4·75 4·75

246 "10" in Lights

247 Abstract

(Des I. Gradevic. Litho)

2004 (26 July). Tenth International Film Festival, Sarajevo. P 13½.

795 **246** 1m.50 vermilion, greenish yellow and black ..... 3·50 3·50

(Des A. Hebib. Litho)

2004 (31 Dec). New Year. P 13½×13.

796 **247** 1m. multicoloured ..... 2·30 2·30

248 Svrzo House (18th—century Ottoman house)

(Des A. Nuhanović. Litho)

2004 (31 Dec). Cultural Heritage. Houses. T **248** and similar horiz design. Multicoloured. P 13½×13.

797	1m. Type **248**	2·40	2·40
798	1m. Despic house (Serbian merchant's house)	2·40	2·40

249 Emblem, "50" and "@"

(Des M. Tvico. Litho)

2004 (31 Dec). 50th Anniv of European Cultural Convention. P 13½.

799 **249** 1m.50 multicoloured ..... 3·50 3·50

250 "Prozori" (window) (Safet Zec)

251 Nikola Šop

(Des H. Zec. Litho)

2004 (31 Dec). Art. P 13.

800 **250** 2m. multicoloured ..... 4·75 4·75

(Des S. Fazlić. Litho)

2004 (31 Dec). Birth Centenary of Nikola Šop (writer). P 13.

801 **251** 3m. multicoloured ..... 7·00 7·00

252 Auditorium

(Des F. Šehić. Litho)

2005 (7 Mar). 50th Anniv of Chamber Theatre 55. P 13.

802 **252** 40f. multicoloured ..... 1·00 1·00

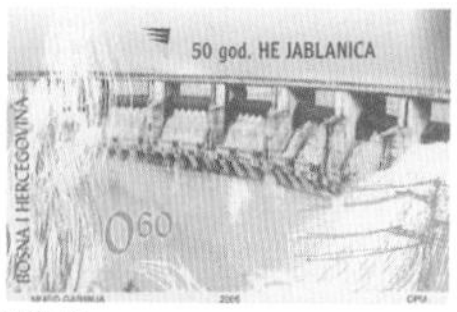

253 Dam

254 Electric Tram

(Des M. Garibija. Litho)

2005 (7 Mar). 50th Anniv of Jablanica Hydroelectric Power Plant. P 13.

803 **253** 60f. multicoloured ..... 1·40 1·40

(Des D. Sehovic. Litho)

2005 (7 Mar). 110th Anniv of Electrification and First Electric Tram. P 13.

804 **254** 2m. multicoloured ..... 4·75 4·75

255 Izet Sarajlic

(Des A. Havizovic. Litho)

2005 (10 Mar). 75th Birth Anniv of Izet Sarajlic (writer). P 13.

805 **255** 1m. multicoloured ..... 2·30 2·30

256 Hasan Kickic   **257** *Rosa damascena*

(Des D. Rehar. Litho)

2005 (10 Mar). Birth Centenary of Hasan Kickic (writer). P 13.
806 **256** 1m.50 multicoloured ... 3·50 3·50

(Des M. Srdija. Litho)

2005 (20 Apr). Roses. T **257** and similar vert design. Multicoloured. P 13.
807 80f. Type **257** ... 1·60 1·60
808 1m.20 *Rosa alba* ... 2·30 2·30

Nos. 807/8 were each issued with a *se-tenant* stamp size label attached at left.

258 Baklava

(Des Mezet/Stapic. Litho)

2005 (20 Apr). Europa. Gastronomy. T **258** and similar horiz designs. Multicoloured. P 13.
809 2m. Type **258** ... 3·50 3·50
810 2m. Sogon Dolma (stuffed onions) ... 3·50 3·50
MS811 115×88 mm. Nos. 809/10 ... 7·00 7·00

The stamps and margin of No. **MS**811 form a composite design of a table laid with food.

259 Partridge (inscr "Tatro urogallus")   **260** Sportsmen

(Des A. Music, S. Alihodzic and S. Hadziabdic. Litho)

2005 (20 Apr). Fauna. T **259** and similar horiz design. Multicoloured. P 13.
812 2m. Type **259** ... 3·50 3·50
813 3m. Beaver (*Castor fiber*) ... 5·25 5·25

(Des A. Začina. Litho)

2005 (20 May). Mediterranean Games, Almeria. P 13.
814 **260** 1m. multicoloured ... 1·80 1·80

261 Composers and Building Façade   **262** Grieving Women

(Des A. Hafizović. Litho)

2005 (31 May). 50th Anniv of Sarajevo Music Academy. P 13.
815 **261** 1m. multicoloured ... 1·80 1·80

(Des M. Berber. Litho)

2005 (1 July). Tenth Anniv of Srebrenica Massacre. P 13.
816 **262** 1m. multicoloured ... 1·80 1·80

263 Sarajevo and Doha

(Des M. Garibija. Litho)

2005 (13 July). P 13.
817 **263** 2m. multicoloured ... 3·50 3·50

A stamp of the same design was issued by Qatar.

264 Emblem and Post Van (EMS)

2005 (1 Sept). Postal Service. T **264** and similar horiz designs. Multicoloured. P 13.
818 10f. Type **264** ... 45 45
819 20f. Emblem and sorter (hybrid mail) ... 60 60
820 30f. Emblem and "IZBOR JE VAS!" (door to door) ... 75 75
821 50f. Emblem and pigeons (philately) ... 1·00 1·00
818/821 *Set of 4* ... 2·50 2·50

265 *Pyrus communis*

(Des O. Krsmanović (1m. and 5m.) or S. Konjhodzic (others). Litho)

2005 (1 Sept). Fruit. T **265** and similar vert designs. Multicoloured. P 13.
822 1m. Type **265** ... 2·10 2·10
823 1m.50 Orange (inscr "Orange carica") ... 3·25 3·25
824 2m. *Ficus carica* ... 4·25 4·25
825 2m.50 *Prunus domestica* ... 5·25 5·25
826 5m. Cherry (inscr "Prunus avium") ... 10·50 10·50
822/826 *Set of 5* ... 23·00 23·00

266 Column and Garden (Hakija Kulenovic)   **267** Dogs and Girl

2005 (5 Sept). Birth Centenary of Hakija Kulenović (artist). Litho. P 13.
827 **266** 2m. multicoloured ... 4·75 4·75

(Des S. Brackovic. Litho)

2005 (15 Sept). Youth Stamps. Sheet 96×72 mm containing T **267** and similar vert design. Multicoloured. P 13.
MS828 50f.×2, Type **267**; Hedgehog windsurfing ... 2·40 2·40

268 Trade Union Building   **269** Stylized Buildings

(Des A. Nuhanović. Litho)

2005 (15 Sept). Centenary of Trade Unions. P 13.
829 **268** 1m. multicoloured ... 2·40 2·40

(Des S. Sakic. Litho)

2005 (15 Sept). Plehan Monastery. P 13.
830 **269** 1m. multicoloured ... 2·40 2·40

270 Aladza Mosque, Foca   **271** King Tvrtko Kotromanić

2005 (15 Sept). Cultural Heritage. T **270** and similar vert design. Multicoloured. P 13.
831 1m. Type **270** ... 2·40 2·40
832 1m. Zitomislici Monastery ... 2·40 2·40

2005 (10 Oct). History. Bogomils. T **271** and similar vert designs. Multicoloured. P 14×13½.
833 50f. Type **271** ... 1·20 1·20
a. Booklet pane. Nos. 833/6 ... 9·75
834 50f. Kulin Ban ... 1·20 1·20
835 1m. Burning man (Inquisition) (stone plaque) ... 2·30 2·30
836 2m. Eugene IV's Papal Bull (1439) ... 4·75 4·75
833/836 *Set of 4* ... 8·50 8·50

272 Decorated Salon   **273** Flowers

2005 (15 Oct). Bosnia Institute. T **272** and similar vert design. Multicoloured. Litho. P 13.
837 70f. Type **272** ... 1·60 1·60
838 4m. Exhibition ... 9·25 9·25

(Des Bojanić and Skocajic. Litho)

2005 (21 Nov). Tenth Anniv of Dayton Agreement. P 14×13½.
839 **273** 1m.50 multicoloured ... 3·50 3·50

274 Emblem   **275** Members Flags and Globe (left)

(Des S. Brackovic. Litho)

2005 (25 Nov). 60th Anniv of End of World War II. P 14×13½.
840 **274** 1m. multicoloured ... 2·40 2·40

2005 (30 Nov). 50th Anniv of Europa Stamps. T **275** and similar horiz designs. Multicoloured. P 14×13½.
841 3m. Type **275** ... 5·00 5·00
a. Horiz pair. Nos. 841/2 ... 10·50 10·50
b. Horiz strip of 4. Nos. 841/4 ... 21·00
842 3m. Globe (right) and members flags ... 5·00 5·00
843 3m. Euro coin and map of Europe ... 5·00 5·00
844 3m. Stars and 1999 chess championships emblem ... 5·00 5·00
841/844 *Set of 4* ... 18·00 18·00
MS845 104×76 mm. Nos. 841/4 ... 19·00 19·00

Nos. 841/2 were issued in horizontal *se-tenant* pairs, within strips of four stamps, in the sheet, each pair forming a composite design.

276 Faces   **277** Slalom Skier

(Des M. Kujovic. Litho)

2005 (3 Dec). World Vision. People with Special Needs Week. P 14×13½.
846 **276** 50f. multicoloured ... 1·60 1·60

(Des S. Brackovic. Litho)

2006 (1 Feb). Winter Olympic Games, Turin. Sheet 88×77 mm containing T **277** and similar horiz design. Multicoloured. P 13½×13.
MS847 1m. Type **277**; 2m. Speed skaters ... 7·00 7·00

278 Treskavica Mountains, Trnovo

(Des S. Brackovic. Litho)

2006 (10 Mar). Tourism. T **278** and similar multicoloured design. P 13½×14 (horiz) or 14×13½ (vert).
848 1m. Type **278** ... 2·30 2·30
849 1m. Rafting, Goradzde (vert) ... 2·30 2·30

279 Mercedes Benz 500K Cabriolet B, 1935

(Des S. Konjhodzic and O. Krsmanovic. Litho)

2006 (20 Mar). Cars. Sheet 104×76 mm containing T **279** and similar horiz designs. Multicoloured. P 13½×13.

MS850 50f.×2 Type **279**; Dodge D11 Graber Cabriolet, 1939; 1m. Mercedes Benz SS Schwarzer, 1929; 2m. Bugatti T **57** Ventoux, 1939 .... 9·50 9·50

280 Crowd

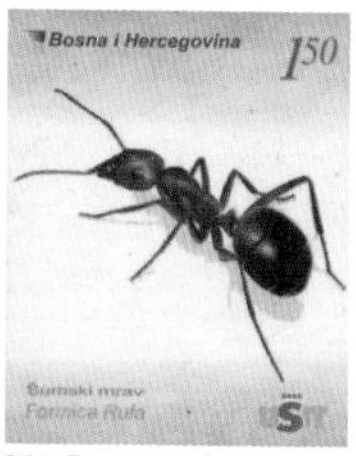

281 *Formica rufa*

(Des M. Garibija. Litho)

2006 (5 Apr). Europa. Integration. T **280** and similar horiz designs. Multicoloured. P 13.

851	2m. Type **280**	5·00	5·00
852	2m. Crowd (different)	5·00	5·00
MS853	115×87 mm. 2m.×2, As Type **280**; As No. 852	16·00	16·00

(Des A. Muslic, S. Alihodzic and M. Uscuplic. Litho)

2006 (20 Apr). Fauna and Flora. T **281** and similar horiz design. Multicoloured. P 14×13½.

854	1m.50 Type **281**	3·50	3·50
855	3m. *Sarcosphaera crassa*	7·00	7·00

282 Prisoners and Barbed Wire

(Des M. Bajrovic. Litho)

2006 (9 May). Prisoner of War Day. P 14×13½.

856	**282**	1m. multicoloured	2·40	2·40

283 Gallery Facade

(Des L. Zukic. Litho)

2006 (20 May). 60th Anniv of National Art Gallery. P 13.

857	**283**	1m. multicoloured	2·40	2·40

284 Illustration from "Zenidba nosaca Samuela"

(Des L. Zukic. Litho)

2006 (20 May). Isak Samokovlija (writer) Commemoration. P 13.

858	**284**	1m. multicoloured	2·40	2·40

284a Mohamed Kadic

(Des D. Fejzic. Litho)

2006 (20 May). Birth Centenaries. T **284a** and similar horiz design. Multicoloured. P 13.

858*a*	1m. Type **284a**	2·40	2·40
858*b*	1m. Mustafa Kamaric	2·40	2·40

285 Team Members

(Des A. Zlotrg. Litho)

2006 (10 June). Football Event and Anniversary. T **285** and similar square design. Multicoloured. P 14.

859	1m. Type **285** (60th anniv of Sarajevo Football Club)	2·40	2·40
	a. Booklet pane. No. 859×2	5·00	
860	3m. Player, globe and flags (World Cup Football Championship, Germany)	7·00	7·00
	a. Booklet pane. No. 860×2	14·50	

Nos. 859/60 were each perforated centrally in a ball shape.

286 Potatoes

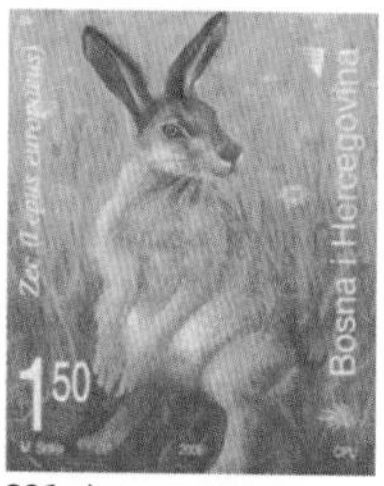

286a *Lepus europaeus*

(Des I. Saracevic. Litho)

2006 (30 June). Vegetables. T **286** and similar horiz designs. Multicoloured. P 13½×14.

861	10f. Type **286**	60	60
862	20f. Cauliflower	80	80
863	30f. Savoy cabbage	95	95
864	40f. Green cabbage	1·20	1·20
865	1m. Carrots	2·50	2·50
861/865 *Set of 5*		5·45	5·45

(Des M. Srdija (866, 868), M. Bajrović (867), Sehović Demo (869) or S. Brackovic (870). Litho)

2006 (30 June). Fauna. T **286a** and similar multicoloured designs. P 13.

866	1m.50 Type **286a**	3·50	3·50
867	2m. *Capreolus capreolus*	4·75	4·75
868	2m.50 *Anas* (mallard) (horiz)	5·75	5·75
869	4m. *Vulpes vulpes*	9·25	9·25
870	5m. *Canis lupus* (horiz)	11·50	11·50
866/870 *Set of 5*		31·00	31·00

287 Emblem

288 Basilica, Breza

(Des A. Suljkanovic. Litho)

2006 (5 July). European Junior Table Tennis Championship. P 13.

871	**287**	1m. multicoloured	2·40	2·40

(Des M. Garibiji (872) or D. Rehar (873). Litho)

2006 (10 Sept). Cultural—Historical Heritage. T **288** and similar multicoloured design. P 13.

872	1m. Type **288**	2·40	2·40
873	1m. Semiz Ali Pasha's Mosque, Prača (vert)	2·40	2·40

289 Orange Bird

290 Girl

(Des F. Sābanović. Litho)

2006 (10 Sept). Youth Philately. Sheet 115×88 mm containing T **289** and similar vert design. Multicoloured. P 13.

MS874 50f.×2, Type **289**; Yellow bird .... 4·75 4·75

(Des Majda Husanovic. Litho)

2006 (6 Oct). Children's Week. Stop Violence against Children Campaign. Self-adhesive. Die-cut.

875	**290**	50f. multicoloured	1·20	1·20

291 School Building

292 Vladimir Prelog (Chemistry, 1975)

(Des M. Gariblia. Litho)

2006 (25 Oct). 300th Anniv of Muslim Secondary School, Travnik. P 13.

876	**291**	1m. multicoloured	2·40	2·40

(Des Mirza Pepić. Litho)

2006 (25 Oct). Nobel Prize Winners. T **292** and similar vert design. Multicoloured. P 13.

877	1m. Type **292**	2·40	2·40
878	2m.50 Iro Andrić (Literature, 1961)	5·75	5·75

293 Emblem

294 Museum Exhibits

(Des R. Šilić. Litho)

2006 (25 Oct). 30th Anniv of Tuzli University. P 14×13½.

879	**293**	1m. multicoloured	2·40	2·40

(Des M. Gerstenhofer. Litho)

2006 (24 Nov). P 13.

880	**294**	1m. multicoloured	2·40	2·40

295 Steam Locomotive

296 Sheep

(Des Mirza Pepić. Litho)

2006 (24 Nov). Railways. T **295** and similar horiz design. Multicoloured. P 13.

881	50f. Type **295**	1·20	1·20
882	1f. Modern locomotive	2·40	2·40

(Des O. Krsmanovic. Litho)

2007 (31 Jan). Domestic Animals. T **296** and similar horiz designs. Multicoloured. P 13.

883	10f. Type **296**	60	60
884	20f. Goat	80	80
885	30f. Cow	95	95
886	40f. Donkey	1·20	1·20
887	70f. Horse (42×35 mm)	1·90	1·90
888	1m. Cat (42×35 mm)	2·40	2·40
883/777 *Set of 6*			

297 Arms

298 Scouts

(Des B. Dursum. Litho)

2007 (15 Feb). 60th Anniv of National Opera Theatre. P 13.

889	**297**	50f. multicoloured	1·30	1·30

(Des S. Brackovic. Litho)

2007 (15 Feb). Europa. Centenary of Scouting. T **298** and similar horiz design. Multicoloured. P 13.

890	2m. Type **298**	4·75	4·75
	a. Sheetlet. Nos. 890/1	9·75	9·75
	b. Booklet pane. Nos. 890/1, each×2	20·00	
891	2m. Scouts by campfire	4·75	4·75

Nos. 890/1 were issued in sheetlets of two stamps with enlarged illustrated margins.

299 Prokos Lake

300 *Knautia travnicensis*

(Des F. Foco. Litho)

2007 (15 Feb). Tourism. P 13.
892 **299** 2m.50 multicoloured .... 6·00 6·00

(Des N. Francic. Litho)

2007 (15 Mar). Fauna and Flora. T **300** and similar multicoloured design. P 13.
893 80f. Type **300** .... 1·70 1·70
894 1m.20 *Sciurus vulgaris* (horiz) .... 3·00 3·00

301 Kozarac

302 Building Façade

(Des E. Blažević. Litho)

2007 (15 Mar). Tourism. P 13.
895 **301** 1m. multicoloured .... 2·40 2·40

(Des H. Topic. Litho)

2007 (10 Apr). 140th Anniv of Cazin Madrasah (Islamic school). P 13.
896 **302** 2m. multicoloured .... 4·75 4·75

302a Fountain, Tuzla

303 Masthead

(Des R. Šilić. Litho)

2007 (10 Apr). Fountains. T **302a** and similar multicoloured designs. P 13.
897 1m.50 Type **302a** .... 3·50 3·50
898 2m. Mostar .... 4·75 4·75
899 2m.50 Sanski Most .... 5·75 5·75
900 4m. Sebilj, Sarajevo (horiz) .... 9·25 9·25
901 5m. Fountain, Bey's Mosque .... 11·50 11·50
897/901 *Set of 5* .... 31·00 31·00

(Des D. Sehovic. Litho)

2007 (16 Apr). Centenary of Gajret Periodical. P 13.
902 **303** 1m. multicoloured .... 2·40 2·40

304 Courtyard

(Des M. Garibija. Litho)

2007 (16 Apr). 30th Anniv of Islamic Science Faculty, Sarajevo. P 13.
903 **304** 2m. multicoloured .... 4·75 4·75

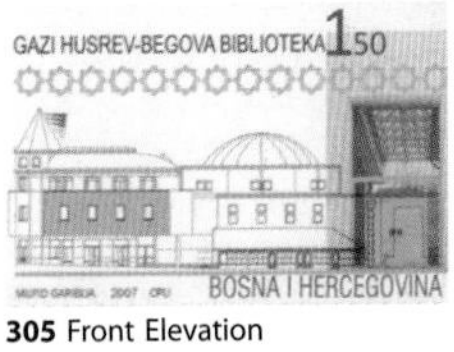

305 Front Elevation

(Des M. Garibija. Litho)

2007 (16 Apr). Gazi Husrev-Begova Library. P 13.
904 **305** 1m.50 multicoloured .... 3·50 3·50

306 Landscape (Ismet Rizvić)

2007 (4 May). Art. T **306** and similar horiz design. Multicoloured. P 13.
905 1m. Počitelj Visual Art Colony .... 2·40 2·40
906 1m.50 Type **306** .... 3·50 3·50

307 '140' and Stylised Building

2007 (4 May). 140th Anniv of Abdulah Nakas Hospital. P 13.
907 **307** 1m.50 deep carmine-red and silver .... 3·50 3·50

308 Bear Figurine

(Des L. Bešić and S. J. Hodović)

2007 (1 June). Museum Exhibit. P 13.
908 **308** 1m. multicoloured .... 2·40 2·40

309 Buildings and Karel Pařík

310 Combatants

(Des L. Bešić and S. J. Hodović)

2007 (6 June). 150th Birth Anniv of Karel Pařík (architect). P 13.
909 **309** 2m.50 multicoloured .... 6·00 6·00

(Des A. Začina)

2007 (2 July). Karate. P 13.
910 **310** 1m. multicoloured .... 2·40 2·40

311 *Self Portrait* (Zuko Džumhur)

312 Building Façade

2007 (2 July). Zuko Džumhur (artist, writer and caricaturist). P 13.
911 **310** 1m. multicoloured .... 2·40 2·40

(Des S. Brackovic)

2007 (2 July). 60th Anniv of Medical Faculty of Sarajevo University. P 13.
912 **312** 1m. multicoloured .... 2·40 2·40

313 Joseph Blatter

(Des Mirza Pepić (913) or B. Fazic (914))

2007 (20 Sept). Honorary Ambassadors for Sport and Culture of Peace. T **313** and similar horiz design. Multicoloured. P 13.
913 2m. Type **313** .... 4·50 4·50
914 2m. Juan Antonio Samaranch (41×27 mm) .... 4·50 4·50

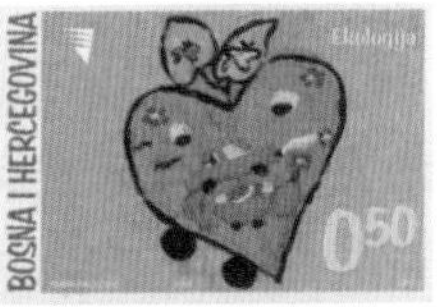

314 Heart (Amira Halilovic)

315 Fortress, Samobor

2007 (28 Sept). Ecology. Children's Drawings. T **314** and similar horiz design. Multicoloured. P 13.
915 50f. Type **314** .... 1·30 1·30
916 50f. Couple holding globe (Maida Hasanic) .... 1·30 1·30
MS916a 75×95 mm. Nos. 915/16 .... 2·50 2·50

(Des M. Bajrovic)

2007 (28 Sept). Cultural Heritage. P 13.
917 **315** 1m. multicoloured .... 2·40 2·40

316 Meat Pie

(Des E. Seleskovic)

2007 (1 Oct). Gastronomy. P 13.
918 **316** 2m. multicoloured .... 4·75 4·75
No. 918 was perforated in a circle contained in an outer perforated square.

317 Stegosaurus

318 Laika

2007 (15 Nov). Pre-History. Dinosaurs. P 13.
919 **317** 2m. multicoloured .... 5·00 5·00

(Des S. Brackovic)

2007 (15 Nov). 50th Anniv of Space Exploration. P 13.
920 **318** 3m. multicoloured .... 7·00 7·00

319 Emblem

320 Player

(Des O. Alić)

2007 (3 Dec). 60th Anniv of University Sports Association. P 13.
921 **319** 50f. multicoloured .... 1·40 1·40
No. 921 was issued in sheetlets of four stamps.

(Des S. Brackovic)

2007 (31 Dec). 60th Anniv of Bosna Handball Club. P 13.
922 **320** 50f. multicoloured .... 1·30 1·30

321 Emblem

(Des Murid Garibija)

2008 (15 Feb). 95th Anniv of Merhamet (Muslim charitable society). P 13×13½.
923 **321** 70f. multicoloured .... 1·80 1·80

322 Candle, Quill and Letter

(Des S. Brackovic)

2008 (8 Mar). Europa. The Letter. T **322** and similar horiz design. Multicoloured. P 13½×14.

924	2m. Type **322**	4·75	4·75
925	3m. Postcard and hand holding pen	7·00	7·00
MS926	88×115 mm. Nos. 924/5	11·50	11·50

STAMP BOOKLETS

The following checklist covers, in simplified form, booklets issued by the Sarajevo Postal Administration of Bosnia and Herzegovina. It is intended that it should be used in conjunction with the main listings and details of stamps and panes listed there are not repeated.

Prices are for complete booklets

Booklet No.	*Date*	*Contents and Cover Price*	*Price*
SB1	12.6.95	Sarajevo Post Office 1 pane, No. 460a (445d.)	5·50
SB2	20.3.98	Old Fortified Towns 1 pane, No. 568a (3m.25)	5·25
SB3	9.5.00	Europa (T **155**) No. 651×4 (8m.)	12·50
SB4	9.5.03	Europa (T **217**) 1 pane, No. 737a (4m.)	19·00
SB5	26.1.04	Zodiac. Self-adhesive. Nos. 756/67 (6m.)	12·00
SB6	26.4.04	Europa. Holidays 1 pane, No. 785b (7m.50)	19·00
SB7	10.10.05	History. Bogomils 1 pane, No. 833a (4m.)	10·00
SB8	10.6.06	Football 1 pane, No. 859a (8m.)	5·25
SB9	15.2.07	Europa. Centenary of Scouting 1 pane, No. 890b	21·00

II. CROATIAN POSTS

Issues made by the Croat administration based in Mostar.

1993. 100 Paras = 1 Croatian Dinar
1994. 100 Lipa = 1 Kuna
1999. 100 Feninga (f) = 1 Marka

Various definitives of Yugoslavia (Tito (No. 1600), Towns (Nos. 1672, 1674, 1676 and 1680) and Postal Services (Nos. 2265/9 and 2278)) exist overprinted with arms and "SUVERENA / BOSNA I / HERCEGOVINA" or "SUVERENA / HERCEG- / BOSNA" in *se-tenant* pairs within the sheet, the overprint often covering the face values of the stamps. These are sometimes found used on covers with issues of Croatia or Croatian Posts in Bosnia but there is no evidence they pre-paid postage.

PRINTER AND PROCESS. The following issues were printed in lithography by Zrinski Printing Company, Čakovec, *unless otherwise stated.*

C **1** Statue and Church

C **2** Silvije Kranjčević (poet)

(Des I. Šiško)

1993 (12 May). Sanctuary of Our Lady Queen of Peace Shrine, Medugorje. P 14.

C1	C **1** 2000d. multicoloured	1·20	1·20

(Des I. Šiško)

1993 (15–20 May). Type C **2** and similar multicoloured designs. P 14.

C2	200d. Type C **2**	20	20
C3	500d. Jajce	35	35
C4	1000d. Mostar (horiz)	75	75
C2/C4	*Set of 3*	1·20	1·20

C **3** Medieval Gravestone

C **4** "Madonna of the Grand Duke" (Raphael)

(Des D. Popović)

1993 (24 May). 250th Anniv of Census in Bosnia and Herzegovina. P 14.

C5	C **3** 100d. multicoloured	40	40

(Des D. Oparić)

1993 (3 Dec). Christmas. P 14.

C6	C **4** 6000d. multicoloured	2·30	2·30

No. C6 was issued in sheets of 20 stamps and five central labels forming an overall design of a cross.

C **5** "Uplands in Bloom"

C **6** Kravica Waterfall

(Des H. Šercar)

1993 (6 Dec). Europa. Contemporary Art. Type C **5** and similar horiz design, each showing paintings by Gabrijel Jurkić. Multicoloured. P 14.

C7	3500d. Type C **5**	4·75	4·75
	a. Pair. Nos. C7/8	10·50	10·50
C8	5000d. "Wild Poppy"	5·25	5·25

Nos. C7/8 were issued together in *se-tenant* pairs within sheets of 16, the stamps in a chessboard arrangement in two blocks of eight separated by four ? stamp-size inscribed labels.

(Des Z. Keser)

1993 (7 Dec). P 14.

C9	C **6** 3000d. multicoloured	1·30	1·30

C **7** Hrvoje (from *Hrvoje's Missal* by Butkó)

C **8** Plehan Monastery

(Des H. Šercar)

1993 (8 Dec). 577th Death Anniv of Hrvoje Vukčić Hrvatinić, Duke of Split, Viceroy of Dalmatia and Croatia and Grand Duke of Bosnia. P 14.

C10	C **7** 1500d. multicoloured	80	80

(Des I. Šiško)

1993 (15 Dec). P 14.

C11	C **8** 2200d. multicoloured	85	85

C **9** Arms

C **10** Bronze Cross, Rama-Šćit (Mile Blažević)

(Des I. Šiško)

1994 (10 Feb). Proclamation (August 1993) of Croatian Community of Herceg Bosna. P 14.

C12	C **9** 10000d. multicoloured	4·00	4·00

No. C12 was issued in sheetlets consisting of two blocks of ten stamps separated by five inscribed labels.

New Currency

1000 (old) Dinars = 1 (new) Kuna

(Des M. Šutej)

1994 (28 Nov). P 14.

C13	C **10** 2k.80 multicoloured	1·20	1·20

No. C13 was issued both in sheets of 20 stamps and in sheetlets of four.

C **11** *Campanula hercegovina*

C **12** Hutovo Swamp

(Des Z. Keser)

1994 (30 Nov). Flora and Fauna. Type C **11** and similar vert design. Multicoloured. P 14.

C14	3k.80 Type C **11**	1·60	1·60
	a. Horiz pair. Nos. C14/15	3·50	3·50
C15	4k. Mountain dog	1·70	1·70

Nos. C14/15 were issued together in horizontal *se-tenant* pairs within sheets of 16.

(Des Z. Keser)

1994 (2 Dec). P 14.

C16	C **12** 80l. multicoloured	45	45

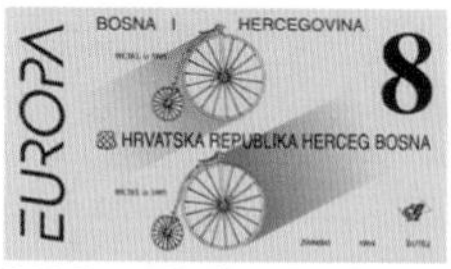

C **13** Penny Farthing Bicycles

C **14** Views of Town and Fortress

(Des M. Šutej)

1994 (5 Dec). Europa. Discoveries and Inventions. Type C **13** and similar horiz design. Multicoloured. P 14.

C17	8k. Type C **13**	4·75	4·75
	a. Horiz pair. Nos. C17/18	11·00	11·00
C18	10k. Mercedes motor cars, 1901	5·75	5·75

Nos. C17/18 were issued together in horizontal *se-tenant* pairs within sheets of 16 stamps.

(Des I. Šiško)

1994 (8 Dec). 550th Anniv of First Written Record of Ljubuški. P 14.

C19	C **14** 1k. multicoloured	50	50

C **15** Hospital and Christ

C **16** Anniversary Emblem

(Des I. Šiško)

1994 (12 Dec). Second Anniv of Dr. Nikolić Franciscan Hospital, Nova Bila. P 14.

C20	C **15** 5k. multicoloured	2·00	2·00

No. C20 was issued both in large sheets and in sheetlets of four stamps.

(Litho PostLine Security Printing, Sweden)

1995 (24 Oct). 50th Anniv of United Nations Organization. Self-adhesive. Rouletted.

C21	C **16** 1k.50 deep ultramarine, rosine and black	60	60
	a. Card. No. C21×10	12·00	

The individual stamps are peeled directly from a card backing. The outer edges of the card are imperforate.

C **17** Crib

C **18** Franciscan Monastery, Kraljeva Sutjeska

(Des I. Lacković Croata)

1995 (4 Dec). Christmas. P 14.

C22	C **17** 5k.40 multicoloured	2·20	2·20

(Des I. Šiško)

1995 (7 Dec). P 14.

C23	C **18** 3k. multicoloured	1·20	1·20

C **19** Srebrenica

C **20** Christ on the Cross

C **21** Statue and Church

(Des H. Šercar)

1995 (12–20 Dec). Towns. Type C **19** and similar vert design. Multicoloured. P 14.

C24	2k. Type C **19** (20.12)	70	70
C25	4k. Franciscan Monastery, Mostar	1·40	1·40

(Des I. Šiško)

1995 (20 Dec). Europa. Peace and Freedom. P 14.

C26	C **20** 6k.50 multicoloured	23·00	23·00

(Des I. Šiško)

1996 (24 June). 15th Anniv of Sanctuary of Our Lady Queen of Peace Shrine, Medugorje. Phosphorescent paper. P 14.

C27	C **21** 10k. multicoloured	4·75	4·75
	a. Booklet pane. No. C27×4	20·00	

The booklet pane has a perforated margin around the strip of stamps.

No. C27 was issued both in large sheets and in sheetlets of four stamps.

C **22** Queen Katarina Kosača Kotromanić

C **23** Monastery

C **24** Virgin Mary

(Des I. Šiško)

1996 (20 July). Europa. Famous Women. Phosphorescent paper. P 14.

C28	C **22**	2k.40 multicoloured	1·90	1·90

(Des H. Šercar)

1996 (23 July). 150th Anniv of Franciscan Monastery and Church, Široki Brijeg. Phosphorescent paper. P 14.

C29	C **23**	1k.40 multicoloured	55	55

(Litho PostLine Security Printing, Sweden)

1996 (14 Aug). Self-adhesive. Rouletted.

(a) POSTAGE

C30	C **24**	2k. multicoloured	60	60
		a. Card. No. C30×10	12·00	

(b) AIR

C31	C **24**	9k. multicoloured	3·00	3·00
		a. Card. No. C31×5 plus five labels	30·00	

The individual stamps are peeled directly from a card backing. No. C30a contains ten stamps and No. C31a contains five stamps and five air mail labels separated by a line of rouletting. The outer edges of the cards are imperforate.

1.10

(C **25**)

C **26** *Madonna and Child* (anon)

1996 (21 Oct). Taipeh '96 International Stamp Exhibition. Nos. C30/1 surch with Type C **25**.

(a) POSTAGE

C32	C **24**	1k.10 on 2k. multicoloured	45	45
		a. Card. No. C32×10	9·00	

(b) AIR

C33	C **24**	1k.10 on 9k. multicoloured	45	45
		a. Card. No. C33×5 plus five labels	9·00	

(Des D. Popović)

1996 (8 Dec). Christmas. Phosphorescent paper. P 14.

C34	C **26**	2k.20 multicoloured	90	90

C **27** St. George and the Dragon

C **28** Pope John Paul II

(Des I. Šiško)

1997 (4 Apr). Europa. Tales and Legends. Type C **27** and similar multicoloured design. P 14.

C35	2k. Type C **27**	95	95
	a. Pair. Nos. C35/6	3·25	3·25
C36	5k. Zeus as bull and Europa (39×34 mm)	2·10	2·10

(Des D. Babić)

1997 (12 Apr). Papal Visit. P 14.

C37	C **28**	3k.60 multicoloured	1·50	1·50
MSC38		90×100 mm. No. C37×4	6·00	6·00

No. **MS**C38 was issued in a folder.

C **29** Chapel, Šamatorje, Gorica

(Des A. Mikulić. Litho)

1997 (20 Apr). P 14.

C39	C **29**	1k.40 multicoloured	55	55

C **30** Purple Heron (*Ardea purpurea*)

(Des I. Šiško (1k.), D. Babić (2k.40))

1997 (19 Nov). Flora and Fauna. Type C **30** and similar vert design. Multicoloured. P 14.

C40	1k. Type C	60	60
C41	2k.40 *Symphyandra hofmannii* (orchid)	1·00	1·00

C **31** "Birth of Christ" (fresco, Giotto)

(Des M. Šutej)

1997 (1 Dec). Christmas. P 14.

C42	C **31**	1k.40 multicoloured	55	55

C **32** Cats

C **33** Seal

(Des Z. Grgić, A. Dizajn and I. Šiško)

1998 (1 Apr). Europa. Animated Film Festival. P 14.

C43	C **32**	6k.50 multicoloured	4·50	4·50

(Des Š. Šutej)

1998 (8 Apr). 550th Anniv of Herzegovina. P 14.

C44	C **33**	2k.30 scarlet-vermilion, black and gold	90	90

C **34** Livno

C **35** *Sibiraea croatica*

(Des I. Šiško)

1998 (9 Apr). 1100th Anniv of Livno. P 14.

C45	C **34**	1k.20 multicoloured	55	55

(Des I. Šiško)

1998 (9 Nov). P 14.

C46	C **35**	1k.40 multicoloured	80	80

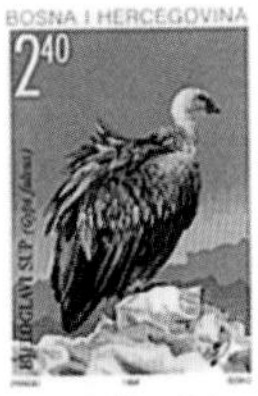

C **36** Griffon Vulture (*Gyps fulvus*)

C **37** Adoration of the Wise Men

(Des I. Šiško)

1998 (16 Nov). P 14.

C47	C **36**	2k.40 multicoloured	1·10	1·10

(Des I. Šiško)

1998 (2 Dec). Christmas. P 14.

C48	C **37**	5k.40 multicoloured	2·20	2·20

Currency Change

100 Feninga (f) = 1 Marka

C **38** Woman, Posavina Region

C **39** Ruins of Bobovac

(Des I. Šiško)

1999 (26 Mar). Regional Costumes. P 14.

C49	C **38**	40l. multicoloured	55	55

(Des Mikulić)

1999 (29 Mar). Old Towns. P 14.

C50	C **39**	10l. multicoloured	25	25

C **40** Šimić

C **41** Blidinje Nature Park

(Des Skoko)

1999 (29 Mar). Birth Centenary (1998) of Antun Šimić (writer). P 14.

C51	C **40**	30f. multicoloured	55	55

(Des Mikulić)

1999 (31 Mar). Europa. Parks and Gardens. P 14.

C52	C **41**	1m.50 multicoloured	4·00	4·00

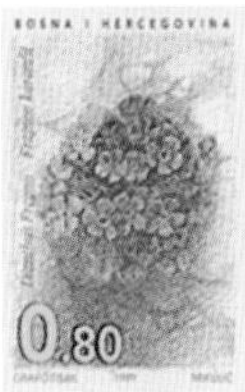

C **42** *Dianthus freynii*

C **43** Pine Marten (*Martes martes*)

(Des A. Mikulić. Litho Grafotisak)

1999 (11 Oct). P 14.

C53	C **42**	80f. multicoloured	1·30	1·30

(Des Skoko. Litho Grafotisak)

1999 (15 Oct). P 14.

C54	C **43**	40f. multicoloured	55	55

C **44** Gradina Ošanici, Stolac

C **45** The Nativity (mosaic)

(Des Vučković. Litho Grafotisak)

1999 (3 Nov). Archaeology. P 14.

C55	C **44**	10f. multicoloured	25	25

(Des Salavarda. Litho Grafotisak)

1999 (22 Nov). Christmas. P 14.

C56	C **45**	30f. multicoloured	55	55

C **46** Šop

C **47** Emblem

(Des M. Palameta. Litho Grafotisak)

2000 (5 Apr). 96th Birth Anniv of Nikola Šop (poet). P 14.

C57	C **46**	40f. multicoloured	60	60

(Litho Grafotisak)

2000 (7 Apr). World Health Day. P 14.

C58	C **47**	40f. multicoloured	60	60

C **48** Ceramic Doves

(Des Studio eRDe. Litho Grafotisak)

2000 (9 May). Europa. P 14.
C59 C **48** 1m.80 multicoloured .... 4·00 4·00

C **49** Chess Board and Emblem

(Des Mirna and E. Cesović and N. Stojanović (No. C60), N. Stojanović , D. Čaušević, B. Paulinović and F. Brkanić (No. C61). Litho Grafotisak)

2000 (16 May–23 Sept). 40th Anniv of Bosnian Chess Association. Chess Events in 2000. Type C **49** and similar horiz design. Multicoloured. P 14.
C60 80f. Type C **49** (30th Chess Olympiad, Sarajevo) .... 1·30 1·30
C61 80f. Octopus holding pawn and emblem (16th European Chess Club Cup, Neum) .... 1·30 1·30

C **50** Brother Karaula
C **51** Oak Tree (*Quercus sessilis*)

(Des N. Šiško and G. Jurmkic. Litho Grafotisak)

2000 (19 May). Birth Bicentenary Anniv of Brother Lovro Karaula. P 14.
C62 C **50** 80f. multicoloured .... 1·30 1·30

(Des A. Mikulić. Litho Grafotisak)

2000 (16 Aug). Chestnut Oak of Široki Brijeg. P 14.
C63 C **51** 1m.50 multicoloured .... 2·20 2·20

C **52** European Eel (*Anguilla anguilla*)

(Des S. Skoko. Litho Grafotisak)

2000 (18 Aug). P 14.
C64 C **52** 80f. multicoloured .... 1·30 1·30

C **53** Franciscan Monastery, Tomislavgrad

(Des Studio eRDe. Litho Grafotisak)

2000 (26 Sept). P 14.
C65 C **53** 1m.50 multicoloured .... 2·20 2·20

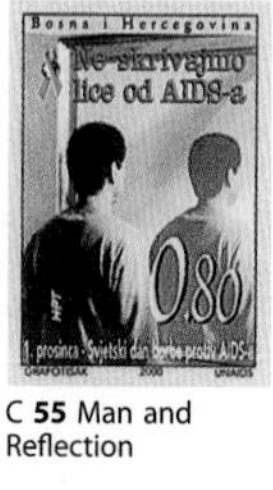

C **54** Woman and Patterned Cloth
C **55** Man and Reflection

(Des Studio eRDe. Litho Grafotisak)

2000 (27 Sept). Traditional Costume from Kraljeve Sutjesmke. P 14.
C66 C **54** 40f. multicoloured 80 80

(Litho Grafotisak)

2000 (1 Dec). A.I.D.S. Awareness Campaign. P 14.
C67 C **55** 80f. multicoloured .... 1·30 1·30

C **56** Nativity
C **57** Chondrostoma phoxinus

(Des M. Vekić. Litho Grafotisak)

2000 (4 Dec). Christmas. P 14.
C68 C **56** 40f. multicoloured 65 65

(Des Ana Tolić. Litho)

2001 (19–22 Feb). Fishes. Type C **57** and similar horiz design. Multicoloured. P 14.
C69 30f. Type C **57** 40 40
C70 1m.50 *Salmo marmoratus* .... 2·20 2·20

C **58** Tihaljina Spring
C **59** Petar Zrinski

(Des N. Vucmkovic (1m.10), Studio eRDe (1m.80). Litho)

2001 (31 Mar). Europa. Water Resources. Type C **58** and similar vert design. Multicoloured. P 14.
C71 1m.10 Type C 58 .... 2·00 2·00
C72 1m.80 Pliva Waterfall .... 3·25 3·25

(Des G. Bouttats. Litho Grafotisak)

2001 (30 Apr). 330th Death Anniversaries. Type C **59** and similar vert design. Multicoloured. P 14.
C73 40f. Type C **59** 60 60
a. Pair. Nos. C73/4 .... 1·30 1·30
C74 40f. Fran Krsto Frankopan 60 60
Nos. C73/4 were issued together in *se-tenant* pairs within the sheet.

C **60** 16th-century Galley Ship
C **61** Boat, Neretva River Valley

(Des M. Vekić. Litho)

2001 (15 June). P 14.
C75 C **60** 1m.80 multicoloured .... 2·75 2·75

(Des A. Naronitana. Litho)

2001 (20 June). P 14.
C76 C **61** 80f. multicoloured .... 1·30 1·30

C **62** Queen of Peace of Medugorje
C **63** Our Lady of Kondžilo (17th-century painting)

(Des I. Šiško. Litho)

2001 (24 June). 20th Anniv of Medugorje. Sheet 90×65 mm. P 14.
MSC77 C **62** 3m.80 multicoloured .... 5·25 5·25

(Litho Grafotisak)

2001 (15 Aug). P 14.
C78 C **63** 80f. multicoloured .... 1·30 1·30

C **64** Binary Digits

(Des R. Alilović. Litho Grafotisak)

2001 (9 Sept). 50th Anniv of Computers. Type C **64** and similar horiz design. Each black and orange-vermilion. P 14.
C79 40f. Type C **64** 65 65
a. Pair. Nos. C70/80 .... 1·40 1·40
C80 40f. Binary forming "50" 65 65
Nos. C79/80 were issued in *se-tenant* pairs within the sheet.

C **65** Mars, Globe and Sisyphus pushing Stone

(Des Eurodesign. Litho)

2001 (9 Sept). Millennium. P 14.
C81 C **65** 1m.50 multicoloured .... 2·00 2·00
No. C81 was issued with ½ stamp-sized se-tenant label.

C **66** Father Slavko Barbaric
C **67** Minnie and Mickey Mouse (Danijela Nedić)

(Des F. Primorac. Litho)

2001 (24 Nov). First Death Anniv of Father Slavko Barbaric. P 14.
C82 C **66** 80f. multicoloured .... 1·30 1·30

(Litho Grafotisam)

2001 (5 Dec). Birth Centenary of Walt Disney (film maker). P 14.
C83 C **67** 1m.50 multicoloured .... 2·40 2·40

C **68** Nativity
C **69** Alfred Nobel

(Des B. Kajić. Litho Grafotisak)

2001 (8 Dec). Christmas. P 14.
C84 C **68** 40f. multicoloured 65 65

(Des Eurodesign. Litho)

2001 (10 Dec). Centenary of the Nobel Prize. P 14.
C85 C **69** 1m.80 multicoloured .... 3·00 3·00

C **70** Skier
C **71** Vran Mountain

(Des Zimonia)

2002 (14 Feb). Winter Olympic Games, Salt Lake City, USA. Fluorescent security markings. P 14.
C86 C **70** 80f. multicoloured .... 1·40 1·40

(Des Studio eRDe. Litho Grafotisak)

2002 (11 Mar). International Year of Mountains. Granite paper. P 14.
C87 C **71** 40f. multicoloured 70 70
No. C87 was issued with a stamp-sized label showing anniversary emblem attached at left.

C **72** Bridge over River Neretva, Mostar

(Des Tofic. Litho Grafotisak)

2002 (3 Apr). 550th Anniv of First Written Record of Mostar. Granite paper. P 14.
C88 C **72** 30f. multicoloured 55 55

C **73** Clown, Lion and Mouse

C **74** Leonardo da Vinci and Designs

(Des Eurodesign)

2002 (5 Apr). Europa. Circus. Type C **73** and similar horiz design. Multicoloured. Fluorescent security markings. P 14.

C89 80f. Type C **73** ... 2·10 2·00
C90 1m.50 Big Top and clowns ... 3·50 3·50

(Des Pavić)

2002 (15 Apr). 550th Birth Anniv of Leonardo da Vinci (artist and designer). Cream paper. Fluorescent security markings. P 14.

C91 C **74** 40f. blackish brown and agate ... 70 70

C **75** Players and Football

C **76** Father Buntić and Children

(Des Jelavić)

2002 (22 May). World Cup Football Championships, Japan and South Korea. Fluorescent security markings. P 14.

C92 C **75** 1m.50 multicoloured ... 2·50 2·40

(Des Jurkić. Litho Grafotisak)

2002 (5 June). 60th Death Anniv of Father Didak Buntić (humanitarian). Granite paper. P 14.

C93 C **76** 80f. multicoloured ... 1·40 1·40

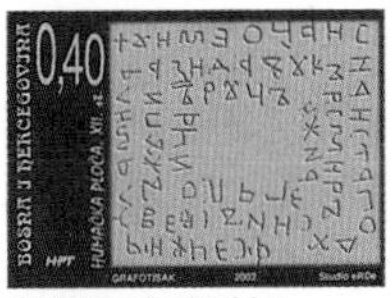

C **77** Inscribed Tablet

(Des Studio eRDe. Litho Grafotisak)

2002 (13 June). 11th-century Inscribed Tablet, Humac. Granite paper. P 14.

C94 C **77** 40f. multicoloured ... 70 70

C **78** Marilyn Monroe

C **79** Elvis Presley

(Des Bečić)

2002 (5 Aug). 40th Death Anniv of Marilyn Monroe (actor). Fluorescent security markings. P 14.

C95 C **78** 40f. multicoloure ... 70 70

(Des Bečić)

2002 (16 Aug). 25th Death Anniv of Elvis Presley (entertainer). Fluorescent security markings. P 14.

C96 C **79** 1m.50 multicoloured ... 2·50 2·40

C **80** Transmitter Tower

C **81** 1905 Postcard

(Des Vekić. Litho Grafotisak)

2002 (7 Sept). 50th Anniv of Television. Granite paper. P 14.

C97 C **80** 1m.50 multicoloured ... 2·50 2·40

(Des Eurodesign. Litho Grafotisak)

2002 (9 Sept). Stamp Day. Granite paper. P 14.

C98 C **81** 80f. multicoloured ... 1·40 1·40

C **82** 1929 Calendar

C **83** Stylized Player

(Des Jurković. Litho Grafotisak)

2002 (14 Sept). Centenary of "Naprodak" (cultural association). Granite paper. P 14.

C99 C **82** 40f. multicoloured ... 70 70

(Des GTG Design. Litho Grafotisak)

2002 (8 Oct). European Bowling Championships, Grude. Granite paper. P 14.

C100 C **83** 1m.50 multicoloured ... 2·50 2·40

C **84** Viola beckiana

C **85** Red Admiral (*Vanessa atalanta*)

(Des Pavić)

2002 (21 Oct). Flowers. Fluorescent security markings. P 14.

C101 C **84** 30f. multicoloured ... 55 55

(Des Pavić)

2002 (25 Oct). Butterflies. Fluorescent security markings. P 14.

C102 C **85** 80f. multicoloured ... 1·40 1·40

C **86** Madonna and Child (painting, Bernardino Luini)

C **87** School Buildings

(Litho Grafotisak)

2002 (4 Dec). Christmas. Granite paper. P 14.

C103 C **86** 40f. multicoloured ... 70 70

(Des Eurodesign. Litho Grafotisak)

2002 (14 Dec). 120th Anniv of Society of Jesuits High School, Travnik. Granite paper. P 14.

C104 C **87** 80f. multicoloured ... 1·40 1·40

C **88** Josip Stadler

C **89** Sirokom Brijegu High School

(Litho Grafotisak)

2003 (24 Jan). 160th Birth Anniv (first archbishop). Granite paper. P 14.

C105 C **88** 50f. multicoloured ... 85 85

(Des Ibrulj. Litho Grafotisak)

2003 (26 Feb). Granite paper. P 14.

C106 C **89** 40f. multicoloured ... 80 80

C **90** Key Box and Letter Holder

C **91** Figures

(Des hercegtisak)

2003 (5 Apr). Europa. Poster Art. Litho. P 14.

C107 C **90** 1m.80 multicoloured ... 4·75 4·75

(Des Skoko. Litho Grafotisak)

2003 (8 Apr). 800th Anniv of the Abjuration at Bilino Polje. Granite paper. P 14.

C108 C **91** 50f. multicoloured ... 95 95

C **92** Mary and Angels

(Des Šiško)

2003 (12 May). Tenth Anniv of HP Mostar. P 14.

C109 C **92** 980f. multicoloured ... 1·60 1·60

C **93** Corkscrews

(Des Alilović)

2003 (25 May). World Wine Day. Litho. P 14.

C110 C **93** 1m.50 multicoloured ... 2·75 2·75

C **94** *Oxytropis prenja*

(Des Frankovic and Vucic)

2003 (10–16 June). Flora and Fauna. Type C**94** and similar vert design. Multicoloured. P 14.

C111 50f. Type C 94 ... 95 95
C112 2m. Rock partridge (*Alectoris graeca*) (16.6) ... 3·75 3·75

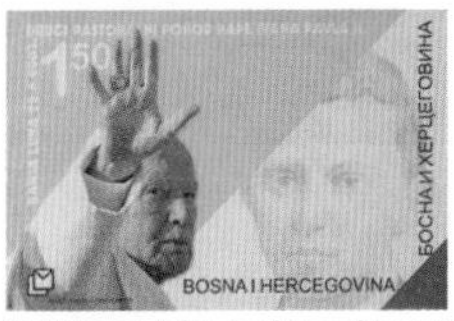

C **95** Pope John Paul II and Ivan Merz

(Des Ragulž and Alikovic. Litho Cartor)

2003 (22 June). Second Visit of Pope John Paul II. P 13½.

C113 C **95** 1m.50 multicoloured ... 2·75 2·75

C **96** Crucifix

C **97** Woman wearing Folk Costume, Rama

(Des Musa. Litho Grafotisak)

2003 (24 June). 440th Birth Anniv of Matija Divkovic (writer). Granite paper. P 14.

C114 C **96** 3m.80 multicoloured ... 7·00 7·00

(Des Musa. Litho Grafotisak)

2003 (20 Aug). Cultural Heritage. Type C **97** and similar multicoloured design. Granite paper. P 14.

C115 50f. Type C **97** ... 95 95
C116 70f. Jewellery, Neum (horiz) ... 1·20 1·20

C **98** Summit Cross

C **99** Stjepan Kotromanić

(Des Jurisic and Vranić)

2003 (14 Sept). 70th Anniv of Summit Cross on Krizevac Mountain. P 14.

C117 C **98** 80f. multicoloured ... 1·60 1·60

(Des Palameta. Litho Grafotisak)

2003 (28 Sept). 650th Death Anniv of Stjepan Kotromanić (King of Bosnia). Granite paper. P 14.

C118 C **99** 20f. multicoloured ... 45 45

C **100** Tele-printer

C **101** Quill and Inkwell

(Des Alilović. Litho Grafotisak)

2003 (9 Oct). World Post Day. Granite paper. P 14.
C119 C **100** 1k.50 black and carmine-red .... 3·25 3·25

(Des Raguž and Barbaric. Litho Grafotisak)

2003 (21 Oct). Birth Bicentenary of Alberto Fortis (writer). Granite paper. P 14.
C120 C **101** 50f. multicoloured .... 1·00 1·00

C **102** Car and Bicycle

C **103** Nativity

(Des Antonio Lovric. Litho Grafotisak)

2003 (20 Nov). Children. Granite paper. P 14.
C121 C **102** 1m. multicoloured .... 2·10 2·10

(Des Vučković)

2003 (4 Dec). Christmas. Granite paper. P 14.
C122 C **103** 50f. multicoloured .... 1·00 1·00

C **104** "100"

(Des Konjhodzic)

2003 (17 Dec). Centenary of Powered Flight. P 14.
C123 C **104** 2m. multicoloured .... 4·25 4·25

C **105** Emblem

C **106** Hearts

(Des Musa. Litho Grafotisak)

2004 (23 Jan). International Investment Conference. P 14½.
C124 C **105** 5m. silver .... 11·50 11·50

(Des Alilović. Litho Grafotisak)

2004 (14 Feb). St. Valentine's Day. P 14½.
C125 C **106** 10f. multicoloured .... 1·00 1·00

C **107** Albert Einstein

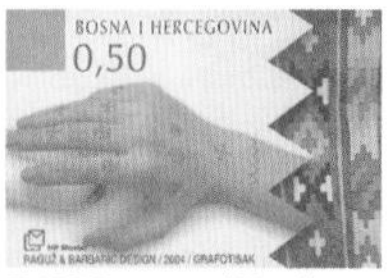

C **108** Decorated Hand

(Litho Grafotisak)

2004 (14 Mar). 125th Birth Anniv of Albert Einstein (physicist). P 14½.
C126 C **107** 50f. multicoloured .... 1·30 1·30

(Litho Grafotisak)

2004 (20 Mar). Tattooing. P 14½.
C127 C **108** 50f. multicoloured .... 1·30 1·30

C **109** *Aquilegia dinarica*

C **110** Skis and Snow Scene

(Des Šantić and Šilić)

2004 (30 Mar). Flora and Fauna. Type C **109** and similar multicoloured design. P 14½.
C128 1m. Type C **109** .... 2·40 2·40
C129 1m.50 *Salamandra atra prenjensis* (horiz) .... 3·50 3·50

(Des Volic)

2004 (5 Apr). Europa. Holidays. Type C **110** and similar vert design. P 14½.
C130 1f.50 Type C **110** .... 3·75 3·75
a. Pair. Nos. C130/1 .... 8·75 8·75
C131 2f. Flippers and beach scene .... 4·75 4·75
Nos. C130/1 were issued in horizontal *se-tenant* pairs within the sheet.

C **111** Andrije Kacica Miosica

C **112** Ball and Boots

(Des Nikolić. Litho Grafotisak)

2004 (17 Apr). 300th Birth Anniv of Andrije Kacica Miosica (writer and theologian). P 14½.
C132 C **111** 70f. chrome yellow and reddish brown .... 1·80 1·80

(Des Musa. Litho Grafotisak)

2004 (12 June). European Football Championship 2004, Portugal. P 14½.
C133 C **112** 2m. multicoloured .... 5·00 5·00

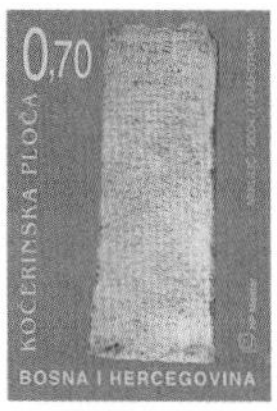

C **113** Kocerin Tablet (carved stone), Široki Brijeg (c.1404)

C **114** Footprint

(Des Mikulić. Litho Grafotisak)

2004 (27 June). P 14½.
C134 C **113** 70f. multicoloured .... 1·50 1·50

(Des Frankovic and Vogic. Litho Grafotisak)

2004 (20 July). 35th Anniv of First Landing on Moon. P 14½.
C135 C **114** 1m. multicoloured .... 2·50 2·50

C **115** Old Bridge, Mostar

C **116** Water Wheel, Buna

(Des Raguž and Barbaric. Litho Grafotisak)

2004 (23 July). Reconstruction of Mostar Bridge. P 14½.
C136 C **115** 50f. multicoloured .... 1·30 1·30

(Des Puljic. Litho Grafotisak)

2004 (9 Sept). P 14½.
C137 C **116** 1f. multicoloured .... 2·50 2·50

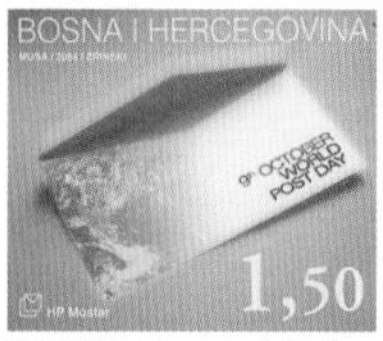

C **117** Envelope and Earth

C **118** Money Box and Hippopotamus

(Des Musa)

2004 (9 Oct). World Post Day. P 14½.
C138 C **117** 1m.50 multicoloured .... 3·75 3·75

(Des Musa. Litho Grafotisak)

2004 (31 Oct). World Savings Day. P 14½.
C139 C **118** 50f. multicoloured .... 1·30 1·30

C **119** Karl Friedrich Benz

(Des Briševac)

2004 (25 Nov). 160th Birth Anniv of Karl Friedrich Benz (German motor pioneer). P 14½.
C140 C **119** 1m.50 multicoloured .... 3·75 3·75

C **120** Flight into Egypt

C **121** Woman wearing Folk Costume, Kupres

(Des Palameta)

2004 (4 Dec). Christmas. Type C **120** and similar horiz design. Multicoloured. P 14½.
C141 50f. Type C **120** .... 1·30 1·30
a. Pair. Nos. C141/2 .... 4·00 4·00
C142 1m. Postman carrying present .... 2·50 2·50
Nos. C141/2 were issued in horizontal *se-tenant* pairs within the sheet.

(Des D. Briševac. Litho Grafotisak)

2005 (20 Feb). Cultural Heritage. P 14½.
C143 C **121** 1m.50 multicoloured .... 3·75 3·75

C **122** *Gentiana dinarica*

C **123** Little Egret (*Egretta garzetta*)

(Des Ivana Marijanovic)

2005 (2 Mar). Flora. Type C **122** and similar vert design. Multicoloured. P 14½.
C144 50f. Type C **122** .... 1·30 1·30
C145 50f. *Petteria ramentacea* .... 1·30 1·30

(Des D. Raic)

2005 (2 Mar). Birds. Type C **123** and similar vert designs. Multicoloured. P 14½.
C146 1m. Type C **123** .... 2·50 2·50
a. Strip of 4. Nos. C146/9 .... 10·50
C147 1m. Black-winged stilt (*Himantopus himantopus*) .... 2·50 2·50
C148 1m. Kingfisher (*Alcedo atthis*) .... 2·50 2·50
C149 1m. European bee eater (*Merops apiaster*) .... 2·50 2·50
C146/C149 *Set of 4* ....
Nos. C146/9 were issued in horizontal *se-tenant* strips of four stamps within the sheet.

C **124** Early Footballers

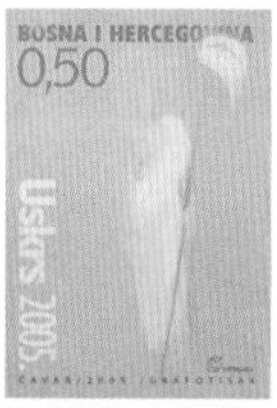

C **125** Figure holding Flag

(Des M. Musa. Litho Grafotisak)

2005 (15 Mar). Centenary of CSC Zrinjski Sports Club. Type C **124** and similar horiz design. P 14½.
C150 3m. Type C **124** .... 7·25 7·25
a. Pair. Nos. C150/1 .... 15·00 15·00
C151 3m. Modern footballers ....
Nos. C150/1 were issued in horizontal *se-tenant* pairs within the sheet.

(Des Ivana Cavar. Litho Grafotisak)

2005 (27 Mar). Easter. P 14½.
C152 C **125** 50f. multicoloured .... 1·30 1·30

C **126** Thumbelina (Hans Christian Andersen)

C **127** Bread, Grapes, Wine, Nuts and Soft Cheese

(Des M. Palmeta)

2005 (2 Apr). Writers Anniversaries. Type C **126** and similar horiz design. Multicoloured. P 14½.
C153 20f. Type C **126** (birth bicentenary) 50 50
a. Pair. Nos. C153/4 .... 1·10 1·10
C154 20f. Tintilinic (Ivana Brlic Mazuranic) (130th (2004) birth anniv) 50 50
Nos. C153/4 were issued in horizontal and vertical *se-tenant* pairs within the sheet.

(Des M. Raguž and S. Barbaric)

2005 (5 Apr). Europa. Gastronomy. Type C **127** and similar horiz design. Multicoloured. P 14½.

C155 2m. Type C **127** .... 5·00 5·00
a. Pair. Nos. C155/6 .... 10·50 10·50
C156 2m. Bread, garlic, meats, glass and flagon .... 5·00 5·00

Nos. C155/6 were issued in horizontal and vertical *se-tenant* pairs within the sheet.

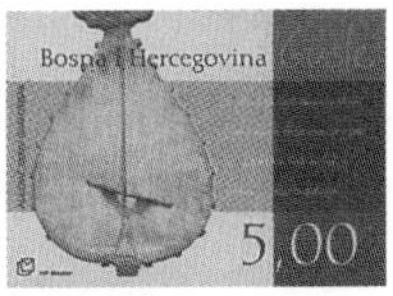

C **128** Gusle

(Des Alilović. Litho Grafotisak)

2005 (10 Apr). Musical Instruments. P 14½.

C157 C **128** 5m. multicoloured .... 12·50 12·50

C **129** Vjetrenica Cave

(Des Raic)

2005 (5 June). International Day of Water. P 14.

C158 C **129** 1m. multicoloured .... 2·50 2·50

C **130** Steam Locomotive

C **131** Virgin Mary (statue) and Crowds

(Des Raic)

2005 (14 June). 120th Anniv of Metkovic—Mostar Railway. P 14.

C159 C **130** 50f. multicoloured .... 1·30 1·30

(Des G. Zovko)

2005 (29 July). Medugorje Youth Festival. P 14.

C160 C **131** 1m. multicoloured .... 2·50 2·50

C **132** Father Grgo Martić

C **133** Trumpet

(Des D. Briševac)

2005 (30 Aug). Birth Centenary of Father Grgo Martić. P 14.

C161 C **132** 1m. multicoloured .... 2·50 2·50

(Des R. Alilović)

2005 (1 Oct). International Music Day. P 14.

C162 C **133** 50f. multicoloured .... 1·00 1·00

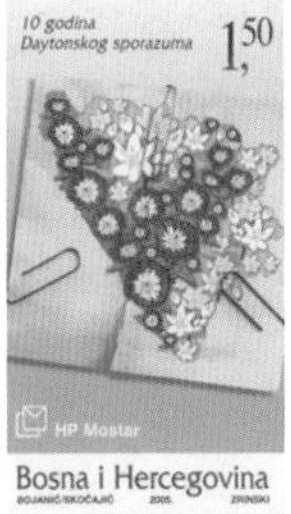

C **134** Flowers

C **135** Slavko Barbaric

(Des Bojanić and Skocajic. Litho)

2005 (21 Nov). Tenth Anniv of Dayton Agreement. P 14.

C163 C **134** 1m.50 multicoloured .... 3·75 3·75

(Des F. Musa. Litho)

2005 (24 Nov). Fifth Death Anniv of Slavko Barbaric (writer). P 14.

C164 C **135** 1m. multicoloured .... 2·50 2·50

C **136** Mary and Jesus

C **137** "50"

(Des Ivana Mikulić. Litho)

2005 (4 Dec). Christmas. Type C **136** and similar vert design. Multicoloured. P 14.

C165 50f. Type C **136** .... 1·30 1·30
C166 50f. Tree .... 1·30 1·30

(Des F. Musa (C167) or Raguž & Barbaric (others). Litho)

2005 (4 Dec). 50th Anniv of Europa Stamps. Type C **137** and similar vert designs. Multicoloured. P 14.

C167 2m. Type C **137** .... 3·75 3·75
a. Horiz strip. Nos. C167/70 .... 16·00 16·00
C168 2m. Sunflowers and envelope .... 3·75 3·75
C169 2m. Map and 2003 1m.80 stamp (No. C107) .... 3·75 3·75
C170 2m. European flags .... 3·75 3·75
C167/C170 *Set of 4* ....
MSC171 90×100 mm. Nos. 167/70 .... 20·00 20·00

Nos. C167/70 were issued in horizontal *se-tenant* strips of four stamps within the sheet.

C **138** Lake and Bearded Tit

(Des Raic. Litho)

2006 (2 Feb). International Swamp Protection Day. P 14.

C172 C **138** 1m. multicoloured .... 2·50 2·50

C **139** Faces

(Des Barbaric. Litho)

2006 (5 Apr). Europa. Integration. Type C **139** and similar horiz design. Multicoloured. P 14.

C173 2m. Type C **139** .... 5·00 5·00
a. Pair. Nos. C173/4 .... 10·50 10·50
C174 2m. "Integration" .... 5·00 5·00

Nos. C173/4 were issued in *se-tenant* pairs within the sheet.

C **140** Sunflower and Globe

C **141** Paper Birds

(Des M. Musa. Litho)

2006 (22 Apr). Earth Day. P 14.

C175 C **140** 1m. multicoloured .... 2·50 2·50

(Des M. Raguž. Litho)

2006 (3 May). World Press Freedom Day. P 14.

C176 C **141** 50f. multicoloured .... 1·30 1·30

C **142** Cable

C **143** Queen of Peace (statue) and Church

(Des R. Alilović. Litho)

2006 (17 May). World Telecommunications Day. P 14.

C177 C **142** 1m. multicoloured .... 2·50 2·50

(Des R. Alilović. Litho)

2006 (16 June). 25th Anniv of Medugorje. Booklet Stamps. Type C **143** and similar vert designs. Multicoloured. P 14.

C178 1m. Type C **143** .... 2·40 2·40
a. Booklet pane. Nos. C178/C182, each×2 .... 25·00
C179 1m. Statue with multicoloured halo amongst rocks .... 2·40 2·40
C180 1m. Cross, Krizevac Hill and statue .... 2·40 2·40
C181 1m. Statue (detail) and church .... 2·40 2·40
C182 1m. Stylized church and crowd .... 2·40 2·40
C178/C182 *Set of 5* .... 11·00 11·00

C **144** Church

C **145** Nikola Tesla

2006 (24 June). 150th Anniv of Uzdol Parish. P 14.

C183 C **144** 50f. multicoloured .... 1·30 1·30

(Des S. Mihaljevic. Litho)

2006 (9 July). 150th Birth Anniv of Nikola Tesla (engineer). P 14.

C184 C **145** 2m. multicoloured .... 5·00 5·00

C **146** Archer and Stag

C **147** Car

(Des Z. Anic. Litho)

2006 (9 Sept). Stećci (medieval tombstones). P 14.

C185 C **146** 20f. multicoloured .... 1·00 1·00

(Des S. Barbaric. Litho)

2006 (22 Sept). Car Free Day. P 14.

C186 C **147** 1m. black, vermilion and orange-yellow .... 2·50 2·50

C **148** Crucifix from Woman's Rosary, Franciscan Monastery, Humac

C **149** *Upupa epops* (hoopoe)

(Des Marin Musa. Litho)

2006 (9 Oct). P 14.

C187 C **148** 5m. multicoloured .... 12·50 12·50

2006 (1 Nov). Birds of Hutovo. Type C **149** and similar vert design. Multicoloured. P 14½.

C188 70f. Type C **149** .... 1·80 1·80
a. Horiz pair. Nos. C188/9 .... 3·75 3·75
C189 70f. *Alauda arvensis* .... 1·80 1·80

Nos. C188/9 were issued in horizontal *se-tenant* pairs within the sheet. Nos. C190/1 have been left for additions to this set.

C **150** Papaver Kerneri

C **151** Door with Wreath

2006 (1 Nov). Flora. Type C **150** and similar horiz design. Multicoloured. P 14×14½.

C192 20f. Type C **150** 50 50
a. Pair. Nos. C192/3 .... 1·10 1·10
C193 20f. *Cerastium dinaricum* 50 50

Nos. C192/3 were issued in *se-tenant* pairs within the sheet.

2006 (1 Dec). Christmas and New Year. Type C **151** and similar horiz design. Multicoloured. P 14½×14.

C194 50f. Type C **151** .... 1·30 1·30
C195 1m. Grass and candles .... 2·50 2·50

C **152** Hearts and Birds

C **153** Head of Dog

(Des Antonija Gudelj)

2007 (14 Feb). St. Valentine's Day. P 14½.

C196 C **152** 10f. multicoloured .... 1·00 1·00

2007 (22 Feb). Dogs. Tornjak. Type C **153** and similar vert design. Multicoloured. P 14½.

C197 70f. Type C **153** .... 1·70 1·70
a. Sheetlet. Nos. C197/C200 .... 7·00

C198 70f. Head of dog, black markings .... 1·70 1·70
C199 70f. Dog with black markings .... 1·70 1·70
C200 70f. Dog with brown markings .... 1·70 1·70
C197/C200 *Set of 4* ....
Nos. C197/C200 were issued in *se-tenant* sheetlets of four stamps.

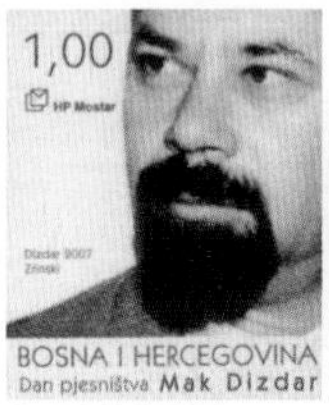

C **154** Mak Dizdar

C **155** Clasped Hands

(Des Bor Dizdar)

2007 (21 Mar). 90th Birth Anniv of Mehmedalija Mak Dizdar (poet). P 14.
C201 C **154** 1m. multicoloured .... 2·50 2·50

2007 (5 Apr). Europa. Centenary of Scouting. Type C **155** and similar horiz design. Multicoloured. P 14½.
C202 3m. Type C **155** .... 6·75 6·75
a. Pair. Nos. C202/3 .... 14·00 14·00
C203 3m. Reef knot s .... 6·75 6·75
Nos. C202/3 were issued in horizontal *se-tenant* pairs within sheetlets of four stamp.

C **156** *Sorbus domestica*

2007 (25 Apr). Tree Day. Sheet 68×91 mm. P 14.
MSC204 C **156** 2k. multicoloured .... 5·25 5·25

C **157** Lion (base relief) and Map

(Des Zdravko Anic)

2007 (12 May). Gabela Archaeological Site, Čapljina. P 14.
C205 C **157** 1m.50 multicoloured .... 3·75 3·75

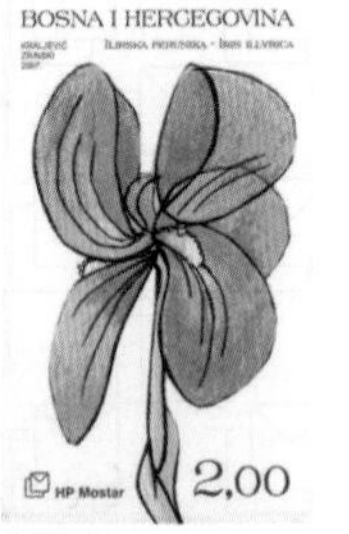

C **158** Iris

C **159** Virgin Mary (statue)

2007 (22 May). *Iris Illyrica*. Type C **158** and similar vert design. Multicoloured. P 14½.
C206 2k. Type C **158** .... 5·00 5·00
MSC207 61×80 mm. 3m. Iris and trireme (24×58 mm) .... 7·75 7·75

(Des Miro Raguž)

2007 (1 June). Medugorje. Booklet Stamps. Type C **159** and similar vert designs. Multicoloured. P 14.
C208 1m. Type C **131** .... 2·40 2·40
a. Booklet pane. Nos. C207/C211, each×2 .... 25·00
C209 1m. Hands holding rosary .... 2·40 2·40
C210 1m. Virgin Mary and pilgrims .... 2·40 2·40
C211 1m. Bronze statue of Friar .... 2·40 2·40
C212 1m. Virgin Mary (statue) and tower .... 2·40 2·40
C208/C212 *Set of 5* ....

C **160** Friar Marko Dobretić

C **161** Duke Vlatko's Tombstone, Boljuni Necropolis

(Des Davorin Briševac)

2007 (13 June). 300th Birth Anniv of Friar Marko Dobretić. P 14.
C213 C **160** 60f. multicoloured .... 1·50 1·50
No. C213 was issued in sheetlets of nine stamps.

(Des Zdravko Anic)

2007 (23 Sept). Cultural Heritage Day. P 14½.
C214 C **161** 20f. multicoloured .... 1·00 1·00

C **162** Emblem

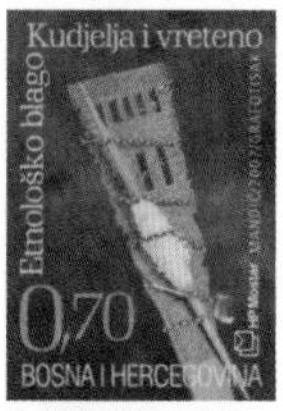

C **163** Hemp and Spindle

(Des Tvrtko Bojic)

2007 (24 Sept). World Bowling Championship, Grude. P 14½.
C215 C **162** 5m. black and scarlet .... 12·50 12·50

(Des Marko Mandic)

2007 (9 Oct). Ethnological Treasures. P 14½.
C216 C **163** 70f. multicoloured .... 1·80 1·80

C **164** *Fulica atra* (coot)

C **165** *Gentiana lutea*

2007 (1 Nov). Birds. Type C **164** and similar horiz designs. Multicoloured. P 14½.
C217 2m. Type C **164** .... 3·75 3·75
a. Block of 4. Nos. C217/20 .... 16·00
C218 2m. *Anas platyrhynchos* (mallard) .... 3·75 3·75
C219 2m. *Anas crecca* (common teal) .... 3·75 3·75
C220 2m. *Streptopella turtur* (turtle dove) .... 3·75 3·75
C217/C220 *Set of 4* ....
Nos. C217/20 were issued in *se-tenant* blocks of four stamps within the sheet.

(Des Drazenko Maric)

2007 (1 Nov). Flora of Blidinje Park. Type C **165** and similar horiz design. Multicoloured. P 14½.
C221 3m. Type C **165** .... 7·75 7·75
MSC222 80×60 mm. 3m. *Vaccinium vitis-idaea* .... 7·75 7·75
The stamp and margins No. **MS**C222 form a composite design.

C **166** Candles

C **167** Friar Andeo Kraljevic

(Des Bozena Dzidic)

2007 (1 Dec). Christmas. Type C **166** and similar horiz design. Multicoloured. P 14½.
C223 50f. Type C 166 .... 1·30 1·30
C224 70f. Decorated trees and doorway .... 1·90 1·90

(Des Mirko Cosic and Marin Musa)

2007 (28 Dec). Birth Bicentenary of Friar Ivan (Andeo) Kraljevic. P 14½.
C225 C **167** 1m. multicoloured .... 2·75 2·75

C **168** Chick and Flowers

C **169** Piano Keys

(Des Igor Filjak)

2008 (23 Mar). Easter. P 14½.
C226 C **168** 70f. multicoloured .... 1·90 1·90

(Des Marin Musa)

2008 (25 Mar). Tenth Anniv of Matica Hrvatska (cultural Institution's) Festival Week. P 14½.
C227 C **169** 10f. black and scarlet vermilion .... 1·00 1·00

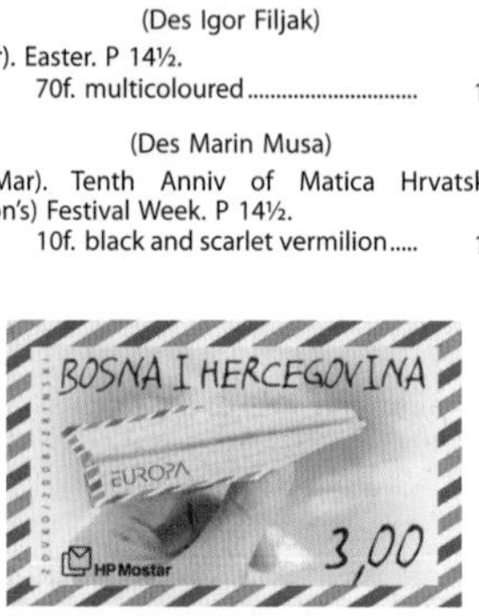

C **170** Hand holding Envelope as Paper Aeroplane

(Des Gordan Zovko)

2008 (5 Apr). Europa. The Letter. Type C **170** and similar horiz design. Multicoloured. P 14½.
C228 3m. Type C **170** .... 7·00 7·00
a. Vert strip of 3. Nos. C228/9 plus label .... 15·00 15·00
b. Pair. Nos. 228/9 .... 14·50 14·50
C229 3m. Pen nib .... 7·00 7·00
Nos. 228/9 were issued both in sheets as vertical strips of two stamps surrounding a central stamp size label and as *se-tenant* pairs within small sheets of four stamps.

C **171** Illyrian Warrior's Helmet, Vranjevo Selo

(Des Ariana Norsic)

2008 (12 May). Archaeology. P 14½.
C230 C **171** 2m.10 multicoloured .... 6·00 6·00

C **172** Grave of Mosha Danon, Rabbi of Sarajevo

(Des Marin Musa)

2008 (21 May). International Day of Diversity. P 14½.
C231 C **172** 1m.50 multicoloured .... 4·25 4·25

C **173** *Achillea millefolium* (milfoil)

C **174** Virgin Mary, Girl and Dove

(Des Davorin Briševac)

2008 (22 May). Myth and Flora. Andrija Šimić and Milfoil. Sheet 80×60 mm. P 14.
MSC232 C **173** 2m.90 multicoloured .... 8·25 8·25

(Des Ariana Norsic)

2008 (1 June). Medugorje. Booklet Stamps. Type C **174** and similar vert designs. Multicoloured. P 14.
C233 1m. Type C **174** .... 2·75 2·75
a. Booklet Pane. Nos. C233/7, each×2 .. 29·00
C234 1m. Church of St. Jacob .... 2·75 2·75
C235 1m. Page, crucified Christ and praying hands .... 2·75 2·75
C236 1m. Virgin Mary (statue) .... 2·75 2·75
C237 1m. Summit Cross .... 2·75 2·75
C233/C237 *Set of 5* ....

C **175** Grapes

(Des Anja Filjak)

2008 (9 Sept). Vintage Days in Brotnjo, 2008. Type C **175** and similar vert design. Multicoloured. P 14.
C238 50f. Type C **175** .... 1·30 1·30
C239 70f. White grapes .... 2·20 4·50

C **176** Building

(Des Mladen Ivesic)

2008 (4 Oct). Zaostrog Monastery. P 14.
C240 C **176** 1m. multicoloured 3·00 3·00

STAMP BOOKLETS

The following checklist covers, in simplified form, booklets issued by the Croat Postal Administration of Bosnia and Herzegovina. It is intended that it should be used in conjunction with the main listings and details of stamps and panes listed there are not repeated.

Prices are for complete booklets

Booklet No.	*Date*	*Contents and Cover Price*	*Price*
SBC1	24.6.96	Our Lady Queen of Peace Shrine, Medugorje (Type C **21**) 1 pane, No. C27a (40k.)	21·00
SBC2	16.6.06	Medugorje 1 pane, No. C178a (10m.)	26·00
SBC3	1.6.07	Medugorje 1 pane, No. C208a (10m.)	26·00
SBC4	1.6.08	Medugorje 1 pane, No. C233a (10m.)	30·00

III. REPUBLIKA SRPSKA

Issued by the Serb administration based in Pale.

1992. 100 Paras = 1 Dinar
1997. 100 Fennig = 1 Mark

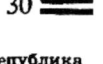

30
Република Српска
(S **1**)

S **2** Stringed Instrument

1992 (26 Oct). Nos. 2586/99 of Yugoslavia surch as Type S **1** (with thin bars over original face value on Nos. S1, S3 and S9). P 12½.
S1 5d. on 10p. bluish violet and bright green 1·10 1·10
S2 30d. on 3d. blue and orange-red £140 £140
S3 50d. on 40p. blue-green and bright purple (thin bars over original face value) 65·00 65·00
a. Perf 13½ 1·10 1·10
b. Thick bars over original face value 3·25 3·25
S4 60d. on 20p. bright crimson and orange-yellow 1·20 1·20
S5 60d. on 30p. light green and reddish orange 1·20 1·20
S6 100d. on 1d. turquoise-blue and bright purple 1·20 1·20
S7 100d. on 2d. new blue and bright crimson 65·00 65·00
a. Perf 13½ 1·20 1·20
S8 100d. on 3d. blue and orange-red 1·20 1·20
S9 300d. on 5d. ultramarine and greenish blue 20·00 20·00
a. Perf 13½ 1·50 1·50
S10 500d. on 50p. blue-green and reddish violet 1·50 1·50
S11 500d. on 60p. bright mauve and orange-vermilion 1·50 1·50
a. Perf 13½ 65·00 65·00
S1/11 *Set of* 11 (cheapest) 70·00 70·00

(Des M. Djorem. Litho The Mint, Belgrade)

1993 (11 Jan). Dated "1992". P 13½.
S12 S **2** 10d. black and orange-yellow 4·50 4·50
S13 20d. black and light new blue 20 20
S14 30d. black and deep salmon-pink 50 50
S15 – 50d. black and vermilion 60 60
S16 – 100d. black and vermilion 1·50 1·50
S17 – 500d. black and light new blue 3·00 3·00
S12/17 *Set of* 6 9·25 9·25
Designs: Vert—50, 100d. Coat of arms. Horiz—500d. Monastery.

1993 (8 June). Dated "1993". P 12½ (6000d.) or 13½ (others).
S18 S **2** 5000d. black and lilac 10 10
S19 6000d. black and yellow 20 20
S20 10000d. black and pale violet-blue 3·50 3·50
a. Perf 12½ 1·60 1·60
S21 – 20000d. black and vermilion 95 95
S22 – 30000d. black and vermilion 1·50 1·50
S23 – 50000d. black and lilac 1·50 1·50
S18/23 *Set of* 6 5·25 5·25
Designs: Vert—20000, 30000d. Coat of arms. Horiz—50000d. Monastery.

референдум
15-16. 05. '93.
7500
(S **3**)

S **4** Symbol of St. John the Evangelist

1993 (15 June). Referendum. Nos. S15/16 surch as Type S **3**.
S24 7500d. on 50d. black and vermilion 2·00 2·00
S25 7500d. on 100d. black and vermilion 2·00 2·00
S26 9000d. on 50d. black and vermilion 2·75 2·75
S24/26 *Set of* 3 6·00 6·00

(Litho The Mint, Belgrade)

1993 (16 Aug). No value expressed. P 13½.
S27 S **4** A vermilion 70 70
No. S27 was sold at the rate for internal letters.

Currency Reform

S **5** Icon of St. Stefan

S **6** King Peter I

(Des M. Djorem. Litho Forum, Novi Sad)

1994 (9 Jan). Republic Day. P 14.
S28 S **5** 1d. multicoloured 7·00 7·00

(Des M. Djorem. Litho Forum, Novi Sad)

1994 (28 May). 150th Birth Anniv of King Peter I of Serbia. P 14.
S29 S **6** 80p. olive-sepia and blackish brown 3·50 3·50
No. S29 was issued in sheets of eight stamps and one central label showing coat of arms.

S **7** Banja Luka

A
(S **8**)

(Des M. Djorem. Litho Forum, Novi Sad)

1994 (18 July). 500th Anniv of Banja Luka. P 14.
S30 S **7** 1d.20 multicoloured 4·00 4·00

1994 (July–Aug). Issued at Doboj. Surch as Type S **8**.

(a) On Nos. S13/16
S31 S **2** A on 20d. black and light new blue
S32 R on 20d. black and light new blue
S33 R on 30d. black and deep salmon-pink
S34 – R on 50d. black and vermilion
S35 – R on 100d. black and vermilion

(b) On Nos. S18/19 and S21/2
S36 S **2** R on 5000d. black and lilac
S37 R on 6000d. black and yellow
S38 – A on 20000d. black and vermilion
S39 – R on 20000d. black and vermilion
S40 – R on 30000d. black and vermilion
S31/40 *Set of* 10 £250
Nos. S31/40 were issued in North-east Bosnia during a period when communications with the remainder of Republika Srpska were disrupted by fighting in the Brčko Corridor. Stamps surcharged "A" were sold at the current rate for internal letters and those surcharged "R" at the rate for internal registered letters. The "R" on No. S32 is reversed.

S **9** "Madonna and Child" (icon)

P
(S **10**)

(Des M. Djorem. Litho Forum, Novi Sad)

1994 (1 Sept). Čajničke Church. P 14.
S41 S **9** 1d. multicoloured 3·50 3·50
No. S41 was issued in sheets of eight stamps and one central label.

1994 (1 Nov). Nos. S18/20 and S23 surch as Type S **10** or Type S **13**.
S42 S **2** A on 5000d. black and lilac 2·00 2·00
S43 R on 6000d. black and yellow 2·00 2·00
S44 40p. on 10000d. black and pale violet-blue 2·00 2·00
a. Perf 12½ 3·50 3·50
S45 – 2d. on 50000d. black and lilac 2·00 2·00
S42/45 *Set of* 4 7·25 7·25
No. S42 was sold at the current rate for internal letters and No. S43, which shows the surcharge as the cyrillic letter resembling "P", at the rate for internal registered letters.

S **11** Tavna Monastery

S **12** *Aquilegia dinarica*

(Des M. Djorem. Litho Forum, Novi Sad)

1994 (11 Nov–31 Dec). Monasteries. Type S **11** and similar multicoloured designs. P 14.
S46 60p. Type S **11** 2·00 2·00
S47 1d. Moštanica (horiz) (31 Dec) 3·00 3·00
S48 1d.20 Žitomislić (28 Dec) 3·50 3·50
S46/48 *Set of* 3 7·75 7·75

(Litho Forum, Novi Sad)

1996 (1 Mar). Nature Protection. Type S **12** and similar horiz designs. Multicoloured. P 14.
S49 1d.20 Type S **12** 2·00 2·00
a. Block of 4. Nos. S49/52 8·25
S50 1d.20 *Edraianthus niveus* (plant) 2·00 2·00
S51 1d.20 Shore lark 2·00 2·00
S52 1d.20 *Dinaromys bogdanovi* (dormouse) 2·00 2·00
S49/52 *Set of* 4 7·25 7·25
Nos. S49/52 were issued together in *se-tenant* blocks of four within sheets of 24 stamps and one central label.

0,70
(S **13**)

S **14** Relay Station, Mt. Kozara

1996 (1 July). Nos. S14/16, S19 and S22 surch as Type S **13**.
S53 S **2** 70p. on 30d. black and deep salmon-pink 60 60
S54 – 1d. on 100d. black and vermilion 70 70
S55 – 2d. on 30000d. black and vermilion 1·30 1·30
S56 – 3d. on 50d. black and vermilion 1·90 1·90
S57 S **2** 5d. on 6000d. black and yellow 3·25 3·25
S53/57 *Set of* 5 7·00 7·00

(Litho Forum, Novi Sad)

1996 (20 Sept). Type S **14** and similar designs. P 14.
S58 A slate-green and olive-bistre 25 25
S59 R plum and chestnut 60 60
S60 1d.20 violet and blue 65 65
S61 2d. reddish lilac and mauve 1·30 1·30
S62 5d. blackish purple and pale blue 2·75 2·75
S63 10d. deep brown and olive-sepia 5·75 5·75
S58/63 *Set of* 6 10·00 10·00
Designs: Vert—R, Kraljica relay station, Mt. Ozren; 2d. Relay station, Mt. Romanija; 5d. Stolice relay station, Mt. Maljevica. Horiz—1d.20, Bridge over R. Drina at Srbinje; 10d. Bridge at Višegrad.
No. S58 was sold at the current rate for an internal letter and No. S59 at the rate for an internal registered letter.

S **15** Orthodox Church, Baščaršiji

S **16** Michael Pupin

(Litho Forum, Novi Sad)

1997 (7 July). P 14.
S64 S **15** 2d.50 multicoloured 1·40 1·40

(Litho Forum, Novi Sad)

1997 (14 July). 62nd Death Anniv of Michael Pupin (physicist and inventor). P 14.
S65 S **16** 2d.50 multicoloured 1·40 1·40

S **17** *Primula kitaibeliana*

S **18** Robert Koch

(Litho Forum, Novi Sad)

1997 (12 Sept). Flowers. Type S **17** and similar vert designs. Multicoloured. P 14.
S66 3d.20 Type S **17** 1·50 1·50
S67 3d.20 *Pedicularis hoermanniana* 1·50 1·50
S68 3d.20 *Knautia sarajevensis* 1·50 1·50
S69 3d.20 *Oxytropis campestris* 1·50 1·50
S66/69 *Set of* 4 5·50 5·50

1997 (14 Sept). OBLIGATORY TAX. Anti-tuberculosis Week. Self-adhesive. Die-cut (straight sides).
S70 S **18** 15f. bright rose-red and dull ultramarine 45 45

S **19** Branko Čopić

S **20** European Otter (*Lutra lutra*)

(Des R. Bojanić. Litho Forum, Novi Sad)

1997 (1 Nov). Writers. Type S **19** and similar square designs. Each deep magenta and yellow. P 14.

S71	A (60p.) Type S **19**	35	35
S72	R (90p.) Jovaî Dučić	60	60
S73	1d.50 Meša Selimović	60	60
S74	3d. Aleksá Šantić	1·40	1·40
S75	5d. Petar Kočić	2·30	2·30
S76	10d. Ivï Andrić	4·75	4·75
S71/76 *Set of 6*		9·00	9·00

(Litho Forum, Novi Sad)

1997 (12 Nov). Nature Protection. Type S **20** and similar vert designs. Multicoloured. P 14.

S77	2d.50 Type S 20	60	60
S78	4d.50 Roe deer (*Capreolus capreolus*)	1·70	1·70
S79	6d.50 Brown bear (*Ursus arctos*)	3·50	3·50
S77/79 *Set of 3*		5·25	5·25

S **21** Two Queens S **22** Diana, Princess of Wales

(Des R. Bojanić. Litho Forum, Novi Sad)

1997 (12 Nov). Europa. Tales and Legends. Type S **21** and similar vert design. Multicoloured. P 14.

S80	2d.50 Type S **21**	9·25	9·25
S81	6d.50 Prince on horseback	20·00	20·00

(Des R. Bojanić. Litho Forum, Novi Sad)

1998 (22 Dec). Diana, Princess of Wales Commemoration. P 14.

S82	S **22** 3d.50 multicoloured ("DIANA" in Roman alphabet)	5·75	5·75
	a. Pair. Nos. S82/3	12·00	12·00
S83	3d.50 multicoloured ("DIANA" in Cyrillic alphabet)	5·75	5·75

New Currency

100 Fennig = 1 Mark

S **23** Cross and Globe S **24** Brazil

1998 (5 May). OBLIGATORY TAX. Red Cross. Self-adhesive. Die-cut (straight sides).

S84	S **23** 90f. carmine-red, azure and ultramarine	1·20	1·20

(Des R. Bojanić. Litho Forum, Novi Sad)

1998 (5 May). World Cup Football Championship, France. Type S **24** and similar vert designs showing flags and players of countries in final rounds. Multicoloured. P 14×13½.

S85	90f. Type S **24**	1·90	1·90
	a. Sheetlet. Nos. S85/92 plus label (groups A and B)	16·00	
S86	90f. Morocco	1·90	1·90
S87	90f. Norway	1·90	1·90
S88	90f. Scotland	1·90	1·90
S89	90f. Italy	1·90	1·90
S90	90f. Chile	1·90	1·90
S91	90f. Austria	1·90	1·90
S92	90f. Cameroun	1·90	1·90
S93	90f. France	1·90	1·90
	a. Sheetlet. Nos. S93/100 plus label (groups C and D)	16·00	
S94	90f. Saudi Arabia	1·90	1·90
S95	90f. Denmark	1·90	1·90
S96	90f. South Africa	1·90	1·90
S97	90f. Spain	1·90	1·90
S98	90f. Nigeria	1·90	1·90
S99	90f. Paraguay	1·90	1·90
S100	90f. Bulgaria	1·90	1·90
S101	90f. Netherlands	1·90	1·90
	a. Sheetlet. Nos. S101/8 plus label (groups E and F)	16·00	
S102	90f. Belgium	1·90	1·90
S103	90f. Mexico	1·90	1·90
S104	90f. South Korea	1·90	1·90
S105	90f. Germany	1·90	1·90
S106	90f. United States of America	1·90	1·90
S107	90f. Yugoslavia	1·90	1·90
S108	90f. Iran	1·90	1·90
S109	90f. Romania	1·90	1·90
	a. Sheetlet. Nos. S109/16 plus label (groups G and H)	16·00	
S110	90f. England (U.K. flag)	1·90	1·90
S111	90f. Tunisia	1·90	1·90
S112	90f. Colombia	1·90	1·90
S113	90f. Argentina	1·90	1·90
S114	90f. Jamaica	1·90	1·90
S115	90f. Croatia	1·90	1·90
S116	90f. Japan	1·90	1·90
S85/116 *Set of 32*		55·00	55·00

Nos. S85/92, S93/100, S101/8 and S109/16 respectively were issued together in *se-tenant* sheetlets of eight stamps and one central label, showing the French cock or a Paris landmark.

S **25** Couple and Musical Instrument S **26** Family walking in Countryside

(Des R. Bojanić. Litho Forum, Novi Sad)

1998 (9 June). Europa. National Festivals. Type S **25** and similar horiz design. Multicoloured. P 14.

S117	7m.50 Type S 25	9·25	9·25
S118	7m.50 Couple from Neretva and musical instrument	9·25	9·25

Nos. S117/18 were issued in sheetlets of eight stamps and one central label showing the design of the other stamp.

1998 (14 Sept). OBLIGATORY TAX. Anti-tuberculosis Week. Photo. P 11.

S119	S **26** 75f. multicoloured	1·20	1·20

S **27** St. Pantelejmon S **28** Bijeljina

(Des R. Bojanić. Litho Forum, Novi Sad)

1998 (24 Dec). 800th Anniv of Hilandar Monastery. Icons. Type S **27** and similar vert designs. Multicoloured. P 14.

S120	50f. Type S **27**	80	80
S121	70f. Jesus Christ	1·20	1·20
S122	1m.70 St. Nikola	2·50	2·50
S123	2m. St. John of Rila	3·00	3·00
S120/123 *Set of 4*		6·75	6·75

(Des R. Bojanić. Litho Forum, Novi Sad)

1999 (15 Mar). Towns. Type S **28** and similar square design. Multicoloured. P 14.

	(a) With face value		
S124	15f. Type S **28**	25	25
S125	20f. Sokolac	35	35
S126	75f. Prijedor	1·20	1·20
S127	2m. Brčko	3·00	3·00
S128	4m.50 Zvornik	6·50	6·50
S129	10m. Doboj	15·00	15·00
	(b) Face value expressed by letter		
S130	A (50f.) Banja Luka	70	70
S131	R (1m.) Trebinje	1·50	1·50
S124/131 *Set of 8*		26·00	26·00

No. S130 was sold at the current rate for an internal letter and No. S131 at the rate for an internal registered letter.

S **29** Airliner over Lake

(Des R. Bojanić. Litho Forum, Novi Sad)

1999 (26 Mar). Founding of Air Srpska (state airline). Type S **29** and similar horiz designs. Multicoloured. P 14.

S132	50f. Type S **29**	70	70
S133	50f. Airliner above clouds	70	70
S134	75f. Airliner over beach	1·20	1·20
S135	1m.50 Airliner over lake (different)	2·20	2·20
S132/135 *Set of 4*		4·25	4·25

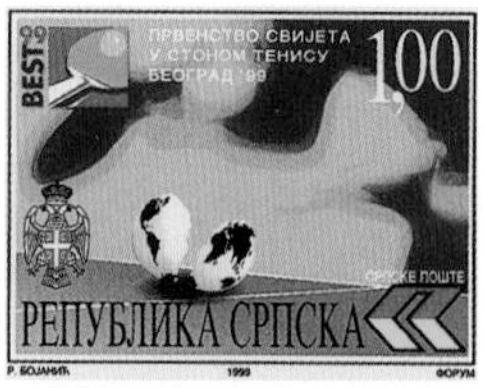

S **30** Table Tennis Ball as Globe

(Des R. Bojanić. Litho Forum, Novi Sad)

1999 (19 Apr). International Table Tennis Championships, Belgrade. Type S **30** and similar horiz design. Multicoloured. P 14.

S136	1m. Type S **30**	1·70	1·70
S137	2m. Table tennis table, bat and ball	3·50	3·50

S **31** Kozara National Park

(Des R. Bojanić. Litho Forum, Novi Sad)

1999 (4 May). Europa. National Parks. Type S **31** and similar vert design. Multicoloured. P 14.

S138	1m.50 Type S **31**	75·00	75·00
S139	2m. Perućica National Park	75·00	75·00

S **32** Open Hands S **33** Manuscript

1999 (8 May). OBLIGATORY TAX. Red Cross. Litho. P 11.

S140	S **32** 10f. multicoloured	45	45

(Des R. Bojanić. Litho Forum, Novi Sad)

1999 (28 May). 780th Anniv of Bosnia and Herzegovina Archbishopric (S142, S144/8) and 480th Anniv of Garažole Printing Works (S141, S143). Type S **33** and similar vert designs. Multicoloured. P 14.

S141	50f. Type S **33**	70	70
	a. Sheetlet. Nos. S141/8 plus label	5·75	
S142	50f. Dobrun Monastery	70	70
S143	50f. "G"	70	70
S144	50f. Zhitomislib Monastery	70	70
S145	50f. Gomionitsa Monastery	70	70
S146	50f. Madonna and Child with angels and prophets (icon, 1578)	70	70
S147	50f. St. Nicolas (icon)	70	70
S148	50f. Wise Men (icon)	70	70
S141/148 *Set of 8*		5·00	5·00

Nos. S141/8 were issued together in *se-tenant* sheetlets of eight stamps and one central label showing a coat of arms.

S **34** Brown Trout (*Salmo trutta morpha fario*) S **35** Lunar Module on Moon's Surface

(Des R. Bojanić. Litho Forum, Novi Sad)

1999 (17 June). Fish. Type S **34** and similar horiz designs. Multicoloured. P 14.

S149	50f. Type S **34**	6·75	1·20
	a. Horiz strip. Nos. S149/52		
S150	50f. Lake trout (*Salmo trutta morpha lacustris*)	1·20	1·20
S151	75f. Huchen (*Hucho hucho*)	1·70	1·70
S152	1m. European grayling (*Thymallus thymallus*)	2·30	2·30
S149/152 *Set of 4*		5·75	5·75

Nos. S149/52 were issued together in horizontal *se-tenant* strips of four stamps and one central label.

(Des R. Bojanić. Litho Forum, Novi Sad)

1999 (21 July). 30th Anniv of First Manned Landing on Moon. Type S **35** and similar vert design. Multicoloured. P 14.

S153	1m. Type S 35	1·90	1·90
S154	2m. Astronaut on Moon	3·00	3·00

S **36** Pencil and Emblem S **36a** Roadway to "2000"

(Des R. Bojanić. Litho Forum, Novi Sad)

1999 (9 Sept). 125th Anniv of Universal Postal Union. Type S **36** and similar horiz design. Multicoloured. P 14.

S155	75f. Type S **36**	1·20	1·20
S156	1m.25 Earth and emblem	2·00	2·00

Nos. S155/6 were each issued in sheets of eight stamps and one central label.

1999 (14 Sept). OBLIGATORY TAX. Tuberculosis Week.

	(a) Ordinary gum. P 11		
S156	10f. Type S **36a**		
	(b) Self-adhesive gum		
S156	10f. As Type S **36a**		

S **37** Madonna and Child S **38** Ancient Egyptians

1999 (29 Oct). Art. Icons. Type S **37** and similar vert designs. Multicoloured. P 14.

S157	50f. Type S **37**	75	75
	a. Sheetlet. Nos. S157/64	6·25	
S158	50f. Madonna, Cajnice	75	75
S159	50f. Madonna, Pelagonitisa	75	75
S160	50f. Holy Kirjak, Otselnik	75	75
S161	50f. Pieta	75	75
S162	50f. Entry of Christ into Jerusalem	75	75
S163	50f. St. Jovan	75	75
S164	50f. Sava and Simeon	75	75
S157/164 *Set of* 8		5·50	5·50

Nos. S157/64 were issued together in *se-tenant* sheetlets of eight stamps and one central label showing a coat of arms.

(Des R. Bojanić. Litho Forum, Novi Sad)

1999 (22 Nov). Millennium (1st series). Sheet 137×86 mm containing Type S **38** and similar horiz designs. Multicoloured. P 14.

MSS170 50f.×4, Type S **38**; Inventions for time keeping; Iron working; Invention of steam engines; 1m. Space exploration .... 10·00 10·00

No. **MS**S170 also contains a stamp size label and was issued in a folder.

See also No. **MS**S202.

S **39** Postal Stage-Coach during Austro-Hungarian Occupation

S **40** Fresco of St. Simeon (Stefan Nemanja) holding Studenica Monastery

(Des R. Bojanić. Litho Forum, Novi Sad)

1999 (23 Dec). 135th Anniv of Postal Service. Type S **39** and similar horiz design. Multicoloured. P 14.

S171	50f. Type S **39**	75	75
MSS172	55×70 mm. 3m. Tatar postmen crossing bridge during Turkish regency	80·00	80·00

No. **MS**S172 also contains a stamp size label.

(Des R. Bojanić. Litho Forum, Novi Sad)

2000 (29 Jan). 800th Death Anniv of Stefan Nemanja (Stephen II). P 14.

S173	S **40** 1m.50 multicoloured	2·20	2·20

S **41** *Prunus domestica* (plum)

S **42** Bridge, Sepk

(Des R. Bojanić. Litho Forum, Novi Sad)

2000 (22 Mar). Trees. Type S **41** and similar vert design. Multicoloured. P 14.

S174	1m. Type S **41**	1·50	1·50
S175	2m. *Corylus avellana* (hazel)	3·00	3·00

(Des R. Bojanić. Litho Forum, Novi Sad)

2000 (12 Apr). Bridges on Drina River. Type S **42** and similar horiz designs. Multicoloured. P 14.

S176	1m. Type S **42**	1·60	1·60
S177	1m. Pavlovica Bridge, Bijeljina	1·60	1·60
S178	1m. Stag and iron bridge, Bratunac	1·60	1·60
S179	1m. Train crossing bridge, Zvornik	1·60	1·60
S176/179 *Set of* 4		5·75	5·75

S **43** Jovaî Dučić

S **44** Construction of Europe

(Des R. Bojanić. Litho Forum, Novi Sad)

2000 (26 Apr). Jovaî Dučić (writer) Commemoration. P 14.

S180	S **43** 20f. multicoloured	35	35

(Des R. Bojanić. Litho Forum, Novi Sad)

2000 (5 May). Europa. Construction of Europe. Type S **44** and similar vert designs. Multicoloured. P 14.

S181	1m.50 Type S **44**	70·00	70·00
S182	2m.50 Children and stars	80·00	80·00

S **45** Girl

S **46** Basilica, Banja Luka (destroyed in 1941)

2000 (8 May). OBLIGATORY TAX. Red Cross Week. Type S **45** and similar vert designs. Multicoloured.

(a) Ordinary gum. P 11

S183	10f. Type S **45**	50	50
S183*a*	10f. Symbols of care (30×41 mm)	50	50

(b) Self-adhesive gum. Die-cut

S183*b*	50f. As No. 183*a* (20×30 mm)	50	50
S183/183*b* *Set of* 3		1·40	1·40

(Des R. Bojanić. Litho Forum, Novi Sad)

2000 (26 May). Centenary of Banja Luka Province. P 14.

S184	S **46** 1m.50 multicoloured	2·20	2·20

S **47** Footballers

S **48** Leaders of Herzegovina Uprising

(Des R. Bojanić. Litho Forum, Novi Sad)

2000 (14 June). Euro 2000—European Football Championships, Belgium and the Netherlands. Type S **47** and similar vert designs. Multicoloured. P 14.

S185	1m. Type S **47**	1·50	1·50
S186	2m. Footballers (different)	3·00	3·00
MSS187	66×83 mm. 6m. Netherlands and Belgium flags as map and footballers (35×42 mm)	12·50	12·50

(Des R. Bojanić. Litho Forum, Novi Sad)

2000 (12 July). 125th Anniv of Herzegovina Rebellion (Nevesinje uprising).

S188	S **48** 1m.50 multicoloured	2·40	2·40

S **49** Outline of Australia and Hurdling

S **50** Toddler

(Des R. Bojanić. Litho Forum, Novi Sad)

2000 (6 Sept). Olympic Games, Sydney. Type S **49** and similar horiz designs. Multicoloured. P 14.

S189	50f. Type S **49**	75	75
S190	50f. Australia and volleyball	75	75
S191	50f. Australia and basketball	75	75
S192	50f. Australia and handball	75	75
S189/192 *Set of* 4		2·75	2·75
MSS193	71×98 mm. 2m. Australia, emu and kangaroo	3·00	3·00

No. **MS**S193 also contains a stamp size label showing Sydney Opera House and Olympic Stadium, the whole forming a composite design.

2000 (14 Sept). OBLIGATORY TAX. Tuberculosis Week. Type S **50** and similar vert design. Multicoloured.

(a) Ordinary gum. P 11

S194	10f. Type S **50**	50	50

(b) Self-adhesive gum. Die-cut

S195	1m. As Type S **50** (20×30 mm)	50	50

S **51** Locomotive, 1848

S **52** *Leontopodium alpinum* (edelweiss)

(Des R. Bojanić. Litho Forum, Novi Sad)

2000 (4 Oct). 175th Anniv of Railways. Type S**51** and similar horiz designs. Multicoloured. P 14.

S196	50f. Type S **51**	2·50	2·50
	a. Pair. Nos. S196/7	5·25	5·25
	b. Strip. Nos. S196/9 plus label	12·00	
S197	50f. Steam locomotive, 1865	2·50	2·50
S198	50f. Steam locomotive, 1930	2·50	2·50
	a. Pair. Nos. S198/9	6·50	6·50
S199	1m. Electric locomotive, 1990	3·75	3·75
S196/199 *Set of* 4		10·00	10·00

Nos. S196/7 and S198/9 were issued in horizontal *se-tenant* pairs, surrounding a central stamp size label, giving a horizontal strip of five.

(Des R. Bojanić. Litho Forum, Novi Sad)

2000 (31 Oct). European Nature Protection. Type S **52** and similar multicoloured design. P 14.

S200	1m. Type S **52**	1·50	1·50
S201	2m. *Proteus anguinus* (olm) (horiz)	3·00	3·00

S **53** Columbus discovering America

S **54** The Assumption of Mary (fresco)

(Des R. Bojanić. Litho Forum, Novi Sad)

2000 (22 Nov). Millennium (2nd series). Two sheets, each 140×86 mm containing Type S **53** and similar horiz designs. Multicoloured. P 14.

MSS202 (a) 50f.×6, Type S **53**; Discovery of glass, iron and steel; First printing press; Industrial revolution; James Watt and steam engine; Hubble telescope and satellite (space exploration). (b) 3m. Exploration by sea (105×55 mm) .... 9·25 9·25

Nos. **MS**S202a/b were issued in a folder.

(Des R. Bojanić. Litho Forum, Novi Sad)

2000 (20 Dec). Icons and Frescoes. Type S **54** and similar vert designs. Multicoloured. P 14.

S203	50f. Type S **54**	75	75
S204	50f. Entry of Christ into Jerusalem (icon)	75	75
S205	1m. Madonna with Child and Angels (icon)	1·50	1·50
S206	1m. Christos Pantocrator (ceiling fresco).	1·50	1·50
S203/206 *Set of* 4		4·00	4·00

S **55** Alexander Graham Bell and Development of Telephones

(Des R. Bojanić. Litho Forum, Novi Sad)

2001 (27 Feb). 125th Anniv of Telephony. P 14.

S207	S **55** 1m. multicoloured	1·50	1·50

S **56** Yuri Gagarin and *Vostok 1*

S **57** Vlado Milosevic

(Des R. Bojanić. Litho Forum, Novi Sad)

2001 (29 Mar). 40th Anniv of First Manned Space Flight. Type S**56** and similar horiz design. Multicoloured. P 14.

S208	1m. Type S **56**	1·50	1·50
MSS209	86×66 mm. 3m. Yuri Gagarin, take off and first flight orbit (53×34 mm)	8·75	8·75

(Des R. Bojanić. Litho Forum, Novi Sad)

2001 (11 Apr). Birth Centenary of Vlado Milosevic (composer and ethnomusicologist).

S210	S **57** 50f. multicoloured	75	75

S **58** Waterfall, Sutjeska River

S **59** *Maniola jurtina*

(Des R. Bojanić. Litho Forum, Novi Sad)

2001 (4 May). Europa. Water Conservation. Type S **58** and similar vert design. Multicoloured. P 14.

S211	1m. Type S **58**	2·75	2·75
	a. Booklet pane. Nos. S211/12, each×3	26·00	
S212	2m. Turjanica river	5·50	5·50

(Des R. Bojanić. Litho Forum, Novi Sad)

2001 (19 June). Butterflies. Type S**59** and similar vert designs. Multicoloured. P 14.

S213	50f. Type S **59**	75	75
S214	50f. *Pyrgus malvae*	75	75
S215	1m. *Papilio machaon*	1·50	1·50
S216	1m. *Lycaena phlaeas* inscr "Lycaena pylaeas"	1·50	1·50
S213/216 *Set of* 4		4·00	4·00

S **60** Women's Costumes, Popovo

S **61** Combatants

(Des R. Bojanić. Litho Forum, Novi Sad)

2001 (17 July). Traditional Costumes. Type S **60** and similar vert designs. Multicoloured. P 14.

S217 50f. Type S 60 ... 75 75
S218 50f. Bridal costume, Zmijanje ... 75 75
S219 1m. Woman's costume, Bileca mountains ... 1·50 1·50
S220 1m. Two women, Lijevce ... 1·50 1·50

(Des R. Bojanić. Litho Forum, Novi Sad)

2001 (5 Sept). Republic of Srpska—Karate World Champion—2001.

S221 S **61** 1m.50 multicoloured ... 2·20 2·20

S **62** Old Castle, Kostajnica

(Des R. Bojanić. Litho Forum, Novi Sad)

2001 (5 Sept–23 Oct). Towns. Type S **62** and similar multicoloured designs. P 14.

S222 25f. Type S **62** ... 35 35
S223 A (50f.) As No. S130 (24×22 mm) (20.9) ... 75 75
S224 1m. Square with monument dedicated to war victims, Srbinje (23.10) ... 1·50 1·50
S222/224 *Set of* 3 ... 2·30 2·30

No. S225 is vacant.

S **63** Emblem

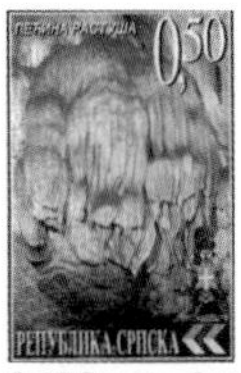
S **64** Rastusa Cave, Teslic

2001 (14 Sept). Obligatory Tax. Anti-Tuberculosis Week. P 14.

S226 S **63** 10f. multicoloured ... 50 50

(Des R. Bojanić. Litho Forum, Novi Sad)

2001 (20 Sept). Caves. Booklet Stamps. Type S **64** and similar vert designs. Multicoloured. P 14×imperf.

S227 50f. Type S **64** ... 75 75
a. Booklet pane. Nos. S227/32 ... 5·00
S228 50f. Vagan cave, Vitorog ... 75 75
S229 50f. Pavlova cave, Petrovo ... 75 75
S230 50f. Orlovaca cave, Pale ... 75 75
S231 50f. Ledana cave, Bobija ... 75 75
S232 50f. Hole, Podovi plateau ... 75 75
S227/232 *Set of* 6 ... 4·00 4·00

S **65** Alfred Nobel (founder)

S **66** Klinje Lake, Gacko

(Des R. Bojanić. Litho Forum, Novi Sad)

2001 (23 Oct). Centenary of Nobel Prizes. Type S **65** and similar vert design. Multicoloured. P 14.

S233 1m. Type S **65** ... 1·50 1·50
S234 2m. Ivi Andrić (winner of Nobel prize for Literature—1961) ... 3·00 3·00

(Des R. Bojanić. Litho Forum, Novi Sad)

2001 (15 Nov). European Nature Protection. Type S **66** and similar horiz design. Multicoloured. P 14.

S235 1m. Type S **66** ... 1·50 1·50
S236 1m. Bardaca Lake, Srbac ... 1·50 1·50

S **67** *Still Life with Parrot* (Jovan Bijelic)

S **68** Birth of Christ (icon, Studenica Monastery)

(Des R. Bojanić. Litho Forum, Novi Sad)

2001 (5 Dec). Art. Type S **67** and similar multicoloured designs. P 14.

S237 50f. Type S **67** ... 75 75
S238 50f. *Djerdap* (Todor Svrakic) ... 75 75
S239 50f. *Suburb of Belgrade* (Kosta Hakman) .. 75 75
S240 50f. *Adela* (Miodrag Vujacic Mirski) (vert) 75 75
S237/240 *Set of* 4 ... 2·75 2·75

(Des R. Bojanić. Litho Forum, Novi Sad)

2001 (5 Dec). Christmas. P 14.

S241 S **68** 1m. multicoloured ... 1·50 1·50

S **69** Player and Club Badge

S **70** National Arms

(Des R. Bojanić. Litho Forum, Novi Sad)

2001 (24 Dec). 75th Anniv of Borac Football Club. P 14.

S242 S **69** 1m.50 multicoloured ... 2·20 2·20

(Des R. Bojanić. Litho Forum, Novi Sad)

2002 (10 Jan). Tenth Anniv of Republic Srpska. Type S **70** and similar multicoloured designs. P 14.

S243 50f. Type S **70** ... 80 80
S243*a* 1m. National flag (horiz) ... 1·60 1·60
MSS243*b* 71×64 mm. 2m. Map (42×35 mm) ... 2·35 2·35

S **71** Hand gripping Cobra

S **72** Ski Jump

(Des R. Bojanić. Litho Forum, Novi Sad)

2002 (29 Jan). Fight against Terrorism. Type S **71** and similar vert design. Multicoloured. P 14.

S244 1m. Type S **71** ... 1·60 1·60
MSS244*a* 68×76 mm. 2m. Eyes enclosed in globe.... 3·25 3·25

(Des R. Bojanić. Litho Forum, Novi Sad)

2002 (13 Feb). Winter Olympic Games, Salt Lake City. Type S **72** and similar vert design. Multicoloured. P 14.

S245 50f. Type S **72** ... 80 80
S246 1m. Two man bobsleigh ... 1·60 1·60

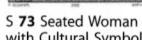

S **73** Seated Woman with Cultural Symbols

S **74** Vasilije Ostroski Church, Sarajevo

(Des R. Bojanić. Litho Forum, Novi Sad)

2002 (5 Mar). Centenary of Prosvjeta Cultural Association. P 14.

S247 S **73** 1m. multicoloured ... 1·60 1·60

(Des R. Bojanić. Litho Forum, Novi Sad)

2002 (5 Mar–17 Apr). Towns. Type S **74** and similar multicoloured design. P 14.

S248 50f. Type S **74** ... 80 80
S249 2m. Oil Refinery, Srpski Brod (horiz) (17.4) ... 3·25 32·00

S **75** Charles Lindbergh and *Spirit of St Louis*

S **76** Horses and Clown

(Des R. Bojanić. Litho Forum, Novi Sad)

2002 (11 Apr). 75th Anniv of First Solo Flight across Atlantic Ocean. P 14.

S250 S **75** 1m. multicoloured ... 1·60 1·60

(Des R. Bojanić. Litho Forum, Novi Sad)

2002 (30 Apr). Europa. Circus. Type S **76** and similar horiz design. Multicoloured. P 14.

S251 1m. Type S **76** ... 1·60 1·60
a. Booklet pane. Nos. S251/2, each×3 .. 12·50
S252 1m.50 Elephants ... 2·40 2·40

S **76a** Rescue Workers

S **77** Footballers

2002 (8 May). OBLIGATORY TAX. Red Cross Week. Type S **76a** and similar horiz design. Multicoloured.

(a) Ordinary gum. P 11

S252*a* 10f. Type S **76a** ... 55 55

(b) Self-adhesive gum. Die-cut

S252*b* 50f. As Type S **76a** plus emblem ... 55 55

(Des R. Bojanić. Litho Forum, Novi Sad)

2002 (31 May). World Cup Football Championships, Japan and South Korea. Type S **77** and similar vert design. Multicoloured. P 14.

S253 50f. Type S **77** ... 80 80
S254 1m. Footballers (different) ... 1·60 1·60

S **78** Slatina

S **79** Greek-Illyrian Helmet (4th—5th century BC)

(Des R. Bojanić. Litho Forum, Novi Sad)

2002 (5 July). Spas. Type S **78** and similar horiz designs. Multicoloured. P 14.

S255 25f. Type S **78** ... 40 40
S256 50f. Mljecanica ... 85 85
S257 75f. Vilina Vlas ... 1·30 1·30
S258 1m. Laktasi ... 1·70 1·70
S259 1m.50 Vrucica ... 2·50 2·50
S260 5m. Dvorovi ... 8·75 8·75
S255/260 *Set of* 6 ... 14·00 14·00

(Des R. Bojanić. Litho Forum, Novi Sad)

2002 (2 Sept). Museum Exhibits. Type S **79** and similar multicoloured designs. P 14.

S261 50f. Type S **79** ... 85 85
S262 50f. Murano glass cup ... 85 85
S263 1m. Headstone of Grd (12th century parish priest) (horiz) ... 1·70 1·70
S264 1m. Silver bracelet (4th–5th century BC) (horiz) ... 1·70 1·70
S261/264 *Set of* 4 ... 4·50 4·50

S **79a** Waterfall and Lungs as Forest

S **80** *Boletus regius*

2002 (14 Sept). OBLIGATORY TAX. Tuberculosis Week. Type S **79a** and similar vert design. Multicoloured.

(a) Ordinary gum. P 11

S264*a* 10f. Type S**79a** ... 55 55

(b) Self-adhesive gum. Die-cut

S264*b* 50f. As Type S**79a** (20×30 mm) ... 55 55

(Des R. Bojanić. Litho Forum, Novi Sad)

2002 (17 Oct). Fungi. Type S **80** and similar horiz designs. Multicoloured. P 14.

S265 50f. Type S **80** ... 85 85
a. Strip. Nos. S265/8 plus label ... 5·25
S266 50f. *Macrolepiota procera* ... 85 85
S267 1m. *Amanita caesarea* ... 1·70 1·70
S268 1m. *Craterellus cornucopoides* ... 1·70 1·70
S265/268 *Set of* 4 ... 4·50 4·50

Nos. S265/8 were issued in horizontal *se-tenant* strips of four stamps surrounding a central stamp size label.

S **81** Maglic Mountain

S **82** *Petar Popović Pecija* (Spiro Bocaric) (1933)

(Des R. Bojanić. Litho Forum, Novi Sad)

002 (26 Nov). European Nature Protection. Type S **81** and similar vert design. Multicoloured. P 14.

269 50f. Type S **81** 85 85
269*a* 1m. Klekovaca Mountain .... 1·70 1·70

(Des R. Bojanić. Litho Forum, Novi Sad)

002 (18 Dec). Art. Type S **82** and similar multicoloured designs. P 14.

270 50f. Type S **82** 85 85
271 50f. Black Lake beneath Durmitor (Lazar Drljaca) (1935) (horiz) 85 85
272 1m. Zembilj Street (Branko Sotra) (1937) (horiz) .... 1·70 1·70
273 1m. Birds and Landscape (Milan Sovilj) (2000) (horiz) .... 1·70 1·70
270/273 *Set of 4* .... 4·50 4·50

Nos. 270/3 were each issued with a *se-tenant* stamp size label nowing a painting.

S **83** Vrbas Canyon (scene from film by Spiro Bocaric) (1937)

(Des R. Bojanić. Litho Forum, Novi Sad)

2003 (13 Feb). Centenary of First Film shown in Republic Srpska. Sheet 92×73 mm. P 14.

MSS274 S **83** 3m. multicoloured .... 5·00 5·00

S **84** Aleksá Šantić

S **85** Crucifixion, Sretenje Monastery

(Des R. Bojanić. Litho Forum, Novi Sad)

2003 (5 Mar). 135th Birth Anniv of Aleksá Šantić (writer). P 14.

S275 S **84** 1m. multicoloured .... 1·80 1·80

(Des R. Bojanić. Litho Forum, Novi Sad)

2003 (28 Mar). Easter. Type S **85** and similar vert designs. Multicoloured. P 14.

S276 50f. Type S **85** 90 90
S277 1m. Resurrection (painting, Altarpiece, Eisenheim by Matias Greenwald) .... 1·80 1·80

S **86** Everest Peaks

S **87** Aviation Poster

(Des R. Bojanić. Litho Forum, Novi Sad)

2003 (16 Apr). 50th Anniv of First Ascent of Mount Everest. Sheet 82×58 mm containing T S 86 and similar vert design. Multicoloured. P 14.

MSS278 1m.50 Type S **86**; 1m.50 Mountaineer through magnifying glass .... 7·25 7·25

The stamps and margin of No. **MS**S278 form a composite design.

(Des R. Bojanić. Litho Forum, Novi Sad)

2003 (5 May). Europa. Poster Art. Type S **87** and similar vert design. Multicoloured. P 14.

S279 1m. Type S **87** .... 1·80 1·80
S280 1m.50 Naval poster .... 2·75 2·75

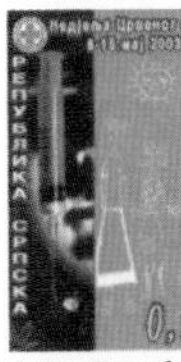

S **87a** Transfusion Equipment and Family

S **88** Arab

2003 (8 May). OBLIGATORY TAX. Red Cross Week. P 11.

S280*a* S **87a** 10f. multicoloured 60 60

(Des R. Bojanić. Litho Forum, Novi Sad)

2003 (9 June). Horses. Type S **88** and similar horiz design. Multicoloured. P 14.

S281 50f. Type S **88** 90 90
S282 50f. Lipizzaner 90 90
S283 1m. Inscr "Bosanko" .... 1·80 1·80
S284 1m. Inscr "Posavatz" .... 1·80 1·80
S281/284 *Set of 4* .... 4·75 4·75

S **89** Pope John Paul II

S **90** Medal of Honour

(Des Nadezda Skocajic and R. Bojanić. Litho Forum, Novi Sad (S285) or Miro Raguz and Robert Alilović. Litho Cartor (S285*a*))

2003 (22 June). Second visit of Pope John Paul II to Bosnia Hercegovina. Type S **89** and similar multicoloured design. P 14.

S285 1m.50 Type S **89** .... 8·25 8·25
S285*a* 1m.50 Pope John Paul II and Ivan Merz (Croatian lay academic, beatified by Pope John-Paul II on Sunday, June 22, 2003 at Banja Luka) (horiz) Stamps of the same design as No. S285a were issued by Bosnia Herzegovina (Sarajevo) and Bosnia Herzegovina (Croatia) .... 3·00 3·00

(Des R. Bojanić. Litho Forum, Novi Sad)

2003 (11 July). Medals. Type S **90** and similar vert design. Multicoloured. P 14.

S286 50f. Type S **90** .... 1·00 1·00
S287 1m. Njegos I medal .... 2·00 2·00

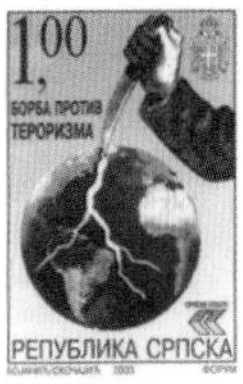

S **91** Dagger piercing Globe

S **91a** "Stop TB"

(Des R. Bojanić. Litho Forum, Novi Sad)

2003 (14 Aug). Fight against Terrorism. P 14.

S288 S **91** 1m. multicoloured .... 2·00 2·00

2003 (14 Sept). OBLIGATORY TAX. Tuberculosis Week. P 11.

S288*a* S **91a** 10f. multicoloured 65 65
a. Imperf 65 65

(b) Self-adhesive. Die-cut

S288*b* 50f. As No. S288*a* (30×20 mm) 65 65

S **92** Leo Tolstoy

S **93** Ugar River Canyon

(Des R. Bojanić. Litho Forum, Novi Sad)

2003 (25 Sept). 175th Birth Anniv of Count Lev Nikolayevich (Leo) Tolstoy (writer, pacifist, Christian anarchist and educational reformer). P 14.

S289 S **92** 1m. multicoloured .... 2·10 2·10

(Des R. Bojanić. Litho Forum, Novi Sad)

2003 (21 Oct). European Nature Protection. Type S **93** and similar vert design. Multicoloured. P 14.

S290 50f. Type S **93** .... 1·10 1·10
S291 1m. Drina River canyon .... 2·10 2·10

S **94** *St. Sava and Martyr Varvara* (Radul)

S **95** Child and Snowman

(Des Nadezda Skocajic and R. Bojanić. Litho Forum, Novi Sad)

2003 (19 Nov). Religious Art. Type S **94** and similar vert designs. Multicoloured. P 14.

S292 50f. Type S **94** .... 1·30 1·30
a. Pair. Nos. S292 and S294 .... 4·25 4·25
b. Strip of 5. Nos. S292/5 plus label .... 8·25
S293 50f. *St. Lazar* (Andrej Raicevic) .... 1·30 1·30
a. Pair. Nos. S293 and S295 .... 4·25 4·25
S294 1m. *Coronation of Madonna with Saints* (Dimitrije Bacevic) .... 2·75 2·75
S295 1m. *Deisis* (intercession of Madonna and Jovan Pretaca) .... 2·75 2·75
S292/295 *Set of 4* .... 7·25 7·25

Nos. S292 and S294, and Nos. S293 and S295, respectively, were issued in horizontal *se-tenant* pairs surrounding a central stamp size label, giving a horizontal strip of five.

(Des Nadezda Skocajic and R. Bojanić. Litho Forum, Novi Sad)

2003 (5 Dec). Christmas and New Year. Type S **95** and similar vert design. Multicoloured.

S296 50f. Type S **95** .... 1·30 1·30
S297 1m. Santa Claus and reindeer .... 2·75 2·75

S **96** Wright Brothers and *Wright Flyer I*

S **97** *Oath of Rebels* (bas relief, memorial fountain, Orasac)

(Des Nadezda Skocajic and R. Bojanić. Litho Forum, Novi Sad)

2003 (17 Dec). Centenary of Powered Flight. Type S **96** and similar horiz design. Multicoloured. P 14.

S298 50f. Type S **96** .... 1·30 1·30
S299 1m. Ferdinand von Zeppelin and air ship LZ 127 *Graf Zeppelin* .... 2·75 2·75

(Des Nadezda Skocajic and R. Bojanić. Litho Forum, Novi Sad)

2004 (5 Feb). Bicentenary of First Serbian Uprising. Sheet 78×62 mm containing Type S **97** and similar vert design. Multicoloured. P 14.

MSS300 1m.50×2, Type S **97**; *Oath of Rebels* (right) .... 8·00 8·00

The stamps of No. **MS**S300 form a composite design.

S **98** Early Greek Chariot Race

(Des Nadezda Skocajic and R. Bojanić. Litho Forum, Novi Sad)

2004 (2 Mar). Olympic Games, Athens. Sheet 100×60 mm containing Type S **98** and similar vert design. Multicoloured. P 14.

MSS301 1m.50×2, Type S **98**; Early Greek chariot race (right) .... 8·50 8·50

The stamps of No. **MS**S301 form a composite design.

S **99** Albert Einstein

S **100** Risen Christ

(Des Nadezda Skocajic and R. Bojanić. Litho Forum, Novi Sad)

2004 (12 Mar). 125th Birth Anniv of Albert Einstein (physicist and 1921 Nobel Prize winner).

S302 S **99** 1m.50 multicoloured .... 4·25 4·25

(Des R. Bojanić. Litho Forum, Novi Sad)

2004 (2 Apr). Easter. Type S **100** and similar vert design. Multicoloured. P 14.

S303 50f. Type S **100** .... 1·40 1·40
S304 1m. Risen Christ (different) .... 2·75 2·75

Nos. S303/4 each have a *se-tenant* stamp size label attached at left.

S **101** Canoeing

S **102** Hands holding Blood Droplet as Gift

(Des Nadezda Skocajic and R. Bojanić. Litho Forum, Novi Sad)

2004 (5 May). Europa. Holidays. Type S **101** and similar vert design. Multicoloured. P 14.

S305 50f. Type S **101** .... 2·75 2·75
a. Booklet pane. Nos. S305/6, each×3 .... 22·00
S306 1m. Hang-gliding .... 4·25 4·25

2004 (8 May). Obligatory Tax. Red Cross. P 11.

S307 S **102** 10f. multicoloured .... 1·00 1·00

S **103** Kulasi

S **104** Milutina Milankovica

(Des Nadezda Skocajic and R. Bojanić. Litho Forum, Novi Sad)

2004 (10 May). Spas. P 14.
S308 S **103** 20f. multicoloured 1·00 1·00

(Des Nadezda Skocajic and R. Bojanić. Litho Forum, Novi Sad)

2004 (28 May). 125th Birth Anniv of Milutina Milankovica. P 14.
S309 S **104** 1m. multicoloured 2·75 2·75

No. S310 and Type S **105** have been left for "EURO 2004", issued on 8 June 2004, not yet received.

Nos. S311/**MS**S314 and Type S **106** have been left for "Olympic Games, Athens (2nd issue)", issued on 12 July 2004, not yet received.

Nos. S315/16 and Type S **107** have been left for "European Nature Protection", issued on 27 August 2004, not yet received.

Nos. S317/20 and Type S **108** have been left for "Minerals", issued on 14 September 2004, not yet received.

No. S321 and Type S **109** have been left for "150th Birth Anniv of Mihalja Pupin", issued on 9 October 2004, not yet received.

No. S322 and Type S **110** have been left for "Fight against Terrorism", issued on 21 October 2004, not yet received.

Nos. S323/4 and Type S **111** have been left for "Spas", issued on 6 December 2004, not yet received.

No. S325 and Type S **112** have been left for "Christmas", issued on 7 December 2004, not yet received.

Nos. S326/7 and Type S **113** have been left for "Art", issued on 7 February 2005, not yet received.

No. S328 and Type S **114** have been left for "International Day of Water", issued on 22 March 2005, not yet received.

S **115** Traditional Hearth

S **117** Pope John Paul II

(Des Nadezda Skocajic and R. Bojanić. Litho Forum, Novi Sad)

2005 (4 Apr). Europa. Gastronomy. Type S **115** and similar square design. Multicoloured. P 14.
S329 1m. Type S **115** 2·75 2·75
a. Booklet pane. Nos. S329/30, each×3 22·00
S330 1m.50 Table laid with food 4·25 4·25

No. S331 and Type S **116** have been left for "Easter", issued on 18 April 2005, not yet received.

(Des Nadezda Skocajic and R. Bojanić. Litho Forum, Novi Sad)

2005 (21 Apr). Pope John Paul II Commemoration. Type S **117** and similar horiz design. Multicoloured. P 14.
S332 1m.50 Type S **117** 4·25 4·25
MSS333 56×49 mm. 5m. St. Peters Basilica and Pope John Paul II 14·00 14·00

S **118** Emblem

S **119** *Vipera berus berus*

2005 (8 May). OBLIGATORY TAX. Red Cross. Self-adhesive. Die-cut.
S334 S **118** 10f. scarlet vermilion and black 1·00 1·00

(Des Nadezda Skocajic and R. Bojanić. Litho Forum, Novi Sad)

2005 (23 June). Snakes. Type S **119** and similar horiz designs. Multicoloured. P 14.
S335 50f. Type S **119** 1·40 1·40
a. Strip. Nos. S335/8 plus label 8·50
S336 50f. *Vipera ursinii* 1·40 1·40
S337 1m. *Vipera berus bosniensis* 2·75 2·75
S338 1m. *Vipera ammodytes* 2·75 2·75
S335/338 *Set of 4* 7·50 7·50

Nos. S335/8 were issued in horizontal *se-tenant* strips of four stamps surrounding a central stamp size label. Nos. S339/40 and

Nos. S339/40 and Type S **120** have been left for "50th Anniv of Disneyland", issued on 15 July 2005, not yet received.

S **121** Fighting Bulls, Grmec

S **122** Prašuma Perućica

(Des Nadezda Skocajic and R. Bojanić. Litho Forum, Novi Sad)

2005 (5 Aug). Traditions. P 14.
S341 S **121** 1m.50 multicoloured 4·25 4·25

(Des Nadezda Skocajic and R. Bojanić. Litho Forum, Novi Sad)

2005 (30 Aug). 50th Anniv of Europa Stamps. Type S **122** and similar vert designs. Multicoloured. P 14.
S342 1m.95 Type S **122** 5·50 5·50
S343 1m.95 Rafting, Odmor 5·50 5·50
S344 1m.95 Mostar bridge 5·50 5·50
S345 1m.95 Drina river 5·50 5·50
S342/345 *Set of 4* 20·00 20·00

Nos. S342/5, respectively, were issued both in sheets and together in *se-tenant* sheetlets of four stamps.

S **123** Landscape and Lungs

S **124** Balls and Belgrade Arena

2005 (14 Sept). OBLIGATORY TAX. Anti-Tuberculosis Week. Die-cut.
S346 S **123** 10f. multicoloured 1·00 1·00

(Des Nadezda Skocajic and R. Bojanić. Litho Forum, Novi Sad)

2005 (16 Sept). European Basketball Championship, Belgrade. Multicoloured, colour wash given. P 14.
S347 S **124** 50f. lilac 1·40 1·40
a. Strip. Nos. S347/51 7·25
S348 50f. yellow 1·40 1·40
S349 50f. yellow green 1·40 1·40
S350 50f. grey lilac 1·40 1·40
S351 50f. cobalt blue 1·40 1·40
S347/351 *Set of 5* 6·25 6·25

Nos. S347/51 were issued in horizontal *se-tenant* strips of five stamps.

S **125** National Museum

S **126** Tunnel, Sargan

(Des Nadezda Skocajic and R. Bojanić. Litho Forum, Novi Sad)

2005 (26 Sept). 75th Anniversaries. Type S **125** and similar multicoloured design. P 14.
S352 1m. Type S **125** 2·75 2·75
S353 1m. National Theatre (horiz) 2·75 2·75

(Des Nadezda Skocajic and R. Bojanić. Litho Forum, Novi Sad)

2005 (3 Oct). Tourism. Makra Gora Railway, Visegard. Sheet 101×54 mm containing Type S **126** and similar vert design. Multicoloured. P 14.
MSS354 50f. Type S **126**; 1m. Station, Makra Gora 4·25 4·25

The stamps and margin of No. **MS**S354 form a composite design.

S **127** *Bleriot XI*

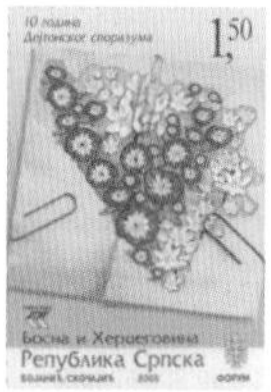

S **128** Flowers

(Des Nadezda Skocajic and R. Bojanić. Litho Forum, Novi Sad)

2005 (14 Oct). Centenary of International Aviation Federation (FAI). P 14.
S355 S **127** 1m.50 multicoloured 4·25 4·25

(Des Nadezda Skocajic and R. Bojanić. Litho Forum, Novi Sad)

2005 (21 Nov). Tenth Anniv of Dayton Agreement. P 14.
S356 S **128** 1m.50 multicoloured 4·25 4·25

No. S356 has a *se-tenant* stamp size label inscribed for the anniversary attached at left.

S **129** Guber

S **130** *Crex crex* (corncrake)

(Des Nadezda Skocajic and R. Bojanić. Litho Forum, Novi Sad)

2005 (23 Nov). Spas. P 14.
S357 S **129** 50f. multicoloured 1·40 1·40

(Des Nadezda Skocajic and R. Bojanić. Litho Forum, Novi Sad)

2005 (25 Nov). European Nature Protection. Birds. Type S **130** and similar vert design. Multicoloured. P 14.
S358 50f. Type S **130** 1·40 1·40
S359 1m. *Platalea leucorodia* (spoonbill) 2·75 2·75

S **131** Monument to Victims

S **132** Mozart

(Des Nadezda Skocajic and R. Bojanić. Litho Forum, Novi Sad)

2005 (15 Dec). 60th Anniv of Liberation of Jasenovac Concentration Camp. P 14.
S360 S **131** 50f. multicoloured 1·40 1·40

(Des Nadezda Skocajic and R. Bojanić. Litho Forum, Novi Sad)

2006 (27 Jan). 250th Birth Anniv of Wolfgang Amadeus Mozart (composer and musician). P 14.
S361 S **132** 1m.50 multicoloured 4·25 4·25

S **133** Branke Sotre

S **134** Biathlete

(Des Nadezda Skocajic and R. Bojanić. Litho Forum, Novi Sad)

2006 (31 Jan). Birth Centenary of Branke Sotre (artist). P 14.
S362 S **133** 1m. multicoloured 2·75 2·75

No. S362 has a *se-tenant* stamp size label showing painting attached at foot.

(Des Nadezda Skocajic and R. Bojanić. Litho Forum, Novi Sad)

2006 (10 Feb). Winter Olympic Games, Turin. Type S **134** and similar horiz design. Multicoloured. P 14.
S363 50f. Type S **134** 1·40 1·40
S364 1m. Alpine skier 2·75 2·75

S **135** Kulasi

S **136** Inscr "Saxifraga prenja"

(Des Nadezda Skocajic and R. Bojanić. Litho Forum, Novi Sad)

2006 (7 Mar). Spas. P 14.
S365 S **135** 20f. multicoloured 1·00 1·00

No. S365 is as No. S308 but redrawn.

(Des Nadezda Skocajic and R. Bojanić. Litho Forum, Novi Sad)

2006 (14 Mar). Flora. Type S **136** and similar horiz designs. Multicoloured. P 14.
S366 50f. Type S **136** 1·40 1·40
S367 50f. *Asperula hercegovina* 1·40 1·40
S368 1m. *Campanula hercegovina* 2·75 2·75
S369 1m. Inscr "Oxtropis prenja" 2·75 2·75
S366/369 *Set of 4* 7·50 7·50

S **137** Basket of Eggs

S **138** "Tear" (Luja Kajkut)

(Des Nadezda Skocajic and R. Bojanić. Litho Forum, Novi Sad)

2006 (14 Apr). Easter. P 14.
S370 S **137** 70f. multicoloured 2·10 2·10

(Des Nadezda Skocajic and R. Bojanić. Litho Forum, Novi Sad)

2006 (15 Apr). Europa. Integration. Type S **138** and similar horiz design. Multicoloured. P 14.
S371 1m. Type S **138** 2·75 2·75
a. Booklet pane. Nos. S371/2, each×3 22·00
S372 1m.50 "Country Dance" (Milica Popic) 4·25 4·25

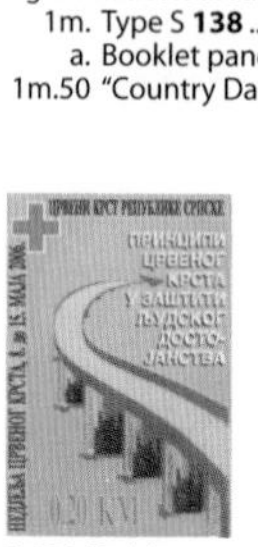
S **139** Emblem

S **140** Legs and Ball

2005 (8 May). OBLIGATORY TAX. Red Cross. P 10.
S373 S **139** 20f. multicoloured 1·00 1·00

(Des Nadezda Skocajic and R. Bojanić. Litho Forum, Novi Sad)

2006 (9 June). World Cup Football Championships, Germany. Type S **140** and similar horiz design. Multicoloured. P 14.

S374 50f. Type S **140** 1·40 1·40
 a. Pair. Nos. S374/5, each×3 4·50 4·50
S375 1m. Stadium and ball 2·75 2·75
MSS376 65×49 mm. 3m. German player and ball 8·25 8·25

Nos. S374/5 were issued in *se-tenant* pairs within the sheet.

S **141** Runner

S **142** Nikola Tesla

(Des Nadezda Skocajic and R. Bojanić. Litho Forum, Novi Sad)

2006 (28 June). Tenth Anniv of Vidovdan Road Race. P 14.

S377 S **141** 1m. multicoloured 2·75 2·75

No. S377 has a *se-tenant* stamp size label showing race course, attached at right.

(Des Nadezda Skocajic and R. Bojanić. Litho Forum, Novi Sad)

2006 (10 July). 150th Birth Anniv of Nikola Tesla (engineer) (1st issue). Sheet 66×60 mm. P 14.

MSS378 S **142** 1m.50 multicoloured 4·25 4·25

The stamps and margin of No. **MS**S378 form a composite design.

S **143** "CTOH TB"

S **144** *Tetrao urogallus* (capercaille)

2006 (14 Sept). OBLIGATORY TAX. Anti-Tuberculosis Week. P 11.

S379 S **143** 20f. multicoloured 1·00 1·00

(Des Nadezda Skocajic and R. Bojanić. Litho Forum, Novi Sad)

2006 (19 Sept). European Nature Protection. Type S **144** and similar horiz design. Multicoloured. P 14.

S380 50f. Type S **144** 1·40 1·40
S381 1m. *Rupicapra rupicapra* (chamois) 2·75 2·75

No. S382 and Type S **145** have been left for "50th Anniv of Children's Theatre", issued on 14 October 2006, not yet received.

S **146** Buckle

S **147** Nikola Tesla

(Des Nadezda Skocajic and R. Bojanić. Litho Forum, Novi Sad)

2006 (28 Nov). Museum Exhibits. Type S **146** and similar horiz design. Multicoloured. P 14.

S383 1m. Type S **146** 2·75 2·75
S384 1m. Curved buckle with red stones 2·75 2·75

(Des Nadezda Skocajic and R. Bojanić. Litho Forum, Novi Sad)

2006 (29 Dec). 150th Birth Anniv of Nikola Tesla (engineer) (2nd issue). P 14.

S385 S **147** 70f. multicoloured 2·10 2·10

S **148** Johann von Goethe

S **149** Decorated Egg

(Des Nadezda Skocajic and R. Bojanić. Litho Forum, Novi Sad)

2007 (22 Mar). 175th Birth Anniv of Johann Wolfgang von Goethe (polymath). P 14.

S386 S **148** 1m.50 multicoloured 4·25 4·25

(Des Smiljana Vekić. Litho Forum, Novi Sad)

2007 (10 Apr). Easter. P 14.

S387 S **149** 70f. multicoloured 2·10 2·10

S **150** Study for *Isabella d`Este*

S **151** Campsite

(Des Nebojsa Djumic and Bozidar Dosenovic. Litho Forum, Novi Sad)

2007 (16 Apr). 555th Birth Anniv of Leonardo da Vinci (artist and polymath). Type S **150** and similar vert design. Multicoloured. P 14.

S388 70f. Type S **150** 2·10 2·10
S389 1m. Study for *The Last Supper* 2·75 2·75

(Des Nebojsa Djumic and Bozidar Dosenovic. Litho Forum, Novi Sad)

2007 (3 May). Europa. Centenary of Scouting. Type S **151** and similar horiz design. Multicoloured.

(a) Sheet stamps. P 14

S390 1m. Type S **151** 2·75 2·75
S391 1m.50 Scouts 4·25 4·25

(b) Booklet stamps. Size 35×45 mm. P 14×imperf

S392 1m. As Type S **151**, with pink upper edge 2·75 2·75
 a. Booklet pane. Nos. S392/7, each×3 22·00
S393 1m. As Type S **151**, with pink lower edge 'EUROPA 100 ANS DU SCOUTISME'/'EUROPA 100 JAHRE PFADFINDERBEWEGUNG' 2·75 2·75
S394 1m. As Type S **151** with pink lower edge 'EUROPA 100 ANS DU SCOUTISME' 2·75 2·75
S395 1m.50 As No. S391, with pink upper edge 4·25 4·25
S396 1m.50 As No. S 391, with pink upper edge 'EUROPA 100 YEARS OF SCOUTING' 4·25 4·25
S397 1m.50 As No. S 391, with pink lower edge 4·25 4·25
S390/397 *Set of 8* 25·00 25·00

Nos. S390/1 were each issued with a *se-tenant* stamp size label illustrating scouts. The booklet pane No. S392a has straight outer edges, giving stamp with either the upper or lower edge imperforate depending on position.

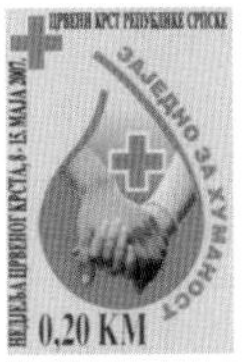

S **152** Clasped Hands

S **153** Liplje Monastery

2007 (8 May). OBLIGATORY TAX. Red Cross. P 10.

S398 S **152** 20f. multicoloured 1·00 1·00
 a. Imperf

2007 (5 June). Monasteries. Type S **153** and similar horiz design. Multicoloured. P 13½×14.

S399 70f. Type S **153** 1·90 1·90
S400 1m. Dobricevo 2·75 2·75

S **154** Koarac

S **155** Serbian Tri-colour Hound

(Des Nebojsa Djumic and Bozidar Dosenovic. Litho Forum, Novi Sad)

2007 (9–20 June). Cities. Type S **154** and similar vert design. Multicoloured. P 14.

S401 20f. Type S **154** 70 70
S402 20f. Derventa 70 70
S403 20f. Prjedor 70 70
S404 20f. Laktasi 70 70
S405 20f. Foca 70 70
S406 20f. Bijelijina 70 70
S407 70f. Srebrenica (20.6) 2·10 2·10
S408 1m.50 Sipovo 4·25 4·25
S409 1m.50 Mrkonjic Grad 4·25 4·25
S410 2m. Trebinje 5·50 5·50
S411 5m. Zvornik 14·00 14·00
S401/411 *Set of 11* 31·00 31·00

(Des Nebojsa Djumic and Bozidar Dosenovic. Litho Forum, Novi Sad)

2007 (5 July). Dogs. Type S **155** and similar vert design. Multicoloured. P 14.

S412 70f. Type S **155** 2·10 2·10
 a. Pair. Nos. S412/13 4·50 4·50
 b. Horiz strip. Nos. S412/15 plus label 8·75
S413 70f. Istarski oštrodlaki gonic (rough coated scent hound) 2·10 2·10
S414 70f. Srpski odbrambeni pas (Serbian guard dog) 2·10 2·10
 a. Pair. Nos. S414/15 4·50 4·50
S415 70f. Tornak (sheep dog) 2·10 2·10
S412/415 *Set of 4* 7·50 7·50

Nos. S412/13 and S414/15 were issued in horizontal *se-tenant* pairs within strips of four stamps surrounding an illustrated stamp size label within the sheet.

S **156** Orthodox Church and Old Post Office

S **157** Ban Milosavljević (statue)

(Des Nebojsa Djumic and Bozidar Dosenovic. Litho Forum, Novi Sad)

2007 (7 July). Centenary of Post Office, Obudovac. P 14.

S416 S **156** 10f. multicoloured 1·00 1·00

(Des Nebojsa Djumic , M. Nikolić and Bozidar Dosenovic. Litho Forum, Novi Sad)

2007 (7 Sept). 125th Birth Anniv of Ban Svetislav Milosavljević (leader 1930–33). P 14.

S417 S **157** 1m.50 multicoloured 4·25 4·25

S **158** Apple containing People

S **159** Early Racquet and Balls

2007 (14 Sept). OBLIGATORY TAX. Anti-Tuberculosis Week. P 10.

S418 S **158** 20f. multicoloured 1·20 1·20
 a. Imperf 1·20 1·20

(Des Nebojsa Djumic and Bozidar Dosenovic. Litho Forum, Novi Sad)

2007 (14 Sept). Centenary of Banja Luca Tennis Club. Sheet 83×58 mm containing Type S **159** and similar horiz design. Multicoloured. P 14.

MSS419 1m.×2 Type S **159**; Modern racquet and ball 5·50 5·50

The stamps and margin of No. **MS**S342 form a composite design.

S **160** Sputnik and Globe

S **161** *Picea abies*

(Des Nebojsa Djumic, G. Bosnic and Bozidar Dosenovic. Litho Forum, Novi Sad)

2007 (4 Oct). 50th Anniv of Space Exploration. P 14.

S420 S **160** 1m.50 multicoloured 4·25 4·25

(Des Nadezda Skocajic and R. Bojanić. Litho Forum, Novi Sad)

2007 (9 Nov). European Nature Protection. Conifers. Type S **161** and similar vert design. Multicoloured. P 14.

S421 70f. Type S **161** 1·90 1·90
S422 1m. *Picea omorica* 2·75 2·75

S **162** Post Office Building

S **163** *Self Portrait*

(Des Nebojsa Djumic and Bozidar Dosenovic)

2008 (28 Feb). 125th Anniv of Šamac Post Office.

S422*a* S **162** 1m.40 multicoloured 4·25 4·25

(Des Nebojsa Djumic and Bozidar Dosenovic. Litho Forum, Novi Sad)

2008 (28 Mar). 155th Birth Anniv of Vincent Van Gogh (artist).

S423 S **163** 1m.50 multicoloured 4·25 4·25

S **164** Player's Foot and Ball

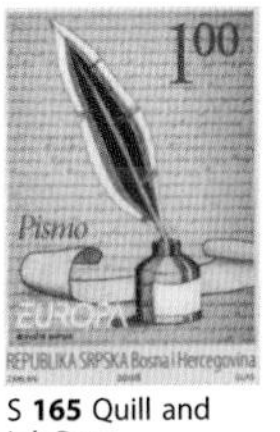

S **165** Quill and Ink Pot

(Des N. Zaklan, Nebojsa Djumic and Bozidar Dosenovic. Litho Forum, Novi Sad)

2008 (18 Apr). Euro 2008—European Football Championship, Austria and Switzerland. Sheet 82×60 mm containing Type S **164** and similar vert design. Multicoloured. P 14.

MSS424 1m.40×2, Type S **164**; Ball and red and white boot 8·25 8·25

The stamps and margins of No. **MS**S424 form a composite design.

(Des N. Zaklan, Nebojsa Djumic and Bozidar Dosenovic. Litho Forum, Novi Sad)

2008 (24 Apr). Europa. The Letter. Type S **165** and similar vert design. Multicoloured. P 14.

S425 1m. Type S **165** 2·75 2·75
S426 2m. Hand holding pencil 5·50 5·50
MSS427 108×82 mm. Nos. S425/6, each×3 26·00 26·00

S **166** Hands

S **167** Children and Microphone

2008 (8 May). OBLIGATORY TAX. Red Cross. P 10.
S428 S **166** 20f. multicoloured .... 1·20 1·20
a. Imperf ....

(Des M. Nikolić, Nebojsa Djumic and Bozidar Dosenovic. Litho Forum, Novi Sad)

2008 (8 May). 15th Children's Song Festival, Djurdjerdan. P 14.
S429 S **167** 1m.50 multicoloured .... 4·25 4·25

S **168** Post Van

(Des Nebojsa Djumic and Bozidar Dosenovic)

2008 (13 May). Personal Stamps. Type S **168** and similar multicoloured design. Self-adhesive gum. Die-cut wavy edge.
S430 70f. Type S **168** .... 2·10 2·10
S431 70f. Post box (vert) .... 2·10 2·10
S432 70f. Hand stamp (vert) .... 2·10 2·10
S433 70f. Post horn .... 2·10 2·10
S430/S433 *Set of 4* .... 7·50 7·50
Nos. S430/3 have wavy edges to simulate perforations. Nos. S430/3 could be personalised by the addition of a photograph or logo.

S **169** Festival Mascot as Postman

S **170** *Gyromitra esculenta*

2008 (15 May). Banja Luka International Festival. P 14.
S434 S **169** 1m.50 multicoloured .... 4·25 4·25

2008 (26 May). Poisonous Fungi. Type S **170** and similar horiz designs. Multicoloured.
S435 70f. Type S **170** .... 2·10 2·10
a. Pair. Nos. S435/6 .... 4·50 4·50
S436 70f. *Amanita muscaria* .... 2·10 2·10
S437 70f. *Amanita pantherina* .... 2·10 2·10
a. Pair. Nos. S437/8 .... 4·50 4·50
S438 70f. *Amanita phalloides* .... 2·10 2·10
S435/S438 *Set of 4* .... 7·50 7·50
Nos. S435/6 and S437/8 were issued in horizontal *se-tenant* pairs within strips of two pairs surrounding a central stamp size label.

S **171** Charles Darwin

S **172** *Gentiana verna*

2008 (1 July). 150th Anniv of Publication of *Theory of Evolution* by Charles Darwin. P 14.
S439 S **171** 1m.50 multicoloured .... 4·25 4·25

(Des Biljana Savic and Miodrag Nikolić)

2008 (7 July). Flowers. Type S **172** and similar multicoloured designs. P 13.
S440 50f. Type S **172** .... 1·60 1·60
S441 1m.50 *Galanthus nivalis* (vert) .... 4·75 4·75
S442 2m. *Viola odorata* .... 6·25 6·25
S443 5m. *Centaurea cyanus* .... 16·00 16·00
S440/S443 *Set of 4* .... 25·00 25·00
Nos. S440, S442/3 have the design to the edge of the stamp, whilst No. S441 has a white border.

S **173** High Jump and National Stadium

S **174** *Ciconia ciconia* (white stork)

(Des Miodrag Nikolić)

2008 (16 July). Olympic Games, Beijing. Type S **173** and similar horiz design. Multicoloured. P 13.
S444 70f. Type **173** .... 2·40 2·40
S445 2m.10 Swimmer and National Aquatic Center, Beijing .... 6·50 6·50
MSS446 3m.10 Gymnast .... 10·00 10·00

2008 (12 Aug). European Nature Protection. Birds. Type S **174** and similar vert design. Multicoloured. P 14.
S448 1m. Type S **174** .... 3·25 3·25
S449 1m. *Strix aluco* (Eurasian tawny owl) .... 3·25 3·25
Nos. S448/9 each have a stamp size label attached at right.

S **175** Tvrdos

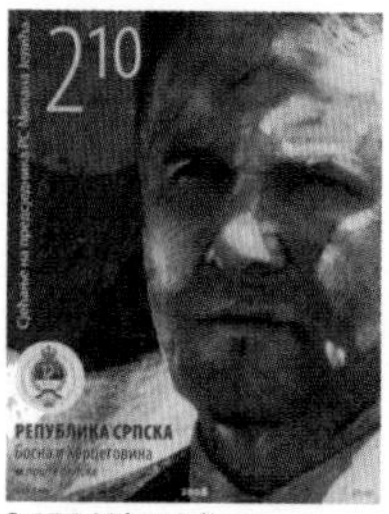

S **176** Milan Jelic

(Des Miodrag Nikolić)

2008 (10 Sept). Monasteries. Type S **175** and similar horiz design. Multicoloured. P 13.
S450 1m. Type S **175** .... 3·25 3·25
S451 1m. Gracanica .... 3·25 3·25

(Des Nikola Zaklan)

2008 (20 Sept). Milan Jelic (President, 2006–7) Commemoration. Sheet 87×64 mm. P 13.
MSS452 S **176** 2m.10 multicoloured .... 6·50 6·50

STAMP BOOKLETS

Prices are for complete booklets

Booklet No.	Date	Contents and Cover Price	Price
SBS1	4.5.01	Europa. Water Conservation 1 pane, No. S211a	27·00
SBS2	20.9.01	Caves 1 pane, No. S227a	5·25
SBS3	30.4.02	Europa. Circus 1 pane, No. S251a	13·00
SBS4	5.5.04	Europa. Holidays 1 pane, No. S305a	23·00
SBS5	4.4.05	Europa. Gastronomy 1 pane, No. S329a	23·00
SBS6	15.4.06	Europa. Integration 1 pane, No. S371a	23·00
SBS7	3.5.07	Europa. Centenary of Scouting 1 pane, No. S392a	23·00

Bulgaria

1879. 100 Centimes = 1 Franc
1881. 100 Stotinki = 1 Lev

Until 1877 Bulgaria was part of the Ottoman Empire but following a revolt and the intervention of Russia, the Treaty of Berlin, 1878, established a Principality north of the Balkan Mts., under Turkish suzerainty, whilst in the south a semi- autonomous administration was granted to Eastern Roumelia. This was incorporated in Bulgaria in 1885.

PRINCIPALITY

Prince Alexander, 24 April 1879–4 Sept 1886

The dates of issue are according to local computation based on the Julian or Gregorian Calendar in use. In the 19th century the Julian Calendar was twelve days behind the Gregorian Calendar. After 1900 the difference was thirteen days. In Bulgaria the Gregorian Calendar was introduced in 1917.

1 Large Lion

2 Large Lion

(Types **1** and **2** Des G. Ya. Kirkov of State Ptg Wks, Sofia. Eng F. Kepler. Typo Russian State Ptg Wks, St. Petersburg)

1879 (1 May). Laid paper. Sheet wmk letters E Z G B (representing initials of the printing house) drawn between symmetrical curved lines, forming a lozenge-shaped pattern. P 14½×15.

1	1	5c. black and orange	£225	75·00
2		5c. black and yellow	£225	75·00
3		10c. black and green	£1000	£200
4		10c. black and deep green	£1000	£200
5		25c. black and lilac	£600	50·00
6		25c. black and purple	£600	50·00
7		50c. black and blue	£850	£170
8	2	1f. black and red	£130	50·00

1881 (10 June). Laid paper. Wmk letters E Z G B etc. P 14½×15. Values in stotinki variously, thus:—

9	1	3st. carmine and grey	43·00	8·25
10		3st. deep carmine and grey	43·00	8·25
11		5st. black and yellow	43·00	8·25
		a. Background inverted	£3250	£1800
12		5st. black and orange	43·00	8·25
13		10st. black and green	£250	26·00
14		10st. black and deep green	£250	26·00
15		15st. deep carmine and green	£250	26·00
16		15st. carmine and pale green	£250	26·00
17		25st. black and lilac	£1000	£130
18		25st. black and purple	£1000	£130
19		30st. deep blue and brown	43·00	21·00
20		30st. blue and pale brown	43·00	21·00

1882 (4 Dec). Colours changed. Laid paper. Wmk letters E Z G B etc. P 14½×15.

21	1	3st. pale orange and yellow	2·20	1·00
		a. Background inverted	£5500	£3750
22		3st. orange and yellow	2·20	1·00
23		5st. grey-green and pale green	16·00	1·60
24		5st. yellow-green and pale green	16·00	1·60
		a. Error. Rose and pale rose	£4000	£3750
25		10st. rose and pale rose	22·00	1·60
26		10st. carmine and pale rose	22·00	1·60
27		10st. scarlet and pale rose	22·00	1·60
28		15st. plum and pale mauve	22·00	1·30
29		15st. purple and pale mauve	22·00	1·30
30		25st. deep blue and pale blue	20·00	2·10
31		25st. blue and pale blue	20·00	2·10
32		30st. deep lilac and green	21·00	1·90
33		30st. purple and green	21·00	1·90
34		50st. blue and rose	21·00	1·90
35		50st. blue and flesh	21·00	1·90

See also Nos. 275/80.

(3) (4) (5) (6)

1884–85. Previous issues surch with T **3** to **6** by State Ptg Wks, Sofia. (i) Typo (1.5.84) (ii) Litho (5.4.85).

(a) In black

37	1	3 on 10st. rose and pale rose (i)	£325	£100
		a. Surch inverted	£1600	£1000
		b. Surch double	—	£2000
38		3 on 10st. carmine and pale rose (ii)	£110	£100
39		5 on 30st. deep blue and brown (i)	£3750	£3000
40	2	50 on 1f. black and red (ii)	£750	£475

Most of the stamps offered with "5" in black on 30st. have forged surcharges.

(b) In carmine (C.) or vermilion (V.)

41	1	5 on 30st. deep blue and brown (i) (C.)	£140	£100
42		5 on 30st. blue and pale brown (i) (C.)	£140	£100
		a. Surch double (Bk.+C.)	£4250	
43		5 on 30st. blue and pale brown (ii) (V.)	£110	£100
44		15 on 25st. deep blue and pale blue (i) (C.)	£1100	£180
		a. Surch inverted	—	£4250
45		15 on 25st. blue and pale blue (ii) (V.)	£200	£140

D 7

A. 1884–92

B. Redrawn 1893

In B the background lines are wider apart and the semicircle of colour over the tablet is larger.

(Litho State Ptg Wks, Sofia)

1884 (1 Sept)–**95**. POSTAGE DUE. Lozenge perf 5 to 7½ and compound.

D46	D 7	5st. orange	£850	£150
		a. Yellow	£550	£130
D47		25st. lake	£450	70·00
D48		50st. deep blue	70·00	50·00
		a. Blue (1895)	65·00	42·00

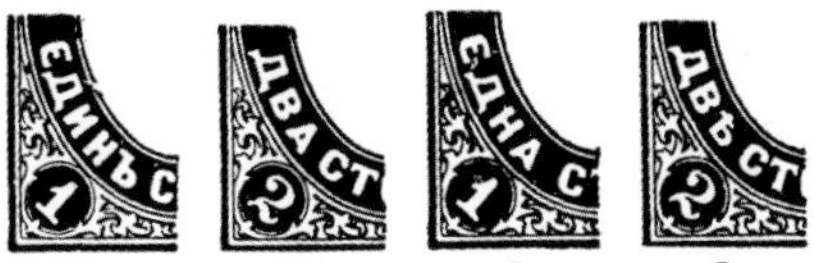

A B Masculine Gender C D Feminine Gender

1885 (25 May). Wmk letters E Z G B etc. P 14½×15.

46	1	1st. slate-violet and drab (A)	38·00	12·50
47		2st. slate-green and drab (B)	37·00	11·50

1886 (13 Aug). As last, but spelling as (C) and (D).

48	1	1st. slate-violet and drab (C)	2·75	50
49		2st. slate-green and drab (D)	2·75	50

1886 (15 Aug). POSTAGE DUE. Litho. Imperf

D50	D 7	5st. orange	£550	26·00
D51		25st. brown-lake	£800	23·00
D52		50st. deep blue	27·00	23·00
		a. Blue	33·00	26·00

Nos. D50/52*a* exist on rough yellowish grey paper and on smooth whiter paper.

1887 (1 Jan). Wmk letters E Z G B etc. P 14½×15.

Value in leva, thus:—

50	2	1l. black and red	75·00	9·50

Prince Ferdinand 1, 14 August 1887–5 October 1908

(Litho State Ptg Wks, Sofia)

1887 (10 Oct). POSTAGE DUE. P 11½.

D53	D 7	5st. orange	80·00	12·50
		a. Yellow	80·00	12·50
D54		25st. brown-lake	27·00	7·75
D55		50st. deep blue	27·00	23·00
		a. Blue	33·00	26·00

7 8 (9) D 10

(Typo Govt Ptg Works, Paris)

1889 (May)–**91**. No wmk. P 13½.

51	7	1st. mauve	2·20	50
52		2st. grey	3·25	1·60
53		3st. bistre-brown	1·10	50
54		5st. green	16·00	40
		a. Imperf (pair)		
55		10st. rose (5.5.89)	16·00	1·00
56		15st. orange	55·00	1·00
57		25st. pale blue (1891)	16·00	1·00
58		30st. brown (1891)	18·00	1·00
59		50st. blue-green	1·10	50
60	8	1l. brick-red (1.8.89)	1·10	1·00

The horizontal perforation of this issue gauges slightly under 13½. See note after No. 100.

1892 (26 Jan). Surch with T **9** at Sofia.

61	7	15 on 30st. brown	55·00	2·10
		a. Surch inverted	£275	£250

(Typo Austrian State Ptg Wks, Vienna or State Ptg Wks, Sofia)

1892–93.

(a) P 10½

62	7	5st. green (1893)	£375	£250
63		10st. rose (1893)	£425	£200
64		15st. orange	49·00	2·10
65		25st. pale blue	16·00	1·60

(b) P 11

66	7	15st. orange	£200	18·00
67		25st. pale blue	49·00	1·60

(c) P 11½

68	7	5st. green (1893)	£325	18·00
69		5st. yellow-green (1893)	£225	18·00
70		10st. rose (1893)	8·25	2·50
71		15st. orange	£140	2·10
72		25st. blue	16·00	1·60

(d) Pelure paper. P 11½

73	7	10st. rose (1893)	11·00	1·00
		a. Imperf (pair)	£160	£160

Early printings of the 15 and 25st. values were made in Vienna and issued 1892. Later printings of these values and all printings of the 5 and 10st. were made at Sofia and issued from 1893 onwards.

1892. POSTAGE DUE. Litho. P 11½×lozenge, perf.

D74	D 7	25st. brown-lake	£550	£450

1893. POSTAGE DUE. Redrawn as B. Thick or thin paper. Litho. P 11½.

D75	D 7	5st. orange	55·00	7·75
		a. Perf 10½	65·00	8·00
		b. Perf 11	£160	26·00
D76		25st. dull lake	27·00	7·75
		a. Perf 10½	70·00	10·50
		b. Perf 11	£160	33·00

1894 (1 Apr). POSTAGE DUE. Larger lettering. Figure of value outlined. Litho. Pelure paper. P 11½.

D77	D 10	5st. orange	65·00	26·00

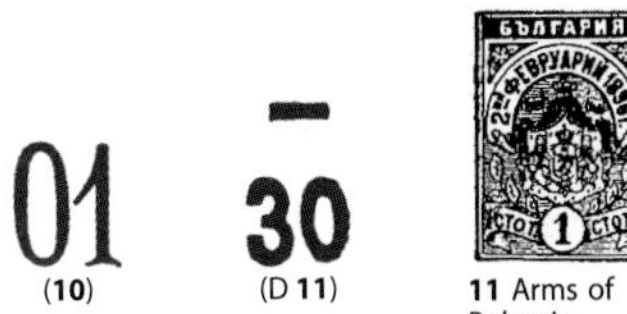

(10) (D 11) 11 Arms of Bulgaria

A B

1895 (25 Oct). No. 49 surch with T **10**.

74		01 on 2st. slate-green and drab (R.)	1·60	50
		a. Surch inverted	13·00	10·50
		b. Pair, one without surcharge	£375	£325
		c. Surch double	£150	£150
		d. Surch on No. 47	£600	£600

1895 (18 Nov). POSTAGE DUE. Surch with Type D **11**, in red.

D78	D 7	30st. on 50st. (No. D52)	80·00	18·00
		a. Surch inverted	£325	£325
		b. Bar double	£100	95·00
		c. Surch inverted and bar double	£600	£600
		d. Blue (D52*a*)	49·00	16·00
D79		30st. on 50st. (D55)	43·00	16·00
		a. Surch inverted	£325	£325
		b. Blue (D55*a*)	55·00	21·00

1896 (2 Feb). Baptism of Prince Boris. Litho.

(a) No wmk. Rough paper. P 13

75	11	1st. green	85	50
76		1st. deep green	85	45
77		15st. violet (A)	6·50	50
77*a*		25st. red	11·00	4·25

(b) Wmk Bulgarian Arms and Inscription (Principality of Bulgaria) in sheet (some stamps without wmk). Smooth paper. P 13

78	11	1st. blue-green	55	30
79		5st. ultramarine	55	30
80		5st. deep blue	55	30
81		15st. violet (B)	65	50
82		25st. red	9·25	3·25

D 12 (12) 13 Cherrywood Cannon used against the Turks

1896 (13 Mar). POSTAGE DUE. Smaller design. Litho. With or without wmk Arms in sheet. P 13×12½.

D83	D 12	5st. orange	27·00	4·25
D84		10st. violet	16·00	3·75
D85		30st. green	13·00	3·25

No. D83 exists in two types differing in the figure of value.

1896 (30 Apr). Wmk Bulgarian Arms and Inscription (Principality of Bulgaria) in sheet (some stamps without wmk). Typo. P 13.

83	8	2l. rose and pale rose	4·25	3·25
		a. Perf 11½	£425	£100
84		3l. black and drab	6·50	7·25
		a. Perf 11½	£425	£140

(Typo State Pty Works, Sofia)

1896–1901. P 13.

85	7	1st. grey-mauve	20	20
86		1st. mauve	20	20
87		1st. dull mauve	20	20
88		2st. drab	1·30	1·00
89		3st. bistre-brown	55	50
90		5st. green	20	20
91		5st. pale green	20	20
92		5st. yellow-green	20	20
93		5st. dull green	20	20
94		10st. rose	1·60	1·00
95		10st. pale rose	1·60	1·00
96		15st. orange	1·10	50
97		15st. brown-orange	1·10	50
98		15st. red-orange	1·10	50
99		15st. yellow	1·10	50
100		25st. dull blue	1·10	50

The perforation in this issue is the same on all sides gauging slightly under 13, a difference which distinguishes it from the Paris printing, Nos. 51, etc. All values exist imperf.

1901. Surch as T **12**.

101	7	5 on 3st. bistre-brown (53) (24 May)	2·75	2·10
102		5 on 3st. bistre-brown (89) (24 May)	3·25	2·30
		a. Surch inverted	£160	£160
		b. Pair, one without surcharge	£225	£180
103		10 on 50st. blue-green (59) (24 Mar)	2·75	2·30
		a. Surch inverted	£160	£160

(Typo State Ptg Wks, Sofia)

1901 (20 Apr). 25th Anniv of Uprising against Turkey. P 13.

104 **13** 5st. carmine ... 2·20 1·60
a. "1878" for "1876" ... 55·00
105 15st. green ... 2·20 1·60
a. "1870" for "1876" ... 55·00

14 Prince Ferdinand

15 Prince Ferdinand

A

B

In Type A the figures "1" in the corners at top have an additional straight serif at right. In Type B this is omitted.

(Des S. Badzhov. Typo Cartographic Bureau, Russian War Department, St. Petersburg)

1901 (1 Oct)–**05**. P 12½.

106 **14** 1st. greenish black and purple ... 35 15
a. Imperf (pair) ... £1300
107 2st. blue and slate-green ... 55 15
a. Imperf (pair) ... £1600
108 3st. black and orange ... 55 15
109 5st. brown and emerald ... 2·20 20
110 10st. sepia and rose ... 3·25 20
111 10st. sepia and vermilion ... 3·25 20
112 10st. sepia and carmine-rose ... 3·25 20
113 15st. greenish black and lake ... 1·60 30
a. Imperf (pair) ... £1600
114 25st. black and blue ... 1·60 15
115 25st. black and deep blue ... 1·60 15
116 30st. black and bistre-brown ... 49·00 1·00
117 50st. brown and deep blue ... 2·20 30
118 **15** 1l. deep green and pale red (A) ... 5·50 40
a. Redrawn (B) (1905) ... £100 4·25
119 2l. black and vermilion ... 11·00 1·60
120 2l. black and rose ... 11·00 1·60
121 2l. black and carmine ... 11·00 1·60
122 2l. black and brick-red ... 11·00 1·60
123 3l. brown-lake and grey ... 16·00 7·25
106/123 *Set of* 12 (cheapest) ... 85·00 10·50

On 22.12.01 the Rustchuk P.O. overprinted current postage stamps (Nos. 109, 110, 113, 116 and 117) with a large "T" in a circle, as shown, to convert them into postage due stamps.

D **16**

16 Fighting at Shipka Pass

10

(**17**)

1901–04. POSTAGE DUE. Typo. P 11½.

D124 D **16** 5st. rose-red ... 1·10 50
D125 10st. green (1902) ... 2·20 65
D126 20st. blue (1904) ... 16·00 65
D127 30st. maroon ... 5·50 70
D128 50st. orange (1902) ... 14·00 12·50
D124/128 *Set of* 5 ... 35·00 13·50

(Des Kh. Tachev. Litho Hungarian State Ptg Works, Budapest)

1902 (29 Aug). 25th Anniv of Battle of Shipka Pass. P 11½.

124 **16** 5st. carmine ... 3·25 1·00
125 10st. green ... 3·25 1·00
126 15st. blue ... 13·00 5·25
124/126 *Set of* 3 ... 18·00 6·50

1903 (1 Oct). No. 113 surch with T **17** at Sofia.

127 **14** 10 on 15st. greenish black and lake ... 60·00 1·60
a. Surch on 10st. (No. 110) ... £900 £750
b. Surch inverted ... £130 £100
c. Surch double ... £130 £100

For this surcharge in blue-black see No. 141.

18 Ferdinand I in 1887 and 1907

(Litho Hungarian State Ptg Wks, Budapest)

1907 (14 Aug). 20th Anniv of Prince Ferdinand's Accession. P 11½.

131 **18** 5st. green ... 22·00 2·10
a. Imperf (pair) ... £120
132 5st. pale green ... 22·00 2·10
133 5st. black-green ... 22·00 2·10
134 10st. brown-rose ... 33·00 2·30
a. Imperf (pair) ... £160
135 10st. deep rose ... 33·00 2·30
136 10st. red-brown ... 33·00 2·30
137 25st. blue ... 75·00 4·25
a. Imperf (pair) ... £225
138 25st. pale blue ... 75·00 4·25
a. Background omitted ... £110
139 25st. deep blue ... 75·00 4·25

INDEPENDENT KINGDOM

Tsar Ferdinand I, 5 October 1908–3 October 1918

Prince Ferdinand proclaimed himself Tsar in 1908 and repudiated Turkish suzerainty; Bulgarian independence was recognised by Turkey in 1909.

1910

1909

5 (**19**)   1909 (**20**)   10 (**21**)   1 (**22**)

(Surch at Sofia)

1909. (a) Nos. 113 and 116 surch as T **19** or **17** (No. 141) (17 June).

140 **14** 5 on 15st. (B.-Bk.) ... 3·25 2·10
a. Surch inverted ... 43·00 42·00
141 10 on 15st. (B.-Bk.) ... 5·50 1·00
a. Surch inverted ... 43·00 42·00
142 25 on 30st. (B.-Bk.) ... £1000 £650
143 25 on 30st. (R.) ... 18·00 2·10
a. "2" omitted ... £160 £160
b. "25" double ... £150 £150

(b) Optd with T **20** (3 July (1st.)–30 Aug (5st.))

144 **7** 1st. mauve (p 13½) ... £110 85·00
145 1st. mauve (p 13) ... 2·20 95
a. Opt inverted ... 43·00 36·00
146 1st. dull mauve (p 13) ... 2·20 95
a. Opt inverted ... 43·00 36·00
b. Opt double, one inverted ... 55·00 50·00
147 5st. green (p 13½) ... £150 £150
148 5st. green (p 11½) ... £160 £160
149 5st. green (p 13) ... 2·20 95
150 5st. dull green (p 13) ... 2·20 95
a. Opt inverted ... 55·00 50·00

(c) Surch as T **21** (30 Aug (Nos. 152/4)–25 Sept (others))

151 **7** 5 on 30st. brown (p 13½) ... 3·75 65
a. Surch double ... 55·00 50·00
b. Date reading "1969" ... £1200
c. Date reading "1990" ... £1100 £950
152 10 on 15st. brown-orange (p 11½) ... £900 £750
153 10 on 15st. orange (p 13) ... 3·75 1·30
a. Surch inverted ... 38·00 36·00
b. Surch double ... 55·00
c. Surch triple ...
d. Date reading "909" ... £110 95·00
154 10 on 15st. yellow (p 13) ... 8·75 1·00
a. Surch inverted ... 55·00 50·00
b. Date reading "909" ... £110 95·00
155 10 on 50st. blue-green (p 13½) ... 55·00 50·00
a. Date reading "1990" ... £1500
156 10 on 50st. blue-green (p 13½) (R.) ... 3·75 1·30
a. Imperf (pair) ... £110 £100
b. Date reading "909" ... 85·00
c. Date reading "1990" ... £110 £100
d. Surch on back in addition ... 55·00

On Nos. 152/4 the height of the surcharge is slightly less than on Nos. 155/6.

1910 (1 Oct). Nos. 108 and 113 surch as T **22** at Sofia.

157 **14** 1 on 3st. black and orange (B.) ... 8·75 2·10
158 5 on 15st. greenish black and lake (B.) ... 2·20 1·60

23 King Asen Tower

24 Tsar in General's Uniform

25 Veliko Turnovo

26 Tsar Ferdinand

27 Tsar in Admiral's Uniform

28 River Isker

29 Tsar Ferdinand

30 Rila Monastery

31 Tsar and Princes (after Ya. Veshin)

32 Tsar in Coronation Robes (after A. Mitov)

33 Monastery of the Holy Trinity, Veliko Turnovo

34 Varna

(Des A. Mitov and G. Evstatiev. Eng Bradbury, Wilkinson, London. Recess Govt Ptg Wks, Rome)

1911 (14 Feb). P 12.

159 **23** 1st. myrtle-green ... 35 15
160 **24** 2st. black and carmine ... 35 15
161 **25** 3st. black and lake ... 85 15
162 **26** 5st. black and green ... 1·60 15
163 **27** 10st. black and red ... 2·75 20
164 **28** 15st. bistre ... 8·25 30
165 **29** 25st. black and ultramarine ... 55 15
166 **30** 30st. black and blue ... 8·25 30
167 **31** 50st. black and ochre ... 43·00 50
a. Centre inverted ... — £7000
168 **32** 1l. brown ... 20·00 30
169 **33** 2l. black and purple ... 3·75 1·30
170 **34** 3l. black and violet ... 22·00 7·75
159/170 *Set of* 12 ... £100 10·50

During the Balkan war of 1912–13 stamps of this issue were obliterated in the occupied territories with the old Turkish cancellations, until these could be superseded by new Bulgarian cancellations.

For similar types see Nos. 181/4*a*, 229/30 and 236/7.

35 Tsar Ferdinand

ОСВОБ. ВОЙНА

1912-1913

(**36**) War of Liberation, 1912–13

(Des S. Badzhov. Typo Austrian State Ptg Wks, Vienna)

1912 (2 Aug). Tsar's Silver Jubilee. Chalk-surfaced paper. P 12½.

171 **35** 5st. greenish grey ... 5·50 2·10
a. Error. Bright green ... £1200 £1200
172 10st. lake ... 7·50 3·75
173 25st. slate-blue ... 11·00 5·75
171/173 *Set of* 3 ... 22·00 10·50

1913 (6 Aug). Victory over the Turks. Optd as T **36** at Sofia.

174 **23** 1st. myrtle-green (R.) ... 55 20
a. "c" for first "o" in first word of overprint ... 9·75 9·75
175 **24** 2st. black and carmine (B.) ... 55 20
176 **25** 3st. black and lake (B. or Bk.) ... 2·20 50
177 **26** 5st. black and green (R.) ... 55 20
178 **27** 10st. black and red (Bk.) ... 55 20
179 **28** 15st. bistre (G.) ... 3·25 1·60
180 **29** 25st. black and ultramarine (R.) ... 8·75 2·50
174/180 *Set of* 7 ... 15·00 4·75

The spacing of the two lines of the overprint differs for each value except the 2st. and 25st. which are the same.

10 СТ.

D **37**

(**37**)

3 СТОТИНКИ (**37a**)

(Litho State Ptg Wks, Sofia)

1915 (12 Apr). POSTAGE DUE. Thin toned paper. P 11½.

D181 D **37** 5st. dull green ... 65 20
D182 10st. violet ... 70 30
D183 20st. rose ... 70 30
D184 30st. orange ... 3·75 1·00
D185 50st. Prussian blue ... 1·30 65
D181/185 *Set of* 5 ... 6·50 2·20

See also Nos. D200/4 and D239/45.

1915 (6 July). Surch with T **37**, in red, at Sofia.

180*a* **29** 10st. on 25st. black and ultramarine ... 1·30 30

(Recess E. Petiti, Rome)

1915 (7 Nov). Types of 1911. Re-engraved plates; colours changed.

(a) P 14.

181 **26** 5st. purple-brown and green ... 4·25 20
181*a* **27** 10st. sepia and red-brown ... 20 15
182 **30** 30st. brown and olive ... 55 20

(b) P 11½

182*a* **23** 1st. slate ... 20 15
183 **28** 15st. grey-olive ... 70 15
184 **29** 25st. black and deep blue ... 35 10
184*a* **32** 1l. deep brown ... 55 30
181/184*a* *Set of* 7 ... 6·00 1·10

Nos. 181 to 184*a* differ considerably in size and details of design from stamps printed from the earlier plates and the designer's initials are omitted in Nos. 181, 181*a* and 184.

1916 (9 Mar). Red Cross Fund. Surch with T **37a** at Sofia.

185	**7**	3 on 1st. mauve (G.)	13·00	12·50
		a. Surch inverted	£150	

38

39 Bulgarian Peasant

40 Soldier and Mt. Sonichka

41 Nish

42 Ohrid and Lake

43 Demir Kapija

44 Gevgeli

(Des S. Badzhov. Typo Austrian State Ptg Works, Vienna)

1917 (14 Aug)–**19**. Liberation of Macedonia. P 13×12½ (30st., 2, 3l.) or 12½ (others).

186	**38**	5st. grey-green	55	40
187	**39**	15st. greenish grey	20	20
		a. Perf 11½	20	20
		b. Imperf (pair)	41·00	
188	**40**	25st. blue	20	20
189	**41**	30st. orange	20	30
190	**42**	50st. violet	1·10	85
191	**43**	2l. chestnut (1919)	1·10	85
192	**44**	3l. claret	1·60	1·40
186/192 *Set of* 7			4·50	3·75

A 1l. value in bluish green showing Bulgaria on the throne (vertical format) was prepared but not issued.

45 Veles

46 Bulgarian Ploughman

47 Monastery of St. John, Ohrid

48 Tsar Ferdinand

(Des D. Gyudzhenov and R. Aleksiev. Typo German State Ptg Wks, Berlin)

1918–19. Liberation of Macedonia. P 13×13½ or 13½×13 (No. 194).

193	**45**	1st. grey	20	10
194	**46**	1st. grey-green (1919)	20	10
195	**47**	5st. green	20	10
193/195 *Set of* 3			55	25

(Des S. Badzhov. Typo Austrian State Ptg Wks, Vienna)

1918 (1 July). 30th Anniv of Tsar Ferdinand's Accession. Chalk-surfaced paper. P 12½×13.

196	**48**	1st. greenish slate	20	15
197		2st. brown	20	15
198		3st. indigo	55	50
199		10st. red	55	50
196/199 *Set of* 4			1·40	1·20

The 1l. indigo in this type is an essay.

Tsar (King) Boris III

3 October 1918–28 August 1943

PRINTERS The following were printed at the State Printing Works, Sofia *except where otherwise stated*.

1919 (19 June). POSTAGE DUE. Litho. Thick white paper. P 12×11½.

D200	D **37**	5st. bright green	55	10
D201		10st. dull violet	55	20
D202		20st. pale rose-red	55	20
D203		30st. red-orange	4·25	4·25
		a. Brick-red	55	20
D204		50st. deep blue	1·80	85
D200/204 *Set of* 5 (cheapest)			3·50	1·40

49 Parliament Building

50 King Boris III

(Des S. Badzhov. Typo)

1919 (3 Oct). P 12 (1st.) or 11½ (2st.).

201	**49**	1st. black	20	15
		a. Imperf between (horiz strip of 3)		
202		2st. olive	20	15

(Des S. Badzhov. Typo)

1919 (3 Oct)–**21**. First Anniv of Enthronement of King Boris III. P 11½.

203	**50**	3st. brown-red (1920)	20	15
		a. Venetian red	20	15
204		5st. green	20	15
		a. Emerald (1921)	20	15
205		10st. rose	20	15
		a. Scarlet (1921)	20	15
206		15st. violet	20	15
207		25st. blue	20	15
208		30st. chocolate (1920)	20	15
209		50st. yellow-brown	20	15
203/209 *Set of* 7			1·30	95

All values exist on thin or thick paper, with pin roulette 12.

(**51**)

(**52**)

(**53**)

1920 (22 June). Prisoners of War Fund. Surch as T **51** (Nos. 210, 218/19), **53** (No. 217) or **52** (others).

210	**49**	1 on 2st. olive	20	15
211	**50**	2½ on 5st. green	20	15
212		5 on 10st. rose	20	15
213		7½ on 15st. violet	20	15
214		12½ on 25st. blue	20	15
215		15 on 30st. chocolate	20	15
216		25 on 50st. yellow-brown	20	15
217	**32**	50 on 1l. deep brown (184*a*)	55	30
		a. Surch double	£100	
		b. Surch in blue	£110	
218	**43**	1(l.) on 2l. chestnut	55	50
		a. Surch inverted	£100	
219	**44**	1½(l.) on 3l. claret	1·60	1·00
210/219 *Set of* 10			3·75	2·50

On No. 219 the surcharge is larger.

These were sold at the original face-value, but only had franking value to half that amount, represented by the surcharge, the surplus being for the prisoners of war fund.

54 Vazov's Birthplace at Sopot and Cherrywood Cannon

55 The Bearfighter (character from *Under the Yoke*)

56 Ivan Vazov in 1870 and 1920

57 Vazov

58 Vazov's Houses in Plovdiv and Sofia

58a Father Paisii Khilendarski (historian)

(Des S. Badzhov and R. Aleksiev. Photo)

1920 (24 Oct). 70th Birthday of Ivan Vazov (writer). P 11½.

220	**54**	30st. carmine	20	15
221	**55**	50st. myrtle	45	20
222	**56**	1l. sepia	75	50
223	**57**	2l. brown	2·20	1·30
224	**58**	3l. deep violet	2·75	1·80
225	**58a**	5l. blue	3·75	2·30
220/225 *Set of* 6			9·00	5·75

59 Aleksandr Nevski Cathedral, Sofia

60 Monument to Alexander II, "The Liberator", Sofia

61 Shipka Pass Monastery

62 King Boris III

63 Harvester

64 King Asen Tower

65 Rila Monastery

(Des S. Badzhov (10st.), R. Aleksiev (20, 75st., 2l.), E. Vake (25st., 1, 10l.), A. Mitov (50st.), G. Evstatiev (3, 5l.). Eng and recess Bradbury, Wilkinson)

1921 (23 Mar)–**23**. T **59** to **65**, and **25** (redrawn). P 12.

226	**59**	10st. slate-violet (7.21)	20	15
227	**60**	20st. green (7.21)	20	15
228	**62**	25st. greenish blue (20.3.22)	20	15
229	**25**	50st. orange (12.21)	45	20
230		50st. deep blue (1.12.23)	9·25	3·50
231	**61**	75st. violet (7.21)	20	15
232		75st. deep blue (1.12.23)	55	20
233	**62**	1l. scarlet (25.8.21)	55	20
234		1l. deep blue (2.12.21)	45	15
235	**63**	2l. brown (1.6.21)	1·60	20
236	**64**	3l. dull purple	1·60	20
237	**65**	5l. blue	8·75	40
238	**62**	10l. maroon (25.7.21)	22·00	4·75
226/238 *Set of* 13			41·00	9·25

1921 (12 May). POSTAGE DUE. Colours changed and new values. Litho. Thick greyish paper. P 11½.

D239	D **37**	5st. yellow-green	1·10	50
		a. Imperf between (horiz pair)	38·00	
D240		10st. bright violet	20	10
D241		20st. pale orange	20	10
D242		50st. milky blue	20	10
D243		1l. pale blue-green	55	10
		a. Imperf between (vert pair)		
D244		2l. carmine	55	20
D245		3l. orange-brown	1·10	40
D239/245 *Set of* 7			3·50	1·40

The 50st. to 3l. values were authorized for use as ordinary postage stamps in November 1923.

66 Tsar Ferdinand and Map

67 Tsar Ferdinand

68 Mt. Shar

69 Bridge over Vardar, at Skopje

70 St. Clement's Monastery, Ohrid

(Des B. Marinov (240), R. Aleksiev (241), D. Gyudzhenov (others). Typo State Ptg Wks, Berlin)

1921 (11 June). P 13×13½ or 13½×13 (T **69**/**70**).

239	**66**	10st. claret	20	15
240	**67**	10st. claret	20	15
241	**68**	10st. claret	20	15
242	**69**	10st. mauve	20	15
243	**70**	20st. blue	85	20
239/243 *Set of* 5			1·50	70

These stamps were prepared in 1915 to commemorate the annexation of Macedonia, but were not issued until 1921. Owing to protests by Yugoslavia they were only on sale for three days and were then withdrawn. An additional 50st. value in violet, showing Bulgarian soldiers in a trench, was not placed on sale at post offices.

71 Bourchier in Bulgarian Costume

72 J. D. Bourchier

73 Rila Monastery, Bourchier's Resting-place

(Eng and recess Bradbury, Wilkinson)

1921 (30 Dec). James Bourchier (*Times* correspondent) Commemoration. P 12.

244	**71**	10st. vermilion	20	20
245		20st. orange	20	20
246	**72**	30st. slate	20	20
247		50st. slate-lilac	20	20
248		1l. purple	55	20
249	**73**	1½l. olive-green	55	40
250		2l. grey-green	55	30
251		3l. grey-blue	1·30	50
252		5l. maroon	2·40	1·20
244/252 *Set of 9*			5·50	3·00

10 СТОТИНКИ (**74**) **3** ЛЕВА (**75**) **6** ЛЕВА (**76**)

1924 (10 Nov–24 Dec). Various types surch.

(a) As T **74**

253	**49**	10st. on 1st. black (p 11½) (R.)	20	15
		a. Imperf between (horiz pair)	43·00	
254	D **37**	10st. on 20st. pale orange (D241)	20	15
255		20st. on 5st. bright green (D200)	27·00	26·00
		a. Imperf between (vert pair)	55·00	
255*b*		20st. on 5st. yellow-green (D239)	20	15
256		20st. on 10st. dull violet (D201)	8·25	7·75
		a. Imperf between (vert pair)	49·00	
256*b*		20st. on 10st. bright violet (D240)	20	15
257		20st. on 30st. red-orange (D203)	20	15
		a. Imperf between (vert pair)	49·00	

(b) As T **75** or **76** (1l. and 6l.)

258	**50**	1l. on 5st. emerald (B.)	35	15
259	**25**	3l. on 50st. deep blue (R.)	1·10	30
260	**62**	6l. on 1l. scarlet (B.)	2·20	65

77

78

79 King Boris III

80 King Boris III

T **80** redrawn. The shoulder does not touch the frame at left, and there are many other differences.

81 Aleksandr Nevski Cathedral, Sofia

82 Harvesters

(Des Kh. Lozev (261/4), G. Zhelezarov (268), S. Krustev (267), D. Zankov (265/6*a*, 267*a*). Typo)

1925–28.

(a) P 13

261	**77**	10st. blue and scarlet/*rose* (15.6.25)	35	20
		a. Perf 11½	45	20
262		15st. orange and deep rose-red/*blue* (20.6.25)	35	20
		a. Perf 11½	45	20
		b. Error. Buff and black	—	£3250
263		30st. buff and black (15.7.25)	35	20
		a. Perf 11½	45	20
264	**78**	50st. chocolate/*green* (1.6.25)	35	20
		a. Perf 11½	45	20

(b) P 11½

265	**79**	1l. olive-green (1.3.25)	1·00	20
266	**80**	1l. dull grey-olive (1926)	1·20	20
266*a*		1l. dull yellowish green (1928)	27·00	50
267	**81**	2l. deep grey-green and buff (15.7.25)	4·25	20
267*a*	**80**	2l. olive-brown (1926)	1·60	20
268	**82**	4l. brown-lake and greenish yellow (1.10.25)	4·25	20
		a. Imperf between (horiz pair)		
261/268 *Set of 9* (excluding 266*a*)			33·00	1·90

83 Proposed Rest-home, Varna

84 Proposed Sanatorium, Bankya

(Des G. Nikolov. Litho)

1925 (1 Sept)–**29**. SUNDAY DELIVERY. Litho. P 11½.

268*b*	**83**	1l. black/*green*	11·00	30
268*c*		1l. brown (1.5.26)	11·00	30
268*d*		1l. orange (1.6.27)	16·00	50
268*e*		1l. pink (1.5.28)	14·00	50
268*f*		1l. violet/*rose* (1.5.29)	16·00	50
268*g*	**84**	2l. green	1·60	30
268*h*		2l. violet (1.6.27)	1·60	30
268*i*		5l. blue	17·00	1·30
268*j*		5l. rose (1.6.27)	17·00	1·30
268*b*/268*j* *Set of 9*			95·00	4·75

For use in addition to normal postage to ensure delivery on Sundays and holidays. The funds raised from the sale of these stamps were to maintain a sanatorium for the benefit of postal, telegraph and telephone employees.

85 St. Nedelya's Cathedral, Sofia, after Bomb Outrage

86 C. Botev (poet)

(Des G. Zhelezarov. Litho)

1926 (15 Mar). P 11½.

269	**85**	50st. olive-black	35	20

(Des Kh. Losev. Litho)

1926 (2 June). 50th Anniv of Death of Botev. P 11½.

270	**86**	1l. olive-green	1·30	50
271		2l. violet-blue	2·75	50
272		4l. claret	3·75	2·50
270/272 *Set of 3*			7·00	3·25

87

(**88** Albatros Biplane)

89 King Boris III

(Des Kh. Losev. Typo, centre embossed)

1926 (1 Oct)–**27**. P 11½.

273	**87**	6l. pale yellow-olive and deep blue (1927)	2·20	30
274		10l. orange-brown and blackish brown	16·00	4·00

1927 (1 Feb)–**35**. As T **1**, but value in stotinki, as for the issue of 1881. P 13.

(a) No wmk

275	10st. carmine and green	20	20
276	15st. black and yellow (1929)	20	20
277	30st. slate and yellow-buff	20	20
278	30st. blue and buff (1928)	20	20
279	50st. black and rose (1928)	20	20

(b) Wmk Vert Wavy Lines

280	10st. carmine and green (5.9.35)	1·10	20
275/280 *Set of 6*		1·90	1·10

1927 (7 Nov)–**28**. AIR. P 11½.

(a) Optd as T **88** (sideways, nose at top) and additionally surch

281	**87**	1 on pale yellow-olive and deep 6l. blue (R.)	2·20	2·10
		a. Surch inverted	£650	£650

(b) Optd wih T **88** (horiz)

282	**80**	2l. olive-brown (R.) (15.4.28)	2·20	2·10
283	**82**	4l. brown-lake and greenish yellow (B.)	3·25	2·10
284	**87**	10l. orange-brown and blackish brown (G.) (15.4.28)	85·00	50·00
281/284 *Set of 4*			85·00	50·00

Nos. 281 and 283/4 but with the surcharge or overprint in brown, green and blue respectively were prepared but not issued.

(Des Kh. Lozev. Typo)

1928 (3 Oct)–**31**. P 12×11½.

285	**89**	1l. bright green	3·25	20
		a. Olive-green (1931)	4·25	20
286		2l. chocolate	4·25	20

90 Saint Clement of Ohrid

91 Monastery of Dryanovo

(Des Ts. Lavrenov (10st., 50st., 1l.), Kh. Lozev (15st., 4l., 6l.), T. Dolapchiev (30st.), S. Velkov (5l.), D. Zankov (2l., 3l.). Typo)

1929 (12 May). 50th Anniv of the Liberation of Bulgaria and Millenary of Tsar Simeon. T **90** (and other portraits) and **91**. P 11½.

287	10st. deep violet	30	10
288	15st. purple	30	10
289	30st. carmine	30	10
290	50st. olive-green	75	20
291	1l. brown-red	1·90	20
292	2l. blue	2·10	20
293	3l. olive-green	5·25	1·0
294	4l. olive-brown	9·50	4
295	5l. red-brown	7·25	1·0
296	6l. greenish blue	9·25	2·5
287/296 *Set of 10*		33·00	5·2

Portraits: 23½×33½ mm—15st. Konstantin Miladinov (poet an folklorist); 1l. Father Paisii Khilendarski (historian); 2l. Tsar Simeon; 4 Vasil Levski (revolutionary); 5l. Georgi Benkovski (revolutionary); 6 Tsar Alexander II of Russia, "The Liberator". 19×28½ mm—30st. Georg Rakovski (writer). 19×26 mm—3l. Lyuben Karavelov (journalist).

98 Convalescent Home, Varna

99

(Des N. Biserov. Litho)

1930–33. SUNDAY DELIVERY. P 11½.

297	**98**	1l. green and claret (1.6.30)	18·00	30
298		1l. yellow and green (1.9.31)	2·10	30
299		1l. bistre-brown and claret (1.6.33)	2·10	30
297/299 *Set of 3*			20·00	80

(Des N. Biserov. Typo)

1930 (12 Nov). Wedding of King Boris and Princess Giovanna of Italy. T **99** and similar horiz design. P 11½.

300	**99**	1l. green	50	40
301	–	2l. purple	85	50
302	**99**	4l. carmine	85	50
303	–	6l. deep blue	1·00	55
300/303 *Set of 4*			3·00	1·80

Design:—2l., 6l. Portraits in two medallions.

A miniature sheet containing Nos. 300/3 exists. Only 55 copies were printed and these were presented to eminent guests attending the wedding.

101 King Boris III

102 King Boris III

(Des K. Shermaten. Typo)

1931 (3 April)–**37**. No wmk.

(a) Without horiz coloured frame lines at top and bottom. P 13

304	**101**	1l. green (12.31)	85	20
		a. Wmk Wavy Lines (7.35)	1·30	20
		b. Emerald (1936)	2·10	20
305		2l. carmine (9.31)	1·30	20
		a. Wmk Wavy Lines (7.35)	80·00	40
306		4l. orange (27.1.34)	1·80	20
307		6l. blue	1·30	20
		a. Wmk Wavy Lines (5.9.35)	1·40	40
308		12l. brown (4.32)	1·00	30

(b) With horiz coloured frame lines at top and bottom. P 12×11½ or 11½ (20l.)

308*a*	**101**	4l. orange (1936)	1·00	20
308*b*		6l. blue (1936)	2·75	20
308*c*		7l. ultramarine (7.3.37)	40	20
308*d*		10l. slate	42·00	2·50
308*e*		14l. chestnut (1.7.37)	95	50
308*f*	**102**	20l. chestnut and purple	2·50	1·00
304/308*f* *Set of 11* (cheapest)			50·00	5·25

103 Gymnastics

104 Football

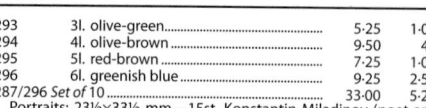

105 The Spirit of Victory

(Des G. Nikolov (6l., 50l.), N. Biserov (others). Typo)

1931 (18 Sept). Balkan Olympic Games. T **103/5** and similar types, dated "1931". P 11½.

309	1l. green	3·25	1·50
310	2l. brown-lake	4·25	2·00
311	4l. carmine	9·50	2·50
312	6l. blue-green	21·00	6·00
313	10l. orange-vermilion	42·00	15·00
314	12l. deep blue	£130	40·00
315	50l. brown	£140	85·00
309/315 *Set of 7*		£325	£140

Designs:—4l. Horse-riding (as T **104**); 6l. Fencing (as T **103**); 10l. Cycling (as T **103**); 12l. Diving (as T **105**).

See also Nos. 326/32.

108

109 Rila Monastery

(Des B. Denev. Typo)

1931 (28 Oct)–**38**. AIR. P 11½.

316	**108**	1l. green	85	30
316*a*		1l. maroon (27.12.38)	50	20
317		2l. maroon	85	30
317*a*		2l. green (27.12.38)	65	30
318		6l. light blue	1·00	50
318*a*		6l. carmine (27.12.38)	1·60	60
319		12l. carmine	2·10	50
319*a*		12l. light blue (27.12.38)	1·80	70
320		20l. violet	2·10	1·00
321		30l. orange	4·25	2·00
322		50l. red-brown	5·75	3·50
316/322 *Set of* 11			19·00	9·00

(Des N. Biserov. Typo)

1932 (9 May). AIR. P 11½.

323	**109**	18l. green	£140	70·00
324		24l. carmine	95·00	45·00
325		28l. ultramarine	50·00	35·00
323/325 *Set of* 3			£250	£140

These stamps were issued for use on mail carried from Sofia to Strasbourg on a flight in connection with a Philatelic Exhibition there.

D **110**

D **111**

D **112**

2
(**110**)

1932 (15 Aug). POSTAGE DUE. Typo. P 11½.

D326	D **110**	1l. bistre	2·10	1·30
D327		2l. lake	2·10	1·30
D328		6l. maroon	4·75	1·50
D326/328 *Set of* 3			8·00	3·75

1933 (5 Jan). Balkan Olympic Games. T **103/5** and similar types. Colours changed, Litho. P 11½.

326	1l. blue-green	4·25	4·00
327	2l. blue	6·25	4·50
328	4l. slate-purple	10·50	5·50
329	6l. carmine	21·00	10·00
330	10l. brown	£160	65·00
331	12l. orange-vermilion	£250	£100
332	50l. claret	£750	£750
326/332 *Set of* 7		£1100	£850

(Des N. Biserov. Typo)

1933 (10 Apr). POSTAGE DUE. P 11½.

D333	D **111**	20st. olive-brown	20	10
D334		40st. blue	20	10
D335		80st. carmine	20	10
D336	D **112**	1l. red-brown	1·00	60
D337		2l. brown-olive	1·00	90
D338		6l. slate-purple	50	40
D339		14l. ultramarine	75	60
D333/339 *Set of* 7			3·50	2·50

For stamps as Type D **112** but larger, see Nos. D646/9.

1934 (27 Jan). T **101** (without frame-line) surcharged with T **110**. No wmk. P 13.

333	2 on 3l. brown-olive (B.)	13·50	1·00

111 Defending the Pass

112 Bulgarian Veteran

(Des D. Gyudzhenov (1l.), V. Staikov (2l.), N. Biserov (3, 7, 14l.), N. Kozhukharov (4l.). Typo)

1934. Unveiling of Shipka Pass Memorial. T **111/12** and similar vert designs. Wmk Wavy Lines.

(a) First issue

A. P 11

334A	1l. green	2·10	1·00
335A	2l. reddish orange	1·60	50
336A	3l. olive-sepia	5·25	3·00
337A	4l. carmine	3·75	1·00
338A	7l. blue	7·25	3·50
339A	14l. deep reddish purple	27·00	18·00

B. P 11½ (26 Aug)

334B	1l. green	2·10	1·00
335B	2l. reddish orange	1·60	50
336B	3l. olive-sepia	5·25	3·00
337B	4l. carmine	3·75	1·00
338B	7l. blue	7·25	3·50
339B	14l. deep reddish purple	27·00	18·00

(b) Second issue

A. P 11×10½ (2l.) or 11 (others)

340A	1l. yellowish green	2·10	1·00
341A	2l. yellow-orange	1·60	50
342A	3l. lemon	5·25	3·00
343A	4l. rose-red	3·75	1·00
344A	7l. new blue	7·25	3·50
345A	14l. ochre	27·00	18·00
334A/345A *Set of* 12		85·00	49·00

B. P 11½ (21 Sept)

340B	1l. yellowish green	2·10	1·00
341B	2l. yellow-orange	1·60	50
342B	3l. lemon	5·25	3·00
343B	4l. rose-red	3·75	1·00
344B	7l. new blue	7·25	3·50
345B	14l. ochre	27·00	18·00
334B/345B *Set of* 12		85·00	49·00

Design:—2l. Shipka Pass Memorial; 3, 7l. Veteran standard-bearer; 14l. Widow showing memorial to orphans.

113 Convalescent Home, Troyan

114 Capt. Georgi Mamarchev

(Des G. Nikolov. Typo)

1935 (9 Feb). SUNDAY DELIVERY. T **113** and similar horiz design. Wmk Wavy Lines. P 11½ (347) or 11 (others).

346	1l. scarlet and chocolate	2·10	30
	a. Perf 11½		
347	1l. ultramarine and green	2·10	30
348	5l. ultramarine and brown-lake	6·75	1·50
346/348 *Set of* 3		9·75	1·90

Design:—5l. Convalescent Home, Bankya.

(Des K. Chokanov and D. Gyudzhenov. Typo)

1935 (5 May). Centenary of Turnovo Insurrection. T **114** and similar vert design. Wmk Wavy Lines. P 11½.

349	1l. steel blue	3·25	80
350	2l. brown-purple	3·25	1·20

Design:—1l. Velcho Atanasov Dzhamdzhiyata.

115 Aleksandr Nevski Cathedral, Sofia

116 Girl Gymnast

117 Janos Hunyadi

(Des N. Balkchiev (1, 50l.), K. Penev (2, 4l.), N. Biserov (7l.), G. Krustev (14l.). Typo)

1935 (14 June). Fifth Balkan Football Tournament. T **115** and various football types. Wmk Wavy Lines. P 11½.

351	1l. green	8·25	6·00
	a. Perf 11		
352	2l. deep blue	12·50	8·00
353	4l. rosine	16·00	10·00
354	7l. greenish blue	29·00	20·00
355	14l. orange	26·00	20·00
	a. Perf 11×10½		
356	50l. chocolate	£475	£400
351/356 *Set of* 6		£500	£425

Designs: Horiz—1l. Match in progress at Yunak Stadium, Sofia; 4l. Footballers. Vert—7l. Herald and Balkan map; 14l. Footballers and trophy; 50l. Trophy.

(Des S. Badzhov. Typo)

1935 (10 July). Eighth Bulgarian Gymnastic Tournament. T **116** and sports types inscr "12–14 VII 1935". Wmk Wavy Lines. P 11½.

357	1l. green	9·50	8·00
358	2l. light blue	10·50	9·00
359	4l. scarlet	13·50	11·00
360	7l. blue	16·00	16·00
361	14l. chocolate	16·00	15·00
362	50l. orange-red	£325	£250
357/362 *Set of* 6		£350	£275

Designs: Vert—1l. Parallel bars; 2l. Male gymnast in uniform; 7l. Pole vault; 50 1. Sports Association Emblem (athlete and lion). Horiz—14l. Yunak Stadium, Sofia.

(Des V. Zakhariev. Typo)

1935 (4 Aug). Unveiling of Monument to Ladislas III of Poland at Varna. T **117** and designs inscr "WARNENCZYK (A)". Wmk Wavy Lines.

A. P 11½

363A	1l. brown-orange	3·25	1·00
364A	2l. maroon	5·25	1·10
365A	4l. vermilion	26·00	7·00
366A	7l. dull blue	4·75	1·90
367A	14l. green	4·75	1·80
363A/367A *Set of* 5		40·00	11·50

B. P 11

363B	1l. brown-orange	4·25	1·20
364B	2l. maroon	5·00	1·50
365B	4l. vermilion	31·00	8·00
366B	7l. dull blue	5·25	2·00
367B	14l. green	5·25	1·80
363B/367B *Set of* 5		46·00	13·00

Designs: Vert—2l. King Ladislas of Hungary enthroned (22×32 mm); 7l. Full length portrait of King Ladislas in armour (20×31 mm). Horiz—4l. Varna Memorial (33×24 mm); 14l. Battle scene (30×25 mm).

Some values also exist perf compound of 10½ and 11½.

118 Dimitur

119

120

(Des N. Balkchiev (1l.), F. Filipov (2l.), K. Penev (4, 7l.), G. Krustev (14l.). Typo)

1935 (11 Oct). 67th Death Anniv of Khadzhi Dimitur (revolutionary). T **118** and similar designs.

A. P 11½

368A	1l. green	3·25	1·00
369A	2l. chocolate	5·25	2·00
370A	4l. carmine	14·50	5·00
371A	7l. blue	21·00	9·00
372A	14l. orange	26·00	10·00
368A/372A *Set of* 5		65·00	24·00

B. P 11

368B	1l. green	4·25	1·50
369B	2l. chocolate	6·25	2·50
370B	4l. carmine	17·00	6·00
371B	7l. blue	21·00	9·00
372B	14l. orange	26·00	10·00
368B/372B *Set of* 5		65·00	26·00

Designs: Vert—1l. Dimitur's monument at Sliven; 7l. Revolutionary Group (dated "1868"). Horiz—4l. Dimitur and Stefan Karadzha (revolutionary); 14l. Dimitur' s birthplace at Sliven.

Stamps also exist perf compound of 10½ and 11½.

1936 (4 Apr)–**39**. Typo. P 13.

373	**119**	10st. vermilion (3.37)	20	15
373*a*		15st. emerald-green (23.5 36)	20	15
374	**120**	30st. maroon	30	15
374*a*		30st. chestnut (1937)	20	15
374*b*		30st. greenish blue (2.38)	20	15
375		50st. ultramarine (8.4.36)	30	15
375*a*		50st. carmine (1.38)	30	15
375*b*		50st. dark green (27.12.39)	20	15
373/375*b* *Set of* 8			1·70	1·10

121 Nesebur

(Des V. Zhakariev. Photo)

1936 (16 Aug). Slav Geographical and Ethnographical Congress, Sofia. T **121** and similar designs. P 11½.

376	1l. violet	4·25	2·00
377	2l. bright blue	4·25	2·00
378	7l. deep blue	8·25	4·00
376/378 *Set of* 3		15·00	7·25

Designs: 25×34 mm—1l. Meteorological Bureau, Mt. Musala. 23×34 mm—2l. Peasant girl.

122 St. Cyril and St. Methodius

123 St. Cyril and St. Methodius

124 Princess Marie Louise

(Des I. Manev (T **122**), E. Rakarov (T **123**). Photo)

1937 (3 June). Millenary of Introduction of Cyrillic Alphabet and Slavonic Liturgy. P 11½.

379	**122**	1l. myrtle-green	75	30
380		2l. bright purple	75	30
381	**123**	4l. vermilion	85	30
382	**122**	7l. bright blue	4·25	2·20
383	**123**	14l. scarlet	4·25	2·30
379/383 *Set of* 5			9·75	4·75

(Des K. Khristov. Photo)

1937 (3 Oct). P 11½.

384	**124**	1l. emerald-green	75	20
385		2l. red	85	20
386		4l. vermilion	85	50
384/386 *Set of* 3			2·20	80

125 King Boris III

126 Harvesting

128 "Attar of Roses"

(Des A. Apostolov. Photo)

1937 (3 Oct). 19th Anniv of Accession. P 11½.

387	**125**	2l. red	1·00	50

MS387*a* 76×115 mm. **125** 2l. (+18l.) ultramarine. Imperf. (22.11.37) 10·50 20·00

(Des B. Angelushev (10, 15, 50st., 7l.), A. Apostolov (30st.), A. Zhendov (1, 3, 4l.), V. Staikov and S. Petrov (2, 14l.). Photo)

1938. Agricultural Products. T **126** and **128** and similar designs. P 13.

388	**126**	10st. orange (25 Oct)	20	10
389		10st. red-orange (25 Oct)	20	10
390	–	15st. crimson (25 Oct)	50	10
391	–	15st. claret (25 Oct)	50	10
392	–	30st. brown (17 May)	40	10
393	–	30st. red-brown (17 May)	45	10
394	–	50st. steel-blue (17 May)	95	10
395	–	50st. black (17 May)	95	10
396	–	1l. green (25 Oct)	1·00	10
397	–	1l. yellow-green (25 Oct)	1·00	10
398	**128**	2l. carmine (22 Mar)	1·00	20
399		2l. lake (22 Mar)	1·00	20
400	–	3l. magenta (25 Oct)	2·10	1·00
401	–	3l. maroon (25 Oct)	2·10	1·00
402	–	4l. brown (30 May)	1·60	50
403	–	4l. bright purple (30 May)	1·60	50
404	–	7l. bluish violet (25 Oct)	3·25	1·00
405	–	7l. bright blue (25 Oct)	3·25	1·00
406	–	14l. red-brown (18 June)	5·25	2·00
407	–	14l. chocolate (18 June)	5·25	2·00
388/407 *Set of* 20			29·00	9·25

Designs: Vert—15st. Sunflower; 30st. Wheat; 50st. Chickens and eggs; 1l. Grapes; 3l. Strawberries; 4l. Girl carrying grapes; 7l. Roses; 14l. Leaves of tobacco.

129 Prince Simeon

130 Prince Simeon

(Des K. Penev (1, 2, 7l.), N. Biserov (4, 14l.). Photo)

1938 (16 June). Heir Apparent's First Birthday. As T **129** and **130** (various portraits). P 13.

408	1l. green	30	20
409	2l. carmine	30	20
410	4l. vermilion	40	25
411	7l. bright blue	1·60	80
412	14l. brown	1·60	80
408/412 *Set of* 5		3·75	2·00

Portraits:—2l. (different frame), 7l. as T **129**; 14l. as T **130** (but slightly larger portrait in simpler frame).

131 King Boris III

132 First Bulgarian Locomotive

(Des K. Penev. Photo)

1938 (3 Oct). 20th Anniv of King's Accession. As T **131** (various uniforms). P 13.

413	1l. green	25	20
414	2l. lake	1·30	30
415	4l. brown	40	30
416	7l. bright blue	65	50
417	14l. magenta	65	50
413/417 *Set of* 5		3·00	1·60

Portraits:—2l. Dated "3.X.1918/3.X.1938"; 4l. Dated "3.X.1918/3.X.1928"; 7l., 14l. Dated "3.X.1938".

(Des B. Angelushev. Photo)

1939 (26 Apr). 50th Anniv of Bulgarian State Railways. T **132** and similar horiz designs. P 13.

418	1l. yellow-green	50	40
419	2l. red-brown	50	40
420	4l. orange	3·25	1·50
421	7l. blue	9·50	5·50
418/421 *Set of* 4		12·50	7·00

Designs:—2l. Modern express train; 4l. Train crossing a viaduct; 7l. King Boris as engine-driver.

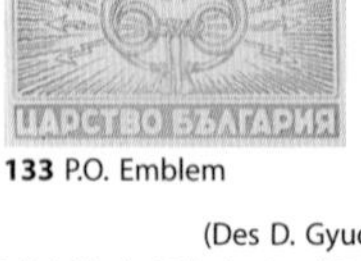

133 P.O. Emblem

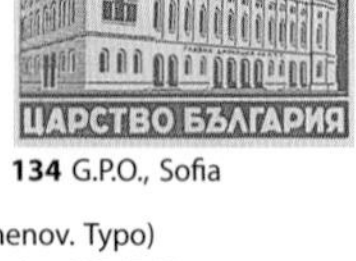

134 G.P.O., Sofia

(Des D. Gyudzhenov. Typo)

1939 (14 May). 60th Anniv of Bulgarian P.O. P 13.

422	**133**	1l. emerald-green	40	10
423	**134**	2l. scarlet	50	15

135 Gymnast

Наводнението
1939
1+1
лева

(**136**) ("Inundation 1939")

E **136** Bicycle Messenger

E **137** Express Delivery Van

(Des S. Badzhov. Photo)

1939 (7 July). Yunak Gymnastic Society's Rally, Sofia. T **135** and similar vert designs. P 13.

424	1l. yellowish green	50	40
425	2l. bright carmine-red	50	40
426	4l. deep orange-brown	1·00	50
427	7l. bright blue	3·25	1·50
428	14l. mauve	16·00	12·00
424/428 *Set of* 5		19·00	13·50

Designs:—2l. Yunak badge; 4l. "The Discus-thrower" (statue by Miron); 7l. Rhythmic dancer; 14l. Athlete holding weight aloft.

(Des D. Uzunov (1, 20l.), G. Apostolov (others). Photo)

1939 (6 Aug). EXPRESS LETTER. Type E **136/7** and similar vert design. P 13.

E429	E **136**	5l. blue	1·80	45
E430	E **137**	6l. brown	85	40
E431	–	7l. brown	1·30	40
E432	E **137**	8l. vermilion	1·60	50
E433	E **136**	20l. carmine	2·50	1·20
E429/433 *Set of* 5			7·25	2·75

Design: As Type E **136**—7l. Motor cyclist and sidecar.

1939 (22 Oct). Sevlievo and Turnovo Floods Relief Fund. Surch as T **136**.

429	**39**	1l. +1l. on 15st.greenish grey (p 12½)	20	45
430	**73**	2l. +1l. on 1½l.olive-green	30	50
431		4l. +2l. on 2l.grey-green	35	60
432		7l. +4l. on 3l.grey-blue	1·00	1·50
433		14l. +7l. on 5l.maroon	1·60	2·50
429/433 *Set of* 5			3·00	5·00

137 Mail 'Plane

138 King Boris III

(Des K. Ikonomov. Photo)

1940 (15 Jan). AIR. T **137** and similar designs. P 13.

434	1l. deep blue-green	20	15
435	2l. scarlet	2·50	15
436	4l. red-orange	20	15
437	6l. blue	40	20
438	10l. sepia	75	30
439	12l. sepia	1·00	50
440	16l. bright violet	1·60	80
441	19l. bright blue	1·70	1·00
442	30l. magenta	2·50	1·50
443	45l. deep violet	6·75	3·75
444	70l. rose-carmine	5·25	4·00
445	100l. deep blue	21·00	14·00
434/445 *Set of* 12		39·00	24·00

Designs: Horiz—6l. Loading mails at aerodrome; 12l. Airplanes over Sofia Palace; 16l. Mt. El Tepe; 19l. Rila lakes and mountains. Vert—Airplane over: 2l. King Asen's Tower; 4l. Bachkovo Monastery; 45l. Aleksandr Nevski Cathedral, Sofia; 70l. Shipka Pass Memorial. Vert—Airplane and: 10l. Mail train and express motor cycle; 30l. Swallow; 100l. Royal cypher.

(Des S. Sharankov. Typo)

1940 (10 Feb). P 13.

445*a*	**138**	1l. dull green	40	20
446		2l. scarlet	50	20

139 First Bulgarian Postage Stamp

(Des N. Biserov. Photo)

1940 (19 May). Centenary of First Adhesive Postage Stamps. T **139** and similar type, but scroll dated "1840–1940". P 13.

447	10l. olive-green	3·25	2·50
448	20l. deep blue	3·25	2·50

140 Grapes

141 Ploughing

142 King Boris III

(Des A. Anev. Typo)

1940 (2 Sept)–**44**. T **140/1** and similar designs and T **142**. P 13.

(a) No wmk

449	**140**	10st. red-orange	20	15
450	–	15st. blue	20	15
451	**141**	30st. brown	20	15
452	–	50st. violet (1941)	20	15
452*a*	–	50st. bright green (1942)	20	15
453	**142**	1l. green	20	15
		a. Perf 10 (1944)	2·50	70
		b. Perf 11½ (1944)	20	15
		c. Perf 10×11½ (1944)	20	15
		d. Perf 11½×10 (1944)	50·00	40·00
454		2l. carmine-red	30	15
		a. Perf 10 (1944)	1·60	20
		b. Perf 11½ (1944)	20	15
		c. Perf 10×11½ (1944)	20	15
		d. Perf 11½×10 (1944)	50·00	40·00
455		4l. orange (7.12.41)	30	15
		a. Perf 11½ (1944)	5·25	4·00
456		6l. bright reddish violet (1944)	50	20
457		7l. blue (1944)	30	15
458		10l. blue-green (7.12.41)	50	20
449/458 *Set of* 11			2·75	1·60

(b) Wmk Wavy Lines (20.11.41)

A. Wmk vert

459A	–	50st. violet	20	15
460A	**142**	1l. green	1·30	20
461A		2l. carmine-red	20	15
462A		7l. blue	30	15
463A		10l. blue-green	50	20
459A/463A *Set of* 5			2·30	75

B. Wmk horiz

459B	–	50st. violet	20	15
460B	**142**	1l. green	1·30	20
461B		2l. carmine-red	20	15
462B		7l. blue	30	15
463B		10l. blue-green	50	20
459B/463B *Set of* 5			2·30	75

Designs: Vert—15st. Beehive. Horiz—50st. Shepherd and flock.

143 Peasant Couple and King Boris

144 King Boris and Map of the Dobrudja

(Des B. Angelushev. Photo)

1940 (20 Sept). Recovery of the Dobrudja from Rumania. T **143/4** and similar design incorporating miniature portrait of King Boris. P 13.

464	**143**	1l. green	20	15
465	–	2l. carmine	30	20
466	**144**	4l. brown	50	30
467		7l. blue	1·00	80
464/467 *Set of* 4			1·80	1·30

Design: Vert—2l. Bulgarian flags and wheatfield.

145 Bee-keeping

(Des P. Morozov and B. Angelushev. Photo)

1940–44. Agricultural Scenes. T **145** and similar designs. P 13.

468	10st. slate-purple (7.10.40)	20	15
469	10st. blue (12.5.41)	20	15
470	15st. deep blue-green (5.12.41)	20	15
471	15st. blackish olive (1.4.43)	20	15
472	30st. orange (7.12.40)	20	15
473	30st. deep green (5.12.41)	20	15
474	50st. slate-violet (5.12.41)	20	15
475	50st. red-purple (12.4.42)	20	15
476	3l. red-brown (1.4.43)	85	20
	a. Red (1944)	1·00	50
477	3l. blackish brown (1944)	1·90	1·00
478	5l. brown (shades) (1943/44)	1·60	80
479	5l. deep blue (1944)	2·10	1·50
468/79 *Set of* 12		7·25	4·25

Designs:—10st. Threshing; 15st. Ploughing with oxen; 50st. Picking apples; 3l. Shepherd; 5l. Cattle.

146 Pencho Slaveikov (poet)

147 St. Ivan Rilski

(Des D. Uzunov (1l.), S. Velkov (2l.), V. Zakhariev (3l.), K. Chokanov (4l.), V. Kotsev (7l.), G. Gerasimov (10l.). Photo)

1940 (23 Nov). National Relief. T **146/7** and similar vert designs. P 13.

480	1l. green	20	15
481	2l. carmine	20	15
482	3l. brown	25	20
483	4l. orange	30	20
484	7l. blue	2·10	1·50
485	10l. brown	3·25	2·00
480/485 *Set of* 6		5·75	3·75

Designs:—2l. Bishop Sofronii of Vratsa; 4l. Marin Drinov (historian); 7l. Chernorisets Khrabur (monk); 10l. Kolo Ficheto (architect).

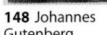

148 Johannes Gutenberg **149** Nikola Karastoyanov

(Des N. Biserov. Photo)

1940 (16 Dec). 500th Anniv of Invention of Printing and Centenary of Bulgarian Printing. P 13.

486	**148**	1l. myrtle green	40	20
487	**149**	2l. chestnut	50	20

150 Botev **151** Arrival in Koslodui

(Des N. Tuzsuzov. Photo)

1941 (3 May). 65th Death Anniv of Khristo Botev (poet and revolutionary). T **150/1** and similar design. P 13.

488	**150**	1l. deep green	20	20
489	**151**	2l. scarlet	50	30
490	–	3l. brown	1·40	1·00
488/490 *Set of* 3			1·90	1·40

Design: Vert—3l. Botev Memorial Cross.

152 National History Museum

(Des P. Morozov (14l.), A. Mutafov (20l.), P. Kurshovski (50l.). Recess)

1941 (2 June)–**43**. Buildings in Sofia. T **152** and similar horiz designs. P 11½.

491	14l. brown (3.43)	75	40
492	20l. green (3.43)	85	50
493	50l. blue	3·75	2·00
491/493 *Set of* 3		4·75	2·50

Designs:—20l. Tsaritsa Ioanna Workers' Hospital; 50l. National Bank.

P 153 Weighing Machine **P 154** Loading Motor Lorry

(Des N. Biserov. Photo)

1941 (1 July). PARCEL POST. Types P **153/154** and similar designs. White chalk-surfaced paper. P 12½×13½ (vert) or 13½×12½ (horiz).

P494	P **153**	1l. deep green	15	10
P495	–	2l. rose-red	15	10
P496	P **154**	3l. bistre-brown	15	10
P497	–	4l. red-orange	15	10
P498	P **153**	5l. deep blue	15	10
P499	–	6l. purple	15	10
P500	P **153**	7l. blue	15	10
P501	P **154**	8l. deep turquoise-green	20	10
P502	–	9l. brown-olive	30	15
P503	–	10l. bright orange	40	15
P504	P **154**	20l. bluish violet	65	20
P505	–	30l. black	1·50	30
P494/505 *Set of* 12			3·75	1·40

Designs: Horiz—2, 9, 30l. Motor cycle combination; 4, 6, 10l. Loading railway mail coach.

153 Thasos Island **154** Ohrid

(Des D. Gyudzhenov (1l.), B. Angelushev (2l., both), V. Zakhariev (4l.), B. Denev (7l.). Photo)

1941 (3 Oct). Reacquisition of Macedonia. T **153/4** and similar designs. P 13.

494	1l. deep green	20	15
495	2l. orange	20	15
496	2l. carmine	20	15
497	4l. brown	20	15
498	7l. blue	95	70
494/498 *Set of* 5		1·60	1·20

Designs: Vert—1l. Macedonian Girl. Horiz—2l. (No. 496) King Boris and map dated "1941"; 4l. Poganovski Monastery.

155 Children on Beach

(Des B. Angelushev. Photo)

1941 (15 Oct). SUNDAY DELIVERY. T **155** and similar horiz designs. P 13.

499	1l. blackish olive	20	15
500	2l. red-orange	30	20
501	5l. deep blue	1·00	40
499/501 *Set of* 3		1·40	70

Designs:—1l. St. Konstantin Sanatorium, Varna; 5l. Sun-bathing terrace, Bankya.

1942 (7 Jan). PARCEL POST. As Nos. P498/505 but colours changed. Greyish ordinary paper. Photo. P 12½×13½ (vert) or 13½×12½ (horiz).

P506	P **153**	5l. bronze green	20	15
P507	–	6l. red-brown	20	15
P508	P **153**	7l. sepia	20	15
P509	P **154**	8l. dull green	20	15
P510	–	9l. blackish olive	20	15
P511	–	10l. reddish orange	20	15
P512	P **154**	20l. slate-violet	60	25
P513	–	30l. brownish black	65	30
P506/513 *Set of* 8			2·20	1·30

156 Bugler at Camp **157** Folk Dancers O **158**

1942 (1 June). "Work and Joy". Designs inscribed as at foot of T **156** (2l., 7l.) or of T **157** (others). Photo. P 13.

502	1l. deep blue-green	20	15
503	2l. red	30	15
504	4l. olive-black	40	20
505	7l. blue	50	30
506	14l. brown	65	40
502/506 *Set of* 5		1·80	1·10

Designs: Vert—1l. Guitarist and accordion player; 2l. Camp orchestra; 4l. Hoisting the flag.

1942 (1 June). OFFICIAL. Type O **158** (and similar type). Typo. P 13.

	(a) Size 15×21 mm		
O507	10st. yellow-green	10	10
O508	30st. red-orange	10	10
O509	50st. yellow-brown	10	10
	(b) Size 19×23 mm		
O510	1l. bright blue	10	10
O511	2l. deep green	15	10
O512	3l. mauve	20	10
O513	4l. pink	30	15
O514	5l. lake	50	20
O507/14 *Set of* 8		1·40	85

See also Nos. O533/4.

158 Wounded Soldier **159** Queen visiting wounded

(Des D. Gyudzhenov and V. Stoilov. Photo)

1942 (7 Sept). War Invalids. Designs inscribed as T **158/9**. P 13½×12½ or 12½×13½ (vert).

507	1l. deep green	20	15
508	2l. carmine	20	15
509	4l. orange	20	15
510	7l. blue	20	15
511	14l. olive-brown	30	15
512	20l. black	65	20
507/512 *Set of* 6		1·60	85

Designs: Horiz—2l. Soldier and family; 4l. First Aid on battlefield; 7l. Widow and orphans at grave; 14l. Unknown Soldier's Memorial.

160 Khan Kubrat (ruled 595–642)

(Des E. Rakarov. Photo)

1942–43. Historical series. T **160** and similar vert designs. P 13.

513	10st. blue-black (22.5.43)	20	15
514	15st. greenish blue (22.5.43)	20	15
515	30st. mauve (22.5.43)	20	15
516	50st. deep blue (22.5.43)	20	15
517	1l. slate-green (12.10.42)	20	15
518	2l. rose-red (12.10.42)	20	15
519	3l. brown (22.5.43)	20	15
520	4l. orange (22.5.43)	20	15
521	5l. blackish green (22.5.43)	20	15
522	7l. blue (22.5.43)	20	15
523	10l. brownish black (22.5.43)	20	15
524	14l. blackish olive (22.5.43)	40	20
525	20l. red-brown (22.5.43)	1·00	70
526	30l. black (22.5.43)	2·10	1·00
513/526 *Set of* 14		5·25	3·25

Designs:—15st. Cavalry charge (Khan Asparukh, 680–701); 30st. Equestrian statue of Khan Krum (803–814); 50st. Baptism of King Boris 1 (852–889); 1l. St. Naum's school; 2l. King Boris crowns his son Tsar Simeon; 3l. Golden Era of Bulgarian literature; 4l. Trial of Bogomil Vasilii; 5l. Proclamation of Second Bulgarian Empire; 7l. Ivan Asen II (1214–81) at Trebizond; 10l. Expulsion of Evtimii, Patriarch of Turnovo; 14l. Wandering minstrels; 20l. Father Paisii Khilendarskí (historian); 30l. Shipka Pass Memorial.

King Simeon II, 28 August 1943–15 Sept 1946

161 King Boris III **162**

(Des D. Gyudzhenov. Photo)

1944 (28 Feb). King Boris Mourning Issue. T **161** (and similar portraits dated "1894–1943"). Frames in black. W **162**.

	A. Imperf		
527A	1l. olive-green	20	20
528A	2l. red-brown	25	25
529A	4l. brown	30	30
530A	5l. violet	85	85
531A	7l. blue	1·00	1·00
527A/531A *Set of* 5		2·30	2·30
	B. P 13		
527B	1l. olive-green	20	20
528B	2l. red-brown	25	25
529B	4l. brown	30	30
530B	5l. violet	85	85
531B	7l. blue	1·00	1·00
527B/531B *Set of* 5		2·30	2·30

ВСИЧКО
ЗА
ФРОНТА

P **163** **163** King Simeon II (**164**)

1944 (21 Mar). PARCEL POST. Typo. Imperf.

P532	P **163**	1l. carmine	20	15
P533		3l. green	20	15
P534		5l. deep green	20	15
P535		7l. mauve	20	15
P536		10l. blue	20	15
P537		20l. brown	20	15
P538		30l. brown-purple	40	20
P539		50l. orange	75	50
P540		100l. blue	1·40	80
P532/540 *Set of* 9			3·50	2·20

(Des A. Anev. Typo)

1944 (12 June).

		A. P 13		
532A	**163**	3l. red-orange	20	10
		B. P 11½		
532B	**163**	3l. red-orange	50	30

1944. OFFICIAL. As Nos. O510/11, but colour and perf changed. P 10½×11½.

O533	1l. blue	1·40	50
O534	2l. vermilion	1·40	50

1945 (25 Jan). "All for the Front". Parcel Post stamps. Type P **163**, optd as T **164**, (No. 534 surch also). P 11½.

533	1l. carmine	20	15
534	4l. on 1l. carmine	20	15
535	7l. purple	20	15
536	20l. brown	30	15
537	30l. brown-purple	40	20
538	50l. orange	75	50
539	100l. blue (R.)	1·80	1·00
533/539 *Set of* 7		3·50	2·10

(**165** Heinkel He 111H) (**166** Arado Ar 240 Bomber) **167**

1945 (15 Feb). AIR.

		(a) Surch as T **165**. P 13		
540	**144**	1l. green (457)	20	15
541		4l. orange (459)	20	15

(b) Surch as T **166**. Imperf

542	P **163**	10 on 100l. yellow (B.)	30	15
543		45 on 100l. yellow (R.)	40	20
544		75 on 100l. yellow (G.)	1·00	60
545		100l. yellow (V.)	1·30	90
540/545 *Set of* 6			3·00	1·90

(Des B. Angelushev. Litho)

1945. Slav Congress.

		A. Imperf (8 Mar)		
546A	**167**	4l. vermilion	20	10
547A		10l. blue	20	10
548A		50l. claret	40	40
546A/548A *Set of* 3			70	55
		B. P 11½ (23 April)		
546B	**167**	4l. vermilion	20	15
547B		10l. blue	20	15

СЪБИРАЙТЕ ВСЪКАКВИ ПАРЦАЛИ (**168** "Collect All Rags")

СЪБИРАЙТЕ СТАРО ЖЕЛЪЗО (**169** "Collect Old Iron")

СЪБИРАЙТЕ ХАРТИЕНИ ОТПАДЪЦИ (**170** "Collect Wastepaper")

1945 (Mar). Savings Campaign. Nos. 453/9 optd with slogans, T **168/70**. P 13.

		A. Type **168**.		
549A	**143**	1l. green	40	30
		a. Perf 11½	30	40
550A		2l. carmine-red (perf 11½)	1·60	20
551A		4l. orange	1·00	40
		B. Type **169**		
549B	**143**	1l. green	30	40
550B		2l. carmine-red	5·25	3·00
		a. Perf 11½	2·30	40
551B		4l. orange	1·00	40
		a. Perf 11½	6·25	6·00
		C. T **170**		
549C	**143**	1l. green	30	40
		a. Perf 11½	65	40
550C		2l. carmine-red (perf 11½)	1·30	40
551C		4l. orange	1·00	40
		a. Perf 11½	5·75	4·00

171

172

I. Wide Crown

II. Narrow Crown

2l. and 4l. Two types of Crown

(Des I. Barov (552, 557/60), B. Angelushev (553, 555/6), St. Kunchev (554, 561/2). Typo)

1945–46. T **171/2** and similar vert designs (small Arms types). P 13.

552	30st. emerald-green (13.12.45)	25	15
553	50st. greenish blue (15.7.45)	25	15
554	1l. deep green (shades) (26.4.45)	25	15
555	2l. brown (I) (26.4.45)	25	15
	a. Type II (15.5.46)	25	15
556	4l. blue (I) (15.5.45)	25	15
	a. Type II (15.5.46)	25	15
557	5 l reddish violet (shades) (25.7 45)	25	15
558	9l. grey (20.7.45)	25	15
559	10l. turquoise-blue (4.6.45)	25	15
560	15l. brown (shades) (4.6.45)	25	15
561	20l. black (21.1.46)	50	15
562	20l. scarlet (21.1.46)	50	15
552/562 *Set of* 11		3·00	1·50

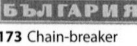

173 Chain-breaker

174 "VE" Day

(Des B. Angelushev (Nos. 563/8), A. Zhendov (Nos. 569/70). Litho)

1945 (4 June). Liberty Loan. T **173** and similar types. Rose, laid paper. Imperf.

563	50l. orange	30	15
564	50l. brown-lake	30	15
565	100l. blue	40	20
566	100l. brown	40	20
567	150l. carmine	1·00	60
568	150l. olive-green	1·00	60
569	200l. grey-olive	1·30	80
570	200l. violet-blue	1·30	80
563/570 *Set of* 8		5·50	3·25

MS570*a* Two blocks 88×123 mm. with the four values imperf (a) in brown-red and (b) in violet .... Pair 16·00 24·00

Designs:—100l. Hand holding coin; 150l. Water-mill, 200l. Coin and symbols of industry and agriculture.

(Des G. Manolov. Typo)

1945 (1 Sept). "Victory in Europe". P 13.

571	**174**	10l. green and brown	20	15
572		50l. green and red	65	30

175

176

(Des I. Barov. Typo)

1945 (7 Sept). First Anniv of Fatherland Front Coalition. P 13.

573	**175**	1l. grey-green	20	15
574		4l. deep blue	20	15
575		5l. mauve	20	15
576	**176**	10l. blue	20	15
577		20l. carmine	20	20
578	**175**	50l. green	1·00	60
579		100l. brown	1·30	1·00
573/579 *Set of* 7			3·00	2·20

O **177**

O **178**

O **179**

(Des I. Barov (O **179**). Typo)

1945–50. OFFICIAL.

		A. P 13 (29/30.10.45)		
O581A	O **177**	2l. turquoise-green	10	10
O582A	O **178**	3l. orange-brown	10	10
O583A		4l. pale ultramarine	10	10
O584A	O **179**	5l. claret (30.10.45)	10	10
O581A/584A *Set of* 4			35	35
		B. Imperf (1.10.46)		
O580B	O **179**	1l. mauve	10	10
O581B	O **177**	2l. turquoise-green	10	10
O582B	O **178**	3l. orange-brown	10	10
O583B		4l. pale ultramarine	10	10
O584B	O **179**	5l. claret (30.10.45)	10	10
O580B/584B *Set of* 5			45	45
		C. P 11, 11½, 11×11½, or 11½×11 (10.10.50)		
O585C	O **179**	5l. deep brown-red	40	20

177 Refugee Children

178 Red Cross Train

(Des B. Angelushev. Typo)

1946 (4 Apr). Red Cross (1st Issue). T **177/8** (and similar designs). Cross in red. P 11½.

580	**177**	2l. deep olive	20	15
581	–	4l. violet	20	15
582	**177**	10l. purple	20	15
583	–	20l. ultramarine	20	15
584	–	30l. brown	30	20
585	**178**	35l. grey-black	50	40
586	–	50l. purple-brown	65	50
587	**178**	100l. slate-brown	2·10	1·80
580/587 *Set of* 8			4·00	3·25

Designs: Horiz—4l., 20l. Soldier on stretcher. Vert—30l., 50l. Nurse and wounded soldier.

For 1947 issue in new colours, see Nos. 645*d/k*.

179 Postal Savings Emblem

180 Savings Bank-Note

(Des B. Angelushev, G. Manolov, A. Poplilov, N. Biserov, respectively. Typo)

1946 (12 Apr). 50th Anniv of Savings Bank. T **179/180** and similar designs dated "1896–1946". P 11½.

588	4l. brownish red	20	15
589	10l. deep olive	20	15
590	20l. blue	20	15
591	50l. grey-black	1·60	1·40
588/591 *Set of* 4		2·00	1·70

Designs: Vert—20l. Child filling money-box; 50l. Postal Savings Bank.

181 Arms of Russia and Bulgaria and Spray of Oak

182 Lion Rampant

(Des L. Nenov. Typo)

1946 (23 May–11 July). Bulgo-Russian Congress. P 11½.

592	**181**	4l. claret	10·00	10·00
593		4l. orange (11.7.46)	20	20
594		20l. light blue	10·00	10·00
595		20l. green (11.7.46)	40	40
592/595 *Set of* 4			19·00	19·00

(Des St. Kunchev. Typo)

1946 (25 May). Stamp Day. Imperf.

596	**182**	20l. blue	85	40

183

184

188

189

190

(Des I. Barov (4, 10, 12, 16, 19l.), A. Poplilov (6l.), I. Penkov (100l.), St. Kunchev (others). Typo)

1946 (15 June). AIR. Inscr "PAR AVION". P 13.

597	**183**	1l. deep dull purple	25	15
598		2l. greenish slate	25	15
599	–	4l. black	25	15
600	–	6l. greenish blue	25	15
601	**184**	10l. blue-green	25	15
602		12l. yellow-brown	25	15
603	–	16l. purple	25	15
		a. Imperf (pair)	£425	£375
604	**184**	19l. rosine	25	15
605	**188**	30l. orange	30	20
606	**189**	45l. olive-green	65	25
607		75l. reddish brown	95	30
608	**190**	100l. vermilion	1·70	50
609	–	100l. slate-green	1·70	50
597/609 *Set of* 13			6·50	2·75

Designs: 23×18 mm—4l. Bird carrying envelope; 18×23 mm—6l. Airplane and envelope; 16l. Winged envelope. 22½×18 mm—100l. Airplane.

192 Stamboliiski

193 Flags of Albania, Bulgaria, Yugoslavia and Rumania

(Des D. Gyudzhenov. Typo)

1946 (13 June). 23rd Death Anniv of Aleksandur Stamboliiski (Prime Minister 1919–23). P 11½.

610	**192**	100l. orange	9·50	9·50

(Des I. Barov. Typo)

1946 (6 July). Balkan Games. P 11½.

611	**193**	100l. black-brown	1·80	1·80
		a. Tête-bêche (pair)	4·25	4·25

194 Grenade Thrower

195 Junkers Ju 87B "Stuka" Dive Bombers

196 Artillery

(Des A. Poplilov (613), A. and B. Tilov (615), B. Angelushev (620, 622), D. Gyudzhenov (others). Typo)

1946 (9 Aug). Military and Air Services. T **194/5** and horiz designs as T **196**. P 11½.

612	–	2l. deep claret	20	15
613	**194**	4l. olive-grey	20	15
614	**196**	5l. Indian red	20	15
615	**195**	6l. bistre-brown	20	15
616	–	9l. magenta	20	15
617	–	10l. dull violet	20	15
618	–	20l. deep bright blue	50	20
619	–	30l. bright orange	65	30
620	–	40l. brown-olive	75	40
621	–	50l. deep green	95	70
622	–	60l. reddish brown	1·30	80
612/622 *Set of* 11			4·75	3·00

Designs: As T **196**—2, 20l. Grenade thrower and machine gunner; 9l. Building pontoon-bridge; 10, 30l. Cavalry charge; 40l. Supply column; 50l. Motor convoy; 60l. Tank.

203 St. Ivan Rilski

204 Rila Monastery

(Des Ts. Lavrenov (623, 626), I. Manev (624), D. Gyudzhenov (625), V. Tomov (627). Typo)

1946 (26 Aug). Death Millenary of St. Ivan Rilski. T **203/4** and similar designs. P 11½.

623	**203**	1l. red-brown	20	15
624	**204**	4l. deep brown	20	15
625	–	10l. deep blue-green	30	20
626	–	20l. deep bright blue	50	25
627	–	50l. dull scarlet	2·10	1·10
623/627 *Set of* 5			3·00	1·70

Designs: Horiz—10l. Monastery entrance; 50l. Cloistered courtyard. Vert—20l. Aerial view of monastery.

PEOPLE'S REPUBLIC

15 September 1946–15 November 1990

208 "New Republic"

(Des B. Angelushev. Typo)

1946 (15 Sept). Referendum. P 11½.

628	**208**	4l. claret	20	15
629		20l. greenish blue	20	15
630		50l. bistre-brown	50	40
628/630 *Set of* 3			80	65

209 Assault

210 Ambuscade

(Des G. Bogdanov (T **209**), A. Poplilov (T **210**), B. Angelushev (633, 637) and St. Kunchev (636). Typo)

1946 (2 Dec). Partisan Activities. As T **209/10** (various designs). P 11½.

631	**209**	1l. maroon	20	15
632	**210**	4l. blue-green	20	15
633	–	5l. chocolate	20	15
634	**210**	10l. scarlet	20	15
635	**209**	20l. bright blue	50	20
636	–	30l. yellow-brown	65	30
637	–	50l. black	85	70
631/637 *Set of* 7			2·50	1·60

Designs: Vert—5l., 50l. Partisan riflemen, 30l. Partisan leader.

211 Nurse and Children

212 Hungry Child

212a Partisans

(Des St. Kunchev and G. Popov (T **211**), A. Poplilov (639/40), B. Angelushev (T **212**) and L. Nenov (643). Typo)

1946 (30 Dec). Winter Relief. T **211/12** and similar designs. P 11½.

638	**211**	1l. brown-violet	20	15
639	–	4l. vermilion	20	15
640	–	9l. brown-olive	20	15
641	**211**	10l. grey	20	15
642	**212**	20l. blue	20	15
643	–	30l. brown-red	40	20
644	**212**	40l. claret	50	40
645	**211**	50l. turquoise-green	95	70
638/645 *Set of* 8			2·50	1·80

Designs: Vert—4l., 9l. Child carrying gifts, 30l. Destitute mother and child.

(Des S. Sotirov. Typo)

1947 (21 Jan). Commemorating anti-fascists of 1923, 1941 and 1944. T **212a** and designs similarly inscr. P 11½.

645*a*	10l. deep brown and orange-brown	75	70
645*b*	20l. deep blue and pale blue	75	70
645*c*	70l. purple-brown and pale claret	47·00	45·00
645*a*/645*c* *Set of* 3		44·00	42·00

Designs: Horiz—10l. Group of fighters. Vert—70l. Soldier addressing crowd.

"BULGARIA" is in Roman characters on the 20l.

1947 (31 Jan). Red Cross (2nd Issue) As Nos. 580/7 but colours changed. Cross in red. P 11½.

645*d*	**177**	2l. yellow-brown	15	15
645*e*	–	4l. blackish olive	15	15
645*f*	**177**	10l. green	20	20
645*g*	–	20l. pale blue	50	50
645*h*	–	30l. yellow-green	65	60
645*i*	**178**	35l. grey-green	75	70
645*j*	–	50l. brown-red	1·00	1·00
645*k*	**178**	100l. blue	1·70	1·60
645*d*/*k* *Set of* 8			4·50	4·50

1947 (10 Feb). POSTAGE DUE. As Type D **112**, but larger (18×24 mm, instead of 16×22 mm). Typo. P 10½.

D646	1l. sepia	20	20
D647	2l. maroon	30	30
D648	8l. orange	20	20
D649	20l. blue	75	30
D646/649 *Set of* 4		1·30	90

213 Olive Branch

214 Dove of Peace

(Des A. Poplilov (T **213**), St. Kunchev (T **214**). Typo)

1947 (28 Feb). Peace. P 11½.

646	**213**	4l. olive-green	20	15
647	**214**	10l. brown-red	20	20
648		20l. blue	50	50
646/648 *Set of* 3			80	75

"BULGARIA" is in Roman characters on the 20l.

215 "U.S.A." and "Bulgaria"

216 Esperanto Emblem and Map of Bulgaria

(Des I. Manev. Typo)

1947 (31 May). AIR. Stamp Day and New York International Philatelic Exhibition. P 11½.

649	**215**	70l. +30l. brown-red	2·10	2·00

(Des I. Barov. Typo)

1947 (16 June). 30th Esperanto Congress, Sofia. P 11½.

650	**216**	20l. +10l. purple and emerald	1·00	1·00

217 G.P.O., Sofia

218 National Theatre, Sofia

219 Parliament Building, Sofia

220 President's Palace

221 G.P.O., Sofia

1947–48. Government Buildings. Typo. P 13.

	(a) T **217**		
651	1l. blue-green (1.7.47)	20	15
	(b) T **218**		
652	50st. yellow-green (28.11.47)	20	15
653	2l. claret (19.8.47)	20	15
654	4l. blue (17.7.47)	20	15
655	9l. carmine (9.1.48)	65	20
	(c) T **219**		
656	50st. yellow-green (7.11.47)	20	15
657	2l. yellow-brown (26.9.47)	20	15
658	4l. blue (26.9.47)	20	15
659	20l. blue (9.1.48)	1·60	1·00
	(d) T **220**		
660	1l. emerald-green (29.12.47)	20	15
	(e) T **221**		
661	1l. emerald-green (29.12.47)	20	15
662	2l. brown-lake (shades) (9.1.48)	20	15
663	4l. blue (9.1.48)	20	15
651/663 *Set of* 13		4·00	2·50

222 Hydro-Electric Power Station and Dam

223 Emblem of Industry

(Des P. Vulkov (4l.), I. Manev (9l., 40l.), S. Kunchev (20l.). Typo)

1947 (6 Aug). Reconstruction. T **222/3** and similar horiz designs. P 11½.

664	4l. grey-green	20	15
665	9l. orange-brown (Miner)	30	25
666	20l. blue	40	35
667	40l. brown-olive (Motor plough)	1·30	1·20
664/667 *Set of* 4		2·00	1·80

224 Exhibition Building

225 Former Residence of the French Poet Lamartine

226 Rose and Grapes

227 Airplane over City

(Des A. Apostolov (4l.), V. Staikov (others). Litho)

1947 (31 Aug). Plovdiv Fair.

		(a) POSTAGE. P 11×11½		
668	**224**	4l. scarlet	15	10
669	**225**	9l. claret	20	10
670	**226**	20l. ultramarine	40	40
		(b) AIR. Imperf		
671	**227**	40l. grey-green	1·60	1·50
668/671 *Set of* 4			2·10	1·90

228 Cycle Racing

229 Basketball

230 Chess

(Des Ts. Kosturkova (2l., 20l.), I. Manev (4l.), S. Kunchev (9l.), P. Vulkov (60l.). Typo)

1947 (29 Sept). Balkan Games. As T **228/30** and vert designs inscr "1947". P 11½.

672	2l. rose-lilac	75	40
673	4l. grey-olive	85	50
674	9l. orange-brown	1·60	60
675	20l. bright blue (Football)	2·10	70
676	60l. claret (Balkan flags)	4·75	3·25
672/676 *Set of* 5		9·00	5·00

231 V. E. Aprilov

232 V. E. Aprilov

(Des Ts. Kosturkova and G. Manolov. Litho)

1947–48. Death Centenary of Vasil Aprilov (educationist).

		(a) P 10½		
677	**231**	40l. blue (19.10.47)	85	50
		(b) P 11½		
678	**232**	4l. claret/*cream* (19.2.48)	30	15

233 Postman

234 Wireless Masts

(Des St. Penchev (40l.), D. Gyudzhenov (others). Typo)

1947 (5 Nov). Postal Employees' Relief Fund. T **233/4** and similar vert designs. P 11½.

679	4l. +2l. brown-olive	15	15
680	10l. +5l. scarlet (Lineman)	20	20
681	20l. +10l. blue (Telephonists)	30	30
682	40l. +20l. brown-purple	1·60	1·50
679/682 *Set of* 4		2·00	1·90

235 Geno Kirov 236 *Rodina* (freighter)

(Des A. Zhendov, St. Kunchev, A. Poplilov and I. Barov. Litho)

1947 (8 Dec). Theatrical Artists Benevolent Fund. As T **235** (portraits). P 10½.

683	50st. brown	10	10
684	1l. pale blue-green	10	10
685	2l. grey-green	10	10
686	3l. blue	10	10
687	4l. scarlet	10	10
688	5l. maroon	10	10
689	9l. +5l. greenish blue	20	15
690	10l. +6l. carmine	20	20
691	15l. +7l. violet	50	35
692	20l. +15l. ultramarine	75	60
693	30l. +20l. purple	1·60	1·30
683/693 *Set of* 11		3·50	3·00

Designs:—1l. Zlatina Nedeva; 2l. Ivan Popov; 3l. Atanas Kirchev; 4l. Elena Snezhina; 5l. Stoyan Buchvarov; 9l. Khristo Ganchev; 10l. Adriana Budevska; 15l. Vasil Kirkov; 20l. Sava Ognyanov; 30l. Krustyu Sarafov.

(Des P. Vulkov. Litho)

1947 (19 Dec). National Shipping Revival. P 10½.

694	**236**	50l. greenish blue/*cream*	1·00	80

237 Worker and Flag 238 Worker and Globe

(Des V. Staikov and A. Poplilov. Photo)

1948 (29 Feb). Second General Workers' Union Congress. P 11½.

(a) POSTAGE

695	**237**	4l. blue/*cream*	20	10

(b) AIR

696	**238**	60l. brown-red/*cream*	85	70

239 240

(Des I. Manev, B. Kotsev, V. Tomov, S. Penchev and P. Vulkov. Litho)

1948 (31 Mar). Leisure and Culture. T **239/40** and similar vert designs. P 10½.

697	4l. carmine	20	15
698	20l. blue	40	20
699	40l. green	75	40
700	60l. chocolate	1·30	80
697/700 *Set of* 4		2·40	1·40

Designs:—40l. Workers' musical interlude; 60l. Sports girl.

241 Nikola Vaptsarov 242 Petlyakov Pe-2 Bomber over Balduin's Tower

(Des S. Sotirov, A. Poplilov, St. Kunchev and I. Barov. Litho)

1948 (18 May). Poets. T **241** and similar vert designs. P 10½.

701	4l. orange-vermilion/*cream*	20	15
702	9l. red-brown/*cream*	25	20
703	15l. claret/*cream*	30	25
704	20l. blue/*cream*	40	35
705	45l. blue-green/*cream*	1·00	90
701/705 *Set of* 5		1·90	1·70

Designs:—9l. Peyu Yavorov; 15l. Khristo Smirnenski; 20l. Ivan Vazov; 45l. Petko Slaveikov.

(Des Ts. Kosturkova. Photo)

1948 (23 May). AIR. Stamp Day. P 11½.

706	**242**	50l. olive-brown/*cream*	2·10	2·00

243 Soldier 244 Peasants and Soldiers

(Des D. Gyudzhenov and N. Biserov. Photo)

1948 (5 July). Soviet Army Monument. As T **243/4**. P 10½.

707	4l. orange-red/*cream*	20	15
708	10l. green/*cream*	25	20
709	20l. blue/*cream*	50	40
710	60l. olive/*cream*	1·30	1·00
707/710 *Set of* 4		2·00	1·60

Designs: Horiz—20l. Soldiers of 1878 and 1944. Vert—60l. Stalin and Spassky Tower, Kremlin.

245 Bath, Gorna Banya 246 Lion Emblem

(Des Ts. Kosturkova (2, 20l.), G. Manolov (3,10l.), A. Anev (4, 20l.), G. Zhelezarov (5, 15l.). Typo)

1948 (20 Aug)–**49**. Designs as T **245**. P 12½.

(a) Bulgarian Mineral Baths

711	2l. claret (13.9.48) (T **245**)	20	15
712	3l. red-orange (7.10.48) (Bankya)	20	15
	a. Perf 11		
713	4l. deep blue (20.8.48) (Sofia)	20	15
714	10l. bright purple (7.10.48) (Bankya)	40	20
715	20l. deep blue (7.10.48) (T **245**)	1·60	30
716	20l. deep blue (5.11.48) (Sofia)	2·30	60

(b) Malyovitsa Peak

717	5l. purple-brown (29.10.48)	75	15
718	15l. olive-green (3.1.49)	1·00	15
711/718 *Set of* 8		6·00	1·70

(Des A. Anev and G. Manolov. Typo)

1948 (20 Aug)–**50**. P 12½.

719	**246**	50st. red-orange (5.11.48)	20	15
719*a*		50st. chestnut (27.9.50)	20	15
720		1l. green (20.8.48)	20	15
721		9l. black (20.8.48)	50	30
719/721 *Set of* 4			1·00	70

247 Dimitur Blagoev 248 Youths Marching

(Des S. Penchev (4l., 9l.), P. Vulkov (20l.), V. Tomov (60l.). Photo)

1948 (6 Sept). 25th Anniv of September Uprising. T **247/8** and similar designs. P 11.

722	4l. brown/*cream*	20	15
723	9l. brown-orange/*cream*	20	15
724	20l. blue/*cream*	30	30
725	60l. brown/*cream*	1·60	1·20
722/725 *Set of* 4		2·10	1·60

Designs: Vert—9l. Gabril Genov. Horiz—20l. Bishop Andrei Monument.

249 Khristo Smirnenski 250 Miner 251 Battle of Grivitsa

(Des A. Anev. Photo)

1948 (2 Oct). 50th Anniv of Birth of Smirnenski (poet and revolutionary). P 11½.

726	**249**	4l. dark blue/*cream*	20	15
727		16l. light brown/*cream*	40	20

(Des A. Zhendov. Typo)

1948 (7 Oct). P 11×11½.

728	**250**	4l. deep blue	40	20

(Des B. Angelushev (20l.), I. Manev (others). Photo)

1948 (1 Nov). Treaty of Friendship with Romania. T **251** and similar designs. P 11½.

(a) POSTAGE

729	20l. deep blue/*cream*	30	20

(b) AIR

730	40l. grey-black/*cream*	50	40
731	100l. mauve/*cream*	1·30	1·20

Designs:—40l. Parliament buildings in Sofia and Bucharest; 100l. Projected Danube Bridge.

252 Botev's House, Kalofer 253 Botev 254 Lenin

(Des V. Staikov (1l., 15l.), A. Apostolov (4l.), B. Angelushev (9l., 20l.), G. Atanasov (40l.), A. Poplilov (50l.). Litho)

1948 (21 Dec)–**49**. Birth Centenary of Khristo Botev (poet and revolutionary). T **252/3** and similar designs. P 11 (1, 15, 50l.) or 11½ (others).

732	1l. deep green/*cream*	20	15
733	4l. purple-brown/*cream*	20	15
734	4l. purple/*cream* (2.6.49)	20	15
735	9l. violet/*cream*	20	15
736	15l. yellow-brown/*cream*	20	15
737	20l. blue/*cream*	30	15
737*a*	20l. deep blue/*cream* (2.6.49)	40	20
738	40l. red-brown/*cream*	75	50
739	50l. brown-olive/*cream*	1·00	70
732/739 *Set of* 9		3·00	2·10

Designs: Horiz—9l. River paddle-steamer *Radetski*; 15l. Village of Kalofer; 40l. Botev's mother and verse of poem. Vert—4l. (2) Type **253**; 20l. Botev in uniform; 50l. Quill, pistol and laurel wreath.

(Des G. Monolov and A. Anev. Litho)

1949 (24 Jan). 25th Death Anniv of Lenin. T **254** and similar type inscr "1924 1949". P 11½.

740	4l. yellow-brown/*cream*	30	20
741	20l. red-brown/*cream*	75	60

Design:—20l. Lenin as an orator (27×37 mm).

255 Road Construction 256 Pleven Mausoleum

(Des D. Gyudzhenov, N. Biserov, P. Vulkov and S. Penchev. Photo)

1949 (6 Apr). National Youth Movement. Designs as T **255**. P 10½.

742	4l. brown-red/*cream*	20	15
743	5l. dark brown/*cream*	40	20
744	9l. blackish green/*cream*	1·00	50
745	10l. violet/*cream*	65	40
746	20l. dull blue/*cream*	1·30	1·00
747	40l. brown/*cream*	2·50	1·20
742/747 *Set of* 6		5·50	3·00

Designs:—5l. Tunnel construction; 9l. Steam locomotive; 10l. Textile worker; 20l. Girl driving tractor; 40l. Workers in lorry.

(Des Ts. Kosturkova. Photo)

1949 (26 June). AIR. Stamp Day. Seventh Philatelic Congress, Pleven. P 11½.

748	**256**	50l. yellow-brown	5·75	5·00

257 G. Dimitrov 258 G. Dimitrov

(Des Ts. Kosturkova (4l.), A. Anev (20l.). Photo)

1949 (10 July). Death of Georgi Dimitrov (Prime Minister 1946–49). P 11½.

749	**257**	4l. red-brown	30	30
750	**258**	20l. blue	1·60	60

259 Hydro-electric Power Station 260 Symbols of Agriculture and Industry

(Des D. Gyudzhenov and N. Biserov (4l., 9l., 50l.), P. Vulkov (15l.), S. Penchev (20l.). Photo)

1949 (5 Aug). Five Year Industrial and Agricultural Plan.

(a) POSTAGE. T **259** and similar designs. P 11½ (9l., 20l.) or 11½×11 (4l., 15l.)

751	**259**	4l. blackish olive	20	15

752	–	9l. brown-red	30	25
753	–	15l. violet	50	30
754	–	20l. blue	1·60	90
		(b) AIR. P 11×11½		
755	**260**	50l. brown	4·50	2·00
751/755 *Set of* 5			6·50	3·25

Designs: Horiz—20l. Tractors in field. Vert—9l. Cement works; 15l. Tractors in garage.

261 Javelin and Grenade Throwing

262 Motor-cyclist and Tractor

(Des P. Vulkov (20l.), O. Bogdanova (others). Photo)

1949 (5 Sept). Physical Culture Campaign. T **261** and similar athletic designs and **262**. P 11 (4l.), 11×11½ (9l., 20l.) or 11½ (50l.).

756	**261**	4l. brown-red	75	40
757	–	9l. deep olive	2·10	90
758	**262**	20l. blue	3·25	1·70
759	–	50l. claret	7·75	4·25
756/759 *Set of* 4			12·50	6·50

Designs: Horiz—9l. Hurdling and leaping barbed-wire. Vert—50l. Two athletes marching.

263 Globe

264 Guardsman and Peasant

265 Guardsman with Dog

(Des P. Vulkov. Photo)

1949 (10 Oct). AIR. 75th Anniv of Founding of Universal Postal Union. P 11½.

760	**263**	50l. blue	3·25	1·70

(Des D. Gyudzhenov and N. Biserov (4l., 20l.), O. Bogdanova (60l.). Litho)

1949 (31 Oct). Frontier Guards. T **264/5** and similar type. P 11×11½ (60l.), 11½l. (others).

		(a) POSTAGE		
761	**264**	4l. orange-brown	50	40
762	–	20l. dull blue	1·60	1·40
		(b) AIR		
763	**265**	60l. deep olive	4·75	4·00
761/763 *Set of* 3			6·25	5·25

Design: Vert—20l. Guardsman on coast.

266 Georgi Dimitrov (Prime Minister 1946–49)

267 "Unanimity"

268 Iosif Stalin

(Des P. Vulkov (4l.), I. Manev (9l.), D. Gyudzhenov and N. Biserov (20l.), S. Penchev (50l.). Litho)

1949 (13 Dec). Fatherland Front. T **266/7** and similar types. P 11½.

764	**266**	4l. red-brown	20	15
765	**267**	9l. violet	85	50
766	–	20l. blue	95	60
767	–	50l. carmine	1·30	1·00
764/767 *Set of* 4			3·00	2·00

Designs:—20l. Man and woman with wheel-barrow and spade; 50l. Young people marching.

(Des V. Tomov. Litho)

1949 (21 Dec). Stalin's 70th Birthday. T **268** and larger type. P 11½.

768	**268**	4l. brown-orange	50	20
769	–	40l. claret	1·60	1·10

Design (25×37 mm):—40l. Stalin as orator.

269 Kharalampi Stoyanov

270 Strikers and Train

(Des V. Tomov (4l.), O. Bogdanova (20l.), A. Zhendov (60l.). Photo)

1950 (15 Feb). 30th Anniv of Railway Strike. T **269/70** and vert type inscr "1919–1949". P 11½.

770	**269**	4l. brown	50	20
771	**270**	20l. blue	65	30
772	–	60l. grey-olive	1·00	80
770/772 *Set of* 3			1·90	1·20

Design:—60l. Two workers and flag.

271 Miner

272 Steam Locomotive

(Des V. Tomov (1l., 5l., 9l.), P. Vulkov (2l., 3l.), S. Penchev (4l., 10l.), O. Bogdanova (15l., 20l.). Photo)

1950. T **271/2** and similar designs. P 11 (10, 15l.), 11×11½ (9, 20l.) or 13 (others).

773	**271**	1l. deep olive-green (23 Feb)	15	10
773*a*		1l. violet (30 Apr)	30	10
774	**272**	2l. black (23 Feb)	1·00	30
774*a*		2l. brown (18 May)	1·00	25
775	–	3l. deep blue (17 Mar)	50	10
776	–	4l. blue-green (17 Mar)	85	20
776*a*	–	4l. grey-green (18 May)	3·25	1·20
777	–	5l. brown-red (17 Mar)	65	10
778	–	9l. grey (1 Dec)	40	15
779	–	10l. reddish purple (1 Dec)	30	10
780	–	15l. brown-carmine (1 Dec)	1·00	30
781	–	20l. blue (1 Dec)	1·20	40
773/781 *Set of* 12			9·50	3·00

Designs: Horiz—4l. Tractor; 5l., 9l. Threshing machines. Vert—3l. Ship under construction; 10l. Power station; 15l., 20l. Woman in factory.

273 Kolarov

274 Stanislas Dospevski (self-portrait)

274a "In the Field" (Khristo Stanchev)

(Des Ts. Kosturkova (4l.), A. Anev (20l.). Photo)

1950 (6 Mar). Death of Vasil Kolarov (Prime Minister 1949–50). T **273** and similar vert design. P 11½.

782		4l. lake-brown	20	15
783		20l. dull ultramarine	85	80

Design: 27½×39½ mm—20l. Same portrait but different frame.

(Des P. Vulkov (4l., 20l.), O. Bogdanova (others). Photo)

1950 (15 Apr). As T **274/274a**, painters and paintings. P 11½.

784	**274**	1l. green	65	40
785	–	4l. orange-red	2·10	60
786	–	9l. chocolate	3·25	80
787	**274a**	15l. brown	4·50	1·00
788	–	20l. deep blue	6·75	3·00
789	–	40l. red-brown	8·25	4·00
790	–	60l. brown-orange	9·00	6·00
784/790 *Set of* 7			31·00	14·00

Designs: Vert—4l. King Kaloyan and Desislava; 9l. Nikolai Pavlovich (self-portrait); 40l. Statue of Debelyanov (Ivan Lazarov); 60l. "Peasant" (Vladimir Dimitrov the Master).

275 Ivan Vazov and Birthplace, Sopot

(Des V. Tomov. Photo)

1950 (26 June). Birth Centenary of Ivan Vazov (poet). P 11½.

791	**275**	4l. olive-green	20	15

276 Dimitrov and Birthplace, Kovachevtsi

276a G. Dimitrov

(Des L. Ivanov (4l.), V. Manski (10l.), V. Tomov (others). Photo)

1950 (2 July). First Death Anniv of Georgi Dimitrov (statesman). As T **276/6a** and similar designs showing Dimitrov and buildings. P 11½.

		(a) POSTAGE		
792		50st. brown	40	15
793		50st. green	40	15
794		1l. red-brown	50	20
795		2l. blue-grey	50	20
796		4l. purple	1·00	30
797		9l. brown-red	1·80	90
798		10l. carmine	2·50	1·20
799		15l. grey	2·50	1·20
800		20l. blue	4·25	2·50
		(b) AIR		
801		40l. yellow-brown	8·25	4·00
792/801 *Set of* 10			20·00	9·75

Designs: Horiz—2l. Dimitrov's house, Sofia; 15l. Dimitrov signing new constitution; 20l. Portrait of Dimitrov; 40l. Mausoleum. Vert—50st. (No. 792), 4l., 9l. and 10l. Dimitrov in various poses.

277 Runners

278 Workers and Tractor

(Des V. Tomov (4l.), E. Poptoshev (9l.), L. Kuleliev (others). Photo)

1950 (21 Aug). Sports. T **277** and similar vert designs. P 10½ (9l.) or 11½ (others).

802		4l. deep green	95	50
803		9l. red-brown (Cycling)	1·00	80
804		20l. deep blue (Putting the shot)	1·30	1·20
805		40l. purple (Volleyball)	3·25	2·50
802/805 *Set of* 4			5·75	4·50

(Des V. Tomov. Photo)

1950 (19 Sept). Second National Peace Congress. T **278** and vertical type. P 11½×10½ (4l.) or 10½×11½ (20l.).

806		4l. brown-red	20	15
807		20l. ultramarine	95	60

Design:—20l. Stalin's portrait on flag and three heads.

278a

278b

279 Children on Beach

1950 (1 Oct). Typo. P 13.

807*a*	**278a**	2l. yellow-brown	20	15
807*b*		3l. carmine	20	15
807*c*	**278b**	5l. claret	20	15
807*d*		9l. turquoise-blue	20	15
807*a*/807*d* *Set of* 4			70	55

Although inscribed "OFFICIAL MAIL" the above were issued as regular postage stamps.

1950 (1 Oct). SUNDAY DELIVERY. Horiz types inscr as T **279**. Litho. P 11 (5l., 10l.) or 13 (others).

808	–	1l. grey-green	20	15
809	**279**	2l. brown-red	30	15
810	–	5l. orange	65	30
811	**279**	10l. blue	1·60	60
808/811 *Set of* 4			2·50	1·10

Designs:—1l. Sanatorium; 5l. Sun-bathing.

280 Molotov. Kolarov, Stalin and Dimitrov

281 Russian and Bulgarian Girls

(Des V. Tomov (4l., 50l.), V. Manski (9l.), B. Kotsev (20l.) Photo)

1950 (10 Oct). Second Anniv of Soviet–Bulgarian Treaty of Friendship. T **280/1** and other vert types. P 11½.

812	**280**	4l. red-brown	20	15
813	–	9l. claret	30	15
814	**281**	20l. blue	65	50
815	–	50l. blue-green	3·25	1·20
812/815 *Set of* 4			4·00	1·80

Designs:—9l. Spassky Tower (Moscow) and flags; 50l. Freighter and tractor.

282 Marshal Tolbukhin

283 Bulgarians Greeting Marshal

(Des V. Tomov (4l.), V. Tomov and L. Ivanov (20l.) Photo)

1950 (10 Dec). Honouring Marshal Tolbukhin. P 11½.

816	**282**	4l. magenta	30	20
817	**283**	20l. deep blue	1·60	80

284 A. S. Popov

285 First Bulgarian Truck

(Des Ts. Kosturkova and A. Anev. Photo)

1951 (10 Feb). 45th Death Anniv of Aleksandr Popov (radio pioneer). P 10½.

818	**284**	4l. lake-brown	75	30
819		20l. blue	1·40	70

(Des P. Vulkov (1l.), V. Tomov (2l.), L. Ivanov and V. Manski (4l.). Photo)

1951. Various designs as T **285**. P 12½.

820	1l. violet/*cream* (25.4)	20	10
821	2l. green/*cream* (15.4)	25	10
822	4l. red-brown/*cream* (15.3)	30	10
820/822 *Set of 3*		70	25

Designs:—1l. First Bulgarian tractor, 2l. Fist Bulgarian steamroller.

286 Georgi Kirkov

287 Nacho Ivanov and Avram Stoyanov

(Des V. Tomov (4l., 9l., 15l.), A. Zhendov (others). Photo)

1951 (25 Mar). Anti-Fascist Heroes. Portrait types as T **286/7**. P 11½.

823	1l. reddish purple	40	20
824	2l. plum	40	20
825	4l. carmine-lake	40	20
826	9l. red-brown	1·20	60
827	15l. olive-brown	2·50	1·10
828	20l. blue	2·50	1·50
829	50l. blackish olive	6·25	2·20
823/829 *Set of 7*		12·50	5·50

Portraits:—1l. Chankova, Adalbert Antonov-Malchika, Sasho Dimitrov and Lilyana Dimitrova; 2l. Stanke Dimitrov; 9l. Anton Ivanov, 15l. Khristo Mikhailov; 20l. Georgi Dimitrov at Leipzig.

288 First Bulgarian Tractor

289 Embroidery

(Des P. Vulkov (1l., 20l.), V. Tomov (2l., 40l.), L. Ivanov and V. Manski (4l.), A. Zhendov, V. Naslednikova and V. Bibina (9l.,15l.) Photo)

1951 (30 Apr). National Occupations. Designs as T **288/9**. P 11×10½ (horiz) or 10½×11 (vert).

830	1l. yellow-brown	30	20
831	2l. violet	40	30
832	4l. red-brown	75	60
833	9l. bright violet	1·30	80
834	15l. reddish purple	2·30	1·50
835	20l. bright blue	5·25	2·20
836	40l. green	7·75	3·25
830/836 *Set of 7*		16·00	8·00

Designs: Horiz—2l. First Bulgarian steamroller; 4l. First Bulgarian truck; 15l. Carpets; 40l. Fruit. Vert—20l. Roses and tobacco.

290 Turkish Attack

(Des P. Vulkov (1l.), V. Staikov (4l.), G. Gerasimov (9l.), V. Tomov (20l., 40l.). Photo)

1951 (3 May). 75th Anniv of April Uprising. T **290** and similar horizontal types inscr "1876–1951". P 11.

837	1l. brown/*cream*	75	35
838	4l. green/*cream*	85	40
839	9l. purple/*cream*	1·30	1·00
840	20l. blue/*cream*	1·90	1·50
841	40l. lake/*cream*	2·50	2·00
837/841 *Set of 5*		6·50	4·75

Designs:—4l. Proclamation of Uprising; 9l. Cannon and cavalry; 20l. Patriots in 1876 and 1944; 40l. Georgi Benkovski and Georgi Dimitrov.

291 Dimitur Blagoev as Orator

(Des V. Staikov. Photo)

1951 (2 Aug). 60th Anniv of First Bulgarian Social Democratic Party Congress, Buzludzha. P 10½×11.

842	**291**	1l. violet	30	20
843		4l. green	1·00	40
844		9l. reddish purple	1·80	1·20
842/844 *Set of 3*			2·75	1·60

292 Babies in Crèche

D **293**

(Des I. Manev (1l.), P. Vulkov (9l.), V. Staikov (others). Photo)

1951 (10 Oct). Children's Day. T **292** and similar horiz designs. P 11.

845	1l. red-brown	30	20
846	4l. reddish purple	75	30
847	9l. blue-green	1·60	60
848	20l. blue	3·25	2·00
845/848 *Set of 4*		5·25	2·75

Designs:—4l. Children building models; 9l. Girl and children's playground; 20l. Boy bugler and children marching.

1951 (15 Oct). POSTAGE DUE. Typo. P 10½, 11½ or compound.

D849	D **293**	1l. sepia	20	15
D850		2l. maroon	30	15
D851		8l. orange	65	50
D852		20l. blue	1·70	1·30
D849/852 *Set of 4*			2·50	1·90

293 Workers

294 Labour Medal (obverse)

295 Labour Medal (reverse)

(Des G. Manolov. Photo)

1951 (29 Dec). Third General Workers' Union Congress. T **293** and similar vert design. P 10½ (4l.) or 11½ (1l.).

849	1l. blackish green	20	15
850	4l. brown	30	20

Design:—4l. Georgi Dimitrov and Vulko Chervenkov (Prime Minister).

(Des Ts. Kosturkova and G. Zhozev. Photo)

1952 (1 Feb). Order of Labour. P 13.

851	**294**	1l. carmine	20	15
852	**295**	1l. brown-lake	20	15
853	**294**	4l. green	20	15
854	**295**	4l. turquoise	20	15
855	–	9l. violet	75	20
856	**295**	9l. deep blue	75	20
851/856 *Set of 6*			2·10	90

Design:—No. 855, as T **294** but value at bottom left.

Currency stabilizied, 12th May, 1952

296 Vasil Kolarov Dam

297 G. Dimitrov and Chemical Works

(Des V. Tomov. Photo)

1952. P 13 and various other perfs.

857	**296**	4st. blackish green (16.5)	20	15
858		12st. reddish violet (17.5)	30	15
859		16st. lake-brown (16.5)	40	15
860		44st. claret (18.5)	1·00	20
861		80st. blue (18.5)	4·50	50
857/861 *Set of 5*			5·75	1·00

(Des V. Tomov. Photo)

1952 (18 June). 70th Birth Anniv of Dimitrov (statesman) T **297** and similar designs inscr "1882–1952". P 11 (80st.) or 11½ (others).

862	16st. brown	95	50
863	44st. chocolate	1·60	1·00
864	80st. blue	2·75	1·50
862/864 *Set of 3*		4·75	2·75

Designs: Horiz—44st. Georgi Dimitrov (Prime Minister 1946–49) and Prime Minister Vulko Chervenkov. Vert—80st. Full-face portrait of Georgi Dimitrov.

298 Republika Power Station

299 N. Vaptsarov

(Des V. Tomov. Photo)

1952 (30 June–4 July). P 13.

866	**298**	16st. sepia	65	20
867		44st. deep reddish purple (4 July)	2·10	30

(Des St. Penchev (16st.), S. Sotirov (44st.), A. Stamenov (80st.). Photo)

1952 (23 July). Tenth Death Anniv of Nikola Vaptsarov (poet and revolutionary). T **299** and similar vert portraits. P 11½ (44st.) or 11 (others).

869	16st. brown-lake	95	70
870	44st. purple-brown	1·90	1·70
871	80st. sepia	4·00	1·90
869/871 *Set of 3*		6·25	3·75

Portraits:—44st. Facing bayonets at right; 80st. Full-face.

300 Congress Delegates

(Des V. Staikov (2st.), D. Gyudzhenov (16st.), V. Tomov (44st.), P. Vulkov (80st.), Photo)

1952 (1 Sept). 40th Anniv of First Workers' Social Democratic Youth League Congress. T **300** and similar horiz designs inscr "1912 r.". P 11×11½.

872	2st. brown-lake	20	15
873	16st. slate-violet	40	30
874	44st. deep green	1·60	85
875	80st. sepia	2·50	1·90
872/875 *Set of 4*		4·25	3·00

Designs:—16st. Young partisans; 44st. Factory and guards, 80st. Dimitrov addressing young workers.

301 Attack on Winter Palace, St. Petersburg

(Des V. Staikov (4st.), G. Zhelezarov (8st.), V. Tomov (16st., 44st.), P. Vulkov (80st.). Photo)

1952 (6 Nov). 35th Anniv of Russian Revolution. T **301** and similar horiz designs inscr "1917 1952". P 11½.

876	4st. brown-lake	40	20
877	8st. deep blue-green	50	30
878	16st. deep blue	1·20	40
879	44st. sepia	1·50	50
880	80st. deep olive-brown	3·00	2·40
876/880 *Set of 5*		6·00	3·50

Designs:—8st. Volga-Don canal; 16st. Dove and globe, 44st. Lenin and Stalin; 80st. Lenin, Stalin and Himlay hydroelectric station.

302

303 Vintagers and Grapes

304 V. Levski

(Des St. Penchev (2st.), V. Tomov (8, 12 and 16st.), I. Manev (others). Photo)

1952–53. National Products (Wood Carvings). Various designs as T **302/3**. P 13.

881	–	2st. grey-brown (6.1.53)	20	15
882	–	8st. deep grey-green (6.1.53)	20	15
883	–	12st. brown (24.12.52)	40	15
884	–	16st. brown-purple (8.12.52)	80	15
885	**302**	28st. bronze-green (31.1.53)	1·10	20
886	–	44st. sepia (11.12.52)	1·50	30
887	**303**	80st. ultramarine (15.1 .53)	1·70	40
888		1l. deep violet-blue (12.11.52)	4·00	60
889		4l. lake (27.1.53)	4·75	3·50
881/889 *Set of 9*			13·00	5·00

Designs: Vert—2st. Numeral in carved frame. Horiz—8st. Gift-offering to idol; 12st. Birds and grapes; 16st. Rosegathering; 44st. "Attar of Roses".

(Des B. Angelushev. Photo)

1953 (19 Feb). 80th Anniv of Execution of Vasil Levski (revolutionary). T **304** and similar horiz design. P 11.

890	16st. brown/*cream*	20	15
891	44st. deep olive-brown/*cream*	60	30

Design:—44st. Levski addressing crowd.

305 Russian Army Crossing R. Danube

306 Mother and Children

(Des G. Bogdanov, E. Poptoshev and I. Tabakov. Photo)

1953 (3 Mar). 75th Anniv of Liberation from Turkey. T **305** and similar designs inscr "1878 1953". P 11.

892	8st. deep turquoise	30	20
893	16st. brown	40	20
894	44st. deep grey-green	95	30
895	80st. lake-brown	3·00	1·50
896	1l. olive-black	3·50	3·00
892/896 *Set of 5*		7·25	4·75

Designs: Vert—16st. Battle of Shipka Pass. Horiz—44st. Peasants welcoming Russian soldiers; 80st. Bulgarians and Russians embracing; 1l. Shipka Pass memorial and Dimitrovgrad.

(Des B. Angelushev. Photo)

1953 (9 Mar). International Women's Day. P 11.

897	**306**	16st. blue	30	10
898		16st. grey-green	30	10

307 Karl Marx

308 May Day Parade

(Des S. Sotirov. Photo)

1953 (30 Apr). 70th Death Anniv of Karl Marx. T **307** and vert design inscr 1883–1953 . P 11.

899		16st. blue	30	20
900		44st. deep brown	70	50

Design:—44st. Book *Das Kapital*.

(Des A. Poplilov. Photo)

1953 (30 Apr). Labour Day. P 13.

901	**308**	16st. brown-red	40	20

309 Stalin

310 Goce Delčev (Macedonian revolutionary)

(Des N. Petkov. Photo)

1953 (23 May). Death of Stalin. P 13.

902	**309**	16st. deep brown	80	30
903		16st. black	80	30

(Des V. Korenev. Photo)

1953. 50th Anniv of Ilinden-Preobrazhenie Rising. T **310** and other designs inscr "1903–1953". P 13.

904		16st. deep brown (8 Aug)	20	15
905		44st. deep violet (19 Aug)	80	50
906		1l. maroon (8 Aug)	1·10	80
904/906 *Set of* 3			1·90	1·30

Designs: Vert—44st. Insurgents and flag facing left. Horiz—1l. Insurgents and flag facing right.

311 Soldier and Insurgents

312 Dimitur Blagoev

(Des P. Penev (16st.), V. Tomov (44st.). Photo)

1953 (18 Sept). Army Day. T **311** and similar horiz design. P 13.

907		16st. crimson	50	20
908		44st. Prussian blue	95	30

Design:—44st. Soldier, factories and combine-harvester.

(Des S. Sotirov and N. Petkov. Photo)

1953 (21 Sept). 50th Anniv of Bulgarian Workers' Social Democratic Party. T **312** and similar vert design. P 13.

909		16st. brown	50	30
910		44st. Venetian red (Dimitrov and Blagoev)	95	30

313 Georgi Dimitrov and Vasil Kolarov

314 Railway Viaduct

(Des B. Angelushev. Photo)

1953 (22 Sept). 30th Anniv of September Uprising. T **313** and similar designs inscr "1923–1953". P 13.

911		8st. greenish black	30	15
912		16st. deep red-brown	40	20
913		44st. carmine	1·30	60
911/913 *Set of* 3			1·80	85

Designs: Horiz—16st. Insurgent and flag; 44st. Crowd of Insurgents.

(Des A. Zhendov. Photo)

1953 (17 Oct). Bulgarian–Russian Friendship. Designs as T **314**. P 13.

914		8st. blue	20	15
915		16st. blackish green	30	20
916		44st. brown-red	80	40
917		80st. red-orange	95	70
914/917 *Set of* 4			2·00	1·30

Designs: Horiz—16st., Welder and industrial plant; 80st. Combine-harvester. Vert—44st. Iron foundry.

315 Dog Rose (*Rosa canis*)

316 Vasil Kolarov Library

317 Singer and Musician

(Des B. Angelushev, St. Kunchev and I. Manev. Photo)

1953 (30 Oct)–**54**. Medicinal Flowers. T **315** and similar vert designs. P 13 (a) or 13½ (b).

918		2st. grey-blue (b)	20	15
919		4st. orange-red (a)	20	15
920		8st. deep turquoise-green (a)	20	15
		a. Perf 13½	20	15
921		12st. myrtle green (a)	20	15
922		12st. orange-red (a)	20	15
		a. Perf 13½	20	15
923		16st. violet-blue/*white* (b)	50	20
923*a*		16st. ultramarine/*cream* (a)	50	20
924		16st. lake-brown/*cream* (a)	50	20
925		20st. carmine/*cream* (a)	80	25
926		28st. slate-green (a)	85	30
927		40st. blue/*cream* (b)	95	50
		a. Perf 11		
928		44st. light brown/*cream* (a)	1·50	60
		a. Perf 13½	1·50	60
929		80st. yellow-brown/*cream* (b)	2·40	1·10
930		1l. chestnut/*cream* (b)	6·75	1·90
		a. Perf 11		
931		2l. deep mauve (b)	9·75	4·00
918/931 *Set of* 15			23·00	9·00
MS931*a* 161×172 mm. Twelve values as above in blue-green (sold at 6l.). Imperf (18.12.53)			70·00	70·00

Designs:—2st. Deadly nightshade (*Atropa belladonna*); 4st. Thorn-apple (*Datura stramonium*); 8st. Sage (*Salvia officinalis*); 16st. Great yellow gentian (*Gentiana lutea*); 20st. Opium poppy (*Papaver somniferum*); 28st. Peppermint (*Mentha pipenta*); 40st. Bearberry (*Uva ursi*); 44st. Coltsfoot (*Tussilago farfara*), 80st. *Primula officinalis*; 1l. Dandelion (*Taraxacum officinalis*); 2l. Foxglove (*Digitalis lanata*).

(Des St. Gospodinova. Photo)

1953 (16 Dec). 75th Anniv of Kolarov Library, Sofia. P 13.

932	**316**	44st. brown	60	40

(Des L. Zidarov (16st.), A. Poplilov (44st.). Photo)

1953 (26 Dec). Amateur Theatricals. T **317** and similar vert design. P 13.

933		16st. purple-brown	30	15
934		44st. bluish green (Folk-dancers)	70	40

318 Airplane over Mountains

319 Lenin and Stalin

(Des S. Sotirov (8st., 20st., 80st., 4l.); V. Yonchev (12st., 16st., 1l.), V. Staikov (28st., 44st., 60st.). Photo)

1954 (12 Feb–1 Apr). AIR. T **318** and similar designs. P 13.

935		8st. deep grey-green	20	15
936		12st. lake-brown	20	15
937		16st. brown	20	15
938		20st. deep orange-red/*cream* (1.4)	20	15
939		28st. blue/*cream* (1.4)	40	20
940		44st. maroon/*cream* (1.4)	50	20
941		60st. red-brown/*cream* (1.4)	85	30
942		80st. green/*cream* (1.4)	95	40
943		1l. deep bluish green/*cream* (1.4)	3·00	85
944		4l. blue	5·25	2·40
935/944 *Set of* 10			10·50	4·50

Designs: Vert—12st. Exhibition buildings, Plovdiv, 80st. Tirnovo, 4l. Partisans' Monument. Horiz—16st. Seaside promenade, Varna; 20st. Combine-harvester in cornfield; 28st. Rila Monastery; 44st. Studena hydroelectric barrage; 60st. Dimitrovgrad; 1l. Sofia University and equestrian statue.

(Des St. Gospodinova, B. Angelushev, T. Bocheva-Paspaleeva and I. Khristov, respectively. Photo)

1954 (13 Mar). 30th Death Anniv of Lenin. T **319** and similar designs inscr "1924–1954". P 13.

945		16st. brown/*cream*	30	15
946		44st. lake/*cream*	70	20
947		80st. blue/*cream*	95	40
948		1l. bronze-green/*cream*	1·90	1·20
945/948 *Set of* 4			3·50	1·80

Designs: Vert—44st. Lenin statue; 80st. Lenin-Stalin mausoleum and Kremlin; 1l. Lenin.

320 Dimitur Blagoev and Crowd

(Des B. Angelushev. Photo)

1954 (28 Apr). 30th Death Anniv of Blagoev. T **320** and similar horiz design inscr "1924 1954". P 13.

949		16st. red-brown/*cream*	20	10
950		44st. sepia/*cream*	80	30

Design:—44st. Blagoev writing at desk.

321 Dimitrov Speaking

322 Steam Locomotive

(Des St. Penchev and O. Bogdanova. Photo)

1954 (11 June). 5th Death Anniv of Dimitrov. T **321** and similar design inscr "1949 1954". P 13.

951		44st. lake/*cream*	50	30
952		80st. brown/*cream*	95	70

Design: Horiz—80st. Dimitrov and blast-furnace.

(Des St. Gospodinova. Photo)

1954 (30 July). Railway Workers' Day. P 13.

953	**322**	44st. deep turquoise-blue/*cream*	1·70	80
954		44st. black/*cream*	1·70	80

323 Miner Operating Machinery

324 Marching Soldiers

(Des L. Zidarov. Photo)

1954 (19 Aug). Miners' Day. P 13.

955	**323**	44st. blackish green/*cream*	50	20

(Des A. Poplilov (12st.), L. Zidarov (80st., 1l.), B. Angelushev (others). Photo)

1954 (4 Sept). Tenth Anniv of Fatherland Front Government. T **324** and similar designs inscr" 1944–1954". P 13.

956		12st. brown red/*cream*	20	15
957		16st. carmine-red/*cream*	20	15
958		28st. deep slate- blue/*cream*	30	20
959		44st. reddish brown/*cream*	60	25
960		80st. blue/*cream*	1·30	50
961		1l. deep green/*cream*	1·50	60
956/961 *Set of* 6			3·75	1·70

Designs: Vert—16st. Soldier and parents; 80st. Girl and boy pioneers; 1l. Dimitrov. Horiz—28st. Industrial plant; 44st. Dimitrov and workers.

325 Academy Building

326 Gymnast

(Des St. Gospodinova. Photo)

1954 (27 Oct). 85th Anniv of Academy of Sciences. P 13.

962	**325**	80st. black/*cream*	1·50	80

(Des V. Tomov. Photo)

1954 (21 Dec). Sports. Designs as T **326**. P 11.

963		16st. deep bluish green/*cream*	1·50	50
964		44st. red/*cream*	1·60	95
965		80st. chestnut/*cream*	3·50	1·90
966		2l. ultramarine/*cream*	5·25	4·00
963/966 *Set of* 4			10·50	6·50

Designs: Vert—44st. Wrestlers; 2l. Ski-jumper. Horiz—80st. Horse-jumper.

327 Velingrad Rest Home

(Des S. Sotirov. Photo)

1954 (28 Dec). 50th Anniv of Trade Union Movement. T **327** and similar designs. P 13.

967		16st. myrtle green/*cream*	30	20
968		44st. Indian red/*cream*	50	30
969		80st. deep blue/*cream*	1·20	95
967/969 *Set of* 3			1·80	1·30

Designs: Vert—44st. Foundryman. Horiz—80st. Georgi Dimitrov, Dimitur Blagoev and Georgi Kirkov.

328 Geese

329 Communist Party Building

(Des N. Tuzsuzov (2st. to 16st.), Zh. Zhelev (28st. to 1l.). Photo)

1955 (19 Feb)–**56**. T **328/9** and simlar horiz designs. P 13½.

970		2st. myrtle green	20	10
		a. Perf 13	20	10
971		4st. bronze green	30	10
		a. Perf 13	30	10
972		12st. chocolate	60	20
973		16st. Indian red	95	30
		a. Perf 13	95	30
974		28st. ultramarine	60	20
975		44st. brown-red	11·50	3·50
975*a*		44st. bright crimson (p 11×13) (20.4.56)	4·75	95
976		80st. chocolate	1·50	50
977		1l. myrtle green	2·40	95
970/977 *Set of* 9			21·00	6·00

Designs:—4st. Rooster and hens; 12st. Sow and piglets; 16st. Ewe and lambs; 28st. Telephone exchange; 80st. Flats; 1l. Cellulose factory.

330 Mill Girl

16 ст.
(331)

332 Rejoicing Crowds

(Des B. Angelushev. Photo)

1955 (5 Mar). International Women's Day. T **330** and similar designs inscr "8. III. 1955". P 13.

978	12st. deep brown	10	10
979	16st. deep myrtle-green	30	15
980	44st. ultramarine	1·10	20
981	44st. carmine-lake	1·10	20
978/981 *Set of 4*		2·30	60

Designs: Horiz—16st. Girl feeding cattle. Vert—44st. (2), Mother and baby.

1955 (8 Mar)–**57**. Stamps as Nos. 820 and 822 but colours changed and surch as T **331**.

981*a*	–	16st. on 1l. violet (R.) (8.4.57)	20	10
982	**285**	16st. on 4l. chocolate (shades) (B.)	1·90	50
		a. Surch 11½ mm. ('56)	1·90	50

(Des V. Staikov Photo)

1955 (23 Apr). Labour Day. T **332** and similar vert design. P 13.

983	16st. carmine	30	20
984	44st. blue (Three workers and globe)	70	30

333 St. Cyril and St. Methodius

334 Sergei Rumyantsev

(Des B. Angelushev. Photo)

1955 (21 May). 1100th Anniv of First Bulgarian Literature. T **333** and similar horiz designs. P 13.

985	4st. blue/*cream*	20	15
986	8st. deep olive/*cream*	20	15
987	16st. black/*cream*	20	15
988	28st. brown-red/*cream*	50	40
989	44st. brown/*cream*	80	50
990	80st. carmine-red/*cream*	1·40	95
991	2l. greenish black/*cream*	3·50	2·10
985/991 *Set of 7*		6·00	4·00

Designs:—8st. Monk writing; 16st. Early printing press; 28st. Khristo Botev (poet); 44st. Ivan Vazov (poet and novelist); 80st. Dimitur Blagoev (writer and editor) and books; 2l. Dimitur Blagoev Polygraphic Complex, Sofia.

(Des S. Gospodinova. Photo)

1955 (30 June). 30th Death Annivs of Bulgarian Poets. T **334** and similar vert portraits inscr "1925–1955". P 13.

992	12st. Indian red/*cream*	40	20
993	16st. orange-brown/*cream*	50	30
994	44st. slate-green/*cream*	1·50	95
992/994 *Set of 3*		2·20	1·30

Designs:—16st. Khristo Yasenov; 44st. Geo Milev.

335 F. Engels and Book

336 Mother and Children

(Des S. Gospodinova and T. Bocheva. Photo)

1955 (30 July). 60th Death Anniv of Engels. P 13.

995	**335**	44st. brown/*cream*	95	80

(Des B. Angelushev. Photo)

1955 (30 July). World Mothers' Congress, Lausanne. P 13.

996	**336**	44st. lake/*cream*	95	80

337 "Youth of the World"

338 Main Entrance in 1892

(Des L. Zidarov. Photo)

1955 (30 July). Fifth World Youth Festival, Warsaw. P 13.

997	**337**	44st. blue/*cream*	95	80

(Des P. Dachev and C. Nikolov (16st.). Photo)

1955 (31 Aug). Sixteenth International Fair, Plovdiv. T **338** and similar designs inscr "1955". P 13.

998	4st. sepia/*cream*	20	15
999	16st. carmine/*cream*	25	15
1000	44st. olive-black/*cream*	50	20
1001	80st. blue/*cream*	1·20	40
998/1001 *Set of 4*		1·90	80

Designs: Vert—16st. Sculptured group; 80st. Fair poster. Horiz—44st. Fruit.

339 Friedrich Schiller (dramatist) (150th death anniv)

340 Industrial Plant

(Des B. Angelushev. Photo)

1955 (31 Oct). Cultural Anniversaries. Vert portraits of famous writers as T **339**. P 13.

1002	16st. reddish brown/*cream*	50	20
1003	44st. brown-red/*cream*	1·10	30
1004	60st. deep turquoise-blue/*cream*	1·40	40
1005	80st. olive-black/*cream*	1·70	60
1006	1l. purple/*cream*	3·50	1·50
1007	2l. deep olive/*cream*	4·50	3·00
1002/1007 *Set of 6*		11·50	5·50

Portraits:—44st. Adam Mickiewicz (poet, death centenary); 60st. Hans Christian Andersen (150th birth anniv); 80st. Baron de Montesquieu (philosopher, death bicentenary); 1l. Miguel de Cervantes (350th anniv of publication of *Don Quixote*); 2l. Walt Whitman (poet) (centenary of publication of *Leaves of Grass*).

Nos. 1006/7 were each issued with *se-tenant* labels bearing the titles of *Don Quixote* and *Leaves of Grass* respectively.

(Des Z. Zhelev (2st., 16st., 80st.), St. Gospodinova (4st., 44st.), M. Rashkov (1l.). Photo)

1955 (1 Dec). Bulgarian–Russian Friendship. Views and portraits (80st., 1l.) inscr as T **340**. P 13.

1008	2st. slate-black/*cream*	20	15
1009	4st. blue/*cream*	20	15
1010	16st. deep blue-green/*cream*	60	20
1011	44st. red-brown/*cream*	80	20
1012	80st. deep green/*cream*	1·20	30
1013	1l. greenish black/*cream*	1·30	70
1008/1013 *Set of 6*		3·75	1·50

Designs: Horiz—4st. Dam; 16st. Danube railway bridge. Vert—44st. Monument; 80st. Ivan Michurin (botanist); 1l. Vladimir Mayakovsky (writer).

341 Emblem

342 Quinces

(Des B. Angelushev. Photo)

1956 (10 Feb). Centenary of Library Reading Rooms. T **341** and similar horiz designs inscr "1856–1956". P 11.

1014	12st. lake/*cream*	20	15
1015	16st. deep brown/*cream*	30	20
1016	44st. slate-green/*cream*	1·20	50
1014/1016 *Set of 3*		1·50	75

Designs:—16st. K. Pishurka writing; 44st. B. Kiro reading.

(Des V. Tomov. Photo)

1956 (14 Apr)–**57**. Fruit. T **342** and similar vert designs. P 13.

1017	4st. scarlet	2·10	30
1017*a*	4st. bright green (13.4.57)	20	10
	ab. Perf 11		
1018	8st. blue-green (Pears)	95	30
1018*a*	8st. Indian red (Pears) (13.4.57)	20	10
1019	16st. bright crimson (Apples)	1·70	40
1019*a*	16st. rosine (Apples) (13.4.57)	60	20
1020	44st. violet (Grapes)	1·90	60
1020*a*	44st. dull orange (Grapes) (13.4.57)	1·20	30
1017/1020*a* *Set of 8*		8·00	2·10

343 Artillerymen

344 Blagoev and Birthplace at Zagorichane

(Des B. Angelushev. Photo)

1956 (28 Apr). 80th Anniv of April Uprising. T **343** and similar horiz design inscr "1876 1956". P 11.

1021	16st. chocolate	40	40
1022	44st. deep grey-green (Cavalry charge)	50	50

(Des N. Petkov. Photo)

1956 (30 May). Birth Centenary of Dimitur Blagoev (socialist writer). P 11.

1023	**344**	44st. deep turquoise-blue	1·50	95

345 Cherries

346 Football

(Des B. Angelushev and S. Penchev. Photo)

1956 (29 June). Fruit. T **345** and similar vert designs. P 13.

1024	2st. carmine-lake	15	10
1025	12st. blue (Plums)	20	10
1026	28st. orange-brown (Greengages)	40	30
	a. Perf 11		
1027	80st. bright carmine-red (Strawberries)	1·20	60
1024/1027 *Set of 4*		1·80	1·00

(Des V. Tomov and L. Zidarov, Photo)

1956 (29 Aug). Olympic Games. T **346** and similar designs inscr "1956". P 11.

1028	4st. bright blue	60	20
1029	12st. light brown-red	70	25
1030	16st. orange-brown	80	30
1031	44st. deep myrtle-green	1·50	60
1032	80st. deep brown	2·40	1·30
1033	1l. crimson	3·50	1·50
1028/1033 *Set of 6*		8·50	3·75

Designs: Vert—4st. Gymnastics; 12st. Throwing the discus; 80st Basketball. Horiz—16st. Pole vaulting; 1l. Boxing.

347 Tobacco and Rose

348 Gliders

(Des D. Krustev. Photo)

1956 (1 Sept). Seventeenth International Fair, Plovdiv. P 13.

1034	**347**	44st. carmine-red	1·50	60
1035		44st. deep green	1·50	60

(Des T. Zakhariev, A. Khadzhiev and I. R. Ivanova. Photo)

1956 (15 Oct). AIR. Thirtieth Anniv of Gliding Club. T **348** and similar horiz designs, inscr as in T **348**. P 13.

1036	44st. blue	40	20
1037	60st. reddish violet	50	30
1038	80st. deep turquoise-green	1·50	95
1036/1038 *Set of 3*		2·20	1·30

Designs:—44st. Launching glider; 60st. Glider over hangar.

349 National Theatre

350 Wolfgang Mozart (composer, birth bicentenary)

(Des T. Zakhariev (16st.), D. Krustev (44st.). Photo)

1956 (16 Nov). Centenary of National Theatre, Sofia T **349** and similar horiz design inscr "1856 1956". P 13.

1039	16st. red-brown	30	20
1040	44st. deep bluish-green	70	60

Design:—44st. Dobri Voinikov and Sava Dobroplodni (dramatists).

(Des B. Angelushev. Photo)

1956 (29 Dec). Cultural Anniversaries. T **350** and similar vert designs. P 13.

1041	16st. bronze green	30	20
1042	20st. brown	50	20
1043	40st. carmine-red	70	25
1044	44st. deep dull purple	80	30
1045	60st. deep slate	95	35
1046	80st. bistre-brown	1·50	80
1047	1l. bluish green	2·40	95
1048	2l. deep greenish blue	4·75	3·00
1041/1048 *Set of 8*		10·50	5·50

Designs:—16st. Benjamin Franklin (U.S. journalist and statesman, 250th birth anniv); 20st. Rembrandt (artist, 350th birth anniv); 44st. Heinrich Heine (poet, death centenary); 60st. George Bernard Shaw (dramatist, birth centenary); 80st. Fyodor Dostoevsky (novelist, 75th death anniv); 1l. Henrik Ibsen (dramatist, 50th death anniv); 2l. Pierre Curie (physicist, 50th death anniv).

351 Cyclists

352 Woman with Microscope

(Des P. Rachev Photo)

1957 (6 Mar). Tour of Egypt Cycle Race. P 11.

1049	**351**	80st. chestnut	1·50	70
1050		80st. deep turquoise-blue	1·50	70

(Des B. Angelushev. Photo)

1957 (8 Mar). International Women's Day T **352** and similar designs inscr "8 MAPT 1957". P 11.

1051	12st. blue	10	10
1052	16st. deep chestnut	30	15
1053	44st. bronze-green	60	30
1051/1053 *Set of 3*		90	50

Designs:—16st. Women and children; 44st. Woman feeding poultry.

353 *New Times*

354 Lisunov Li-2 Airliner

(Des I. Zakhariev. Photo)

1957 (8 Mar). 60th Anniv of *New Times* (review). P 11.
1054 **353** 16st. carmine-red 40 20

(Des St. Kunchev. Photo)

1957 (21 May). AIR. Tenth Anniv of Bulgarian Airways. P 13.
1055 **354** 80st. blue 1·50 50

355 St. Cyril and St. Methodius

356 Basketball

357 Girl in National Costume

(Des B. Angelushev. Photo)

1957 (22 May). Centenary of Canonization of St. Cyril and St. Methodius (founders of Cyrillic Alphabet). P 11.
1056 **355** 44st. deep olive-green and pale buff 1·50 60

(Des St. Penchev. Photo)

1957 (20 June). Tenth European Basketball Championships. P 11.
1057 **356** 44st. deep green 2·40 70

(Des V. Korenev. Photo)

1957 (18 July). Sixth World Youth Festival, Moscow. P 13.
1058 **357** 44st. pale blue 80 30

358 G. Dimitrov

359 V. Levski

(Des B. Angelushev. Photo)

1957 (18 July). 75th Birth Anniv of Georgi Dimitrov (statesman). P 13.
1059 **358** 44st. carmine-red 1·50 50

(Des N. Petkov. Photo)

1957 (18 July). 120th Birth Anniv of Vasil Levski (revolutionary). P 11.
1060 **359** 44st. blackish green 95 30

360 View of Turnovo and Ludwig Zamenhof (inventor)

361 Soldiers in Battle

(Des M. Velev and St. Kunchev. Photo)

1957 (27 July). 70th Anniv of Esperanto (invented language) and 50th Anniv of Bulgarian Esperanto Association. P 13.
1061 **360** 44st. bronze green 1·50 50

(Des I. Petrov and V. Barakov. Photo)

1957 (13 Aug). 80th Anniv of Liberation from Turkey. T **361** and similar vert design inscr "1878–1958". P 13.
1062 16st. deep bluish green 20 10
1063 44st. brown 80 25
Design:—16st. Old and Young soldiers.

362 Woman Planting Tree

363 Two Hemispheres

(Des V. Staikov and V. Barakov. Photo)

1957 (16 Sept). Reafforestation Campaign. T **362** and simlar designs. P 13.
1064 2st. deep blue-green 20 15
1065 12st. deep brown 20 15
1066 16st. greenish blue 20 15
1067 44st. deep bluish green 70 30
1068 80st. green 1·20 60
1064/1068 *Set of 5* 2·30 1·20
Designs: Horiz—12st. Red deer in forest; 16st. Dam and trees; 44st. Polikarpov Po-2 biplane over forest; 80st. Trees and cornfield.

(Des T. Zakhariev. Photo)

1957 (4 Oct). Fourth World Trade Unions Congress, Leipzig. P 13.
1069 **363** 44st. greenish blue 80 30

364 Lenin

365 Youth and Girl

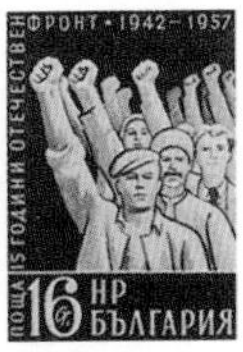
366 Partisans

(Des B. Angelushev (60st.), V. Tomov and S. Sotirov (others). Photo)

1957 (29 Oct). 40th Anniv of Russian Revolution. T **364** and similar vert designs inscr "1917–1957". P 11.
1070 12st. chocolate 60 30
1071 16st. deep turquoise-blue 1·30 80
1072 44st. blue 2·75 95
1073 60st. carmine-lake 3·00 1·50
1074 80st. myrtle-green 9·75 3·50
1070/1074 *Set of 5* 16·00 6·25
Designs:—16st. Cruiser *Aurora*; 44st. Dove of Peace over Europe; 60st. Revolutionaries; 80st. Oil refinery.

(Des D. Krustev. Photo)

1957 (28 Dec). Tenth Anniv of National Youth Movement. P 11.
1075 **365** 16st. carmine 30 20

(Des B. Angelushev. Photo)

1957 (28 Dec). 15th Anniv of Fatherland Front. P 11.
1076 **366** 16st. chocolate 30 20

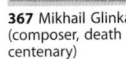

367 Mikhail Glinka (composer, death centenary)

368 Hotel Vasil Kolarov

(Des B. Angelushev, N. Petkov, St Kunchev and L. Zidarov. Photo)

1957 (30 Dec). Cultural Anniversaries. T **367** and similar vert designs. P 13.
1077 12st. deep brown 60 20
1078 16st. bronze green 70 25
1079 40st. deep greenish blue 1·60 30
1080 44st. brown-lake 1·70 40
1081 60st. Indian red 1·90 80
1082 80st. maroon 3·00 2·75
1077/1082 *Set of 6* 8·50 4·25
Designs:—16st. Jan Comenius (educationist) (300th anniv of publication of *Didactica Opera Omnia*); 40st. Carl Linnaeus (botanist, 250th birth anniv); 44st. William Blake (writer, birth bicentenary); 60st. Carlo Goldoni (dramatist, 250th birth anniv); 80st. Auguste Comte (philosopher, death centenary).

(Des B. Angelushev, T. Danov, St. Kunchev and M. Velve. Photo)

1958 (20 Jan–5 July). Holiday Resorts. T **368** and similar horiz designs. P 13.
1083 4st. deep blue (5.7) 20 15
1084 8st. orange-brown (5.7) 20 15
1085 12st. deep green (5.7) 20 15
1086 16st. myrtle green 20 15
a. Perf 11
1087 44st. deep bluish green 50 20
1088 60st. blue 80 30
1089 80st. dull scarlet 95 40
1090 1l. purple-brown (5.7) 1·20 50
1083/1090 *Set of 8* 3·75 1·80
Designs:—4st. Skis and Pirin Mountains; 8st. Old house in Koprivshtitsa; 12st. Hostel at Velingrad; 44st. Hotel at Momin-Prokhod; 60st. Seaside hotel and peninsula, Nesebur; 80st. Beach scene, Varna; 1l. Modern hotels, Varna.

IMPERFORATE STAMPS. Some Bulgarian stamps issued from 1958 (No. 1091) to 1965 exist imperforate from limited printings, sometimes in different colours.

369 Brown Hare

370 Marx and Lenin

(Des V. Korenev (2st., 80st.), V. Tomov (others). Photo)

1958 (5 April). Forest Animals. Designs as T **369**. P 11.
1091 2st. deep olive and light yellow-green 70 20
1092 12st. chestnut and bronze-green 1·20 30
1093 16st. brown and slate-green 1·60 40
1094 44st. yellow-brown and blue 1·90 60
1095 80st. deep brown and yellow-ochre 2·40 80
1096 1l. sepia and slate-blue 3·00 1·20
1091/1096 *Set of 6* 9·75 3·25
Designs: Vert—12st. Roe deer. Horiz—16st. Red deer stag; 44st. Chamois; 80st. Brown bear; 1l. Wild boar.

(Des B. Angelushev. Photo)

1958 (2 June). Seventh Bulgarian Communist Party Congress. T **370** and similar horiz designs. P 11.
1097 12st. sepia 50 20
1098 16st. brown-red 80 30
1099 44st. deep blue 1·60 95
1097/1099 *Set of 3* 2·50 1·30
Designs:—16st. Workers marching with banners; 44st. Lenin blast furnaces.

371 Wrestlers

372 Chessmen and "oval chessboard"

(Des V. Tomov. Photo)

1958 (20 June). Wrestling Championships. P 11.
1100 **371** 60st. brown-lake 2·10 1·50
1101 80st. sepia 2·40 1·90

(Des St. Kunchev. Photo)

1958 (18 July). Fifth World Students' Team Chess Championship, Sofia. P 11.
1102 **372** 80st. blue-green and pale green 11·50 10·50

373 Russian Pavilion

374 Swimmer

(Des P. Rachev. Photo)

1958 (14 Sept). Eighteenth International Fair, Plovdiv. P 11.
1103 **373** 44st. crimson 95 70

(Des I. R. Ivanova (28st.), V. Tomov (others). Photo)

1958 (19 Sept). Bulgarian Students' Games. T **374** and similar designs inscr "1958". P 11.
1104 16st. blue 30 15
1105 28st. bright orange-brown 60 20
1106 44st. bright emerald 85 50
1104/1106 *Set of 3* 1·60 75
Designs: Vert—28st. Dancer; 44st. Volleyball players at net.

375 Onions

376 Insurgent with Rifle

(Des V. Korenev (2st., 16st.), S. Georgiev (12st.), Ana and M. Velev (others). Photo)

1958 (20 Sept). "Agricultural Propaganda". Vert designs as T **375**. P 13.
1107 2st. orange-brown 20 15
1108 12st. deep turquoise 20 15
1109 16st. dull yellowish green 30 20
1110 44st. deep rose-red 50 25
1111 80st. myrtle green 1·20 40
1112 1l. reddish violet 1·60 50
1107/1112 *Set of 6* 3·50 1·50
Designs:—12st. Garlic; 16st. Peppers; 44st. Tomatoes; 80st. Cucumbers; 1l. Aubergines.

(Des S. Sotirov. Photo)

1958 (23 Sept). 35th Anniv of September Uprising. T **376** and similar vert design. P 11.
1113 16st. orange-red 50 30
1114 44st. brown-purple 95 70
Design:—44st. Insurgent helping wounded comrade.

377 Conference Emblem

378 Exhibition Emblem

(Des D. Krustev. Photo)

1958 (24 Sept). First World Trade Unions Young Workers' Conference, Prague. P 11.
1115 **377** 44st. blue 95 70

(Des B. Angelushev. Photo)

1958 (13 Oct). Brussels International Exhibition. P 11.
1116 **378** 1l. blue and black 9·75 9·75

379 Sputnik over Globe

(Des D. Krustev. Photo)

1958 (28 Nov). AIR. International Geophysical Year. P 11.
1117 **379** 80st. turquoise-blue .... 6·75 5·75

380 Running

381 Young Gardeners

(Des L. Zidarov (16st., 44st.), A. Poplilov (others). Photo)

1958 (29 Nov). Balkan Games. Sporting designs as T **380** inscr "1958". P 11.
1118 16st. orange-brown/*flesh* 85 40
1119 44st. olive/*yellow* 95 60
1120 60st. blue/*blue* .... 1·60 70
1121 80st. emerald/*yellow-green* .... 1·90 95
1122 4l. lake/*mauve* .... 11·50 7·25
1118/1122 *Set of* 5 .... 15·00 9·00
Designs: Horiz—44st. Throwing the javelin; 60st. High-jumping; 80st. Hurdling. Vert—4l. Putting the shot.

(Des L. Marinov (8st., 40st.), V. Korenev (12st., 16st.), D. Krustev (44st.). Photo)

1958 (29 Nov). Fourth Dimitrov National Youth Movement Congress. T **381** and similar designs inscr "1958". P 11.
1123 8st. bronze-green 20 15
1124 12st. brown 20 15
1125 16st. brown-purple 20 15
1126 40st. greenish blue 80 20
1127 44st. crimson .... 1·20 50
1123/1127 *Set of* 5 .... 2·30 1·00
Designs: Horiz—12st. Farm girl with cattle; 40st. Youth with wheel-barrow. Vert—16st. Youth with pickaxe and girl with spade; 44st. Communist Party Building.

382 Smirnenski

383 First Cosmic Rocket

(Des B. Angelushev. Photo)

1958 (22 Dec). 60th Birth Anniv of Khristo Smirnenski (poet and revolutionary). P 11.
1128 **382** 16st. brown-red 40 20

(Des D. Krustev. Photo)

1959 (28 Feb). AIR. Launching of First Cosmic Rocket. P 11.
1129 **383** 2l. yellow-brown and blue .... 9·75 9·75

384 Footballers

385 U.N.E.S.C.O. Headquarters, Paris

(Des C. Nikolov. Photo)

1959 (25 Mar). Youth Football Games, Sofia. P 11.
1130 **384** 2l. brown/*cream* .... 3·50 2·40

(Des P. Rachev. Photo)

1959 (28 Mar). Inauguration of Headquarters Building of United Nations Educational, Scientific and Cultural Organization, Paris. P 11.
1131 **385** 2l. purple/*cream* .... 3·50 2·40

386 Skier

45 CT.

(387)

388 Military telegraph linesmen

(Des V. Staikov. Photo)

1959 (28 Mar). Forty Years of Skiing in Bulgaria. P 11.
1132 **386** 1l. blue/*cream* .... 2·40 95

1959 (1 Apr). No. 1110 surch with Type **387**.
1133 45st. on 44st. deep rose-red (B.) .... 1·50 50

(Des St. Kunchev (60st.), G. Kovachev (1l.), A. Poplilov (2l.), M. Peikova (others). Photo)

1959 (4 May). 80th Anmv of First Bulgarian Postage Stamp. Vert designs as T **388** inscr "1879–1959". P 11.
1134 12st. yellow and deep green 20 15
1135 16st. mauve and purple 50 20
1136 60st. yellow and olive-brown 85 40
1137 80st. salmon and brown-red 95 50
1138 1l. light blue and blue .... 2·40 60
1139 2l. chocolate .... 4·75 2·40
1134/1139 *Set of* 6 .... 8·50 3·75
MS1139*a* 91×121 mm. 60st. (+4l.40) orange-yellow and black (as 1136). Imperf (16.5.59) .... 75·00 75·00
MS1139*b* 125×125 mm. Remaining values in different colours (sold at 5l.). Imperf (16.5.59) .... 75·00 75·00
Designs: Horiz—16st. 19th-century mailcoach; 80st. Early postal car; 2l. Riot scene. Vert—60st. First Bulgarian stamp of 1879; 1l. Radio tower.

389 Great Tits

390 Cotton-picking

(Des G. Kovachev (16st.), M. Peikova (45st.), V. Korenev (others). Photo)

1959 (30 June). Birds. Designs as T **389**. P 11.
1140 2st. slate-green and yellow-olive 40 20
1141 8st. bronze-green and brown-orange 70 30
1142 16st. sepia and brown 80 35
1143 45st. black-green and yellow-brown .... 1·80 70
1144 60st. slate-grey and blue .... 3·50 1·20
1145 80st. grey-brown & deep turq-green .... 4·75 1·90
1140/1145 *Set of* 6 .... 11·00 4·25
Birds: Horiz—8st. Hoopoe; 60st. Rock partridge; 80st. European cuckoo. Vert—16st. Great spotted woodpecker; 45st. Grey partridge.

(Des L. Yotov, C. Nikolov, D. Krustev and L. Marinov. Photo)

1959–61. Five Year Plan. Designs as T **390** inscr "1959". P 11 (2l.) or 13 (others).
1146 2st. Indian red (15.6.60) 20 15
1147 4st. yellow-brown (6.61) 20 15
1148 5st. deep green (3.7.59) 20 15
1149 10st. reddish brown (6.61) 20 15
1150 12st. reddish brown (26.9.59) 20 15
1151 15st. deep magenta (9.7.60) 20 15
1152 16st. violet (12.3.60) 20 15
1153 20st. bright orange (25.7.59) 30 20
1154 25st. blue (16.6.60) 30 20
1155 28st. emerald (25.7.59) 40 20
1156 40st. deep turquoise-blue (20.5.60) 50 20
1157 45st. chocolate (12.6.60) 50 20
1158 60st. vermilion (20.5.60) 95 40
1159 80st. bistre (9.6.60) .... 1·70 30
1160 1l. brown-lake (6.7.59) 95 50
a. Perf 11 ....
1161 1l.25 Prussian blue (6.61) .... 3·00 95
a. Perf 11 ....
1162 2l. carmine-red (22.2.60) .... 1·80 60
1146/1162 *Set of* 17 .... 10·50 4·25
Designs: Horiz—2st. Children at play; 10st. Dairymaid milking cow; 16st. Industrial plant; 20st. Combine-harvester; 40st. Hydroelectric barrage; 60st. Furnaceman; 1l.25, Machinist. Vert—4st. Woman doctor examining child; 12st. Tobacco harvesting; 15st. Machinist; 25st. Power linesman; 28st. Tending sunflowers; 45st. Miner; 80st. Fruit picker; 1l. Workers with symbols of agriculture and industry; 2l. Worker with banner.

391 Patriots

392 Piper

(Des B. Angelushev. Photo)

1959 (8 Aug). 300th Anniv of Batak. P 11.
1163 **391** 16st. chocolate 50 20

(Des V. Tomov (16st.), L. Grozeva (1l.), V. Korenev (others). Photo)

1959 (29 Aug). Spartacist Games. Designs as T **392** inscr "1958–1959". P 11.
1164 4st. deep olive/*cream* 20 15
1165 12st. scarlet/*yellow* 20 15
1166 16st. lake/*salmon* 30 20
1167 20st. blue/*pale blue* 50 25
1168 80st. blue-green/*pale green* .... 1·50 60
1169 1l. orange-brown/*orange* .... 1·60 1·10
1164/1169 *Set of* 6 .... 3·75 2·20
Designs: Vert—12st. Gymnasts; 1l. Urn. Horiz—16st. Girls exercising with hoops; 20st. Dancers leaping; 80st. Ballet dancers.

393 Soldiers in Lorry

394 Footballer

(Des B. Angelushev. Photo)

1959 (8 Sept). 15th Anniv of Fatherland Front Government. T **393** and similar designs inscr "1944–1959". P 11.
1170 12st. slate-blue and red 20 15
1171 16st. black-purple and red 20 15
1172 45st. blue and red 40 20
1173 60st. bronze-green and red 50 30
1174 80st. yellow-brown and red 80 40
1175 1l.25 brown and red .... 1·60 70
1170/1175 *Set of* 6 .... 3·25 1·70
Designs: Horiz—16st. Partisans meeting Red Army soldiers; 45st. Blast furnaces; 60st. Tanks; 80st. Combine-harvester in cornfield. Vert—1l.25, Pioneers with banner.

(Des B. Angelushev. Photo)

1959 (10 Oct). 50th Anniv of Football in Bulgaria. P 11.
1176 **394** 1l.25 deep green/*yellow* .... 7·75 7·75

395 Tupolev Tu-104A Jetliner and Statue of Liberty

396 Globe and Letter

(Des B. Angelushev. Photo)

1959 (11 Nov). AIR. Visit of Nikita Khrushchev (Russian Prime Minister) to the United States. P 11.
1177 **395** 1l. pink and blue .... 4·00 4·00

(Des B. Angelushev (45st.), St. Kunchev (1l.25). Photo)

1959 (23 Nov). International Correspondence Week. T **396** and similar vert design inscr "5–11 OKT. 1959". P 11.
1178 45st. black and green 70 20
1179 1l.25 red, black and blue .... 1·30 50
Design:—1l.25, Pigeon and letter.

397 Parachutist

398 N. Vaptsarov

(Des M. Popov. Photo)

1959 (3 Dec). Third Voluntary Defence Congress. P 11.
1180 **397** 1l.25, cream & deep bluish green .... 3·50 1·60

(Des N. Petkov and St. Kunchev. Photo)

1959 (5 Dec). 50th Birth Anniv of Nikola Vaptsarov (poet and revolutionary). P 11.
1181 **398** 80st. brown and yellow-green 95 50

399 Dr. L. Zamenhof

400

(Des B. Angelushev. Photo)

1959 (14 Dec). Birth Centenary of Dr. Ludwig Zamenhof (inventor of Esperanto). P 11.
1182 **399** 1l.25 deep green and apple green .... 1·50 95

(Des St. Kunchev. Photo)

1960 (23 Feb). 50th Anniv of State Opera. T **400** and similar vert design inscr "1908 1958". P 11.
1183 80st. black and green 95 60
1184 1l.25 black and red (Lyre) .... 1·50 85

401 Trajectory of "Lunik 3" around the Moon

(Des B. Angelushev. Photo)

1960 (28 Mar). Flight of "Lunik 3". P 11.
1185 **401** 1l.25 greenish yellow and Prussian blue .... 7·25 5·75

402 Skier

403 Vela Blagoeva

(Des V. Tomov. Photo)

1960 (15 Apr). Winter Olympic Games. P 11.
1186 **402** 2l. brown, blue and black .... 1·50 1·50

(Des B. Angelushev, N. Petkov, L. Zidarov and St. Kunchev. Photo)

1960 (26 Apr). 50th Anniv of International Women's Day. T **403** and similar vert portrait designs inscr "1910–1960". P 11.
1187 16st. deep chestnut and pink 20 15
1188 28st. deep yellow-olive and olive-yellow.. 20 15
1189 45st. blackish green and olive-green........ 40 20
1190 60st. Prussian blue and pale blue 50 30
1191 80st. red-brown and orange-red........ 80 40
1192 1l.25 olive and yellow-ochre 95 80
1187/1192 *Set of* 6........ 2·75 1·80
Portraits:—28st. Anna Maimunkova; 45st. Vela Piskova; 60st. Rosa Luxemburg; 80st. Clara Zetkin; 1l.25, Nadezhda Krupskaya.

404 Lenin

406 Basketball Players

(Des B. Angelushev. Photo)

1960 (10 May). 90th Birth Anniv of Lenin. T **404** and similar horiz design inscr "1870–1960". P 11.
1193 16st. flesh and deep chestnut........ 1·90 80
1194 45st. black and rose-pink........ 3·50 1·60
Design:—45st. "Lenin at Smolny" (writing in chair).

(Des B. Angelushev. Litho)

1960 (3 June). Seventh European Women's Basketball Championships. P 11.
1195 **406** 1l.25 black and yellow .... 1·90 95

407 Moon Rocket

408 Parachutist

(Des St. Goristanova. Litho)

1960 (23 June). AIR. Landing of Russian Rocket on Moon. P 11.
1196 **407** 1l.25 black, yellow and blue........ 7·25 5·75

(Des M. Popov. Photo)

1960 (29 June). World Parachuting Championships, 1960. T **408** and similar design inscr "1960". P 11.
1197 16st. deep violet-blue and lilac........ 60 55
1198 1l.25 claret and greenish blue........ 3·00 1·20
Design:—1l.25, Parachutists descending.

409 Great Yellow Gentian (*Gentiana lutea*)

410 Football

(Des V. Tomov, S. Goristanova and V. Purpov. Photo)

1960 (27 July). Flowers. Vert designs as T **409**. P 11.
1199 2st. yellow-orange, green and drab........ 20 15
1200 5st. carmine, green and yellow-green 80 20
1201 25st. orange, green and salmon........ 85 25
1202 45st. magenta, green and lilac........ 95 30
1203 60st. orange-red, green and buff........ 1·50 40
1204 80st. ultramarine, green and olive-grey .... 1·90 1·50
1199/1204 *Set of* 6........ 5·50 2·50
Flowers:—5st. *Tulipa rhodopea*; 25st. *Lilium jankae*; 45st. *Rhododendron ponticum*; 60st. Lady's slipper (*Cypripedium calceolus*); 80st. *Haberlea rhodopensis*.

(Des B. Angelushev, S. Kunchev, L. Zidarov and T. Danov. Photo)

1960 (29 Aug). Olympic Games. Horiz designs as T **410** inscr "1960". P 11.
1205 8st. pink and brown........ 20 15
1206 12st. pink and violet........ 20 15
1207 16st. pink and turquoise-blue........ 40 20
1208 45st. pink and purple........ 50 25
1209 80st. pink and blue........ 1·10 70
1210 2l. pink and deep green........ 1·50 95
1205/1210 *Set of* 6........ 3·50 2·20
Designs:—12st. Wrestling; 16st. Weightlifting; 45st. Gymnastics; 80st. Canoeing; 2l. Running.

411 Racing Cyclists

(Des B. Angelushev. Litho)

1960 (22 Sept). Tour of Bulgaria Cycle Race. P 11.
1211 **411** 1l. black, yellow and red........ 1·90 1·50

412 Globes

(Des I. Boyadzhiev. Photo)

1960 (12 Oct). 15th Anniv of World Federation of Trades Unions. P 11.
1212 **412** 1l.25 cobalt and blue........ 95 60

413 Popov

414 Y. Veshin

(Des St. Kunchev. Litho)

1960 (12 Oct). Birth Centenary of Aleksandr Popov (Russian radio pioneer). P 11.
1213 **413** 90st. black and greenish blue........ 1·50 95

(Des B. Angelushev. Photo)

1960 (22 Nov). Birth Centenary of Yaroslav Veshin (painter). P 11.
1214 **414** 1l. deep olive and olive-yellow........ 5·75 3·00

415 U.N. Headquarters. New York

416 Boyana Church

(Des D. Krustev. Photo)

1961 (14 Jan). 15th Anniv of United Nations Organization. P 11.
1215 **415** 1l. cream and brown........ 2·40 2·40
MS1215*a* 74×57 mm. **415** 1l. (+ 1l.) rose and olive. Imperf........ 13·50 13·50

(Des St. Kunchev. Photo)

1961 (28 Jan). 700th Anniv of Boyana Murals (1959). T **416** and similar horiz designs. P 11.
1216 60st. black, emerald-green and yellow-green........ 95 40
1217 80st. blackish green, cream and orange.... 1·50 50
1218 1l.25 crimson, cream and yellow-green..... 1·90 95
1216/1218 *Set of* 3........ 4·00 1·70
Designs:—Frescoes of: 80st. Theodor Tiron; 1l.25, Desislava.

417 Cosmic Rocket and Dogs Belka and Strelka

419 Pleven Costume

(Des P. Rachev. Photo)

1961 (28 Jan). AIR. Russian Cosmic Rocket Flight of August, 1960. P 11.
1219 **417** 1l.25 greenish blue and red........ 6·75 6·75

(Des V. Korenev. Litho)

1961 (28 Jan). Provincial Costumes. Vert designs as T **419**. P 11.
1220 12st. yellow, blackish green & salmon........ 20 10
1221 16st. chocolate, buff and lilac........ 20 10
1222 28st. rose, black and turquoise-green........ 40 15
1223 45st. deep blue, vermilion and pale violet-blue........ 80 20
1224 60st. yellow, blue and light blue........ 1·10 30
1225 80st. rose, black-green and yellow .... 1·30 70
1220/1225 *Set of* 6........ 3·50 1·40
Designs:—Costumes of: 12st. Kyustendil; 28st. Sliven; 45st. Sofia; 60st. Rhodope; 80st. Karnobat.

420 Clock Tower, Vratsa

421 Dalmatian Pelican (*Pelecanus crispus*)

(Des B. Angelushev and S. Kunchev (16, 45, 60, 80st.), M. Peikova and G. Kovachev (others). Photo)

1961 (25 Feb). Bulgarian Museums and Monuments. Designs as T **420**. Star and figure of value in red. P 11.
1226 8st. bronze-green........ 20 15
1227 12st. violet........ 20 15
1228 16st. red-brown........ 20 15
1229 20st. blue........ 20 15
1230 28st. greenish blue........ 30 20
1231 40st. red-brown........ 40 25
1232 45st. olive-brown........ 50 30
1233 60st. black........ 70 40
1234 80st. deep yellow-olive........ 1·20 50
1235 1l. deep bluish green........ 1·90 95
1226/1235 *Set of* 10........ 5·25 3·00
Designs: Vert—12st. Clock Tower, Bansko; 20st. "Agushev" building, Mogilitsa (Smolensk). Horiz—28st. Oslekov House, Koprivshtitsa; 40st. Pasha's House, Melnik. 26½×26½ mm—16st. Wine jug; 45st. Lion (bas-relief); 60st. "Horseman of Madara"; 80st. Part of fresco, Bachkovo Monastery; 1l. Coin of Tsar Konstantin-Asen (13th century).

(Des M. Velev (4st.), V. Tomov (80st., 2l.), V. Korenev (others). Photo)

1961 (31 Mar). Birds. Designs as T **421**. P 11.
1236 2st. greenish blue, black and salmon-red........ 25 15
1237 4st. orange, black and apple-green........ 30 20
1238 16st. orange, deep brown and light green 40 30
1239 80st. yellow, deep brown and light turquoise-green........ 3·00 1·10
1240 1l. yellow, deep chocolate and light blue........ 3·50 1·70
1241 2l. yellow, red-brown and light grey-blue........ 4·75 1·90
1236/1241 *Set of* 6........ 11·00 4·75
Birds:—2st. Capercaillie (*Tetrao urogallus*); 16st. Ring-necked pheasant (*Phasianus colchicus*); 80st. Great bustard (*Otis tarda*); 1l. Lammergeier (*Gypaetus barbatus*); 2l. Hazel grouse (*Tetrastes bonasia*).

422 "Communications and Transport"

423 Gagarin and Rocket

(Des P. Rusinov. Photo)

1961 (1 Apr). 50th Anniv of Transport Workers' Union. P 11.
1242 **422** 80st. bluish green and black........ 95 50

(Des V. Popov. Photo)

1961 (26 Apr). AIR. World's First Manned Space Flight. P 11.
1243 **423** 4l. greenish blue, black and red...... 6·75 4·25

424 Shevchenko (poet)

425 Throwing the Discus

(Des P. Rusinov. Photo)

1961 (27 Apr). Death Centenary of Taras Shevchenko (Ukrainian poet). P 11.
1244 **424** 1l. black-brown and yellow-olive ... 6·25 4·25

(Des B. Angelushev and St. Kunchev. Photo)

1961 (15 May). World Students' Games. T **425** and similar designs inscr "FISU 1961". P 11.
1245 4st. cobalt and black........ 20 15
1246 5st. vermilion and black........ 20 15
1247 16st. olive and black........ 30 20
1248 45st. slate-blue and black........ 50 30
1249 1l.25 yellow-brown and black .... 1·70 50
1250 2l. bright reddish violet and black .... 1·90 1·30
1245/1250 *Set of* 6........ 4·25 2·30
MS1250*a* 66×66 mm. 5l. ultramarine, yellow and green (Sports Palace and inscriptions). Imperf...... 19·00 19·00
Designs: Horiz—5st. Tennis; 16st. Fencing; 1l.25, Sports Palace, Sofia. Vert—4st. Water polo; 2l. Basketball.

426 Sea-horse

427 "Space" Dogs

(Des V. Tomov and N. Tuzsuzov. Photo)

1961 (19 June). Black Sea Fauna. T **426** and similar designs. P 11.

1251 2st. deep sepia and green 20 15
1252 12st. pink and greenish blue 20 15
1253 16st. deep violet-blue and cobalt 25 20
1254 45st. brown and light blue 1·50 95
1255 1l. deep slate-blue and green 4·00 1·50
1256 1l.25 red-brown and light blue 4·75 2·40
1251/1256 *Set of 6* 9·75 4·75

Designs: Horiz—2st. Mediterranean monk seals; 12st. Lung jellyfish; 16st. Common dolphins; 1l. Starred sturgeons; 1l.25, Thornback ray.

(Des P. Rusinov (1257), L. Yotov (1258). Photo)

1961. AIR. Space Exploration. T **427** and another design inscr "12.11.1961". P 11.

1257 **427** 2l. slate and brown-purple (29.6) 5·75 4·25
1258 – 2l. blue, yellow and orange (28.6) 10·50 6·75

Design: Vert (24×41½ mm.)—No. 1258, "Venus" rocket in flight.

428 Dimitur Blagoev as Orator

429 Hotel

(Des V. Staikov. Photo)

1961 (5 Aug). 70th Anniv of First Bulgarian Social Democratic Party Congress, Buzludzha. P 11.

1259 **428** 45st. brown-red and cream 30 20
1260 80st. deep blue and pink 70 50
1261 2l. sepia and pale green 1·50 1·20
1259/1261 *Set of 3* 2·30 1·70

(Des T. Danov, V. Yonchev and B. Angelushev. Photo)

1961 (25 Aug). Tourist Issue. T **429** and other vert designs. P 11.

1262 4st. cream, black and yellow-green 10 10
1263 12st. cream, black and light blue (Hikers) 10 10
1264 16st. cream, black and bluish green (Tents) 20 15
1265 1l.25 cream, black and bistre (Climber) 1·20 30
1262/1265 *Set of 4* 1·40 60

430 "The Golden Girl"

431 Major Titov in Space-suit

(Des V. Korenev, L. Zidarov and St. Kunchev. Photo)

1961 (10 Oct). Bulgarian Fables. T **430** and similar horiz designs. P 11.

1266 2st. black, yellow, grey and blue 20 15
1267 8st. grey, black and bright purple 20 15
1268 12st. pink, black and blue-green 25 20
1269 16st. grey, black, light blue and red 95 50
1270 45st. pink, black, grey and olive 1·90 80
1271 80st. crimson, black, grey and yellow-brown 2·40 95
1266/1271 *Set of 6* 5·25 2·50

Designs:—8st. Man and woman ("The Living Water"), 12st. Archer and dragon ("The Golden Apple"); 16st. Horseman ("Krali Marko"; national hero); 45st. Female archer on stag ("Samovila-Vila": fairy); 80st. "Tom Thumb" and cockerel.

(Des P. Rusinov and G. Popov. Photo)

1961 (20 Nov). AIR. Second Russian Manned Space Flight. T **431** and similar horiz design. P 11.

1272 75st. flesh, pale blue and deep olive 4·00 3·00
1273 1l.25 pink, pale blue and violet-blue 4·75 4·00

Design:—1l.25, "Vostok-2" in flight.

432 Caesar's Mushroom (*Amanita caesarea*)

433 Dimitur and Konstantin Miladinov (authors)

(Des M. Parpulova and St. Kunchev. Photo)

1961 (20 Dec). Fungi. T **432** and similar vert designs. Values in black. P 11.

1274 2st. red and bistre 20 15
1275 4st. red-brown and olive-green 20 15
1276 12st. red-brown and bistre 20 15
1277 16st. red-brown and mauve 20 20
1278 45st. red, yellow and orange 30 30
1279 80st. orange and sepia 80 60
1280 1l.25 lavender and chocolate 1·60 80
1281 2l. brown and yellow-brown 2·10 1·90
1274/1281 *Set of 8* 5·00 3·75

Designs:—4st. Red-staining mushroom (*Psalliota silvatica*); 12st. Larch bolete (*Boletus elegans*); 16st. Cep (*Boletus edulis*); 45st. Saffron milk cap (*Lactarius deliciosus*); 80st. Parasol mushroom (*Lepiota procera*); 1l.25, Oyster mushroom (*Pleurotus ostreatus*); 2l. Honey fungus (*Armillariella mellea*).

(Des B. Angelushev. Photo)

1961 (21 Dec). Centenary of Publication of Bulgarian Popular Songs. P 11.

1282 **433** 1l.25 black and olive-green 1·50 95

Currency revaluation

1 New Lev = 10 Old Leva

3 СТ. (**434**)

2 СТ. (**435**)

1962 (1 Jan). Various stamps surch as T **434** or with T **435** (No. 1288).

1283 1st. on 10st. (No. 1149) 20 15
1284 1st. on 12st. (No. 1150) 20 15
1285 2st. on 15st. (No. 1151) 20 15
1286 2st. on 16st. (No. 1152) (R.) 20 15
1287 2st. on 20st. (No. 1153) 20 15
1288 2st. on 20st. (No. 1153) 30 15
1289 3st. on 25st. (No. 1154) (R.) 20 15
a. Surch in black 19·00 19·00
1290 3st. on 28st. (No. 1155) (R.) 20 15
1291 5st. on 44st. (No. 1087) (R.) 30 15
1292 5st. on 44st. (No. 1110) (V.) 30 15
1293 5st. on 45st. (No. 1157) 40 20
1294 10st. on 1l. (No. 1160) (perf 13) 60 30
1295 20st. on 2l. (No. 1162) 1·20 70
1296 40st. on 4l. (No. 889) (V.) 3·00 1·50
1283/1296 *Set of 14* 6·75 3·75

436 Isker River

437 Freighter *Varna*

(Des V. Staikov. Photo)

1962 (3 Feb). AIR. Horiz designs as T **436**. P 13.

1297 1st. deep bluish green and lavender 20 15
1298 2st. deep blue and reddish purple 20 15
1299 3st. red-brown and orange-yellow 20 20
1300 10st. black-green and yellow-bistre 60 25
1301 40st. black-green, blue-green and deep olive 2·30 1·10
1297/1301 *Set of 5* 3·25 1·70

Designs:—2st. Yacht at Varna; 3st. Melnik; 10st. Turnovo; 40st. Pirin Mountains.

(Des M. Velev, N. Tuzsuzov, V. Tomov and V. Popov. Photo)

1962 (1 Mar). Bulgarian Merchant Navy. T **437** and similar horiz designs. Photo. P 11.

1302 1st. turquoise-green and blue 20 10
1303 5st. light blue and green 50 15
1304 20st. violet-blue and greenish blue 1·30 50
1302/1304 *Set of 3* 1·80 70

Ships:—5st. Tanker *Komsomols*; 20st. Liner *Georgi Dimitrov*.

438 Rila Mountains

439 Georgi Dimitrov as Typesetter

(Des V. Korenev, V. Tomov and N. Tuzsuzov. Photo)

1962 (13 Mar)–**63**. T **438** and similar horiz designs. P 13.

1305 1st. deep turquoise-green 20 15
1306 2st. greenish blue 20 15
a. Perf 10½
1307 6st. bright turquoise-blue 40 20
1308 8st. deep bright mauve 60 30
1309 13st. deep olive 1·20 70
1310 1l. myrtle green (6.63) 6·75 1·90
1305/1310 *Set of 6* 8·50 3·00

Designs:—2st. Pirin Mountains; 6st. Fishing boats, Nesebur; 8st. Danube shipping; 13st. Viden Castle; 1l. Rhodope Mts.

(Des M. Peikova (2st.), St. Kunchev (13st.). Photo)

1962 (19 Mar). 80th Anniv of State Printing Office. T **439** and similar vert design inscr "1881–1961". P 11.

1311 2st. red, black and yellow 20 15
1312 13st. black, red-orange and yellow 80 40

Design:—13st. Emblem of Printing Office.

440 Pink Roses

441 "The World United against Malaria"

(Des A. Tuzsuzova and N. Tuzsuzov. Litho)

1962 (28 Mar). Bulgarian Roses. T **440** and similar vert designs. P 11.

1313 1st. pink, green and violet 20 15
a. Perf 10½
1314 2st. carmine-red, green and orange-buff 20 15
1315 3st. carmine-red, green and pale blue 40 20
1316 4st. yellow, blue-green and green 60 25
1317 5st. pink, green and blue 95 30
1318 6st. carmine-red, green and turquoise-green 1·30 70
1319 8st. carmine-red, green and light yellow-green 3·00 1·30
1320 13st. yellow, green and black 5·25 3·75
1313/1320 *Set of 8* 10·50 6·00

(Des B. Angelushev. Photo)

1962 (19 Apr). Malaria Eradication. T **441** and similar horiz design P 11.

1321 5st. yellow, black and orange-brown 60 20
1322 20st. yellow, green and black 1·80 80

Design:—20st. Campaign Emblem.

442 Lenin and Front Page of *Pravda*

443 Text-book and Blackboard

(Des A. Poplilov. Photo)

1962 (5 May). 50th Anniv of *Pravda* Newspaper. P 10.

1323 **442** 5st. indigo, rose-red and black 1·90 1·20

(Des B. Angelushev. Photo)

1962 (21 May). Bulgarian Teachers' Congress. P 10.

1324 **443** 5st. black, yellow and blue 50 20

444 Footballer

445 Dimitrov

(Des V. Tomov. Photo)

1962 (26 May). World Football Championship, Chile. P 11.

1325 **444** 13st. orange-brown, blue-green and black 1·90 95

(Des L. Yotov. Photo)

1962 (18 June). 80th Birth Anniv of Georgi Dimitrov (Prime Minister 1946–49). P 11.

1326 **445** 2st. olive-green 50 20
1327 5st. grey-blue 95 40

446 Bishop

XXXV КОНГРЕС
1962

13 =

(**447**)

(Des St. Kunchev. Litho)

1962 (7 July). 15th Chess Olympiad, Varna. T **446** and similar vert designs inscr "1962". P 11.

1328 1st. green, black and grey 20 15
1329 2st. bistre, black and grey 30 20
1330 3st. reddish violet, black and grey 40 25
1331 13st. brown-orange, black and grey 1·90 80
1332 20st. blue, black and grey 2·50 1·50
1328/1332 *Set of 5* 4·75 2·50
MS1332*a* 76×66 mm. 20st. (+30st.) scarlet and grey-green (Chess pieces). Imperf 14·50 14·50

Designs (chess pieces):—2st. Rook; 3st. Queen; 13st. Knight; 20st. Pawn.

1962 (14 July). 35th Esperanto Congress, Burgas. No. 1061 surch with T **447** in red.

1333 **360** 13st. on 44st. bronze-green 4·75 3·50

448 Festival Emblem

449 Ilyushin Il-18 Airliner

(Des St. Kunchev. Photo)

1962 (18 Aug). World Youth Festival, Helsinki. T **448** and similar horiz design inscr "1962". P 11.

1334 5st. light blue, pink and blue-green 40 20
1335 13st. light blue, reddish violet and grey 1·10 30

Design:—13st. Girl and emblem.

(Des D. Rusinov. Photo)

1962 (18 Aug). AIR. 15th Anniv of TABSO Airline. P 11.

1336 **449** 13st. blue, deep ultramarine and black 1·50 50

450 Apollo (*Parnassius apollo*) **451** K. E. Tsiolkovsky (scientist)

(Des V. Tomov (1st. to 3st.), A. Khof, V. Kantardzhieva, M. Velev and A. Balkanski (others). Photo)

1962 (13 Sept). Butterflies and Moths. T **450** and similar horiz designs. Multicoloured. P 11.

1337 1st. Type **450** ... 20 15
1338 2st. Eastern festoon (*Thais cerisyi*) ... 25 15
1339 3st. Meleager's blue (*Lycaena meleager*). 30 15
1340 4st. Camberwell beauty (*Vanessa antiopa*) ... 40 20
1341 5st. Crimson underwing (*Catocala dilecta*) ... 50 30
1342 6st. Hebe tiger moth (*Arctia hebe*) ... 95 40
1343 10st. Danube clouded yellow (*Colias balcanica*) ... 3·50 1·30
1344 13st. Cardinal (*Argynnis pandora*) ... 4·75 2·40
1337/1344 *Set of* 8 ... 9·75 4·50

(Des P. Rusinov and L. Marinov. Photo)

1962 (24 Sept). AIR. 13th International Astronautics Congress. T **451** and similar horiz design inscr "1962". P 11.

1345 5st. drab and green ... 4·75 1·90
1346 13st. blue and yellow ... 1·90 95
Design:—13st. Moon rocket.

452 Combine Harvester **453** Cover of *History of Bulgaria*

(Des V. Tomov (3st.), V. Korenev (others). Photo)

1962 (1 Nov). Eighth Bulgarian Communist Party Congress. T **452** and similar horiz designs. P 11½.

1347 1st. deep olive and blue-green ... 20 15
1348 2st. greenish blue and bright blue ... 25 20
1349 3st. red-brown and carmine-red ... 30 20
1350 13st. sepia, red and purple ... 1·20 60
1347/1350 *Set of* 4 ... 1·80 1·00
Designs:—2st. Electric train; 3st. Steel furnace; 13st. Blagoev and Dimitrov.

(Des A. Poplilov. Recess)

1962 (9 Dec). Bicentenary of Paisii Khilendarski's *History of Bulgaria*. T **453** and similar design. P 11.

1351 2st. black and olive-green ... 20 15
1352 5st. sepia and chestnut ... 50 20
Design: Horiz—5st. Father Paisii at work on book.

454 Andrian Nikolaev and "Vostok 3" **455** Parachutist

(Des K. Mikhailov and L. Yotov. Photo)

1962 (9 Dec). AIR. First "Team" Manned Space Flight. T **454** and similar horiz designs inscr "1962". P 11.

1353 1st. deep olive, blue and black ... 30 20
1354 2st. deep olive, blue-green and black ... 70 30
1355 40st. pink, greenish blue and black ... 4·00 2·10
1353/1355 *Set of* 3 ... 4·50 2·30
Designs:—2st. Pavel Popovich and "Vostok 4"; 40st. "Vostok 3" and "4" in flight.

(Des K. Mikhailov and L. Yotov. Photo)

1963 (20 Feb)–**64**. T **455** and similar designs.

A. P 10½ (20.2.63)

1356A 1st. lake-red ... 20 10
1357A 1st. deep orange-brown ... 20 10
1358A 1st. deep blue-green ... 20 10
1359A 1st. deep green ... 20 10
1360A 1st. blue ... 20 10
1356A/1360A *Set of* 5 ... 90 45

B. P 11½ (1964)

1356B 1st. lake-red ... 20 10
1357B 1st. deep orange-brown ... 20 10
1358B 1st. deep blue-green ... 20 10
1359B 1st. deep green ... 20 10
1360B 1st. blue ... 20 10
1356B/1360B *Set of* 5 ... 90 45
Designs: Vert—No. 1356, State crest. Horiz—No. 1357, Sofia University; No. 1358, "Vasil Levski" Stadium, Sofia; No. 1359, "The Camels" (archway), Hisar; No. 1360, T **455**.

456 A. Konstantinov **457** Mars and "Mars 1" Space Probe

(Des B. Angelushev. Photo)

1963 (5 Mar). Centenary of Birth of Aleko Konstantinov (author). P 11½.

1361 **456** 5st. deep bluish green, black and red ... 50 30

No. 1361 was issued in sheets with brown *se-tenant* label portraying Bai Ganyu, hero of Konstantinov's works.

(Des L. Yotov and P. Rusinov. Photo)

1963 (5 Mar). AIR. Launching of Soviet Space Station, "Mars 1". T **457** and similar horiz design. P 11½.

1362 5st. rose, pale turquoise-green, black and violet-blue ... 95 50
1363 13st. light salmon, yellow, black and light blue ... 1·90 95
Design:—13st. Release of probe from rocket.

458 Orpheus Restaurant, "Sunny Beach" **459** V. Levski

(Des V. Tomov. Photo)

1963 (12 Mar). Black Sea Coast Resorts. T **458** and similar horiz designs. P 13.

1364 1st. blue (6.63) ... 20 15
1365 2st. vermilion (6.63) ... 95 20
1365*a* 2st. carmine (12.63) ... 7·25 20
b. Perf 11 ...
1366 3st. yellow-brown (6.63) ... 30 20
1367 5st. purple ... 50 20
1368 13st. turquoise (6.63) ... 1·50 40
1369 20st. green (6.63) ... 1·90 50
1364/1369 *Set of* 7 ... 11·50 1·70
Designs: "Sunny Beach"—5st. The Dunes Restaurant; 20st. Hotel. "Golden Sands"—2st., 3st., 13st. Various hotels.

(Des N. Petkov. Photo)

1963 (11 Apr). 90th Anniv of Execution of Vasil Levski (revolutionary). P 10½.

1370 **459** 13st. greenish blue and pale yellow ... 1·90 75

460 Dimitrov, Boy and Girl **461** Eurasian Red Squirrel

(Des V. Tomov. Photo)

1963 (25 Apr). Tenth Dimitrov Communist Youth League Congress, Sofia. T **460** and similar vert design. P 11½.

1371 2st. red-brown, red and black ... 20 15
1372 13st. yellow-brown, turquoise & black ... 80 45
Design:—13st. Girl and youth holding book and hammer aloft.

(Des L. Zidarov, St. Kunchev and B. Angelushev. Litho)

1963 (30 Apr). Woodland Animals. T **461** and similar designs. Figures of value in red. P 11½.

1373 1st. brown and green/*blue-green* ... 20 15
1374 2st. black and green/*yellow* ... 25 15
1375 3st. sepia and olive/*olive-drab* ... 30 20
1376 5st. red-brown and ultramarine/*violet-blue* ... 95 35
1377 13st. black and brown-red/*pink* ... 3·50 65
1378 20st. sepia and blue/*light blue* ... 4·75 1·10
1373/1378 *Set of* 6 ... 9·00 2·30
Animals: Horiz—2st. East European hedgehog; 3st. Marbled polecat; 5st. Beech marten; 13st. Eurasian badger. Vert—20st. European otter.

462 Wrestling **463** Congress Emblem and Allegory

(Des L. Marinov and V. Popov. Photo)

1963 (31 May). 15th International Open Wrestling Championships, Sofia. T **462** and similar design. P 11½.

1379 5st. bistre and black ... 50 20
1380 20st. orange-brown and black ... 1·50 85
Design: Horiz—20st. As T **462** but different hold.

(Des V. Korenev. Photo)

1963 (24 June). World Women's Congress, Moscow. P 11½.

1381 **463** 20st. light blue and black ... 1·50 55

464 Esperanto Star and Sofia Arms **465** Rocket, Globe and Moon

(Des St. Kunchev. Photo)

1963 (29 June). 48th World Esperanto Congress, Sofia. P 11½.

1382 **464** 13st. multicoloured ... 1·50 55

(Des P. Rusinov and V. Popov. Photo)

1963 (22 July). Launching of Soviet Moon Rocket "Luna 4". T **465** and similar vert designs inscr "2.IV.1963". P 11½.

1383 1st. pale ultramarine ... 20 10
1384 2st. bright purple ... 20 10
1385 3st. greenish blue ... 20 10
1383/1385 *Set of* 3 ... 55 25
Designs:—2st. Tracking equipment; 3st. Sputniks.

MOSTRA EUROPEISTICA·1963
RICCIONE

466 Valery Bykovsky in Spacesuit (**467**)

(Des V. Tomov, N. Tuzsuzov, V. Korenev and St. Goristanova. Photo)

1963 (26 Aug). AIR. Second "Team" Manned Space Flights. T **466** and similar horiz designs. P 11½.

1386 1st. greenish blue and lilac ... 20 10
1387 2st. brown and light yellow ... 30 15
1388 5st. red and light red ... 50 20
1389 20st. +10st. olive-green and light blue ... 2·40 1·10
1386/1389 *Set of* 4 ... 3·00 1·40
MS1389*a* 79×68 mm. 50st. purple and red-brown (Spassky Tower and Globe). Imperf ... 4·75 4·25
Designs:—2st. Valentina Tereshkova in spacesuit; 5st. Globe; 20st. Bykovsky and Tereshkova.

1963 (31 Aug). Europa Fair, Riccione (Italy). Nos. 1314/15 and 1318 (Roses) optd as T **467** or additionally surch.

1390 2st. carmine-red, green and orange-buff (G.) ... 50 20
1391 5st. on 3st. carmine-red, green and pale blue (B.) ... 70 35
1392 13st. on 6st. carmine-red, green and turquoise-green ... 1·70 55
1390/1392 *Set of* 3 ... 2·50 1·00

468 Relay-racing

(Des V. Tomov. Photo)

1963 (13 Sept). Balkan Games. T **468** and similar horiz designs. Flags in red, yellow, blue, green and black. P 11½.

1393 1st. green ... 10 10
1394 2st. violet ... 15 10
1395 3st. greenish blue ... 20 15
1396 5st. brown-red ... 95 20
1397 13st. brown ... 4·00 3·00
1393/1397 *Set of* 5 ... 4·75 3·25
MS1397*a* 74×69 mm. 50st. black and olive (as T **468**). Imperf ... 7·00 7·00
Designs:—2st. Throwing the hammer; 3st. Long jumping; 5st. High jumping; 13st. Throwing the discus. Each design includes the flags of the competing countries.

469 Slavonic Scroll **470** Insurgents

(Des B. Angelushev. Litho)

1963 (19 Sept). Filth International Slav Congress, Sofia. P 10½.

1398 **469** 5st. vermilion, pale yellow and deep olive-green ... 50 20

(Des V. Korenev. Litho)

1963 (21 Sept). 40th Anniv of September Uprising. P 11½.

1399 **470** 2st. black and vermilion ... 30 15

471 *Aquilegia aurea*

472 Khristo Smirnenski

(Des D. Rusinov. Litho)

1963 (9 Oct). Nature Protection. T **471** and similar vert floral designs. Flowers in natural colours; background colours below. P 11½ (1st.) or 10½ (others).

1400	1st. greenish blue	20	15
1401	2st. grey-olive	20	15
1402	3st. olive-yellow	20	15
1403	5st. blue	40	20
1404	6st. bright purple	50	35
1405	8st. light grey	95	45
1406	10st. light mauve	1·90	85
1407	13st. deep yellow-olive	3·50	1·10
1400/1407	*Set of 8*	7·00	3·00

Flowers:—2st. Edelweiss (*Leontopodium alpinum*); 3st. *Primula deorum*; 5st. White water-lily (*Nimphaea alba*); 6st. Tulip (*Tulipa urumovii*); 8st. *Viola delphinantha*; 10st. Alpine clematis (*Clematis alpina*). 13st. *Anenome narcissiflora*.

(Des L. Yotov. Litho)

1963 (28 Oct). 65th Anniv of Birth of Smirnenski (poet and revolutionary). P 10½.

1408	**472** 13st. black and lilac	95	45

473 Chariot Horses (wall-painting)

474 Hemispheres and Centenary Emblem

(Des S. Kunchev, R. Stanoeva and A. Sertev. Litho)

1963 (28 Dec). Thracian Tombs, Kazanlik. Vert designs as T **473**. P 10½.

1409	1st. red, yellow and grey	20	15
1410	2st. reddish violet, yellow and grey	20	15
1411	3st. greenish blue, yellow and grey	20	15
1412	5st. brown, yellow and dull green	40	35
1413	13st. black, yellow and dull green	1·10	55
1414	20st. reddish purple, yellow and dull green	1·90	85
1409/1414	*Set of 6*	3·50	2·00

Designs (wall-paintings on tombs):—2st. Chariot race; 3st. Flautists; 5st. Tray-bearer; 13st. Funeral feast; 20st. Seated woman.

ZARSKA BULGARSKA POSTA. Labels with this inscription are bogus issues produced in Madrid in 1963–64.

(Des B. Angelushev. Litho)

1964 (27 Jan). Red Cross Centenary. T **474** and similar horiz designs. Cross in red. P 10½.

1415	1st. olive-yellow and black	20	15
1416	2st. bright blue and black	20	15
1417	3st. slate-blue, black and grey	20	15
1418	5st. greenish blue and black	30	20
1419	13st. black and yellow-orange	1·30	55
1415/1419	*Set of 5*	2·00	1·10

Designs:—2st. Blood donation; 3st. Bandaging wrist; 5st. Nurse; 13st. Henri Dunant.

475 Speed-skating

476 Head (2nd cent)

(Des R. Stanoeva, A. Sertev and D. Vlaev. Photo)

1964 (21 Feb). Winter Olympic Games, Innsbruck. Various horiz designs as T **475**. P 10½.

1420	1st. deep blue, orange-brown and light blue	20	15
1421	2st. olive-green, mauve and black	20	15
1422	3st. deep bluish green, orange-brown and black	20	15
1423	5st. multicoloured	40	20
1424	10st. red-orange, black and brownish grey	80	45
1425	13st. olive, red and grey	95	55
1420/1425	*Set of 6*	2·50	1·50
MS1425*a*	64×67 mm. 50st. red, turquoise-blue and greenish grey (Girl skater). Imperf	6·50	6·50

Designs:—2st. Figure skating; 3st. Cross-country skiing; 5st. Ski jumping. Ice hockey—10st. Goalkeeper; 13st. Players.

(Des B. Angelushev and St. Kunchev. Photo)

1964 (14 Mar). 2,500 Years of Bulgarian Art. T **476** and similar horiz designs. Borders in grey. P 10½.

1426	1st. deep bluish green and red	20	15
1427	2st. deep olive-black and red	20	15
1428	3st. bistre-brown and red	20	15
1429	5st. greenish blue and red	30	20
1430	6st. orange-brown and red	60	25
1431	8st. brown-red and red	85	35
1432	10st. yellow-olive and red	95	40
1433	13st. olive and red	1·20	1·00
1426/1433	*Set of 8*	4·00	2·40

Designs:—2st. Horseman (1st to 4th cent); 3st. Jug (19th cent); 5st. Buckle (19th cent); 6st. Pot (19th cent); 8st. Angel (17th cent); 10st. Animals (8th to 10th cent); 13st. Peasant woman (20th cent).

477 "The Unborn Maid"

478 Turkish Lacewing (*Ascalaphus otomanus*)

(Des St. Kunchev and V. Korenev. Photo)

1964 (17 Apr). Folk Tales. T **477** and similar horiz designs. Multicoloured. P 10½.

1434	1st. Type **477**	20	15
	a. Perf 11½		
1435	2st. "Grandfather's Glove"	20	15
1436	3st. "The Big Turnip"	20	15
1437	5st. "The Wolf and the Seven Kids"	30	20
1438	8st. "Cunning Peter"	60	35
1439	13st. "The Loaf of Corn"	1·60	55
1434/1439	*Set of 6*	2·75	1·40

(Des M. Peikova and V. Vasileva. Photo)

1964 (16 May). Insects. T **478** and similar designs. P 11½.

1440	1st. black yellow and Venetian red	20	15
1441	2st. black, yellow-brown and deep bluish green	20	15
1442	3st. deep green, black and drab	25	20
1443	5st. violet, black and yellow-olive	90	35
1444	13st. yellow-brown black and bluish violet	1·80	55
1445	20st. orange-yellow, black and slate-blue	3·00	75
1440/1445	*Set of 6*	5·75	1·90

Insects: Vert—2st. Thread lacewing fly (*Nemoptera coa*); 5st. Alpine longhorn beetle (*Rosalia alpina*); 13st. Cockchafer (*Anisoplia austriaca*). Horiz—3st. Cricket (*Saga natalia*); 20st. Hunting wasp (*Scolia flavitrons*).

479 Football

(Des St. Kunchev and V. Korenev. Photo)

1964 (8 June). 50th Anniv of Levski Physical Culture Association. Multicoloured. P 11½.

1446	2st. Type **479**	20	10
1447	13st. Handball	1·20	55
MS1447*a*	60×60 mm. 60st. grey-green and orange-yellow (Cup and Map of Europe). Imperf	4·50	4·25

480 Title Page and Petur Beron (author)

(Des B. Angelushev. Photo)

1964 (22 June). 140th Anniv of First Bulgarian Primer. P 11½.

1448	**480** 20st. black and orange-brown	2·20	2·20

481 Stephenson's *Rocket*

(Des M. Peikova and V. Vasileva. Photo)

1964 (1 July). Railway Transport. T **481** and similar horiz designs. Multicoloured. P 11½.

1449	1st. Type **481**	20	15
1450	2st. Steam locomotive	20	15
1451	3st. Diesel locomotive	20	15
1452	5st. Electric locomotive	35	20
1453	8st. Steam train on bridge	90	45
1454	13st. Diesel train emerging from tunnel	1·30	1·10
1449/1454	*Set of 6*	2·75	2·00

482 Alsatian

(483)

(Des B. Angelushev, M. Peikova and V. Vasileva. Photo)

1964 (20 Aug). Dogs. Various horiz designs as T **482**. Multicoloured. P 11½.

1455	1st. Type **482**	20	15
1456	2st. Setter	25	15
1457	3st. Poodle	35	20
1458	4st. Pomeranian	45	25
1459	5st. St. Bernard	60	35
1460	6st. Fox terrier	90	55
1461	10st. Pointer	3·50	1·60
1462	13st. Dachshund	4·50	3·25
1455/1462	*Set of 8*	9·75	5·75

1964 (22 Aug). AIR. International Cosmic Exhibition, Riccione (Italy). No. 1386 surch with T **483** and No. 1387 with similar surch in Italian.

1463	10st. on 1st. greenish blue and lilac (C.)	45	45
1464	20st. on 2st. brown & light yellow (G.)	1·30	65

484 Partisans and Flag

(Des A. Poplilov Photo)

1964 (9 Sept). 20th Anniv of Fatherland Front Government. T **484** and similar horiz designs. Flag in red. P 11½.

1465	1st. blue and light blue	20	15
1466	2st. olive-brown and light bistre	20	15
1467	3st. lake and mauve	20	15
1468	4st. bluish violet and lavender	20	15
1469	5st. red-brown and yellow-orange	20	15
1470	6st. blue and light greenish blue	35	20
1471	8st. blue-green and light grey-green	70	35
1472	13st. red-brown and salmon-pink	90	55
1465/1472	*Set of 8*	2·75	1·70

Designs:—2st. Greeting Soviet troops; 3st. Soviet Aid—arrival of goods; 4st. Industrial plant, Kremikovtsi; 5st. Combine-harvester; 6st "Peace" campaigners; 8st. Soldier of National Guard; 13st. Blagoev and Dimitrov. All with flag as T **484**.

(485)

486 "Transport"

1964 (13 Sept). 21st International Fair, Plovdiv. No. 1020*a* surch with T **485**.

1473	20st. on 44st. dull orange	1·80	75

(Des St. Kunchev. Photo)

1964 (3 Oct). First National Stamp Exhibition, Sofia. P 11½.

1474	**486** 20st. light blue	1·60	1·10

No. 1474 was issued in sheets of 12 stamps, 12 labels depicting a woman's head with inscription, and one centre label depicting a stylized bird.

487 Gymnastics

488 Vrattsata

(Des B. Angelushev. Photo)

1964 (10 Oct). Olympic Games, Tokyo T **487** and similar designs. Rings and values in red. P 11½.

1475	1st. deep green and light green	20	15
1476	2st. ultramarine and lavender	20	15
1477	3st. brown and turquoise-blue	20	15
1478	5st. violet and rose-pink	35	20
1479	13st. turquoise-blue and light blue	1·20	35
1480	20st. deep green and yellow-buff	1·30	75
1475/1480	*Set of 6*	3·00	1·60
MS1480*a*	61×67 mm. 40st.+20st. ochre, vermilion and new blue (Rings, track, etc.). Imperf	5·75	5·50

Designs:—2st. Long jump; 3st. Swimmer on starting block; 5st. Football; 13st. Volleyball; 20st. Wrestling.

(Des V. Popov, L. Marinov and P. Rusinov Photo)

1964 (26 Oct). Landscapes. T **488** and similar vert designs. P 12½×13½.

1481	1st. deep slate-green	20	15
1482	2st. light brown	20	15
1483	3st. blue	20	15
1484	4st. red-brown	25	15
1485	5st. deep bluish green	45	20
1486	6st. deep bluish violet	70	35
1481/1486	*Set of 6*	1·80	1·00

Views:—2st. The Ritli; 3st. Maliovitsa; 4st. Broken rocks, 5st. Erkyupria; 6st. Rhodope mountain pass.

489 Paper and Cellulose Factory, Bukovtsi

490 Rila Monastery

(Des M. Peikova and V. Vasileva. Photo)

1964 (7 Dec). AIR. Industrial Buildings. T **489** and similar horiz designs. P 13.

1487	8st. greenish blue	45	15
1488	10st. bright purple	60	20
1489	13st. violet	70	25
1490	20st. Prussian blue	1·30	55
1491	40st. bronze-green	2·20	75
1487/1491 *Set of 5*		4·75	1·70

Designs:—10st. Metal works, Plovdiv; 13st. Metallurgical works, Kremikovtsi; 20st. Petrol refinery, Burgas; 40st. Fertiliser factory, Stara-Zagora.

(Des V. Staikov. Photo)

1964 (22 Dec). Philatelic Exhibition for Franco-Bulgarian Amity. T **490** and similar design. P 11½.

1492	5st. black and drab	55	25
1493	13st. black and cobalt	1·30	65

Design:—13st. Nôtre-Dame, Paris (inscriptions in French).

491 500-year-old Walnut

492

(Des V. Staikov. Photo)

1964 (28 Dec). Ancient Trees. T **491** and similar vert designs. Values and inscriptions in black. P 11½.

1494	1st. Venetian red and pale cream	20	15
1495	2st. maroon and pale salmon	20	15
1496	3st. bistre-brown and pale yellow	20	15
1497	4st. grey-blue and pale blue	20	15
1498	10st. green and pale green	90	35
1499	13st. deep olive-green & pale yell-grn	1·30	45
1494/1499 *Set of 6*		2·75	1·30

Trees:—2st. Plane (1000 yrs.); 3st. Plane (600 yrs.); 4st. Poplar (800 yrs.); 10st. Oak (800 yrs.); 13st. Fir (1200 yrs.).

(Des S. Markov. Photo)

1964 (30 Dec). Eighth Congress of International Union of Students, Sofia. P 11½.

1500	**492**	13st. black and pale blue	90	55

493 Bulgarian Veteran and Soviet Soldier (sculpture by T. Zlatarev)

494 "Gold Medal"

(Des L. Marinov. Photo)

1965 (15 Jan). 30 Years of Bulgarian–Russian Friendship. P 11½.

1501	**493**	2st. red and black	45	20

(Des S. Sotirov. Photo)

1965 (27 Jan). Olympic Games, Tokyo (1964). P 11½.

1502	**494**	20st. black, gold and orange-brown	1·30	75

495 Vladimir Komarov

(Des L. Yotov and P. Rusinov. Photo)

1965 (15 Feb). Flight of "Voskhod 1". T **495** and similar designs. Multicoloured. P 11½.

1503	1st. Type **495**	20	15
1504	2st. Konstantin Feoktistov	20	15
1505	5st. Boris Yegorov	25	20
1506	13st. The three astronauts	1·10	35
1507	20st. "Voskhod 1"	1·30	55
1503/1507 *Set of 5*		2·75	1·30

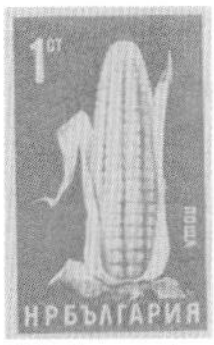
496 Corn-cob

497 "Victory against Fascism"

(Des V. Tomov and M. Velev. Photo)

1965 (1 Apr). Agricultural Products. T **496** and similar vert designs. P 12½×13½.

1508	1st. orange-yellow	15	10
1509	2st. light blue-green	20	10
1510	3st. red-orange	25	10
1511	4st. yellow-olive	35	15
1512	5st. cerise	40	15
1513	10st. turquoise-blue	45	20
1514	13st. bistre	1·30	35
1508/1514 *Set of 7*		2·75	1·00

Designs:—2st. Ears of wheat; 3st. Sunflowers; 4st. Sugar beet; 5st. Clover; 10st. Cotton; 13st. Tobacco.

(Des D. Rusinov and B. Dimitrov. Photo)

1965 (16 Apr). 20th Anniv of "Victory of 9 May, 1945". T **497** and similar horiz design. P 11½.

1515	5st. black, bistre and grey	20	10
1516	13st. blue, black and grey	70	45

Design:—13st. Globes on dove ("Peace").

498 Bullfinch (*Pyrrhula pyrrhula*)

499 Transport, Globe and Whale

(Des St. Kunchev and V. Korenev. Litho)

1965 (20 Apr). Song Birds. T **498** and similar vert designs. Multicoloured. P 11½.

1517	1st. Type **498**	20	15
1518	2st. Golden oriole (*Oriolus oriolus*)	25	15
1519	3st. Rock thrush (*Monticola saxatilis*)	35	15
1520	5st. Barn swallows (*Hirundo rustica*)	60	20
1521	8st. Common roller (*Coracias garrulus*)	70	55
1522	10st. Goldfinch (*Carduelis carduelis*)	2·50	90
1523	13st. Rose-coloured starling (*Pastor roseus*)	2·75	1·70
1524	20st. Nightingale (*Luscinia megarhynchos*)	3·75	3·50
1517/1524 *Set of 8*		10·00	6·50

(Des St. Kunchev. Photo)

1965 (30 Apr). Fourth International Transport Conference, Sofia. P 11½.

1525	**499**	13st. silver, blue, magenta and yellow	1·90	1·10

500 I.C.Y. Emblem

501 I.T.U. Emblem and Symbols

(Des St. Kunchev. Litho)

1965 (15 May). International Co-operation Year. P 11½.

1526	**500**	20st. red-orange, olive and black	1·40	80

(Des St. Kunchev. Photo)

1965 (17 May). Centenary of International Telecommunications Union. P 11½.

1527	**501**	20st. yellow, green and light blue	1·40	80

502 Pavel Belyaev and Aleksei Leonov

(Des S. Sotirov and V. Tomov. Litho)

1965 (20 May). Space Flight of "Voskhod 2". T **502** and similar horiz designs inscr "18 III 1965". P 11½.

1528	2st. deep purple, deep bluish green and light drab	45	20
1529	20st. slate-violet, black, ol-grn & grey	3·75	1·50

Design:—20st. Leonov in space.

503 Sting Ray

504 Marx and Lenin

(Des D. Rusinov and B. Dimitrov. Litho)

1965 (10 June). Fishes. T **503** and similar horiz designs. Borders in grey. P 11½.

1530	1st. gold, black and orange	10	10
1531	2st. silver, indigo and bright blue	20	10
1532	3st. gold, black and green	30	15
1533	5st. gold, black and carmine	45	20
1534	10st. silver, indigo and bright turquoise-blue	2·00	1·00
1535	13st. gold, black and Venetian red	2·50	1·30
1530/1535 *Set of 6*		5·00	2·50

Fishes:—2st. Belted bonito; 3st. Scorpion-fish; 5st. Gurnard; 10st. Horse mackerel; 13st. Turbot.

(Des V. Tomov. Photo)

1965 (30 June). Organization of Socialist Countries' Postal Ministers' Conference, Peking. P 10½.

1536	**504**	13st. brown and orange-red	1·40	90

505 Film and Screen

506 Quinces

(Des R. Stanoeva and A. Sertev. Photo)

1965 (30 June). Balkan Film Festival, Varna. P 10½.

1537	**505**	13st. black, silver-gilt and greenish blue	95	35

(Des Z. Taseva. Photo)

1965 (1 July). Fruits, etc. T **506** and similar vert designs. P 13.

1538	1st. red-orange	10	10
1539	2st. yellow-olive (Grapes)	10	10
1540	3st. yellow-bistre (Pears)	20	10
1541	4st. yellow-orange (Plums)	30	10
1542	5st. carmine (Strawberries)	35	20
1543	6st. yellow-brown (Walnuts)	45	35
1538/1543 *Set of 6*		1·40	85

507 Ballerina

508 Dove, Emblem and Map

(Des R. Stanoeva and A. Sertev. Photo)

1965 (10 July). Ballet Competitions, Varna. P 10½.

1544	**507**	5st. black and magenta	1·90	1·10

(Des St. Kunchev. Photo)

1965 (23 July–7 Aug). Balkanphila Stamp Exhibition, Varna. T **508** and similar horiz designs. P 10½.

1545	1st. silver, ultramarine and greenish yellow	10	10
1546	2st. silver, reddish violet and greenish yellow	15	10
1547	3st. gold, blue-green and greenish yellow	30	20
1548	13st. gold, brown-red and greenish yellow	1·40	1·30
1549	20st. bistre-brown, light blue and silver (7 Aug)	1·90	1·70
1545/1549 *Set of 5*		3·50	3·00
MS1550	71×62 mm. 40st. gold and greenish blue (T **508**). Imperf	4·25	4·00

Designs: As T **508**—2st. Yacht emblem; 3st. Stylized fish and flowers; 13st. Stylized sun, planet and rocket. 45×25½ mm—20st. Cosmonauts Pavel Belyaev and Aleksei Leonov.

509 Escapers in Boat

(510)

(Des St. Kunchev. Photo)

1965 (23 July). 40th Anniv of Political Prisoners' Escape from "Bolshevik Island". P 10½.

1551	**509**	2st. black and slate	45	20

1965 (12 Aug). National Folklore Competition. No. 1084 surch with T **510**.

1552	2st. on 8st. orange-brown	2·20	2·20

511 Gymnast

512 Dressage

(Des M. Peikova and G. Kovachev. Photo)

1965 (14 Aug). Balkan Games. T **511** and similar vert designs. P 10½.

1553	1st. black and scarlet	20	15
1554	2st. deep purple, black and reddish purple	20	15
1555	3st. brown-purple, black and cerise	20	15
1556	5st. orange-brown, black and light red	30	20
1557	10st. deep purple, black and magenta	1·00	45
1558	13st. purple, black & lt reddish purple	1·10	55

1553/1558 *Set of 6* .... 2·75 1·50
Designs:—2st. Gymnastics on bars; 3st. Weightlifting; 5st. Rally car and building; 10st. Basketball; 13st. Rally car and map.

(Des S. Sotirov. Photo)

1965 (30 Sept). Horsemanship. T **512** and similar horiz designs. P 10½.

1559 1st. plum, black & light greyish blue 20 15
1560 2st. brown-red, black and ochre 20 15
1561 3st. crimson, black and light greyish brown 20 15
1562 5st. lake-brown, deep green and sage-green 65 20
1563 10st. deep lake-brown, black and pale grey .... 2·75 1·30
1564 13st. deep lake-brown, deep bluish green and orange-brown .... 3·25 1·70
1559/1564 *Set of 6* .... 6·50 3·25
MS1565 80×80 mm. 40+20st. plum and pale bluish grey (as 13st.). Imperf .... 6·00 5·50
Designs:—5st. Horse-racing; others, Horse-jumping (various).

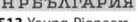

513 Young Pioneers

514 Junkers Ju 52/3m over Turnovo

(Des Z. Taseva. Photo)

1965 (24 Oct). Dimitrov Septembrist Pioneers Organization. T **513** and similar vert designs. P 10½.

1566 1st. yellow-green and turquoise-blue 20 15
1567 2st. mauve and bluish violet 20 15
1568 3st. yellow-bistre and yellow-olive 20 15
1569 5st. yellow-ochre and blue 30 20
1570 8st. orange and bistre-brown 95 45
1571 13st. reddish violet and crimson .... 1·40 80
1566/1571 *Set of 6* .... 3·00 1·70
Designs:—2st. Admitting recruit; 3st. Camp bugler; 5st. Flying model airplane; 8st. Girls singing; 13st. Young athlete.

(Des D. Rusinov and B. Dimitrov. Photo)

1965 (25 Nov). Bulgarian Civil Aviation. T **514** and similar horiz designs. P 10½.

1572 1st. black, grey, new blue and red 20 15
1573 2st. black, grey, reddish lilac and red 20 15
1574 3st. black, grey, light blue and red 20 15
1575 5st. black, grey, orange-yellow and red 35 20
1576 13st. black, grey, ochre and red .... 1·10 45
1577 20st. black, grey, emerald and red .... 1·90 80
1572/1577 *Set of 6* .... 3·50 1·70
Designs:—2st. Ilyushin Il-14M airliner over Plovdiv; 3st. Mil Mi-4 helicopter over Dimitrovgrad; 5st. Tupolev Tu-104A jetliner over Ruse; 13st. Ilyushin Il-18 airliner over Varna; 20st. Tupolev Tu-114 airliner over Sofia.

515 Women of N. and S. Bulgaria

516 I.Q.S.Y. Emblem and Earth's Radiation Zones

(Des S. Sotirov. Photo)

1965 (6 Dec). 80th Anniv of Union of North and South Bulgaria (Eastern Roumelia). P 10½.

1578 **515** 13st. black and bright green 95 80

(Des St. Kunchev. Photo)

1965 (15 Dec). International Quiet Sun Year. T **516** and similar horiz designs. P 10½.

1579 1st. yellow, grey-green and bright blue 20 15
1580 2st. yellow, lake-brown, red and light purple 20 15
1581 13st. yellow, blue-green, black and greenish blue .... 1·20 45
1579/1581 *Set of 3* .... 1·40 70
Designs:—I.Q.S.Y. emblem and—2st. Sun and solar flares; 13st. Total eclipse of the Sun.

517 "Spring Greetings"

518 Byala Bridge

(Des Neva and Nikola Tuzsuzov. Photo)

1966 (10 Jan). "Spring". National Folklore. T **517** and similar vert designs. P 10½.

1582 1st. mauve, ultramarine and olive-grey 20 15
1583 2st. red, black and drab 20 15
1584 3st. violet, red and olive-grey 20 15
1585 5st. red, light reddish violet and black 30 20
1586 8st. purple, purple-brown & light pur 55 30
1587 13st. mauve, black and new blue .... 1·10 35
1582/1587 *Set of 6* .... 2·30 1·20
Designs:—2st. Drummer; 3st. "Birds" (stylized); 5st. Folk dancer; 8st. Vase of flowers; 13st. Bagpiper.

(Des V. Korenev. Photo)

1966 (10 Feb). Ancient Monuments. T **518** and similar horiz designs. P 13.

1588 1st. turquoise-blue 20 15
1589 1st. emerald 20 15
1590 2st. olive-green 20 15
1591 2st. brown-purple 20 15
1592 8st. lake-brown 55 20
1593 13st. deep blue 95 45
1588/1593 *Set of 6* .... 2·10 1·10
Designs:—No. 1588, Type **518**; 1589, Svilengrad Bridge; 1590, Fountain, Samokov; 1591, Ruins of Matochina Castle, Khaskovo; 1592, Cherven Castle, Ruse; 1593, Café, Bozhentsi, Gabrovo.

519 "Christ" (from fresco, Boyana Church)

520 "The First Gunshot" at Koprivshtitsa

(Des adapted by S. Kunchev. Litho Kultura, Budapest)

1966 (25 Feb). "2,500 Years of Culture". T **519** and similar designs. P 11½.

1594 1st. multicoloured .... 3·75 3·25
1595 2st. multicoloured 35 35
1596 3st. multicoloured 45 40
1597 4st. multicoloured 55 45
1598 5st. multicoloured 65 55
1599 13st. multicoloured .... 95 1·00
1600 20st. multicoloured .... 1·40 1·10
1594/1600 *Set of 7* .... 7·25 6·50
Designs: Horiz—2st. "Destruction of the Idols" (from fresco, Boyana Church); 4st. Zemen Monastery. Vert—3st. Bachkovo Monastery; 5st. John the Baptist Church, Nesebur; 13st. "Nativity" (icon, Aleksandr Nevski Cathedral, Sofia); 20st. "Virgin and Child" (icon, Archaeological Museum, Sofia).

(Des M. Peikova and G. Kovachev. Photo)

1966 (3 Mar). 90th Anniv of April Uprising. T **520** and similar horiz designs. Central designs in black. P 10½.

1601 1st. lake-brown and gold 20 15
1602 2st. red and gold 20 15
1603 3st. olive-green and gold 20 15
1604 5st. turquoise-blue and gold 25 15
1605 10st. bright purple and gold 65 20
1606 13st. bluish violet and gold 75 55
1601/1606 *Set of 6* .... 2·00 1·20
Designs:—2st. Georgi Benkovski and Todor Kableshkov; 3st. "Showing the flag" at Panagyurishte; 5st. Vasil Petleshkov and Tsanko Dyustabanov; 10st. Landing of Khristo Botev's detachment at Kozlodui; 13st. Panayot Volov and Ilarion Dragostinov.

521 Luna reaching for the Moon

(Des A. Denkov. Photo)

1966 (29 Apr). Moon Landing of "Luna 9". Sheet 70×50 mm. Imperf.
MS1607 **521** 60st. silver, black and crimson .... 5·50 5·50

522 W.H.O. Building

523 Worker

(Des St. Kunchev. Photo)

1966 (3 May). Inauguration of World Health Organization Headquarters, Geneva. P 10½.

1608 **522** 13st. blue and silver .... 1·10 55

(Des S. Sotirov. Photo)

1966 (9 May). Sixth Trade Unions Congress, Sofia. P 10½.

1609 **523** 20st. grey-black and pink .... 1·40 80

524 Indian Elephant

525 Boy and Girl holding Banners

(Des Z. Taseva. Litho and photo)

1966 (23 May). Sofia Zoo Animals. T **524** and similar horiz designs. Multicoloured. P 10½.

1610 1st. Type **254** 20 15
1611 2st. Tiger 20 15
1612 3st. Chimpanzee 20 15
1613 4st. Ibex 30 20
1614 5st. Polar bear 95 35
1615 8st. Lion .... 1·10 55
1616 13st. American bison .... 3·25 1·70
1617 20st. Eastern grey kangaroo .... 4·25 2·20
1610/1617 *Set of 8* .... 9·50 5·00

(Des Zh. Kosturkova and N. Petkov. Photo)

1966 (25 May). Third Congress of Bulgarian Sports Federation. P 10½.

1618 **525** 13st. greenish blue, red-orange and light blue 95 55

526 River Paddle-steamer *Radetski* and Pioneer

527 Standard-bearer Simov-Kuruto

(Des I. Kosev. Photo)

1966 (28 May). 90th Anniv of Khristo Botev's Seizure of Paddle-steamer *Radetski*. P 10½.

1619 **526** 2st. multicoloured 30 20

(Des Ts. Kosturkova. Litho and photo)

1966 (30 May). 90th Death Anniv of Nikola Simov-Kuruto (hero of the Uprising against Turkey). P 10½.

1620 **527** 5st. multicoloured 45 20

528 Federation Emblem

529 U.N.E.S.C.O. Emblem

(Des V. Tomov. Photo)

1966 (6 June). Seventh International Youth Federation Assembly, Sofia. P 10½.

1621 **528** 13st. new blue and black 95 35

(Des I. Kosev. Photo)

1966 (8 June). 20th Anniv of United Nations Educational, Scientific and Cultural Organization. P 10½.

1622 **529** 20st. ochre, orange-vermilion, and black .... 1·10 55

530 Footballer with Ball

(Des Zh. Kosturkova and N. Petkov. Photo)

1966 (27 June). World Cup Football Championship, London.

(a) T **530** and similar horiz designs showing players in action. Borders in pale grey. P 10½

1623 1st. black and yellow-brown 20 15
1624 2st. black and rosine 20 15
1625 5st. black and yellow-bistre 30 20
1626 13st. black and blue 85 45
1627 20st. black and greenish blue 95 55
1623/1627 *Set of 5* .... 2·30 1·40

531 Jules Rimet Cup

(b) Sheet 60×65½ mm. T **531**. Imperf

MS1628 50st. gold, cerise and grey .... 4·25 3·75

532 Wrestling

(Des Zh. Kosturkova and N. Petkov. Photo)

1966 (29 July). 3rd International Wrestling Championships, Sofia. P 10½.

1629 **532** 13st. sepia, yellow-green and light brown 95 55

533 Throwing the Javelin

(Des Zh. Kosturkova and N. Petkov. Photo)

1966 (10 Aug). Third Republican Spartakiad. T **533** and similar horiz design. P 10½.

1630 2st. green, red and yellow 20 15
1631 13st. deep bluish green, red and yellow (Running) 75 40

534 Map of Balkans, Globe and U.N.E.S.C.O. Emblem

535 Children with Construction Toy

(Des St. Kunchev. Photo)

1966 (26 Aug). International Balkan Studies Congress, Sofia. P 10½.

1632 **534** 13st. light emerald, pink and blue 95 55

(Des B. Stoev and S. Anastasov. Photo)

1966 (1 Sept). Children's Day. T **535** and similar horiz designs. P 10½.

1633 1st. black, yellow-orange and carmine 10 10
1634 2st. black, red-brown and emerald 10 10
1635 3st. black, orange-yellow and ultram 20 15
1636 13st. black, mauve and blue .... 1·50 35
1633/1636 *Set of 4* .... 1·70 65

Designs:—2st. Rabbit and Teddy Bear; 3st. Children as astronauts; 13st. Children with gardening equipment.

536 Yuri Gagarin and "Vostok 1"

(Des S. Sotirov. Photo)

1966 (29 Sept). Russian Space Exploration. T **536** and similar horiz designs. Backgrounds in deep and light grey. P 11½×11.

1637 1st. slate 10 10
1638 2st. purple 10 10
1639 3st. orange-brown 10 10
1640 5st. brown-lake 20 10
1641 8st. blue 35 20
1642 13st. greenish blue .... 1·10 35
1643 20 +10st. reddish violet .... 1·90 65
1637/1643 *Set of 7* .... 3·50 1·40
MS1644 70×62½ mm. 30+10st. black, light red and light grey. Imperf .... 4·25 3·75

Designs:—2st. German Titov and "Vostok 2"; 3st. Andrian Nikolaev, Pavel Popovich and "Vostok 3" and "4"; 5st. Valentina Tereshkova, Valery Bykovsky and "Vostok 5" and "6"; 8st. Vladimir Komarov, Boris Yegorov, Konstantin Feoktistov and "Voskhod 1"; 13st. Pavel Belyaev, Aleksei Leonov and "Voskhod 2"; 20st. Gagarin, Leonov and Tereshkova; 30st. Rocket and Globe.

537 St. Clement (14th-century wood-carving)

538 Metodi Shatorov

(Des V. Zakhariev. Photo)

1966 (27 Oct). 1050th Death Anniv of St. Clement of Ohrid. P 11½×11.

1645 **537** 5st. bistre-brown, red and pale drab 95 55

(Des M. Peikova and G. Kovachev. Photo)

1966 (8 Nov). Anti-Fascist Fighters. T **538** and similar horiz designs. Frames in gold; values in black. P 11×11½.

1646 2st. bluish violet and red 10 10
1647 3st. deep olive-brown and magenta 20 10
1648 5st. deep blue and red 30 15
1649 10st. olive-brown and orange 65 20
1650 13st. brown and vermilion 75 35
1646/1650 *Set of 5* .... 1·80 80

Portraits:—3st. Vlado Trichkov; 5st. Vulcho Ivanov; 10st. Raiko Daskalov; 13st. Gen. Vladimir Zaimov.

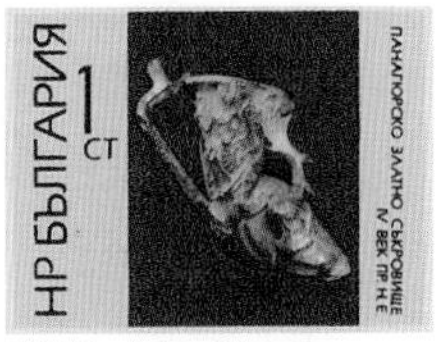

539 Georgi Dimitrov (statesman)

540 Deer's-head Vessel

(Des S. Sotirov. Photo)

1966 (14 Nov). Ninth Bulgarian Communist Party Congress, Sofia. T **539** and similar vert design. P 11½×11.

1651 2st. black and crimson 20 10
1652 20st. black, brown-red and pale grey .... 1·70 45

Design:—20st. Furnaceman and steelworks.

(Des A. Mechkuev. Photo "Kultura", Budapest)

1966 (28 Nov). The Gold Treasures of Panagyurishte. T **540** and similar horiz designs. Multicoloured. P 12×11½.

1653 1st. Type **540** 20 15
1654 2st. Amazon 25 15
1655 3st. Ram 30 15
1656 5st. Plate 35 15
1657 6st. Venus 45 20
1658 8st. Roe-buck 95 35
1659 10st. Amazon (different) .... 1·10 45
1660 13st. Amphora .... 1·40 55
1661 20st. Goat .... 2·30 1·10
1653/1661 *Set of 9* .... 6·50 3·00

Except for the 5st. and 13st. the designs show vessels with animal heads.

541 Bansko Hotel

542 Christmas Tree

(Des V. Tomov. Photo)

1966 (29 Nov). Tourist Resorts. T **541** and similar horiz designs. P 11×11½.

1662 1st. blue 20 15
1663 2st. deep green 20 15
1664 2st. brown-lake 20 15
1665 20st. purple .... 1·10 45
1662/1665 *Set of 4* .... 1·50 80

Designs:—No. 1663, Belogradchik; 1664, Tryavna; 1665, Malovitsa, Rila.

(Des St. Kunchev. Photo)

1966 (12 Dec). New Year. T **542** and similar horiz design. Multicoloured. P 11×11½.

1666 2st. Type **542** 20 15
1667 13st. Money-box 85 45

543 Pencho Slaveikov (poet)

544 Dahlias (*Dahlia variabilis*)

(Des M. Peikova and G. Kovachev. Photo)

1966 (15 Dec). Cultural Celebrities. T **543** and similar vert designs. P 11×11½.

1668 1st. bistre, new blue and orange 20 15
1669 2st. brown, orange and grey 20 15
1670 3st. new blue, bistre and orange 20 15
1671 5st. light purple-brown, drab and orange 30 20
1672 8st. olive-grey, reddish purple and new blue 65 30
1673 13st. bluish violet, new blue and bright purple 75 35
1668/1673 *Set of 6* .... 2·10 1·20

Celebrities: Writers (with pen emblem)—2st. Dimcho Debelyanov (poet); 3st. Petko Todorov. Painters (with brush emblem)—5st. Dimitur Dobrovich; 8st. Ivan Murkvichka; 13st. Iliya Beshkov.

(Des St. Goristanova. Photo)

1966 (29 Dec). Flowers. T **544** and similar vert designs. Multicoloured. P 11×11½.

1674 1st. Type **544** 15 10
1675 1st. *Clematis integrifolia* 20 10
1676 2st. Poet's narcissus (*Narcissus poeticus*) 25 10
1677 2st. Foxgloves (*Digitalis purpurea*) 30 15
1678 3st. Snowdrops (*Galanthus nivalis*) 45 20
1679 5st. Petunias (*Petunia hibrida*) 55 30
1680 13st. Tiger lilies (*Lilium tigrinum*) .... 1·10 35
1681 20st. Canterbury bells (*Campanula media*) .... 1·40 55
1674/1681 *Set of 8* .... 4·00 1·70

545 Ring-necked Pheasant

546 "Philately"

(Des V. Korenev. Photo)

1967 (28 Jan). Hunting. T **545** and similar horiz designs. P 11½×11.

1682 1st. yellow-orange, deep red-brown and light blue 30 20
1683 2st. slate-green & pale yellow-green 30 20
1684 3st. pale buff, slate-green and light blue 35 20
1685 5st. deep sepia and pale green 95 45
1686 8st. yellow-brown, blackish brown and pale turquoise-green .... 2·50 90
1687 13st. brown, deep sepia and light turquoise-blue .... 2·75 1·60
1682/1687 *Set of 6* .... 6·50 3·25

Designs:—2st. Chukar partridge; 3st. Grey partridge; 5st. Brown hare; 8st. Roe deer; 13st. Red deer stag.

(Des St. Kunchev. Photo)

1967 (4 Feb). Tenth Bulgarian Philatelic Federation Congress, Sofia. P 10½.

1688 **546** 10st. yellow, black and green .... 2·30 1·70

547 6th-century B.C. Coin of Thrace

548 Partisans listening to Radio

(Des M. Peikova and V. Vasileva. Photo)

1967 (30 Mar). Ancient Bulgarian Coins. T **547** and similar designs. Coins in silver on black background except 13st. (gold on black). Frame colours given. P 11½×11.

1689 1st. yellow-brown 20 15
1690 2st. bright purple 20 15
1691 3st. yellow-green 20 15
1692 5st. orange-brown 45 35
1693 13st. turquoise-blue .... 1·40 90
1694 20st. violet .... 2·30 1·70
1689/1694 *Set of 6* .... 4·25 3·00

Coins: Square—2st. 2nd-century B.C. Macedonian tetradrachm; 3st. 2nd century B.C. Odessos (Varna) tetradrachm; 5st. 4th-century B.C. Macedonian coin of Philip II. Horiz (38×25 mm)—13st. Obverse and reverse of 4th-century B.C. coin of King Sevt (Thrace); 20st. Obverse and reverse of 5th-century B.C. coin of Apollonia (Sozopol).

(Des V. Staikov. Photo)

1967 (20 Apr). 25th Anniv of Fatherland Front. T **548** and similar horiz design. P 11×11½.

1695 1st. multicoloured 20 15
1696 20st. multicoloured .... 1·30 45

Design:—20st. Dimitrov speaking at rally.

549 Nikola Kofardzhiev

550 "Cultural Development"

(Des M. Peikova and G. Kovachev. Photo)

1967 (24 Apr). Anti-Fascist Fighters. T **549** and similar horiz designs. P 11½×11.

1697 1st. deep brown-red, black and pale blue 20 15
1698 2st. olive-green, black and pale blue 20 15
1699 5st. deep ochre, black and pale blue 20 15
1700 10st. deep blue, black and pale lilac 65 30
1701 13st. purple, blue and pale grey 95 35
1697/1701 *Set of 5* .... 2·00 1·00

Portraits:—2st. Petko Napetov; 5st. Petko Petkov; 10st. Emil Markov; 13st. Traicho Kostov.

(Des St. Kunchev. Photo)

1967 (18 May). First Cultural Conference, Sofia. P 11½×11.

1702 **550** 13st. yellow, light emerald and gold 95 55

551 Angora Kitten

552 "Golden Sands" Resort

(Des M. Peikova and V. Vasileva. Photo)

1967 (27 May). Cats. T **551** and similar designs. Multicoloured. P 11½×11 (vert) or 11×11½ (horiz).

1703 1st. Type **551** 20 15
1704 2st. Siamese (horiz) 30 15
1705 3st. Abyssinian 45 20
1706 5st. European black and white .... 1·50 35
1707 13st. Persian (horiz) .... 1·90 65
1708 20st. European tabby .... 2·30 1·70
1703/1708 *Set of 6* .... 6·00 3·00

(Des V. Korenev. Photo)

1967 (12 June). International Tourist Year. T **552** and similar horiz designs. P 11×11½.

1709 13st. blackish green, pale yellow, black and bright blue 45 20
1710 20st. blackish green, buff, black and turquoise-blue 95 45
1711 40st. blackish green, buff, black and light blue-green 2·30 1·00
1709/1711 *Set of 3* 3·25 1·50

Designs:—20st. Pamporovo; 40st. Old Church, Nesebur.

553 Scene from Iliev's Opera *The Master of Boyana*

554 G. Kirkov

(Des B. Kitanov. Photo)

1967 (18 June). Third International Young Opera singers Competition, Sofia. T **553** and similar design. P 11½×11 (5st.) or 11×11½ (13st.).

1712 5st. cerise, blue and grey 20 15
1713 13st. red, deep blue, grey and light grey 75 45

Design: Vert—13st. "Vocal Art" (songbird on piano-key).

(Des V. Tomov. Pnoto)

1967 (24 June). Birth Centenary of Georgi Kirkov (patriot). P 11×11½.

1714 **554** 2st. bistre-brown and rose-red 20 15

555 Roses and Distillery

556 D.K.M.S. Emblem

(Des Z. Taseva. Photo)

1967 (15 July). Economic Achievements. T **555** and similar horiz designs. Multicoloured. P 11×11½.

1715 1st. Type **555** 20 15
1716 1st. Chick and incubator 20 15
1717 2st. Cucumbers and glasshouses 20 15
1718 2st. Lamb and farm building 20 15
1719 3st. Sunflower and oil-extraction plant (24.7) 20 15
1720 4st. Pigs and piggery (24.7) 25 15
1721 5st. Hops and vines (24.7) 30 15
1722 6st. Grain and irrigation canals (24.7) 35 15
1723 8st. Grapes and "Bulgar" tractor (24.7) 40 15
1724 10st. Apples and tree 45 20
1725 13st. Honey bees and honey 95 45
1726 20st. Honey bee on flower, and hives 1·20 55
1715/1726 *Set of 12* 4·50 2·30

(Des S. Kunchev. Photo)

1967 (28 July). 11th Anniv of Dimitrov Communist Youth League. P 11½×11.

1727 **556** 13st. black, red and blue 95 35

557 Map and Spassky Tower, Moscow Kremlin

558 Scenic "Fish" and Rod

(Des V. Staikov. Photo)

1967 (25 Aug). 50th Anniv of October Revolution. T **557** and similar horiz designs. P 11.

1728 1st. multicoloured 20 15
1729 2st. blackish olive and deep reddish purple 20 15
1730 3st. slate-violet and deep reddish purple 20 15
1731 5st. red and purple 20 15
1732 13st. light ultramarine and deep reddish purple 65 35
1733 20st. blue and deep reddish purple 1·40 55
1728/1733 *Set of 6* 2·50 1·40

Designs:—2st. Lenin directing revolutionaries; 3st. Revolutionaries; 5st. Marx, Engels and Lenin; 13st. Soviet oil refinery; 20st. "Molniya" satellite and Moon (Soviet space research).

(Des St. Kunchev. Photo)

1967 (28 Aug). Seventh World Angling Championships, Varna. P 11.

1734 **558** 10st. bright green, gold, light blue and black 75 45

559 Cross-country Skiing

560 Bogdan Peak, Sredna Mts

(Des V. Korenev and St. Goristanova. Photo)

1967 (20 Sept). Winter Olympic Games, Grenoble (1968). T **559** and similar horiz designs. P 11.

1735 1st. black, red and turquoise-blue 20 15
1736 2st. black, bistre and bright blue 20 15
1737 3st. black, light blue and brown-purple 20 15
1738 5st. black, yellow and bluish green 30 20
1739 13st. black, buff and ultramarine 1·40 45
1740 20st. +10st. black, light red, pale drab and greenish blue 2·40 90
1735/1740 *Set of 6* 4·25 1·80
MS1741 98×98 mm (diamond) 40st.+10st. black, yellow-ochre and turquoise-blue. Imperf 3·75 3·25

Designs:—2st. Ski jumping; 3st. Biathlon; 5st. Ice hockey; 13, 40st. Ice skating (pairs); 20st. Men's slalom.

(Des V. Zakhariev. Recess and photo)

1967 (25 Sept). Tourism. Mountain Peaks. T **560** and similar horiz designs. P 11½.

1742 1st. myrtle-green and light yellow 20 15
1743 2st. sepia and pale blue 20 15
1744 3st. deep blue and light blue 20 15
1745 5st. blackish green and light blue 30 15
1746 10st. lake-brown and light blue 40 20
1747 13st. black and light blue 45 40
1748 20st. deep blue & light reddish purple 95 80
1742/1748 *Set of 7* 2·40 1·80

Designs: Horiz—2st. Cherni Vruh, Vitosha; 5st. Persenk, Rhodopes; 10st. Botev, Stara-Planina; 20st. Vikhren, Pirin. Vert—3st. Ruen, Osogovska Planina; 13st. Musala, Rila.

561 G. Rakovski

563 Railway Bridge over Yantra River

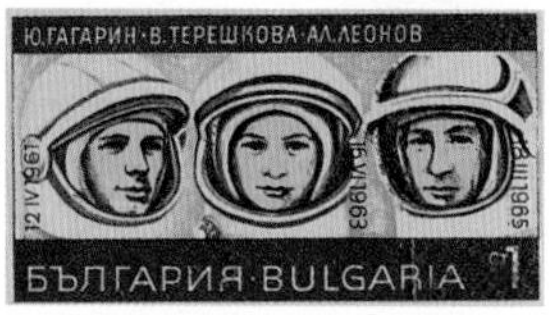

562 Yuri Gagarin, Valentina Tereshkova and Aleksei Leonov

(Des N. Petkov. Photo)

1967 (20 Oct). Death Centenary of Georgi Rakovski (newspaper editor and revolutionary). P 11.

1749 **561** 13st. black and yellow-green 95 55

(Des Zh. Kosturkova. Photo)

1967 (20 Oct). Space Exploration. T **562** and similar horiz designs. Multicoloured. P 11.

1750 1st. Type **562** 20 15
1751 2st. John Glenn and Edward White 20 15
1752 5st. "Molniya 1" 30 20
1753 10st. "Gemini 6" and "7" 95 35
1754 13st. "Luna 13" 1·00 55
1755 20st. "Gemini 10" docking with "Agena" 1·20 1·10
1750/1755 *Set of 6* 3·50 2·30

(Des V. Staikov. Photo)

1967 (5 Dec). Views of Turnovo (ancient capital). T **563** and similar vert views. P 11.

1756 1st. black, drab and blue 20 15
1757 2st. multicoloured 20 15
1758 3st. multicoloured 20 15
1759 5st. black, slate and red 45 25
1760 13st. multicoloured 75 35
1761 20st. black, light yellow-orange and lavender 95 55
1756/1761 *Set of 6* 2·50 1·40

Designs:—2st. Hadji Nikola's Inn; 3st. Houses on hillside; 5st. Town and river; 13st. "House of the Monkeys"; 20st. Gurko street.

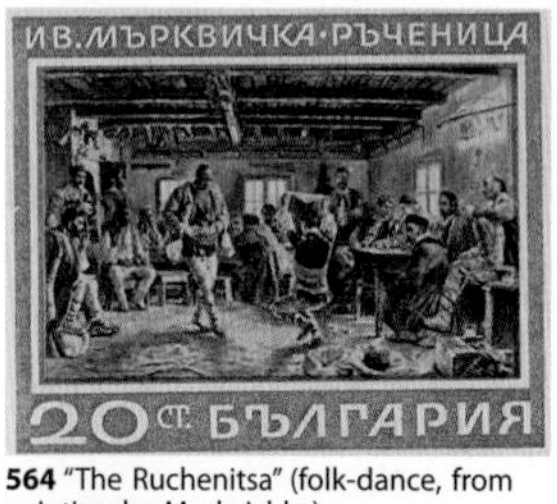

564 "The Ruchenitsa" (folk-dance, from painting by Murkvichka)

(Des St. Kunchev. Photo)

1967 (8 Dec). Belgian–Bulgarian Painting and Philately Exhibition, Brussels. P 11.

1762 **564** 20st. bronze-green and gold 1·90 1·70

No. 1762 was issued in sheets of 8 (4×2) with *se-tenant* commemorative labels in the upper and lower margins inscr in Bulgarian, Flemish and French.

565 "The Shepherd" (Zlatko Boyadzhiev)

566 Linked Satellites "Cosmos 186" and "188"

(Des O. and V. Ionchev. Litho Kultura, Budapest)

1967 (25 Dec). Paintings in the National Gallery, Sofia. T **565** and similar designs. Multicoloured. P 12 (3st.) or 11½ (others).

1763 1st. Type **565** 10 10
1764 2st. "The Wedding" (Vladimir Dimitrov) (vert) 10 10
1765 3st. "The Partisans" (Ilya Petrov) (55×35 mm) 45 20
1766 5st. "Anastasia Penchovich" (Nikolai Pavlovich) (vert) 95 35
1767 13st. "Self-portrait" (Zakharii Zograf) (vert) 1·90 1·00
1768 20st. "Old Town of Plovdiv" (Tsanko Lavrenov) 2·30 1·10
1763/1768 *Set of 6* 5·25 2·50
MS1769 65×85 mm. 60st. "St. Clement of Ohrid" (Anton Mitov) 6·75 6·75

(Des Zh. Kosturkova. Photo)

1967 (30 Dec). "Cosmic Activities". T **566** and similar design. P 11.

1770 20st. multicoloured 95 55
1771 40st. multicoloured 2·30 1·10

Design: Horiz—40st. "Venus 4" and orbital diagram.

567 "Crossing the Danube" (Orenburgski)

(Des A. Poplilov. Photo)

1968 (25 Jan). 90th Anniv of Liberation from Turkey. Paintings as T **567**. Inscr and borders in black and gold; centre colours below. P 11.

1772 1st. blackish green 20 15
1773 2st. indigo 20 15
1774 3st. red-brown 20 15
1775 13st. chalky blue 1·10 55
1776 20st. deep turquoise 1·40 65
1772/1776 *Set of 5* 2·75 1·50

Designs: Vert—2st. "Flag of Samara" (Veshin); 13st. "Battle of Orlovo Gnezdo" (Popov). Horiz—3st. "Battle of Pleven" (Orenburgski); 20st. "Greeting Russian Soldiers" (Goudienov).

568 Karl Marx

569 Gorky

(Des V. Tomov. Photo)

1968 (20 Feb). 150th Birth Anniv of Karl Marx. P 11.

1777 **568** 13st. brownish grey, vermilion and black 95 35

(Des M. Peikova and G. Kovachev. Photo)

1968 (20 Feb). Birth Centenary of Maksim Gorky (writer). P 11.

1778 **569** 13st. blackish green, red-orange and black 95 35

570 Dancers

(Des D. Rusinov. Photo)

1968 (20 Mar). Ninth World Youth and Students' Festival, Sofia. T **570** and similar horiz designs. Multicoloured. P 11.

1779 2st. Type **570** 20 15
1780 5st. Running 20 15
1781 13st. "Doves" 85 35
1782 20st. "Youth" (symbolic design) 95 55
1783 40st. Bulgarian 5c. stamp of 1879 under magnifier, and Globe 1·60 1·30
1779/1783 *Set of 5* 3·50 2·30

571 *Campanula alpina*

572 "The Unknown Hero" (Ran Bosilek)

(Des V. Tomov. Photo)

1968 (25 Apr). Wild Flowers. T **571** and similar vert designs. Multicoloured. P 11.

1784 1st. Type **571** ... 20 15
1785 2st. Trumpet gentian (*Gentiana acaulis*) ... 20 15
1786 3st. *Crocus veluchensis* ... 20 15
1787 5st. Siberian iris (*Iris sibirica*) ... 45 20
1788 10st. Dog's-tooth violet (*Erythronium dens-canis*) ... 65 20
1789 13st. Houseleek (*Sempervivum leucanthum*) ... 1·10 35
1790 20st. Burning bush (*Dictamnus albus*) ... 1·40 55
1784/1790 *Set of 7* ... 3·75 1·60

(Des L. Zidarov. Photo)

1968 (25 Apr). Bulgarian–Danish Stamp Exhibition. Fairy Tales. T **572** and similar horiz design. Multicoloured. P 10½.

1791 13st. Type **572** ... 45 35
1792 20st. "The Witch and the Young Man" (Hans Andersen) ... 95 80

573 Memorial Temple, Shipka

574 Copper Rolling-mill, Medet

(Des St. Kunchev. Photo)

1968 (3 May). Bulgarian–West Berlin Stamp Exhibition. P 10½.

1793 **573** 13st. multicoloured ... 95 55

No. 1793 was issued in sheets with *se-tenant* stamp-sized label inscr in Bulgarian and German.

(Des M. Peikova and V. Vasileva. Photo)

1968 (6 May). AIR. P 13.

1794 **574** 1l. rosine ... 3·25 80

575 Lake Smolyan

576 Gymnastics

(Des St. Goristanova. Photo)

1968. T **575** and similar vert designs, showing landscapes. P 13.

1795 1st. deep bluish green (17.5) ... 20 15
1796 2st. deep green (19.8) ... 20 15
1797 3st. sepia (26.8) ... 20 15
1798 8st. olive-green (27.9) ... 35 15
1799 10st. brown (13.9) ... 40 20
1800 13st. blackish olive (27.9) ... 45 30
1801 40st. greenish blue (26.8) ... 1·40 35
1802 2l. olive-brown (2.9) ... 6·50 2·20
1795/1802 *Set of 8* ... 8·75 3·25

Designs:—2st. River Ropotamo; 3st. Lomnitza Gorge, Erma River; 8st. River Isker; 10st. Cruise ship *Die Fregatte*; 13st. Cape Kaliakra; 40st. Sozopol; 2l. Mountain road, Kamchia River.

(Des S. Sotirov. Photo)

1968 (24 June). Olympic Games, Mexico. T **576** and similar vert designs. P 10½.

1803 1st. grey-black and bright red ... 20 15
1804 2st. black, lake-brown and grey ... 20 15
1805 3st. grey-black and deep magenta ... 20 15
1806 10st. grey-black, olive-yellow and deep turquoise-blue ... 65 20
1807 13st. grey-black, pink and deep ultramarine ... 1·40 55
1808 20st. grey, light pink and deep blue +10st. ... 1·90 65
1803/1808 *Set of 6* ... 4·00 1·70
MS1809 74×76 mm. 50st. +10st. black, slate and deep turquoise-blue. Imperf ... 4·75 4·50

Designs:—2st. Horse-jumping; 3st. Fencing; 10st. Boxing; 13st. Throwing the discus; 20st. Rowing; 50st. Stadium and communications satellite.

577 Dimitur on Mt. Buzludzha, 1868

578 Human Rights Emblem

(Des N. Mirchev. Photo)

1968 (1 July). Centenary of Exploits of Khadzhi Dimitur and Stefan Karadzha (revolutionaries). T **577** and similar horiz design. P 10½.

1810 2st. chestnut and silver ... 20 10
1811 13st. blackish green and gold ... 75 45

Design:—13st. Dimitur and Karadzha.

(Des St. Kunchev. Photo)

1968 (8 July). Human Rights Year. P 10½.

1812 **578** 20st. gold and blue ... 1·10 55

579 European Black Vulture

580 Battle Scene

(Des V. Korenev. Photo)

1968 (29 July). 80th Anniv of Sofia Zoo. T **579** and similar vert design. P 10½.

1813 1st. black, cinnamon and blue ... 20 20
1814 2st. black, greenish yellow and orange-brown ... 25 20
1815 3st. black and yellow-green ... 30 20
1816 5st. black, yellow and brown-lake ... 65 35
1817 13st. black, bistre and bluish green ... 2·40 1·10
1818 20st. black, light yellow-green and greenish blue ... 3·25 1·70
1813/1818 *Set of 6* ... 6·25 3·50

Designs:—2st. South African crowned crane; 3st. Common zebra; 5st. Leopard; 13st. Python; 20st. Crocodile.

(Des N. Mirchev. Photo)

1968 (22 Aug). 280th Anniv of Chiprovtsi Rising. P 10½.

1819 **580** 13st. olive, orange-yellow, emerald and light grey ... 95 20

581 Caterpillar-hunter (*Calosoma sycophanta*)

582 Flying Swans

(Des M. Peikova and V. Vasileva. Photo)

1968 (26 Aug). Insects. T **581** and similar designs. P 12½×13 (vert) or 13×12½ (horiz).

1820 1st. blackish green ... 30 10
1821 1st. olive-brown ... 30 10
1822 1st. deep blue ... 30 10
1823 1st. chestnut ... 30 10
1824 1st. reddish purple ... 30 10
1820/1824 *Set of 5* ... 1·40 45

Designs: Vert—No. 1820, Type **581**; 1821, Stag beetle (*Lucanus cervus*); 1822, *Procerus scabrosus* (ground beetle). Horiz—No. 1823, European rhinoceros beetle (*Oryctes nasicornis*); 1824, *Perisomena caecigena* (moth).

(Des D. Rusinov. Photo)

1968 (12 Sept). "Co-operation with Scandinavia". T **582** and similar horiz designs. P 10½.

1825 2st. ochre and deep green (22.11) ... 1·90 1·70
a. Strip. Nos. 1825 and 1828 plus label ... 4·00 3·75
1826 5st. Prussian blue, light grey and black ... 1·90 1·70
a. Strip. Nos. 1826/7 plus label ... 4·00 3·75
1827 13st. reddish purple and maroon ... 1·90 1·70
1828 20st. light grey and bright violet (22.11) ... 1·90 1·70
1825/1828 *Set of 4* ... 6·75 6·00

Designs:—2st. Wooden flask; 13st. Rose; 20st. Viking ships.

Nos. 1825 and 1828 and 1826/7 respectively were issued together *se-tenant* with intervening double stamp-size label showing a "bridge" of flags (inscribed in either Bulgarian or Swedish) within sheets of 20 stamps and 10 labels.

583 Congress Building and Emblem

(Des St. Kunchev. Photo)

1968 (17 Sept). International Dental Congress, Varna. P 10½.

1829 **583** 20st. gold, yellow-green and red ... 95 35

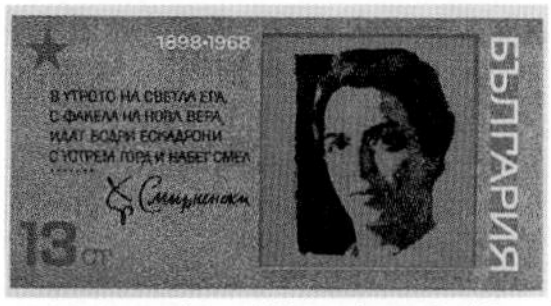

584 Smirnenski and Verse from *Red Squadrons*

(Des G. Kovachev. Photo)

1968 (28 Sept). 70th Birth Anniv of Khristo Smirnenski (poet). P 10½.

1830 **584** 13st. black, red-orange and gold ... 95 35

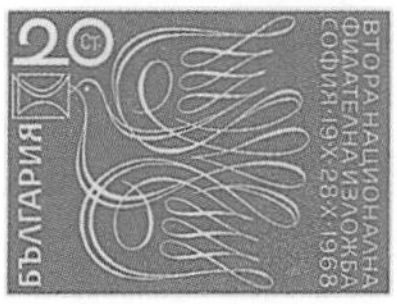

585 Dove with Letter

586 Dalmatian Pelican (*Pelecanus crispus*)

(Des St. Kunchev. Photo)

1968 (19 Oct). National Stamp Exhibition, Sofia and 75th Anniv of "National Philately". P 10½.

1831 **585** 20st. emerald ... 1·90 1·70

No. 1831 was issued in small sheets containing 4 stamps and 5 *se-tenant* stamp-size labels in two designs, (a) "Arms", in gold and carmine; (b) "magnifier and tweezers", in bright scarlet.

(Des Z. Taseva. Photo)

1968 (28 Oct). Srebirna Wildlife Reservation. Birds. T **586** and similar horiz designs. Multicoloured. P 10½.

1832 1st. Type **586** ... 35 20
1833 2st. Little egret (*Egretta garzetta*) ... 45 30
1834 3st. Great crested grebe (*Podiceps cristatus*) ... 55 35
1835 5st. Common tern (*Sterna hirundo*) ... 65 45
1836 13st. White spoonbill (*Platalea leucorodia*) ... 2·00 1·50
1837 20st. Glossy ibis (*Plegadis falcinellus*) ... 4·25 2·20
1832/1837 *Set of 6* ... 7·50 4·50

587 Silistra Costume

588 "St. Arsenius" (icon)

(Des N. Tuzsuzova. Litho German Bank Note Ptg Co, Leipzig)

1968 (20 Nov). Provincial Costumes. T **587** and similar vert designs. Multicoloured. P 13½.

1838 1st. Type **587** ... 20 15
1839 2st. Lovech ... 20 15
1840 3st. Yambol ... 20 15
1841 13st. Chirpan ... 75 35
1842 20st. Razgrad ... 1·10 65
1843 40st. Ikhtiman ... 2·40 90
1838/1843 *Set of 6* ... 4·25 2·20

(Des St. Kunchev. Photo Kultura, Budapest)

1968 (25 Nov). Rila Monastery. Icons and murals. T **588** and similar multicoloured designs. P 12½×11½ (2st.) or 11½×12½ (others).

1844 1st. Type **588** ... 20 15
1845 2st. "Carrying St. Ivan Rilski's Relics" (horiz) ... 20 15
1846 3st. "St. Michael torments the Rich Man's Soul" ... 30 20
1847 13st. "St. Ivan Rilski" ... 1·10 65
1848 20st. "Prophet Joel" ... 1·70 90
1849 40st. "St. George" ... 2·75 1·50
1844/1849 *Set of 6* ... 5·75 3·25
MS1850 100×74 mm. 1l. "Arrival of Relics at Rila Monastery". Imperf ... 7·50 7·25

589 *Matricaria chamomilla*

590 Silkworms and Spindles

(Des St. Goristanova and V. Korenev. Photo)

1969 (2 Jan). Medicinal Plants. T **589** and similar horiz designs. Multicoloured. P 10½.

1851 1st. Type **589** ... 20 15
1852 1st. *Mespilus oxyacantha* ... 20 15
1853 2st. Lily of the valley (*Convallaria majalis*) ... 20 15
1854 3st. Deadly nightshade (*Atropa belladonna*) ... 20 15
1855 5st. Common mallow (*Malva silvestris*) ... 30 15
1856 10st. Yellow pheasant's-eye (*Adonis vernalis*) ... 65 20
1857 13st. Common poppy (*Papaver rhoeas*) ... 75 35
1858 20st. Wild thyme (*Thymus serpyllum*) ... 1·10 55
1851/1858 *Set of 8* ... 3·25 1·70

(Des St. Goristanova and V. Korenev. Photo)

1969 (30 Jan). Silk Industry. T **590** and similar horiz designs. Multicoloured. P 11.

1859	1st. Type **590**	20	15
1860	2st. Worm, cocoons and pattern	20	15
1861	3st. Cocoons and spinning wheel	20	15
1862	5st. Cocoons and pattern	20	15
1863	13st. Moth, cocoon and spindles	75	20
1864	20st. Moth, eggs and shuttle	1·10	35
1859/1864	*Set of* 6	2·40	1·00

591 "Death of Ivan Asen"

592 "Saints Cyril and Methodius" (mural, Troyan Monastery)

(Des O. and V. Yonchev. Photo German Bank Note Ptg Co, Leipzig)

1969 (20 Mar). Manasses Chronicle (1st series). T **591** and similar vert designs. Multicoloured. P 14×13½.

1865	1st. Type **591**	20	15
1866	2st. "Emperor Nicephorus invading Bulgaria"	20	15
1867	3st. "Khan Krum's Feast"	20	15
1868	13st. "Prince Sviatoslav invading Bulgaria"	1·10	45
1869	20st. "The Russian invasion"	1·60	55
1870	40st. Jesus Christ, Tsar Ivan Alexander and Constantine Manasses	2·30	1·10
1865/1870	*Set of* 6	5·00	2·30

See also Nos. 1911/16.

(Des O. and V. Yonchev. Photo German Bank Note Ptg Co, Leipzig)

1969 (23 Mar). Saints Cyril and Methodius Commemoration. P 14×13½.

1871	**592**	28st. multicoloured	1·90	1·10

593 Galleon

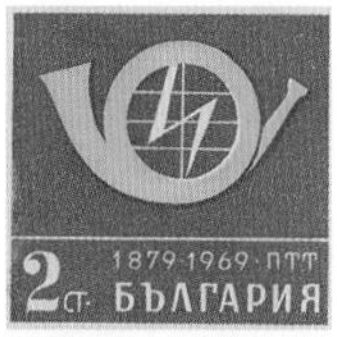

594 Posthorn Emblem

(Des St. Kunchev. Photo)

1969 (31 Mar). AIR. SOFIA 1969 International Stamp Exhibition. Transport. T **593** and similar vert designs. Multicoloured. P 13½×12½.

1872	1st. Type **593**	20	15
1873	2st. Mail coach	20	15
1874	3st. Steam locomotive	20	15
1875	5st. Early motor-car	20	15
1876	10st. Montgolfier balloon and Henri Giffard's steam-powered dirigible airship	35	20
1877	13st. Early flying machines	65	35
1878	20st. Modern aircraft	1·10	45
1879	40st. Rocket and planets	2·00	1·10
1872/1879	*Set of* 8	4·50	2·40
MS1880	57×55 mm. 1l. gold and red-orange. Imperf	4·75	4·50

Design:—1l. Postal courier.

(Des A. Poplilov. Photo)

1969 (15 Apr). 90th Anniv of Bulgarian Postal Services. T **594** and similar horiz designs. P 11.

1881	2st. yellow and blue-green	20	15
1882	13st. multicoloured	65	20
1883	20st. pale blue and blue	1·10	55
1881/1883	*Set of* 3	1·80	80

Designs:—13st. Bulgarian stamps of 1879 and 1946; 20st. Post Office workers' strike, 1919.

595 I.L.O. Emblem

596 "Fox and Rabbit"

(Des M. Peikova. Photo)

1969 (15 Apr). 50th Anniv of International Labour Organization. P 11.

1884	**595**	13st. black and light bluish green	65	35

(Des L. Zidarov. Photo)

1969 (21 Apr). Children's Book Week. T **596** and similar horiz designs. P 11.

1885	1st. black, red-orange and emerald	20	15
1886	2st. black, light blue and orange-red	20	15
1887	13st. black, yellow-olive and light blue	75	35
1885/1887	*Set of* 3	1·00	60

Designs:—2st. Boy with "hedgehog" and "squirrel"; 13st. "The Singing Lesson".

597 Hand with Seedling

598 "St. George" (14th Century)

(Des V. Vasileva. Photo)

1969 (28 Apr). "10,000,000 Hectares of New Forests". P 11.

1888	**597**	2st. black, olive-green and reddish purple	20	10

(Des St. Kunchev. Photo State Ptg Office, Budapest)

1969 (30 Apr). Religious Art. Vert designs as T **598**. Multicoloured. P 11×12.

1889	1st. Type **598**	20	15
1890	2st. "The Virgin and St. John Bogoslov" (14th-century)	20	15
1891	3st. "Archangel Michael" (17th-century)	20	15
1892	5st. "Three Saints" (17th-century)	30	15
1893	8st. "Jesus Christ" (17th-century)	35	15
1894	13st. "St. George and St. Dimitr" (19th-century)	75	20
1895	20st. "Christ, the Universal" (19th-century)	95	45
1896	60st. "The Forty Martyrs" (19th-century)	2·75	1·70
1897	80st. "The Transfiguration" (19th-century)	3·75	2·20
1889/1897	*Set of* 9	8·50	4·75
MS1898	103×165 mm. 40st.×4, "St. Dimitur" (17th-century). P 12½	9·25	9·00

599 Roman Coin

600 St. George and the Dragon

(Des St. Kunchev. Photo)

1969 (25–31 May). SOFIA 1969 International Stamp Exhibition. "Sofia Through the Ages". T **599** and similar vert designs. P 13×12½.

1899	1st. silver, greenish blue and gold	10	10
1900	2st. silver, bronze-green and gold	10	10
1901	3st. silver, brown-lake and gold	10	10
1902	4st. silver, reddish violet and gold	15	10
1903	5st. silver, purple and gold	20	10
1904	13st. silver, blue-green and gold	45	15
1905	20st. silver, ultramarine and gold	75	35
1906	40st. silver, carmine and gold	1·40	65
1899/1906	*Set of* 8	3·00	1·50
MS1907	78×72 mm. 1l. multicoloured. Imperf (31 May)	6·50	5·50

Designs: As T **599**—2st. Roman coin showing Temple of Aesculapius; 3st. Church of St. Sophia; 4st. Boyana Church; 5st. Parliament Building; 13st. National Theatre; 20st. Aleksandr Nevski Cathedral; 40st. Sofia University. 44×44 mm—1l. Arms.

(Des V. Staikov. Photo)

1969 (9 June). 38th International Philatelic Federation Congress, Sofia. P 11.

1908	**600**	40st. black, pale salmon and silver	2·30	1·10

601 St. Cyril

602 Partisans

(Des I. Kiosev. Photo)

1969 (20 June). 1,100th Death Anniv of St. Cyril. T **601** and similar vert design. P 11.

1909	2st. deep green and red/*silver*	20	10
1910	28st. deep blue and red/*silver*	1·60	65

Design:—28st. St. Cyril and procession.

Nos. 1909/10 were each issued in sheets vertically *se-tenant* with half stamp-size labels.

(Des O. and V. Yonchev. Photo German Bank Note Ptg Co, Leipzig)

1969 (5 Aug). Manasses Chronicle (2nd series). Designs as T **591**, but all horiz. Multicoloured. P 14.

1911	1st. "Nebuchadnezzar II and Balthasar of Babylon, Cyrus and Darius of Persia"	10	10
1912	2st. "Cambyses, Gyges and Darius"	10	10
1913	5st. "Prophet David and Tsar Ivan Alexander"	30	10
1914	13st. "Rout of the Byzantine Army, 811"	95	35
1915	20st. "Christening of Khan Boris"	1·90	45
1916	60st. Tsar Simeon's attack on Constantinople"	2·75	1·90
1911/1916	*Set of* 6	5·50	2·75

(Des A. Poplilov. Photo)

1969 (8 Aug). 25th Anniv of Fatherland Front Government. T **602** and similar horiz designs. P 11.

1917	1st. slate-lilac, light red and black	20	15
1918	2st. ochre, light red and black	20	15
1919	3st. bluish green, light red and black	20	15
1920	5st. brown-lake, light red and black	20	15
1921	13st. greenish blue, light red and black	65	20
1922	20st. purple-brown, emerald, light red and black	1·20	55
1917/1922	*Set of* 6	2·40	1·20

Designs:—2st. Combine-harvester; 3st. Dam; 5st. Folk singers; 13st. Petroleum Refinery; 20st. Lenin, Dimitrov and flags.

603 Gymnastics

604 "Construction" and Soldier

(Des V. Tomov. Photo)

1969 (1 Sept). Third Republican Spartakiad. T **603** and similar horiz design. Multicoloured. P 11.

1923	2st. Type **603**	20	10
1924	20st. Wrestling	95	65

(Des V. Koronev. Photo)

1969 (5 Sept). 25th Anniv of Army Engineers. P 13.

1925	**604**	6st. black and bright blue	30	15

605 T. Tserkovski

606 "Woman" (Roman Statue)

(Des A. Poplilov. Photo)

1969 (6 Sept). Birth Centenary of Tsanko Tserkovski (poet). P 11.

1926	**605**	13st. multicoloured	75	35

(Des M. Kefsizova. Photo)

1969 (22 Sept). 1,800th Anniv of Silistra. T **606** and similar design. P 11.

1927	2st. brownish grey, ultram & silver	20	15
1928	13st. drab, deep bluish green & silver	1·00	45

Design: Horiz—13st. "Wolf" (bronze).

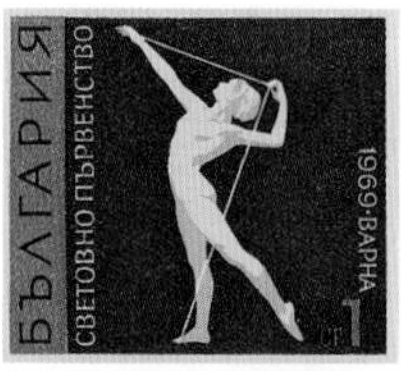

607 Skipping-rope Exercise

608 Mann Drinov (founder)

(Des St. Goristanova and V. Korenev. Photo)

1969 (27 Sept). World Gymnastics Competition, Varna, T **607** and similar horiz designs. P 11.

1929	1st. grey, deep blue and blue-green	20	15
1930	2st. grey, chalky blue and greenish blue.	20	15
1931	3st. grey, deep myrtle-green and bright emerald	20	15
1932	5st. grey, plum and vermilion	20	15
1933	13st. grey, deep violet-blue and magenta +5st.	1·10	55
1934	20st. grey, deep bluish green and deep +10st. olive-yellow	1·40	65
1929/1934	*Set of* 6	3·00	1·60

Designs:—2st. Hoop exercise (pair); 3st. Hoop exercise (solo); 5st. Ball exercise (pair); 13st. Ball exercise (solo); 20st. Solo gymnast.

(Des D. Rusinov. Photo)

1969 (1 Oct). Centenary of Bulgarian Academy of Sciences. P 11.

1935	**608**	20st. black and red	95	45

609 "Neophit Rilski" (Zakharii Zograf)

610 Pavel Banya

(Des S. Kunchev. Photo Kultura, Budapest)

1969 (3 Oct). Paintings in National Art Gallery, Sofia. T **609** and similar multicoloured designs. P 12½×11½ (horiz) or 11½×12½ (vert).

1936	1st. Type **609**	10	10
1937	2st. "German's Mother" (Vasil Stoikov)	20	10
1938	3st. "Worker's Family" (Nenko Balkanski) (horiz)	30	10
1939	4st. "Woman Dressing" (Ivan Nenov)	35	10
1940	5st. "Portrait of a Woman" (Nikolai Pavlovich)	45	20
1941	13st. "Krustyu Sarafov as Falstaff" (Dechko Uzunov)	95	30
1942	20st. "Artist's Wife" (N. Mikhailov) (horiz)	1·30	45
1943	20st. "Worker's Lunch" (Stoyan Sotirov) (horiz)	1·40	55
1944	40st. "Self-portrait" (Tseno Todorov)	1·90	80
1936/1944 *Set of* 9		6·25	2·40

(Des K. Gogov. Photo)

1969 (14 Oct)–**70**. Sanatoria. T **610** and similar horiz designs. P 11.

1945	2st. new blue (9.1.70)	20	10
1946	5st. bright blue	20	10
	a. Perf 12½	20	10
1947	6st. myrtle green (3.11.69)	35	10
	a. Perf 12½	35	10
	b. Perf 14×13½		
1948	20st. light emerald	75	35
	a. Perf 12½	75	35
1945/1948 *Set of* 4		1·40	60

Sanatoria:—5st. Khisar; 6st. Kotel; 20st. Narechen Polyclinic.

611 Deep-sea Trawler

(Des M. Peikova and G. Kovachev. Photo)

1969 (30 Oct). Ocean Fisheries. T **611** and similar horiz designs, showing fish. P 11.

1949	1st. grey, blue and blackish blue	20	15
1950	1st. pale green, olive-green and black	20	15
1951	2st. pale violet, violet and black	20	15
1952	3st. light blue, violet-blue and black	20	15
1953	5st. pale mauve, mauve and black	30	20
1954	10st. pale grey, grey and black	1·50	45
1955	13st. pale flesh, salmon and black	2·30	80
1956	20st. light buff, ochre and black	3·00	1·10
1949/1956 *Set of* 8		7·00	2·75

Designs:—1st. (No. 1950), Cape hake (*Merluccius capensis*); 2st. Scad (*Trachurus trachurus*); 3st. Pilchard (*Sardinops sagax*); 5st. Large-eyed sea bream (*Dentex macrophthalmus*); 10st. Chub mackerel (*Scomber colias*); 13st. Croaker (*Otolithes macrognathus*); 20st. Big-toothed leerfish (*Lichia vadigo*).

612 Trapeze Act

613 V. Kubasov, Georgi Shonin and "Soyuz 6"

(Des V. Vasileva and A. Denkov. Photo)

1969 (29 Nov). Circus. Vert designs as T **612**. Multicoloured. P 11.

1957	1st. Type **612**	10	10
1958	2st. Acrobats	10	10
1959	3st. Balancing act with hoops	10	10
1960	5st. Juggler, and bear on cycle	20	10
1961	13st. Equestrian act	65	35
1962	20st. Clowns	1·40	55
1957/1962 *Set of* 6		2·30	1·20

(Des S. Sotirov. Photo)

1969 (25 Dec). Space Flights of "Soyuz 6, 7 and 8". Vert designs as T **613**. P 11.

1963	1st. multicoloured	10	10
1964	2st. multicoloured	10	10
1965	3st. multicoloured	20	15
1966	28st. pink, new blue and chalky blue	1·50	55
1963/1966 *Set of* 4		1·70	80

Designs:—2st. Viktor Gorbatko, Vladislav Volkov, Anatoly Filipchenko and "Soyuz 7"; 3st. Aleksei Elseev, Vladimir Shatalov and "Soyuz 8"; 28st. Three "Soyuz" spacecraft in orbit.

614 Khan Asparuch and "Old-Bulgars" crossing the Danube, 679

(Des V. Vasileva and A. Denkov. Photo)

1970 (28 Jan). History of Bulgaria (1st series). T **614** and similar horiz designs. Multicoloured. P 10½.

1967	1st. Type **614**	20	15
1968	2st. Khan Krum and defeat of Emperor Nicephorus, 811	20	15
1969	3st. Conversion of Khan Boris I to Christianity, 865	20	15
1970	5st. Tsar Simeon and Battle of Akhelo, 917	30	15
1971	8st. Tsar Samuel and defeat of Byzantines, 976	35	15
1972	10st. Tsar Kaloyan and victory over Emperor Baldwin, 1205	55	20
1973	13st. Tsar Ivan Asen II and defeat of Komnine of Epirus, 1230	95	35
1974	20st. Coronation of Tsar Ivailo, 1277	1·40	55
1967/1974 *Set of* 8		3·75	1·70

See also No. 2274/81.

615 Bulgarian Pavilion

(Des D. Rusinov. Photo)

1970 (20 Feb). Expo 70 World's Fair, Osaka, Japan (1st issue). P 12½.

1975	**615**	20st. silver, yellow and brown	1·90	1·10

See also Nos. 2009/12.

616 Footballers

(Des V. Vasileva and A. Denkov Litho)

1970 (4 Mar). World Football Cup, Mexico. T **616** and similar designs. P 12½.

1976	1st. multicoloured	10	10
1977	2st. multicoloured	10	10
1978	3st. multicoloured	10	10
1979	5st. multicoloured	20	15
1980	20st. multicoloured	1·60	55
1981	40st. multicoloured	2·00	75
1976/1981 *Set of* 6		3·75	1·60
MS1982 55×99 mm. 80st.+20st. mult. Imperf		4·75	4·50

Designs: Horiz—2st. to 40st. Various football scenes. Vert (45×69 mm.)—80st. Football and inscription.

617 Lenin

618 *Tephrocactus Alexanderi v. bruchi*

(Des A. Poplilov. Photo)

1970 (28 Mar). Birth Centenary of Lenin. Square designs as T **617**. Multicoloured. P 12½.

1983	2st. Type **617**	20	15
1984	13st. Full-face portrait	75	35
1985	20st. Lenin writing	1·60	65
1983/1985 *Set of* 3		2·30	1·00

(Des R. Stanoeva and A. Sertev. Photo)

1970 (30 Apr). Flowering Cacti. T **618** and similar vert designs. Multicoloured. P 12½.

1986	1st. Type **618**	20	15
1987	2st. *Opuntia drummondii*	20	15
1988	3st. *Hatiora cilindrica*	20	15
1989	5st. *Gymnocalycium vatteri*	30	20
1990	8st. *Heliantho cereus grandiflorus*	45	35
1991	10st. *Neochilenia andreaeana*	2·20	80
1992	13st. *Peireskia vargasii v. longispina*	2·30	90
1993	20st. *Neobesseya rosiflora*	2·75	1·10
1986/1993 *Set of* 8		7·75	3·50

619 Rose

620 Union Badge

(Des V. Tomov and Zh. Tishev. Litho German Bank Note Ptg Co, Leipzig)

1970 (5 June). Bulgarian Roses. Vert designs as T **619** showing different varieties. P 13½.

1994	1st. multicoloured	20	15
1995	2st. multicoloured	20	15
1996	3st. multicoloured	30	15
1997	4st. multicoloured	40	15
1998	5st. multicoloured	45	20
1999	13st. multicoloured	95	45
2000	20st. multicoloured	1·90	1·10
2001	28st. multicoloured	3·25	1·90
1994/2001 *Set of* 8		7·00	3·75

(Des M. Peikova and G. Kovachev. Photo)

1970 (8 June). 70th Anniv of Agricultural Union. P 12½.

2002	**620**	20st. black, gold and red-orange	1·40	45

621 Gold Bowl

(Des M. Peikova. Photo)

1970 (15 June). Gold Treasures of Thrace. T **621** and similar square designs. P 12½.

2003	1st. black, blue and gold	20	15
2004	2st. black, lilac and gold	20	15
2005	3st. black, red and gold	20	15
2006	5st. black, green and gold	30	20
2007	13st. black, orange and gold	1·40	55
2008	20st. black, violet and gold	1·90	1·10
2003/2008 *Set of* 6		3·75	2·10

Designs:—2st. Three small bowls; 3st. Plain lid; 5st. Pear-shaped ornaments; 13st. Large lid with pattern; 20st. Vase.

622 Rose, and Woman with Baskets of Produce

(Des V. Tomov. Photo)

1970 (20 June). Expo 70 World's Fair, Osaka, Japan (2nd issue). T **622** and horiz designs. Multicoloured. P 12½.

2009	1st. Type **622**	20	15
2010	2st. Three dancers	20	15
2011	3st. Girl in national costume	20	15
2012	28st. Dancing couples	1·70	80
2009/2012 *Set of* 4		2·10	1·10
MS2013 75×90 mm. 40st. Bulgarian pavilion. Imperf		1·90	1·90

623 U.N. Emblem

(Des D. Rusinov. Photo)

1970 (14 July). 25th Anniv of United Nations. P 12½.

2014	**623**	20st. gold, turquoise-blue and greenish blue	95	55

624 I. Vasov

625 Edelweiss Sanatorium, Borovets

(Des M. Peikova and G. Kovachev. Photo)

1970 (15 July). 120th Birth Anniv of Ivan Vasov (writer). P 12½.

2015	**624**	13st. chalky blue	85	35

(Des St. Goristanova and V. Korenev. Photo)

1970 (30 July). Health Resorts. T **625** and similar horiz designs. P 13.

2016	1st. bluish green (2.10.70)	20	15
2017	2st. deep olive (5.8.70)	20	15
2018	4st. bright blue (26.10.70)	20	15
2019	8st. greenish blue (9.12.70)	45	15
2020	10st. turquoise-blue	65	20
2016/2020 *Set of* 5		1·50	70

Designs:—2st. Panorama Hotel, Pamporovo; 4st. Yachts, Albena; 8st. Harbour scene, Rusalka; 10st. Shtastlivetsa Hotel, Mt. Vitosha.

626 Hungarian Retriever

627 Fireman with Hose

(Des V. Tomov and Zh. Tishev. Photo)

1970 (10 Aug). Dogs. T **626** and similar multicoloured designs. P 12½.

2021	1st. Type **626**	20	15
2022	2st. Retriever (vert)	30	15

2023 3st. Great Dane (vert) 35 15
2024 4st. Boxer (vert) 45 20
2025 5st. Cocker spaniel (vert) 55 30
2026 13st. Dobermann pinscher (vert) .... 1·40 80
2027 20st. Scottish terrier (vert) .... 2·75 1·20
2028 28st. Russian hound .... 3·25 1·70
2021/2028 *Set of* 8 .... 8·25 4·25

(Des S. Goristanova and V. Korenev. Photo)

1970 (3 Sept). Fire Protection. T **627** and similar horiz design. P 12½.
2029 1st. grey, yellow and black 20 10
2030 3st. vermilion, grey and black 30 20
Design:—3st. Fire-engine.

628 Congress Emblem

629 Two Male Players

(Des St. Kunchev. Photo)

1970 (14 Sept). 7th World Sociological Congress, Varna. P 12½.
2031 **628** 13st. multicoloured 75 20

(Des Zh. Kosturkova. Photo)

1970 (20–22 Sept). World Volleyball Championships. T **629** and similar vert designs. P 12½.
2032 2st. greenish blue, black and chocolate .. 20 15
2033 2st. pale orange, black & blue (22.9) 20 15
2034 20st. yellow, black and blue-green .... 1·20 55
2035 20st. bright green, yellow, black and greenish blue (22.9) .... 1·40 65
2032/2035 *Set of* 4 .... 2·75 1·40
Designs:—2st. (No. 2033), Two female players; 20st. (No. 2034), Male player; (No. 2035), Female player.

630 Cyclists

632 Beethoven

631 Enrico Caruso and Scene from *Il Pagliacci*

(Des V. Korenev. Photo)

1970 (30 Sept). 20th Round-Bulgaria Cycle Race. P 12½.
2036 **630** 20st. mauve, olive-yellow and myrtle-green 95 55

(Des V. Tomov. Photo German Bank Note Ptg Co, Leipzig)

1970 (15 Oct). Opera Singers. T **631** and similar horiz designs. Multicoloured. P 14.
2037 1st. Type **631** 20 15
2038 2st. Khristina Morfova and *The Bartered Bride* 20 15
2039 3st. Petur Raichev and *Tosca* 20 15
2040 10st. Tsvetana Tabakova and *The Flying Dutchman* 35 25
2041 13st. Katya Popova and *The Masters* 45 35
2042 20st. Fyodor Chaliapin and *Boris Godunov* 2·30 1·30
2037/2042 *Set of* 6 .... 3·25 2·10

(Des A. Poplilov. Photo)

1970 (15 Oct). Birth Bicentenary of Ludwig von Beethoven (composer). P 12½.
2043 **632** 28st. steel blue and reddish purple .... 2·75 2·20

633 Ivan Asen II Coin

(Des D. Rusinov. Photo)

1970 (2 Nov). Bulgarian Coins of the 14th Century. T **633** and similar horiz designs. Multicoloured. P 12½.
2044 1st. Type **633** 20 15
2045 2st. Theodor Svetoslav 20 15
2046 3st. Mikhail Shishman 20 15
2047 13st. Ivan Alexander and Mikhail Asen 45 20
2048 20st. Ivan Sratsimir .... 1·40 45
2049 28st. Ivan Shishman (initials) .... 1·90 65
2044/2049 *Set of* 6 .... 4·00 1·60

634 "Luna 16"

635 Engels

(Des A. Denkov. Photo)

1970 (14 Nov). Moon Mission of "Luna 16". Sheet 51×70 mm. Imperf.
MS2050 **634** 1l. red, silver and deep ultramarine. 7·50 7·25

(Des A. Poplilov. Photo)

1970 (28 Nov). 150th Birth Anniv of Friedrich Engels. P 12½.
2051 **635** 13st. yellow-brown, blackish brown and vermilion 95 55

636 Snow Crystal

(Des St. Kunchev. Photo)

1970 (15 Dec). New Year. P 12½×13.
2052 **636** 2st. multicoloured 20 10

637 "Lunokhod 1" on Moon

638 "Girl's Head" (Zheko Spiridonov)

(Des A. Denkov. Photo)

1970 (18 Dec). Moon Mission of "Lunokhod 1". Sheet 60×72 mm. Imperf.
MS2053 **637** 80st. silver, black, pur & light bl .... 7·25 5·50

(Des St. Kunchev. Photo)

1970 (28 Dec). Modern Bulgarian Sculpture. T **638** and similar vert designs. P 12½.
2054 1st. violet and gold 20 15
2055 2st. bronze-green and gold 20 15
2056 3st. brown-lake and gold 20 15
2057 13st. slate-green and gold 65 20
2058 20st. brown-red and gold .... 1·30 45
2059 28st. bistre-brown and gold .... 1·40 65
2054/2059 *Set of* 6 .... 3·50 1·60
MS2060 61×72 mm. 1l. chestnut and gold. Imperf .. 4·75 4·75
Sculptures: As T **638**—2st. "Third Class Carriage" (Ivan Funev); 3st. "Elin Pelin" (Marko Markov); 13st. "Nina" (Andrei Nikolov); 20st. "Kneeling Woman" (Yavorov monument, Ivan Lazarov); 28st. "Engineer" (Ivan Funev). 36½×41 mm—1l. "Refugees" (Sekul Krumov).

639 Birds and Flowers

(Des St. Kunchev. Photo)

1971 (25 Jan). Spring. T **639** and similar horiz designs showing birds and flowers. P 12½×13.
2061 1st. multicoloured 10 10
2062 2st. multicoloured 10 10
2063 3st. multicoloured 10 10
2064 5st. multicoloured 10 10
2065 13st. multicoloured 45 20
2066 20st. multicoloured .... 1·00 45
2061/2066 *Set of* 6 .... 1·70 95

640 "Khan Asparuch crossing Danube" (Boris Angelushev)

(Des M. Peikova. Photo German Bank Note Ptg Co, Leipzig)

1971 (6 Mar). Bulgarian History. Paintings. T **640** and similar horiz designs. Multicoloured. Photo. P 13½×14.
2067 2st. Type **640** 20 15
2068 3st. "Ivailo in Turnovo" (Ilya Petrov) 20 15
2069 5st. "Cavalry Charge, Benkovski" (P. Morozov) 45 20
2070 8st. "Gen. Gurko entering Sofia, 1878" (D. Gyudzhenov) 95 30
2071 28st. "Greeting Red Army" (Stefan Venev) 3·75 2·00
2067/2071 *Set of* 5 .... 5·00 2·50
MS2072 137×131 mm. Nos. 2067/70 .... 1·90 1·70

641 Running

(Des Zh. Kosturkova. Photo)

1971 (13 Mar). 2nd European Indoor Track and Field Championships. T **641** and similar horiz design. Multicoloured. P 12½×13.
2073 2st. Type **641** 20 15
2074 20st. Putting the shot .... 1·90 55

642 School Building

(Des Z. Taseva. Photo)

1971 (16 Mar). Foundation of first Bulgarian Secondary School, Bolgrad, 1858. T **642** and similar horiz design. P 12½.
2075 2st. green, yellow-brown and silver 20 15
2076 20st. violet, yellow-brown and silver .... 1·30 45
Design:—20st. Dimitur Mutev, Prince Bogoridi and Sava Radulov (founders).

643 Communards

(Des S. Goristanova and V. Korenev. Photo)

1971 (18 Mar). Centenary of Paris Commune. P 12½×13.
2077 **643** 20st. black and claret 95 55

644 Georgi Dimitrov challenging Hermann Goering (photo-montage, J. Hartfield)

646 G. Rakovski

645 Gagarin and Space Scenes

(Des D. Rusinov. Photo)

1971 (11 Apr). 20th Anniv of "Fédération Internationale des Résistants". P 12½.
2078 **644** 2st. multicoloured 20 15
2079 13st. multicoloured .... 1·40 55

(Des D. Rusinov. Photo)

1971 (12 Apr). Tenth Anniv of First Manned Space Flight. Sheet 80×53 mm. Imperf.
MS2080 **645** 40st. +20st. multicoloured .... 4·75 4·00

(Des A. Poplilov. Photo)

1971 (14 Apr). 150th Birth Anniv of Georgi Rakovski (politician and revolutionary). Photo. P 12½.
2081 **646** 13st. blackish brown, pale cream and light olive-green 75 20

647 Worker and Banner ("People's Progress")

648 Pipkov and Music

(Des A. Denkov. Photo)

1971 (20 Apr). Tenth Bulgarian Communist Party Congress. T **647** and similar multicoloured designs. P 12½.

2082 1st. Type **647** ... 20 15
2083 2st. Symbols of "Technical Progress" (horiz) ... 20 15
2084 13st. Men clasping hands ("Bulgarian-Soviet Friendship") ... 1·40 45
2082/2084 *Set of 3* ... 1·60 70

(Des K. Kotseva and V. Dokev. Photo)

1971 (20 May). Birth Centenary of Panaiot Pipkov (composer). P 12½.

2085 **648** 13st. black, bright green and silver ... 95 55

649 "Three Races"

650 Mammoth

(Des V. Korenev. Photo)

1971 (20 May). Racial Equality Year. P 12½.

2086 **649** 13st. multicoloured ... 95 55

(Des A. Denkov. Photo)

1971 (29 May). Prehistoric Animals. Multicoloured designs as T **650**. P 12½.

2087 1st. Type **650** ... 20 20
2088 2st. Bear (vert) ... 20 20
2089 3st. Hipparion ... 20 20
2090 13st. Mastodon ... 1·90 65
2091 20st. Dinotherium (vert) ... 2·75 1·70
2092 28st. Sabre-toothed tiger ... 3·25 2·20
2087/2092 *Set of 6* ... 7·75 4·75

651 Façade of Ancient Building

652 Weights Emblem on Map of Europe

(Des K. Gogov. Photo)

1971 (10 June). Ancient Buildings of Koprivshtitsa. T **651** and similar horiz designs showing different façades. P 12½.

2093 1st. myrtle-green, red-brown and light yellow-green ... 10 10
2094 2st. red-brown, myrtle-green and buff ... 10 10
2095 6st. violet, brown-lake and blue ... 35 15
2096 13st. carmine-red, blue and yellow-orange ... 95 45
2093/2096 *Set of 4* ... 1·40 70

(Des S. Nenov. Photo)

1971 (19 June). 30th European Weightlifting Championships, Sofia. T **652** and similar vert design. Multicoloured. P 12½.

2097 2st. Type **652** ... 20 15
2098 13st. Figures XXX supporting weights ... 1·40 45

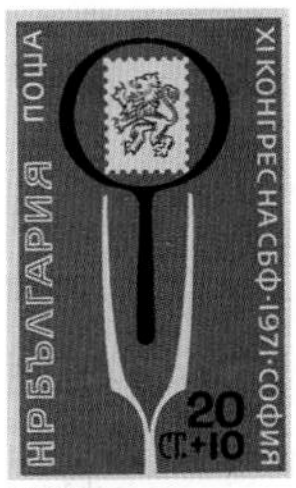

653 Frontier Guard and Dog

654 Tweezers, Magnifying Glass and "Stamp"

(Des V. Tomov. Photo)

1971 (26 June). 25th Anniv of Frontier Guards. Photo. P 12½.

2099 **653** 2st. olive-green, green and pale blue-green ... 20 10

(Des V. Korenev. Photo)

1971 (10 July). 9th Congress of Bulgarian Philatelic Federation. P 12½.

2100 **654** 20st. +10st. olive-brown, black and orange-red ... 1·90 80

655 Congress Meeting (sculpture)

(Des L. Marinov. Photo)

1971 (31 July). 80th Anniv of Bulgarian Social Democratic Party, Buzludzha. P 12½.

2101 **655** 2st. emerald, cream and carmine-red ... 20 10

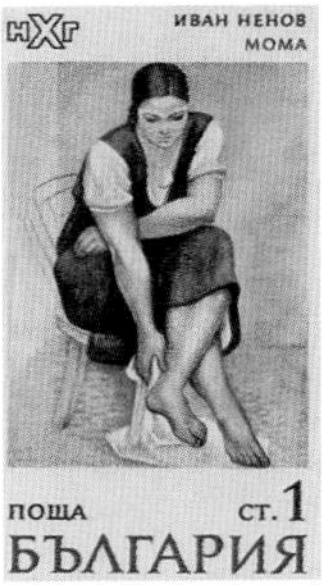

656 "Mother" (Ivan Nenov)

657 Factory, Botevgrad

(Des V. and O. Ionchev. Photo German Bank Note Ptg Co, Leipzig)

1971 (2 Aug). Paintings from the National Art Gallery (1st series). T **656** and similar vert designs. Multicoloured. P 14×13½.

2102 1st. Type **656** ... 20 15
2103 2st. "Lazarova" (Stefan Ivanov) ... 20 15
2104 3st. "Portrait of Yu. Kh." (Kiril Tsonev) ... 35 20
2105 13st. "Portrait of a Lady" (Dechko Uzunov) ... 95 35
2106 20st. "Young Woman from Kalotina" (Vladimir Dimitrov) ... 1·40 80
2107 40st. "Goryanin" (Stoyan Venev) ... 1·90 1·30
2102/2107 *Set of 6* ... 4·50 2·75

See also Nos. 2145/50.

(Des M. Peikova. Photo)

1971 (25 Aug). Industrial Buildings. T **657** and similar designs. P 13.

2108 1st. bright violet ... 10 10
2109 2st. bright orange-red ... 10 10
2110 10st. blackish violet ... 35 15
2111 13st. cerise ... 55 20
2112 40st. chocolate ... 1·90 45
2108/2112 *Set of 5* ... 2·75 90

Designs: Vert—2st. Petro-chemical plant, Pleven. Horiz—10st. Chemical works, Vratsa; 13st. "Maritsa-Istok" plant, Dimitrovgrad; 40st. Electronics factory, Sofia.

658 Free-style Wrestling

659 Posthorn Emblem

(Des St. Goristanova and V. Korenev. Photo)

1971 (27 Aug). European Wrestling Championships. T **658** and similar horiz design. P 12½.

2113 2st. black, turquoise-blue and bright emerald ... 10 10
2114 13st. black, turquoise-blue and bright vermilion ... 95 45

Design:—13st. Greco-Roman wrestling.

(Des St. Kunchev. Photo)

1971 (15 Sept). Eighth Organization of Socialist Countries' Postal Administrations Congress. P 12½.

2115 **659** 20st. gold and emerald ... 95 55

660 Entwined Ribbons

(Des D. Rusinov. Photo)

1971 (20 Sept). Seventh European Biochemical Congress, Varna. P 12½.

2116 **660** 13st. rosine, purple-brown and black ... 95 55

661 "New Republic" Statue

662 Cross-country Skiing

(Des St. Kunchev. Photo)

1971 (20 Sept). 25th Anniv of People's Republic. T **661** and similar vert design. P 13×12½.

2117 2st. scarlet, yellow and gold ... 10 10
2118 13st. dull green, vermilion and gold ... 95 45

Design:—13st. Bulgarian flag.

(Des S. Goristanova and V. Korenev. Photo)

1971 (25 Sept). Winter Olympic Games, Sapporo, Japan. T **662** and similar horiz designs. Multicoloured. P 12½.

2119 1st. Type **662** ... 20 15
2120 2st. Downhill skiing ... 20 15
2121 3st. Ski jumping ... 20 15
2122 4st. Figure skating ... 20 15
2123 13st. Ice hockey ... 95 65
2124 28st. Slalom skiing ... 1·90 1·10
2119/2124 *Set of 6* ... 3·25 2·10
MS2125 60×70 mm. 1l. Olympic flame and stadium. Imperf ... 4·75 3·00

663 Brigade Members

664 U.N.E.S.C.O. Emblem and Wreath

(Des V. Tomov. Photo)

1971 (13 Oct). 25th Anniv of Youth Brigades Movement. P 13.

2126 **663** 2st. deep violet-blue ... 20 10

(Des I. Kosev. Photo)

1971 (4 Nov). 25th Anniv of United Nations Educational, Scientific and Cultural Organization. P 12½.

2127 **664** 20st. multicoloured ... 95 55

665 "The Footballer"

(Des St. Kunchev. Photo State Printing Works, Budapest)

1971 (10 Nov). 75th Birth Anniv of Kiril Tsonev (painter). T **665** and similar multicoloured designs, showing his paintings. P 12×11½ (2, 20st.) or 11½×12 (others).

2128 1st. Type **665** ... 20 15
2129 2st. "Landscape" (horiz) ... 20 15
2130 3st. Self-portrait ... 30 20
2131 13st. "Lilies" ... 95 35
2132 20st. "Woodland Scene" (horiz) ... 1·40 65
2133 40st. "Portrait of a Young Woman" ... 1·90 90
2128/2133 *Set of 6* ... 4·50 2·20

666 "Salyut" Space-station

(Des A. Denkov. Photo)

1971 (20 Dec). Russian Space Programme. "Soyuz 11" Mission. T **666** and similar horiz designs. Multicoloured. P 12½.

2134 2st. Type **666** ... 20 15
2135 13st. "Soyuz 11" ... 45 30
2136 40st. Docking of "Salyut" & "Soyuz 11" ... 2·30 80
2134/2136 *Set of 3* ... 2·75 1·10
MS2137 70×74 mm. 80st. Cosmonauts G. Dobrovolsky, Vladislav Volkov and V. Patsaev (victims of "Soyuz 11" disaster). Imperf ... 3·25 2·75

667 *Vikhren* (ore carrier)

(Des M. Peikova. Photo)

1972 (8 Jan). Construction of One Million Tons of Shipping in Bulgaria. P 12½.

2138 **667** 18st. lilac, magenta and black .... 1·40 55

668 Goce Delčev

670 Bulgarian Worker

669 Gymnast with Ball

(Des G. Nedyalkov. Photo)

1972 (21 Jan). Birth Centenaries of Macedonian Revolutionaries. T **668** and similar horiz portraits. P 12½.

2139 2st. black and orange-red 10 10
2140 5st. black and yellow-green 20 10
2141 13st. black and olive-yellow 65 35
2139/2141 *Set of* 3 .... 85 50

Designs:—5st. Jan Sandanski; 13st. Dame Gruev (centenary in 1971).

(Des I. Kiosev. Photo)

1972 (10 Feb). Fifth World Gymnastics Championships, Havana, Cuba. T **669** and similar horiz designs. Multicoloured. P 12½.

2142 13st. Type **669** 95 35
2143 18st. Gymnast with hoop .... 1·40 65
MS2144 61×74 mm. 70st. Team with hoops. Imperf 4·75 4·50

(Des O. and V. Ionchev. Photo German Bank Note Ptg Co, Leipzig)

1972 (20 Feb). Paintings from the National Gallery (2nd series). Horiz designs similar to T **656**. Multicoloured. P 13½×14.

2145 1st. "Melnik" (Petur Mladenov) 20 15
2146 2st. "Ploughman" (Pencho Georgiev) 20 15
2147 3st. "By the Death-bed" (Aleksandur Zhendov) 30 20
2148 13st. "Family" (Vladimir Dimitrov) .... 1·20 35
2149 20st. "Family" (Nenko Balkanski) .... 1·50 45
2150 40st. "Father Paisii" (Koyu Denchev) .... 1·70 55
2145/2150 *Set of* 6 .... 4·50 1·70

(Des T. Momchilov. Photo)

1972 (7 Mar). Seventh Bulgarian Trade Unions Congress. P 12½.

2151 **670** 13st. multicoloured 65 20

671 "Singing Harvesters"

672 Heart and Tree Emblem

(Des I. Kosev. Photo State Ptg Wks, Budapest)

1972 (29 Mar). 90th Birth Anniv of Vladimir Dimitrov, the Master (painter). T **671** and similar multicoloured designs. P 12×11½ (3, 13st.) or 11½×12 (others).

2152 1st. Type **671** 20 15
2153 2st. "Farm Worker" 20 15
2154 3st. "Women Cultivators" (horiz) 30 15
2155 13st. "Peasant Girl" (horiz) 45 20
2156 20st. "My Mother" .... 1·40 90
2157 40st. Self-portrait .... 1·90 1·30
2152/2157 *Set of* 6 .... 4·00 2·50

(Des A. Stareishinski. Photo)

1972 (30 Apr). World Heart Month. P 12½.

2158 **672** 13st. multicoloured .... 1·40 80

673 St. Mark's Cathedral

675 Lamp of Learning and Quotation

674 Dimitrov at Typesetting Desk

(Des St. Kunchev. Photo)

1972 (6 May). U.N.E.S.C.O. "Save Venice" Campaign. T **673** and similar vert design. P 13×12½.

2159 2st. pale turquoise-blue, turquoise-green and bronze-green 30 20
2160 13st. pale turquoise-green, slate-violet and Venetian red .... 1·20 55

Design:—13st. Palace of the Doge.

(Des I. Kiosev. Photo)

1972 (8 May). 90th Birth Anniv of Georgi Dimitrov (statesman) (1st issue). T **674** and similar horiz designs. Multicoloured. P 12½.

2161 1st. Type **674** 20 15
2162 2st. September Uprising of 1923 .... 20 15
2163 3st. Dimitrov at Leipzig Trial 20 15
2164 5st. Dimitrov addressing workers 20 15
2165 13st. Dimitrov with Bulgarian crowd 35 35
2166 18st. Addressing young people 45 45
2167 28st. Dimitrov with children 95 65
2168 40st. Dimitrov's mausoleum .... 1·90 1·00
2169 80st. Portrait head (olive-green and gold centre) .... 5·50 2·10
2161/2169 *Set of* 9 .... 9·00 4·75
MS2170 87×84 mm. As No. 2169, but centre in brown-red and gold. Imperf .... 8·25 7·75

For 80st. imperforate and with different coloured centre see No. 2173.

(Des A. Stareishinski. Photo)

1972 (12 May). 250th Birth Anniv of Father Paisii Khilendarski (historian). T **675** and similar vert design. P 12½.

2171 2st. sepia, blue-green and gold 20 10
2172 13st. sepia, blue-green and gold .... 1·20 45

Design:—13st. Paisii writing.

(Des I. Kosev. Photo)

1972 (18 June). 90th Birth Anniv of Georgi Dimitrov (statesman) (2nd issue). As No. 2169, but centre in red and gold. Imperf.

2173 80st. multicoloured .... 11·00 11·00

676 Canoeing

(Des A. Denkov and St. Kunchev. Photo)

1972 (25 June). Olympic Games, Munich. T **676** and similar horiz designs. Multicoloured. P 12½.

2174 1st. Type **676** 20 15
2175 2st. Gymnastics 20 15
2176 3st. Swimming 20 15
2177 13st. Volleyball 45 35
2178 18st. Hurdling 95 55
2179 40st. Wrestling .... 1·90 1·10
2174/2179 *Set of* 6 .... 3·50 2·20
MS2180 64×60 mm. 80st. Running track and sports. Imperf .... 4·75 4·50

677 Angel Kunchev

678 "Golden Sands"

(Des I. Kosev. Photo)

1972 (30 June). Death Centenary of Angel Kunchev (patriot). P 12½.

2181 **677** 2st. maroon, gold and purple 20 15

(Des V. Vasileva. Photo)

1972 (16 Sept). Hotels at Black Sea Resorts. T **678** and similar vert designs. Multicoloured. P 12½.

2182 1st. Type **678** 20 15
2183 2st. Druzhba 20 15
2184 3st. "Sunny Beach" 20 15
2185 13st. Primorsko 65 20
2186 28st. Rusalka .... 1·20 45
2187 40st. Albena .... 1·40 55
2182/2187 *Set of* 6 .... 3·50 1·50

679 Canoeing (Bronze Medal)

680 Subi Dimitrov

(Des St. Kunchev and A. Stareishinski. Photo)

1972 (28 Sept). Bulgarian Medal Winners, Olympic Games, Munich. T **679** and similar horiz designs. Multicoloured. P 12½.

2188 1st. Type **679** 20 15
2189 2st. Long-jumping (Silver Medal) 20 15
2190 3st. Boxing (Gold Medal) 20 15
2191 18st. Wrestling (Gold Medal) .... 1·40 45
2192 40st. Weightlifting (Gold Medal) .... 1·70 90
2188/2192 *Set of* 5 .... 3·25 1·60

(Des M. Peikova and G. Kovachev. Photo)

1972 (30 Oct). Resistance Heroes. T **680** and similar vert portraits. Multicoloured. P 13.

2193 1st. Type **680** 10 10
2194 2st. Tsvyatko Radoinov 10 10
2195 3st. Iordan Lyutibrodski 10 10
2196 5st. Mito Ganev 30 15
2197 13st. Nedelcho Nikolov 95 35
2193/2197 *Set of* 5 .... 1·40 70

681 Commemorative Text

682 *Lilium rhodopaeum*

(Des St. Kunchev. Photo)

1972 (3 Nov). 50th Anniv of U.S.S.R. P 12½×13½.

2198 **681** 13st. red, yellow and gold 75 35

(Des V. Vasileva. Photo)

1972 (25 Nov). Protected Flowers. T **682** and similar vert designs. Multicoloured. P 12½.

2199 1st. Type **682** 20 15
2200 2st. Marsh gentian (*Gentiana pneumonanthe*) 20 15
2201 3st. Sea lily (*Pancratium maritimum*) 20 15
2202 4st. Globe flower (*Trollius europaeus*) 30 20
2203 18st. *Primula frondosa* 95 45
2204 23st. Pale pasque flower (*Pulsatilla vernalis*) .... 1·40 65
2205 40st. *Fritillaria stribrnyi* .... 1·90 1·00
2199/2205 *Set of* 7 .... 4·75 2·50

СВЕТОВЕН ПЪРВЕНЕЦ

(**683**)

684 Dobri Chintulov

1972 (27 Nov). "Bulgaria, World Weightlifting Champions". No. 2192 optd with T **683**, in red.

2206 40st. multicoloured .... 2·30 1·10

(Des K. Kunev and M. Rashkov. Photo)

1972 (28 Nov). 150th Birth Anniv of Dobri Chintulov (poet). P 12½.

2207 **684** 2st. multicoloured 35 20

685 Forehead Ornament (19th-century)

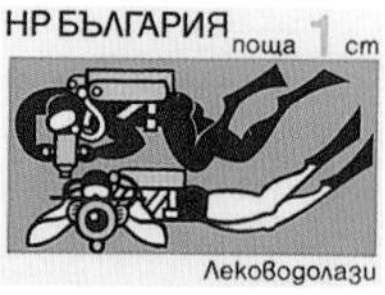

686 Divers with Cameras

(Des I. Kiosev. Recess German Bank Note Ptg Co, Leipzig)

1972 (27 Dec). Antique Jewellery. T **685** and similar horiz designs. P 14×13½.

2208 1st. black and red-brown 20 15
2209 2st. black and blue-green 20 15
2210 3st. black and greenish blue 20 15
2211 8st. black and brown-red 45 20
2212 23st. black and chestnut .... 1·20 55
2213 40st. black and violet .... 1·90 1·30
2208/2213 *Set of* 6 .... 3·75 2·30

Designs:—2st. Belt-buckle (19th-century); 3st. Amulet (18th-century); 8st. Pendant (18th-century); 23st. Earrings (14th-century); 40st. Necklace (18th-century).

(Des A. Denkov, K. Kunev and A. Stareishinski. Photo)

1973 (24 Jan). Underwater Research in Black Sea. T **686** and similar designs. P 12½.

2214 1st. black, yellow and light blue 20 20
2215 2st. black, yellow and new blue 20 20
2216 18st. black, yellow-orange and greenish blue 95 65
2217 40st. black, yellow-orange and bright blue .... 1·90 80
2214/2217 *Set of* 4 .... 3·00 1·70
MS2218 118×98 mm. 20st. ×4. Designs as Nos 2214/17, but background colours changed. Imperf (sold at 1l.) .... 8·75 8·50

Designs: Horiz—2st. Divers with *Shelf 1* (underwater research vessel). Vert—18st. Diver with diving bell *NIV 100*; 40st. Lifting balloon.

687 "The Hanging of Vasil Levski" (Boris Angelushev)

688 Elhovo Mask

(Des St. Kunchev. Photo)

1973 (19 Feb). Death Centenary of Vasil Levski (patriot). T **687** and similar vert design. P 13×12½.

2219	2st. deep bluish green and claret	20	10
2220	20st. brown, pale cream and light grey-green	1·70	80

Design:—20st. "Vasil Levski" (Georgi Danchov).

(Des V. Vasileva. Photo)

1973 (26 Feb). "Kukeris" Carnival Masks. T **688** and similar vert designs. Multicoloured. P 12½.

2221	1st. Type **688**	20	15
2222	2st. Breznik	20	15
2223	3st. Khisar	20	15
2224	13st. Radomir	65	35
2225	20st. Karnobat	95	65
2226	40st. Pernik	4·75	4·25
2221/2226 *Set of* 6		6·25	5·25

689 Copernicus

690 Vietnamese Girl

(Des K. Kunev and P. Rashkov. Photo)

1973 (21 Mar). 500th Birth Anniv of Nicolas Copernicus. P 12½.

2227 **689**	28st. brown-purple, black and buff	2·30	1·60

1973 (3 Apr). "Visit Bulgaria by Air". No. **MS**2072 surch with various airline emblems and new sheet value.

MS2228	137×131 mm. Nos. 2067/70 surch with new sheet value of 1l.	30·00	30·00

Although originally issued on 3 April it is understood that most of the sheets were not distributed until much later.

(Des A. Stareishinski. Photo)

1973 (16 Apr). Vietnam Peace Treaty. P 12½.

2229 **690**	18st. multicoloured	75	55

1973 (4 May). IBRA 73 Stamp Exhibition, Munich. No. **MS**1907 optd with "IBRA" and Olympic symbols, in green.

MS2230	78×72 mm. 1l. multicoloured	£140	£140

This sheet also exists with the overprint in grey from a limited printing.

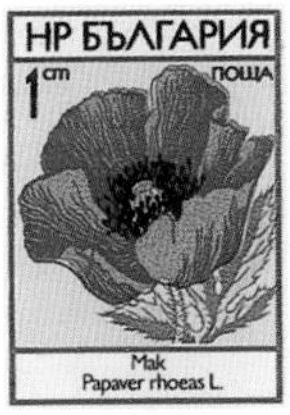

691 Common Poppy (*Papaver rhoeas*)

692 Botev (after T. Todorov)

(Des L. Chekhlarov. Photo)

1973 (15 May). Wild Flowers. T **691** and similar vert designs. Multicoloured. P 13.

2231	1st. Type **691**	20	15
2232	2st. Ox-eye daisy (*Leucanthemum vulgare*)	20	15
2233	3st. Peony (*Paeonia peregrina*)	20	15
2234	13st. Cornflower (*Centaurea cyanus*)	65	35
2235	18st. Corn cockle (*Agrostemma githago*)	6·50	4·50
2236	28st. Meadow buttercup (*Ranunculus acer*)	1·90	1·20
2231/2236 *Set of* 6		8·75	5·75

(Des St. Kunchev. Photo)

1973 (2 June). 125th Birth Anniv of Khristo Botev (poet and revolutionary). P 13.

2237 **692**	2st. brown, stone and metallic grey-green	20	15
2238	18st. bronze green, pale sage green and bronze	1·40	1·10

693 Asen Khalachev and Insurgents

(Des M. Peikova and G. Kovachev. Photo)

1973 (6 June). 50th Anniv of June Uprising at Pleven. T **693** and similar horiz design. P 13.

2239	1st. black, vermilion and gold	10	10
2240	2st. black, yellow-orange and gold	10	10

Design:—2st. "Wounded Worker" (illustration by Boris Angelushev to the poem "September" by Geo Milev).

694 Stamboliiski (from sculpture by A. Nikolov)

(Des I. Kosev. Photo)

1973 (14 June). 50th Death Anniv of Aleksandur Stamboliiski (Prime Minister 1919–23). P 12½.

2241 **694**	18st. deep brown and orange	65	55
2242	18st. bright orange	5·00	4·25

695 Muskrat

696 Turnovo

(Des M. Peikova and G. Kovachev. Photo)

1973 (29 June). Bulgarian Fauna. T **695** and similar multicoloured designs. P 13×12½ (3, 12st.) or 12½×13 (others).

2243	1st. Type **695**	20	15
2244	2st. Racoon-dog	20	15
2245	3st. Mouflon (vert)	20	15
2246	12st. Fallow deer (vert)	65	45
2247	18st. European bison	1·90	1·10
2248	40st. Elk	6·50	4·25
2243/2248 *Set of* 6		8·75	5·75

(Des V. Vasileva. Photo)

1973 (30 July). AIR. Views of Bulgarian Cities. T **696** and similar vert designs. Multicoloured. P 13.

2249	2st. Type **696**	20	15
2250	13st. Rusalka	65	25
2251	20st. Plovdiv	3·75	3·25
2252	28st. Sofia	95	85
2249/2252 *Set of* 4		5·00	4·00

697 "Insurgents on the March" (Boris Angelushev)

698 Congress Emblen

(Des St. Kunchev. Photo)

1973 (20 Aug). 50th Anniv of September Uprising. T **697** and similar designs. P 12½.

2253	2st. multicoloured	20	15
2254	5st. bluish violet, pale pink and lake	30	20
2255	13st. multicoloured	65	35
2256	18st. blackish olive, pale cream and lake	1·40	1·10
2253/2256 *Set of* 4		2·30	1·60

Designs: Horiz—5st. "Armed Train" (Boris Angelushev); 18st. Georgi Dimitrov and Vasil Kolarov. Vert—13st. Patriotic poster by N. Mirchev.

(Des S. Kamenov. Photo)

1973 (27 Aug). Eighth World Trade Union Congress, Varna. P 12½.

2257 **698**	2st. multicoloured	20	20

699 "Sun" Emblem and Olympic Rings

700 "Prince Kaloyan"

(Des St. Kunchev and A. Stareishinski. Photo)

1973 (29 Aug). Olympic Congress, Varna. T **699** and similar multicoloured designs. P 13.

2258	13st. Type **699**	1·90	75
2259	28st. Lion emblem of Bulgarian Olympic Committee	2·30	1·60
MS2260	61×77 mm. 80st. Footballers (40×25 mm.)	6·00	5·50

No. **MS**2260 has a new blue frame to both the stamp and the sheet. The sheet also exists imperforate, and imperforate with this frame colour changed to reddish purple, both from limited printings.

(Des St. Kunchev. Photo German Bank Note Ptg Co, Leipzig)

1973 (24 Sept). Frescoes from Boyana Church. T **700** and similar square portraits. Multicoloured. P 13.

2261	1st. Type **700**	20	15
2262	2st. "Desislava"	20	15
2263	3st. "Saint"	30	20
2264	5st. "St. Eustratius"	55	25
2265	10st. "Tsar Constantine Asen"	95	55
2266	13st. "Deacon Laurentius"	1·10	65
2267	18st. "Virgin Mary"	1·30	85
2268	20st. "St. Ephraim"	1·50	1·10
2269	28st. "Jesus Christ"	4·75	1·60
2261/2269 *Set of* 9		9·75	5·00
MS2270	56×76 mm. 80st. "Scribes". Imperf	8·75	8·75

701 Smirnenski and Cavalry Charge

(Des A. Stareishinski. Photo)

1973 (29 Sept). 75th Birth Anniv and 50th Death Anniv of Khristo Smirnenski (poet). P 12½.

2271 **701**	1st. greenish blue, red and gold	20	10
2272	2st. ultramarine, red and gold	45	20

702 Human Rights Emblem

704 "Finn" Class Dinghy

703 Tsar Todor Svetoslav and Byzantine Embassy, 1307

(Des St. Kunchev. Photo)

1973 (10 Oct). 25th Anniv of Declaration of Human Rights. P 12½.

2273 **702**	13st. gold, red and ultramarine	65	55

(Des P. Kulekov. Photo)

1973 (23 Oct). History of Bulgaria (2nd series). T **703** and similar horiz designs. Multicoloured. P 13½.

2274	1st. Type **703**	20	15
2275	2st. Tsar Mikhail Shishman in battle against the Byzantines, 1328	20	15
2276	3st. Battle of Rosokastro, 1332, and Tsar Ivan Aleksandur	20	15
2277	4st. Defence of Turnovo, 1393, and Patriarch Evtimii	20	15
2278	5st. Tsar Ivan Shishman's attack on the Turks	30	20
2279	13st. Momchil attacks Turkish ships at Umur, 1344	65	35
2280	18st. Meeting of Tsar Ivan Sratsimir and King Sigismund of Hungary's Crusaders, 1396	95	45
2281	28st. Embassy of Empress Anne of Savoy meets Boyars Balik, Teodor and Dobrotitsa	2·30	1·60
2274/2281 *Set of* 8		4·50	3·00

(Des A. Stareishinski. Litho German Bank Note Ptg Co, Leipzig)

1973 (29 Oct). Sailing. T **704** and similar vert designs, showing various yachts and dinghies. Multicoloured. P 13.

2282	1st. Type **704**	20	15
2283	2st. "Flying Dutchman" class	20	15
2284	3st. "Soling" class	20	15
2285	13st. "Tempest" class	65	35
2286	20st. "470" class	95	65
2287	40st. "Tornado" class	4·75	4·25
2282/2287 *Set of* 6		6·25	5·25

Nos. 2282/7 also exist imperforate from a limited printing with different coloured backgrounds.

705 "Balchik" (Bencho Obreshkhov)

(Des St. Kunchev. Litho State Security Ptg Works, Moscow)

1973 (10 Nov). 25th Anniv of Bulgarian National Gallery, and 150th Birth Anniv of Stanislav Dospevski (artist) (No. **MS**2294). T **705** and similar multicoloured designs, showing paintings. P 12.

2288 1st. Type **705** ... 20 20
2289 2st. "Mother and Child" (Stoyan Venev) ... 20 20
2290 3st. "Rest" (Tsenko Boyadzhiev) ... 20 20
2291 13st. "Vase with Flowers" (Sirak Skitnik) (vert) ... 75 35
2292 18st. "Mary Kuneva" (Iliya Petrov) (vert) ... 95 45
2293 40st. "Winter in Plovdiv" (Zlatyu Boyadzhiev) (vert) ... 4·25 3·75
2288/2293 *Set of 6* ... 6·00 4·75
MS2294 100×95 mm. 50st. "Domnika Lambreva" (S. Dospevski) (vert); 50st. Self-portrait (S. Dospevski) (vert) ... 6·00 4·25

706 Footballers and Emblem

707 Old Testament Scene (wood carving)

(Des St. Kunchev. Photo)

1973 (12 Dec). World Cup Football Championship, Munich (1974). Sheet 62×94 mm. P 13.

MS2295 **706** 28st. multicoloured (sold at 1l.) ... 6·50 6·50

A restricted issue of No. **MS**2295 overprinted with "ARGENTINA 78" etc. appeared in 1978.

(Des K. Kunev and P. Rashkov. Photo)

1974 (15 Jan). Wood Carvings from Rozhen Monastery. T **707** and similar vert designs. P 13.

2296 1st. brown, cream and brown-lake ... 20 15
a. Horiz strip of 3. Nos. 2296/8 ... 65
2297 2st. brown, cream and brown-lake ... 20 15
2298 3st. brown, cream and brown-lake ... 20 15
2299 5st. blackish olive, cream and green ... 30 15
a. Horiz pair. Nos. 2299/2300 ... 70 40
2300 8st. blackish olive, cream and green ... 35 20
2301 13st. olive-brown, cream and chestnut ... 55 40
a. Horiz pair. Nos. 2301/2 ... 1·80 1·20
2302 28st. olive-brown, cream and chestnut ... 1·10 65
2296/2302 *Set of 7* ... 2·50 1·70

Designs:—1, 2, 3st. "Passover Table"; 5, 8st. "Abraham and the Angel"; 13, 28st. "The Expulsion from Eden".

Nos. 2296/8, 2299/2300 and 2301/2 respectively were issued together *se-tenant* within their sheets, forming three composite designs.

708 "Lenin" (N. Mirchev)

(Des M. Peikova and G. Kovachev. Litho State Ptg Works, Moscow)

1974 (28 Jan). 50th Death Anniv of Lenin. T **708** and similar horiz design. Multicoloured. P 12.

2303 2st. Type **708** ... 20 15
2304 18st. "Lenin with Workers" (V. Serov) ... 95 65

709 "Blagoev addressing Meeting" (G. Kovachev)

(Des M. Peikova and G. Kovachev. Litho State Ptg Works, Moscow)

1974 (28 Jan). 50th Death Anniv of Dimitur Blagoev (founder of Bulgarian Social Democratic Party). P 12.

2305 **709** 2st. multicoloured ... 20 15

710 Sheep

711 Social Economic Integration Emblem

(Des V. Vasileva. Photo)

1974 (1 Feb). Domestic Animals. T **710** and similar horiz designs. P 13.

2306 1st. purple-brown, buff and bright green ... 20 15
2307 2st. dull purple, slate-violet and carmine-red ... 20 15
2308 3st. brown, pink and deep emerald ... 20 15
2309 5st. brown, buff and deep turquoise-blue ... 20 15
2310 13st. black, violet-blue and orange-brown ... 1·10 35
2311 20st. red-brown, pink and ultramarine ... 3·00 1·80
2306/2311 *Set of 6* ... 4·50 2·50

Designs:—2 st Goat; 3st. Pig; 5st. Cow; 13st. Buffalo; 20st. Horse.

(Des A. Mechkuev. Photo)

1974 (11 Feb). 25th Anniv of the Council for Mutual Economic Aid. P 13.

2312 **711** 13st. multicoloured ... 75 55

712 Footballers

(Des V. Vasileva and A. Stareishinski. Photo)

1974 (25 Mar). World Cup Football Championship, Munich. T **712** and similar horiz designs, showing footballers. P 13½×13.

2313 1st. multicoloured ... 20 15
2314 2st. multicoloured ... 20 15
2315 3st. multicoloured ... 20 15
2316 13st. multicoloured ... 55 20
2317 28st. multicoloured ... 95 55
2318 40st. multicoloured ... 2·30 1·60
2313/2318 *Set of 6* ... 4·00 2·50
MS2319 66×78 mm. 1l. multicoloured (55×30 mm) ... 4·75 4·25

No. **MS**2319 also exists imperforate from a restricted printing.

713 Folk-singers

714 "Cosmic Research" (Penko Bambov)

(Des A. Stareishinski. Photo)

1974 (25 Apr). Festival of Amateur Arts and 4th Republican Sports Day. T **713** and similar vert designs. Multicoloured. P 13.

2320 1st. Type **713** ... 20 15
2321 2st. Folk-dancers ... 20 15
2322 3st. Piper and drummer ... 20 15
2323 5st. Wrestling ... 20 15
2324 13st. Athletics ... 95 85
2325 18st. Gymnastics ... 1·10 55
2320/2325 *Set of 6* ... 2·50 1·80

(Des St. Kunchev. Photo German Bank Note Ptg Co, Leipzig)

1974 (20 May). Mladost '74 Youth Stamp Exhibition, Sofia. T **714** and similar square designs. Multicoloured. P 13.

2326 1st. Type **714** ... 15 10
2327 2st. "Salt Production" (Mariana Bliznakova) ... 20 10
2328 3st. "Fire-dancer" (Detelina Lalova) ... 55 10
2329 28st. "Friendship" (Vanya Boyanova) ... 2·75 2·40
2326/2329 *Set of 4* ... 3·25 2·40
MS2330 70×70 mm. 60st. "Spring" (Vladimir Kunchev) (40×40 mm) ... 4·25 4·25

A further miniature sheet, face value 80st. showing a horseman, was issued on 23 May in a restricted printing.

715 Motor-cars

(Des St. Kunchev. Photo)

1974 (25 May). World Automobile Federation's Spring Congress, Sofia. P 13.

2331 **715** 13st. multicoloured ... 65 45

716 Period Architecture

(Des St. Kunchev. Photo)

1974 (20 June). United Nations Educational, Scientific and Cultural Organization's Executive Council's 94th Session, Varna. P 13.

2332 **716** 18st. multicoloured ... 65 45

717 Chinese Aster

718 19th-Century Post-boy

(Des M. Yoich. Photo)

1974 (22 June). Bulgarian Flowers. T **717** and similar horiz designs. Multicoloured. P 13.

2333 1st. Type **717** ... 20 20
2334 2st. Mallow ... 20 20
2335 3st. Columbine ... 20 20
2336 18st. Tulip ... 95 35
2337 20st. Marigold ... 1·10 45
2338 28st. Pansy ... 2·75 1·80
2333/2338 *Set of 6* ... 4·75 3·00
MS2339 80×60 mm. 80st. Gaillarde (44×33 mm) ... 3·75 3·25

(Des K. Kunev and P. Rashkov. Photo)

1974 (5 Aug). Centenary of the Universal Postal Union. T **718** and similar horiz designs. P 13½×13.

2340 2st. violet and pale yellow-orange ... 20 15
2341 18st. dull yellsh grn & pale yell-orge ... 95 45
MS2342 80×58 mm. 28st. pale turquoise-blue and pale yellow-orange (sold at 80st.) ... 3·25 3·25

Designs:—18st. 19th-century mail coach; 28st. U.P.U. emblem.

No. **MS**2342 also exists imperforate from a restricted printing.

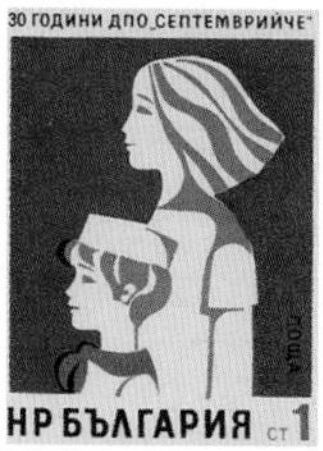

719 Young Pioneer and Komsomol Girl

720 Communist Soldiers with Flag

(Des M. Konstantinova. Photo)

1974 (12 Aug). 30th Anniv of Dimitrov Septembrist Pioneers Organization. T **719** and similar vert designs. Multicoloured. P 13.

2343 1st. Type **719** ... 15 10
2344 2st. Pioneer with doves ... 15 10
MS2345 60×84 mm. 60st. Emblem with portrait of Dimitrov (34×44 mm) ... 2·50 2·20

(Des P. Rashkov. Photo)

1974 (29 Aug). 30th Anniv of Fatherland Front Government. T **720** and similar vert designs. Multicoloured. P 13.

2346 1st. Type **720** ... 20 15
2347 2st. Soviet Liberators ... 20 15
2348 5st. Industrialisation ... 20 15
2349 13st. Modern Agriculture ... 55 20
2350 18st. Science and Technology ... 1·00 65
2346/2350 *Set of 5* ... 1·90 1·20

721 Stockholm and Emblems

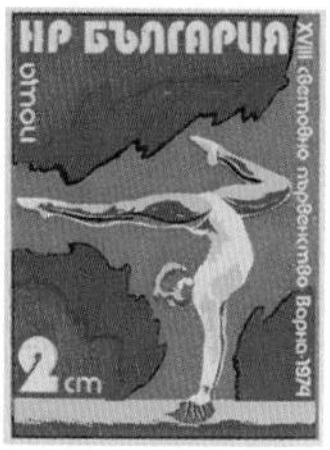

722 Gymnast on Beam

(Des St. Kunchev. Photo)

1974 (18 Sept). Stockholmia '74 International Stamp Exhibition. Sheet 65×72 mm. P 13.

MS2351 **721** 40st. bright blue, emerald and bistre-yellow ... 7·50 7·50

(Des L. Chekhlarov. Photo)

1974 (19 Oct). 18th World Gymnastics Championships, Varna. T **722** and similar vert design. Multicoloured. P 13.

2352 2st. Type **722** ... 15 10
2353 13st. Gymnast on horse ... 65 55

723 Doves on Script

724 Envelope with Arrow pointing to Postal Code

(Des St. Kunchev. Photo)

1974 (29 Oct). European Security and Co-operation Conference. Sheet 97×117 mm containing T **723** and similar vert designs. P 13×13½.

MS2354 13st. chrome-yellow, blue and chestnut (Type **723**); 13st. blue, mauve and chestnut (Map of Europe and script); 13st. emerald, light blue and chestnut (Leaves on script); 13st. multicoloured (Commemorative text) (sold at 60st.) ... 3·50 3·50

No. **MS**2354 also exists imperforate from a restricted printing.

A restricted issue of No. **MS**2354 with each stamp overprinted "EUROPA" appeared in 1979.

(Des K. Kunev. Photo)

1974 (20 Nov). Introduction of the Postal Coding System (1975). P 13.
2355 **724** 2st. yellowish green, yellow and black ... 20 15

725 "Sourovachka" (twig decorated with coloured ribbons)

726 Icon of St. Theodor Stratilat

(Des St. Kunchev. Photo)

1974 (5 Dec). New Year. P 13.
2356 **725** 2st. multicoloured ... 20 15

(Des M. Peikova and G. Kovachev. Photo)

1974 (28 Dec). Bulgarian History. T **726** and similar vert designs. P 13.
2357 1st. multicoloured ... 20 15
2358 2st. bluish grey, mauve and black ... 20 15
2359 3st. grey, pale greenish blue and black ... 20 15
2360 5st. grey, slate-lilac and black ... 20 15
2361 8st. black, gold and vermilion ... 30 15
2362 13st. grey, bright green and black ... 45 20
2363 18st. black, gold and vermilion ... 75 35
2364 28st. grey, bright blue and black ... 2·20 1·10
2357/2364 *Set of 8* ... 4·00 2·20
Designs:—2st. Bronze medallion; 3st. Carved capital; 5st. Silver bowl of Sivin Jupan: 8st. Clay goblet; 13st. Lioness (torso); 18st. Gold tray; 28st. Double-headed eagle.

727 Apricot

728 Peasant with Flag

(Des L. Chekhlarov. Photo)

1975 (3 Feb). Fruit Tree Blossoms. T **727** and similar vert designs. Multicoloured. P 13.
2365 1st. Type **727** ... 20 15
2366 2st. Apple ... 20 15
2367 3st. Cherry ... 20 15
2368 19st. Pear ... 65 35
2369 28st. Peach ... 1·60 55
2365/2369 *Set of 5* ... 2·50 1·20

(Des St. Kunchev and A. Stareishinski. Photo)

1975 (20 Feb). 75th Anniv of Bulgarian People's Agrarian Union. Sheet 104×95 mm containing T **728** and similar vert designs. P 13.
MS2370 2st. reddish brown, bright orange and yellowish green; 5st. yellow-brown, bright orange and yellowish green; 13st. sepia, bright-orange and yellowish green; 18st. chestnut, bright orange and yellowish green ... 1·60 1·60
Designs:—5st. Rebels keeping watch during 1923 September Uprising; 13st. Dancing; 18st. Woman harvesting fruit.

729 Spanish 6c. Stamp of 1850 and "España" Emblem

730 Star and Arrow

(Des St. Kunchev. Photo)

1975 (24 Feb). España 1975 International Stamp Exhibition, Madrid. Sheet 68×100 mm. P 13.
MS2371 **729** 40st. multicoloured ... 8·00 7·50

(Des P. Petrov. Photo)

1975 (20 Mar). 30th Anniv of "Victory in Europe" Day. T **730** and similar vert designs. P 13.
2372 2st. rosine, black and gold ... 20 15
2373 13st. greenish blue, black and gold ... 75 35
Design:—13st. Peace dove and broken sword.

731 "Weights and Measures"

732 Tree and Open Book

(Des P. Petrov. Photo)

1975 (21 Mar). Centenary of the Metre Convention. P 13×13½.
2374 **731** 13st. black, deep mauve and silver ... 30 20

(Des P. Petrov. Photo)

1975 (25 Mar). 50th Anniv of the Bulgarian Forestry School. P 13.
2375 **732** 2st. multicoloured ... 20 15

733 Michelangelo

734 Festival Emblem

(Des A. Stareishinski. Photo)

1975 (28–31 Mar). 500th Birth Anniv of Michelangelo. T **733** and similar designs. P 13.
2376 2st. brown-purple and deep grey-blue ... 20 15
2377 13st. chalky blue and deep mauve ... 55 35
2378 18st. sepia and deep green ... 1·10 65
2376/2378 *Set of 3* ... 1·70 1·00
MS2379 70×84 mm. **733** 2st. yellow-olive and red (sold at 60st.) (31.3) ... 2·20 2·20
Designs: Horiz (sculptures from Giuliano de Medici's tomb)—13st. "Night"; 18st. "Day".

(Des St. Kunchev. Photo)

1975 (15 May). Festival of Humour and Satire, Gabrovo. P 13.
2380 **734** 2st. multicoloured ... 20 15

735 Woman's Head and Emblem

736 Vasil and Sava Kokareshkov

(Des St. Kunchev. Photo)

1975 (20 May). International Women's Year. P 13.
2381 **735** 13st. multicoloured ... 45 20

(Des G. Nedyalkov. Photo)

1975 (30 May). "Young Martyrs to Fascism." T **736** and similar horiz designs. P 13½×13.
2382 1st. black, turquoise-green and gold ... 10 10
2383 2st. black, deep magenta and gold ... 10 10
2384 5st. black, rose-carmine and gold ... 15 10
2385 13st. black, bright blue and gold ... 55 45
2382/2385 *Set of 4* ... 80 70
Designs:—2st. Mitko Palauzov and Ivan Vasilev; 5st. Nikola Nakev and Stefcho Kraichev; 13st. Ivanka Pashkulova and Detelina Mincheva.

737 "Mother feeding Child" (Jean Millet)

738 Gabrovo Costume

(Des St. Kunchev. Recess and photo State Ptg Wks, Moscow)

1975 (6 June). World Graphic Exhibition, Sofia. Celebrated Drawings and Engravings. T **737** and similar multicoloured designs. P 11½×12 (40st.) or 12×11½ (others).
2386 1st. Type **737** ... 20 15
2387 2st. "Mourning a dead Daughter" (Goya) ... 20 15
2388 3st. "The Reunion" (Iliya Beshkov) ... 20 15
2389 13st. "Seated Nude" (Auguste Renoir) ... 45 20
2390 20st. "Man in a Fur Hat" (Rembrandt) ... 65 55
2391 40st. "The Dream" (Honoré Daumier) (horiz) ... 2·30 1·20
2386/2391 *Set of 6* ... 3·50 2·20

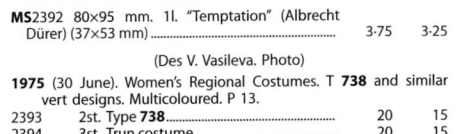

MS2392 80×95 mm. 1l. "Temptation" (Albrecht Dürer) (37×53 mm) ... 3·75 3·25

(Des V. Vasileva. Photo)

1975 (30 June). Women's Regional Costumes. T **738** and similar vert designs. Multicoloured. P 13.
2393 2st. Type **738** ... 20 15
2394 3st. Trun costume ... 20 15
2395 5st. Vidin costume ... 20 15
2396 13st. Goce Delčev costume ... 75 35
2397 18st. Ruse costume ... 1·70 55
2393/2397 *Set of 5* ... 2·75 1·20

739 "Bird" (manuscript illumination)

740 Ivan Vazov

(Des K. Kunev. Litho State Ptg Wks, Moscow)

1975 (8 July). Original Bulgarian Manuscripts. Decorated Lettering. T **739** and similar square designs. Multicoloured. P 11.
2398 1st. Type **739** ... 20 15
2399 2st. "Head" ... 20 15
2400 3st. Abstract design ... 20 15
2401 8st. "Pointing finger" ... 35 20
2402 13st. "Imaginary creature" ... 75 35
2403 18st. Abstract design ... 1·30 45
2398/2403 *Set of 6* ... 2·75 1·30

(Des G. Nedyalkov. Photo)

1975 (9 July). 125th Birth Anniv of Ivan Vazov (writer). T **740** and similar vert design. Multicoloured. P 13.
2404 2st. Type **740** ... 20 10
2405 13st. Vazov seated ... 55 20

741 "Soyuz" and Aleksei Leonov

(Des St. Kunchev and A. Stareishinski. Photo)

1975 (15 July). "Apollo"–"Soyuz" Space Link. T **741** and similar horiz designs. P 13.
2406 13st. bright blue, pale brownish grey and deep rose-red ... 45 20
2407 18st. bluish violet, pale brownish grey and deep rose-red ... 95 35
2408 28st. dull ultramarine, pale brownish grey and deep rose-red ... 1·90 65
2406/2408 *Set of 3* ... 3·00 1·10
MS2409 76×84 mm. 1l. deep ultramarine, pale, brownish grey and deep rose-red ... 4·25 3·25
Designs:—18st. "Apollo" and Thomas Stafford; 28st. The Link-up; 1l. "Apollo" and "Soyuz" after docking procedure.

742 Ryukyu Sailing Boat, Map and Emblems

(Des St. Kunchev. Photo)

1975 (5 Aug). International Exposition, Okinawa. P 13.
2410 **742** 13st. multicoloured ... 45 20

743 St. Cyril and St. Methodius

744 Footballer

(Des St. Kunchev. Photo)

1975 (21 Aug). Balkanphila V. Stamp Exhibition, Sofia. T **743** and similar designs. P 13.
2411 2st. blackish brown, stone and red ... 20 10
2412 13st. blackish brown, stone and deep green ... 55 20
MS2413 90×86 mm. 50st. sepia, orange-brown and reddish orange ... 2·20 2·20
Designs: Vert—13st. St. Constantine and St. Helene; Horiz—50st. Sophia Church, Sofia (53×43 mm).

(Des Kh. Khristov. Photo)

1975 (21 Sept). 8th Inter-Toto (Football Pools) Congress, Varna. P 13.
2414 **744** 2st. multicoloured ... 20 15

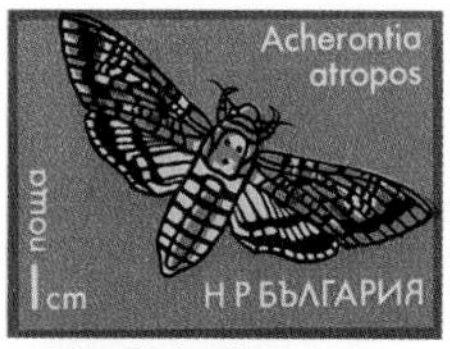

745 Death's-head Hawk Moth (*Acherontia atropos*)

746 U.N. Emblem

(Des A. Stareishinski. Photo)

1975 (23 Oct). Hawk Moths. T **745** and similar horiz designs. Multicoloured. P 13.

2415 1st. Type **745** ... 20 15
2416 2st. Oleander hawk moth (*Daphnis nerii*) ... 20 15
2417 3st. Eyed hawk moth (*Smerinthus ocellata*) ... 20 15
2418 10st. Mediterranean hawk moth (*Deilephila nicea*) ... 55 20
2419 13st. Elephant hawk moth (*Choerocampa elpenor*) ... 95 45
2420 18st. Broad-bordered bee hawk moth (*Macroglossum fuciformis*) ... 1·90 75
2415/2420 *Set of 6* ... 3·50 1·70

(Des B. Ikonomov. Photo)

1975 (24 Oct). 30th Anniv of the United Nations Organization. P 13.

2421 **746** 13st. deep carmine, stone and black ... 45 20

747 Map of Europe on Peace Dove

748 D. Khristov

(Des St. Kunchev. Photo)

1975 (29 Oct). European Security and Co-operation Conference, Helsinki. P 13.

2422 **747** 18st. rose-lilac, ultramarine and greenish yellow ... 85 85

The stamp was issued in sheets of five, with four *se-tenant* labels.

(Des A. Stareishinski. Photo)

1975 (11 Nov). Birth Centenary of Dobri Khristov (composer). P 13.

2423 **748** 5st. red-brown, greenish yellow and emerald ... 20 10

749 Constantine's Rebellion against the Turks

(Des B. Stoev. Photo)

1975 (27 Nov). Bulgarian History. T **749** and similar horiz designs. Multicoloured. P 13.

2424 1st. Type **749** ... 20 15
2425 2st. Vladislav III's campaign ... 20 15
2426 3st. Battle of Turnovo ... 20 15
2427 10st. Battle of Chiprovtsi ... 30 20
2428 13st. 17th-century partisans ... 75 35
2429 18st. Return of banished peasants ... 1·00 55
2424/2429 *Set of 6* ... 2·40 1·40

750 "First Aid"

(Des N. Kovachev. Photo)

1975 (5 Dec). 90th Anniv of the Bulgarian Red Cross. T **750** and similar horiz design. P 13×13½.

2430 2st. Venetian red, black and scarlet ... 15 10
2431 13st. deep turquoise-green, blk & scar ... 55 20

Design:—13st. "Peace and International Co-operation".

751 Ethnographical Museum, Plovdiv

(Des St. Kunchev. Photo)

1975 (17 Dec). European Architectural Heritage Year. P 13.

2432 **751** 80st. purple-brown, chrome-yellow and bronze-green ... 2·75 2·75

The stamp was issued in sheets of three, with three *se-tenant* labels.

752 Christmas Lanterns

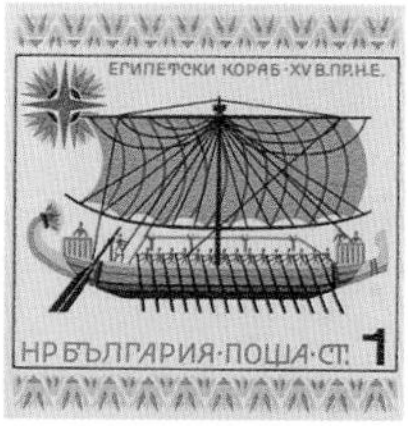

753 Egyptian Galley

(Des St. Kunchev. Photo)

1975 (22 Dec). Christmas and New Year. T **752** and similar horiz design. Multicoloured. P 13.

2433 2st. Type **752** ... 20 10
2434 13st. Stylized peace dove ... 45 35

(Des St. Kunchev. Photo German Bank Note Ptg Co, Leipzig)

1975 (25 Dec). Historic Ships (1st series). T **753** and similar square designs. Multicoloured. P 13.

2435 1st. Type **753** ... 10 10
2436 2st. Phoenician galley ... 10 10
2437 3st. Greek trireme ... 10 10
2438 5st. Roman galley ... 20 10
2439 13st. *Mora* (Norman ship), 1066 ... 55 35
2440 18st. Venetian galley ... 1·10 55
2435/2440 *Set of 6* ... 1·90 1·20

See also Nos. 2597/2602, 2864/9, 3286/91 and 3372/7.

754 Modern Articulated Tramcar

(Des I. Bogdanov. Photo)

1976 (12 Jan). 75th Anniv of the Sofia Tramways. T **754** and similar horiz design. Multicoloured. P 13½×13.

2441 2st. Type **754** ... 20 10
2442 13st. Early 20th-century tramcar ... 85 40

755 Skiing

(Des A. Stareishinski. Photo)

1976 (30 Jan). Winter Olympic Games, Innsbruck. T **755** and similar multicoloured designs. P 13.

2443 1st. Type **755** ... 20 15
2444 2st. Cross-country skiing (vert) ... 20 15
2445 3st. Ski jumping ... 20 15
2446 13st. Biathlon (vert) ... 55 35
2447 18st. Ice hockey (vert) ... 65 55
2448 23st. Speed skating (vert) ... 1·90 75
2443/2448 *Set of 6* ... 3·25 1·90

MS2449 70×80 mm. 80st. Ice skating (pairs) (30×55 mm) ... 3·25 2·75

756 Stylized Bird

757 Alexander Graham Bell and early Telephone

(Des A. Stareishinski. Photo)

1976 (1 Mar). 11th Bulgarian Communist Party Congress. T **756** and similar vert designs. Multicoloured. P 13.

2450 2st. Type **756** ... 10 10
2451 5st. "1956–1976, Fulfilment of the Five Year Plans" ... 20 15
2452 13st. Hammer and Sickle ... 45 20
2450/2452 *Set of 3* ... 70 40

MS2453 55×65 mm. 50st. Georgi Dimitrov (Prime Minister and Party secretary-general, 1945–49) (33×43 mm) ... 1·90 1·60

(Des N. Kovachev. Photo)

1976 (10 Mar). Telephone Centenary. P 13.

2454 **757** 18st. brown-ochre, yellow-brown and deep purple-brown ... 65 35

758 Mute Swan (*Cygnus olor*)

(Des L. Chekhlarov. Photo State Ptg Works, Moscow)

1976 (27 Mar). Water-fowl. T **758** and similar horiz designs. Multicoloured. P 11½×12.

2455 1st. Type **758** ... 20 15
2456 2st. Ruddy shelduck (*Tadorna ferruginea*) ... 20 15
2457 3st. Common shelduck (*Tadorna tadorna*) ... 30 20
2458 5st. Garganey (*Anas querquedula*) ... 1·10 35
2459 13st. Mallard (*Anas platyrhynchas*) ... 1·40 85
2460 18st. Red-crested pochard (*Netta rufina*) ... 3·75 2·75
2455/2460 *Set of 6* ... 6·25 4·00

759 Guerrillas' Briefing

760 Kozlodui Atomic Energy Centre

(Des B. Stoev. Photo)

1976 (5 Apr). Centenary of April Uprising (1st issue). T **759** and similar horiz designs. Multicoloured. P 13.

2461 1st. Type **759** ... 10 10
2462 2st. Peasants briefing ... 10 10
2463 5st. Krishina, horse and guard ... 20 10
2464 13st. Rebels with cannon ... 55 35
2461/2464 *Set of 4* ... 85 60

See also Nos. 2529/**MS**2534.

(Des J. Minchev. Photo)

1976 (7 Apr). Five Year Plan. Modern Industrial Installations. T **760** and similar vert designs. P 13.

2465 5st. dull blue-green ... 20 15
2466 8st. lake ... 30 20
2467 10st. myrtle green ... 45 25
2468 13st. bluish violet ... 55 30
2469 20st. emerald ... 75 35
2465/2469 *Set of 5* ... 2·00 1·10

Designs:—8st. Bobovdol plant; 10st. Sviloza chemical works; 13st. Devnya chemical works; 20st. Sestrimo dam.

761 Guard with Patrol-dog

(Des P. Ferdzhanov. Photo)

1976 (15 May). 30th Anniv of Frontier Guards. T **761** and similar horiz design. Multicoloured. P 13.

2470 2st. Type **761** ... 20 15
2471 13st. Mounted guards ... 45 20

762 Worker with Spade

763 Botev

(Des P. Ferdzhanov. Photo)

1976 (20 May). 30th Anniv of Youth Brigades Movement. P 13.

2472 **762** 2st. multicoloured ... 20 15

(Des St. Kunchev and A. Stareishinski. Photo)

1976 (25 May). Death Centenary of Khristo Botev (poet). P 13.

2473 **763** 13st. bronze green and ochre ... 65 35

No. 2473 was issued with *se-tenant* label bearing a quotation from Botev's poetry.

764 "Martyrs of First Congress" (relief)

765 Dimitur Blagoev

(Des P. Petrov. Photo)

1976 (28 May). 85th Anniv of First Bulgarian Social Democratic Party Congress, Buzludzha. T **764** and similar vert design. Multicoloured. P 13.

2474 2st. Type **764** ... 15 10
2475 5st. Modern memorial, Buzludzha Peak ... 20 10

(Des P. Petrov. Photo)

1976 (28 May). 120th Birth Anniv of Dimitur Blagoev (founder of Bulgarian Social Democratic Party). P 13.

2476 **765** 13st. blue-black, dull vermilion and gold ... 65 20

766 "Thematic Stamps"

(Des St. Kunchev. Photo)

1976 (5 June). 12th Bulgarian Philatelic Federation Congress. Sheet 73×103 mm. P 13.

MS2477 **766**	50st. multicoloured	3·25	2·75

767 Children Playing

(Des N. Stoyanov. Photo)

1976 (15 June). Child Welfare. T **767** and similar horiz designs, showing children at play. P 13.

2478	1st. multicoloured	20	15
2479	2st. multicoloured	20	15
2480	5st. multicoloured	20	15
2481	23st. multicoloured	95	55
2478/2481 *Set of 4*		1·40	90

Designs:—2st. Girls with pram and boy on rocking horse; 5st. Playing ball; 23st. Dancing.

768 Wrestling

(Des A. Stareishinski. Photo)

1976 (25 June). Olympic Games, Montreal. T **768** and similar multicoloured designs. P 13.

2482	1st. Type **768**	20	15
2483	2st. Boxing (vert)	20	15
2484	3st. Weightlifting (vert)	20	15
2485	13st. Canoeing (vert)	45	20
2486	18st. Gymnastics (vert)	65	35
2487	28st. Diving (vert)	1·00	55
2488	40st. Athletics (vert)	1·40	65
2482/2488 *Set of 7*		3·75	2·00
MS2489 70×80 mm. 1l. Weightlifting (vert)		3·25	3·25

769 Belt Buckle, Vidin

(Des St. Kunchev. Photo)

1976 (30 July). Thracian Art (8th–4th-centuries BC). T **769** and similar vert designs. Multicoloured. P 13.

2490	1st. Type **769**	20	15
2491	2st. Brooch, Durzhanitsa	20	15
2492	3st. Mirror handle, Chukarka	20	15
2493	5st. Helmet cheek guard, Gurlo	20	15
2494	13st. Gold decoration, Orizovo	45	20
2495	18st. Decorated horse-harness, Brezovo	65	30
2496	20st. Greave, Mogilanska Mogila	85	35
2497	28st. Pendant, Bukovtsi	95	55
2490/2497 *Set of 8*		3·25	1·80

770 "Partisans at Night" (Petrov)

(Des K. Kunev. Photo German Bank Note Ptg Co, Leipzig)

1976 (11 Aug). Paintings by Iliya Petrov and Tsanko Lavrenov from the National Gallery. T **770** and similar multicoloured designs. P 14.

2498	2st. Type **770**	20	15
2499	5st. "Kurshum-Khan" (Lavrenov)	20	15
2500	13st. "Seated Woman" (Petrov) (vert)	45	20
2501	18st. "Boy seated in Chair" (Petrov) (vert)	95	35
2502	28st. "Old Plovdiv" (Lavrenov) (vert)	1·10	45
2498/2502 *Set of 5*		2·50	1·20
MS2503 60×82 mm. 80st. "Self-portrait" (Petrov) (vert)		2·75	2·75

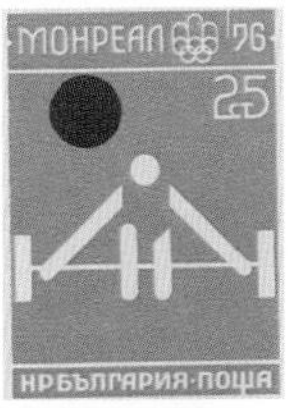

771 Weightlifting

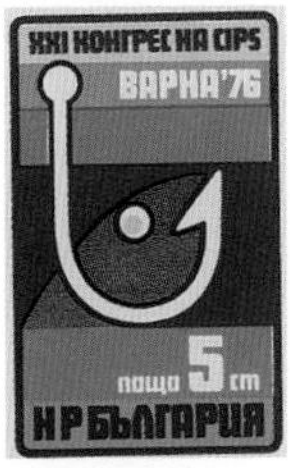

772 Fish on Line

(Des St. Kunchev. Photo)

1976 (6 Sept). Gold Medal Winners, Montreal Olympic Games. Sheet 98×116 mm, containing vert designs as T **771**, each with medal in brown-red and gold. P 13.

MS2504 25st. yellow (Type **771**); 25st. new blue (Rowing); 25st. emerald (Running); 25st. scarlet (Wrestling)	3·25	3·25

(Des P. Petrov. Photo)

1976 (21 Sept). World Sports Fishing Congress, Varna. P 13.

2505 **772**	5st. multicoloured	30	20

773 "The Pianist"

774 St. Theodor

(Des Y. Petrov. Photo)

1976 (30 Sept). 75th Birth Anniv of A. Zhendov (caricaturist). P 13×13½.

2506	2st. bottle green, pale cinnamon and blue-green	10	10
2507	5st. deep violet, pale lilac and bright violet	30	15
2508	13st. black, rose and deep claret	45	20
2506/2508 *Set of 3*		75	40

Designs:—5st. "Trick or Treat"; 13st. "The Leader".

(Des St. Kunchev. Litho State Ptg Works, Moscow)

1976 (4 Oct). Zemen Monastery. Frescoes. T **774** and similar vert designs. Multicoloured. P 12×12½.

2509	2st. Type **774**	20	15
2510	3st. St. Paul the Apostle	20	15
2511	5st. St. Joachim	30	15
2512	13st. Prophet Melchisadek	55	20
2513	19st. St. Porphyrius	75	35
2514	28st. Queen Doya	95	45
2509/2514 *Set of 6*		2·75	1·30
MS2515 60×76 mm. 1l. Holy Communion		3·25	3·25

775 Legal Document

776 Horse Chestnut (*Aesculus hippocastanum*)

(Des S. Kamenov. Photo)

1976 (5 Oct). 25th Anniv of State Archives. P 13.

2516 **775**	5st. black, lake-brown and new blue	30	20

(Des V. Vasileva. Photo)

1976 (14 Oct). Plants. T **776** and similar vert designs. Multicoloured. P 13.

2517	1st. Type **776**	20	15
2518	2st. Shrubby cinquefoil (*Potentilla fruticosa*)	20	15
2519	5st. Holly (*Ilex aquifolium*)	20	15
2520	8st. Yew (*Taxus baccata*)	30	20
2521	13st. *Daphne pontica*	45	35
2522	23st. Judas tree (*Cercis siliquastrum*)	1·20	55
2517/2522 *Set of 6*		2·30	1·40

777 Cloud over Sun

778 Dimitur Polyanov

(Des A. Stareishinski. Photo)

1976 (10 Nov). Protection of the Environment. T **777** and similar horiz design. Multicoloured. P 13.

2523	2st. Cloud over tree	20	15
2524	18st. Type **777**	65	35

(Des N. Kovachev. Photo)

1976 (19 Nov). Birth Centenary of Dimitur Polyanov (poet). P 13.

2525 **778**	2st. deep reddish lilac and pale orange	20	15

779 Congress Emblem

780 Warrior with Horses (vase painting)

(Des Y. Petrov. Photo)

1976 (28 Nov). 33rd Bulgarian People's Agrarian Union Congress. T **779** and similar vert design. Multicoloured. P 13.

2526	2st. Type **779**	20	10
2527	13st. Flags	55	35

(Des St. Kunchev. Photo)

1976 (3 Dec). 30th Anniv of United Nations Educational, Scientific and Cultural Organization. Sheet 71×81 mm. P 13.

MS2528 **780**	50st. multicoloured	2·75	2·75

781 "Khristo Botev" (Zlatyu Boyadzhiev)

(Des V. Vasileva. Photo German Bank Note Ptg Co, Leipzig)

1976 (8 Dec). Centenary of April Uprising (2nd issue). T **781** and similar square designs. Multicoloured. P 13.

2529	1st. Type **781**	20	15
2530	2st. "Partisan carrying Cherrywood Cannon" (Iliya Petrov)	20	15
2531	3st. "Necklace of Immortality" (Dechko Uzunov)	20	15
2532	13st. "April 1876" (Georgi Popov)	45	20
2533	18st. "Partisans" (Stoyan Venev)	75	45
2529/2533 *Set of 5*		1·60	1·00
MS2534 45×82 mm. 60st. "The Oath" (Svetlin Rusev). Imperf		2·20	2·20

782 "Tobacco Workers"

(Des St. Kunchev. Photo)

1976 (16 Dec). 70th Birth Anniv of Veselin Staikov (artist). T **782** and similar horiz designs. Multicoloured. P 13.

2535	1st. Type **782**	10	10
2536	2st. "Melnik"	15	10
2537	13st. "Boat Builders"	55	25
2535/2537 *Set of 3*		70	40

783 "Snowflake"

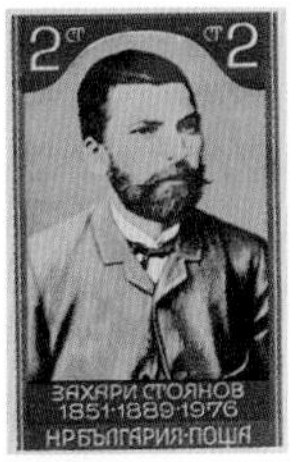

784 Zakhari Stoyanov

(Des St. Kunchev. Photo)

1976 (20 Dec). New Year. P 13.

2538 **783**	2st. multicoloured	20	10

(Des St. Kunchev. Photo)

1976 (30 Dec). 125th Birth Anniv of Zakhari Stoyanov (writer). P 13.

2539 **784**	2st. reddish brown, brown-red and gold	20	10

785 Bronze Coin of Septimus Severus

(Des Kh. Khristov. Photo)

1977 (28 Jan). Coins Struck in Serdica. T **785** and similar horiz designs. Multicoloured. P 14.

2540		1st. Type **785**	20	15
2541		2st. Bronze coin of Caracalla	20	15
2542		13st. Bronze coin of Caracalla (diff)	30	20
2543		18st. Bronze coin of Caracalla (diff)	55	35
2544		23st. Copper coin of Diocletian	95	55
2540/2544		*Set of 5*	2·00	1·30

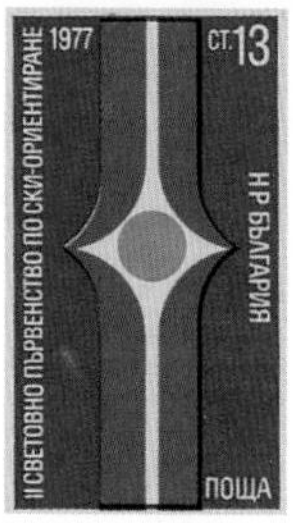

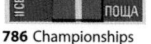

786 Championships Emblem

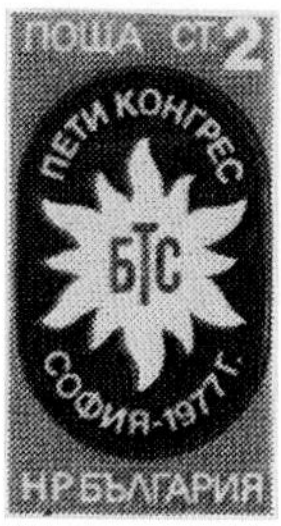

787 Congress Emblem

(Des S. Kamenov. Photo)

1977 (14 Feb). World Ski-Orienteering Championships. P 13.

2545	**786**	13st. pale blue, orange-vermilion and ultramarine	55	20

(Des S. Kamenov. Photo)

1977 (24 Feb). Fifth Congress of Bulgarian Tourist Associations. P 13.

2546	**787**	2st. multicoloured	20	10

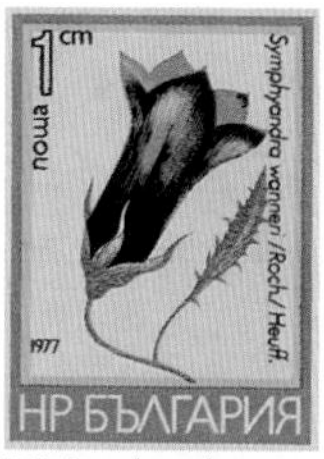

788 *Symphyandra wanneri*

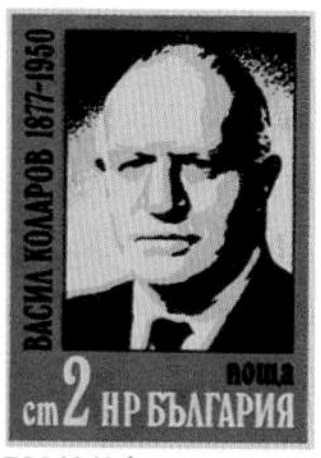

789 V. Kolarov

(Des L. Chekhlarov. Photo)

1977 (2 Mar). Mountain Flowers. T **788** and similar vert designs. Multicoloured. P 13.

2547		1st. Type **788**	20	15
2548		2st. *Petcovia orphanidea*	20	15
2549		3st. *Campanula lanata*	20	15
2550		13st. *Campanula scutellata*	55	35
2551		43st. Nettle-leaved bellflower (*Campanula trachelium*)	1·90	75
2547/2551		*Set of 5*	2·75	1·40

(Des N. Kovachev. Photo)

1977 (21 Mar). Birth Centenary of Vasil Kolarov (Prime Minister 1949–50). P 13.

2552	**789**	2st. pale grey, black and new blue	20	10

790 Congress Emblem

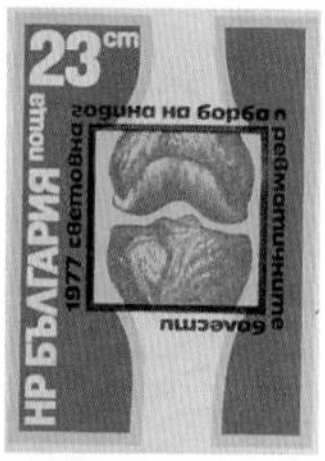

791 Joint

(Des S. Kamenov. Photo)

1977 (25 Mar). Eighth Bulgarian Trade Unions Congress. P 13.

2553	**790**	2st. multicoloured	20	10

(Des L. Chekhlarov. Photo)

1977 (31 Mar). World Rheumatism Year. P 13.

2554	**791**	23st. multicoloured	95	55

792 Wrestling

(Des V. Vasileva. Photo)

1977 (15 Apr). World University Games, Sofia (1st issue). T **792** and similar horiz designs. Multicoloured. P 13.

2555		2st. Type **792**	20	20
2556		13st. Running	45	25
2557		23st. Handball	85	45
2558		43st. Gymnastics	1·40	85
2555/2558		*Set of 4*	2·50	1·60

See also No. **MS**2591.

793 Ivan Vazov National Theatre

794 Congress Emblem

(Des Yu. Minchev. Photo)

1977 (30 Apr). Buildings in Sofia. T **793** and similar horiz designs. P 13.

2559		12st. brown-red/*pale grey-brown*	35	20
2560		13st. chestnut/*pale grey-brown*	45	25
2561		23st. deep turq-blue/*pale grey-brown*	75	35
2562		30st. deep green/*pale grey-brown*	1·10	45
2563		80st. violet/*pale grey-brown*	1·90	1·20
2564		1l. red-brown/*pale grey-brown*	2·40	1·50
2559/2564		*Set of 6*	6·25	3·50

Designs:—13st. Party Building; 23st. People's Army Building; 30st. Clement of Ohrid University; 80st. National Art Gallery; 1l. National Assembly Building.

(Des B. Yonov. Photo)

1977 (9 May). 13th Dimitrov Communist Youth League Congress. P 13.

2565	**794**	2st. bright scarlet, bright green and gold	20	10

795 "St. Nicholas", Nesebur

(Des St. Kunchev. Photo German Bank Note Ptg Co, Leipzig)

1977 (10 May). Bulgarian Icons. T **795** and similar square designs. Multicoloured. P 13.

2566		1st. Type **795**	20	15
2567		2st. "Old Testament Trinity", Sofia	20	15
2568		3st. "The Royal Gates", Veliko Turnovo	20	15
2569		5st. "Deisis", Nesebur	20	15
2570		13st. "St. Nicholas", Elena	45	20
2571		23st. "The Presentation of the Blessed Virgin", Rila Monastery	75	35
2572		35st. "The Virgin Mary with Infant", Varna	1·10	75
2573		40st. "St. Demetrius on Horseback", Provadiya	2·40	1·10
2566/2573		*Set of 8*	5·00	2·75
MS2574		100×99 mm. 1l. "The Twelve Festival Days", Rila Monastery. Imperf	4·25	3·25

796 Wolf (*Canis lupus*)

(Des A. Stareiskinski. Litho State Ptg Wks, Moscow)

1977 (16 May). Wild Animals. T **796** and similar horiz designs. Multicoloured. P 12.

2575		1st. Type **796**	20	15
2576		2st. Red fox (*Vulpes vulpes*)	20	15
2577		10st. Weasel (*Mustela nivalis*)	45	20
2578		13st. Wild cat (*Felis silvestris*)	65	55
2579		23st. Golden jackal (*Canis aureus*)	1·90	1·10
2575/2579		*Set of 5*	3·00	1·90

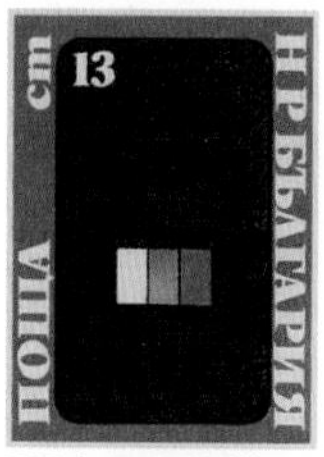

797 Congress Emblem

798 "Crafty Peter riding a Donkey" (drawing by Iliya Beshkov)

(Des D. Tasev. Photo)

1977 (17 May). Third Bulgarian Culture Congress. P 13.

2580	**797**	13st. multicoloured	45	20

(Des St. Kunchev. Photo)

1977 (19 May). 11th Festival of Humour and Satire, Gabrovo. P 13.

2581	**798**	2st. multicoloured	20	10

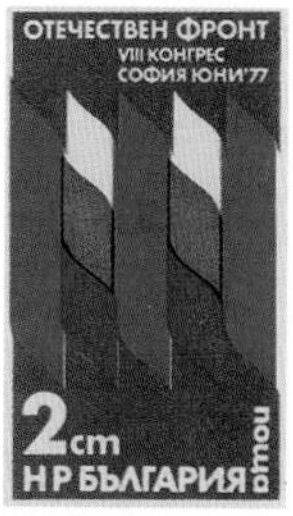

799 Congress Emblem

800 Newspaper Masthead

(Des S. Kamenov. Photo)

1977 (26 May). Eighth Congress of the Popular Front, Sofia. P 13.

2582	**799**	2st. multicoloured	20	10

(Des P. Petrov. Photo)

1977 (3 June). Centenary of Bulgarian Daily Press. P 13.

2583	**800**	2st. multicoloured	20	10

801 St. Cyril

(Des B. Yonov. Photo)

1977 (7 June). 1150th Birth Anniv of St. Cyril. Sheet 106×87 mm. P 13.

MS2584	**801**	1l. multicoloured	3·75	3·75

802 Conference Emblem

(Des St. Kunchev. Photo)

1977 (7 June). International Writers Conference, Sofia. P 13.

2585	**802**	23st. new blue, light blue and pale yellow-green	1·40	1·10

Printed in sheets of eight stamps and four different labels.

803 Map of Europe

(Des St. Kunchev. Photo)

1977 (10 June). 21st Congress of European Organization for Quality Control, Varna. P 13.

2586	**803**	23st. multicoloured	95	55

804 Basketball

805 Weightlifter

(Des B. Ikonomov. Photo)

1977 (15 June). Women's European Basketball Championships. P 13.

2587	**804**	23st. multicoloured	95	55

(Des S. Nenov. Photo)

1977 (15 June). World Junior Weightlifting Championships, Sofia. P 13.

2588	**805**	13st. multicoloured	45	20

806 Georgi Dimitrov

807 Tail Section of Tupolev Tu-154 Jetliner

(Des St. Kunchev. Photo)

1977 (17 June). 95th Birth Anniv of Georgi Dimitrov (statesman). P 13.
2589 **806** 13st. purple-brown and orange-vermilion ... 65 35

(Des St. Kunchev. Photo)

1977 (29 June). 30th Anniv of Balkanair (Bulgarian Airline). P 13.
2590 **807** 35st. multicoloured ... 1·70 85
Issued in sheets of 6 stamps and 3 labels bearing Balkanair's emblem.

808 Games Emblem

(Des St. Kunchev. Photo)

1977 (10 Aug). World University Games, Sofia (2nd issue). Sheet 84×76 mm. P 13.
MS2591 **808** 1l. multicoloured ... 3·25 2·75

809 T.V. Towers, Berlin and Sofia

810 Elin Pelin, *alias* Dimitur Stoyanov (writer)

(Des P. Petrov. Photo)

1977 (12 Aug). Sozphilex '77 Stamp Exhibition, East Berlin. P 13.
2592 **809** 25st. new blue and royal blue ... 95 55

(Des St. Kunchev and A. Stareishinski. Photo)

1977 (26 Aug). Writers and Painters. T **810** and similar vert designs. P 13.
2593 2st. reddish brown and gold ... 20 20
2594 5st. deep olive and gold ... 20 20
2595 13st. reddish purple and gold ... 35 25
2596 23st. ultramarine and gold ... 1·10 55
2593/2596 *Set of 4* ... 1·70 1·10
Designs:—5st. Peyu Yavorov (poet); 13st. Boris Angelushev (painter and illustrator); 23st. Tseno Todorov (painter).
Nos. 2593/6 were each issued in sheets of 8 stamps and 8 labels depicting an illustration.

(Des St. Kunchev. Photo German Bank Note Ptg Co, Leipzig)

1977 (29 Aug). Historic Ships (2nd series). Square designs as T **753**. Multicoloured. P 13.
2597 1st. Hansa kogge ... 20 15
2598 2st. Caravelle *Santa Maria* ... 20 15
2599 3st. Drake's ship *Golden Hind* ... 20 15
2600 12st. Carrack *Santa Catherina* ... 40 20
2601 13st. Galleon *Corona* ... 45 25
2602 43st. Mediterranean galley ... 1·90 65
2597/2602 *Set of 6* ... 3·00 1·40

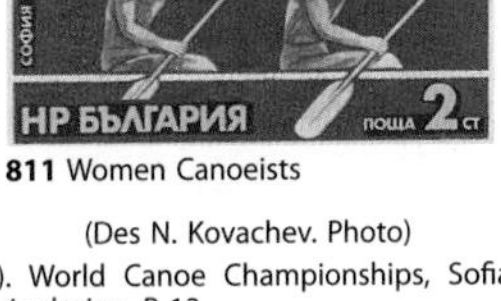

811 Women Canoeists

(Des N. Kovachev. Photo)

1977 (1 Sept). World Canoe Championships, Sofia. T **811** and similar horiz design. P 13.
2603 2st. new blue and olive-yellow ... 20 15
2604 23st. ultramarine and turquoise-green ... 95 45
Design:—23st. Men canoeists.

812 Balloon over Plovdiv

813 Presidents Zhivkov and Brezhnev

(Des S. Kamenov. Photo)

1977 (3 Sept). AIR. 85th Anniv of "Panair" International Aviation Exhibition, Plovdiv. P 13.
2605 **812** 25st. red-orange, yellow and reddish brown ... 95 55

(Des Kh. Khristov. Photo)

1977 (7 Sept). Soviet Bulgarian Friendship. P 13.
2606 **813** 18st. purple-brown, bright scarlet and gold ... 55 45
Issued in sheets of 3 stamps and 3 labels arranged chessboard fashion.

814 Conference Building

(Des Kh. Khristov. Photo)

1977 (12 Sept). 64th International Parliamentary Conference, Sofia. P 13.
2607 **814** 23st. yellowish green, salmon-pink and rose-red ... 95 45

815 Newspaper Mastheads

816 "The Union of Earth and Water"

(Des St. Kunchev. Photo)

1977 (12 Sept). 50th Anniv of Official Newspaper *Rabotnichesko Delo* (Workers' Press). P 13.
2608 **815** 2st. bright rose-red, yellow-green and grey ... 20 10

(Des St. Kunchev. Litho State Ptg Wks, Moscow)

1977 (23 Sept). 400th Birth Anniv of Rubens. T **816** and similar vert designs. Multicoloured. P 11½.
2609 13st. Type **816** ... 55 20
2610 23st. "Venus and Adonis" (detail) ... 1·10 1·10
2611 40st. "Amorous Shepherd" (detail) ... 2·20 1·60
2609/2611 *Set of 3* ... 3·50 2·50
MS2612 71×87 mm. 1l. "Portrait of a Chambermaid" 4·75 3·75

817 Cossack with Bulgarian Child (Angelushev)

818 Albena, Black Sea

(Des L. Chekhlarov. Photo)

1977 (30 Sept). Centenary of Liberation from Turkey (1978) (1st issue). Posters. T **817** and similar vert designs. P 13.
2613 2st. multicoloured ... 30 15
2614 13st. green, dull ultramarine and carmine-vermilion ... 45 20
2615 23st. royal blue, red and green ... 85 45
2616 25st. multicoloured ... 95 50
2613/2616 *Set of 4* ... 2·30 1·20
Designs:—13st. Bugler (Chekhlarov); 23st. Mars (god of war) and Russian soldiers (Petrov); 25st. Flag of Russian Imperial Army (Iliev).
See also No. **MS**2636.

(Des L. Chekhlarov. Photo)

1977 (5 Oct). Tourism. T **818** and similar horiz design. P 13.
2617 35st. greenish blue, deep blue-green and reddish brown ... 1·30 55
2618 43st. pale yellow, deep green and royal blue ... 1·40 65
Design:—43st. Rila Monastery.
Nos. 2617/18 were issued in sheets containing 4 of each design plus one centre label.

819 Dr. Nikolai Pirogov (Russian surgeon)

821 Soviet Emblems and Decree (D. Ivanov)

820 Space-walking

(Des N. Kovachev. Photo)

1977 (14 Oct). Centenary of Dr. Pirogov's Visit to Bulgaria. P 13.
2619 **819** 13st. brown, brown-ochre and olive-green ... 45 35

(Des T. Aleksieva and Zh. Aleksiev. Photo)

1977 (14 Oct). AIR. 20th Anniv of First Artificial Satellite. T **820** and similar horiz designs. Multicoloured. P 13.
2620 12st. Type **820** ... 45 20
2621 25st. Space probe over Mars ... 95 45
2622 35st. Space probe "Venus-4" over Venus ... 1·40 55
2620/2622 *Set of 3* ... 2·50 1·10

(Des St. Kunchev. Photo)

1977 (21 Oct). 60th Anniv of Russian Revolution. T **821** and similar vert designs showing posters. P 13.
2623 2st. bright rose-red, black and stone ... 30 20
2624 13st. dull vermilion and deep purple ... 55 25
2625 23st. dull vermilion and reddish violet ... 1·00 35
2623/2625 *Set of 3* ... 1·70 70
Designs:—13st. Lenin (Kh. Belchev); 23st. "1977" as flame (St. Kunchev).

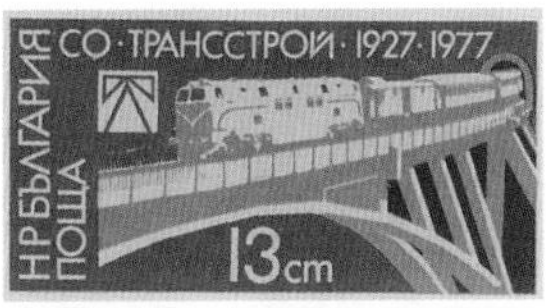

822 Diesel Train on Bridge

(Des B. Yonov. Photo)

1977 (9 Nov). 50th Anniv of Transport, Bridges and Highways Organisation. P 13.
2626 **822** 13st. pale yellow, sage green and emerald ... 75 55

823 Petko Slaveikov

824 Decorative Initials of New Year Greeting

(Des St. Kunchev and A. Stareishinski. Photo)

1977 (15 Nov). Birth Anniv of Petko Slaveikov (poet). P 13.
2627 **823** 8st. chocolate and gold ... 30 20
Issued in sheets of 8 stamps and 8 labels.

(Des St. Kunchev. Photo)

1977 (1 Dec). New Year. T **824** and similar horiz design. Multicoloured. P 13.
2628 2st. Type **824** ... 20 10
2629 13st. "Fireworks" ... 45 15

825 Footballer

826 Baba Vida Fortress, Vidin

(Des S. Nenov. Photo)

1978 (30 Jan). World Cup Football Championship, Argentina. T **825** and similar vert designs. Multicoloured. P 13.

2630 13st. Type **825** 45 35
2631 23st. Shooting the ball 1·40 85
MS2632 77×61 mm. 50st. Struggle for ball 2·50 2·20

(Des St. Kunchev. Photo)

1978 (9 Feb). AIR. "The Danube—European River". T **826** and similar horiz design. Multicoloured. P 13.

2633 25st. Type **826** 75 55
2634 35st. Friendship Bridge 1·40 1·20

Issued in sheets containing 5 stamps of each value plus 2 labels, one showing a map of the Danube, the other a hydrofoil and fishes.

827 Television Mast, Moscow

828 Shipka Monument

(Des R. Serteva and A. Sertev. Photo)

1978 (1 Mar). 20th Anniv of Organization of Socialist Countries' Postal Administrations (O.S.S.). P 13.

2635 **827** 13st. multicoloured 45 20

(Des St. Kunchev. Photo)

1978 (3 Mar). Centenary of Liberation from Turkey (2nd issue). Sheet 55×73 mm. P 13.

MS2636 **828** 50st. multicoloured 1·60 1·60

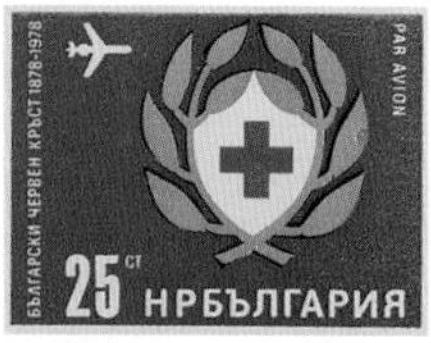

829 Red Cross in Laurel Wreath

(Des S. Nenov. Photo)

1978 (15 Mar). AIR. Centenary of Bulgarian Red Cross. P 13.

2637 **829** 25st. bright scarlet, brown-ochre and blue 95 55

830 "XXX" formed from Bulgarian and Russian National Colours

831 Leo Tolstoy (Russian writer)

(Des S. Kamenov. Photo)

1978 (18 Mar). 30th Anniv of Bulgarian-Soviet Friendship. P 13.

2638 **830** 2st. multicoloured 20 15

(Des A. Stareishinski. Photo)

1978 (28 Mar). Famous Personalities. T **831** and similar vert designs. P 13.

2639 2st. olive-green and yellow 30 15
2640 5st. reddish brown and olive-bistre 30 15
2641 13st. deep bluish green and dull mauve 35 20
2642 23st. red-brown and brownish grey 40 35
2643 25st. blackish brown and sage green 45 40
2644 35st. violet and pale blue 1·40 55
2639/2644 *Set of 6* 3·00 1·60

Designs:—5st. Fyodor Dostoevsky (Russian writer); 13st. Ivan Turgenev (Russian writer); 23st. Vassily Vereshchagin (Russian artist); 25st. Giuseppe Garibaldi (Italian patriot); 35st. Victor Hugo (French writer).

832 Nikolai Roerich (artist)

833 Bulgarian Flag and Red Star

(Des. St. Kunchev. Photo)

1978 (5 Apr). Nikolai Roerich Exhibition, Sofia. P 13.

2645 **832** 8st. stone, grey-green and deep carmine 45 20

(Des B. Yonov. Photo)

1978 (18 Apr). Communist Party National Conference, Sofia. P 13.

2646 **833** 2st. multicoloured 20 10

834 Goddess

835 "Spirit of Nature"

(Des V. Vasileva. Photo)

1978 (26 Apr). Philaserdica 79 International Stamp Exhibition (1st issue). Ancient Ceramics. T **834** and similar horiz designs. Multicoloured. P 13.

2647 2st. Type **834** 20 15
2648 5st. Mask with beard 20 15
2649 13st. Decorated vase 45 20
2650 23st. Vase with scallop design 75 65
2651 35st. Head of Silenus 1·10 1·10
2652 53st. Cockerel 4·00 1·60
2647/2652 *Set of 6* 6·00 3·50

See also Nos. 2674/9, 2714/**MS**2719, 2721/5, **MS**2752, 2753 and 2754.

(Des St. Kunchev. Photo)

1978 (29 Apr). Birth Centenary of Andrei Nikolov (sculptor). P 13.

2653 **835** 13st. grey-blue, mauve and reddish violet 45 20

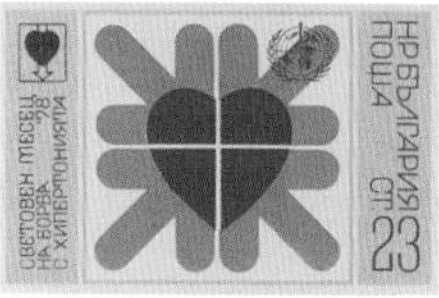

836 Heart and Arrows

(Des Kh. Khristov. Photo)

1978 (12 May). World Hypertension Month. P 13.

2654 **836** 23st. orange-red, yellow-orange and brownish-grey 95 45

837 *Kor Karoli* and Map of Route

(Des St. Kunchev. Photo)

1978 (19 May). Georgi Georgiev's World Voyage. P 13.

2655 **837** 23st. new blue, magenta and emerald 1·90 85

838 Doves

(Des B. Yonov. Photo)

1978 (31 May). 11th World Youth and Students' Festival, Havana. P 13.

2656 **838** 13st. multicoloured 45 20

839 "Portrait of a Young Man" (Dürer)

840 *Fritillaria stribrnyi*

(Des St. Kunchev. Photo German Bank Note Ptg Co, Leipzig)

1978 (19 June). Paintings. T **839** and similar square designs. Multicoloured. P 13.

2657 13st. Type **839** 30 20
2658 23st. "Bathsheba at the Fountain" (Rubens) 45 35
2659 25st. "Signor de Moret" (Hans Holbein the Younger) 55 40
2660 35st. "Self Portrait with Saskia" (Rembrandt) 75 45
2661 43st. "Lady in Mourning" (Tintoretto) 95 55
2662 60st. "Old Man with a Beard" (Rembrandt) 1·20 75
2663 80st. "Man in Armour" (Van Dyck) 2·75 1·80
2657/2663 *Set of 7* 6·25 4·00

(Des T. Aleksieva and Zh. Aleksiev. Photo)

1978 (27 June). Flowers. T **840** and similar vert designs. Multicoloured. P 13.

2664 1st. Type **840** 20 15
2665 2st. *Fritillaria drenovskyi* 20 15
2666 3st. *Lilium rhodopaeum* 20 15
2667 13st. *Tulipa urumoffi* 45 20
2668 23st. *Lilium jankae* 55 35
2669 43st. *Tulipa rhodopaea* 1·90 1·10
2664/2669 *Set of 6* 3·25 1·90

841 Varna

(Des T. Momchilov. Photo)

1978 (13 July). 63rd Esperanto Congress, Varna. P 13.

2670 **841** 13st. orange, carmine and dull yellowish-green 75 45

842 Delčev

843 Freedom Fighters

(Des B. Stoev. Photo)

1978 (1 Aug). 75th Death Anniv of Goce Delčev (Macedonian revolutionary). P 13.

2671 **842** 13st. multicoloured 55 20

(Des B. Stoev. Photo)

1978 (1 Aug). 75th Anniv of Ilinden-Preobrazhenie Rising. P 13.

2672 **843** 5st. black and rose-red 20 10

844 "The Sleeping Venus" (Giorgione)

(Des St. Kunchev. Photo German Bank Note Ptg Co, Leipzig)

1978 (17 Aug). World Masters of Art. Sheet 71×71 mm. Imperf.

MS2673 **844** 1l. multicoloured 2·20 2·20

845 "Market" (Naiden Petkov)

846 Black Woodpecker (*Drycopus martius*)

(Des K. Kunev. Litho State Ptg Wks, Moscow)

1978 (28 Aug). Philaserdica 79 International Stamp Exhibition (2nd issue). Paintings of Sofia. T **845** and similar horiz designs. Multicoloured. P 12.

2674 2st. Type **845** 20 20
2675 5st. "View of Sofia" (Emil Stoichev) 20 20
2676 13st. "View of Sofia" (Boris Ivanov) 30 20
2677 23st. "Tolbukhin Boulevard" (Nikola Tanev) 75 35
2678 35st. "National Theatre" (Nikola Petrov) 85 45
2679 53st. "Market" (Anton Mitov) 95 85
2674/2679 *Set of 6* 3·00 2·00
MS2679*a* 186×106 mm. Nos. 2674/9 7·00 7·00

(Des L. Chekhlarov. Photo)

1978 (1 Sept). Woodpeckers. T **846** and similar vert designs. Multicoloured. P 13.

2680 1st. Type **846** 20 15
2681 2st. Syrian woodpecker (*Dendrocopos syriacus*) 20 15
2682 3st. Three-toed woodpecker (*Picoides tridactylus*) 20 15
2683 13st. Middle spotted woodpecker (*Dendrocopos medius*) 95 55
2684 23st. Lesser spotted woodpecker (*Dendrocopos minor*) 1·40 75
2685 43st. Green woodpecker (*Picus viridis*) 3·75 2·40
2680/2685 *Set of 6* 6·00 3·75

847 Ivan Vazov National Theatre, Sofia

848 "Elka 55" Computer

(Des T. Aleksieva and Zh. Aleksiev. Recess and photo Postal Ptg Wks, Prague)

1978 (1 Sept). Praga 78 and Philaserdica 79 International Stamp Exhibitions. Sheet 153×110 mm, containing T **847** and similar horiz designs. Multicoloured. P 11½×11.

MS2686 (a) 40st. Type **847**; (b) 40st. Festival Hall, Sofia; (c) 40st. Charles Bridge, Prague; (d) 40st. Belvedere Palace, Prague .... 3·25 3·25

(Des B. Yotov. Photo)

1978 (3 Sept). Plovdiv International Fair. Fluorescent overprint of Philaserdica 79 emblems. P 13.

2687 **848** 2st. multicoloured 20 10

849 "September 1923" (Boris Angelushev)

850 Khristo Danov

(Des P. Petrov. Photo)

1978 (5 Sept). 55th Anniv of September Uprising. P 13.

2688 **849** 2st. scarlet vermilion and brown-lake 20 10

(Des A. Stareishinski. Photo)

1978 (18 Sept). 150th Birth Anniv of Khristo Danov (first Bulgarian publisher). P 13.

2689 **850** 2st. pale orange and lake 20 10

Issued in sheets of 10 stamps and 10 labels depicting printing press.

851 "The People of Vladaya" (Todor Panaiotov)

852 Hands supporting Rainbow

(Des St. Kunchev. Photo)

1978 (20 Sept). 60th Anniv of Vladaya Mutiny. P 13.

2690 **851** 2st. pale lilac, reddish brown and light crimson 20 10

(Des V. Kitanov. Photo)

1978 (3 Oct). International Anti-Apartheid Year. P 13.

2691 **852** 13st. multicoloured 45 20

853 Pipeline and Flags

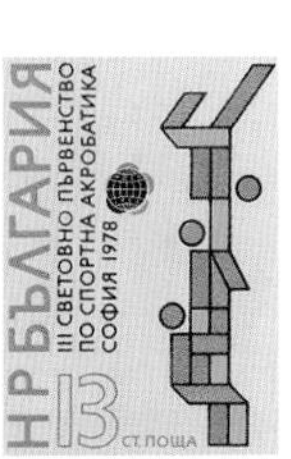

854 Acrobats

(Des V. Kitanov. Photo)

1978 (3 Oct). Inauguration of Orenburg–U.S.S.R. Natural Gas Pipeline. P 13.

2692 **853** 13st. multicoloured 45 20

(Des K. Gogov. Photo)

1978 (4 Oct). Third World Sports Acrobatics Championships, Sofia. P 13.

2693 **854** 13st. multicoloured 45 20

855 Salvador Allende

856 Human Rights Emblem

(Des St. Kunchev. Photo)

1978 (11 Oct). 70th Birth Anniv of Salvador Allende (Chilean politician). P 13.

2694 **855** 13st. deep brown and vermilion 45 20

(Des St. Kunchev. Photo)

1978 (18 Oct). 30th Anniv of Declaration of Human Rights.

2695 **856** 23st. greenish yellow, vermilion and deep ultramarine 95 55

857 "Levski and Matei Mitkaloto" (Kalina Taseva)

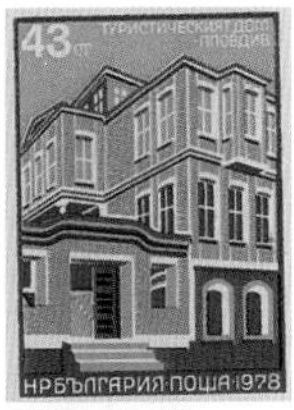

858 Tourist Home, Plovdiv

(Des N. Kovachev. Litho State Ptg Wks, Moscow)

1978 (25 Oct). History of Bulgaria. Paintings. T **857** and similar designs. Multicoloured. P 12.

2696 1st. Type **857** 20 15

2697 2st. "Give Strength to my Arm" (Zlatyu Boyadzhiev) 20 15

2698 3st. "Rumena Voevoda" (Nikola Mirchev) (horiz) 20 15

2699 13st. "Kolyu Ficheto" (Elza Goeva) 45 35

2700 23st. "A Family of the National Revival Period" (Naiden Petkov) .... 1·00 65

2696/2700 *Set of* 5 .... 1·80 1·30

(Des St. Kunchev. Photo)

1978 (1 Nov). European Architectural Heritage. T **858** and similar vert design. Multicoloured. P 13.

2701 43st. Type **858** .... 1·50 55

a. Pair. Nos. 2701/2 .... 3·25 1·20

2702 43st. Tower of the Prince, Rila Monastery . 1·50 55

Nos. 2701/2 were issued in small sheets containing three of No. 2701, two of No. 2702 and one label bearing a decorative motif.

859 *Geroi Plevny* and Route Map

860 Mosaic Bird (Santa Sofia Church)

(Des V. Petrov. Photo)

1978 (1 Nov). Opening of Varna–Ilichovsk Ferry Service. P 13.

2703 **859** 13st. bright violet-blue, dull scarlet and yellow-green 45 35

(Des St. Kunchev. Photo)

1978 (20 Nov). Bulgaria 78 National Stamp Exhibition, Sofia. P 13.

2704 **860** 5st. multicoloured 35 20

Issued in sheets of 8 stamps and 8 labels bearing the exhibition emblem.

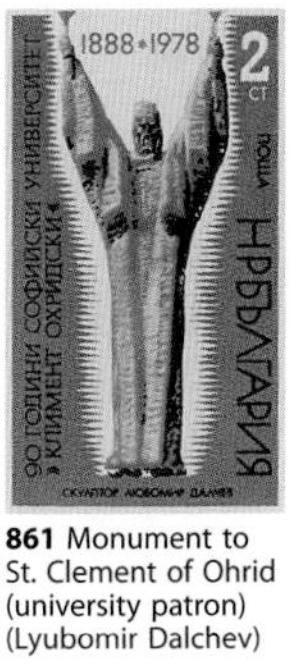

861 Monument to St. Clement of Ohrid (university patron) (Lyubomir Dalchev)

862 Nikola Karastoyanov

(Des A. Sertev. Photo)

1978 (8 Dec). 90th Anniv of Sofia University. P 13.

2705 **861** 2st. slate-lilac, black and yellow-olive 20 10

(Des K. Kunev and V. Konovalov. Photo)

1978 (12 Dec). 200th Birth Anniv of Nikola Karastoyanov (first Bulgarian printer). P 13.

2706 **862** 2st. brown, pale stone and chestnut 35 20

Issued in sheets of 8 stamps and 8 labels depicting a printing press.

863 Initial from 13th Century Bible Manuscript

864 Ballet Dancers

(Des Kh. Khristov. Photo)

1978 (15 Dec). Centenary of Cyril and Methodius People's Library. T **863** and similar vert designs. Multicoloured. P 13½ (23st.) or 13 (others).

2707 2st. Type **863** 20 15

2708 13st. Monk writing (from a 1567 manuscript) 45 20

2709 23st. Decorated page from 16th century manuscript Bible 85 45

2707/2709 *Set of* 3 .... 1·40 70

MS2710 63×94 mm. 80st. Seated saint with attendant (from 13th century manuscript Bible) .. 2·20 2·20

(Des A. Sertev and R. Stanoeva. Photo)

1978 (22 Dec). 50th Anniv of Bulgarian Ballet. P 13.

2711 **864** 13st. bronze-green, magenta and lavender 45 35

865 Tree of Birds

866 1961 Communist Congress Stamp

(Des St. Kunchev. Photo)

1978 (22 Dec). New Year. T **865** and similar horiz design. Multicoloured. P 13.

2712 2st. Type **865** 20 10

2713 13st. Posthorn 30 15

(Des St. Kunchev. Photo)

1978 (30 Dec). Philaserdica 79 International Stamp Exhibition (3rd issue) and Bulgarian Stamp Centenary (1st issue). T **866** and similar designs dated "1978". P 13.

2714 2st. scarlet and yellowish green 20 15

2715 13st. claret and ultramarine 20 15

2716 23st. bronze-green and bright magenta... 30 20

2717 35st. deep brownish grey and new blue.... 95 45

2718 53st. deep dull green and rosine .... 1·70 65

2714/2718 *Set of* 5 .... 3·00 1·40

MS2719 62×87 mm. 1l. black, orange-yellow and bluish green .... 2·20 2·20

Designs: Horiz—2st. 1901 "Cherrywood Cannon" Stamp; 3st. 1946 "New Republic" Stamp; 23st. 1957 Canonisation of St. Cyril and St. Methodius stamp; 1l. First Bulgarian stamp. Vert—53st. 1962 Dimitrov stamp.

No. **MS**2719 also exists imperf from a restricted printing.

See also Nos. 2721/5 and **MS**2755.

867 Council Building, Moscow and Flags

(Des A. Mechnev. Photo)

1979 (25 Jan). 30th Anniv of Council of Mutual Economic Aid. P 13.

2720 **867** 13st. multicoloured 45 20

(Des St. Kunchev. Photo)

1979 (30 Jan). Philaserdica 79 International Stamp Exhibition (4th issue) and Bulgarian Stamp Centenary (2nd issue). As Nos. 2714/18, but inscr "1979" and colours changed. P 13.

2721 2st. scarlet and greenish blue 20 15

2722 13st. claret and bright yellowish green...... 45 20

2723 23st. deep green, pale yellow and Indian red 55 35

2724 35st. deep brownish grey and deep brown-red 95 45

2725 53st. brown-olive and bright violet .... 1·20 65

2721/2725 *Set of* 5 .... 3·00 1·60

868 National Bank

868a

(Des S. Nenov. Photo)

1979 (13 Feb). Centenary of Bulgarian National Bank. P 13.

2726	**868**	2st. grey, deep grey and orange-yellow	20	10

1979 (26 Feb). Coil stamps. T **868a** and similar vert design. Photo. P 14.

2726*a*	2st. dull ultramarine	10	10
2726*b*	5st. deep carmine	20	10

Design:—5st. Similar to T **868a** but with different pattern.

Nos. 2726*a*/*b* have every fifth stamp numbered on the back.

869 Stamboliiski

870 Child's Head as Flower

(Des A. Stareishinski. Photo)

1979 (28 Feb). Birth Centenary of Aleksandur Stamboliiski (Prime Minister 1919–23).

2727	**869**	2st. bistre-brown and yellow-orange	20	10

(Des. V. Kantardzhieva. Photo)

1979 (8 Mar). International Year of the Child. P 13.

2728	**870**	23st. multicoloured	95	45

871 Profiles

872 "75" and Emblem

1979 (20 Mar). Eighth World Congress for the Deaf, Varna. Photo. P 13.

2729	**871**	13st. blackish green and cobalt	45	20

1979 (20 Mar). 75th Anniv of Bulgarian Trade Unions. Photo. P 13.

2730	**872**	2st. deep green and pale orange	20	10

873 Soviet War Memorial

874 Rocket

(Des Kh. Khristo. Photo)

1979 (2 Apr). Centenary of Sofia as Capital of Bulgaria. Sheet 106×105 mm containing T **873** and similar vert designs. Multicoloured. P 13.

MS2731 2st. Type **873**; 5st. Mother and child (sculpture); 13st., 23st., 25st. Bas-relief from Monument to the Liberators of 1876 ... 2·20 2·20

The 13, 23 and 25st. values form a composite design.

(Des St. Kunchev. Photo)

1979 (11 Apr). Soviet–Bulgarian Space Flight. T **874** and similar designs. Multicoloured. P 13.

2732	2st. Georgi Ivanov (horiz) (14.5)	20	15
2733	12st. Type **874**	35	20
2734	13st. Nikolai Rukavishnikov and Ivanov (horiz) (14.5)	75	25
2735	25st. Link-up with "Salyut" space station (horiz)	95	45
2736	35st. Capsule descending by parachute	1·10	55
2732/2736 *Set of 5*		3·00	1·40

MS2737 67×86 mm. 1l. Globe and orbiting space craft (horiz) ... 2·75 2·75

No. **MS**2737 also exists imperforate from a restricted printing.

875 Carrier Pigeon and Tupolev Tu-154 Jetliner over Hemispheres

(Des St. Kunchev. Photo)

1979 (8 May). Centenary of Bulgarian Post and Telegraph Services. T **875** and similar horiz design. Multicoloured. P 13.

2738	2st. Type **875**	20	15
2739	5st. Old and new telephones	20	15
2740	13st. Morse apparatus and teleprinter	45	20
2741	23st. Old radio transmitter and aerials	65	35
2742	35st. TV tower and satellite	95	45
2738/2742 *Set of 5*		2·20	1·20

MS2743 64×69 mm. 50st. Ground receiving station (38×28 mm) ... 2·75 2·75

No. **MS**2743 also exists imperf from a restricted printing.

876 Running

878 First Bulgarian Stamp and 1975 European Security Conference Stamp

877 Thracian Gold Leaf Collar

1979 (15 May). Olympic Games, Moscow (1980) (1st issue). Athletics. T **876** and similar multicoloured designs. Photo. P 13.

2744	2st. Type **876**	30	25
2745	13st. Pole vault (horiz)	65	55
2746	25st. Discus	1·10	75
2747	35st. Hurdles (horiz)	1·40	1·10
2748	43st. High jump (horiz)	1·90	1·30
2749	1l. Long jump	2·75	2·20
2744/2749 *Set of 6*		7·25	5·50

MS2750 90×65 mm. 2l. Shot put ... 9·75 9·75

See also Nos. 2773/**MS**2779, 2803/**MS**2809, 2816/**MS**2822, 2834/**MS**2840 and 2851/**MS**2857.

(Des St. Kunchev. Photo)

1979 (16 May). 48th International Philatelic Federation Congress, Sofia. Sheet 77×86 mm. P 13.

MS2751 **877** 1l. multicoloured ... 4·50 4·50

(Des St. Kunchev. Photo)

1979 (18 May). Philaserdica 79 International Stamp Exhibition, Sofia (5th issue). Sheet 63×61 mm. P 13.

MS2752 **878** 1l. multicoloured ... 7·50 7·50

879 Hotel Vitosha-New Otani

880 "Good Morning, Little Brother" (illus by Kukuliev of folktale)

(Des St. Kunchev. Photo)

1979 (20 May). Philaserdica 79 International Stamp Exhibition, Sofia (6th issue), and Bulgaria Day. P 13.

2753	**879**	2st. pink and ultramarine	20	10

(Des V. Korenev. Photo)

1979 (23 May). Philaserdica 79 International Stamp Exhibition, Sofia (7th issue), and Bulgarian–Russian Friendship. P 13.

2754	**880**	2st. multicoloured	20	10

881 First Bulgarian Stamp

882 Man on Donkey (Boris Angelushev)

(Des St. Kunchev. Photo)

1979 (23 May). Centenary of First Bulgarian Stamp (3rd issue). Sheet 91×121 mm. P 13.

MS2755 **881** 5l. black, orange-yellow and carmine vermilion ... 60·00 60·00

(Des St. Kunchev. Photo)

1979 (23 May). Festival of Humour and Satire, Gabrovo. P 13½.

2756	**882**	2st. multicoloured	20	15

883 "Four Women"

884 Clocktower, Byala Cherkva

(Recess and litho German Bank Note Ptg Co, Leipzig)

1979 (31 May). 450th Death Anniv of Albrecht Dürer (artist). T **883** and similar multicoloured designs. P 14×13½.

2757	13st. Type **883**	20	20
2758	23st. "Three Peasants talking"	55	35
2759	25st. "The Cook and his Wife"	75	45
2760	35st. "Portrait of Eobanus Hessus"	1·10	65
2757/2760 *Set of 4*		2·30	1·50

MS2761 80×81 mm. 80t. "Rhinoceros" (horiz). Imperf ... 2·20 2·20

(Des St. Kunchev. Photo State Ptg Wks, Moscow)

1979 (5 June). AIR. Clocktowers (1st series). T **884** and similar vert designs. Multicoloured. P 12×12½.

2762	13st. Type **884**	35	20
2763	23st. Botevgrad	45	35
2764	25st. Pazardzhik	55	45
2765	35st. Gabrovo	65	65
2766	53st. Tryavna	1·40	1·10
2762/2766 *Set of 5*		3·00	2·50

See also Nos. 2891/5.

885 Petko Todorov (birth centenary)

886 Congress Emblem

1979 (26 June). Bulgarian Writers. T **885** and similar vert designs. Photo. P 13.

2767	2st. agate, orange-brown and bistre-yellow	25	20
2768	2st. grey-green and greenish yellow	25	20
2769	2st. crimson and orange-yellow	25	20
2767/2769 *Set of 3*		70	55

Designs:—No. 2768, Dimitur Dimov (70th birth anniv); 2769, Stefan Kostov (birth centenary).

Nos. 2767/9 were each issued *se-tenant* with label depicting the title page of one of the author's works.

1979 (8 July). 18th Congress of International Theatrical Institute, Sofia. Photo. P 13.

2770	**886**	13st. cobalt, blue and black	35	20

887 House of Journalists, Varna

888 Children of Different Races

(Des V. Kantardzhieva. Photo)

1979 (17 July). 20th Anniv of House of Journalists (holiday home), Varna. P 13.

2771	**887**	8st. yellow-orange, black and bright blue	20	10

1979 (17 July). "Banners for Peace" Children's Meeting, Sofia. Photo. P 13.

2772	**888**	2st. multicoloured	20	10

889 Parallel Bars

890 "Virgin and Child" (Nesebur)

1979 (31 July). Olympic Games, Moscow (1980) (2nd issue). Gymnastics. T **889** and similar multicoloured designs. Photo. P 13.

2773	2st. Type **889**	30	25
2774	13st. Horse exercise (horiz)	55	35
2775	25st. Rings exercise	75	55
2776	35st. Beam exercise	95	85
2777	43st. Uneven bars	1·40	1·20
2778	1l. Floor exercise	2·75	2·40
2773/2778 *Set of 6*		6·00	5·00
MS2779 65×88 mm. 2l. Horizontal bar		9·75	9·75

(Des St. Kunchev. Photo State Ptg Wks, Moscow)

1979 (7 Aug). Icons of the Virgin and Child. T **890** and similar square designs. Multicoloured. P 12.

2780	13st. Type **890**	45	20
2781	23st. Nesebur (different)	55	35
2782	35st. Sozopol	65	45
2783	43st. Sozopol (different)	75	65
2784	53st. Samokov	1·40	1·10
2780/2784 *Set of 5*		3·50	2·50

891 Anton Bezenshek

892 Mountaineer

(Des I. Kiosev. Photo)

1979 (9 Aug). Centenary of Bulgarian Stenography. P 13.

2785	**891**	2st. pale yellow and deep greenish grey	20	10

(Des L. Chekhlarov. Photo)

1979 (28 Aug). 50th Anniv of Bulgarian Alpine Club. P 13.

2786	**892**	2st. multicoloured	20	10

893 Commemorative Inscription

894 Rocket and Flowers

(Des D. Rusinov. Photo)

1979 (31 Aug). Centenary of Bulgarian Public Health Services. P 13×13½.

2787	**893**	2st. black, silver and deep green	20	20

No. 2787 was issued *se-tenant* with half stamp-size labels depicting Dr. Mollov.

(Des D. Tasev. Photo)

1979 (4 Sept). 35th Anniv of Fatherland Front Government. T **894** and similar vert designs. Multicoloured. P 13.

2788	2st. Type **894**	10	10
2789	5st. Russian and Bulgarian flags	15	10
2790	13st. "35" in national colours	35	20
2788/2790 *Set of 3*		55	35

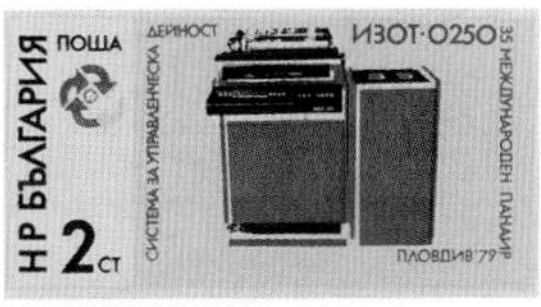

895 "IZOT-0250" Computer

(Des V. Popov. Photo)

1979 (8 Sept). 35th Plovdiv Fair. P 13.

2791	**895**	2st. multicoloured	20	10

896 Games Emblem

897 Footballer

(Des St. Kunchev. Photo)

1979 (20 Sept). World University Games, Mexico. P 13.

2792	**896**	5st. indian red, pale orange-yellow and deep grey-blue	20	10

(Des K. Gogov. Photo)

1979 (2 Oct). 50th Anniv of DFS Lokomotiv Football Team. P 13.

2793	**897**	2st. orange-vermilion and black	20	10

898 Lyuben Karavelov

899 Cross-country Skiing

(Des I. Bogdanov. Photo)

1979 (4 Oct). Death Centenary of Lyuben Karavelov (newspaper editor and President of Bulgarian Revolutionary Committee). P 13.

2794	**898**	2st. grey-olive and new blue	20	10

(Des A. Stareishinski. Photo)

1979 (25 Oct). Winter Olympics, Lake Placid (1980). T **899** and similar vert designs. P 13.

2795	2st. bright crimson, violet and black	20	15
2796	13st. red-orange, violet-blue and black	35	20
2797	23st. deep turquoise-green, dull blue and black	65	35
2798	43st. bluish violet, greenish blue and black	1·70	55
2795/2798 *Set of 4*		2·50	1·10
MS2799 68×77 mm. 1l. blue-green, light greenish blue and black. Imperf.		3·25	3·25

Designs:—13st. Speed skating; 23st. Skiing; 43st. Luge; 1l. Skiing (different).

The miniature sheet as No. **MS**2799 but also depicting satellites on the margin comes from a limited printing.

900 "Woman from Thrace"

901 Canoeing (Canadian pairs)

(Des St. Kunchev. Photo German Bank Note Ptg Co, Leipzig)

1979 (31 Oct). 80th Birth Anniv of Dechko Uzunov (artist). T **900** and similar vert designs. Multicoloured. P 14×13½.

2800	12st. "Figure in Red"	35	15
2801	13st. Type **900**	35	20
2802	23st. "Composition II"	1·10	65
2800/2802 *Set of 3*		1·60	90

A miniature sheet for the 1982 World Cup Football Championship, containing Nos. 1981 and 2316, was issued 28 November 1979 in a limited printing.

1979 (30 Nov). Olympic Games, Moscow (1980) (3rd issue). Water Sports. T **901** and similar multicoloured designs. Photo. P 13.

2803	2st. Type **901**	35	35
2804	13st. Swimming (freestyle)	65	55
2805	25st. Swimming (backstroke) (horiz)	1·10	75
2806	35st. Kayak (horiz)	1·40	1·10
2807	43st. Diving	1·90	1·30
2808	1l. Springboard diving	2·75	2·20
2803/2808 *Set of 6*		7·25	5·75
MS2809 64×88 mm. 2l. Water polo		9·75	9·75

902 Nikola Vaptsarov

903 "Dawn in Plovdiv" (Ioan Leviev)

1979 (7 Dec). 70th Birth Anniv of Nikola Vaptsarov (writer). Photo. P 13.

2810	**902**	2st. rose and lake	30	20

No. 2810 was issued *se-tenant* with a label depicting one of Vaptsarov's works.

1979 (10 Dec). History of Bulgaria. Paintings. T **903** and similar horiz designs. Multicoloured. Litho. P 12×12½ (35st.) or 12½×12 (others).

2811	2st. "The First Socialists" (Boyan Petrov)	20	15
2812	13st. "Dimitur Blagoev as Editor of *Rabotnik*" (Dimitur Gyudzhenov)	35	20
2813	25st. "Workers' Party March" (Stoyan Sotirov)	75	45
2814	35st. Type **903**	1·10	85
2811/2814 *Set of 4*		2·20	1·50

904 Doves in Girl's Hair

(Des St. Kunchev. Photo)

1979 (14 Dec). New Year. P 13.

2815	**904**	13st. multicoloured	35	20

905 Shooting

906 Procession with Relics of Saints

1979 (22 Dec). Olympic Games, Moscow (1980) (4th issue). T **905** and similar multicoloured designs. Photo. P 13.

2816	2st. Type **905**	35	25
2817	13st. Judo (horiz)	65	55
2818	25st. Wrestling (horiz)	1·10	85
2819	35st. Archery	1·40	1·10
2820	43st. Fencing (horiz)	1·90	1·20
2821	1l. Fencing (different)	2·75	2·20
2816/2821 *Set of 6*		7·25	5·50
MS2822 65×89 mm. 2l. Boxing		9·75	9·75

(Des St. Kunchev. Photo German Bank Note Ptg Co, Leipzig)

1979 (25 Dec). Frescoes of Saints Cyril and Methodius in St. Clement's Basilica, Rome. T **906** and similar square designs. Multicoloured. P 13.

2823	2st. Type **906**	20	15
2824	13st. Cyril and Methodius received by Pope Adrian II	30	20
2825	23st. Burial of Cyril the Philosopher	55	35
2826	25st. St. Cyril	75	45
2827	35st. St. Methodius	1·10	65
2823/2827 *Set of 5*		2·50	1·60

907 Television Screen showing Emblem

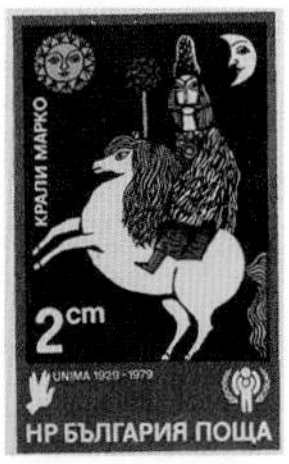

908 Puppet of Krali Marko (national hero)

(Des N. Kovachev. Photo)

1979 (29 Dec). 25th Anniv of Bulgarian Television. P 13½.

2828	**907**	5st. new blue and deep ultramarine	30	20

No. 2828 was issued with *se-tenant* half stamp-size label depicting Sofia television tower.

(Des A. Stareishinski. Photo)

1980 (22 Jan). 50th Anniv of International Puppet Theatre Organization (U.N.I.M.A.) (1979). P 13.

2829	**908**	2st. multicoloured	20	10

909 Thracian Rider (3rd-century votive tablet)

910 "Meeting of Lenin and Dimitrov" (Aleksandur Poplilov)

(Des N. Kovachev. Photo)

1980 (29 Jan). Centenary of National Archaeological Museum, Sofia. T **909** and similar vert design. P 13.

2830	2st. bistre-brown, copper and purple-brown	20	10
2831	13st. bistre-brown, gold and bottle-green	35	20

Design:—13st. Grave stele of Deines (5th–6th century).

During 1980 miniature sheets were issued for the European Security and Co-operation Conference, Madrid (2 sheets, one at 50st., one containing 13st.×6), the World Cup Football Championship, Spain (50st.) and for Nature Protection and 49th F.I.P. Congress, Essen (containing 5, 13, 25, 35 and 43st.). Supplies and distribution of these sheets were restricted, and it is understood they were not available at face value.

(Des N. Kovachev. Litho State Ptg Wks, Moscow)

1980 (28 Mar). 110th Birth Anniv of Lenin. P 12.
2832 **910** 13st. multicoloured ... 35 20

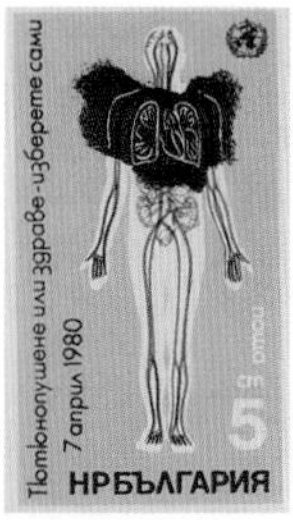

911 Diagram of Blood Circulation with Lungs obscured by Smoke

912 Basketball

(Des V. Kantardzhieva. Photo)

1980 (7 Apr). World Health Day. Anti-smoking Campaign. P 13.
2833 **911** 5st. multicoloured ... 20 10

1980 (10 Apr). Olympic Games, Moscow (5th issue). T **912** and similar vert designs. Multicoloured. Photo. P 13.

2834	2st. Type **912**	35	25
2835	13st. Football	65	55
2836	25st. Hockey	1·10	75
2837	35st. Cycling	1·40	1·10
2838	43st. Handball	1·90	1·30
2839	1l. Volleyball	2·75	2·20
2834/2839	*Set of 6*	7·25	5·50
MS2840	66×90 mm. 2st. Weightlifting	9·75	9·75

913 Emblem, Cosmonauts and Space Station

(Des St. Kunchev. Litho State Ptg Wks, Moscow)

1980 (22 Apr). "Intercosmos" Space Programme. Sheet 111×102 mm. P 12.
MS2841 **913** 50st. multicoloured ... 2·20 2·20

914 Peno Penev

915 Penny Black

(Des St. Kunchev. Photo)

1980 (22 Apr). 50th Birth Anniv of Peno Penev (poet). P 13½.
2842 **914** 5st. agate, orange-red and blue-green ... 30 20

No. 2842 was issued with *se-tenant* half stamp-size label bearing extract from poem.

1980 (24 Apr). London 1980 International Stamp Exhibition. Photo. P 13.
2843 **915** 25st. agate and brown red ... 1·10 75

Issued in sheets of 6 stamps and 3 labels depicting Sir Rowland Hill.

A further limited printing of the sheetlet was issued with additional marginal inscription, each sheetlet being numbered; this was re-issued in 1982 with the stamps and marginal inscription overprinted for 19th U.P.U. Congress, Hamburg, the sheetlet surcharged 2l. and renumbered.

916 Dimitur Khr. Chorbadzhiiski-Chudomir (self-portrait)

(Des Zh. Kosturkova. Photo)

1980 (29 Apr). 90th Birth Anhiv of Dimitur Khr. Chorbadzhiiski Chudomir (artist). T **916** and similar horiz design. P 13.
2844 5st. pink, bistre-brown and deep turquoise-blue ... 20 10
2845 13st. black, pale blue & dp blue-green ... 35 35

Design:—13st. "Our People".

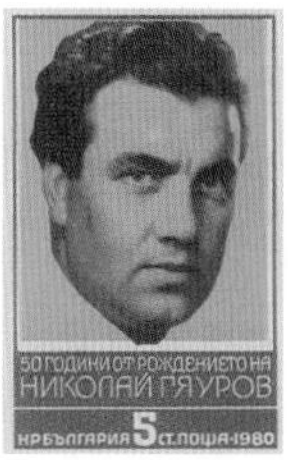

917 Nikolai Gyaurov

918 Soviet Soldiers raising Flag on Berlin Reichstag

(Des A. Stareishinski. Photo)

1980 (30 Apr). 50th Birth Anniv of Nikolai Gyaurov (opera singer). P 13.
2846 **917** 5st. orange-yellow, orange-brown and bright green ... 30 20

No. 2846 was issued with *se-tenant* stamp-size label depicting scene from *Boris Godunov*.

(Des P. Petrov. Photo)

1980 (6 May). 35th Anniv of "Victory in Europe" Day. T **918** and similar vert design. P 13.
2847 5st. gold, purple-brown and black ... 20 10
2848 13st. gold, purple-brown and black ... 35 20

Design:—13st. Soviet Army Memorial, Berlin-Treptow.

919 Open Book and Sun

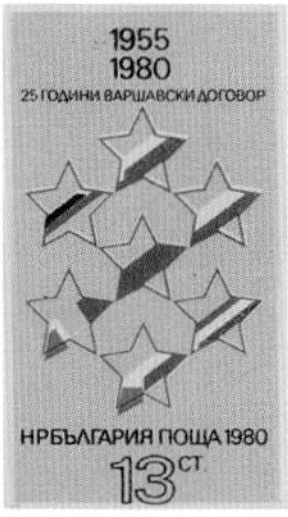

920 Stars representing Member Countries

(Des B. Yonov. Photo)

1980 (12 May). 75th Anniv of Bulgarian Teachers' Union. P 13.
2849 **919** 5st. deep reddish purple and orange-yellow ... 20 10

(Des K. Gogov. Photo)

1980 (14 May). 25th Anniv of Warsaw Pact. P 13.
2850 **920** 13st. multicoloured ... 45 20

921 Greek Girl with Olympic Flame

922 Ballerina

(Des A. Stareishinski. Photo)

1980 (10 June). Olympic Games, Moscow (6th issue). T **921** and similar vert designs. Multicoloured. P 13.

2851	2st. Type **921**	35	25
2852	13st. Spartacus monument, Sandanski	65	55
2853	25st. Liberation monument, Sofia (detail)	1·10	85
2854	35st. Liberation monument, Plovdiv	1·40	1·00
2855	43st. Liberation monument, Shipka Pass	1·90	1·30
2856	1l. Liberation monument, Ruse	2·75	2·20
2851/2856	*Set of 6*	7·25	5·50
MS2857	66×92 mm. 2l. Athlete with Olympic flame, Moscow	9·75	9·75

(Des R. Stanoeva and A. Sertev. Photo)

1980 (1 July). Tenth International Ballet Competition, Varna. P 13.
2858 **922** 13st. multicoloured ... 45 20

923 Europa Hotel, Sofia

924 Parachute Descent

(Des Kh. Khristov. Photo)

1980 (11 July). Hotels. T **923** and similar multicoloured designs. P 13.

2859	23st. Type **923**	55	35
2860	23st. Bulgaria Hotel, Burgas (vert)	55	35
2861	23st. Plovdiv Hotel, Plovdiv	55	35
2862	23st. Riga Hotel, Ruse (vert)	55	35
2863	23st. Varna Hotel, Druzhba	55	35
2859/2863	*Set of 5*	2·50	1·60

(Des St. Kunchev. Photo German Bank Note Ptg Co, Leipzig)

1980 (14 July). Historic Ships (3rd series). Square designs as T **753**. Multicoloured. P 13.

2864	5st. Hansa kogge *Jesus of Lübeck*	20	15
2865	8st. Roman galley	30	15
2866	13st. *Eagle* (galleon)	35	20
2867	23st. *Mayflower*	55	35
2868	35st. Maltese galleon	1·00	45
2869	53st. *Royal Louis* (galleon)	1·50	1·10
2864/2869	*Set of 6*	3·50	2·20

(Des L. Chekhlarov. Photo)

1980 (6 Aug). 15th World Parachute Championships, Kazanluk. T **924** and similar vert design. Multicoloured. P 13.
2870 13st. Type **924** ... 35 20
2871 25st. Parachutist in free fall ... 75 35

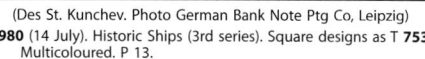

925 Clown and Children

926 Assembly Emblem

(Des V. Kantardzhieva. Litho)

1980 (1 Sept). First Anniv of "Banners for Peace" Children's Meeting. T **925** and similar multicoloured designs. P 12.

2872	3st. Type **925**	20	15
2873	5st. "Cosmonauts in Spaceship" (vert)	20	15
2874	8st. "Picnic"	20	15
2875	13st. "Children with Ices"	30	20
2876	25st. "Children with Cat" (vert)	45	35
2877	35st. "Crowd"	1·00	45
2878	43st. "Banners for Peace" monument (vert)	1·50	65
2872/2878	*Set of 7*	3·50	1·90

(Des Y. Petrov. Photo)

1980 (4 Sept). Assembly of People's Parliament for Peace, Sofia. P 13.
2879 **926** 25st. multicoloured ... 55 45

927 Iordan Iovkov

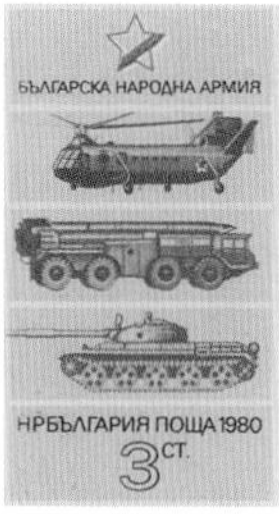

928 Yakovlev Yak-24 Helicopter, Missile Launcher and Tank

(Des T. Aleksieva. Photo)

1980 (19 Sept). Birth Centenary of Iordan Iovkov (writer). P 13½.
2880 **927** 5st. multicoloured ... 30 25

No. 2880 was issued with *se-tenant* half stamp-size label depicting drawing by T. Panaiotov of scene from Iovkov's work *Over the Wire*.

(Des K. Gogov. Photo)

1980 (23 Sept). Bulgarian Armed Forces. T **928** and similar vert designs. Multicoloured. P 13.

2881	3st. Type **928**	10	10
2882	5st. Mikoyan Gurevich MiG-21 jet fighter, radar antennae and missile transporter	20	15
2883	8st. Mil Mi-24 helicopter, missile boat and *Ropucha* (landing ship)	35	20
2881/2883	*Set of 3*	60	40

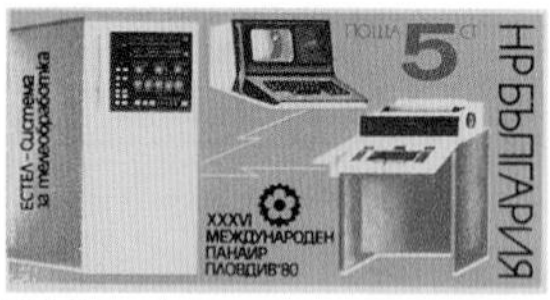

929 Computer

(Des R. Stanoeva and A. Sertev. Photo)

1980 (24 Sept). 36th Plovdiv Fair. P 13.
2884 **929** 5st. multicoloured ... 20 10

930 "Virgin and Child with St. Anne"

931 *Parodia saint-pieana*

(Des A. Stareishinski. Photo)

1980 (10 Oct). Paintings by Leonardo da Vinci. T **930** and similar square designs. Multicoloured. P 13.

2885	5st. Type **930**	20	15
2886	8st. Angel (detail "The Annunciation")	20	15
2887	13st. Virgin (detail "The Annunciation")	35	20
2888	25st. "Adoration of the Kings" (detail)	65	45
2889	35st. "Woman with Ermine"	1·10	55
2885/2889 *Set of 5*		2·30	1·40
MS2890 57×80 mm. 50st. "Mona Lisa". Imperf		1·60	1·60

(Des St. Kunchev. Litho State Ptg Wks, Moscow)

1980 (22 Oct). AIR. Clocktowers (2nd series). Vert designs as T **884**. Multicoloured. P 12×12½.

2891	13st. Byala	35	20
2892	23st. Razgrad	45	35
2893	25st. Karnobat	55	45
2894	35st. Sevlievo	95	55
2895	53st. Berkovitsa	1·90	85
2891/2895 *Set of 5*		3·75	2·20

(Des M. Konstantinova. Photo)

1980 (4 Nov). Cacti. T **931** and similar vert designs. Multicoloured. P 13.

2896	5st. Type **931**	20	15
2897	13st. *Echinopsis bridgesii*	35	20
2898	25st. *Echinocereus purpureus*	75	45
2899	35st. *Opuntia bispinosa*	1·10	85
2900	53st. *Mamillopsis senilis*	2·30	1·10
2896/2900 *Set of 5*		4·25	2·50

932 U.N. Building and Bulgarian Arms

(Des St. Kunchev. Photo)

1980 (25 Nov). 25th Anniv of United Nations Membership. Sheet 64×86 mm. P 13.

MS2901 **932** 60st. multicoloured ... 4·25 4·25

933 Przewalski's Horse

(Des V. Korenev and S. Goristanova. Litho State Ptg Wks, Moscow)

1980 (27 Nov). Horses. T **933** and similar horiz designs. Multicoloured. P 12½×12.

2902	3st. Type **933**	20	35
2903	5st. Tarpan	20	35
2904	13st. Arabian	55	55
2905	23st. Anglo-Arabian	1·50	1·10
2906	35st. Draught horse	3·25	2·75
2902/2906 *Set of 5*		5·25	4·50

934 Vasil Stoin

(Des E. Klincharov. Photo)

1980 (5 Dec). Birth Centenary of Vasil Stoin (collector of folk songs). P 13.

2907 **934** 5st. reddish violet, yellow-ochre and gold ... 20 10

935 Armorial Lion   **936** Red Star

(Des St. Kunchev. Photo)

1980 (8 Dec). New Year. 1300th Anniv of Bulgarian State. T **935** and similar horiz design. Multicoloured. P 13.

2908	5st. Type **935**	20	10
2909	13st. Dish and dates "681/1981"	35	15

(Des St. Kunchev. Photo)

1980 (26 Dec). 12th Bulgarian Communist Party Congress (1st issue). P 13.

2910 **936** 5st. orange-yellow and rosine ... 20 10

See also Nos. 2920/**MS**2923.

During 1981 miniature sheets were issued for Olympic Games medal winners (50st.), World Cup Football Championship, Spain (50st.), 125th Anniv of Danube Commission (2 sheets, one containing 25st.×2, the other 35st.×8) and the European Security and Co-operation Conference, Madrid (35st.×2). Supplies and distribution of these sheets were restricted, and it is understood they were not available at face value.

937 Cross-country Skier

(Des Kh. Aleksiev. Photo)

1981 (15 Jan). World Ski-racing Championship, Velingrad. P 13.

2911 **937** 43st. red-orange, bright blue and black ... 1·10 65

938 Midland Hawthorn (*Crataegus oxyacantha*)   **939** Skier

(Des V. Kantardzhieva. Photo)

1981 (22 Jan). Useful Plants. T **938** and similar vert designs. Multicoloured. P 13.

2912	3st. Type **938**	20	15
2913	5st. Perforate St. John's wort (*Hypericum perforatum*)	20	15
2914	13st. Elder (*Sambucus nigra*)	45	20
2915	25st. Dewberry (*Rubus caesius*)	85	35
2916	35st. Lime (*Tilia argentea*)	1·00	55
2917	43st. Dog rose (*Rosa canina*)	1·60	1·10
2912/2917 *Set of 6*		3·75	2·30

(Des Kh. Aleksiev. Photo)

1981 (27 Feb). Alpine Skiing World Championships, Borovets. P 13.

2918 **939** 43st. yellow, black and blue ... 1·10 65

940 Nuclear Traces

(Des K. Gogov. Photo)

1981 (10 Mar). 25th Anniv of Nuclear Research Institute, Dubna, U.S.S.R. P 13.

2919 **940** 13st. black and silver ... 35 15

941 "XII" formed by Flag

(Des P. Petrov. Photo)

1981 (12 Mar). 12th Bulgarian Communist Party Congress (2nd issue). T **941** and similar horiz designs. P 13×13½.

2920	5st. multicoloured	20	15
2921	13st. rosine, brownish blk & dp ultram	35	20
2922	23st. rosine, brownish blk & dp ultram	65	55
2920/2922 *Set of 3*		1·10	80
MS2923 68×86 mm. 50st. multicoloured		1·60	1·60

Designs:—13st. Stars; 23st. Computer tape; 50st. Georgi Dimitrov and Dimitur Blagoev.

Nos. 2920/2 were each issued with *se-tenant* half stamp-size inscribed label.

942 Palace of Culture

(Des St. Kunchev. Photo)

1981 (13 Mar). Opening of Palace of Culture, Sofia. P 13.

2924 **942** 5st. deep olive, light green and vermilion ... 20 10

HAVE YOU READ THE NOTES AT THE BEGINNING OF THIS CATALOGUE?
These often provide answers to the enquiries we receive

943 "Self-portrait"   **944** Squacco Heron (*Ardeola ralloides*)

(Des K. Gogov. Litho State Ptg Wks, Moscow)

1981 (23 Mar). 170th Birth Anniv (1980) of Zakharii Zograf (artist). T **943** and similar multicoloured designs. P 12×12½ (vert) or 12½×12 (horiz).

2925	5st. Type **943**	20	15
2926	13st. "Portrait of Khristiania Zografska"	45	20
2927	23st. "The Transfiguration" (icon from Preobrazhenie Monastery)	75	35
2928	25st. "Doomsday" (detail) (horiz)	95	55
2929	35st. "Doomsday" (different detail) (horiz)	1·40	1·10
2925/2929 *Set of 5*		3·50	2·10

(Des L. Chekhlarov. Litho State Ptg Wks, Moscow)

1981 (7 Apr). Birds. T **944** and similar vert designs. Multicoloured. P 12.

2930	5st. Type **944**	20	15
2931	8st. Eurasian bittern (*Botaurus stellaris*)	45	20
2932	13st. Cattle egret (*Ardeola ibis*)	65	35
2933	25st. Great egret (*Casmerodius albus*)	1·50	65
2934	53st. Black stork (*Ciconia nigra*)	2·75	1·60
2930/2934 *Set of 5*		5·00	2·75

945 Liner *Georgi Dimitrov*

(Des Kh. Khristov. Photo)

1981 (15 Apr). Centenary of Bulgarian Shipbuilding. T **945** and similar horiz designs. Multicoloured. P 13.

2935	35st. Type **945**	95	35
2936	43st. Freighter *Petimata ot RMS*	1·40	55
2937	53st. Tanker *Khan Asparukh*	1·90	85
2935/2937 *Set of 3*		3·75	1·60

946 Hofburg Palace, Vienna   **947** "XXXIV"

(Des St. Kunchev. Photo)

1981 (15 May). WIPA 1981 International Stamp Exhibition, Vienna. P 13.

2938 **946** 35st. crimson, vermilion and deep green ... 95 65

(Des Y. Petrov. Photo)

1981 (18 May). 34th Bulgarian People's Agrarian Union Congress. T **947** and similar horiz designs. P 13½.

2939	5st. multicoloured	20	15
2940	8st. yellow-orange, black and ultramarine	30	20
2941	13st. multicoloured	55	35
2939/2941 *Set of 3*		95	65

Designs:—8st. Flags; 13st. Bulgarian Communist Party and Agrarian Union flags.

948 Wild Cat

(Des A. Stareishinski. Photo)

1981 (27 May). International Hunting Exhibition, Plovdiv. T **948** and similar horiz designs. P 13½.

2942	5st. stone, black and chestnut	20	15
2943	13st. black, chestnut and pale olive-sepia	45	20
2944	23st. orange-brown, black and pale orange	95	45
2945	25st. black, chestnut and dull purple	1·10	55
2946	35st. orange-brown, black and grey-brown	1·50	65
2947	53st. brown-ochre, black and dull green	2·30	1·10
2942/2947 *Set of 6*		5·75	2·75
MS2948 78×103 mm. 1l. brown-ochre, black and dull yellow-green (52×42 mm). P 13		3·25	3·25

Designs:—13st. Wild boar; 23st. Mouflon; 25st. Chamois; 35st. Roebuck; 53st. Fallow deer; 1l. Red deer.

Nos. 2942/7 were each issued with *se-tenant* half stamp-size label depicting an ornamental hunting gun.

949 "Crafty Peter" (sculpture, Georgi Chapkanov)

950 Bulgarian Arms and U.N.E.S.C.O. Emblem

(Des St. Kunchev. Photo)

1981 (28 May). Festival of Humour and Satire, Gabrovo. P 13.
2949 **949** 5st. multicoloured ... 20 10

(Des St. Kunchev. Photo)

1981 (11 June). 25th Anniv of United Nations Educational, Scientific and Cultural Organization Membership. P 13.
2950 **950** 13st. multicoloured ... 35 20

951 Deutsche Flugzeugwerke D.F.W.C.V. Biplane

(Des Zh. Aleksiev. Litho State Ptg Wks, Moscow)

1981 (24 June). AIR. Aircraft. T **951** and similar horiz designs. Multicoloured. P 12½×12.
2951 5st. Type **951** ... 20 15
2952 12st. LAS-7 monoplane ... 30 15
2953 25st. LAS-8 monoplane ... 75 45
2954 35st. DAR-1 biplane ... 95 55
2955 45st. DAR-3 biplane ... 1·10 85
2956 55st. DAR-9 biplane ... 1·40 1·10
2951/2956 *Set of* 6 ... 4·25 3·00

952 "Eye"

953 Veliko Turnovo Hotel

(Des N. Kovachev. Photo)

1981 (9 July). Centenary of State Statistical Office. P 13.
2957 **952** 5st. multicoloured ... 20 10

(Des Kh. Khristov. Photo)

1981 (13 July). Hotels. P 13.
2958 **953** 23st. multicoloured ... 55 35

954 "Flying Figure"

(Des R. Stanoeva and A. Sertev. Photo)

1981 (16 July). 90th Anniv of First Bulgarian Social Democratic Party Congress, Buzludzha. T **954** and similar horiz designs showing sculptures by Velichko Minekov. P 13.
2959 5st. light blue, black and apple green ... 20 15
2960 13st. cinnamon, black and reddish orange ... 35 20
Design:—13st. "Advancing Female".

955 Animal-shaped Dish

(Des St. Kunchev. Photo German Bank Note Ptg Co, Leipzig)

1981 (21 July). Golden Treasure of Old Saint Nicholas. T **955** and similar square designs. Multicoloured. P 13.
2961 5st. Type **955** ... 20 15
2962 13st. Jug with decorated neck ... 35 20
2963 23st. Jug with loop pattern ... 55 45
2964 25st. Jug with bird pattern ... 75 55
2965 35st. Decorated vase ... 95 75
2966 53st. Decorated dish ... 1·90 1·30
2961/2966 *Set of* 6 ... 4·25 3·00

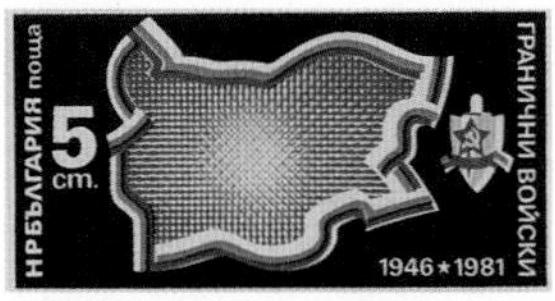

956 Badge and Map of Bulgaria

(Des K. Gogov. Photo)

1981 (28 July). 35th Anniv of Frontier Guards. P 13.
2967 **956** 5st. multicoloured ... 20 10

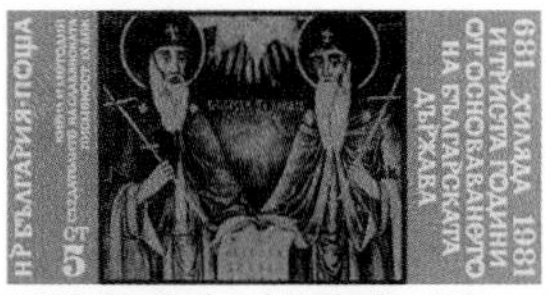

957 Saints Cyril and Methodius (9th century)

(Des I. Kosev. Photo)

1981 (10 Aug). 1300th Anniv of Bulgarian State. T **957** and similar horiz designs. P 13.
2968 5st. deep dull green and greyish green ... 20 15
2969 5st. blackish brown and yellow ... 20 15
2970 8st. violet and deep lilac ... 20 15
2971 12st. mauve and reddish purple ... 30 15
2972 13st. dull slate-purple and agate ... 35 15
2973 13st. dull yellowish green and black ... 35 15
2974 16st. emerald and myrtle green ... 45 20
2975 23st. black and light blue ... 65 35
2976 25st. bottle green and turquoise-green ... 75 45
2977 35st. brown and ochre ... 1·00 55
2978 41st. deep rose-red and rose-pink ... 1·20 65
2979 43st. deep carmine and rose ... 1·20 65
2980 53st. chocolate and light brown ... 1·30 70
2981 55st. myrtle green and pale blue-green ... 1·40 75
2968/2981 *Set of* 14 ... 8·50 4·75
MS2982 Two sheets, each 83×74 mm. (a) 50st. olive-grey and blackish olive; (b) 1l. grey-brown, brownish black and light brown ... 5·00 5·00
Designs:—5st. (No. 2968), Madara horsemen (8th century); 8st. Plan of Round Church at Veliki Preslav (10th century); 12st. Four Evangelists of Ivan Aleksandur (1356); 13st. (2972), Column of Ivan Asen II (13th century); 13st. (2973), Manasses Chronicle (14th century); 16st. Rising of April 1876; 23st. Arrival of Russian liberation troops, 1877; 25st. Foundation ceremony of Bulgarian Social Democratic Party, 1891; 35st. Rising of September 1923; 41st. Formation of Fatherland Front Government, 9 September 1944; 43st. Bulgarian Communist Party Congress, 1948; 50st. Bas-relief of lion at Stara Zagora (10th century); 53st. Tenth Communist Party Congress, 1971; 55st. Kremikovtsi metallurgical combine; 1l. Leonid Brezhnev and Todor Yovkov.

958 Volleyball Players

959 "Pegasus" (bronze sculpture)

1981 (16 Sept). European Volleyball Championships. Photo. P 13.
2983 **958** 13st. bright crimson, deep ultramarine and black ... 35 20

1981 (2 Oct). Day of the Word. Photo. P 13.
2984 **959** 5st. pale yellow and dull olive ... 20 10

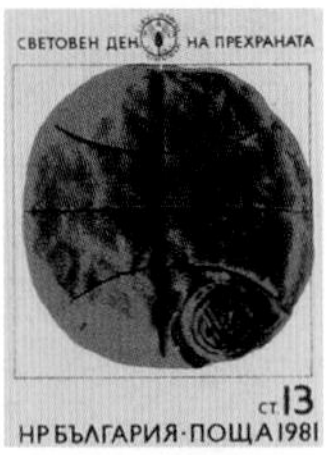

960 Loaf of Bread

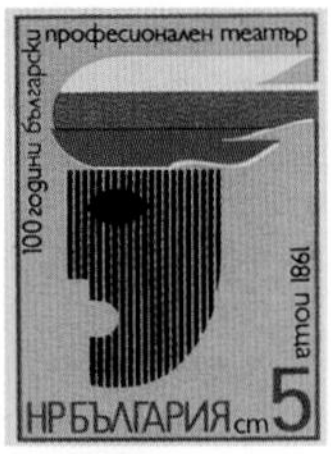

961 Mask

1981 (16 Oct). World Food Day. Photo. P 13.
2985 **960** 13st. black, orange-brown and myrtle green ... 35 20

(Des L. Chekhlarov. Photo)

1981 (30 Oct). Centenary of Bulgarian Professional Theatre. P 13.
2986 **961** 5st. multicoloured ... 20 15

962 Examples of Bulgarian Art

963 Footballer

(Des St. Kunchev. Photo)

1981 (21 Nov). Cultural Heritage Day. P 13.
2987 **962** 13st. yellow-green and brown-red ... 95 20
See also No. **MS**2993.

(Des Kh. Aleksiev. Photo)

1981 (25 Nov). World Cup Football Championship, Spain (1982). T **963** and similar vert designs. Multicoloured. P 13.
2988 5st. Type **963** ... 20 15
2989 13st. Player heading ball ... 30 20
2990 43st. Goalkeeper catching ball ... 95 65
2991 53st. Player kicking ball ... 1·10 1·00
2988/2991 *Set of* 4 ... 2·30 1·80

964 Dove encircled by Barbed Wire

965 "Mother" (Lilyana Ruseva)

(Des P. Rashkov. Photo)

1981 (2 Dec). Anti-apartheid Campaign. P 13.
2992 **964** 5st. black, deep carmine and orange-yellow ... 20 10

1981 (11 Dec). 13th Bulgarian Philatelic Federation Congress. Sheet 51×72 mm containing design as T **962** but inscr "XIII KONGRES NA SBF SOFIYA" at foot. P 13.
MS2993 60st. blue and bright crimson ... 9·25 8·25

(Des V. Kantardzhieva. Litho German Bank Note Ptg Co, Leipzig)

1981 (16 Dec). 35th Anniv of United Nations Children's Fund (U.N.I.C.E.F.). T **965** and similar vert designs. Multicoloured. P 14.
2994 53st. Type **965** ... 1·70 55
2995 53st. "Bulgarian Madonna" (Vasil Stoilov) . 1·70 55
2996 53st. "Village Madonna" (Ivan Milev) ... 1·70 55
2997 53st. "Mother" (Vladimir Dimitrov) ... 1·70 55
2994/2997 *Set of* 4 ... 6·00 2·00

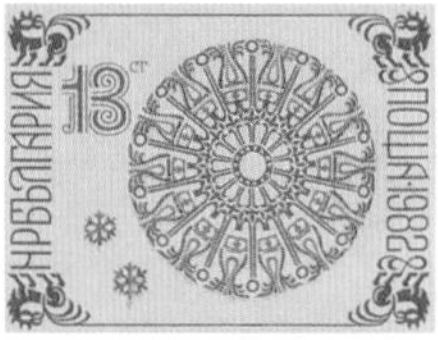

966 8th-century Ceramic from Pliska

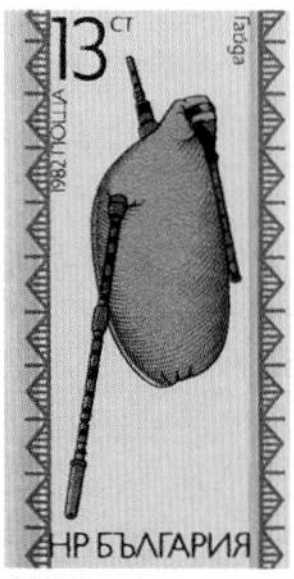

967 Bagpipes

(Des St. Kunchev. Photo)

1981 (22 Dec). New Year. T **966** and similar horiz design. Multicoloured. P 13.
2998 5st. Armorial lion ... 20 10
2999 13st. Type **966** ... 35 15

(Des L. Chekhlarov. Photo)

1982 (14 Jan). Musical Instruments. T **967** and similar vert designs. Multicoloured. P 13.
3000 13st. Type **967** ... 30 20
3001 25st. Single and double flutes ... 55 25
3002 30st. Rebec ... 65 35
3003 35st. Flute and pipe ... 75 45
3004 44st. Mandolin ... 1·50 55
3000/3004 *Set of* 5 ... 3·50 1·60

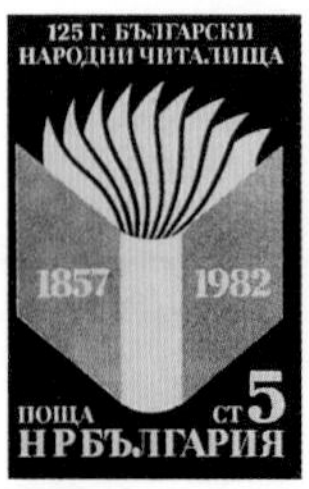

968 Book

969 "Sofia Plains"

1982 (20 Jan). 125th Anniv of Public Libraries. Photo. P 13.
3005 **968** 5st. dull green and deep green ... 20 10

1982 (10 Feb). Birth Centenary of Nikola Petrov (artist). T **969** and similar square designs. Multicoloured. Litho. P 12½.
3006 5st. Type **969** ... 20 15
3007 13st. "Girl embroidering" ... 35 20
3008 30st. "Fields of Peshtera" ... 1·00 55
3006/3008 *Set of* 3 ... 1·40 80

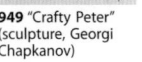

970 Woman's Head and Dove

971 "Peasant Woman"

1982 (8 Mar). International Decade of Women. Sheet 66×76 mm. Photo. P 13.
MS3009 **970** 1l. multicoloured .... 2·75 2·75

1982 (25 Mar). Birth Centenary of Vladimir Dimitrov (artist). T **971** and similar multicoloured designs. Litho. P 14.

3010	5st. Figures in a landscape (horiz)	20	15
3011	8st. Town and harbour (horiz)	20	15
3012	13st. Town scene (horiz)	45	20
3013	25st. "Reapers"	55	35
3014	30st. Woman and child	65	45
3015	35st. Type **971**	95	50
3010/3015	*Set of 6*	2·75	1·60
MS3016	65×58 mm. 50st. "Self-portrait" (horiz)	1·60	1·60

972 Georgi Dimitrov

973 Summer Snowflake (*Leucojum aestivum*)

(Des T. Momchilov. Photo)

1982 (5 Apr). Ninth Bulgarian Trade Unions Congress, Sofia. T **972** and similar horiz design. P 13½.

3017	5st. cinnamon, chocolate and lake-brown	10	10
3018	5st. chestnut and deep new blue	20	10

Design:—No. 3018, Palace of Culture, Sofia.

Nos. 3017/18 were each issued with *se-tenant* half stamp-size label showing congress emblem and text.

(Des V. Kitanov. Photo)

1982 (10 Apr). Flowers. T **973** and similar vert designs. Multicoloured. P 13.

3019	3st. Type **973**	20	15
3020	5st. Chicory (*Cichorium intybus*)	20	15
3021	8st. Rosebay willowherb (*Chamaenerium angustifolium*)	30	15
3022	13st. Solomon's seal (*Polygonatum officinale*)	45	20
3023	25st. Sweet violet (*Viola odorata*)	85	35
3024	35st. *Ficaria verna*	1·40	55
3019/3024	*Set of 6*	3·00	1·40

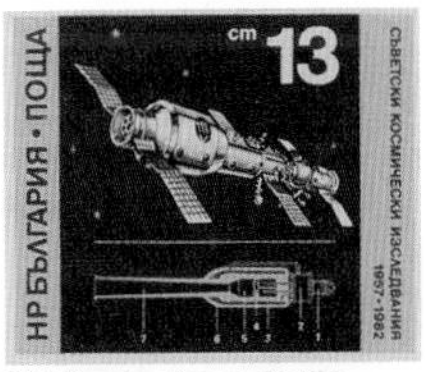
974 Russian Space Station

1982 (12 Apr). 25th Anniv of First Soviet Artificial Satellite. Photo. P 13½.
3025 **974** 13st. multicoloured 35 20

No. 3025 was issued with *se-tenant* half stamp-size label depicting K. Tsiolkovski (space pioneer).

975 Georgi Dimitrov

(Des K. Gogov. Photo)

1982 (7 May). Sozphilex '82 Stamp Exhibition, Veliko Tirnovo. Sheet 61×82 mm. P 13.
MS3026 **975** 50st. vermilion and black .... 3·25 3·25

976 Dimitrov and Congress Emblem

978 Abstract with Birds

977 First French and Bulgarian Stamps

(Des St. Chakarov. Photo)

1982 (25 May). 14th Dimitrov Communist Youth League Congress, Sofia. P 13.
3027 **976** 5st. multicoloured 20 10

(Des P. Petrov. Photo)

1982 (28 May). Philexfrance 82 International Stamp Exhibition, Paris. P 13½×13.
3028 **977** 42st. multicoloured 95 55

(Des St. Kunchev. Litho)

1982 (8 June). Alafrangi Frescoes from 19th-century Houses. T **978** and similar vert designs showing flower and bird patterns. P 11½.

3029	5st. multicoloured	20	15
3030	13st. multicoloured	30	20
3031	25st. multicoloured	45	35
3032	30st. multicoloured	55	45
3033	42st. multicoloured	95	55
3034	60st. multicoloured	1·90	65
3029/3034	*Set of 6*	4·00	2·10

During 1982 sets were issued for World Cup Football Championship, Spain (5, 13, 30st., **MS**2×50st.), Tenth Anniv of First European Security and Co-operation Conference (5, 13, 25, 30st., **MS**1l.), World Cup Results (5, 13, 30st., **MS**2×50st.) and Tenth Anniv (1983) of European Security and Co-operation Conference, Helsinki (5, 13, 25, 30st., **MS**1l.). Supplies and distribution of these stamps were restricted and it is understood they were not available at face value.

979 Georgi Dimitrov

980 Georgi Dimitrov

(Des A. Stareishinski. Photo)

1982 (15 June). Birth Centenary of Georgi Dimitrov (statesman). Sheet 76×52 mm. P 13.
MS3035 **979** 50st. multicoloured .... 1·60 1·60

1982 (21 June). Ninth Fatherland Front Congress, Sofia. Photo. P 13.
3036 **980** 5st. multicoloured 20 10

981 Airplane

982 Atomic Bomb Mushroom-cloud

(Des P. Feredzhanov. Photo)

1982 (29 June). 35th Anniv of Balkanair (state airline). P 13.
3037 **981** 42st. deep new blue, light green and vermilion .... 1·00 65

No. 3037 was issued with *se-tenant* label bearing airline emblem and inscription.

(Des N. Nikolov. Photo)

1982 (15 July). Nuclear Disarmament Campaign. P 13.
3038 **982** 13st. multicoloured 45 20

983 Lyudmila Zhivkova

984 Emblem

(Des St. Kunchev. Photo)

1982 (26 July–4 Aug). 40th Birth Anniv of Lyudmila Zhivkova (founder of "Banners for Peace" Children's Meetings). P 13.

3039	**983**	5st. multicoloured (4.8)	20	10
3040		13st. multicoloured (4.8)	35	15
MS3041		62×67 mm. **983** 1l. multicoloured	2·20	2·20

(Des I. Bogdanov. Photo)

1982 (27 July). Tenth Anniv of United Nations Environment Programme. P 13.
3042 **984** 13st. emerald and deep new blue 35 20

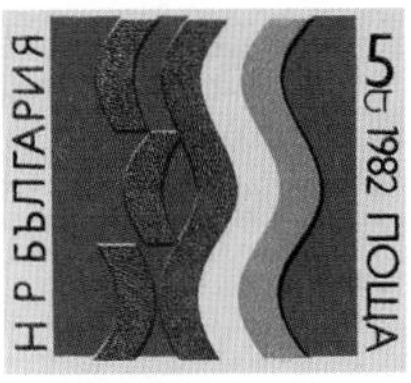
985 Wave Pattern

(Des D. Tasev. Photo)

1982 (27 July). Fifth Bulgarian Painters' Association Congress. P 13½.
3043 **985** 5st. multicoloured 25 20

No. 3043 was issued with *se-tenant* half stamp-size inscribed label.

986 Child Musicians

(Des St. Kunchev and A. Stareishinski. Litho German Bank Note Ptg Co, Leipzig)

1982 (10 Aug). Second "Banners for Peace" Children's Meeting (1st issue). T **986** and similar horiz designs showing children's paintings. Multicoloured. P 14.

3044	3st. Type **986**	10	10
3045	5st. Children skating	20	10
3046	8st. Adults, children and flowers	30	15
3047	13st. Children with flags	35	20
3044/3047	*Set of 4*	85	50
MS3048	70×110 mm. 50st. Children in "Sun" balloon (vert). Perf or imperf	2·20	2·20

See also Nos. 3057/**MS**3063.

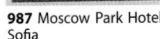

987 Moscow Park Hotel, Sofia

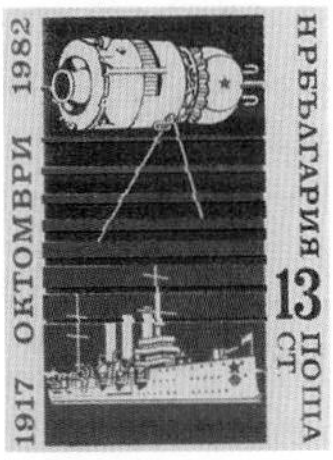
988 Cruiser *Aurora* and Satellite

(Des Kh. Khristov. Photo)

1982 (20 Oct). Hotels. T **987** and similar vert design. Multicoloured. P 13.

3049	32st. Type **987**	85	45
3050	32st. Black Sea Hotel, Varna	85	45

(Des K. Gogov. Photo)

1982 (4 Nov). 65th Anniv of Russian October Revolution. P 13.
3051 **988** 13st. bright scarlet and violet-blue 35 25

989 Hammer and Sickle

990 "The Piano"

(Des K. Gogov. Photo)

1982 (9 Dec). 60th Anniv of U.S.S.R. P 13.
3052 **989** 13st. bright scarlet, gold and bluish violet 35 20

(Des T. Vardzhiev. Litho State Ptg Wks, Budapest)

1982 (23 Dec). Birth Centenary of Pablo Picasso (artist). T **990** and similar vert designs. Multicoloured. P 11½×12½.
3053 13st. Type **990** 45 25
3054 30st. "Portrait of Jacqueline" 65 55
3055 42st. "Maternity" .... 1·40 85
3053/3055 *Set of 3* .... 2·30 1·50
MS3056 61×79 mm. 1l. "Self-portrait" .... 2·75 2·75

991 Boy and Girl

(Des St. Kunchev and A. Stareishinski. Litho German Bank Note Ptg Co, Leipzig)

1982 (28 Dec). Second "Banners for Peace" Children's Meeting (2nd issue). T **991** and similar multicoloured designs. P 14.
3057 3st. Type **991** 20 15
3058 5st. Market place 20 15
3059 8st. Children in fancy dress (vert) 20 15
3060 13st. Chickens (vert) 35 20
3061 25st. Interlocking heads 75 35
3062 30st. Lion 85 45
3057/3062 *Set of 6* .... 2·30 1·30
MS3063 70×109 mm. 50st. Boy and girl in garden (vert). Perf or imperf .... 2·20 2·20

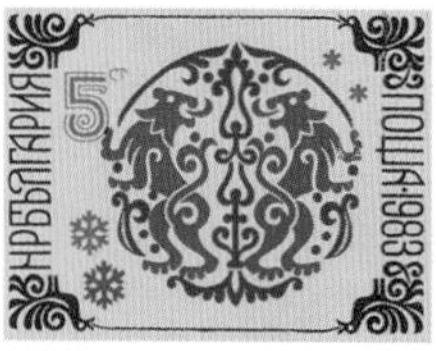

992 Lions

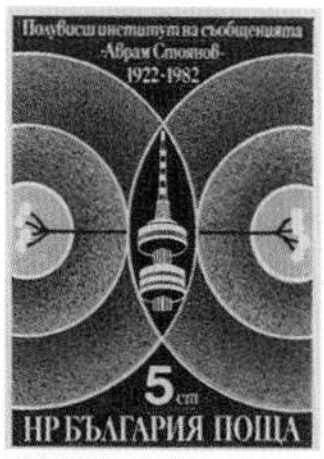

993 Broadcasting Tower

(Des St. Kunchev. Photo)

1982 (28 Dec). New Year. T **992** and similar horiz design. Multicoloured. P 13.
3064 5st. Type **992** 20 10
3065 13st. Decorated letters 35 15

(Des V. Kantardzhieva. Photo)

1982 (29 Dec). 60th Anniv of Avram Stoyanov Broadcasting Institute. P 13.
3066 **993** 5st. ultramarine 20 15

994 Dr. Robert Koch

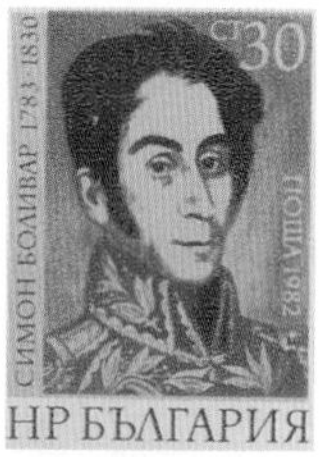

995 Simón Bolívar (bicentenary)

(Des T. Tonchev. Photo)

1982 (30 Dec). Centenary of Discovery of Tubercule Bacillus. P 13.
3067 **994** 25st. yellow and olive-green 65 35

(Des T. Vardzhiev. Photo)

1982 (30 Dec). Birth Anniversaries. T **995** and similar vert design. P 13.
3068 30st. pale yellow-olive and olive-grey 75 45
3069 30st. pale yellow and yellow-brown 75 45
Design:—No. 3069, Rabindranath Tagore (philosopher, 120th anniv).

996 Vasil Levski

997 Skier

(Des I. Bogdanov. Photo)

1983 (10 Feb). 110th Death Anniv of Vasil Levski (revolutionary). P 13×13½.
3070 **996** 5st. yellow-brown and blackish green 20 10

(Des A. Stareishinski. Photo)

1983 (15 Feb). "Universiade '83" University Games, Sofia. P 13.
3071 **997** 30st. multicoloured 75 45

998 Pike (*Esox lucius*)

(Des A. Stareishinski. Photo)

1983 (24 Mar). Freshwater Fish. T **998** and similar horiz designs. Multicoloured. P 13½×13.
3072 3st. Type **998** 20 15
3073 5st. Sturgeon (*Huso huso*) 20 15
3074 13st. Chub (*Leuciscus cephalus*) 35 20
3075 25st. Perch (*Lucioperca lucioperca*) 75 35
3076 30st. Catfish (*Silurus glanis*) 85 45
3077 42st. Trout (*Salmo trutta fario*) .... 2·40 55
3072/3077 *Set of 6* .... 4·25 1·70

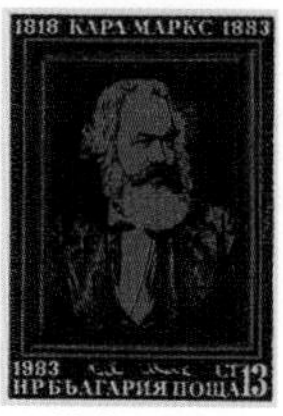

999 Karl Marx

1000 Hašek and Illustrations from *The Good Soldier Schweik*

(Des I. Kiosev. Photo)

1983 (5 Apr). Death Centenary of Karl Marx. P 13×13½.
3078 **999** 13st. bright scarlet, deep purple and lemon 45 20

(Des I. Kiosev. Photo)

1983 (20 Apr). Birth Centenary of Jaroslav Hašek (Czech writer). P 13.
3079 **1000** 13st. reddish brown, pale brownish grey and deep olive 35 20

1001 Martin Luther

(Des I. Kiosev. Photo)

1983 (10 May). 500th Birth Anniv of Martin Luther (Protestant reformer). P 13½×13.
3080 **1001** 13st. pale bluish grey, blackish brown and chestnut 45 20

1002 People forming Initials

(Des P. Petrov. Photo)

1983 (13 May). 55th Anniv of Young Workers' Union. P 13½×13.
3081 **1002** 5st. vermilion, black and salmon 20 15

1003 Khaskovo Costume

1004 Old Man feeding Chicken

(Des V. Vasileva. Litho)

1983 (17 May). Costumes. T **1003** and similar vert designs. Multicoloured. P 14.
3082 5st. Type **1003** 25 15
3083 8st. Pernik 30 15
3084 13st. Burgas 35 20
3085 25st. Tolbukhin 75 35
3086 30st. Blagoevgrad 85 45
3087 42st. Topolovgrad .... 2·40 55
3082/3087 *Set of 6* .... 4·50 1·70

(Des I. Bogdanov. Photo)

1983 (20 May). Sixth International Festival of Humour and Satire, Gabrovo. P 13.
3088 **1004** 5st. multicoloured 20 10

During 1983 sets were issued for European Security and Co-operation Conference, Budapest (5, 13, 25, 30st., **MS**1l.), Olympic Games, Los Angeles (5, 13, 30, 42st., **MS**2×50st.), Winter Olympic Games, Sarajevo (horiz designs, 5, 13, 30, 42st., **MS**1l.) and European Security and Co-operation Conference, Madrid (5, 13, 30, 42st., **MS**1l.). Supplies and distribution of these stamps were restricted, and it is understood they were not available at face value.

1005 Smirnenski

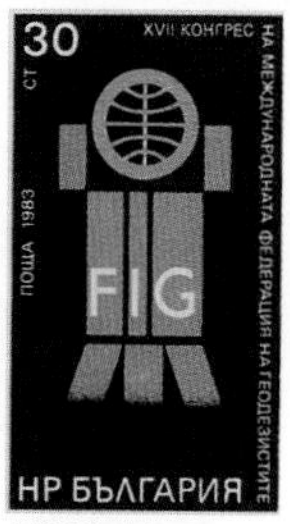

1006 Emblem

(Des P. Petrov. Photo)

1983 (25 May). 85th Birth Anniv of Khristo Smirnenski (poet). P 13.
3089 **1005** 5st. orange-red, sepia and olive-yellow 20 20

(Des V. Kitanov. Photo)

1983 (27 May). 17th International Geodesy Federation Congress. P 13.
3090 **1006** 30st. bright green, deep ultramarine and orange-yellow 65 45

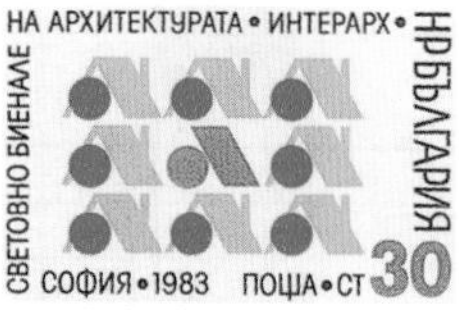

1007 Stylized Houses

1008 Chessmen on Map of Europe

(Des Kh. Khristov. Photo)

1983 (6 June). Interarch '83 World Architecture Biennale, Sofia. P 13.
3091 **1007** 30st. multicoloured 75 45

(Des Maglena Konstantinova. Photo)

1983 (20 June). Eighth European Chess Team Championship, Plovdiv. P 13.
3092 **1008** 13st. multicoloured 45 20

1009 Brazilian and Bulgarian Football Stamps

(Des S. Gruev. Photo)

1983 (24 June). Brasiliana 83 International Stamp Exhibition, Rio de Janeiro. Sheet 73×103 mm. P 13.
MS3093 **1009** 1l. slate-green, reddish brown and gold .... 2·75 2·75

1010 Valentina Tereshkova

1011 Television Mast, Tolbukhin

(Des Tekla Aleksieva. Photo)

1983 (28 June). AIR. 20th Anniv of First Woman in Space. Sheet 121×75 mm containing T **1010** and similar vert design, each deep ultramarine and chestnut. P 13.
MS3094 50st. Type **1010**; 50st. Svetlana Savitskaya, 1982 cosmonaut .... 3·25 3·25

(Des L. Chekhlarov. Photo)

1983 (20 July). AIR. World Communications Year. T **1011** and similar vert designs. P 13.
3095 5st. pale blue and lake 20 15
a. Strip of 3. Nos. 3095/7 .... 1·20
3096 13st. pale magenta and lake 35 20
3097 30st. bright lemon and lake 55 35
3095/3097 *Set of 3* .... 1·00 65
Designs:—13st. Postwoman; 30st. Radio tower, Mount Botev.
Nos. 3095/7 were issued together in *se-tenant* strips of three within the sheet.

1012 Lenin addressing Congress

(Des P. Petrov. Photo)

1983 (29 July). 80th Anniv of Second Russian Social Democratic Workers' Party Congress. P 13.

3098 **1012** 5st. plum, deep reddish purple and gold 20 10

1013 Pistol and Dagger on Book

1014 Crystals and Hammers within Gearwheel

(Des T. Vardzhiev. Photo)

1983 (29 July). 80th Anniv of Ilinden-Preobrazhenie Rising. P 13.

3099 **1013** 5st. greenish yellow and blackish green 20 10

(Des St. Kunchev. Photo)

1983 (10 Aug). 30th Anniv of Mining and Geology Institute, Sofia. P 13.

3100 **1014** 5st. olive-grey, blackish purple and dull blue 20 10

1015 Georgi Dimitrov and Revolution Scenes

(Des I. Kiosev. Photo)

1983 (18 Aug). 60th Anniv of September Uprising. T **1015** and similar horiz design. Multicoloured. P 13½×13.

3101 5st. Type **1015** 20 10
3102 13st. Wreath and revolution scenes 35 15

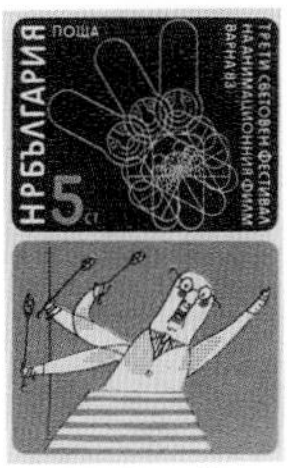

1016 Animated Drawings

1017 Angora

(Des K. Gogov. Photo)

1983 (15 Sept). Third Animated Film Festival, Varna. P 14×13½.

3103 **1016** 5st. multicoloured 20 10

(Des V. Kitanov. Photo)

1983 (26 Sept). Cats. T **1017** and similar multicoloured designs. P 13.

3104 5st. Type **1017** 25 20
3105 13st. Siamese 45 20
3106 20st. Abyssinian (vert) 65 35
3107 25st. European 95 45
3108 30st. Persian (vert) .... 1·10 65
3109 42st. Khmer .... 1·90 1·10
3104/3109 *Set of 6* .... 4·75 2·75

1018 Trevithick's Locomotive, 1803

1019 Liberation Monument, Plovdiv

(Des St. Kunchev. Photo)

1983 (20 Oct). Locomotives (1st series). T **1018** and similar horiz designs. Multicoloured. P 13.

3110 5st. Type **1078** 20 10
3111 13st. Blenkinsop's rack locomotive *Prince Royal*, 1810 .... 45 35
3112 42st. Hedley's *Puffing Billy*, 1812 .... 2·00 1·10
3113 60st. *Der Adler* (first German locomotive), 1835 .... 3·25 1·60
3110/3113 *Set of 4* .... 5·25 2·75

See also Nos. 3159/63.

(Des Veni Kantardzhieva. Photo)

1983 (4 Nov). 90th Anniv of Bulgarian Philatelic Federation and Fourth National Stamp Exhibition, Plovdiv. Sheet 65×79 mm. P 13.

MS3114 **1019** 50st. grey, royal blue and scarlet-vermilion .... 1·60 1·60

1020 Mask and Laurel as Lyre

1021 Ioan Kukuzel

(Des Ralitsa Stanoeva. Photo)

1983 (2 Dec). 75th Anniv of National Opera, Sofia. P 13×13½.

3115 **1020** 5st. brown-lake, black and gold 20 10

(Des I. Kiosev. Photo)

1983 (5 Dec). Bulgarian Composers. T **1021** and similar vert designs. P 13×13½.

3116 5st. pale yellow, chocolate and grey-olive 20 15
3117 8st. pale yellow, chocolate and dull vermilion 20 15
3118 13st. pale yellow, chocolate and bottle green 30 20
3119 20st. pale yellow, chocolate and royal blue 35 25
3120 25st. pale yellow, chocolate and brownish grey 45 35
3121 30st. pale yellow, chocolate and red-brown 55 45
3116/3121 *Set of 6* .... 1·80 1·40

Designs:—8st. Georgi Atanasov; 13st. Petko Stainov; 20st. Veselin Stoyanov; 25st. Lyubomir Pipkov; 30st. Pancho Vladigerov.

Nos. 3116/21 were each issued with *se-tenant* label depicting the score of one of the composer's works.

1022 Snowflake

1023 "Angelo Donni"

(Des St. Kunchev. Photo)

1983 (10 Dec). New Year. P 13.

3122 **1022** 5st. bright emerald, blue and gold 20 10

(Des St. Kunchev. Photo German Bank Note Ptg Co, Leipzig)

1983 (22 Dec). 500th Birth Anniv of Raphael (artist). T **1023** and similar vert designs. Multicoloured. P 14.

3123 5st. Type **1023** 20 15
3124 13st. "Portrait of a Cardinal" 35 20
3125 30st. "Baldassare Castiglioni" 45 45
3126 42st. "Woman with a Veil" 95 55
3123/3126 *Set of 4* .... 1·80 1·20
MS3127 59×98 mm. 1l. "Sistine Madonna" .... 2·40 2·40

1024 Eurasian Common Shrew (*Sorex araneus*)

1025 Karavelov

(Des B. Kitanov. Photo)

1983 (30 Dec). Protected Mammals. T **1024** and similar horiz designs. Multicoloured. P 13.

3128 12st. Type **1024** 45 35
3129 13st. Greater horseshoe bat (*Rhinolophus ferrum equinum*) 65 35
3130 20st. Common long-eared bat (*Plecotus auritus*) .... 1·00 45
3131 30st. Forest dormouse (*Dryomys nitedula*) .... 1·60 65
3132 42st. Fat dormouse (*Glis glis*) .... 3·25 1·10
3128/3132 *Set of 5* .... 6·25 2·60

(Des I. Bogdanov. Photo)

1984 (31 Jan). 150th Birth Anniv of Lyuben Karavelov (poet). P 13×13½.

3133 **1025** 5st. deep violet-blue, olive-bistre and reddish brown 20 10

During 1984 sets were issued for European Confidence- and Security-building Measures and Disarmament Conference, Stockholm (5, 13, 30, 42st., **MS**1l.) and Winter Olympic Games, Sarajevo (vert designs, 5, 13, 30, 42st., **MS**1l.). Supplies and distribution of these stamps were restricted and it is understood that they were not available at face value.

1026 Mendeleev and Formulae

(Des I. Kiosev. Photo)

1984 (14 Mar). 150th Birth Anniv of Dmitry Mendeleev (chemist). P 13.

3134 **1026** 13st. multicoloured 35 20

1027 *Gen. Vl. Zaimov* (bulk carrier)

(Des M. Peikova. Photo)

1984 (21 Mar). Ships. T **1027** and similar horiz designs. Multicoloured. P 13½×14.

3135 5st. Type **1027** 20 10
3136 13st. *Mesta* (tanker) 35 15
3137 25st. *Veleka* (tanker) 65 35
3138 32st. *Geroite na Odesa* (ferry) 80 45
3139 42st. *Rozhen* (bulk carrier) .... 1·40 55
3135/3139 *Set of 5* .... 3·00 1·40

1028 World Cup Stamps

1029 Pigeon with Letter over Globe

(Des Ralitsa Stanoeva. Photo)

1984 (18 Apr). España 84 International Stamp Exhibition, Madrid. Sheet 89×110 mm. P 13.

MS3140 **1028** 2l. multicoloured .... 8·25 8·25

(Des Maglena Konstantinova. Photo)

1984 (24 Apr). Mladost '84 Youth Stamp Exhibition, Pleven (1st issue). P 13.

3141 **1029** 5st. multicoloured 20 10

See also Nos. 3171/2 and **MS**3176.

1030 Wild Cherries (*Prunus avium*)

(Des L. Chekhlarov. Photo)

1984 (5 May). Fruit. T **1030** and similar vert designs. Multicoloured. P 13.

3142 5st. Type **1030** 20 15
3143 8st. Wild strawberries (*Fragaria vesca*) 20 15
3144 13st. Dewberries (*Rubus caesius*) 35 20
3145 20st. Raspberries (*Rubus idaeus*) 55 35
3146 42st. Medlars (*Mespilus germanica*) .... 1·70 55
3142/3146 *Set of 5* .... 2·75 1·30

1031 "Vitosha Conference" (K. Buyukliiski and P. Petrov)

(Des D. Karapantev. Photo)

1984 (17 May). 60th Anniv of Bulgarian Communist Party Conference, Vitosha. P 13½×13.

3147 **1031** 5st. blackish purple, pale cinnamon and rosine 20 10

1032 Security Conference 1980 13st. Stamp

(Des St. Kunchev. Photo)

1984 (22 May). Fifth International Stamp Fair, Essen. Sheet 94×147 mm containing T **1032** and similar horiz design. Multicoloured. P 13.

MS3148	1l.50 Type **1032**; 1l.50 Security Conference 1981 35st. stamp	8·75	8·75

1033 Athlete and Doves

1034 Mt. Everest

(Des A. Stareishinski. Photo)

1984 (23 May). Sixth Republican Spartakiad. P 13.

3149	**1033**	13st. multicoloured	35	20

(Des Kh. Khristov. Photo)

1984 (31 May). Bulgarian Expedition to Mt. Everest. P 13.

3150	**1034**	5st. multicoloured	20	10

1035 Kogge

(Des Tekla Aleksieva. Photo)

1984 (11 June). Universal Postal Union Congress Philatelic Salon, Hamburg. Sheet 100×107 mm. P 13.

MS3151	**1035**	3l. multicoloured	7·50	7·50

1036 Drummer

1037 Seal

(Des A. Stareishinski. Photo)

1984 (12 June). Sixth Amateur Performers Festival. P 13.

3152	**1036**	5st. multicoloured	20	10

(Des T. Momchilov. Photo)

1984 (27 June). 50 Years of Bulgarian–U.S.S.R. Diplomatic Relations. P 13.

3153	**1037**	13st. multicoloured	35	20

1038 Rock Dove (*Columba livia*)

1039 Production Quality Emblem

(Des B. Kitanov. Litho German Bank Note Ptg Co, Leipzig)

1984 (6 July). Pigeons and Doves. T **1038** and similar horiz designs. Multicoloured. P 14.

3154	5st. Type **1038**	20	10
3155	13st. Stock dove (*Columba oenas*)	35	20
3156	20st. Wood pigeon (*Columba palumbus*)	55	35
3157	30st. Turtle dove (*Streptopelia turtur*)	95	45
3158	42st. Domestic pigeon (*Columba var. domestica*)	1·20	55
3154/3158	*Set of 5*	3·00	1·50

(Des B. Kitanov. Photo)

1984 (31 July). Locomotives (2nd series). Horiz designs as T **1018**. Multicoloured. P 13.

3159	13st. *Best Friend*, Charleston, U.S.A., 1830	35	20
3160	25st. *Saxonia*, Dresden, 1836	65	35
3161	30st. *Lafayette*, U.S.A., 1837	85	45
3162	42st. *Borsig*, Germany, 1841	1·20	60
3163	60st. *Philadelphia*, U.S.A., 1843	2·00	85
3159/3163	*Set of 5*	4·50	2·20

(Des P. Petrov. Photo)

1984 (8 Aug). 40th Anniv of Fatherland Front Government. T **1039** and similar vert designs. P 13.

3164	5st. vermilion, deep emerald and yellowish green	20	15
3165	20st. orange-vermilion and bright violet	55	25
3166	30st. orange-vermilion and deep new blue	85	45
3164/3166	*Set of 3*	1·40	75

Designs:—20st. Monument to Soviet Army, Sofia; 30st. Figure nine and star.

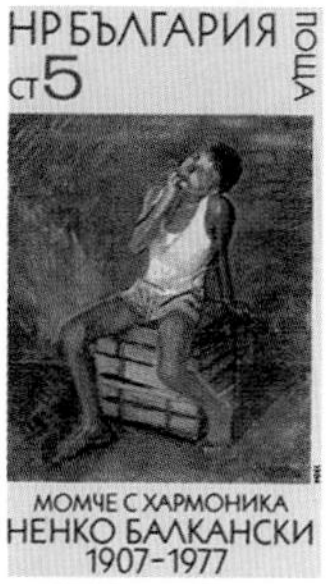

1040 "Boy with Harmonica"

1041 Mausoleum of Russian Soldiers

(Des K. Kunev. Photo German Bank Note Ptg Co, Leipzig)

1984 (7 Sept). Paintings by Nenko Balkanski. T **1040** and similar multicoloured designs. P 14.

3167	5st. Type **1040**	20	15
3168	30st. "Window in Paris"	85	45
3169	42st. "Portrait of Two Women" (horiz)	1·60	55
3167/3169	*Set of 3*	2·40	1·00
MS3170	65×110 mm. 1l. "Self-portrait"	2·75	2·75

1984 (20 Sept). Mladost '84 Youth Stamp Exhibition, Pleven (2nd issue). T **1041** and similar vert design. Photo. P 13.

3171	5st. multicoloured	20	10
3172	13st. black, deep green and orange-red	35	15

Design:—13st. Panorama building.

1042 Pioneers saluting

(Des Tekla Aleksieva. Photo)

1984 (21 Sept). 40th Anniv of Dimitrov Septembrist Pioneers Organization. P 13.

3173	**1042**	5st. multicoloured	20	10

1043 Vaptsarov (after D. Nikolov)

1984 (2 Oct). 75th Birth Anniv of Nikola I. Vaptsarov (poet). Photo. P 13.

3174	**1043**	5st. yellow-ochre and brown-lake	20	10

1044 Goalkeeper saving goal

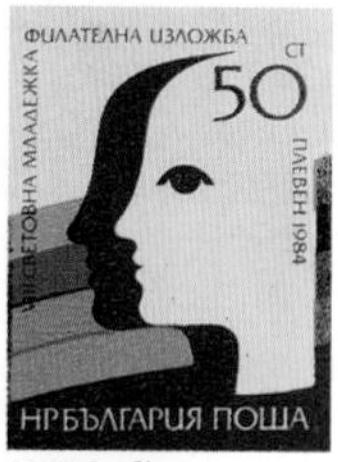

1045 Profiles

(Des D. Tasev. Photo)

1984 (3 Oct). 75th Anniv of Bulgarian Football. P 13.

3175	**1044**	42st. multicoloured	95	55

1984 (5 Oct). Mladost '84 Youth Stamp Exhibition, Pleven (3rd issue). Sheet 50×76 mm. Photo. P 13.

MS3176	**1045**	50st. multicoloured	1·60	1·60

1046 Devil's Bridge, River Arda

(Des Kh. Aleksiev. Photo)

1984 (5 Oct). Bridges. T **1046** and similar horiz designs. Multicoloured. P 13½×13.

3177	5st. Type **1046**	30	20
3178	13st. Kolo Ficheto Bridge, Byala	55	45
3179	30st. Asparukhov Bridge, Varna	95	85
3180	42st. Bebresh Bridge, Botevgrad	2·00	1·50
3177/3180	*Set of 4*	3·50	2·75

Nos. 3177/80 were each issued in sheetlets of six stamps.

A miniature sheet, 1l. depicting Friendship Bridge, Ruse, exists but supply and distribution were limited.

1047 Olympic Emblem

(Des Kh. Khristov. Photo)

1984 (24 Oct). 90th Anniv of International Olympic Committee. P 13.

3181	**1047**	13st. multicoloured	35	20

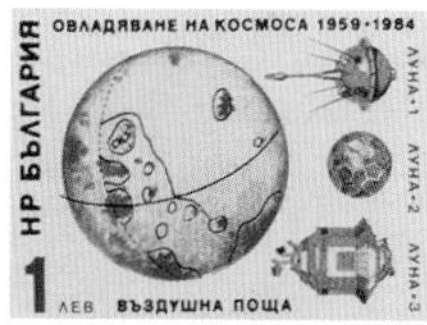

1048 Moon and "Luna I", "II" and "III"

1049 Dalmatian Pelican with Chicks

(Des Tekla Aleksieva. Photo)

1984 (24 Oct). 25th Anniv of First Moon Rocket. Sheet 79×57 mm. P 13.

MS3182	**1048**	1l. multicoloured	3·25	3·25

(Des A. Stareishinski. Photo)

1984 (2 Nov). Wildlife Protection. Dalmatian Pelican (*Pelecanus crispus*). T **1049** and similar vert designs. P 13.

3183	5st. multicoloured	45	20
3184	13st. lavender, black and orange-brown	95	45
3185	20st. multicoloured	1·40	1·10
3186	32st. multicoloured	3·25	1·60
3183/3186	*Set of 4*	5·50	3·00

Designs:—13st. Two pelicans; 20st. Pelican on water; 32st. Pelican in flight.

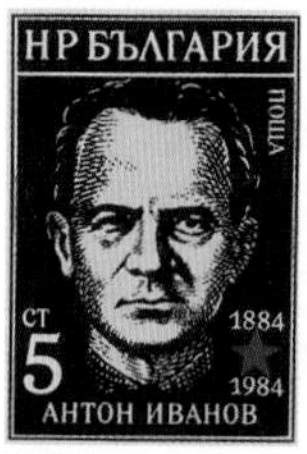

1050 Anton Ivanov

1051 Girl's Profile with Text as Hair

(Des I. Bogdanov. Photo)

1984 (2 Nov). Birth Centenary of Anton Ivanov (revolutionary). P 13.

3187	**1050**	5st. pale yellow, lake-brown and scarlet-vermilion	20	10

(Des Ralitsa Stanoeva. Photo)

1984 (9 Nov). 70th Anniv of Bulgarian Women's Socialist Movement. P 13.

3188	**1051**	5st. multicoloured	20	10

1052 Snezhanka Television Tower

1053 Birds and Posthorns

(Des Kh. Khristov. Photo)

1984 (23 Nov). Television Towers. T **1052** and similar vert design. P 13.

3189	5st. deep ultramarine, deep grey-green and bright mauve	20	15
3190	1l. deep brown, bright mauve and olive-bistre	2·30	1·10

Design:—1l. Orelek television tower.

(Des St. Kunchev. Photo)

1984 (5 Dec). New Year. T **1053** and similar horiz design. Multicoloured. P 13.

3191	5st. Type **1053**	20	10
3192	13st. Decorative pattern	35	15

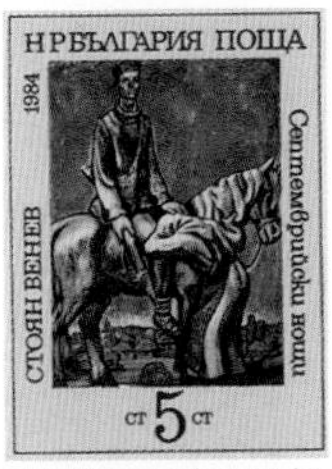

1054 "September Nights"

1055 Peacock (*Inachis io*)

(Des V. Vasileva. Litho)

1984 (10 Dec). 80th Birth Anniv of Stoyan Venev (artist). T **1054** and similar vert designs. Multicoloured. P 13.

3193 5st. Type **1054** 20 15
3194 30st. "Man with Three Orders" 85 45
3195 42st. "The Hero" .... 1·40 55
3193/3195 *Set of 3* .... 2·20 1·00

(Des L. Chekhlarov. Litho)

1984 (14 Dec). Butterflies. T **1055** and similar horiz designs. Multicoloured. P 11½.

3196 13st. Type **1055** 35 20
3197 25st. Swallowtail (*Papilio machaon*) 65 35
3198 30st. Great banded grayling (*Brintesia circe*) 85 45
3199 42st. Orange-tip (*Anthocharis cardamines*) 1·20 55
3200 60st. Red admiral (*Vanessa atalanta*) .... 2·00 75
3196/3200 *Set of 5* .... 4·50 2·10
MS3201 75×60 mm. 1l. Poplar admiral (*Limenitis populi*) .... 2·75 2·75

1056 Augusto Sandino

1057 Tupolev Tu-154 Jetliner

(Des G. Nikolov. Photo)

1984 (18 Dec). 50th Death Anniv of Augusto Sandino (Nicaraguan revolutionary). P 13×13½.

3202 **1056** 13st. black, scarlet-vermilion and lemon 35 20

(Des Tekla Aleksieva. Photo)

1984 (21 Dec). 40th Anniv of International Civil Aviation Organization. P 13½×13.

3203 **1057** 42st. multicoloured 95 55

1058 "The Three Graces" (detail)

1060 Eastern Hog-nosed Skunk (*Conepatus leuconotus*)

1059 *Sofia*

1984 (28 Dec). 500th Birth Anniv (1983) of Raphael (artist) (2nd issue). T **1058** and similar vert designs. Multicoloured. Litho. P 14.

3204 5st. Type **1058** 25 20
3205 13st. "Cupid and the Three Graces" (detail) 30 25
3206 30st. "Original Sin" (detail) 65 45
3207 42st. "La Fornarina" .... 1·30 50
3204/3207 *Set of 4* .... 2·30 1·30
MS3208 106×95 mm. 1l. "Galatea" (detail) .... 2·50 2·50

Nos. 3204/7 were each issued in separate sheetlets of six stamps and also together in *se-tenant* sheetlets of four.

(Des D. Tasev. Photo)

1984 (29 Dec). Maiden Voyage of Danube Cruise Ship *Sofia*. P 13.

3209 **1059** 13st. deep blue, new blue and lemon 35 20

A miniature sheet for Tenth Anniv of European Security and Co-operation Conference, Helsinki, containing 3×50st., was issued in 1985 in a limited quantity.

(Des A. Stareishinski. Photo)

1985 (17 Jan). Mammals. T **1060** and similar horiz designs. P 13.

3210 13st. black, grey-blue and yellow-orange. 30 15
3211 25st. black, light brown and yellowish green 65 35
3212 30st. black, brown and lemon 75 40
3213 42st. multicoloured .... 1·10 55
3214 60st. multicoloured .... 1·90 85
3210/3214 *Set of 5* .... 4·25 2·10

Designs:—25st. Banded linsang (*Prionodon linsang*); 30st. Zorilla (*Ictonix striatus*); 42st. Banded palm civet (*Hemigalus derbyanus*); 60st. Broad-striped galidia (*Galidictis fasciata*).

1061 Nikolai Liliev

(Des D. Nikolov. Photo)

1985 (25 Jan). Birth Centenary of Nikolai Liliev (poet). P 13.

3215 **1061** 30st. buff, deep yellow-brown and gold 65 45

1062 Tsvyatko Radoinov

1063 Asen Zlatarov

(Des D. Nikolov. Photo)

1985 (29 Jan). 90th Birth Anniv of Tsvyatko Radoinov (resistance fighter). P 13.

3216 **1062** 5st. reddish brown and scarlet-vermilion 20 10

(Des T. Vardzhiev. Photo)

1985 (14 Feb). Birth Centenary of Asen Zlatarov (biochemist). P 13.

3217 **1063** 5st. brown-purple, pale yellow and green 20 10

1064 Research Ship *Akademik*

1065 Lenin Monument, Sofia

(Des Tekla Aleksieva. Photo)

1985 (1 Mar). 13th General Assembly and 25th Anniv of Intergovernmental Oceanographic Commission. Sheet 90×60 mm. P 13.

MS3218 **1064** 80st. multicoloured .... 2·20 2·20

(Des S. Gruev. Photo)

1985 (12 Mar). 115th Birth Anniv of Lenin. Sheet 55×87 mm. P 13.

MS3219 **1065** 50st. multicoloured .... 1·30 1·30

1066 Olive Branch and Sword Blade

1067 Bach

(Des R. Kolev. Photo)

1985 (19 Mar). 30th Anniv of Warsaw Pact. P 13.

3220 **1066** 13st. multicoloured 30 20

(Des A. Stareishinski. Photo)

1985 (25 Mar). Composers. T **1067** and similar vert designs. P 13.

3221 42st. deep steel blue and orange-vermilion .... 1·40 65
3222 42st. bluish violet and light green .... 1·40 65
3223 42st. stone, lake-brown and bright orange 1·40 65
3224 42st. stone, reddish brown and orange-red .... 1·40 65
3225 42st. stone, bottle green and new blue ..... 1·40 65
3226 42st. stone, deep reddish purple and yellowish green .... 1·40 65
3221/3226 *Set of 6* .... 7·50 3·50

Designs:—No. 3222, Mozart; 3223, Tchaikovsky; 3224, Modest Petrovich Musorgsky; 3225, Giuseppe Verdi; 3226, Filip Kutev.

1068 Girl with Birds

(Des St. Kunchev. Litho German Bank Note Ptg Co, Leipzig)

1985 (26 Mar). Third "Banners for Peace" Children's Meeting, Sofia. T **1068** and similar multicoloured designs showing children's paintings. P 14.

3227 5st. Type **1068** 20 15
3228 8st. Children painting 20 15
3229 13st. Girl among flowers 30 20
3230 20st. Children at market stall 45 25
3231 25st. Circle of children 55 35
3232 30st. Nurse 65 45
3227/3232 *Set of 6* .... 2·10 1·40
MS3233 70×110 mm. 50st. Children dancing (vert). Perf or imperf .... 2·20 2·20

Nos. 3227/32 were issued both in separate sheets and together in *se-tenant* sheetlets of six (*Price of sheetlet*: £2.20 *un*).

1069 Saint Methodius

1070 Soldiers and Nazi Flags

(Des S. Gruev. Photo)

1985 (6 Apr). 1100th Death Anniv of Saint Methodius. P 13.

3234 **1069** 13st. multicoloured 65 35

(Des D. Nikolov. Photo)

1985 (30 Apr). 40th Anniv of V.E. ("Victory in Europe") Day. T **1070** and similar horiz designs. Multicoloured. P 13½.

3235 5st. Type **1070** 20 15
3236 13st. 11th Infantry parade, Sofia 35 25
3237 30st. Soviet soldier with orphan 75 35
3235/3237 *Set of 3* .... 1·20 70
MS3238 90×123 mm. 50st. Soldier raising Soviet flag .... 1·60 1·60

Nos. 3235/7 were each issued with *se-tenant* half stamp-size label depicting an Order.

Nos. 3235/7 were issued both in separate sheets and together in *se-tenant* sheetlets of six stamps and six labels (*Price for sheetlet*: £3 *un*).

1071 Woman carrying Child and Man on Donkey

(Des S. Dukov. Photo)

1985 (30 Apr). Seventh International Festival of Humour and Satire, Gabrovo. P 13½.

3239 **1071** 13st. black, lemon and dull vermilion 30 20

No. 3239 was issued with *se-tenant* half stamp-size label bearing festival emblem.

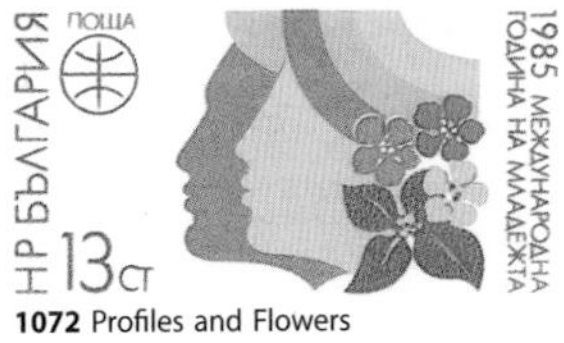

1072 Profiles and Flowers

(Des I. Bogdanov. Photo)

1985 (21 May). International Youth Year. P 13.

3240 **1072** 13st. multicoloured 30 20

1073 Ivan Vazov

1074 Monument to Unknown Soldier and City Arms

(Des P. Petrov. Photo)

1985 (30 May). 135th Birth Anniv of Ivan Vazov (poet). P 13½.

3241 **1073** 5st. blackish brown and stone 20 10

No. 3241 was issued with *se-tenant* half stamp-size label depicting Vazov's birthplace, Vazovgrad.

(Des K. Gogov. Photo)

1985 (1 June). Millenary of Khaskovo. P 13.

3242 **1074** 5st. multicoloured 20 10

1075 Festival Emblem

1076 Indira Gandhi

(Des D. Tashev. Photo)

1985 (25 June). 12th World Youth and Students' Festival, Moscow. P 13.

3243 **1075** 13st. multicoloured 30 20

(Des D. Nikolov. Photo)

1985 (26 June). Indira Gandhi (Indian Prime Minister) Commemoration. P 13.

3244 **1076** 30st. deep brown, reddish orange and lemon 65 35

1077 Vasil E. Aprilov (founder)

1078 Congress Emblem

(Des I. Bogdanov. Photo)

1985 (30 June). 150th Anniv of New Bulgarian School, Gabrovo. P 13.

3245 **1077** 5st. dull violet-blue, maroon and olive-green 20 10

(Des Kh. Khristov. Photo)

1985 (30 June). 36th International Shorthand and Typing Federation Congress ("Intersteno"), Sofia. P 13.

3246 **1078** 13st. multicoloured 30 20

1079 Aleksandr Nevski Cathedral, Sofia

1080 State Arms and U.N. Flag

(Des R. Kolev. Photo)

1985 (9 July). Sixth General Assembly of World Tourism Organization, Sofia. P 13.

3247 **1079** 42st. green, royal blue and yellow-orange 95 55

(Des St. Kunchev. Photo)

1985 (16 July). 40th Anniv of United Nations Organization (3248) and 30th Anniv of Bulgaria's Membership (3249). T **1080** and similar horiz design. Multicoloured. P 13.

3248 13st. Doves around U.N. emblem 30 20
3249 13st. Type **1080** 30 20

1081 Rosa "Trakijka"

1082 Peace Dove

(Des I. Bogdanov. Litho National Ptg Wks, Havana)

1985 (20 July). Roses. T **1081** and similar vert designs. Multicoloured. P 13.

3250 5st. *Rosa damascena* 20 15
3251 13st. Type **1081** 30 20
3252 20st. "Radiman" 45 25
3253 30st. "Marista" 55 35
3254 42st. "Valentina" 95 45
3255 60st. "Maria" .... 1·40 55
3250/3255 *Set of 6* .... 3·50 1·80

Nos. 3250/5 were issued both in separate sheets and together in *se-tenant* sheetlets of six (*Price of sheetlet*: £3.75 *un*).

(Des St. Kunchev. Photo)

1985 (1 Aug). Tenth Anniv of European Security and Cooperation Conference, Helsinki. P 13.

3256 **1082** 13st. multicoloured 30 20

1083 Water Polo

1084 Edelweiss

(Des Kh. Aleksiev. Litho National Ptg Wks, Havana)

1985 (2 Aug). European Swimming Championships, Sofia. T **1083** and similar multicoloured designs. P 12½.

3257 5st. Butterfly stroke (horiz) 20 15
3258 13st. Type **1083** 30 20
3259 42st. Diving .... 1·10 55
3260 60st. Synchronised swimming (horiz) .... 1·90 75
a. Inscr and face value inverted .... 9·00 9·00
3257/3260 *Set of 4* .... 3·25 1·50

On No. 3260/a the swimmer's head is at the foot of the stamp.

(Des L. Chekhlarov. Photo)

1985 (15 Aug). 90th Anniv of Bulgarian Tourist Organization. P 13.

3261 **1084** 5st. multicoloured 20 10

1085 State Arms

1086 Footballers

(Des S. Gruev. Photo)

1985 (29 Aug). Centenary of Union of E. Roumelia and Bulgaria. P 14×13½.

3262 **1085** 5st. black, reddish orange and deep yellow-green 20 10

(Des D. Tashev. Photo)

1985 (29 Aug). World Cup Football Championship, Mexico (1986) (1st issue). T **1086** and similar designs showing footballers. P 13.

3263 5st. multicoloured 20 15
3264 13st. multicoloured 30 20
3265 30st. multicoloured 65 45
3266 42st. multicoloured .... 1·40 55
3263/3266 *Set of 4* .... 2·30 1·20
MS3267 54×76 mm. 1l. multicoloured (horiz) .... 2·30 2·30

See also Nos. 3346/**MS**3352.

1087 Computer Picture of Boy

(Des L. Chekhlarov. Photo)

1985 (24 Sept). International Young Inventors' Exhibition, Plovdiv. T **1087** and similar horiz designs. Multicoloured. P 13.

3268 5st. Type **1087** 20 15
3269 13st. Computer picture of youth 30 20
3270 30st. Computer picture of cosmonaut 75 35
3268/3270 *Set of 3* .... 1·10 65

1088 St. John's Church, Nesebur

1089 Lyudmila Zhivkova Palace of Culture

(Des K. Kunev. Litho National Ptg Wks, Havana)

1985 (25 Sept). 40th Anniv of United Nations Educational, Scientific and Cultural Organization. T **1088** and similar multicoloured designs. P 12½.

3271 5st. Type **1088** 20 15
3272 13st. Rila Monastery 30 20
3273 35st. Soldier (fresco, Ivanovo Rock Church) 95 45
3274 42st. Archangel Gabriel (fresco, Boyana Church) .... 1·10 55
3275 60st. Thracian woman (fresco, Kazanlak tomb) .... 1·90 75
3271/3275 *Set of 5* .... 4·00 1·90
MS3276 100×83 mm. 1l. Madara horseman (horiz). Imperf .... 2·20 2·20

(Des K. Kunev. Litho National Ptg Wks, Havana)

1985 (8 Oct). 23rd United Nations Educational, Scientific and Cultural Organization General Session, Sofia. Sheet 62×95 mm. P 13.

MS3277 **1089** 1l. multicoloured .... 2·20 2·20

1090 Colosseum, Rome

1091 Gladiolus

(Des St. Kunchev. Photo)

1985 (15 Oct). Italia '85 International Stamp Exhibition, Rome. P 13½.

3278 **1090** 42st. multicoloured 95 55

No. 3278 was issued with *se-tenant* half stamp-size label showing the exhibition emblem.

(Des G. Gadelev. Photo)

1985 (22 Oct)–**86**. Flowers. T **1091** and similar vert designs. P 13×13½.

3279 5st. rose-red and rosine 20 15
3280 5st. royal blue and grey-blue 20 15
3281 5st. bright reddish violet and dull violet 20 15
3282 8st. light new blue and new blue (29.7.86) 20 15
3283 8st. reddish orange and brown-red (29.7.86) 20 15
3284 32st. yellow-orange and ochre (29.7.86) 65 35
3279/3284 *Set of 6* .... 1·50 1·00

Designs:—No. 3280, Garden iris (*Iris germanica*); 3281, Dwarf morning glory (*Convolvulus tricolor*); 3282, Morning glory (*Ipomoea tricolor*); 3283, *Anenome coronaria*; 3284, Golden-rayed lily (*Lilium auratum*).

1092 St. Methodius

1093 Cologne Cathedral

(Des St. Kunchev. Photo)

1985 (22 Oct). Cultural Congress of European Security and Co-operation Conference, Budapest. Sheet 105×93 mm containing T **1092** and similar vert designs. Multicoloured. P 13.

MS3285 50st. St. Cyril; 50st. Map of Europe (imperf×p 13); 50st. Type **1092** .... 4·25 4·25

No. **MS**3285 also exists imperforate from a limited printing.

(Des St. Kunchev. Photo German Bank Note Ptg Co, Leipzig)

1985 (28 Oct). Historic Ships (4th series). 17th-century Ships. Square designs as T **753**. Multicoloured. P 13.

3286 5st. Dutch fly 20 10
3287 12st. *Sovereign of the Seas* (English galleon) 30 15
3288 20st. Mediterranean polacca 45 20
3289 25st. *Prince Royal* (English warship) 55 35
3290 42st. Xebec .... 1·00 65
3291 60st. English warship .... 1·90 75
3286/3291 *Set of 6* .... 4·00 2·00

(Des P. Petrov. Photo)

1985 (4 Nov). Philatelia '85 International Stamp Exhibition, Cologne. Sheet 109×56 mm containing T **1093** and similar vert design, each black, bright new blue and scarlet. Imperf.

MS3292 30st. Type **1093**; 30st. Aleksandr Nevski Cathedral, Sofia .... 1·60 1·60

1094 Bacho Kiro

1095 Hands, Sword and Bible

(Des T. Vardzhiev. Photo)

1985 (6 Nov). Revolutionaries. T **1094** and similar vert design. P 13.

3293 5st. ochre, deep bistre-brown and deep violet-blue 20 10
3294 5st. sage green, maroon and deep bistre-brown 20 10

Design:—No. 3294, Georgi S. Rakovski.

(Des T. Vardzhiev. Photo)

1985 (6 Nov). 150th Anniv of Turnovo Uprising. P 13.

3295 **1095** 13st. grey-brown, deep blue and brown-purple 30 20

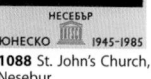

1096 "1185 Revolution" (G. Bogdanov)

1097 Emblem

(Des Kh. Khristov. Photo (1l.), litho (others))

1985 (15 Nov). 800th Anniv of Liberation from Byzantine Empire. T **1096** and similar horiz designs. Multicoloured. P 13.

3296	5st. Type **1096**	20	15
3297	13st. "1185 Revolution" (Al. Terziev)	35	20
3298	30st. "Battle of Klakotnitsa, 1230" (B. Grigorov and M. Ganovski)	45	35
3299	42st. "Veliko Turnovo" (Ts. Lavrenov)	1·40	55
3296/3299	*Set of 4*	2·20	1·10
MS3300	74×80 mm. 1l. Church of St. Dimitrius, Veliko Turnovo (38×28 mm). Imperf	2·20	2·20

(Des P. Petrov. Photo)

1985 (29 Nov). Balkanfila '85 Stamp Exhibition, Vratsa. Sheet 55×80 mm. P 13.

MS3301 **1097** 40st. greenish blue, black and deep greenish blue ... 1·10 1·10

1098 Emblem and Globe

(Des St. Kunchev. Photo)

1985 (2 Dec). International Development Programme for Posts and Telecommunications. P 13.

3302 **1098** 13st. multicoloured ... 30 20

1099 Popov

(Des A. Stareishinski. Photo)

1985 (11 Dec). 70th Birth Anniv of Anton Popov (revolutionary). P 13.

3303 **1099** 5st. brown-lake ... 20 10

1100 Doves around Snowflake

(Des St. Kunchev. Photo)

1985 (11 Dec). New Year. T **1100** and similar horiz design. Multicoloured. P 13.

3304	5st. Type **1100**	20	10
3305	13st. Circle of stylized doves	30	15

1101 Pointer and Chukar Partridge

(Des A. Stareishinski. Litho National Ptg Wks, Havana)

1985 (27 Dec). Hunting Dogs. T **1101** and similar horiz designs. Multicoloured. P 13×12½.

3306	5st. Type **1101**	20	20
3307	8st. Irish setter and European pochard	25	20
3308	13st. English setter and mallard	30	20
3309	20st. Cocker spaniel and woodcock	35	25
3310	25st. German pointer and rabbit	55	35
3311	30st. Bulgarian bloodhound and boar	75	40
3312	42st. Dachshund and fox	1·50	55
3306/3312	*Set of 7*	3·50	1·90

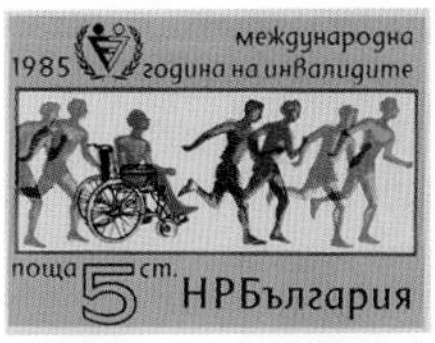

1102 Person in Wheelchair and Runners

(Des K. Gogov. Photo)

1985 (30 Dec). International Year of Disabled Persons (1984). P 13.

3313 **1102** 5st. multicoloured ... 20 10

1103 Georgi Dimitrov (statesman)

(Des K. Gogov. Photo)

1985 (30 Dec). 50th Anniv of Seventh Communist International Congress, Moscow. P 13.

3314 **1103** 13st. brown-lake ... 35 20

1104 Emblem within "40"

(Des D. Tasev. Photo)

1986 (21 Jan). 40th Anniv of United Nations Children's Fund. P 13.

3315 **1104** 13st. bright new blue, gold and black ... 35 20

1105 Blagoev

1106 Hands and Dove within Laurel Wreath

(Des A. Stareishinski. Photo)

1986 (28 Jan). 130th Birth Anniv of Dimitur Blagoev (founder of Bulgarian Social Democratic Party). P 13.

3316 **1105** 5st. maroon and orange-red ... 20 10

(Des K. Gogov. Photo)

1986 (31 Jan). International Peace Year. P 13½×13.

3317 **1106** 5st. multicoloured ... 20 10

1107 *Dactylorhiza romana*

(Des L. Chekhlarov. Litho National Ptg Wks, Havana)

1986 (12 Feb). Orchids. T **1107** and similar horiz designs. Multicoloured. P 13×12½.

3318	5st. Type **1107**	20	15
3319	13st. *Epipactis palustris*	30	20
3320	30st. *Ophrys cornuta*	40	25
3321	32st. *Limodorum abortivum*	45	35
3322	42st. *Cypripedium calceolus*	85	45
3323	60st. *Orchis papilionacea*	1·40	55
3318/3323	*Set of 6*	3·25	1·80

Nos. 3318/23 were issued both in individual sheets and together in *se-tenant* sheetlets (*Price for sheetlet*: £7 *un*).

Nos. 3318/23 exist imperforate from a limited printing.

1108 Angora Rabbit

1110 Neptune and Comet Position, 1980

1109 Front Page and Ivan Bogorov

(Des A. Stareishinski. Litho State Ptg Wks, Moscow)

1986 (24 Feb). Rabbits. T **1108** and similar horiz designs. P 12½×12.

3324	5st. greenish slate, black and chestnut	20	15
3325	25st. bright carmine-red and black	45	20
3326	30st. olive-sepia, yellow and black	55	25
3327	32st. dull orange and black	65	35
3328	42st. dull vermilion and black	85	45
3329	60st. new blue and black	1·40	55
3324/3329	*Set of 6*	3·75	1·80

Designs:—5st. French grey; 30st. English lop-eared; 32st. Belgian; 42st. English spotted; 60st. Dutch black and white rabbit.

Nos. 3324/9 exist imperforate from a limited printing.

(Des I. Bogdanov. Photo)

1986 (28 Feb). 140th Anniv of Bulgarian Eagle. P 13.

3330 **1109** 5st. multicoloured ... 20 10

(Des K. Gogov. Photo)

1986 (7 Mar). Appearance of Halley's Comet. Sheet 120×114 mm containing T **1110** and similar horiz designs, each blackish violet, new blue and yellow. P 13½×13.

MS3331 25st. Type **1110**; 25st. Sun, Earth, Mars, Saturn and comet positions, 1985 and 1910/86; 25st. Uranus and comet positions, 1960, 1926, 1948 and 1970; 25st. Jupiter and comet position, 1911 ... 2·20 2·20

No. **MS**3331 exists imperforate from a limited printing.

1111 Bashev

1112 Wave Pattern

(Des A. Stareishinski. Photo)

1986 (12 Mar). 50th Birth Anniv (1985) of Vladimir Bashev (poet). P 13×13½.

3332 **1111** 5st. royal blue and new blue ... 20 10

(Des P. Petrov. Photo)

1986 (17 Mar). 13th Bulgarian Communist Party Congress. T **1112** and similar vert designs. P 13.

3333	5st. deep blue, emerald and rosine	10	15
3334	8st. dp new blue & scarlet-vermilion	25	15
3335	13st. dp new bl, scar-verm & lt new bl	30	20
3333/3335	*Set of 3*	60	45
MS3336	60×77 mm. 50st. multicoloured. Imperf	1·00	1·10

Designs:—8st. Printed circuit as tail of shooting star; 13st. Computer picture of man; 50st. Steel construction tower.

1113 "Vostok 1"

(Des K. Gogov. Photo)

1986 (28 Mar). 25th Anniv of First Man in Space. Sheet 105×100 mm containing T **1113** and similar horiz design, each blackish blue and turquoise-blue. P 13½×13.

MS3337 50st. Type **1113**; 50st. Yuri Gagarin ... 2·20 2·20

No. **MS**3337 exists imperforate from a limited printing.

1114 Monument, Panagyurishte

1115 Gymnast

(Des D. Karapantev. Photo)

1986 (30 Mar). 110th Anniv of April Uprising. T **1114** and similar vert design. P 13.

3338	5st. black, stone and deep emerald	20	10
3339	13st. black, stone and bright scarlet	30	15

Design:—13st. Statue of Khristo Botev, Vratsa.

(Des Kh. Aleksiev. Photo)

1986 (12 May). 75th Anniv of Levski-Spartak Sports Club. Sheet 81×65 mm. Imperf.

MS3340 **1115** 50st. multicoloured ... 1·00 1·10

1116 Stylized Ear of Wheat

1117 Transport Systems

(Des B. Ikonomov and O. Funev. Photo)

1986 (19 May). 35th Bulgarian People's Agrarian Union Congress. T **1116** and similar vert designs. P 13.

3341	5st. gold, reddish orange and black	10	10
3342	8st. gold, new blue and black	20	10
3343	13st. multicoloured	30	15
3341/3343	*Set of* 3	55	30

Designs:—8st. Stylized ear of wheat on globe; 13st. Flags.

(Des St. Kunchev. Photo)

1986 (27 May). Socialist Countries' Transport Ministers Conference. P 13.

3344 **1117** 13st. multicoloured ... 30 20

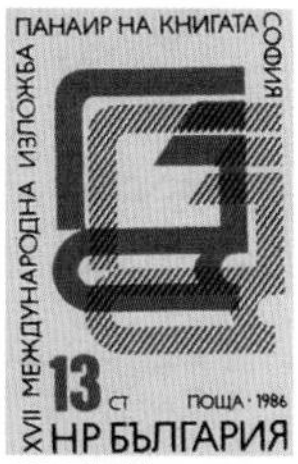

1118 Emblem

1119 Player with Ball

(Des O. Khristov. Photo)

1986 (28 May). 17th International Book Fair, Sofia. P 13.

3345 **1118** 13st. olive-grey, bright scarlet and black ... 30 20

(Des S. Krustev. Photo)

1986 (30 May). World Cup Football Championship, Mexico (2nd issue). T **1119** and similar multicoloured designs. P 13½.

3346	5st. Type **1119**	20	15
3347	13st. Player tackling (horiz)	30	20
3348	20st. Player heading ball (horiz)	35	25
3349	30st. Player kicking ball (horiz)	65	35
3350	42st. Goalkeeper (horiz)	95	45
3351	60st. Player with trophy	1·50	65
3346/3351	*Set of* 6	3·50	1·80

MS3352 95×75 mm. 1l. Azteca Stadium (42×31 mm). P 13 ... 2·20 2·20

Nos. 3346/51 were each issued with *se-tenant* half stamp-size label depicting a landmark in Mexico.

Nos. 3346/**MS**3352 exist imperforate from limited printings both in separate sheets and together in *se-tenant* sheetlets of six stamps and six labels.

1120 Square Brooch

(Des Kh. Khristov. Litho German Bank Note Ptg Co, Leipzig)

1986 (7 July). Treasures of Preslav. T **1120** and similar multicoloured designs. P 13½×13.

3353	5st. Type **1120**	20	15
3354	13st. Pendant (vert)	30	20
3355	20st. Wheel-shaped pendant	35	25
3356	30st. Breast plate decorated with birds and chalice	65	35
3357	42st. Pear-shaped pendant (vert)	95	45
3358	60st. Enamelled cockerel on gold base	1·40	55
3353/3358	*Set of* 6	3·25	1·60

1121 Fencers with Sabres

(Des A. Sertev. Photo)

1986 (25 July). World Fencing Championships, Sofia. T **1121** and similar horiz designs. Multicoloured. P 13.

3359	5st. Type **1121**	20	10
3360	13st. Fencers	30	15
3361	25st. Fencers with rapiers	55	35
3359/3361	*Set of* 3	95	55

1122 Stockholm Town Hall

1123 White Stork (*Ciconia ciconia*)

(Des St. Kunchev. Photo)

1986 (25 Aug). "Stockholmia 86" International Stamp Exhibition. P 13.

3362 **1122** 42st. deep brown, Venetian red and carmine-lake ... 75 65

No. 3362 was issued in sheetlets of three stamps and three labels depicting various Viking stone carvings.

(Des A. Stareishinski. Litho German Bank Note Ptg Co, Leipzig)

1986 (29 Aug). Nature Protection. Sheet 138×90 mm containing T **1123** and similar vert designs. Multicoloured. P 14.

MS3363 30c. Type **1123**; 30c. Yellow water-lily (*Nuphar lutea*); 30c. Fire salamander (*Salamandra salamandra*); 30c. White water-lily (*Nymphaea alba*) ... 5·00 4·25

The miniature sheet contains the four stamps arranged around a central label depicting the oldest oak tree in Bulgaria at Granit village, Stara Zagora.

No. **MS**3363 also exists imperforate from a limited printing.

1124 Arms and Parliament Building, Sofia

(Des St. Kunchev. Photo)

1986 (15 Sept). 40th Anniv of People's Republic. P 13.

3364 **1124** 5st. bright turquoise-green, scarlet-vermilion and bright green ... 20 10

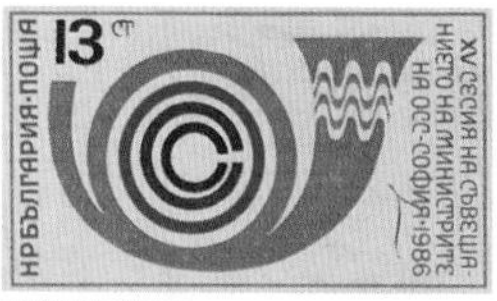

1125 Posthorn

1126 "All Pull Together"

(Des St. Kunchev. Photo)

1986 (24 Sept). 15th Organization of Socialist Countries' Postal Administrations Session, Sofia. P 13.

3365 **1125** 13st. multicoloured ... 30 20

(Des Kh. Khristov. Photo)

1986 (3 Oct). 40th Anniv of Voluntary Brigades. P 13.

3366 **1126** 5st. multicoloured ... 20 10

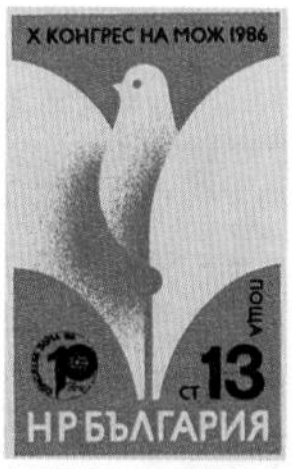

1127 Dove and Book as Pen Nib

1128 Wrestlers

(Des Veni Kantardzhieva. Photo)

1986 (13 Oct). Tenth International Journalists Association Congress, Sofia. P 13.

3367 **1127** 13st. greenish-blue and deep blue ... 30 20

(Des Kh. Aleksiev. Photo)

1986 (Oct). 75th Anniv of Levski-Spartak Sports Club. P 13.

3368 **1128** 5st. multicoloured ... 20 10

1129 Saints Cyril and Methodius with Disciples (fresco)

(Des K. Kunev. Photo)

1986 (28 Oct). 1100th Anniv of Arrival in Bulgaria of Pupils of Saints Cyril and Methodius. P 13½.

3369 **1129** 13st. reddish brown and buff ... 30 20

No. 3369 was issued with *se-tenant* half stamp-size inscribed label.

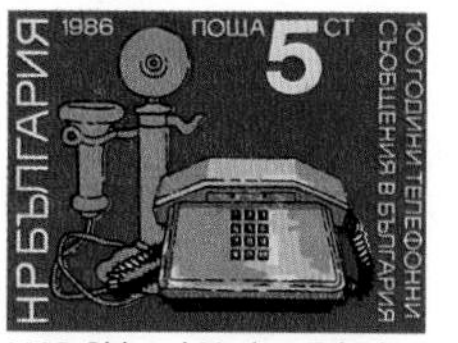

1130 Old and Modern Telephones

(Des S. Krustev. Photo)

1986 (5 Nov). Centenary of Telephone in Bulgaria. P 13.

3370 **1130** 5st. multicoloured ... 20 10

1131 Weightlifter

(Des L. Chekhlarov. Photo)

1986 (6 Nov). World Weightlifting Championships, Sofia. P 13.

3371 **1131** 13st. multicoloured ... 30 20

(Des St. Kunchev. Photo German Bank Note Ptg Co, Leipzig)

1986 (20 Nov). Historic Ships (5th series). 18th-century ships. Square designs as T **753**. Multicoloured. P 13.

3372	5st. *King of Prussia*	10	10
3373	13st. Indiaman	20	15
3374	25st. Xebek	45	25
3375	30st. *Sv. Pavel*	55	35
3376	32st. Top-sail schooner	65	45
3377	42st. *Victory*	1·40	55
3372/3377	*Set of* 6	3·00	1·70

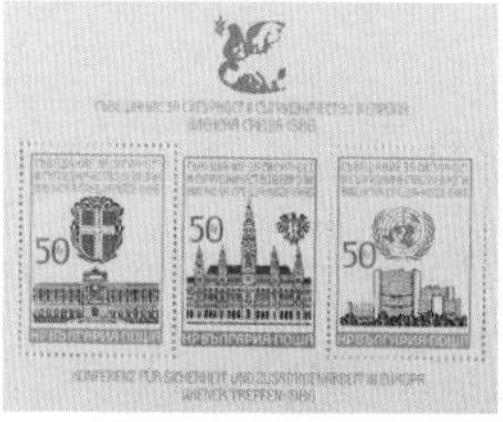

1132 Hofburg Conference Centre, Vienna (13-size illustration)

1133 Silver Jug decorated with seated Woman

(Des St. Kunchev. Photo)

1986 (27 Nov). European Security and Co-operation Conference Review Meeting, Vienna. Sheet 109×86 mm containing T **1132** and similar vert designs. P 13.

MS3378 50st. brown-olive, bright orange and bright green; 50st. dull yellowish green, bright orange and new blue (imperf×p 13) (Vienna Town Hall); 50st. multicoloured (United Nations Centre, Vienna) ... 4·25 4·25

No. **MS**3378 also exists imperforate from a limited printing.

(Des St. Gruev. Photo)

1986 (5 Dec). 14th Congress of Bulgarian Philatelic Federation and 60th Anniv of International Philatelic Federation. T **1133** and similar vert design showing repoussé work found at Rogozen. P 13.

3379	10st. slate-black, black and bright turquoise-blue	30	20
	a. Block. Nos. 3379/80 plus 2 labels	65	45
3380	10st. slate-green, black and scarlet-vermilion	30	20

Design:—No. 3380, Silver jug decorated with sphinx.

Nos. 3379/80 were printed in alternate horizontal rows within the same sheet, No. 3379 with *se-tenant* label showing the Congress emblem and No. 3380 with *se-tenant* label showing the F.I.P. anniversary emblem.

Nos. 3379/80 also exist imperforate from a limited printing.

1134 Doves between Pine Branches

(Des St. Kunchev. Photo)

1986 (9 Dec). New Year. T **1134** and similar horiz design. P 13.

3381	5st. carmine-vermilion, yellowish green and new blue	20	10
3382	13st. bright magenta, new blue and violet	30	20

Design:—13st. Fireworks and snowflakes.

1135 Earphones as "60" on Globe

(Des V. Kitanov. Photo)

1986 (10 Dec). 60th Anniv of Bulgarian Amateur Radio. P 13.
3383 **1135** 13st. multicoloured 30 20

1136 "The Walnut Tree" (Danail Dechev)

(Des B. Mavrodinov. Litho German Bank Note Ptg Co, Leipzig)

1986 (10 Dec). 90th Anniv of Sofia Art Academy. Modern Paintings. Sheet 146×102 mm containing T **1136** and similar horiz designs. Multicoloured. P 14.
MS3384 25st. Type **1136**; 25st. "Resistance Fighters and Soldiers" (Iliya Beshkov); 30st. "Melnik" (Veselin Staikov); 30st. "The Olive Grove" (Kiril Tsonev) .... 3·25 3·25

1137 Gen. Augusto Sandino and Flag

(Des St. Kunchev. Photo)

1986 (16 Dec). 25th Anniv of Sandinista National Liberation Front of Nicaragua. P 13.
3385 **1137** 13st. multicoloured 30 20

1138 Dimitur and Konstantin Miladinov (authors)

1139 Pencho Slaveikov (poet)

(Des T. Vardzhiev. Photo)

1986 (17 Dec). 125th Anniv of Publication of Bulgarian Popular Songs. P 13.
3386 **1138** 10st. deep blue, buff and brown-red 20 10

(Des I. Bogdanov (3387/9), T. Vardzhiev (3390). Photo)

1986 (17 Dec). Writers' Birth Annivs. T **1139** and similar vert designs. Multicoloured. P 13.
3387 5st. Type **1139** (125th anniv) 20 10
3388 5st. Stoyan Mikhailovski (130th anniv) 20 10
3389 8st. Nikola Atanasov (dramatist) (centenary) 20 10
3390 8st. Ran Bosilek (children's author) (centenary) 20 10
3387/3390 *Set of 4* 70 35

1140 Raiko Daskalov

1141 "Girl with Fruit"

(Des T. Vardzhiev. Photo)

1986 (22 Dec). Birth Centenary of Raiko Daskalov (politician). P 13.
3391 **1140** 5st. purple-brown 20 10

(Des St. Kunchev. Litho German Bank Note Ptg Co, Leipzig)

1986 (23 Dec). 500th Birth Anniv of Titian (painter). T **1141** and similar vert designs. Multicoloured. P 14.
3392 5st. Type **1141** 20 15
3393 13st. "Flora" 30 15
3394 20st. "Lucretia and Tarquin" 35 20
3395 30st. "Caiphas and Mary Magdalene" (detail) 50 25
3396 32st. "Toilette of Venus" (detail) 55 35
3397 42st. "Self-portrait" .... 1·10 45
3392/3397 *Set of 6* .... 2·75 1·40
MS3398 105×75 mm. 1l. "Danae" (32×54 mm) .... 3·00 2·75
Nos. 3392/7 were issued both in separate sheets and also together in *se-tenant* sheetlets (*Price of sheetlet*: £6 *un*).

1142 Fiat, 1905

(Des E. Stankev. Litho North Korean Stamp Ptg Wks, Pyongyang)

1986 (30 Dec). Racing Cars. T **1142** and similar horiz designs. P 13½.
3399 5st. deep brown, rosine and black 20 15
3400 10st. brown-red, vermilion and black 20 15
3401 25st. yellowish green, rosine and black 45 20
3402 32st. deep brown, rosine and black 55 35
3403 40st. bright violet, vermilion and black 95 40
3404 42st. deep grey, black and scarlet-vermilion .... 1·20 45
3399/3404 *Set of 6* .... 3·25 1·50
Designs:—10st. Bugatti, 1928; 25st. Mercedes, 1936; 32st. Ferrari, 1952; 40st. Lotus, 1985; 42st. Maclaren, 1986.

1143 Steam Locomotive

(Des Maglena Konstantinova. Litho North Korean Stamp Ptg Wks, Pyongyang)

1987 (19 Jan). 120th Anniv of Ruse–Vama Railway. P 13½.
3405 **1143** 5st. multicoloured 20 20

1144 Debelyanov

(Des D. Nikolov. Photo)

1987 (20 Jan). Birth Centenary of Dimcho Debelyanov (poet). P 13.
3406 **1144** 5st. deep bright blue, greenish yellow and greenish blue 20 10

1145 Lazarus Ludwig Zamenhof (inventor)

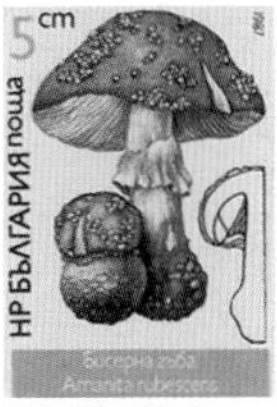

1146 The Blusher (*Amanita rubescens*)

(Des D. Karapantev. Photo)

1987 (12 Feb). Centenary of Esperanto (invented language). P 13.
3407 **1145** 13st. deep violet-blue, greenish yellow and emerald 30 20

(Des L. Chekhlarov. Litho North Korean Stamp Ptg Wks, Pyongyang)

1987 (26 Feb). Edible Fungi. T **1146** and similar vert designs. Multicoloured. P 11½.
3408 5st. Type **1146** 20 15
3409 20st. Royal boletus (*Boletus regius*) 30 20
3410 30st. Red-capped scaber stalk (*Leccinum aurantiacum*) 45 35
3411 32st. Shaggy ink cap (*Coprinus comatus*) 65 40
3412 40st. Bare-toothed russula (*Russula vesca*) 75 45
3413 60st. Chanterelle (*Cantharellus cibarius*) 85 55
3408/3413 *Set of 6* .... 3·00 1·90
Nos. 3408/13 were issued both in separate sheets and also together in *se-tenant* sheetlets (*Price of sheetlet*: £3.75 *un*).

1147 Worker

1148 Silver-gilt Plate with Design of Hercules and Auge

(Des S. Krustev. Photo)

1987 (25 Mar). Tenth Trade Unions Congress, Sofia. P 13.
3414 **1147** 5st. blue-violet and carmine-vermilion 20 10

(Des T. Vardzhiev. Photo German Bank Note Ptg Co, Leipzig)

1987 (31 Mar). Treasure of Rogozen. T **1148** and similar square designs. Multicoloured. P 13.
3415 5st. Type **1148** 20 15
3416 8st. Siver-gilt jug with design of lioness attacking stag 20 15
3417 20st. Silver-gilt plate with quatrefoil design 30 20
3418 30st. Silver-gilt jug with design of horse rider 35 25
3419 32st. Silver-gilt pot with palm design 45 30
3420 42st. Silver jug with chariot and horses design 55 35
3415/3420 *Set of 6* .... 1·80 1·30

1149 Ludmila Zhivkova Festival Complex, Varna

1150 Wrestlers

(Des Kh. Khristov. Photo)

1987 (7 Apr). Modern Architecture. Sheet 107×100 mm containing T **1149** and similar horiz designs. Multicoloured. P 13½×13.
MS3421 30st. Type **1149**; 30st. Ministry of Foreign Affairs building, Sofia; 30st. Interpred building, Sofia; 30st. Hotel, Sandanski .... 2·20 2·20
No. **MS**3421 also exists imperforate from a limited printing.

(Des S. Gruev. Photo)

1987 (22 Apr). 30th European Freestyle Wrestling Championships, Turnovo. T **1150** and similar vert design. P 13.
3422 5st. deep lilac, rose-carmine and violet 10 10
3423 13st. deep turquoise-blue, rose-carmine and blue 20 10
Design:—13st. Wrestlers (different).

1151 Totem Pole

1152 "X" and Flags

(Des St. Kunchev. Photo)

1987 (24 Apr). Capex'87 International Stamp Exhibition, Toronto. P 13.
3424 **1151** 42st. multicoloured 75 45

(Des D. Tasev. Photo)

1987 (11 May). Tenth Fatherland Front Congress. P 13.
3425 **1152** 5st. emerald, orange-vermilion and deep ultramarine 20 10

1153 Georgi Dimitrov and Profiles

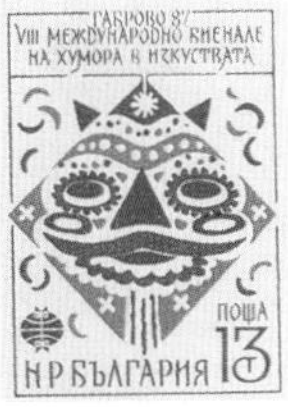

1154 Mask

(Des Kh. Aleksiev. Photo)

1987 (13 May). 15th Dimitrov Communist Youth League Congress. P 13.
3426 **1153** 5st. brown-purple, emerald and bright scarlet 20 10

(Des I. Bogdanov. Photo)

1987 (15 May). Eighth International Festival of Humour and Satire, Gabrovo. P 13×13½.
3427 **1154** 13st. multicoloured 30 20

1155 Mastheads

1156 Mariya Gigova

(Des P. Petrov. Photo)

1987 (28 May). 60th Anniv of *Rabotnichesko Delo* (newspaper). P 13.
3428 **1155** 5st. bright crimson and black 20 10

(Des A. Stareishinski. Photo)

1987 (29 May–5 Aug). 13th World Rhythmic Gymnastics Championships, Varna. T **1156** and similar vert designs. P 13.
3429 5st. deep ultramarine and yellow-ochre (5.8.87) 20 15
a. Perf 13×13½ 20 15
3430 8st. bright crimson and yellow-ochre (5.8.87) 20 15

a. Perf 13×13½ 20 15
3431 13st. turquoise-blue and stone (5.8.87) 30 20
a. Perf 13×13½ 30 20
3432 25st. carmine-lake and yellow-ochre (5.8.87) 45 25
3433 30st. new blue and greenish yellow (5.8.87) 55 30
a. Perf 13×13½ 55 30
3434 42st. deep magenta and yellow-ochre (5.8.87) 75 35
a. Perf 13×13½ 75 35
3429/3434 *Set of 6* 2·20 1·30
MS3435 78×87 mm 1l. reddish violet and yellow-ochre. P 13×13½ 2·20 2·20

Designs:—8st. Iliana Raeva; 13st. Aneliya Ralenkova; 25st. Dilyana Georgieva; 30st. Liliya Ignatova; 42st. Bianka Panova; 1l. Neshka Robeva.

1157 Man breaking Chains around Globe and Kolarov

(Des D. Nikolov. Photo)

1987 (3 June). 110th Birth Anniv of Vasil Kolarov (Prime Minister 1949–50). P 13.
3436 **1157** 5st. multicoloured 20 10

1158 Stela Blagoeva

1159 Levski

(Des P. Petrov. Photo)

1987 (4 June). Birth Centenary of Stela Blagoeva. P 13.
3437 **1158** 5st. deep reddish brown and rose-pink 20 20

(Des T. Varadzhiev. Photo)

1987 (19 June). 150th Birth Anniv of Vasil Levski (revolutionary). T **1159** and similar horiz design. P 13.
3438 5st. lake-brown and bronze green 10 10
3439 13st. bronze green and chestnut 20 10

Design:—13st. Levski and Bulgarian Revolutionary Central Committee emblem.

1160 Roe Deer (*Capreolus capreolus*)

1161 Barbed Wire as Dove

(Des K. Gogov. Litho Cuban National Ptg Wks, Havana)

1987 (23 June). Stags. T **1160** and similar multicoloured designs. P 13.
3440 5st. Type **1160** 20 15
3441 10st. Elk (*Alces alces*) (horiz) 20 15
3442 32st. Fallow deer (*Dama dama*) 55 25
3443 40st. Sika deer (*Cervus nippon*) 65 35
3444 42st. Red deer (*Cervus elaphus*) (horiz) 75 45
3445 60st. Reindeer (*Rangifer tarandus*) 1·00 55
3440/3445 *Set of 6* 3·00 1·70
MS3445*a* 145×131 mm. Nos. 3340/5. Imperf 3·75 3·75

(Des S. Krustev. Photo)

1987 (8 July). International Namibia Day. P 13.
3446 **1161** 13st. black, scarlet-vermilion and bright yellow-orange 25 10

1162 Kirkov

1163 *Phacelia tanacetifolia*

(Des A. Stareishinski. Photo)

1987 (17 July). 120th Birth Anniv of Georgi Kirkov (pseudonym: Maistora) (politician). P 13×13½.
3447 **1162** 5st. brown-lake and dull brown-rose 20 10

(Des Ralitsa Stanoeva. Litho Cuban National Ptg Wks, Havana)

1987 (29 July). Flowers. T **1163** and similar vert designs. Multicoloured. Litho. P 13.
3448 5st. Type **1163** 20 15
3449 10st. Sunflower (*Helianthus annuus*) 20 15
3450 30st. False acacia (*Robinia pseudoacacia*) 50 30
3451 32st. Dutch lavender (*Lavandula vera*) 55 35
3452 42st. Small-leaved lime (*Tilia parvifolia*) 75 45
3453 60st. *Onobrychis sativa* 1·10 55
3448/3453 *Set of 6* 3·00 1·80

Nos. 3448/53 were issued both in separate sheets of 40 stamps and together in *se-tenant* sheetlets of six stamps (*Price of sheetlet*: £3.75 *un*).

1164 Mil Mi-8 Helicopter, Tupolev Tu-154 Jetliner and Antonov An-12 Transport

1987 (25 Aug). 40th Anniv of Balkanair. Photo. P 13.
3454 **1164** 25st. multicoloured 55 20

1165 1879 5c. Stamp

1166 Copenhagen Town Hall

(Des St. Kunchev. Photo)

1987 (3 Sept). Bulgaria '89 International Stamp Exhibition, Sofia (1st issue). P 13.
3455 **1165** 13st. multicoloured 20 10

See also Nos. 3569, 3579/82 and 3602/5.

(Des Kh. Khristov. Photo)

1987 (8 Sept). Hafnia '87 International Stamp Exhibition, Copenhagen. P 13.
3456 **1166** 42st. multicoloured 75 55

No. 3456 was issued in sheetlets of three stamps and three inscribed labels.

1167 "Portrait of Girl" (Stefan Ivanov)

1168 Battle Scene

(Des St. Kunchev. Litho German Bank Note Ptg Co, Leipzig)

1987 (15 Sept). Paintings in Sofia National Gallery. T **1167** and similar vert designs. Multicoloured. P 14.
3457 5st. Type **1167** 20 15
3458 8st. "Woman carrying Grapes" (Bencho Obreshkov) 20 15
3459 20st. "Portrait of a Woman wearing a Straw Hat" (David Perez) 35 20
3460 25st. "Women listening to Marimba" (Kiril Tsonev) 45 30
3461 32st. "Boy with Harmonica" (Nenko Balkanski) 65 35
3462 60st. "Rumyana" (Vasil Stoilov) 1·20 55
3457/3462 *Set of 6* 2·75 1·50

1987 (15 Sept). 75th Anniv of Balkan War. Photo. P 13½×13.
3463 **1168** 5st. black, stone and orange-red 20 10

1169 Emblem

1171 Winter Wren (*Troglodytes troglodytes*)

1170 Mastheads

1987 (15 Sept). 30th Anniv of International Atomic Energy Agency. Photo. P 13½×13.
3464 **1169** 13st. new blue, light green and bright scarlet 35 20

(Des I. Bogdanov. Photo)

1987 (24 Sept). 95th Anniv of Rabotnik, 90th Anniv of *Rabotnicheski Vestnik* and 60th Anniv of *Rabotnichesko Delo* (newspapers). P 13.
3465 **1170** 5st. deep rose-red, deep Prussian blue and gold 20 10

(Des I. Bogdanov. Litho North Korean Stamp Ptg Wks, Pyongyang)

1987 (12 Oct). Birds. T **1171** and similar vert designs. Multicoloured. P 12.
3466 5st. Type **1171** 20 15
3467 13st. Yellowhammer (*Emberiza citrinella*) 20 15
3468 20st. European nuthatch (*Sitta europaea*) 45 20
3469 30st. Blackbird (*Turdus merula*) 65 35
3470 42st. Hawfinch (*Coccothraustes coccothraustes*) 1·00 45
3471 60st. Dipper (*Cinclus cinclus*) 1·40 55
3466/3471 *Set of 6* 3·50 1·70

Nos. 3466/71 were issued both in separate sheets and together in *se-tenant* sheetlets (*Price of sheetlet*: £4.25 *un*).

1172 "Vega" Automatic Space Station

(Des S. Gruev. Photo)

1987 (16 Oct–24 Dec). 30th Anniv of Soviet Space Exploration. Sheet 98×98 mm containing T **1172** and similar horiz design. P 13½×13.
MS3472 50st. deep violet-blue, reddish orange and blackish purple (Type **1172**); 50st. deep violet-blue, blue and blackish purple ("Soyuz" spacecraft docking with "Mir" space station) 2·75 2·75

No. **MS**3472 exists imperforate from a limited printing.

The spaceship in the bottom margin of No. **MS**3472 is inscribed "1961 BOCTOK" and was issued in December. In the initial printing issued in October the inscription read "1964 BOCTOK"; only a very small quantity was issued, perforated and imperforate.

1173 Lenin and Revolutionary

1174 Biathlon

(Des A. Stareishinski. Litho)

1987 (22 Oct). 70th Anniv of Russian Revolution. T **1173** and similar horiz design. P 13.
3473 5st. brown-purple and orange-red 10 10
3474 13st. deep ultramarine and orange-red 20 10

Design:—13st. Lenin and cosmonaut.

(Des Kh. Aleksiev. Litho German Bank Note Ptg Co, Leipzig)

1987 (27 Oct). Winter Olympic Games, Calgary. T **1174** and similar vert designs. Multicoloured. P 13×13½.
3475 5st. Type **1174** 20 15
3476 13st. Slalom 20 15
3477 30st. Figure skating (women's) 55 35
3478 42st. Four-man bobsleigh 85 55
3475/3478 *Set of 4* 1·60 1·10
MS3479 65×87 mm. 1l. Ice hockey 2·20 2·20

No. **MS**3479 also exists imperforate from a limited printing.

1175 "Socfilex" Emblem within Folk-design Ornament

(Des St. Kunchev. Photo)

1987 (25 Dec). New Year. T **1175** and similar horiz design. Multicoloured. P 13.
3480 5st. Type **1175** 10 10
3481 13st. Emblem within flower ornament 20 10

1176 Helsinki Conference Centre

1177 Kabakchiev

(Des St. Kunchev. Photo)

1987 (30 Dec). European Security and Co-operation Conference Review Meeting, Vienna. Sheet 140×100 mm containing T **1176** and similar vert designs. P 13.

MS3482 50st. lavender, red-brown and bright Indian red; 50st. multicoloured (Map of Europe) (imperf×p 13); 50st. multicoloured (Vienna Conference Centre) 5·00 5·00

No. **MS**3482 also exists imperforate from a limited printing.

(Des Tekla Aleksieva. Photo)

1988 (20 Jan). 110th Birth Anniv of Khristo Kabakchiev (Communist Party official). P 13×13½.

3483 **1177** 5st. multicoloured 20 10

1178 *Scilla bythynica*

1179 Commander on Horseback

(Des B. Kitanov. Litho North Korean Stamp Ptg Wks, Pyongyang)

1988 (25 Jan). Marsh Flowers. T **1178** and similar vert designs. Multicoloured. P 12.

3484 5st. Type **1178** 10 10
3485 10st. *Geum rhodopaeum* 15 10
3486 13st. *Caltha polypetala* 20 10
3487 25st. Fringed water-lily (*Nymphoides peltata*) 45 20
3488 30st. *Cortusa matthioli* 55 30
3489 42st. Water soldier (*Stratiotes aloides*) 65 45
3484/3489 *Set of* 6 1·90 1·10

Nos. 3484/9 were issued both in separate sheets and together in *se-tenant* sheetlets (*Price of sheetlet*: £2.20 *un*).

(Des S. Krustev. Photo)

1988 (15 Feb). 110th Anniv of Liberation from Turkey. T **1179** and similar horiz design. Multicoloured. P 13.

3490 5st. Type **1179** 10 10
3491 13st. Soldiers 20 10

1180 Emblem

(Des P. Petrunov. Photo)

1988 (22 Mar). Public Sector Workers' Eighth International Congress, Sofia. P 13.

3492 **1180** 13st. multicoloured 20 10

1181 *Yantra*, 1888

(Des Maglena Konstantinova. Litho North Korean Stamp Ptg Wks, Pyongyang)

1988 (25 Mar). Centenary of State Railways. Locomotives. T **1181** and similar horiz designs. Multicoloured. P 11.

3493 5st. Type **1181** 15 10
3494 13st. *Khristo Botev*, 1905 20 15
3495 25st. Steam locomotive No. 807, 1918 55 20
3496 32st. Steam locomotive, 1943 65 35
3497 42st. Diesel locomotive, 1964 85 45
3498 60st. Electric locomotive, 1979 1·40 55
3493/3498 *Set of* 6 3·50 1·60

Nos. 3493/8 were issued both in individual sheets and together in *se-tenant* sheetlets (*Price of sheetlet*: £4.25 *un*).

1182 Ivan Nedyalkov (Shablin)

1183 Traikov

(Des A. Stareishinski. Photo)

1988 (31 Mar). Post Office Anti-fascist Heroes. T **1182** and similar horiz designs. P 13½×13.

3499 5st. pale cinnamon and lake-brown 10 10
3500 8st. bluish grey and royal blue 10 10
3501 10st. sage green and olive-green 15 10
3502 13st. pink and carmine-lake 20 10
3499/3502 *Set of* 4 50 35

Designs:—8st. Delcho Spasov; 10st. Nikola Ganchev (Gudzho); 13st. Ganka Rasheva (Boika).

(Des E. Stankev. Litho)

1988 (8 Apr). 90th Birth Anniv of Georgi Traikov (politician). P 13×13½.

3503 **1183** 5st. bright orange and reddish brown 20 10

1184 Red Cross, Red Crescent and Globe

1185 Girl

(Des D. Tasev. Photo)

1988 (26 Apr). 125th Anniv of International Red Cross. P 13.

3504 **1184** 13st. multicoloured 20 10

(Des St. Kunchev. Litho German Bank Note Ptg Co, Leipzig)

1988 (28 Apr). Fourth "Banners for Peace" Children's Meeting, Sofia. T **1185** and similar multicoloured designs showing children's paintings. P 14.

3505 5st. Type **1185** 10 10
3506 8st. Artist at work 20 10
3507 13st. Circus (horiz) 35 15
3508 20st. Kite flying (horiz) 45 20
3509 32st. Accordion player 55 30
3510 42st. Cosmonaut 65 35
3505/3510 *Set of* 6 2·10 1·10
MS3511 86×90 mm. 50st. Emblem within film frame (Youth Film Festival) (horiz) 1·10 1·10

No. **MS**3511 also exists imperforate from a limited printing.

1186 Marx

1187 Herring Gull (*Larus argentatus*)

(Des A. Stareishinski. Litho)

1988 (5 May). 170th Birth Anniv of Karl Marx. P 13.

3512 **1186** 13st. vermilion, black and greenish yellow 20 10

1988 (6 May). Birds. T **1187** and similar vert designs. Multicoloured. Litho. P 13×13½.

3513 5st. Type **1187** 20 10
3514 5st. White stork (*Ciconia ciconia*) 20 10
3515 8st. Grey heron (*Ardea cinerea*) 40 15
3516 8st. Carrion crow (*Corvus corone*) 40 15
3517 10st. Northern goshawk (*Accipiter gentillis*) 55 20
3518 42st. Eagle owl (*Bubo bubo*) 1·60 45
3513/3518 *Set of* 6 3·00 1·00

1188 African Elephant (*Loxodonta africana*)

1189 "Soyuz TM" Spacecraft, Flags and Globe

(Des L. Chekhlarov. Litho Cuban National Ptg Wks, Havana)

1988 (20 May). Centenary of Sofia Zoo. T **1188** and similar horiz designs. Multicoloured. P 13.

3519 5st. Type **1188** 10 10
3520 13st. White rhinoceros (*Ceratotherium simum*) 20 10
3521 25st. Hunting dog (*Lycaon pictus*) 55 20
3522 30st. Eastern white pelican (*Pelecanus onocrotalus*) 65 35
3523 32st. Abyssinian ground hornbill (*Bucorvus abissinicus*) 75 45
3524 42st. Snowy owl (*Nyctea scandiaca*) 1·00 65
3519/3524 *Set of* 6 3·00 1·70

Nos. 3519/24 were issued both in separate sheets and also together in *se-tenant* sheetlets (*Price of sheetlet*: £3.50 *un*).

(Des D. Tasev. Photo)

1988 (7 June). Second Soviet–Bulgarian Space Flight. T **1189** and similar vert design. Multicoloured. P 13.

3525 5st. Type **1189** 10 10
3526 13st. Rocket on globe 20 10

1190 Young Inventor

(Des St. Kunchev. Litho)

1988 (7 June). International Young Inventors' Exhibition, Plovdiv. P 13½×13.

3527 **1190** 13st. multicoloured 20 10

1191 1856 Handstamp of Russian Duchy of Finland

1192 Player taking Corner Kick

1988 (7 June). Finlandia '88 International Stamp Exhibition, Helsinki. Litho. P 13.

3528 **1191** 30st. blue and vermilion 45 35

No. 3528 was issued in sheetlets of three stamps and three labels bearing the Exhibition emblems of Finlandia '88 and Bulgaria '89 exhibitions.

An imperforate sheetlet with additional marginal inscriptions was issued in March 1989 in a limited printing.

(Des I. Bogdanov. Litho)

1988 (10 June). Eighth European Football Championship, West Germany. T **1192** and similar multicoloured designs. P 13.

3529 5st. Type **1192** 10 10
3530 13st. Goalkeeper and player 20 15
3531 30st. Referee and player 65 35
3532 42st. Player with trophy 85 45
3529/3532 *Set of* 4 1·60 95
MS3533 90×69 mm. 1l. Stadium (horiz) 2·20 2·20

No. **MS**3533 also exists imperforate from a limited printing.

1193 "Portrait of Child"

1194 Valentina Tereshkova

(Des K. Kunev. Litho German Bank Note Ptg Co, Leipzig)

1988 (14 June). Second Death Anniv of Dechko Uzunov (painter). T **1193** and similar vert designs. Multicoloured. P 13×13½.

3534 5st. Type **1193** 10 10
3535 13st. "Portrait of Mariya Vasileva" 35 15
3536 30st. "Self-portrait" 65 20
3534/3536 *Set of* 3 1·00 40

(Des A. Stareishinski. Photo)

1988 (16 June). 25th Anniv of First Woman in Space. Sheet 87×56 mm. P 13½×13.

MS3537 **1194** 1l. pink and royal blue 2·20 2·20

No. **MS**3537 also exists imperforate from a limited printing.

1195 "St. John"

1196 High Jumping

1988 (27 June). Icons from Kurdzhali. T **1195** and similar vert design. Multicoloured. Litho. P 13×13½.

3538 5st. Type **1195** 20 10
3539 8st. "St. George and Dragon" 20 10

1988 (25 July). Olympic Games, Seoul. T **1196** and similar vert designs. Multicoloured. Litho. P 13.

3540 5st. Type **1196** 10 10
3541 13st. Weightlifting 20 10
3542 30st. Wrestling 55 30
3543 42st. Gymnastics 85 35
3540/3543 *Set of* 4 1·50 80
MS3544 115×75 mm. 1l. Volleyball 2·20 2·20

No. **MS**3544 also exists imperforate from a limited printing.

1197 Dimitur and Karadzha

1988 (25 July). 120th Death Anniv of Khadzhi Dimitur and Stefan Karadzha (revolutionaries). P 13.
3545 **1197** 5st. deep green, black and chestnut 20 10

1198 Magazines

1199 "The Dead Tree" (Roland Udo)

1988 (26 July). 30th Anniv of Problems of Peace and Socialism (magazine). P 13.
3546 **1198** 13st. multicoloured 20 10

(Litho German Bank Note Ptg Co, Leipzig)

1988 (27 July). Paintings in Lyudmila Zhivkova Art Gallery. T **1199** and similar vert designs. Multicoloured. P 14.
3547 30st. Type **1199** 55 35
3548 30st. "Algiers Harbour" (Albert Marque) 55 35
3549 30st. "Portrait of Hermine David" (Jule Pasquin) 55 35
3550 30st. "Madonna and Child with Two Saints" (Giovanni Rosso) 55 35
3547/3550 *Set of 4* .... 2·00 1·30

1200 University Building

(Des D. Karapantev. Litho)

1988 (22 Aug). Centenary of St. Clement of Ohrid University, Sofia. P 13.
3551 **1200** 5st. black, greenish yellow and yellowish green 20 10

1201 Czechoslovakia 1918 Stamp Design

(Des St. Kunchev. Litho)

1988 (22 Aug). Praga '88 International Stamp Exhibition, Prague. P 13.
3552 **1201** 25st. rosine and bright royal blue 45 35
No. 3552 was issued in sheetlets of three stamps and three labels bearing the emblems of Praga '88 and Bulgaria '89 exhibitions.
An imperforate sheetlet with additional marginal inscriptions was issued in March 1989 in a limited printing.

1202 Korea 1884 5m. Stamp

1203 Anniversary Emblem

(Des St. Kunchev. Litho)

1988 (1 Sept). Olymphilex '88 Olympic Stamps Exhibition, Seoul. P 13.
3553 **1202** 62st. carmine-vermilion and emerald 1·30 1·10
No. 3553 was issued in sheetlets of three stamps and three labels bearing the emblems of Olymphilex '88 and Bulgaria '89 exhibitions.

(Des G. Dobroslavov. Litho)

1988 (15 Sept). 25th Anniv of Kremikovtsi Steel Mills. P 13.
3554 **1203** 5st. deep blue-violet, rosine and cobalt 20 10

1204 Parliament Building, Sofia, and Map

1205 Chalice, Glinena

(Des St. Kunchev. Litho)

1988 (16 Sept). 80th Interparliamentary Conference, Sofia. P 13.
3555 **1204** 13st. blue and carmine-vermilion 35 15

(Des L. Chekhlarov. Litho)

1988 (20 Sept). Kurdzhali Culture. T **1205** and similar multicoloured design. P 13.
3556 5st. Type **1205** 20 10
3557 8st. Part of ruined fortifications, Perperikon (vert) 20 10

1206 Soldiers

(Des D. Ushtavaliiski. Litho)

1988 (23 Sept). 300th Anniv of Chiprovtsi Rising. P 13.
3558 **1206** 5st. multicoloured 20 10

1207 Brown Bear (*Ursus arctos*)

(Des V. Tsenov. Litho Cuban National Ptg Wks, Havana)

1988 (26 Sept). Bears. T **1207** and similar horiz designs. Multicoloured. P 12½.
3559 5st. Type **1207** 10 10
3560 8st. Polar bear (*Thalassarctos maritimus*) 10 10
3561 13st. Sloth bear (*Melursus ursinus*) 20 10
3562 20st. Sun bear (*Helarctos malayanus*) 45 20
3563 32st. Asiatic black bear (*Selenarctos thibetanus*) 65 30
3564 42st. Spectacled bear (*Tremarctos ornatus*) .... 1·10 35
3559/3564 *Set of 6* .... 2·30 1·00
Nos. 3559/64 were issued both in separate sheets and together in *se-tenant* sheetlets of six (*Price of sheetlet*: £2.75 *un*).

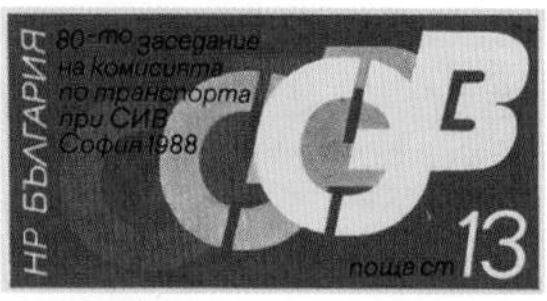

1208 Emblem

(Des A. Stareishinski. Litho)

1988 (17 Oct). 80th Council of Mutual Economic Aid Transport Commission Meeting, Sofia. P 13½×13.
3565 **1208** 13st. bright crimson and black 35 15

1209 Emblem

(Des Kh. Khristov. Litho)

1988 (29 Oct). World Ecoforum. P 13.
3566 **1209** 20st. multicoloured 45 20

1210 Amphitheatre, Plovdiv

1211 Transmission Towers

(Des Kh. Khristov. Litho)

1988 (2 Nov). Plovdiv '88 National Stamp Exhibition. P 13.
3567 **1210** 5st. pale lemon, deep brown and rosine 20 10
An imperforate sheetlet containing six examples of No. 3567 and with marginal inscriptions was issued in March 1989 in a limited printing.

(Des Kh. Khristov. Litho)

1988 (17 Nov). 25th Anniv of Radio and Television. P 13.
3568 **1211** 5st. bronze green, ultramarine and brown-ochre 20 10

1212 1879 5c. Stamp

(Des St. Kunchev. Litho)

1988 (22 Nov). Bulgaria '89 International Stamp Exhibition (2nd issue). P 13.
3569 **1212** 42st. yellow-orange, black and deep mauve 65 55
No. 3569 was issued with *se-tenant* label showing the exhibition emblem.
An imperforate sheetlet containing three stamps and three labels and with marginal inscriptions was issued in March 1989 in a limited printing.

1213 *Ruse* (river boat)

(Des Kh. Khristov. Litho)

1988 (25 Nov). 40th Anniv of Danube Commission. Sheet 104×124 mm containing T **1213** and similar horiz design. Multicoloured. P 13½×13.
MS3570 1l. Type **1213**; 1l. *Al. Stamboliiski* (river cruiser) .... 4·25 4·50
No. **MS**3570 also exists imperforate from a limited printing.

1214 Children and Cars

(Des D. Tasev. Litho)

1988 (28 Nov). Road Safety Campaign. P 13½×13.
3571 **1214** 5st. multicoloured 20 10

1215 Rila Hotel, Borovets

1216 Tree Decoration

(Des Tekla Aleksieva. Litho)

1988 (19 Dec). Hotels. T **1215** and similar horiz designs. Multicoloured. P 13.
3572 5st. Type **1215** 20 15
3573 8st. Pirin Hotel, Bansko 20 15
3574 13st. Shtastlivetsa Hotel, Vitosha 35 20
3575 30st. Perelik Hotel, Pamporovo 55 30
3572/3575 *Set of 4* .... 1·20 70

(Des St. Kunchev. Litho)

1988 (20 Dec). New Year. T **1216** and similar vert design. Multicoloured. P 13.
3576 5st. Type **1216** 10 10
3577 13st. Bulgaria '89 emblem, tree and decorations 20 10

1217 Space Shuttle *Buran*

(Des Emiliya Stankeva. Litho)

1988 (28 Dec). Energiya–Buran Space Flight. Sheet 102×67 mm. P 13½×13.
MS3578 **1217** 1l. deep dull blue .... 2·20 2·00
No. **MS**3578 also exists imperforate from a limited printing.

1218 Mail Coach

1988 (29 Dec). Bulgaria '89 International Stamp Exhibition, Sofia (3rd issue). Mail Transport. T **1218** and similar horiz designs. Multicoloured. Litho. P 13½×13.
3579 25st. Type **1218** 55 20
3580 25st. Paddle-steamer 55 20
3581 25st. Lorry 55 20
3582 25st. Biplane 55 20
3579/3582 *Set of 4* .... 2·00 70
Five imperforate sheetlets, four each containing four examples of one design and the fifth containing all four designs, were issued in March 1989 in a limited printing.

1219 India 1947 1½a. Independence Stamp

(Des St. Kunchev. Litho)

1989 (14 Jan). India '89 International Stamp Exhibition, New Delhi. P 13.

3583 **1219** 62st. olive-green and red-orange ... 1·10 90

No. 3583 was issued in sheetlets of three stamps and three labels bearing the emblems of India '89 and Bulgaria '89 exhibitions.

An imperforate sheetlet was issued in May 1989 in a limited printing.

1220 France 1850 10c. Ceres Stamp

1221 Slalom

(Des St. Kunchev. Litho)

1989 (23 Jan). Philexfrance '89 International Stamp Exhibition, Paris. P 13.

3584 **1220** 42st. ochre and ultramarine ... 65 55

No. 3584 was issued in sheetlets of three stamps and three labels bearing the emblems of Philexfrance '89 and Bulgaria '89 exhibitions.

An imperforate sheetlet was issued in May 1989 in a limited printing.

(Des Kh. Aleksiev. Litho)

1989 (30 Jan). Sofia '89 University Winter Games, Sofia. Sheet 84×142 mm containing T **1221** and similar vert designs. Multicoloured. Imperf.

MS3585 25st. Type **1221**; 25st. Ice hockey; 25st. Biathlon; 25st. Speed skating ... 2·20 2·20

No. **MS**3585 has simulated perforations. The sheet also exists without this simulation from a limited printing.

1222 Don Quixote (sculpture, House of Humour and Satire)

1223 *Ramonda serbica*

(Des I. Bogdanov. Litho)

1989 (7 Feb). International Festival of Humour and Satire, Gabrovo. P 13½×13.

3586 **1222** 13st. multicoloured ... 35 15

(Des B. Kitanov. Litho)

1989 (22 Feb). Flowers. T **1223** and similar vert designs. Multicoloured. P 13×13½.

3587	5st. Type **1223**	10	10
3588	10st. *Paeonia maskula*	20	10
3589	25st. *Viola perinensis*	45	20
3590	30st. *Dracunculus vulgaris*	55	35
3591	42st. *Tulipa splendens*	85	45
3592	60st. *Rindera umbellata*	1·10	55
3587/3592	*Set of 6*	3·00	1·60

Nos. 3587/92 were issued both in separate sheets and together in *se-tenant* sheetlets of six (*Price of sheetlet*: £3.50 *un*).

1224 Common Noctule Bat (*Nyctalus noctula*)

(Des G. Drummond. Litho)

1989 (27 Feb). Bats. T **1224** and similar horiz designs. Multicoloured. P 13.

3593	5st. Type **1224**	20	15
3594	13st. Greater horseshoe bat (*Rhinolophus ferrumequinum*)	35	20
3595	30st. Large mouse-eared bat (*Myotis myotis*)	1·10	45
3596	42st. Particoloured frosted bat (*Vespertilio murinus*)	1·60	1·30
3593/3596	*Set of 4*	3·00	1·90

Nos. 3593/6 were issued both in separate sheets and together in *se-tenant* sheetlets of four (*Price of sheetlet*: £3.50 *un*).

1225 Stamboliiski

1226 Launch of "Soyuz 33"

(Des Milena Ioich and P. Rashkov. Litho)

1989 (1 Mar). 110th Birth Anniv of Aleksandur Stamboliiski (Prime Minister 1919–23). P 13.

3597 **1225** 5st. black and orange ... 20 10

(Des S. Gruev. Litho)

1989 (10 Apr). Tenth Anniv of Soviet–Bulgarian Space Flight. Sheet 130×90 mm containing T **1226** and similar vert design. Multicoloured. P 13.

MS3598 50st. Type **1226**; 50st. Cosmonauts Nicolai Rukavishnikov and Georgi Ivanov ... 2·20 2·20

No. **MS**3598 also exists imperforate from a limited printing.

1227 Young Inventor

(Des Kh. Aleksiev. Litho)

1989 (20 Apr). International Young Inventors' Exhibition, Plovdiv. P 13½×13.

3599 **1227** 5st. multicoloured ... 20 10

1228 Stanke Dimitrov-Marek (Party activist)

1229 "John the Baptist" (Toma Vishanov)

(Des Milena Ioich and P. Rashkov. Litho)

1989 (28 Apr). Birth Centenaries. T **1228** and similar design. P 13.

3600	5st. bright carmine-red and black	20	10
3601	5st. bright rose-red and black	20	10

Design: Horiz—No. 3601, Petko Yenev (revolutionary).

(Des Tekla Aleksieva and Zh. Aleksiev. Litho)

1989 (28 Apr). Bulgaria '89 International Stamp Exhibition, Sofia (4th issue). Icons. T **1229** and similar vert designs. Multicoloured. P 13×13½.

3602	30st. Type **1229**	55	20
3603	30st. "St. Dimitur" (Ivan Terziev)	55	20
3604	30st. "Archangel Michael" (Dimitur Molerov)	55	20
3605	30st. "Madonna and Child" (Toma Vishanov)	55	20
3602/3605	*Set of 4*	2·00	70

Five imperforate sheetlets, four containing four examples of one design and the fifth containing all four designs, were issued in May 1989 in a limited printing.

1230 Fax Machine and Woman reading Letter

1231 "Nike in Quadriga" (relief)

(Des Tekla Aleksieva and Zh. Aleksiev. Litho)

1989 (5 May). 110th Anniv of Bulgarian Post and Telegraph Services. T **1230** and similar vert designs. Multicoloured. P 13×13½.

3606	5st. Type **1230**	20	15
3607	8st. Telex machine and old telegraph machine	20	15
3608	35st. Modern and old telephones	65	45
3609	42st. Dish aerial and old radio	85	55
3606/3609	*Set of 4*	1·70	1·20

Three imperforate sheetlets, each containing six examples of one design (Nos. 3606, 3607 or 3608), were issued in a limited printing.

(Des Tekla Aleksieva and Zh. Aleksiev. Litho)

1989 (22 May). 58th International Philatelic Federation Congress, Sofia. Sheet 87×120 mm. P 13.

MS3610 **1231** 1l. multicoloured ... 2·20 2·20

No. **MS**3610 also exists imperforate from a limited printing.

1232 A. P. Aleksandrov, A. Ya. Solovov and V. P. Savinikh

(Des I. Bogdanov. Litho)

1989 (7 June). AIR. Soyuz TM5 Soviet–Bulgarian Space Flight. P 13½×13.

3611 **1232** 13st. multicoloured ... 35 20

1233 Party Programme

1234 Sofronii Vrachanski (250th anniv)

(Des S. Krustev. Litho)

1989 (15 June). 70th Anniv of First Bulgarian Communist Party Congress, Sofia. P 13×13½.

3612 **1233** 5st. black, vermilion and brown-lake ... 20 10

(Des T. Vardzhiev. Litho)

1989 (15 June). Writers' Birth Anniversaries. T **1234** and similar vert designs. P 13.

3613	5st. pale green, bistre-brown and black	20	10
3614	5st. pale olive-green, bistre and black	20	10

Design:—No. 3614, Iliya Bluskov (150th anniv).

1235 Birds

(Des V. Konovalov and K. Kunev (30, 42st.). Litho)

1989 (26 June). Bicentenary of French Revolution. T **1235** and similar horiz designs. Each black, bright scarlet and deep ultramarine. P 13.

3615	13st. Type **1235**	35	15
3616	30st. Jean-Paul Marat	55	20
3617	42st. Maximilien Robespierre	75	35
3615/3617	*Set of 3*	1·50	65

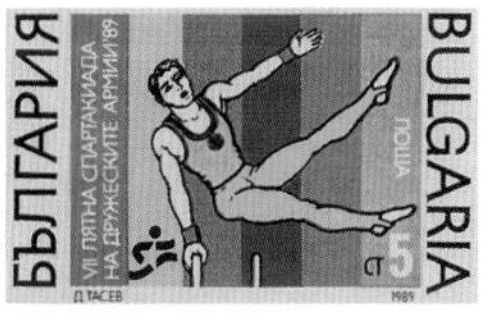

1236 Gymnastics

1237 Aprilov

(Des D. Tasev. Litho)

1989 (30 June). Seventh Friendly Armies Summer Spartakiad. T **1236** and similar horiz designs. Multicoloured. P 13.

3618	5st. Type **1236**	10	10
3619	13st. Show-jumping	35	15
3620	30st. Long jumping	55	20
3621	42st. Shooting	75	45
3618/3621	*Set of 4*	1·60	90

(Des T. Vardzhiev. Litho)

1989 (1 Aug). Birth Bicentenary of Vasil Aprilov (educationist). P 13.

3622 **1237** 8st. azure, deep violet-blue and black ... 20 10

1238 Zagorchinov

1239 Woman in Kayak

(Des T. Vardzhiev. Litho)

1989 (5 Aug). Birth Centenary of Stoyan Zagorchinov (writer). P 13.
3623 **1238** 10st. deep turquoise, pale grey-brown and black 20 10

(Des D. Tashev. Litho)

1989 (11 Aug). Canoeing and Kayak Championships, Plovdiv. T **1239** and similar vert designs. Multicoloured. P 13.
3624 13st. Type **1239** 35 20
3625 30st. Man in kayak 75 35

1240 Felix Nadar taking Photograph from his Balloon *Le Géant* (1863) and Airship *Graf Zeppelin* over Aleksandr Nevski Cathedral, Sofia

(Des Kh. Aleksiev. Litho)

1989 (29 Aug). 150th Anniv of Photography. P 13½×13.
3626 **1240** 42st. black, stone and lemon .... 1·10 45

1241 Lammergeier and Lynx **1242** Soldiers

(Des I. Bogdanov. Litho)

1989 (29 Aug). Centenary of Natural History Museum. P 13.
3627 **1241** 13st. multicoloured 35 30

(Des D. Nikolov. Litho)

1989 (30 Aug). 45th Anniv of Fatherland Front Government. T **1242** and similar vert designs. Multicoloured. P 13.
3628 5st. Type **1242** 10 10
3629 8st. Welcoming officers 10 10
3630 13st. Crowd of youths 35 15
3628/3630 *Set of* 3 .... 50 30

1243 Lyubomir Dardzhikov **1244** Yasenov

(Des A. Stareishinski. Litho)

1989 (22 Sept). 48th Death Anniversaries of Post Office War Heroes. T **1243** and similar vert designs. Multicoloured. P 13.
3631 5st. Type **1243** 10 10
3632 8st. Ivan Bankov Dobrev 10 10
3633 13st. Nestor Antonov 35 15
3631/3633 *Set of* 3 .... 50 30

(Des T. Vardzhiev. Litho)

1989 (25 Sept). Birth Centenary of Khristo Yasenov (writer). P 13.
3634 **1244** 8st. grey-brown, red-brown and black 20 10

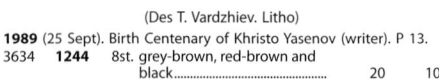

1245 Lorry leaving Weighbridge **1246** Nehru

(Des M. Chankov. Litho)

1989 (25 Sept). 21st Transport Congress, Sofia. P 13.
3635 **1245** 42st. new blue and royal blue .... 1·10 65

(Des Tekla Aleksieva and Zh. Aleksiev. Litho)

1989 (10 Oct). Birth Centenary of Jawaharlal Nehru (Indian statesman). P 13.
3636 **1246** 13st. stone, brown and black 35 20

1247 Cranes flying **1248** Javelin Sand Boa (*Eryx jaculus turcicus*)

(Des Tekla Aleksieva and Zh. Aleksiev. Litho)

1989 (12 Oct). Ecology Congress of European Security and Co-operation Conference, Sofia. Sheet 130×85 mm containing T **1247** and similar vert design. Multicoloured. P 13.
MS3637 50st. Type **1247**; 1l. Cranes flying (different) 4·25 4·50
No. **MS**3637 also exists imperforate from a limited printing.

(Des L. Cheklarov. Litho)

1989 (20 Oct). Snakes. T **1248** and similar horiz designs. Multicoloured. P 13.
3638 5st. Type **1248** 10 10
3639 10st. Aesculapian snake (*Elaphe longissima*) 20 15
3640 25st. Leopard snake (*Elaphe situla*) 55 35
3641 30st. Four-lined rat snake (*Elaphe quatuorlineata*) 65 45
3642 42st. Cat snake (*Telescopus fallax*) .... 1·00 55
3643 60st. Whip snake (*Coluber rubriceps*) .... 1·30 65
3638/3643 *Set of* 6 .... 3·50 2·00
Nos. 3638/43 were issued both in separate sheets and together in *se-tenant* sheetlets (*Price of sheetlet*: £4 un).

1249 Tiger and Balloon of Flags **1250** Boy on Skateboard

(Des I. Konstantinov. Litho)

1989 (4 Nov). Young Inventors' Exhibition, Plovdiv. P 13.
3644 **1249** 13st. multicoloured 35 20

(Des D. Tasev. Litho)

1989 (10 Nov). Children's Games. Sheet 100×120 mm containing T **1250** and similar vert designs. Multicoloured. P 13×13½.
MS3645 30st.+15st. Type **1250**; 30st.+15st. Girl with ball and doll; 30st.+15st. Girl jumping over ropes; 30st.+15st. Boy with toy train .... 3·75 4·00
No. **MS**3645 also exists imperforate from a limited printing.

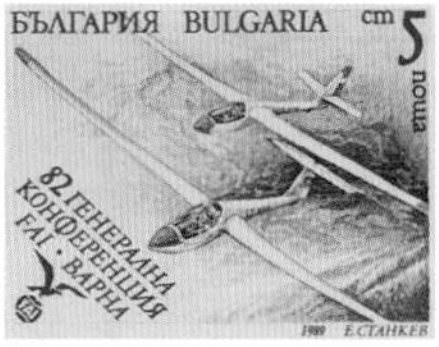

1251 Goalkeeper saving Ball **1252** Gliders

(Des G. Gadelev. Litho)

1989 (1 Dec). World Cup Football Championship, Italy (1990) (1st issue). T **1251** and similar vert designs. Multicoloured. P 13.
3646 5st. Type **1251** 10 10
3647 13st. Player tackling 20 10
3648 30st. Player heading ball 55 35
3649 42st. Player kicking ball .... 1·30 55
3646/3649 *Set of* 4 .... 1·90 1·00
MS3650 109×54 mm. 50st. Player tackling; 50st. Players .... 2·20 2·00
No. **MS**3650 also exists imperforate from a limited printing.
See also Nos. 3675/**MS**3679.

(Des E. Stankev. Litho)

1989 (8 Dec). 82nd International Airsports Federation General Conference, Varna. Aerial Sports. T **1252** and similar horiz designs. Multicoloured. P 13.
3651 5st. Type **1252** 10 10
3652 13st. Hang gliding 35 20
3653 30st. Parachutist landing 75 40
3654 42st. Free falling parachutist 85 45
3651/3654 *Set of* 4 .... 1·80 1·00

1253 Children on Road Crossing **1254** Santa Claus's Sleigh

(Des Ralitsa Stanoeva. Litho)

1989 (12 Dec). Road Safety. P 13.
3655 **1253** 5st. multicoloured 20 10

(Des St. Kunchev. Litho)

1989 (25 Dec). New Year. T **1254** and similar vert design. Multicoloured. P 13.
3656 5st. Type **1254** 20 15
3657 13st. Snowman 35 20

1255 European Shorthair **1256** Christopher Columbus and *Santa Maria*

(Des D. Karapantev. Litho)

1989 (26 Dec). Cats. T **1255** and similar designs. P 13×13½ (vert) or 13½×13 (horiz).
3658 5st. black and bistre-yellow 20 15
3659 5st. black and light grey 20 15
3660 8st. black and yellow 20 15
3661 10st. black and orange-brown 35 20
3662 10st. black and cobalt 35 20
3663 13st. black and rose-red 45 25
3658/3663 *Set of* 6 .... 1·60 1·00
Designs: Horiz—No. 3659, Persian; 3660, European shorthair (different); 3662, Persian (different). Vert—3661, Persian (different); 3663, Siamese.

(Des A. Stareishinski. Litho)

1989 (17 Jan). Navigators and their Ships. T **1256** and similar horiz designs. Multicoloured. P 13.
3664 5st. Type **1256** 20 20
3665 8st. Vasco da Gama and *São Gabriel* 20 20
3666 13st. Ferdinand Magellan and *Vitoria* 25 20
3667 32st. Francis Drake and *Golden Hind* 65 45
3668 42st. Henry Hudson and *Discoverie* .... 1·00 55
3669 60st. James Cook and H.M.S. *Endeavour* .... 1·30 65
3664/3669 *Set of* 6 .... 3·25 2·00
Nos. 3664/9 were issued both in separate sheets and together in *se-tenant* sheetlets of six stamps (*Price of sheetlet*: £3.75 *un*).

1257 Banner **1258** "Portrait of Madeleine Rono" (Maurice Brianchon)

(Des P. Petrunov. Litho)

1990 (23 Feb). Centenary of Esperanto (invented language) in Bulgaria. P 13.
3670 **1257** 10st. stone, emerald and black 20 10

(Des St. Kunchev. Litho)

1990 (23 Mar). Paintings. T **1258** and similar vert designs. Multicoloured. P 14.
3671 30st. Type **1258** 75 45
3672 30st. "Still Life" (Suzanne Valadon) 75 45
3673 30st. "Portrait of a Woman" (Moise Kisling) 75 45
3674 30st. "Portrait of a Woman" (Giovanni Boltraffio) 75 45
3671/3674 *Set of* 4 .... 2·75 1·60

1259 Players

(Des S. Krustev. Litho)

1990 (26 Mar). World Cup Football Championship, Italy (2nd issue). T **1259** and similar horiz designs showing various match scenes. P 13.
3675 5st. multicoloured 20 15
3676 13st. multicoloured 35 20
3677 30st. multicoloured 65 35
3678 42st. multicoloured .... 1·10 45
3675/3678 *Set of* 4 .... 2·10 1·00
MS3679 80×125 mm. 2×50st. multicoloured .... 2·75 2·50
No. **MS**3679 exists imperforate from a limited printing.

1260 Bavaria 1849 1k. Stamp

(Des St. Kunchev. Litho)

1990 (6 Apr). Essen '90 International Stamp Fair. P 13.

3680 **1260** 42st. black and red 85 80

No. 3680 was issued in sheetlets of three stamps and three different labels.

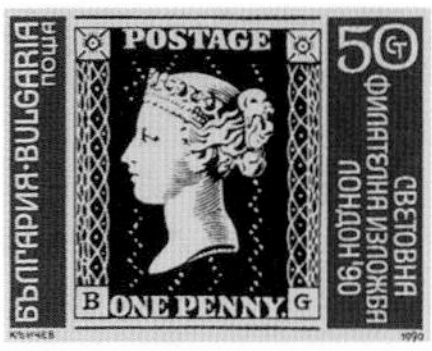

1261 Penny Black

(Des St. Kunchev. Litho)

1990 (10 Apr). Stamp World London '90 International Stamp Exhibition. Sheet 90×140 mm containing T **1261** and similar horiz design. P 13.

MS3681 50st. black and deep new blue (Type **1261**); 50st. black and bright scarlet (Sir Rowland Hill (instigator of postage stamps)) .... 2·20 2·10

1262 "100" and Rainbow

(Des D. Tasev. Litho)

1990 (17 Apr). Centenary of Co-operative Farming. P 13.

3682 **1262** 5st. multicoloured 20 10

1263 "Elderly Couple at Rest" **1264** Map

(Des D. Nikolov. Litho)

1990 (24 Apr). Birth Centenary of Dimitur Chorbadzhiiski-Chudomir (artist). P 13.

3683 **1263** 5st. multicoloured 20 10

(Des Kh. Khristov. Litho)

1990 (1 May). Centenary of Labour Day. P 13×13½.

3684 **1264** 10st. multicoloured 20 15

1265 Emblem

(Des A. Stareishinski. Litho)

1990 (13 May). 125th Anniv of International Telecommunications Union. P 13½×13.

3685 **1265** 20st. bright blue, bright scarlet and black 55 35

1266 Belgium 1849 10c. "Epaulettes" Stamp **1267** Lamartine and his House

(Des St. Kunchev. Litho)

1990 (23 May). Belgica '90 International Stamp Exhibition, Brussels. P 13.

3686 **1266** 30st. olive-brown and emerald 65 55

No. 3686 was issued in sheetlets of three stamps and three different labels.

(Des Maglena Konstantinova. Litho)

1990 (15 June). Birth Bicentenary of Alphonse de Lamartine (poet). P 13½×13.

3687 **1267** 20st. multicoloured 55 35

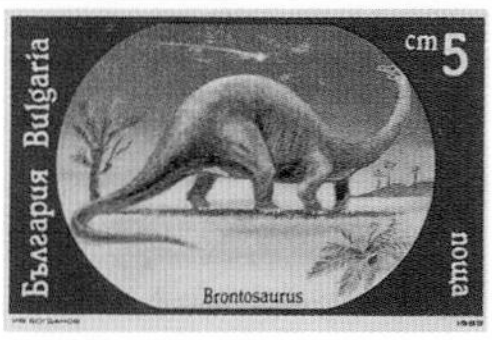

1268 Brontosaurus

(Des I. Bogdanov. Litho Cuban National Ptg Wks, Havana)

1990 (19 June). Prehistoric Animals. T **1268** and similar horiz designs. Multicoloured. P 12½.

3688 5st. Type **1268** 20 15
3689 8st. Stegosaurus 20 15
3690 13st. Edaphosaurus 35 20
3691 25st. Rhamphorhynchus 65 45
3692 32st. Protoceratops 85 55
3693 42st. Triceratops .... 1·30 65
3688/3693 *Set of 6* .... 3·25 1·90

Nos. 3688/93 were issued both in individual sheets and together in *se-tenant* sheetlets (*Price of sheetlet*: £3.75 *un*).

1269 Swimming

(Des E. Stankev. Litho)

1990 (13 July). Olympic Games, Barcelona (1992) (1st issue). T **1269** and similar horiz designs. Multicoloured. P 13½×13.

3694 5st. Type **1269** 10 10
3695 13st. Handball 35 20
3696 30st. Hurdling 65 40
3697 42st. Cycling .... 1·10 45
3694/3697 *Set of 4* .... 2·00 1·00

MS3698 77×117 mm. 50st. Tennis player serving; 50st. Tennis player waiting to receive ball .... 2·75 2·20

No. **MS**3698 also exists imperforate from a limited printing.

See also Nos. 3840/**MS**3844.

1270 Southern Festoon (*Zerynthia polyxena*) **1272** Iosif I

1271 Airbus Industrie A310 Jetliner

(Des T. Vardzhiev. Litho Cuban National Ptg Wks, Havana)

1990 (8 Aug). Butterflies and Moths. T **1270** and similar vert designs. Multicoloured. P 13.

3699 5st. Type **1270** 20 15
3700 10st. Jersey tiger moth (*Panaxia quadripunctaria*) 20 15
3701 20st. Willow-herb hawk moth (*Proserpinus proserpina*) 45 20
3702 30st. Striped hawk moth (*Hyles lineata*) 65 45
3703 42st. *Thecla betulae* 75 65
3704 60st. Cynthia's fritillary (*Euphydryas cynthia*) .... 1·30 90
3699/3704 *Set of 6* .... 3·25 2·30

Nos. 3699/3704 were issued both in separate sheets and together in *se-tenant* sheetlets of six stamps (*Price of sheetlet*: £3.75 *un*).

(Des D. Tasev. Litho)

1990 (30 Aug). Aircraft T **1271** and similar horiz designs. Multicoloured. P 13½×13.

3705 5st. Type **1271** (wrongly inscr "A300") 20 15
3706 10st. Tupolev Tu-204 jetliner 20 15
3707 25st. Concorde supersonic jetliner 55 35
3708 30st. Douglas DC-9 jetliner 60 40
3709 42st. Ilyushin Il-86 jetliner 75 55
3710 60st. Boeing 747-300/400 jetliner .... 1·30 90
3705/3710 *Set of 6* .... 3·25 2·30

Nos. 3705/10 were issued both in separate sheets and together in *se-tenant* sheetlets of six stamps (*Price of sheetlet*: £3.75 *un*).

(Des Ralitsa Stanoeva. Litho)

1990 (27 Sept). 150th Birth Anniv of Exarch Iosif I. P 13.

3711 **1272** 5st. bright mauve, black and green 20 10

1273 Road and U.N. Emblem within Triangles **1274** Putting the Shot

(Des St. Kunchev. Litho)

1990 (9 Oct). International Road Safety Year. P 13.

3712 **1273** 5st. multicoloured 20 10

(Des Kh. Aleksiev. Litho)

1990 (16 Oct). Olymphilex '90 Olympic Stamps Exhibition, Varna. T **1274** and similar vert designs. Multicoloured. P 13×13½.

3713 5st. Type **1274** 20 15
3714 13st. Throwing the discus 20 15
3715 42st. Throwing the hammer 75 55
3716 60st. Throwing the javelin .... 1·10 90
3713/3716 *Set of 4* .... 2·00 1·60

Nos. 3713/16 also exist in *se-tenant*, imperforate sheetlets of four stamps from a limited printing.

1275 "Sputnik" (first artificial satellite, 1957)

(Des I. Bogdanov. Litho)

1990 (22 Oct). Space Research. T **1275** and similar multicoloured designs. P 13½×13.

3717 5st. Type **1275** 10 10
3718 8st. "Vostok" and Yuri Gagarin (first manned flight, 1961) 20 15
3719 10st. Aleksei Leonov spacewalking from "Voskhod 2" (first spacewalk, 1965) .. 25 20
3720 20st. "Soyuz"–"Apollo" link, 1975 .... 45 35
3721 42st. Space shuttle *Columbia*, 1981 .... 1·10 55
3722 60st. Space probe "Galileo" .... 1·30 90
3717/3722 *Set of 6* .... 3·00 2·00

MS3723 90×71 mm. 1l. Neil Armstrong from "Apollo 11" on lunar surface (first manned moon landing, 1969) (28×53 mm). P 13×13½ .... 2·20 2·20

No. **MS**3723 also exists imperforate from a limited printing.

REPUBLIC

15 November 1990

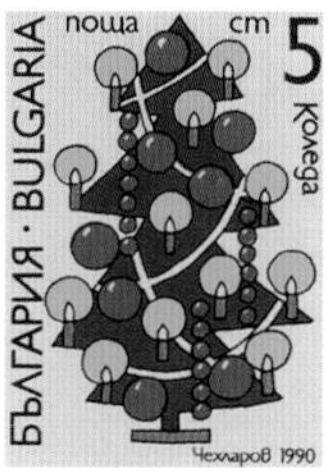

1276 St. Clement of Ohrid **1277** Tree

(Des A. Poplilov. Litho)

1990 (29 Nov). 1150th Birth Anniv of St. Clement of Ohrid, Bishop of Velitsa. P 13.

3724 **1276** 5st. chestnut, black and deep green 20 10

(Des L. Chekhlarov. Litho)

1990 (25 Dec). Christmas. T **1277** and similar vert design. Multicoloured. P 13.

3725 5st. Type **1277** 20 10
3726 20st. Father Christmas 45 20

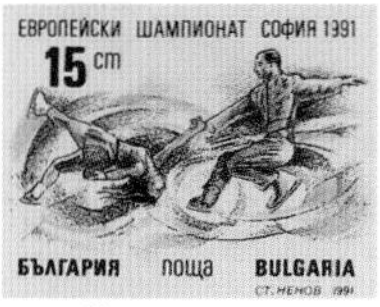

1278 Skaters **1279** Chicken

(Des S. Nenov. Litho)

1991 (18 Jan). European Figure Skating Championships, Sofia. P 13½×13.

3727 **1278** 15st. multicoloured 35 20

(Des T. Vardzhiev. Litho)

1991 (11 Feb)–**92**. Farm Animals. T **1279** and similar horiz designs. Chalk-surfaced paper. P 13½ (95st.) or 14×13½ (others).

3728 20st. olive-sepia and black (21.8.91) 20 10
3729 25st. deep violet-blue and black (21.8.91) 20 10
3730 30st. red-brown and black 20 10
3731 40st. purple-brown and black (21.8.91) 35 20
3732 62st. deep bluish green and black 55 45
3733 86st. lake and black (21.8.91) 75 45
3734 95st. deep mauve and black (5.5.92) 80 50
3735 1l. sepia and black (21.8.91) 85 55
3736 2l. deep dull green and black .... 1·60 1·10
3737 5l. blue-violet and black .... 2·75 2·00
3738 10l. deep violet-blue and black (22.2.91) .... 5·00 2·75
a. Ordinary paper .... 5·00 2·75
3728/3738 *Set of 11* .... 12·00 7·50

Designs:—20st. sheep; 25st. Goose; 40st. Horse; 62, 95st. Billy goat; 86st. Sow; 1l. Donkey; 2l. Bull; 5l. Common turkey; 10l. Cow.

No. 3738a is on whiter paper with creamier gum.

Nos. 3739/45 are vacant.

1280 Death Cap (*Amanita phalloides*)

1281 "Good Day" (Paul Gauguin)

(Des A. Stareishinski. Litho Cuban National Ptg Wks, Havana)

1991 (19 Mar). Fungi. T **1280** and similar vert designs. Multicoloured. P 12½×13.

3746 5st. Type **1280** ... 10 10
3747 10st. *Amanita verna* ... 25 20
3748 20st. Panther cap (*Amanita pantherina*) ... 25 20
3749 32st. Fly agaric (*Amanita muscaria*) ... 35 25
3750 42st. Beefsteak morel (*Gyromitra esculenta*) ... 45 35
3751 60st. Satan's mushroom (*Boletus satanas*). 1·20 50
3746/3751 *Set of 6* ... 2·30 1·40

Nos. 3746/51 were issued both in separate sheets and together in *se-tenant* sheetlets of six stamps (*Price of sheetlet*: £2.75 *un*).

(Des St. Kunchev. Litho)

1991 (1 Apr). Paintings. T **1281** and similar vert designs. Multicoloured. P 13.

3752 20st. Type **1281** ... 25 20
3753 43st. "Madame Dobini" (Edgar Degas) ... 35 25
3754 62st. "Peasant Woman" (Camille Pissarro). 60 35
3755 67st. "Woman with Black hair" (Edouard Manet) ... 70 50
3756 80st. "Blue Vase" (Paul Cézanne) ... 1·00 70
3757 2l. "Madame Samari" (Pierre Auguste Renoir) ... 2·00 1·10
3752/3757 *Set of 6* ... 4·50 2·75
MS3758 65×90 mm. 3l. "Self-portrait" (Vincent van Gogh) ... 3·00 3·00

1282 Map

1284 "Meteosat" Weather Satellite

1283 Postman on Bicycle, Envelopes and Paper

(Des St. Kunchev. Litho)

1991 (11 Apr). 700th Anniv of Swiss Confederation. P 13.

3759 **1282** 62st. vermilion and bright reddish violet ... 70 50

(Des M. Chankov. Litho)

1991 (7 May). 100 Years of Philatelic Publications in Bulgaria. P 13.

3760 **1283** 30st. multicoloured ... 35 25

(Des S. Krustev. Litho)

1991 (10 May). Europa. Europe in Space. T **1284** and similar vert design. Multicoloured. P 13×13½.

3761 43st. Type **1284** ... 1·20 60
3762 62st. "Ariane" rocket ... 1·70 85

1285 Przewalski's Horse

(Des Kh. Aleksiev. Litho Cuban National Ptg Wks, Havana)

1991 (21 May). Horses. T **1285** and similar horiz designs. Multicoloured. P 13×12½.

3763 5st. Type **1285** ... 25 20
3764 10st. Tarpan ... 25 20
3765 25st. Black arab ... 30 25
3766 35st. White arab ... 35 30
3767 42st. Shetland pony ... 45 35
3768 60st. Draught horse ... 1·20 60
3763/3768 *Set of 6* ... 2·50 1·70

Nos. 3763/8 were issued both in separate sheets and together in *se-tenant* sheetlets of six stamps (*Price of sheetlet*: £3 *un*).

1286 Expo '91

(Des Konstantina Konstantinova. Litho)

1991 (6 June). Expo '91 Exhibition, Plovdiv. P 13½×13.

3769 **1286** 30st. multicoloured ... 35 25

1287 Mozart

(Des Maglena Konstantinova. Litho)

1991 (2 July). Death Bicentenary of Wolfgang Amadeus Mozart (composer). P 13.

3770 **1287** 62st. multicoloured ... 70 50

1288 Astronaut and Rear of Space Shuttle *Columbia*

1289 Luge

(Des M. Chankov. Litho)

1991 (23 July). Space Shuttles. T **1288** and similar multicoloured designs. P 13.

3771 12st. Type **1288** ... 15 10
3772 32st. Satellite and *Challenger* ... 25 20
3773 50st. *Discovery* and satellite ... 45 25
3774 86st. Satellite and *Atlantis* (vert) ... 60 35
3775 1l.50 Launch of *Buran* (vert) ... 1·40 60
3776 2l. Satellite and *Atlantis* (different) (vert) ... 1·70 60
3771/3776 *Set of 6* ... 4·00 1·90
MS3777 86×74 mm. 3l. Earth, *Atlantis* and Moon ... 3·00 3·00

No. **MS**3777 also exists imperforate from a limited printing.

(Des Konstantina Konstantinova. Litho)

1991 (7 Aug). Winter Olympic Games, Albertville (1992). T **1289** and similar vert designs. Multicoloured. P 13×13½.

3778 30st. Type **1289** ... 35 25
3779 43st. Skiing ... 45 30
3780 67st. Ski jumping ... 70 50
3781 2l. Biathlon ... 2·30 1·40
3778/3781 *Set of 4* ... 3·50 2·20
MS3782 128×86 mm. 3l. Two-man bobsleigh ... 3·00 3·00

No. **MS**3782 also exists imperforate from a limited printing.

1290 Sheraton Hotel Balkan, Sofia

1291 Japanese Chin

(Des E. Stankev. Litho)

1991 (6 Sept). P 13.

3783 **1290** 62st. multicoloured ... 60 50

No. 3783 was issued both in large sheets and in sheetlets of three stamps and three labels showing world map (*Price of sheetlet*: £1.90 *un*).

(Des Kh. Aleksiev. Litho)

1991 (11 Oct). Dogs. T **1291** and similar vert designs. Multicoloured. P 13×13½.

3784 30st. Type **1291** ... 25 25
3785 43st. Chihuahua ... 35 25
3786 62st. Miniature pinscher ... 45 30
3787 80st. Yorkshire terrier ... 60 35
3788 1l. Mexican hairless ... 80 60
3789 3l. Pug ... 2·30 1·20
3784/3789 *Set of 6* ... 4·25 2·75

Nos. 3784/9 were issued both in separate sheets and together in *se-tenant* sheetlets of six stamps (*Price of sheetlet*: £5 *un*).

1292 Arms

(Des St. Kunchev. Litho)

1991 (21 Oct). Philatelia '91 Stamp Fair, Cologne. P 13.

3790 **1292** 86st. multicoloured ... 70 60

No. 3790 was issued in sheetlets of three stamps and three different labels.

1293 Brandenburg Gate

(Des Kh, Khristov. Litho)

1991 (23 Oct). Bicentenary of Brandenburg Gate, Berlin. Sheet 90×70 mm. P 13.

MS3791 **1293** 4l. bottle green and cobalt ... 3·00 2·75

No. **MS**3791 also exists imperforate from a limited printing.

1294 Japan 1871 48mon "Dragon" Stamp

(Des St. Kunchev. Litho)

1991 (11 Nov). Phila Nippon '91 International Stamp Exhibition, Tokyo. P 13.

3792 **1294** 62st. black, brown and bright turquoise-blue ... 45 35

No. 3792 was issued in sheetlets of three stamps and three labels each bearing the exhibition emblem and a different motif.

1295 Early Steam Locomotive and Tender

(Des Veni Kantardzhieva. Litho)

1991 (30 Nov). 125th Anniv of the Railway in Bulgaria. T **1295** and similar horiz design. Multicoloured. P 13.

3793 30st. Type **1295** ... 35 25
3794 30st. Early passenger carriage ... 35 25

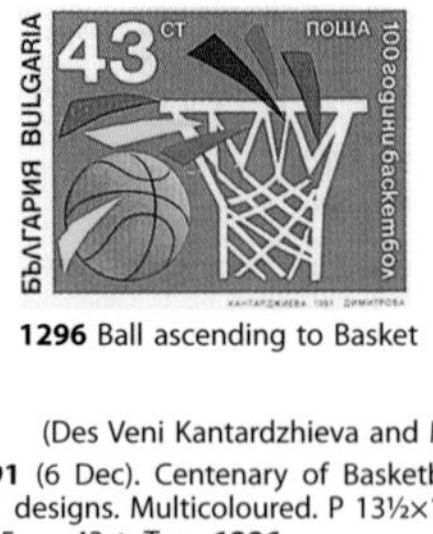

1296 Ball ascending to Basket

1297 "Christ carrying the Cross"

(Des Veni Kantardzhieva and Mariya Dimitrova. Litho)

1991 (6 Dec). Centenary of Basketball. T **1296** and similar horiz designs. Multicoloured. P 13½×13.

3795 43st. Type **1296** ... 35 20
3796 62st. Ball level with basket mouth ... 45 25
3797 90st. Ball entering basket ... 60 35
3798 1l. Ball in basket ... 70 50
3795/3798 *Set of 4* ... 1·90 1·20

(Des St. Kunchev. Litho)

1991 (13 Dec). 450th Birth Anniv of El Greco (painter). T **1297** and similar vert designs. Multicoloured. P 13.

3799 43st. Type **1297** ... 25 15
3800 50st. "Holy Family with St. Anna" ... 30 20
3801 60st. "St. John of the Cross and St. John the Evangelist" ... 45 25
3802 62st. "St. Andrew and St. Francis" ... 60 30
3803 1l. "Holy Family with Magdalene" ... 70 35
3804 2l. "Cardinal Fernando Niño de Guevara" ... 1·20 50
3799/3804 *Set of 6* ... 3·25 1·60
MS3805 68×86 mm. 3l. Detail of "Holy Family with St. Anna" (different) (39×50 mm). P 13 ... 2·10 1·40

1298 Snowman, Moon, Candle, Bell and Heart

(Des L. Chekhlarov. Litho)

1991 (18 Dec). Christmas. T **1298** and similar horiz design. Multicoloured. P 13.

3806	30st. Type **1298**	25	15
3807	62st. Star, clover, angel, house and Christmas tree	45	25

1299 Small Pasque Flower (*Pulsatilla pratensis*)

(Des Maglena Konstantinova. Litho)

1991 (20 Dec). Medicinal Plants. T **1299** and similar horiz designs. Multicoloured. P 13.

3808	30st. (+15st.) Pale pasque flower (*Pulsatilla vernalis*)	15	10
3809	40st. Type **1299**	25	10
3810	55st. *Pulsatilla halleri*	30	15
3811	60st. *Aquilegia nigricans*	35	20
3812	1l. Sea buckthorn (*Hippophae rhamnoides*)	60	25
3813	2l. Blackcurrant (*Ribes nigrum*)	1·20	50
3808/3813	*Set of 8*	2·50	1·20

No. 3808 includes a *se-tenant* premium-carrying label for 15st. inscribed "ACTION 2000. For Environment Protection".

Nos. 3808/13 were issued both in separate sheets and together in *se-tenant* sheetlets of six stamps without the label but with the 15st. premium included in the purchase price (*Price of sheetlet*: £3 *un*).

1300 Greenland Seals (*Phogophoca graenlandica*)

(Des E. Stankev. Litho)

1991 (24 Dec). Marine Mammals. T **1300** and similar horiz designs. Multicoloured. P 13.

3814	30st. Type **1300**	15	10
3815	43st. Killer whales (*Orcinus orca*)	25	15
3816	62st. Walruses (*Odobenus rosmarus*)	30	20
3817	68st. Bottle-nosed dolphins (*Tursiops truncatus*)	35	25
3818	1l. Mediterranean monk seals (*Monachus monachus*)	60	35
3819	2l. Common porpoises (*Phocaena phocaena*)	1·20	50
3814/3819	*Set of 6*	2·50	1·40

Nos. 3814/19 were issued both in separate sheets and together in *se-tenant* sheetlets of six stamps (*Price of sheetlet*: £3 *un*).

1301 Synagogue

1302 Rossini, *The Barber of Seville* and Figaro

(Des St. Kunchev. Litho)

1992 (5 Mar). 500th Anniv of Jewish Settlement in Bulgaria. P 13.

3820	**1301**	1l. multicoloured	60	25

(Des T. Vardzhiev. Litho)

1992 (11 Mar). Birth Bicentenary of Gioacchino Rossini (composer). P 13.

3821	**1302**	50st. multicoloured	35	20

1303 Plan of Fair

(Des G. Stareishinski. Litho)

1992 (25 Mar). Centenary of Plovdiv Fair. P 13.

3822	**1303**	1l. black and stone	60	25

1304 Volvo "740"

(Des K. Krustev (3823, 3827), I. Panaiotov (3824), Kh. Stoyanov (others). Litho)

1992 (26 Mar). Motor Cars. T **1304** and similar horiz designs. Multicoloured. P 13½×13.

3823	30st. Type **1304**	25	10
3824	45st. Ford "Escort"	30	15
3825	50st. Fiat "Croma"	35	20
3826	50st. Mercedes Benz "600"	35	20
3827	1l. Peugeot "605"	80	25
3828	2l. B.M.W. "316"	1·40	50
3823/3828	*Set of 6*	3·00	1·30

1305 Amerigo Vespucci

1306 Granada

(Des E. Stankev. Litho)

1992 (22 Apr). Explorers. T **1305** and similar vert designs. Multicoloured. P 13.

3829	50st. Type **1305**	25	20
3830	50st. Francisco de Orellana	25	20
3831	1l. Ferdinand Magellan	70	35
3832	1l. Jiménez de Quesada	70	35
3833	2l. Sir Francis Drake	1·20	55
3834	3l. Pedro de Valdivia	1·70	60
3829/3834	*Set of 6*	4·25	2·00
MS3835	121×83 mm. 4l. Christopher Columbus	3·00	2·50

(Des St. Kunchev. Litho)

1992 (23 Apr). Granada '92 International Stamp Exhibition. P 13.

3836	**1306**	62st. multicoloured	35	25

No. 3836 was issued in sheetlets of three stamps and three labels bearing the exhibition emblem and different motifs.

1307 *Santa Maria*

(Des S. Gruev. Litho)

1992 (24 Apr). Europa. 500th Anniv of Discovery of America by Columbus. T **1307** and similar horiz design. Multicoloured. P 13.

3837	1l. Type **1307**	1·70	60
	a. Horiz pair. Nos. 3837/8	5·00	1·60
3838	2l. Christopher Columbus	3·00	85

Nos. 3837/8 were issued together in horizontal *se-tenant* pairs within the sheet, each pair forming a composite design.

1308 House

(Des D. Tasev. Litho)

1992 (12 June). SOS Children's Village. P 13.

3839	**1308**	1l. multicoloured	70	25

1309 Long Jumping

(Des Kh. Aleksiev. Litho)

1992 (15 July). Olympic Games, Barcelona (2nd issue). T **1309** and similar multicoloured designs. P 13.

3840	50st. Type **1309**	35	20
3841	50st. Swimming	35	20
3842	1l. High jumping	60	35
3843	3l. Gymnastics	1·90	60
3840/3843	*Set of 4*	3·00	1·20
MS3844	52×75 mm. 4l. Olympic Torch (vert)	2·30	1·80

1310 1902 Laurin and Klement Motor Cycle

(Des A. Radevski. Litho)

1992 (30 July). Motor Cycles. T **1310** and similar horiz designs. Multicoloured. P 13.

3845	30st. Type **1310**	25	10
3846	50st. 1928 Puch "200 Luxus"	35	15
3847	50st. 1931 Norton "CS 1"	35	15
3848	70st. 1950 Harley Davidson	45	20
3849	1l. 1986 Gilera "SP 01"	70	25
3850	2l. 1990 BMW "K 1"	1·40	50
3845/3850	*Set of 6*	3·25	1·20

1311 Genoa

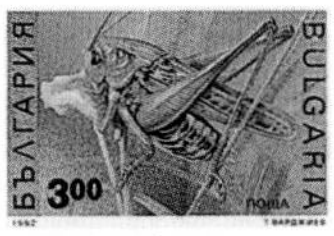

1312 Grasshopper

(Des St. Kunchev. Litho)

1992 (18 Sept). Genova '92 International Thematic Stamp Exhibition. P 13.

3851	**1311**	1l. multicoloured	70	25

(Des T. Vardzhiev. Litho)

1992 (25 Sept)–**93**. Insects. T **1312** and similar horiz designs. Multicoloured. P 13½×14.

3852	1l. Four-spotted libellula (15.12.93)	10	10
3853	2l. *Raphidia notata* (15.12.93)	35	20
3854	3l. Type **1312** (30.11.92)	80	25
3855	4l. Stag beetle (15.12.93)	1·20	35
3856	5l. Fire bug (15.12.93)	1·40	50
3857	7l. Ant	2·30	1·20
3858	20l. Wasp	5·75	1·80
3859	50l. Praying mantis (30.11.92)	14·00	3·50
3852/3859	*Set of 8*	23·00	7·00

Nos. 3860/1 are vacant.

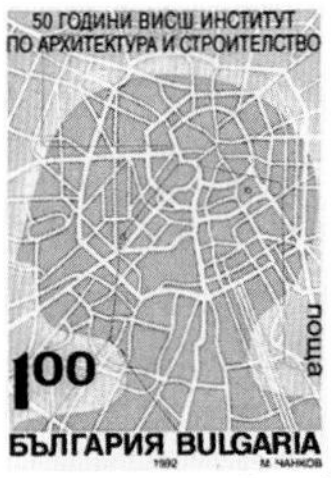

1313 Silhouette of Head on Town Plan

1314 Oak (*Quercus mestensis*)

(Des M. Chankov. Litho)

1992 (30 Sept). 50th Anniv of Institute of Architecture and Building. P 13.

3862	**1313**	1l. deep rose-red and black	70	25

(Des Konstantina Konstantinova. Litho)

1992 (16 Oct). Trees. T **1314** and similar vert designs. Multicoloured. P 13.

3863	50st. Type **1314**	20	15
3864	50st. Horse chestnut (*Aesculus hippocastanum*)	20	15
3865	1l. Oak (*Quercus thracica*)	60	25
3866	1l. Macedonian pine (*Pinus peuce*)	60	25
3867	2l. Maple (*Acer heldreichii*)	1·40	35
3868	3l. Pear (*Pyrus bulgarica*)	1·70	60
3863/3868	*Set of 6*	4·25	1·60

1315 Embroidered Flower

(Des V. Paskalev. Litho)

1992 (23 Oct). Centenary of Folk Museum, Sofia. P 13.

3869	**1315**	1l. multicoloured	70	25

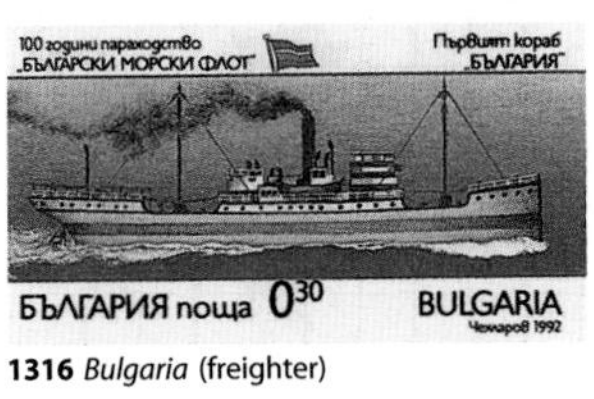

1316 *Bulgaria* (freighter)

(Des L. Chekhlarov. Litho)

1992 (30 Oct). Centenary of National Shipping Fleet. T **1316** and similar horiz designs. Multicoloured. P 13.

3870 30st. Type **1316** ... 10 10
3871 50st. *Kastor* (tanker) ... 25 15
3872 1l. *Geroite na Sebastopol* (ferry) ... 70 25
3873 2l. *Aleko Konstantinov* (tanker) ... 1·20 50
3874 2l. *Bulgaria* (tanker) ... 1·20 50
3875 3l. *Varna* (container ship) ... 1·90 70
3870/3875 *Set of 6* ... 4·75 2·00

1317 Council Emblem

(Des S. Gruev and D. Dosev. Litho)

1992 (6 Nov). Admission to Council of Europe. P 13.

3876 **1317** 7l. multicoloured ... 4·75 2·40

1318 Family exercising on Beach

1319 "Father Christmas" (Ani Bacheva)

(Des Konstantina Konstantinova. Litho)

1992 (17 Nov). Fourth World Sport for All Congress, Varna. Sheet 58×75 mm. P 13.

MS3877 **1318** 4l. multicoloured ... 2·50 2·50

(Des V. Paskalev. Litho)

1992 (1 Dec). Christmas. T **1319** and similar horiz design showing children's drawings. Multicoloured. P 13½×13.

3878 1l. Type **1319** ... 60 25
3879 7l. "Madonna and Child" (Georgi Petkov) 3·75 1·60

1320 Leopard (*Panthera pardus*)

1321 Cricket

(Des Olga Paskaleva. Litho)

1992 (18 Dec). Big Cats. T **1320** and similar vert designs. Multicoloured. P 13.

3880 50st. Type **1320** ... 35 10
3881 50st. Cheetah (*Acinonyx jubatus*) ... 35 10
3882 1l. Jaguar (*Panthera onca*) ... 70 25
3883 2l. Puma (*Felis concolor*) ... 1·40 60
3884 2l. Tiger (*Panthera tigris*) ... 1·40 60
3885 3l. Lion (*Panthera leo*) ... 1·70 70
3880/3885 *Set of 6* ... 5·25 2·10

(Des S. Krustev. Litho)

1992 (18 Dec). Sport. T **1321** and similar horiz designs. Multicoloured. P 13.

3886 50st. Type **1321** ... 35 15
3887 50st. Baseball ... 35 15
3888 1l. Pony and trap racing ... 70 25
3889 1l. Polo ... 70 25
3890 2l. Hockey ... 1·40 60
3891 3l. American football ... 1·70 70
3886/3891 *Set of 6* ... 4·75 1·90

1322 Tengmalm's Owl (*Aegolius funereus*)

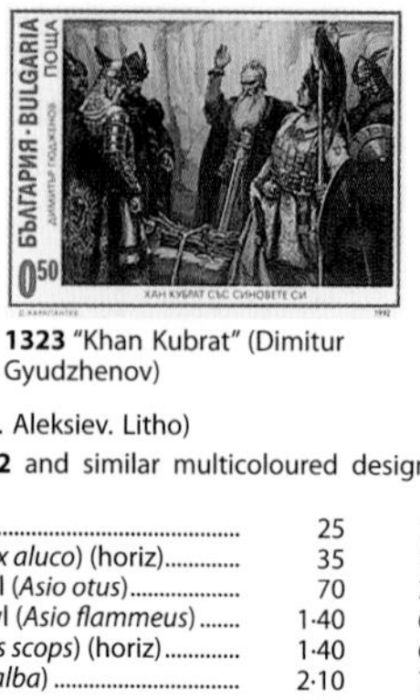

1323 "Khan Kubrat" (Dimitur Gyudzhenov)

(Des Kh. Aleksiev. Litho)

1992 (23 Dec). Owls. T **1322** and similar multicoloured designs. P 13.

3892 30st. Type **1322** ... 25 15
3893 50st. Tawny owl (*Strix aluco*) (horiz) ... 35 15
3894 1l. Long-eared owl (*Asio otus*) ... 70 25
3895 2l. Short-eared owl (*Asio flammeus*) ... 1·40 60
3896 2l. Scops owl (*Otus scops*) (horiz) ... 1·40 60
3897 3l. Barn owl (*Tyto alba*) ... 2·10 70
3892/3897 *Set of 6* ... 5·50 2·20

(Des D. Karapantev. Litho)

1992 (28 Dec). Historical Paintings. T **1323** and similar multicoloured designs. P 13.

3898 50st. Type **1323** ... 35 15
3899 1l. "Khan Asparukh" (Nikolai Pavlovich) 70 25
3900 2l. "Khan Tervel at Tsarigrad" (Dimitur Panchev) ... 1·20 60
3901 3l. "Prince Boris" (Nikolai Pavlovich) ... 1·90 95
3898/3901 *Set of 4* ... 3·75 1·80
MS3902 75×90 mm. 4l. "The Warrior" (Mito Ganovski) (vert) ... 2·50 2·50

1324 Sculpted Head

1325 Shooting

(Des St. Kunchev. Litho)

1993 (1 Jan). Centenary of National Archaeological Museum, Sofia. P 13×13½.

3903 **1324** 1l. multicoloured ... 70 25

(Des E. Stankev. Litho)

1993 (5 Feb). Borovets '93 Biathlon Championship. T **1325** and similar vert design. Multicoloured. P 13×13½.

3904 1l. Type **1325** ... 70 35
3905 7l. Cross-country skiing ... 4·75 2·00

1326 Rilski

1327 "Morning" (sculpture, Georgi Chapkunov)

(Des I. Kosev. Litho)

1993 (22 Apr). Birth Bicentenary of Neofit Rilski (compiler of Bulgarian grammar and dictionary). P 13½×13.

3906 **1326** 1l. bistre and Indian red ... 70 25

(Des St. Kunchev. Litho)

1993 (29 Apr). Europa. Contemporary Art. T **1327** and similar vert design. Multicoloured. P 13×13½.

3907 3l. Type **1327** ... 1·70 60
3908 8l. "Composition" (D. Buyukliiski) ... 3·00 1·80

1328 Goldfish

(Des L. Chekhlarov. Litho)

1993 (29 June). Fish. T **1328** and similar horiz designs. Multicoloured. P 13.

3909 1l. Type **1328** ... 25 15
3910 2l. Yucatan sailfish (*Mollienesia velifera*) 45 20
3911 3l. Two-striped killifish (*Aphyosemion bivittatum*) ... 70 25
3912 3l. Angelfish (*Pterophyllum eimekei*) ... 70 25
3913 4l. Discus (*Symphysodon discus*) ... 1·00 35
3914 8l. Pearl gourami (*Trichogaster leeri*) ... 2·10 70
3909/3914 *Set of 6* ... 4·75 1·70

1329 Apple (*Malus domestica*)

1330 Monteverdi

(Des Konstantina Konstantinova. Litho)

1993 (8 July). Fruits. T **1329** and similar vert designs. Multicoloured. P 13×13½.

3915 1l. Type **1329** ... 25 10
3916 2l. Peach (*Persica vulgaris*) ... 45 15
3917 2l. Pear (*Pyrus sativa*) ... 45 15
3918 3l. Quince (*Cydonia oblonga*) ... 70 25
3919 5l. Pomegranate (*Punica granatum*) ... 1·40 35
3920 7l. Fig (*Ficus carica*) ... 2·10 60
3915/3920 *Set of 6* ... 4·75 1·40

(Des I. Kosev. Litho)

1993 (20 July). 350th Death Anniv of Claudio Monteverdi (composer). P 13½×13.

3921 **1330** 1l. bronze green, yellow and orange-red ... 25 15

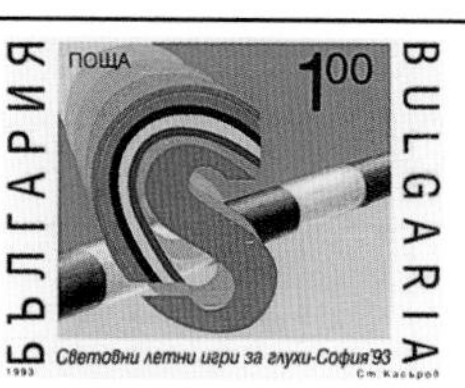

1331 High Jumping

(Des S. Kasurov. Litho)

1993 (20 July). International Games for the Deaf, Sofia. T **1331** and similar horiz designs. Multicoloured. P 13.

3922 1l. Type **1331** ... 25 15
3923 2l. Swimming ... 45 20
3924 3l. Cycling ... 80 25
3925 4l. Tennis ... 85 35
3922/3925 *Set of 4* ... 2·10 85
MS3926 86×75 mm. 5l. Football ... 1·20 1·20

1332 Baptism (from Manasses Chronicle)

1333 Prince Alexander

(Des V. Paskalev (T **1332**), T. Vardzhiev (Boris I), S. Gruev (Simeon I), K. Gogov (Cavalry). Litho)

1993 (16 Sept). 1100th Anniv of Preslav and Introduction of Cyrillic Script. Sheet 113×110 mm containing T **1332** and similar horiz designs. Multicoloured. P 13½.

MS3927 5l. Type **1332**; 5l. Prince Boris I (after Dimitur Gyudzhenov); 5l. Tsar Simeon I (after Dimitur Gyudzhenov); 5l. Cavalry charge (from Manasses Chronicle) ... 4·75 4·75

(Des I. Bogdanov. Litho)

1993 (23 Sept). Death Centenary of Prince Alexander I. P 13×13½.

3928 **1333** 3l. multicoloured ... 70 25

1334 Tchaikovsky

1335 Crossbow

(Des L. Metodiev. Litho)

1993 (30 Sept). Death Centenary of Pyotr Tchaikovsky (composer). P 13½×13.

3929 **1334** 3l. multicoloured ... 70 25

(Des Konstantina Konstantinova. Litho)

1993 (22 Oct). Weapons. T **1335** and similar vert designs. Multicoloured. P 13½×14.

3930 1l. Type **1335** ... 25 15
3931 2l. 18th-century flintlock pistol ... 45 20
3932 3l. Revolver ... 70 25
3933 3l. Luger pistol ... 70 25
3934 5l. Mauser rifle ... 1·30 40
3935 7l. Kalashnikov assault rifle ... 1·90 70
3930/3935 *Set of 6* ... 4·75 1·80

1336 Newton

1337 "100" on Stamps and Globe

(Des S. Gruev. Litho)

1993 (29 Oct). 350th Birth Anniv of Sir Isaac Newton (mathematician). P 13½×13.

3936 **1336** 1l. multicoloured ... 25 15

(Des Kh. Aleksiev. Litho)

1993 (16 Nov). Centenary of Bulgarian Philately. P 13½×13.

3937 **1337** 1l. multicoloured ... 25 15

1338 "Ecology" in Cyrillic Script

1339 Mallard (*Anas platyrhynchos*)

(Des T. Likho. Litho)

1993 (17 Nov). Ecology. T **1338** and similar horiz design. Multicoloured. P 13½×13.

3938 1l. Type **1338** ... 25 15
3939 7l. "Ecology" in English ... 1·90 60

(Des R. Iliev. Litho)

1993 (25 Nov). Hunting. T **1339** and similar horiz designs. Multicoloured. P 13½×13.

3940	1l. Type **1339**	15	10
3941	1l. Ring-necked pheasant (*Phasianus colchicus*)	15	10
3942	2l. Red fox (*Vulpes vulpes*)	35	20
3943	3l. Roe deer (*Capreolus capreolus*)	60	25
3944	6l. European brown hare (*Lepus europaeus*)	1·20	50
3945	8l. Wild boar (*Sus scrofa*)	1·70	70
3940/3945	*Set of* 6	3·75	1·70

1340 "Taurus", "Gemini" and "Cancer"

1341 Sofia Costume

(Des N. Gogova. Litho)

1993 (1 Dec). Christmas. T **1340** and similar horiz designs showing signs of the zodiac. Multicoloured. P 13½×13.

3946	1l. Type **1340**	10	10
	a. Vert pair. Nos. 3946/7	25	25
3947	1l. "Leo", "Virgo" and "Libra"	10	10
3948	7l. "Aquarius", "Pisces" and "Aries"	1·40	50
	a. Vert pair. Nos. 3948/9	3·00	1·10
3949	7l. "Scorpio", "Sagittarius" and "Capricorn"	1·40	50
3946/3949	*Set of* 4	2·75	1·10

Nos. 3946/7 and 3948/9 respectively were issued together in vertical *se-tenant* pairs within their sheets. When placed together the four stamps form a composite design.

(Des Tekla Aleksieva. Litho)

1993 (16 Dec). Costumes. T **1341** and similar vert designs. Multicoloured. P 13½×14.

3950	1l. Type **1341**	25	10
3951	1l. Plovdiv	25	10
3952	2l. Belograd	35	15
3953	3l. Oryakhovo	45	20
3954	3l. Shumen	45	20
3955	8l. Kurdzhali	1·40	60
3950/3955	*Set of* 6	2·75	1·20

1342 Freestyle Skiing

1343 "Self-portrait" and "Tsar Simeon"

(Des T. Vardzhiev. Litho)

1994 (8 Feb). Winter Olympic Games, Lillehammer, Norway. T **1342** and similar vert designs. Multicoloured. P 13.

3956	1l. Type **1342**	10	10
3957	2l. Speed skating	35	15
3958	3l. Two-man luge	60	20
3959	4l. Ice hockey	95	25
3956/3959	*Set of* 4	1·80	65
MS3960	59×90 mm. 5l. Speed skiing	95	95

(Des I. Kosev. Litho)

1994 (16 Feb). Death Centenary of Nikolai Pavlovich (artist). P 13½×13.

3961	**1343**	3l. multicoloured	60	25

1344 Plesiosaurus

(Des Konstantina Konstantinova. Litho)

1994 (27 Apr). Prehistoric Animals. T **1344** and similar horiz designs. Multicoloured. P 13.

3962	2l. Type **1344**	35	10
3963	3l. Archaeopteryx	60	20
3964	3l. Iguanodon	60	20
3965	4l. Edmontonia	80	25
3966	5l. Styracosaurus	95	35
3967	7l. Tyrannosaurus	1·40	50
3962/3967	*Set of* 6	4·25	1·40

1345 Players (Chile, 1962)

1346 Photoelectric Analysis (Georgi Nadzhakov)

(Des T. Likho. Litho)

1994 (28 Apr). World Cup Football Championship, U.S.A. T **1345** and similar multicoloured designs. P 13.

3968	3l. Type **1345**	60	25
3969	6l. Players (England, 1966)	1·20	35
3970	7l. Goalkeeper making save (Mexico, 1970)	1·30	50
3971	9l. Player kicking (West Germany, 1974)	1·60	70
3968/3971	*Set of* 4	4·25	1·60
MS3972	90×123 mm. 5l. Player punching air (Mexico, 1986) (vert); 5l. Player tackling (U.S.A., 1994)	2·50	2·50

(Des Konstantina Konstantinova. Litho)

1994 (29 Apr). Europa. Discoveries. T **1346** and similar horiz design. Multicoloured. P 14×13½.

3973	3l. Type **1346**	1·20	60
3974	15l. Cardiogram and heart (Prof. Ivan Mitev)	4·00	1·80

1347 Khristov

1348 Sleeping Hamster

(Des P. Vulchev. Litho)

1994 (18 May). 80th Birth Anniv of Boris Khristov (actor). P 13.

3975	**1347**	3l. multicoloured	60	25

(Des G. Vásárhelyi. Litho)

1994 (23 Sept). The Common Hamster (*Cricetus cricetus*). T **1348** and similar vert designs. Multicoloured. P 13.

3976	3l. Type **1348**	60	25
3977	7l. Hamster looking out of burrow	1·00	60
3978	10l. Hamster sitting up in grass	1·70	85
3979	15l. Hamster approaching berry	2·50	1·30
3976/3979	*Set of* 4	5·25	2·75

1349 Space Shuttle, Satellite and Dish Aerial

1350 Baron Pierre de Coubertin (founder of modern games)

(Des T. Vardzhiev. Litho)

1994 (4 Nov). North Atlantic Co-operation Council (North Atlantic Treaty Organization and Warsaw Pact members). P 13.

3980	**1349**	3l. multicoloured	60	35

(Des K. Ivanov. Litho)

1994 (7 Nov). Centenary of International Olympic Committee. P 13×13½.

3981	**1350**	3l. multicoloured	60	35

1351 "Christ Pantocrator"

1352 Vechernik

(Des V. Aleksandrov and M. Enev. Litho)

1994 (24 Nov). Icons. T **1351** and similar vert designs. Multicoloured. P 13×13½.

3982	2l. Type **1351**	25	10
3983	3l. "Raising of Lazarus"	45	20
3984	5l. "Passion of Christ"	60	25
3985	7l. "Archangel Michael"	1·20	50
3986	8l. "Sts. Cyril and Methodius"	1·40	60
3987	15l. "Madonna Enthroned"	3·00	70
3982/3987	*Set of* 6	6·25	2·10

(Des K. Karamfilov. Litho)

1994 (1 Dec). Christmas. Breads. T **1352** and similar vert design. Multicoloured. P 13×13½.

3988	3l. Type **1352**	60	25
3989	15l. Bogovitsa	3·00	1·60

1353 "Golden Showers"

БЪЛГАРИЯ - С БРОНЗОВИ МЕДАЛИ

(**1354**)

(Des A. Yaneva. Litho)

1994 (12 Dec). Roses. T **1353** and similar horiz designs. Multicoloured. P 13.

3990	2l. Type **1353**	35	10
3991	3l. "Caen Peace Monument"	60	25
3992	5l. "Theresa of Lisieux"	95	35
3993	7l. "Zambra 93"	1·40	60
3994	10l. "Gustave Courbet"	2·00	65
3995	15l. "Honoré de Balzac"	3·00	1·20
3990/3995	*Set of* 6	7·50	2·75

1994 (15 Dec). Bulgaria's Fourth Place in World Cup Football Championship. No. MS**3972** optd with T **1354** in the margin.

MS3996	90×123 mm. 5l. multicoloured; 5l. multicoloured	22·00	22·00

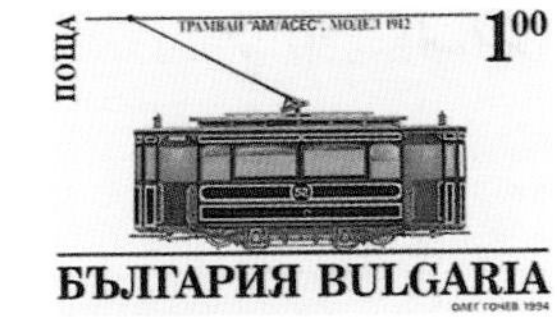

1355 "AM/ASES", 1912

(Des O. Gochev. Litho)

1994 (29 Dec). Trams. T **1355** and similar horiz designs. Multicoloured. P 13.

3997	1l. Type **1355**	10	10
3998	2l. "AM/ASES", 1928	35	15
3999	3l. "M.A.N./AEG", 1931	60	25
4000	5l. "D.T.O.", 1942	95	35
4001	8l. "Republika", 1951	1·70	70
4002	10l. "Kosmonavt" articulated tram-car, 1961	2·10	85
3997/4002	*Set of* 6	5·25	2·20

1356 Petleshkov and Flag

1357 Daisy growing through Cracked Helmet

(Des K. Ivanov. Litho)

1995 (27 Feb). 150th Birth Anniv of Vasil Petleshkov (leader of 1876 April uprising). P 13½×13.

4003	**1356**	3l. multicoloured	60	35

(Des Ya. Vasev. Litho)

1995 (3 May). Europa. Peace and Freedom. T **1357** and similar vert design. Multicoloured. P 13.

4004	3l. Type **1357**	1·20	60
4005	15l. Dove with olive branch on rifle barrel	4·00	1·80

1358 Player

(Des T. Likho. Litho)

1995 (25 May). Centenary of Volleyball. Sheet 92×75 mm containing T **1358** and similar multicoloured design. P 13.
MS4006 10l. Type **1358**; 15l. Player hitting ball (vert) .... 4·25 4·25

1359 Sea Lily (*Pancratium maritimum*)

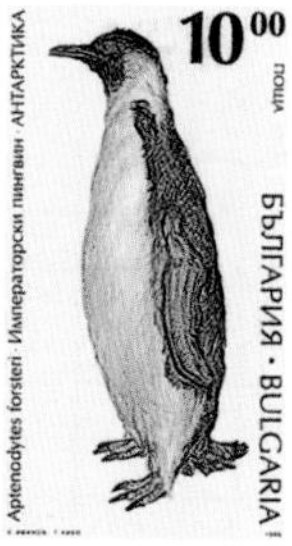

1360 Emperor Penguin (*Aptenodytes forsteri*)

(Des Krasimira Despotova. Litho)

1995 (23 June). European Nature Conservation Year. Sheet 70×99 mm containing T **1359** and similar horiz design. Multicoloured. P 13.
MS4007 10l. Type **1359**; 15l. Imperial eagle (*Aquila heliaca*) .... 5·50 5·50

(Des E. Ivanov and T. Likho. Litho)

1995 (29 June). Antarctic Animals. T **1360** and similar multicoloured designs. P 13.

4008	1l. Shrimp (*Euphausia superba*) (horiz) ..	15	10
4009	2l. Ice fish (*Chaenocephalus*) (horiz)	35	15
4010	3l. Sperm whale (*Physeter catodon*) (horiz)	45	25
4011	5l. Weddell's seal (*Leptonychotes weddelli*) (horiz)	80	35
4012	8l. Arctic skua (*Stercorarius skua*) (horiz)	1·40	70
4013	10l. Type **1360**	1·70	85
4008/4013 *Set of 6*	....	4·25	2·20

1361 Stambolov

(Des P. Vulchev. Litho)

1995 (6 July). Death Centenary of Stefan Stambolov (politician). P 13.
4014 **1361** 3l. multicoloured 60 35

1362 Pole Vaulting

1363 Pea (*Pisum sativum*)

(Des E. Stankev. Litho)

1995 (17 July). Olympic Games, Atlanta (1996) (1st issue). T **1362** and similar horiz designs. Multicoloured. P 13.

4015	3l. Type **1362**	45	15
4016	7l. High jumping	1·20	50
4017	10l. Long jumping	1·70	60
4018	15l. Triple jumping	2·50	85
4015/4018 *Set of 4*	....	5·25	1·90

See also Nos. 4083/**MS**4087.

(Des Tekla Aleksieva. Litho)

1995 (31 July). Food Plants. T **1363** and similar vert designs. Multicoloured. P 13.

4019	2l. Type **1363**	25	15
4020	3l. Chickpea (*Cicer arietinum*)	45	25
4021	3l. Soya bean (*Glicine max*)	45	25
4022	4l. Spinach (*Spinacia oleracea*)	70	35
4023	5l. Peanut (*Arachis hypogaea*)	80	50
4024	15l. Lentil (*Lens esculenta*)	2·30	85
4019/4024 *Set of 6*	....	4·50	2·10

1364 "100"

1365 "Ivan Nikolov-Zograf"

(Des Konstantina Konstantinova. Litho)

1995 (21 Aug). Centenary of Organized Tourism. P 13.
4025 **1364** 3l. multicoloured 60 25

(Des St. Kunchev. Litho)

1995 (4 Sept). Birth Centenary of Vasil Zakhariev (painter). T **1365** and similar vert designs. P 13.

4026	2l. multicoloured	35	15
4027	3l. multicoloured	60	25
4028	5l. black, grey-brown and yellow-green	95	50
4029	10l. multicoloured	1·70	95
4026/4029 *Set of 4*	....	3·25	1·70

Designs:—3l. "Rila Monastery"; 5l. "Self-portrait"; 10l. "Raspberry Collectors".

1366 "Dove-Hands" holding Globe

(Des I. Klimentov. Litho)

1995 (12 Sept). 50th Anniv of United Nations Organization. P 13.
4030 **1366** 3l. multicoloured 60 25

1367 Polikarpov Po-2 Biplane

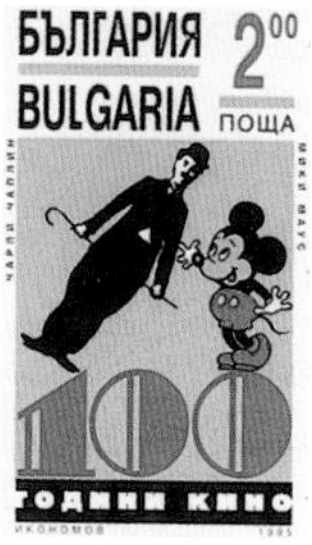

1368 Charlie Chaplin and Mickey Mouse

(Des S. Iliev and G. Todorov. Litho)

1995 (26 Sept). Aircraft. T **1367** and similar horiz designs. Multicoloured. P 13.

4031	3l. Type **1367**	45	25
4032	5l. Lisunov Li-2 airliner	80	35
4033	7l. Junkers Ju 52	1·20	60
4034	10l. Focke Wulf Fw 58	1·70	70
4031/4034 *Set of 4*	....	3·75	1·70

(Des Ikonomov. Litho)

1995 (16 Oct). Centenary of Motion Pictures. T **1368** and similar vert designs. Multicoloured. P 13.

4035	2l. Type **1368**	35	15
4036	3l. Marilyn Monroe and Marlene Dietrich	45	25
4037	5l. Nikolai Cherkasov and Humphrey Bogart	60	30
4038	8l. Sophia Loren and Liza Minelli	1·50	35
4039	10l. Gérard Philipe and Toshiro Mifune....	1·70	50
4040	15l. Katya Paskaleva and Nevena Kokanova	2·30	85
4035/4040 *Set of 6*	....	6·25	2·20

1369 Agate

(Des Ts. Ostoich. Litho)

1995 (20 Nov). Minerals. T **1369** and similar horiz designs. Multicoloured. P 13½×13.

4041	1l. Type **1369**	15	10
4042	2l. Sphalerite	35	15
4043	5l. Calcite	95	25
4044	7l. Quartz	1·20	30
4045	8l. Pyromorphite	1·40	35
4046	10l. Almandine	1·90	60
4041/4046 *Set of 6*	....	5·25	1·60

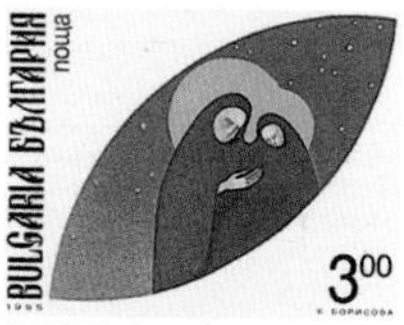

1370 Mary and Joseph

(Des K. Borisova. Litho)

1995 (8 Dec). Christmas. T **1370** and similar horiz design. Multicoloured. P 13½×13.

4047	3l. Type **1370**	60	25
4048	15l. Three wise men approaching stable	2·30	1·30

1371 "Polynesian Woman with Fruit"

(Des K. Kunev. Litho)

1996 (25 Jan). Birth Centenary of Kiril Tsonev (painter). P 13.
4049 **1371** 3l. multicoloured 60 25

1372 Luther (after Lucas Cranach the elder)

1373 Preobrazhenie

(Des K. Gogov. Litho)

1996 (5 Feb). 450th Death Anniv of Martin Luther (Protestant reformer). P 13.
4050 **1372** 3l. multicoloured 60 25

(Des Tekla Aleksieva and Zh. Aleksiev. Litho)

1996 (28 Feb). Monasteries. T **1373** and similar horiz designs. P 14×13½.

4051	3l. blue-green	15	10
4052	5l. carmine	35	20
4053	10l. deep ultramarine	45	25
4054	20l. yellow-orange	1·20	50
4055	25l. chestnut	1·40	70
4056	40l. bright purple	2·30	1·20
4051/4056 *Set of 6*	....	5·25	2·75

Designs:—5l. Arapov; 10l. Dryanovo; 20l. Bachkov; 25l. Troyan; 40l. Zograf.

Nos. 4057/62 are vacant.

1374 Bulgarian National Bank

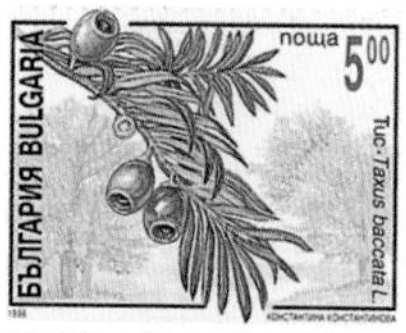

1375 Yew (*Taxus baccata*)

(Des St. Kunchev. Litho)

1996 (15 Apr). Fifth Anniv of European Reconstruction and Development Bank. T **1374** and similar vert design. P 13.

4063	7l. dull green, vermilion and deep ultramarine	60	35
4064	30l. deep ultramarine, vermilion and bright purple	2·30	85

Design:—30l. Palace of Culture, Sofia.

(Des Konstantina Konstantinova. Litho)

1996 (23 Apr). Conifers. T **1375** and similar horiz designs. Multicoloured. P 13½×13.

4065	5l. Type **1375**	25	10
4066	8l. Silver fir (*Abies alba*)	45	20
4067	10l. Norway spruce (*Picea abies*)	60	25
4068	20l. Scots pine (*Pinus silvestris*)	1·20	35
4069	25l. *Pinus heldreichii*	1·40	50
4070	40l. Juniper (*Juniperus excelsa*)	2·30	1·20
4065/4070 *Set of 6*	....	5·50	2·30

1376 Battle Scene and Mourning Women

1377 Modern Officer's Parade Uniform

(Des I. Bogdanov. Litho)

1996 (1 May). 120th Anniversaries. T **1376** and similar multicoloured design. P 13×13½ (10l.) or 13½×13 (40l.).

4071	10l. Type **1376** (April uprising)	60	25
4072	40l. Khristo Botev and script (poet, death anniv) (horiz)	2·30	1·20

(Des A. Vuchkov. Litho)

1996 (6 May). Military Uniforms. T **1377** and similar vert designs. Multicoloured. P 13.

4073	5l. Type **1377**	20	10
4074	8l. Second World War combat uniform.	30	15
4075	10l. Balkan War uniform	40	20
4076	20l. Guard officer's ceremonial uniform..	95	50
4077	25l. Serbo–Bulgarian War officer's uniform	1·20	60
4078	40l. Russo–Turkish War soldier's uniform	1·70	1·20
4073/4078 *Set of 6*	....	4·25	2·50

1378 Monument

1379 Elisaveta Bagryana (poet)

(Des Ts. Ostoich. Litho)

1996 (13 May). 50th Anniv of the Republic. P 13×13½.
4079 **1378** 10l. multicoloured 60 35

(Des P. Vulchev. Litho)

1996 (29 May). Europa. Famous Women. T **1379** and similar horiz design. Multicoloured. P 13.
4080 10l. Type **1379** .... 2·30 1·20
4081 40l. Katya Popova (opera singer) .... 3·00 1·80

1380 Player

1381 Nikola Stanchev (wrestling, Melbourne 1956)

(Des S. Despodov. Litho)

1996 (4 June). European Football Championship, England. Sheet 71×86 mm containing T **1380** and similar vert design. Multicoloured. P 13.
MS4082 10l. Type **1380**; 15l. Player (different) .... 2·50 2·50

(Des E. Stankev. Litho)

1996 (4 July). Olympic Games, Atlanta (2nd issue). Bulgarian Medal Winners. T **1381** and similar vert designs. Multicoloured. P 13.
4083 5l. Type **1381** 20 10
4084 8l. Boris Georgiev (boxing, Helsinki 1952) 45 20
4085 10l. Ivanka Khristova (putting the shot, Montreal 1976) 70 25
4086 25l. Z. Iordanova and S. Otsetova (double sculls, Montreal 1976) .... 1·50 60
4083/4086 *Set of 4* .... 2·50 1·00
MS4087 89×68 mm. 15l. Olympic stadium, Athens 1896 .... 1·70 1·70

1382 "The Letter" (detail)

1383 Water Flea (*Gammarus arduus*)

(Des A. Sertev. Litho)

1996 (9 July). 250th Birth Anniv of Francisco Goya (painter). T **1382** and similar multicoloured designs. P 13.
4088 5l. Detail of fresco 20 10
4089 8l. Type **1382** 60 35
4090 26l. "3rd of May 1808 in Madrid" (detail) .... 1·50 70
4091 40l. "Neighbours on a Balcony" (detail) ... 2·30 1·20
4088/4091 *Set of 4* .... 4·25 2·10
MS4092 99×73 mm. 10l. "Clothed Maja" (50×26 mm); 15l. "Naked Maja" (50×26 mm). P 13½×13 .... 1·70 1·70

(Des T. Vardzhiev. Litho)

1996 (30 July). Aquatic Life. T **1383** and similar horiz designs. Multicoloured. P 13½×13.
4093 5l. Type **1383** 20 10
4094 10l. Common water louse (*Asellus aquaticus*) 45 20
4095 12l. European river crayfish (*Astacus astacus*) 60 25
4096 25l. Prawn (*Palaemon serratus*) .... 1·00 35
4097 30l. *Cumella limicola* .... 1·20 60
4098 40l. Mediterranean shore crab (*Carcinus mediterraneus*) .... 3·00 1·20
4093/4098 *Set of 6* .... 5·75 2·50

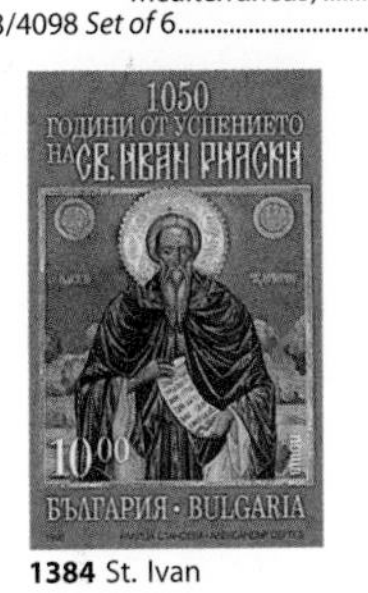

1384 St. Ivan

1385 Tryavna

(Des Ralitsa Stanoeva and A. Sertev. Litho)

1996 (3 Sept). 1050th Death Anniv of Ivan Rilski (founder of Rila Monastery). Sheet 56×87 mm. P 13.
MS4099 **1384** 10l. multicoloured .... 1·00 1·00

(Des Maya Buyukliiska. Litho)

1996 (12 Sept). Houses. T **1385** and similar horiz designs. P 14×13½.
4100 10l. bistre-brown and stone 35 15
4101 15l. bright crimson and chrome yellow... 45 20
4102 30l. deep green and olive-yellow 95 50
4103 50l. bright violet and bright mauve .... 1·60 85
4104 60l. blue-green and bright apple green.. 2·10 1·20
4105 100l. ultramarine and turquoise-blue .... 3·25 1·80
4100/4105 *Set of 6* .... 7·75 4·25
Designs:—15l. Nesebur; 30l. Tryavna (different); 50l. Koprivshtitsa; 60l. Plovdiv; 100l. Koprivshtitsa (different).

1386 *Philadelphia*, 1836

(Des L. Chekhlarov. Litho)

1996 (24 Sept). Steam Locomotives. T **1386** and similar horiz designs. Multicoloured. P 13.
4106 5l. Type **1386** 25 20
4107 10l. *Jenny Lind*, 1847 .... 60 25
4108 12l. *Liverpool*, 1848 .... 70 35
4109 26l. *Anglet*, 1876 .... 1·50 70
4106/4109 *Set of 4* .... 2·75 1·40

1387 Anniversary Emblem and Academy

(Des P. Vulchev. Litho)

1996 (14 Oct). Centenary of National Arts Academy. P 13.
4110 **1387** 15l. black and orange-yellow 95 35

1388 Sword and Miniature from *Chronicle of Ivan Skilitsa*

(Des S. Gruev. Litho)

1996 (21 Oct). 1100th Anniv of Tsar Simeon's Victory over the Turks. T **1388** and similar horiz design. Multicoloured. P 13.
4111 10l. Type **1388** 60 25
a. Horiz pair. Nos. 4111/12 .... 3·25 1·60
4112 40l. Dagger and right-hand detail of miniature .... 2·30 1·20
Nos. 4111/12 were issued together in horizontal *se-tenant* pairs within the sheet, each pair forming a composite design.

1389 Fish and Diver (Dilyana Lokmadzhieva)

1390 Christmas Tree

(Des M. Kolchev. Litho)

1996 (18 Nov). 50th Anniv of United Nations Children's Fund. Children's Paintings. T **1389** and similar horiz designs. Multicoloured. P 13.
4113 7l. Type **1389** 45 25
4114 15l. Circus (Velislava Dimitrova) 95 50
4115 20l. Man and artist's pallet (Miglena Nikolova) .... 1·30 60
4116 60l. Family meal (Darena Dencheva) .... 3·75 1·90
4113/4116 *Set of 4* .... 5·75 3·00

(Des Maiya Cholakova. Litho)

1996 (26 Nov). Christmas. T **1390** and similar vert design. Multicoloured. P 13×13½.
4117 15l. Type **1390** 80 35
4118 60l. Star over basilica and Christmas tree 3·50 1·80

1391 "Zograf Monastery"

1392 Pointer

(Des S. Kasurov. Litho)

1996 (11 Dec). Birth Centenary of Tsanko Lavrenov (painter). P 13.
4119 **1391** 15l. multicoloured 80 35

(Des V. Paunov. Litho)

1997 (25 Feb). Puppies. T **1392** and similar horiz designs. Multicoloured. P 13.
4120 5l. Type **1392** 25 25
4121 7l. Chow chow 35 20
4122 25l. Carakachan dog .... 1·20 60
4123 50l. Basset hound .... 2·30 1·20
4120/4123 *Set of 4* .... 3·75 2·00

1393 Bell

1394 Man drinking

(Des Krasimira Despotova. Litho)

1997 (10 Mar). 150th Birth Anniv of Alexander Graham Bell (telephone pioneer). P 13.
4124 **1393** 30l. multicoloured 95 50

(Des K. Kunev. Litho)

1997 (20 Mar). Birth Centenary of Ivan Milev (painter). T **1394** and similar vert designs showing murals from Kazaluk. Multicoloured. P 13.
4125 5l. Type **1394** 20 15
4126 15l. Woman praying 45 25
4127 30l. Reaper 60 50
4128 60l. Mother and child .... 1·70 95
4125/4128 *Set of 4* .... 2·75 1·70

1395 Lady March (symbol of spring)

1396 Konstantin Kisimov in Character

(Des Tekla Aleksieva. Litho)

1997 (14 Apr). Europa. Tales and Legends. T **1395** and similar vert design. Multicoloured. P 13×13½.
4129 120l. Type **1395** .... 3·00 1·20
4130 600l. St. George (national symbol) .... 2·30 1·20

(Des I. Bogdanov. Litho)

1997 (16 Apr). Birth Centenary of Konstantin Kisimov (actor). P 13.
4131 **1396** 120l. multicoloured 25 25

1397 Heinrich von Stephan

1398 Old Town, Nesebur

(Des M. Kolchev. Litho)

1997 (21 Apr). Death Centenary of Heinrich von Stephan (founder of Universal Postal Union). P 13.
4132 **1397** 60l. multicoloured 25 25

(Des Maya Buyukliiska. Litho)

1997 (2 May). Historic Sights. T **1398** and similar vert designs. P 13½×14.
4133 80l. reddish brown and black 10 10
4134 200l. bright violet and black 25 10
4135 300l. yellow and black 35 25
4136 500l. dull yellowish green and black 60 35
4137 600l. yellow and black 80 50
4138 1000l. orange and black .... 1·40 85

4133/4138	*Set of* 6	3·25	1·90

Designs:—200l. Sculpture, Ivanovské Church; 300l. Christ (detail of icon), Boyana Church; 500l. Horseman (stone relief), Madara; 600l. Figure of woman (carving from sarcophagus), Sveshary; 1000l. Tomb decoration, Kazanlak.

1399 Gaetano Donizetti

(Des P. Bulchev. Litho)

1997 (29 May). Composers' Anniversaries. T **1399** and similar horiz designs. Multicoloured. P 13½×13.

4139	120l. Type **1399** (birth bicentenary)	45	35
	a. Sheetlet of 4. Nos. 4139/42	1·90	
4140	120l. Franz Schubert (birth bicentenary)	45	35
4141	120l. Felix Mendelssohn-Bartholdy (150th death anniv)	45	35
4142	120l. Johannes Brahms (death centenary)	45	35
4139/4142	*Set of* 4	1·60	1·30

Nos. 4139/42 were issued together in *se-tenant* sheetlets of four stamps.

1400 *Trifolium rubens*

1401 Anniversary Emblem

(Des Mladena Elezova. Litho)

1997 (24 June). Flowers in the Red Book. T **1400** and similar horiz designs. Multicoloured. P 13.

4143	80l. Type **1400**	25	10
4144	100l. *Tulipa hageri*	35	10
4145	120l. *Inula spiraeifolia*	35	25
4146	200l. Thin-leafed peony (*Paeonia tenuifolia*)	80	35
4143/4146	*Set of* 4	1·60	70

(Des S. Iliev and G. Todorov. Litho)

1997 (29 June). 50th Anniv of Civil Aviation. P 13.

4147	**1401**	120l. multicoloured	35	25

1402 Evlogii Georgiev

1403 Show Jumping and Running

(Des A. Sertev. Litho)

1997 (3 July). Death Centenary of Evlogii Georgiev. P 13.

4148	**1402**	120l. multicoloured	35	25

(Des T. Vardzhiev. Litho)

1997 (25 July). World Modern Pentathlon Championship, Sofia. T **1403** and similar horiz designs. Multicoloured. P 13.

4149	60l. Type **1403**	35	10
4150	80l. Fencing and swimming	35	25
4151	100l. Running and fencing	45	25
4152	120l. Shooting and swimming	60	35
4153	200l. Show jumping and shooting	70	50
4149/4153	*Set of* 5	2·20	1·30

1404 St. Basil's Cathedral

1405 D 2500 M Boat Engine

(Des Konstantina Konstantinova. Litho)

1997 (30 July). 850th Anniv of Moscow and Moskva 97 International Stamp Exhibition. Sheet 87×96 mm. P 13.

MS4154 **1404**	120l. multicoloured	80	60

No. **MS**4154 also contains a label which forms a composite design with the stamp.

(Des O. Gochev. Litho)

1997 (8 Sept). Centenary of Diesel Engine. T **1405** and similar horiz designs. Multicoloured. P 13½×13.

4155	80l. Type **1405**	35	10
4156	100l. D 2900 T tractor engine	50	25
4157	120l. D 3900 A truck engine	60	35
4158	200l. D 2500 K fork-lift truck engine	1·00	50
4155/4158	*Set of* 4	2·20	1·10

1406 Goddess with Mural Crown

(Des T. Vardzhiev. Litho)

1997 (2 Oct). 43rd General Assembly of Atlantic Club, Sofia. T **1406** and similar horiz designs. P 13.

4159	120l. magenta, new blue and bright ultramarine	50	35
	a. Sheetlet of 4. Nos. 4159/62	2·10	
4160	120l. emerald, new blue and bright ultramarine	50	35
4161	120l. bistre-brown, new blue and bright ultramarine	50	35
4162	120l. bright violet, new blue and bright ultramarine	50	35
4159/4162	*Set of* 4	1·80	1·30

Designs:—No. 4160, Eagle on globe; 4161, Venue; 4162, Venue (different).

Nos. 4159/62 were issued together in *se-tenant* sheetlets of four stamps.

1407 Cervantes and Don Quixote with Sancho

(Des S. Deslodov. Litho)

1997 (15 Oct). 450th Birth Anniv of Miguel de Cervantes (writer). P 13.

4163	**1407**	120l. multicoloured	50	25

1408 Asen Raztsvetnikov

1409 Fragment of Tombstone

(Des P. Petrunov. Litho)

1997 (5 Nov). Birth Centenary of Asen Raztsvetnikov (writer and translator). P 13.

4164	**1408**	120l. multicoloured	50	25

(Des K. Gogov. Litho)

1997 (18 Nov). Millenary of Coronation of Tsar Samuel. T **1409** and similar horiz design. Multicoloured. P 13½×13.

4165	120l. Type **1409**	50	25
	a. Horiz pair. Nos. 4165/6	3·25	1·60
4166	600l. Tsar Samuel and knights in battle	2·40	1·20

Nos. 4165/6 were issued together in horizontal *se-tenant* pairs within the sheet.

1410 Star and Houses forming Christmas Tree

1411 Speed Skating

(Des I. Ugrinova. Litho)

1997 (8 Dec). Christmas. T **1410** and similar vert design. Multicoloured. P 13×13½.

4167	120l. Type **1410**	50	25
4168	600l. Stable with Christmas tree roof	2·20	1·20

(Des E. Stankev. Litho)

1997 (17 Dec). Winter Olympic Games, Nagano, Japan (1998). T **1411** and similar horiz designs. Multicoloured. P 13½×13.

4169	60l. Type **1411**	25	10
4170	80l. Skiing	35	20
4171	120l. Shooting (biathlon)	50	25
4172	600l. Ice skating	3·00	1·90
4169/4172	*Set of* 4	3·75	2·20

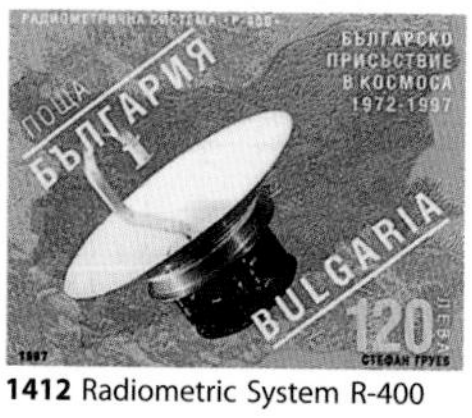

1412 Radiometric System R-400

(Des S. Gruev. Litho)

1997 (22 Dec). 25th Anniv of Bulgarian Space Experiments. Sheet 87×68 mm. P 13.

MS4173 **1412**	120l. multicoloured	1·20	1·20

1413 State Arms

1414 Khristo Botev (after B. Petrov)

(Des K. Gogov. Litho)

1997 (22 Dec). P 13½×13.

4174	**1413**	120l. multicoloured	40	25

(Des B. Mavrodinov. Litho)

1998 (6 Jan). 150th Birth and 120th Death (1996) Anniv of Khristo Botev (poet and revolutionary). P 13.

4175	**1414**	120l. multicoloured	40	25

1415 Bertolt Brecht

1416 Arrows

(Des S. Deslodov. Litho)

1998 (10 Feb). Birth Centenary of Bertolt Brecht (playwright).

4176	**1415**	120l. multicoloured	40	25

(Des P. Petrunov. Litho)

1998 (13 Feb). Centenary of Bulgarian Telegraph Agency. P 13.

4177	**1416**	120l. multicoloured	40	25

1417 Swallow at Window

1418 Tsar Alexander II

(Des B. Kitanov. Litho)

1998 (24 Feb). 120th Birth Anniv of Aleksandur Bozhinov (children's illustrator). T **1417** and similar horiz designs. P 13½×13.

4178	120l. Type **1417**	40	15
	a. Sheetlet of 4. Nos. 4178/81	1·70	
4179	120l. Blackbird with backpack on branch	40	15
4180	120l. Father Frost and children	40	15
4181	120l. Maiden Rositsa in field holding hands up to rain	40	15
4178/4181	*Set of* 4	1·40	55

Nos. 4178/81 were issued together in *se-tenant* sheetlets of four stamps.

(Des N. Pekarev. Litho)

1998 (27 Feb). 120th Anniv of Liberation from Turkey. T **1418** and similar vert design. Multicoloured. P 13.

4182	120l. Type **1418**	40	15
	a. Pair. Nos. 4182/3	2·75	1·20
4183	600l. Independence monument, Ruse	2·00	95

Nos. 4182/3 were issued together in *se-tenant* pairs within the sheet.

1419 Christ ascending and Hare pulling Cart of Eggs

1420 Torch Bearer

(Des V. Vulkanov. Litho)

1998 (27 Mar). Easter. P 13×13½.

4184	**1419**	120l. multicoloured	40	25

(Des Maya Buyukliiska. Litho)

1998 (30 Mar). 75th Anniv of Bulgarian Olympic Committee. P 13.

4185	**1420**	120l. multicoloured	40	25

1421 Map of Participating Countries

(Des S. Krustev. Litho)

1998 (24 Apr). Phare International Programme for Telecommunications and Post. P 13.

4186 **1421** 120l. multicoloured 40 25

1422 Girls in Folk Costumes

ПЪРВИ
ЗЛАТЕН МЕДАЛ
ЗА БЪЛГАРИЯ

Е. ДАФОВСКА
(**1423**)

(Des M. Konstantinova. Litho)

1998 (27 Apr). Europa. National Festivals. T **1422** and similar horiz design. Multicoloured. P 13.

4187 120l. Type **1422** .... 1·40 70
4188 600l. Boys wearing dance masks .... 3·50 2·75

1998 (29 Apr). Winning of Gold Medal in 15km Biathlon by Ekaterina Dafovska at Winter Olympic Games, Nagano. No. 4171 optd with T **1423**.

4189 **1423** 120l. multicoloured .... 4·00 4·00

1424 "Dante and Virgil in Hell"

1425 Footballer and Club Badge

(Des A. Sertev. Litho)

1998 (30 Apr). Birth Bicentenary of Eugène Delacroix (artist). P 13½×13.

4190 **1424** 120l. multicoloured 40 25

(Des Ts. Ostoich. Litho)

1998 (15 May). 50th Anniv of TsSKA Football Club. P 13.

4191 **1425** 120l. multicoloured 40 25

1426 European Tabby

1427 "Oh, You are Jealous!"

(Des Konstantina Konstantinova. Litho)

1998 (28 May). Cats. T **1426** and similar vert designs. Multicoloured. P 13×13½.

4192 60l. Type **1426** 15 10
4193 80l. Siamese 25 15
4194 120l. Exotic shorthair 40 25
4195 600l. Birman .... 2·20 1·10
4192/4195 *Set of 4* .... 2·75 1·40

(Des R. Kolev. Litho)

1998 (4 June). 150th Birth Anniv of Paul Gauguin (artist). P 13.

4196 **1427** 120l. multicoloured 40 25

1428 Neofit Khilendarski-Bozveli

1429 Tackling

(Des Ralitsa Stanoeva. Litho)

1998 (4 June). 150th Death Anniv of Neofit Khilendarski-Bozveli (priest and writer). P 13.

4197 **1428** 120l. multicoloured 40 25

(Des O. Gochev. Litho)

1998 (10 June). World Cup Football Championship, France. T **1429** and similar horiz designs. Multicoloured. P 13½×13.

4198 60l. Type **1429** 15 10
4199 80l. Players competing for ball 25 15
4200 120l. Players and ball 40 25
4201 600l. Goalkeeper .... 2·20 1·10
4198/4201 *Set of 4* .... 2·75 1·40
MS4202 68×91 mm. 120l. Lion, ball and Eiffel Tower 1·40 1·40

1430 A. Aleksandrov

(Des P. Petrunov. Litho)

1998 (17 June). Tenth Anniv of Second Soviet–Bulgarian Space Flight. P 13.

4203 **1430** 120l. multicoloured 55 25

1431 Vasco da Gama

(Des Ya. Gyuzelev. Litho)

1998 (23 June). Expo '98 World's Fair, Lisbon. 500th Anniv of Vasco da Gama's Voyage to India. T **1431** and similar horiz design. Multicoloured. P 13.

4204 600l. Type **1431** .... 2·30 70
a. Sheetlet. Nos. 4204/5 plus two labels 4·75 1·50
4205 600l. *São Gabriel* (Vasco da Gama's ship) ... 2·30 70

Nos. 4204/5 were issued together in sheetlets of two stamps and two labels, forming a composite design.

1432 Focke Wulf FW 61, 1937

(Des E. Stankev. Litho)

1998 (7 July). Helicopters. T **1432** and similar horiz designs. Multicoloured. P 13.

4206 80l. Type **1432** 25 10
4207 100l. Sikorsky R-4, 1943 .... 40 15
4208 120l. Mil Mi-V12, 1970 .... 55 25
4209 200l. McDonnell-Douglas MD-900, 1995 .. 80 40
4206/4209 *Set of 4* .... 1·80 80

1433 Mediterranean Monk Seal (*Monachus monachus*)

(Des Krasimira Despotova. Litho)

1998 (14 July). International Year of the Ocean. Sheet 67×88 mm. P 13.

MS4210 **1433** 120l. multicoloured .... 4·75 4·75

1434 Dimitur Talev

1435 Aleksandur Malinov (Prime Minister, 1931)

(Des S. Daskalov. Litho)

1997 (14 Sept). Birth Centenary of Dimitur Talev (writer). P 13.

4211 **1434** 180l. multicoloured 70 40

(Des Kh. Zhablyanov. Litho)

1998 (22 Sept). 90th Anniv of Independence. P 13.

4212 **1435** 180l. black, slate-blue and lemon ... 70 40

1436 *Limenitis redukta* and *Ligularia sibirica*

1437 Khristo Smirnenski

(Des Z. Stoyanov. Litho)

1998 (24 Sept). Butterflies and Flowers. T **1436** and similar vert designs. Multicoloured. P 13.

4213 60l. Type **1436** 10 10
4214 180l. Painted lady (*Vanessa cardui*) and *Anthemis macrantha* 70 25
4215 200l. Red admiral (*Vanessa atalanta*) and *Trachelium jacquinii* 80 40
4216 600l. *Anthocharis gruneri* and *Geranium tuberosum* .... 2·20 1·20
4213/4216 *Set of 4* .... 3·50 1·80

(Des Kh. Zhablyanov. Litho)

1998 (29 Sept). Birth Centenary of Khristo Smirnenski (writer). P 13.

4217 **1437** 180l. multicoloured 70 40

1438 Silhouette of Man

(Des Ya. Vasev. Litho)

1998 (26 Oct). 50th Anniv of Universal Declaration of Human Rights. P 13.

4218 **1438** 180l. multicoloured 70 40

1439 Giordano Bruno

(Des T. Ushev. Litho)

1998 (26 Oct). 450th Birth Anniv of Giordano Bruno (scholar). P 13.

4219 **1439** 180l. multicoloured 70 40

1440 Man diving through Heart ("I Love You")

(Des B. Dimovski. Litho)

1998 (1 Nov). Greetings Stamps. T **1440** and similar multicoloured designs. P 13.

4220 180l. Type **1440** 70 40
4221 180l. Making wine (holiday) (vert) 70 40
4222 180l. Man in chalice (birthday) (vert) 70 40
4223 180l. Waiter serving wine (name day) (vert) 70 40
4220/4223 *Set of 4* .... 2·50 1·40

1441 Madonna and Child

1442 Ivan Geshov

(Des M. Tsvetkova and Maria Aimitrova. Litho)

1998 (2 Dec). Christmas. P 13½×13.

4224 **1441** 180l. multicoloured 70 40

(Des St. Kunchev and L. Metodiev. Litho)

1999 (8 Feb). 150th Birth Anniv of Ivan Evstratiev Geshov (politician). P 13.

4225 **1442** 180l. multicoloured 70 40

1443 National Assembly Building, Sofia

(Des G. Yankov (4226), S. Krustev (4227), N. Tsachev (4228), N. Pekarev (4229), O. Gochev (4230), Ya. Zhablyanov (4231). Litho)

1999 (10 Feb). 120th Anniv of Third Bulgarian State. T **1443** and similar horiz designs. Multicoloured. P 13.

4226	180l. Type **1443**	70	40
	a. Sheetlet of 6. Nos. 4226/31	4·50	
4227	180l. Council of Ministers	70	40
4228	180l. Statue of Justice (Supreme Court of Appeal)	70	40
4229	180l. Coins (National Bank)	70	40
4230	180l. Army	70	40
4231	180l. Lion emblem of Sofia and lamp post	70	40
4226/4231 *Set of 6*		3·75	2·20

Nos. 4226/31 were issued together in *se-tenant* sheetlets of six stamps.

1444 Georgi Karakashev (stage designer) and Set of *Kismet*

(Des T. Ushev (180l.), L. Metodiev (200l.), Ya. Gyuzelev (300l.), G. Atanasov (600l.). Litho)

1999 (12 Mar). Birth Centenaries. T **1444** and similar horiz designs. Multicoloured. P 13.

4232	180l. Type **1444**	55	25
4233	200l. Bencho Obreshkov (artist) and "Lodki"	70	35
4234	300l. Score and Asen Naidenov (conductor of Sofia Opera)	80	40
4235	600l. Pancho Vladigerov (composer) and score of *Vardar*	1·90	95
4232/4235 *Set of 4*		3·50	1·80

1445 Rainbow Lory (*Trichoglossus haematodus*)

(Des E. Stankev. Litho)

1999 (15 Mar). Bulgaria '99 European Stamp Exhibition. Parrots. Sheet 100×110 mm containing T **1445** and similar vert designs. Multicoloured. P 13×13½.

MS4236 600l. Type **1445**; 600l. Eastern rosella (*Platycercus eximius*); 600l. Budgerigar (*Melopsittacus undulates*) 600l. Green-winged macaw (*Ara chloroptera*) ..... 12·00 12·00

1446 Sun and Emblem

(Des T. Likho. Litho)

1999 (29 Mar). 50th Anniv of North Atlantic Treaty Organisation. P 13.

4237	**1446**	180l. multicoloured	55	25

1447 Decorated Eggs

(Des Maglena Konstantinova. Litho)

1999 (1 Apr). Easter. P 13½×13.

4238	**1447**	180l. multicoloured	55	25

1448 Duck and Ropotamo Reserve

(Des Mladena Elezova. Litho)

1999 (13 Apr). Europa. Parks and Gardens. T **1448** and similar horiz design. Multicoloured. P 13.

4239	180l. Type **1448**	95	40
4240	600l. Central Balkan National Park	2·40	2·00

1449 Albrecht Dürer (self-portrait) and Nuremberg

(Des R. Kolev. Litho)

1999 (15 Apr). iBRA '99 International Stamp Exhibition, Nuremberg, Germany. P 13.

4241	**1449**	600l. multicoloured	2·00	95

No. 4241 was issued in sheetlets of three stamps and three labels showing Bavaria 1849 1k. stamp and different engravings of a town.

1450 Anniversary Emblem

(Des S. Daskalov. Litho)

1999 (5 May). 50th Anniv of Council of Europe. P 13.

4242	**1450**	180l. multicoloured	1·40	70

1451 Honoré de Balzac (novelist)

(Des V. and Marina Kitanov. Litho)

1999 (18 May). Birth Anniversaries. T **1451** and similar horiz designs. Multicoloured. P 13.

4243	180l. Type **1451** (bicentenary)	55	15
4244	200l. Johann Wolfgang von Goethe (poet and playwright) (250th anniv)	95	25
4245	300l. Aleksandr Pushkin (poet) (bicentenary)	1·10	55
4246	600l. Diego de Silva Velázquez (painter) (400th anniv)	2·00	95
4243/4246 *Set of 4*		4·25	1·70

1452 Penny Farthing

1453 Sts. Cyril and Methodius

(Des Kh. Zhablyanov. Litho)

1999 (1 June). Bicycles. T **1452** and similar horiz designs. Multicoloured. P 13.

4247	180l. Type **1452**	55	10
4248	200l. Road racing bicycles	70	15
4249	300l. Track racing bicycles	1·10	40
4250	600l. Mountain bike	2·00	70
4247/4250 *Set of 4*		4·00	1·20

(Des Ivelina Velinova. Litho)

1999 (15 June). Bulgaria '99 European Stamp Exhibition, Sofia. 19th-century Icons of Sts. Cyril and Methodius. Sheet 100×110 mm containing T **1453** and similar vert designs. Multicoloured. P 13×13½.

MS4251 600l. Type **1453**; 600l. St. Cyril with scroll and staff and St. Methodius; 600l. Sts. Cyril and Methodius with scrolls; 600l. St. Cyril with crucifix, St. Methodius and Christ ..... 11·00 11·00

See also Nos. **MS**4265 and **MS**4272.

Currency Reform

1000 (old) Lev = 1 (new) Lev

1454 Sopot Monastery Fountain

1455 *Oxytropis urumovii*

(Des P. Petrunov. Litho)

1999 (5 July)–**2003**. Fountains. T **1454** and similar vert designs. P 13½×14.

4252	1st. light brown	15	10
	a. Perf 12½ (with one diamond-shaped hole on each horiz side) (11.02)	15	10
4254	8st. deep blue-green and black (22.11.99)	15	10
	a. Perf 12½ (with one diamond-shaped hole on each horiz side) (3.03)	15	10
4255	10st. deep brown	40	10
	a. Perf 12½ (with one diamond-shaped hole on each horiz side) (11.02)	40	10
4257	18st. new blue	55	15
	a. Perf 12½ (with one diamond-shaped hole on each horiz side) (11.02)	55	15
4258	20st. bright blue (3.8.99)	55	25
	a. Perf 12½ (with one diamond-shaped hole on each horiz side) (11.02)	55	25
4262	60st. lake-brown and black (22.11.99)	1·60	70
	a. Perf 12½ (with one diamond-shaped hole on each horiz side) (3.03)	3·00	1·30
4252/4262 *Set of 6*		5·75	2·40

Designs:—8st. Peacock Fountain, Karlovo; 10st. Peev Fountain, Kopivshtitsa; 18st. Sandanski Fountain; 20st. Eagle Owl Fountain, Karlovo; 60st. Fountain, Sokolski Monastery.

Numbers have been left for additions to this series.

(Des Krasimira Despotova. Litho)

1999 (20 July). Bulgaria '99 European Stamp Exhibition, Sofia (2nd issue). Flowers in Pirin National Park. Sheet 109×100 mm containing T **1455** and similar horiz designs. Multicoloured. P 13½×13.

MS4265 60st. Type **1455**; 60st. Bellflower (*Campanula transsilvanica*); 60st. Iris (*Iris reichenbachii*); 60st. Spotted gentian (*Gentiana punctata*) ..... 13·50 13·50

1456 Cracked Green Russula (*Russula virenscens*)

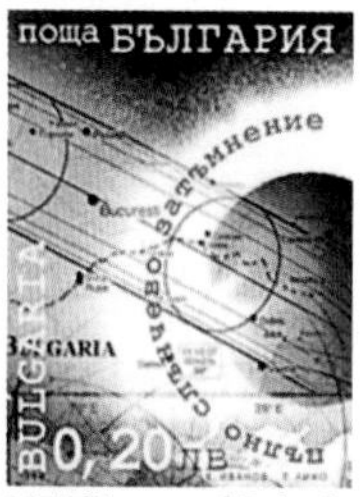

1457 Diagram of Path of Eclipse

(Des Konstantina Konstantinova. Litho)

1999 (27 July). Fungi. T **1456** and similar horiz designs. Multicoloured. P 13½×13.

4266	10st. Type **1456**	40	10
	a. Sheetlet of 4. Nos. 4266/9	4·25	
4267	18st. Field mushroom (*Agaricus campestris*)	55	15
4268	20st. *Hygrophorus russula*	80	25
4269	60st. Wood blewit (*Lepista nuda*)	2·20	55
4266/4269 *Set of 4*		3·50	95

Nos. 4266/9 were issued together in *se-tenant* sheetlets of four stamps.

(Des E. Ivanov and T. Likho. Litho)

1999 (10 Aug). Solar Eclipse (11 Aug 1999). Sheet 90×90 mm. P 13.

MS4270 **1457** 20st. multicoloured ..... 2·00 2·00

1458 Four-leaved Clover

1459 1884 25st. Postage Due Stamp

(Des Ralitza Karapanteva. Litho)

1999 (23 Sept). Centenary of Organised Peasant Movement. P 13.

4271	**1458**	18st. multicoloured	40	25

(Des O. Gochev. Litho)

1999 (5 Oct). Bulgaria '99 European Stamp Exhibition, Sofia (3rd issue). 125th Anniv of Universal Postal Union. Sheet 110×102 mm containing T **1459** and similar vert designs. Multicoloured. P 13×13½.

MS4272 60st. Type **1459**; 60st. Dove and hand with letter; 60st. Globe and left half of messenger; 60st. Right half of messenger with letter and globe ..... 11·00 11·00

The stamps form a composite design of the Bulgarian lion.

1460 Lesser Grey Shrike (*Lanius minor*)

1461 Greek Tortoise (*Testudo graeca*)

(Des Z. Stoyanov. Litho)

1999 (6 Oct). Song Birds and their Eggs. T **1460** and similar vert designs. Multicoloured. P 13.

4273	8st. Type **1460**	25	10
4274	18st. Mistle thrush (*Turdus viscivorus*)	55	15
4275	20st. Dunnock (*Prunella modularis*)	70	25
4276	60st. Ortolan bunting (*Emberiza hortulana*)	1·90	80
4273/4276 *Set of 4*		3·00	1·20

(Des P. Petrunov. Litho)

1999 (8 Oct). Reptiles. T **1461** and similar horiz designs. Multicoloured. P 13.

4277	10st. Type **1461**	40	10
4278	18st. Swamp turtle (*Emys orbicularis*)	55	15
4279	30st. Hermann's tortoise (*Testudo hermanni*)	95	40
4280	60st. Caspian turtle (*Mauremys caspica*)	1·90	80
4277/4280 *Set of 4*		3·50	1·30

1462 Boxing (16 medals)

(Des G. Gadelev. Litho)

1999 (10 Oct). Bulgarian Olympic Medal Winning Sports. T **1462** and similar horiz designs. Multicoloured. P 13.

4281	10st. Type **1462**	40	10
4282	20st. High jumping (17 medals)	70	25
4283	30st. Weightlifting (31 medals)	95	40
4284	60st. Wrestling (60 medals)	1·90	80
4281/4284 *Set of 4*		3·50	1·40

1463 Police Light and Emblem

1464 Jug

(Des M. Chankov. Litho)

1999 (8 Nov). Tenth European Police Conference. P 13.

4285	**1463**	18st. multicoloured	40	25

(Des Maiya Cholakova. Litho)

1999 (15 Nov)–**2002**. Gold Artefacts from Panagyurishte. T **1464** and similar vert designs. P 13½×14.

4286	2st. yellow-brown and deep green	10	10
	a. Perf 12½ (with one diamond-shaped hole on each horiz side) (11.02)	10	10
4287	3st. yellow-brown and deep turquoise-green	10	10
	a. Perf 12½ (with one diamond-shaped hole on each horiz side) (11.02)	10	10
4288	5st. yellow-brown and deep ultramarine	10	10
	a. Perf 12½ (with one diamond-shaped hole on each horiz side) (11.02)	10	10
4289	30st. yellow-brown and reddish violet	70	25
	a. Perf 12½ (with one diamond-shaped hole on each horiz side) (11.02)	70	25
4290	1l. yellow-brown and deep rose-red	2·40	1·40
	a. Perf 12½ (with one diamond-shaped hole on each horiz side) (2.02)	2·40	1·40
4286/4290 *Set of 5*		3·00	1·80

Designs:—3st. Human figures around top of drinking horn; 5st. Bottom of chamois-shaped drinking horn; 30st. Decorated handle and spout; 1l. Head-shaped jug.

1465 Virgin and Child

1466 Scout beside Fire

(Des K. Andreev. Litho)

1999 (22 Nov). Christmas. Religious Icons. T **1465** and similar vert design. Multicoloured. P 13.

4291	18st. Type **1465**	40	25
4292	60st. Jesus Christ	1·80	80

(Des Tekla Aleksieva. Litho)

1999 (6 Dec). Scouts. T **1466** and similar horiz designs. Multicoloured. P 13.

4293	10st. Type **1466**	40	15
4294	18st. Scout helping child	55	25
4295	30st. Scout saluting	80	40
4296	60st. Girl and boy scouts	1·60	80
4293/4296 *Set of 4*		3·00	1·40

1467 Emblem

1468 Emblem and Flag

(Des T. Likho. Litho)

1999 (21 Dec). Expo 2005 World's Fair, Aichi, Japan. P 13.

4297	**1467**	18st. multicoloured	55	25

(Des S. Daskalov. Litho)

2000 (15 Feb). Bulgarian Membership of European Union. P 13.

4298	**1468**	18st. multicoloured	1·40	70

1469 White Stork (*Ciconia ciconia*)

1470 Peter Beron and Scientific Instruments

(Des V. Paunov. Litho)

2000 (22 Mar). Endangered Species. Sheet 80×60 mm. P 13.

MS4299	**1469**	60st. multicoloured	2·75	2·75

(Des S. Petrunov (4300), L. Karaleev (4301) and A. Atanasov (4302). Litho)

2000 (30 Mar). Birth Anniversaries. T **1470** and similar horiz designs. Multicoloured. P 13.

4300	10st. Type **1470** (scientist, bicentenary)	40	15
4301	20st. Zakhari Stoyanov (writer, 150th anniv)	70	25
4302	50st. Kolyo Ficheto (architect, bicentenary)	1·40	55
4300/4302 *Set of 3*		2·30	85

1471 Madonna and Child with Circuit Board

(Des R. Kolev. Litho)

2000 (26 Apr). Europa. T **1471** and similar horiz designs. Multicoloured. P 13.

4303	18st. Type **1471**	1·40	70
4304	60st. Madonna and Child (Leonardo da Vinci) with circuit board	2·75	2·50

1472 Judo

(Des B. Filchev. Litho)

2000 (28 Apr). Olympic Games, Sydney. T **1472** and similar horiz designs. Multicoloured. P 13.

4305	10st. Type **1472**	25	10
4306	18st. Tennis	40	15
4307	20st. Pistol shooting	55	25
4308	60st. Long jump	1·60	80
4305/4308 *Set of 4*		2·50	1·20

1473 *Puss in Boots* (Charles Perrault)

1474 "Friends" (detail) (Assen Vasiliev)

(Des Al. Aleksov. Litho)

2000 (23 May). Children's Fairytales. T **1473** and similar horiz designs. Multicoloured. P 13½×13.

4309	18st. Type **1473**	55	40
	a. Sheetlet of 3. Nos. 4309/11 plus 3 labels	1·80	
4310	18st. *Little Red Riding Hood* (Brothers Grimm)	55	40
4311	18st. *Thumbelina* (Hans Christian Andersen)	55	40
4309/4311 *Set of 3*		1·50	1·10

Nos. 4309/11 were issued together in *se-tenant* sheetlets of three stamps and three labels.

(Des M. Kolchev. Litho)

2000 (23 May). Artists' Birth Centenaries. T **1474** and similar horiz designs. Multicoloured. P 13.

4312	18st. Type **1474**	55	25
4313	18st. "All Soul's Day (detail) (Pencho Georgiev)	55	25
4314	18st. "Veliko Turnovo" (detail) (Ivan Khristov)	55	25
4315	18st. "At the Fountain" (sculpture) (detail) (Ivan Funev)	55	25
4312/4315 *Set of 4*		2·00	90

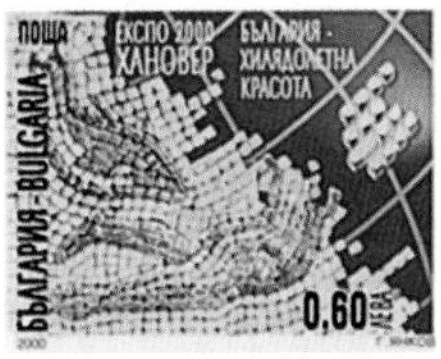

1475 Roman Mosaic (detail), Stara Zagora

(Des G. Yankov. Litho)

2000 (31 May). EXPO 2000, World's Fair, Hanover, Germany. P 13.

4316	**1475**	60st. multicoloured	1·80	70

No. 4316 was issued with a *se-tenant* label.

1476 Johannes Gutenberg (inventor of printing press) and Printed Characters

(Des I. Bogdanov. Litho)

2000 (20 June). Anniversaries. T **1476** and similar horiz designs. Multicoloured. P 13.

4317	10st. Type **1476** (600th birth anniv)	25	10
4318	18st. Johann Sebastian Bach (composer, 250th death anniv)	40	15
4319	20st. Guy de Maupassant (writer, 150th birth anniv)	70	25
4320	60st. Antoine de Saint-Exupéry (writer and aviator, birth centenary)	2·00	55
4317/4320 *Set of 4*		3·00	95

1477 *La Jaune* (Lebaudy-Juillot airship) and Eiffel Tower, 1903

(Des Kh. Aleksiev. Litho)

2000 (3 July). Centenary of First Zeppelin Flight. Airship Development. T **1477** and similar vert designs. Multicoloured. P 13.

4321	10st. Type **1477**	25	10
4322	18st. LZ-13 *Hansa* (Zeppelin airship) over Cologne	40	15
4323	20st. N-1 *Norge* over Rome	70	25
4324	60st. *Graf Zeppelin* over Sofia	2·00	80
4321/4324 *Set of 4*		3·00	1·20

1478 Ivan Vazov and Text

(Des L. Metodiev. Litho)

2000 (9 July). 150th Birth Anniv of Ivan Vazov (writer). P 13.

4325	**1478**	18st. multicoloured	55	25

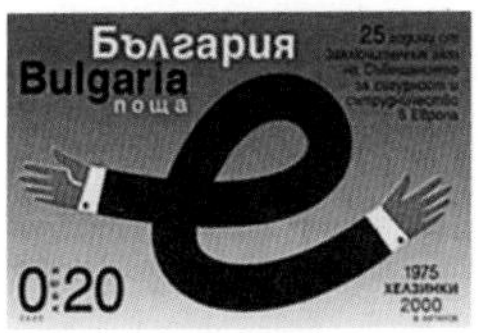

1479 Letter "e" with Hands

1480 St. Atanasii Church, Startsevo

(Des V. Kitanov. Litho)

2000 (19 July). 25th Anniv of Organization for Security and Co-operation in Europe Helsinki Final Act (establishing governing principles). Sheet 68×92 mm containing T **1479** and other similar horiz design. Multicoloured. P 13.

MS4326 20st. Type **1479**; 20st. Three "e's" .... 2·75 2·00

(Des I. Gazdov. Litho)

2000 (1 Sept). Churches. T **1480** and similar horiz designs. P 14×13½.

4327 22st. black and new blue 55 10
a. Perf 12½ (with one diamond-shaped hole on each vert side) (11.02) 55 10
4328 24st. black and bright mauve 70 15
a. Perf 12½ (with one diamond-shaped hole on each vert side) (11.02) 70 15
4329 50st. black and yellow .... 1·40 40
a. Perf 12½ (with one diamond-shaped hole on each vert side) (11.02) .... 1·40 40
4330 65st. black and bright green .... 1·80 70
a. Perf 12½ (with one diamond-shaped hole on each vert side) (11.02) .... 1·80 70
4331 300st. black and pale orange .... 6·75 2·75
4332 500st. black and rose .... 11·00 4·75
4327/4332 *Set of 6* .... 20·00 8·00

Designs:— 24st. St. Clement of Ohrid, Sofia; 50st. Mary of the Ascension, Sofia; 65st. St. Nedelya, Nedelino; 3l. Mary of the Ascension, Sofia, (different); 5l. Mary of the Ascension, Pamporovo.

1481 Ibex (*Capra ibex*)

(Des T. Vardzhiev. Litho)

2000 (25 Sept). Animals. T **1481** and similar horiz designs. Multicoloured. P 13.

4333 10st. Type **1481** 25 10
4334 22st. Argali (*Ovis ammon*) 55 20
4335 30st. European bison (*Bison bonasus*) 70 25
4336 65st. Yak (*Bos grunniens*) .... 1·90 55
4333/4336 *Set of 4* .... 3·00 1·00

1482 Field Gladiolus (*Gladiolus segetum*)

(Des Z. Stoyanov. Litho)

2000 (17 Oct). Spring Flowers. T **1482** and similar vert designs. Multicoloured. P 13×13½.

4337 10st. Type **1482** 25 10
4338 22st. Liverwort (*Hepatica nobilis*) 55 20
4339 30st. Pheasant's eye (*Adonis vernalis*) 80 25
4340 65st. Peacock anemone (*Anemone pavonina*) .... 1·90 55
4337/4340 *Set of 4* .... 3·25 1·00

1483 Crowd and Emblem

1484 Order of Gallantry, 1880

(Des P. Petrunov. Litho)

2000 (3 Nov). 50th Anniv of European Convention on Human Rights. P 13½×13.

4341 **1483** 65st. multicoloured .... 2·00 1·40

(Des S. Kunchev and A. Apostolov. Litho)

2000 (28 Nov). Medals. T **1484** and similar vert designs. Multicoloured. P 13.

4342 12st. Type **1484** 25 10
4343 22st. Order of St. Aleksandur, 1882 .... 70 20
4344 30st. Order of Merit, 1891 .... 80 25
4345 65st. Order of Cyril and Methodius, 1909 .... 2·00 55
4342/4345 *Set of 4* .... 3·50 1·00

1485 Prince Boris-Mihail

1486 Seal

(Des K. Andreev. Litho)

2000 (28 Nov). Bimillenary of Christianity. Sheet 105×83 mm containing T **1485** and similar horiz designs. Multicoloured. P 13½×13.

4346 22st. Type **1485** 70 25
a. Sheetlet of 4. Nos. 4346/9 .... 5·75
4347 22st. St. Sofroni Vrachanski 70 25
4348 65st. Mary and Child (detail) .... 2·00 55
4349 65st. Antim I .... 2·00 55
4346/4349 *Set of 4* .... 4·75 1·40

(Des P. Rashkov. Litho)

2000 (8 Dec). 120th Anniv of Supreme Audit Office. P 13×13½.

4350 **1486** 22st. multicoloured 70 25

1487 Microchip, Planets and "The Proportions of Man" (Leonardo da Vinci)

(Des B. Filichev. Litho)

2001 (8 Jan). New Millennium. Paper with fluorescent fibres. P 13.

4351 **1487** 22st. multicoloured 70 25

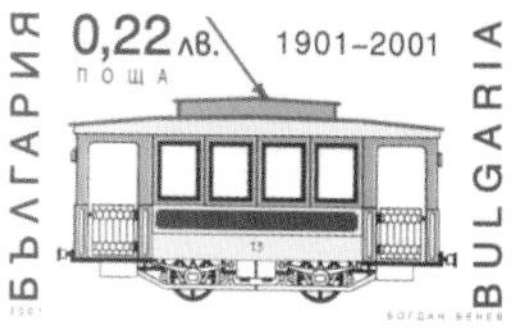

1488 Tram

(Des B. Benev. Litho)

2001 (12 Jan). Centenary of the Electrification of Bulgarian Transport. T **1488** and similar horiz design. Multicoloured. P 13.

4352 22st. Type **1488** 70 25
a. Sheetlet of 4. Nos. 4352/3 each×2 .... 5·75
4353 65st. Train carriages .... 2·00 55

Nos. 4352/3 each×2 were issued together in *se-tenant* sheetlets of four stamps.

1489 Muscat Grapes and Evsinograd Palace

(Des S. Daskaov. Litho)

2001 (7 Feb). Viticulture. T **1489** and similar vert designs. Multicoloured. Paper with fluorescent fibres. P 13.

4354 12st. Type **1489** 25 10
4355 22st. Gumza grapes and Baba Vida Fortress 70 20
4356 30st. Shiroka Melnishka Loza grapes and Melnik Winery 80 25
4357 65st. Mavrud grapes and Asenova Krepost Fortress .... 2·00 55
4354/4357 *Set of 4* .... 3·50 1·00

1490 "@" and Microcircuits

(Des K. Andreev. Litho)

2001 (1 Mar). Information Technology. Sheet 82×95 mm containing T **1490** and similar horiz design. Multicoloured. Paper with fluorescent fibres. P 13.

MS4358 Type **1490**; 65st. John Atanasoff (computer pioneer) and ABC .... 34·00 34·00

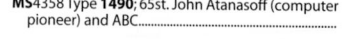

1491 Southern Europe and Emblem

(Des T. Vardzhiev. Litho)

2001 (4 Apr). Tenth Anniv of the Atlantic Club of Bulgaria. Sheet 87×67 mm. Paper with fluorescent fibres. P 13.

MS4359 **1491** 65st. multicoloured .... 5·50 4·00

1492 Eagle and Lakes, Rila

(Des A. Apostolov. Litho)

2001 (18 Apr). Europa. Water Resources. T **1492** and similar vert design. Multicoloured. Paper with fluorescent fibres. P 13.

4360 22st. Type **1492** .... 1·40 1·10
4361 65st. Cave and waterfall, Rhodope .... 26·00 23·00

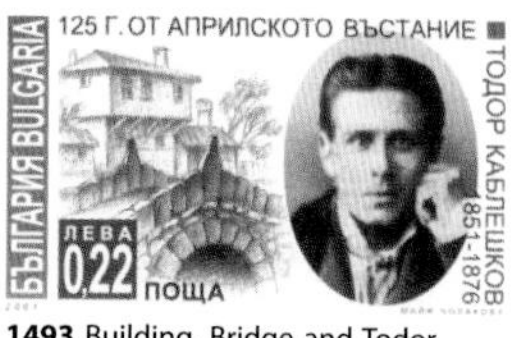

1493 Building, Bridge and Todor Kableschkov

(Des Maiya Cholakova. Litho)

2001 (1 May). 125th Anniversary of the April Uprising and 150th Birth Anniv of Todor Kableschkov (revolutionary leader). Paper with fluorescent fibres. P 13.

4362 **1493** 22st. multicoloured 70 40

1494 Juvenile Egyptian Vulture in Flight

(Des S. Dechev. Litho)

2001 (21 May). Endangered Species. Egyptian Vulture (*Neophron perconpterus*). T **1494** and similar horiz designs. Multicoloured. Paper with fluorescent fibres. P 13.

4363 12st. Type **1494** 40 10
4364 22st. Juvenile landing 70 25
4365 30st. Adult and chick 80 40
4366 65st. Adult and eggs .... 1·90 55
4363/4366 *Set of 4* .... 3·50 1·20

1495 Georgi (Gundy) Asparuchov (footballer)

1496 Rainbow and People

(Des L. Metodiev. Litho)

2001 (29 June). Sportsmen. T **1495** and similar horiz designs. Multicoloured. Paper with fluorescent fibres. P 13.

4367 22st. Type **1495** 70 40
a. Sheetlet of 6. Nos. 4367/9 plus 3 labels .... 7·00
4368 30st. Dancho (Dan) Kolev (wrestler) 80 50
4369 65st. Gen. Krum Lekarski (equestrian) .... 1·90 1·10
4367/4369 *Set of 3* .... 3·00 1·80

Nos. 4367/9 were issued together in *se-tenant* sheetlets of three stamps plus three labels, the stamps arranged in a checkerboard fashion with a label showing each sportsman at left (No. 4368) or right (others).

(Des N. Pekarev. Litho)

2001 (11 July). 50th Anniv United Nations High Commissioner for Refugees. Paper with fluorescent fibres. P 13.

4370 **1496** 65st. multicoloured .... 1·90 65

1497 Alexander Zhendov

(Des I. Bogdanov. Litho)

2001 (24 July). Artists' Birth Centenaries. T **1497** and similar horiz design. Multicoloured. Paper with fluorescent fibres. P 13.

4371 22st. Type **1497** 70 40
4372 65st. Ilya Beshkov .... 2·00 1·20

1498 Court Seal

(Des N. Tachev. Litho)

2001 (3 Oct). Tenth Anniv of Constitutional Court. Paper with fluorescent fibres. P 14×13.

4373 **1498** 25st. multicoloured 70 40

1499 Flags

1500 Children encircling Globe

(Des T. Vardzhiev. Litho)

2001 (5 Oct). North Atlantic Treaty Organization Summit, Sofia. Sheet 116×111 mm containing T **1499** and similar horiz designs. Paper with fluorescent fibres. P 13½×13.

MS4374 12st. Type **1499**; 24st. Streamer of flags; 25st. Flags in upper right semi-circle; 65st. Flags in upper left semi-circle .... 6·75 5·75

(Des M. Doncheva. Litho)

2001 (9 Oct). United Nations Year of Dialogue among Civilizations. Paper with fluorescent fibres. P 13.

4375 **1500** 65st. multicoloured .... 1·80 80

1501 Black Sea Turbot (*Scopthalmus maeoticus*)

1502 The Nativity

(Des Krasimira Despotova. Litho)

2001 (31 Oct). International Day for the Protection of the Black Sea. Sheet 73×91 mm. Paper with fluorescent fibres. P 13.

MS4376 **1501** 65st. multicoloured .... 2·75 2·00

(Des V. Vulkanov. Litho)

2001 (19 Nov). Christmas. Paper with fluorescent fibres. P 13.

4377 **1502** 25st. multicoloured 70 40

1503 Cape Shabla Lighthouse

1504 Icon

(Des B. Kitanov. Litho)

2001 (19 Nov)–**03**. Lighthouses. T **1503** and similar horiz design. Paper with fluorescent fibres. P 14.

4378 25st. scarlet-vermilion and dark green 70 40

a. Perf 12½ (with one diamond-shaped hole on each vert side) (3.03) 70 40

4379 32st. deep blue and chrome-yellow 80 50

a. Perf 12½ (with one diamond-shaped hole on each vert side) (2.03) 80 50

Designs:—32st. Kaliakra Cape lighthouse.

(Des M. Enev. Litho)

2001 (27 Nov). Zographu Monastery, Mount Athos. Sheet 85×105 mm containing T **1504** and similar horiz design. Multicoloured. Paper with fluorescent fibres. P 13.

MS4380 25st. Monastery Buildings; 65st. Type **1504** .... 2·75 2·00

1505 Father Christmas (from film by Al. Zahariev)

2001 (12 Dec). Bulgarian Animation. Paper with fluorescent fibres. Litho. P 13½×13.

4381 **1505** 25c. multicoloured 80 50

No. 4381 was issued in sheetlets of three stamps and three labels.

1506 Vincenzo Bellini

(Des S. Dechev. Litho)

2001 (17 Dec). Birth Bicentenary of Vincenzo Bellini (composer). Paper with fluorescent fibres. P 13.

4382 **1506** 25st. multicoloured 80 50

1507 Crowd and Ancient Calendar

(Des P. Vulchev. Litho)

2001 (21 Dec). Founders of Bulgarian State (1st Series). T **1507** and similar horiz designs. Multicoloured. Paper with fluorescent fibres. P 13.

4383 10st. Type **1507** 25 10

4384 25st. Khans, Kubrat and Asparuh 80 50

4385 30st. Khans, Krum and Omurtag 95 55

4386 65st. King Boris and Tsar Simeon .... 2·00 1·20

4383/4386 *Set of* 4 .... 3·50 2·10

See also Nos. 4424/7, 4456/9, 4511/14, 4559/62 and 4610/13.

1508 "€" Symbol and Stars

(Des V. Kitanov. Litho)

2002 (3 Jan). The Euro (European currency). Paper with fluorescent fibres. P 14×13.

4387 **1508** 65l. multicoloured .... 2·00 1·20

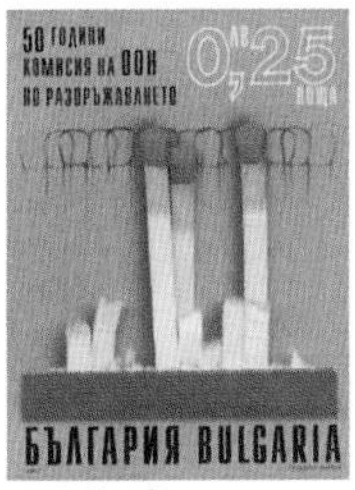

1509 Matches

1510 Limestone Arch

(Des T. Likho. Litho)

2002 (21 Jan). 50th Anniv of United Nations Disarmament Commission. Paper with fluorescent fibres. P 13×14.

4388 **1509** 25f. multicoloured 80 50

(Des Elena Panatsomova. Litho)

2002 (29 Jan). BALKANMAX '02 International Stamp Exhibition. Sheet 95×87 mm containing T **1510** and similar vert design. Multicoloured. Paper with fluorescent fibres. P 13.

MS4389 25f. Type **1510**; 65f. Long-legged buzzard (*Buteo rufinus*) .... 34·00 33·00

1511 Figure Skater

(Des N. Atanasov. Litho)

2002 (5 Feb). Winter Olympic Games, Salt Lake City. T **1511** and similar horiz design. Multicoloured. Paper with fluorescent fibres. P 13.

4390 25f. Type **1511** 80 50

4391 65f. Speed skater .... 2·00 1·20

1512 Station Building and Bearded Penguins

(Des T. Vardzhiev. Litho)

2002 (20 Mar). Tenth National Antarctic Expedition. P 13½×13.

4392 **1512** 25f. multicoloured 80 50

No. 4392 was issued in sheetlets of three stamps plus three labels, the stamps arranged checkerboard fashion.

1513 Performing Elephant

(Des E. Stankev. Litho)

2002 (22 Mar). Europa. Circus. T **1513** and similar horiz design. Multicoloured. Paper with fluorescent fibres. P 13.

4393 25f. Type **1513** 95 55

4394 65f. Clown .... 2·40 1·50

1514 Veselin Stojano

1515 "Illustrated Landscape" (Vasil Barakov)

(Des A. Atanasov. Litho)

2002 (27 Mar). Birth Centenaries. T **1514** and similar horiz design. Multicoloured. paper with fluorescent fibres. P 13.

4395 25f. Type **1514** (composer) 80 50

4396 65f. Angel Karaliechev (writer) 95 55

(Des D. Trendafilov. Litho)

2002 (17 Apr). Art. T **1515** and similar multicoloured designs. Paper with fluorescent fibres. P 13.

4397 10st. Type **1515** 25 10

4398 25st. Book illustration from "Under the Yoke" (novel by Ivan Vazov) (Boris Angulshev) (horiz) 80 50

4399 65st. "The Balcony and Canary" (Ivan Nenov) .... 2·00 1·20

4397/4399 *Set of* 3 .... 2·75 1·60

1516 Stefan Kanchev

(Des D. Tassev. Litho)

2002 (26 Apr). First Death Annivs of Stamp Designers. T **1516** and similar horiz design. Multicoloured. P 13.

4400 25c. Type **1516** 80 50

4401 65c. Alex Popilov .... 2·00 1·20

1517 Melon (*Cucumis melo*)

(Des S. Dechev. Litho)

2002 (8 May). Fruits. T **1517** and similar horiz designs. Multicoloured. Paper with fluorescent fibres. P 13.

4402 10st. Type **1517** 40 25

4403 25st. Watermelon (*Citrullus lanatus*) 80 50

4404 27st. Pumpkin (*Cucurbita pepo*) 90 55

4405 65st. Calabash (*Lagenaria siceraria*) .... 2·00 1·20

4402/4405 *Set of* 4 .... 3·75 2·30

1518 Cock Bird

1519 Pope John Paul II and Monument to Cyril & Methodius

(Des Z. Stoyanov. Litho)

2002 (10 May). Poultry. T **1518** and similar multicoloured designs. Paper with fluorescent fibres. P 13.

4406 10st. Type **1518** 40 25

4407 20st. Leghorn pair (horiz) 70 40

4408 25st. Two cocks fighting (horiz) 80 50

4409 65st. Plymouth Rock pair (inscr "Plimouth Rock") .... 2·00 1·20

4406/4409 *Set of* 4 .... 3·50 2·10

(Des Z. Stoyanov. Litho)

2002 (24 May). Pope John Paul II's Visit to Bulgaria. Paper with fluorescent fibres. P 13.

4410	**1519**	65st. multicoloured	2·00	1·20

1520 Chess Pieces

1521 Flag and Stars

(Des I. Gazdov. Litho)

2002 (27 May). Chess. Sheet 91×71 mm containing T **1520** and similar vert design. Paper with fluorescent fibres. P 13.

MS4411 25c. chocolate, pale cinnamon and black (Type **1520**); 65c. multicoloured (Hand holding pawn) ... 2·75 2·00

(Des S. Daskalov. Litho)

2002 (29 May). Tenth Anniv of Bulgaria's Admission to Council of Europe. Paper with fluorescent fibres. P 13.

4412	**1521**	25st. multicoloured	80	50

1522 Rabbit

1523 *Marie-Luisa* (1st ocean-going liner)

(Des A. Appostolov. Litho)

2002 (12 Aug)–**08**. Woodcarvings by Peter Kuschlev. T **1522** and similar horiz designs. Paper with fluorescent fibres. P 14.

4413	6st. light brown and black	15	10
	a. Perf 12½ (with one diamond-shaped hole on each vert side) (11.02)	15	10
	b. Ordinary paper. Imperf×p13×4 (3.08)	15	10
4414	12st. dull orange and black	40	25
	a. Perf 12½ (with one diamond-shaped hole on each vert side) (11.02)	40	25
	b. Ordinary paper. Imperf×p13×4 (3.08)	40	25
4415	36st. yellow-olive and black	1·10	65
	a. Perf 12½ (with one diamond-shaped hole on each vert side) (11.02)	1·10	65
	b. Ordinary paper. Imperf×p13×4 (3.08)	1·10	65
4416	44st. brown-rose and black	1·40	80
	a. Perf 12½ (with one diamond-shaped hole on each vert side) (11.02)	1·40	80
	b. Ordinary paper. Imperf×p13×4 (3.08)	1·40	80
4413/4416	*Set of* 4	2·75	1·60

Designs:—6st. Type **1522**; 12st. Deer; 36st. Bird; 44st. Boar.

(Des Maglena Konstantinova. Litho)

2002 (18 Oct). Merchant Ships. T **1523** and similar horiz designs. Multicoloured. Paper with fluorescent fibres. P 13.

4417	12st. Type **1523**	40	25
4418	36st. *Persenk* (cargo ship)	1·10	65
4419	49st. *Kaliakra* (sail training ship)	1·60	1·00
4420	65st. *Sofia* (container ship)	2·00	1·20
4417/4420	*Set of* 4	4·50	2·75

1524 Father Christmas and Sun

(Des Bagryana Tasseva. Litho)

2002 (20 Nov). Christmas. Paper with fluorescent fibres. P 13½×13.

4421	**1524**	36st. multicoloured	1·10	65

1525 Flag and NATO Emblem

(Des Ivellina Velinova. Litho)

2002 (21 Nov). Bulgaria's Participation in NATO Conference, Prague. Sheet 85×65 mm. Paper with fluorescent fibres. P 13.

MS4422 **1525** 65st. multicoloured ... 4·00 3·00

1526 Paper Bird

(Des R. Kolev. Litho)

2002 (22 Nov). 30th Anniv of Security and Co-operation in Europe Conference. Sheet 85×60 mm. Paper with fluorescent fibres. P 13.

MS4423 **1526** 65st. multicoloured ... 3·50 2·75

1527 Tsar Samuil

(Des Dea Vulcheva. Litho)

2002 (6 Dec). Founders of Bulgarian State (2nd series). T **1527** and similar horiz designs. Multicoloured. Paper with fluorescent fibres. P 13.

4424	18st. Type **1527**	55	35
4425	36st. Tsars Peter II and Assen	1·10	65
4426	49st. Tsar Kaloyan	1·40	80
4427	65st. Tsar Ivan Assen II	1·90	1·10
4424/4427	*Set of* 4	4·50	2·50

1528 Exhibition Emblem

(Des B. Ionov. Litho)

2003 (10 Jan). Europalia Cultural Exhibition, Belgium. P 13.

4428	**1528**	65l. multicoloured	2·00	1·20

1529 "Rose Pickers" (Stoyan Sotirov)

1530 Space Construction surrounding Earth

(Des K. Gogov. Litho)

2003 (28 Jan). Artists' Birth Centenaries. T **1529** and similar horiz designs. Multicoloured. P 13.

4429	18l. Type **1529**	55	35
4430	36l. "The Blind Fiddler" (Illya Petrov)	1·10	65
4431	65l. "Swineherd" (Zlatyo Boyadjiev)	1·90	1·10
4429/4431	*Set of* 3	3·25	1·90

(Des K. Andreev. Litho)

2003 (7 Feb). Space Exploration. Sheet 104×85 mm. Fluorescent security markings. P 13.

MS4432 **1530** 65l. multicoloured ... 2·75 2·00

1531 Statue of Russian and Bulgarian Soldiers

(Des P. Rashkov. Litho)

2003 (28 Feb). 125th Anniv of Bulgarian State. P 13.

4433	**1531**	36l. multicoloured	1·10	65

1532 Exarch Stefan I, Menorah Candlestick and Dimitar Peshev

(Des T. Vardzhiev. Litho)

2003 (10 Mar). 60th Anniv of Rescue of Bulgarian Jews. P 13.

4434	**1532**	36l. multicoloured	1·10	65

1533 Silhouettes of Birds and Woman

(Des I. Gazdov. Litho)

2003 (17 Mar). Europa. Poster Art. T **1533** and similar horiz design. Multicoloured. P 13.

4435	36l. Type **1533**	1·10	65
	a. Pair. Nos. 4435/6	3·25	1·90
4436	65l. Chicken, legs and farm animals	1·90	1·10

Nos. 4435/6 were issued in vertical *se-tenant* pairs within the sheet.

1534 "Vase with Fifteen Sunflowers"

1535 Pterodactylus

(Des N. Mladenov. Litho)

2003 (19 Mar). 150th Birth Anniv of Vincent van Gogh (artist). Sheet 70×90 mm. P 13.

MS4437 **1534** 65l. multicoloured ... 1·90 1·50

(Des Z. Stoyanov. Litho)

2003 (24 Apr). Dinosaurs. T **1535** and similar horiz designs. Multicoloured. P 13.

4438	30st. Type **1535**	80	50
	a. Horiz strip. Nos. 4438/41	5·50	
4439	36st. Gorgosaurus	1·10	65
4440	49st. Mesosaurus	1·50	90
4441	65st. Monoclonius	1·90	1·10
4438/4441	*Set of* 4	4·75	2·75

Nos. 4438/41 were issued in horizontal *se-tenant* strips of four stamps within the sheet.

1536 *Nymphoides peltata*

(Des B. Kitanov. Litho)

2003 (15 May). Water Plants (1st issue). T **1536** and similar horiz designs. Multicoloured. P 13.

4442	**1536**	36st. multicoloured	1·10	65

See also Nos. 4447/50.

1537 Honey Bee (*Apis mellifera*)

1538 *Butomus umbellatus*

(Des H. Kourouch. Litho)

2003 (17 June). Bees. T **1537** and similar horiz designs. Multicoloured. P 13.

4443	20st. Type **1537**	55	35
4444	30st. *Anthidium manicatum*	80	50
4445	36st. Bumble bee (*Bombus subterraneus*)	95	55
4446	65st. Blue carpenter bee (*Xylocopa violacea*)	1·80	1·10
4443/4446	*Set of* 4	3·75	2·30

(Des Elena Panaiotova. Litho)

2003 (25 July). Water Plants (2nd issue). T **1538** and similar vert designs. Multicoloured. P 13.

4447	20st. Type **1538**	55	35
4448	36st. *Sagirraria sagittifolia*	1·10	65
4449	50st. *Menyanthes trifoliata*	1·50	90
4450	65st. *Iris pseudoacorus*	1·90	1·10
4447/4450	*Set of* 4	4·50	2·75

1539 Gotze Delchev

(Des I. Bogdanov. Litho)

2003 (1 Aug). Death Centenary of Gotze Delchev (revolutionary). Centenary of Macedonian Uprising. P 13.

4451	**1539**	36st. multicoloured	1·10	65

1540 Mountains

(Des L. Methodiev. Litho)

2003 (19 Sept). International Year of Mountains. P 13.
4452 **1540** 65st. multicoloured .... 6·00 4·50
No. 4452 was issued in sheetlets of three stamps and three stamp-size labels showing rivers.

1541 Bulgarian and USA Flags as Bowtie

1542 John Atanasoff

(Des T. Licho. Litho)

2003 (19 Sept). Centenary of Bulgaria–USA Diplomatic Relations. P 13.
4453 **1541** 65st. multicoloured .... 1·90 1·10

(Des H. Aleksiev. Litho)

2003 (3 Oct). Birth Centenary of John Atanasoff (computer pioneer). P 13.
4454 **1542** 65st. multicoloured .... 1·90 1·10
No. 4454 was issued with *se-tenant* stamp-size label.

1543 Pawn and Buildings

1544 Tsar Ivan Alexander

(Des E. Stankev. Litho)

2003 (10 Oct). European Chess Championship, Plovdiv. P 13.
4455 **1543** 65st. multicoloured .... 1·90 1·10

(Des P. Vulcheva. Litho)

2003 (18 Oct–23 Dec). Founders of Bulgarian State (3rd series). T **1544** and similar horiz designs. Multicoloured. P 13.
4456 30st. Type **1544** (23.12) 80 50
4457 45st. Despot Dobrotitsa (23.12) .... 1·20 75
4458 65st. Tsar Ivan Shishman .... 1·90 1·10
4459 89st. Tsar Ivan Sratsimir (23.12) .... 2·20 1·30
4456/4459 *Set of 4* .... 5·50 3·25

1545 Taekwondo

1546 Father Christmas

(Des S. Nenov. Litho)

2003 (27 Oct). 80th Anniv of National Olympic Committee. T **1545** and similar vert designs. Multicoloured. P 13.
4460 20st. Type **1545** 55 35
4461 36st. Mountain biking .... 1·10 65
4462 50st. Softball .... 1·50 90
4463 65st. Canoe slalom .... 1·90 1·10
4460/4463 *Set of 4* .... 4·50 2·75

(Des D. Trendafilov. Litho)

2003 (24 Nov). Christmas. P 13.
4464 **1546** 65st. multicoloured .... 1·90 1·10

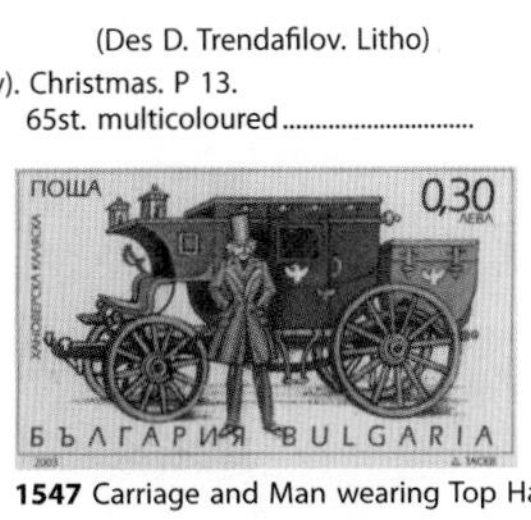

1547 Carriage and Man wearing Top Hat

(Des D. Tasev. Litho)

2003 (28 Nov). Carriages. T **1547** and similar horiz designs. Multicoloured. P 13.
4465 30st. Type **1547** 80 50
4466 36st. Closed carriage with woman passenger .... 1·10 65
4467 50st. State coach, woman and dog .... 1·50 90
4468 65st. Couple and large carriage .... 1·90 1·10
4465/4468 *Set of 4* .... 4·75 2·75

1548 FIFA Centenary Emblem

1549 Eye, Square, Compass and Statue

(Des M. Yaranov. Litho)

2003 (12 Dec). Centenary of FIFA (Fédèration Internationale de Football Association). T **1548** and similar multicoloured designs. P 13.
4469 20st. Type **1548** 55 35
4470 25st. Early players 70 40
4471 36st. Early players and rules .... 1·10 65
4472 50st. FIFA fair play trophy (vert) .... 1·40 80
4473 65st. FIFA world player trophy (vert) .... 1·90 1·10
4469/4473 *Set of 5* .... 5·00 3·00

(Des E. Ivanov and L. Pavlov. Litho)

2003 (22 Dec). Tenth Anniv of Re-establishment of Masonic Activity in Bulgaria. P 13.
4474 **1549** 80st. multicoloured .... 2·20 1·30

1550 *Noctua tertia*

1551 Mask

(Des S. Detchev. Litho)

2004 (15 Jan). Moths. T **1550** and similar horiz designs. Multicoloured. P 12½ (with one diamond-shaped hole on each vert side).
4475 40st. Type **1550** .... 1·10 65
a. Without gum. P 14×13½ (10.04) .... 9·50 9·50
4476 45st. *Rethera komarovi* .... 1·20 75
a. Without gum. P 14×13½ (10.04) .... 9·50 9·50
4477 55st. *Symtomis marjana* .... 1·50 90
a. Without gum. P 14×13½ (10.04) .... 9·50 9·50
4478 80st. *Arctia caja* .... 2·20 1·30
a. Without gum. P 14×13½ (10.04) .... 9·50 9·50
4475/4478 *Set of 4* .... 5·50 3·25
Nos. 4475a/8a were issued without gum. The issue was limited to approximately 3000.

(Des L. Vesselinov. Litho)

2004 (23 Jan). SERVA, International Masquerade Festival, Pernik. P 13.
4479 **1551** 80st. multicoloured .... 2·20 1·40
No. 4479 was issued in *se-tenant* sheetlets of three stamps and three stamp-size labels showing bells.

1552 OSCE Emblem and Bridge

(Des S. Gruev. Litho)

2004 (30 Jan). Bulgaria, Chair of Organization for Security and Co-operation in Europe. P 13.
4480 **1552** 80st. multicoloured .... 2·10 1·30

1553 Theatre Façade

(Des S. Despodov. Litho)

2004 (19 Feb). Centenary of Ivan Vazov National Theatre, Sofia. P 13.
4481 **1553** 45st. multicoloured .... 1·30 80
No. 4481 was issued with a *se-tenant* stamp size label showing an early play bill.

1554 Atanas Dalchev

(Des S. Petrunov. Litho)

2004 (25 Mar). Birth Centenaries. T **1554** and similar horiz design. Multicoloured. P 13.
4482 45st. Type **1554** (poet) .... 1·30 80
4483 80st. Lubomir Pipkov (composer) .... 2·20 1·40

1555 NATO Emblem and National Colours

(Des T. Vardjiev. Litho)

2004 (2 Apr). Accession to Full Membership of NATO. P 13.
4484 **1555** 80st. multicoloured .... 2·75 1·80

1556 Georgi Ivanov

1557 Cover of Document

(Des B. Benev. Litho)

2004 (15 Apr). 25th Anniv of First Bulgarian in Space. Sheet 84×68 mm. P 13.
MS4485 **1556** 80st. multicoloured .... 2·20 1·90

(Des Ivelina Velinova. Litho)

2004 (16 Apr). 125th Anniv of Turnovska Constitution and Restoration of Bulgarian State. Sheet 86×67 mm. P 13.
MS4486 **1557** 45st. multicoloured .... 7·00 5·25

1558 Globe surmounted by Mortar Board

1559 Salvador Dali (sculpture)

(Des M. Todorov. Litho)

2004 (3 May). "Bulgarian Dream" (graduate assistance) Programme. P 13.
4487 **1558** 45st. multicoloured .... 1·30 80

(Des P. Trendafilov. Litho)

2004 (12 May). Birth Centenary of Salvador Dali (artist). Sheet 85×65 mm. P 13.
MS4488 **1559** 80st. multicoloured .... 4·25 3·50

1560 Luben Dimitrov (sculptor) and Boris Ivanov (cinema director)

(Des A. Attanassov. Litho)

2004 (21 May). Birth Centenaries. T **1560** and similar horiz design. Multicoloured. P 13.
4489 45st. Type **1560** .... 1·40 90
4490 80st. Vassil Stoilov and Stoyan Venev (artists) .... 2·20 1·40

1561 Mountains and Skiers

(Des Elaena Panayotova. Litho)

2004 (27 May). Europa. Holidays. T **1561** and similar horiz design. Multicoloured. P 13.

4491 45st. Type **1561** .... 1·40 90
4492 80st. Beach scene .... 2·20 1·40

1562 Christo Stoychkov

(Des R. Toshev. Litho)

2004 (2 June). Bulgarian Footballers. T **1562** and similar horiz designs. Multicoloured. P 13.

4493 45st. Type **1562** .... 1·40 90
a. Block of 4. Nos. 4493/6 .... 5·75
4494 45st. Georgi Asparuchov .... 1·40 90
4495 45st. Krassimir Balakov .... 1·40 90
4496 45st. Nikola Kotkov .... 1·40 90
4493/4496 *Set of 4* .... 5·00 3·25

Nos. 4493/6 were issued in *se-tenant* blocks of four stamps within the sheet.

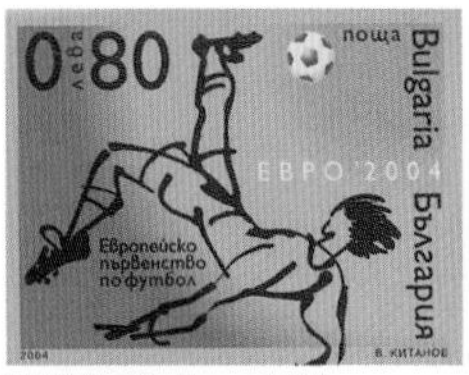

1563 Footballer and Ball

1564 Seal

(Des V. Kitanov. Litho)

2004 (11 June). European Football Championship 2004, Portugal. Sheet 85×67 mm. P 13.

MS4497 **1563** 80st. multicoloured .... 2·20 1·90

(Des C. Alexiev. Litho)

2004 (23 June). 125th Anniv of Bulgaria–Austria Diplomatic Relations. P 13.

4498 **1564** 80st. multicoloured .... 2·20 1·40

1565 Lion (statue), Flag and Document

(Des S. Krustev. Litho)

2004 (26 June). 125th Anniv of Ministry of Interior. P 13.

4499 **1565** 45st. multicoloured .... 1·40 90

1566 De Dion Button Post Car (1905)

1567 Red Kite (*Milvus milvus*)

(Des Natalia Kuruch. Litho)

2004 (16 July). 125th Anniv of Postal Service. Sheet 93×80 mm. P 13.

MS4500 **1566** 45st. multicoloured .... 7·00 5·75

No. **MS**4500 contains a *se-tenant* stamp size label, which with the stamp forms a composite design.

(Des Krassimira Despotova. Litho)

2004 (28 July). Endangered Species. Preservation of the Black Sea. Sheet 86×86 mm containing T **1567** and similar horiz design. Multicoloured. P 13.

MS4501 45st. Type **1567**; 80st. *Blennius ocellaris* .... 3·75 3·00

1568 Runner holding Torch and Olympic Flame (Berlin, 1936)

(Des I. Gazdov. Litho)

2004 (5 Aug). Olympic Games, Athens. T **1568** and similar horiz designs showing runner and Olympic flame. Multicoloured. P 13.

4502 10st. Type **1568** 30 20
4503 20st. Munich, 1972 .... 55 35
4504 45st. Moscow, 1980 .... 1·40 90
4505 80st. Athens, 2004 .... 2·20 1·40
4502/4505 *Set of 4* .... 4·00 2·50

1569 *Krum* (steamer)

(Des E. Stankev. Litho)

2004 (6 Aug). 125th Anniv of Bulgarian Navy. T **1569** and similar horiz designs. Multicoloured. P 13.

4506 10st. Type **1569** 30 20
4507 25st. *Druski* (torpedo boat) 70 45
4508 45st. *Christo Botev* (mine-sweeper) .... 1·40 90
4509 80st. *Smeli* (frigate) .... 2·20 1·40
4506/4509 *Set of 4* .... 4·25 2·75

1570 Square and Compass

(Des I. Bogdanov. Litho)

2004 (20 Sept). 125th Anniv of Bulgarian Masonic Movement. P 13.

4510 **1570** 45st. multicoloured .... 7·00 5·25

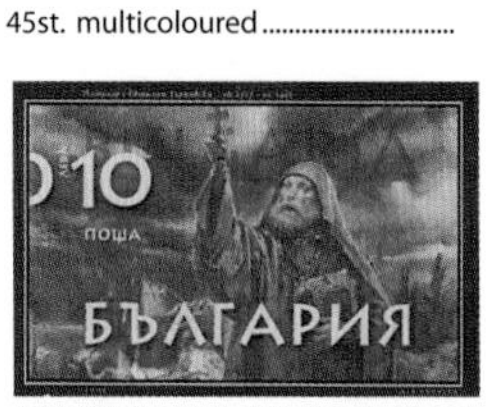

1571 Patriarch Ephtimius Turnovski

(Des P. Vulcheva. Litho)

2004 (15 Nov). Founders of Bulgarian State (4th series). T **1571** and similar horiz designs. Multicoloured. P 13.

4511 10st. Type **1571** 30 20
4512 20st. Kniaz Fruzhin and Kniaz Constantine 70 45
4513 45st. Georgi Peyachevich and Peter Partchevich .... 1·40 90
4514 80st. Piessii Hilendarski .... 2·50 1·60
4511/4514 *Set of 4* .... 4·50 2·75

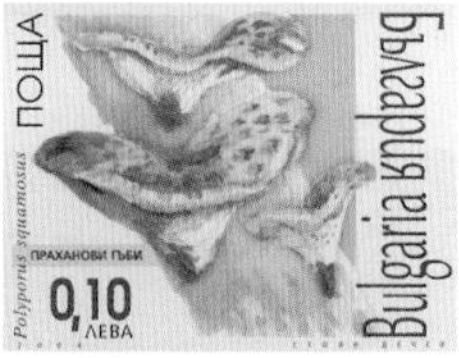

1572 *Polyporus squamosus*

(Des S. Dechev. Litho)

2004 (17 Nov). Fungi. Sheet 125×93 mm containing T **1572** and similar horiz designs. Multicoloured. P 13.

MS4515 10st. Type **1572**; 20st. *Fomes fomentarius*; 45st. *Piptoporus betulinus*; 80st. *Laetiporus sulphureus* .... 5·00 3·75

1573 Two Sturgeon

(Des Z. Stoyanov. Litho)

2004 (18 Nov). Sturgeon (*Huso huso*). T **1573** and similar horiz designs showing sturgeon. Multicoloured. P 13.

4516 80st. Type **1573** .... 2·50 1·60
a. Horiz strip of 4. Nos. 4516/19 .... 10·50
4517 80st. From below .... 2·50 1·60
4518 80st. Looking down .... 2·50 1·60
4519 80st. Eating .... 2·50 1·60
4516/4519 *Set of 4* .... 9·00 5·75

Nos. 4516/19 were issued in horizontal *se-tenant* strips of four stamps within the sheet.

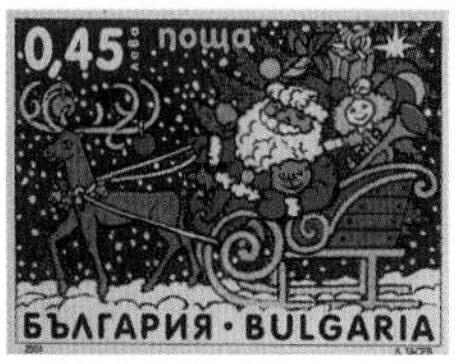

1574 Father Christmas

(Des D. Tassev. Litho)

2004 (24 Nov). Christmas. P 13.

4520 **1574** 45st. multicoloured .... 1·40 90

1575 Hands

(Des T. Varjiev. Litho)

2004 (6 Dec). 12th Organization for Security and Co-operation in Europe (OSCE) Council, Sofia. Sheet 84×67 mm. P 13.

MS4521 **1575** 80st. multicoloured .... 2·10 1·90

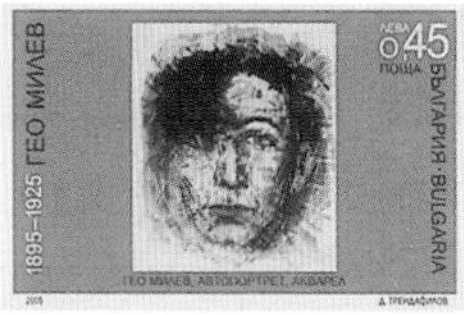

1576 Geo Milev

1577 Emblem

(Des D. Trendafilov. Litho)

2005 (17 Jan). Birth Centenary of Georghi Milev Kassabov (Geo Milev) (writer and revolutionary). P 13½.

4522 **1576** 45st. multicoloured .... 1·50 1·10

(Des V. Attanassov. Litho)

2005 (23 Feb). Centenary of Rotary International (charitable organization). P 13.

4523 **1577** 80st. multicoloured .... 2·40 1·70

1578 Charlie Chaplin in "Gold Rush" (1925)

1579 "The Monument" (lithograph) (Nickolai Pavlovitch)

(Des C. Alexiev. Litho)

2005 (25 Feb). History of Cinema. Sheet 88×118 mm containing T **1578** and similar vert designs. Multicoloured. P 13½.

MS4524 10st. Type **1578**; 20st. Scene from "Battleship Potemkin (Bronenoset Potemkin)" (1925); 45st. Marlene Dietrich in "Blue Angel (Der Baue Engel)" (1930); 80st. Vassil Ghendov in "Bulgarian is a Gallant Man" (first Bulgarian film) .... 4·75 4·25

(Des S. Daskalov. Litho)

2005 (11 Mar). 135th Anniv of Exarchate (independent Bulgarian ecclesiastical organisation). Sheet 68×88 mm. P 13.

MS4525 **1579** 45st. multicoloured .... 2·20 1·80

1580 European Stars and Bulgarian Flag

1581 Panayot Hitov and Philip Totyo

(Des L. Vesselinov. Litho)

2005 (16 Mar). Volunteers for Europe (educational campaign). P 13½.

4526 **1580** 80st. multicoloured .... 2·40 1·70

(Des R. Toshev. Litho)

2005 (21 Mar). 175th Birth Anniv of Panayot Hitov and Philip Totyo (revolutionaries). P 13½.

4527 **1581** 45st. multicoloured .... 1·50 1·10

1582 Robert Peary

(Des T. Alexieva. Litho)

2005 (23 Mar). Polar Explorers. Sheet 64×95 mm containing T **1582** and similar horiz design. Multicoloured. P 13½.
MS4528 45st. Type **1582** (American) (North Pole, 1909); 80st. Roald Amundsen (Norwegian) (South Pole, 1911) .... 3·75 3·25

1583 Peugeot (1936)

(Des D. Tassev. Litho)

2005 (20 Apr). Fire Engines. Sheet 136×77 mm containing T **1583** and similar horiz design. Multicoloured. P 13½.
MS4529 10st. Type **1583**; 20st. Mercedes (1935); 45st. Magirus (1934); 80st. Renault (1925) .... 4·75 4·00

1584 Hans Christian Andersen

(Des I. Gazdov. Litho)

2005 (20 May). Birth Bicentenary of Hans Christian Andersen (writer). Sheet 87×78 mm. P 13½.
MS4530 **1584** 80st. multicoloured .... 2·40 2·00

1585 Hand holding Scroll

(Des C. Gogov. Litho)

2005 (24 May). Cyrillic Alphabet. Sheet 88×59 mm. P 13½.
MS4531 **1585** 80st. multicoloured .... 2·40 2·00

1586 Electric Locomotive 46

(Des Krassimira Despotova. Litho)

2005 (26 May). Railways. T **1586** and similar horiz design. Multicoloured. P 13½.

4532	45st. Type **1586**	1·50	1·10
	a. Pair. Nos. 4532/3	9·00	6·75
4533	80st. Modern locomotive DMV 10	7·25	5·50

Nos. 4532/3 were issued in horizontal and vertical *se-tenant* pairs within the sheet.

1587 *Radetski* (revolutionary ship) (Georgi Dimov)

2005 (27 May). Children's Painting. P 13½.
4534 **1587** 45st. multicoloured .... 1·50 1·10

1588 Blinis

1589 Stylized Figures

(Des T. Vardjiev. Litho)

2005 (28 May). Europa. Gastronomy. T **1588** and similar horiz design. Multicoloured. P 13½.

4535	45st. Type **1588**	1·50	1·10
	a. Horiz pair. Nos. 4535/6	4·25	3·00
	b. Booklet pane. Nos. 4535/6, each×2	8·50	
4536	80st. Bread, kebab and tomatoes	2·40	1·70

Nos. 4535/6 were issued in horizontal *se-tenant* pairs within sheets of ten stamps.

(Des Svetlin Belezdrov. Litho)

2005 (28 May). 50th Anniv of Europa–CEPT Postage Stamps. T **1589** and similar vert design. P 13½.

4537	45st. reddish violet, bright green and black	1·50	1·10
4538	80st. new blue, magenta and black	2·40	1·70

Designs:—45st. Type **1589**; 80st. Square of figures.

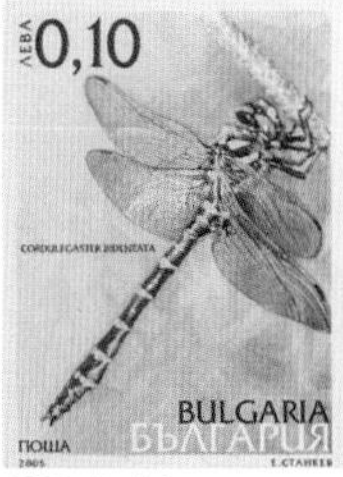

1590 *Cordulegaster bidentata*

1591 Elias Canetti

(Des E. Stankev. Litho)

2005 (29 June). Dragonflies. T **1590** and similar multicoloured designs. P 13×13½ (vert) or 13½×13 (horiz).

4539	10st. Type **1590**	30	20
4540	20st. *Erythromma najas* (horiz)	60	45
4541	45st. *Sympetrum pedemontanum* (horiz)	1·30	1·00
4542	80st. *Brachytron pratense*	2·50	1·80
4539/4542	*Set of 4*	4·25	3·00

(Des Ivelina Velinova. Litho)

2005 (25 July). Birth Centenary of Elias Canetti (writer). P 13.
4543 **1591** 80st. multicoloured .... 2·50 1·80

1592 *Synema globosum*

1593 Flag as Tree Bark

(Des S. Dechev. Litho)

2005 (29 July). Spiders. T **1592** and similar vert designs. Multicoloured. P 13×13½.

4544	10st. Type **1592**	30	20
4545	20st. *Argiope bruennichi*	60	45
4546	45st. *Eresus cinnaberinus*	1·30	1·00
4547	80st. *Araneus diadematus*	2·50	1·80
4544/4547	*Set of 4*	4·25	3·00

(Des T. Licho. Litho)

2005 (26 Aug). 110th Anniv of Organized Tourism. P 13½×13.
4548 **1593** 45st. multicoloured .... 1·20 90

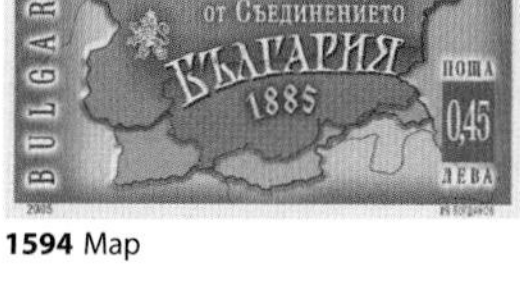

1594 Map

1595 Girl wearing Traditional Costume, Sofia

(Des I. Bogdanov. Litho)

2005 (6 Sept). 120th Anniv of Unification of Bulgaria. P 13×13½.
4549 **1594** 45st. multicoloured .... 1·20 90

(Des Anna Tuzsuzova. Litho)

2005 (5 Oct). Women's Traditional Costumes. T **1595** and similar vert designs. Multicoloured. P 13½×13.

4550	20st. Type **1595**	50	40
4551	25st. Pleven	70	55
4552	45st. Sliven	1·20	90
4553	80st. Stara Zagora	2·00	1·60
4550/4553	*Set of 4*	4·00	3·00

1596 Stamen Grigoroff (discoverer)

1597 Chess Board and Antoaneta Steffanova (Women's World Chess Champion)

(Des Natalya Kuruch. Litho)

2005 (31 Oct). Centenary of Discovery of *Lactobacillus bulgaricus Grigoroff* (yoghurt bacilli) (1st issue). Sheet 94×81 mm. P 13½×13.
MS4554 **1596** 80st. multicoloured .... 2·20 1·70
See also No. **MS**4557.

(Des B. Benev. Litho)

2005 (10 Nov). Chess. P 13×13½.
4555 **1597** 80st. multicoloured .... 2·00 1·60

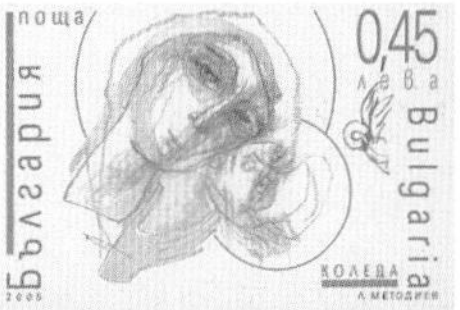

1598 Virgin and Child

1599 Stamen Grigoroff (discoverer)

(Des L. Metodiev. Litho)

2005 (30 Nov). Christmas. P 13×13½.
4556 **1598** 45st. multicoloured .... 1·20 90

(Des Natalya Kuruch. Litho)

2005 (2 Dec). Centenary of Discovery of *Lactobacillus bulgaricus Grigoroff* (yoghurt bacilli) (2nd issue). Sheet 94×81 mm. Imperf.
MS4557 **1599** 80st. multicoloured .... 20·00 18·00
The design of No. **MS**4557 is as Type **1596** with the addition of an owl in the top right corner. The sheets include a perforated number.

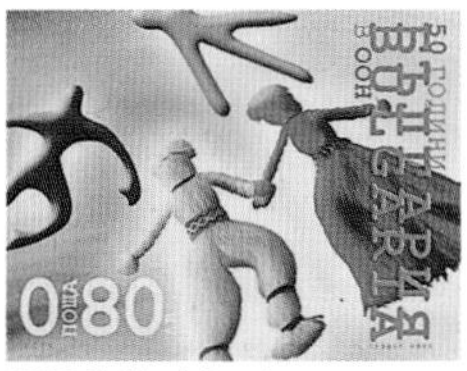

1600 Stylized Couple

(Des T. Licho. Litho)

2005 (14 Dec). 50th Anniv of Membership of United Nations. Sheet 86×88 mm. P 13.
4558 **1600** 80st. multicoloured .... 2·20 1·70

1601 Patriarchs Illarion Makariopolski and Antim I

1602 *Rosa pendulina*

(Des P. Vulcheva. Litho)

2005 (20 Dec). Founders of Bulgarian State (5th series). T **1601** and similar horiz designs. P 13.

4559	10st. chocolate and dull green	35	25
4560	20st. brown and dull green	50	40
4561	45st. deep claret and dull green	1·20	90
4562	80st. brown-purple and dull green	2·00	1·60
4559/4562	*Set of 4*	3·75	2·75

Designs:—10st. Type **1601**; 20st. Georgi Rakovski and Vassil Levski; 45st. Luben Karavelov and Christo Botev; 80st. Panayot Volov and Pavel Bobekov.

(Des D. Damyanov. Litho)

2006 (23 Jan). Roses. T **1602** and similar vert designs. Multicoloured. P 13 (with large indented perf on each horiz side).

4563	54st. Type **1602**	1·40	1·10
4564	1l.50 *Rosa gallica*	3·75	3·00
4565	2l. *Rosa spinosissima*	5·00	4·00
4566	10l. *Rosa arvensis*	24·00	18·00
4563/4566	*Set of 4*	31·00	23·00

1603 Wolfgang Amadeus Mozart

1604 Ellin Pellin (writer)

(Des A. Appostolov. Litho)

2006 (27 Jan). 250th Birth Anniv of Wolfgang Amadeus Mozart. P 13.
4567 **1603** 1l. multicoloured .... 8·50 8·00
No. 4567 has a *se-tenant* stamp size label inscribed for the anniversary attached at right.

(Des L. Methodiev. Litho)

2006 (31 Jan). 115th Anniv of National Philatelic Press. Bulgarian Philatelists. T **1604** and similar horiz designs. Multicoloured. P 13.
4568 35st. Type **1604** 85 80
4569 55st. Lazar Dobritch (circus artiste) .... 1·40 1·20
4570 60st. Boris Christov (opera singer) .... 1·50 1·30
4571 1l. Bogomil Nonev (writer) .... 2·50 2·10
4568/4571 *Set of 4* .... 5·75 4·75
Nos. 4568/71 were each issued with a *se-tenant* stamp size label showing a stamp attached at right.

1605 Snowboarder

1606 Sextant

(Des C. Alexiev. Litho)

2006 (10 Feb). Winter Olympic Games, Turin. Sheet 86×118 mm containing T **1605** and similar vert design. Multicoloured. P 13.
MS4572 55st. Type **1605**; 1l. Ice dancers .... 4·00 3·75

(Des T. Vardjiev. Litho)

2006 (28 Feb). Tenth Anniv of Bulgarian Antarctic Cartography. Sheet 86×69 mm. P 13.
MS4573 **1606** 1l. multicoloured .... 2·50 2·20

1607 Ship (15th Century manuscript)

(Des T. Licho. Litho)

2006 (14 Mar). 610th Anniv of Battle at Nikopol. P 13.
4574 **1607** 1l.50 multicoloured .... 3·50 2·75

1608 *Martes martes*

(Des S. Dechev. Litho)

2006 (28 Mar). Ecology. Sheet 86×118 mm containing T **1608** and similar horiz design. Multicoloured. P 13.
MS4575 55st. Type **1608**; 1l.50 *Ursus arctos* .... 4·75 4·25
The stamps of No. **MS**4575 overlap and share a central area containing a leaf enclosed in a heart.

1609 Stylized Figure and Stars

(Des S. Balazdrov. Litho)

2006 (25 Apr). Europa. Integration. T **1609** and similar horiz design. Multicoloured. P 13 (with large indented perf on each horiz side).
4576 55st. Type **1609** .... 1·70 1·30
4577 1l. Star as flower .... 3·50 2·75
Nos. 4576/7 were each issued with a *se-tenant* stamp size label attached at right.

1610 Emblem

1611 Mastheads

(Des T. Vardjiev. Litho)

2006 (27 Apr). Meeting of NATO Foreign Ministers, Sofia. Sheet 87×70 mm. P 13.
MS4578 **1610** 1l.50 multicoloured .... 3·50 3·25

(Des L. Vesselinov. Litho)

2006 (28 Apr). 70th Anniv of Trud Newspaper. P 13.
4579 **1611** 55st. multicoloured .... 2·50 2·00

1612 Vesselin Topalov

(Des B. Benev. Litho)

2006 (4 May). Vesselin Topalov–World Chess Champion. Sheet 87×71 mm. P 13.
MS4580 **1612** 1l.50 multicoloured .... 3·50 3·25
No. **MS**4580 also exist imperforate.

1613 Building Façade

(Des R. Kolev. Litho)

2006 (5 May). 25th Anniv of National Palace of Culture. P 13.
4581 **1613** 55st. multicoloured .... 1·70 1·50
No. 4581 was issued with a *se-tenant* stamp size label.

1614 *Circus aeruginosus*

(Des L. Chehlarov. Litho)

2006 (9 May). Raptors. T **1614** and similar horiz designs. Multicoloured. P 13.
4582 10st. Type **1614** 35 25
4583 35st. *Circus cyaneus* 85 65
4584 55st. *Circus macrourus* .... 1·20 90
4585 1l. *Circus pygargus* .... 2·75 2·10
4582/4585 *Set of 4* .... 4·75 3·50

1615 Building Façade, Ship and Sailor

(Des Magdalena Konstantinova. Litho)

2006 (20 May). 125th Anniv of Nikola Vaptsarov Naval Academy, Varna. P 13.
4586 **1615** 55st. multicoloured .... 1·20 90

1616 Players

(Des S. Petrunov. Litho)

2006 (9 June). World Cup Football Championship, Germany. Sheet 87×87 mm. P 13.
MS4587 **1616** 1l. multicoloured .... 2·20 2·00

1617 Emblem

1618 Gena Dimitrova

(Des V. Kitanov. Litho)

2006 (29 June). 50th Anniv of Bulgaria in UNESCO. P 13.
4588 **1617** 1l. multicoloured .... 2·20 1·70

(Des V. Kitanov. Litho)

2006 (18 July). 65th Birth Anniv and First Death Anniv of Gena Dimitrova (opera singer). P 13.
4589 **1618** 1l. multicoloured .... 2·20 1·70

1619 *Saponaria stranjensis*

1620 Rover Maestro

(Des Z. Stoyanov. Litho)

2006 (28 July). Flora. T **1619** and similar vert designs. Multicoloured. P 13.
4590 10st. Type **1619** 35 25
a. Strip. Nos. 4590/93 .... 5·50
4591 35st. *Trachystemon orientalis* 85 65
4592 55st. *Hypericum calycinum* .... 1·20 90
4593 1l. *Rhododendron ponticum* .... 2·75 2·10
4590/4593 *Set of 4* .... 4·75 3·50
Nos. 4590/93 were issued in horizontal *se-tenant* strips of four stamps within the sheet.

(Des I. Gazdov. Litho)

2006 (29 Sept). Bulgaria Automobile Industry. T **1620** and similar vert designs. Multicoloured. P 13.
4594 10st. Type **1620** 35 25
4595 35st. Moskovitch 85 65
4596 55st. Bulgaralpine .... 1·20 90
4597 1l. Bulgarrnault .... 2·75 2·10
4594/4597 *Set of 4* .... 4·75 3·50

1621 "Return of the Prodigal Son"

1622 "All Soul's Day" (Ivan Murkvitchka)

(Des S. Gruev. Litho)

2006 (25 Oct). 400th Birth Anniv of Rembrandt Harmenszoon van Rijn. Sheet 65×84 mm. P 13.
MS4598 **1621** 1l. multicoloured .... 2·75 2·40

(Des D. Trendaffilov. Litho)

2006 (27 Oct). Art Anniversaries. T **1622** and similar vert designs. Multicoloured. P 13.
4599 10st. Type **1622** (150th birth anniv) 35 25
4600 35st. "Sozopol—Houses" (Vesselin Statkov) (birth centenary) .... 1·00 80
4601 55st. "Sofia in Winter" (Nikola Petrov) (90th death anniv) .... 1·50 1·20
4602 1l. "T. Popova" (John Popov) (birth centenary) .... 2·75 2·10
4599/4602 *Set of 4* .... 5·00 4·00

1623 Competitors

1624 Post Van

(Des S. Nenov. Litho)

2006 (3 Nov). World Sambo Championship, Sofia. P 13.
4603 **1623** 55st. multicoloured .... 1·50 1·20

(Des Ivelina Velinova. Litho)

2006 (17 Nov). Post Europ. Sheet 85×75 mm. P 13.
MS4604 **1624** 1l. multicoloured .... 15·00 14·50

1625 Angel

(Des Deya Vulcheva. Litho)

2006 (24 Nov). Christmas. P 13.
4605 **1625** 55st. multicoloured .... 1·50 1·20

1626 Ballot Box and Flags

(Des S. Târlea (4606) or S. Balezdrov (4607). Litho)

2006 (29 Nov). Bulgaria and Romania's Membership of European Union. T **1626** and similar horiz design. Multicoloured. P 13.

4606 55st. Type **1626** .... 1·50 1·20
4607 1l.50 "EU" .... 4·00 3·25
MS4608 97×87 mm. Nos. 4606/7 .... 5·75 5·50

Stamps of a similar design were issued by Romania.

1627 Peter Dimkov

(Des V. Attanassov. Litho)

2006 (20 Dec). 120th Birth Anniv of Peter Dimkov (naturopath). P 13.
4609 **1627** 55st. multicoloured .... 1·50 1·20

1628 Generals Danail Nikolaev and Racho Petrov

(Des P. Vulcheva. Litho)

2006 (21 Dec). Founders of Bulgarian State (6th series). T **1628** and similar horiz designs. Multicoloured.

4610 10st. Type **1628** 35 25
4611 35t. Petko Karavelov and Marin Drinov ... 1·00 80
4612 55st. Konstantin Stoylov and Stephan Stambolov .... 1·50 1·20
4613 1l. Prince Albert I of Bulgaria .... 2·75 2·10
4610/4613 *Set of 4* .... 5·00 4·00

1629 Aircraft and Terminal Building

(Des D. Damyanov. Litho)

2006 (27 Dec). New Airport Terminal, Sofia. Sheet 87×72 mm. P 13.
MS4614 **1629** 55st. multicoloured .... 1·50 1·30

No. **MS**4615 and Type **1630** have been left for "Membership of EU", issued on 31 January 2007, not yet received.

1631 Emilian Stanev

(Des A. Apostolov. Litho)

2007 (28 Feb). Birth Centenary of Nikola Stoyanov Stanev (Emilian Stanev) (writer). P 13.
4616 **1631** 55st. multicoloured .... 1·40 1·10

No. 1631 was issued with a *se-tenant* stamp size label.

1632 Flags as Stars

(Des P. Alexandrov. Litho)

2007 (23 Mar). 50th Anniv of Treaty of Rome. P 13.
4617 **1632** 1l. multicoloured .... 2·50 2·00

1633 Ivan Dimov

(Des L. Metodiev. Litho)

2007 (27 Mar). Theatre Personalities. T **1633** and similar horiz designs. Multicoloured. P 13.

4618 10st. Type **1633** 35 25
4619 55st. Sava Ognyanov .... 1·40 1·10
4620 1l. Krustyo Sarfov .... 2·50 2·00
4618/4620 *Set of 3* .... 3·75 3·00

1634 Sputnik

(Des K. Andreev. Litho)

2007 (25 Apr). 50th Anniv of First Manmade Satellite. Sheet 87×56 mm. P 13.
MS4621 **1634** 1l. multicoloured .... 2·50 2·40

1635 Campfire

(Des E. Stankev. Litho)

2007 (26 Apr). Europa. Centenary of Scouting. T **1635** and similar horiz designs. Multicoloured.

(a) Sheet stamps. P 13 (with one large indented perf on each horiz side)

4622 55st. Type **1635** .... 1·40 1·10
4623 1l.50 Route finding .... 3·75 3·00

(b) Booklet stamps. Size 31×23 mm. P 13

4624 1l. As Type **1635** .... 1·40 1·10
4625 1l. As No. 4623 .... 3·75 3·00
4622/4625 *Set of 4* .... 9·25 7·50

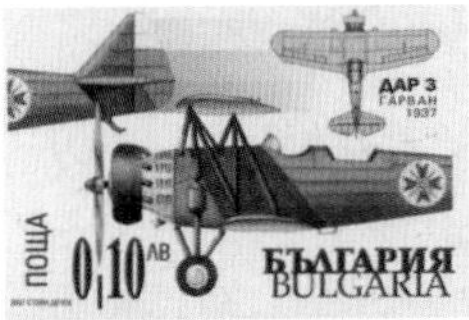

1636 DAR-3 Garvan II (1937)

(Des E. Stankev. Litho)

2007 (27 Apr). Military Aircraft. T **1636** and similar horiz designs. Multicoloured. P 13.

4626 10st. Type **1636** 35 25
4627 35st. DAR-9 Siniger (1939) 85 65
4628 55st. Kaproni Bulgarski KB-6 Papagal (1939) .... 1·40 1·10
4629 1l. Kaproni Bulgarski KB-11A Fanzan ..... 2·50 2·00
4626/4629 *Set of 4* .... 4·50 3·50

1637 Boris I

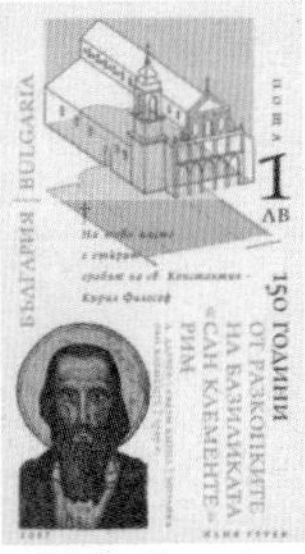

1637a Basilica and Saint Cyril

(Des S. Krustev. Litho)

2007 (2 May). 1100th Death Anniv of Knyaz (Prince) Boris I (Michael). P 13.
4630 **1637** 55st. multicoloured .... 1·40 1·10

(Des Iliya Gruev. Litho)

2007 (21 May). 150th Anniv of Excavation of San Clement Basilica, Rome. P 13.
4630*a* **1637a** 1l. multicoloured .... 2·75 2·10

1638 Dimcho Debelyanov

1639 St. Spass Monastery, Lozenski

(Des Christo Alekiev. Litho)

2007 (23 May). Birth Anniversaries. T **1638** and similar vert designs. Multicoloured. P 13.

4631 10st. Type **1638** (poet) (120th) 35 25
4632 35st. Nenko Balkanski (artist) (centenary) 85 65
4633 55st. Vera Lukova (artist) (centenary) .... 1·20 90
4634 1l. Theodor Trayanov (poet) (125th) .... 2·75 2·10
4631/4634 *Set of 4* .... 4·75 3·50

(Des Anatoliy Stankulov. Litho)

2007 (30 May). Monasteries. T **1639** and similar vert designs. Multicoloured. P 13 (with large indented perf on each horiz side).

4635 63st. Type **1639** .... 1·70 1·30
4636 75st. St. Mina, Obradovski .... 2·00 1·60
4637 1l.20 St. George the Victor, Kremikovski .... 3·25 2·50
4638 2l.20 Three Saints, Chepinski .... 6·00 4·50
4635/4638 *Set of 4* .... 11·50 9·00

1640 Symbols of Transport

(Des Teodor Liho. Litho)

2007 (30 May). International Transport Forum, Sofia. P 13.
4639 **1640** 1l. multicoloured .... 2·75 2·10

1641 Presidents of Bulgaria and Azerbaijan

1642 *Onosma thracica*

(Des Dimitar Tassev. Litho)

2007 (1 June). 15th Anniv of Bulgaria–Azerbaijan Diplomatic Relations. Sheet 86×64 mm. P 13.
MS4640 **1641** 1l. multicoloured .... 2·75 2·50

(Des Dimitar Tassev. Litho)

2007 (6 July). Flora. T **1642** and similar vert designs. Multicoloured. P 13 (with large indented perf on each horiz side).

4641 10st. Type **1642** 35 25
4642 45st. *Astracantha aitosensis* .... 1·20 90
4643 55st. *Veronica krumovii* .... 1·50 1·20
4644 1l. *Verbascum adrianopolitanum* .... 2·75 2·10
4641/4644 *Set of 4* .... 5·25 4·00

1643 Vassal Levski

1644 Sailor

(Des Cyril Gogov. Litho)

2007 (18 July). 170th Birth Anniv of Vassal Levski (revolutionary leader). P 13.
4645 **1643** 55st. multicoloured .... 1·50 1·20

(Des Stephan Nenov. Litho)

2007 (21 July). Junior World Sailing Championship, Olympian Class 470, Burgas. P 13.
4646 **1644** 1l. multicoloured .... 2·75 2·10

1645 Lt. Colonel Pavel Kalitin (painting) and 'Battle at Stara Zagora' (Nikola Kozhuharov)

(Des Natalya Kuroch. Litho)

2007 (31 July). 130th Anniv of Battle at Stara Zagora. P 13.
4647 **1645** 55st. multicoloured ... 1·50 1·20

1646 Players

(Des Razvigor Kolev. Litho)

2007 (5 Sept). Rugby. 50th (2005) Anniv of Locomotiv Rugby Club, Sofia. World Rugby Championship–2007, France. P 13.
4648 **1646** 55st. multicoloured ... 1·50 1·20

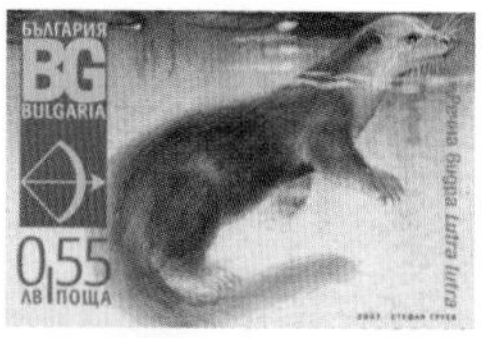

1647 *Lutra lutra* (otter)

(Des Stephan Gruev. Litho)

2007 (10 Sept). Ecology. 15th Anniv of Ropotamo Reserve. Sheet 85×85 mm containing T **1647** and similar horiz design. Multicoloured. P 13.
MS4649 55st. Type **1647**; 1l. *Haliaeetus albicilla* (white tailed eagle) ... 4·25 4·00
The stamps and margins of No. **MS**4649 form a composite design.

1648 *Alcedo atthis* (kingfisher)

1649 Emblem

(Des Zdravko Stoyanov. Litho)

2007 (11 Sept). Endangered Species. Birds. Sheet 97×130 mm containing T **1648** and similar horiz design. Multicoloured. P 13.
MS4650 10st. Type **1648**; 35st. *Tichodroma muraria* (wall creeper); 55st. *Bombycilla garrulous* (waxwing); 1l. *Phoenicopterus ruber* (flamingo) ... 5·50 5·25

(Des Valentin Attanassov. Litho)

2007 (21 Sept). Tenth Anniv Grand Lodge of the Ancient Freemasons. P 13.
4651 **1649** 55st. multicoloured ... 1·50 1·20

1650 Centre Building

(Des Deya Vulcheva. Litho)

2007 (9 Oct). Inauguration of Exchange and Sorting Centre, Sofia. Sheet 87×63 mm. P 13.
MS4652 **1650** 55st. multicoloured ... 1·50 1·40

1651 Ivan Hadjiski

1652 Woman holding Offerings

(Des Dimitar Trendaffilov. Litho)

2007 (12 Oct). Birth Centenary of Ivan Hadjiski (social psychologist). P 13.
4653 **1651** 55st. multicoloured ... 1·50 1·20

(Des Rumen Statkov. Litho)

2007 (27 Nov). Christmas. P 13.
4654 **1652** 55st. multicoloured ... 1·50 1·20

1653 Rumyana Neykova (European 2000m. skiff rowing champion)

1654 '100' and Soldier

(Des Razvigor Kolev. Litho)

2007 (19 Dec). Women Sports Personalities. T **1653** and similar horiz designs. Multicoloured. P 13.

4655	10st. Type **1653**	35	25
4656	35st. Stanka Zlateva (World freestyle wrestling champion)	85	65
4657	1l. Stefka Kostadinova (World record high jump (30.8.1987))	2·75	2·10
4655/4657	*Set of 3*	3·50	2·75

(Des Svetlin Belezdrov. Litho)

2007 (20 Dec). Centenary of Military Reconnaissance. P 13.
4658 **1654** 55st. multicoloured ... 1·50 1·20

1655 Hristo Botev

(Des Ivan Bogdanov. Litho)

2008 (6 Jan). 150th Birth Anniv of Hristo Botev (poet and revolutionary). P 13.
4659 **1655** 55st. multicoloured ... 1·50 1·20

1656 Polar Bear

1657 Volleyball Player

(Des Todor Vardjiev. Litho)

2008 (10 Jan). International Polar Year. 20th Anniv of Bulgarian Antarctic Expedition. Sheet 115×85 mm containing T **1656** and similar horiz design. Multicoloured. P 13.
MS4660 55st. Type **1656**; 1l. Skua stealing penguin chick ... 4·25 4·00
The stamps and margins of No. **MS**4660 form a composite design.

(Des Christo Alexiev)

2008 (25 Feb). Olympic Games, Beijing. Sheet 88×109 mm containing T **1657** and similar vert design. Multicoloured. P 13.
MS4661 55st. Type **1657**; 1l. Two players ... 4·25 4·00
The stamps of No. **MS**4661 form a composite design of a volley ball match.

1658 Arms of Bulgaria

(Des Atanass Atanassov)

2008 (29 Feb). 130th Anniv of San Stefano Peace Treaty (treaty between Russia and the Ottoman Empire at the end of the Russo-Turkish War (setting up an autonomous self-governing tributary principality of Bulgaria)). P 13.
4662 **1658** 55st. multicoloured ... 1·50 1·20

1659 Envelope as Postman

(Des Stoyan Dechev)

2008 (22 Apr). Europa. The Letter. T **1659** and similar horiz designs. Multicoloured (background colour given). P 13.

4663	55st. Type **1659**	1·50	1·20
4664	55st. As Type **1659** (purple)	1·50	1·20
	a. Booklet pane. No. 4664×4	6·25	
4665	1l. Envelope as pigeon (bright blue)	2·75	2·10
4666	1l. As No. 4665 (yellow)	2·75	2·10
	a. Booklet pane. No. 4666×4	11·50	
4663/4666	*Set of 4*	9·00	7·00

Nos. 4663 and 4665, respectively, were issued in blocks of four stamps within sheets of eight, the two blocks laid tête-bêche to each other and separated by a gutter of two stamp size labels. The booklet panes Nos. 4664a and 4666a have the stamps arranged with first stamp in the top row upright and the second stamp upside down and the first stamp in bottom row upside down and the second stamp upright. Giving two tête-bêche pairs.

1660 Captain Dimiter Spissarevski

(Des Lyidmil Metodiev)

2008 (25 Apr). History of Military Aviation. Pilots' Birth Anniversaries. T **1660** and similar horiz design. Multicoloured. P 13.

4667	55st. Type **1660** (90th birth anniv)	1·50	1·20
	a. Pair. Nos. 4667/8	4·50	3·50
4668	1l. General Stoyan Stoyanov (95th birth anniv)	2·75	2·10

Nos. 4667/8 were issued in horizontal *se-tenant* pairs within the sheet, each pair forming a composite design.

1661 Women from the Rhodopes (Boris Kotsev)

(Des Ivelina Velinova)

2008 (7 May). Artists' Birth Centenaries. T **1661** and similar horiz designs. Multicoloured. P 13.

4669	10st. Type **1661**	35	25
4670	35st. Nude (Eliezer Alsheh)	85	65
4671	55st. Nude (Vera Nedova)	1·50	1·20
4672	1l. Maritsa (Assen Peykov)	2·75	2·10
4669/4672	*Set of 4*	5·00	3·75

1662 Club Members

(Des Anatoli Stankulov)

2008 (7 May). 60th Anniv of CSKA Central Sports Club. Sheet 90×58 mm. P 13½.
MS4673 **1662** 55st. multicoloured ... 1·70 1·60

1663 White-headed Marmoset (*Callithrix geoffroyi*)

1664 Alexander Alexandrov

(Des Lyudmil Chehlarov)

2008 (14 May). 120th Anniv of Zoological Gardens, Sofia. Two sheets containing T **1663** and similar vert designs. Multicoloured. P 13.
MS4674 (a) 126×130 mm 10st. Type **1663**; 20st. Hippopotamus (*Hippopotamus amphibius*); 35st. Bactrian camel (*Camelus bactrianus*); 55st. Meerkat (*Suricata suricatta*); 60st. Blue-and-yellow macaw (*Ara ararauna*); 1l. Eurasian lynx (*Lynx lynx*); (b) 66×85 mm 55st. Meerkat (*Suricata suricatta*). Imperf ... 7·25 7·25

(Des Rumen Stakov)

2008 (9 June). 20th Anniv of Alexander Alexandrov's Flight in Orbital Space Station MIR. Sheet 85×61 mm. P 13.
MS4675 **1664** 1l. multicoloured ... 2·75 2·75

1665 BMW R12 Single Carb, 1935

(Des Nenko Atanassov)

008 (16 June). 70th Anniv of Union of Bulgarian Philatelists. P 13.
676 **1665** 60st. multicoloured .... 1·70 1·30
S4677 106×92 mm. 60st. As Type **1665**. Imperf .... 1·90 1·90

1666 *Canis aureus* (golden jackal)

(Des Zdravko Stoyanov)

008 (21 July). Strandja Nature Park. Sheet 104×79 mm containing T **1666** and similar multicoloured design. P 13.
4S4678 60st. Type **1666**; 1l.50 *Aquila pomarina* (lesser spotted eagle) (vert) .... 5·50 5·50
The stamps and margins of No. **MS**4678 form a composite esign.

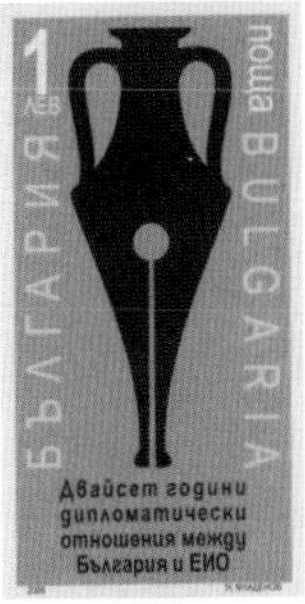

1667

(Des Nikolay Mladenov)

008 (30 July). 20th Anniv of Bulgaria–European Economic Community. P 13.
679 **1667** 1l. black and olive-yellow .... 2·75 2·10

1668 Wagons Lits (sleeping car)

(Des Stephan Gruev)

2008 (11 Sept). 120th Anniv of Orient Express. T **1668** and similar horiz design. Multicoloured. P 13.
4680 60st. Type **1668** .... 1·70 1·30
a. Horiz pair. Nos. 4680/1 .... 6·00 5·00
4681 1l.50 Steg Wien locomotive No. 5 .... 3·75 3·00
Nos. 4680/1 were issued in horizontal *se-tenant* pairs within the sheet.
The stamps also show the arms of cities enroute and the emblems of the Orient Express (60st.) or the Bulgarian State Railways (1l.50).

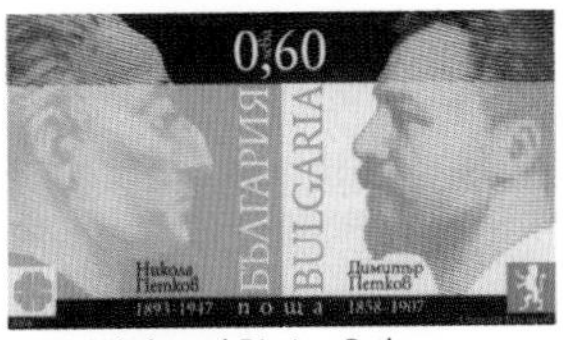

1669 Nikola and Dimitar Petkov

(Des Svetlin Balezdrov)

2008 (18 Sept). Birth Anniversaries of Dimitar Petkov (Prime Minister 1906–1907) (150th) and Nikola Petkov (politician, son of Dimitar Petkov and leader of Bulgarian Agrarian National Union) (115th). P 13.
4682 **1669** 60st. multicoloured .... 1·70 1·30

1670 Tsar Ferdinand

1671 Arms of the Templars

(Des Simeon Krustev)

2008 (22 Sept). Centenary of Proclamation of Independence. Sheet 48×87 mm. P 13.
MS4683 **1670** 60st. multicoloured .... 1·90 1·90

(Des Valetin Atanasov)

2008 (30 Sept). 700th Anniv (2007) of Disbanding of Knights Templar (Order of the Temple) by King Philip IV of France. P 13.
4684 **1671** 1l. multicoloured .... 2·75 2·10

1672 Race Car (2008)

(Des Emilyan Stankev)

2008 (16 Oct). Ferrari Cars. T **1672** and similar horiz designs. Multicoloured. P 13.
4685 60st. Type **1672** .... 1·70 1·30
a. Pair. Nos. 4685/6....................................... 4·75 3·75
4686 1l. Race car (1952) .... 2·75 2·10
Nos. 4685/6 were issued in horizontal *se-tenant* pairs within the sheet.
No. 4687 has been left for miniature sheet, not yet received.

1673 Arms

(Des Theodor Licho)

2008 (24 Oct). 130th Anniv of Bulgarian Red Cross Societies. P 13.
4688 **1673** 60st. multicoloured .... 1·70 1·30

1674 Virgin Mary, Rila Monastery (12th-century)

(Des Natalia Kuruch. Litho)

2008 (21 Nov). Bulgarian Icons. T **1674** and similar vert designs. Multicoloured. P 13.
4689 50st. Type **1674** .... 1·40 1·10
a. Strip of 3. Nos. 4689/91 .... 6·00
4690 60st. Virgin and Child, Troyan Monastery (18th-century).. 1·70 1·30
4691 1l. Virgin and Child, Bachkovo Monastery (14th-century).................... 2·75 2·10
4689/4691 *Set of* 3 .... 5·25 4·00
Nos. 4689/91 were issued in *se-tenant* strips of three stamps within the sheet.

1675 Virgin and Child

1676 Saint Clement of Ohrid (St. Kliment Ohridski)

(Des Ivan Gazdov. Litho)

2008 (21 Nov). Christmas. P 13.
4692 **1675** 60st. multicoloured .... 1·70 1·30

(Des Damyan Damyanov. Litho)

2008 (25 Nov). 120th Anniv of Sofia University, St. Kliment Ohridski. P 13.
4693 **1676** 60st. multicoloured .... 1·70 1·30

1677 Andranik Ozanyan (Armenian general in Balkan Wars of Independence)

(Des Onnil Karanfilyan. Litho)

2008 (10 Dec). Nationalist Liberation Movements of Bulgaria and Armenia. T **1677** and similar horiz design. Multicoloured. P 13.
4694 60st. Type **1677** .... 1·70 1·30
a. Pair. Nos. 4694/5....................................... 4·75 3·75
4695 1l.50 Peyo Yavorov (Bulgarian poet and revolutionary) .... 2·75 2·10
Nos. 4694/5 were issued in *se-tenant* pairs within the sheet.

Eastern Roumelia and South Bulgaria

40 Paras = 1 Piastre

A. EASTERN ROUMELIA

The Congress of Berlin, 1878, decided that Eastern Roumelia, south of the Balkan Mts, should become semi-autonomous, and remain in the Turkish Empire.

(1)

(2)

3

1880. Stamps of Turkey, handstamped with T **1**, in blue.

(a) Issue of Jan 1876

1	½ pre. on 20pa. green (78)	65·00	55·00

(b) T **9**

2	20pa. plum and green	85·00	65·00
3	2pi. black and flesh	£110	95·00
4	5pi. rose and pale blue	£425	£475

The 10pa. was prepared but not issued (*Price £34 un*).

1880. T **9** of Turkey handstamped with T **1** and further handstamped with T **2** (both in blue), in Philippopolis.

5	10pa. black and mauve	95·00	90·00

The 10pa. overprinted with Type **2** only was prepared but not issued (*Price £55 un*).

(Typo Constantinople)

1881. P 13½.

6	**3**	5pa. black and olive-green	11·00	1·30
7		10pa. black and blue-green	19·00	1·30
		a. Error. 10pa. black and carmine	£600	
8		20pa. black and carmine	1·70	1·10
9		1pi. black and pale blue	5·50	4·25
		b. Black and lilac-blue	5·50	4·25
10		5pi. red and grey-blue	55·00	80·00

The error consisting of No. 9 *se-tenant* with a 1pi. stamp of Turkey, formerly No. 9a, is listed under Turkey No. 93a.

Stamps of the above series perf 11½, tête-bêche pairs and imperforate stamps are from unissued remainder stocks.

1884. Colours changed. P 11½.

11	**3**	5pa. deep lilac and pale lilac	55	55
		a. Perf 13½	1·10	3·25
12		10pa. bright green and pale green	20	55
		a. Perf 13½	17·00	16·00

The following were prepared but not issued. Prices un.

	Perf 11½	Perf 13½	Perf 11½×13
20 pa. rose	55	19·00	†
1 pi. blue	1·10	19·00	1·70
5 pi. brown	£400	£450	†

B. SOUTH BULGARIA

Following a revolt in favour of union with Bulgaria in Philippopolis (Plovdiv), the chief town of E. Roumelia, the following stamps were issued by the new régime, the name being changed to South Bulgaria.

The dates of issue are according to the Julian Calendar then in use. In the 19th century the Julian Calendar was twelve days behind the Gregorian Calendar.

(4)

(5)

Type **4**. Lion with four toes on each leg. Height from end of claw on left leg to top of crown, 14 mm.

Type **5**. Lion with three toes on each leg. Height of lion 15 to 16 mm.

There are many dangerous forgeries of these overprints, and collectors are warned to purchase only from responsible firms.

1885 (10 Sept). T **3** optd.

A. With T **4**

(i) Stamps of 1881. P 13½

(a) In dull blue or blue

13	5pa. black and olive-green	£325	£375
14	10pa. black and blue-green	£850	£800
15	20pa. black and carmine	£325	
16	1pi. black and blue	17·00	38·00
17	5pi. red and grey-blue	£1100	

(b) In black

18	1pi. black and blue	55·00	£110

(ii) Stamps of 1884. P 11½

(a) In dull blue or blue

19	5pa. deep lilac and pale lilac	34·00	80·00
20	10pa. bright green and pale green	55·00	£110
21	20pa. rose and pale rose	£325	£375

(b) In black

22	10pa. bright green and pale green (p 13½)	55·00	£110
23	20pa. rose and pale rose	55·00	80·00

B. With T **5**

(i) Stamps of 1881. P 13½

(a) In dull blue or blue

24	20pa. black and carmine	£325	
25	1pi. black and blue	80·00	95·00
26	5pi. red and grey-blue	£550	

(b) In black

27	1pi. black and blue	65·00	80·00
28	5pi. red and grey-blue	£650	

(ii) Stamps of 1884. P 11½.

(a) In dull blue or blue

29	5pa. deep lilac and pale lilac	22·00	55·00
	a. Perf 13½	85·00	95·00
30	10pa. bright green and pale green	40·00	75·00
31	20pa. rose and pale rose	£275	£325

(b) In black

32	5pa. deep lilac and pale lilac	55·00	65·00
	a. Perf 13½	39·00	65·00
33	10pa. bright green and pale green	65·00	
34	20pa. rose and pale rose	55·00	65·00

Many of the above are found with inverted or double overprint.

(6)

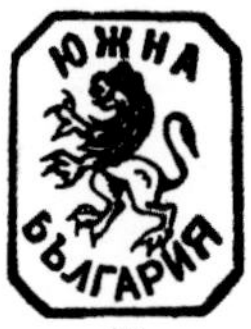

(7)

Inscription = "South Bulgaria"

Type **6**. Circular "O" at top.

Type **7**. Oval "O" at top

1885 (11 Sept). T **3** optd.

A. With T **6**

(i) Stamps of 1881. P 13½

35	5pa. black and olive-green		
36	10pa. black and blue-green		
37	20pa. black and carmine	£130	£160
38	1pi. black and blue	85·00	£110
39	5pi. red and grey-blue		

(ii) Stamps of 1884. P 11½

40	5pa. deep lilac and pale lilac	£225	£275
	a. Perf 13½	25·00	43·00
41	10pa. bright green and pale green	28·00	35·00
42	20pa. rose and pale rose	28·00	49·00

B. With T **7**

(i) Stamps of 1881. P 13½

43	5pa. black and olive-green		
44	10pa. black and blue-green		
45	20pa. black and carmine	25·00	43·00
46	1pi. black and blue	85·00	£110
47	5pi. red and grey-blue		

(ii) Stamps of 1884. P 11½

48	5pa. deep lilac and pale lilac	£225	£275
	a. Perf 13½	22·00	43·00
49	10pa. bright green and pale green	55·00	55·00
50	20pa. rose and pale rose	28·00	27·00

Many of the above are known with inverted or double overprint.

Some of these stamps are known with red overprints, and with double overprints, one of each type, or in different colours, but these are extremely rare.

Bulgarian stamps were used in South Bulgaria from 1 October 1885.

Croatia

Croatia was an independent kingdom in the early Middle Ages; : became part of Hungary in 1393. From 1918 it was part of the ingdom of the Serbs, Croats and Slovenes, known as Yugoslavia 'om 1929. For stamps issued in 1918–19 before general issues for ne Kingdom, see under Yugoslavia.

A. KINGDOM OF CROATIA

12.4.1941. 100 Paras = 1 Dinar
7.7.1941. 100 Banicas = 1 Kuna

German and Italian troops invaded Yugoslavia on 6 April 1941 and n 10 April the independence of Croatia was proclaimed. In theory : was a kingdom, but it was ruled by the Poglavnik, or leader, Ante avelić. From 7 July 1941 Croatia comprised Bosnia and Herzegovina, ne Dalmatian coast from Crikvenica to Cavtat inclusive (except for ne Italian enclave of Zara) and all territory south of the Drava and as ar west as Varaždin, including Zagreb as capital. In September 1943 ibenik was taken over from the Italians.

King Tomislav

18 May 1941–September 1943

King Tomislav renounced all claims in 1943. Although Croatia emained technically a Kingdom no successor was appointed.

(1)

(2)

(3)

(Nos. 1/25 and D26/30 optd by State Ptg Wks, Zagreb)

1941. T **99** of Yugoslavia (King Petar) optd or surch.

(a) With T **1** (12 Apr)

1	50p. orange	3·75	4·25
2	1d. green	3·75	4·25
3	1d.50 scarlet	4·25	2·20
4	2d. carmine-rose	5·00	3·25
5	3d. red-brown	8·25	8·75
6	4d. ultramarine	9·75	9·75
7	5d. blue	9·75	9·75
8	5d.50 dull violet	11·00	12·00
1/8 *Set of* 8		50·00	49·00

(b) With T **2** (21 Apr)

9	25p. black	55	65
10	50p. orange	55	65
11	1d. green	55	65
12	1d.50 scarlet	85	65
13	2d. carmine-rose	85	65
14	3d. red-brown	1·10	1·30
15	4d. ultramarine	1·30	1·80
16	5d. blue	2·00	1·80
17	5d.50 dull violet	2·20	1·80
18	6d. deep blue	2·75	3·25
19	8d. chocolate	3·75	3·25
20	12d. violet	5·00	4·25
21	16d. purple	5·50	6·50
22	20d. light blue	7·00	7·50
23	30d. pink	10·50	14·00
9/23 *Set of* 15		40·00	44·00

(c) Surch as T **3** (16 May)

24	1d. on 3d. red-brown	45	55
25	2d. on 4d. ultramarine	45	55

(4)

(5)

(6)

1941 (26 Apr). POSTAGE DUE. Nos. D259/63 II of Yugoslavia optd as T **2**, but "NEZAVISNA/DRZAVA/HRVATSKA" above shield.

D26	50p. violet	1·10	85
D27	1d. magenta	1·10	85
D28	2d. blue	22·00	27·00
D29	5d. orange	3·25	2·75
D30	10d. chocolate	16·00	16·00
D26/30 *Set of* 5		35·00	43·00

1941 (10 May). Founding of Croatian Army. T **99** of Yugoslavia (King Peter) optd with T **4**.

25*a*	25p. black (R.)	38·00	40·00
25*b*	50p. orange (B.)	38·00	41·00
25*c*	1d. green (R.)	38·00	43·00
25*d*	1d.50 scarlet (B.)	43·00	50·00
25*e*	2d. carmine-rose (B.)	49·00	50·00
25*f*	3d. red-brown (B.)	49·00	55·00
25*g*	4d. ultramarine (R.)	38·00	43·00
25*h*	5d. blue (R.)	43·00	45·00
25*i*	5d.50 dull violet (R.)	43·00	45·00
25*j*	6d. deep blue (R.)	49·00	50·00
25*k*	8d. chocolate (R.)	43·00	43·00
25*l*	12d. violet (R.)	43·00	45·00
25*m*	16d. purple (B.)	43·00	50·00
25*n*	20d. light blue (R.)	43·00	45·00
25*o*	30d. pink (B.)	49·00	50·00
25*a/o* *Set of* 15		£600	£600

Sold at double face value.

1941 (10 May). Nos. 456/7 of Yugoslavia (Slav Brod National Philatelic Exhibition), optd as T **5**, in gold.

26	1d.50+1d.50 blue-black	22·00	27·00
	a. Perf 9½ at right	£160	£170
27	4d.+3d. chocolate	22·00	27·00
	a. Perf 9½ at right	£160	£170

1941 (17 May). Postage Due stamps of Yugoslavia, Nos. D259 II and D261/3 II, optd with T **6** and used for postage.

28	50p. violet	55	55
29	2d. blue	1·60	1·60
30	5d. orange	2·20	1·60
31	10d. chocolate	2·75	2·20
28/31 *Set of* 4		6·50	5·25

7 Mt. Ozalj

8 Banja Luka

(Des O. Antonini. Photo Tipografija, Zagreb)

1941–42. As T **7** (pictorial designs) and T **8** (100k.). P 11.

32	25b. brown-red (11.41)	20	10
	a. Tête-bêche (pair)	2·40	4·00
33	50b. deep Prussian blue (15.8.41)	20	10
	a. Tête-bêche (pair)	2·75	4·25
34	75b. olive-green (7.9.42)	20	10
35	1k. blue-green (1941)	20	10
	a. Tête-bêche (pair)	2·75	5·00
36	1k.50 myrtle green (15.8.41)	20	10
	a. Tête-bêche (pair)	3·75	6·50
37	2k. claret (15.8.41)	20	10
	a. Tête-bêche (pair)	5·00	7·50
38	3k. brown-lake (13.7.42)	20	10
39	4k. ultramarine (11.41)	20	20
	a. Tête-bêche (pair)	5·00	8·25
40	5k. black (1.9.41)	2·75	1·60
	a. Tête-bêche (pair)	6·50	9·75
41	5k. greenish blue (7.9.42)	35	20
42	6k. brown-olive (1941)	35	20
	a. Tête-bêche (pair)	5·50	8·75
43	7k. orange-red (1.9.41)	35	20
	a. Tête-bêche (pair)	6·00	9·25
44	8k. red-brown (1941)	65	35
	a. Tête-bêche (pair)	6·50	10·50
45	10k. brown-violet (15.8.41)	1·30	65
	a. Tête-bêche (pair)	7·00	12·00
46	12k. olive-brown (7.9.42)	1·70	75
47	20k. brown	1·30	55
	a. Tête-bêche (pair)	8·25	13·00
48	30k. purple-brown	1·70	75
	a. Tête-bêche (pair)	9·25	14·00
49	50k. blackish green	3·25	2·20
	a. Tête-bêche (pair)	16·00	16·00
50	100k. violet (13.6.42)	5·50	4·50
32/50 *Set of* 19		19·00	11·50

Views:—50b. Waterfall at Jajce; 75b. Varaždin; 1k. Mt. Velebit; 1k.50, Zelenjak; 2k. Zagreb Cathedral; 3k. Church at Osijek; 4k. R. Drina; 5k. (No. 40) Konjic Bridge; 5k. (No. 41) Modern Building at Zemun; 6k. Dubrovnik; 7k. R. Save in Slavonia; 8k. Mosque at Sarajevo; 10k. Lake Plitvice; 12k. Klis Fortress near Split; 20k. Hvar; 30k. Harvesting in Syrmia; 50k. Senj.

D **9**

9 Croat (Sinj) Costume

10 Emblems of Germany, Croatia and Italy

(Des O. Antonini. Litho Tipografija, Zagreb)

1941 (12 Sept). POSTAGE DUE. P 11.

D51	D **9** 50b. claret	55	65
D52	1k. claret	55	65
D53	2k. claret	75	1·00
D54	5k. claret	1·30	1·40
D55	10k. claret	1·60	2·00
D51/55 *Set of* 5		4·25	5·25

(Des O. Antonini. Litho Tipografija, Zagreb)

1941 (12 Oct). Red Cross. Various national costumes as T **9**. Cross in red. P 10½×10.

51	1k.50+1k.50 blue	1·10	1·30
52	2k.+2k. brown (Travnik)	1·10	1·40
53	4k.+4k. claret (Turopolje)	2·75	3·25
51/53 *Set of* 3		4·50	5·25

Each issued in sheets of 20 stamps and five labels, four bearing a red cross and one the Croatian arms. The labels were arranged in a cross.

(Des Brili. Litho Tipografija, Zagreb)

1941 (3 Dec). Eastern Volunteer Fund. P 11½×11.

54	**10** 4k.+2k. blue	3·75	4·25

O **11**

O **12**

11 Glider

(Des V. Kirin. Litho State Ptg Wks, Zagreb)

1942 (5 Feb)–**43**. OFFICIAL.

A. P 11½

O55A	O **11** 25b. claret	20	10
O56A	50b. slate-grey	20	10
O57A	75b. green	20	10
O58A	1k. orange-brown	20	10
O59A	2k. turquoise-blue	20	10
O60A	3k. vermilion	20	10
O61A	3k.50 carmine (1943)	20	10
O62A	4k. purple-brown	20	10
O63A	5k. ultramarine	55	65
O64A	6k. violet	20	10
O65A	10k. yellow-green	35	45
O66A	12k. brown-red	45	55
O67A	12k.50 orange (1943)	20	10
O68A	20k. dark blue	55	65
O69A	O **12** 30k. brown-violet and grey	45	55
O70A	40k. violet-black and grey	55	65
O71A	50k. carmine and grey	1·30	1·60
O72A	100k. black and salmon	1·30	1·60

B. P 10½

O55B	O **11** 25b. claret	20	10
O56B	50b. slate-grey	20	10
O57B	75b. green	55	20
O58B	1k. orange-brown	20	10
O59B	2k. turquoise-blue	2·20	2·75
O60B	3k. vermilion	20	10
O62B	4k. purple-brown	20	10
O63B	5k. ultramarine	2·20	2·40
O64B	6k. violet	3·25	3·50
O65B	10k. yellow-green	20	10
O66B	12k. brown-red	3·00	3·25
O68B	20k. dark blue	3·00	3·25
O69B	O **12** 30k. brown-violet and grey	45	55
O70B	40k. violet-black and grey	55	65
O71B	50k. carmine and grey	1·50	1·60
O72B	100k. black and salmon	1·50	1·60

Some printings of 25, 50, 75b., 1, 2, 3, 3k.50, 5, 6 and 12k.50, all perf 11½, were made on very thin paper.

(Des R. Valić. Photo State Ptg Wks, Zagreb)

1942 (25 Mar). Aviation Fund. T **11** and similar designs. P 11½×11 (vert) or 11×11½ (horiz).

55	2k.+2k. brown	1·10	1·60
	a. Imperf vert (horiz pair)		
56	2k.50+2k.50 green	1·60	1·80
57	3k.+3k. lake	2·00	2·20
58	4k.+4k. blue	2·75	3·25
55/58 *Set of* 4		6·75	8·00
MS58 Two sheets, each 124×110 mm, comprising Nos. 55 and 57 but colours changed and with higher premiums (No. 57 also larger)			
	a. 2k.+8k. blue; 3k.+12k. lake. Imperf	65·00	65·00
	b. 2k.+8k. lake; 3k.+12k. blue. P 11	65·00	65·00

Designs: Horiz—2k.50, Glider (different); 4k. Seaplane glider. Vert—3k. Boy with model glider.

(**12**)

(**13**)

14 Trumpeters

1942 (10 Apr). 1st Anniv of Croat Independence. As Nos. 37, 40 and 45 (new colours), variously optd as T **12**, by Tipografija, Zagreb).

59	2k. purple-brown	55	75
60	5k. lake (Br.)	85	1·10
61	10k. blue-green	1·60	2·00
59/61 *Set of* 3		2·75	3·50

1942 (13 June). Banja Luka Philatelic Exhibition. As No. 50, but inscr "F.I." in top right corner. P 11.

62	**8** 100k. violet	5·50	6·00

1942 (23 June). No. 37 surch as T **13**, by State Ptg Wks, Zagreb.

63	"0.25Kn" on 2k. claret (Br.)	55	75
	a. Tête-bêche (pair)	3·25	4·25

(Des O. Antonini. Photo Tipografija, Zagreb)

1942 (5 July). National Relief Fund. As T **14** (inscr "POMOC"). P 11½.

64	3k.+1k. brown-lake	1·50	1·60
65	4k.+2k. chocolate	2·10	2·20
66	5k.+5k. greenish blue	3·00	3·25
64/66 *Set of* 3		6·00	6·25

Designs: Vert (25×31 mm)—5k. Mother and child. Horiz (31×25 mm)—4k. Procession beneath Triumphal Archways.

D 15 **15** Šestine (Croatia) **15a** Red Cross Sister

(Des V. Kirin. Typo or litho State Ptg Wks, Zagreb)

1942–44. POSTAGE DUE. Network background in second colour.

(a) Typo. Size 25×24¾ mm. P 11½ (1942)

D67 **D 15** 50b. grey-olive and pale blue (24.8). 45 55
D68 1k. grey-olive and pale blue (30.7). 55 65
a. Perf 10½ 55 65
D69 2k. grey-olive and pale blue (30.7). 55 65
a. Perf 10½ 1·70 1·80
D70 5k. grey-olive and pale blue (5.8) 55 65
a. Perf 10½ 1·50 1·60
D71 10k. deep blue and pale blue (5.8) 1·60 1·70
a. Perf 10½ 1·70 1·80
D72 20k. deep blue and pale blue (5.8) 2·30 2·40
a. Perf 10½ 3·50 3·75

(b) Litho. Size 24¼×24 mm. P 12½ (50b., 1k., 4k.) or 11½ (others) (1943–44)

D73 **D 15** 50b. grey-brown and light blue (4.43) 10 20
a. Perf 12×10 22·00 27·00
D74 1k. grey-brown and light blue (4.43.) 10 20
D75 2k. grey-brown and light blue (4.43) 20 35
D76 4k. grey-brown and light blue (10.2.44) 35 55
D77 5k. grey-brown and light blue (19.5.43) 45 65
D78 6k. grey-brown and light blue (24.11.43) 35 55
D79 10k. indigo and blue 45 75
D80 15k. indigo and blue 45 75
D81 20k. indigo and blue (1944) 1·70 2·20

(Des O. Antonini. Photo Tipografija, Zagreb)

1942 (4 Oct). Red Cross Fund. T **15** and similar vert designs showing girls in costumes. Cross in red. P 11½.

67 **15** 1k.50+0k.50 orange-brown 2·00 2·10
68 – 3k.+1k. violet (Slavonia) 2·10 2·20
69 – 4k.+2k. blue (Bosnia) 2·75 3·00
70 – 10k.+5k. olive-bistre (Dalmatia) 3·50 3·75
71 **15** 13k.+6k. claret 7·25 7·50
67/71 *Set of* 5 16·00 17·00

Each issued in sheets of 24 stamps and one centre label bearing the date, coat of arms and a red cross.

(Des O. Antonini. Litho Tipografija, Zagreb)

1942 (4 Oct). CHARITY TAX. Red Cross Fund. Cross in red. P 11½.

71*a* **15a** 1k. green 85 90

16 M. Gubec **17**

(Des Baldasar and Vulpe. Photo State Ptg Wks, Vienna)

1942 (22 Nov). Croat ("Ustascha") Youth Fund. T **16** and similar type. P 14½.

72 3k.+6k. brown-lake 85 1·10
73 4k.+7k. sepia 85 1·10

Miniature sheet (81×95 mm)

MS73*a* 5k.+20k. indigo. P 12 30·00 35·00
MS73*b* 5k.+20k. indigo. Imp 30·00 35·00

Nos. 72/3 were each issued in sheets of 16 stamps arranged in four blocks of 4, the blocks separated by nine labels each inscribed with the name of a fighter killed at Senj.

(Des R. Auer. Litho Tipografija, Zagreb)

1943 (17 Jan). Labour Front. T **17** and similar designs showing workers. Lozenge wmk. P 11½.

74 2k.+1k. sepia and olive 5·25 5·50
75 3k.+3k. sepia and purple-brown 5·25 5·50
76 7k.+4k. sepia and blue-grey 5·50 6·00
74/76 *Set of* 3 14·50 15·00

19 Arms of Zagreb **20** Trakošćan Castle

(Des O. Antonini. Photo Tipografija, Zagreb)

1943 (23 Mar). Seventh Centenary of Foundation of Zagreb. P 11.

77 **19** 3k.50(+6k.50) blue 5·50 6·00

(Des O. Antonini. Photo Tipografija, Zagreb)

1943–44. Castles. T **20** and similar design.

(a) Pelure paper. P 11

78 3k.50 deep crimson (28.3.43) 75 1·00
79 12k.50 black (14.4.43) 1·10 1·30

(b) Ordinary paper. P 12

79*a* 3k.50 purple-brown (5.44) 65 1·30

Design:—12k.50, Veliki Tabor.

21 A. Pavelić **22** Krsto Frankopan

(Photo State Ptg Works, Vienna)

1943 (10 Apr). Croat ("Ustascha") Youth Fund. P 14.

80 **21** 5k.+3k. brown-red 65 1·10
81 7k.+5k. green 75 1·10

Miniature sheet (81×94 mm). (17.5.43)

MS81*a* **21** 12k.+8k. deep ultramarine. P 12 35·00 40·00
MS81*b* 12k.+8k. deep ultramarine. Imperf 35·00 40·00

Nos. 80/1 were each issued both in sheets of 16 stamps and 9 inscribed labels, and in sheets of 100.

(Des I. Režek. Eng K. Seizinger. Recess State Ptg Wks, Vienna)

1943 (7 June). Famous Croats. As T **22** (portraits). P 12×12½.

82 1k. blue (Katarina Zrinska) 55 55
83 2k. olive-green 55 55
84 3k.50 carmine (Petar Zrinski) 65 75
82/84 *Set of* 3 1·60 1·70

23 Croat Sailor and Motor Torpedo Boats **24** St. Mary's Church and Cistercian Monastery 1650

(Des R. Valić. Litho Tipografija, Zagreb)

1943 (1 July). Croat Legion Relief Fund. As T **23** (inscr "HRVATSKA LEGIJA"). P 11½.

85 1k.+0k.50 green 35 45
86 2k.+1k. carmine 35 45
87 3k.50+1k.50 blue 35 45
88 9k.+4k.50 red-brown 35 45
85/88 *Set of* 4 1·30 1·60

Designs:—2k. Pilot and Heinkel He 111H bomber; 3k.50, Infantrymen; 9k. Mechanised column.

Miniature sheet (102×89 mm). Nos. 85/8 but colours changed. P 11½.

MS88*a* 1k.+0k.50 blue; 2k.+1k. green; 3k.50+1k.50 red-brown; 9k.+4k.50 grey-black 7·50 8·25
MS88*b* As last but imperf 7·50 8·25

(Des after V. Kirin. Eng K. Seizinger. Recess State Ptg Works, Vienna)

1943 (12 Sept). Philatelic Exhibition, Zagreb. P 14.

89 **24** 18k.+9k. slate-blue 7·00 7·50
MS89*a* 99×132 mm. **24** 18k.+9k. brownish black. P 12½ 20·00 20·00

1943 (12 Sept). Return of Šibenik to Croatia. No. 89 optd HRVATSKO MORE/8, IX./1943.

90 **24** 18k.+9k. slate-blue (R.) 14·00 15·00

25 Mother and Children **26** Nurse and Patient **26a**

(Des I. Režek. Litho, cross typo Tipografija, Zagreb)

1943 (3 Oct). Red Cross Fund. Cross in red. P 11.

91 **25** 1k.+0k.50 greenish blue 55 75
92 2k.+1k. carmine 55 75
93 3k.50+1k.50 blue 55 75
94 **26** 8k.+3k. red-brown 75 1·10
95 9k.+4k. yellow-green 85 1·10
96 **25** 10k.+5k. violet 1·20 1·30
97 **26** 12k.+6k. ultramarine 1·40 1·60
98 **25** 12k.50+6k. chocolate 1·80 2·00
99 **26** 18k.+8k. brown-orange 3·00 3·25
100 32k.+ 12k. grey 4·25 4·50
91/100 *Set of* 10 13·50 15·00

(Des I. Režek. Litho, cross typo Tipografija, Zagreb)

1943 (3 Oct). CHARITY TAX. Red Cross Fund. Cross in red. P 11.

100*a* **26a** 2k. blue 75 90

27 A. Pavelić **28** Ruder Bosković

(Des K. Seizinger. Litho State Ptg Wks, Zagreb)

1943–44.

(a) Size 20½×26 mm. P 12½ or 14 (32k.)

101 **27** 0k.25 brown-red (17.1.44) 35 2
102 0k.75 bronze-green (8.5.44) 35 2
103 5k. ultramarine (8.5.44) 35 2
104 32k. chocolate (13.4.44) 1·10 5

(b) Size 22×28 mm. P 12½ (3k., 8k. and 9k.), or P 14 (others)

105 **27** 0k.50 dull blue (9.2.44) 35 2
106 1k. bright green (17.5.44) 35 2
107 1k.50 slate-purple (8.5.44) 35 2
108 2k. claret (24.11.43) 35 2
109 3k. brown-lake (13.4.44) 35 2
110 3k.50 blue (20.2.44) 35 2
a. Perf 11½ (13.6.43) 3·75 4·2
111 4k. bright purple (8.5.44) 35 2
112 8k. orange-brown (13.4.44) 35 2
113 9k. carmine (17.5.44) 35 2
114 10k. maroon (8.5.44) 45 3
115 12k. olive-bistre (13.4.44) 45 3
116 12k.50 black (28.1.44) 55 3
117 **7** 18k. brown (13.4.44) 65 5
118 50k. bluish green (13.4.44) 1·60 5
119 70k. orange (13.4.44) 2·20 1·1
120 100k. violet (18.5.44) 3·25 2·2
101/120 *Set of* 20 13·00 8·0

No. 110a was issued in 1943 on the occasion of Pavelić birthday.

(Des I. Režek. Eng K. Seizinger. Recess State Ptg Works, Vienna)

1943 (13 Dec). Honouring Ruder Bosković (astronomer). P 11.

121 **28** 3k.50 brown-lake 65 5
122 12k.50 brown-purple 75 8

29 Posthorn **30** St. Sebastian

(Des I. Režek. Litho Tipografija, Zagreb)

1944 (1 Feb). Postal and Railway Employees' Relief Fund. Symbolical designs as T **29**. P 11.

123 7k.+3k.50 brown-red and bistre 70 8
124 16k.+8k. blue and light blue 75 8
125 24k.+12k. carmine and rose 1·00 1·1
126 32k.+16k. black and scarlet 1·50 1·6
123/126 *Set of* 4 3·50 4·0

Designs: Horiz—32k. Winged wheel. Vert—16k. Dove, aeroplan and globe; 24k. Mercury.

(Des I. Režek. Litho Tipografija, Zagreb)

1944 (15 Feb). War Invalids Relief Fund. Designs as T **30**. P 11.

127 7k.+3k.50 claret, red and rose 75 8
128 16k.+8k. blue-green and yellow-green 1·00 1·1
129 24k.+12k. yellow, brown and red 1·10 1·3
130 32k.+16k. blue and light blue 2·00 2·2
127/130 *Set of* 4 4·25 5·0

Designs: Vert—24k. Mediæval statuette. Horiz—16k. Blind man an cripple; 32k. Death of Petar Svavić, 1094.

Each issued in sheets of 8 stamps and one centre label.

31 The Legion in Action **32** Jure-Ritter Francetić

(Des O. Antonini. Photo State Ptg Works, Vienna)

1944 (22 May). Croat Youth Fund. T **31**, **32** and similar vert design. Imperf.

131 **31** 3k.50+1k.50 red-brown 15 20
132 – 12k.50+6k.50 blue 15 20
133 **32** 18k.+9k. blackish brown 15 20
131/133 *Set of* 3 40 55

Design:—12k.50, Sentries on the Drina.

1944 (22 May). Honouring Jure-Ritter Francetić. As No. 133 but new value and colour. P 14½.

134 **32** 12k.50+287k.50 black 14·00 18·00

33

(Des O. Antonini. Eng K. Seizinger. Recess State Ptg Works, Vienna)

1944 (20 Aug). Labour Front. Designs as T **33** inscr "D.R.S.". P 12½.

135	3k.50+1k. scarlet	10	20
	a. Perf 14½	9·75	13·00
	b. Perf 11	65	75
136	12k.50+6k. sepia (Digging)	35	55
	a. Perf 14½	13·00	16·00
	b. Perf 11	1·60	1·80
137	18k.+9k. blue (Instruction)	35	45
	a. Perf 14½	20·00	22·00
	b. Perf 11	1·20	1·30
138	32k.+16k. green ("On parade")	45	55
135/138 *Set of 4*		1·10	1·60
MS138*a* 74×100 mm. 32k.+16k. (as No. 138) grey-brown/yellow		5·50	6·50

Nos. 135/8 were issued in sheets of 8 stamps and one label.

34 Bombed Home

35 War Victim

(Des B. Muhamed. Litho State Pig Wks, Zagreb)

1944 (1 Jan–19 June). CHARITY TAX. War Victims. P 12.

138*b*	**34**	1k. blue-green (1 Jan)	20	35
138*c*	**35**	2k. claret (1 Jan)	20	35
138*d*		5k. blackish green (15 June)	35	45
138*e*		10k. blue (15 June)	55	65
138*f*		20k. brown (19 June)	1·30	1·40
138*b*/138*f* *Set of 5*			2·30	3·00

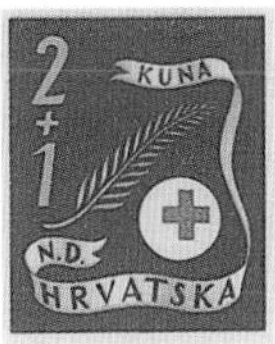

36

37 Storm Division Soldiers

(Des I. Režek. Litho Tipografija, Zagreb)

1944 (12 Nov). Red Cross. Cross in red. P 11½.

139	**36**	2k.+1k. green	45	55
140		3k.50+1k.50 crimson	55	65
141		12k.50+6k. blue	65	75
139/141 *Set of 3*			1·50	1·80

1945 (9 Jan). Creation of Croatian Storm Division on 9th Oct, 1944. T **37** and similar horiz designs. Grey network background. Litho. P 11½.

142	50k.+50k. red	£180	£225
143	70k.+70k. sepia	£180	£225
144	100k.+100k. blue	£180	£225
142/144 *Set of 3*		£475	£600
MS144*a* 216×134 mm. Nos. 142/4		£2000	£2500

Designs:—70k. Storm Division soldiers in action; 100k. Divisional emblem.

38

39

1945. Postal Employees' Fund. Designs as T **38**. Photo. P 11½.

145	3k.50+1k.50 grey	20	35
146	12k.50+6k. reddish purple	35	45
147	24k.+12k. green	45	55
148	50k.+25k. purple	65	85
145/148 *Set of 4*		1·50	2·00
MS148*a* 99×110 mm. 100k.+50k. brown-red		11·00	13·00

Designs:—12k.50, Telegraph linesman; 24k. Telephone switchboard; 50k., 100k. The Postman calls.

(Photo Tipografija, Zagreb)

1945 (1 May). Labour Day. P 12.

149	**39**	3k.50 red-brown	1·10	2·00

After Yugoslav partisans and Russian troops had gained complete control of Croatia early in 1945, Croatia became a state in the new Federal People's Republic of Yugoslavia.

The issues made in 1945 before the resumption of Yugoslav issues for the whole country are listed under Yugoslavia.

A "Croatian Government in Exile" has produced numerous stamps since 1951 but these are regarded as propaganda labels.

B. REPUBLIC OF CROATIA

April 1991. 100 Paras = 1 (Yugoslav) Dinar
23 December 1991. 100 Paras = 1 (Croatian) Dinar
1994. 100 Lipa = 1 Kuna

Following the break-up of the Federation of Yugoslavia, Croatia declared itself independent on 26 June 1991 and had received widespread international recognition by January 1992. Yugoslav stamps became invalid on 16 January 1992.

BOGUS STAMPS. Yugoslav stamps overprinted with Croatian arms are bogus.

PRINTER AND PROCESS. The following issues from No. 150 to 457 were printed in lithography by Zrinski Printing Company, Čakoveć, *unless otherwise stated*.

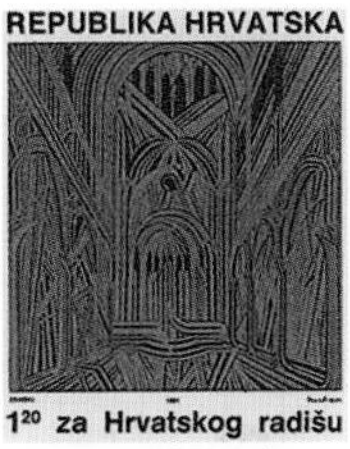

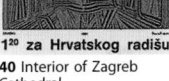

40 Interior of Zagreb Cathedral

41 Statue of the Virgin and Shrine

(Des B. Bućan)

1991 (1–15 Apr). OBLIGATORY TAX. Workers' Fund. Mass for Croatia. P 13½×14.

150	**40**	1d.20 gold and black	75	65
		a. Perf 11	16·00	14·00
		b. Perf 11×10½	85	75
		c. Imperf (15 Apr)	1·20	1·10

No. 150 was for compulsory use on mail during April.

OBLIGATORY TAX STAMPS. Nos. 150/3, 157/8, 160/5 and 168 were each issued in sheets of 30 (5×6) containing 25 stamps and five labels. One label, showing the Croatian arms, appears on R. 3/3 and the design of each issue is repeated across four further labels at R. 5/4–5 and R. 6/4–5.

Imperforate examples of these stamps were originally intended for philatelic sale but were available at face value from post offices and were used on mail when supplies of the perforated stamps became exhausted.

(Des M. Veža)

1991 (16 May). OBLIGATORY TAX. Workers' Fund. 700th Anniv of Shrine of the Virgin, Trsat. P 10½×11.

151	**41**	1d.70 multicoloured	55	55
		a. Imperf	85	75

No. 151 was for compulsory use on mail from 16 to 31 May.

42 State Arms

43 Members of Parliament

(Des M. Šutej)

1991 (1–3 July). OBLIGATORY TAX. Workers' Fund. Rally in Ban Jelačić Square, Zagreb. P 11×10½.

152	**42**	2d.20 multicoloured	55	55
		a. Imperf (3 July)	85	75

No. 152 was for compulsory use on mail during July.

For similar 10d. design but inscription at foot replaced by "HPT" emblem, see No. 170.

(Des B. Ljubičić)

1991 (1 Aug). OBLIGATORY TAX. Workers' Fund. First Multiparty Session of Croatian Parliament, 30 May 1990. P 11×10½.

153	**43**	2d.20 multicoloured	55	55
		a. Imperf	85	75

No. 153 was for compulsory use on mail during August.

44 Sud Aviation SE 210 Caravelle Jetliner over Zagreb Cathedral and Dubrovnik

(Des Z. Jakuš (1d.), B. Ljubičić (2d.), Z. Tišljar (3d.))

1991 (9 Sept)–**92**. AIR. T **44** and similar horiz designs. P 11×10½.

154	1d. new blue, black and scarlet	35	35
	a. Perf 14 (24.6.92)	20	20
155	2d. multicoloured (9.10.91)	35	35
	a. Perf 14 (14.4.92)	20	20
156	3d. multicoloured (20.11.91)	35	35
154/156 *Set of 3*		95	95

Designs:—2d. Bell tower and ruins of Diocletian's Palace, Split; 3d. Sud Aviation SE 210 Caravelle jetliner over Zagreb Cathedral and Pula amphitheatre.

Nos. 154/6 were originally intended to pay the additional airmail fee of 1d. per 10 grams, but, in the event, were widely used on other mail.

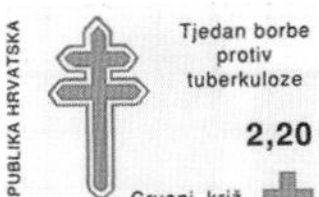

45 Anti-tuberculosis Emblem

46 Ban Jelačić Statue

1991 (14 Sept). OBLIGATORY TAX. Anti-tuberculosis Week. P 11.

157	**45**	2d.20 rose-red and ultramarine	35	35

No. 157 was for compulsory use on mail from 14 to 21 September.

(Des Z. Tišljar)

1991 (1 Nov). OBLIGATORY TAX. Workers' Fund. Re-erection of Ban Josip Jelačić Equestrian Statue, Zagreb. P 11×10½.

158	**46**	2d.20 multicoloured	55	55
		a. Imperf	85	75

No. 158 was for compulsory use on mail during November.

(**47**)

48 First Article of Constitution in Croatian

1991 (Nov). No. 150/b surch with T **47** in black on gold.

159	**40**	4d. on 1d.20 gold and black (p 13½×14)	55	55
		a. Perf 11	6·50	6·50
		b. Perf 11×10½	55	55

(Des B. Ljubičić)

1991 (1 Dec). OBLIGATORY TAX. Workers' Fund. First Anniv of New Constitution. T **48** and similar vert designs. Multicoloured. P 11×10½.

160	2d.20 Type **48**	60	55
	a. Sheet of 30. Nos. 160×15, 161/5 each×2 and 5 labels	20·00	
	b. Imperf	2·75	2·20
	ba. Sheet of 30. Nos. 160b×15, 161b/5b each×2 and 5 labels	£225	
161	2d.20 Text in English	1·40	1·30
	b. Imperf	13·00	12·00
162	2d.20 Text in French	1·40	1·30
	b. Imperf	13·00	12·00
163	2d.20 Text in German	1·40	1·30
	b. Imperf	13·00	12·00
164	2d.20 Text in Russian	1·40	1·30
	b. Imperf	13·00	12·00
165	2d.20 Text in Spanish	1·40	1·30
	b. Imperf	1·40	1·30
160/165 *Set of 6*		8·00	7·50

Nos. 160/5 were issued, *se-tenant*, in the sheet format described beneath No. 150. No. 161 occurs on R. 1/1–2, No. 162 on R. 2/1–2, No. 163 on R. 4/1–2, No. 164 on R. 5/1–2 and No. 165 on R. 6/1–2 with the remaining stamps being No. 160.

Nos. 160/5 were for compulsory use on mail during December.

49 Book of Croatian Independence

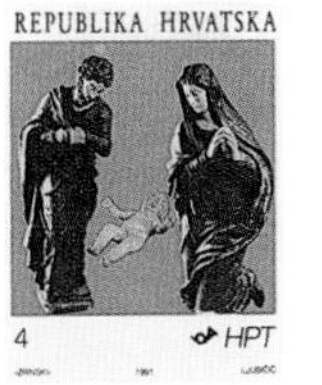

50 17th-century Crib Figures, Kosljun Monastery, Krk

(Des Z. Tišljar)

1991 (10 Dec). Recognition of Independence. P 12.

166	**49**	30d. multicoloured	1·30	1·30

No. 166 also exists imperforate from a souvenir folder.

(Des B. Ljubičić)

1991 (11 Dec). Christmas. P 12.

167	**50**	4d. multicoloured	85	85

No. 167 also exists imperforate from a souvenir folder.

New Currency

51 "VUKOVAR" and Barbed Wire

52 Ban Josip Jelačić

(Des B. Ljubičić)

1992 (1 Jan). OBLIGATORY TAX. Vukovar Refugees' Fund. P 11×10½.

168	**51**	2d.20 reddish brown and black	75	75
		a. Imperf	1·10	1·10

No. 168 was for compulsory use on mail during January.

1992 (3 Jan). No. 151 surch as T **47** in black on gold.

169	**41**	20d. on 1d.70 multicoloured	6·50	6·50

1992 (15 Jan–July). Design as No. 152 but redrawn with new value and "HPT" emblem replacing obligatory tax inscr at foot. P 11×10½.

170	**42**	10d. multicoloured	45	45
		a. Perf 14 (26 July)	20	20

(Des R. Labaš and M. Šutej)

1992 (1 Feb–2 Apr). Famous Croatians. T **52** and similar vert designs. Multicoloured. P 11×10½ (Nos. 171/2) or 14 (No. 173).

171 4d.+2d. Type **52** ... 50 50
172 4d.+2d. Dr. Ante Starčević (founder of Party of the Right) (4 Mar) ... 45 45
173 7d.+3d. Stjepan Radić (founder of Croatian Peasant Party) (2 Apr) ... 45 45
171/173 *Set of 3* ... 1·30 1·30

The premiums on Nos. 171/3 initially represented an obligatory tax charge on all internal and overseas mail. From 15 May 1992 all three stamps were declared valid for postage at their full face values, 6d. or 10d.

53 Olympic Rings

54 Osijek Cathedral on Paper Dart

(Des B. Ljubičić)

1992 (4 Feb). Winter Olympic Games, Albertville, France. P 11×10½.

174 **53** 30d. multicoloured ... 1·00 1·00

(Des B. Bućan)

1992 (14 Feb). AIR. P 11×10½.

175 **54** 4d. multicoloured ... 35 35

55 Knin

56 Statue of King Tomislav, Zagreb

(Des I. Šiško)

1992 (28 Feb–July). Croatian Towns (1st series). T **55** and similar horiz designs. P 11×10½. (20d.) or 14 (others).

176 6d. multicoloured (18 Apr) ... 20 20
177 7d. multicoloured (8 Apr) ... 35 35
178 20d. deep ultramarine, carmine-red and orange-yellow ... 95 80
a. Perf 14 (26 July) ... 45 45
179 30d. multicoloured (21 May) ... 55 55
180 45d. yellow-brown, violet and scarlet (14 Apr) ... 65 65
181 50d. multicoloured (28 Apr) ... 75 75
182 300d. multicoloured (26 June) ... 3·25 3·25
176/182 *Set of 7* ... 6·75 6·75

Designs:—7d. Von Eltz Castle, Lukovar; 20d. St. Francis's Church, Ilok; 30d. Dr. Ante Starčević Street, Gospić; 45d. Rector's Palace, Dubrovnik; 50d. St. Jakov's Cathedral, Šibenik; 300d. Sokak Street, Beli Manastir.

See also Nos. 208/14, 382/7, 523/24, 636 and 639.

(Des and eng Z. Jakuš. Recess Stamp Ptg Office, Stockholm)

1992 (5 May). Coil stamp. P 12½×imperf.

183 **56** 10d. deep green ... 20 20

The coils have every tenth stamp numbered on the reverse.

57 Red Cross Emblems on Globe

58 Map of Croatia on Red Cross

59 Railway Station, Zagreb

1992 (8 May). OBLIGATORY TAX. Red Cross Week. P 11.

184 **57** 3d. scarlet and black ... 35 35

For compulsory use from 8 to 15 May.

1992 (1 June). OBLIGATORY TAX. Solidarity Week. P 11.

185 **58** 3d. bright rose-red and black ... 35 35

For compulsory use from 1 to 7 June.

(Des M. Šutej and V. Žiljak)

1992 (30 June). Centenary of Zagreb Main Railway Station. P 14.

186 **59** 30d. multicoloured ... 35 35

60 Society Imprint

61 Bishop Josip Strossmayer (patron) and Academy Building

(Des F. Paro)

1992 (8 July). 150th Anniv of Matica Hrvatska (Croatian language society). P 14.

187 **60** 20d. gold and bright scarlet ... 25 25

(Des R. Labaš and F. Paro)

1992 (9 July). 125th Anniv of Croatian Academy of Sciences and Arts. P 14.

188 **61** 30d. multicoloured ... 35 35

62 Olympic Rings on Computer Pattern

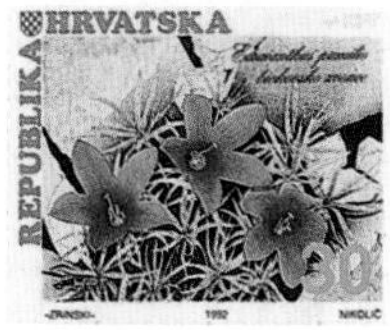

63 Bellflowers (*Edraianthus pumilio*)

(Des M. Šutej and V. Žiljak (40d.), Z. Keser (105d.))

1992 (25 July). Olympic Games, Barcelona. T **62** and similar horiz design. Multicoloured. P 14.

189 40d. Type **62** ... 35 35
190 105d. Rings and symbolic sports ... 85 85

(Des T. Nikolić)

1992 (28 July). Flowers. T **63** and similar multicoloured design. P 14.

191 30d. Type **63** ... 30 30
192 85d. Degenia (*Degenia velebitica*) (vert) ... 75 75

64 Blue Rock Thrush (*Monticola solitarius*)

65 15th-century Carrack, Dubrovnik

(Des D. Cifrek)

1992 (30 July). Environmental Protection. T **64** and similar horiz design. Multicoloured. P 14.

193 40d. Type **64** ... 35 35
194 75d. Red-spot snake (*Elaphe situla*) ... 75 75

(Des Z. Borić (30d.), B. Ljubičić (75d.))

1992 (31 July). Europa. 500th Anniv of Discovery of America by Columbus (1st issue). T **65** and similar horiz design. P 14.

195 30d. multicoloured ... 55 55
196 75d. black and vermilion ... 1·10 1·10

Designs:—75d. "Indian Horseman" (bronze statue in Chicago by Ivan Meštrović).

See also Nos. 198/9.

66 "Madonna of Bistrica"

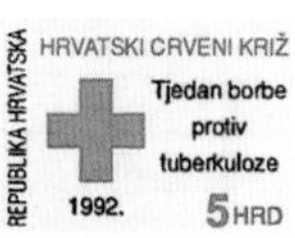

67 Red Cross

(Des D. Šimunković. Photo)

1992 (1 Aug). OBLIGATORY TAX. Fund for National Shrine to Madonna of Bistrica. P 14.

197 **66** 5d. gold and deep new blue ... 35 35

For compulsory use from 1 to 8 August.

1992 (4 Sept). Europa. 500th Anniv of Discovery of America by Columbus (2nd issue). As Nos. 195/6 but new face values and with additional C.E.P.T. posthorns emblem in gold. P 14.

198 **65** 60d. multicoloured ... 1·10 1·10
199 – 130d. black, vermilion and gold (as No. 196) ... 2·75 2·75

1992 (14 Sept). OBLIGATORY TAX. Anti-tuberculosis Week. P 11.

200 **67** 5d. rosine and black ... 45 45

For compulsory use from 14 to 21 September.

68 "25"

69 Dove and Coat of Arms

(Des B. Ljubičić)

1992 (2 Oct). Croatian Language Anniversaries. T **68** and similar horiz design. Multicoloured. P 14.

201 40d. Type **68** (25th anniv of Croatian Language Declaration) ... 35 35
202 130d. "100" (centenary of Croatian Orthography by Dr. Ivan Broz) ... 55 55

(Des H. Šercar)

1992 (16 Oct). 750th Anniv of Grant of Royal City Charter to Samobor. P 14.

203 **69** 90d. multicoloured ... 55 55

70 Remains of Altar Screen from Uzdoije Church

71 St. George and the Dragon

(Des Z. Keser)

1992 (30 Oct). 1100th Anniv of Duke Mucimir's Donation (judgement in ecclesiastical dispute). P 14.

204 **70** 60d. multicoloured ... 35 35

(Des O. Berberović and D. Eljuga)

1992 (4 Nov). OBLIGATORY TAX. Croatian Anti-cancer League. P 14.

205 **71** 15d. multicoloured ... 35 35

For compulsory use from 4 to 11 November.

See also No. 255.

72 Seal of King Béla IV

73 "Croatian Christmas" (Ljubo Babić)

(Des Z. Keser)

1992 (16 Nov). 750th Anniv of Zagreb's Charter from King Béla IV. P 14.

206 **72** 180d. multicoloured ... 70 70

(Des J. Biffel)

1992 (7 Dec). Christmas. P 14.

207 **73** 80d. multicoloured ... 45 45

FLUORESCENT BURELAGE. Many stamps issued from 1993 have a fluorescent burelage forming an intricate network. This can be seen only under an ultra-violet lamp. Apart from the following set, this burelage occurs on various issues between No. 230 and No. 343 plus No. 362.

74 Former Town Hall, Vinkovci

75 Lorković

(Des I. Šiško)

1992 (14 Dec)–**94**. Croatian Towns (2nd series). T **74** and similar multicoloured designs. Fluorescent burelage (Nos. 209 and 212/14). P 14.

208 100d. Type **74** ... 35 20
209 200d. Castle, Pazin (vert) (9.4.93) ... 45 35
210 500d. Jelačić Square, Slavonski Brod (9.2.93) ... 1·00 85
211 1000d. Town Hall, Ban Josip Jelačić Square, Varaždin (15.3.93) ... 1·40 1·10
212 2000d. Zorin cultural centre, Karlovac (20.5.93) ... 1·60 1·60
213 5000d. St. Donat's Church and bell tower of St. Stošija's Cathedral, Zadar (vert) (24.9.93) ... 2·40 2·00
214 10000d. Pirovo peninsula and Franciscan monastery, Vis (22.2.94) ... 3·50 3·00
208/214 *Set of 7* ... 9·75 8·25

Nos. 215/17 are vacant.

(Des Z. Čular)

1992 (21 Dec). Death Centenary of Blaž Lorković (political economist). P 14.

218 **75** 250d. multicoloured ... 85 85

76 Coiled National Colours

77 Bunić-Vučić

(Des Z. Čular)

1992 (22 Dec). 150th Anniv of *Kolo* (literary magazine). P 14.

219 **76** 300d. multicoloured ... 1·10 1·10

(Des Z. Keser)

1992 (29 Dec). 400th Birth Anniv of Ivan Bunić-Vučić (poet). P 14.

220 **77** 350d. multicoloured ... 1·20 1·20

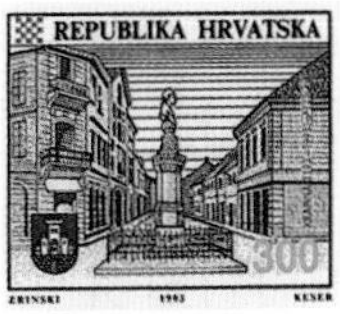

78 Ljudevit Gaj Square, Krapina

79 Tesla

(Des Z. Keser)

1993 (15 Jan). 800th Anniv of Krapina. P 14.
221 **78** 300d. multicoloured 85 85

(Des Nada Žiljak)

1993 (30 Jan). 50th Death Anniv of Nikola Tesla (physicist). P 14.
222 **79** 250d. multicoloured 70 70

80 Quiquerez (self-portrait)

81 Red Deer (*Cervus elaphus*)

(Des J. Biffel)

1993 (10 Feb). Death Centenary of Ferdo Quiquerez (painter). P 14.
223 **80** 100d. multicoloured 35 35

(Des D. Cifrek)

1993 (23 Feb). Animals of the Kopački Rit Swamp. T **81** and similar horiz design. Multicoloured. P 14.
224 500d. Type **81** .... 1·20 1·20
225 550d. White-tailed sea eagle (*Haliaeetus albicilla*) .... 1·30 1·30

82 Šulentić (self-portrait)

83 Kursalon, Lipik

(Des J. Biffel)

1993 (16 Mar). Birth Centenary of Zlatko Šulentić (painter). P 14.
226 **82** 350d. multicoloured 60 60

(Des Nada Žiljak)

1993 (25 Mar). Centenary of Lipik Spa. P 14.
227 **83** 400d. multicoloured 65 65

84 Kovačić. (statue, Vojin Bakić)

85 Minčeta Fortress, Dubrovnik

(Des J. Biffel)

1993 (16 Apr). 50th Death Anniv of Ivan Goran Kovačić (writer). P 14.
228 **84** 200d. multicoloured 40 40

(Des H. Šercar)

1993 (19 Apr). 59th P.E.N. Literary Congress, Dubrovnik. P 14.
229 **85** 800d. multicoloured .... 1·50 1·50
No. 229 was issued both in sheets of 20 stamps and in sheetlets of six stamps and six inscribed labels.

86 Ivan Kukuljević (writer)

87 Mask and Split Theatre

(Des J. Biffel)

1993 (2 May). 150th Anniv of First Speech in Croatian Language made to Croatian Parliament. Fluorescent burelage. P 14.
230 **86** 500d. multicoloured 75 75

(Des P. Jakelić)

1993 (6 May). Centenary of Split Theatre. P 14.
231 **87** 600d. multicoloured 85 85

88 Boy and Ruined House

89 Pag in 16th Century

1993 (8 May). OBLIGATORY TAX. Red Cross Week. P 11.
232 **88** 80d. black and scarlet 35 35
For compulsory use from 8 to 15 May.

(Des F. Paro)

1993 (18 May). 550th Anniv of Refoundation of Pag. Fluorescent burelage. P 14.
233 **89** 800d. multicoloured .... 1·00 1·00

90 Dove

91 Girl at Window

(Des Z. Keser)

1993 (22 May). First Anniv of Croatia's Membership of United Nations. Fluorescent burelage. P 14.
234 **90** 500d. multicoloured 60 60

1993 (1 June). OBLIGATORY TAX. Solidarity Week. P 11.
235 **91** 100d. black and bright scarlet 35 35
For compulsory use from 1 to 7 June.

92 "In the Café" (Ivo Dulčić)

(Des J. Biffel)

1993 (5 June). Europa. Contemporary Art. T **92** and similar horiz designs. Multicoloured. Fluorescent burelage. P 14.
236 700d. Type **92** .... 1·20 1·20
237 1000d. "The Waiting Room" (Miljenko Stančić) .... 2·50 2·50
238 1100d. "Two Figures" (Ljubo Ivančić) .... 3·75 3·75
236/238 *Set of* 3 .... 6·75 6·75
Nos. 236/8 were issued both in separate sheets of 20 stamps and together in *se-tenant* sheetlets of six containing two examples of each value (*Price of sheetlet*: £16).

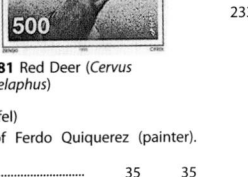

93 "Homodukt" (Milivoj Bijelić)

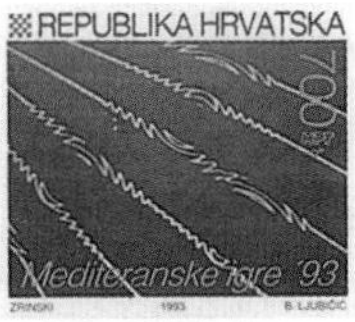

94 Swimming Pool

(Des J. Biffel)

1993 (10 June). 45th Art Biennale, Venice. T **93** and similar vert designs. Multicoloured. Fluorescent burelage (Nos. 239/40). P 14.
239 250d. Type **93** 35 35
240 600d. "Snails" (Ivo Deković) 85 85
241 1000d. "Esa carta de mi flor" (Željko Kipke) .... 1·20 1·20
239/241 *Set of* 3 .... 2·20 2·20
Nos. 239/41 were each issued both in separate sheets of 20 stamps and in separate sheetlets of four.

(Des B. Ljubičić)

1993 (15 June). 12th Mediterranean Games, Agde and Roussillon (Languedoc), France. Fluorescent burelage. P 14.
242 **94** 700d. multicoloured 80 80

95 "Slavonian Oaks"

(Des J. Biffel)

1993 (16 June). 150th Birth Anniv of Adolf Waldinger (painter). Fluorescent burelage. P 14.
243 **95** 300d. multicoloured 40 40

96 Battle of Krbava, 1493

(Des J. Biffel)

1993 (6 July). Anniversaries of Famous Battles. T **96** and similar horiz design showing 16th-century engravings. Fluorescent burelage. P 14.
244 800d. Type **96** 90 90
245 1300d. Battle of Sisak, 1593 .... 1·50 1·50

97 Krleža (after Marija Ujević)

98 Cardinal Stepinac

(Des J. Biffel)

1993 (7 July). Birth Centenary of Miroslav Krleža (writer). Fluorescent burelage. P 14.
246 **97** 400d. multicoloured 60 60

(Des D. Šimunković)

1993 (15 July). OBLIGATORY TAX. Cardinal Stepinac Foundation. Fluorescent burelage. P 14.
247 **98** 150d. black, bright magenta and gold 40 40
For compulsory use from 15 to 22 July.

99 Croatian Postman

100 Paljetak

(Des B. Bućan)

1993 (20 July). First Anniv of Croatia's Membership of Universal Postal Union. Fluorescent burelage. P 14.
248 **99** 1800d. multicoloured .... 1·40 1·40

(Des R. Labaš and J. Biffel)

1993 (7 Aug). Birth Centenary of Vlaho Paljetak (singer-songwriter). Fluorescent burelage. P 14.
249 **100** 500d. multicoloured 55 55

101 Peter Zrinski and Krsto Frankopan

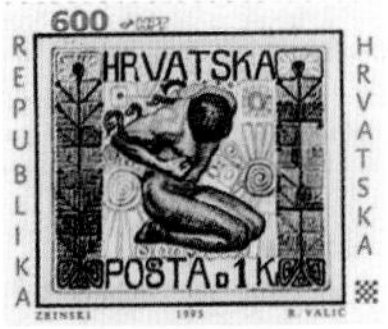

102 "Freedom of Croatia" (central motif of 1918 stamp)

(Des D. Popović, D. Zglavnik and O. Franković)

1993 (12 Aug). OBLIGATORY TAX. Zrinski-Frankopan Foundation. Fluorescent burelage. P 14.
250 **101** 200d. ultramarine and bluish grey 40 40
For compulsory use from 12 to 19 August.

(Des J. Biffel)

1993 (9 Sept). Stamp Day. Fluorescent burelage. P 14.
251 **102** 600d. multicoloured 70 70

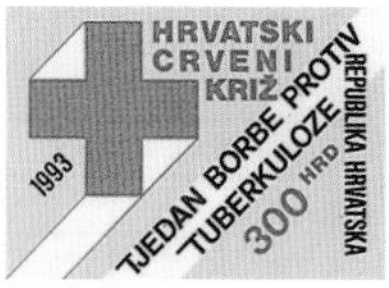

103 Red Cross

104 Antonio Magini's Map of Istria, 1620

1993 (14 Sept). OBLIGATORY TAX. Anti-tuberculosis Week. Fluorescent burelage. P 11.
252 **103** 300d. sage green, black and scarlet..... 40 40
For compulsory use from 14 to 21 September.

(Des F. Paro)

1993 (20 Sept). 50th Anniv of Incorporation of Istria, Rijeka and Zadar into Croatia. Fluorescent burelage. P 14.
253 **104** 2200d. multicoloured.............................. 1·60 1·60

105 Smičiklas

106 Allegory of Birth of Croatian History on Shores of the Adriatic

(Des D. Popović, D. Zglavnik and O. Franković)

1993 (1 Oct). 150th Birth Anniv of Tadija Smičiklas (historian). Fluorescent burelage. P 14.
254 **105** 800d. black, gold and scarlet.................. 70 70

(Des O. Berberović and D. Eljuga)

1993 (11 Oct). OBLIGATORY TAX. Croatian Anti-cancer League. As No. 205 but face value changed. Fluorescent burelage. P 14.
255 **71** 400d. multicoloured.................................. 40 40
For compulsory use from 11 to 31 October.

(Des B. Bućan)

1993 (27 Oct). Centenary of National Archaeological Museum, Split. P 14.
256 **106** 1000d. multicoloured.............................. 80 80

107 Girl in Heart

108 Croatian and French Flags and Soldiers

(Des Nada Žiljak)

1993 (1 Nov). OBLIGATORY TAX. Save Croatian Children Fund. P 14.
257 **107** 400d. scarlet, new blue and black........ 40 40

(Des Nada Žiljak)

1993 (17 Nov). 50th Anniv of Uprising of 13th Pioneer Battalion, Villefranche-de-Rouergue, France. Fluorescent burelage. P 14.
258 **108** 3000d. multicoloured.............................. 2·00 2·00

109 Tomić

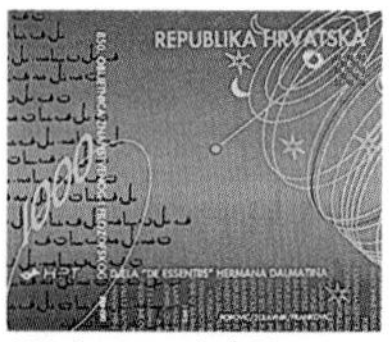

110 Astronomical Diagram

(Des R. Labaš)

1993 (18 Nov). 150th Birth Anniv of Josip Eugen Tomić (writer). Fluorescent burelage. P 14.
259 **109** 900d. deep brown, pale sage green and scarlet.. 55 55

(Des D. Popović, D. Zglavnik and O. Franković)

1993 (30 Nov). 850th Anniv of Publication of De Essentiis by Herman Dalmatin. Fluorescent burelage. P 14.
260 **110** 1000d. multicoloured.............................. 55 55

111 Christmas on the Battlefield

112 Skiers

(Des M. Šutej (1000d.), J. Biffel (4000d.))

1993 (3 Dec). Christmas. T **111** and similar vert design. Multicoloured. Fluorescent burelage. P 14.
261 1000d. Type **111**.. 55 55
262 4000d. "Nativity" (fresco, St. Mary's Church, Dvigrad).. 2·40 2·40

(Des Z. Keser)

1993 (15 Dec). Centenary of Competitive Skiing in Croatia. Fluorescent burelage. P 14.
263 **112** 1000d. multicoloured.............................. 80 80

113 Decorations and Badge

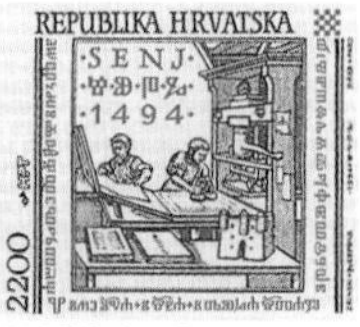

114 Printing Press

(Des I. Šiško)

1993 (22 Dec). 125th Anniv of Croatian Militia. P 14.
264 **113** 1100d. multicoloured.............................. 80 80

(Des F. Paro)

1994 (29 Jan). 500th Anniv of Printing of First Croatian Book (a Glagolitic missal), Senj. P 14.
265 **114** 2200d. chocolate and orange-red........ 1·10 1·10
No. 265 has an underprinting showing an extract from the book. This can be seen very faintly by eye but is more visible under an ultra-violet lamp.

115 Skier

116 Iguanodon

(Des L. Artuković)

1994 (12 Feb). Winter Olympic Games, Lillehammer, Norway. Fluorescent burelage. P 14.
266 **115** 4000d. multicoloured.............................. 2·20 2·20

(Des T. Nikolić)

1994 (7 Mar). Croatian Dinosaur Fossils from West Istria. T **116** and similar vert design. Multicoloured. Fluorescent burelage. P 14.
267 2400d. Type **116**.. 1·40 1·40
a. Horiz pair. Nos. 267/8.......................... 3·75 3·75
268 4000d. Iguanodon, skeleton and map......... 2·75 2·75
Nos. 267/8 were issued together in horizontal *se-tenant* pairs within the sheet, each pair forming a composite design.

117 Masthead

118 University, Emperor Leopold I's Seal and Vice-chancellor's Chain

(Des L. Artuković)

1994 (15 Mar). 150th Anniv of Zora Dalmatinska (literary periodical). Fluorescent burelage. P 14.
269 **117** 800d. multicoloured.................................. 55 55

(Des N. Mihanović and I. Šiško)

1994 (19 Apr). 325th Anniv of Croatian University, Zagreb. Fluorescent burelage. P 14.
270 **118** 2200d. multicoloured.............................. 1·10 1·10

119 Wolf (*Canis lupus*)

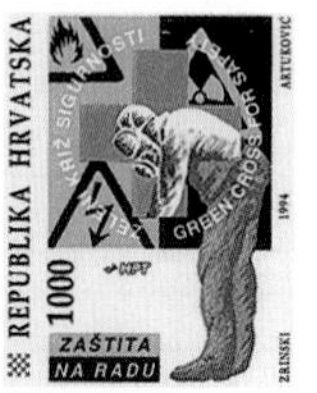

120 Safety Signs and Worker wearing Protective Clothing

(Des D. Žilić)

1994 (22 Apr). Planet Earth Day. Fluorescent burelage. P 14.
271 **119** 3800d. multicoloured.............................. 2·00 2·00

(Des L. Artuković)

1994 (2 May). 75th Anniv of International Labour Organization and 50th Anniv of Philadelphia Declaration (social charter). Fluorescent burelage. P 14.
272 **120** 1000d. multicoloured.............................. 70 70

121 Globe and Map

122 Flying Man (17th-century idea by Faust Vrančić)

1994 (8 May). OBLIGATORY TAX. Red Cross Week. P 11.
273 **121** 500d. black, yellow-ochre and bright scarlet.. 40 40
For compulsory use from 8 to 15 May.

(Des H. Šercar)

1994 (16 May). Europa. Inventions. T **122** and similar multicoloured design. Fluorescent burelage. P 14.
274 3800d. Type **122**.. 4·00 4·00
275 4000d. Quill and pencil writing surname (technical pencil by Slavoljub Penkala, 1906) (32×28 mm)............... 4·00 4·00

New Currency
1000 (old) Dinars = 1 (new) Kuna

123 Red Cross

124 Croatian Iris (*Iris croatica*)

1994 (1 June). OBLIGATORY TAX. Solidarity Week. P 11.
276 **123** 50l. scarlet-vermilion, black and greenish slate.................................. 40 40
For compulsory use from 1 to 7 June.

(Des Z. Keser)

1994 (3 June). Flowers. T **124** and similar vert design. Multicoloured. Fluorescent burelage. P 14.
277 2k.40 Type **124**.. 1·10 1·10
278 4k. Meadow saffron (*Colchicum visianii*) 1·90 1·90

125 Petrović

126 Plitvice Lakes

(Des D. Popović)

1994 (7 June). First Death Anniv of Dražen Petrović (basketball player). Fluorescent burelage. P 14.
279 **125** 1k. multicoloured.................................. 70 70

(Des M. Šutej and V. Žiljak)

1994 (15 June). 150th Anniv of Tourism in Croatia. T **126** and similar square designs. Multicoloured. With or without fluorescent burelage (283, 285/6), with burelage (others). P 14.
280 80l. Type **126**.. 25 25
281 1k. River Krka.. 40 40
282 1k.10 Kornati Islands.. 70 70
283 2k.20 Kopački Tršćak ornithological reserve.. 95 95
284 2k.40 Opatija Riviera.. 1·40 1·40
285 3k.80 Brijuni Islands.. 1·60 1·60
286 4k. Trakošćan Castle, Zagorje.................... 2·20 2·20
280/286 *Set of 7*.. 6·75 6·75
Nos. 280/6 were issued both in separate sheets of 40 and in *se-tenant* sheetlets of seven stamps and two inscribed labels (*Price of sheetlet*: £7.75).

127 Baranović at Keyboard

128 Monstrance

(Des Z. Keser (289), H. Šercar (others))

1994 (20 June). Musical Anniversaries. T **127** and similar designs. Fluorescent burelage. P 14.
287 1k. multicoloured.................................. 55 55
288 2k.20 silver, black and rose-red.................... 1·10 1·10
289 2k.40 multicoloured.................................. 1·20 1·20
287/289 *Set of 3*.. 2·50 2·50

Designs: Vert—1k. Type **127** (birth centenary of Krešimir Baranović (composer and conductor/director of Croatian National Theatre Opera, Zagreb, 1915–40)); 2k.20, Vatroslav Lisinski (composer, 175th birth anniv). Horiz—2k.40, Score and harp player (350th anniv of Pauline songbook).

(Des D. Šimunković)

1994 (15 July). OBLIGATORY TAX. Ludbreg Shrine. Fluorescent burelage. P 14.

290 **128** 50l. multicoloured 40 40

For compulsory use from 15 to 28 July.

129 Men dressed in Croatian and American Colours

130 Mother and Children

(Des L. Artuković)

1994 (15 Aug). Centenary of Croatian Brotherhood in U.S.A. Fluorescent burelage. P 14.

291 **129** 2k.20 multicoloured .... 2·00 2·00

(Des Nada Žiljak. Litho FS & HTZ)

1994 (16 Aug). OBLIGATORY TAX. Save Croatian Children Fund. P 14.

292 **130** 50l. multicoloured 40 40

For compulsory use from 16 to 29 August.

131 Family

132 St. George and the Dragon

(Des B. Ljubičić)

1994 (31 Aug). International Year of the Family. Fluorescent burelage. P 14.

293 **131** 80l. multicoloured 70 70

(Des Nada Žiljak and D. Eljuga. Litho FS & HTZ)

1994 (1 Sept). OBLIGATORY TAX. Croatian Anti-cancer, League. Phosphorescent security markings. P 14.

294 **132** 50l. multicoloured 40 40

The phosphorescent markings consist of "HRVATSKA LIGA PROTIV RAKA" in the top left-hand corner and the League emblem in the bottom corners.

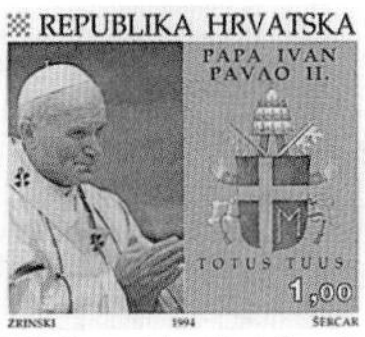

133 Pope John Paul II and his Arms

134 Franjo Bučar (Committee member, 1920–46)

(Des H. Šercar)

1994 (10 Sept). Papal Visit. Fluorescent burelage. P 14.

295 **133** 1k. multicoloured 70 70

No. 295 was issued in sheets of 16 stamps and four labels in two different designs.

(Des D. Popović)

1994 (10 Sept). Centenary of International Olympic Committee. Fluorescent burelage. P 14.

296 **134** 1k. multicoloured 70 70

135 Red Cross on Leaf

136 The Little Prince (book character)

1994 (14 Sept). OBLIGATORY TAX. Anti-tuberculosis Week. P 11.

297 **135** 50l. bright scarlet, emerald and black 40 40

For compulsory use from 14 to 21 September.

(Des H. Šercar)

1994 (20 Sept). 50th Death Anniv of Antoine de Saint-Exupéry (writer). Fluorescent burelage. P 14.

298 **136** 3k.80 multicoloured .... 1·90 1·90

137 "Resurrection" (lunette, Gati near Omiš)

138 "Still Life with Fruits and Basket" (Marino Tartaglia)

(Des H. Šercar and D. Popović)

1994 (23 Sept). 13th International Convention on Christian Archaeology, Split and Poreč. Fluorescent burelage. P 14.

299 **137** 4k. multicoloured .... 2·00 2·00

No. 299 was issued with *se-tenant* half stamp-size inscribed label.

(Des D. Popović)

1994 (12 Oct). Paintings. T **138** and similar horiz designs. Multicoloured. Fluorescent burelage. P 14.

300 2k.40 Type **138** .... 1·20 1·20

301 3k.80 "In the Park" (Milan Steiner) .... 2·00 2·00

302 4k. "Self-portrait" (Vilko Gecan) .... 2·20 2·20

300/302 *Set of 3* .... 4·75 4·75

Nos. 300/2 were each issued both in separate sheets of 24 stamps and in separate sheetlets of four.

139 Plan of Fortress

140 I.O.C. Centenary Emblem and Flame

(Des M. Arsovski. Litho HTZ)

1994 (15 Oct). OBLIGATORY TAX. 750th Anniv of Slavonski Brod. P 14.

303 **139** 50l. bistre-yellow, black and bright scarlet 40 40

For compulsory use from 15 to 28 October.

(Des I. Lacković and Librić (304/5), Z. Jakuš (others))

1994 (2 Nov). OBLIGATORY TAX. National Olympic Committee. T **140** and similar multicoloured designs incorporating either the National Olympic Committee emblem or the International Olympic Committee centenary emblem. Fluorescent burelage. P 14.

304 50l. Type **140** 40 40

a. Vert pair. Nos. 304/5 .... 85 85

305 50l. As T **140** but with National Olympic Committee emblem 40 40

306 50l. Tennis and national emblem (vert) 40 40

a. Sheetlet of 16. Nos. 306/21 .... 6·75

307 50l. Football and centenary emblem (vert) 40 40

308 50l. As No. 306 but with centenary emblem 40 40

309 50l. As No. 307 but with national emblem 40 40

310 50l. Basketball and centenary emblem (vert) 40 40

311 50l. Handball and national emblem (vert) 40 40

312 50l. As No. 310 but with national emblem 40 40

313 50l. As No. 311 but with centenary emblem 40 40

314 50l. Kayaks and national emblem (vert) 40 40

315 50l. Water polo and centenary emblem (vert) 40 40

316 50l. As No. 314 but with centenary emblem 40 40

317 50l. As No. 315 but with national emblem 40 40

318 50l. Running and centenary emblem (vert) 40 40

319 50l. Gymnastics and national emblem (vert) 40 40

320 50l. As No. 318 but with national emblem 40 40

321 50l. As No. 319 but with centenary emblem 40 40

304/321 *Set of 18* .... 6·50 6·50

Nos. 304/5 were issued together in vertical *se-tenant* pairs within sheetlets of eight stamps which exist in two versions, either with No. 304 in the top row or with No. 305 at the top; the two versions were also issued as a combined sheetlet of 16 stamps.

Nos. 306/21 were issued together in sheetlets of 16 divided into two blocks of eight separated by a gutter; the two blocks of eight were also available as separate sheetlets.

For compulsory use from 2 to 15 November.

141 Cover of *Gazophylacium*

142 St. Mark's Church and Gas Lamp

(Des D. Popović)

1994 (9 Nov). 400th Birth Anniv of Ivan Belostenec (lexicographer). Fluorescent burelage. P 14.

322 **141** 2k.20 multicoloured .... 1·10 1·10

(Des D. Popović, S. Kirinić and O. Franković)

1994 (16 Nov). 900th Anniversaries of Zagreb (323/5) and Zagreb Bishopric (326). T **142** and similar horiz designs. Multicoloured. Fluorescent burelage. P 14.

323 1k. Type **142** 40 40

a. Horiz strip of 4. Nos. 323/6 .... 3·25

324 1k. Street scene from early film, Maxi Cat (cartoon character) and left side of Zagreb Exchange 40 40

325 1k. Right side of Zagreb Exchange, Slavoljub Penkala's biplane and Cibona building 40 40

326 4k. 15th-century bishop's crosier and 17th-century view of Zagreb by Valvasor .... 1·80 1·80

323/326 *Set of 4* .... 2·75 2·75

MS327 79×59 mm. 13k.50, Penkala's biplane and street scene from early film (23×47 mm) .... 6·50 6·50

Nos. 323/6 were issued together in horizontal *se-tenant* strips of four stamps within the sheet, each strip forming a composite design.

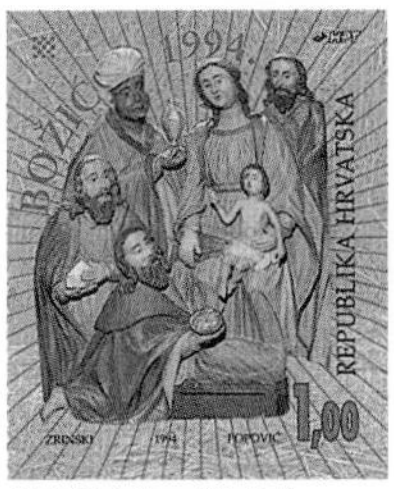

143 "Epiphany" (relief, Vrhovac Church)

144 "Translation of the Holy House" (Giovanni Battista Tiepolo)

(Des D. Popović)

1994 (1 Dec). Christmas. Fluorescent burelage. P 14.

328 **143** 1k. multicoloured 70 70

(Des D. Popović)

1994 (10 Dec). 700th Anniv of St. Mary's Sanctuary, Loreto. Fluorescent burelage. P 14.

329 **144** 4k. multicoloured .... 1·90 1·90

145 Modern Tie

146 St. Catherine's Church and Monastery, Zagreb, and Jesuit

(Des L. Artuković)

1995 (19 Jan). Ties. T **145** and similar vert designs. Multicoloured. Fluorescent burelage. P 14.

330 1k.10 Type **145** 40 40

331 3k.80 English dandy, 1810 .... 1·80 1·80

332 4k. Croatian soldier, 1630 .... 1·90 1·90

330/332 *Set of 3* .... 3·75 3·75

MS333 109×88 mm. Nos. 330/2 .... 4·75 4·75

(Des L. Artuković)

1995 (16 Feb). Monasteries. T **146** and similar horiz design. Multicoloured. Fluorescent burelage. P 14.

334 1k. Type **146** (350th anniv) 55 55

335 2k.40 St. Paul's Monastery, Visovac, and Franciscan monk (550th anniv) .... 1·40 1·40

PHOSPHORESCENT SECURITY MARKINGS. From No. 336 to 404 many stamps have phosphorescent security markings. These consist of lines forming a geometric pattern and solid yellow lozenges.

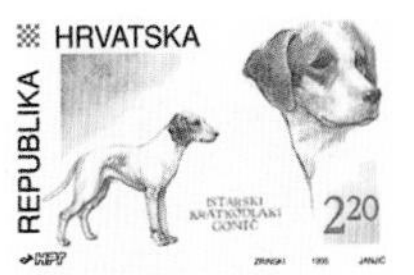

147 Istrian Short-haired Hunting Dog

148 Rowing

(Des R. Janjić)

1995 (9 Mar). Dogs. T **147** and similar horiz designs. Multicoloured. Phosphorescent security markings. P 14.

336 2k.20 Type **147** .... 1·40 1·40

337 2k.40 Posavinian hunting dog .... 1·50 1·50

338 3k.80 Istrian wire-haired hunting dog .... 2·00 2·00

336/338 *Set of 3* .... 4·50 4·50

(Des Z. Jakuš)

1995 (17 Apr). OBLIGATORY TAX. National Olympic Committee. T **148** and similar horiz designs. Multicoloured. Fluorescent burelage. P 14.

339 50l. Type **148** ... 40 40
a. Horiz strip of 5. Nos. 339/43 ... 2·10
340 50l. Pétanque ... 40 40
341 50l. Monument to Dražen Petrović, Olympic Park, Lausanne ... 40 40
342 50l. Tennis ... 40 40
343 50l. Basketball ... 40 40
339/343 *Set of 5* ... 1·80 1·80

Nos. 339/43 were issued together in horizontal *se-tenant* strips of five stamps within the sheet.
For compulsory use from 17 to 30 April.

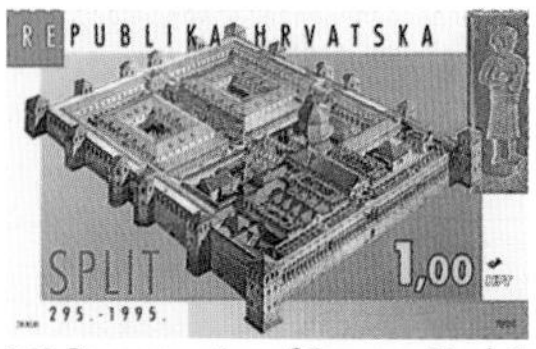

149 Reconstruction of Emperor Diocletian's Palace

(Des D. Popović)

1995 (20 Apr). 1700th Anniv of Split. T **149** and similar horiz designs. Multicoloured. Phosphorescent security markings. P 14.

344 1k. Type **149** ... 55 55
a. Horiz strip of 3. Nos. 344/6 ... 4·25
345 2k.20 "Split Harbour" (Emanuel Vidović) ... 1·20 1·20
346 4k. View of city and bust of Marko Marulić (Ivan Meštrović) ... 2·30 2·30
344/346 *Set of 3* ... 3·75 3·75
MS347 90×60 mm. 13k.40, Aerial view (23×47 mm) 6·50 6·50

Nos. 344/6 were issued together in horizontal *se-tenant* strips of three stamps within the sheet.

150 Player

151 Woman's Head

(Des D. Popović)

1995 (4 May). World Handball Championship, Iceland. Phosphorescent security markings. P 14.

348 **150** 4k. multicoloured ... 2·00 2·00

1995 (8 May). OBLIGATORY TAX. Red Cross Week. P 11.

349 **151** 50l. black and bright scarlet ... 40 40

For compulsory use from 8 to 15 May.

152 Storm Clouds and Clear Sky

153 Shadow behind Cross

(Des B. Ljubičić)

1995 (9 May). Europa. Peace and Freedom. T **152** and similar horiz design. Multicoloured. Phosphorescent security markings. P 14.

350 2k.40 Type **152** ... 2·75 2·75
351 4k. Angel (detail of sculpture, Francesco Robba) ... 5·50 5·50

(Des B. Ljubičić)

1995 (15 May). 150th Anniv of July Riots (352) and 50th Anniv of Croatian Surrender at Bleiburg (353). T **153** and similar horiz design. Multicoloured. Phosphorescent security markings. P 14.

352 1k.10 Type **153** ... 80 80
353 3k.80 Sunrise behind cross ... 1·80 1·80

154 Arms and Hand holding Rose

155 Hands

(Des M. Šutej)

1995 (30 May). Independence Day. Phosphorescent paper. P 14.

354 **154** 1k.10 multicoloured ... 70 70

No. 354 was issued in sheets of 25 stamps and five labels, four of the latter forming an enlarged version of the stamp design.

1995 (1 June). OBLIGATORY TAX. Solidarity Week. Litho. P 11.

355 **155** 50l. multicoloured ... 40 40

For compulsory use from 1 to 7 June.

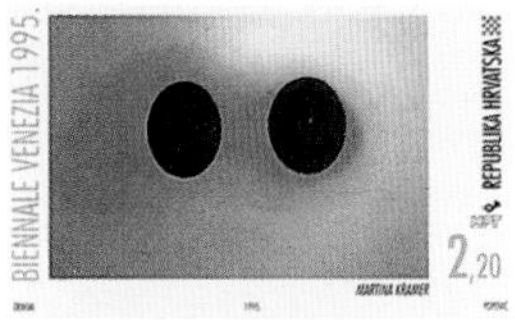

156 "Installation" (detail) (Martina Kramer)

(Des D. Popović)

1995 (8 June). 46th Art Biennale, Venice. T **156** and similar multicoloured designs showing work by Croatian artists. Phosphorescent security markings. P 14.

356 2k.20 Type **156** ... 1·20 1·20
357 2k.40 "Paraćelsus Paraduchamps" (Mirko Zrinščak) (vert) ... 1·40 1·40
358 4k. "Shadows/136" (Goran Petercol) ... 2·30 2·30
356/358 *Set of 3* ... 4·50 4·50

Nos. 356/8 were each issued both in separate sheets of 20 stamps and in separate sheetlets of four stamps.

157 "St. Antony" (detail of polyptych by Ljubo Babić, St. Antony's Sanctuary, Zagreb)

158 Loggerhead Turtle (*Caretta caretta*)

(Des J. Biffel)

1995 (13 June). 800th Birth Anniv of St. Antony of Padua. Phosphorescent paper. P 14.

359 **157** 1k. multicoloured ... 55 55

(Des D. Cifrek)

1995 (29 June). Animals. T **158** and similar horiz design. Phosphorescent security markings. P 14.

360 2k.40 Type **158** ... 1·20 1·20
361 4k. Bottle-nosed dolphin (*Tursiops truncatus*) ... 2·20 2·20

159 Osijek Cathedral

160 "Croatian Pietà"

(Des D. Šimunković)

1995 (17 July). OBLIGATORY TAX. Restoration of Sts. Peter and Paul's Cathedral, Osijek. Fluorescent burelage. P 14.

362 **159** 65l. multicoloured ... 40 40

For compulsory use from 17 to 30 July.

(Des I. Lacković (363), N. Bašić (364). Litho Graphoart Jakuš)

1995 (14 Aug). OBLIGATORY TAX. "Holy Mother of Freedom" War Memorial. T **160** and similar horiz design. P 14.

363 **160** 65l. on 50l. black, bright scarlet and dull violet-blue ... 2·00 2·00
364 65l. black, bright scarlet and dull violet-blue ... 70 70
365 – 65l. deep violet-blue and pale yellow ... 70 70
363/365 *Set of 3* ... 3·00 3·00

Design:—No. 365, Projected memorial church.
No. 363 was not issued without surcharge.
For compulsory use from 14 to 27 August.
Nos. 364/5 were issued in sheets of 20 stamps. Booklets containing two panes of 10 (one for each design) were produced for collectors only.

161 Town and Fortress

162 Electric Power Plant

(Des I. Šiško)

1995 (16 Aug). Liberation of Knin. Phosphorescent security markings. P 14.

366 **161** 1k.30 multicoloured ... 70 70

(Des R. Janjić),

1995 (28 Aug). Centenary of Jaruga Hydro-electric Power Station, River Krka. Phosphorescent security markings. P 14.

367 **162** 3k.60 multicoloured ... 1·60 1·60

163 Postman

(Des I. Lacković)

1995 (9 Sept). Stamp Day. Phosphorescent security markings. P 14.

368 **163** 1k.30 multicoloured ... 70 70

No. 369 has been left for reported Obligatory Tax stamp.

165 Suppé and Heroine of *The Fair Galatea* (operetta)

166 Petrinja Fortress (after Valvasor) and Cavalrymen

(Des A. Böcskör)

1995 (15 Sept). Death Centenary of Franz von Suppé (composer). Phosphorescent security markings. P 14.

370 **165** 6k.50 multicoloured ... 3·00 3·00

(Des H. Šercar)

1995 (21 Sept). 400th Anniv of Habsburg Capture of Petrinja. Phosphorescent security markings. P 14.

371 **166** 2k.20 multicoloured ... 1·40 1·40

No. 371 was issued in sheets of 25 stamps and five labels, four of the latter forming an enlarged version of the stamp design.

167 No Tijardović

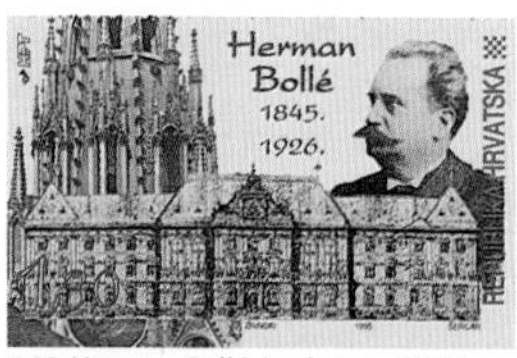

168 Herman Bollé (architect, 150th birth)

(Des Z. Keser)

1995 (23 Sept). Composers' Anniversaries. T **167** and similar vert designs. Multicoloured. Phosphorescent security markings. P 14.

372 1k.20 Type **167** (birth centenary) ... 70 70
373 1k.40 Lovro von Matačić (tenth death) ... 80 80
374 6k.50 Jakov Gotovac (birth centenary) ... 3·25 3·25
372/374 *Set of 3* ... 4·25 4·25

(Des H. Šercar)

1995 (14 Oct). Anniversaries. T **168** and similar horiz designs. Phosphorescent paper. P 14.

375 1k.30 Type **168** ... 95 95
376 2k.40 Izidor Kršnjavi (artist and art administrator, 150th birth) ... 1·20 1·20
377 3k.60 Gala curtain by Vlaho Bukovac (centenary of National Theatre) ... 2·20 2·20
375/377 *Set of 3* ... 4·00 4·00

169 Children in Nest

170 Left-hand Detail of Curtain

(Des Nada Žiljak. Litho FS & HTZ)

1995 (16 Oct). OBLIGATORY TAX. Save Croatian Children Fund. P 14.

378 **169** 65l. multicoloured ... 40 40

For compulsory use from 16 to 29 October.

(Des D. Popović)

1995 (16 Oct). OBLIGATORY TAX. Centenary of National Theatre, Zagreb. T **170** and similar vert designs showing details of gala curtain by Vlaho Bukovac. Multicoloured. Phorescent security markings. P 14.

379 65l. Type **170** ... 40 40
a. Horiz strip of 3. Nos. 379/81 ... 1·30
380 65l. Central detail ... 40 40
381 65l. Right-hand detail ... 40 40
379/381 *Set of 3* ... 1·10 1·10

Nos. 379/81 were issued together in horizontal *se-tenant* strips of three stamps within the sheet, each strip forming a composite design.
For compulsory use from 16 to 29 October.

171 Zagrebačka Street, Bjelovar

172 "50"

(Des I. Šiško)

1995 (20 Oct). Croatian Towns (3rd series). T **171** and similar multicoloured designs. P 14.

382	1k. Type **171**	40	40
383	1k.30 Sts. Peter and Paul's Cathedral, Osijek (vert)	70	70
384	1k.40 Castle, Čakoveć (vert)	80	80
385	2k.20 Rovinj	1·10	1·10
386	2k.40 Korčula	1·20	1·20
387	3k.60 Town Hall, Županja	1·50	1·50
382/387	*Set of* 6	5·25	5·25

Nos. 388/94 are vacant.

(Des B. Ljubičić)

1996 (24 Oct). 50th Anniversaries. T **172** and similar horiz design. Multicoloured. Phosphorescent security markings. P 14.

395	3k.60 Type **172** (United Nations Organization)	1·60	1·60
	a. Pair. Nos. 395/6	3·50	3·50
396	3k.60 "5" and "FAO" within biscuit forming "50" (Food and Agriculture Organization)	1·60	1·60

Nos. 395/6 were issued together in *se-tenant* pairs within the sheet.

173 Špiro Brusina (zoologist)

174 Birds flying through Sky

(Des H. Šercar (1k.), R. Janjić (2k.20), D. Jakić (6k.50))

1995 (30 Oct). Anniversaries. T **173** and similar vert designs. Multicoloured. Phosphorescent security markings. P 14.

397	1k. Type **173** (150th birth)	70	70
398	2k.20 Bogoslav Šulek (philologist, death centenary)	1·20	1·20
399	6k.50 Faust Vrančić's Dictionary of Five Most Noble European Languages (400th anniv of publication)	3·00	3·00
397/399	*Set of* 3	4·50	4·50

(Des S. Bernarda and H. Šercar)

1995 (6 Nov). OBLIGATORY TAX. Anti-drugs Campaign. P 14.

400	**174** 65l. multicoloured	40	40

For compulsory use from 6 to 19 November.

175 Breast Screening

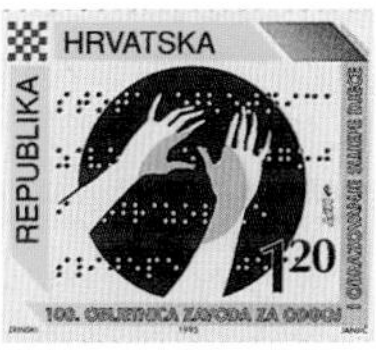

176 Hands reading Braille

(Des M. Mikulić and D. Eljuga. Litho SGI & HTZ)

1995 (20 Nov). OBLIGATORY TAX. Croatian Anti-cancer League. Breast Screening Campaign. Phosphorescent paper. P 14×13½.

401	**175** 65l. multicoloured	40	40

For compulsory use from 20 to 30 November.

(Des R. Janjić)

1995 (23 Nov). Centenary of Institute for Blind Children, Zagreb. Phosphorescent security markings. P 14.

402	**176** 1k.20 scarlet, bright lemon and black.	75	75

177 Animals under Christmas Tree

178 Polo, Animals in Boat and Court of Kublai Khan

(Des I. Lovrenčić)

1995 (1 Dec). Christmas. P 14.

403	**177** 1k.30 multicoloured	80	80

(Des H. Šercar)

1995 (7 Dec). 700th Anniv of Marco Polo's Return from China. Phosphorescent security markings. P 14.

404	**178** 3k.60 multicoloured	1·80	1·80

179 Hrvatska Kostajnica

180 Lectionary of Bernardin of Split, 1495 (first printed book using Cakavian dialect)

(Des I. Šiško)

1995 (16 Dec). Liberated Towns. T **179** and similar multicoloured designs. P 14.

405	20l. Type **179**	25	25
406	30l. Slunj	25	25
407	50l. Gračac	40	40
408	1k.20 Drniš (vert)	55	55
409	6k.50 Glina	2·75	2·75
410	10k. Obrovac (vert)	4·00	4·00
405/410	*Set of* 6	7·50	7·50

Nos. 411/19 are vacant.

(Des F. Paro)

1995 (28 Dec). Incunabula. T **180** and similar vert design. Multicoloured. Phosphorescent paper. P 14.

420	1k.40 Type **180**	80	80
421	3k.60 Callipers and last page of *Spovid Općena* (manual for confessors), 1496 (first book printed in Croatia)	2·00	2·00

181 Crucifix

182 Breast Cancer Campaign

(Des L. Artuković)

1996 (18 Jan). Events and Anniversaries. T **181** and similar vert designs. Multicoloured. P 14.

422	1k.30 St. Marko Križevčanin (detail of mosaic (Ante Starčević), St. Marko's Church, Zagreb) (canonization)	55	55
	a. Strip of 3. Nos. 422/4	1·80	
423	1k.30 Type **181** (700th anniv of veneration of miraculous crucifix, St. Guido's Church, Rijeka)	55	55
424	1k.30 Ivan Merz (teacher and Catholic youth worker, birth centenary)	55	55
422/424	*Set of* 3	1·50	1·50

Nos. 422/4 were issued together in *se-tenant* strips of three stamps within the sheet.

(Des Nada Žiljak and D. Eljuga. Litho FS & HTZ)

1996 (15 Feb). OBLIGATORY TAX. 30th Anniv of Croatian Anti-cancer League. P 14×13½.

425	**185** 65l. multicoloured	40	40

For compulsory use from 15 to 28 February.

183 Eugen Kvaternik (125th anniv of Rakovica Uprising)

184 Madonna and Child and Church

(Des N. Arbanas)

1996 (28 Feb). Anniversaries. T **183** and similar multicoloured designs. P 14.

426	1k.20 Type **183**	55	55
427	1k.40 Ante Starčević (founder of Party of the Right, death centenary) (vert)	70	70
428	2k.20 Stjepan Radić (founder of Croatian Peasant Party) (125th birth anniv and 75th anniv of Peasant Republic constitution) (vert)	1·10	1·10
429	3k.60 Collage (75th anniv of Labin Republic) (vert)	1·80	1·80
426/429	*Set of* 4	3·75	3·75

(Des H. Šercar)

1996 (18 Mar). OBLIGATORY TAX. St. Mary of Bistrica Sanctuary. Phosphorescent paper. P 14.

430	**184** 65l. multicoloured	40	40

For compulsory use from 18 to 31 March.

185 Julije Domac (founder) and Culture

186 Score

(Des D. Popović)

1996 (23 Mar). Centenary of Pharmacology Institute, University of Zagreb. Phosphorescent paper. P 14.

431	**185** 6k.50 multicoloured	2·75	2·75

(Des B. Ljubičić)

1996 (28 Mar). Music Anniversaries. T **186** and similar horiz designs. Multicoloured. Phosphorescent paper. P 14.

432	2k.20 Type **186** (400th birth anniv of Vinko Jelic, composer)	95	95
	a. Horiz strip of 4. Nos. 432/5	4·00	
433	2k.20 "O" over musical bars (150th anniv of *Love and Malice* (first Croatian opera) by Vatroslav Lisinski)	95	95
434	2k.20 Josip Slavenski (composer, birth centenary)	95	95
435	2k.20 "Lijepa naša domovino" (birth bicentenary of Antun Mihanović and 175th birth anniv of Josip Runjanin (composers of National Anthem))	95	95
432/435	*Set of* 4	3·50	3·50

Nos. 432/5 were issued together in horizontal *se-tenant* strips of four stamps within the sheet.

187 Cvijeta Zuzorić (beauty)

188 Olympic Rings

(Des H. Šercar)

1996 (11 Apr). Europa. Famous Women. T **187** and similar vert design. Multicoloured. Phosphorescent paper. P 14.

436	2k.20 Type **187**	2·30	2·30
437	3k.60 Ivana Brlić-Mažuranić (writer)	3·75	3·75

(Des D. Popović)

1996 (17 Apr). OBLIGATORY TAX. National Olympic Committee. P 14.

438	**188** 65l. multicoloured	40	40

For compulsory use from 17 to 30 April.

189 Nikola Šubić Zrinski of Sziget (Ban of Croatia)

190 Child outside House

(Des L. Artuković)

1996 (30 Apr). 16th and 17th-century Members of Zrinski and Frankopan Families. T **189** and similar vert designs. Multicoloured. Phosphorescent paper. P 14.

439	1k.30 Type **189**	70	70
440	1k.40 Nikola Zrinski (Ban of Croatia)	70	70
441	2k.20 Petar Zrinski (Ban of Croatia)	1·40	1·40
442	2k.40 Katarina Zrinski (wife of Petar and sister of Fran Krsto Frankopan)	1·50	1·50
443	3k.60 Fran Krsto Frankopan (writer and revolutionary)	1·60	1·60
439/443	*Set of* 5	5·25	5·25
MS444	117×172 mm. Nos. 439/43	6·00	6·00

1996 (8 May). OBLIGATORY TAX. Red Cross Week. P 11.

445	**190** 65l. black and scarlet	40	40

For compulsory use from 8 to 15 May.

191 Soldier carrying Child

192 Istrian Bellflower (*Campanula istriaca*)

(Des D. Popović)

1996 (28 May). Fifth Anniv of National Guard. Phosphorescent paper. P 14.

446	**191** 1k.30 multicoloured	70	70

(Des Z. Keser)

1996 (5 June). Flowers. T **192** and similar vert design. Multicoloured. Phosphorescent paper. P 14.

447 2k.40 Type **192** .... 1·10 1·10
448 3k.60 Dubrovnik cornflower (*Centaurea ragusina*) .... 1·60 1·60

193 Child with Red Cross Parcel

194 Football

1996 (6 June). OBLIGATORY TAX. Solidarity Week. P 11.

449 **193** 65l. black and scarlet 40 40
For compulsory use from 5 to 7 June.

(Des I. Belinić)

1996 (8 June). European Football Championship, England. Phosphorescent paper. P 14.

450 **194** 2k.20 black and rose-vermilion .... 1·20 1·20

195 Konšćak's Map of California

196 Children sitting outside House

(Des L. Artuković)

1996 (10 June). 250th Anniv of Father Ferdinand Konšćak's Expedition to Lower California. Phosphorescent paper. P 14.

451 **195** 2k.40 multicoloured .... 1·40 1·40

(Des Nada Žiljak. Litho FS & HTZ)

1996 (14 June). OBLIGATORY TAX. Save Croatian Children Fund. P 14×13½.

452 **196** 65l. multicoloured 40 40

197 Anniversary Emblem

198 Man holding Dumb-bell and Falcon

(Des I. Doroghy)

1996 (3 July). OBLIGATORY TAX. 800th Anniv of Osijek. Phosphorescent paper. P 14.

453 **197** 65l. blue, orange-yellow and brownish grey 40 40
For compulsory use from 3 to 16 July.

(Des Z. Keser)

1996 (4 July). 150th Birth Anniv of Josip Fon (founder of Croatian Falcon gymnastics society). Phosphorescent paper. P 14.

454 **198** 1k.40 multicoloured 70 70

199 Olympic Colours and Rings

200 Cathedral

(Des I. Belinić)

1996 (4 July). Olympic Games, Atlanta, and Centenary of Modern Olympics. Phosphorescent paper. P 14.

455 **199** 3k.60 multicoloured .... 1·80 1·80

(Des D. Šimunković)

1996 (17 July). OBLIGATORY TAX. Restoration of Dakovo Cathedral. P 14.

456 **200** 65l. multicoloured 40 40
For compulsory use from 17 to 30 July.

201 "Church Tower"

202 Crucifix

(Des B. Ljubičić)

1996 (1 Aug). OBLIGATORY TAX. 1700th Anniv of Split. P 14.

457 **201** 65l. deep ultramarine and bright new blue 40 40
For compulsory use from 1 to 14 August.

PRINTER AND PROCESS. From No. 458 onwards all stamps were printed in lithography by AKD-HTZ Stamp Printing Works, Zagreb, *unless otherwise stated.*

1996 (16 Aug). OBLIGATORY TAX. Vukovar. P 14×13½.

458 **202** 65l. multicoloured 40 40
For compulsory use from 16 to 29 August.

203 Lighted Candle, Shell and Lilies

204 Tweezers holding Stamp

(Des S. Bernardica. Litho Zrinski Ptg Co, Čakovec)

1996 (1 Sept). OBLIGATORY TAX. Anti-drugs Campaign. Phosphorescent paper. P 14.

459 **203** 65l. multicoloured 40 40
For compulsory use from 1 to 12 September.

(Des B. Ljubičić)

1996 (9 Sept). Stamp Day. Fifth Anniv of Issue of First Postage Stamp by Independent Croatia. Phosphorescent paper. P 14.

460 **204** 1k.30 multicoloured 70 70
No. 460 was issued in sheets of 16 stamps and four inscribed labels.

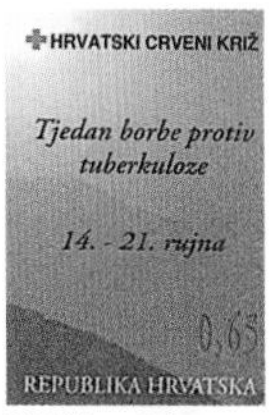

205 Mountains

206 St. Elias's Chapel, Žumberak

1996 (14 Sept). OBLIGATORY TAX. Anti-tuberculosis Week. P 11.

461 **205** 65l. multicoloured 40 40
For compulsory use from 14 to 21 September.

(Des Z. Keser)

1996 (14 Sept). 700th Anniv of First Written Reference to Žumberak. Phosphorescent paper. P 14.

462 **206** 2k.20 multicoloured 95 95

207 Illuminated Page

208 Fish and Spear

(Des Z. Keser)

1996 (19 Sept). Early Middle Ages. T **207** and similar vert design. Multicoloured. Phosphorescent paper. P 14.

463 1k.20 Type **207** (900th anniv of *Vekenega's Book of Gospels*) 55 55
464 1k.40 Gottschalk (Benedictine abbot) (1150th anniv of Gottschalk's visit to Duke of Trpimir) 70 70

(Des Z. Keser)

1996 (19 Sept). Millenary of First Written Reference to Fishing in Croatia. Phosphorescent paper. P 14.

465 **208** 1k.30 multicoloured 70 70

209 Gjuro Pilar (geologist, 150th anniv)

210 Sir Frederick Banting and Charles Best (discoverers)

(Des N. Arbanas)

1996 (4 Oct). Scientists' Birth Anniversaries. T **209** and similar horiz designs. Multicoloured. Phosphorescent paper. P 14.

466 2k.40 Type **209** 95 95
a. Horiz strip of 3. Nos. 466/8 .... 3·00
467 2k.40 Frane Bulić (archaeologist, 150th anniv) 95 95
468 2k.40 Ante Šercer (otolaryngologist, centenary) 95 95
466/468 *Set of* 3 .... 2·50 2·50
Nos. 466/8 were issued together in horizontal *se-tenant* strips of three stamps within the sheet.

(Des N. Pepeonik)

1996 (10 Oct). OBLIGATORY TAX. Croatian Diabetic Council. 75th Anniv of Discovery of Insulin. P 14.

469 **210** 65l. gold, yellow and black 40 40
For compulsory use from 10 to 17 October.

211 Laws of Dominican Nuns, Zadar

(Des D. Popović)

1996 (16 Oct). 600th Anniv of Founding of Dominican General High School (university), Zadar. Phosphorescent paper. P 13½.

470 **211** 1k.40 multicoloured 70 70

212 "Rain" (Menci Crncic)

213 "Mother of God of Remete", Zagreb

(Des J. Biffel)

1996 (7 Nov). 20th-Century Paintings. T **212** and similar horiz designs. Multicoloured. Phosphorescent paper. P 14.

471 1k.30 Type **212** 70 70
472 1k.40 "Pelješac-Korčula Channel" (Mato Medovic) 80 80
473 3k.60 "Pink Dream" (Vlaho Bukovac) .... 1·60 1·60
471/473 *Set of* 3 .... 2·75 2·75

(Des Henc)

1996 (11 Nov). OBLIGATORY TAX. P 14.

474 **213** 65l. multicoloured 40 40
For compulsory use from 11 to 24 November.

214 Children of Different Races

215 Sts. Peter and Paul's Cathedral

(Des I. Belinić)

1996 (15 Nov). 50th Anniv of United Nations Children's Fund. Phosphorescent paper. P 14.

475 **214** 3k.60 multicoloured .... 1·60 1·60

(Des L. Artuković)

1996 (2 Dec). 800th Anniv of First Written Reference to Osijek. T **215** and similar vert design. Multicoloured. Phosphorescent paper. P 14.

476 2k.20 Type **215** .... 1·10 1·10
a. Horiz pair. Nos. 476/7 .... 2·30 2·30
477 2k.20 Riverbank and view down street .... 1·10 1·10
Nos. 476/7 were issued together in horizontal *se-tenant* pairs within the sheet.

216 Nativity

217 Bond and Bank

(Des J. Botteri Dini)

1996 (3 Dec). Christmas. Phosphorescent paper. P 14.

478 **216** 1k.30 multicoloured 70 70

(Des N. Arbanas)

1996 (14 Dec). Anniversaries. T **217** and similar horiz designs. Multicoloured. Phosphorescent paper. P 14.

479 2k.40 Type **217** (150th anniv of founding of First Croatian Savings Bank, Zagreb) .... 1·10 1·10
480 3k.60 Frontispiece (bicentenary of publication of *The Principles of the Corn Trade* by Josip Šipuš) .... 1·80 1·80

218 Mihanović

219 *Professor Baltazar* (Zagreb School of Animated Film)

(Des H. Šercar. Litho Zrinski Ptg Co, Čakoveć)

1997 (6 Jan). OBLIGATORY TAX. Birth Bicentenary (1996) of Antun Mihanović. P 14.

481 **218** 65l. multicoloured 40 40

For compulsory use from 6 to 26 January.

(Des D. Popović)

1997 (16 Jan). Centenary of Croatian Films. T **219** and similar horiz designs. Multicoloured. Phosphorescent paper. P 14.

482 1k.40 Oktavijan Miletić (cameraman and director) filming *Vatroslav Lisinski* (first Croatian sound film), 1944 .... 95 95

a. Vert strip of 3. Nos. 482/4 .... 3·00

483 1k.40 Type **219** 95 95

484 1k.40 Mirjana Bohanec-Vidović and Relja Bašić in *Who Sings Means No Harm*, 1970 .... 95 95

482/484 *Set of 3* .... 2·50 2·50

Nos. 482/4 were issued together in vertical *se-tenant* strips of three stamps within the sheet.

220 Dr. Ante Starčevićs House

221 Don Quixote and Windmill

(Des K. Čop)

1997 (27 Jan). OBLIGATORY TAX. P 14.

485 **220** 65l. multicoloured 40 40

For compulsory use from 27 January to 14 February.

(Des Z. Keser (2k.20), B. Ljubičić (3k.60))

1997 (7 Feb). Birth Anniversaries. T **221** and similar multicoloured design. Phosphorescent paper. P 14.

486 2k.20 Type **221** (450th anniv of Miguel de Cervantes (author of *Don Quixote*)) 95 95

487 3k.60 Metal type (600th anniv of Johannes Gutenberg (inventor of printing)) (horiz) .... 1·60 1·60

222 Woman

223 *Big Joseph* by Vladimir Nazor (illus. Saša Santel)

(Des Nada Žiljak and D. Eljuga)

1997 (15 Feb). OBLIGATORY TAX. Croatian Anti-cancer League. P 14.

488 **222** 65l. multicoloured 40 40

For compulsory use from 15 to 28 February.

(Des N. Arbanas)

1997 (6 Mar). Europa. Tales and Legends. T **223** and similar design. Phosphorescent paper. P 14.

489 1k.30 multicoloured .... 1·40 1·40

490 3k.60 red, black and gold .... 3·50 3·50

Design: Horiz—1k.30, Elves from *Stribor's Forest* by Ivana Brlić-Mažuranić (illus. Cvijeta Job).

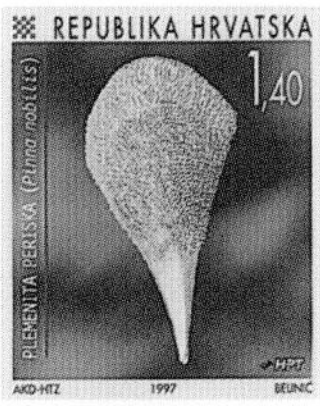

224 Noble Pen Shell (*Pinna nobilis*)

225 Comforting Hand

(Des I. Belinić)

1997 (22 Apr). Molluscs and Insects. T **224** and similar vert designs. Multicoloured. Phosphorescent paper. P 14.

491 1k.40 Type **224** 70 70

492 2k.40 *Radziella styx* (cave beetle) .... 1·10 1·10

493 3k.60 Giant tun (*Tonna galea*) .... 1·80 1·80

491/493 *Set of 3* .... 3·25 3·25

1997 (8 May). OBLIGATORY TAX. Red Cross Week. P 10½×11.

494 **225** 65l. multicoloured 40 40

a. Perf 10½ 40 40

For compulsory use from 8 to 15 May.

226 Pres. Franjo Tudjman

227 Ludwig Zamenhof (inventor)

(Des I. Belinić)

1997 (22 May). Fifth Anniv of Croatia's Membership of United Nations. Phosphorescent paper. P 14.

495 **226** 6k.50 multicoloured .... 2·75 2·75

No. 495 was issued in sheets of 10 stamps and two different labels.

(Des E. Kokot)

1997 (31 May). Croatian Esperanto (invented language) Conference. Phosphorescent paper. P 14.

496 **227** 1k.20 multicoloured 55 55

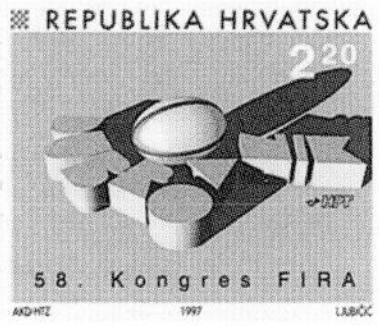

228 Congress Emblem

(Des B. Ljubičić)

1997 (6 June). 58th Congress of International Amateur Rugby Federation, Dubrovnik. P 14.

497 **228** 2k.20 multicoloured .... 1·10 1·10

229 "Vukovar" (Zlatko Atač)

1997 (8 June). Rebuilding of Vukovar. P 14.

498 **229** 6k.50 multicoloured .... 2·75 2·75

No. 498 was issued in sheets of six stamps.

230 King Petar Svačić (1095–97)

231 16th-century Dubrovnik Courier (after Nicole de Nicolai)

(Des Kokot)

1997 (3 July). Kings of Croatia. Multicoloured. P 14.

499 1k.30 Type **230** (900th death anniv) 55 55

500 2k.40 King Stjepan Držislav (996–97) 95 95

(Des N. Arbanas)

1997 (9 Sept). Stamp Day. P 14.

501 **231** 2k.30 multicoloured .... 1·10 1·10

232 Tennis

233 Turkish Attack on Šibenik, 1647

(Des Z. Keser)

1997 (10 Sept). Olympic Medal Winners. T **232** and similar vert designs. Multicoloured. P 14.

502 1k. Type **232** (Goran Ivanišević–bronze (singles and doubles), Barcelona 1992) 40 40

503 1k.20 Basketball (silver, Barcelona 1992) 55 55

504 1k.40 Water polo (silver, Atlanta 1996) (27×31 mm) 70 70

505 2k.20 Handball (gold, Atlanta 1996) (27×31 mm) .... 1·10 1·10

502/505 *Set of 4* .... 2·50 2·50

(Des Z. Keser)

1997 (18 Sept). Defence of Šibenik. T **233** and similar horiz design. Multicoloured. P 14.

506 1k.30 Type **233** (350th anniv of defence against the Turks) 55 55

a. Pair. Nos. 506/7 .... 1·20 1·20

507 1k.30 Air attack on Šibenik, 1991 .... 55 55

Nos. 506/7 were issued together in *se-tenant* pairs within the sheet.

234 Frane Petric (philosopher)

235 Parliamentary Session (after Ivan Zasche) and Ivan Kukuljević (politician)

(Des D. Popović)

1997 (17 Oct). Anniversaries. T **234** and similar horiz designs. Multicoloured. P 14.

508 1k.40 Type **234** (400th death anniv) 70 70

a. Horiz strip of 4. Nos. 508/11 .... 3·00

509 1k.40 "Madonná and Child" (detail from the polyptich of St. Michael in Franciscan Church, Cavtat) (500th anniv of first recorded work of Vicko Lovrin (artist)) 70 70

510 1k.40 Frano Kršinić (sculptor, birth centenary) 70 70

511 1k.40 Dubravko Dujšin (actor, 50th death anniv) 70 70

508/511 *Set of 4* .... 2·50 2·50

Nos. 508/11 were issued together in horizontal *se-tenant* strips of four stamps within the sheet.

(Des N. Arbanas)

1997 (23 Oct). Anniversaries. T **235** and similar vert design. Multicoloured. P 14.

512 2k.20 Type **235** (150th anniv of promulgation of Croatian as official language) .... 1·10 1·10

513 3k.60 Zagreb and elevation of school (centenary of Croatian Grammar School, Zadar) .... 1·60 1·60

236 Primordial Elephant (*Gomphoterium angustidens*)

237 "Painter in the Pond" (Nikola Mašič)

(Des Z. Keser)

1997 (6 Nov). Palaeontological Finds. T **236** and similar horiz design. Multicoloured. P 14.

514 1k.40 Type **236** 55 55

515 2k.40 Fossil of *Viviparus novskaensis* (periwinkle) 95 95

(Des D. Popović)

1997 (14 Nov). Paintings. T **237** and similar horiz designs. Multicoloured. P 14.

516 1k.30 Type **237** 55 55

517 2k.20 "Angelus" (Emanuel Vidović) 95 95

518 3k.60 "Tree in the Snow" (Slava Raškaj) .... 1·50 1·50

516/518 *Set of 3* .... 2·75 2·75

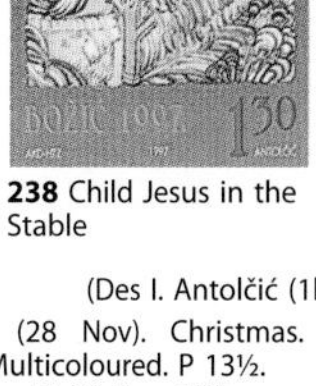

238 Child Jesus in the Stable

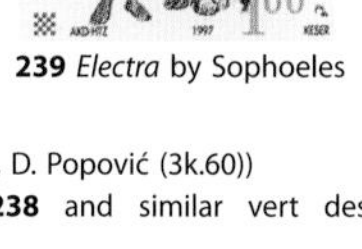

239 *Electra* by Sophoeles

(Des I. Antolčić (1k.30), D. Popović (3k.60))

1997 (28 Nov). Christmas. T **238** and similar vert design. Multicoloured. P 13½.

519 1k.30 Type **238** 55 55

520 3k.60 "Birth of Jesus" (Isidoò Kršnjavi) (33×59 mm) .... 1·40 1·40

No. 520 was issued in sheetlets of four stamps.

(Des Z. Keser)

1997 (18 Dec). Literary Anniversaries. T **239** and similar vert design. Multicoloured. P 14.

521 1k. Type **239** (400th anniv of publication of collected translations by Dominkï Zlatarić) 40 40

522 1k.20 Closed book (300th birth anniv of Filip Grabovac and 250th anniv of publication of his *Best of Folk Speech and the Illyric or Croatian Language*) . 55 55

NOTE. The obligatory use of charity stamps was discontinued in 1997. Such stamps produced after June 1997 were for voluntary use only and are not therefore eligible for listing.

240 Ilok

241 Score and Varaždin (Baroque Evenings)

(Des I. Šiško. Litho Zrinski Ptg Co. Čakovec)

1998 (2–5 Jan). Croatian Towns (4th series). T **240** and similar horiz designs. Fluorescent burelage. P 14.

523 5l. violet, cinnamon and scarlet 15 15
524 10l. yellow brown, reddish violet and scarlet (5.1.98) 30 30

Designs:—10l. Dubrovnik.

Numbers have been left for possible additions to this series.

(Des H. Šercar. Litho)

1998 (23 Jan). Europa. National Festivals. T **241** and similar vert design. Multicoloured. Phosphorescent paper. P 13½.

531 1k.45 Type **241** .... 1·40 1·40
532 4k. Dubrovnik (Summer Festival) .... 3·50 3·50

242 Olympic Rings and Japanese Red Sun

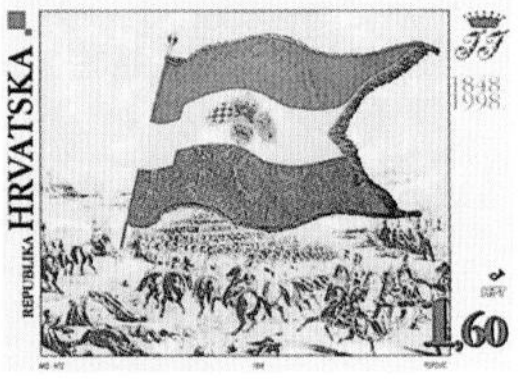

243 Jelačićs Flag and Battle near Moor (lithograph)

(Des Z. Keser. Litho)

1998 (7 Feb). Winter Olympic Games, Nagano, Japan. Phosphorescent paper. P 14.

533 **242** 2k.45 multicoloured .... 1·10 1·10

(Des D. Popović. Litho)

1998 (25 Mar). Historical Events of 1848. T **243** and similar multicoloured designs. Phosphorescent paper. P 14.

534 1k.60 Type **243** 85 85
a. Horiz strip of 3. Nos. 534/6 .... 4·00
535 1k.60 "Croatian Assembly in Session" (Dragutin Weingärtner) 85 85
536 4k. Ban Josip Jelačić (after Ivan Zasche) (21×31 mm) .... 2·00 2·00
534/536 *Set of* 3 .... 3·25 3·25

Nos. 534/6 were issued together in horizontal *se-tenant* strips of three stamps within the sheet.

244 Ante Topić Mimara

245 Caesar's Mushroom (*Amanita caesarea*)

(Des N. Šiško. Litho)

1998 (7 Apr). Birth Centenary of Ante Topić Mimara (art collector). Phosphorescent paper. P 14.

537 **244** 2k.65 multicoloured .... 1·10 1·10

(Des D. Popović. Litho)

1998 (22 Apr). Fungi. T **245** and similar vert designs. Multicoloured. Phosphorescent paper. P 14.

538 1k.30 Type **245** 70 70
a. Horiz strip of 3. Nos. 538/40 .... 5·50
539 1k.30 Saffron milk cup (*Lactarius deliciosus*) 70 70
540 7k.20 *Morchella conica* .... 3·75 3·75
538/540 *Set of* 3 .... 4·75 4·75

Nos. 538/40 were issued together in horizontal *se-tenant* strips of three stamps within the sheet.

246 Stepinac

247 Magnifying Glass over Fingerprint and Dubrovnik

(Des D. Jakić)

1998 (8 May). Birth Centenary of Cardinal Alojzije Stepinac (Archbishop of Zagreb). P 14.

541 **246** 1k.50 multicoloured 70 70

(Des N. Šiško)

1998 (13 May). 27th European Regional Conference of Interpol, Dubrovnik. P 14.

542 **247** 2k.45 multicoloured .... 1·10 1·10

248 *Falkuša* (fishing boat)

(Des D. Popović. Litho Zrinski Ptg Co, Čakovec)

1998 (3 June). Expo '98 World's Fair, Lisbon. Sheet 97×80 mm. P 14.

MS543 **248** 14k.85 multicoloured .... 6·75 6·75

249 Football

250 Title Page of *Slavonic Fairy*

(Des N. Šiško)

1998 (10 June). World Cup Football Championship, France. P 14.

544 **249** 4k. multicoloured .... 1·80 1·80

(Des N. Šiško)

1998 (13 June). Writers' Anniversaries. T **250** and similar horiz designs. Multicoloured. P 14.

545 1k.20 Type **250** (450th birth anniv of Juraj Baraković (poet)) 55 55
546 1k.50 Milan Begović (50th death anniv) 70 70
547 1k.60 Mate Balota (birth centenary) 85 85
548 2k.45 Antun Gustav Matoš (125th birth anniv) .... 1·00 1·00
549 2k.65 Matija Antun Relković (death bicentenary) .... 1·10 1·10
550 4k. Antun Branko Šimić (birth centenary) .... 1·80 1·80
545/550 *Set of* 6 .... 5·50 5·50

251 Text on Water

252 Betlheim

(Des D. Popović. Litho)

1998 (15 June). 19th Danube Countries Conference, Osijek. P 14.

551 **251** 1k.80 multicoloured 70 70

(Des D. Popović)

1998 (22 July). Birth Centenary of Dr. Stjepan Betlheim (psychoanalyst). P 14.

552 **252** 1k.50 multicoloured 70 70

253 Team Member

(Des D. Popović. Litho Zrinski Ptg Co, Čakovec)

1998 (24 July). Winning of Bronze Medal by Croatia in World Cup Football Championship. Sheet 112×82 mm containing T **253** and similar horiz designs. Multicoloured. P 14.

MS553 4k.×4, Composite design of Croatian World Cup squad .... 7·00 7·00

254 Liburnian Sewn Boat (1st century B.C.)

255 Mail Coach and Posthorn

(Des N. Šiško. Litho Zrinski Ptg Co, Čakovec)

1998 (27 Aug). Croatian Ships. T **254** and similar horiz designs. Multicoloured. P 14.

554 1k.20 Type **254** 55 55
555 1k.50 Condura (11th–12th centuries) 65 65
556 1k.60 Ragusan (Dubrovnik) carrack (16th century) 70 70
557 1k.80 Istrian bracera 85 85
558 2k.45 River Neretva sailing barge .... 1·10 1·10
559 2k.65 Barque .... 1·30 1·30
560 4k. *Vila Velebita* (sail/steam cadet ship) .. 1·80 1·80
561 7k.20 *Amorela* (car ferry) .... 3·50 3·50
562 20k. *King Petar Krešimir IV* (missile corvette) .... 9·00 9·00
554/562 *Set of* 9 .... 18·00 18·00

Nos. 554/62 were issued both in separate sheets of 50 and together in *se-tenant* sheetlets of nine stamps and three labels showing different ships.

(Des D. Popović)

1998 (9 Sept). Stamp Day. 150th Anniv of Creation of Croatian Supreme Postal Administration. P 14.

563 **255** 1k.50 multicoloured 70 70

256 Font and Cathedral

(Des D. Popović)

1998 (29 Sept). 700th Anniv of Šibenik Bishopric and Proclamation of Šibenik as a Free Borough. P 14.

564 **256** 4k. multicoloured .... 1·50 1·50

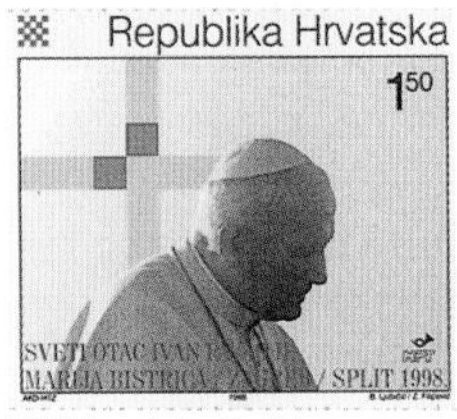

257 Pope John Paul II

258 Horse Tram, Osijek

(Des B. Ljubičić)

1998 (2 Oct). Second Papal Visit. P 14.

565 **257** 1k.50 multicoloured 70 70

No. 565 was issued in sheetlets of 12 stamps and four labels showing Cardinal Alojzije Stepinac.

(Des D. Popović)

1998 (23 Oct). Transport. T **258** and similar multicoloured designs. P 14.

566 1k.50 Type **258** 70 70
a. Horiz strip of 5. Nos. 566/70 .... 6·00
567 1k.50 First motor car in Zagreb, 1901 .... 70 70
568 1k.50 Electric train, Karlovac–Rijeka line (125th anniv) 70 70
569 1k.50 Aerial view of Oštrovica–Delnice section of Zagreb–Rijeka motorway 70 70
570 7k.20 Zagreb funicular railway (19×23 mm) .... 3·00 3·00
566/570 *Set of* 5 .... 5·25 5·25

Nos. 566/70 were issued together in horizontal *se-tenant* strips of five stamps within the sheet.

259 "Adoration of the Shepherds" (detail, from breviary Officinum Virginis illus by Klović)

260 Ibrišimović

(Des D. Popović. Litho Enschedé)

1998 (21 Nov). Christmas. 500th Birth Anniv of Julije Klović (artist). P 14×13½.

571 **259** 1k.50 multicoloured 70 70

(Des N. Šiško)

1998 (30 Nov). 300th Death Anniv of Father Luka Ibrišimović (revolutionary). P 14.

572 **260** 1k.90 multicoloured 85 85

261 Distorted Tree bound to Stake

262 "Cypress" (Frano Šimunović)

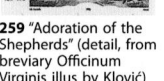

(Des N. Arbanas)

998 (10 Dec). 50th Anniv of Universal Declaration of Human Rights. P 14.
73 **261** 5k. multicoloured .... 2·10 2·10

(Des D. Popović)

998 (15 Dec). 20th-century Art. T **262** and similar multicoloured designs. P 14.
74 1k.90 "Paromlin Road" (Josip Vaništa) (horiz) .... 1·00 1·00
75 2k.20 Type **262** .... 1·10 1·10
76 5k. "Coma" (interactive video installation, Dalibor Martinis) .... 2·10 2·10
74/576 *Set of* 3 .... 3·75 3·75

263 Flags

264 Haulik

(Des B. Ljubičić. Litho)

999 (21 Jan). Zagreb Fair. P 14.
77 **263** 1k.80 multicoloured .... 1·00 1·00

(Des J. Baláš. Eng M. Činovský. Recess and photo Czech Post Office Ptg Wks)

999 (28 Jan). 130th Death Anniv of Cardinal Juraj Haulik (first Archbishop of Zagreb). Phosphorescent paper. P 11½.
78 **264** 5k. multicoloured .... 2·10 2·10

265 Mljet Island National Park

266 Viper

(Des N. Šiško)

1999 (12 Mar). Europa. Parks and Gardens. T **265** and similar horiz design. Multicoloured. Phosphorescent paper. P 14.
579 1k.80 Type **265** .... 2·10 2·10
580 5k. River Lonja Basin Nature Park .... 5·00 5·00

(Des O. Bell and D. Popović)

1999 (27 Apr). The Orsini's Viper (*Vipera ursinii*). T **266** and similar horiz designs. Multicoloured. Phosphorescent paper. P 14.
581 2k.20 Type **266** .... 1·10 1·10
a. Strip of 4. Nos. 581/4 .... 4·75
582 2k.20 Viper on alert .... 1·10 1·10
583 2k.20 Two vipers .... 1·10 1·10
584 2k.20 Viper's head .... 1·10 1·10
581/584 *Set of* 4 .... 4·00 4·00
Nos. 581/4 were issued in horizontal and vertical *se-tenant* strips of four stamps within sheets of 16.

267 Anniversary Emblem

268 Orlando's Pillar with Mask

(Des D. Popović)

1999 (5 May). 50th Anniv of Council of Europe. Phosphorescent paper. P 14.
585 **267** 2k.80 multicoloured .... 1·40 1·40

(Des Z. Keser)

1999 (8 May). 19th Foundation of European Carnival Cities Convention, Dubrovnik. Phosphorescent paper. P 14.
586 **268** 2k.30 multicoloured .... 1·10 1·10

269 1 Kreutzer Coin, 1849

270 Vladimir Nazor (writer)

(Des D. Popović)

1999 (30 May). 150th Anniv of Minting of Jelačić Kreutzer (587) and Fifth Anniv of Croatian Kuna (588). T **269** and similar multicoloured design. P 14.
587 2k.30 Type **269** .... 1·00 1·00
a. Horiz pair. Nos. 587/8 .... 3·25 3·25
588 5k. 1 kuna coin .... 2·10 2·10
Nos. 587/8 were issued together in horizontal *se-tenant* pairs within the sheet.

(Des D. Popović)

1999 (18 June). Anniversaries. T **270** and similar vert designs. Multicoloured. P 14.
589 1k.80 Type **270** (50th death anniv) 70 70
590 2k.30 Ferdo Livadić (composer, birth bicentenary) .... 1·00 1·00
591 2k.50 Ivan Rendić (sculptor, 150th birth anniv) .... 1·10 1·10
592 2k.80 Milan Lenuci (urban planner, 150th birth anniv) .... 1·30 1·30
593 3k.50 Vjekoslav Klaić (historian, 150th birth anniv) .... 1·40 1·40
594 4k. Emilij Laszowski (historian, 50th death anniv) .... 1·70 1·70
595 5k. Antun Kanižlić (religious writer and poet, 300th birth anniv) .... 2·10 2·10
589/595 *Set of* 7 .... 8·25 8·25

271 Basilicá and Mosaics of Bishop Euphrasius, St. Maurus and Fish

(Des H. Šercar)

1999 (25 June). Euphrasian Basilicá, Poreč. P 14.
596 **271** 4k. multicoloured .... 1·70 1·70

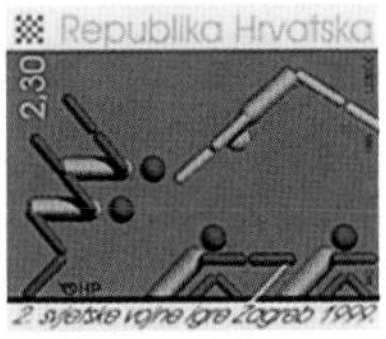
272 Swimming, Diving and Rowing

273 Reconstruction of Woman, Skull Fragments and Stone Tools

(Des B. Ljubičić)

1999 (7 Aug). Second World Military Games, Zagreb. Phosphorescent paper. P 14.
597 **272** 2k.30 multicoloured 85 85

(Des N. Šiško)

1999 (23 Aug). Centenary of Discovery of Remains of Early Man in Krapina. T **273** and similar vert design. Multicoloured. Phosphorescent paper. P 14.
598 1k.80 Type **273** 85 85
a. Horiz pair. Nos. 598/9 .... 2·75 2·75
599 4k. Dragutin Gorjanović-Kramberger (palaeontologist and discoverer of remains) and bone fragments .... 1·70 1·70
Nos. 598/9 were issued together in *se-tenant* pairs within the sheet, each pair forming a composite design.

274 UPU Emblem and Clouds

275 Lace, "Jesus expelling the Merchants from the Temple" (detail of fresco, Ivan Ranger), and Angel, St. Mary's Church

(Des D. Popović)

1999 (9 Sept). World Post Day. 125th Anniv of Universal Postal Union. Phosphorescent paper. P 14.
600 **274** 2k.30 multicoloured .... 1·10 1·10

(Des N. Šiško)

1999 (11 Sept). 600th Anniv of Founding of Paulist Monastery of the Blessed Virgin Mary in Lepoglava. T **275** and similar horiz designs. Multicoloured. Phosphorescent paper. P 14.
601 5k. Type **275** .... 2·20 2·20
a. Horiz strip of 3. Nos. 601/3 .... 6·75
602 5k. Altar angel and façade of St. Mary's Church .... 2·20 2·20
603 5k. St. Elizabeth (statue), detail of choir gallery and lace .... 2·20 2·20
601/603 *Set of* 3 .... 6·00 6·00
Nos. 601/3 were issued together in horizontal *se-tenant* strips of three stamps within the sheet.

276 Josip Jelačić, Ban of Croatia (after C. Lanzelli)

277 Cloud and Chemical Symbol for Ozone

(Des H. Šercar)

1999 (16 Sept). 150th Anniv of Composing of the Jelačić March by Johann Strauss, the elder. P 14.
604 **276** 3k.50 multicoloured .... 1·80 1·80

(Des I. Belanić. Litho Zrinski Ptg Co, Čakovec)

1999 (16 Sept). World Ozone Layer Protection Day. P 14.
605 **277** 5k. multicoloured .... 2·10 2·10

278 Pazin Grammar School

279 Andrija Hebrang

(Des I. Belanić)

1999 (15 Oct). School Anniversaries. T **278** and similar horiz design. Multicoloured. Phosphorescent paper. P 14.
606 2k.30 Type **278** (centenary) .... 1·00 1·00
607 3k.50 Požega Grammar School (300th anniv) .... 1·50 1·50

(Des H. Šercar)

1999 (21 Oct). Birth Centenary of Andrija Hebrang (politician). Phosphorescent paper. P 14.
608 **279** 1k.80 multicoloured .... 1·10 1·10

280 "Madonna of the Rose-garden" (Blaž Jurjev of Trogir)

281 "Nativity for my Children" (plaster relief, Mila Wood)

(Des N. Šiško)

1999 (28 Oct). "Croats—Christianity, Culture, Art" Exhibition, Vatican City. Phosphorescent paper. P 14.
609 **280** 5k. multicoloured .... 2·10 2·10

(Des D. Popović)

1999 (24 Nov). Christmas. Phosphorescent paper. P 14.
610 **281** 2k.30 multicoloured .... 1·10 1·10

282 "Winter Landscape" (Gabrijel Jurkić)

283 Tudjman

(Des D. Popović)

1999 (15 Dec). Modern Art. T **282** and similar multicoloured designs. Phosphorescent paper. P 14.
611 2k.30 Type **282** .... 1·00 1·00
612 3k.50 "Klek" (Oton Postružnik) .... 1·40 1·40
613 5k. "Stone Table" (Ignjat Job) (vert) .... 2·10 2·10
611/613 *Set of* 3 .... 4·00 4·00

(Des D. Popović)

1999 (16 Dec). Death Commemoration of President Franjo Tudjman. Phosphorescent paper. P 14.
614 **283** 2k.30 black and orange-vermilion .... 1·00 1·00
615 5k. deep ultramarine, black and orange-vermilion .... 2·10 2·10

284 Angel

285 Woman's Face

(Des Z. Lončarić)

2000 (1 Jan). Holy Year 2000. Phosphorescent paper. P 14.
616 **284** 2k.30 multicoloured .... 1·70 1·70

(Des Z. Lončarić)

2000 (1 Feb). St. Valentines Day. Phosphorescent paper. P 14.
617 **285** 2k.30 multicoloured .... 1·40 1·40

286 Latin Text, Building and Archbishop Stjepan Cosmi (founder)

287 Typewriter

(Des L. Artuković. Litho Zrinski Ptg Co, Čakovec)

2000 (25 Mar). 300th Anniv of Split Grammar School. Phosphorescent security markings. P 14.
618 **286** 2k.80 multicoloured .... 2·40 2·40

(Des O. Franković. Litho Zrinski Ptg Co, Čakovec)

2000 (22 Apr). Centenary of Association of Croatian Writers. Phosphorescent security markings. P 14.
619 **287** 2k.30 black and bright scarlet .... 2·10 2·10

288 "The Lamentation" (Andrija Medulić)

289 Map of Croatia and European Union Stars

(Des H. Šercar (1k.80, 2k.80, 5k.), Z. Keser (2k.30, 3k.50). Litho Zrinski Ptg Co, Čakovec)

2000 (22 Apr). Anniversaries. T **288** and similar multicoloured designs. Phosphorescent security markings. P 14.
620 1k.80 Type **288** (artist, 500th birth anniv) .. 85 85
621 2k.30 Matija Petar Katančić (poet, 250th birth anniv) .... 1·00 1·00
622 2k.80 Marija Ružička-Strozzi (actress, 150th birth anniv) .... 1·10 1·10
623 3k.50 Statue of Marko Marulić (writer, 550th birth anniv) .... 1·50 1·50
624 5k. "Madonna with the Child and Saints" (Blaž Jurjev Trogiranin) (artist, 550th death anniv) (47×25 mm) .... 2·50 2·50
620/624 *Set of* 5 .... 6·25 6·25

(Des Z. Lončarić (2k.30), J.-P. Cousin (5k.). Litho Zrinski Ptg Co, Čakovec)

2000 (9 May). Europa. 50th Anniv of Schuman Plan (proposal for pooling the coal and steel industries of France and West Germany. T **289** and similar multicoloured design. Phosphorescent security markings. P 14.
625 2k.30 Type **289** .... 2·10 2·10
626 5k. "Building Europe" (vert) .... 3·50 3·50

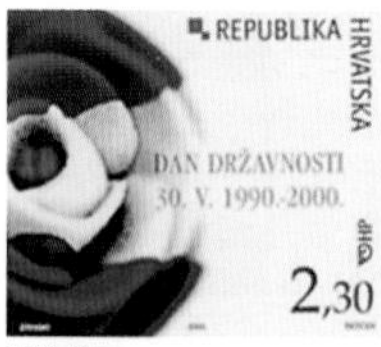

290 Flag

291 Pavilion Building

(Des S. Rešček. Litho Zriniski Ptg Co, Čakovec)

2000 (30 May). Tenth Anniv of Independence. Phosphorescent security markings. P 14.
627 **290** 2k.30 multicoloured .... 1·70 1·70

(Des N. Dogan. Litho Zriniski Ptg Co, Čakovec)

2000 (1 June). EXPO 2000 World's Fair, Hanover. Sheet 100×74 mm. P 14.
MS628 **291** 14k.40 multicoloured .... 6·25 6·25

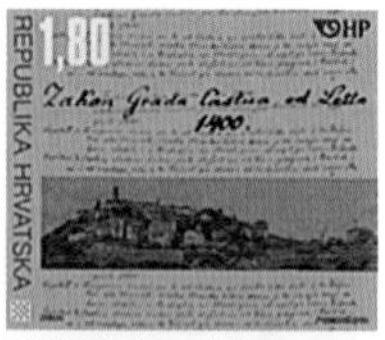

292 *Micromeria croatica*

293 Statute and Postcard of Kastav

(Des D. Popović. Litho Zrinski Ptg Co, Čakovec)

2000 (5 June). Flowers. T **292** and similar vert designs. Multicoloured. P 14.
629 3k.50 Type **292** .... 1·50 1·50
a. Pair. Nos. 629/30 .... 3·75 3·75
b. Booklet pane. No. 629×10 .... 16·00
630 5k. *Geranium dalmaticum* .... 2·10 2·10
b. Booklet pane. No. 630×10 .... 22·00
Nos. 629/30 were issued together in *se-tenant* pairs within the sheet.

(Des O. Franković. Litho Zrinski Ptg Co, Čakovec)

2000 (6 June). 600th Anniv of the Kastav Statute. P 14.
631 **293** 1k.80 multicoloured .... 1·10 1·10

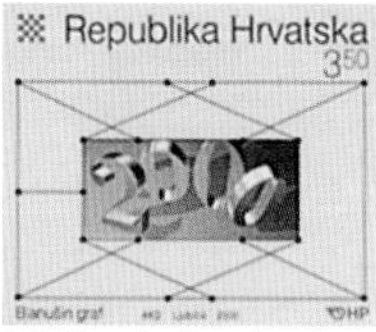

294 Blanuša Gospel and "2000"

295 Angels (fresco), St. George's Church, Purga

(Des B. Ljubičić. Litho)

2000 (15 June). World Mathematics Year. P 14.
632 **294** 3k.50 multicoloured .... 1·80 1·80

(Des O. Franković. Litho)

2000 (19 June). 300th Birth Anniv of Ivan Ranger (artist). P 14.
633 **295** 1k.80 multicoloured .... 1·10 1·10

296 Stone Tablet

(Des N. Šiško. Litho Zrinski Ptg Co, Čakovec)

2000 (24 June). 900th Anniv of Baška Stone Tablet (early Croatian written record). Sheet 95×67 mm. Phosphorescent security markings. P 14.
MS634 **296** 16k.70 multicoloured .... 7·75 7·75

297 Latin Text

298 Vis

(Des O. Franković. Litho)

2000 (10 July). 800th Birth Anniv of Toma, Archdeacon of Split. Phosphorescent paper. P 14.
635 **297** 3k.50 black, silver and ultramarine ...... 1·80 1·80

(Des I. Šiško. Litho Zrinski Ptg Co, Čakovec)

2000 (1 Aug)–**05**. Croatian Towns (5th series). Phosphorescent security markings. Multicoloured. P 14.
636 2k.30 Makarska (30.3.01) .... 1·10 1·10
639 3k.50 Type **298** .... 1·80 1·80
639*a* 3k.50 Rijeka (vert) (10.11.05) .... 1·80 1·80
640 5k. Virovitica (16.8.04) .... 2·75 2·75
636/640 *Set of* 4 .... 6·75 6·75
Numbers have been left for possible additions to this series.

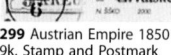

299 Austrian Empire 1850 9k. Stamp and Postmark

300 Basketball, Football, Handball, Water-polo and Tennis Balls

(Des N. Šiško. Litho)

2000 (9 Sept). World Post Day. T **299** and similar horiz design. Multicoloured. Phosphorescent paper. P 14.
641 2k.30 Type **299** (150th anniv of first stamp in territory of Croatia) .... 1·10 1·10
a. Pair. Nos. 641/2 .... 2·50 2·50
642 2k.30 Automatic sorting machine (introduction of automatic sorting system) .... 1·10 1·10
Nos. 641/2 were issued together in *se-tenant* pairs within the sheet.

(Des B. Ljubičić. Litho)

2000 (15 Sept). Olympic Games, Sydney. Phosphorescent paper. P 14.
643 **300** 5k. multicoloured .... 2·75 2·75

301 "Nativity" (relief, Church of the Blessed Virgin Mary, Ogulin)

302 "Korčula" (Vladimir Varlaj)

(Des D. Popović. Litho Zrinski Ptg Co, Čakovec)

2000 (23 Nov). Christmas. Phosphorescent security markings. P 14.
644 **301** 2k.30 multicoloured .... 1·10 1·10
a. Booklet pane. No. 644×10, with margins all round .... 11·50

(Des D. Popović. Litho Zrinski Ptg Co, Čakovec)

2000 (1 Dec). Paintings (1st series). T **302** and similar horiz designs. Multicoloured. Phosphorescent security markings. P 14.
645 1k.80 Type **302** .... 1·00 1·00
646 2k.30 "Brusnik" (Đuro Tiljak) .... 1·10 1·10
647 5k. "Boats" (Ante Kaštelančić) .... 2·75 2·75
645/647 *Set of* 3 .... 4·25 4·25
See also Nos. 675/7, 711/13, 746/8, 779/81, 826/8, 872/4 and 908/10.

303 White Dove, Ship and Village

304 Charles the Great (statue)

(Des V. Radoičić. Litho Zrinski Ptg Co, Čakovec)

2001 (1 Jan). New Millennium. Phosphorescent security markings. P 14.
648 **303** 2k.30 multicoloured .... 1·70 1·70

(Des H. Šercar. Litho Zrinski Ptg Co, Čakovec)

2001 (19 Jan). 1200th Anniv of the Coronation of Charlemagne as Emperor of the Romans. Sheet 92×78 mm. Phosphorescent security markings. P 14.
MS649 **304** 14k.40 multicoloured .... 7·00 7·00

305 Scene from *Radmio and Ljubmir* (poem)

(Des L. Artuković. Litho Zrinski Ptg Co, Čakovec)

2001 (15 Mar). 500th Death Anniv of Džore Držić (playwright). Phosphorescent security markings. P 14.
650 **305** 2k.80 multicoloured .... 1·50 1·50

306 Black Rider (comic strip character)

307 Goran Ivanišević

(Des D. Popović. Litho Zrinski Ptg Co, Čakovec)

2001 (29 Mar). Birth Centenary of Andrija Maurović (comic strip illustrator). Phosphorescent security markings. P 14.
651 **306** 5k. multicoloured .... 2·30 2·30

(Des D. Popović. Litho Zrinski Ptg Co, Čakovec)

2001 (19 Apr–31 Aug). Croatian Sporting Victories. T **307** and similar horiz design. Multicoloured. Phosphorescent security markings. P 14.
652 2k.50 Type **307** (Wimbledon Men's Champion) (31.8) .... 1·80 1·80
653 2k.80 Janica Kostelić (Alpine Skiing World Cup Women's Champion) .... 2·00 2·00

308 Olive Tree, Kaštel Štafilić

309 Water (green splash to left)

(Des D. Popović. Litho Zrinski Ptg Co, Čakovec)

2001 (20 Apr). Phosphorescent security markings. P 14.
654 **308** 1k.80 multicoloured 90 90

(Des M. Franić. Litho Zrinski Ptg Co, Čakovec)

2001 (9 May). Europa. Water Resources. T **309** and similar horiz design. Phosphorescent security markings. Multicoloured. P 14.
655 3k.50 Type **309** .... 1·50 1·50
a. Horiz pair. Nos. 655/6 .... 4·75 4·75
656 5k. Water (blue splash to right) .... 3·00 3·00
Nos. 655/6 were issued together in *se-tenant* pairs within the sheet, each pair forming a composite design.

310 Poster (Mikele Janko)

311 Apollo (*Parnassius apollo*)

(Litho Zrinski Ptg Co, Čakovec)

2001 (31 May). World No Smoking Day. Phosphorescent security markings. P 14.
657 **310** 2k.50 multicoloured ... 1·20 1·20

(Des Z. Keser. Litho Zrinski Ptg Co, Čakovec)

2001 (5 June). Butterflies. T **311** and similar vert designs. Multicoloured. Phosphorescent security markings. P 14.
658 2k.50 Type **311** ... 1·10 1·10
659 2k.80 Scarce large blue (*Maculinea teleius*) 1·20 1·20
660 5k. False ringlet (*Coenonympha oedippus*) ... 2·30 2·30
658/660 *Set of 3* ... 4·25 4·25

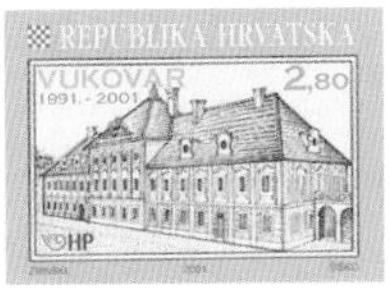

312 Vukovar

(Des I. Šiško. Litho Zrinski Ptg Co, Čakovec)

2001 (21 June). Phosphorescent security markings. P 14.
661 **312** 2k.80 multicoloured ... 1·80 1·80

313 Statues and Flames

(Des D. Popović. Litho Zrinski Ptg Co, Čakovec)

2001 (12 July). Trsteno Arboretum. Sheet 95×76 mm. Phosphorescent security markings. P 14.
MS662 **313** 14k.40 multicoloured ... 7·50 7·50

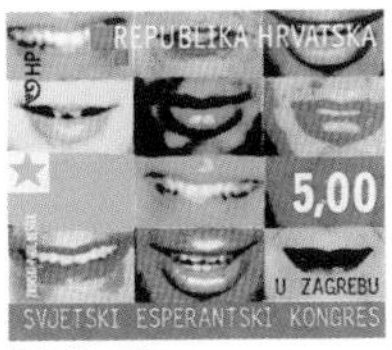

314 Mouths

315 Woman and Wall

(Des S. Rešček. Litho Zrinski Ptg Co, Čakovec)

2001 (21 July). World Esperanto Congress, Zagreb. Phosphorescent security markings. P 14.
663 **314** 5k. multicoloured ... 3·00 3·00

(Des B. Ljubičić. Litho Zrinski Ptg Co, Čakovec)

2001 (28 July). 50th Anniv of United Nations Commissioner for Refugees (No. 664) and I.O.M. International Organization for Migration (No. 665). T **315** and similar horiz design. Multicoloured. Phosphorescent security markings. P 14.
664 1k.80 Type **315** ... 1·10 1·10
665 5k. Refugees and 50IOM ... 2·75 2·75

316 Perforated Blocks of Colour

317 Croatian Sheep Dog

(Des O. Franković. Litho Zrinski Ptg Co, Čakovec)

2001 (9 Sept). Stamp Day. Phosphorescent security markings. P 14.
666 **316** 2k.50 multicoloured ... 1·10 1·10
No. 666 was issued in sheetlets consisting of two blocks of eight stamps separated by a gutter of four labels inscribed "CROATIA PHILA 2001".

(Des R. Janjić. Litho Zrinski Ptg Co, Čakovec)

2001 (4 Oct). Dog Breeds. T **317** and similar horiz design. Multicoloured. Phosphorescent security markings. P 14.
667 1k.80 Type **317** ... 1·10 1·10
668 5k. Dalmatian ... 2·75 2·75

318 Head of "Our Lady of Konavle" (statue)

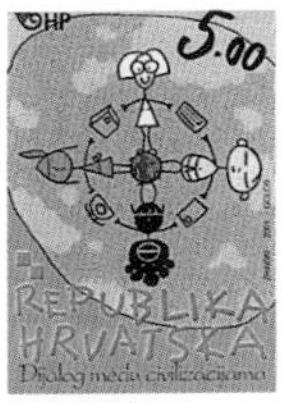

319 Children encircling Globe

(Des D. Popović. Litho Zrinski Ptg Co, Čakovec)

2001 (8 Oct). Tenth Anniv of Republic of Croatia. Phosphorescent security markings. P 14.
669 **318** 2k.30 multicoloured ... 1·10 1·10
No. 669 was issued in sheets of 25 stamps and five labels.

(Des Urska Golob and S. Gradec. Litho Zrinski Ptg Co, Čakovec)

2001 (9 Oct). U.N. Year of Dialogue among Civilizations. Phosphorescent security markings. P 14.
670 **319** 5k. multicoloured ... 2·75 2·75

320 Klis (16th-century)

(Des D. Popović. Litho Zrinski Ptg Co, Čakovec)

2001 (26 Oct). Fortresses (1st series). T **320** and similar horiz designs. Multicoloured. Phosphorescent security markings. P 14.
671 1k.80 Type **320** ... 90 90
672 2k.50 Ston (14th-century) ... 1·20 1·20
673 3k.50 Sisak (16th-century) ... 1·70 1·70
671/673 *Set of 3* ... 3·50 3·50
See also Nos. 705/7, 734/6, 776/8, 817/19 and 867/9.

321 Adoration of the Magi (altarpiece), The Visitation of Mary Church, Cučerje

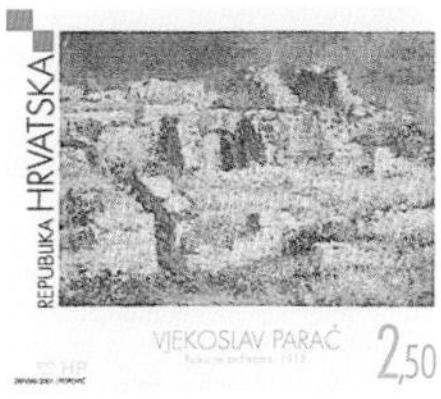

322 "Amphitheatre Ruins" (Vjekoslav Parać)

(Des D. Popović. Litho Zrinski Ptg Co, Čakovec)

2001 (22 Nov). Christmas. Phosphorescent security markings. P 14.
674 **321** 2k.30 multicoloured ... 1·20 1·20
a. Booklet pane. No. 674×10, with margins all round ... 12·50

(Des D. Popović. Litho Zrinski Ptg Co, Čakovec)

2001 (1 Dec). Paintings (2nd series). T **322** and similar multicoloured designs. Phosphorescent security markings. P 14.
675 2k.50 Type **322** ... 1·20 1·20
676 2k.50 "Maternité du Port-Royal" (Leo Junek) ... 1·20 1·20
677 5k. "Nude with a Baroque Figure" (Slavko Šohaj) (vert) ... 2·30 2·30
675/677 *Set of 3* ... 4·25 4·25

323 Lavoslav Ružička (Chemistry, 1939)

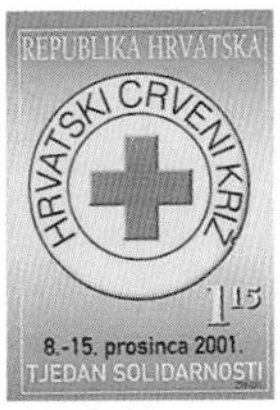

323a Emblem

(Des D. Popović. Litho Zrinski Ptg Co, Čakovec)

2001 (5 Dec). Nobel Prize Winners. T **323** and similar vert designs. Multicoloured. Phosphorescent security markings. P 14.
678 2k.80 Type **323** ... 1·50 1·50
679 3k.50 Vladimir Prelog (Chemistry, 1975) ... 2·30 2·30
680 5k. Ivo Andrić (Literature, 1961) ... 3·00 3·00
678/680 *Set of 3* ... 6·00 6·00

2001 (8 Dec). OBLIGATORY TAX. Solidarity Week. Litho. P 14.
680*a* **323a** 1k.15 orange-vermilion and black ... 60 60
For compulsory use from 8 to 15 December.

324 Ivan Gučetić

(Des O. Franković. Litho Zrinski Ptg Co, Čakovec)

2002 (24 Jan). Anniversaries. T **324** and similar horiz designs. Multicoloured. P 14.
681 1k.80 Type **324** (writer, 500th death anniv) ... 90 90
682 2k.30 Dobriša Cesarić (writer, birth centenary) ... 1·10 1·10
683 2k.50 Juraj Rattkay (historian, 350th anniv of publication of *Memoria Regum et Banorum Regnorum Dalmatia, Croatiae et Sclavoniae Ab Origine sua usque ad praesentem Annum 1652 deducta* (history of Croatia)) ... 1·20 1·20
684 2k.80 Franjo Vranjanin Laurana (sculptor, 500th death anniv) ... 1·50 1·50
685 3k.50 Augustin Kažotić (Bishop of Zagreb, 300th anniv of beatification) ... 2·30 2·30
686 5k. Matko Laginja (politician and writer, 150th birth anniv) ... 3·00 3·00
681/686 *Set of 6* ... 9·00 9·00

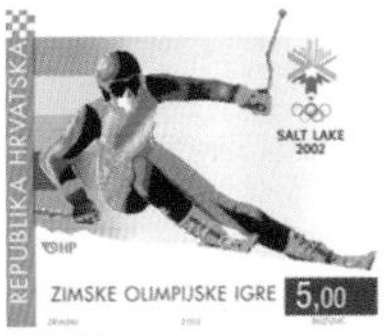

325 Skier

326 Barcode and "Reaper" (drawing, Robert Frangeš Mihanović)

(Des V. Buzolić. Litho Zrinski Ptg Co, Čakovec)

2002 (8 Feb). Winter Olympic Games, Salt Lake City, U.S.A. P 14.
687 **325** 5k. multicoloured ... 3·00 3·00

(Des Nevenka Arbanas. Litho Zrinski Ptg Co, Čakovec)

2002 (16 Feb). 150th Anniv of Croatian Chamber of Economy. P 14.
688 **326** 2k.50 multicoloured ... 1·50 1·50

327 9th-century Gable bearing Prince Trpimir's Name (detail, altar partition, Rižinice Church)

(Des H. Šercar. Litho and embossed Zrinski Ptg Co, Čakovec)

2002 (4 Mar). 1150th Anniv of Prince Trpimir's Deed of Gift of Land to Archbishop of Salona. Sheet 116×59 mm. P 14.
MS689 **327** 14k.40 multicoloured ... 7·50 7·50

328 Kuharić

(Des B. Ljubičić. Litho Zrinski Ptg Co, Čakovec)

2002 (25 Mar). Cardinal Franjo Kuharić (Archbishop of Zagreb) Commemoration. P 14.
690 **328** 2k.30 multicoloured ... 1·20 1·20

329 "Divan"

(Des J. Solpera. Eng V. Fajt. Recess and litho)

2002 (23 Apr). 80th Death Anniv of Vlaho Bukovac (artist). P 12×11½.
691 **329** 5k. multicoloured ... 2·50 2·50
No. 691 was issued with a *se-tenant* ½ stamp-sized label.
A stamp in a similar design was issued by Czech Republic.

330 Arms

331 Façade

(Des D. Zglavnik. Litho Zrinski Ptg Co, Čakovec)

2002 (24 Apr). 750th Anniv of Royal Borough of Križevci. P 14.
692 **330** 1k.80 multicoloured ... 90 90

(Des D. Popović. Litho Zrinski Ptg Co, Čakovec)

2002 (26 Apr). Centenary of Post Office Building, Varaždin. P 14.
693 **331** 2k.30 multicoloured ... 1·20 1·20

332 Clown with Umbrella

333 Stylized Player and Ball

(Des I. Molnar. Litho Zrinski Ptg Co, Čakovec)

2002 (9 May). Europa. Circus. T **332** and similar horiz design. Multicoloured. P 14.

694 **332** 3k.50 multicoloured ... 1·80 1·80

a. Pair. Nos. 694/5 ... 4·75 4·75

695 5k. multicoloured ... 2·75 2·75

Nos. 694/5 were issued in horizontal *se-tenant* pairs within the sheet.

(Des B. Benčina. Litho Zrinski Ptg Co, Čakovec)

2002 (15 May). World Cup Football Championship, Japan and South Korea. T **333** and similar vert design. Multicoloured. P 14.

696 3k.50 Type **333** ... 1·50 1·50

a. Pair. Nos. 696/7 ... 4·00 4·00

697 5k. Stylized player, ball at right ... 2·30 2·30

Nos. 696/7 were issued in horizontal *se-tenant* pairs within the sheet.

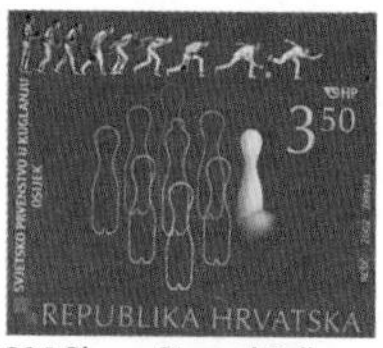

334 Player, Pin and Ball

335 Common Oak (*Quercus robur*)

(Des Sabina Rešić. Litho Zrinski Ptg Co, Čakovec)

2002 (18 May). World Ten-pin Bowling Championship, Osijek. P 14.

698 **334** 3k.50 multicoloured ... 2·30 2·30

(Des V. Zečić. Litho Zrinski Ptg Co, Čakovec)

2002 (5 June). Trees. T **335** and similar vert designs. Multicoloured. P 14.

699 1k.80 Type **335** ... 90 90

a. Booklet pane. No. 699×10, with margins all round ... 9·25

700 2k.50 Sessile oak (*Quercus petraea*) ... 1·40 1·40

a. Booklet pane. No. 700×10, with margins all round ... 14·50

701 2k.80 Holly oak (*Quercus ilex*) ... 1·50 1·50

a. Booklet pane. No. 701×10, with margins all round ... 16·00

699/701 *Set of 3* ... 3·50 3·50

336 Mouse and Moon

337 Pag Lacework

(Des S. Reščček. Litho Zrinski Ptg Co, Čakovec)

2002 (18 June). 15th World Animated Film Festival, Zagreb. P 14.

702 **336** 5k. multicoloured ... 3·00 3·00

(Des O. Franković. Litho Malines)

2002 (13 July). Lace-making. T **337** and similar vert design. Multicoloured. P 11½.

703 3k.50 Type **337** ... 2·30 2·30

704 5k. Liedekerke lacework and statue of lace-maker ... 3·00 3·00

Stamps of a similar design were issued by Belgium.

(Des D. Popović. Litho Zrinski Ptg Co, Čakovec)

2002 (20 Sept). Fortresses (2nd series). Horiz designs as T **320**. Multicoloured. Phosphorescent security markings. P 14.

705 2k.50 Skočibuha family summer villa, Šipan (16th-century) ... 1·40 1·40

706 2k.50 Nehaj (16th-century) ... 1·40 1·40

707 5k. Veliki Tabor (16th-century) ... 2·75 2·75

705/707 *Set of 3* ... 5·00 5·00

338 Slavonic Script

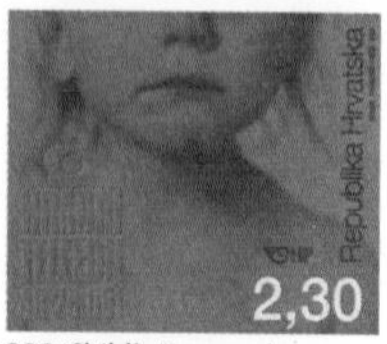

339 Child's Face and Emblem

(Des D. Stanišljević and M. Baus. Litho and die-stamped Zrinski Ptg Co, Čakovec)

2002 (3 Oct). Centenary of Krk Slavic Academy. Phosphorescent security markings. P 14.

708 **338** 4k. black and bright scarlet ... 4·25 4·25

(Des O. Franković and I. Vučić. Litho Zrinski Ptg Co, Čakovec)

2002 (15 Oct). Children's Telephone Helpline. P 14.

709 **339** 2k.30 multicoloured ... 1·40 1·40

340 "Our Lady and the Saints" (detail) (polyptych, Nikola Božidarević), Danče Church, Dubrovnik

(Des O. Franković and I. Vučić. Litho Zrinski Ptg Co, Čakovec)

2002 (21 Nov). Christmas. Phosphorescent security markings. P 14.

710 **340** 2k.30 multicoloured ... 1·40 1·40

a. Booklet pane. No. 710×10, with margins all round ... 14·50

(Des D. Popović. Litho Zrinski Ptg Co, Čakovec)

2002 (3 Dec). Paintings (3rd series). Multicoloured designs as T **322**. Phosphorescent security markings. P 14.

711 2k.50 "Girl in the Boat" (Milivoj Uzelac) (vert) ... 1·40 1·40

712 2k.50 "Flowers on the Window" (Antun Motika) (vert) ... 1·40 1·40

713 5k. "On the Drava River" (Krsto Hegedušić) ... 2·75 2·75

711/713 *Set of 3* ... 5·00 5·00

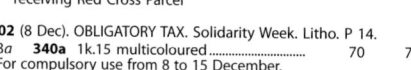

340a Elderly Woman receiving Red Cross Parcel

341 Zagreb Cathedral

2002 (8 Dec). OBLIGATORY TAX. Solidarity Week. Litho. P 14.

713*a* **340a** 1k.15 multicoloured ... 70 70

For compulsory use from 8 to 15 December.

(Des H. Šercar. Litho Zrinski Ptg Co, Čakovec)

2002 (11 Dec). 150th Anniv of Zagreb Archbishopric. Phosphorescent security markings. P 14.

714 **341** 2k.80 multicoloured ... 1·40 1·40

342 Pavao Vitezović

343 Column Capitals, Bell Tower, St. Mary's Church, Zadar

(Des Dubravka Zglavnik-Horvat. Litho Zrinski Ptg Co, Čakovec)

2002 (13 Dec). 350th Birth Anniv of Pavao Ritter Vitezović (writer). Phosphorescent security markings. P 14.

715 **342** 2k.30 multicoloured ... 1·70 1·70

(Des D. Popović. Litho Zrinski Ptg Co, Čakovec)

2002 (14 Dec). 900th Anniv of Accession of Hungarian King Koloman to Croatian Throne. Phosphorescent security markings. P 14.

716 **343** 3k.50 multicoloured ... 2·00 2·00

344 Kosjenka (Regoč)

345 Heart enclosed in Jigsaw Puzzle

(Des Sanja Reščček. Litho Zrinski Ptg Co, Čakovec)

2003 (15 Jan). Fairy Stories. T **344** and similar horiz design showing characters from stories by Ivana Brlić Mažuranić. Multicoloured. Phosphorescent security markings. P 14.

717 2k.30 Type **344** ... 1·20 1·20

a. Pair. Nos. 717/18 ... 2·75 2·75

718 2k.80 Malik Tintilinić (Šuma Striborova) ... 1·40 1·40

Nos. 717/18 were issued in *se-tenant* pairs within sheets of 20 stamps.

(Des Sanja Reščček. Litho Zrinski Ptg Co, Čakovec)

2003 (1 Feb). St. Valentine's Day. Phosphorescent security markings. P 14.

719 **345** 2k.30 multicoloured ... 1·20 1·20

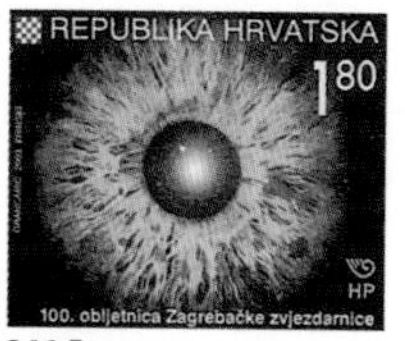

346 Eye

347 Players and Coach

(Des K. Grancarić. Litho Zrinski Ptg Co, Čakovec)

2003 (17 Feb). Centenary of Zagreb Astronomical Observatory (1k.80). 150th Anniv of Meteorological Measurements and 50th Anniv of Meteorological Station on Zavižan (3k.50). T **346** and similar horiz design. Multicoloured. Phosphorescent security markings. P 14.

720 1k.80 Type **346** ... 85 85

a. Pair. Nos. 720/1 ... 2·75 2·75

721 3k.50 Eye and lightning ... 1·70 1·70

Nos. 720/1 were issued in *se-tenant* vertical and horizontal pairs within sheetlets of ten stamps.

(Des D. Popović. Litho Zrinski Ptg Co, Čakovec)

2003 (20 Feb). Croatia, World Handball Champions, Portugal 2003. Sheet 112×83 mm containing T **347** and similar vert designs showing team. Phosphorescent security markings. P 14.

MS722 4k. Type **347**; 4k. Eight players; 4k. Six players; 4k. Four players ... 7·75 7·75

348 Building Façade and Monks

349 Page from Missal

(Des Sabina Rešić. Litho Zrinski Ptg Co, Čakovec)

2003 (1 Mar). 500th Anniv of the Paulist (White Friars) Secondary School, Lepoglava. Phosphorescent security markings. P 14.

723 **348** 5k. multicoloured ... 2·40 2·40

(Des I. Molnar. Litho Zrinski Ptg Co, Čakovec)

2003 (25 Mar). 600th Anniv of Duke Hrvoje's *Glagolitic Missal* (illuminated book). Phosphorescent security markings. P 14.

724 **349** 5k. multicoloured ... 2·40 2·40

350 Prosthetic Leg

351 Janica Kostelić

(Des Maja Pecanic. Litho Zrinski Ptg Co, Čakovec)

2003 (8 Apr). Anti-Landmine Campaign. Phosphorescent security markings. P 14.

725 **350** 2k.30 multicoloured ... 1·00 1·00

(Des D. Popović. Litho Zrinski Ptg Co, Čakovec)

2003 (16 Apr). World Cup Alpine Skiing Gold Medallists, St. Moritz 2003. T **351** and similar horiz design. Multicoloured. Phosphorescent security markings. P 14.

726 3k.50 Type **351** ... 1·50 1·50

727 3k.50 Ivica Kostelić ... 1·50 1·50

Nos. 726/7 were issued in *se-tenant* sheetlets of eight stamps and two labels showing portraits of the skiers.

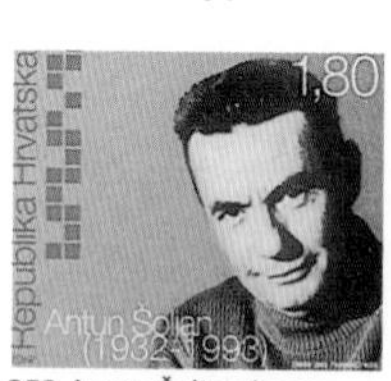

352 Antun Šoljan (poet, tenth anniv)

353 St. Jerome

(Des Orsat Franković. Litho Zrinski Ptg Co, Čakovec)

2003 (22 Apr). Death Anniversaries. T **352** and similar horiz designs. Multicoloured. Phosphorescent security markings. P 14.

728 1k.80 Type **352** ... 85 85

729 2k.30 Hanibal Lučić (poet, 450th anniv) ... 1·00 1·00

730 5k. Federiko Benković (artist, 250th anniv) ... 2·20 2·20

728/730 *Set of 3* ... 3·75 3·75

(Des I. Molnar. Litho Zrinski Ptg Co, Čakovec)

2003 (22 Apr). 550th Anniv of St. Jerome Papal Institutions, Rome. Phosphorescent security markings. P 14.

731 **353** 2k.80 multicoloured ... 1·40 1·40

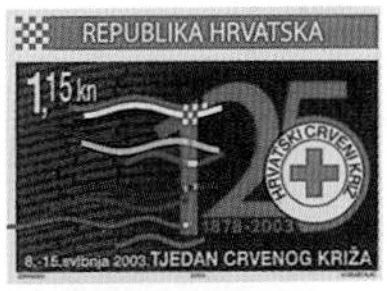

353a "125"

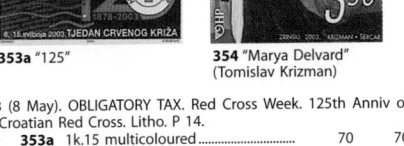

354 "Marya Delvard" (Tomislav Krizman)

2003 (8 May). OBLIGATORY TAX. Red Cross Week. 125th Anniv of Croatian Red Cross. Litho. P 14.
731*a* **353a** 1k.15 multicoloured 70 70
For compulsory use from 8 to 15 May.

(Des H. Šercar. Litho Zrinski Ptg Co, Čakovec)

2003 (9 May). Europa. Poster Art. T **354** and similar multicoloured design. Phosphorescent security markings. P 14.
732 3k.50 Type **354** .... 2·00 2·00
733 5k. "The Firebird" (Boris Bućan) (35×35 mm) .... 3·00 3·00

(Des D. Popović. Litho Zrinski Ptg Co, Čakovec)

2003 (13 May). Fortresses (3rd series). Horiz designs as T **320**. Multicoloured. Phosphorescent security markings. P 14.
734 1k.80 Kostajnica, (15th-century) 85 85
735 2k.80 Slavonski, Brod (18th-century) .... 1·40 1·40
736 5k. Minčeta, Dubrovnik (15th-century) .... 2·20 2·20
734/736 *Set of 3* .... 4·00 4·00

355 Pope John Paul II

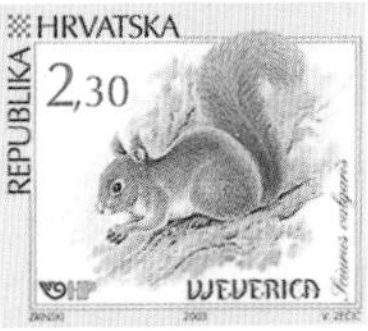

356 Squirrel (*Sciurus vulgaris*)

(Des D. Popović. Litho Zrinski Ptg Co, Čakovec)

2003 (2 June). Pope John Paul II's Third Visit to Croatia. Phosphorescent security markings. P 14.
737 **355** 2k.30 multicoloured .... 1·00 1·00

(Des V. Zečić. Litho Zrinski Ptg Co, Čakovec)

2003 (5 June). Fauna. T **356** and similar horiz designs. Multicoloured. Phosphorescent security markings. P 14.
738 2k.30 Type **356** .... 1·00 1·00
739 2k.80 Dormouse (*Glis glis*) .... 1·40 1·40
740 3k.50 Beaver (*Castor fiber*) .... 1·50 1·50
738/740 *Set of 3* .... 3·50 3·50

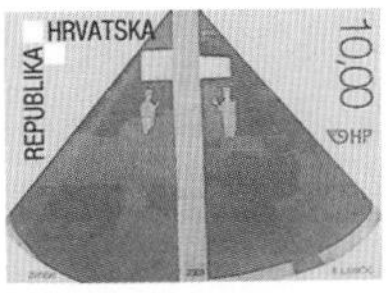

357 Cape

358 Letter Box, Envelopes and Stamp

(Des B. Ljubičić. Litho Zrinski Ptg Co, Čakovec)

2003 (13 June). King Ladislaus' Cape (11th-century). Sheet 95×70 mm. P 12.
MS741 **357** 10k. multicoloured .... 4·75 4·75

(Litho Zrinski Ptg Co, Čakovec)

2003 (9 Sept). Stamp Day. 50th Anniv of Post Museum, Zagreb. P 14.
742 **358** 2k.30 multicoloured .... 1·20 1·20

358a "tjedan borbe protiv TBC"

359 Vines and Paths

2003 (14 Sept). OBLIGATORY TAX. Anti-Tuberculosis Week. Litho. P 14.
742*a* **358a** 1k.15 scarlet-vermilion and light green 70 70
For compulsory use from 14 to 21 September.

(Litho Zrinski Ptg Co, Čakovec)

2003 (19 Sept). UNESCO World Heritage Site. Primošten Vineyard. Sheet 110×78 mm. P 14.
MS743 **359** 10k. multicoloured .... 4·75 4·75

360 Mother of Mercy (statue) and Nativity Church, Varaždin

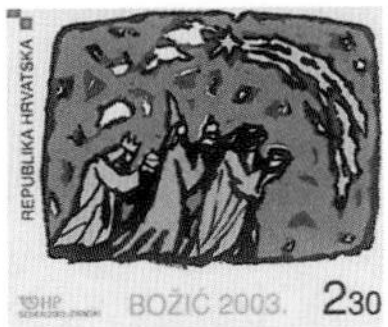

361 Three Wise Men

(Des S. Reščec. Litho Zrinski Ptg Co, Čakovec)

2003 (20 Oct). 300th Anniv of Ursuline Religious Order in Croatia. P 14.
744 **360** 2k.50 multicoloured .... 1·20 1·20

(Des D. Seder. Litho Zrinski Ptg Co, Čakovec)

2003 (20 Nov). Christmas. Fluorescent security markings. P 14.
745 **361** 2k.30 multicoloured .... 1·20 1·20

(Des D. Popović. Litho Zrinski Ptg Co, Čakovec)

2003 (21 Nov). Paintings (4th series). Multicoloured designs as T **322**. P 14.
746 1k.80 "Flower Girl II" (Slavko Kopač) 90 90
747 3k.50 "Dry Stone Wall" (Oton Gliha) (vert) .... 1·80 1·80
748 3k.50 "Pont Des Art" (Josip Račić) (vert) .... 1·80 1·80
746/748 *Set of 3* .... 4·00 4·00

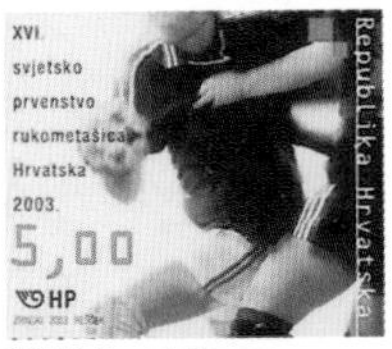

362 Ball and Players

362a Snow-covered House and Tree

(Des S. Reščec. Litho Zrinski Ptg Co, Čakovec)

2003 (1 Dec). 16th Women's World Handball Championships. P 14.
749 **362** 5k. multicoloured .... 3·00 3·00

2003 (8 Dec). OBLIGATORY TAX. Solidarity Week. Litho. P 14.
749*a* **362a** 1k.15 multicoloured .... 1·00 1·00
For compulsory use from 8 to 15 December.

363 Josip Hatze

(Des Dubravka Zglavnik Horvat. Litho Zrinski Ptg Co, Čakovec)

2004 (5 Jan). Musical Anniversaries. T **363** and similar vert design. Multicoloured. P 14.
750 5k. Type **363** (125th birth anniv of Josip Hatze (composer)) .... 3·00 3·00
a. Pair. Nos. 750/1 .... 6·25 6·25
751 5k. Violin bridge and strings (50th anniv of Zagreb Soloists ensemble) .... 3·00 3·00
Nos. 750/1 were issued in *se-tenant* pairs within the sheet.

364 Manuscript Page

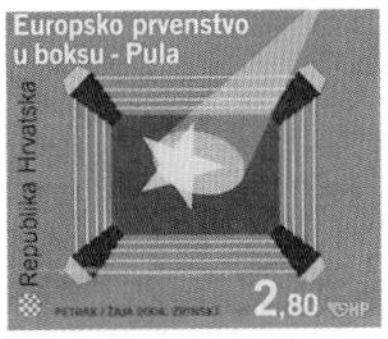

365 Stylized Boxing Ring

(Des Dubravka Zglavnik Horvat. Litho Zrinski Ptg Co, Čakovec)

2004 (22 Jan). 600th Anniv of Hval's Manuscript. P 14.
752 **364** 2k.30 multicoloured .... 1·50 1·50

(Des Ana Žaja and M. Petrak. Litho Zrinski Ptg Co, Čakovec)

2004 (19 Feb). European Boxing Championship, Pula. P 14.
753 **365** 2k.80 multicoloured .... 1·70 1·70

366 Adult Heron

367 Frontispiece of "De Regno Dalmatiae et Croatie" and Ivan Lučić

(Des Z. Keser. Litho Zrinski Ptg Co, Čakovec)

2004 (22 Mar). Purple Heron (*Ardea puruorea*). T **366** and similar vert designs. Multicoloured. P 14.
754 5k. Type **366** .... 3·00 3·00
a. Strip of 4. Nos. 754/7 .... 12·50
755 5k. Adult and chick .... 3·00 3·00
756 5k. Adults flying .... 3·00 3·00
757 5k. Adult in reed bed .... 3·00 3·00
754/757 *Set of 4* .... 11·00 11·00
Nos. 754/7 were issued in horizontal or vertical *se-tenant* strips of four stamps within sheets of 16.

(Des V. Buzolić. Litho Zrinski Ptg Co, Čakovec)

2004 (22 Apr). Anniversaries. T **367** and similar vert designs. Multicoloured. P 14.
758 2k.30 Type **367** (writer and historian) (400th birth anniv) .... 1·70 1·70
759 3k.50 Antun Vrančić (writer) (500th birth anniv) .... 2·30 2·30
760 3k.50 St. Jerome (sculpture) (Andrija Alesi) (500th death anniv) .... 2·30 2·30
761 10k. Frontispiece Croatian grammar (Bartol Kasic) (400th anniv of first publication) .... 6·25 6·25
758/761 *Set of 4* .... 11·50 11·50

368 Wild Flowers

(Des D. Popović. Litho Zrinski Ptg Co, Čakovec)

2004 (22 Apr). Risnjak National Park. Sheet 99×74 mm. P 14.
MS762 **368** 10k. multicoloured .... 6·00 6·00

369 Martyrdom of St. Domnius

369a Elderly Man and Child

(Des Ivana Vučić and O. Franković. Litho Zrinski Ptg Co, Čakovec)

2004 (7 May). 700th Anniv of the Martyrdom of St. Domnius. P 14.
763 **369** 3k.50 multicoloured .... 2·30 2·30

2004 (8 May). OBLIGATORY TAX. Red Cross Week. Litho. P 14.
763*a* **369a** 1k.15 multicoloured .... 1·00 1·00
For compulsory use from 8 to 15 May.

370 Toboggan, Skater, Ski Poles and Skis

(Des Z. Keser. Litho Zrinski Ptg Co, Čakovec)

2004 (9 May). Europa. Holidays. T **370** and similar horiz design. Multicoloured. P 14.
764 3k.50 Type **370** .... 2·20 2·20
765 3k.50 Deck chair, beach ball and sunglasses .... 2·20 2·20

371 Football and Emblem

372 Dog Rose (*Rosa canina*)

(Des D. Popović. Litho Zrinski Ptg Co, Čakovec)

2004 (21 May). Centenary of FIFA (Fédération Internationale de Football Association). P 14.
766 **371** 2k.50 multicoloured .... 1·50 1·50

(Des D. Popović. Litho Zrinski Ptg Co, Čakovec)

2004 (5 June). Medicinal Plants. T **372** and similar vert designs. Multicoloured. Phosphorescent security markings. P 14.
767 2k.30 Type **372** .... 1·70 1·70
a. Booklet pane. No. 767×10 .... 18·00
768 2k.80 Sweet violet (*Viola odorata*) .... 2·00 2·00
a. Booklet pane. No. 768×10 .... 21·00
769 3k.50 Peppermint (*Mentha piperita*) .... 2·40 2·40
a. Booklet pane. No. 769×10 .... 25·00
767/769 *Set of 3* .... 5·50 5·50

373 Puppets forming "UNIMA"

374 Multicoloured Football

(Des D. Popović. Litho Zrinski Ptg Co, Čakovec)

2004 (6 June). World UNIMA (puppeteers) Conference, Opatija. International Puppetry Festival, Rijeka. P 14.
770 **373** 3k.50 multicoloured .... 2·30 2·30

(Des Ana Žaja and M. Petrak. Litho Zrinski Ptg Co, Čakovec)

2004 (12 June). European Football Championship 2004, Portugal. P 14.
771 **374** 3k.50 multicoloured .... 2·30 2·30
No. 771 was perforated in a circle contained in an outer perforated square.

375 Mostar Bridge

376 Dicus Throwing

(Des D. Popović. Litho Zrinski Ptg Co, Čakovec)

2004 (23 July). Reconstruction of Ottoman Bridge at Mostar. P 14.
772 **375** 3k.50 multicoloured .... 2·30 2·30

(Des D. Popović. Litho Zrinski Ptg Co, Čakovec)

2004 (13 Aug). Olympic Games, Athens. P 14.
773 **376** 3k.50 multicoloured .... 2·30 2·30

377 Building Façade

377a Hand-washing

(Des Ana Žaja and M. Petrak. Litho Zrinski Ptg Co, Čakovec)

2004 (9 Sept). Centenary of Post Office, Zagreb. P 14.
774 **377** 2k.30 multicoloured .... 1·50 1·50

2004 (14 Sept). OBLIGATORY TAX. Anti-Tuberculosis Week. Litho. P 14.
774*a* **377a** 1k.15 multicoloured .... 1·00 1·00
For compulsory use from 14 to 21 September.

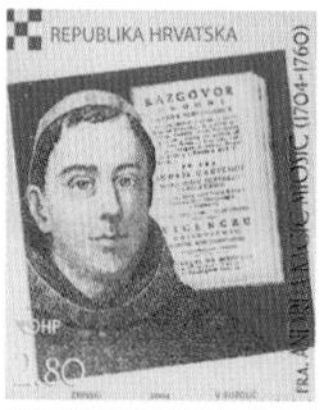

378 Andrija Miosic

379 Christmas Wheat

(Des V. Stegu. Litho Zrinski Ptg Co, Čakovec)

2004 (15 Sept). 300th Birth Anniv of Father Andrija Kacic Miosic (writer). P 14.
775 **378** 2k.80 multicoloured .... 1·80 1·80

(Des D. Popović. Litho Zrinski Ptg Co, Čakovec)

2004 (29 Sept). Fortresses (4th series). Horiz designs as T **320**. Multicoloured. P 14.
776 3k.50 Dubovac (15th-century) .... 2·40 2·40
777 3k.50 Valpovo (15th–18th-century) .... 2·40 2·40
778 3k.50 Gripe (17th-century) .... 2·40 2·40
776/778 *Set of* 3 .... 6·50 6·50

(Des D. Popović. Litho Zrinski Ptg Co, Čakovec)

2004 (15 Nov). Paintings (5th series). Multicoloured designs as T **322**. P 14.
779 2k.30 "Parisian Suburb" (Juraj Plancic) (vert) .... 1·70 1·70
780 2k.30 "Noon in Supetar" (Jerolim Mise) (vert) .... 1·70 1·70
781 2k.30 "Self-portrait" (Miroslav Kraljevic) (vert) .... 1·70 1·70
779/781 *Set of* 3 .... 4·50 4·50

(Des Ana Žaja and M. Petrak. Litho Zrinski Ptg Co, Čakovec)

2004 (25 Nov). Christmas. P 14.
782 **379** 2k.30 multicoloured .... 1·50 1·50

379a Children, Red Cross Parcel and Elderly Woman

380 Antun and Stjepan Radić (founders)

2004 (8 Dec). OBLIGATORY TAX. Solidarity Week. Litho. P 14.
782*a* **379a** 1k.15 multicoloured .... 1·00 1·00
For compulsory use from 8 to 15 December.

(Des H. Šercar. Litho Zrinski Ptg Co, Čakovec)

2004 (22 Dec). Centenary of Croatian Peoples Peasants' Party (HPSS). P 14.
783 **380** 7k.20 turquoise and black .... 4·25 4·25

381 Halugica

382 "@" and Circuit Board

(Des Sanja Rešček. Litho Zrinski Ptg Co, Čakovec)

2005 (14 Jan). Fairy Stories. T **381** and similar horiz design showing characters from stories by Vladimir Nazor. Multicoloured. P 14.
784 5k. Type **381** .... 3·00 3·00
a. Pair. Nos. 784/5 .... 6·25 6·25
785 5k. Longbeard Mannikin ("Grujo the Pioneer") .... 3·00 3·00
Nos. 784/5 were issued in *se-tenant* pairs within sheets of 20 stamps.

(Des Sabina Rešić. Litho Zrinski Ptg Co, Čakovec)

2005 (10 Feb). World Conferences on Information Technology, Geneva and Tunis. P 14.
786 **382** 2k.80 multicoloured .... 1·80 1·80

383 Livia Drusilla (Oxford—Opuzen Livia) (statue)

384 Circle enclosing Square

(Des Maja Danica Pecanic. Litho Zrinski Ptg Co, Čakovec)

2005 (24 Feb). Roman Archaeological Site, Narona. Joint British–Croatian Roman Exhibitions, 2004–2005. Sheet 110×71 mm. P 14.
MS787 **383** 10k. multicoloured .... 8·00 8·00

(Des D. Fabijanic. Litho Zrinski Ptg Co, Čakovec)

2005 (25 Mar). EXPO 2005 World Exhibition, Aichi, Japan. Sheet 97×80 mm. P 14.
MS788 **384** 10k. vermilion and silver .... 8·00 8·00

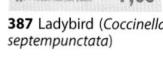

385 Pope John Paul II

386 Keyboard

(Des S. Rešček. Litho Zrinski Ptg Co, Čakovec)

2005 (8 Apr). Pope John Paul II Commemoration. P 14.
789 **385** 2k.30 multicoloured .... 1·50 1·50

(Des D. Zglavnik-Horvat. Litho Zrinski Ptg Co, Čakovec)

2005 (15 Apr). Croatian Music. T **386** and similar horiz design. P 14.
790 2k.30 Type **386** (Music Biennale (festival), Zagreb) .... 1·50 1·50
791 2k.30 Stjepan Šulek (composer) .... 1·50 1·50

387 Ladybird (*Coccinella septempunctata*)

388 Tank

(Des Ana Žaja and M. Petrak. Litho Zrinski Ptg Co, Čakovec)

2005 (22 Apr). Insects. T **387** and similar vert designs Multicoloured. P 14.
792 1k.80 Type **387** .... 1·30 1·3
793 2k.30 *Rosalia alpine* .... 1·70 1·7
794 3k.50 Stag beetle (*Lucanus cervus*) .... 2·30 2·3
792/794 *Set of* 3 .... 4·75 4·7

(Des D. Popović. Litho)

2005 (1 May). Tenth Anniv of Military Action. P 14.
795 **388** 1k.80 multicoloured .... 1·00 1·0

389 Josip Buturac

389a Kiss

(Des O. Franković and I. Vučić. Litho)

2005 (6 May). Birth Centenary of Josip Buturac (historian and writer). P 14.
796 **389** 2k.80 multicoloured .... 1·80 1·8

2005 (8 May). OBLIGATORY TAX. Red Cross Week. Litho. P 14.
796*a* **389a** 1k.15 multicoloured .... 1·00 1·0
For compulsory use from 8 to 15 May.

390 Bread

391 Rock, Sea and Cliff

(Des O. Franković and I. Vučić. Litho)

2005 (9 May). Europa. Gastronomy. T **390** and similar horiz design Multicoloured. P 14.
797 3k.50 Type **390** .... 2·00 2·0
a. Pair. Nos. 797/8 .... 4·25 4·2
798 3k.50 Glass of wine .... 2·00 2·0
Nos. 797/8 were issued in horizontal *se-tenant* pairs within the sheet.

(Des O. Franković and I. Vučić. Litho Zrinski Ptg Co, Čakovec)

2005 (24 May). Tourism. Booklet Stamps. T **391** and similar horiz design. Multicoloured. P 14.
799 1k.80 Type **391** .... 1·20 1·2
a. Booklet pane. Nos. 799/808 .... 18·00
800 1k.80 Branches, cliff and sea .... 1·20 1·2
801 1k.80 Sea and rock .... 1·20 1·2
802 1k.80 Canoe, rock and sea .... 1·20 1·2
803 1k.80 Sea surrounding rock .... 1·20 1·2
804 3k.50 Trees .... 2·20 2·2
805 3k.50 Trees and cliff .... 2·20 2·2
806 3k.50 Cliff and rocks .... 2·20 2·2
807 3k.50 Cliff and sunken rocks .... 2·20 2·2
808 3k.50 Rock point and sea .... 2·20 2·2
799/808 *Set of* 10 .... 15·00 15·0

392 Krešimir Cosic

393 Coral surrounding Sponge

(Des D. Popović. Litho Zrinski Ptg Co, Čakovec)

2005 (25 May). Tenth Death Anniv of Krešimir Cosic (basketball player). P 14½.
809 **392** 3k.50 multicoloured .... 2·30 2·30

(Des Ana Žaja and M. Petrak. Litho and thermography Zrinski Ptg Co, Čakovec)

2005 (2 June). Endangered Species. P 14½.
810 **393** 3k.50 multicoloured .... 2·30 2·30

394 Building Façade

395 St. Florian (statue)

(Des H. Šercar. Litho Zrinski Ptg Co, Čakovec)

2005 (20 June). Varaždinske Toplice Spa. P 14½.
811 **394** 1k.80 multicoloured .... 1·10 1·10

(Des D. Popović. Litho Zrinski Ptg Co, Čakovec)

2005 (15 July). International Fire Brigade Olympics, Varaždin. P 14½.

812	**395** 2k.30 multicoloured	1·50	1·50

(Des Z. Borić (813) or B. Ljubičić (814). Litho Zrinski Ptg Co, Čakovec)

2005 (8 Sept). 50th Anniv of Europa Stamps. Horiz design as T **65**. Multicoloured. P 14½.

813	7k.20 As No. 195	4·00	4·00
814	8k. Stylized bird	4·50	4·50
MS815	92×78 mm. Nos. 813/14	60·00	60·00

396 Morse Code Machine

396a Running

(Des Sabina Rešić. Litho Zrinski Ptg Co, Čakovec)

2005 (9 Sept). 155th Anniv of First Overhead Telegraph Lines. P 14½.

816	**396** 2k.30 multicoloured	1·50	1·50

2005 (14 Sept). OBLIGATORY TAX. Anti-Tuberculosis Week. Litho. P 14.

816*a*	**396a** 1k.15 multicoloured	1·00	1·00

For compulsory use from 14 to 21 September.

(Des D. Popović. Litho Zrinski Ptg Co, Čakovec)

2004 (29 Sept). Fortresses (5th series). Multicoloured designs as T **320**. P 14.

817	1k. Ilok (14th–15th-century)	80	80
818	3k.50 Motovun (13th–15th-century) (vert)	1·60	1·60
819	3k.50 St. Nicholas Fortress, Šibenik (16th-century)	2·20	2·20
817/819 *Set of* 3		4·25	4·25

397 Adam Baltazar Krcelic (writer) (290th birth anniv)

398 "Our Lady with Child and Saints" (detail)

(Des Sabina Rešić. Litho Zrinski Ptg Co, Čakovec)

2005 (4 Nov). Personalities. T **397** and similar vert designs. Multicoloured. P 14½.

820	1k. Type **397**	90	90
821	2k.30 Dragutin Tadijanovic (writer) (100th birthday)	1·70	1·70
822	2k.30 Augustin (Tin) Ujević (writer) (50th death anniv)	1·70	1·70
823	2k.80 "Madonna and Child" (Juraj Culinovic) (400th death anniv (2004))	2·00	2·00
820/823 *Set of* 4		5·75	5·75

(Des D. Popović. Litho Zrinski Ptg Co, Čakovec)

2005 (22 Nov). Christmas.

(a) Ordinary gum. P 14½

824	**398** 2k.30 multicoloured	1·00	1·00

(b) Self-adhesive Booklet stamp. Die-cut wavy edge

825	**398** 2k.30 multicoloured	1·00	1·00

(Des D. Popović. Litho Zrinski Ptg Co, Čakovec)

2005 (1 Dec). Paintings (6th series). Multicoloured designs as T **322**. P 14.

826	1k.80 "Zader" (Edo Mutric)	1·20	1·20
827	5k. "Meander" (Julije Knifer)	3·00	3·00
828	10k. "Drawing" (Miroslav Šutej) (vert)	6·00	6·00
826/828 *Set of* 3		9·25	9·25

399 Team and Trophy

399a Elderly Man receiving Red Cross Parcel

(Des D. Popović. Litho Zrinski Ptg Co, Čakovec)

2005 (22 Dec). Croatia—Winner of Davis Cup (tennis championship)—2005. P 14.

829	**399** 5k. multicoloured	3·00	3·00

2005 (8 Dec). OBLIGATORY TAX. Solidarity Week. Litho. P 14.

829*a*	**399a** 1k.15 multicoloured	3·00	3·00

For compulsory use from 8 to 15 December.

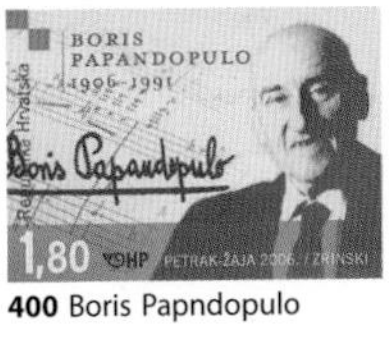

400 Boris Papndopulo

401 Crossed Skis

(Des Ana Žaja and M. Petrack. Litho Zrinski Ptg Co, Čakovec)

2006 (17 Jan). Musicians' Birth Centenaries. T **400** and similar horiz designs. Multicoloured. P 14.

830	1k.80 Type **400**	1·00	1·00
831	2k.30 Milo Cipra	1·60	1·60
832	2k.80 Ivan Brkanovic	1·80	1·80
830/832 *Set of* 3		4·00	4·00

(Litho Zrinski Ptg Co, Čakovec)

2006 (10 Feb). Winter Olympic Games, Turin. P 14.

833	**401** 3k.50 multicoloured	2·10	2·10

402 "Self-portrait with Velvet Cap with Plume"

403 Josip Kozarac (writer) (death centenary)

(Des J. Biffel. Litho Zrinski Ptg Co, Čakovec)

2006 (7 Mar). 400th Birth Anniv of Rembrandt Harmenszoon Van Rijn (Rembrandt) (artist). P 14½×14.

834	**402** 5k. multicoloured	3·00	3·00

(Des Irena Frantal. Litho Zrinski Ptg Co, Čakovec)

2006 (7 Mar). Anniversaries. T **403** and similar horiz designs. Multicoloured. P 14 (diamond-shaped hole on each horiz side).

835	1k. Type **403**	65	65
836	1k. Andrija Ljudevit Adamic (entrepreneur) (240th birth anniv)	65	65
837	5k. Ljubo Karaman (art historian) (120th birth anniv)	3·00	3·00
838	7k.20 Vanja Radaus (artist and writer) (birth centenary)	4·25	4·25
835/838 *Set of* 4		7·75	7·75

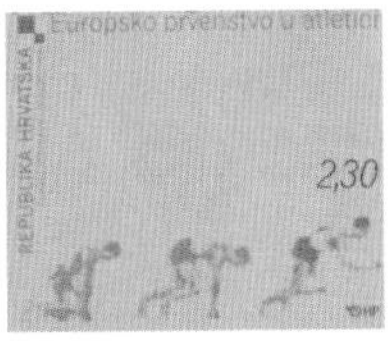

404 Runner

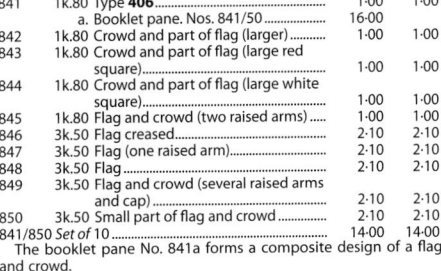

405 Stylized Player

(Des Ivana Cukelj and Tatjana Strinavić. Litho Zrinski Ptg Co, Čakovec)

2006 (4 Apr). European Athletics Championship, Göteburg. P 14 (diamond-shaped hole on each horiz side).

839	**404** 2k.30 multicoloured	1·50	1·50

(Litho Zrinski Ptg Co, Čakovec)

2006 (4 Apr). World Cup Football Championship, Germany. P 14 (diamond-shaped hole on each vert side).

840	**405** 2k.80 multicoloured	1·80	1·80

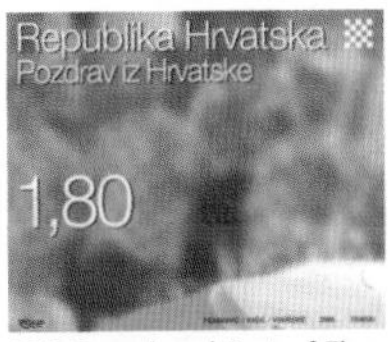

406 Crowd and Part of Flag

407 Boy carrying Red Cross Bag

(Litho Zrinski Ptg Co, Čakovec)

2006 (25 Apr). Tourism. Booklet Stamps. T **406** and similar horiz designs showing parts of the Croatian flag. Multicoloured. P 14 (diamond-shaped hole on each horiz side).

841	1k.80 Type **406**	1·00	1·00
	a. Booklet pane. Nos. 841/50	16·00	
842	1k.80 Crowd and part of flag (larger)	1·00	1·00
843	1k.80 Crowd and part of flag (large red square)	1·00	1·00
844	1k.80 Crowd and part of flag (large white square)	1·00	1·00
845	1k.80 Flag and crowd (two raised arms)	1·00	1·00
846	3k.50 Flag creased	2·10	2·10
847	3k.50 Flag (one raised arm)	2·10	2·10
848	3k.50 Flag	2·10	2·10
849	3k.50 Flag and crowd (several raised arms and cap)	2·10	2·10
850	3k.50 Small part of flag and crowd	2·10	2·10
841/850 *Set of* 10		14·00	14·00

The booklet pane No. 841a forms a composite design of a flag and crowd.

2006 (8 May). OBLIGATORY TAX. Red Cross Week. Litho. P 14.

851	**407** 1k.15 multicoloured	1·00	1·00

For compulsory use from 8 to 15 May.

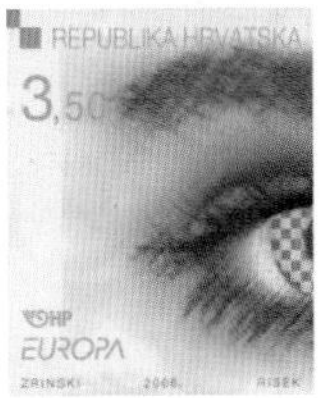

408 Eye containing Squares

409 Little Tern

(Des Iva Risek. Litho Zrinski Ptg Co, Čakovec)

2006 (9 May). Europa. Integration. T **408** and similar vert design. Multicoloured. P 14 (with one diamond shaped hole on each vert side).

852	3k.50 Type **408**	2·10	2·10
	a. Horiz pair. Nos. 852/3	4·50	4·50
853	3k.50 Eye containing stars	2·10	2·10

Nos. 852/3 were issued in horizontal *se-tenant* pairs within the sheet, each pair forming a composite design of an eye.

(Des D. Popović. Litho Zrinski Ptg Co, Čakovec)

2006 (23 May). Little Tern (*Sterna albifrons*). T **409** and similar horiz designs. Multicoloured. P 14 (with one diamond shaped hole on each horiz side).

854	5k. Type **409**	3·00	3·00
	a. Strip. Nos. 854/7	12·50	
855	5k. Diving	3·00	3·00
856	5k. Facing right	3·00	3·00
857	5k. Sitting on eggs	3·00	3·00
854/857 *Set of* 4		11·00	11·00

Nos. 854/7 were issued in horizontal and vertical *se-tenant* strips of four stamps within sheets of 16.

410 Elmore (1905)

(Des Maja Pecanic. Litho Zrinski Ptg Co, Čakovec)

2006 (1 June). Centenary of Croatian Motor Club (HAK). P 14 (with one diamond shaped hole on each horiz side).

858	**410** 5k. multicoloured	3·00	3·00

411 *Nymphaea alba*

412 Nikola Tesla

(Des V. Buzolić. Litho Zrinski Ptg Co, Čakovec)

2006 (5 June). Flora. T **411** and similar horiz designs. Multicoloured. P 14 (with one diamond shaped hole on each horiz side).

859	2k.30 Type **411**	1·60	1·60
860	2k.80 *Nuphar lutea*	1·80	1·80
	a. Booklet pane. No. 860×10	19·00	
861	3k.50 *Menyanthes trifoliata*	2·30	2·30
859/861 *Set of* 3		5·25	5·25

(Des D. Popović. Litho Zrinski Ptg Co, Čakovec)

2006 (10 July). 150th Birth Anniv of Nikola Tesla (scientist). P 14 (with one diamond shaped hole on each vert side).

862	**412** 3k.50 multicoloured	2·30	2·30

413 Clock Tower

414 Post Box

(Des H. Šercar. Litho Zrinski Ptg Co, Čakovec)

2006 (22 Aug). 250th Anniv of Bjelovar. P 14 (with one diamond shaped hole on each horiz side).

863	**413** 2k.80 multicoloured	1·60	1·60

(Des Ariana Norsic. Litho and embossed Zrinski Ptg Co, Čakovec)

2006 (9 Sept). Statehood. P 14 (with one diamond shaped hole on each vert side).

864	**414** 2k.30 multicoloured	1·40	1·40

415 "Tjedan borbe protiv TBC-a"

416 Synagogue and Menorah

2006 (14 Sept). OBLIGATORY TAX. Anti-Tuberculosis Week. Litho. P 14.

865 **415** 1k.15 multicoloured .... 1·00 1·00

For compulsory use from 14 to 21 September.

(Des H. Šercar. Litho Zrinski Ptg Co, Čakovec)

2006 (15 Sept). Bicentenary of Jewish Community, Zagreb. P 14 (with one diamond shaped hole on each vert side).

866 **416** 5k. multicoloured .... 3·00 3·00

(Des D. Popović. Litho Zrinski Ptg Co, Čakovec)

2006 (21 Sept). Fortresses (6th series). Horiz designs as T **320**. Multicoloured. P 14 (with one diamond shaped hole on each horiz side).

867 1k. Sudurad, Sipan (16th-century) 75 75

868 1k. St. Mary of Mercy, Vrboska (16th-century) 75 75

869 7k.20 Francopan Citadel, Ogulin (16th-century) .... 4·50 4·50

867/869 *Set of 3* .... 5·50 5·50

417 "DAN BIJELOG ŠTAPA 2006"

(Des H. Šercar. Litho and embossed Zrinski Ptg Co, Čakovec)

2006 (15 Oct). White Stick Day. P 14 (with one diamond shaped hole on each vert side).

869*a* **417** 1k.80 black and scarlet vermillion .... 1·10 1·10

No. 869*a* has "White Cane Safety Day" embossed in Braille on its surface.

418 "Nativity" (Pantaleone)

419 Santa on Skis

(Des D. Popović. Litho Zrinski Ptg Co, Čakovec)

2006 (27 Nov). Christmas.

(a) Ordinary gum. P 14 (with one diamond shaped hole on each vert side)

870 **418** 2k.30 multicoloured .... 1·40 1·40

(b) Self-adhesive booklet. Die-cut wavy edge

871 **418** 2k.30 multicoloured .... 1·40 1·40

(Des D. Popović. Litho Zrinski Ptg Co, Čakovec)

2006 (1 Dec). Paintings (7th series). Multicoloured designs as T **322**. P 14 (with one diamond shaped hole on each vert (871/2) or horiz side (873)).

872 1k. "Still Life" (Vladimir Becić) 85 85

873 1k.80 "Composition Tyma 3" (Ivan Picelj) .... 1·50 1·50

874 10k. "Self Portrait Hunter" (Nasta Rojc) (vert) .... 6·25 6·25

872/874 *Set of 3* .... 7·75 7·75

2006 (8 Dec). OBLIGATORY TAX. Solidarity Week. Litho. P 14.

875 **419** 1k.15 multicoloured .... 1·00 1·00

For compulsory use from 8 to 15 December.

420 Emblem

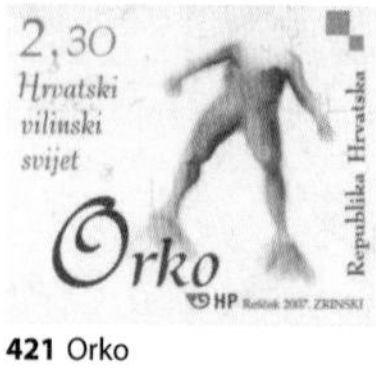

421 Orko

(Des B. Ljubičić. Litho Zrinski Ptg Co, Čakovec)

2007 (9 Jan). 400th Anniv of Classical Gymnasium, Zagreb. P 14 (with one diamond shaped perf on each vert side).

876 **420** 5k. multicoloured .... 3·00 3·00

For compulsory use from 8 to 15 December.

(Des Sanja Rešček. Litho Zrinski Ptg Co, Čakovec)

2007 (18 Jan). Fairy Stories. T **421** and similar horiz design. Multicoloured. P 14 (with one diamond shaped hole on each horiz side).

877 2k.30 Type **421** .... 1·30 1·30

a. Pair. Nos. 877/8 .... 2·75 2·75

878 2k.30 Macic ("Grujo the Pioneer") .... 1·30 1·30

Nos. 877/8 were issued in *se-tenant* pairs within the sheet.

422 Building Façade

423 *Palinurus elephas*

(Litho Zrinski Ptg Co, Čakovec)

2007 (22 Feb). 400th Anniv of National and University Library, Zagreb. P 14 (with one diamond shaped perf on each horiz side).

879 **422** 5k. multicoloured .... 3·00 3·00

(Des Ana Žaja Petrak and M. Petrak. Litho Zrinski Ptg Co, Čakovec)

2007 (15 Mar). Fauna. T **423** and similar horiz designs. Multicoloured. P 14 (with one diamond shaped hole on each horiz side).

880 1k.80 Type **423** .... 1·20 1·20

a. Booklet pane. No. 880×10 .... 12·50

881 2k.30 *Nephrops norvegicus* .... 1·70 1·70

a. Booklet pane. No. 881×10 .... 18·00

882 2k.80 *Astacus astacus* .... 1·90 1·90

a. Booklet pane. No. 882×10 .... 20·00

880/882 *Set of 3* .... 4·25 4·25

424 Istrian Ox

425 Emblem

(Des Ana Žaja Petrak and M. Petrak. Litho Zrinski Ptg Co, Čakovec)

2007 (15 Mar). Autochthonous Breeds. T **424** and similar horiz designs. Multicoloured. P 14 (with one diamond shaped hole on each horiz side).

883 2k.80 Type **424** .... 1·90 1·90

884 3k.50 Posavina horse .... 2·50 2·50

885 5k. Dalmatian donkey .... 3·25 3·25

883/885 *Set of 3* .... 7·00 7·00

(Des Alenka Lalić. Litho Zrinski Ptg Co, Čakovec)

2007 (15 Mar). Europa. Centenary of Scouting. T **425** and similar vert design. Multicoloured. P 14 (with one diamond shaped hole on each vert side).

886 3k.50 Type **425** .... 2·10 2·10

a. Pair. Nos. 886/7 .... 4·50 4·50

887 3k.50 Neckerchief .... 2·10 2·10

Nos. 886/7 were issued in *se-tenant* pairs within the sheet.

426 Andrija Mohorovičić

427 Team Members

(Des Hrvoje Šercar. Litho Zrinski Ptg Co, Čakovec)

2007 (23 Apr). Anniversaries. T **426** and similar vert design. Multicoloured. P 14 (with one diamond shaped hole on each vert side).

888 5k. Type **426** (mathematician and seismologist) (150th birth anniv) .... 3·00 3·00

889 7k.20 Đuro Baglivi (medical scientist) (300th birth anniv) .... 4·50 4·50

2007 (3 May). Croatia—World Water Polo Champions, Melbourne 2007. Sheet 105×68 mm containing T **427** and similar vert designs. Multicoloured. P 14½ (with one diamond shaped perf on each vert side).

MS890 5k.×3, Type **427**; Ten team members; Flag and team members .... 9·25 9·25

The stamps and margins of No. **MS**890 form a composite design of the winning team and trainers.

428 Red Cross, Red Crescent and Proposed New Emblems

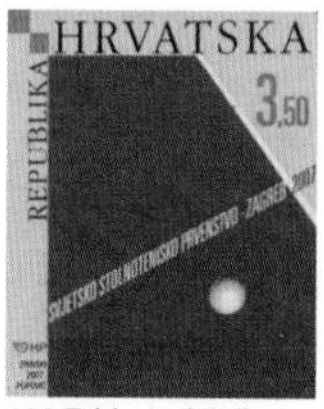

429 Table and Ball

2007 (8 May). OBLIGATORY TAX. Red Cross Week. Litho. P 14.

891 **428** 1k.15 multicoloured .... 1·00 1·00

For compulsory use from 8 to 15 May.

NOTE: On No. 892 the stamps were printed on paper with phosphorescent security markings showing postal emblem.

(Des Danijel Popović. Litho Zrinski Ptg Co, Čakovec)

2007 (21 May). World Table Tennis Championship, Zagreb—2007. P 14 (with one diamond shaped hole on each vert side).

892 **429** 3k.50 multicoloured .... 2·30 2·30

430 'China' engraved in Glagolitic Script

431 Women in Window (17th-century Trompe L'Oeil)

(Des Boris Ljubičić. Litho Zrinski Ptg Co, Čakovec)

2007 (30 May). 15th Anniv of Croatia—China Diplomatic Relations. T **430** and similar horiz design. Multicoloured. P 14.

893 5k. Type **430** .... 3·00 3·00

a. Pair. Nos. 893/4 .... 6·25 6·25

894 5k. 'Hrvatska' written in Chinese script .... 3·00 3·00

Nos. 893/4 were issued in *se-tenant* pairs within the sheet.

(Des Dubravka Zglavnik Horvat. Litho Zrinski Ptg Co, Čakovec)

2007 (31 May). Centenary of City Museum, Zagreb. P 14 (with one diamond shaped hole on each vert side).

895 **431** 2k.30 multicoloured .... 1·50 1·50

432 Lake and Cliff

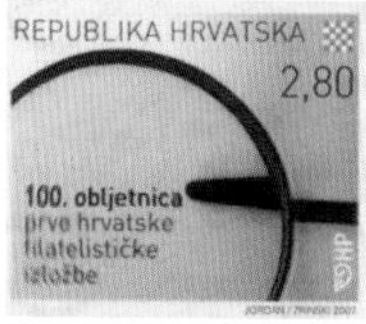

433 Magnifying Glass

(Des Dubravka Zglavnik Horvat. Litho Zrinski Ptg Co, Čakovec)

2007 (8 June). Red Lake. Sheet 112×72 mm. P 14½ (with one diamond shaped perf on each vert side).

MS896 **432** 10k. multicoloured .... 6·25 6·25

The stamp and margins of No. **MS**896 form a composite design of the Red Lake and surrounding area.

(Des Zeljka Jordan. Litho and embossed Zrinski Ptg Co, Čakovec)

2007 (9 Sept). Centenary of First National Philatelic Exhibition. Phosphorescent security markings. P 14½ (with one diamond shaped perf on each horiz side).

897 **433** 2k.80 multicoloured .... 1·80 1·80

433a "Tjedan borbe protiv TBC-a"

434 Sv. Ivan na pucini (St. John at open sea)

2007 (14 Sept). OBLIGATORY TAX. Anti-Tuberculosis Week. Litho. P 14.

897*a* **433a** 1k.15 multicoloured .... 1·00 1·00

For compulsory use from 14 to 21 September.

(Des Z. Boras, O. Franković and I. Vučić. Litho Zrinski Ptg Co, Čakovec)

2007 (14 Sept). Lighthouses. T **434** and similar horiz designs. Multicoloured. Phosphorescent security markings. P 14 (with one diamond shaped hole on each horiz side).

898 5k. Type **434** .... 3·50 3·50

899 5k. Savudrija .... 3·50 3·50

900 5k. Porer .... 3·50 3·50

898/900 *Set of 3* .... 9·50 9·50

435 Fragment of Statute

436 Omiš

(Des Hrvoje Šercar. Litho and embossed Zrinski Ptg Co, Čakovec)

2007 (2 Oct). 500th Anniv of *Veprinac Statute* (oldest Croatian legal document). Phosphorescent security markings. P 14½ (with one diamond shaped perf on each vert side).

901 **435** 2k.70 multicoloured .... 1·80 1·80

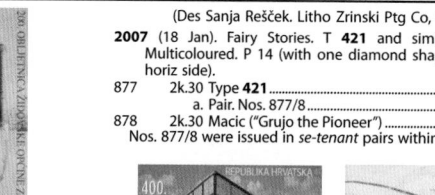

(Des Hrvoje Šercar. Litho Zrinski Ptg Co, Čakovec)

2007 (30 Oct). Towns. T **436** and similar designs. P 14½ (with one diamond shaped perf on each vert side (vert) or on each horiz side (horiz)).

902 1k.80 bistre-brown, bistre and scarlet-vermilion ... 1·10 1·10
903 2k.30 red-brown, brown-rose and scarlet-vemilion (horiz) ... 1·50 1·50
904 2k.80 multicoloured ... 2·00 2·00
902/904 *Set of 3* ... 4·25 4·25

Designs: 1k.80 Type **436**; 2k.30 Koprivnica; 2k.80 Krk.

437 Blanka Vlasic

438 Nativity (painting, Bishop's Palace, Požega)

(Des Vladimir Buzolić. Litho Zrinski Ptg Co, Čakovec)

2007 (8 Nov). Blanka Vlasic. Women's High Jump World Champion—2007. Phosphorescent security markings. P 14½ (with one diamond shaped perf on each horiz side).

905 **437** 2k.30 multicoloured ... 1·50 1·50

(Litho Zrinski Ptg Co, Čakovec)

2007 (15 Nov). Christmas. Phosphorescent security markings.

(a) Ordinary gum. P 14 (with one diamond-shaped perf on each horiz side)

906 **438** 2k.30 multicoloured ... 1·60 1·60

(b) Self-adhesive Booklet stamp. Die-cut wavy edge

906*a* **438** 2k.30 multicoloured ... 1·60 1·60

439 Marija Zagorka

440 Angel (Vedran Damjanovic Maglica)

(Litho Zrinski Ptg Co, Čakovec)

2007 (16 Nov). 50th Death Anniv of Marija Juric Zagorka (writer). Phosphorescent security markings. P 14 (with one diamond shaped perf on each horiz side).

907 **439** 7k.20 multicoloured ... 4·75 4·75

(Des D. Popović. Litho Zrinski Ptg Co, Čakovec)

2007 (1 Dec). Paintings (8th series). Multicoloured designs as T **322**. P 14 (with one diamond shaped hole on each vert side.

908 2k.80 *Area by the River Sava* (Branko Senoa) ... 2·50 2·50
909 5k. *Bridgeport* (Ivan Benokovic) ... 3·50 3·50
910 5k. *Pegasus's Garden* (Ferdinand Kulmer) ... 3·50 3·50
908/910 *Set of 3* ... 8·50 8·50

(Litho Zrinski Ptg Co, Čakovec)

2007 (5 Dec). New Year. Phosphorescent security markings. P 14 (with one diamond shaped perf on each horiz side).

911 **440** 1k.80 multicoloured ... 1·30 1·30

441 Gifts

442 Igor Kuljeric

2007 (8 Dec). OBLIGATORY TAX. Solidarity Week. Litho. P 14.

912 **441** 1k.15 multicoloured ... 1·00 1·00

For compulsory use from 8 to 15 December.

(Des Ana Žaja Petrak and Mario Petrack. Litho Zrinski Ptg Co, Čakovec)

2008 (22 Jan). Croatian Composers. T **442** and similar horiz design. Multicoloured. Phosphorescent security markings. P 14 (with one diamond shaped perf on each horiz side).

913 2k.30 Type **442** (70th birth anniv) ... 1·60 1·60
914 2k.30 Krsto Odak (120th birth anniv) ... 1·60 1·60

443 Cover and Frontispiece

(Des Sabina Rešić. Litho Zrinski Ptg Co, Čakovec)

2008 (25 Jan). 250th Anniv of *Arithmetika Horvatszka* (mathematical handbook). Phosphorescent security markings. P 14 (with one diamond shaped perf on each horiz side).

915 **443** 3k.50 multicoloured ... 2·30 2·30

444 Steam Locomotive MÁV 651/JŽ 31

(Des Tatjana Strinavić. Litho Zrinski Ptg Co, Čakovec)

2008 (15 Feb). Steam Locomotives made by MÁV Gépgyár, Budapest. T **444** and similar horiz design. Multicoloured. Phosphorescent security markings. P 14 (with one diamond shaped perf on each horiz side).

916 5k. Type **444** ... 3·50 3·50
917 5k. MÁV 601/JŽ 32 ... 3·50 3·50

(Des Hrvoje Šercar. Litho Zrinski Ptg Co, Čakovec)

2008 (3 Mar). Towns. Horiz design as T **436**. Multicoloured. P 14½ (with one diamond shaped perf on each horiz side).

918 7k.20 St. Nicholas Church, Cavtat ... 4·75 4·75

445 Stylized Athletes

446 *Hellborus niger* (Christmas rose)

(Des Sanja Reščeк. Litho Zrinski Ptg Co, Čakovec))

2008 (11 Mar). Olympic Games, Beijing. P 14½ (with one diamond shaped perf on each vert side).

919 **445** 5k. multicoloured ... 3·25 3·25

2008 (20 Mar). Flora. T **446** and similar vert designs. Multicoloured. P 14½ (with one diamond shaped perf on each vert side).

920 1k.80 Type **446** ... 1·40 1·40
a. Booklet pane. No. 920×10 ... 14·50
921 2k.80 *Onosma stellulata* (star flower) ... 2·10 2·10
a. Booklet pane. No. 921×10 ... 22·00
922 3k.50 *Lonicera glutinosa* (honeysuckle) ... 2·50 2·50
a. Booklet pane. No. 922×10 ... 26·00
920/922 *Set of 3* ... 5·50 5·50

447 Petar Zoranic

448 Rocks and Water

(Des Sabina Rešić. Litho Zrinski Ptg Co, Čakovec)

2008 (22 Apr). Personalities. T **447** and similar vert designs. Multicoloured. P 14 (with one diamond shaped perf on each horiz side).

923 2k.30 Type **447** (writer) (500th birth anniv) ... 1·60 1·60
924 2k.80 Silvije Strahimir Kranjcevic (writer) (death centenary) ... 1·90 1·90
925 7k.20 Marin Držić (dramatist) (500th birth anniv) ... 4·75 4·75
923/925 *Set of 3* ... 7·50 7·50

(Des Ivana Vučić and Orsat Franković. Litho Zrinski Ptg Co, Čakovec)

2008 (25 Apr). Tourism. Booklet Stamps. T **448** and similar horiz designs showing parts of Cascades, Plitvice. Multicoloured.

926 3k.50 Type **448** ... 2·30 2·30
a. Booklet pane. Nos. 926/35 ... 24·00
927 3k.50 Rocks and water pouring left ... 2·30 2·30
928 3k.50 Cascade, central weed covered rock ... 2·30 2·30
929 3k.50 Rocks and water pouring right ... 2·30 2·30
930 3k.50 Rocks, water and small trees ... 2·30 2·30
931 3k.50 Rocks and water pouring left, two rocks central ... 2·30 2·30
932 3k.50 Cascade, waterweed at left ... 2·30 2·30
933 3k.50 Cascade, large plume, lower right ... 2·30 2·30
934 3k.50 Water, waterweeds and grass covered rock, lower right ... 2·30 2·30
935 3k.50 Grass covered rock, lower left and water ... 2·30 2·30
926/935 *Set of 10* ... 21·00 21·00

The booklet pane No. 926a forms a composite design of the cascades and waterfall.

The covers of the booklet can be used as postcards.

449 Children

450 Volkswagen Beetle

(Litho Zrinski Ptg Co, Čakovec)

2008 (8 May). OBLIGATORY TAX. 130th Anniv of Croatian Red Cross. P 14.

936 **449** 1k.15 multicoloured ... 1·00 1·00

(Litho Zrinski Ptg Co, Čakovec)

2008 (8 May). P 14 (with one diamond shaped perf on each horiz side).

937 **450** 2k.30 multicoloured ... 1·60 1·60

No. 937 was issued in sheetlets of ten stamps and ten labels.

451 Envelope sealed with Wax

452 Footballs

(Des Ariana Norsic. Litho, embossed (5k.) and thermography (3k.50) Zrinski Ptg Co, Čakovec)

2008 (9 May). Europa. The Letter. T **451** and similar horiz design. Multicoloured. P 14 (with one diamond shaped perf on each horiz side).

938 3k.50 Type **451** ... 2·30 2·30
939 5k. Airmail envelope ... 3·25 3·25

No. 939 has the outline of an aircraft embossed at upper right.

(Des Ana Žaja Petrak and Mario Petrak. Litho Zrinski Ptg Co, Čakovec)

2008 (14 May). European Football Championship, Austria and Switzerland. P 14.

940 **452** 3k.50 multicoloured ... 2·30 2·30

No. 940 was perforated in a circle contained in an outer perforated rectangle.

453 Sails

454 Ivan Vucetica

(Litho Zrinski Ptg Co, Čakovec)

2008 (16 May). Adris. P 14 (with one diamond shaped perf on each horiz side).

941 **453** 2k.30 multicoloured ... 1·60 1·60

No. 937 was issued in sheetlets of ten stamps and ten labels, each pair of stamp and label forming a composite design.

(Des Klara Mikulić. Litho Zrinski Ptg Co, Čakovec)

2008 (20 May). 150th Birth Anniv of Ivan Vucetica (fingerprint identification pioneer). Sheet 112×73 mm. P 14½ (with one diamond shaped perf on each vert side).

MS942 **454** 10k. multicoloured ... 7·00 7·00

The stamp and margins of No. **MS**942 form a composite design.

455 Water

456 Rijeka and Mountains

(Litho and die-stamped silver foil Zrinski Ptg Co, Čakovec)

2008 (14 June). Zaragoza 2008 International Water and Sustainable Development Exhibition. Sheet 112×72 mm. P 14½ (with one diamond shaped perf on each vert side).

MS943 **455** 10k. multicoloured ... 7·00 7·00

(Des Danijel Popović. Litho Zrinski Ptg Co, Čakovec)

2008 (14 June). Bicentenary of Louisiana Road (from Rijeka to Karlovac). Sheet 95×80 mm containing T **456** and similar vert designs showing map of route. Multicoloured. P 14½ (with one diamond shaped perf on each vert side).

MS944 5k.×3, Type **456**; 'Delnice', 'Skrad' and 'Vrbovsko'; 'Bosiljevo' and 'Karlovac' ... 10·00 10·00

The stamp and margins of No. **MS**944 form a composite design.

457 Globes

458 Stylized Postmen as Athletes

(Des BarBarShop. Litho Zrinski Ptg Co, Čakovec)

2008 (11 July). 150th Anniv of Western Union. P 14 (with one diamond shaped perf on each horiz side).
945 **457** 3k.50 multicoloured .... 2·40 2·40
No. 945 has a *se-tenant* stamp size label attached at right and was issued in sheets of ten stamps and ten labels.

(Des Sandra Turic. Litho Zrinski Ptg Co, Čakovec)

2008 (9 Sept). Post Employees' Sports Meeting. P 14.
946 **458** 2k.80 multicoloured .... 2·00 2·00

459 Pinida

459a Pinida

(Litho Zrinski Ptg Co, Čakovec)

2008 (12 Sept). Lighthouses. T **459** and similar vert designs. Multicoloured. P 14 (with one diamond shaped hole on each vert side).
947 5k. Type **459** .... 3·75 3·75
948 5k. Vnetak .... 3·75 3·75
949 5k. Zaglav .... 3·75 3·75
947/949 *Set of 3* .... 10·00 10·00

(Litho Zrinski Ptg Co, Čakovec)

2008 (14 Sept). OBLIGATORY TAX. Anti-Tuberculosis Week. Litho. P 14.
949*a* **459a** 5k. multicoloured .... 1·00 1·00
For compulsory use from 14 to 21 September.

460 St. Clare Porziuncola (fresco)

461 Embroidered Flowers (Sunja)

(Des Sabina Rešić. Litho Zrinski Ptg Co, Čakovec)

2008 (16 Sept). 700th Anniv of Order of Poor Clare Sisters in Split. P 14.
950 **460** 2k.80 multicoloured .... 2·00 2·00

(Des Sabina Rešić. Litho Zrinski Ptg Co, Čakovec)

2008 (30 Sept). Cultural Heritage. Folk Costume Designs. Sheet 118×102 mm containing T **461** and similar vert designs. Multicoloured. P 14 (with one diamond shaped hole on each vert side).
951 10l. Type **461** 20 20
952 20l. Beaded strands (Bistra) 30 30
953 50l. Woollen fringes and pierced embroidered cloth (Bizovac) 50 50
954 1k. Fringed cloth (Ravni Kotari) .... 1·00 1·00
955 10k. Lace (Pag) .... 6·75 6·75
951/955 *Set of 5* .... 8·00 8·00
MS956 10l. Type **461**; 20l. Beaded strands (Bistra); 50l. Woollen fringes and pierced embroidered cloth (Bizovac); 1k. Fringed cloth (Ravni Kotari); 10k. Lace (Pag) .... 8·00 8·00

462 Sun and Skyline

463 Frontispiece

(Litho Zrinski Ptg Co, Čakovec)

2008 (17 Oct). 20th Anniv of Healthy Cities Movement in Europe. P 14 (with one diamond shaped hole on each vert side).
957 **462** 2l.80 multicoloured .... 2·00 2·00

(Des Hrvoje Šercar. Litho Zrinski Ptg Co, Čakovec)

2008 (22 Oct). 550th Anniv of *The Book on the Art of Trading* by Benedict Kotruljevic. P 14 (with one diamond shaped hole on each vert side).
958 **463** 2l.80 multicoloured .... 2·00 2·00

464 College Façade

465 Map, Radio Waves and Globe

(Des Hrvoje Šercar. Litho Zrinski Ptg Co, Čakovec)

2008 (7 Nov). 350th Anniv of Collegium Ragusinum. P 14 (with one diamond shaped hole on each vert side).
959 **464** 7l.20 multicoloured .... 4·50 4·50

(Des Sabina Rešić. Litho Zrinski Ptg Co, Čakovec)

2008 (14 Nov). International Amateur Radio Union Conference, Cavtat. P 14 (with one diamond shaped hole on each vert side).
960 **465** 3l.50 multicoloured .... 2·50 2·50

466 Boy and Sleigh (leo Zivica)

467 *Christmas Interior* (Emanuel Vidović)

(Litho Zrinski Ptg Co, Čakovec)

2008 (21 Nov). New Year. Winning Design in Children's Painting Competition. P 14 (with one diamond shaped hole on each horiz side).
961 **466** 1l.80 multicoloured .... 1·20 1·20

(Litho Zrinski Ptg Co, Čakovec)

2008 (27 Nov). Christmas. P 14 (with one diamond shaped hole on each horiz side).
962 **467** 2l.80 multicoloured .... 2·00 2·00

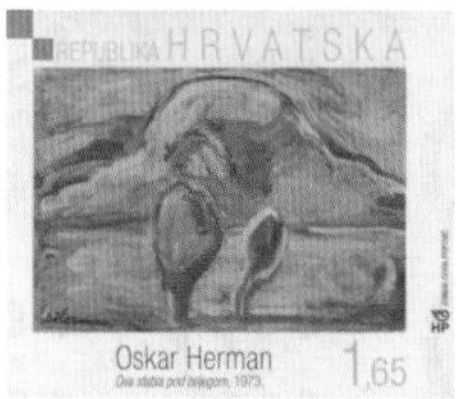

468 *Two Trees at Foot of Hill* (Oskar Herman)

469 Zorin dom Karlovac Theatre and Lyre

(Litho Zrinski Ptg Co, Čakovec)

2008 (1 Dec). Art. T **468** and similar horiz designs. Multicoloured. P 14 (with one diamond shaped hole on each vert side).
963 1l.65 Type **468** .... 1·20 1·20
964 1l.80 *Carousel* (Nevenka Đorđevic) .... 1·50 1·50
965 6l.50 *Still Life* (Ivo Režek) .... 4·50 4·50
963/965 *Set of 3* .... 6·50 6·50

(Des Hrvoje Šercar. Litho Zrinski Ptg Co, Čakovec)

2008 (5 Dec). 150th Anniv of 'Zora' Choral Society. P 14 (with one diamond shaped hole on each vert side).
966 **469** 1l.65 multicoloured .... 1·20 1·20

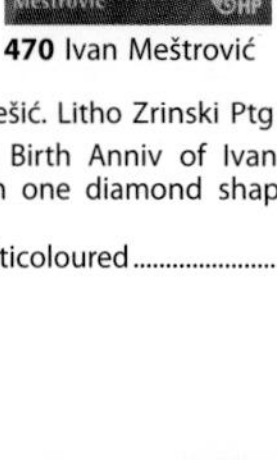

470 Ivan Meštrović

(Des Sabina Rešić. Litho Zrinski Ptg Co, Čakovec))

2008 (17 Dec). 125th Birth Anniv of Ivan Meštrović (artist and writer). P 14 (with one diamond shaped hole on each vert side).
967 **470** 5l. multicoloured .... 3·50 3·50

STAMP BOOKLETS

The following checklist covers, in simplified form, booklets issued by Croatia. It is intended that it should be used in conjunction with the main listings and details of the stamps and panes listed there are not repeated.

Prices are for complete booklets

Booklet No.	*Date*	*Contents and Cover Price*	*Price*
SB1	23.11.00	Christmas (T **301**) 1 pane, No. 644a (23k.)	12·00
SB2	22.11.01	Christmas (T **321**) 1 pane, No. 674a (23k.)	13·00
SB3	5.6.02	Trees (T **335**) 1 pane, No. 699a (18k.)	9·50
SB4	5.6.02	Trees 1 pane, No. 700a (25k.)	15·00
SB5	5.6.02	Trees 1 pane, No. 701a (28k.)	17·00
SB6	22.11.02	Christmas (T **340**) 1 pane, No. 710a (23k.)	15·00
SB7	5.6.04	Dog Rose No. 767a (23k.)	19·00
SB8	5.6.04	Sweet Violet No. 768a. (28k.)	22·00
SB9	5.6.04	Peppermint No. 769a (35k.)	26·00
SB10	24.5.05	Tourism 1 pane. 799a. (26k.50)	19·00
SB11	22.11.05	Christmas No. 825×10	11·00
SB12	25.4.06	Tourism No. 841a (23k.)	17·00
SB13	5.6.06	Flora No. 860a (28k.)	20·00
SB14	27.11.06	Christmas No. 871×10	16·00
SB15	15.3.07	Fauna No. 880a	13·00
SB16	15.3.07	Fauna No. 881a	19·00
SB17	15.3.07	Fauna No. 882a	21·00
SB18	15.11.07	Christmas No. 906a×10	17·00
SB19	20.3.08	Flora 1 pane 920a	15·00
SB20	20.3.08	Flora 1 pane 921a	23·00
SB21	20.3.08	Flora 1 pane 922a	26·00
SB22	25.4.08	Tourism No. 926a	25·00

Where the same design, or subject, appears more than once in a set only the first number is given. Scenes and buildings are listed under the town or geographical area in which they are situated. Portraits are listed under surnames only. In cases of difficulty part of the inscription has been used to identify the stamp.

SERBIAN POSTS IN CROATIA

100 Paras = 1 Dinar

REPUBLIC OF SRPSKA KRAJINA

Following Croatia's declaration of independence from Yugoslavia on 30 May 1991 fighting broke out between Serb inhabitants, backed by units of the Yugoslav Federal Army, and Croatian forces. By January 1992, when a ceasefire sponsored by the United Nations and the European Community became effective, the Croatian Serbs and their allies controlled 30% of the country organized into the districts of the Krajina, Western Slavonia and Eastern Slavonia. These were declared peacekeeping zones under United Nations supervision and the Yugoslav Army withdrew. In 1993 the Serbs proclaimed the Republic of Srpska Krajina, covering all three areas, and elections for a separate president and parliament were held in January 1994.

K 1 Stag, Kopačevo Marsh

5000

(K 2)

K 3 Coat of Arms

(Litho The Mint, Belgrade)

1993 (24 Mar). Type K **1** and similar vert designs. P 13½.

K1	200d. deep yellow-green and orange-yellow	50	50
K2	500d. black and vermilion	1·20	1·20
K3	1000d. deep yellow-green and orange-yellow	2·30	2·30
K4	1000d. deep yellow-green and orange-yellow	2·30	2·30
K5	2000d. black and vermilion	4·75	4·75
K1/5 *Set of 5*		10·00	10·00

Designs:—No. K2, Krka Monastery; K3, Town walls, Knin; K4, Ruined house, Vukovar; K5, Coat of arms.

For 100000d. in same design as No. K2 see No. K12.

1993 (May). Issued at Knin. Nos. 2594a/5a of Yugoslavia surch as Type K **2**. P 13½.

K6	5000d. on 3d. black and orange-red	1·90	1·90
K7	10000d. on 2d. new blue and bright crimson	1·90	1·90
	a. Perf 12½	25·00	25·00

Nos. K6/7 were used at Knin between May and August 1993 when lines of communication to Belgrade were disrupted by fighting in the Brčko Corridor.

Subsequently similar 5000d. surcharges on the 20, 30, 50 and 60p. values from the same set (Nos. 2588/9, 2591/2 of Yugoslavia) appeared, but these were not used for postal purposes during the period when normal issues were unavailable. All of these additional surcharges were on stamps perforated 12½, except for the 60p. which is known perforated either 12½ or 13½.

(Litho The Mint, Belgrade)

1993 (15 June). P 13½.

K8	K **3**	A deep ultramarine and vermilion	95	95

No. K8 was sold at the internal letter rate.

K 4 Citadel, Knin

A

(K 5)

K 6 Helmet and Swords

(Litho The Mint, Belgrade)

1993 (15 June). Type K **4** and similar vert designs. P 13½.

K9	5000d. turquoise-green and scarlet	50	50
K10	10000d. turquoise-green and scarlet	95	95
K11	50000d. deep ultramarine and scarlet	1·90	1·90
K12	100000d. ultramarine and scarlet	2·40	2·40
K9/12 *Set of 4*		5·25	5·25

Designs:—10000d. Heron, Kopačevo Marsh; 50000d. Icon and church, Vukovar; 100000d. Krka Monastery.

Currency Reform

1993 (1 Nov). No. K8 surch with Type K **5** (Cyrillic letter "D") in ultramarine.

K13	K **3**	"D" on A deep ultramarine and vermilion	1·50	1·50

No. K13 was sold at the new internal letter rate.

1993 (1 Nov). Nos. K9/12 surch with Type K **5** (Cyrillic letter "D") in ultramarine.

K14	K **4**	"D" on 5000d. turquoise-green and scarlet	50	50
K15	–	"D" on 10000d. turquoise-green and scarlet	95	95
K16	–	"D" on 50000d. deep ultramarine and scarlet	4·25	4·25
K17	–	"D" on 100000d. ultramarine and scarlet	12·50	12·50
K14/17 *Set of 4*			16·00	16·00

(Litho The Mint, Belgrade)

1993 (22 Nov). P 13½.

K18	K **6**	R bright blue	1·50	1·50

No. K18 was sold at the internal registered letter rate.

K 7 St. Simeon

K 8 Cup-and-saucer (*Cobaea scandens*)

(Litho The Mint, Belgrade)

1994 (26 Feb). Serb Culture and Tradition. Type K **7** and similar multicoloured designs. P 13½.

K19	50p. Type K **7**	95	95
K20	80p. Krajina coat of arms (vert)	1·90	1·90
K21	1d. "The Vučedol Dove" (carving) (vert)	3·00	3·00
K19/21 *Set of 3*		5·25	5·25

PRINTER AND PROCESS. The following issues were printed in lithography by Forum at Novi Sad, *unless otherwise stated*.

1994 (6 July). Climbing Plants. Type K **8** and similar vert designs. Multicoloured. P 14.

K22	30p. Type K **8**	80	80
K23	40p. *Dipladenia*	1·00	1·00
K24	60p. Black-eyed Susan (*Thunbergia alata*)	1·70	1·70
K25	70p. Climbing rose	1·90	1·90
K22/25 *Set of 4*		4·25	4·25

Nos. K22/5 were each issued in sheets of eight stamps with different centre labels showing butterflies.

K 9 Krka Monastery

K 10 "The Flower of Life" (memorial to Jasenovac Concentration Camp victims)

1994 (10 Dec). Type K **9** and similar vert designs. P 14.

K26	5p. deep carmine	10	10
K27	10p. deep brown	25	25
K28	20p. brown-olive	50	50
K29	50p. Indian red	1·30	1·30
K30	60p. reddish violet	1·60	1·60
K31	1d. dull ultramarine	2·75	2·75
K26/31 *Set of 6*		5·75	5·75

Designs:—10p. Carin; 20p. Vukovar; 50p. Monument, Batina; 60p. Ilok; 1d. Lake, Plitvice.

During early May 1995 an offensive by the Croatian Army drove Serbian forces from Western Slavonia which was then reincorporated into the Republic of Croatia.

1995 (9 May). 50th Anniv of End of Second World War. P 14.

K32	K **10**	60p. multicoloured	2·10	2·10

No. K32 was issued in sheets of eight stamps and a centre label showing the entrance to Jasenovac Concentration Camp.

K 11 "A" over Mosaic

K 12 Krčić Waterfall, Knin

1995 (20 June). P 14.

K33	K **11**	A vermilion	1·00	1·00

No. K33 was sold at the internal letter rate.

1995 (28 June). Type K **12** and similar vert designs. P 14.

K34	10p. greenish blue	10	10
K35	20p. ochre	20	20
K36	40p. rosine	50	50
K37	2d. deep blue	2·50	2·50
K38	5d. yellow-brown	5·75	5·75
K34/38 *Set of 5*		8·25	8·25

Designs:—20p. Benkovac; 40p. Citadel, Knin; 2d. Petrinja; 5d. Pakrac.

In a three-day operation starting on 4 August 1995 the Croatian army occupied the Krajina and the area was reincorporated into the Republic of Croatia. The only surviving part of the Serbian territories, Eastern Slavonia, was, by agreement, placed under temporary United Nations administration in November 1995 and was subsequently called Sremsko Baranjska Oblast (Srem and Baranya Region).

SREMSKO BARANJSKA OBLAST

K 13 Common Cormorant (*Phalacrocorax carbo*), Kopačevo Marsh

K 14 St. Dimitriev's Church, Dalj

1995 (30 Aug). Protected Species. Type K **13** and similar vert design. Multicoloured. P 14.

K39	80p. Type K **13**	3·25	3·25
K40	80p. Chamois (*Rupicapra rupicapra*), Lika	3·25	3·25

No. K40 is wrongly inscr "Rupricapra".

Nos. K39/40 were each issued in sheets of eight stamps with different centre labels showing habitats.

1995 (28 Dec). Churches (1st series). Type K **14** and similar vert designs. P 14.

K41	5p. myrtle green	10	10
K42	10p. carmine-lake	20	20
K43	30p. bright mauve	65	65
K44	50p. red-brown	1·20	1·20
K45	1d. royal blue	2·10	2·10
K41/45 *Set of 5*		3·75	3·75

Designs:—10p. St. Peter and St. Paul's Church, Bolman; 30p. St. Nicholas's Church, Mirkovci; 50p. St. Nicholas's Church, Tenja; 1d. St. Nicholas's Church, Vukovar.

See also Nos. K48/53.

K 15 Vukovar Marina, River Danube

K 16 The Workers' Hall, Vukovar

1996 (6 Feb). River Danube Co-operation. P 14.

K46	K **15**	1d. multicoloured	3·25	3·25

No. K46 was issued in sheets of eight stamps and a centre label showing the "Vučedol Dove".

1996 (14 May). P 14.

K47	K **16**	A vermilion	30	30

No. K47 was sold at the internal letter rate.

K 17 Archangel Church, Darda

K 18 Nikola Tesla

1996 (14 May). Churches (2nd series). Type K **17** and similar vert designs. P 14.

K48	10p. red-brown	10	10
K49	50p. reddish violet	40	40
K50	1d. deep turquoise-green	85	85
K51	2d. olive-green	1·70	1·70
K52	5d. steel-blue	4·25	4·25
K53	10d. deep ultramarine	8·25	8·25
K48/53 *Set of 6*		14·00	14·00

Designs:—50p. St. George's Church, Kneževo; 1d. St. Nicholas's Church, Jagodnjak; 2d. Archangel Gabriel's Church, Bršadin; 5d. St. Stephen's Church, Borovo Selo; 10d. St. Nicholas's Church, Pačetin.

1996 (10 July). 140th Birth Anniv of Nikola Tesla (inventor). P 14.

K54	K **18**	1d.50 multicoloured	3·25	3·25

No. K54 was issued in sheets of eight stamps and a centre label showing Tesla's transformer.

K 19 Milica Stojadinović-Srpkinja (1830–1878) (poetess)

K 20 Jasna Šekarić (Olympic gold medal winner)

1996 (10 Oct). Europa. Famous Women. Type K **19** and similar vert design. Multicoloured. P 14.

K55	1d.50 Type K **19**	26·00	26·00
K56	1d.50 Mileva Marić-Einstein (1875–1948) (mathematician)	26·00	26·00

Nos. K55/6 were each issued in sheets of eight stamps and different centre labels symbolising their achievements.

1996 (5 Dec). Centenary of Modern Olympic Games. P 14.

K57	K **20**	1d.50 multicoloured	3·25	3·25

No. K57 was issued in sheets of eight stamps and a centre label showing ancient Greek athletes.

K 21 Milutin Milanković

K 22 "Madonna and Child" (icon)

1996 (16 Dec). Milutin Milanković (geophysicist) Commemoration (1879–1958). P 14.

K58	K **21**	1d.50 multicoloured	3·25	3·25

No. K58 was issued in sheets of eight stamps and a centre label showing calculation.

1996 (20 Dec). Christmas. P 14.

K59	K **22**	1d.50 multicoloured	3·25	3·25

No. K59 was issued in sheets of eight stamps and a centre label showing St. Nicholas's Church, Vukovar.

K **23** Pigeon

XXXXXX
XX 20.00
XXXXXXXX
(K **24**)

1997 (8 Feb). Domestic Pets. Type K **23** and similar vert designs. Multicoloured. P 14.

K60		1d. Type K **23**	1·00	1·00
K61		1d. Budgerigar	1·00	1·00
K62		1d. Cat	1·00	1·00
K63		1d. Black labrador	1·00	1·00
K60/63 *Set of* 4			3·50	3·50

Nos. K60/3 were each issued in sheets of eight stamps with different centre labels.

1997 (15 Feb). No. K18 surch or optd (No. K67) as Type K **24**.

K64	K **6**	10p. on R blue (R.)	10	10
K65		20p. on R blue (R.)	20	20
K66		30p. on R blue (R.)	40	40
K67		R (90p.) blue (R.)	1·20	1·20
K68		1d. on R blue (R.)	1·30	1·30
K69		1d.50 on R blue (Blk.)	1·90	1·90
K70		2d. on R blue (Blk.)	2·50	2·50
K71		5d. on R blue (Blk.)	6·25	6·25
K72		10d. on R blue (Blk.)	12·50	12·50
K73		20d. on R blue (Blk.)	26·00	26·00
K64/73 *Set of* 10			47·00	47·00

K **25** St. Peter and St. Paul's Cathedral, Orolik

K **26** Prince Marko and the Turks

1997 (22 Feb). Restoration of Orthodox Church, Ilok. Type K **25** and similar vert designs. P 14.

K74		50p. +50p. new blue	50	50
K75		60p. +50p. bright mauve	60	60
K76		1d.20 +50p. scarlet	1·00	1·00
K74/76 *Set of* 3			1·90	1·90

Designs:—60p. St. George's Church, Tovarnik; 1d.20, Church, Negoslavci.

1997 (12 Apr). Europa. Tales and Legends. Type K **26** and similar vert design. Multicoloured. P 14.

K77		1d. Type K **26**	6·75	6·75
K78		1d. Emperor Trajan	6·75	6·75

Nos. K77/8 were each issued in sheets of eight stamps with different centre labels.

The postal administration of the Srem and Baranya Region was reincorporated into that of the Republic of Croatia on 19 May 1997 when Croatian kuna became the only legal currency. A 10d. miniature sheet had been prepared by the Serb postal administration to mark the "Pacific 97" International Stamp Exhibition at San Francisco between 29 May and 8 June 1997. This miniature sheet, which exists both perforate and imperforate, was available at the exhibition, but was not sold for postal purposes in Srem and Baranya Region.

Eastern Slavonia was returned to Croat control on 15 January 1998.

Epirus

100 Lepta = 1 Drachma

A. PROVISIONAL GOVERNMENT

At the end of 1913, after the Powers had decided that Epirus was to be included in Albania, the population, who were largely Greek, set up a Provisional Government and declared their autonomy.

1

1914 (10 Feb). Issued at Chimara. Handstamped. Seal in blue, value in second colour. Imperf. No gum.

1	**1**	1l. black and blue	£225	£150
2		5l. blue and red	£225	£150
3		10l. red and black	£225	£150
4		25l. blue and red	£225	£150
1/4 *Set of* 4			£800	£550

The majority of stamps on the market are forgeries.

1914 (2 Mar). Issued at Argyrocastro. Stamps of Turkey variously surch "ΑΥΤΟΝΟΜΟΣ ΗΠΕΙΡΟΣ" and value vertically reading up or down. (Types of Turkey are illustrated at beginning of Albania).

(a) On issue of 1908 (T **25**). P 12

5	1d. on 2½pi. black-brown (R.)	8·00	8·00
	a. Perf 13½		
6	2d. on 2½pi. black-brown (R.)	10·00	10·00
	a. Perf 13½		
7	5d. on 25pi. myrtle green	65·00	65·00
8	5d. on 50pi. brown	£150	£150

(b) On issue of 1908, T **25** optd with T **26**. P 12

9	40l. on 2pi. black (R.)	75·00	75·00
10	80l. on 2pi. black (R.)	75·00	75·00

(c) On issue of 1909–11 (T **28**). P 12

11	5l. on 10pa. green (R.)	2·00	2·00
12	10l. on 20pa. rose-carmine ("10" italic)	2·00	2·00
	a. Larger surch with "10" upright	2·00	2·00
13	20l. on 1pi. bright blue (R.)	2·00	2·00
14	25l. on 1pi. bright blue (R.)	2·00	2·00
15	30l. on 2pa. olive-green	2·00	2·00
16	40l. on 2pi. blue-black (R.)	2·00	2·00
17	50l. on 2pa. olive-green	2·30	2·30
18	80l. on 2pi. blue-black (R.)	2·50	2·50
19	1d. on 5pi. slate-purple	8·00	8·00
20	2d. on 5pi. slate-purple	10·00	10·00
21	5d. on 10pi. dull red	50·00	50·00
22	5d. on 50pi. brown	£130	£130

Surcharges on other stamps are trials.

Dangerous forgeries exist.

The following stamps were printed together in sheets: Nos. 5 and 6; 5a and 6a; 9 and 10; 12 and 12a; 13 and 14; 15 and 17; 16 and 18; 19 and 20. *Se-tenant* pairs may therefore be found.

2

3

ΕΛΛΗΝΙΚΗ
1914
ΧΕΙΜΑΡΡΑ
(**4**)

(Litho Aspiotis, Corfu)

1914. Zigzag roulette 14.

(a) T **2** (inscr "Epirus") (5 Mar)

23	**2**	10l. carmine-red	50	50
24		25l. blue	60	60

(b) T **3** (Inscr "ΑΥΤΟΝΟΜΟΣ ΗΠΕΙΡΟΣ") (26 Mar)

25	**3**	1l. orange	50	50
26		5l. green	50	50
27		50l. brown	80	80
28		1d. violet	2·00	2·00
29		2d. grey-black	12·00	12·00
30		5d. olive-green	15·00	15·00
23/30 *Set of* 8			29·00	29·00

1914 (24 Aug). Issued at Chimara. Types of Greece (2l. and 3l. engraved, others litho) optd with T **4**, with or without Greek initials "S.S." (= S Spiromilos) in manuscript in black.

31	**29**	1l. green	20·00	20·00
32	**30**	2l. carmine	20·00	20·00
33	**29**	3l. vermilion	25·00	25·00
34	**31**	5l. green	25·00	25·00
35	**29**	10l. carmine	25·00	25·00
36	**30**	20l. grey-lilac	50·00	50·00
37		25l. ultramarine	80·00	80·00
38	**31**	50l. indigo-purple	£100	£100
31/38 *Set of* 8			£300	£300

Dangerous forgeries exist.

5

ΚΟΡΥΤΣΑ
(**6**)

(Litho Aspiotis, Corfu)

1914 (28 Aug). Zigzag roulette 14.

39	**5**	1l. brown and blue	70	1·70
40		5l. yellow-green and blue	70	1·70
41		10l. rose and blue	70	1·70
42		25l. indigo and blue	70	1·70
43		50l. violet and blue	70	1·70
44		1d. carmine and blue	5·00	8·00
45		2d. yellow and blue	1·50	3·00
46		5d. deep green and blue	8·00	10·00
39/46 *Set of* 8			16·00	27·00

1914 (25 Sept). Issued at Koritza. Nos. 42/3 optd with T **6** in blue.

47	**5**	25l. indigo and blue	5·00	5·00
48		50l. violet and blue	15·00	15·00

7 King Constantine I of Greece

(Litho Papachrysantu, Athens)

1914 (25 Oct). Issued at Chimara. P 11½.

49	**7**	1l. yellow-green	£100	55·00
50		2l. orange-brown	50·00	40·00
51		5l. grey-blue	£100	40·00
52		10l. orange-brown	50·00	40·00
53		20l. carmine	50·00	40·00
54		25l. grey-blue	£100	55·00
55		50l. yellow-green	£110	60·00
56		1d. carmine	£100	60·00
57		2d. yellow-green	£150	80·00
58		5d. orange-brown	£250	£180
49/58 *Set of* 10			£950	£600

The stamps in the same colours were printed together in the sheet and it is possible to find stamps of different values se-tenant, but unused stamps are very scarce.

A

B

1, 2, 3, 5, 10, 25, 30, 40 and 50l. values in design A and 1, 2, 3, 5, 10 and 25d. values as design B (with different centres showing ancient coins) were privately produced, probably in early 1914, and are believed to have been printed in France. Following the seizure by Epirots of Moschopolis (Voskopojë) in June 1914 the commander of the local forces was persuaded to issue the stamps.

The majority of known covers are dated October or November 1914, are addressed to various stamp dealers and contained offers or shipments of the stamps. There is little evidence that the stamps were actually available to the general public for postal purposes. After the occupation of Epirus by Greek troops the remaining stock was sent to Athens where it was destroyed in 1931. (*Price for set of 15: £40 un; £75 c.t.o.*).

All values are known imperforate. Some values exist in different colours or with inverted centres. All except the 10 and 25d. values can be found with a two-line overprint.

Various other purported issues of Epirus are considered to be bogus.

B. NORTHERN EPIRUS

GREEK OCCUPATION

In December 1914 the Powers agreed to a provisional occupation of Epirus by Greek troops. This was the same area as that which had declared its autonomy but it was now known as Northern Epirus.

"Β. ΗΠΕΙΡΟΣ"
(**8**) (= Northern Epirus)

1914 (8 Dec)–**15**. Types of Greece optd with T **8** horizontally.

59	**35**	1l. brown	1·00	1·00
		a. Opt inverted	20·00	
		b. Opt double	20·00	
		c. Opt double, one inverted	30·00	
60	**36**	2l. scarlet	1·50	1·50
		a. Opt inverted	20·00	
		b. Opt double	20·00	
		c. Carmine (1915)	2·50	2·50
		ca. Opt double	25·00	
		cb. Opt double, one inverted	30·00	
61		3l. orange	1·00	1·00
		a. Opt inverted	18·00	
		b. Opt double	18·00	
62	**35**	5l. green	1·50	1·50
		a. Opt double, one inverted	30·00	
63		10l. rose-red	3·00	3·00
		a. Opt inverted	35·00	
64		20l. bright violet	8·50	8·50
		a. Opt inverted	60·00	
65	**36**	25l. pale blue	3·00	3·00
		a. Opt inverted		
		b. Opt double		
66	**35**	30l. green	12·00	12·00
67	**36**	40l. indigo	15·00	15·00
68	**35**	50l. deep blue	17·00	17·00
69	**36**	1d. dull purple	85·00	85·00
		a. Opt inverted	£250	
		b. Opt double	£200	

Nos. 59/62 optd in red were not issued.

1915. Stamps of Greece, 1911–13, optd with T **8** sideways (reading downwards on 5d., upwards on other values).

(a) Engraved

70	**29**	3l. vermilion	9·00	9·00
71	**31**	30l. carmine-red	65·00	65·00
72	**32**	1d. ultramarine	60·00	60·00
73		2d. vermilion	70·00	70·00
74		3d. carmine	80·00	80·00
75		5d. grey-blue	£450	£500
		a. Opt double	£650	

(b) Lithographed

76	**29**	1l. green	1·00	1·00
		a. "I" omitted	18·00	
77	**30**	2l. carmine	1·00	1·00
		a. "I" omitted	18·00	
		b. No point after "B"	18·00	
78	**29**	3l. vermilion	7·50	7·50
		a. No point after "B"	35·00	
		b. Pair, one with opt omitted		
79	**31**	5l. green	1·20	1·20
		a. "I" omitted	20·00	
		b. No point after "B"	20·00	
		c. Opt double	25·00	
80	**29**	10l. carmine	2·00	2·00
81	**30**	20l. purple-grey	2·75	2·75
82		25l. blue	3·00	3·00
		a. No point after "B"	30·00	
83	**31**	30l. carmine-red	8·50	8·50
84	**30**	40l. deep blue	10·00	10·00
85	**31**	50l. brown-purple	15·00	15·00

The "I omitted" error occurs on position 28 and the "No point after B" on position 52 of the sheet of 100.

In June 1916 Northern Epirus was taken over by Italian troops and after the war it was incorporated in Albania. For issues for this area made in 1940–41, see under Albania (Greek Occupation).

Greece

1861. 100 Lepta = 1 Drachma
2002. 100 Cents = 1 Euro

KINGDOM

King Otho

6 February 1833–23 October 1862

King Otho was deposed, and a Provisional Government ruled Greece until Prince William of Denmark was chosen as King George I of the Hellenes.

The dates of issue are according to local computation on the Julian or Gregorian Calendar in use. In the 19th century the Julian Calendar was twelve days behind the Gregorian Calendar. After 1900 the difference was thirteen days. In Greece the Gregorian Calendar was introduced on 16 February 1923 which became 1 March.

Unoverprinted Greek stamps were used in Greek Post Offices in the Turkish Empire until their closure in 1881. Until 1863 the numbered cancellations noted in brackets were used, after that date town cancellations were also used: Constantinople (95), Smyrna (96), Alexandria (97), Salonika (98), Ioannina (99), Galatz (100), Ibraila (101), Bucharest (102), Larissa (103), Preveza (104), Arta (105) and Volos (135). There were also post offices in Crete at Canea (open Mar–Nov 1881, number 162), Rethymnon (open 1881–85, number 163) and Iraklion (open 1881–82, number 164). Larissa, Arta and Volos became domestic post offices in 1881 after the cession of Thessaly to Greece.

PRICES.—The prices for early Greek stamps are for fine specimens, with original gum if unused. Inferior specimens, both unused and used, are worth much less.

1 Hermes

Paris print

(Eng A. Barre. Electrotypes. Ptd first by E. Meyer, Paris, later at Athens)

1861 (1 Oct). Type **1** Paris print. Imperf. On cream paper unless otherwise stated.

(i) Without figures at back

1	1l. chocolate	£500	£400
	a. Red-brown	£650	£475
2	2l. olive-bistre	55·00	65·00
	a. Brown-buff/buff	55·00	65·00
3	5l. emerald/*greenish*	£650	£130
4	20l. blue/*bluish*	£800	95·00
	a. Deep blue/bluish	£1000	£180
	b. Pelure paper	£1300	£750
5	40l. mauve/*blue*	£250	£120
6	80l. carmine	£200	£120

(ii) With large figures 8 mm high at back

7	10l. red-orange/*blue*	£800	£550
	a. "0" of "10" inverted	—	£1500
	b. "1" of "10" inverted	—	£1900
	c. "10" inverted		
	d. Without "10" at back	£1000	

The figures on the back are outlined more thickly on the right-hand outer edge with the "0" also on the left inner curve. Inverted numerals can be identified by the thicker outer edge being wrongly on the left side. Only two examples of No. 7c are known.

The Paris-printed stamps have the shading on cheek and neck of Mercury made up of fine lines and dots. In those printed in Athens the lines are unbroken and thicker.

Trial impressions of Paris exist in many different shades, of which some are indistinguishable from those of the issued stamps. These are often found with false gum which is thin and smooth, differing greatly from that on the issued stamps, which is generally thick, often brownish, and always "crackly". Stamps with false gum are worth about the same as those without gum. The variety No. 7d comes from proof sheets. There is an essay of the 10l. in orange-red/*blue*, which is also without figures at the back.

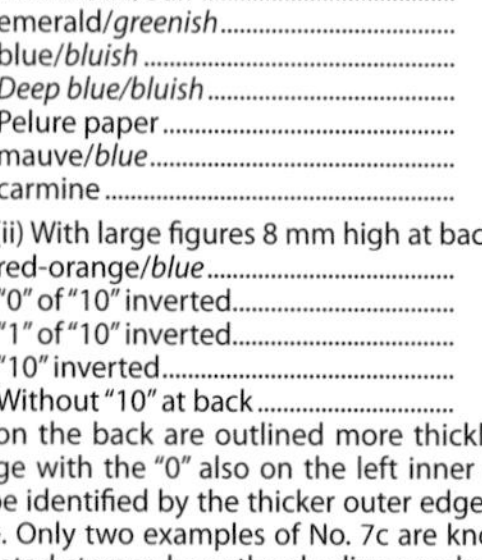

Athens print

(I) (II)

1861 (Nov)–**62**. First Athens print. On cream paper *unless otherwise stated.*

A. Coarse print

(i) Without figures at back

9A	2l. grey-brown (*shades*)/*straw*	75·00	£100
	a. Deep bistre-brown/cream	—	—
	c. Brown/straw	—	—
10A	20l. deep blue/*bluish* (*shades*) (*quadrillé background*)	—	—
	a. Ultramarine/bluish (shades)	—	—
	b. Ultramarine/bluish (thin paper)	£5000	—

B. Fine print

8B	1l. deep chocolate	£850	£900
	a. Pale chocolate	£425	£400
	b. Yellowish chocolate	£350	£350
9B	2l. grey-brown (*shades*)/*straw*	40·00	48·00
	a. Deep bistre-brown/cream	—	—
	b. Dull yellow-brown/cream	55·00	70·00

(ii) With figures 6 mm high at back Figure at back of 5l., Type I

11A	5l. green (*shades*)/*greenish*	£250	£120
	a. Yellow-green to olive-green/greenish.	£250	£130
	b. Blue-green/greenish	£250	£110
	c. Emerald-green/greenish	£300	£140
	d. Double "5" at back	—	£2500
12A	10l. yellow-orange/*bluish*	£750	£140
	a. Ochre/bluish green	£1400	£200
	b. Vermilion/bluish green	£1800	£325
	d. "1" of "10" at back inverted	—	£1700
	e. "0" of "10" at back inverted	—	£1700
13A	20l. deep blue/*bluish*	£7000	£450
	a. Indigo-blue/bluish	£8500	£475
	b. Pale Prussian blue/bluish	£5500	£225
	c. Deep dull chalky blue/bluish	£8000	£425
	d. "0" of "20" at back inverted	—	£1600
	e. "20" at back double	—	£2250
14A	40l. mauve/*bluish*	£7000	£475
	a. Dull mauve/bluish	£7000	£500

B. Fine print

11B	5l. green (*shades*)/*greenish*	£225	95·00
	a. Yellow-green to olive-green/greenish.	£225	95·00
	b. Blue-green/greenish	£275	£140
	c. Emerald-green/greenish	£275	£140
	d. Double "5" at back	—	£1600
12B	10l. yellow-orange/*bluish*	£550	£100
	b. Vermilion/bluish green	£800	£170
	c. Red-orange/bluish	£1100	£200
	d. "1" of "10" at back inverted	—	£1700
	e. "0" of "10" at back inverted	—	£2500
13B	20l. deep blue/*bluish*	£3250	£160
	d. "0" of "20" at back inverted	—	£1600
	e. "20" at back double	—	
14B	40l. mauve/*bluish*	£3750	£375
	a. Dull mauve/bluish	£3750	£375
15B	80l. rose	£1100	£160
	a. Carmine	£1200	£150
	b. Deep carmine-red	£1200	£160

All values of the First Athens issue frequently present a cloudy whitish contour outlining various parts of the Hermes head, usually on one of the sides.

The 20l. without figures on the back (the earliest known printing in Athens), is known only with the postmarks "1", "13" and "44", whereas the Paris print in deep blue (No. 4*a*) is only known with the postmark "9".

The following characteristics are also helpful for distinguishing these printings from subsequent ones:

(*a*) These stamps, with the exception of the 80l., were printed with the "hard" method of printing (like the Paris and 1870 issues). They do not, therefore, present any reliefs of the white parts of the Hermes head.

(*b*) The control numbers on the back are very delicate, sometimes presenting a peculiar dotting appearance.

The 5, 10, 20 and 40l. values in both the coarse and fine prints sometimes show a yellow wash on the surface of the paper, either on the front or more rarely on the back, and exceptionally on both sides of the stamp. Stamps with the wash on the front are worth about twice the value of the normals, both unused and used. With the wash on the back they are worth about three times normal and with it on both sides, about four times.

The 80l. stamp is of a very fine print and has thin and delicately designed red-orange figures on the back. All the later 80l. prints have carmine figures. This stamp was printed with the newly adopted "soft" method of printing when a piece of cloth, known as a "blanket" was used on the printing screen. This caused an accentuated relief on the white parts of the stamps. A faint vertical lining of the background is often visible.

See first note below No. 7 on how to identify inverted figures at back.

1862–**67**. Second Athens print. Printings made at Athens before the plates were cleaned in 1867. On cream paper *unless otherwise stated.* With figures at back except on the 1l. and 2l.

Figure at back of 5l., Type II

16	1l. chocolate-brown (*solid background*)	43·00	42·00
	a. Chocolate-brown (vert line background)	60·00	60·00
	b. Chocolate-brown (horiz line background)	60·00	60·00
	c. Olive-brown	65·00	65·00
	d. Chocolate brown (smudgy print)	43·00	42·00
	e. Red-brown (smudgy print)	£110	£100
	f. Purple-brown (coarse print)	£110	£100
	g. Deep purple-brown (coarse print)	£110	£100
17	2l. yellow-bistre	12·50	35·00
	a. Pale yellow-bistre	12·50	30·00
	b. Dull bistre (smooth print)	65·00	75·00
18	5l. yellowish green/*greenish*	£300	70·00
	a. Bluish green/greenish	£300	42·00
	b. Yellow-green/greenish (coarse print)..	£200	17·00
	c. "5" at back double	—	£2000
19	10l. yellowish orange/*bluish*	£550	80·00
	a. Pale orange-yellow/bluish	£300	42·00
	b. Orange/blue	£550	80·00
	ba. "10" on face instead of at back (on 19*b*)	—	£17000
	c. Red-orange/blue	£475	19·00
	d. "01" instead of "10"	£6500	£130
20	20l. blue/*bluish*	£275	16·00
	a. Pale blue/bluish (very fine print)	£275	16·00
	b. Deep bright bl/bluish (very fine print).	£400	38·00
	c. Dull greenish blue/bluish	£275	16·00
	d. Cobalt/bluish (coarse print)	£1200	26·00
	e. Blue/greenish	£1500	26·00
	f. Indigo-blue/bluish	£3250	90·00
	g. "80" at back (on 20*a*)	—	£1600
	h. Double "20" at back	—	£1000
21	40l. mauve/*blue*	£400	26·00
	a. Bright mauve/blue	£400	26·00
	b. Rose-mauve/lilac	£2250	£160
	c. Double figures at back	—	£1600
22	80l. carmine	90·00	50·00
	a. Deep carmine	65·00	18·00
	b. Rose-carmine	65·00	17·00
	c. "8" at back inverted	—	£375

Most of these stamps vary more or less in shade. Nos. 16*c* and 17*a* are exceedingly fine prints. In this group the numerals at back are thin and delicate as compared with those on later issues.

King George I

31 October 1863–18 March 1913

1867–**69**. Printings made in Athens after the plates were cleaned. On cream paper unless otherwise stated. With figures at back except the 1 and 2l.

23	1l. reddish brown	49·00	60·00
	a. Deep red-brown	49·00	50·00
	b. Fawn	85·00	80·00
24	2l. yellowish bistre	24·00	35·00
25	5l. bright green/*greenish*	£4750	£100
	a. Yellow-green/greenish	£4750	£100
26	10l. orange-vermilion/*bluish*	£1200	26·00
	a. "10" at back inverted	—	£1600
27	20l. pale bright blue/*bluish*	£650	16·00
	a. Double "20" at back	—	£1000
	b. Double print		
28	40l. rosy mauve/*blue*	£250	26·00
	a. Dull rosy mauve/blue	£250	26·00
	b. "20" at back corrected to "40"	£1900	
29	80l. carmine-rose	£170	£180

The stamps of this period show none of the blots and specks of colour which distinguish the later printings of the preceding set. No. 23*a* has rather short lines of shading on the cheek.

1870. Special printing made in Athens under the supervision of German workmen. Very fine impressions.

30	1l. fawn	£130	£190
	a. Deep fawn	£150	£200
31	20l. pale blue/*bluish*	£1500	18·00
	a. Bright blue/bluish	£1500	18·00
	b. "02" at back	—	£1500
	c. Inverted "20" at back	—	£1400

The 1l. has short lines of shading on the cheek and clear spandrels. The 20l. has short dotted lines of shading on cheek, resembling the Paris print, and very pale spandrels.

1870–**71**. Later printings from the cleaned plates. On cream paper unless otherwise stated. With figures at back except the 1 and 2l.

32	1l. dull brown	£250	£225
	a. Red-brown	£250	£225
33	2l. pale yellow-bistre/*deep cream*	14·50	31·00
34	5l. yellow-green/*greenish*	£5000	85·00
35	10l. pale red-orange/*greenish*	£1100	37·00
36	20l. dull blue/*bluish*	£1100	16·00
	a. Deep dull blue/bluish	£1400	21·00
	b. "02" at back	—	£425
	c. "20" at back double	—	£950
37	40l. pale salmon/*greenish*	£600	80·00
	a. Lilac-rose (solferino)/greenish		
38	80l. carmine-rose	£140	£170
	a. Deep carmine-red	£140	£170
	b. "80" at back inverted	—	£2750
	c. "8" for "80" at back	—	£1300

The 5l. is on thin transparent paper without any pronounced mesh, and must not be confused with No. 40*a*. The 10l. has coarse orange, instead of vermilion, figures. The 40l. was printed in a fugitive colour and is found in reddish salmon, salmon and, in the worst cases, a dirty yellow; the prices quoted are for stamps of good colour. No. 37*a*, of which only a few examples are known, was used only at Piraeus, from 12–14 July 1871; in colour it is the exact shade of the numerals at the back of the pale salmon stamps. The 80l. (Nos. 38 and 38*a*) are believed to have been printed in 1869, but were only used during this period; they are characterized by their pale and delicate spandrels. The stamps of this set have thick, coarse figures at back.

1872–**75**. Thin transparent paper. With figures at the back except on the 1l. and 2l.

39	1l. grey-brown/*buff*	38·00	50·00
	a. Deep reddish brown/buff	60·00	80·00
	b. Red-brown/buff	60·00	80·00
	c. Grey-brown/straw	43·00	60·00
39*d*	2l. brownish bistre	£275	£325
40	5l. green/*greenish*	£500	21·00
	a. Sage-green/greenish	£1300	50·00
	b. Deep bright green/greenish	£500	21·00
	c. Emerald-green/greenish	£1300	50·00
	d. "5" at back double	—	£150
41	10l. red-orange/*pale greenish*	£700	23·00
	a. Without numerals at back	£7000	£1500
	b. "10" at back inverted	—	£1500
	c. "0" for "10" at back	—	£375
	d. Orange-vermilion/lavender	£5500	£100
	da. "0" for "10" at back (on 41*d*)	—	£375
42	20l. deep bright blue/*bluish*	£1000	21·00
	aa. "20" at back inverted		
	a. Deep indigo-blue/bluish	£1700	38·00
	b. Pale bright blue/bluish	£1700	44·00
	c. Grey-blue/bluish	£1300	38·00
	d. Deep blue/blue	£1000	21·00
43	40l. dull rosy mauve/*blue*	£700	65·00
	a. Deep bright purple/blue	—	£750
	b. Rosy mauve/blue	£600	50·00
	ba. Red-lilac, figures at back bistre	—	£225
	c. Double "40" at back	—	£1000
	d. Bistre/blue	33·00	47·00
	e. Bistre-brown/blue	33·00	47·00
	f. Pale dull olive-green/blue	70·00	65·00
44	80l. carmine-rose	£150	£170

The paper of this series varies from medium to very thin, and, except on the 1l., shows a pronounced mesh when looked through in a strong light.

1875–80. On cream paper (except No. 48*a*). With figures at back except on the 1l. and 2l.

45	1l. red-brown	38·00	42·00
	a. Black-brown	55·00	65·00
	b. Dark red-brown	33·00	42·00
	c. Pale red-brown	33·00	42·00
	d. Grey-brown	55·00	65·00
	e. Double print		
46	2l. bistre	22·00	21·00
	a. Stone	22·00	21·00
47	5l. yellow-green	£150	21·00
	a. Deep yellow-green	£225	31·00
	b. Emerald-green		
	c. Clear bright green	£425	47·00
48	10l. orange	£170	16·00
	a. Orange/yellow	£300	31·00
	aa. On yellow, no figures at back		
	b. Orange-vermilion	£170	16·00
	ba. Orange-vermilion double print		
	c. "00" at back	£850	£100
	d. "1" instead of "10" at back	—	£375
	e. "0" for "10" at back	—	£160
	f. "01" instead of "10" at back	—	£375
	g. Double "10" at back	—	£550
49	20l. Prussian blue	£2500	50·00
	a. Deep blue	£200	16·00
	b. Royal blue	£375	42·00
	c. Ultramarine	£120	16·00
	d. Double "20" at back	—	£550
	e. "02" at back	—	£325
	f. "20" at back inverted	—	£2000
	g. "2" of "20" at back inverted	—	£1200
50	40l. rose-buff	22·00	65·00
	a. Pale buff	22·00	65·00

The impressions in this issue are generally coarse, though the first printings of the 5l., 10l. and 20l. (Nos. 47, 48 and 49), which are on highly surfaced paper, are very good prints. No. 47*c* is always a remarkably fine clear print. No. 48aa, of which very few specimens exist, is only known with postmark of Smyrna dated 1877.

1876. Without figures at back.

(i) Paris print

51	30l. olive-brown/*cream*	£200	42·00
	a. Brown/cream	£350	95·00
52	60l. deep green/*green*	27·00	80·00

(ii) Athens print

53	30l. grey-brown/*cream*	55·00	8·25
	a. Grey-brown/buff	55·00	8·25
	b. Dark red-brown/cream	55·00	8·25
54	60l. deep green/*buff*	£450	47·00

1881–87. Without figures at back.

(i) On cream paper. Imperf

55	5l. yellow-green	16·00	2·10
	a. Green	16·00	2·10
	b. Pale yellow-green	16·00	2·10
56	10l. orange	16·00	2·10
	a. Yellow-orange	16·00	2·10
	b. Bright orange-vermilion	£2500	33·00
	c. Orange-red	£2750	47·00
57	20l. ultramarine	£275	£100
58	20l. carmine-lake	£200	6·25
59	20l. bright rosine	2·20	2·10
	a. Pale rosine	4·25	2·10
60	30l. ultramarine	£150	7·25
	a. Deep ultramarine	£140	7·25
	b. Dull ultramarine	£140	7·25
61	40l. mauve	43·00	7·25
	a. Deep mauve	65·00	21·00

(ii) On thin buff paper. Imperf (1882)

62	1l. red-brown	11·00	5·25
63	5l. deep bright green	80·00	42·00
64	10l. orange	65·00	37·00

(iii) On cream paper. P 11½ (1881)

65	1l. red-brown	27·00	9·50
66	2l. bistre	33·00	21·00

(iv) On cream paper. Pin perf 15–15½ (1887)

67	1l. grey-brown (45*d*)	30·00	37·00
	a. Red-brown (45)	30·00	37·00
68	2l. bistre (46)	30·00	37·00
	a. Pale yellow-bistre (33)	30·00	37·00
69	5l. pale yellow-green (55*b*)	27·00	31·00
70	10l. yellow-orange (56*a*)	33·00	39·00
71	20l. rosine (59)	27·00	31·00
72	40l. mauve (61)	£100	85·00
	a. Deep mauve (61*a*)	£100	85·00

The other values formerly listed with the 11½ perforation are now omitted as they were not issued to the public. They were perforated at the head post office in Athens on request, entirely for philatelic purposes, and at a time when the stamps of the first type had been superseded for some years.

The pin perforations were the work of the Postmaster of Corfu, who in 1887, perforated all his remaining stock of obsolete stamps and issued them in the ordinary way. They are found with the postmark "KERKYRA" in a circle with date in the centre.

The rouletted stamps formerly listed were entirely unofficial.

D **2** Small letters above numeral

D **3** Larger letters above numeral

(Litho Austrian State Ptg Wks, Vienna)

1875 (1 Mar). POSTAGE DUE. Type D **2**. Centres in black.

A. Perf 10–11

D73A	1l. green	1·90	2·10
D74A	2l. green	2·40	2·10
D75A	5l. green	2·40	2·10
D76A	10l. green	2·40	1·30
D77A	20l. green	£120	40·00
D78A	40l. green	18·00	18·00
D79A	60l. green	75·00	37·00
D80A	70l. green	18·00	18·00
D81A	80l. green	22·00	21·00
D82A	90l. green	18·00	18·00
D83A	1d. green	18·00	18·00
	g. Centre inverted	£550	
	h. Broad "M"	£100	95·00
D84A	2d. green	27·00	26·00
	g. Centre inverted		£275

B. Perf 10–11×12½–13

D73B	1l. green	1·90	3·25
D74B	2l. green	£110	55·00
D75B	5l. green	4·50	2·50
D76B	10l. green	8·50	5·25
D77B	20l. green	75·00	42·00
D78B	40l. green	38·00	21·00
D79B	60l. green	75·00	37·00
D80B	70l. green	13·00	12·50
D81B	80l. green	22·00	31·00
D82B	90l. green	38·00	44·00
D83B	1d. green	38·00	44·00
	g. Centre inverted		—
	h. Broad "M"	£325	£325
D84B	2d. green	38·00	37·00
	g. Centre inverted		—

C. Perf 12½–13

D73C	1l. green	1·90	2·40
D74C	2l. green	2·40	3·25
D75C	5l. green	16·00	16·00
D76C	10l. green	13·00	7·75
D77C	20l. green	75·00	44·00
D78C	40l. green	75·00	25·00
D79C	60l. green	75·00	44·00
D80C	70l. green	39·00	38·00
D81C	80l. green	24·00	23·00
D82C	90l. green	38·00	37·00
D83C	1d. green	38·00	37·00
	ch. Broad "M"	£325	£325
D84C	2d. green	38·00	37·00

D. Perf 8½–9½

D73D	1l. green	3·50	5·00
D74D	2l. green	3·00	4·50
D75D	5l. green	7·50	4·75
D76D	10l. green	16·00	5·50
D77D	20l. green	55·00	60·00
D78D	40l. green	33·00	21·00
D79D	60l. green	75·00	75·00
D80D	70l. green	21·00	20·00
D81D	80l. green	39·00	38·00
D82D	90l. green	33·00	31·00
D83D	1d. green	33·00	31·00
	h. Broad "M"	£325	£325
D84D	2d. green	38·00	37·00

E. Perf 8½–9½×10–11

D73E	1l. green		
D74E	2l. green	27·00	26·00
D75E	5l. green	20·00	20·00
D76E	10l. green	18·00	11·50
D77E	20l. green	75·00	42·00
D78E	40l. green	27·00	21·00
D79E	60l. green	75·00	37·00
D80E	70l. green	17·00	14·00
D81E	80l. green	£110	37·00
D82E	90l. green	38·00	44·00
D83E	1d. green	38·00	44·00
	h. Broad "M"		
D84E	2d. green	£200	£200

F. Perf 8½–9½×12½–13

D74F	2l. green	£160	£160
D75F	5l. green	£160	£160
D77F	20l. green	£170	£170

The imperforate varieties are now regarded as of doubtful status with the possible exception of the 40l. and 1d.

The variety on the 1d. shows a broad, short "M" in "ΔΡΑΧΜΗ".

In this issue there is a wide range of shades of green.

(Litho Austrian State Ptg Wks, Vienna)

1876 (June). POSTAGE DUE. Type D **3**. Centres in black.

(a) Perf 12–13

D85	1l. yellow-green	1·30	1·30
	a. Green	1·30	1·30
D86	2l. yellow-green	1·30	1·30
	a. Green	1·30	1·30
D87	5l. grey-green	2·75	2·50
	a. Green	£350	£275
D88	10l. yellow-green	1·30	1·30
	a. Blue-green	1·30	1·30
	b. Green	4·00	3·25
D89	20l. yellow-green	2·75	2·50
	a. Blue-green	2·75	2·50
	b. Green	5·50	5·25
D90	40l. green	65·00	50·00
D91	60l. blue-green	9·75	9·50
D92	70l. green	£275	
D93	80l. green	£200	
D94	100l. green	14·00	13·50
D95	200l. green	16·00	12·50

(b) Perf 10½ (x), 10½–11 (y) or 11 (z)

D96	1l. yellow-green (x)	£250	£225
	a. Green (y)	£250	£225
D97	2l. yellow-green (x)	£250	£225
	a. Green (y)	£250	£225
D98	5l. grey-green (z)	4·25	2·50
	a. Green (y)	£400	£350
D99	10l. green (y)	5·50	2·10
	a. Perf 10½–11×12–13. Yellow-green	55·00	21·00
D100	20l. green (y)	2·75	2·10
D101	40l. green (y)	75·00	70·00
	a. Grey-green (x)	16·00	16·00
D102	60l. grey-green (x)	38·00	16·00
	a. Green (y)	46·00	22·00
D103	70l. green (y)	33·00	26·00
D104	80l. green (y)	33·00	26·00
D105	90l. green (y)	24·00	19·00
D106	100l. green (y)	33·00	26·00
D107	200l. green (y)	33·00	26·00

(c) Perf 11½

D108	1l. yellow-green	8·75	8·25
D109	2l. yellow-green	8·75	8·25
D110	5l. grey-green	5·50	3·25
D111	40l. grey-green	90·00	90·00
D112	60l. grey-green	46·00	

(d) Perf 9–9½

D113	20l. green	20·00	26·00
D114	60l. green	33·00	26·00
D115	70l. green	39·00	38·00
D116	80l. green	46·00	44·00

2 Hermes

(Des H. Hendrickx. Eng A. Doms. Electrotypes. Ptd first at the Belgian Stamp Printing Works, Malines; later at Athens)

1886–88. Belgian print.

(a) Imperf

73	2	1l. pale brown (2.88)	3·00	2·10
74		2l. pale ochre (8.88)	8·25	£150
75		5l. bright green (2.88)	11·00	2·40
76		10l. yellow-orange (5.88)	15·00	2·10
77		20l. carmine (2.88)	33·00	2·10
78		25l. dull blue (4.86)	£140	1·00
79		40l. bright mauve (2.88)	90·00	21·00
80		50l. grey-green (4.86)	11·00	4·75
81		1d. grey (4.86)	£110	3·75

(b) P 11½

81*a*	2	1l. pale brown	8·25	5·75
82		40l. bright mauve	£140	£140
83		50l. grey-green	16·00	5·75
84		1d. grey	£160	6·25

The Belgian-printed stamps may be distinguished from those of Athens by the impression being smoother and finer, and by the paper being more highly surfaced.

The stamps perforated 13½ and most of the lower values with the 11½ perforation are now omitted as they were never officially issued. They were perforated, by the official machines, to the order of private individuals for philatelic purposes. See note following No. 72.

1889–95. Athens print.

(a) Imperf

85	2	1l. brown	2·20	1·00
		a. Black-brown	5·50	2·10
		b. Yellow-brown	2·20	1·00
86		2l. stone	1·10	1·30
		a. Pale bistre	3·25	3·25
		b. Pale ochre	1·20	1·30
87		5l. yellow-green	6·50	2·10
		a. Bright green	14·00	2·10
		b. Green	2·40	1·60
		c. Emerald	22·00	3·25
88		10l. orange-yellow	85·00	3·25
		a. Orange	£110	4·25
		b. Red-orange	£200	5·25
89		20l. carmine	33·00	1·00
		a. Aniline rose	80·00	4·25
		b. Scarlet	60·00	1·00
		c. Rose-pink	33·00	1·00
		d. Pink	60·00	1·00
90		25l. dull blue	75·00	2·10
		a. Deep blue	75·00	2·10
		b. Ultramarine	£110	7·25
		c. Bright blue	75·00	12·50
		d. Pale blue	65·00	1·00
91		25l. purple (1893)	11·00	2·10
		a. Pale purple	11·00	2·10
92		40l. purple (1891)	£120	21·00
93		40l. blue (1893)	7·50	2·10
94		1d. grey (1895)	£375	6·25

(b) P 13½

95	2	1l. yellow-brown	22·00	26·00
		a. Black-brown	22·00	26·00
96		2l. stone	1·10	8·25
		a. Pale ochre	1·10	8·25
97		10l. orange-yellow	80·00	12·50
		a. Red-orange	80·00	12·50
98		20l. carmine-rose	65·00	26·00
		a. Scarlet	65·00	21·00
99		40l. purple	£100	37·00

Other values, perf 13½, were not issued.

(c) P 11½

100	2	1l. brown	2·20	1·00
		a. Black-brown	6·50	2·10
		b. Yellow-brown	5·50	2·10
101		2l. stone	1·10	1·00
		a. Pale ochre	2·20	2·10
102		5l. yellow-green	8·75	1·00
		a. Bright green	8·75	1·00
		b. Green	11·00	1·00
		c. Emerald	£160	21·00
		d. Pale green	8·75	1·00
103		10l. orange-yellow	75·00	2·10
		a. Red-orange	£250	3·25
		b. Orange	38·00	2·10
104		20l. carmine-rose	80·00	1·60
		a. Carmine	43·00	2·10
		b. Scarlet	£140	8·25
		c. Pink	85·00	5·25
105		25l. dull blue	85·00	2·10
		a. Deep blue	£130	16·00
		b. Ultramarine	£250	65·00
		c. Bright blue	£100	8·25
		d. Pale blue	£100	8·25
106		25l. purple	16·00	3·25
		a. Pale purple	11·00	2·10
107		40l. purple	£120	31·00
108		40l. blue	13·00	3·25
109		1d. grey	£500	8·25

Pairs of all values, imperf between, are frequently found. They are worth about 50% above the price for two normal singles.

The early printings of some values are to be found with a watermark, "ΧΑΡΤΗΣ ΔΗΜΟΣΙΑΣ ΥΠΗΡΕΣΙΑΣ" (paper for the Public Services), across the middle and bottom of the sheet, in double-lined capitals about 36 mm. high. In the middle of each pane (i.e. six times in each sheet) appear the letters "E.X." about 14 mm. high.

All values may be found perforated 8½–9¼ by the postmaster at Astakos and with a rough pin-perforation by the postmaster at Amphissa. Normally stamps with the official 11½ perforation were issued only in Athens and neighbourhood, the provinces being supplied with imperf stamps.

3 Wrestlers

4 Discus-thrower

5 Vase depicting Pallas Athene

6 Quadriga or Chariot-driving

7 Acropolis and Stadium

8 "Hérmes", after the statue by Praxiteles

9 "Victory", after the statue by Pæonius

(Des Prof Gillieron. Eng E. Mouchon. Typo French Govt Ptg Wks, Paris)

1896 (25 Mar). First International Olympic Games. P 13½×14 (T **5**, **8/9**) or 14×13½ (others).

110	3	1l. ochre	2·20	1·80
111		2l. pink	2·75	2·10
		a. Without engraver's name at foot	27·00	19·00
112	4	5l. mauve	11·00	3·25
113		10l. slate	11·00	4·50
114	5	20l. red-brown	24·00	4·75
115	6	25l. red	30·00	6·00
116	5	40l. pale violet	13·00	7·25
117	6	60l. grey-black	41·00	21·00
118	7	1d. blue	£100	20·00
119	8	2d. bistre	£300	80·00
		a. Imperf between (pair)		
120	9	5d. green	£550	£450
121	–	10d. brown	£600	£500
110/121 *Set of 12*			£1500	£1000

Design: As T **6**—10d. Parthenon.

ΛΕΠΤΑ
20
(**11**)

ΔΡΑΧΜΗ
1
(**12**)

1900 (Sept). Surch as T **11** or **12** (dr. values).

I. T **2**. Athens print of 1889–95

(a) Imperf

122	2	20l. on 25l. blue	3·25	1·00
		a. Deep blue	43·00	42·00
		b. Ultramarine	85·00	50·00
123		1d. on 40l. purple	16·00	6·25
124		2d. on 40l. purple	£475	

(b) P 11½

125	2	20l. on 25l. blue	3·25	1·00
		a. Deep blue	70·00	70·00
		b. Ultramarine	85·00	85·00
		c. Perf 13½	£110	£100
126		1d. on 40l. purple	22·00	10·50
		a. Perf 13½	65·00	50·00
127		2d. on 40l. purple	£250	
		a. Perf 13½	11·00	12·50

II. T **2**. Belgian print

128	2	2d. on 40l. bright mauve (Imperf)	£300	
129		2d. on 40l. bright mauve (P 11½)	£325	

Pairs imperf between are frequently found in these provisionals and are worth about 50% more than the price of two normal stamps.

III. T **1**. Athens print.

(a) Imperf

130	1	30l. on 40l. deep mauve (61*a*)	6·50	6·25
		a. Mauve (61)	16·00	16·00
		b. "A" for "Λ" in "ΛΕΠΤΑ"	£130	£130
131		40l. on 2l. pale yellow-bistre/*deep cream* (33)	8·75	8·25
		a. "A" for "Λ" in "ΛΕΠΤΑ"	£160	£160
132		50l. on 40l. rose-buff (50)	6·50	6·25
		a. "A" for "Λ" in "ΛΕΠΤΑ"	£140	£130
133		3d. on 10l. orange/*cream* (56)	55·00	50·00
		a. Yellow-orange/*cream* (56*a*)	55·00	£600
134		5d. on 40l. dull rosy mauve/*blue* (28*a*)	£140	£160
		a. Rosy mauve/blue (28)	£160	£190
		b. Rosy mauve/blue (thin paper) (43b)	£500	
		c. "20" at back corrected to "40"	£2000	

(b) P 11½

135	1	30l. on 40l. deep mauve	11·00	10·50
		a. Mauve	18·00	18·00
		b. "A" for "Λ" in "ΛΕΠΤΑ"	£160	£180
136		40l. on 2l. stone	16·00	16·00
		a. "A" for "Λ" in "ΛΕΠΤΑ"	£190	£180
137		50l. on 40l. rosy buff	11·00	10·50
		a. "A" for "Λ" in "ΛΕΠΤΑ"	£225	£200
138		3d. on 10l. orange	60·00	60·00
		a. Yellow-orange	60·00	60·00
139		5d. on 40l. dull rosy mauve/*blue*	£160	£170
		a. Rosy mauve/blue	£180	£200
		b. Rosy mauve/blue (thin paper)	£550	
		c. "20" at back corrected to "40"	£2000	

In the 30, 40 and 50l. there are two types of surcharge: (1) Narrow figure "0" as illustrated (97 times in sheet of 150); (2) Wider "0" (53 times).

Nos. 130b, 131a, 132a, 135b, 136a, 137a occur in positions 35 and 50, in conjunction with narrow "0". This error with wide "0" is a forgery.

On Nos. 130/9 the distance between the word and figures of the surcharge varies within the sheet between 1½ and 4 mm.

Pairs imperf between. The note after No. 129 also applies here.

A M
ΛΕΠΤΑ
25
(**13**)

A M
ΔΡΑΧΜΗ
1
(**14**)

"A M" = "Axia Metallike" (see note after No. 182)

1900 (Oct)–**01** (Jan). Surch as T **13** or **14**.

I. On T **2**, Belgian print, in black

(a) Imperf

140	2	25l. on 40l. bright mauve	5·50	10·50
141		50l. on 25l. dull blue	27·00	26·00

(b) P 11½

142	2	25l. on 40l. bright mauve	11·00	16·00
143		50l. on 25l. dull blue	55·00	65·00

II. On T **1**, Athens print, in black

(a) Imperf

144	1	1d. on 40l. bistre/*blue* (thin paper)	£110	£160
145		2d. on 5l. green/*cream*	16·00	26·00

(b) P 11½

146	1	1d. on 40l. bistre/*blue* (thin paper)	£150	£170
147		2d. on 5l. green/*cream*	22·00	37·00

Pairs, imperf between. The note after No. 129 also applies here.

(Dec 1900–Jan 1901)

III. On Olympic Games issue of 1896, in red.

148	5l. on 1d. blue	22·00	31·00
	a. Surcharge double	£275	£225
149	25l. on 40l. pale violet	£110	85·00
	a. With 50l. surch in black in addition	£550	£500
150	50l. on 2d. bistre	£100	75·00
151	1d. on 5d. green	£350	£225
	a. "Δ" for "A" in "ΔΡΑΧΜΗ"	£900	£650
152	2d. on 10d. brown	75·00	£120
	a. "Δ" for "A" in "ΔΡΑΧΜΑΙ"	£425	£325
148/152 *Set of 5*		£600	£475

The note below No. 139*b* regarding the two types of "0" also applies to Nos. 149a and 150.

15

16

17

Hermes, after the "Mercury" of Giovanni da Bologna

18

I 1l. II

I 2l. II

I 3l. II

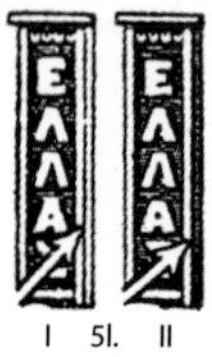

I 5l. II

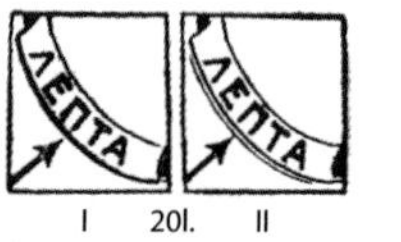

I 20l. II

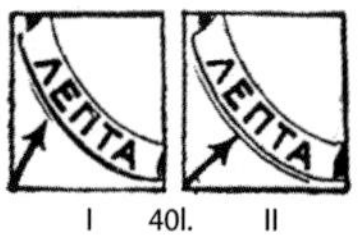

I 40l. II

I 50l. II

DIFFERENCES BETWEEN THE DIES

1l. I. Reticulated shading in rectangular ornaments below words "ΛΕΠΤΟΝ" faint. II. Shading stands out clearly.

2l. I. The curved line below "ΛΕΠΤΑ" at left is doubled by a thinner line starting below the "E". II. The thin line starts to the left of the "Λ".

3l. I. Reticulated shading in rectangular ornament below words "ΛΕΠΤΑ" clear. II. Shading faint.

5l. I. Outer vertical margin of panels containing "ΕΛΛΑΣ" hardly shaded at all. II. Bold horizontal shading.

20l. I. Single thick line below "ΛΕΠΤΑ" at left. II. Two thinner lines below "ΛΕΠΤΑ".

40l. I. Curved line below "ΛΕΠΤΑ" at left doubled below "ΛΕ". II. Curved line doubled throughout.

50l. I. Vertical line outlining right forearm of Hermes at left doubled near elbow; vertical lines of shading at each end of bands containing "ΛΕΠΤΑ" clear and bold. II. Line on arm single throughout. Shading in bands faint.

(Printed by Perkins, Bacon. 1l. to 1d. recess; 2d. to 5d. litho)

1901 (1 July)–**02**. W **18** (sideways on the 1d. thin paper). P 13½ (lepta values) or 12½ (others).

I. Thick paper

153	15	1l. brown (I)	75	30
		a. Imperf (pair)	28·00	
154		2l. grey (I)	75	30
155		3l. orange (I)	85	50
156	16	5l. green (I)	85	30
		a. Imperf (pair)	39·00	
157		10l. rose-carmine	2·20	40
158	15	20l. mauve (I)	5·50	30
159	16	25l. blue	6·50	40
160	15	30l. violet	13·00	1·60
		a. Imperf (pair)	£325	
161		40l. dark brown (I)	49·00	3·25
		a. Die II	43·00	3·25
		b. Dies I and II in pair	£200	42·00
162		50l. brown-lake (I)	33·00	3·25
163	17	1d. black	40·00	2·10
164		2d. bronze	11·00	8·25
165		3d. silver	15·00	10·50
		a. Imperf (pair)	£1700	
166		5d. gold	17·00	10·50

II. Thin paper

A. Die I

167A	15	1l. brown	65	20
		a. Perf 11½	£140	—
		b. Imperf (pair)	20·00	—
168A		2l. grey	75	20
		a. Imperf (pair)	27·00	—
169A		3l. yellow-orange	85	30
		a. Imperf (pair)	27·00	—
170A	16	5l. green	75	30
		a. Imperf (pair)	20·00	—
		b. Yellow-green	75	30
171A		10l. carmine (shades)	1·10	30
		a. Aniline red	1·10	30
		b. Imperf (pair)	30·00	—
172A	15	20l. mauve	1·10	30
		a. Imperf (pair)	27·00	
173A	16	25l. blue	2·00	30
		a. Imperf (pair)	27·00	
174A	15	30l. purple	20·00	4·25
		a. Imperf (pair)	—	£325
175A		40l. black-brown	2·75	1·90
		a. Dark red-brown	20·00	1·00
		c. Dies I & II in pair	11·00	—
176A		50l. brown-lake	20·00	1·00
177A	17	1d. black (p 14×12½)	65·00	42·00
		a. Perf 12½	70·00	55·00
		b. Perf 14	65·00	49·00
		c. Perf 14×imperf (pr)	£550	—
		d. Imperf (pair)	£550	—

II. Thin paper

B. Die II

167B	15	1l. brown	75	30
		a. Perf 11½	£225	—
		b. Imperf (pair)	20·00	—
		c. Dark red-brown	75	30
168B		2l. grey	85	30
		a. Imperf (pair)	24·00	—
169B		3l. yellow-orange	1·10	30
		a. Imperf (pair)	24·00	—
170B	16	5l. green	25	25
		b. Yellow-green	1·10	30
172B	15	20l. mauve	1·60	30
		a. Imperf (pair)	24·00	
175B		40l. black-brown	1·60	30
		a. Dark red-brown	15·00	75
		c. Dies I & II in pair	75·00	—
176B		50l. brown-lake	20·00	4·25

There was only one plate for the 40l. on which the first four vertical rows were Die I and the other six Die II. This is the only value which contained both dies on the same sheet. Unlike all the others the second die of the 5 lepta is actually the original one retouched. The 10l. die was also retouched for later plates, but the difference is too slight for inclusion in this catalogue.

Though we have included all the known imperforate varieties, it appears doubtful whether all of them were actually issued in that state. On the other hand some are only known used.

19 Head of Hermes

D **20**

(Recess Perkins, Bacon & Co.)

902 (1 Jan). P 13½.

78	**19**	5l. orange	2·30	1·00
		a. Imperf (pair)	£110	
79		25l. emerald-green	35·00	2·40
80		50l. bright blue	35·00	2·40
		a. Imperf (pair)	£900	
81		1d. scarlet	35·00	10·00
82		2d. chestnut	65·00	44·00
78/182 *Set of 5*			£150	55·00

The letters "AM" stand for "Axia Metallike" = "metal (i.e. gold) value". ne stamps were intended for use on foreign parcels and had to be aid for at the "gold" rate.

The remainders of this issue were used as Postage Due stamps for short time in 1913.

(Printed by Perkins, Bacon & Co. 1l. to 1d. recess; 2d. to 5d. litho)

902 (Mar). POSTAGE DUE. W **18**. P 13½.

)183	D **20**	1l. brown	55	35
)184		2l. grey	55	35
		a. Imperf (pair)	70·00	
)185		3l. orange	55	35
		a. Imperf (pair)	70·00	
)186		5l. green	55	35
		a. Imperf (pair)	70·00	
)187		10l. scarlet	55	35
)188		20l. pale purple	55	35
)189		25l. blue	9·50	5·25
		a. Imperf (pair)	£100	
)190		30l. deep purple	65	35
		a. Imperf (pair)	80·00	
)191		40l. black-brown	80	50
)192		50l. brown-lake	65	40
		a. Imperf (pair)	£120	
)193		1d. black	1·60	85
		a. Imperf (pair)	£120	
)194		2d. bronze	2·40	3·25
)195		3d. silver	3·75	7·25
)196		5d. gold	6·00	22·00
)183/196 *Set of 14*			25·00	37·00

The 3l. in purple is a colour trial.

See also Nos. D269/83, D451/8, D480/1 and D595/8.

20 Athlete throwing Discus

21 Jumper

22 Victory

23 Atlas offering the Apples of Hesperides to Hercules

24 Struggle between Hercules and Antaeus

25 Wrestlers

26 "Daemon" or God of the Games

27 Race, Ancient Greeks

28 Offerings for the Olympic Games

(Recess Perkins Bacon & Co.)

1906 (25 Mar). Second Olympic Games Issue, Athens. W **18**. P 13½–14.

183	**20**	1l. brown	55	30
		a. Imperf (pair)	£375	
184		2l. grey	60	30
		a. Imperf (pair)	£375	
185	**21**	3l. orange	70	30
		a. Imperf (pair)	£140	
186		5l. green	1·20	50
		a. Imperf (pair)	£140	
187	**22**	10l. carmine-red	3·25	50
		a. Imperf (pair)	£375	
188	**23**	20l. purple	5·50	50
		a. Imperf (pair)	£650	
189	**24**	25l. ultramarine	5·75	65
		a. Imperf (pair)	£650	
190	**25**	30l. deep purple	6·50	3·25
		a. Double impression	£1100	
191	**26**	40l. sepia	6·50	3·25
192	**23**	50l. brown-lake	15·00	3·25
193	**27**	1d. grey-black	75·00	19·00
		a. Imperf (pair)	£1200	
194		2d. rose	£130	41·00
195		3d. yellow-olive	£150	£140
196	**28**	5d. slate-blue	£200	£150
183/196 *Set of 14*			£550	£325

29 Head of Hermes

30 Iris

31 Hermes

32 Hermes and Arcas

33 Head of Hermes

(Eng T. Macdonald. Aspiotis)

1911–23. Zigzag roulette 13–13½.

(a) Recess (1911–21)

197	**29**	1l. green (shades)	30	25
		a. Imperf (pair)	£120	£120
198	**30**	2l. carmine	40	25
199	**29**	3l. vermilion	60	25
		a. Imperf (pair)	£500	£300
200	**31**	5l. green	1·80	25
		a. Yellow-green	1·80	25
		b. Imperf (pair)	40·00	40·00
201	**29**	10l. carmine	11·00	25
		a. Imperf (pair)	70·00	70·00
202	**30**	20l. lilac	4·00	1·10
		a. Imperf (pair)	£300	£300
203		25l. bright ultramarine	17·00	80
		a. Prussian blue	£250	75·00
		b. Rouletted in black	£250	£250
		c. Imperf (pair)	£425	
204	**31**	30l. carmine-red	3·50	1·80
205	**30**	40l. deep blue	13·00	3·50
		a. Imperf (pair)	£500	
206	**31**	50l. deep purple	18·00	3·25
		a. Imperf (pair)	£500	
		Design (1d. to 10d.), 20×26½ mm.		
207	**32**	1d. ultramarine	24·00	65
		a. Imperf (pair)	£500	
208		2d. vermilion	33·00	1·30
		a. Imperf (pair)	£500	
209		3d. carmine	33·00	1·30
		a. Imperf (pair)	£500	
		b. Design 20¼×25¼ mm. (1921)	£160	95·00
210		5d. grey-blue	35·00	5·75
		a. Imperf (pair)	£325	
		b. Design 20¼×25¼ mm. (1921)	£300	31·00
211		10d. deep blue	£350	£100
		a. Imperf (pair)	£2250	
		b. Design 20¼×25¼ mm. (1921)	80·00	50·00
212	**33**	25d. deep blue	65·00	27·00
		a. Imperf (pair)	£3000	
		(b) Litho (Jan 1913–1923)		
213	**29**	1l. green (shades)	20	20
		a. No stop after "ΕΛΛΑΣ"	85·00	85·00
		b. Imperf (pair)	75·00	
214	**30**	2l. carmine	20	20
		a. Imperf (pair)	£130	
215	**29**	3l. vermilion	20	20
		a. Imperf (pair)	£190	
216	**31**	5l. green	20	20
		a. Imperf (pair)	65·00	
217	**29**	10l. carmine	20	20
		a. Imperf (pair)	75·00	
218	**30**	15l. dull blue (3.18)	55	30
219		20l. purple-grey	65	20
		a. Imperf (pair)	£100	
220		25l. ultramarine	6·50	65
		a. Blue	65	20
		b. Imperf (pair)	£190	
		c. Double impression		
221	**31**	30l. carmine-red (4.14)	85	30
		a. Imperf (pair)	£190	
222	**30**	40l. deep blue (1.14)	2·75	65
223	**31**	50l. brown-purple (shades) (1.14)	5·50	20
		a. Imperf (pair)	£350	
		b. Imperf between (pair)		
224		80l. brown-purple (6.23)	7·50	1·40
		a. Imperf (pair)	£110	
225	**32**	1d. ultramarine (10.19)	8·75	50
226		2d. vermilion (10.19)	8·75	65
		a. Imperf (pair)	£140	
227		3d. carmine (10.20)	14·00	65
		a. Imperf (pair)	£350	
228		5d. pale grey-blue (6.22)	17·00	75
		a. Imperf (pair)	£425	
		b. Imperf between (pair)	£425	
229		10d. deep grey-blue (1922)	17·00	1·00
230	**33**	25d. slate-blue (5.22)	17·00	2·30

The 25l., 40l. and 1d. were also printed, during 1926, by a Vienna firm. The size and the rouletting of stamps of this printing vary slightly from the usual.

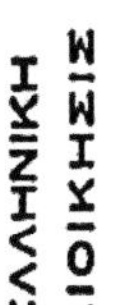

(**34** "Greek Administration")
(*reading up*)

VARIETIES

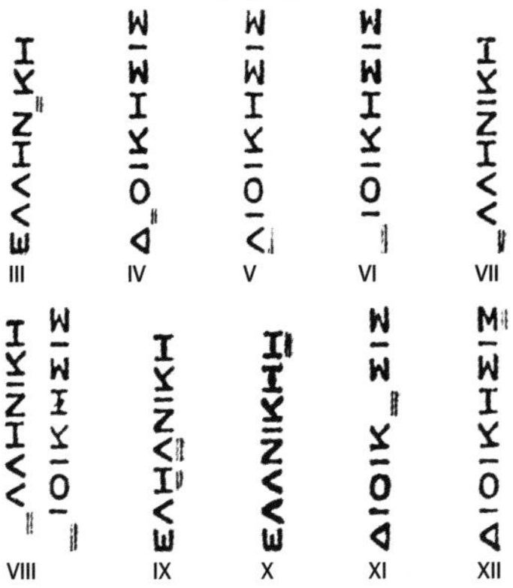

1912 (Oct)–**13**. Optd with T **34**. For use in the territories acquired as a result of the Balkan Wars.

A. Optd in black

X. Reading up

	(i) On stamp of 1901. Type **15**		
231AX	20l. mauve (172B)	65	65
	b. Opt double	33·00	—
	e. Variety V	13·00	12·50
	(ii) On stamps of 1911, recess. Types **29/33**		
232AX	1l. green	65	65
	ab. Opt double	13·00	
	ac. Variety III	11·00	10·50
	ad. Variety IV	11·00	10·50
	ae. Variety V	11·00	10·50
233AX	2l. carmine	65	65
	ab. Opt double	27·00	23·00
	ac. Variety III	11·00	10·50
	ad. Variety IV	11·00	10·50
	ae. Variety V	11·00	10·50
	af. Variety VI	11·00	10·50
	ag. Variety VII	11·00	10·50
	ah. Variety VIII	11·00	10·50
234AX	3l. vermilion	65	65
	ab. Opt double	22·00	21·00
	ac. Variety III	11·00	10·50
	ad. Variety IV	13·50	13·00
	ae. Variety V	13·50	13·00
	af. Variety VI	11·00	10·50
	ag. Variety VII	11·00	10·50
	ah. Variety VIII	11·00	10·50
235AX	5l. green	1·10	1·00
	ab. Opt double	11·00	8·25
	ac. Variety III	11·00	10·50
	ad. Variety IV	11·00	10·50
	ae. Variety V	11·00	10·50
	af. Variety VI	11·00	10·50
	ag. Variety VII	11·00	10·50
	ah. Variety VIII	11·00	10·50
236AX	10l. carmine	1·60	1·60
	ab. Opt double	13·50	13·00
	ac. Variety III	11·00	10·50
	ad. Variety IV	11·00	10·50
	ae. Variety V	11·00	10·50
237AX	20l. lilac	2·75	2·10
	aa. Imperf (pair)	£1300	—
	ab. Opt double	24·00	24·00
	ac. Variety III	13·50	13·00
	ad. Variety IV	13·50	13·00
238AX	25l. bright ultramarine	2·75	2·50
	ab. Opt double	27·00	23·00
	ac. Variety III	11·00	10·50
	ad. Variety IV	16·00	16·00
	ae. Variety V	16·00	16·00
239AX	30l. carmine-red	3·25	2·50
	ab. Opt double	38·00	31·00
	ac. Variety III	13·50	13·00
	ad. Variety IV	19·00	18·00
	ae. Variety V	13·50	13·00
240AX	40l. deep blue	5·50	4·25
	ab. Opt double	38·00	31·00
	ac. Variety III	27·00	26·00
	ad. Variety IV	33·00	31·00
	ae. Variety V	33·00	31·00
241AX	50l. deep purple	6·00	5·25
	ab. Opt double	49·00	37·00
	ac. Variety III	38·00	31·00
	ad. Variety IV	41·00	34·00
	ae. Variety V	43·00	42·00
242AX	1d. ultramarine	14·00	2·50
	ab. Opt double	£110	£100
	ac. Variety III	38·00	37·00
	ad. Variety IV	41·00	39·00
	ae. Variety V	43·00	42·00
243AX	2d. vermilion	60·00	31·00
	ab. Opt double	£140	£130
	ac. Variety III	£350	
	ad. Variety IV	£350	
	ae. Variety V	£1000	
	ai. Variety IX	£1000	—
	aj. Variety X	£1000	—
	ak. Variety XI	£1500	—
244AX	3d. carmine	£130	£130
	ac. Variety III	£350	—
	ad. Variety IV	£350	
245AX	5d. grey-blue	27·00	31·00
	ab. Opt double	49·00	—
	ac. Variety III	£130	
	ad. Variety IV	£130	
	ai. Variety IX	£800	—
	aj. Variety X	£800	—
	ak. Variety XI	£1600	—
246AX	10d. deep blue	£325	£325
	ab. Opt double	£1200	—
	ac. Variety III	£1500	—
	ad. Variety IV	£1500	—
247AX	25d. deep blue (opt horiz)	£325	£325
	al. Variety XII	£1600	

(iii) On stamps of 1911, litho. Types **29**/**31**
248AX 1l. green 65 65
aa. On No. 213a £130 —
ab. Opt double 33·00 —
af. Variety VI 13·00 12·50
ag. Variety VII 13·00 12·50
ah. Variety VIII 13·00 12·50
249AX 5l. green 1·10 1·00
ab. Opt double 13·50 —
ae. Variety V 11·00 10·50
af. Variety VI 11·00 10·50
ag. Variety VII 11·00 10·50
ah. Variety VIII 11·00 10·50
250AX 10l. carmine 1·60 1·60
ab. Opt double 11·00 —
ae. Variety V 13·50 13·00
251AX 25l. ultramarine 5·50 2·50
ab. Opt double 27·00 —
ae. Variety V 16·00

Y. Reading down

(i) On stamp of 1901. Type **15**
231AY 20l. mauve (172B) 8·75 7·25

(ii) On stamps of 1911, recess. Types **29**/**33**
232AY 1l. green 27·00 26·00
ac. Variety III
ad. Variety IV
ae. Variety V
233AY 2l. carmine 2·20 2·10
ab. Opt double
ac. Variety III
ad. Variety IV
ae. Variety V
af. Variety VI £180 £180
ag. Variety VII £180 £180
ah. Variety VIII £180 £180
234AY 3l. vermilion 1·60 1·60
ac. Variety III
ad. Variety IV
ae. Variety V
af. Variety VI 6·50 6·25
ag. Variety VII 6·50 6·25
ah. Variety VIII 6·50 6·25
235AY 5l. green 2·20 2·10
ab. Opt double
ac. Variety III
ad. Variety IV
ae. Variety V
af. Variety VI 16·00 16·00
ag. Variety VII 16·00 16·00
ah. Variety VIII 16·00 16·00
236AY 10l. carmine £160 £160
ac. Variety III
ad. Variety IV
ae. Variety V
237AY 20l. lilac 8·75 7·25
ab. Opt double £200
ac. Variety III 85·00 85·00
ad. Variety IV 85·00 85·00
238AY 25l. bright ultramarine £110 £100
ac. Variety III
ad. Variety IV
ae. Variety V
239AY 30l. carmine-red £425 £425
ac. Variety III
ad. Variety IV
ae. Variety V
240AY 40l. deep blue £250 £180
ac. Variety III
ad. Variety IV
ae. Variety V
241AY 50l. deep purple £425 £375
ab. Opt double £800
ac. Variety III £2250 23·00
ad. Variety IV
ae. Variety V
242AY 1d. ultramarine 85·00 85·00
ac. Variety III £1000 35·00
ad. Variety IV
ae. Variety V
243AY 2d. vermilion £160 £150
ac. Variety III
ad. Variety IV
ae. Variety V
244AY 3d. carmine £110 £100
ac. Variety III
ad. Variety IV
245AY 5d. grey-blue £600 £500
ac. Variety III
ad. Variety IV
247AY 25d. deep blue (opt horiz) £275 £250
al. Variety XII £1800

(iii) On stamps of 1911, litho. Types **29**/**31**
248AY 1l. green 3·25 3·25
ab. Opt double
af. Variety VI £180 12·00
ag. Variety VII £180 12·00
ah. Variety VIII £180 12·00
249AY 5l. green 1·10 1·00
ab. Opt double £140
ae. Variety V
af. Variety VI 11·00 10·50
ag. Variety VII 11·00 10·50
ah. Variety VIII 11·00 10·50
250AY 10l. carmine 2·20 2·50
ae. Variety V
af. Variety VI 16·00
ag. Variety VII 16·00
ah. Variety VIII 16·00
251AY 25l. ultramarine 70·00 70·00
ab. Opt double 55·00
ae. Variety V

B. Optd in red, reading up. On stamps of 1911

(i) Recess
232B **29** 1l. green 55 50
bc. Variety III 8·25 7·75
233B **30** 2l. carmine 13·00 12·50
bb. Opt double 38·00
234B **29** 3l. vermilion 11·00 10·50
235B **31** 5l. green 55 50
bc. Variety III 8·25 7·75
237B **30** 20l. lilac 16·00 16·00
bb. Opt double £110
bc. Variety III £110 £100
238B 25l. bright ultramarine 75·00 70·00
239B **31** 30l. carmine-red 85·00 85·00
bb. Opt double £225
240B **30** 40l. deep blue 2·75 4·25
bc. Variety III 27·00 26·00
241B **31** 50l. deep purple 3·25 3·25
bc. Variety III 27·00 26·00
242B **32** 1d. ultramarine 16·00 16·00
bc. Variety III 38·00
243B 2d. vermilion £110 £130
bb. Opt double £100
bc. Variety III £375
bj. Variety X £1100
bk. Variety XI £1100
244B 3d. carmine 33·00 31·00
bc. Variety III £160
245B 5d. grey-blue £275 £250
bb. Opt double
bc. Variety III £1700
bj. Variety X £1700
bk. Variety XI £1700
246B 10d. deep blue 49·00 70·00
bc. Variety III £375
247B **33** 25d. deep blue £600 £650
ba. Opt double (reading up) £1400
c. Opt reading down £425
d. Opt horiz 75·00 £190

(ii) Litho
248B **29** 1l. green 9·75 9·50
ba. On No. 213a £250
c. Opt reading down £800
ca. On No. 213a, reading down £7000
249B **31** 5l. green 55 50
bc. Variety III 8·25 7·75
250B **29** 10l. carmine 80·00 85·00
251B **30** 25l. ultramarine 2·20 2·10
bc. Variety III 16·00 16·00
c. Opt reading down £275
cc. Variety III £2250

1912 (Dec). POSTAGE DUE. Nos. D183/96 optd with T **34**.

(a) In black, reading up
D252A D **20** 1l. brown 65 65
aa. Opt double 16·00
ab. Variety III 11·00 10·50
b. Opt reading down 1·10 10·50
c. Opt double, one reading up, one down 22·00
D253A 2l. grey 65 65
aa. Opt double 16·00
ab. Variety III 11·00 10·50
b. Opt reading down 4·25 4·25
c. Opt double, one reading up, one down 22·00
D254A 3l. orange 35 30
aa. Opt double 16·00
ab. Variety III 11·00 10·50
D255A 5l. green 35 30
aa. Opt double 16·00
ab. Variety III 16·00 16·00
D256A 10l. scarlet 1·40 1·40
aa. Opt double 18·00
ab. Variety III 16·00 16·00
D257A 20l. pale purple 1·40 1·40
ab. Variety III 22·00 21·00
D258A 30l. deep purple 4·25 4·25
ab. Variety III 24·00 23·00
D259A 40l. black-brown 8·75 8·25
aa. Opt double £100
ab. Variety III 43·00 42·00
D260A 50l. brown-lake 12·00 11·50
ab. Variety III 55·00 50·00
D261A 1d. black 38·00 37·00
D262A 2d. bronze
b. Opt reading down 27·00 26·00
D263A 3d. silver
b. Opt reading down 85·00 85·00
D264A 5d. gold
b. Opt reading down £140 £160

(b) In red, reading up
D252D D **20** 1l. brown 85 85
db. Variety III 13·00 12·50
D253D 2l. grey 85 85
da. Opt double 43·00
db. Variety III 16·00 16·00
D255D 5l. green 85 85
db. Variety III 16·00 16·00
D256D 10l. scarlet
D257D 20l. pale purple 85 85
db. Variety III 18·00 18·00
D258D 30l. deep purple 6·00 5·75
db. Variety III 80·00 80·00
e. Opt reading down 35·00 33·00
eb. Variety III £110 £100
D259D 40l. black-brown 85 85
db. Variety III 22·00 21·00
D260D 50l. brown-lake 85 85
db. Variety III 22·00 21·00
D261D 1d. black 11·00 10·50
D262D 2d. bronze 14·00 13·50
D263D 3d. silver 24·00 23·00
D264D 5d. gold 38·00 37·00

(c) In carmine, reading down
D253F D **20** 2l. grey 4·25 4·25
fb. Variety IV 15·00 14·50
fc. Variety VI 15·00 14·50
fd. Variety VII 15·00 14·50
fe. Variety VIII 15·00 14·50
g. Opt reading up 4·25 6·25
gc. Variety VI 55·00 50·00
gd. Variety VII 55·00 50·00
ge. Variety VIII 55·00 50·00
D254F 3l. orange 8·75 8·25
fb. Variety IV 20·00 19·00
fc. Variety VI 20·00 19·00
fd. Variety VII 20·00 19·00
fe. Variety VIII 20·00 19·00
g. Opt reading up 75·00 95·00
gc. Variety VI £500
gd. Variety VII £500
ge. Variety VIII £500
D255F 5l. green 8·75 8·25
fb. Variety IV 15·00 14·50
fc. Variety VI 15·00 14·50
fd. Variety VII 15·00 14·50
fe. Variety VIII 15·00 14·50
D256F 10l. scarlet 8·75 8·25
fb. Variety IV 15·00 14·50
fc. Variety VI 15·00 14·50
fd. Variety VII 15·00 14·50
fe. Variety VIII 15·00 14·50
D261F 1d. black 35·00 33·00
fa. Opt double £225
g. Opt reading up 43·00 47·00
D262F 2d. bronze 70·00 70·00
g. Opt reading up £160 £150
D263F 3d. silver £250 £250
D264F 5d. gold £550 £500

A minor variety with large "E" in "ΕΛΛΗΝΙΚΗ" is found in all values.

King Constantine I

18 March 1913–12 June 1917

35 Vision of Constantine over Athens and Salamis

36 Victorious Eagle over Mt. Olympus

(Litho Aspiotis)

1913 (16 Apr)–**15**. Victory stamps, used only in newly acquired territories in Macedonia, Epirus and the Aegean Islands.

A. Zigzag roulette 13–13½.
252A **35** 1l. brown 55 50
253A **36** 2l. scarlet 55 50
a. Carmine (1915) 1·40 1·40
254A 3l. orange 55 50
255A **35** 5l. green 1·30 75
256A 10l. rose-red 9·75 50
257A 20l. bright violet 27·00 5·25
258A **36** 25l. pale blue 3·25 1·00
a. Prussian blue 6·00 1·00
259A **35** 30l. green 85·00 3·25
260A **36** 40l. indigo 15·00 5·25
261A **35** 50l. deep blue 5·50 3·25
262A **36** 1d. dull purple 27·00 5·25
263A **35** 2d. grey-brown 60·00 8·25
a. Yellow-brown — 10·50
264A **36** 3d. grey-blue £250 42·00
265A **35** 5d. drab £250 48·00
266A **36** 10d. rose-carmine £275 £375
267A **35** 25d. grey-black £275 £375
252A/267A *Set of 16* £1200 £800

B. Imperf (pairs)
252B **35** 1l. brown £650 —
253B **36** 2l. scarlet £650 —
a. Carmine (1915) £850 —
254B 3l. orange £500 —
255B **35** 5l. green £200 —
256B 10l. rose-red £250 —
257B 20l. bright violet £2000 —
258B **36** 25l. pale blue £2500 —
259B **35** 30l. green £2500 —
260B **36** 40l. indigo £2500 —
264B 3d. grey-blue £4000 —

Dangerous forgeries exist of the 10d. and 25d.

The Mt. Athos opt (see after D283*a*) was also applied to Nos. 252/267 which were surcharged in addition. These stamps were not issued.

37 Hoisting the Greek Flag at Suda Bay, 1 May 1913

(Recess Bradbury, Wilkinson & Co.)

1913 (15 Nov). Union of Crete with Greece. P 14½.
268 **37** 25l. black and blue 12·00 5·25
a. Imperf (pair) £1300

This stamp was used only in Crete.

(Litho Aspiotis)

1913 (Dec)–**26**. POSTAGE DUE. Lithographed. Zigzag roulette.
D269 D **20** 1l. green 10 10
D270 2l. carmine 10 10
D271 3l. vermilion 10 10
D272 5l. green 10 10
a. "o" for "p" in word at foot 3·25 3·25
b. Imperf (pair) £425
c. Double impression 65·00
d. Imperf between (pair) £425
D273 10l. carmine 35 30
D274 20l. slate-grey 35 30
D275 25l. ultramarine 35 30
D276 30l. scarlet 35 30
D277 40l. slate-blue 35 30
D278 50l. brown 35 30
a. "o" for "p" in word at foot 65·00 65·00
D279 80l. brown-purple (10.5.24) 55 50
D280 1d. ultramarine 20·00 11·50
a. Blue 6·50 1·00
D281 2d. vermilion 6·50 3·25
D282 3d. carmine 12·00 8·25

283		5d. pale blue	43·00	14·50
		a. Slate-blue (3.26)	11·00	5·25

The 5l., 10l., 20l., 1d., 2d. and 3d. values exist in a re-drawn pe in which there is no accent shown on the first "O" of ΡΑΜΜΑΤΟΣΗΜΟΝ".

In 1916 No. D186 and all values except the 80l. and the 3 and 5d. ere overprinted in Greek "I(era) Koinotis Ag(iou) Orous", for the Mt. thos Monastery district, but were never issued.

During 1922–23 several values of the unoverprinted stamps were sed as ordinary postage stamps during a shortage of the latter. At e same period some Mt. Athos stamps were used up as postage ue stamps, without being noticed; D186, D273 and D275 are known sed (*Price* £190 *each*).

OMPULSORY CHARITY TAX STAMPS. These were for compulsory dditional use at certain periods of the year for various funds. They are iven C numbers. They were all ithographed by Aspiotis (later Aspiotika) of Corfu, *unless otherwise stated.*

C **38** Dying Soldier, Widow and Child

C **39** Red Cross, Nurses, Wounded and Bearers

(Des Matheopoulo)

914 (31 Mar)–**15**. Zigzag roulette 13½.

269	C **38**	2l. scarlet vermilion	65	40
		a. Carmine (1915)	65	40
		ab. Imperf (pair)	£200	
270		5l. blue	75	50
		a. Imperf (pair)	£450	

915 (Sept). Red Cross. Zigzag roulette 13½.

271	C **39**	(5l.) Red and blue	21·00	2·40
		a. Imperf (pair)	£160	

C **40** Greek Women's Patriotic League Badge

(**38**)

915 (Sept). Greek Women's Patriotic League. P 11½.

272	C **40**	(5l.) Red and blue	1·40	1·30
		a. Imperf (pair)	65·00	

Nos. C271/2 were not for compulsory use on certain days. They vere supplied by the charity bodies to certain postal officials who vere allowed to retain 10% of the amount sold over the counter and he balance was paid by the G.P.O. to the charities.

See also Nos. C344/7.

On 29 September 1916, Eleftherios Venizelos, who had broken with ing Constantine because of the sympathy of the king for the Central owers, set up a Provisional Government, favourable to the Allies, rst in Crete, and on 9 October at Salonika. Nos. 269/85 were used in outhern and central Greece, which were under Royalist control.

"E.T." = Greek Post

916 (1 Nov). Royalist issue. Optd with T **38**.

(a) Lithographed

69	**29**	1l. green (R.)	35	20
		a. Opt double, one inverted	27·00	14·50
70	**30**	2l. rose-red	35	30
		a. Opt inverted	38·00	29·00
71	**29**	3l. vermilion	55	50
		a. Opt inverted	60·00	47·00
72	**31**	5l. green (R.)	80	40
		a. Opt inverted	55·00	39·00
		b. Opt double	60·00	47·00
		c. Opt double, one inverted	60·00	47·00
73	**29**	10l. carmine	1·60	30
		a. Opt inverted	55·00	37·00
74	**30**	20l. purple-grey (R.)	2·10	30
		a. Opt inverted	£110	70·00
75		25l. blue (R.)	1·60	30
		a. Opt inverted	27·00	19·00
76	**31**	30l. carmine-red	2·40	1·00
		a. Opt inverted	22·00	10·50
77	**30**	40l. slate-blue (R.)	19·00	6·00
78	**31**	50l. purple-brown (R.)	65·00	3·00

(b) Engraved

79	**29**	3l. vermilion	75	40
		a. Opt inverted	60·00	50·00
80	**31**	30l. carmine-red	2·40	1·20
81	**32**	1d. ultramarine (R.)	60·00	5·75
		a. Rouletted in black	£475	
82		2d. vermilion	34·00	5·00
83		3d. carmine	20·00	3·75
84		5d. grey blue (R.)	80·00	12·50
85		10d. deep blue (R.)	31·00	21·00
		a. Opt inverted	£450	£350

Nos. 286/96 were used in northern Greece and the Greek slands, which were under the control of the Venizelist Provisional Government.

39 Iris

(Litho Perkins, Bacon & Co.)

1917 (5 Feb). Venizelist issue. Sheet wmk "SPECIAL POSTAGE PAPER LONDON".

A. P 14

286A	**39**	1l. green	35	30
287A		5l. yellow-green	35	30
288A		10l. rose-carmine	75	30
289A		25l. light blue	75	30
290A		50l. grey-purple	6·50	2·30
291A		1d. ultramarine	4·25	1·00
292A		2d. dull vermilion	5·50	1·70
293A		3d. claret	22·00	4·25
294A		5d. slate-blue	8·75	5·25
295A		10d. deep blue	75·00	21·00
296A		25d. slate	£130	£150

B. Imperf (pairs)

286B	**39**	1l. green	16·00	—
287B		5l. yellow-green	16·00	—
288B		10l. rose-carmine	16·00	—
289B		25l. light blue	27·00	—
290B		50l. grey-purple	39·00	—
291B		1d. ultramarine	39·00	—
292B		2d. dull vermilion	39·00	—
293B		3d. claret	75·00	—
294B		5d. slate-blue	75·00	—
295B		10d. deep blue	£150	—
296B		25d. slate	£250	—

A 4d., in grey-brown, was only used fiscally (*Price* £7.50 *un.*).

Κ. Π.
λεπτοῦ
1
(C **41**)
(Thick "K. Π.")

Κ. Π.
λεπτοῦ
1
(C **42**)
(Taller, thinner "K. Π.")

The letters "K. Π." stand for "Kolnonike Pronea" or "Social Providence". This represented an extra tax, part of the proceeds of which went to those who had suffered from the war blockade.

The following minor varieties exist:—

No stop after "K" (all values).
No stop after "Π" (all values).
Stop raised after "Π" (all values).
Stop before "Π" (Nos. C303/9).
Comma after "K" (Nos. C303/5).
Comma after "Π" (Nos. C303/5).

These are worth three to four times the prices for the normal stamps.

1917 (Apr).

(a) Surch as Type C **41**. Thin paper. Die II (C297/300).

C297	**15**	1l. on 1l. brown	1·10	4·25
		a. "—" on "ü"	3·25	12·50
		b. Surch double, one inverted	11·00	
		c. Brown surch	16·00	31·00
C298		1l. on 3l. orange	20	65
		a. "—" over "ü"	3·25	3·25
		b. "λεπτο"	3·25	3·25
		c. "λεπτ"	3·25	3·25
		d. "λεπ οῦ"	3·25	3·25
		e. "λεπτρῦ"	3·25	3·25
		f. "λεπτοΰ"	3·25	3·25
C299		5l. on 1l. brown	2·20	2·10
		a. Surch inverted	27·00	
		b. Surch double	22·00	
		c. Surch double, one inverted	22·00	
C300		5l. on 20l. mauve	35	2·50
		a. Surch inverted	22·00	
		b. Surch double	16·00	
		c. Surch double, one inverted	16·00	
		d. Die I	20	1·00
C301		10l. on 30l. purple	65	2·10
		a. Surch double	22·00	
		c. Surch double, one inverted	22·00	
		d. Thick paper	80	2·50
C302		30l. on 30l. purple	1·10	2·30
		a. Surch inverted	22·00	
		b. Surch double	22·00	
		c. Surch double, one inverted	22·00	9·00
		d. Thick paper	1·30	3·25
		da. Surch treble, one inverted	27·00	

(b) Surch as Type C **42**

(i) On T **15** and **17**

C303	**15**	1l. on 3l. orange (thin paper, Die II)	35	65
		a. "K. M." in top line	16·00	21·00
		b. Surch inverted	7·00	
		c. Surch double	7·00	
		d. Surch double, one inverted	7·00	
		e. Thin paper, Die I	2·75	
		ea. "K. M." in top line	55·00	
C304		5l. on 40l. deep brown (thick paper, Die I)	60	1·60
		a. Thick paper, Die II	65	1·60
		ab. Dies I and II in pair	13·00	42·00
		b. Thin paper, Die I	85	1·30
		ba. Thin paper, Die II	85	1·30
		bb. Dies I and II in pair	20·00	
		bc. Surch double	22·00	
		c. Deep red-brown (I)	55	1·60
		ca. Die II	55	1·60
		cb. Dies I and II in pair	22·00	
C305		5l. on 50l. lake (II)	55	1·60
		a. Surch inverted	16·00	
		b. Surch double, one inverted	16·00	
C306	**17**	5l. on 1d. black (thick paper)	1·10	4·25
		a. Thin paper. Perf 12×14	3·75	10·50
		ab. Perf 14	3·75	10·50
		ac. Imperf (pair)		
		ad. Surch inverted	33·00	
		ae. Surch double	33·00	

No. C306 with red surcharge is an essay.

(ii) On T **35/6**.

C307	**36**	5l. on 25l. pale blue	20	50
		a. Surch inverted	22·00	
		b. Surch double	20·00	
		c. Surch double, one inverted	20·00	
C308		5l. on 40l. dull blue	20	30
		a. Surch inverted	22·00	
		b. Surch double	20·00	
		c. Surch double, one inverted	20·00	
C309	**35**	5l. on 50l. deep blue	22·00	31·00
		a. Surch inverted	22·00	
		b. Surch double	20·00	
		c. Surch double, one inverted	20·00	

Similar surcharges on Nos. 183 and 185 were unauthorized.

C **43**

Κ. Π.
λεπτοῦ
1
(C **44**)

Κ. Π.
5 λεπι. 5
(C **45**)

Κ.Π.
10 ΛΕΠΤΑ 10
(C **46**)

Κ. Π.
5 Λεπτὰ 5
(C **47**)

1917. Social Providence Fund. Fiscal stamps, Type C **43**, surch. Zigzag roulette 13.

(a) As Type C **44**, in brownish red

C310		1l. on 10l. blue	1·10	2·10
C311		1l. on 80l. blue	1·10	2·10
C312		5l. on 60l. blue	8·75	10·50
C313		5l. on 80l. blue	4·25	3·25
		a. Surch inverted	—	75·00
C314		10l. on 70l. blue	38·00	65·00
C315		10l. on 90l. blue	22·00	50·00
C316		20l. on 20l. blue	£8000	£7000
C317		20l. on 30l. blue	11·00	12·50
C318		20l. on 40l. blue	27·00	31·00
C319		20l. on 50l. blue	13·00	16·00
C320		20l. on 60l. blue	£550	
C321		20l. on 80l. blue	£130	
C322		20l. on 90l. blue	7·50	12·50
		a. Surch inverted	—	£140

As last, p 11½ vertically through centre of stamps

C323		5l. on 10l. blue	22·00	37·00
C324		5l. on 60l. blue	11·00	19·00
C325		5l. on 80l. blue	14·00	26·00
C326		10l. on 70l. blue	11·00	26·00
C327		10l. on 90l. blue	27·00	44·00

(b) As Type C **45**, in red-brown (Br.) or black

C328		1l. on 50l. purple (Bk.)	1·10	2·10
C329		5l. on 10l. blue (Br.)	1·10	2·10
		a. Surch inverted	£110	
		b. "5" at left inverted	£110	
C330		5l. on 10l. purple (Br.)	1·10	2·10
C331		10l. on 50l. purple (Br.)	12·00	19·00
C332		10l. on 50l. purple (Bk.)	49·00	42·00
C333		20l. on 2d. blue (Bk.)	15·00	26·00
		a. "30" for "20" at right	85·00	

(c) As Type C **46**, in black, but thin double lines through old value (Corfu issue)

C334		1l. on 10l. blue	1·60	1·60
C335		5l. on 50l. blue	70·00	£120
C336		10l. on 50l. blue	£750	£425
C337		20l. on 50l. blue	£2750	

(d) As Type C **46**, in black (bar through old value)

C338		10l. on 50l. blue	15·00	12·50
C339		20l. on 50l. blue	35·00	29·00
C340		30l. on 50l. blue	26·00	21·00

(e) As Type C **47**, in black

C341		5l. on 10l. purple and red	13·00	18·00
		a. "K" with serifs	22·00	

Type C **43** with surcharges higher than 30l. are fiscal stamps.

King Alexander

12 June 1917–25 October 1920

C **48** Wounded Soldier

C **49**

1918 (June). Red Cross. Zigzag roulette 13½.

C342	C **48**	5l. scarlet, blue and yellow	11·00	1·60

1918. No. C342 optd "Π.Ι.Π." (= P.I.P. initials of the Patriotic Charity League).

C343	C **48**	5l. scarlet, blue and yellow	16·00	1·60

King Constantine 1 (restored)

20 December 1920–27 September 1922

1922. Greek Women's Patriotic League. Surch in red as in Type C **49**. P 11½.

C344 C **49** 5l. on 10l. red and blue £375 16·00
C345 5l. on 20l. red and blue £120 80·00
C346 5l. on 50l. red and blue £375 £275
C347 5l. on 1d. red and blue 11·00 75·00

Nos. C344/7 were not issued without surcharge. Dangerous forgeries exist of Nos. C344/6.

Examples of the 10, 20 and 50l. without surcharge are found (*Price 50p. each*).

King George II

27 September 1922–25 March 1924

(**46** "Revolution, 1922")

1923 (8 May). Revolution of 1922. Various stamps of Greece and Crete, optd or surch as T **46**.

I. On stamps of Greece

(a) T **35** and **36**

340 5l. on 3l. orange 70 70
341 10l. on 20l. bright violet 3·00 2·50
342 10l. on 25l. pale blue 1·60 1·60
343 10l. on 30l. green 1·90 1·60
a. Imperf (pair) £750
344 10l. on 40l. indigo 2·75 2·40
345 50l. on 50l. deep blue 90 90
346 2d. on 2d. grey-brown £120 £110
347 3d. on 3d. grey-blue 8·75 8·25
a. Imperf (pair) £900
348 5d. on 5d. drab 8·75 8·25
349 10d. on 1d. dull purple 20·00 19·00
350 10d. on 10d. rose-carmine £1900

(b) T **39**

351 5l. on 10l. rose-carmine 65 65
352 50l. on 50l. grey-purple 70 70
353 1d. on 1d. ultramarine 70 70
354 2d. on 2d. dull vermilion 80 80
355 3d. on 3d. claret 3·75 3·75
356 5d. on 5d. slate-blue 5·00 3·75
357 25d. on 25d. slate 55·00 55·00

II. On stamps of Crete

(a) Pictorials of 1900

358 5l. on 1l. chocolate (1) 75·00
359 10l. on 10l. scarlet (3) 65 65
360 10l. on 25l. blue (5B) £190
361 10l. on 25l. blue (15) 70 70
362 50l. on 50l. deep lilac (16) 80 1·30
363 50l. on 50l. ultramarine (14) 16·00 18·00
364 50l. on 1d. indigo-violet (17) 7·50 8·25
365 50l. on 5d. black and green (19) 70·00

(b) Pictorials of 1905

366 10l. on 20l. blue-green £250 £225
367 10l. on 25l. ultramarine 70 70
a. Surch double 85·00
368 50l. on 50l. brown 70 70
369 50l. on 1d. sepia and carmine 6·00 7·75
370 3d. on 3d. black and orange 28·00 26·00
371 5d. on 5d. black and olive-green 19·00 21·00

No. 366 is found with forged overprint, used.

(c) Stamps of 1907–8.

372 10l. on 10l. dull carmine* 70 70
373 10l. on 25l. black and blue (30) 2·75 2·50
374 50l. on 1d. black and green (31) 8·25 7·75

*No. 372 is on Crete No. 36 but without opt T **22**.

(d) Stamps with overprint T **22**, **28** or **30**.

375 5l. on 1l. chocolate (58) 70 70
376 5l. on 5l. green (60) 70 70
377 10l. on 10l. dull carmine (61) 70 70
378 10l. on 20l. blue-green (62) 70 70
379 10l. on 25l. ultramarine (63) 70 70
380 50l. on 50l. brown (39) £1600
381 50l. on 50l. brown (64) 1·10 1·00
382 50l. on 1d. sepia and carmine (65) 9·25 10·50
383 3d. on 3d. black and orange (56) 38·00 44·00
384 3d. on 3d. black and orange (66) 28·00 34·00
385 5d. on 5d. black and olive-green (67) £550 £425

(e) Postage Due stamps, Type D **8**

386 5l. on 5l. red 70 70
387 5l. on 10l. red 70 70
388 10l. on 20l. red 24·00 18·00
389 10l. on 40l. red 75 1·00
390 50l. on 50l. red 75 1·00
391 50l. on 1d. red 1·00 1·60
392 50l. on 1d. on 1d. red (No. D18) 19·00 21·00
393 2d. on 2d. red 1·60 2·50

(f) Postage Due stamps with overprint T **22**

394 5l. on 5l. red 7·50 9·50
395 5l. on 10l. red 2·40 2·50
a. Cretan opt inverted (No. D46a)
396 10l. on 20l. red £100 £110

(g) Postage Due stamps with overprint T **30**

397 5l. on 5l. red 65 65
398 5l. on 10l. red 65 65
399 10l. on 20l. red 75 75
400 50l. on 50l. red 90 90
401 50l. on 1d. red 8·25 9·00
402 2d. on 2d. red 15·00 16·00

The Postage Due stamps with overprint Type **46** were sold as ordinary postage stamps.

Nos. 350, 358, 360, 365 and 380 were not issued.

FIRST REPUBLIC

25 March 1924–25 November 1935

47 Lord Byron **48** Byron at Missolonghi

(Recess Bradbury, Wilkinson)

1924 (16 Apr). Byron Centenary. P 12.

403 **47** 80l. indigo 1·00 30
404 **48** 2d. black and violet 3·50 95

C **50** Wounded Soldier and Family **49** Grave of Marco Botzaris

1924 (12 June)–**26**. Red Cross Fund.

(a) P 13½×12½ (Aspiotis)

C405 C **50** 10l. scarlet, blue and yellow 3·75 1·00

(b) P 11½ (M. Erginos, Athens) ('26)

C406 C **50** 10l. scarlet, blue and yellow 80 50
a. Imperf (pair) 65·00

(Litho Aspiotis)

1926 (24 Apr). Centenary of Fall of Missolonghi. Zigzag roulette.

405 **49** 25l. mauve 2·20 65

50 Fortress

(Des A. Gavallas. Litho in Milan)

1926 (21 Oct). AIR. Aeroespresso Co. issue. T **50** and similar horiz designs, each showing a Savoia Marchetti S-55C flying boat. Multicoloured. P 11½.

406 2d. Type **50** 5·50 3·75
a. Imperf between (pair) £1300
407 3d. Acropolis 43·00 13·00
408 5d. Map of Greece and Mediterranean 6·00 2·10
409 10d. Colonnade 43·00 16·00
406/409 *Set of 4* 90·00 31·00

Nos. 406 and 408 were issued both in sheets of 15 and of 25. No. 407 was issued both in sheets of 15 stamps and one blank label and in sheets of 25.

51 Corinth Canal **52** Dodecanese Costume

53 Temple of Theseus, Athens **54** Acropolis

I

II

I

II

I

II

(Original dies and plates eng by T. Macdonald, London. Re-engraved dies of 1933–35 and No. 419*e* by De La Rue. Recess Aspiotis; 1d. later by Perkins, Bacon; 3 and 15d. later in Poland)

1927 (1 Apr)–**35**. T **51** to **54** and similar types. P 12½, 13 an compound (*Aspiotis*); 13¾ (P.B.); 11½, 11½×11, 11½×12¾ an 12¾×11½ (Polish).

410 5l. deep green 20 1
a. Imperf between (pair) £425 £19
411 10l. scarlet 55 1
a. Imperf between (pair) £425 £19
412 20l. violet (to purple) 75 1
a. Imperf between (pair) £500 £20
413 25l. blue-green 75 1
a. Imperf between (pair) £500 £20
414 40l. blue-green 1·10 1
415 50l. violet (to purple) 3·25 1
a. Imperf between (pair) £500 £20
b. Re-engraved (1933) 8·75 1·0
416 80l. black and indigo 2·20 3
a. Imperf (pair) £2750
417 1d. brown and blue (shades) (I) 3·25 2
a. Imperf (pair) £500 £25
b. Centre inverted — £1900
c. Centre double £850 £47
d. Frame double £850 £47
e. Perkins, Bacon ptg. P 13½ (II) (24.12.31) 29·00 3
f. Aspiotis (re-engraved) (1933) 6·50 1·0
418 2d. black and blue-green 26·00 2
a. Imperf (pair) £2750 £200
b. Re-engraved. Black and deep green ('33) 4·25 2
419 3d. black and purple 27·00 2
a. Centre double £850 £47
b. Centre inverted — £1900
c. Imperf (pair) £3250 £225
d. Polish ptg (1934) 11·00 3
419*e* 4d. brown (1.11.35) 49·00 1·0
420 5d. black and orange 43·00 1·3
a. Imperf (pair) £2750 £225
b. Centre inverted — £1100
421 10d. black and claret (I) £150 6·5
a. Re-engraved (II) (1935) £150 2·0
422 15d. black and yellow-green £225 12·5
a. Polish ptg (1934) £350 22·0
423 25d. black and green (I) £300 12·5
a. Re-engraved (II) (1935) £150 16·0
410/423 *Set of* 15 (cheapest) £600 27·0

Designs: Vert (18×25 mm.)—20l. Macedonian costume; 25l Monastery of Simon Peter, Athos; 40l. White Tower, Salonika; 50l and 80l. Corinth Canal. Horiz (25×18 mm.)—2d. Acropolis; 3d. Cruise *Averoff*; 4d. Mistra Cathedral (32×22 mm.)—5d. and 15d. Academy o Sciences, Athens: 10d. Temple of Theseus, Athens.

Printings.—50l. In the 1927 printing the white markings forming the bow of the ship appear as a faint cross. In the 1933 redrawing there is a white mark to left of the vertical line of the bows only.

1d. Illustrations I and II show the difference in the figures of value in the 1927 and Perkins Bacon printings. In the 1933 redrawing the figures are similar to I, but the left-hand "1" has very little serif to the left of the base, giving it a lop-sided appearance. The lines slantin down to the right from the peak of the roof are much more clearl defined in the Perkins, Bacon and 1933 types than in the 192 issue.

2d. In the 1927 issue the heavy shading of the ground in the foreground extends to below the trees to the right of the left-han group of buildings at the foot of the hill. In the 1933 issue the heav shading does not extend to the left much beyond the right-hanc group of buildings.

Generally speaking, the shading and details of the 50l., 1d. and 2d of 1933 are much clearer than those of 1927.

Polish printings. Apart from the difference of perf, the lines o shading, etc, in the Polish printings are much sharper than in the Aspiotis printing.

10d. and 25d. Illustrations I and II show the differences between the figures of value in the 1927 and 1935 printings. In the re-engravec issue of 1935 the details of the design are much sharper.

A 1l. brown in T **52** was prepared but not issued, most of the stock being destroyed. (*Price un*., £450).

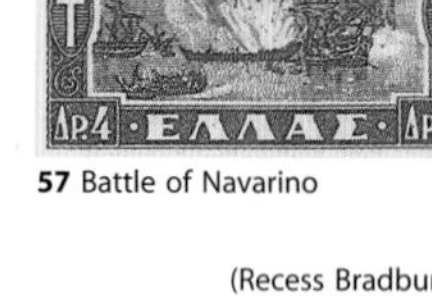

55 General Favier and Acropolis **56** Navarino Bay and Pylos

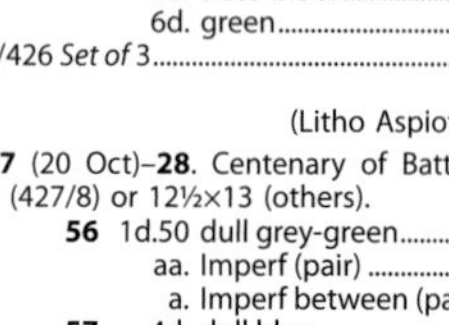

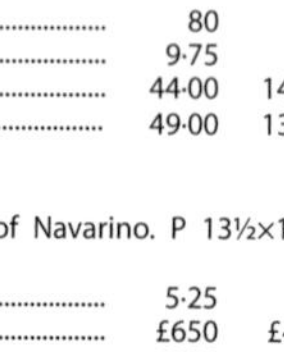

57 Battle of Navarino **58** Sir Edward Codrington

(Recess Bradbury, Wilkinson)

1927 (1 Aug). Centenary of Liberation of Athens from the Turks. P 12.

424 **55** 1d. scarlet 80 35
425 3d. slate-blue 9·75 70
426 6d. green 44·00 14·00
424/426 *Set of* 3 49·00 13·50

(Litho Aspiotis)

1927 (20 Oct)–**28**. Centenary of Battle of Navarino. P 13½×12½ (427/8) or 12½×13 (others).

427 **56** 1d.50 dull grey-green 5·25 45
aa. Imperf (pair) £650 £475
a. Imperf between (pair) £850
428 **57** 4d. dull blue 24·00 1·70
a. Imperf (pair) — £3250
429 **58** 5d. grey and brown ("Sir Codrington") (1st ptg) 13·50 4·75
a. Black and brown (2nd ptg) 13·50 4·75
430 5d. black and brown ("Sir Edward Codrington") 95·00 13·00
431 – 5d. black and ultram (De Rigny) 85·00 11·00

432	–	5d. black and carmine (Van der Heyden)	49·00	10·00
427/432 *Set of* 6			£250	37·00

Small quantities of the 1d.50 and 5d. (No. 429) were issued at Navarino on 20 Oct 1927. The other values appeared on 17 March 1928.

59 Righas Ferreo

60 Patriarch Gregory V

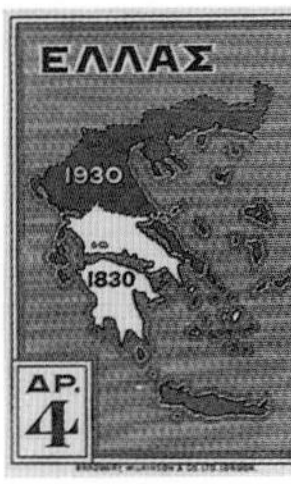
61 Greece in 1830 and 1930

62 Declaration of Independence

63 Sortie from Missolonghi

(Recess Perkins, Bacon (P) or Bradbury, Wilkinson (B))

1930 (1 Apr). Centenary of Independence. Various portraits (except 4, 25 and 50d.) and T **61** to **63** all dated "1830–1930". Perkins, Bacon values, P 13½; Bradbury, Wilkinson, P 12.

433	10l. brown (P)	20	10
	a. Imperf between (pair)	£400	
434	20l. black (B)	20	15
435	40l. blue-green (B)	25	20
436	50l. vermilion (P)	35	30
437	50l. blue (B)	35	30
438	1d. carmine (P)	50	30
439	1d. brown-orange (B)	50	30
440	1d.50 light blue (P)	90	20
	a. Imperf (pair)	£650	
441	1d.50 scarlet (B)	85	25
442	2d. red-orange (P)	1·00	30
443	3d. purple-brown (B)	1·90	65
444	4d. deep blue (B)	7·00	70
445	5d. violet (P)	3·50	1·40
446	10d. black (P)	21·00	7·00
447	15d. yellow-green (P)	35·00	11·00
448	20d. bluish slate (P)	70·00	14·00
449	25d. slate-grey (B)	65·00	22·00
450	50d. brown-lake (B)	£120	60·00
433/450 *Set of* 18		£300	£110

Designs (P 20×29 mm. B 21½×30 mm.):—40l. A. Ypsilanti, 50l. (436) Lascarina Bouboulina; (437) Ath. Diakos; 1d. (438) Th. Kolokotronis; (439) C. Kanaris; 1d.50, (440) Karaiskakis; (441) M. Botzaris; 2d. A. Miaoulis; 3d. L. Kondouriotis; 5d. Count Capodistria; 10d. P. Mavromikhalis; 15d. Solomos; 20d. Korais.

(Litho Aspiotis)

1930 (5 Nov). POSTAGE DUE. P 13½×12½–13½.

D451	D **20**	50l. brown	45	40
D452		1d. pale blue	45	40
D453		2d. vermilion	45	40
D454		3d. carmine-red	55·00	32·00
D455		5d. slate-blue	45	40
D456		10d. green	45	1·00
D457		15d. red-brown	45	1·60
D458		25d. vermilion	1·10	2·50
		a. No accent on last "e" of word in lowest tablet	55·00	50·00
D451/458 *Set of* 8			55·00	35·00

See also Nos. D480/1 and D595/8.

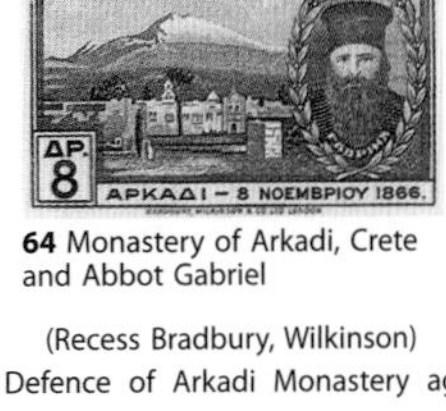
64 Monastery of Arkadi, Crete and Abbot Gabriel

(Recess Bradbury, Wilkinson)

1930 (8 Nov). Defence of Arkadi Monastery against the Turks. P 12.

451	**64**	8d. violet	70·00	1·30

The monastery was blown up by the Abbot on 8 November 1866.

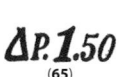

ΔP.1.50
(**65**)

66 Airship *Graf Zeppelin* and Acropolis

1932 (24 Apr–7 Aug). Surch as T **65** in red.

452	–	1d.50 on 5d. black and ultramarine	5·50	20
453	–	1d.50 on 5d. black and carmine	5·50	20
		a. Surcharge double	£225	
454	**55**	2d. on 3d. slate-blue (7.8)	6·00	35
455	**58**	2d. on 5d. black and brown (429*a*) (7.8)	9·25	20
456		2d. on 5d. black and brown (430) (7.8	23·00	20
457	**55**	4d. on 6d. green	6·00	1·00
452/457 *Set of* 6			50·00	1·90

(Des A. Gavallas. Litho Aspioti-Elka)

1933 (2 May). AIR. Aeroespresso Co. issue. P 13×12½.

458	**66**	30d. carmine-red	55·00	24·00
459		100d. dull blue	£160	50·00
460		120d. brown	£160	50·00
458/460 *Set of* 3			£350	£110

67 Swinging the Propeller

68 "Flight"

69 Italy–Greece–Rhodes–Turkey Air Routes

70 Hermes and Marina Fiat MF.5 Flying Boat

(Recess Bradbury, Wilkinson)

1933 (10 Oct). AIR. Aeroespresso Co. issue. T **67** to **70** and other designs all inscr "ΕΝΑΕΡ ΤΑΧΥΔΡ" etc. P 12.

461	50l. orange and green	70	50
462	1d. red-orange and deep blue	1·10	65
463	3d. chestnut and purple	1·70	1·00
464	5d. blue and orange	23·00	8·25
465	10d. black and scarlet	2·40	2·50
466	20d. green and black	42·00	12·50
467	50d. indigo and brown	£140	80·00
461/467 *Set of* 7		£190	95·00

Designs: Horiz—1d. Temple of Neptune, Corinth; 3d. Marina Fiat MF.5 flying boat over Hermoupolis. Vert—50d. Woman and Marina Fiat MF.5 flying boat.

The 1d. is known used, bisected.

PRINTERS. In the following postage stamps, *unless otherwise stated*, the recess-printed stamps as well as those printed by recess and litho combined, were executed by De La Rue & Co., in conjunction with Aspiotis, Corfu (later Aspioti-Elka); the lithographed issues were made by Aspioti-Elka. From the beginning of 1953 both lithographed and engraved issues were printed by Aspioti-Elka, *unless otherwise stated.*

71 Greece

73 Junkers G.24 Airplane and Acropolis

1933 (2 Nov). AIR. Govt issue. Recess. Perfs as shown.

468	**71**	50l. green (p 13×13½)	1·10	65
469		1d. claret (p 13×12½)	2·40	75
470	–	2d. bright violet (p 13×13½)	3·00	1·40
471	**73**	5d. bright blue (p 12½×13)	21·00	6·25
		a. Imperf (pair)		
472	–	10d. carmine (p 13×12½)	27·00	10·50
473	**71**	25d. deep blue (p 13×13½)	90·00	26·00
474	**73**	50d. brown (p 13½×13)	£130	65·00
		a. Imperf (pair)	£2500	
468/474 *Set of* 7			£250	£100

Design: As T **71**—2d., 10d. Ikarian Is.

74 Admiral Kondouriotis and cruiser *Averoff*

75 "Greece"

76 Statue (Youth of Marathon)

C **77** St. Demetrius

1933. Recess. P 13½×13 (50d.) or 13×13½ (others).

475	**74**	50d. grey-blue and black (16.12)	£160	4·25
476	**75**	75d. purple-lake and black (2.11)	£350	£190
		a. Imperf (pair)	£2000	
477	**76**	100d. grey-green and brown (16.12)	£1600	38·00
475/477 *Set of* 3			£1900	£200

(Litho Kontogony, Athens)

1934 (22 Sept). Salonika International Exhibition Fund. P 11½.

C478	C **77**	20l. red-brown	65	20
		a. Imperf between (pair)	22·00	
		b. Imperf (pair)	22·00	

78 Athens Stadium, Entrance

C **78** Allegory of Health

(Des L. Sowinski. Eng Wl. Vacek. Recess, in Poland)

1934 (10 Dec). P 11½.

479	**78**	8d. blue	£225	2·10
		a. Perf 13×11½	£250	2·10

1934 (28 Dec). Postal Staff Anti-tuberculosis Fund. P 13½ (50l.) or 13½×13 (others).

C480	C **78**	10l. orange and blue-green	25	20
C481		20l. orange and blue	55	30
C482		50l. orange and green	4·50	3·75
C480/482 *Set of* 3			4·75	3·75

(Recess Aspiotis)

1935 (1 Nov). POSTAGE DUE. P 12½×13.

D480	D **20**	50d. orange	85	5·25
D481		100d. blue-green	85	5·25

79 Sun Chariot

80 Hermes

(Des M. Biskinis. Recess)

1935–39. AIR. Mythological designs as T **79/80**. P 13×12½, 12½×13 or 13½×13 (5d.).

(a) Grey-white paper. Size 34×23½ or 23½×34 mm. (10 Nov 1935)

480	1d. scarlet	2·75	95
481	2d. grey-blue	4·25	1·20
482	5d. mauve	49·00	10·50
483	7d. ultramarine	75·00	12·50
484	10d. brown	9·75	4·25
485	25d. rose-carmine	11·00	10·50
486	30d. green	2·40	3·25
487	50d. mauve	11·00	16·00
488	100d. brown	3·25	9·50
480/488 *Set of* 9		£150	60·00

(b) White paper. Size 34¼×24 or 24×34¼ mm. (1937–39)

488*a*	1d. scarlet	55	30
488*b*	2d. grey-blue	55	30
488*c*	5d. mauve	55	40
488*d*	7d. ultramarine	55	40
488*e*	10d. orange-red (1.3.39)	7·50	7·25
488*a/e* *Set of* 5		8·75	7·75

Designs: Horiz—2d. Iris; 30d. Triptolemus; 100d. Phrixus and Helle. Vert—5d. Daedalus and Icarus: 7d. Minerva; 25d. Zeus and Ganymede; 50d. Bellerophon on Pegasus.

King George II (restored)
25 November 1935–1 April 1947

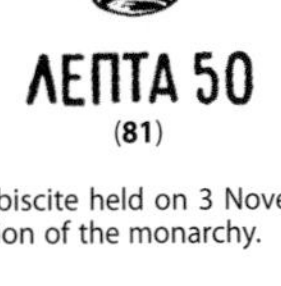

(**81**)

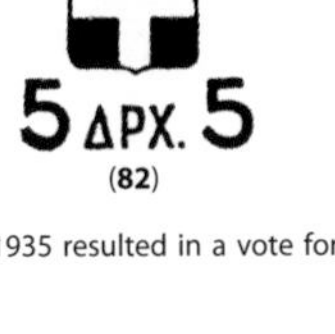

(**82**)

A plebiscite held on 3 November 1935 resulted in a vote for the restoration of the monarchy.

1935 (24 Nov). Restoration of Greek Monarchy. Surch as T **81** or **82**.

489	**81**	50l. on 40l. (D277) (Br.)	55	30
490		3d. on 3d. (D282) (B.)	2·20	1·30
491		3d. on 3d. (D454) (B.)	6·50	1·60
492	**82**	5d. on 100d. (477) (Br.)	4·25	1·60
493		15d. on 75d. (476) (B.)	22·00	6·75
489/493 *Set of* 5			32·00	10·50

1935 (13 Dec)–**39**. As Nos. C480/2, but inscr "ΕΛΛΑΣ" at top. P 13×13½, 13 (No. C494) or 12½ (No. C497).

C494	**C 78**	10l. orange and blue-green ('35)	65	50
C495		20l. orange and blue ('35)	1·10	80
C496		50l. orange and green ('35)	2·75	2·50
C497		50l. orange and brown (2.12.39)	75	45
C494/497 *Set of* 4			4·75	3·75

83 King Constantine

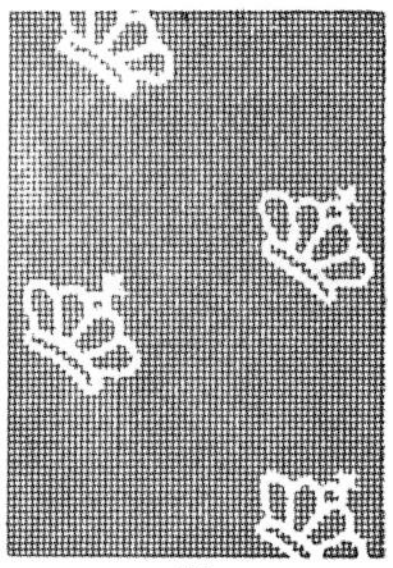

84

(Portrait, recess; frame, litho)

1936 (18 Nov). Re-interment of King Constantine and Queen Sophia. W **84**. P 12½×13½.

494	**83**	3d. brown and black	1·10	30
495		8d. blue and black	2·75	1·80

ΠΡΟΝΟΙΑ

(C **85**)

85 Pallas Athene (Minerva)

1937 (20 Jan–June). Nos. D273 and 415b optd as Type C **85**.

C498		10l. carmine (B.)	1·90	30
		a. Opt inverted	55·00	
C499		50l. violet (R.)	1·80	30
		a. Opt inverted (16.2.37)	1·20	30
C500		50l. violet (G.) (16.6.37)	1·10	30
C498/500 *Set of* 3			4·25	80

No. C498 exists in the two types mentioned in the first footnote after No. D283*a*. No. C498*a* occurs on the original type with accent.

On one or two sheets of No. C499 the overprint was accidentally inverted and these stamps were sold at post offices before the mistake was discovered. To prevent speculation the Postal Authorities deliberately printed a supply with inverted overprint and put them on sale at the chief post offices.

(Recess Bradbury, Wilkinson)

1937 (17 Apr). Centenary of Athens University. P 12.

496	**85**	3d. orange-brown	1·10	50

86 Bull-leaping

87 Zeus and Thunderbolt

88 Amphictyonic Coin

89 King George II

89a Statue of King Constantine

90 St. Paul on Mt. Areopagus

91 Leo III (the Isaurian) destroying the Saracens

92 "Glory" of Psara

1937–38. As T **86/92** (various designs). Nos. 497/502 and 514, litho; Nos. 503/13 and 515/16, recess.

(a) W **84**. P 13½×12½ (horiz); 12½×13½ (vert) or 13×12 (T **89**).

497	**86**	5l. greenish blue and red-brown (1.11.37)	10	10
498	–	10l. red-brown and light blue (inscr "TYPIN" etc) (1.11.37)	10	10
499	**87**	20l. blue-green and black (1.11.37)	10	10
500	**88**	40l. black and blue-green (1.11.37)	10	10
501	–	50l. black and bistre-brown (1.11.37)	10	10
502	–	80l. brown and dull violet (1.11.37)	10	10
503	**89**	1d. green (24.1.37)	35	10
504	–	2d. ultramarine (1.11.37)	20	20
505	**89**	3d. red-brown (24.1.37)	55	20
506	–	5d. scarlet (1.11.37)	20	20
507	–	6d. olive-brown (1.11.37)	35	25
508	**90**	7d. chocolate (1.11.37)	1·80	1·60
509	**89**	8d. deep blue (24.1.37)	1·80	50
510	–	10d. red-brown (1.11.37)	35	25
511	**91**	15d. blue-green (1.11.37)	45	30
512	**92**	25d. deep blue (1.11.37)	35	30
513	**89**	100d. lake (24.1.37)	31·00	14·00

As No. 498, but correctly inscr "TIPYN", etc, instead of "TYPIN", etc.

514	–	10l. red-brown and light blue (1938)	55	50

(b) No wmk. P 12½×13½

515	**89a**	1d.50 green (9.10.38)	75	30
516		30d. brown-red (9.10.38)	5·25	4·25
497/516 *Set of* 20			40·00	21·00

Designs: Vert—10l. (Nos. 498, 514) Court lady of Tiryns; 80l. Venus of Milo. Horiz—50l. Chairing Diagoras of Rhodes; 2d. Battle of Salamis; 5d. Panathenaic chariot; 6d. Alexander the Great at Battle of Issus; 10d. Temple of St. Demetrius, Salonika.

For other values in Type **92**, but smaller, see Nos. 609/16.

93 Prince Paul and Princess Frederika Louise

94 Arms of Greece, Rumania, Turkey and Yugoslavia

1938. Royal Wedding. Recess. W **84**. P 13½×12½.

517	**93**	1d. green (8.2.38)	25	25
518		3d. red-brown (9.1.38)	70	25
519		8d. blue (24.1.38)	2·00	1·40
517/519 *Set of* 3			2·75	1·70

1938 (8 Feb). Balkan Entente. Litho. P 12½.

520	**94**	6d. blue	16·00	2·40

Λ.50
ΠΡΟΝΟΙΑ

(C **95**)

(**95**)

C **96** Queens Olga and Sophia

1938. Nos. D272 and D274 surch with Type C **95**.

C521	**D 20**	50l. on 5l. green (B.) (1.6.38)	7·50	1·00
		a. Imperf between (vert pair)	£200	
		b. "o" for "p" in word at foot	85·00	42·00
C522		50l. on 20l. slate-grey (B.) (18.7.38)	7·50	1·00

Nos. C521/2 exist in the two types mentioned in the first footnote after D283*a*.

1938–39. AIR. Nos. D278 and D451 optd with T **95** (Junkers G.24 airplane).

521	**D 20**	50l. brown (R.) (8.8.38)	20	30
		a. "o" for "p" in word at foot	22·00	21·00
522		50l. brown (R.) (26.6.39)	20	30

For other values, see Nos. 554/60.

1938 (13 Sept). No. 412 surch as Type C **95**, but size 15×17 mm.

C523		50l. on 20l. (V.)	1·10	85

1939 (1 Feb). P 13½×12.

C524	**C 96**	10l. carmine/*rose*	20	10
C525		50l. green/*pale green*	35	15
C526		1d. blue/*pale blue*	55	30
C524/526 *Set of* 3			1·00	50

96 Arms of Ionian Islands

97 Corfu Bay and Citadel

98 King George I of Greece and Queen Victoria

1939 (21 May). 75th Anniv of Cession of Ionian Islands. Recess P 12½ (1d.) or 13½×12½ (others).

523	**96**	1d. blue	1·90	5
524	**97**	4d. green	7·50	2·5
525	**98**	20d. orange	45·00	24·0
526		20d. blue	45·00	24·0
527		20d. carmine	45·00	24·0
523/527 *Set of* 5			£130	70·0

99 Javelin-thrower

100 Arms of Greece, Rumania, Turkey and Yugoslavia

1939 (1 Oct). 10th Pan-Balkan Games, Athens. Vert designs as T **99**. Litho. P 12½×13½.

528	50l. myrtle/*green* (Runner)	45	35
529	3d. carmine/*pink*	1·50	40
530	6d. red-brown/*pale orange* (Discus-thrower)	8·75	3·25
531	8d. blue/*grey* (Jumper)	9·00	4·25
528/531 *Set of* 4		18·00	7·50

1940 (27 May). Balkan Entente. Litho. W **84**. P 13×12½.

532	**100**	6d. pale blue	27·00	2·10
533		8d. bluish slate	24·00	2·40

101 Greek Youth Badge

102 Youths on Parade

103 Meteora Monasteries

1940 (3 Aug). Fourth Anniv of Greek Youth Organization. Designs as T **101/3**. Litho. W **84**. Nos. 534 and 543, perf 13½×12½; others perf 12½.

(a) POSTAGE

534	3d. blue, red and silver	2·20	1·00
535	5d. black and blue	13·50	5·50
536	10d. black and orange	16·00	11·50
537	15d. black and green	£120	70·00
538	20d. black and lake	90·00	41·00
539	25d. black and blue	90·00	50·00
540	30d. black and purple	90·00	50·00
541	50d. black and lake	£150	60·00
542	75d. gold, brown and blue	£150	60·00
543	100d. blue, red and silver	£200	95·00
534/543 *Set of* 10		£850	£400

(b) AIR

544	2d. black and orange	3·25	80
545	4d. black and green	19·00	3·50
546	6d. black and lake	24·00	6·25
547	8d. black and blue	50·00	10·50
548	16d. black and purple	80·00	24·00
549	32d. black and orange	£140	60·00
550	45d. black and green	£160	65·00
551	55d. black and carmine	£160	65·00
552	65d. black and blue	£160	65·00
553	100d. black and purple	£190	75·00
544/553 *Set of* 10		£900	£350

Designs: Postage. Horiz—3d., 100d. Greek Youth badge. Vert—5d. Boy, and 10d. girl members; 15d. Javelin-thrower; 20d., 50d. Youths on parade; 25d. Standard-bearer and buglers; 30d. Three youths in uniform; 75d. Coat of Arms.

Air. (Vert. Landscapes with aeroplanes above)—2d. Meteora monasteries, Thessaly; 4d. Simon Peter Monastery, Mt. Athos; 6d., 16d. Isle of Santorin (Thira); 8d. Pantanassa Church, Mistra; 32d. Ponticonissi, Corfu; 45d. The Acropolis; 55d. The Erechtheum; 65d. The Temple of Nike, Athens; 100d. The Temple of Zeus.

ΠΡΟΣΤΑΣΙΑ ΦΥΜΑΤΙΚΩΝ ΤΤΤ

(C **104**)

1 ΔΡ.

(**104**)

1940 (1 Dec). Postal Staff Anti-Tuberculosis Fund. No. C525 optd with Type C **104**.

C554	C **96**	50l. green/*pale green* (R.)	45	30
		a. Opt inverted	55·00	

1941 (15 Mar–1 July). AIR. Postage Due stamps surch or optd only, as in T **104**, in red.

		(a) Rouletted. Litho		
554	D **20**	1d. on 2d. pale red (D281) (1.7)	15	30
		a. Surch inverted	55·00	
		b. Surch double	£130	
555		5d. slate-blue (D283*a*)	£160	£160
		(b) Perf. Litho		
556	D **20**	1d. on 2d. vermilion (D453)	25	30
		a. Surch inverted	55·00	
557		5d. grey-blue (D455)	20	30
		a. Opt double	55·00	
		b. Vert pair, one without opt	£325	
		c. Opt inverted	60·00	
558		10d. green (D456) (1.7)	20	30
		a. Opt inverted	27·00	
		b. Imperf (pair)	£600	
559		25d. scarlet (D458) (1.7)	1·40	3·00
		a. No accent (D458a)	55·00	65·00
		b. Opt inverted	£225	
		(c) Perf. Recess		
560	D **20**	50d. orange (D480) (1.7)	1·50	3·25
545/560 *Set of* 7			3·25	6·75

For red airplane overprint on 50l. brown, see Nos. 521/2.

GERMAN AND ITALIAN OCCUPATION

April 1941-October 1944

The Axis invasion began on 6 April 1941 and was completed by the capture of Crete on 31 May 1941.

(C **105**)

(C **106**)

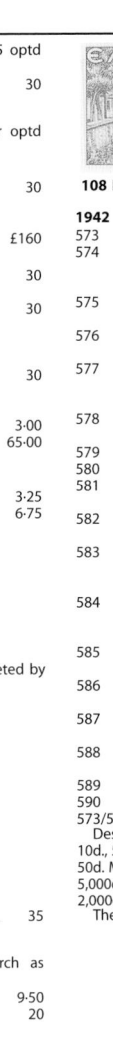

1941 (1 Nov). Social Funds. No. 410 surch with Type C **105**.

C561	**51**	50l. on 5l. deep green (R.)	45	35
		a. Surch inverted	55·00	

1941 (15 Nov). Postal Staff Anti-Tuberculosis Fund. Surch as Type C **106**.

C562	C **78**	50 on 10l. (C480)	2·10	9·50
C563		50 on 10l. (C494)	40	20
		a. Surch inverted	65·00	

(D **105**)

105 "Boreas"

(C **107**)

1942 (1 Jan). POSTAGE DUE. No. D276 surch with Type D **105**.

D564	D **20**	50 on 30l. scarlet	6·50	13·00

1942 (15 Aug)–**43**. AIR. Winds (symbolic designs). T **105** and similar horiz designs. Litho. W **84**. P 12½.

	(a) First issue (15.8.42)		
561	2d. emerald and pale green	25	50
	a. No wmk	11·00	
562	5d. orange-red and pale orange	35	50
	a. Imperf (pair)	£400	
563	10d. red-brown and orange-brown	45	50
564	20d. dull ultramarine and pale blue	90	1·00
565	25d. red-orange and pale orange	55	1·00
566	50d. grey-black and bluish grey	2·30	2·10
	a. Double impression	£150	
	(b) Second issue (15.9.43)		
567	10d. carmine-red and salmon	20	30
	a. Imperf (pair)	£130	
568	25d. deep bluish green and pale grey	20	30
	a. Imperf (pair)	£130	
569	50d. violet-blue and dull violet-blue	20	30
	a. Imperf (pair)	£130	
570	100d. slate-black and bluish grey	35	30
	a. Imperf (pair)	£130	
571	200d. claret and brown-rose	35	30
	a. Imperf (pair)	£130	
572	400d. slate-green and violet-blue	35	30
	a. Imperf (pair)	£130	
561/572 *Set of* 12		5·75	6·75

Designs:—2d., 100d. "Boreas" (North wind); 5d. "Notos" (South); 10d. "Apiliotis" (East); 20d. "Lips" (South-west); 25d. "Zephyr" (West); 50d. "Kekias" (North-east); 200d. "Evros" (South-east); 400d. "Skiron" (North-west).

1942 (1 Sept). Sample Fair, Salonika. No. C478 surch with Type C **107**.

C573	C **77**	1d. on 20l. red-brown (G.)	45	10
		a. Surch double	38·00	

106 Windmills on Mykonos Island

107 Houses on Hydra Island

108 Edessa

No. 574b

1942 (1 Sept)–**44**. Designs as T **106/8**. Litho. W **84**. P 12½.

573	2d. reddish brown	10	20
574	5d. blue-green (1.12.42)	10	20
	a. Imperf (pair)	£160	
	b. Square "O" for Greek "P"	11·00	11·00
575	10d. pale blue	10	20
	a. Imperf (pair)	£160	
576	15d. bright purple	10	20
	a. Imperf (pair)	£160	
577	25d. brown-orange	10	20
	a. Imperf (pair)	£110	
	b. Double impression	16·00	31·00
578	50d. blue	10	20
	a. Imperf (pair)	£110	
579	75d. carmine (1.12.42)	10	20
580	100d. black (1.12.42)	10	20
581	200d. ultramarine (1.12.42)	10	20
	a. Without printer's imprint	11·00	11·00
582	500d. olive-brown (15.3.44)	10	20
	a. Imperf (pair)	£110	
583	1,000d. red-brown (15.3.44)	20	20
	a. Imperf (pair)	£140	
	b. Double impression	33·00	50·00
584	2,000d. blue (15.3.44)	20	20
	a. Imperf (pair)	£140	
	b. Double impression	33·00	50·00
585	5,000d. scarlet (1.7.44)	20	20
	a. Imperf (pair)	£140	
586	15,000d. bright purple (1.7.44)	20	20
	a. Imperf (pair)	£140	
587	25,000d. green (1.7.44)	20	20
	a. Imperf (pair)	£140	
588	500,000d. blue (15.9.44)	40	50
	a. Imperf (pair)	£140	
589	2,000,000d. turquoise-green (15.9.44)	55	1·30
590	5,000,000d. lake (15.9.44)	55	1·30
573/590 *Set of* 18		3·25	5·50

Designs: (31×21 mm.)—5d., 5,000,000d. Burzi Fortress, Nauplion; 10d., 500,000d. Katokhi on Aspropotamos River; 15d. Heraklion, Crete; 50d. Meteora Monastery; 100d., 200d. Monastery on Mt. Athos; 500d., 5,000d. Konitza Bridge; 1,000d., 15,000d. Ekatontapiliani Church, Paros; 2,000d., 25,000d. Kerkyra (Corfu) Island; 2,000,000d. T **106**.

The error No. 574b occurs on position 15 in part of the printing.

(C **109**)

110 Child

1942 (1 Dec)–**43**. Postal Staff Anti-Tuberculosis Fund. Nos. 410 and 413 surch as Type C **109**.

C591	**51**	10d. on 5l. deep green (R.) (1.12.43)	35	25
		a. Surch inverted	65·00	
C592	–	10d. on 25l. blue-green (R.)	35	25
		a. Surch inverted	65·00	

1943 (1 Oct). Children's Welfare Fund. T **110** and similar designs. Litho. W **84**. P 12×13½.

592	25d. +25d. green	40	35
	a. Imperf (pair)	80·00	
593	100d. +50d. bright purple	40	35
	a. Imperf (pair)	80·00	
594	200d. + 100d. brown	45	40
592/594 *Set of* 3		1·10	1·00

Designs:—100d. Mother and Child; 200d. Madonna and Child.

1943 (11 Oct). POSTAGE DUE. Litho. W **84**. P 12½.

D595	D **20**	10d. orange-red	35	3·00
D596		25d. blue	35	3·00
D597		100d. sepia	35	3·00
D598		200d. reddish violet	35	3·00
D595/598 *Set of* 4			1·30	11·00

(C **111**)

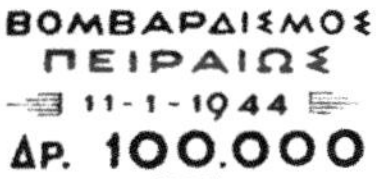

(**111**)

1944 (15 Mar). Postal Staff Anti-Tuberculosis Fund. No. 580 optd with Type C **111**.

C599	100d. black (R.)	25	25
	a. Opt. double	22·00	
	b. Opt. inverted	11·00	

1944 (11 June). Fund for Victims of Piraeus Air Raid. Nos. 576/580 and 567/71 surch with T **111**, in blue.

	(a) POSTAGE		
594*a*	100,000d. on 15d. bright purple	1·10	1·10
594*b*	100,000d. on 25d. brown-orange	1·10	1·10
594*c*	100,000d. on 50d. blue	1·10	1·10
594*d*	100,000d. on 75d. carmine	1·10	1·10
594*e*	100,000d. on 100d. black	1·10	1·10
	(b) AIR		
594*f*	100,000d. on 10d. carmine	1·10	1·10
594*g*	100,000d. on 25d. blue-green	1·10	1·10
594*h*	100,000d. on 50d. ultramarine	1·10	1·10
594*i*	100,000d. on 100d. blue-black	1·10	1·10
594*j*	100,000d. on 200d. claret	1·10	1·10
594*a/j* *Set of* 10		10·00	10·00

(C **112**)

(**112**)

1944 (1 July). Postal Staff Anti-Tuberculosis Fund. No. 579 surch with Type C **112**.

C600	5,000d. on 75d. carmine (B.)	25	40

1944 (20 July). Children's Convalescent Camp Fund. Surch as T **112**, in blue.

	(a) POSTAGE. Nos. 573/7		
595	50,000 +450,000d. on 2d.	1·00	1·00
596	50,000 +450,000d. on 5d.	1·00	1·00
597	50,000 +450,000d. on 10d.	1·00	1·00
598	50,000 +450,000d. on 15d.	1·00	1·00
599	50,000 +450,000d. on 25d.	1·00	1·00
	a. Surch inverted	39·00	
	(b) AIR. Nos. 567/71		
600	50,000 +450,000d. on 10d.	1·00	1·00
	a. Surch inverted	39·00	
601	50,000 +450,000d. on 25d.	1·00	1·00
	a. Surch inverted	39·00	
602	50,000 +450,000d. on 50d.	1·00	1·00
	a. Surch inverted	39·00	
603	50,000 +450,000d. on 100d.	1·00	1·00
	a. Surch inverted	39·00	
604	50,000 +450,000d. on 200d.	1·00	1·00
	a. Surch inverted	39·00	
595/604 *Set of* 10		9·00	9·00

(C **113**)

1944 (1 Aug). Postal Staff Anti-Tuberculosis Fund. No. 573 surch with Type C **113**.

C605	**106**	25,000d. on 2d. reddish brown (B.)	60	70
		a. Surch double	46·00	
		b. Additional surch on back	£150	

INDEPENDENCE REGAINED

October 1944

(**113** Trans. "New drachmas")

1944 (11 Nov)–**45**. Nos. 501, 504 and 506/7, optd with T **113**, in blue.

605	50l. black and bistre-brown	30	30
	a. Opt double	35·00	
606	2d. ultramarine	30	30
607	5d. scarlet	30	30
	a. Opt inverted	35·00	
608	6d. olive-brown (15.5.45)	30	30
605/608 *Set of* 4		1·10	1·10

REGENCY

30 December 1944–27 September 1946

1945 (1 Mar–10 Aug). As T **92**, but reduced to 22½×33 mm. Litho. W **84**. P 12½×13½.

609	**92**	1d. purple	40	20
610		3d. claret	40	20
		a. Imperf (pair)	£180	
611		5d. ultramarine	40	20
		a. Imperf (pair)	£180	
612		10d. chocolate	45	20
		a. Imperf (pair)	£180	
613		20d. violet	80	20
		a. Imperf (pair)	£180	
614		50d. blue-green (10.8.45)	1·70	50
615		100d. greenish blue (10.8.45)	17·00	10·50
		a. Imperf (pair)	£225	
616		200d. blackish green (10.8.45)	12·00	2·50
		a. Imperf (pair)	£200	
609/616 *Set of* 8			30·00	13·00

114 "*OXI*"=No!

115 President Roosevelt

(**116**)

1945 (28 Oct). Resistance to Italian Ultimatum. Litho. P 12½×13½.

617	**114**	20d. orange-red	40	25
		a. Imperf (pair)	£130	
618		40d. blue	45	30
		a. Imperf (pair)	£130	

1945 (8 Nov). Postal Staff Anti-Tuberculosis Fund. No. 500 surch as Type C **113**.

C619	**88**	1d. on 40l. black and blue-green (B.)	25	15
		a. Surch double	33·00	
C620		2d. on 40l. black and blue-green (R.)	25	15
		a. Surch inverted	46·00	

1945 (21 Dec). Roosevelt Mourning issue. Borders in black. Litho. P 12×13½.

619	**115**	30d. brown-purple	50	20
		a. Centre inverted	90·00	
		b. Imperf (pair)	65·00	

620 60d. blue-grey 50 20
a. Centre inverted 90·00
b. Imperf (pair) 65·00
621 200d. slate-violet 50 20
a. Imperf (pair) 65·00
b. Centre inverted 90·00
619/621 *Set of 3* 1·40 55

1946 (10 Feb)–**47**. Variously surch as T **116**.
622 10d. on 10d. (567) (6.3.46) 35 20
a. Surch inverted £150
623 10d. on 2000d. (584) (R.) (20.7.46) 35 20
624 20d. on 50d. (569) (R.) (6.3.46) 35 20
a. Surch inverted £200
625 20d. on 500d. (582) (R.) (5.47) 35 20
a. Surch double £110
626 20d. on 1000d. (583) (8.7.46) 35 20
627 30d. on 5d. (574) (R.) (5.47) 35 20
a. On No. 574b £130 75·00
628 50d. on 50d. (578) (R.) (22.9.47) 35 20
629 50d. on 25,000d. (587) (R.) (6.3.46) 55 20
630 100d. on 10d. (575) (R.) (21.12.47) 1·90 20
631 100d. on 2,000,000d. (589) (R.) 6.3.46) 1·20 20
632 130d. on 20l. (499) (R.) (10.2.46) 1·10 30
633 250d. on 20l. (499) (R.) (8.7.46) 1·10 30
a. Surch double £120
634 300d. on 80l. (502) (10.2.46) 1·10 40
a. Surch in red-brown 22·00 21·00
635 450d. on 75d. (579) (21.12.47) 2·30 45
636 500d. on 5,000,000d. (590) (6.3.46) 4·25 75
a. Surch inverted £130
637 1000d. on 500,000d. (588) (R.) (6.3.46) 18·00 1·60
a. Surch double
638 2000d. on 5000d. (585) (28.3.46) 60·00 6·50
639 5000d. on 15,000d. (586) (28.3.46) £250 43·00
a. Surch in blue £275 £275
622/639 *Set of 18 (cheapest)* £300 50·00

All the above are postage stamps despite the fact that some air stamps were used for surcharging.

A 150d. on 20l. is fraudulent.

(C **117**)

117 E. Venizelos

1946. Postal Staff Anti-Tuberculosis Fund. Surch as Type C **117**, in red.
C640 **86** 20d. on 5l. (No. 497) (20.7) 1·60 65
C641 **88** 20d. on 40l. (No. 500) (11.3) 65 20

1946 (25 Mar). Tenth Death Anniv of Venizelos (statesman). Litho. W **84**. P 12½×13½.
640 **117** 130d. sage-green 55 30
641 300d. red-brown 55 30

1946 (20 June)–**49**. Red Cross. No. C525 surch as Type C **117** in red.
C642 C **96** 50d. on 50l. green/*pale green* (surch 22½ mm wide) 70 30
a. Surch 21¼ mm (9.49)

1946 (20 Sept). Social Funds. No. C526 surch as Type C **117** in red.
C643 C **96** 50d. on 1d. blue/*pale blue* 55 30

King George II (restored)
27 September 1946–1 April 1947

A plebiscite held on 1 September 1946 resulted in a vote for the return of the King of Greece.

1-9-1946

(**118**)

1946 (28 Sept). Restoration of Monarchy. Surch as T **118**, in shades of blue.
642 **89** 50d. on 1d. green 80 20
643 250d. on 3d. red-brown 1·60 25
a. Surch inverted 49·00
644 600d. on 8d. deep blue 14·00 1·60
a. Additional surch on back (inverted) £170
b. Surch in red £250
645 3000d. on 100d. lake 30·00 1·30
642/645 *Set of 4* 42·00 3·00

119 Women carrying Munitions, Pindos Mountains

120 Torpedoing of Cruiser *Helle*

1946 (28 Oct)–**47**. First Victory Issue. As T **119/20** (war episodes). Recess. P 12½.
646 50d. green (1.5.47) 45 20
647 100d. ultramarine (1.5.47) 65 20
648 250d. yellow-green 90 20
649 500d. red-brown (1.5.47) 1·40 30
650 600d. chocolate (1.5.47) 1·60 80
651 1000d. violet (1.5.47) 7·50 40
652 2000d. ultramarine (1.5.47) 41·00 3·00
653 5000d. carmine (1.5.47) 50·00 1·90
a. Imperf (pair) £1800
646/653 *Set of 8* 95·00 6·25

Designs: Horiz—50d. Convoy; 500d. Column of infantry; 1000d. Supermarine Spitfire Mk IIB fighter plane and pilot; 2000d. Torpedo-boat *Hyacinth* towing submarine *Perla*. Vert—600d. Badge, Alpine troops and outlined map of Italy; 5000d. Monument at El Alamein.

See also No. 682.

121 Panayiotis Tsaldaris

(**122**)

1946 (15 Nov). Tenth Death Anniv of P. Tsaldaris (statesman). Litho. P 12×13½.
654 **121** 250d. red-brown and salmon 6·50 1·00
a. Imperf (pair) £120
655 600d. deep blue and pale blue 6·50 1·60
a. Imperf (pair) £120

King Paul I
1 April 1947–6 March 1964

1947 (Apr). King George II Mourning Issue. Surch as T **122**.
656 **89** 50d. on 1d. green (15 Apr) 1·40 25
a. Surch double 85·00
657 250d. on 3d. red-brown (6 Apr) 2·40 25
a. Surch double 85·00
b. Pair, one without surch £110
658 600d. on 8d. deep blue (15 Apr) 7·00 95
a. Surch double £100
656/658 *Set of 3* 9·75 1·30

ΔP. —— 50

(C **123**)

124 Castelrosso Fortress

125 Dodecanese Vase

126 Apollo (Type K **1** of Dodecanese Is)

C **127** St. Demetrius

1947 (11 Aug). Postal Staff Anti-Tuberculosis Fund. Surch with Type C **123** in red.
C659 C **96** 50d. on 50l. (C525) 70·00
C660 50d. on 50l. (C554) 4·50 50

1947 (20 Nov)–**51**. Restoration of Dodecanese Islands to Greece. T **124/6** and similar designs. Litho. W **84**. P 13½×12 (horiz) or 12×13½ (vert).
659 **124** 20d. ultramarine 45 10
a. Imperf (pair) £350
660 **125** 30d. flesh and brown-black 45 10
a. Imperf (pair) £350
661 – 50d. blue 45 10
662 – 100d. deep olive and pale olive 45 10
a. Imperf (pair) £350
663 – 200d. brown-orange (5.11.50) 1·60 10
664 – 250d. grey 1·40 10
a. Imperf (pair) £350
665 – 300d. yellow-orange (15.9.50) 1·80 10
666 – 400d. light blue (5.11.50) 2·40 10
667 **126** 450d. blue (12.1.48) 3·00 10
668 – 450d. blue and pale blue (1.7.48) 2·40 10
a. Imperf (pair) £350
669 **126** 500d. vermilion 2·20 10
670 – 600d. brown-purple 3·00 25
a. Imperf (pair) £375
671 – 700d. magenta (20.8.50) 4·00 20
a. Imperf (pair) £375
672 – 700d. turquoise-green (10.4.51) 33·00 20
a. Imperf (pair) £375
673 – 800d. green and violet (5.11.50) 5·25 20
674 – 1000d. brown-olive 3·25 30
a. Imperf (pair) £325
675 **126** 1300d. carmine (15.9.50) 27·00 20
676 **124** 1500d. orange-brown (1.12.50) £140 40
677 **125** 1600d. greenish blue and ultramarine (5.9.50) 9·75 20
678 2000d. salmon and brown (5.4.50) 75·00 30
a. Imperf (pair) £190
679 – 2600d. green (5.9.50) 16·00 1·20
680 – 5000d. violet (5.4.50) 75·00 75
681 – 10,000d. ultramarine (5.4.50) £130 85
659/681 *Set of 23* £475 5·50

Designs: Horiz—100, 400d. St. John's Convent, Patmos. Vert—50, 300d. Woman in national costume; 200, 250d. Emmanuel Xanthos; 600, 700 (2), 5000d. Statue of Hippocrates; 450d. (No. 668), 800d. Casos Is. and 19th-century frigate; 1000, 2600, 10000d. Colossus of Rhodes.

1948 (25 Jan). Church Restoration Fund. P 12×13½.
C682 C **127** 50d. yellow-brown 35 25

128 Battle of Crete

129 Column of Women and Children

(Recess Bradbury, Wilkinson, London)

1948 (15 Sept). Second Victory Issue. W **84**. P 13×13½.
682 **128** 1000d. blue-green 7·75 65

1949 (1 Feb). Abduction of Greek Children to neighbouring countries. T **129** and similar types. Litho. W **84**. P 13½×12 (horiz) or 12×13½ (vert).
683 450d. violet and mauve 9·25 1·00
684 1000d. brown and sepia 17·00 65
685 1800d. lake and buff 12·00 65
683/685 *Set of 3* 34·00 2·10

Designs: Vert—1000d. Captive children and map of Greece; 1800d. Hand menacing woman and child.

1950 (1 Mar). Postal Staff Anti-tuberculosis Fund. Surch as Type C **117** (21½ mm) sideways (reading upwards) in blue.
C686 50d. on 10l. (498) 2·50 50
a. Surch reading down 39·00 31·00
C687 50d. on 10l. (514) 1·50 30
a. Surch reading down 39·00 31·00

130 Map and Flags

131 "Youth of Marathon"

1950 (28 Apr). Battle of Crete. Recess. W **84**. P 13½×13.
686 **130** 1000d. blue 21·00 50
a. Imperf (pair) £2000

1950 (21 May). 75th Anniv of Universal Postal Union. Recess. W **84**. P 13×13½.
687 **131** 1000d. green/*buff* 3·25 50
a. Imperf (pair) £1600

132 "To the Unknown God"

133 St. Paul

134 St. Paul

135 "Industry"

(Des Jean Kefalinos. Recess)

1951 (15 June). Nineteenth Centenary of St. Paul's Travels in Greece. T **132/4** and similar type inscr "51–1951". P 13½×12½ (700d. and 1600d.), 12½×13½ (others).
688 **132** 700d. bright purple 4·00 50
689 **133** 1600d. greenish blue 22·00 3·00
690 **134** 2600d. yellow-brown 30·00 3·75
691 – 10,000d. brown-lake £250 95·00
688/691 *Set of 4* £275 90·00

Design: Vert—as T **134**: 10,000d. St. Paul preaching to Athenians.

1951 (20 Sept). Reconstruction Issue. T **135** and similar vert designs. Recess. W **84**. P 13×13½.
692 700d. orange 4·25 30
693 800d. blue-green 8·50 35
694 1300d. turquoise 13·00 35
695 1600d. olive-green 38·00 40
696 2600d. grey-violet £110 2·10
697 5000d. purple £120 45
692/697 *Set of 6* £275 3·50

Designs:—800d. Fish and trident ("Fishing"); 1300d. Workmen and column ("Reconstruction"), 1600d. Ceres and tractors ("Agriculture"); 2600d. Women and loom ("Home Crafts"); 5000d. Map and stars ("Electrification").

‡

ΠΡΟΝΟΙΑ
ΤΑΧ. ΥΠΑΛΛΗΛΩΝ
ΔΡΑΧΜΑΙ 50

(C 136)

50

(C 137)

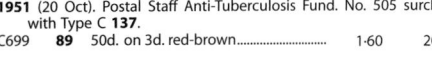

1951. Postal Staff Welfare Funds. No. 497 surch with Type C **136**, in red.

C698	**86**	50d. on 5l. greenish blue and red-brown	3·00	40

1951 (20 Oct). Postal Staff Anti-Tuberculosis Fund. No. 505 surch with Type C **137**.

C699	**89**	50d. on 3d. red-brown	1·60	20

136 Blessing before Battle

137 King Paul

138 "Spirit of Greece"

(Des Prof Ghalanis. Recess)

1952 (29 Aug). AIR. Anti-Communist Campaign. T **136** and similar designs. W **84**. P 12½×13½.

698	1000d. deep blue	1·40	30
699	1700d. deep bluish green	9·25	1·00
700	2700d. brown	20·00	3·50
701	7000d. deep green	60·00	14·50
698/701 *Set of 4*		80·00	17·00

Designs: Vert—1700d. "Victory" over mountains; 2700d. Infantry attack; 7000d. "Victory" and soldiers.

(Des Prof Ghalanis. Recess)

1952 (14 Dec). 50th Birthday of King Paul. Recess. W **84**. P 13×12½.

702	**137**	200d. deep emerald	1·90	30
703		1000d. carmine-red	6·50	35
704	**138**	1400d. pale blue	26·00	1·40
705	**137**	10,000d. reddish purple	75·00	12·50
702/705 *Set of 4*			£100	13·00

ΠΡΟΣΘΕΤΟΝ
ΔΡ. 100

(C 139)

1952 (15 Dec). State Welfare Fund. No. 509 surch with Type C **139**, in red.

C706	**89**	100d. on 8d. deep blue	1·80	20

PRINTERS. From 1953 to 1983 all stamps (litho or recess) were printed by Aspioti-Elka, *unless otherwise stated*.

139 "Oranges"

C **140** Argostoli, Cephalonia

1953 (1 July). National Products. T **139** and similar allegorical designs. Recess. W **84**. P 13×14 (vert) or 14×13 (horiz).

706	500d. orange and carmine-red	1·90	20
707	700d. yellow-ochre and deep brown	2·40	20
	a. Imperf (pair)		
708	1000d. dull green and deep blue	5·00	20
	a. Imperf (pair)		
709	1300d. yellow-brown and maroon	9·25	30
710	2000d. pale blue-green and deep brown	27·00	40
	a. Imperf (pair)		
711	2600d. olive-bistre and slate-lilac	35·00	1·20
712	5000d. apple-green and deep brown	49·00	65
706/712 *Set of 7*		£120	2·75

Designs: Vert—700d. "Tobacco" (tobacco plant); 1300d. "Wine" (wineglass and vase); 2000d. "Figs" (basket of figs); 2600d. "Dried Fruit" (grapes and currant bread); 5000d. "Grapes" (male figure holding grapes). Horiz—1000d. "Olive oil" (Pallas Athene and olive branch).

(Litho Government Mint)

1953 (15 Nov). Ionian Is. Earthquake Fund. Type C **140** and similar vert design. W **84**. P 12½.

C713	300d. indigo and grey-green	3·25	15
C714	500d. deep brown and buff	3·50	90

Design:—300d. Church of Faneromeni, Zante.

140 Bust of Pericles

141 Alexander the Great

142 Hunting Wild Boar

1954 (15 Jan). Ancient Greek Art. Designs showing sculptures, etc, as T **140/2**. Litho. W **84**. P 13×12½ (large vert designs) or 13 (others).

713	**140**	100d. chestnut	55	15
714	–	200d. black	55	15
715	–	300d. blue-violet	1·10	15
716	–	500d. green	1·60	15
717	–	600d. rose	1·90	15
718	**141**	1000d. black and deep blue	2·75	15
719	–	1200d. olive-green	3·00	15
720	–	2000d. orange-brown	12·00	20
721	**142**	2400d. greenish blue	12·00	35
		a. Double impression	£200	
722	–	2500d. deep bluish green	18·00	30
723	–	4000d. claret	38·00	40
724	–	20,000d. reddish purple	£275	1·30
713/724 *Set of 12*			£325	3·25

Designs:—As T **140**—200d. Mycenaean oxhead vase; 1200d. Head of charioteer of Delphi; 2000d. Vase of Dipylon; 2500d. Man carrying calf; 20,000d. Two pitcher-bearers. As T **141**—300d. Bust of Homer; 500d. Zeus of Istiaea; 600d. Youth's head; 4000d. Dish depicting voyage of Dionysus.

See also Nos. 733*a*/41.

143 Athlete Bearing Torch

144 Extracts from *Hansard* (Parliamentary Debates)

(Des A. Tassos. Recess)

1954 (15 May). AIR. Fifth Anniv of North Atlantic Treaty Organization. T **143** and similar vert designs. W **84**. P 13×13½.

725	1200d. orange	5·00	35
726	2400d. deep green	55·00	3·00
727	4000d. deep blue	90·00	4·00
725/727 *Set of 3*		£140	6·50

Designs:—2400d. Amphictyonic coin; 4000d. Pallas Athene.

Currency revalued: 1000 old Drachmai = 1 new Drachma

(Litho State Bank)

1954 (22–24 Sept). "Enosis" (Union of Cyprus with Greece). W **84**. P 12½.

728	**144**	1d.20 black and pale yellow (24.9)	4·25	40
729		2d. black and salmon	23·00	4·25
730		2d. black and light blue	23·00	4·25
731		2d.40 black and lavender	23·00	3·00
732		2d.50 black and pink	23·00	3·00
733		4d. black and pale yellow-green	70·00	4·75
728/733 *Set of 6*			£150	18·00

On No. 728 the text of the report is in Greek, on Nos. 730 and 731 in French, and in English on the others.

I.

II.

Two types of 2d.50:—

Type I. Ten dots at upper righthand corner.
Type II. Only nine dots at corner.

1955–60. As Nos. 713/24 but colours changed and new values.

733*a*	**140**	10l. light emerald (12.1.59)	40	15
734	–	20l. deep bluish green (10.7.55)	55	15
734*a*	–	20l. bright reddish purple (29.12.58)	45	15
735	**140**	30l. yellow-brown (10.7.55)	80	20
736	–	50l. lake (14.4.55)	1·40	20
736*a*	–	50l. turquoise-green (12.1.59)	80	10
736*b*	–	70l. red-orange (2.1.59)	55	10
737	–	1d. turquoise-green (10.7.55)	2·40	15
737*a*	–	1d. red-brown (27.12.58)	3·00	10
737*b*	–	1d.50 light blue (3.1.59)	27·00	20
738	**141**	2d. black and bistre-brown (10.7.55)	14·00	15
738*a*		2d.50 black and deep magenta (I) (14.3.59)	24·00	20
		ab. Type II	33·00	1·00
739	**142**	3d. orange-red (10.7.55)	11·00	20
739*a*	–	3d. cobalt (1.9.60)	3·50	35
740	–	3d.50 rose-carmine (10.7.55)	22·00	65
741	–	4d. bright blue (10.7.55)	95·00	40
733*a*/741 *Set of 16*			£190	£300

Designs: As T **140**—20l. (2) Mycenaean ox-head vase; 70l. Head of charioteer of Delphi; 1d.50, Two pitcher bearers; 3d. (739*a*), Man carrying calf. As T **141**—50l. (2) Zeus of Istiaea; 1d. (2) Youth's head; 3d.50, Bust of Homer; 4d. Dish depicting voyage of Dionysus.

No. 738ab occurs in five positions on the sheet, printed from one particular plate.

145 Samian Coin depicting Pythagoras

146 Rotary Emblem and Globe

1955 (20 Aug). Pythagorean Congress. T **145** and similar designs. Litho. W **84**. P 13½×12 (6d.) or 12×13½ (others).

742	**145**	2d. green	5·25	40
743	–	3d.50 black	15·00	3·00
744	**145**	5d. reddish purple	70·00	2·10
745	–	6d. blue	55·00	39·00
742/745 *Set of 4*			£130	40·00

Designs: Vert—3d.50, Representation of Pythagorean theorem. Horiz—6d. Map of Samos.

1956 (15 May). 50th Anniv of Rotary International. Litho. W **84**. P 12×13½.

746	**146**	2d. ultramarine	21·00	70

147 King George I

C **148** Zeus (Macedonian Coin of Philip II)

148 Dionysios Solomos

(Des A. Tassos. Eng H. Woyty-Wimmer (1d.50, 3d., 10d.), D.L.R. (others). Recess Aspioti-Elka)

1956 (21 May). Royal Family. T **147** and similar portraits. W **84**. P 12½×13½ (vert) or 13½×12½ (horiz).

747	10l. deep slate-violet	20	10
748	20l. deep reddish purple	20	10
749	30l. sepia	20	10
750	50l. red-brown	55	10
751	70l. ultramarine	85	20
752	1d. light blue	1·10	20
753	1d.50 slate-blue	4·50	20
754	2d. black	5·50	20
755	3d. deep brown	4·25	10
756	3d.50 chestnut	16·00	30
757	4d. deep dull green	16·00	30
758	5d. carmine	11·00	30
759	7d.50 ultramarine	11·00	2·00
760	10d. deep blue	65·00	80
747/760 *Set of 14*		£120	4·50

Portraits: Horiz—10l. King Alexander; 5d. King Paul and Queen Frederika; 10d. King and Queen and Crown Prince Constantine. Vert—20l. Crown Prince Constantine; 50l. Queen Olga; 70l. King Otto; 1d. Queen Amalia; 1d.50, King Constantine; 2d. King Paul; 3d. King George II; 3d.50, Queen Sophia; 4d. Queen Frederika; 7d.50, King Paul.

See also Nos. 764/77.

(Litho Perivolaraki-Lykogianni and Aspioti-Elka, Athens)

1956 (6–26 Sept). Macedonian Cultural Fund. Type C **148** and similar vert portrait. W **84**. P 13½.

C761	50l. crimson	1·90	60
	a. Imperf (pair)	£425	
C762	1d. blue (Aristotle) (26.9)	6·25	1·50

This was the last of the Compulsory Charity Tax stamps.

(Des A. Tassos. Litho)

1957 (26 Mar). Death Centenary of D. Solomos (national poet). T **148** and similar horiz designs. W **84**. P 12×13½ (3d.50) or 13½×12 (others).

761	2d. buff and lake-brown	6·50	40
762	3d.50 greenish grey and blue	6·50	2·50
763	5d. bistre and deep bluish green	11·50	10·50
761/763 *Set of 3*		22·00	12·00

Designs:—2d. D. Solomos and K. Mantzaros (composer); 5d. Zante landscape and D. Solomos.

1957 (15 Nov). As Nos. 747/60 but colours changed.

764	10l. claret	20	15
765	20l. orange	20	15
766	30l. black	20	15
767	50l. deep grey-green	40	15
768	70l. reddish purple	85	35
769	1d. deep rose-red	1·50	15
770	1d.50 yellow-green	2·75	15
771	2d. carmine-red	5·75	15
772	3d. deep blue	6·75	20
773	3d.50 slate-purple	13·50	20
774	4d. red-brown	16·00	20
775	5d. deep grey-blue	14·50	20
776	7d.50 orange-yellow	3·25	1·50
777	10d. deep emerald	85·00	80
764/777 *Set of 14*		£140	4·00

149 *Argo* (5th Century, B.C.)

150 The Piraeus (Port of Athens)

(Des A. Tassos. Litho)

1958 (30 Jan). Greek Merchant Marine Commemoration. T **149** and similar horiz ship designs. W **84**. P 13½×12½.

778	50l. red, black, grey and dull blue	40	10

779 1d. ochre, black, pale blue and bright blue ... 45 20
a. Black (portholes) omitted ... £275
780 1d.50 red, black, light blue and blue ... 1·90 1·20
781 2d. brown, black, pale blue and deep violet-blue ... 55 30
782 3d.50 black, red, light blue and blue ... 2·75 1·50
a. Double impression of black ... £225
783 5d. red, black, light blue and blue-green 14·00 11·50
778/783 *Set of* 6 ... 18·00 13·50

Designs:—50l. *Michael Carras* (tanker); 1d. *Queen Frederika* (liner); 1d.50, Full-rigged sailing ship of 1821; 2d. Byzantine galley; 3d.50, 6th-century B.C. galley.

(Des A. Tassos. Litho)

1958 (1 July). AIR. Greek Ports. Various horiz designs as T **150**. W **84**. P 13½×13.

784 10d. brown-red, blue, black and pale grey 22·00 20
785 15d. brown-red, slate-blue, black and grey-drab ... 2·40 30
786 20d. ultramarine, black, brown-red and dull turquoise-blue ... 22·00 20
787 25d. brown-red, black, ultramarine and slate-grey ... 3·00 65
788 30d. brown-red, black, slate-blue and turquoise-green ... 1·90 70
789 50d. ultramarine, black and brown ... 7·50 70
790 100d. bright blue, black and yellow-brown 60·00 2·75
784/790 *Set of* 7 ... £110 5·00

Designs:—Ports of: 15d. Salonika; 20d. Patras; 25d. Hermoupolis (Syra); 30d. Volos (Thessaly); 50d. Kavalla; 100d. Heraklion (Crete).

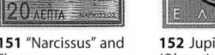

151 "Narcissus" and Flower

152 Jupiter's Head and Eagle (Olympia 4th Century B.C. coin)

(Des A. Tassos. Litho)

1958 (15 Sept). International Congress for Protection of Nature, Athens. T **151** and various mythological and floral vert designs. W **84**. P 13×13½ (20l. to 70l.), 13×12½ (1d.) or 12½×13½ (others).

791 20l. multicoloured ... 20 15
792 30l. multicoloured ... 20 15
793 50l. multicoloured ... 25 15
794 70l. multicoloured ... 35 20
795 1d. multicoloured ... 35 25
796 2d. multicoloured ... 75 50
797 3d.50 multicoloured ... 70 45
a. Imperf (pair) ... £550
798 5d. multicoloured ... 6·50 6·75
791/798 *Set of* 8 ... 8·25 7·75

Designs:—30l. "Daphne and Apollo"; 50l. "Venus and Adonis" (Venus and hibiscus); 70l. "Pan and the Nymph" (Pan and pine cones). 21½×26mm.—1d. Crocus. 22×32mm.—2d. Iris; 3d.50, Tulip; 5d. Cyclamen.

(Des A. Tassos. Litho Perivolaraki-Lykogianni)

1959 (24 Mar). Ancient Greek coins. Designs as T **152** showing both sides of each coin. W **84**. P 14×14½ (1d., 4d.50, 6d., 8d.50) or 14½×14 (others).

799 10l. grey-green, black and red-brown ... 40 10
800 20l. grey, black and blue ... 40 10
801 50l. grey, black and purple ... 45 10
802 70l. grey, black and ultramarine ... 55 20
803 1d. drab, black and carmine ... 2·00 10
804 1d.50 grey, black and yellow-brown ... 2·50 10
805 2d.50 drab, black and cerise ... 3·50 10
806 4d.50 grey, black and deep bluish green ... 8·50 50
807 6d. pale blue, black and olive ... 31·00 20
808 8d.50 drab, black and carmine-red ... 8·25 1·80
799/808 *Set of* 10 ... 50·00 3·00

Designs: Horiz—Coins showing: 20l. Athene's head and owl (Athens 5th cent B.C.); 50l. Nymph Arethusa and chariot (Syracuse 5th cent B.C.); 70l. Hercules and Jupiter (Alexander the Great 4th cent B.C.); 1d.50, Griffin and squares (Abdera, Thrace 5th cent B.C.); 2d.50, Apollo and lyre (Chalcidice, Macedonia 4th cent B.C.). Vert—1d. Helios and rose (Rhodes 4th cent B.C.); 4d.50, Apollo and labyrinth (Crete 3rd cent B.C.); 6d. Venus and Apollo (Paphos, Cyprus 4th cent B.C.); 8d.50, Ram's heads and incised squares (Delphi 5th cent B.C.).

See also Nos. 909/17.

153 Amphitheatre, Delphi

154 "Victory" and Greek soldiers through the ages

(Des A. Tassos. Litho)

1959 (20 June). Ancient Greek Theatre. Designs as T **153**. W **84**. P 13½×13 (3d.50, 4d.50) or 13×13½ (others).

809 20l. orange-brown, black, light brown and light blue ... 40 15
810 50l. red-brown, sepia and light olive-drab 40 20
811 1d. brown, yellow-brown, grey and green 45 25
812 2d.50 brown and light blue ... 85 40
813 3d.50 brown, green, grey and red ... 17·00 16·00
814 4d.50 orange-brown and black ... 2·00 90
815 6d. orange-brown, grey and black ... 2·40 1·20
809/815 *Set of* 7 ... 21·00 17·00

Designs: Vert—20l. Ancient theatre audience (after a Pharsala, Thessaly, vase of 580 B.C.); 50l. Clay mask of 3rd cent B.C.; 1d. Flute, drum and lyre; 2d.50, Actor (3rd cent statuette); 6d. Performance of a satirical play (after a mixing bowl of 410 B.C.). Horiz—3d.50, T **153**; 4d.50, Performance of Euripides' "Andromeda" (after vase of 4th cent B.C.).

1959 (29 Aug). Tenth Anniv of Greek Anti-Communist Victory. Litho. W **84**. P 13×13½.

816 **154** 2d.50 light blue, blue, black and red-brown ... 6·50 45

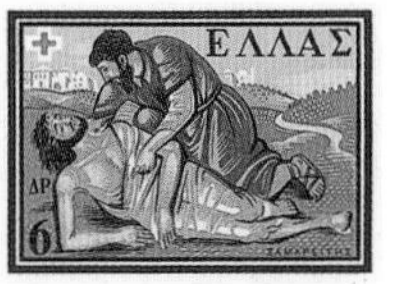

155 "The Good Samaritan"

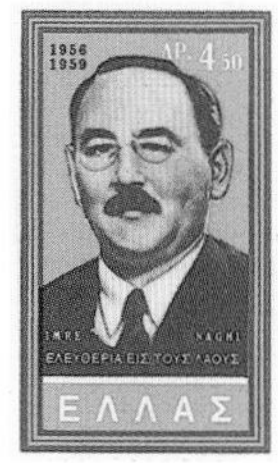

156 Imre Nagy (former Prime Minister of Hungary)

(Des A. Tassos. Litho)

1959 (21 Sept). Red Cross Commemoration. Designs as T **155**. Cross in red. W **84**. P 13½×12½ (20l., 3d., 6d.) or 12½×13½ (others).

817 20l. multicoloured ... 20 20
818 50l. deep olive-grey, red, blue and deep blue ... 35 20
819 70l. black, red-brown, yellow-brown and blue ... 50 40
820 2d.50 black, orange-brown, grey- brown and red-brown ... 85 60
821 3d. multicoloured ... 10·50 10·00
822 4d.50 black, orange-brown and red-brown 2·00 1·30
823 6d. multicoloured ... 2·20 1·00
817/823 *Set of* 7 ... 15·00 12·50

Designs: Horiz—20l. Hippocrates Tree, Cos; 6d. T **155**. Vert—50l. Bust of Aesculapius; 70l. St. Basil (after mosaic in Hosios Loukas Monastery, Boeotia); 2d.50, Achilles and Patroclus (from vase of 6th century B.C.); 3d. (32×47½ mm.) Red Cross, globe, infirm people and nurses; 4d.50, J. H. Dunant.

1959 (8 Dec). Third Anniv of Hungarian Revolt. Litho. W **84**. P 13×13½.

824 **156** 4d.50 sepia, light orange-brown and brown-red ... 2·00 2·00
825 6d. black, light blue and ultramarine 2·00 2·00

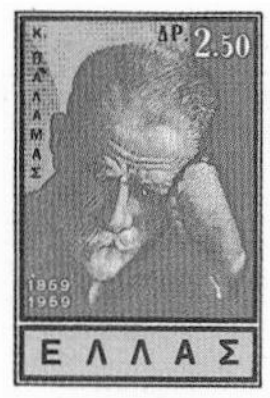

157 Kostes Palamas

158 Brig in Storm

(Des A. Tassos. Litho)

1960 (25 Jan). Birth Centenary of Palamas (poet). W **84**. P 12½×13½.

826 **157** 2d.50 magenta, pale mauve, grey and deep maroon ... 8·25 50

(Des A. Tassos. Litho)

1960 (7 Apr). World Refugee Year. T **158** and similar horiz design. W **84**. P 13½×13.

827 2d.50 multicoloured ... 70 20
828 4d.50 multicoloured ... 2·00 95

Design:—4d.50, Ship in calm waters.

159 Scout emulating St. George

160 Sprinting

(Des A. Tassos. Litho)

1960 (23 Apr). 50th Anniv of Greek Boy Scout Movement. Designs as T **159**. W **84**. P 13×13½ (20l., 30l., 40l., 2d.50) or 13½×13 (others).

829 20l. multicoloured ... 25 20
830 30l. multicoloured ... 25 20
831 40l. multicoloured ... 25 20
832 50l. multicoloured ... 25 20
833 70l. multicoloured ... 35 20
834 1d. multicoloured ... 75 30
835 2d.50 multicoloured ... 2·20 85
836 6d. multicoloured ... 3·25 2·40
829/836 *Set of* 8 ... 6·75 4·00

Designs: Vert—30l. Ephebi Oath and Scout Promise; 40l. Scouts in fire rescue work; 2d.50, Crown Prince Constantine in uniform of Chief Greek Scout. Horiz—50l. Scouts planting tree; 70l. Scouts with map; 1d. Scouts on beach; 6d. Greek Scout flag and medal.

(Des A. Tassos. Litho)

1960 (12 Aug). Olympic Games. Designs as T **160**. W **84**. P 13×13½ (20l., 70l., 2d.50, 5d.) or 13½×13 (others).

837 20l. red-brown, black and blue ... 25 20
838 50l. red-brown, brown and black ... 35 25
839 70l. red-brown, black, light green and bronze-green ... 35 25
840 80l. red-brown, black, grey and drab ... 35 25
a. Imperf (pair) ... £750
841 1d. red-brown, black, buff and blue ... 50 35
842 1d.50 red-brown, black, orange and deep brown ... 55 40
843 2d.50 red-brown, black, ultramarine and light blue ... 1·40 65
844 4d.50 red-brown, black, ultramarine, yellow and brown ... 1·60 1·00
a. Double impression of black ... £650 £750
845 5d. red-brown, black, green and turquoise ... 3·50 1·40
846 6d. red-brown, black, brown and violet-blue ... 3·50 1·40
847 12d.50 black, buff, grey, brn-red & brn ... 21·00 17·00
837/847 *Set of* 11 ... 30·00 21·00

Designs: Vert—20l. Official holding plaque; 70l. Athlete taking oath; 2d.50, Discus-throwing; 5d. Javelin-throwing. Horiz—50l. Olympic flame; 80l. Cutting olive branches; 1d. Entrance of judges; 1d.50, Long-jumping; 4d.50, T **160**; 6d. Crowning the victor; 12d.50, Quadriga or chariot-driving.

161 Conference Emblem

162 Crown Prince Constantine and *Nirefs*

(Des P. Rahikainen. Litho)

1960 (19 Sept). First Anniv of European Postal and Telecommunications Conference. W **84**. P 13½×12½.

848 **161** 4d.50 ultramarine ... 11·00 2·50

(Des A. Tassos. Litho)

1961 (18 Jan). Victory of Crown Prince in Dragon Class Yacht-races. Olympic Games. W **84**. P 13½×13.

849 **162** 2d.50 multicoloured ... 1·20 50

163 Kastoria

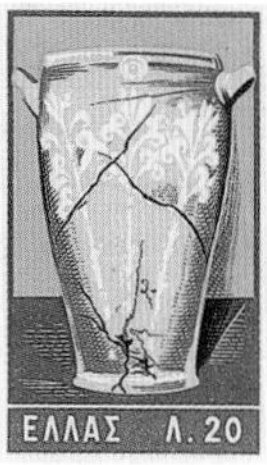

164 Lilies Vase of Knossos

(Des A. Tassos. Recess)

1961 (15 Feb). Tourist Publicity. T **163** and similar designs. W **84**. P 13½×12.

850 10l. indigo ... 15 10
851 20l. plum ... 15 10
852 50l. blue ... 15 10
853 70l. deep purple ... 20 10
854 80l. ultramarine ... 60 20
855 1d. red-brown ... 80 10
856 1d.50 emerald ... 1·40 10
857 2d.50 carmine-red ... 3·75 10
858 3d.50 reddish violet ... 1·90 50
859 4d. deep green ... 13·50 10
860 4d.50 deep blue ... 1·60 15
861 5d. lake ... 13·50 15
862 6d. myrtle-green ... 3·25 15
863 7d.50 black ... 80 20
864 8d. deep ultramarine ... 7·00 20
865 8d.50 orange-red ... 8·25 50
866 12d.50 sepia ... 2·75 95
850/866 *Set of* 17 ... 55·00 3·50

Designs: Horiz—20l. The Meteora Monasteries; 50l. Hydra; 70l. Acropolis, Athens; 80l. Mykonos; 1d. Salonika; 1d.50, Olympia; 2d.50, Knossos; 3d.50, Rhodes; 4d. Epidavros; 4d.50, Sounion; 5d. Temple of Zeus, Athens; 7d.50, Yannina; 12d.50, Delos. Vert—6d. Delphi; 8d. Mount Athos; 8d.50, Santorini.

(Des A. Tassos. Litho)

1961 (30 June). Minoan Art. T **164** and similar designs. W **84**. P 13×13½ (20l., 1d.50, 4d.50) or 13½×13 (others).

867 20l. multicoloured ... 50 15
868 50l. multicoloured ... 50 15
869 1d. multicoloured ... 70 20
870 1d.50 multicoloured ... 1·60 20
871 2d.50 multicoloured ... 8·25 20
872 4d.50 multicoloured ... 3·25 2·30
873 6d. multicoloured ... 15·00 1·60
874 10d. multicoloured ... 15·00 9·50
867/874 *Set of* 8 ... 40·00 13·00

Designs: Vert—1d.50, Knossos rhyton-bearer; 4d.50, Part of Hagia Trias sarcophagus. Horiz—50l. Partridge and fig-pecker (Knossos frieze); 1d. Kamares fruit dish; 2d.50, Ladies of Knossos Palace (painting); 6d. Knossos dancer (painting); 10d. Kamares prochus and pithos with spout.

165 Reactor Building

166 Doves

(Des A. Tassos. Litho)

1961 (31 July). Inauguration of "Democritus" Nuclear Research Centre, Aghia Paraskevi. T **165** and similar horiz design. W **84**. P 13½×13.

875 2d.50 deep magenta and mauve ... 80 35
876 4d.50 deep blue and light grey-blue ... 1·60 95

Design:—4d.50, Democritus and atomic symbol.

(Des T. Kurpershoek. Litho)

1961 (18 Sept). Europa. W **84**. P 13½×12.

877	**166** 2d.50 red and pink	40	35
	a. Pink underprint omitted	12·00	17·00
878	4d.50 ultramarine and pale blue	1·00	70

167 Emperor Nicephorus Phocas

168 "Hermes" 1l. stamp of 1861

(Des A. Tassos. Litho)

1961 (22 Sept). Millenary of Liberation of Crete from the Saracens. W **84**. P 13½×12½.

879	**167** 2d.50 multicoloured	1·10	60

1961 (20 Dec). Centenary of First Greek Postage Stamps. T **168** and similar vert designs showing "Hermes" stamps of 1861. Multicoloured. Litho. W **84**. P 13×13½.

880	20l. Type **168**	25	15
881	50l. "2l."	25	15
882	1d.50 "5l."	35	20
883	2d.50 "10l."	35	20
884	4d.50 "20l."	75	30
885	6d. "40l."	1·20	65
886	10d. "80l."	3·00	2·10
880/886 *Set of* 7		5·50	3·50

169 Ptolemais Steam Plant

170 Zappion Building

(Des A. Tassos. Litho)

1962 (14 Apr). Electrification Project. T **169** and similar designs. Multicoloured. W **84**. P 13×13½ (20l., 50l.), or 13½×13 (others).

887	20l. Tauropos Dam (vert)	20	20
888	50l. Ladhon River hydro-electric plant (vert)	25	20
889	1d. Type **169**	35	20
890	1d.50 Louros River Dam	40	20
891	2d.50 Aliverion steam plant	1·30	20
892	4d.50 Salonika hydro-electric sub-station	1·50	1·10
893	6d. Agra River power station	4·50	3·50
887/893 *Set of* 7		7·75	5·00

(Des A. Tassos. Litho)

1962 (3 May). North Atlantic Treaty Organization Ministers' Conference, Athens. T **170** and similar designs. W **84**. P 13½×12½ (2d.50), 13½×14 (6d.) or 12½×13½ (others).

894	2d.50 sepia, green, red and light blue	40	20
895	3d. sepia, brown and buff	40	20
896	4d.50 black and blue	60	40
897	6d. black and brown-red	60	40
894/897 *Set of* 4		1·80	1·10

Designs: Vert—3d. Ancient Greek warrior with shield; 4d.50, Soldier kneeling (after Marathon tomb); 6d. (21×37 mm.) Soldier (statue in Temple of Aphea, Aegina).

171 Europa "Tree"

172 "Protection"

(Des L. Weyer. Litho)

1962 (17 Sept). Europa. W **84**. P 13½×12½.

898	**171** 2d.50 red and black	1·10	35
899	4d.50 bright blue and black	3·00	1·20

1962 (30 Oct). Greek Farmers' Social Insurance Scheme. Litho. W **84** (sideways). P 13×13½.

900	**172** 1d.50 black, yellow-brown and carmine	50	20
901	2d.50 black, yellow-brown and emerald-green	70	20

173 Demeter, Goddess of Corn

174 Kings of the Greek Dynasty

(Des A. Tassos. Litho)

1963 (25 Apr). Freedom from Hunger. T **173** and similar vert design. Multicoloured. W **84**. P 12½×13½.

902	2d.50 Type **173**	50	20
903	4d.50 Wheat ears and Globe	1·10	60

(Des A. Tassos. Recess)

1963 (29 June). Centenary of Greek Royal Dynasty. W **84**. P 13½×13.

904	**174** 50l. carmine	25	10
905	1d.50 deep green	75	15
906	2d.50 red-brown	1·50	15
907	4d.50 ultramarine	3·00	80
908	6d. violet	4·00	40
904/908 *Set of* 5		8·50	1·40

1963 (5 July). As Nos. 799/808 (Ancient Greek coins), but colours changed and new values.

909	50l. drab, black and deep violet-blue (801)	20	15
910	80l. drab, black and bright purple (802)	25	20
911	1d. grey, black and green (803)	40	15
912	1d.50 drab, black and cerise (804)	1·50	15
913	3d. drab, black and olive (799)	1·00	15
914	3d.50 grey, black and red (800)	1·00	35
915	4d.50 grey, black and red-brown (806)	1·00	20
916	6d. grey, black and blue-green (807)	1·00	20
917	8d.50 grey, black and blue (808)	2·20	90
909/917 *Set of* 9		7·75	2·20

175 "Athens at Dawn" (after watercolour by Lord Baden-Powell)

176 Delphi

(Des A. Tassos. Litho)

1963 (1 Aug). 11th World Scout Jamboree, Marathon. T **175** and similar designs. W **84** (sideways on vert format). P 13½×13 (horiz) or 13×13½ (others).

918	1d. salmon, blue, olive, light brown and pale blue	35	20
919	1d.50 yellow-orange, black and deep blue	35	20
920	2d.50 flesh, black, bistre, blue, lake and grey	1·50	20
921	3d. black, cinnamon and deep green	90	65
922	4d.50 yellow-brown, brn, blk, bl & lt bl	1·70	85
918/922 *Set of* 5		4·25	1·90

Designs: Vert—1d.50, Jamboree badge; 2d.50, Crown Prince Constantine, Chief Scout of Greece; 4d.50, Scout bugling with Atlantic trumpet triton. Horiz—3d. A. Lefkadites (founder of Greek Scout Movement) and Lord Baden-Powell.

(Des A. Tassos. Litho)

1963 (16 Sept). Red Cross Centenary. T **176** and similar vert designs. Multicoloured. W **84**. P 12½×13½.

923	1d. Type **176**	65	35
924	2d. Centenary emblem	25	15
925	2d.50 Queen Olga	35	20
926	4d.50 Henri Dunant	1·20	85
923/926 *Set of* 4		2·20	1·40

177 "Co-operation"

178 Great Lavra Church

(Des A. Holm. Litho)

1963 (16 Sept). Europa. W **84**. P 13½×12½.

927	**177** 2d.50 deep green	4·25	50
928	4d.50 bright purple	8·25	3·25

(Des A. Tassos. Litho)

1963 (5 Dec). Millenary of Mt. Athos Monastic Community. T **178** and similar designs. W **84**. Multicoloured. P 13½×13 (1d., 6d.) or 13×13½ (others).

929	30l. Vatopediou Monastery	40	10
930	80l. Dionysion Monastery	40	10
931	1d. Protaton Church, Karyae	45	10
932	2d. Stavronikita Monastery	1·60	10
933	2d.50 Cover of Nicephorus Phocas Gospel, Great Lavra Church	3·50	10
934	3d.50 St. Athanasius the Athonite (fresco)	1·60	95
935	4d.50 11th-century papyrus, Iviron Monastery	1·40	45
936	6d. Type **178**	1·60	40
929/936 *Set of* 8		9·75	2·10

The 1d. and 6d. are horiz, the rest vert.

King Constantine II, 6 March 1964–1 June 1973

179 King Paul

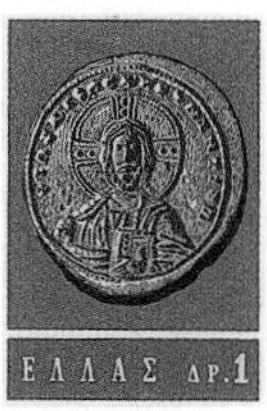

180 Gold Coin

(Des A. Tassos. Litho)

1964 (6 May). Death of Paul I. W **84**. P 12×13½.

937	**179** 30l. brown	20	10
938	50l. bright violet	25	10
939	1d. bronze-green	1·10	10
940	1d.50 red-orange	50	10
941	2d. blue	85	10
942	2d.50 deep dull purple	85	10
943	3d.50 brown-purple	1·40	20
944	4d. ultramarine	2·20	20
945	4d.50 indigo	2·40	95
946	6d. cerise	3·75	20
937/946 *Set of* 10		12·00	1·90

(Des A. Tassos. Litho)

1964 (10 June). Byzantine Art Exhibition, Athens. T **180** and similar vert designs. Multicoloured. W **84**. P 12×13½.

947	1d. Type **180**	20	10
	a. Imperf (pair)	£250	
948	1d.50 "Two Saints"	20	15
	a. Imperf (pair)	£250	
949	2d. "Archangel Michael"	20	15
	a. Imperf (pair)	£250	
950	2d.50 "Young Lady"	40	15
	a. Imperf (pair)	£250	
951	4d.50 "Angel"	1·50	90
	a. Imperf (pair)	£250	
947/951 *Set of* 5		2·30	1·30

Design origins:—1d. reign of Emperor Basil II (976–1025); 1d.50, from Harbaville's 10th-century ivory triptych (Louvre); 2d. 14th-century Constantinople icon (Byzantine Museum, Athens); 2d.50, from 14th-century fresco "The Birth of the Holy Virgin" by Panselinos (Protaton Church, Mt. Athos); 4d.50, from 11th-century mosaic (Daphne Church, Athens).

181 Trident of Paxi

182 Child

(Des A. Tassos. Litho)

1964 (20 July). Centenary of Union of Ionian Islands with Greece. T **181** and similar horiz designs inscr "1864–1964". W **84**. P 13½×12.

952	20l. greenish grey, deep greenish grey and dull blue-green	20	10
953	30l. multicoloured	20	10
954	1d. deep brown, light brown and red-brown	20	10
955	2d. multicoloured	20	10
956	2d.50 dull green, blackish olive and deep dull green	50	10
957	4d.50 multicoloured	1·30	90
958	6d. multicoloured	1·20	40
952/958 *Set of* 7		3·50	1·60

Designs:—30l. Venus of Cythera; 1d. Ulysses of Ithaca; 2d. St. George of Levkas; 2d.50, Zakynthos of Zante; 4d.50, Cephalus of Cephalonia; 6d. War galley emblem of Corfu.

(Des A. Tassos. Litho)

1964 (10 Sept). 50th Anniv of National Institution of Social Welfare (P.I.K.P.A.). W **84**. P 13½×12.

959	**182** 2d.50 multicoloured	1·10	40

183 Europa "Flower"

184 King Constantine II and Queen Anne-Marie

(Des G. Bétemps. Litho)

1964 (14 Sept). Europa. W **84**. P 13×13½.

960	**183** 2d.50 brown-red and light emerald	3·25	80
961	4d.50 brown and light drab	5·50	1·30

(Des A. Tassos. Recess)

1964 (18 Sept). Royal Wedding. W **84**. P 13½×14.

962	**184** 1d.50 deep green	35	15
963	2d.50 carmine	25	15
964	4d.50 ultramarine	70	35
962/964 *Set of* 3		1·20	60

185 Peleus and Atalanta (amphora)

186 "Christ stripping off His garments"

187 Aesculapius Theatre, Epidauros

(Des A. Tassos. Litho)

1964 (24 Oct). Olympic Games, Tokyo. T **185** and similar designs. Multicoloured. W **84**. P 12½×13½ (vert) or 13½×12½ (horiz).

965	10l. Type **185**	15	10
966	1d. Running (bowl)	20	10
967	2d. Jumping (pot)	20	10
968	2d.50 Throwing the discus	40	10

969 4d.50 Chariot-racing (sculpture) .... 1·00 60
970 6d. Boxing (vase) 45 25
971 10d. Apollo (part of frieze, Zeus Temple, Olympia) .... 1·00 50
965/971 *Set of 7* .... 3·00 1·60
The 1d., 2d., 4d.50 and 6d. are horiz.

(Des A. Tassos. Litho)

1965 (6 Mar). 350th Death Anniv of El Greco (painter). T **186** and similar designs. Multicoloured. W **84**. P 13½×12 (1d.50) or 12×13½ (others).
972 50l. Type **186** 25 20
973 1d. "Angels' Concert" 25 20
974 1d.50 El Greco's signature (horiz) 25 20
975 2d.50 Self-portrait 25 20
976 4d.50 "Storm-lashed Toledo" 60 45
972/976 *Set of 5* .... 1·40 1·20

1965 (30 Apr). Greek Artistic Festivals. T **187** and similar vert design. Multicoloured. Litho. W **84**. P 12×13½.
977 1d.50 Type **187** 40 30
978 4d.50 Herod Atticus Theatre, Athens 70 35

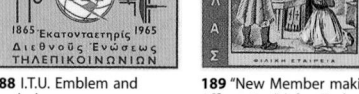

188 I.T.U. Emblem and Symbols

189 "New Member making Affirmation" (after Tsokos)

1965 (30 Apr). Centenary of International Telecommunications Union. Litho. W **84**. P 13½×12.
979 **188** 2d.50 red, deep blue and bluish grey 65 20

(Des A. Tassos. Litho)

1965 (31 May). 150th Anniv of "Philiki Hetaeria" ("Friends' Society"). T **189** and similar horiz design. Multicoloured. W **84**. P 13½×12½.
980 1d.50 Type **189** 20 10
981 4d.50 Society flag 60 30

190 AHEPA Emblem

191 Venizelos as Revolutionary

(Des A. Tassos. Litho)

1965 (30 June). American Hellenic Educational Progressive Association (AHEPA) Congress, Athens. W **84** (sideways). P 13½×12.
982 **190** 6d. black, yellow-olive and light blue 65 35

(Des and eng A. Tassos. Recess)

1965 (30 June). Birth Centenary of E. Venizelos (statesman). T **191** and similar vert designs. W **84**. P 12×13½.
983 1d.50 bronze-green 35 20
984 2d. deep blue 55 45
985 2d.50 brown 25 20
983/985 *Set of 3* .... 1·00 75
Designs:—2d. Venizelos signing Treaty of Sèvres (1920); 2d.50, Venizelos.

192 Games' Flag

193 Symbols of the Planets

(Des A. Tassos. Litho)

1965 (11 Sept). Balkan Games, Athens. T **192** and similar designs. Multicoloured. W **84**. P 13×13½ (2d.) or 13½×13 (others).
986 1d. Type **192** 20 20
987 2d. Victor's medal (vert) 20 20
988 6d. Karaiskakis Stadium, Athens 45 30
986/988 *Set of 3* 75 65

(Des A. Tassos. Litho)

1965 (11 Sept). International Astronautic Conference, Athens. T **193** and similar vert designs Multicoloured. W **84**. P 12×13½.
989 50l. Type **193** 20 20
990 2d.50 Astronaut in space 20 20
991 6d. Rocket and space-ship 45 30
989/991 *Set of 3* 75 65

194 Europa "Sprig"

195 Hipparchus (astronomer) and Astrolabe

(Des H. Karlsson. Litho)

1965 (21 Oct). Europa. W **84**. P 13½×12½.
992 **194** 2d.50 deep blue, black and pale slate-violet .... 1·90 35
993 4d.50 green, black and yellow-olive .... 2·20 70

(Des A. Tassos. Litho)

1965 (21 Oct). Opening of Evghenides Planetarium, Athens. W **84**. P 13½×12½.
994 **195** 2d.50 black, crimson & turq-grn 65 20

196 Carpenter Ants

197 St. Andrew's Church, Patras

198 T. Brysakes

(T **196/8** des A. Tassos. Litho)

1965 (30 Nov). 50th Anniv of P.O. Savings Bank. T **196** and similar vert design. Multicoloured. P 12½×13½.
995 10l. Type **196** 20 20
996 2d.50 Savings Bank and book 50 20

1965 (30 Nov). Restoration of St. Andrew's Head to Greece. T **197** and similar vert design. Multicoloured. P 12½×13½.
997 1d. Type **197** 20 20
998 5d. St. Andrew, after 11th-century mosaic, Hosios Loukas Monastery, Boeotia 40 20

1966 (28 Feb). Modern Greek Painters. Vert portraits as T **198**. Multicoloured. W **84**. P 12×13½.
999 80l. Type **198** 20 15
1000 1d. N. Lytras 20 15
1001 2d.50 C. Volonakes 20 15
1002 4d. N. Gyses 35 20
1003 5d. G. Jacobides 35 20
999/1003 *Set of 5* .... 1·10 75

199 Greek 25d. Banknote of 1867

200 Geannares (revolutionary leader)

(Des A. Tassos. Recess)

1966 (30 Mar). 125th Anniv of Greek National Bank. T **199** and similar designs. W **84**. P 12½×13½.
1004 1d.50 bronze-green 25 10
1005 2d.50 brown 25 10
1006 4d. royal blue 35 15
1007 6d. black 55 30
1004/1007 *Set of 4* .... 1·30 60
Designs: Vert (23×33½ mm.)—1d.50, J.-G. Eynard; 2d.50, G. Stavros (founders). Horiz (As T **199**)—4d. National Bank headquarters, Athens.

(Des A. Tassos. Litho)

1966 (18 Apr). Centenary of Cretan Revolt. T **200** and similar designs. Multicoloured. W **84**. P 12×13½ (2d.) or 13½×12 (others).
1008 2d. Type **200** 25 15
1009 2d.50 Explosion of gun-powder machine, Arkadi Monastery (horiz) 25 15
1010 4d.50 Map of Crete (horiz) 40 30
1008/1010 *Set of 3* 80 55

201 "Movement of Water" (Decade of World Hydrology)

202 Tragedian's Mask of 4th Century B.C.

(Des A. Tassos. Litho)

1966 (18 Apr). United Nations Events. T **201** and similar designs. W **84**. P 13½×12 (5d.) or 12×13½ (others).
1011 1d. grey-blue, orange-brown and black 25 15
1012 3d. multicoloured 25 15
1013 5d. black, new blue and brown-red 40 30
1011/1013 *Set of 3* 80 55
Designs: Vert—3d. United Nations Educational, Scientific and Cultural Organization emblem (20th anniv). Horiz—5d. World Health Organization building (inauguration of headquarters, Geneva).

(Des A. Tassos. Litho)

1966 (26 May). 2,500th Anniv of Greek Theatre. T **202** and similar designs. W **84**. P 12×13½ (vert) or 13½×12 (horiz).
1014 1d. yellow-green, black, blue and grey 20 15
1015 1d.50 black, red and orange-brown 20 15
1016 2d.50 black, green and pale yellow-green 20 15
1017 4d.50 red, flesh, black and reddish lilac 50 30
1014/1017 *Set of 4* .... 1·00 70

Designs: Horiz—1d.50, Dionysus in a Thespian ship-chariot (vase painting, 500–480 B.C.); 2d.50, Theatre of Dionysus, Athens. Vert—4d.50, Dionysus dancing (after vase painting by Kleophrades, circa 500 B.C.).

203 Boeing 707 Jetliner crossing Atlantic Ocean

204 Tending Plants

(Des A. Tassos. Litho)

1966 (26 May). Inauguration of Greek Airways' Transatlantic Flights. W **84**. P 13½×13.
1018 **203** 6d. deep blue, new blue and light blue 60 35

(Des A. Tassos. Litho)

1966 (19 Sept). Greek Tobacco. T **204** and similar vert design. Multicoloured. W **84**. P 12×13½.
1019 1d. Type **204** 25 15
1020 5d. Sorting leaf 70 40

205 Europa "Ship"

206 Horseman (embroidery)

(Des G. and J. Bender. Litho)

1966 (19 Sept). Europa. W **84**. P 12×13½.
1021 **205** 1d.50 olive-black, yellow-olive and light yellow-olive .... 1·10 35
1022 4d.50 deep red-brown, light red-brown and pale red-brown .... 3·00 65

(Des A. Tassos. Litho)

1966 (21 Nov). Greek "Popular" Art. T **206** and similar designs. Multicoloured. W **84**. P 12×13½ (vert) or 13½×12 (horiz).
1023 10l. Knitting-needle boxes 20 10
1024 30l. Type **206** 20 10
1025 50l. Cretan lyre 20 10
1026 1d. "Massa" (Musical instrument) 20 10
1027 1d.50 "Cross and Angels" (bas-relief after Melios) 20 10
1028 2d. "Sts. Constantine and Helen" (icon) .... 1·20 10
1029 2d.50 Carved altar-screen, St. Nicholas' Church, Galaxidion 25 10
1030 3d. 19th-century ship of Skyros (embroidery) 25 10
1031 4d. "Psiki" (wedding procession) (embroidery) .... 1·10 10
1032 4d.50 Distaff 50 25
1033 5d. Earrings and necklace 90 10
1034 20d. Detail of handwoven cloth .... 2·75 60
1023/1034 *Set of 12* .... 7·25 1·70
The 10l., 50l., 1d., 1d.50, 2d. 2d.50, 4d.50 and 5d. designs are vertical.

207 Princess Alexia

208 "Woodcutter" (after D. Filippotes)

(Des A. Tassos. Recess)

1966 (19 Dec). Princess Alexia's First Birthday (July 10th, 1966). T **207** and similar vert designs. W **84**. P 13½×14.
1035 2d. green 30 15
1036 2d.50 chocolate 35 15
1037 3d.50 ultramarine 65 30
1035/1037 *Set of 3* .... 1·20 55
Portraits:—2d.50, Royal Family; 3d.50, Queen Anne-Marie with Princess Alexia.

(Des A. Tassos. Litho)

1967 (28 Feb). Greek Sculpture. T **208** and similar designs. Multicoloured. W **84**. P 12×13½ (vert) or 13½×12 (horiz).
1038 20l. "Night" (I. Cossos) 15 10
1039 50l. "Penelope" (L. Drossos) 15 10
1040 80l. "Shepherd" (G. Phitalis) 15 10
1041 2d. "Woman's Torso" (K. Demetriades) 35 10
1042 2d.50 "Kolokotronis" (L. Sochos) 25 10
1043 3d. "Girl Sleeping" (I. Halepas) 90 35
1044 10d. Type **208** 60 30
1038/1044 *Set of 7* .... 2·30 1·00
The 20l. to 2d.50 are vert designs.

209 Olympic Rings ("Olympic Day")

210 Cogwheels

(Des A. Tassos. Litho)

1967 (6 Apr). Sports Events. T **209** and similar multicoloured designs. W **84**. P 12×13½ (5d.) or 13½×12 (others).

1045	1d. Type **209**	25	10
1046	1d.50 Marathon Cup, first Olympics (1896)	25	10
1047	2d.50 Hurdling	35	15
1048	5d. "The Discus-thrower", after C. Demietriades	65	45
1049	6d. Ancient Olympic stadium	1·00	30
1045/1049 *Set of 5*		2·30	1·00

The 2d.50 commemorates the European Athletics Cup, 1967; the 5d. (vert), the European Highest Award Championships, 1968; and the 6d. the Inauguration of "International Academy" buildings, Olympia.

(Des O. Bonnevalle. Litho)

1967 (2 May). Europa. W **84**. P 12×13½.

1050	**210**	2d.50 brown, light brown, black and pale brown	1·40	30
1051		4d.50 bronze-green, light green, black and pale green	3·50	1·00

211 *Lonchi* (destroyer) and Sailor

212 The Plaka, Athens

(Des A. Tassos. Litho)

1967 (26 June). Nautical Week. T **211** and similar designs. W **84**. P 12×13½ (1d.) or 13½×12 (others).

1052	20l. multicoloured	25	15
1053	1d. multicoloured	25	15
1054	2d.50 multicoloured	25	15
1055	3d. multicoloured	80	50
1056	6d. multicoloured	60	35
1052/1056 *Set of 5*		1·90	1·20

Designs: Vert—1d. *Eugene Eugenides* (cadet ship). Horiz—2d.50, Merchant Marine Academy, Aspropyrgos, Attica; 3d. *Averoff* (cruiser) and Naval School, Poros; 6d. *Australis* (liner) and figurehead.

(Des A. Tassos. Litho)

1967 (26 June). International Tourist Year. T **212** and similar designs. W **84**. P 12×13½ (6d.) or 13½×12 (others).

1057	2d.50 multicoloured	20	10
1058	4d.50 multicoloured	1·00	30
1059	6d. multicoloured	80	20
1057/1059 *Set of 3*		1·80	55

Designs: Horiz—2d.50, Island of Skopelos; 4.d.50, Apollo's Temple, Bassai, Peloponnese.

213 Soldier and Phoenix

214 Industrial Skyline

(Design suggested by A. Skylitses, Mayor of Piraeus. Litho)

1967 (30 Aug). National Revolution of 21 April (1967). W **84**. P 12×13½.

1060	**213**	2d.50 multicoloured	15	10
1061		3d. multicoloured	20	15
1062		4d.50 multicoloured	65	45
1060/1062 *Set of 3*			90	65

1967 (29 Nov). First Convention of UN. Industrial Development Organization, Athens. Litho. W **84**. P 13½×14.

1063	**214**	4d.50 ultramarine, black and light blue	65	40

215 "Seaside Scene" (A. Pelaletos)

216 Throwing the Javelin

(Des by schoolchildren (names in brackets). Litho)

1967 (20 Dec). Children's Drawings. T **215** and similar horiz designs. Multicoloured. W **84**. P 13½×12½.

1064	20l. Type **215**	20	10
1065	1d.50 "Steamer and Island" (L. Tsirikas)	20	10
1066	3d.50 "Country Cottage" (K. Ambeliotis)	60	50
1067	6d. "The Church on the Hill" (N. Frangos)	50	20
1064/1067 *Set of 4*		1·40	80

(Des G. Velissarides (50l., 1d., 6d.), S.E.G.A.S. Bureau (others). Litho)

1968 (28 Feb). Sports Events, 1968. T **216** and similar designs. W **84**. P 12½.

1068	50l. multicoloured	25	10
1069	1d. multicoloured	25	10
1070	1d.50 multicoloured	25	10
1071	2d.50 multicoloured	40	10
1072	4d. multicoloured	50	30
1073	4d.50 multicoloured	1·20	60
1074	6d. multicoloured	60	20
1068/1074 *Set of 7*		3·00	1·40

Designs: Horiz—1d. Long-jumping; 4d. Olympic rings (Olympic Day). Vert—1d.50, "Apollo's Head", Temple of Zeus; 2d.50, Olympic scene on Attic vase; 4d.50, "Throwing the Discus", sculpture by Demetriades (European Athletic Championships, 1969); 6d. Long-distance running.

The 50l., 1d. and 6d. publicise the Balkan Games and the 1d.50 and 2d.50 the Olympic Academy Meeting.

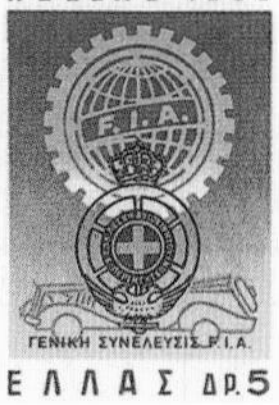

217 F.I.A. and E.L.P.A. Emblems

218 Europa "Key"

(Des Greek Auto & Touring Club (E.L.P.A.). Litho)

1968 (29 Mar). General Assembly of International Automobile Federation (F.I.A.), Athens. W **84**. P 13½×14.

1075	**217**	5d. blue and orange-brown	1·10	40

(Des H. Schwarzenbach. Litho)

1968 (29 Mar). Europa. W **84**. P 13½×12.

1076	**218**	2d.50 bistre, brown, black and brown-red	1·90	40
1077		4d.50 bistre, brown, black and bluish-violet	3·00	1·20

219 "Athene defeats Alkyoneus" (from frieze, Altar of Zeus, Pergamos)

1968 (27 Apr). "Hellenic Fight for Civilization" Exhibition, Athens. T **219** and similar multicoloured designs. Litho. W **84**. P 13½×13 (10l., 1d.50), 13½×14 (20l., 50l., 2d.50) or 13×13½ (3d., 4d.50, 6d.).

1078	10l. Type **219**	20	10
1079	20l. Athene attired for battle (bronze from Piraeus)	20	10
1080	50l. Alexander the Great (from sarcophagus of Alexander of Sidon)	25	10
1081	1d.50 Emperors Constantine and Justinian making offerings to the Holy Mother (Byzantine mosaic)	30	20
1082	2d.50 Emperor Constantine Paleologos (lithograph by D.Tsokos)	30	15
1083	3d. "Greece in Missolonghi" (painting by Delacroix)	30	20
1084	4d.50 "Evzone" (Greek soldier, painting by G.B. Scott)	55	40
1085	6d. "Victory of Samothrace" (statue)	60	45
1078/1085 *Set of 8*		2·50	1·50

The 1d.50 is horiz as T **219**, the 20l., 50l., and 2d.50 are 24×37 mm, and the remainder 28×40 mm.

220 "The Unknown Priest and Teacher" (Rhodes monument)

221 Congress Emblem

(Des G. Velissarides (2d.), P. Gravalos (5d.). Litho)

1968 (11 July). 20th Anniv of Dodecanese Union with Greece. T **220** and similar multicoloured design. W **84**. P 14×13½ (2d.) or 13½×14 (5d.).

1086	2d. Type **220**	50	10
1087	5d. Greek flag on map (vert)	1·50	75

(Des P. Gravalos. Litho)

1968 (11 July). 19th Biennial Congress of Greek Orthodox Archdiocese of North and South America. W **84**. P 13½×14.

1088	**221**	6d. multicoloured	1·00	40

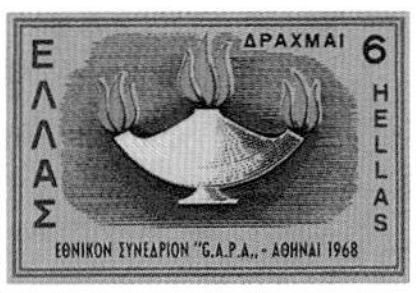

222 GAPA Emblem

223 "Hand of Aesculapius" (fragment of bas relief; from Asclepios Temple, Athens)

(Des G. Velissarides. Litho)

1968 (11 July). Regional Congress of Greek-American Progressive Association (GAPA). W **84**. P 14×13½.

1089	**222**	6d. multicoloured	1·00	40

(Des by Congress committee. Litho)

1968 (8 Sept). Fifth European Cardiological Congress, Athens. W **84**. P 13½×14.

1090	**223**	4d.50 black, orange-yellow and brown-lake	1·90	1·00

224 Panathenaic Stadium

225 P.Z.L. P.24 1 ramming Savoia Marchetti S.M.79-11 Sparviero Bomber

(Des P. Gravalos. Litho)

1968 (25 Sept). Olympic Games, Mexico. T **224** and similar multicoloured designs. W **84**. P 13×14 (10d.) or 14×13½ (others).

1091	2d.50 Type **224**	50	20
1092	5d. Ancient Olympia	90	25
1093	10d. One of Pindar's odes	2·10	90
1091/1093 *Set of 3*		3·25	1·20

The 10d. is vert (28×40 mm.).

(Des G. Velissarides (2d.50), P. Gravalos (others). Litho)

1968 (8 Nov). Royal Hellenic Air Force. T **225** and similar multicoloured designs. W **84**. P 13½×14 (8d.) or 14×13½ (others).

1094	2d.50 Type **225**	35	10
1095	3d.50 Mediterranean flight in Breguet 19 bomber, 1928	50	20
1096	8d. Farman H.F.111 biplane and Lockheed F-104G Super Starfighter (vert)	1·10	70
1094/1096 *Set of 3*		1·80	90

226 Goddess "Hygeia"

227 St. Zeno, the Letter-carrier

(Des G. Velissarides. Litho)

1968 (8 Nov). 20th Anniv of World Health Organization. W **84**. P 13½×14.

1097	**226**	5d. multicoloured	1·20	40

(Des P. Gravalos. Litho)

1969 (10 Feb). Greek Post Office Festival. W **84**. P 13½×14.

1098	**227**	2d.50 multicoloured	80	40

228 "Workers Festival Parade" (detail from Minoan vase)

229 Yacht Harbour, Vouliagmeni

(Des G. Velissarides (1d.50), P. Gravalos (10d.). Litho)

1969 (10 Feb). 50th Anniv of International Labour Organization. T **228** and similar horiz design. Multicoloured. W **84**. P 13½×12½.

1099	1d.50 "Hephaestus and Cyclops" (detail from ancient bas-relief)	40	10
1100	10d. Type **228**	1·30	75

(Des P. Gravalos (1d.), G. Velissarides (others). Litho)

1969 (12 Mar). Tourism. T **229** and similar multicoloured designs. W **84**. P 13×13½ (5d.) or 13½×13 (others).

1101	1d. Type **229**	35	10
1102	5d. "Chorus of Elders" (Ancient drama) (vert)	1·30	80
1103	6d. View of Astypalia	45	20
1101/1103 *Set of 3*		1·90	1·00

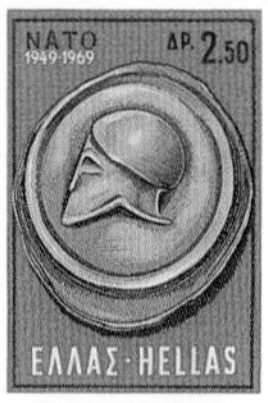

230 Ancient Coin of Kamarina **231** Colonnade

(Des G. Velissarides (2d.50), P. Gravalos (4d.50). Litho)

1969 (4 Apr). 20th Anniv of North Atlantic Treaty Organization. T **230** and similar multicoloured design. W **84**. P 12½×13½ (2d.50) or 13½×12½ (4d.50).

1104 2d.50 Type **230** 45 20
1105 4d.50 "Going into Battle" (from Corinthian vase) (horiz) ..... 1·20 90

(Des L. Gasbarra and G. Belli. Litho)

1969 (5 May). Europa. W **84**. P 13½×12.

1106 **231** 2d.50 multicoloured ..... 4·25 30
1107 4d.50 multicoloured ..... 7·50 1·60

232 Gold Medal **233** "19th-century Brig and Steamship" (I. Poulakas)

(Des G. Velissarides (20l.), P. Gravalos (others). Litho)

1969 (5 May). Ninth European Athletic Championships, Athens. T **232** and similar multicoloured designs. W **84**. P 12×13½ (vert) or 13½×12 (horiz).

1108 20l. Type **232** 20 15
1109 3d. Pole-vaulting, and ancient pentathlon contest 35 20
1110 5d. Relay-racing, and Olympic race *c.*525 B.C. (horiz) 45 20
1111 8d. Throwing the discus, modern and *c.*480 B.C. ..... 2·10 95
1108/1111 *Set of* 4 ..... 2·75 1·40

(Des L. Montesantou (2d., 4d.50), P. Gravalos (others). Litho)

1969 (28 June). Navy Week and Merchant Marine Year. T **233** and similar multicoloured designs. W **84**. P 12×13½ (80l.), 13½×12 (2d., 4d.50) or 13½×12½ (others).

1112 80l. Type **233** 20 10
1113 2d. *Olympic Garland* (tanker) (horiz) 20 10
1114 2d.50 "*Themistocles* and *Karteria*, War of Independence, 1821" (anon) (41×29 mm) 35 10
1115 4d.50 *Velos* (modern destroyer) (horiz) ..... 1·30 45
1116 6d. "The Battle of Salamis" (K. Volonakis) (41×29 mm) ..... 1·80 85
1112/1116 *Set of* 5 ..... 3·50 1·40

234 Raising the Flag on Mt. Grammos

(Des P. Gravalos, from Army photograph. Litho)

1969 (31 Aug). 20th Anniv of Communists' Defeat on Mounts Grammos and Vitsi. W **84**. P 12½×13½.

1117 **234** 2d.50 multicoloured ..... 1·10 40

235 Athena Promachos **236** Demetrius Karatasios (statue by G. Demetriades)

(Des P. Gravalos. Litho)

1969 (12 Oct). 25th Anniversary of the Liberation. T **235** and similar vert designs. Multicoloured. W **84**. P 13½×14 (5d.) or 12½×13½ (others).

1118 4d. Type **235** 35 10
1119 5d. "Resistance" (21×37 mm.) ..... 1·80 80
1120 6d. Map of Eastern Mediterranean theatre 50 10
1118/1120 *Set of* 3 ..... 2·40 90

(Des G. Velissarides (1d.50, 2d.50), P. Gravalos (others). Litho)

1969 (12 Nov). Heroes of Macedonia's Fight for Freedom. T **236** and similar vert designs. Multicoloured. W **84**. P 12×13½.

1121 1d.50 Type **236** 20 10
1122 2d.50 Emmanuel Pappas (statue by N. Perantinos) 20 10
1123 3d.50 Pavlos Melas (from painting by P. Mathiopoulos) 25 25
1124 4d.50 Capetan Kolas ..... 1·00 75
1121/1124 *Set of* 4 ..... 1·50 1·10

237 Dolphin Mosaic, Delos. (110 B.C.) **238** Overwhelming the Cretan Bull (sculpture)

(Des G. Velissarides (1d.50, 5d.), P. Gravalos (others) Litho)

1970 (16 Jan). Greek Mosaics. T **237** and similar multicoloured designs. W **84**. P 13½×12½ (1d.), 12½×13½ (6d.) or 12×13½ (others).

1125 20l. "Angel of the Annunciation", Daphne (11th-century) (vert) 20 10
1126 1d. Type **237** 20 10
1127 1d.50 "The Holy Ghost", Hosios Loukas Monastery (11th-century) (vert) 25 20
1128 2d. "Hunter", Pella (4th-century B.C.) (vert) 55 10
1129 5d. "Bird", St. George's Church, Salonika (5th-century) (vert) 65 20
1130 6d. "Christ", Nea Moni Church, Khios (5th-century) (vert) ..... 1·40 1·00
1125/1130 *Set of* 6 ..... 3·00 1·50

Nos. 1125 and 1127/9 are smaller, 23×34 mm.

(Des G. Velissarides (1d., 1d.50, 2d.), P. Gravalos (others). Litho)

1970 (16 Mar). "The Labours of Hercules". T **238** and similar designs. W **84**. P 13½×12 (horiz) or 12×13½ (vert).

1131 20l. multicoloured 20 10
1132 30l. multicoloured 20 10
1133 1d. black, pale blue and slate-blue 45 10
1134 1d.50 agate, sage-green & yell-ochre 45 10
1135 2d. multicoloured ..... 2·75 10
1136 2d.50 sepia, dull scarlet and buff 40 10
1137 3d. multicoloured ..... 2·75 10
1138 4d.50 multicoloured 40 20
1139 5d. multicoloured 55 15
1140 6d. multicoloured 55 15
1141 20d. multicoloured ..... 2·30 70
1131/1141 *Set of* 11 ..... 10·00 1·70

Designs: Horiz—30l. Hercules and Cerberus (from decorated pitcher); 1d.50, The Lernean Hydra (from stamnos); 2d. Hercules and Geryon (from amphora); 4d.50, Combat with the River-god Achelous (from pitcher); 5d. Overwhelming the Nemean Lion (from amphora); 6d. The Stymphalian Birds (from vase); 20d. Wrestling with Antaeus (from bowl). Vert—1d. Golden Apples of the Hesperides (sculpture); 2d.50, The Erymanthine Boar (from amphora); 3d. The Centaur Nessus (from vase).

239 "Flaming Sun" **240** Satellite and Dish Aerial

(Des P. Gravalos (3d.), L. le Brocquy (others). Litho)

1970 (21 Apr). Europa. T **239** and similar design. W **84**. P 12×13½ (3d.) or 13½×12 (others).

1142 **239** 2d.50 orange-yellow and cerise ..... 3·25 65
1143 – 3d. deep blue and new blue ..... 3·25 70
1144 **239** 4d.50 orange-yellow and ultramarine ..... 10·50 2·40
1142/1144 *Set of* 3 ..... 15·00 3·50

Design: Vert—3d. "Owl" and C.E.P.T. emblem.

(Des G. Velissarides. Litho)

1970 (21 Apr). Satellite Earth Telecommunications Station, Thermopylae. W **84**. P 13½×12.

1145 **240** 2d.50 multicoloured 55 25
1146 4d.50 multicoloured ..... 1·50 1·00

241 Saints Cyril and Methodius with Emperor Michael III (from 12th-century wall-painting) **242** Cephalonian Fir

(Des G. Velissarides (5d.), P. Gravalos (others). Litho)

1970 (17 May). Saints Cyril and Methodius Commemoration. T **241** and similar vert designs. Multicoloured. W **84**. P 13½×14 (50l.), 12½×13½ (5d.) or 12×13½ (others).

1147 50l. Saints Demetrius, Cyril and Methodius (mosaic) (21×37 mm) 20 15
1148 2d. St. Cyril (Russian miniature) (25×32 mm) 85 65
a. Horiz pair. Nos. 1148 and 1150 ..... 1·80 80
1149 5d. Type **241** 55 20
1150 10d. St. Methodius (Russian miniature) (25×32 mm) 90 65
1147/1150 *Set of* 4 ..... 2·30 1·50

Nos. 1148 and 1150 were issued together in horizontal *se-tenant* pairs within the sheet, each pair forming a composite design.

(Des G. Velissarides (2d.50), P. Gravalos (others). Litho)

1970 (1 June). Nature Conservation Year. T **242** and similar multicoloured designs. W **84**. P 12×13½ (2d.50), 13½×12½ (6d.) or 12½×13½ (others).

1151 80l. Type **242** 45 40
1152 2d.50 *Jankaea heldreichii* (plant) ..... 1·70 30
1153 6d. Rock partridge (horiz) ..... 2·75 50
1154 8d. Wild goat ..... 3·75 3·00
1151/1154 *Set of* 4 ..... 7·75 3·25

No. 1152 is smaller, 23×34 mm.

243 "Cultural Links" **244** New U.P.U. Headquarters Building, Berne (Opening)

(Des G. Velissarides. Litho)

1970 (1 Aug). American-Hellenic Educational Progressive Association Congress, Athens. W **84**. P 13½×12½.

1155 **243** 6d. multicoloured ..... 1·50 40

(Des G. Velissarides (50l., 4d.50), P. Gravalos (others). Litho)

1970 (7 Oct). Anniversaries. T **244** and similar multicoloured designs. W **84**. P 13½×12 (50l.), 12×13½ (3d.50, 4d.) or 12½×13½ (others).

1156 50l. Type **244** 15 10
1157 2d.50 Emblem (Int Education Year) (vert) 55 10
1158 3d.50 Mahatma Gandhi (birth cent) (vert) 25 20
1159 4d. "25" (25th anniv of United Nations) (vert) ..... 1·10 10
1160 4d.50 Beethoven (birth bicentenary) (vert) ..... 2·30 1·40
1156/1160 *Set of* 5 ..... 4·00 1·70

Nos. 1157 and 1160 are larger, 28½×41 mm.

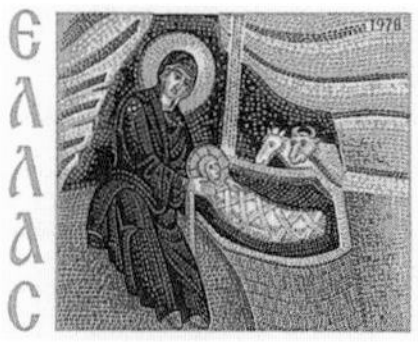

245 "The Nativity"

(Des G. Velissarides (2d.), P. Gravalos (others). Litho)

1970 (5 Dec). Christmas. Scenes from "The Mosaic of the Nativity", Hosios Loukas Monastery. T **245** and similar multicoloured designs. W **84**. P 13½×12½ (6d.) or 12½×13½ (others).

1161 2d. "The Shepherds" (vert) 30 20
1162 4d.50 "The Magi" (vert) 55 35
1163 6d. Type **245** ..... 1·30 90
1161/1163 *Set of* 3 ..... 1·90 1·30

246 "Death of Bishop of Salona in Battle, Alamana" (lithograph)

(Des G. Velissarides (50l., 2d.), P. Gravalos (others). Litho)

1971 (8 Feb). 150th Anniv of War of Independence (1st Issue). The Church. T **246** and similar multicoloured designs. W **84**. P 13×13½ (50l., 2d.) or 12×13½ (others).

1164 50l. Warriors taking the oath (medal) (vert) 20 20
1165 2d. Patriarch Gregory V (statue by Phitalis) (vert) 25 20
1166 4d. Type **246** 35 20
1167 10d. "Bishop Germanos blessing the Standard" (Vryzakis) ..... 1·60 1·10
1164/1167 *Set of* 4 ..... 2·20 1·50

See also Nos. 1168/73, 1178/80, 1181/6 and 1187/9.

(Des G. Velissarides (6d.), P. Gravalos (others). Litho)

1971 (15 Mar). 150th Anniv of War of Independence (2nd Issue). The War at Sea. Horiz designs dated as T **246**. Multicoloured. W **84**. P 13½×12½ (3d., 6d.) or 13½×13 (others).

1168 20l. *Leonidas* (warship) (37×24 mm) 25 20
1169 1d. *Pericles* (warship) (37×24 mm) 35 20
1170 1d.50 *Terpsichore* (warship) (from painting by Roux) (37×24 mm) 35 20
1171 2d.50 *Karteria* (warship) (from painting by Hastings) (37×24 mm) 35 20
1172 3d. "Battle of Samos" (contemporary painting) (40×28 mm) 95 40
1173 6d. "Turkish Frigate ablaze, Battle of Yeronda" (Michalis) (40×28 mm) ..... 2·00 95
1168/1173 *Set of* 6 ..... 3·75 1·90

247 Spyridon Louis winning Marathon, Athens 1896

(Des P. Gravalos (3d.), G. Velissarides (8d.). Litho)

1971 (10 Apr). 75th Anniversary of Olympic Games Revival. T **247** and similar multicoloured design. W **84**. P 13½×13 (3d.) or 13×13½ (8d.).

1174 3d. Type **247** 80 20
1175 8d. P. de Coubertin and Memorial, Olympia (vert) .... 2·20 1·10

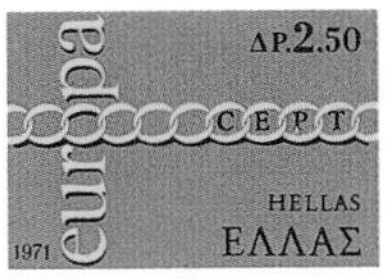

248 Europa Chain

249 Kaltetsi Monastery and Seal of Peloponnesian Senate

(Des H. Haflidason. Litho)

1971 (18 May). Europa. W **84**. P 13½×12.

1176 **248** 2d.50 yellow, emerald and black .... 3·25 40
1177 5d. yellow, orange and black .... 9·75 1·90

(Des P. Gravalos (15d.), G. Velissarides (others). Litho)

1971 (21 June). 150th Anniv of War of Independence (3rd Issue). "Teaching the People". Multicoloured designs dated as T **246**. W **84**. P 12×13½.

1178 50l. Eugenius Voulgaris 25 10
1179 2d.50 Dr. Adamantios Korais 25 20
1180 15d. "The Secret School" (N. Ghyzis) .... 1·90 1·20
1178/1180 *Set of 3* .... 2·20 1·40

Sizes:—50l., 2d.50, 23×34 mm. 15d. as T **246**.

(Des G. Velissarides (1d., 9d.), P. Gravalos (others). Litho)

1971 (21 Sept). 150th Anniv of War of Independence (4th Issue). The War on Land. Multicoloured designs dated as T **246**. W **84**. P 12×13½ (6d.50, 9d.), 13½×12½ (2d.) or 12½×13½ (others).

1181 50l. "Battle of Corinth" (Krazeisen) 35 20
1182 1d. "Sacrifice of Kapsalis" (Vryzakis) 35 20
1183 2d. "Suliot Women in Battle" (Deneuville) 35 20
1184 5d. "Battle of Athens" (Zographos) 40 20
1185 6d.50 "Battle of Maniaki" (lithograph) 60 20
1186 9d. "Death of Markos Botsaris at Karpenisi" (Vryzakis) .... 1·40 95
1181/1186 *Set of 6* .... 3·00 1·80

Sizes:—50l., 1d., 5d. 25×50 mm. 2d.40×25 mm. 6d.50, 9d. as T **246**.

(Des G. Velissarides (20d.), P. Gravalos (others). Litho)

1971 (19 Oct). 150th Anniv of War of Independence (5th Issue). Government. T **249** and similar horiz designs. W **84**. P 13½×12½.

1187 2d. black, light green and yellow-brown 40 20
1188 2d.50 black, light blue and blue 40 20
1189 20d. black, light olive-yellow and sepia .... 2·50 1·70
1187/1189 *Set of 3* .... 3·00 1·90

Designs:—2d.50, National Assembly Memorial, Epidavros, and Seal of Provincial Administration; 20d. Signature and seal of John Capodistria, first President of Greece.

250 Hosios Loukas Monastery, Boeotia

251 Cretan Costume

(Des P. Gravalos. Litho)

1972 (17 Jan). Greek Monasteries and Churches. T **250** and similar horiz designs. Multicoloured. W **84**. P 14×13½.

1190 50l. Type **250** 15 10
1191 1d. Daphni Church, Attica 15 10
1192 2d. Monastery of St. John the Divine, Patmos 20 10
1193 2d.50 Panaghia Koumbelidiki Church, Kastoria 20 10
1194 4d.50 Panaghia ton Chalkeon, Salonika 30 20
1195 6d.50 Panaghia Paregoritissa Church, Arta 30 20
1196 8d.50 St. Paul's Monastery, Mount Athos .... 1·80 1·50
1190/1196 *Set of 7* .... 2·75 2·10

(Des G. Velissarides (2, 3 and 4d.50), P. Gravalos (others). Litho)

1972 (1 Mar). Greek Regional Costumes (1st series). Exhibits from Benaki Museum. T **251** and similar vert designs inscr "1972". Multicoloured. W **84**. P 12×13½.

1197 50l. Type **251** 15 10
1198 1d. Pindus bride 15 10
1199 2d. Warrior-chief, Missolonghi 15 10
1200 2d.50 Sarakatsan woman, Attica 15 10
a. "1972" omitted .... 11·00 2·10
1201 3d. Nisiros woman 20 10
1202 4d.50 Megara woman 25 10
1203 6d.50 Trikeri woman 35 10
1204 10d. Pylaia woman, Macedonia .... 4·00 1·40
1197/1204 *Set of 8* .... 4·75 1·90

No. 1200a occurs on R1/5 on sheets from the end of the printing.

See also Nos. 1232/48 and 1282/96.

252 Flag and Map

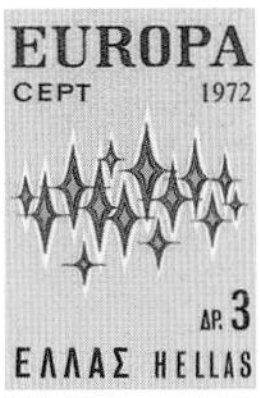

253 "Communications"

(Des G. Velissarides (2d.50) and P. Gravalos (others). Litho)

1972 (21 Apr). Fifth Anniv of 1967 Revolution. T **252** and similar multicoloured designs. W **84**. P 13×13½.

1205 2d.50 Commemorative medal (horiz) 20 10
1206 4d.50 Type **252** 45 25
1207 5d. Facets of modern development 60 40
1205/1207 *Set of 3* .... 1·10 70

(Des P. Huovinen. Litho)

1972 (2 May). Europa. W **84**. P 12½×13½.

1208 **253** 3d. multicoloured .... 1·40 35
1209 4d.50 multicoloured .... 3·50 1·50

254 Acropolis, Athens

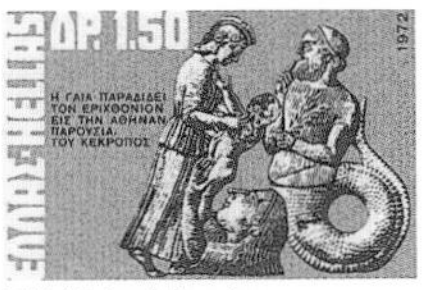

255 "Gaia delivering Erecthonius to Athene"

(Des P. Gravalos. Litho)

1972 (26 May). 20th Anniv of Acropolis Motor Rally. T **254** and similar horiz design. Multicoloured. W **84**. P 13½×12½.

1210 4d.50 Type **254** 90 65
1211 5d. Emblem and map 90 65

(Des I. Svoronos. Litho)

1972 (26 June). Greek Mythology. Museum Pieces (1st series). T **255** and similar horiz designs. W **84**. P 14×13½.

1212 1d.50 black and yellow-olive 25 10
a. Horiz strip of 4. Nos. 1212/15 .... 1·80
1213 2d. black and Prussian blue 25 20
1214 2d.50 black and orange-brown 25 20
1215 5d. black and deep brown 90 50
1212/1215 *Set of 4* .... 1·50 90

Designs:—2d. "Uranus" (altar-piece); 2d.50, "The Gods repulsing the Giants"; 5d. "Zeus".

Nos. 1212/15 were issued together in horizontal *se-tenant* strips of four within the sheet of 40 stamps. The three low values were also each issued in separate sheets of 50 stamps (*Price per horiz pair of one value: £36 un, £35 used*).

See also Nos. 1252/5 and 1271/4.

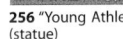

256 "Young Athlete" (statue)

257 Young Stamp Collector

(Des P. Gravalos. Litho)

1972 (28 July). Olympic Games, Munich. Ancient Olympics. T **256** and similar multicoloured designs. W **84**. P 13½×14 (vert) or 14×13½ (horiz).

1216 50l. Type **256** 25 15
1217 1d.50 "Wrestlers" (bas-relief) (horiz) 25 15
1218 3d.50 "Female athlete" (statuette) 55 15
1219 4d.50 "Ball game" (bas-relief) (horiz) 75 20
1220 10d. "Runners" (amphora) (horiz) .... 2·10 90
1216/1220 *Set of 5* .... 3·50 1·40

(Des P. Gravalos. Litho)

1972 (15 Nov). Stamp Day. W **84**. P 13×13½.

1221 **257** 2d.50 multicoloured 20 20

258 "The Birth of Christ"

259 University Buildings

(Des G. Velissarides. Litho)

1972 (15 Nov). Christmas. T **258** and similar vert design. Multicoloured. W **84**. P 13½×14.

1222 2d.50 "Pilgrimage of the Magi" 25 20
a. Horiz pair. Nos. 1222/3 .... 55 45
1223 4d.50 Type **258** 25 20

Nos. 1222/3 were issued together in horizontal *se-tenant* pairs within the sheet, each pair forming a composite design.

(Des V. Constantinea. Litho)

1973 (30 Mar). Centenary of National Polytechnic University, Athens. W **84**. P 13½×13.

1224 **259** 2d.50 multicoloured 40 20

260 "Spring" (wall fresco)

261 Europa "Posthorn"

(Des P. Gravalos. Litho)

1973 (30 Mar). Archaeological Discoveries, Island of Thera. T **260** and similar multicoloured designs. W **84**. P 13×13½ (vert) or 13½×13 (horiz).

1225 10l. Type **260** 20 15
1226 20l. "Barley" (jug) 20 15
1227 30l. "Blue Apes" (fresco) (horiz) 20 15
1228 1d.50 "Bird" (jug) 20 15
1229 2d.50 "Swallows" (detail, "Spring" fresco) (horiz) 20 20
1230 5d. "Wild Goats" (fresco) (horiz) 20 20
1231 6d.50 "Wrestlers" (detail, fresco) (horiz) .... 1·10 95
1225/1231 *Set of 7* .... 2·10 1·80

(Des G. Velissarides (10l., 20l., 1d.50, 3d.50 and 8d.50) and P. Gravalos (others). Litho)

1973 (18 Apr). Greek Regional Costumes (2nd series). Vert designs similar to T **251** but inscr "1973". Multicoloured. W **84**. P 12½×13½.

1232 10l. Peloponnese 10 10
1233 20l. Central Greece 10 10
1234 30l. Locris (Livanates) 10 10
1235 50l. Skyros (male) 10 10
1236 1d. Spetsai 10 10
1237 1d.50 Almyros 10 10
1238 2d.50 Macedonia (Roumlouki) 10 10
1239 3d.50 Salamis 20 10
1240 4d.50 Epirus (Souli) 20 10
1241 5d. Lefkas (Santa Maura) 35 10
1242 6d.50 Skyros (female) 45 10
1243 8d.50 Corinth 60 20
1244 10d. Corfu (Garitsa) 60 10
1245 15d. Epirus 70 10
1246 20d. Thessaly (Karagouniko) .... 1·90 10
1247 30d. Macedonia (Episkopi) .... 2·40 10
1248 50d. Thrace (Makra Gefyra) .... 5·75 3·75
1232/1248 *Set of 17* .... 12·50 5·00

(Des L. F. Anisdahl. Litho)

1973 (2 May). Europa. W **84**. P 13½×12½.

1249 **261** 2d.50 blue and new blue 70 20
1250 3d. rosine, orange and lake .... 1·20 25
1251 4d.50 buff, bronze-green and grey-green .... 3·00 95
1249/1251 *Set of 3* .... 4·50 1·30

SECOND REPUBLIC

1 June 1973

262 "Olympus" (from photograph by Boissonnas)

263 Dr. G. Papanicolaou

(Des P. Gravalos. Litho)

1973 (25 June). Greek Mythology (2nd series). T **262** and similar horiz designs. W **84**. P 14×13½.

1252 1d. black and grey 35 25
a. Horiz strip of 4. Nos. 1252/5 .... 1·80
1253 2d. multicoloured 35 25
1254 2d.50 black, grey and buff 35 25
1255 4d.50 multicoloured 65 45
1252/1255 *Set of 4* .... 1·50 1·10

Designs:—2d. "Zeus in combat with Typhoeus" (amphora); 2d.50, "Zeus at Battle of Giants" (altar relief); 4d.50, "The Punishment of Atlas and Prometheus" (vase).

Nos. 1252/5 were issued together in horizontal *se-tenant* strips of four within the sheet of 40.

(Des V. Constantinea. Litho)

1973 (10 Aug). Honouring Dr. George Papanicolaou (cancer specialist). W **84**. P 13×13½.

1256 **263** 2d.50 multicoloured 15 10
1257 6d.50 multicoloured 45 35

264 "Our Lady of the Annunciation"

265 "Triptolemus in a Chariot" (vase)

(Des V. Constantinea. Litho)

1973 (10 Aug). 150th Anniv of Discovery of Miraculous Icon of Our Lady of the Annunciation, Tinos. W **84**. P 13×13½.

1258 **264** 2d.50 multicoloured ... 40 30

(Des V. Constantinea. Litho)

1973 (22 Oct). European Transport Ministers' Conference, Athens. W **84**. P 13×13½.

1259 **265** 4d.50 multicoloured ... 45 35

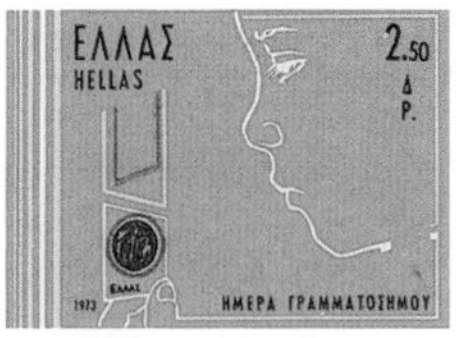

266 Child examining Stamp

267 G. Averof

(Des V. Constantinea. Litho)

1973 (15 Nov). Stamp Day. W **84**. P 13½×13.

1260 **266** 2d.50 multicoloured ... 25 20

(Des and eng Aspioti-Elka. Recess)

1973 (15 Nov). National Benefactors (1st series). T **267** and similar vert portraits. W **84**. P 13×13½.

1261 1d.50 purple-brown ... 15 10
1262 2d. carmine ... 15 10
1263 2d.50 green ... 15 10
1264 4d. reddish lilac ... 25 15
1265 6d.50 black ... 55 35
1261/1265 *Set of 5* ... 1·10 70

Portraits:—2d. A. Arsakis; 2d.50, C. Zappas; 4d. A. Syngros; 6d.50, I. Varvakis.

See also Nos. 1315/18.

268 "Lord Byron in Suliot Costume" (Thomas Phillips)

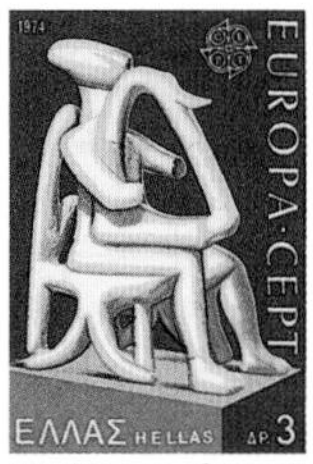

269 "Harpist of Keros"

(Des P. Gravalos and V. Constantinea. Litho)

1974 (4 Apr). 150th Death Anniv of Lord Byron. T **268** and similar vert design. Multicoloured. W **84**. P 13×13½.

1266 2d.50 Type **268** ... 20 15
1267 4d.50 "Byron taking the Oath at the Grave of Markos Botsaris" (lithograph) ... 25 20

(Des P. Gravalos and V. Constantinea. Litho)

1974 (10 May). Europa. Ancient Greek Sculptures. T **269** and similar vert designs. Multicoloured. W **84**. P 13×13½.

1268 3d. Type **269** ... 65 15
1269 4d.50 "Athenian Maiden" ... 1·00 25
1270 6d.50 "Charioteer of Delphi" (bronze) ... 3·00 90
1268/1270 *Set of 3* ... 4·25 1·20

270 "Theocracy of Zeus" (vase)

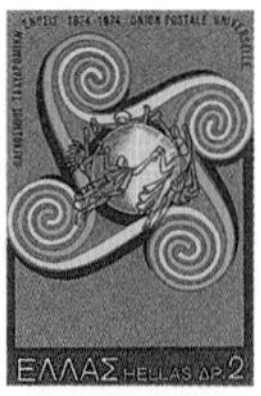

271 U.P.U. Emblem within Mycenaean Vase Design

(Des P. Gravalos and V. Constantinea. Litho)

1974 (25 June). Greek Mythology (3rd series). T **270** and similar designs. W **84**. P 13×13½ (vert) or 13½×13 (horiz).

1271 1d.50 black and yellow-orange ... 15 10
1272 2d. blackish brown, Venetian red and yellow-orange ... 15 10
1273 2d.50 black, red-brown and yellow-orange ... 15 10
1274 10d. blackish brown, brown-red and yellow-orange ... 45 30
1271/1274 *Set of 4* ... 80 55

Designs: Horiz—2d. "Athena's Birth" (vase); 2d.50, "Artemis, Apollo and Lito" (vase). Vert—10d. "Hermes" (vase).

(Des P. Gravalos and V. Constantinea. Litho)

1974 (14 Sept). Centenary of Universal Postal Union. T **271** and similar multicoloured designs. W **84**. P 12×13½ (vert) or 13½×12 (horiz).

1275 2d. Type **271** ... 15 10
1276 4d.50 Hermes (horiz) ... 15 10
1277 6d.50 Woman reading letter ... 45 35
1275/1277 *Set of 3* ... 70 50

272 Crete 1d. Stamp, 1905

273 Joseph

(Des P. Gravalos and V. Constantinea. Litho)

1974 (15 Nov). Stamp Day. W **84**. P 13½×13.

1278 **272** 2d.50 black, carmine-red and blackish lilac ... 20 20

(Des P. Gravalos and V. Constantinea. Litho)

1974 (15 Nov). Christmas. T **273** and similar vert designs. Multicoloured. W **84**. P 13½×14.

1279 2d. Type **273** ... 20 15
a. Horiz strip of 3. Nos. 1279/81 ... 65
1280 4d.50 Virgin and Child on donkey ... 20 15
1281 8d.50 Jacob ... 20 15
1279/1281 *Set of 3* ... 55 40

Nos. 1279/81 were issued together in horizontal *se-tenant* strips of three stamps within the sheet, each strip forming a composite design.

(Des P. Gravalos and V. Constantinea. Litho)

1974 (5 Dec). Greek Regional Costumes (3rd series). Vert designs similar to T **251** but inscr "1974". Multicoloured. W **84**. P 12×13½.

1282 20l. Megara costume ... 10 10
1283 30l. Salamis costume ... 10 10
1284 50l. Edipsos costume ... 10 10
1285 1d. Kymi costume ... 10 10
1286 1d.50 Sterea Hellas costume ... 10 10
1287 2d. Desfina costume ... 10 10
1288 3d. Epirus costume ... 10 10
1289 3d.50 Naousa costume ... 10 10
1290 4d. Hasia costume ... 10 10
1291 4d.50 Thasos costume ... 10 10
1292 5d. Skopelos costume ... 10 10
1293 6d.50 Epirus costume ... 10 10
1294 10d. Pelion costume ... 35 10
1295 25d. Kerkyra costume ... 90 10
1296 30d. Boeotia (Tanagra) costume ... 2·30 1·80
1282/1296 *Set of 15* ... 4·25 3·00

274 Secret Assembly, Vostitsa

275 Roses in Vase

(Des P. Gravalos and V. Constantinea. Litho)

1975 (24 Mar). 150th Death Anniv of Grigorios Dikeos-Papaflessas (soldier). T **274** and similar designs. W **84**. P 13½×12 (horiz) or 12×13½ (vert).

1297 4d. brownish black, brown and stone ... 10 10
1298 7d. multicoloured ... 15 10
1299 11d. multicoloured ... 45 35
1297/1299 *Set of 3* ... 65 50

Designs: Vert—7d. Papaflessas in uniform. Horiz—11d. Aghioi Apostoli (Chapel), Kalamata.

(Des P. Gravalos and V. Constantinea. Litho)

1975 (10 May). Europa. T **275** and similar vert designs. Multicoloured. W **84**. P 13×13½.

1300 4d. Type **275** ... 70 20
1301 7d. Erotokritos and Aretussa ... 1·40 45
1302 11d. Girl and sheep ... 4·00 1·20
1300/1302 *Set of 3* ... 5·50 1·70

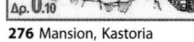

276 Mansion, Kastoria

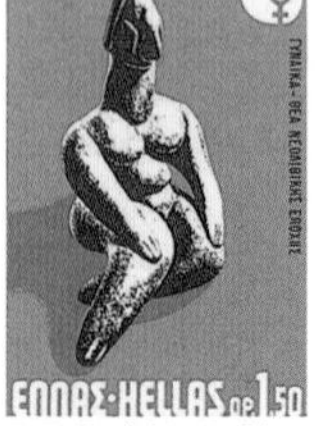

277 Neolithic Goddess (sculpture)

(Des P. Gravalos and V. Constantinea. Litho)

1975 (26 June). National Architecture. T **276** and similar horiz designs. W **84**. P 13½×12½.

1303 10l. black and new blue ... 15 15
1304 40l. black and red ... 20 15
1305 4d. black and bistre ... 20 15
1306 6d. black and ultramarine ... 20 15
1307 11d. black and red-orange ... 40 30
1303/1307 *Set of 5* ... 1·00 80

Designs:—40l. House, Arnea, Halkidiki; 4d. House, Veria; 6d. Mansion, Siatista; 11d. Mansion, Ambelakia, Thessaly.

(Des P. Gravalos and V. Constantinea. Litho)

1975 (29 Sept). International Women's Year. T **277** and similar vert designs. W **84**. P 13×13½.

1308 1d.50 agate, deep mauve and mauve ... 15 10
1309 8d.50 black, maroon and ochre ... 15 10
1310 11d. black, deep slate-blue and light greenish blue ... 45 35
1308/1310 *Set of 3* ... 70 50

Designs:—8d.50, Confrontation between Antigone and Creon; 11d. Women "Looking to the Future".

278 Alexandros Papanastasiou (founder) and University Buildings

279 Greek 100d. Stamp, 1933

(Des P. Gravalos and V. Constantinea. Litho)

1975 (29 Sept). 50th Anniv of Thessaloniki University. T **278** and similar horiz designs. W **84**. P 13½×13.

1311 1d.50 sepia and pale olive-sepia ... 15 10
1312 4d. multicoloured ... 15 10
1313 11d. multicoloured ... 45 35
1311/1313 *Set of 3* ... 70 50

Designs:—4d. Original University building; 11d. Plan of University city.

(Des P. Gravalos and V. Constantinea Litho)

1975 (15 Nov). Stamp Day. W **84**. P 13×13½.

1314 **279** 11d. brown, cream and bronze-green ... 45 35

280 Evangelos Zappas and Zappeion Building

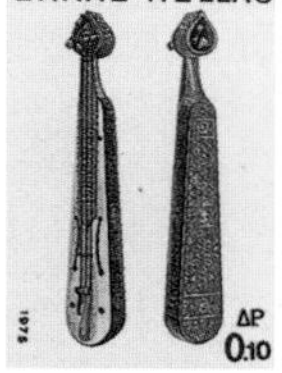

281 Pontos Lyre

(Des P. Gravalos and V. Constantinea. Litho)

1975 (15 Nov). National Benefactors (2nd series). T **280** and similar horiz designs. W **84**. P 13½×13.

1315 1d. black, olive-grey and deep green ... 15 10
1316 4d. black, deep grey and red-brown ... 15 10
1317 6d. black, brown-grey and orange ... 20 10
1318 11d. black, brownish grey & Venetian red ... 45 35
1315/1318 *Set of 4* ... 85 60

Designs:—4d. Georgios Rizaris and Rizarios Ecclesiastical School; 6d. Michael Tositsas and Metsovion Technical University; 11d. Nicolaos Zosimas and Zosimea Academy.

(Des P. Gravalos and V. Constantinea. Litho)

1975 (15 Dec). Musical Instruments. T **281** and similar multicoloured designs. W **84**. P 12×13½ (vert) or 13½×12 (horiz).

1319 10l. Type **281** ... 10 10
1320 20l. Musicians (Byzantine mural) ... 10 10
1321 1d. Cretan lyre ... 10 10
1322 1d.50 Tambourine ... 10 10
1323 4d. Cithern-player (from amphora) (horiz) ... 10 10
1324 6d. Bagpipes ... 10 10
1325 7d. Lute ... 10 10
1326 10d. Barrel-organ ... 10 10
1327 11d. Pipes and zournades ... 35 10
1328 20d. "Praising God" (Byzantine mural) (horiz) ... 50 10
1329 25d. Drums ... 55 10
1330 30d. Kanonaki (horiz) ... 1·80 1·00
1319/1330 *Set of 12* ... 3·50 1·90

282 Early Telephone and Globe

283 Battle of Missolonghi

(Des P. Gravalos and V. Constantinea. Litho)

1976 (23 Mar). Telephone Centenary. T **282** and similar horiz design. Multicoloured. W **84**. P 13½×12.

1331 7d. Type **282** ... 30 20
a. Horiz pair. Nos. 1331/2 ... 65 45
1332 11d. Modern telephone and globe ... 30 20

Nos. 1331/2 were issued together in horizontal *se-tenant* pairs within the sheet, each pair forming a composite design.

(Des P. Gravalos and V. Constantinea. Litho)

1976 (23 Mar). 150th Anniv of Battle of Missolonghi. W **84**. P 13½×13.

1333 **283** 4d. multicoloured ... 25 20

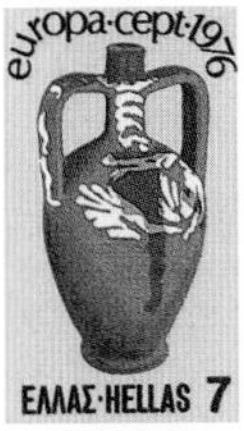

284 Florina Jug

285 Lion attacking Bull

(Des P. Gravalos and V. Constantinea. Litho)

1976 (10 May). Europa. T **284** and similar vert designs. Multicoloured. W **84**. P 12½×12 (8d.50) or 13×13½ (others).

1334 7d. Type **284** ... 55 25
1335 8d.50 Plate with bird design (25×30 mm) ... 55 25
1336 11d. Egina pitcher ... 2·40 85
1334/1336 *Set of* 3 ... 3·25 1·20

(Des P. Gravalos and V. Constantinea. Litho)

1976 (10 May). Ancient Sealing-stones. T **285** and similar multicoloured designs. W **84**. P 13×13½ (8d.50), 13½×13 (11d.) or 12½×12 (others).

1337 2d. Type **285** ... 15 10
1338 4d.50 Water birds ... 15 10
1339 7d. Wounded bull ... 15 10
1340 8d.50 Head of Silenus (27×40 mm) ... 20 15
1341 11d. Cow feeding Calf (40×27 mm) ... 40 25
1337/1341 *Set of* 5 ... 95 65

286 Long-jumping

287 Lemnos

(Des P. Gravalos and V. Constantinea. Litho)

1976 (25 June). Olympic Games, Montreal. T **286** and similar horiz designs. Multicoloured. W **84**. P 12×13½ (11d.) or 13½×13 (others).

1342 50l. Type **286** ... 15 10
1343 2d. Hand-ball ... 15 10
1344 3d.50 Wrestling ... 15 10
1345 4d. Swimming ... 20 10
1346 11d. Athens and Montreal stadiums (52×37 mm) ... 25 20
1347 25d. "The Olympic flame" ... 1·50 1·10
1342/1347 *Set of* 6 ... 2·20 1·50

(Des P. Gravalos and V. Constantinea. Litho)

1976 (26 July). Tourist Publicity. T **287** and similar horiz designs. Multicoloured. W **84**. P 13×13½ (30d.) or 13½×13 (others).

1348 30d. Type **287** ... 45 10
1349 50d. Lesbos ... 1·00 10
1350 75d. Chios ... 1·30 15
1351 100d. Samos ... 2·40 1·50
1348/1351 *Set of* 4 ... 4·75 1·70

288 "The Magi speaking to the Jews"

289 Lascaris Book of Grammar, 1476

(Des P. Gravalos and V. Constantinea. Litho)

1976 (8 Dec). Christmas. T **288** and similar vert design, showing illustrations from manuscripts at Esfigmenou Monastery. Multicoloured. W **84**. P 13×13½.

1352 4d. Type **288** ... 20 15
1353 7d. "Adoration of the Magi" ... 35 25

(Des P. Gravalos and V. Constantinea. Litho)

1976 (8 Dec). 500th Anniv of First Book printed in Greek. W **84**. P 13½×13.

1354 **289** 4d. multicoloured ... 25 20

290 Heinrich Schliemann

291 "Patients visiting Aesculapius" (relief)

(Des P. Gravalos and V. Constantinea. Litho)

1976 (8 Dec). Centenary of Schliemann's Excavation of the Royal Graves, Mycenae. T **290** and similar multicoloured designs. W **84**. P 13½×13 (4d., 7d.) or 13×13½ (others).

1355 2d. Type **290** ... 20 10
1356 4d. Gold bracelet (horiz) ... 20 10
1357 5d. Silver and gold brooch ... 20 15
1358 7d. Gold diadem (horiz) ... 35 15
1359 11d. Gold mask ... 80 50
1355/1359 *Set of* 5 ... 1·60 90

(Des P. Gravalos and V. Constantinea. Litho)

1977 (15 Mar). International Rheumatism Year. T **291** and similar vert designs. W **84**. P 12×13½ (50l., 20d.) or 12½×12 (others).

1360 50l. black, stone and brown-red ... 15 10
1361 1d. black, yellow-orange and red ... 15 10
1362 1d.50 black, stone and brown-red ... 15 10
1363 2d. black, yellow-orange and red ... 15 10
1364 20d. black, stone and brown-red ... 40 25
1360/1364 *Set of* 5 ... 90 60

Designs: 22×27 mm—1d. Ancient clinic; 1d.50, "Aesculapius curing a young man" (relief); 2d. Hercules and nurse. 23×34 mm—"Cured patient offering model of leg" (relief).

292 Fortresses of Mani

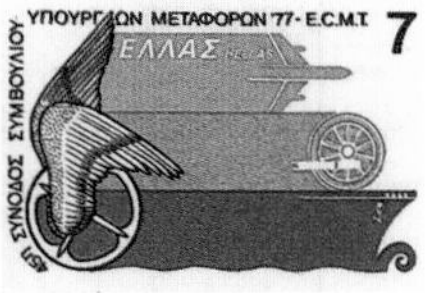

293 Emblem and Transport

(Des P. Gravalos and V. Constantinea. Litho)

1977 (16 May). Europa. T **292** and similar multicoloured designs. P 13×14 (7d.) or 14×13 (others).

1365 5d. Type **292** ... 90 15
1366 7d. Santorin (vert) ... 1·00 20
1367 15d. Lassithi Plain, Crete ... 3·50 60
1365/1367 *Set of* 3 ... 4·75 85

(Des P. Gravalos and V. Constantinea. Litho)

1977 (16 May). 45th European Conference of Ministers of Transport. P 14×13.

1368 **293** 7d. multicoloured ... 25 20

294 Alexandria Lighthouse (Roman coin)

(Des P. Gravalos and V. Constantinea. Litho)

1977 (23 July). "The Civilizing Influence of Alexander the Great". T **294** and similar horiz designs. Multicoloured. P 13½×13.

1369 50l. Type **294** ... 20 10
1370 1d. "Placing the Works of Homer in Achilles' Tomb" (fresco, Raphael) ... 20 10
1371 1d.50 Descending to sea bed in special ship (Flemish miniature) ... 20 10
1372 3d. In search of water of life (Hindu plate) ... 25 10
1373 7d. Alexander the Great on horseback (Coptic carpet) ... 25 10
1374 11d. Listening to oracle (Byzantine manuscript) ... 40 10
1375 30d. Death of Alexander the Great (Persian miniature) ... 85 45
1369/1375 *Set of* 7 ... 2·10 95

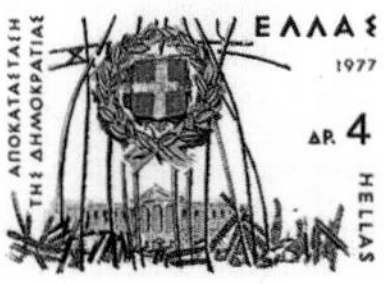

295 Wreath in Front of University

296 Archbishop Makarios

(Des. G. Varlamos (4d.), P. Gravalos and V. Constantinea (7d.), L. Orfanos (20d.). Litho)

1977 (23 July). Restoration of Democracy. T **295** and similar designs. P 13½×12 (4d.), 12×12½ (7d.) or 12½×12 (20d.).

1376 4d. blue, pale brown-olive and black ... 15 10
1377 7d. multicoloured ... 20 10
1378 20d. multicoloured ... 55 35
1376/1378 *Set of* 3 ... 80 50

Designs: 26×22 mm—7d. Demonstrators in front of University. 22×26 mm—20d. Flags, University and hand with olive branch.

1977 (10 Sept). Archbishop Makarios Commemoration. T **296** and similar horiz design. Litho. P 13×13½ (4d.) or 13½×13 (7d.).

1379 4d. black and brownish grey ... 20 15
1380 7d. black, sepia and pale stone ... 25 25

Design:—7d. Makarios and map of Cyprus.

297 Melas Building, Athens (former post office)

1977 (22 Sept). 19th-century Hellenic Architecture. T **297** and similar horiz designs. Litho. P 13½×13.

1381 50l. black, stone and Venetian red ... 15 10
1382 1d. black, stone and turquoise-green ... 15 10
1383 1d.50 black, stone and light blue ... 15 10
1384 2d. black, stone and pale yellow-olive ... 20 10
1385 5d. black, stone and bistre-yellow ... 20 10
1386 50d. black, stone and salmon ... 75 50
1381/1386 *Set of* 6 ... 1·40 90

Designs:—1d. Institution for the Blind, Thessalonika; 1d.50, Town Hall of Hermoupolis, Syros; 2d. Branch Office of National Bank, Piraeus; 5d. Ilissia (Palace of Duchess of Plakentia), Athens; 50d. Municipal Theatre, Patras.

298 Battle of Navarino

299 Parthenon and Industrial Complex

(Des P. Gravalos and V. Constantinea. Litho)

1977 (20 Oct). 150th Anniv of Battle of Navarino. T **298** and similar horiz design. P 13½×13.

1387 4d. pale yellow, black and brown ... 20 15
1388 7d. multicoloured ... 25 20

Design:—7d. Admirals Van der Heyden, Sir Edward Codrington and Comte de Rigny.

(Des P. Gravalos and V. Constantinea (1390/2). Litho)

1977 (20 Oct). Environmental Protection. T **299** and similar multicoloured designs. P 14×13½ (4d., 7d.) or 13½×14 (others).

1389 3d. Type **299** ... 20 10
1390 4d. Birds and fish (horiz) ... 20 10
1391 7d. Living and dead trees (horiz) ... 20 10
1392 30d. Head of Erechtheum caryatid and chimneys ... 65 50
1389/1392 *Set of* 4 ... 1·10 70

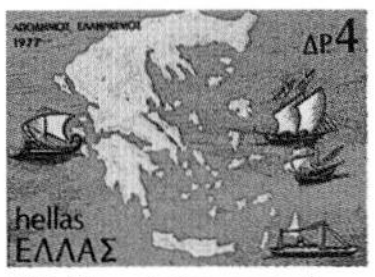

300 Map of Greece and Ships

301 "The Port of Kalamata" (C. Parthenis)

(Des L. Orfanos (5d.), P. Gravalos and V. Constantinea (others). Litho)

1977 (15 Dec). "Greeks Abroad". T **300** and similar horiz designs. Multicoloured. P 13½×12.

1393 4d. Type **300** ... 15 10
1394 5d. Globe and Greek flag ... 15 10
1395 7d. Globe and swallows ... 15 10
1396 11d. Envelope with flags ... 20 15
1397 13d. Map of the World ... 50 35
1393/1397 *Set of* 5 ... 1·00 70

(Des P. Gravalos and V. Constantinea. Litho)

1977 (15 Dec). Greek Paintings. T **301** and similar multicoloured designs. P 13×13½ (2d.50, 11d.) or 13½×13 others).

1398 1d.50 Type **301** ... 20 10
1399 2d.50 "Arsanas" (S. Papaloucas) (vert) ... 20 10
1400 4d. "Santorin" (C. Maleas) ... 20 10
1401 7d. "The Engagement" (N. Gyzis) ... 20 10
1402 11d. "The Straw Hat" (N. Lytras) (vert) ... 20 10
1403 15d. "Spring" (G. Iacovidis) ... 40 30
1398/1403 *Set of* 6 ... 1·30 70

302 *Ebenus cretica*

303 Horse Postman and Pre-stamp Cancel

(Des P. Gravalos and V. Constantinea, from paintings by N. Goulandris. Litho)

1978 (30 Mar). Greek Flora. T **302** and similar vert designs. Multicoloured. P 13×13½.

1404 1d.50 Type **302** ... 15 10
1405 2d.50 *Fritillaria rhodokanakis* ... 15 10
1406 3d. *Campanula oreadum* ... 15 10
1407 4d. *Lilium heldreichii* ... 15 10
1408 7d. *Viola delphinantha* ... 20 15
1409 25d. *Paeonia rhodia* ... 60 45
1404/1409 *Set of* 6 ... 1·30 90

(Des P. Gravalos and V. Constantinea. Litho)

1978 (15 May–Sept). 150th Anniv of Postal Service. T **303** and similar horiz designs. Multicoloured. P 13½×12.

1410 4d. Type **303** ... 15 10
1411 5d. *Maximilianos* (passenger steamer) and Greek "Hermes" stamp ... 15 10
1412 7d. Mail train and 1896 Olympic Games stamp ... 20 10

1413 30d. Postmen on motor cycles and 1972 "Stamp Day" commemorative 60 45
1410/1413 *Set of 4* .... 1·00 70
MS1414 101×92 mm. Nos. 1410/13 (sold at 60d.) (25.9.78) .... 1·40 1·20

304 Lighting the Olympic Flame

305 St. Sophia, Salonika

(Des P. Gravalos and V. Constantinea. Litho)

1978 (15 May). 80th International Olympic Committee Session, Athens. T **304** and similar vert design. Multicoloured. P 13½×14.
1415 7d. Type **304** 80 35
1416 13d. Start of 100 m. race .... 1·40 85

(Des P. Gravalos and V. Constantinea. Litho)

1978 (15 May). Europa. T **305** and similar vert design. Multicoloured. P 14×13½ (4d.) or 13½×14 (7d.).
1417 4d. Type **305** .... 1·10 30
1418 7d. Lysicrates' Monument, Athens .... 2·20 75

306 Bust of Aristotle

307 Rotary Emblem (50th anniv)

(Des P. Gravalos and V. Constantinea. Litho)

1978 (10 July). 2300th Death Anniv of Aristotle. T **306** and similar vert designs. Multicoloured. P 13×14 (20d.) or 13×13½ (others).
1419 2d. Type **306** 20 15
1420 4d. "The School of Athens" (Raphael, detail) 20 15
1421 7d. Map of Chalkidiki and statue plinth . 35 20
1422 20d. "Aristotle the Wise" (Byzantine fresco) (21×37 mm) 55 35
1419/1422 *Set of 4* .... 1·20 75

(Des P. Gravalos and V. Constantinea. Litho)

1978 (21 Sept). Anniversaries and Events. T **307** and similar multicoloured designs. P 12½.
1423 1d. Type **307** 25 20
1424 1d.50 Surgery (11th Greek Surgery Congress) (vert) 25 20
1425 2d.50 Ugo Foscolo (poet, birth bicentenary) 25 20
1426 5d. Bronze head (25th anniv of European Convention on Human Rights) 25 20
1427 7d. Hand with reins (Conference of Ministers of Culture of Council of Europe countries) (vert) 25 20
1428 13d. *Wright Flyer I* and Daedalus and Icarus (75th anniv of first powered flight) (vert) 55 40
1423/1428 *Set of 6* .... 1·60 1·30

308 The Poor Woman with Five Children

309 Grafted Plant and Circulation Diagram

(Des C. Kourabas. Litho)

1978 (6 Nov). "The Twelve Months" (Greek fairy tale). T **308** and similar horiz designs. Multicoloured. P 14×13.
1429 2d. Type **308** 15 10
1430 3d. The poor woman and the twelve months 15 10
1431 4d. The poor woman and the gold coins 20 15
1432 20d. The poor woman with her children and the rich woman with the snakes 40 30
1429/1432 *Set of 4* 80 60

(Des P. Gravalos and V. Constantinea. Litho)

1978 (6 Nov). Transplants. T **309** and similar vert design. Multicoloured. P 12×13½.
1433 4d. Type **309** 20 10
1434 10d. "The Miracle of Sts. Cosmas and Damian" (Alonso de Sedano) 35 20

310 "Virgin and Child"

311 First Academy, Nauplion, and Cadet

(Des P. Gravalos and V. Constantinea. Litho)

1978 (15 Dec). Christmas. Icons from Stavronikita Monastery, Mount Athos. T **310** and similar vert design. Multicoloured. P 13×13½.
1435 4d. Type **310** 20 10
1436 7d. "The Baptism of Christ" 25 20

(Des P. Gravalos and V. Constantinea. Litho)

1978 (15 Dec). 150th Anniv of Military Academy. T **311** and similar multicoloured designs. P 12×13½ (2d.) or 13½×12 (others).
1437 1d.50 Type **311** 15 10
1438 2d. Academy coat of arms (vert) 15 10
1439 10d. Modern Academy, Athens, and cadet 40 30
1437/1439 *Set of 3* 65 45

312 Destroyer

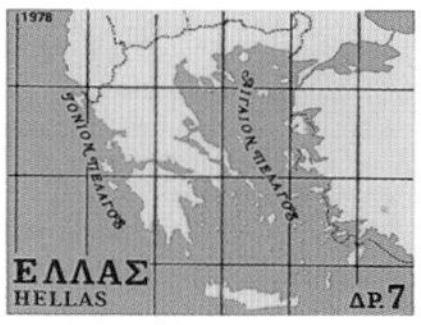

313 Map of Greece

(Des P. Gravalos and V. Constantinea. Litho)

1978 (15 Dec). Greek Naval Ships. T **312** and similar horiz designs. Multicoloured. P 13½×12.
1440 50l. Type **312** 15 10
1441 1d. *Andromeda* (motor torpedo-boat) 15 10
1442 2d.50 *Papanicolis* (submarine) 15 10
1443 4d. *Psara* (cruiser) 15 10
1444 5d. *Madonna of Hydra* (armed sailing caique) 20 10
1445 7d. Byzantine dromon 20 15
1446 50d. Athenian trireme 75 45
1440/1446 *Set of 7* .... 1·60 1·00

(Des P. Gravalos and V. Constantinea. Litho)

1978 (28 Dec). The Greek State. P 14×13½.
1447 **313** 7d. multicoloured 15 10
1448 11d. multicoloured 20 10
1449 13d. multicoloured 40 30
1447/1449 *Set of 3* 70 45

314 Kitsos Tsavellas

315 Figurine found at Amoraos

(Des P. Gravalos and V. Constantinea. Litho)

1979 (12 Mar). "The Struggle of the Souliots". T **314** and similar designs. P 12½×13½ (1d.50, 20d.) or 13½×12½ (others).
1450 1d.50 cinnamon, black and brown 15 10
1451 3d. multicoloured 15 10
1452 10d. multicoloured 20 15
1453 20d. pale ochre, black and brown 35 25
1450/1453 *Set of 4* 75 55
Designs: Horiz—3d. Souli Castle; 10d. Fighting Souliots. Vert—20d. The dance of Zalongo.

(Des P. Gravalos and V. Constantinea. Litho)

1979 (26 Apr). Art of the Aegean. P 13×14.
1454 **315** 20d. multicoloured 45 35

316 Cretan Postmen

317 Nicolas Skoufas

(Des P. Gravalos and V. Constantinea. Litho)

1979 (12 May). Europa. T **316** and similar vert design. Multicoloured. P 13×14.
1455 4d. Type **316** 80 15
a. Horiz pair. Nos. 1455/6 .... 1·70 45
1456 7d. Mounted postman 80 25
Nos. 1455/6 were issued together in horizontal *se-tenant* pairs within the sheet, each pair forming a composite design.

(Des P. Gravalos and V. Constantinea. Litho)

1979 (12 May). Anniversaries and Events. T **317** and similar multicoloured designs. P 14×13 (2d., 4d.) or 13×14 (others).
1457 1d.50 Type **317** (founder of Friendly Society, birth bicentenary) 25 20
1458 2d. Locomotives (75th anniv of railway) (horiz) 25 20
1459 3d. Basketball (European Basketball Championship) 25 20
1460 4d. Fossil moonfish *Mene psarianos* (seventh International Congress of Mediterranean Neogene) (horiz) 25 20
1461 10d. Greek church (Balkan Tourist Year) 25 20
1462 20d. Victory of Paeonius and flags (50th anniv of Balkan Sports) 40 35
1457/1462 *Set of 6* .... 1·50 1·20

318 Flags of Member States forming Ear of Wheat

319 "Girl with Dove" (classic statue)

(Des P. Gravalos and V. Constantinea. Litho)

1979 (28 May). Signing of Treaty of Accession of Greece to European Community. T **318** and similar horiz design. Multicoloured. P 13×13½ (7d.) or 13½×13 (30d.).
1463 7d. Type **318** 20 15
1464 30d. European Parliament 50 35

(Des P. Gravalos and V. Constantinea. Litho)

1979 (27 June). International Year of the Child. T **319** and similar vert designs. Multicoloured. P 13×13½.
1465 5d. Type **319** 15 10
1466 8d. Girl with doves 20 15
1467 20d. "Mother and Children" (Iacovides, detail) 35 25
1465/1467 *Set of 3* 65 45

320 Head of Philip of Macedonia

321 Purple Heron (*Ardea purpurea*)

(Des P. Gravalos and V. Constantinea. Litho)

1979 (15 Sept). Archaeological Discoveries from Vergina. T **320** and similar designs. Multicoloured. P 14×13 (14d.) or 13×14 (others).
1468 6d. Type **320** 15 10
1469 8d. Gold wreath 15 10
1470 10d. Copper vessel 20 10
1471 14d. Golden casket (horiz) 25 10
1472 18d. Silver ewer 25 10
1473 20d. Detail of decoration of golden quiver 25 15
1474 30d. Iron cuirass 75 50
1468/1474 *Set of 7* .... 1·80 1·00

(Des N. Goulandris. Litho)

1979 (15 Oct). Endangered Birds. T **321** and similar designs. Multicoloured. P 12½×13½ (vert) or 13½×12½ (horiz).
1475 6d. Type **321** 15 15
1476 8d. Audouin's gull (*Larus audouini*) 15 15
1477 10d. Eleonora's falcon (*Falco eleonorae*) (horiz) 15 15
1478 14d. Common kingfisher (*Alcedo athis*) (horiz) 15 15
1479 20d. Eastern white pelican (*Pelecanus onocrotalus*) 35 15
1480 25d. White-tailed sea eagle (*Haliaetus albicila*) .... 1·20 80
1475/1480 *Set of 6* .... 1·90 1·40

322 Agricultural Bank of Greece (50th anniv)

323 Parnassos

(Des P. Gravalos and V. Constantinea. Litho)

1979 (24 Nov). Anniversaries and Events. T **322** and similar designs. P 13½×14 (vert) or 14×13½ (horiz).
1481 3d. black, olive-yellow and deep olive 20 20
1482 4d. multicoloured 20 20
1483 6d. multicoloured 25 20
1484 8d. multicoloured 25 20
1485 10d. multicoloured 25 20
1486 12d. multicoloured 25 20
1487 14d. multicoloured 25 20
1488 18d. multicoloured 40 25

489 25d. multicoloured ... 75 50
481/1489 *Set of 9* ... 2·50 1·90

Designs and events: Vert—4d. Cosmas the Aetolian (death centenary); 6d. Basil the Great (1600th death anniv); 8d. Magnifying ass and map of Balkan countries (Balkanfila '79 stamp exhibition); 2d. Aristotelis Valaoritis (poet, death centenary); 14d. Golfer (World olfing Championship); 18d. Bust of Hippocrates (International ippocratic Foundation, Kos). Horiz—10d. Ionic column and map of alkans (Balkanfila '79 stamp exhibition); 25d. Parliamentary meeting 04th anniv of Greek parliament).

(Des P. Gravalos and V. Constantinea. Litho)

979 (15 Dec). Landscapes. T **323** and similar designs. Multicoloured. P 12½×13½ (vert) or 13½×12½ (horiz).

490 50l. Type **323** ... 20 10
491 1d. Tempi (horiz) ... 20 10
492 2d. Milos ... 20 10
493 4d. Vikos Gorge ... 20 10
494 5d. Missolonghi (horiz) ... 20 10
495 6d. Louros Aqueduct ... 20 10
496 7d. Samothrace ... 20 10
497 8d. Sithonia, Chalkidike (horiz) ... 20 10
498 10d. Samaria Gorge ... 20 10
499 12d. Sifnos ... 20 10
500 14d. Kymi (horiz) ... 25 10
501 18d. Ios ... 45 10
502 20d. Thassos ... 50 10
503 30d. Paros (horiz) ... 85 10
504 50d. Cephalonia ... 1·60 70
490/1504 *Set of 15* ... 5·00 1·90

324 Gate of Galerius

325 Aegosthena Castle

(Des P. Gravalos and V. Constantinea. Litho)

980 (15 Mar). First Hellenic Nephrology Congress, Thessalonika. P 13½×12½.

505 **324** 8d. azure, black and brown-red ... 30 20

(Des P. Gravalos and V. Constantinea. Litho)

980 (15 Mar). Castles, Caves and Bridges. T **325** and similar multicoloured designs. P 12½×13½ (vert) or 13½×12½ (horiz).

506 4d. Type **325** ... 15 10
507 6d. Byzantine castle, Thessalonika (horiz) ... 15 10
508 8d. Perama cave, Ioannina ... 15 10
509 10d. Dyros cave, Mani ... 15 10
510 14d. Arta bridge (horiz) ... 25 15
511 20d. Kalogiros bridge, Epirus (horiz) ... 40 20
506/1511 *Set of 6* ... 1·10 70

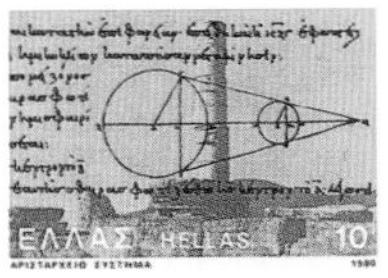
326 Aristarchus's Theorem and Temple of Hera

327 George Seferis (writer)

(Des P. Gravalos and V. Constantinea. Litho)

980 (5 May). 2300th Birth Anniv of Aristarchus of Samos (astronomer). T **326** and similar horiz design. P 13½×12½.

512 10d. salmon, black and deep grey-brown ... 20 15
513 20d. multicoloured ... 50 30

Design:—20d. Heliocentric system.

(Des P. Gravalos and V. Constantinea. Litho)

1980 (5 May). Europa. T **327** and similar horiz design. P 13½×12½.

1514 8d. bistre-brn, pale greenish bl & blk ... 1·10 15
1515 14d. light brown, black and cream ... 1·60 50

Design:—14d. Maria Callas (opera singer).

328 Open Book

329 Fire-fighting

(Des P. Gravalos and V. Constantinea. Litho)

1980 (5 May). Energy Conservation. T **328** and similar vert design. Multicoloured. P 13½×12½ (8d.) or 12½×13½ (20d.).

1516 8d. Type **328** ... 20 10
1517 20d. Lightbulb as a candle ... 50 35

(Des P. Gravalos and V. Constantinea. Litho)

1980 (14 July). Anniversaries and Events. T **329** and similar multicoloured designs. P 12½.

1518 4d. Type **329** (50th anniv of fire brigade) ... 25 20
1519 6d. St. Demetrius (mosaic) (1700th birth anniv) (vert) ... 25 20
1520 8d. Revolutionaries (75th anniv of Theriso revolution) ... 25 20
1521 10d. Ancient vase and olive branch (World Olive Oil Year) (vert) ... 25 20
1522 14d. International press emblem (15th International Journalists Federation congress) (vert) ... 25 20
1523 20d. Constantinos Ikonomos (cleric and scholar, birth bicentenary) (vert) ... 40 30
1518/1523 *Set of 6* ... 1·50 1·20

330 Olympia and Coin of Elia

331 Asbestos

(Des P. Gravalos and V. Constantinea. Litho)

1980 (11 Aug). Olympic Games, Moscow. T **330** and similar horiz designs showing Greek stadia. Multicoloured. P 13½×13.

1524 8d. Type **330** ... 20 10
1525 14d. Delphi and Delphic coin ... 55 40
1526 18d. Epidaurus and coin of Olympia ... 20 15
1527 20d. Rhodes and coin of Kos ... 35 15
1528 50d. Panathenaic stadium and First Olympic Games medal ... 1·20 65
1524/1528 *Set of 5* ... 2·30 1·30

(Des P. Gravalos and V. Constantinea. Litho)

1980 (22 Sept). Minerals. T **331** and similar multicoloured designs. P 12½×13½ (vert) or 13½×12½ (horiz).

1529 6d. Type **331** ... 15 10
1530 8d. Gypsum (vert) ... 15 10
1531 10d. Copper ... 15 10
1532 14d. Barite (vert) ... 50 30
1533 18d. Chromite ... 15 10
1534 20d. Mixed sulphides (vert) ... 35 15
1535 30d. Bauxite (vert) ... 60 40
1529/1535 *Set of 7* ... 1·90 1·10

332 Dassault Mirage III Jet Fighter

333 Left Detail of Poulakis's Painting

(Des P. Gravalos and V. Constantinea. Litho)

1980 (31 Oct). Anniversaries and Events. T **332** and similar multicoloured designs. P 12½.

1536 6d. Breakdown truck (20th anniv of Automobile and Touring Club of Greece road assistance service) (horiz) ... 25 20
1537 8d. Type **332** (50th anniv of Air Force) ... 25 20
1538 12d. Piper PA-18 Super Cub light airplane outside hangar (50th anniv of Thessalonika Flying Club) (horiz) ... 25 20
1539 20d. Harbour scene (50th anniv of Piraeus Port Organization) ... 40 30
1540 25d. Association for Macedonian Studies headquarters (40th anniv) ... 55 35
1536/1540 *Set of 5* ... 1·50 1·10

(Des P. Gravalos and V. Constantinea. Litho)

1980 (10 Dec). Christmas. T **333** and similar vert designs showing details from "He is Happy Thanks to You" by T. Poulakis (in St. John's Monastery, Patmos). Multicoloured. P 13½×14.

1541 6d. Type **333** ... 20 20
a. Horiz strip of 3. Nos. 1541/3 ... 80
1542 14d. Virgin and Child (centre) ... 25 20
1543 20d. Right detail ... 30 25
1541/1543 *Set of 3* ... 70 60

Nos. 1541/3 were issued together in horizontal *se-tenant* strips of three within sheets of 12 stamps, each strip forming a composite design.

334 Fresh and Canned Vegetables

335 "Kira Maria" (Alexandrian folk dance)

(Des P. Gravalos and V. Constantinea. Litho)

1981 (16 Mar). Exports. T **334** and similar vert designs. Multicoloured. P 12½.

1544 9d. Type **334** ... 15 10
1545 17d. Fruit ... 20 15
1546 20d. Cotton ... 25 20
1547 25d. Marble ... 50 30
1544/1547 *Set of 4* ... 1·00 70

(Des P. Gravalos and V. Constantinea. Litho)

1981 (4 May). Europa. T **335** and similar horiz design. Multicoloured. P 13½×12½.

1548 12d. Type **335** ... 80 10
1549 17d. "Sousta" (Cretan dance) ... 1·50 40

336 Olympic Stadium, Kalogreza

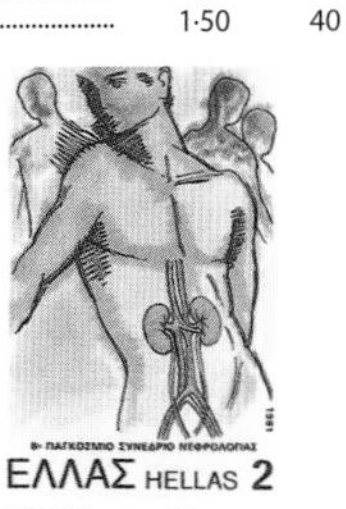
337 Human Figure showing kidneys

(Des P. Gravalos and V. Constantinea. Litho)

1981 (4 May). European Athletics Championships, Athens (1982) (1st issue). T **336** and similar horiz design. P 14×13½.

1550 12d. grey-blue, black and new blue ... 30 10
1551 17d. multicoloured ... 55 30

Design:—17d. Athletes converging on Greece.

See also Nos. 1586/8.

(Des P. Gravalos and V. Constantinea. Litho)

1981 (22 May). Anniversaries and Events. T **337** and similar designs. P 13½×14 (vert) or 14×13½ (horiz).

1552 2d. multicoloured ... 25 20
1553 3d. multicoloured ... 25 20
1554 6d. multicoloured ... 25 20
1555 9d. yellow-ochre, black and red-brown ... 25 20
1556 12d. multicoloured ... 25 20
1557 21d. multicoloured ... 40 30
1558 40d. rosine, brt ultram & dull ultram ... 65 50
1552/1558 *Set of 7* ... 2·10 1·90

Designs and events: Vert—2d. Type **337** (eighth World Nephrology Conference, Athens); 3d. Potez 25 biplane, glider, parachutist, model glider and emblem (50th anniv of Greek National Air Club); 6d. Meteora Monasteries, Thessaly, and Konitsa Bridge, Epirus (International Historical Symposium, Volos, and centenary of incorporation of Thessaly and Epirus into Greece); 12d. Oil rig (first Greek oil production); 40d. Heart (15th World Cardiovascular Surgery Conference, Athens). Horiz—9d. Bowl with "eye" decoration (50th anniv of Greek Ophthalmological Society); 21d. Globes, plant and coin (foundation in Athens of World Association for International Relations).

338 Variable Scallops

339 Aegean Island Bell Tower

(Des P. Gravalos and V. Constantinea. Litho)

1981 (30 June). Shells, Fishes and Butterflies. T **338** and similar horiz designs. Multicoloured. P 14×13½.

1559 4d. Type **338** ... 20 10
1560 5d. Painted comber (fish) ... 20 10
1561 12d. Mediterranean parrot fishes ... 20 10
1562 15d. Dentex (fish) ... 20 10
1563 17d. Apollo (*Parnassius apollo*) (butterfly) ... 60 50
1564 50d. Pale clouded yellow (*Colias hyale*) (butterfly) ... 1·40 95
1559/1564 *Set of 6* ... 2·50 1·70

(Des P. Gravalos and V. Constantinea. Litho)

1981 (30 Sept). Bell Towers and Altar Screens. T **339** and similar multicoloured designs. P 12½×13½ (vert) or 13½×12½ (horiz).

1565 4d. Type **339** ... 20 10
1566 6d. Altar gate, St. Paraskevi Church, Metsovo ... 20 10
1567 9d. Altar gate, Pelion (horiz) ... 20 10
1568 12d. Bell tower, Saints Constantine and Helen Church, Halkiades, Epirus ... 20 10
1569 17d. Altar screen, St. Nicholas Church, Velvendos (horiz) ... 20 15
1570 30d. Icon of St. Jacob and stand, Alexandroupolis Church Museum ... 45 20
1571 40d. Upper section of altar gate, St. Nicholas Church, Makrinitsa ... 85 70
1565/1571 *Set of 7* ... 2·10 1·30

340 Town Scene

341 Old Parliament Building (museum)

(Des P. Gravalos and V. Constantinea. Litho)

1981 (20 Nov). Anniversaries and Events. T **340** and similar multicoloured designs. P 13½×14 (vert) or 14×13½ (horiz).

1572 3d. Type **340** (Council of Europe Urban Renaissance campaign) ... 25 20
1573 9d. St. Simeon, Archbishop of Thessalonika (miniature) (Canonization in Greek Orthodox Church) (vert) ... 25 20
1574 12d. Child Jesus (detail of Byzantine icon) (Breast feeding campaign) (vert) ... 40 30
1575 17d. Gina Bachauer (pianist, 5th death anniv) (vert) ... 45 30
1576 21d. Constantine Broumidis (artist, 175th birth anniv) (vert) ... 45 30
1577 50d. "Phoenix" banknotes, 1831 (150th anniv of first Greek banknotes) ... 85 70
1572/1577 *Set of 6* ... 2·40 1·80

(Des A. Tassos (21d.), P. Gravalos and V. Constantinea (others). Litho)

1982 (15 Mar). Anniversaries and Events. T **341** and similar multicoloured designs. P 12½×13½ (vert) or 13½×12½ (horiz).

1578 2d. Type **341** (centenary of Historical and Ethnological Society) ... 25 20
1579 9d. Angelos Sikelianos (poet, 31st death anniv) (vert) ... 25 20
1580 15d. Harilaos Tricoupis (politician, 150th birth anniv) (vert) ... 25 20
1581 21d. Mermaid (History of Aegean Islands exhibition) (vert) ... 40 30
1582 30d. Airbus Industrie A300 jetliner and emblem (25th anniv of Olympic Airways) ... 55 40

1583 50d. Skull of Petralona man and Petralona cave (Third European Congress of Anthropology, Petralona) (vert) ... 80 60
1578/1583 *Set of* 6 ... 2·30 1·70

342 "Flight from Missolonghi"

343 Pole Vaulter and Wreath

(Des P. Gravalos and V. Constantinea. Litho)

1982 (10 May). Europa. T **342** and similar vert design. Multicoloured. P 13½×14.
1584 21d. Bust of Miltiades and shield (Battle of Marathon) ... 3·50 35
1585 30d. Type **342** ... 5·75 95

(Des P. Gravalos and V. Constantinea. Litho)

1982 (10 May). European Athletic Championships, Athens (2nd issue). T **343** and similar multicoloured designs. P 13½×14 (25d.) or 14×13½ (others).
1586 21d. Type **343** ... 25 15
1587 25d. Women runners (vert) ... 40 15
1588 40d. Athletes at start of race, shot putter, high jumper and hurdler ... 85 65
1586/1588 *Set of* 3 ... 1·40 85

344 Lectionary Heading

345 "Karaiskakis's Camp" in Piraeus (detail, von Krazeisen)

(Des P. Gravalos and V. Constantinea. Litho)

1982 (28 June). Byzantine Book Illustrations. T **344** and similar multicoloured designs. P 12½×13½ (vert) or 13½×12½ (horiz).
1589 4d. Type **344** ... 20 10
1590 6d. Initial letter E (vert) ... 20 10
1591 12d. Initial letter T (vert) ... 25 10
1592 15d. Canon-table of Gospel readings (vert) ... 25 15
1593 80d. Heading of zoology book ... 1·30 80
1589/1593 *Set of* 5 ... 2·00 1·10

(Des V. Constantinea (12k.), P. Gravalos (50d.). Litho)

1982 (20 Sept). Birth Bicentenary of Georges Karaiskakis (revolutionary leader). T **345** and similar vert design. P 13×14.
1594 12d. pale yellow-olive, black & ultram ... 35 15
1595 50d. multicoloured ... 95 70
Design:—50d. Karaiskakis meditating.

346 Cypriot "Disappearances" Demonstration

347 "Demonstration in Athens, 25 March 1942" (P. Zachariou)

(Des V. Constantinea (15d.), P. Gravalos (75d.). Litho)

1982 (20 Sept). Amnesty International Year of "Disappearances". T **346** and similar vert design. Multicoloured. P 13½×14.
1596 15d. Type **346** ... 25 20
1597 75d. Victims, barbed wire and candle ... 1·40 1·00

(Des P. Gravalos. Litho)

1982 (8 Nov). National Resistance, 1941–44. T **347** and similar multicoloured designs. P 12½.
1598 1d. Type **347** ... 20 10
1599 2d. "Kalavryta's Sacrifice" (S. Vasiliou) ... 20 10
1600 5d. "Resistance in Thrace" (A. Tassos) (vert) ... 20 10
1601 9d. "The Onset of the Struggle in Crete" (P. Gravalos) (vert) ... 35 10
1602 12d. Resistance fighters (vert) ... 25 10
1603 21d. "Gorgopotamos" (A. Tassos) (vert) ... 55 30
1604 30d. "Kaisariani, Athens" (G. Sikeliotis) ... 55 30
1605 50d. "Struggle in Northern Greece" (V. Katraki) ... 1·50 95
1598/1605 *Set of* 8 ... 3·50 1·80
MS1606 Two sheets (a) 90×81 mm. Nos. 1598/9 and 1604/5; (b) 81×90 mm. Nos. 1600/3 ... 6·00 3·75

348 Mary and Jesus

349 Figurehead from Tsamados's *Ares* (brig)

(Des V. Constantinea and P. Gravalos. Litho)

1982 (6 Dec). Christmas. T **348** and similar horiz design showing early Christian bas reliefs. Multicoloured. P 13½×12½.
1607 9d. Type **348** ... 20 15
1608 21d. Jesus in manger ... 50 35
Nos. 1607/8 were printed together in *se-tenant* pairs within the sheet.

(Des P. Gravalos. Litho)

1983 (14 Mar). 25th Anniv of International Maritime Organization. Ships' Figureheads. T **349** and similar multicoloured designs. P 14×13½ (horiz) or 13½×14 (vert).
1609 11d. Type **349** ... 20 10
1610 15d. Miaoulis's *Ares* (full-rigged ship) (vert) ... 20 10
1611 18d. Topsail schooner from Sphakia (vert) ... 40 15
1612 25d. Bouboulina's *Spetses* (full-rigged ship) (vert) ... 55 30
1613 40d. Babas's *Epameinondas* (brig) (vert) ... 80 40
1614 50d. *Carteria* (steamer) ... 1·50 1·00
1609/1614 *Set of* 6 ... 3·25 1·80

350 Letter and Map of Greece showing Postcode Districts

351 Archimedes

(Des V. Constantinea (15d.), P. Gravalos (25d.). Litho)

1983 (14 Mar). Inauguration of Postcode. T **350** and similar vert design. Multicoloured. P 12½.
1615 15d. Type **350** ... 20 15
1616 25d. Hermes' head within posthorn ... 65 35

(Des V. Constantinea (25d.), P. Gravalos (80d.). Litho)

1983 (28 Apr). Europa. T **351** and similar horiz design. Multicoloured. P 12½×13½ (25d.) or 13×14 (80d.).
1617 25d. Acropolis, Athens (49×34 mm) ... 2·75 50
1618 80d. Type **351** ... 6·00 1·60

352 Rowing

353 Marinos Antypas (farmers' leader)

(Des V. Constantinea (50, 80d.), P. Gravalos (others). Litho)

1983 (28 Apr). Sports. T **352** and similar multicoloured designs. P 14×13½ (horiz) or 13½×14 (vert).
1619 15d. Type **352** ... 20 10
1620 18d. Water skiing (vert) ... 35 10
1621 27d. Windsurfing (vert) ... 90 65
1622 50d. Ski lift (vert) ... 70 40
1623 80d. Skiing ... 2·10 1·30
1619/1623 *Set of* 5 ... 3·75 2·30

(Des V. Constantinea (20, 32d.), A. Tassos (27d.), G. Varlamos (40d.),P. Gravalos (others). Litho)

1983 (11 July). Personalities. T **353** and similar vert designs. P 13½×14.
1624 6d. multicoloured ... 20 10
1625 9d. multicoloured ... 20 10
1626 15d. multicoloured ... 20 10
1627 20d. multicoloured ... 35 10
1628 27d. multicoloured ... 45 15
1629 32d. multicoloured ... 65 35
1630 40d. pale yellow, deep chocolate and black ... 85 35
1631 50d. multicoloured ... 1·10 85
1624/1631 *Set of* 8 ... 3·50 1·90
Designs:—9d. Nicholas Plastiras (soldier and statesman); 15d. George Papandreou (statesman); 20d. Constantin Cavafy (poet); 27d. Nikos Kazantzakis (writer); 32d. Manolis Calomiris (composer); 40d. George Papanicolaou (medical researcher); 50d. Despina Achladioti, "Matron of Rho" (patriot).

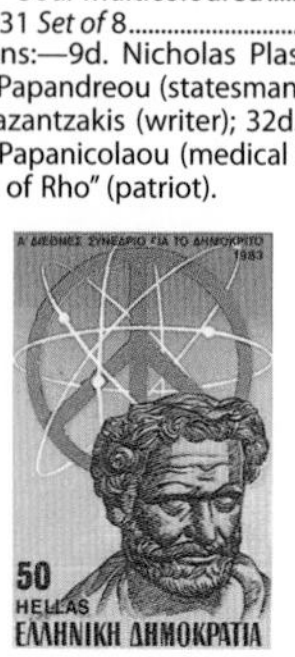
354 Democritus

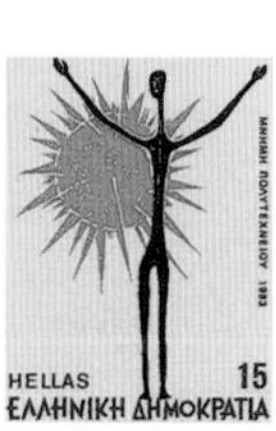
355 Poster by V. Katraki

(Des P. Gravalos. Litho Alexandros Matsoukis, Athens)

1983 (26 Sept). First International Democritus Congress, Xanthe. P 13½×13.
1632 **354** 50d. multicoloured ... 90 5

(Des P. Gravalos (30d.). Litho Alexandros Matsoukis, Athens)

1983 (17 Nov). Tenth Anniv of Polytechnic School Uprising. T **355** and similar vert design. Multicoloured. P 13½×13.
1633 15d. Type **355** ... 20 1
1634 30d. Students leaving Polytechnic ... 55 3

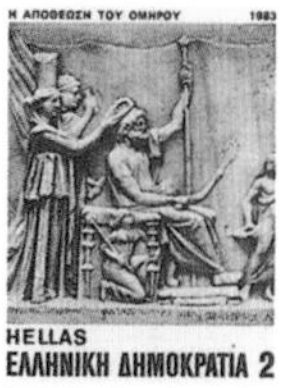
356 Deification of Homer

357 Horse's Head, Chariot of Selene

(Des V. Constantinea. Litho Alexandros Matsoukis, Athens)

1983 (19 Dec). Homeric Odes. T **356** and similar multicoloured designs. P 13×13½ (vert) or 13½×13 (horiz).
1635 2d. olive-sepia and deep brown ... 20 10
1636 3d. reddish brown, pale orange and orange ... 20 10
1637 4d. pale yellow, orange-brown and deep reddish brown ... 20 10
1638 5d. multicoloured ... 20 10
1639 6d. yellow-orange and deep reddish brown ... 20 10
1640 10d. pale orange, reddish brown and orange ... 20 10
1641 14d. orange, pale orange and reddish brown ... 20 10
1642 15d. pale orange, orange and deep reddish brown ... 25 10
1643 20d. bistre, greenish black and deep reddish brown ... 25 10
1644 27d. deep reddish brown, pale orange and orange ... 40 15
1645 30d. reddish brown, pale orange and orange ... 50 10
1646 32d. orange, deep reddish brown and pale orange ... 60 15
1647 50d. reddish brown, pale orange and orange ... 85 10
1648 75d. reddish brown, pale orange and brown-red ... 1·20 10
1649 100d. olive-sepia, sage green and deep brown ... 2·75 95
1635/1649 *Set of* 15 ... 7·50 2·20
Designs: Horiz—3d. Abduction of Helen by Paris (pot); 4d. Wooden horse; 5d. Achilles throwing dice with Ajax (jar); 14d. Battle between Ajax and Hector (dish); 15d. Priam requesting body of Hector (pot); 27d. Ulysses escaping from Polyphemus's cave; 32d. Ulysses and Sirens; 50d. Ulysses slaying suitors; 75d. Heroes of Iliad (cup). Vert—6d. Achilles; 10d. Hector receiving arms from his parents (vase), 20d. Blinding of Polyphemus; 30d. Ulysses meeting Nausica; 100d. Homer (bust).

(Des V. Constantinea. Litho Alexandros Matsoukis, Athens)

1984 (15 Mar). Parthenon Marbles. T **357** and similar horiz designs. Multicoloured. P 14½×14.
1650 14d. Type **357** ... 75 15
1651 15d. Dionysus ... 45 15
1652 20d. Hestia, Dione and Aphrodite ... 65 35
1653 27d. Ilissus ... 90 35
1654 32d. Lapith and Centaur ... 1·90 1·00
1650/1654 *Set of* 5 ... 4·25 1·80
MS1655 105×81 mm. 15d. Horseman (left); 21d. Horseman (right); 27d. Heroes (left); 32d. Heroes (right). P 13×13½ ... 8·75 7·25

358 Bridge

359 Ancient Stadium, Olympia

(Des J. Larrivière. Litho Alexandros Matsoukis, Athens)

1984 (30 Apr). Europa. 25th Anniv of European Post and Telecommunications Conference. P 14½×14.
1656 **358** 15d. multicoloured ... 80 25
a. Pair. Nos. 1656/7 ... 3·25 1·70
1657 25d. multicoloured ... 2·20 1·30
Nos. 1656/7 were issued both in separate sheets and together in sheets containing 20 *se-tenant* pairs. They were also issued in booklets containing two *se-tenant* pairs.

(Des P. Gravalos. Litho Alexandros Matsoukis, Athens)

1984 (30 Apr). Olympic Games, Los Angeles. T **359** and similar vert designs. Multicoloured. P 14×14½.
1658 14d. Type **359** ... 25 20
1659 15d. Athletes preparing for training ... 35 10
1660 20d. Flute player, discus thrower and long jumper ... 55 25
1661 32d. Athletes training ... 1·00 60
1662 80d. K. Vikelas and Panathenaic Stadium. ... 3·00 1·50
1658/1662 *Set of* 5 ... 4·75 2·40
Nos. 1658/62 were issued both in separate sheets and together in sheets containing four *se-tenant* strips and in booklets containing one *se-tenant* strip (*Price ofse-tenantstrip:* £5.50 *un*).

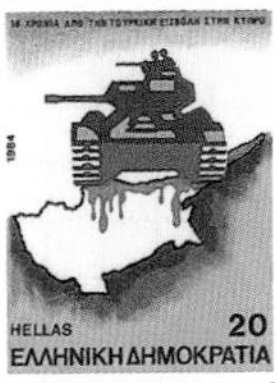

360 Tank on Map of Cyprus

361 Pelion Train

(Des P. Gravalos. Litho Alexandros Matsoukis, Athens)

1984 (10 July). Tenth Anniv of Turkish Invasion of Cyprus. T **360** and similar horiz design. Multicoloured. P 13½×13 (20d.) or 13×13½ (32d.).

1663	20d. Type **360**	35	20
1664	32d. Hand grasping barbed wire and map of Cyprus	80	65

(Des P. Gravalos. Litho Alexandros Matsoukis, Athens)

1984 (20 July). Railway Centenary. T **361** and similar multicoloured designs. P 13×13½ (horiz) or 13½×13 (vert).

1665	15d. Type **361**	85	30
1666	20d. Steam goods train on Papadia Bridge (vert)	2·20	1·00
1667	30d. Piraeus-Peloponnese steam train	1·00	60
1668	50d. Cogwheel railway, Kalavryta (vert)	2·50	1·10
1665/1668 *Set of* 4		6·00	2·75

362 Athens 5th Cent. B.C. Silver Coin on Plan of City

363 "10" enclosing Arms

(Des M. Amarantos (15d.), P.-E. Mela (100d.). Litho Alexandros Matsoukis, Athens)

1984 (12 Oct). 150th Anniv of Athens as Capital. T **362** and similar horiz design. Multicoloured. P 13½×13 (15d.) or 13×13½ (100d.).

1669	15d. Type **362**	50	20
1670	100d. Symbols of ancient Athens and skyline of modern Athens	1·80	1·10

(Des P. Gravalos. Litho Alexandros Matsoukis, Athens)

1984 (12 Oct). Tenth Anniv of Revolution. P 13×13½.

1671	**363**	95d. multicoloured	1·70	60

364 "Annunciation"

365 Running

(Des V. Constantinea. Litho Alexandros Matsoukis, Athens)

1984 (6 Dec). Christmas. T **364** and similar vert designs showing scenes from Hagion Panton icon by Athanasios Tountas. Multicoloured. P 13½×13.

1672	14d. Type **364**	70	40
	a. Block of 4. Nos. 1672/5	3·75	
1673	20d. "Nativity"	80	50
1674	25d. "Presentation in Temple"	80	50
1675	32d. "Baptism of Christ"	1·10	80
1672/1675 *Set of* 4		3·00	2·00

Nos. 1672/5 were issued together in *se-tenant* blocks of four within sheets of 16 or 40 stamps. A booklet containing one *se-tenant* block was also issued.

(Des P. Gravalos. Litho Alexandros Matsoukis, Athens)

1985 (1 Mar). 16th European Indoor Athletics Championships, New Phaleron. T **365** and similar horiz designs. Multicoloured. P 13×13½.

1676	12d. Type **365**	20	20
1677	15d. Putting the shot	25	15
1678	20d. Sports stadium (37×24 mm)	50	25
1679	25d. Hurdling	70	20
1680	80d. High jumping	1·40	85
1676/1680 *Set of* 5		2·75	1·50

366 Catacomb Niche

(Des P. Gravalos. Litho Alexandros Matsoukis, Athens)

1985 (29 Apr). Catacombs of Melos. T **366** and similar horiz designs. Multicoloured. P 14½×14.

1681	15d. Type **366**	25	15
1682	20d. Martyrs' altar and niches, central passageway	40	20
1683	100d. Niches	1·60	1·20
1681/1683 *Set of* 3		2·00	1·40

367 Apollo and Marsyas

(Des P. Gravalos. Litho Alexandros Matsoukis, Athens)

1985 (29 Apr). Europa. T **367** and similar horiz design. Multicoloured. P 14×14½.

1684	27d. Type **367**	80	70
	a. Pair. Nos. 1684/5	3·00	1·70
1685	80d. Nikos Skalkotas and Dimitris Mitropoulos (composers)	1·90	90

Nos. 1684/5 were issued both in separate sheets and together in sheets containing ten *se-tenant* pairs. They were also issued in booklets.

368 Coin (315 B.C.) and "Salonika" (relief)

369 Urn on Map of Cyprus

(Des P. Gravalos. Litho Alexandros Matsoukis, Athens)

1985 (24 June). 2300th Anniv of Salonika. T **368** and similar horiz designs. Multicoloured. P 14×14½ (5, 95d.) or 14½×14 (others).

1686	1d. Type **368**	20	15
1687	5d. Saints Demetrius and Methodius (mosaics) (49×34 mm)	50	20
1688	15d. Galerius's Arch (detail) (Roman period)	40	15
1689	20d. Salonika's eastern walls (Byzantine period)	50	15
1690	32d. Upper City, Salonika	50	15
1691	50d. Greek army liberating Salonika, 1912	85	15
1692	80d. Soldier's legs and Salonika (German occupation 1941–44)	1·80	35
1693	95d. Contemporary views of Salonika (60th annivs of Aristotelian University and International Trade Fair) (49×34 mm)	3·00	1·60
1686/1693 *Set of* 8		7·00	2·50

(Des P. Gravalos. Litho Alexandros Matsoukis, Athens)

1985 (24 June). 25th Anniv of Republic of Cyprus. P 13×13½.

1694	**369**	32d. multicoloured	70	45

370 "Democracy crowning the City" (relief)

371 Children of different Races

(Des P. Gravalos. Litho Alexandros Matsoukis, Athens)

1985 (7 Oct). Athens, "Cultural Capital of Europe". T **370** and similar designs. P 13½×13 (vert) or 13×13½ (horiz).

1695	15d. multicoloured	25	10
1696	20d. black, light grey and turquoise-blue	35	20
1697	32d. multicoloured	75	25
1698	80d. multicoloured	2·20	1·30
1695/1698 *Set of* 4		3·25	1·70

Designs: Horiz—20d. Tritons and dolphins (mosaic floor, Roman Baths, Hieratis); 80d. Capodistrian University, Athens. Vert—32d. Angel (fresco, Pentelis Cave).

(Des P. Gravalos. Litho Alexandros Matsoukis, Athens)

1985 (7 Oct). International Youth Year (1st issue) (15, 25d.) and 40th Anniv of United Nations Organization (27, 100d.). T **371** and similar vert designs. Multicoloured. P 14.

1699	15d. Type **371**	20	10
1700	25d. Doves and youths	40	20
1701	27d. Interior of U.N. General Assembly	75	20
1702	100d. U.N. building, New York, and U.N. emblem	1·60	1·20
1699/1702 *Set of* 4		2·75	1·50

See also No. **MS**1703.

372 Girl with Flower Crown

(Des P. Gravalos. Litho Aspioti-Elka)

1985 (22 Nov). International Youth Year (2nd issue). "Piraeus '85" Stamp Exhibition. Sheet 87×62 mm. P 14×13.

MS1703	**372**	100d. multicoloured	2·50	2·50

373 Folk Dance

374 Hestia

(Des P. Gravalos. Litho Aspioti-Elka)

1985 (9 Dec). Pontic Culture. T **373** and similar multicoloured designs. P 12½×13½ (27d.) or 13½×12½ (others).

1704	12d. Type **373**	25	20
1705	15d. Monastery of Our Lady of Soumela	25	20
1706	27d. Women's costumes (vert)	65	25
1707	32d. Trapezus High School	70	25
1708	80d. Sinope Castle	1·30	95
1704/1708 *Set of* 5		2·75	1·70

(Des P. Gravalos. Litho Alexandros Matsoukis, Athens)

1986 (17 Feb). Gods of Olympus. T **374** and similar horiz designs.

A. P 13

1709A	5d. salmon, black and olive-sepia	20	15
1710A	18d. salmon, black and olive-sepia	20	15
1711A	27d. salmon, black and blue	50	20
1712A	32d. salmon, black and carmine-red	60	25
1713A	35d. salmon, black and dull reddish brown	60	30
1714A	40d. salmon, black and carmine-red	70	30
1715A	50d. salmon, black and greenish grey	90	30
1716A	110d. salmon, black and dull reddish brown	1·50	30
1717A	150d. salmon, black and greenish grey	2·50	30
1718A	200d. salmon, black and blue	3·75	30
1719A	300d. salmon, black and deep violet-blue	6·25	1·00
1720A	500d. salmon, black and deep violet-blue	13·50	3·25
1709A/1720A *Set of* 12		28·00	6·00

B. P 13×imperf

1709B	5d. salmon, black and olive-sepia	25	15
1710B	18d. salmon, black and olive-sepia	25	15
1711B	27d. salmon, black and blue	60	15
1712B	32d. salmon, black and carmine-red	70	15
1713B	35d. salmon, black and dull reddish brown	70	15
1714B	40d. salmon, black and carmine-red	70	15
1715B	50d. salmon, black and greenish grey	90	15
1716B	110d. salmon, black and dull reddish brown	2·00	20
1717B	150d. salmon, black and greenish grey	4·50	20
1718B	200d. salmon, black and blue	5·00	20
1719B	300d. salmon, black and deep violet-blue	7·50	20
1720B	500d. salmon, black and deep violet-blue	14·50	4·25
1709B/1720B *Set of* 12		34·00	5·50

Designs:—18d. Hermes: 27d. Aphrodite; 32d. Ares; 35d. Athene; 40d. Hephaestus; 50d. Artemis; 110d. Apollo; 150d. Demeter; 200d. Poseidon; 300d. Hera; 500d. Zeus.

Nos. 1709A/20A were each issued in sheets of 50; Nos. 1709B/20B were each issued in strips of five within packets of 100 stamps.

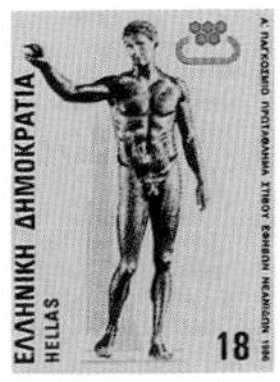

375 "Ephebos of Antikythera"

376 Fastening Seat Belt

377 Intelpost

(Des P. Gravalos. Litho Aspioti-Elka)

1986 (3 Mar). Sports Events and Anniversaries. T **375** and similar designs. P 12½.

1721	18d. olive-green, black and light grey	50	20
1722	27d. yellow, black and orange-red	1·20	55
1723	32d. multicoloured	1·70	80
1724	35d. olive-green, black and pale bistre	2·40	1·00
1725	40d. multicoloured	1·70	95
1726	50d. multicoloured	1·70	50
1727	110d. multicoloured	6·50	2·10
1721/1727 *Set of* 7		14·00	5·50

Designs: Vert—18d. Type **375** (1st World Junior Athletics Championships); 32d. Footballers (Pan-European Junior Football Finals); 35d. "Wrestlers" (sculpture) (Pan-European Freestyle and Greco-Roman Wrestling Championships); 50d. Cyclists (6th International Round Europe Cycling Meet. Horiz—27d. "Diadoumenos" (sculpture by Polycleitus) (1st World Junior Athletics Championships); 40d. Volleyball players (Men's World Volleyball Championships); 110d. "Victory" (unadopted design by Nikephoros Lytras for first Olympic Games commemoratives, 1896) (90th anniv of modern Olympic Games).

(Des P. Gravalos. Litho Aspioti-Elka)

1986 (3 Mar). European Road Safety Year. T **376** and similar vert designs. Multicoloured. P 12½×13½.

1728	18d. Type **376**	40	10
1729	27d. Motorcyclist in traffic	1·00	70
1730	110d. Child strapped in back seat of car and speed limit signs	2·75	1·60
1728/1730 *Set of* 3		3·75	2·20

(Des Post Office Advertising Dept. Litho Aspioti-Elka)

1986 (23 Apr). New Postal Services. T **377** and similar horiz design. Multicoloured. P 13½×14 (18d.) or 14×13½ (110d.).

1731	18d. Type **377**	45	20
1732	110d. "Express Mail" banner around globe	1·80	1·60

378 Sapling between Hands and burning Forest

379 Victims' Memorial and Workers

(Des V. Constantinea. Litho Aspioti-Elka)

1986 (23 Apr). Europa. T **378** and similar horiz design. P 14×13½.
1733 35d. yellowish green, black and dull orange ... 4·50 2·40
a. Pair. Nos. 1733/4 ... 9·25 5·25
b. Imperf×p 13½. Booklets ... 10·50 5·50
bb. Booklet pane. Nos. 1733b×2 and 1734a×2 ... 43·00
1734 110d. ultramarine, black and yellowish green ... 4·50 2·50
a. Imperf×p 13½. Booklets ... 10·50 5·50
Design:—110d. Prespa Lake.
Nos. 1733/4 were issued together in *se-tenant* pairs within the sheet.

(Des V. Constantinea. Litho Aspioti-Elka)

1986 (23 Apr). Centenary of Chicago May Day Strike. P 12½.
1735 **379** 40d. multicoloured ... 90 50

380 Swearing-in of Venizelos Government

(Des V. Constantinea. Litho Aspioti-Elka)

1986 (30 June). 50th Death Anniv of Eleftherios Venizelos (politician) (18d.) and Sixth International Crete Conference, Hania (110d.). T **380** and similar horiz design. Multicoloured. P 14×12½.
1736 18d. Type **380** ... 45 25
1737 110d. Hania harbour ... 1·80 1·30

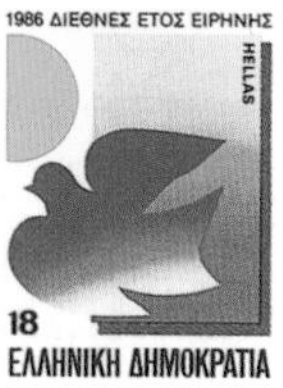

381 Dove and Sun

382 "Madonna and Child"

(Des S. Karachristos (18d.), P. Gravalos (35d.), P.-C. Sotiriou (110d.). Litho Aspioti-Elka)

1986 (6 Oct). International Peace Year. T **381** and similar multicoloured designs. P 12½.
1738 18d. Type **381** ... 35 25
1739 35d. Dove holding olive branch with flags as leaves ... 65 50
1740 110d. Dove with olive branch flying out of globe (horiz) ... 1·70 1·30
1738/1740 *Set of* 3 ... 2·40 1·80

(Des V. Constantinea. Litho Aspioti-Elka)

1986 (1 Dec). Christmas. T **382** and similar vert designs showing icons. Multicoloured. P 12½ (46d.) or 13½×14 (others).
1741 22d. Type **382** ... 25 10
1742 46d. "Adoration of the Magi" (24×32 mm) ... 90 65
1743 130d. "Christ enthroned with St. John the Evangelist" ... 2·00 1·00
1741/1743 *Set of* 3 ... 2·75 1·60
Nos. 1741 and 1743 depict the centre and one side panel of a triptych.

383 "The Fox and the Grapes"

384 "Composition" (Achilleas Apergis)

(Des P. Gravalos. Litho M. A. Moatsos, Athens)

1987 (5 Mar). Aesop's Fables. T **383** and similar horiz designs. Multicoloured.

A. P 12½×13

1744A 2d. Type **383** ... 35 15
1745A 5d. "The North Wind and the Sun" ... 35 15
1746A 10d. "The Stag at the Spring and the Lion" ... 55 15
1747A 22d. "Zeus and the Snake" ... 1·10 15
1748A 32d. "The Crow and the Fox" ... 1·50 30
1749A 40d. "The Woodcutter and Hermes" ... 2·40 85
1750A 46d. "The Ass in a Lion's Skin and the Fox" ... 3·25 85
1751A 130d. "The Hare and the Tortoise" ... 6·75 1·30
1744A/1751A *Set of* 8 ... 14·50 3·50

B. P 13½×imperf

1744B 2d. Type **383** ... 40 10
1745B 5d. "The North Wind and the Sun" ... 45 10
1746B 10d. "The Stag at the Spring and the Lion" ... 85 15
1747B 22d. "Zeus and the Snake" ... 2·75 15
1748B 32d. "The Crow and the Fox" ... 3·25 20
1749B 40d. "The Woodcutter and Hermes" ... 4·00 20
1750B 46d. "The Ass in a Lion's Skin and the Fox" ... 6·50 30
1751B 130d. "The Hare and the Tortoise" ... 29·00 1·00
1744B/1751B *Set of* 8 ... 42·00 2·00
Nos. 1744A/51A were each issued in sheets of 50 and Nos. 1744B/51B each in strips of five within packets of 100 stamps.

(Des P. Gravalos. Litho Aspioti-Elka, Athens)

1987 (4 May). Europa. Sculptures. T **384** and similar horiz design. Multicoloured. P 12½.
1752 40d. Type **384** ... 4·00 2·10
a. Pair. Nos. 1752/3 ... 8·25 4·50
b. Imperf×p 12½. Booklets ... 4·50 2·10
bb. Booklet pane. Nos. 1752b×2 and 1753a×2 ... 19·00
1753 130d. "Delphic Light" (Gerasimos Sklavos) ... 4·00 2·10
a. Imperf×p 12½. Booklets ... 4·50 2·10

385 Player shooting Goal and Indoor Court

386 Banner and Students

(Des T. Katsoulidis (**MS**1757), V. Constantinea (others). Litho Aspioti-Elka, Athens)

1987 (4 May–June). 25th European Men's Basketball Championship, Athens. T **385** and similar multicoloured designs. P 12½ (25d.) or 13½×14 (others).
1754 22d. Type **385** ... 80 50
1755 25d. Emblem and spectators (32×24 mm) ... 45 20
1756 130d. Players ... 2·30 1·50
1754/1756 *Set of* 3 ... 3·25 2·00
MS1757 113×63 mm. 40d. Players; 60d. Players around goal; 100d. Player shooting goal (each 28×40 mm). P 13×14 (3.6) ... 8·25 7·25

(Des P. Gravalos. Litho Aspioti-Elka, Athens)

1987 (4 May). 150th Anniversaries of Athens University (3, 23d.) and National Metsovio Polytechnic Institute (others). T **386** and similar multicoloured designs. P 14×13½ (horiz) or 13½×14 (vert).
1758 3d. Type **386** ... 25 15
1759 23d. Medal and owl ... 40 15
1760 40d. Building façade, measuring instruments and computer terminal (vert) ... 70 50
1761 60d. Students outside building (vert) ... 1·30 1·00
1758/1761 *Set of* 4 ... 2·40 1·60

387 Ionic and Corinthian Capitals, Temple of Apollo, Phigaleia-Bassae

388 Hands holding Cup Aloft

(Des V. Constantinea. Litho Aspioti-Elka, Athens)

1987 (1 July). Classical Architecture Capitals. T **387** and similar horiz designs. Multicoloured. P 13½×12½.
1762 2d. Type **387** ... 15 10
1763 26d. Doric capital, Parthenon ... 50 25
1764 40d. Ionic capital, The Erechtheum ... 70 40
1765 60d. Corinthian capital, The Tholos, Epidaurus ... 2·00 1·30
1762/1765 *Set of* 4 ... 3·00 1·80

(Des P. Gravalos. Litho M. A. Moatsos, Athens)

1987 (1 Oct). Greek Victory in European Basketball Championship. P 13×14.
1766 **388** 40d. multicoloured ... 1·10 95

389 Diploma Engraving (Yiannis Kephalinos)

390 Angel and Christmas Tree (left half)

(Des P. Gravalos. Litho M. A. Moatsos, Athens)

1987 (1 Oct). 150th Anniv of Fine Arts High School (1767) and 60th Anniv of Panteios Political Science High School (1768). T **389** and similar multicoloured design. P 12½×13½ (26d.) or 13½×12½ (60d.).
1767 26d. Type **389** ... 45 15
1768 60d. School campus (horiz) ... 1·20 95

(Des P. Gravalos. Litho M. A. Moatsos, Athens)

1987 (2 Dec). Christmas. T **390** and similar vert design. P 13×12½
1769 26d. Type **390** ... 65 4
a. Horiz pair. Nos. 1769/70 ... 1·40 9
1770 26d. Angel and christmas tree (right half) ... 65 4
Nos. 1769/70 were issued together in horizontal *se-tenant* pai within the sheet, each pair forming a composite design.

391 Eleni Papadaki in *Hecuba* (Euripides) and Philippi Amphitheatre

392 *Codonellina* sp. (polyzoan)

(Des V. Constantinea. Litho M. A. Moatsos, Athens)

1987 (2 Dec). Greek Theatre. T **391** and similar horiz designs. Multicoloured. P 14×13½.
1771 2d. Type **391** ... 20 1
1772 4d. Christopher Nezer in *The Wasps* (Aristophanes) and Dodona amphitheatre ... 20 1
1773 7d. Emilios Veakis in *Oedipus Rex* (Sophocles) and Delphi amphitheatre ... 20 1
1774 26d. Marika Kotopouli in *The Shepherdess's Love* (Dimitris Koromilas) ... 60 4
1775 40d. Katina Paxinou in *Abraham's Sacrifice* (Vitzentzos Comaros) ... 1·00 4
1776 50d. Kyveli in *Countess Valeraina's Secret* (Gregory Xenopoulos) ... 1·10 6
1777 60d. Karolos Koun and stage set ... 2·00 7
1778 100d. Dimitris Rontiris teaching National Theatre dancers an ancient dance ... 3·25 5
1771/1778 *Set of* 8 ... 7·75 2·7

(Des V. Constantinea. Litho M. A. Moatsos, Athens)

1988 (2 Mar). Marine Life. T **392** and similar horiz designs. Multicoloured.

A. P 13½×12½

1779A 30d. Type **392** ... 1·30 4
1780A 40d. *Diaperoecia major* (polyzoan (clump-forming animals)) and rainbow wrasse ... 1·30 4
1781A 50d. *Artemia* (marine animal) ... 1·50 4
1782A 60d. *Posidonia oceanica* (plant) and Marmora sea bream ... 3·75 1·5
1783A 100d. *Padina pavonica* (plant) ... 7·00 2·3
1779A/1783A *Set of* 5 ... 13·50 4·5

B. Imperf×p 12½

1779B 30d. Type **392** ... 5·50 3
1780B 40d. *Diaperoecia major* (polyzoan (clump-forming animals)) and rainbow wrasse ... 6·25 3
1781B 50d. *Artemia* (marine animal) ... 6·50 3
1782B 60d. *Posidonia oceanica* (plant) and Marmora sea bream ... 13·50 1·6
1783B 100d. *Padina pavonica* (plant) ... 19·00 9
1779B/1783B *Set of* 5 ... 46·00 3·2
Nos. 1779A/83A were each issued in sheets of 50 an Nos. 1779B/83B each in strips of five within packets of 100 stamps.

393 Ancient Olympia

394 Satellite and Fax Machine

(Des Lee Hea Ok (170d.), T. Katsoulidis (others). Litho M. A. Moatsos, Athens)

1988 (6 May). Olympic Games, Seoul. T **393** and similar horiz designs. Multicoloured.

A. P 13½×12½

1784A 4d. Type **393** ... 60 20
c. Horiz strip of 5. Nos. 1784A/8A ... 21·00 —
1785A 20d. Ancient athletes in Gymnasium ... 1·20 20
1786A 30d. Modern Olympics centenary emblem ... 3·00 95
1787A 60d. Ancient athletes training ... 5·25 3·25
1788A 170d. Runner with Olympic flame ... 9·75 2·50
1784A/1788A *Set of* 5 ... 18·00 6·50

B. Imperf×p 12½

1784B 4d. Type **393** ... 1·60 30
c. Horiz strip of 5. Nos. 1784B/8B ... 27·00
1785B 20d. Ancient athletes in Gymnasium ... 2·40 65
1786B 30d. Modern Olympics centenary emblem ... 4·25 1·20
1787B 60d. Ancient athletes training ... 6·50 2·50
1788B 170d. Runner with Olympic flame ... 11·50 3·25
1784B/1788B *Set of* 5 ... 24·00 7·00
Nos. 1784A/8A were issued together in horizontal *se-tenant* strips of five within sheets of 20 stamps. Nos. 1784B/8B were issued together in *se-tenant* strips of five in booklets and separately in post office packets of 100; the set price for Nos. 1784B/8B is for a set of singles.

(Des P. Gravalos. Litho M. A. Moatsos, Athens)

1988 (6 May). Europa. Transport and Communications. T **394** and similar vert design. Multicoloured.

A. P 12½

1789A 60d. Type **394** ... 5·50 2·40
c. Pair. Nos. 1789A/90A ... 16·00 5·25
1790A 150d. Modern express and commuter trains ... 9·25 2·50

B. Imperf×p 14

1789B 60d. Type **394** ... 6·00 1·90
c. Pair. Nos. 1789B/90B ... 19·00 4·50
d. Booklet pane. No. 1789cB×2 ... 20·00
1790B 150d. Modern express and commuter trains ... 12·00 2·30

Nos. 1789A/90A were issued together in *se-tenant* pairs within sheets of 16 stamps. Nos. 1789B/90B were issued together in *se-tenant* pairs in booklets and separately in post office packets of 100.

395 Katarraktis Falls

396 Emblem

(Des S.-P. Metaxas. Litho M. A. Moatsos, Athens)

1988 (4 July). European Campaign for Rural Areas. Waterfalls. T **395** and similar vert designs. Multicoloured.

A. P 12½×13½

1791A 10d. Type **395** ... 2·75 40
1792A 60d. Edessa waterfalls ... 7·00 3·25
1793A 100d. River Edessaios cascades ... 8·75 2·50
1791A/1793A *Set of* 3 ... 17·00 5·50

B. Imperf×p 14

1791B 10d. Type **395** ... 8·25 90
1792B 60d. Edessa waterfalls ... 20·00 1·70
1793B 100d. River Edessaios cascades ... 31·00 3·75
1791B/1793B *Set of* 3 ... 55·00 5·75

Nos. 1791A/3A were each issued in sheets of 50 and Nos. 1791B/3B each in strips of five within packets of 100 stamps.

(Des P. Gravalos. Litho M. A. Moatsos, Athens)

1988 (4 July). 20th European Postal Workers Trade Unions Congress.

A. P 12½

1794A **396** 60d. multicoloured ... 9·75 3·00

B. Imperf×p 14

1794B **396** 60d. multicoloured ... 23·00 1·30

No. 1794A was issued in sheets of 50 and No. 1974B in strips of five within packets of 100 stamps.

397 Mytilene Harbour, Lesbos (painting by Theophilos)

398 Eleftherios Venizelos, Map and Flag

(Des P. Gravalos. Litho Alexandros Matsoukis, Athens)

1988 (7 Oct). Prefecture Capitals (1st series). T **397** and similar multicoloured designs.

A. P 13

1795A 2d. Type **397** ... 15 10
c. Booklet pane. Nos. 1795A×4, 1798A×4, 1801A×4 and 1802A×4 ... 3·50 —
1796A 3d. Alexandroupolis lighthouse, Evros (vert) ... 15 10
1797A 4d. St. Nicholas's bell-tower, Kozani (vert) ... 15 10
1798A 5d. Workmen's centre, Hermoupolis, Cyclades (vert) ... 15 10
1799A 7d. Sparta Town Hall, Lakonia ... 15 10
1800A 8d. Pegasus, Leukas ... 20 10
1801A 10d. Castle of the Knights, Rhodes, Dodecanese (vert) ... 20 10
1802A 20d. Acropolis, Athens (vert) ... 25 10
1803A 25d. Aqueduct, Kavala ... 40 15
1804A 30d. Castle and statue of Athanasios Diakos, Lamia, Phthiotis (vert) ... 40 15
1805A 50d. Preveza Cathedral bell-tower and clock (vert) ... 80 20
1806A 60d. Esplanade, Corfu ... 1·00 70
1807A 70d. Aghios Nikolaos, Lassithi ... 1·30 25
1808A 100d. Six Springheads, Polygyros, Khalkidiki ... 3·25 35
1809A 200d. Church of Paul the Apostle, Corinth, Corinthia ... 7·25 75
1795A/1809A *Set of* 15 ... 14·00 3·00

B. P 13×imperf (horiz) or imperf×p 13 (vert)

1795B 2d. Type **397** ... 15 10
1796B 3d. Alexandroupolis lighthouse, Evros (vert) ... 15 10
1797B 4d. St. Nicholas's bell-tower, Kozani (vert) ... 20 10
1798B 5d. Workmen's centre, Hermoupolis, Cyclades (vert) ... 20 10
1799B 7d. Sparta Town Hall, Lakonia ... 20 10
1800B 8d. Pegasus, Leukas ... 30 10
1801B 10d. Castle of the Knights, Rhodes, Dodecanese (vert) ... 30 10
1802B 20d. Acropolis, Athens (vert) ... 35 15
1803B 25d. Aqueduct, Kavala ... 40 15
1804B 30d. Castle and statue of Athanasios Diakos, Lamia, Phthiotis (vert) ... 50 15
1805B 50d. Preveza Cathedral bell-tower and clock (vert) ... 1·20 20
1806B 60d. Esplanade, Corfu ... 1·60 45
1807B 70d. Aghios Nikolaos, Lassithi ... 3·00 25
1808B 100d. Six Springheads, Polygyros, Khalkidiki ... 5·50 30
1809B 200d. Church of Paul the Apostle, Corinth, Corinthia ... 6·50 65
1795B/1809B *Set of* 15 ... 18·00 2·75

Nos. 1795A/1809A were each issued in sheets of 50 and Nos. 1795B/1809B each in strips of five within packets of 100 stamps.

The outer edges of the booklet pane are imperforate, giving stamps with one side imperforate.

See also Nos. 1848/62, 1911/22 and 1955/64.

(Des P. Gravalos. Litho M. A. Moatsos, Athens)

1988 (7 Oct). 75th Anniversaries of Union of Crete and Greece (30d.) and Liberation of Epirus and Macedonia (70d.). T **398** and similar horiz design. Multicoloured.

A. P 12½

1810A 30d. Type **398** ... 1·10 35
1811A 70d. Flags, map and "Liberty" ... 2·20 1·20

B. P 14×imperf

1810B 30d. Type **398** ... 4·25 50
1811B 70d. Flags, map and "Liberty" ... 6·50 1·30

Nos. 1810A/11A were each issued in sheets of 50 and Nos. 1810B/11B each in strips of five within packets of 100 stamps.

399 "Adoration of the Magi" (El Greco)

400 Map of E.E.C. and Castle of the Knights, Rhodes

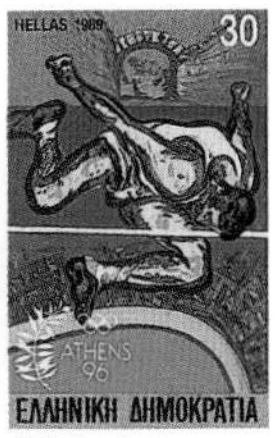

401 Ancient Olympia and High Jumper

(Des V. Constantinea. Litho M. A. Moatsos, Athens)

1988 (2 Dec). Christmas. T **399** and similar multicoloured design. P 12½.

1812 30d. Type **399** ... 1·40 50
a. Booklet pane. No. 1812×10 ... 15·00
1813 70d. "The Annunciation" (Kostas Parthenis) (horiz) ... 1·90 1·20
a. Imperf×p 14 ... 7·50 1·20

The outer edges of the booklet pane are imperforate, giving stamps with one side imperforate.

No. 1813a was issued in strips of five within packets of 100 stamps.

(Des P. Gravalos. Litho M. A. Moatsos, Athens)

1988 (2 Dec). European Economic Community Meeting of Heads of State, Rhodes. T **400** and similar vert design. Multicoloured.

A. P 12½

1814A 60d. Type **400** ... 2·75 1·60
1815A 100d. Members' flags and coin ... 3·25 1·00

B. P 14×imperf

1814B 60d. Type **400** ... 5·50 1·40
1815B 100d. Members' flags and coin ... 8·25 1·00

Nos. 1814A/15A were each issued in sheets of 50 and Nos. 1814B/15B each in strips of five within packets of 100 stamps.

(Des P. Gravalos (170d.), T. Patraskidis (others). Litho M. A. Moatsos, Athens)

1989 (17 Mar). Centenary (1996) of Modern Olympic Games (1st issue). T **401** and similar vert designs. Multicoloured.

A. P 13½×14

1816A 30d. Type **401** ... 70 35
c. Strip of 4. Nos. 1816A/19A ... 9·00 —
1817A 60d. Wrestlers and Delphi ... 1·70 1·20
1818A 70d. Acropolis, Athens, and swimmers ... 2·20 1·50
1819A 170d. Stadium and Golden Olympics emblem ... 4·25 2·10
1816A/1819A *Set of* 4 ... 8·00 4·75

B. Imperf×p 13½

1816B 30d. Type **401** ... 75 35
c. Strip of 4. Nos. 1816B/19B ... 9·50
1817B 60d. Wrestlers and Delphi ... 1·70 1·00
1818B 70d. Acropolis, Athens, and swimmers ... 2·50 1·20
1819B 170d. Stadium and Golden Olympics emblem ... 4·25 1·00
1816B/1819B *Set of* 4 ... 8·25 3·25

Nos. 1816A/19A were issued together in *se-tenant* strips of four within sheets of 16 stamps.

Nos. 1816B/19B were issued together in *se-tenant* strips in booklets and separately in post office packets of 100; the set price for Nos. 1816B/19B is for a set of singles.

See also Nos. 1863/7, **MS**1995 and 1998/2001.

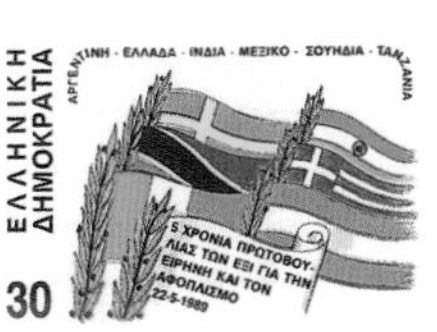

402 Flags

403 Whistling Bird

(Des P. Gravalos. Litho M. A. Moatsos, Athens)

1989 (22 May). International Anniversaries. T **402** and similar horiz designs. Multicoloured.

A. P 14×13½

1820A 30d. Type **402** (fifth anniv of Six-nation Initiative for Peace and Disarmament) ... 1·10 50
1821A 50d. Flag and "Liberty" (bicentenary of French Revolution) ... 1·40 80
1822A 60d. Flag and ballot box (third direct European Parliament elections) ... 3·00 1·60
1823A 70d. Coins (centenary of Interparliamentary Union) ... 3·75 1·60
1824A 200d. Flag (40th anniv of Council of Europe) ... 7·25 1·80
1820A/1824A *Set of* 5 ... 15·00 5·75

B. P 13½×imperf

1820B 30d. Type **402** (fifth anniv of Six-nation Initiative for Peace and Disarmament) ... 3·25 40
1821B 50d. Flag and "Liberty" (bicentenary of French Revolution) ... 9·25 2·40
1822B 60d. Flag and ballot box (third direct European Parliament elections) ... 15·00 3·25
1823B 70d. Coins (centenary of Interparliamentary Union) ... 16·00 3·25
1824B 200d. Flag (40th anniv of Council of Europe) ... 17·00 4·75
1820B/1824B *Set of* 5 ... 55·00 12·50

Nos. 1820A/4A were each issued in sheets of 50 stamps and Nos. 1820B/4B each in strips of five within packets of 100 stamps.

(Des D. Mytaras. Litho M. A. Moatsos, Athens)

1989 (22 May). Europa. Children's Toys. T **403** and similar vert design. Multicoloured.

A. P 12½×13½

1825A 60d. Type **403** ... 4·00 1·70
c. Pair. Nos. 1825A/6A ... 8·25 3·75
1826A 170d. Butterfly ... 4·00 1·70

B. Imperf×p 13½

1825B 60d. Type **403** ... 5·00 2·50
c. Pair. Nos. 1825B/6B ... 10·50 5·25
d. Booklet pane. No. 1825cB×2 ... 22·00
1826B 170d. Butterfly ... 5·00 2·50

Nos. 1825A/6A were issued together in *se-tenant* pairs within sheets of 16 stamps. Nos. 1825B/6B were issued together in booklets and separately in strips of five within post office packets of 100 stamps.

404 Magnifying Glass and Bird

405 Dog Roses

(Des V. Constantinea. Litho M. A. Moatsos, Athens)

1989 (25 Sept). Balkanfila XII International Stamp Exhibition, Salonika. T **404** and similar horiz designs. Multicoloured. P 13½×12½.

1827 60d. Type **404** ... 1·00 45
1828 70d. Eye looking through magnifying glass ... 1·10 75
MS1829 86×61 mm. 200d. Stamp collectors (42×30 mm). P 14×13 ... 4·25 4·25

(Des V. Constantinea. Litho M. A. Moatsos, Athens)

1989 (8 Dec). Wild Flowers. T **405** and similar horiz designs. Multicoloured. P 13½×12½.

1830 8d. Type **405** ... 25 15
1831 10d. Common myrtle ... 25 15
1832 20d. Common poppies ... 45 20
1833 30d. Anemones ... 60 25
1834 60d. Dandelions and chicory ... 90 40
1835 70d. Mallow ... 1·40 40
1836 200d. Thistles ... 3·25 1·70
1830/1836 *Set of* 7 ... 6·50 3·00

406 Brown Bear (*Ursus arctos*)

407 Gregoris Lambrakis

(Des V. Constantinea. Litho M. A. Moatsos, Athens)

1990 (16 Mar). Endangered Animals. T **406** and similar horiz designs. Multicoloured. P 13½×12½.

1837 40d. Type **406** ... 80 20
1838 70d. Loggerhead turtle (*Caretta caretta*) ... 80 50
1839 90d. Mediterranean monk seal (*Monachus monachus*) ... 1·60 60
1840 100d. Lynx (*Lynx lynx*) ... 3·00 1·30
1837/1840 *Set of* 4 ... 5·50 2·30

(Des V. Constantinea. Litho M. A. Moatsos, Athens)

1990 (11 May). Politicians' Death Anniversaries. T **407** and similar vert design. Multicoloured. P 12½×13½.

1841 40d. Type **407** (27th anniv) ... 70 50
1842 40d. Pavlos Bakoyiannis (first anniv) ... 70 50

408 Clasped Hands, Roses and Flag

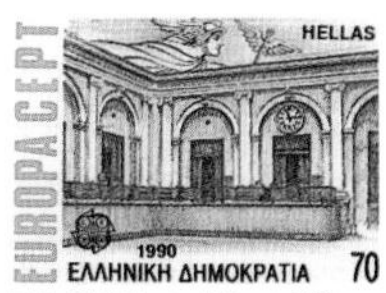

409 Old Central Post Office Interior

(Des P. Gravalos (70d.), Y. Papadakis (others). Litho M. A. Moatsos, Athens)

1990 (11 May). National Reconciliation. T **408** and similar vert designs. Multicoloured. P 12½×13½.

1843 40d. Type **408** ... 55 15
1844 70d. Dove with banner ... 1·00 50
1845 100d. Map and hands holding roses ... 1·50 1·30
1843/1845 *Set of* 3 ... 2·75 1·80

(Des P. Gravalos. Litho M. A. Moatsos, Athens)

1990 (11 May). Europa. Post Office Buildings. T **409** and similar horiz designs. P 13½×12½.

1846 70d. Type **409** ... 4·00 1·60
a. Pair. Nos. 1846/7 ... 8·25 3·50
b. Imperf×p 12½. Booklets ... 5·00 2·10
ba. Booklet pane. Nos. 1846b×2 and 1847a×2 ... 21·00

1847 210d. Exterior of modern post office 4·00 1·60
a. Imperf×p 12½. Booklets 5·00 3·75

Nos. 1846/7 were issued together in *se-tenant* pairs within sheets of 16 stamps.

410 "Animal Fair" (D. Gioldassi) (Karditsa)

411 Yachting

(Des P. Gravalos. Litho M. A. Moatsos, Athens)

1990 (20 June). Prefecture Capitals (2nd series). T **410** and similar multicoloured designs.

A. P 13×12½ (vert) or 12½×13 (horiz)

1848A 2d. Type **410** 35 15
1849A 5d. Fort, Trikala (horiz) 35 15
1850A 8d. Street, Veroia (Imathia) 35 15
1851A 10d. Monument to Fallen Heroes, Missolonghi (Aetolia) (horiz) 35 15
1852A 15d. Harbour, Chios (horiz) 40 20
1853A 20d. Street, Tripolis (Arcadia) (horiz) 40 20
1854A 25d. "City and Town Hall" (woodcut, A. Tasou) (Volos, Magnesia) (horiz) 70 35
1855A 40d. Town Hall, Kalamata (Messenia) (horiz) 80 35
1856A 50d. Market, Pyrgos (Elia) (horiz) 95 35
1857A 70d. Lake and island, Yiannina (horiz) 1·00 35
1858A 80d. Harbour sculpture, Rethymnon 1·70 45
1859A 90d. Argostoli (*Cephalonia*) (horiz) 1·70 40
1860A 100d. Citadel and islet, Nauplion (*Argolis*) (horiz) 1·70 40
1861A 200d. Lighthouse, Patras (*Akhaia*) 4·00 50
1862A 250d. Street, Florina (horiz) 6·00 80
1848A/1862A *Set of* 15 19·00 4·50

B. Imperf×p 13½ (vert) or p 13½×imperf (horiz)

1848B 2d. Type **410** 20 10
1849B 5d. Fort, Trikala (horiz) 20 10
1850B 8d. Street, Veroia (Imathia) 20 10
1851B 10d. Monument to Fallen Heroes, Missolonghi (Aetolia) (horiz) 25 10
1852B 15d. Harbour, Chios (horiz) 25 10
1853B 20d. Street, Tripolis (Arcadia) (horiz) 35 10
1854B 25d. "City and Town Hall" (woodcut, A. Tasou) (Volos, Magnesia) (horiz) 60 30
1855B 40d. Town Hall, Kalamata (Messenia) (horiz) 60 30
1856B 50d. Market, Pyrgos (Elia) (horiz) 75 30
1857B 70d. Lake and island, Yiannina (horiz) 85 50
1858B 80d. Harbour sculpture, Rethymnon 1·50 35
1859B 90d. Argostoli (*Cephalonia*) (horiz) 1·50 50
1860B 100d. Citadel and islet, Nauplion (*Argolis*) (horiz) 1·60 35
1861B 200d. Lighthouse, Patras (*Akhaia*) 3·50 45
1862B 250d. Street, Florina (horiz) 5·75 45
1848B/1862B *Set of* 15 16·00 3·75

Nos. 1848A/62A were each issued in sheets of 50 stamps and Nos. 1848B/62B each in strips of five within packets of 100 stamps.

(Des P. Gravalos. Litho M. A. Moatsos, Athens)

1990 (13 July). Centenary (1996) of Modern Olympic Games (2nd issue). T **411** and similar vert designs. Multicoloured. P 12½×13½.

1863 20d. Type **411** 60 20
1864 50d. Wrestling 85 35
1865 80d. Running 1·20 90
1866 100d. Handball 1·70 80
1867 250d. Football 5·00 1·50
1863/1867 *Set of* 5 8·50 3·50

Nos. 1863/7 were issued both in separate sheets of 50 and together in *se-tenant* strips of five within sheets of 20 stamps (*Price for se-tenant strip: £9.75 un*).

412 Schliemann and Lion Gate, Mycenae

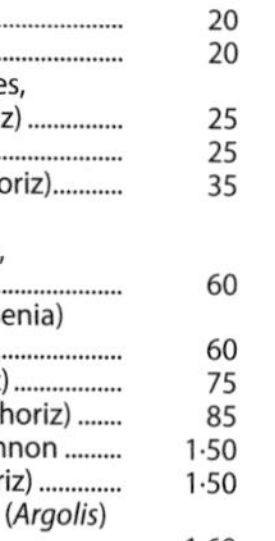

413 "Woman knitting" (lithograph, Vasso Katraki)

(Des E. Jünger. Litho M. A. Moatsos, Athens)

1990 (11 Oct). Death Centenary of Heinrich Schliemann (archaeologist). P 14×13½.

1868 **412** 80d. multicoloured 8·50 4·25

(Des P. Gravalos. Litho M. A. Moatsos, Athens)

1990 (11 Oct). 50th Anniv of Greek–Italian War. T **413** and similar vert designs. Multicoloured. P 12½.

1869 50d. Type **413** 80 40
1870 80d. "Virgin Mary protecting Army" (lithograph, George Gounaropoulou) 1·10 80
1871 100d. "Women's War Work" (lithograph, Kosta Grammatopoulou) 1·30 95
1869/1871 *Set of* 3 3·00 1·90

414 Hermes

(Des P. Gravalos. Litho M. A. Moatsos, Athens)

1990 (14 Dec). Stamp Day. Sheet 87×62 mm. P 14×13.

MS1872 **414** 300d. multicoloured 15·00 15·00

415 Calliope, Euterpe and Erato

(Des P. Gravalos. Litho M. A. Moatsos, Athens)

1991 (11 Mar). The Nine Muses. T **415** and similar horiz designs. Multicoloured. P 12½.

1873 50d. Type **415** 85 40
1874 80d. Terpsichore, Polyhymnia and Melpomene 1·60 90
1875 250d. Thalia, Clio and Urania 4·25 1·20
1873/1875 *Set of* 3 6·00 2·30

416 Battle Scene (Ioannis Anousakis)

(Des I. Mylonas (300d.). Litho M. A. Moatsos, Athens)

1991 (20 May). 50th Anniv of Battle of Crete. T **416** and other horiz design. Multicoloured. P 12½×14 (60d.) or 12½ (300d.).

1876 60d. Type **416** 2·20 75
1877 300d. Map and flags of allied nations (32×24 mm) 5·00 2·10

417 Icarus pushing Satellite

418 Swimming

(Des P. Gravalos. Litho M. A. Moatsos, Athens)

1991 (20 May). Europa. Europe in Space. T **417** and similar horiz design. Multicoloured. P 12½.

1878 80d. Type **417** 4·00 2·40
a. Pair. Nos. 1878/9 9·50 6·25
b. Imperf×p 12½. Booklets 5·00 3·25
ba. Booklet pane. Nos. 1878b×2 and 1879a×2 24·00
1879 300d. Chariot of the Sun 5·25 3·50
a. Imperf×p 12½. Booklets 6·50 3·75

Nos. 1878/9 were issued together in *se-tenant* pairs within the feet.

(Des P. Gravalos. Litho M. A. Moatsos, Athens)

1891 (25 June). 11th Mediterranean Games, Athens. T **418** and similar vert designs. Multicoloured. P 13½×14.

1880 10d. Type **418** 35 20
1881 60d. Basketball 80 35
1882 90d. Gymnastics 1·50 35
1883 130d. Weightlifting 2·10 65
1884 300d. Throwing the hammer 4·75 2·50
1880/1884 *Set of* 5 8·50 3·75

419 Pillar of Democracy

420 Europa and Zeus as Bull (from Attic vase)

(Des P. Gravalos. Litho M. A. Moatsos, Athens)

1991 (20 Sept). 2500th Anniv of Birth of Democracy. P 13½×14.

1885 **419** 100d. black, stone and bright blue 1·70 90

(Des V. Constantinea. Litho M. A. Moatsos, Athens)

1991 (20 Sept). Greek Presidency of European Postal and Telecommunications Conference. Sheet 81×62 mm. P 14×13.

MS1886 **420** 300d. multicoloured 19·00 19·00

421 Pres. Konstantinos Karamanlis signing Treaty of Athens

422 Emblem and Speed Skaters

(Des P. Gravalos. Litho M. A. Moatsos, Athens)

1991 (9 Dec). Tenth Anniv of Greek Admission to European Community. T **421** and similar vert design. Multicoloured. P 13×14.

1887 50d. Type **421** 80 35
1888 80d. Map of Europe and Pres. Karamanlis 1·40 65

(Des T. Katsoulidis. Litho M. A. Moatsos, Athens)

1991 (9 Dec). Winter Olympic Games, Albertville. T **422** and similar vert design. Multicoloured. P 12½×13½.

1889 80d. Type **422** 1·90 1·00
a. Pair. Nos. 1889/90 6·00 2·75
1890 300d. Slalom skier 3·75 1·60

Nos. 1889/90 were issued together in *se-tenant* pairs within the sheet.

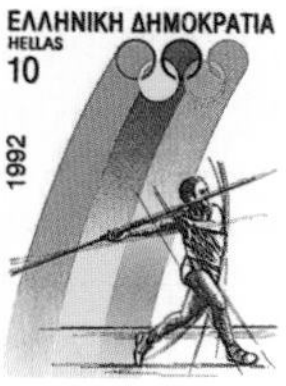

423 Throwing the Javelin

424 Couple beneath Umbrella

(Des A. Rouhier (90d.), K. Michotas (340d.), P. Gravalos (others). Litho M. A. Moatsos, Athens)

1992 (3 Apr). Olympic Games, Barcelona. T **423** and similar multicoloured designs. P 14×13½ (90, 340d.) or 12½ (others).

1891 10d. Type **423** 40 20
1892 60d. Show jumping 1·40 45
1893 90d. Runner (37×24 mm) 2·10 95
1894 120d. Gymnastics 3·50 75
1895 340d. Runners' heads forming Olympic rings (37×24 mm) 6·50 1·90
1891/1895 *Set of* 5 12·50 3·75

(Des V. Constantinea. Litho M. A. Moatsos, Athens)

1992 (22 May). Health. T **424** and similar vert designs. Multicoloured. P 12½.

1896 60d. Type **424** (anti-AIDS campaign) 65 25
1897 80d. Doctor examining child (1st European Gastroenterology Week) 1·20 40
1898 90d. Crab killing flower on healthy plant (anti-cancer campaign) 1·40 50
1899 120d. Hephaestus's forge (from 6th-century B.C. urn) (European Year of Social Security, Hygiene and Health in the Workplace) 1·60 1·00
1900 280d. Alexandros Onassis Cardiosurgical Centre, Athens 5·50 2·10
1896/1900 *Set of* 5 9·25 3·75

425 *Santa Maria*, Map and Columbus

(Des P. Gravalos. Litho M. A. Moatsos, Athens)

1992 (22 May). Europa. 500th Anniv of Discovery of America by Columbus. T **425** and similar horiz design. Multicoloured. P 13½×12½.

1901 90d. Type **425** 4·00 2·10
a. Pair. Nos. 1901/2 9·50 5·50
b. Imperf×p 12½. Booklets 4·50 2·10
ba. Booklet pane. Nos. 1901b×2 and 1902a×2 22·00
1902 340d. Chios in late 15th century 5·25 3·25
a. Imperf×p 12½. Booklets 5·75 3·50

Nos. 1901/2 were issued together in *se-tenant* pairs within the sheet.

426 Proetus, Bellerophon and Pegasus

427 Head of Hercules in Lion Skin (relief)

(Des K. Michotas. Litho M. A. Moatsos, Athens)

1992 (8 June). European Transport Ministers' Conference, Athens. Sheet 85×59 mm. P 14×13.

MS1903 **426** 300d. multicoloured 11·00 11·00

(Des P. Gravalos (10, 80, 340d.), V. Constantinea (60, 90, 120d.). Litho M. A. Moatsos, Athens)

1992 (17 July). Macedonia. T **427** and similar multicoloured designs. P 12½.

1904 10d. Type **427** ... 35 10
1905 20d. Map of Macedonia and bust of Aristotle (horiz) ... 45 10
1906 60d. Alexander the Great at Battle of Issus (mural) (horiz) ... 1·00 15
1907 80d. Tomb of Philip II at Vergina and Manolis Andronikos (archaeologist). 1·50 50
1908 90d. Deer hunt (mosaic, Pella) ... 2·20 50
1909 120d. Macedonian coin ... 3·00 1·00
1910 340d. 4th-century church at Philippi and Apostle Paul ... 8·75 3·25
1904/1910 *Set of 7* ... 16·00 5·00

428 Piraeus

429 Column, Map, Flags and European Community Emblem

(Des P. Gravalos. Litho Alexandros Matsoukis, Athens)

1992 (12 Oct). Prefecture Capitals (3rd series). T **428** and similar multicoloured designs.

A. P 13

1911A 10d. Type **428** ... 15 10
1912A 20d. Amphissa (Phocis) ... 20 10
1913A 30d. The Heraion, Samos ... 30 15
1914A 40d. Canea ... 45 15
1915A 50d. Zakynthos ... 55 15
1916A 60d. Karpenisi (Evrytania) ... 65 30
1917A 70d. Cave, Kilkis (vert) ... 70 30
1918A 80d. Door of Town Hall, Xanthi (vert) ... 1·10 50
1919A 90d. Macedonian Struggle Museum,Thessaloniki ... 1·40 50
1920A 120d. Tsanakleous School, Komotini (Rhodope) ... 2·40 85
1921A 340d. Spring, Drama ... 5·25 2·10
1922A 400d. Pinios Bridge, Larissa ... 6·50 2·50
1911A/1922A *Set of 12* ... 18·00 7·00

B. P 10½×imperf (horiz) or imperf×p 10½ (vert)

1911B 10d. Type **428** ... 15 10
1912B 20d. Amphissa (Phocis) ... 20 10
1913B 30d. The Heraion, Samos ... 25 10
1914B 40d. Canea ... 40 10
1915B 50d. Zakynthos ... 55 20
1916B 60d. Karpenisi (Evrytania) ... 65 20
1917B 70d. Cave, Kilkis (vert) ... 80 20
1918B 80d. Door of Town Hall, Xanthi (vert) ... 1·60 20
1919B 90d. Macedonian Struggle Museum,Thessaloniki ... 1·90 30
1920B 120d. Tsanakleous School, Komotini (Rhodope) ... 2·75 50
1921B 340d. Spring, Drama ... 6·00 1·30
1922B 400d. Pinios Bridge, Larissa ... 7·75 2·10
1911B/1922B *Set of 12* ... 21·00 4·75

Nos. 1911A/22A were each issued in sheets of 50 stamps and Nos. 1911B/22B each in strips of five within packets of 100 stamps.

(Des V. Constantinea. Litho M. A. Moatsos, Athens)

1992 (12 Oct). European Single Market. P 14×13.

1923 **429** 90d. multicoloured ... 1·20 1·00

430 Headstone (4th century B.C.)

431 Georgakis Olympios at Sekkou Monastery, 1821

(Des V. Constantinea. Litho M. A. Moatsos, Athens)

1993 (26 Feb). 2400th Anniv of Rhodes. T **430** and similar vert designs. Multicoloured. P 13×14.

1924 60d. Type **430** ... 1·10 40
1925 90d. "Aphrodite bathing" (statue) ... 1·90 90
1926 120d. "St. Irene" (from St. Catherine's church) ... 1·40 80
1927 250d. St. Paul's Gate, Naillac Mole ... 5·50 2·10
1924/1927 *Set of 4* ... 9·00 3·75

(Des V. Constantinea and K. Michotas. Litho M. A. Moatsos, Athens)

1993 (25 May). Historical Events. T **431** and similar multicoloured designs. P 13×14 (vert) or 14×13 (horiz).

1928 10d. Type **431** (War of Independence) ... 45 10
1929 30d. Theodore Kolokotronis (War of Independence) ... 60 20
1930 60d. Pavlos Melas (military hero) ... 1·00 35
1931 90d. "Glory crowns the Casualties" (Balkan Wars, 1912–13) ... 2·30 90
1932 120d. Soldiers of Sacred Company, El Alamein, 1942 (horiz) ... 3·75 1·00
1933 150d. Sacred Company on Aegean Island, 1943–45 (horiz) ... 4·25 1·40
1934 200d. Victims' Monument, Kalavryta (destruction of village, 1943) ... 8·25 2·40
1928/1934 *Set of 7* ... 19·00 5·75

432 "The Benefits of Transportation" (Konstantinus Parthenis) (left half)

433 Athens Concert Hall

(Des K. Michotas. Litho M. A. Moatsos, Athens)

1993 (25 May). Europa. Contemporary Art. T **432** and similar vert design. Multicoloured. P 13×14.

1935 90d. Type **432** ... 3·50 2·10
a. Horiz pair. Nos. 1935/6 ... 9·00 6·00
b. Imperf×p 13½. Booklets ... 3·75 2·50
ba. Booklet pane. No. 1935b×2 and 1936a×2 ... 20·00
1936 350d. "The Benefits of Transportation" (right half) ... 5·25 3·75
a. Imperf×p 13½. Booklets ... 5·50 4·00

The two values were issued in horizontal *se-tenant* pairs in sheets and booklets, each pair forming a composite design.

(Des V. Constantinea (30, 200d.), K. Michotas (others). Litho Alexandros Matsoukis, Athens)

1993 (4 Oct). Modern Athens. T **433** and similar horiz designs. Multicoloured. P 14.

1937 30d. Type **433** ... 1·10 20
1938 60d. Iliou Melathron (former house of Heinrich Schliemann (archaeologist), now Numismatic Museum) ... 1·60 30
1939 90d. National Library ... 1·90 50
1940 200d. Athens Eye Hospital ... 5·25 1·80
1937/1940 *Set of 4* ... 8·75 2·50

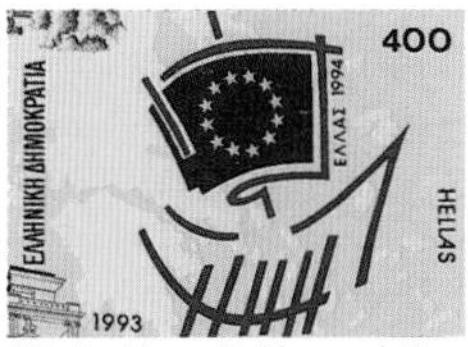

434 Presidency Emblem and Map

(Des V. Constantinea. Litho Alexandros Matsoukis, Athens)

1993 (20 Dec). Greek Presidency (1994) of European Union (1st issue). Sheet 84×60 mm. P 14.

MS1941 **434** 400d. multicoloured ... 7·50 7·50

See also Nos. 1953/4.

435 "Hermes leading Selene's Chariot" (Boeotian vase)

436 "Last Supper" (icon by Michael Damaskinou, St. Catherine's Church, Heraklion, Crete)

(Des V. Constantinea. Litho Alexandros Matsoukis, Athens)

1994 (7 Mar). Second Pan-European Transport Conference. P 13×13½.

1942 **435** 200d. multicoloured ... 3·50 1·60

(Des V. Constantinea. Litho Alexandros Matsoukis, Athens)

1994 (8 Apr). Easter. T **436** and similar multicoloured designs. P 14.

1943 30d. Type **436** ... 55 10
1944 60d. "Crucifixion" (detail of wall painting, Great Meteoron) ... 80 20
1945 90d. "Burial of Christ" (icon, Church of the Presentation of the Lord, Patmos) (horiz) ... 1·10 40
1946 150d. "Resurrection" (detail, illuminated manuscript from Mt. Athos) (horiz) ... 2·75 1·00
1943/1946 *Set of 4* ... 4·75 1·50

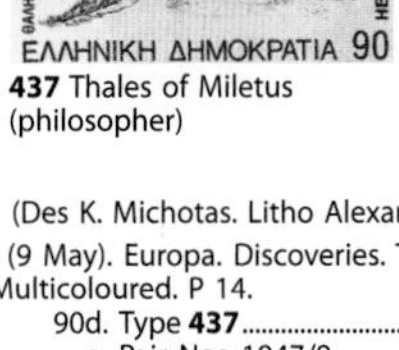

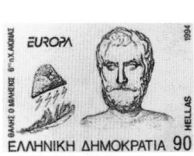

437 Thales of Miletus (philosopher)

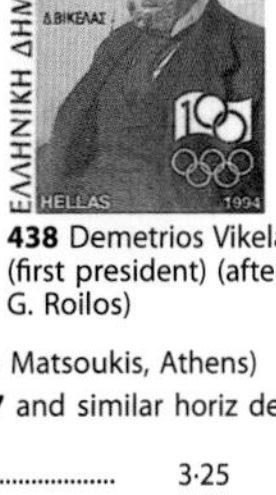

438 Demetrios Vikelas (first president) (after G. Roilos)

(Des K. Michotas. Litho Alexandros Matsoukis, Athens)

1994 (9 May). Europa. Discoveries. T **437** and similar horiz design. Multicoloured. P 14.

1947 90d. Type **437** ... 3·25 2·10
a. Pair. Nos. 1947/8 ... 9·00 5·50
b. Imperf×p 14. Booklets ... 3·25 2·10
ba. Booklet pane. Nos. 1947b×2 and 1948a×2 ... 19·00
1948 350d. Konstantinos Karatheodoris (mathematician) and equations ... 5·50 3·25
a. Imperf×p 14. Booklets ... 5·50 3·25

Nos. 1947/8 were issued together in *se-tenant* pairs within the sheet.

(Des M. Angelopoulos and V. Constantinea (120d.), P. Gravalos (400d.), V. Constantinea (others). Litho Alexandros Matsoukis, Athens)

1994 (6 June). Sports Events and Anniversary. T **438** and similar multicoloured designs. P 14.

1949 60d. Type **438** (centenary of International Olympic Committee) ... 1·00 25
1950 90d. Modern footballer and ancient relief (World Cup Football Championship, U.S.A.) (horiz) ... 1·10 70
1951 120d. Ball, net and laurel (World Volleyball Championship, Piraeus and Salonika) ... 3·25 70
1949/1951 *Set of 3* ... 4·75 1·50

MS1952 68×70 mm. 400d. Modern footballers, Statue of Liberty and ancient relief (World Cup) (41×51 mm) ... 8·25 8·25

439 "Greece" driving E.U. Chariot

440 Parigoritissas Byzantine Church, Arta

(Des K. Michotas. Litho Alexandros Matsoukis, Athens)

1994 (21 June). Greek Presidency of European Union (2nd issue). T **439** and similar horiz design. Multicoloured. P 13×13½.

1953 90d. Type **439** ... 1·40 85
1954 120d. Doric columns and E.U. flag ... 2·20 95

(Des K. Michotas. Litho Alexandros Matsoukis, Athens)

1994 (5 Oct). Prefecture Capitals (4th series). T **440** and similar multicoloured designs.

A. P 13

1955A 10d. Tsalopoulou mansion house, Katerini (Pieria) (vert) ... 15 10
1956A 20d. Type **440** ... 15 10
1957A 30d. Bridge and tower, Levadia (Boeotia) (vert) ... 35 15
1958A 40d. Koumbelidikis church, Kastoria ... 35 20
1959A 50d. Outdoor theatre, Grevena ... 50 25
1960A 60d. Waterfall, Edessa (Pella) ... 60 25
1961A 80d. Red House, Chalkida (Euboea) ... 1·20 35
1962A 90d. Government House, Serres ... 1·50 40
1963A 120d. Town Hall, Heraklion ... 1·50 70
1964A 150d. Church of Our Lady of the Annunciation, Igoumenitsa (Thesprotia) (vert) ... 2·20 70
1955A/1964A *Set of 10* ... 7·75 3·00

B. Imperf×p 10½ (vert) or 10½×imperf (horiz)

1955B 10d. Tsalopoulou mansion house, Katerini (Pieria) (vert) ... 15 10
1956B 20d. Type **440** ... 15 10
1957B 30d. Bridge and tower, Levadia (Boeotia) (vert) ... 35 10
1958B 40d. Koumbelidikis church, Kastoria ... 45 10
1959B 50d. Outdoor theatre, Grevena ... 60 20
1960B 60d. Waterfall, Edessa (Pella) ... 70 20
1961B 80d. Red House, Chalkida (Euboea) ... 1·10 25
1962B 90d. Government House, Serres ... 1·80 35
1963B 120d. Town Hall, Heraklion ... 1·80 65
1964B 150d. Church of Our Lady of the Annunciation, Igoumenitsa (Thesprotia) (vert) ... 2·75 65
1955B/1964B *Set of 10* ... 8·75 2·40

Nos. 1955A/64A were each issued in sheets of 50 stamps and Nos. 1955B/64B each in strips of five within packets of 100 stamps.

441 "Declaration of Constitution" (detail, Karl Haupt)

442 Mercouri and Demonstrators (fighter for Democracy)

(Des V. Constantinea. Litho Alexandros Matsoukis, Athens)

1994 (21 Nov). 150th Anniv of Constitution. T **441** and similar multicoloured designs. P 13×14 (60d.) or 14×13 (others).

1965 60d. Type **441** ... 55 20
1966 150d. Ioannis Makrygiannis, Andreas Metaxas and Dimitrios Kallergis (from *Neos Aristophanes* (magazine)) (horiz) ... 1·40 50
1967 200d. "The Night of 3rd September, 1843" (anon) (horiz) ... 3·75 1·00
1968 340d. Article 107 of 1844 Constitution and Parliament Seal (horiz) ... 6·50 2·10
1965/1968 *Set of 4* ... 11·00 3·50

(Des K. Michotas (60d.), V. Constantinea (others). Litho Alexandros Matsoukis, Athens)

1995 (7 Mar). Melina Mercouri (actress and Minister of Culture) Commemoration. T **442** and similar multicoloured designs. P 13×14 (340d.) or 14×13 (others).

1969 60d. Type **442** ... 80 20
1970 90d. Mercouri and Acropolis (politician) ... 90 50
1971 100d. Mercouri in three roles (actress) ... 2·75 95
1972 340d. Mercouri with flowers (vert) ... 7·50 2·10
1969/1972 *Set of 4* ... 11·00 3·50

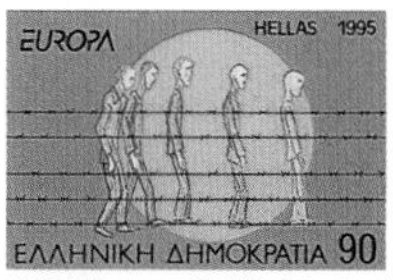

443 Prisoners behind Barbed Wire

444 Emblem

(Des K. Michotas. Litho Alexandros Matsoukis, Athens)

1995 (3 May). Europa. Peace and Freedom. T **443** and similar horiz design. Multicoloured. P 14.

1973	90d. Type **443**	3·00	2·50
	a. Horiz pair. Nos. 1973/4	8·50	5·25
	b. Imperf×p 13½. Booklets	3·00	2·50
	ba. Booklet pane. Nos. 1973b×2 and 1974a×2	18·00	
1974	340d. Doves flying from crushed barbed wire	5·25	2·50
	a. Imperf×p 13½. Booklets	5·25	2·50

The two values were issued together in horizontal *se-tenant* pairs in sheets and booklets, each pair forming a composite design.

(Des D. Mitaras (10, 300d.), M. Vardopoulou (others). Litho Alexandros Matsoukis, Athens)

1995 (21 June). Anniversaries and Events. T **444** and similar multicoloured designs. P 13×13½ (horiz) or 13½×13 (vert).

1975	10d. Type **444** (fifth World Junior Basketball Championship)	55	10
1976	70d. Agriculture University, Athens (75th anniv) (horiz)	1·10	15
1977	90d. Delphi (50th anniv of United Nations Organization)	1·40	30
1978	100d. Greek flag and returning soldier (50th anniv of end of Second World War)	1·60	50
1979	120d. "Peace" (statue by Kifisodotos) (50th anniv of United Nations Organization)	1·60	70
1980	150d. Dolphins (European Nature Conservation Year) (horiz)	2·75	90
1981	200d. Old telephone and modern key-pad (centenary of telephone in Greece)	4·25	1·00
1982	300d. Owl sitting on ball (29th European Basketball Championship)	8·75	1·90
1975/1982	*Set of* 8	20·00	5·00

445 "The First Vision of the Apocalypse" (icon, Thomas Bathas)

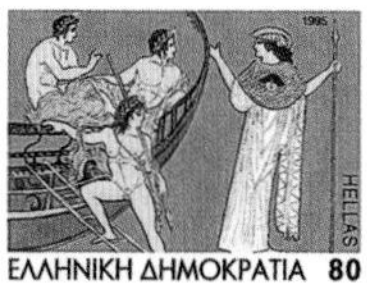

446 Goddess Athene with Argonauts

(Des M. Vardopoulou. Litho Alexandros Matsoukis, Athens)

1995 (18 Sept). 1900th Anniv of the Apocalypse of St. John. T **445** and similar multicoloured designs. P 14.

1983	80d. Type **445**	1·90	40
1984	110d. St. John dictating to Prochoros in front of the Cave of the Apocalypse (miniature from the Four Gospels, Codex 81 of library of Patmos Monastery)	1·90	85
1985	300d. Trumpet of the First Angel (gilded Gospel cover) (horiz)	5·00	2·10
1983/1985	*Set of* 3	8·00	3·00

(Des V. Constantinea. Litho Alexandros Matsoukis, Athens)

1995 (6 Nov). Jason and the Argonauts. T **446** and similar horiz designs. Multicoloured. P 13×13½.

1986	80d. Type **446**	80	35
1987	120d. Phineas (blind seer), god Hermes and the Voreadae pursuing Harpies	1·60	50
1988	150d. Medea, Nike and Jason taming bull	1·60	70
1989	200d. Jason and Medea killing snake and taking the Golden Fleece	3·00	1·00
1990	300d. Jason presenting Golden Fleece to Pelias	6·00	1·70
1986/1990	*Set of* 5	11·50	3·75

447 Psyttaleia

448 1l. Stamp

(Des G. Papageorgiou. Litho Alexandros Matsoukis, Athens)

1995 (18 Dec). Lighthouses. T **447** and similar vert designs. Multicoloured. P 14.

1991	80d. Type **447**	1·10	50
1992	120d. Sapientza	1·60	75
1993	150d. Kastri, Othonoi	3·25	2·40
1994	500d. Zourva, Hydra	6·50	3·25
1991/1994	*Set of* 4	11·00	6·25

(Des M. Vardopoulou. Litho Alexandros Matsoukis, Athens)

1996 (25 Mar). Centenary of Modern Olympic Games (3rd issue). Reproduction of Olympic Games issue of 1896. Three sheets, each 88×88 mm, containing designs as T **448**. Inscriptions in brown, backgrounds flesh; colour of reproduction listed below. P 13½×13 (vert) or 13×13½ (horiz).

MS1995 3 sheets. (a) 80d. ochre (Type **448**); 120d. pink (2l.); 150d. purple-brown (5l.); 650d. brown-olive (10d.). (b) 80d. Venetian red (25l.); 120d. blue-black (60l.); 150d. Prussian blue (1d.); 650d. reddish brown (10d.). (c) 80d. orge-brn (20l.); 120d. grey-lilac (40l.); 150l. bistre-brn (2d.); 650d. dp grey-grn (5d.) 45·00 45·00

No. **MS**1995 was issued in a presentation folder.

449 Sappho (poet)

450 Running

(Des M. Vardopoulou. Litho Alexandros Matsoukis, Athens)

1996 (22 Apr). Europa. Famous Women. T **449** and similar vert design. P 14.

1996	120d. multicoloured	4·25	3·25
	a. Pair. Nos. 1996/7	12·50	8·75
	b. Imperf×p 14. Booklets	4·25	3·25
	ba. Booklet pane. Nos. 1996b×2 and 1997a×2	25·00	
1997	430d. orange-brown, black and ultramarine	7·50	5·25
	a. Imperf×p 14. Booklets	7·50	5·25

Design:—430d. Amalia Fleming.

Nos. 1996/7 were issued in *se-tenant* pairs within the sheet.

(Des M. Vardopoulou. Litho Alexandros Matsoukis, Athens)

1996 (4 June). Centenary of Modern Olympic Games (4th issue). T **450** and similar multicoloured designs. P 13½.

1998	10d. Type **450**	2·20	35
1999	80d. Throwing the discus	1·60	70
2000	120d. Weightlifting	2·75	1·00
2001	200d. Wrestling (horiz)	5·50	2·40
1998/2001	*Set of* 4	11·00	4·00

451 Hippocrates

452 Mytilene

(Des K. Michotas. Litho Alexandros Matsoukis, Athens)

1996 (8 July). First International Medical Olympiad, Athens. T **451** and similar vert design. P 13½×13.

2002	80d. orange-brown, flesh and black	2·75	1·30
2003	120d. olive-brown, turquoise-green and black	3·25	1·80

Design:—120d. Galen.

(Des K. Michotas. Litho Alexandros Matsoukis, Athens)

1996 (7 Oct). Castles (1st series). T **452** and similar horiz designs. Multicoloured.

A. P 13×13½

2004A	10d. Type **452**	20	10
2005A	20d. Lindos	25	10
2006A	30d. Rethymnon	35	15
2007A	70d. Assos Cephalonia	60	35
2008A	80d. Castle of the Serbs	1·10	65
2009A	120d. Monemvasia	1·90	80
2010A	200d. Didimotihon	3·50	1·00
2011A	430d. Vonitsas	7·50	2·40
2012A	1000d. Nikopolis	15·00	6·50
2004A/2012A	*Set of* 9	27·00	11·00

B. Imperf×p 13½

2004B	10d. Type **452**	20	10
2005B	20d. Lindos	25	10
2006B	30d. Rethymnon	35	15
2007B	70d. Assos Cephalonia	60	20
2008B	80d. Castle of the Serbs	1·10	50
2009B	120d. Monemvasia	1·90	65
2010B	200d. Didimotihon	3·50	1·00
2011B	430d. Vonitsas	7·50	1·50
2012B	1000d. Nikopolis	15·00	5·75
2004B/2012B	*Set of* 9	27·00	9·00

Nos. 2004A/12A were each issued in sheets of 50 stamps and Nos. 2004B/12B each in strips of five within packets of 100 stamps.

See also Nos. 2069/78.

453 Puppets

(Des V. Constantinea. Litho Alexandros Matsoukis, Athens)

1996 (15 Nov). Shadow Puppets. T **453** and similar horiz designs. Multicoloured. P 14.

2013	80d. Type **453**	1·60	70
2014	100d. Men courting woman	1·10	80
2015	120d. Soldiers	2·40	1·00
2016	200d. Men fighting dragon	4·25	1·60
2013/2016	*Set of* 4	8·50	3·75

454 Inscription on Wine Jug (720 B.C.)

455 Papandreou, Cap, Degree and Books

(Des K. Michotas. Litho Alexandros Matsoukis, Athens)

1996 (18 Dec). The Greek Language. T **454** and similar horiz designs. Multicoloured. P 13×13½.

2017	80d. Type **454**	80	65
2018	120d. Homer's *Iliad* (papyrus scroll, 436–45)	1·60	75
2019	150d. Psalm (6th century)	2·20	1·00
2020	350d. Dionysios Solomos (writer) and verse of poem (1824)	9·00	3·25
2017/2020	*Set of* 4	12·00	5·00

(Des T. Toumbas. Litho Alexandros Matsoukis, Athens)

1997 (12 Feb). Andreas Papandreou (Prime Minister, 1981–89 and 1993–96) Commemoration. T **455** and similar horiz designs. Multicoloured. P 13×13½.

2021	80d. Type **455** (Doctorate in Economics, Harvard University, 1943)	1·10	50
2022	120d. Return from exile, 1974, and smoking pipe	1·60	75
2023	150d. Parliament building and Papandreou	2·75	95
2024	500d. State flag, dove and Papandreou wearing glasses	7·00	3·50
2021/2024	*Set of* 4	11·00	5·25

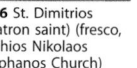

456 St. Dimitrios (patron saint) (fresco, Aghios Nikolaos Orphanos Church)

457 Trikomo

(Des K. Michotas. Litho Alexandros Matsoukis, Athens)

1997 (26 Mar). Thessaloniki, Cultural Capital of Europe. T **456** and similar multicoloured designs. P 13½.

2025	80d. Type **456**	80	35
2026	100d. Hippocratic Hospital (horiz)	1·90	65
2027	120d. Marble statue pedestal (2nd century) and circular relief of woman's head	1·90	80
2028	150d. Mosaic (detail) in cupola of Rotunda	2·75	85
2029	300d. 14th-century chalice (horiz)	7·00	2·40
2025/2029	*Set of* 5	13·00	4·50

(Des M. Vardopoulou. Litho Alexandros Matsoukis, Athens)

1997 (24 Apr). Macedonian Bridges. T **457** and similar horiz designs. Multicoloured. P 14.

2030	80d. Type **457**	1·10	40
2031	120d. Portitsa	1·40	65
2032	150d. Ziakas	2·75	95
2033	350d. Kastro	5·50	2·50
2030/2033	*Set of* 4	9·75	4·00

458 Prometheus the Fire-stealer

459 Running

(Des M. Vardopoulou. Litho Alexandros Matsoukis, Athens)

1997 (19 May). Europa. Tales and Legends. T **458** and similar horiz design. Multicoloured. P 14.

2034	120d. Type **458**	3·25	2·40
	a. Pair. Nos. 2034/5	8·50	5·25
	b. Imperf×p 13½. Booklets	3·50	2·50
	ba. Booklet pane. Nos. 2034b×2 and 2035a×2	19·00	
2035	430d. Knights (Digenis Akritas)	5·00	2·50
	a. Imperf×p 13½. Booklets	5·25	3·00

(Des P. Gravalos. Litho Alexandros Matsoukis, Athens)

1997 (11 July). Sixth World Athletics Championships, Athens. T **459** and similar horiz designs. Multicoloured. P 13×13½.

2036	20d. Type **459**	45	25
2037	100d. "Nike" (statue)	1·20	60
2038	140d. High jumping	2·20	85
2039	170d. Hurdling	2·75	1·50
2040	500d. Stadium, Athens	8·25	3·00
2036/2040	*Set of* 5	13·50	5·50

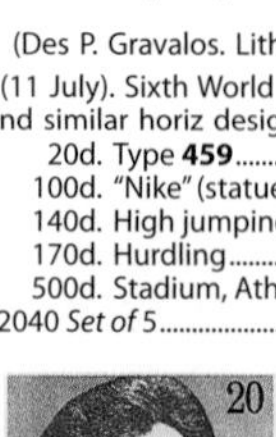

460 Alexandros Panagoulis (resistance leader)

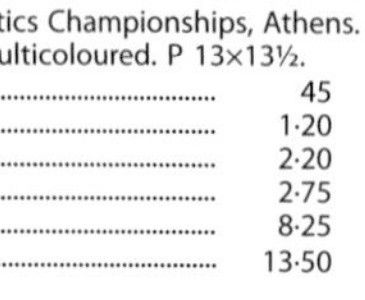

461 Vassilis Avlonitis

(Des M. Vardopoulou. Litho Alexandros Matsoukis, Athens)

1997 (31 Oct). Anniversaries. T **460** and similar multicoloured designs. Multicoloured. P 13×13½ (horiz) or 13½×13 (vert).

2041 20d. Type **460** (20th death anniv (1996)) . 60 50
2042 30d. Grigorios Xenopoulos (writer, 130th birth anniv) 60 50
2043 40d. Odysseaó Elytió (poet, first death anniv) (horiz) 60 50
2044 50d. Panayiotis Kanellopoulos (Prime Minister, 1945 and 1967, tenth death anniv (1996)) 1·20 50
2045 100d. Harilaos Trikoupis (Prime Minister 1881–85, death centenary (1996)) (horiz) 2·50 95
2046 170d. Maria Callas (opera singer, 20th death anniv) (horiz) 4·00 1·50
2047 200d. Rigas Velestinlis-Feraios (revolutionary writer, death bicentenary (1998)) 5·00 1·90
2041/2047 *Set of* 7 13·00 5·75

(Des M. Vardopoulou. Litho Alexandros Matsoukis, Athens)

1997 (17 Dec). Greek Actors. T **461** and similar horiz designs. Multicoloured. P 13×13½.

2048 20d. Type **461** 60 45
2049 30d. Vassilis Argyropoulos 60 45
2050 50d. Georgia Vassileiadou 60 45
2051 70d. Lambros Constantaras 60 45
2052 100d. Vassilis Logothetidis 1·70 1·40
2053 140d. Dionysis Papagiannopoulos 2·10 1·70
2054 170d. Nikos Stavrides 2·30 1·90
2055 200d. Mimis Fotopoulos 7·50 6·00
2048/2055 *Set of* 8 14·50 11·50

462 "Greece", Greek Flag and Colossus of Rhodes

463 Aghia Sofia Hospital, Athens

(Des K. Michotas. Litho Alexandros Matsoukis, Athens)

1998 (27 Feb). 50th Anniv of Incorporation of Dodecanese Islands into Greece. T **462** and similar vert designs. Multicoloured. P 13½×13.

2056 100d. German commander signing surrender to British and Greek military authorities at Simi, 1945 1·70 1·40
2057 140d. Type **462** 2·10 1·70
2058 170d. Greek and British military representatives as transfer ceremony, Rhodes, 1947 2·30 1·90
2059 500d. Raising Greek flag, Kasos, 1947 7·00 5·50
2056/2059 *Set of* 4 12·00 9·50

1998 (30 Apr). Anniversaries and Events. T **463** and similar multicoloured designs. Litho. P 13×13½ (horiz) or 13½×13 (vert).

2060 20d. Type **463** (centenary of Aghia Sofia Children's Hospital) 10 10
2061 100d. St. Xenophon's Monastery (millenary) (vert) 1·20 95
2062 140d. Woman in traditional costume (4th International Thracian Congress, Nea Orestiada) (vert) 1·70 1·40
2063 150d. Parthenon and congress emblem (International Cardiography Research Congress, Rhodes) 1·70 1·40
2064 170d. Sculpture of man and young boy (Cardiography Congress) (vert) 2·30 1·90
2065 500d. Emblem (50th anniv of Council of Europe) (vert) 8·25 6·50
2060/2065 *Set of* 6 13·50 11·00

464 Ancient Theatre, Epidavros

466 Ierapetra, Crete

465 Players

(Litho Alexandros Matsoukis, Athens)

1998 (29 May). Europa. National Festivals. T **464** and similar horiz design. Multicoloured. P 14.

2066 140d. Type **464** 1·70 1·40
a. Pair. Nos. 2066/7 10·50 8·25
b. Imperf×p 13½. Booklets 1·70 1·40
ba. Booklet pane. Nos. 2066b×2 and 2067a×2 21·00
2067 500d. Festival in Herod Atticus Theatre, Athens 8·25 6·50
a. Imperf×p 13½. Booklets 8·25 6·50

1998 (15 June). World Basketball Championship, Athens. Sheet 70×68 mm containing T **465**. Litho. P 14×14½.

MS2068 **465** 300d. multicoloured 4·00 3·25

1998 (15 July). Castles (2nd series). T **466** and similar multicoloured designs. Litho. P 13×13½.

2069 30d. Type **466** 10 10
a. Imperf×p 13½ 10 10
2070 50d. Corfu 35 30
a. Imperf×p 13½ 35 30
2071 70d. Limnos 45 35
a. Imperf×p 13½ 45 35
2072 100d. Argolis 60 45
a. Imperf×p 13½ 60 45
2073 150d. Iraklion, Crete 1·00 85
a. Imperf×p 13½ 1·00 85
2074 170d. Naupaktos (vert) 1·20 95
a. Perf 13½×imperf 1·20 95
2075 200d. Ioannina (vert) 1·30 1·00
a. Perf 13½×imperf 1·30 1·00
2076 400d. Platamona 2·50 2·00
a. Imperf×p 13½ 2·50 2·00
2077 550d. Karitainas (vert) 3·75 3·00
a. Perf 13½×imperf 3·75 3·00
2078 600d. Fragkokastello, Crete 4·00 3·25
a. Imperf×p 13½ 4·00 3·25
2069/2078 *Set of* 10 13·50 11·00

The stamps perforated on all four sides were each issued in sheets of 50 stamps; those perforated on two sides only were each issued in strips of five within packets of 100 stamps.

467 "Church of St. George of the Greeks (18th-century copperplate)

(Des M. Vardopoulou. Litho Alexandros Matsoukis, Athens)

1998 (26 Oct). 500th Anniv of Greek Orthodox Community in Venice. T **467** and similar multicoloured designs. P 14.

2079 30d. Type **467** 25 20
2080 40d. "Christ Pantocrator" (icon) (vert) 60 45
2081 140d. Illuminated script of hymn "Epi Soi hairei" by Georgios Klontzas (vert) 1·70 1·40
2082 230d. "St. George of the Greeks" (illuminated manuscript, 1640) 3·00 2·30
2079/2082 *Set of* 4 5·00 4·00

468 Homer (poet)

469 Ancient Trireme and Circulation of Mediterranean Sea Currents

(Des I. Gourzis. Litho Alexandros Matsoukis, Athens)

1998 (18 Dec). Ancient Greek Writers. T **468** and similar vert designs. P 13½×13.

2083 20d. lake-brown and gold 25 20
2084 100d. purple-brown and gold 1·70 1·40
2085 140d. brown-red and gold 2·30 1·90
2086 200d. black and gold 3·50 2·75
2087 250d. deep brown and gold 4·00 3·25
2083/2087 *Set of* 5 10·50 8·50

Designs:—No. 2084, Sophocles (poet); 2085, Thucydides (historian); 2086, Plato (philosopher); 2087, Demosthenes (orator).

(Des M. Vardopoulou. Litho Alexandros Matsoukis, Athens)

1999 (19 Feb). International Year of the Ocean. T **469** and similar horiz designs. Multicoloured. P 13×13½.

2088 40d. Type **469** 25 20
2089 100d. Galleon (detail of icon "Thou art Great, O Lord" by I. Kornaros) 1·20 95
2090 200d. *Aigaio* (oceanographic vessel), astrolabe and seismic sounding of seabed 2·30 1·90
2091 500d. Apollo on ship (3rd-century B.C. silver tetradrachmon coin of Antigonus Dosonos) 4·75 3·75
2088/2091 *Set of* 4 7·75 6·00

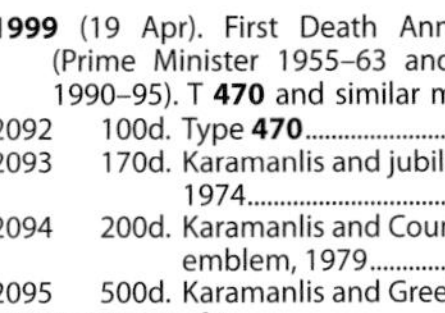

470 Konstantinos Karamanlis

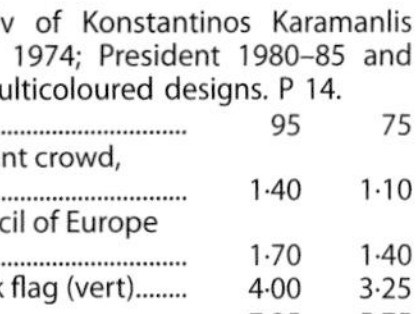

471 Mt. Olympus and Flowers

1999 (19 Apr). First Death Anniv of Konstantinos Karamanlis (Prime Minister 1955–63 and 1974; President 1980–85 and 1990–95). T **470** and similar multicoloured designs. P 14.

2092 100d. Type **470** 95 75
2093 170d. Karamanlis and jubilant crowd, 1974 1·40 1·10
2094 200d. Karamanlis and Council of Europe emblem, 1979 1·70 1·40
2095 500d. Karamanlis and Greek flag (vert) 4·00 3·25
2092/2095 *Set of* 4 7·25 5·75

(Des M. Vardopoulou. Litho Alexandros Matsoukis, Athens)

1999 (24 May). Europa. Parks and Gardens. T **471** and similar horiz design. Multicoloured. P 14.

2096 170d. Type **471** 1·40 1·10
a. Horiz pair. Nos. 2096/7 6·75 5·25
b. Imperf×13. Booklets 1·40 1·10
ba. Booklet pane. Nos. 2096b×2 and 2097a×2 13·50
2097 550d. Mt. Olympus and flowers (different). 5·00 4·00
a. Imperf×13. Booklets 5·00 4·00

Nos. 2096/7 were issued together in *se-tenant* pairs within the sheet, each pair forming a composite design.

472 Ancient Greek and Japanese Noh Theatre Masks

473 Temple of Hylates Apollo, Kourion

(Des M. Vardopoulou. Litho Alexandros Matsoukis, Athens)

1999 (28 June). Centenary of Diplomatic Relations between Greece and Japan. P 14.

2098 **472** 120d. multicoloured 1·20 95

(Des A. Ladommatos. Litho Alexandros Matsoukis, Athens)

1999 (28 June). 4000 Years of Greek Culture. T **473** and similar vert designs. Multicoloured. P 13½×13.

2099 120d. Type **473** 95 75
a. Block of 4. Nos. 2099/2102 4·00
2100 120d. Mycenaean pot depicting warriors (Athens) 95 75
2101 120d. Mycenaean amphora depicting horse (Nicosia) 95 75
2102 120d. Temple of Apollo, Delphi 95 75
2099/2102 *Set of* 4 3·50 2·75

Nos. 2099/2102 were issued together in *se-tenant* blocks of four stamps within the sheet, each block having a composite design of a rosette at the centre.

474 Trains

475 Helicopter and Commandos in Inflatable Boat

(Des M. Vardopoulou. Litho Alexandros Matsoukis, Athens)

1999 (8 Nov). Fifth Anniv of Community Support Programme. T **474** and similar horiz designs. Multicoloured. P 13×13½.

2103 20d. Type **474** (modernization of railways) 25 20
2104 120d. Bridge over River Antirrio 95 75
2105 140d. Compact disk, delivery lorries and conveyor belt (modernization of Post Office) 1·20 95
2106 250d. Athens underground train 1·70 1·40
2107 500d. Control tower, Eleftherios Venizelos airport, Athens 4·00 3·25
2103/2107 *Set of* 5 7·25 6·00

(Des K. Michotas. Litho Alexandros Matsoukis, Athens)

1999 (13 Dec). Armed Forces. T **475** and similar horiz designs. Multicoloured. P 13½.

2108 20d. Type **475** 25 20
2109 30d. Missile corvette 30 25
2110 40d. Two F-16 aircraft 35 30
2111 50d. CL-215 aircraft dispersing water on forest fire 45 35
2112 70d. Destroyer 60 45
2113 120d. Forces distributing aid in Bosnia 1·20 95
2114 170d. Dassault Mirage 2000 jet fighter above Aegean 1·70 1·40
2115 250d. Helicopters, tanks and soldiers on joint exercise 2·30 1·90
2116 600d. Submarine *Okeanos* 4·75 3·75
2108/2116 *Set of* 9 10·50 8·50

476 Birth of Christ

477 "Building Europe"

(Des I. Mitrakas. Litho Alexandros Matsoukis, Athens)

2000 (1 Jan). Birth Bimillenary of Jesus Christ. Icons. T **476** and similar multicoloured designs. P 14×14½ (170d.), 13½ (200d.), 13½×14 (500d.) or 14½×14 (others).

2117 20d. Type **476** 25 20
2118 50d. Discussion between men of different denominations 60 45
2119 120d. Angels praising God 95 75

2120 170d. Epiphany (horiz) 1·70 1·40
2121 200d. Communion (35×35 mm) 2·10 1·70
2122 500d. Heavenly beings above priests and worshippers (27×57 mm) 4·00 3·25
2117/2122 *Set of* 6 8·75 7·00

(Des J.-P. Cousin. Litho Alexandros Matsoukis, Athens)

2000 (9 May). Europa. P 13½×13.
2123 **477** 170d. multicoloured 3·50 2·75
a. Imperf×13. Booklets 3·50 2·75
ab. Booklet pane. No. 2123a×4 14·50

478 *Ilissos* (steamship)

479 Rainbow over Village (Spyros Dalakos)

(Des G. Papageorgiou. Litho Alexandros Matsoukis, Athens)

2000 (26 June). Ships. T **478** and similar horiz designs. Multicoloured. P 14½×14.
2124 10d. Type **478** 35 30
2125 120d. *Adrias* (destroyer) 80 65
2126 170d. *Ia II* (steamship) 1·70 1·40
2127 400d. *Vas Olga* (destroyer) 4·75 3·75
2124/2127 *Set of* 4 6·75 5·50

(Des M. Vardopoulou. Litho Alexandros Matsoukis, Athens)

2000 (26 June). Stampin the Future. Winning Entries in Children's International Painting Competition. T **479** and similar horiz designs. Multicoloured. P 14½×14.
2128 130d. Type **479** 80 65
2129 180d. Robots (Moshovaki-Chaiger Ornella) 1·20 95
2130 200d. Cars and house (Zisis Zariotis) 2·10 1·70
2131 620d. Children astride rocket (Athina Limioudi) 5·25 4·25
2128/2131 *Set of* 4 8·50 6·75

480 Torch and Flag

481 Emblem and Olympic Rings

(Des Lynda Warner. Litho Alexandros Matsoukis, Athens)

2000 (15 Sept). Olympic Games, Sydney. T **480** and similar vert design. Multicoloured. P 13½.
2132 200d. Type **480** 1·70 1·40
2133 650d. Torch, flag and Sydney Opera House 5·25 4·25

(Litho Alexandros Matsoukis, Athens)

2000 (7 Nov). Olympic Games, Athens (2004) (1st issue). T **481** and similar vert designs all showing the Olympic Rings and emblem. P 14×14½.
2134 10d. multicoloured 25 20
2135 50d. multicoloured 60 45
2136 130d. multicoloured 80 65
2137 180d. multicoloured 1·70 1·40
2138 200d. multicoloured 2·30 1·90
2139 650d. multicoloured 4·75 3·75
2134/2139 *Set of* 6 9·25 7·50

The backgrounds of Nos. 2134/9 show progressively, an enlarged portion of the emblem from the second to the eighth pair of leaves.

See also Nos. **MS**2169, 2191/3, 2207/10, **MS**2211, 2216/21, **MS**2222, 2234/8, **MS**2239, 2246/51, 2252/8, 2259/63, 2264/**MS**2270, **MS**2271, **MS**2272, 2275/**MS**2279, **MS**2285 and 2286/**MS**2288.

482 Crete 1901 1d. Stamp

483 Orpheus Christ (sculpture)

(Des M. Vardopoulou. Litho Alexandros Matsoukis, Athens)

2000 (18 Dec). Centenary of First Crete Stamp. Sheet 104×73 mm containing T **482** and similar vert design. Multicoloured. P 14×14½.
MS2140 200d. Type **482**; 650d. Crete 1901 6d. stamp 17·00 16·00

(Des I. Papadakis. Litho Alexandros Matsoukis, Athens)

2000 (18 Dec). Birth Bimillenary of Jesus Christ. T **483** and similar multicoloured designs. P 14×14½ (vert) or 14½×14 (horiz).
2141 20d. Type **483** 10 10
2142 30d. The Good Shepherd (sculpture) 25 20
2143 40d. Christ Pantocrator (mosaic, Holy Monastery of Sina) 35 30
2144 100d. Anapeson in the Protato of Mount Athos (fresco, Manuel Panselinos) (horiz) 60 45
2145 130d. Christ (icon) 80 65
2146 150d. Christ (icon) 95 75
2147 180d. Christ Pantocrator (Encaustic icon) 1·20 95
2148 1000d. Christ Pantocrator (Byzantine coin) (horiz) 8·75 7·00
2141/2148 *Set of* 8 11·50 9·25

484 Mother and Child holding Money Box

485 Dried Earth

(Des M. Vardopoulou. Litho Alexandros Matsoukis, Athens)

2001 (15 May). Anniversaries and Events. T **484** and similar multicoloured designs. P 13½×14 (vert) or 14×13½ (horiz).
2149 20d. Type **484** (centenary of Post Office Savings Bank) 25 20
2150 130d. Euro currency and emblem (centenary of Post Office Savings Bank) (horiz) 1·20 95
2151 140d. Refugees (50th anniv of United Nations High Commission for Refugees) (horiz) 1·50 1·20
2152 180d. Emblem and crowd (75th anniv of Thessalonika International Trade Fair) 1·70 1·40
2153 200d. University façade (75th anniv of Aristotle University, Thessalonika) (horiz) 2·00 1·60
2154 500d. Academy building (75th anniv of Academy of Athens) (horiz) 4·00 3·25
2155 700d. Ioannis Zigdis (politician, third death anniv) 7·00 5·50
2149/2155 *Set of* 7 16·00 13·00

(Des M. Vardopoulou. Litho Alexandros Matsoukis, Athens)

2001 (15 May). Europa. Water Resources. T **485** and similar horiz design. Multicoloured. P 14½×14.
2156 180d. Type **485** 2·30 1·90
a. Pair. Nos. 2156/7 8·25 6·75
b. Imperf×p 13½ 2·30 1·90
ba. Booklet pane. Nos. 2156b×2 and 2157a×2 17·00
2157 650d. Pool of water and droplet 5·75 4·75
a. Imperf×p 13½ 5·75 4·75

486 Little Egret

(Des M. Vardopoulou. Litho Alexandros Matsoukis, Athens)

2001 (27 June). Flora and Fauna. T **486** and similar multicoloured designs. P 13½×14 (140, 150d.) or 14×13½ (others).
2158 20d. Type **486** 10 10
2159 50d. White storks 35 30
2160 100d. Bearded vulture 70 55
2161 140d. Orchid (vert) 95 75
2162 150d. Dalmatian pelican (vert) 1·00 85
2163 200d. Lily, Plastina Lake, Karditsa 1·40 1·10
2164 700d. Egyptian vulture 4·75 3·75
2165 850d. Black vulture 11·50 9·25
2158/2165 *Set of* 8 19·00 15·00

487 Emblem

488 "The Annunciation" (13th-century minature) (detail)

(Des K. Michotas. Litho Alexandros Matsoukis, Athens)

2001 (8 Sept). New Name of Hellenic Post. P 13.
2166 **487** 140d. deep new blue and yellow 95 75
a. Sheetlet of 10 plus 10 labels. Nos. 2166/7 25·00
2167 200d. deep new blue 1·40 1·10

Nos. 2166/7 were issued in horizontal pairs together with *se-tenant* half stamp-size labels within sheets of ten stamps and ten labels.

Sheets could also be "Personalized" by the addition of a portrait photograph in place of the logo on the labels for the cost of 3,400d. per sheetlet available only from ELTA Post Office Pavilion, Thessaloniki International Trade Fair.

(Des K. Michotas. Litho Alexandros Matsoukis, Athens)

2001 (5 Dec). 1700th Anniv of Christianity in Armenia. Sheet 63×85 mm. P 13.
MS2168 **488** 850d. multicoloured 8·75 7·00

489 Figures of Swimmers from Amphora

490 Kamakaki, Salamina

(Des G. Varlamos. Litho Alexandros Matsoukis, Athens)

2001 (5 Dec). Olympic Games, Athens (2004) (2nd issue). Sheet 80×70 mm. P 14.
MS2169 **489** 1200d. multicoloured 11·50 9·25

New Currency

2002. 100 Cents = 1 Euro

(Des M. Vardopoulou. Litho Alexandros Matsoukis, Athens)

2002 (2 Jan). Traditional Dances. T **490** and similar horiz designs. Multicoloured. P 13×13½ (horiz) or 13½×13 (vert).
2170 2c. Type **490** 10 10
a. Imperf×p 13½ 10 10
2171 3c. Prikia (bride's dowry) 10 10
a. Imperf×p 13½ 10 10
2172 5c. Zagorissios, Epirus (vert) 10 10
a. Perf 13×imperf 10 10
2173 10c. Balos, Aegean Islands 25 20
a. Imperf×p 13½ 25 20
2174 15c. Synkathistos, Thrace 35 30
a. Imperf×p 13½ 35 30
2175 20c. Tsakonikos, Peloponnese (vert) 45 35
a. Perf 13×imperf 45 35
2176 30c. Pyrrichios (Sera) (Pontian Greek) 70 55
a. Imperf×p 13½ 70 55
2177 35c. Fourles, Kythnos (vert) 80 65
a. Perf 13×imperf 80 65
2178 40c. Apokriatos, Skyros 95 75
a. Imperf×p 13½ 95 75
2179 45c. Kotsari (Pontian Greek) 1·00 85
a. Imperf×p 13½ 1·00 85
2180 50c. Pentozalis, Crete (vert) 1·20 95
a. Perf 13×imperf 1·20 95
2181 55c. Karagouna, Thessaly 1·30 1·00
a. Imperf×p 13½ 1·30 1·00
2182 60c. Hassapiko, Smyrneikos 1·40 1·10
a. Imperf×p 13½ 1·40 1·10
2183 65c. Zalistos, Naoussa 1·50 1·20
a. Imperf×p 13½ 1·50 1·20
2184 85c. Pogonissios, Epirus 2·00 1·60
a. Imperf×p 13½ 2·00 1·60
2185 €1 Kalamtianos, Peloponnese 2·30 1·90
a. Imperf×p 13½ 2·30 1·90
2186 €2 Maleviziotis, Crete 4·75 3·75
a. Imperf×p 13½ 4·75 3·75
2187 €2.15 Tsamikos, Roumeli 5·00 4·00
a. Imperf×p 13½ 5·00 4·00
2188 €2.60 Zeibekikos (vert) 6·00 4·75
a. Perf 13×imperf 6·00 4·75
2189 €3 Nyfiatikos, Corfou 7·00 5·50
a. Imperf×p 13½ 7·00 5·50
2190 €4 Paschaliatikos 9·25 7·50
a. Imperf×p 13½ 9·25 7·50
2170/2190 *Set of* 21 42·00 33·00

The stamps perforated on all four sides were each issued in sheets of 25 stamps; those perforated on two sides only were each issued in strips of five within books of 100 stamps.

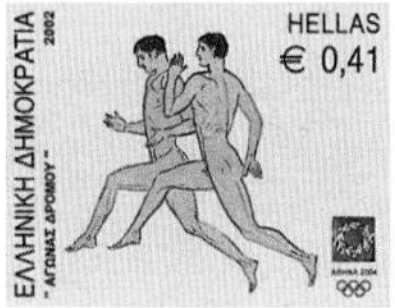

491 Runners (vase painting)

492 Performing Elephant

(Des P. Gravalos (**MS**2196), G. Varlamos (others). Litho Alexandros Matsoukis, Athens)

2002 (15 Mar). Olympic Games, Athens (2004) (3rd issue). T **491** and similar horiz designs. Multicoloured. P 13½×14 (Nos. 2192, 2194) or 14×13½ (others).
2191 41c. Type **491** 1·20 95
2192 59c. Charioteer (8th-century bronze statuette) (vert) 1·70 1·40
2193 80c. Javelin thrower (vase painting) 2·00 1·60
2194 €2.05 Doryphoros ("Spear Bearer") (statue, Polycleitos) (vert) 4·75 3·75
2195 €2.35 Weightlifter (vase painting) 5·75 4·75
2191/2195 *Set of* 5 14·00 11·00
MS2196 121×80 mm. €5 "Crypt of the ancient Olympic stadium, Olympia" (49×29 mm). P 13 13·00 12·00

(Des D. Mytaras. Litho Alexandros Matsoukis, Athens)

2002 (9 May). Europa. Circus. T **492** and similar vert design. Multicoloured. P 13½×14.
2197 60c. Type **492** 2·30 1·90
a. Horiz pair. Nos. 2197/8 11·00 8·75
b. Imperf×13½. Booklets 2·30 1·90
ba. Booklet pane. No. 2197b×2 and No. 2198a×2 22·00
2198 €2.60 Equestrian acrobat 8·25 6·50
a. Imperf×13½. Booklets 8·25 6·50

Nos. 2197/8 were issued together in *se-tenant* pairs within the sheet.

493 Navy Scout

(Des M. Vardopoulou. Litho Alexandros Matsoukis, Athens)

2002 (26 June). Scouts. T **493** and similar horiz designs. Multicoloured. P 13×13½.
2199 45c. Type **493** 1·00 85
2200 60c. Scout and World Conference emblem 1·40 1·10
2201 70c. Air scout and Cub scouts planting tree 1·60 1·30
2202 €2.15 Scouts, mountains and map 5·25 4·25
2199/2202 *Set of* 4 8·25 6·75

494 Fragment of 5th-century B.C. Tablet, Acropolis, Athens

495 Man wearing Olive Wreath holding Two Ears of Corn

(Des P. Katsoulidis. Litho Alexandros Matsoukis, Athens)

2002 (23 Sept). The Greek Language. T **494** and similar multicoloured designs. P 13½.

2203	45c. Type **494**	1·00	85
2204	60c. 13th-century B.C. Linear B script tablet, Glay	1·40	1·10
2205	90c. Manuscript and General Makrygiannis (writer)	2·10	1·70
2206	€2.15 Manuscript and page from 11th-century Byzantine manuscript, Mount Athos	5·00	4·00
2203/2206 *Set of* 4		8·50	7·00

(Des A. Fassianos. Litho Alexandros Matsoukis, Athens)

2002 (30 Oct). Olympic Games, Athens (2004) (4th issue). T **495** and similar vert designs. Multicoloured. P 13½.

2207	45c. Type **495**	1·00	85
2208	60c. Man wearing wreath and chewing ear of corn	1·40	1·10
2209	€2.15 Man beside column wearing wreath and chewing ear of corn	5·00	4·00
2210	€2.60 Man beside tilted column holding wreath	6·00	4·75
2207/2210 *Set of* 4		12·00	9·75

Nos. 2207/10 were issued separately in sheets of 25 stamps and together in *se-tenant* sheetlets of eight (2×4).

496 Façade

(Des M. Vardopoulou. Litho Alexandros Matsoukis, Athens)

2002 (30 Oct). Olympic Games, Athens (2004) (5th issue). Early Stadia. Sheet 120×75 mm. P 13.

MS2211 **496** €6 multicoloured .... 14·00 11·00

497 Chrysostomos Papadopoulos (1923–38)

498 Discus

(Des Katerina Papadimitropoulou. Litho Alexandros Matsoukis, Athens)

2002 (10 Dec). Archbishops of Athens. T **497** and similar horiz designs. Multicoloured. P 13×13½.

2212	10c. Type **497**	25	20
2213	45c. Chrysanthos Philippides (1938–41)	1·20	95
2214	€2.15 Damaskinos Papandreou (1941–49)	5·75	4·75
2215	€2.60 Seraphem Tikas (1974–98)	9·25	7·50
2212/2215 *Set of* 4		15·00	12·00

(Des K. Tsoklis. Litho Alexandros Matsoukis, Athens)

2003 (11 Feb). Olympic Games, Athens (2004) (6th issue). T **498** and similar vert designs. Multicoloured. P 14.

2216	2c. Type **498**	10	10
2217	5c. Shot put	10	10
2218	47c. Javelin	1·20	95
2219	65c. High jump	1·50	1·20
2220	€2.17 Hurdles	5·00	4·00
2221	€2.85 Dumbbells	6·75	5·25
2216/2221 *Set of* 6		13·00	10·50

499 Athena (Girl Mascot)

500 Globe

(Litho Alexandros Matsoukis, Athens)

2003 (11 Feb). Olympic Games, Athens (2004) (7th issue). Sheet 128×82 mm containing T **499** and similar horiz design. Multicoloured. P 13×13½.

MS2222 €2.50 Type **499**; €2.85 Phevos (boy mascot) .... 14·00 13·00

(Des M. Vardopoulou (**MS**2223b), Katerina Papadimitropoulou (**MS**2223a,d,e,h/l); Pin Communication (**MS**2223f) or A. Fassianos (**MS**2223c,g). Litho Alexandros Matsoukis, Athens)

2003 (18 Mar). Greetings Stamps. Sheet 123×124 containing T **500** and similar square designs. Multicoloured. P 14.

MS2223 47c. (a) Type **500** (corporate); 47c. (b) 2004 Olympic emblem (sponsor); 47c. (c) Man wearing wreath (Greece); 47c. (d) Roses (wedding); 47c. (e) Grid and skyline (corporate); 47c. (f) Stylized train (children); 47c. (g) Couple (social occasion); 65c. (h) Statue head (Greece); 65c. (i) Acropolis (Greece) .... 16·00 15·00

Nos. **MS**2223 were each available individually printed on gummed A4 sheets of 15 stamps and 15 labels, which could be personalised by the addition of a photograph or company logo, from the Central Philatelic Office, at double face value.

501 Swallow and European Stars

502 Stylized Figure

(Des P. Xenikopdakis (47c.), M. Papadimitriou (65c.), M. Vardopoulou (€2.85), E. Apostolou 47, 65c., €2.17). Litho Alexandros Matsoukis, Athens)

2003 (16 Apr). Greek Presidency of the European Union. T **501** and similar square designs. Multicoloured. P 14.

2224	47c. Type **501**	1·20	95
2225	65c. White Tower, Thessaloniki formed from letters	1·70	1·40
2226	€2.17 Swallows (fresco, Thera)	5·25	4·25
2227	€2.85 Stars and flags of member countries as jigsaw puzzle	7·00	5·50
2224/2227 *Set of* 4		13·50	11·00

(Des I. Moralis. Litho Alexandros Matsoukis, Athens)

2003 (8 May). Europa. Poster Art. T **502** and similar vert design. Multicoloured. P 13½.

2228	65c. Type **502**	1·70	1·40
	a. Horiz pair. Nos. 2228/9	9·00	7·25
	b. Imperf×13½. Booklets	1·70	1·40
	ba. Booklet pane. No. 2228b×2 and No. 2229a×2	18·00	
2229	€2.85 House with flag pole and veranda	7·00	5·50
	a. Imperf×13½. Booklets	7·00	5·50

Nos. 2228/9 were issued in *se-tenant* pairs within the sheet.

503 Apple floating in Space and Trees

504 High Jump

(Des D. Nalbadis. Litho Alexandros Matsoukis, Athens)

2003 (5 June). Environmental Protection. T **503** and similar vert designs. Multicoloured. P 13½.

2230	15c. Type **503**	35	30
2231	47c. Apple floating in water	1·20	95
2232	65c. Wreath above waves	1·60	1·30
2233	€2.85 Planet above apple tree	6·75	5·50
2230/2233 *Set of* 4		9·00	7·25

(Des Mina Valyraki. Litho Alexandros Matsoukis, Athens)

2003 (9 Sept). Olympic Games, Athens (2004) (8th issue). T **504** and similar multicoloured designs. P 13½.

2234	5c. Type **504**	10	10
2235	47c. Wrestlers	1·20	95
2236	65c. Runners	1·50	1·20
2237	80c. Cyclists (vert)	1·90	1·50
2238	€4 Windsurfer (vert)	9·25	7·50
2234/2238 *Set of* 5		12·50	10·00

505 Athena (Girl Mascot)

506 Stair Maker

(Litho Alexandros Matsoukis, Athens)

2003 (9 Sept). Olympic Games, Athens (2004) (9th issue). Sheet 128×80 mm containing T **505** and similar horiz design. Multicoloured. P 13×13½.

MS2239 €2.50 Type **505**; €2.85 Phevos (boy mascot) .... 14·00 13·00

(M. Vardopoulou. Litho Alexandros Matsoukis, Athens)

2003 (17 Oct). Traditional Trades and Crafts. T **506** and similar horiz designs. Multicoloured. P 13½.

2240	3c. Type **506**	10	10
2241	10c. Shoemaker	25	20
2242	50c. Smith	1·20	1·10
2243	€1 Type setter	2·50	2·20
2244	€1.40 Sponge diver	3·50	3·25
2245	€4 Hand weaver	10·00	9·00
2240/2245 *Set of* 6		16·00	14·50
MS2245*a* 115×149 mm. Nos. 2240/5		16·00	16·00

507 Weightlifting

508 Volos

(Des A. Fassianos. Litho Alexandros Matsoukis, Athens)

2003 (28 Nov). Olympic Games 2004, Athens (10th issue). Athletes. T **507** and similar vert designs. Multicoloured. P 13½.

2246	20c. Type **507**	55	50
2247	30c. Throwing javelin	80	75
2248	40c. Charioteers	1·10	1·00
2249	47c. Soldier carrying spear and shield	1·30	1·20
2250	€2 Running	5·25	5·00
2251	€2.85 Throwing discus	7·50	7·00
2246/2251 *Set of* 6		15·00	14·00

(Des T. Katsouldis. Litho Alexandros Matsoukis, Athens)

2004 (15 Jan). Olympic Games 2004, Athens (11th issue). Cities. T **508** and similar horiz designs. Multicoloured. P 13×13½.

2252	1c. Type **508**	10	10
2253	2c. Patra	10	10
2254	5c. Herakleio, Crete	10	10
2255	47c. Athens	1·20	1·20
2256	€1.40 Thessalonika	3·50	3·25
2257	€4 Athens	10·00	9·25
2252/2257 *Set of* 6		13·50	12·50
MS2258 120×135 mm. Nos. 2252/7		12·50	12·00

509 Spiros Louis

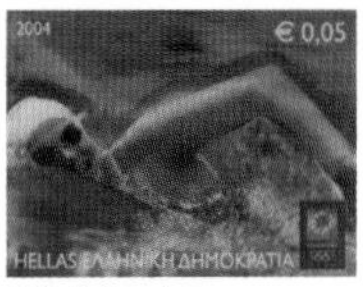

510 Swimming

(Des Myrsini Vardopoulou. Litho and embossed)

2004 (15 Jan). Olympic Games 2004, Athens (12th issue). Greek Olympic Champions. T **509** and similar horiz designs. Multicoloured. P 13×13½.

2259	3c. Type **509** (marathon, 1896)	10	10
2260	10c. Aristides Konstantinides (cycling, 1896)	25	25
2261	€2 Ioannis Fokianos (modern Olympic pioneer)	5·00	4·75
2262	€2.17 Ioannis Mitropoulos (gymnast, 1896)	5·50	5·00
2263	€3.60 Konstantinos Tsiklitiras (long jump, 1912)	9·25	8·50
2259/2263 *Set of* 5		18·00	17·00

(Des Myrsini Vardopoulou. Litho and embossed)

2004 (24 Mar). Olympic Games 2004, Athens (13th issue). Sport Disciplines. T **510** and similar multicoloured designs. P 13½.

2264	5c. Type **510**	10	10
2265	10c. Hands applying Rosin	25	25
2266	20c. Canoeing	45	40
2267	47c. Relay race	1·10	1·00
2268	€2 Gymnastics floor exercise (vert)	5·00	4·75
2269	€5 Gymnastics ring exercise (vert)	12·50	12·00
2264/2269 *Set of* 6		17·00	17·00
MS2270 162×140 mm. Nos. 2264/9		17·00	17·00

511 Woman holding Torch

512 Dove and Olympic Rings

(Des G. Stathopoulos. Litho Alexandros Matsoukis, Athens)

2004 (4 May). Olympic Games 2004, Athens (14th issue). Greetings Stamps. Sheet 90×75 mm containing T **511** and similar square design. Multicoloured. P 14.

MS2271 47c. Type **511**; €2.50 Woman and buildings .... 6·75 6·75

No. **MS**2271 (Type **511**) was also available printed on gummed A4 sheets of 15 stamps and 15 labels, which could be personalised by the addition of a photograph or company logo, from the Central Philatelic Office, for €15.

(Des AlterVision. Litho Alexandros Matsoukis, Athens)

2004 (4 May). Olympic Games 2004, Athens (15th issue). Sheet 128×81 mm containing T **512** and similar horiz design. Multicoloured. P 14.

MS2272 47c. Type **512**; €2.50 Dove and children .... 6·75 6·75

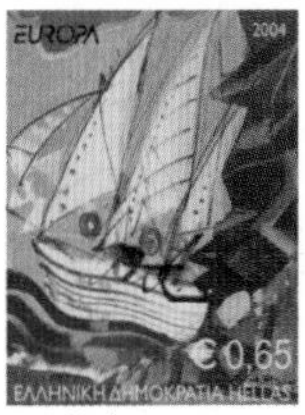

513 Yacht

514 Obverse and Reverse of 3 Drachma Coin (480–450 BC)

(Des D. Mytaras. Litho Alexandros Matsoukis, Athens)

2004 (4 May). Europa. Holidays. T **513** and similar vert design. Multicoloured. P 14.

2273 65c. Type **513** 1·40 1·30
a. Pair. Nos. 2273/4 7·75 7·00
2274 €2.85 Hot air balloon 6·00 5·50

Nos. 2273/4 were issued in horizontal *se-tenant* pairs within the sheet.

(Des M. Vardopoulou. Litho Alexandros Matsoukis, Athens)

2004 (15 June). Olympic Games, Athens 2004 (16th issue). Ancient Coins. T **514** and similar horiz designs. Multicoloured. P 13½.

2275 47c. Type **514** 1·20 1·10
2276 65c. Philip of Macedonia gold stater 1·60 1·50
2277 €2 Obverse and reverse of 2 drachma coin (460 BC) 4·75 4·50
2278 €2.17 Obverse and reverse of 4 drachma coin 5·25 5·00
2275/2278 *Set of 4* 11·50 11·00
MS2279 140×120 mm. Nos. 2275/8 12·00 11·00

515 Championship Trophy

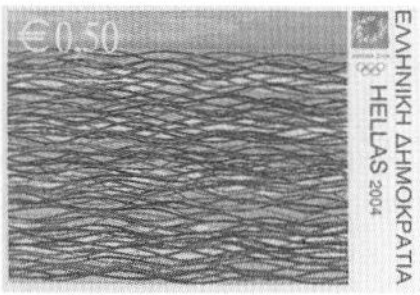

516 Sea

(Des M. Vardopoulou and A. Lygka. Litho Alexandros Matsoukis, Athens)

2004 (16 July). Greece–European Football Champions, 2004 T **515** and similar horiz designs. Multicoloured. P 13×13½.

2280 47c. Type **515** 1·20 1·10
2281 65c. Team members 1·60 1·50
2282 €1 Team members with raised arms 2·40 2·20
2283 €2.88 Outstretched hands and trophy 7·00 6·50
2280/2283 *Set of 4* 11·00 10·00
MS2284 160×135 mm. Nos. 2280/3 11·00 11·00

No. 2280 was also available printed on gummed A4 sheets of 15 stamps and 15 labels, which could be personalised by the addition of a photograph or company logo, from the Central Philatelic Office, for €15.

(Des M. Vardopoulou. Litho Alexandros Matsoukis, Athens)

2004 (23 July). Olympic Games, Athens 2004 (17th issue). Modern Art. Three sheets containing T **516** and similar multicoloured designs. P 13×13½ (horiz) or 13½×13 (vert).

MS2285 (a) 120×80 mm. 50c. Type **516**; €2.50 Rainbow. (b) 120×80 mm. €1 Multicoloured paint brush and glass; €2 Roller making Greek flag. (c) 135×163 mm. As Nos. **MS**2285a/b 27·00 27·00

517 Temple of Heaven, Beijing

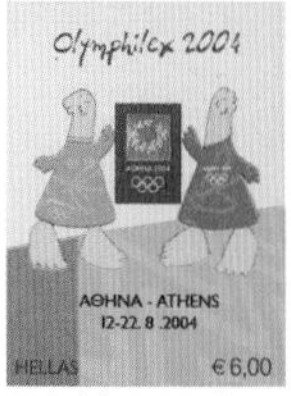

518 Athena and Phevos holding Athens 2004 Emblem

(Des M. Vardopoulou. Litho Alexandros Matsoukis, Athens)

2004 (13 Aug). Olympic Games, Athens 2004 (18th issue). Athens 2004–Beijing 2008. T **517** and similar square designs. Multicoloured. P 14.

2286 50c. Type **517** 1·20 1·10
2287 65c. Parthenon, Athens 1·60 1·50
MS2288 90×120 mm. Nos. 2286/7 11·00 11·00

(Des Eleni Apostolou. Litho Alexandros Matsoukis, Athens)

2004 (13 Aug). Olymphilex 2004, International Olympic Stamp and Memorabilia Exhibition. Sheet 81×70 mm. P 13½.

MS2289 **518** €6 multicoloured 13·50 13·50

519 Thomas Bimis and Nikos Siranidis

520 Horse Riders

2004 (17 Aug–Sept). Greek Olympic Medal Winners. T **519** and similar square designs. Multicoloured. Litho. P 13.

2290 65c. Type **519** (gold) (synchronised diving) 1·50 1·40
a. Digital print (17.8) 1·50 1·40
b. Sheetlet of 16. Nos. 2290; 2292/2306 24·00
2292 65c. Ilias Iliadis (gold) (judo) 1·50 1·40
a. Digital print (18.8) 1·50 1·40
2293 65c. Emilia Tsoulfa and Sofia Bekatorou (gold) (women's sailing) 1·50 1·40
a. Digital print (22.8) 1·50 1·40
2294 65c. Pyrros Dimas (bronze) (weight lifting) 1·50 1·40
a. Digital print (22.8) 1·50 1·40
2295 65c. Dimosthenis Tabacos (gold) (gymnastics) 1·50 1·40
a. Digital print (23.8) 1·50 1·40
2296 65c. Anastasia Kelesidou (silver) (discus) 1·50 1·40
a. Digital print (23.8) 1·50 1·40
2297 65c. Vasilis Polymeros and Nikos Skiathitis (bronze) (rowing) 1·50 1·40
a. Digital print (23.8) 1·50 1·40
2298 65c. Athanasia Tzoumeleka (gold) (20km. walk) 1·50 1·40
a. Digital print (24.8) 1·50 1·40
2299 65c. Chrysopigi Devezi (silver) (triple jump) 1·50 1·40
a. Digital print (24.8) 1·50 1·40
2300 65c. Fani Chalkia (gold) (400m. hurdles) 1·50 1·40
a. Digital print (26.8) 1·50 1·40
2301 65c. Nikos Kaklamanakis (silver) (sailing) 1·50 1·40
a. Digital print (26.8) 1·50 1·40
2302 65c. Artiom Kiourgian (bronze) (Greco-roman wrestling) 1·50 1·40
a. Digital print (26.8) 1·50 1·40
2303 65c. Women's water polo team (silver) 1·50 1·40
a. Digital print (27.8) 1·50 1·40
2304 65c. Mirela Maniani (bronze) (women's javelin) (Sept) 1·50 1·40
a. Digital print (28.8) 1·50 1·40
2305 65c. Elisavet Mystakidou (silver) (women's Taekwondo) (Sept) 1·50 1·40
a. Digital print (29.8) 1·50 1·40
2306 65c. Alexandros Nikolaidis (silver) (men's Taekwondo) (Sept) 1·50 1·40
a. Digital print (30.8) 1·50 1·40
2290/2306 *Set of 16* 22·00 20·00

Nos. 2290a/2306a were printed digitally in sheetlets of ten stamps at the main post office where the event shown was held, each sheet inscribed in bottom right hand corner with an emblem of the relevant city. The stamps were then printed in litho, also in sheetlets of ten stamps, a few days later.

Nos. 2290; 2292/2306, respectively, were issued individually in sheetlets of ten and together in sheetlets of 16 stamps.

No. 2291 was left for a stamp that was later withdrawn from circulation when the athlete, Leonidas Sampanis, was stripped of his medal after failing a drug test.

(Des A. Fassianos. Litho Alexandros Matsoukis, Athens)

2004 (22 Sept). Paralympics. T **520** and similar vert designs. Multicoloured. P 13½.

2307 20c. Type **519** 50 50
2308 49c. Disabled runner 1·30 1·20
2309 €2 Wheelchair basket ball players 5·00 4·75
2310 €2.24 Wheelchair archer 6·00 5·50
2307/2310 *Set of 4* 11·50 11·00

521 Santorini

(Des Myrsini Vardopoulou. Litho)

2004 (27 Dec). Tourism. Greek Islands. T **521** and similar horiz designs. Multicoloured. P 14.

2311 2c. Type **521** 15 10
2312 3c. Karpathos 15 10
2313 5c. Crete-Vai 15 10
2314 10c. Mykonos 25 25
2315 49c. Chania 1·30 1·20
2316 50c. Kastelorizo 1·30 1·20
2317 €1 Astypalaia 2·50 2·40
2318 €2 Serifos 5·00 4·75
2319 €2.24 Milos 5·75 5·50
2320 €4 Skiathos 10·00 9·50
2311/2320 *Set of 10* 24·00 23·00

Nos. 2311/20, respectively, were issued in sheets of 25 stamps. The stamps were also available in packs of 100 stamps from Central Post Offices and the Central Philatelic Office. It is reported that these stamps exist perf 13×imperf.

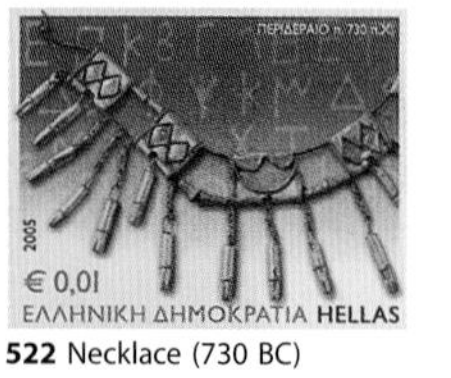

522 Necklace (730 BC)

523 Formula Diagram and "E=mc²" (75th anniv of State Laboratory)

(Des Myrsini Vardopoulou. Litho Alexandros Matsoukis, Athens)

2005 (25 Feb). Jewellery. T **522** and similar multicoloured designs. P 14×13½ (horiz) or 13½×14 (vert).

2321 1c. Type **522** 15 10
2322 15c. Snake-shaped bracelet (2nd–3rd century BC) (vert) 40 35
2323 30c. Necklace with bulls head pendant (5th century) 75 70
2324 49c. Central part of crown (2nd century) 1·30 1·20
2325 $4 Earring (8th century BC) (vert) 10·00 9·50
2321/2325 *Set of 5* 11·50 10·50

(Des Anthoula Lygka. Litho Alexandros Matsoukis, Athens)

2005 (5 Apr). Anniversaries and Events. T **523** and similar multicoloured designs. P 14×13½ (horiz) or 13½×14 (vert).

2326 1c. Type **523** 15 10
2327 4c. Sugar cubes and stop sign (41st European Association for Diabetes Meeting) (horiz) 15 10
2328 5c. Electrocardiogram chart and heart (54th European Society for Cardiovascular Surgery Congress) (horiz) 15 10
2329 40c. I. Kondilakis (first president) (90th anniv of ESIA (journalists' union of Athens) 1·00 95
2330 49c. Emblem (2005–Year of Economic Competitiveness) 1·30 1·20
2331 €1.40 Woman examining breast (25th anniv of Senologic Hellenic Society) 3·50 3·25
2332 €3.50 Angel (painting, Alekos Kontopoylos) (birth centenary) (horiz) 9·25 8·75
2326/2332 *Set of 7* 14·00 13·00

524 *Gladiolus illyricus*

525 Agiorgitiko Peloponnese

(Des Myrsini Vardopoulou. Litho Alexandros Matsoukis, Athens)

2005 (5 Apr). Flowers. T **524** and similar vert designs. P 13½×14.

2333 20c. Type **524** 50 50
2334 40c. *Crocus sieberi* 1·00 95
2335 49c. *Narcissus tazetta* 1·30 1·20
2336 €1.40 *Rhododendron luteum* 3·50 3·25
2337 €3 *Tulipa boetica* 7·75 7·25
2333/2337 *Set of 5* 12·50 12·00

(Des C. Garoufalis. Litho Alexandros Matsoukis, Athens)

2005 (19 May). Wine. T **525** and similar horiz designs showing grape varieties. Multicoloured. P 14.

2338 20c. Type **525** 50 50
2339 49c. White grapes on cloth (Assyrtiko Santorini) 1·30 1·20
2340 65c. Black grapes and coin (Xinomavro Macedonia) 1·70 1·60
2341 €2.24 White grapes and barrel (Robola Kefalonia) 5·75 5·50
2342 €2.40 Black grapes (Moschofilero Peloponnese) 6·25 5·75
2338/2342 *Set of 5* 14·00 13·00

526 Dakos

527 Blackboard

(Des Myrsini Vardopoulou. Litho Alexandros Matsoukis, Athens)

2005 (19 May). Europa. Gastronomy. T **526** and similar horiz design. P 14½×14.

2343 65c. Type **526** 1·70 1·60
a. Horiz pair. Nos. 2343/4 8·00 7·50
b. Imperf×13½. Booklets 1·70 1·60
ba. Booklet pane. No. 2343b×2 and No. 2344a×2 16·00
2344 €2.35 Rusk, tomato, herbs, oil and feta cheese 6·00 5·75
a. Imperf ×13½. Booklets 6·00 5·75

Nos. 2343/4 were issued in horizontal *se-tenant* pairs within the sheet, each pair forming a composite design.

(Des Anthoula Lygka (2346/7) or Eleni Apostolou (2348/53). Litho Alexandros Matsoukis, Athens)

2005 (15 July). Greetings Stamps. T **527** and similar square designs. Multicoloured. P 14.

2345 49c. Type **527** 1·30 1·20
2346 49c. Envelopes 1·30 1·20
2347 49c. Girl reading 1·30 1·20
2348 49c. Globe and stamp 1·30 1·20
2349 49c. Grid 1·30 1·20
2350 49c. Flowers 1·30 1·20
2351 49c. Figures 1·30 1·20
2352 65c. Church 1·70 1·60
2345/2352 *Set of 8* 9·75 9·00

Nos. 2345/52, respectively, were each available printed on gummed A4 sheets of stamps and labels which could be personalised by the addition of a photograph or company logo, from the Central Philatelic Office. Nos. 2345/7 in sheets of ten stamps and labels priced €10, Nos. 2348/51 in sheets of 15 stamps and labels priced €15 and No. 2352 in sheets of ten stamps and ten labels priced €13.

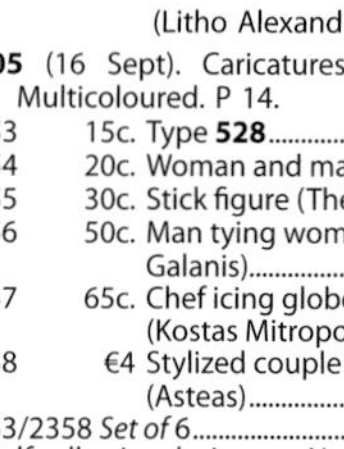

528 Rocket and Mountaineers (Fokion Dimitriadis)

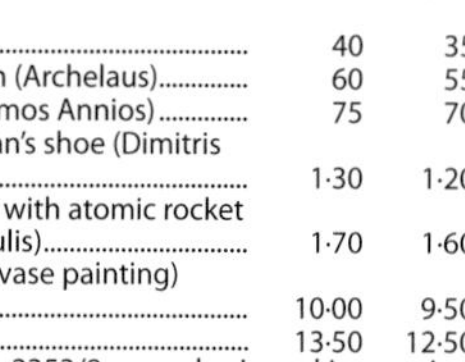

529 Two Players, Referee and Ball

(Litho Alexandros Matsoukis, Athens)

2005 (16 Sept). Caricatures. T **528** and similar vert designs. Multicoloured. P 14.

2353 15c. Type **528** 40 35
2354 20c. Woman and man (Archelaus) 60 55
2355 30c. Stick figure (Themos Annios) 75 70
2356 50c. Man tying woman's shoe (Dimitris Galanis) 1·30 1·20
2357 65c. Chef icing globe with atomic rocket (Kostas Mitropoulis) 1·70 1·60
2358 €4 Stylized couple (vase painting) (Asteas) 10·00 9·50
2353/2358 *Set of 6* 13·50 12·50

Self-adhesive designs as Nos. 2353/8 were also issued in premium stamp booklets sold at €9.90.

(Des Myrsini Vardopoulou. Litho Alexandros Matsoukis, Athens)

2005 (7 Oct). Greece–European Basketball Champions, 2005 (Eurobasket 2005, Belgrade). T **529** and similar horiz designs. Multicoloured. P 14.

2359	30c. Type **529**	75	70
2360	50c. Trophy	1·30	1·20
2361	65c. Team members	1·70	1·60
2362	€3.65 Holding trophy aloft	9·00	8·50
2359/2362 *Set of 4*		11·50	11·00
MS2363 165×138 mm. Nos. 2359/62		11·50	11·50

530 Mini Cooper

531 Ethnikos Sports Club Emblem

(Des Anthoula Lygka. Litho Alexandros Matsoukis, Athens)

2005 (11 Nov). Cars. T **530** and similar horiz designs. Multicoloured. P 14.

2364	1c. Type **530**	15	10
	a. Booklet pane. Nos. 2364/8	16·00	
2365	30c. Fiat 500	75	70
2366	50c. Citroen 2CV	1·30	1·20
2367	€2.25 Volkswagen Beetle	5·75	5·50
2368	€2.85 Ford Model T	7·50	7·00
2364/2368 *Set of 5*		14·00	13·00

Booklet pane Nos. 2364a was issued with 14 pages of text in premium stamp booklets.

(Litho Alexandros Matsoukis, Athens)

2005 (30 Nov). Sports Clubs. T **531** and similar square designs. Multicoloured. P 14.

2369	30c. Type **531**	75	70
2370	50c. Panionios Football Club	1·30	1·20
2371	50c. Iraklis Football Club	1·30	1·20
2372	50c. Panathinakos Football Club	1·30	1·20
2373	65c. PAOK Football Club	1·70	1·60
2374	65c. Panellinios Sports Club	1·70	1·60
2375	€4 Omilos Ereton Athletics Club	10·00	9·50
2369/2375 *Set of 7*		16·00	15·00

532 Virgin and Child ("Hodeghetria")

533 Building Façade

(Des Myrsini Vardopoulou. Litho Alexandros Matsoukis, Athens)

2005 (20 Dec). Christmas. T **532** and similar vert designs showing icons. Multicoloured. P 14.

2376	1c. Type **532**	25	25
2377	20c. "Kardiotissa"	50	50
2378	70c. "Glykophiloussa"	1·80	1·70
2379	€3.20 Virgin, Child and symbols of the Passion	8·25	7·75
2376/2379 *Set of 4*		9·75	9·25

(Des Myrsini Vardopoulou. Litho Alexandros Matsoukis, Athens)

2006 (10 Jan). 50th Anniv of Europa Stamps. Sheet 105×81 mm containing T **533** and similar horiz design. P 14.

MS2380 €1.50 Type **533**; €2.50 As No. 1617 .... 13·00 12·00

534 "Ancient Drama" (Dionisis Fotopoulos)

535 Kouros of Anavissos (National Archaeological Museum)

(Des Myrsini Vardopoulou. Litho Alexandros Matsoukis, Athens)

2006 (28 Feb). Patras–European Capital of Culture–2006. T **534** and similar multicoloured designs. P 13×13½ (horiz) or 13½×13 (vert).

2381	1c. Type **534**	15	10
2382	15c. "Travelling" (Dimitris Milionis)	25	25
2383	20c. "Child and Art" (Rania Kapeliari)	50	50
2384	50c. "Carnival" (Charis Pressas)	1·30	1·20
	a. Size 30×30 mm. Perf 14	2·50	2·40
2385	65c. Patras–2006 emblem (vert)	1·70	1·60
	a. Size 30×30 mm. Perf 14	3·25	3·00
2386	€2.25 "Poetry and Music" (Kelly Mendrinou)	5·50	5·25
2387	€2.30 Icon (vert)	5·75	5·50
2381/2387 *Set of 7*		13·50	13·00

(Des Myrsini Vardopoulou. Litho Alexandros Matsoukis, Athens)

2006 (7 Apr). Museum Exhibits. T **535** and similar multicoloured designs. P 14.

2388	5c. Type **535**	15	10
2389	20c. Marble seated figure (Museum of Cycladic Art, Athens)	50	50
2390	50c. Spiral (29×30 mm)	1·30	1·20
2391	65c. Parthenon pediment (Acropolis Museum) (horiz)	1·70	1·60
2392	€1.40 Antinopolis (painting) (Benaki Museum, Athens)	3·50	3·25
2393	€2.25 "Concert of the Angels" (Domenicos Theotokopoulos) (National Art Gallery) (horiz)	5·75	5·50
2388/2393 *Set of 6*		11·50	11·00

536 As Type **21**

537 Moon and Multicoloured Twisted Strands

(Des Anthi Lygka. Litho Alexandros Matsoukis, Athens)

2006 (7 Apr). Centenary of Intercalated Olympic Games, Athens. T **536** and similar horiz designs showing 1906 stamps "Second Olympic Games Issue, Athens". Multicoloured. P 14.

MS2394 Two sheets, each 105×81 mm. (a) 20c. Type **536**; 30c. As Type **25**; 50c. As Type **22**; €2. As Type **26**. (b) 50c. As Type **23**; 65c. As Type **27**; 85c. As Type **28**; €1. As Type **24** .... 13·50 13·50

(Des Myrsini Vardopoulou. Litho Alexandros Matsoukis, Athens)

2006 (15 May). Europa. Integration. T **537** and similar vert design. P 14×14½.

2395	65c. Type **537**	1·50	1·40
	a. Horiz pair. Nos. 2395/6	8·75	8·25
	b. Imperf×13½. Booklets	1·50	1·40
	ba. Booklet pane. No. 2395b×2 and No. 2396a×2	18·00	
2396	€3 Green twisted strands and sun	7·00	6·50
	a. Imperf ×13½. Booklets	7·00	6·50

Nos. 2395/6 were issued in horizontal *se-tenant* pairs within the sheet.

538 Book and Archive Building (90th anniv of state archives)

539 Lesvos

(Des Eleni Apostolou (2397/99 and 2401/2) or Myrsini Vardopoulou (2400). Litho Alexandros Matsoukis, Athens)

2006 (15 May). Anniversaries and Events. T **538** and similar square designs. Multicoloured. P 14.

2397	15c. Type **538**	40	35
2398	20c. European stars (25th anniv of membership of EU)	50	50
2399	50c. Circle of squares (Eurovision Song Contest, Athens)	1·30	1·20
2400	65c. Olive tree (2006–Year of Olive Oil and Olives)	1·70	1·60
2401	€1.40 Tinia (god)	3·50	3·25
2402	€3 Council chamber (Greece's participation in UN Security Council 2005–2006)	7·00	6·50
2397/2402 *Set of 6*		13·00	12·00

Nos. 2400 was available printed on gummed A4 sheets of ten stamps and ten labels which could be personalised by the addition of a photograph or company logo, priced €13, from the Central Philatelic Office.

(Des Myrsini Vardopoulou. Litho)

2006 (16 June). Tourism. Greek Islands. T **539** and similar horiz designs. Multicoloured. P 14.

2403	1c. Type **539**	15	10
	a. Imperf×p 13½	15	10
2404	3c. Hydra	15	10
	a. Imperf×p 13½	15	10
2405	10c. Sifnos	15	10
	a. Imperf×p 13½	15	10
2406	20c. Lefkada	20	20
	a. Imperf×p 13½	20	20
2407	40c. Samothrace	1·00	95
	a. Imperf×p 13½	1·00	95
2408	50c. Syros	1·30	1·20
	a. Imperf×p 13½	1·30	1·20
	b. Size 30×30 mm	2·50	2·40
2409	65c. Rhodes	1·70	1·60
	a. Imperf×p 13½	1·70	1·60
	b. Size 30×30 mm	3·25	3·00
2410	85c. Cephalonia	2·20	2·00
	a. Imperf×p 13½	2·20	2·00
2411	€2.25 Corfu	5·00	4·75
	a. Imperf×p 13½	5·00	4·75
2412	€5 Naxos	11·50	11·00
	a. Imperf×p 13½	11·50	11·00
2403/2412 *Set of 10*		21·00	20·00

The stamps perforated on all four sides were issued in sheets of 25 stamps, those perforated on two sides only, were only available in packs of 100 stamps from Central Post Offices and the Central Philatelic Office.

Nos. 2408, sold at €10, and 2409, sold at €13, were also available printed on gummed A4 sheets of ten stamps and ten labels which could be personalised by the addition of a photograph or company logo.

Nos. 2408b/2409b were issued with a *se-tenant* stamp size label which could be personalized with the addition of a photograph or a logo.

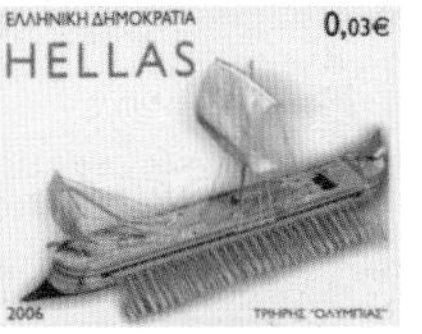

540 "Olympias" (trireme)

(Des Myrsini Vardopoulou. Litho)

2006 (14 Sept). Ancient Technology. T **540** and similar multicoloured designs. P 14.

2413	3c. Type **540**	15	10
2414	5c. 1st-century odometer (Heron of Alexandria)	15	10
2415	50c. 3rd-century piston water pump (Ktesibius) (vert)	1·30	1·20
2416	65c. The Antikythera mechanism, 80 B.C. (vert)	1·70	1·60
2417	€3.80 1st-century automatic temple gates (Heron of Alexandria) (vert)	9·50	9·00
2413/2417 *Set of 5*		11·50	11·00

541 Team members (left)

542 Apollon Kalamarias

(Des Myrsini Vardopoulou. Litho Alexandros Matsoukis, Athens)

2006 (16 Oct). Greece–World Basketball Championship Silver Medallists. Sheet 105×81 mm containing T **541** and similar horiz designs. Multicoloured. P 14.

MS2418 50c. Medal; €2 Type **541**; €3 Team members (right) .... 12·50 12·50

The stamps and margins of No. **MS**2417 form a composite design.

(Des Eleni Apostolou. Litho Alexandros Matsoukis, Athens)

2007 (12 Mar). Sports Clubs. T **542** and similar square designs. Multicoloured. P 14.

2419	2c. Type **542**	15	10
2420	3c. Atromitos Athinon	15	10
2421	52c. Aris Thessalonikis	1·30	1·20
2422	€2.27 Ethnikos Peiraio	5·75	5·50
2423	€3.20 Apollon Smirnis	8·25	7·75
2419/2423 *Set of 5*		14·00	13·00

543 Bleuette (doll, 1905)

544 Faces

(Des Myrsini Vardopoulou. Litho Alexandros Matsoukis, Athens)

2006 (22 Dec). Children's Toys. T **543** and similar multicoloured designs. P 14.

2424	5c. Type **543**	10	10
2425	15c. Wooden aircraft (1940–5)	35	35
2426	30c. Paper Mache head dolls (1925–30)	70	65
2427	40c. Wheeled horses and cat (1920–90)	95	90
2428	52c. Clockwork cat, wheeled duck and dominoes (1930–60)	1·30	1·20
2429	72c. Parachutist (c 1950) (vert)	1·80	1·70
2430	€2.27 Airplane carousel (c. 1950) (vert)	6·75	6·25
2431	€4 Puppet show of the Resistance (1941–5) (vert)	9·50	9·00
2424/2431 *Set of 8*		19·00	18·00

(Des Eleni Apostolou. Litho Alexandros Matsoukis, Athens)

2007 (12 Mar). Greetings Stamps. T **544** and similar square designs. Multicoloured. P 14.

2432	52c. Type **544**	1·30	1·20
2433	52c. Crescents	1·30	1·20
2434	52c. Artemis	1·30	1·20
2435	52c. Earth from space	1·30	1·20
2436	52c. Globe	1·30	1·20
2437	65c. Parthenon	1·60	1·50
2438	65c. Kore Phrasikleia	1·60	1·50
2432/2438 *Set of 7*		8·75	8·00
MS2439 118×122 mm. Nos. 2432/8		12·00	11·00

Nos. 2432/6 were available printed on gummed A4 sheets of ten or 15 stamps and ten or 15 labels which could be personalised by the addition of a photograph or company logo, priced €10 or €15.

Nos. 2437/8 were available only in sheets of ten stamps and ten labels. All sheets could be purchased from the Central Philatelic Office.

545 Costis Palamas (poet and critic) (engraving by Giannis Gourzis)

546 Scorpio

(Des Myrsini Vardopoulou. Litho Alexandros Matsoukis, Athens)

2007 (25 Apr). Anniversaries and Events. T **545** and similar square designs. Multicoloured. P 14.

2440	2c. Type **545**	10	10
2441	10c. Poseidon and head with gold mask (Year of Greece in China) (horiz)	20	20
2442	20c. Emblem (1st Symposium of Seven Wise Men in Cardiovascular Surgery, Athens and Delphi)	45	40
2443	52c. Figures with arms raised (2nd UNI Postal Global Union World Conference, Athens) (horiz)	1·20	1·20
2444	65c. Rainbow and stars (50th anniv of Treaty of Rome)	1·50	1·40
2445	85c. Georgios Kotzias (30th death anniv)	1·90	1·80
2446	€1 Rigas Velestinlis (revolutionary) (engraving by Giannis Gourzis) (250th birth anniv)	2·20	2·10
2447	€2.27 Light bulb as air balloon (2007–year of innovation)	5·00	4·75
2448	€3 Blind justice (125th anniv of Legal Council of State) (horiz)	6·75	6·25
2440/2448 *Set of* 9		17·00	16·00

(Des Maria Zissimopoulou and Eleni Apostolou. Litho Alexandros Matsoukis, Athens)

2007 (25 May). Western Zodiac. T **546** and similar multicoloured designs. P 14.

2449	2c. Type **546**	10	10
2450	3c. Cancer	10	10
2451	5c. Capricorn	10	10
2452	10c. Taurus	20	20
2453	20c. Sagittarius (vert)	45	40
2454	40c. Leo (vert)	90	85
2455	52c. Virgo (vert)	1·20	1·20
2456	65c. Aries	1·50	1·40
2457	85c. Aquarius	1·90	1·80
2458	€1 Libra	2·20	2·10
2459	€2.27 Pisces	5·00	4·75
2460	€2.80 Gemini	6·25	5·75
2449/2460 *Set of* 12		18·00	17·00

547 Emblem and Part of Dove

548 Asclepius (statue) (Ampuria Museum, Spain)

(Des Myrsini Vardopoulou. Litho Alexandros Matsoukis, Athens)

2007 (25 May). Europa. Centenary of Scouting. T **547** and similar horiz designs. Multicoloured. P 14½×14.

2461	65c. Type **547**	1·50	1·40
	a. Horiz pair. Nos. 2461/2	8·75	8·25
	b. Imperf×p 14. Booklets	1·50	1·40
	ba. Booklet pane. Nos. 2461b×2 and 2462a×2	18·00	
2462	€3.15 Part of Dove and scouts	7·00	6·50
	a. Imperf×p 14. Booklets	7·00	6·50

Nos. 2461/2 were issued in horizontal *se-tenant* pairs within the sheet, each pair forming a composite design.

(Des Myrsini Vardopoulou. Litho Alexandros Matsoukis, Athens)

2007 (28 June). Asclepius (demigod of *medicine*). Sheet 120×76 mm containing T **548** and similar vert design. Multicoloured. P 14.

MS2463 €2.50×2, Type **548**; Asclepius (head) (National Archaeological Museum) ... 11·00 11·00

549 Basilica of San Clemente, Rome

550 Ergotelis Sports Club

(Litho Alexandros Matsoukis, Athens)

2007 (28 Sept). Anniversaries and Events. T **549** and similar multicoloured designs. P 14.

2464	2c. Type **549** (150th anniv of excavation and discovery of St. Cyril's grave)	10	10
2465	3c. Emblem (50th anniv of University of Macedonia)	10	10
2466	€4 Konstantinos Tsatsos (politician and writer) (president 1975–1980) (50th death anniv) (vert)	10·50	9·75
2464/2466 *Set of* 3		9·75	9·00

(Des Myrsini Vardopoulou (54c.) or Eleni Apostolou (others). Litho Alexandros Matsoukis, Athens)

2007 (2 Nov). Sports Clubs. T **550** and similar square designs. P 14.

2467	2c. Type **550**	10	10
2468	4c. OFI Football Club	10	10
2469	54c. Olympiacos Club of Fans of Piraeus (umbrella organization)	1·30	1·20
2470	€2.29 Doxa Dramas Sports Club	5·75	5·25
2471	€5 Mytilini Nautical Club	12·00	11·00
2467/2471 *Set of* 5		17·00	16·00

551 Aphrodite (Greek)

552 Chios

(Des Myrsini Vardopoulou. Litho Giesecke & Devrient Matsoukis, Athens)

2007 (14 Dec). Statues. T **551** and similar vert design. Multicoloured. P 14×13½.

2472	54c. Type **551**	1·40	1·30
2473	€2.40 Anahit (Armenian)	6·00	5·50

Stamps of the same design were issued by Armenia.

2008 (27 Feb). Islands. T **552** and similar horiz designs. Multicoloured. P 14½×14.

2474	2c. Type **552**	10	10
2475	5c. Amorgos	10	10
2476	10c. Nissiros	25	20
2477	20c. Paxi	50	45
2478	40c. Leros	95	90
2479	54c. Kalymnos	1·30	1·20
2480	67c. Kos	1·70	1·60
2481	€1 Simi	2·40	2·20
2482	€2.29 Zakynthos	5·50	5·25
2483	€4 Inousses	9·50	9·00
2474/2483 *Set of* 10		20·00	19·00

Nos. 2484/93 have been left for coil stamps not yet received.

553 Discus Thrower

554 Heart

(Des Alekos Fassianos and Anthi Lygka)

2008 (14 Mar). Olympic Games, Beijing. T **553** and similar multicoloured designs. P 13½×13 (vert) or 13×13½ (horiz).

2494	3c. Type **553**	15	15
2495	35c. Lighting Olympic flame	95	90
2496	67c. Cyclist (horiz)	1·90	1·80
2497	67c. Torch relay	1·90	1·80
2494/2497 *Set of* 4		4·50	4·25

(Des Anthi Lygka)

2008 (21 Apr). Personal Stamps. T **554** and similar square designs. Multicoloured. P 13.

2498	54c. Type **554**	1·60	1·50
2499	54c. Kites	1·60	1·50
2500	54c. Digital symbols	1·60	1·50
2501	54c. Letter	1·60	1·50
2502	67c. Flag	2·00	1·90
2503	67c. Pillar and capitol	2·00	1·90
2498/2503 *Set of* 6		9·25	8·75
MS2504 120×122 mm. Nos. 2498/503		9·50	9·00

555 Ink bottle, Pen and Letters

556 Emblem

(Des Anthi Lygka)

2008 (26 May). Europa. The Letter. T **555** and similar horiz design. Multicoloured. P 14×14½ (sheet stamps) or imperf×14 (booklet stamps).

2505	67c. Type **555**	1·90	1·80
	a. Pair. Nos. 2505/6	10·50	9·75
	b. Booklet pane. Nos. 2505/6, each×2	21·00	
2506	€3.17 Letter, script and pen	8·25	7·75

Nos. 2505/6 were issued in horizontal *se-tenant* pairs, each pair forming a composite design.

(Des Anthi Lygka)

2008 (20 June). Anniversaries and Events. T **556** and similar vert designs. Multicoloured. P 13½×14.

2507	3c. Type **556** (180th anniv of Hellenic Post)	15	15
2508	5c. Symbols of Greece (180th anniv of Hellenic Post)	15	15
2509	10c. Ioannis Kapodistrias (180th anniv of his election as first head of state of newly-liberated Greece)	25	25
2510	57c. Dimitris Rodopoulos (M. Karagatsis) (writer) (birth centenary)	1·60	1·50
2511	70c. Fish (International Year of Planet Earth)	2·00	1·90
2512	€1.85 '50' (50th anniv of National Hellenic Reseach Foundation)	5·50	5·00
2513	€3 Emblem (centenary of National Council of Women)	8·25	7·75
2507/2513 *Set of* 7		16·00	15·00

557 Feta Cheese

558 Diagoras Rhodos Sports Club

(Des Apostolos Chatzaras)

2008 (19 Sept). Traditional Products. T **557** and similar vert designs. Multicoloured. P 13½×14 (vert) or 14×13½ (horiz).

2514	3c. Type **557**	15	15
2515	5c. Mastic gum from Chios	15	15
2516	20c. Olive oil (horiz)	55	50
2517	57c. Ouzo spirit	1·60	1·50
2518	€1 Pistachio nuts from Aigina	3·00	2·75
2519	€4 Honey	11·00	10·00
2514/2519 *Set of* 6		15·00	13·50

(Des Eleni Apostolou)

2008 (20 Oct). Sports Clubs. T **558** and similar square designs. Multicoloured. P 13½×14.

2520	40c. Type **558**	1·40	1·30
2521	57c. AEK Football Club	1·90	1·80
2522	70c. Asteras Tripolis Football Club	2·30	2·20
2523	€2 Panserraikos Football Club	6·25	6·00
2524	€3 Keriraikos Sports Club	8·75	8·25
2520/2524 *Set of* 5		19·00	18·00

MACHINE LABELS

All Greek Frama labels were printed in red.

A

1984 (26 Mar). Type **A** in red. Number in the bottom frame indicates issuing machine.

Face values 1 to 999d. in 1d. steps.

26.3.84 Nos. 2/3 and 6/9
28.6.84 Nos. 1, 4/5 and 10

Machine Number		
	001	Rhodes airport (withdrawn November 1987)
	002	Athens East Airport (withdrawn 26.1.88)
	003	Thessaloniki Central P.O.(withdrawn 28.1.88)
	004	Heraklion Airport (withdrawn November 1987)
	005	Corfu Airport (withdrawn November 1987)
	006	Piraeus Central P.O. (withdrawn November 1987)
	007	Syntagma Square P.O., Athens (withdrawn January 1988)
	008	Athens Sorting Centre (withdrawn May 1986)
	009	Athens Central P.O. (withdrawn December 1987)
	010	Athens Railway Station (withdrawn November 1987)

B

1991 (29 Apr). Type **B** in red. Number in the bottom frame indicates issuing machine.

Face values 5 to 1000d. in 5d. steps.

23.3.92	01	Kypseli P.O., Athens
29.4.91	02	Athens East Airport
26.10.91	03	Thessaloniki Central P.O
23.3.92	04	Ampelokipi P.O., Athens
23.3.92	05	Pagrali P.O., Athens
26.10.01	06	Piraeus Central P.O.
29.4.91	07	Syntagma Square P.O., Athens
23.3.92	08	Athens East Airport
29.4.91	09	Eolou P.O., Athens
23.3.92	10	Acropolis P.O., Athens

Commemorative labels with special designs were available from machines at the following exhibitions:

22 Nov–1 Dec 1985	Piraeus '85
6–15 June 1986	Philatelic Literature Exhibition, Athens
25 Oct–2 Nov 1986	Heraklion '86
7–15 Nov 1987	Heraklion '87
27 Nov–6 Dec 1987	Athens '87
27 Mar–3 Apr 1988	Ioannina '88
4–11 Nov 1988	Maxhellas '88, Athens
15–23 June 1991	Hellas-Cyprus '91, Heraklion
26 Oct–3 Nov 1991	Mytilini '91
20–27 May 1992	Philatelic '92, Athens
23–31 Oct 1993	Rhodes '93
5–9 Nov 1994	Panhellenic '94, Kifisia
22–28 Nov 1995	Athens Piraeus '95
25 Mar–6 April 1996	Centenary of the Modern Olympic Games

998 (13 July). Multicoloured designs showing a Greek galleon. Number in right hand frame indicates issuing machine. Face values 5 to 1000d. in 5d. steps.

Fixed values: 13.7.98 100d., 130d., 140d., 170d. 100d., 140d., 170d., 400d., 450d.
1.9.98 100d., 160d., 170d., 200d.
2.2.2000 50d., 120d., 170d., 200d., 500d., 600d.

000 (2 Jan). Multicoloured designs showing a Greek galleon but face values in Euros. Number in right hand frame indicates issuing machine. Face values 1c. to €5 in 1c. steps.

Fixed values 2.2.2000

STAMP BOOKLETS

The following checklist covers, in simplified form, booklets issued y Greece. It is intended that it should be used in conjunction with he main listings and details of stamps and panes listed there are ot repeated.

From 1976 for several years sachets of stamps were available from ending machines. Stamps to the value of 10 or 20d. were torn from ormal sheets in stock at the post offices and folded inside cardboard overs. These are not included in the list below.

Also excluded from this list are the Post Office packets containing 00 stamps in strips of five issued from 1986 onwards.

Prices are for complete booklets

ooklet o.	*Date*	*Contents and Cover Price*	*Price*
B1	1930	Centenary of Independence 1 pane, No. 433×10; 1 pane, No. 434×10; 1 pane, No. 436×10; 1 pane, No. 440×10 (23d.)	—
B2	1930	Centenary of Independence 1 pane, No. 433×10; 1 pane, No. 434×10; 1 pane, No. 437×10; 1 pane, No. 440×10 (23d.)	—
B3	1930	Centenary of Independence 1 pane, No. 433×10; 1 pane, No. 434×10; 1 pane, No. 437×10; 1 pane, No. 441×10 (23d.)	—
B4	30.8.67	Greek "Popular" Art 2 panes, No. 1026×4; 2 panes, No. 1027×4; 1 pane, No. 1029×4 (30d.)	£250
B5	30.8.67	Greek "Popular" Art 1 pane, No. 1026×4; 4 panes, No. 1027×4; 1 pane, No. 1029×4; 1 pane, No. 1030×4 (50d.)	£300
B6	2.1.84	Homeric Odes 1 pane, No. 1642×10 (150d.)	20·00
B7	30.4.84	Europa 1 pane, No. 1656a×2 (84d.)	7·25
B8	30.4.84	Olympic Games 1 pane, Nos. 1658/62 (161d.)	5·50
B9	10.7.84	Tenth Anniv of Turkish Invasion of Greece 1 pane, No. 1663×2; 1 pane, No. 1664×2 (104d.)	6·00
B10	6.12.84	Christmas 1 pane, No. 1672a (91d.)	4·00
B11	29.4.85	Europa 1 pane, Nos. 1684×2 and 1685 (134d.)	3·75
B12	23.4.86	Europa 1 pane, No. 1733bb (290d.)	44·00
SB13	4.5.87	Europa 1 pane, No. 1752bb (340d.)	20·00
SB14	4.5.87	Athens University 1 pane, No. 1759×10 (230d.)	10·00
SB15	2.12.87	Christmas 1 pane, No. 1769a×5 (260d.)	7·50
SB16	6.5.88	Olympic Games, Seoul 1 pane, No. 1784cB (284d.)	28·00
SB17	6.5.88	Europa 1 pane, No. 1789dB (420d.)	21·00
SB18	7.10.88	Prefecture Capitals 1 pane, No. 1795cA (152d.)	3·75
SB19	2.12 .88	Christmas (T **399**) 1 pane, No. 1812a (300d.)	16·00
SB20	17.3.89	Centenary of Modern Olympics 1 pane, No. 1816cB (330d.)	10·00
SB21	22.5.89	Europa 1 pane, No. 1825dB (460d.)	23·00
SB22	11.5.90	Europa 1 pane, No. 1846ba (560d.)	22·00
SB23	20.5.91	Europa 1 pane, No. 1878ba (760d.)	25·00
SB24	22.5.92	Europa 1 pane, No. 1901ba (860d.)	22·00
SB25	25.5.93	Europa 1 pane, No. 1935ba (880d.)	21·00
SB26	9.5.94	Europa 1 pane, No. 1947ba (880d.)	20·00
SB27	3.5.95	Europa 1 pane, No. 1973ba (860d.)	19·00
SB28	22.4.96	Europa 1 pane, No. 1996ba (1100d.)	26·00
SB29	19.5.97	Europa 1 pane, No. 2034ba (1100d.)	20·00
SB30	29.5.98	Europa 1 pane, No. 2066ba (1280d.)	22·00
SB31	24.5.99	Europa 1 pane, No. 2095ba (1440d.)	14·00
SB32	9.5.00	Europa 1 pane, No. 2123ab (680d.)	15·00
SB33	15.5.01	Europa 1 pane, No. 2156ba (1660d.)	18·00
SB34	9.5.02	Europa 1 pane, No. 2197ba (€6.40)	23·00
SB35	8.5.03	Europa 1 pane, No. 2228ba (€7)	19·00
SB36	19.5.05	Europa. Gastronomy 1 pane, No. 2343ba (€6)	17·00
SB37	15.5.06	Europa. Integration 1 pane, No. 2395ba (€7.30)	19·00
SB38	25.5.07	Europa. Centenary of Scouting 1 pane, No. 2461ba (€7.60)	19·00
SB39	26.5.08	Europa. The Letter 1 pane, No. 2505a (€7.68)	22·00

Where the same design, or subject, appears more than once in a set only the first number is given. Scenes and buildings are listed under the town or geographical area in which they are situated. Portraits are listed under surnames only. In cases of difficulty part of the inscription has been used to identify the stamp.

BALKAN WAR ISSUES

100 Lepta = 1 Drachma

All except Kavalla were united to Greece by the Treaty of London,) May 1913.

IKARIA

(Icaria, Nicaria)

A. FREE STATE

This island declared its independence from Turkey, as a free state, the end of July 1912.

1 Hermes, from an old Coin

(Litho Grundmann & Co., Athens)

912 (8 Oct). P 11½.

	1	2l. orange	2·20	3·25
		5l. green	2·20	3·25
		10l. rose	2·20	3·25
		25l. blue	2·20	3·25
		50l. deep lilac	3·25	4·50
		1d. brown	4·50	10·50
		2d. carmine	5·50	13·50
		5d. grey	7·75	27·00
/8 *Set of* 8			27·00	60·00

B. GREEK OCCUPATION

The island was occupied by Greek troops on 4 (17) November 1912 nd at first used the Greek stamps overprinted "ΕΛΛΗΝΙΚΗ ΔΙΟΙΚΗΣΙΣ" ireece Type **34**.

ΕΛΛΗΝΙΚΗ
ΔΙΟΙΚΗΣΙΣ

(**2** "Greek Administration")

913. Stamps of Greece, 1911–13, handstamped with T **2**.

(a) Engraved

	30	2l. carmine	65·00	43·00
0	**29**	3l. vermilion	65·00	43·00
		(b) Lithographed		
1	**29**	1l. green	65·00	43·00
2		3l. vermilion	65·00	43·00
3	**31**	5l. green	65·00	43·00
4	**29**	10l. carmine	65·00	43·00
/14 *Set of* 6			£350	£225

KAVALLA

Kavalla was taken by the Greeks in June 1913.

ΕΛΛΗΝΙΚΗ
ΔΙΟΙΚΗΣΙΣ
10
ΛΕΠΤΑ

(**1** Trans "Greek Administration")

1913 (1 July). Stamps of Bulgaria of 1911 surch as T **1**, in red (vert on Nos. 3, 6 and 9/11).

1	**23**	5l. on 1st. myrtle-green	34·00	32·00
2	**27**	10l. on 10st. black and red	£650	£550
3	**28**	10l. on 15st. bistre	95·00	65·00
4	**29**	10l. on 25st. black and ultramarine	55·00	43·00
5	**24**	15l. on 2st. black and carmine	95·00	65·00
6	**25**	20l. on 3st. black and lake	95·00	65·00
7	**26**	25l. on 5st. black and green	95·00	65·00
8	**27**	50l. on 10st. black and red	28·00	16·00
		a. Surch in blue	28·00	27·00
9	**28**	1d. on 15st. bistre	£325	£275
10	**30**	1d. on 30st. black and blue	£130	£130
11	**31**	1d. on 50st. black and ochre	£200	£190

Extensive forgeries of the above exist.

For French Post Offices in Kavalla (Cavalle), see under French Post Offices in the Turkish Empire in Parts 6 (France) or 16 (Central Asia) of this catalogue.

KHIOS

(Chios)

Khios was occupied by Greek forces on 11 (24) November 1912.

1913 (May). T **30** (litho) of Greece, opt "Ε*Δ".

1	25l. ultramarine (R.)	75·00	55·00
	a. Greek "L" for "D" in opt	£300	£160
	b. Opt inverted	£325	£190

The overprint was made because of the absence of the overprint "ΕΛΛΗΝΙΚΗ ΔΙΟΙΚΗΣΙΣ", Greece (Type **34**) on a supply of 25l. stamps sent to Khios.

LESVOS

(Lesbos)

This island was formerly called Mytilene, from the name of the chief town. It was occupied by Greek forces on 8 (21) November 1912.

Types of Turkey are illustrated at beginning of Albania.

Ἑλληνικὴ
Κατοχὴ
Μυτιλήνης

(**1** "Greek Possession Mytilene")

1912 (9 Nov). Stamps of Turkey, optd with T **1**, in black, reading up or down.

1	**28**	2pa. olive-green	3·25	3·25
2		5pa. brown-ochre	3·25	3·25
3		10pa. green (Pl. II)	3·25	3·25
4		20pa. rose-carmine (Pl. II)	3·25	3·25
5		1pi. ultramarine (Pl. II)	6·75	6·50
6		2pi. blue-black	31·00	30·00
7	**25**	2½pi. brown	15·00	14·50
8	**28**	5pi. slate-purple	34·00	32·00
9		10pi. dull red	£150	£150
		a. Opt in blue	£150	£150

1912. Stamps of Turkey with opt T **26** in red, optd with T **1**, in black, reading up or down.

10	**28**	10pa. green (Pl. II)	11·00	11·00
10*a*		20pa. rose-carmine	11·00	11·00
		b. Opt in blue	65·00	65·00
10*c*		1pi. ultramarine	11·00	11·00
11	**25**	2pi. black	75·00	70·00

ΛΕΠΤΑ 25 (**2**) ΔΡΑΧΜΗ (**3**) ΔΙΔΡΑΧΜΟΝ (**4**)

1912 (Nov). Stamps as above surch with values in Greek, as T **2/4**, in blue (Nos. 12/13) or black (others).

12	**28**	25l. on 2pa. olive-green. (No. 1)	13·50	13·00
13		50l. on 20pa. rose-carmine (No. 4)	15·00	14·50
14		1d. on 20pa. rose-carmine (No. 10b)	55·00	55·00
15		2d. on 1pi. ultramarine (No. 5)	34·00	32·00

1912. Postage Due stamp of Turkey, 1908, optd with T **1** for postal use.

16	**25**	1pi. black/*crimson*	75·00	70·00

There are large numbers of forgeries of these provisionals, nearly all with forged postmarks.

LIMNOS

(Lemnos)

Limnos was occupied by Greek marines on 7 (20) October 1912.

ΛΗΜΝΟΣ

(**1**)

VARIETIES OF OVERPRINT

I. "ΔΗΜΝΟΣ" II. "ΑΗΜΝΟΣ"

Variety I occurs in position 95, variety II in position 69.

1912–13. Stamps of Greece optd with T **1**.

		(a) On stamp of 1901		
1	**15**	20l. mauve	12·00	10·00
		a. Variety I	55·00	55·00
		(b) On stamps of 1911, engraved		
2	**29**	1l. green	65	65
		a. Variety I	4·00	4·00
		b. Variety II	6·75	7·50
		c. Opt double	17·00	
		d. Opt inverted	17·00	
3	**30**	2l. carmine	80	75
		a. Variety I	4·00	4·00
		b. Variety II	6·75	7·50
		c. Opt double	17·00	
		d. Opt inverted	17·00	
		g. Opt in red	3·25	3·25
4	**29**	3l. vermilion	80	75
		a. Variety I	4·00	4·00
		b. Variety II	6·75	7·50
		c. Opt double	19·00	
		d. Opt inverted	19·00	
		g. Opt in red	3·25	3·25
5	**31**	5l. green	80	75
		a. Variety I	7·25	7·25
		b. Variety II	11·50	11·50
		c. Opt double	19·00	
6	**29**	10l. carmine	1·10	1·10
		a. Variety I	12·00	12·00
		b. Variety II	16·00	16·00
		c. Opt double	19·00	
		d. Opt inverted	19·00	
7	**30**	20l. lilac	2·20	2·20
		a. Variety I	12·00	12·00
		b. Variety II	16·00	16·00
		c. Opt double	28·00	
		d. Opt inverted	28·00	
		g. Opt in red	13·50	13·00
8		25l. ultramarine	2·00	1·90
		b. Variety II	18·00	17·00
		c. Opt double	28·00	
9	**31**	30l. carmine-red	3·25	3·25
		a. Variety I	13·50	13·50
		b. Variety II	22·00	22·00
		d. Opt inverted	55·00	
		g. Opt in red	6·75	6·50
10	**30**	40l. deep blue	5·00	4·75
		a. Variety I	20·00	20·00
		b. Variety II	36·00	36·00
		g. Opt in red	2·20	2·20
		ga. Variety I	31·00	31·00
11	**31**	50l. deep purple	5·00	4·75
		b. Variety II	36·00	36·00
		g. Opt in red	2·20	2·20
		ga. Variety I	31·00	31·00
12	**32**	1d. ultramarine	6·75	6·50
		b. Variety II	36·00	36·00
		c. Opt double	60·00	
		g. Opt in red	3·25	3·25
		ga. Variety I	31·00	31·00
13		2d. vermilion	22·00	22·00
		b. Variety II	65·00	65·00
		g. Opt in red	£325	£300
14		3d. carmine (209)	25·00	24·00
		b. Variety II	65·00	65·00
		g. Opt in red	17·00	16·00
		ga. Variety I	60·00	60·00
15		5d. grey-blue (210)	29·00	28·00
		b. Variety II	60·00	60·00
		c. Opt double	85·00	
		g. Opt in red	65·00	65·00
		ga. Variety I	85·00	85·00
16		10d. deep blue (211)	90·00	85·00
		b. Variety II	£275	£275
		g. Opt in red	£130	£110
		ga. Variety I	£400	£400
17	**33**	25d. deep blue (212)	£170	£160
		g. Opt in red	£200	£160
		(c) On stamps of 1913, lithographed		
18	**29**	1l. green	65	65
		a. Variety I	5·50	5·50
		c. Opt double	28·00	
		e. On No. 213a	£275	
		g. Opt in red	2·20	2·20
		ga. On No. 213a	£425	
19	**31**	5l. green	5·50	5·50
		a. Variety I	39·00	39·00
		g. Opt in red	3·25	3·25
		ga. Variety I	24·00	24·00
20	**29**	10l. carmine	80	75
		a. Variety I	22·00	23·00
		c. Opt double	19·00	
		d. Opt inverted	19·00	
		g. Opt in red	4·50	4·25
21	**30**	25l. ultramarine	3·25	3·25
		a. Variety I	12·50	12·50
		g. Opt in red	2·20	2·20
		ga. Variety I	6·75	6·75
		(d) On No. 248 (with opt T **34**)		
22	**29**	1l. green	39·00	39·00

SAMOS

From 1832 to 1912 an independent principality under Turkish suzerainty with British, French and Russian protection. For stamps of French Post Office in Vathy, the capital, used between 1893 and 1914, see French Post Offices in the Turkish Empire in Parts 6 (France) or 16 (Central Asia) of this catalogue.

Between 1878 and 1911 various local issues were prepared but their use was forbidden by the Turkish authorities and it is doubtful if many were postally used.

A. PROVISIONAL GOVERNMENT

Following a revolt in September 1912, and the withdrawal of the Turkish garrison, a provisional government under Themistocles Sophoulos declared for union with Greece on 11 (24) November 1912.

The dates of issue are expressed first in the Julian calendar and then in the Gregorian calendar.

1 Map of Samos

2 Hermes

(Handstruck. Govt. Building, Vathy)

1912 (14–27 Nov). Imperf.

1	**1**	5l. dull green	28·00	9·75
		a. Tête-bêche (pair)	£600	£425
2		10l. red	22·00	9·75
		a. Tête-bêche (pair)	£600	£425
3		25l. blue	55·00	19·00
		a. Tête-bêche (pair)	£3250	£1900
		b. Error. Dull green	£650	£550

Nos. 1/3 in other colours are colour trials.

(Litho. G. Stangel & Co., Athens)

1912 (29 Nov–12 Dec).

		(A) P 11½		
4A	**2**	1l. grey	2·20	1·60
5A		5l. yellow-green	2·20	1·60
6A		10l. carmine	3·25	1·90
7A		25l. pale blue	9·00	2·20
8A		50l. brown-purple	20·00	6·50
		(B) Imperf (singles)		
4B	**2**	1l. grey	22·00	16·00
5B		5l. yellow-green	22·00	16·00
6B		10l. carmine	22·00	16·00
7B		25l. pale blue	22·00	16·00
8B		50l. brown-purple	22·00	16·00

ΕΛΛΑΣ

(**3**)

4 Scene of Turkish Repulse, 1824

1912 (22 Dec–4 Jan). T **2** redrawn, optd with T **3** in Athens.

9 1l. grey 1·40 1·40
a. Imperf (pair) £120
10 5l. green 1·40 1·40
a. Imperf (pair) £120
11 10l. rose-pink 1·70 1·40
a. Imperf (pair) £120
12 25l. deep blue 2·50 1·90
13 50l. chocolate 14·00 7·75
a. Imperf (pair) £120
14 1d. orange 17·00 14·00

Nos. 6 and 11 were officially used bisected as 5l. stamps.

(Des Ramphos. Litho G. Travlos, Samos)

1913 (Jan). Turkish Evacuation Commemoration. Signed T.S., in black ink (25d.) or red ink (others). P 12.

15 **4** 1d. brown 22·00 12·00
a. Imperf (pair) £300
16 2d. blue 22·00 12·00
a. Imperf (pair) £300
17 5d. olive-green 45·00 26·00
a. Imperf (pair) £450
18 10d. yellow-green £150 £140
a. Imperf (pair) £1800
b. Imperf between (pair) £1500
19 25d. red £120 £140
a. Imperf (pair) £1800
b. Imperf between (pair) £1500

The initials are those of the local President, Themistocles Sophoulis. Stamps may be found without them. Nos. 15/17 were issued on 4/17 Jan. and Nos. 18/19 on 24 Jan./6 Feb. Forgeries exist.

B. GREEK ADMINISTRATION

Samos was united to Greece by the Treaty of London on 30 May 1913.

ΕΛΛΑΣ
(5)

1914 (1–14 Feb). Nos. 4/8 optd at Vathy with T **5**.

20 **2** 1l. grey 9·00 6·50
21 5l. yellow-green 9·00 6·50
22 10l. carmine 9·00 6·50
a. Opt double
23 25l. pale blue 13·00 11·50
24 50l. chocolate 10·00 8·75
a. Opt double £130

The Provisional Government was dissolved at the end of 1914, after which the stamps of Greece were placed on sale. The following stamps were authorised by the Greek Governor, with the agreement of the Ministry of Finance in Athens.

(6)

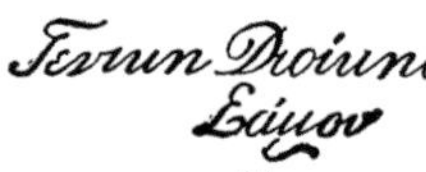
(7)

1915 (17–30 Jan). Vathy Hospital Fund.

(a) Nos. 9/14 optd with T **6**, No. 26 additionally surch "ΛΕΙΠΤΟΝ"

25 1l. grey (R.) 20·00 24·00
a. Black opt £190 £180
26 1l. on 1d. orange (R.) 22·00 25·00
a. Surch inverted £325
b. Surch double £325
27 5l. green 2·20 2·75
a. Opt double £225
b. Red opt £170 £170
28 10l. rose-pink 2·20 2·75
a. Opt inverted £150
b. Red opt £170 £170
29 25l. deep blue 2·20 2·75
a. Red opt £170 £170
30 50l. chocolate 2·20 2·75
a. Red opt £170 £160
31 1d. orange (R.) 3·25 3·25
a. Opt inverted £225
b. Black opt £190 £180
ba. Black opt double £225 £225

(b) Nos. 15/19 optd with T **7**

32 **4** 1d. brown (R.) 28·00 22·00
33 2d. blue (R.) 34·00 32·00
a. Opt double
34 5d. olive-green (R.) 34·00 32·00
35 10d. yellow-green 36·00 32·00
a. Opt inverted £1500
36 25d. red £850 £700

Nos. 25/36 are also embossed with a cross within a circular pattern and inscription, with or without initials.
Nos. 30/34 were also used on Icaria.

BRITISH FIELD OFFICE IN SALONIKA

These overprints were originally prepared for use by a civilian post office to be set up on Mount Athos, Northern Greece. When the project was abandoned they were placed on sale at the Army Field Office in Salonika.

Levant
(S 1)

1916 (end Feb–9 Mar). George V stamps of Gt. Britain, optd with Type S **1** by Army Printing Office, Salonika.

S1 **105** ½d. green 50·00 £250
a. Opt double £3250 £4000
b. Vert pair, one without opt £1600 £2000
S2 **104** 1d. scarlet 50·00 £250
a. Opt double £2000 £2500
S3 **106** 2d. reddish orange (Die I) £150 £375
S4 3d. bluish violet £120 £375
a. Opt double
S5 4d. grey-green £150 £375
S6 **107** 6d. reddish purple, **C** 85·00 £325
a. Vert pair, one without opt £1900 £2500
S7 **108** 9d. agate £325 £600
a. Opt double £11000 £8500
S8 1s. bistre-brown £275 £500
S1/8 *Set of 8* £1100 £2750

There are numerous forgeries of this overprint.
All values can be found with an additional albino overprint, inverted on the gummed side.

ITALIAN OCCUPATION OF CORFU

31 August–27 September 1923

As a sequel to the murder on Greek soil of Italian officers on a Greco-Albanian Boundary Commission, Italian warships bombarded Corfu and troops occupied the town on 31 August 1923.

100 Centesimi = 1 Lira
100 Lepta = 1 Drachma

CORFÙ
(1)

CORFÙ
Lepta 60
(2)

1923 (20 Sept). Stamps of Italy (*various portraits of Victor Emmanuel III*) optd with T **1**.

1 **37** 5c. green 9·50 9·75
2 **38** 10c. rose 9·50 9·75
3 **37** 15c. slate 9·50 9·75
4 **41** 20c. orange (No. 105) 9·50 9·75
5 **39** 30c. orange-brown 9·50 9·75
6 **40** 50c. mauve 9·50 9·75
7 **39** 60c. blue 9·50 9·75
8 **34** 1l. brown and green 9·50 9·75
1/8 *Set of 8* 70·00 70·00

1923 (24 Sept). Stamps of Italy surch as T **2**.

9 **38** 25l. on 10c. rose £100 43·00
10 **39** 60l. on 25c. blue 28·00
11 70l. on 30c. orange-brown 28·00
12 **40** 1d.20l. on 50c. mauve 50·00 43·00
13 **34** 2d.40l. on 1l. brown and green 50·00 43·00
14 4d.75l. on 2l. myrtle and orange 22·00

Nos. 10, 11 and 14 were not sent to Corfu as the island was evacuated by Italian troops on 27 September, before they could arrive.

ITALIAN OCCUPATION OF CORFU AND PAXOS

1941–1943

Issues made during the occupation of the Ionian Islands by Italian troops.

100 Lepta = 1 Drachma

CORFU
(1)

1941 (5 June). Stamps of Greece optd with T **1**.

(a) On Postage issue of 1937–38. Nos. 497/516

1 **86** 5l. greenish blue and red-brown 6·75 4·25
2 – 10l. red-brown and light blue (498) 3·25 3·25
3 – 10l. red-brown and light blue (514) £850 £750
4 **87** 20l. blue-green and black 3·25 3·25
5 **88** 40l. black and blue-green 3·25 3·25
6 – 50l. black and bistre-brown 3·25 3·25
7 – 80l. brown and dull violet 3·25 6·50
8 **89** 1d. green 11·00 16·00
9 **89a** 1d.50 green 11·00 11·00
10 – 2d. ultramarine 8·50 7·50
11 **89** 3d. red-brown 8·50 7·50
12 – 5d. scarlet 8·50 7·50
13 – 6d. olive-brown 8·50 7·50
14 **90** 7d. chocolate 11·00 7·50
15 **89** 8d. deep blue 28·00 27·00
16 – 10d. red-brown £600 £225
17 **91** 15d. blue-green 31·00 27·00
18 **92** 25d. deep blue 22·00 27·00
19 **89a** 30d. brown-red £100 £110
20 **89** 100d. lake £350 £225
1/20 *Set of 20* £1800 £1300

No. 2 is inscr "TYPIN" and No. 3 is corrected to "TIPYN".

(b) On Air stamps, Nos. 521/2 and 480/8

21 **D 20** 50l. brown (*rouletted*) 65·00 32·00
22 50l. brown (*perf*) 12·50 11·00
23 **79** 1d. scarlet £800 £300
24 – 2d. grey-blue 12·50 7·50
a. Opt double
25 – 5d. mauve 17·00 13·00
26 – 7d. ultramarine 17·00 15·00
27 **80** 10d. brown £900 £425
28 10d. orange-red 80·00 49·00
29 – 25d. rose-carmine £100 65·00
30 – 30d. green £120 90·00
31 – 50d. mauve £120 80·00
32 – 100d. brown £1200 £800

(c) On Charity Tax Stamps, Nos. C524/6

33 **C 96** 10l. carmine/*rose* 3·25 6·50
34 50l. green/*pale green* 3·25 6·50
35 1d. blue/*pale blue* 39·00 35·00

(d) On Postage Due stamps, Nos. D273, D275, D279, D452/3, D455/8 and D480/1

D36 **D 20** 10l. carmine 4·50 5·50
D37 25l. ultramarine 6·75 5·50
D38 80l. brown-purple £1100 £400
D39 1d. pale blue £1800 £850
D40 2d. vermilion 11·00 16·00
D41 5d. slate-blue 25·00 27·00
D42 10d. green 22·00 27·00
D43 15d. red-brown 25·00 27·00
D44 25d. vermilion 25·00 27·00
D45 50d. orange 25·00 27·00
D46 100d. blue-green £650 £550

These issues were superseded by the general issues made for the Italian Occupation of the Ionian Islands.

ITALIAN OCCUPATION OF CEPHALONIA AND ITHACA

1941–43

Issues made during the occupation of the Ionian Islands by Italia[n] troops.

100 Lepta = 1 Drachma

I T A L I A

Occupazione Militare
Italiana isole
Cefalonia e Itaca
(1)

PRICES. Prices are for unsevered pairs except where overprint wa[s] applied to single stamps. Single stamps from severed pairs are wort[h] ⅓ unused and ½ used prices.

1941 (20 May–Aug). Stamps of Greece optd with T **1** across [a] pair of stamps, sideways (reading downwards) on horizonta[l] designs and horizontally on vertical designs.

(a) On Postage issue of 1937–8. Nos. 497 etc

1 **86** 5l. blue and red-brown 28·00 27·0
a. Reading upwards 32·00 31·0
2 – 10l. red-brown and light blue (514) 28·00 27·0
a. On No. 498 34·00 32·0
3 **87** 20l. green and black 28·00 27·0
4 **88** 40l. black and green 28·00 27·0
a. Reading upwards 34·00 32·0
5 – 50l. black and bistre-brown 28·00 27·0
a. Reading upwards 34·00 32·0
6 – 80l. brown and violet 43·00 38·0
7 **89** 1d. green £325 £19
8 **89a** 1d.50 green £200 £12
9 – 2d. ultramarine 34·00 43·0
a. Reading upwards 45·00 43·0
10 – 5d. scarlet £100 49·0
a. Reading upwards £150 £11
11 – 6d. olive-brown £100 49·0
a. Reading upwards £160 75·0
12 **90** 7d. chocolate £100 49·0
a. Reading upwards £160 75·0
13 **89** 8d. deep blue £225 £12
14 – 10d. red-brown £100 49·0
a. Reading upwards £150 £11
15 **91** 15d. blue-green £200 95·0
a. Reading upwards £250 £18
16 **92** 25d. deep blue £225 £14
17 **89a** 30d. brown-red £1000 £60

(b) On Air stamps. Nos. 521, 488a/d and 485/8

18 **D 20** 50l. brown 75·00 £19
a. On No. 521a £400 £40
19 **79** 1d. scarlet 75·00 £11
a. On No. 480 £160 £22
20 – 2d. grey-blue 28·00 43·0
a. Reading upwards 28·00 43·0
b. Horiz opt on horiz pair £750 £70
c. Horiz opt on single stamp £600 £60
d. On No. 481 55·00 43·0
21 – 5d. mauve 55·00 75·0
a. Reading down on single stamp £750 £70
b. Reading up on single stamp £750 £70
22 – 7d. ultramarine 65·00 £11
a. On No. 483 £225 £32
23 – 25d. rose-carmine £325 £37
24 – 30d. green £400 £47
a. Reading upwards £475 £55
b. Horiz opt on single stamp £550 £55
25 – 50d. mauve £2000 £275
26 – 100d. brown £1000 £130
a. Reading upwards £1100 £150

(c) On Charity Tax stamps

27 10l. carmine (No. C498) 34·00 32·0
28 10l. carmine/*rose* (No. C524) 45·00 32·0
a. Horiz opt on horiz pair £325 £32
b. Horiz opt on single stamp 34·00 27·0
29 50l. green/*pale green* (No C525) 34·00 27·0
a. Reading upwards 50·00 40·0
b. Horiz opt on horiz pair 34·00 32·0
c. Horiz opt on single stamp 65·00 43·0
30 50l. green/*pale green* (No. C554) £900 £65
a. Reading upwards £900
31 1d. blue/*pale blue* (No. C526) 90·00 60·0
a. Reading upwards £180 £12

Nos. 1 to 31a. A wrong fount "C" exists in all values optd in pairs.
Contemporary stamps were also overprinted similarly with a hand-stamp but the word "isole" is spelt "isola". There was another type o[f] overprint issued in Ithaca arranged in four lines: "occupazione/ (o[r] Occupazione) Militare Italiana/Isole/Cefalonia e Itaca". All these are rare and outside the scope of this catalogue.

These issues were superseded by the general issues made for the Italian Occupation of the Ionian Islands.

ITALIAN OCCUPATION OF THE IONIAN ISLANDS

1941–1943

The Ionian Islands consist of Corfu (Kerkira), Paxos (Paxoi) Santa Maura (Levkas), Ithaca (Ithaki), Cephalonia (Kefalinia) and Zante (Zakinthos).
After the armistice between the Greek forces on the mainland of Greece and those of the Axis powers on 23 April 1941, Italian troops occupied the islands.

100 Centesimi = 1 Lira

ISOLE JONIE
(1)

1941 (1 Sept). Stamps of Italy optd with T **1**.

(a) On Postage stamps of 1929–42, Nos. 239 etc

	98	5c. brown (R.) (Romulus, Remus and wolf)	55	2·75
	100	10c. sepia (R.) (Augustus the Great)	55	2·75
	99	20c. carmine (Julius Caesar)	55	2·75
	102	25c. green (Victor Emmanuel III)	55	2·75
	103	30c. brown (R.) (Victor Emmanuel III)	55	2·75
		50c. bright violet (R.)	55	2·75
	102	75c. carmine	55	2·75
		1l.25 blue (R.)	1·10	5·50

(b) On Air stamp of 1930, No. 271

	110	50c. sepia (Pegasus)	1·10	6·50

(c) On Postage Due stamps of 1934, Nos. D396 etc. (Arms)

10	D **141**	10c. blue	1·50	4·25
11		20c. carmine	1·50	4·25
12		30c. orange-vermilion	1·50	4·25
13	D **142**	1l. orange	1·50	4·25

Stamps as above further optd or surch "BOLLO" are fiscals.

On the island of Cerigo (Kithyra), which is off the south coast of Greece, stamps of Greece without overprint continued to be used during the occupation.

The following overprints on Greek stamps are bogus: "CERIGO/Occupazione Militare/Italiana"; "ISOLA ITALIANA DI/PAXO/ANNO XIXo"; "ITALIA/SANTA MAURA".

GERMAN OCCUPATION OF ZANTE

1943–1944

In September 1943, after the armistice between the Kingdom of Italy and the Allies, German troops took over control of the Ionian Islands from Italian forces.

The following issue was made by the local administration.

100 Centesimi = 1 Lira = 8 Drachma

ΕΛΛΑΣ
2·X·43

(**1**)

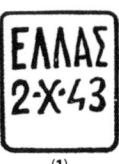

1943 (22 Oct). Stamps of Italian Occupation of Ionian Islands (optd "ISOLE JONIE") further handstamped with T **1** in black.

(a) POSTAGE. Nos. 4 and 6

1		25c. green	31·00	46·00
		a. Optd with Type **1** in red	55·00	70·00
2		50c. bright violet	31·00	46·00
		a. Optd with Type **1** in red	55·00	70·00

(b) AIR. No. 9

3		50c. sepia	44·00	50·00
		a. Optd with Type **1** in red	£275	£300

The 10c. value exists with handstamp in black and in red but was not issued.

Inverted handstamps exist.

Nos. 1/3 were used from 22 to 29 October.

In 1941 whilst under Italian military occupation contemporary Greek stamps were handstamped "OCCUPAZIONE/MILITARE DI/ZANTE/1-5-XIX". These are rare and outside the scope of this catalogue.

Castelrosso

A. FRENCH OCCUPATION

100 Centimes = 1 Franc = 4 Piastres

This island off the coast of Asia Minor was occupied by the French Navy on 27 December 1915 and at first used stamps of French Post Offices in the Turkish Empire (see Part 6 or 16 of this catalogue) with special cancellations.

B. N. F.

CASTELLORIZO

(F **1**) "B.N.F."=Base Navale Française

1920 (19 June). Stamps of 1902–20 of French Post Offices in the Turkish Empire (inscr "LEVANT") optd with Type F **1** (sideways reading down on Nos. 10/13).

F1	**11**	1c. grey	60·00	60·00
F2		2c. claret	60·00	60·00
F3		3c. orange-red	60·00	60·00
F4		5c. yellow-green	75·00	70·00
F5	**14**	10c. carmine	75·00	70·00
F6		15c. pale red	£110	£100
F7		20c. purple-brown	£120	£120
F8		1pi. on 25c. blue	£120	£120
F9		30c. deep lilac	£130	£130
F10	**13**	40c. red and pale blue	£225	£225
F11		2pi. on 50c. brown and lavender	£250	£250
F12		4pi. on 1f. lake and yellow-green	£325	£325
F13		20pi. on 5f. deep blue and buff	£900	£850
F1/13 *Set of 13*			£2250	£2250

All values exist with "S" instead of "Z" in "CASTELLORIZO"; Nos. F1/9 exist with "CASTELLORIZO" inverted; Nos. F10/13 exist without stop after "N". Double and inverted overprints also exist.

O. N. F.
Castellorizo
(F **2**)

O F
CASTELLORISO
(F **3**)

"O.N.F."=Occupation Navale Française
"O.F."=Occupation Française

1920 (July). Stamps as last but optd with Type F **2**.

F14	**11**	1c. grey	50·00	50·00
F15		2c. claret	50·00	50·00
F16		3c. orange-red	50·00	50·00
F17		5c. yellow-green (R.)	50·00	50·00
F18	**14**	10c. carmine	55·00	55·00
F19		15c. pale red	65·00	65·00
F20		20c. purple-brown	£130	£130
F21		1pi. on 25c. blue (R.)	£130	£120
F22		30c. deep lilac (R.)	£120	£120
F23	**13**	40c. red and pale blue	£120	£120
F24		2pi. on 50c. brown and lavender	£120	£120
F25		4pi. on 1f. lake and yellow-green	£150	£150
F26		20pi. on 5f. deep blue and buff	£550	£500
F14/26 *Set of 13*			£1500	£1400

An 8pi. on 2f. was prepared but not issued.

Nos. F14/22 exist with the errors "CASETLLORIZO" and "ASTELLORIZO"; also without dot over "i" and broken "F".

1920 (June). Nos. 358 and 364 of France optd with Type F **2**.

F27	**18**	10c. red	55·00	32·00
F28		25c. blue	55·00	32·00

The above exist with overprint inverted and also without dot over "i" and broken "F".

The 5, 15, 20, 30, 40 and 50c. and 1f. and 5f. of the 1916–19 issue of France also exist with this overprint but are only known unused and it is doubtful if they were issued.

1920 (July). Stamps of France optd with Type F **3**.

F29	**18**	5c. blue-green (357)	£300	£275
F30		10c. red (358)	£300	£275
F31		20c. brown-lake (337)	£300	£275
F32		25c. blue (364)	£300	£275
F33	**13**	50c. cinnamon and lavender (368)	£1600	£1600
F34		1f. lake and yellow-green (306)	£1600	£1600
F29/34 *Set of 6*			£4000	£4000

The 5, 10, 15, 20c., 1pi. on 25c., 40c., 2pi. on 50c. and 4pi. on 1f. of French Post Offices in the Turkish Empire with this overprint were prepared but not issued.

On 21 August 1920 the French forces withdrew and the island was occupied by the Italians.

B. ITALIAN OCCUPATION

100 Centesimi = 1 Lira

In accordance with the Treaty of Sèvres on 10 August 1920 Castelrosso was awarded to Italy. After a temporary transference to Italian naval administration on 1 March 1921, it came later under the rule of the Governor of the Dodecanese Islands and Castelrosso.

CASTELROSSO

(**1**)

2

1922 (11 July). Contemporary stamps of Italy (various portraits of Victor Emmanuel III) optd with T **1**.

1	**37**	5c. green	6·25	24·00
2	**38**	10c. rose-red	2·75	24·00
3	**37**	15c. slate	4·50	24·00
4	**41**	20c. orange (No. 105)	2·75	24·00
5	**39**	25c. blue	2·75	24·00
6	**40**	40c. brown	60·00	27·00
7		50c. violet	60·00	27·00
8	**39**	60c. carmine-red	60·00	38·00
9		85c. red-brown	6·25	43·00
1/9 *Set of 9*			£180	£225

1923 (Jan). Typo. Wmk Crown. P 14.

10	**2**	5c. green	4·00	18·00
11		10c. carmine	4·00	18·00
12		25c. blue	4·00	18·00
13		50c. dull purple	4·00	18·00
14		1l. brown	4·00	18·00
10/14 *Set of 5*			18·00	80·00

CASTELROSSO
(**3**)

CASTELROSSO
(**4**)

1924 (Mar). Contemporary stamps of Italy optd with T **3**.

15	**37**	5c. green	2·20	27·00
16	**38**	10c. rose-red	2·20	27·00
17	**37**	15c. slate	2·20	38·00
18	**41**	20c. orange (No. 105)	2·20	38·00
19	**39**	25c. blue	2·20	30·00
20	**40**	40c. brown	2·20	30·00
21		50c. violet	2·20	38·00
22	**39**	60c. carmine-red	2·20	43·00
23		85c. red-brown	2·75	55·00
24	**34**	1l. brown and green	2·75	55·00
15/24 *Set of 10*			21·00	£350

1930 (20 Oct). "Ferrucci" issue of Italy (colours changed) optd with T **4**.

25	**114**	20c. bright violet (R.)	8·50	7·50
26	**115**	25c. deep green (R.)	8·50	13·00
27		50c. black (R.)	8·50	7·50
28		1l.25 blue (R.)	8·50	15·00
29	**116**	5l.+2l. carmine-red (B.)	39·00	75·00
25/29 *Set of 5*			65·00	£110

1931 (28 Aug). T **128/9** and similar types (Garibaldi) of Italy with colours changed optd with T **4**.

30		10c. sepia (R.)	34·00	55·00
31		20c. lake-brown (B.)	34·00	55·00
32		25c. green (R.)	34·00	55·00
33		30c. slate-blue (R.)	34·00	55·00
34		50c. purple (B.)	34·00	55·00
35		75c. lake (B.)	34·00	55·00
36		1l.25c. deep blue (R.)	34·00	55·00
37		1l.75 +25c. sepia (R.)	34·00	55·00
38		2l.55 +50c. orange-vermilion (B.)	34·00	55·00
39		5l. +1l. violet (R.)	34·00	55·00
30/39 *Set of 10*			£300	£500

Castelrosso was transferred to Greece with the Dodecanese Islands by the Treaty of Paris, which came into force on 15 September 1947. It is now called Kastellorizon.

Crete

After many rebellions against Turkish rule, Crete was made autonomous, under Turkish suzerainty, in November 1898, and British, French, Italian and Russian troops were stationed in four separate zones there until July 1908. On 7 October 1908, the Cretan Assembly proclaimed union with Greece, but this was not recognised until Turkey ceded the island by the Treaty of London on 30 May 1913.

I. BRITISH ADMINISTRATION

CANDIA PROVINCE

(Now Iraklion)

40 Paras = 1 Piastre

The British postal service operated from 25 November 1898 until the end of 1899.

Overseas mail franked with Nos. 1/5 were forwarded through the Austrian post office at Canea, being additionally franked with stamps of the Austro-Hungarian Post Offices in the Turkish Empire.

B 1

B 2

1998 (25 Nov). Handstruck locally. Imperf.

B1	B 1	20pa. bright violet	£425	£225

(Litho M. Grundmann, Athens)

1998 (3 Dec). P 11½.

B2	B 2	10pa. blue	8·00	19·00
		a. Imperf (pair)	£250	
B3		20pa. green	14·00	17·00
		a. Imperf (pair)	£250	

1899. P 11½.

B4	B 2	10pa. brown	8·50	26·00
		a. Imperf (pair)	£250	
B5		20pa. rose	19·00	15·00
		a. Imperf (pair)	£250	

II. RUSSIAN ADMINISTRATION

RETHYMNON PROVINCE

4 Metallik = 1 Grosion (Turkish piastre)

The Russian postal service operated from 1 May to 29 July 1899.

R 1

R 2

1899 (May). Handstruck locally and with violet or blue control handstamp. Wove or laid paper. Imperf.

R1	R 1	1m. blue (1 May)	55·00	15·00
R2	R 2	1m. green	12·00	9·75
R3		2m. rose (1 May)	£250	£150
R4		2m. green-black	12·00	9·75

R 3

R 4

(Litho Grohmann & Stangel, Athens)

1899. Control mark of Russian double eagle in a circle, in violet. P 11½.

(a) Without stars in oval (27 May)

R5	R 3	1m. rose	60·00	33·00
R6		2m. rose	60·00	33·00
R7		1g. rose	60·00	33·00
R8		1m. blue	60·00	33·00
R9		2m. blue	60·00	33·00
R10		1g. blue	60·00	33·00
R11		1m. green	60·00	33·00
R12		2m. green	60·00	33·00
R13		1g. green	60·00	33·00
R14		1m. claret	60·00	33·00
R15		2m. claret	60·00	33·00
R16		1g. claret	60·00	33·00
R17		1m. orange	60·00	33·00
R18		2m. orange	60·00	33·00
R19		1g. orange	60·00	33·00
R20		1m. yellow	60·00	33·00
R21		2m. yellow	60·00	33·00
R22		1g. yellow	60·00	33·00
R23		1m. black	—	£600
R24		2m. black	—	£600
R25		1g. black	—	£600
		a. Perf 10½×10½×12×12		

Nos. R23/5 may not have been authorised for issue, but used copies are known.

(b) Star at each side. Figures at foot shaded (8 June)

R26	R 4	1m. rose	35·00	20·00
R27		2m. rose	15·00	9·75
R28		1g. rose	11·00	9·75
R29		1m. blue	23·00	13·00
R30		2m. blue	15·00	9·75
R31		1g. blue	11·00	8·50
R32		1m. green	17·00	13·00
R33		2m. green	15·00	9·75
R34		1g. green	11·00	8·50
R35		1m. claret	20·00	13·00
R36		2m. claret	15·00	9·75
R37		1g. claret	11·00	8·50

Many of the above can be supplied unused without the control mark.

Dangerous forgeries exist.

III. PROVISIONAL GOVERNMENT OF CRETE

High Commissioner: Prince George of Greece

21 December 1898–25 September 1906

100 Lepta = 1 Drachma

1 Hermes

2 Hera

3 Prince George of Greece

4 Talos

5 Minos

6 St. George and the Dragon

(Recess Bradbury, Wilkinson)

1900 (1 Mar). P 14.

(a) Without opt

1	1	1l. chocolate	55	30
2	2	5l. green	2·20	30
3	3	10l. scarlet	1·70	45
4	2	20l. rose	5·50	1·10

ΠΡΟΣΩΡΙΝΟΝ
(7) ("Provisional")

(b) Optd with T **7**. P 14

A. In vermilion

5A	3	25l. blue	1·10	85
6A	1	50l. deep lilac	2·20	1·30
7A	4	1d. indigo-violet	13·50	13·00
8A	5	2d. brown	34·00	27·00
9A	6	5d. black and green	£170	£160

B. In black

5B	3	25l. blue	2·20	55
6B	1	50l. deep lilac	2·20	1·60
7B	4	1d. indigo-violet	11·00	6·50
		a. Opt inverted		
8B	5	2d. brown	29·00	19·00
9B	6	5d. black and green	90·00	85·00

D **8**

1 ΔΡΑΧΜΗ
(D **9**)

(Litho Bradbury, Wilkinson)

1901 (Feb). POSTAGE DUE. P 14.

D10	D 8	1l. red	35	30
D11		5l. red	55	30
D12		10l. red	80	45
D13		20l. red	1·10	55
D14		40l. red	11·00	11·00
D15		50l. red	11·00	11·00
D16		1d. red	22·00	22·00
D17		2d. red	14·00	11·00

1901 (June). POSTAGE DUE. Surch with Type D **9**.

D18	D 8	1d. on 1d. red	11·00	9·25

ΠΡΟΣΩΡΙΝΟΝ
(8)

5 **5**
(9)

1901. Optd locally with T **8**.

10	3	25l. blue (Grey-Blk.)	28·00	1·10
		a. First letter of opt inverted	£400	£250
11		25l. blue (Blk.)	28·00	1·10
		a. "Σ" of opt omitted	£170	75·00

1901. Without opt. Colours changed. P 14.

12	1	1l. olive-yellow	80	8
13	2	20l. orange	3·25	8
14	1	50l. ultramarine	13·50	13·0

No. 12 is a revenue stamp which was authorised for postal use fo about 14 days in 1901 and again in 1904. Other values in olive-yellov are revenue stamps without postal validity.

1901–02. As Nos. 5/9 but without opt.

15	3	25l. blue	11·00	5
16	1	50l. deep lilac	39·00	27·0
17	4	1d. indigo-violet	45·00	27·0
18	5	2d. brown	14·50	11·5
19	6	5d. black and green	18·00	13·0

1904 (Dec). No. 13 surch with T **9**.

20	2	5 on 20l. orange	3·25	1·1
		a. "5" with straight top	£170	£16

10 Rhea

11 Europa

12 Prince George of Greece

13 Miletus

14 Triton

15 Ariadne

16 Europa and Jupiter

17 Minos Ruins

18 View of Mount Ida, etc.

(Recess Bradbury, Wilkinson)

1905 (9 Feb). P 14.

21	10	2l. slate-lilac	1·70	20
22	11	5l. green	2·20	20
23	12	10l. red	2·20	1·10
24	13	20l. blue-green	6·25	65
25	14	25l. ultramarine	7·75	1·10
26	15	50l. brown	9·00	3·25
27	16	1d. sepia and carmine	65·00	43·00
28	17	3d. black and orange	39·00	30·00
29	18	5d. black and olive-green	18·00	17·00

Date quoted is that of earliest use seen.

High Commissioner: Alexander Zaimis

25 September 1906

19 High Commissioner A. T. A. Zaimis

20 Landing of Prince George of Greece at Suda

(Recess Bradbury, Wilkinson)

1907 (28 Aug). P 14.

30	19	25l. black and blue	45·00	1·10
31	20	1d. black and green	11·00	7·50

O **21**

O **22**

(Litho Bradbury, Wilkinson)

1908 (14 Jan). OFFICIAL. P 14.

O32	O 21	10l. dull claret	22·00	1·10
O33	O 22	30l. slate-blue	45·00	1·10

21 Hermes

ΕΛΛΑΣ
(22)

Varieties

A. "Σ" inverted reading "ΕΛΛΑ Σ"
B. "Δ" instead of "Α", reading "ΕΛΔΣ"
C. "Ε" omitted, reading "ΛΛΑΣ"
D. "Α" and "Λ" transposed, reading "ΕΛΑΛΣ"
E. First "Λ" omitted, reading "Ε ΛΑΣ"
F. "Σ" omitted, reading "ΕΛΛΑ"

1908 (21 Sept). Optd with T **22** ("GREECE").

32	**1**	1l. chocolate (No. 1)	65	45
		a. Variety A	13·50	13·00
		b. Variety B	13·50	13·00
		g. Opt inverted	28·00	27·00
33	**10**	2l. slate-lilac (No. 21)	65	45
		a. Variety A	17·00	16·00
		b. Variety B	17·00	16·00
		g. Opt inverted	34·00	33·00
		h. Opt double	34·00	33·00
		i. Pair, one without opt	65·00	65·00
34	**11**	5l. green (No. 22)	65	45
		a. Variety A	17·00	16·00
		b. Variety B	17·00	16·00
		c. Variety C	25·00	24·00
		d. Variety D	17·00	16·00
		e. Variety E	£325	£325
		f. Variety F	25·00	24·00
		g. Opt inverted	28·00	27·00
		i. Pair, one without opt	65·00	65·00
35	**3**	10l. scarlet (No. 3)	1·30	85
		c. Variety C	80·00	75·00
		d. Variety D	55·00	55·00
		f. Variety F	80·00	75·00
		g. Opt inverted	80·00	75·00
36	**21**	10l. dull carmine	3·25	85
		a. Variety A	65·00	65·00
		b. Variety B	65·00	65·00
		i. Pair, one without opt	80·00	75·00
37	**13**	20l. blue-green (No. 24)	3·25	1·10
		f. Variety F	34·00	32·00
		i. Pair, one without opt	55·00	55·00
38	**19**	25l. black and blue (No. 30)	9·00	2·20
		d. Variety D	50·00	49·00
		f. Variety F	45·00	43·00
39	**15**	50l. brown (No. 26)	12·50	4·25
		g. Opt inverted	£170	£160
40	**16**	1d. sepia and carmine (No. 27)	£100	65·00
		f. Variety F	£300	£300
41	**5**	2d. brown (No. 18)	11·00	8·75
		f. Variety F	45·00	45·00
42	**17**	3d. black and orange (No. 28)	39·00	36·00
43	**18**	5d. black and olive-green (No. 29)	34·00	32·00

The above were issued before the (unrecognised) proclamation of union with Greece.

Varieties

A. "Σ" inverted, reading "ΕΛΛΑ Σ"
B. "Δ" instead of "Α" reading "ΕΛΔΣ"
C. "Α" inverted, reading "ΕΛΛ∀Σ"
D. "Σ" omitted, reading "ΕΛΛΑ"

1908 (Sept). POSTAGE DUE. Optd with T **22**.

D44	**D 8**	1l. red	35	30
		a. Variety A	6·75	6·75
		c. Variety C		
		d. Variety D	34·00	34·00
		e. Opt inverted	17·00	17·00
		f. Pair, one without opt	65·00	65·00
D45		5l. red	65	65
		a. Variety A	9·00	9·00
		d. Variety D	27·00	27·00
		e. Opt inverted	40·00	40·00
D46		10l. red	65	65
		a. Variety A	10·00	10·00
		e. Opt inverted	40·00	40·00
		f. Pair, one without opt	80·00	
D47		20l. red	1·70	1·60
		a. Variety A	28·00	28·00
D48		40l. red	7·75	6·50
		a. Variety A	95·00	90·00
		b. Variety B	65·00	65·00
		e. Opt inverted	£120	£120
D49		50l. red	10·00	8·75
		e. Opt inverted	£110	£110
		f. Pair, one without opt	£150	£150
D50		1d. red (No. D16)	£325	£325
		b. Variety B	—	£650
		f. Pair, one without opt		
D51		1d. on 1d. red (No. D18)	11·00	8·75
		a. Variety A	£130	£130
		b. Variety B	£130	£130
		e. Opt inverted	£275	£275
D52		2d. red	18·00	11·00
		a. Variety A	£130	£130
		b. Variety B	£130	£130
		e. Opt inverted	£275	£275

1908. OFFICIAL. Optd with T **22**.

O44	**O 21**	10l. dull claret	17·00	1·10
		a. "Σ" inverted	65·00	27·00
		b. "Δ" for "Α"	65·00	27·00
O45	**O 22**	30l. slate-blue	34·00	1·10
		a. Opt inverted	£170	£160
		b. "Σ" inverted	95·00	49·00
		c. "Δ" for "Α"	95·00	55·00

ΕΛΛΑΣ 2 ΠΡΟΣΩΡΙΝΟΝ
(23)

ΠΡΟΣΩΡΙΝΟΝ ΕΛΛΑΣ
(24)

ΕΛΛΑΣ 2 ΠΡΟΣΩΡΙΝΟΝ
(25)

ΠΡΟΣΩΡΙΝΟΝ 5 5
(26)

1909. Optd or surch with T **23/26** for postal use.

44	**23**	1l. olive-yellow (12)	1·70	1·30
45		1l. red (D10)	4·50	4·25
46	**24**	2 on 20l. red (D47)	1·70	1·30
		a. Surch inverted	90·00	90·00
		b. "D" for first "P"	45·00	45·00
47	**25**	2 on 20l. red (D13)	1·70	1·40
48	**26**	5 on 20l. rose (4)	£180	£180
49		5 on 20l. orange (13)	1·70	1·40

ΕΛΛΑΣ
(27)

ΕΛΛΑΣ
(28)

ΕΛΛΑΣ
(29)

ΕΛΛΑΣ
(30)

1909. Optd with T **27/29**.

50	**27**	10l. dull carmine (T **21**)	3·25	1·10
		a. Opt inverted	90·00	
51		20l. blue-green (24)	5·50	1·10
52	**29**	25l. black and blue (30)	5·50	2·20
53	**27**	50l. brown (26)	9·00	4·25
54	**28**	1d. black and green (31)	13·50	7·50
55	**27**	2d. brown (18)	13·50	11·00
56	**28**	3d. black and orange (28)	£110	£100
57	**29**	5d. black and olive-green (29)	45·00	43·00

1909 (Mar)–**10**. Optd as T **30**.

58		1l. chocolate (R.) (1)	45	20
59		2l. slate-lilac (R.) (21)	45	30
60		5l. green (R.) (22)	45	30
61		10l. dull carmine (T **21**) (1.2.10)	65	65
62		20l. blue-green (R.) (24) (1.2.10)	1·80	65
63		25l. ultramarine (R.) (25) (1.2.10)	3·00	65
64		50l. brown (R.) (26) (1.2.10)	6·75	1·50
65		1d. sepia and carmine (27) (5.10)	80·00	75·00
66		3d. black and orange (R.) (28) (5.10)	65·00	65·00
67		5d. black and olive-green (R.) (29) (5.10)	45·00	43·00

1910 (Feb). OFFICIAL. Optd as T **30**.

O68	**O 21**	10l. dull claret	2·20	1·10
O69	**O 22**	30l. slate-blue	2·20	1·10

1910 (April). POSTAGE DUE. Optd as T **30**.

D70	**D 8**	1l. red	45	30
D71		5l. red	1·10	30
D72		10l. red	1·10	45
D73		20l. red	3·00	1·60
D74		40l. red	11·00	4·75
D75		50l. red	17·00	11·00
D76		1d. red	28·00	27·00
D77		2d. red	28·00	27·00

The 1l. is found overprinted "ΧΑΡΤΟΣΗΜΟΝ", = Revenue, and has no postal significance.

After Greece officially took over Crete on 10 December 1913, Greek stamps were placed on sale. The remainders of Cretan stamps were overprinted and issued in Greece in 1923 (see Greece Nos. 358/402).

During the Italian Occupation of the eastern part of Crete in 1941–43 stamps of the Dodecanese Islands were used there.

IV. REVOLUTIONARY ASSEMBLY

March-November, 1905

In March, 1905, a revolt in favour of union with Greece began, organised by Venizelos with Headquarters at Theriso, south of Canea. The revolt collapsed in November, 1905.

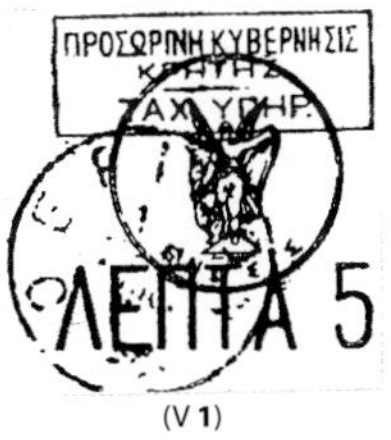

(V **1**)

(Handstamped by Kokinakis, Stangel, Athens)

1905 (1 Sept). Type V **1** and similar type, but with Greek characters meaning "drachma" for No. R5.

V1	5l. carmine-rose and blue-green	17·00	8·75
V2	10l. green and rose	17·00	8·75
V3	20l. blue and carmine-rose	17·00	8·75
V4	50l. green and violet	17·00	8·75
V5	1d. carmine-rose and blue	17·00	8·75

Many varieties are to be found such as "tête-bêche," "semi-tête-bêche", "without the circular control", "control inverted, "stamps overlapping", "double print", etc, etc. We believe that most of these are bogus varieties.

V **2** Crete enslaved

V **3** King George of Greece

(Litho Kokinakis, Athens)

1905 (5 Oct). P 11½.

V6	V **2**	5l. orange	90	85
V7		10l. grey	90	85
V8		20l. mauve	90	85
V9		50l. blue	1·70	1·70
V10	V **3**	1d. violet and red	4·50	4·25
V11		2d. brown and green	6·75	6·50

These stamps imperf are reprints.

V **4** Map of Crete

1905. Imperf.

V12	V **4**	5l. green	17·00
V13		10l. red	17·00
V14		20l. blue	34·00

The above were prepared but not issued. They also exist tête-bêche.

AUSTRO-HUNGARIAN POST OFFICES

Postal agencies opened by the Austrian Lloyd Company at Canea, Candia and Rethymnon had by the 1890s become Post Offices. Stamps issued for Lombardy and Venetia and for Austro-Hungarian Post Offices in the Turkish Empire (the latter denominated in either Turkish or French currency) were used in these offices but such use can only be identified by the postmarks. For listings of these stamps see Part 2 (*Austria & Hungary*) or Part 16 (*Central Asia*) of this catalogue.

These post offices closed on 15 December 1914.

FRENCH POST OFFICES

100 Centimes = 1 Franc
25 Centimes = 1 Piastre

French Post Offices were opened at Canea, Rethymnon, Candia, San Nicolo (Ayios Nikolaos), Sitia and Hierapetra in July 1897.

1902 (Oct)–**03**. Blanc (**11**), Mouchon (**14**) and Merson (**13**), types of France, Inscr CRETE. P 14×13½.

1	**11**	1c. grey	2·75	1·20
2		2c. claret	35	75
3		3c. orange-red	1·70	3·00
4		4c. brown	2·75	4·50
5		5c. green	2·50	2·20
6	**14**	10c. carmine (12.02)	3·25	3·00
7		15c. pale red (2.03)	3·50	5·00
8		20c. purple-brown (3.03)	2·75	6·00
9		25c. blue (9.03)	5·75	3·50
10		30c. mauve (5.03)	8·50	14·00
11	**13**	40c. red and pale blue	19·00	23·00
12		50c. brown and lavender	13·50	25·00
13		1f. lake and yellow-green	21·00	23·00
14		2f. deep lilac and buff	50·00	60·00
15		5f. deep blue and buff	60·00	60·00
1/15 *Set of* 15			£180	£200

1 PIASTRE 1
(1)

2 PIASTRES
(2)

1903 (Feb–Mar). Nos. 9 and 12/15, surch with values in Turkish currency, as T **1/2**.

16	**14**	1pi. on 25c. blue (Mar)	60·00	60·00
17	**13**	2pi. on 50c. brown and lavender	65·00	65·00
18		4pi. on 1f. lake and green	£120	£130
19		8pi. on 2f. deep lilac and buff	£130	£140
20		20 pi on 5f. deep blue and buff	£160	£160
16/20 *Set of* 5			£475	£500

The French post offices at Ayios Nikolaos, Sitia and Hierapetra were closed at the end of 1899 and the three others on 13 October 1914.

ITALIAN POST OFFICES

1900. 40 Paras = 1 Piastre
1906. 100 Centesimi = 1 Lira

A military post office using unoverprinted Italian stamps operated in 1899. A civil post office opened 15 January 1900 and closed 31 December 1914.

Italian stamps surcharged or overprinted

LA CANEA
1 PIASTRA 1
(1)

LA CANEA
(2)

1900 (10 July). Stamp of 1893 (Umberto I) surch as T **1** but without "LA CANEA".

1	**27**	1pi. on 25c. blue (R.)	13·50	55·00

1901 (1 July). Stamp of 1901 (Victor Emmanuel III) surch with T **1**.

2	**33**	1pi. on 25c. blue	18·00	11·00

1906 (5 Nov). EXPRESS LETTER. No. E73 optd with T **2**.

E1	E **35**	25c. rose	18·00	19·00

1906 (15 Nov). Stamps of 1901 and 1905 (Arms (T **30**) or portraits of Victor Emmanuel III (others)) optd with T **2**.

3	**30**	1c. brown	2·20	3·25
4	**31**	2c. orange-brown	2·20	3·25
5	**32**	5c. green	34·00	4·25
6	**33**	10c. lake	£170	£110
7		15c. on 20c. orange (73)	3·25	43·00
8		25c. blue	9·00	11·00
9		40c. brown	9·00	11·00
10		45c. grey-green	9·00	11·00
11		50c. mauve	9·00	11·00
12	**34**	1l. brown and green	45·00	65·00
13		5l. blue and rose	£225	£275
3/13 *Set of* 11			£450	£500

1907–12. Stamps of 1906–09 (portraits of Victor Emmanuel III) optd with T **2**.

14	**37**	5c. green (7.07)	2·20	2·20
		a. Opt inverted	£325	
15	**38**	10c. rose (3.07)	2·20	2·20
16	**41**	15c. slate-black (V.) (1.12)	3·25	5·50
17	**39**	25c. blue (4.09)	3·25	3·25
18	**40**	40c. pale brown (1910)	34·00	38·00
19		50c. mauve (6.09)	5·50	11·00
14/19 *Set of* 6			45·00	55·00

Dodecanese Islands

A. ITALIAN OCCUPATION

These islands (literally, in Greek, the "Twelve Islands") consist of twelve small islands in the south-east Aegean Sea, with the larger island of Rhodes. In 1912 they declared their independence from Turkey, but they were occupied by Italy in May of that year, during the Turco-Italian War; her possession of them was not recognised until the Greco-Italian Agreement of 10 August 1920. Castelrosso was placed under the same administration in 1921.

100 Centesimi = 1 Lira

1912 (22 Sept). Nos. 77 and 79 of Italy optd "EGEO".

1	**39**	25c. blue	55·00	37·00
		a. Opt inverted	£170	£170
2	**40**	50c. violet	55·00	37·00
		a. Opt inverted	£170	£170

1912 (1 Dec)–**21**. Stamps of Italy (Arms (T **31**) or various portraits of Victor Emmanuel III (others)) optd for the individual islands (in capitals on Nos. 6 and 10, in upper and lower case on others).

A. Calimno

3A	**31**	2c. orange-brown	9·25	6·50
4A	**37**	5c. green	2·75	6·50
5A	**38**	10c. rose-red	55	6·50
6A	**49**	15c. slate (90, no wmk) (V.)	55·00	17·00
7A	**37**	15c. slate (104, wmkd) (10.21)	12·00	48·00
8A	**49**	20c. on 15c. slate (100) (1.1.16)	26·00	32·00
9A	**41**	20c. orange (101, no wmk) (6.17)	£130	£160
10A		20c. orange (105, wmkd) (9.21)	12·00	48·00
11A	**39**	25c. blue	17·00	6·50
12A	**40**	40c. brown	55	6·50
13A		50c. violet	55	11·50
3A/13A *Set of* 12			£225	£300

B. Caso

3B	**31**	2c. orange-brown	9·25	6·50
4B	**37**	5c. green	5·00	6·50
5B	**38**	10c. rose-red	55	6·50
6B	**49**	15c. slate (90, no wmk) (V.)	55·00	17·00
7B	**37**	15c. slate (104, wmkd) (10.21)	8·00	48·00
8B	**49**	20c. on 15c. slate (100) (1.1.16)	4·00	27·00
9B	**41**	20c. orange (101, no wmk) (6.17)	£190	£160
10B		20c. orange (105, wmkd) (9.21)	8·00	48·00
11B	**39**	25c. blue	55	6·50
12B	**40**	40c. brown	55	6·50
13B		50c. violet	55	11·50
3B/13B *Set of* 12			£250	£300

C. Cos

3C	**31**	2c. orange-brown	9·25	8·50
4C	**37**	5c. green	£110	8·50
5C	**38**	10c. rose-red	4·75	8·50
6C	**49**	15c. slate (90, no wmk) (V.)	55·00	17·00
7C	**37**	15c. slate (104, wmkd) (10.21)	8·00	65·00
8C	**49**	20c. on 15c. slate (100) (1.1.16)	2·75	27·00
9C	**41**	20c. orange (101, no wmk) (6.17)	£190	£160
10C		20c. orange (105, wmkd) (9.21)	8·00	48·00
11C	**39**	25c. blue	65	6·50
12C	**40**	40c. brown	65	6·50
13C		50c. violet	65	11·50
3C/13C *Set of* 12			£350	£325

D. Karki

3D	**31**	2c. orange-brown	9·25	6·50
4D	**37**	5c. green	3·25	6·50
5D	**38**	10c. rose-red	55	6·50
6D	**49**	15c. slate (90, no wmk) (V.)	55·00	17·00
7D	**37**	15c. slate (104, wmkd) (10.21)	4·00	32·00
8D	**49**	20c. on 15c. slate (100) (1.1.16)	4·00	32·00
9D	**41**	20c. orange (101, no wmk) (6.17)	£190	£160
10D		20c. orange (105, wmkd) (9.21)	8·00	48·00
11D	**39**	25c. blue	65	6·50
12D	**40**	40c. brown	65	6·50
13D		50c. violet	65	11·50
3D/13D *Set of* 12			£250	£300

E. Leros

3E	**31**	2c. orange-brown	9·25	6·50
4E	**37**	5c. green	2·75	6·50
5E	**38**	10c. rose-red	65	6·50
6E	**49**	15c. slate (90, no wmk) (V.)	£100	17·00
7E	**37**	15c. slate (104, wmkd) (10.21)	8·00	43·00
8E	**49**	20c. on 15c. slate (100) (1.1.16)	26·00	32·00
9E	**41**	20c. orange (101, no wmk) (6.17)	80·00	£170
10E		20c. orange (105, wmkd) (9.21)	£225	£110
11E	**39**	25c. blue	40·00	6·50
12E	**40**	40c. brown	6·50	6·50
13E		50c. violet	65	11·50
3E/13E *Set of* 12			£700	£700

F. Lipso

3F	**31**	2c. orange-brown	4·00	6·50
4F	**37**	5c. green	4·00	6·50
5F	**38**	10c. rose-red	2·00	6·50
6F	**49**	15c. slate (90, no wmk) (V.)	55·00	17·00
7F	**37**	15c. slate (104, wmkd) (10.21)	8·00	43·00
8F	**49**	20c. on 15c. slate (100) (1.1.16)	2·75	32·00
9F	**41**	20c. orange (101, no wmk) (6.17)	£110	£170
10F		20c. orange (105, wmkd) (9.21)	8·00	48·00
11F	**39**	25c. blue	55	6·50
12F	**40**	40c. brown	2·00	6·50
13F		50c. violet	55	11·50
3F/13F *Set of* 12			£180	£300

G. Nisiros

3G	**31**	2c. orange-brown	9·25	6·50
4G	**37**	5c. green	2·75	6·50
5G	**38**	10c. rose-red	55	6·50
6G	**49**	15c. slate (90, no wmk) (V.)	55·00	16·00
7G	**37**	15c. slate (104, wmkd) (10.21)	40·00	48·00
8G	**49**	20c. on 15c. slate (100) (1.1.16)	2·75	32·00
9G	**41**	20c. orange (101, no wmk) (6.17)	£190	£160
10G		20c. orange (105, wmkd) (9.21)	£140	£130
11G	**39**	25c. blue	2·75	6·50
12G	**40**	40c. brown	1·30	6·50
13G		50c. violet	8·00	11·50
3G/13G *Set of* 12			£400	£400

H. Patmos

3H	**31**	2c. orange-brown	9·25	6·50
4H	**37**	5c. green	1·30	6·50
5H	**38**	10c. rose-red	1·30	6·50
6H	**49**	15c. slate (90, no wmk) (V.)	55·00	17·00
7H	**37**	15c. slate (104, wmkd) (10.21)	8·00	48·00
8H	**49**	20c. on 15c. slate (100) (1.1.16)	26·00	43·00
9H	**41**	20c. orange (101, no wmk) (6.17)	£160	£180
10H		20c. orange (105, wmkd) (9.21)	£225	£170
11H	**39**	25c. blue	55	6·50
12H	**40**	40c. brown	2·75	6·50
13H		50c. violet	1·30	11·50
3H/13H *Set of* 12			£450	£450

I. Piscopi

3I	**31**	2c. orange-brown	9·25	6·50
4I	**37**	5c. green	3·25	6·50
5I	**38**	10c. rose-red	65	6·50
6I	**49**	15c. slate (90, no wmk) (V.)	55·00	17·00
7I	**37**	15c. slate (104, wmkd) (10.21)	26·00	45·00
8I	**49**	20c. on 15c. slate (100) (1.1.16)	2·75	32·00
9I	**41**	20c. orange (101, no wmk) (6.17)	£110	£160
10I		20c. orange (105, wmkd) (9.21)	75·00	90·00
11I	**39**	25c. blue	55	6·50
12I	**40**	40c. brown	55	6·50
13I		50c. violet	55	11·50
3I/13I *Set of* 12			£170	£225

J. Rodi*

3J	**31**	2c. orange-brown	1·30	5·25
4J	**37**	5c. green	2·75	5·25
5J	**38**	10c. rose-red	1·30	5·25
6J	**49**	15c. slate (90, no wmk) (V.)	60·00	21·00
7J	**37**	15c. slate (104, wmkd) (10.21)	£225	£140
8J	**49**	20c. on 15c. slate (100) (1.1.16)	£190	£170
9J	**41**	20c. orange (101, no wmk) (6.17)	£190	£160
10J		20c. orange (105, wmkd) (9.21)	10·50	21·00
11J	**39**	25c. blue	4·00	5·25
12J	**40**	40c. brown	10·00	5·25
13J		50c. violet	1·30	13·00
3J/13J *Set of* 12			£600	£500

*Dates of issue of Nos. 7, 9 and 10 with the "Rodi" overprint were 4.22, 5.17 and 8.19 respectively.

K. Scarpanto

3K	**31**	2c. orange-brown	9·25	6·50
4K	**37**	5c. green	2·75	6·50
5K	**38**	10c. rose-red	55	6·50
6K	**49**	15c. slate (90, no wmk) (V.)	50·00	17·00
7K	**37**	15c. slate (104, wmkd) (10.21)	26·00	37·00
8K	**49**	20c. on 15c. slate (100) (1.1.16)	2·75	32·00
9K	**41**	20c. orange (101, no wmk) (6.17)	£190	£170
10K		20c. orange (105, wmkd) (9.21)	75·00	55·00
11K	**39**	25c. blue	9·25	6·50
12K	**40**	40c. brown	55	6·50
13K		50c. violet	2·75	11·50
3K/13K *Set of* 12			£325	£325

L. Simi

3L	**31**	2c. orange-brown	9·25	6·50
4L	**37**	5c. green	3·25	6·50
5L	**38**	10c. rose-red	55	6·50
6L	**49**	15c. slate (90, no wmk) (V.)	80·00	17·00
7L	**37**	15c. slate (104, wmkd) (10.21)	£170	75·00
8L	**49**	20c. on 15c. slate (100) (1.1.16)	17·00	27·00
9L	**41**	20c. orange (101, no wmk) (6.17)	95·00	£120
10L		20c. orange (105, wmkd) (9.21)	£100	43·00
11L	**39**	25c. blue	4·00	6·50
12L	**40**	40c. brown	55	6·50
13L		50c. violet	55	11·50
3L/13L *Set of* 12			£425	£300

M. Stampalia

3M	**31**	2c. orange-brown	9·25	6·50
4M	**37**	5c. green	55	6·50
5M	**38**	10c. rose-red	55	6·50
6M	**49**	15c. slate (90, no wmk) (V.)	65·00	17·00
7M	**37**	15c. slate (104, wmkd) (10.21)	18·00	32·00
8M	**49**	20c. on 15c. slate (100) (1.1.16)	2·75	27·00
9M	**41**	20c. orange (101, no wmk) (6.17)	£130	£130
10M		20c. orange (105, wmkd) (9.21)	65·00	55
11M	**39**	25c. blue	1·30	6·50
12M	**40**	40c. brown	4·00	6·50
13M		50c. violet	55	11·50
3M/13M *Set of* 12			£275	£225

1916–**24**. Nos. 66, 110 and 71 of Italy optd "Rodi".

14	**33**	20c. orange (1.16)	10·50	21·00
15	**39**	85c. red-brown (9.22)	£100	£110
16	**34**	1l. brown and green (24)	6·50	

1 Rhodian Windmill

2 Knight kneeling before the Holy City

(Des F. Di Fausto. Litho (A) by Bestelli & Tuminelli, Milan, (B) by Govt Ptg Wks, Rome)

1929 (19 May)–**32**. King of Italy's Visit to the Aegean Islands. T **1/2** (and similar types).

A. Without printers' imprint. No wmk. P 11

17A	5c. claret	6·50	1·60
18A	10c. sepia	6·50	1·40
19A	20c. scarlet	6·50	75
20A	25c. green	6·50	1·10
21A	30c. deep blue	6·50	2·10
22A	50c. chocolate	6·50	2·10
23A	1l.25 deep blue	6·50	2·10
24A	5l. claret	65·00	55·00
25A	10l. olive-green	£190	90·00
17A/25A *Set of* 9		£275	£140

B. With imprint (8.32). Wmk Crown. P 14

17B	5c. claret	2·00	30
18B	10c. sepia	2·00	30
19B	20c. scarlet	2·00	30
20B	25c. green	2·00	30
21B	30c. deep blue	2·00	30
22B	50c. chocolate	2·00	30
23B	1l.25 deep blue	2·00	30
24B	5l. claret	2·00	5·00
25B	10l. olive-green	4·00	4·25
17B/25B *Set of* 9		18·00	10·00

Designs: Vert—10c. Galley of Knights of St. John; 20, 25c. Knight defending Christianity; 50c., 1l.25, A Knight's tomb. As Type **2**: 30c., 5l.

Although these stamps are inscribed "RODI" they were issued for general use in all the Dodecanese Islands.

Nos. 17B/25B and 124/7 were also used in eastern Crete during its Italian occupation, 1941–43.

XXI
Congresso
Idrologico
(**3**)

ISOLE ITALIANE
DELL'EGEO
(**4**)

1930 (25 Sept). Twenty-first Hydrological Congress. Nos. 17A/25A optd with T **3**.

26	5c. claret	20·00	19·00
27	10c. sepia	22·00	19·00
28	20c. scarlet	37·00	19·00
29	25c. green	46·00	19·00
30	30c. deep blue	22·00	19·00
31	50c. chocolate	£700	65·00
32	1l.25 deep blue	£475	95·00
33	5l. claret	£250	£400
34	10l. olive-green	£250	£450
26/34 *Set of* 9		£1600	£1000

1930 (20 Oct). "Ferrucci" issue of Italy (colours changed), optd in capital letters for the individual islands.

A. CALINO	F. LISSO	J. RODI
B. CASO	G. NISIRO	K. SCARPANTO
C. COO	H. PATMO	L. SIMI
D. CALCHI	I. PISCOPI	M. STAMPALIA
E. LERO		

Same prices for each island

35	**114**	20c. bright violet (R.)	6·50	8·50
36	**115**	25c. deep green (R.)	6·50	8·50
37		50c. black (R.)	6·50	16·00
38		1l.25 blue (R.)	6·50	16·00
39	**116**	5l. +2l. carmine-red (B.)	10·00	30·00
35/39 *Set of* 5			33·00	48·00

See also Castelrosso Nos. 25/9.

1930 (20 Oct). AIR. "Ferrucci" air stamps of Italy (colours changed), optd with T **4**.

40	**117**	50c. purple (B.)	10·00	21·00
41		1l. deep blue (R.)	10·00	21·00
42		5l. +2l. carmine-red (B.)	20·00	60·00
40/42 *Set of* 3			36·00	90·00

ISOLE ITALIANE DELL'EGEO
(**5**)

1931
CONGRESSO
EUCARISTICO
ITALIANO
(**6**)

1930 (1 Dec). Virgil. Nos. 290/302 of Italy optd as T **5**. Colours changed.

(a) POSTAGE. As T **118**

43	15c. slate-violet (R.)	3·25	10·50
44	20c. chestnut (B.)	3·25	10·50
45	25c. blue-green (R.)	3·25	4·25
46	30c. brown (B.)	3·25	4·25
47	50c. purple (R.)	3·25	4·25
48	75c. carmine-red (B.)	3·25	10·50
49	1l.25 greenish blue (R.)	3·25	16·00
50	5l. +1l.50 purple (R.)	3·25	32·00
51	10l. +2l.50 brown (B.)	3·25	32·00

(b) AIR. T **119**

52	50c. blue-green (R.)	4·00	19·00
53	1l. carmine-red (B.)	4·00	21·00
54	7l.70 +1l.30 brown (R.)	8·00	27·00
55	9l. +2l. slate-blue (R.)	8·00	43·00
43/55 *Set of* 13		48·00	£200

1931 (16 Sept). Italian Eucharistic Congress. Nos. 17A/23A optd with T **6**.

56	5c. claret (B.)	8·25	16·00
57	10c. sepia (R.)	8·00	16·00
58	20c. scarlet (B.)	8·00	21·00
	a. Opt inverted	£275	
59	25c. green (R.)	8·00	21·00
60	30c. deep blue (R.)	8·00	21·00
61	50c. chocolate (R.)	65·00	55·00
62	1l.25, deep blue (R.)	55·00	90·00
56/62 *Set of* 7		£140	£220

1932 (21 Feb). T **121/2** and similar types of Italy (St. Anthony) optd as T **4**. Colours changed.

63	20c. slate-purple (B.)	33·00	19·00
64	25c. green (R.)	33·00	19·00
65	30c. red-brown (B.)	33·00	23·00
66	50c. purple (B.)	33·00	16·00
67	75c. carmine-rose (B.)	33·00	29·00
68	1l.25 light blue (R.)	33·00	32·00
69	5l. +2l.50 orange (B.)	33·00	£130
63/69 *Set of* 7		£200	£250

ISOLE ITALIANE
DELL' EGEO
(**7**)

1932 (May–Nov). Dante. Nos. 314/32 of Italy optd as T **7**. Colours changed.

(a) POSTAGE. As T **124**

70	10c. olive-green	2·00	6·50
71	15c. violet-slate	2·00	6·50
72	20c. chestnut	2·00	6·50
73	25c. green	2·00	6·50
74	30c. orange-vermilion	2·00	6·50
75	50c. purple	2·00	2·10
76	75c. carmine-red	2·00	8·50
77	1l.25 blue	2·00	4·25
78	1l.75 sepia	2·75	6·50
79	2l.75 carmine	2·75	6·50

80		5l. +2l. bright violet	4·00	10·50
81		10l. +2l.50 chocolate	4·00	16·00
70/81 *Set of* 12			18·00	80·00

(b) AIR

82	**125**	50c. carmine	2·00	6·50
83	**126**	1l. green	2·00	6·50
84		3l. purple	2·00	8·50
85		5l. orange-vermilion	2·00	8·50
86	**125**	7l.70 +2l.sepia	4·00	21·00
87	**126**	10l. +2l.50 deep blue	4·00	32·00

Inscr "ISOLE ITALIANE DELL'EGEO".

88	**127**	100l. olive-green and blue (Nov)	25·00	85·00
82/88 *Set of* 7			37·00	£150

1932 (28 Aug). Garibaldi issue (T **128/9** and similar types) of Italy, optd in capital letters for the individual islands. Colours changed.

A. CALINO, B. CASO, C. COO, D. CALCHI, E. LERO, F. LISSO, G. NISIRO, H. PATMO, I. PISCOPI, J. RODI, K. SCARPANTO, L. SIMI, M. STAMPALIA

Same prices for each island

89	10c. sepia (R.)	20·00	21·00
90	20c. lake-brown (B.)	20·00	21·00
91	25c. green (R.)	20·00	21·00
92	30c. slate-blue (R.)	20·00	21·00
93	50c. purple (B.)	20·00	21·00
94	75c. lake (B.)	20·00	21·00
95	1l.25c. deep blue (R.)	20·00	21·00
96	1l.75 +25c. sepia (R.)	20·00	21·00
97	2l.55 +50c. orange-vermilion (B.)	20·00	21·00
98	5l. +1l. deep violet (R.)	20·00	21·00
89/98 *Set of* 10		£180	£190

See also Castelrosso Nos. 30/9.

1932 (28 Aug). AIR. Garibaldi air stamps as T **130** optd as T **4**. Colours changed.

99	50c. olive-green (R.)	60·00	85·00
100	80c. lake (B.)	60·00	85·00
101	1l. +25c. deep blue (R.)	60·00	85·00
102	2l. +50c. lake-brown (B.)	60·00	85·00
103	5l. +1l. slate (R.)	60·00	85·00
99/103 *Set of* 5		£275	£375

1932 (28 Aug). AIR EXPRESS. Garibaldi Air Express stamps as T **131** optd as T **4**. Colours changed.

E104	2l.25 +1l. carmine and blue (B.)	75·00	95·00
E105	4l.50 +1l.50 grey and yellow (Y.)	75·00	95·00

8

9

(Litho Bestelli & Tuminelli, Milan)

1932 (Oct). 20th Anniv of Italian Occupation of Dodecanese Islands. Wmk Crown. P 11.

106	**8**	5c. scarlet, black and emerald	13·00	21·00
107		10c. scarlet, black and blue	13·00	16·00
108		20c. scarlet, black and yellow	13·00	16·00
109		25c. scarlet, black and violet	13·00	16·00
110		30c. scarlet, black and rose	13·00	16·00
111	**9**	50c. scarlet, black and pale blue	13·00	16·00
112		1l.25 scarlet, maroon and pale blue	13·00	32·00
113		5l. scarlet, blue and pale blue	40·00	85·00
114		10l. scarlet, green and pale blue	£110	£150
115		25l. scarlet, chocolate and pale blue	£550	£1300
106/115 *Set of* 10			£700	£1000

10 Airship *Graf Zeppelin*

11 Wing from the Arms of Francesco Sans

(Des G. Rondini. Photo)

1933 (12 May). AIR. Wmk Crown. P 14.

116	**10**	3l. brown	75·00	£110
117		5l. purple	75·00	£110
118		10l. blue-green	75·00	£170
119		12l. blue	75·00	£180
120		15l. carmine	75·00	£180
121		20l. black	75·00	£180
116/121 *Set of* 6			£400	£850

1933 (20 May). AIR. Balbo Transatlantic Mass Formation Flight. As T **135/6** of Italy, without the pilot's name, optd as T **5** (smaller) on both left and right sides. Centres in slate-blue.

122	5l.25 +19l.75 scarlet and green/green/scarlet	55·00	£110
123	5l.25 +44l.75 green and scarlet/scarlet/green	55·00	£110

(Des B. Bramanti. Typo)

1934 (Jan). AIR. Wmk Crown. P 14.

124	**11**	50c. black and yellow	55	20
125		80c. black and carmine	8·00	3·50
126		1l. black and green	5·25	20
127		5l. black and magenta	13·00	7·75
124/127 *Set of* 4			24·00	10·00

See note below No. 25.

1934 (15 June). World Football Championship. As Nos. 413/21 of Italy optd "ISOLE ITALIANE DELL'EGEO" as T **5**, but smaller. Colours changed.

(a) POSTAGE

128	20c. lake-red	95·00	75·00
129	25c. green (R.)	95·00	75·00
130	50c. bright violet (R.)	£375	43·00
131	1l.25 deep blue (R.)	95·00	£130
132	5l. +2l.50 bright blue (R.)	95·00	£300

(b) AIR

133	50c. brown (R.)	13·00	32·00
134	75c. carmine-red	13·00	32·00
135	5l. +2l.50 orange-vermilion	45·00	65·00
136	10l. +5l.green (R.)	45·00	£110
128/136 *Set of* 9		£800	£800

P **12** Galley and Rose

P **13** Stag and St. Paul's Gate, Rhodes

(Des B. Bramanti. Photo)

1934 (1 July). PARCEL POST. Wmk Crown. P 13½.

			Un pair	*Used pair*	*Used half*
P137	P **12**	5c. orange	4·75	5·25	3·25
P138		10c. scarlet	4·75	5·25	3·25
P139		20c. green	4·75	5·25	3·25
P140		25c. bright violet	4·75	5·25	3·25
P141		50c. deep blue	4·75	5·25	3·25
P142		60c. black	4·75	5·25	3·25
P143	P **13**	1l. orange	4·75	5·25	3·25
P144		2l. scarlet	4·75	5·25	3·25
P145		3l. green	4·75	5·25	3·25
P146		4l. bright violet	4·75	5·25	3·25
P147		10l. deep blue	4·75	5·25	3·25
P137/147 *Set of* 11			47·00	50·00	32·00

The left-hand portion is affixed to the packet-card, the right-hand portion to the receipt. Prices in the first column are for unused complete pairs, in the second column for used pairs (usually cancelled-to-order) and in the third column for the left half used.

D **14** Badge of the Knights of St. John

D **15** Immortelle

(Des B. Bramanti. Photo)

1934 (1 July). POSTAGE DUE. Wmk Crown. P 14.

D148	D **14**	5c. orange	4·50	3·25
D149		10c. scarlet	4·50	3·25
D150		20c. green	4·50	2·10
D151		30c. bright violet	4·50	2·10
D152		40c. deep blue	4·50	5·25
D153	D **15**	50c. orange	4·50	2·10
D154		60c. scarlet	4·50	10·50
D155		1l. green	4·50	8·50
D156		2l. bright violet	4·50	5·25
D148/156 *Set of* 9			36·00	38·00

1934 (Dec). Military Medal Centenary. As Nos. 424/41 of Italy, optd "ISOLE ITALIANE DELL'EGEO" as T **5**, but smaller. Colours changed.

(a) POSTAGE

157	10c. slate (R.)	60·00	70·00
158	15c. brown	60·00	70·00
159	20c. orange-vermilion	60·00	70·00
160	25c. green (R.)	60·00	70·00
161	30c. claret	60·00	70·00
162	50c. olive-green	60·00	70·00
163	75c. carmine-red	60·00	70·00
164	1l.25 blue (R.)	60·00	70·00
165	1l.75 +1l. bright violet (R.)	46·00	43·00
166	2l.55 +2l. lake	46·00	43·00
167	2l.75 +2l. chestnut	46·00	43·00
157/167 *Set of* 11		£550	£600

(b) AIR

168	25c. green	75·00	85·00
169	50c. brown-black (R.)	75·00	85·00
170	75c. rose-carmine	75·00	85·00
171	80c. brown	75·00	85·00
172	1l. +50c. olive-green	55·00	85·00
173	2l. +1l. blue (R.)	55·00	85·00
174	3l. +2l. bright violet (R.)	55·00	85·00

(c) AIR EXPRESS

E175	2l. +1l.25 blue	55·00	85·00
E176	4l.50 +2l. green	55·00	85·00
E168/E176 *Set of* 9		£500	£700

16

E **17**

(Des B. Bramanti. Photo)

1935 (Apr). Holy Year. Wmk Crown. P 14.

177	**16**	5c. orange	20·00	16·00
178		10c. brown	20·00	16·00
179		20c. carmine	20·00	19·00
180		25c. green	20·00	19·00
181		30c. purple	20·00	19·00
182		50c. chestnut	20·00	19·00
183		1l.25 blue	20·00	65·00
177/183 *Set of* 7			£130	£150

A 5l. value was prepared but not issued (*Price* £300 *un*).

(Des B. Bramanti. Photo)

1935 (6 Dec). EXPRESS LETTER. Wmk Crown. P 14.

E184	E **17**	1l.25 green	2·75	3·25
E185		2l.50 orange	4·00	5·25

ISOLE
ITALIANE
DELL'EGEO
(**18**)

1938 (10 May). Augustus Bimillenary. As Nos. 506/20 of Italy, optd with T **18**. Colours changed.

(a) POSTAGE

186	10c. olive-brown (B.)	5·25	8·50
187	15c. bright violet (R.)	5·25	8·50
188	20c. red-brown (B.)	5·25	8·50
189	25c. grey-green (R.)	5·25	8·50
190	30c. purple (B.)	5·25	8·50
191	50c. deep blue-green (R.)	5·25	16·00
192	75c. carmine (B.)	5·25	16·00
193	1l.25 deep blue (R.)	5·25	16·00
194	1l.75 +1l. orange (B.)	8·00	27·00
195	2l.55 +2l. sepia (R.)	8·00	27·00
186/195 *Set of* 10		60·00	£140

(b) AIR

196	25c. slate-violet (R.)	6·50	8·50
197	50c. green (R.)	6·50	8·50
198	80c. blue (R.)	6·50	27·00
199	1l.+1l. purple (B.)	9·25	32·00
200	5l.+1l. scarlet (B.)	13·00	65·00
196/200 *Set of* 5		37·00	£130

1938 (20 Aug). 600th Death Anniv of Giotto (painter). Nos. 527 and 530 of Italy optd with T **18**.

201	1l.25 blue (R.)	1·30	2·10
202	2l.75 +2l. brown (R.)	3·25	8·50

19 Dante House, Rhodes

20 Roman Wolf Statue

21 Crown and Maltese Cross

22 Savoia Marchetti S.M.75 over Statues, Rhodes Harbour

(Des G. Rondini. Photo)

1940 (3 June). Colonial Exhibition. T **19/22** and similar design inscr "TRIENNALE D'OLTREMARE". Wmk Crown. P 14.

(a) POSTAGE

203	**20**	5c. brown	55	2·10
204	**21**	10c. orange	55	2·10
205	**19**	25c. green	2·00	3·25
206	**20**	50c. violet	2·00	3·25
207	**21**	75c. carmine	2·00	4·25
208	**19**	1l.25. blue	2·00	4·25
209	**21**	2l. +75c. pink	2·00	27·00

(b) AIR

210	**22**	50c. sepia	2·75	4·25
211	–	1l. violet	2·75	4·25
212	**22**	2l. +75c. deep blue	2·75	10·50
213	–	5l. +2l.50 red-brown	2·75	16·00
203/213 *Set of* 11			20·00	75·00

Design: Horiz—1, 5l. Savoia Marchetti S.M.75 airplane and Government House, Rhodes.

CENT. 20
PRO
ASSISTENZA
EGEO
(**23**)

LRE 2,50 PRO
ASSISTENZA EGEO
(E **24**)

1943 (15 Nov). Relief Fund.

(a) POSTAGE. Nos. 17B/24B surch with premium as T **23**

214	5c. +5c. claret	2·00	1·10
215	10c. +10c. sepia	2·00	1·10
216	20c. +20c. scarlet	2·00	1·10
217	25c. +25c. green	2·00	1·10
	a. Inverted opt	£130	
218	30c. +30c. deep blue (R.)	2·75	1·10
219	50c. +50c. chocolate	2·75	2·10
220	1l.25 +1l.25 deep blue (R.)	5·25	3·25
221	5l.+5l. claret	£150	£110
214/221 *Set of* 8		£150	£110

(b) EXPRESS. Surch with premium as Type E **24**

E222	E **17**	1l.25 +1l.25 green (R.)	55·00	43·00
E223		2l.50 +2l.50 orange (R.)	80·00	55·00

(25)

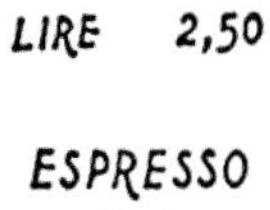

(E 26)

1944 (16 July). War Victims' Relief. Nos. 17B/20B and 22B/23B surch with premium as T **25**.

224	5c. +3l. claret	2·75	3·25
225	10c. +3l. sepia (R.)	2·75	3·25
226	20c. +3l. scarlet	2·75	3·25
227	25c. +3l. green (R.)	4·00	3·25
228	50c. +3l. chocolate (R.)	4·00	3·25
229	1l.25 +5l. deep blue (R.)	40·00	43·00
224/229 *Set of* 6		50·00	55·00

1944. EXPRESS LETTER. Nos. 19B/20B surch as Type E **26**.

E230	1l.25 on 25c. green	55	1·10
E231	2l.50 on 20c. scarlet	55	1·10

(27)

(28)

1944 (11 Oct). AIR. War Victims' Relief. Surch with premium as T **27**, in silver.

232	**11**	50c. +2l. black and yellow	13·00	6·50
233		80c. +2l. black and carmine	17·00	10·50
234		1l. +2l. black and green	23·00	13·00
235		5l. +2l. black and magenta	85·00	£110
232/235 *Set of* 4			£120	£130

1945 (18 Feb). Red Cross Fund. Nos. 24B/25B surch with premium as T **28**.

236	+10 on 5l. claret (R.)	13·00	6·50
237	+10 on 10l. olive-green (R.)	13·00	6·50

In October 1944 the Dodecanese Islands were occupied by the British and Great Britain stamps overprinted "M.E.F." were used (see British Occupation of Italian Colonies in *Commonwealth & British Empire* catalogue) until 31 March 1947 when they were transferred to Greek administration.

The islands are now known as Kalimnos, Kasos, Kos, Khalki, Leros, Lipsoi, Nisiros, Patmos, Tilos (Piskopi), Rhodes (Rodos), Karpathos, Simi and Astipalaia.

B. ISLAND COMMITTEE FOR UNION WITH GREECE

100 Lepta = 1 Drachma

K **1** Apollo

(Litho Aspiotis)

1912 (21 May). Serrated roul 13½.

K1	K **1**	1l. blue-green	2·30
K2		5l. deep blue	2·30
K3		10l. red	2·30

This issue was prepared by the Island Committee for Union with Greece but the Italian Military Administration in Rhodes forbade its use. However, it was placed on sale in Kalimnos and a few postally used copies are known. Copies are known cancelled by favour from Kasos, Leros, Patmos, Simi and Astipalaia and forged postmarks exist. This design appears on the Greek issue of 1947 commemorating the transfer of the Dodecanese Islands to Greece.

C. GREEK MILITARY ADMINISTRATION

100 Lepta = 1 Drachma

The Dodecanese Islands were transferred to Greek administration on 31 March 1947.

1947. Optd "ΣΔΔ".

(a) Horiz, in silver or red on Nos. 623, 625 and 627 of Greece

G1	10d. on 2000d. blue (Sil.) (1 Apr)	55	1·10
G2	10d. on 2000d. blue (R.) (2 Apr)	55	1·10
G3	20d. on 500d. olive-brown (R.)	55	1·10
G4	30d. on 5d. blue-green (R.)	55	1·10
	a. On No. 627a	33·00	33·00

(b) Vert, in black, on stamps as Nos. 642/3 of Greece, but with T **118** within a narrow frame also in black

G5	50d. on 1d. green (20 Apr)	1·00	1·60
	a. Surch inverted	£110	
G6	250d. on 3d. red-brown (20 Apr)	1·00	1·60
	a. Surch inverted	£110	

Nos. G1/2 although surcharged "10" were sold at and had a franking value of 100 drachmas.

(G **1**)

1947 (21 Sept). Stamps of Greece surch as Type G **1**.

G7	50d. on 2d. reddish brown (No. 573)	1·00	1·60
G8	250d. on 10d. red-brown (No. 510)	1·30	2·10
G9	400d. on 15d. blue-green (No. 511) (R.)	2·00	3·25
	a. Surch inverted	£110	
G10	1000d. on 200d. ultramarine (No. 581) (R.)	1·70	2·75
	a. On No. 581a	20·00	32·00
G7/10 *Set of* 4		5·50	8·75

The islands came under Greek sovereignty on 15 September 1947.

Stamps of Greece have been used since 20 November 1947.

Thrace

A. GREEK OCCUPATION, 1913

Dedeagatz was occupied by Greek troops during the Second Balkan War from 11 July to 21 August and from 1 September to 1 October 1913. Gumultsina was occupied from 16 July to 8 August 1913.

ISSUES FOR DEDEAGATZ

(Now Alexandroupolis)

ΕΛΛΗΝΙΚΗ
ΔΙΟΙΚΗΣΙΣ
ΔΕΔΕΑΓΑΤΣ
ΔΕΚΑ ΛΕΠΤΑ
(1) (10l.)

ΕΛΛΗΝΙΚΗ
ΔΙΟΙΚΗΣΙΣ
ΔΕΔΕΑΓΑΤΣ
10
ΛΕΠΤΑ
(2)

(Trans: "Greek Administration Dedeagatz")

1913 (18 July). Typeset as T **1**. Circular control cachet with Greek inscription, crown and anchor in carmine (only part on each stamp). No gum. P 11½.

1		ΠΕΝΤΕ l. = 5l. black	65·00	37·00
2		ΔΕΚΑ l. = 10l. black	7·75	5·25
		a. Tête-bêche	65·00	43·00
		b. Second "I" of second word omitted	65·00	43·00
3		25l. black	8·75	7·50

This issue was printed in sheets of 8, containing one 5l., four 10l. (incl. one tête-bêche pair) and three 25l. with one blank space.

1913 (24 July). Stamps of Bulgaria, 1911, surch as T **2**.

4	**23**	5l. on 1st. myrtle-green (R.)	90·00	48·00
5	**27**	10l. on 10st. black and red (B.)	39·00	23·00
6	**26**	25l. on 5st. black and green (B.)	50·00	30·00
7	**24**	50l. on 2st. black and carmine (B.)	90·00	55·00
8	**29**	1d. on 25st. black and ultramarine (R.)	£120	70·00

The above were overprinted in a setting of 8, the value being altered for each. In position 6 there is a Greek "L" instead of 'D" for the third letter of the third word.

The 25l. was applied in error to 8 copies of the 25st. of Bulgaria, No. 165, of which only three copies are known.

ΠΡΟΣΩΡΙΝΟΝ
ΕΛΛΗΝΙΚΗ
ΔΙΟΙΚΗΣΙΣ
ΔΕΔΕΑΓΑΤΣ
2 ΛΕΠΤΑ 2
(3)

ΠΡΟΣΩΡΙΝΟΝ
ΕΛΛΗΝΙΚΗ
ΔΙΟΙΚΗΣΙΣ
ΔΕΔΕΑΓΑΤΣ
1 ΛΕΠΤΟΝ 1
(4)

1913 (15 Sept). Type-set as T **3** on white paper. Ungummed. Circular control cachet in blue. P 11½.

9		1l. blue	£325	95·00
10		2l. blue	£325	95·00
11		3l. blue	£325	95·00
12		5l. blue	£325	95·00
13		10l. blue	£325	95·00
14		25l. blue	£325	95·00
15		40l. blue	£325	95·00
16		50l. blue	£325	95·00

Printed in sheets of 8, one of each value.

1913 (25 Sept). Type-set as T **4** on bluish paper. Ungummed. Circular control cachet in blue. P 11½.

17		1l. blue/*blue*	£250	50·00
18		5l. blue/*blue*	£250	50·00
19		10l. blue/*blue*	£250	50·00
20		25l. blue/*blue*	£250	75·00
21		30l. blue/*blue*	£250	75·00
22		50l. blue/*blue*	£250	75·00

Printed in sheets of 6, one of each value.

For French Post Offices in Dedeagatz (Dédéagh), see under French Post Offices in the Turkish Empire in Parts 6 (*France*) or 16 (*Central Asia*) of this catalogue.

ISSUE FOR GUMULTSINA

(Now Komotini)

(1)

1913 (7 Aug). Stamps of Turkey, 1909–10, surch as T **1**.

1	**28**	10l. on 20pa. rose-carmine (B.)	60·00	60·00
2		25l. on 10pa. green (R.)	90·00	90·00
3		25l. on 20pa. rose-carmine (B.)	90·00	90·00
4		25l. on 1pi. ultramarine (R.)	£130	£130

B. AUTONOMOUS GOVERNMENT OF WESTERN THRACE

The area known as Western Thrace was the territory bounded by the Rhodope Mts., the Aegean Sea and the Nestos and Evros (formerly Maritza) rivers. In Turkey until 1912, it was occupied by Bulgarian troops in the First Balkan War that year.

In October 1913 the Moslem inhabitants of Western Thrace drove out the Bulgarian troops and set up an autonomous régime.

40 Paras = 1 Piastre or Grush

1

1913 (Oct). Litho. Imperf.

(a) Size 23×27 mm. (11 Oct)

1	**1**	1pi. blue	22·00	16·00
2		2pi. violet	22·00	16·00
		(b) Size 19½×29½ mm		
3	**1**	10pa. vermilion	39·00	27·00
4		20pa. blue	39·00	27·00
5		1pi. violet	50·00	32·00

Nos. 1/2 were impressed on envelopes handed in by the public and are known with or without control mark.

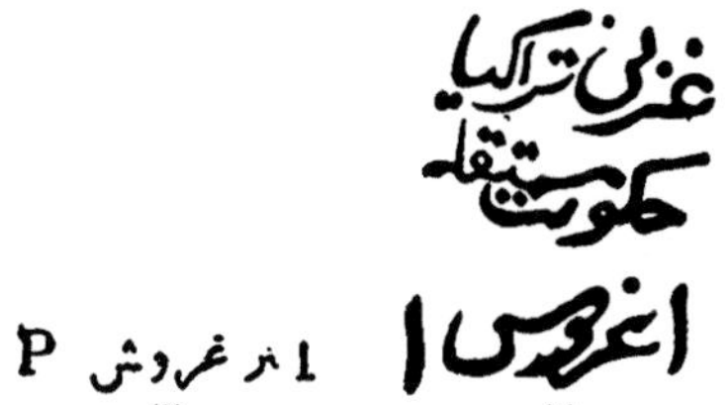
(2) (3)

1913 (Oct). Stamps of Turkey (G.P.O., Constantinople) surch with T **2**.

6	**30**	1pi. on 2pa. olive-green (R.)	33·00	32·00
		a. Surch in black	33·00	32·00
7		1pi. on 5pa. bistre	33·00	32·00
		a. Surch in red	33·00	32·00
8		1pi. on 20pa. rose	39·00	37·00
9		1pi. on 5pi. purple (R.)	85·00	80·00
		a. Surch in black	85·00	80·00
10		1pi. on 10pi. vermilion	£130	£130
11		1pi. on 25pi. deep green	£600	£600

1913 (Oct). Stamps of Greece handstamped as T **3** for use in Dedeagatz.

(a) No. 252

12	**35**	10pa. on 1l. brown (B.)	33·00	32·00
13		20pa. on 1l. brown (B.)	33·00	32·00
14		1pi. on 1l. brown (B.)	33·00	32·00
		(b) 1911 issue (recess)		
15	**29**	10pa. on 1l. green (R.)	28·00	27·00
		a. Surch in blue	28·00	27·00
16	**30**	10pa. on 25l. ultramarine	22·00	22·00
17		20pa. on 2l. carmine (B.)	28·00	27·00
18	**29**	1pi. on 3l. vermilion (B.)	28·00	27·00
19	**31**	2pi. on 5l. green (R.)	75·00	75·00
20	**29**	2½pi. on 10l. carmine (B.)	75·00	75·00
21	**30**	5pi. on 40l. deep blue (R.)	£140	£140

1913 (10 Oct). Stamps of Bulgaria, 1911, handstamped as T **3** for use in Gumultsina.

22	**23**	10pa. on 1st. myrtle-green (R.)	28·00	27·00
23	**24**	20pa. on 2st. black and carmine (B.)	28·00	27·00
24	**26**	1pi. on 5st. black and green (R.)	28·00	27·00
25	**25**	2pi. on 3st. black and lake (B.)	39·00	37·00
26	**27**	2½pi. on 10st. black and red (B.)	50·00	48·00
27	**28**	5pi. on 15st. bistre (B.)	90·00	85·00

By the Treaty of Bucharest, 1913, Bulgaria acquired Western Thrace.

C. ALLIED OCCUPATION, 1919–20

After the defeat of Bulgaria in October 1918, Allied troops occupied Western Thrace.

100 Stotinki = 1 Leva

THRACE
INTERALLIÉE
(4)

THRACE INTERALLIEE
(5)

1920 (7 Jan). Stamps of Bulgaria handstamped with T **4**, sideways reading up on 5st. to 25st. and 1l.

28	**49**	1st. black (R.)	35	30
29		2st. olive	35	30
30	**50**	5st. green	35	30
31		10st. rose	35	30
32		15st. violet	35	30
33	**29**	25st. black and deep blue	35	30
34	**32**	1l. deep brown	5·50	5·25
35	**43**	2l. chestnut	8·75	8·50
36	**44**	3l. claret	13·00	13·00
28/36 *Set of 9*			26·00	26·00

1920 (9 Jan). POSTAGE DUE. Postage Due stamps of Bulgaria handstamped with T **4**, sideways reading up. P 12×11½.

D37	**D 37**	5st. bright green	55	55
D38		10st. dull violet	1·10	1·10
D39		50st. deep blue	3·25	2·10
D37/39 *Set of 3*			4·50	3·50

Minor varieties occur in the opt, T **4**: Second "L" of "INTERALLIEE" inverted: "INTERALLIEF".

1920 (11 Jan). Contemporary stamps of Bulgaria handstamped diagonally inverted with T **5**.

40	**49**	1st. black	3·25	2·10
41		2st. olive	3·25	2·10
42	**50**	5st. green	1·10	55
43		10st. rose	1·10	55
44		15st. violet	1·10	55
45	**29**	25st. black and deep blue	1·10	55
40/45 *Set of 6*			10·00	5·75

Thrace Interalliée
(6)

THRACE OCCIDENTALE
(7)

1920 (10 Apr). Stamps of Bulgaria optd with T **6**.

46	**50**	5st. green	35	30
47		10st. rose	35	30
48		15st. violet	35	30
49		50st. yellow-brown	1·70	1·60
		a. Opt reading down	28·00	32·00
46/49 *Set of 4*			2·50	2·20

Varieties "r" for "n" in "Interalliée" and last "e" inverted occur in this overprint.

1920 (19 Apr). Stamps of Bulgaria optd as T **7**, but 15½ mm. between lines. P 11½, or imperf (30st.).

50	**50**	5st. green	35	30
		a. Opt inverted	45·00	
51		10st. rose	35	30
52		15st. violet	35	30
53		25st. blue	35	30
54		30st. chocolate	1·70	1·60
55		50st. yellow-brown	35	30
50/55 *Set of 6*			3·00	2·75

1920 (21 Apr). POSTAGE DUE. Postage Due stamps of Bulgaria optd with T **7**.

(a) Imperf

D56	**D 37**	5st. bright green	35	30
D57		10st. dull violet	2·20	2·10
D58		20st. red-orange	55	55
D59		50st. deep blue	1·70	1·60
		(b) P 12×11½		
D60	**D 37**	10st. dull violet	1·30	85
D56/60 *Set of 5*			5·50	5·00

Except for No. D60 the above were supplied to Thrace imperforate. All values are known perforated (including the 10st. in gauges other than that listed) but their status is uncertain.

D. GREEK OCCUPATION, 1920

At the Spa Conference Greece was given a mandate to administer both Western and Eastern Thrace.

The area known as Eastern Thrace was the territory bounded by the Bulgarian frontier of 1913, the Black Sea, the Chataldja lines to the west of Constantinople (Istanbul), the Sea of Marmora and the Evros river (formerly Maritza). It included the city of Adrianople (now Edirne), the Gallipoli peninsula and the island of Imbros (now Imroz).

100 Lepta = 1 Drachma

Διοίκησις
Δυτικῆς
Θράκης
(8)

ΔΙΟΙΚΗΣΙΣ
ΔΥΤΙΚΗΣ
ΘΡΑΚΗΣ
(9)

("Administration of Western Thrace")

1920 (June). Stamps of Greece optd with T **8** or **9** (25d.).

(a) On issue of 1911, recess

61	**30**	2l. carmine	1·70	75
62	**29**	3l. vermilion	1·70	75
63	**32**	1d. ultramarine	55·00	55·00
64		2d. vermilion	19·00	13·00
65		3d. carmine	65·00	48·00
66		5d. grey-blue	33·00	27·00
67		10d. deep blue	22·00	21·00
68	**33**	25d. deep blue	75·00	55·00
61/68 *Set of 8*			£250	£200
		(b) On issue of 1913, lithographed		
69	**29**	1l. green	35	85
70	**30**	2l. carmine	35	55
71	**29**	3l. vermilion	35	55
72	**31**	5l. green	35	55
73	**29**	10l. carmine	55	1·10
74	**30**	15l. dull blue	35	55
75		25l. ultramarine	55	1·10
76	**31**	30l. carmine-red	33·00	43·00
77	**30**	40l. deep blue	1·70	2·10
78	**31**	50l. brown-purple	8·75	10·50
79	**32**	1d. ultramarine	8·75	10·50
80		2d. vermilion	33·00	37·00
69/80 *Set of 12*			80·00	95·00

Faked overprints have appeared on the 20l. value.

(c) On Royalist issue of 1916 with "E.T." and Crown overprint

81	**29**	1l. green	5·50	5·25
82	**30**	2l. rose-red	35	55
83	**29**	10l. carmine	55	85
84	**30**	20l. purple-grey	55	85
85	**31**	30l. carmine-red (No. 276)	55	85
86	**32**	2d. vermilion	40·00	55·00
87		3d. carmine	55·00	32·00
88		5d. grey-blue	46·00	65·00
89		10d. deep blue	33·00	60·00
81/89 *Set of 9*			£160	£200

Double and inverted overprint errors occur in the above issue.

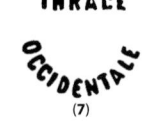

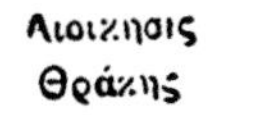

(**10** "Administration of Thrace")

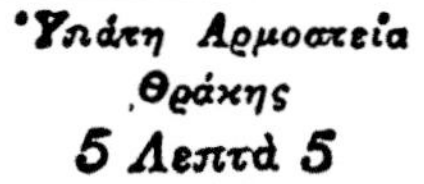

(**11** Trans "High Commission of Thrace")

1920 (July). Stamps of Greece optd with T **10**.

(a) On 1911 issue, recess

89*a*	**30**	2l. carmine	2·20	4·25
90	**29**	3l. vermilion	2·20	4·25
91	**30**	20l. lilac	6·50	10·50
92	**33**	25d. deep blue	65·00	95·00
89*a*/92 *Set of* 4			70·00	£100

(b) On 1913 issue, lithographed

93	**29**	1l. green	35	1·10
94	**30**	2l. carmine	35	55
95	**29**	3l. vermilion	35	55
96	**31**	5l. green	35	55
97	**29**	10l. carmine	55	85
98	**30**	20l. purple-grey	55	85
99		25l. ultramarine	1·10	1·60
100		40l. deep blue	1·70	3·25
101	**31**	50l. brown-purple	1·70	2·10
102	**32**	1d. ultramarine	17·00	21·00
103		2d. vermilion	33·00	37·00
93/103 *Set of* 11			50·00	60·00

(c) On Royalist issue of 1916 with "E.T." and Crown overprint

103*a*	**29**	1l. green	11·00	11·00
104	**30**	2l. rose-red	35	55
105	**31**	5l. green	8·75	16·00
106	**30**	20l. purple-grey	35	55
107	**31**	30l. carmine-red (No. 276)	35	55
108	**32**	3d. carmine	14·50	21·00
109		5d. grey-blue	28·00	43·00
110		10d. deep blue	44·00	65·00
104/110 *Set of* 7			85·00	£130

Double and inverted overprint errors occur in the above issue. Other stamps exist with this overprint but were not issued in Thrace.

1920 (Aug). Occupation of Adrianople. Stamps of Turkey surch as T **11** (vert downwards on 1d. and 3d.).

111	**72**	1l. on 5pa. orange (No. 917a) (B.)	55	55
112	**40**	5l. on 3pi. blue (No. 965)	55	55
113	**38**	20l. on 1pi. dp blue-green (No. 964)	75	75
114	**69**	25l. on 5pi. on 2pa. greenish blue (No. 923) (R.)	75	75
115	**78**	50l. on 5pi. sepia and greenish blue (No. 922a) (R.)	5·50	5·25
116	**74**	1d. on 20pa. carmine (No. 948) (B.)	2·75	2·10
117	**30**	2d. on 10pa. on 2pa. olive-green (No. 946) (R.)	2·75	2·75
118	**85**	3d. on 1pi. indigo (No. 940) (R.)	13·00	13·00
119	**31**	5d. on 20pa. red	11·00	10·50
111/119 *Set of* 9			34·00	32·00

By the Treaty of Sèvres, 10 August 1920, all of Thrace was incorporated into Greece. After the Greek defeat by the Turks in Asia Minor in 1922 Eastern Thrace was returned to Turkey by the Treaty of Lausanne, 24 July 1923; Western Thrace remained part of Greece.

Macedonia

Formerly part of the Turkish Empire, the area of Macedonia was, after the Balkan Wars of 1912–13, divided among Serbia, Bulgaria and Greece. In 1918, when the Kingdom of the Serbs, Croats and Slovenes (later Yugoslavia) was set up, Serbia incorporated its section as South Serbia.

A. GERMAN OCCUPATION, 1944

During the Second World War Bulgaria, in April 1941, occupied Yugoslav Macedonia as far as a line running south and east of Bela Palanka, Lescovac and Gnjilane; this included Pirot, Skopje, Prilep, Bitola and Ohrid. Stamps of Bulgaria were used.

On 8 September 1944 Bulgaria signed an armistice and Macedonia was occupied by German troops and declared its independence, which lasted until German troops left on 13 November.

100 Stotinki = 1 Lev

Македония
8. IX. 1944
1 лв.
(G 1)

МАКЕДОНИЯ
8. IX. 1944
30 лв.
(G 2)

1944 (28 Oct). Stamps of Bulgaria, 1940–44, surch by A. D. Krainichanets, Skopje.

	(a) As Type G **1**		
G1	1l. on 10st. orange (449) (B.)	2·40	15·00
G2	3l. on 15st. blue (450) (R.)	2·40	15·00
	(b) As Type G **2**		
G3	6l. on 10st. blue (469) (R.)	2·75	25·00
G4	9l. on 15st. deep blue-green (470) (R.)	3·75	25·00
G5	9l. on 15st. blackish olive (471) (R.)	5·25	30·00
G6	15l. on 4l. olive-black (504) (R.)	18·00	60·00
G7	20l. on 7l. blue (505) (R.)	26·00	60·00
G8	30l. on 14l. brown (506) (B.)	32·00	£110
G1/8 *Set of* 8		85·00	£300

Numerous errors and varieties occur in these surcharges including two types of "9" in "1944" and the 20l. on 7l. with or without bar over the original face value.

Nos. G1/8 are known with genuine postmarks of Skopje and Kumanovo from 28 October to early November 1944.

On the reconstitution of Yugoslavia as a Federal People's Republic in 1945, Serbian Macedonia became a constituent republic.

B. INDEPENDENT REPUBLIC

The former Yugoslav republic of Macedonia was declared independent, following a referendum, on 8 September 1991.

1991. 100 Paras = 1 Dinar
1992. 100 Deni (de.) = 1 Denar (d.)

SURCHARGED STAMPS. Yugoslav definitive issues exist surcharged "1991–1992", "Macedonia" in Cyrillic letters and new value. There is no evidence that these were official issues.

1 Trumpeters

2 Emblems and Inscriptions

(Litho Institute for the Production of Bank Notes, Belgrade)

1991 (30 Dec). OBLIGATORY TAX. Independence. P 13½.

1	**1**	2d.50 brownish black and yellow-orange	35	35

No. 1 was in use throughout Macedonia between 30 December 1991 and 8 September 1992 and from rural post offices until the end of March 1993. Covers exist showing the stamp cancelled with a Skopje postmark dated 8 September 1991, the actual date of Independence.

(Des Zh. Matejevic. Litho)

1992 (1 Mar). OBLIGATORY TAX. Anti-cancer Week. P 10.

	(a) T **2** and similar vert designs showing Red Cross symbol at bottom left		
2	5d. magenta, blue and black	70	70
	a. Block of 4. Nos. 2/5	3·00	
3	5d. multicoloured	70	70
4	5d. multicoloured	70	70
5	5d. multicoloured	70	70

Designs:—No. 3, Flowers, columns and scanner; 4, Scanner and couch; 5, Computer trolley.

	(b) As T **2** but with right-hand inscr reading down instead of up, and similar vert designs without Red Cross symbol		
6	5d. magenta, blue and black	25	25
	a. Block of 4. Nos. 6/9	1·10	
7	5d. multicoloured (as No. 3)	25	25
8	5d. multicoloured (as No. 4)	25	25
9	5d. multicoloured (as No. 5)	25	25
2/9 *Set of* 8		3·50	3·50

Nos. 2/5 and 6/9 were each issued together in *se-tenant* blocks of four within their sheets. Nos. 6/9 also exist as perforate and imperforate miniature sheets containing a *se-tenant* block of four.

For compulsory use from 1 to 8 March.

New Currency

100 Deni (de.) = 1 Denar (d.)

3 Red Cross Aircraft dropping Supplies

4 "Skopje Earthquake"

1992 (8 May). OBLIGATORY TAX. Red Cross Week. T **3** and similar horiz designs. Multicoloured. Litho. P 10.

10	10d. Red Cross slogans (dated "08–15 MAJ 1992")	15	15
	a. Block of 4. Nos. 10/13	65	
11	10d. Type **3**	15	15
12	10d. Treating road accident victim	15	15
13	10d. Evacuating casualties from ruined building	15	15
10/13 *Set of* 4		55	55

Nos. 10/13 were issued together in *se-tenant* blocks of four within the sheet; the three pictorial designs are taken from children's paintings. They also exist as perforate and imperforate miniature sheets containing a *se-tenant* block of four.

For compulsory use from 8 to 15 May.

(Des Zh. Matejevic. Litho)

1992 (1 June). OBLIGATORY TAX. Solidarity Week. T **4** and similar vert designs. P 10.

14	20d. black and magenta	15	15
	a. Block of 4. Nos. 14/17	65	
15	20d. multicoloured	15	15
16	20d. multicoloured	15	15
17	20d. multicoloured	15	15
14/17 *Set of* 4		55	55

Designs:—No. 15, Red Cross nurse with child; 16, Mothers carrying toddlers at airport; 17, Family at airport.

Nos. 14/17 were issued together in *se-tenant* blocks of four within the sheet. They were accompanied by perforate and imperforate 130d. miniature sheets showing a woman and child in front of a control tower.

For compulsory use from 1 to 7 June.

5 "Wood-carvers Petar and Makarie" (icon), St. Joven Bigorski Monastery, Debar

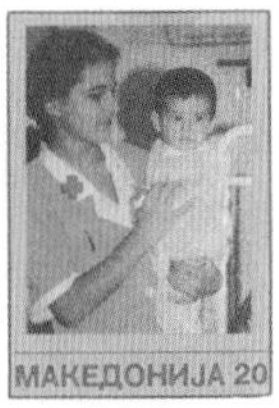

6 Nurse with Baby

(Des M. Dameski. Litho)

1992 (8 Sept). First Anniv of Independence. P 13½×13.

18	**5**	30d. multicoloured	55	55

For 40d. in same design see No. 33.

1992 (14 Sept). OBLIGATORY TAX. Anti-tuberculosis Week. T **6** and similar vert designs. Multicoloured. Litho. P 10.

19	20d. Anti-tuberculosis slogans (dated "14–21.IX.1992")	15	15
	a. Block of 4. Nos. 19/22	65	
20	20d. Type **6**	15	15
21	20d. Nurse giving oxygen	15	15
22	20d. Baby in cot	15	15
19/22 *Set of* 4		55	55

Nos. 19/22 were issued together in *se-tenant* blocks of four within the sheet. They were accompanied by perforate and imperforate 200d. miniature sheets showing a child undergoing treatment; these sheets exist with country name and top marginal inscription in magenta or red.

For compulsory use from 14 to 21 September.

7 "The Nativity" (fresco, Slepce Monastery)

8 Mixed Bouquet

(Des M. Dameski. Litho)

1992 (10 Dec). Christmas. T **7** and similar vert design. Multicoloured. P 13×13½.

23	100d. Type **7**	1·40	1·40
24	500d. "Madonna and Child" (fresco), Zrze Monastery	3·25	3·25

(Des A. Popovski and N. Tozi. Litho)

1993 (1 Feb). OBLIGATORY TAX. Red Cross Fund. T **8** and similar horiz designs. Multicoloured with country name (25/8) and background (26/8) in gold. P 10.

25	20d. Red Cross slogans	15	15
	a. Block of 4. Nos. 25/8	65	
26	20d. Marguerites	15	15
27	20d. Carnations	15	15
28	20d. Type **8**	15	15
25/28 *Set of* 4		55	55

Nos. 25/8 were issued together in *se-tenant* blocks of four within the sheet. They were accompanied by a 500d. miniature sheet, perforate or imperforate, containing a *se-tenant* block of four with country name (25/8) and background (26/8) in either gold or silver.

For compulsory use from 1 February to 31 March.

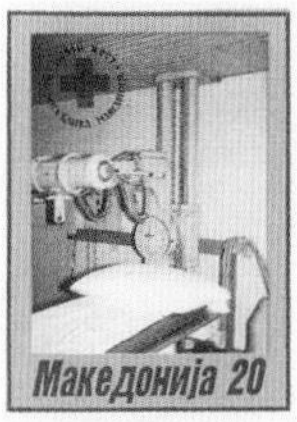

9 Radiography Equipment

10 Macedonian Flag

1993 (1 Mar). OBLIGATORY TAX. Anti-cancer Week. T **9** and similar vert designs. Multicoloured with country name (29) and background (30/32) in silver. Litho. P 10.

29	20d. Anti-cancer slogans (dated "1–8 MART 1993")	15	15
	a. Block of 4. Nos. 29/32	65	
30	20d. Type **9**	15	15
31	20d. Overhead treatment unit	15	15
32	20d. Scanner	15	15
29/32 *Set of* 4		55	55

Nos. 29/32 were issued together in *se-tenant* blocks of four within the sheet. They also exist as 500d. miniature sheets, perforate or imperforate, containing a *se-tenant* block of four with the country inscription (as No. 29) and background (as Nos. 30/32) in gold.

For compulsory use from 1 to 8 March.

1993 (15 Mar). As No. 18 but changed face value shown in black. P 10.

33	**5**	40d. multicoloured	60	60

(Des M. Dameski. Litho)

1993 (15 Mar). P 13½×13.

34	**10**	10d. multicoloured	35	35
35		40d. multicoloured	1·40	1·40
36		50d. multicoloured	1·80	1·80
34/36 *Set of* 3			3·25	3·20

11 Macedonian Roach (*Rutilus macedonicus*)

12 Crucifix, St. George's Monastery

(Des M. Dameski. Litho)

1993 (15 Mar). Fishes from Lake Ohrid. T **11** and similar horiz design. Multicoloured. P 10.

37	50d. Type **11**	25	25
38	100d. Ohrid salmon (*Salmothymus ochridanus*)	35	35
39	1000d. Type **11**	3·50	3·50
40	2000d. As No. 38	4·75	4·75
37/40 *Set of* 4		8·00	8·00

(Des M. Dameski. Litho)

1993 (16 Apr). Easter. P 10.

41	**12**	300d. multicoloured	3·00	3·00

13 Diagram of Telecommunications Cable and Map

14 Red Cross Worker with Baby

(Des M. Dameski. Litho)

1993 (6 May). Opening of Trans-Balkan Telecommunications Line. P 10.

42	**13**	500d. new blue, black and lemon	1·80	1·80

1993 (8 May). OBLIGATORY TAX. Red Cross Week. T **14** and similar horiz designs. Multicoloured with country name (43) or frame (others) in silver. Litho. P 10.

43	50d. Red Cross inscriptions (dated "08–15 MAJ 1993")	15	15
	a. Block of 4. Nos. 43/6	65	
44	50d. Type **14**	15	15
45	50d. Physiotherapist and child in wheelchair	15	15
46	50d. Stretcher party	15	15
43/46 *Set of* 4		55	55

Nos. 43/6 were issued together in *se-tenant* blocks of four within the sheet. They were accompanied by a 700d. miniature sheet, perforate or imperforate, containing a *se-tenant* block of four with inscription (as No. 43) or frames (others) in yellow.

For compulsory use from 8 to 15 May.

For 1d. value in Type **14**, see No. 73.

Currency Reform

1 (new) Denar = 100 (old) Denar

15 Unloading U.N.I.C.E.F. Supplies from Lorry

16 U.N. Emblem and Rainbow

1993 (1 June). OBLIGATORY TAX. Solidarity Week. T **15** and similar horiz designs. Litho. P 10.

47	–	50de. black, magenta and silver	15	15
		a. Block of 4. Nos. 47/50	65	
48	**15**	50de. multicoloured (silver frame)	15	15
49	–	50de. multicoloured (silver frame)	15	15
50	–	50de. multicoloured (silver frame)	15	15
47/50 *Set of 4*			55	55

Designs:—No. 47, "Skopje Earthquake"; 49, Labelling parcels in warehouse; 50, Consignment of parcels on fork-lift truck.

Nos. 47/50 were issued together in *se-tenant* blocks of four within the sheet. They were accompanied by a 7d. miniature sheet, perforate or imperforate, containing a *se-tenant* block of four with country name (as No. 47) or frames (others) in gold.

For compulsory use from 1 to 7 June.

For 1d. value as No. 50, see No. 72.

(Des R. Lazeska. Litho)

1993 (28 July). Admission to United Nations Organization. P 10.

51	**16**	10d. multicoloured	1·40	1·40

17 "Insurrection" (detail, B. Lazeski)

18 Children in Meadow

1993 (2 Aug). 90th Anniv of Macedonian Insurrection. Litho. P 10.

52	**17**	10d. multicoloured	1·40	1·40
MS53		116×73 mm. 30d. multicoloured. Imperf	4·25	4·25

(Des R. Shapkar. Litho)

1993 (14 Sept). OBLIGATORY TAX. Anti-tuberculosis Week. T **18** and similar horiz designs. Multicoloured. P 10.

54	50de. Anti-tuberculosis slogans (dated "14–21.09.1993")	15	15
	a. Block of 4. Nos. 54/7	65	
	ab. Block of 4. Yellow omitted	2·00	
55	50de. Type **18**	15	15
56	50de. Bee on flower	15	15
57	50de. Goat behind boulder	15	15
54/57 *Set of 4*		55	55

Nos. 54/7 were issued together in *se-tenant* blocks of four within the sheet. They were accompanied by a 15d. miniature sheet, perforate or imperforate, containing a *se-tenant* block of four with designer's name omitted from designs as Nos. 55/7.

For compulsory use from 14 to 21 September.

For 1d. value in Type **18** see No. 71.

19 Tapestry

20 "The Nativity" (fresco from St. George's Monastery, Rajcica)

(Des A. Jordanova and M. Dameski. Litho)

1993 (4 Nov). Centenary of Founding of Inner Macedonia Revolutionary Organization. T **19** and similar multicoloured design. P 10.

58		4d. Type **19**	60	60
MS59		90×75 mm. 40d. Two motifs as Type **19**. Imperf	4·25	4·25

(Des M. Dameski. Litho A. D. Printers)

1993 (31 Dec). Christmas. T **20** and similar square design. Multicoloured. P 10.

60	2d. Type **20**	50	50
61	20d. "The Three Kings" (fresco from Slepce Monastery)	3·50	3·50

21 Lily

2

(**22**)

(Des R. Shapkar. Litho)

1994 (1 Mar). OBLIGATORY TAX. Anti-cancer Week. T **21** and similar horiz designs. Multicoloured with background (No. 62) or frame (others) in silver. P 10.

62	1d. Red Cross and anti-cancer emblems	15	15
	a. Block of 4. Nos. 62/5	65	
63	1d. Type **21**	15	15
64	1d. Caesar's mushroom	15	15
65	1d. Mute swans on lake	15	15
62/65 *Set of 4*		55	55

Nos. 62/5 were issued together in *se-tenant* blocks of four within the sheet. They were accompanied by a 20d. miniature sheet, perforate or imperforate, containing a *se-tenant* block of four without the silver.

For compulsory use from 1 to 8 March.

1994 (2 Apr). Nos. 1, 18 and 34 surch as T **22**.

66	**5**	2d. on 30d. multicoloured	25	25
67	**1**	8d. on 2d.50 brownish black and yellow-orange	95	95
68	**10**	15d. on 10d. multicoloured	1·90	1·90
66/68 *Set of 3*			2·75	2·75

Nos. 67/8 show smaller numerals in the surcharge with the 8d. including an oblong over the original value.

See also Nos. 95/6.

23 Decorated Eggs

24 Kosta Racin (writer)

(Des M. Serafimovski. Litho)

1994 (29 Apr). Easter. P 10.

69	**23**	2d. multicoloured	60	60

1994 (8 May). OBLIGATORY TAX. Red Cross Week. As previous designs but values, and date (70), changed. Multicoloured. Litho. P 10.

70	1d. Red Cross inscriptions (dated "8–15 MAJ 1994")	15	15
	a. Block of 4. Nos. 70/3	65	
71	1d. Type **18**	15	15
72	1d. As No. 50	15	15
73	1d. Type **14**	15	15
70/73 *Set of 4*		55	55

Nos. 70/3 were issued together in *se-tenant* blocks of four within the sheet. They were accompanied by a 30d. miniature sheet, perforate or imperforate, containing a *se-tenant* block of four with face values removed.

For compulsory use from 8 to 15 May.

(Des M. Dameski. Litho)

1994 (23 May). Revolutionaries. T **24** and similar vert designs showing portraits by Dimitar Kondovski. Multicoloured. P 10.

74	8d. Type **24**	60	60
75	15d. Grigor Prlicev (writer)	1·20	1·20
76	20d. Nikola Vaptsarov (Bulgarian poet)	1·80	1·80
77	50d. Goce Delcev (founder of Internal Macedonian–Odrin Revolutionary Organization)	4·25	4·25
74/77 *Set of 4*		7·00	7·00

25 "Skopje Earthquake"

26 Tree and Family

(Des Zh. Matejevik. Litho)

1994 (1 June). OBLIGATORY TAX. Solidarity Week. P 10.

78	**25**	1d. black, bright scarlet and silver	35	35

For compulsory use from 1 to 7 June.

1994 (21 June). Census. Litho. P 10.

79	**26**	2d. multicoloured	60	60

27 St. Prohor Pcinski Monastery (venue)

28 Swimmer

1994 (2 Aug). 50th Anniv of Macedonian National Liberation Council. Litho. P 10.

80	**27**	5d. multicoloured	60	60
MS81		108×73 mm. 50d. Aerial view of Monastery. Imperf	4·25	4·25

1994 (22 Aug). Swimming Marathon, Ohrid. Litho. P 10.

82	**28**	8d. multicoloured	85	85

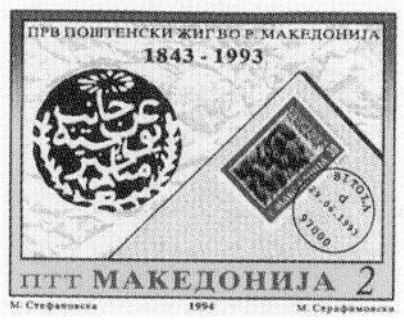

29 Turkish Cancellation and 1992 30d. Stamp on Cover

30 Mastheads

(Des M. Stefanovska and M. Serafimovski. Litho)

1994 (12 Sept). 150th Anniv (1993) of Postal Service in Macedonia. P 10.

83	**29**	2d. multicoloured	60	60

(Des M. Veljkovik-Misho. Litho)

1994 (13 Sept). 50th Anniversaries of *Nova Makedonija*, *Mlad Borec* and *Makedonka* (newspapers). P 10.

84	**30**	2d. multicoloured	60	60

31 Open Book

(Des K. Fidanovski. Litho)

1994 (29 Sept). 50th Anniv of St. Clement of Ohrid Library. T **31** and similar multicoloured design. P 10.

85	2d. Type **31**	25	25
86	10d. Page of manuscript (vert)	1·60	1·60

32 Globe

33 Wireless and Gramophone Record

1994 (1 Dec). OBLIGATORY TAX. Anti-AIDS Week. T **32** and similar horiz designs. Litho. P 10.

87	2d. scarlet and black	15	15
	a. Block of 4. Nos. 87/90	65	
88	2d. black, scarlet and bright blue	15	15
89	2d. black, greenish yellow and scarlet	15	15
90	2d. black and scarlet	15	15
87/90 *Set of 4*		55	55

Designs:—No. 87, Inscriptions in Cyrillic (dated "01–08.12.1994"); 88, Type **32**; 89, Exclamation mark in warning triangle; 90, Safe sex campaign emblem.

Nos. 87/90 were issued together in *se-tenant* blocks of four stamps within the sheet. They were accompanied by a 40d. miniature sheet, perforate or imperforate, depicting the motif in Type **32**.

For compulsory use from 1 to 8 December.

(Des K. Fidanovski. Litho)

1994 (26 Dec). 50th Anniv of Macedonian Radio. P 10.

91	**33**	2d. multicoloured	60	60

34 Macedonian Pine (*Pinus peluse*)

2

(**35**)

36 Emblems and Inscriptions

(Des R. Lezeska. Litho)

1994 (26 Dec). Flora and Fauna. T **34** and similar horiz design. Multicoloured. P 10.

92	5d. Type **34**	60	60
93	10d. Lynx (*Lynx lynx martinoi*)	1·20	1·20

1995 (13 Mar). Nos. 35 and 33 surch with T **35** (94) or as T **22** (95/6).

94	**10**	2d. on 40d. multicoloured	1·20	1·20
95		2d. on 40d. multicoloured	60	60
96	**5**	5d. on 40d. multicoloured (Gold)	70	70
94/96 *Set of 3*			2·30	2·30

(Des V. Pulevski. Litho)

1995 (10 Apr). OBLIGATORY TAX. Anti-cancer Week. T **36** and similar vert designs. Multicoloured. P 10.

97	1d. Type **36**	15	15
	a. Block of 4. Nos. 97/100	65	
98	1d. White lilies	15	15
99	1d. Red lilies	15	15
100	1d. Red roses	15	15
97/100 *Set of 4*		55	55

Nos. 97/100 were issued together in *se-tenant* blocks of four within the sheet. They were accompanied by a 30d. miniature sheet, perforate or imperforate, containing designs as Type **36** and No. 100 but with country inscription, face value and dates omitted.

For compulsory use from 10 to 16 April. The stamps are however dated "01-08 MART 1995".

37 Fresco

(Des M. Dameski. Litho 11 Oktombri)

1995 (23 Apr). Easter. P 10.
101 **37** 4d. multicoloured ... 60 60
No. 101 was issued in sheets of 24 stamps and one label.

38 Voluntary Workers **39** Troops on Battlefield

(Des Zh. Matejevik and V. Pulevski. Litho)

1995 (8 May). OBLIGATORY TAX. Red Cross Week. T **38** and similar vert designs. Multicoloured. P 10.
102 1d. Cross and inscriptions in Cyrillic (dated "8–15 MAJ 1995") ... 15 15
a. Horiz strip of 4. Nos. 102/5 ... 65
103 1d. Type **38** ... 15 15
104 1d. Volunteers in t-shirts ... 15 15
105 1d. Globe, red cross and red crescent ... 15 15
102/105 *Set of* 4 ... 55 55
Nos. 102/5 were issued together in horizontal *se-tenant* strips of four stamps within the sheet. They were accompanied by a 30d. miniature sheet, perforate or imperforate, containing design as No. 105 but with inscriptions replacing date and face value.
For compulsory use from 8 to 15 May.

(Des T. Ivanovski and M. Dameski. Litho 11 Oktombri)

1995 (9 May). 50th Anniv of End of Second World War. P 10.
106 **39** 2d. multicoloured ... 1·20 1·20

40 Anniversary Emblem **41** Röntgen and X-Ray Lamp

1995 (20 May). 50th Anniv of Macedonian Red Cross. Litho. P 10.
107 **40** 2d. multicoloured ... 1·20 1·20

(Des M. Dameski. Litho 11 Oktombri)

1995 (31 May). Centenary of Discovery of X-Rays by Wilhelm Röntgen. P 10.
108 **41** 2d. multicoloured ... 1·40 1·40

42 "Skopje Earthquake" **43** Černodrinski (dramatist)

(Des Zh. Matejevik and V. Puleski. Litho)

1995 (1 June). OBLIGATORY TAX. Solidarity Week. P 10.
109 **42** 1d. black, vermilion and gold ... 15 15
No. 109 was accompanied by a 30d. miniature sheet, perforate or imperforate, containing design as Type **42** but without bottom panel.
For compulsory use from 1 to 7 June.

(Des M. Dameski. Litho 11 Oktombri)

1995 (8 June). 50th Anniv of Vojdan Černodrinski Theatre Festival. P 10.
110 **43** 10d. multicoloured ... 1·20 1·20

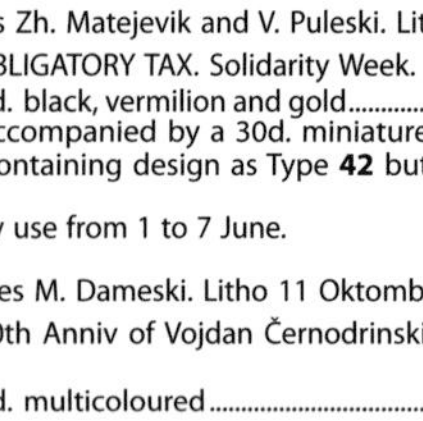

44 Kraljevic (fresco, Markov Monastery, Skopje)

(Des M. Dameski. Litho 11 Oktombri)

1995 (22 June). 600th Death Anniv of Marko Kraljevic (Serbian Prince). P 10.
111 **44** 20d. multicoloured ... 1·60 1·60

45 Puleski **46** Manuscript, Bridge and Emblem

(Des M. Dameski. Litho 11 Oktombri)

1995 (8 July). Death Centenary of Gorgi Puleski (linguist and revolutionary). P 10.
112 **45** 2d. multicoloured ... 1·20 1·20

(Des M. Dameski. Litho 11 Oktombri)

1995 (23 Aug). Writers' Festival, Struga. P 10.
113 **46** 2d. multicoloured ... 1·20 1·20

47 Robert Koch (discoverer of tubercule bacillus) **48** Child holding Parents' Hands

(Des V. Pulevski and Zh. Matejevik. Litho)

1995 (14 Sept). OBLIGATORY TAX. Anti-tuberculosis Week. P 10.
114 **47** 1d. orange-brown, black and scarlet-vermilion ... 35 35
No. 114 was accompanied by a 30d. miniature sheet, perforate or imperforate, containing design as Type **47** but without top inscription, country name or face value.
For compulsory use from 14 to 21 September.

1995 (2 Oct). OBLIGATORY TAX. Children's Week. Litho. Self-adhesive. Die-cut.
115 **48** 2d. ultramarine ... 35 35
For compulsory use from 2 to 8 October.

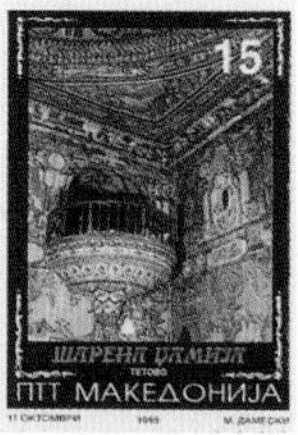

49 Maleshevija **50** Interior of Mosque

(Des M. Dameski and P. Namichev. Litho 11 Oktombri)

1995 (4 Oct). Buildings. T **49** and similar square design. Multicoloured. P 10.
116 2d. Type **49** ... 20 20
117 20d. Krakornica ... 1·40 1·40

(Des M. Dameski. Litho 11 Oktombri)

1995 (4 Oct). Tetovo Mosque. P 10.
118 **50** 15d. multicoloured ... 1·20 1·20

51 Lumière Brothers (inventors of cine-camera)

(Des M. Dameski. Litho 11 Oktombri)

1995 (6 Oct). Centenary of Motion Pictures. T **51** and similar horiz design. Multicoloured. P 10 (3 sides).
119 10d. Type **51** ... 1·20 1·20
a. Horiz pair. Nos. 119/20 ... 2·50 2·50
120 10d. Milton and Janaki Manaki (Macedonian cinematographers) ... 1·20 1·20
Nos. 119/20 were issued together in horizontal *se-tenant* pairs within the sheet, each pair forming a composite design. The outer vertical edges of the pair are imperforate giving stamps with one side imperf.

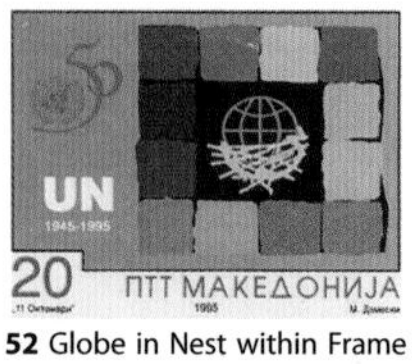

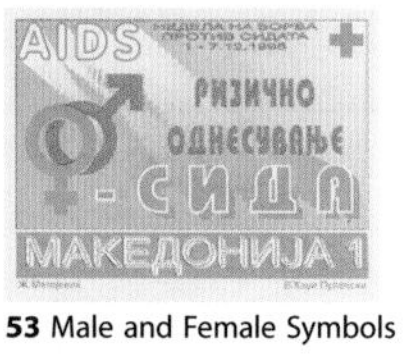

52 Globe in Nest within Frame **53** Male and Female Symbols

(Des M. Dameski. Litho 11 Oktombri)

1995 (24 Oct). 50th Anniv of United Nations Organization. T **52** and similar horiz design. Multicoloured. P 10.
121 20d. Type **52** ... 95 95
122 50d. Sun within frame ... 2·75 2·75

(Des Zh. Matejevik and V. Pulevski. Litho)

1995 (1 Dec). OBLIGATORY TAX. Anti-AIDS Week. P 10.
123 **53** 1d. multicoloured ... 35 35

No. 123 was accompanied by a 30d. miniature sheet, perforate or imperforate, containing design as T **53** but without top inscription, country name or face value.
For compulsory use from 1 to 7 December.

54 Madonna and Child **55** Dalmatian Pelican (*Pelecanus crispus*)

(Des B. Damevska. Litho 11 Oktombri)

1995 (13 Dec). Christmas. P 10.
124 **54** 15d. multicoloured ... 1·40 1·40

(Des B. Damevska. Litho 11 Oktombri)

1995 (14 Dec). Birds. T **55** and similar horiz design. Multicoloured. P 10.
125 15d. Type **55** ... 1·20 1·20
126 40d. Lammergeier (*Gypaetus barbatus*) ... 2·40 2·40

56 Letters of Alphabet and Jigsaw Pieces **57** St. Clement of Ohrid (detail of fresco)

(Des S. Kozhukharova. Litho 11 Oktombri)

1995 (18 Dec). 50th Anniv of Alphabet Reform. P 10.
127 **56** 5d. multicoloured ... 60 60

(Des M. Dameski. Litho 11 Oktombri)

1995 (19 Dec). 700th Anniv of Fresco, St. Bogorodica's Church, Ohrid. P 10.
128 **57** 8d. multicoloured ... 70 70
MS129 85×67 mm. **57** 50d. multicoloured. Imperf ... 60·00 60·00

58 Postal Headquarters, Skopje **59** Zip joining Flags

1995 (27 Dec). Second Anniv of Membership of Universal Postal Union. Litho. P 10.
130 **58** 10d. multicoloured ... 70 70

(Des S. Kozhukharova, Stankoski and M. Dameski. Litho 11 Oktombri)

1995 (27 Dec). Entry to Council of Europe and Organization for Security and Co-operation in Europe. P 10.
131 **59** 20d. multicoloured ... 1·60 1·60

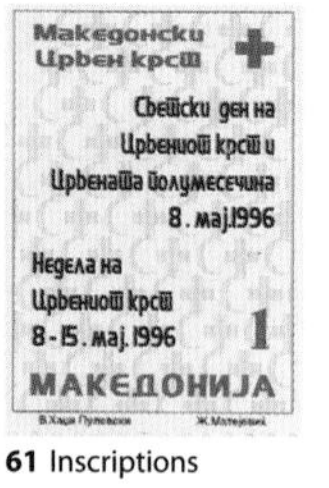

60 Hand holding out Apple **61** Inscriptions

(Des V. Pulevski. Litho)

1996 (1 Mar). OBLIGATORY TAX. Anti-cancer Week. P 10.
132 **60** 1d. bright scarlet, black and yellowish green ... 35 35
No. 132 was accompanied by a 30d. miniature sheet, perforate or imperforate, containing design as Type **60** but without top inscription and bottom panel.
For compulsory use from 1 to 8 March.

(Des V. Pulevski and Zh. Matejevik. Litho)

1996 (8 May). OBLIGATORY TAX. Red Cross Week. T **61** and similar vert designs. Each bright scarlet, black and lemon. P 10.
133 1d. Type **61** ... 15 15
a. Strip of 5. Nos. 133/7 ... 80
134 1d. Red Cross principles in Macedonian ... 15 15
135 1d. Red Cross principles in English ... 15 15
136 1d. Red Cross principles in French ... 15 15
137 1d. Red Cross principles in Spanish ... 15 15
133/137 *Set of* 5 ... 70 70
Nos. 133/7 were issued together in *se-tenant* strips of five stamps within the sheet. They were accompanied by a 30d. miniature sheet, perforate or imperforate, containing a design combining the motifs of Nos. 133/7.
For compulsory use from 8 to 15 May.

62 Canoeing

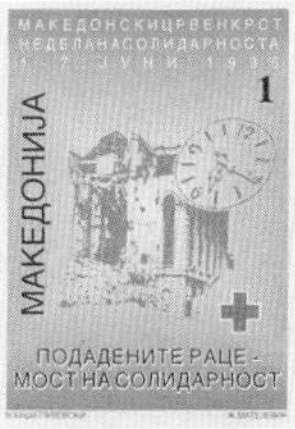
63 "Skopje Earthquake"

(Des B. Damevska. Litho 11 Oktombri)

996 (20 May). Olympic Games, Atlanta. T **62** and similar multicoloured designs showing statue of discus thrower and sport. P 10.

38 2d. Type **62** 35 35
39 8d. Basketball (vert) 50 50
40 15d. Swimming 85 85
41 20d. Wrestling .... 1·30 1·30
42 40d. Boxing (vert) .... 2·75 2·75
43 50d. Running (vert) .... 3·25 3·25
38/143 *Set of* 6 .... 8·00 8·00

(Des V. Pulevski and Zh. Matejevik. Litho)

996 (1 June). OBLIGATORY TAX. Solidarity Week. P 10.

44 **63** 1d. gold, bright rose-red and black 35 35

No. 144 was accompanied by a 30d. miniature sheet, perforate or imperforate, containing design as Type **63** but without country name and face value.

For compulsory use from 1 to 7 June.

64 Scarecrow Drug Addict

65 Boy

(Des M. Dameski. Litho 11 Oktombri)

1996 (11 July). United Nations Anti-drugs Decade. Litho. P 10.

145 **64** 20d. multicoloured .... 1·20 1·20

996 (15 July). Children's Week. T **65** and similar vert design showing children's drawings. Multicoloured. Litho. P 10.

146 2d. Type **65** 25 25
147 8d. Girl 60 60

66 Fragment from Tomb and Tsar Samuel (after Dimitar Kondovski)

67 Petrov

1996 (19 July). Millenary of Crowning of Tsar Samuel (ruler of Bulgaria and Macedonia). Litho. P 10.

148 **66** 40d. multicoloured .... 2·20 2·20

(Des M. Dameski. Litho 11 Oktombri)

1996 (2 Aug). 75th Death Anniv of Gorce Petrov (revolutionary). P 10.

149 **67** 20d. multicoloured .... 1·20 1·20

68 Ohrid Seal, 1903, and State Flag

69 Lungs on Globe

(Des M. Dameski. Litho 11 Oktombri)

1996 (8 Sept). Fifth Anniv of Independence. P 10.

150 **68** 10d. multicoloured 60 60

(Des V. Pulevski. Litho)

1996 (14 Sept). OBLIGATORY TAX. Anti-tuberculosis Week. P 10.

151 **69** 1d. bright scarlet, blue and black..... 50 50

No. 151 was accompanied by a 30d. miniature sheet, perforate or imperforate, containing design as Type **69** but without all inscriptions.

For compulsory use from 14 to 21 September.

70 Vera Ciriviri-Trena (freedom fighter)

71 Hand holding Syringe

(Des S. Kozhukharova (20d.), B. Damevska (40d.). Litho BNF)

1996 (22 Nov). Europa. Famous Women. T **70** and similar vert design. Multicoloured. P 13×13½.

152 20d. Type **70** .... 8·50 8·50
153 40d. Mother Teresa (Nobel Peace Prize winner and founder of Missionaries of Charity) .... 12·00 12·00

(Des V. Pulevski. Litho)

1996 (1 Dec). OBLIGATORY TAX. Anti-AIDS Week. P 10.

154 **71** 1d. black, scarlet and yellow 35 35

No. 154 was accompanied by a 30d. miniature sheet, perforate or imperforate, containing design as Type **71** but without bottom panel and inscription.

For compulsory use from 1 to 7 December.

72 Candle, Nuts and Fruit

73 "Daniel in the Lions' Den"

1996 (14 Dec). Christmas. T **72** and similar vert design. Multicoloured. Litho. P 10.

155 10d. Type **72** 70 70
a. Pair. Nos. 155/6 .... 1·50 1·50
156 10d. Tree and carol singers 70 70

Nos. 155/6 were issued together in *se-tenant* pairs within the sheet.

1996 (19 Dec). Early Christian Terracotta Reliefs. T **73** and similar vert designs. Litho. P 10.

(a) Yellow-olive backgrounds

157 4d. Type **73** 25 25
a. Block of 4. Nos. 157/60 .... 5·25
158 8d. St. Christopher and St. George 50 50
159 20d. Joshua and Caleb .... 1·20 1·20
160 50d. Unicorn .... 3·00 3·00

(b) Turquoise-blue backgrounds

161 4d. Type **73** 25 25
a. Block of 4. Nos. 161/4 .... 5·25
162 8d. As No. 158 .... 50 50
163 20d. As No. 159 .... 1·20 1·20
164 50d. As No. 160 .... 3·00 3·00
157/164 *Set of* 8 .... 9·00 9·00

Nos. 157/60 and 161/4 respectively were issued together in *se-tenant* blocks of four stamps within their sheets.

74 Nistrovo

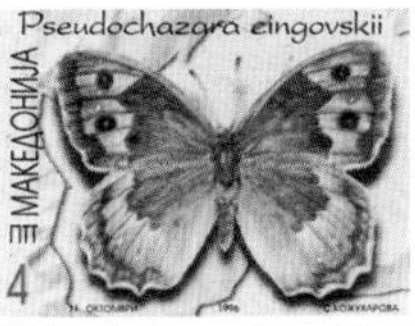
75 *Pseudochazara cingovskii*

(Litho 11 Oktombri)

1996 (20–25 Dec). Traditional Houses. T **74** and similar square designs. Multicoloured. P 10.

165 2d. Type **74** (25 Dec) 25 25
166 8d. Brodec 70 70
167 10d. Nivište (25 Dec) 85 85
165/167 *Set of* 3 .... 1·60 1·60

(Des S. Kozhukharova. Litho 11 Oktombri)

1996 (21 Dec). Butterflies. T **75** and similar horiz design. Multicoloured. P 10.

168 4d. Type **75** 25 25
169 40d. Danube clouded yellow (*Colias balcanica*) .... 3·00 3·00

76 U.N.I.C.E.F. Coach

(Des M. Dameski (40d.). Litho Courvoisier)

1996 (31 Dec). 50th Anniversaries. T **76** and similar horiz design. Multicoloured. P 14½×15.

170 20d. Type **76** (United Nations Children's Fund) .... 1·20 1·20
171 40d. Church in Mtskheta, Georgia (United Nations Educational, Scientific and Cultural Organization) .... 2·40 2·40

77 Skier

(Des M. Dameski. Litho 11 Oktombri)

1997 (7 Feb). 50 Years of Ski Championships at Šar Planina. P 10.

172 **77** 20d. multicoloured .... 1·40 1·40

78 Bell

(Des Lj. Ivanovski. Litho 11 Oktombri)

1997 (12 Mar). 150th Birth Anniv of Alexander Graham Bell (telephone pioneer). P 10.

173 **78** 40d. multicoloured .... 2·40 2·40

79 Family and Healthy Foodstuffs

(Des V. Pulevski. Litho)

1997 (1 Mar). OBLIGATORY TAX. Anti-cancer Week. P 10.

174 **79** 1d. multicoloured .... 1·80 1·80

For compulsory use from 1 to 8 March.

80 Hound

81 Red Cross on Globe

(Des M. Dameski. Litho 11 Oktombri)

1997 (26 Mar). Roman Mosaics from Heraklia. T **80** and similar horiz designs. Multicoloured. P 10.

175 2d. Type **80** 25 25
176 8d. Steer 50 50
177 20d. Lion .... 1·10 1·10
178 40d. Leopard with prey .... 2·40 2·40
175/178 *Set of* 4 .... 3·75 3·75
MS179 85×60 mm. 50d. Deer and plant tub. Imperf 4·75 4·75

(Des V. Pulevski. Litho)

1997 (8 May). OBLIGATORY TAX. Red Cross Week. P 10.

180 **81** 1d. multicoloured 35 35

For compulsory use from 8 to 15 May.

82 Gold Plate

83 Schoolchildren

(Des F. Unkovski and D. Drakalski. Litho 11 Oktombri)

1997 (24 May). 1100th Anniv of Cyrillic Alphabet. T **82** and similar horiz design. Multicoloured.

181 10d. Type **82** 70 70
a. Pair. Nos. 181/2 .... 1·50 1·50
182 10d. Sts. Cyril and Methodius 70 70

(Des V. Pulevski. Litho)

1997 (1 June). OBLIGATORY TAX. Solidarity Week. P 10.

183 **83** 1d. multicoloured 35 35

For compulsory use from 1 to 7 June.

84 Mountain Flowers

85 Itar Pejo

(Des. A. Jankovik. Litho 11 Oktombri)

1997 (5 June). Fifth Anniv of Ecological Association. P 10.

184 **84** 15d. multicoloured .... 1·20 1·20

(Des B. Damevska. Litho Courvoisier)

1997 (6 June). Europa. Tales and Legends. T **85** and similar vert design. Multicoloured. P 15×14½.

185 20d. Type **85** .... 7·25 7·25
186 40d. Stork-men .... 13·00 13·00

86 St. Naum and St. Naum's Church, Ohrid

(Des Lj. Ivanovski. Litho 11 Oktombri)

1997 (3 July). 1100th Birth Anniv of St. Naum. P 10.

187 **86** 15d. multicoloured .... 1·20 1·20

87 Diseased Lungs

88 Stibnite

(Des V. Pulevski. Litho 11 Oktombri)

1997 (14 Sept). OBLIGATORY TAX. Anti-tuberculosis Week. P 10.

188 **87** 1d. multicoloured 35 35
For compulsory use from 14 to 21 September.

(Des B. Damevska. Litho 11 Oktombri)

1997 (10 Oct). Minerals. T **88** and similar vert designs. Multicoloured. P 10.

189 27d. Type **88** .... 1·80 1·80
190 40d. Lorandite .... 2·40 2·40

89 Dove and Sun above Child in Open Hand

(Des M. Veljkovik. Litho 11 Oktombri)

1997 (11 Oct). International Children's Day. P 10.

191 **89** 27d. multicoloured .... 1·70 1·70

90 Chanterelle (*Cantharellus cibarius*)

91 Group of Children

(Des I. Stevkovski. Litho 11 Oktombri)

1997 (7 Nov). Fungi. T **90** and similar horiz designs. Multicoloured. P 10.

192 2d. Type **90** 35 35
193 15d. Bronze boletus (*Boletus aereus*) 85 85
194 27d. Caesar's mushroom (*Amanita caesarea*) .... 1·60 1·60
195 50d. *Morchella conica* .... 2·75 2·75
192/195 *Set of* 4 .... 5·00 5·00

(Des V. Pulevski. Litho 11 Oktombri)

1998 (14 Jan). OBLIGATORY TAX. Anti-AIDS Week. P 10.

196 **91** 1d. multicoloured 35 35
For compulsory use from 14 to 21 January.

92 Mahatma Gandhi

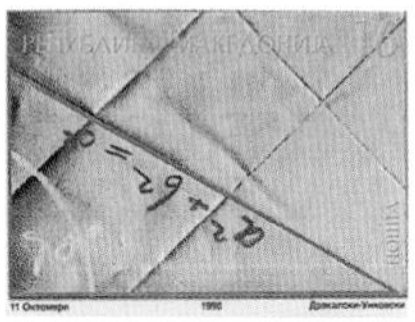

93 Formula of Pythagoras's Theory

(Des M. Dameski. Litho 11 Oktombri)

1998 (4 Feb). 50th Death Anniv of Mahatma Gandhi (Indian independence campaigner). P 13½.

197 **92** 30d. multicoloured .... 1·40 1·40

(Des D. Unkovski. Litho 11 Oktombri)

1998 (6 Feb). 2500th Death Anniv of Pythagoras (philosopher and mathematician). P 13½.

198 **93** 16d. multicoloured 85 85

94 Alpine Skiing

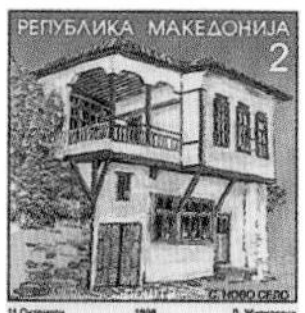

95 Novo Selo

(Des I. Stevkovski. Litho 11 Oktombri)

1998 (7 Feb). Winter Olympic Games, Nagano, Japan. T **94** and similar horiz design. Multicoloured. P 13½.

199 4d. Type **94** 10 10
200 30d. Cross-country skiing .... 1·40 1·40

(Des M. Dameski (1, 4, 5, 30d.), I. Stevkovski (6d.), Lj Ivanovski (16d.), L. Zhivkovska (others). Litho 11 Oktombri)

1998 (9 Feb)–**02**. Traditional Houses. T **95** and similar square designs. Multicoloured. P 13½.

201 1d. Bogomila (5.11.99) 10 10
202 2d. Type **95** 10 10
203 3d. Jachintse (5.11.02) 20 20
204 4d. Jablanica 25 25
205 4d. Svekani (1.2.99) 30 30
206 5d. Teovo (25.2.99) 30 30
207 6d. Zdunje (28.7.00) 35 35
208 6d. Mitrasinci (25.6.01) 35 35
209 9d. Ratevo (5.11.02) 50 50
210 16d. Kiselica (10.6.98) 65 65
211 20d. Konopnica (12.2.98) 85 85
212 30d. Ambar .... 1·40 1·40
213 50d. Galicnik (12.2.98) .... 2·40 2·40
201/213 *Set of* 13 .... 7·00 7·00

96 "Exodus" (Kole Manev)

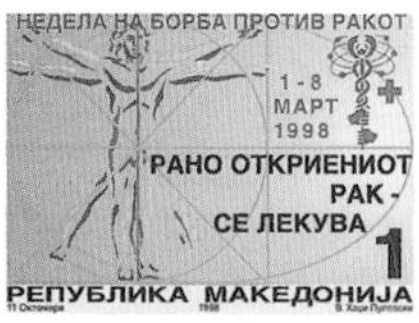

97 "Proportions of Man" (Leonardo da Vinci)

(Des M. Dameski. Litho 11 Oktombri)

1998 (11 Feb). 50th Anniv of Exodus of Children during Greek Civil War. P 13½.

215 **96** 30d. multicoloured .... 1·40 1·40

(Des V. Pulevski. Litho 11 Oktombri)

1998 (1 Mar). OBLIGATORY TAX. Anti-cancer Week. P 13½.

216 **97** 1d. multicoloured 50 50
For compulsory use from 1 to 8 March.

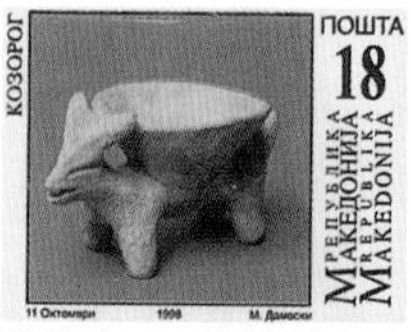

98 Bowl supported by Animal

99 Football Pitch

(Des M. Dameski. Litho 11 Oktombri)

1998 (27 Apr). Archaeological Finds from Nedit. T **98** and similar horiz designs. Multicoloured. P 13½.

217 4d. Carafes 25 25
218 18d. Type **98** 70 70
219 30d. Sacred female figurine .... 1·40 1·40
220 60d. Stemmed cup .... 2·75 2·75
217/220 *Set of* 4 .... 4·50 4·50

(Des A. Prilepchanski. Litho 11 Oktombri)

1998 (30 Apr). World Cup Football Championship, France. T **99** and similar horiz design. Multicoloured. P 13½.

221 4d. Type **99** 25 25
222 30d. Globe and football pitch .... 1·60 1·60

100 Folk Dance

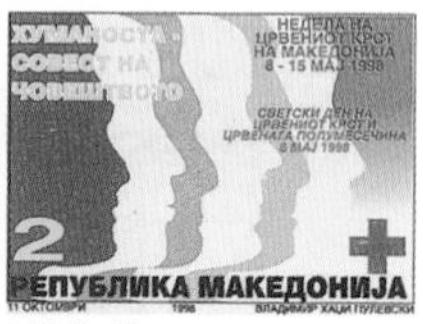

101 Profiles

(Des T. Pocevska and A. Stojkovik. Litho 11 Oktombri)

1998 (5 May). Europa. National Festivals. T **100** and similar horiz design. Multicoloured. P 13½.

223 30d. Type **100** .... 3·00 3·00
224 40d. Carnival .... 4·25 4·25

(Des V. Pulevski. Litho 11 Oktombri)

1998 (8 May). OBLIGATORY TAX. Red Cross Week. P 13½.

225 **101** 2d. multicoloured 50 50
For compulsory use from 8 to 15 May.

102 Carnival Procession

103 Hands and Red Cross

(Des A. Mikhailov. Litho 11 Oktombri)

1998 (10 May). 18th Congress of Carnival Towns, Strumica. P 13½.

226 **102** 30d. multicoloured .... 1·40 1·40

(Des V. Pulevski. Litho 11 Oktombri)

1998 (1 June). OBLIGATORY TAX. Solidarity Week. P 13½.

227 **103** 2d. multicoloured 50 50
For compulsory use from 1 to 7 June.

104 Flower

105 Dimitrija Cupovski

(Des D. Drakalski (4d.); D. Mikhajlov (30d.). Litho 11 Oktombri)

1998 (5 June). Environmental Protection. T **104** and similar vert design. Multicoloured. P 13½.

228 4d. Type **104** 25 25
229 30d. Polluting chimney uprooting tree .... 1·30 1·30

(Des D. Andonova. Litho 11 Oktombri)

1998 (30 June). 120th Birth Anniv of Dimitrija Cupovski. P 13½.

230 **105** 16d. multicoloured 70 70

106 Steam Locomotive and Station

107 Doctor and Patient

(Des D. Isailovski (30d.); S. Sharovik (60d.). Litho 11 Oktombri)

1997 (9 Aug). 150th Anniv of Railways in Macedonia. T **106** and similar multicoloured design. P 13½.

231 30d. Type **106** .... 1·80 1·80
232 60d. Steam locomotive, 1873 (horiz) .... 3·50 3·50

(Des V. Pulevski. Litho 11 Oktombri)

1998 (14 Sept). OBLIGATORY TAX. Anti-tuberculosis Week. P 13½.

233 **107** 2d. multicoloured 50 50

108 *Ursus spelaeus*

109 Atanos Badev (composer) and Score

(Des P. Namicev. Litho 11 Oktombri)

1998 (17 Sept). Fossilized Skulls. T **108** and similar horiz designs. Multicoloured. P 13½.

234 4d. Type **108** 25 25
235 8d. *Mesopithecus pentelici* 35 35
236 18d. *Tragoceros* 95 95
237 30d. *Acaratherium incsivum* .... 1·40 1·40
234/237 *Set of* 4 .... 2·75 2·75

(Des I. Markovska. Litho 11 Oktombri)

1998 (21 Sept). Centenary of Zlatoustova Liturgy. P 13½.

238 **109** 25d. multicoloured .... 1·20 1·20

110 Child with Kite

111 *Cerambyx cerdo* (longhorn beetle)

(Des G. Bliznakovski. Litho 11 Oktombri)

998 (5 Oct). Children's Day. P 13½.
9 **110** 30d. multicoloured .... 1·40 1·40

(Des Lj. Ivanovski. Litho 11 Oktombri)

998 (20 Oct). Insects. T **111** and similar horiz designs. Multicoloured. P 13½.
0 4d. Type **111** 25 25
1 8d. Alpine longhorn beetle (*Rosalia alpina*) 50 50
2 20d. European rhinoceros beetle (*Oryctes nasicornis*) 95 95
3 40d. Stag beetle (*Lucanus cervus*) .... 1·90 1·90
0/243 *Set of* 4 .... 3·25 3·25

112 Reindeer and Snowflakes

113 Ribbon and Gender Symbols

(Des L. Zhivkovska (4d.), A. Bartling (30d.). Litho 11 Oktombri)

998 (20 Nov). Christmas and New Year. T **112** and similar horiz design. Multicoloured. P 13½.
4 4d. Type **112** 25 25
5 30d. Bread and oak leaves .... 1·60 1·60

(Des V. Pulevski. Litho 11 Oktombri)

998 (1 Dec). OBLIGATORY TAX. Anti-AIDS Week. P 13½.
6 **113** 2d. multicoloured 50 50

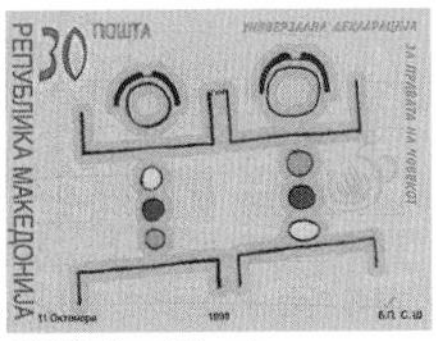

114 Stylized Couple

(Des V. Pulevski and S. Sharovik. Litho 11 Oktombri)

998 (10 Dec). 50th Anniv of Universal Declaration of Human Rights. P 13½.
47 **114** 30d. multicoloured .... 1·40 1·40

115 Sharplaninec

116 Girl's Face

(Des I. Stevkovski. Litho 11 Oktombri)

999 (20 Jan). Dogs. P 13½.
48 **115** 15d. multicoloured .... 1·20 1·20

(Des V. Pulevski. Litho 11 Oktombri)

999 (1 Mar). OBLIGATORY TAX. Anti-cancer Week. P 13½.
49 **116** 2d. multicoloured 50 50
For compulsory use from 1 to 8 March.

117 "The Annunciation" (Demir Hisar, Slepce Monastery)

118 Dimitar Pandilov and "Hay Harvest"

(Des Lj. Ivanovski. Photo Courvoisier)

999 (3 Mar). Icons. T **117** and similar vert designs. Multicoloured. P 11½.
50 4d. Type **117** 35 35
51 8d. "Saints" (St. Nicholas's Church, Ohrid) 50 50
52 18d. "Madonna and Child" (Demir Hisar, Slepce Monastery) 85 85
53 30d. "Christ the Redeemer" (Zrze Monastery, Prilep) .... 1·30 1·30
50/253 *Set of* 4 .... 2·75 2·75
MS254 53×74 mm. 50d. "Christ and Archangels" (Archangel Michael Church, Lesnovo Monastery, Probištip) .... 3·00 3·00

(Des M. Dameski. Litho 11 Oktombri)

999 (14 Mar). Birth Centenary of Dimitar Pandilov (painter). P 13½.
55 **118** 4d. multicoloured 25 25

119 Telegraph Apparatus

(Des G. Bliznakovski. Litho 11 Oktombri)

1999 (22 Apr). Centenary of the Telegraph in Macedonia. P 13½.
256 **119** 4d. multicoloured 25 25

120 University and Sts. Cyril and Methodius

(Des I. Stevkovski. Litho 11 Oktombri)

1999 (24 Apr). 50th Anniv of Sts. Cyril and Methodius University. P 13½.
257 **120** 8d. multicoloured 35 35

121 Anniversary Emblem and Map of Europe

122 Pelister National Park

(Des A. Bartling. Litho 11 Oktombri)

1999 (5 May). 50th Anniv of Council of Europe. P 13½.
258 **121** 30d. multicoloured .... 1·40 1·40

(Des Lj. Ivanovski. Litho 11 Oktombri)

1999 (5 May). Europa. Parks and Gardens. T **122** and similar horiz design. Multicoloured. P 13½.
259 30d. Type **122** .... 3·00 3·00
260 40d. Mavrovo National Park .... 4·25 4·25

123 Figures linking Raised Arms

124 People running round Globe

(Des V. Pulevski. Litho 11 Oktombri)

1999 (8 May). OBLIGATORY TAX. Red Cross Week. P 13½.
261 **123** 2d. multicoloured 60 60
For compulsory use from 8 to 15 May.

(Des V. Pulevski. Litho 11 Oktombri)

1999 (1 June). OBLIGATORY TAX. Solidarity Week. P 13½.
262 **124** 2d. multicoloured 60 60
For compulsory use from 1 to 7 June.

125 Tree

126 Tsar Petur Delyan

(Des M. Markovska. Litho 11 Oktombri)

1999 (5 June). Environmental Protection. P 13½.
263 **125** 30d. multicoloured .... 1·40 1·40

1999 (25 June). Medieval Rulers of Macedonia. T **126** and similar horiz designs. Multicoloured. Litho. P 13½.
264 4d. Type **126** 10 10
a. Block of 4. Nos. 264/7 .... 3·00
265 8d. Prince Gjorgji Vojteh 35 35
266 18d. Prince Dobromir Hrs 85 85
267 30d. Prince Strez .... 1·40 1·40
264/267 *Set of* 4 .... 2·40 2·40
Nos. 264/7 were issued together in *se-tenant* blocks of four stamps within the sheet, each block forming a composite design.

127 Kuzman Shaikarev (author)

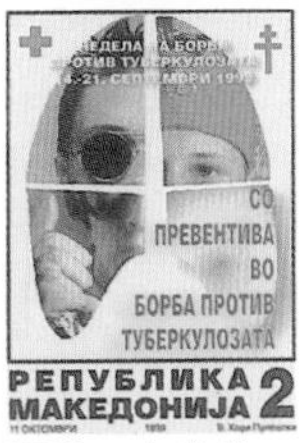

128 Faces in Outline of Lungs

(Des S. Sharovik. Litho 11 Oktombri)

1999 (1 Sept). 125th Anniv of First Macedonian Language Primer. P 13½.
268 **127** 4d. multicoloured 25 25

(Des V. Pulevski. Litho 11 Oktombri)

1999 (14 Sept). OBLIGATORY TAX. Anti-tuberculosis Week. P 13½.
269 **128** 2d. multicoloured 60 60
For compulsory use from 14 to 21 September.

129 *Crocus scardicus*

130 Child

(Des I. Stevkovski. Litho 11 Oktombri)

1999 (16 Sept). Flowers. T **129** and similar vert designs. Multicoloured. P 13½.
270 4d. Type **129** 25 25
271 8d. *Astragalus mayeri* 35 35
272 18d. *Campanula formanekiana* 95 95
273 30d. *Viola kosaninii* .... 1·40 1·40
270/273 *Set of* 4 .... 2·75 2·75

(Des A. Stojkovik. Litho 11 Oktombri)

1999 (4 Oct). Children's Week. P 13½.
274 **130** 30d. multicoloured .... 1·40 1·40

131 Emblem

132 Men on Horseback

(Des T. Pocevska. Litho 11 Oktombri)

1999 (9 Oct). 125th Anniv of Universal Postal Union. T **131** and similar horiz design. Multicoloured. P 13½.
275 5d. Type **131** 25 25
276 30d. Emblem (different) .... 1·60 1·60

(Des I. Stevkovski. Litho 11 Oktombri)

1999 (27 Oct). 1400th Anniv of Slavs in Macedonia. P 13½.
277 **132** 5d. multicoloured 25 25

133 Krste Petkov Misirkov

134 Pine Needles

(Des L. Zhivkovska. Litho 11 Oktombri)

1999 (18 Nov). 125th Birth Anniv (2000) of Krste Petkov Misirkov (writer). P 13½.
278 **133** 5d. multicoloured 25 25

(Des T. Pocevska (5d.), I. Stevkovski (30d.). Litho 11 Oktombri)

1999 (24 Nov). Christmas. T **134** and similar multicoloured design. P 13½.
279 5d. Type **134** 35 35
280 30d. Traditional pastry (vert) .... 1·40 1·40

135 Stylized Figures supporting Globe

136 Altar Cross (19th-century), St. Nikita Monastery

(Des V. Khadzipulevski. Litho 11 Oktombri)

1999 (1 Dec). OBLIGATORY TAX. Anti-AIDS Week. P 13½.
281 **135** 2d.50 multicoloured 60 60
For compulsory use from 1 to 7 December.

(Litho 11 Oktombri)

2000 (19 Jan). Bimillenary of Christianity. T **136** and similar multicoloured designs. P 13½.
282 5d. Type **136** 35 35
283 10d. "Akathist of the Holy Mother of God" (14th-century fresco), Marko's Monastery (horiz) 60 60
284 15d. "St. Clement" (14th-century icon), Ohrid 70 70
285 30d. "Paul the Apostle" (14th-century fresco), St. Andrew's Monastery .... 1·30 1·30
282/285 *Set of 4* .... 2·75 2·75
MS286 70×50 mm. 50d. Cathedral Church of St. Sophia (11th-century), Ohrid (29×31 mm) .... 2·40 2·40
The stamp in No. **MS**286 has the top edge imperforate.

137 "2000"

138 Globe Unravelling and Medical Symbols

(Des G. Bliznakovski. Litho 11 Oktombri)

2000 (16 Feb). New Year. T **137** and similar horiz design. Multicoloured. P 13½.
287 5d. Type **137** 25 25
a. Pair. Nos. 287/8 .... 1·60 1·60
288 30d. Religious symbols .... 1·20 1·20
Nos. 287/8 were issued together in *se-tenant* pairs within the sheetlet.

(Des V. Pulevski. Litho 11 Oktombri)

2000 (1 Mar). OBLIGATORY TAX. Anti-Cancer Week. P 13½.
289 **138** 1d.50 multicoloured 60 60
For compulsory use from 1 to 8 March.

139 Jewelled Brooch with Icon, Orhid

140 Magnifying Glass and Perforation Gauge

(Des T. Potsevska. Litho 11 Oktombri)

2000 (1 Mar). Jewellery. T **139** and similar vert designs. Multicoloured. P 13½.
290 5d. Type **139** 25 25
291 10d. Bracelet, Bitola 35 35
292 20d. Earrings, Ohrid 95 95
293 30d. Butterfly brooch, Bitola .... 1·40 1·40
290/293 *Set of 4* .... 2·75 2·75

(Des T. Potsevska. Litho 11 Oktombri)

2000 (19 Mar). 50th Anniv of Philately in Macedonia. P 13½.
294 **140** 5d. multicoloured 25 25

141 Globe and Emblem

142 Men with Easter Eggs

(Des I. Stevkovski. Litho 11 Oktombri)

2000 (23 Mar). 50th Anniv of World Meteorological Organization. P 13½.
295 **141** 30d. multicoloured .... 1·40 1·40

(Litho 11 Oktombri)

2000 (21 Apr). Easter. P 13½.
296 **142** 5d. multicoloured 25 25

143 Stylized Figures

(Des V. Pulevski. Litho 11 Oktombri)

2000 (8 May). OBLIGATORY TAX. Red Cross Week. P 13½.
297 **143** 2d.50 multicoloured 60 60
For compulsory use from 8 to 15 May.

144 "Building Europe"

(Des J.- P. Cousin. Litho)

2000 (9 May). Europa. P 14.
298 **144** 30d. multicoloured .... 3·00 3·00

145 Running

(Des I. Stevkovski. Litho 11 Oktombri)

2000 (17 May). Olympic Games, Sydney. T **145** and similar horiz designs. Multicoloured. P13½.
299 5d. Type **145** 25 25
300 30d. Wrestling .... 1·60 1·60

146 Cupped Hands

147 Flower and Globe

(Des. V. Pulevski. Litho 11 Oktombri)

2000 (1 June). OBLIGATORY TAX. Solidarity Week. P 13½.
301 **146** 2d.50 multicoloured 60 60
For compulsory use from 1 to 7 June.

(Des K. Zarkovska. Litho 11 Oktombri)

2000 (5 June). International Environmental Protection Day. P 13½.
302 **147** 5d. multicoloured 25 25

148 Teodosija Sinaitski (printing pioneer)

(Des T. Potsevska. Litho 11 Oktombri)

2000 (28 July). Printing. T **148** and similar vert design. Multicoloured. P 13½.
303 6d. Type **148** 25 25
304 30d. Johannes Gutenberg (inventor of printing press) .... 1·40 1·40

149 Mother Teresa

(Des I. Stevkovski. Photo 11 Oktombri)

2000 (28 Aug). Third Death Anniv of Mother Teresa (founder of Order of Missionaries of Charity). P 13½.
305 **149** 6d. multicoloured 25 25

150 Faces and Hands

151 Little Egret (*Egretta garzetta*)

(Des V. Pulevski. Litho 11 Oktombri)

2000 (14 Sept). OBLIGATORY TAX. Red Cross Week. P 13½.
306 **150** 3d. multicoloured 60 6
For compulsory use from 14 to 21 September.

(Des I. Stevkovski. Litho 11 Oktombri)

2000 (14 Sept). Birds. T **151** and similar vert designs Multicoloured. P 13½.
307 6d. Type **151** 35 3
308 10d. Grey heron (*Ardea cinerea*) 50 5
309 20d. Purple heron (*Adrea purpurea*) .... 1·10 1·1
310 30d. Glossy ibis (*Plegadis falcinellus*) .... 1·70 1·7
307/310 *Set of 4* .... 3·25 3·2

152 Children and Tree

153 Dimo Dimov

(Des K. Zarkovska. Litho 11 Oktombri)

2000 (2 Oct). Children's Week. P 13½.
311 **152** 6d. multicoloured 25 2

(Des I. Stevkovski. Litho 11 Oktombri)

2000 (20 Oct). 125th Birth Anniv of Dimo Hadži Dimov (revolutionary). P 13½.
312 **153** 6d. multicoloured 25 2

154 Emblem

155 Church and Frontispiece

(Des T. Pocevska. Litho 11 Oktombri)

2000 (1 Nov). 50th Anniv of Faculty of Economics, St. Cyril and St. Methodius University, Skopje. P 13½.
313 **154** 6d. multicoloured 25 2

(Des Lj. Ivanovski. Litho 11 Oktombri)

2000 (8 Nov). 250th Birth Anniv of Joakim Krčovski (writer) P 13½.
314 **155** 6d. multicoloured .... 1·00 1·0

156 Nativity

157 Hand holding Condom

(Des Lj. Ivanovski. Litho 11 Oktombri)

2000 (22 Nov). Christmas. P 13½.
315 **156** 30d. multicoloured .... 1·50 1·50

(Des V. Pulevski. Litho 11 Oktombri)

2000 (1 Dec). OBLIGATORY TAX. Anti-AIDS Week. P 13½.
316 **157** 3d. multicoloured 65 65
For compulsory use from 1 to 7 December.

158 Handprints and Emblem

(Des K. Zarkovska. Litho 11 Oktombri)

2001 (10 Jan). 50th Anniv of United Nations Commissioner for Human Rights. T **158** and similar multicoloured design. P 13½.
317 6d. Type **158** 25 25
318 30d. Hands forming Globe (vert) .... 1·70 1·70

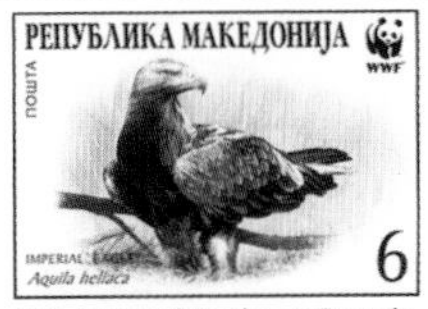

159 Imperial Eagle on Branch

001 (1 Feb). Endangered Species. The Imperial Eagle (*Aquila heliaca*). T **159** and similar horiz designs. Multicoloured. P 14.

19 6d. Type **159** ... 25 25
a. Block of 4. Nos. 319/22 ... 2·75
20 8d. With chick ... 40 40
21 10d. Flying ... 50 50
22 30d. Head ... 1·40 1·40
19/322 *Set of 4* ... 2·30 2·30

Nos. 319/22 were issued together in *se-tenant* blocks of four stamps, within sheets of eight.

160 Partenja Zografski

161 Emblem

(Des T. Pocevska. Litho 11 Oktombri)

2001 (6 Feb). 125th Death Anniv of Partenja Zografski (historian). P 13½.

23 **160** 6d. multicoloured ... 25 25

(Des V. Pulevski. Litho 11 Oktombri)

2001 (1 Mar). OBLIGATORY TAX. Anti-Cancer Week. P 13½.

24 **161** 3d. multicoloured ... 65 65

For compulsory use from 1 to 8 March.

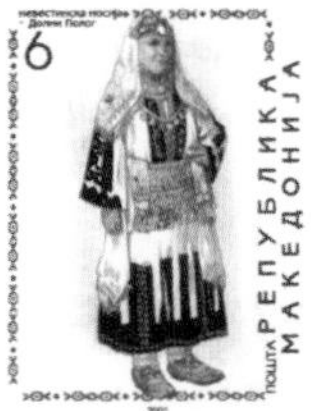

162 Woman in Costume

2001 (1 Mar). Regional Costumes. T **162** and similar vert designs. Multicoloured. P 13½.

325 6d. Type **162** ... 40 40
326 12d. Couple in costume ... 65 65
327 18d. Woman in costume ... 90 90
328 30d. Couple in costume ... 1·40 1·40
325/328 *Set of 4* ... 3·00 3·00
MS329 76×64 mm. 50d. Women working (30×30 mm). Imperf ... 2·50 2·50

163 Landscape

2001 (26 Mar). Birth Centenary of Lazar Licenoski (artist). Litho. P 13½.

330 **163** 6d. multicoloured ... 40 40

164 Text

165 Jesus and Sick Man

2001 (1 Apr). 50th Anniv of State Archives. Litho. P 13½.

331 **164** 6d. multicoloured ... 40 40

2001 (15 Apr). Easter. Litho. P 13½.

332 **165** 6d. multicoloured ... 40 40

166 Children

2001 (8 May). OBLIGATORY TAX. Red Cross Week. Litho. P 13½.

333 **166** 3d. multicoloured ... 65 65

For compulsory use from 8 to 15 May.

167 Lake and Island

2001 (16 May). Europa. Water Resources. T **167** and similar horiz design. Multicoloured. Paper with fluorescent fibres. Litho. P 13½.

334 18d. Type **167** ... 1·00 1·00
a. Pair. Nos. 334/5 ... 3·50 3·50
335 36d. Right-side of lake and island ... 2·20 2·20

Nos. 334/5 were issued together in horizontal *se-tenant* pairs within the sheet, each pair forming a composite design.

168 Dimitri Berovski (nationalist leader) and Flag

169 Man carrying Red Cross Boxes

2001 (20 May). 125th Anniversary of Razlovci Village Uprising. Litho. P 13½.

336 **168** 6d. multicoloured ... 40 40

2001 (1 June). OBLIGATORY TAX. Red Cross Week. Litho. P 13½.

337 **169** 3d. multicoloured ... 65 65

For compulsory use from 1 to 7 June.

170 Championship Emblem

171 Boats on Lake

2001 (1 June). Second Individual Chess Championship, Ohrid. Litho. P 13½.

338 **170** 36d. multicoloured ... 1·90 1·90

2001 (5 June). Environment Protection. Lake Dojran. Litho. P 13½.

339 **171** 6d. multicoloured ... 40 40

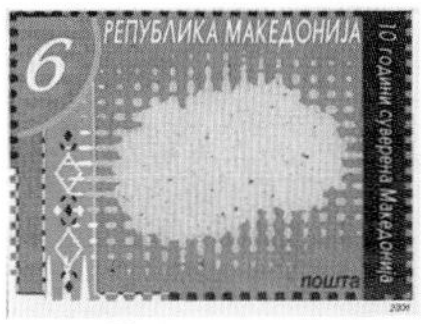

172 Emblem

2001 (8 Sept). Tenth Anniv of Independence. Litho. P 13½.

340 **172** 6d. multicoloured ... 40 40

173 Juniper (*Juniperus exelsa*)

2001 (12 Sept). Trees. T **173** and similar horiz designs. Multicoloured. Litho. P 13½.

341 6d. Type **173** ... 40 40
342 12d. Macedonian oak (*Quercus macedonica*) ... 65 65
343 24d. Strawberry tree (*Arbutus andrachne*) ... 1·20 1·20
344 36d. Kermes oak (*Quercus coccifera*) ... 1·70 1·70
341/344 *Set of 4* ... 3·50 3·50

174 Man with raised Arms

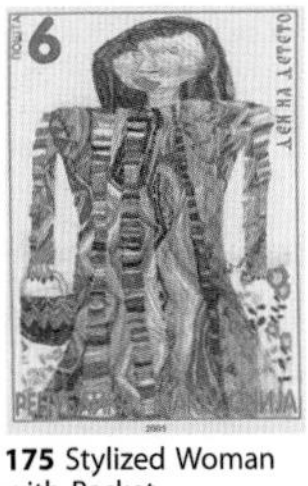

175 Stylized Woman with Basket

2001 (14 Sept). OBLIGATORY TAX. Anti-Tuberculosis Week. Litho. P 13½.

345 **174** 3d. multicoloured ... 65 65

For compulsory use from 14 to 21 September.

2001 (1 Oct). Children's Day. Litho. P 13½.

346 **175** 6d. multicoloured ... 40 40

176 Children encircling Globe

177 Fox and Cubs

(Urska Golob. Litho)

2001 (9 Oct). United Nations Year of Dialogue among Civilizations. P 13½.

347 **176** 36d. multicoloured ... 2·20 2·20

2001 (26 Oct). 75th Anniv of Zoological Museum. Litho. P 13½.

348 **177** 6d. multicoloured ... 50 50

178 Icon

179 Faces

2001 (22 Nov). Christmas. Litho. P 13½.

349 **178** 6d. multicoloured ... 50 50

2001 (1 Dec). OBLIGATORY TAX. Anti-AIDS Week. Litho. P 13½.

350 **179** 3d. multicoloured ... 65 65

For compulsory use from 1 to 7 December.

180 Alfred Nobel

2001 (10 Dec). Centenary of First Nobel Prize. Litho. P 13½.

351 **180** 36d. multicoloured ... 1·90 1·90

181 Skier

2002 (16 Jan). Winter Olympic Games, Salt Lake City, USA. T **181** and similar horiz design. Multicoloured. Litho. P 14.

352 6d. Type **181** ... 40 40
353 36d. Skier (different) ... 1·50 1·50

182 Sunrise

2002 (1 Mar). OBLIGATORY TAX. Anti-Cancer Week. Litho. P 13½.

354 **182** 3d. multicoloured ... 65 65

For compulsory use from 1 to 8 March.

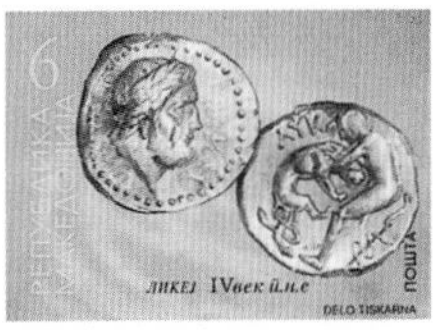

183 Likej (coin)

2002 (1 Mar). Ancient Coins. T **183** and similar horiz designs showing coins. Multicoloured. Litho. P 14.

355 6d. Type **183** ... 40 40
356 12d. Alexander III tetradrachm ... 65 65
357 24d. Lichnidos ... 1·20 1·20
358 36d. Philip II gold coin (stater) ... 1·70 1·70
355/358 *Set of 4* ... 3·50 3·50
MS359 85×62 mm. 50d. Coin ... 3·25 3·25

184 Painting and Petar Mazev

185 "The Risen Christ"

2002 (15 Apr). Artists Birth Anniversaries. T **184** and similar horiz designs. Multicoloured. Litho. P 14.

360	6d. Type **184** (75th anniv)	50	50
361	6d. Triptych, 1978 (Dimitar Kondovski, 75th anniv)	50	50
362	36d. Mona Lisa (La Gioconda) and Leonardo da Vinci (550th anniv)	1·90	1·90
360/362 *Set of 3*		2·50	2·50

2002 (24 Apr). Easter. P 14.

363	**185**	6d. multicoloured	50	50

186 Red Cross and Red Crescent Flags

2002 (8 May). OBLIGATORY TAX. Red Cross Week. Litho. P 13½.

364	**186**	3d. multicoloured	65	65

For compulsory use from 8 to 15 May.

187 Acrobat, Bicycle, Sea Lion and Ball

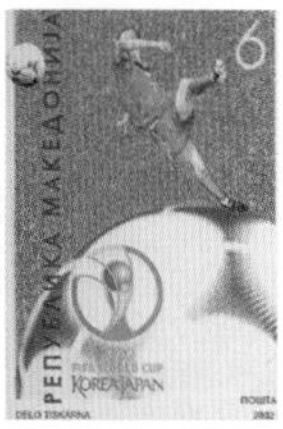

188 Championship Emblem, Ball and Player

2002 (9 May). Europa. Circus. T **187** and similar horiz design. Multicoloured. Litho. P 14.

365	6d. Type **187**	65	65
366	36d. Circles, bicycle and ball	1·90	1·90

2002 (15 May). World Cup Football Championship, Japan and South Korea. Litho. P 14.

367	**188**	6d. multicoloured	2·30	2·30

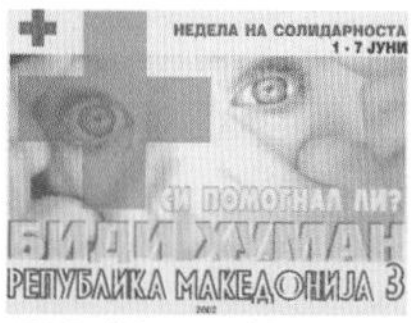

189 Red Cross and Face

2002 (1 June). OBLIGATORY TAX. Solidarity Week. Litho. P 13½.

368	**189**	3d. multicoloured	65	65

For compulsory use from 1 to 7 June.

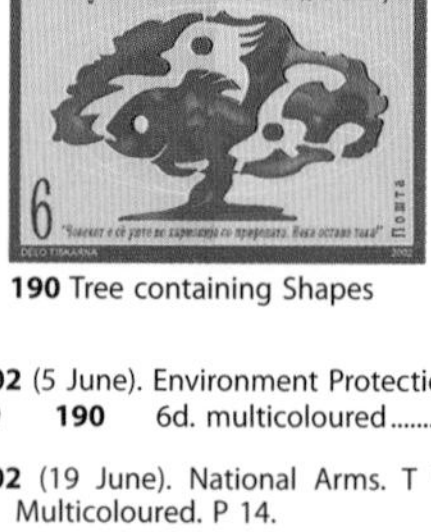

190 Tree containing Shapes

191 1595 Korenic Neonic Coat of Arms

2002 (5 June). Environment Protection. Litho. P 14.

369	**190**	6d. multicoloured	50	50

2002 (19 June). National Arms. T **191** and similar vert design. Multicoloured. P 14.

370	10d. Type **191**	65	65
371	36d. 1620 Coat of Arms	1·90	1·90

192 House, Kruševo

2002 (28 June). City Architecture. T **192** and similar horiz design. Multicoloured. Litho. P 13½.

372	36d. Type **192**	1·30	1·30
373	50d. House, Bitola	2·50	2·50

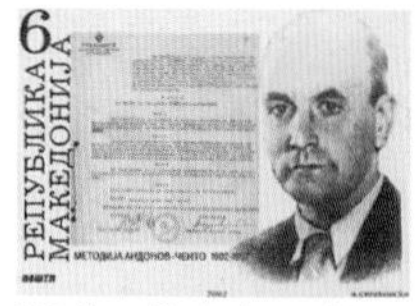

193 Metodija Andonov-Cento

194 Nikola Karev

(Des I. Stevkovski. Litho)

2002 (18 Aug). Birth Centenary of Metodija Andonov-Cento (first Macedonian president). P 13½.

374	**193**	6d. multicoloured	50	50

(Des L. Donev. Litho)

2002 (18 Aug). 125th Birth Anniv of Nikola Karev (revolutionary leader). P 13½.

375	**194**	18d. multicoloured	1·00	1·00

195 Grey Partridge (*Perdix perdix*)

(Des I. Stevkovski. Litho)

2002 (11 Sept). Fauna. T **195** and similar horiz designs. Multicoloured. P 14.

376	6d. Type **195**	25	25
	a. Block of 4. Nos. 376/9	3·50	
377	12d. Wild Pig (*Sus scrofa*)	50	50
378	24d. Chamois (*Rupicapra rupicapra*)	1·00	1·00
379	36d. Rock Partridge (*Alectoris graeca*)	1·50	1·50
376/379 *Set of 4*		3·00	3·00

Nos. 376/9 were issued in *se-tenant* blocks of four stamps within the sheet.

196 Face

2002 (14 Sept). OBLIGATORY TAX. Anti-Tuberculosis Week. Litho. P 13½.

380	**196**	3d. multicoloured	65	65

For compulsory use from 14 to 21 September.

197 House and People (child's drawing)

198 Mary and Jesus (14th-century icon)

(Des L. Zhivkovska. Litho)

2002 (1 Oct). Children's Day. P 14.

381	**197**	6d. multicoloured	50	50

2002 (20 Nov). Christmas. P 13½.

382	**198**	9d. multicoloured	50	50

199 Clock, Numbers and Face

2002 (1 Dec). OBLIGATORY TAX. Anti-AIDS Week. Litho. P 13½.

383	**199**	3d. multicoloured	65	65

For compulsory use from 1 to 7 December.

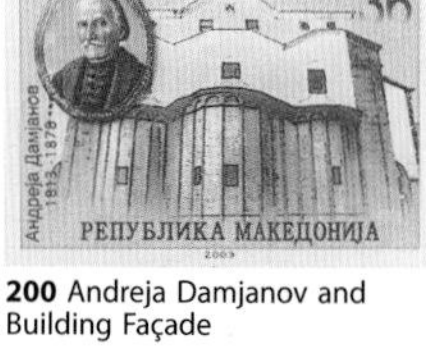

200 Andreja Damjanov and Building Façade

201 Gajga

2003 (2 Jan). 125th Death Anniv of Andreja Damjanov (architect). Litho. P 13½.

384	**200**	36d. multicoloured	1·90	1·90

2003 (18 Feb). Traditional Musical Instruments. T **201** and simila vert designs. Multicoloured. Litho. P 13½.

385	9d. Type **201**	40	4
386	10d. Tambura	40	4
387	20d. Kemene	1·30	1·3
388	50d. Tapan	2·50	2·5
385/388 *Set of 4*		4·25	4·2

202 Scouts and Campsite

203 Face surrounded by Petals

2003 (22 Feb). 50th Anniv of Scouting in Macedonia. P 13½.

389	**202**	9d. multicoloured	60	6

2003 (1 Mar). OBLIGATORY TAX. Anti-Cancer Week. Litho. P 13½.

390	**203**	4d. multicoloured	75	7

For compulsory use from 1 to 8 March.

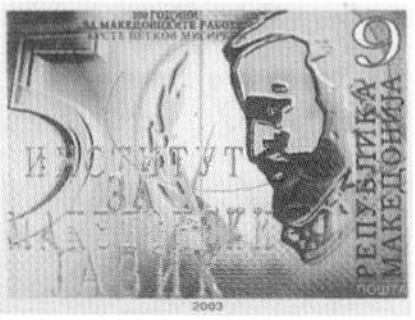

204 Krste Petkov Misirkov (founder)

205 Red Ribbon with Red Cross and Red Crescent Emblems

2003 (5 Mar). 50th Anniv of Krste Petkov Misirkov Macedonia Language Institute. P 13½.

391	**204**	9d. multicoloured	60	6

2003 (8 May). OBLIGATORY TAX. Red Cross Week. Litho. P 13½.

392	**205**	3d. multicoloured	75	7

For compulsory use from 8 to 15 May.

206 International Graphic Art Triennial, Bitola (1994)

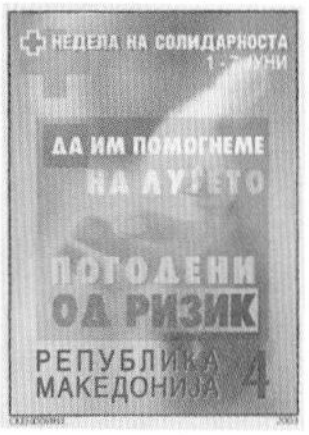

207 Outstretched Hand

2003 (9 May). Europa. Poster Art. T **206** and similar vert design Multicoloured. P 13½.

393	36d. Type **206**	2·30	2·3
394	36d. "Ohrider Sommer" (1966)	2·30	2·3

2003 (1 June). OBLIGATORY TAX. Solidarity Week. Litho. P 13½.

395	**207**	4d. multicoloured	75	75

For compulsory use from 1 to 7 June.

208 Brown Bear (*Ursus arctos*)

2003 (5 June). P 13½.

396	**208**	9d. multicoloured	60	60

2003 (16 June). City Architecture. Horiz designs as T **192**. Multicoloured. Litho. P 13½.

397	10d. House, Skopje	60	60
398	20d. House, Resen	1·20	1·20

2003 (23 June). National Arms. Vert designs as T **191**. Multicoloured. Litho. P 14.

399	9d. 17th-century arms	60	60
400	36d. 1694 Coat of Arms	2·40	2·40

209 Handball Player

210 Seal and Revolutionaries

2003 (30 July). World Youth Handball Championships. P 13½.

401	**209**	36d. multicoloured	2·30	2·30

2003 (2 Aug). Centenary of Ilinden Uprising. T **210** and similar horiz designs. Multicoloured. Litho. P 13½.

402	9d. Type **210**	60	60
403	36d. Leaders and Mechen Kamen monument	2·40	2·40
MS404	60×75 mm. 50d. Revolutionaries (different)	3·00	3·00

211 "Self Portrait" (Nikola Martinovski)

2003 (18 Aug). Artists' Anniversaries. T **211** and similar multicoloured design. Litho. P 13½.

405	9d. Type **211** (birth centenary)	60	60
406	36d. "Moulin de Galette" (Vincent van Gogh) (150th birth anniv) (horiz)	2·10	2·10

212 Stylized Figure

213 Colchicum (*Colchicum macedonicum*)

2003 (14 Sept). OBLIGATORY TAX. Anti-Tuberculosis Week. Litho. P 13½.

407	**212**	4d. multicoloured	75	75

For compulsory use from 14 to 21 September.

2003 (25 Sept). Flowers. T **213** and similar vert designs. Multicoloured. Litho. P 13½.

408	9d. Type **213**	80	80
409	20d. Viola (*Viola allchariensis*)	1·60	1·60
410	36d. *Tulipa mariannae*	2·75	2·75
411	50d. *Thymus oehmianus*	4·00	4·00
408/411	*Set of* 4	8·25	8·25

214 Said Najdeni

215 Family sheltering under Umbrella

2003 (30 Sept). Death Centenaries. T **214** and similar horiz design. Multicoloured. P 13½.

412	9d. Type **214** (Albanian writer and reformer)	70	70
413	9d. Jeronim de Rada (Italian-Albanian writer)	70	70

(Des L. Zhivkovska. Litho)

2003 (6 Oct). Children's Day. P 13½.

414	**215**	9d. multicoloured	1·00	1·00

216 Seal and Armed Revolutionaries

2003 (17 Oct). 125th of Kresna Uprising. Litho. P 13½.

415	**216**	9d. multicoloured	1·00	1·00

217 Dimitir Vlahov

2003 (8 Nov). 50th Death Anniv of Dimitir Vlahov (politician). Litho. P 13½.

416	**217**	9d. multicoloured	1·00	1·00

218 Mary and Jesus (fresco)

219 Ribbon

2003 (19 Nov). Christmas. Litho. P 13½.

417	**218**	9d. multicoloured	1·00	1·00

2003 (1 Dec). OBLIGATORY TAX. Anti-AIDS Week. Litho. P 13½.

418	**219**	4d. scarlet vermilion	1·00	1·00

For compulsory use from 1 to 7 December.

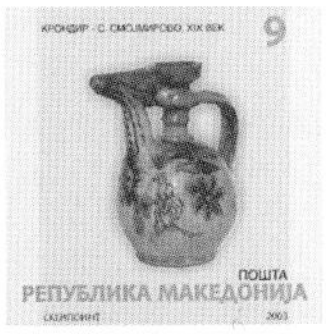

220 19th-century Jug, Smojmirovo

2003 (16 Dec)–**06**. Cultural Artifacts. T **220** and similar horiz designs. Multicoloured. Litho. P 13½.

419	3d. Amphora (4.6.04)	40	40
420	3d. 18th–19th century lidded jug (p 13) (30.8.06)	40	40
421	4d. 19th century coffee pot (horiz) (p 13) (30.11.06)	50	50
422	5d. Tassel, Vrutok (25.1.04)	60	60
423	5d. 20th century circular flask (p 13) (30.11.06)	60	60
424	6d. 18th–19th century jug and ewer (p 13) (30.8.06)	70	70
425	9d. Type **220**	80	80
426	10d. Kettle, Ohrid (20.1.04)	80	80
427	10d. 18th century hand-bell (p 13) (30.11.06)	80	80
428	12d. Albastron (alabaster incense pot) (4.6.04)	1·00	1·00
429	12d. 18th–19th century pot with cover (p 13) (30.11.06)	1·40	1·40
430	20d. Chest decoration, Galicnik (25.1.04)	2·30	2·30
419/430	*Set of* 12	9·25	9·25

Numbers have been left for additions to this series.

221 Wilbur and Orville Wright and Wright *Flyer*

2003 (17 Dec). Centenary of Powered Flight. P 13½.

440	**221**	50d. multicoloured	3·75	3·75

222 Street Scene (Tomo Vladimirski)

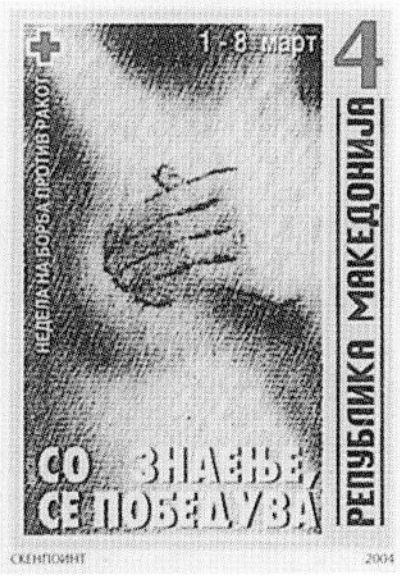

223 Breast Examination

2004 (14 Feb). Artists' Birth Centenaries. T **222** and similar multicoloured design. Litho. P 13½.

441	9d. Type **222**	65	65
442	9d. Ohrid Street (Vangel Kodzoman)	65	65

2004 (1 Mar). OBLIGATORY TAX. Anti-Cancer Week. Litho. P 13½.

443	**223**	4d. multicoloured	1·00	1·00

For compulsory use from 1 to 8 March.

224 Knives and Armour

225 Carpet

2004 (10 Mar). Cultural Heritage. Weapons. T **224** and similar vert designs. Multicoloured. Litho. P 13½.

444	10d. Type **224**	1·00	1·00
445	20d. 19th-century sword	1·80	1·80
446	36d. 18th-century pistol	2·75	2·75
447	50d. 18th-century rifle	3·75	3·75
444/447	*Set of* 4	8·50	8·50

2004 (24 Mar). Traditional Carpets. T **225** and similar vert design. Multicoloured. Litho. P 13½.

448	36d. Type **225**	2·50	2·50
449	50d. Carpet (different)	3·75	3·75

226 Kostandin Kristoforidhi (writer)

227 House, Kratovo

2004 (19 Apr). Centenary of Publication of First Albanian Dictionary in Macedonia. Litho. P 13½.

450	**226**	36d. multicoloured	2·50	2·50

2004 (23 Apr). City Architecture. Litho. P 13½.

451	**227**	20d. multicoloured	1·50	1·50

228 Parasol and Woman Reading

229 Profiles

2004 (7 May). Europa. Holidays. T **228** and similar vert design. Multicoloured. P 13½.

452	50d. Type **228**	3·50	3·50
	a. Pair. Nos. 452/3	7·25	7·25
453	50d. Yacht and island	3·50	3·50

Nos. 452/3 were issued in *se-tenant* pairs within the sheet, each pair forming a composite design of a beach scene.

2004 (8 May). OBLIGATORY TAX. Red Cross Week. Litho. P 13½.

454	**229**	4d. multicoloured	1·00	1·00

For compulsory use from 8 to 15 May.

230 Stars

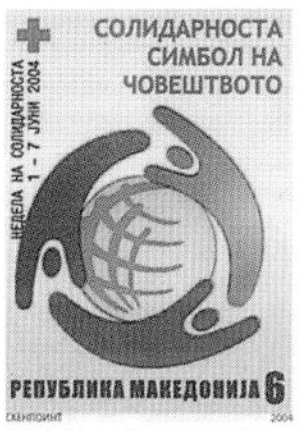

231 Hands enclosing Globe

2004 (9 May). Application to join European Union. Litho. P 13½.

455	**230**	36d. multicoloured	2·50	2·50

2004 (1 June). OBLIGATORY TAX. Solidarity Week. Litho. P 13½.

456	**231**	6d. multicoloured	1·00	1·00

For compulsory use from 1 to 7 June.

232 Pelican and Lake

233 Flags as Interlocking Rings

2004 (5 June). Prespa National Park. Litho. P 13½.

457	**232**	36d. multicoloured	2·50	2·50

2004 (16 June). Olympic Games, Athens. T **233** and similar horiz design. Multicoloured. P 13½.

458	50d. Type **233**	3·50	3·50
	a. Pair. Nos. 458/9	7·25	7·25
459	50d. Rings (different)	3·50	3·50

Nos. 458/9 were issued in horizontal *se-tenant* pairs within the sheet, each pair forming a composite design of Olympic rings.

234 Sami Frasheri

235 Emblem, Feet and Ball

2004 (18 June). Death Centenary of Sami Frasheri (Albanian writer). Litho. P 13½.
460 **234** 12d. multicoloured .... 1·00 1·00

2004 (3 July). Centenary of FIFA (Fédèration Internationale de Football Association). Litho. P 13½.
461 **235** 100d. multicoloured .... 7·25 7·25

236 Marko Cepenkov

2004 (1 Sept). Anniversaries. T **236** and similar multicoloured design. Litho. P 13½.
462 12d. Type **236** (writer) (175th birth) .... 1·00 1·00
463 12d. Vasil Glavinov (politician) (75th death) (vert) .... 1·00 1·00

237 Child blowing Bubbles

238 Bohemian Waxwing (*Bombycilla garrulous*)

2004 (14 Sept). OBLIGATORY TAX. Anti-Tuberculosis Week. Litho. P 13½.
464 **237** 4d. multicoloured .... 1·00 1·00
For compulsory use from 14 to 21 September.

2004 (25 Sept). Birds. T **238** and similar vert designs. Multicoloured. Litho. P 13½.
465 12d. Type **238** .... 1·00 1·00
466 24d. Woodchat shrike (*Lanius senator*) .... 2·10 2·10
467 36d. Rock thrush (*Monticola saxatilis*) .... 2·75 2·75
468 48d. Northern bullfinch (*Pyrrhula pyrrhula*) .... 4·00 4·00
465/468 *Set of* 4 .... 8·75 8·75
MS469 86×61 mm. 60d. Wall creeper (*Tichodroma muraria*). Imperf .... 4·50 4·50

239 Children

240 Binary Code

2004 (4 Oct). Children's Day. Litho. P 13½.
470 **239** 12d. multicoloured .... 1·00 1·00

2004 (16 Oct). World Summit on Information Technology Society (WSIS). Litho. P 13½.
471 **240** 36d. multicoloured .... 2·50 2·50

241 Manuscript

2004 (27 Oct). Millenary of Publication of Asseman Gospel (Glagolitic (early Slavonic language) liturgical gospel). Litho. P 13½.
472 **241** 12d. multicoloured .... 1·00 1·00

242 Marco Polo

243 Star, Ribbons, Snowflakes and Holly

2004 (10 Nov). 750th Birth Anniv of Marco Polo (traveller). Litho. P 13½.
473 **242** 36d. multicoloured .... 2·50 2·50

2004 (24 Nov). Christmas. Litho. P 13½.
474 **243** 12d. multicoloured .... 1·00 1·00

244 Hands

245 Konstantin Miladinov

2004 (1 Dec). OBLIGATORY TAX. Anti-AIDS Week. Litho. P 13½.
475 **244** 6d. multicoloured .... 1·00 1·00
For compulsory use from 1 to 7 December.

2005 (4 Feb). 175th Birth Anniv of Konstantin Miladinov (writer). Litho. P 13½.
476 **245** 36d. multicoloured .... 2·50 2·50

246 Ash Tray

247 Manuscript (16th—17th century)

2005 (1 Mar). OBLIGATORY TAX. Anti-Cancer Week. Litho. P 13½.
477 **246** 6d. multicoloured .... 1·00 1·00
For compulsory use from 1 to 8 March.

2005 (9 Mar). Illuminated Manuscripts. T **247** and similar vert designs. Multicoloured. Litho. P 13½.
478 12d. Type **247** .... 1·00 1·00
479 24d. Illustration (16th century) .... 1·80 1·80

248 Embroidered Cloth (19th century)

2005 (9 Mar). Embroidery. T **248** and similar horiz design. Multicoloured. Litho. P 13½.
480 36d. Type **248** .... 2·50 2·50
481 50d. Embroidery (20th century) .... 3·75 3·75

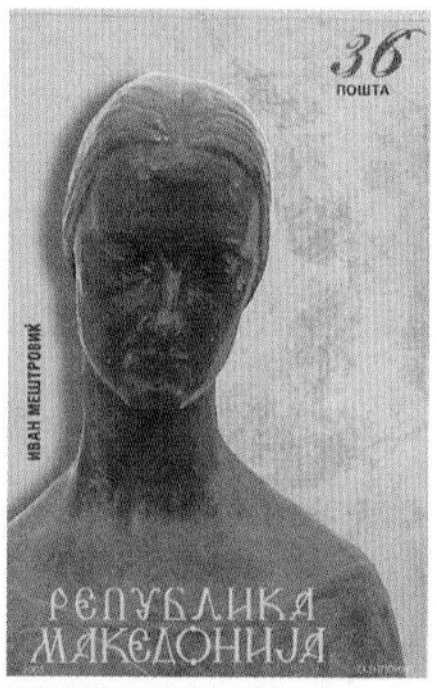

249 Woman's Head (sculpture) (Ivan Mestrovic)

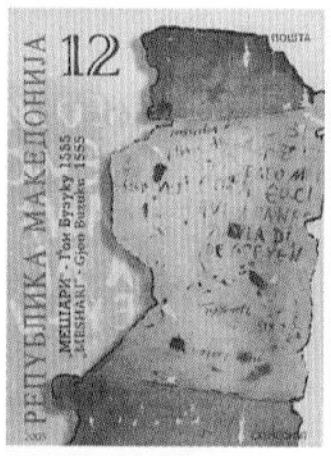

250 Fragment

2005 (6 Apr). Art. T **249** and similar multicoloured design. Litho. P 13½.
482 36d. Type **249** .... 2·50 2·50
483 50d. Portrait of Woman (painting) (Paja Jovanovic) (horiz) .... 3·75 3·75

2005 (27 Apr). 450th Anniv of *The Missal* by Gjon Buzuku (first book written and published in Albanian). Litho. P 13½.
484 **250** 12d. multicoloured .... 1·00 1·00

251 Skanderbeg

252 Henry Dunant (Red Cross founder)

2005 (27 Apr). 600th Birth Anniv of Gjergj Kastrioti (Skanderbeg) (Albanian leader). Litho. P 13½.
485 **251** 36d. multicoloured .... 2·50 2·50

2004 (8 May). OBLIGATORY TAX. Red Cross Week. Litho. P 13½.
486 **252** 6d. multicoloured .... 1·00 1·00
For compulsory use from 8 to 15 May.

253 Grain, Cake and Bread

2005 (9 May). Europa. Gastronomy. T **253** and similar horiz design. Multicoloured. Litho. P 13½.
487 36d. Type **253** .... 2·50 2·50
a. Horiz pair. Nos. 487/8 .... 6·75 6·75
488 60d. Roasted meat with peppers .... 4·00 4·00
Nos. 487/8 were issued in horizontal *se-tenant* pairs within the sheet.

254 Building and Script

2005 (23 May). Centenary of National Day of Vlachs (Aromanians) (imperial decree, issued by Ottoman Sultan Abdual Hamid II, which gave Vlachs their first collective rights). Litho. P 13½.
489 **254** 12d. multicoloured .... 1·00 1·00

No. 490 and Type **255** have been left for "OBLIGATORY TAX. Solidarity Week" issued 1 June not yet received.

256 Globe as Tree

257 Figure (16th century)

2005 (5 June). Environmental Protection. Litho. P 13½.
491 **256** 36d. multicoloured .... 2·50 2·50

2005 (8 June). Carvings. T **257** and similar vert designs. Multicoloured. Litho. P 13½.
492 3d. Type **257** 20 20
493 4d. Ten-sided stars shape (15th century) 40 40
494 6d. Winged serpents (16th century) 60 60
495 8d. Diamond shaped design (1883—4) 80 80
496 12d. Figure, snake and animals (16th century) .... 1·00 1·00
492/496 *Set of* 5 .... 2·75 2·75

258 Ford (1905)

2005 (15 June). Transport Anniversaries. T **258** and similar horiz design. Multicoloured. Litho. P 13½.
497 12d. Type **258** (centenary of first car) .... 1·00 1·00
498 36d. Glider (50th anniv of Macedonia aircraft) .... 2·50 2·50

259 Albert Einstein and Emblem

260 Cross of Lorraine

2005 (30 June). International Year of Physics. Centenary of Publication of "Theory of Special Relativity". Litho. P 13½.
499 **259** 60d. multicoloured .... 4·50 4·50

2005 (14 Sept). OBLIGATORY TAX. Anti-Tuberculosis Week. Litho. P 13½.
500 **260** 6d. multicoloured .... 1·00 1·00
For compulsory use from 14 to 21 September.

261 *Malus* (apples)

262 Smolarski Waterfall

2005 (14 Sept). Fruit. T **261** and similar multicoloured designs. P 13½.

501	12d. Type **261**	1·00	1·00
502	24d. *Prunus persica* (peaches)	2·10	2·10
503	36d. *Prunus avium*	3·00	3·00
504	48d. *Prunus* (plums)	3·75	3·75
501/504 *Set of 4*		8·75	8·75
MS505	97×65 mm. 100d. *Pyrus* (pears) (vert)	7·25	7·25

2005 (14 Sept). Litho. P 13½.
506 **262** 24d. multicoloured 1·80 1·80

263 Hans Christian Andersen

2005 (3 Oct). Birth Bicentenary of Hans Christian Andersen (writer). Litho. P 13½.
507 **263** 12d. multicoloured 1·00 1·00

264 Kozjak Dam

2005 (25 Oct). Litho. P 13½.
508 **264** 12d. multicoloured 1·00 1·00

265 "1880—8"

266 Delegates

2005 (25 Oct). 125th Anniv of Brsjai Rebellion. Litho. P 13½.
509 **265** 12d. multicoloured 1·00 1·00

2005 (28 Oct). Centenary of Rila Congress. Litho. P 13½.
510 **266** 12d. multicoloured 1·00 1·00

267 2002 36d. Stamp (as Type **187**)

268 Candle

2005 (14 Nov). 50th Anniv of Europa Stamps. T **267** and similar horiz designs. Multicoloured. Litho. P 13½.

511	60d. Type **267**	4·00	4·00
	a. Block of 4. Nos. 511/14	55·00	
512	170d. 1999 30d. stamp (as Type **122**)	11·50	11·50
513	250d. 1997 20d. stamp (as Type **85**)	17·00	17·00
514	350d. 1996 40d. stamp (as No. **153**)	24·00	24·00
511/514 *Set of 4*		50·00	50·00
MS515	66×132 mm. Nos. 511/14	80·00	80·00

Nos. 511/14 were issued in *se-tenant* blocks of four stamps within the sheet.

2005 (23 Nov). Christmas. Litho. P 13½.
516 **268** 12d. multicoloured 1·00 1·00

269 White Water Kayaking

270 Hand holding Condom

2005 (23 Nov). Litho. P 13½.
517 **269** 36d. multicoloured 2·75 2·75

2005 (1 Dec). OBLIGATORY TAX. Anti-AIDS Week. Litho. P 13½.
518 **270** 6d. multicoloured 1·00 1·00
For compulsory use from 1 to 7 December.

271 Postal Emblem

272 Skier

2005 (14 Dec). Litho. P 13½.
519 **271** 12d. multicoloured 1·00 1·00

2006 (25 Jan). Winter Olympic Games, Turin. T **272** and similar vert design. Multicoloured. Litho. P 13½.

520	36d. Type **272**	2·50	2·50
521	60d. Ice hockey player	4·00	4·00

273 Woman examining Breast

274 Fresco, Monastic Church, Matejce

2006 (1 Mar). OBLIGATORY TAX. Anti-Cancer Week. Litho. P 13½.
522 **273** 6d. multicoloured 1·00 1·00
For compulsory use from 1 to 8 March.

2006 (8 Mar). Cultural Heritage. T **274** and similar vert design. Multicoloured. Litho. P 13½.

523	12d. Type **274**	80	80
524	24d. Isaac Celebi Mosque, Bitola	1·60	1·60

275 Leopold Senghor

276 Wooden Pattens

2006 (20 Mar). Birth Centenary of Leopold Sedar Senghor (Senegalese politician). Litho. P 13½.
525 **275** 36d. multicoloured 2·75 2·75

2006 (22 Mar). Craftwork. Mother of Pearl Inlays. T **276** and similar vert design. Multicoloured. Litho. P 13½.

526	12d. Type **276**	1·00	1·00
527	24d. Pipes	2·10	2·10

277 Woodcarving, Church of the Holy Saviour, Skopje

2006 (5 Apr). Birth Bicentenary of Makarie Negriev Frckovski. Litho. P 13½.
528 **277** 12d. multicoloured 1·00 1·00

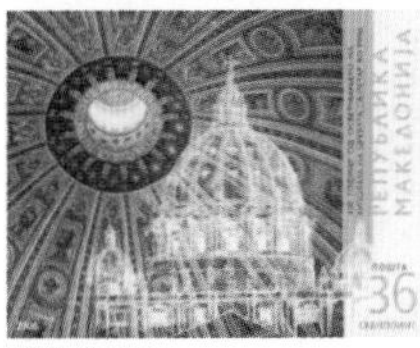

278 Cupola

279 Zhivko Firkov

2006 (5 Apr). 450th Anniv of Cupola, Church of St Peter, Rome. P 13½.
529 **278** 36d. multicoloured 2·75 2·75

2006 (26 Apr). Birth Centenary of Zhivko Firkov (composer). P 13½.
530 **279** 24d. multicoloured 1·80 1·80

280 Mozart, Score and Violins

281 Stylized Figure

2006 (26 Apr). 250th Birth Anniv of Wolfgang Amadeus Mozart (composer). P 13½.
531 **280** 60d. multicoloured 4·50 4·50

2006 (8 May). OBLIGATORY TAX. Red Cross Week. Litho. P 13½.
532 **281** 6d. multicoloured 1·00 1·00
For compulsory use from 8 to 15 May.

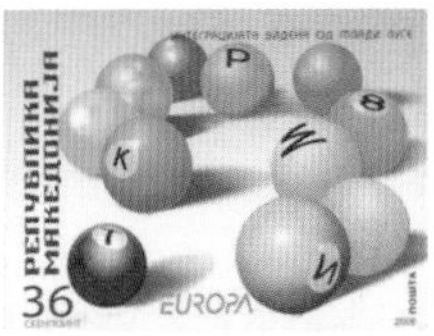

282 Coloured Balls

283 Pope John Paul II

2006 (9 May). Europa. Integration. T **282** and similar vert design. Multicoloured. Litho. P 13½.

533	36d. Type **282**	2·50	2·50
534	60d. Coloured building blocks	4·50	4·50

2006 (9 May). Tenth Anniv of Europa Stamps in Macedonia. Sheet 80×70 mm containing T **283** and similar vert design. Multicoloured. Litho. P 13½.
MS535 60d.×2, Type **283**; Mother Teresa 8·75 8·75

284 Greenery running to Sand through Hourglass

2006 (5 June). International Year of Deserts and Desertification. Litho. P 13½.
536 **284** 12d. multicoloured 1·00 1·00

285 Chequered Flag

2006 (14 June). Centenary of Grand Prix Motor Race. Litho. P 13½.
537 **285** 36d. multicoloured 2·75 2·75

286 Nikola Tesla

2006 (28 June). 150th Birth Anniv of Nikola Tesla (inventor). Litho. P 13½.
538 **286** 24d. multicoloured 1·80 1·80

287 *Santa Maria*

288 *Ancylus scalariformis*

2006 (28 June). 500th Death Anniv of Christopher Columbus. Litho. P 13½.
539 **287** 36d. multicoloured 2·75 2·75

2006 (6 Sept). Shells. T **288** and similar vert designs. Multicoloured. Litho. P 13½.

540	12d. Type **288**	1·10	1·10
541	24d. *Macedopyrgula pavlovici*	2·00	2·00
542	36d. *Gyraulus trapezoides*	3·00	3·00
543	48d. *Valvata hirsutecostata*	4·00	4·00

540/543 *Set of 4* ... 9·00 9·00
MS544 80×70 mm. 72d. *Ochridopyrgula macedonica* ... 5·75 5·75

289 Child

290 Girl drawing

2006 (14 Sept). OBLIGATORY TAX. Anti-Tuberculosis Week. Litho. P 13½.
545 **289** 6d. multicoloured ... 1·00 1·00
For compulsory use from 14 to 21 September.

2006 (2 Oct). 60th Anniv of UNICEF. Litho. P 13½.
546 **290** 12d. multicoloured ... 1·00 1·00

291 National Park, Galicica

2006 (2 Oct). Litho. P 13½.
547 **291** 24d. multicoloured ... 1·80 1·80

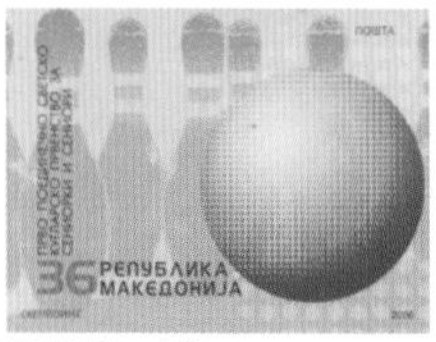

292 Ball and Pins

293 Frang Bardhi (author of the first Albanian dictionary)

2006 (20 Oct). World Ten-Pin Bowling Championship, Skopje. Litho. P 13½.
548 **292** 36d. multicoloured ... 2·75 2·75

2006 (25 Oct). Personalities. T **293** and similar vert designs. Multicoloured. Litho. P 13½.
549 12d. Type **293** ... 90 90
550 24d. Boris Trajkovski (president, 1999—2004) ... 90 90
551 36d. Mustafa Kemel Attaturk (founder of Turkish Republic) ... 2·00 2·00
552 48d. Dositheus II (Metropolitan of Macedonia) ... 2·00 2·00
549/552 *Set of 4* ... 5·25 5·25

294 Stars

2006 (22 Nov). Christmas. Litho. P 13½.
553 **294** 12d. multicoloured ... 1·00 1·00

295 Emblem

296 Carved Stone

2006 (1 Dec). OBLIGATORY TAX. Anti-AIDS Week. Litho. P 13½.
554 **295** 6d. multicoloured ... 1·00 1·00
For compulsory use from 1 to 7 December.

2007 (31 Jan). Kokino Megalithic Observatory. T **296** and similar vert design. Multicoloured. Litho. P 13½.
555 12d. Type **296** ... 90 90
556 36d. Sunrise ... 2·75 2·75

297 Slivnik Monastery (400th anniv)

2007 (31 Jan). Monasteries' Anniversaries. T **297** and multicoloured design. Litho. P 13½.
557 12d. Type **297** ... 90 90
558 36d. St. Nikita (700th anniv) (vert) ... 2·75 2·75

298 18th—19th century Metal Cap

2007 (14 Feb). Crafts. T **298** and horiz design. Multicoloured. Litho. P 13½.
559 12d. Type **297** ... 90 90
560 36d. 19th century decorated box ... 2·75 2·75

299 *Cobitis vardarensis*

(Des I. Stefkovski. Litho)

2006 (28 Feb). Fish. T **299** and horiz design. Multicoloured. P 13½.
561 12d. Type **299** ... 1·10 1·10
562 36d. *Zingel balcanicus* ... 2·75 2·75
563 60d. *Chondrostoma vardarense* ... 4·50 4·50
564 100d. *Barbus macedonicus* ... 7·50 7·50
561/564 *Set of 4* ... 14·50 14·50
MS565 60×71 mm. 100d. *Leuciscus cephalus* ... 7·50 7·50

299a Woman

300 "Epos of Freedom" (mosaic, detail) (Borko Lazeski)

2007 (1 Mar). OBLIGATORY TAX. Anti-Cancer Week. Litho. P 13½.
565a **299a** 6d. multicoloured ... 1·00 1·00
For compulsory use from 1 to 8 March.

(Des I. Stefkovski. Litho)

2007 (14 Mar). Art. Centenary of Cubism. T **300** and similar multicoloured design. Litho. P 13½.
566 36d. Type **300** ... 2·75 2·75
567 100d. "Head of a Woman" (Pablo Picasso) (vert) ... 7·50 7·50

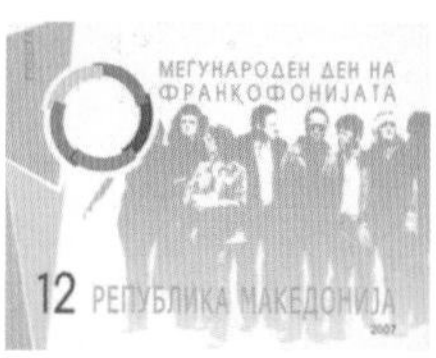

301 Emblem and People talking

302 Cat

(Des I. Stefkovski. Litho)

2007 (20 Mar). International Day of Francophonie (organization of French speaking communities). P 13½.
568 **301** 12d. multicoloured ... 1·00 1·00

(Des G. Boev. Litho)

2007 (9 Apr). Pets. P 13½.
569 **302** 12d. multicoloured ... 1·00 1·00

302a Hands and Globe

303 Camp

2007 (8 May). OBLIGATORY TAX. Red Cross Week. Litho. P 13½.
569a **302a** 6d. multicoloured ... 1·00 1·00
For compulsory use from 8 to 15 May.

(Des I. Stefkovski. Litho)

2006 (9 May). Europa. Centenary of Scouting. T **303** and similar multicoloured designs. P 13½.
570 60d. Type **303** ... 5·00 5·00
571 100d. Scout (vert) ... 7·75 7·75
MS572 60×70 mm. 160d. Emblem ... 32·00 32·00

303a Fresco, Basilica of San Clemente (detail)

(Des Igor Stevkovski)

2007 (23 May). 150th Anniv of Discovery of St. Cyril's Grave. P 13½.
572a **303a** 50d. multicoloured ... 1·00 1·00

304 Globe, Chimneys and Clock

305 Dimitri Ivanovich Mendeleev

(Des I. Najdenovski Litho)

2007 (5 June). Pollution Awareness. P 13½.
573 **304** 12d. multicoloured ... 1·00 1·00

(Des M. Georgievski. Litho)

2007 (20 June). Scientific Personalities. T **305** and similar multicoloured design. P 13½.
574 36d. Type **305** (chemist and creator of first periodic tables) (death centenary) ... 3·00 3·00
575 36d. Carl von Linné (Linnaeus) (scientist and plant and animal classification deviser) (300th birth anniv) (vert) ... 3·00 3·00

306 NATO and EPAC Emblems

307 Yachts

(Des L. Zivkovska Donev. Litho)

2007 (28 June). Euro—Atlantic Security Forum, Ohrid. P 13½.
576 **306** 60d. multicoloured ... 5·50 5·50

(Des I. Stevkovski. Litho)

2007 (31 July). Centenary of Yacht Racing Union. P 13½.
577 **307** 36d. multicoloured ... 3·00 3·00

308 Child and Dandelion

309 Maminska River Waterfall

2007 (14 Sept). OBLIGATORY TAX. Anti-Tuberculosis Week. Litho. P 13½.
578 **308** 6d. multicoloured ... 1·00 1·00
For compulsory use from 14 to 21 September.

(Des L. Zivkovska Donev. Litho)

2007 (19 Sept). Natural Heritage. P 13½.
579 **309** 12d. multicoloured ... 1·00 1·00

310 Dhimitër Pasko (Mitrush Kuteli)

(Des I. Stevkovski. Litho)

2007 (25 Sept). Personalities. T **310** and similar vert design. Multicoloured. P 13½.
580 12d. Type **310** (writer) (birth centenary) ... 1·00 1·00
581 12d. Theofan (Fan) Stilian Noli (nationalist) (125th birth anniv) ... 1·00 1·00

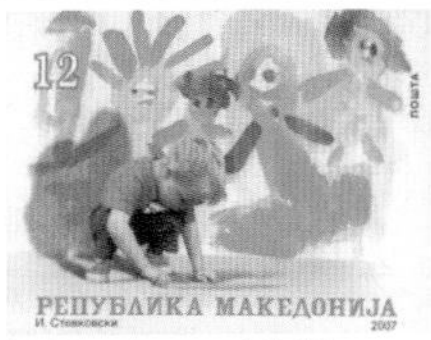

311 Drawings and Child

312 Sputnik

(Des I. Stevkovski. Litho)

2007 (1 Oct). Children's Day. P 13½.
582 **311** 12d. multicoloured .... 1·00 1·00

(Des I. Stevkovski. Litho)

2007 (4 Oct). 50th Anniv of Space Exploration. P 13½.
583 **312** 36d. multicoloured .... 3·00 3·00

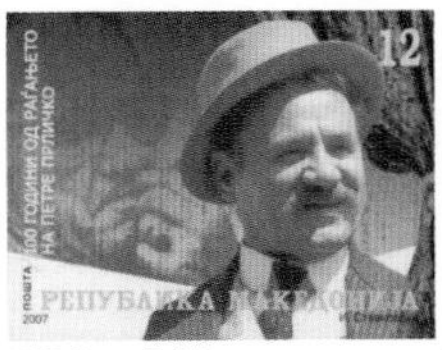

313 Petre Prlicko

314 Jordan Dzinot

(Des I. Stevkovski. Litho)

2007 (31 Oct). Petre Prlicko (actor) Commemoration. P 13½.
584 **313** 12d. multicoloured .... 1·00 1·00

(Des L. Zivkovska Donev. Litho)

2007 (31 Oct). Jordan Hadzi-Konstantinov Dzinot (educator) Commemoration. P 13½.
585 **314** 12d. multicoloured .... 1·00 1·00

315 Textile

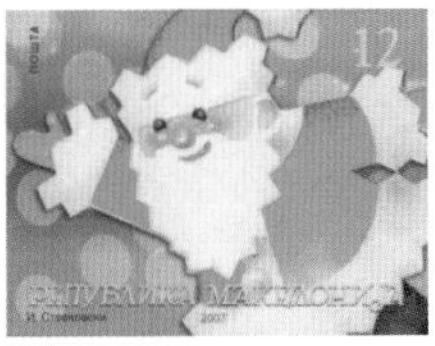

316 Santa Claus

(Des L. Zivkovska Donev)

2007 (9 Nov). P 13½.
586 **315** 12d. multicoloured .... 1·00 1·00

(Des I. Stevkovski. Litho)

2007 (21 Nov). Christmas. P 13½.
587 **316** 12d. multicoloured .... 1·00 1·00

317 AIDS Ribbon

318 Tose Proeski

2007 (1 Dec). OBLIGATORY TAX. Anti-AIDS Week. Litho. P 13½.
588 **317** 6d. multicoloured .... 1·00 1·10
For compulsory use from 1 to 7 December.

(Des D. Moraitov and I. Stevkovski)

2007 (15 Dec). Tose Proeski (singer) Commemoration. P 13½.
589 **318** 12d. multicoloured .... 1·00 1·00

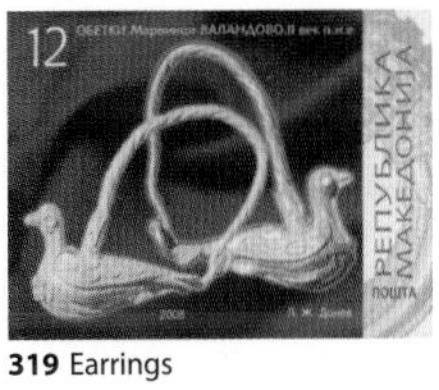

319 Earrings

(Des L. Zivkovska Donev)

2008 (23 Jan). Cultural Heritage. Jewellery. T **319** and similar multicoloured design. P 13½.
590 12d. Type **319** .... 1·00 1·00
591 24d. Lion headed earring (vert) .... 2·00 2·00

No. 592 and Type **320** have been left for '50th Anniv of Space Exploration', issued on 31 January 2008, not yet received.

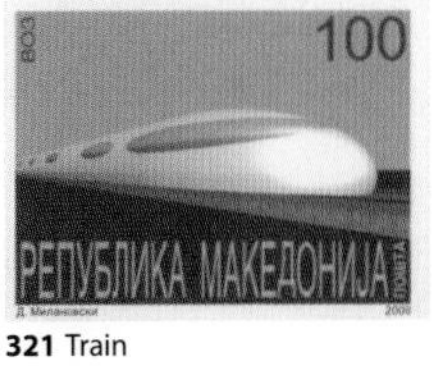

321 Train

(Des D. Milanovski)

2008 (27 Feb). Transportation. P 13½.
593 **321** 100d. multicoloured .... 7·50 7·50

322 Child and Cigarette

2008 (1 Mar). OBLIGATORY TAX. Anti-Cancer Week. Litho. P 13½.
594 **322** 6d. multicoloured .... 1·00 1·00
For compulsory use from 1 to 8 March.

323 Hoopoe

(Des Igor Stevkovski)

2008 (28 Mar). Hoopoe (*Upupa epops*). T **323** and similar horiz designs. Multicoloured. P 13½.
595 12d. Type **323** .... 1·00 1·00
a. Block of 4. Nos. 595/8 .... 12·50
596 24d. Head .... 2·00 2·00
597 48d. Facing left .... 3·75 3·75
598 60d. Facing right .... 5·00 5·00
595/598 *Set of* 4 .... 10·50 10·50
Nos. 595/8 were issued in *se-tenant* blocks of four stamps within the sheet.

324 Bull Dog

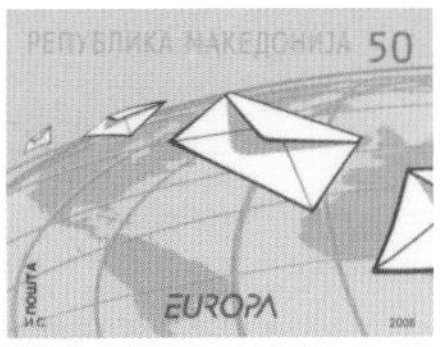

325 Envelope and Globe

(Des Igor Stevkovski)

2008 (16 Apr). Pets. P 13½.
599 **324** 30d. multicoloured .... 2·30 2·30

(Des Igor Stevkovski)

2008 (2 May). Europa. The Letter. T **325** and similar horiz designs. Multicoloured, background colours given. P 13½.
600 50d. Type **325** .... 1·20 1·20
a. Pair. Nos. 600/1 .... 2·50 2·50
b. Booklet pane. Nos. 600/3 .... 5·00
601 50d. Envelopes and globe .... 1·20 1·20
602 50d. As Type **325** (cobalt) .... 1·20 1·20
a. Pair. Nos. 602/3 .... 2·50 2·50
603 50d. As No. 601 (cobalt) .... 1·20 1·20
604 50d. As Type **325** (deep grey-blue) .... 1·20 1·20
a. Pair. Nos. 604/5 .... 3·75 3·75
605 100d. As No. 601 (deep grey-blue) .... 2·40 2·40
600/605 *Set of* 6 .... 7·50 7·50
Nos. 600/1, 602/3 and 604/5, respectively were printed in horizontal *se-tenant* pairs, each pair forming a composite design.
The booklet pane No. 600b has blue margins.

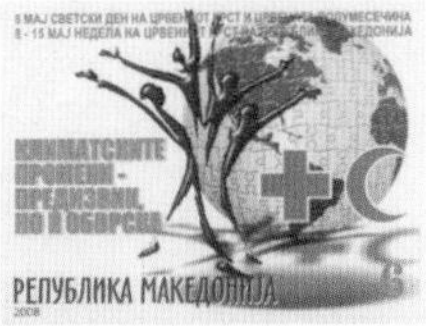

326 Stylized Figures and Globe as Jigsaw Puzzle

327 Robert Schuman (one of founders of EU)

2008 (8 May). OBLIGATORY TAX. Red Cross Week. Litho. P 13½.
606 **326** 6d. multicoloured .... 1·00 1·00
For compulsory use from 8 to 15 May.

(Des I. Stevkovski. Litho)

2008 (22 May). European Union. T **327** and similar multicoloured designs. P 13½.
607 36d. Type **327** .... 3·00 3·00
608 50d. Eiffel Tower (horiz) .... 4·00 4·00
609 50d. Ljubljana (horiz) .... 4·00 4·00
607/609 *Set of* 3 .... 10·00 10·00

328 Cupped Hands and Water

329 Rudolf Diesel

(Des I. Stevkovski. Litho)

2008 (5 June). Environmental Protection. P 13½.
610 **328** 12d. multicoloured .... 3·75 3·75

(Des I. Stevkovski. Litho)

2008 (18 June). 150th Birth Anniv of Rudolf Diesel (German engineer and inventor of the diesel engine). P 13½.
611 **329** 30d. multicoloured .... 8·00 8·00

330 Sailing

(Des M. Micova)

2008 (25 June). Olympic Games, Beijing. T **330** and similar horiz designs showing stylized athletes. Multicoloured. P 13½.
612 12d. Type **330** .... 3·75 3·75
613 18d. Gymnastics .... 5·75 5·75
614 20d. Tennis .... 6·00 6·00
615 36d. Equestrian .... 6·50 6·50
612/615 *Set of* 4 .... 20·00 20·00

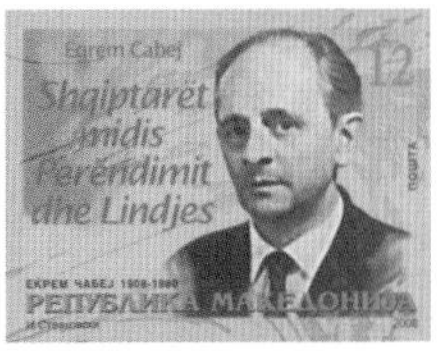

331 Eqrem Cabej

(Des I. Stevkovski. Litho)

2008 (6 Aug). Birth Centenary of Eqrem Cabej. P 13½.
616 **331** 12d. multicoloured .... 3·75 3·75

Montenegro

1874. 100 Novcic = 1 Florin
1900. 100 Heller = 1 Krone
1907. 100 Para = 1 Krone
1910. 100 Para = 1 Perper
2003. 100 Cents = 1 Euro

Montenegro became independent under the name Crna Gora (the Black Mountain) in 1452.

Nicholas I, Prince, 14 August 1860–28 August 1910
King, 28 August 1910–26 November 1918

PRINTERS. All stamps of Montenegro were printed at the State Printing Works, Vienna.

1 Prince Nicholas

(2)

1874–98. Typo.

I. Wmk "BRIEF-MARKEN" in double-lined capitals, in one line, across the middle of a double-width sheet. Measures 428 mm.

(a) Medium wove paper. P 10½-11, irregular large holes (1 May–Dec 1874).

1	1	2n. dull yellow	45·00	55·00
2		3n. bluish green	65·00	55·00
		a. Yellow-green (12.74)	65·00	55·00
3		5n. dull rose-red	55·00	55·00
4		7n. pale violet	55·00	43·00
5		10n. pale blue	£170	£110
6		15n. yellow-brown	£190	£160
7		25n. grey-purple	£400	£275

A second printing of the 2n., 3n. (No. 2*a*) and 5n. was made in December, 1874 on a thicker, softer paper showing no transparency.

(b) Thick to medium paper. Thick white gum (1876–81)

A. P 13

8A	1	2n. pale yellow	13·50	8·75
		a. Perf 13×10½	£225	£160
9A		3n. green	11·00	7·00
10A		5n. dull red	11·00	7·00
12A		10n. pale blue	22·00	9·25
		a. Perf 12×10½–11	£200	£130

B. P 12, irregular

8B	1	2n. pale yellow	31·00	24·00
9B		3n. green	60·00	49·00
10B		5n. dull red	36·00	28·00
11B		7n. pale Venetian red	11·00	7·00
12B		10n. pale blue	55·00	38·00
13B		15n. yellow-ochre	85·00	43·00
14B		25n. grey-brown	85·00	60·00

The "Montenegrin perforations", due to use of worn perforators showing as irregular spacing and alignment, occur most frequently in these printings.

II. Wmk "BRIEF-MARKEN" as before but letters wider. Measures 480 mm. Medium wove paper. Gum clear and penetrating causing transparency (1883–89). P 12.

15	1	2n. dull yellow	5·50	3·75
		b. Perf 13	13·50	8·75
		c. Perf 12½	5·50	3·75
		d. Perf 12×12½ or 12½×12	13·50	8·75
		e. Perf 12×13	34·00	
16		3n. green	5·50	3·75
		b. Perf 13	11·00	7·00
		c. Perf 12½	6·75	4·25
		d. Perf 12×12½. or 12½×12	17·00	16·00
		e. Perf 12×13	—	35·00
		f. Perf 12½×13	35·00	35·00
17		5n. red (*shades*)	6·75	4·25
		b. Perf 13	6·75	4·25
		c. Perf 12½	6·75	5·50
		d. Perf 12×12½	11·00	7·00
		e. Perf 12×13	35·00	
18		7n. pale Venetian red	22·00	14·00
19		7n. dull purple	90·00	65·00
20		7n. dull rose	4·00	2·75
		c. Perf 12½	5·50	3·75
		d. Perf 12×12½. or 12½×12	11·00	7·50
		e. Perf 12×13	—	35·00
		f. Perf 12½×13	—	35·00
21		10n. blue (*shades*)	5·50	3·75
		b. Perf 13	22·00	9·25
		c. Perf 12½	5·50	3·75
		d. Perf 12×12½ or 12½×12	55·00	38·00
		f. Perf 12½×13	55·00	
22		15n. ochre (*shades*)	13·50	11·00
		d. Perf 12×12½ or 12½×12	65·00	15·00
23		25n. brown (*shades*) (p 13)	55·00	60·00
		c. Perf 12½	34·00	22·00
		d. Perf 12½×12	85·00	55·00
		e. Perf 12×13	13·50	13·50
		f. Perf 12½×13	39·00	

III. Wmk "ZEITUNGS-MARKEN" in double-lined capitals in one line, across the middle of a double-width sheet.

(i) Stamps 2–2½ mm apart (as earlier printings). Thin paper. Arabic transparent gum. P 11½, small holes and often not clear cut (early 1893).

24	1	2n. dull yellow	5·50	3·75
25		3n. green (*shades*)	5·50	3·75
26		5n. red	6·75	4·25
27		7n. claret	4·00	2·75
28		10n. Prussian blue (*shades*)	5·50	3·75
29		15n. ochre	5·50	4·25
30		25n. dull brown	6·75	5·50

(ii) Stamps 2¾–3¼ mm apart. Clichés made from cleaned dies giving clear impressions and brighter colours (mid 1893).

A. P 10½

31A	1	2n. lemon-yellow	5·50	3·75
		a. Perf 11	39·00	27·00
32A		3n. bright yellow-green	5·50	3·75
33A		5n. rose-red	4·00	2·75
34A		7n. dark rose	4·00	2·75
		a. Perf 11	17·00	16·00
35A		10n. Prussian blue (*shades*)	5·50	3·75
36A		15n. pale ochre	5·50	4·25
37A		25n. chocolate (*shades*)	6·75	5·50
		a. Perf 11½×10½	£150	—
		b. Red-brown (*shades*)	6·75	5·50

B. P 11½

31B	1	2n. lemon-yellow	5·50	3·75
32B		3n. bright yellow-green	5·50	3·75
33B		5n. rose-red	4·00	2·75
35B		10n. Prussian blue (*shades*)	5·50	3·75
36B		15n. pale ochre	5·50	4·25
37B		25n. chocolate (*shades*)	6·75	5·50

(iii) Stamps 2½ mm apart. Plates constructed from electrotypes in horizontal blocks of ten. Blurred or heavy impressions and dull colours (late 1893).

A. P 10½

38A	1	2n. yellow	4·50	4·25
39A		3n. dull green	1·10	1·10
40A		5n. orange-red	1·10	1·10
		ab. Perf 10½×11½	£150	
41A		7n. light rose	1·10	1·10
42A		10n. Prussian blue	1·10	1·10
		ab. P 11½×10½	—	95·00
43A		15n. bright ochre	2·50	2·50
44A		25n. brown	1·10	6·50

B. P 11½, small holes

38B	1	2n. yellow	5·50	3·75
39B		3n. dull green	1·20	1·20
40B		5n. orange-red	1·20	1·20
41B		7n. light rose	1·20	1·20
42B		10n. Prussian blue	2·00	2·20
43B		15n. bright ochre	2·40	1·90
44B		25n. brown	1·20	3·25

C. P 11½, large holes

38C	1	2n. yellow	17·00	17·00
39C		3n. dull green	2·50	2·50
40C		5n. orange-red	2·50	2·50
41C		7n. light rose	2·50	2·50
43C		15n. bright ochre	9·00	9·00
44C		25n. brown	3·00	3·00

(iv) New values (10.2.94)

A. P 10½

45A	1	1n. grey-blue	80	80
46A		20n. orange-brown	80	80
47A		30n. brown-purple	80	80
48A		50n. ultramarine	80	80
49A		1f. blue-green	1·10	5·50
50A		2f. brown-lake	1·70	16·00

B. P 11½, small holes

45B	1	1n. grey-blue	65	70
46B		20n. orange-brown	75	75
47B		30n. brown-purple	75	1·10
48B		50n. ultramarine	90	1·60
49B		1f. blue-green	2·20	3·75
50B		2f. brown-lake	2·20	4·75

C. P 11½, large holes

45C	1	1n. grey-blue	55	55
46C		20n. orange-brown	55	55
47C		30n. brown-purple	55	65
48C		50n. ultramarine	3·25	75
49C		1f. blue-green	5·00	7·50
50C		2f. brown-lake	5·00	22·00

(v) Colours changed (1.5.98)

A. P 10½

51A	1	2n. blue-green	55	55
52A		3n. bright red	55	55
		ad. Aniline red	55	85
53A		5n. brown-orange	3·25	75
54A		7n. lilac-grey	65	1·10
55A		10n. claret	80	1·10
56A		15n. lake-brown	55	75
57A		25n. slate-blue	55	75

B. P 11½, small holes

51B	1	2n. blue-green	80	75
52B		3n. bright red	80	75
		d. Aniline red	9·50	1·60
53B		5n. brown-orange	1·30	1·30
54B		7n. lilac-grey	1·70	1·30
55B		10n. claret	1·70	1·60
56B		15n. lake-brown	1·30	1·60
57B		25n. slate-blue	1·30	1·60

C. P 11½, large holes

51C	1	2n. blue-green	2·75	2·50
52C		3n. bright red	80	75
		d. Aniline red	2·40	3·25
53C		5n. brown-orange	9·50	1·60
54C		7n. lilac-grey	1·30	1·30
55C		10n. claret	1·70	1·30
56C		15n. lake-brown	1·30	1·60
57C		25n. slate-blue	1·30	1·60

1893 (25 July). 400th Anniv of Introduction of Printing into Montenegro. Optd with T **2** at Cetinje in panes of 25.

(a) On stamps of 1883–89. P 12 or 12½ (25n.)

58	1	7n. dull purple	£750	£800
		a. Opt inverted	£1500	
59		7n. dull rose	£130	85·00
		a. Opt inverted	£325	£325
60		15n. ochre	£170	£110
		a. Opt inverted	—	£300
61		25n. brown (Verm.)	†	£325

(b) On stamps of early 1893 (Nos. 24/30). P 11½

62	1	2n. dull yellow	39·00	9·25
		a. Opt inverted	—	75·00
		b. "1494" for "1493"	£120	£120
63		3n. green (*shades*)	4·50	2·75
		a. Opt inverted	75·00	
		b. "1494" for "1493"	£120	£120
64		5n. red	5·50	3·25
		a. Opt inverted	75·00	
		b. "1494" for "1493"	£120	£130
65		7n. claret	6·75	5·50
		a. Opt double	—	55·00
66		10n. Prussian blue (*shades*)	6·75	5·50
		a. Opt inverted	—	
67		10n. Prussian blue (*shades*) (R.)	10·00	7·50
		a. Opt inverted	—	70·00
		b. Opt double	—	75·00
68		15n. ochre	5·00	4·25
		a. Opt inverted	—	75·00
		b. Opt double	—	75·00
69		15n. ochre (R.)	£3250	£2250
70		25n. dull brown	5·50	4·25
71		25n. dull brown (R.)	10·00	6·50
		a. Opt inverted	—	75·00
		b. Opt double	—	75·00

(c) On stamps of mid 1893 (Nos. 31/7)

A. P 10½

72A	1	2n. lemon-yellow	39·00	9·25
		a. Opt inverted	80·00	80·00
		d. Perf 11	90·00	38·00
73A		3n. bright yellow-green	39·00	8·00
		a. Opt inverted	85·00	60·00
		b. Pair, one with opt inverted	95·00	75·00
		c. "1495" for "1493"	—	85·00
74A		5n. rose-red	28·00	8·75
		a. Opt inverted	65·00	
75A		7n. dark rose	8·50	4·25
		a. Perf 11	39·00	22·00
		b. Do. "1495" for "1493"	—	£180
		c. Perf 11 (R.)	55·00	27·00
76A		10n. Prussian blue	11·00	6·50
		a. Opt double	80·00	80·00
		b. "1495" for "1493"	80·00	90·00
77A		10n. Prussian blue (R.)	45·00	6·50
		a. Opt inverted	45·00	32·00
		b. "1495" for "1493"	—	95·00
78A		15n. pale ochre	45·00	6·50
79A		25n. chocolate	45·00	6·00
80A		25n. chocolate (R.)	28·00	11·00
		a. Opt double	65·00	—
		b. Do. (R. and Bk.)	£200	£275

B. P 11½

72B	1	2n. lemon-yellow	50·00	11·00
		a. Opt inverted	80·00	75·00
		b. Pair, one with opt inverted	—	£130
		c. "1495" for "1493"	—	95·00
73B		3n. bright yellow-green	34·00	6·50
		a. Opt inverted	—	35·00
		c. "1495" for "1493"	—	75·00
74B		5n. rose-red	39·00	5·50
		a. Opt inverted	60·00	32·00
		b. "1495" for "1493"	—	65·00
		c. Do. Opt inverted	£170	—
76B		10n. Prussian blue	39·00	5·50
77B		10n. Prussian blue (R.)	45·00	8·00
		a. Opt inverted	39·00	39·00
78B		15n. pale ochre	45·00	6·50
79B		25n. chocolate	45·00	6·50
		a. Opt inverted	65·00	55·00
		b. Pair, one with opt inverted	—	£140
		c. Opt double	65·00	65·00
		d. "1495" for "1493"	—	85·00
		e. Do. Opt inverted	—	£130
80B		25n. chocolate (R.)	47·00	7·50

(d) On stamps of late 1893 (Nos. 38/44)

A. P 10½

81A	1	2n. yellow	43·00	3·75
		b. Opt double	—	75·00
82A		3n. dull green	4·50	2·75
83A		5n. orange-red	3·25	2·20
		a. Opt double	34·00	34·00
84A		7n. light rose	4·50	2·75
		a. Opt inverted	—	49·00
		b. Opt double	34·00	—
85A		10n. Prussian blue	5·50	4·25
		a. Opt double	45·00	—
86A		10n. Prussian blue (R.)	8·50	5·50
		a. P 10½×11½	45·00	—
87A		15n. bright ochre	6·25	4·25
88A		25n. brown	5·50	3·25
		a. Opt double	17·00	—
89A		25n. brown (R.)	6·75	5·50
		a. Opt double	45·00	—

B. P 11½, small holes

81B	1	2n. yellow	50·00	11·00
		a. Opt inverted	—	65·00
		b. Opt double	—	65·00
		c. P 11½, large	50·00	11·00
82B		3n. dull green	4·50	2·75
		a. Opt double	50·00	—
		b. P 11½, large	14·00	14·00
83B		5n. orange-red	5·50	3·25
		b. P 11½, large	14·50	14·50
84B		7n. light rose	6·75	5·50
85B		10n. Prussian blue	6·75	5·50
86B		10n. Prussian blue (R.)	10·00	7·50
87B		15n. bright ochre	5·00	4·25
88B		25n. brown	5·50	4·25
		b. P 11½, large	6·75	18·00
89B		25n. brown (R.)	5·50	4·25
		a. Opt double	50·00	
		b. P 11½, large	7·75	9·75

Many minor varieties exist due to broken or worn type and also missing letters or figures and when repairs were made wrong founts were sometimes used. Shifted overprints are also known.

In this issue the red overprints vary from vermilion to carmine.

The majority of Nos. 81/9 in used condition on the market have remainder cancellations. Our prices are for genuine postally cancelled stamps.

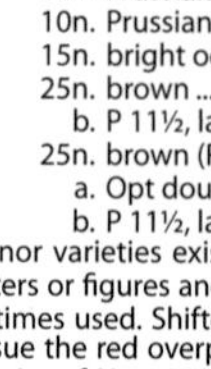

D **3**

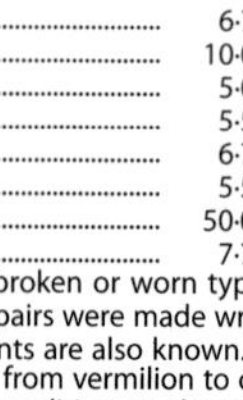

A **3**

1894 (Nov). POSTAGE DUE. Wmk "ZEITUNGS-IVIARKEN" in sheet. Typo. P 10½.

D90 D **3** 1n. rose-red 4·50 4·25
a. Imperf (pair) 50·00
b. Perf 11½ 4·50 4·25
c. Perf 11 8·50 8·00
D91 2n. yellow-green 1·70 1·60
b. Perf 11½ 1·70 1·60
c. Perf 11 5·50 5·50
D92 3n. yellow-orange 1·10 1·10
a. Double print 10·00
b. Perf 11½ 1·10 1·10
c. Perf 11 6·75 6·50
D93 5n. yellow-olive 80 75
b. Perf 11½ 80 75
D94 10n. purple 80 75
b. Perf 11½ 80 75
c. Perf 11 4·50 4·25
D95 20n. grey-blue 80 75
a. Double print 65·00
b. Perf 11½ 80 75
c. Perf 11 4·50 4·25
D96 30n. emerald 80 75
a. Double print 65·00
b. Perf 11½ 80 75
c. Perf 11 6·75 6·50
D97 50n. greenish grey 80 75
b. Perf 11½ 80 75
c. Perf 11 6·75 6·50

1895 (Oct). ACKNOWLEDGMENT OF RECEIPT. Wmk "ZEITUNGS-MARKEN" in sheet. Typo.

A90 A **3** 10n. ultramarine and rose (p 10½) 1·30 1·30
A91 10n. ultramarine and rose (p 11½) 1·30 1·30

3 Monastery near Cetinje, Royal Mausoleum

1896 (1 Sept). Bicentenary of Dynasty of Petrovich Njegush. Litho. No wmk.

A. P 10½

90A **3** 1n. pale brown and blue 55 1·60
91A 2n. yellow and reddish purple 55 1·60
a. Centre inverted 60·00 —
92A 3n. light green and chestnut 55 1·60
a. Centre inverted 60·00 —
b. Centre double 50·00 —
93A 5n. ochre and emerald 55 1·60
a. Centre inverted 60·00 —
b. Centre double 50·00 —
c. Frame double 75·00 —
94A 10n. ultramarine and yellow 55 1·60
a. Centre inverted £110 —
b. Centre double 75·00 —
95A 15n. green and blue 55 1·60
96A 20n. ultramarine and green 65 1·80
a. Centre inverted £110 —
97A 25n. yellow and indigo 65 1·80
98A 30n. pale brown and reddish purple 80 1·80
99A 50n. blue and lake 80 1·80
100A 1f. blue and rose 1·30 2·20
101A 2f. black and brown 1·90 2·75
a. Centre double 65·00 —

B. P 11½

90B **3** 1n. pale brown and blue 1·10 2·75
91B 2n. yellow and reddish purple 1·10 2·75
92B 3n. light green and chestnut 1·10 2·75
93B 5n. ochre and emerald 1·10 2·75
94B 10n. ultramarine and yellow 55 1·60
95B 15n. green and blue 85·00 £130
96B 20n. ultramarine and green 55·00 80·00
97B 25n. yellow and indigo 1·70 3·25
98B 30n. pale brown and reddish purple 1·70 3·25
99B 50n. blue and lake 1·70 3·25
100B 1f. blue and rose 2·50 4·25
101B 2f. black and brown 3·25 6·50

4

D 4

A 4

1902 (12 July). New Currency. Typo. P 12½ (1h.) and 13×12½ or 13 (others).

102 **4** 1h. ultramarine 55 55
103 2h. mauve 55 55
a. Error. Blackish brown £110
104 5h. green 55 55
a. Imperf (pair) 6·75
105 10h. rosine 55 55
106 25h. blue 1·10 1·30
a. Perf 12½ 5·50
b. Error. Indigo-blue 75·00
107 50h. grey-green 1·10 1·30
108 1k. purple-brown 1·10 1·10
109 2k. yellow-brown 1·10 1·30
110 5k. cinnamon 1·30 3·25

Other imperf stamps of this issue come from printers' waste.

1902 (15 July). POSTAGE DUE. Typo. P 12½.

D111 D **4** 5h. yellow-orange 55 75
D112 10h. yellow-olive 55 75
D113 25h. purple-brown 55 75
D114 50h. emerald 55 75
D115 1k. greenish grey 1·10 1·80

1902 (Oct). ACKNOWLEDGMENT OF RECEIPT. Typo. P 12½.

A111 A **4** 25h. orange and rosine 1·30 1·30
a. Double print 34·00
b. Imperf (pair) 55·00

(**5**)

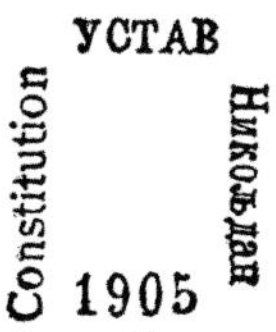

(**6**)

1905 (5 Dec). Granting of Constitution. Optd with T **5** at Cetinje.

(a) POSTAGE

111 **4** 1h. ultramarine (R.) 55 55
a. Opt double 17·00 17·00
112 2h. mauve 55 55
a. Opt double 17·00
113 5h. green (R.) 1·10 1·10
a. Opt double 17·00 17·00
b. Opt inverted 45·00
114 10h. rosine 1·70 1·30
a. Opt double 17·00
115 25h. blue (R.) 80 75
a. Opt double 17·00
116 50h. grey-green (R.) 80 75
a. Opt double 17·00
117 1k. purple-brown (R.) 80 75
a. Opt double 17·00 17·00
b. Opt inverted 45·00
118 2k. yellow-brown (R.) 1·10 1·10
a. Opt double 20·00 20·00
119 5k. cinnamon 1·70 1·60
a. Opt double 20·00

(b) POSTAGE DUE

D120 D **4** 5h. yellow-orange 80 1·60
a. Opt inverted 45·00
b. Opt double 20·00
D121 10h. yellow-olive (R.) 1·10 3·25
a. Opt double 20·00
D122 25h. purple-brown 80 1·60
a. Opt inverted 45·00
b. Opt double 20·00
D123 50h. emerald 80 1·60
a. Opt inverted 45·00
b. Opt double 17·00
D124 1k. greenish grey 1·10 2·20
a. Opt double 17·00

(c) ACKNOWLEDGEMENT OF RECEIPT

A120 A **4** 25h. orange and rosine 1·30 1·30
a. Opt inverted £100
b. Opt double 28·00

Types **5** and **6** also exist overprinted in other colours but these come from trial printings although some are known postally used.

The 1 to 50h. values may be found in pairs *se-tenant* with overprint T **6** at left.

Shifted overprints account for pairs of double and normal overprints and also with and without overprint.

УСТАВ (I) (8¼×1½ mm) УСТАВ (II) (9¾×2 mm)

УСТАВ (III) (10¼×2½ mm) УСТАВ (IV) (11¼×2 mm)

1906. As Nos. 111/19 but optd with T **6** ("Constitution" 16½ mm instead of 15 mm). Four types of "YCTAB".

120 **4** 1h. ultramarine (R.) (II) 55 55
b. Type III 3·25 3·25
c. Type IV 1·10 1·10
ca. "Constitutton" 26·00
cb. "Coustitution" 26·00
121 2h. mauve (I) 55·00 55·00
a. Type II 55 55
b. Type III 3·25 3·25
c. Type IV 1·10 1·10
ca. "Constitutton" 26·00
cb. "Coustitution" 26·00
d. Opt double (I–IV) 22·00
e. Opt inverted (I–IV) 55·00
122 5h. green (R.) (II) 1·10 1·10
b. Type III 6·75 6·50
c. Type IV 2·75 2·75
ca. "Constitutton" 26·00
cb. "Coustitution" 26·00
d. Opt double (II–IV) 22·00
123 10h. rosine (I) £400
a. Type II 1·30 1·30
b. Type III 8·50 8·00
c. Type IV 4·00 3·75
ca. "Constitutton" 26·00
cb. "Coustitution" 26·00
e. Opt inverted (II–IV) 55·00
124 25h. blue (R.) (I) 34·00 32·00
a. Type II 80 75
b. Type III 4·50 4·25
c. Type IV 2·20 2·20
ca. "Constitutton" 45·00
cb. "Coustitution" 45·00
d. Opt double (I–IV) 22·00
e. Opt inverted (I–IV) 55·00
125 50h. grey-green (R.) (I) 34·00 32·00
a. Type II 80 75
b. Type III 4·50 4·25
c. Type IV 2·75 2·75
ca. "Constitutton" 45·00
cb. "Coustitution" 45·00
d. Opt double (I–IV) 22·00
126 1k. purple-brown (R.) (I) 34·00 32·00
a. Type II 80 75
b. Type III 4·50 4·25
c. Type IV 2·75 2·75
ca. "Constitutton" 55·00
cb. "Coustitution" 55·00
127 2k. yellow-brown (R.) (I) 34·00 32·00
a. Type II 1·10 1·10
b. Type III 5·50 5·50
c. Type IV 4·00 3·75
ca. "Constitutton" 55·00
cb. "Coustitution" 55·00
e. Opt inverted (I–IV) 55·00
128 5k. cinnamon (I) 34·00 32·00
a. Type II 1·70 1·60
b. Type III 6·75 6·50
c. Type IV 4·50 4·25
ca. "Constitutton" 55·00
cb. "Coustitution" 55·00
e. Opt inverted (I–IV) 65·00

There were three settings of Type **6**:

1st setting—2h. and 10h. to 5k.: 2×Type I, 61×Type II, 12×Type III, 25×Type IV.

2nd setting—1 to 10h.: 63×Type II, 12×Type III, 25×Type IV.

3rd setting—1 and 10h.: 62×Type II, 16×Type III, 22×Type IV.

The "Constitutton" error occurs on position 79 and Coustitution" on position 86, both of which are Type IV. Other minor varieties exist in Type IV while in Type II there is a variety of a large "0" in "1905".

The prices quoted for double and inverted overprints are for Type II. These errors are also known for other Types indicated and their prices will be proportionately higher.

1906. POSTAGE DUE. Optd with T **6**.

D129 D **4** 10h. olive-yellow (II) 2·20 4·75
D130 10h. olive-yellow (III) 2·20 4·75
D131 10h. olive-yellow (IV) 6·75 8·00
a. "Constitutton" 45·00
b. "Coustitution" 45·00
129/131 *Set of* 3

Only the second setting was used of this overprint.

1906. ACKNOWLEDGMENT OF RECEIPT. Optd with T **6**.

A129 A **4** 25h. orange and rosine (I) 39·00 43·00
A130 25h. orange and rosine (II) 1·70 2·20
A131 25h. orange and rosine (III) 6·75 7·50
A132 25h. orange and rosine (IV) 4·00 4·25
a. "Constitutton" 26·00
b. "Coustitution" 26·00

Only the first setting was used of this overprint.

7

D 8

A 8

1907 (1 June). New Currency. Recess. P 12½.

129 **7** 1pa. ochre 45 30
130 2pa. black 45 30
131 5pa. pale green 1·90 20
132 10pa. rose-red 3·25 20
133 15pa. blue 55 55
134 20pa. red-orange 55 55
135 25pa. indigo 55 55
136 35pa. pale brown 80 55
137 50pa. lilac 80 75
138 1k. carmine 80 75
139 2k. green 80 75
140 5k. Venetian red 1·70 1·30
129/140 *Set of* 12 11·50 6·00

1907 (1 June). POSTAGE DUE. Typo. P 13×12½.

D141 D **8** 5pa. chestnut 55 1·60
D142 10pa. lavender 55 1·60
D143 25pa. carmine 55 1·60
D144 50pa. dull green 55 1·60
D141/144 *Set of* 4 2·00 5·75

1907 (1 June). ACKNOWLEDGMENT OF RECEIPT. Recess. P 12½.

A141 A **8** 25pa. drab 1·10 1·60

KINGDOM

9 King Nicholas when a Youth

10 King Nicholas and Queen Milena

11 Prince Nicholas

(Des K. Moser. Eng F. Schirnböck. Recess)

1910 (28 Aug). New Currency. Proclamation of Kingdom and 50th Anniv of Reign of Prince Nicholas. T **9/11** and similar portraits of King Nicholas. P 12½.

141 1pa. black 90 55
142 2pa. chocolate 90 55
143 5pa. bronze-green 90 55
144 10pa. rose-carmine 90 55
145 15pa. slate-blue 90 55
146 20pa. olive-green 1·10 75
147 25pa. blue 1·10 75
148 35pa. chestnut 1·70 1·10
149 50pa. violet 1·70 1·10
150 1per. lake 1·70 1·10
151 2per. yellow-green 2·00 1·30
152 5per. sky-blue 2·20 1·60
a. Perf 10 30·00
141/152 *Set of* 12 14·50 9·50

Designs: As T **9**—5pa., 10pa., 25pa., 35pa. In 1910; 15pa. In 1878; 50pa., 1per., 2per. In profile: As T **10**—20pa. King and Queen in different frame.

12

D **13** Nicholas I

A **13**

1913 (1 Apr). Typo. P 12½.

153	**12**	1pa. yellow-orange	55	75
154		2pa. crimson	55	75
155		5pa. deep green	60	75
156		10pa. rose-carmine	60	75
157		15pa. grey-blue	65	75
158		20pa. brown	65	75
159		25pa. blue	1·10	1·10
160		35pa. vermilion	80	75
161		50pa. pale blue	55	1·10
162		1per. pale brown	1·10	1·60
163		2per. slate-purple	1·10	1·60
164		5per. yellow-green	1·10	1·60
153/164 *Set of* 12			8·50	11·00

1913 (1 Apr). POSTAGE DUE. Typo. P 12½.

D165	D **13**	5pa. grey	1·70	2·20
D166		10pa. slate-lilac	1·10	1·60
D167		25pa. dull blue	1·10	1·60
D168		50pa. rose-lake	1·70	2·20
D165/168 *Set of* 4			5·00	6·75

1913 (1 Apr). ACKNOWLEDGMENT OF RECEIPT. Typo. P 12½.

A169	A **13**	25pa. yellow-olive	1·10	4·00

Montenegro was occupied by Austrian troops in January 1916 and the King went to Bordeaux. On 26 November 1918 he was deposed by a council of men with Serbian sympathies and the country was declared to be united with Serbia. The union was not recognised by the Powers until 13 July 1922. In the meantime stamps of Serbia and Yugoslavia were in use.

REPUBLIC

100 Cents = 1 Euro

These issues were only for sale within Montenegro.

M **14** Quay, Budva, Montenegro

M **15** Candle and Baubles

(Des M. Kalezić. Litho)

2003 (15 Sept). Tourism. Type M **14** and similar multicoloured designs. P 13.

M170	25c. Type M **14**	90	85
M171	40c. Durmitor national park (vert)	1·30	1·30

(Des M. Kalezić. Litho)

2003 (5 Dec). Christmas. P 13½.

M172	M **15**	25c. multicoloured	90	85
		a. Booklet pane. Nos. M172×10	9·25	

M **16** Map of Montenegro

2005 (15 Dec). State Symbols. Type M **16** and similar horiz designs. Multicoloured. Litho. P 13½.

M173	25c. Type M **16**	90	85
M174	40c. First Houses of Parliament	1·30	1·30
M175	50c. State emblem	1·70	1·60
M176	60c. State flag	2·75	2·75
M173/M176 *Set of* 4		6·00	5·75

M **17** Shellfish

2005 (30 Dec). Europa. Gastronomy. Type M **17** and similar horiz designs. Multicoloured. Litho. P 13½.

M177	25c. Type M **17**	3·25	3·25
M178	50c. Smoked ham and olives	6·75	6·50
MSM179	110×50 mm. 25c. Bee and honey; 50c. Wine and grapes	22·00	22·00

M **18** Montenegro 1913 2pa. Stamp (No. 154) and Emblem

2006 (3 Jan). 50th Anniv of Europa Stamps. Type M **18** and similar horiz designs. Multicoloured. Litho. P 13½.

M180	50c. Type M **18**	1·10	1·10
	a. Horiz strip. Nos. M180/3	13·00	
M181	€1 Montenegro 1913 5pa. Stamp (No. 155) and doves	2·20	2·20
M182	€2 Montenegro 1913 10pa. Stamp (No. 156) and bee	4·50	4·25
M183	€2 Montenegro 1913 25pa. Stamp (No. 159) and Europa emblem	4·50	4·25
M180/M183 *Set of* 4		11·00	10·50
MSM184	107×92 mm. Nos. M180/3	22·00	22·00
MSM185	103×76 mm. €5.50 Map of Europe highlighting Montenegro. Imperf	22·00	22·00

Nos. M180/3 were issued in horizontal *se-tenant* strips of four stamps within the sheet.

M **19** Figure Skater

(Des M. Kalezić. Litho)

2006 (7 Feb). Winter Olympic Games, Turin. Type M **19** and similar horiz design. Multicoloured. P 13½.

M186	60c. Type M **19**	1·30	1·30
M187	90c. Ski jumper	2·00	1·90

M **20** *Petteria ramentacea*

(Des A. Kostic. Litho)

2006 (15 Mar). Flora. Type M **20** and similar horiz design. Multicoloured. P 13½.

M188	25c. Type M **20**	55	55
M189	50c. *Viola nikolai*	1·10	1·10

M **21** 1 para Coin and Central Banking

(Des M. Kalezić. Litho)

2006 (27 Apr). Coins. Type M **21** and similar horiz design. Multicoloured. P 13½.

M190	40c. Type M **21**	90	85
M191	50c. 20 para coin and bank	1·10	1·10

M **22** Player

2006 (30 May). World Cup Football Championship, Germany. Type M **22** and similar vert designs. Multicoloured. Litho. P 13½.

M192	60c. Type M **22**	1·30	1·30
M193	90c. Player wearing short-sleeved jersey.	2·00	1·90
MSM194	100×72 mm. 60c. Player leaning right; 90c. Player facing left	3·25	3·25

The stamps and margins of No. **MS**M194 form a composite design.

Montenegro declared independence from Serbia on 3 June 2006, from this date all stamps were issued as Montenegro.

GOVERNMENT IN EXILE AT BORDEAUX, 1916–18

(B **1** "S. P. du M.=Service Postal du Montenégro")

1916 (6 June). OFFICIAL. Stamps of France optd with Type B **1**.

B1	**18**	5c. deep green	22·00
B2		10c. orange-red	28·00
B3	**15**	15c. slate-green	£400
B4	**18**	20c. brown-lake	£400
B5		25c. deep blue	34·00
B6		30c. yellow-orange	55·00
B7		35c. violet	65·00
B8	**13**	40c. red and pale blue	65·00
B9		45c. deep green and blue	65·00
B10		50c. cinnamon and lavender	£110
B11		1f. lake and yellow-green	£130
B1/11 *Set of* 11			£1200

The above were in use from 6 to 28 June 1916.

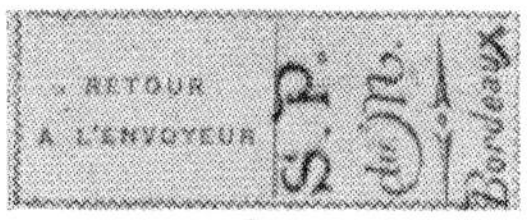

R **1**

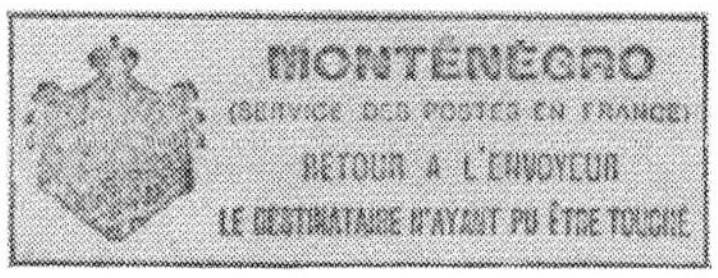

R **2** (Actual size 29×83 mm)

1916. RETURN LETTER. Imperf.

BR1	R **1**	(–) Black/*blue*	45·00
BR2	–	(–) Black/*red*	55·00
BR3	R **2**	(–) Blue	85·00
1/3 *Set of* 3			

No. BR2 is inscribed "LE DESTINATAIRE N'A PU ETRE ATTEINT".

A set of twelve stamps depicting the King wearing a laurel wreath, usually overprinted "Slobodna Crna Gora" in Cyrillic letters, and postage due and acknowledgement of receipt stamps depicting a crown were not used. Red Cross stamps showing Queen Milena are private productions.

AUSTRO-HUNGARIAN MILITARY POST IN MONTENEGRO

Austro-Hungarian troops occupied Montenegro from January 1916 to October 1918.

100 Heller = 1 Krone

K. U. K. MILIT.
VERWALTUNG
MONTENEGRO
(1)

Montenegro
(2)

1917 (1 Mar). Nos. 28 and 30 of General issues of Austro Hungarian Military Post (Francis Joseph I) optd.

(a) With T **1**

1	10h. light blue	20·00	16·00
2	15h. rose-scarlet	20·00	16·00

(b) With T **2**

3	10h. light blue	55·00	
4	15h. rose-scarlet	2·20	

Nos. 3 and 4 were not put into use.

OCCUPATION OF MONTENEGRO, 1941–1945

A. ITALIAN OCCUPATION

Following the capitulation of Yugoslav forces during the Second World War, an Italian Governorship was formed on 3 October 1941 consisting of the Montenegro of 1913 with additions west of Novi Pazar but without the Pec and Dakovica areas.

Yugoslav and Italian Currency

Montenegro
Црна Гора
17-IV-41-XIX
(1)

ЦРНА ГОРА
(2)

1941 (16 June). Nos. 414, etc., of Yugoslavia (1939 King Peter II issue), optd with T **1**.

1	**99**	25p. black	1·10	1·80
2		1d. green	1·10	1·80
3		1d.50 scarlet	1·10	1·80
4		2d. carmine-rose	1·10	1·80
5		3d. red-brown	1·10	1·80
6		4d. bright blue	1·10	1·80
7		5d. blue	4·50	5·50
8		5d.50 dull violet	4·50	5·50
9		6d. deep blue	4·50	5·50
10		8d. chocolate	4·50	6·50
11		12d. violet	4·50	5·50
12		16d. purple	4·50	5·50
13		20d. light blue	£275	£325
14		30d. pink	£110	£130
1/14 *Set of* 14			£375	£450

1941 (16 June). AIR. Nos. 360/7 of Yugoslavia, (pictorial air stamps), optd with T **1**. P 12½, 12½×11½ or 11½×12½.

15	50p. brown	11·00	11·00
16	1d. bright green	8·50	11·00
17	2d. slate-blue	8·50	11·00
18	2d.50 carmine	11·00	11·00
19	5d. violet	65·00	80·00
20	10d. lake	65·00	80·00
21	20d. bluish green	£140	£150
22	30d. bright blue	80·00	80·00
15/22 *Set of* 8		£350	£400

1941 (16 June). POSTAGE DUE. Nos. D259/63 II of Yugoslavia optd with T **1**.

D23	D **56**	50p. violet	1·90	2·75
D24		1d. magenta	1·90	2·75
D25		2d. blue	1·90	2·75
D26		5d. orange	£130	£140
D27		10d. chocolate	11·00	14·00
D23/27 *Set of* 5			£130	£150

1941 (June). Stamps of Italy optd with T **2**.

(a) POSTAGE. Nos. 239, etc

28	**98**	5c. brown (R.)	90	1·30
29	**100**	10c. sepia	90	1·30
30	**101**	15c. blue-green (R.)	90	1·30
31	**99**	20c. carmine	90	1·30
32	**102**	25c. green	90	1·30
33	**103**	30c. brown (R.)	90	1·30
34		50c. bright violet (R.)	90	1·30
35	**102**	75c. carmine	90	1·30
36		1l.25 blue (R.)	90	1·30

(b) AIR. No. 271

37	**110**	50c. sepia	90	1·30
28/37 *Set of* 10			8·00	11·50

1942 (June). POSTAGE DUE. Nos. D396, etc. of Italy, optd with T **2**.

D38	D **141**	10c. blue	2·20	3·25
D39		20c. bright carmine	2·20	3·25
D40		30c. orange-vermilion	2·20	3·25
D41		50c. bright violet	2·20	3·25
D42		1l. orange	2·20	3·25
D38/42 *Set of* 5			10·00	14·50

Governatorato
del
Montenegro

Valore
LIRE

(**3**)

1942. Nos. 416, etc. of Yugoslavia (1939 King Peter II issue), optd with T **3**.

A. In red

43A	**99**	1d. green	2·75	3·75
44A		1d.50 scarlet	£200	£275
45A		3d. red-brown	2·75	3·75
46A		4d. bright blue	2·75	3·75
47A		5d.50 dull violet	2·75	3·75
48A		6d. deep blue	2·75	3·75
49A		8d. chocolate	2·75	3·75
50A		12d. violet	2·75	3·75
51A		16d. purple	2·75	3·75
43A/51 *Set of* 9			£200	£275

B. In black

43B	**99**	1d. green	2·75	3·75
44B		1d.50 scarlet	£130	85·00
45B		3d. red-brown	2·75	3·75
46B		4d. bright blue	2·75	3·75
47B		5d.50 dull violet	2·75	3·75
48B		6d. deep blue	2·75	3·75
49B		8d. chocolate	2·75	3·75
50B		12d. violet	2·75	3·75
51B		16d. purple	2·75	3·75
43B/51 *Set of* 9			£140	£100

1942 (9 Jan). AIR. Air stamps of Yugoslavia, 1937, Nos. 360/7, optd "Governatorato/del/Montenegro/Valore in Lire" in four lines.

A. In red

52A	0.50l. brown	£225	£250
53A	1l. bright green	£225	£250
54A	2l. slate-blue	£225	£250
55A	2.50l. carmine	£225	£250
56A	5l. violet	£225	£250
57A	10l. lake	£225	£250
58A	20l. bluish green	£225	£250
59A	30l. bright blue	£225	£250
52A/59 *Set of* 8		£1600	£1800

B. In black

52B	0.50l. brown	7·75	8·75
53B	1l. bright green	7·75	8·75
54B	2l. slate-blue	7·75	8·75
55B	2.50l. carmine	7·75	8·75
56B	5l. violet	7·75	8·75
57B	10l. lake	7·75	8·75
58B	20l. bluish green	£300	£375
59B	30l. bright blue	60·00	70·00
52B/59 *Set of* 8		£375	£450

4 Prince Bishop Peter Njegoš and View **5** Cetinje

(Des P. Pocek. Photo)

1943 (9 May). National Poem Commemoratives. T **4** and similar designs, each with a fragment of poetry inscribed at back. P 14.

60	5c. violet	3·25	5·50
61	10c. olive-green	3·25	5·50
62	15c. brown	3·25	5·50
63	20c. brown-orange	3·25	5·50
64	25c. green	3·25	5·50
65	50c. rose-magenta	3·25	5·50
66	1l.25 blue	3·25	5·50
67	2l. blue-green	5·00	8·00
68	5l. carmine/*buff*	11·00	14·00
69	20l. purple/*grey*	22·00	30·00
60/69 *Set of* 10		55·00	80·00

Designs: Horiz—10c. Meadow near Mt. Lovcen; 15c. Country chapel; 20c. Chiefs' Meeting; 25c. and 50c. Folk dancing; 1l.25 Taking the Oath; 2l. Moslem wedding procession; 5l. Watch over wounded standard-bearer. Vert—20l. Prince Bishop Peter Njegoš.

(Des P. Pocek. Photo)

1943. AIR. T **5** and similar designs with Junkers G.31 airplane (2, 20l.) or Fokker F.VIIa/3m airplane (others).

70	50c. brown	1·70	3·50
71	1l. ultramarine	1·70	3·50
72	2l. rose-magenta	2·20	3·50
73	5l. green	2·75	4·25
74	10l. purple/*buff*	14·50	20·00
75	20l. indigo/*pink*	34·00	43·00
70/75 *Set of* 6		50·00	70·00

Designs: Horiz—1l. Coastline; 2l. Budva; 5l. Mt. Lovcen; 10l. Lake of Scutari. Vert—20l. Mt. Durmitor.

B. GERMAN OCCUPATION

In September 1943 Italy ended hostilities with the Allies and German forces took over Montenegro.

Italian and German Currency

Deutsche
Militaer-
Verwaltung
Montenegro

0.50 LIRE

(**1**)

1943 (22 Nov). Nos. 419/20 of Yugoslavia (1939 King Peter II issue), surch as T **1**.

76	**99**	50c. on 3d. red-brown	5·25	30·00
77		1l. on 3d. red-brown	5·25	30·00
78		1l.50 on 3d. red-brown	5·25	30·00
79		2l. on 3d. red-brown	6·75	60·00
80		4l. on 3d. red-brown	6·75	60·00
81		5l. on 4d. bright blue	6·75	60·00
82		8l. on 4d. bright blue	18·00	£120
83		10l. on 4d. bright blue	26·00	£190
84		20l. on 4d. bright blue	55·00	£425
76/84 *Set of* 9			£120	£900

1943. Appointment of National Administrative Committee. Optd "Nationaler/Verwaltungsausschuss/10.xi.1943".

(a) POSTAGE. On Nos. 64/8 of Italian Occupation (National Poem Commemoratives)

85	25c. green	13·00	£200
86	50c. rose-magenta	13·00	£200
87	1l.25 blue	13·00	£200
88	2l. blue-green	13·00	£200
89	5l. carmine/*buff*	£275	£2500

(b) AIR. On Nos. 70/74 of Italian Occupation

90	50c. brown	13·00	£200
91	1l. ultramarine	13·00	£200
92	2l. rose-magenta	13·00	£200
93	5l. green	13·00	£200
94	10l. purple/*buff*	£2250	£22000

Flücht-
lingshilfe
Montenegro

0,15 + 0,85 RM.

(**2**)

Flüchtlingshilfe
Montenegro

0,15 + 1,35 RM.

(**3**)

1944 (22 May). Refugees' Fund. Surch as T **2** or **3** in German Currency.

(a) With T **2** on Nos. 419/20 of Yugoslavia

95	0.15 +0.85Rm. on 3d. red-brown	12·50	£250
96	0.15 +0.85Rm. on 4d. bright blue	12·50	£250

(b) As T **2** on Nos. 64/7 of Italian Occupation

97	0.15 +0.85Rm. on 25c. green	12·50	£250
98	0.15 +1.35Rm. on 50c. rose-magenta	12·50	£250
99	0.25 +1.75Rm. on 1l.25 blue	12·50	£250
100	0.25 +1.75Rm. on 2l. blue-green	12·50	£250

(c) AIR. As T **3** on Nos. 70/2 of Italian Occupation

101	0.15 +0.85Rm. on 50c. brown	12·50	£250
102	0.25 +1.25Rm. on 1l. ultramarine	12·50	£250
103	0.50 +1.50Rm. on 2l. rose-magenta	12·50	£250
95/103 *Set of* 9		£100	£2000

+
Crveni krst
Montenegro

0.50+2.50 RM.

(**4**)

+
Crvèni krst
Montenegro

0.25 + 2.75 RM.

(**5**)

1944 (Aug). Red Cross. Surch as T **4** or **5** in German currency in red.

(a) With T **4** on Nos. 419/20 of Yugoslavia

104	0.50 +2.50Rm. on 3d. red-brown	9·50	£190
105	0.50 +2.50Rm. on 4d. bright blue	9·50	£190

(b) As T **5** on Nos. 64/5 of Italian Occupation

106	0.15 +0.85Rm. on 25c. green	9·50	£190
107	0.15 +1.35Rm. on 50c. rose-magenta	9·50	£190

(c) AIR. As T **5** on Nos. 70/2 of Italian Occupation

108	0.25 +1.75Rm. on 50c. brown	9·50	£190
109	0.25 +2.75Rm. on 1l. ultramarine	9·50	£190
110	0.50 +2Rm. on 2l. rose-magenta	9·50	£190
104/110 *Set of* 7		60·00	£1200

In 1945, following the defeat of Germany, Yugoslavia was reconstituted as a democratic federation with Montenegro as a constituent republic.

Romania

1858. 40 Parale = 1 Piastre
1867. 100 Bani = 1 Leu

I. MOLDAVIA

Moldavia and Wallachia, the two Danubian principalities which later united to form Romania, were in 1858 under the suzerainty of the Sultan of Turkey.

The dates of issue are according to local computation based on the Julian or Gregorian Calendar in use. In the 19thcentury the Julian Calendar was twelve days behind the Gregorian Calendar. After 1900 the difference was thirteen days. In Romania the Gregorian Calendar was introduced on 18 January 1919.

1

2

3

(Types **1** to **3**. Dies eng Dettmer. Handstruck at Security Printers, Jassy)

1858 (21 July). Wove paper (81p.) or laid papers (others). Imperf.
1 **1** 27p. black/*rose* £42000 £16000
a. Tête-bêche (vert pair)
2 54p. blue/*green* £21000 £6500
3 81p. blue/*blue* £40000 £44000
4 108p. blue/*pink* £30000 £14000

Prices quoted are for stamps cut square; those cut to shape are worth approximately 50% less than quoted prices.

Only one (used) example of No. 1a is known. Sheet formation was probably same as for Nos. 5/22.

The only genuine cancellers used on Nos. 1/4 were double-circle datestamps. Other obliterations are fakes.

1858–61. Imperf.

(a) Bluish wove paper (1.11.58–61)
5 **2** 5p. black (7.11.58) £27000 £16000
6 **3** 40p. blue (1.11.58) £325 £250
7 80p. red (1861) £12000 £1200

Tête-bêche (vert pairs)
8 **2** 5p. black
9 **3** 40p. blue £1800 £3750
10 80p. red

(b) White wove paper (1858 (80p.)–1.6.59 (others))
11 **2** 5p. black (I) £24000 £16000
12 5p. black (II) £200
13 **3** 40p. blue £200 £225
a. Greenish blue £225 £225
14 80p. red (5.11.58) £650 £400

Tête-bêche (vert pairs)
15 **2** 5p. black (I)
16 5p. black (II) £800
17 **3** 40p. blue £1800 £3750
a. Greenish blue £850 £3250
18 80p. red £650 £400

(c) Yellowish wove paper
19 **3** 40p. greenish blue £225 £225
20 80p. red £1300 £1300
a. Brown-red £1300 £1300

Tête-bêche (vert pairs)
21 **3** 40p. greenish blue £1800
22 80p. red £2000 £3750

Individual dates in brackets are those of earliest known cancellations.

The 5p. paid the rate for newspapers. Only three uncancelled examples of No. 5 are known, one on newspaper in the German Post Archives. In Type II of the 5p. there is a break in the bottom frame-line below the "A". This was not issued, although examples are known used on a newspaper wrapper.

Nos. 5/22 were printed in sheets of 32 (8×4) with the bottom two horizontal rows inverted.

Reprints from the original dies were made at various times, in the same colours, in black on white and in completely different colours.

On 1 May 1862 a new uniform postal tariff for the whole of Romania was introduced. Stampless mail was used in May and June 1862.

On 19 August 1858 a Conference in Paris decided to establish the United Principalities of Moldavia and Wallachia; each principality was to have a prince (Hospodar) elected for life, and a separate legislature. On 17 January 1859 Moldavia elected Colonel Alexandru Cuza as Hospodar, and on 5 February Wallachia made the same choice. On 23 December 1861 the union of the two principalities as the Principality of Romania was proclaimed; Alexandru Cuza had been recognised by the Sultan as Prince of Romania on 5 December.

II. ROMANIA

Prince Cuza (Alexandru Ioan I)

6 December 1861–23 February 1866

4

1862 (26 June–Oct). Handstruck from single dies. Imperf.

(a) Horizontally laid paper
23 **4** 3p. yellow £375 £3250
a. Orange-yellow £375 £3250
24 6p. red £375 £600
a. Carmine £400 £400
25 30p. pale blue £120 £140
a. Deep blue £120 £140

Tête-bêche (pairs)
26 **4** 3p. orange-yellow £1900
27 6p. carmine £1800 £2000
28 30p. blue £250 £1900

(b) Wove paper (Oct.)
29 **4** 3p. yellow £120 £325
a. Orange-yellow £130 £325
b. Lemon-yellow £375 £500
30 6p. vermilion £100 £300
a. Double print £600
b. Carmine £120 £325
c. Red £100 £325
31 30p. pale blue 75·00 85·00
a. Deep blue £120 £140

Tête-bêche (vert pairs)
32 **4** 3p. yellow £325 £1600
a. Orange-yellow £325 £1600
b. Lemon-yellow £1000
33 6p. carmine £250 £850
a. Red £250 £850
34 30p. pale blue £250 £1000
a. Deep blue £250 £1000

The above were printed in four rows of 8, the two lower rows being inverted.

1864 (May–Sept). Printed from plates, forty varieties on the sheet. Imperf.

(a) White wove paper
35 **4** 3p. yellow £130 £1600
a. Orange-yellow £160 £1600
36 6p. pale dull rose 26·00
a. Rose-carmine 26·00
37 30p. pale blue 21·00 £130
a. Deep blue 21·00 £130

Tête-bêche (horiz pairs)
38 **4** 3p. yellow £425
a. Orange-yellow £500
39 6p. pale dull rose 95·00
a. Rose-carmine 95·00
40 30p. pale blue £100
a. Deep blue £100

Stamp turned sideways (pair)
41 **4** 3p. yellow £225
a. Orange-yellow £250
42 6p. rose-carmine 65·00
43 30p. pale blue 85·00
a. Deep blue 85·00

(b) Bluish wove paper
44 **4** 30p. deep blue £275 £325

5

Two types of 20p.

A. Central oval does not touch inner rectangular frame at bottom; "1" of "DECI" is too tall.
B. Central oval touches frame and "1" is normal height.

(Litho S. Sander & Co, Bucharest)

1865 (9 Jan). Imperf.

(a) White wove paper
45 **5** 2p. yellow 95·00 £375
a. Orange 85·00 £325
b. Ochre £130 £400
46 5p. pale blue 50·00 £325
a. Deep blue 50·00 £325
47 20p. scarlet (A) 42·00 50·00
a. Rose-red 42·00 50·00
48 20p. scarlet (B) 42·00 50·00
a. Rose-red 42·00 50·00

(b) White vert laid paper
49 **5** 2p. yellow £120
a. Orange 75·00 £325
50 5p. blue £130 £500

The 2p. exists in ochre but was not issued (*price £160 un*).

(c) Bluish wove paper
51 **5** 2p. yellow £425
52 20p. deep red (A) £425
53 20p. deep red (B) £425

(d) Bluish laid paper
54 **5** 2p. orange £650

2p. yellow, 5p. blue and 20p. red stamps showing Prince Cuza facing right in a circle (instead of an oval) were prepared in 1864 but not issued (*Price: each £10·50 un*).

Prince Carol

(Prince Karl of Hohenzollern-Sigmaringen)

14 April 1866–23 May 1881

Prince Cuza was forced to abdicate in February 1866.

Under Prince Carol's rule the full independence of Romania was recognised by the Treaty of Berlin, 13 July 1878.

6

A Aa B

Types of 20p.

(Litho S. Sander & Co, Bucharest)

1866–67. Imperf.

(i) Thick paper (27.7.66)
55 **6** 2p. black/*yellow* 80·00 £475
56 5p. black/*blue* 85·00 £650
a. Black/grey-blue 85·00 £650
57 20p. black/*rose* (A) £160 80·00
58 20p. black/*rose* (Aa) £225 £130
59 20p. black/*rose* (B) £180 £100

(ii) Thin paper (1.2.67)
60 **6** 2p. black/*yellow* 42·00 £120
61 5p. black/*grey-blue* 75·00 £900
a. Black/bright blue £130 £1300
62 20p. black/*deep rose* (A) 37·00 31·00
63 20p. black/*deep rose* (Aa) £500 £325
64 20p. black/*deep rose* (B) 37·00 31·00

New Currency

7

8 No Beard

9 With Beard

(Litho S. Sander & Co, Bucharest)

1868–70. Imperf.

(i) Thick paper (20.1.68)

(a) White wove paper
65 **7** 2b. yellow 47·00 50·00
a. Red-orange 31·00 31·00
b. Orange-yellow 40·00 40·00
c. "FOSTA" for "POSTA" £250
66 4b. pale blue 85·00 60·00
a. Retouch. Right lower spandrel dotted and value partially redrawn £600 £325
b. Blue 85·00 60·00
c. Deep blue 80·00 75·00
67 18b. rose £250 37·00
a. Rose-red £275 37·00
b. Salmon £300 42·00

(b) Yellowish toned paper
68 **7** 2b. deep orange
69 4b. deep blue £140 £100
70 18b. red £275 60·00

(ii) Thinner paper (5.70)

(a) White wove paper
71 **7** 2b. bright orange 50·00 42·00
72 3b. mauve 65·00 47·00
a. Bright mauve 65·00 47·00

(b) Yellowish wove paper
73 **7** 3b. mauve £160 £100

The 2b. is known bisected and the 3b. trisected.

The 3b. exists privately perforated.

Nos. 23 to 70 were valid for use only on internal mail. The foreign postal service came into use with the following issue on 1 April 1869.

(Des Sander. Litho Socecu, Sander & Co, Bucharest)

1869 (1 April). Imperf.

(a) White wove paper
74 **8** 5b. orange-yellow 90·00 50·00
a. Orange 90·00 50·00
b. Deep red-orange £425 £200
75 10b. dull blue 47·00 42·00
a. Double print
b. Deep Prussian blue £100 75·00
c. Ultramarine 95·00 65·00
76 15b. red 47·00 42·00
a. Rose 60·00 47·00
b. Vermilion 70·00 50·00
c. Reversed "N" in "CINCIS" — £325
d. Bright scarlet 47·00 42·00
77 25b. blue and yellow 47·00 31·00
a. Deep blue and yellow 50·00 31·00
b. Blue and orange 47·00 31·00
c. Deep blue and orange 45·00 31·00
78 50b. red and pale blue £190 60·00
a. Red and blue £200 65·00
b. Red and deep blue £225 70·00
c. Head double, one inverted

(b) White vert laid paper
79 **8** 15b. rose £1800

(c) Yellowish toned paper
80 **8** 10b. indigo 95·00 65·00
81 15b. vermilion 95·00 60·00
a. Reversed "N" in "CINCIS" — £475
82 50b. red and blue £500 65·00

Two types of 10b.

A. Fine impression with the head central and three coloured vertical lines separating figures at left from "BANI".
B. New stones (also used for 50b.) but much coarser impression. The head is more to the right with the back closer to "ROM" and the chin further from "PO". Four indistinct coloured lines separate figures from "BANI" and the lettering at top and bottom is generally thicker.

(Des Sander. Litho Socecu, Sander & Co, Bucharest)

1871–72.

A. Imperf (1871–72)

(a) White wove paper
83 **9** 5b. red (4.71) 50·00 42·00
a. Scarlet 50·00 42·00
b. Rose 60·00 47·00
c. Rose-carmine 60·00 47·00
84 10b. orange-yellow (A) (4.71) 75·00 47·00
b. Orange 75·00 47·00
85 10b. blue (A) (12.71) £180 85·00
86 15b. carmine-red (3.72) £275 £250
a. Rose-red £275 £250
87 25b. olive-brown (12.71) 65·00 60·00
a. "CINCI" redrawn, reading "CINSI" £140

(b) Rose-tinted wove paper
88 **9** 5b. carmine 65·00 50·00

(c) Yellowish toned wove paper
89 **9** 5b. scarlet £130 50·00

90		10b. orange (A)	£150	65·00
91		25b. olive-brown	70·00	65·00
		(d) Laid paper		
92	9	10b. yellow (A)	£500	£500
		B. P 12½ (March–April 1872)		
		(a) White wove paper		
93	9	5b. rose-red	85·00	50·00
		a. Imperf between (vert pair)		
		b. Deep rose-carmine	85·00	50·00
		c. Vermilion	£1600	£850
94		10b. blue (A)	85·00	50·00
		a. Imperf vert (horiz pair)		
		b. Bright ultramarine	£150	70·00
95		25b. sepia	60·00	50·00
		(b) Yellowish wove paper		
96	9	5b. red	90·00	
97		10b. blue (A)	95·00	50·00
		a. Bright ultramarine	£200	95·00
98		25b. sepia	60·00	60·00
		C. Imperf. New stones (8.72)		
		(a) White wove paper		
99		10b. ultramarine (B)	50·00	65·00
		a. Greenish blue	£160	£180
100		50b. red and blue (B)	£225	£250
		a. Vermilion and blue	£250	£300
		(b) White vert laid paper		
101	9	10b. ultramarine (B)	£180	£300
		(c) Yellowish wove paper		
102	9	10b. ultramarine (B)	£180	£190
		(d) Yellowish vert laid paper		
103	9	10b. ultramarine (B)		

10

(Typo A. Hulot, Paris)

1872 (15 Oct). Tinted paper. P 14×13½.

104	10	1½b. bronze-green	31·00	6·25
105		3b. emerald	47·00	7·25
106		5b. bistre	26·00	5·75
107		10b. blue/*white*	26·00	6·25
109		15b. Venetian red	£170	20·00
110		25b. orange-buff	£180	23·00
		a. Deep orange	£190	37·00
111		50b. carmine-rose	£200	50·00

Two types of 10b.

A. Paris plate. Coloured line in upper right-hand arc of circle (typical of Paris plates for all values except 15b.)

B. Bucharest plate. No extra coloured line

Two types of 15b.

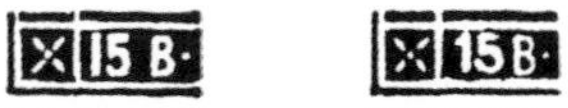

C. Paris plate. No serif to "1"

D. Bucharest plate. "1" with serif

(Typo in Bucharest from Paris plates (1½, 5b., 10b. (A), 15b.) or new plates made locally (10b. (B), 30b.))

1876 (Oct)–**79**.

		(a) P 11		
112	10	1½b. olive-green	7·75	5·25
		a. Olive-slate	6·25	5·25
		b. Printed both sides	—	80·00
113		5b. deep bistre	21·00	4·25
		a. Yellow-bistre	24·00	4·25
		b. Imperf between (horiz pair)	£250	
		c. Printed both sides	—	£250
114		10b. blue (A) (9.77)	31·00	6·25
		b. Pale greenish blue	31·00	6·25
		ba. Imperf between (vert pair)	—	80·00
		c. Deep blue	50·00	8·25
		d. Ultramarine (7.78)	60·00	6·25
114*e*		10b. blue (B) (1.79)	70·00	9·50
		ea. Error. 5b. blue	£500	£600
115		15b. Venetian red (C)	90·00	11·50
		a. Deep brown-red	95·00	12·50
116		30b. orange-red (p 11) (12.78)	£225	65·00
		a. Printed both sides	£425	

The error No. 114ea occurred in the sheet of the 10b. In 1882 it was reprinted in full sheets in deep blue, perf 11½.

		(b) P 13½		
117	10	1½b. olive-green	7·75	5·75
118		5b. olive-bistre	26·00	4·25
		a. Printed both sides	—	£250
		b. Yellow-bistre	21·00	4·25
		c. Brown-bistre	21·00	4·25
119		15b. brownish rose (C)	95·00	12·50
		a. Deep brown-red	95·00	12·50
		b. Imperf between (horiz pair)		
		(c) Perf compound of 11 and 13½		
120	10	1½b. olive-green		
121		5b. bistre	—	£100
122		10b. blue (A)	—	£130
123		15b. brownish rose (C)	—	£130

(Typo Bucharest from Paris plates (3b., 15b. (C), 25, 50b.) or local plates (1½, 5, 10b., 15b. (D))

1879 (1 April)–**80**. Colours changed and new values.

		(a) P 11 or 11½		
124	10	1½b. black	7·75	3·25
		a. Imperf between (vert pair)	—	80·00
		b. Imperf (pair)	—	£100
125		3b. olive-green (12.79)	21·00	16·00
126		5b. emerald-green	8·25	4·25
		a. Blue-green	18·00	5·25
127		10b. pale rose (B) (7.79)	17·00	3·25
		a. Error. 5b. pale rose (p 11)	£475	£950
		b. Imperf horiz (vert pair)	—	£200
		c. Rose-red	16·00	3·25
		d. Crimson (1880)	18·00	4·25
128		15b. orange-red (C)	£250	47·00
		a. Pale red	42·00	12·50
129		15b. rosine (D) (1880)	65·00	21·00
130		25b. blue (10.79)	£170	31·00
		a. Imperf (pair)	—	£170
131		50b. bistre-buff (7.79)	£150	42·00
		a. Deep bistre	£150	42·00
		b. Yellow-bistre	£150	42·00

The error No. 127a occurred in the sheet of the 10b. In 1882 it was reprinted in full sheets in deep carmine, perf 11½.

		(b) P 13½		
133	10	1½b. black	7·75	4·25
134		10b. crimson (B)	21·00	7·25
135		15b. pale red (C)		
136		15b. rosine (D)		
137		25b. blue		
		(c) Perf compound of 11½ and 13½		
138	10	1½b. black	14·00	7·25
139		3b. olive-green	—	19·00
140		5b. blue-green	—	12·50
141		10b. pale rose (B)	33·00	7·25
142		15b. pale red (C)		
143		15b. rosine (D)		
144		25b. blue		
145		50b. bistre-buff		

PRINTERS. The issues of 1880 to 1902 were typographed at the Government Printing Works, Bucharest.

11

D 12

1880 (July).

		(a) P 11 or 11½		
146	11	15b. cinnamon	16·00	3·25
		a. Red-brown	14·50	3·25
		b. Deep brown	14·50	3·25
147		25b. blue	29·00	4·25
		a. Imperf (pair)	£150	
		(b) P 13½		
148	11	15b. red-brown	£130	12·50
		a. Deep brown	£325	
149		25b. blue	29·00	3·75
		(c) Perf compound of 11½ and 13½		
150	11	15b. red-brown	14·50	3·25
151		25b. blue	29·00	4·25

1881 (1 May). POSTAGE DUE.

		(a) P 11 or 11½		
D152	D **12**	2b. deep brown	5·25	4·25
D153		5b. deep brown	26·00	6·25
		a. Tête-bêche (pair)	£225	95·00
D154		10b. deep brown	31·00	4·25
D155		30b. deep brown	37·00	4·25
D156		50b. deep brown	21·00	7·25
D157		60b. deep brown	26·00	10·50
		(b) P 13½		
D158	D **12**	2b. deep brown		
D159		10b. deep brown		
		(c) Perf compound of 11½ and 13½		
D160	D **12**	30b. deep brown	37·00	4·25

See also Nos. D200/15, D234/50, D357/73, D448/63 and D550/60.

King Carol I

23 May 1881–10 October 1914

Prince Carol was proclaimed King on 23 May 1881.

12

13

14

1885 (Aug)–**88**. No wmk.

		(a) P 13½		
161	12	1½b. black	4·25	2·10
162		1½b. black/*bluish* (12.88)	6·25	2·10
163		3b. pea-green/*bluish*	6·25	2·10
164		3b. violet/*greenish* (2.87)	6·25	2·10
165		3b. violet (2.88)	6·25	2·10
		a. Purple	6·25	2·10
166		5b. blue-green/*bluish*	6·25	2·10
167		5b. blue-green (2.88)	95·00	26·00
168		10b. red/*yellowish* (15.4.86)	6·25	3·25
169		15b. red-brown	18·00	3·25
170		15b. red-brown/*buff* (12.88)	23·00	3·75
		a. Chocolate/buff	23·00	3·75
171		25b. blue	21·00	7·25
		a. Ultramarine	21·00	7·25
172		25b. blue/*yellowish* (12.88)	23·00	7·25
		a. Indigo/yellowish	23·00	7·25
173		50b. ochre/*yellowish*	95·00	26·00
		(b) P 11½		
174	12	1½b. black	4·75	2·10
175		1½b. black/*bluish*	12·50	9·50
176		3b. pea-green/*bluish*	9·50	3·75
177		3b. violet/*greenish*	9·50	3·75
178		3b. violet	9·00	2·10
		a. Purple	9·00	2·50
179		5b. blue-green/*bluish*	9·00	2·10
180		5b. blue-green	—	26·00
181		10b. red/*yellowish*	9·00	2·10
182		15b. red-brown	33·00	4·25
183		15b. red-brown/*buff*	37·00	5·25
184		25b. blue	31·00	2·50
185		25b. blue/*yellowish*	44·00	9·50
186		50b. ochre/*yellowish*	95·00	26·00
		(c) Perf compound of 11½ and 13½		
187	12	1½b. black	4·75	2·10
188		1½b. black/*bluish*	5·25	2·30
189		3b. pea-green/*bluish*	9·50	4·25
190		3b. violet/*greenish*	9·50	2·10
191		3b. violet	9·50	2·30
192		5b. blue-green/*bluish*	8·25	2·10
193		5b. blue-green	95·00	26·00
194		10b. red/*yellowish*	9·00	2·10
195		15b. red-brown	33·00	6·25
196		15b. red-brown/*buff*	33·00	6·25
		a. Chocolate/buff	23·00	3·75
197		25b. blue	31·00	8·25
198		25b. blue/*yellowish*	23·00	7·25
		a. Indigo/yellowish	42·00	7·25
199		50b. ochre/*yellowish*	95·00	26·00

1885. POSTAGE DUE. Colour changed.

		(a) P 13½		
D200	D **12**	10b. red-brown	10·50	1·00
D201		30b. red-brown	10·50	1·00
		(b) P 11½		
D202	D **12**	10b. red-brown	11·50	1·20
		a. Imperf between (vert pr)	—	95·00
D203		30b. red-brown	11·50	1·20
		(c) Perf compound of 11½ and 13½		
D204	D **12**	10b. red-brown	85·00	10·50
D205		30b. red-brown	47·00	8·25

1887 (6 Dec)–**90**. POSTAGE DUE. Colour changed. No wmk.

		A. On white paper (6.12.87)		
		(a) P 13½		
D206A	D **12**	2b. green	5·25	2·10
D207A		5b. green	10·50	7·25
D208A		10b. green	10·50	7·25
D209A		30b. green	10·50	2·10
		B. On yellowish paper (1888–90)		
		(a) P 13½		
D206B	D **12**	2b. green	1·00	1·00
D207B		5b. green	3·25	2·50
D208B		10b. green	23·00	4·25
D209B		30b. green	18·00	1·60
		A. On white paper (6.12.87)		
		(b) P 11½		
D211A	D **12**	30b. green	26·00	5·25
		B. On yellowish paper (1888–90)		
		(b) P 11½		
D210B	D **12**	5b. green	25·00	21·00
D211B		30b. green	25·00	6·25
		A. On white paper (6.12.87)		
		(c) Perf compound of 11½ and 13½		
D212A	D **12**	2b. green	35·00	21·00
D213A		5b. green	35·00	29·00
D214A		10b. green	35·00	7·25
D215A		30b. green	16·00	7·25
		B. On yellowish paper (1888–90)		
		(c) Perf compound of 11½ and 13½		
D212B	D **12**	2b. green	9·50	9·50
D213B		5b. green	—	—
D214B		10b. green	—	—
D215B		30b. green	18·00	7·25

1889 (14 Oct). W **13** impressed in the paper.

		(a) P 13½		
216	12	1½b. black	37·00	7·25
217		3b. violet	26·00	7·25
218		5b. dull green	26·00	7·25
219		10b. dull rose	26·00	7·25
220		15b. chestnut	90·00	16·00
221		25b. deep blue	60·00	12·50
		(b) P 11½		
222	12	1½b. black	£190	70·00
223		3b. violet	75·00	26·00
		a. Imperf between (horiz pr)	£350	
224		5b. dull green	47·00	16·00
225		10b. dull rose	26·00	7·25
226		15b. chestnut	85·00	26·00
227		25b. deep blue	47·00	12·50
		(c) Perf compound of 11½ and 13½		
228	12	1½b. black	40·00	14·00
229		3b. violet	26·00	7·25
230		5b. dull green	26·00	7·25
231		10b. dull rose	39·00	7·25
232		15b. chestnut	85·00	14·50
233		25b. deep blue	49·00	8·25

1990–96. POSTAGE DUE. W **13** impressed in the paper.

		(a) P 13½		
D234	D **12**	2b. emerald	2·10	75
D235		5b. emerald	1·00	75
D236		10b. emerald	1·60	75
D237		30b. emerald	2·50	75
D238		50b. emerald (1893)	8·25	1·60
D239		60b. emerald (1896)	11·50	5·25
		(b) P 11½		
D240	D **12**	2b. emerald	2·10	75
D241		5b. emerald	5·25	2·30
D242		10b. emerald	2·10	75

D243		30b. emerald	5·25	85
D244		50b. emerald	8·25	1·60
D245		60b. emerald	11·00	4·75

(c) Perf compound of 11½ and 13½

D246	D **12**	2b. emerald		
D247		5b. emerald	4·25	1·40
D248		10b. emerald	6·75	1·40
D249		30b. emerald	12·50	1·60
D250		50b. emerald	21·00	5·25

1890 (Jan). W **13** impressed in the paper.

(a) P 13½

251	**14**	1½b. lake	6·25	2·10
252		3b. mauve	31·00	4·25
		a. Violet	26·00	3·75
253		5b. emerald	14·50	2·50
254		10b. brick-red	16·00	6·25
		a. Carmine	21·00	8·25
255		15b. grey-brown	26·00	4·75
256		25b. blue	21·00	4·25
		a. Ultramarine	21·00	4·25
257		50b. orange	75·00	42·00

(b) P 11½

258	**14**	1½b. lake	26·00	26·00
259		3b. mauve	£100	26·00
		a. Violet	£130	31·00
260		5b. emerald	£100	24·00
261		10b. brick-red	£140	26·00
		a. Carmine	£140	26·00
262		15b. grey-brown	26·00	6·75
263		25b. ultramarine	50·00	7·75

(c) Perf compound of 11½ and 13½

264	**14**	1½b. lake	6·75	4·25
265		3b. mauve	50·00	7·75
		a. Violet	26·00	6·75
266		5b. emerald	42·00	23·00
267		10b. brick-red	60·00	16·00
		a. Carmine	95·00	19·00
268		15b. grey-brown	31·00	23·00
269		25b. ultramarine	37·00	20·00
270		50b. orange	—	75·00

1890 (Sept). No wmk. Thin semi-transparent or thicker opaque paper.

(a) P 13½

271	**14**	1½b. dull rose	2·10	1·60
272		3b. pale lilac	2·50	2·10
		a. Indigo-lilac	2·50	2·50
		b. Printed both sides	£200	£200
273		5b. green	4·25	2·10
274		10b. brick-red	26·00	2·10
		a. Printed both sides	£225	£225
275		15b. grey-brown	16·00	1·60
276		25b. ultramarine	12·50	2·10
277		50b. orange	£100	16·00

(b) P 11½

278	**14**	1½b. dull rose	5·25	1·60
		a. Printed both sides	—	£130
279		3b. dull lilac	3·00	2·10
		a. 5b. printed on back	£100	80·00
		b. Indigo-lilac	4·25	2·10
280		5b. green	5·25	1·80
281		10b. brick-red	27·00	3·75
		a. Printed both sides	£130	80·00
282		15b. grey-brown	16·00	1·60
283		25b. ultramarine	13·50	2·10
284		50b. orange	—	33·00

(c) Perf compound of 11½ and 13½

285	**14**	1½b. dull rose	4·00	2·10
286		3b. pale lilac	4·75	2·10
		a. Indigo-lilac	4·50	2·10
287		5b. green	4·00	2·30
288		10b. brick-red	16·00	3·25
289		15b. grey-brown	16·00	1·60
290		25b. ultramarine	13·00	2·10
291		50b. orange	£100	16·00

See also Nos. 304/15.

15

16

1891 (10 May). Silver Jubilee: 25 Years' Reign. No wmk.

(a) P 13½

292	**15**	1½b. rose-lake	26·00	26·00
293		3b. mauve	7·25	8·25
294		5b. emerald	9·50	10·50
295		10b. brick-red	9·50	10·50
296		15b. grey-brown	9·50	8·25

(b) P 11½

297	**15**	3b. mauve		
298		5b. emerald		
299		10b. brick-red		

(c) Perf compound of 11½ and 13½

300	**15**	1½b. rose-lake	7·25	8·25
301		3b. mauve	10·50	10·50
302		5b. emerald		
303		15b. grey-brown	9·50	8·25

1894 (Jan). W **16**.

(a) P 13½

304	**14**	3b. bright violet	16·00	16·00
305		5b. pale green	11·50	6·25
306		25b. pale ultramarine	17·00	7·75
		a. Imperf between (horiz pr)	—	£350
307		50b. orange	33·00	16·00

(b) P 11½

308	**14**	3b. bright violet	27·00	7·50
309		5b. pale green	50·00	12·50
310		25b. pale ultramarine		
311		50b. orange		

(c) Perf compound of 11½ and 13½

312	**14**	3b. bright violet	11·50	3·75
313		5b. pale green	10·50	3·25
314		25b. pale ultramarine	50·00	7·25
315		50b. orange	80·00	19·00

17

18

19

20

21

22

23

P **24**

WATERMARKS. The following issue exists with the watermark "PR" in several sizes. W **16** (letters 11 mm. tall) was introduced in 1893/4; a second type (13½–14½ mm. tall) in 1895 and again in 1897/8; a third type (12–12½ mm. tall) in 1897 and finally W **23** (15½ mm. tall) in 1899. This last type usually occurs reversed but all types are found sideways, inverted etc.

1893–99. Wmk "P R" in various sizes. Various types of paper.

(a) P 13½

316	**17**	1b. pale brown (1895)	1·60	1·00
		a. Brown (1897)	1·60	1·00
317		1½b. black	1·60	90
318	**18**	3b. chocolate (1895)	2·10	90
		a. Red-brown	2·10	90
319	**19**	5b. blue	2·50	1·30
		a. Error. 25b. blue	£180	£200
320	**20**	10b. emerald	4·50	1·30
321	**21**	15b. rose	5·25	2·10
		a. Carmine-pink (1899)	6·25	2·30
322	**19**	25b. bright mauve	5·25	1·60
323		40b. blue-green	26·00	4·25
324		50b. orange	21·00	2·50
		a. Lemon (1895)	21·00	2·50
325	**22**	1l. rose and pale brown	37·00	2·50
326		2l. brown and orange	42·00	4·25

(b) P 11½

327	**17**	1b. pale brown	1·60	1·00
		a. Brown	1·60	1·00
328		1½b. black	1·60	90
329	**18**	3b. chocolate	2·50	1·00
		a. Red-brown	2·50	1·00
330	**19**	5b. blue	3·75	1·50
		a. Error. 25b. blue	£180	£200
331	**20**	10b. emerald	6·25	1·60
332	**21**	15b. rose	6·25	1·60
		a. Carmine-pink	7·25	3·25
333	**19**	25b. bright mauve	6·25	1·60
334		50b. orange	21·00	2·50
		a. Lemon	21·00	2·50
335	**22**	1l. rose and pale brown	42·00	4·25

(c) Perf compound of 11½ and 13½

336	**17**	1b. pale brown	2·10	90
		a. Brown	2·10	90
337		1½b. black	26·00	5·25
338	**18**	3b. chocolate	2·50	1·00
		a. Red-brown	2·50	1·00
339	**19**	5b. blue	3·75	1·50
		a. Error. 25b. blue	£190	£225
340	**20**	10b. emerald	6·25	1·60
341	**21**	15b. rose	6·25	1·60
		a. Carmine-pink	7·25	1·80
342	**19**	25b. bright mauve	8·25	2·10
343		40b. blue-green	50·00	8·25
344		50b. orange	47·00	3·25
345	**22**	1l. rose and pale brown		
346		2l. brown and orange		

Nos. 319a, 330a and 339a were caused by the insertion of a 25b. cliché in the plate of the 5b. with which it is known *se-tenant*.

The 3b. in *orange-yellow*, 10b. in *light brown*, 15b. in *black* and 25b. in *light green* are proofs.

See also Nos. 374/447, 532/47, 625*a*/*b* and 685, etc.

1895 (15 Sept)–**96**. PARCEL POST. W **13** impressed in the paper.

(a) P 13½

P347	P **24**	25b. red-brown	11·50	1·80
P348		25b. vermilion (1896)	16·00	2·40

(b) P 11½

P349	P **24**	25b. red-brown	10·50	2·50
P350		25b. vermilion	10·50	2·50

(c) Perf compound of 11½ and 13½

P351	P **24**	25b. red-brown	12·00	3·25
P352		25b. vermilion	16·00	4·25

See also Nos. P353/6, P479/80 and P548/9.

1898 (Oct). PARCEL POST. Wmk "P R".

(a) P 13½

P353	P **24**	25b. red-brown	8·25	1·00
		a. Tête-bêche (pair)		
P354		25b. vermilion	8·25	1·00

(b) Perf compound of 11½ and 13½

P355	P **24**	25b. red-brown	8·25	1·00
P356		25b. vermilion	11·50	2·10

All the above exist with the watermark 13½–14½ mm. tall and the vermilion stamps also 15½ mm tall, issued in 1899.

1898. POSTAGE DUE. Wmk "P R".

(a) P 13½

D357	D **12**	2b. bright green	75	65
D358		5b. bright green	1·00	50
D359		10b. bright green	1·60	50
D360		30b. bright green	2·10	50
D361		50b. bright green	5·25	1·60
D362		60b. bright green	6·25	3·25

(b) P 11½

D363	D **12**	2b. bright green	75	65
D364		5b. bright green	1·30	50
D365		10b. bright green	2·10	50
D366		30b. bright green	5·75	1·00
D367		50b. bright green	5·25	1·80

(c) Perf compound of 11½ and 13½

D368	D **12**	2b. bright green	2·10	80
D369		5b. bright green	2·10	50
D370		10b. bright green	1·60	50
D371		30b. bright green	1·90	50
D372		50b. bright green	19·00	4·25
D373		60b. bright green		

All the above exist with the watermark 13½–14½ mm. and 15½ mm. tall, except No. D373 which only exists 15½ mm tall.

1899 (July). Colours changed to comply with U.P.U. Colour Convention. W **23** (upright or sideways).

(a) P 13½

374	**19**	5b. emerald	7·25	4·00
375	**20**	10b. rose-red	6·75	3·25
376	**21**	15b. black	6·25	3·25
377	**19**	25b. blue	10·50	3·25

(b) P 11½

378	**19**	5b. emerald	6·25	3·75
379	**20**	10b. rose-red	7·25	3·25
380	**21**	15b. black	7·25	2·50
381	**19**	25b. blue	11·50	4·25

(c) Perf compound of 11½ and 13½

382	**19**	5b. emerald	5·75	4·25
383	**20**	10b. rose-red	6·25	3·25
384	**21**	15b. black	6·75	3·25
385	**19**	25b. blue	11·50	4·25

24

(Reduced size illustration covering 25 stamps)

1900 (5 July). Thin paper, tinted pink at back. W **24** in sheet. P 11½.

386	**17**	1 bani, pale brown	12·50	6·25
387	**18**	3b. red-brown	12·50	6·75
		a. Compound perf		
388	**19**	5b. emerald	14·50	5·25
		a. Perf 13½		
		b. Compound perf		
389	**20**	10b. rose-red	19·00	7·25
		a. Compound perf		
390	**21**	15b. black	21·00	9·00
		a. Compound perf		
391	**19**	25b. deep blue	23·00	16·00
392		40b. deep green	37·00	19·00
		a. Perf 13½		
		b. Compound perf		
393		50b. orange	37·00	19·00
		a. Perf 13½		
		b. Compound perf		
394	**22**	1l. rose and grey-brown	42·00	21·00
		a. Perf 13½		
395		2l. brown and orange	50·00	26·00

1900. Thin paper, tinted pink at back. No wmk.

(a) P 11½

396	**17**	1 bani, pale brown	2·10	1·30
		a. Deep brown	2·10	1·30
397	**18**	3b. maroon	2·20	1·30
		a. Red-brown	2·30	1·30
398	**19**	5b. blue-green	3·25	1·00
		a. Emerald	3·25	1·00
399	**20**	10b. rose-red	3·75	1·60
400	**21**	15b. black	3·25	1·00
401	**19**	25b. blue	4·25	1·30
		a. Deep blue	4·25	1·30
402		40b. blue-green	10·50	1·90
403		50b. orange	21·00	2·10
404	**22**	1l. rose and grey-brown	42·00	3·75
405		2l. brown and orange	31·00	4·75

(b) P 13½

06 **17** 1 bani, pale brown 19·00 3·75
a. Deep brown 19·00 3·75
07 **18** 3b. maroon 2·10 1·30
a. Red-brown 2·10 1·30
08 **19** 5b. blue-green 3·75 1·60
a. Emerald 3·75 1·60
09 **20** 10b. rose-red 4·25 1·30
10 **21** 15b. black 17·00 5·25
11 **19** 25b. blue 4·25 1·70
a. Deep blue 4·25 1·70
12 40b. blue-green 20·00
13 50b. orange 21·00 1·40
14 **22** 1l. rose and grey-brown 37·00 4·00

(c) Perf compound of 11½ and 13½

15 **17** 1 bani, pale brown 9·00 3·75
a. Deep brown 20·00 4·00
16 **18** 3b. maroon 2·10 1·30
a. Red-brown 2·10 1·30
17 **19** 5b. blue-green 3·75 1·60
a. Emerald 3·75 1·60
18 **20** 10b. rose-red 3·75 1·60
19 **21** 15b. black 8·75 1·60
20 **19** 25b. blue 4·00 1·60
a. Deep blue 4·00 1·60
21 40b. blue-green 12·50 1·90
22 50b. orange 37·00 4·00
23 **22** 1l. rose and grey-brown

(d) P 9×10

24 **19** 25b. blue — 37·00
25 50b. orange — 37·00

In the above and following issue stamps bearing part of the papermaker's watermark "JOHANNOT & Cie ANNONAY" are worth about ten times the prices quoted.

For the 1908 printings of this and the following issue on white paper, see Nos. 532/47.

1901–03. Colours changed. 1b. inscr "BAN" instead of "BANI". Thin paper, tinted pink at back. No wmk.

(a) P 11½

26 **17** 1 ban, red-brown 2·10 1·60
a. Deep brown 2·10 1·60
27 1 ban, black (1903) 2·10 1·60
a. Grey 2·10 1·60
28 **19** 5b. yellow-green (1903) 3·75 1·30
29 **20** 10b. bright rose (1903) 3·75 1·30
a. Carmine 3·50 1·30
30 **21** 15b. drab 3·50 1·30
31 15b. dull violet (1903) 3·75 1·30
32 **22** 1l. black and blue-green (1903) 42·00 3·75
33 2l. black and brown (1903) 31·00 4·75

(b) P 13½

34 **17** 1 ban, red-brown 3·50 1·50
a. Deep brown 3·50 1·50
35 1 ban, black 2·30 1·30
a. Grey 2·30 1·30
36 **19** 5b. yellow-green 3·50 1·30
37 **20** 10b. bright rose 40·00 14·50
a. Carmine 29·00 5·50
38 **21** 15b. drab 12·50 3·75
39 15b. dull violet 12·50 3·75
40 **22** 1l. black and blue-green 28·00 3·75

(c) Perf compound of 11½ and 13½

41 **17** 1 ban, red-brown 3·50 1·50
a. Deep brown 3·50 1·50
42 1 ban, black 2·30 1·30
a. Grey 2·30 1·30
43 **19** 5b. yellow-green 3·50 1·30
44 **20** 10b. bright rose 3·50 1·30
a. Carmine 3·50 1·30
45 **21** 15b. drab 4·00 1·30
46 **22** 1l. black and blue-green 42·00 3·75

(d) P 9×10

47 **21** 15b. dull violet — 19·00

See also Nos. 532/47.

1902–10. POSTAGE DUE. Thin paper, tinted pink at back. No. wmk.

(a) P 11½

D448 D **12** 2b. green 75 20
D449 5b. green 50 20
D450 10b. green 50 20
D451 30b. green 50 20
D452 50b. green 2·30 1·00
D453 60b. green (1910) 5·25 2·50

(b) P 13½

D454 D **12** 2b. green 9·00 1·30
D455 5b. green 3·25 45
D456 10b. green 3·25 85
D457 30b. green 3·25 85
D458 50b. green 5·25 1·40

(c) Perf compound of 11½ and 13½

D459 D **12** 2b. green 1·50 1·30
D460 5b. green 1·60 20
D461 10b. green 1·40 20
D462 30b. green 1·40 20
D463 50b. green 6·50 1·40

Shades range between pale green and emerald-green.

For 1908 printings on white paper, see Nos. D550/60.

25 Four-in-hand Postal Coach

26 New Post Office, Bucharest

(Eng A. Thévenin (T **25**), M. Popescu (T **26**). Typo French Govt Ptg Wks, Paris)

1903 (1 May). Opening of New Post Office (1901). No wmk.

(a) Pink-surfaced paper. P 14×13½

464 **25** 1b. pale brown 2·10 1·80
465 3b. claret 4·25 2·10
466 5b. pale green 7·75 3·25
467 10b. rose 6·25 3·25
468 15b. black 6·25 4·25
469 25b. blue 21·00 12·50
470 40b. dull green 31·00 16·00
471 50b. orange 38·00 21·00
464/471 *Set of* 8 £100 60·00

Stamps bearing portions of the papermaker's watermark "JOHANNOT & Cie ANNONAY" are rare.

See No. 1275 for 16l. in green.

(b) Thick toned wove paper. P 13½×14

472 **26** 15b. black 5·25 4·25
473 25b. blue 12·50 7·75
474 40b. green 21·00 10·50
475 50b. orange 23·00 12·50
476 1l. brown 18·00 10·50
477 2l. red-orange £160 80·00
a. Error. Yellow-orange £200 £180
478 5l. lilac £190 £130
472/478 *Set of* 7 £375 £225

Beware of forgeries, particularly of the high values.

1905. PARCEL POST. Thin paper, tinted pink at back. No wmk.

(a) P 11½

P479 P **24** 25b. vermilion 6·25 2·10

(b) Perf compound of 11½ and 13½

P480 P **24** 25b. vermilion 10·50 2·50

Stamps bearing portions of the papermaker's watermark "JOHANNOT & Cie ANNONAY" are scarce.

27 Queen of Romania spinning

28 Queen of Romania weaving

(Typo Govt Ptg Wks, Bucharest)

1906 (1 Jan). Welfare Fund. Motto: "God guide our Hand". Typo. P 11½.

481 **27** 3(+7)b. red-brown 7·75 5·25
a. Perf compound of 11½ and 13½
482 5(+10)b. green 7·75 5·25
a. Perf compound of 11½ and 13½
483 10(+10)b. carmine 37·00 16·00
a. Perf compound of 11½ and 13½
484 15(+10)b. purple 31·00 10·50
a. Perf compound of 11½ and 13½
481/484 *Set of* 4 75·00 33·00

(Des C. Petrescu. Typo Govt Ptg Wks, Bucharest)

1906 (5 Mar). Welfare Fund. Motto: "Woman weaves the Future of the Country". Typo. P 11½.

485 **28** 3(+7)b. red-brown 7·75 5·25
a. Perf compound of 11½ and 13½ 7·75 5·25
486 5(+10)b. green 7·75 5·25
a. Perf compound of 11½ and 13½ 7·75 5·25
487 10(+10)b. carmine 42·00 16·00
a. Perf compound of 11½ and 13½ 42·00 16·00
488 15(+10)b. lilac 26·00 10·50
a. Perf compound of 11½ and 13½ 26·00 10·50
485/488 *Set of* 4 75·00 33·00

29 Queen of Romania nursing Wounded Soldier

30

(Typo Govt Ptg Wks, Bucharest)

1906 (10 Mar). Welfare Fund. Motto: "The Wounds dressed and the Tears wiped away". Typo. P 11½.

489 **29** 3(+7)b. red-brown 7·75 5·25
a. Perf compound of 11½ and 13½ 7·75 5·25
490 5(+10)b. green 7·75 5·25
a. Perf compound of 11½ and 13½ 7·75 5·25
491 10(+10)b. carmine 42·00 16·00
a. Perf compound of 11½ and 13½ 42·00 16·00
492 15(+10)b. purple 26·00 10·50
a. Perf compound of 11½ and 13½ 26·00 10·50
489/492 *Set of* 4 75·00 33·00

(Des S. Pompilian. Recess Bradbury, Wilkinson & Co.)

1906 (June). 25th Anniv of the Kingdom. P 12.

493 **30** 1b. black and bistre 1·00 50
494 3b. black and red-brown 2·50 1·00
495 5b. black and green 1·60 75
496 10b. black and carmine 1·60 75
497 15b. black and violet 1·60 75
498 25b. black and blue 14·50 7·75
a. Head inverted
499 40b. black and deep brown 6·25 1·60
500 50b. black and yellow-brown 6·25 1·60
501 1l. black and vermilion 6·25 1·60
502 2l. black and orange 6·25 1·60
493/502 *Set of* 10 43·00 16·00

31 Prince Carol at Battle of Calafat

32

(Des S. Pompilian. Recess Bradbury, Wilkinson & Co.)

1906 (July). Forty Years' Rule of the Prince and King. T **31** and similar types inscr "1866–1906". P 12.

503 1b. black and bistre 75 50
504 3b. black and brown 1·60 50
505 5b. black and green 1·80 50
506 10b. black and carmine 1·30 50
507 15b. black and indigo-lilac 1·30 50
508 25b. black and blue 7·75 6·25
a. Error. Black and sage-green 9·25 6·25
509 40b. black and deep brown 2·10 1·60
510 50b. black and yellow-brown 2·30 1·60
511 1l. black and vermilion 2·30 1·80
512 2l. black and orange 2·50 2·50
503/512 *Set of* 10 21·00 14·50

Designs:—1b. Prince Carol taking oath of allegiance in 1866; 3b. Prince in royal carriage; 10b. Meeting of Prince Carol and Osman Pasha in 1878; 15b. Carol when Prince in 1866 and King in 1906; 25b. Romanian Army crossing Danube, 1877; 40b. Triumphal entry into Bucharest, 1878; 50b. Prince Carol and his Army in 1877; 1l. King Carol at Cathedral in 1896; 2l. King Carol at shrine of St. Nicholas, 1904.

(Typo Bradbury, Wilkinson)

1906 (Aug). Welfare Fund. Motto: "But Glory, Honour and Peace to All that do Good". P 12.

513 **32** 3(+7)b. brown and red-brown 4·25 2·10
514 5(+10)b. green, rose and bistre 4·25 2·10
515 10(+10)b. carmine, bistre and blue 6·25 4·25
516 15(+10)b. violet, bistre and blue 17·00 5·25
513/516 *Set of* 4 29·00 12·50

33 Peasant ploughing and Angel

(Des C. Stengel. Typo Govt Ptg Wks, Bucharest (15 to 75b.) or A. Baer, Bucharest (others))

1906 (29 Oct). Jubilee Exhibition, Bucharest. T **33** and similar designs inscr "EXPOSITIA GENERALA". P 12.

517 5b. black and yellow-green 5·25 1·60
518 10b. black and carmine 5·25 1·60
519 15b. black and violet 7·75 2·50
520 25b. black and blue 7·75 2·50
521 30b. sepia and red 10·50 2·50
522 40b. sepia and blue-green 11·50 3·25
523 50b. black and orange 10·50 3·75
524 75b. sepia and light brown 9·50 3·75
525 1l.50 sepia and reddish mauve £120 50·00
526 2l.50 brown and yellow 42·00 31·00
527 3l. brown and orange-brown 31·00 31·00
517/527 *Set of* 11 £225 £120

Designs: Horiz—10b. T **33**; 15b., 25b. Exhibition Building. Vert—30b., 40b. Farmhouse; 50b., 75b. (different), Royal Family pavilion; 1l.50, 2l.50, King Carol on horseback; 3l. Queen Elisabeth (Carmen Sylva).

The above issue was only on sale and valid for three days. Stamps sold at the Exhibition were overprinted in black with "S E" ("Servicul Expositiei") as Exhibition Official stamps. Remainders were sold by the exhibition authorities, both unused and cancelled to order.

34 Princess Maria and her Children receiving Poor Family conducted by an Angel

(Recess Bradbury, Wilkinson)

1907 (Jan). Welfare Fund. P 11.

528 **34** 3(+7)b. brown and red-brown 5·25 2·10
529 5(+10)b. brown and green 5·25 2·10
530 10(+10)b. brown and carmine 5·25 2·10
531 15(+10)b. brown and indigo-blue 5·25 2·10
528/531 *Set of* 4 19·00 7·50

1908. White paper. No wmk.

(a) P 11½

532 **17** 1 ban, grey 40 30
a. Black 40 30
533 **18** 3b. red-brown 1·00 40
a. Orange-brown 1·00 40
534 **19** 5b. yellow-green 2·10 50
a. Grass-green 3·75 50
535 **20** 10b. carmine 2·10 50
536 **21** 15b. bright violet 2·50 50
537 **19** 25b. deep blue 2·40 50
538 40b. deep green 10·50 2·10

(b) P 13½

539	17	1 ban, black		
540	21	15b. bright violet	—	13·00

(c) Perf compound of 11½ and 13½

541	17	1 ban, grey	40	30
		a. Black	40	30
542	18	3b. red-brown	1·00	40
		a. Orange-brown	1·00	40
543	19	5b. yellow-green	2·10	50
		a. Grass-green	3·75	50
544	20	10b. carmine	2·10	50
545	21	15b. bright violet	2·50	50
546	19	25b. deep blue	2·40	50
547		40b. deep green	10·50	2·10

For 1½b. value see Nos. 625*a*/*b*.

1908. PARCEL POST. White paper. No wmk.

(a) P 11½

P548	P **24**	25b. vermilion		

(b) Perf compound of 11½ and 13½

P549	P **24**	25b. vermilion	10·50	2·10

1908–11. POSTAGE DUE. White paper. No wmk.

(a) P 11½

D550	D **12**	2b. green (1911)	2·50	40
D551		5b. green	75	40
		a. Tête-bêche (pair)	16·00	16·00
D552		10b. green	2·50	20
		a. Tête-bêche (pair)	21·00	21·00
D553		30b. green	65	20
		a. Tête-bêche (pair)	12·50	12·50
D554		50b. green	2·50	1·00

(b) P 13½

D555	D **12**	5b. green	—	6·25
D556		30b. green	3·75	1·00

(c) Perf compound of 11½ and 13½

D557	D **12**	5b. green	75	40
		a. Tête-bêche (pair)	16·00	16·00
D558		10b. green	50	20
		a. Tête-bêche (pair)	12·50	12·50
D559		30b. green	1·00	50
		a. Tête-bêche (pair)	17·00	17·00
D560		50b. green	2·50	1·80

Shades vary in this issue.

35

36

37

(Des J. Pompilian. Eng G. Popescu. Recess Govt Ptg Wks, Bucharest)

1908 (April)–**09**.

(a) P 11½

561	35	5b. emerald	3·25	30
		a. Yellow-green	3·25	30
562		10b. rose-carmine	50	20
		a. Bright carmine	50	20
563	36	15b. dull violet	12·00	3·75
		a. Deep violet	6·25	2·40
		b. Bluish violet	6·75	2·40
564	35	25b. deep blue	2·10	20
565		40b. blue-green (28.8.08)	50	20
566		50b. orange	75	20
		a. Yellow-orange	1·00	20
567		1l. sepia (28.8.08)	2·50	50
568		2l. red (28.8.08)	9·50	2·50
		a. Vermilion	9·50	2·50

(b) P 13½

569	35	10b. rose-carmine	85	10
570		25b. deep blue	1·00	20
571		40b. blue-green	1·40	30
		a. Emerald	3·00	80
572		50b. orange	50	20
		a. Yellow-orange	1·00	20
573		1l. sepia	3·25	85
		a. Bistre-brown	4·25	85
574		2l. red	10·50	3·25
		a. Vermilion	10·50	3·25

(c) Perf compound of 11½ and 13½

575	35	5b. emerald	3·25	30
		a. Yellow-green	3·25	30
576		10b. rose-carmine	50	20
		a. Bright carmine	50	20
577	36	15b. deep violet	6·25	2·40
		a. Bluish violet	6·75	2·40
578	35	25b. deep blue	2·10	20
579		40b. blue-green	75	20
		a. Emerald	1·00	20
580		50b. orange	75	20
		a. Yellow-orange	75	20
581		1l. sepia	2·30	50
		a. Bistre-brown	2·30	50
582		2l. red	9·50	2·50
		a. Vermilion	9·50	2·50

See also Nos. 686 etc.

PERF 13½. At the end of 1911 a new comb perforator which gauged 13.4×13.7 was introduced and this became the norm. However, the old line perforator, measuring approximately 13.4 all round, continued to be used. The difference is too small to warrant separate listing but as a rule the stamps with line perforation are scarcer.

(Des J. Pompilian. Typo Govt Ptg Wks, Bucharest)

1909–14.

(a) P 11½

583	37	1b. grey-black	50	10
584		3b. red-brown	1·00	10
585		5b. yellow-green	50	10
586		10b. carmine (1914)	1·60	10
587		15b. dull violet	26·00	16·00
588		15b. sage-green	1·00	10

(b) P 13½

589	37	1b. grey-black	50	10
590		3b. red-brown	1·00	10
591		5b. yellow-green	50	10
592		10b. carmine	50	10
593		15b. dull violet	28·00	20·00
594		15b. sage-green	1·00	10

(c) Perf compound of 11½ and 13½

595	37	1b. grey-black	50	10
596		3b. red-brown	1·00	10
597		5b. yellow-green	50	10
598		10b. carmine	50	10
599		15b. dull violet	11·50	10·50
600		15b. sage-green	1·00	10

See also Nos. 684, 692 and 700.

D **38**

F **38**

Two types of 20b.:
A. Wide head to "2" as in Type D **38**.
B. Narrow head to "2".

(Typo Govt Ptg Wks, Bucharest)

1911 (7 May). POSTAGE DUE Wmk "P R" in monogram, impressed in the paper.

(a) P 11½

D601	D **38**	2b. blue/*greenish yellow*		
D602		5b. blue/*greenish yellow*	—	50
D603		10b. blue/*greenish yellow*	50	10
D604		15b. blue/*greenish yellow*	40	10
D605		20b. blue/*greenish yellow* (A)	10	
		a. Type B		
D606		30b. blue/*greenish yellow*	1·00	20
D607		50b. blue/*greenish yellow*	1·60	20
D608		60b. blue/*greenish yellow*	1·80	50
D609		2l. blue/*greenish yellow*	2·10	85

(b) P 13½

D610	D **38**	2b. blue/*greenish yellow*	50	10
D611		5b. blue/*greenish yellow*	50	10
D612		10b. blue/*greenish yellow*	50	10
D613		20b. blue/*greenish yellow* (A)	50	10
		a. Type B		
D614		30b. blue/*greenish yellow*	1·60	20
D615		50b. blue/*greenish yellow*	3·25	1·00
D616		60b. blue/*greenish yellow*		

(c) Perf compound of 11½ and 13½

D617	D **38**	2b. blue/*greenish yellow*	50	10
D618		5b. blue/*greenish yellow*	50	10
D619		10b. blue/*greenish yellow*	50	10
D620		15b. blue/*greenish yellow*	50	10
D621		20b. blue/*greenish yellow* (A)	50	10
		a. Type B	50	10
D622		30b. blue/*greenish yellow*	1·00	20
D623		50b. blue/*greenish yellow*	1·60	20
D624		60b. blue/*greenish yellow*	1·80	50
D625		2l. blue/*greenish yellow*		

The 5, 10 and 20b., perf 13½ and compound of 11½ and 13½, may be found on greenish paper as well as on the greenish yellow.

See also Nos. D714/36, D984/1014 and D1547/8.

1911 (July). New value. White paper. No wmk.

(a) P 11½

625*a*	17	1½b. olive-yellow	9·50	

(b) Perf compound of 11½ and 13½

625*b*	17	1½b. olive-yellow	3·25	2·50

1913. FRANK. Silistra Commemoration Committee. Typo. P 11½.

F626	F **38**	(–) red-brown	7·75	9·50

38

39 Troops crossing Danube

(Des L. Basarab. Typo Govt Ptg Wks, Bucharest)

1913 (25 Dec). Acquisition of Southern Dobruja. T **38/9** and similar designs. P 11½×13½ (vert) or 13½×11½ (horiz).

626	–	1b. grey-black	1·00	50
627	38	3b. brown and grey	2·50	1·00
628	39	5b. black and green	2·10	50
		a. Perf 13½	—	2·10
629	–	10b. black and orange	1·00	50
630	–	15b. violet and bistre	2·50	1·00
631	–	25b. brown and blue	3·75	1·60
632	39	40b. claret and bistre	7·25	6·25
633	38	50b. blue and yellow	16·00	8·25
634		1l. grey and blue	29·00	19·00
635		2l. rose and vermilion	42·00	26·00
626/635 *Set of 10*			95·00	60·00

Designs: Vert—1b. "Dobruja" holding flag. Horiz—10b. View of Constantza; 25b. Church and school, Dobruja. 24×16 mm—15b. Mircea the Great and King Carol.

King Ferdinand

10 October 1914–20 July 1927

POSTAL TAX STAMPS. These were for compulsory use at certain times on inland mail to raise money for various funds. In some instances where the stamps were not applied the appropriate Postal Tax Postage Due stamps were applied.

Other denominations exist but these were purely for revenue purposes and were not applied to postal matter.

TIMBRU DE AJUTOR
(T **40**)

T **41** The Queen weaving

TD **42**

1915 (11 Jan). POSTAL TAX. Soldiers' Families Fund. Optd with Type T **40**.

(a) P 11½

T636	37	5b. yellow-green	6·25	1·00
T637		10b. carmine	6·25	1·00

(b) P 13½

T638	37	5b. yellow-green	30	10
T639		10b. carmine	75	30

(c) Perf compound of 11½ and 13½

T640	37	5b. yellow-green	1·00	50
T641		10b. carmine	1·00	50

1915. POSTAL TAX POSTAGE DUE. Optd with Type T **40**.

(a) P 11½

TD642	D **38**	10b. blue/*greenish yellow*		

(b) P 13½

TD643	D **38**	5b. blue/*greenish yellow*	65	30
		a. Opt double		
TD644		10b. blue/*greenish yellow*	85	50

(c) Perf compound of 11½ and 13½

TD645	D **38**	5b. blue/*greenish yellow*	65	30
TD646		10b. blue/*greenish yellow*	2·10	50

(Typo Govt Ptg Wks, Bucharest)

1916. POSTAL TAX.

(a) P 11½

T647	T **41**	5b. black	9·50	6·75
T648		10b. chocolate	21·00	9·50

(b) P 13½

T649	T **41**	5b. black	30	30
T650		10b. chocolate	75	50

(c) Perf compound of 11½ and 13½

T651	T **41**	5b. black	1·60	50
T652		10b. chocolate	5·25	1·00

The above also exist on coarse greyish war-time paper.

For 5b. green and 10b. black, see Nos. T708/13.

(Typo Govt Ptg Wks, Bucharest)

1916. POSTAL TAX POSTAGE DUE. No wmk.

(a) P 13½

TD653	TD **42**	5b. brown/*greenish*	5·25	5·25
TD654		10b. red/*greenish*	30	30

(b) Perf compound of 11½ and 13½

TD655	TD **42**	5b. brown/*greenish*	75	30
TD656		10b. red /*greenish*	30	30

See also Nos. TD737/46, TD968/77 and TD1015/20.

Romania entered the war against the Central Powers on 27 August 1916; after early successes her troops were defeated and by January 1917 all Romania S.E. of the River Sereth was in German, Austro-Hungarian or Bulgarian occupation and the government had moved to Jassy in Moldavia.

Issues made by the occupying powers are listed at the end of Romania.

In 1917 stamps showing King Ferdinand (25×34 mm) in the values 5, 10, 25, 35, 40, 50b., 1 and 2l. both perforated 11½ and imperforate were prepared but not issued. There were also 5 and 10b. Postal Tax stamps showing two people standing in front of a house as well as a 10b. Postal Tax Postage Due stamp in a design showing lines and arabesques.

Type **40** and the overprints, Types **41** and D **43** were applied at Jassy for use in the unoccupied areas.

25 BANI
(**40**)

1918
(**41**)

TAXA DE PLATĂ
(D **43**)

1918 (1 May). Provisional issue. Surch with T **40**, in red.

657	37	25b. on 1b. grey-black (p 11½)	2·10	1·00
		a. Surch inverted		
		b. "BAN" for "BANI"		
658		25b. on 1b. grey-black (compound perf)	5·25	5·25
659		25b. on 1b. grey-black (p 13½)	1·00	85
		a. Surch inverted	5·25	5·25

1918. Optd with T **41**.

(a) P 11½

660	37	5b. yellow-green	75	50
		a. Opt inverted	12·50	12·50
661		10b. carmine	75	50

(b) P 13½

662	37	5b. yellow-green	75	50
		a. Opt inverted	10·50	10·50
663		10b. carmine	75	50
		a. Opt inverted	16·00	16·00
		b. Dull claret/greyish		

(c) Perf compound of 11½ and 13½

664	37	5b. yellow-green	75	50
		a. Opt inverted	16·00	16·00
665		10b. carmine	3·50	3·50
		a. Dull claret/greyish		

1918. POSTAL TAX. Optd with T **41**.

(a) P 11½

T666 **T 41** 10b. chocolate (opt inverted) 37·00 37·00

(b) P 13½

T667 **T 41** 5b. black (R.) 1·00 50
a. Opt inverted 21·00 21·00
b. Opt in black 2·10 2·10
T668 10b. chocolate 1·60 1·00
a. Opt inverted 21·00 21·00
b. Opt double 50·00 50·00

(c) Perf compound of 11½ and 13½

T669 **T 41** 5b. black (R.) 21·00 10·50
T670 10b. chocolate 16·00 7·75

1918. POSTAL TAX. Nos. T638/9 optd with T **41**.

T671 **37** 5b. yellow-green (R.) 47·00 47·00
T672 10b. carmine 47·00 47·00

Some sheets of Nos. T638/9 were overprinted with T **41** in error and were sold to the public and used on mail.

1918. POSTAGE DUE. Optd as Type D **43**.

(a) P 11½

D673 **37** 5b. yellow-green 21·00 21·00
D674 10b. carmine 6·25 6·75

(b) P 13½

D675 **37** 5b. yellow-green 3·00 1·00
a. Opt inverted 7·75 7·75
D676 10b. carmine 3·00 1·00
a. Opt inverted 16·00 16·00

(c) Perf compound of 11½ and 13½

D677 **37** 10b. carmine 5·75 2·10
a. Opt inverted 18·00 18·00

In Type D **43** there are variations in the relative positions of "TAXA" and "DE PLATA", and in the thickness of the letters.

1918. POSTAL TAX POSTAGE DUE. Optd as Type D **43**.

(a) P 11½

TD678 **T 41** 5b. black (R.)
TD679 10b. chocolate
a. Opt inverted

(b) P 13½

TD680 **T 41** 5b. black (R.) 50 30
a. Opt inverted 9·50 9·50
TD681 10b. chocolate 50 30
a. Opt inverted 4·50 4·50
b. Opt in blue 9·50 9·50
ba. Blue opt vert 37·00 37·00

(c) Perf compound of 11½ and 13½

TD682 **T 41** 5b. black (R.) 16·00
a. Opt inverted 70·00 70·00
TD683 10b. chocolate 4·75 4·75
a. Opt inverted 10·00 10·00

The following issues were made at Jassy for use in the unoccupied part of Moldavia. In November 1918 the Romanian Post Office resumed control in the whole of Romania.

(T **35** recess, others typo at Jassy)

1918–19. Colours changed. No wmk.

(a) P 11½

684 **37** 15b. red-brown 2·40 85
685 **19** 25b. steel-blue 3·25 1·00
686 **35** 40b. sepia 5·75 2·50
687 **19** 40b. grey-brown (1919) 10·00 4·25
688 **35** 50b. orange-rose 2·10 1·00
689 **19** 50b. rose (1919) 4·25 1·60
690 **22** 1l. grey-green 2·50 1·00
691 2l. yellow 23·00 23·00

(b) P 13½

692 **37** 15b. red-brown 1·00 50
693 **19** 25b. steel-blue 6·00 30
694 **35** 40b. sepia 16·00 10·50
695 **19** 40b. grey-brown 10·00 4·25
696 **35** 50b. orange-rose — 4·75
697 **19** 50b. rose 2·10 1·00
698 **22** 1l. grey-green — 10·50
699 2l. yellow 9·75 1·60

(c) Perf compound of 11½ and 13½

700 **37** 15b. red-brown 3·50 50
701 **19** 25b. steel-blue 1·00 30
702 **35** 40b. sepia 5·75 2·50
703 **19** 40b. grey-brown 1·80 1·00
704 **35** 50b. orange-rose 2·10 1·00
705 **19** 50b. rose 1·80 1·00
706 **22** 1l. grey-green 2·40 95
707 2l. orange 3·25 1·00

Coarse greyish paper was used but later printings of the 15b. were on white paper. This may have been the lithographic printing made at the Government map-printing establishment, the impression being less clear and the colour of a more orange tone.

1918. POSTAL TAX. As stamps of 1916 but colours changed.

(a) P 11½

T708 **T 41** 5b. green 4·25 65
T709 10b. black 6·75 2·10

(b) P 13½

T710 **T 41** 5b. green 1·00 40
T711 10b. black 1·00 40

(c) Perf compound of 11½ and 13½

T712 **T 41** 5b. green 1·30 40
T713 10b. black 1·30 40

Early printings were on coarse war-time paper and later printings on greyish paper.

1918–19. POSTAGE DUE. Colours changed.

(i) Wmk "P R" in monogram, impressed (1918)

(a) P 11½

D714 **D 38** 5b. black/*greenish* 20 20
D715 10b. black/*greenish* — 50
D716 20b. black/*greenish* (A) 5·25 1·00
a. Type B 3·25 85
D717 30b. black/*greenish* 2·30 2·30

(b) P 13½

D718 **D 38** 10b. black/*greenish* — 3·25
D719 30b. black/*greenish* — —
D720 50b. black/*greenish* 8·25 4·25

(c) Perf compound of 11½ and 13½

D721 **D 38** 5b. black/*greenish* 20 10
D722 10b. black/*greenish* 20 10
D723 20b. black/*greenish* (A) 65 85
a. Type B 5·25 1·00
D724 30b. black/*greenish* 75 50
D725 50b. black/*greenish* 1·60 1·00

(ii) No wmk (1919)

(a) P 11½

D726 **D 38** 5b. black/*greenish* — 50
D727 10b. black/*greenish*
D728 20b. black/*greenish* (A)
a. Type B
D729 30b. black/*greenish*

(b) P 13½

D730 **D 38** 30b. black/*greenish* 1·00 1·00
D731 50b. black/*greenish*

(c) Perf compound of 11½ and 13½

D732 **D 38** 5b. black/*greenish* 20 10
D733 10b. black/*greenish* 20 10
D734 20b. black/*greenish* (A)
a. Type B 65 30
D735 30b. black/*greenish* 75 30
D736 50b. black/*greenish* 85 85

See also Nos. D974/1004.

1918. POSTAL TAX POSTAGE DUE. Colours changed.

(i) Wmk "P R" in monogram, impressed

(a) P 11½

TD737 **TD 42** 10b. brown/*green* — 1·60

(b) P 13½

TD738 **TD 42** 5b. red/*green* 1·00 50
TD739 10b. brown/*green* — 1·60

(c) P 13½×11½

TD740 **TD 42** 5b. red/*green* — 3·25
TD741 10b. brown/*green* 1·00 50

(ii) No wmk

(a) P 11½

TD742 **TD 42** 10b. brown/*green* — 85

(b) P 13½

TD743 **TD 42** 5b. red/*green* 65 65
TD744 10b. brown/*green* — 85

(c) P 13½×11½

TD745 **TD 42** 5b. red/*green* 65 65
TD746 10b. brown/*green* 6·25 65

For white paper, see Nos. TD1015/20.

TRANSYLVANIA

On 1 December 1918 the union of Transylvania, the Eastern portion of Hungary, and Romania was proclaimed and the final frontiers were determined by the Treaty of Trianon on 4 June 1920.

The following overprints were made to convert to Romanian use the stocks of Hungarian stamps found in post offices in Transylvania; the stamps were valid for use throughout Romania.

(**42**) "Kingdom of Romania" (**43**)

(The "F" monogram stands for King Ferdinand and "P.T.T." for Posts, Telegraphs and Telephones)

The values "BANI", "LEU" or "LEI" appear above or below the monogram and prices are the same for either state except where the alternative is listed.

A. Issues for Cluj (Kolozsvar or Klausenburg)

1919 (26 July). Various stamps of Hungary optd as T **42** (values in capital letters).

(a) Flood Relief Charity stamps of 1913 (T **7/8** with label as T **12**)

747 **7** 1l. on 1f. grey-black 21·00 18·00
748 1l. on 2f. olive-yellow £120 85·00
749 1l. on 3f. orange 50·00 42·00
750 1l. on 5f. emerald 2·50 1·60
751 1l. on 10f. rose-red 2·50 1·60
752 1l. on 12f. lilac/yellow 9·00 5·75
753 1l. on 16f. deep blue-green 4·75 3·25
754 1l. on 25f. blue 50·00 42·00
755 1l. on 35f. purple 5·25 3·25
756 **8** 1l. on 1k. red 65·00 50·00

(b) War Charity stamps of 1916–17

757 **20** 10(+2)b. carmine 30 20
a. Opt inverted 16·00 21·00
b. "BANI" at top 21·00
758 **21** 15(+2)b. deep violet 30 20
a. Opt inverted 42·00
759 **22** 40(+2)b. lake 40 30

(c) Harvester and Parliament Types

760 **18** 2b. yellow-brown 20 20
761 3b. dull claret 30 20
762 5b. green 30 20
763 6b. greenish blue 30 20
764 10b. rose-red £140 £100
765 **17** 15b. violet 5·00 3·75
766 **18** 15b. violet 20 10
767 25b. blue 20 10
768 35b. brown 20 10
769 40b. olive-green 20 10
a. Opt inverted
770 **19** 50b. dull purple 30 20
771 75b. turquoise-blue 40 30
772 80b. yellow-green 40 30
773 1l. lake 40 30
a. "LFU" for "LEU" 8·25
774 2l. bistre-brown 55 40
a. "LFI" for "LEI" 8·25
775 3l. grey and dull violet 3·50 2·50
a. "LFI" for "LEI" 26·00
b. Opt inverted 70·00
776 5l. pale brown and brown 2·75 2·10
a. "LFI" for "LEI" 21·00
777 10l. magenta and chocolate 3·50 2·50
a. "LFI" for "LEI" 29·00

T **7** has white figures of value, T **18** coloured.

(d) Charles and Zita stamps

778 **27** 10b. rose 30·00 21·00
779 15b. violet 11·50 7·75
a. Opt inverted 80·00
780 20b. deep brown 50 30
a. Gold opt 70·00 70·00
b. Silver opt 70·00 70·00
781 25b. blue 85 50
a. Opt Inverted 95·00
782 **28** 40b. olive-green 50 30
a. Opt inverted
b. "BANI" at top 5·25 7·25

1919 (26 July). NEWSPAPER. No. N136 of Hungary optd as T **42**.

N783 **N 9** 2b. orange 2·50 2·10

1919 (26 July). EXPRESS LETTER. No. E245 of Hungary optd as T **42**.

E784 **E 18** 2b. olive and red 30 45

1919 (26 July). SAVINGS BANK. No. B199 of Hungary optd as T **42**.

B785 **B 17** 10b. dull purple 50 75
a. Opt inverted

1919 (3 Aug). POSTAGE DUE. Nos. D190 etc. of Hungary optd as T **42**.

D786 **D 9** 1b. red and green £275 £275
D787 2b. red and green 55 55
D788 5b. red and green 75·00 75·00
D789 10b. red and green 30 30
D790 15b. red and green 12·50 12·50
D791 20b. red and green 25 25
D792 30b. red and green 19·00 19·00
D793 50b. red and green 13·00 13·00

A number of errors are known in this overprint; BANIL for "BANI", "N" with diagonal stroke straight instead of curved or "B" of "BANI" omitted.

B. Issues for Oradea (Nagyvarad or Grosswardein)

1919 (25 Oct). Various stamps of Hungary optd as T **43** (values in italic capital and lower case letters).

(a) "Turul" Type

794 **7** 2b. olive-yellow 5·25 4·75
795 3b. orange 9·75 8·50
796 6b. drab 95 50
797 16b. deep blue-green 21·00 12·50
798 50b. lake/*blue* 1·30 1·00
799 70b. brown/*green* 20·00 18·00

(b) Flood Relief Charity stamps of 1913 (T **7** with label as T **12**)

800 **7** 1l. on 1f. grey-black 1·20 1·10
801 1l. on 2f. olive yellow 4·75 4·50
802 1l. on 3f. orange 1·60 1·30
803 1l. on 5f. emerald 30 20
804 1l. on 6f. drab 1·20 1·10
805 1l. on 10f. rose-red 30 20
806 1l. on 12f. lilac/*yellow* 50·00 46·00
807 1l. on 16f. deep blue-green 1·50 1·30
808 1l. on 20f. brown 6·50 6·25
809 1l. on 25f. blue 4·50 3·25
810 1l. on 35f. purple 4·50 3·25

(c) War Charity stamp of 1915–16

811 **7** 5(+2)b. emerald (No. 173) 11·50 11·50

(d) War Charity stamps of 1916–17

812 **20** 10(+2)b. carmine 70 70
813 **21** 15(+2)b. deep violet 30 20
814 **22** 40(+2)b. lake 30 30

(e) Harvester and Parliament Types

815 **18** 2b. yellow-brown 20 20
816 3b. dull claret 20 20
817 5b. green 30 20
818 6b. greenish blue 90 65
819 10b. rose-red 1·60 1·00
820 **17** 15b. violet £130 £100
821 **18** 15b. violet 15 10
822 20b. grey-brown 15·00 9·50
823 25b. blue 30 20
824 35b. brown 35 20
825 40b. olive-green 30 20
826 **19** 50b. dull purple 40 30
827 75b. turquoise-blue 20 20
828 80b. yellow-green 30 30
829 1l. lake 55 40
830 2l. bistre-brown 20 20
831 3l. grey and dull violet 4·50 4·25
832 5l. pale brown and brown 2·75 2·50
833 10l. magenta and chocolate 1·60 1·50

(f) Charles and Zita stamps

834 **27** 10b. rose 2·75 2·10
835 20b. deep brown 20 20
836 25b. blue 45 30
837 **28** 40b. olive-green 70 50

(g) Various types optd "KOZTARSASÀG", T **29**

(i) Harvesters and Parliament Types

838 **18** 2b. yellow-brown 2·10 1·30
839 3b. dull claret 40 30
840 4b. slate 30 20
841 5b. green 40 30
842 6b. greenish blue 2·30 1·60
843 10b. rose-red 21·00 17·00
844 20b. grey-brown 1·90 1·30
845 40b. olive-green 40 30
846 **19** 1l. lake 30 20
847 3l. grey and dull violet 1·20 85
848 5l. pale brown and brown 4·75 3·75

(ii) Charles and Zita stamps

849 **27** 10b. rose £130 £130
850 20b. deep brown 2·75 2·10
851 25b. blue 70 40
852 **28** 50b. purple 30 20
a. Opt inverted

(h) Harvesters and Parliament Types inscr "MAGYAR POSTA"
853 **30** 5b. green 20 20
854 10b. rose-red 20 20
855 20b. grey-brown 25 20
856 25b. blue 1·00 50
857 40b. olive-green 1·00 75
858 **31** 5l. pale brown and brown 8·75 6·50

1919 (Oct). NEWSPAPER. No. N136 of Hungary optd as T **43**.
N859 N **9** 2b. orange 50 70

1919 (Oct). EXPRESS LETTER. No. E245 of Hungary optd as T **43**.
E860 E **18** 2b. olive and red 40 70

1919 (Oct). SAVINGS BANK. No. B199 of Hungary optd as T **43**.
B861 B **17** 10b. dull purple 50 70

1919 (Oct). POSTAGE DUE. Nos. D190, etc. of Hungary optd as T **43**.
D861 D **9** 1b. red and green 26·00 26·00
D862 2b. red and green 20 20
D863 5b. red and green 5·75 5·75
D864 6b. red and green 3·75 3·75
D865 10b. red and green 30 30
D866 12b. red and green 80 80
D867 15b. red and green 80 80
D868 20b. red and green 20 20
D869 30b. red and green 85 85
Hungarian stamps are also known overprinted "Ocupatiunea Romana B.-Pesta 1919". These are bogus.

(**44**) King Ferdinand's Monogram

45 King Ferdinand

1919. Optd with T **44**. Coarse greyish or smooth white paper.
(a) P 11½
870 **37** 1b. black (R.) 30 20
871 5b. yellow-green 4·25 4·25
a. Pale green 4·25 4·25
872 10b. carmine 4·25 4·25
a. Dull claret 1·00 1·00
ab. Opt inverted 5·25 5·25
ac. Opt double 5·25 5·25
(b) P 13½
873 **37** 1b. black (R.) 30 20
a. Opt inverted 1·60 1·60
b. Opt double 3·75 3·75
c. Opt in black
874 5b. yellow-green 40 50
a. Pale green 30 20
ab. Opt inverted 5·25 5·25
ac. Opt double 12·50 12·50
875 10b. carmine 1·00 50
a. Dull claret
(c) Perf compound of 11½ and 13½
876 **37** 1b. black (R.) 30 20
a. Opt in black
877 5b. yellow-green 30 20
a. Pale green 20 20
ab. Opt inverted
ac. Opt double 5·25 5·25
878 10b. carmine 75 20
a. Dull claret 20 20
ab. Opt inverted 4·25 4·25
ac. Opt double 4·25 4·25

(Typo Govt Ptg Wks, Bucharest)
1920 (Jan)–**22**. Coarse greyish or smooth white paper.
(a) P 11½
879 **45** 1b. black 20 10
880 5b. green 20 10
a. Granite paper (1921) 3·25 1·00
881 10b. dull carmine 20 10
a. Granite paper (1921) 3·75 75
b. Very thin paper 6·25 3·25
882 15b. red-brown 75 30
883 25b. blue 1·60 50
a. Granite paper (1921) 85·00 21·00
884 25b. brown (5.21) 50 30
885 40b. grey-brown 1·30 50
886 50b. salmon 50 30
887 1l. green 1·60 30
888 1l. rosine (5.21) 3·25 2·10
a. Very thin paper 8·25 4·25
889 2l. orange 2·10 50
890 2l. deep blue (5.21) — 31·00
(b) P 13½
891 **45** 1b. black 20 15
892 5b. green 20 15
a. Very thin paper 3·25 1·00
b. Granite paper (1921)
893 10b. dull carmine 20 15
a. Granite paper (1921) £100 21·00
b. Very thin paper
894 15b. red-brown 1·00 50
895 25b. blue 30 30
a. Granite paper (1921) £100 21·00
896 25b. brown 30 30
897 40b. grey-brown 9·50 5·75
898 50b. salmon 85 20
899 1l. green 9·50 9·50
900 1l. rosine 40 30
a. Very thin paper
901 2l. orange 12·50 1·60
902 2l. deep blue 1·00 35
903 2l. carmine (1.22) 3·25 2·10
(c) Pert compound of 11½ and 13½
904 **45** 1b. black 30 20
905 5b. green 50 30
a. Granite paper (1921) 2·10 1·00
b. Very thin paper 8·25 3·25
906 10b. dull carmine 50 20
a. Granite paper (1921)
b. Very thin paper
907 15b. red-brown 1·00 30
a. Granite paper (1921)
908 25b. blue 1·00 50
909 25b. brown 1·60 50
910 40b. grey-brown 65 20
911 50b. salmon 1·00 30
912 1l. green 1·60 30
913 1l. rosine 50 20
914 2l. orange 2·10 30
915 2l. deep blue 3·25 50
(d) P 10½×11½
916 **45** 1b. black
917 15b. red-brown
(e) Imperf (pairs)
918 **45** 1b. black 50·00
919 5b. green 50·00
920 10b. dull carmine 50·00
921 15b. red-brown 50·00
922 25b. brown
There are numerous shades in this issue.
The 5b., 1l. (green and rosine) and 2l. (deep blue and carmine) exist on white paper with watermark of horizontal lines; the 10b. exists on white paper with this watermark vertical. This watermark resulted from the process used in the manufacture of the paper and was not made deliberately.

46

A B C

A. "5" has a large ball, end of top bar straight and to left of peak in shield; bottom of "0" pointed and over "N", interior of "0" wide.
B. "5" has small ball, end of top bar rounded; bottom of "0" over "NI", interior narrow.
C. "5" has large ball, end of top bar straight but under peak of shield; bottom of "0" rounded and over "N", interior narrow.

D E F G H

D. Small "U". E. Large "U".
F. Thin "2". G. Very thick "2". H. Medium "2". "LEI" also differs in each case.

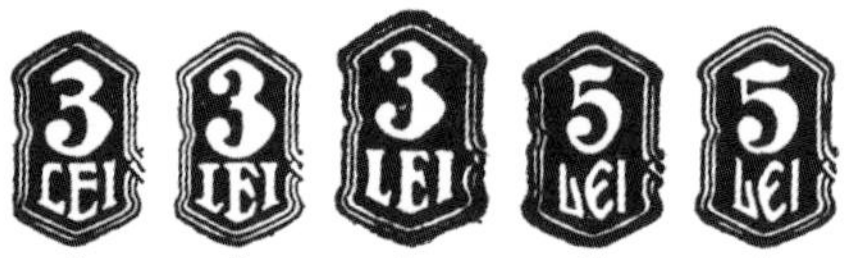
J K L M N

J. Blunt end to top curve of "3"; "LEI" thin.
K. Large ball to top curve of "3"; "LEI" thicker.
L. Smaller ball to top curve of "3"; "LEI" even more thick.
M. Short top and thin body to "5".
N. Longer top and thick body to "5".

(Typo Govt Ptg Wks, Bucharest)
1920–**27**. White paper.
(a) P 13½
923 **46** 3b. black 20 10
a. Very thin paper 1·00 50
924 5b. black (1922) 10 10
a. Very thin paper 1·00 50
925 10b. green (1925) 20 10
926 25b. brown (1922) 20 10
927 25b. rose-red (1925) 30 10
928 30b. reddish violet 30 10
a. Very thin paper 5·25 1·00
929 50b. orange (A) (1922) 50 30
a. Very thin paper 5·25 1·00
b. Type B 50 30
c. Type C
930 60b. green (1922) 1·50 75
931 1l. purple (D) (1922) 40 10
a. Very thin paper 5·25 1·00
b. Type E
932 2l. rose (F) (1922) 2·10 20
a. Very thin paper 7·25 1·00
b. Claret 50·00 50·00
933 2l. light green (F) (1924) 1·30 50
a. Type G (1926) 65 20
b. Type H (1927) 75 30
934 3l. blue (J) (1922) 3·25 1·00
935 3l. brown (J) (1924) 31·00 3·25
a. Type K 3·25 1·00
b. Types J and K, *se-tenant* £130
936 3l. flesh (J) (1924) 2·10 1·60
a. Type K 37·00 10·50
b. Types J and K, *se-tenant* £130
c. Orange-red (L) 1·60 50
cd. Very thin paper 7·25 1·00
937 3l. carmine-rose (L) (1925) 1·20 10
a. Very thin paper 7·25 1·00
938 5l. emerald-green (M) 2·75 1·00
939 5l. buff (M) (1925) 1·60 75
a. Very thin paper 7·25 1·00
b. Red-brown (N) (1926) 1·00 10
940 6l. blue (1923) 4·50 1·60
a. Very thin paper 7·25 1·00
941 6l. carmine (1924) 8·25 4·25
a. Very thin paper 16·00 8·25
942 6l. olive-green (1926) 4·50 1·00
943 7l.50 pale blue (1925) 4·25 50
a. Very thin paper 9·50 2·50
944 10l. blue (1925) 4·25 50
(b) P 11½
945 **46** 3b. black 20 10
a. Granite paper — 4·25
946 5b. black 65·00 10·50
947 25b. light brown 1·80 80
948 30b. reddish violet 30 10
a. Granite paper 8·25 1·00
949 50b. orange (A) 1·00 50
950 60b. green 14·50 9·50
951 1l. purple (D) £120 21·00
952 2l. light green (H)
953 3l. blue (J) 5·25 1·00
954 5l. emerald-green 10·50 1·00
(c) Perf compound of 11½ and 13½
955 **46** 3b. black 50 10
a. Granite paper 2·10 80
956 5b. black 30 10
957 10b. green 1·30 80
958 25b. light brown 1·30 25
959 30b. reddish violet 30 10
a. Granite paper 2·10 50
b. Very thin paper 10·50 2·50
960 50b. orange (A) 50 30
961 60b. green 1·60 75
962 1l. purple (D) 2·50 30
963 2l. rose (F) 2·40 50
964 3l. blue (J) 4·75 80
965 5l. emerald-green (M) 23·00 3·25
966 5l. buff (M) 7·25 7·00
a. Orange-brown (N)
967 6l. blue — 10·50
There are numerous marked shades in this issue but the 10b. olive-green (perf 13½ and compound) was not issued.
Most values exist on thick carton paper. Also on paper with horizontal lines watermark (see notes after No. 922).

1920. POSTAL TAX POSTAGE DUE. Greyish paper ranging from grey-green to grey-blue.
(i) Wmk "P R" in monogram, impressed
(a) P 13½
TD968 TD **42** 5b. red 50 20
TD969 10b. brown 50 20
(b) P 11½
TD970 TD **42** 10b. brown 1·00 50
(c) P 13½×11½
TD971 TD **42** 5b. red 1·00 50
TD972 10b. brown 1·00 50
(ii) No wmk
(a) P 13½
TD973 TD **42** 5b. red 50 20
TD974 10b. brown 50 20
(b) P 11½
TD975 TD **42** 10b. brown 1·00 50
(c) P 13½×11½
TD976 TD **42** 5b. red 80 30
TD977 10b. brown 80 30
For white paper, see Nos. TD1015/20.

T **47** "Charity"

1921–**24**. POSTAL TAX. Social Welfare. No wmk.
(a) P 13½
T978 T **47** 10b. green 20 10
T979 25b. black (1924) 20 10
(b) P 11½
T980 T **47** 10b. green 3·25 1·30
T981 25b. black 7·75 4·75
(c) Perf compound of 11½ and 13½
T982 T **47** 10b. green 85 30
T983 25b. black 5·25 4·75
Shades exist. These also exist on thick carton paper and on chalk-surfaced paper.
See also No. T1079.

1921–**26**. POSTAGE DUE. No wmk.
(i) White or greyish paper, ranging from grey-green to grey-blue (1921–26)
(a) Perf 13½
D984 D **38** 10b. black 20 10
D985 20b. black (A) 20 10
a. Type B 30 10
D986 30b. black 30 10
D987 50b. black 85 30
D988 60b. black 20 10
D989 1l. black 1·30 50
D990 2l. black 1·50 30
D991 3l. black (1926) 20 10
D992 6l. black (1926) 50 10
(b) P 11½
D993 D **38** 5b. black 20 10
D994 10b. black 20 10
D995 20b. black (A) 20 10
a. Type B 20 10
D996 30b. black 30 10
D997 50b. black 1·80 30
D998 60b. black 20 10
D999 1l. black 40 10
D1000 2l. black 2·10 50
(c) Perf compound of 11½ and 13½
D1001 D **38** 5b. black 20 10
D1002 10b. black 20 10
D1003 20b. black (A) 40 10
a. Type B 65 3·25

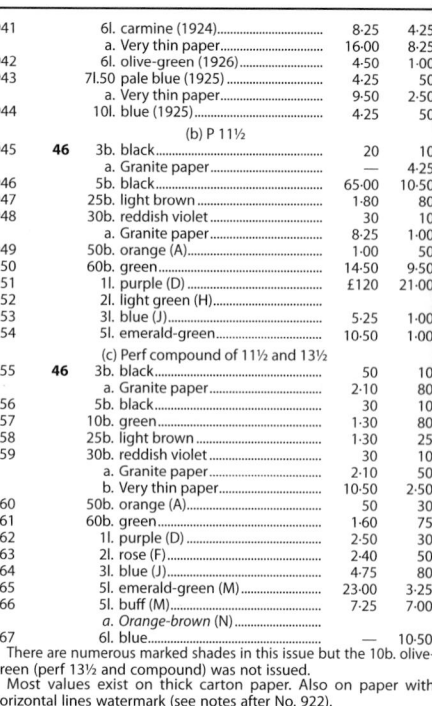

D1004		30b. black	50	20
D1005		50b. black	30	20
D1006		60b. black	20	10
D1007		1l. black	40	20
D1008		2l. black	2·10	50

The 10b. exists imperforate and the 5b. to 2l. on paper with horizontal lines watermark.

(ii) Yellowish paper (1924)

(a) Perf 13½

D1009	D **38**	1l. black	50	20
D1010		2l. black	75	30
D1011		3l. black	2·10	1·00
D1012		6l. black	3·25	1·00

(b) Perf compound of 11½ and 13½

D1013	D **38**	1l. black	6·25	
D1014		2l. black	6·25	

See also Nos. D1198/9.

1921. POSTAL TAX POSTAGE DUE. White paper. No wmk.

(a) P 13½

TD1015	TD **42**	5b. red	50	20
TD1016		10b. brown	50	20

(b) P 11½

TD1017	TD **42**	5b. red	1·00	1·00
TD1018		10b. brown	65	50

(c) P 13½×11½

TD1019	TD **42**	5b. red	85	30
TD1020		10b. brown	1·50	1·50

1922–26. POSTAL TAX POSTAGE DUE. As Type TD **42** but inscr "ASSISTENTA SOCIALA" instead of "TIMBRU DE AJUTOR".

(i) White paper (1922–26)

(a) P 13½

TD1021	10b. brown	50	50
TD1022	20b. brown	50	50
TD1023	25b. brown (1926)	30	50
TD1024	50b. brown (1926)	30	50

(b) P 11½

TD1025	10b. brown	1·80	1·00

(c) P 13½×11½

TD1026	10b. brown	—	85
TD1027	20b. brown	50	50

(ii) Greenish paper. P 13½ (1923–25)

TD1028	10b. brown	20	20
TD1029	20b. brown	20	20
TD1030	25b. brown (1925)	30	30
TD1031	50b. brown	30	30

47 Cathedral of Alba Julia

48 King Ferdinand

49 State Arms

50 Queen Marie as Nurse

51 Michael the Brave and King Ferdinand

52 King Ferdinand

53 Queen Marie

(Des L. Basarab. Photo A. Bruckmann, Munich)

1922 (15 Oct). Coronation. Wmk Wavy Lines (horiz on vert stamps or vert on horiz designs).

(a) P 13½

1032	**47**	5b. black	50	30
		a. Without designer's name	4·25	5·25
1033	**48**	25b. purple-brown	1·30	50
1034	**49**	50b. green	1·30	75
1035	**50**	1l. deep olive-green	1·60	1·00
1036	**51**	2l. carmine	1·60	1·00
1037	**52**	3l. blue	3·25	1·60
1038	**53**	6l. violet	8·75	7·00
1032/1038 *Set of 7*			16·00	11·00

(b) P 11½

1039	**47**	5b. black	21·00	16·00
		a. Without designer's name		
1040	**48**	25b. purple-brown	6·25	2·10
1041	**49**	50b. green	3·25	1·00
1042	**50**	1l. deep olive-green	4·25	2·10
1043	**51**	2l. carmine	11·50	9·50
1044	**52**	3l. blue	4·25	1·70
1045	**53**	6l. violet	11·50	10·50

(c) Perf compound of 11½ and 13½

1046	**47**	5b. black	50	30
		a. Without designer's name	3·25	4·25
1047	**49**	50b. green	1·30	75
1048	**50**	1l. deep olive-green	1·30	75
1049	**51**	2l. carmine	1·60	1·00
1050	**53**	6l. violet	8·75	7·00

The 5b. is known with the watermark vertical and the 25b., 50b. and 3l. with it horizontal.

All values exist imperforate.

54 King Ferdinand

55 Map of Romania

56 Stephen the Great

57 Michael the Brave

58 Carol and Ferdinand

59 The Adam Clisi Monument

(Des L. Basarab. Photo A. Bruckmann, Munich)

1926 (1 July). King Ferdinand's 60th Birthday. P 11.

1051	**54**	10b. yellow-green	75	50
1052		25b. orange	75	50
1053		50b. chestnut	75	50
1054		1l. violet-blue	75	50
1055		2l. deep blue-green	75	50
1056		3l. carmine	75	1·00
1057		5l. sepia	75	1·00
1058		6l. deep olive-green	75	1·00
		a. Error. Bright blue	£200	£225
1059		9l. slate-blue	75	1·00
1060		10l. bright blue	75	1·00
		a. Error. Carmine	£200	£225
1051/1060 *Set of 10*			6·75	6·75

In the lei values the value tablet is at the right.

All values exist imperforate.

(Des L. Basarab. Typo Govt Ptg Wks, Bucharest)

1927 (15 Mar). 50th Anniv of Romanian Geographical Society. No wmk. P 13½.

1061	**55**	1l. +9l. violet	5·25	2·10
1062	**56**	2l. +8l. green	5·25	2·10
1063	**57**	3l. +7l. carmine	5·25	2·10
1064	**58**	5l. +5l. blue	5·25	2·10
1065	**59**	6l. +4l. olive	7·75	3·25
1061/1065 *Set of 5*			26·00	10·50

King Michael

20 July 1927–8 June 1930

60 King Carol and King Ferdinand

61

62

FACTAJ
5
LEI

(P **63**)

(Des G. Chirovici. Photo Helio Vaugirard, Paris)

1927 (1 Aug). 50th Anniv of Romanian Independence. P 13½.

1066	**60**	25b. plum	1·00	20
1067	**61**	30b. black	1·00	30
1068	**62**	50b. deep green	1·00	30
1069	**60**	1l. greenish blue	1·00	30
1070	**61**	2l. green	1·00	40
1071		3l. purple	1·00	50
1072	**62**	4l. brown	1·00	65
1073		4l.50 brown-red	3·25	2·10
1074	**61**	5l. chestnut	1·00	50
1075	**62**	6l. carmine-lake	2·10	1·20
1076	**60**	7l.50 greenish blue	1·00	50
1077		10l. blue	3·25	1·00
1066/1077 *Set of 12*			16·00	7·25

1928. PARCEL POST. Surch as Type P **63**. P 13½.

P1078	**46**	5l. on 10b. yellow-green (C.) (A)	2·10	85
		a. Type B	2·10	85
		b. Type C	3·25	1·00

In Type A the surcharge is 16 mm. high and "LEI" is 10 mm. long; Type B 15½ mm. high, "LEI" 11½ mm.; Type C 17½ mm. high, "LEI" 9½ mm.

This issue also exists with horizontal lines watermark.

1928. POSTAL TAX. Wmk Wavy Lines. P 13½.

T1079	T **47**	25b. black	1·60	1·00

In 1930 the Social Welfare stamps were withdrawn.

63 King Michael

64 King Michael

(Des L. Basarab. Typo (T **63**) or photo Govt Ptg Wks, Bucharest)

1928 (16 Mar)–**29**. T **64** size 18½×24½ mm. P 13½.

(i) No wmk

1080	**63**	25b. black	50	20
1081		30b. rose-pink (5.29)	1·00	20
1082		50b. olive-green	50	20
1083	**64**	1l. purple	1·00	20
1084		2l. green	1·30	20
1085		3l. carmine-pink	1·60	20
1086		5l. chocolate-brown	2·50	20
1087		7l.50 ultramarine	11·50	1·30
1088		10l. blue	9·50	50
1080/1088 *Set of 9*			26·00	3·00

(ii) Wmk Wavy Lines (1.9.28)

1089	**63**	25b. black	50	20
1090	**64**	7l.50 ultramarine	5·75	1·00
1091		10l. blue	4·75	50

See also Nos. 1129/33 for Type **64** in smaller size.

PRINTERS. From this point all stamps were printed by the Government Printing Works, Bucharest, unless otherwise stated. Until 1955 they were printed in photogravure. From No. 2413 onwards the process is indicated.

65 Bessarabian Parliament House

(Des L. Basarab)

1928 (29 Apr). 10th Anniv of Annexation of Bessarabia. T **65** and similar designs. Wmk Wavy Lines. P 13½.

1092	**65**	1l. green	2·30	1·00
1093		2l. chocolate	2·30	1·00
1094	–	3l. sepia	2·30	1·00
1095	–	5l. claret	2·75	1·30
1096	–	7l.50 ultramarine	2·75	1·30
1097	–	10l. greenish blue	7·25	3·25
1098	–	20l. slate-violet	9·50	4·25
1092/1098 *Set of 7*			26·00	12·00

Designs:—3l., 5l., 20l. Hotin Fortress; 7l.50, 10l. Fortress Cetatea Alba.

66 Blériot SPAD 33 Biplane

(Des L. Basarab)

1928 (4 Sept). AIR. Wmk Wavy Lines. P 13½.

A. Wmk vert

1099A	**66**	1l. red-brown	7·75	5·25
1100A		2l. bright blue	7·75	5·25
1101A		5l. carmine	7·75	5·25
1099A/1101A *Set of 3*			21·00	14·00

B. Wmk horiz

1099B	**66**	1l. red-brown	12·50	7·25
1100B		2l. bright blue	12·50	7·25
1101B		5l. carmine	12·50	7·25
1099B/1101B *Set of 3*			34·00	20·00

67 King Carol and King Michael

(Des L. Basarab)

1928 (25 Oct). 50th Anniv of Acquisition of Northern Dobruja. T **67** and similar horiz designs. Wmk Wavy Lines. P 13½.

1102	**67**	1l. green	1·80	65
1103	–	2l. red-brown	1·80	65
1104	**67**	3l. brownish grey	2·50	65
1105	–	5l. magenta	3·25	75
1106	–	7l.50 ultramarine	3·75	85
1107	–	10l. blue	5·25	2·10
1108	–	20l. carmine	9·00	2·50
1102/1108 *Set of 7*			25·00	7·25

Designs:—2l. Constantza Harbour and Carol Lighthouse; 5l., 7l.50, Adam Clisi Monument; 10l., 20l. Cernavoda Bridge over the Danube.

68 Ferdinand I, Stephen the Great, Michael the Brave, Janos Hunyadi and Constantine Brancoveanu

69 The Union

70 Bran Castle

O 71 Romanian Eagle and National Flag

(Des L. Basarab)

1929 (10 May). 10th Anniv of Union of Romania and Transylvania. T **68/70** and similar types. Wmk Wavy Lines. P 13½.

1109	1l. slate-purple	4·25	2·10
1110	2l. green	4·25	2·10
1111	3l. chocolate	4·75	2·10
1112	4l. carmine	4·75	2·50
1113	5l. orange	6·25	2·50
1114	10l. blue	7·75	5·25
1109/1114 *Set of* 6		29·00	15·00

Designs: Vert—3l. Avram Jancu; 4l. King Michael the Brave. Horiz—10l. Ferdinand I.

1929 (1 Dec). OFFICIAL. Photo. Wmk Wavy Lines.

(a) P 13½

O1115	O **71**	25b. vermilion	20	10
O1116		50b. brown	20	10
O1117		1l. deep violet	20	10
O1118		2l. green	20	10
O1119		3l. bright carmine	30	10
O1120		4l. brownish black	50	15
O1121		6l. slate-blue	1·70	40
O1122		10l. deep ultramarine	85	50
O1123		25l. brown-lake	2·50	1·60
O1124		50l. bright violet	7·75	4·25
O1115/1124 *Set of* 10			13·00	6·75

(b) P 14½×14

O1125	O **71**	2l. green	20	10
O1126		3l. bright carmine	30	10
O1127		6l. slate-blue	85	20
O1128		10l. deep ultramarine	1·60	40

1930. Photo. Size 18×23 mm. No wmk. P 14½×14.

1129	**64**	1l. purple	1·00	20
1130		2l. green	1·60	20
1131		3l. carmine	3·25	20
1132		7l.50 ultramarine	6·25	1·60
1133		10l. blue	21·00	10·50
1129/1133 *Set of* 5			30·00	11·50

King Carol II

8 June 1930–6 September 1940

8 IUNIE 1930

(**71**)

1930 (8 June)–**31**. Stamps of King Michael optd with T **71** (date of Accession of King Carol II).

(a) Large format. Typo

(i) No wmk

1134	**63**	25b. black	50	20
1135		30b. rose-pink	1·00	20
1136		50b. olive-green	1·00	20
1137	**64**	5l. chocolate-brown	2·10	20
1138		10l. blue	4·25	1·00

(iii) Wmk Wavy Lines

1139	**63**	25b. black (1931)	1·60	50
1140	**64**	7l.50 ultramarine	5·25	1·00
1141		10l. blue	37·00	
1134/1138, 1140 *Set of* 6			12·50	2·50

(b) Small format. Photo. Wmk Wavy Lines

1142	**64**	1l. purple	50	20
1143		2l. green	50	20
1144		3l. carmine	65	20
1145		7l.50 ultramarine	4·25	85
1146		10l. blue	3·50	80
1142/1146 *Set of* 5			8·50	2·00

1930. AIR. Nos. 1099/1101 optd with T **71**.

A. Wmk vert (8 June)

1147A	**66**	1l. red-brown	£100	£140
1148A		2l. bright blue	£100	£140
1149A		5l. carmine	£100	£140
1147A/1149A *Set of* 3			£275	£375

B. Wmk horiz (1 Aug)

1147B	**66**	1l. red-brown	21·00	10·50
1148B		2l. bright blue	21·00	10·50
1149B		5l. carmine	21·00	10·50
1147B/1149B *Set of* 3			60·00	28·00

1930 (8 June)–**31**. OFFICIAL. Optd with T **71**.

(i) Wmk Wavy Lines

(a) P 13½

O1150	O **71**	25b. vermilion	50	20
		a. Opt inverted	26·00	
O1151		50b. brown	50	20
O1152		1l. deep violet	50	20
O1153		2l. green	50	20
		a. Opt inverted	50·00	
O1154		4l. brownish black	75	20
		a. Opt inverted	31·00	
O1155		6l. slate-blue	85	40
		a. Opt inverted	31·00	
O1156		25l. brown-lake	5·25	1·80
O1157		50l. bright violet	10·50	3·75

(b) P 14½×14

O1158	O **71**	2l. green	50	20
O1159		3l. bright carmine	50	20
O1160		6l. slate-blue	50	20
O1161		10l. deep ultramarine	1·60	30

(ii) No wmk

(a) P 14½×14

O1162	O **71**	25b. vermilion	50	30
		a. Opt omitted	12·50	
O1163		50b. brown	50	30
		a. Opt omitted	12·50	
O1164		1l. deep violet	50	30
O1165		3l. bright carmine	50	30

(b) P 13½

O1166	O **71**	25b. vermilion	50	30
O1167		50b. brown	50	30

1930. POSTAGE DUE. Nos. D989/92 on white paper optd with T **71**.

D1168	D **38**	1l. black	40	20
D1169		2l. black	40	20
		a. Opt inverted	50·00	21·00
D1170		3l. black	50	40
D1171		6l. black	1·60	1·00
		a. On yellowish paper (D1012)		
D1168/1171 *Set of* 4			2·50	1·60

IMPERFORATE STAMPS. Many of the issues of the reign of King Carol II exist imperforate. Nos. 1172/82 and 1191/3 were put on sale at the Philatelic Bureau, but others were clandestine.

72

73
King Carol II

74

75

76

(Des L. Basarab and A. Murnu)

1930. W **75**. P 13½–14½.

1172	**72**	25b. black	50	10
1173		50b. chocolate	1·30	65
1174		1l. deep violet	50	10
1175		2l. green	1·00	10
1176	**73**	3l. carmine	2·00	10
1177		4l. vermilion	2·30	10
1178		6l. brown-lake	2·75	10
1179		7l.50 bright ultramarine	3·25	30
1180	**74**	10l. blue	7·75	10
1181		16l. blue-green	18·00	30
1182		20l. orange	21·00	85
1172/1182 *Set of* 11			31·00	2·50

See also Nos. 1233/42.

(Des L. Basarab)

1930 (4 Oct). AIR. No wmk. P 13½.

1183	**76**	1l. violet/*azure*	3·25	5·00
1184		2l. green/*azure*	4·00	5·25
1185		5l. chocolate/*azure*	7·25	5·25
1186		10l. blue/*azure*	15·00	6·75
1183/1186 *Set of* 4			27·00	20·00

77 Map of Romania

78 Woman with Census Form

79 King Carol II

(Des S. Constantinescu)

1930 (24 Dec). National Census. No wmk. P 13½.

1187	**77**	1l. slate-violet	1·80	50
1188	**78**	2l. green	3·00	60
1189		4l. vermilion	3·50	40
1190		6l. claret	8·25	65
1187/1190 *Set of* 4			15·00	1·90

(Des A. Murnu. Recess Bradbury, Wilkinson & Co)

1931. No wmk. P 12.

1191	**79**	30l. blue and olive	1·40	75
1192		50l. blue and scarlet	2·75	1·30
1193		100l. blue and green	5·75	2·75
1191/1193 *Set of* 3			9·00	4·25

O 80

80 King Carol II

81 King Carol I

82 Kings Carol II, Ferdinand I and Carol I

(Des A. Murnu)

1931. OFFICIAL. Typo. W **75**. P 14×14½ or 13½ (2l.).

O1194	O **80**	25b. black	15	15
O1195		1l. purple	25	25
O1196		2l. green	55	40
O1197		3l. carmine	60	40
O1194/1197 *Set of* 4			95	1·10

See also Nos. O1243/7.

1931. POSTAGE DUE Typo. W **75**.

(a) P 13½

D1198	D **38**	2l. black	1·10	75

(b) P 14½×13½

D1199	D **38**	2l. black	1·10	75

(Des L. Basarab and A. Murnu (10l.))

1931 (10 May). 50th Anniv of Romanian Monarchy. T **80/2** and similar types inscr "1881–1931". W **75**. P 13½.

1200	**80**	1l. slate-violet	3·75	1·90
1201	**81**	2l. green	5·75	1·90
1202	–	6l. lake	13·00	3·00
1203	**82**	10l. blue	19·00	5·75
1204	–	20l. orange	23·00	7·50
1200/1204 *Set of* 5			60·00	18·00

Designs: Horiz (as T **80**)—6l. King Carol II facing right. Vert (as T **81**)—20l. King Ferdinand I.

83 *Mircea* (cadet ship)

(Des D. Stiubei)

1931 (10 May). 50th Anniv of Romanian Navy. As T **83** (ship types inscr "1881–1931"). W **75**. P 13½.

1205	6l. lake	6·75	4·25
1206	10l. blue	9·00	4·50
1207	16l. blue-green	38·00	5·00
1208	20l. orange	17·00	9·00
1205/1208 *Set of* 4		65·00	20·00

Designs:—10l. *Lascar Catargiu* and *Mihail Kogalniceanu* (monitors); 16l. *Ardeal* (monitor); 20l. *Regelè Ferdinand* (destroyer).

84 Bayonet attack

85 Infantryman, 1870

87 King Carol I

88 Infantry attack

89 King Ferdinand I

90 King Carol II

(Des A. Murnu (25b.) and L. Basarab (1l., 7l.50, 16l.))

1931 (10 May). Centenary of Romanian Army. W **75**. P 13½.

1209	**84**	25b. black	2·30	1·10
1210	**85**	50b. chocolate	3·00	1·50
1211	–	1l. slate-violet	3·75	1·90
1212	**87**	2l. green	6·00	2·30
1213	**88**	3l. carmine	13·00	6·75
1214	**89**	7l.50 ultramarine	17·00	15·00
1215	**90**	16l. blue-green	20·00	6·75
1209/1215 *Set of* 7			60·00	32·00

Design: As T **90**—1l. Infantry.

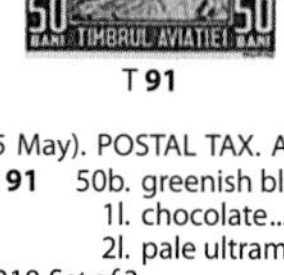

T 91

TIMBRUL
AVIAŢIEI

(TD **92**)

1931 (15 May). POSTAL TAX. Aviation Fund. No wmk. P 13½×14½.

T1216	T **91**	50b. greenish blue	75	30
T1217		1l. chocolate	1·50	30
T1218		2l. pale ultramarine	2·30	30
T1216/1218 *Set of* 3			4·00	80

1931 (15 May). POSTAL TAX POSTAGE DUE. Optd with Type TD **92**. W **75**. P 13½.

TD1219	D **38**	1l. black (C.)	40	25
TD1220		2l. black (C.)	40	25

91 Scouts Encampment

92 King Carol II in Scoutmaster's Uniform

(Des A. Murnu (6l.))

1931 (8 June). Romanian Boy Scouts, Exhibition Fund. T **91/2** and similar types. W **75**. P 13½.

1221	1l. +1l. carmine	5·75	3·75
1222	2l. +2l. green	7·50	4·50
1223	3l. +3l. pale ultramarine	9·00	5·75
1224	4l. +4l. sepia	11·50	7·50
1225	6l. +6l. chocolate	15·00	7·50
1221/1225 *Set of 5*		44·00	26·00

Designs: As T **91**—3l. Recruiting. As T **92**—(2l. slightly smaller)—2l. Rescue work; 4l. Prince Nicholas.

92a Farman F.121 Jaribu

93 Formation Flying

94

(Des L. Basarab and G. Chirovici (20l.))

1931 (4 Nov). AIR. T **92a** (various views and aircraft) and **93**. W **94**. P 13½.

1226	2l. green	1·90	1·00
1227	3l. carmine	3·00	1·30
1228	5l. chocolate	3·75	1·70
1229	10l. blue	9·00	3·75
1230	20l. slate-violet	23·00	5·25
1226/1230 *Set of 5*		37·00	11·50

Designs:—3l. Farman F.300 and biplane; 5l. Farman F.60 Goliath; 10l. Fokker F.XII.

95 Kings Carol II, Ferdinand I and Carol I

96 Alexander the Good

(Des A. Murnu)

1931 (Nov). W **94**. P 13½.

1231	**95**	16l. blue-green	15·00	90

(Des L. Basarab)

1932 (May). 5th Death Centenary of Alexander I, Prince of Moldavia. W **94**. P 13½.

1232	**96**	6l. brown-lake	17·00	11·50

1932. W **94**. P 13½–14½.

1233	**72**	25b. black	75	15
1234		50b. chocolate	1·90	15
1235		1l. deep violet	2·30	15
1236		2l. green	3·00	15
1237	**73**	3l. carmine	3·75	15
1238		4l. vermilion	7·50	25
1239		6l. brown-lake	13·00	25
1240		7l.50 bright ultramarine	20·00	1·10
1241	**74**	10l. blue	£170	1·50
1242		20l. orange	£170	15·00
1233/1242 *Set of 10*			£350	17·00

1932. OFFICIAL. W **94**. P 13½.

O1243	O **80**	25b. black	20	10
O1244		1l. purple	20	10
O1245		2l. green	75	20
O1246		3l. carmine	1·20	30
O1247		6l. claret	1·90	75
O1243/1247 *Set of 5*			3·75	1·30

The use of official stamps was discontinued on 15 March 1932.

97 King Carol II

D **98**

T **98**

1932. W **94**. P 13½.

1248	**97**	10l. blue	17·00	75

1932–37. POSTAGE DUE. Typo. W **94**. P 13½ (1l., 2l.) or 14½×13½ (others).

D1249	D **98**	1l. black	10	10
D1250		2l. black	10	10
D1251		3l. black (1937)	20	10
D1252		6l. black (1937)	20	10
D1249/1252 *Set of 4*			55	35

See also Nos. D1835/44.

1932. POSTAL TAX. Aviation Fund. W **94**. P 14½×14.

T1253	T **98**	50b. turquoise-blue	75	30
		a. Perf 13½	75	30
		b. Perf 14½×13½	75	30
T1254		1l. chocolate	1·10	30
		a. Perf 13½	1·10	30
		b. Perf 14½×13½	1·10	30
T1255		2l. bright blue	1·20	30
		a. Perf 13½	1·20	30
T1253/1255 *Set of 3*			2·75	80

10 and 20b. and 3 and 5l. values in this design were for fiscal use but are occasionally found used on letters.

98 Semaphore Signaller

99 Cantacuzino and Gregory Chika

1932 (8 June). Boy Scouts' Jamboree Fund. T **98** and similar designs. W **94**. P 13½.

1256	25b. +25b. blue-green	4·50	1·90
1257	50b. +50b. blue	5·75	3·75
1258	1l. +1l. green	6·50	5·75
1259	2l. +2l. vermilion	11·50	7·50
1260	3l. +3l. greenish blue	27·00	15·00
1261	6l. +6l. black-brown	30·00	23·00
1256/1261 *Set of 6*		75·00	5·25

Designs: Vert as T **98**—25b. Scouts in camp; 1l. On the trail; 3l. King Carol II; 6l. King Carol II and King Michael when a Prince. Horiz (20×15 mm)—2l. Camp fire.

1932 (Sept). Ninth International Medical Congress. T **99** and similar horiz types inscr "IX Congress International de Istoria Medicinei". W **94**. P 13½.

1262	1l. carmine	9·75	7·50
1263	6l. orange	24·00	11·50
1264	10l. blue	42·00	19·00
1262/1264 *Set of 3*		70·00	34·00

Designs:—6l. Congress in session; 10l. Aesculapius and Hygeia.

100 Tuberculosis Sanatorium

101 King Carol II

(Des L. Basarab)

1932 (1 Nov). Postal Employees' Fund. T **100** and similar designs. W **94**. P 13½.

1265	4l. +1l. green	9·00	4·50
1266	6l. +1l. chocolate	10·00	5·50
1267	10l. +1l. blue	18·00	9·00
1265/1267 *Set of 3*		33·00	17·00

Designs: Vert—6l. War Memorial Tablet; Horiz—10l. Convalescent home.

1932 (20 Nov). International Philatelic Exhibition, Bucharest (EFIRO). Sheet 100×125 mm. No wmk. Imperf.

MS1267*a*	**101**	6l.+5l. deep olive	85·00	70·00

102 "Bulls head"

103 Dolphins

104 Arms

1932 (20 Nov). 75th Anniv of First Postage Stamps in Moldavia. Various Arms inscr "1858–1933". Typo. W **94**. Imperf.

1268	**102**	25b. black	2·40	45
1269	–	1l. purple	4·00	95
1270	**103**	2l. green	4·25	1·10
1271	–	3l. carmine	4·75	1·40
1272	**104**	6l. claret	5·75	1·60
1273	–	7l.50 light blue	7·25	2·30
1274	–	10l. blue	9·75	3·75
1268/1274 *Set of 7*			34·00	10·50

Designs as T **103**:—1l. Lion rampant and bridge, 3l. Eagle and castles; 7l.50 Eagle; 10l. Bull's head.

1932 (20 Nov). 30th Anniv of Opening of G.P.O., Bucharest. T **25** reduced to 37×22½ mm. Typo. W **94**. P 13½.

1275	16l. green	21·00	9·25

T **105**

TD **106**

1932–34. POSTAL TAX. Cultural Fund. No wmk (1276) or W **94** (1277). P 13½ or 13½×14½.

T1276	T **105**	2l. blue	1·50	65
T1277		2l. brown (1934)	1·20	55

These were for compulsory use on postcards.

1932. POSTAL TAX POSTAGE DUE. Recess. No wmk. P 13½.

TD1278	TD **106**	3l. grey-black	1·60	95

105 Ruins of Trajan's Bridge; Arms of Turnu-Severin and Towers of Severus

106 Trajan's Bridge

(Des S. Constantinescu (2l.))

1933 (2 June). Centenary of Founding of Turnu-Severin. T **105/6** and similar horiz designs. W **94**. P 14½×14.

1279	25b. olive-green	1·50	40
1280	50b. blue	1·90	60
1281	1l. sepia	3·50	95
1282	2l. blackish green	4·75	1·50
1279/1282 *Set of 4*		10·50	3·00

Designs:—50b. Trajan at the completion of bridge over the Danube; 1l. Arrival of Prince Carol at Turnu-Severin.

107 Carmen Sylva and Carol I

1933 (Aug). 50th Anniv of Construction of Pelesch Castle, Sinaia. T **107** and similar designs inscr "CASTELUL PELES". W **94**. P 14½×14.

1283	1l. violet	3·50	2·40
1284	3l. brown	4·00	3·50
1285	6l. vermilion	4·75	4·00
1283/1285 *Set of 3*		11·00	9·00

Designs: Horiz—3l. Eagle and medallion portraits of Kings Carol I, Ferdinand I and Carol II; 6l. Pelesch castle.

F **108** Mail Coach and Biplane

108 Wayside Shrine

1933. FRANK. For free postage on book 75th Anniv of Introduction of First Romanian Postage Stamp. Imperf.

F1286	F **108**	(–) green	5·75	4·75

1934 (16 Apr). Romanian Women's Exhibition Fund. T **108** and similar designs. W **94**. P 13½.

1286	1l. +1l. sepia	3·50	2·40
1287	2l. +1l. blue	4·75	3·00
1288	3l. +1l. green	6·25	4·25
1286/1288 *Set of 3*		13·00	8·75

Designs: Horiz—2l. Weaver. Vert—3l. Woman spinning.

(**109**) Arms of Constantza

110 King Carol II

111 King Carol II

1934 (8 July). Mamaia Jamboree Fund. Nos. 1256/61 optd with T **109**.

1289	25b. +25b. blue-green	7·25	4·75
1290	50b. +50b. blue (Gold)	9·75	5·75
1291	1l. +1l. green	11·50	9·25
1292	2l. +2l. vermilion	14·50	10·50
1293	3l. +3l. greenish blue (Gold)	31·00	18·00
1294	6l. +6l. black-brown (Gold)	35·00	24·00
1289/1294 *Set of 6*		£100	65·00

1934 (Aug–Dec). T **110/11** and similar portrait. W **94**. P 13½.

1295	–	50b. brown (1.12)	1·90	60
1296	**110**	2l. green	3·50	60

1297		4l. scarlet-vermilion	5·75	60
1298	**111**	6l. brown-lake (1.12)	14·50	60
1295/1298 *Set of 4*			23·00	2·25

Design:—50b. Profile portrait of King Carol II in civilian clothes.

112 "Grapes for Health"

113 Crisan, Horia and Closca

(Des A. Murnu)

1934 (14 Sept). Bucharest Fruit Exhibition. T **112** (and another "Eat more Fruit" type similarly inscr showing a woman holding a basketful of fruit). W **94**. P 13½.

1299		1l. green	7·25	4·00
1300		2l. purple-brown	7·25	4·00

(Des S. Constantinescu)

1935 (28 Feb). 150th Death Anniv of Three Romanian Martyrs. T **113** (and similar portrait types inscr "MARTIR AL NEAMULUI/1785"). W **94**. P 13½.

1301		1l. violet	1·20	70
1302		2l. green (Crisan)	1·60	95
1303		6l. chocolate-brown (Closca)	4·25	1·60
1304		10l. bright blue (Horia)	7·25	3·50
1301/1304 *Set of 4*			13·00	6·00

114 Boy Scouts

115 King Carol II

116

117

(Des D. Stiubei)

1935 (8 June). 5th Anniv of Accession of Carol II. T **114** and similar designs inscr "O.E.T.R.". W **94**. P 13½.

1305		25b. olive-black	5·75	4·00
1306		1l. violet	9·75	6·75
1307		2l. green	11·50	9·75
1308		6l. +1l. purple-brown	14·50	11·50
1309		10l. +2l. bright blue	31·00	29·00
1305/1309 *Set of 5*			65·00	55·00

Designs: Vert—25b. Scout saluting; 1l. Bugler; 6l. King Carol II. Horiz—10l. Colour party.

1935 (1 July)–**40**. T **115/17** and as T **110/11** but additionally inscr "POSTA". W **94**. P 13½.

1310	**115**	25b. olive-black (8.35)	20	10
1311	**116**	50b. brown (10.10.35)	20	10
1312	**117**	1l. violet (8.35)	50	10
1313	**110**	2l. green (1.7.35)	95	10
1314		2l. blue-green (22.5.40)	1·50	20
1315	**116**	3l. carmine (8.35)	1·50	10
1316		3l. greenish blue (14.5.40)	1·90	30
1317	**110**	4l. scarlet-vermilion (1936)	3·00	10
1318	**117**	5l. rose-carmine (25.4.40)	2·40	70
1319	**111**	6l. brown-lake (8.35)	3·00	10
1320	**117**	7l.50 ultramarine (8.35)	3·50	70
1321	**116**	8l. magenta (22.5.40)	3·50	70
1322	**110**	9l. bright blue (10.5.40)	4·75	80
1323	**116**	10l. light blue (1936)	1·90	30
1324	**111**	12l. slate-blue (1940)	3·00	1·30
1325	**115**	15l. sepia (10.5.40)	3·00	95
1326	**111**	16l. blue-green (1936)	4·00	60
1327		20l. orange (1936)	2·40	80
1328		24l. rose-carmine (10.5.40)	4·75	95
1310/1328 *Set of 19*			41·00	8·00

See also No. **MS**1367.

118 King Carol II

119 Oltenia Peasant Girl

120 Brasov Jamboree Badge

(Des from portrait by Julietta)

1936 (13 May). Bucharest Exhibition and 70th Anniv of Hohenzollern-Sigmaringen Dynasty. W **94**. P 13½.

1329	**118**	6l. +1l. carmine	2·40	1·20

(Des S. Constantinescu (2, 3 and 4l.), D. Stiubei (others))

1936 (8 June). 6th Anniv of Accession of Carol II. As T **119** (provincial costume types, inscr "O.E.T.R. 8 IUNIE 1936"). W **94**. P 13½.

1330		50b. +50b. chocolate	1·90	95
1331		1l. +1l. violet	1·50	95
1332		2l. +1l. grey-green	1·60	1·20
1333		3l. +1l. carmine	2·40	1·50
1334		4l. +2l. vermilion	3·00	1·50
1335		6l. +3l. olive-grey	4·00	1·90
1336		10l. +5l. blue	6·25	4·00
1330/1336 *Set of 7*			19·00	11·00

Designs (costumes of the following districts): Vert—24×30 mm., 1l. Banat and 6l. Neamtz; 22×38 mm., 4l. Gorj. Horiz—30×25 mm., 2l. Saliste; 3l. Hateg; 10l. Suceava (Bukovina).

1936 (20 Aug). National Boy Scout Jamboree, Brasov. As T **120** (Boy Scout emblems inscr ("JAMBOREEA NATIONALA BRASOV 1936"). W **94**. P 13½.

1337		1l. +1l. blue	9·75	8·25
1338		3l. +3l. olive-grey	14·50	8·25
1339		6l. +6l. carmine	19·00	8·25
1337/1339 *Set of 3*			39·00	22·00

Designs:—1l. National Scout Badge; 3l. Tenderfoot Badge.

T **121** "Aviation"

121 *Transylvania* (liner)

(Des S. Constantinescu)

1936 (10 Oct). POSTAL TAX. Aviation Fund. W **94**. P 13½–14½.

T1340	T **121**	50b. blue-green	50	40
T1341		1l. deep red-brown	95	40
T1342		2l. bright blue	95	40
T1340/1342 *Set of 3*			2·20	1·10

Other stamps inscr. "FONDUL AVIATIEI" were only for fiscal use.

(Des D. Stiubei)

1936 (19 Oct). First Marine Exhibition, Bucharest. As T **121** (naval designs inscr "PRIMA EXPOZITIE MARINAREASCA"). W **94**. P 13½.

1343		1l. +1l. violet	11·50	5·25
1344		3l. +2l. bright blue	9·75	5·75
1345		6l. +3l. carmine	12·50	8·25
1343/1345 *Set of 3*			30·00	17·00

Designs: Horiz—1l. *Delfinul* (submarine); 3l. *Mircea* (cadet ship).

CEHOSLOVACIA
YUGOSLAVIA
1920·1936
(**122**)

123 Creanga's Birthplace

1936 (5 Dec). 18th Anniv of Annexation of Transylvania and 16th Anniv of Foundation of the "Little Entente". Optd with T **122**, in red.

1346	**117**	7l.50 ultramarine	7·25	5·75
1347	**116**	10l. light blue	7·25	5·75

1937 (15 May). Birth Centenary of Ion Creanga (poet). T **123** and similar design. W **94**. P 13½.

1348	**123**	2l. green	1·90	95
1349	–	3l. carmine	2·40	1·10
1350	**123**	4l. violet	3·00	1·40
1351	–	6l. chocolate	7·25	3·00
1348/1351 *Set of 4*			13·00	5·75

Design:—3l., 6l. Portrait of Creanga (37×22 mm).

124 Footballers

125 King Carol II

126 Rowers

127 Curtea de Arges Cathedral

128 Hurdling

(Des I. Basarab (2l.) and D. Stiubei (others))

1937 (8 June). 7th Anniv of Accession of Carol II. As T **124/6** (sports types inscr "8 IUNIE 1937" and "U.F.S.R."). W **94**. P 13½.

1352		25b. +25b. olive-black	1·90	30
1353		50b. +50b. chocolate	1·90	50
1354		1l. +50b. violet	2·40	70
1355		2l. +1l. slate-green	3·00	80
1356		3l. +1l. claret	4·75	95
1357		4l. +1l. vermilion	7·75	1·10
1358		6l. +2l. lake	9·75	1·60
1359		10l. +4l. blue	11·50	2·40
1352/1359 *Set of 8*			39·00	7·50

Designs: Horiz (38×24 mm)—50b. Swimmer; 10l. Inaugural meeting of U.F.S.R. Vert (25×33 mm)—1l. Javelin thrower; 2l. Skier; 6l. Steeplechaser.

Premium in aid of the Federation of Romanian Sports Clubs (U.F.S.R.).

1937 (1 July). "Little Entente". W **94**. P 13½.

1360	**127**	7l.50 ultramarine	3·00	1·50
1361		10l. blue	4·00	95

(Des I. Basarab)

1937 (1 Sept). Eighth Balkan Games, Bucharest. As T **128** (sports types inscr "BALCANIADA VIII ATLETISM 1937"). W **94**. P 13½.

1362		1l. +1l. violet	1·90	1·20
1363		2l. +1l. green	2·40	1·60
1364		4l. +1l. vermilion	3·00	2·10
1365		6l. +1l. chocolate	3·50	2·40
1366		10l. +1l. blue	10·50	4·25
1362/1366 *Set of 5*			19·00	10·50

Designs:—1l. Sprinting; 2l. Throwing the javelin; 6l. Breasting the tape; 10l. High jumping.

1937 (25 Oct). 16th Birthday of Crown Prince Michael and his Promotion to Rank of Sub-lieutenant. Sheet 125×152 mm containing four stamps of 1935–40 surch.

MS1367 2l. on 20l. (No. 1327); 6l. on 10l. (No. 1323); 10l. on 6l. (No. 1319); 20l. on 2l. (No. 1313) ... 14·50 16·00

129 Arms of Romania, Greece, Turkey and Yugoslavia

130 King Carol II

(Des I. Basarab)

1938 (10 Feb). Balkan Entente. W **94**. P 13½.

1368	**129**	7l.50 bright blue	2·40	1·30
1369		10l. pale blue	3·50	1·10

1938 (10 May). New Constitution. T **130** and other profile portraits of King Carol II inscr "27 FEBRUARIE 1938". W **94**. P 13½.

1370		3l. carmine	1·50	80
1371		6l. red-brown	2·40	80
1372		10l. blue	3·50	1·60
1370/1372 *Set of 3*			6·75	3·00

Portraits: 25×24 mm—6l. Right profile and royal arms. 25×26 mm—10l. Right profile.

131 King Carol II and Provincial Arms

1938 (24 May). Fund for Bucharest Exhibition celebrating 20th Anniv of Union of Romanian Provinces. W **94**. P 13½.

1373	**131**	6l. +1l. magenta	1·90	95

132 Dimitrie Cantemir

133 Queen Elisabeth

134 "The Spring"

(Des D. Stiubei (25b., 1l., 3l., 4l., 6l.), A. Bordenache (others))

1938 (8 June). 8th Anniv of Accession of Carol II and Boy Scouts' Fund. As T **132/3** (portrait types inscr "STRAJA TARII 8 IUNIE 1938"). W **94**. P 13½.

1374		25b. +25b. blackish olive	95	60
1375		50b. +50b. brown	1·50	60
1376		1l. +1l. deep violet	1·50	60
1377		2l. +2l. emerald-green	1·60	60
1378		3l. +2l. magenta	1·60	60
1379		4l. +2l. red	1·60	60
1380		6l. +2l. red-brown	1·90	70
1381		7l.50 grey-blue	2·40	95
1382		10l. light blue	3·00	95
1383		16l. slate-green	4·00	3·00
1384		20l. red	5·75	3·00
1374/1384 *Set of 11*			23·00	11·00

Portraits (25×30 mm)—50b. Maria Doamna; 1l. Mircea the Great; 2l. Constantin Brancoveanu; 3l. Stephen the Great; 4l. Prince Cuza; 6l. Michael the Brave; 10l. King Carol II; 16l. King Ferdinand I; 20l. King Carol I.

1938 (23 June). Birth Centenary of Nicholas Grigorescu (painter). As T **134** (reproductions of paintings inscr "1838 N(ICOLAE) GRIGORESCU 1938"). W **94**. P 13½.

1385		1l. +1l. blue	3·00	95
1386		2l. +1l. green	3·00	1·90
1387		4l. +1l. vermilion	3·00	1·90
1388		6l. +1l. claret	4·00	3·00
1389		10l. +1l. blue	8·75	4·00
1385/1389 *Set of 5*			20·00	10·50

Designs: Horiz—2l. "Escorting Prisoners" (Russo-Turkish War, 1877–78); 4l. "Returning from Market". Vert—6l. "Rodica, The Water Carrier"; 10l. Self-portrait.

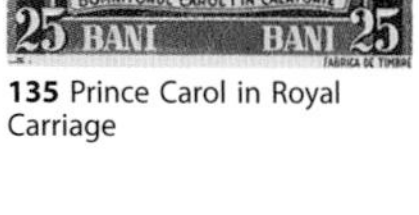

135 Prince Carol in Royal Carriage

136 Romanian Pavilion, N.Y. World's Fair

(Des A. Bordenache (15l.), D. Stiubei (25b., 50b., 1l.50, 3l., 7l.))

1939 (10 Apr). Birth Centenary of King Carol I. As T **135** (designs dated "1839 1939"). W **94**. P 14×13½ (25b., 50b., 1l.50, 15l.), 13½×14 (16l.) or 13 (others).

1390	25b. olive-black	20	10
1391	50b. purple-brown	20	10
1392	1l. violet	50	10
1393	1l.50 green	20	10
1394	2l. blue-green	20	10
1395	3l. vermilion	20	10
1396	4l. claret	20	10
1397	5l. grey	20	10
1398	7l. olive-brown	20	10
1399	8l. grey-blue	50	30
1400	10l. magenta	95	30
1401	12l. light blue	95	30
1402	15l. bright blue	1·90	30
1403	16l. blue-green	1·90	80
1390/1403 *Set of* 14		7·50	2·50

Designs: Horiz (37–38×21½–22½ mm)—50b. Prince Carol at Battle of Calafat; 1l.50, Views of Sigmaringen and Pelesch Castles; 15l. Carol I, Queen Elisabeth and Arms of Romania. Vert (23½–25×29–30 mm)—1l. Examining plans for restoration of Curtea de Arges Monastery; 2l. Nuptial portraits of Carol I and Queen Elisabeth; 3l. Carol I at 8 years of age; 4l. In 1866; 5l. In 1877; 7l. Equestrian statue; 8l. Leading troops in 1878; 10l. In General's uniform; 12l. Bust. (22×37½ mm)—16l. Restored monastery at Curtea de Arges.

1939 (Apr)–**40**. As last but in miniature sheet form. P 14×13½ (horiz) or 13½×14 (vert).

MS1404 141×116 mm. Nos. 1390/1 and 1393. P 14½×13½ (sold at 20l.)	4·75	14·50
a. Imperf (7.2.40)	9·75	19·00
MS1405 126×146 mm. Nos. 1394 and 1398/1400. P 13½×15½ (sold at 50l.)	4·75	14·50
a. Imperf (7.2.40)	9·75	19·00
MS1406 126×146 mm. Nos. 1395/7 and 1401. P 13½×15½ (sold at 50l.)	4·75	14·50
a. Imperf (7.2.40)	9·75	19·00

See also Nos. **MS**1452/4.

1939 (8 May). New York World's Fair. As T **136** (views of Romanian Pavilion inscr "EXPOZITIA INTERNATIONALA NEW YORK"). W **94**. P 14×13½ (6l.) or 13½ (12l.).

1407	6l. brown-lake	1·50	80
1408	12l. bright blue	1·50	80

137 Mihail Eminescu, after a painting by Joano Basarab

138 St. George and Dragon

1939 (22 May). 50th Death Anniv of Mihail Eminescu (poet). As T **137** (portrait types inscr "1850 EMINESCU 1889"). W **94**. P 13½.

1409	5l. olive-black	1·50	80
1410	7l. brown-lake (Eminescu in later years)	1·50	80

1939 (8 June). 9th Anniv of Accession of Carol II and Boy Scouts' Fund. W **94**. P 13½.

1411	**138**	25b. +25b. olive-grey	95	70
1412		50b. +50b. brown	95	70
1413		1l. +1l. violet-blue	1·10	70
1414		2l. +2l. yellow-green	1·20	70
1415		3l. +2l. bright purple	1·50	70
1416		4l. +2l. vermilion	1·90	95
1417		6l. +2l. carmine	2·10	95
1418		8l. blue-grey	2·40	95
1419		10l. light blue	2·50	1·20
1420		12l. ultramarine	3·00	1·90
1421		16l. blue-green	4·00	2·40
1411/1421 *Set of* 11			19·00	10·50

139 Railway Locomotives of 1869 and 1939

140 Torch and Arms of Romania, Greece, Turkey and Yugoslavia

(Des G. Chiriac. Die eng A. H. Nedelescu. Typo)

1939 (10 June). 70th Anniv of Romanian Railways. As T **139** (inscr "CEFERIADA 1869–1939"). W **94**. P 14×13½ (1l., 4l., 15l.) or 13½×14 (others).

1422	1l. reddish violet	2·10	80
1423	4l. carmine-red	2·10	80
1424	5l. blue-grey	2·10	80
1425	7l. mauve	2·10	80
1426	12l. blue	4·00	2·10
1427	15l. green	4·25	3·00
1422/1427 *Set of* 6		15·00	7·50

Designs: Horiz—4l. Steam train crossing railway bridge; 15l. Railway Headquarters, Budapest. Vert—5l. and 7l. Steam train leaving station; 12l. Diesel train crossing railway bridge.

1940 (27 May). Balkan Entente. W **94**. P 13½.

1428	**140**	12l. blue	1·50	95
1429		16l. deep blue	1·50	95

141 King Carol II

142 King Carol II

143 King Carol II

1940 (1 June). Aviation Fund. T **141** (1l., 2l.50, 3l.50) and similar type (others). W **94**. P 13½.

1430	1l. +50b. dark green	40	30
1431	2l.50 +50b. green	60	50
1432	3l. +1l. carmine	80	60
1433	3l.50 +50b. chocolate	85	70
1434	4l. +1l. orange-brown	1·10	80
1435	6l. +1l. light blue	1·60	50
1436	9l. +1l. bright blue	1·90	1·50
1437	14l. +1l. blue-green	2·30	1·90
1430/1437 *Set of* 8		8·50	6·00

1940 (8 June). 10th Anniv of Accession, and Aviation Fund. Portraits of King Carol II, dated "1930 1940 8 IUNIE". W **94**. P 13½.

1438	**142**	1l. +50b. violet	1·50	50
1439		4l. +1l. brown-red	1·50	70
1440	–	6l. +1l. blue	1·50	95
1441	**143**	8l. lake	1·90	1·20
1442	–	16l. ultramarine	2·40	1·50
1443	–	32l. violet-brown	3·50	2·40
1438/1443 *Set of* 6			11·00	6·50

Portraits: Vert—6l., 16l. In helmet (25×27½ mm); 32l. In flying costume (24½×30 mm).

144 The Iron Gate of the Danube

1940 (8 June). 10th Anniv of Accession of King Carol II and Boy Scouts' Fund. T **144** and views inscr "STRAJA TARII 8 IUNIE 1940". W **94**. P 13½.

1444	1l. +1l. violet	95	70
1445	2l. +1l. red-brown	1·10	80
1446	3l. +1l. yellow-green	1·20	95
1447	4l. +1l. greenish black	1·30	1·10
1448	5l. +1l. vermilion	1·50	1·20
1449	8l. +1l. lake	1·90	1·30
1450	12l. +2l. ultramarine	2·40	1·50
1451	16l. +2l. blue-grey	4·25	3·00
1444/1451 *Set of* 8		13·00	9·50

Designs: Horiz—3l. Fortress of Hotin; 4l. Monastery of Hurez. Vert—2l. Greco-Roman ruins; 5l. Church in Suceava; 8l. Cathedral of Alba Julia; 12l. Village church in Transylvania; 16l. Triumphal Arch in Bucharest.

1940 (July). Armaments Fund. Nos. **MS**1404/6 optd "PRO PATRIA 1940".

A. Perf

MS1452A on No. **MS**1404	24·00	29·00
MS1453A on No. **MS**1405	29·00	48·00
MS1454A on No. **MS**1406	39·00	75·00

B. Imperf

MS1452B on No. **MS**1404	80·00	£120
MS1453B on No. **MS**1405	24·00	39·00
MS1454B on No. **MS**1406	95·00	£150

King Michael
6 September 1940–30 December 1947

145 King Michael

146 King Michael

1940 (20 Oct)–**42**. W **94**. P 13½.

1455	**145**	25b. blue-green	10	10
1456		50b. deep green (1.4.42)	10	10
1457		1l. purple	10	10
1458		2l. orange	10	10
1459		4l. blue-grey (1.4.42)	10	10
1460		5l. pink	10	10
1461		7l. blue (1.4.42)	10	10
1462		10l. magenta	50	10
1463		12l. grey-blue	10	10
1464		13l. blackish violet (1.4.42)	10	10
1465		16l. deep blue-green	70	10
1466		20l. brown	1·90	10
1467		30l. yellow-green	30	10
1468		50l. grey-olive	30	10
1469		100l. lake	95	10
1455/1469 *Set of* 15			5·00	1·40

See also Nos. 1604/23.

1940 (20 Oct)–**42**. Aviation Fund. W **94**. P 13½.

1470	**146**	1l. +50b. yellow-green	10	10
1471		2l. +50b. yellow-green (1.4.42)	10	10
1472		2l.50 +50b. blue-green	10	10
1473		3l. +1l. violet	10	10
1474		3l.50 +50b. pink	20	20
1475		4l. +50b. orange-red (1.4.42)	20	10
1476		4l. +1l. brown	10	10
1477		5l. +1l. claret (1.4.42)	1·50	50
1478		6l. +1l. ultramarine	10	10
1479		7l. +1l. grey-green (1.4.42)	50	20
1480		8l. +1l. violet (1.4.42)	30	10
1481		12l. +1l. purple-brown (1.4.42)	50	30
1482		14l. +1l. blue	50	10
1483		19l. +1l. magenta (1.4.42)	1·20	50
1470/1483 *Set of* 14			5·00	2·30

147 Codreanu (founder)

148 Codreanu (founder)

(Des S. Zainea)

1940. "Iron Guard" Fund. W **94**. P 13½.

(a) POSTAGE

1484	**147**	7l. +30l. green (8.11)	8·25	7·75

(b) AIR

1485	**148**	20l. +5l. blue-green (30.11)	4·75	5·75

149 Ion Mota

150 Library

1941 (13 Jan). Marin and Mota (legionaries killed in Spain). T **149** and similar portrait type. W **94**. P 13½.

1486 7l. +7l. carmine/brown (Vasile Marin)	4·75	4·75
1487 15l. +15l. blue	6·75	6·75
MS1487*a* 89×35 mm. As Nos. 1486/7 both in blue-green. Imperf (sold at 300l.)	£120	£150

1941 (9 May). Carol I Endowment Fund. As T **150** (horiz designs inscr "1891 1941"). W **94**. P 13½.

1488	1l.50 +43l.50 violet	2·40	2·40
1489	2l. +43l. brown-lake	2·40	2·40
1490	7l. +38l. carmine	2·40	2·40
1491	10l. +35l. blackish green	2·75	2·75
1492	16l. +29l. chocolate	3·00	3·00
1488/1492 *Set of* 5		11·50	11·50

Designs:—1l.50 Ex-libris; 7l. Foundation building and equestrian statue; 10l. Foundation stone; 16l. Kings Michael and Carol I.

CERNAUTI
5 Iulie 1941
(**151**)

CHIŞINAU
16 Iulie 1941
(**152**)

1941 (Aug). Occupation of Cernauti. Nos. 1488/92 optd with T **151**.

1493	1l.50 +43l.50 violet (R.)	4·75	4·75
1494	2l. +43l. brown-lake	4·75	4·75
1495	7l. +38l. carmine	4·75	4·75
1496	10l. +35l. blackish green (R.)	4·75	4·75
1497	16l. +29l. chocolate	5·00	5·00
1493/1497 *Set of* 5		22·00	22·00

1941 (Aug). Occupation of Chisinau. Nos. 1488/92 optd with T **152**.

1498	1l.50 +43l.50 violet (R.)	4·75	4·75
1499	2l. +43l. brown-lake	4·75	4·75
1500	7l. +38l. carmine	4·75	4·75
1501	10l. +35l. blackish green (R.)	4·75	4·75
1502	16l. +29l. chocolate	5·00	5·00
1498/1502 *Set of* 5		22·00	22·00

153 "Charity"

1941 (Aug). Red Cross. Cross in red. W **94**. P 13½.

1503	**153**	1l.50 +38l.50 violet	1·90	1·20
1504		2l. +38l. carmine	1·90	1·20
1505		5l. +35l. olive	1·90	1·20
1506		7l. +33l. chocolate	1·90	1·20
1507		10l. +30l. blue	2·40	2·20
1503/1507 *Set of* 5			9·00	6·25
MS1508 105×73 mm. Nos. 1506/7. Imperf. No gum (sold at 200l.)			29·00	31·00

154 Prince Voda

155 King Michael and Stephen the Great

1941 (6 Oct). Conquest of Transdniestria. W **94**. P 13½.

1509	**154**	6l. brown	50	50
1510		12l. violet	95	1·00
1511		24l. blue	1·50	1·60
1509/1511 *Set of* 3			2·75	2·75

Nos. 1509/11 were valid in Transdniestria only.

Nos. 1509/11 each exist in imperf ungummed sheets of four with marginal inscriptions including the date "1943". These were prepared by the civil government of Transdniestria for sale at 300l. each in aid of the Red Cross but were not recognised by the Bucharest government.

See also Nos. 1572/5.

Transdniestria, the area of the Soviet Union between the rivers Dniester and Bug, including Odessa, was incorporated in Romania by the decree of 8 October 1941, after conquest by Romanian troops. It was reconquered by the Soviet army in 1944.

1941 (11 Oct). Anti-Bolshevik Crusade. Horiz designs inscr "RAZBOIUL SFANT CONTRA BOLSEVISMULUI" as T **155**. W **94**. P 14.

1512 10l. +30l. blue 3·00 4·75
1513 12l. +28l. brown-red 3·00 4·75
1514 16l. +24l. brown 4·00 5·25
1515 20l. +20l. violet 4·00 5·25
1512/1515 *Set of* 4 12·50 18·00
MS1516 105×73 mm. 16l. slate-blue (emblems and angel with sword); 20l. brown-red (helmeted soldiers and eagle). Imperf. No gum (sold at 200l.) 14·50 21·00

ODESA
16 Oct.1941
(**156**)

157 Hotin

1941 (16 Oct). Fall of Odessa. Nos. 1512/15 and **MS**1516 optd with T **156**.

1517 10l. +30l. blue 3·00 4·75
1518 12l. +28l. brown-red 3·00 4·75
1519 16l. +24l. brown 4·00 5·25
1520 20l. +20l. brown-violet 4·00 5·25
1517/1520 *Set of* 4 12·50 18·00
MS1521 (No. **MS**1516) 24·00 26·00

1941 (1 Dec). Restoration of Bessarabia and Bukovina (Suceava). Pictorial types as T **157** inscr "BASARABIA" or "BUCOVINA" in bottom of frame. W **94**. P 13½.

1522 0l.25 carmine 10 10
1523 0l.50 red-brown 10 10
1524 1l. violet 10 10
1525 1l.50 green 10 10
1526 2l. orange-brown 10 10
1527 3l. olive 30 10
1528 5l. olive 50 20
1529 5l.50 brown 50 20
1530 6l.50 magenta 1·20 75
1531 9l.50 grey 1·20 75
1532 10l. brown-purple 80 20
1533 13l. grey-blue 85 40
1534 17l. red-brown 1·10 30
1535 26l. grey-green 1·30 65
1536 39l. greenish blue 2·30 85
1537 130l. orange-yellow 7·25 5·25
1522/1537 *Set of* 16 16·00 9·25

Views: Vert—0l.25, 5l. Paraclis Hotin; 3l. Dragomirna; 13l. Milisauti. Horiz—0l.50, T **157**; 1l., 17l. Sucevita; 1l.50, Soroca; 2l., 5l.50, Tighina; 6l.50, Cetatea Alba; 10l., 130l. Putna; 26l. St. Nicolae, Suceava; 39l. Monastery, Rughi.

1941 (1 Dec). Winter Relief Fund for Bessarabia and Bukovina. As T **157**. W **94**. P 13½.

1538 3l. +0l.50 lake 60 30
1539 5l.50 +0l.50 orange-red 95 85
1540 5l.50 +1l. black 95 85
1541 6l.50 +1l. brown 1·20 1·20
1542 8l. +1l. light blue 95 50
1543 9l.50 +1l. grey-blue 1·20 1·00
1544 10l.50 +1l. blue 1·30 50
1545 16l. +1l. mauve 1·50 1·20
1546 25l. +1l. grey 1·60 1·30
1538/1546 *Set of* 9 9·25 7·00

Views: Horiz—3l. Sucevita; 5l.50 (1539), Monastery, Rughi; 5l.50 (1540), Tighina; 6l.50, Soroca; 8l. St. Nicolae, Suceava; 10l.50, Putna; 16l. Cetatea Alba; 25l. Hotin. Vert—9l.50, Milisauti.

The Soviet Union had forced Romania to give up Bessarabia and Northern Bukovina on 28 June 1940. They were reconquered by Romanian troops in June and July 1941, and retaken by the Soviet army in 1944.

1942. POSTAGE DUE. W **94**. P 13½.

D1547 D **38** 50l. black 50 20
D1548 100l. black 70 30

158 Titu Maiorescu

159 Coat-of-Arms of Bukovina

1942 (5 Oct). Prisoners of War Relief Fund through International Education Office, Geneva. W **94**. P 13½.

1549 **158** 9l. +11l. violet 95 1·30
1550 20l. +20l. brown 2·40 3·25
1551 20l. +30l. blue 2·75 3·50
1549/1551 *Set of* 3 5·50 7·25
MS1552 128×81 mm. Nos. 1549/51. Imperf. No gum (sold at 200l.) 11·50 13·50

1942 (1 Nov). First Anniv of Liberation of Bukovina. As T **159** (armorial designs inscr "BUCOVINA/UN AN DE LA DESROBIRE"). W **94**. P 13½.

1553 9l. +41l. vermilion 4·00 5·25
1554 18l. +32l. blue (Castle) 4·00 5·25
1555 20l. +30l. carmine (Mounds and crosses) 4·00 5·25
1553/1555 *Set of* 3 11·00 14·00

160 Map of Bessarabia, King Michael, Antonescu, Hitler and Mussolini

161 Statue of Miron Costin

162 Andrei Muresanu

1942. First Anniv of Liberation of Bessarabia. Designs inscr "BASARABIA/UN AN DE LA DESROBIRE" as T **160**. W **94**. P 13½.

1556 9l. +41l. red-brown 4·00 5·25
1557 18l. +32l. olive-brown 4·00 5·25
1558 20l. +30l. blue 4·00 5·25
1556/1558 *Set of* 3 11·00 14·00

Designs: Vert—18l. King Michael and Marshal Antonescu below miniature of King Stephen. Horiz—20l. Marching soldiers and miniature of Marshal Antonescu.

1942 (Dec). First Anniv of Incorporation of Transdniestria. W **94**. P 13½.

1559 **161** 6l. +44l. sepia 2·40 4·25
1560 12l. +38l. grey-violet 2·40 4·25
1561 24l. +26l. greenish blue 2·40 4·25
1559/1561 *Set of* 3 6·50 11·50

Nos. 1559/61 were only valid in Transdniestria.

1942 (30 Dec). Eightieth Death Anniv of A. Muresanu (novelist). W **94**. P 13½.

1562 **162** 5l. +5l. violet 1·50 1·60

163 Statue of Avram Iancu

164 Nurse and Wounded Soldier

1943 (15 Feb). Fund for Statue of Iancu (national hero). W **94**. P 13½.

1563 **163** 16l. +4l. sepia 1·50 1·70

1943 (1 Mar). Red Cross. Cross in red. W **94**. P 13½.

1564 **164** 12l. +88l. lake-brown 1·20 1·30
1565 16l. +84l. ultramarine 1·20 1·30
1566 20l. +80l. olive-brown 1·20 1·30
1564/1566 *Set of* 3 3·25 3·50
MS1567 100×60 mm. Nos. 1565/6 (different shades). Imperf. No gum (sold at 500l.) 9·75 12·50

165 Sword and Shield

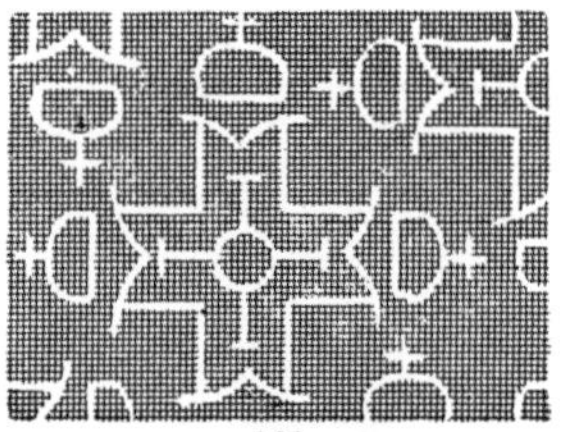
166

1943 (22 June). Second Year of War. Symbolical designs inscr "22 JUNIE 1941/22 JUNIE 1943" as T **165**. W **166**. P 13½.

1568 36l. +164l. brown 4·00 5·25
1569 62l. +138l. blue 4·00 5·25
1570 76l. +124l. red 4·00 5·25
1568/1570 *Set of* 3 11·00 14·00
MS1571 90×65 mm. Nos. 1569/70 (different shades). Imperf. No gum (sold at 600l.) 24·00 26·00

Designs: Vert—62l. Sword severing chain; 76l. Angel protecting soldier and family.

1943 (July). Conquest of Transdniestria (2nd issue). W **166**. P 13½.

1572 **154** 3l. orange-red 50 1·00
1573 6l. brown 50 1·00
1574 12l. violet 95 1·60
1575 24l. blue 1·50 2·10
1572/1575 *Set of* 4 3·00 5·25

Nos. 1572/5 were only valid in Transdniestria.

167 P. Maior

168 Horia, Closca and Crisan

1943 (15 Aug). Transylvanian Refugees' Fund (1st issue). T **168** and vert portraits as T **167**. W **166**. P 13½.

1576 16l. +134l. red 95 1·00
1577 32l. +118l. blue (G. Sincai) 95 1·00
1578 36l. +114l. purple-brown (T. Cipariu) 95 1·00
1579 62l. +138l. carmine 95 1·00
1580 91l. +109l. brown (G. Cosbuc) 95 1·00
1576/1580 *Set of* 5 4·25 4·50

See also Nos. 1584/8.

Northern Transylvania had been surrendered to Hungary by Romania, under pressure from Hitler and Mussolini, on 30 August 1940.

169 King Michael and Marshal Antonescu

170 Sports Shield

1943 (6 Sept). Third Anniv of King Michael's Reign. W **166**. P 13½.

1581 **169** 16l. +24l. blue 3·50 3·75

1943 (26 Sept). Sports Week. W **166**. P 13½.

1582 **170** 16l. +24l. ultramarine 1·30 1·00
1583 16l. +24l. red-brown 1·30 1·00

1943 (15 Oct). Transylvanian Refugees' Fund (2nd issue). Vert portraits as T **167**. W **166**. P 13½.

1584 16l. +134l. magenta (S. Micu) 1·00 1·00
1585 51l. +99l. orange-red (G. Lazar) 1·00 1·00
1586 56l. +144l. carmine (O. Goga) 1·00 1·00
1587 76l. +124l. indigo (S. Barnutiu) 1·00 1·00
1588 77l. +123l. brown (A. Saguna) 1·00 1·00
1584/1588 *Set of* 5 4·50 4·50

T **171** King Michael

171 Calafat, 1877

1943. POSTAL TAX. General Revenue Fund. W **166**. P 14.

T1589 T **171** 50b. orange-vermilion 40 40
T1590 1l. lilac 40 40
T1591 2l. brown 40 40
T1592 4l. ultramarine 40 40
T1593 5l. violet 40 40
T1594 8l. green 40 40
T1595 10l. sepia 40 40
T1589/1595 *Set of* 7 2·50 2·50

1943 (10 Nov). National Artillery Centenary. As T **171** (inscr "1843–1943"). W **166**. P 13½.

1596 1l. +1l. red-brown 50 50
1597 2l. +2l. violet 50 50
1598 3l.50 +3l.50 ultramarine 50 50
1599 4l. +4l. magenta 50 50
1600 5l. +5l. red-orange 1·50 1·60
1601 6l.50 +6l.50 greenish blue 1·50 1·60
1602 7l. +7l. purple 1·90 2·10
1603 20l. +20l. scarlet 3·00 3·25
1596/1603 *Set of* 8 9·00 9·50

Designs: Horiz—(2l. to 7l. inscribed battle scenes). 2l. "1916–1918"; 3l.50, Stalingrad; 4l. Crossing the R. Tisza; 5l. Odessa; 6l.50, Caucasus; 7l. Sevastopol; 20l. Bibescu and King Michael.

1943–45. W **166**. P 13½.

1604 **145** 25b. blue-green 10 10
1605 50b. deep blue-green 10 10
1606 1l. purple 10 10
1607 2l. orange 10 10
1608 3l. red-brown (1.12.43) 10 10
1609 3l.50 red-brown (1.12.43) 10 10
1610 4l. blue-grey 10 10
1611 4l.50 brown (1.12.43) 10 10
1612 5l. pink 10 10
1613 6l.50 violet (1.12.43) 10 10
1614 7l. blue 10 10
1615 10l. magenta 10 10
1616 11l. ultramarine (1.12.43) 10 10
1617 12l. grey-blue 10 10
1618 15l. blue (1.12.43) 20 10
1619 16l. deep blue-green 10 10
1620 20l. brown 20 10
1621 29l. blue (1945) 1·60 1·30
1622 30l. yellow-green 70 20
1623 50l. grey-olive 95 30
1604/1623 *Set of* 20 4·75 3·25

In 1945 redrawn types were issued of the 2l., 3l.50, 4l.50, 6l.50, 11l. and 15l. values, with the figures of value ½ mm. further apart.

172 Association Insignia

173 Motor-cycle and Delivery Van

(Des A. Murnu)

1943 (19 Dec). 25th Anniv of National Engineers' Association. W **166**. P 14.

1624 **172** 21l. +29l. sepia 1·50 1·60

1944. Postal Employees' Relief Fund and Bicent of National Postal Service. Designs as T **173**. W **166**. P 14.

(a) Without opt (1 Feb)

1625 1 +49l. red 3·00 3·25
1626 2 +48l. magenta 3·00 3·25
1627 4 +46l. blue 3·00 3·25

1628 10 +40l. purple-brown .... 3·00 3·25
1625/1628 *Set of 4* .... 11·00 11·50
MS1629 143×86 mm. Nos. 1625/7 but in orange-red. P 13½ at sides, imperf between stamps (sold at 200l.) .... 9·75 10·50
MS1630 As last but in violet and imperf .... 9·75 10·50

(b) Optd "1744 1944" (28 Feb)

1631 1 +49l. red .... 6·25 6·75
1632 2 +48l. magenta .... 6·25 6·75
1633 4 +46l. blue .... 6·25 6·75
1634 10 +40l. purple-brown .... 6·25 6·75
1631/1634 *Set of 4* .... 23·00 24·00
MS1635 (No. **MS**1629) .... 24·00 31·00
MS1636 (No. **MS**1630) .... 24·00 31·00

Designs: Horiz—2l. Mail van and eight horses; 4l. Chariot. Vert—10l. Horseman and Globe.

174 Dr. Cretzulescu

175 Rugby Player

(Des I. Basarab)

1944 (1 Mar). Centenary of Medical Teaching in Romania. W **166**. P 14.

1637 **174** 35l. +65l. ultramarine .... 1·50 1·60

1944 (16 Mar). 30th Anniv of Foundation of National Rugby Football Association. W **166**. P 14.

1638 **175** 16l. +184l. carmine-red .... 6·25 6·75

176 Stefan Tomsa Church, Radaseni

177 Fruit Pickers

(Des A. Murnu)

1944. Cultural Fund. Town of Radaseni. As T **176/7** (inscr "RADASENI"). W **166**. P 14.

1639 5l. +145l. blue .... 1·30 1·30
1640 12l. +138l. carmine .... 1·30 1·30
1641 15l. +135l. red .... 1·30 1·30
1642 32l. +118l. sepia .... 1·30 1·30
1639/1642 *Set of 4* .... 4·75 4·75

Designs: Horiz—12l. Agricultural Institution; 32l. School.

178 Queen Helen

179 King Michael and Carol I Foundation, Bucharest

(Portrait and Cross typo; frame photo)

1945 (10 Feb). Red Cross Relief Fund. Cross in red. W **166**. P 13½.

1643 **178** 4l.50 +5l.50 black, buff and violet 50 50
1644 10l. +40l. black, buff and brown 70 75
1645 15l. +75l. black, buff and blue .... 95 1·00
1646 20l. +80l. black, buff and brown-red .... 1·50 1·60
1643/1646 *Set of 4* .... 3·25 3·50

1945 (10 Feb). King Carol I Foundation Fund. W **166**. P 13.

1647 **179** 20l. +180l. orange 70 75
1648 25l. +175l. slate 70 75
1649 35l. +165l. purple-brown 70 75
1650 75l. +125l. violet 70 75
1647/1650 *Set of 4* .... 2·50 2·75
MS1651 74×60 mm. 200l.+1000l. blue (as T **179** but portrait of King Carol I). Imperf. No gum .... 9·75 9·75

Nos. 1647/50 were printed in sheets of four.

180 A. Saguna

181 A. Muresanu

(Des I. Basarab)

1945 (Feb). Liberation of Northern Transylvania. As T **180/1** (inscr "1944"). W **166**. P 14.

1652 25b. carmine .... 95 1·00
1653 50b. orange .... 50 1·00
1654 4l.50 chocolate .... 50 1·00
1655 11l. ultramarine .... 50 1·00
1656 15l. blue-green .... 50 1·00
1657 31l. violet .... 50 1·00
1658 35l. blue-grey .... 50 1·00
1659 41l. grey-olive .... 50 1·00
1660 55l. red-brown .... 50 1·00
1661 61l. magenta .... 50 1·00
1662 75l. +75l. sepia .... 50 1·00
1652/1662 *Set of 11* .... 5·25 10·00

Designs (views and miniature portraits): Horiz—4l.50, S. Micu; 31l. G. Lazar; 55l. Horia, Closca and Crisan; 61l. P. Maior; 75l. Kings Ferdinand and Michael. Vert—11l. G. Sincai; 15l. Prince Michael; 41l. S. Barnutiu; 35l. A. Iancu.

Northern Transylvania, allotted to Hungary by the "Vienna Award" of 30 August 1940, was regained after Romania had gone over to the side of the Allies in August 1944.

182

183

King Michael

184

185

186 N. Jorga

(Des S. Wladimir)

1945 (Mar)–**47**. White (W) or grey (G) paper. W **166**. P 14.

1663 **182** 50b. slate (W) 10 10
1664 **183** 1l. olive-brown (W) 10 10
1665 2l. violet (W) 10 10
1666 **182** 2l. sepia (G) (15.12.45) 10 10
1667 **183** 4l. green (W) 10 10
1668 **184** 5l. magenta (G) (15.12.45) 10 10
1669 **182** 10l. blue (W) 10 10
1670 10l. red-brown (G) (15.12.45) 10 10
1671 **183** 10l. red-brown (G) (1947) 10 10
1672 **182** 15l. magenta (W) 10 10
1673 20l. blue (WG) 10 10
1674 20l. lilac (G) (15.12.45) 10 10
1675 **184** 20l. bright crimson (G) (1947) 10 10
1676 25l. vermilion (WG) 10 10
1677 35l. brown (W) 10 10
1678 40l. carmine (W) 30 10
1679 **183** 50l. ultramarine (G) (15.12.45) 10 10
1680 55l. scarlet (G) (15.12.45) 30 10
1681 **184** 75l. blue-green (W) 50 10
1682 **185** 80l. orange (WG) 50 10
1683 80l. grey-blue (G) (15.12.45) 10 10
1684 **182** 80l. blue (G) (1947) 10 10
1685 **185** 100l. red-brown (WG) 10 10
1686 **182** 137l. olive-green (G) (1946) 50 10
1687 **185** 160l. green (G) (1946) 10 10
1688 160l. grey-blue (G) (1947) 50 10
1689 200l. olive-green (WG) 50 10
1690 200l. red (G) (1946) 10 10
1691 **183** 200l. red (G) (1947) 10 10
1692 **185** 300l. grey-blue (G) (1946) 10 10
1693 360l. brown (G) (1946) 50 10
1694 400l. violet-blue (G) (1946) 10 10
1695 **183** 400l. orange-red (G) (1946) 10 10
1696 **185** 480l. red-brown (G) (1946) 50 10
1697 **182** 500l. magenta (W) (1947) 50 10
1698 **185** 600l. olive (G) (1946) 10 10
1699 **184** 860l. violet-brown (W) (1947) 80 20
1700 **185** 1000l. deep green (G) (1946) 50 10
1701 **182** 1500l. blue-green (G) (1946) 50 10
1702 **185** 2400l. lilac (G) (1946) 95 10
1703 **183** 2500l. ultramarine (W) (1947) 50 10
1704 **185** 3700l. grey-blue (G) (1947) 95 10
1705 **182** 5000l. slate-grey (W) (1947) 40 10
1706 8000l. green (W) (1947) 95 20
1707 **185** 10000l. chocolate (W) (1947) .... 1·20 30
1663/1707 *Set of 45* .... 12·50 4·50

(Des I. Cova and I. Molnar)

1945 (30 Apr). War Victims' Relief Fund. As T **186** (inscr "VICTIMELE TEROAREI HITLERISTE"). W **166**. P 14 or 13½ (20l.).

1708 12l. +188l. blue .... 95 1·00
1709 16l. +184l. brown .... 95 1·00
1710 20l. +180l. sepia .... 95 1·00
1711 32l. +168l. scarlet .... 95 1·00
1712 35l. +165l. greenish blue .... 95 1·00
1713 36l. +164l. violet .... 95 1·00
1708/1713 *Set of 6* .... 5·25 5·50
MS1714 76×60 mm. Nos. 1711/12 but mauve. Imperf (sold at 1000l.) .... 29·00 31·00

Portraits:—12l. Ion Gheorghe Duca (Prime Minister, 1933); 16l. Virgil Madgearu (politician); 32l. Ilie Pintilie (communist); 35l. Bernath Andrei (communist); 36l. Filimon Sârbu (saboteur).

187 Books and Torch

188 Karl Marx

(Des I. Cova and I. Molnar)

1945 (20 May). First Romanian-Soviet Congress Fund. As T **187** (inscr "ARLUS"). W **166**. P 14.

1715 20l. +80l. olive-green 60 65
1716 35l. +165l. carmine 60 65
1717 75l. +225l. blue 60 65
1718 80l. +420l. red-brown 60 65
1715/1718 *Set of 4* .... 2·20 2·30
MS1719 60×75 mm. As Nos. 1716/17 but orange-red. Imperf (sold at 900l.) .... 11·50 12·50

Designs: Vert—35l. Soviet and Romanian Flags; 75l. Drawn curtain revealing Kremlin; 80l. T. Vladimirescu and A. Nevsky.

1945 (30 June). Trades Union Congress, Bucharest. Portraits as T **188** inscr "CONFEDERATIA GENERALA A MUNCII". W **166**.

(a) P 13½

1720 75l. +425l. carmine .... 4·00 4·25
1721 120l. +380l. blue .... 4·00 4·25
1722 155l. +445l. purple-brown .... 4·00 4·25

(b) Colours changed. Imperf.

1723 75l. +425l. blue .... 11·50 12·50
1724 120l. +380l. purple-brown .... 11·50 12·50
1725 155l. +445l. carmine .... 11·50 12·50
1720/1725 *Set of 6* .... 42·00 45·00

Portraits: 75l. Marx; 120l. Engels; 155l. Lenin.

Nos. 1723/5 were each printed in sheets of four.

189 Postman

1945 (20 July). Postal Employees. Designs as T **189** inscr "MUNCA P.T.T.". W **166**. P 13.

1726 100l. brown .... 95 1·00
1727 100l. olive .... 95 1·00
1728 150l. brown .... 1·50 1·60
1729 150l. carmine .... 1·50 1·60
1730 250l. olive .... 2·40 2·50
1731 250l. blue .... 2·40 2·50
1732 500l. magenta .... 19·00 21·00
1726/1732 *Set of 7* .... 26·00 28·00

Designs: Horiz—150l. Telegraphist; 250l. Linesman; 500l. Post Office, Bucharest.

The above were printed in sheets of four.

190 Discus Throwing

191 Flying

(Des I. Cova and I. Molnar)

1945 (5 Aug). Vert sports designs inscr "O.S.P." in shield as T **190**. W **166**. P 13.

A. POSTAGE

1733 12l. +188l. olive-grey .... 3·50 3·75
1734 16l. +184l. ultramarine .... 3·50 3·75
1735 20l. +180l. green .... 3·50 3·75
1736 32l. +168l. magenta .... 3·50 3·75
1737 35l. +165l. blue .... 3·50 3·75
1733/1737 *Set of 5* .... 16·00 17·00

(b) Colours changed. Imperf

1738 12l. +188l. orange-red .... 3·50 3·75
1739 16l. +184l. purple-brown .... 3·50 3·75
1740 20l. +180l. violet .... 3·50 3·75
1741 32l. +168l. yellow-green .... 3·50 3·75
1742 35l. +165l. olive-green .... 3·50 3·75
1738/1742 *Set of 5* .... 16·00 17·00

Designs:—16l. Diving; 20l. Skiing; 32l. Volleyball; 35l. "Sport and work".

B. AIR

1743 **191** 200l. +1000l. blue .... 29·00 31·00

No. 1743 was issued in sheets of 30 stamps and 10 labels, the labels alternating with the stamps in the second and fourth horizontal rows.

Nos. 1733/42 were each issued in sheetlets of nine stamps.

192 Agricultural and Industrial Workers

193 T. Vladimirescu

(Des A. Murnu)

1945 (23 Aug). First Anniv of Romanian Armistice with Russia. As T **192** inscr "23 AUGUST 1944/23 AUGUST 1945". W **166**. P 14.

1744 100l. +400l. red .... 1·20 1·30
1745 200l. +800l. blue .... 1·20 1·30

Design: Horiz—200l. King Michael, "Agriculture" and "Industry".

(Des A. Murnu)

1945 (23 Aug). Patriotic Defence Fund. As T **193** inscr "APARAREA PATRIOTICA". W **166**. P 13.

1746	20l. +580l. chocolate	8·75	11·50
1747	20l. +580l. magenta	8·75	11·50
1748	40l. +560l. blue	8·75	11·50
1749	40l. +560l. slate-green	8·75	11·50
1750	55l. +545l. red	8·75	11·50
1751	55l. +545l. purple-brown	8·75	11·50
1752	60l. +540l. ultramarine	8·75	11·50
1753	60l. +540l. chocolate	8·75	11·50
1754	80l. +520l. red	8·75	11·50
1755	80l. +520l. magenta	8·75	11·50
1756	100l. +500l. slate-green	8·75	11·50
1757	100l. +500l. red-brown	8·75	11·50
1746/1757 *Set of* 12		95·00	£120

Designs: Horiz—20l. "Political Amnesty"; 40l. "Military Amnesty"; 55l. "Agrarian Amnesty"; 100l. King Michael and "Reconstruction". Vert—80l. Nicholas Horia.

This issue, printed in sheets of four, exists on white paper and on coarse grey paper without gum.

194 Destitute Children

195 I. Ionescu, G. Titeica, A. G. Idachimescu and V. Cristescu

1945 (23 Aug). Child Welfare Fund. W **166**. P 14.

1758	**194**	40l. blue	95	50

1945 (5 Sept). 50th Anniv of Founding of Journal of Mathematics. T **195** and similar horiz design. W **166**. P 13.

1759	2l. blackish brown	20	10
1760	80l. deep slate-blue (Allegory of Learning)	70	75

196 Cernavoda Bridge

197 Electric Train

198

1945 (26 Sept). 50th Anniv of Building of Cernavoda Bridge. W **166**. P 14.

1761	**196**	80l. blue-black	95	50

1945. 16th Congress of Romanian Engineers. Inscr "AL XVI CONGRES ASOCIATIA GENERALA A INGINERILOR DIN ROMANIA". W **166**.

(a) POSTAGE. As T **197**

(i) P 14 (1 Oct)

1762	10l. +490l. olive-green	95	1·00
1763	20l. +480l. red-brown	95	1·00
1764	25l. +475l. brown-purple	95	1·00
1765	55l. +445l. ultramarine	95	1·00
1766	100l. +400l. brown	95	1·00

(ii) Colours changed. Imperf (21 Oct)

1767	10l. +490l. blue	95	1·00
1768	20l. +480l. violet	95	1·00
1769	25l. +475l. blue-green	95	1·00
1770	55l. +445l. grey	95	1·00
1771	100l. +400l. magenta	95	1·00

Designs: Horiz—20l. Coats of Arms; 25l. Arterial road; 35l. Oil wells; 100l. "Agriculture".

(b) AIR. As T **198**. Imperf (1 Oct)

1772	80l. +420l. grey	2·40	2·50
1773	200l. +800l. ultramarine	2·40	2·50
1762/1773 *Set of* 12		13·00	13·50
MS1774 75×55 mm. 80l. bright purple (as 1772). Imperf (11 Oct)		14·50	19·00
MS1775 75×55 mm. 80l. myrtle-green (as 1773). P 12½ (21 Oct)		24·00	27·00

Design:—200l. Icarus and Lockheed 14 Super Electra airplane.

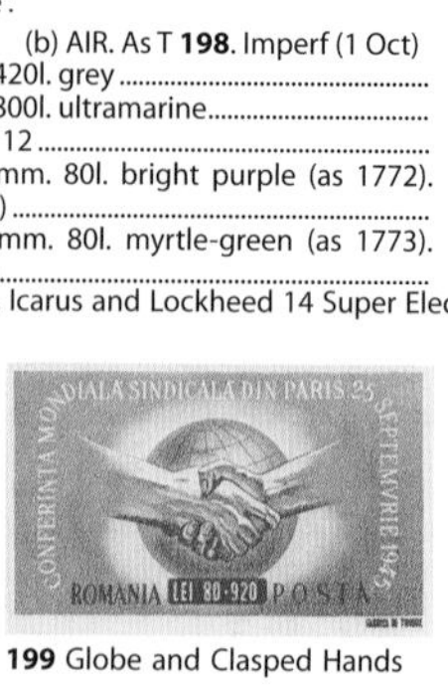

199 Globe and Clasped Hands

1945 (5 Dec). World Trade Union Congress, Paris. Symbolical designs inscr as T **199**. W **166**. P 14.

1776	80l. +920l. magenta	24·00	26·00
1777	160l. +1840l. orange-brown	24·00	26·00
1778	320l. +1680l. violet	24·00	26·00
1779	440l. +2560l. yellow-green	24·00	26·00
1776/1779 *Set of* 4		85·00	95·00

Designs: Horiz—160l. Globe and Dove of Peace; Hand and hammer; 440l. Scaffolding and flags.

1946 (Feb). Nos. 1444/5 surch with new values.

1780	10l.+90l. on 100l.+400l. red	1·90	2·10
1781	10l.+90l. on 200l.+800l. blue (R.)	1·90	2·10
1782	20l.+80l. on 100l.+400l. red (G.)	1·90	2·10
1783	20l.+80l. on 200l.+800l. blue	1·90	2·10
1784	80l.+120l. on 100l.+400l. red (B.)	1·90	2·10
1785	80l.+120l. on 200l.+800l. blue	1·90	2·10
1786	100l.+150l. on 100l.+400l. red	1·90	2·10
1787	100l.+150l. on 200l.+800l. blue (R.)	1·90	2·10
1780/1787 *Set of* 8		13·50	15·00

200 Sower

201 Distribution of Title Deeds

(Des A. Murnu)

1946. Agrarian Reform. As T **200/1** (inscr "REFORMA AGRARA"). W **166**. P 14.

(a) POSTAGE (6 March)

1788	80l. light blue	60	65
1789	50l. +450l. scarlet	60	65
1790	100l. +900l. purple	60	65
1791	200l. +800l. orange	60	65
1792	400l. +1600l. green	60	65
1788/1792 *Set of* 5		2·75	3·00

(b) AIR. (4 May)

MS1793 75×60 mm. 80l. blue (as No. 1789 but larger) (sold at 100l.)	19·00	21·00

Designs: Vert—80l. Blacksmith and ploughman. Horiz— 200l. Ox-drawn farm wagon; 400l. Plough and tractor.

202

203 Building Worker

(Des O. Adler)

1946 (26 Apr). 25th Anniv of Bucharest Philharmonic Orchestra. As T **202** inscr "FILARMONICA". W **166**. P 13½.

1794	10l. blue	20	10
1795	20l. red-brown	20	10
1796	55l. blue-green	20	10
1797	80l. violet	20	10
	a. Tête-bêche (pair)	95	1·00
1798	160l. orange	20	10
1799	200l. +800l. red	1·50	1·60
1800	350l. +1650l. blue	1·90	2·10
1794/1800 *Set of* 7		4·00	3·75
MS1801	No. 1799×12+4 labels	60·00	65·00
MS1802	No. 1800×12+4 labels	60·00	65·00

Designs: 20, 55 and 160l. "XXV" and musical score; 80l. 350l. G. Enescu; 200l. T **202**.

Nos. 1799/1800 only come from the miniature sheets.

(Des C. Müller)

1946 (1 May). Labour Day. T **203** (and similar types inscr "ZIUA MUNCII"). W **166**. P 13½.

1803	10l. claret (Type **203**)	20	10
1804	10l. green (Mechanic)	95	1·00
1805	20l. blue (Peasant)	95	1·00
1806	20l. brown (Peasant woman)	20	10
1807	200l. scarlet (Students)	50	50
1803/1807 *Set of* 5		2·50	2·50

204 Sky-writing

(F **205**)

1946 (1 May). AIR. Labour Day. Sheet 70×63 mm. W **166**. P 13.

MS1808	**204**	200l. blue and vermilion (sold at 10,000l.)	19·00	21·00

1946 (May). FRANK. For Internees' Mail via Red Cross. Nos. T1589/95 optd with Type F **205** in red.

F1809	T **171**	(–) on 50b. orange-vermilion	1·50	1·60
F1810		(–) on 1l. lilac	1·50	1·60
F1811		(–) on 2l. brown	1·50	1·60
F1812		(–) on 4l. ultramarine	1·50	1·60
F1813		(–) on 5l. violet	1·50	1·60
F1814		(–) on 8l. green	1·50	1·60
F1815		(–) on 10l. sepia	1·50	1·60
F1809/1815 *Set of* 7			9·50	10·00

205 Sower

206 Aviator and Aircraft

1946 (28 July). Youth Issue. W **166**.

(a) POSTAGE. As T **205**. P 11½

1809	10l. +100l. vermilion and brown	50	50
1810	10l. +200l. purple-brown and greenish blue	50	50
1811	80l. +200l. brown and maroon	50	50
1812	80l. +300l. dull magenta and red-brown	50	50
1813	200l. +400l. vermilion and deep turquoise-green	50	50

(b) AIR. As T **206**. P 13½×13

1814	200l. blue and yellow-green	4·75	5·25
1815	500l. dull blue and orange	4·75	5·25
1809/1815 *Set of* 7		11·00	11·50

Designs:—No. 1810, Hurdler; 1811, Student; 1812, Worker and factory; 1813, Marching with flag; 1814, Airplane on ground.

Issued in sheets of four.

207 Football

208 "Traditional Ties"

1946 (1 Sept). Sports. T **207** and similar vert designs. W **166**.

A. P 11½

(a) POSTAGE

1816A	10l. deep blue	50	50
1817A	20l. vermilion	50	50
1818A	50l. slate-violet	50	50
1819A	80l. chocolate	50	50
1820A	160l. +1340l. deep bluish green	50	50

(b) AIR. Inscr "POSTA AERIANA"

1821A	300l. rosine	1·90	2·50
	a. Pair. Nos. 1821A/2A	4·00	5·25
1822A	300l. +1200l. blue	1·90	2·50
1816A/1822A *Set of* 7		5·75	6·75

B. Imperf

(a) POSTAGE

1816B	10l. deep blue	50	50
1817B	20l. vermilion	50	50
1818B	50l. slate-violet	50	50
1819B	80l. chocolate	50	50
1820B	160l. +1340l. deep bluish green	50	50
MS1823 58×64 mm. 300l. crimson (as No. 1821 but larger). Imperf (sold at 1300l.)		21·00	23·00

(Des O. Adler)

1946 (20 Oct). Romanian Soviet Friendship Pact. T **208** and similar vert designs. W **166**. P 13½.

1824	80l. sepia	50	50
1825	100l. blue ("Cultural ties")	50	50
1826	300l. blue-black ("Economic ties")	50	50
1827	300l. +1200l. bright scarlet (Dove)	95	1·00
	a. Imperf		
1824/1827 *Set of* 4		2·20	2·30
MS1828 70×65 mm. 1000l. scarlet (as No. 1827). P 14 (sold at 6000l.)		9·75	10·50

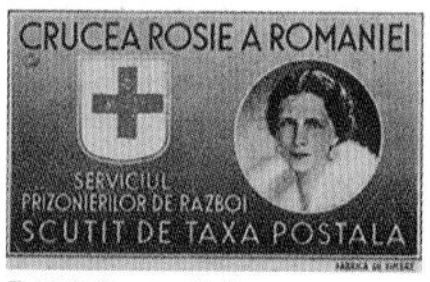

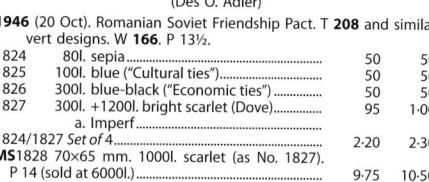

F **209** Queen Helen

1946 (Nov). FRANK. For Internees' Mail via Red Cross. Grey or white paper. W **166**. Photo.

A. P 13½

F1829A	F **209**	(–) bronze green and carmine-red	70	75
F1830A		(–) dull purple and carmine-red	70	75
F1831A		(–) brown-red and carmine-red.	70	75
F1829A/1831A *Set of* 3			1·90	2·00

B. Imperf

F1829B	F **209**	(–) bronze green and carmine-red	1·20	1·30
F1830B		(–) dull purple and carmine-red	1·20	1·30
F1831B		(–) brown-red and carmine-red.	1·20	1·30
F1829B/1831B *Set of* 3			3·25	3·50

209 Banat Girl holding Distaff

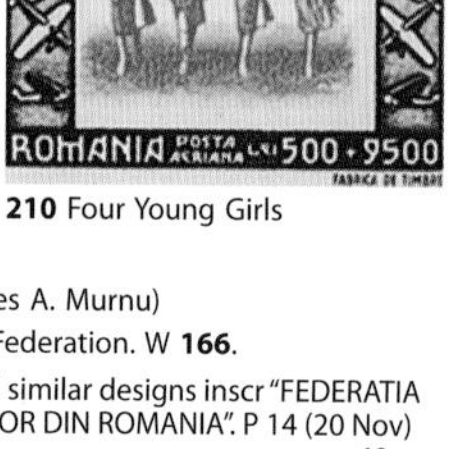

210 Four Young Girls

(Des A. Murnu)

1946. Women's Democratic Federation. W **166**.

(a) POSTAGE. T **209** and similar designs inscr "FEDERATIA DEMOCRATA A FEMEILOR DIN ROMANIA". P 14 (20 Nov)

1829	80l. olive-brown	40	40
1830	80l. +320l. vermilion	40	40
1831	140l. +360l. orange	40	40
1832	300l. +450l. deep olive-green	40	40
1833	600l. +900l. blue	40	40
1829/1833 *Set of* 5		1·80	1·80

Designs: Vert—80l. (No. 1829), Girl and handloom; 140l. Wallachian girl and wheatsheaf; 300l. Transylvanian horsewoman; 600l. Moldavian girl carrying water.

(b) AIR. T **210** Imperf (20 Dec)

MS1834 80×65 mm. 500l.+9500l. vermilion and chocolate .... 9·75 10·50

1946–47. POSTAGE DUE. With imprint below designs. P 14.

(a) No wmk

D1835	D **98**	20l. black	20	10
D1836		100l. black (1947)	70	30
D1837		200l. black	1·50	75

(b) W **166**

D1838	D **98**	20i. black	20	10
D1839		50l. black	20	15
D1840		80l. black	40	20
D1841		100l. black	60	30
D1842		200l. black	95	65
D1843		500l. black	1·50	1·00
D1844		5000l. black (19.6.47)	2·40	1·60
D1835/1844 *Set of* 10			7·75	4·50

211 King Michael and Food Transport

212 Mother and Children

(Des A. Murnu)

1947 (15 Jan). Social Relief Fund. W **166**. T **211** and symbolic designs inscr "AJUTOR INFORMETATILOR SI ASISTENTEI SOCIALE". P 14.

1845	300l. blackish olive	50	50
1846	600l. reddish purple	50	50
1847	1500l. +3500l. red-orange	50	50
1848	3700l. +5300l. slate-violet	50	50
1845/1848 *Set of* 4		1·80	1·80

MS1849 52×36 mm. **212** 5000l.+5000l. ultramarine. No gum. Imperf .... 9·75 10·50

Designs: Vert—300l. Loaf of bread and hungry child; 1500l. Angel bringing food and clothing to destitute people; 3700l. Loaf of bread and starving family.

213 King Michael and Chariot

(Des A. Murnu)

1947 (25 Feb). Peace. T **213** and designs inscr "PACEA 10 FEBRUARIE 1947". W **166**. P 14.

1850	300l. dull purple	50	50
1851	600l. red-brown	50	50
1852	3000l. blue	50	50
1853	7200l. grey-green	50	50
1850/1853 *Set of* 4		1·80	1·80

Designs: Vert—600l. Winged figure of Peace; 3000l. Flags of four Allied Nations; 7200l. Dove of Peace.

214 Symbols of Labour and **215** Clasped Hands

216 Worker and Torch

1947 (Mar). Trades Union Congress. W **166**.

(a) POSTAGE. P 13½

1854	**214**	200l. blue	70	75
		a. Horiz strip of 6. Nos. 1854/6, each×2	8·75	
1855		300l. orange	70	75
1856		600l. scarlet	70	75

(b) AIR. P 13×14 (1000l.) or imperf (3000l.)

1857	**215**	1100l. blue	95	1·00
1858	**216**	3000l. +7000l. chocolate	95	1·00
1854/1858 *Set of* 5			3·50	3·75

Nos. 1854/6 were issued in sheets of 18 comprising three blocks of 6, giving horizontal *se-tenant* strips (No. 1854a).

No. 1857 was issued in sheets of 15 and No. 1858 in sheets of four.

217 Girls' School

218 Symbolical of "Learning"

1947 (5 Mar). As T **217/18** inscr "CASA SCOALELOR SI A CULTURII POPORULUI 1896/1946"). W **166**. P 14.

1859	200l. +200l. violet-blue	20	30
1860	300l. +300l. red-brown	20	30
1861	600l. +600l. grey-green	20	30
1862	1200l. +1200l. ultramarine	20	30
1863	1500l. +1500l. claret	20	30
1859/1863 *Set of* 5		90	1·40

MS1864 64×80 mm. 3700l.+3700l. grey-blue and yellow-brown (as T **218**). Imperf .... 3·00 3·75

Designs: Horiz—200l. Boys' reading class; 600l. Engineering classroom; 1200l. School building.

219 King Michael

220 N. Grigorescu

221 Lisunov Li-2 Airliner

(Des A. Murnu)

1947 (Mar). W **166**. P 13½.

(a) 18×21½ mm

1865	**219**	1000l. slate-blue	20	20
1866		5500l. green	30	30
1867		20000l. olive-brown	70	40
1868		50000l. red-orange	1·30	65

(b) 25×30 mm

1869	**219**	3000l. blue	30	30
1870		7200l. mauve	30	30
1871		15000l. bright blue	50	30
1872		21000l. magenta	50	30
1873		36000l. violet	95	85
1865/1873 *Set of* 9			4·50	3·25

(Des I. Cova)

1947 (June). As T **220** (various portraits). Frames inscr "INSTITUTUL DE STUDII ROMANO SOVIETIC 1947". W **166**.

(a) POSTAGE. P 14

1874	1500l. +1500l. purple	40	40
1875	1500l. +1500l. red-orange	40	40
1876	1500l. +1500l. slate-green	40	40
1877	1500l. +1500l. grey-blue	40	40
1878	1500l. +1500l. ultramarine	40	40
1879	1500l. +1500l. brown-lake	40	40
1880	1500l. +1500l. carmine	40	40
1881	1500l. +1500l. brown	40	40

(b) AIR. Imperf

1882	**221** 15000l. +15000l. grey-green	95	1·00
1874/1882 *Set of* 9		3·75	3·75

Portraits:—Petru Movila, V. Babes, M. Eminescu, N. Grigorescu, P. Tchaikovsky, M. Lomonosov, A. Pushkin and I. Y. Repin.

No. 1882 was printed in sheets of four.

222 Miner

223 Air Force Monument

224 Douglas DC-4 Airliner over Black Sea

(Des I. Molnar)

1947 (15 June). Labour Day. W **166**.

(a) POSTAGE. As T **222**. P 14.

1883	1000l. +1000l. olive-brown	40	40
1884	1500l. +1500l. lake-brown	40	40
1885	2000l. +2000l. blue	40	40
1886	2500l. +2500l. purple	40	40
1887	3000l. +3000l. carmine	40	40

Designs:—1500l. Peasant; 2000l. Peasant woman; 2500l. "Intellectual"; 3000l. Factory worker.

(b) AIR. As T **223**. P 11½

1888	3000l. vermilion	50	50
1889	3000l. greenish grey	50	50
1890	3000l. black-brown	50	50

Designs:—No. 1888, "1 MAI" suspended from four parachutes; 1889, Type **223**; 1890, Douglas DC-4 airliner over landscape.

Nos. 1888/90 were each issued in sheets of four.

(c) AIR. T **224**. P 14×13

1891	3000l. +12000l. blue	95	1·00
1883/1891 *Set of* 9		4·00	4·00

New Currency. 15 August 1947

1 (new) Leu = 100 (old) Lei

225 King Michael and Timber Barges

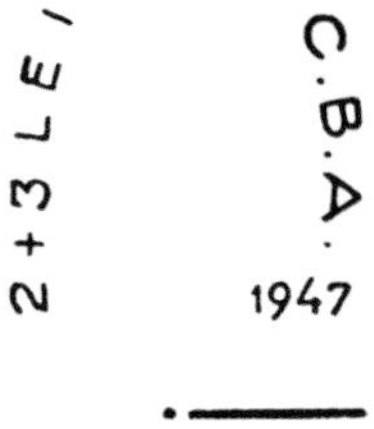

(226)

(Des A. Murnu)

1947 (from 15 Aug). Designs with medallion portrait of King Michael as T **225**. W **166**. P 14.

1892	50b. orange	20	10
1893	1l. red-brown	20	10
1894	2l. greenish blue	20	10
1895	3l. rose	50	20
1896	5l. violet-blue	50	20
1897	10l. blue	70	30
1898	12l. violet	95	30
1899	15l. ultramarine	1·50	30
1900	20l. brown	2·40	50
1901	32l. purple-brown	6·25	2·50
1902	36l. lake	6·25	2·50
1892/1902 *Set of* 11		18·00	6·50

Designs: Horiz—50b. Harvesting; 2l. River Danube; 3l. Reshitza Industries; 5l. Curtea de Arges Cathedral; 10l. Royal Palace, Bucharest; 12l., 36l. Cernavoda Bridge; 15l., 32l. Liner *Transylvania* in Port of Constantza; 20l. Oil Wells, Prahova.

1947 (6 Sept). Balkan Games. No. 1873 surch with T **226**, in red.

1903	**219**	2+3l. on 36000l. violet	1·50	1·60

F **227** King Michael

F **228** Torch and Book

PRIN AVION

F **228a**

1947. FRANK. King Michael's Fund. Types F **227/228** and similar design. W **166**. Photo.

A. P 14×13½ (F1906) or 13½ (others)

(a) POSTAGE (Sept)

F1904A	F **227**	(–) slate-purple	50	50
F1905A	F **228**	(–) deep grey-blue	50	50
F1906A	–	(–) reddish brown	50	50

B. Imperf

(a) POSTAGE (Sept)

F1904B	F **227**	(–) slate-purple	95	1·00
F1905B	F **228**	(–) deep grey-blue	95	1·00
F1906B	–	(–) reddish brown	95	1·00

A. P 14×13½ (F1906) or 13½ (others)

(b) AIR. No. F1904 optd with F **228a** "PRIN AVION" (1 Dec)

F1907A	F **227**	(–) slate-purple (Blk.)	70	75
		c. Opt in red	70	75
F1904A/1907A *Set of* 4			2·00	2·00

B. Imperf

(b) AIR. No. F1904 optd with F **228a** "PRIN AVION" (1 Dec)

F1907B	F **227**	(–) slate-purple (Blk.)	70	75
		c. Opt in red	70	75
F1904B/1907B *Set of* 4			3·25	3·50

Design: As Type F **227** but horiz—No. F1906, Man writing and couple reading.

(227)

ARLUS +5
1-7.XI.
1947

(228)

1947 (1 Oct). 17th Congress of General Association of Romanian Engineers. As T **227** (vert designs with the letters "A G I R" interwoven in a monogram). W **166**. P 14.

(a) POSTAGE

1904	1l. +1l. claret	20	10
1905	2l. +2l. sepia	20	10
1906	3l. +3l. violet	20	10
1907	4l. +4l. grey-olive	30	30

(b) AIR. Inscr "POSTA AERIANA"

1908	5l. +5l. blue	1·10	1·20
1904/1908 *Set of* 5		1·80	1·60

Designs:—2l. Sawmill; 3l. Refinery; 4l. Steel mill; 5l. Gliders over mountains.

1947 (30 Oct). Romanian-Soviet Amity. As No. 1896 (but imperf), surch with T **228**.

1909	5l. +5l. violet-blue (R.)	95	75

229 Beehive

230 Food Convoy

1947 (31 Oct). Savings Day. W **166**. P 13½.

1910	**229**	12l. rose	95	50

1947 (7 Nov). Patriotic Defence. As T **230** (symbolic designs inscr "APARAREA PATRIOTICA"). W **166**. P 14.

1911	1l. +1l. blue	50	50
1912	2l. +2l. sepia	50	50
1913	3l. +3l. claret	50	50
1914	4l. +4l. deep bright blue	50	50
1915	5l. +5l. rose-red	50	50
1911/1915 *Set of 5*		2·30	2·30

Designs and mottoes: Horiz—2l. Soldiers' parcels ("Everything for the front"); 3l. Modern hospital ("Heal the wounded"); 4l. Hungry children ("Help famine-stricken regions"). Vert—5l. Manacled wrist and flag.

Nos. 1911/15 were each issued in sheetlets of eight stamps, arranged in two blocks of four divided by a gutter.

231 Allegory of Work

232 Lisunov Li-2 Airliner over Demonstration

1947 (10 Nov). Trades' Union Congress, Bucharest. W **166**. P 14.

(a) POSTAGE. As T **231**

1916		2l. +10l. lake	50	50
1917		7l. +10l. greenish black	50	50
		(b) AIR. Photo (banner typo)		
1918	**232**	11l. red and blue	95	1·00
1916/1918 *Set of 3*			1·80	1·80

Design:—2l. Industrial and agricultural workers.

D 233

I
O
V
R **1** LEU

(T 233)

1947. POSTAGE DUE. Type D **233** perforated down centre (without overprint). W **166**. Typo. P 14½×14.

		Un pair
D1919	2l. red	50
D1920	4l. grey-blue	95
D1921	5l. black	1·50
D1922	10l. red-brown	2·40
D1919/1922 *Set of 4 pairs*		4·75

The left half showing Crown of Nos. D1919/22 served as a receipt and was stuck in the postman's book and so does not come postally used.

1947 (8 Dec). POSTAL TAX. Invalids, Widows and Orphans Fund. Fiscal stamps (22×18½ mm showing King's head on right side and on left side seal (T1923) or inscription (T1924)) perf vert through centre, surch as Type T **233**. Typo. P 14×14½.

T1923	1l. on 2l. carmine	20	20
	a. Surch inverted	25·00	27·00
T1924	5l. on 1l. green	95	1·00

PEOPLE'S REPUBLIC

30 December 1947–26 December 1989

233 Map of Romania

234 Printing Works and Press

(Des A. Murnu)

1948 (25 Jan). Census of 1948. W **166**. P 14.

1925	**233**	12l. blue	95	30

(Des I. Dumitrana)

1948 (12 Feb–20 May). 75th Anniv of Romanian State Stamp Printing Works. W **166**. P 14.

1926	**234**	6l. rose-carmine (20 May)	2·40	1·60
1927		7l.50 deep green	1·50	20
		a. Tête-bêche (pair)		

235 Discus Thrower

R·P·R·

(236 R.P.R.= Republica Populara Romana)

T 237 "Hope"

(Des I. Juster)

1948 (20 Feb). Balkan Games 1947 Sports designs as T **235** inscr "JOCURILE BALCANICE 1947". W **166**.

(a) POSTAGE. P 13½

1928	1l. +1l. sepia	70	85
1929	2l. +2l. claret	95	1·30
1930	5l. +5l. blue	1·50	2·10
	(b) AIR. Inscr "POSTA AERIANA". P 13½×14 or imperf (10l.)		
1931	7l. +7l. dull violet	2·40	2·10
1932	10l. +10l. grey-green	3·50	4·25
1928/1932 *Set of 5*		8·25	9·50

Designs:—2l. Runner; 5l. Heads of two young athletes; 7, 10l. Airplane over running track.

No. 1932 was issued in sheets of four.

1948 (Mar). Nos. 1892/1902 optd with T **236**.

1933	50b. orange	50	30
1934	1l. red-brown	50	20
1935	2l. greenish blue	1·20	30
1936	3l. rose	1·20	30
1937	5l. violet-blue	1·90	40
1938	10l. blue	2·40	50
1939	12l. violet	3·00	50
1940	15l. ultramarine	3·00	65
1941	20l. brown	4·00	75
1942	32l. purple-brown	9·75	4·25
1943	36l. lake	9·75	4·25
1933/1943 *Set of 11*		33·00	11·00

1948. POSTAGE DUE. Nos. D1919/22 optd as in Type D **233**.

		Un pair	Us pair
D1944	2l. red	40	20
D1945	4l. grey-blue	60	30
D1946	5l. black	95	65
D1947	10l. red-brown	1·90	85
D1944/1947 *Set of 4 pairs*		3·50	1·80

1948. POSTAL TAX. Invalids', Widows' and Orphans' Fund. Typo. P 14.

(a) No wmk

T1948	**T 237**	1l. rose	30	50
T1949		1l. violet (Oct)	70	50
T1950		2l. blue	95	75
T1951		5l. yellow	4·75	3·25
T1948/1951 *Set of 4*			6·00	4·50

237 Industrial Worker

238 Youths bearing Filimon Sarbu Banner

239 Barn Swallows and Airplane

(Des I. Molnar)

1948 (15 Mar). Young Workers' Union. W **166**. Imperf (No. 1957), P 13½ (others).

(a) POSTAGE

1954	**237**	2l. +2l. deep blue	50	1·00
1955	–	3l. +3l. grey-green	60	1·00
1956	–	5l. +5l. red-brown	70	1·00
1957	**238**	8l. +8l. carmine	85	1·00
		(b) AIR. Inscr "POSTA AERIANA"		
1958	**239**	12l. +12l. blue	2·10	3·25
1954/1958 *Set of 5*			4·25	6·50

Designs: As T **237**—3l. Peasant girl and wheatsheaf; 5l. Student and book.

No. 1957 was issued in sheets of four.

240 "Friendship"

241 "New Constitution"

(T **240/1** des A. Murnu)

1948 (28 Mar). Romanian-Bulgarian Amity. W **166**. P 14.

1959	**240**	32l. brown	1·90	1·00

See also No. 1995.

1948 (8 Apr). New Constitution. W **166**. P 14.

1960	**241**	1l. rose-carmine	70	50
1961		2l. orange	95	75
1962		12l. blue	3·00	1·30
1960/1962 *Set of 3*			4·25	2·30

242 Globe and Banner

243 Aviator and Heinkel He 116A

(Des I. Dumitrana (8l.), S. Wladimir (others))

1948 (1 May). Labour Day. W **166**. P 14.

(a) POSTAGE

1963	**242**	8l. +8l. red	2·40	3·75
1964	–	10l. +10l. olive-green	3·50	5·25
1965	–	12l. +12l. red-brown	4·75	6·25
		(b) AIR		
1966	**243**	20l. +20l. blue	8·25	10·50
1963/1966 *Set of 4*			17·00	23·00

Designs: As T **242**—10l. Peasants and mountains; 12l. Worker and factory.

No. 1966 was issued in sheets of nine.

244 Barbed Wire Entanglement

(Des I. Molnar)

1948 (9 May). Army Day. Military designs as T **244** inscr "23 Aug 1944 9 Mai 1945". W **166**. P 14.

(a) POSTAGE

1967	1l.50 +1l.50 red	60	65
1968	2l. +2l. reddish purple	60	65
1969	4l. +4l. red-brown	1·10	1·20
1970	7l.50 +7l.50 greenish black	1·90	2·10
1971	8l. +8l. violet	2·10	2·30
	(b) AIR. Inscr "POSTA AERIANA"		
1972	3l. +3l. deep ultramarine	9·75	10·50
1973	5l. +5l. blue	14·50	16·00
1967/1973 *Set of 7*		27·00	30·00

Designs: Horiz—4l. Artillery; 7l.50, Tank; 8l. Destroyer. Vert—1l.50, Infantry; 3l. Ilyushin Il-2M3 Stormovik fighter planes; 5l. Petlyakov Pe-2 dive bombers.

Nos. 1972/3 were each issued in sheets of nine.

245 Balcescu, Ipatescu, Radulescu, Sapea and Magheru

246 Proclamation of Islaz

247 Emblem of Republic

(Des A. Damian)

1948 (1 June). Centenary of 1848 Revolution. Designs inscr "1848 1948". W **166**. P 13½ (5l.), 14½ (others).

1974	–	2l. +2l. reddish purple	60	95
1975	**245**	5l. +5l. violet	80	95
1976	**246**	11l. red	1·20	1·90
1977	–	10l. +10l. olive-green	1·10	95
1978	–	36l. +18l. blue	2·50	4·00
1974/1978 *Set of 5*			5·50	8·00

Designs: (22×38 mm) Vert—2l. Nicolas Balcescu; 36l. Portraits of Balcescu, Kogalniceanu, Alecsandri and Cuza. Horiz—10l. Portraits of Balcescu, Petöfi, Iancu, Barnutiu, Baritiu and Murcu.

(Des A. Murnu)

1948 (8 July–Oct). W **166**. P 14.

1979	**247**	0.50 B. vermilion	70	70
1980		0.50 L. vermilion (Oct)	50	20
1981		1l. lake-brown	50	10
1982		2l. green	50	10
1983		3l. slate-green	70	20
1984		4l. deep brown	70	20
1985		5l. ultramarine	70	20
1986		10l. dull blue	1·90	20
1979/1986 *Set of 8*			5·50	1·70

No. 1979 is inscribed "BANI 0.50" (=½ bani) and in No. 1980 this was corrected to "LEI 0.50".

See also Nos. 2023/9 and **MS**2039.

248 Monimoa Gliders

249 Yachts

(Des D. Stiubei)

1948 (26 July). Air Force and Navy Day. W **166**. P 14.

(a) Air Force. As T **248**

1987	2l. +2l. blue	1·90	1·90
1988	5l. +5l. violet	1·90	1·90
1989	8l. +8l. red	3·00	3·00
1990	10l. +10l. brown	4·00	4·00

(b) Navy. As T **249**

991 2l. +2l. green 1·90 1·90
992 5l. +5l. grey 1·90 1·90
993 8l. +8l. blue 3·00 3·00
994 10l. +10l. orange-red 4·00 4·00
987/1994 *Set of 8* 19·00 19·00

Designs: Air Force—5l. Aurel Vlaicu's No. 1 "Crazy Fly" airplane; 8l. isunov Li-2 airliner and tractor; 10l. Lisunov Li-2 airliner. Navy—5l. Aircea (cadet ship); 8l. *Romana Mare* (Danube river steamer); 10l. *ransylvania* (liner).

31

LEI

(250)

251 Newspapers and Torch

948 (17 Aug). No. 1959 surch with T **250**.
995 **240** 31l. on 32l. brown 1·50 50

948 (12 Sept). Press Week. T **251** and similar designs. W **166**.

A. P 14

996A **251** 10l. chocolate 50 10
997A 5l. +5l. rosine 95 95
998A – 10l. +10l. slate-violet 1·50 1·50
999A – 15l. +15l. blue 1·90 1·90
996A/1999A *Set of 4* 4·50 4·00

B. Imperf

996B **251** 10l. chocolate 50 10
997B 5l. +5l. rosine 95 95
998B – 10l. +10l. slate-violet 1·50 1·50
999B – 15l. +15l. blue 1·90 1·90
996B/1999B *Set of 4* 4·50 4·00

Designs: Horiz—10l. (1998), Flag, torch and inkwell. Vert—15l. Alex ahia (journalist).

252 Soviet Soldiers' Monument

253 Lisunov Li-2 Airplane

(Des I. Cova)

948 (29 Oct). Romanian-Russian Amity. W **166**. P 14.

(a) POSTAGE. As T **252**

2000 10l. red 95 95
2001 10l. +10l. green 4·00 4·75
2002 15l. +15l. blue 4·75 7·25

(b) AIR. T **253**

2003 20l. +20l. blue 14·50 19·00
2000/2003 *Set of 4* 22·00 29·00

Designs: Vert—10l. (No. 2001) Badge of Arius, 15l. Kremlin. Nos. 2000/1 were each issued with *se-tenant* inscribed label.

No. 2003 was issued as a triptych with two *se-tenant* half stamp-size labels, that at the left showing a view of Bucharest and that at the right a view of Moscow.

MULTIPLE RPR WATERMARK TYPE 254.

There are four types of this watermark as illustrated but they are not easy to distinguish on single stamps. Some stamps exist with more than one type of watermark. We have not attempted to list these but give below the catalogue numbers of stamps that are known to exist for each type.

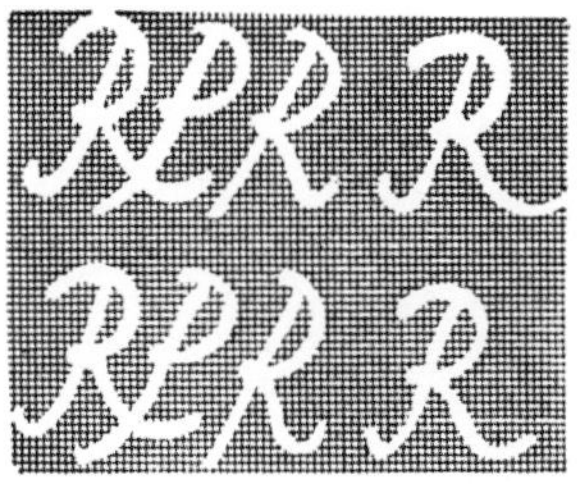

254 Type I

Type I (1948–51)

Nos. 2004/2065, D2070/6, 2077/2123, 2125, 2132, 2136/8.

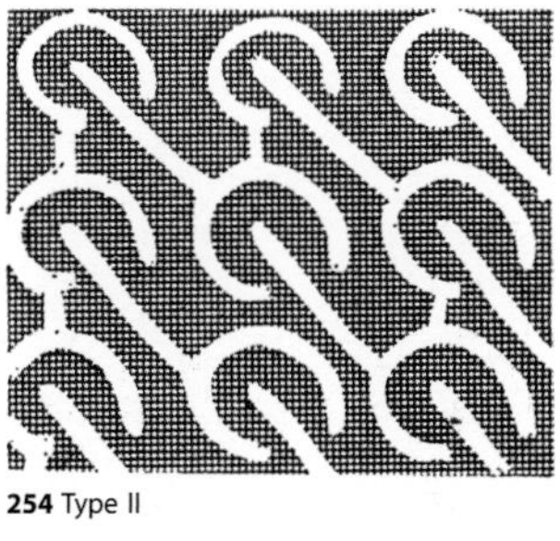

254 Type II

Type II (1951–59)

Nos. 2124/35, 2139/2412, 2419/52, 2454/7, 2474/89, 2524/6, 2529, 2561, 2694.

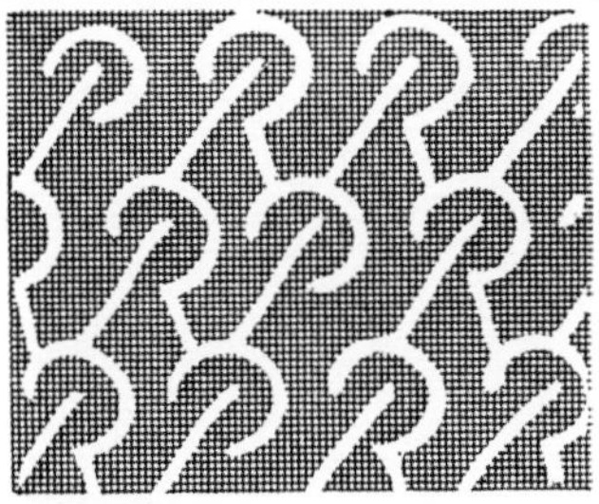

254 Type III

Type III (1957–67)

Nos. 2358/67, 2369, 2492/D2512, 2521/3, 2527/8, 2531/4, 2537/9, 2543/62, 2567/75, 2627/8, 2639/46, 2681, 2709/16, 2723/30, 2754/6, 2760/8, 2794/5, 2850/1, 2882/7, 2939/47, D3436/41.

254 Type IV

Type IV (1957–60)

Nos. 2359/61, 2363/8, 2529/30, 2532/46, 2549, 2693, 2695/2701.

255 Emblem of Republic

256 Lorry

(Des A. Murnu)

1948 (22 Nov)–**50**. AIR. T **255** and similar horiz designs. W **254**. P 14.

2004 30l. carmine 95 20
a. Red (10.5.50) 1·90 50
2005 50l. olive-green 1·50 70
2006 100l. blue 4·75 1·90
2004/2006 *Set of 3* 6·50 2·50

Designs:—50l. Workers in field; 100l. Steam train, airplane and liner.

(Des D. Stiubei)

1948 (10 Dec). Work on Communications. As T **256**. W **254**. P 14½×14.

2007 1l. +1l. black and green 95 1·90
2008 3l. +3l. black and red-brown 1·30 1·90
2009 11l. +11l. black and blue 5·25 4·75
2010 15l. +15l. black and red 6·75 7·75
2007/2010 *Set of 4* 13·00 14·50

MS2011 110×85 mm. Nos. 2007/10 but in brown and red, blue, blue and red respectively. Imperf. No gum 34·00 39·00

Designs:—1l. Dockers loading freighter; 11l. Lisunov Li-2 airliner on ground and in air; 15l. Steam train.

257 Nicolas Balcescu

258 Hands Breaking Chain

(Des A. Murnu)

1948 (20 Dec). W **254**. P 14.
2012 **257** 20l. red 1·50 50

(Des D. Stiubei)

1948 (30 Dec). First Anniv of People's Republic. W **254**. P 13½.
2013 **258** 5l. carmine 95 50

259 Runners

260 Lenin

(Des I. Juster)

1948 (31 Dec). National Sports Organisation. Sporting designs as T **259**. W **254**.

I. P 13×13½ vert or 13½×13 horiz

(a) POSTAGE

2014 5l. +5l. green 4·75 4·75
2015 10l. +10l. violet 7·25 7·25

(b) AIR

2016 20l. +20l. blue 24·00 24·00

II. Imperf. Colours changed

(a) POSTAGE

2017 5l. +5l. brown 4·75 4·75
2018 10l. +10l. red 7·25 7·25

(b) AIR

2019 20l. +20l. blue-green 24·00 24·00
2014/2019 *Set of 6* 65·00 65·00

Designs: Horiz—10l. Parade of athletes with flags. Vert—20l. Boy flying model airplane.

Nos. 2014/19 were each issued in sheetlets of four.

(Des A. Murnu)

1949 (21 Jan). 25th Anniv of Lenin's Death. W **254**. P 13½×13.
2020 **260** 20l. black 95 50
a. Imperf 1·50 95

261 Dancers

262 I. C. Frimu, and Revolutionaries

(Des A. Murnu)

1949 (24 Jan). 90th Anniv of Union of Romanian Principalities. W **254**. P 13×13½.
2021 **261** 10l. blue 95 50

(Des D. Stiubei)

1949 (22 Mar). 30th Death Anniv of Ion Frimu (union leader and journalist). W **254**. P 14.
2022 **262** 20l. vermilion 95 50
a. Imperf 1·50 95

1949–50. W **254**. P 14.
2023 **247** 0.50l. vermilion 50 30
2024 1l. lake-brown 50 10
2025 2l. green 50 10
2026 3l. slate-green 70 20
2027 5l. ultramarine 70 20
2028 5l. violet (1950) 95 10
2029 10l. dull blue 1·20 30
2023/2029 *Set of 7* 4·50 1·20

See also No. **MS**2039.

263 A. S. Pushkin

264 Globe and Posthorn

265 Forms of Transport

266 Russians entering Bucharest

(Des C. Müller)

1949 (20 May). 150th Birth Anniv of A. S. Pushkin (Russian poet). W **254**. P 14.
2030 **263** 11l. carmine 1·50 85
2031 30l. blue-green 1·90 95

(Des D. Stiubei (20l.) and I. Dumitrana (30l.))

1949 (30 June). 75th Anniv of Universal Postal Union. W **254**. P 13½ (20l.) or 14 (30l.).
2032 **264** 20l. yellow-brown 2·40 1·50
2033 **265** 30l. blue 4·75 2·40

(Des D. Stiubei)

1949 (23 Aug). Fifth Anniv of Russian Army's Entry into Bucharest. W **254**. P 14.
2034 **266** 50l. reddish brown and green 1·20 1·20
a. Imperf 2·40 2·40

267 "Romanian-Soviet Amity"

(Des D. Stiubei)

1949 (1 Nov). Romanian-Soviet Friendship Week. W **254**. P 13½×14 or imperf.

2035	**267**	20l. deep carmine	95	50

268 Forms of Transport

269 Stalin

(Des C. Müller)

1949 (10 Dec). International Congress of Transport Unions. W **254**. P 13½.

2036	**268**	11l. blue	1·20	1·20
		a. Imperf	1·50	1·50
2037		20l. bright scarlet	1·70	1·70
		a. Imperf	1·90	1·90

Nos. 2036/7 were each issued with *se-tenant* inscribed label.

(Des I. Dumitrana)

1949 (21 Dec). 70th Birth Anniv of Iosif Stalin. W **254**. P 13½.

2038	**269**	31l. blackish green	95	50
		a. Imperf	1·90	1·90

(Des C. Müller)

1950 (27 Jan). Philatelic Exhibition, Bucharest. Sheet 110×80 mm. comprising T **1** and **247**. W **254**. Imperf. No gum.

MS2039 81(p.) grey-blue and blue; 10l. carmine and rose (sold at 50l.) 7·25 4·75

270 "The Third Letter"

271 Mihail Eminescu

(Des E. Droczay (T **271**) and D. Stiubei (others))

1950 (26 Feb). Birth Centenary of Mihail Eminescu (poet). T **270** and similar designs inscr "MIHAIL EMINESCU 1850 1950", and **271**. W **254**. P 13½.

2040	**270**	11l. green	1·50	50
2041	–	11l. lake-brown	2·40	95
2042	–	11l. rose-magenta	1·50	50
2043	–	11l. violet	1·50	50
2044	**271**	11l. blue	1·50	50
2040/2044 *Set of 5*			7·50	2·75

Designs:—Scenes representing poems: "Angel and Demon" (2041); "Ruler and Proletariat" (2042); "Life" (2043).

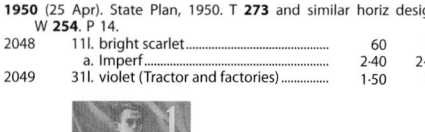

272 "Dragaica Fair"

273 Factory and Graph

(Des C. Müller)

1950 (25 Mar). Birth Centenary of Ion Andreescu (painter). T **272** and similar designs. W **254**. P 14.

2045		5l. blackish olive	1·50	95
2046		11l. blue	2·40	95
		a. Imperf	4·75	4·75
2047		20l. deep chestnut	3·00	1·90
2045/2047 *Set of 3*			6·25	3·50

Designs: Vert—11l. Andreescu. Horiz—20l. "The Village Well".

(Des E. Taru)

1950 (25 Apr). State Plan, 1950. T **273** and similar horiz design. W **254**. P 14.

2048		11l. bright scarlet	60	30
		a. Imperf	2·40	2·40
2049		31l. violet (Tractor and factories)	1·50	70

274 Worker and Flag

275 Emblem of Republic

(Des I. Cova)

1950 (1 May). Labour Day. W **254**. P 14.

2050	**274**	31l. vermilion	80	10
		a. Imperf	1·50	1·50

(Des C. Müller)

1950 (1 May–Aug). W **254**. P 12½.

2051	**275**	50b. black	30	20
2052		1l. red	20	10
2053		2l. olive-grey	20	10
2054		3l. purple	30	10
2055		4l. magenta	20	10
2056		5l. lake-brown	30	10
2057		6l. deep green	30	10
2058		7l. purple-brown	30	10
2059		7l.50 light blue	50	10
2060		10l. brown	80	10
2061		11l. carmine (1 May)	80	10
2062		15l. deep blue	60	10
2063		20l. blue-green	60	10
2064		31l. grey-green (1 May)	95	10
2065		36l. orange-brown	1·90	80
2051/2065 *Set of 15*			7·50	2·10

For similar design, but with white figures of value, see Nos. 2240/54 and with star at top of emblem, Nos. 2277/8.

D **276** Badge Postwoman

276 Trumpeter and Drummer

1950. POSTAGE DUE. P 14½×14.

(a) No wmk

			Un pair	*Us pair*
D2066	D **276**	2l. vermilion	1·50	1·50
D2067		4l. blue	1·50	1·50
D2068		5l. grey-green	2·40	2·40
D2069		10l. orange-brown	3·00	3·00
D2066/2069 *Set of 4 pairs*			7·50	7·50

(b) W **254**

D2070	D **276**	2l. vermilion	1·20	1·20
D2071		4l. blue	1·20	1·20
D2072		5l. grey-green	1·60	1·60
D2073		10l. orange-brown	2·40	2·40
D2070/2073 *Set of 4 pairs*			5·75	5·75

(Des N. Pavlin, A. Rosenblum and N. Popescu respectively)

1950 (25 May). First Anniv of Romanian Pioneers Organisation. T **276** and similar types inscr "UN AN DELA INFIINNTAREA ORGANIZATIILOR DE PIONIERI IN R.P.R.". W **254**. P 14.

2074		8l. blue	1·90	95
2075		11l. purple	2·40	1·50
2076		31l. vermilion	4·25	3·00
2074/2076 *Set of 3*			7·75	5·00

Designs:—11l. Three children reading; 31l. Youth parade.

277 Engineer

278 Aurel Vlaicu and his Airplane No. 1 "Crazy Fly"

279 Mother and Child

(Des L. Corda)

1950 (20 July). Industrial Nationalisation. W **254**. P 14.

2077	**277**	11l. rose-red	70	50
2078		11l. blue	1·20	50
2079		11l. reddish brown	1·20	50
2080		11l. blackish olive	70	30
2077/2080 *Set of 4*			3·50	1·60

(Des L. Nazarov)

1950 (22 Aug). 40th Anniv of First Flight by A. Vlaicu. W **254**. P 12½.

2081	**278**	3l. blue-green	50	20
2082		6l. deep blue	85	30
2083		8l. bright blue	95	50
2081/2083 *Set of 3*			2·10	90

(Des L. Nazarov)

1950 (9 Sept). Peace Congress, Bucharest. T **279** and similar type. W **254**. P 13½.

2084		11l. rose-carmine	50	30
2085		20l. blackish brown	60	30

Design:—20l. Lathe operator and graph.

280 Statue and Flags

TRĂIASCĂ
PRIETENIA
ROMÂNO-
MAGHIARĂ

(**281**)

(Des A. Valerian)

1950 (6 Oct). Romanian-Soviet Amity. W **254**. P 14.

2086	**280**	30l. lake-brown	95	50

1950 (6 Oct). Romanian-Hungarian Amity. No. 2062 optd with T **281**, in red.

2087	**275**	15l. deep blue	1·60	50

282 Young People and Badge

(Des L. Nazarov)

1950 (30 Oct). GMA Complex Sports Facilities. T **282** and similar types including badge. W **254**. P 14.

2088	–	3l. carmine	1·90	1·90
2089	**282**	5l. lake-brown	1·50	1·50
2090		5l. blue	1·50	1·50
2091	–	11l. green	1·50	1·50
2092	–	31l. olive	3·50	3·50
2088/2092 *Set of 5*			9·00	9·00

Designs:—3l. Agricultural and industrial work; 11l. Runners; 31l. Gymnasts.

283

284 Ski-jumper

(Des N. Popescu)

1950 (2 Nov). Third Congress of "ARLUS". W **254**. P 13½.

2093	**283**	11l. orange/*orange*	70	50
2094		11l. blue/*blue*	70	50

(Des D. Stiubei and N. Popescu)

1951 (28 Jan). Winter Sports. T **284** and similar types inscr "A IX EDITIE A JOCURILOR MONDIALE UNIVERSITARE DE IARNA". W **254**. P 13½.

2095		4l. brown	1·90	1·90
2096		5l. pale scarlet (Skater)	1·50	1·50
2097		11l. blue (Skier)	1·50	1·50
2098		20l. brown (Ice hockey)	1·50	1·50
2099		31l. deep green (Tobogganing)	3·50	3·50
2095/2099 *Set of 5*			9·00	9·00

285 Worker and Machine

286 Peasant and Tractor

(Des D. Stiubei)

1951 (12 Feb). Agricultural and Industrial Exhibition. W **254**. P 14.

2100	**285**	11l. lake-brown	50	50
		a. Imperf	95	95
2101	**286**	31l. deep blue	95	50
		a. Imperf	1·50	1·50

287 Star of the Republic, Class I-II

288 Youth Camp

(Des C. Müller)

1951 (26 Apr). Orders and Medals. T **287** and similar vert designs. W **254**.

A. P 13½

2102A		2l. blackish olive	30	30
2103A		4l. blue	50	50
2104A		11l. carmine-red	80	80
2105A		35l. orange-brown	1·10	1·10
2102A/2105A *Set of 4*			2·40	2·40

B. Imperf

2102B		2l. blackish olive	50	50
2103B		4l. blue	60	60
2104B		11l. carmine-red	85	85
2105B		35l. orange-brown	1·20	1·20
2102B/2105B *Set of 4*			2·75	2·75

Designs:—2l. Medal of Work; 4l. Star of the Republic, Class III-V; 11l. Order of Work.

(Des I. Dumitrana)

1951 (8 May). Second Anniv of Romanian Pioneers Organization. T **288** and similar designs. W **254**. P 14.

2106		1l. blue-green	1·50	90
2107		11l. blue	1·50	90
2108		35l. vermilion	1·90	1·30
2106/2108 *Set of 3*			4·50	2·75

Designs: Vert—11l. Children meeting Stalin. Horiz—35l. Decorating boy on parade.

289 Woman and Flags

290 Ion Negulici

(Des A. Alexe)

1951 (18 May). International Women's Day. W **254**. P 14×14½.
2109 **289** 11l. orange-brown ... 95 45
a. Imperf ... 95 90

(Des O. Adler)

1951 (20 June). Death Centenary of Negulici (painter). W **254**. P 14×14½.
2110 **290** 35l. carmine ... 4·75 3·00

291 Cyclists

292 F. Sarbu

(Des D. Stiubei)

1951 (9 July). Romanian Cycle Race. W **254**. P 14.
2111 **291** 11l. reddish brown ... 3·00 1·30
a. Tête-bêche (vert pair) ... 7·75 7·75

(Des I. Dumitrana)

1951 (21 July). Tenth Death Anniv of F. Sarbu (patriot). W **254**. P 14.
2112 **292** 11l. sepia ... 95 45

293 "Revolutionary Romania"

294 Students

(Des O. Adler)

1951 (23 July). Death Centenary of C. D. Rosenthal (painter). T **293** and similar design showing painting, inscr "C. D. ROSENTHAL 1820–1851". W **254**. P 14.
2113 **293** 11l. blue-green ... 2·40 90
2114 11l. orange ... 2·40 90
2115 – 11l. brown ... 2·40 90
2116 – 11l. reddish violet ... 2·40 90
2113/2116 *Set of* 4 ... 8·75 3·25
Design: Vert—11l. (2) "Romania calls to the masses".

(Des C. Müller)

1951 (1 Aug). Third World Youth Festival, Berlin. T **294** and vert designs inscr "AL III-LEA FESTIVAL MONDIAL", etc. W **254**. P 13½.
2117 1l. carmine ... 95 60
2118 5l. blue ... 1·90 60
2119 11l. purple ... 3·00 1·30
2117/2119 *Set of* 3 ... 5·25 2·30
Designs:—5l. Girl, boy and flag; 11l. Young students around globe.

295 *Scânteia* Building

296 Soldier and Pithead

(Des I. Dumitrana)

1951 (15 Aug). 20th Anniv of *Scânteia* (Communist newspaper). W **254**. P 14.
2120 **295** 11l. blue ... 95 45

(Des O. Adler)

1951 (21 Aug). Miners' Day. T **296** and similar vert type inscr "ZIUA MINERULUI 1951". W **254**. P 14.
2121 5l. blue ... 80 35
2122 11l. mauve (Miner and pithead) ... 1·10 45

297 Order of Defence

298 Oil Refinery

(Des O. Adler)

1951 (23 Aug). Liberation Day. W **254**. P 14.
2123 **297** 10l. carmine ... 70 45

(Des A. Radulescu)

1951–52. Five Year Plan. T **298** and similar vert designs inscr "1951 1955". W **254**. P 13½.

(a) POSTAGE
2124 1l. blackish olive (22.9.51) ... 95 20
2125 2l. chocolate (8.51) ... 50 20
2126 3l. scarlet (10.51) ... 95 55
2127 4l. reddish brown (12.51) ... 70 20
2128 5l. green (22.9.51) ... 70 20
2129 6l. blue (12.51) ... 2·40 1·30
2130 7l. emerald-green (12.51) ... 1·50 55
2131 8l. lake-brown (12.51) ... 1·20 45
2132 11l. blue (8.51) ... 1·20 35
2133 35l. violet (12.51) ... 1·50 90

(b) AIR
2134 30l. deep green ... 4·00 2·75
2135 50l. red-brown (1.52) ... 5·75 3·75
2124/2135 *Set of* 12 ... 19·00 10·50
Designs:—2l. Miner and pithead; 3l. Soldier and pylons; 4l. Steel furnace; 5l. Combine-harvester; 6l. Canal construction; 7l. Threshing machine; 8l. Sanatorium; 11l. Dam and pylons; 30l. Potato planting; 35l. Factory; 50l. Liner, steam locomotive and Lisunov Li-2 airliner.

299 Orchestra and Dancers

300 Soldier and Arms

(Des I. Dumitrana)

1951 (22 Sept). Music Festival. Designs as T **299**. W **254**. P 13½.
2136 11l. reddish brown (Type **299**) ... 70 45
2137 11l. blue (Mixed choir) ... 95 60
2138 11l. mauve (Lyre and dove, vert) ... 70 45
2136/2138 *Set of* 3 ... 2·10 1·40

(Des D. Stiubei)

1951 (2 Oct). Army Day. W **254**. P 13½.
2139 **300** 11l. blue ... 95 45

301 Arms of U.S.S.R. and Romania

302 P. Tcancenco

(Des D. Stiubei)

1951 (11 Oct). Romanian-Soviet Friendship. W **254**. P 13½.
2140 **301** 4l. brown/*buff* ... 50 45
2141 35l. red-orange ... 95 90

(Des C. Müller)

1951 (15 Dec). 25th Death Anniv of Tcancenco (revolutionary). W **254**. P 14.
2142 **302** 10l. blackish olive ... 95 90

Currency Revaluation

20 Old Lei = 1 New Leu

303 Open Book "1907"

304 I. L. Caragiale

20
Bani
(305)

3 BANI
(306)

(Des O. Adler)

1952 (28 Jan–6 Apr). Birth Centenary of Ion Caragiale (dramatist). W **254**. P 13½ (T **304**) or 14 (others).

(a) Unissued values as T **303/4** surch as T **305**. (28 Jan)
2143 **303** 20b. on 11l. scarlet ... 1·60 70
2144 – 55b. on 11l. green (R.) ... 2·10 1·00
2145 **304** 75b. on 11l. blue (R.) ... 3·75 1·20

(b) T **303/4** and similar designs inscr "1852–1952". (28 Jan– 6 Apr)
2146 **303** 55b. scarlet ... 4·00 60
2147 – 55b. green ... 4·00 60
2148 **304** 55b. blue ... 4·00 60
2149 – 1l. red-brown (28 Jan) ... 5·75 2·20
2143/2149 *Set of* 7 ... 23·00 6·25
Designs as T **303**—55b. (2144, 2147) Profile of Caragiale; 1l. Caragiale addressing assembly.

1952 (28 Jan)–**53**. Earlier issues surch as T **306** or with similar types in one or two lines.

On 1948 Census issue (No. 1925)
2150 **233** 55b. on 12l. blue (R.) ... 4·00 2·30

On 1948 New Constitution issue (No. 1962)
2151 **241** 50b. on 12l. blue (R.) ... 5·25 1·50

On 1948 Revolution issue (Nos. 1974/8)
2152 – 1l.75 on 2l.+2l. ... 19·00 5·75
2153 **245** 1l.75 on 5l.+5l. (R.) ... 19·00 5·75
2154 **246** 1l.75 on 11l. red ... 19·00 5·75
2155 – 1l.75 on 10l.+10l. (R.) ... 19·00 5·75
2156 – 1l.75 on 36l.+18l. (R.) ... 19·00 5·75
2152/2156 *Set of* 5 ... 85·00 26·00

On 1948–50 Air stamps (Nos. 2004/6)
2157 **255** 3b. on 30l. carmine (B.) ... 21·00 14·50
a. on 30l. *red* (B.) ... 5·25 3·50
2158 – 3b. on 50l. olive-green (R.) ... 2·10 1·00
2159 – 3b. on 100l. blue (R.) ... 3·00 1·30

On 1949 Pushkin issue (Nos. 2030/1)
2160 **263** 10b. on 11l. carmine ... 5·25 2·00
2161 10b. on 30l. blue-green (R.) ... 5·25 2·00

AIR. On 1949 U.P.U. issue (Nos. 2032/3) additionally optd with aeroplane and "AERIANA"
2162 **264** 3l. on 20l. yellow-brown (B.) ... 29·00 23·00
2163 **265** 5l. on 30l. blue (R.) ... 44·00 31·00

On 1950 Eminescu issue (Nos. 2040/4)
2164 **270** 10b. on 11l. green (R.) ... 4·00 2·30
2165 – 10b. on 11l. lake-brown (R.) ... 4·00 2·30
2166 – 10b. on 11l. rose-magenta ... 4·00 2·30
2167 – 10b. on 11l. violet ... 4·00 2·30
2168 **271** 10b. on 11l. blue (R.) ... 4·00 2·30
2164/2168 *Set of* 5 ... 18·00 10·50

On 1950 Andreescu issue (Nos. 2045/6)
2169 **272** 55b. on 5l. blackish olive (R.) ... 12·50 4·00
2170 – 55b. on 11l. light blue (R.) ... 12·50 4·00

On 1950 State Plan issue (Nos. 2048/9)
2171 **273** 20b. on 11l. red ... 4·75 1·50
2172 – 20b. on 31l. violet (R.) ... 4·75 1·50

On 1950 Labour Day Issue (No. 2050)
2173 **274** 55b. on 31l. vermilion ... 6·25 4·00

On 1950 definitive issue (Nos. 2051/65)
2174 **275** 3b. on 1l. red ... 3·00 1·30
2175 3b. on 2l. olive-grey ... 3·00 1·30
2176 3b. on 4l. magenta ... 3·00 1·30
2177 3b. on 5l. lake-brown ... 3·00 1·30
2178 3b. on 7l.50 light blue ... 3·00 1·30
2179 3b. on 10l. brown ... 3·00 1·30
2180 55b. on 50b. black (R.) ... 8·75 2·20
2181 55b. on 3l. purple (R.) ... 8·75 2·20
2182 55b. on 6l. deep green (R.) ... 8·75 2·20
2183 55b. on 7l. purple-brown (R.) ... 8·75 2·20
2184 55b. on 15l. deep blue (R.) ... 11·50 2·20
2185 55b. on 20l. blue-green (R.) ... 8·75 2·20
2186 55b. on 31l. grey-green (R.) ... 8·75 2·20
2187 55b. on 36l. orange-brown (R.) ... 11·50 2·20
2174/2187 *Set of* 14 ... 85·00 23·00

On 1950 Pioneers issue (Nos. 2074/6)
2188 **276** 55b. on 8l. blue (R.) ... 11·50 5·25
2189 – 55b. on 11l. purple (R.) ... 11·50 5·25
2190 – 55b. on 31l. vermilion ... 11·50 5·25
2188/2190 *Set of* 3 ... 31·00 14·00

On 1950 Vlaicu issue (Nos. 2081/3)
2191 **278** 10b. on 3l. blue-green (R.) ... 4·00 1·30
2192 10b. on 6l. deep blue (R.) ... 4·00 1·30
2193 10b. on 8l. bright blue (R.) ... 4·00 1·30
2191/2193 *Set of* 3 ... 11·00 3·50

On 1950 Peace Congress issue (No. 2085)
2194 – 20b. on 20l. blackish brown (R.) ... 4·75 2·20

On 1950 Sports Facilities issue (No. 2088)
2195 – 55b. on 3l. carmine ... 29·00 18·00

On 1951 Winter Sports issue (Nos. 2098/9)
2196 – 55b. on 20l. brown ... 44·00 18·00
2197 – 55b. on 31l. deep green (R.) ... 44·00 18·00

On 1951 Agricultural Exhibition issue (No. 2101)
2198 **286** 55b. on 31l. deep blue (R.) ... 7·25 4·50

On 1951 Orders and Medals issue (Nos. 2102A/5A)
2199 – 20b. on 2l. blackish olive (R.) ... 6·25 2·75
2200 – 20b. on 4l. blue (R.) ... 6·25 2·75
2201 – 20b. on 11l. carmine-red ... 6·25 2·75
2202 **287** 20b. on 35l. orange-brown ... 6·25 2·75
2199/2202 *Set of* 4 ... 23·00 10·00

On 1951 Romanian Pioneers issue (No. 2108)
2203 – 55b. on 35l. vermilion ... 10·50 5·75

On 1951 Miners' Day issue (No. 2121)
2204 **295** 55b. on 5l. blue (R.) ... 7·25 3·25

On 1951 Liberation Day issue (No. 2123)
2205 **297** 55b. on 10l. carmine ... 7·25 3·25

On 1951–52 Five Year Plan issue

(a) POSTAGE. (Nos. 2124/33)
2206 35b. on 1l. blackish olive (R.) ... 3·00 1·30
2207 35b. on 2l. chocolate (R.) ... 3·00 1·30
2208 35b. on 3l. scarlet ... 5·75 2·75
2209 35b. on 4l. reddish brown ... 6·75 3·00
a. Surch in red ... 25·00 20·00
2210 35b. on 5l. green (R.) ... 5·75 4·50
2211 1l. on 6l. blue (R.) ... 7·75 6·25
2212 1l. on 7l. emerald-green (R.) ... 7·75 3·00
2213 1l. on 8l. lake-brown (R.) ... 7·75 6·25
2214 1l. on 11l. blue (R.) ... 7·75 3·50
2215 1l. on 35l. violet (R.) ... 10·50 3·00

(b) AIR. (Nos. 2134/5)
2216 1l. on 30l. deep green (R.) ... 12·50 2·75
2217 1l. on 50l. red-brown (R.) ... 12·50 2·75
2206/2217 *Set of* 12 ... 80·00 36·00

On 1951 Romanian-Soviet Friendship issue (Nos. 2140/1)
2218 **301** 10b. on 4l. brown/*buff* ... 3·00 1·40
2219 10b. on 35l. red-orange ... 3·00 1·40

On 1951 Tcancenco issue (No. 2142)
2220 **302** 10b. on 10l. blackish olive (R.) ... 3·00 1·40
A number of these issues exist with surcharge inverted and other varieties.

1952 (Feb). POSTAGE DUE. Nos. D2066/73 surch as T **306** but in capital and lower case letters.

(a) No wmk

			Un pair	*Us pair*
D2221	D **276**	4b. on 2l. vermilion	95	90
D2222		10b. on 4l. blue (R.)	95	90
D2223		20b. on 5l. grey-green (R.)	2·40	2·20
D2224		50b. on 10l. orange-brown	3·00	2·75
D2221/4 *Set of 4 pairs*			6·50	6·00

(b) W **254**

D2225	D **276**	4b. on 2l. vermilion	1·20	1·10
D2226		10b. on 4l. blue (R.)	1·20	1·10
D2227		20b. on 5l. grey-green (R.)	1·90	1·80
D2228		50b. on 10l. orange-brown	1·90	1·80
D2225/8 *Set of 4 pairs*			5·50	5·25

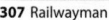

307 Railwayman

308 Gogol and character from *Taras Bulba*

(Des C. Müller)

1952 (16 Feb). Railway Day. W **254**. P 13½.

2229	**307**	55b. brown	4·00	45

(Des C. Müller)

1952 (4 Mar). Death Centenary of Nikolai Gogol (Russian writer). T **308** and similar vert design. W **254**. P 14.

2230	55b. blue	3·00	45
2231	1l.75 blackish olive	4·75	60

Design—1l.75, Gogol and open book.

309 Maternity Medal

310 I. P. Pavlov

311 Hammer and Sickle Medal

(Des I. Dumitrana)

1952 (8 Mar). International Women's Day. T **309** and similar vert designs. W **254**. P 13½.

2232	20b. indigo and purple	1·20	20
2233	55b. brown and chestnut	2·40	55
2234	1l.75 yellow-brown and carmine-red	5·75	75
2232/2234 *Set of 3*		8·50	1·40

Designs:—55b. "Glory of Maternity" medal; 1l.75, "Mother Heroine" medal.

(Des D. Stiubei)

1952 (22 Apr). Romanian-Soviet Medical Congress. W **254**. P 13½.

2235	**310**	1l. brown-lake	4·00	45

(Des C. Müller)

1952 (29 Apr). Labour Day. W **254**. P 13½.

2236	**311**	55b. reddish brown	3·50	45

312 Boy and Girl Pioneers

313 Emblem of Republic

314 "Smirdan" (after Grigorescu)

(Des N. Pavlin)

1952 (17 May). Third Anniv of Romanian Pioneers Organization. T **312** and similar designs. W **254**. P 14.

2237	20b. chestnut	1·90	20
2238	55b. green	4·75	30
2239	1l.75 blue	9·75	65
2237/2239 *Set of 3*		15·00	1·00

Designs: Horiz—1l.75, Worker and pioneers. Vert—55b. Pioneer nature-study group.

1952 (May–June). As T **275** but figures of value, etc in white. W **254**. P 12½.

(a) Size 20¼×24¼ mm

2240	**313**	3b. red-orange	70	30
2241		5b. scarlet	95	20
2242		7b. emerald	1·20	30
2243		10b. red-brown	1·50	20
2244		20b. blue	1·90	20
2245		35b. blackish brown	3·50	20
2246		50b. green	4·00	20
2247		55b. violet	8·75	20

(b) Size 24½×29½ mm

2248	**313**	1l.10 red-brown	7·75	45
2249		1l.75 violet	31·00	65
2250		2l. olive	8·25	75
2251		2l.35 brown	9·75	65
2252		2l.55 red-orange	11·50	65
2253		3l. green	12·50	65
2254		5l. red	16·00	1·10
2240/2254 *Set of 15*			£110	6·00

For similar design, but with star at top of emblem, see Nos. 2277/8.

1952 (10 June). 75th Anniv of Independence. T **314** and similar design inscr "1877–1952". W **254**. P 13½.

2255	50b. lake	1·50	10
2256	1l.10 blue	2·40	55

Design:—1l.10, Romanian and Russian soldiers.

315 Leonardo da Vinci

316 Miner

317 Students' Union Badge

(Des C. Müller)

1952 (20 June). Fifth Centenary of Birth of Leonardo da Vinci. W **254**. P 13½.

2257	**315**	55b. reddish violet	6·75	65

(Des N. Popescu)

1952 (15 Aug). Miners' Day. W **254**. P 13½.

2258	**316**	20b. scarlet	3·00	55
2259		55b. reddish violet	3·00	55

(Des Druga, Alamaru and Costescu)

1952 (5 Sept). International Students' Union Council, Bucharest. T **317** and similar designs inscr "CONSILIUL UNIUNII INTERNATIONALE", etc. W **254**. P 14 (20b.) or 13½ (others).

2260	10b. blue	70	10
2261	20b. orange	4·00	45
2262	55b. blue-green	4·00	65
2263	1l.75 carmine-red	7·25	1·40
2260/2263 *Set of 4*		14·50	2·30

Designs—As T **317**: Vert—55b. Students playing football. Horiz—1l.75, Six students dancing; Larger (35½×22 mm) 20b. Student in laboratory.

318 Soldier, Sailor and Airman

319 Statue and Flags

320 Workers and Views of Russia and Romania (after N. Parlius)

(Des L. Nazarov)

1952 (1 Oct). Army Day. W **254**. P 14.

2264	**318**	55b. blue	2·40	45

(Des Druga, Alamaru and Costescu (55b.) and L. Nazarov (1l.75))

1952 (7 Oct). Romanian-Soviet Friendship. W **254**. P 13½.

2265	**319**	55b. red	1·60	10
2266	**320**	1l.75 deep olive-brown	4·00	65

321 Rowing

322 N. Balcescu (after C. Tattarescu)

(Des A. Alexandru)

1952 (20 Oct). Physical Culture. T **321** and similar horiz design. W **254**. P 13½.

2267	20b. blue	7·75	45
2268	1l.75 carmine-red	16·00	1·20

Design:—1l.75, Parade of athletes.

(Des I. Dumitrana)

1952 (27 Nov). Death Centenary of Balcescu (revolutionary). W **254**. P 13½.

2269	**322**	55b. greenish grey	4·75	20
2270		1l.75 olive-bistre	11·50	1·20

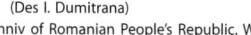

323 Emblem and Flags

324

(Des Druga, Alamaru and Costescu)

1952 (5 Dec). New Constitution. W **254**. P 13½.

2271	**323**	55b. deep green	4·00	45

(Des I. Dumitrana)

1952 (30 Dec). Fifth Anniv of Romanian People's Republic. W **254**. P 12½×13½.

2272	**324**	55b. blue, green, yell & brn-red	4·75	65

325 Millo, Caragiale and Mme. Romanescu

326 Foundry Worker

(Des D. Stiubei)

1953 (24 Jan). Centenary of Caragiale National Theatre. W **254**. P 13½.

2273	**325**	55b. bright blue	4·75	45

(Des Druga, Alamaru and Costescu)

1953 (25 Jan). Third Industrial and Agricultural Congress. T **326** and similar designs inscr "AL III-LEA CONGRES" etc. W **254**. P 13½.

2274	**326**	55b. deep green	1·50	20
2275	–	55b. red-orange	1·50	20
2276	–	55b. deep olive-brown	1·90	65
2274/2276 *Set of 3*			4·50	95

Designs: Horiz—No. 2275, Farm workers and tractor; No. 2276, Workman, refinery and oil wells.

1953 (7 Feb). As T **313** but with five-pointed star added at top of emblem. W **254**. P 12½.

2277	5b. scarlet	95	20
2278	55b. purple	1·60	30

327 "The Strikers of Grivitsa" (after Nazarev)

328

(Des L. Nazarov)

1953 (13 Feb). Twentieth Anniv of Strike of Grivitsa. W **254**. P 13½.

2279	**327**	55b. brown	4·00	45

(Des I. Ursa)

1953 (20 Mar). Fifth Anniv of Treaty of Friendship with Russia. W **254**. P 14.

2280	**328**	55b. red-brown/*blue*	4·00	45

329 Table Tennis Badge

330 Oltenian Carpet

331 Karl Marx

(Des F. Finkelstein)

1953 (23 Mar). Twentieth World Table Tennis Championship, Bucharest. W **254**. P 14.

2281	**329**	55b. deep grey-green	9·75	1·60
2282		55b. red-brown	9·75	1·60

(Des D. Stiubei and F. Finkelstein)

1953. Designs as T **330** inscr "ARTA POPULARA ROMANEASCA". W **254**. P 14.

2283	10b. deep grey-green (May)	1·90	10
2284	20b. red-brown (May)	3·00	10
2285	35b. deep reddish violet (6.9)	3·50	20
2286	55b. bright blue (May)	6·25	20
2287	1l. reddish purple (22.4)	11·50	45
2283/2287 *Set of 5*		24·00	95

Designs: Vert—10b. Pottery; 20b. Campulung peasant girl; 55b. Apuseni Mountains peasant girl. Horiz—35b. National dance.

(Des F. Finkelstein)

1953 (11 May). 70th Death Anniv of Karl Marx. W **254**. P 13½.

2288	**331**	1l.55 deep olive-brown	4·75	55

332 Pioneers Planting Tree

333 Women and Flags

334

(Des E. Kuscenko)

1953 (21 May). Fourth Anniv of Romanian Pioneers Organization. T **332** and similar designs. W **254**. P 14.

2289	**332**	35b. deep grey-green	2·40	30
2290	–	55b. blue	3·00	35
2291	–	1l.75 deep orange-brown	6·75	85
2289/2291 *Set of 3*			11·00	1·40

Designs: Vert—55b. Pioneers flying model gliders. Horiz— 1l.75, Pioneers and instructor.

(Des Druga, Alamaru and Costescu)

1953 (16 June). Third World Congress of Women. W **254**. P 13½.

2292 **333** 55b. red-brown .... 3·00 45

(Des C. Müller and O. Adler)

1953 (11 July). Fourth World Youth Festival. Designs as T **334** inscr "BUCURETIS 2-16 AUGUST 1953". W **254**. P 14.

2293 20b. orange .... 1·50 45
2294 55b. blue .... 2·40 95
2295 65b. rose-red .... 3·50 1·40
2296 1l.75 purple .... 9·75 2·75
2293/2296 *Set of 4* .... 15·00 5·00

Designs: Vert—55b. Students releasing dove over globe. Horiz—65b. Girl presenting bouquet; 1l.75, Folk dancers.

335 Cornfield and Forest

336 V. V. Mayakovsky

(Des L. Nazarov)

1953 (29 July). Forestry Month. T **335** and similar designs. W **254**. P 13½.

2297 20b. bright blue .... 1·60 20
2298 38b. green .... 4·75 1·40
2299 55b. pale brown .... 5·75 45
2297/2299 *Set of 3* .... 11·00 1·80

Designs: Vert—20b. Waterfall and trees; 55b. Forestry worker.

(Des I. Dumitrana)

1953 (22 Aug). 60th Birth Anniv of Vladimir Mayakovsky (Russian poet). W **254**. P 13½.

2300 **336** 55b. deep orange-brown .... 3·50 65

337 Miner

(Des L. Kuscenko)

1953 (3 Sept). Miners' Day. W **254**. P 14.

2301 **337** 1l.55 slate-black .... 5·25 45

338 Telephonist, G.P.O. and P.O. Worker

339

(Des O. Adler and Triscu)

1953 (30 Sept). 50th Anniv of Construction of G.P.O. T **338** and similar horiz designs inscr "1903 1953". W **254**. P 14.

2302 20b. deep red-brown 50 10
2303 55b. deep olive 95 10
2304 1l. blue .... 2·40 30
2305 1l.55 lake .... 3·50 75
2302/2305 *Set of 4* .... 6·50 1·10

Designs:—55b. Postwoman and G.P.O.; 1l. G.P.O., radio transmitter and map; 1l.55, Telegraphist, G.P.O. and teletypist.

1953 (30 Sept). Ninth Anniv of Liberation. W **254**. P 13½.

2306 **339** 55b. reddish brown .... 2·40 45

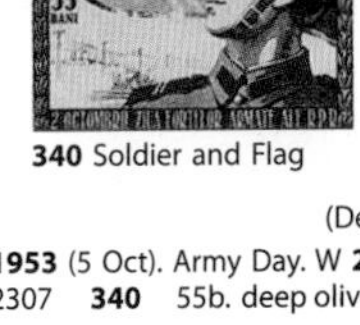

340 Soldier and Flag

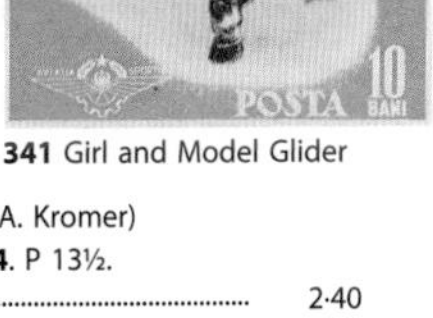

341 Girl and Model Glider

(Des A. Kromer)

1953 (5 Oct). Army Day. W **254**. P 13½.

2307 **340** 55b. deep olive .... 2·40 45

(Des I. Schiffer, I. Avramescu and J. Vintila)

1953 (Oct). Aerial Sports. Horiz designs as T **341**. W **254**. P 14.

2308 10b. deep green and orange .... 4·25 55
2309 20b. blackish olive and chestnut .... 8·75 30
2310 55b. purple and deep rose-red .... 16·00 95
2311 1l.75, brown and purple .... 19·00 1·40
2308/2311 *Set of 4* .... 43·00 3·00

Designs:—20b. Parachutists; 55b. Glider and pilot; 1l.75, Zlin Z-22 monoplane.

342 Workman, Girl and Flags

343 "Unity"

(Des I. Dumitrana)

1953 (7 Oct). Romanian-Soviet Friendship. T **342** and similar horiz design inscr "7 OCT–7 NOV' 1953". W **254**. P 13½.

2312 55b. brown .... 1·30 20
2313 1l.55 lake .... 3·00 55

Design:—1l.55, Spassky Tower (Moscow Kremlin) and Volga-Don canal.

(Des L. Kuscenko and F. Constantin)

1953 (9 Oct). Third World Trades' Union Congress. T **343** and vert design inscr "AL III—LEA CONGRES MONDIAL" etc. W **254**. P 14.

2314 55b. deep olive-green .... 1·20 30
2315 1l.25 carmine-red .... 3·00 95

Design:—1l.25, Workers, flags and globe.

344 C. Porumbescu

345 Agricultural Machinery

(Des I. Dumitrana)

1953 (17 Nov). Birth Centenary of Porumbescu (composer). W **254**. P 14.

2316 **344** 55b. deep reddish lilac .... 11·50 45

(Des Druga, Alamaru and Costescu)

1953 (17 Nov). Agricultural designs as T **345**. W **254**. P 13½.

2317 10b. deep olive-brown 50 10
2318 35b. deep myrtle-green 70 10
2319 2l.55 reddish brown .... 5·75 1·20
2317/2319 *Set of 3* .... 6·25 1·30

Designs: Horiz—35b. Tractor drawing disc harrows; 2l.55, Cows grazing.

346 Vlaicu and his Airplane No. 1 "Crazy Fly"

347 Lenin

(Des D. Stiubei)

1953 (17 Dec). 40th Death Anniv of Aurel Vlaicu (pioneer aviator). W **254**. P 14.

2320 **346** 50b. dull ultramarine .... 2·50 45

(Des L. Nazarov)

1954 (21 Jan). 30th Death Anniv of Lenin. W **254**. P 13½.

2321 **347** 55b. deep red-brown .... 3·00 45

348 Red Deer Stag

349 Calimanesti

(Des L. Nazarov)

1954 (1 Apr). Forestry Month. T **348** and similar vert designs. W **254**. P 13½.

2322 20b. black-brown/*lemon* .... 4·75 55
2323 55b. reddish violet/*lemon* .... 4·00 55
2324 1l.75 blue/*greenish yellow* .... 5·75 1·10
2322/2324 *Set of 3* .... 13·00 2·00

Designs:—55b. Pioneers planting tree; 1l.75, Forest scene.

(Des I. Schiffer, I. Vintila and S. Victor)

1954 (15 Apr). Workers' Rest Homes. T **349** and similar horiz designs. W **254**. P 14.

2325 5b. black/*yellow* 70 20
2326 1l.55 grey-black/*blue* (Siniai) .... 3·00 30
2327 2l. deep blue-green/*pink* (Predeal) .... 4·75 45
2328 2l.35 black-brown/*green* (Tusnad) .... 4·50 1·40
2329 2l.55 red-brown/*green* (Govora) .... 6·25 1·90
2325/2329 *Set of 5* .... 17·00 3·75

350 O. Bancila

351 Child and Dove of Peace

(Des C. Stroe after N. Popa)

1954 (26 May). Tenth Anniv of Death of Bancila (painter). W **254**. P 13½.

2330 **350** 55b. slate-green and chocolate .... 5·75 2·75

(Des I. Dumitrana)

1954 (1 June). International Children's Day. W **254**. P 13½.

2331 **351** 55b. brown .... 2·40 45

352 Girl Pioneer feeding Calf

353 Stephen the Great

(Des I. Dumitrana)

1954 (3 July). Fifth Anniv of Romanian Pioneer Organization. T **352** and similar horiz designs. W **254**. P 14.

2332 20b. greenish black 70 20
2333 55b. chalky blue .... 1·20 45
2334 1l.75 carmine .... 4·00 95
2332/2334 *Set of 3* .... 5·25 1·40

Designs:—55b. Girl Pioneers harvesting; 1l.75, Young Pioneers examining globe.

(Des A. Ionescu)

1954 (10 July). 450th Anniv of Death of Stephen the Great. W **254**. P 14.

2335 **353** 55b. purple-brown .... 4·00 55

354 Miner Operating Coal-cutter

355 Dr. V. Babes

(Des L. Nazarov)

1954 (8 Aug). Miners' Day. W **254**. P 13½.

2336 **354** 1l.75 violet-black .... 4·00 85

(Des O. Adler)

1954 (15 Aug). Birth Centenary of Babes (pathologist). W **254**. P 14.

2337 **355** 55b. pale carmine-red .... 3·00 45

356 Sailor, Flag and Destroyer

357 Dedication Tablet

(Des D. Stiubei)

1954 (19 Aug). Navy Day. W **254**. P 13½.

2338 **356** 55b. blue .... 2·40 45

(Des L. Nazarov)

1954 (20 Aug). Fifth Anniv of Mutual Aid Organization. T **357** and similar vert design inscr "1949–AUGUST–1954". W **254**. P 14.

2339 20b. deep violet 70 20
2340 55b. lake-brown .... 1·20 45

Design:—20b. Man receiving money from counter clerk.

358 Liberation Monument

359 Recreation Centre

(Des Druga, Almaru and Costesco)

1954 (21 Aug). Tenth Anniv of Liberation. W **254**. P 13½.

2341 **358** 55b. reddish violet and scarlet .... 1·90 45

(Des H. Kalman)

1954 (31 Aug). Liberation Anniv Celebrations. T **359** and other designs inscr "ZECE ANI DELA ELIBERARE". W **254**. P 14 (20b., 55b.) or 13½ (others).

2342 20b. bright blue 70 10
2343 38b. violet .... 1·20 45
2344 55b. brown-purple .... 1·50 30
2345 1l.55b. red-brown .... 3·50 55
2342/2345 *Set of 4* .... 6·25 1·30

Designs: Horiz (as T **359**)—55b. "Scanteia" offices. Vert (24½×30 mm)—38b. Opera House, Bucharest; 1l.55b. Radio Station.

360 Pilot and Mikoyan Gurevich MiG-15 Jet Fighters

361 Chemical Plant Oil Derricks

(Des I. Dumitrana)

1954 (7 Sept). Aviation Day. W **254**. P 13½.

2346	**360**	55b. blue		4·00	45

(Des R. Negru)

1954 (17 Sept). International Chemical and Petroleum Workers' Conference, Bucharest. W **254**. P 13½.

2347	**361**	55b. slate-black		3·50	65

362 Dragon Pillar, Peking

363 T. Neculuta

(Des L. Nazarov)

1954 (7 Oct). Chinese Culture Week. W **254**. P 14.

2348	**362**	55b. grey-black/*yellow*	3·50	65

(Des C. Müller)

1954 (15 Oct). 50th Death Anniv of Dumitru Theodor Neculuta (poet). W **254**. P 13½.

2349	**363**	55b. reddish violet	3·00	45

364 ARLUS Badge

365 Friendship

(Des L. Nazarov (55b.) and I. Cova (65b.))

1954 (22 Oct). Tenth Anniv of ARLUS and Romanian-Russian Friendship. W **254**. P 14.

2350	**364**	55b. pale crimson	95	30
2351	**365**	65b. deep purple	1·50	45

366 G. Tattarescu

367 B. Iscovescu

368 Teleprinter

(Des N. Ean)

1954 (24 Oct). 60th Death Anniv of Gheorghe Tattarescu (painter). W **254**. P 13½.

2352	**366**	55b. bright crimson	3·50	45

(Des O. Adler)

1954 (3 Nov). Death Centenary of Barbu Iscovescu (painter). W **254**. P 14.

2353	**367**	1l.75 purple-brown	4·75	95

(Des A. Gesticone)

1954 (31 Dec). Centenary of Telecommunications in Romania. W **254**. P 13½.

2354	**368**	50b. deep reddish lilac	2·40	45

369 Wild Boar

370 Airman

371 Clasped Hands

(Des H. Meschendörfer)

1955 (15 Mar). Forestry Month. T **369** and similar vert designs. W **254**. P 13½.

2355	35b. bistre-brown	2·10	20
2356	65b. deep turquoise-green	2·50	45
2357	1l.20 carmine-red	5·75	95
2355/2357 *Set of* 3		9·25	1·40

Designs:—65b. Planting trees; 1l.20, Lumberjack poling logs.

1955 (29 Mar)–**56**. Various designs as T **370**. W **254**. P 14.

2358	3b. blue	50	10
2359	5b. violet	30	10
2360	10b. chocolate	50	10
2361	20b. magenta	70	10
2362	30b. ultramarine (1956)	1·20	30
2363	35b. turquoise-blue	95	10
2364	40b. deep blue (11.55)	1·90	30
2365	55b. blackish olive	1·90	10
2366	1l. reddish violet	2·40	10
2367	1l.55 lake	4·00	10
2368	2l.35 yellow-brown	5·25	95
2369	2l.55 slate-green	7·75	65
2358/2369 *Set of* 12		25·00	2·75

Designs:—3b. Scientist; 5b. Foundryman; 20b. Miner, 30b. Tractor driver; 35b. Schoolboy; 40b. Girl student; 55b. Bricklayer; 1l. Sailor; 1l.55, Mill girl; 2l.35, Soldier; 2l.55, Telegraph linesman.

1955 (5 Apr). International Conference of Postal Municipal Workers, Vienna. W **254**. P 13½.

2370	**371**	25b. carmine-red	95	45

372 Lenin

373 Dove and Globe

(Des O. Adler)

1955 (22 Apr). 85th Birth Anniv of Lenin. T **372** and similar vert portraits. W **254**. P 14.

2371	20b. sepia and pale bistre-brown	95	30
2372	55b. red-brown (Full-face)	1·90	45
2373	1l. deep carmine-red and pale red (Half-length)	3·00	55
2371/2373 *Set of* 3		5·25	1·20

1955 (7 May). Peace Congress, Helsinki. W **254**. P 13½.

2374	**373**	55b. ultramarine	2·40	45

374 War Memorial, Berlin

375 Children and Dove

1955 (9 May). Tenth Anniv of Victory over Germany. W **254**. P 14.

2375	**374**	55b. blue	1·90	45

1955 (1 June). International Children's Day. W **254**. P 14.

2376	**375**	55b. brown	2·10	45

376 "Service"

377 People's Art Museum

1955 (17 June). European Volleyball Championships. T **376** and similar vert designs. W **254**. P 14.

2377	55b. deep mauve and pink	7·25	1·40
2378	1l.75 cerise and pale yellow	16·00	1·40

Design:—55b. Volleyball players.

1955 (28 June). Bucharest Museums. T **377** and similar horiz designs. W **254**. P 14 (55b., 1l.75) or 13½ (others).

2379	20b. magenta	50	20
2380	55b. bistre-brown	95	20
2381	1l.20 black	2·40	95
2382	1l.75 deep grey-green	4·00	95
2383	2l.55 deep reddish purple	6·75	1·10
2379/2383 *Set of* 5		13·00	3·00

Designs: (30×24½ mm)—20b. Theodor Aman Museum; 2l.55, Simu Museum. (34×23 mm)—55b. Lenin-Stalin Museum; 1l.75, Republican Art Museum.

378 Mother and Child

379 "Nature Study"

1955 (7 July). First World Mothers Congress, Lausanne. W **254**. P 14.

2384	**378**	55b. ultramarine	2·40	45

1955 (18 July). Fifth Anniv of Pioneer Headquarters, Bucharest. T **379** and similar vert designs inscr "PALATUL PIONIERILOR". W **254**. P 12½.

2385	10b. ultramarine	95	10
2386	20b. deep turquoise-green	1·90	10
2387	55b. deep claret	4·25	45
2385/2387 *Set of* 3		6·50	60

Designs:—10b. Model railway; 55b. Headquarters building.

380 Coxed Four

381 Anton Pann (folklorist)

(Des O. Adler)

1955 (22 Aug). Women's European Rowing Championships, Snagov. T **380** and similar horiz designs inscr "SNAGOV 4–7 AUGUST 1955". W **254**. P 13½.

2388	55b. bronze-green	11·50	1·10
2389	1l. blue	19·00	1·50

Design:—1l. Woman sculler.

(Des O. Adler)

1955 (5 Sept). Romanian Writers. T **381** and similar horiz portrait designs. W **254**. P 13½.

2390	55b. ultramarine	1·90	45
2391	55b. slate	1·90	45
2392	55b. brown-olive	1·90	45
2393	55b. violet	1·90	45
2394	55b. deep reddish purple	1·90	45
2390/2394 *Set of* 5		8·50	2·00

Designs:—No. 2390, Dimitrie Cantemir (historian); 2391, Metropolitan Dosoftei (religious writer); 2392, Type **381**; 2393, Constantin Cantacuzino (historian); 2394, Ienachita Vacarescu (poet, grammarian and historian).

382 Marksman

383 Fire Engine

(Des O. Adler)

1955 (10 Sept). European Sharpshooting Championships, Bucharest. W **254**. P 13½.

2395	**382**	1l. dp purple-brn and pale bis-brn	8·75	95

1955 (12 Sept). Firemen's Day. W **254**. P 13½.

2396	**383**	55b. carmine	2·50	65

384

385 Spraying Fruit Trees

(Des O. Adler)

1955 (1 Oct). Tenth Anniv of World Federation of Trades' Unions. T **384** and another vert design inscr "1945 OCT. 1955". W **254**. P 13½.

2397	55b. grey-olive	70	20
2398	1l. ultramarine	1·20	45

Design:—1l. Workers and flag.

1955 (15 Oct). Fruit and Vegetable Cultivation. T **385** and similar horiz designs. W **254**. P 14.

2399	10b. emerald	1·30	20
2400	20b. magenta	1·50	45
2401	55b. deep ultramarine	4·00	45
2402	1l. purple-brown	5·25	1·40
2399/2402 *Set of* 4		11·00	2·30

Designs:—20b. Fruit picking; 55b. Harvesting grapes; 1l. Gathering vegetables.

386

387 I. V. Michurin

1955 (20 Oct). Fourth ARLUS Congress. W **254**. P 13½.

2403	**386**	20b. ultramarine and buff	1·50	45

(Des C. Müller)

1955 (29 Oct). Birth Centenary of Ivan Michurin (Russian botanist). W **254**. P 13½×14.

2404	**387**	55b. greenish blue	2·40	45

388 Cotton

389 Sheep and Shepherd blowing Bucium

1955 (10 Nov). T **388** and similar vert designs. W **254**. P 13½.

2405	10b. reddish purple (Sugar beet)	85	30
2406	20b. deep grey-green	1·20	30
2407	55b. ultramarine (Linseed)	3·00	85
2408	1l.55 chocolate (Sunflower)	5·75	1·50
2405/2408	*Set of* 4	9·75	2·75

(Des D. Stiubei)

1955 (10 Dec). T **389** and similar horiz designs. W **254**. P 14.

2409	5b. deep brown and green	1·20	20
2410	10b. violet and bistre-brown	1·60	30
2411	35b. chocolate and pale brown-red	3·50	75
2412	55b. deep brown and bistre-brown	5·75	1·00
2409/2412	*Set of* 4	11·00	2·00

Designs:—10b. Pigs and farm girl; 35b. Cows and dairy maid; 55b. Horses and groom.

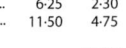

390 Johann von Schiller (novelist)

391 Bank and Book

(Des S. Zainea. Recess)

1955 (17 Dec). Literary Anniversaries. T **390** and similar vert portraits. No wmk. P 14.

2413	20b. indigo	70	10
2414	55b. dull ultramarine	1·60	35
2415	1l. blackish olive	3·00	45
2416	1l.55 red-brown	5·25	1·40
2417	1l.75 slate-violet	6·25	1·40
2418	2l. brown-purple	7·25	2·30
2413/2418	*Set of* 6	22·00	5·50

Designs:—20b. Hans Christian Andersen (children's writer, 150th birth anniv); 55b. Adam Mickiewicz (poet, death centenary); 1l. Type **390** (150th death anniv); 1l.55, Baron de Montesquieu (philosopher, death bicentenary); 1l.75, Walt Whitman (centenary of publication of *Leaves of Grass*); 2l. Miguel de Cervantes (350th anniv of publication of *Don Quixote*).

1955 (29 Dec). Savings Bank. Photo. W **254**. P 14.

2419	**391**	55b. blue	3·00	45
2420		55b. bluish violet	9·75	5·50

392 Family

393 Brown Hare

(Des C. Müller (55b.), I. Dumitrana (1l.75). Photo)

1956 (3 Feb). National Census. T **392** and another horiz design inscr "RECENSAMINTUL POPULATIEI". W **254**. P 13½.

2421	55b. orange	70	20
2422	1l.75 red-brown and emerald	3·00	95
	a. Centre inverted		

Design:—55b. "21 FEBRUARIE 1956" in circle.

(Des I. Dumitrana. Photo)

1956 (28 Mar). Wild Life. T **393** and similar designs. W **254**. P 14.

2423	20b. black and green	3·00	95
2424	20b. black and yellow-olive	3·00	95
2425	35b. black and blue	3·00	95
2426	50b. black-brown and deep blue	3·00	95
2427	55b. blackish green and bistre	3·00	95
2428	55b. deep brown and deep turq-grn	3·00	95
2429	1l. red-brown and deep green	6·25	1·90
2430	1l.55 red-brown and pale blue	6·25	1·90
2431	1l.75 black-brown and grey-green	6·25	1·90
2432	2l. black-brown and cobalt	29·00	23·00
2433	3l.25 brown-black and pale blue-green	29·00	23·00
2434	4l.25 brown-black and brown-orange	29·00	23·00
2423/2434	*Set of* 12	£110	70·00

Designs: Vert—20b. (2424), Great bustard; 35b. Brown trout; 1l.55, Eurasian red squirrel; 1l.75, Capercaillie; 4l.25, Red deer. Horiz—50b. Wild boar; 55b. (2427), Ring-necked pheasant; 55b. (2428), Brown bear; 1l. Lynx; 2l. Chamois; 3l.25, Pintail.

See also Nos. 2474/85.

394 Insurgents

395 Boy and Globe

396 Red Cross Nurse

(Des C. Stroe. Photo)

1956 (29 May). 85th Anniv of Paris Commune. W **254**. P 13½.

2435	**394**	55b. vermilion	2·40	65

(Des Aida Tasgian. Photo)

1956 (1 June). International Children s Day. W **254**. P 14.

2436	**395**	55b. violet	3·50	45

No. 2436 was printed in sheets of 100 containing ten *se-tenant* labels bearing the word "PEACE" in ten languages.

1956 (7 June). Second Romanian Red Cross Congress. Photo. W **254**. P 14.

2437	**396**	55b. brown-olive and scarlet	4·00	45

397 Tree

398 Woman Speaking

(Des A. Bratescu-Voinesti. Photo)

1956 (11 June). Forestry Month. T **397** and similar vert design inscr "LUNA PADURII 1956". W **254**. P 14.

2438	20b. slate-green/*green*	1·90	30
2439	55b. black/*green* (Lumber train)	5·75	45

1956 (14 June). International Women's Conference, Bucharest. Photo. W **254**. P 14.

2440	**398**	55b. blackish green	2·40	45

399 Academy Buildings

(Des I. Dumitrana. Photo)

1956 (19 June). Nineteenth Anniv of Romanian People's Academy. W **254**. P 14.

2441	**399**	55b. blackish green and buff	2·40	45

400 Vuia, Biplane, Vuia No. 1 and Yakovlev Yak-25 Jet Fighters

401 Georgescu and Statues

(Des C. Stroe. Photo)

1956 (21 June). 50th Anniv of First Flight by Traian Vuia (pioneer airman). W **254**. P 13½.

2442	**400**	55b. deep brown and blackish olive.	3·00	45

(Des I. Dumitrana. Photo)

1956 (25 June). Birth Centenary of Ion Georgescu (sculptor). W **254**. P 14.

2443	**401**	55b. reddish brown and deep bluish green	4·00	45

402 Farm Girl

403 Black-veined White (*Aporia crataegi*)

(Des L. Nazarov. Photo)

1956. Collective Farming. W **254**. P 14.

(a) Inscr "1951–1956" (23 July)

2444	**402**	55b. plum	11·50	11·00

(b) Inscr "1949–56" (18 Oct)

2445	**402**	55b. plum	2·10	45

1956 (30 July). Insect Pests. T **403** and similar designs. Photo. W **254**. P 14.

2446	10b. cream, black and violet	4·75	55
2447	55b. yellow-orange and brown-black	7·25	75
2448	1l.75 lake and yellow-olive	19·00	14·00
2449	1l.75 deep brown and olive-green	16·00	1·60
2446/2449	*Set of* 4	42·00	15·00

Designs: Horiz—55b. Colorado potato beetle (*Leptinotarsa decemlineata*). Vert—1l.75 (2), May beetle (*Melolontha melolontha*).

404 Striker

405

406 Gorky

(T **404/5** des L. Nazarov. Photo)

1956 (6 Aug). 50th Anniv of Dockers' Strike at Galatz. W **254**. P 14.

2450	**404**	55b. brown/*flesh*	2·40	45

1956 (13 Aug). 25th Anniv of *Scânteia* (Communist newspaper). W **254**. P 13½.

2451	**405**	55b. bright blue	1·90	45

(Des S. Zainea. Photo)

1956 (29 Aug). Twentieth Anniv of Death of Maksim Gorky. W **254**. P 14.

2452	**406**	55b. brown	2·40	45

407 T. Aman

408 Snowdrops and Polyanthus

409 Janos Hunyadi

(Des L. Nazarov. Recess)

1956 (23 Sept). 125th Anniv of Birth of Aman (painter). No wmk. P 14.

2453	**407**	55b. deep grey-green	4·00	95

(Des I. Dumitrana. Photo)

1956 (26 Sept). Various vert floral designs as T **408**. W **254**. P 14.

2454	5b. multicoloured	95	45
2455	55b. multicoloured	3·50	85
2456	1l.75 multicoloured	7·75	1·10
2457	3l. multicoloured	11·50	1·80
2454/2457	*Set of* 4	21·00	3·75

Designs:—55b. Daffodil and violets; 1l.75, Antirrhinums and campanulas; 3l. Poppies and lilies of the valley.

1956 (15 Oct). 500th Death Anniv of Hunyadi. Photo. No wmk. P 14.

2458	**409**	55b. bright violet	2·40	55

410 Olympic Flame

411 George Bernard Shaw (dramatist)

(Des V. Grigorescu. Photo)

1956 (25 Oct). Olympic Games. T **410** and similar vert designs. No wmk. P 13½×14.

2459	20b. rose-red	95	35
2460	55b. bright blue (Water-polo)	1·50	40
2461	1l. magenta (Ice-skating)	3·00	55
2462	1l.55b. turquoise-green (Canoeing)	4·00	65
2463	1l.75b. reddish violet (High-jumping)	5·25	95
2459/2463	*Set of* 5	13·00	2·50

(Des S. Zainea. Photo)

1956. Cultural Anniversaries. Vert portrait designs as T **411**. No wmk. P 13½×14.

2464	20b. violet-blue (1 Nov)	60	20
2465	35b. claret (28 Dec)	80	20
2466	40b. chocolate (1 Nov)	85	20
2467	50b. black-brown (28 Dec)	1·10	20
2468	55b. deep olive (1 Nov)	1·20	20
2469	1l. deep turquoise-green (1 Nov)	2·10	30
2470	1l.55 reddish violet (1 Nov)	3·00	30
2471	1l.75 blue (1 Nov)	4·00	30
2472	2l.55 reddish purple (28 Dec)	5·25	45
2473	3l.25 deep grey-blue (28 Dec)	5·75	1·10
2464/2473	*Set of* 10	22·00	3·00

Designs:—20b. Benjamin Franklin (U.S. statesman and journalist, 250th birth anniv); 35b. Toyo Oda (painter, 450th death anniv); 40b. Type **411** (birth centenary); 50b. Ivan Franco (writer, birth centenary); 55b. Pierre Curie (physicist, 50th death anniv); 1l. Henrik Ibsen (dramatist, 50th death anniv); 1l.55, Fyodor Dostoevsky (novelist, 75th death anniv); 1l.75, Heinrich Heine (poet, death centenary); 2l.55, Wolfgang Amadeus Mozart (composer, birth bicentenary); 3l.25, Rembrandt (artist, 350th birth anniv).

1956 (12 Dec). Wild Life. As Nos. 2423/34 but colours changed. W **254**. Imperf.

2474	20b. black-brown and grey-green	6·75	6·50
2475	20b. brown-black and blue	6·75	6·50
2476	35b. brown-black and deep turq-blue	6·75	6·50
2477	50b. brown-black and deep brown	6·75	6·50
2478	55b. brown-black and bluish violet	6·75	6·50
2479	55b. deep brown and pale blue-green	6·75	6·50
2480	1l. red-brown and violet-blue	6·75	6·50
2481	1l.55 red-brown and yellow-brown	6·75	6·50
2482	1l.75 deep purple and olive-green	6·75	6·50
2483	2l. black and greenish blue	6·75	6·50
2484	3l.25 red-brown and yellow-green	6·75	6·50
2485	4l.25 deep brown and grey-violet	6·75	6·50
2474/2485	*Set of* 12	75·00	70·00

412 Ilyushin Il-18 Airliner over City

413 Georgi Enescu

(Des I. Dumitrana. Photo)

1956 (15 Dec). AIR. T **412** and similar horiz designs. Multicoloured. W **254**. P 14½×14.

2486	20b. Type **412**	95	65
2487	55b. Ilyushin Il-18 over mountains	1·50	95
2488	1l.75 Ilyushin Il-18 over cornfield	4·25	1·40
2489	2l.55 Ilyushin Il-18 over seashore	6·25	2·30
2486/2489	*Set of* 4	11·50	4·75

(Des S. Zainea. Recess)

1956 (29 Dec). 75th Birth Anniv of Enescu (musician). T **413** and similar portrait. No wmk. P 13½×14.

2490 55b. deep blue .... 1·90 45
2491 1l.75 brown-purple .... 4·00 65

Design:—55b. Enescu when a child, holding violin.

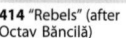

414 "Rebels" (after Octav Băncilă)

415 Stephen the Great

(Des S. Zainea. Photo)

1957 (28 Feb). 50th Anniv of Peasant Revolt. W **254**. P 14×14½.

2492 **414** 55b. blue-grey .... 2·40 45

(Des S. Zainea. Photo)

1957 (24 Apr). 500th Anniv of Accession of Stephen the Great. W **254**. P 14×14½.

2493 **415** 55b. brown .... 1·90 55
2494 55b. blackish olive .... 1·50 95

416 Gheorghe Marinescu (neurologist) and Institute of Medicine

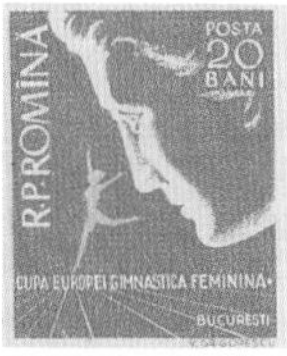

417 Gymnast and Spectator

(Des I. Dumitrana. Photo)

1957 (5 May). National Congress of Medical Sciences, Bucharest, and Centenary of Medical and Pharmaceutical Teaching in Bucharest (1l.75). T **416** and similar horiz designs. W **254**. P 14½×14.

2495 20b. deep bluish green 70 30
2496 35b. purple-brown 95 45
2497 55b. reddish lilac .... 1·60 65
2498 1l.75 scarlet and ultramarine .... 6·25 2·30
2495/2498 *Set of 4* .... 8·50 3·25

Designs: As T **416**—35b. Ioan Cantacuzino (bacteriologist) and Cantacuzino Institute; 55b. Victor Babes (pathologist and bacteriologist) and the Babes Institute. 66×23 mm—1l.75, Nicolae Kretzulescu and Carol Davila (physicians) and Faculty of Medicine, Bucharest.

(Des V. Grigorescu. Photo)

1957 (20 May). First European Women's Gymnastic Championships, Bucharest. T **417** and similar designs inscr "CUPA EUROPEI GIMNASTICA FEMININA BUCURESTI". W **254**. P 13½.

2499 20b. light emerald-green 95 20
2500 35b. vermilion .... 1·50 30
2501 55b. blue .... 3·00 45
2502 1l.75 bright reddish lilac .... 8·25 1·10
2499/2502 *Set of 4* .... 12·50 1·80

Designs showing gymnast: Horiz—35b. On asymmetric bars; 55b. Vaulting over horse. Vert—1l.75, On beam.

418 Emblems of Atomic Energy

419 Dove and Handlebars

(Des V. Palade. Photo)

1957 (29 May). Second A.S.I.T. Congress. W **254**. P 14×14½.

2503 **418** 55b. red-brown .... 1·90 30
2504 55b. deep blue .... 2·40 45

(Des V. Grigorescu. Photo)

1957 (30 May). Tenth International Cycle Race. T **419** and similar horiz design. W **254**. P 13½.

2505 20b. ultramarine 70 20
2506 55b. sepia (Racing cyclist) .... 1·90 45

D **420**

G.P.O., Bucharest Posthorn

(Des I. Dumitrana. Photo)

1957 (31 May). POSTAGE DUE. W **254**. P 14.

				Un pair	*Us pair*
D2507	D **420**	3b. black		20	10
D2508		5b. red-orange		20	10
D2509		10b. bright purple		20	10
D2510		20b. bright red		20	10
D2511		40b. deep turquoise-green		40	20
D2512		1l. bright blue		95	30
D2507/2512		*Set of 6 pairs*		1·90	80

420 Rhododendron

421 N. Grigorescu

(Des H. Meschendörfer. Litho)

1957 (22 June). Flowers of the Carpathian Mountains. T **420** and similar vert designs. No wmk. P 14×14½.

2513 5b. rose-carmine and grey 50 10
2514 10b. deep green and grey 70 20
2515 20b. orange-red and grey 80 20
2516 35b. olive-green and grey .... 1·50 30
2517 55b. bright blue and grey .... 1·60 30
2518 1l. scarlet and grey .... 3·75 1·00
2519 1l.55 greenish yellow and grey .... 4·00 55
2520 1l.75 deep reddish violet and grey .... 7·25 65
2513/2520 *Set of 8* .... 18·00 3·00

Flowers:—10b. Daphne; 20b. Lily; 35b. Edelweiss; 55b. Gentian; 1l. Dianthus; 1l.55, Primula; 1l.75, Anemone.

(Des S. Zainea. Photo)

1957 (29 June). 50th Death Anniv of Nicolae Grigorescu (painter). T **421** and similar designs. W **254**. P 13½.

2521 20b. deep bluish green 95 20
2522 55b. brown .... 2·40 30
2523 1l.75 grey-blue .... 8·75 1·10
2521/2523 *Set of 3* .... 11·00 1·40

Designs: Horiz—20b. "Ox-cart"; 1l.75, "Attack on Smirdan".

422 Festival Visitors

423 Festival Emblem

(Des I. Dumitrana. Photo)

1957 (28 July). Sixth World Youth Festival, Moscow. T **422/3** and various designs inscr "AL VI-LEA FESTIVAL MONDIAL AL TINERETU UI SI STUDENTILOR MOSCOVA 1957". W **254**. P 12½×14 (1l.), 13½×12½ (1l.75) or 14×14½ (others).

2524 **422** 20b. bright purple 30 10
2525 – 55b. emerald-green 80 20
2526 **423** 1l. red-orange .... 1·60 65
2527 – 1l.75 bright blue .... 3·00 45
2524/2527 *Set of 4* .... 5·25 1·30

Designs: Vert—55b. (22×38 mm) Girl with flags. Horiz— 1l.75 (49×20 mm) Dancers.

The 1l. was printed in sheets containing twenty *se-tenant* labels inscr "PEACE AND FRIENDSHIP" in twenty languages.

424 *Stalingrad* (destroyer)

425 "The Trumpeter" (after N. Grigorescu)

(Des I. Dumitrana. Photo)

1957 (3 Aug). Navy Day. W **254**. P 13½.

2528 **424** 1l.75 deep turquoise-blue .... 2·40 45

(Des L. Nazarov. Photo)

1957 (30 Aug). 80th Anniv of War of Independence. W **254**. P 14×14½.

2529 **425** 20b. reddish violet .... 2·40 45

426 Soldiers Advancing

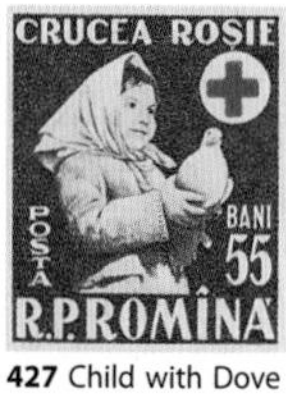

427 Child with Dove

(Des I. Dumitrana. Photo)

1957 (31 Aug). 40th Anniv of Battle of Marasesti. W **254**. P 14½×14.

2530 **426** 1l.75 brown .... 3·00 45

(Des I. Dumitrana. Photo)

1957 (3 Sept). Red Cross. W **254**. P 13½.

2531 **427** 55b. deep blue-green and red .... 2·40 45

428 Sprinter and Bird

429 Ovid

(Des V. Grigerescu. Photo)

1957 (14 Sept). International Athletic Championships, Bucharest. T **428** and similar designs. W **254**. P 13½.

2532 20b. black and blue 70 10
2533 55b. black and yellow .... 2·10 30
2534 1l.75 black and vermilion .... 5·75 75
2532/2534 *Set of 3* .... 7·75 1·00

Designs:—55b. Javelin-thrower and bull; 1l.75, Runner and stag.

(Des S. Zainea. Photo)

1957 (20 Sept). Bimillenary of Birth of Ovid (Latin poet). W **254**. P 13½.

2535 **429** 1l.75 deep grey-blue .... 4·25 95

430 Congress Emblem

431 Oil Refinery, 1957

(Des I. Dumitrana. Photo)

1957 (28 Sept). Fourth World Federation of Trade Unions Congress, Leipzig. W **254**. P 14.

2536 **430** 55b. ultramarine .... 1·50 45

(Des D. Stiubei. Photo)

1957 (5 Oct). Centenary of Romanian Petroleum Industry. T **431** and similar horiz design. W **254**. P 13½.

2537 **431** 20b. purple-brown 70 10
2538 20b. deep blue 70 10
2539 – 55b. deep slate-purple .... 1·50 65
2537/2539 *Set of 3* .... 2·50 75

Design:—55b. Oil production, 1857 (horse-operated borer).

432 Lenin, Youth and Girl

433 Artificial Satellite encircling Globe

(Des I. Dumitrana. Photo)

1957 (6 Nov). 40th Anniv of Russian Revolution. T **432** and similar designs inscr "1917 1957". W **254**. P 14.

2540 10b. scarlet 50 10
2541 35b. reddish purple 95 20
2542 55b. brown .... 1·50 55
2540/2542 *Set of 3* .... 2·75 75

Designs: Horiz—35b. Lenin and flags. Vert—55b. Statue of Lenin.

(Des I. Dumitrana and D. Stiubei. Photo)

1957 (6 Nov). AIR. Launching of Artificial Satellite by Russia. T **433** and similar vert design. W **254**. P 14×14½.

2543 **433** 25b. turquoise-blue 70 20
a. Strip. Nos. 2543/4 plus label .... 20·00
2544 – 3l.75 turquoise-blue .... 4·00 75
a. Tête-bêche (vert pair) .... 15·00
2545 **433** 25b. ultramarine 70 20
a. Strip. Nos. 2545/6 plus label .... 20·00
2546 – 3l.75 ultramarine .... 4·00 75
a. Tête-bêche (vert pair) .... 15·00
2543/2546 *Set of 4* .... 8·50 1·70

Design:—3l.75 (2), Satellite's orbit around globe.

Nos. 2543/4 and 2545/6 respectively were issued together in sheets of 81 (9×9) containing 27 of each value plus 27 inscribed labels arranged to give horizontal and vertical triptyches. The centre three horiz rows are inverted so that rows 3/4 and 6/7 are vertically tête-bêche.

See also Nos. 2593/6.

434 Peasant Soldiers

435 Endre Ady

(Des I. Murnu (50b.), C. Gustav (55b.). Photo)

1957 (30 Nov). 520th Anniv of Bobîlna Revolution. T **434** and similar design but vert. W **254**. P 14.

2547 50b. maroon 60 20
2548 55b. deep slate (Bobîlna Memorial) 80 45

(Des L. Rosianu. Photo)

1957 (5 Dec). 80th Birth Anniv of Endre Ady (poet). W **254**. P 14.

2549	**435**	55b. olive-brown	1·90	45

436 Laika and "Sputnik 2"

437 Black-winged Stilt

(Des I. Dumitrana. Photo)

1957 (10 Dec). Space Flight of Laika (dog). W **254**. P 14.

2550	**436**	1l.20 turquoise-blue and reddish brown	4·75	95
2551		1l.20 blue and reddish brown	4·75	95

(Des I. Dumitrana. Photo)

1957 (24 Dec). Fauna of the Danube Delta. Various designs as T **437**. W **254**. P 14.

(a) POSTAGE

2552	5b. grey and light red-brown	30	10
2553	10b. yellow-orange and light emerald	40	10
2554	20b. buff and scarlet	50	10
2555	50b. orange and blue-green	95	10
2556	55b. blue and maroon	1·50	20
2557	1l.30 orange and deep reddish violet	2·40	20

(b) AIR. Inscr "POSTA AERIANA"

2558	3l.30 grey and blue	4·75	1·10
2559	5l. orange and carmine-red	7·25	1·60
2552/2559 *Set of 8*		16·00	3·25

Designs: Vert—10b. Great egret; 20b. White spoonbill; 50b. Stellate sturgeon. Horiz—55b. Stoat; 1l.30, Eastern white pelican; 3l.30, Black-headed gull; 5l. White-tailed sea eagle.

438 Emblem of Republic and Flags

(Des S. Raslog. Photo)

1957 (30 Dec). Tenth Anniv of People's Republic. T **438** and similar horiz designs. W **254**. P 13½.

2560	25b. buff, red and blue	50	20
2561	55b. yellow-ochre	95	30
2562	1l.20 bright red	1·90	65
2560/2562 *Set of 3*		3·00	1·00

Designs:—55b. Emblem, Industry and Agriculture; 1l.20, Emblem, the Arts and Sport.

439 Republican Flag

440 "Telecommunications"

(Des D. Stiubei. Photo)

1958 (15 Feb). 25th Anniv of Strike at Grivitsa. No wmk. P 13½.

2563	**439**	1l. scarlet and deep brown/*buff*	1·50	45
2564		1l. scarlet and deep blue/*buff*	1·50	45

(Des D. Stiubei. Photo)

1958 (21 Mar). Socialist Countries' Postal Ministers Conference, Moscow. T **440** and similar horiz design. No wmk. P 14×13½.

2565	55b. bluish violet	70	35
2566	1l.75 deep claret	1·60	45

Design:—1l.75, Telegraph pole and pylons carrying lines.

441 Nicolae Balcescu (historian)

442 Fencer

(Des S. Zainea. Photo)

1958 (31 Mar). Romanian Writers. Vert portraits as T **441**. W **254**. P 14.

2567	5b. indigo	60	20
2568	10b. black	70	30
2569	35b. deep blue	80	35
2570	55b. chocolate	1·10	45
2571	1l.75 brownish black	2·75	65
2572	2l. blackish green	4·00	75
2567/2572 *Set of 6*		9·00	2·40

Designs:—10b. Ion Creanga (folklorist); 35b. Alexandru Vlahuta (poet); 55b. Mihail Eminescu (poet); 1l.75, Vasile Alecsandri (poet and dramatist); 2l. Barbu Delavrancea (short-story writer and dramatist).

(Des V. Grigorescu. Photo)

1958 (5 Apr). World Youth Fencing Championships, Bucharest. W **254**. P 14.

2573	**442**	1l.75 bright magenta	3·00	45

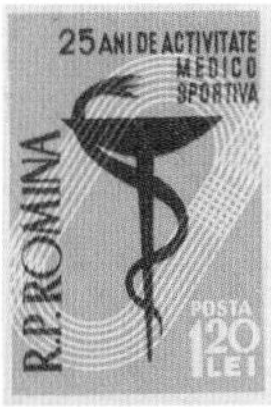

443 Symbols of Medicine and Sport

444

(Des V. Grigorescu. Photo)

1958 (16 Apr). 25th Anniv of Sports Doctors' Service. W **254**. P 14.

2574	**443**	1l.20 brown-red and light emerald	3·00	45

(Des L. Rosianu. Photo)

1958 (15 May). Fourth Interational Congress of Democratic Women. W **254**. P 14.

2575	**444**	55b. blue	1·60	45

445 Linnaeus (botanist)

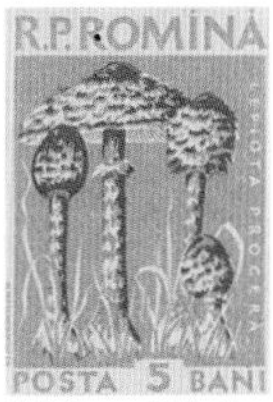

446 Parasol Mushroom (*Lepiota procera*)

(Des S. Zainea. Photo)

1958 (31 May). Cultural Anniversaries (1957). T **445** and similar vert designs. No wmk. P 14×14½.

2576	10b. turquoise-blue	30	20
2577	20b. brown	60	20
2578	40b. deep mauve	95	30
2579	55b. blue	1·50	20
2580	1l. deep bright magenta	1·90	30
2581	1l.75 violet-blue	2·40	55
2582	2l. olive-brown	4·25	65
2576/2582 *Set of 7*		10·50	2·20

Designs:—10b. Type **445** (250th birth anniv); 20b. Auguste Comte (philosopher, death centenary); 40b. William Blake (poet and artist, birth bicentenary); 55b. Mikhail Glinka (composer, death centenary); 1l. Henry Longfellow (poet, 150th birth anniv); 1l.75, Carlo Goldoni (dramatist, 250th birth anniv); 2l. John Komensky, Comenius (educationist, 300th death anniv).

(Des H. Meschendörfer. Litho)

1958 (12–30 July). Fungi. Vert designs as T **446**. No wmk. P 14×14½.

2583	5b. brown, light brown and light grey-blue	30	20
2584	10b. red-brown, orange-yellow and brown-olive	30	20
2585	20b. red, yellow and light grey	70	20
2586	30b. orange-brown, orange and deep yellow-green	95	30
2587	35b. brown, light brown and light blue	1·10	20
2588	55b. deep sepia, Venetian red and yellow-green (30.7)	1·50	20
2589	1l. deep brown, yellow-brown and blue-green (30.7)	2·40	30
2590	1l.55 brown-red, drab and deep grey (30.7)	3·50	45
2591	1l.75 brown, yellow-brown and light emerald (30.7)	4·00	55
2592	2l. orange-yellow, brown and bluish green (30.7)	5·75	65
2583/2592 *Set of 10*		18·00	3·00

Designs:—10b. *Clavaria aurea*; 20b. Caesar's mushroom (*Amanita caesarea*); 30b. Saffron milk cap (*Lactarius deliciosus*); 35b. Honey fungus (*Armillaria mellea*); 55b. Shaggy ink cap (*Coprinus comatus*); 1l. *Morchella conica*; 1l.55, Field mushroom (*Psalliota campestris*); 1l.75, Cep (*Boletus edulis*); 2l. Chanterelle (*Cantharellus cibarius*).

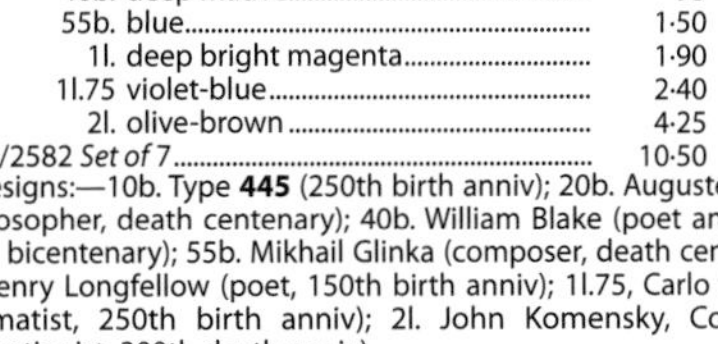

A B C

(**447**)

1958 (20 July). Brussels International Exhibition. Nos. 2543/4 and 2545/6, each pair printed with *se-tenant* labels, with three-part opt, T **447**, in red.

2593	25b. green	4·75	1·90
	a. Opt inverted	29·00	
	b. Horiz strip. Nos. 2593/4 plus label	60·00	
2594	3l.75 green	24·00	14·00
	a. Opt inverted	55·00	
	b. Tête-bêche (vert pair, Nos. 2594 and 2594a)	£110	
2595	25b. ultramarine	4·75	1·90
	a. Opt inverted	29·00	
	b. Horiz strip. Nos. 2595/6 plus label	60·00	
2596	3l.75 ultramarine	24·00	14·00
	a. Opt inverted	55·00	
	b. Tête-bêche (vert pair, Nos. 2596 and 2596a)	£110	
2593/2596 *Set of 4*		50·00	29·00

Nos. 2593/6 and the inverted overprints occur with each of the three parts of the overprint (same price any section). The tête-bêche pairs occur with sections A or C only.

The overprint was the same way up in all positions of the setting; stamps from the middle three rows of the sheet therefore have the overprint inverted.

448 Racovita, Antarctic Map and *Belgica* (Gerlache expedition, 1897)

449 Sputnik encircling Globe

(Des H. Meschendörfer. Photo)

1958 (28 July). Tenth Death Anniv (1957) of Emil Racovita (naturalist and explorer). T **448** and similar horiz design. No wmk. P 14½×14.

2597	55b. deep blue and dull blue	1·60	35
2598	1l.20 yellow-olive and dp reddish violet	4·00	45

Design:—1l.20, Racovita and grotto.

(Des I. Dumitrana. Photo)

1958 (20 Sept). AIR. Launching of Third Artificial Satellite by Russia. No wmk. P 14½×14.

2599	**449**	3l.25 orange-buff and indigo	7·25	1·90

450 Servicemen's Statue

451 Costumes of Oltenia **452**

(Des D. Stiubei. Photo)

1958 (2 Oct). Army Day. Vert designs as T **450**. No wmk. P 13½.

(a) POSTAGE

2600	55b. yellow-brown	50	20
2601	75b. purple-lake	70	20
2602	1l.75 blue	1·60	30

(b) AIR

2603	3l.30 violet	3·00	75
2600/2603 *Set of 4*		5·25	1·30

Designs:—75b. Soldier guarding industrial plant; 1l.75, Sailor hoisting flag and destroyer; 3l.30, Pilot and Mikoyan Gurevich MiG-17 jet fighters.

(Des H. Meschendörfer. Litho)

1958 (25 Oct). Provincial Costumes. Vert designs as T **451/2**. No Wmk. P 14.

2604	35b. red, black and yellow (female)	50	30
	a. Horiz strip. Nos. 2604/5 plus label	1·20	
2605	35b. red, black and yellow (male)	50	30
2606	40b. carmine, brown and light brown (female)	60	35
	a. Horiz strip. Nos. 2606/7 plus label	1·30	
2607	40b. carmine, brown and light brown (male)	60	35
2608	50b. brown, carmine and reddish lilac (female)	70	30
	a. Horiz strip. Nos. 2608/9 plus label	1·60	
2609	50b. brown, carmine and reddish lilac (male)	70	30
2610	55b. carmine, bistre-brown and drab (female)	95	35
	a. Horiz strip. Nos. 2610/11 plus label	2·10	
2611	55b. carmine, bistre-brown and drab (male)	95	35
2612	1l. carmine, brown and Venetian red (female)	1·90	45
	a. Horiz strip. Nos. 2612/13 plus label	4·25	
2613	1l. carmine, brown and Venetian red (male)	1·90	45
2614	1l.75 carmine, brown and greenish blue (female)	2·50	65
	a. Horiz strip. Nos. 2614/15 plus label	5·50	
2615	1l.75 carmine, brown and greenish blue (male)	2·50	65
2604/2615 *Set of 12*		16·00	4·25

Designs:—40b. Tara Oasului; 50b. Transylvania; 55b. Muntenia; 1l. Banat, 1l.75, Moldova.

Stamps of the same value were issued together *se-tenant* with intervening stamp-size label with inscription and decorative patterns.

This set exists imperforate from a limited printing.

453 Stamp Printer

(Des S. Zainea. Recess)

1958 (15 Nov). Centenary of First Romanian Postage Stamps. Horiz designs as T **453** inscr "1858–1958". No wmk. P 14½×14.

(a) POSTAGE

2617	35b. deep ultramarine	60	20
2618	55b. brown	85	20
2619	1l.20 Prussian blue	1·50	40
2620	1l.30 plum	1·90	45
2621	1l.55 sepia	2·40	30
2622	1l.75 claret	2·50	35

2623 2l. deep slate-violet 3·00 65
2624 3l.30 lake-brown 4·00 95
2617/2624 *Set of* 8 15·00 3·25

(b) AIR
MS2625 80×89 mm. 10l. blue/*pale blue* (p. 11½) 60·00 55·00
MS2626 80×89 mm. 10l. red (imperf) 80·00 75·00

Designs:—55b. Scissors and Moldavian stamps of 1858; 1l.20, Driver with whip, and mail coach; 1l.30, Postman with horn, and mounted courier. Moldavian stamps of 1858: 1l.55, "27p."; 1l.75, "54p.; 2l. "81p.; 3l.30, "108p.; 10l. tête-bêche pair of "27p.".

Nos. 2617/24 exist imperforate.

See also No. **MS**2632.

454 Runner

455 Revolutionary Emblem

(Des V. Grigorescu. Photo)

1958 (9 Dec). Third Youth Spartacist Games. W **254**. P 14.
2627 **454** 1l. brown 1·90 45

(Des I. Dumitrana. Photo)

1958 (13 Dec). 40th Anniv of Workers' Revolution. W **254**. P 14.
2628 **455** 55b. crimson 1·20 45

456 Boy Bugler

457 Alexandru Cuza

(T **456/7** des I. Dumitrana. Photo)

1958 (20 Dec). Tenth Anniv of Education Reform. No wmk. P 13½.
2629 **456** 55b. rose-red 1·20 45

1959 (23 Jan). Centenary of Union of Romanian Provinces. No wmk. P 14½×14.
2630 **457** 1l.75 indigo 2·40 45

458 First Cosmic Rocket

459 Charles Darwin (naturalist)

(Des Aida Tasgian. Photo)

1959 (3 Feb). AIR. Launching of First Cosmic Rocket. No wmk. P 14½×14.
2631 **458** 3l.25 deep violet-blue/*salmon* 16·00 2·30

1959 (27 Apr). AIR. Tenth Anniv of State Philatelic Services. No. **MS**2625 optd "10 ANI DE COMERT FILATELIC DE STAT 1949–1959", in red.
MS2632 10l. blue/*pale blue* £225 £200

(Des S. Zainea. Photo)

1959 (28 Apr). Cultural Anniversaries. T **459** and similar vert designs. No wmk. P 14×14½.

(a) POSTAGE
2633 55b. black 95 20
2634 55b. slate-blue 95 20
2635 55b. carmine-red 95 20
2636 55b. purple 95 20
2637 55b. bistre-brown 95 20

(b) AIR. Inscr "POSTA AERIANA"
2638 3l.25 ultramarine 4·75 95
2633/2638 *Set of* 6 8·50 1·80

Designs:—No. 2633, Type **459** (150th birth anniv); 2634, Robert Burns (poet, birth bicentenary); 2635, Aleksandr Popov (radio pioneer, birth centenary); 2636, Sholem Aleichem (writer, birth centenary); 2637, Frederick Handel (composer, death bicentenary); 2638, Frédéric Joliot-Curie (nuclear physicist, 10th anniv of World Peace Council).

460 Maize

461 Rock Thrush

(Des I. Dumitrana. Photo)

1959 (29 May). Tenth Anniv of Collective Farming in Romania. Various agricultural designs as T **460**. No wmk (5l.), W **254** (others). P 14×14½ (Nos. 2639/41) or 14½×14 (others).
2639 55b. blue-green 60 30
2640 55b. orange-red 60 30
2641 55b. bright purple 60 30
2642 55b. deep yellow-olive 60 30
2643 55b. red-brown 60 30
2644 55b. yellow-brown 60 30
2645 55b. grey-blue 60 30
2646 55b. bistre-brown 60 30
2647 5l. crimson 4·75 1·00
2639/2647 *Set of* 9 8·50 3·00

Designs: Vert—No. 2639, T **460**; 2640, Sunflower with bee; 2641, Sugar beet. Horiz—2642, Sheep; 2643, Cattle; 2644, Rooster and hens; 2645, Farm tractor; 2646, Farm wagon and horses; 2647 (38×26½ mm), Farmer and wife, and wheatfield within figure "10".

(Des H. Meschendörfer. Typo)

1959 (20 June). AIR. Various birds as T **461**. Multicoloured on coloured papers. No wmk. P 14½×14 (horiz) or 14×14½ (vert).
2648 10b. Type **461** 30 20
2649 20b. Golden oriole 30 20
2650 35b. Lapwing (vert) 40 20
2651 40b. Barn swallow (vert) 50 20
2652 55b. Great spotted woodpecker (vert) 70 20
2653 55b. Goldfinch (vert) 70 20
2654 55b. Great tit (vert) 70 20
2655 1l. Bullfinch (vert) 2·40 30
2656 1l.55 Long-tailed tit 3·00 30
2657 5l. Wallcreeper 7·75 2·75
2648/2657 *Set of* 10 15·00 4·25

462 Young Couple

(Des O. Adler and I. Cova. Photo)

1959 (18 July). Seventh World Youth Festival, Vienna, T **462** and similar vert design inscr "26 VII–4 VIII 1959". No wmk. P 14×14½.
2658 1l. blue 1·20 30
2659 1l.60 rose-carmine 1·60 35

Design—1l.60, Folk-dancer in national costume.

463 Workers and Banners

464

(Des P. Nazarie (55b.), I. Molnar (1l.20). Litho)

1959 (20 Aug). 15th Anniv of Liberation. No wmk.

(a) P 13½×14
2660 **463** 55b. blue, brown, yellow and red 95 45

(b) Sheet 39×72 mm. Imperf. No gum
MS2661 **464** 1l.20 multicoloured 3·00 1·40

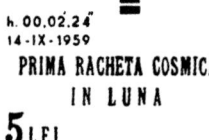

h. 00,02,24
14-IX-1959
PRIMA RACHETA COSMICA
IN LUNA
5 LEI

(**465**)

(**466**)

1959 (14 Sept). AIR. Landing of Russian Rocket on the Moon. No. 2631 surch with T **465**, in red.
2662 **458** 5l. on 3l.25 dp violet-blue/*salmon* 14·50 4·25

1959 (17 Sept). Eighth Balkan Games. No. 2627 optd with T **466**, in silver.
2663 **454** 1l. brown 16·00 16·00

467 Prince Vlad Tepes and Charter

(Des S. Zainea. Photo)

1959 (20 Sept). 500th Anniv of Bucharest. Designs as T **467** inscr "500 ANI BUCURESTI 1459–1959". No wmk. P 13½×14½ or 11½ (20l.).

(a) POSTAGE
2664 20b. black and blue 95 35
2665 40b. black and brown 1·80 35
2666 55b. black and deep bistre 3·00 55
2667 55b. black and reddish purple 3·50 55
2668 1l.55 black and deep lilac 5·75 1·50
2669 1l.75 black and bluish green 6·25 2·00
2664/2669 *Set of* 6 19·00 4·75

(b) AIR
MS2670 66×87 mm. 20l. chocolate £190 £190

Designs: Horiz—40b. Peace Building, Bucharest; 55b. (No. 2666) Atheneum; 55b. (2667) "Scanteia" Printing House; 1l.55, Opera House; 1l.75, "23 August" Stadium. Vert—20l. As T **467** but arranged vert.

468 Football

469 *Lenin*

(Des V. Grigorescu. Typo)

1959 (25 Sept–5 Oct). International Sport. Designs as T **468**. Multicoloured. No wmk. P 13½.

(a) POSTAGE
2671 20b. Type **468** 50 20
2672 35b. Motor-cycle racing 60 20
2673 40b. Ice-hockey 80 30
2674 55b. Handball 95 20
2675 1l. Horse-jumping 1·50 20
2676 1l.50 Boxing 3·00 30
2677 1l.55 Rugby football (25.9) 3·00 20
2678 1l.60 Tennis 3·50 45

(b) AIR. Inscr "POSTA AERIANA"
2679 2l.80 Hydroplaning 4·25 1·20
2671/2679 *Set of* 9 16·00 3·00

The 35b., 40b., 1l.55, 1l.60 and 2l.80 values are horizontal designs.

(Des Aida Tasgian. Photo)

1959 (25 Oct). Launching of Russian Atomic Ice-breaker *Lenin*. No wmk. P 14½×14.
2680 **469** 1l.75 bluish violet 3·50 65

STAMP DAY ISSUES. The annual issues for Stamp Day in November together with the stamp issued on 30 March 1963 for the Romanian Philatelists' Conference are now the only stamps which carry a premium which is expressed on *se-tenant* labels. This was for the Association of Romanian Philatelists. These labels were at first separated by a vertical perforation but in the issues from 1963 to 1971 the label is an integral part of the stamp.

470 Stamp Album and Magnifier

471 Foxglove (*Digitalis purpurea*)

(Des I. Dumitrana. Photo)

1959 (15 Nov). Stamp Day. W **254**. P 14×14½.
2681 **470** 1l.60 (+40b.) deep ultramarine 95 45

(Des H. Meschendörfer. Typo)

1959 (25 Nov). Medicinal Flowers. T **471** and similar vert designs. Multicoloured. No wmk. P 14.
2682 20b. Type **471** 30 10
2683 40b. Peppermint (*Mentha piperita*) 60 30
2684 55b. False chamomile (*Matricaria chamomilla*) 80 20
2685 55b. Cornflower (*Centaurea cyanus*) 1·10 20
2686 1l. Meadow saffron (*Colchicum autumnale*) 1·50 30
2687 1l.20 Monkshood (*Aconitum napellus*) 1·60 30
2688 1l.55 Common poppy (*Papaver rhoeas*) 2·40 45
2689 1l.60 Silver lime (*Tilia tomentosa*) 2·40 55
2690 1l.75 Dog rose (*Rosa canina*) 2·50 55
2691 3l.20 Yellow pheasant's-eye (*Adonis vernalis*) 4·00 75
2682/2691 *Set of* 10 15·00 3·25

472 Cuza University

473 Rocket, Dog and Rabbit

(Des Maria Panin. Photo)

1959 (26 Nov). Centenary of Cuza University, Jassy. W **254**. P 14½×14.

2692 **472** 55b. deep chocolate 95 45

(Des Aida Tasgian. Photo)

1959 (15 Dec). AIR. Cosmic Rocket Flight. T **473** and similar designs. W **254**. P 13½ (1l.60) or 14×14½ (others).

2693	1l.55 deep blue	4·75	45
2694	1l.60 deep ultramarine/*cream*	5·25	75
2695	1l.75 deep blue	5·25	75
2693/2695 *Set of 3*		13·50	1·80

Designs:—Horiz (52×29½ mm)—1l.60, Picture of "invisible" side of the Moon, with lists of place names in Romanian and Russian. Vert (as T **473**)—1l.75, Lunik 3's trajectory around the Moon.

474 G. Cosbuc

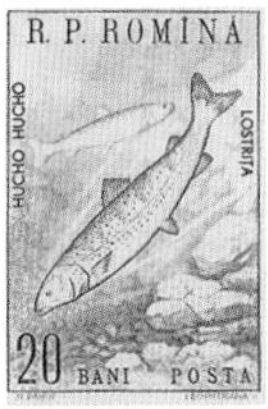

475 Huchen (Danube salmon)

(Des S. Zainea. Photo)

1960 (20 Jan). Romanian Authors. Vert portraits as T **474**. W **254**. P 14.

2696	20b. indigo	50	35
2697	40b. purple (I. L. Caragiale)	95	35
2698	50b. brown (G. Alexandrescu)	1·20	35
2699	55b. purple-brown (A. Donici)	1·20	35
2700	1l. violet (C. Negruzzi)	2·10	45
2701	1l.55 deep violet-blue (D. Bolintineanu)	3·50	55
2696/2701 *Set of 6*		8·50	2·20

(Des Maria Panin. Eng I. Dumitrana. Recess)

1960 (1 Feb). Romanian Fauna. Vert designs as T **475**. No wmk. P 14×14½.

(a) POSTAGE

2702	20b. blue	50	20
2703	55b. chocolate (Tortoise)	95	20
2704	1l.20 deep lilac (Common shelduck)	2·10	65

(b) AIR. Inscr "POSTA AERIANA"

2705	1l.30 deep bright blue (Golden eagle)	2·40	65
2706	1l.75 bronze-green (Black grouse)	2·40	65
2707	2l. brown-red (Lammergeier)	2·50	95
2702/2707 *Set of 6*		9·75	3·00

476 Woman and Dove

477 Lenin (after painting by M. A. Gerasimov)

(Des Aida Tasgian. Photo)

1960 (7 Mar). 50th Anniv of International Women's Day. No wmk. P 14×14½.

2708 **476** 55b. ultramarine .... 1·50 65

(Des S. Zainea. Photo)

1960 (20 Apr). 90th Birth Anniv of Lenin. T **477** and similar vert designs. W **254**. P 13½.

2709	40b. reddish purple	80	30
2710	55b. deep violet-blue	1·10	30
MS2711 65×75 mm. 1l.55, red. P 11½		5·75	3·75

Designs:—55b. Statue of Lenin by Boris Carogea; 1l.55, Lenin (sculpture by C. Baraschi).

478 "Victory"

479 Rocket Flight

(Des Grant-Alexe-Druga team. Photo)

1960 (9 May). 15th Anniv of Victory. T **478** and similar vert design inscr. "Ziua Victoriei 1945–1960". W **254**.

(a) P 13½×14½

2712	40b. violet-blue	70	30
2713	55b. violet-blue	70	30

(b) Colours changed. Imperf

2714	40b. deep purple	3·50	3·75
2715	55b. deep purple	3·50	3·75
2712/2715 *Set of 4*		7·50	7·25

Design:—55b. Statue of soldier with flag.

Nos. 2712/13 and 2714/15 were each issued in sheets with a *se-tenant* stamp-size label inscribed "ANIVERSARE A VICTORIEI", etc. in purple.

(Des I. Dumitrana. Photo)

1960 (8 June). AIR. Launching of Soviet Rocket. W **254**. P 14½×14.

2716 **479** 55b. blue .... 4·75 65

480 Diving

481 Gymnastics

(Des H. Meschendörfer. Litho)

1960 (11 June). Olympic Games, Rome (1st issue). T **480** and similar horiz designs. Multicoloured. No wmk.

A. P 14½×14

2717A	40b. Type **480**	2·40	2·30
	c. Horiz strip of 3. Nos. 2717A/19A	11·50	—
2718A	55b. Gymnastics	2·40	2·30
2719A	1l.20 High jumping	2·40	2·30
2720A	1l.60 Boxing	2·40	2·30
	c. Horiz strip. Nos. 2720A/1A plus 2 labels	11·50	—
2721A	2l.45 Canoeing	2·40	2·30
2717A/2721A or 2722A *Set of 5*		13·00	12·50

B. Imperf

2717B	40b. Type **480**	4·75	2·75
	c. Horiz strip of 3. Nos. 2717B/19B	14·50	—
2718B	55b. Gymnastics	4·75	2·75
2719B	1l.20 High jumping	4·75	2·75
2720B	1l.60 Boxing	5·75	4·75
	d. Horiz strip. Nos. 2720B and 2722B plus 2 labels	14·50	—
2722B	3l.70 Canoeing	6·25	4·75
2717B/20B and 2722B *Set of 5*		29·00	20·00

Nos. 2717/19 were issued together in horizontal *se-tenant*, strips of three in the top half of the sheet; the bottom half, which was separated from the top by a gutter, consisted of horizontal strips of two stamps, No. 2720A plus No. 2721A in the perforated sheets or No. 2722B in the imperforate sheets, together with two half stamp-size labels showing the Olympic torch and rings. When placed together the two strips form a composite design of the Olympic rings.

(Des H. Meschendörfer. Photo)

1960 (11 June). Olympic Games, Rome (2nd issue). T **481** and similar vert designs. W **254**. P 14×14½.

2723	20b. grey-blue (Diving)	20	10
2724	40b. purple-brown (Type **481**)	60	20
2725	55b. bright blue (High-jumping)	85	10
2726	1l. carmine-red (Boxing)	1·20	20
2727	1l.60 reddish purple (Canoeing)	1·60	30
2728	2l. deep lilac (Football)	2·50	55
2723/2728 *Set of 6*		6·25	1·30
MS2729 90×69 mm. 5l. ultramarine (p 11½)		19·00	19·00
MS2730 90×69 mm. 6l. red (imperf)		34·00	33·00

Design:—5l., 6l. Olympic flame and stadium.

482 Industrial Scholars

483 Vlaicu and his Airplane No. 1 "Crazy Fly"

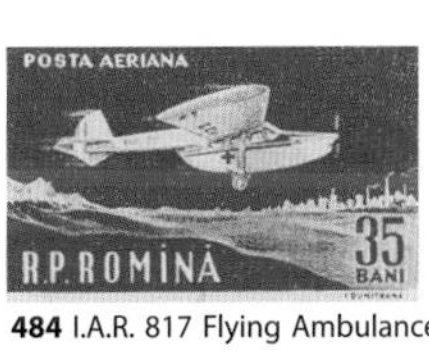

484 I.A.R. 817 Flying Ambulance

485 Pilot and Mikoyan Gurevich MiG-17 Jet Fighters

(Des Grant-Alexe-Druga team. Photo)

1960 (11 June–July). Cream paper. W **254**. P 14.

(a) POSTAGE

2731	3b. magenta (5.7)	10	10
2732	5b. olive-brown	10	10
2733	10b. slate-purple (5.7)	20	10
2734	20b. deep violet-blue	20	10
	a. White paper		
2735	30b. vermilion (5.7)	30	10
2736	35b. carmine-red (5.7)	30	10
2737	40b. yellow-brown (5.7)	30	10
	a. White paper		
2738	50b. bluish violet (5.7)	30	10
2739	55b. blue (5.7)	40	10
	a. White paper		
2740	60b. emerald-green (5.7)	40	10
2741	75b. olive-green (5.7)	50	10
2742	1l. carmine	70	10
	a. White paper		
2743	1l.20 black	60	10
	a. White paper		
2744	1l.50 reddish purple	1·50	10
	a. White paper		
2745	1l.55 deep bluish green	80	10
2746	1l.60 deep blue (5.7)	95	10
	a. White paper		
2747	1l.75 red-brown	1·20	10
	a. White paper		
2748	2l. deep olive-brown	1·50	30
2749	2l.40 bright reddish violet (5.7)	1·60	20
2750	3l. grey-blue (5.7)	1·90	30

(b) AIR. Inscr "POSTA AERIANA"

2751	3l.20 bright blue	3·00	10
2731/2751 *Set of 21*		15·00	2·30

Designs: Vert—5b. Diesel train; 10b. Dam; 20b. Miner; 30b. Doctor; 35b. Textile-worker; 50b. Children at play; 55b. Timber tractor; 1l. Atomic reactor; 1l.20, Petroleum refinery; 1l.50, Iron-works; 1l.75, Mason; 2l. Road-roller; 2l.40, Chemist; 3l. Radio communications and television. Horiz—40b. Grand piano and books; 60b. Combine-harvester; 75b. Cattle-shed; 1l.55, Dock scene; 1l.60, Runner; 3l.20, Baneasa Airport, Bucharest.

The stamps on white paper are thought to be from a later printing, but the actual date of issue is unknown. Other values may exist on this paper.

(Des H. Meschendörfer (10b., 20b.), I. Dumitrana (others). Photo (35b., 40b., 45b.), litho (others))

1960 (15 June). AIR. 50th Anniv of First Flight by A. Vlaicu and Aviation Day (55b.). W **254** (35b., 40b., 55b.) or no wmk (others). P 14½×14 or 14×14½ (55b.).

2752	**483**	10b. chocolate and orange-yellow	20	10
2753	–	20b. chocolate and red-orange	30	10
2754	**484**	35b. bright carmine	50	10
2755	–	40b. bluish violet	70	10
2756	**485**	55b. bright blue	95	10
2757	–	1l.60 multicoloured	2·40	45
2758	–	1l.75 multicoloured	3·00	65
2752/2758 *Set of 7*			7·25	1·40

Designs: As T **484**—20b. Vlaicu in flying helmet and his airplane No. 2; 40b. Antonov An-2 biplane spraying crops. 59×22 mm—1l.60, Ilyushin Il-18 airliner and Baneasa airport control tower; 1l.75, Parachute descents.

486 Worker and Emblem

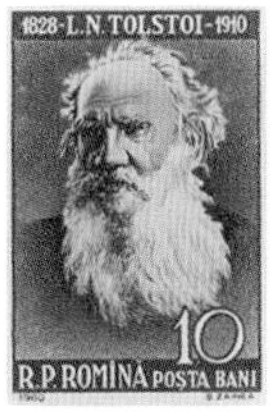

487 Leo Tolstoy (writer)

(Des I. Molnar. Litho)

1960 (20 June). Third Workers Party Congress. No wmk. P 13½.

2759 **486** 55b. orange-red and carmine .... 1·50 45

(Des S. Zainea. Photo)

1960 (2 Aug). Anniversaries. T **487** and similar vert designs. W **254**. P 14×14½.

2760	10b. slate-purple	20	10
2761	20b. olive-brown	40	10
2762	35b. blue	50	10
2763	40b. grey-green	60	20
2764	55b. chocolate	95	20
2765	1l. deep bluish green	1·50	45
2766	1l.20 claret	1·60	20
2767	1l.55 slate	1·90	30
2768	1l.75 light brown	3·00	55
2760/2768 *Set of 9*		9·50	2·00

Designs:—10b. Type **487** (50th death anniv); 20b. Mark Twain (writer, 50th death anniv); 35b. Katsushika Hokusai (painter, birth bicentenary); 40b. Alfred de Musset (poet, 150th birth anniv); 55b. Daniel Defoe (writer, 300th birth anniv); 1l. János Bolyai (mathematician, death centenary); 1l.20, Anton Chekhov (writer, birth centenary); 1l.55, Robert Koch (bacteriologist, 50th death anniv); 1l.75, Frédéric Chopin (composer, 150th birth anniv).

488 Tomis (Constantza)

489 Globe and Flags

(Des Grant-Alexe-Druga team. Litho)

1960 (2 Aug). Black Sea Resorts. Horiz designs as T **488**. Multicoloured. P 14½×14.

(a) POSTAGE

2769	20b. Type **488**	50	10
2770	35b. Constantza	70	10
2771	40b. Vasile Roaita	70	20
2772	55b. Mangalia	95	20
2773	1l. Eforie (South)	1·50	45
2774	1l.60 Eforie (North)	2·40	30

(b) AIR. Inscr "POSTA AERIANA"

2775	2l. Mamaia	3·00	95
2769/2775 *Set of 7*		8·75	2·10

(Des Ella Conovici. Typo)

1960 (15 Sept). International Puppet Theatre Festival, Bucharest. T **489** and various vert designs of puppets. Multicoloured. P 14×14½ (20b.) or 13½ (others).

2776	20b. Type **489**	30	10
2777	40b. Petrushka	50	10
2778	55b. Punch	60	10
2779	1l. Kaspar	1·10	20

2780	1l.20 Tindarica	1·30	20
2781	1l.75 Vasilache	1·90	30
2776/2781	*Set of* 6	5·25	90

Nos. 2777/81 are smaller (24×28½ mm).

490 Viennese Emperor Moth (*Saturnia pyri*)
491 Children tobogganing

(Des Aida Tasgian. Typo)

1960 (10 Oct). AIR. Butterflies and Moths. T **490** and similar designs. Multicoloured. P 13½ (10b.), 14×12½ (20, 40b.), 14×14½ (55b., 1l.60) or 14½×14 (1l.75).

2782	10b. Type **490**	30	10
2783	20b. Poplar admiral (*Limenitis populi*)	30	10
2784	40b. Scarce copper (*Chrisophanus virgaureae*)	50	10
2785	55b. Swallowtail (*Papilio machaon*)	95	20
2786	1l.60 Death's-head hawk moth (*Acherontia atropus*)	3·00	45
2787	1l.75 Purple emperor (*Apatura iris*)	4·00	55
2782/2787	*Set of* 6	8·25	1·40

Sizes: Triangular (36½×21½ mm)—20, 40b. Vert (23½×34 mm)—55b., 1l.60. Horiz (34×23½ mm)—1l.75.

(Des Constantza Marinescu. Litho)

1960 (15 Oct). Village Children's Games. T **491** and similar designs. Multicoloured. No wmk. P 14.

2788	20b. Type **491**	20	10
2789	35b. "Oina" (ball game) (horiz)	30	10
2790	55b. Ice-skating (horiz)	60	10
2791	1l. Running	1·20	20
2792	1l.75 Swimming (horiz)	2·50	30
2788/2792	*Set of* 5	4·25	70

492 Striker and Flag

(Des I. Dumitrana. Litho)

1960 (20 Oct). 40th Anniv of General Strike. P 14½×13.

2793	**492**	55b. orange-red and carmine-lake	95	45

493 Compass Points and Ilyushin Il-18 Airliner
494 "XV", Globe and "Peace" Banner

(Des Grant-Alexe-Druga team. Photo)

1960 (1 Nov). AIR. Stamp Day. W **254**. P 14×14½.

2794	**493**	55b. (+45b.) blue	95	45

(Des Aida Tasgian. Photo)

1960 (5 Nov). 15th Anniv of World Democratic Youth Federation. W **254**. P 14×14½.

2795	**494**	55b. yellow and blue	95	45

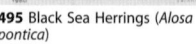

495 Black Sea Herrings (*Alosa pontica*)
496 Woman tending Vine (*Cotnari*)

(Des H. Meschendörfer. Typo)

1960 (30 Nov). Fishes. T **495** and similar horiz designs. P 14½×13.

2796	10b. brown, yellow and turquoise-green	20	10
2797	20b. multicoloured	50	10
2798	40b. brown, yellow-brown and greenish yellow	70	10
2799	55b. slate, new blue and orange	95	10
2800	1l. multicoloured	1·60	20
2801	1l.20 multicoloured	2·40	30
2802	1l.60 multicoloured	3·00	45
2796/2802	*Set of* 7	8·50	1·20

Designs:—10b. Common carp (*Cyprinus carpio*); 20b. Zander (*Lucioperca lucioperca*); 40b. Black Sea turbot (*Scophthalmus maeoticus*); 1l. Wels (*Silurus glanis*); 1l.20, Sterlet (*Acipenser ruthenus*); 1l.60, Beluga (*Huso huso*).

(Des Grant-Alexe-Druga team. Litho)

1960 (10 Dec). Romanian Vineyards. T **496** and similar designs showing vineyard workers and inscriptions. Multicoloured. P 14.

2803	20b. Drăgăsani	20	10
2804	30b. Dealul Mare (horiz)	50	10
2805	40b. Odobesti (horiz)	70	10
2806	55b. Type **496**	95	20
2807	75b. Tirnave	1·60	30
2808	1l. Minis	2·40	45
2809	1l.20 Murfatlar	3·00	75
2803/2809	*Set of* 7	8·50	1·80
MS2810	95×115 mm. 5l. Antique wine jug. Imperf. No gum	5·75	3·75

497 "Furnaceman" (after I. Irimescu)
498 Slalom Racer
499 Petru Poni (chemist)

(Des N. Grant and I. Druga. Photo)

1961 (16 Feb). Romanian Sculptures. T **497** and similar designs. P 14×13½ (55b.) or 13½×14 (others).

2811	5b. carmine-red	10	10
2812	10b. bluish violet	20	10
2813	20b. blackish brown	30	10
2814	40b. bistre-brown	70	10
2815	50b. deep chocolate	80	10
2816	55b. brown-red	1·10	10
2817	1l. purple	1·50	20
2818	1l.55 ultramarine	2·40	30
2819	1l.75 slate-green	3·00	30
2811/2819	*Set of* 9	9·00	1·30

Sculptures: Vert—10b. "Gh. Doja" (I. Vlad) ; 20b. "Reunion" (B. Caragea); 40b. "Enescu" (G. Anghel); 50b. "Eminescu" (C. Baraschi); 1l. "Peace" (I. Jalea); 1l.55, "Constructive Socialism" (C. Medrea); 1l.75, "Birth of An Idea" (A. Szobotka). Horiz—55b. "Peasant Uprising, 1907" (M. Constantinescu).

(Des H. Meschendörfer. Photo)

1961. AIR. 50th Anniv of Romanian Winter Sports. T **498** and similar designs inscr "1961".

(a) P 14½×13 (horiz) or 13×14½ (vert) (18 Mar)

2820	10b. olive and grey	30	10
2821	20b. brown-red and grey	40	10
2822	25b. turquoise and grey	70	10
2823	40b. violet and grey	80	10
2824	55b. bright blue and grey	95	20
2825	1l. crimson and grey	1·40	30
2826	1l.55 brown and grey	2·10	35
2820/2826	*Set of* 7	6·00	1·10

(b) Imperf (20 Apr)

2827	10b. bright blue and grey	20	10
2828	20b. brown and grey	50	30
2829	25b. olive and grey	70	45
2830	40b. crimson and grey	80	75
2831	55b. turquoise and grey	95	95
2832	1l. violet and grey	1·50	1·40
2833	1l.55 brown-red and grey	2·10	2·00
2827/2833	*Set of* 7	6·00	5·25

Designs: Horiz—Skier: 10b. Racing; 55b. Jumping; 1l.55, Walking. Vert—25b. Skiers climbing slope; 40b. Toboggan; 1l. Rock-climber.

(Des V. Grigorescu. Litho)

1961 (30 Mar). Romanian Scientists. T **499** and similar vert portrait designs inscr "1961". P 13½.

2834	10b. black-brown, ultramarine and pink	10	20
2835	20b. black-brown, maroon and olive-yellow	30	20
2836	55b. black-brown, red and light blue	70	20
2837	1l.55 black-brown, violet and brown-orange	2·40	55
2834/2837	*Set of* 4	3·25	1·00

Portraits:—20b. Anghel Saligny (engineer) and Saligny Bridge, Cernavoda; 55b. Constantin Budeanu (electrical engineer); 1l.55, Gheorghe Titeica (mathematician).

500 Yuri Gagarin in Capsule
501 Freighter *Galati*

(Des I. Dumitrana. Photo)

1961 (12 Apr). AIR. World's First Manned Space Flight. T **500** and similar design inscr "12.IV.1961". P 14×14½ (2838), 14½×14 (2839) or imperf (2840).

2838	–	1l.35 blue (Yuri Gagarin) (vert)	1·40	35
2839	**500**	3l.20 ultramarine	3·50	1·00
2840		3l.20 carmine	11·50	4·25
2838/2840		*Set of* 3	15·00	5·00

(Des D. Stiubei. Typo)

1961 (25 Apr). Merchant Navy. T **501** and similar horiz designs. Multicoloured. P 14½×13.

2841	20b. Type **501**	50	10
2842	40b. *Oltenita* (Danube passenger vessel)	50	10
2843	55b. *Tomis* (hydrofoil)	70	10
2844	1l. *Arad* (freighter)	1·50	20
2845	1l.55 *N. Cristea* (tug)	2·40	30
2846	1l.75 *Dobrogea* (freighter)	3·00	45
2841/2846	*Set of* 6	7·75	1·10

502 Red Flag with Marx, Engels and Lenin
503 Eclipse over Scanteia Building, and Observatory

(Des I. Dumitrana. Litho)

1961 (29 Apr). 40th Anniv of Romanian Communist Party. T **502** and similar horiz design inscr "1921–1961". P 14½×13½.

2847	35b. red, blue and ochre	95	30
2848	55b. lake, grey, red and yellow	1·50	30
MS2849	114×80 mm. 1l. multicoloured. Imperf. No gum	3·50	1·60

Designs:—55b. Two bill-posters; 1l. "Industry and Agriculture" and Party Emblem.

(Des I. Dumitrana. Photo)

1961 (13 June). AIR. Solar Eclipse. T **503** and similar horiz design inscr "ECLIPSA DE SOARE 15-11-1961", etc. W **254**. P 14½×14.

2850	1l.60 ultramarine	2·10	30
2851	1l.75 deep blue	2·50	30

Design:—1l.60, Eclipse over Palace Square, Bucharest.

504 Roe Deer
505 George Enescu

(Des I. Dumitrana. Litho)

1961 (22 June). Forest Animals. T **504** and similar designs inscr "1961". Multicoloured. P 13½×14½ (20, 35, 40. 75b.) or 14½×13½ (others).

2852	10b. Type **504**	20	20
2853	20b. Lynx (horiz)	50	20
2854	35b. Wild boar (horiz)	70	30
2855	40b. Brown bear (horiz)	1·20	30
2856	55b. Red deer stag	1·50	30
2857	75b. Red fox (horiz)	1·60	30
2858	1l. Chamois	1·90	30
2859	1l.55 Brown hare	2·40	45
2860	1l.75 Eurasian badger	3·00	55
2861	2l. Roebuck	3·50	95
2852/2861	*Set of* 10	15·00	3·50

(Des H. Meschendörfer. Litho)

1961 (5 Sept). Second International George Enescu Festival. P 14½×13.

2862	**505**	3l. lavender and chocolate	3·00	65

506 Yuri Gagarin and German Titov
507 *Iris brandzae*

(Des I. Cova and C. Müller (55b.), I. Dumitrana (others). Photo)

1961 (11 Sept). AIR. Second Soviet Space Flight. T **506** and similar designs but vert. P 14½×13½ (1l.75) or 13½×14½ (others).

2863	55b. blue ("Vostok 2")	95	10
2864	1l.35 violet (Titov)	1·50	30
2865	1l.75 carmine-red	2·40	45
2863/2865	*Set of* 3	4·25	75

(Des N. Grant and I. Druga. Litho)

1961 (15 Sept). Centenary of Bucharest Botanical Gardens. Floral designs as T **507**. Flowers in natural colours; background and inscription colours below. P 14½×13½ (horiz) or 13½×14½ (vert).

2866	10b. greenish yellow and brown	10	10
2867	20b. yellow-green and crimson	20	10
2868	25b. pale blue, green and red	30	10
2869	35b. reddish lilac and slate	50	10
2870	40b. yellow and violet	70	10
2871	55b. light blue and ultramarine	95	10
2872	1l. yellow-orange and deep blue	1·60	20
2873	1l.20 cobalt and brown	1·90	20
2874	1l.55 light orange-brown and lake	2·40	20
2866/2874	*Set of* 9	7·75	1·10
MS2875	125×92 mm 1l.75, black, dull green and carmine. Imperf. No gum	7·25	4·25

Designs: Horiz—10b. *Primula minima L*; 35b. *Opuntia vulgaris*: 1l. *Hepatica transsilvanica*. Vert—20b. *Dianthus callizonus*; 25b. *Paeonia romanica*; 40b. T **507**; 55b. *Ranunculus carpaticus*; 1l.20, *Papaver pyrenaicum*; 1l.55, *Gentiana frigida*; 1l.75, C. Davila, D. Brindza and Botanical Gardens Buildings.

Nos. 2866/74 also exist imperforate.

508 Cobza Player

509 Heraclitus (Greek philosopher)

510 Olympic Flame

(Des Aida Tasgian. Photo)

1961 (20 Sept). Musicians. T **508** and similar designs. Multicoloured on coloured papers. P 14½×13½ (20b.) or 13½×14½ (others).

2876	10b. Panpiper	10	10
2877	20b. Alpenhorn player (horiz)	20	10
2878	40b. Flute player	50	10
2879	55b. Type **508**	1·10	10
2880	60b. Bagpiper	1·30	20
2881	1l. Cembalo player	1·70	45
2876/2881 *Set of 6*		4·50	95

(Des V. Grigorescu. Litho)

1961 (2 Oct). Cultural Anniversaries. T **509** and similar vert designs. W **254**. P 13½.

2882	10b. maroon	70	30
2883	20b. brown	70	30
2884	40b. deep bluish green	70	30
2885	55b. cerise	1·20	30
2886	1l.35 blue	1·50	30
2887	1l.75 reddish violet	1·90	30
2882/2887 *Set of 6*		6·00	1·60

Designs:—20b. Sir Francis Bacon (philosopher and statesman, 400th birth anniv); 40b. Rabindradrath Tagore (poet and philosopher, birth centenary); 55b. Domingo Sarmiento (writer, 150th birth anniv); 1l.35, Heinrich von Kleist (dramatist, 150th death anniv); 1l.75, Mikhail Lomonosov (writer, 250th birth anniv).

(Des H. Meschendörfer and V. Grigorescu. Photo)

1961 (30 Oct). Olympic Games, 1960, Gold Medal Awards. T **510** and various designs inscr "MELBOURNE 1956" or "ROMA 1960". P 14×14½ (Nos. 2889/90, 2893/4) or 11 (others).

2888	10b. deep greenish blue and ochre	20	15
2889	20b. red	20	15
2890	20b. blue-grey	20	15
2891	35b. brown and ochre	50	15
2892	40b. reddish purple and ochre	60	15
2893	55b. ultramarine	70	20
2894	55b. blue	70	20
2895	55b. brown-red and ochre	70	20
2896	1l.35 bright blue and ochre	2·40	30
2897	1l.75 carmine and yellow-brown	3·50	40
2888/2897 *Set of 10*		8·75	2·00
MS2898 109×86 mm. 4l. multicoloured. Imperf. No gum		14·50	11·00

Designs: *Diamond*—10b. Boxing; 35b. Pistol-shooting; 40b. Rifle-shooting; 55b. (2895) Wrestling; and 1l.35, High-jumping medals. Vert—20b. (2889), T **510**; 20b (2890), Diving; 55b. (2893), Water-polo; 55b. (2894). Women's high-jumping. Horiz (45×33 mm)—1l.75, Canoeing medals. *Larger*—4l. Gold Medals of Melbourne and Rome.

Nos. 2888, 2891/2 and 2895/7 also exist imperforate.

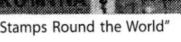

511 "Stamps Round the World"

512 Tower Building, Republic Palace Square, Bucharest

(Des Constantza Marinescu. Litho)

1961 (15 Nov). AIR. Stamp Day. P 13½×14.

2899	**511**	55b. (+45b.) blue, brown and red	1·50	65

(Des Aida Tasgian. Typo and litho)

1961 (20 Nov). AIR. Modern Romanian Architecture. T **512** and similar designs but horiz. Multicoloured. P 13×14½ (20b.) or 14½×13 (others).

2900	20b. Type **512**	30	10
2901	40b. Constantza railway station	50	20
2902	55b. Congress Hall, Republic Palace, Bucharest	60	20
2903	75b. Rolling mill, Hunedoara	70	20
2904	1l. Apartment blocks, Bucharest	95	20
2905	1l.20 Circus building, Bucharest	1·20	45
2906	1l.75 Workers' club, Mangalia	1·90	30
2900/2906 *Set of 7*		5·50	1·50

513 U.N. Emblem

514 Workers with Flags

515 Cock and Savings Book

(Des H. Meschendörfer. Typo and litho)

1961 (27 Nov). 15th Anniv of United Nations Organization. T **513** and similar vert designs bearing U.N. emblem. P 13½×14½.

2907	20b. multicoloured	30	10
2908	40b. multicoloured	70	20
2909	55b. multicoloured	1·20	30
2907/2909 *Set of 3*		2·00	55

Designs:—20b. Peace dove over Eastern Europe, 40b. Peace dove and youths of three races.

Nos. 2907/8 were issued in sheets of 50 with *se-tenant* stamp-size labels inscr "UN TRATAT DE INTELEGERE" etc. in blue on yellow background (20b.), or "TINARA GENERATIE" etc. in chocolate on pale yellow background (40b.).

This issue also exists imperforate.

(Des I. Dumitrana. Photo)

1961 (4 Dec). Fifth World Federation of Trade Unions Congress, Moscow. P 14×14½.

2910	**514**	55b. carmine	1·20	45

(Des C. Ciuvetescu, (40b.), E. Boboia, (55b.). Typo)

1962 (15 Feb). Savings Day. T **515** and similar vert design inscr "1962". P 13½.

2911	40b. multicoloured	50	30
2912	55b. multicoloured	70	30

Design:—55b. Savings Bank book, bee and "honeycombs" of agriculture, housing and industry.

516 Footballer

517 Ear of Corn, Map and Tractor

518 Handball player

(Des H. Meschendörfer after I. Molnar. Litho)

1962 (20 Apr). European Junior Football Competition, Bucharest. P 13×14.

2913	**516**	55b. chestnut and yellow-green	1·90	45

(Des E. Palade, I. Dumitrana, A. Predescu. Litho)

1962 (27 Apr). Completion of Agricultural Collectivization Project. T **517** and similar vert designs inscr "1962". P 13½×14.

2914	40b. carmine and orange	30	10
2915	55b. carmine-lake and yellow	50	10
2916	1l.55 yellow, red and greenish blue	1·20	45
2914/2916 *Set of 3*		1·80	60

Designs:—55b. Commemorative medal; 1l.55, Wheatsheaf, and hammer and sickle emblem.

(Des H. Meschendörfer after V. Grigorescu. Litho)

1962 (12 May). Women's World Handball Championships, Bucharest. P 13×14.

2917	**518**	55b. bluish violet and yellow	1·90	45

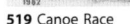

519 Canoe Race

520 Jean Jacques Rousseau

(Des D. Stiubei. Photo)

1962 (15 May). Boating and Sailing. Horiz designs as T **519** inscr "1962".

(a) P 14×13

2918	10b. blue and magenta	30	10
2919	20b. blue and olive-brown	40	10
2920	40b. blue and red-brown	60	10
2921	55b. blue and ultramarine	70	20
2922	1l. blue and scarlet	1·40	20
2923	1l.20 blue and purple	1·60	20
2924	1l.55 blue and orange-red	1·90	20
2925	3l. blue and reddish violet	3·00	55
2918/2925 *Set of 8*		9·00	1·20

(b) Colours changed. Imperf

2926	10b. blue and ultramarine	30	30
2927	20b. blue and magenta	50	30
2928	40b. blue and orange-red	80	55
2929	55b. blue and olive-brown	95	75
2930	1l. blue and red-brown	1·60	95
2931	1l.20 blue and reddish violet	1·80	1·00
2932	1l.55 blue and scarlet	2·10	1·10
2933	3l. blue and purple	4·00	1·90
2926/2933 *Set of 8*		11·00	6·25

Designs:—20b. Kayak; 40b. Racing "eight"; 55b. Sculling; 1l. Yachting; 1l.20, Power boats; 1l.55, Yachting (different); 3l. Canoe slalom.

(Des S. Zainea. Photo)

1962 (9 June). Cultural Anniversaries (writers). T **520** and similar vert designs inscr "MARILE ANIVERSARI CULTIRALE 1962". P 13½×14½ or 11½ (3l.30).

2934	40b. deep olive	40	20
2935	55b. reddish purple	50	30
2936	1l.75 blue	1·10	20
2934/2936 *Set of 3*		1·80	65
MS2937 91×122 mm. 3l.30, brown		7·25	5·50

Designs: As T **520**—40b. Type **520** (250th birth anniv); 55b. Ion Caragiale (dramatist, 50th death anniv); 1l.75, Aleksandr Herzen (150th birth anniv). 32×55 mm—3l.30, Caragiale (full-length portrait).

521 Flags and Globes

522 Traian Vuia (aviator)

(Des H. Meschendörfer. Typo and litho)

1962 (6 July). World Youth Festival, Helsinki. P 11.

2938	**521**	55b. blue, red, yellow and green	1·50	45

(Des S. Zainea. Photo)

1962 (20 July). Romanian Celebrities. T **522** and similar vert portraits. W **254**. P 13½×14½.

2939	15b. brown	20	20
2940	20b. brownish lake	30	20
2941	35b. bright purple	50	20
2942	40b. deep blue	60	20
2943	55b. greenish blue	70	20
2944	1l. ultramarine	1·20	20
2945	1l.20 rose-red	1·50	30
2946	1l.35 deep bluish green	1·60	30
2947	1l.55 reddish violet	1·90	20
2939/2947 *Set of 9*		7·75	1·80

Portraits:—20b. Alexandru Davila (writer); 35b. Vasile Pirvan (archaeologist); 40b. Ion Negulici (painter); 55b. Grigore Cobilcescu (geologist); 1l. Dr. Gheorghe Marinescu (neurologist); 1l.20, Dr. Ion Cantacuzino (bacteriologist); 1l.35, Dr. Victor Babes (bacteriologist and pathologist); 1l.55, Dr. Constantin Levaditi (medical researcher).

523 Anglers by Pond

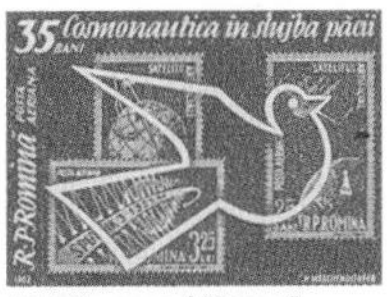

524 Dove and "Space" stamps of 1957/58

(Des I. Untch. Litho)

1962 (25 July). Fishing Sport. T **523** and similar horiz designs. Multicoloured. P 14½×13½.

2948	10b. Rod-fishing from punts	10	10
2949	25b. Line-fishing in mountain pool	20	10
2950	40b. Type **523**	50	15
2951	55b. Anglers on beach	60	15
2952	75b. Line-fishing in mountain stream	95	15
2953	1l. Shore-fishing	1·10	20
2954	1l.75 Freshwater-fishing	1·70	20
2955	3l.25 Fishing in Danube delta	3·00	25
2948/2955 *Set of 8*		7·25	1·20

(Des H. Meschendörfer. Litho)

1962 (27 July). AIR. Cosmic Flights. T **524** and similar designs. P 14½×13½.

2956	35b. yellow-brown	20	10
2957	55b. green	50	20
2958	1l.35 blue	1·20	30
2959	1l.75 carmine-red	1·90	35
2956/2959 *Set of 4*		3·50	85
MS2960 107×79 mm. Nos. 2956/9 but imperf and colours changed: 35b. blue; 55b. yellow-brown; 1l.35, carmine-red; 1l.75, green		5·25	1·90

Designs:—Dove and: 55b. "Space" stamps of 1959; 1l.35, "Space" stamps of 1957 ("Laika"), 1959 and 1960; 1l.75, "Spacemen" stamps of 1961. Dove faces left on 55b. and 1l.75.

1962
Campioană
Europeană
2 lei
(525)

Campioană
Mondială
5 lei
(526)

527 "Vostok 3" and "4" in Orbit

1962 (31 July). Romanian Victory in European Junior Football Competition, Bucharest. No. 2913 surch with T **525**, in blue.

2961	**516**	2l. on 55b. chestnut and yellow-green	4·00	3·75

1962 (31 July). Romanian Victory in Women's World Handball Championships, Bucharest. No. 2917 surch with T **526**, in ultramarine.

2962	**518**	5l. on 55b. bluish violet and yellow	7·25	4·75

(Des I. Dumitrana. Photo)

1962 (20 Aug). AIR. First "Team" Manned Space Flight. T **527** and similar vert designs. P 13½×14.

2963	55b. reddish violet	50	20
2964	1l.60 deep ultramarine	1·50	40
2965	1l.75 reddish purple	1·90	45
2963/2965 *Set of 3*		3·50	95

Designs:—55b. Andrian Nikolaev (cosmonaut); 1l.75, Pavel Popovich (cosmonaut).

528 Child and Butterfly

529 Pottery

(Des H. Meschendörfer. Litho)

1962 (25 Aug). Children. Vert designs as T **528**. P 13½×14 (vert) or 14×13½ (horiz).

No.	Type	Description	Unused	Used
2966		20b. greenish blue, brown and orange-red	30	10
2967		30b. orange-yellow, light blue and brown-red	35	10
2968		40b. grey-blue, orange-red and turquoise-blue	40	10
2969		55b. yellow-olive, light blue and red	70	10
2970		1l.20 carmine, sepia and deep ultramarine	1·90	25
2971		1l.55 ochre, ultramarine and red	3·00	30
2966/2971		*Set of 6*	6·00	85

Designs: Vert—30b. Girl feeding dove; 40b. Boy with model yacht; 1l.20, Boy violinist and girl pianist. Horiz—55b. Girl teaching boy to write; 1l.55, Pioneers around camp-fire.

(Des A. Lucaci, R. Veluda, I. Schön and I. Dúmitrana (1l.60). Litho)

1962 (12 Oct). Fourth Sample Fair, Bucharest. T **529** and similar designs inscr "AL IV—LEA PAVILION DE MOSTRE—BUCURESTI 1962". Multicoloured.

(a) POSTAGE. P 13½×14½

No.	Type	Description	Unused	Used
2972		5b. Type **529**	60	15
2973		10b. Preserved foodstuffs	70	15
2974		20b. Chemical products	80	15
2975		40b. Ceramics	85	10
2976		55b. Leather goods	1·10	10
2977		75b. Textiles	1·30	10
2978		1l. Furniture and Fabrics	1·50	10
2979		1l.20 Office equipment	1·90	10
2980		1l.55 Needlework	2·50	10
		(b) AIR. Inscr "POSTA AERIANA". P 14½×13½		
2981		1l.60 Fair pavilion (horiz)	3·00	30
2972/2981		*Set of* 10	13·00	1·20

530 Lenin and Red Flag

532 Lamb

531 "The Coachmen" (after Szatmary)

(Des I. Dumitrana. Litho)

1962 (7 Nov). 45th Anniv of Russian Revolution. P 11.

No.	Type	Description	Unused	Used
2982	**530**	55b. yellow-brown, red and bright blue	1·50	45

(Des M. Vasiliu. Litho)

1962 (15 Nov). AIR. Stamp Day and Centenary of First Romanian Stamps. P 13½×14½.

No.	Type	Description	Unused	Used
2983	**531**	55b. (+45b.) black and light blue	1·90	55

(Des I. Untch. Litho)

1962 (20 Nov). Prime Farm Stock. T **532** and similar livestock designs. P 14×13.

No.	Type	Description	Unused	Used
2984		20b. black and blue	20	10
2985		40b. deep brown, pale yellow and greenish blue	30	10
2986		55b. grey-green, buff and yellow-orange	50	10
2987		1l. red-brown, pale buff and grey	80	10
2988		1l.35 red-brown, black and grey-green	1·20	20
2989		1l.55 sepia, black and red	1·30	30
2990		1l.75 orange-brown, cream and deep blue	1·90	65
2984/2990		*Set of* 7	5·50	1·40

Designs: Horiz—40b. Ram; 1l.55, Heifer; 1l.75, Sows. Vert—55b. Bull; 1l. Pig; 1l.35, Cow.

533 Arms, Industry, and Agriculture

534 Strikers

(Des I. Dumitrana. Litho)

1962 (30 Dec). 15th Anniv of People's Republic. P 14½×13½.

No.	Type	Description	Unused	Used
2991	**533**	1l.55 multicoloured	1·90	45

(Des I. Schön. Litho)

1963 (16 Feb). 30th Anniv of Grivitsa Strike. P 14½×13½.

No.	Type	Description	Unused	Used
2992	**534**	1l.75 blue-violet, bistre and red	1·90	45

535 Tractor-driver

(Des I. Dumitrana. Photo)

1963 (21 Mar). Freedom from Hunger. T **535** and similar horiz designs, each with F.A.O. emblem. P 14½×13½.

No.	Type	Description	Unused	Used
2993		40b. ultramarine	30	10
2994		55b. bistre-brown	60	10
2995		1l.55 red	1·50	20
2996		1l.75 grey-green	1·60	30
2993/2996		*Set of* 4	3·50	65

Designs:—55b. Girl harvester; 1l.55, Child with beaker of milk; 1l.75, Girl vintager.

(536)

537 Sighisoara Glass Factory

1963 (30 Mar). AIR. Romanian Philatelists' Conference, Bucharest. No. 2983 optd with T **536** in violet.

No.	Type	Description	Unused	Used
2997	**531**	55b. (+45b.) black and light blue	6·25	6·00

(Des D. Stiubei. Photo)

1963 (10 Apr). AIR. Socialist Achievements. T **537** and similar horiz designs inscr "1963". P 14×13.

No.	Type	Description	Unused	Used
2998		30b. blue and red	30	10
2999		40b. grey-green and reddish violet	50	15
3000		55b. claret and ultramarine	70	15
3001		1l. violet and red-brown	1·10	20
3002		1l.55 vermilion and blue	1·30	25
3003		1l.75 ultramarine and reddish purple	1·50	30
2998/3003		*Set of* 6	4·75	1·00

Designs:—40b. Govora soda works; 55b. Tirgul-Jiu wood factory; 1l. Savinesti chemical works; 1l.55, Hunedoara metal works; 1l.75, Brazi thermic power station.

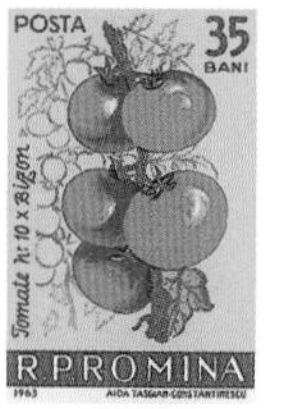

538 Tomatoes

539 Moon Rocket "Luna 4"

(Des Aida Tasgian-Constantinescu. Litho)

1963 (25 Apr). Vegetable Culture. T **538** and similar designs. Multicoloured. P 13½×14½.

No.	Type	Description	Unused	Used
3004		35b. Type **538**	30	10
3005		40b. Hot peppers	60	10
3006		55b. Radishes	70	15
3007		75b. Aubergines	95	20
3008		1l.20 Mild peppers	1·50	30
3009		3l.25 Cucumbers (horiz)	3·00	45
3004/3009		*Set of* 6	6·25	1·20

(Des I. Dumitrana. Photo)

1963 (29 Apr). AIR. Launching of Soviet Moon Rocket "Luna 4". P 13½×14 or imperf (1l.75).

No.	Type	Description	Unused	Used
3010	**539**	55b. red and ultramarine	60	30
3011		1l.75 red and violet	1·90	30

540 Chick

541 Diving

(Des I. Dumitrana. Litho)

1963 (23 May). Domestic Poultry. Designs as T **540**. P 11.

No.	Type	Description	Unused	Used
3012		20b. yellow, blue and deep blue	30	10
3013		30b. red, blue and drab	50	10
3014		40b. deep blue, orange and orange-brown	60	10
3015		55b. red, bistre, blue and turquoise-green	70	10
3016		70b. light blue, orange-red, blue and purple	80	10
3017		1l. red, slate-violet, light blue and deep blue	95	15
3018		1l.35 bright red, deep blue and yellow-ochre	1·10	20
3019		3l.20 red, violet, deep blue and light green	2·10	35
3012/3019		*Set of* 8	6·25	1·10

Poultry:—30b. Cockerel; 40b. Duck; 55b. White Leghorn, 70b. Goose; 1l. Rooster; 1l.35, Turkey (cock); 3l.20, Turkey (hen).

(Des V. Crivat and R. Veluda. Litho)

1963 (15 June). Swimming. T **541** and similar designs. Bodies in drab. P 13½×14½ (vert) or 14½×13½ (horiz).

No.	Type	Description	Unused	Used
3020		25b. green and yellow-brown	20	10
3021		30b. yellow and olive-green	30	10
3022		55b. orange-red and greenish blue	50	10
3023		1l. red and green	80	15
3024		1l.35 magenta and blue	95	15
3025		1l.55 yellow-orange and reddish violet	1·70	20
3026		2l. yellow and magenta	1·70	45
3020/3026		*Set of* 7	5·50	1·10

Designs: Horiz—Swimming: 30b. Crawl; 55b. Butterfly; 1l. Back-stroke; 1l.35, Breast-stroke. Vert—1l.55, Swallow-diving; 2l. Water-polo.

542 Congress Emblem

543 Valery Bykovsky and Globe

(Des Aida Tasgian-Constantinescu. Photo)

1963 (15 June). International Women's Congress, Moscow. P 14½×13.

No.	Type	Description	Unused	Used
3027	**542**	55b. ultramarine	95	45

(Des Aida Tasgian-Constantinescu (**MS**3030), I. Dumitrana (others). Photo)

1963 (6 July). AIR. Second "Team" Manned Space Flights. T **543** and similar designs. P 14½×13.

No.	Type	Description	Unused	Used
3028		55b. blue	70	20
3029		1l.75 scarlet	2·40	45
MS3030		118×80 mm. 1l.20, 1l.60, bright blue. P 13×14½	4·75	2·30

Designs: As T **543**—1l.75, Valentina Tereshkova and globe. 25×41 mm—1l.20, Bykovsky; 1l.60, Tereshkova.

The stamps in No. **MS**3030 form a composite design.

544 Steam Locomotive

545 William Thackeray (novelist)

(Des I. Dumitrana. Litho)

1963 (10 July). AIR. Transport. Horiz designs as T **544**. Multicoloured. P 14½×13½.

No.	Type	Description	Unused	Used
3031		40b. Type **544**	60	20
3032		55b. Diesel freight locomotive	70	20
3033		75b. Trolley bus	95	30
3034		1l.35 *Oltenita* (Danube passenger vessel)	2·10	35
3035		1l.75 Airliner	3·00	45
3031/3035		*Set of* 5	6·50	1·40

(Des S. Zainea. Photo)

1963 (10 Aug). Cultural Anniversaries. T **545** and similar horiz portraits inscr "MARILE ANNIVERSARI CULTURALE 1963". P 14×13½.

No.	Type	Description	Unused	Used
3036		40b. black and lilac	30	15
3037		50b. black and yellow-brown	60	15
3038		55b. black and yellow-olive	80	15
3039		1l.55 black and brown-red	1·60	15
3040		1l.75 black and violet-blue	1·90	30
3036/3040		*Set of* 5	4·75	80

Portraits:—40b. Type **545** (death centenary); 50b. Eugène Delacroix (painter, death centenary); 55b. Gheorghe Marinescu (neurologist, birth centenary); 1l.55, Giuseppe Verdi (composer, 150th birth anniv); 1l.75, Konstantin Stanislavsky (actor and stage director, birth centenary).

546 Walnuts

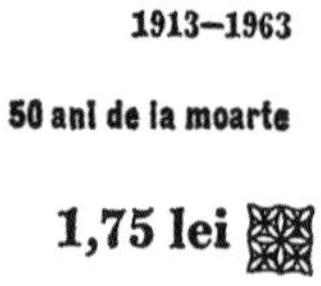

(547)

(Des I. Schön. Litho)

1963 (15 Sept). Fruits and Nuts. Horiz designs as T **546**. Multicoloured. P 14½×13½.

No.	Type	Description	Unused	Used
3041		10b. Type **546**	50	10
3042		20b. Plums	50	10
3043		40b. Peaches	80	10
3044		55b. Strawberries	1·10	10
3045		1l. Grapes	1·20	15
3046		1l.55 Apples	1·60	20
3047		1l.60 Cherries	2·10	30
3048		1l.75 Pears	2·50	30
3041/3048		*Set of* 8	9·25	1·20

1963 (15 Sept). AIR. 50th Death Anniv of Aurel Vlaicu (aviation pioneer). No. 2752 surch with T **547**.

No.	Type	Description	Unused	Used
3049	**483**	1l.75 on 10b. chocolate and orange-yellow	4·75	1·90

548 Volleyball

549 Romanian 1l.55 "Centenary" stamp of 1958

550 U.P.U. Monument, Berne, Globe, Map of Romania and Aircraft (2/3-size illustration)

(Des V. Crivat and R. Veluda. Litho)

1963 (21 Oct). European Volleyball Championships. T **548** and similar vert designs. P 13½×14½.

3050	5b. magenta and grey	50	10
3051	40b. ultramarine and grey	70	10
3052	55b. turquoise-blue and grey	95	15
3053	1l.75 chestnut and grey	1·90	30
3054	3l.20 violet and grey	3·00	45
3050/3054	*Set of* 5	6·25	1·00

Designs:—40b., 55b., 1l.75, Various scenes of play at net; 3l.20, European Cup.

(Des I. Untch. Photo)

1963 (15 Nov). AIR. Stamp Day and 15th Universal Postal Union Congress. T **549** and similar horiz designs and T **550**. P 14½×13½.

3055	20b. sepia and light blue	20	10
3056	40b. blue and magenta	25	10
3057	55b. deep magenta and blue	30	10
3058	1l.20 violet and buff	70	15
3059	1l.55 olive and orange-red	1·10	20
3060	1l.60 +50b. emer, orge-red, bis & grey	2·10	45
3055/3060	*Set of* 6	4·25	1·00

Designs: Romanian stamps—40b. (1l.20) "Laika", 1957 (blue); 55b. (3l.20) "Gagarin", 1961; 1l.20, (55b.) "Nikolaev" and (1l.75) "Popovich", 1962; 1l.55, (55b.) "Post-woman", 1953.

551 Ski Jumping

552 Cone, Fern and Conifer

(Des I. Dumitrana. Litho)

1963 (25 Nov). Winter Olympic Games, Innsbruck, 1964. T **551** and similar designs.

(a) P 14½

3061	10b. blue and orange-red	50	20
3062	20b. red-brown and blue	70	20
3063	40b. red-brown and light green	85	10
3064	55b. red-brown and bluish violet	1·10	20
3065	60b. blue and orange-brown	1·20	30
3066	75b. blue and magenta	1·50	45
3067	1l. ultramarine and yellow-bistre	1·90	45
3068	1l.20 ultramarine and turquoise-blue	2·40	65
3061/3068	*Set of* 8	9·25	2·30

(b) Colours changed. Imperf

3069	10b. red-brown and light green	1·50	95
3070	20b. red-brown and bluish violet	1·50	95
3071	40b. blue and orange-red	1·50	95
3072	55b. red-brown and blue	1·50	95
3073	60b. ultramarine and turquoise-blue	1·50	95
3074	75b. ultramarine and yellow-bistre	1·50	95
3075	1l. blue and magenta	1·50	95
3076	1l.20 blue and orange-brown	1·50	95
3069/3076	*Set of* 8	11·00	6·75
MS3077	120×80 mm. 1l.50, ultramarine and red	11·50	9·25

Designs:—20b. Speed skating; 40b. Ice hockey; 55b. Figure skating; 60b. Slalom; 75b. Biathlon; 1l. Bobsleighing; 1l.20, Cross-country skiing. Horiz—1l.50, Stadium, Innsbruck.

(Des I. Dumitrana. Photo)

1963 (5 Dec). 18th Anniv of Reafforestation Campaign. T **552** and similar horiz design. P 13½.

3078	55b. deep green	30	20
3079	1l.75 deep blue (Chestnut trees)	1·20	30

553 Silkworm Moth

554 Carved Pillar

(Des N. Grant and I. Druga. Litho)

1963 (12 Dec). Bee-keeping and Silkworm-breeding. T **553** and similar designs. Multicoloured. P 13½×14½ (vert) or 14½×13½ (horiz).

3080	10b. Type **553**	50	10
3081	20b. Moth emerging from chrysalis	70	10
3082	40b. Silkworm	85	15
3083	55b. Honey bee (horiz)	95	20
3084	60b. Honey bee on flower	1·20	30
3085	1l.20 Honey bee approaching orange flowers	1·60	45
3086	1l.35 Honey bee approaching pink flowers	2·10	55
3087	1l.60 Honey bee and sunflowers	2·40	65
3080/3087	*Set of* 8	9·25	2·30

(Des Aida Tasgian-Constantinescu. Eng I. Dumitrana. Recess)

1963 (25 Dec). Village Museum, Bucharest. T **554** and similar designs. P 13½.

3088	20b. purple	30	10
3089	40b. greenish blue	50	10
3090	55b. slate-violet	60	10
3091	75b. green	80	10
3092	1l. claret and brown	1·20	10
3093	1l.20 bronze-green	1·50	15
3094	1l.75 light ultramarine and brown	2·40	15
3088/3094	*Set of* 7	6·50	70

Designs:—Various Romanian peasant houses.
The 40b. and 55b. are horizontal, the rest vertical.

555 Yuri Gagarin

556 George Stephanescu (composer)

(Des D. Stiubei. Litho)

1964 (15 Jan). AIR. Space Navigation. T **555** and similar portrait designs. Soviet flag, red and yellow; U.S. flag, red and blue; backgrounds, light blue; portrait and inscription colours below.

(a) P 14

3095	5b. ultramarine	30	10
3096	10b. violet	50	10
3097	20b. bronze-green	60	10
3098	35b. slate-blue	65	10
3099	40b. bluish violet	70	15
3100	55b. bluish violet	85	20
3101	60b. sepia	95	30
3102	75b. blue	1·20	35
3103	1l. reddish purple	1·60	45
3104	1l.40 reddish purple	1·90	95
3095/3104	*Set of* 10	8·25	2·50

(b) Colours changed. Imperf

3105	5b. violet	10	10
3106	10b. ultramarine	10	10
3107	20b. slate-blue	40	15
3108	35b. bronze-green	85	45
3109	40b. reddish purple	1·20	55
3110	55b. reddish purple	1·60	65
3111	60b. blue	1·60	95
3112	75b. sepia	2·10	1·30
3113	1l. bluish violet	2·50	1·60
3114	1l.40 bluish violet	3·25	2·40
3105/3114	*Set of* 10	12·50	7·50
MS3115	120×80 mm. 2l. multicoloured	11·50	9·25

Portraits (with flags of their countries): As T **555**—10b. German Titov; 20b. John Glenn; 35b. Scott Carpenter; 60b. Walter Schirra; 75b. Gordon Cooper. 35½×33½ mm—40b. Andrian Nikolaev; 55b. Pavel Popovich; 1l. Valery Bykovsky; 1l.40, Valentina Tereshkova. 59×43 mm—2l. Globe, orbits, laurel sprigs and commemorative dates.

(Des S. Zainea. Photo)

1964 (20 Jan). Romanian Opera Singers and their Stage Roles. T **556** and similar vert designs. Portraits in brown. P 13½.

3116	10b. olive-green	50	10
3117	20b. ultramarine	60	10
3118	35b. deep blue-green	70	10
3119	40b. greenish blue	80	10
3120	55b. magenta	95	10
3121	75b. reddish violet	1·10	10
3122	1l. new blue	1·20	20
3123	1l.35 violet	1·50	20
3124	1l.55 vermilion	2·40	30
3116/3124	*Set of* 9	8·75	1·20

Designs:—20b. Elena Teodorini in *Carmen*; 35b. Ion Bajenaru in *Petru Rares*; 40b. Dimitrie Popovici-Bayreuth as Alberich in *Ring of the Nibelung*; 55b. Hariclea Darclée in *Tosca*; 75b. George Folescu in *Boris Godunov*; 1l. Jean Athanasiu in *Rigoletto*; 1l.35, Traian Grosavescu as Duke in *Rigoletto*; 1l.55, Nicolae Leonard as Hoffmann in *The Tales of Hoffmann*.

HAVE YOU READ THE NOTES AT THE BEGINNING OF THIS CATALOGUE?
These often provide answers to the enquiries we receive

557 Prof. G. M. Murgoci

558 *Ascalaphus macaronius* (owl-fly)

(Des I. Untch. Photo)

1964 (5 Feb). Eighth International Soil Congress, Bucharest. P 13×13½.

3125	**557**	1l.60 deep blue, ochre and blue	1·20	45

(Des Aida Tasgian-Constantinescu. Litho)

1964 (20 Feb). Insects. T **558** and similar horiz designs. Multicoloured. P 14½×13½.

3126	5b. Type **558**	20	10
3127	10b. *Ammophila sabulosa* (digger wasp)	30	10
3128	35b. *Scolia maculata* (dagger wasp)	50	10
3129	40b. Swamp tiger moth (*Rhyparioides metelkana*)	60	10
3130	55b. Gypsy moth (*Lymantria dispar*)	70	15
3131	1l.20 Great banded grayling (*Kanetisa circe*)	1·10	20
3132	1l.55 *Carabus fabricii malachiticus* (ground beetle)	1·60	20
3133	1l.75 *Procerus gigas* (ground beetle)	2·10	30
3126/3133	*Set of* 8	6·40	1·10

559 *Nicotiana alata*

560 Cross Country

(Des N. Grant and I. Drugă Litho)

1964 (25 Mar). Romanian Flowers. Vert designs as T **559**. Multicoloured. P 13×14.

3134	10b. Type **559**	30	15
3135	20b. *Pelargonium*	50	15
3136	40b. *Fuchsia gracilis*	60	15
3137	55b. *Chrysanthemum indicum*	70	15
3138	75b. *Dahlia hybrida*	80	15
3139	1l. *Lilium croceum*	1·50	20
3140	1l.25 *Hosta ovata*	1·60	30
3141	1l.55 *Tagetes erectus*	1·90	30
3134/3141	*Set of* 8	7·00	1·40

(Des I. Dumitrana. Photo)

1964 (25 Apr). Horsemanship. T **560** and similar designs. P 13½.

3142	40b. crimson, black, light purple and light blue	50	10
3143	55b. brown, red and reddish lilac	70	20
3144	1l.35 brown, red and emerald-green	1·60	30
3145	1l.55 deep magenta, grey-blue and yellbis	2·40	45
3142/3145	*Set of* 4	4·25	95

Designs: Horiz—40b. Dressage; 1l.55, Horse-race. Vert—1l.35, Show jumping.

561 Brown Scorpion Fish (*Scorpaena porcus*)

562 Mihail Eminescu (poet)

(Des S. Zarimba. Litho)

1964 (10 May). Constantza Aquarium. T **561** and similar square designs. Multicoloured. P 14.

3146	5b. Type **561**	10	10
3147	10b. Peacock blenny (*Blennius pavo*)	10	10
3148	20b. Black Sea horse-mackerel (*Trachurus mediterraneus*)	20	10
3149	40b. Russian sturgeon (*Acipenser güldenstaedti*)	50	10
3150	50b. Short-snouted seahorse (*Hippocampus hippocampus*)	60	20
3151	55b. Tub gurnard (*Trigla lucerna*)	70	20
3152	1l. Beluga (*Huso huso*)	1·20	20
3153	3l.20 Common stingray (*Trygon pastinaca*)	4·00	45
3146/3153	*Set of* 8	6·50	1·30

(Des A. Ionescu and I. Mihaiescu. Photo)

1964 (20 June). Cultural Anniversaries. T **562** and similar vert designs. Portraits in brown. P 13½.

3154	5b. green	20	10
3155	20b. bright crimson	20	10
3156	35b. vermillion	50	10
3157	55b. bistre	70	10
3158	1l.20 blue	1·50	20
3159	1l.75 violet	1·90	45
3154/3159	*Set of* 6	4·50	95

Designs:—Type **562** (75th death anniv); 20b. Ion Creanga (folklorist, 75th death anniv); 35b. Emil Girleanu (writer, 50th death anniv); 55b. Michelangelo (artist, 400th death anniv); 1l.20, Galileo Galilei (astronomer, 400th birth anniv); 1l.75, William Shakespeare (dramatist, 400th birth anniv).

563 Cheile Bicazului (gorge)

564 High Jumping

(Des and eng A. Ionescu and I. Mihaiescu. Recess)

1964 (29 June). Mountain Resorts. T **563** and similar designs. P 13½.

3160	40b. lake	50	10
3161	55b. blue	70	10
3162	1l. maroon	95	10
3163	1l.35 sepia	1·20	15
3164	1l.75 blue-green	1·90	20
3160/3164 *Set of 5*		4·75	60

Designs: Vert—55b. Cabin on Lake Bilea; 1l. Poiana Brasov ski-lift; 1l.75, Alpine Hotel. Horiz—1l.35, Lake Bicaz.

(Des S. Zarimba. Litho (1l.55). Des M. Giurca and S. Zarimba. Photo (others))

1964 (28 July). Balkan Games. T **564** and similar vert designs. Multicoloured. P 12×12½ (1l.55) or 13½ (others).

3165	30b. Type **564**	30	10
3166	40b. Throwing the javelin	30	10
3167	55b. Running	60	10
3168	1l. Throwing the discus	1·20	15
3169	1l.20 Hurdling	1·20	15
3170	1l.55 Flags of competing countries (24×44 mm)	1·40	20
3165/3170 *Set of 6*		4·50	70

565 Arms and Flag

(Des I. Ursa. Photo)

1964 (23 Aug). 20th Anniv of Liberation. T **565** and similar designs. Multicoloured. P 13½.

3171	55b. Type **565**	40	10
3172	60b. Industrial plant	50	15
3173	75b. Harvest scene	60	20
3174	1l.20 Apartment houses	1·10	30
3171/3174 *Set of 4*		2·30	70
MS3175 131×94 mm. 2l. "Agriculture and Industry". Imperf. No gum		4·25	2·75

Nos. 3172/4 are horizontal designs.

566 High Jumping

(Des D. Stiubei and I. Ruso. Litho)

1964 (1 Sept). Olympic Games, Tokyo. T **566** and similar designs. Multicoloured.

(a) P 13½

3176	20b. Type **566**	30	10
3177	30b. Wrestling	50	10
3178	35b. Volleyball	60	15
3179	40b. Canoeing	70	20
3180	55b. Fencing	95	20
3181	1l.20 Gymnastics	1·10	30
3182	1l.35 Football	1·50	45
3183	1l.55 Rifle-shooting	1·90	55
3176/3183 *Set of 8*		6·75	1·80

(b) Imperf. Colours changed and new values

3184	20b. Type **566**	40	10
3185	30b. Wrestling	50	10
3186	35b. Volleyball	80	15
3187	40b. Canoeing	85	20
3188	55b. Fencing	1·70	55
3189	1l.60 Gymnastics	3·50	1·50
3190	2l. Football	3·75	1·90
3191	2l.40 Rifle-shooting	4·50	2·75
3184/3191 *Set of 8*		14·50	6·50
MS3192 80×110 mm. 3l.25, Runner (no gum)		11·50	7·00

567 George Enescu

568 Python

(Des and eng I. Dumitrana. Recess)

1964 (5 Sept). Third International George Enescu Festival. T **567** and similar vert designs. P 13×13½.

3193	10b. deep bluish green	20	10
3194	55b. deep maroon	60	20
3195	1l.60 brown-purple	1·60	65
3196	1l.75 deep blue	2·10	45
3193/3196 *Set of 4*		4·00	1·30

Portraits of Enescu:—55b. At piano; 1l.60, Medallion; 1l.75, When an old man.

(Des I. Untch. Litho)

1964 (28 Sept). Bucharest Zoo. T **568** and similar horiz designs. Multicoloured. P 14×13.

3197	5b. Type **568**	10	10
3198	10b. Black swans	40	10
3199	35b. Ostriches	50	10
3200	40b. Crowned cranes	70	20
3201	55b. Tigers	80	20
3202	1l. Lions	1·40	20
3203	1l.55 Grevy's zebras	2·10	20
3204	2l. Bactrian camels	3·00	45
3197/3204 *Set of 8*		8·00	1·40

569 Brincoveanu, Cantacuzino, Lazar and Academy

570 Soldier

(Des I. Untch (55b.), I. Dumitrana (others). Photo)

1964 (14 Oct). Anniversaries. T **569** and similar designs. Multicoloured. P 13½.

3205	20b. Type **569**	10	10
3206	40b. Cuza and seal	20	10
3207	55b. Emblems of the Arts	30	15
3208	75b. Laboratory workers and class	50	20
3209	1l. Savings Bank building	80	45
3205/3209 *Set of 5*		1·70	90

Events, etc.: Horiz—20b. 270th Anniv of Domneasca Academy; 40b., 75b. Bucharest University Centenary; 1l. Savings Bank Centenary. Vert—55b. "Fine Arts" Centenary (emblems are masks, curtains, piano keyboard, harp, palette and brushes).

1964 (25 Oct). Army Day. Litho. P 12×12½.

3210	**570**	55b. ultramarine and light blue	80	45

571 Post Offices of 19th and 20th Centuries

(Des and eng I. Dumitrana. Recess)

1964 (15 Nov). AIR. Stamp Day. P 13½.

3211	**571**	1l.60 +40b. blue, brn-red and yell	1·90	95

572 Canoeing Medal (1956)

573 Strawberries

(Des I. Ursa. Photo, 10l. typo and embossed)

1964 (30 Nov). Olympic Games—Romanian Gold Medal Awards. T **572** and similar designs. Medals in brown and bistre-yellow, Nos. 3218/19, 3226/7, sepia and gold.

(a) P 13½

3212	20b. rose-red and blue	50	10
3213	30b. yellow-green and blue	60	15
3214	35b. turquoise and blue	70	20
3215	40b. lilac and blue	95	25
3216	55b. orange and blue	1·20	30
3217	1l.20 olive-green and blue	1·50	35
3218	1l.35 yellow-brown and blue	1·90	45
3219	1l.55 mauve and blue	2·40	45
3212/3219 *Set of 8*		8·75	2·00

(b) Imperf. Colours changed and new values

3220	20b. orange and blue	20	20
3221	30b. turquoise and blue	50	35
3222	35b. yellow-green and blue	50	35
3223	40b. olive-green and blue	80	55
3224	55b. rose-red and blue	80	55
3225	1l.60 lilac and blue	2·40	1·90
3226	2l. mauve and blue	3·00	2·40
3227	2l.40 yellow-brown and blue	4·00	3·25
3220/3227 *Set of 8*		11·00	8·50
MS3228 140×110 mm. 10l. gold, pale blue and deep blue (no gum)		14·50	11·00

Medals: As T **572**—30b. Boxing (1956); 35b. Pistol-shooting (1956); 40b. High jumping (1960); 55b. Wrestling (1960); 1l.20, 1l.60, Rifle-shooting (1960); 1l.35, 2l. High jumping (1964), 1l.55, 2l.40, Throwing the javelin (1964). Horiz—10l. Tokyo gold medal and world map.

(Des Aida Tasgian-Constantinescu. Litho)

1964 (20 Dec). Forest Fruits. T **573** and similar vert designs. Multicoloured. P 13½×14.

3229	5b. Type **573**	20	10
3230	35b. Blackberries	30	10
3231	40b. Raspberries	50	15
3232	55b. Rosehips	60	15
3233	1l.20 Blueberries	1·20	20
3234	1l.35 Cornelian cherries	1·50	20
3235	1l.55 Hazel nuts	1·60	20
3236	2l.55 Cherries	2·10	30
3229/3236 *Set of 8*		7·25	1·30

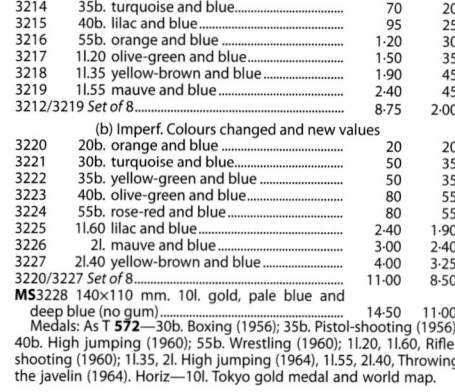

574 "Syncom 3"

575 U.N. Headquarters, New York

(Des M. Giurca. Litho)

1965 (5 Jan). Space Navigation. T **574** and similar designs. Multicoloured. P 13½ (5l.), 13×14½ (30b., 40b.) or 14½×13 (others).

3237	30b. Type **574**	30	10
3238	40b. "Syncom 3" (different)	50	10
3239	55b. "Ranger 7" (horiz)	80	15
3240	1l. "Ranger 7" (different) (horiz)	95	20
3241	1l.20 "Voskhod 1" (horiz)	1·50	20
3242	5l. Konstantin Feoktistov, Vladimir Komarov and Boris Yegorov (cosmonauts) and "Voskhod 1" (52×29 mm)	3·50	1·20
3237/3242 *Set of 6*		6·75	1·80

(Des D. Galin (55b.), C. Grigoriu (1l.60). Litho)

1965 (25 Jan). 20th Anniv of United Nations Organization. T **575** and similar vert design. P 12×12½.

3243	55b. gold, blue and red	70	20
3244	1l.60 gold, blue, yellow and red	1·20	45

Design:—1l.60, Arms and U.N. emblem on Romanian flag.

576 Spur-thighed Tortoise (*Testudo graeca*)

(Des Aida Tasgian-Constantinescu. Litho)

1965 (25 Feb). Reptiles. T **576** and similar diamond-shaped designs. Multicoloured. P 13½.

3245	5b. Type **576**	15	10
3246	10b. Crimean lizard (*Lacerta taurica*)	20	10
3247	20b. Three-lined lizard (*Lacerta trilineata*)	20	10
3248	40b. Snake-eyed skink (*Ablepharus kitaibelii*)	40	10
3249	55b. Slow worm (*Anguis fragilis*)	50	10
3250	60b. Sand viper (*Vipera ammodytes*)	70	10
3251	1l. Arguta (*Eremias arguta*)	85	20
3252	1l.20 Orsini's viper (*Vipera ursinii*)	95	20
3253	1l.35 European whip snake (*Coluber jugularis*)	1·50	20
3254	3l.25 Four-lined rat snake (*Elaphe quatuorlineata*)	3·00	45
3245/3254 *Set of 10*		7·50	1·50

577 Tabby Cat

(Des I. Dumitrana. Litho)

1965 (20 Mar). Domestic Cats. T **577** and similar designs. Multicoloured. P 13½.

3255	5b. Type **577**	20	10
3256	10b. Ginger tomcat	30	10
3257	40b. White Persians	50	20
3258	55b. Kittens with shoe	70	10
3259	60b. Kitten with ball of wool	1·10	10
3260	75b. Cat and two kittens	1·50	15
3261	1l.35 Siamese	1·90	30
3262	3l.25 Heads of three cats	3·50	95
3255/3262	*Set of* 8	8·75	1·80

The 40b. to 1l.35 are vertical designs and the 3l.25 is larger (62×29 mm).

RANGER 9
24-3-1965

5 Lei

(**578**)

1965 (25 Apr). Space Flight of "Ranger 9" (24.3.65). No. 3240 surch with T **578** in blue.

3263	5l. on 1l. multicoloured	29·00	29·00

579 Ion Bianu (philologist)

580 I.T.U. Emblem and Symbols

(Des S. Zainea. Photo)

1965 (10 May). Cultural Anniversaries. T **579** and similar vert portraits. Portraits in blackish sepia. P 13½.

3264	40b. blue	40	10
3265	55b. yellow-ochre	40	10
3266	60b. reddish purple	50	10
3267	1l. brown-red	70	15
3268	1l.35 yellow-olive	95	20
3269	1l.75 orange-red	1·60	45
3264/3269	*Set of* 6	4·00	1·00

Portraits:—40b. Type **579** (30th death anniv); 55b. Anton Bacalbasa (writer, birth centenary); 60b. Vasile Conta (philosopher, 120th birth anniv); 1l. Jean Sibelius (composer, birth centenary); 1l.35, Horace (Roman poet, birth bimillenary); 1l.75, Dante Alighieri (poet, 700th birth anniv).

(Des Aida Tasgian-Constantinescu. Eng I. Dumitrana. Recess)

1965 (15 May). Centenary of International Telecommunications Union. P 13½.

3270	**580**	1l.75 blue	1·60	45

581 Derdap Gorge (The Iron Gate)

582 Rifleman

(Des B. Lazarević, E. Palade (No. **MS**3273). Litho)

1965 (20 May). Inauguration of Derdap Hydro-Electric Project. T **581** and similar horiz designs. P 12½×12.

3271	30b. (25d.) deep green and light grey	30	20
3272	55b. (50d.) lake-red and light grey	50	30

MS3273 103×80 mm. 80b., 1l.20, 100d., 150d. mult (p 13) (sold at 4l. or 500d.) 4·75 4·75

Designs:—55b. Derdap Dam; No. **MS**3273, Arms of Romania and Yugoslavia on alternate stamps with outline of dam superimposed over the four stamps.

Nos. 3271/2 and the miniature sheet were issued simultaneously in Yugoslavia. They are inscribed with both currencies; No. **MS**3273 comprises two Romanian and two Yugoslavian stamps.

(Des A. Dascalescu. Litho)

1965 (30 May). European Shooting Championships, Bucharest. T **582** and similar designs. Multicoloured.

(a) P 12×12½ (20b.), 13½ (2l.) or 12½×12 (others)

3274	20b. Type **582**	20	10
3275	40b. Prone rifleman	30	15
3276	55b. Pistol-shooting	50	10
3277	1l. "Free" pistol-shooting	95	20
3278	1l.60 Standing rifleman	1·50	20
3279	2l. Various marksmen	1·90	65
3274/3279	*Set of* 6	4·75	1·30

(b) Imperf. Colours changed and new values

3280	40b. Prone rifleman	20	10
3281	55b. Pistol-shooting	30	20
3282	1l. "Free" pistol-shooting	70	30
3283	1l.60 Standing rifleman	1·10	45
3284	3l.25 Type **582**	1·90	95
3285	5l. Various marksmen	3·50	1·60
3280/3285	*Set of* 6	7·00	3·25

Apart from T **582** the designs are horizontal, the 2l. and 5l. being larger (51½×28½ mm).

583 "Fat-Frumos and the Beast"

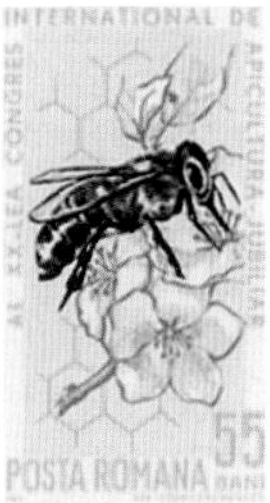

584 Honey Bee on Flowers

(Des S. Zarimba. Photo)

1965 (25 June). Romanian Fairy Tales. T **583** and similar designs. Multicoloured. P 13½.

3286	20b. Type **583**	40	10
3287	40b. "Fat-Frumos and Ileana Cosinzeana"	40	10
3288	55b. "Harap Alb" (horseman and bear)	50	10
3289	1l. "The Moralist Wolf"	95	10
3290	1l.35 "The Ox and the Calf"	1·50	20
3291	2l. "The Bear and the Wolf" (drawing a sledge)	1·90	35
3286/3291	*Set of* 6	5·00	85

(Des Aida Tasgian-Constantinescu. Litho)

1965 (28 July). 20th International Bee-keeping Association Federation ("Apimondia") Congress, Bucharest. T **584** and similar design. P 12×12½ (55b.) or 12½×12 (1l.60).

3292	55b. black, rose-red and yellow	70	20
3293	1l.60 black, light green, buff and new blue	1·70	30

Design: Horiz—1l.60, Congress Hall.

585 Pavel Belyaev, Aleksei Leonov, "Voskhod 2" and Leonov in Space

586 Marx and Lenin

(Des S. Zarimba (1l.75, 3l.20), I. Druga (2l.40), I. Druga and G. Bozianu (others). Litho)

1965 (25 Aug–25 Dec). Space Achievements. T **585** and similar designs. Multicoloured. P 12½×12 (10b., 5l.) or 12×12½ (others).

3294	5b. "Proton 1" (25.12)	30	15
3295	10b. "Sonda 3" (horiz) (25.12)	40	30
3296	15b. "Molnia 1" (25.12)	50	35
3297	1l.75 Type **585**	1·60	20
3298	2l.40 "Early Bird" satellite	2·40	30
3299	3l.20 "Gemini 3" and astronauts in capsule	4·00	45
3300	3l.25 "Mariner 4" (25.12)	4·25	65
3301	5l. "Gemini 5" (horiz) (25.12)	4·75	1·90
3294/3301	*Set of* 8	16·00	3·75

1965 (6 Sept). Socialist Countries' Postal Ministers' Congress, Peking. Photo. P 13½.

3302	**586**	55b. multicoloured	95	45

587 Common Quail (*Coturnix*)

588 V. Alecsandri

(Des F. Ivanus. Photo)

1965 (10 Sept). Migratory Birds. T **587** and similar designs. Multicoloured. P 13½.

3303	5b. Type **587**	20	10
3304	10b. Woodcock (*Scolopax rusticola*)	30	10
3305	20b. Common snipe (*Capella gallinago*)	40	10
3306	40b. Turtle dove (*Streptopelia turtur*)	50	10
3307	55b. Mallard (*Anas platyrhinchos*)	60	10
3308	60b. White-fronted goose (*Anser albifrons*)	70	15
3309	1l. Common crane (*Grus grus*)	95	20
3310	1l.20 Glossy ibis (*Plegadis falcinellus*)	1·20	20
3311	1l.35 Mute swan (*Cygnus olor*)	1·50	30
3312	3l.25 Eastern white pelican (*Pelecanus onocrotalus*) (32×73 mm)	3·00	95
3303/3312	*Set of* 10	8·50	2·10

(Des I. Druga and G. Bozianu. Photo)

1965 (9 Oct). 75th Death Anniv of Vasile Alecsandri (poet). P 13½.

3313	**588**	55b. multicoloured	95	45

589 Zanzibar Water-lily (*Nymphaea zanzibariensis*)

590 Running

(Des Aida Tasgian-Constantinescu. Litho)

1965 (25 Oct). Cluj Botanical Gardens. T **589** and similar designs. Multicoloured. P 12×12½ (vert), 12½×12 (horiz) or 13½ (2l.30).

3314	5b. Bird-of-paradise flower (*Strelitzia reginae*) (vert)	15	10
3315	10b. *Stanhopea tigrina* (orchid) (vert)	20	10
3316	20b. *Paphiopedilum insigne* (orchid) (vert)	25	10
3317	30b. Type **589**	30	10
3318	40b. *Ferocactus glaucescens* (cactus)	50	10
3319	55b. Tree-cotton (*Gossypium arboreum*)	70	15
3320	1l. *Hibiscus rosa sinensis*	95	20
3321	1l.35 *Gloxinia hibrida* (vert)	1·50	20
3322	1l.75 Amazon water-lily (*Victoria amazonica*)	2·40	25
3323	2l.30 *Hibiscus*, water-lily, bird-of-paradise flower and botanical building (52×30 mm)	3·00	65
3314/3323	*Set of* 10	9·00	1·80

(Des E. Palade (55b., 2l.), E. Palade and F. Ivanus (others). Litho)

1965 (10 Nov). Spartacist Games. T **590** and similar designs. Multicoloured. P 13½.

3324	55b. Type **590**	50	20
3325	1l.55 Football	1·20	30
3326	1l.75 Diving	1·40	35
3327	2l. Mountaineering (inscr "TURISM")	1·50	45
3328	5l. Canoeing (inscr "CAMPIONATELE EUROPENE 1965") (horiz)	2·50	95
3324/3328	*Set of* 5	6·50	2·00

591 Pigeon and Horseman

592 Pigeon on TV Aerial

(Des I. Dumitrana. Recess)

1965 (15 Nov). Stamp Day. T **591**, **592** and similar horiz design. P 13½.

3329	**591**	55b. +45b. blue and magenta	70	10
3330	**592**	1l. chocolate and blue-green	80	30
3331	–	1l.75 chocolate and yellow-green (Pigeon in flight)	1·90	45
3329/3331		*Set of* 3	3·00	75

593 Chamois

(Des F. Ivanus. Photo)

1965 (10 Dec). Hunting Trophies. T **593** and similar horiz designs. P 13½.

3332	55b. brown, pale yellow and mauve	50	10
3333	1l. red-brown, light emerald and red	95	20
3334	1l.60 brown, cobalt and orange	1·60	30
3335	1l.75 blackish brown, red and emerald	1·90	35
3336	3l.20 sepia, gold, orange and light sage-green	2·40	85
3332/3336	*Set of* 5	6·50	1·60

Designs: As T **593**—1l. Brown bear; 1l.60, Red deer stag; 1l.75, Wild boar. 49×37½ mm—3l.20, Trophy and antlers of red deer.

594 Dachshund

595 Pawn and Globe

(Des I. Dumitrana. Photo)

1965 (28 Dec). Hunting Dogs. T **594** and similar designs. Multicoloured. P 13½.

3337	5b. Type **594**	10	10
3338	10b. Spaniel	20	10
3339	40b. Retriever with woodcock	40	10
3340	55b. Fox terrier	60	10
3341	60b. Red setter	95	20
3342	75b. White setter	1·50	20
3343	1l.55 Pointers	2·40	45
3344	3l.25 Duck-shooting with retriever	3·50	1·60
3337/3344	*Set of* 8	8·75	2·50

Sizes: Diamond (47½×47½ mm)—10b. to 75b.; Horiz (43½×29 mm)—1l.55, 3l.25.

(Des A. Dascalescu. Litho)

1966 (25 Feb). World Chess Championships, Cuba. T **595** and similar designs. Multicoloured. P 13½.

3345	20b. Type **595**	50	10
3346	40b. Jester and bishop	60	10
3347	55b. Knight and rook	85	15
3348	1l. Knight and rook	1·50	20
3349	1l.60 Type **595**	2·40	30
3350	3l.25 Jester and bishop	4·00	1·90
3345/3350	*Set of* 6	8·75	2·50

596 Tractor, Corn and Sun

597 G. Gheorghiu-Dej

(Des S. Zarimba. Litho)

1966 (5 Mar). Co-operative Farming Union Congress. P 13½.

3351	**596**	55b. green and orange-yellow	70	45

(Des I. Druga. Photo)

1966 (15 Mar). First Death Anniv of Gheorghe Gheorghiu-Dej (President 1961–65). P 13½.

3352	**597**	55b. black and gold	70	45

MS3353 90×100 mm. 5l. Portrait as in Type **597**. Imperf. No gum ... 5·75 5·75

598 Congress Emblem

(Des I. Dumitrana. Litho)

1966 (21 Mar). Communist Youth Union Congress. P 13×14½.

3354	**598**	55b. red and yellow	70	45

599 Dance of Moldova

(Des S. Zainea. Recess)

1966 (5 Apr). Romanian Folk-dancing. T **599** and similar horiz designs. P 13½.

3355	30b. black and purple	50	10
3356	40b. black and orange-red	70	35
3357	55b. black and turquoise-green	95	10
3358	1l. black and lake-brown	1·30	10
3359	1l.60 black and blue	1·90	30
3360	2l. black and yellow-green	4·25	2·30
3355/3360	*Set of* 6	8·75	3·00

Dances of:—40b. Oltenia; 55b. Maramures; 1l. Muntenia; 1l.60, Banat; 2l. Transylvania.

600 Footballers

601 "Agriculture and Industry"

(Des A. Alexe. Litho)

1966 (25 Apr–June). World Cup Football Championship, England. T **600** and similar vert designs. P 13½×13.

3361	5b. multicoloured	30	10
3362	10b. multicoloured	40	10
3363	15b. multicoloured	60	15
3364	55b. multicoloured	1·10	20
3365	1l.75 multicoloured	2·50	45
3366	4l. multicoloured	4·50	4·50
3361/3366	*Set of* 6	8·50	5·00

MS3367 85×100 mm. 10l. gold, black and blue. Imperf (20.6) ... 11·50 11·50

Designs: As T **600**—10b. to 1l.75, Various footballing scenes; 4l. Jules Rimet Cup. 33×46 mm—10l. As No. 3366.

(Des A. Popescu. Photo)

1966 (14 May). Trade Union Congress, Bucharest. P 13½.

3368	**601**	55b. red, blue, yellow and grey	70	45

602 Red-breasted Flycatcher (*Muscicapa parva*)

603 "Venus 3"

(Des I. Druga and G. Bozianu. Photo)

1966 (30 May). Song Birds. T **602** and similar vert designs. Multicoloured. P 13½.

3369	5b. Type **602**	30	10
3370	10b. Red crossbill (*Loxia curvirostra*)	50	10
3371	15b. Great reed warbler (*Acrocephalus arundinaceus*)	70	10
3372	20b. Redstart (*Phoenicurus phoenicurus*)	80	15
3373	55b. European robin (*Erithacus rubecula*)	1·30	15
3374	1l.20 Bluethroat (*Luscinia svecica*)	1·60	20
3375	1l.55 Yellow wagtail (*Motacilla flava*)	2·40	35
3376	3l. Penduline tit (*Remiz pendulinus*)	4·25	2·75
3369/3376	*Set of* 8	10·50	3·50

(Des I. Druga and G. Bozianu. Photo)

1966 (25 June). Space Achievements. T **603** and similar vert designs. Multicoloured. P 13½.

3377	10b. Type **603**	50	10
3378	20b. "FR 1" satellite	60	20
3379	1l.60 "Luna 9"	3·50	30
3380	5l. "Gemini 6" and "Gemini 7"	5·75	2·30
3377/3380	*Set of* 4	9·25	2·50

604 Urechia Nestor (historian)

606 *Hottonia palustris*

605 "House" (after Petrascu)

(Des V. Stoianov. Photo)

1966 (28 June–12 Sept). Cultural Anniversaries. T **604** and similar vert designs. P 13½.

3381	5b. ultramarine, blk and yell-grn (12.9)	10	10
3382	10b. myrtle-green, black and crim (12.9)	10	10
3383	20b. purple, black and bluish green	10	10
3384	40b. brown, black and violet-blue	30	10
3385	55b. deep bluish grn, blk and orge-brn	40	10
3386	1l. bluish violet, black and yellow-brn	85	20
3387	1l.35 blackish olive, black and new blue	1·20	30
3388	1l.60 slate-purple, black and emer-grn	1·90	55
3389	1l.75 slate-pur, blk and yell-orge (12.9)	1·20	30
3390	3l.25 lake, black and grnish blue (12.9)	1·90	55
3381/3390	*Set of* 10	7·25	2·20

Portraits:—5b. George Cosbuc (poet, birth centenary); 10b. Gheorghe Sincai (historian, 150th death anniv); 20b. Type **604** (birth centenary); 40b. Aron Pumnul (linguist, death centenary); 55b. Stefan Luchian (painter, 50th death anniv); 1l. Sun Yat-sen (Chinese statesman, birth centenary); 1l.35, Gottfried Leibniz (philosopher, 250th death anniv); 1l.60, Romain Rolland (writer, birth centenary); 1l.75, Ion Ghica (revolutionary and diplomat, 150th birth anniv); 3l.25, Constantin Cantacuzino (historian, 250th death anniv).

(Des I. Druga and G. Bozianu. Photo)

1966 (25 July). Paintings in National Gallery, Bucharest. T **605** and similar designs. Multicoloured. P 13½.

3391	5b. Type **605**	15	15
3392	10b. "Peasant Girl" (Grigorescu)	20	15
3393	20b. "Midday Rest" (Rescu)	50	20
3394	55b. "Portrait of a Man" (Van Eyck)	1·20	30
3395	1l.55 "The 2nd Class Compartment" (Daumier)	4·75	55
3396	3l.25 "The Blessing" (El Greco)	6·75	6·00
3391/3396	*Set of* 6	12·00	6·50

The 10b., 55b. and 3l.25 are vertical designs.

(Des F. Ivanus. Litho)

1966 (25 Aug). Aquatic Flora. T **606** and similar vert designs. Multicoloured. P 13½ (3l.25) or 13½×13 (others).

3397	5b. Type **606**	20	10
3398	10b. *Ceratophyllum submersum*	30	10
3399	20b. *Aldrovanda vesiculosa*	40	10
3400	40b. *Callitriche verna*	60	10
3401	55b. *Vallisneria spiralis*	70	15
3402	1l. *Elodea canadensis*	1·50	20
3403	1l.55 *Hippuris vulgaris*	2·10	35
3404	3l.25 *Myriophyllum spicatum* (28×49½ mm)	4·00	2·30
3397/3404	*Set of* 8	8·75	3·00

607 Diagram showing one metre in relation to quadrant of Earth

608 Putna Monastery

(Des V. Stoianov. Photo)

1966 (10 Sept). Centenary of Metric System in Romania. T **607** and similar horiz design. P 13½.

3405	55b. ultramarine and orange-brown	50	10
3406	1l. violet and dull green	80	35

Design:—1l. Metric abbreviations and globe.

(Des I. Dumitrana. Photo)

1966 (15 Sept). 500th Anniv of Putna Monastery. P 13½.

3407	**608**	2l. multicoloured	1·60	55

609 "Medicine"

610 Crayfish (*Astacus astacus*)

(Des S. Zarimba (40b., 55b.), Aida Tasgian-Constantinescu (1l.), I. Dumitrana (3l.). Photo)

1966 (30 Sept). Centenary of Romanian Academy. T **609** and similar designs. P 12½.

3408	40b. black, gold, blue and pale lilac	20	10
3409	55b. red, bistre-brown, gold & grey	30	15
3410	1l. brown, gold and bright blue	60	20
3411	3l. brown, gold and yellow	2·10	1·40
3408/3411	*Set of* 4	3·00	1·70

Designs. As T **609**—55b. "Science" (formula). 22½×33½ mm—1l. Gold medal. 67×27 mm—3l. Ion Radulescu (writer), Mihail Kogalniceanu (historian) and Traian Savulescu (biologist).

(Des Aida Tasgian-Constantinescu. Photo)

1966 (15 Oct). Crustaceans and Molluscs. T **610** and similar designs. Multicoloured. P 13½.

3412	5b. Type **610**	20	10
3413	10b. Netted nassa (*Nassa reticulata*)	30	10
3414	20b. Marbled rock crab (*Pachigrapsus marmoratus*)	40	10
3415	40b. *Campylaea trizona* (snail)	50	15
3416	55b. Lucorum helix (*Helix lucorum*)	70	20
3417	1l.35 Mediterranean blue mussel (*Mytilus galloprovincialis*)	1·70	30
3418	1l.75 Stagnant pond snail (*Lymnaea stagnalis*)	2·10	35
3419	3l.25 Swan mussel (*Anodonta cygnaea*)	3·50	2·30
3412/3419	*Set of* 8	8·50	3·25

611 Bucharest and Mail-coach

(Des G. Galin. Eng I. Dumitrana. Recess)

1966 (20 Oct). Stamp Day. P 13½.

3420	**611**	55b. +45b. purple, orange-yellow, green and blue	1·50	75

612 *Ursus spelaeus*

613 "Sputnik 1" orbiting Globe

(Des V. Stoianov. Photo)

1966 (25 Nov). Prehistoric Animals. T **612** and similar horiz designs. P 13½.

3421	5b. ultramarine, red-brn & bl-grn	30	10
3422	10b. violet, bistre-brown & yell-grn	40	10
3423	15b. olive-brn, pur-brn & light grn	50	15
3424	55b. reddish vio, bis-brn & yell-grn	95	20
3425	1l.55 bright bl, yell-brn & light grn	2·50	30
3426	4l. deep magenta, bis-brn & grn	4·75	2·30
3421/3426	*Set of* 6	8·50	2·75

Animals:—10b. *Mamuthus trogontherii*; 15b. *Bison priscus*; 55b. *Archidiscodon*; 1l.55, *Megaceros eurycerus*. (43×27 mm)—4l. *Deinotherium gigantissimum*.

(Des I. Druga and G. Bozianu. Photo)

1967 (15 Feb). Ten Years of Space Achievements. T **613** and similar designs but vert. Multicoloured. P 13½.

(a) POSTAGE

3427	10b. Type **613**	20	10
3428	20b. Yuri Gagarin and "Vostok 1"	30	10
3429	25b. Valentina Tereshkova ("Vostok 6")	40	10
3430	40b. Andrian Nikolaev and Pavel Popovich ("Vostok 3" and "Vostok 4")	60	10
3431	55b. Aleksei Leonov in space ("Voskhod 2")	85	15

(b) AIR. Inscr "POSTA AERIANA"

3432	1l.20 "Early Bird"	1·20	30
3433	1l.55 Photo transmission ("Mariner 4")	1·50	30
3434	3l.25 Space rendezvous ("Gemini 6" and "Gemini 7")	1·90	75
3435	5l. Space link-up ("Gemini 8")	3·00	2·75
3427/3435	*Set of* 9	9·00	4·25

D **614**

1967 (25 Feb). POSTAGE DUE. Photo. W **254**. P 13½.

			Un pair	*Us pair*
D3436	D **614**	3b. emerald	20	10
D3437		5b. new blue	20	10
D3438		10b. magenta	20	10
D3439		20b. rosine	20	10
D3440		40b. brown	70	30
D3441		1l. violet	2·40	45
D3436/3441		*Set of* 6 *pairs*	3·50	1·00

See also Nos. D3708/13 for this design without watermark.

Postage stamps handstamped "T" in a circle were used at P.O.s when stocks of Postage Due stamps ran short.

614 Barn Owl (*Tyco alba*)

(Des F. Ivanus. Photo)

1967 (20 Mar). Birds of Prey. T **614** and similar multicoloured designs. P 13½.

3442	10b. Type **614**	50	10
3443	20b. Eagle owl (*Bubo bubo*)	60	10
3444	40b. Saker falcon (*Falco cherrug*)	60	10
3445	55b. Egyptian vulture (*Neophron percnopterus*)	70	10
3446	75b. Osprey (*Pandion haliaetus*)	80	20
3447	1l. Griffon vulture (*Gyps fulvus*)	1·60	20
3448	1l.20 Lammergeier (*Gypaetus barbatus*)	1·90	45
3449	1l.75 European black vulture (*Aegypius monachus*)	2·40	1·90
3442/3449	*Set of* 8	8·25	2·75

615 "Washerwomen" (after I. Steriadi)

(Des I. Druga and G. Bozianu. Photo)

1967 (30 Mar). Paintings. T **615** and similar designs. P 13½.

3450	10b. blue, gold and red	20	10
3451	20b. deep green, gold and ochre	30	20
3452	40b. rose-red, gold and light blue	60	20
3453	1l.55 purple, gold and new blue	1·20	45
3454	3l.20 brown, gold and emerald	3·00	65
3455	5l. olive-brown, gold and orange	4·25	3·00
3450/3455	*Set of* 6	8·50	4·25

Paintings: Vert—10b. "Model in Fancy Dress" (I. Andreescu); 40b. "Peasants Weaving" (S. Dimitrescu); 1l.55, "Venus and Cupid" (L. Cranach); 5l. "Haman beseeching Esther" (Rembrandt). Horiz—3l.20, "Hercules and the Lion" (Rubens).

616 Woman's Head

(Des E. Palade. Photo)

1967 (27 Apr). Tenth Death Anniv of C. Brancusi (sculptor). T **616** and similar designs showing sculptures. P 13½.

3456	5b. blackish brown, ochre-yell & red	10	10
3457	10b. blk, light bl-grn & reddish vio	20	10
3458	20b. black, light blue-green and red	25	10
3459	40b. black, red and emerald	30	20
3460	55b. black, light yellow-olive and blue	70	30
3461	1l.20 ol-brn, lt bluish vio & yell-orge	1·60	35
3462	3l.25 black, green and magenta	3·00	1·40
3456/3462	*Set of* 7	5·50	2·30

Designs: Horiz—10b. Sleeping muse; 40b. "The Kiss"; 3l.25, Gate of Kisses, Targujiu. Vert—20b. "The Endless Column"; 55b. Seated woman; 1l.20, "Miss Pogany".

617 Copper and Silver Coins of 1867

(Des Aida Tasgian-Constantinescu. Photo)

1967 (4 May). Centenary of Romanian Monetary System. T **617** and similar horiz design. P 13½.

3463	55b. multicoloured	50	45
3464	1l.20 multicoloured	1·10	1·00

Design:—1l.20, Obverse and reverse of modern silver coin (1966).

618 "Infantryman" (Nicolae Grigorescu)

619 Peasants attacking (after Octav Bancila)

(Des I. Dumitrana. Photo)

1967 (9 May). 90th Anniv of Independence. P 13½.

3465	618	55b. multicoloured	1·60	1·60

(Des I. Dumitrana. Photo)

1967 (20 May). 60th Anniv of Peasant Rising. T **619** and similar design. P 13½.

3466	40b. multicoloured	70	65
3467	1l.55 multicoloured	1·60	1·60

Design: Horiz—1l.55, Peasants marching (after S. Luchian).

620 *Centaurea pinnatifida*

621 Towers, Sibiu

622 Map and I.T.Y. Emblem (Illustration reduced. Actual size 100×89 mm)

(Des Aida Tasgian-Constantinescu. Photo)

1967 (10 June). Carpathian Flora. T **620** and similar designs. Multicoloured. P 13½.

3468	20b. Type **620**	20	20
3469	40b. *Erysimum transsilvanicum*	30	20
3470	55b. *Aquilegia transsilvanica*	50	20
3471	1l.20 Alpine violet (*Viola alpina*)	1·50	10
3472	1l.75 Bellflower (*Campanula carpatica*)	1·70	20
3473	4l. Mountain avens (*Dryas octopetala*) (horiz)	4·00	2·30
3468/3473	*Set of* 6	7·50	3·00

(Des V. Stoianov. Photo)

1967 (29 June). Historic Monuments and International Tourist Year. T **621** and similar designs and T **622**. P 13½.

3474	20b. Type **621**	50	20
3475	40b. Castle at Cris	70	20
3476	55b. Wooden church, Plopis	95	20
3477	1l.60 Ruins, Neamtului	1·60	30
3478	1l.75 Mogosoaia Palace, Bucharest	1·90	35
3479	2l.25 Church, Voronet (48½×36 mm)	3·00	1·90
3474/3479	*Set of* 6	7·75	2·75
MS3480	101×89 mm. **622** 5l. blue, black and light greenish blue. Imperf	4·75	4·75

623 "Battle of Marasesti" (E. Stoica)

624 Dinu Lipatti (composer and pianist)

(Des I. Dumitrana. Photo)

1967 (24 July). 50th Anniv of Battles of Marasesti, Marasti and Oituz. P 13½.

3481	**623**	55b. bistre-brown, turquoise-blue and grey	95	65

(Des E. Palade. Photo)

1967 (29 July). Cultural Anniversaries. T **624** and similar horiz designs. P 13½.

3482	10b. reddish violet, bright blue and black	10	10
3483	20b. blue, light red-brown and black	15	10
3484	40b. chestnut, turquoise and black	20	10
3485	55b. deep olive-brown, rose and black	30	10
3486	1l.20 brown, yellow-olive and black	50	30
3487	1l.75 turquoise-green, blue and black	1·10	85
3482/3487	*Set of* 6	2·10	1·40

Designs:—10b. Type **624** (50th birth anniv); 20b. Alexandru Orascu (architect, 150th birth anniv); 40b. Grigore Antipa (biologist, birth centenary); 55b. Mihail Kogalniceanu (politician and historian, 150th birth anniv); 1l.20, Jonathan Swift (satirist, 300th birth anniv); 1l.75, Marie Curie (physicist, birth centenary).

625 Wrestling

626 Inscription on Globe

(Des I. Hasiganu. Photo)

1967 (29 July). World Wrestling Championships, Bucharest. T **625** and similar designs showing wrestlers and globes. P 13½.

3488	10b. multicoloured (T **625**)	10	10
3489	20b. multicoloured (horiz)	20	10
3490	55b. multicoloured	30	10
3491	1l.20 multicoloured	95	20
3492	2l. multicoloured (horiz)	1·60	1·00
3488/3492	*Set of* 5	2·75	1·40

(Des A. Popescu. Photo and litho)

1967 (28 Aug). International Linguists' Congress, Bucharest. P 13½.

3493	**626**	1l.60 ultramarine, crim & lt blue	1·50	45

627 Academy

(Des V. Stoianov. Litho)

1967 (25 Sept). Centenary of Book Academy, Bucharest. P 13½.

3494	**627**	55b. slate, orange-brown & blue	1·50	45

628 Dancing on Ice

629 Curtea de Arges Monastery

(Des A. Popescu. Photo)

1967 (28 Sept). Winter Olympic Games, Grenoble (1968). T **628** and similar vert designs. Multicoloured. P 13½.

3495	20b. Type **628**	10	10
3496	40b. Skiing	20	10
3497	55b. Bobsleighing	30	10
3498	1l. Downhill skiing	70	20
3499	1l.55 Ice hockey	95	30
3500	2l. Games emblem	1·50	45
3501	2l.30 Ski jumping	1·90	1·10
3495/3501	*Set of 7*	5·00	4·50
MS3502	80×100 mm. 5l. Bobsleighing. Imperf	6·25	6·00

(Des I. Dumitrana. Photo)

1967 (1 Nov). 450th Anniv of Curtea de Arges Monastery. P 13½.

3503	**629**	55b. multicoloured	95	45

630 Karl Marx and Title Page

631 Lenin

(Des V. Stoianov. Photo)

1967 (4 Nov). Centenary of Karl Marx's Das Kapital. P 13½.

3504	**630**	40b. black, yellow and crimson	70	45

(Des I. Druga and G. Bozianu. Photo)

1967 (4 Nov). 50th Anniv of October Revolution. P 13½.

3505	**631**	1l.20 black, gold and red	1·20	45

632 Arms of Romania

633 Telephone Dial and Map

(T **632** des I. Dumitrana; recess. Others des I. Druga; photo)

1967–69. P 13½.

(a) T **632**. (6.11.67)

3506	**632**	40b. ultramarine	50	10
3507		55b. yellow	70	20
3508		1l.60 rose-red	1·60	30

(b) T **633** and similar designs.

3509	5b. olive-green (6.2.68)	10	10
3510	10b. brown-red (6.2.68)	10	10
3511	20b. olive-grey (6.2.68)	10	10
3512	35b. indigo (6.2.68)	10	10
3513	40b. ultramarine (10.1.69)	20	10
3514	50b. orange (6.2.68)	20	10
3515	55b. rosine (10.1.69)	30	10
3516	60b. orange-brown (6.2.68)	30	10
3517	1l. bright green (20.1.68)	40	10
3518	1l.20 bright reddish violet (20.1.68)	50	10
3519	1l.35 new blue (6.2.68)	60	10
3520	1l.50 rose-red (20.1.68)	70	10
3521	1l.55 brown (20.1.68)	80	10
3522	1l.75 emerald (20.1.68)	85	10
3523	2l. olive-yellow (6.2.68)	95	10
3524	2l.40 deep blue (6.2.68)	1·10	10
3525	3l. greenish blue (20.12.67)	1·20	20
3526	3l.20 yellow-ochre (6.2.68)	1·40	20
3527	3l.25 ultramarine (6.2.68)	1·60	20
3528	4l. magenta (6.2.68)	1·60	20
3529	5l. violet (6.2.68)	1·90	20
3506/3529	*Set of 24*	16·00	3·00

Designs: 23×17 mm—5b. "Carpati" lorry; 20b. Railway Travelling Post Office coach; 35b. Zlin Z-226A Akrobat plane; 60b. Electric parcels truck. As T **633**—1l.20, Motorcoach; 1l.35, Mil Mi-4 helicopter; 1l.75, Lake-side highway; 2l. Postal van; 3l. Type **633**; 3l.20, Ilyushin Il-18 airliner; 4l. Electric train; 5l. Telex instrument and world map. 17×23 mm—10b. Posthorn and telephone emblem; 40b. Power pylons; 50b. Telephone handset; 55b. Dam. As T **633** but vert—1l. Diesel train; 1l.50, Trolley-bus; 1l.55, Radio station; 2l.40, T.V. relay station; 3l.25, Liner *Transylvania*.

No. 3525 also commemorates the 40th Anniv of the Automatic Telephone Service.

See also Nos. 3842/57.

634 "Crossing the River Buzau" (lithograph by Raffet) (Illustration reduced. Actual size 93×30 mm)

(Des and eng I. Dumitrana. Recess)

1967 (15 Nov). Stamp Day. P 13½.

3530	**634**	55b. +45b. indigo and yell-ochre	1·50	65

635 Monorail Train and Globe

636 Arms and Industrial Scene

(Des I. Druga and G. Bozianu. Photo)

1967 (28 Nov). World Fair, Montreal. T **635** and similar square designs. Multicoloured. P 13½.

3531	55b. Type **635**	20	10
3532	1l. Expo emblem within atomic symbol	50	10
3533	1l.60 Gold cup and world map	70	20
3534	2l. Expo emblem	1·30	75
3531/3534	*Set of 4*	2·40	1·00

(Des V. Stoianov. Photo)

1967 (26 Dec). 20th Anniv of Republic. T **636** and similar vert designs. Multicoloured. P 13½.

3535	40b. Type **636**	20	10
3536	55b. Arms of Romania	30	10
3537	1l.60 Romanian flag (34×48 mm)	95	30
3538	1l.75 Arms and cultural emblems	1·80	1·20
3535/3538	*Set of 4*	3·00	1·50

637 I.A.R. 817 Flying Ambulance

(Des P. Grant. Litho)

1968 (28 Feb). AIR. Romanian Aviation. T **637** and similar designs. P 12×12½ (vert) or 12½×12 (horiz).

3539	40b. multicoloured	20	10
3540	55b. multicoloured	30	10
3541	1l. multicoloured	50	10
3542	2l.40 multicoloured	1·60	65
3539/3542	*Set of 4*	2·30	85

Designs: Vert—40b. Antonov An-2 biplane spraying crops; 1l. "Aviasan" emblem and airliner; 2l.40, Mircea Zorileanu (pioneer aviator) and biplane.

638 "Angelica and Medor" (S. Ricci)

(Des I. Dumitrana. Photo)

1968 (28 Mar). Paintings in Romanian Galleries. T **638** and similar designs but vert. Multicoloured. P 13½.

3543	40b. "Young Woman" (Misu Pop)	50	20
3544	55b. "Little Girl in Red Scarf" (N. Grigorescu)	70	30
3545	1l. "Old Nicolas, the Cobza-player" (S. Luchian)	1·20	45
3546	1l.60 "Man with Skull" (Dierick Bouts)	1·50	45
3547	2l.40 Type **638**	1·90	65
3548	3l.20 "Ecce Homo" (Titian)	4·00	5·00
3543/3548	*Set of 6*	8·75	6·25
MS3549	75×90 mm. 5l. As 3l.20. Imperf	11·50	11·50

See also Nos. 3583/8, 3631/37, 3658/64, 3756/62.

639 "Anemones" (Luchian)

1968 (30 Mar). Birth Centenary of Stefan Luchian (painter). Sheet 90×100 mm. Litho. Imperf.

MS3550	**639**	10l. multicoloured	11·50	11·50

640 Human Rights Emblem

641 W.H.O. Emblem

(Des S. Zarimba. Photo)

1968 (9 May). Human Rights Year. P 13½.

3551	**640**	1l. multicoloured	1·20	45

(Des S. Zarimba. Photo)

1968 (14 May). 20th Anniv of World Health Organization. P 13½.

3552	**641**	1l.60 multicoloured	1·60	45

642 "The Hunter" (after N. Grigorescu)

(Des I. Dumitrana. Photo)

1968 (17 May). Hunting Congress, Mamaia. P 13½.

3553	**642**	1l.60 multicoloured	1·60	45

643 Pioneers and Liberation Monument

1968 (9 June). Young Pioneers. T **643** and similar horiz designs, showing pioneers. Multicoloured. Photo. P 13½.

3554	5b. Type **643**	20	10
3555	40b. Receiving scarves	25	10
3556	55b. With models	30	10
3557	1l. Operating radio sets	60	10
3558	1l.60 Folk-dancing	95	30
3559	2l.40 In camp	1·30	75
3554/3559	*Set of 6*	3·25	1·30

644 Prince Mircea

645 Ion Ionescu de la Brad (scholar)

(Des I. Dumitrana. Photo)

1968 (22 June). 550th Death Anniv of Prince Mircea (the Old). P 13½.

3560	**644**	1l.60 multicoloured	1·60	45

(Des I. Dumitrana. Photo)

1968 (24 June). Cultural Anniversaries. T **645** and similar vert design. P 13½.

3561	40b. multicoloured	30	20
3562	55b. multicoloured	60	30

Portraits and anniversaries:—40b. T **645** (150th birth anniv); 55b. Emil Racovita (scientist: birth centenary).

646 *Pelargonium zonale*

(Des V. Stoianov. Photo)

1968 (20 July). Garden Geraniums. T **646** and similar vert designs. Multicoloured. P 13½.

3563	10b. Type **646**	10	10
3564	20b. *Pelargonium zonale* (orange)	15	10
3565	40b. *Pelargonium zonale* (red)	20	10
3566	55b. *Pelargonium zonale* (pink)	30	10
3567	60b. *Pelargonium grandiflorum* (red)	50	10
3568	1l.20 *Pelargonium peltatum* (red)	70	20
3569	1l.35 *Pelargonium peltatum* (pink)	95	20
3570	1l.60 *Pelargonium grandiflorum* (pink)	1·50	95
3563/3570	*Set of* 8	4·00	1·70

647 "Nicolae Balcescu" (Gheorghe Tattarescu)

(Des I. Dumitrana. Photo)

1968 (25 July). 120th Anniv of 1848 Revolution. Paintings. T **647** and similar horiz designs. Multicoloured. P 13½.

3571	55b. Type **647**	60	10
3572	1l.20 "Avram Iancu" (B. Iscovescu)	1·10	20
3573	1l.60 "Vasile Alecsandri" (N. Livaditti)	2·10	95
3571/3573	*Set of* 3	3·50	1·10

648 Throwing the Javelin

649 F.I.A.P. Emblem within "Lens"

(Des A. Popescu. Photo)

1968 (28 Aug). Olympic Games, Mexico. T **648** and similar vert designs. Multicoloured. P 13½×13.

3574	10b. Type **648**	10	10
3575	20b. Diving	10	10
3576	40b. Volleyball	20	15
3577	55b. Boxing	40	15
3578	60b. Wrestling	60	15
3579	1l.20 Fencing	70	20
3580	1l.35 Punting	95	30
3581	1l.60 Football	1·60	45
3574/3581	*Set of* 8	4·25	1·40
MS3582	77×90 mm. 5l. Running. Imperf	5·75	5·75

1968 (28 Sept). Paintings in the Fine Arts Museum, Bucharest. Multicoloured designs as T **638**. Photo. P 13½.

3583	10b. "The Awakening of Romania" (G. Tattarescu)	10	10
3584	20b. "Composition" (Teodorescu Síonion)	20	10
3585	35b. "The Judgement of Paris" (H. van Balen)	30	10
3586	60b. "The Mystical Betrothal of St. Catherine" (L. Sustris)	60	20
3587	1l.75 "Mary with the Child Jesus" (J. van Bylert)	1·90	45
3588	3l. "The Summer" (J. Jordaens)	4·25	2·30
3583/3588	*Set of* 6	6·50	3·00

Sizes: Vert (28×49 mm)—10b. As T **638**: Vert—1l.75. Horiz—others.

(Des I. Druga. Litho)

1968 (4 Oct). 20th Anniv of International Federation of Photographic Art (F.I.A.P.). P 13½.

3589	**649**	1l.60 multicoloured	1·50	45

650 Academy and Harp

651 "Triumph of Tarjan" (Roman metope)

(Des I. Druga. Litho)

1968 (20 Oct). Centenary of Georgi Enescu Philharmonic Academy. P 12×12½.

3590	**650**	55b. multicoloured	80	45

(Des Aida Tasgian-Constantinescu (10b., 55b.), I. Dumitrana (others). Recess)

1968 (25 Nov). Historic Monuments. T **651** and similar designs. P 13½.

3591	10b. bronze-green, blue and light red	20	10
3592	40b. greenish blue, brown and carmine	30	10
3593	55b. slate-violet, brown and olive-green	50	10
3594	1l.20 brown-purple, slate and ochre	95	20
3595	1l.55 grey-blue, green and purple	1·50	30
3596	1l.75 blackish brn, bistre & red-orge	1·90	95
3591/3596	*Set of* 6	4·75	1·60

Designs: Horiz—40b. Monastery Church, Moldovita; 55b. Monastery Church, Cozia; 1l.20, Tower and Church, Tirgoviste; 1l.55, Palace of Culture, Jassy; 1l.75, Corvinus Castle, Hunedoara.

652 "Old Bucharest" (L. Mayer)

(Des Aiga Tasgian-Constantinescu. Photo)

1968 (15 Dec). Stamp Day. P 13½.

3597	**652**	55b. +45b. multicoloured	1·70	95

653 Mute Swan (*Cygnus olor*)

654 "Entry of Michael the Brave into Alba Julia" (E. Stoica)

(Des H. Meschendörfer. Photo)

1968 (20 Dec). Fauna of Nature Reservations. T **653** and similar horiz designs, Multicoloured. P 13½.

3598	10b. Type **653**	10	10
3599	20b. Black-winged stilt (*Himantopus himantopus*)	20	10
3600	40b. Common shelduck (*Tadorna tadorna*)	30	10
3601	55b. Great egret (*Egretta alba*)	50	10
3602	60b. Golden eagle (*Aquila chrysaetos*)	70	10
3603	1l.20 Great bustard (*Otis tarda*)	95	30
3604	1l.35 Chamois (*Rupicapra rupicapra*)	1·20	30
3605	1l.60 European bison (*Bison bonasus*)	1·90	65
3598/3605	*Set of* 8	5·25	1·60

1968 (24 Dec). 50th Anniv of Union of Transylvania with Romania. T **654** and similar horiz designs. Multicoloured. Litho. P 13½.

3606	55b. Type **654**	40	20
3607	1l. "Union Dance" (T. Aman)	80	20
3608	1l.75 "Alba Julia Assembly"	1·50	55
3606/3608	*Set of* 3	2·40	85
MS3609	121×111 mm. Nos. 3606/8. Imperf (Sold at 4l.)	4·00	4·00

655 Neamtz Costume (female)

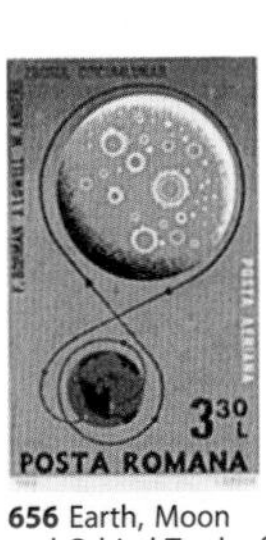

656 Earth, Moon and Orbital Track of "Apollo 8"

(Des Aida Tasgian-Constantinescu. Litho)

1968 (28 Dec). Provincial Costumes (1st series). T **655** and similar vert designs. Multicoloured. P 12×12½.

3610	5b. Type **655**	10	10
3611	40b. Neamtz (male)	30	10
3612	55b. Hunedoara (female)	70	15
3613	1l. Hunedoara (male)	95	20
3614	1l.60 Brasov (female)	1·50	30
3615	2l.40 Brasov (male)	2·10	1·40
3610/3615	*Set of* 6	5·00	2·00

See also Nos. 3617/22.

(Des I. Druga. Photo)

1969 (17 Jan). AIR. Flight of "Apollo 8" Around the Moon. P 13½.

3616	**656**	3l.30 black, silver and blue	2·40	2·30

No. 3616 was issued in sheets of four with decorative margins.

(Des Aida Tasgian-Constantinescu. Litho)

1969 (15 Feb). Provincial Costumes (2nd series). Vert designs as T **655**. Multicoloured. P 12×12½.

3617	5b. Doli (female)	10	10
3618	40b. Doli (male)	30	10
3619	55b. Arges (female)	70	15
3620	1l. Arges (male)	95	20
3621	1l.60 Timisoara (female)	1·50	30
3622	2l.40 Timisoara (male)	2·10	1·40
3617/3622	*Set of* 6	5·00	2·00

657 Fencing

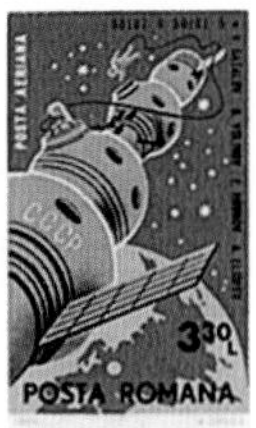

658 "Soyuz 4" and "Soyuz 5"

(Des V. Grigorescu. Photo)

1969 (10 Mar). Sports. T **657** and similar horiz designs. P 13½.

3623	10b. grey, black and light bistre-brown	10	10
3624	20b. grey, black and violet	10	10
3625	40b. grey, black and blue	15	10
3626	55b. grey, black and deep red	20	10
3627	1l. grey, black and olive-green	40	10
3628	1l.20 grey, black and new blue	50	15
3629	1l.60 grey, black and magenta	80	30
3630	2l.40 grey, black and bluish green	1·50	95
3623/3630	*Set of* 8	3·50	1·70

Designs:—20b. Throwing the javelin; 40b. Canoeing; 55b. Boxing; 1l. Volleyball; 1l.20, Swimming; 1l.60, Wrestling; 2l.40, Football.

(Des I. Dumitrana. Photo)

1969 (22 Mar). Nude Paintings in the National Gallery, Bucharest. Multicoloured designs as T **638**. P 13½.

3631	10b. "Nude" (G. Tattarescu)	10	10
3632	20b. "Nude" (T. Pallady)	10	10
3633	35b. "Nude" (N. Tonitza)	20	10
3634	60b. "Venus and Cupid" (Flemish School)	50	20
3635	1l.75 "Diana and Endymion" (M. Liberi)	1·90	95
3636	3l. "The Three Graces" (J. H. von Achen)	4·00	2·30
3631/3636	*Set of* 6	6·00	3·50
MS3637	73×91 mm. 5l. Design as 1l.75. Imperf	5·50	5·50

Sizes: Vert (36×49 mm)—10b., 35b., 60b., 1l.75. (27×49 mm)—3l. Horiz (49×36 mm)—20b.

(Des I. Druga. Photo)

1969 (28 Mar). AIR. Space Link-up of "Soyuz 4" and "Soyuz 5". P 13½.

3638	**658**	3l.30 multicoloured	2·40	2·30

No. 3638 was issued in sheets of four with decorative margins.

659 I.L.O. Emblem

660 Stylized Head

(Des Aida Tasgian-Constantinescu. Photo)

1969 (9 Apr). 50th Anniversary of International Labour Office. P 13½.

3639	**659**	55b. multicoloured	95	45

(Des I. Druga. Photo)

1969 (28 Apr). Inter-European Cultural and Economic Co-operation. P 13½.

3640	**660**	55b. multicoloured	50	45
3641		1l.50 multicoloured	1·90	1·90

661 Posthorn

662 Referee introducing Boxers

(Des V. Stoianov. Photo)

1969 (15 May). Postal Ministers' Conference, Bucharest. P 13½.

3642	**661**	55b. deep ultramarine and light turquoise-blue	70	45

(Des A. Popescu. Photo)

1969 (24 May). European Boxing Championships, Bucharest. T **662** and similar square designs. Multicoloured. P 13½.

3643	35b. Type **662**	20	10
3644	40b. Sparring	30	10
3645	55b. Leading with punch	50	10
3646	1l.75 Declaring the winner	1·50	95
3643/3646	*Set of* 4	2·30	1·10

663 "Apollo 9" and Module over Earth

664 Lesser Purple Emperor (*Apatura ilia*)

(Des I. Druga. Photo)

1969 (15 June). AIR. "Apollo" Moon Flights. T **663** and similar multicoloured design. P 13½.

3647 60b. Type **663** ... 30 10
3648 2l.40 "Apollo 10" and module approaching Moon (vert) ... 1·90 35

(Des V. Stoianov. Photo)

1969 (25 June). Butterflies and Moths. T **664** and similar horiz designs. Multicoloured. P 13½.

3649 5b. Type **664** ... 10 10
3650 10b. Willow-herb hawk moth (*Prosperpinus prosperina*) ... 10 10
3651 20b. Eastern pale clouded yellow (*Colias erate*) ... 10 10
3652 40b. Large tiger moth (*Pericallia matronula*) ... 20 10
3653 55b. Pallas's fritillary (*Argynnis laodice*) ... 50 10
3654 1l. Jersey tiger moth (*Callimorpha quadripunctaria*) ... 60 10
3655 1l.20 Orange-tip (*Anthocaris cardamines*) ... 95 30
3656 2l.40 Meleager's blue (*Meleageria daphnis*) ... 2·40 1·60
3649/3656 *Set of* 8 ... 4·50 2·30

665 Astronaut and Module on Moon

666 Communist Flag

(Des I. Druga. Photo)

1969 (24 July). AIR. First Man on the Moon. P 13½.

3657 **665** 3l.30 multicoloured ... 2·40 2·30

No. 3657 was only issued in small sheets of four stamps *se-tenant* with four illustrated or inscribed stamp-sized labels.

(Des I. Dumitrana. Photo)

1969 (28 July–Sept). Paintings in the National Gallery, Bucharest. Multicoloured designs similar to T **638**. P 13½.

3658 10b. "Venetian Senator" (School of Tintoretto) ... 10 10
3659 20b. "Sofia Kretzulescu" (Tattarescu) ... 10 10
3660 35b. "Philip IV" (Velasquez) ... 30 10
3661 60b. "Man Reading" (Memling) ... 70 15
3662 1l.75 "Lady D'Aguesseau" (Vigée-Lebrun) ... 1·50 30
3663 3l. "Portrait of a Woman" (Rembrandt) ... 3·50 1·90
3658/3663 *Set of* 6 ... 5·50 2·40
MS3664 91×78 mm. 5l. "Return of the Prodigal Son" (Licino). Imperf (28 July) ... 4·75 4·75

Nos. 3658/63 were issued on 29 Sept, and are all vert. No **MS**3664 is horiz.

(Des I. Druga. Photo)

1969 (6 Aug). Tenth Romanian Communist Party Congress. P 13½.

3665 **666** 55b. multicoloured ... 80 45

667 Symbols of Learning

668 Liberation Emblem

669 Juggling on Trick-cycle

(Des V. Stoianov. Photo)

1969 (10 Aug). National Economic Achievements Exhibition, Bucharest. T **667** and similar vert designs. Multicoloured. P 13½.

3666 35b. Type **667** ... 20 10
3667 40b. Symbols of Agriculture and Science ... 30 10
3668 1l.75 Symbols of Industry ... 1·50 35
3666/3668 *Set of* 3 ... 1·80 50

(Des E. Palade. Photo)

1969 (23 Aug). 25th Anniversary of Liberation. T **668** and similar vert designs. Multicoloured. P 13½.

3669 10b. Type **668** ... 20 10
3670 55b. Crane and trowel ... 30 15
3671 60b. Flags on scaffolding ... 50 20
3669/3671 *Set of* 3 ... 90 40

(Des F. Ivanus. Photo)

1969 (20 Sept). Romanian State Circus. T **669** and similar vert designs. Multicoloured. P 13½.

3672 10b. Type **669** ... 10 10
3673 20b. Clown ... 10 10
3674 35b. Trapeze artists ... 30 10
3675 60b. Equestrian act ... 50 10
3676 1l.75 High-wire act ... 95 20
3677 3l. Performing tiger ... 1·90 1·10
3672/3677 *Set of* 6 ... 3·50 1·50

670 Forces' Memorial

(Des M. Stiplosek. Photo)

1969 (25 Oct). Army Day and 25th Anniversary of People's Army. P 13½.

3678 **670** 55b. black, gold and red ... 70 45

671 Trains of 1869 and 1969

(Des I. Dumitrana. Photo)

1969 (31 Oct). Centenary of Romanian Railways. P 13½.

3679 **671** 55b. multicoloured ... 80 45

672 "Courtyard" (M. Bouquet)

(Des I. Dumitrana. Photo)

1969 (15 Nov). Stamp Day. P 13½.

3680 **672** 55b. +45b. multicoloured ... 1·50 95

673 Branesti Mask

674 "Apollo 12" above Moon

(Des Aida Tasgian-Constantinescu. Photo)

1969 (20 Nov). Folklore Masks. T **673** and similar vert designs. Multicoloured. P 13½.

3681 40b. Type **673** ... 30 10
3682 55b. Tudora mask ... 40 10
3683 1l.55 Birsesti mask ... 95 30
3684 1l.75 Rudaria mask ... 1·30 75
3681/3684 *Set of* 4 ... 2·75 1·10

(Des G. Bozianu. Photo)

1969 (24 Nov). Moon Landing of "Apollo 12". P 13½.

3685 **674** 1l.50 multicoloured ... 1·50 1·40

No. 3685 was only issued in small sheets of four stamps, *se-tenant* with four illustrated or inscribed stamp-sized labels.

675 "Three Kings" (Voronet Monastery)

676 "Old Mother Goose" Capra

(Des I. Dumitrana. Photo)

1969 (15 Dec). Frescoes from Northern Moldavian Monasteries (1st series). T **675** and similar multicoloured designs. P 13½.

3686 10b. Type **675** ... 10 10
3687 20b. "Three Kings" (Sucevita) ... 20 10
3688 35b. "Holy Child in Manger" (Voronet) ... 30 10
3689 60b. "Ship" (Sucevita) (vert) ... 60 15
3690 1l.75 "Walled City" (Moldovita) ... 1·70 35
3691 3l. "Pastoral Scene" (Voronet) (vert) ... 3·50 1·90
3686/3691 *Set of* 6 ... 5·75 2·40

See also Nos. 3736/42 and 3872/8.

(Des D. Danila. Photo)

1969 (25 Dec). New Year. Children's Celebrations. T **676** and similar vert designs. Multicoloured. P 13½.

3692 40b. Type **676** ... 20 10
3693 55b. Decorated tree, Sorcova ... 30 10
3694 1l.50 Drummers, Buhaiul ... 1·20 20
3695 2l.40 Singer and bell-ringer, Plugusorul ... 1·50 75
3692/3695 *Set of* 4 ... 3·00 1·00

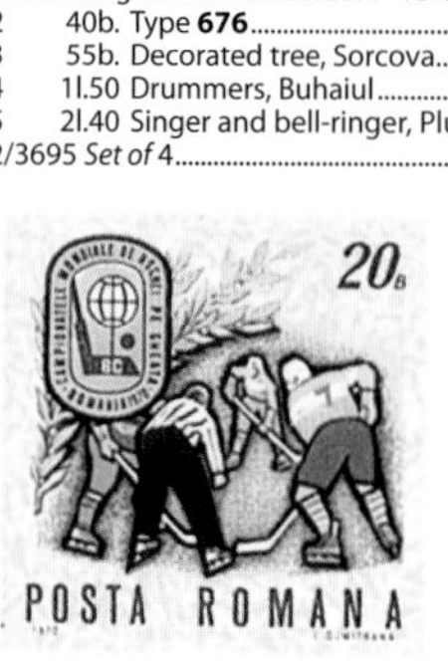

677 Players and Emblem

678 Small Pasque Flower (*Pulsatilla pratensis*)

(Des I. Dumitrana. Photo)

1970 (20 Jan). World Ice Hockey Championships (Groups B and C), Bucharest. T **677** and similar square designs. Multicoloured. P 13½.

3696 20b. Type **677** ... 10 10
3697 55b. Goal-keeper ... 30 10
3698 1l.20 Two players ... 85 15
3699 2l.40 Goal-mouth melee ... 1·60 95
3696/3699 *Set of* 4 ... 2·50 1·20

(Des I. Druga. Photo)

1970 (25 Feb). Flowers. T **678** and similar vert designs. Multicoloured. P 13½.

3700 5b. Type **678** ... 10 10
3701 10b. Yellow pheasant's-eye (*Adonis vernalis*) ... 10 10
3702 20b. Musk thistle (*Carduus nutans*) ... 10 10
3703 40b. Dwarf almond (*Amygdalus nana*) ... 10 10
3704 55b. Dwarf bearded iris (*Iris pumilla*) ... 10 10
3705 1l. Flax (*Linum hirsutum*) ... 50 10
3706 1l.20 Sage (*Salvia aethiopis*) ... 70 10
3707 2l.40 Peony (*Paeonia tenuifolia*) ... 3·00 1·10
3700/3707 *Set of* 8 ... 4·25 1·60

1970 (10 Mar). POSTAGE DUE. As Nos. D3436/41, but without watermark. P 13½.

			Un pair	*Us pair*
D3708	D **614**	3b. emerald	20	20
D3709		5b. new blue	20	20
D3710		10b. magenta	20	20
D3711		20b. rosine	20	20
D3712		40b. brown	40	20
D3713		1l. violet	80	20
D3708/3713 *Set of* 6 pairs			1·80	1·10

679 Japanese Woodcut

681 Lenin

680 B.A.C. One Eleven Series 475 Jetliner and Silhouettes of Aircraft

(Des I. Dumitrana. Photo)

1970 (24 Mar–28 Nov). World Fair, Osaka, Japan. Expo 70. T **679** and similar multicoloured design. P 13½.

3714 20b. Type **679** ... 20 20
3715 1l. Japanese pagoda ... 1·20 65
MS3716 182×120 mm. 5l. As design of 1l. (28 Nov) ... 5·75 5·75

The design of 1l. and 5l. is vert, 29×92 mm. On No. **MS**3716 the face value appears on the sheet and not the stamp.

(Des I. Dumitrana. Photo)

1970 (6 Apr). AIR. 50th Anniv of Romanian Civil Aviation. T **680** and similar horiz design. Multicoloured. P 13½.

3717 60b. Type **680** ... 50 20
3718 2l. Tail of B.A.C. One Eleven Series 475 and control tower at Otopeni Airport, Bucharest ... 1·20 55

(Des I. Dumitrana. Photo)

1970 (15 Apr). Birth Centenary of Lenin. P 13½.

3719 **681** 40b. multicoloured ... 70 45

682 "Camille" (Monet), and Maximum Card

683 "Prince Alexander Cuza" (Szathmary)

(Des I. Dumitrana. Photo)

1970 (19 Apr). Maximafila Franco-Romanian Philatelic Exhibition, Bucharest. P 13½.

3720 **682** 1l.50 multicoloured ... 1·90 5·50

(Des I. Dumitrana. Photo)

1970 (20 Apr). 150th Birth Anniv of Prince Alexandru Cuza. P 13½.

3721 **683** 55b. multicoloured ... 1·10 45

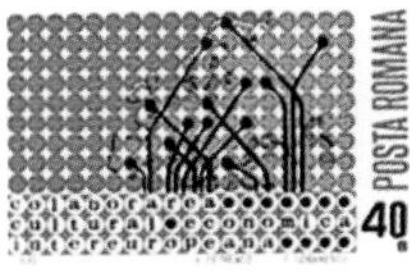

684 "Co-operation" Map

685 Victory Monument, Bucharest

(Des A. Petrenco and F. Goranescu. Photo)

1970 (28 Apr). Inter-European Cultural and Economic Co-operation. P 13½.

3722 **684** 40b. blue-green, chestnut and black 50 45
3723 1l.50 bright blue, yell-brn and blk 95 95

(Des Aida Tasgian-Constantinescu. Photo)

1970 (9 May). 25th Anniversary of Liberation. P 13½.

3724 **685** 55b. multicoloured 95 45

686 Greek Silver Drachma, 5th-cent B.C.

(Des Aida Tasgian-Constantinescu. Photo)

1970 (15 May). Ancient Coins. T **686** and similar designs. P 13½.

3725 10b. black and ultramarine 10 10
3726 20b. black and deep orange-red 20 10
3727 35b. bronze and deep green 30 10
3728 60b. black and brown 50 10
3729 1l.75 black and new blue 1·20 10
3730 3l. black and deep cerise 2·40 1·10
3725/3730 *Set of* 6 4·25 1·40

Designs: Horiz—20b. Getic-Dacian silver didrachm, 2nd–1st-cent B.C.; 35b. Copper sestertius of Trajan, 106 A.D.; 60b. Mircea ducat, 1400; 1l.75, Silver groschen of Stephen the Great, 1460. Vert—3l. Brasov klippe-thaler, 1601.

687 Footballers and Ball

688 "Apollo 13" Splashdown

(Des A. Popescu. Photo)

1970 (26 May). World Cup Football Championship, Mexico. T **687** and similar square designs showing football scenes. P 13½.

3731 40b. multicoloured 20 10
3732 55b. multicoloured 30 10
3733 1l.75 multicoloured 1·20 35
3734 3l.30 multicoloured 2·10 1·00
3731/3734 *Set of* 4 3·50 1·40
MS3735 110×110 mm. 6l. Four designs with face values of 1l.20, 1l.50, 1l.55 and 1l.75 4·75 4·75

The designs within No. **MS**3735 differ from Type **687** in having no frame-line. The miniature sheet has a central football emblem, part of which falls on each stamp.

(Des E. Palade. Photo)

1970 (29 June). Frescoes from Northern Moldavian Monasteries (2nd series). Multicoloured designs as T **675**. P 13½.

3736 10b. "Prince Petru Rares and Family" (Moldovita) (vert) 10 10
3737 20b. "Metropolitan Grigore Rosca" (Voronet) (vert) 20 10
3738 40b. "Alexander the Good and Family" (Sucevita) (vert) 30 10
3739 55b. "The Last Judgement" (Voronet) (vert) 50 10
3740 1l.75 "The Last Judgement (different) (Voronet) 1·20 30
3741 3l. "St. Anthony" (Voronet) (vert) 2·50 1·60
3736/3741 *Set of* 6 4·25 2·10
MS3742 90×77 mm. 5l. "Byzantine Manor" (Arbore) 4·75 4·75

The 20b. is smaller, 28×48 mm. Others as Type **675**.

(Des G. Bozianu. Photo)

1970 (29 June). AIR. Space Flight of "Apollo 13". P 13½.

3743 **688** 1l.50 multicoloured 95 95

No. 3743 was only issued in small sheets of four stamps *se-tenant* with four illustrated stamp-size labels.

689 Engels

690 Exhibition Hall

(Des Aida Tasgian-Constantinescu. Photo)

1970 (10 July). 150th Birth Anniv of Friedrich Engels. P 13½.

3744 **689** 1l.50 multicoloured 1·50 45

(Des V. Stoianov. Photo)

1970. National Events. T **690** and similar horiz designs. Multicoloured. P 13½.

3745 35b. "Iron Gates" Dam (13 July) 20 10
3746 55b. Freighter and flag (17 July) 30 10
3747 1l.50 Type **690** (13 July) 1·10 20
3745/3747 *Set of* 3 1·10 35

Events:—35b. Danube navigation projects; 55b. 75th Anniversary of Romanian Merchant Marine; 1l.50, 1st International Fair, Bucharest.

691 New Headquarters Building

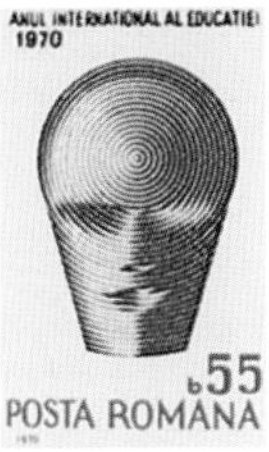

692 Education Year Emblem

(Des Aida Tasgian-Constantinescu. Photo)

1970 (17 Aug). New Universal Postal Union Headquarters Building, Berne. P 13½.

3748 **691** 1l.50 turquoise-blue and ultramarine 1·60 45

1970 (17 Aug). International Education Year. Photo. P 13½.

3749 **692** 55b. plum, black and red 95 45

693 "Iceberg"

694 "Spaniel and Pheasant" (J. B. Oudry)

(Des V. Stoianov. Photo)

1970 (21 Aug). Roses. T **693** and similar vert designs. Muticoloured. P 13½.

3750 20b. Type **693** 10 10
3751 35b. "Wiener Charme" 10 10
3752 55b. "Pink Lustre" 20 10
3753 1l. "Piccadilly" 95 15
3754 1l.50 "Orange Delbard" 1·20 20
3755 2l.40 "Sibelius" 2·10 1·40
3750/3755 *Set of* 6 4·25 1·80

(Des Aida Tasgian-Constantinescu. Photo)

1970 (20 Sept). Paintings in Romanian Galleries. T **694** and similar multicoloured designs. P 13½.

3756 10b. "The Hunt" (D. Brandi) (vert) 10 10
3757 20b. Type **694** 10 10
3758 35b. "The Hunt" (Jan Fyt) (vert) 20 10
3759 60b. "After the Chase" (Jordaens) 50 10
3760 1l.75 "The Game Dealer" (F. Snyders) (horiz) 1·20 30
3761 3l. "The Hunt" (A. de Gryeff) 2·10 95
3756/3761 *Set of* 6 3·75 1·50
MS3762 90×78 mm. 5l. Design as 1l.75 4·75 4·75

Sizes:—60b., 3l. as Type **694**; others larger, 38×50 or 50×38 mm.

695 Refugee Woman and Child

696 U.N. Emblem

(Des E. Palade. Photo)

1970 (25 Sept). Danube Flood Victims (1st issue). T **695** and similar vert designs. P 13½.

(a) POSTAGE

3763 55b. black, Prussian blue and yellow-olive 20 10
a. Strip of 3. Nos. 3763/4 and 3766 1·50
3764 1l.50 multicoloured 80 30
3765 1l.75 multicoloured 1·50 75

(b) AIR. Inscr "POSTA AERIANA"

3766 60b. black, pale drab and slate-blue 40 10
3763/3766 *Set of* 4 2·50 1·10

Designs:—60b. Helicopter rescue; 1l.50, Red Cross post; 1l.75, Building reconstruction.

Nos. 3763/4 and 3766 were issued together in *se-tenant* strips of three within the sheet.

See also Nos. 3777/8.

(Des E. Palade. Photo)

1970 (28 Sept). 25th Anniv of United Nations Organization. P 13½.

3767 **696** 1l.50 multicoloured 1·50 45

697 Arab Horse

698 Beethoven

(Des E. Palade. Photo)

1970 (25 Oct). Horses. T **697** and similar horiz designs. Multicoloured. P 13½.

3768 20b. Type **697** 10 10
3769 35b. American trotter 10 10
3770 55b. Ghidran 40 10
3771 1l. Hutul 95 10
3772 1l.50 Thoroughbred 1·50 30
3773 2l.40 Lippizaner 4·00 1·90
3768/3773 *Set of* 6 6·25 2·30

(Des Aida Tasgian-Constantinescu. Photo)

1970 (2 Nov). Birth Bicentenary of Ludwig van Beethoven (composer). P 13½.

3774 **698** 55b. multicoloured 1·60 45

699 "Mail-cart in the Snow" (E. Volkers)

1970 (15 Nov). Stamp Day. Photo. P 13½.

3775 **699** 55b. +45b. multicoloured 1·60 1·10

700 Henri Coanda's Model Airplane

(Des I. Dumitrana. Photo)

1970 (1 Dec). AIR. 60th Anniv of First Experimental Turbine-powered Airplane. P 13½.

3776 **700** 60b. multicoloured 1·60 45

701 "The Flood" (abstract, Joan Miró)

1970 (10 Dec). Danube Flood Victims (2nd issue). Photo. P 13½.

3777 **701** 3l. multicoloured 3·00 2·75
MS3778 79×95 mm. **701** 5l. multicoloured. Imperf. 7·25 7·25

No. 3777 was issued in sheets of five stamps and one stamp-sized label with artist's signature.

702 "Sight" (G. Coques)

703 Vladimirescu (after Theodor Aman)

(Des I. Dumitrana. Photo)

1970 (15 Dec). Paintings from the Bruckenthal Museum, Sibiu. T **702** and similar multicoloured designs. P 13½.

3779 10b. Type **702** 10 10
3780 20b. "Hearing" 10 10
3781 35b. "Smell" 20 10
3782 60b. "Taste" 50 10
3783 1l.75 "Touch" 95 20
3784 3l. Bruckenthal Museum 2·40 1·10
3779/3784 *Set of* 6 3·75 1·50
MS3785 90×78 mm. 5l. "View of Sibiu, 1808" (lithograph) (horiz) Imperf 5·75 5·75

Nos. 3779/83 show a series of pictures by Coques entitled "The Five Senses".

(Des I. Dumitrana. Photo)

1971 (20 Feb). 150th Death Anniv of Tudor Vladimirescu (Wallachian revolutionary). P 13½.
3786 **703** 1l.50 multicoloured ... 1·60 45

704 "Three Races"

705 Alsatian

(Des I. Dumitrana. Photo)

1971 (23 Feb). Racial Equality Year. P 13½.
3787 **704** 1l.50 multicoloured ... 1·60 45

(Des E. Palade. Photo)

1971 (25 Feb). Dogs. T **705** and similar vert designs. Multicoloured. P 13½.
3788 20b. Type **705** ... 10 10
3789 35b. Bulldog ... 10 10
3790 55b. Fox terrier ... 20 10
3791 1l. Setter ... 95 10
3792 1l.50 Cocker spaniel ... 1·50 45
3793 2l.40 Poodle ... 4·25 2·40
3788/3793 *Set of 6* ... 6·50 3·00

706 "Luna 16" leaving Moon

707 Proclamation of the Commune

(Des Aida Tasgian-Constantinescu. Photo)

1971 (5 Mar). AIR. Moon Missions of "Luna 16" and "Luna 17". T **706** and similar horiz design. Multicoloured. P 13½.
3794 3l.30 Type **706** ... 2·40 2·30
a. Pair. Nos. 3794/5 ... 5·00 4·75
3795 3l.30 "Lunokhod 1" on Moon ... 2·40 2·30

Nos. 3794/5 were issued together in *se-tenant* pairs within sheets of four stamps and four different labels.

(Des Aida Tasgian-Constantinescu. Photo)

1971 (15 Mar). Centenary of Paris Commune. P 13½.
3796 **707** 40b. multicoloured ... 95 45

708 Astronaut and Moon Trolley

709 "Three Fists" Emblem and Flags

(Des Aida Tasgian-Constantinescu. Photo)

1971 (20 Mar). AIR. Moon Mission of "Apollo 14". P 13½.
3797 **708** 3l.30 multicoloured ... 2·40 2·30

No. 3797 was issued in small sheets of four stamps and four stamp-size labels depicting astronauts and emblem.

(Des A. Popescu. Photo)

1971 (23 Mar). Trade Union Congress, Bucharest. P 13½.
3798 **709** 55b. multicoloured ... 95 45

710 "Toadstool" Rocks, Babele

(Des V. Stoianov. Photo)

1971 (15 Apr). Tourism. T **710** and similar multicoloured designs. P 13½.
3799 10b. Gorge, Cheile Bicazului (vert) ... 10 10
3800 40b. Type **710** ... 10 10
3801 55b. Winter resort, Poiana Brasov ... 20 10
3802 1l. Fishing punt and tourist launch, Danube delta ... 80 10
3803 1l.50 Hotel, Baile Sovata ... 1·40 20
3804 2l.40 Venus, Jupiter and Neptune Hotels, Black Sea (77×29 mm) ... 1·90 1·10
3799/3804 *Set of 6* ... 4·00 1·50

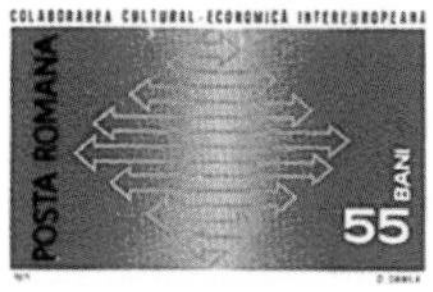

711 "Arrows"

712 Museum Building

(Des D. Danila. Photo)

1971 (28 Apr). Inter-European Cultural and Economic Co-operation. T **711** and similar horiz design. Multicoloured. P 13½.
3805 55b. Type **711** ... 95 95
3806 1l.75 Stylized map of Europe ... 1·90 1·90

(Des I. Dumitrana. Photo)

1971 (7 May). Historical Museum, Bucharest. P 13½.
3807 **712** 55b. multicoloured ... 70 45

713 "The Secret Printing-Press" (S. Szonyi)

714 "Motra Tone" (Kole Idromeno)

(Des Aida Tasgian-Constantinescu. Photo)

1971 (8 May). 50th Anniversary of Romanian Communist Party. T **713** and similar multicoloured designs. P 13½.
3808 35b. Type **713** ... 20 10
3809 40b. Emblem and red flags (horiz) ... 20 10
3810 55b. "The Builders" (A. Anastasiu) ... 40 10
3808/3810 *Set of 3* ... 70 25

(Des I. Dumitrana. Photo)

1971 (27 May). Balkanfila III International Stamp Exhibition, Bucharest. T **714** and similar multicoloured designs, showing paintings. P 13½.
3811 1l.20 +60b. Type **714** ... 1·20 1·10
a. Sheetlet. Nos. 3811/16 plus 6 labels ... 7·50
3812 1l.20 +60b. "Maid" (Vladimir Dimitrov-Maistora) ... 1·20 1·10
3813 1l.20 +60b. "Rosa Botzaris" (Joseph Stieler) ... 1·20 1·10
3814 1l.20 +60b. "Portrait of a Lady" (Katarina Ivanovic) ... 1·20 1·10
3815 1l.20 +60b. "Argeseanca" (C. Popp de Szathmary) ... 1·20 1·10
3816 1l.20 +60b. "Woman in Modern Dress" (Çalli Ibrahim) ... 1·20 1·10
3811/3816 *Set of 6* ... 6·50 6·00
MS3817 90×79 mm. 5l. "Dancing the Hora" (Theodor Aman) (horiz) ... 4·75 4·75

Nos. 3811/16 were issued together in *se-tenant* sheetlets of six stamps and six premium-carrying labels (as shown in Type **714**).

715 Pomegranate (*Punica granatum*)

716 "Nude" (J. Iser)

(Des Aida Tasgian-Constantinescu. Photo)

1971 (20 June). Flowers. T **715** and similar multicoloured designs. P 13½.
3818 20b. Type **715** ... 10 10
3819 35b. *Calceolus speciosum* ... 10 10
3820 55b. *Life jagra* ... 20 10
3821 1l. Blood-drop emlets (*Mimulus luteus*) ... 60 20
3822 1l.50 Dwarf morning glory (*Convolvulus tricolor*) ... 95 35
3823 2l.40 *Phyllocactus phyllanthoides* (horiz) ... 1·90 55
3818/3823 *Set of 6* ... 3·50 1·30

(Des Aida Tasgian-Constantinescu. Photo)

1971 (25 July). Paintings of Nudes. T **716** and similar multicoloured designs. P 13½.
3824 10b. Type **716** ... 10 10
3825 20b. "Nude" (C. Ressu) ... 10 10
3826 35b. "Nude" (N. Grigorescu) ... 10 10
3827 60b. "Odalisque" (Delacroix) (horiz) ... 20 10
3828 1l.75 "Nude in a Landscape" (Renoir) ... 1·20 30
3829 3l. "Venus and Cupid" (Il Vecchio) (horiz) ... 2·10 95
3824/3829 *Set of 6* ... 3·50 1·50
MS3830 90×78 mm. 5l. "Venus and Amour" (Il Bronzino) (horiz) Imperf ... 7·25 7·25

The 20b. is smaller, 29×50 mm.

717 Cosmonauts Patsaev, Dobrovolsky and Volkov

(Des Aida Tasgian-Constantinescu. Litho)

1971 (26 July). AIR. "Soyuz 11" Commemoration. P 13½.
MS3831 101×81 mm. **717** 6l. black and violet blue ... 11·50 11·50

A second miniature sheet as Type **717**, but larger, 130×90 mm., also exists in black and turquoise-blue, imperforate. This was from a restricted printing.

718 Astronauts and Lunar Rover on Moon

720 "Neagoe Basarab" (fresco, Curteá de Arges)

719 "Fishing-boat" (M. W. Arnold)

(Des I. Dumitrana. Photo)

1971 (28 Aug). AIR. Moon Flight of "Apollo 15". P 13½.
3833 **718** 1l.50 mult (blue background) ... 2·40 2·30

Issued in small sheets of four, together with four stamp-size labels showing astronauts and emblem.

No. 3833 also exists imperforate, with background colour changed to green, from a restricted printing.

(Des I. Dumitrana. Photo)

1971 (15 Sept). Marine Paintings. T **719** and similar multicoloured designs. P 13½.
3835 10b. "Coastal Storm" (B. Peters) ... 10 10
3836 20b. "Seascape" (L. Backhuysen) ... 10 10
3837 35b. "Boat in Stormy Seas" (A. van de Eertvelt) ... 30 10
3838 60b. Type **719** ... 50 10
3839 1l.75 "Seascape" (I. K. Aivazovsky) ... 1·20 35
3840 3l. "Fishing-boats, Braila" (J. A. Steriadi) ... 2·50 75
3835/3840 *Set of 6* ... 4·25 1·40
MS3841 78×90 mm. 5l. "Venetian Fishing- boats" (N. Darascu) (vert) ... 5·75 5·75

(Des I. Druga. Photo)

1971. As Nos. 3517/29 and three new designs, but all in the smaller format, 17×23 or 23×17 mm. P 13½.
3842 1l. bright green ... 40 20
3843 1l.20 bright reddish violet ... 50 20
3844 1l.35 new blue ... 60 20
3845 1l.50 rose-red ... 65 20
3846 1l.55 brown ... 70 20
3847 1l.75 emerald ... 80 20
3848 2l. olive-yellow ... 85 20
3849 2l.40 deep blue ... 1·10 20
3850 3l. greenish blue ... 1·30 20
3851 3l.20 yellow-ochre ... 1·40 20
3852 3l.25 ultramarine ... 1·50 20
3853 3l.60 bright blue ... 1·60 20
3854 4l. magenta ... 1·70 20
3855 4l.80 greenish blue ... 1·90 20
3856 5l. violet ... 2·10 20
3857 6l. deep magenta ... 2·50 20
3842/3857 *Set of 16* ... 18·00 3·00

New designs: Vert—3l.60, Clearing letter-box; 4l.80, Postman on round; 6l. Postal Ministry, Bucharest.

(Des I. Dumitrana. Photo)

1971 (20 Sept). 450th Death Anniv of Prince Neagoe Basarab, Regent of Wallachia. P 13½.

3858 **720** 60b. multicoloured 80 45

721 "T. Pallady" (self-portrait)

722 Persian Text and Seal

(Des Aida Tasgian-Constantinescu. Photo)

1971 (12 Oct). Artists' Anniversaries. T **721** and similar vert designs. P 13½.

3859	40b. multicoloured	10	10
3860	55b. black, stone and gold	20	10
3861	1l.50 black, stone and gold	70	10
3862	2l.40 multicoloured	1·60	45
3859/3862	*Set of* 4	2·30	70

Designs (self-portraits):—40b. Type **721** (birth centenary); 55b. Benvenuto Cellini (400th death anniv); 1l.50, Jean Watteau (250th death anniv); 2l.40, Albrecht Dürer (500th birth anniv).

(Des V. Stoianov. Photo)

1971 (12 Oct). 2500th Anniversary of Persian Empire. P 13½.

3863 **722** 55b. multicoloured 95 45

723 Figure-skating

724 "Lady with Letter" (Sava Hentia)

(Des E. Palade. Photo)

1971 (25 Oct). Winter Olympic Games, Sapporo, Japan (1972). T **723** and similar vert designs. Multicoloured. P 13½.

3864	10b. Type **723**	10	10
	a. Strip of 3. Nos. 3864/6	35	
3865	20b. Ice hockey	10	10
3866	40b. Biathlon	10	10
3867	55b. Bobsleighing	20	10
	a. Pair. Nos. 3867/8	1·50	45
3868	1l.75 Downhill skiing	1·20	30
3869	3l. Games emblem	4·00	1·40
3864/3869	*Set of* 6	5·25	1·90
MS3870	78×90 mm. 5l. Symbolic flame (38×50 mm). Imperf	4·75	4·75

Nos. 3864/6 and 3867/8 respectively were issued together *se-tenant* within their sheets.

(Des I. Dumitrana. Photo)

1971 (15 Nov). Stamp Day. P 13½.

3871 **724** 1l.10 +90b. multicoloured .... 1·90 1·10

(Des E. Palade. Photo)

1971 (30 Nov). Frescoes from Northern Moldavian Monasteries (3rd series). Multicoloured designs similar to T **675**. P 13½.

3872	10b. "St. George and the Dragon" (Moldovita) (vert)	10	10
3873	20b. "Three Kings and Angel" (Moldovita) (vert)	10	10
3874	40b. "The Crucifixion" (Moldovita) (vert)	10	10
3875	55b. "Trial" (Voronet) (vert)	20	10
3876	1l.75 "Death of a Martyr" (Voronet) (vert)	1·50	30
3877	3l. "King and Court" (Arborea)	3·00	1·90
3872/3877	*Set of* 6	4·50	2·30
MS3878	78×90 mm. 5l. Wall of frescoes, Voronet (vert). Imperf	4·75	4·75

725 Matei Millo (dramatist, 75th Death Anniv)

726 Magellan and Ships (450th Death Anniv)

(Des V. Stoianov. Photo)

1971 (20 Dec). Famous Romanians. T **725** and similar vert portrait. Multicoloured. P 13½.

3879	55b. Type **725**	30	20
3880	1l. Nicolae Iorga (historian, birth centenary)	70	30

(Des V. Stoianov. Photo)

1971 (20 Dec). Scientific Anniversaries. T **726** and similar horiz designs. P 13½.

3881	40b. reddish mauve, chalky blue and deep bluish green	20	10
3882	55b. blue, grey-green and reddish lilac	20	10
3883	1l. multicoloured	60	10
3884	1l.50 emerald, new blue and chestnut	85	30
3881/3884	*Set of* 4	1·70	55

Designs:—55b. Kepler and observatory (400th birth anniv); 1l. Gagarin, rocket and Globe (10th anniv of first manned space flight); 1l.50, Lord Rutherford and atomic symbol (birth centenary).

727 Lynx Cubs

(Des N. Saftoiu. Photo)

1972 (10 Mar). Young Wild Animals. T **727** and similar horiz designs. Multicoloured. P 13½.

3885	20b. Type **727**	10	10
3886	35b. Red fox cubs	10	10
3887	55b. Roe deer fawns	20	10
3888	1l. Wild piglets	60	20
3889	1l.50 Wolf cubs	95	20
3890	2l.40 Brown bear cubs	3·00	1·60
3885/3890	*Set of* 6	4·50	2·10

728 U.T.C. Emblem

729 Wrestling

(Des R. Coteanu. Photo)

1972 (10 Mar). 50th Anniversary of Communist Youth Union (U.T.C.). P 13½.

3891 **728** 55b. multicoloured 70 45

(Des A. Popescu. Litho)

1972 (25 Apr). Olympic Games, Munich (1st issue). T **729** and similar horiz designs, showing sports. Multicoloured. P 13½.

(a) POSTAGE

3892	10b. Type **729**	10	10
3893	20b. Canoeing	20	10
3894	55b. Football	30	10
3895	1l.55 High-jumping	80	15
3896	2l.90 Boxing	1·60	20
3897	6l.70 Volleyball	4·00	2·30
3892/3897	*Set of* 6	6·25	2·75

(b) AIR

MS3898 100×81 mm. 6l. Runner with Olympic Torch .... 16·00 16·00

Design of 6l. value is larger, 39×51 mm.

An imperforate miniature sheet, 131×91 mm, depicting Show Jumping, exists from a restricted printing.

See also Nos. 3914/**MS**3920 and 3926.

730 Stylized Map of Europe

731 Astronauts in Lunar Rover

(Des D. Danila. Photo)

1972 (28 Apr). Inter-European Cultural and Economic Co-operation. T **730** and similar horiz design. P 13½.

3899	1l.75 gold, black and bright magenta	1·50	1·40
	a. Pair. Nos. 3899/3900	3·75	3·50
3900	2l.90 gold, black and emerald	1·90	1·90

Design:—2l.90, "Crossed Arrows" symbol.

Nos. 3899/3900 were issued together in *se-tenant* pairs within sheets of ten stamps.

(Des R. Coteanu. Photo)

1972 (10 May). AIR. Moon Flight of "Apollo 16". P 13½.

3901 **731** 3l. deep blue, sage-green and rose .... 1·90 1·90

Issued in small sheets of four, together with four stamp-size labels showing astronauts and emblem.

732 Modern Trains and Symbol

(Des D. Danila. Photo)

1972 (20 May). 50th Anniversary of International Railway Union. P 13½.

3902 **732** 55b. multicoloured .... 1·50 45

733 "Summer" (P. Brueghel)

734 *Paeonia romanica*

(Des I. Dumitrana. Photo)

1972 (20 May). Belgica 72 Stamp Exhibition, Brussels. Sheet 89×76 mm. P 13½.

MS3903 **733** 6l. multicoloured .... 5·75 5·75

(Des V. Stoianov. Photo)

1972 (5 June). Scarce Romanian Flowers. T **734** and similar vert designs. P 13½.

3904	20b. multicoloured	10	10
3905	40b. magenta, bright green and chocolate	20	10
3906	55b. olive-bistre and blue	30	10
3907	60b. bright crimson, bright green and deep bluish green	50	15
3908	1l.35 multicoloured	95	20
3909	2l.90 multicoloured	2·10	65
3904/3909	*Set of* 6	3·75	1·20

Designs:—40b. *Dianthus callizonus*; 55b. Edelweiss (*Leontopodium alpinum*); 60b. Vanilla orchid (*Nigritella rubra*); 1l.35, *Narcissus stellaris*; 2l.90, Lady's slipper (*Cypripedium calceolus*).

735 Saligny Bridge, Cernavoda

(Des V. Stoianov. Photo)

1972 (25 June). Danube Bridges. T **735** and similar horiz designs. Multicoloured. P 13½.

3910	1l.35 Type **735**	60	10
3911	1l.75 Giurgeni Bridge, Vadul Oii	95	20
3912	2l.75 Prieteniei Bridge, Giurgiu-Ruse	1·90	45
3910/3912	*Set of* 3	3·00	70

736 North Railway Station, Bucharest, 1872

(Des Aida Tasgian-Constantinescu. Photo)

1972 (4 July). Centenary of North Railway Station, Bucharest. P 13½.

3913 **736** 55b. multicoloured .... 1·20 45

737 Water-polo

738 Rotary Stamp-Printing Press

(Des V. Grigorescu. Photo)

1972 (15 July–Sept). Olympic Games, Munich (2nd issue). T **737** and similar vert designs: Multicoloured. P 13½.

(a) POSTAGE

3914	10b. Type **737**	10	10
3915	20b. Pistol-shooting	20	10
3916	55b. Throwing the discus	30	10
3917	1l.55 Gymnastics	85	20
3918	2l.75 Canoeing	1·90	30
3919	6l.40 Fencing	3·50	1·90
3914/3919	*Set of* 6	6·25	2·40

(b) AIR. Inscr "posta aeriana"

MS3920 90×78 mm. 6l. Football (29.9) ... 14·50 14·50

An imperforate miniature sheet, 130×90 mm., depicting a Satellite, exists from a restricted printing.

(Des I. Dumitrana. Photo)

1972 (25 July). Centenary of State Stamp-Printing Works. P 13½.

3921 **738** 55b. multicoloured ... 95 45

739 "E. Stoenescu" (Stefan Popescu)

(Des I. Dumitrana. Photo)

1972 (10 Aug). Romanian Art. Portraits. T **739** and similar vert designs. Multicoloured. P 13½.

3922	55b. Type **739**	10	10
3923	1l.75 Self-portrait (Octav Bancila)	50	10
3924	2l.90 Self-portrait (Gheorghe Petrascu)	1·10	20
3925	6l.50 Self-portrait (Ion Andreescu)	2·10	65
3922/3925	*Set of 4*	3·50	95

740 Runner with Torch

741 Aurel Vlaicu, his Airplane No. 1 "Crazy Fly" and Silhouette of Boeing 707 Jetliner

(Des I. Dumitrana. Photo)

1972 (13 Aug). Olympic Games, Munich (3rd issue). P 13½.

3926 **740** 55b. purple, blue and silver ... 1·50 45

(Des I. Dumitrana. Photo)

1972 (15 Aug). AIR. Romanian Aviation Pioneers. T **741** and similar horiz design. Multicoloured. P 13½.

3927	60b. Type **741**	20	10
3928	3l. Traian Vuia, Vuia No. 1 and silhouette of Boeing 707 jetliner	1·90	95

742 Cluj Cathedral

743 Satu Mare

(Des Aida Tasgian-Constantinescu and I. Dumitrana. Photo)

1972 (15 Sept–Dec). T **742** and similar designs. P 13½.

(a) POSTAGE

3929	1l.85 reddish violet (20.12)	25	10
3930	2l.75 slate	50	10
3931	3l.35 crimson	70	10
3932	3l.45 greyish green	70	10
3933	5l.15 bright blue	95	10
3934	5l.60 greenish blue (20.12)	1·10	10
3935	6l.20 magenta	1·20	10
3936	6l.40 sepia	1·30	10
3937	6l.80 red (20.12)	1·40	10
3938	7l.05 black	1·50	10
3939	8l.45 rose-red	1·60	10
3940	9l.05 slate-green (20.12)	1·60	10
3941	9l.10 bright blue (20.12)	1·60	10
3942	9l.85 myrtle-green (20.12)	1·90	10
3943	10l. purple-brown	2·00	10
3944	11l.90 indigo (20.12)	2·10	20
3945	12l.75 violet (20.12)	2·20	20
3946	13l.30 Venetian red (20.12)	2·40	20
3947	16l.20 olive-green	3·00	20

(b) AIR. Inscr "POSTA AERIANA"

3948	14l.60 new blue (20.12)	2·50	55
3929/3948	*Set of 20*	27·00	2·50

Designs: Vert (17×24 mm)—3l.35, Heroes' Monument, Bucharest; 5l.60, Iasi-Biserica; 6l.20, Bran Castle; 7l.05, Black Church, Brasova; 8l.45, Atheneum, Bucharest; 9l.85, Decebal's statue, Cetatea Deva; (20×30 mm)—10l. City Hall Tower, Sibiu; 12l.75, TV Building, Bucharest; 16l.20, Clock Tower, Sighisoara. Horiz (24×17 mm)—2l.75, Sphinx Rock, Mt. Bucegi; 3l.45, Sinaia Castle; 5l.15, Hydro-electric power station, Arges; 6l.40, Hunidoara Castle; 6l.80, Bucharest Polytechnic complex; 9l.05, Coliseum, Sarmisegetuza; 9l.10, Hydro-electric power station, Iron Gates; (30×20 mm)—11l.90, Palace of the Republic, Bucharest; 13l.30, City Gate, Alba Julia; 14l.60, Otopeni Airport, Bucharest.

(Des V. Stoianov. Photo)

1972 (5 Oct). Millennium of Satu Mare. P 13½.

3949 **743** 55b. multicoloured ... 95 45

744 Davis Cup on Racquet

(Des I. Dumitrana. Photo)

1972 (10 Oct). Final of Davis Cup Men's Team Tennis Championship, Bucharest. P 13½.

3950 **744** 2l.75 multicoloured ... 2·40 65

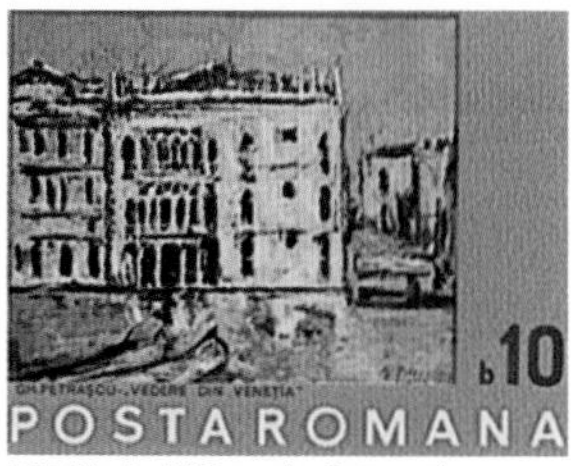

745 "Venice" (Gheorghe Petrascu)

(Des Aida Tasgian-Constantinescu. Photo)

1972 (20 Oct). U.N.E.S.C.O. "Save Venice" Campaign. Paintings of Venice. T **745** and similar designs. Multicoloured. P 13½.

3951	10b. Type **745**	10	10
3952	20b. Gondolas (N. Darascu)	10	10
3953	55b. Palace (Petrascu)	20	10
3954	1l.55 Bridge (Marius Bunescu)	50	10
3955	2l.75 Palace (Darascu) (vert)	1·20	20
3956	6l.40 Canal (Bunescu)	2·50	1·20
3951/3956	*Set of 6*	4·25	1·60
MS3957	91×79 mm. 6l. Old houses (Petrascu)	5·75	5·75

746 Fencing and Bronze Medal

748 Flags and "25"

747 "Travelling Romanies" (E. Volkers)

(Des I. Dumitrana (No. **MS**3964), S. Zarimba (others). Litho (**MS**3964) or photo (others))

1972 (28 Oct). Munich Olympic Games Medals. T **746** and similar designs. Multicoloured. P 13½.

(a) POSTAGE

3958	10b. Type **746**	10	10
3959	20b. Handball and Bronze Medal	20	10
3960	35b. Boxing and Silver Medal	30	10
3961	1l.45 Hurdling and Silver Medal	85	10
3962	2l.75 Shooting, Silver and Bronze Medals	1·80	20
3963	6l.20 Wrestling and two Gold Medals	4·25	2·30
3958/3963	*Set of 6*	6·75	2·75

(b) AIR. Inscr "posta aeriana"

MS3964 90×80 mm. 6l. Gold and Silver Medals (horiz) ... 14·50 14·50

Design of 6l. value is larger, 50×38 mm.

An imperforate miniature sheet, 130×90 mm, depicting a Gold Medal, exists from a restricted printing.

(Des I. Dumitrana. Photo)

1972 (15 Nov). Stamp Day. P 13½.

3965 **747** 1l.10 +90b. multicoloured ... 1·70 95

No. 3965 was issued *se-tenant* with a premium-carrying tab as shown in Type **747**.

(Des A. Popescu. Photo)

1972 (10 Dec). 25th Anniv of Proclamation of Republic. T **748** and similar vert designs. Multicoloured. P 13½.

3966	55b. Type **748**	30	10
3967	1l.20 Arms and "25"	70	20
3968	1l.75 Industrial scene and "25"	1·10	30
3966/3968	*Set of 3*	1·90	55

749 "Apollo 1", "2" and "3"

750 European Bee Eater (*Merops apiaster*)

(Des V. Stoianov. Photo)

1972 (27 Dec). "Apollo" Moon Flights. T **749** and similar multicoloured designs. P 13½.

(a) POSTAGE

3969	10b. Type **749**	10	10
3970	35b. Grissom, Chaffee and White	10	10
3971	40b. "Apollo 4, 5, 6"	10	10
3972	55b. "Apollo 7 and 8"	30	10
3973	1l l. "Apollo 9 and 10"	50	10
3974	1l.20 "Apollo 11 and 12"	75	10
3975	1l.85 "Apollo 13 and 14"	1·00	15
3976	2l.75 "Apollo 15 and 16"	1·80	20
3977	3l.60 "Apollo 17"	3·25	1·50
3969/3977	*Set of 9*	7·00	2·20

(b) AIR. Inscr "POSTA AERIANA". Horiz design 49×38 mm.

MS3978 89×77 mm. 6l. Astronauts and Lunar Rover on Moon ... 18·00 18·00

An imperforate miniature sheet, 104×80 mm, depicting a Moon map, exists from a restricted printing.

(Des V. Stoianov. Photo)

1973 (5 Feb). Nature Protection. T **750** and similar vert designs. Multicoloured. P 13½.

(a) Birds

3979	1l.40 Type **750**	50	10
	a. Strip of 3. Nos. 3979/81	2·75	
3980	1l.85 Red-breasted goose (*Branta ruficollis*)	75	20
3981	2l.75 Penduline tit (*Remiz pendulinus*)	1·30	50

(b) Flowers

3982	1l.40 Globe flower (*Trollius europaeus*)	50	10
	a. Strip of 3. Nos. 3982/4	2·75	
3983	1l.85 Martagon lily (*Lilium martagon*)	75	20
3984	2l.75 Gentian (*Gentiana excisa*)	1·30	50
3979/3984	*Set of 6*	4·50	1·40

Nos. 3979/81 and 3982/4 respectively were issued in *se-tenant* strips of three stamps within their sheets.

751 Copernicus

752 Suceava Costume (female)

(Des I. Dumitrana. Photo)

1973 (19 Feb). 500th Birth Anniv of Copernicus (astronomer). P 13½.

3985 **751** 2l.75 multicoloured ... 1·30 50

No. 3985 was issued *se-tenant* with a stamp-size label showing the town hall and arms of Poznan, publicising the "Polska '73" Stamp Exhibition.

(Des D. Danila. Photo)

1973 (15 Mar). Regional Costumes. T **752** and similar vert designs. Multicoloured. P 13½.

3986	10b. Type **752**	10	10
3987	40b. Suceava (male)	10	10
3988	55b. Harghila (female)	20	10
3989	1l.75 Harghila (male)	85	10
3990	2l.75 Gorj (female)	1·30	30
3991	6l.40 Gorj (male)	2·50	1·50
3986/3991	*Set of 6*	4·50	2·00

753 Dimitrie Paciurea (sculptor)

754 Map of Europe

(Des I. Dumitrana. Photo)

1973 (26 Mar). Anniversaries. T **753** and similar vert designs. Multicoloured. P 13½.

3992	10b. Type **753** (birth centenary)	10	10
3993	40b. Ioan Slavici (writer, 125th birth anniv)	10	10
3994	55b. Gheorghe Lazar (educationist, death centenary)	30	10
3995	6l.40 Alexandru Flechtenmacher (composer, birth centenary)	3·25	1·50
3992/3995	*Set of 4*	3·50	1·60

(Des R. Coteanu. Photo)

1973 (28 Apr). Inter-European Cultural and Economic Co-operation. T **754** and similar horiz design. P 13½.

3996	3l.35 multicoloured	1·00	1·00
	a. Pair. Nos. 3996/7	3·25	3·25
3997	3l.60 gold and bright magenta	2·10	2·00

Design:—No. 3997, Emblem.

Nos. 3996/7 were issued together in *se-tenant* pairs within sheets of ten stamps.

755 "The Rape of Proserpine" (Hans von Aachen)

(Des Aida Tasgian-Constantinescu. Photo)

1973 (5 May). IBRA 73 Stamp Exhibition, Munich. Sheet 90×78 mm. P 13½.

MS3998 **755**	12l. multicoloured	12·50	12·50

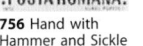

756 Hand with Hammer and Sickle

757 W.M.O. Emblem and Weather Satellite

(Des V. Stoianov (1l.75), A. Popescu (others). Photo)

1973 (28 May). Anniversaries. T **756** and similar vert designs. Multicoloured. P 13½.

3999	40b. Type **756**	65	30
4000	55b. Flags and bayonets	75	40
4001	1l.75 Prince Cuza	1·60	50
3999/4001 *Set of 3*		2·75	1·10

Events:—40b. 25th anniv of Romanian Workers and Peasants Party; 55b. 40th anniv of National Anti-Fascist Committee; 1l.75, Death centenary of Prince Alexandru Cuza.

(Des S. Zarimba. Photo)

1973 (15 June). Centenary of World Meteorological Organization. P 13½.

4002 **757**	2l. multicoloured	1·60	50

758 "Dimitri Ralet" (anon)

759 Prince Dimitri Cantemir

1973 (20 June). Socfilex III Stamp Exhibition, Bucharest. Portraits. T **758** and similar vert designs. Multicoloured. Photo. P 13½.

4003	40b. Type **758**	10	10
4004	60b. "Enacheta Vacarescu" (A. Chladek)	20	10
4005	1l.55 "Dimitri Aman" (C. Lecca)	65	10
4006	4l. +2l. "Barbat at his Desk" (B. Iscovescu)	2·50	1·50
4003/4006 *Set of 4*		3·00	1·60
MS4007	78×89 mm. 6l.+2l. "The Poet Alecsandri and his Family" (N. Livaditti)	6·25	6·25

Design of 6l.+2l. value is larger, 38×51 mm.

(Des. I. Dumitrana. Photo)

1973 (25 June). 300th Birth Anniversary of Dimitri Cantemir, Prince of Moldavia (writer). P 13½.

4008 **759**	1l.75 multicoloured	1·60	50
MS4009	77×90 mm. 6l. multicoloured	6·25	6·25

Design: (38×51 mm)—6l. Miniature of Cantemir.

760 Fibular Brooches

(Des Aida Tasgian-Constantinescu. Photo)

1973 (25 July). 4th-century treasures of Pietroasa. T **760** and similar multicoloured designs. P 13½.

4010	10b. Type **760**	10	10
4011	20b. Golden figurine and bowl (horiz)	10	10
4012	55b. Gold oil flask	20	10
4013	1l.55 Brooch and bracelets (horiz)	85	10
4014	2l.75 Gold platter	1·30	20
4015	6l.80 Filigree cup-holder (horiz)	2·50	1·50
4010/4015 *Set of 6*		4·50	1·90
MS4016	78×91 mm. 12l. Jewelled breastplate	6·25	6·25

761 Map within "Flower"

762 Oboga Jar

(Des Aida Tasgian-Constantinescu. Photo)

1973 (2 Oct). European Security and Co-operation Conference, Helsinki. Sheet 152×81 mm. containing T **761** and similar horiz design. Multicoloured. P 13½.

MS4017	2l.75×2 Type **761**; 5l.×2 Europa "Tree"	4·25	4·25

No. **MS**4017 also contains two stamp-size labels depicting Conference Hall, Helsinki, and Palais des Nations, Geneva.

(Des V. Stoianov. Photo)

1973 (15 Oct). Romanian Ceramics. T **762** and similar horiz designs. Multicoloured. P 13½.

4018	10b. Type **762**	10	10
4019	20b. Vama dish and jug	10	10
4020	55b. Maginea bowl	10	10
4021	1l.55 Sibiu Saschiz jug and dish	85	15
4022	2l.75 Pisc pot and dish	1·30	20
4023	6l.80 Oboga "bird" vessel	2·50	70
4018/4023 *Set of 6*		4·50	1·20

763 "Postilion" (A. Verona)

764 "Textile Workers" (G. Saru)

(Des I. Dumitrana. Photo)

1973 (15 Nov). Stamp Day. P 13½.

4024 **763**	1l.10 +90b. multicoloured	1·00	1·00

No. 4024 was issued in sheets with half stamp-size *se-tenant* labels, carrying the premium.

(Des S. Zarimba. Photo)

1973 (15 Nov). Paintings showing Workers. T **764** and similar multicoloured designs. P 13½.

4025	10b. Type **764**	10	10
4026	20b. "Construction Site" (M. Bunescu) (horiz)	10	10
4027	55b. "Shipyard Workers" (H. Catargi) (horiz)	20	10
4028	1l.55 "Working Man" (H. Catargi)	50	15
4029	2l.75 "Miners" (A. Phoebus)	1·00	20
4030	6l.80 "The Spinner" (N. Grigorescu)	2·50	80
4025/4030 *Set of 6*		4·00	1·30
MS4031	90×77 mm. 12l. "Harvest Meal" (S. Popescu) (horiz)	6·25	6·25

765 Town Hall, Craiova

D **766** Postal Emblems and Postman

(Des I. Untsch. Photo)

1973 (15 Dec)–**74**. T **765** and similar designs. P 13½.

(a) Buildings (15.12.73)

4032	5b. brown-lake	10	10
4033	10b. new blue	10	10
4034	20b. red-orange	10	10
4035	35b. myrtle-green	10	10
4036	40b. deep bluish violet	10	10
4037	50b. blue	10	10
4038	55b. orange-brown	20	10
4039	60b. scarlet	20	10
4040	1l. ultramarine	30	10
4041	1l.20 bronze-green	30	20

(b) Ships (28.1.74)

4042	1l.35 black	30	10
4043	1l.45 greenish blue	30	10
4044	1l.50 rose-carmine	30	10
4045	1l.55 ultramarine	40	10
4046	1l.75 blackish olive	40	10
4047	2l.20 new blue	50	10
4048	3l.65 slate-lilac	95	20
4049	4l.70 dull purple	1·40	30
4032/4049 *Set of 18*		5·50	2·00

Designs: Vert—10b. "Column of Infinity", Tirgu Jiu; 40b. Romanesque church, Densus; 50b. Reformed Church, Dej; 1l. Curtea de Arges Monastery. Horiz—20b. Heroes' Monument, Marasesti; 35b. Citadel, Risnov; 55b. Castle, Maldarasti; 60b. National Theatre, Jassy; 1l.20, Fortress and church, Tigru Mures; 1l.35, *Impingator* (tug) and barges, R. Danube; 1l.45, *Dimbovita* (freighter); 1l.50, *Muntenia* (Danube passenger vessel); 1l.55, *Mircea* (cadet barque); 1l.75, *Transylvania* (liner); 2l.20, *Oltul* (bulk carrier); 3l.65, *Mures* (trawler); 4l.70, *Arges* (tanker).

1974 (10 Jan). POSTAGE DUE. Type D **766** and similar horiz designs. Photo. P 13½.

			Un pair	*Us pair*
D4050	D **766**	5b. new blue	20	20
D4051		10b. olive-green	20	20
D4052	–	20b. bright magenta	20	20
D4053	–	40b. violet	50	20
D4054	–	50b. orange-brown	50	20
D4055	–	1l. yellow-orange	1·00	20
D4050/4055 *Set of 6 pairs*			2·30	1·10

Designs:—20, 40b. Dove with letter and Hermes with posthorn; 50b., 1l. G.P.O. Bucharest and emblem with mail-van.

See also Nos. D4761/6.

767 "Boats at Honfleur" (C. Monet)

1974 (18 Mar). Impressionist Paintings. T **767** and similar multicoloured designs. Photo. P 13½.

4056	20b. Type **767**	10	10
4057	40b. "Moret Church" (A. Sisley) (vert)	10	10
4058	55b. "Orchard in Blossom" (C. Pissarro)	20	10
4059	1l.75 "Jeanne" (C. Pissarro) (vert)	75	10
4060	2l.75 "Landscape" (A. Renoir)	1·30	30
4061	3l.60 "Portrait of a Girl" (P. Cezanne) (vert)	2·30	60
4056/4061 *Set of 6*		4·25	1·20
MS4062	78×84 mm. 10l. "Women Bathing" (Renoir) (vert)	6·25	6·25

768 Trotting with Sulky

769 Nicolas Titulescu (Romanian League of Nations Delegate)

(Des E. Palade. Photo)

1974 (5 Apr). Centenary of Horse-racing in Romania. T **768** and similar horiz designs. Multicoloured. P 13½.

4063	40b. Type **768**	10	10
4064	55b. Three horses racing	20	10
4065	60b. Horse galloping	30	15
4066	1l.55 Two trotters racing	65	20
4067	2l.75 Three trotters racing	1·60	30
4068	3l.45 Two horses racing	2·30	60
4063/4068 *Set of 6*		4·75	1·30

(Des Aida Tasgian-Constantinescu. Photo)

1974 (16 Apr). Interparliamentary Congress Session, Bucharest. P 13½.

4069 **769**	1l.75 multicoloured	1·00	50

770 Roman Monument

1974 (20 Apr). 1850th Anniv of Cluj (Napoca). Sheet 78×91 mm. Photo. P 13½.

MS4070 **770**	10l. black and orange-brown	6·25	6·25

771 "Anniversary Parade" (Pepene Cornelia)

(Des A. Popescu. Photo)

1974 (25 Apr). 25th Anniv of Romanian Pioneers Organization. P 13½.
4071 **771** 55b. multicoloured .... 1·00 50

ROMÂNIA
CAMPIOANĂ
MONDIALĂ
1974

772 "Europe"

175L

(**773**)

(Des D. Danila. Photo)

1974 (27 Apr). Inter-European Cultural and Economic Cooperation. T **772** and similar horiz design. Multicoloured. P 13½.
4072 2l.20 Type **772** .... 1·00 1·00
a. Pair. Nos. 4072/3 .... 3·25 3·25
4073 3l.45 Satellite over Europe .... 2·10 2·00
Nos. 4071/2 were issued together in *se-tenant* pairs within sheets of ten stamps.

1974 (13 May). Romania's Victory in World Handball Championships. No. 3959 surch with T **773**.
4074 1l.75 on 20b. multicoloured .... 5·25 5·00

774 Postal Motor Boat

775 Footballers

(Des E. Palade. Photo)

1974 (15 May). Centenary of Universal Postal Union. T **774** and similar horiz designs. Multicoloured. P 13½.
4075 20b. Type **774** 10 10
4076 40b. Loading mail train 10 10
4077 55b. Loading Ilyushin Il-62M mail plane ... 20 15
4078 1l.75 Rural postman delivering letter 95 20
4079 2l.75 Town postman delivering letter .... 1·20 30
4080 3l.60 Young stamp collectors .... 1·80 50
4075/4080 *Set of 6* .... 4·00 1·20
MS4081 90×78 mm. 4l. Postman clearing post-box; 6l. Letters and G.P.O., Bucharest (each 28×22 mm) .... 6·25 6·25
An imperforate miniature sheet, 107×80 mm, depicting the U.P.U. Monument, Berne, exists from a limited printing.

(Des V. Stoianov. Photo)

1974 (15 June). World Cup Football Championship, West Germany. T **775** and similar designs showing football scenes. P 13½.
4082 20b. multicoloured 10 10
4083 40b. multicoloured 10 10
4084 55b. multicoloured 20 10
4085 1l.75 multicoloured 50 20
4086 2l.75 multicoloured .... 1·00 30
4087 3l.60 multicoloured .... 1·60 50
4082/4087 *Set of 6* .... 3·25 1·20
MS4088 90×78 mm. 10l. Three footballers (horiz, 50×38 mm) .... 6·25 6·25
An imperforate miniature sheet, 108×80 mm, depicting a "World" football, exists from a restricted printing.

776 Anniversary Emblem

777 U.N. and World Population Emblems

(Des V. Stoianov. Photo)

1974 (17 June). 25th Anniv of Council for Mutual Economic Aid. P 13½.
4089 **776** 55b. multicoloured 85 50

(Des D. Danila. Photo)

1974 (25 June). World Population Year Conference, Bucharest. P 13½.
4090 **777** 2l. multicoloured .... 1·30 50

778 Emblem on Map of Europe

779 Hand drawing Peace Dove

(Des R. Coteanu. Photo)

1974 (25 June). Euromax 1974 International Stamp Exhibition, Bucharest. P 13½.
4091 **778** 4l. +3l. greenish yellow, ultramarine and red .... 3·25 70

(Des G. Bozianu and S. Popescu. Photo)

1974 (28 June). 25th Anniv of World Peace Movement. P 13½.
4092 **779** 2l. multicoloured .... 1·30 50

780 Prince John of Wallachia (400th birth anniv)

781 Romanian and Soviet Flags as "XXX"

(Des I. Untsch (1l.), I. Dumitrana and L. Catach (others). Photo)

1974 (10–23 July). Anniversaries. T **780** and similar designs. Photo. P 13½.
4093 20b. deep greenish blue (23.7) 10 10
4094 55b. carmine (23.7) 20 10
4095 1l. deep turquoise-blue 30 10
4096 1l.10 deep brown-olive (23.7) 40 10
4097 1l.30 brown-purple (23.7) 65 10
4098 1l.40 deep violet (23.7) 75 20
4093/4098 *Set of 6* .... 2·20 65
Designs: Horiz—55b. Soldier guarding industrial installations (30th anniv of Romanian Peoples Army). Vert—1l. Blast furnace (220th anniv of Hunedoara iron and steel works); 1l.10, Avram Iancu (revolutionary) (150th birth anniv); 1l.30, Dr. C. I. Parhon (birth centenary); 1l.40, Dosoftei (metropolitan) (350th birth anniv).

(Des E. Palade. Photo)

1974 (20 Aug). 30th Anniv of Liberation. T **781** and similar multicoloured design. P 13½.
4099 40b. Type **781** 20 10
4100 55b. People of Romania and flags (horiz). 30 20

782 View of Stockholm

783 *Centaurea nervosa*

(Des R. Coteanu. Photo)

1974 (10 Sept). Stockholmia 1974 International Stamp Exhibition. Sheet 91×78 mm. P 13½.
MS4101 **782** 10l. multicoloured .... 6·25 6·25

(Des Aida Tasgian-Constantinescu. Photo)

1974 (15 Sept). Nature Conservation. Wild Flowers. T **783** and similar vert designs. Multicoloured. P 13½.
4102 20b. Type **783** 10 10
4103 40b. *Fritillaria montana* 10 10
4104 55b. Yew (*Taxus baccata*) 20 15
4105 1l.75 *Rhododendron kotschyi* 75 20
4106 2l.75 Alpine forgetmenot (*Eritrichium nanum*) .... 1·00 30
4107 3l.60 Pink (*Dianthus spiculifolius*) .... 1·60 50
4102/4107 *Set of 6* .... 3·50 1·20

784 Bust of Isis

(Des Aida Tasgian-Constantinescu. Photo)

1974 (20 Oct). Roman Archaeological Finds. Sculpture. T **784** and similar vert designs. Multicoloured. P 13½.
4108 20b. Type **784** 10 10
4109 40b. "Glykon" serpent 20 10
4110 55b. Head of Emperor Decius 30 15
4111 1l.75 Romanian woman 65 20
4112 2l.75 Mithras .... 1·00 30
4113 3l.60 Roman senator .... 1·70 50
4108/4113 *Set of 6* .... 3·50 1·20

785 Sibiu Market Place

EXPOZIŢIA FILATELICĂ „NAŢIONALA '74"
15–24 noiembrie
Bucureşti

(**786**)

1974 (15 Nov). Stamp Day. Photo. P 13½.
4114 **785** 2l.10 +1l.90 multicoloured .... 2·30 60

1974 (15 Nov). Nationala 1974 Stamp Exhibition. No. 4114 optd with T **786**, in red. P 13½.
4115 **785** 2l.10 +1l.90 multicoloured .... 4·25 4·25

787 Party Emblem

(Des Aida Tasgian-Constantinescu. Photo)

1974 (20 Nov). 11th Romanian Communist Party Congress, Bucharest. T **787** and similar vert design showing party emblem. P 13½.
4116 55b. multicoloured 20 10
4117 1l. multicoloured 50 30

788 "The Discus-thrower" (Myron)

(Des A. Popescu. Photo)

1974 (1 Dec). 60th Anniv of Romanian Olympic Committee. P 13½.
4118 **788** 2l. multicoloured .... 1·60 50

789 "Skylab"

790 Dr. Albert Schweitzer

(Des G. Bozianu. Photo)

1974 (16 Dec). "Skylab" Space Laboratory Project. P 13½.
4119 **789** 2l.50 multicoloured .... 1·60 1·50
Issued in small sheets of four, together with four different stamp-size labels.
An imperforate miniature sheet, 80×108 mm, depicting "Skylab", exists from a restricted printing.

(Des I. Dumitrana. Photo)

1974 (20 Dec). Birth Centenary of Dr. Albert Schweitzer (Nobel Peace Prize-winner). P 13½.

4120 **790** 40b. agate 50 50

791 Handball

792 "Rocks and Birches"

(Des A. Popescu. Photo)

1975 (4 Jan). World Universities' Handball Championships, Romania. T **791** and similar designs showing handball games. P 13½.

4121	55b. multicoloured	20	10
4122	1l.75 multicoloured (vert)	65	20
4123	2l.20 multicoloured	95	30
4121/4123	*Set of 3*	1·60	55

(Des I. Dumitrana. Photo)

1975 (25 Jan). Paintings by Ion Andreescu. T **792** and similar multicoloured designs. P 13½.

4124	20b. Type **792**	10	10
4125	40b. "Peasant Woman with Green Kerchief"	10	10
4126	55b. "Winter in the Forest"	20	15
4127	1l.75 "Winter in Barbizon" (horiz)	50	20
4128	2l.75 "Self-portrait"	1·00	50
4129	3l.60 "Main Road" (horiz)	1·60	80
4124/4129	*Set of 6*	3·25	1·70

793 Torch and Inscription

794 "Battle of High Bridge" (O. Obedeanu)

(Des G. Bozianu. Photo)

1975 (10 Feb). 10th Anniv of Romanian Socialist Republic. P 13½.

4130 **793** 40b. multicoloured 50 30

(Des D. Danila. Photo)

1975 (25 Feb). 500th Anniv of Victory over the Ottomans at High Bridge. P 13½.

4131 **794** 55b. multicoloured 65 30

795 "Peasant Woman Spinning" (Nicolae Grigorescu)

796 "Self-portrait"

(Des Govt Ptg Wks, Bucharest. Photo)

1975 (8 Mar). International Women's Year. P 13½.

4132 **795** 55b. multicoloured 65 30

(Des V. Stoianov. Photo)

1975 (15 Mar). 500th Birth Anniv of Michelangelo. P 13½.

4133 **796** 5l. multicoloured .... 2·50 50

797 Escorial Palace, Madrid

(Des R. Coteanu. Photo)

1975 (25 Mar). Espana 1975 International Stamp Exhibition, Madrid. Sheet 90×78 mm. P 13½.

MS4134 **797** 10l. multicoloured .... 5·25 5·25

798 Mitsui Children's Science Pavilion, Okinawa

(Des V. Stoianov. Photo)

1975 (10 Apr). International Exposition, Okinawa. P 13½.

4135 **798** 4l. multicoloured .... 2·30 60

799 "Peonies" (Nicolae Tonitza)

(Des Aida Tasgian-Constantinescu. Photo)

1975 (28 Apr). Inter-European Cultural and Economic Co-operation. Floral Paintings. T **799** and similar horiz design. Multicoloured. P 13½.

4136	2l.20 Type **799**	1·00	1·00
	a. Pair. Nos. 4136/7	2·75	2·75
4137	3l.45 "Chrysanthemums" (Stefan Luchian)	1·60	1·50

Nos. 4136/7 were issued together in *se-tenant* pairs within sheets of ten stamps.

800 Dove with Coded Letter

(Des D. Danila. Photo)

1975 (2 May). Introduction of Postal Coding. P 13½.

4138 **800** 55b. multicoloured 65 30

801 Convention Emblem on "Globe"

(Des E. Palade. Photo)

1975 (20 May). Centenary of the International Metre Convention. P 13½.

4139 **801** 1l.85 multicoloured .... 1·30 50

802 Mihail Eminescu and Museum

(Des I. Untsch. Photo)

1975 (20 May). 125th Birth Anniv of Mihail Eminescu (poet). P 13½.

4140 **802** 55b. multicoloured 65 30

803 Roman Coins and Stone Inscription

(Des V. Stoianov. Photo)

1975 (27 May). Bimillenary of Alba Julia. P 13½.

4141 **803** 55b. multicoloured 65 30

804 "On the Banks of the Seine" (Th. Pallady)

805 Ana Ipatescu

(Des D. Danila. Photo)

1975 (29 May). Arphila 1975 International Stamp Exhibition, Paris. Sheet 76×90 mm. P 13½.

MS4142 **804** 10l. multicoloured .... 5·25 5·25

(Des I. Untsch. Photo)

1975 (5 June). Death Centenary of Ana Ipatescu (revolutionary). P 13½.

4143 **805** 55b. carmine 65 30

806 Turnu-Severin

(Des A. Constantinescu. Photo)

1975 (26 June). European Architectural Heritage Year. Roman Antiquities. T **806** and similar designs. P 13½.

4144	55b. black and chestnut	20	10
4145	1l.20 black, new blue and royal blue	30	20
4146	1l.55 black and dull yellowish green	50	30
4147	1l.75 black and claret	75	40
4148	2l. black and yellow-ochre	85	50
4149	2l.25 black and new blue	1·60	80
4144/4149	Set of 6	3·75	2·10
MS4150	79×91 mm. 10l. multicoloured	3·25	3·25

Designs: Vert—55b. Emperor Trajan; 1l.20, Trajan's Column, Rome; 1l.55, Decebalus (sculpture); 10l. Roman remains, Gradiste. Horiz—1l.75, Imperial Monument, Adam Clissi; 2l.25, Trajan's Bridge.

An imperforate miniature sheet, 80×108 mm, depicting Romulus, Remus and the Wolf, exists from a restricted printing.

807 "Apollo" and "Soyuz" Spacecraft

(Des V. Stoianov. Photo)

1975 (14 July). AIR. "Apollo"–"Soyuz" Space Link. T **807** and similar horiz design. Multicoloured. P 13½.

4151	1l.75 Type **807**	1·60	1·50
	a. Pair. Nos. 4151/2	4·00	3·75
4152	3l.25 "Apollo" and "Soyuz" linked together	2·10	2·00

Nos. 4151/2 were issued together in *se-tenant* pairs within sheets of four stamps and four labels showing the link emblem.

808 "Michael the Brave" (Aegidius Sadeler)

(Des Govt Ptg Wks, Bucharest. Photo)

1975 (15 July). 375th Anniv of First Political Union of Romanian States. T **808** and similar multicoloured designs. P 13½.

4153	55b. Type **808**	20	10
4154	1l.20 "Ottoman Envoys bringing gifts to Michael the Brave" (Theodov Aman) (horiz)	50	10
4155	2l.75 "Michael the Brave at Calugareni" (T. Aman)	1·20	30
4153/4155	*Set of 3*	1·70	45

An imperforate miniature sheet, 84×104 mm, depicting a statue of Michael the Brave and issued on 20 Sept. 1975, exists from a restricted printing.

809 Map of Europe

810 Larkspur (*Delphinium consolida*)

(Des D. Danila. Photo)

1975 (30 July). European Security and Co-operation Conference, Helsinki. Sheet 111×81 mm containing T **809** and similar horiz designs. Multicoloured. P 13½.

MS4156	(a) POSTAGE. 2l.75 Type **809**; 5l. Open book; 5l. Children playing; (b) AIR. Inscr. "posta aeriana". 2l.75 Peace doves	2·50	2·50

An imperforate miniature sheet, 84×104 mm, depicting a map of Europe, exists from a restricted printing.

(Des G. Bozianu. Photo)

1975 (15 Aug). International Botanical Conference, Romania. Wild Flowers. T **810** and similar vert designs. Multicoloured. P 13½.

4157	20b. Type **810**	10	10
4158	40b. Long-headed poppy (*Papaver dubium*)	10	10
4159	55b. Common immortelle (*Xeranthemum annuum*)	20	10
4160	1l.75 Common rock-rose (*Helianthemum nummularium*)	65	20
4161	2l.75 Meadow clary (*Salvia pratensis*)	1·30	30
4162	3l.60 Chicory (*Cichorium intybus*)	1·60	50
4157/4162	*Set of* 6	3·50	9·25

Tirg internațional
de mărci poștale

Riccione — Italia
23–25 august 1975

(**811**)

812 Policeman using Walkie-talkie

813 Text on Map of Pelendava

1975 (23 Aug). International Philatelic Fair, Riccione. No. 4133 optd with T **811** in red.

4163	**796**	5l. multicoloured	5·25	5·00

(Des R. Coteanu. Photo)

1975 (1 Sept). Road Safety. P 13½.

4164	**812**	55b. blue	65	30

(Des A. Popescu. Photo)

1975 (20 Sept). First Documentary Attestations of Daco-Getian Settlements of Pelendava (1750th Anniv) and Craiova (500th Anniv). T **813** and similar multicoloured designs. P 13½.

4165	20b. Type **813**	15	10
	a. Horiz strip of 3. Nos. 4165/7	80	
4166	55b. Map of Pelendava showing location of Craiova (82×33 mm)	20	10
4167	1l. Text on Map of Pelendava	40	15
4165/4167	*Set of* 3	70	30

Nos. 4165/7 were issued together in *se-tenant* strips of three stamps within the sheet, each strip forming a composite design.

814 Muntenia Carpet

(Des. "Vlasto". Photo)

1975 (5 Oct). Romanian Traditional Carpets. T **814** and similar horiz designs. Multicoloured. P 13½.

4168	20b. Type **814**	10	10
4169	40b. Banat carpet	10	10
4170	55b. Oltenia carpet	20	10
4171	1l.75 Moldova carpet	85	20
4172	2l.75 Oltenia carpet	1·20	30
4173	3l.60 Maramures carpet	1·50	50
4168/4173	*Set of* 6	3·50	1·20

815 T.V. "12 M" Minibus

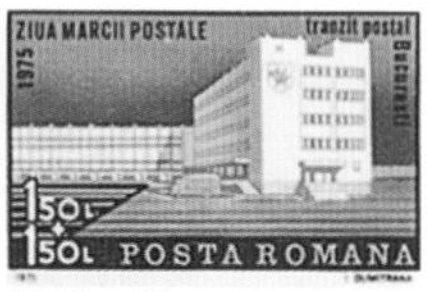

816 Postal Transit Centre, Bucharest

(Des I. Dumitrana. Photo)

1975 (5 Nov). Romanian Motor Vehicles. T **815** and similar horiz designs. Multicoloured. P 13½.

4174	20b. Type **815**	10	10
4175	40b. L.K.W. "19 A.L.P." Oil tanker	10	10
4176	55b. A.R.O. "240" Field car	20	10
4177	1l.75 L.K.W. "R 8135 F" Truck	85	20
4178	2l.75 P.K.W. "Dacia 1300" Saloon car	1·20	30
4179	3l.60 L.K.W. "R 19215 D.F.K." Tipper truck	1·50	50
4174/4179	*Set of* 6	3·50	1·20

(Des I. Dumitrana (1l.50), I. Untsch (2l.10). Photo)

1975 (15 Nov). Stamp Day. T **816** and similar horiz design showing the postal transit centre, Bucharest. P 13½.

4180	1l.50 +1l.50 multicoloured	2·10	1·00
4181	2l.10 +1l.90 multicoloured	3·75	1·50

817 "Winter" (Pieter Brueghel)

(Des R. Coteanu. Photo)

1975 (25 Nov). Themabelga 1975 International Stamp Exhibition, Brussels. Sheet 90×78 mm. P 13½.

MS4182	**817**	10l. multicoloured	5·75	5·75

818 Tobogganing

(Des R. Coteanu. Photo)

1976 (12 Jan). Winter Olympic Games, Innsbruck. T **818** and similar multicoloured designs. P 13½.

4183	20b. Type **818**	10	10
4184	40b. Rifle-shooting (vert)	20	15
4185	55b. Skiing	40	20
4186	1l.75 Ski jumping	75	30
4187	2l.75 Figure skating	1·40	50
4188	3l.60 Ice hockey	1·50	1·10
4183/4188	*Set of* 6	4·00	2·10
MS4189	91×78 mm. 10l. Bobsleighing	9·00	9·00

An imperforate miniature sheet, 108×80 mm, depicting slalom skiing, exists from a restricted printing.

819 "Washington at Valley Forge" (W. Trego)

(Des I. Dumitrana. Photo)

1976 (25 Jan). Bicentenary of American Revolution, and Interphil '76 International Stamp Exhibition, Philadelphia. Paintings. T **819** and similar multicoloured designs. P 13½.

4190	20b. Type **819**	10	10
4191	40b. "Washington at Trenton" (J. Trumbull) (vert)	10	10
4192	55b. "Washington crossing the Delaware" (E. Leutze)	20	10
4193	1l.75 "Capture of the Hessians" (J. Trumbull)	50	20
4194	2l.75 "Jefferson" (T. Sully) (vert)	1·00	30
4195	3l.60 "Surrender of Cornwallis at Yorktown" (J. Trumbull)	1·30	40
4190/4195	*Set of* 6	3·00	1·10
MS4196	91×78 mm. 10l. "Signing of Declaration of Independence" (J. Trumbull)	5·25	5·25

Nos. 4190/5 were each issued in sheets of 20 stamps and 5 labels bearing the Bicentenary emblem.

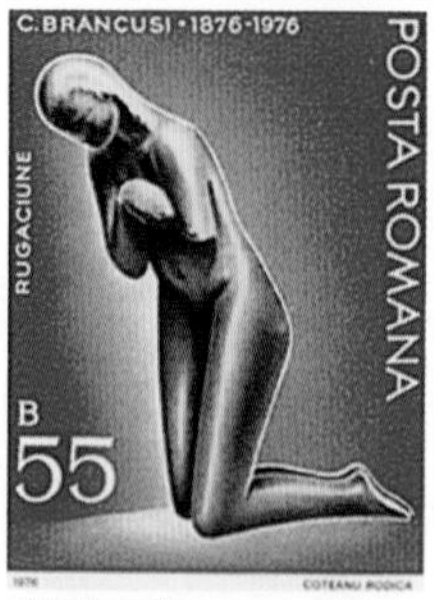

820 "Prayer"

821 Anton Davidoglu (mathematician) (Birth centenary)

(Des R. Coteanu. Photo)

1976 (15 Feb). Birth Centenary of Constantin Brancusi (sculptor). T **820** and similar vert designs. P 13½.

4197	55b. blackish brown, greenish yellow and deep mauve	20	10
4198	1l.75 bistre-brown, stone and greenish blue	50	30
4199	3l.60 multicoloured	1·80	50
4197/4199	*Set of* 3	2·30	80

Designs:—1l.75, Architectural assembly, Tg. Jiu; 3l.60, C. Brancusi.

(Des I. Untch. Photo)

1976 (25 Feb). Anniversaries. T **821** and similar vert designs. Multicoloured. P 13½.

4200	40b. Type **821**	20	10
4201	55b. Vlad Tepes (warrior) (500th death anniv)	20	10
4202	1l.20 Costache Negri (patriot) (Death centenary)	40	10
4203	1l.75 Gallery (50th Anniv of Archives Museum)	65	20
4200/4203	*Set of* 4	1·30	45

822 Inscribed Tablets, Tibiscum (Banat)

(Des Aida Tasgian-Constantinescu. Photo)

1976 (25 Mar). Daco-Roman Archaeological Finds. T **822** and similar designs. P 13½.

4204	20b. multicoloured	10	10
4205	40b. black, grey and red	20	10
4206	55b. multicoloured	30	15
4207	1l.75 multicoloured	85	20
4208	2l.75 black, grey and Venetian red	1·00	30
4209	3l.60 black, grey and turquoise-green	1·70	70
4204/4209	*Set of* 6	3·75	1·40
MS4210	78×91 mm. 10l. multicoloured	6·25	6·25

Designs: Horiz—40b. Sculptures (Banat); 55b. Inscribed tablet, coins and cup (Crisana); 1l.75, Pottery (Crisana); 2l.75, Altar and spears, Maramures (Banat); 3l.60, Vase and spears, Maramures. Vert—10l. Vase and coins (Crisana).

An imperforate miniature sheet, 80×108 mm, depicting a flask and coins, exists from a restricted printing.

823 Dr. Carol Davila

824 King Decebalus Vase

(Des D. Danila. Photo)

1976 (20 Apr). Centenary of Romanian Red Cross. T **823** and similar vert designs. Multicoloured. P 13½.

(a) POSTAGE

4211	55b. Type **823**	20	10
4212	1l.75 Nurse and patient	50	10
4213	2l.20 First aid	75	10

(b) AIR. Inscr "posta aeriana"

4214	3l.35 Blood donors	1·30	20
4211/4214	*Set of* 4	2·50	45

(Des A. Popescu. Photo)

1976 (13 May). Inter-European Cultural and Economic Co-operation. Vases from Cluj-Napoca porcelain factory. T **824** and similar vert design. Multicoloured. P 13½.

4215	2l.20 Type **824**	50	50
4216	3l.45 King Michael the Brave vase	1·20	1·00

Issued in small sheets of four stamps.

825 Romanian Arms **826** de Havilland D.H.9C

(Des I. Dumitrana. Litho)

1976 (12 June). P 13½.
4217 **825** 1l.75 multicoloured .... 1·30 50

(Des A. Popescu. Photo)

1976 (24 June). AIR. 50th Anniv of Romanian Airline. T **826** and similar horiz designs. Multicoloured. P 13½.

4218	20b. Type **826**	10	10
4219	40b. I.C.A.R. Commercial	15	10
4220	60b. Douglas DC-3	20	10
4221	1l.75 Antonov An-24	75	15
4222	2l.75 Ilyushin Il-62 jetliner	1·00	30
4223	3l.60 Boeing 707 jetliner	1·60	50
4218/4223	*Set of 6*	3·50	1·10

827 Gymnastics **828** Spiru Haret

(Des I. Dumitrana (20b., 40b., 55b., 1l.75, 2l.75, 3l.60), A. Popescu (10l.). Photo)

1976 (25 June). Olympic Games, Montreal. T **827** and similar multicoloured designs. P 13½.

4224	20b. Type **827**	10	10
4225	40b. Boxing	20	10
4226	55b. Handball	40	10
4227	1l.75 Rowing (horiz)	75	20
4228	2l.75 Gymnastics (horiz)	1·00	30
4229	3l.60 Canoeing (horiz)	1·60	40
4224/4229	*Set of 6*	3·75	1·10
MS4230	91×78 mm. 10l. Gymnastics (55×42 mm)	6·25	6·25

An imperforate miniature sheet, 105×79 mm, depicting the Olympic stadium, exists from a restricted printing.

(Des D. Danila. Photo)

1976 (25 June). 125th Birth Anniv of Spiru Haret (mathematician). P 13½.
4231 **828** 20b. multicoloured 50 30

EXPOZIŢIA FILATELICĂ
BUCUREŞTI
12–19.IX.1976

1,80
+

829 Daco-Getian Sculpture on Map of Buzau (**830**)

(Des A. Popescu. Photo)

1976 (25 Aug). 1600th Anniv of Buzau State. P 13½.
4232 **829** 55b. multicoloured 65 30

1976 (12 Sept). Philatelic Exhibition, Bucharest. No. 4199 optd with T **830**. P 13½.
4233 3l.60 multicoloured .... 7·75 7·75

831 Red Deer

(Des E. Palade. Photo)

1976 (20 Sept). Game Animals. T **831** and similar horiz designs. Multicoloured. P 13½.

4234	20b. Type **831**	10	10
4235	40b. Brown bear	20	10
4236	55b. Chamois	30	10
4237	1l.75 Wild boar	50	15
4238	2l.75 Red fox	1·00	30
4239	3l.60 Lynx	1·60	50
4234/4239	*Set of 6*	3·25	1·10

832 Cathedral, Milan

(Des V. Micu. Photo)

1976 (20 Oct). Italia 1976 International Stamp Exhibition, Milan. P 13½.
4240 **832** 4l.75 multicoloured .... 1·80 50

833 D. Grecu (gymnast) and Bronze Medal

(Des "Vlasto". Photo)

1976 (20 Oct). Olympic Games, Montreal. Romanian Medal-winners. T **833** and similar multicoloured designs. P 13½.

4241	20b. Type **833**	10	10
4242	40b. Romanian fencers and bronze medal	10	10
4243	55b. G. Megeles (javelin-thrower) and bronze medal	20	10
4244	1l.75 Romanian handball players and silver medal	40	15
4245	2l.75 Romanian boxers, silver and bronze medals	85	20
4246	3l.60 S. Rusu and P. Codreanu (wrestlers), silver and bronze medals	1·30	50
4247	5l.70 Nadia Comaneci (bronze, silver and triple gold medallist for gymnastics) (27×42 mm)	3·75	1·80
4241/4247	*Set of 7*	6·00	2·75
MS4248	90×78 mm. 10l. D. Vasile (canoeist) and gold and silver medals (42×54 mm)	6·25	6·25

An imperforate miniature sheet, 108×80 mm, depicting Nadia Comaneci and medals, exists from a restricted printing.

834 "Carnations and Oranges" **835** "Elena Cuza" (Theodor Aman)

(Des Aida Tasgian-Constantinescu. Photo)

1976 (5 Nov). Floral Paintings by Stefan Luchian. T **834** and similar horiz designs. Multicoloured. P 13½.

4249	20b. Type **834**	10	10
4250	40b. "Flower Arrangement"	10	10
4251	55b. "Immortelles"	10	10
4252	1l.75 "Roses in a Vase"	50	15
4253	2l.75 "Cornflowers"	75	20
4254	3l.60 "Carnations in a Vase"	1·40	30
4249/4254	*Set of 6*	2·75	85

(Des M. Veniamin. Photo)

1976 (15 Nov). Stamp Day. P 13½.
4255 **835** 2l.10 +1l.90 multicoloured .... 2·30 1·70

836 Arms of Alba **837** "Ox Cart"

(Des I. Dumitrana. Photo)

1976 (20 Dec). Arms (1st series). Districts. T **836** and similar vert designs. Multicoloured. P 13½.

4256	55b. Type **836**	30	10
	a. Horiz strip of 10. Nos. 4256/60, each×2	3·25	
4257	55b. Arad	30	10
4258	55b. Arges	30	10
4259	55b. Bacau	30	10
4260	55b. Bihor	30	10
4261	55b. Bistrita Nasaud	30	10
	a. Horiz strip of 10. Nos. 4261/5, each×2	3·25	
4262	55b. Botosani	30	10
4263	55b. Brasov	30	10
4264	55b. Braila	30	10
4265	55b. Buzau	30	10
4266	55b. Caras-Severin	30	10
	a. Horiz strip of 10. Nos. 4266/70, each×2	3·25	
4267	55b. Cluj	30	10
4268	55b. Constanta	30	10
4269	55b. Cavasna	30	10
4270	55b. Dimbovita	30	10
4256/4270	*Set of 15*	4·00	1·40

Nos. 4256/60, 4261/5 and 4266/70 respectively were issued together in *se-tenant* sheets of 50 stamps (10×5), each horizontal row containing a pair of each design. The mint set price is for 15 single stamps.

See also Nos. 4307/31, 4496/4520 and 4542/63.

(Des D. Grigoriu. Photo)

1977 (20 Jan). Paintings by Nicolae Grigorescu. T **837** and similar multicoloured designs. P 13½.

4271	55b. Type **837**	20	10
4272	1l. "Self-portrait" (vert)	30	10
4273	1l.50 "Shepherdess"	40	10
4274	2l.15 "Girl with Distaff"	85	15
4275	3l.40 "Shepherd" (vert)	1·00	30
4276	4l.80 "Halt at the Well"	1·60	50
4271/4276	*Set of 6*	4·00	1·10

838 Telecommunications Station, Cheia

(Des D. Grigoriu. Photo)

1977 (1 Feb). P 13½.
4277 **838** 55b. multicoloured 50 30

839 I.C.A.R. 1

(Des V. Stoianov. Photo)

1977 (20 Feb). AIR. Romanian Gliders. T **839** and similar horiz designs. Multicoloured. P 13½.

4278	20b. Type **839**	10	10
4279	40b. IS-3d	10	10
4280	55b. R.G.-5	20	10
4281	1l.50 IS-11	50	15
4282	3l. IS-29D	1·00	30
4283	3l.40 IS-28B	1·80	50
4278/4283	*Set of 6*	3·25	1·10

840 Red Deer (*Cervus elephus*)

(Des F. Ivănuş. Photo)

1977 (20 Mar). Endangered Animals. T **840** and similar vert designs. Multicoloured. P 13½.

4284	55b. Type **840**	20	10
4285	1l. Mute swan (*Cygnus olor*)	30	10
4286	1l.50 Egyptian vulture (*Neophron percnopterus*)	50	10
4287	2l.15 European bison (*Bison bonasus*)	75	15
4288	3l.40 White-headed duck (*Oxyura leucocephala*)	1·30	30
4289	4l.80 Common kingfisher (*Alcedo atthis*)	1·60	50
4284/4289	*Set of 6*	4·25	1·10

841 "The Infantryman" (Oscar Obedeanu)

1977 (25 Apr). Centenary of Independence. Paintings. T **841** and similar multicoloured designs. Photo. P 13.

4290	55b. Type **841**	20	10
4291	1l. "Artillery Battery at Calafat" (Sava Hentia) (horiz)	40	10
4292	1l.50 "Soldiers Attacking" (Stefan Luchian)	50	10
4293	2l.15 "The Battle of Plevna" (horiz)	95	15
4294	3l.40 "The Artillerymen" (Nicolae Grigorescu) (horiz)	1·30	30
4295	4l.80 +2l. "Battle of Rahova" (horiz)	2·75	1·20
4290/4295	*Set of* 6	5·50	1·80
MS4296	90×78 mm. 10l. "Battle of Grivitza"	5·25	5·25

An imperforate miniature sheet, 80×108 mm, depicting the painting "Romanian Troops Crossing the Dobrudja", exists from a restricted printing.

842 Sinaia, Carpathians

843 Petru Rares, Prince of Moldavia

1977 (17 May). Inter-European Cultural and Economic Co-operation. Views. T **842** and similar horiz design. Multicoloured. Photo. P 13½.

4297	2l. Type **842**	65	30
4298	2l.40 Auroa, Black Sea	85	50

Nos. 4297/8 were each issued in small sheets of four stamps.

(Des I. Untch. Photo)

1977 (10 June). Anniversaries. T **843** and similar vert design. Multicoloured. P 13½.

4299	40b. Type **843** (450th anniv of accession)	50	30
4300	55b. Ion Caragiale (dramatist, 125th birth anniv)	50	30

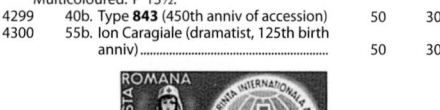

844 Nurse with Children and Emblems

(Des R. Coteanu. Photo)

1977 (10 June). 23rd International Red Cross Conference, Bucharest. P 13.

4301	**844**	1l.50 multicoloured	75	50

845 Triumphal Arch, Bucharest

(Des R. Coteanu. Photo)

1977 (10 June). 60th Anniversaries of Battles of Marasti, Marasesti and Oituz. P 13½.

4302	**845**	2l.15 multicoloured	1·40	50

846 Boeing 707 Jetliner over Bucharest Airport

(Des A. Popescu. Photo)

1977 (28 June). European Security and Co-operation Conference, Belgrade. Sheet 80×70 mm. P 13.

MS4303	**846**	10l. greenish yellow, carmine and new blue	2·50	2·50

An imperforate miniature sheet, 90×75 mm, depicting a Yugoslav airliner en-route from Bucharest to Belgrade, exists from a restricted printing.

847 Postwoman with Letters

1977 (25 July–10 Sept). AIR. T **847** and similar horiz design. Multicoloured. Photo. P 13.

4304	20l. Type **847**	5·25	1·50
4305	30l. Douglas DC-10 jetliner and mail (10.9)	7·75	2·50

848 Mount Titano Castle, San Marino

1977 (28 Aug). Centenary of San Marino Postage Stamps. P 13.

4306	**848**	4l. multicoloured	2·30	50

(Des I. Dumitrana. Photo)

1977 (5 Sept). Arms (2nd series). Districts. Vert designs similar to T **836**. Multicoloured. P 13.

4307	55b. Doji	30	10
	a. Horiz strip of 10. Nos. 4307/11, each×2	3·25	
4308	55b. Galati	30	10
4309	55b. Gorj	30	10
4310	55b. Harghita	30	10
4311	55b. Hunedoara	30	10
4312	55b. Ialomita	30	10
	a. Horiz strip of 10. Nos. 4312/16, each×2	3·25	
4313	55b. Iasi	30	10
4314	55b. Ilfov	30	10
4315	55b. Maramures	30	10
4316	55b. Mehedinti	30	10
4317	55b. Mures	30	10
	a. Horiz strip of 10. Nos. 4317/21, each×2	3·25	
4318	55b. Neamt	30	10
4319	55b. Olt	30	10
4320	55b. Prahova	30	10
4321	55b. Salaj	30	10
4322	55b. Satu Mare	30	10
	a. Horiz strip of 10. Nos. 4322/6, each×2	3·25	
4323	55b. Sibiu	30	10
4324	55b. Suceava	30	10
4325	55b. Teleorman	30	10
4326	55b. Timis	30	10
4327	55b. Tulcea	30	10
	a. Horiz strip of 10. Nos. 4327/31, each×2	3·25	
4328	55b. Vaslui	30	10
4329	55b. Vilcea	30	10
4330	55b. Vrancea	30	10
4331	55b. Romanian postal emblem	30	10
4307/4331	*Set of* 25	6·75	2·30

Nos. 4307/11, 4312/16, 4317/21, 4322/6 and 4327/31 respectively were issued together in *se-tenant* sheets of 50 stamps (10×5), each horizontal row containing a pair of each design. The mint set price is for 25 single stamps.

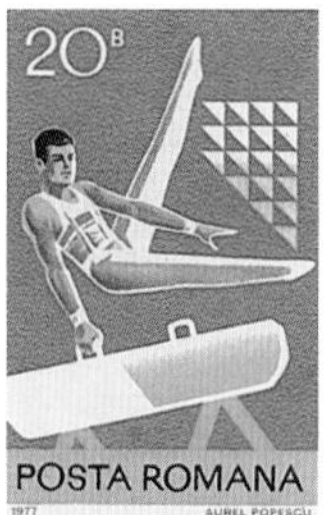

849 Gymnast on Vaulting Horse

850 Despatch Rider and Army Officer

(Des A. Popescu. Photo)

1977 (25 Sept). Gymnastics. T **849** and similar vert designs. Multicoloured. P 13.

4332	20b. Type **849**	10	10
4333	40b. Floor exercise	10	10
4334	55b. Gymnast on parallel bars	20	10
4335	1l. Somersault on bar	40	15
4336	2l.15 Gymnast on rings	85	30
4337	4l.80 Gymnastic exercise	2·50	1·00
4332/4337	*Set of* 6	3·75	1·60

(Des R. Coteanu. Photo)

1977 (5 Nov). Stamp Day. P 13.

4338	**850**	2l.50 +1l.90 multicoloured	2·10	2·00

851 Two Dancers with Sticks

1977 (28 Nov). Calusarii Folk Dance. T **851** and similar vert designs. Multicoloured. Photo. P 13.

4339	20b. Type **851**	10	10
4340	40b. Leaping dancer with stick	10	10
4341	55b. Two dancers	20	10
4342	1l. Dancer with stick	40	15
4343	2l.15 Leaping dancers	85	30
4344	4l.80 Leaping dancer	2·50	1·00
4339/4344	*Set of* 6	3·75	1·60
MS4345	81×71 mm. 10l. Two children in costume	5·25	5·25

852 *Carpati* at Cazane

1977 (28 Dec). European Navigation on the Danube. T **852** and similar horiz designs. Multicoloured. Photo. P 13.

4346	55b. Type **852**	20	10
4347	1l. *Mircesti* near Orsova	25	10
4348	1l.50 *Oltenita* near Calafat	35	20
4349	2l.15 Hydrofoil at Giurgiu port	50	30
4350	3l. *Herculani* at Tulcea	85	40
4351	3l.40 *Muntenia* at Sulina	1·00	50
4352	4l.80 Map of Danube delta	2·10	1·00
4346/4352	*Set of* 7	4·75	2·40
MS4353	81×71 mm. 10l. River god Danubius (relief from Trajan's Column) (vert)	3·25	3·25

An imperforate miniature sheet, 93×75 mm, depicting a satellite map of the Danube, exists from a restricted printing.

853 Arms and Flag of Romania

(Des R. Coteanu. Photo)

1977 (30 Dec). 30th Anniv of the Republic. T **853** and similar horiz designs. Multicoloured. P 13.

4354	55b. Type **853**	20	15
4355	1l.20 Romanian-built computers	55	20
4356	1l.75 National Theatre, Craiova	1·10	40
4354/4356	*Set of* 3	1·70	70

854 Firiza Dam

(Des "Vlasto". Photo)

1978 (10 Mar). Romanian Dams and Hydro-electric Installations. T **854** and similar horiz designs. Multicoloured. P 13.

4357	20b. Type **854**	10	10
4358	40b. Negovanu dam	10	10
4359	55b. Piatra Neamt power station	20	10
4360	1l. Izvorul Muntelui-Bicaz dam	35	10
4361	2l.15 Vidraru dam	65	20
4362	4l.80 Barrage and navigation system on Danube at Iron Gates	1·70	50
4357/4362	*Set of* 6	2·75	1·00

855 LZ-1 over Lake Constance

(Des V. Stoianov. Photo)

1978 (20 Mar). AIR. Airships. T **855** and similar horiz designs. Multicoloured. P 13.

4363	60b. Type **855**	20	10
4364	1l. Santos Dumont's *Ballon No. 6* over Paris	35	10
4365	1l.50 Beardmore airship R-34 over Manhattan Island	55	10
4366	2l.15 *Italia* at North Pole	80	15
4367	3l.40 *Graf Zeppelin* over Brasov	1·30	30
4368	4l.80 *Graf Zeppelin* over Sibiu	2·20	65
4363/4368	*Set of* 6	4·75	1·30
MS4369	80×70 mm. 10l. *Graf Zeppelin* over Bucharest (50×38 mm)	5·50	5·50

856 Footballers and Emblem

857 King Decebalus of Dacia

(Des A. Popescu. Photo)

1978 (15 Apr). World Cup Football Championship, Argentina. T **856** and similar vert designs. Centres multicoloured, background colour given. P 13.

4370 55b. new blue ... 20 10
4371 1l. yellow-orange ... 20 10
4372 1l.50 bright apple green ... 35 10
4373 2l.15 vermilion ... 65 10
4374 3l.40 blue-green ... 1·20 20
4375 4l.80 magenta ... 2·20 30
4370/4375 *Set of 6* ... 4·25 80
MS4376 80×70 mm. 10l. blue (38×50 mm) ... 5·50 5·50

An imperforate miniature sheet, 90×75 mm, exists from a restricted printing.

1978 (22 May). Inter-European Cultural and Economic Co-operation. T **857** and similar horiz design. Multicoloured. Photo. P 13.

4377 1l.30 Type **857** ... 55 50
4378 3l.40 King Mircea the Elder ... 1·70 1·60

Nos. 4377/8 were each issued in small sheets of four stamps.

858 Worker and Factory

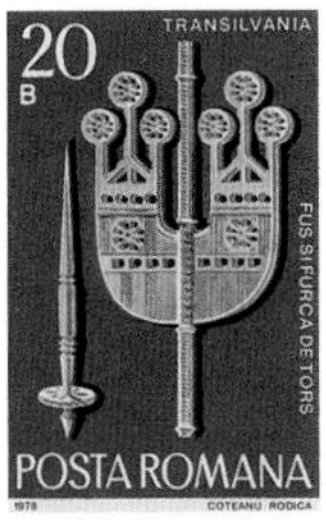

859 Spindle and Fork Handle, Transylvania

(Des F. Ivănuş. Photo)

1978 (11 June). 30th Anniv of Nationalization of Industry. P 13.

4379 **858** 55b. multicoloured ... 55 30

(Des R. Coteanu. Photo)

1978 (20 June). Wood-carving. T **859** and similar vert designs. Multicoloured. P 13½.

4380 20b. Type **859** ... 10 10
4381 40b. Cheese mould, Muntenia ... 20 10
4382 55b. Spoons, Oltenia ... 35 10
4383 1l. Barrel, Moldavia ... 45 15
4384 2l.15 Ladle and mug, Transylvania ... 80 20
4385 4l.80 Water bucket, Oltenia ... 1·70 65
4380/4385 *Set of 6* ... 3·25 1·20

860 Danube Delta

(Des E. Palade. Photo)

1978 (20 July). Tourism. T **860** and similar multicoloured designs. P 13.

4386 55b. Type **860** ... 10 10
4387 1l. Bran Castle (vert) ... 20 10
4388 1l.50 Moldavian village ... 45 10
4389 2l.15 Muierii caves ... 65 15
4390 3l.40 Cable car at Boiana Brasov ... 1·10 20
4391 4l.80 Mangalia (Black Sea resort) ... 1·90 40
4386/4391 *Set of 6* ... 4·00 95
MS4392 80×70 mm. 10l. Strehaia Fortress and Monastery (37×49 mm) ... 6·75 6·75

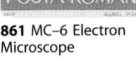

861 MC–6 Electron Microscope

862 Polovraci Cave

(Des A. Popescu. Photo)

1978 (15 Aug). Romanian Industry. T **861** and similar multicoloured designs. P 13.

4393 20b. Type **861** ... 10 10
4394 40b. Hydraulic excavator ... 10 10
4395 55b. Power station control room ... 35 10
4396 1l.50 Oil drillheads ... 55 15
4397 3l. C-12 combine harvester (horiz) ... 90 20
4398 3l.40 Petro-chemical combine, Pitesti ... 1·10 30
4393/4398 *Set of 6* ... 2·75 85

(Des S. Stoianov and C. Lascu. Photo)

1978 (25 Aug). Caves and Caverns. T **862** and similar vert designs. Multicoloured. P 13.

4399 55b. Type **862** ... 10 10
4400 1l. Topolnita cave ... 20 10
4401 1l.50 Ponoare cave ... 45 10
4402 2l.15 Ratei cave ... 65 15
4403 3l.40 Closani cave ... 1·20 20
4404 4l.80 Epuran cave ... 1·90 50
4399/4404 *Set of 6* ... 4·00 1·00

863 Gymnastics

864 Zoomorphic Gold Plate

(Des E. Palade. Photo)

1978 (15 Sept). Daciada Romanian Games. T **863** and similar vert designs. Multicoloured. P 13.

4405 55b. Type **863** ... 10 10
4406 1l. Running ... 20 10
4407 1l.50 Skiing ... 45 10
4408 2l.15 Horse jumping ... 65 15
4409 3l.40 Football ... 1·20 20
4410 4l.80 Handball ... 1·90 40
4405/4410 *Set of 6* ... 4·00 95

(Des D. Grigoriu. Photo)

1978 (25 Sept). Daco-Roman Archaeology. T **864** and similar multicoloured designs. P 13.

4411 20b. Type **864** ... 10 10
4412 40b. Gold armband ... 20 10
4413 55b. Gold cameo ring ... 35 10
4414 1l. Silver bowl ... 55 15
4415 2l.15 Bronze eagle (vert) ... 90 20
4416 4l.80 Silver armband ... 1·20 50
4411/4416 *Set of 6* ... 3·00 1·00
MS4417 74×89 mm. 10l. Gold helmet (38×50 mm). Imperf ... 19·00 19·00

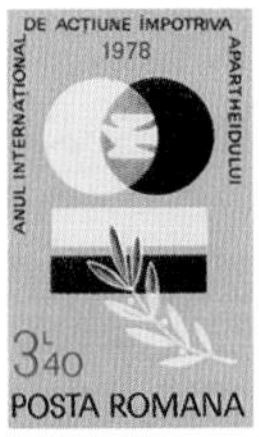

865 Symbols of Equality

866 Romulus, Remus and Wolf

(Des A. Popescu. Photo)

1978 (28 Sept). International Anti-Apartheid Year. P 13.

4418 **865** 3l.40 black, yellow and red ... 1·30 1·00

1978 (16 Oct). International Stamp Exhibition, Essen. Sheet 75×90 mm. Photo. Imperf.

MS4419 **866** 10l. multicoloured ... 14·50 16·00

867 Ptolemaic Map of Dacia (2000th anniv of first record of Ziridava)

(Des A. Popescu. Photo)

1978 (21 Oct). Events in the History of Arad. T **867** and similar horiz designs. Multicoloured. P 13.

4420 40b. Type **867** ... 10 10
a. Strip of 3. Nos. 4420/2 ... 80
4421 55b. National Romanian Central Council building (60th anniv of unified Romanian state) ... 10 10
4422 1l.75 Ceramic pots (950th anniv of first documentary attestation of Arad) ... 55 30
4420/4422 *Set of 3* ... 70 45

Nos. 4420/2 were issued together in *se-tenant* strips of three within the sheet.

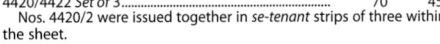

868 Dacian Warrior

(Des S. Stoianov. Photo)

1978 (5 Nov). Stamp Day. P 13.

4423 **868** 6l. (+3l.) multicoloured ... 1·70 1·00

No. 4423 was issued *se-tenant* with a premium-carrying tab, as shown in Type **868**.

869 Assembly at Alba Julia

870 Wright Brothers and Wright Type A

(Des V. Stoianov. Photo)

1978 (1 Dec). 60th Anniv of National Unity. T **869** and similar vert design. Multicoloured. P 13.

4424 55b. Type **869** ... 20 10
4425 1l. Open book, flag and sculpture ... 35 20

(Des V. Stoianov. Photo)

1978 (18 Dec). AIR. Pioneers of Aviation. T **870** and similar horiz designs. Multicoloured. P 13.

4426 55b. Type **870** ... 10 10
4427 1l. Louis Blériot and Blériot XI monoplane ... 20 10
4428 1l.50 Anthony Fokker and Fokker F.VIIa/3m *Josephine Ford* ... 45 10
4429 2l.15 Andrei Tupolev and Tupolev ANT-25 ... 65 15
4430 3l. Otto Lilienthal and Lilienthal monoplane glider ... 80 20
4431 3l.40 Traian Vuia and Vuia No. 1 ... 90 25
4432 4l.80 Aurel Vlaicu and No. 1 "Crazy Fly" ... 1·00 30
4426/4432 *Set of 7* ... 3·75 1·10
MS4433 79×70 mm. 10l. Henri Coanda and turbine-powered model airplane ... 5·50 5·50

871 Dacian Warrior

872 "The Heroes of Vaslui"

(Des S. Stoianov. Photo)

1978 (18 Dec). 2050th Anniv of Independent Centralized Dacic State (1st issue). T **871** and similar vert design, showing details from Trajan's Column. Multicoloured. P 13.

4434 55b. Type **871** ... 20 10
4435 1l.50 Dacian warrior on horseback ... 55 30

See also Nos. 4564/5, **MS**4593 and 4609.

1979 (1 Mar). International Year of the Child (1st issue). T **872** and similar designs, showing children's paintings. Multicoloured. Photo. P 13.

4436 55b. Type **872** ... 10 10
4437 1l. "Building Houses" ... 20 10
4438 1l.50 "Folk Group from Tica" ... 45 10
4439 2l.15 "Industrial Region" (horiz) ... 55 15
4440 3l.40 "Winter Holiday" (horiz) ... 1·00 20
4441 4l.80 "Pioneer Festival" (horiz) ... 1·30 30
4436/4441 *Set of 6* ... 3·25 85

See also Nos. 4453/6.

873 Championship Emblem

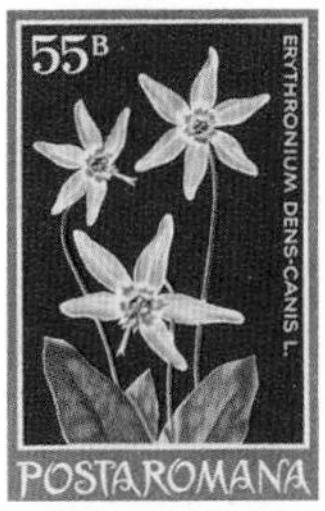

874 Dog's-tooth, Violet (*Erythronium dens-canis*)

1979 (16 Mar). European Junior Ice Hockey Championship, Miercurea-Ciuc, and World Championship, Galati. T **873** and similar vert design. Multicoloured. Photo. P 13.
4442 1l.30 Type **873** 35 10
a. Pair. Nos. 4442/3 .... 1·50 45
4443 3l.40 Championship emblem (different) ... 1·00 30
Nos. 4442/3 were issued in *se-tenant* pairs within the sheet.

1979 (25 Apr). Protected Flowers. T **874** and similar vert designs. Multicoloured. Photo. P 13.
4444 55b. Type **874** 10 10
4445 1l. Alpine violet (*Viola alpina*) 20 10
4446 1l.50 *Linum borzaeanum* 45 10
4447 2l.15 *Convolvulus persicus* 55 15
4448 3l.40 Auricula (*Primula auricula*) .... 1·00 20
4449 4l.80 *Aquilegia transsylvanica* .... 1·30 30
4444/4449 *Set of 6* .... 3·25 85

875 Street with Mail Coach and Post-rider

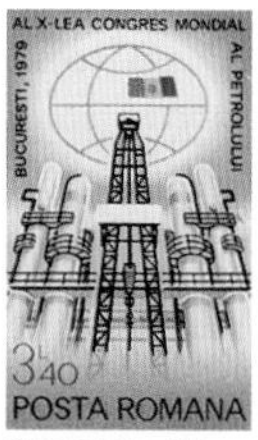

876 Oil Derrick

1979 (3 May). Inter-European Cultural and Economic Co-operation. T **875** and similar horiz design. Multicoloured. Photo. P 13.
(a) POSTAGE
4450 1l.30 Type **875** 55 30
(b) AIR. Inscr "POSTA AERIANA"
4451 3l.40 Modern postal transport 90 50
Nos. 4450/1 were each issued in small sheets of four stamps.

(Des A. Popescu. Photo)

1979 (24 May). International Petroleum Congress, Bucharest. P 13.
4452 **876** 3l.40 multicoloured .... 1·00 50

877 Children with Flowers

878 Young Pioneer

1979 (18 June). International Year of the Child (2nd issue). T **877** and similar horiz designs. Multicoloured. Photo. P 13.
4453 40b. Type **877** 10 10
4454 1l. Children at creative play 35 10
4455 2l. Children with hare 55 20
4456 4l.60 Young pioneers .... 1·50 30
4453/4456 *Set of 4* .... 2·30 65

1979 (20 June). 30th Anniv of Romanian Young Pioneers. Photo. P 13.
4457 **878** 55b. multicoloured 55 30

879 "Woman in Garden"

881 Stefan Gheorghiu

880 Brasov University

(Des S. Petruşel. Photo)

1979 (16 July). Paintings by Gh. Tattarescu. T **879** and similar vert designs. Multicoloured. P 13.
4458 20b. Type **879** 10 10
4459 40b. "Muntenian Woman" 10 10
4460 55b. "Muntenian Man" 10 10
4461 1l. "General Gh. Magheru" 45 15
4462 2l.15 "Artist's Daughter" 80 20
4463 4l.80 "Self-portrait" .... 1·70 50
4458/4463 *Set of 6* .... 3·00 1·00

1979 (25 July). Contemporary Architecture. T **880** and similar horiz designs. Multicoloured. Photo. P 13.
4464 20b. State Theatre, Tirgu Mures 10 10
4465 40b. Type **880** 10 10
4466 55b. Administrative Centre, Baia Mare 10 10
4467 1l. Stefan Gheorghiu Academy, Bucharest 35 15
4468 2l.15 Administrative Centre, Botosani 65 20
4469 4l.80 House of Culture, Tirgoviste .... 1·50 50
4464/4469 *Set of 6* .... 2·50 1·00

(Des V. Stamate. Photo)

1979 (27 July). Anniversaries. T **881** and similar vert designs. Multicoloured. P 13.
4470 40b. Type **881** (birth centenary) 45 20
4471 55b. Statue of Gheorghe Lazàr (poet, birth bicentenary) 55 30
4472 2l.15 Monument to fallen workers (50th anniv of strike at Lupeni) 65 40
4470/4472 *Set of 3* .... 1·50 80

882 Moldavian and Wallachian Women and Monument to Union

883 Party and National Flags

(Des A. Popescu. Photo)

1979 (27 July). 120th Anniv of Union of Moldavia and Wallachia. P 13.
4473 **882** 4l.60 multicoloured .... 1·70 50

(Des "Vlasto". Photo)

1979 (20 Aug). 35th Anniv of Liberation. T **883** and similar horiz design. Multicoloured. P 13.
4474 55b. Type **883** 20 10
4475 1l. "Workers' Militia" (L. Suhar) 45 20

884 *Galati* (freighter)

885 "Snapdragons"

(Des V. Stoianov. Photo)

1979 (27 Aug). Merchant Navy. T **884** and similar horiz designs. Multicoloured. P 13.
4476 55b. Type **884** 10 10
4477 1l. *Bucuresti* (freighter) 35 10
4478 1l.50 *Resita* (bulk carrier) 45 10
4479 2l.15 *Tomis* (bulk carrier) 65 15
4480 3l.40 *Dacia* (tanker) .... 1·00 20
4481 4l.80 *Independenta* (tanker) .... 1·50 30
4476/4481 *Set of 6* .... 3·75 85

(Des S. Stoianov. Photo)

1979 (27 Aug). Socfilex '79 International Stamp Exhibition, Bucharest. T **885** and similar vert designs showing paintings by Stefan Luchian. Multicoloured. P 13.
4482 40b. Type **885** 10 10
4483 60b. "Carnations" 20 10
4484 1l.55 "Stairs with flowers" 45 10
4485 4l. +2l. "Field Flowers" .... 1·90 1·00
4482/4485 *Set of 4* .... 2·40 1·20
MS4486 79×70 mm. 10l.+5l. "Roses" .... 6·75 6·75

886 Gymnast

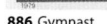

887 Party and National Flags

(Des V. Stoianov. Photo)

1979 (25 Sept). Fourth European Sports Conference, Berchtesgaden. Sheet 90×75 mm. Imperf.
MS4487 **886** 10l. multicoloured .... 17·00 17·00

1979 (15 Oct). 12th Romanian Communist Party Congress. Sheet 70×80 mm. P 13.
MS4488 **887** 5l. multicoloured .... 4·50 4·50

888 Olympic Stadium, Melbourne (1956 Games)

889 Costume of Maramureş (female)

(Des V. Stoianov. Photo)

1979 (23 Oct). Olympic Games, Moscow (1980). T **888** and similar horiz designs showing Olympic Stadia. Multicoloured. P 13.
4489 55b. Type **888** 10 10
4490 1l. Rome (1960) 35 10
4491 1l.50 Tokyo (1964) 45 10
4492 2l.15 Mexico (1968) 65 15
4493 3l.40 Munich (1972) .... 1·00 20
4494 4l.80 Montreal (1978) .... 1·50 30
4489/4494 *Set of 6* .... 3·75 85
MS4495 79×69 mm. 10l. Moscow (1980) .... 6·75 6·50
An imperforate miniature sheet, 90×74 mm, depicting Athens Stadium, exists from a restricted printing.

1979 (25 Oct). Arms (3rd series). Cities. Vert designs similar to T **836**. Multicoloured. Photo. P 13.
4496 1l.20 Alba Julia 35 10
a. Horiz strip of 10. Nos. 4496/4500, each×2 .... 3·75
4497 1l.20 Arad 35 10
4498 1l.20 Bacau 35 10
4499 1l.20 Baia Mare 35 10
4500 1l.20 Birlad 35 10
4501 1l.20 Botosani 35 10
a. Horiz strip of 10. Nos. 4501/5, each×2 .... 3·75
4502 1l.20 Brasov 35 10
4503 1l.20 Braila 35 10
4504 1l.20 Buzau 35 10
4505 1l.20 Calarasi 35 10
4506 1l.20 Cluj 35 10
a. Horiz strip of 10. Nos. 4506/10, each×2 .... 3·75
4507 1l.20 Constanta 35 10
4508 1l.20 Craiova 35 10
4509 1l.20 Dej 35 10
4510 1l.20 Deva 35 10
4511 1l.20 Drobeta Turnu Severin 35 10
a. Horiz strip of 10. Nos. 4511/15, each×2 .... 3·75
4512 1l.20 Focsani 35 10
4513 1l.20 Galati 35 10
4514 1l.20 Gheorghe Gheoghiu Dej 35 10
4515 1l.20 Giurgiu 35 10
4516 1l.20 Hunedoara 35 10
a. Horiz strip of 10. Nos. 4516/20, each×2 .... 3·75
4517 1l.20 Iasi 35 10
4518 1l.20 Lugoj 35 10
4519 1l.20 Medias 35 10
4520 1l.20 Odorheiu Secuiesc 35 10
4496/4520 *Set of 25* .... 8·00 2·30
Nos. 4496/4500, 4501/5. 4506/10, 4511/15 and 4516/20 respectively were issued together in *se-tenant* sheets of 50 stamps (10×5), each horizontal row containing a pair of each design. The mint set price is for 25 single stamps.

(Des D. Danila. Photo)

1979 (27 Oct). Costumes. T **889** and similar vert designs. Multicoloured. P 13.
4521 20b. Type **889** 10 10
4522 40b. Maramures (male) 10 10
4523 55b. Vrancea (female) 10 10
4524 1l.50 Vrancea (male) 45 10
4525 3l. Padureni (female) 90 30
4526 3l.40 Padureni (male) .... 1·00 40
4521/4526 *Set of 6* .... 2·40 1·00

890 Postal Coding Desks

891 Figure Skating

1979 (15 Nov). Stamp Day. Photo. P 13.
4527 **890** 2l.10 +1l.90 multicoloured .... 1·20 50

(Des A. Popescu. Photo)

1979 (27 Dec). Winter Olympics, Lake Placid (1980). T **891** and similar vert designs. Multicoloured. P 13.
4528 55b. Type **891** 10 10
4529 1l. Skiing 35 10
4530 1l.50 Cross-country skiing 45 10

4531 2l.15 Two-man bobsleigh 65 15
4532 3l.40 Speed skating 1·00 20
4533 4l.80 Ice hockey 1·50 30
4528/4533 *Set of 6* 3·75 85
MS4534 70×78 mm. 10l. Ice hockey (different) (37×49 mm) 5·50 5·50

An imperforate miniature sheet, 90×75 mm, depicting four-man bobsleigh, exists from a restricted printing.

892 Locomotive No. 43 *Călugăreni*

893 Dacian Warrior

(Des. G. Bozianu. Photo)

1979 (29 Dec). International Transport Exhibition, Hamburg. T **892** and similar horiz designs. Multicoloured. P 13½.

4535 55b. Type **892** 10 10
4536 1l. Locomotive No. 458 *Orleans* 35 10
4537 1l.50 Locomotive No. 1059 45 10
4538 2l.15 Locomotive No. 150211 65 15
4539 3l.40 Locomotive No. 231085 "Pacific" type 1·00 20
4540 4l.80 Electric locomotive "060-EA" 1·50 30
4535/4540 *Set of 6* 3·75 85
MS4541 80×70 mm. 10l. Diesel locomotive (50×38 mm) 6·75 6·75

(Des I. Dumitrana. Photo)

1980 (5 Jan). Arms (4th series). Cities. Vert designs as T **836**. Multicoloured. P 13½.

4542 1l.20 Oradea 35 10
4543 1l.20 Petroşani 35 10
4544 1l.20 Piatra Neamţ 35 10
4545 1l.20 Piteşti 35 10
4546 1l.20 Ploiesti 35 10
4547 1l.20 Reşiţa 35 10
4548 1l.20 Rîmnicu Vîlcea 35 10
4549 1l.20 Roman 35 10
4550 1l.20 Satu Mare 35 10
4551 1l.20 Sibiu 35 10
4552 1l.20 Sighetu Marmaţiei 35 10
4553 1l.20 Sighişoara 35 10
4554 1l.20 Suceava 35 10
4555 1l.20 Tecuci 35 10
4556 1l.20 Timişoara 35 10
4557 1l.20 Tîrgovişte 35 10
4558 1l.20 Tîrgu Jiu 35 10
4559 1l.20 Tîrgu-Mureş 35 10
4560 1l.20 Tulcea 35 10
4561 1l.20 Turda 35 10
4562 1l.20 Turna Măgurele 35 10
4563 1l.20 Bucharest 35 10
4542/4563 *Set of 22* 7·00 2·00

(Des G. Bozianu. Photo)

1980 (9 Feb). 2050th Anniv of Independent Centralized Dacic State (2nd issue). T **893** and similar vert design. Multicoloured. P 13½.

4564 55b. Type **893** 10 10
4565 1l.50 Dacian warriors with flag 45 20

894 Common Kingfisher (*Alcedo atthis*)

895 Scarborough Lily (*Vallota purpurea*)

(Des E. Palade. Photo)

1980 (25 Mar). European Nature Protection Year. T **894** and similar multicoloured designs. P 13½.

4566 55b. Type **894** 25 10
4567 1l. Great egret (*Egretta alba*) (vert) 35 10
4568 1l.50 Red-breasted goose (*Branta ruficollis*) 40 10
4569 2l.15 Red deer (*Cervus elaphus*) (vert) 50 15
4570 3l.40 Roe deer fawn (*Capreolus capreolus*) 60 20
4571 4l.80 European bison (*Bison bonasus*) (vert) 1·20 30
4566/4571 *Set of 6* 3·00 85
MS4572 90×78 mm. 10l. Eastern white pelicans (*Pelecanus onocrotalus*) (38×50 mm) 3·00 3·00

An imperforate miniature sheet, 105×79 mm, depicting brown bears (*Ursus arctos*), exists from a restricted printing.

(Des R. Coteanu. Photo)

1980 (10 Apr). Exotic Flowers. T **895** and similar vert designs. Multicoloured. P 13½.

4573 55b. Type **895** 10 10
4574 1l. Floating water hyacinth (*Eichhornia crasipes*) 35 10
4575 1l.50 Jacobean lily (*Sprekelia formosissima*) 50 10
4576 2l.15 Rose of Sharon (*Hypericum calycinum*) 70 15
4577 3l.40 Camellia (*Camellia japonica*) 1·10 20
4578 4l.80 Lotus (*Nelumbo nucifera*) 1·60 35
4573/4578 *Set of 6* 4·00 90

896 Tudor Vladimirescu

897 George Enescu playing Violin

(Des E. Palade. Photo)

1980 (25 Apr). Anniversaries. T **896** and similar vert designs. Multicoloured. P 13½.

4579 40b. Type **896** (revolutionary leader, birth bicentenary) 10 10
4580 55b. Mihail Sadoveanu (writer, birth centenary) 10 10
4581 1l.50 Battle of Posada (650th anniv) 50 15
4582 2l.15 Tudor Arghezi (poet, birth centenary) 70 20
4583 3l. Horea (leader of Transylvanian uprising, 250th birth anniv) 95 35
4579/4583 *Set of 5* 2·10 80

(Des I. Untsch. Photo)

1980 (6 May). Inter-European Cultural and Economic Co-operation. Two sheets, each 107×81 mm, containing horiz designs as T **897**. Inscriptions in gold and grey-black. P 13½.

MS4584 Two sheets (a) 1l.30×4: emerald (Type **897**); carmine-red (Enescu conducting); violet (Enescu at piano); blue (Enescu composing) (b) 3l.40×4: emerald (Beethoven at piano); carmine-red(Beethoven conducting); violet (Beethoven at piano (different)); blue (Beethoven composing). Two sheets 8·50 8·50

898 Dacian Fruit Dish and Cup

899 Throwing the Javelin

(Des S. Philipovici. Photo)

1980 (8 May). Bimillenary of Dacian Fortress Petrodava (now Piatra Neamt). P 13½.

4585 **898** 1l. multicoloured 60 35

(Des A. Popescu. Photo)

1980 (20 June). Olympic Games, Moscow. T **899** and similar vert designs. Multicoloured. P 13½.

4586 55b. Type **899** 10 10
4587 1l. Fencing 35 10
4588 1l.50 Pistol shooting 50 10
4589 2l.15 Single kayak 70 15
4590 3l.40 Wrestling 1·10 20
4591 4l.80 Single skiff 1·60 35
4586/4591 *Set of 6* 4·00 90
MS4592 90×78 mm. 10l. Handball (38×50 mm) 4·75 4·75

An imperforate miniature sheet, 104×79 mm, depicting a gymnast, exists from a restricted printing.

900 Postman handing Letter to Woman

(Des E. Palade. Photo)

1980 (1 July). 2050th Anniv of Independent Centralized Dacic State National Stamp Exhibition. Sheet 78×90 mm. P 13½.

MS4593 **900** 5l.+5l. multicoloured 4·75 4·75

901 Congress Emblem

902 Fireman carrying Child

(Des V. Stoianov. Photo)

1980 (10 Aug). 15th International Congress of Historical Sciences, Bucharest. P 13½.

4594 **901** 55b. bright blue and new blue 60 35

(Des V. Stoianov. Photo)

1980 (25 Aug). Fireman's Day. P 13½.

4595 **902** 55b. multicoloured 60 35

903 Chinese and Romanian Stamp Collectors

904 National Assembly Building, Bucharest

(Des R. Coteanu. Photo)

1980 (18 Sept). Romanian-Chinese Philatelic Exhibition, Bucharest. P 13½.

4596 **903** 1l. multicoloured 95 55

(Des E. Palade. Photo)

1980 (30 Sept). European Security and Co-operation Conference, Madrid. Sheet 78×90 mm. P 13½.

MS4597 **904** 10l. multicoloured 3·00 3·00

An imperforate miniature sheet, 106×79 mm, depicting Plaza de España in Madrid, exists from a restricted printing.

905 Rooks and Chessboard

906 Dacian Warrior

(Des E. Keri. Photo)

1980 (10 Oct). Chess Olympiad, Malta. T **905** and similar horiz designs. Multicoloured. P 13½.

4598 55b. Knights and chessboard 10 10
4599 1l. Type **905** 35 10
4600 2l.15 Male head and chessboard 70 15
4601 4l.80 Female head and chessboard 1·60 35
4598/4601 *Set of 4* 2·50 65

(Des V. Stoianov. Photo)

1980 (15 Oct). Military Uniforms. T **906** and similar vert designs. Multicoloured. P 13½.

4602 20b. Type **906** 10 10
4603 40b. Moldavian soldier (15th century) 10 10
4604 55b. Wallachian horseman (17th century) 10 10
4605 1l. Standard bearer (19th century) 35 10
4606 1l.50 Infantryman (19th century) 50 15
4607 2l.15 Lancer (19th century) 70 20
4608 4l.80 Hussar (19th century) 1·60 45
4602/4608 *Set of 7* 3·00 1·10

907 Burebista (sculpture, P. Mercea)

908 George Oprescu

1980 (5 Nov). Stamp Day and 2050th Anniv of Independent Centralized Dacic State. Photo. P 13½.

4609 **907** 2l. multicoloured 60 35

(Des E. Keri. Photo)

1981 (20 Feb). Celebrities' Birth Anniversaries. T **908** and similar vert designs. Multicoloured. P 13½.

4610 1l.50 Type **908** (historian and art critic, centenary) 50 10
4611 2l.15 Marius Bunescu (painter, centenary) 70 15
4612 3l.40 Ion Georgescu (sculptor, 125th anniv) 1·20 20
4610/4612 *Set of 3* 2·20 40

909 St. Bernard

910 *Ştefan cel Mare* (Danube paddle-steamer)

(Des E. Palade. Photo)

1981 (15 Mar). National Canine Exhibition. T **909** and similar multicoloured designs. P 13½.

4613	40b. Mountain sheepdog (horiz)	10	10
4614	55b. Type **909**	10	10
4615	1l. Fox terrier (horiz)	35	10
4616	1l.50 Alsatian (horiz)	50	15
4617	2l.15 Boxer	70	20
4618	3l.40 Dalmatian (horiz)	1·20	35
4619	4l.80 Poodle	1·80	55
4613/4619	*Set of* 7	4·25	1·40

(Des V. Stoianov. Photo)

1981 (27 Mar). 125th Anniv of Danube Commission. T **910** and similar horiz designs. Multicoloured. P 13½.

4620	55b. Type **910**	25	10
4621	1l. Danube Commission steam launch	30	20
4622	1l.50 *Tudor Vladimirescu* (Danube paddle-steamer)	35	30
4623	2l.15 *Sulina* (dredger)	50	35
4624	3l.40 *Republica Populară Română* (Danube paddle-steamer)	60	45
4625	4l.80 Freighter in Sulina Channel	1·20	90
4620/4625	*Set of* 6	3·00	2·10
MS4626	90×78 mm. 10l. *Moldova* (tourist ship) sailing past Galati (49×38 mm)	3·00	3·00

An imperforate miniature sheet, 105×80 mm, depicting a map of the Danube, exists from a restricted printing.

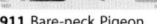

911 Bare-neck Pigeon

912 Party Flag and Oak Leaves

(Des F. Ivănuş. Photo)

1981 (15 Apr). Pigeons. T **911** and similar horiz designs. Multicoloured. P 13½.

4627	40b. Type **911**	10	10
4628	55b. Orbetan pigeon	20	10
4629	1l. Craiovan chestnut pigeon	35	10
4630	1l.50 Timişoara pigeon	50	15
4631	2l.15 Homing pigeon	70	20
4632	3l.40 Salonta giant pigeon	1·20	35
4627/4632	*Set of* 6	2·75	90

(Des G. Bozianu. Photo)

1981 (20 Apr). 60th Anniv of Romanian Communist Party. P 13½.

4633	**912**	1l. multicoloured	60	35

913 "Învîrtita" Dance, Oas-Maramures

(Des R. Coteanu. Photo)

1981 (4 May). Inter-European Cultural and Economic Cooperation. Two sheets, each 107×81 mm, containing horiz designs as T **913**. Multicoloured. P 13½.

MS4634 Two sheets. (a) 2l.50×4: Type **913**; "Hora" dance, Dobrogea; "Brîuleţul" dance, Oltenia; "Arderleana" dance, Crisana. (b) 2l.50×4: "Tărăneasca" dance, Moldavia; "Învîrtita Sibiană' dance, Transylvania; "Jocul de 2" dance, Banat; "Căluşul" dance, Muntenia. Two sheets ... 4·75 4·75

914 "Soyuz 40"

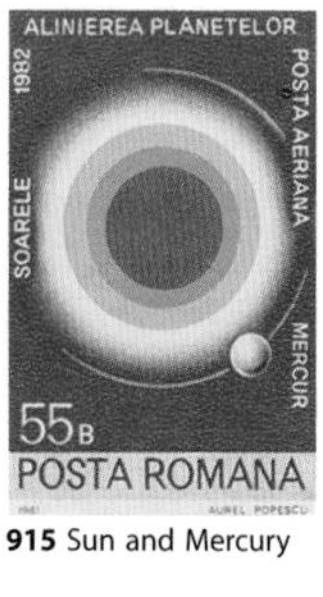

915 Sun and Mercury

(Des V. Stoianov. Photo)

1981 (14 May). AIR. Soviet-Romanian Space Flight. T **914** and similar horiz designs. Multicoloured. P 13½.

4635	55b. Type **914**	10	10
4636	3l.40 "Soyuz" linking with "Salyut" space station	1·20	45
MS4637	78×90 mm. 10l. Cosmonauts and space complex (49×38 mm)	4·75	4·75

(Des A. Popescu. Photo)

1981 (30 June). AIR. The Planets. T **915** and similar vert designs. Multicoloured. P 13½.

4638	55b. Type **915**	10	10
4639	1l. Venus, Earth and Mars	25	20
4640	1l.50 Jupiter	50	45
4641	2l.15 Saturn	60	55
4642	3l.40 Uranus	1·10	1·00
4643	4l.80 Neptune and Pluto	1·60	1·50
4638/4643	*Set of* 6	3·75	3·50
MS4644	90×77 mm. 10l. Earth seen from the Moon (38×49 mm)	4·75	4·75

An imperforate miniature sheet, 106×80 mm, depicting the planets orbiting the sun, exists from a restricted printing.

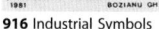

916 Industrial Symbols

917 Book and Flag

(Des G. Bozianu. Photo)

1981 (15 July). Singing Romania National Festival. T **916** and similar vert designs. Multicoloured. P 13½.

4645	55b. Type **916**	25	10
4646	1l.50 Technological symbols	60	15
4647	2l.15 Agricultural symbols	85	20
4648	3l.40 Cultural symbols	1·20	55
4645/4648	*Set of* 4	2·50	90

(Des L. Radu. Photo)

1981 (17 July). Universiada Games, Bucharest. T **917** and similar multicoloured designs. P 13½.

4649	1l. Type **917**	25	10
4650	2l.15 Games emblem	60	35
4651	4l.80 Stadium (horiz)	1·40	1·10
4649/4651	*Set of* 3	2·00	1·40

918 "Woman in an Interior"

919 "The Thinker of Cernavoda" (polished stone sculpture)

1981 (28 July). 150th Birth Anniv of Theodor Aman (painter). T **918** and similar multicoloured designs. Photo. P 13½.

4652	40b. "Self-portrait"	10	10
4653	55b. "Battle of Giurgiu" (horiz)	10	10
4654	1l. "Family Picnic" (horiz)	25	10
4655	1l.50 "The Painter's Studio" (horiz)	60	15
4656	2l.15 Type **918**	70	20
4657	3l.40 Aman Museum, Bucharest (horiz)	1·20	30
4652/4657	*Set of* 6	2·75	85

(Des R. Coteanu. Photo)

1981 (30 July). 16th International Congress of Historical Sciences. P 13½.

4658	**919**	3l.40 multicoloured	1·20	1·10

920 Blood Donation

921 Central Military Hospital

(Des E. Keri. Photo)

1981 (1 Sept). Blood Donor Campaign. P 13½.

4659	**920**	55b. multicoloured	60	35

(Des A. Popescu. Photo)

1981 (1 Sept). 150th Anniv of Central Military Hospital, Bucharest. P 13½.

4660	**921**	55b. multicoloured	60	35

922 Paul Constantinescu

923 Children at Stamp Exhibition

(Des E. Palade. Photo)

1981 (20 Sept). Romanian Musicians and Composers. T **922** and similar vert designs. Multicoloured. P 13½.

4661	40b. George Enescu	10	10
4662	55b. Type **922**	10	10
4663	1l. Dinu Lipatti	35	10
4664	1l.50 Ionel Perlea	50	15
4665	2l.15 Ciprian Porumbescu	70	20
4666	3l.40 Mihail Jora	1·20	45
4661/4666	*Set of* 6	2·75	1·00

A miniature sheet, containing 3×5l. and commemorating the European Security and Co-operation Conference, Madrid, was issued in October 1981 in a restricted printing.

(Des S. Petruşel. Photo)

1981 (15 Nov). Stamp Day. P 13½.

4667	**923**	2l. multicoloured	60	35

924 Hopscotch

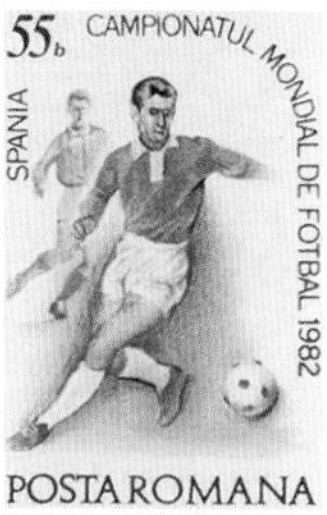

925 Football Players

(Des E. Palade. Photo)

1981 (26 Nov). Children's Games and Activities. T **924** and similar vert designs. Multicoloured. P 13½.

(a) POSTAGE

4668	40b. Type **924**	10	10
4669	55b. Football	10	10
4670	1l. Children with hobby horse and balloons	25	15
4671	1l.50 Fishing	35	20
4672	2l.15 Dog looking through school window at child	60	35
4673	3l. Child on stilts	85	55
4674	4l. Child tending sick dog	1·20	90

(b) AIR. Inscr "POSTA AERIANA"

4675	4l.80 Children with model gliders	1·40	1·10
4668/4675	*Set of* 8	4·25	3·00

Nos. 4671/5 show illustrations by Norman Rockwell.

(Des E. Palade. Photo)

1981 (28 Dec). World Cup Football Championship, Spain (1982). T **925** and similar vert designs. Multicoloured. P 13½.

4676	55b. Type **925**	10	10
4677	1l. Goalkeeper saving ball	25	10
4678	1l.50 Player heading ball	35	20
4679	2l.15 Player kicking ball over head	60	35
4680	3l.40 Goalkeeper catching ball	85	55
4681	4l.80 Player kicking ball	1·20	90
4676/4681	*Set of* 6	3·00	2·00
MS4682	90×78 mm. 10l. Goalkeeper catching ball headed by player (38×50 mm)	4·75	4·75

An imperforate miniature sheet, 106×79 mm, depicting a referee, a player and a satellite, exists from a restricted printing.

926 Alexander the Good, Prince of Moldavia

927 Entrance to Union Square Station

(Des R. Coteanu. Photo)

1982 (30 Jan). Anniversaries. T **926** and similar vert designs. Multicoloured. P 13½.

4683	1l. Type **926** (550th death anniv)	35	15
4684	1l.50 Bogdan P. Hasdeu (historian, 75th death anniv)	50	20
4685	2l.15 Nicolae Titulescu (diplomat and politician, birth centenary)	85	35
4683/4685	*Set of* 3	1·50	65

(Des E. Keri. Photo)

1982 (25 Feb). Inauguration of Bucharest Underground Railway. T **927** and similar horiz design. Multicoloured. P 13½.

4686	60b. Type **927**	25	10
4687	2l.40 Platforms and train at Heroes Square station	85	35

928 Dog rescuing Child from Sea

929 Dove, Banner and Crowd

(Des E. Palade. Photo)

1982 (27 Mar). Dog, Friend of Mankind. T **928** and similar multicoloured designs. P 13½.

4688	55b.	Type **928**	10	10
4689	1l.	Shepherd and sheepdog (vert)	35	15
4690	3l.	Gundog (vert)	95	20
4691	3l.40	Huskies	1·10	20
4692	4l.	Dog carrying woman's basket (vert)	1·20	35
4693	4l.80	Dog guiding blind person (vert)	1·40	35
4694	5l.	Dalmatian and child with doll (vert)	1·60	45
4695	6l.	St. Bernard	1·80	45
4688/4695		*Set of* 8	7·75	2·00

(Des A. Dumitrache. Photo)

1982 (29 Mar–2 May). 60th Anniv of Communist Youth Union. T **929** and similar vert designs. Multicoloured. P 13½.

4696	1l.	Type **929**	25	15
4697	1l.20	Construction worker (2.5)	25	15
4698	1l.50	Farm workers (2.5)	35	15
4699	2l.	Laboratory worker and students (2.5)	60	20
4700	2l.50	Labourers	85	30
4701	3l.	Choir, musicians and dancers (2.5)	95	35
4696/4701		*Set of* 6	3·00	1·20

930 Bran

1982 (6 May). Inter-European Cultural and Economic Co-operation. Two sheets, each 108×80 mm, containing horiz designs as T **930**. Multicoloured. P 13½.

MS4702 Two sheets. (a) 2l.50×4; Type **930**; Hunedoara; Sinaia; Iasi. (b) 2l.50×4; Neuschwanstein; Stolzenfels; Katz-Loreley: Linderhof. Two sheets ... 7·25 7·25

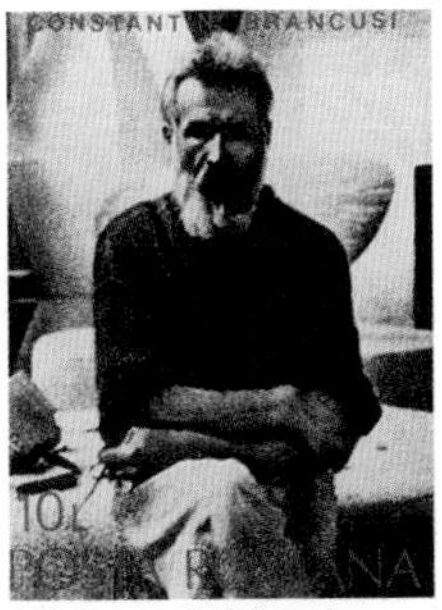

931 Constantin Brâncuşi (sculptor)

(Des D. Drăguşin. Photo)

1982 (5 June). Philexfrance '82 International Stamp Exhibition, Paris. Sheet 71×81 mm. P 13½.

MS4703 **931** 10l. multicoloured ... 4·75 4·75

932 Harvesting Wheat

(Des V. Stoianov. Photo)

1982 (28 June). 20th Anniv of Agricultural Co-operatives. T **932** and similar horiz designs. Multicoloured. P 13½.

(a) POSTAGE

4704	50b.	Type **932**	10	10
4705	1l.	Cows and milking equipment	25	10
4706	1l.50	Watering apple trees	35	15
4707	2l.50	Cultivator in vineyard	70	30
4708	3l.	Irrigating vegetables	95	35

(b) AIR. Inscr "POSTA AERIANA"

4709	4l.	Helicopter spraying cereal crop	1·20	45
4704/4709		*Set of* 6	3·25	1·30

MS4710 68×80 mm. 10l. Aerial view of new village (50×37 mm) ... 4·75 4·75

933 Vladimir Nicolae's Standard 1 Hang-glider

934 Băile Felix

(Des A. Mihai. Photo)

1982 (30 July). AIR. Hang-gliders. T **933** and similar horiz designs. Multicoloured. P 13½.

4711	50b.	Type **933**	10	10
4712	1l.	Excelsior D	25	10
4713	1l.50	Dedal-1	35	20
4714	2l.50	Entuziast	85	35
4715	4l.	AK-22	1·20	55
4716	5l.	Grifrom	1·60	65
4711/4716		*Set of* 6	4·00	1·80

(Des D. Drăguşin. Photo)

1982 (30 Aug). Spas and Health Resorts. T **934** and similar multicoloured designs. P 13½.

4717	50b.	Type **934**	10	10
4718	1l.	Predeal (horiz)	25	10
4719	1l.50	Băile Herculane	50	15
4720	2l.50	Eforie Nord (horiz)	70	30
4721	3l.	Olimp (horiz)	85	35
4722	5l.	Neptun (horiz)	1·60	55
4717/4722		*Set of* 6	3·50	1·40

935 "Legend"

(Des S. Petruşel. Photo)

1982 (6 Sept). Paintings by Sabin Bălaşa. T **935** and similar multicoloured designs. P 13½.

4723	1l.	Type **935**	35	15
4724	1l.50	"Contrasts"	50	20
4725	3l.50	"Peace Relay"	1·30	55
4726	4l.	"Genesis of the Romanian People" (vert)	1·40	65
4723/4726		*Set of* 4	3·25	1·40

A 10l. miniature sheet commemorating tenth anniv of European Security and Co-operation Conference was issued 25 September 1982 in a restricted printing.

936 Vlaicu Monument, Băneşti-Prahova

937 "Cheerful Peasant Woman"

(Des A. Popescu. Photo)

1982 (27 Sept). AIR. Birth Centenary of Aurel Vlaicu (aviation pioneer). T **936** and similar multicoloured designs. P 13½.

4727	50b.	Vlaicu's glider, 1909 (horiz)	10	10
4728	1l.	Type **936**	35	20
4729	2l.50	Air Heroes Monument	95	55
4730	3l.	Vlaicu's No. 1 airplane "Crazy Fly", 1910 (horiz)	1·10	65
4727/4730		*Set of* 4	2·30	1·40

(Des S. Petruşel. Photo)

1982 (30 Sept). 75th Death Anniv of Nicolae Grigorescu (artist). Sheet 70×80 mm. P 13½.

MS4731 **937** 10l. multicoloured ... 4·75 4·75

938 Central Exhibition Pavilion

939 Young Pioneer with Savings Book and Books

(Des V. Stoianov. Photo)

1982 (2 Oct). Tib '82 International Fair, Bucharest. P 13½.

4732	**938**	2l. multicoloured	70	35

(Des A. Popescu. Photo)

1982 (25 Oct). Savings Week. T **939** and similar vert design. Multicoloured. P 13½.

4733	1l.	Type **939**	35	15
4734	2l.	Savings Bank advertisement (Călin Popovici)	70	20

940 Postwoman delivering Letters

941 *Brave Young Man and the Golden Apples* (Petre Ispirescu)

(Des R. Coteanu. Photo)

1982 (10 Nov). Stamp Day. T **940** and similar vert design. Multicoloured. P 13½.

4735	1l.	Type **940**	35	15
4736	2l.	Postman	70	20

(Des F. Ivănus. Photo)

1982 (30 Nov). Fairy Tales. T **941** and similar vert designs. Multicoloured. P 13½.

4737	50b.	Type **941**	10	10
4738	1l.	*Bear tricked by the Fox* (Ion Creanga)	25	10
4739	1l.50	Warrior fighting bird (*Prince of Tears* (Mihai Eminescu))	50	15
4740	2l.50	Hen with bag (*Bag with Two Coins* (Ion Creangă))	70	20
4741	3l.	Rider fighting three-headed dragon (*Ileana Simziana* (Petre Ispirescu))	85	35
4742	5l.	Man riding devil (*Dănilă Prepeleac* (Ion Creangă))	1·60	55
4737/4742		*Set of* 6	3·50	1·30

942 Symbols of Industry, Party Emblem and Programme

943 Wooden Canteen from Suceava

944 Wheat, Cogwheel, Flask and Electricity Emblem

(Des A. Popescu. Photo)

1982 (16 Dec). Romanian Communist Party National Conference, Bucharest. T **942** and similar vert design. Multicoloured. P 13½.

4743	1l.	Type **942**	35	15
4744	2l.	Wheat, symbols of industry and Party emblem and open programme	70	20

(Des A. Popescu. Photo)

1982 (22 Dec)–**89**. Household Utensils. T **943** and similar designs. P 13½.

4745	50b.	orange-red	10	10
		a. Orange-vermilion. Wmkd (1989)	60	20
4746	1l.	violet-blue	35	10
		a. Wmkd (1989)	1·20	55
4747	1l.50	dull orange	60	10
4748	2l.	new blue	70	10
		a. Wmkd (1989)	2·00	90
4749	3l.	olive-bistre	1·10	10
4750	3l.50	myrtle green	1·30	10
4751	4l.	yellow-brown	1·60	10
		a. Wmkd (1989)	4·25	1·90
4752	5l.	slate-blue	1·90	10
4753	6l.	bright blue	2·30	10
4754	7l.	bright crimson	2·75	10
4755	7l.50	bright mauve	2·75	10
4756	8l.	light green	3·00	10
4757	10l.	carmine-red	3·00	10
		a. Bright rose-red. Wmkd (1989)	12·00	5·50
4758	20l.	bright violet	4·25	20
4759	30l.	greenish blue	7·25	35
4760	50l.	reddish brown	12·00	45
4745/4760		*Set of* 16	40·00	2·10

Designs: As T **943**. Vert—1l. Ceramic plates from Rădăuti; 2l. Jug and plate from Vama-Maramures; 3l. Wooden churn and pail from North Moldavia; 4l. Wooden spoons and ceramic plate from Cluj; 5l. Ceramic bowl and pot from Marginea-Suceava. Horiz—1l.50, Wooden dipper from Valea Mare; 3l.50, Ceramic plates from Leheceni-Crişana. 29×23 mm—10l. Wooden tubs from Hunedoara and Suceava; 30l. Wooden spoons from Alba. 23×29 mm—6l. Ceramic pot and jug from Bihor; 7l. Distaff and spindle from Transylvania; 7l.50, Double wooden pail from Suceava; 8l. Pitcher and ceramic plate from Oboga and Horezu; 20l. Wooden canteen and six glasses from Horezu; 50l. Ceramic plates from Horezu.

The watermark consists of the multiple initials "RSR".

(Des I. Dumitrana (25b., 1l.), V. Stoianov (50b., 3l.), A. Constantinescu (2, 4l.). Photo)

1982 (23 Dec). POSTAGE DUE. Type D **766** and similar horiz designs. P 13½.

		Un pair	*Us pair*
D4761	25b. bright violet	25	10
D4762	50b. orange-yellow	35	10
D4763	1l. rose-vermilion	60	10
D4764	2l. light green	1·20	15
D4765	3l. chestnut	1·80	15
D4766	4l. ultramarine	3·00	20
D4761/4766 *Set of* 6 pairs		6·50	70

Designs:—25b., 1l. Dove with letter and Hermes with posthorn; 50b., 3l. Type D **766**; 2, 4l. G.P.O., Bucharest, and emblem with mail van.

The left-hand stamp of the pair was put on insufficiently franked mail, the right-hand stamp on associated documents.

(Des V. Stoianov. Photo)

1982 (27 Dec). 35th Anniv of People's Republic. T **944** and similar vert design. Multicoloured. P 13½.

4767 1l. Type **944** 35 15
4768 2l. National flag and oak leaves 70 35

945 H. Coandă and Diagram of Jet Engine

(Des A. Mihai. Photo)

1983 (24 Jan). AIR. 25 Years of Space Exploration. T **945** and similar multicoloured designs. P 13½.

4769 50b. Type **945** 10 10
4770 1l. H. Oberth and diagram of rocket 35 10
4771 1l.50 "Sputnik 1", 1957 (first artificial satellite) 60 15
4772 2l.50 "Vostok 1", 1961 (first manned flight) 85 20
4773 4l. "Apollo 11", 1969 (first Moon landing) 1·40 35
4774 5l. Space shuttle *Columbia* 1·80 55
4769/4774 *Set of* 6 4·50 1·30
MS4775 93×80 mm. 10l. Earth (41×53 mm) 7·25 7·25

946 Rombac One Eleven 500 Jetliner

947 Matei Millo in *The Discontented* by Vasile Alecsandri

(Des A. Mihai. Photo)

1983 (25 Jan). AIR. First Romanian-built Jetliner. P 13½.

4776 **946** 11l. deep turquoise-blue 4·25 80

(Des E. Palade. Photo)

1983 (28 Feb). Romanian Actors. T **947** and similar vert designs. P 13½.

4777 50b. maroon and grey-black 10 10
4778 1l. blackish green and grey-black 35 10
4779 1l.50 deep mauve and grey-black 60 10
4780 2l. reddish brown and grey-black 70 10
4781 2l.50 olive-green and grey-black 95 15
4782 3l. Prussian blue and grey-black 1·20 20
4783 4l. bronze green and grey-black 1·40 35
4784 5l. rose-lilac and grey-black 1·80 45
4777/4784 *Set of* 8 7·50 1·40

Designs:—1l. Mihail Pascaly in *Director Millo* by Vasile Alecsandri; 1l.50, Aristizza RoMânescu in *The Dogs* by H. Lecca; 2l. C. I. Nottara in *Blizzard* by B. S. Delavrancea; 2l.50, Grigore Manolescu in *Hamlet* by William Shakespeare; 3l. Agatha Bîrsescu in *Medea* by Lebouvet; 4l. Ion Brezeanu in *The Lost Letter* by I. L. Caragiale; 5l. Aristide Demetriad in *The Despotic Prince* by Vasile Alecsandri.

948 Hugo Grotius

949 Aro "10"

(Des M. Totan. Photo)

1983 (30 Apr). 400th Birth Anniv of Hugo Grotius (Dutch jurist). P 13½.

4785 **948** 2l. brown 95 55

(Des C. Şuteu. Photo)

1983 (3 May). Romanian-built Vehicles. T **949** and similar horiz designs. Multicoloured. P 13½.

4786 50b. Type **949** 25 10
4787 1l. Dacia "1300 Break" 50 10
4788 1l.50 Aro "242" 70 15
4789 2l.50 Aro "244" 1·20 20
4790 4l. Dacia "1310" 1·90 35
4791 5l. Oltcit "Club" 2·40 55
4786/4791 *Set of* 6 6·25 1·30

950 Johannes Kepler (astronomer)

951 National and Communist Party Flags

(Des F. Ivănuş. Photo)

1983 (16 May). Inter-European Cultural and Economic Co-operation. Two sheets, each 110×80 mm, containing horiz designs as T **950**. Multicoloured. P 13½.

MS4792 Two sheets. (a) 3l.×4: Type **950**; Alexander von Humboldt (explorer) and *Pizarro*; J. W. von Goethe (writer); Richard Wagner (composer). (b) 3l.×4: Ion Andreescu (artist); George Constantinescu (engineer); Tudor Arghezi (writer); C. I. Parhon (physician). Two sheets 7·25 7·25

(Des V. Stoianov. Photo)

1983 (22 July). 50th Anniv of 1933 Workers' Revolution. P 13½.

4793 **951** 2l. multicoloured 95 55

952 Loading Mail into Boeing 707

953 Bluethroat (*Luscinia svecica*)

(Des A. Mihai. Photo)

1983 (25 July). AIR. World Communications Year. P 13½.

4794 **952** 2l. multicoloured 95 55

(Des M. Vămăşescu. Photo)

1983 (1 Aug). Birds of the Danube Delta. T **953** and similar vert designs. Multicoloured. P 13½.

4795 50b. Type **953** 25 10
4796 1l. Rose-coloured starling (*Sturnus roseus*) 50 10
4797 1l.50 Common roller (*Coracias garrulus*) 70 15
4798 2l.50 European bee eater (*Merops apiaster*) 1·20 20
4799 4l. Reed bunting (*Emberiza schoeniclus*) 1·90 35
4800 5l. Lesser grey shrike (*Lanius minor*) 2·40 45
4795/4800 *Set of* 6 6·25 1·20

954 Kayak

955 Postman on Bicycle

(Des N. Saftoiu. Photo)

1983 (16 Sept). Water Sports. T **954** and similar horiz designs. Multicoloured. P 13½.

4801 50b. Type **954** 25 10
4802 1l. Water polo 50 10
4803 1l.50 Canoeing 70 15
4804 2l.50 Diving 1·20 20
4805 4l. Rowing 1·90 35
4806 5l. Swimming (start of race) 2·40 45
4801/4806 *Set of* 6 6·25 1·20

(Des A. Popescu. Photo)

1983 (24 Oct). Stamp Day. T **955** and similar multicoloured designs. P 13½.

(a) POSTAGE

4807 1l. Type **955** 35 15
4808 3l.50 (+3l.) National flag as stamp 1·40 1·10

(b) AIR. Inscr "POSTA AERIANA"

MS4809 90×79 mm. 10l. Unloading mail from Rombac One Eleven 500 at Bucharest airport (38×50 mm) 7·25 7·25

No. 4808 was issued *se-tenant* with a premium-carrying tab showing the Philatelic Association's emblem.

956 *Geum reptans*

957 Girl with Feather

(Des V. Gheorghita. Photo)

1983 (28 Oct). European Flora and Fauna. T **956** and similar horiz designs. Multicoloured. P 13½.

4810 1l. Type **956** 70 45
a. Vert strip of 5. Nos. 4810/14 3·75
4811 1l. Long-headed poppy (*Papaver dubium*) 70 45
4812 1l. Stemless carline thistle (*Carlina acaulis*) 70 45
4813 1l. *Paeonia peregrina* 70 45
4814 1l. *Gentiana excisa* 70 45
4815 1l. Eurasian red squirrel (*Sciurus vulgaris*) 70 45
a. Vert strip of 5. Nos. 4815/19 3·75
4816 1l. *Grammia quenselii* (moth) 70 45
4817 1l. Middle spotted woodpecker (*Dendrocopos medius*) 70 45
4818 1l. Lynx (*Lynx lynx*) 70 45
4819 1l. Wallcreeper (*Tichodroma muraria*) 70 45
4810/4819 *Set of* 10 6·25 4·00

Nos. 4810/14 and 4815/19 respectively were issued together in vertical *se-tenant* strips of five within sheets of fifteen stamps, each strip being differently arranged.

1983 (3 Nov). Paintings by Corneliu Baba. T **957** and similar multicoloured designs. Photo. P 13½.

4820 1l. Type **957** 50 15
4821 2l. "Congregation" 95 20
4822 3l. "Farm Workers" (horiz) 1·40 35
4823 4l. "Rest in the Fields" (horiz) 1·90 45
4820/4823 *Set of* 4 4·25 1·00

A 10l. imperforate miniature sheet commemorating European Security and Co-operation Conference, Madrid, was issued 28 November 1983 in a restricted printing.

958 Flag and Oak Leaves

959 Postman and Post Office

(Des A. Popescu. Photo)

1983 (30 Nov). 65th Anniv of Union of Transylvania and Romania. T **958** and similar vert design. Multicoloured. P 13½.

4824 1l. Type **958** 50 20
4825 2l. National and Communist Party flags and Parliament building, Bucharest 95 35

(Des A. Popescu. Photo)

1983 (17 Dec). Balkanfila IX '83 Stamp Exhibition, Bucharest. T **959** and similar vert designs. Multicoloured. P 13½.

4826 1l. Type **959** 50 20
4827 2l. Postwoman and Athenaeum Concert Hall 95 35
MS4828 90×78 mm. 10l. Balkan flags and Athenaeum Concert Hall (37×50 mm) 4·75 4·75

960 "Orient Express" at Bucharest, 1883

(Des A. Mihai. Photo)

1983 (30 Dec). Centenary of "Orient Express". Sheet 90×78 mm. P 13½.

MS4829 **960** 10l. multicoloured 7·25 7·25

961 Cross-country Skiing

(Des V. Stoianov. Photo)

1984 (14 Jan). Winter Olympic Games, Sarajevo. T **961** and similar vert designs. Multicoloured. P 13½.

4830 50b. Type **961** 10 10
4831 1l. Biathlon 35 15
4832 1l.50 Ice skating 50 20
4833 2l. Speed skating 70 35
4834 3l. Ice hockey 95 45
4835 3l.50 Bobsleigh 1·20 55
4836 4l. Luge 1·40 65
4837 5l. Downhill skiing 1·80 85
4830/4837 *Set of* 8 6·25 3·00

A 10l. imperforate miniature sheet, 107×81 mm, depicting a ski jumper, exists from a restricted printing.

962 Prince Cuza and Arms

(Des A. Popescu. Photo)

1984 (24 Jan). 125th Anniv of Union of Moldavia and Wallachia. Sheet 90×78 mm. P 13½.

MS4838 **962** 10l. multicoloured .... 4·75 4·75

963 Palace of Udrişte Năsturel (Chancery official)

964 Chess Game

(Des V. Stoianov. Photo)

1984 (8 Feb). Anniversaries. T **963** and similar vert designs dated "1983". Multicoloured. P 13½.

4839 50b. deep dull green, dull rose and silver 25 10
4840 1l. violet, dull green and silver 50 10
4841 1l.50 multicoloured 70 15
4842 2l. olive-brown, dull violet-blue and silver 95 20
4843 3l.50 multicoloured .... 1·70 40
4844 4l. multicoloured .... 1·90 45
4839/4844 *Set of* 6 .... 5·50 1·30

Designs:—50b. Type **963** (325th death anniv); 1l. Miron Costin (poet, 350th birth anniv); 1l.50, Crişan (Giurgiu Marcu) (leader of peasant revolt, 250th birth anniv); 2l. Simion Bărnuţiu (scientist, 175th birth anniv); 3l.50, Diuliu Zamfirescu (writer, 125th birth anniv); 4l. Nicolae Milescu at Great Wall of China (explorer, 275th death anniv).

(Des Victoria Gheorghită. Photo)

1984 (20 Feb). 15th Balkan Chess Championships, Băile Herculane. Sheet 107×80 mm, containing T **964** and similar horiz designs. Multicoloured. P 13½.

MS4845 3l.×4, various chess games .... 7·25 7·25

965 Orsova Bridge

(Des F. Ivănuş. Photo)

1984 (24 Apr). Inter-European Cultural and Economic Co-operation. Two sheets, each 108×81 mm, containing horiz designs as T **965**. Multicoloured. P 13½.

MS4846 Two sheets. (a) 3l.×4: Type **965**; Arges Bridge; Basarabi Bridge; Ohaba Bridge, all in Romania. (b) 3l.×4: Köhlbrand Bridge, Hamburg; Bosphorus Bridge, Istanbul; Europa Bridge, Innsbruck; Tower Bridge, London. Two sheets .... 7·25 7·25

966 Sunflower

967 Flowering Rush (*Butomus umbellatus*)

(Des F. Ivănuş. Photo)

1984 (26 Apr). Protection of Environment. T **966** and similar horiz designs. Multicoloured. P 13½.

4847 1l. Type **966** 50 10
4848 2l. Red deer stag 95 20
4849 3l. Carp .... 1·40 45
4850 4l. Jay .... 1·90 55
4847/4850 *Set of* 4 .... 4·25 1·20

(Des Eliza Palade. Photo)

1984 (30 Apr). Flowers of the Danube. T **967** and similar multicoloured designs. P 13½.

4851 50b. Arrowhead (*Sagittaria sagittifolia*) 25 10
4852 1l. Yellow iris (*Iris pseudacorus*) 50 10
4853 1l.50 Type **967** 70 15
4854 3l. White water-lily (*Nymphaea alba*) (horiz) .... 1·40 30
4855 4l. Fringed water-lily (*Nymphoides peltata*) (horiz) .... 1·90 35
4856 5l. Yellow water-lily (*Nuphar luteum*) (horiz) .... 2·40 55
4851/4856 *Set of* 6 .... 6·50 1·40

968 Crowd with Banners

969 High Jumping

(Des A. Popescu. Photo)

1984 (30 Apr). 45th Anniv of Anti-Fascist Demonstration. P 13½.

4857 **968** 2l. multicoloured .... 1·20 55

(Des V. Stoianov. Photo)

1984 (25 May). Olympic Games, Los Angeles (1st issue). T **969** and similar horiz designs. Multicoloured. P 13½.

4858 50b. Type **969** 10 10
4859 1l. Swimming 35 15
4860 1l.50 Running 50 20
4861 3l. Handball .... 1·10 50
4862 4l. Rowing .... 1·30 60
4863 5l. Canoeing .... 1·90 90
4858/4863 *Set of* 6 .... 4·75 2·20

A 10l. imperforate miniature sheet, 82×106 mm, depicting a gymnast (vert), exists from a restricted printing.

See also Nos. 4866/73.

970 Congress Emblem

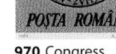

971 Footballers and Romanian Flag

(Des A. Bulacu. Photo)

1984 (30 May). 25th Ear, Nose and Throat Association Congress, Bucharest. P 13½.

4864 **970** 2l. multicoloured 95 55

(Des E. Palade. Photo)

1984 (7 June). European Cup Football Championship. Two sheets, each 109×81 mm, containing horiz designs as T **971** showing footballers and national flag. Multicoloured. P 13½.

MS4865 Two sheets. (a) 3l.×4: Type **971**; West Germany; Portugal; Spain. (b) 3l.×4: France; Belgium; Yugoslavia; Denmark. Two sheets .... 12·00 12·00

(Des V. Stoianov. Photo)

1984 (2 July). Olympic Games, Los Angeles (2nd issue). Horiz designs as T **969**. Multicoloured. P 13½.

4866 50b. Boxing 10 10
4867 1l. Rowing 25 10
4868 1l.50 Handball 40 15
4869 2l. Judo 50 20
4870 3l. Wrestling 85 40
4871 3l.50 Fencing 95 45
4872 4l. Kayak .... 1·10 50
4873 5l. Swimming .... 1·40 65
4866/4873 *Set of* 8 .... 5·00 2·30

Two 10l. imperforate miniature sheets, each 107×80 mm, depicting a long jumper or a gymnast (horiz), exist from a restricted printing.

972 Mihai Ciucă (bacteriologist, centenary)

973 Lockheed 14 Super Electra

(Des V. Stoianov. Photo)

1984 (28 July). Birth Anniversaries, T **972** and similar vert designs, dated "1983". P 13½.

4874 1l. purple, blue and silver 35 15
4875 2l. blue, yellow-brown and silver 70 20
4876 3l. myrtle green, lake-brown and silver 1·10 45
4877 4l. deep purple, blue-green and silver .. 1·40 55
4874/4877 *Set of* 4 .... 3·25 1·20

Designs:—2l. Petre S. Aurelian (agronomist, 150th anniv); 3l. Alexandru Vlahută (Writer, 125th anniv); 4l. Dimitrie Leonida (engineer, centenary).

(Des A. Mihai. Photo)

1984 (15 Aug). AIR. 40th Anniv of International Civil Aviation Organization. T **973** and similar horiz designs. Multicoloured. P 13½.

4878 50b. Type **973** 25 10
4879 1l.50 Britten Norman Islander 70 20
4880 3l. Rombac One Eleven 500 jetliner .... 1·40 45
4881 6l. Boeing 707 jetliner .... 3·00 55
4878/4881 *Set of* 4 .... 4·75 1·20

974 Flags, Flame and Power Station.

975 Lippizaner

(Des A. Popescu. Photo)

1984 (17 Aug). 40th Anniv of Liberation. P 13½.

4882 **974** 2l. multicoloured .... 1·20 55

(Des E. Palade. Photo)

1984 (30 Aug). Horses. T **975** and similar horiz designs. Multicoloured. P 13½.

4883 50b. Type **975** 25 10
4884 1l. Hutul 50 10
4885 1l.50 Bukovina 70 15
4886 2l.50 Nonius .... 1·20 20
4887 4l. Arab .... 1·90 35
4888 5l. Romanian halfbreed .... 2·40 45
4883/4888 *Set of* 6 .... 6·25 1·20

976 V. Racila (women's singles sculls, gold)

977 Memorial, Alba Julia

(Des V. Stoianov and M. Mănescu. Photo)

1984 (29 Oct). Romanian Olympic Games Medal Winners. Two sheets, each 125×129 mm, containing horiz designs as T **976**. Multicoloured. P 13½.

MS4889 Two sheets. (a) 3l.×6: Type **976**; P. Becheru and N. Vlad (weightlifting, gold); D. Melinte (800m.) and M. Puica (3000m. women's running, gold); Men's canoeing (Canadian pairs, gold); Fencing (silver); Women's modern rhythmic gymnastics (silver). (b) 3l.×6: Women's team gymnastics (gold); Women's kayak fours (gold); A. Stanciu (women's long jump, gold); I. Draica and V. Andrei (wrestling, gold); Judo (bronze); Pistol shooting (silver). Two sheets .... 18·00 18·00

1984 (1 Nov). Bicentenary of Horea, Closça and Crişan Uprisings. Photo. P 13½.

4890 **977** 2l. multicoloured 70 45

978 "Portrait of a Child" (Th. Aman)

979 Stage Coach and Romanian Philatelic Association Emblem

1984 (10 Nov). Paintings of Children. T **978** and similar vert designs. Multicoloured. Photo. P 13½.

4891 50b. Type **978** 10 10
4892 1l. "The Little Shepherd" (N. Grigorescu) 35 10
4893 2l. "Lica with an Orange" (St. Luchian) ... 70 15
4894 3l. "Portrait of a Child" (N. Tonitza) .... 1·10 20
4895 4l. "Portrait of a Boy" (S. Popp) .... 1·60 35
4896 5l. "Portrait of Young Girl" (I. Tuculescu) 2·00 45
4891/4896 *Set of* 6 .... 5·25 1·20

1984 (15 Nov). Stamp Day. Photo. P 13½.

4897 **979** 2l. (+1l.) multicoloured 95 55

No. 4897 was issued with *se-tenant* premium-carrying label, as shown in T **979**.

980 Flags and Party Emblem **981** Dalmatian Pelicans

(Des A. Popescu. Photo)

1984 (17 Nov). 13th Romanian Communist Party Congress, Bucharest. Sheet 90×78 mm. P 13½.

MS4898 **980** 10l. multicoloured .... 8·50 8·50

(Des M. Vămăşescu. Photo)

1984 (15 Dec). Protected Animals. Dalmatian Pelicans (*Pelecanus crispus*). T **981** and similar vert designs. Multicoloured. P 13½.

4899	50b. Type **981**	25	15
4900	1l. Pelican on nest	60	35
4901	1l. Pelicans on lake	60	35
4902	2l. Pelicans roosting	95	55
4899/4902	*Set of* 4	2·20	1·30

982 Dr. Petru Groza (former President) **983** Generator

(Des M. Tohatan. Photo)

1984 (26 Dec). Anniversaries. T **982** and similar vert designs. Multicoloured. P 13½.

4903	50b. Type **982** (birth centenary)	10	10
4904	1l. Alexandru Odobescu (writer, 150th birth anniv)	35	10
4905	2l. Dr. Carol Davila (physician, death centenary)	60	15
4906	3l. Dr. Nicolae Gh. Lupu (physician, birth centenary)	1·10	20
4907	4l. Dr. Daniel Danielopolu (physician, birth centenary)	1·30	35
4908	5l. Panait Istrati (writer, birth centenary)	1·80	45
4903/4908	*Set of* 6	4·75	1·20

1984 (29 Dec). Centenary of Power Station and Electric Street Lighting in Timisoara. T **983** and similar vert design. Multicoloured. P 13½.

4909	1l. Type **983**	35	20
4910	2l. Street lamp	70	35

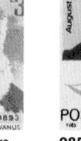

984 Gounod and Paris Opera House **985** August Treboniu Laurian (linguist and historian)

(Des F. Ivănuş. Photo)

1985 (28 Mar). Inter-European Cultural and Economic Co-operation. Composers. Two sheets, each 110×80 mm, containing horiz designs as T **984**. P 13½.

MS4911 Two sheets. (a) 3l.×4: blue-green and reddish violet (Type **984**); carmine-red and deep dull blue (Strauss and Munich Opera House); reddish violet and blue-green (Mozart and Vienna Opera House); deep dull blue and carmine-red (Verdi and La Scala, Milan). (b) 3l.×4: reddish violet and blue-green (Tchaikovsky and Bolshoi Theatre, Moscow); deep dull blue and carmine-red (Enescu and Bucharest Opera House); blue-green and reddish violet (Wagner and Dresden Opera House); carmine-red and deep dull blue (Moniuszko and Warsaw Opera House). Two sheets .... 7·25 7·25

(Des E. Palade. Photo)

1985 (29 Mar). Anniversaries. T **985** and similar vert designs. Multicoloured. P 13½.

4912	50b. Type **985** (75th birth anniv)	10	10
4913	1l. Grigore Alexandrescu (writer, death centenary)	25	10
4914	1l.50 Gheorghe Pop de Băseşti (politician, 150th birth anniv)	50	15
4915	2l. Mateiu Caragiale (writer, birth centenary)	70	20
4916	3l. Gheorghe Ionecu-Sişeşti (scientist, birth-centenary)	95	35
4917	4l. Liviu Rebreanu (writer, birth centenary)	1·40	55
4912/4917	*Set of* 6	3·50	1·30

986 Students in Science Laboratory **987** Racoon Dog (*Nyctereutes procyonoides*)

(Des M. Mănescu. Photo)

1985 (15 Apr). International Youth Year. T **986** and similar multicoloured designs. P 13½.

4918	1l. Type **986**	35	20
4919	2l. Students on construction site	70	35
MS4920	91×79 mm. 10l. Students with banner and dove (53×41 mm)	4·75	4·75

(Des Z. Silviu and D. Ionel. Photo)

1985 (6 May). Protected Animals. T **987** and similar vert designs. Multicoloured. P 13½.

4921	50b. Type **987**	25	10
4922	1l. Grey partridge (*Perdix perdix*)	50	10
4923	1l.50 Snowy owl (*Nyctea scandiaca*)	70	10
4924	2l. Pine marten (*Martes martes*)	95	15
4925	3l. Eurasian badger (*Meles meles*)	1·30	20
4926	3l.50 European otter (*Lutra lutra*)	1·40	30
4927	4l. Capercaillie (*Tetrao urogallus*)	1·70	35
4928	5l. Great bustard (*Otis tarda*)	2·00	45
4921/4928	*Set of* 8	8·00	1·60

988 Flags and Victory Monument, Bucharest **989** Union Emblem

(Des A. Popescu. Photo)

1985 (9 May). 40th Anniv of Victory in Europe Day. P 13½.

4929	**988**	2l. multicoloured	1·20	55

(Des Z. Silviu. Photo)

1985 (14 May). Communist Youth Union Congress. P 13½.

4930	**989**	2l. multicoloured	70	55

A 10l. imperforate miniature sheet commemorating tenth anniv of signing of final European Security and Co-operation Conference document was issued 3 June 1985 in a restricted printing.

990 Route Map and Canal **991** Brown Pelican (*Pelecanus occidentalis*)

(Des M. Mănescu (10l.) and A. Mihai (others). Photo)

1986 (7 June). Danube–Black Sea Canal. T **990** and similar horiz designs. Multicoloured. P 13½.

4931	1l. Type **990**	50	10
4932	2l. Canal and bridge, Cernavodă	95	15
4933	3l. Road bridge over canal, Medgidia	1·40	20
4934	4l. Canal control tower, Agigea	1·80	35
4931/4934	*Set of* 4	4·25	70
MS4935	90×79 mm. 10l. Opening ceremony (53×39 mm)	9·00	9·00

(Des M. Mănescu. Photo)

1985 (26 June). Birth Bicentenary of John J. Audubon (ornithologist). T **991** and similar multicoloured designs. P 13½.

4936	50b. American robin (*Turdus migratorius*) (horiz)	25	10
4937	1l. Type **991**	50	10
4938	1l.50 Yellow-crowned night heron (*Nyctanassa violacea*)	70	15
4939	2l. Northern oriole (*Icterus galbula*)	95	20
4940	3l. Red-necked grebe (*Podiceps grisegena*)	1·40	35
4941	4l. Mallard (*Anas platyrhynchos*) (horiz).	1·90	45
4936/4941	*Set of* 6	5·25	1·20

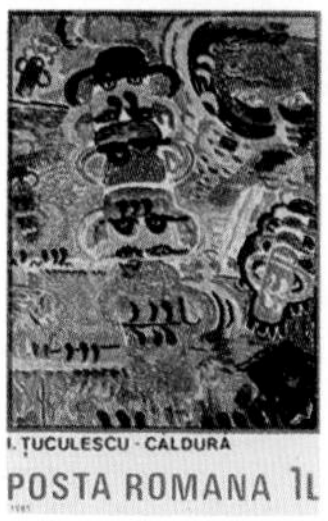

992 "Fire" **993** Peacock (*Inachis io*)

(Des D. Mihălţeanu. Photo)

1985 (13 July). Paintings by Ion Tuculescu. T **992** and similar multicoloured designs. P 13½.

4942	1l. Type **992**	25	10
4943	2l. "Circulation"	60	20
4944	3l. "Interior of Peasant's Home" (horiz)	85	35
4945	4l. "Sunset" (horiz)	1·20	55
4942/4945	*Set of* 5	2·50	1·10

(Des E. Palade. Photo)

1985 (15 July). Butterflies and Moths. T **993** and similar horiz designs. Multicoloured. P 13½.

4946	50b. Type **993**	10	10
4947	1l. Swallowtail (*Papilio machaon*)	35	10
4948	2l. Red admiral (*Vanessa atalanta*)	70	15
4949	3l. Emperor moth (*Saturnia pavonia*)	1·20	20
4950	4l. Hebe tiger moth (*Ammobiota festiva*)	1·60	35
4951	5l. Eyed hawk moth (*Smerinthus ocellatus*)	1·90	45
4946/4951	*Set of* 6	5·25	1·20

994 Transfăgărăşan Mountain Road **995** Romanian Crest, Symbols of Agriculture and "XX"

(Des A. Philipovici. Photo)

1985 (29 July). 20th Anniv of Election of General Secretary Nicolae Ceauşescu at Ninth Communist Party Congress. T **994** and similar vert designs. Multicoloured. P 13½.

4952	1l. Type **994**	60	20
4953	2l. Danube–Black Sea Canal	1·20	35
4954	3l. Bucharest underground railway	1·80	55
4955	4l. Irrigating fields	2·40	80
4952/4955	*Set of* 4	5·50	1·70

(Des A. Popescu. Photo)

1985 (5 Aug). 20th Anniv of Romanian Socialist Republic. T **995** and similar vert design. Multicoloured. P 13½.

4956	1l. Type **995**	60	25
4957	2l. Crest, symbols of industry and "XX"	1·20	35

996 Daimler's Motor Cycle, 1885 **997** *Senecio glaberrimus*

(Des M. Mănescu. Photo)

1985 (22 Aug). Centenary of Motor Cycle. Sheet 91×79 mm. P 13½.

MS4958	**996**	10l. multicoloured	4·75	4·75

(Des M. Vămăşescu. Photo)

1985 (29 Aug). 50th Anniv of Retezat National Park. T **997** and similar vert designs. Multicoloured. P 13½.

4959	50b. Type **997**	25	10
4960	1l. Chamois (*Rupicapra rupicapra*)	50	15
4961	2l. *Centaurea retezatensis*	95	20
4962	3l. Violet (*Viola dacica*)	1·20	25
4963	4l. Alpine marmot (*Marmota marmota*)	1·70	35
4964	5l. Golden eagle (*Aquila chrysaëtos*)	2·00	55
4959/4964	*Set of* 6	6·00	1·40
MS4965	91×80 mm. 10l. Lynx (*Lynx lynx*)	6·00	6·00

998 Universal "530 DTC"

999 Costume of Muscel (female)

(Des D. Drăguşin. Photo)

1985 (10 Sept). Romanian Tractors. T **998** and similar horiz designs. Multicoloured. P 13½.

4966	50b. Type **998**	10	10
4967	1l. Universal "550 M HC"	35	15
4968	1l.50 Universal "650 Super"	50	20
4969	2l. Universal "850"	70	25
4970	3l. Universal "S 1801 IF" tracked front loader	1·20	35
4971	4l. Universal "A 3602 IF" front loader	1·80	55
4966/4971	*Set of 6*	4·25	1·40

(Des A. Tasgian. Photo)

1985 (28 Sept). Costumes (1st series). T **999** and similar vert designs. Multicoloured. P 13½.

4972	50b. Type **999**	10	10
	a. Pair. Nos. 4972/3	25	25
4973	50b. Muscel (male)	10	10
4974	1l.50 Bistriţa-Năsăud (female)	50	20
	a. Pair. Nos. 4974/5	1·10	45
4975	1l.50 Bistriţa-Năsăud (male)	50	20
4976	2l. Vrancea (female)	70	35
	a. Pair. Nos. 4976/7	1·50	75
4977	2l. Vrancea (male)	70	35
4978	3l. Vilcea (female)	95	45
	a. Pair. Nos. 4978/9	2·00	95
4979	3l. Vilcea (male)	95	45
4972/4979	*Set of 8*	4·00	2·00

The two stamps of each value were issued together in *se-tenant* pairs within their sheets, each pair forming a composite design.

See also Nos. 5143/50.

1000 Footballer attacking Goal

1001 U.N. Emblem and "40"

(Des A. Popescu. Photo)

1985 (15 Oct). World Cup Football Championship, Mexico (1986) (1st issue). T **1000** and similar horiz designs. Multicoloured. P 13½.

4980	50b. Type **1000**	10	10
4981	1l. Player capturing ball	35	15
4982	1l.50 Player heading ball	50	20
4983	2l. Player about to tackle	70	25
4984	3l. Player heading ball and goalkeeper	1·20	35
4985	4l. Player kicking ball over head	1·80	55
4980/4985	*Set of 6*	4·25	1·40

A 10l. imperforate miniature sheet, 106×80 mm, depicting two footballers, exists from a restricted printing.

See also Nos. 5038/43.

(Des V. Stoianov. Photo)

1985 (21 Oct). 40th Anniv of United Nations Organization (4986) and 30th Anniv of Romanian Membership (4987). T **1001** and similar horiz design. Multicoloured. P 13½.

4986	2l. Type **1001**	60	45
4987	2l. U.N. building, New York, U.N. emblem and Romanian crest	60	45

1002 Copper

1003 Posthorn

(Des D. Mihălţeanu. Photo)

1985 (28 Oct). Minerals. T **1002** and similar vert designs. Multicoloured. P 13½.

4988	50b. Quartz and calcite	10	10
4989	1l. Type **1002**	25	15
4990	2l. Gypsum	70	20
4991	3l. Quartz	95	25
4992	4l. Stibium	1·30	35
4993	5l. Tetrahedrite	1·80	55
4988/4993	*Set of 6*	4·50	1·40

(Des V. Stoianov. Photo)

1985 (29 Oct). Stamp Day. P 13½.

4994	**1003**	2l. (+1l.) multicoloured	1·20	1·10

No. 4994 was issued *se-tenant* with premium-carrying tab, as shown in Type **1003**.

1004 Goofy as Hank waking to find himself at Camelot

(Des Walt Disney Productions. Photo)

1985 (28 Nov). 150th Birth Anniv of Mark Twain (writer). Scenes from *A Connecticut Yankee in King Arthur's Court*. T **1004** and similar vert designs. Multicoloured. P 13½.

4995	50b. Type **1004**	3·00	2·20
4996	50b. Hank at the stake and Merlin (Mickey Mouse)	3·00	2·20
4997	50b. Hank being hoisted onto horseback in full armour	3·00	2·20
4998	50b. Pete as Sir Sagramor on horseback	3·00	2·20
4995/4998	*Set of 4*	11·00	8·00
MS4999	122×96 mm. 5l. Hank at the tournament against Sir Sagramor	24·00	24·00

(Des Walt Disney Productions. Photo)

1985 (28 Nov). Birth Bicentenaries of Grimm Brothers (folklorists). Scenes from *The Three Brothers*. Horiz designs as T **1004**. Multicoloured. P 13½.

5000	1l. Father (Donald Duck) bidding farewell to the brothers (Huey, Louie and Dewey)	7·25	6·75
5001	1l. Louie as fencing master brother practising	7·25	6·75
5002	1l. Louie keeping rain off his father with sword	7·25	6·75
5003	1l. Huey as blacksmith brother shoeing galloping horse	7·25	6·75
5004	1l. Dewey as barber brother shaving Brer Rabbit on the run	7·25	6·75
5000/5004	*Set of 5*	33·00	30·00
MS5005	120×95 mm. 5l. Brothers playing music	24·00	24·00

1005 Wright Brothers (aviation pioneers) and Wright Flyer 1

1985 (25 Dec). Explorers and Pioneers. T **1005** and similar horiz designs. Multicoloured. Photo. P 13½.

5006	1l. Type **1005**	35	10
5007	1l.50 Jacques Yves Cousteau (undersea explorer) and *Calypso*	50	10
5008	2l. Amelia Earhart (first woman trans-Atlantic flyer) and Fokker F.VIIb/3m seaplane *Friendship*	70	15
5009	3l. Charles Lindbergh (first solo trans-Atlantic flyer) and Ryan NYP Special *Spirit of St. Louis*	1·10	20
5010	3l.50 Sir Edmund Hillary (first man to reach summit of Everest)	1·20	25
5011	4l. Robert Peary and Emil Racovita (polar explorers)	1·40	30
5012	5l. Richard Byrd (polar explorer and aviator) and polar supply ship	1·80	40
5013	6l. Neil Armstrong (first man on Moon) and Moon	1·90	45
5006/5013	*Set of 8*	8·00	1·80

1006 Edmond Halley and Comet

(Des M. Mănescu. Photo)

1986 (27 Jan). AIR. Appearance of Halley's Comet. T **1006** and similar horiz design. P 13½.

5014	2l. Type **1006**	70	25
5015	4l. Comet, orbit and space probes	1·70	45

No. 5014 is wrongly inscr "Edmund".

A 10l. imperforate miniature sheet, 104×81 mm depicting a space probe and the tail of the comet, exists from a restricted printing.

1007 "Nina in Green"

1008 Wild Cat (*Fells silvestris*)

1986 (12 Mar). Paintings by Nicolae Tonitza. T **1007** and similar vert designs. Multicoloured. Photo. P 13½.

5016	1l. Type **1007**	35	10
5017	2l. "Irina"	70	20
5018	3l. "Forester's Daughter"	1·10	35
5019	4l. "Woman on Veranda"	1·40	55
5016/5019	*Set of 4*	3·25	1·10

1986 (25 Mar). Inter-European Cultural and Economic Co-operation. Two sheets, each 110×81 mm, containing horiz designs as T **1008**. Multicoloured. Photo. P 13½.

MS5020	Two sheets. (a) 3l.×4: Type **1008**; Stoat (*Mustela erminea*); Capercaillie (*Tetrao urogallus*); Brown bear (*Ursus arctos*). (b) 3l.×4: Dianthus callizonus; Arolla pine (*Pinus cembra*); Willow (*Salix* sp.); *Rosa pendulina*. Two sheets	7·25	7·25

1009 Goofy playing Clarinet

(Des Walt Disney Productions. Photo)

1986 (10 Apr). 50th Anniv of Colour Animation. T **1009** and similar horiz designs showing scenes from Band Concert (cartoon film). P 13½.

5021	50b. Type **1009**	3·00	2·20
5022	50b. Clarabelle playing flute	3·00	2·20
5023	50b. Mickey Mouse conducting	3·00	2·20
5024	50b. Paddy and Peter Pig playing euphonium and trumpet	3·00	2·20
5025	1l. Conductor Mickey and flautist Donald Duck	7·25	6·75
5026	1l. Donald caught in trombone slide	7·25	6·75
5027	1l. Horace playing drums	7·25	6·75
5028	1l. Donald selling ice cream	7·25	6·75
5029	1l. Mickey and euphonium caught in tornado	7·25	6·75
5021/5029	Setof 9	43·00	38·00
MS5030	120×95 mm. 5l. Instruments and musicians in tree	24·00	24·00

1010 Hotel Diana, Băile Herculane

1986 (23 Apr). Spa Hotels. T **1010** and similar vert designs. Multicoloured. Photo. P 13½.

5031	50b. Type **1010**	10	10
5032	1l. Hotel Termal, Băile Felix	25	15
5033	2l. Hotels Delfin, Meduza and Steaua de Mare, North Eforie	60	20
5034	3l. Hotel Căciulata, Călimăneşti-Căciulata	95	25
5035	4l. Villa Palas, Slănic Moldova	1·30	35
5036	5l. Hotel Brădet, Sovata	1·90	55
5031/5036	*Set of 6*	4·50	1·40

1011 Ceauşescu and Red Flag

(Des A. Popescu. Photo)

1986 (8 May). 65th Anniv of Romanian Communist Party. P 13½.

5037	**1011**	2l. multicoloured	1·90	1·10

1012 Italy v Bulgaria

(Des A. Philipovici. Photo)

1986 (9 May). World Cup Football Championship, Mexico (2nd issue). T **1012** and similar horiz designs. Multicoloured. P 13½.

5038	50b. Type **1012**	10	10
5039	1l. Mexico v Belgium	25	15
5040	2l. Canada v France	60	20
5041	3l. Brazil v Spain	85	25
5042	4l. Uruguay v W. Germany	1·40	35
5043	5l. Morocco v Poland	1·90	55
5038/5043 *Set of 6*		4·50	1·40

A 10l. imperforate miniature sheet, 120×94 mm depicting Azteca Stadium, exists from a restricted printing.

1013 Alexandru Papana's Bucker Bu 133 Jungmeister Biplane (Aerobatics Champion, 1936)

(Des A. Mihai. Photo)

1986 (15 May). AIR. Ameripex '86 International Stamp Exhibition, Chicago. Sheet 120×95 mm. P 13½.

MS5044	**1013**	10l. multicoloured	4·75	4·75

1014 *Tulipa gesneriana*

1015 Mircea the Great and Horsemen

(Des Eliza Palade. Photo)

1986 (15 June). Garden Flowers. T **1014** and similar vert designs. Multicoloured. P 13½.

5045	50b. Type **1014**	10	10
5046	1l. *Iris hispanica*	35	15
5047	2l. *Rosa hybrida*	70	20
5048	3l. *Anemone coronaria*	1·10	25
5049	4l. *Freesia refracta*	1·40	35
5050	5l. *Chrysanthemum indicum*	1·90	55
5045/5050 *Set of 6*		5·00	1·40

(Des A. Popescu. Photo)

1986 (17 July). 600th Anniv of Mircea the Great's Accession. P 13½.

5051	**1015**	2l. multicoloured	70	45

1016 Thatched House with Veranda, Alba

(Des M. Vămăşescu. Photo)

1986 (21 July). 50th Anniv of Museum of Historic Dwellings, Bucharest. T **1016** and similar horiz designs. Multicoloured. P 13½.

5052	50b. Type **1016**	10	10
5053	1l. Stone built house, Argeş	35	15
5054	2l. House with veranda, Constanţa	70	20
5055	3l. House with tiled roof and steps, Timiş	1·10	25
5056	4l. House with porch to veranda, Neamt	1·60	35
5057	5l. Two storey house with first floor veranda; Gorj	1·90	55
5052/5057 *Set of 6*		5·25	1·40

1017 Julius Popper (Tierra del Fuego, 1886–93)

(Des S. Avram. Photo)

1986 (23 July). Polar Research. T **1017** and similar horiz designs. Multicoloured. P 13½.

5058	50b. Type **1017**	10	10
5059	1l. Bazil Gh. Assan (Spitzbergen, 1896)	35	15
5060	2l. Emil Racovita and *Belgica* (barque) (Antarctic, 1897–99)	70	20
5061	3l. Constantin Dumbrava (Greenland, 1927–28)	1·10	25
5062	4l. Romanian participation in 17th Soviet Antarctic Expedition, 1971–72	1·60	35
5063	5l. 1977 *Sinoe* and 1979–80 *Tirnava* krill fishing expeditions	1·90	55
5058/5063 *Set of 6*		5·25	1·40

1018 Dove and Map on Globe

(Des E. Palade. Photo)

1986 (25 July). International Peace Year. Sheet 89×77 mm. P 13½.

MS5064	**1018**	5l. multicoloured	3·50	3·50

1019 The Blusher (*Amanita rubescens*)

1020 Group of Cyclists

(Des A. Philipovici. Photo)

1986 (15 Aug). Fungi. T **1019** and similar vert designs. Multicoloured. P 13½.

5065	50b. Type **1019**	10	10
5066	1l. Oak mushroom (*Boletus luridus*)	35	15
5067	2l. Peppery milk cap (*Lactarius piperatus*)	70	20
5068	3l. Shield fungus (*Lepiota clypeolaria*)	1·10	25
5069	4l. The charcoal burner (*Russula cyanoxantha*)	1·60	35
5070	5l. *Tremiscus helvelloides*	1·90	55
5065/5070 *Set of 6*		5·25	1·40

(Des A. Popescu. Photo)

1986 (29 Aug). Cycle Tour of Romania. T **1020** and similar vert designs. Multicoloured. P 13½.

5071	1l. Type **1020**	35	15
5072	2l. Motorcycle following cyclist	70	20
5073	3l. Jeep following cyclists	1·10	35
5074	4l. Winner	1·40	45
5071/5074 *Set of 4*		3·25	1·00
MS5075 90×78 mm. 10l. Cyclist (38×51 mm)		4·75	4·75

A 10l. imperforate miniature sheet commemorating European Security and Co-operation Conference, Vienna, was issued 28 October 1986 in a limited printing.

1021 Emblem

1022 Petru Maior (historian)

(Des A. Popescu. Photo)

1986 (10 Nov). 40th Anniv of United Nations Educational, Scientific and Cultural Organization and 30th Anniv of Romanian Membership. P 13½.

5076	**1021**	4l. multicoloured	1·30	55

(Des V. Stoianov. Photo)

1986 (10 Nov). Birth Anniversaries. T **1022** and similar vert designs. P 13½.

5077	50b. brown-purple, gold and deep bluish green	10	10
5078	1l. bottle green, gold and deep magenta	25	10
5079	2l. carmine-lake, gold and blue	70	10
5080	3l. grey-blue, gold, and reddish brown	1·20	20
5077/5080 *Set of 4*		2·00	45

Designs:—50b. Type **1022** (225th anniv); 1l. George Topîrceanu (writer, centenary); 2l. Henri Coandă (engineer, centenary); 3l. Constantin Budeanu (electical engineer, centenary).

1023 Coach and Horses

(Des V. Stoianov. Photo)

1986 (15 Nov). Stamp Day. P 13½.

5081	**1023**	2l. (+1l.) multicoloured	1·20	1·10

No. 5081 includes the *se-tenant* premium-carrying tab shown in Type **1023**.

1024 F 300 Oil Drilling Rigs

1025 "Goat"

1986 (28 Nov). Industry. T **1024** and similar multicoloured designs. Photo. P 13½.

5082	50b. Type **1024**	10	10
5083	1l. "Promex" excavator (horiz)	35	15
5084	2l. Petrochemical refinery, Piteşti	70	20
5085	3l. Tipper "110 t" (horiz)	1·10	25
5086	4l. "Coral" computer	1·60	35
5087	5l. 350 m.w. turbine (horiz)	1·90	55
5082/5087 *Set of 6*		5·25	1·40

(Des M. Mănescu. Photo)

1986 (26 Dec). New Year Folk Customs. T **1025** and similar horiz designs. Multicoloured. P 13½.

5088	50b. Type **1025**	10	10
5089	1l. Sorcova	35	15
5090	2l. Pluguşorul	70	20
5091	3l. Buhaiul	1·10	25
5092	4l. Căiuţii	1·60	35
5093	5l. Urătorii	1·90	55
5088/5093 *Set of 6*		5·25	1·40

1026 Tin Can and Motor Car ("Re-cycle metals")

1027 Flags and Young People

1986 (30 Dec). "Save Waste Materials". T **1026** and similar vert design. Photo. P 13½.

5094	1l. deep claret and bright orange	35	20
5095	2l. bright green and blackish green	85	35

Design:—2l. Trees and hand with newspaper ("Re-cycle waste paper").

(Des M. Mănescu. Photo)

1987 (18 Mar). 65th Anniv of Communist Youth Union. T **1027** and similar vert designs. Multicoloured. P 13½.

5096	1l. Type **1027**	35	10
5097	2l. Anniversary emblem	85	35
5098	3l. Flags and young people (different)	1·10	55
5096/5098 *Set of 3*		2·10	90

1028 Anniversary Emblem

1029 Administrative Building, Satu Mare

(Des M. Mănescu. Photo)

1987 (25 Apr). 25th Anniv of Agricultural Co-operatives. P 13½.

5099	**1028**	2l. multicoloured	70	55

(Des S. Mircea. Photo)

1987 (18 May). Inter-European Cultural and Economic Co-operation. Two sheets, each 110×80 mm, containing horiz designs as T **1029**. Multicoloured. P 13½.

MS5100 Two sheets. (a) 3l.×4: Type **1029**; House of Young Pioneers, Bucharest; Valahia Hotel, Tirgovişte; Căciulata Hotel, Căciulata. (b) 3l.×4: Exhibition Pavilion, Bucharest; Intercontinental Hotel, Bucharest; Europa Hotel, Eforie Nord; Polytechnic Institute, Bucharest. Two sheets .... 8·50 8·50

1030 "Birch Trees by Lake" (Ion Andreescu)

1987 (28 May). Paintings. T **1030** and similar multicoloured designs. Photo. P 13½.

5101	50b. Type **1030**	10	10
5102	1l. "Young Peasent Girls spinning" (Nicolae Grigorescu)	35	15
5103	2l. "Washerwoman" (Ştefan Luchian)	70	20
5104	3l. "Interior" (Ştefan, Dimitrescu)	1·10	25
5105	4l. "Winter Landscape" (Alexandru Ciucurencu)	1·60	35
5106	5l. "Winter in Bucharest" (Nicolae Tonitza) (vert)	1·90	55
5101/5106 *Set of 6*		5·25	1·40

1031 "1907" and Peasants

1032 Players

(Des M. Mănescu. Photo)

1987 (30 May). 80th Anniv of Peasant Uprising. P 13½.

5107	**1031**	2l. multicoloured	70	55

(Des A. Popescu. Photo)

1987 (15 July). Tenth Students World Men's Handball Championship. T **1032** and similar designs showing various match scenes. P 13½.

5108	50b. multicoloured	10	10
5109	1l. multicoloured (horiz)	35	15
5110	2l. multicoloured	70	20
5111	3l. multicoloured (horiz)	1·10	25
5112	4l. multicoloured	1·60	35
5113	5l. multicoloured (horiz)	1·90	55
5108/5113 *Set of 6*		5·25	1·40

1033 1 Leu Coin

1034 Eastern White Pelicans in the Danube Delta

(Des S. Mircea. Photo)

1987 (15 July). Currency. T **1033** and similar horiz design. Multicoloured. P 13½.

5114	1l. Type **1033**	60	35
MS5115	90×78 mm. 10l. 10 lei banknote (53×41 mm)	4·75	4·75

1987 (31 July). Tourism. T **1034** and similar vert designs. Multicoloured. Photo. P 13½.

5116	50b. Type **1034**	10	10
5117	1l. Cable car above Transfăgărăşan mountain road	35	15
5118	2l. Cheile Bicazului	70	20
5119	3l. Ceahlău mountains	1·10	30
5120	4l. Lake Capra, Făgărăş mountains	1·60	35
5121	5l. Borşa orchards	1·90	55
5116/5121 *Set of 6*		5·25	1·50

1035 Henri August's Glider, 1909

(Des A. Mihai. Photo)

1987 (10 Aug). AIR. Aircraft. T **1035** and similar horiz designs. Multicoloured. P 13½.

5122	50b. Type **1035**	10	10
5123	1l. IS-28B2 glider and sky diver	35	15
5124	2l. IS-29 D2 glider	70	20
5125	3l. IS-32 glider	1·10	30
5126	4l. I.A.R. 35 light airplane	1·60	35
5127	5l. IS-28 M2 aircraft	1·90	55
5122/5127 *Set of 6*		5·25	1·50

1036 Youth on Winged Horse

(Des M. Mănescu. Photo)

1987 (25 Sept). Fairy Tales by Petre Ispirescu. T **1036** and similar multicoloured designs. P 13½.

5128	50b. Type **1036**	10	10
5129	1l. King and princesses (*Salt in the Food*)	35	15
5130	2l. Girl on horse fighting lion (*Ileana Simziana*)	70	20
5131	3l. Youth with bow and arrow aiming at bird (*The Youth and the Golden Apples*)	1·10	30
5132	4l. George and dead dragon (*George the Brave*)	1·60	35
5133	5l. Girl looking at sleeping youth (*The Enchanted Pig*)	1·90	55
5128/5133 *Set of 6*		5·25	1·50
MS5134	90×79 mm. 10l. Youth holding sun and moon (*Greuceanu*) (41×53 mm)	4·75	4·75

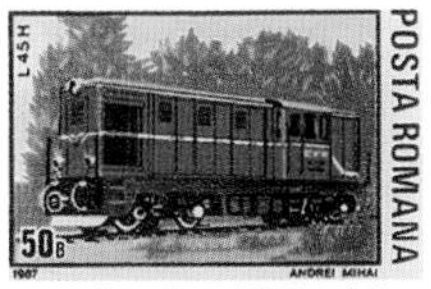

1037 Class "L 45 H" Diesel Shunter

(Des A. Mihai. Photo)

1987 (15 Oct). Railway Locomotives. T **1037** and similar horiz designs. Multicoloured. P 13½.

5135	50b. Type **1037**	10	10
5136	1l. Class "LDE 125" diesel goods locomotive	35	15
5137	2l. Class "LDH 70" diesel goods locomotive	70	20
5138	3l. Class "LDE 2100" diesel locomotive	1·10	30
5139	4l. Class "LDE 3000" diesel locomotive	1·60	35
5140	5l. Class "LE 5100" diesel locomotive	1·90	55
5135/5140 *Set of 6*		5·25	1·50

1038 Alpine Columbine (*Aquilegia alpina*)

1039 Bucharest Municipal Arms

(Des F. Ivănuş. Photo)

1987 (16 Oct). Nature Reserves in Europe. Two sheets, each 150×135 mm, containing horiz designs as T **1038**. Multicoloured. P 13½.

MS5141 Two sheets. (a) 1l.×12: Type **1038**; Pasque flower (*Pulsatilla vernalis*); Alpine aster (*Aster alpinus*); *Soldanella pusilla*; Orange lily (*Lilium bulbiferum*); Alpine bearberry (*Arctostaphylos uva-ursi*); *Crocus vernus*; Golden hawksbeard (*Crepis aurea*); Lady's slipper (*Cypripedium calceolus*); *Centaurea nervosa*; Mountain avens (*Dryas octopetala*); *Gentiana excisa*. (b) 1l.×12: Pine marten (*Martes martes*); Lynx (*Felis lynx*); Polar bear (*Ursus maritimus*); European otter (*Lutra lutra*); European bison (*Bison bonasus*); Red-breasted goose (*Branta ruficollis*); Greater flamingo (*Phoenicopterus ruber*); Great bustard (*Otis tarda*); Black grouse (*Lyrurus tetrix*); Lammergeier (*Gypäetus barbatus*); Marbled polecat (*Vormela peregusna*); White-headed duck (*Oxyura leucocephala*). Two sheets .... 16·00 16·00

(Des S. Mircea. Photo)

1987 (19 Oct). "Philatelia'87" International Stamp Fair, Cologne. Sheet 79×109 mm containing T **1039** and similar vert design. Multicoloured. P 13½.

MS5142 3l. Type **1039**; 3l. Cologne arms .... 4·75 4·75

No. **MS**5142 contains the two stamps and two labels bearing the Exhibition emblem in a chessboard design.

(Des R. Coteanu. Photo)

1987 (7 Nov). Costumes (2nd series). Vert designs as T **999**. Multicoloured. P 13½.

5143	1l. Tirnave (female)	35	15
	a. Pair. Nos. 5143/4	75	35
5144	1l. Tirnave (male)	35	15
5145	2l. Buzau (female)	70	20
	a. Pair. Nos. 5145/6	1·50	45
5146	2l. Buzau (male)	70	20
5147	3l. Dobrogea (female)	1·10	30
	a. Pair. Nos. 5147/8	2·30	65
5148	3l. Dobrogea (male)	1·10	30
5149	4l. Ilfov (female)	1·40	35
	a. Pair. Nos. 5149/50	3·00	75
5150	4l. Ilfov (male)	1·40	35
5143/5150 *Set of 8*		6·50	1·80

The two stamps of each value were issued together in *se-tenant* pairs within their sheets.

1040 Postal Services

(Des M. Mănescu. Photo)

1987 (15 Nov). Stamp Day. P 13½.

5151	**1040**	2l. (+1l.) multicoloured	1·20	1·10

No. 5151 includes the *se-tenant* premium-carrying tab shown in Type **1040**, the stamp and tab forming a composite design.

1041 Honey Bee on Flower

(Des M. Vămăşescu. Photo)

1987 (16 Nov). Bee-keeping. T **1041** and similar horiz designs. Multicoloured. P 13½.

5152	1l. Type **1041**	35	15
5153	2l. Honey bee, sunflowers and hives	85	20
5154	3l. Hives in Danube delta	1·20	35
5155	4l. Apiculture Complex, Bucharest	1·70	45
5152/5155 *Set of 4*		3·75	1·00

1042 Car behind Boy on Bicycle

(Des F. Ivănuş. Photo)

1987 (10 Dec). Road Safety. T **1042** and similar vert designs. Multicoloured. P 13½.

5156	50b. Type **1042**	10	10
5157	1l. Children using school crossing	35	15
5158	2l. Driver carelessly opening car door	70	20
5159	3l. Hand holding crossing sign and family using zebra crossing	1·10	30
5160	4l. Speedometer and crashed car	1·60	35
5161	5l. Child's face and speeding car	1·90	55
5156/5161 *Set of 6*		5·25	1·50

1043 Red Flag and Lenin

(Des A. Philipovici. Photo)

1987 (26 Dec). 70th Anniv of Russian Revolution. P 13½.
5162 **1043** 2l. multicoloured .... 1·20 55

1044 Biathlon

1045 Crest and National Colours

(Des V. Stoianov. Photo)

1987 (28 Dec). Winter Olympic Games, Calgary (1988). T **1044** and similar vert designs. Multicoloured. P 13½.
5163 50b. Type **1044** 10 10
5164 1l. Slalom 25 10
5165 1l.50 Ice hockey 35 10
5166 2l. Luge 50 15
5167 3l. Speed skating 85 20
5168 3l.50 Figure skating 95 35
5169 4l. Downhill skiing .... 1·20 40
5170 5l. Two-man bobsleigh .... 1·40 55
5163/5170 *Set of 8* .... 5·00 1·80
A 10l. imperforate miniature sheet, 106×81 mm depicting ski jumping, exists from a limited printing.

(Des M. Mănescu. Photo)

1987 (30 Dec). 40th Anniv of People's Republic. P 13½.
5171 **1045** 2l. multicoloured 95 55

1046 Pres. Ceauşescu and Flags

(Des V. Stoianov. Photo)

1988 (26 Jan). 70th Birthday and 55 Years of Revolutionary Activity of Pres. Nicolae Ceauşescu. P 13½.
5172 **1046** 2l. multicoloured .... 1·40 80

1047 Wide-necked Pot, Marginea

(Des V. Stoianov. Photo)

1988 (26 Feb). Pottery. T **1047** and similar horiz designs. Multicoloured. P 13½.
5173 50b. Type **1047** 10 10
5174 1l. Flask, Oboga 35 15
5175 2l. Jug and saucer, Horezu 70 20
5176 3l. Narrow-necked pot, Curtea de Arges .... 1·10 30
5177 4l. Jug, Birsa .... 1·60 35
5178 5l. Jug and plate, Varna .... 1·90 55
5173/5178 *Set of 6* .... 5·25 1·50

1048 *Santa Maria*

1049 Ceramic Clock

(Des A. Mihai. Photo)

1988 (27 Apr). Inter-European Cultural and Economic Co-operation. Two sheets, each 110×80 mm, containing horiz designs as T **1048**. Multicoloured. P 13½.
MS5179 Two sheets. (a) 3l.×4: Type **1048**; Dish aerials, Cheia earth station; Bucharest underground train; Airbus Industrie A320 jetliner. (b) 3l.×4: Mail coach and horses; "ECS" satellite; Oltcit motor car; "ICE" express train. Two sheets .... 8·50 8·50

1988 (20 May). Clocks in Ploieşti Museum. T **1049** and similar vert designs. Multicoloured. Photo. P 13½.
5180 50b. Type **1049** 10 10
5181 1l.50 Gilt clock with sun at base 35 15
5182 2l. Clock with pastoral figure 70 20
5183 3l. Gilt clock surmounted with figure 95 30
5184 4l. Vase-shaped clock .... 1·60 35
5185 5l. Clock surmounted with porcelain figures .... 1·90 55
5180/5185 *Set of 6* .... 5·00 1·50

1050 West German Flag and Player kicking Ball into Net

1051 Constantin Brîncoveanu

(Des A. Mihai. Photo)

1988 (9 June). European Football Championship, West Germany. Two sheets, each 110×80 mm, containing horiz designs as T **1050**. Multicoloured. P 13½.
MS5186 Two sheets. (a) 3l.×4: Type **1050**; Goalkeeper diving to save ball and Spanish flag; Italian flag and player; Players and Danish flag. (b) 3l.×4: English flag, referee and player; Players and Netherlands flag; Irish flag and players; Players and flag of U.S.S.R. Two sheets .... 12·00 12·00
Each horizontal pair within the sheets forms a composite design.

(Des A. Popescu. Photo)

1988 (20 June). 300th Anniv of Election of Constantin Brîncoveanu as Ruler of Wallachia. P 13½.
5187 **1051** 2l. multicoloured 70 55

1052 Gymnastics

1053 Postal Emblems and Roses

(Des E. Palade. Photo)

1988 (28 June). Olympic Games, Seoul (1st issue). T **1052** and similar vert designs. Multicoloured. P 13½.
5188 50b. Type **1052** 10 10
5189 1l.50 Boxing 35 15
5190 2l. Lawn tennis 70 20
5191 3l. Judo 95 30
5192 4l. Running .... 1·60 35
5193 5l. Rowing .... 1·90 55
5188/5193 *Set of 6* .... 5·00 1·50
A 10l. imperforate miniature sheet, 107×80 mm depicting swimming, exists from a limited printing.
See also Nos. 5197/5204.

(Des M. Mănescu. Photo)

1988 (5 Aug). Romanian–Chinese Stamp Exhibition, Bucharest. P 13½.
5194 **1058** 2l. multicoloured 70 55

1054 Player and Wimbledon Centre Court

(Des A. Popescu. Photo)

1988 (22 Aug). "Grand Slam" Tennis Championships. Two sheets, each 110×80 mm, containing horiz designs as T **1054**. P 13½.
MS5195 Two sheets. (a) 3l.×4; Type **1054**; Wimbledon match; Flushing Meadow match; Flushing Meadow centre courts, New York. (b) 3l.×4; Melbourne centre court; Melbourne match; Roland Garros match; Roland Garros centre court, Paris. Two sheets .... 12·00 12·00
Each horizontal pair within the sheets forms a composite design.

1055 "Bowl of Flowers" (Ştefan Luchian)

1988 (26 Aug). Praga '88 International Stamp Exhibition. Sheet 90×78 mm. Photo. P 13½.
MS5196 **1055** 5l. multicoloured .... 3·50 3·50

1056 Running

(Des V. Stoianov. Photo)

1988 (1 Sept). Olympic Games, Seoul (2nd issue). T **1056** and similar horiz designs. Multicoloured. P 13½.
5197 50b. Type **1056** 10 10
5198 1l. Canoeing 25 10
5199 1l.50 Gymnastics 35 10
5200 2l. Double kayak 50 15
5201 3l. Weightlifting 85 20
5202 3l.50 Swimming 95 35
5203 4l. Fencing .... 1·20 40
5204 5l. Double sculls .... 1·40 45
5197/5204 *Set of 8* .... 5·00 1·70
A 10l. imperforate miniature sheet, 105×80 mm depicting gymnastics, exists from a limited printing.

1057 *Oncidium lanceanum*

(Des M. Mănescu. Photo)

1988 (24 Oct). Orchids. Two sheets, each 150×137 mm, containing horiz designs as T **1057**. Multicoloured. P 13½.
MS5205 Two sheets. (a) 1l.×12: Type **1057**; *Cattleya trianae; Sophronitis cernua; Bulbophyllum lobbii; Lycaste cruenta; Mormolyce ringens; Phragmipedium schlimii; Angraecum sesquipedale; Laelia crispa; Encyclia atropurpurea; Dendrobium nobile; Oncidium splendidurn.* (b) 1l.×12: *Brassavola perrinii; Paphiopedilum maudiae; Sophronitis coccinea; Vandopsis lissochiloides; Phalaenopsis lueddemanniana; Chysis bractescens; Cochleanthes discolor; Phalaenopsis amabilis; Pieione pricei; Sobralia macrantha; Aspasia lunata; Cattleya citrina.* Two sheets .... 14·50 14·00

1058 Past and Present Postal Services

(Des M. Mănescu. Photo)

1988 (13 Nov). Stamp Day. P 13½.
5206 **1058** 2l. (+1l.) multicoloured 95 90
No. 5206 includes the *se-tenant* premium-carrying tab shown in T **1058**.

1059 Gymnastics and Three Gold Medals

1060 State Arms

(Des M. Mănescu. Photo)

1988 (7 Dec). Seoul Olympic Games Romanian Medal Winners. Two sheets, each 110×80 mm, containing horiz designs as T **1059**. Multicoloured. P 13½.

MS5207 Two sheets. (a) 3l.×4: Type **1059**; Pistol shooting and gold medal; Weightlifting and silver medal; Boxing and silver medal. (b) 3l.×4: Athletics and gold and silver medals; Swimming and silver medal; Wrestling and gold medal; Rowing and gold medal. Two sheets........ 12·00 12·00

The miniature sheets are each inscribed in the margins with the total medal tally.

1988 (29 Dec). 70th Anniv of Union of Transylvania and Romania. Photo. P 13½.

5208	**1060**	2l. multicoloured	1·20	1·10

1061 Athenaeum Concert Hall, Bucharest (centenary)

(Des M. Mănescu. Photo)

1988 (30 Dec). Romanian History. T **1061** and similar horiz designs. Multicoloured. P 13½.

5209	50b. Type **1061**	10	10
5210	1l.50 Roman coin showing Drobeta Bridge	35	15
5211	2l. Ruins (600th anniv of Suceava as capital of Moldavian feudal state)	70	20
5212	3l. Scroll, arms and town (600th anniv of first documentary reference to Pitesti)	95	30
5213	4l. Dacian warriors from Trajan's Column	1·60	35
5214	5l. Thracian gold helmet from Cotofeneşti-Prahova	1·90	55
5209/5214	*Set of 6*	5·00	1·50

1062 Zapodeni, 17th century

1063 Red Cross Worker

(Des M. Vămăşescu. Photo)

1989 (18 Feb). Traditional House Architecture. T **1062** and similar horiz designs. Multicoloured. P 13½.

5215	50b. Type **1062**	10	10
5216	1l.50 Berbeşti, 18th century	35	15
5217	2l. Voitinel, 18th century	70	20
5218	3l. Chiojdu Mic, 18th century	95	30
5219	4l. Cîmpanii de Sus, 19th century	1·60	35
5220	5l. Năruja, 19th century	1·90	55
5215/5220	*Set of 6*	5·00	1·50

(Des E. Palade. Photo)

1989 (25 Feb). Life-saving Services. T **1063** and similar multicoloured designs. P 13½.

5221	50b. Type **1063**	10	10
5222	1l. Red Cross orderlies giving first aid to girl (horiz)	35	10
5223	1l.50 Fireman carrying child	60	10
5224	2l. Rescuing child from earthquake-damaged building	70	15
5225	3l. Mountain rescue team transporting casualty on sledge (horiz)	1·10	20
5226	3l.50 Rescuing climber from cliff face	1·20	30
5227	4l. Rescuing child from river	1·30	35
5228	5l. Lifeguard in rowing boat and children playing in sea (horiz)	1·60	45
5221/5228	*Set of 8*	6·25	1·60

1064 Taşca Bicaz Cement Factory

(Des A. Mihai. Photo)

1989 (10 Apr). Industrial Achievements. T **1064** and similar horiz designs. Multicoloured. P 13½.

5229	50b. Type **1064**	10	10
5230	1l.50 New railway bridge, Cernavodă	50	15
5231	2l. Synchronous motor, Resita	70	20
5232	3l. Bucharest underground	95	30
5233	4l. Mangalia–Constanţa train ferry	1·30	35
5234	5l. Gloria (oil drilling platform)	1·60	55
5229/5234	*Set of 6*	4·75	1·50

1065 Flags and Symbols of Industry and Agriculture

(Des A. Popescu. Photo)

1989 (1 May). 50th Anniv of Anti-Fascist Demonstration. T **1065** and similar vert design. Multicoloured. P 13½.

5235	2l. Type **1065**	1·20	55
MS5236	90×78 mm. 10l. Flag and demonstrators	7·75	7·75

1066 Roses

(Des M. Mănescu. Photo)

1989 (20 May). Bulgaria '89 International Stamp Exhibition, Sofia. Sheet 90×78 mm. P 13½.

MS5237	**1066**	10l. multicoloured	4·75	4·75

1067 Girls playing with Dolls

(Des E. Palade. Photo)

1989 (15 June). Inter-European Cultural and Economic Co-operation. Children. Two sheets, each 110×80 mm, containing horiz designs as T **1067**. P 13½.

MS5238 Two sheets. (a) 3l.×4: Type **1067**; Playing football; On beach; Playing with toy cars. (b) 3l.×4: Playing in sea; On slides; At playground; Flying kites. Two sheets........ 8·50 8·50

1068 Ion Creangă (writer, death centenary)

1069 State and Communist Party Flags and Symbols of Industry and Agriculture

(Des V. Stoianov. Photo)

1989 (18 Aug). Anniversaries. T **1068** and similar vert designs. Multicoloured. P 13½.

5239	1l. Type **1068**	35	10
5240	2l. Mihai Eminescu (poet, death centenary)	85	35
5241	3l. Nicolae Teclu (scientist, 150th birth anniv)	1·20	55
5239/5241	*Set of 3*	2·20	90

(Des A. Popescu. Photo)

1989 (21 Aug). 45th Anniv of Liberation. P 13½.

5242	**1069**	2l. multicoloured	1·20	55

1070 *Pin-Pin*

1989 (25 Sept). Romanian Cartoon Films. T **1070** and similar horiz designs. Multicoloured. Photo. P 13½.

5243	50b. Type **1070**	10	10
5244	1l. *Maria*	35	10
5245	1l.50 *Gore and Grigore*	60	15
5246	2l. *Pisoiul, Bălănel, Manole, Monk*	70	20
5247	3l. *Gruia lui Novac*	1·10	30
5248	3l.50 *Mihaela*	1·20	35
5249	4l. *Harap Alb*	1·30	40
5250	5l. *Homo Sapiens*	1·60	45
5243/5250	*Set of 8*	6·25	1·80

1071 Globe, Letter and Houses

(Des V. Stoianov. Photo)

1989 (7 Oct). Stamp Day. P 13½.

5251	**1071**	2l. (+1l.) multicoloured	1·20	1·10

No. 5251 includes the *se-tenant* premium-carrying tab shown in Type **1071**; it was issued with *se-tenant* ½ stamp-size label showing a posthorn.

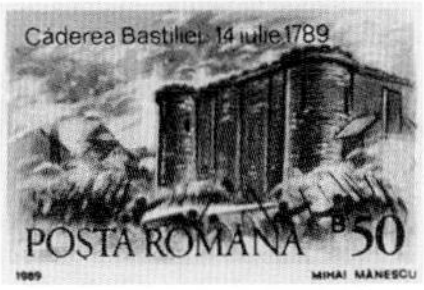

1072 Storming of the Bastille

(Des M. Mănescu. Photo)

1989 (14 Oct). Bicentenary of French Revolution. T **1072** and similar horiz designs. Multicoloured. P 13½.

5252	50b. Type **1072**	10	10
5253	1l.50 Street boy and Marianne	60	15
5254	2l. Maximilien de Robespierre	70	20
5255	3l. Rouget de Lisle singing the *Marseillaise*	1·10	30
5256	4l. Denis Diderot (encyclopaedist)	1·40	45
5257	5l. Crowd with banner	1·80	55
5252/5257	*Set of 6*	5·25	1·60
MS5258	90×78 mm. 10l. Philexfrance 89 International Stamp Exhibition emblem and Eiffel Tower (50×39 mm)	6·00	6·00

1073 Conrad Haas and Diagram

(Des A. Mihai. Photo)

1989 (25 Oct). AIR. Space Pioneers. T **1073** and similar horiz designs. Multicoloured. P 13½.

5259	50b. Type **1073**	10	10
5260	1l.50 Konstantin Tsiolkovski and diagram.	60	15
5261	2l. Hermann-Oberth and equation	70	20
5262	3l. Robert Goddard and diagram	1·10	35
5263	4l. Sergei Korolev, Earth and satellite	1·40	45
5264	5l. Wernher von Braun and landing module	1·80	55
5259/5264	*Set of 6*	5·25	1·60

A 10l. imperforate miniature sheet, 105×80 mm depicting Neil Armstrong walking on the Moon, exists from a limited printing.

1074 Horse-drawn Mail Coach

1075 State and Party Flags and Emblem

(Des A. Popescu. Photo)

1989 (17 Nov). AIR. World Stamp Expo '89 International Stamp Exhibition, Washington D.C. Sheet 90×77 mm. P 13½.

MS5265	**1074**	5l. multicoloured	3·75	3·75

(Des A. Popescu (2l.), M. Vămăşescu (10l.). Photo)

1989 (20 Nov). 14th Communist Party Congress, Bucharest. P 13½.

5266	**1075**	2l. multicoloured	1·20	55
MS5267		77×89 mm. 10l. multicoloured	7·25	7·25

Design:—10l. Party emblem and "XIV".

REPUBLIC

26 December 1989

1076 Date, Flag, Victory Sign and Candles

1077 Flags and Footballers

1990 (8 Jan). Popular Uprising (1st issue). Photo. P 13½.

5268	**1076**	2l. multicoloured	85	55

See also Nos. 5294/**MS**5302.

(Des M. Mănescu. Photo)

1990 (19 Mar). World Cup Football Championship, Italy (1st issue). T **1077** and similar horiz designs showing flags and footballers. P 13½.

5269	50b. multicoloured	10	10
5270	1l.50 multicoloured	60	15
5271	2l. multicoloured	70	20
5272	3l. multicoloured	1·10	35
5273	4l. multicoloured	1·40	45
5274	5l. multicoloured	1·80	55
5269/5274 *Set of 6*		5·25	1·60

A 10l. imperforate miniature sheet, 115×80 mm depicting footballers with a referee, exists from a limited printing.

See also Nos. 5276/83.

1078 Penny Black and Moldavian 27p. Stamp

(Des A. Popescu. Photo)

1990 (2 May). Stamp World London '90 International Stamp Exhibition. Sheet 90×78 mm. P 13½.

MS5275	**1078**	10l. multicoloured	4·75	4·75

1079 Footballers

(Des M. Mănescu. Photo)

1990 (7 Mar). World Cup Football Championship, Italy (2nd issue). T **1079** and similar horiz designs showing footballing scenes. P 13½.

5276	50b. multicoloured	10	10
5277	1l. multicoloured	35	10
5278	1l.50 multicoloured	60	15
5279	2l. multicoloured	70	20
5280	3l. multicoloured	1·10	30
5281	3l.50 multicoloured	1·20	35
5282	4l. multicoloured	1·30	40
5283	5l. multicoloured	1·60	45
5276/5283 *Set of 8*		6·25	1·80

A 10l. imperforate miniature sheet, 120×95 mm depicting Olympia Stadium, Rome, exists from a limited printing.

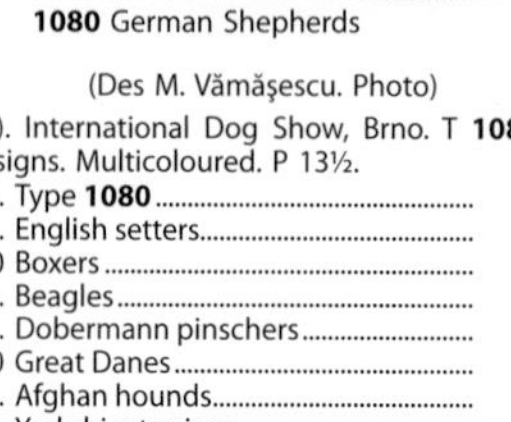

1080 German Shepherds

(Des M. Vămăşescu. Photo)

1990 (6 July). International Dog Show, Brno. T **1080** and similar horiz designs. Multicoloured. P 13½.

5284	50b. Type **1080**	10	10
5285	1l. English setters	35	10
5286	1l.50 Boxers	60	10
5287	2l. Beagles	70	15
5288	3l. Dobermann pinschers	1·20	20
5289	3l.50 Great Danes	1·40	30
5290	4l. Afghan hounds	1·60	35
5291	5l. Yorkshire terriers	2·00	40
5284/5291 *Set of 8*		7·25	1·50

1081 Fountain, Brunnen

(Des A. Philipovici. Photo)

1990 (24 Aug). Riccione '90 International Stamp Fair. P 13½.

5292	**1081**	2l. multicoloured	90	60

1082 Athenaeum Concert Hall, Bucharest, and Chinese Temple

(Des A. Popescu. Photo)

1990 (8 Sept). Romanian–Chinese Stamp Exhibition, Bucharest. P 13½.

5293	**1082**	2l. multicoloured	90	60

1083 Soldiers and Crowd at Television Headquarters, Bucharest

1084 "Nicolae Cobzarul" (Ştefan Luchian)

(Des M. Mănescu. Photo)

1990 (1 Oct). Popular Uprising (2nd issue). T **1083** and similar multicoloured designs. P 13½.

5294	50b. +50b. Republic Palace ablaze, Bucharest (horiz)	25	10
5295	1l. +1l. Crowd in Opera Square, Timişoara (horiz)	65	15
5296	1l.50 +1l. Soldiers joining crowd in Town Hall Square, Tirgu Mureş (horiz)	90	20
5297	2l. +1l. Type **1083**	1·00	25
5298	3l. +1l. Mourners at funeral, Timişoara (horiz)	1·30	30
5299	3l.50 +1l. Crowd celebrating, Braşov	1·50	35
5300	4l. +1l. Crowd with banners, Sibiu (horiz)	1·70	35
5301	5l. +2l. Cemetery, Bucharest (horiz)	2·20	40
5294/5301 *Set of 8*		8·50	1·90
MS5302	90×78 mm. 5l.+2l. Foreign aid (53×41 mm)	3·75	3·75

1990 (25 Oct). Paintings damaged during the Uprising. T **1084** and similar multicoloured designs. P 13½.

5303	50b. Type **1084**	15	10
5304	1l.50 "Woman in White" (Ion Andreescu)	40	10
5305	2l. "Florist" (Luchian)	65	15
5306	3l. "Vase of Flowers" (Jan Brueghel, the elder)	90	25
5307	4l. "Spring" (Pieter Brueghel, the elder) (horiz)	1·30	35
5308	5l. "Madonna and Child" (G. B. Paggi)	1·50	50
5303/5308 *Set of 6*		4·50	1·30

1085 Flag Stamps encircling Globe

(Des V. Stoianov. Photo)

1990 (10 Nov). Stamp Day. P 13½.

5309	**1085**	2l. (+1l.) multicoloured	1·30	1·20

No. 5309 includes the *se-tenant* premium-carrying tab shown in Type **1085**.

1086 Constantin Cantacuzino (historian)

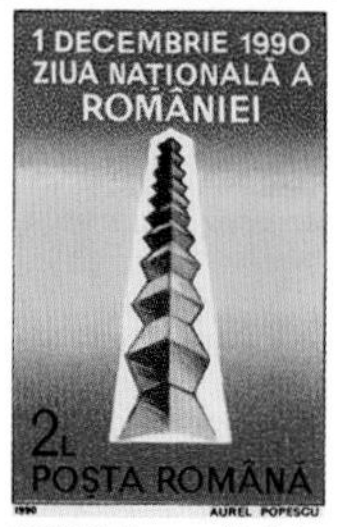

1087 Column of Infinity

(Des V. Stoianov. Photo)

1990 (27 Nov). Anniversaries. T **1086** and similar vert designs. P 13½.

5310	50b. sepia and blue	15	10
5311	1l.50 emerald and deep mauve	40	10
5312	2l. brown-lake and blue	65	15
5313	3l. blue and orange-brown	90	25
5314	4l. reddish brown and deep bright blue	1·30	35
5315	5l. bright reddish violet and emerald	1·50	50
5310/5315 *Set of 6*		4·50	1·30

Designs:—50b. Type **1086** (350th birth anniv); 1l.50, Ienachiţă Văcărescu (writer, 250th birth anniv); 2l. Titu Maiorescu (politician, 150th birth anniv); 3l. Nicolae Iorga (historian, 50th death anniv); 4l. Martha Bibescu (writer, birth centenary); 5l. Ştefan Procupiu (scientist, birth centenary).

(Des A. Popescu. Photo)

1990 (1 Dec). National Day. P 13½.

5316	**1087**	2l. multicoloured	75	60

(**1088**)

1990 (22 Dec). First Anniv of Popular Uprising. No. 5268 surch with T **1088** in chocolate.

5317	**1076**	4l. on 2l. multicoloured	1·50	60

1089 "Irises"

1991 (29 Mar). Death Centenary of Vincent van Gogh (painter). T **1089** and similar multicoloured designs. Photo. P 13½.

5318	50b. Type **1089**	15	10
5319	2l. "The Artist's Room"	25	10
5320	3l. "Illuminated Coffee Terrace" (vert)	50	15
5321	3l.50 "Orchard in Blossom"	65	20
5322	5l. "Sunflowers" (vert)	90	25
5318/5322 *Set of 5*		2·20	70

1090 Great Black-backed Gull (*Larus marinus*)

1091 Crucifixion

(Des A. Popescu. Photo)

1991 (3 Apr). Water Birds. T **1090** and similar vert designs. P 13½.

5323	50b. ultramarine	10	10
5324	1l. deep bluish green	15	10
5325	1l.50 olive-bistre	20	10
5326	2l. deep turquoise-blue	25	10
5327	3l. deep blue-green	40	10
5328	3l.50 myrtle green	50	10
5329	4l. reddish violet	65	10
5330	5l. red-brown	75	10
5331	6l. orange-brown	1·40	10
5332	7l. new blue	1·50	25
5323/5332 *Set of 10*		5·25	1·00

Designs:—1l. Common tern (*Sterna hirundo*); 1l.50, Avocet (*Recurvirostra avosetta*); 2l. Pomarine skua (*Stercorarius pomarinus*); 3l. Lapwing (*Vanellus vanellus*); 3l.50, Red-breasted merganser (*Mergus serrator*); 4l. Little egret (*Egretta garzetta*); 5l. Dunlin (*Calidris alpina*); 6l. Black-tailed godwit (*Limosa limosa*); 7l. Whiskered tern (*Chlidonias hybrida*).

1991 (5 Apr). Easter. Photo. P 13½.
5333 **1091** 4l. multicoloured 65 60

1092 "Eutelsat 1" Communications Satellite

1093 Posthorn

(Des D. Petre. Photo)

1991 (10 May). Europa. Europe in Space. P 13½.
5334 **1092** 4l.50 multicoloured .... 5·00 1·20

1991 (24 May). Photo. P 13½.
5335 **1093** 4l.50 new blue 75 60

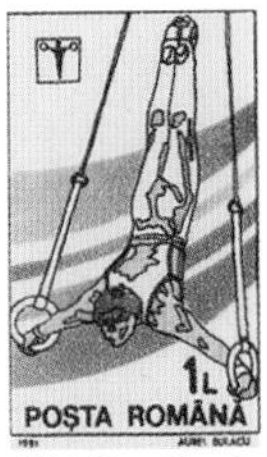

1094 Rings Exercise

1095 Curtea de Argeş Monastery

(Des A. Bulacu. Photo)

1991 (14 June). Gymnastics. T **1094** and similar vert designs. Multicoloured. P 13½.
5336 1l. Type **1094** 15 10
5337 1l. Parallel bars 15 10
5338 4l.50 Vaulting 50 10
5339 4l.50 Asymmetric bars 50 10
5340 8l. Floor exercises 90 15
5341 9l. Beam .... 1·20 20
5336/5341 *Set of 6* .... 3·00 70
For similar design to No. 5341, surcharged 90l. on 5l., see No. 5431.

1991 (4 July). Monasteries. T **1095** and similar multicoloured designs. Photo. P 13½.
5342 1l. Type **1095** 15 10
5343 1l. Putna 15 10
5344 4l.50 Văratec 50 10
5345 4l.50 Agapia (horiz) 50 10
5346 8l. Golia (horiz) 90 10
5347 9l. Suceviţa (horiz) .... 1·20 10
5342/5347 *Set of 6* .... 3·00 55

No. 5348 is vacant.

1096 Hotel Continental, Timişoara

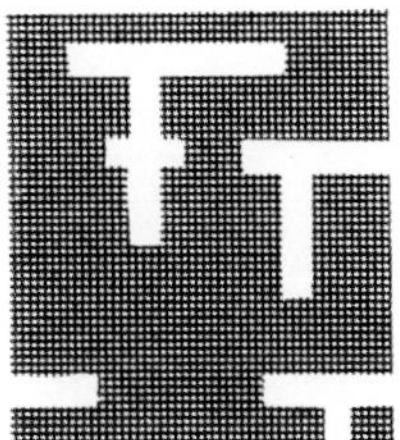
1096a

(Des P. Vasile and M. Vămăşescu. Photo)

1991 (27 Aug)–**97**. Hotels. T **1096** and similar designs. Matt paper. No wmk. P 13½.
5349 1l. royal blue 15 10
5350 2l. deep green (8.10.91) 15 10
5351 4l. carmine-red (8.10.91) 25 10
5352 5l. slate-violet 50 10
5353 6l. bistre-brown (14.11.91) 25 25
5354 8l. brown (14.11.91) 25 25
5355 9l. brown-lake .... 1·20 35
5356 10l. yellow-green .... 1·00 35
5357 18l. rose-red (8.10.91) .... 1·30 35
5358 20l. reddish orange (14.11.91) .... 1·40 35
a. Orange .... 1·40 35
5359 25l. greenish blue (8.10.91) .... 1·70 60
5360 30l. deep reddish purple (8.10.91) .... 2·20 70
5361 45l. ultramarine (14.11.91) .... 1·90 50
5362 60l. olive-brown (14.11.91) .... 2·50 85
5363 80l. bluish violet (14.11.91) .... 3·25 95
a. Wmk **1096a** (1994) .... 3·75 1·20
5364 120l. ultramarine and grey (5.12.91) .... 3·75 25
a. Wmk **1096a** (1994) .... 6·50 60
b. Glazed paper (no wmk) (1997) .... 3·75 25
5365 160l. vermilion and brown-rose (5.12.91) . 5·00 35
5366 250l. blue and bluish grey (5.12.91) .... 6·50 50
a. Wmk **1096a** (1994) .... 9·00 85
5367 400l. brown and brown-ochre (5.12.91) .... 8·25 60
a. Wmk **1096a** (1995) .... 11·50 1·20
5368 500l. deep blue-green and dull green (5.12.91) .... 9·50 70
a. Wmk **1096a** (1994) .... 15·00 1·40
5369 800l. magenta and flesh (5.12.91) .... 11·50 95
a. Wmk **1096a** (1996) .... 19·00 1·60
5349/5369 *Set of 21* .... 55·00 8·25

Designs: As T **1096**. Horiz—2l. Valea Caprei Chalet, Mt. Făgăraş; 5l. Hotel Lebăda, Crişan; 6l. Muntele Roşu Chalet, Mt. Ciucaş; 8l. Transilvania Hotel, Cluj-Napoca; 9l. Hotel Orizont, Predeal; 20l. Alpin Hotel, Poiana Braşov; 25l. Constanţa Casino; 30l. Mioriţa Chalet, Mt. Bucegi; 45l. Sura Dacilor Chalet, Poiana Braşov; 60l. Valea Drăganului Tourist Complex; 80l. Hotel Florica, Venus. Vert—4l. Intercontinental Hotel, Bucharest; 10l. Hotel Roman, Băile Herculane; 18l. Rarău Chalet, Mt. Rarău. 26×40 mm—120l. International Complex, Băile Felix, 160l. Hotel Egreta, Tulcea. 40×26 mm—250l. Valea de Peşti Motel, Jiului Valley; 400l. Băişoara Tourist Complex; 500l. Bradul Hotel, Covasna; 800l. Goej Hotel, Tirgu Jiu.
Nos. 5362/9 have no frame.
Several values exist on both greyish paper with yellow gum and whiter paper with white gum.

Nos. 5370/80 are vacant.

1097 Gull and Sea Shore

(Des C. Decebal. Photo)

1991 (27 Aug). Europa '91 Stamp Exhibition, Riccione, Italy. P 13½.
5381 **1097** 4l. multicoloured 65 60

1098 Vase decorated with Scarlet and Military Macaws

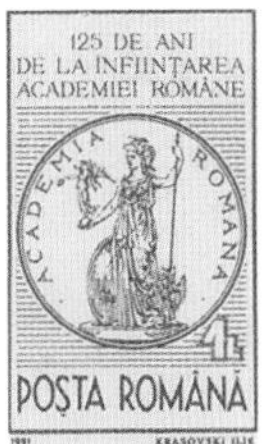

1099 Academy Emblem

1100 "Flowers" (Nicu Enea)

(Des Aida Tasgian Philipovici. Photo)

1991 (12 Sept). Romanian–Chinese Stamp Exhibition. T **1098** and similar vert design. Multicoloured. P 13½.
5382 5l. Type **1098** 50 35
a. Pair. Nos. 5382/3 .... 1·10 75
5383 5l. Vase with peony decoration 50 35
Nos. 5382/3 were issued together in *se-tenant* pairs within the sheet. For similar design to Type **1098**, see No. 5430.

(Des I. Krasovski. Photo)

1991 (17 Sept). 125th Anniv of Romanian Academy. P 13½.
5384 **1099** 1l. greenish blue 65 60

1991 (20 Sept). Balcanfila '91 Stamp Exhibition, Bacau. T **1100** and similar multicoloured designs. P 13½.
5385 4l. Type **1100** 65 25
5386 5l. (+2l.) "Peasant Girl of Vlaşca" (Georghe Tattarescu) 75 35
MS5387 90×77 mm. 20l. Exhibition venue (53×41 mm) .... 2·50 2·50
No. 5386 includes a *se-tenant* premium-carrying label showing the Exhibition emblem.

1101 Red-Billed Blue Magpie (*Cissa erythrorhyncha*)

1102 Map with House and People

(Des M. Mănescu. Photo)

1991 (7 Oct). Birds. Two sheets, each 136×150 mm, containing vert designs as T **1101**. Multicoloured. P 13½.
MS5388 Two sheets. (a) 2l.×12: Type **1101**; Grey-headed bush shrike (*Malaconotus blanchoti*); Eastern bluebird (*Sialia sialis*); Western meadowlark (*Sturnella neglecta*); Malabar trogon (*Harpactes fasciatus*); Hoopoe (*Upupa epops*); Blue wren (*Malurus cyaneus*); Scaly ground roller (*Brachypteracias squamigera*); Blue vanga (*Leptopterus madagascariensis*); White- headed wood hoopoe (*Phoeniculus bollei*); Red-headed woodpecker (*Melanerpes erythrocephalus*); Scarlet minivet (*Pericrocotus flammeus*). (b) 2l.×12: Golden backed honeyeater (*Melithreptus laetior*); Kagu (*Rhynochetos jubata*); American robin (*Turdus migratorius*); Magpie robin (*Copsychus saularis*); Rock thrush (*Monticola saxatilis*); Yellow-headed blackbird (*Xanthocephalus xanthocephalus*); Pel's fishing owl (*Scotopelia peli*); Long-tailed silky flycatcher (*Ptilogonys caudatus*); Puerto Rican tody (*Todus mexicanus*); White-rumped shama (*Copsychus malabaricus*); Mangrove redheaded honeyeater (*Myzomela erythrocephala*); Montezuma oropendola (*Gymnostinops montezuma*). Two sheets .... 9·25 9·25

(Des D. Stănescu. Photo)

1991 (15 Oct). Population and Housing Census. P 13½.
5389 **1102** 5l. multicoloured 65 60

1103 Bridge

(Des C. Decebal. Photo)

1991 (13 Nov). Phila Nippon '91 International Stamp Exhibition, Tokyo. T **1103** and similar horiz design. P 13½.
5390 **1103** 10l. yellow-ochre, agate and rosine .... 1·30 35
5391 – 10l. multicoloured .... 1·30 35
Design:—No. 5391, Junk.

1104 Isabel (*Graëllsia isabellae*)

1105 Running

(Des M. Vămăşescu. Photo)

1991 (20 Nov). Butterflies and Moths. Two sheets, each 155×136 mm containing horiz designs as T **1104**. Multicoloured. P 13½.
MS5392 Two sheets. (a) 3l.×12: Type **1104**; Orange-tip (*Antocharis cardamines*); Hebe tiger moth (*Ammobiota festiva*); Comma (*Polygonia c-album*); *Catocala promisa*; Purple tiger moth (*Rhyparia purpurata*); *Arctia villica*; *Polyommatus daphnis*; Southern festoon (*Zerynthia polyxena*); Oleander hawk moth (*Daphnis nerii*); *Licaena dispar rutila*; *Pararge roxelana*. (b) 3l.×12: Paradise birdwing (*Ornithoptera paradisea*); Bhutan glory (*Bhutanitis lidderdalii*); *Morpho helena*; *Ornithoptera croesus*; Red-splashed sulphur (*Phoebis avellaneda*); Queen Victoria's birdwing (*Ornithoptera victoriae*); Kaiser-i-hind (*Teinopalpus imperialis*); *Hypolimnas dexithea*; *Dabasa payeni*; *Morpho achilleana*; *Heliconius melpomene*; *Agrias claudina sardanapalus*. Two sheets .... 13·00 13·00

(Des E. Palade. Photo)

1991 (21 Nov). World Athletics Championships, Tokyo. T **1105** and similar vert designs. Multicoloured. P 13½.
5393 1l. Type **1105** 25 10
5394 4l. Long jumping 50 10
5395 5l. High jumping 65 10
5396 5l. Athlete in starting blocks 65 10
5397 9l. Hurdling .... 1·20 20
5398 10l. Throwing the javelin .... 1·30 20
5393/5398 *Set of 6* .... 4·00 70

1106 Mihail Kogălniceanu (politician and historian)

1107 Library Building

(Des V. Stoianov. Photo)

1991 (10 Dec). Anniversaries. T **1106** and similar vert designs. P 13½.
5399 1l. deep yellow-brown, greenish blue and deep greenish blue 25 10
5400 4l. yellowish green, bright lilac and reddish violet 50 10
5401 5l. olive-brown, dull ultram & ultram 65 10
5402 5l. dull ultramarine, chestnut and brown-lake 65 10
5403 9l. brown-lake, turquoise-blue and deep turquoise-blue .... 1·20 20
5404 10l. slate-black, light reddish brown and reddish brown .... 1·30 20
5399/5404 *Set of 6* .... 4·00 70
Designs:—No. 5399, Type **1106** (death centenary); 5400, Nicolae Titulescu (politician and diplomat, 50th death anniv); 5401, Andrei Mureşeanu (poet, 175th birth anniv); 5402, Aron Pumnul (writer, 125th death anniv); 5403, George Bacovia (writer, 110th birth anniv); 5394, Perpessicius (literature critic, birth centenary).

(Des I. Krasovski. Photo)

1991 (23 Dec). Centenary of Central University Library, Bucharest. P 13½.
5405 **1107** 8l. lake-brown .... 1·00 60

1108 Mail Coach and Horses

(Des M. Vămăşescu. Photo)

1991 (24 Dec). Stamp Day. P 13½.
5406 **1108** 8l. (+2l.) multicoloured ... 1·30 1·20
No. 5406 includes the *se-tenant* premium-carrying tab shown in Type **1108**.

1109 "Nativity" (17th-century icon)

1110 Biathlon

(Des D. Grigoriu. Photo)

1991 (25 Dec). Christmas. P 13½.
5407 **1109** 8l. multicoloured ... 1·00 60

(Des M. Vămăşescu. Photo)

1992 (1 Feb). Winter Olympic Games, Albertville. T **1110** and similar vert designs. Multicoloured. P 13½.

(a) POSTAGE

5408 4l. Type **1110** ... 15 10
5409 5l. Downhill skiing ... 20 10
5410 8l. Cross-country skiing ... 25 10
5411 10l. Two-man luge ... 40 10
5412 20l. Speed skating ... 75 10
5413 25l. Ski jumping ... 90 20
5414 30l. Ice hockey ... 1·20 20
5415 45l. Men's figure skating ... 1·50 30
5408/5415 *Set of 8* ... 4·75 1·10

(b) AIR. Inscr "POŞTA AERIANĂ"

MS5416 95×78 mm. 75l. Women's figure skating (37×52 mm) ... 4·00 4·00
A 125l. imperforate miniature sheet, 106×78 mm depicting four-man bobsleigh, exists from a limited printing.

D **1111**

1992 (3 Feb). POSTAGE DUE. Photo. P 13½.
D5417 D **1111** 4l. scarlet ... 1·00 35
D5418 8l. new blue ... 1·30 60

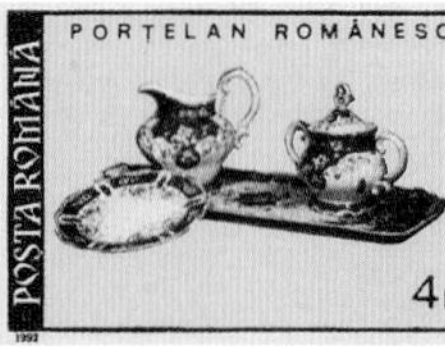

1112 Jug, Plate, Tray and Bowl

1992 (20 Feb). Romanaian Porcelain from Cluj Napoca. T **1112** and similar multicoloured designs. Photo. P 13½.
5419 4l. Type **1112** ... 15 10
5420 5l. Tea set ... 15 10
5421 8l. Jug and goblet (vert) ... 20 10
5422 30l. Tea set (different) ... 1·00 20
5423 45l. Vase (vert) ... 1·50 35
5419/5423 *Set of 5* ... 2·75 75

1113 Atlantic Mackerels (*Scomber scombrus*)

1114 Vase decorated with Scarlet and Military Macaws

(Des M. Vămăşescu. Photo)

1992 (28 Feb). Fish. T **1113** and similar horiz designs. Multicoloured. P 13½.
5424 4l. Type **1113** ... 15 10
5425 5l. Tench (*Tinca tinca*) ... 15 10
5426 8l. Brook charr (*Salvelinus fontinalis*) ... 20 10
5427 10l. Riffle perch (*Romanichthys valsanicola*) ... 25 10
5428 30l. Nase (*Chondrostoma nasus*) ... 90 25
5429 45l. Black Sea red mullet (*Mullus barbatus ponticus*) ... 1·40 40
5424/5429 *Set of 6* ... 2·75 95

1992 (11 Mar). Apollo Art Gallery. Unissued stamp surch in red as in T **1114**. Photo. P 13½.
5430 **1114** 90l. on 5l. multicoloured ... 3·25 60
For similar design to Type **1114**, see No. 5382.

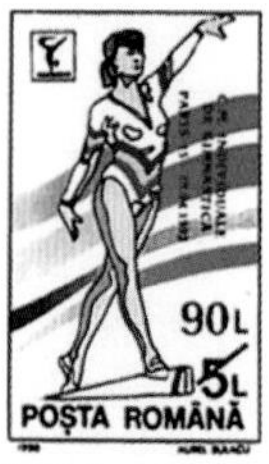

1115 Gymnast on Beam

1116 Dressage

(Des A. Bulacu. Photo)

1992 (11 Mar). World Individual Gymnastic Championships, Paris. Unissued stamp surch as in T **1115**. P 13½.
5431 **1115** 90l. on 5l. multicoloured ... 3·25 60
For similar 9l. value, see No. 5341.

(Des M. Chirnoaga. Photo)

1992 (17 Mar). Horses. T **1116** and similar multicoloured designs. P 13½.
5432 6l. Type **1116** ... 15 10
5433 7l. Racing (horiz) ... 15 10
5434 10l. Rearing ... 25 10
5435 25l. Jumping gate ... 75 15
5436 30l. Stamping foot (horiz) ... 1·00 20
5437 50l. Winged horse ... 1·50 25
5432/5437 *Set of 6* ... 3·50 80

1117 Columbus and *Santa Maria*

(Des M. Vămăşescu. Photo)

1992 (22 Apr). Europa. 500th Anniv of Discovery of America by Columbus. Sheet 130×88 mm containing T **1117** and similar horiz designs. P 13½.
MS5438 35l. Type **1117**; 35l. Columbus (hatless) and *Niña* at sea; 35l. Columbus (in hat) and *Pinta*; 35l. Columbus, *Santa Maria* and island ... 38·00 38·00

1118 "Descent into Hell" (icon)

1119 Emblem

1992 (24 Apr). Easter. Photo. P 13½.
5439 **1118** 10l. multicoloured ... 65 50

(Des Aida Tasgian Philipovici. Photo)

1992 (24 Apr). Granada'92 International Thematic Stamp Exhibition. Sheet 122×72 mm containing T **1119** and similar vert designs. P 13½.
MS5440 10l. carmine-vermilion, emerald and black; 25l. multicoloured; 30l. multicoloured ... 2·50 2·50
Designs:—25l. Spanish 1850 6c. and Moldavian 1858 27p. stamps; 30l. Courtyard, Alhambra.

1120 Tower and Hand Pump

1121 Filipino Vinta and Rook

(Des L. Carmen. Photo)

1992 (2 May). Centenary of Bucharest Fire Tower. P 13½.
5441 **1120** 10l. multicoloured ... 65 50

(Des M. Vămăşescu. Photo)

1992 (7 June). 30th Chess Olympiad, Manila, Philippines. T **1121** and similar multicoloured designs. P 13½.
5442 10l. Type **1121** ... 40 25
5443 10l. Exterior of venue and chessmen ... 40 25
MS5444 91×79 mm. 75l. Chessboard on beach (41×53 mm) ... 3·25 3·25

1122 Post Rider approaching Town

1992 (15 July). Stamp Day. P 13½.
5445 **1122** 10l. +4l. pink, slate-violet and greenish blue ... 65 50

1123 Pistol Shooting

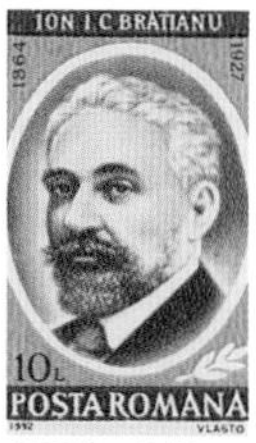

1124 Ion Brătianu

(Des E. Mülthaler. Photo)

1992 (17 July). Olympic Games, Barcelona. T **1123** and similar multicoloured designs. P 13½.
5446 6l. Type **1123** ... 10 10
5447 7l. Weightlifting ... 10 10
5448 9l. Two-man kayak (horiz) ... 15 10
5449 10l. Handball ... 25 10
5450 25l. Wrestling (horiz) ... 40 10
5451 30l. Fencing (horiz) ... 50 15
5452 50l. Running ... 90 25
5453 55l. Boxing (horiz) ... 1·00 30
5446/5453 *Set of 8* ... 3·00 1·10
MS5454 90×79 mm. 100l. Rowing (50×39 mm) ... 2·50 2·50
A 200l. imperforate miniature sheet, 106×81 mm depicting a gymnast, exists from a limited printing.

(Des V. Stoianov. Photo)

1992 (27 July). 130th Anniv of Foreign Ministry. T **1124** and similar vert designs showing former Ministers. P 13½.
5455 10l. bright violet, grey-green and deep grey-green ... 10 10
5456 25l. brown-purple, bright blue and blue ... 25 10
5457 30l. blue, brown-purple and purple-brown ... 30 10
5455/5457 *Set of 3* ... 60 25
Designs:—25l. Ion Duca; 30l. Grigore Gafencu.

1125 "The Thinker of Cernavodă" (sculpture)

(Des C. Decebal (6, 100l.), G. Leahu (15, 25, 30l.), S. Ionescu (30, 90l.). Photo)

1992 (1 Sept). "Expo 92" World's Fair, Seville. "Era of Discovery". T **1125** and similar multicoloured designs. P 13½.
5458 6l. Type **1125** ... 10 10
5459 7l. Trajan's bridge, Turnu-Severin ... 10 10
5460 10l. House on stilts ... 10 10
5461 25l. Saligny Bridge, Cernavodă ... 25 10
5462 30l. Traian Vuia's No. 1 airplane ... 40 10
5463 55l. Hermann Oberth's rocket ... 65 20
5458/5463 *Set of 6* ... 1·40 65
MS5464 79×91 mm. 100l. "Kneeling Figure" (sculpture, Constantin Brâncuşi) (41×49 mm) ... 1·30 1·30

1126 Doves posting Letters in Globe

(Des V. Stoianov. Photo)

1992 (9 Oct). World Post Day. P 13½.
5465 **1126** 10l. multicoloured ... 65 50

1127 *Santa Maria* and Bust of Columbus

(Des M. Vămăşescu. Photo)

1992 (30 Oct). 500th Anniv of Discovery of America by Columbus. T **1127** and similar multicoloured designs. P 13½.

5466	6l. Type **1127**	15	10
5467	10l. *Niña*	15	10
5468	25l. *Pinta*	50	15
5469	55l. Columbus claiming New World	90	25
5466/5469	*Set of 4*	1·50	55

MS5470 91×79 mm. 100l. Columbus and *Santa Maria* (38×51 mm) 2·50 2·50

1128 Post Office Emblem

1129 Jacob Negruzzi (writer, 150th birth anniv)

(Des V. Stoianov. Photo)

1992 (5 Nov). First Anniv of Establishment of R. A. Posta Romana (postal organization). P 13½.

5471	**1128**	10l. multicoloured	65	50

(Des V. Stoianov. Photo)

1992 (9 Nov). Anniversaries. T **1129** and similar vert designs. P 13½.

5472	6l. yellow-green and violet	10	10
5473	7l. deep magenta, purple and emerald	10	10
5474	9l. indigo and deep mauve	10	10
5475	10l. yellow-brown, bistre-brown and ultramarine	10	10
5476	25l. blue and red-brown	25	10
5477	30l. slate-green and blue	50	10
5472/5477	*Set of 6*	1·00	55

Designs:—7l. Grigore Antipa (biologist, 125th birth anniv); 9l. Alexe Mateevici (poet, 75th death anniv); 10l. Cezar Petrescu (writer, birth centenary); 25l. Octav Onicescu (mathematician, birth centenary); 30l. Ecaterina Teodoroiu (first world war fighter, 75th death anniv).

1130 American Bald Eagle (*Haliaeetus leucocephalus*)

1131 Arms

1992 (16 Nov). Animals. T **1130** and similar multicoloured designs. Photo. P 13½.

5478	6l. Type **1130**	10	10
5479	7l. Spotted owl (*Strix occidentalis*)	10	10
5480	9l. Brown bear (*Ursos arctos*)	15	10
5481	10l. American black oystercatcher (*Haematopus bachmani*) (horiz)	15	10
5482	25l. Wolf (*Canis lupus*) (horiz)	25	10
5483	30l. White-tailed deer (*Odocoileus virginianus*) (horiz)	40	10
5484	55l. Elk (*Alces alces*) (horiz)	90	25
5478/5484	*Set of 7*	1·80	75

MS5485 91×80 mm. 100l. Killer whale (*Orcinus orca*) (horiz) 1·90 1·90

1992 (1 Dec). New State Arms. Photo. P 13½.

5486	**1131**	15l. multicoloured	65	50

1132 Buildings and Street, Mogoşoaiei

1133 Nativity

(Des M. Muntenescu. Photo)

1992 (3 Dec). Anniversaries. T **1132** and similar horiz designs. Multicoloured. P 13½.

5487	7l. Type **1132** (300th anniv)	10	10
5488	9l. College building and statue, Roman (600th anniv)	10	10
5489	10l. Prince Basarai, monastery and Princess Despina (475th anniv of Curtea de Argeş Monastery)	10	10
5490	25l. Bucharest School of Architecture (80th anniv)	20	10
5487/5490	*Set of 4*	45	35

1992 (15 Dec). Christmas. Photo. P 13½.

5491	**1133**	15l. multicoloured	65	50

1134 Globe and Key-pad on Telephone

1135 Women's Gymnastics (two gold medals)

1992 (28 Dec). New Telephone Number System. Photo. P 13½.

5492	**1134**	15l. black, bright carmine and blue	65	50

(Des C. Decebal. Photo)

1992 (30 Dec). Romanian Medals at Olympic Games, Barcelona. Two sheets, each 110×80 mm, containing horiz designs as T **1135**. Multicoloured. P 13½.

MS5493 Two sheets. (a) 35l.×4: Type **1135**; Rowing (two gold medals); Fencing and bronze medal; High jumping and silver medal. (b) 35l.×4: Shooting and bronze medal; Bronze medal and wrestling; Weightlifting and bronze medal; Bronze medal and boxing. Two sheets 3·75 3·75

1136 Mihai Vodă Monastery

(Des G. Leahu. Photo)

1993 (11 Feb). Destroyed Bucharest Buildings. T **1136** and similar horiz designs. Multicoloured. P 13½.

5494	10l. Type **1136**	10	10
5495	15l. Văcăreşti Monastery	10	10
5496	25l. Unirii Hall	20	10
5497	30l. Mina Minovici Medico-legal Institute	50	10
5494/5497	*Set of 4*	80	35

1137 Parseval Sigsfeld Kite-type Observation Balloon *Draken*

(Des S. Ionescu. Photo)

1993 (26 Feb). AIR. Balloons. T **1137** and similar horiz design. Multicoloured. P 13½.

5498	30l. Type **1137**	25	15
5499	90l. Caquot observation balloon, 1917	1·70	35

1138 Crucifixion

1139 Hawthorn (*Crataegus monogyna*)

(Des G. Makara. Photo)

1993 (25 Mar). Easter. P 13½.

5500	**1138**	15l. multicoloured	65	50

(Des A. Popescu. Photo)

1993 (30 Mar). Medicinal Plants. T **1139** and similar vert designs. Multicoloured. P 13½.

5501	10l. Type **1139**	10	10
5502	15l. Gentian (*Gentiana phlogifolia*)	10	10
5503	25l. Sea buckthorn (*Hippophaë rhamnoides*)	45	10
5504	30l. Bilberry (*Vaccinium myrtillus*)	50	10
5505	50l. Arnica (*Arnica Montană*)	1·00	20
5506	90l. Dog rose (*Rosa canina*)	1·90	25
5501/5506	*Set of 6*	3·75	75

1140 Stănescu

1141 Mounted Courier

1993 (31 Mar). 60th Birth Anniv of Nichita Stănescu (poet). Photo. P 13½.

5507	**1140**	15l. multicoloured	65	50

(Des V. Munteanu. Photo)

1993 (26 Apr). Stamp Day. P 13½.

5508	**1141**	15l. +10l. multicoloured	65	50

1142 Exhibition Venue

(Des V. Stoianov. Photo)

1993 (28 Apr). Polska'93 International Stamp Exhibition, Poznan. Sheet 90×78 mm. P 13½.

MS5509 **1142** 200l. multicoloured 2·50 2·50

1143 Magpie (*Pica pica*)

1144 Long-hair

(Des Aida Tasgian Philipovici. Photo)

1993 (30 Apr)–**97**. Birds. T **1143** and similar designs. Cream matt paper. No wmk. P 13½.

5510	5l. black and yellow-green	15	10
5511	10l. black and brown-red	15	10
5512	15l. black and vermilion	15	10
5513	20l. black and yellow-brown	25	10
	a. White paper. W **1096a** (1995)	1·30	60
	b. White matt paper (1995)	25	10
	c. White glazed paper (1997)	25	10
5514	25l. black and scarlet	25	10
	a. White paper. W **1096a** (1995)	1·30	60
	b. White matt paper (1995)	25	10
5515	50l. black and chrome-yellow	40	10
	a. White paper. W **1096a** (1995)	1·90	60
	b. White matt paper (1995)	40	10
	c. White glazed paper (1997)	40	10
5516	65l. black and scarlet	50	10
5517	90l. black and scarlet	75	10
5518	160l. black and greenish blue	1·30	15
5519	250l. black and magenta	1·70	25
	a. White matt paper (1995)	3·25	60
	b. White glazed paper (1997)	1·70	25
5510/5519	*Set of 10*	5·00	1·10

Designs: Horiz—10l. Golden eagle (*Aquila chrysaëtos*). Vert—15l. Bullfinch (*Pyrrhula pyrrhula*); 20l. Hoopoe (*Upupa epops*); 25l. Great spotted woodpecker (*Dendrocopos major*); 50l. Golden oriole (*Oriolus oriolus*); 65l. White-winged crossbill (*Loxia leucoptera*); 90l. Barn swallows (*Hirundo rustica*); 160l. Azure tit (*Parus cyanus*); 250l. Rose-coloured starling (*Sturnus roseus*).

(Des Z. Nicolae. Photo)

1993 (24 May). Cats. T **1144** and similar vert designs. Multicoloured. P 13½.

5520	10l. Type **1144**	25	20
5521	15l. Tabby-point long-hair	25	20
5522	30l. Red long-hair	40	20
5523	90l. Blue Persian	90	20
5524	135l. Tabby	1·20	20
5525	160l. Long-haired white Persian	1·50	25
5520/5525	*Set of 6*	4·00	1·10

1145 "Lola, Artist's Sister" (Pablo Picasso)

1146 Adder (*Vipera berus*)

1993 (31 May). Europa. Contemporary Art. Sheet 75×105 mm containing T **1145** and similar vert designs. Multicoloured. Photo. P 13½.

MS5526 280l. Type **1145**; 280l. "World Inception" (sculpture, Constantin Brâncuşi); 280l. "Girl with Idol" (sculpture, Ion Irimescu); 280l. "Woman in Grey" (Alexandra Ciucurencu) 6·50 6·50

(Des Aida Tasgian Philipovici. Photo)

1993 (30 June). Protected Animals. T **1146** and similar multicoloured designs. P 13½.

5527 10l. Type **1146** ... 25 15
5528 15l. Lynx (*Lynx lynx*) (vert) ... 25 15
5529 25l. Common shelduck (*Tadorna tadorna*) ... 40 15
5530 75l. Huchen (*Hucho hucho*) ... 90 15
5531 105l. Poplar admiral (*Limenitis populi*) ... 1·20 20
5532 280l. Alpine longhorn beetle (*Rosalia alpina*) ... 1·50 35
5527/5532 *Set of 6* ... 4·00 1·00

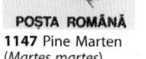

1147 Pine Marten (*Martes martes*)

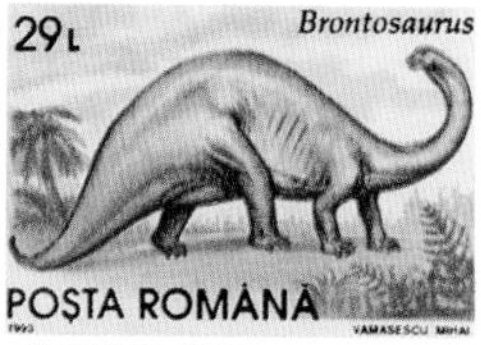
1148 Brontosaurus

(Des Aida Tasgian Philipovici. Photo)

1993 (30 June)–**95**. Mammals. T **1147** and similar designs. Cream matt paper. No wmk. P 13½.

5533 10l. black and yellow ... 25 10
a. White glazed paper ... 1·30 60
5534 15l. black and yellow-brown ... 25 10
5535 20l. vermilion and black ... 25 10
a. White glazed paper ... 1·30 60
5536 25l. black and orange-brown ... 40 10
5537 30l. black and orange-red ... 40 10
a. White paper. W **1096a** (1995) ... 1·30 60
5538 40l. black and vermilion ... 40 10
5539 75l. black and yellow ... 65 10
5540 105l. black and chestnut ... 1·00 10
5541 150l. black and yellow-orange ... 1·20 15
a. White glazed paper ... 1·90 60
5542 280l. black and orange-yellow ... 2·50 25
5533/5542 *Set of 10* ... 6·50 1·10

Designs: Horiz—15l. Common rabbit (*Oryctolagus cuniculus*); 30l. Red fox (*Vulpes vulpes*); 150l. Stoat (*Mustela erminea*); 280l. Egyptian mongoose (*Herpestes ichneumon*). Vert—20l. Eurasian red squirrel (*Sciurus vulgaris*); 25l. Chamois (*Rupicapra rupicapra*); 40l. Argali (*Ovis ammon*); 75l. Small-spotted genet (*Genetta genetta*); 105l. Garden dormouse (*Eliomys quercinus*).

(Des M. Vămăşescu. Photo)

1993 (30 July). Prehistoric Animals. T **1148** and similar horiz designs. Multicoloured. P 13½.

5543 29l. Type **1148** ... 15 15
5544 46l. Plesiosaurus ... 50 15
5545 85l. Triceratops ... 75 15
5546 171l. Stegosaurus ... 1·70 20
5547 216l. Tyrannosaurus ... 1·90 25
5548 319l. Archaeopteryx ... 2·50 35
5543/5548 *Set of 6* ... 6·75 1·10

1149 "Woman selling Eggs" (Marcel Iancu)

1150 St. Stefan the Great, Prince of Moldavia

(Des Aida Tasgian Philipovici. Photo)

1993 (21 Aug). Telafila 93 Israel–Romania Stamp Exhibition, Tel Aviv. Sheet 90×78 mm. P 13½.

MS5549 **1149** 535l. multicoloured ... 3·25 3·25

1993 (31 Aug). Icons. T **1150** and similar vert designs. Multicoloured. Photo. P 13½.

5550 75l. Type **1150** ... 25 10
5551 171l. Prince Constantin Brancoveanu of Wallachia with his sons Constantin, Stefan, Radu and Matei and Adviser Ianache Văcărescu ... 65 15
5552 216l. St. Antim Ivireanul, Metropolitan of Wallachia ... 1·50 25
5550/5552 *Set of 3* ... 2·20 45

Riccione '93
3–5 septembrie

1151 Mounted Officers

171 L

(1152)

1993 (1 Sept). Centenary of Rural Gendarmerie Law. Photo. P 13½.

5553 **1151** 29l. multicoloured ... 65 50

1993 (3 Sept). Riccione '93 International Stamp Fair. No. 5292 surch with T **1152** in red.

5554 **1081** 171l. on 2l. multicoloured ... 1·30 60

1153 Temple Roof

1154 George Bariţiu (politician and historian)

(Des C. Decebal. Photo)

1993 (20 Sept). Bangkok 1993 International Stamp Exhibition. Sheet 79×90 mm. P 13½.

MS5555 **1153** 535l. multicoloured ... 3·25 3·25

(Des M. Vămăşescu. Photo)

1993 (8 Oct). Anniversaries. T **1154** and similar vert designs. P 13½.

5556 29l. flesh, black and rose-lilac ... 10 10
5557 46l. flesh, black and new blue ... 15 10
5558 85l. flesh, black and blue-green ... 40 10
5559 171l. flesh, black and claret ... 75 15
5560 216l. flesh, black and light blue ... 90 20
5561 319l. flesh, black and grey ... 1·50 25
5556/5561 *Set of 6* ... 3·50 80

Designs:—29l. Type **1154** (death centenary); 46l. Horia Creangă (architect, 50th death anniv); 85l. Armand Călinescu (leader of Peasant National Party, birth centenary); 171l. Dr. Dumitru Bagdasar (neurosurgeon, birth centenary); 216l. Constantin Brăiloiu (musician, birth centenary); 319l. Iuliu Maniu (Prime Minister 1927–30 and 1932–33, 40th death anniv).

35 ANI DE ACTIVITATE AFR-FFR
1958–1993

70L + 45L

(**1155**)

1993 (9 Nov). 35th Anniversaries of Romanian Philatelic Association and Romanian Philatelic Federation. No. 5445 surch with T **1155** in red.

5562 **1122** 70l.+45l. on 10l.+4l. pink, slate-violet and greenish blue ... 65 50

1156 Map, National Flag and Council Emblem

(Des M. Vămăşescu. Photo)

1993 (26 Nov). Admission to Council of Europe. Sheet 90×78 mm. P 13½.

MS5563 **1156** 1590l. multicoloured ... 7·75 7·75

1157 Iancu Flondor (Bukovinan politician)

(Des Aida Tasgian Philipovici. Photo)

1993 (1 Dec)–**94**. 75th Anniv of Union of Bessarabia, Bukovina and Transylvania with Romania. T **1157** and similar vert designs. P 13½.

5564 115l. yellow-brown, new blue and black ... 65 25
5565 245l. bright reddish violet, yellow and emerald ... 1·30 30
5566 255l. multicoloured ... 1·40 30
5567 325l. yellow-brown, rose and deep brown ... 1·90 35
5564/5567 *Set of 4* ... 4·75 1·10
MS5568 90×78 mm. 1060l. multicoloured (map in several shades of brown) (41×53 mm) ... 15·00 15·00
a. Map in one shade (2.94) ... 4·50 4·50

Designs:—245l. Ionel Brătianu (Prime Minister 1918–19, 1922–26 and 1927); 255l. Iuliu Maniu (Prime Minister, 1927– 30 and 1932–33); 325l. Panteleimon Halippa (Bessarabian politician); 1060l. King Ferdinand I and map.

The first printing of No. **MS**5568 had the king's portrait in royal blue and the eastern provinces on the map picked out in different shades of brown; this printing was withdrawn at the end of December as territory now part of Ukraine and Moldova was highlighted. At the end of February 1994 a revised printing (No. **MS**5568a) was issued with the king's portrait in blue-violet and the same map but without the territories highlighted.

1158 Emblem

1159 "Nativity" (17th-century icon)

(Des Aida Tasgian Philipovici. Photo)

1993 (15 Dec). Anniversaries. T **1158** and similar vert designs. Multicoloured. P 13½.

5569 115l. Type **1158** (75th anniv of General Association of Romanian Engineers) 65 25
5570 245l. Statue of Johannes Honterus (450th anniv of Romanian Humanist School) ... 1·30 30
5571 255l. Bridge, arms on book spine and seal (625th anniv of first documentary reference to Slatina) ... 1·40 30
5572 325l. Map and town arms (625th anniv of first documentary reference to Braila) ... 1·50 35
5569/5572 *Set of 4* ... 4·25 1·10

1993 (20 Dec). Christmas. Photo. P 13½.

5573 **1159** 45l. multicoloured ... 65 50

1160 *Clivina subterranea*

(Des Art Design. Photo)

1993 (27 Dec). Movile Cave Animals. T **1160** and similar multicoloured designs. P 13½.

5574 29l. Type **1160** ... 10 10
5575 46l. *Nepa anophthalma* ... 15 10
5576 85l. *Haemopis caeca* ... 50 15
5577 171l. *Lascona cristiani* ... 90 25
5578 216l. *Semisalsa dobrogica* ... 1·30 30
5579 319l. *Armadilidium tabacarui* ... 1·90 35
5574/5579 *Set of 6* ... 4·25 1·10
MS5580 90×78 mm. 535l. Diver exploring cave (41×53 mm) ... 2·50 2·50

1161 Prince Alexandru Ioan Cuza and Seal

1162 Opera House

(Des C. Decebal. Photo)

1994 (24 Jan). 130th Anniv of Court of Accounts. P 13½.

5581 **1161** 45l. multicoloured ... 65 50

(Des G. Leahu. Photo)

1994 (7 Feb). Destroyed Buildings of Bucharest. T **1162** and similar multicoloured designs. P 13½.

5582 115l. Type **1162** ... 40 15
5583 245l. Church of Văcăreşti Monastery (vert) ... 90 25
5584 255l. St. Vineri's Church ... 1·30 35
5585 325l. Cloisters of Văcăreşti Monastery ... 1·40 40
5582/5585 *Set of 4* ... 3·50 1·00

D **1163**

(Des B. Marinela. Photo)

1994 (10 Feb). POSTAGE DUE. P 13½.
D5586 D **1163** 10l. yellow-brown 65 50
D5587 45l. orange 65 50

1164 Speed Skating

1165 Sarichioi Windmill, Tulcea

(Des M. Vămăşescu. Photo)

1994 (12 Feb). Winter Olympic Games, Lillehammer, Norway. T **1164** and similar vert designs. Multicoloured. P 13½.

(a) POSTAGE

5588	70l. Type **1164**	10	10
5589	115l. Skiing	50	10
5590	125l. Bobsleighing	65	10
5591	245l. Cross-country skiing	90	15
5592	255l. Ski jumping	1·00	20
5593	325l. Figure skating	1·40	25
5588/5593	*Set of* 6	4·00	80

(b) AIR. Inscr "POŞTA AERIANĂ"

MS5594 90×78 mm. 1590l. Single luge (41×53 mm) .... 5·75 5·75

(Des G. Leahu. Photo)

1994 (31 Mar). Mills. T **1165** and similar multicoloured designs. P 13½.

5595	70l. Type **1165**	10	10
5596	115l. Nucarilor Valley windmill, Tulcea	25	10
5597	125l. Caraorman windmill, Tulcea	40	10
5598	245l. Romanii de Jos watermill, Vâlcea	75	15
5599	255l. Enisala windmill, Tulcea (horiz)	90	20
5600	325l. Nistoreşti watermill, Vrancea	1·30	25
5595/5600	*Set of* 6	3·25	80

1166 Călin the Backward

1167 "Resurrection of Christ" (17th-century icon)

(Des V. Munteanu. Photo)

1994 (8 Apr). Fairy Tales. T **1166** and similar vert designs. Multicoloured. P 13½.

5601	70l. Type **1166**	25	10
5602	115l. Ileana Cosânzeana flying	60	10
5603	125l. Ileana Cosânzeana seated	65	10
5604	245l. Ileana Cosânzeana and castle	1·00	15
5605	255l. Agheran the Brave	1·20	20
5606	325l. The Enchanted Wolf carrying Ileana Cosânzeana	1·50	25
5601/5606	*Set of* 6	4·75	80

1994 (21 Apr). Easter. Photo. P 13½.
5607 **1167** 60l. multicoloured 65 50

1168 *Struthiosaurus transylvanicus*

(Des E. Palade. Photo)

1994 (30 Apr). Prehistoric Animals. T **1168** and similar horiz designs. Multicoloured. P 13½.

5608	90l. Type **1168**	25	10
5609	130l. Megalosaurus	40	10
5610	150l. Parasaurolophus	65	15
5611	280l. Stenonychosaurus	1·00	20
5612	500l. Camarasaurus	1·30	25
5613	635l. Gallimimus	1·50	30
5608/5613	*Set of* 6	4·50	1·00

1169 Hermann Oberth (rocket designer)

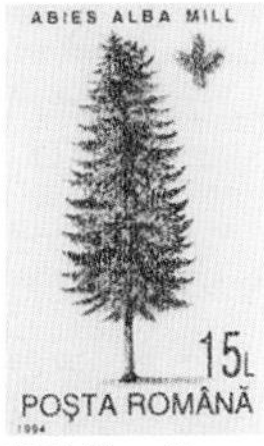

1170 Silver Fir (*Abies alba*)

(Des A. Mihai. Photo)

1994 (25 May). Europa. Inventions. Sheet 109×78 mm containing T **1169** and similar horiz design. P 13½.

MS5614 240l. new blue, indigo and black; 2100l. new blue and black .... 6·50 6·50
Design:—2100l. Henri Coandă (airplane designer).

(Des G. Aniko. Photo)

1994 (27 May). Trees. T **1170** and similar vert designs. Each turquoise-green and black. W **1096a**. P 13½.

5615	15l. Type **1170**	10	10
5616	35l. Scots pine (*Pinus sylvestris*)	10	10
5617	45l. White poplar (*Populus alba*)	15	10
5618	60l. Pedunculate oak (*Quercus robur*)	20	10
5619	70l. European larch (*Larix decidua*)	25	10
5620	125l. Beech (*Fagus sylvatica*)	50	10
5621	350l. Sycamore (*Acer pseudoplatanus*)	1·00	10
5622	940l. Ash (*Fraxinus excelsior*)	3·25	35
5623	1440l. Norway spruce (*Picea abies*)	4·50	50
5624	3095l. Large-leaved lime (*Tilia platyphyllos*)	9·00	60
5615/5624	*Set of* 10	17·00	1·90

1171 Players and Flags of U.S.A., Switzerland, Colombia and Romania

1172 Torch-bearer and Centenary Emblem

(Des C. Decebal. Photo)

1994 (17 June). World Cup Football Championship, U.S.A. T **1171** and similar vert designs showing various footballing scenes and flags of participating countries. Multicoloured. P 13½.

5625	90l. Type **1171** (Group A)	10	10
5626	130l. Brazil, Russia, Cameroun and Sweden (Group B)	40	10
5627	150l. Germany, Bolivia, Spain and South Korea (Group C)	65	10
5628	280l. Argentina, Greece, Nigeria and Bulgaria (Group D)	1·00	20
5629	500l. Italy, Ireland, Norway and Mexico (Group E)	1·30	25
5630	635l. Belgium, Morocco, Netherlands and Saudi Arabia (Group F)	1·50	35
5625/5630	*Set of* 6	4·50	1·00

MS5631 91×78 mm. 2075l. Goalkeeper stopping goal attempt (53×41 mm) .... 5·00 5·00

(Des C. Decebal. Photo)

1994 (23 June). Centenary of International Olympic Committee. T **1172** and similar multicoloured designs showing Ancient Greek athletes. P 13½.

5632	150l. Type **1172**	40	10
5633	280l. Discus-thrower and International Sports Year emblem	90	25
5634	500l. Wrestlers and Olympic Peace emblem	1·30	30
5635	635l. Arbitrator and "Paris 1994" centenary congress emblem	2·50	35
5632/5635	*Set of* 4	4·50	90

MS5636 90×78 mm. 2075l. Athletes, National Olympic Committee emblem and wreath (80th anniv of Romanian membership of Olympic movement) (53×41 mm) .... 5·00 5·00

1173 National History Museum (former Postal Headquarters), Bucharest

1174 Death Trumpet (*Craterellus cornucopioides*)

(Des G. Leahu. Photo)

1994 (15 July). Stamp Day. P 13½.
5637 **1173** 90l. +60l. multicoloured 65 50

(Des G. Aniko. Photo)

1994 (9 Aug). Edible (**MS**5638a) and Poisonous (**MS**5638b) Fungi. Two sheets, each 155×72 mm, containing vert designs as T **1147**. Multicoloured. P 13½.

MS5638 Two sheets. (a) 30l. Type **1174**; 60l. Wood blewit (*Lepista nuda*); 150l. Cep (*Boletus edulis*); 940l. Common puff-ball (*Lycoperdon perlatum*). (b) 90l. Satan's mushroom (*Boletus satanas*); 280l. Death cap (*Amanita phalloides*); 350l. Red-staining inocybe (*Inocybe patouillardii*, wrongly inscr "*patonillardi*"); 500l. Fly agaric (*Amanita muscana*). Two sheets .... 6·50 6·50

1175 Traian Vuia's Airplane No. 1, 1906

1176 Tuning Fork

(Des A. Mihai. Photo)

1994 (12 Aug). AIR. 50th Anniv of International Civil Aviation Organization. T **1175** and similar horiz designs. Matt paper. W **1096a**. P 13½.

5639	110l. brown-ochre, black and grey-blue	25	25
5640	350l. multicoloured	1·30	25
	a. Glazed paper. No wmk	1·30	25
5641	500l. multicoloured	1·90	30
	a. Glazed paper. No wmk	1·90	30
5642	635l. black, ultramarine and blue	2·50	30
5639/5642	*Set of* 4	5·25	1·00

Designs:—350l. Rombac One Eleven; 500l. Boeing 737-300; 635l. Airbus Industrie A310.

(Des C. Decebal. Photo)

1994 (16 Aug). Philakorea 1994 International Stamp Exhibition, Seoul. T **1176** and similar vert design. P 13½.

5643 **1176** 60l. black, dull orange and magenta 65 50
MS5644 78×91 mm. 2075l. multicoloured .... 4·50 4·50
Design: 38×52 mm—2075l. Korean drummer.

1177 Beluga (*Huso huso*)

150L
Echipa României
Compioană Europeană
Stockholm 1994

(**1178**)

(Des Simona Bucan. Photo)

1994 (31 Aug). Environmental Protection of Danube Delta. T **1177** and similar horiz designs. Multicoloured. P 13½.

5645	150l. Type **1177**	50	10
5646	280l. Orsini's viper (*Opera ursini*)	90	15
5647	500l. White-tailed sea eagle (*Haliaeetus albicilla*)	1·50	20
5648	635l. European mink (*Mustela lutreola*)	1·70	25
5645/5648	*Set of* 4	4·25	65

MS5649 90×78 mm. 2075l. *Periploca gracca* (plant) (50×38 mm) .... 5·00 5·00

1994 (9 Sept). Victory of Romanian Team in European Gymnastics Championships, Stockholm. Nos. 5338/9 surch as T **1178**.

5650 150l. on 4l.50 multicoloured (5338) 65 35
5651 525l. on 4l.50 multicoloured (5339) .... 1·90 50
On No. 5651 "Stockholm 1994" reads downwards.

1179 Elephant

(Des Ioana Pârvan. Photo)

1994 (15 Sept). The Circus. T **1179** and similar multicoloured designs. P 13½.

5652	90l. Type **1179**	25	10
5653	130l. Balancing bear (vert)	40	10
5654	150l. Cycling monkeys	65	15
5655	280l. Tiger jumping through hoop	1·30	20
5656	500l. Clown on tightrope balancing dogs	1·70	25
5657	635l. Clown on horseback	2·20	35
5652/5657	*Set of* 6	6·00	1·00

150LEI
1994
Poşta - cea mai buna alegere

(**1180**)

1994 (7 Oct). World Post Day. No. 5465 surch with T **1180**. P 13½.
5658 **1126** 150l. on 10l. multicoloured 65 50

1181 Emblem

1182 Sterlet (*Acipenser ruthenus*)

1994 (10 Oct). 20th International Fair, Bucharest. Photo. P 13½.
5659 **1181** 525l. multicoloured .... 1·90 60

(Des G. Vasarhelyi. Photo)

1994 (28 Oct). Sturgeons. T **1182** and similar horiz designs. P 13½.
5660 150l. Type **1182** 65 10
5661 280l. Russian sturgeon (*Acipenser güldenstaedti*) .... 1·30 15
5662 500l. Stellate sturgeon (*Acipenser stellatus*) .... 1·90 20
5663 635l. Common sturgeon (*Acipenser sturio*) 2·50 25
5660/5663 *Set of 4* .... 5·75 65
Nos. 5660/3 were each issued in sheetlets of ten stamps.

1183 Snake

1184 Early Steam Train, Bucharest–Giurgiu Line

(Des Tută Corina. Photo)

1994 (29 Oct). Romanian–Chinese Stamp Exhibition, Timişoara and Cluj-Napoca. T **1183** and similar vert design. Multicoloured. P 13½.
5664 150l. Type **1183** 65 25
a. Pair. Nos. 5664/5 .... 5·50 80
5665 1135l. Dragon .... 4·50 50
Nos. 5664/5 were issued together in *se-tenant* pairs within the sheet; each horizontal row in the sheet contained two pairs, each pair separated by a label showing the Great Wall of China.

(Des Horia Serbănescu. Photo)

1994 (31 Oct). 125th Anniv of Romanian Railway Administration. P 13½.
5666 **1184** 90l. multicoloured 65 50

1185 Alexandru Orăscu (architect and mathematician)

1186 Nativity

(Des Simona Bucan. Photo)

1994 (30 Nov). Anniversaries. T **1185** and similar vert designs. Multicoloured. P 13½.
5667 30l. Type **1185** (death centenary) 25 15
5668 60l. Gheorghe Polizu (physician, 175th birth anniv) 40 15
5669 150l. Iulia Haşdeu (writer, 125th birth anniv) 65 15
5670 280l. S. Mehedinţi (scientist, 125th birth anniv) 75 15
5671 350l. Camil Petrescu (writer, birth centenary) .... 1·20 25
5672 500l. N. Paulescu (physician, 125th birth anniv) .... 1·30 35
5673 940l. L. Grigorescu (painter, birth centenary) .... 3·25 50
5667/5673 *Set of 7* .... 7·00 1·50
See also No. 5684.

(Des I. Ştefan. Photo)

1994 (14 Dec). Christmas. P 13½.
5674 **1186** 60l. multicoloured 65 50

1187 St. Mary's Church, Cleveland, U.S.A.

(Des Art Design. Photo)

1994 (21 Dec). P 13½.
5675 **1187** 610l. multicoloured .... 1·90 60

1188 Anniversary Emblem

1189 Military Aviation Medal, 1938

(Des B. Munteanu. Photo)

1994 (22 Dec). 20th Anniv of World Tourism Organization. P 13½.
5676 **1188** 525l. greenish blue, yellow-orange and black .... 1·90 60

(Des Horia Serbănescu. Photo)

1994 (23 Dec). Military Decorations. Sheet 73×104 mm containing T **1189** and similar vert designs. Multicoloured. P 13½.
MS5677 30l. Type **1189**; 60l. "For Valour" Cross, Third Class, 1916; 150l. Military Medal, First Class, 1880; 940l. Romanian Star, 1877 .... 3·25 3·25

1190 Kittens

1191 Emblem

(Des Art Design. Photo)

1994 (27 Dec). Young Domestic Animals. T **1190** and similar vert designs. Multicoloured. P 13½.
5678 90l. Type **1190** 15 25
5679 130l. Puppies 25 25
5680 150l. Kid 40 25
5681 280l. Foal 75 25
5682 500l. Rabbit kittens .... 1·50 35
5683 635l. Lambs .... 1·90 50
5678/5683 *Set of 6* .... 4·50 1·70

(Des Simona Bucan. Photo)

1994 (28 Dec). Death Centenary of Gheorghe Tattarescu (painter). Vert design as T **1185**. Multicoloured. P 13½.
5684 90l. Tattarescu 65 50

1995 (31 Jan). Save the Children Fund. Photo. P 13½.
5685 **1191** 60l. ultramarine 65 50

1192 Tânăr

1193 Hand and Barbed Wire

(Des M. Vămăşescu. Photo)

1995 (25 Feb). Braşov Youth. T **1192** and similar vert designs showing neighbourhood group leaders. Multicoloured. P 13½.
5686 40l. Type **1192** 15 25
5687 60l. Bătrân 25 25
5688 150l. Curcan 40 25
5689 280l. Dorobant 75 25
5690 350l. Braşovechean .... 1·30 25
5691 500l. Roşior .... 1·50 35
5692 635l. Albior .... 1·90 50
5686/5692 *Set of 7* .... 5·75 1·90

(Des Simona Bucan. Photo)

1995 (24 Mar). 50th Anniv of Liberation of Concentration Camps. P 13½.
5693 **1193** 960l. black and bright crimson .... 1·30 60

1194 Emblems of French and Romanian State Airlines

(Des A. Mihai. Photo)

1995 (31 Mar). AIR. 75th Anniv of Founding of Franco-Romanian Air Company. T **1194** and similar horiz design. P 13½.
5694 60l. new blue and bright scarlet 25 10
5695 960l. greenish blue and black .... 1·70 35
Design:—960l. Potez IX biplane and Paris–Bucharest route map.

1195 Ear of Wheat

1196 "Resurrection" (icon)

(Des Simona Bucan. Photo)

1995 (12 Apr). 50th Anniversaries. T **1195** and similar horiz designs. Multicoloured. P 13½.
5696 675l. Type **1195** (Food and Agriculture Organization) .... 1·30 25
5697 960l. Anniversary emblem (United Nations Organization) .... 1·90 35
5698 1615l. Hand holding pen showing members' flags (signing of United Nations Charter) .... 2·50 55
5696/5698 *Set of 3* .... 5·25 1·00

1995 (14 Apr). Easter. Photo. P 13½.
5699 **1196** 60l. multicoloured 65 50

1197 *Youth without Age and Life without Death*

(Des Ioana Pârvan. Photo)

1995 (20 Apr). Fairy Tales. T **1197** and similar multicoloured designs. P 13½.
5700 90l. Type **1197** 15 20
5701 130l. *The Old Man's Servant and the Old Woman's Servant* (vert) 20 20
5702 150l. *The Prince with the Golden Hair* 25 20
5703 280l. *Son of the Red King* 90 20
5704 500l. *Praslea the Brave and the Golden Apples* (vert) .... 1·70 20
5705 635l. *King Dafin* (drawn by golden horses) 2·50 25
5700/5705 *Set of 6* .... 5·25 1·10

1198 Enescu

(Des Simona Bucan. Photo)

1995 (5 May). 40th Death Anniv of George Enescu (composer). P 13½.
5706 **1198** 960l. pale orange and black .... 1·40 60

1199 Dove with Section of Rainbow

1200 Blaga

(Des D. Petre. Photo)

1995 (8 May). Europa. Peace and Freedom. T **1199** and similar vert design. Multicoloured. P 13½.
5707 150l. Type **1199** 15 10
5708 4370l. Dove wings forming "EUROPA" around rainbow .... 9·50 9·00

(Des D. Petre. Photo)

1995 (9 May). Birth Centenary of Lucian Blaga (poet). P 13½.
5709 **1200** 150l. multicoloured 65 50
See also Nos. 5745/9.

Nos. 5710/11 are vacant.

1201 Bucharest Underground Railway, 1979

1202 *Dacia* (liner)

(Des A. Mihai. Photo)

1995 (30 May–Nov). Transport. T **1201** and similar designs. P 13½.

(a) POSTAGE

5712 470l. lemon and black ... 65 10
5713 630l. bright scarlet and new blue (16.11) ... 90 10
5714 675l. bright scarlet and black ... 90 10
5715 755l. new blue and black (16.11) ... 1·00 10
5716 1615l. blue-green and black (16.11) ... 1·90 50
5717 2300l. blue-green and black ... 3·00 25
5718 2550l. black and bright scarlet ... 3·25 25

(b) AIR. Inscr "POŞTA AERIANĂ"

5719 285l. grey-olive and black (16.11) ... 25 10
5720 715l. bright scarlet and deep grey-blue (16.11) ... 90 10
5721 965l. black and blue ... 3·00 10
5722 1575l. blue-green and black (16.11) ... 2·30 35
5723 3410l. blue and black ... 4·50 60
5712/5723 *Set of* 12 ... 20·00 2·40

Designs: Horiz—285l. I.A.R. 80 aircraft (70th anniv of Romanian aeronautical industry); 630l. *Mesagerul* (post boat); 715l. I.A.R. 316 Red Cross helicopter; 755l. *Razboieni* (container ship); 965l. Sud Aviation SA 330 Puma helicopter; 1575l. I.A.R. 818H seaplane; 2300l. Trolleybus, 1904; 2550l. Steam train, 1869; 3410l. Boeing 737-300 airliner (75th anniv of Romanian air transport). Vert—675l. Cable-car, Braşov; 1615l. Electric tram, Bucharest, 1894.

Nos. 5724/34 are vacant.

(Des A. Mihai. Photo)

1995 (31 May). Centenary of Romanian Maritime Service. T **1202** and similar multicoloured designs. P 13½.

5735 90l. Type **1202** ... 25 20
5736 130l. *Impăratul Traian* (Danube steamer) (horiz) ... 25 20
5737 150l. *România* (Danube steamer) (horiz) ... 25 20
5738 280l. *Costineşti* (tanker) (horiz) ... 40 20
5739 960l. *Caransebeş* (container ship) (horiz) ... 1·30 25
5740 3410l. *Tutova* (car ferry) (horiz) ... 4·50 85
5735/5740 *Set of* 6 ... 6·25 1·70

1203 Fallow Deer (*Dama dama*)

1204 Youths and Torch-bearer

(Des Simona Bucan. Photo)

1995 (5 June). European Nature Conservation Year. T **1203** and similar vert designs. Multicoloured. P 13½.

5741 150l. Type **1203** ... 25 25
5742 280l. Great bustard (*Otis tarda*) ... 40 25
5743 960l. Lady's slipper (*Cypripedium calceolus*) ... 1·90 60
5744 1615l. Stalagmites ... 2·50 1·20
5741/5744 *Set of* 4 ... 4·50 2·10

(Des D. Petre. Photo)

1995 (26 June). Anniversaries. Vert designs as T **1200**. Multicoloured. P 13½.

5745 90l. D. Roşca (birth centenary) ... 25 25
5746 130l. Vasile Conta (150th birth anniv) ... 25 25
5747 280l. Ion Barbu (birth centenary) ... 25 25
5748 960l. Iuliu Haţieganu (110th birth anniv) ... 1·20 30
5749 1650l. Dimitrie Brândză (botanist) (death centenary) ... 2·00 40
5745/5749 *Set of* 5 ... 3·50 1·30

1995 (10 July). European Youth Olympic Days. Photo. P 13½.

5750 **1204** 1650l. multicoloured ... 2·50 60

1205 Post Wagon (½-size illustration)

(Des Şt. Avram and M. Dragoteanu. Photo)

1995 (15 July). Stamp Day. Centenary of Upper Rhine Local Post. P 13½.

5751 **1205** 960l. (+715l.) multicoloured ... 2·50 60

No. 5751 includes the *se-tenant* premium-carrying tab shown in Type **1205**.

1206 Saligny Bridge

1207 Mallard (*Anas platyrhynchos*)

(Des A. Mihai. Photo)

1995 (27 July). Centenary of Saligny Bridge, Cernavodă. P 13½.

5752 **1206** 675l. multicoloured ... 1·30 60

(Des Carmen Paraschivescu. Photo)

1995 (31 July). Domestic Birds. T **1207** and similar vert designs. Multicoloured. P 13½.

5753 90l. Type **1207** ... 25 20
5754 130l. Red junglefowl (*Gallus gallus*) (hen) ... 25 20
5755 150l. Helmet guineafowl (*Numida meleagris*) ... 25 20
5756 280l. Common turkey (*Meleagris gallopavo*) ... 65 20
5757 960l. Greylag goose (*Anser anser*) ... 1·50 25
5758 1650l. Red junglefowl (*Gallus gallus*) (cock) ... 2·30 35
5753/5758 *Set of* 6 ... 4·75 1·30

1208 General Dr. Victor Anastasiu

1209 Battle Scene

(Des D. Petre. Photo)

1995 (4 Aug). 75th Anniv of Institute of Aeronautics Medicine. P 13½.

5759 **1208** 960l. ultramarine, pale blue and bright crimson ... 1·90 60

(Des B. Molea. Photo)

1995 (13 Aug). 400th Anniv of Battle of Călugăreni. P 13½.

5760 **1209** 100l. multicoloured ... 65 50

1210 Giurgiu Castle

1211 Moldoviţa Monastery

(Des G. Leahu. Photo)

1995 (28 Aug). Anniversaries. T **1210** and similar multicoloured designs. P 13½.

5761 250l. Type **1210** (600th anniv) ... 40 15
5762 500l. Neamţului Castle (600th anniv) (vert) ... 65 15
5763 960l. Sebeş-Alba Mill (750th anniv) ... 1·30 20
5764 1615l. Dorohoi Church (500th anniv) (vert) ... 1·90 30
5765 1650l. Military Observatory, Bucharest (centenary) (vert) ... 2·30 35
5761/5765 *Set of* 5 ... 6·00 1·00

(Des G. Leahu. Photo)

1995 (31 Aug). U.N.E.S.C.O. World Heritage Sites. T **1211** and similar multicoloured designs. P 13½.

5766 675l. Type **1211** ... 65 25
5767 960l. Hurez Monastery ... 1·30 35
5768 1615l. Biertan Castle (horiz) ... 1·90 50
5766/5768 *Set of* 3 ... 3·50 1·00

1212 Racket

1213 Ion Ionescu (editor)

1995 (8 Sept). Fifth International Open Tennis Championships, Bucharest. Photo. P 13½.

5769 **1212** 1020l. multicoloured ... 1·90 60

1995 (15 Sept). Centenary of Mathematics Gazette. Photo. P 13½.

5770 **1213** 100l. flesh and reddish brown ... 65 50

1214 *Albizzia julibrissin*

1215 St. John's Church

(Des Carmen Paraschivescu. Photo)

1995 (29 Sept). Plants from Bucharest Botanical Garden. T **1214** and similar horiz designs. Multicoloured. P 13½.

5771 50l. Type **1214** ... 15 10
5772 100l. Yew (*Taxus baccata*) ... 15 10
5773 150l. *Paulownia tomentosa* ... 15 10
5774 500l. Bird of Paradise flower (*Strelitzia reginae*) ... 75 10
5775 960l. Amazon water-lily (*Victoria amazonica*) ... 1·50 35
5776 2300l. Azalea (*Rhododendron indicum*) ... 2·75 50
5771/5776 *Set of* 6 ... 5·00 1·10

(Des G. Leahu. Photo)

1995 (1 Oct). 600th Anniv of First Documentary Reference to Piatra-Neamt. P 13½.

5777 **1215** 250l. multicoloured ... 1·30 1·20

1216 George Apostu (sculptor)

1217 Running

(Des E. Palade. Photo)

1995 (9 Nov). Anniversaries. T **1216** and similar vert designs. P 13½.

5778 150l. dull blue-green and black ... 25 20
5779 250l. cobalt and black ... 50 20
5780 500l. yellow-brown, grey-brown and black ... 75 20
5781 960l. brown-rose, maroon and black ... 1·50 25
5782 1650l. brown-ochre and black ... 2·30 50
5778/5782 *Set of* 5 ... 4·75 1·20

Designs:—150l. Type **1216** (tenth death anniv (1996)); 250l. Emil Cioran (philosopher, death in 1995); 500l. Eugen Ionescu (writer, first death anniv); 960l. Elena Văcărescu (poetess, 130th birth anniv (1996)); 1650l. Mircea Eliade (philosopher, tenth death anniv (1996)).

(Des C. Decebal. Photo)

1995 (8 Dec). Olympic Games, Atlanta (1996) (1st issue). T **1217** and similar multicoloured designs. P 13½.

5783 50l. Type **1217** ... 15 15
5784 100l. Gymnastics ... 15 15
5785 150l. Canoeing ... 15 15
5786 500l. Fencing ... 90 15
5787 960l. Rowing ... 1·50 25
5788 2300l. Boxing ... 3·50 60
5783/5788 *Set of* 6 ... 5·75 1·30

MS5789 78×92 mm. 2610l. Gymnastics (different) (41×53 mm) ... 3·75 3·75

See also Nos. 5829/**MS**5834.

1218 Nativity

1219 Masked Person

1995 (15 Dec). Christmas. Photo. P 13½.

5790 **1218** 100l. multicoloured ... 65 50

(Des Emanuela Bolgar. Photo)

1996 (31 Jan). Folk Masks of Maramureş; (250l.) and Moldavia (others). T **1219** and similar designs showing different masks. P 13½.

5791 **1219** 250l. multicoloured ... 65 25
5792 – 500l. multicoloured ... 1·00 25
5793 – 960l. multicoloured (vert) ... 1·70 35
5794 – 1650l. multicoloured (vert) ... 2·50 50
5791/5794 *Set of* 4 ... 5·25 1·20

1220 Tristan Tzara

1221 "Resurrection" (icon)

(Des Silvia and M. Muntenescu. Photo)

1996 (27 Mar). Writers' Birth Anniversaries. T **1220** and similar vert design. Multicoloured. P 13½.

5795	150l. Type **1220** (centenary)	25	10
5796	1500l. Anton Pann (bicentenary)	2·30	35

1996 (29 Mar). Easter. Photo. P 13½.

5797	**1221** 150l. multicoloured	65	50

1222 National History Museum

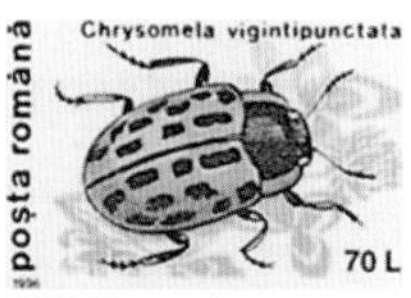

1223 *Chrysomela vigintipunctata* (leaf beetle)

(Des Mihaela Stoican (150l.). Photo)

1996 (5 Apr). Romfilex '96 Romanian–Israeli Stamp Exhibition. Sheet 124×73 mm containing T **1222** and similar vert designs. P 13½.

MS5798 150l. red-brown and black; 370l. multicoloured; 1500l. multicoloured ... 10·00 10·00

Designs:—370l. "On the Terrace at Sinaia" (Theodor Aman); 1500l. "Old Jerusalem" (Reuven Rubin).

(Des Aida Tasgian Philipovici. Photo)

1996 (16 Apr–10 June). Beetles. T **1223** and similar horiz designs. P 13½.

5799	70l. yellow and black (10.6)	20	10
5800	220l. dull scarlet and black	20	10
5801	370l. orange-brown and black (10.6)	40	10
5802	650l. black, vermilion and brownish grey (10.6)	65	10
5803	700l. dull verm, blk & sage grn (10.6)	75	10
5804	740l. black and olive-yellow	90	10
5805	960l. black and dull vermilion	1·20	10
5806	1000l. orange-yellow and black	1·20	10
5807	1500l. black and chestnut	1·90	25
5808	2500l. dull scarlet, black and grey-olive (10.6)	2·50	50
5799/5808	*Set of* 10	9·00	1·40

Designs:—220l. *Cerambyx cerdo* (longhorn beetle); 370l. *Entomoscelis adonidis*; 650l. Ladybird (*Coccinella bipunctata*); 700l. Caterpillar-hunter (*Calosoma sycophanta*); 740l. *Hedobia imperialis*; 960l. European rhinoceros beetle (*Oryctes nasicornis*); 1000l. Bee chafer (*Trichius fasciatus*); 1500l. *Purpuricenus kaehleri* (longhorn beetle); 2500l. *Anthaxia salicis*.

1224 Dumitru Prunariu (first Romanian cosmonaut)

(Des C. Prunariu. Photo)

1996 (22 Apr). Espamer Spanish–Latin American and Aviation and Space Stamp Exhibitions, Seville, Spain. Sheet 91×78 mm. P 13½.

MS5809 **1224** 2720l. multicoloured ... 2·50 2·50

1225 Arbore Church

1226 Ana Aslan (doctor)

(Des G. Leahu. Photo)

1996 (24 Apr). U.N.E.S.C.O. World Heritage Sites. T **1225** and similar horiz designs. Multicoloured. P 13½.

5810	150l. Type **1225**	25	25
5811	1500l. Voroneţ Monastery	1·70	35
5812	2550l. Humor Monastery	3·25	60
5810/5812	*Set of* 3	4·75	1·10

(Des E. Palade. Photo)

1996 (6 May). Europa. Famous Women. T **1226** and similar vert design. Multicoloured. P 13½.

5813	370l. Type **1226**	40	35
	a. Strip. Nos. 5813/14 and 2 labels	7·00	6·25
5814	4140l. Lucia Bulandra (actress)	6·25	5·75

Nos. 5813/14 were issued together in *se-tenant* strips of two stamps and two labels showing a symbol of each woman's work.

1227 "Mother and Children" (Oana Negoită)

1996 (25 May). 50th Anniv of United Nations Children's Fund. T **1227** and similar multicoloured designs showing prize-winning children's paintings. P 13½.

5815	370l. Type **1227**	40	35
5816	740l. "Winter Scene" (Cosmin Badea)	90	35
5817	1500l. "Children and Sun over House" (Nicoleta Georgescu)	1·50	50
5818	2550l. "House on Stilts" (Biborka Bartha) (vert)	2·30	70
5815/5818	*Set of* 4	4·50	1·70

1228 Goalkeeper with Ball

1229 Metropolitan Toronto Convention Centre (venue)

(Des M.A.C.S. Photo)

1996 (27 May). European Football Championship, England. T **1228** and similar vert designs. Multicoloured. P 13½.

5819	220l. Type **1228**	10	10
	a. Horiz strip of 5. Nos. 5819/23	5·00	
5820	370l. Player with ball	25	10
5821	740l. Two players with ball	65	15
5822	1500l. Three players with ball	1·40	25
5823	2550l. Player dribbling ball	2·40	50
5819/5823	*Set of* 5	4·25	1·00
MS5824	90×78 mm. 4050l. Balls and two players (41×53 mm)	3·75	3·75

Nos. 5819/23 were issued together in horizontal *se-tenant* strips of five stamps within the sheet, each strip forming a composite design of the pitch and stadium.

(Des Simona Bucan. Photo)

1996 (29 May). Capex'96 International Stamp Exhibition, Toronto, Canada. T **1229** and similar vert design. Multicoloured. P 13½.

5825	150l. Type **1229**	65	50
MS5826	78×90 mm. 4050l. View of city (41×52 mm)	3·75	3·75

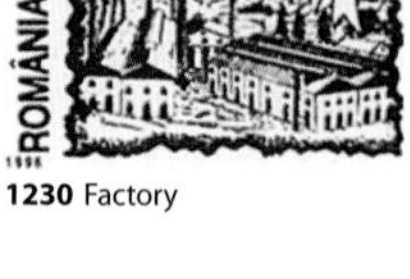

1230 Factory

1232 Boxing

1996 - 5 ANI DE LA ÎNFIINTARE

L150 ═══

(**1231**)

1996 (20 June). 225th Anniv of Resita Works. Photo. P 13½.

5827	**1230** 150l. lake-brown	65	50

1996 (22 June). Fifth Anniv of Establishment of R. A. Posta Romana (postal organization). No. 5471 surch with T **1231** in crimson.

5828	**1128** 150l. on 10l. multicoloured	65	60

(Des C. Decebal. Photo)

1996 (12 July). Centenary of Modern Olympic Games and Olympic Games, Atlanta (2nd issue). T **1232** and similar multicoloured designs. P 13½.

(a) POSTAGE

5829	220l. Type **1232**	25	10
5830	370l. Running	40	10
5831	740l. Rowing	90	15
5832	1500l. Judo	1·70	35
5833	2550l. Gymnastics (asymmetrical bars)	2·75	50
5829/5833	*Set of* 5	5·50	1·10

(b) AIR. Inscr "Poşta Aeriană"

MS5834	90×78 mm. 4050l. Gymnastics (beam) (53×41 mm)	3·75	3·75

No. **MS**5834 also commemorates Olymphilex'96 sports stamp exhibition, Atlanta.

1233 Postman, Keyboard and Stamp under Magnifying Glass

(Des C. Decebal. Photo)

1996 (15 July). Stamp Day. P 13½.

5835	**1233** 1500l. (+650l.) multicoloured	1·90	60

No. 5835 includes the *se-tenant* premium-carrying tab shown in Type **1233**.

1234 White Spruce (*Picea glauca*)

1235 Grass Snake (*Natrix natrix*)

(Des Adriana Dobra. Photo)

1996 (1 Aug). Coniferous Trees. T **1234** and similar horiz designs. Multicoloured. P 13½.

5836	70l. Type **1234**	15	10
5837	150l. Serbian spruce (*Picea omorica*)	15	10
5838	220l. Blue Colorado spruce (*Picea pungens*)	15	10
5839	740l. Sitka spruce (*Picea sitchensis*)	90	10
5840	1500l. Scots pine (*Pinus sylvestris*)	1·70	25
5841	3500l. Maritime pine (*Pinus pinaster*)	3·75	60
5836/5841	*Set of* 6	6·00	1·10

(Des P. Comisarschi. Photo)

1996 (12 Sept). Animals. T **1235** and similar multicoloured designs. P 13½.

5842	70l. Type **1235**	15	10
5843	150l. Hermann's tortoise (*Testudo hermanni*)	15	10
5844	220l. Sky lark (*Alauda arvensis*). (horiz)	15	10
5845	740l. Red fox (*Vulpes vulpes*) (horiz)	90	10
5846	1500l. Common porpoise (*Phocoena phocoena*) (wrongly inscr "Phocaena")	1·70	25
5847	3500l. Golden eagle (*Aquila chrysaëtos*) (horiz)	3·75	60
5842/5847	*Set of* 6	6·00	1·10

1236 Madonna and Child

1237 Stan Golestan (composer, 40th)

1996 (27 Nov). Christmas. Photo. P 13½.

5848	**1236** 150l. multicoloured	65	50

(Des M. Lungu. Photo)

1996 (29 Nov). Death Anniversaries. T **1237** and similar vert designs. P 13½.

5849	100l. bright rose and black	25	25
5850	150l. brown-purple and black	40	35
5851	370l. dull orange and black	65	60
5852	1500l. vermilion and black	2·00	1·90
5849/5852	*Set of* 4	3·00	2·75

Designs:—150l. Corneliu Coposu (politician, first); 370l. Horia Vintilă (writer, fourth); 1500l. Alexandru Papană (test pilot, 50th).

1238 Ford "Spider", 1930

(Des M. Lungu (**MS**5853a), Mihaela Stoican and Bejenaru (**MS**5853b). Photo)

1996 (19 Dec). Motor Cars. Two sheets containing horiz designs as T **1238**. Multicoloured. P 13½.

MS5853	Two sheets. (a) 110×78 mm. 70l. Type **1238**; 150l. Citroen, 1932; 220l. Rolls Royce, 1936; 280l. Mercedes Benz, 1933. (b) 113×80 mm. 120l. Jaguar SS 100, 1937; 2500l. Bugatti Type **59**, 1934; 2550l. Mercedes Benz 500K Roadster, 1936; 2550l. Alfa Romeo 8C, 1931	10·00	10·00

1239 Deng Xiaoping and Margaret Thatcher

1997 (20 Jan). Hong Kong '97 Stamp Exhibition. Sheet 92×78 mm. P 13½.

MS5854	**1239** 1500l. multicoloured	1·90	1·90

1240 Stoat (*Mustela erminea*)

1241 Bow

(Des Adriana Dobra. Photo)

1997 (14 Feb). Fur-bearing Mammals. T **1240** and similar horiz designs. Multicoloured. P 13½.

5855	70l. Type **1240**	25	25
5856	150l. Arctic fox (*Alopex lagopus*)	25	25
5857	220l. Racoon-dog (*Nyctereutes procyonoides*)	25	25
5858	740l. European otter (*Lutra lutra*)	40	30
5859	1500l. Muskrat (*Ondatra zibethica*)	75	35
5860	3500l. Pine marten (*Martes martes*)	1·90	60
5855/5860	*Set of* 6	3·50	1·80

1997 (6 Mar). 26th Anniv of Greenpeace (environmental organization). T **1241** and similar vert designs showing the *Rainbow Warrior* (campaign ship). Multicoloured. Photo. P 13½.

5861	150l. Type **1241**	25	25
5862	370l. Ship and ice	25	25
5863	1940l. Ship cruising past beach	1·00	35
5864	2500l. Rainbow and ship	1·70	35
5861/5864	*Set of* 4	3·00	1·10
MS5865	90×77 mm. 4050l. Ship carrying banner (49×38 mm)	3·25	3·25

1242 Thomas Edison (inventor)

(Des P. Comisarschi. Photo)

1997 (27 Mar). Birth Anniversaries. T **1242** and similar horiz designs. Multicoloured. P 13½.

5866	200l. Type **1242** (150th anniv)	25	25
5867	400l. Franz Schubert (composer, bicentenary)	40	30
5868	3600l. Miguel de Cervantes Saavedra (writer, 450th anniv)	2·50	60
5866/5868	*Set of* 3	2·75	1·00

1243 Emblem

1244 Şurdeşti

1997 (7 Apr). Inauguration of Mobile Telephone Network in Romania. Photo. P 13½.

5869	**1243** 400l. multicoloured	65	50

1997 (21 Apr). Churches. T **1244** and similar vert designs. Each brown, agate and bottle green. Photo. P 13½.

5870	200l. Type **1244**	25	20
5871	400l. Plopiş	25	20
5872	450l. Bogdan Vodă	25	20
5873	850l. Rogoz	50	25
5874	3600l. Călineşti	1·70	30
5875	6000l. Bîrsana	2·75	50
5870/5875	*Set of* 6	5·25	1·50

1245 Al. Demetrescu Dan in *Hamlet*, 1916

1246 Vlad Tepeş Dracula (Voivode of Wallachia)

(Des L. Irimescu. Photo)

1997 (23 Apr). Second Shakespeare Festival, Craiova. T **1245** and similar vert designs. Multicoloured. P 13½.

5876	200l. Type **1245**	15	10
	a. Sheetlet. Nos. 5876/9 plus 4 labels	3·75	
5877	400l. Constantin Serghie in *Othello*, 1855	15	10
5878	2400l. Gheorghe Cozorici in *Hamlet*, 1957	1·30	1·20
5879	3600l. Ion Manolescu in *Hamlet*, 1924	1·90	1·80
5876/5879	*Set of* 4	3·25	3·00

Nos. 5876/9 were issued together in *se-tenant* sheetlets of four stamps and four labels showing different portraits of Shakespeare.

(Des P. Comisarschi. Photo)

1997 (5 May). Europa, Tales and Legends. Dracula. T **1246** and similar vert design. Multicoloured. P 13½.

5880	400l. Type **1246**	25	10
	a. Pair. Nos. 5880/1	3·50	2·75
5881	4250l. Dracula the myth	3·00	2·40

Nos. 5880/1 were issued together in *se-tenant* pairs within sheets of 12 stamps and eight labels showing views of a castle.

1247 *Dolichothele uberiformis*

1248 National Theatre, Cathedral and Statue of Mihai Viteazul

(Des C. Furnea. Photo)

1997 (27 June). Cacti. T **1247** and similar horiz designs. Multicoloured. P 13½.

5882	100l. Type **1247**	25	25
5883	250l. *Rebutia*	25	25
5884	450l. *Echinofossulocactus lamellosus*	25	25
5885	500l. *Ferocactus glaucescens*	25	25
5886	650l. *Thelocactus*	25	25
5887	6150l. *Echinofossulocactus albatus*	5·00	1·20
5882/5887	*Set of* 6	5·75	2·20

(Des I. Daniliuc. Photo)

1997 (27 June). Balcanmax'97 Maximum Cards Exhibition, Cluj-Napoca. P 13½.

5888	**1248** 450l. multicoloured	65	60

1249 19th-century Postal Transport

1997 (15 July). Stamp Day. Photo. P 13½.

5889	**1249** 3600l. (+1500l.) multicoloured	3·25	1·80

No. 5889 includes the *se-tenant* premium-carrying tab shown in Type **1249**.

250 Lei
(**1250**)

1251 Archway of Vlad Tepeş Dracula's House

1997 (17 July). Nos. 5349/55 and 5357 surch as T **1250**.

5890	250l. on 1l. royal blue (Crim.)	25	25
5891	250l. on 2l. deep green (Crim.)	25	25
5892	250l. on 4l. carmine-red	25	25
5893	450l. on 5l. slate-violet (Crim.)	25	25
5894	450l. on 6l. bistre-brown (Crim.)	25	25
5895	450l. on 18l. rose-red	25	25
5896	950l. on 9l. brown-lake	40	25
5897	3600l. on 8l. brown (Crim.)	1·90	35
5890/5897	*Set of* 8	3·50	1·90

(Des G. Leahu. Photo)

1997 (31 July). Sighişoara. T **1251** and similar vert designs. Multicoloured. P 13½.

5898	250l. Type **1251**	25	15
5899	650l. Town Hall clocktower	40	15
5900	3700l. Steps leading to fortress and clocktower	2·00	1·20
5898/5900	*Set of* 3	2·40	1·40

1252 Tourism Monument

1253 Printing Works

(Des D. Tăran. Photo)

1997 (3 Aug). Rusca Montană, Banat. P 13½.

5901	**1252** 950l. multicoloured	40	25

(Des G. Leahu. Photo)

1997 (13 Aug). 125th Anniv of Stamp Printing Works. P 13½.

5902	**1253** 450l. bright crimson, deep brown and greenish blue	65	40

1254 Emil Racovita (biologist) and *Belgica* (polar barque)

1050 L
AEROMFILA '97
Braşov
(**1255**)

(Des C. Furnea. Photo)

1997 (18 Aug). Centenary of Belgian Antarctic Expedition. T **1254** and similar vert designs. P 13½.

5903	450l. royal blue, bluish grey and black	25	10
5904	650l. deep rose-red, greenish yellow and black	25	10
5905	1600l. yellowish green, pale carmine-rose and black	75	15
5906	3700l. sepia, greenish yellow and black	2·50	1·60
5903/5906	*Set of* 4	3·50	1·80

Designs:—650l. Frederick Cook (anthropologist and photographer) and *Belgica* at sea; 1600l. Roald Amundsen and *Belgica* in port; 3700l. Adrien de Gerlache (expedition Commander) and *Belgica* ice-bound.

1997 (27 Sept). Aeromfilá '97 Stamp Exhibition, Braşov. No. 5334 surch with T **1255** in bright scarlet.

5907	**1092** 1050l. on 4l.50 multicoloured	65	40

1256 Campsite

500 L
(**1257**)

(Des Cornelia Petrescu. Photo)

1997 (25 Oct). Romanian Scout Association. T **1256** and similar vert designs. Multicoloured. P 13½.

5908	300l. Type **1256**	15	10
	a. Horiz strip of 5. Nos. 5908/12	3·75	
5909	700l. Romanian Scout Association emblem	25	15
5910	1050l. Joined hands	50	30
5911	1750l. Carvings	75	45
5912	3700l. Scouts around campfire	1·80	1·10
5908/5912	*Set of* 5	3·00	1·90

Nos. 5908/12 were issued together in horizontal *se-tenant* strips of five within the sheet, each strip forming a composite design.

1997 (28 Oct). Ninth Romanian–Chinese Stamp Exhibition, Bucharest. No. 5293 surch with T **1257** in red.
5913 **1082** 500l. on 2l. multicoloured 65 40

1258 Ion Mihalache (politician)

1259 Rugby

1997 (8 Nov). Anniversaries. T **1258** and similar vert designs. Multicoloured. Photo. P 13½.
5914 500l. Type **1258** (34th death anniv) 25 15
5915 1050l. King Carol I (131st anniv of accession) (black inscriptions and face value) 65 40
a. Strip of 4. Nos. 5915/18 .... 2·75
5916 1050l. As No. 5915 but cerise inscriptions and face value 65 40
5917 1050l. As No. 5915 but light blue inscriptions and face value 65 40
5918 1050l. As No. 5915 but lake-brown inscriptions and face value 65 40
5914/5918 *Set of 5* .... 2·50 1·60
Nos. 5915/18 were issued together in *se-tenant* strips of four stamps within the sheet.

(Des P. Comisarschi. Photo)

1997 (21 Nov). Sports. T **1259** and similar multicoloured designs. P 13½.
5919 500l. Type **1259** 25 15
5920 700l. American football (vert) 40 25
5921 1750l. Oină (Romanian bat and ball game) 75 45
5922 3700l. Mountaineering (vert) .... 2·50 1·60
5919/5922 *Set of 4* .... 3·50 2·20

1260 New Building

1998 (29 Jan). 130th Anniv of Bucharest Chamber of Commerce and Industry. Photo. P 13½.
5923 **1260** 700l. multicoloured 65 40
No. 5923 was issued with *se-tenant* half stamp-size label showing the old Chamber building.

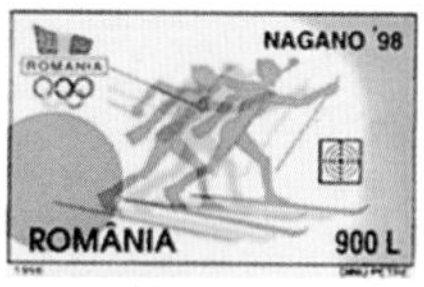

1261 Biathlon

(Des D. Petre. Photo)

1998 (5 Feb). Winter Olympic Games, Nagano, Japan. T **1261** and similar horiz design. Multicoloured. P 13½.
5924 900l. Type **1261** 60 40
5925 3900l. Figure skating .... 2·30 1·60

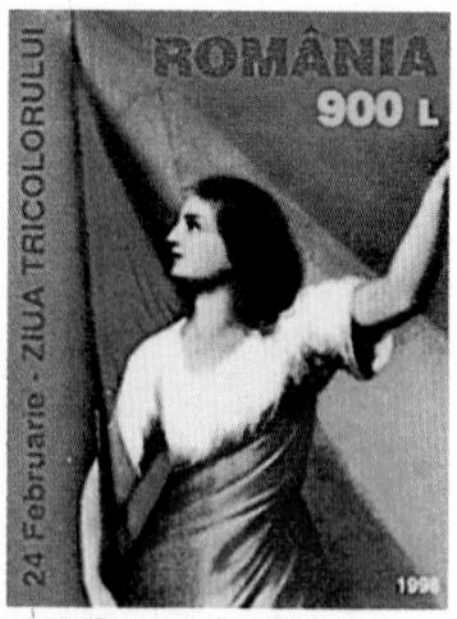

1262 "Romania breaking the Chains on Libertătii Plain" (C. D. Rosenthal)

1263 Four-leaved Clover (Good luck and Success)

1998 (24 Feb). National Tricolour Flag Day. Sheet 78×90 mm. Photo. P 13½.
MS5926 **1262** 900l. multicoloured .... 1·20 1·20

(Des C. Furnea. Photo)

1998 (26 Feb). Europa. National Festivals. T **1263** and similar vert designs. P 13½.
5927 900l. emerald and scarlet .... 1·20 80
5928 3900l. scarlet, dull vermilion and emerald .. 28·00 19·00
Design:—3900l. Butterfly (youth and suaveness).

1264 Alfred Nobel

1265 Shrine, Cluj

(Des Elena Caracenţev. Photo)

1998 (31 Mar). The 20th Century (1st series). T **1264** and similar horiz designs. Multicoloured. P 13½.
5929 700l. Type **1264** (establishment of Nobel Foundation, 1901) 45 30
5930 900l. Guglielmo Marconi (first radio-telegraphic trans-Atlantic link, 1901) 60 40
5931 1500l. Albert Einstein (elaboration of Theory of Relativity, 1905) 70 45
5932 3900l. Traian Vuia (his first flight, 1906) .... 2·30 1·60
5929/5932 *Set of 4* .... 3·75 2·50
See also Nos. 5991/5, 6056/9, 6060/3, 6128/31, 6133/6, 6205/8 and 6230/3.

(Des G. Leahu. Photo)

1998 (17 Apr). Roadside Shrines. T **1265** and similar vert designs. Multicoloured. P 13½.
5933 700l. Type **1265** 35 25
5934 900l. Crucifixion, Prahova 45 30
5935 1500l. Shrine, Argeş .... 1·20 80
5933/5935 *Set of 3* .... 1·80 1·20

ISRAEL '98
900 L

(**1266**)

1267 Dr. Thomi Ionescu (founder) and Coltea Hospital, Bucharest

1998 (12 May). Israel '98 International Stamp Exhibition, Tel Aviv. No. **MS**5798 with each stamp surch as T **1266** in red.
MS5936 700l. on 150l. red-brown and black; 900l. on 370l. multicoloured; 3900l. on 1500l. multicoloured .... 3·50 3·50
The surcharge on the 150l. also included the exhibition emblem.

1998 (18 May). Centenary of Romanian Surgery Society. Photo. P 13½.
5937 **1267** 1050l. bluish grey, light brown and scarlet-vermilion 60 40

50 L

(**1268**)

1269 Player

1998 (21 May). Nos. 5350/1, 5353/4 and 5357 surch as T **1268**.
5938 50l. on 2l. deep green (R.) 45 30
5939 100l. on 8l. brown (G.) 45 30
5940 200l. on 4l. carmine-red 45 30
5941 400l. on 6l. bistre-brown (V.) 45 30
5942 500l. on 18l. rose-red (B.) 45 30
5938/5942 *Set of 5* .... 2·00 1·40

(Des D. Cojoc. Photo)

1998 (10 June). World Cup Football Championship, France. Sheet 74×104 mm containing T **1269** and similar vert designs. Each dull ultramarine, red-brown and green. P 13½.
MS5943 800l. Type **1269**; 1050l. Player in air; 1850l. Player bouncing ball off knee; 4150l. Player preparing to kick ball .... 4·75 4·75

700 L (**1270**) 1500 L (**1271**)

1998 (30 June). Nos. 5615/17 and 5620 surch as T **1270**.
5944 700l. on 125l. turquoise-green and black (Mag.) 60 40
5945 800l. on 35l. turquoise-green and black (B.) 60 40
5946 1050l. on 45l. turquoise-green and black 60 40
5947 4150l. on 15l. turquoise-green and black (R.) 60 40
5944/5947 *Set of 4* .... 2·20 1·40

1998 (6 July). Nos. 5352 and 5355 surch as T **1271**.
5948 1000l. on 9l. brown-lake 60 40
5949 1500l. on 5l. slate-violet (R.) 60 40

1272 Brown Kiwi (*Apteryx australis*)

350 L

(**1273**)

(Des P. Comisarschi. Photo)

1998 (12 Aug). Nocturnal Birds. T **1272** and similar multicoloured designs. P 13½.
5950 700l. Type **1272** 45 30
5951 1500l. Barn owl (*Tyto alba*) 60 40
5952 1850l. Water rail (*Rallus aquaticus*) 70 45
5953 2450l. European nightjar (*Caprimulgus europaeus*) .... 1·70 1·20
5950/5953 *Set of 4* .... 3·00 2·10

1998 (15 Sept). No. 5361 surch as T **1273**, the old value cancelled by a sign of the zodiac.
5954 **1273** 250l. on 45l. ultramarine (Aries) (B.) 60 40
5955 350l. on 45l. ultramarine (Taurus) ... 60 40
5956 400l. on 45l. ultramarine (Gemini) (G.) 60 40
5957 450l. on 45l. ultramarine (Cancer) (Mag.) 60 40
5958 850l. on 45l. ultramarine (Leo) (O.) .. 60 40
5959 900l. on 45l. ultramarine (Aquarius) (V.) 60 40
5960 1000l. on 45l. ultramarine (Libra) (G.) 60 40
5961 1600l. on 45l. ultramarine (Scorpio) (Br.) .... 1·20 80
5962 2500l. on 45l. ultramarine (Sagittarius) (R.) .... 4·75 3·50
5954/5962 *Set of 9* .... 9·25 6·50

1274 81p. Stamp and Waslui Cancellation

1998 (17 Sept). 140th Anniv of Bull's Head Issue of Moldavia. T **1274** and similar horiz design. Multicoloured. Photo. P 13½.
5963 700l. Type **1274** 60 40
5964 1050l. 27p. stamp and Jassy cancellation 70 45
MS5965 130×80 mm. 4150l.+850l. 54 and 108p. stamps and Galatz cancellation (53×41 mm) .... 3·50 3·50
Nos. 5963/4 were each also issued in booklets of four stamps.

1275 Soldiers and Revolutionaries fighting

1276 Nikolaus Lenau (poet)

1998 (28 Sept). 150th Anniv of the 1848 Revolutions. Photo. P 13½.
5966 **1275** 1050l. black, olive-yellow and scarlet 60 40

(Des D. Tăran. Photo)

1998 (16 Oct). German Personalities of Banat. T **1276** and similar vert designs. P 13½.
5967 800l. pale orange, black and pink 45 35
5968 1850l. pale orange, black and apple green . 80 65
5969 4150l. pale orange, black and light blue ...... 1·70 1·40
5967/5969 *Set of 3* .... 2·75 2·50
Design:—1850l. Stefan Jäger (artist); 4150l. Adam Müller-Guttenbrunn (writer).
Nos. 5967/9 were each issued in sheets of eight stamps and one label.

1277 Diver and Marine Life

50L

(**1278**)

(Des Silvia Cumpătă. Photo)

1998 (4 Nov). International Year of the Ocean. P 13½.
5970 **1277** 1100l. multicoloured 60 45

1998 (10 Nov). Nos. 5336/7 surch as T **1278**, the old value cancelled by a sporting emblem.

5971	50l. on 1l. multicoloured (Type **1278**) (G.)	60	45
5972	50l. on 1l. multicoloured (Trophy)	60	45

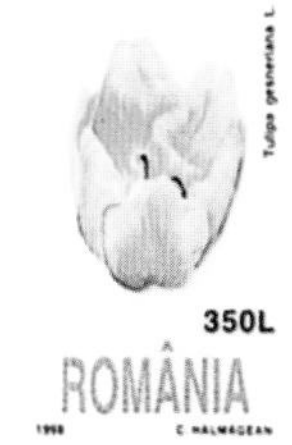

1279 *Tulipa gesneriana*

(**1280**)

(Des C. Hâlmăgean. Photo)

1998 (25 Nov). Flowers. T **1279** and similar vert designs. Multicoloured. P 13½.

5973	350l. Type **1279**	25	20
5974	850l. *Dahlia variabilis* "Rubin"	45	35
5975	1100l. Martagon lily (*Lilium martagon*)	60	45
5976	4450l. *Rosa centifolia*	2·30	1·90
5973/5976 *Set of 4*		3·25	2·50

No. 5975 commemorates the 50th anniv of the Horticulture Institute, Bucharest.

Nos. 5973/6 were each issued in sheets of ten stamps and two labels illustrating the relevant plant.

1998 (27 Nov). Various stamps surch as T **1280**.

(a) Nos. 5399/5404, the old value cancelled by a transport emblem

5977	50l. on 1l. deep yellow-brown, greenish blue and deep greenish blue (Type **1280**)	25	20
5978	50l. on 4l. yellowish green, bright lilac and reddish violet (Steam locomotive) (R.)	25	20
5979	50l. on 5l. olive-brown, dull ultramarine and ultramarine (Lorry) (R.)	25	20
5980	50l. on 5l. dull ultramarine, chestnut and brown-lake (Helicopter)	25	20
5981	50l. on 9l. brown-lake, turquoise-blue and deep turquoise blue (Airplane)	25	20
5982	50l. on 10l. slate-black, light reddish brown and reddish brown (Ship) (R.)	25	20

(b) Nos. 5472/5 and 5477, the old value cancelled by a bird emblem

5983	50l. on 6l. yellow-green and violet (Cockerel) (Mag.)	25	20
5984	50l. on 7l. deep magenta, purple and emerald (Duck) (Ult.)	25	20
5985	50l. on 9l. indigo and deep mauve (Swan)	25	20
5986	50l. on 10l. yellow-brown, bistre-brown and ultramarine (Dove) (G.)	25	20
5987	50l. on 30l. slate-green and blue (Swallow) (R.)	25	20
5977/5987 *Set of 11*		2·50	2·00

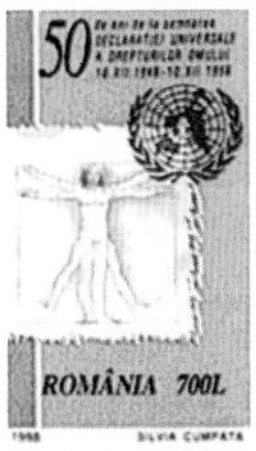

1281 "Proportions of Man" (Leonardo Da Vinci)

1282 Paciurea

(Des Silvia Cumpătă. Photo)

1998 (10 Dec). 50th Anniv of Universal Declaration of Human Rights. P 13½.

5988	**1281**	50l. multicoloured	60	45

(Des E. Palade. Photo)

1998 (11 Dec). 125th Birth Anniv of Dimitrie Paciurea (sculptor). P 13½.

5989	**1282**	850l. multicoloured	60	45

1283 Eclipse

(Des N. Nobilescu. Photo)

1998 (17 Dec). Total Eclipse of the Sun (11 Aug 1999). P 13½.

5990	**1283**	1100l. multicoloured	60	45

No. 5990 was issued with *se-tenant* half stamp-size label showing a diagram of the eclipse.

See also No. 6050.

1284 Sinking of *Titanic* (liner), 1912

(**1285**)

(Des S. Zamşa. Photo)

1998 (22 Dec). The 20th Century (2nd series). T **1284** and similar horiz designs. P 13½.

5991	350l. black, pale blue and vermilion	25	20
5992	1100l. multicoloured	45	35
5993	1600l. multicoloured	60	45
5994	2000l. multicoloured	70	55
5995	2600l. black, grey and vermilion	1·40	1·10
5991/5995 *Set of 5*		3·00	2·40

Designs:—1100l. Henri Coandă and his turbine-powered model airplane, 1910; 1600l. Louis Blériot and his Blériot XI airplane (first powered flight across English Channel, 1909); 2000l. Freighter in locks and map of American sea routes (opening of Panama Canal, 1914); 2600l. Prisoners in courtyard (Russian October revolution, 1917).

1998 (22 Dec). Nos. 5491 and 5674 surch as T **1285**, the old value cancelled by a Christmas emblem.

5996	2000l. on 15l. multicoloured (Type **1285**) (G.)	95	75
5997	2600l. on 60l. multicoloured (Father Christmas) (R.)	95	75

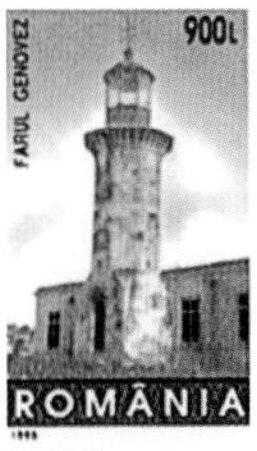

1286 Gonovez Lighthouse

1287 Arnota Monastery

1998 (28 Dec). Lighthouses. T **1286** and similar vert designs. Multicoloured. Photo. P 13½.

5998	900l. Type **1286**	25	20
5999	1000l. Constanţa	35	30
6000	1100l. Sfântu Gheorghe	45	35
6001	2600l. Sulina	1·60	1·30
5998/6001 *Set of 4*		2·40	1·90

(Des G. Leahu. Photo)

1999 (15 Jan). Monasteries. T **1287** and similar horiz designs. Multicoloured. P 13½.

6002	500l. Type **1287**	25	20
6003	700l. Bistrita	35	30
6004	1100l. Dintr'un Lemn	45	35
6005	2100l. Govora	60	45
6006	4850l. Tismana	1·70	1·40
6002/6006 *Set of 5*		3·00	2·40

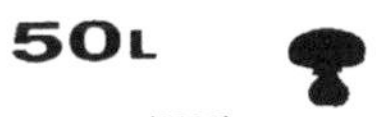

(**1288**)

(**1289**)

1999 (15 Jan). No. 5492 surch as T **1288**, the previous value cancelled by a different fungus emblem.

6007	**1288**	50l. on 15l. black, bright carmine and blue (Blk.)	25	20
6008		50l. on 15l. black, bright carmine and blue (R.)	25	20
6009		400l. on 15l. black, bright carmine and blue (G.)	25	20
6010		2300l. on 15l. black, bright carmine and blue (Br.)	60	45
6011		3200l. on 15l. black, bright carmine and blue (Dp V.)	1·20	95
6007/6011 *Set of 5*			2·30	1·80

1999 (10 Feb). No. 5384 surch as T **1289**, the previous value cancelled by a musical instrument.

6012	100l. on 1l. greenish blue (Type **1289**) (R.)	25	20
6013	250l. on 1l. greenish blue (saxophone) (Blk.)	35	30

1290 *Magnolia soulangiana*

L50

(D **1291**)

(Des Claudia Tache. Photo)

1999 (15 Feb). Shrubs. T **1290** and similar horiz designs. Multicoloured. P 13½.

6014	350l. Type **1290**	10	10
6015	1000l. *Stewartia malacodendron*	25	20
6016	1100l. *Hibiscus rosa-sinensis*	35	30
6017	5350l. *Clematis patens*	2·30	1·90
6014/6017 *Set of 4*		2·75	2·30

1999 (12 Mar). POSTAGE DUE. Nos. D4762/4 and D4766 surch as Type D **1291** on both stamps in the pair.

D6018	50l. on 50b. orange-yellow (G.)	25	20
D6019	50l. on 1l. rose-vermilion (B.)	25	20
D6020	100l. on 2l. light green	25	20
D6021	700l. on 1l. rose-vermilion	25	20
D6022	1100l. on 4l. ultramarine	25	20
D6018/6022 *Set of 5*		1·10	90

On No. D6018 the surcharge reads "L50".

1292 Easter Eggs

(Des Claudia Tache. Photo)

1999 (15 Mar). Easter. P 13½.

6023	**1292**	1100l. multicoloured	60	45

(**1293**) (Brontosaurus)

1294 Girdle of Keys (Pădureni)

1999 (22 Mar). No. 5799 surch as T **1293**, the previous value cancelled by a dinosaur emblem.

6024	**1293**	100l. on 70l. yellow and black (Type **1293**) (Mag.)	25	20
6025		100l. on 70l. yellow and black (Iguanodon) (R.)	25	20
6026		200l. on 70l. yellow and black (Allosaurus) (Dp V.)	25	20
6027		1500l. on 70l. yellow and black (Diplodocus) (Blk.)	30	25
6028		1600l. on 70l. yellow and black (Tyrannosaurus) (G.)	35	30
6029		3200l. on 70l. yellow and black (Stegosaurus) (B.)	80	65
6030		6000l. on 70l. yellow and black (Plateosaurus) (G.)	1·50	1·20
6024/6030 *Set of 7*			3·25	2·75

(Des Stela Lie. Photo)

1999 (29 Mar). Jewellery. T **1294** and similar multicoloured designs. P 13½.

6031	1200l. Type **1294**	25	20
6032	2100l. Pendant of keys (Ilia, Hunedoara)	45	35
6033	2600l. Jewelled bib (Maramureş)	60	45
6034	3200l. Necklace (Banat) (horiz)	1·70	1·40
6031/6034 *Set of 4*		2·75	2·20

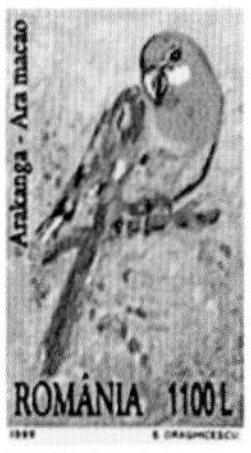

1295 Scarlet Macaw (*Ara macao*)

1296 Council Flag and Headquarters, Strasbourg

(Des Sylvia Drăghicescu. Photo)

1999 (26 Apr). Birds. T **1295** and similar vert designs. Multicoloured. P 13½.

6035	1100l. Type **1295**	25	20
6036	2700l. White peafowl (*Pavo albus*)	60	45
6037	3700l. Common peafowl (*Pavo cristatus*)	80	65
6038	5700l. Sulphur-crested cockatoo (*Cacatua galerita*)	1·30	1·00
6035/6038 *Set of 4*		2·75	2·10

(Des O. Penda. Photo)

1999 (5 May). 50th Anniv of Council of Europe. P 13½.

6039	**1296**	2300l. multicoloured	1·20	95

No. 6039 was issued with *se-tenant* half stamp-size label which continues the design.

1297 St. Peter's Cathedral, Rome

1298 Common Shoveler (*Anas clypeata*)

(Des C. Furnea. Photo)

1999 (7 May). Papal Visit. T **1297** and similar vert designs. P 13½.

6040	1300l. dull mauve and black	95	75
	a. Sheetlet. Nos. 6040/1, 6042×2, 6043×2 plus 2 labels	4·75	
6041	1600l. dull mauve and black	1·00	85
6042	2300l. multicoloured	1·20	95
6043	6300l. multicoloured	1·30	1·00
6040/6043 *Set of 4*		4·00	3·25

Designs:—1600l. Patriarchal Cathedral, Bucharest; 2300l. Father Teoctist (patriarch of Romanian Orthodox church); 6300l. Pope John Paul II (after Dina Bellotti).

Nos. 6040/3 were issued together in *se-tenant* sheetlets containing Nos. 6040/1, two examples each of Nos. 6042/3 and two labels showing either the Papal arms or the arms of the Romanian Orthodox Church.

(Des Silvia Cumpătă. Photo)

1999 (17 May). Europa. Parks and Gardens. The Danube Delta Nature Reserve. T **1298** and similar vert design. Multicoloured. P 13½.

6044 1100l. Type **1298** ... 60 45
6045 5700l. Black stork (*Ciconia nigra*) ... 1·70 1·40

Nos. 6044/5 were each issued in sheetlets of six stamps and two labels showing silhouettes of birds.

1299 Gheorghe Cârtan (historian, 150th birth anniv)

(Des O. Penda. Photo)

1999 (31 May). Anniversaries. T **1299** and similar horiz designs. P 13½.

6046 600l. green, black and scarlet ... 10 10
6047 1100l. blackish purple, black and scarlet ... 25 20
6048 2600l. turquoise, black and scarlet ... 45 35
6049 7300l. reddish brown, black and scarlet ... 2·00 1·60
6046/6049 *Set of 4* ... 2·50 2·00

Designs:—1100l. George Călinescu (critic and novelist, birth centenary); 2600l. Johann Wolfgang von Goethe (dramatist, 250th birth anniv); 7300l. Honoré de Balzac (novelist, birth bicentenary).

1300 Moon Eclipsing Sun

(Des O. Penda. Photo)

1999 (21 June). Total Eclipse of the Sun (11 August) (2nd issue). P 13½.

6050 **1300** 1100l. multicoloured ... 60 45

No. 6050 was issued with *se-tenant* half stamp-size label.

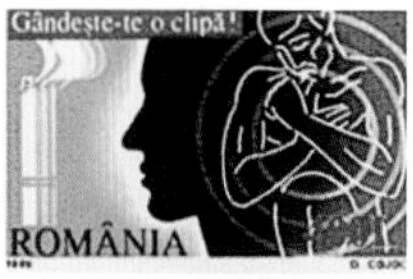

1301 Cigarette and Man with Arms Crossed

(Des D. Cojoc. Photo)

1999 (29 July). Public Health Awareness Campaign. T **1301** and similar horiz designs. Multicoloured. P 13½.

6051 400l. Type **1301** (anti-smoking) ... 10 10
6052 800l. Bottles and man cradling glass and bottle (alcohol abuse) ... 25 20
6053 1300l. Cannabis leaf, pills and man injecting arm (drugs) ... 35 30
6054 2500l. Profiles and man on intravenous drip (HIV) ... 45 35
6051/6054 *Set of 4* ... 1·00 85

1302 Eclipse and Pavarotti

(Des Liliana Ignat. Photo)

1999 (9 Aug). Luciano Pavarotti's (opera singer) Concert on Day of Eclipse (11 August), Bucharest. P 13½.

6055 **1302** 8100l. multicoloured ... 3·00 2·30

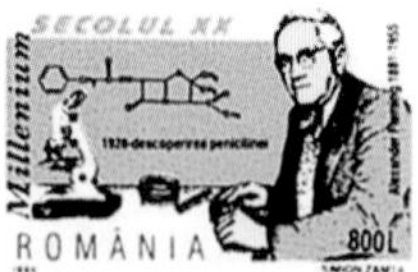

1303 Alexander Fleming (bacteriologist)

(Des S. Zamşa. Photo)

1999 (30 Aug). The 20th Century (3rd series). T **1303** and similar horiz designs. Multicoloured. P 13½.

6056 800l. Type **1303** (discovery of penicillin, 1928) ... 25 20
6057 3000l. "Swords into Ploughshares" (sculpture) and map of Europe, Africa and Asia (foundation of League of Nations, 1920) ... 60 45
6058 7300l. Harold Clayton Urey (chemist) (discovery of heavy water, 1932) ... 1·50 1·20
6059 17000l. Deep sea drilling (first oil platform, Beaumont, Texas, 1934) ... 4·00 3·25
6056/6059 *Set of 4* ... 5·75 4·50

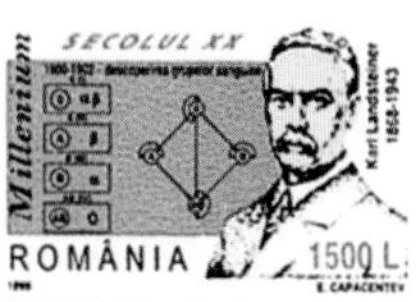

1304 Karl Landsteiner (pathologist)

1305 Posthorn in Envelope and Berne

(Des Elena Caracenţev. Photo)

1999 (24 Sept). The 20th Century (4th series). T **1304** and similar horiz designs. P 13½.

6060 1500l. red-orange, black and yellow ... 25 20
6061 3000l. ochre, black and pale chestnut ... 60 45
6062 7300l. multicoloured ... 1·50 1·20
6063 17000l. multicoloured ... 4·00 3·25
6060/6063 *Set of 4* ... 5·75 4·50

Designs:—1500l. Type **1304** (discovery of blood groups, 1900–02); 3000l. Nicolae Paulescu (biochemist) (discovery of insulin, 1921); 7300l. Otto Hahn (radiochemist) (discovery of nuclear fission, 1938); 17000l. Ernst Ruska (electrical engineer) (designer of first electron microscope, 1931).

(Des O. Penda. Photo)

1999 (9 Oct). 125th Anniv of Universal Postal Union. P 13½.

6064 **1305** 3100l. multicoloured ... 1·70 1·40

1306 Grigore Vasiliu Birlic

1307 Monastery

(Des Liliana Ignat. Photo)

1999 (21 Oct). Comic Actors. T **1306** and similar designs. Each slate-purple, black and red. P 13½.

6065 900l. Type **1306** ... 25 20
6066 1500l. Toma Caragiu ... 35 30
6067 3100l. Constantin Tănase ... 60 45
6068 7950l. Charlie Chaplin ... 1·70 1·40
6069 8850l. Stan Laurel and Oliver Hardy (horiz) ... 2·30 1·90
6065/6069 *Set of 5* ... 4·75 3·75

(Des Simona Bucan. Photo)

1999 (29 Oct). 275th Anniv of Stavropoleos Church. P 13½.

6070 **1307** 2100l. reddish brown, stone and black ... 60 45

1308 Snowboarding

1309 Christmas Tree and Bell

(Des I. Pâcev. Photo)

1999 (10 Nov). New Olympic Sports. T **1308** and similar horiz designs. Multicoloured. P 13½.

6071 1600l. Type **1308** ... 50 40
6072 1700l. Softball ... 60 45
6073 7950l. Taekwondo ... 1·70 1·40
6071/6073 *Set of 3* ... 2·50 2·00

(Des Rodica Coteanu. Photo)

1999 (29 Nov). Christmas. T **1309** and similar vert design. Multicoloured. P 13½.

6074 1500l. Type **1309** ... 35 30
6075 3100l. Father Christmas with presents ... 60 45

1310 Child as Flower (Antonela Vieriu)

1311 Diana, Princess of Wales

1999 (30 Nov). Tenth Anniv of UN Convention on the Rights of the Child. T **1310** and similar multicoloured designs. Photo. P 13½.

6076 900l. Type **1310** ... 25 20
6077 3400l. Girl writing numbers (Ana-Maria Bulete) (vert) ... 60 45
6078 8850l. Group of people (Maria-Luiza Rogojeanu) ... 2·10 1·70
6076/6078 *Set of 3* ... 2·75 2·10

1999 (2 Dec). Diana, Princess of Wales Commemoration. Photo. P 13½.

6079 **1311** 6000l. multicoloured ... 1·70 1·40

No. 6079 was issued in sheetlets of four stamps with an enlarged top margin.

1312 Ferrari 365 GTB/4, 1968

1999 (17 Dec). Birth Centenary (1998) of Enzo Ferrari (car designer). T **1312** and similar horiz designs. Multicoloured. Photo. P 13½.

6080 1500l. Type **1312** ... 25 20
6081 1600l. Dino 246 GT, 1970 ... 35 30
6082 1700l. 365 GT/4BB, 1973 ... 60 45
6083 7950l. Mondial 3.2, 1985 ... 1·70 1·40
6084 8850l. F 355, 1994 ... 1·90 1·50
6085 14500l. 456 MGT, 1998 ... 3·50 2·75
6080/6085 *Set of 6* ... 7·50 6·00

1313 Child with Romanian Flag

(Des O. Penda. Photo)

1999 (21 Dec). Tenth Anniv of Popular Uprising. P 13½.

6086 **1313** 2100l. multicoloured ... 60 45

1314 European Union Flag

(Des D.C. Communication. Photo)

2000 (13 Jan). European Union Membership Negotiations. P 13½.

6087 **1314** 6100l. multicoloured ... 1·70 1·40

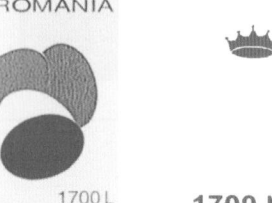

1315 Mihail Eminescu

1316 Cupid

(Des E. Karacentev. Photo)

2000 (15 Jan). 150th Birth Anniv of Mihail Eminescu (poet). Sheet 120×92 mm containing T **1315** and similar horiz designs. Each olive-grey, agate and black. P 13½.

MS6088 3400l. Type **1315**; 3400l. Eminescu and people seated at table; 3400l. Eminescu and star shining over woman; 3400l. Eminescu and three men ... 4·75 4·75

(Des D. Cojoc. Photo)

2000 (1 Feb). Valentine's Day. T **1316** and similar vert design. Multicoloured. P 13½.

6089 1500l. Type **1316** ... 60 45
6090 7950l. Couple ... 1·70 1·40

Designs of the same value were arranged in two horizontal tête-bêche rows throughout the sheet.

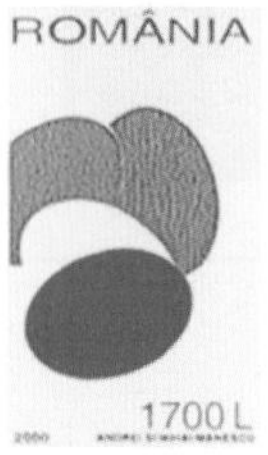

1317 Easter Eggs

1700 L

(**1318**)

(Des A. and M. Mănescu. Photo)

2000 (29 Feb). Easter. P 13½.

6091 **1317** 1700l. new blue, bright yellowish green and bright orange ... 60 45

2000 (13–14 Mar). Nos. 5855 and 5842 surch as T **1318** in red, the old value cancelled by a different emblem.

6092 1700l. on 70l. multicoloured (Type **1318**) ... 60 45
6093 1700l. on 70l. multicoloured (snake) (14.3.00) ... 60 45

1900 L

1319 Greater Bird of Paradise (*Paradisaea apoda*)

(**1320**)

(Des C. Dénes. Photo)

2000 (20 Mar). Birds of Paradise. T **1319** and similar horiz designs. Multicoloured. P 13½.

6094	1700l. Type **1319**	60	45
6095	2400l. Magnificent bird of paradise (*Diphyllodes magnificus*)	1·20	95
6096	9050l. Superb bird of paradise (*Lophorina superba*)	1·70	1·40
6097	10050l. King bird of paradise (*Cicinnurus regius*)	2·30	1·90
6094/6097	*Set of 4*	5·25	4·25

2000 (31 Mar). Nos. 5342/3 surch with T **1320** in carmine.

6098	1900l. on 1l. multicoloured	60	45
6099	2000l. on 1l. multicoloured	60	45

(**1321**)

1322 Cineraria (*Senecio cruentus*)

2000 (12 Apr). Nos. 5310/14 surch in black as T **1321**, the previous value cancelled by various book and quill emblems.

6100	1700l. on 50b. sepia and black	45	35
6101	1700l. on 1l.50 emerald and deep mauve	45	35
6102	1700l. on 2l. brown-lake and blue	45	35
6103	1700l. on 3l. blue and orange-brown	45	35
6104	1700l. on 4l. reddish brown and deep bright blue	45	35
6100/6104	*Set of 5*	2·00	1·60

(Des Elena Karacentev. Photo)

2000 (20 Apr). Flowers. T **1322** and similar vert designs. Multicoloured. P 13½.

6105	1700l. Type **1322**	25	20
6106	3100l. Indoor lily (*Clivia miniata*)	45	35
6107	5800l. Plumeria (*Plumeria rubra*)	1·40	1·10
6108	10050l. Fuschia (*Fuschia hybrida*)	2·10	1·70
6105/6108	*Set of 4*	3·75	3·00

1700 L

(**1323**)

1324 "Building Europe"

2000 (24 Apr). Nos. 5303/7 surch in black as T **1323**, the previous value cancelled by an easel with palette emblem.

6109	1700l. on 50b. multicoloured	45	35
6110	1700l. on 1l.50 multicoloured	45	35
6111	1700l. on 2l. multicoloured	45	35
6112	1700l. on 3l. multicoloured	45	35
6113	1700l. on 4l. multicoloured	45	35
6109/6113	*Set of 5*	2·00	1·60

(Des J.-P. Cousin. Photo)

2000 (9 May). Europa. P 13½.

6114	**1324** 10150l. multicoloured	3·50	2·75

1700 L

(**1325**)

1700 L

(**1326**)

2000 (17 May). Death Centenary of Vincent van Gogh (artist). Nos. 5318 and 5321 surch in carmine-vermilion with T **1325**.

6115	1700l. on 50b. multicoloured	60	45
6116	1700l. on 3l.50 multicoloured	60	45

2000 (19 May). No. 5642 surch in carmine-vermilion as T **1326**, the previous value cancelled by an airship.

6117	1700l. on 635l. black, ultramarine and blue	60	45
6118	2000l. on 635l. black, ultramarine and blue	1·20	95
6119	3900l. on 635l. black, ultramarine and blue	1·20	95
6120	9050l. on 635l. black, ultramarine and blue	1·20	95
6117/6120	*Set of 4*	3·75	3·00

1327 Mihai the Brave and Soldiers

(Des N. Nobilescu (6122). Photo)

2000 (19 May). Anniversaries. T **1327** and similar multicoloured design. P 13½.

6121	3800l. Type **1327** (400th anniv of first union of the Romanian provinces (Wallachia, Transylvania and Moldavia))	95	75
6122	9050l. Printing press (550th anniv of the 42 line Bible (first Bible printed in Latin)) (36×23 mm)	2·00	1·60

10000 L

(**1328**)

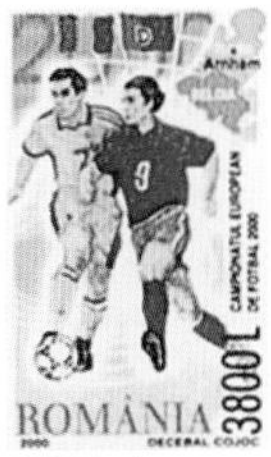

1329 Arnhem, Players and Flags of Romania and Portugal

2000 (31 May). No. 5801 surch in carmine-vermilion as T **1328**, the previous value cancelled by a flower.

6123	10000l. on 370l. orange-brown and black	1·70	1·40
6124	19000l. on 370l. orange-brown and black	3·50	2·75
6125	34000l. on 370l. orange-brown and black	6·50	5·00
6123/6125	*Set of 3*	10·50	8·25

(Des D. Cojoc. Photo)

2000 (20 June). European Football Championship, The Netherlands and Belgium. Sheet 82×121 mm containing T **1329** and similar vert designs, each showing a map of Europe pinpointing the named town. Multicoloured. P 13½.

MS6126 3800l. Type **1329**; 3800l. Players, Charleroi and English and Romanian flags; 10150l. Players, Liege and Romanian and German flags; 10150l. Goalkeeper and Rotterdam 5·75 5·75

1330 Ferdinand von Zeppelin and Airship

(Des S. Zamşa. Photo)

2000 (12 July). Centenary of First Zeppelin Flight. P 13½.

6127	**1330** 2100l. multicoloured	60	45

1331 Enrico Fermi (physicist) and Mathematical Equation

(**1332**)

(Des E. Cartis. Photo)

2000 (24 July). The 20th Century (5th series). T **1331** and similar horiz designs. P 13½.

6128	2100l. black, greenish grey and bright carmine	45	35
6129	2200l. black and brownish grey	75	60
6130	2400l. deep rose-red and black	80	65
6131	6000l. multicoloured	85	70
6128/6131	*Set of 4*	2·50	2·10

Designs:—2100l. Type **1331** (construction of first nuclear reactor, 1942); 2200l. United Nations Charter (signing of charter, 1945); 2400l. Edith Piaf (singer) (release of *La Vie en Rose* (song), 1947); 6131l. Sir Edmond Percival Hillary (mountaineer) (conquest of Mt. Everest, 1953).

2000 (31 July). No. 5365 surch with T **1332** in green.

6132	1700l. on 160l. vermilion and brown-rose	60	45

1333 Globe and "Sputnik 1" Satellite

(Des E. Cartis. Photo)

2000 (28 Aug). The 20th Century (6th series). T **1333** and similar horiz designs. P 13½.

6133	1700l. multicoloured	35	30
6134	3900l. multicoloured	1·40	1·10
6135	6400l. black and bright carmine	1·50	1·20
6136	11300l. multicoloured	1·60	1·30
6133/6136	*Set of 4*	4·25	3·50

Designs:—1700l. Type **1333** (launch of first man-made satellite, 1957); 3900l. Yuri Gagarin (first manned space flight, 1961); 6400l. Surgeons operating (first heart transplant operation, 1967); 11300l. Edwin E. Aldrin and moon (first manned landing on moon, 1969).

1334 Boxing

1335 Gabriela Szabo (athlete) and Emblem

(Des I. Pîcev. Photo)

2000 (7 Sept). Olympic Games, Sydney. T **1334** and similar multicoloured designs. P 13½.

6137	1700l. Type **1334**	45	35
6138	2200l. High jump	50	40
6139	3900l. Weightlifting	60	45
6140	6200l. Gymnastics	1·50	1·20
6137/6140	*Set of 4*	2·75	2·20
MS6141	89×78 mm. 11300l. Athletics (41×53 mm)	3·00	3·00

2000 (8 Sept). Olymphilex 2000 International Olympic Stamp Exhibition, Sydney. Sheet 81×60 mm. Photo. Imperf.

MS6142	**1335** 14100l. multicoloured	3·50	3·50

1336 Palace of Agriculture Ministry

(Des V. Pogolsa. Photo)

2000 (29 Sept). Bucharest Palaces. T **1336** and similar designs. P 13½.

6143	1700l. black and bluish grey	45	35
6144	2200l. black and stone (horiz)	50	40
6145	2400l. black and pale sage-green (horiz)	60	45
6146	3900l. black and light olive-sepia (horiz)	70	55
6143/6146	*Set of 4*	2·00	1·60

Designs:—2200l. Cantacuzino Palace (now George Enescu Museum); 2400l. Grigore Ghica Palace; 3900l. Stirbei Palace (now Museum of Ceramics and Glass).

300L

(**1337**)

2000 (11 Oct). No. 5836 surch with T **1337** in lake-brown.

6147	300l. on 70l. multicoloured	60	45

(**1338**)

2000L

(**1339**)

2000 (26 Oct). No. 5349 surch with T **1338** in deep ultramarine.

6148	300l. on 1l. royal blue	60	45

2000 (27 Oct). AIR. No. 5695 surch in scarlet as T **1339**.

6149	2000l. on 960l. greenish blue and black	25	20
6150	4200l. on 960l. greenish blue and black	60	45
6151	4600l. on 960l. greenish blue and black	95	75
6152	6500l. on 960l. greenish blue and black	1·20	95
6149/6152	*Set of 4*	2·75	2·10

1340 Ilie Ilascu (political prisoner)

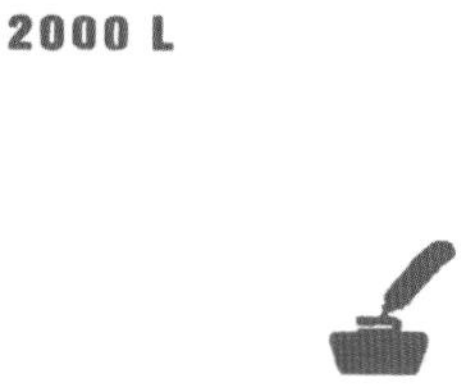

(**1341**)

(Des A. Mănescu. Photo)

2000 (3 Nov). 50th Anniv of United Nations Convention on Human Rights. P 13½.

6153	**1340** 11300l. multicoloured	3·00	2·30

2000 (3 Nov). No. 5700 surch in deep magenta with T **1341**.

6154	2000l. on 90l. multicoloured	60	45

(**1342**)

2000 (28 Nov). No. 5556 surch in black with T **1342**.

6155	2000l. on 29l. flesh, black and rose-lilac	60	45

1343 Leopard (*Panthera pardus*)

1344 Camil Ressu

(Des Silvia Cumpătă. Photo)

2000 (29 Nov). Big Cats. T **1343** and similar horiz designs. P 13½.

6156	1200l. multicoloured	10	10
6157	2000l. new blue and black	25	20
6158	2200l. multicoloured	30	25
6159	2300l. multicoloured	35	30
6160	4200l. brown, slate-blue and black	60	45
6161	6500l. multicoloured	1·70	1·40
6156/6161	*Set of 6*	3·00	1·50
MS6162	90×78 mm. 14100l. multicoloured	3·50	3·50

Designs: As Type **1343**—2000l. Snow leopard (*Panthera uncia*); 2200l. Lion (*Panthera leo*); 2300l. Bobcat (*Lynx rufus*); 4200l. Mountain lion (*Puma concolor*); 6500l. Tiger (*Panthera tigris*); 53×41 mm—14100l. Lions.

2000 (8–13 Dec). Self-portraits. T **1344** and similar vert designs. Multicoloured. Photo. P 13½.

6163	2000l. Type **1344**	25	20
6164	2400l. Jean Al Steriadi (13.12)	35	30
6165	4400l. Nicolae Tonitza (13.12)	60	45
6166	15000l. Nicolae Grigorescu (13.12)	3·00	2·30
6163/6166	*Set of 4*	3·75	3·00

1345 Christmas Tree

1346 Jesus Christ and Angel

(Des A. and M. Mănescu. Photo)

2000 (15 Dec). Christmas. P 13½.

6167	**1345** 4400l. multicoloured	60	45

2000 (22 Dec). Birth Bimillenary of Jesus Christ. T **1346** and similar vert design. Multicoloured. Photo. P 13½.

6168	2000l. Type **1346**	25	20
6169	7000l. Jesus Christ and dove (22×38 mm)	1·50	1·20

(**1347**)

2000 (28 Dec). No. 5624 surch in lake-brown as T **1347**, the previous value cancelled by different animals.

6170	7000l. on 3095l. Large-leaved lime (Type **1347**)	2·00	1·60
6171	10000l. on 3095l. Large-leaved lime (bear)	2·00	1·60
6172	11500l. on 3095l. Large-leaved lime (cow)	2·00	1·60
6170/6172	*Set of 3*	5·50	4·25

(D **1348**)

2001 (17 Jan). POSTAGE DUE. Nos. D5417 and D5587 surch as Type D **1348** on both stamps in the pair.

D6173	500l. on 4l. scarlet	10	10
D6174	1000l. on 4l. scarlet	25	20
D6175	2000l. on 45l. orange	45	35
D6173/6175	*Set of 3*	70	60

1349 Globe and Fireworks

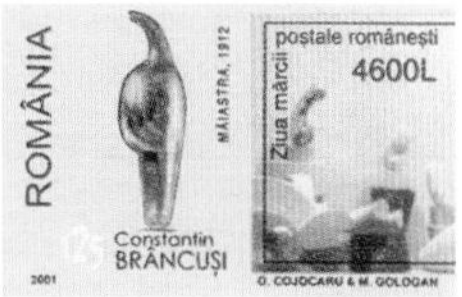

1350 Sculpture

(Des O. Cojocaru. Photo)

2001 (17 Jan). New Millennium. P 13½.

6176	**1349** 11500l. multicoloured	2·30	1·90

(Des O. Cojocaru and M. Gologan. Photo)

2001 (2 Feb). 125th Birth Anniv of Constantin Brancuşi (sculptor). T **1350** and similar horiz design. Multicoloured. P 13½.

6177	4600l. Type **1350**	70	55
	a. Horiz pair. Nos. 6177/8	1·80	1·50
6178	7200l. Display of sculptures	1·00	85

Nos. 6177/8 were issued together in horizontal *se-tenant* pairs, each pair forming a composite design.

(**1351**)

1352 Ribbons forming Heart

2001 (9 Feb). No. 5542 surch as T **1351**, the previous value cancelled by different snakes.

6179	7400l. on 280l. black and orange-yellow (B.)	1·20	95
6180	13000l. on 280l. black and orange-yellow (C.)	2·30	1·90

(Des F. Ciuca (2200l.), A. Tintu (11500l.). Photo)

2001 (15 Feb). Valentine's Day. T **1352** and similar vert design. Each bright scarlet and greenish slate. P 13½.

6181	2200l. Type **1352**	25	20
6182	11500l. Pierced heart	1·60	1·30

(**1353**)

2001 (21 Feb). Nos. 5595/6 and 5598 surch as T **1353**, the previous value cancelled by an ear of corn.

6183	1300l. on 245l. multicoloured (C.)	25	20
6184	2200l. on 115l. multicoloured (C.)	35	30
6185	5000l. on 115l. multicoloured (G.)	70	55
6186	16500l. on 70l. multicoloured (C.)	3·00	2·30
6183/6186	*Set of 4*	3·75	3·00

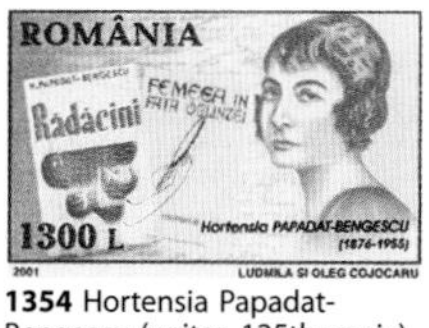

1354 Hortensia Papadat-Bengescu (writer, 125th anniv)

1355 Chick inside Egg

(Des Ludmila and O. Cojocaru. Photo)

2001 (9–15 Mar). Birth Anniversaries. T **1354** and similar horiz designs. Multicoloured. P 13½.

6187	1300l. Type **1354** (15.3)	25	20
6188	2200l. Eugen Lovinescu (writer, 120th anniv)	30	25
6189	2400l. Ion Minulescu (poet, 120th anniv) (15.3)	35	30
6190	4600l. André Malraux (writer, centenary)	60	45
6191	7200l. George H. Gallup (opinion pollster and journalist, centenary)	1·50	1·20
6192	35000l. Walt Disney (artist and film producer, centenary) (15.3)	6·50	5·50
6187/6192	*Set of 6*	8·50	7·00

(Des N. Nobilescu. Photo)

2001 (23 Mar). Easter. P 13½.

6193	**1355** 2200l. multicoloured	60	45

1356 Sloe (*Prunus spinosa*)

1357 George Hagi

(Des S. Târlea. Photo)

2001 (12 Apr). Berries. T **1356** and similar vert designs. Multicoloured. P 13½.

6194	2200l. Type **1356**	25	20
6195	4600l. Red currant (*Ribes rubrum L.*)	60	45
6196	7400l. Gooseberry (*Ribes uva-crispa*)	1·70	1·40
6197	11500l. Mountain cranberry (*Vaccinium vitis-idaea L.*)	2·10	1·70
6194/6197	*Set of 4*	4·25	3·50

2001 (23 Apr). Retirement of George Hagi (footballer). Photo. P 13½.

6198	**1357** 2200l. multicoloured	60	45

No. 6198 was issued with a *se-tenant* label.

A 35000l. imperforate miniature sheet, inscr "POŞTA AERIANĂ" and depicting Hagi, exists from a limited printing.

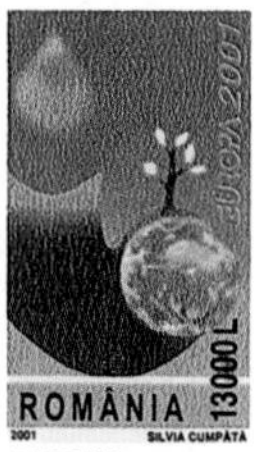

1358 Water Droplet and Globe surmounted by Tree

1359 Collie

(Des Sylvia Cumpătă. Photo)

2001 (4 May). Europa. Water Resources. P 13½.

6199	**1358** 13000l. multicoloured	2·30	1·90

(Des N. Nobilescu. Photo)

2001 (16 June). Dogs. T **1359** and similar horiz designs. Multicoloured. P 13½.

6200	1300l. Type **1359**	25	20
6201	5000l. Basset hound	80	65
6202	8000l. Siberian husky	1·20	95
6203	13500l. Ciobănesc mioritic	2·00	1·60
6200/6203	*Set of 4*	3·75	3·00

1360 Goddess Europa

1361 *Mariner 9* (spacecraft) and Mars

(Des O. Penda. Photo)

2001 (6 July). Romanian Presidency of Organization for Security and Co-operation in Europe. P 13½.

6204 **1360** 11500l. multicoloured ... 2·30 1·90

(Des O. Cojocaru and M. Gologan. Photo)

2001 (13 July). The 20th Century (7th series). T **1361** and similar horiz designs. Multicoloured. P 13½.

6205 1300l. Type **1361** (first orbit of Mars, 1979) 25 20
6206 2400l. Bull (discovery of Paleolithic cave paintings, Ardèche, 1994) ... 60 45
6207 5000l. Nadia Comăneci (gymnast) (first "10" for gymnastics, Olympic Games, Montreal, 1976) ... 95 75
6208 8000l. Wall (fall of the Berlin wall, 1989) ... 1·20 95
6205/6208 *Set of 4* ... 2·75 2·10

1362 George Palade (Nobel Prize winner for medicine, 1974)

(**1363**)

(Des Ludmila and O. Cojocaru. Photo)

2001 (26 July). 50th Anniv of United Nations High Commissioner for Refugees. P 13½.

6209 **1362** 13500l. multicoloured ... 2·30 1·90

2001 (20–31 Aug). Various stamps surch as T **1363**. Previous values cancelled by various emblems as stated.

6210 **1100** 300l. on 4l. multicoloured (Type **1363**) (31.8) ... 25 20
6211 **1110** 300l. on 4l. multicoloured (bob sled) (R.) (31.8) ... 25 20
6212 **1132** 300l. on 7l. multicoloured (harp) (R.) (31.8) ... 25 20
6213 – 300l. on 9l. multicoloured (No. 5488) (lyre) (R.) (31.8) ... 25 20
6214 **1168** 300l. on 90l. multicoloured (lizard) (28.8) ... 25 20
6215 **1190** 300l. on 90l. multicoloured (computer mouse) (G.) (31.8) . 25 20
6216 **1202** 300l. on 90l. multicoloured (fish) (28.8) ... 25 20
6217 – 300l. on 90l. multicoloured (No. 5745) (chess knight) (29.8) ... 25 20
6218 **1207** 300l. on 90l. multicoloured (fungi) (G.) (31.8) ... 25 20
6219 **1157** 300l. on 115l. yellow-brown, new blue and black (scroll) (R.) ... 25 20
6220 **1158** 300l. on 115l. multicoloured (train) (R.) (24.8) ... 25 20
6221 **1162** 300l. on 115l. multicoloured (rectangle) (29.8) ... 25 20
6222 – 300l. on 115l. multicoloured (No. 5602) (kite) (G.) (31.8) ... 25 20
6210/6222 *Set of 13* ... 3·00 2·30

(**1364**)

2001 (20 Aug). Nos. 5715/16 and 5720 surch as T **1364**, the previous values cancelled by a sign of the zodiac.

(a) Postage

6223 2500l. on 755l. new blue and black (Pisces) (B.) ... 35 30
6224 2500l. on 1615l. blue-green and black (Capricorn) ... 35 30

(b) AIR. Inscr "POŞTA AERIANĂ"

6225 2500l. on 715l. bright scarlet and deep grey-blue (Aquarius) (R.) ... 35 30
6223/6225 *Set of 3* ... 95 80

1365 Trap Racing

(Des Simona Bucan. Photo)

2001 (21 Aug). Equestrian Competitive Events. T **1365** and similar horiz designs. Multicoloured. P 13½.

6226 1500l. Type **1365** ... 35 30
6227 2500l. Dressage ... 45 35
6228 5300l. Show jumping ... 70 55
6229 8300l. Flat racing ... 1·40 1·10
6226/6229 *Set of 4* ... 2·50 2·10

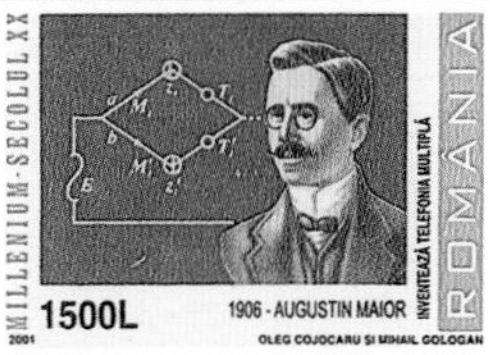

1366 Augustin Maior and Drawing

(Des O. Cojocaru and M. Gologan. Photo)

2001 (25 Sept). The 20th Century (8th series). T **1366** and similar horiz designs. Multicoloured. P 13½.

6230 1500l. Type **1366** (invention of multiple telephony, 1906) ... 35 30
6231 5300l. Pioneer 10 (satellite) (launched, 1972) ... 80 65
6232 13500l. Microchip (introduction of first microprocessor, 1971) ... 1·70 1·40
6233 15500l. Hubble space telescope (launched, 1990) ... 2·30 1·90
6230/6233 *Set of 4* ... 4·75 3·75

1367 Finger Coral (*Porites porites*)

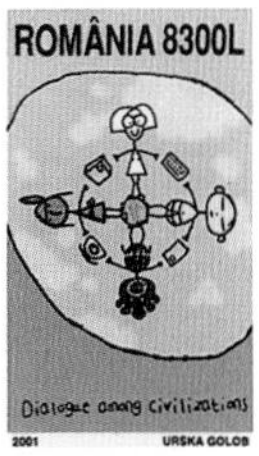

1368 Children encircling Globe

(Des O. Cojocaru. Photo)

2001 (27 Sept). Corals and Sea Anemones (1st series). T **1367** and similar horiz designs. Multicoloured. P 13½.

6234 2500l. Type **1367** ... 25 20
a. Sheetlet of 4. Nos. 6234/7 ... 8·00
6235 8300l. Giant sea anemone (*Condylactis gigantia*) ... 95 75
6236 13500l. Northern red anemone (*Anemonia telia*) ... 1·70 1·40
6237 37500l. Common sea fan (*Gorgonia ventalina*) ... 4·75 4·00
6234/6237 *Set of 4* ... 7·00 5·75

Nos. 6234/7 were issued together in *se-tenant* sheetlets of four stamps.

See also No. **MS**6260.

(Des Urska Golob. Photo)

2001 (9 Oct). United Nations Year of Dialogue among Civilizations. P 13½.

6238 **1368** 8300l. multicoloured ... 1·20 95

1369 King, Bear and Cat

(Des Cătălin Ilinca. Photo)

2001 (31 Oct). Comic Strip Cartoons. T **1369** and similar horiz designs. Multicoloured. P 13½.

6239 13500l. Type **1369** ... 1·50 1·20
a. Horiz strip of 5. Nos. 6239/43 ... 7·75
6240 13500l. Fox beating drum and kicking cat... 1·50 1·20
6241 13500l. King sleeping and fox beating drum ... 1·50 1·20
6242 13500l. Cat giving fox drum ... 1·50 1·20
6243 13500l. Drum exploding ... 1·50 1·20
6239/6243 *Set of 5* ... 6·75 5·50

Nos. 6239/43 were issued together in horizontal *se-tenant* strips of five stamps within the sheet.

1370 Top of Wreath with Baubles

(Des Simona Bucan. Photo)

2001 (5 Nov). Christmas. T **1370** and similar triangular design. Multicoloured. P 13½.

6244 2500l. Type **1370** ... 60 45
a. *se-tenant* pair. Nos. 6244/5 ... 1·30 95
6245 2500l. Bottom of wreath with stars ... 60 45

Nos. 6244/5 were issued together in *se-tenant* pairs within the sheet, each pair forming a composite design of a wreath.

Nos. 6244/5 were also issued in booklets of ten stamps (five pairs) and eight labels bearing a Christmas greeting in Romanian or English.

1371 Scorpio

(Des N. Nobilescu. Photo)

2001 (23 Nov). Signs of the Zodiac (1st series). T **1371** and similar horiz designs. Multicoloured. P 13½.

6246 1500l. Type **1371** ... 25 20
6247 2500l. Libra ... 35 30
6248 5500l. Capricorn ... 60 45
6249 9000l. Pisces ... 1·20 95
6250 13500l. Aquarius ... 1·70 1·40
6251 16500l. Sagittarius ... 2·30 1·90
6246/6251 *Set of 6* ... 5·75 4·75

See also Nos. 6254/9.

1372 Building

2001 (18 Dec). Centenary of Central Post Headquarters, Bucharest. T **1372** and similar multicoloured design. P 13½.

6252 5500l. Type **1372** ... 70 55
a. Pair. Nos. 6252/3 ... 1·50 1·20
6253 5500l. Obverse of medal showing building, 1901 (vert) ... 70 55

Nos. 6252/3 were issued together in *se-tenant* pairs within the sheet.

(Des N. Nobilescu. Photo)

2002 (4 Jan). Signs of the Zodiac (2nd series). Designs as T **1371**. Multicoloured. P 13½.

6254 1500l. Aries ... 25 20
6255 2500l. Taurus ... 35 30
6256 5500l. Gemini ... 60 45
6257 8700l. Cancer ... 1·00 85
6258 9000l. Leo ... 1·10 90
6259 23500l. Virgo ... 2·75 2·20
6254/6259 *Set of 6* ... 5·50 4·40

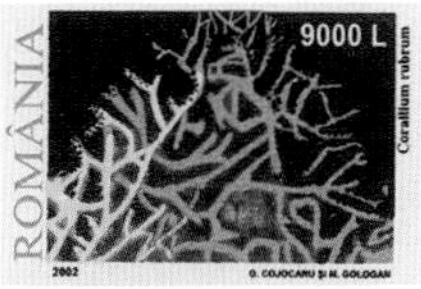

1373 Red Coral (*Corallum rubrum*)

(Des O. Cojocaru and M. Gologan. Photo)

2002 (31 Jan). Corals and Sea Anemones (2nd series). Sheet 106×77 mm containing T **1373** and similar horiz designs. Multicoloured. P 13½.

MS6260 9000l. Type **1373**; 9000l. Elkhorn coral (*Acropora palmata*); 16500l. Beadlet anemone (*Actinia equina*); 16500l. Pulmose anemone (*Metridium senile*) ... 6·50 6·50

1374 Emanuil Gojdu

(Des O. Penda. Photo)

2002 (6 Feb). Birth Bicentenary of Emanuil Gojdu (nationalist). P 13½.

6261 **1374** 2500l. black, pale blue and deep dull blue ... 60 45

1375 Mice

(Des Cătălin Ilinca. Photo)

2002 (8 Feb). St. Valentine's Day. T **1375** and similar horiz design. Multicoloured. P 13½.

6262 5500l. Type **1375** ... 70 55
6263 43500l. Elephants ... 5·25 4·75

1376 Ion Mincu

1377 Flag and Statue of Liberty

(Des Cătălin Ilinca. Photo)

2002 (1 Mar). Birth Anniversaries. T **1376** and similar horiz designs. P 13½.

6267 1500l. sage-green and black ... 25 20
6268 2500l. multicoloured ... 35 30
6269 5500l. multicoloured ... 70 55
6270 9000l. multicoloured ... 1·00 85
6271 16500l. multicoloured ... 2·00 1·60
6272 34000l. multicoloured ... 4·00 3·50
6267/6272 *Set of* 6 ... 7·50 6·25

Designs:—Type **1376** (architect) (150th); 2500l. Costin Nenitescu (chemist) (centenary); 5500l. Alexander Dumas (writer) (bicentenary); 9000l. Şerban Cioculescu (literary historian) (centenary); 16500l. Leonardo da Vinci (artist) (550th); 34000l. Victor Hugo (writer) (bicentenary).

(Des O. Penda. Photo)

2002 (22 Mar). "United We Stand". T **1377** and similar vert design. Multicoloured. P 13½.

6273 25500l. Type **1377** ... 3·00 2·30
a. Pair. Nos. 6273/4 ... 6·25 4·75
6274 25500l. Flags and monument ... 3·00 2·30

Nos. 6273/4 were issued together in horizontal *se-tenant* pairs within sheets of 20 stamps, each pair forming a composite design.

1378 Fortified Church and Tower, Saschiz

1379 Crucifixion (Picu Pătrut)

(Des Gh. Leahu. Photo)

2002 (4 Apr). Germanic Fortresses and Churches in Translyvania. T **1378** and similar multicoloured designs. P 13½.

6275 1500l. Type **1378** ... 25 20
6276 2500l. Church staircase, Darjiu ... 35 30
6277 6500l. Fortress, Viscri (horiz) ... 70 55
6278 10500l. Fortified church, Vorumloc (horiz) ... 1·20 95
6279 13500l. Tower gate, Câlnic ... 1·60 1·30
6280 17500l. Fortified church, Prejmer ... 2·00 1·60
6275/6280 *Set of* 6 ... 5·50 4·50

2002 (12 Apr). Easter. T **1379** and similar vert design showing miniatures by Picu Pătrut. Multicoloured. Photo. P 13½.

6281 2500l. Type **1379** ... 35 30
6282 10500l. Resurrection ... 1·40 1·10

1380 Clown

1381 "Dorobantul" (Nicolae Grigorescu)

(Des N. Nobilescu. Photo)

2002 (9 May). Europa. Circus. T **1380** and similar vert design. Multicoloured. P 13½.

6283 17500l. Type **1380** ... 2·30 1·90
6284 25500l. Clown (different) ... 3·50 2·75

2002 (9 May). 125th Anniv of Independence. Sheet 77×91 mm. Photo. P 13½.

MS6285 **1381** 25500l. multicoloured ... 4·75 4·75

1382 Post Mark

1383 Mountains

2002 (10 June). 50th Anniv of International Federation of Stamp Dealers' Association (IFSDA). Sheet 105×75 mm containing T **1382** and similar horiz designs. Multicoloured. Photo. P 13½.

MS6286 10,000l. Type **1382**; 10,000l. IFSDA emblem; 27,500l. World Trade Centre, Bucharest; 27500l. Philatelic shop, Bucharest ... 8·75 8·75

(Des Art Design. Photo)

2002 (14 June). Year of Mountains (2000l.) and Year of Eco-tourism (3000l.). T **1383** and similar multicoloured design. P 13½.

6287 2000l. Type **1383** ... 25 20
a. Tête-bêche pair. Nos. 6287/8 ... 65 55
6288 3000l. Landscape and recycling symbol (32×24 mm) ... 35 30

Nos. 6287/8 were issued in tête-bêche pairs throughout the sheet.

1384 Cricket

(Des O. Cojocaru and M. Golgan. Photo)

2002 (11 July). Sport. T **1384** and similar horiz designs. Multicoloured. P 13½.

6289 7000l. Type **1384** ... 80 65
6290 11000l. Polo ... 1·30 1·00
6291 15500l. Golf ... 1·70 1·40
6292 19500l. Baseball ... 2·20 1·80
6289/6292 *Set of* 4 ... 5·50 4·25

1385 Ion Luca Caragiale

(Des A. Sainciuc. Photo)

2002 (15 July). Anniversaries. T **1385** and similar horiz design. Multicoloured. P 13½.

6293 10000l. Type **1385** (playwright) (150th birth anniv) ... 1·20 95
a. Pair. Nos. 6293/4 ... 2·50 2·00
6294 10000l. National Theatre, Bucharest (150th anniv) ... 1·20 95

Nos. 6293/4 were issued in *se-tenant* pairs, each pair forming a composite design within the sheet.

1386 Financial Postal Service Emblem

2002 (9 Aug–1 Oct). Postal Services. T **1386** and similar horiz designs. Photo. P 13½.

6295 2000l. multicoloured ... 25 20
6296 3000l. vermilion, greenish yellow and new blue ... 35 30
6297 8000l. multicoloured (1.10) ... 95 75
6298 10000l. brown-purple and chocolate ... 1·20 95
6299 13000l. brown-red, brownish grey and black (1.10) ... 1·40 1·10
6300 15500l. multicoloured ... 1·70 1·40
6301 20500l. bright mauve, new blue and black (1.10) ... 2·30 1·90
6302 27500l. multicoloured ... 3·25 2·50
6295/6302 *Set of* 8 ... 10·50 8·25

Designs:—2000l. Type **1386**; 3000l. Romania Post emblem; 8000l. Direct mailing centre emblem; 10000l. Post building (130th anniv); 13000l. Direct marketing emblem; 15500l. Rapid post emblem; 20500l. Priority post emblem; 27500l. Globe and stamp album (Romafilatelia).

Numbers have been left for additions to this series.

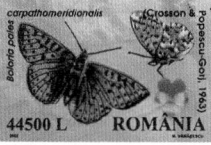

1387 *Boloria pales carpathomeridionalis*

(Des M. Vămăşescu. Photo)

2002 (2 Sept). Butterflies. Sheet 101×71 mm containing T **1387** and similar horiz designs. Multicoloured. P 13½.

MS6310 44500l. Type **1387**; 44500l. *Erebia pharte romaniae*; 44500l. *Peridea korbl herculana*; 44500l. *Tomares nogelii dobrogensis* ... 19·00 19·00

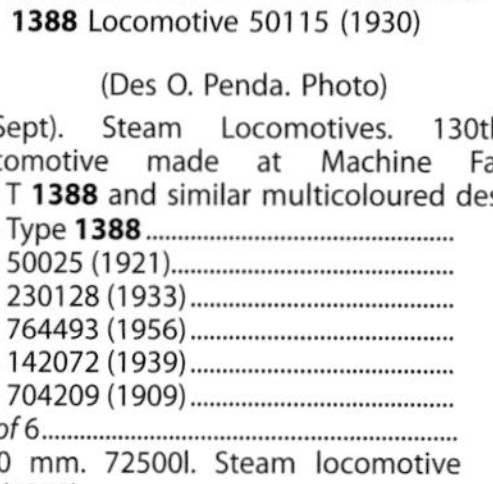

1388 Locomotive 50115 (1930)

(Des O. Penda. Photo)

2002 (22 Sept). Steam Locomotives. 130th Anniv of First Locomotive made at Machine Factory, Resita (**MS**6317). T **1388** and similar multicoloured designs. P 13½.

6311 4500l. Type **1388** ... 45 35
6312 6500l. 50025 (1921) ... 70 55
6313 7000l. 230128 (1933) ... 80 65
6314 11000l. 764493 (1956) ... 1·20 95
6315 19500l. 142072 (1939) ... 2·10 1·70
6316 44500l. 704209 (1909) ... 4·75 4·25
6311/6316 *Set of* 6 ... 9·00 7·50

MS6317 75×90 mm. 72500l. Steam locomotive (42×54 mm) (1872) ... 8·25 8·25

1389 Knight and Bishop

1390 Quince (*Cydonia oblonga*)

(Des M. Vămăşescu. Photo)

2002 (23 Oct). 35th Chess Olympiad, Bled, Slovenia. Sheet 102×62 mm containing T **1389** and similar vert designs. Multicoloured. P 13½.

MS6318 20500l. Type **1389**; 20500l. King and knight; 20500l. Queen and rook ... 7·00 7·00

(Des O. Cojocaru and M. Golgan. Photo)

2002 (5 Nov). Fruit. T **1390** and similar vert designs. Multicoloured. P 13½.

6319 15500l. Type **1390** ... 1·70 1·40
6320 20500l. Apricot (*Armeniaca vulgaris*) ... 2·30 1·90
6321 44500l. Cherries (*Cerasus vulgaris*) ... 4·75 4·25
6322 73500l. Mulberry (*Morus nigra*) ... 8·25 7·50
6319/6322 *Set of* 4 ... 15·00 13·50

1391 Father Christmas carrying Parcels

(Des Simona Bucan. Photo)

2002 (19 Nov). Christmas. T **1391** and similar horiz design. Multicoloured. P 13½.

6323 3000l. Type **1391** ... 35 30
6324 15500l. Father Christmas and computer ... 1·70 1·40

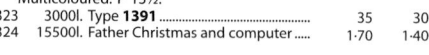

1392 Eagle (Romanian emblem), Flags and NATO Emblem

(Des O. Penda. Litho and holography Cartor)

2002 (22 Nov). Romanian Invitation to join North Atlantic Treaty Organization (NATO). Sheet 168×106 mm containing T **1392**. P 13½.

MS6325 131000l.×2, Type **1392**×2 ... 29·00 29·00

No. **MS**6325 contains a central label showing NATO emblem.

1393 "Braila Harbour" (Jean-Alexandru Steriadi)

2003 (22 Jan). Art. T **1393** and similar multicoloured designs. Litho. P 13½.

6326 4500l. Type **1393** ... 45 35
6327 6500l. "Balcic" (Nicolae Darascu) ... 70 55
6328 30500l. "Conversation" (Nicolae Vermont) ... 3·25 2·75
6329 34000l. "Dalmatia" (Nicolae Darascu) ... 3·75 3·25
6330 46500l. "Fishing Boats" (Jean-Alexandru Steriadi) ... 5·25 4·75
6331 53000l. "Nude" (Bogdan Pietris) ... 5·75 5·25
6326/6331 *Set of* 6 ... 17·00 15·00

MS6332 75×91 mm. "Woman on Seashore" (Nicolae Grigorescu) (42×54 mm) ... 9·25 9·25

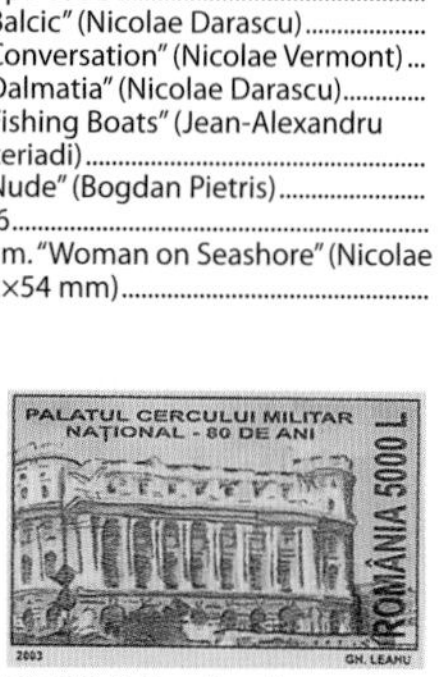

1394 Building Façade

(Des Gh. Leahu. Litho)

2003 (28 Jan). 80th Anniv of National Military Palace, Bucharest. P 13½.

6333 **1394** 5000l. multicoloured ... 60 45

1395 Ladybird

(Des A. Ciubotariu. Litho)

2003 (14 Feb). March Amulet (good luck). T **1395** and similar multicoloured design. P 13½.

6334 3000l. Type **1395** 45 35
6335 5000l. Chimney sweep (vert) 70 55

Nos. 6334/5 respectively were issued in sheetlets of eight stamps surrounding a central stamp size label.

1396 "10"

(Des E. Varga. Litho)

2003 (20 Feb). Tenth Anniv of Romania signing European Agreement (precursor to joining EU). P 13½.

6336 **1396** 142000l. multicoloured .... 14·00 14·00

1397 Ion Irimescu **1398** Post Palace

(Des Cătălin Ilinca. Litho)

2003 (27 Feb). Birth Anniversaries. T **1397** and similar vert designs. P 13½.

6337 6000l. Type **1397** (sculptor) (centenary) 60 45
6338 18000l. Hector Berlioz (composer) (bicentenary) .... 1·70 1·40
6339 20000l. Vincent van Gogh (artist) (150th) .... 2·00 1·60
6340 36000l. Groeges de Bellio (doctor and art collector) (175th) .... 3·50 3·00
6337/6340 *Set of 4* .... 7·00 5·75

(Des Gh. Leahu. Litho)

2003 (27 Mar). Architecture. T **1398** and similar multicoloured designs. P 13½.

6341 4500l. Type **1398** 45 35
6342 5500l. Central Savings House 55 45
6343 10000l. National Bank (horiz) 85 75
6344 15500l. Stock Exchange .... 1·40 1·20
6345 20500l. Carol I University .... 1·80 1·60
6346 46500l. Athenium .... 4·00 3·50
6341/6346 *Set of 6* .... 8·25 7·00
MS6347 76×91 mm. 73500l. Palace of Justice (42×54 mm) .... 6·50 6·50

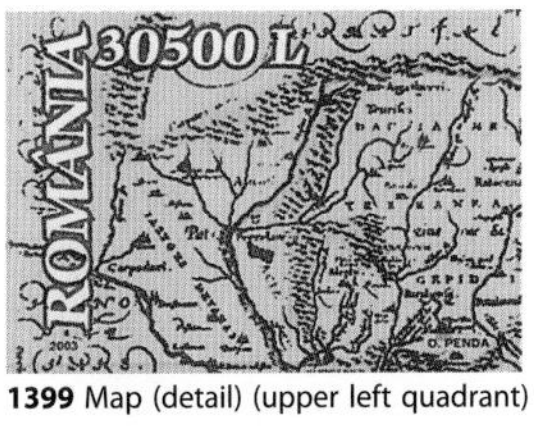

1399 Map (detail) (upper left quadrant)

(Des O. Penda. Litho)

2003 (4 Apr). Pieter van den Keere (Petrus Kærius Cælavit) (cartographer) Commemoration. Two sheets containing T **1399** and similar multicoloured designs. P 13½.

MS6348 (a) 120×90 mm. 30500l.×4 "Vetus description Daciarum" (description of Dacia); (b) 76×91 mm. 46500l. National Map and Book Museum (42×54 mm) .... 15·00 15·00

1400 Rabbit carrying Egg and Envelope **1401** Eurasian Scops Owl (*Otus scops*)

(Des A. Ciubotariu. Litho)

2003 (10 Apr). Easter. P 13½.

6349 **1400** 3000l. multicoloured 55 45

(Des Cătălin Ilinca. Litho)

2003 (25 Apr). Owls. T **1401** and similar vert designs. Multicoloured. P 13½.

6350 5000l. Type **1401** 45 35
6351 8000l. Ural owl (*Strix uralensis*) 65 55
6352 10000l. Eurasian pygmy owl (*Glaucidium passerinum*) 85 75
6353 13000l. Short-eared owl (*Asio flammeus*) .... 1·10 95
6354 15500l. Long-eared owl (*Asio otus*) .... 1·30 1·10
6355 20500l. Tengmalm's owl (*Aegolius funereus*) 2·20 1·90
6350/6355 *Set of 6* .... 6·00 5·00

1402 Butterfly emerging from Cocoon **1403** Dumltru Staniloae

(Des D. Grebu. Litho)

2003 (9 May). Europa. Poster Art. T **1402** and similar vert design. Multicoloured. P 13½.

6356 20500l. Type **1402** .... 2·20 1·90
6357 73500l. Figure holding Painting .... 6·50 5·50

No. 6356/7 respectively were issued in *se-tenant* sheetlets of three stamps.

(Des Cătălin Ilinca. Litho)

2003 (6 June). Birth Centenaries. T **1403** and similar vert designs. Multicoloured. P 13½.

6358 4500l. Type **1403** (theologian) 45 35
6359 8000l. Alexandru Ciucurencu (artist) 65 55
6360 30500l. Ilarie Voronca (poet) .... 2·50 2·20
6361 46500l. Victor Brauner (artist) .... 4·00 3·50
6358/6361 *Set of 4* .... 6·75 6·00

1404 "Fantastic Animals"

2003 (24 June). Birth Centenary of Victor Brauner (artist). Sheet 175×129 mm containing T **1404** and similar multicoloured designs showing paintings. Litho. P 13½.

MS6362 10000l.×12. Type **1404**; "Self Portrait" ×3 (24×33 mm); "Heron of Alexandria" (24×33 mm); "Surrealist Composition"; "Drobegea Landscape"; "Nude" (24×33 mm); "Drobegea Landscape" (different); "Courteous Passivity"; "Ion Minulescu Portrait" (abstract) (24×33 mm); "Dragon" .... 11·00 11·00

1405 Nostradamus and Astrolabe

(Des Cătălin Ilinca. Litho)

2003 (2 July). 500th Birth Anniv of Nostradamus (prophet). T **1405** and similar horiz design. Multicoloured. P 13.

6363 73500l. Type **1405** .... 6·00 5·00
a. Pair. Nos. 6363/4 .... 12·50 10·50
6364 73500l. Astrolabe, diagram and Nostradamus .... 6·00 5·00

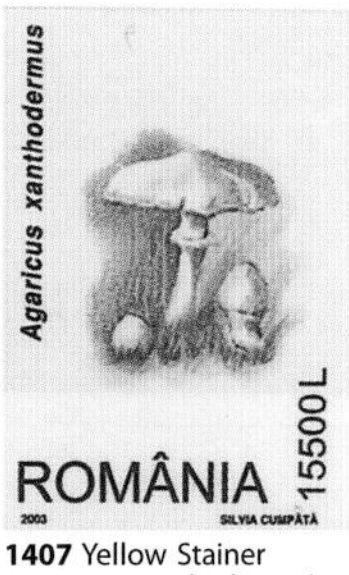

1406 Magnifying Glass, Building and Emblem **1407** Yellow Stainer (*Agaricus xanthodermus*)

(Des Cătălin Ilinca. Litho)

2003 (15 July). Post Day. Centenary of Timişoara Philatelic Association. P 13½.

6365 **1406** 5000l. multicoloured 55 45

(Des Sylvia Cumpătă. Litho)

2003 (19 Sept). Fungi. Two sheets each 126×75 mm containing T **1407** and similar vert designs. Multicoloured. P 13½.

MS6366 (a) 15500l.×3 Type **1407**; Basket fungus (*Clathrus ruber*); Panther cap (*Amanita pantherina*); (b) 20500l.×3 Red-capped scaber stalk (*Leccinum aurantiacum*); Chicken mushroom (*Laetiporus sulphurous*); *Russula xerampelina* .... 11·00 11·00

1408 Skydiving **1409** Green Lizard (*Lacerta viridis*)

(Des M. Gologan and O. Cojocaru. Litho)

2003 (30 Sept). Extreme Sports. T **1408** and similar multicoloured designs. P 13½.

6367 5000l. Type **1408** 45 35
6368 8000l. Windsurfing (horiz) 65 55
6369 10000l. Motor cycle racing (horiz) 85 75
6370 30500l. Skiing .... 2·50 2·20
6367/6370 *Set of 4* .... 4·00 3·50

(Des M. Vămăşescu. Litho)

2003 (28 Oct). Amphibians. Sheet 125×105 mm containing T **1409** and similar vert designs. P 13½.

MS6371 8000l.×4 Type **1409**; Green tree frog (*Hyla arborea*); Snake-eyed skink (*Ablepharus kitaibelii*); Common frog (*Rana temporaria*) .... 7·50 7·50

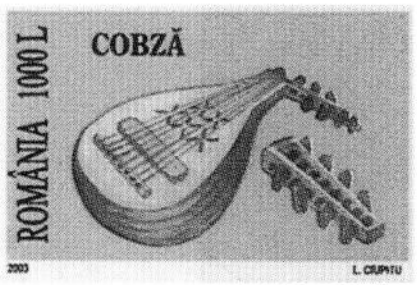

1410 Cobza (stringed instrument)

(Des L. Ciupitu. Litho)

2003 (31 Oct). Traditional Instruments. T **1410** and similar horiz designs. Multicoloured. P 13½.

6372 1000l. Type **1410** 10 10
6373 4000l. Bucium (wind) 35 30
6374 6000l. Vioara cu Goarna (violin with horn) .. 55 45
6372/6374 *Set of 3* 90 75

1411 Map and Statue

2003 (11 Nov). 125th Anniv of Berlin Treaty returning Dobrudja to Romania. P 13½.

6375 **1411** 16000l. multicoloured .... 1·30 1·10

1412 Pope John Paul II and Teoctist, Romanian Patriarch

2003 (29 Nov). 25th Anniv of Pontificate of Pope John Paul II. T **1412** and similar horiz design. Multicoloured. P 13½.

6376 16000l. Type **1412** .... 1·30 1·10
a. Horiz strip. Nos. 6376/7 plus 2 labels .... 2·75 2·30
6377 16000l. Pope John Paul II and Teoctist (different) .... 1·30 1·10

Nos. 6376/7 were issued in sheets of eight stamps and eight labels, comprising of two vertical strips of four stamps separated by two strips of four labels giving four horizontal *se-tenant* strips of two stamps and two labels.

1413 Father Christmas

1414 Woman wearing Suit and Cloche Hat (1921/1930)

(Des A. Ciubotariu. Litho)

2003 (5 Dec). Christmas. T **1413** and similar vert design. P 13½.

6378 4000l. black, rosine and reddish orange 45 40
a. Pair. Nos. 6378/9 ...... 1·00 85
6379 4000l. black and reddish orange 45 40

Design:—No. 6379 Snowman.

Nos. 6378/9 were issued in horizontal *se-tenant* pairs within the sheet, each pair forming a composite design.

(Des Simona Bucan. Litho)

2003 (13 Dec). 20th-century Women's Fashion. T **1414** and similar vert designs. Multicoloured. P 13½.

6380 4000l. Type **1414** 45 40
6381 4000l. Wearing coat with fur collar (1931/1940) 45 40
6382 21000l. Wearing hat and carrying muff (1901/1910) ...... 1·70 1·40
6383 21000l. Wearing caped coat and hat (1911/1920) ...... 1·70 1·40
6380/6383 *Set of* 4 ...... 4·00 3·25

1415 Early Woman Footballer

2003 (22 Dec). Centenary of FIFA (Fédération Internationale de Football Association). T **1415** and similar horiz designs. Multicoloured. P 13½.

6384 3000l. Type **1415** 25 20
6385 4000l. Players and film camera 35 30
6386 6000l. Heads and newsprint 50 40
6387 10000l. Boots, pad and ball 85 70
6388 34000l. Rule book and pitch ...... 3·00 2·40
6384/6388 *Set of* 5 ...... 4·50 3·50

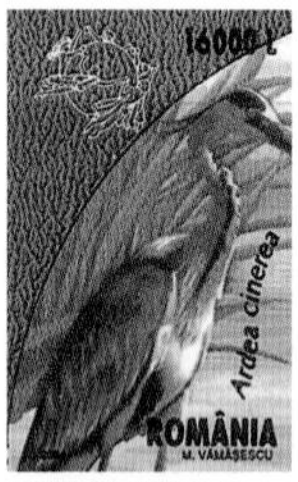

1416 Grey Heron (*Ardea cinerea*)

1417 Globe, Satellite and Disc

(Des M. Vămăşescu. Litho)

2004 (23 Jan). Water Birds. Sheet 94×96 mm containing T **1416** and similar vert designs. Multicoloured. P 13½.

MS6389 16000l.×4 Type **1416**; Mallard (*Anas platyrhynchos*); Great crested grebe (*Podiceps cristatus*); Eastern white pelican (*Pelecanus onocrotalus*) ...... 5·25 5·25

(Des M. Vămăşescu. Litho)

2004 (26 Jan). Information Technology. Sheet 93×69 mm containing T **1417** and similar horiz design. Multicoloured. P 13½.

MS6390 20000l.×4 Type **1417**; Computer screen; Satellite dish; Computer keyboard ...... 6·50 6·50

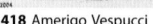

1418 Amerigo Vespucci

1419 Couple

(Des Cătălin Ilinca. Litho)

2004 (31 Jan). 550th Birth Anniv of Amerigo Vespucci (explorer). T **1418** and similar horiz design. Multicoloured. P 13½.

6391 16000l. Type **1418** ...... 1·30 1·10
6392 31000l. Sailing ship ...... 2·75 2·20

(Des Sorin Tarlea. Litho)

2004 (10 Feb). St. Valentine. P 13½.

6393 **1419** 21000l. multicoloured ...... 1·80 1·50

1420 UPU Emblem

1421 Easter Egg and Rabbit holding Envelope

(Des G. Ursachi. Litho)

2004 (20 Feb). Universal Postal Union Congress, Bucharest (1st issue). T **1420** and similar horiz design. Multicoloured. P 13½.

6394 31000l. Type **1420** ...... 2·40 2·00
a. Pair. Nos. 6394/5 ...... 5·00 4·25
6395 31000l. Bird holding envelope ...... 2·40 2·00

Nos. 6394/5 were issued in horizontal *se-tenant* pairs within the sheet, each pair forming a composite design.

See also Nos. 6445/50.

(Des A. Ciubotariu. Litho)

2004 (1 Mar). Easter. P 13½.

6396 **1421** 4000l. multicoloured 60 50

1422 *Bullet* Locomotive, Japan

(Des Cătălin Ilinca. Litho)

2004 (11 Mar). Modern Locomotives. T **1422** and similar horiz designs. Multicoloured. P 13½.

6397 4000l. Type **1422** 40 35
6398 6000l. *TGV*, France 55 45
6399 10000l. *KTX*, South Korea 90 75
6400 16000l. *AVE*, Spain ...... 1·40 1·20
6401 47000l. *ICE*, Germany ...... 4·00 3·25
6402 56000l. *Eurostar*, UK and France ...... 5·00 4·25
6397/6402 *Set of* 6 ...... 11·00 9·25

MS6403 92×77 mm. 77000l. *Blue Arrow* (Sageti Albastre), Romania (54×42 mm) ...... 6·50 6·50

1423 NATO Headquarters

1424 Pierre de Coubertin

2004 (24 Mar). Romania's Accession to NATO. Litho. P 13½.

6404 **1423** 4000l. multicoloured ...... 1·00 85

(Des L. Pascanu. Litho)

2004 (25 Mar). 90th Anniv of Romanian Olympic Committee. Sheet 120×86 mm containing T **1424** and similar multicoloured designs. P 13½.

MS6405 16000l.+5000l.×3, Type **1424** (founder of modern Olympics); Olympic stadium, Athens, 1896 (54×42 mm); George Bibescu (founder member) ...... 5·00 5·00

(Des Simona Bucan. Litho)

2004 (31 Mar). 20th-century Women's Fashion. Vert designs as T **1414** showing women's clothes. Multicoloured. P 13½.

6406 4000l. Calf length suit and hat (1941/1950) 50 40
a. Pair. Nos. 6406/7 ...... 1·10 85
6407 4000l. Knee length coat (1951/1960) 50 40
6408 21000l. Dress and jacket (1981/1990) ...... 1·90 1·60
a. Pair. Nos. 6408/9 ...... 4·00 3·50
6409 21000l. Sleeveless dress (1991/2000) ...... 1·90 1·60
6410 31000l. Mini skirted coat (1961/1970) ...... 2·75 2·20
a. Pair. Nos. 6410/11 ...... 5·75 4·75
6411 31000l. Trouser suit (1971/1980 ...... 2·75 2·20
6406/6411 *Set of* 6 ...... 9·25 7·50

Nos. 6406/7, 6408/9 and 6410/11, respectively, were issued in *se-tenant* pairs within the sheet, each pair forming a composite design.

1425 Marksman

1426 Sun and Shoreline

(Des M. Vămăşescu. Litho)

2004 (24 Apr). 51st International Council for Game and Wildlife Conservation General Assembly. T **1425** and similar multicoloured designs. P 13½.

6412 16000l. Type **1425** ...... 1·30 1·10
a. Horiz strip of 5. Nos. 6412/16 ...... 6·75
6413 16000l. Dog's head and pheasant ...... 1·30 1·10
6414 16000l. Stag ...... 1·30 1·10
6415 16000l. Ibex ...... 1·30 1·10
6416 16000l. Bear ...... 1·30 1·10
6412/6416 *Set of* 5 ...... 5·75 5·00

MS6417 99×87 mm. 16000l. Stag (54×42 mm) ...... 1·30 1·30

Nos. 6412/16 were issued in horizontal *se-tenant* strips of five stamps, each strip forming a composite design.

(Des D. Grebu. Litho)

2004 (7 May). Europa. Holidays. T **1426** and similar horiz design. Multicoloured. P 13½.

6418 21000l. Type **1426** ...... 1·80 1·50
6419 77000l. Sun and snowy mountains ...... 6·25 5·25

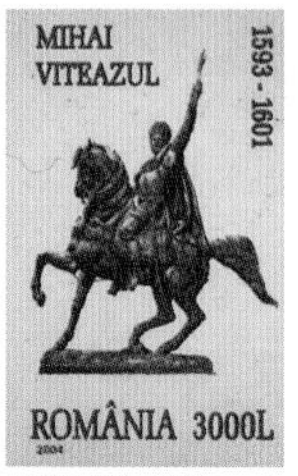

1427 Mihai Viteazul (Michael the Brave) (statue)

1428 Façade

2004 (17 May). P 13½.

6420 **1427** 3000l. multicoloured ...... 1·00 85

2004 (21 May). National Philatelic Museum. Litho. P 13½.

6421 **1428** 4000l. multicoloured ...... 1·00 85

1429 Bram Stoker

1430 Anghel Saligny

(Des R. Oltean. Litho)

2004 (21 May). *Dracula* (novel by Bram Stoker). Sheet 142×84 mm containing T **1429** and similar vert designs. Multicoloured. P 13½.

MS6422 31000l.×4, Type **1429**; Dracula and cross; Dracula carrying woman; Dracula in coffin ...... 10·00 10·00

(Des G. Ursachi. Litho)

2004 (27 May). Anniversaries. T **1430** and similar horiz designs. Multicoloured. P 13½.

6423 4000l. Type **1430** (engineer) (150th birth) 25 25
6424 16000l. Gheorgi Anghel (sculptor) (birth centenary) ...... 1·00 95
6425 21000l. George Sand (Aurore Dupin) (writer) (birth bicentenary) ...... 1·30 1·20
6426 31000l. Oscar Wilde (writer) (150th birth) .... 1·90 1·70
6423/6426 *Set of* 4 ...... 4·00 3·75

1431 Roman Temple, Bucharest

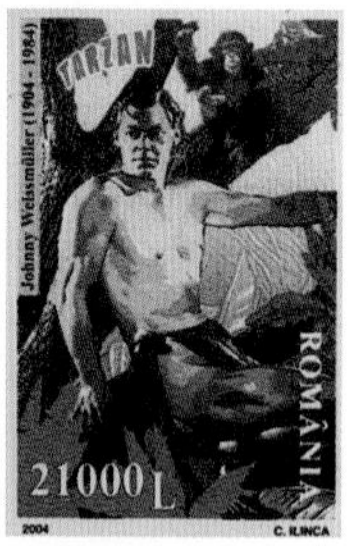

1432 Johnny Weissmuller

2004 (28 May). Litho. P 13½.

6427 **1431** 10000l. yellow olive and deep green ...... 1·00 95

(Des C. Ilinca. Litho)

2004 (2 June). Birth Centenary of Johnny Weissmuller (athlete and actor). P 13½.

6428 **1432** 21000l. multicoloured ...... 1·20 1·10

1433 Aircraft and Emblem

2004 (7 June). 50th Anniv of TAROM Air Transport. Litho. P 13½.

6429 **1433** 16000l. multicoloured ...... 1·30 1·20

1434 Footballs and Anniversary Emblem

(Des M. Vămăşescu. Litho)

2004 (15 June). Centenary of FIFA (Fédération Internationale de Football Association). P 13½.
6430 **1434** 31000l. multicoloured .... 2·30 2·10

1435 Stefan III (fresco), Dobrovat Monastery (²/₃-size illustration)

2004 (16 June). 500th Death Anniv of Stefan III (Stefan cel Mare) (Moldavian ruler). Two sheets, each 173×62 mm, containing T **1435** and similar horiz designs. Multicoloured (**MS**6431a). P 13½.
MS6431 (a). 10000l.×3, Type **1435**; Ruins of Sucevei; Stefan III (embroidered panel). (b) 16000l. pale brown; 16000l. multicoloured; 16000l. pale brown .... 5·75 5·75
Designs:—**MS**6431b. 16000l.×3, Putna monastery; Stefan III (painting); Neamt fortress.

1436 Alexandru Macedonski

(Des G. Ursachi. Litho)

2004 (30 June). Anniversaries. T **1436** and similar horiz designs. Multicoloured. P 13½.
6432 2000l. Type **1436** (writer) (150th birth) 20 20
6433 3000l. Victor Babes (scientist) (150th birth) 35 30
6434 6000l. Arthur Rimbaud (writer) (150th birth) 45 40
6435 56000l. Salvador Dali (artist) (birth centenary) .... 4·50 4·00
6432/6435 *Set of* 4 .... 5·00 4·50

1437 King Ferdinand and First Stamp Exhibition Poster

2004 (15 July). Post Day. 80th Anniv of First National Stamp Exhibition. P 13½.
6436 **1437** 21000l. +10000l. multicoloured .... 2·20 2·00
a. Sheetlet. No. 6436×4. Perf and imperf .... 9·00

1438 Zeppelin LZ-127 and Buildings
1439 Bank Building

(Des C. Ilinca. Litho)

2004 (29 July). 75th Anniv of Zeppelin LZ-127's Flight over Braşov. P 13½.
6437 **1438** 31000l. multicoloured .... 2·30 2·10

2004 (30 July). 140th Anniv of National Savings Bank (Casa de Economii si Consemnatiuni). P 13½.
6438 **1439** 5000l. multicoloured .... 1·00 90

1440 Firemen and Engine
1441 Woman Rower

(Des G. Ursachi. Litho)

2004 (12 Aug). 24th International CTIF (International Fire-fighters Association) Symposium, Braşov. T **1440** and similar horiz design. Multicoloured. P 13½.
6439 12000l. Type **1440** 85 75
a. Pair. Nos. 6438/9 .... 1·80
6440 12000l. Firemen fighting fire 85 75
Nos. 6439/40 were issued in *se-tenant* pairs within the sheet, each pair with a *se-tenant* half stamp-size label inscribed for CTIF, attached at either left or right.

(Des M. Vămăşescu. Litho)

2004 (20 Aug). Olympic Games, Athens. T **1441** and similar vert designs. Multicoloured. P 13½.
6441 7000l. Type **1441** 55 50
6442 12000l. Fencers .... 1·00 90
6443 21000l. Swimmer .... 1·80 1·60
6444 31000l. +9000l. Gymnast .... 3·25 2·75
6441/6444 *Set of* 4 .... 6·00 5·25

1442 23rd Conference Emblem and 2004 Romania Stamp

2004 (10 Sept). Universal Postal Union Congress, Bucharest (2nd issue). T **1442** and similar horiz designs showing emblem and stamps commemorating congresses. Multicoloured. Litho. P 13½.
6445 8000l. Type **1442** 60 55
6446 10000l. 1974 Switzerland 75 65
6447 19000l. 1994 South Korea .... 1·70 1·50
6448 31000l. 1990 China .... 2·50 2·20
6449 47000l. 1989 USA .... 4·00 3·50
6450 77000l. 1979 Brasil .... 6·25 5·50
6445/6450 *Set of* 6 .... 14·00 12·50

1443 "L'appel"
1444 Bronze Age Cucuteni Pot

2004 (20 Sept). Tenth Death Anniv of Idel Ianchelevici (sculptor). T **1443** and similar vert design showing statues. Multicoloured. P 13½.
6451 21000l. Type **1443** .... 1·60 1·40
6452 31000l. "Perennis perdurat poeta" .... 2·20 2·00
Nos. 6451/2 were each issued with a *se-tenant* stamp size label inscribed for the joint issue.
Stamps of the same design were issued by Belgium.

(Des C. Ilinca (6453) or Wang Huming (6454))

2004 (22 Sept). Cultural Heritage. T **1444** and similar vert design. Multicoloured. P 13½.
6453 5000l. Type **1444** 50 45
a. Pair. Nos. 6453/4 .... 1·10 95
6454 5000l. Drum supported by phoenixes and tigers 50 45
Nos. 6453/4 were issued in *se-tenant* pairs within the sheet. Stamps of the same design were issued by China.

1445 Gerard Kremer (Geradus Mercator) and Jodocus Hondius

(Des Penda. Litho Cartor)

2004 (22 Sept). European Anniversaries. Sheet 158×144 mm containing T **1445** and similar horiz designs. Multicoloured. P 13½.
MS6455 18000l.×3, Type **1445** (cartographers) (450th anniv of Mercator's map of Europe and 400th anniv of Hondius-Mercator atlas); UPU monument, Berne (23rd UPU congress, Bucharest); Amerigo Vespucci (explorer) (550th birth anniv) .... 26·00 26·00

1446 Roman Riders and Foot Soldiers

2004 (15 Oct). Fragments of Trajan's Column (Roman monument) (1st issue). T **1446** and similar horiz designs. Litho. P 13½.
6456 7000l. greenish grey and dull ultramarine 55 50
6457 12000l. yellow-brown and dull ultramarine .... 1·00 90
6458 19000l. orange and dull ultramarine .... 1·60 1·40
6459 56000l. rose carmine and dull ultramarine .... 4·50 4·00
6456/6459 *Set of* 4 .... 7·00 6·00
Designs:—Type **1446**; 12000l. Neptune and soldiers embarking on ships; 19000l. Fortress and soldier holding cauldron in stream; 56000l. Chariot in moat and soldiers attacking fortress.
See also Nos. 6468/70.

1447 "Simfonia" (Symphony) Rose
1448 Ilie Nastase

(Des A. Bartos. Litho)

2004 (25 Oct). Roses. T **1447** and similar horiz designs. Multicoloured. P 13½.
6460 8000l. Type **1447** 65 60
6461 15000l. "Foc de Tabara" (Camp fire) .... 1·20 1·10
6462 25000l. "Golden Elegance" .... 2·00 1·80
6463 36000l. "Doamna in mov" (Lady in mauve) .... 3·00 2·50
6460/6463 *Set of* 4 .... 6·25 5·50
MS6464 120×90 mm. Nos. 6460/3 .... 6·50 6·50

(Des M. Vămăşescu. Litho)

2004 (16 Nov). Ilie Nastase (tennis player). T **1448** and similar vert designs. P 13½.
6465 10000l. Type **1448** .... 1·00 90
MS6466 Two sheets. (a) 110×200 mm. 72000l. Ilie Nastase (42×52 mm). (b) 91×110 mm. As No. **MS**6466a. Imperf .... 10·00 9·00

1449 Father Christmas
1450 Scouts Emblem

(Des E. Multhaler. Litho)

2004 (4 Dec). Christmas. P 13½.
6467 **1449** 5000l. multicoloured .... 1·00 90

2004 (4 Dec). Fragments of Trajan's Column (Roman monument) (2nd issue). Horiz designs as T **1446**. Litho. P 13½.
6468 21000l. deep turquoise green and dull ultramarine .... 1·70 1·50
6469 31000l. grey-black and dull ultramarine .... 2·50 2·20
6470 145000l. carmine-vermilion and dull ultramarine .... 12·00 10·50
6468/6470 *Set of* 3 .... 14·50 13·00
Designs:—21000l. Ritual sacrifice; 31000l. Soldiers, trees, water and heads on posts; 145000l. Stone encampment.

2004 (8 Dec). International Organizations. T **1450** and similar multicoloured designs showing emblems. Litho. P 13½.
6471 12000l. Type **1450** .... 1·00 90
6472 16000l. Lions International .... 1·30 1·20
6473 19000l. Red Cross and Red Crescent .... 1·60 1·40
6471/6473 *Set of* 3 .... 3·50 3·25
MS6474 90×78 mm. 87000l. Dimitrie Cantemir (writer and linguist) (Freemasonry) (42×52 mm) .... 6·50 6·50

1451 Iolanda Balas-Soter
1452 "Tristan Tzara" (M. H. Maxy)

(Des M. Vămăşescu. Litho)

2004 (15 Dec). Olympic Games, Athens. Women Athletes. T **1451** and similar square designs. Each grey-black and gold. P 13½.

6475 5000l. Type **1451** (high jump) 55 50
6476 33000l. Elsabeta Lipa (rowing) 3·25 2·75
6477 77000l. Ivan Patzaichin (kayaking) 6·50 5·75
6475/6477 *Set of 3* 9·25 8·00

Nos. 6475/7 were each perforated in a circle enclosed in an outer perforated square.

2004 (16 Dec). Modern Art. Two sheets, each 129×78 mm containing T **1452** and similar vert designs. Multicoloured. Litho. P 13½.

MS6478 (a) 7000l.×3, Type **1452**; "Baroneasa" (Merica Ramniceanu); "Portret de Femeie" (Jean David). (b) 12000l.×3, "Compozitie" (Marcel Ianescu); "Femeie care viseaza II" (Victor Brauner); "Compozitie" (Hans Mattis-Teutsch) 4·50 4·50

1453 Gheorghe Magheru

(Des G. Mandriscanu. Litho)

2005 (20 Jan). Anniversaries (1st issue). T **1453** and similar horiz designs. Multicoloured. P 13½.

6479 15000l. Type **1453** (revolutionary leader) (125th death anniv) 1·20 1·10
6480 25000l. Christian Dior (dress designer) (birth centenary) 2·00 1·80
6481 35000l. Henry Fonda (actor) (birth centenary) 3·00 2·50
6482 72000l. Greta Garbo (actress) (birth centenary) 5·50 5·00
6483 77000l. George Valentin Bibescu (aviation pioneer) (125th birth anniv) 6·25 5·50
6479/6483 *Set of 5* 16·00 14·50

See also Nos. 6512/16.

1454 Emblem

1455 Wedding Pitcher (Oboga-Olt)

2005 (23 Feb). Centenary of Rotary International (charitable organization.). Litho. P 13½.

6484 **1454** 21000l. multicoloured 7·00 6·25

2005 (24 Feb). Pottery (1st issue). T **1455** and similar vert designs. Multicoloured. Litho. P 13½.

6485 3000l. Type **1455** 35 20
6486 5000l. Jugs and pitchers (Sacel-MaraMureş) 45 30
6487 12000l. Pitcher (Horezu-Valcea) 1·10 90
6488 16000l. Wedding pitcher (Corund-Harghita) 1·30 1·10
6485/6488 *Set of 4* 3·00 2·30

See also Nos. 6498/500, 6591/7, 6605/6, 6639/42, 6650/3, 6684/7, 6781/4, 6794/7, 6817/24, 6842/5 and 6873/6.

1456 Elopteryx nopcsai

1457 *Carassius auratus*

(Des R. Oltean. Litho)

2005 (25 Feb). Dinosaurs. T **1456** and similar horiz designs. Multicoloured. P 13½.

6489 21000l. Type **1456** 2·00 1·90
6490 31000l. Telmatosaurus transylvanicus (inscr "transsylvanicus") 3·00 2·75
6491 35000l. Struthiosaurus transilvanicus 3·25 3·00
6492 47000l. Hatzegopteryx thambema 4·25 4·00
6489/6492 *Set of 4* 11·50 10·50
MS6493 125×120 mm. Nos. 6489/92 11·50 11·50

2005 (1 Mar). Fish. T **1457** and similar vert designs. Multicoloured. Litho. P 13½.

6494 21000l. Type **1457** 2·00 1·90
a. Block of 8. Nos. 6494/7 plus 4 labels 26·00
6495 31000l. *Symphysodon discus* 3·00 2·75
6496 36000l. *Labidochromis* 3·25 3·00
6497 47000l. *Betta splendens* 4·25 4·00
6494/6497 *Set of 4* 11·50 10·50
MS6497*a* 120×103 mm. Nos. 6494/7 12·00 12·00

Nos. 6494/7 were each issued with a *se-tenant* stamp-size label attached at either left or right. Each block of four stamps and four labels forming a composite design.

2005 (24 Mar). Pottery (2nd issue). Vert designs as T **1455**. Multicoloured. Litho. P 13½.

6498 7000l. Wedding pitchers (Romana-Olt) 65 60
6499 8000l. Jug (Vadul Crisului-Bihor) 80 75
6500 10000l. Jug (Tara Barsei-Braşov) 90 85
6498/6500 *Set of 3* 2·10 2·00

1458 "Castle of the Carpathians"

1459 Last Supper (icon) (Matei Purcariu)

(Des W. Reiss. Litho)

2005 (29 Mar). Death Centenary of Jules Verne (writer). T **1458** and similar vert designs. Multicoloured. P 13½.

6501 19000l. Type **1458** 1·70 1·60
6502 21000l. "The Danube Pilot" 2·00 1·90
6503 47000l. "Claudius Bombarnac" 4·25 4·00
6504 56000l. "The Stubborn Keraban" 5·25 5·00
6501/6504 *Set of 4* 12·00 11·50
MS6505 120×116 mm. Nos. 6501/4 12·00 12·00

2005 (1 Apr). Easter. T **1459** and similar square designs. Multicoloured. Litho. P 13½.

6506 5000l. Type **1459** 40 35
a. Horiz strip of 3. Nos. 6506/8 1·30
6507 5000l. Crucifixion 40 35
6508 5000l. Resurrection 40 35
6506/6508 *Set of 3* 1·10 95

No. 6507 was perforated in a circle around the design, contained in an outer perforated square.

Nos. 6506/8 were issued in horizontal *se-tenant* strips of three stamps within the sheet.

1460 Pope John Paul II and Stylized Dove

2005 (8 Apr). Pope John Paul II Commemoration. T **1460** and similar horiz design. Multicoloured. Litho. P 13½.

6509 5000l. Type **1460** 40 35
6510 21000l. Vatican 2·00 1·90
MS6511 106×78 mm. Nos. 6509/10 each×2 4·50 4·50

(Des G. Mandriscanu. Litho)

2005 (18 Apr). Anniversaries (2nd issue). Horiz designs as T **1453**. Multicoloured. P 13½.

6512 3000l. Hans Christian Andersen (writer) (birth bicentenary) 25 25
6513 5000l. Jules Verne (writer) (death centenary) 55 50
6514 12000l. Albert Einstein (physicist) (50th death anniv) 1·10 1·00
6515 21000l. Dimitrie Gusti (sociologist and philosopher) (50th death anniv) 2·00 1·90
6516 22000l. George Enescu (musician) (50th death anniv) 2·10 2·00
6512/6516 *Set of 5* 5·50 5·00

1461 Map of Romania and European Stars

(**1461a**)

2005 (25 Apr). Signing of Treaty of Accession to European Union. T **1461** and similar horiz design. Multicoloured. Litho. P 13½.

6517 5000l. Type **1461** 50 50
a. Pair. Nos. 6517/18 1·10 1·10
6518 5000l. As No. 6516 but map and vertical band silver 50 50

Nos. 6517/18 were issued in horizontal and vertical *se-tenant* pairs within sheetlets of four and in sheets of 36 stamps.

2005 (9 May). No. 5623 surch as T **1461a**. P 13½.

6519 5000l. on 50l. 55 50
a. Surch 1 mm to left 55 50

1462 Archer on Horseback and Casserole

(Des O. Penda. Litho)

2005 (9 May). Europa. Gastronomy. T **1462** and similar horiz design. Multicoloured. P 13½.

6520 21000l. Type **1462** 1·80 1·70
6521 77000l. Retriever, fowl, vegetables and wine glass 6·50 6·25
MS6522 120×90 mm. Nos. 6520/1, each×2 17·00 17·00

1463 Grasa de Cotnari Grapes

1464 Fire Supervision

(Des O. Penda. Litho)

2005 (27 May). Viticulture. T **1463** and similar square designs showing grape varieties. Multicoloured. P 13½.

6523 21000l. Type **1463** 1·70 1·60
a. Sheetlet. Nos. 6523/6 plus 2 labels 7·00
6524 21000l. Feteasca neagra 1·70 1·60
6525 21000l. Feteasca alba 1·70 1·60
6526 21000l. Victoria 1·70 1·60
6523/6526 *Set of 4* 6·00 5·75

Nos. 6523/6 were issued in *se-tenant* sheetlets of four stamps and two stamp size labels.

(Des S. Tarlea. Litho)

2005 (15 June). Romania Scouts. T **1464** and similar horiz designs. Multicoloured. P 13½.

6527 22000l. Type **1464** 1·80 1·70
a. Horiz strip of 4. Nos. 6527/30 7·50
b. Sheetlet. Nos. 6527/30 7·75
6528 22000l. Orienteering 1·80 1·70
6529 22000l. Trail marking 1·80 1·70
6530 22000l. Rock climbing 1·80 1·70
6527/6530 *Set of 4* 6·50 6·00

Nos. 6527/30, respectively, were issued in sheets of 50, together in horizontal *se-tenant* strips of four within sheets of 12, and also together in *se-tenant* sheetlets of four stamps.

On 1 July 2005 the currency of Romania was simplified so that now 1 new leu equals 10000 old leu.

New Currency

10000 Leu (l.) = 1 Leu (l.)

1465 1 bani Coin

(Des M. Vămăşescu. Litho)

2005 (1 July). New Currency. T **1465** and similar horiz designs showing old and new currency. Multicoloured. P 13½.

6531 30b. Type **1465** 35 30
a. Vert pair. Nos. 6531/2 75 65
6532 30b. As No. 6531 but design reversed 35 30
6533 50b. 1 leu bank note 55 50
a. Vert pair. Nos. 6533/4 1·20 1·10
6534 50b. As No. 6533 but design reversed 55 50
6535 70b. 5 bani coin 65 60
a. Vert pair. Nos. 6535/6 1·40 1·30
6536 70b. As No. 6535 but design reversed 65 60
6537 80b. 5 lei note 75 70
a. Vert pair. Nos. 6537/8 1·60 1·50
6538 80b. As No. 6537 but design reversed 75 70
6539 1l. 10 lei note 1·00 90
a. Vert pair. Nos. 6539/40 2·10 1·90
6540 1l. As No. 6539 but design reversed 1·00 90
6541 1l.20 50 lei note 1·10 1·00
a. Vert pair. Nos. 6541/2 2·30 2·10
6542 1l.20 As No. 6541 but design reversed 1·10 1·00
6543 1l.60 100 lei note 1·40 1·30
a. Vert pair. Nos. 6543/4 3·00 2·75
6544 1l.60 As No. 6543 but design reversed 1·40 1·30
6545 2l.10 10 bani coin 1·80 1·70
a. Vert pair. Nos. 6545/6 3·75 3·75
6546 2l.10 As No. 6545 but design reversed 1·80 1·70
6547 2l.20 500 lei note 2·10 1·90
a. Vert pair. Nos. 6547/8 4·50 4·00
6548 2l.20 As No. 6547 but design reversed 2·10 1·90
6549 3l.10 50 bani coin 3·00 2·75
a. Vert pair. Nos. 6549/50 6·25 5·75
6550 3l.10 As No. 6549 but design reversed 3·00 2·75
6531/6550 *Set of 20* 23·00 21·00

Nos. 6531/2, 6533/4, 6535/6, 6537/8, 6539/40, 6541/2, 6543/4, 6545/6, 6547/8 and 6549/50, respectively, were issued in vertical *se-tenant* pairs within the sheet.

1466 *Constanţa* (teaching ship)

(Des C. Ilinca. Litho)

2005 (15 July). Stamp Day. Ships. T **1466** and similar horiz designs. Multicoloured. P 13½.

6551 2l.20 Type **1466** 1·80 1·70
a. Vert strip of 4. Nos. 6551/4 7·50
b. Sheetlet. Nos. 6551/4 7·75
6552 2l.20 *Counter Admiral Horia Macellariu* (corvette) 1·80 1·70
6553 2l.20 *Mihail Kogălniceanu* 1·80 1·70
6554 2l.20 *Marasesti* (frigate) 1·80 1·70
6551/6554 *Set of 4* 6·50 6·00

Nos. 6551/4 were issued in vertical *se-tenant* strips of four within sheets of 12, and in *se-tenant* sheetlets of four stamps.

1467 Rainbow and Sphinx

1468 Cardinal Joseph Ratzinger

(Des M. Vămăşescu. Litho)

2005 (2 Aug). Floods–July 2005 (1st issue). P 13½.

6555 **1467** 50b. multicoloured 1·00 90

See also Nos. 6563/6.

(Des G. Ursachi. Litho)

2005 (18 Aug). Enthronement of Benedict XVI. T **1468** and similar vert designs. P 13½.

6556 1l.20 Type **1468** 1·00 90
6557 2l.10 Pope Benedict XVI 1·70 1·60
MS6558 122×98 mm. Nos. 6556/7 2·75 2·75

1469 Christopher Columbus

1470 "The Forest Mailman" (Bianca Paul)

(Des M. Vămăşescu. Litho)

2005 (22 Aug). 50th Anniv of Europa Stamps. 500th Death Anniv of Christopher Columbus (2006). T **1469** and similar horiz designs. Multicoloured. P 13½.

6559 4l.70 Type **1469** 3·75 3·50
a. Horiz strip of 4. Nos. 6559/62 16·00
b. Sheetlet. Nos. 6559/62 17·00
6560 4l.70 *Santa Maria* at left and Columbus 3·75 3·50
6561 4l.70 *Santa Maria* at right and Columbus 3·75 3·50
6562 4l.70 Christopher Columbus wearing wig and hat 3·75 3·50
6559/6562 *Set of 4* 13·50 12·50

Nos. 6559 and 6562 were perforated in a hexagon around the design, enclosed in an outer perforated rectangle.

Nos. 6559/62 were issued in horizontal *se-tenant* strips of four within sheets of 28, and together in horizontal *se-tenant* strips of two stamps plus one label within sheetlets of four stamps and two labels, the strips separated by a gutter showing Christopher Columbus' ships.

2005 (31 Aug). Floods–July 2005 (2nd issue). Winning Entries in Children's Design a Stamp Competition. T **1470** and similar multicoloured designs. Litho. P 13½.

6563 30b. Type **1470** 25 25
6564 40b. "The Road to You" (Daniel Ciornei) 35 30
6565 60b. "A Messenger of Peace" (Stefan Ghiliman) (horiz) 65 60
6566 1l. "Good News for Everybody" (Adina Elena Mocanu) (horiz) 85 80
6563/6566 *Set of 4* 1·90 1·80

(1471)

1472 Jagd Terrier

(Des Penda. Litho Cartor)

2005 (26 Sept). International Philatelic Exhibition, Bucharest. No. **MS**6455 overprinted as T **1471**. P 13½.

MS6567 11l.80×3 on 118000l.×3, multicoloured 30·00 30·00

(Des R. Oltean. Litho)

2005 (28 Sept). Hunting Dogs. T **1472** and similar vert designs. Multicoloured. P 13½.

6568 2l.20 Type **1472** 1·80 1·70
a. Block of 6. Nos. 6568/73 11·50
b. Sheetlet. Nos. 6568/73 12·00
6569 2l.20 Rhodesian ridgeback 1·80 1·70
6570 2l.20 Munsterlander 1·80 1·70
6571 2l.20 Bloodhound 1·80 1·70
6572 2l.20 Copoi ardelenesc (Transylvanian hound) 1·80 1·70
6573 2l.20 Pointer 1·80 1·70
6568/6573 *Set of 6* 9·75 9·25

Nos. 6568/73 were issued in *se-tenant* blocks of six stamps within sheets of 36, and in *se-tenant* sheetlets of six stamps.

1473 Bull's Head

(Des D. Grebu. Litho)

2005 (30 Sept). First Anniv of National Philatelic Museum. P 13½.

6574 **1473** 40b. multicoloured 1·00 90

1474 Emblem

2005 (10 Oct). World Information Society Summit, Tunis. P 13½.

6575 **1474** 5l.60 multicoloured 4·00 3·75

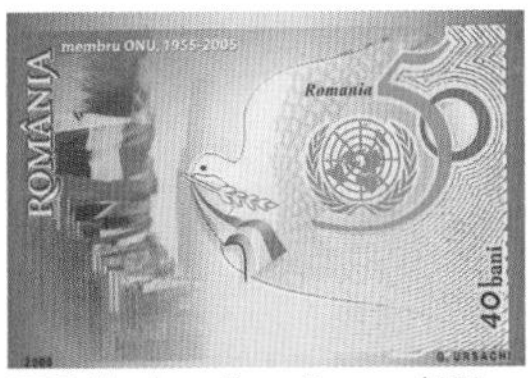

1475 Members Flags, Dove and UN Emblem (50th anniv of Romania's membership)

(Des G. Ursachi. Litho)

2005 (24 Oct). United Nations Anniversaries. T **1475** and similar horiz designs. Multicoloured. P 13½.

6576 40b. Type **1475** 55 50
6577 1l.50 Council chamber (Romania's membership of Security Council, 2004–5 and Presidency, October 2005) 1·40 1·30
6578 2l.20 UN building and dove (60th anniv of UN) 2·00 1·80
6576/6578 *Set of 3* 3·50 3·25
MS6579 164×76 mm. Nos. 6576/8 3·50 3·50

1476 Birthplace and Society Emblem (Illustration further reduced. Actual size 72×33 mm)

(Des L. Pascanu. Litho)

2005 (4 Nov). 160th Birth Anniv of Dimitrie Butculescu (1st president of Romanian Philatelic Society). T **1476** and similar multicoloured designs. P 13½.

6580 50b. Type **1476** 50 45
a. Horiz pair. Nos. 6580/1 1·10 95
6581 50b. Romanian Philatelic Society gazette and Dimitrie Butculescu 50 45
MS6582 114×82 mm. 9l. Dimitrie Butculescu. Imperf 7·50 7·50

Nos. 6580/1 were issued in horizontal *se-tenant* pairs within sheets of six stamps and six labels, the label attached at either left (6580) or right (6581).

1477 Library Building

(Des M. Vămăşescu. Litho)

2005 (10 Nov). 110th Anniv of Central University Library (formerly Carol I University Foundation). T **1477** and similar multicoloured design. P 13½.

6583 60b. Type **1477** 50 45
a. Horiz pair. Nos. 6583/4 1·10 95
6584 60b. Horse and rider (statue) (21×30 mm) 50 45
MS6585 137×96 mm. Nos. 6583/4 1·00 1·00

Nos. 6583/4 were issued in horizontal *se-tenant* pairs within the sheet.

1478 Gusat Englez (English Pouter)

(Des. S. Cumpătă. Litho)

2005 (18 Nov). Domestic Pigeons. T **1478** and similar square designs. Multicoloured. P 13½.

6586 2l.50 Type **1478** 2·10 1·90
a. Sheetlet. Nos. 6586/9 8·75
6587 2l.50 Jucator pestrit (Parlour roller) 2·10 1·90
6588 2l.50 Calator tip standard (Standard carrier) 2·10 1·90
6589 2l.50 Zburator de Andaluzia (Andalusian) 2·10 1·90
6586/6589 *Set of 4* 7·50 6·75

Nos. 6586/9 were issued in *se-tenant* sheetlets of four stamps.

1479 "Thinker of Hamangia" and "Sitting Woman" (Neolithic sculptures)

(Des G. Mandriscanu. Litho)

2005 (21 Nov). 60th Anniv of UNESCO. P 13½.

6590 **1479** 2l.10 multicoloured 1·80 1·70

No. 6590 was issued with a *se-tenant* stamp size label inscribed for the anniversary.

2005 (24 Nov). Pottery (3rd issue). Vert designs as T **1455**. Multicoloured. Litho. P 13½.

6591 30b. Jug (Leheceni, Bihor) 35 30
6592 50b. Pitcher (Vladesti, Valcea) 55 50
6593 1l. Pitcher (Curtea de Argeş, Argeş) 85 80
6594 1l.20 Jug (Vama, Satu Mare) 1·10 1·00
6595 2l.20 Jug (Barsa, Arad) 1·80 1·70
6596 2l.50 Wide-necked pitcher (Corund, Harghita) 2·20 2·00
6597 14l.50 Wide-necked pitcher (Valea Izei, MaraMureş) 11·50 10·50
6591/6597 *Set of 7* 17·00 15·00

1480 The Annunciation

1481 "Inscripti" (Virgil Preda)

(Des M. Vămăşescu. Litho)

2005 (2 Dec). Christmas. T **1480** and similar multicoloured designs showing icons. P 13½.

6598 50b. Type **1480** 40 35
a. Imperf 40 35
b. Horiz strip. Nos. 6598/600 1·30
c. Sheetlet. No. 6598b×3 1·40
6599 50b. The Nativity (48×83 mm) 40 35
a. Imperf 40 35
6600 50b. Madonna and Child 40 35
a. Imperf 40 35
6598/6600 *Set of 3* 1·10 95

Nos. 6598/600 were issued in horizontal *se-tenant* strips of three in sheetlets of nine and in sheets of 54 stamps. Nos. 6598a/600a were only available in sheetlets of nine stamps.

2005 (12 Dec). Contemporary Romanian Art. T **1481** and similar multicoloured designs. Litho. P 13½.

6601 1l.50 Type **1481** 1·20 1·10
a. Strip of 4. Nos. 6601/4 5·00
6602 1l.50 "Gradina suspendata (Alin Gheorghiu) (horiz) 1·20 1·10

6603 1l.50 "Still Life" (Constantin Ceraceanu) (horiz) 1·20 1·10
6604 1l.50 "Monstru 1" (Cristian Paleologu) 1·20 1·10
6601/6604 *Set of 4* 4·25 4·00

Nos. 6601/4 were issued in horizontal *se-tenant* strips of four stamps, with Nos. 6602 and 6603 laid at right angles.

2005 (19 Dec). Pottery (4th issue). Vert designs as T **1455**. Multicoloured. Litho. P 13½.
6605 4l.70 Jug (Targu Neamt) 4·00 3·75
6606 5l.60 Jug and lidded jug (Poiana Deleni) 4·75 4·25

1482 Norwegian Forest Cat

(Des Simona Bucan. Litho)

2006 (20 Jan). Cats. T **1482** and similar square designs. Multicoloured. P 13½.
6607 30b. Type **1482** 25 25
6608 50b. Turkish Van 50 45
6609 70b. Siamese 60 60
6610 80b. Ragdoll 75 70
6611 1l.20 Persian 1·10 1·00
6612 1l.60 Birman (Inscr "Sacred cat of Burma") 1·50 1·40
6607/6612 *Set of 6* 4·25 4·00
MS6613 144×108 mm. As No. 6607/12. Imperf 4·25 4·25

1483 Wolfgang Amadeus Mozart (composer) (250th birth anniv)

(Des R. Popescu. Litho)

2006 (27 Jan). Anniversaries. T **1483** and similar horiz designs. Multicoloured. P 13½.
6614 50b. Type **1483** 50 45
6615 1l.20 Ion Brătianu (politician) (185th birth anniv) 1·10 1·00
6616 2l.10 Grigore Moisii (mathematician) (birth centenary) 2·00 1·90
6614/6616 *Set of 3* 3·25 3·00

1484 Ice Dance

1486 Crucifixion

1485 1868 Charles I 20lei

(Des Simona Bucan. Litho)

2006 (1 Feb). Winter Olympic Games, Turin. Sheet 123×92 mm containing T **1484** and similar square designs. Multicoloured. P 13½.
MS6617 1l.60×4, Type **1484**; 1l.60 Downhill skiing; Bobsleigh; Biathlon 6·25 6·25

No. **MS**6617 has an enlarged illustrated central gutter showing Elisabeta Lipa holding the Olympic torch.

Nos. 6618/20 are vacant.

2006 (22 Feb). Gold Coins. T **1485** and similar horiz designs. Multicoloured. Litho. P 13½.
6621 30b. Type **1485** 25 25
6622 50b. 1906 Charles I 50lei 50 45
6623 70b. 1906 Charles I 100lei 60 60
6624 1l. 1922 Ferdinand I 50lei 1·00 95
6625 1l.20 1939 Charles II 100lei 1·10 1·00
6626 2l.20 1940 Charles II 100lei 2·10 2·00
6621/6626 *Set of 6* 5·00 4·75

Nos. 6621/6, respectively, were issued both in sheets of 16 and in small sheets of seven stamps and two labels.

2006 (22 Feb). Easter. Icons. T **1486** and similar square designs. Multicoloured. Litho. P 13½.
6627 50b. Type **1486** 50 45
6628 50b. Mary grieving 50 45
6629 50b. Mary grieving (different) 50 45
6630 50b. Removing Christ from the Cross 50 45
6631 50b. Ascension to heaven 50 45
6627/6631 *Set of 5* 2·30 2·00
MS6632 132×132 mm. Nos. 6627/31 2·50 2·50

1487 Traian Vuia and Drawing

1488 Leopold Senghor

(Des Vămăşescu. Litho)

2006 (18 Mar). Centenary of Traian Vuia's First Powered Flight. T **1487** and similar multicoloured designs. P 13½.
6633 70b. Type **1487** 60 60
6634 80b. *Vuia I* 75 70
6635 1l.60 *Vuia II* 1·50 1·40
6633/6635 *Set of 3* 2·50 2·40
MS6636 114×91 mm. Nos. 6633/5 plus label 2·50 2·50
MS6637 116×84 mm. 4l.70 Traian Vuia seated on *Vuia I* (42×52 mm) 4·00 4·00

(Des G. Ursachi. Litho)

2006 (20 Mar). Birth Centenary of Léopold Sédar Senghor (writer and president of Senegal, 1960–1980). P 13½.
6638 **1488** 2l.10 multicoloured 1·80 1·70

No. 6638 was issued both in large sheets of 50 and small sheets of four stamps with enlarged central margin inscribed for the anniversary.

2006 (30 Mar). Pottery (5th issue). Wedding Pots. Vert designs as T **1455**. Multicoloured. Litho. P 13½.
6639 60b. Jug with animal spout (Poienita Argeş) 50 45
6640 70b. Complex pot with storks (Oboga Olt) 60 60
6641 80b. Jug with raised decoration (Oboga Olt) 75 70
6642 1l.60 Figure as jug (Romana Olt) 1·40 1·30
6639/6642 *Set of 4* 3·00 2·75

1489 Turkestanica

1490 House and Children

(Des Cătălin Ilinca. Litho)

2006 (14 Apr). Tulips. T **1489** and similar multicoloured designs. P 13½.
6643 30b. Type **1489** 25 25
a. Block of 6. Nos. 6643/8 7·50
6644 50b. Ice Follies 35 35
6645 1l. Cardinal 75 70
6646 1l.50 Yellow Empress (47×33 mm) 1·10 1·00
6647 2l.10 Donna Bella 1·70 1·60
6648 3l.60 Don Quixote (47×33 mm) 3·00 2·75
6643/6648 *Set of 6* 6·50 6·00
MS6649 112×122 mm. As No. 6643/8 7·50 7·50

Nos. 6643/5 and 6647, respectively, were issued in sheets of 72, Nos. 6646 and 6648, in sheets of 36, and all six stamps were issued together in *se-tenant* blocks of six within sheets of 12 stamps.

2006 (20 Apr). Pottery (6th issue). Vert designs as T **1455**. Multicoloured. Litho. P 13½.
6650 30b. Jug with snakes and frog (Oboga Olt) 35 35
6651 40b. Jug with pig's head spout (Radauti Suceava) 50 45
6652 2l.50 Jar with handle and raised decoration (Vladesti Valcea) 2·40 2·20
6653 3l.10 Jar with four handles (Jupanesti, Timis) 2·50 2·40
6650/6653 *Set of 4* 5·25 4·75

2006 (4 May). Europa. Integration. T **1490** and similar horiz design. Multicoloured. Litho. P 13½.
6654 2l.10 Type **1490** 1·90 1·70
a. Pair. Nos. 6654/5 4·50 4·25
6655 3l.10 Adult and child approaching house 2·40 2·20

Nos. 6654/5 were issued in horizontal and vertical *se-tenant* pairs within sheets of four stamps.

1491 1866 Carol I 2p. Stamp (As Type **6**)

1493 Opening Ceremony

1492 Christopher Columbus (500th death anniv)

2006 (8 May). 140th Anniv of Romanian Dynasty. 125th Anniv of Proclamation of Romanian Kingdom. Two sheets containing T **1491** and similar multicoloured designs. Litho. P 13½.
6656 30b. Type **1491** 35 35
6657 1l. 1920 Ferdinand I 1b. stamp (As No. 879) 85 80
6658 2l.10 1930 Carol II 7l.50 (As No. 1179) 1·90 1·70
6659 2l.50 1940 Michael I 20l. stamp (As No. 1466) 2·40 2·20
6656/6659 *Set of 4* 5·00 4·50
MS6660 140×145 mm. Nos. 6656/9 5·25 5·25
MS6661 125×90 mm. 4l.70 1906 Carol I 15b. stamp (As No. 507) (horiz) 4·00 4·00

(Des R. Popescu. Litho)

2006 (17 May). Anniversaries. T **1492** and similar multicoloured designs. P 13½.
6662 50b. Type **1492** 45 40
6663 1l. Paul Cezanne (death centenary) 95 85
6664 1l.20 Henrik Ibsen (composer) (death centenary) 1·20 1·10
6662/6664 *Set of 3* 2·30 2·10

2006 (17 May). Dimitrie Gusti National Village Museum. Litho. P 13½.
6665 **1493** 2l.20 multicoloured 1·90 1·70

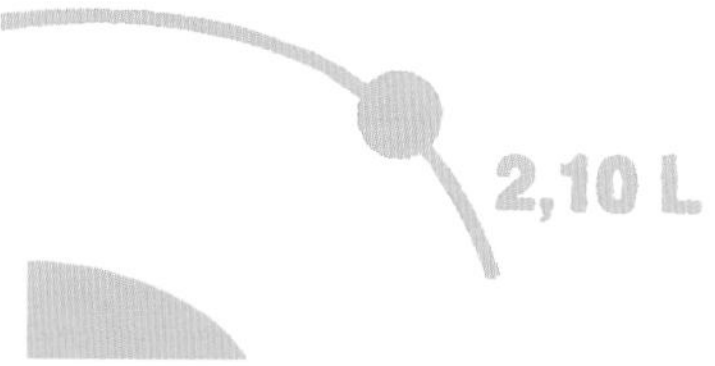

(**1494**)

2006 (19 May). 25th Anniv of First Romanian Astronaut. No. **MS**5809 surch as T **1494** in gold or silver. Litho. P 13½.
MS6666 **1224** 2l.10 on 2720l. multicoloured 1·80 1·70

The margins of No. **MS**6666 were additionally overprinted for the anniversary.

1495 Main Entrance, Charles I Park

2006 (6 June). Centenary of General Expo and Charles I Park, Bucharest. T **1495** and similar horiz designs. Multicoloured. Litho. P 13½.
6667 30b. Type **1495** 30 30
6668 50b. Tepeş Castle 45 40
6669 1l. Post Office pavilion 85 80
6670 1l.20 Danube European Commission pavilion 1·10 1·00
6671 1l.60 Palace of Industry 1·50 1·40
6672 2l.20 Roman arenas 2·10 2·00
6667/6672 *Set of 6* 5·75 5·25
MS6673 160×130 mm. Nos. 6667/72 5·75 5·75
MS6674 115×85 mm. 2l.20 Palace of Art 1·90 1·90

1496 Béla Bartók

1497 Trophy

(Des G. Ursachi. Litho)

2006 (8 June). Composers' 125th Birth Anniversaries. T **1496** and similar horiz design. Multicoloured. P 13½.
6675 1l.20 Type **1496** 95 85
a. Horiz pair. Nos. 6675/6 2·00 1·80
6676 1l.20 George Inescu 95 85
MS6677 95×82 mm. Nos. 6675/6 2·00 2·00

Nos. 6675/6 were issued in horizontal *se-tenant* pairs within the sheet.

Stamps of a similar design were issued by Hungary.

(Des O. Cojocari. Litho)

2006 (9 June). World Cup Football Championship, Germany. T **1497** and similar square designs. Multicoloured. P 13½.

6678 30b. Type **1497** ... 35 30
6679 50b. Ball in net ... 45 40
6680 1l. Player ... 90 85
6681 1l.20 Hands holding trophy ... 1·10 1·00
6678/6681 *Set of 4* ... 2·50 2·30
MS6682 93×93 mm. Nos. 6678/81 ... 2·50 2·50

1498 Young People

2006 (26 June). International Day against Drug Abuse and Illegal Drug Trafficking. Litho. P 13½.

6683 **1498** 2l.20 multicoloured ... 1·90 1·80

2006 (10 July). Pottery (7th issue). Vert designs as T **1455**. Multicoloured. Litho. P 13½.

6684 30b. Jar with handle and central decoration (Golesti-Argeş) ... 35 30
6685 70b. Jug with spout and raised decoration (Romana-Olt) ... 65 65
6686 1l. Ornate jug with bird's head spout and circular base of birds (Oboga-Olt) ... 90 85
6687 2l.20 White bodied jar with handle and floral decoration (Vama-Satu Mare) .. 1·90 1·80
6684/6687 *Set of 4* ... 3·50 3·25

1499 Woman and Accoutrements

(Des O. Penda. Litho)

2006 (15 July). Stamp Day. 1900th Death Anniv of Decebalus (Decebal), King of Dacia. T **1499** and similar horiz designs. Multicoloured. P 13½.

6688 30b. Type **1499** ... 35 30
6689 50b. Man, facing left ... 55 50
6690 1l.20 Helmet (c. 150 A.D.) ... 1·10 1·00
6691 3l.10 Man standing ... 2·75 2·50
6688/6691 *Set of 4* ... 4·25 3·75
MS6692 116×87 mm. Nos. 6688/91 ... 4·50 4·50

1500 Fluorite

2006 (7 Aug). Minerals. T **1500** and similar diamond-shaped designs. Multicoloured. Litho. P 13½.

6693 30b. Type **1500** ... 35 30
6694 50b. Quartz ... 45 40
6695 1l. Agate ... 90 85
6696 1l.20 Zinc blende (sphalerite) ... 1·10 1·00
6697 1l.50 Amethyst ... 1·50 1·40
6698 2l.20 Stibnite ... 2·00 1·90
6693/6698 *Set of 6* ... 5·75 5·25
MS6699 168×85 mm. Nos. 6693/8 ... 5·75 5·75

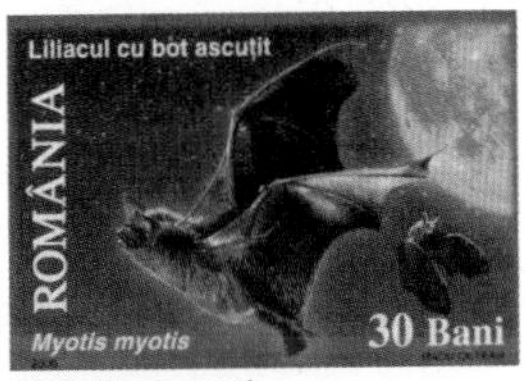

1501 *Myotis myotis*

(Des R. Oltean. Litho)

2006 (15 Aug). Bats. T **1501** and similar horiz designs. Multicoloured. P 13½.

6700 30b. Type **1501** ... 35 30
6701 50b. *Rhinolophus hipposideros* ... 45 40
6702 1l. *Plecotus auritus* ... 90 85
6703 1l.20 *Pipistrellus pipistrellus* ... 1·10 1·00
6704 1l.60 *Nycatalus lasiopterus* ... 1·50 1·40
6705 2l.20 *Barbastella barbastella* ... 2·00 1·90
6700/6705 *Set of 6* ... 5·75 5·25
MS6706 116×140 mm. Nos. 6700/5 ... 5·75 5·75

The stamps and margins of No. **MS**6706 form a composite design.

1502 Wartberg Type 1B-n2 (1854)

(Des R. Popescu. Litho)

2006 (23 Aug). 150th Anniv of First Railway Line from Oravita–Bazias. T **1502** and similar horiz designs. Multicoloured. P 13½.

6707 30b. Type **1502** ... 35 30
6708 50b. Ovidiu Type C-n2 (1860) ... 45 40
6709 1l. Curierulu Type 1B-n2 (1869) ... 90 85
6710 1l.20 Berlad Type 1A1-n2 (1869) ... 1·10 1·00
6711 1l.50 Unirea Type 1B-n2 (1877) ... 1·30 1·30
6712 1l.60 Fulger King Charles I Pullman Express (1933) ... 1·50 1·40
6707/6712 *Set of 6* ... 5·00 4·75
MS6713 138×108 mm. 2l.20 Steyerdorf Type CB-2nf (72×33 mm) ... 2·00 2·00

1503 1858 27p. Stamp (As Type **1**)

1504 Goddess of Fortune

2006 (30 Aug). EFIRO 2008, International Stamp Exhibition, Bucharest (1st isssue). T **1503** and similar vert designs showing first Romanian Stamps. Multicoloured. Litho. P 13½.

6714 30b. Type **1503** ... 35 30
6715 50b. As No. 2 ... 45 40
6716 1l.20 As No. 3 ... 1·10 1·00
6717 1l.60 As No. 4 ... 1·50 1·40
6714/6717 *Set of 4* ... 3·00 2·75
MS6718 100×123 mm. 2l.20 Bull's head (42×52 mm) ... 1·90 1·90

Nos. 6714/17 were each issued with a different *se-tenant* stamp size label, inscribed for the exhibition, attached at left.

See also Nos. 6826/**MS**6829 and 6893/**MS**6899.

2006 (14 Sept). Centenary of National Lottery. Litho. P 13½.

6719 **1504** 1l. multicoloured ... 1·00 95

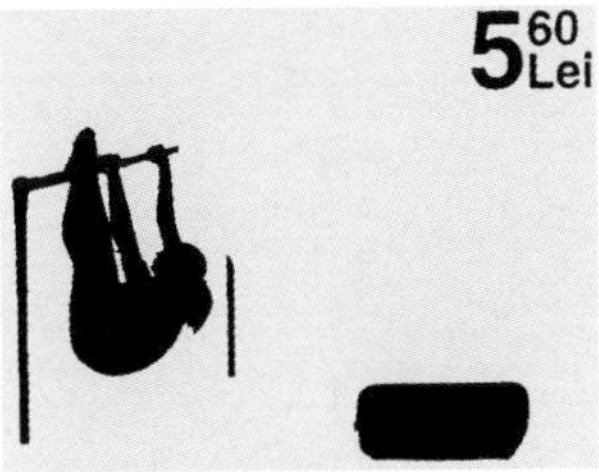

(1505)

2006 (16 Sept). Gymnastics. No. **MS**5834 surch as T **1505**. Litho. P 13½.

6720 5l.60 on 4050l. multicoloured ... 4·75 4·75

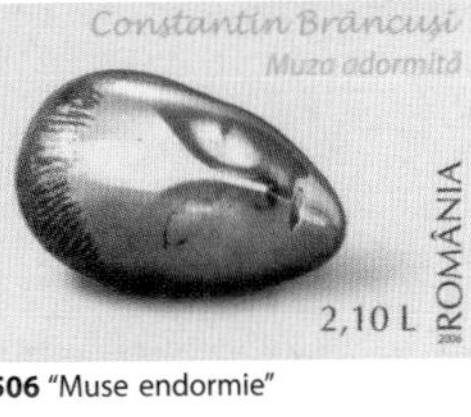

1506 "Muse endormie"

2006 (25 Sept). 130th Birth Anniv of Constantin Brancuşi (sculptor). T **1506** and similar horiz design. Multicoloured. Litho. P 13½.

6721 2l.10 Type **1506** ... 1·80 1·70
6722 3l.10 "Le sommeil" ... 2·75 2·50
MS6723 130×94 mm. Nos. 6721/2 ... 4·50 4·50

Stamps of a similar design were issued by France.

1507 "Thinker of Hamangia" (Neolithic sculpture)

2006 (28 Sept). 11th La Francaphone (French speaking countries and organizations) Meeting, Bucharest. Litho. P 13½.

6724 **1507** 1l.20 multicoloured ... 1·00 95
MS6725 90×95 mm. **1507** (42×52 mm) 5l.60 multicoloured ... 4·75 4·75

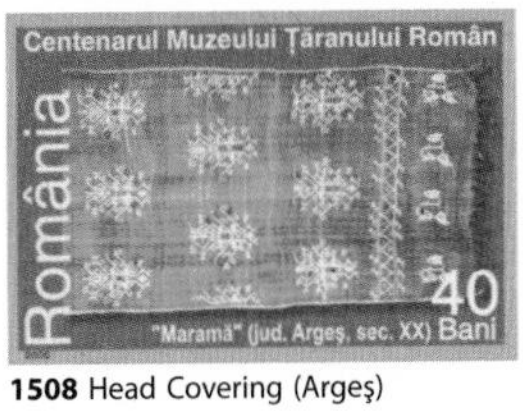

1508 Head Covering (Argeş)

2006 (5 Oct). Centenary of Peasant Museum. T **1508** and similar horiz designs. Multicoloured. Litho. P 13½.

6726 40b. Type **1508** ... 35 30
6727 70b. Necklace (Dobruja) ... 65 65
6728 1l.60 Coin necklace (Bucovina) ... 1·50 1·40
6729 3l.10 Alexandru Tzigara-Samurcas (founder) ... 3·00 2·75
6726/6729 *Set of 4* ... 5·00 4·50

1509 Alexandru Ioan Cuza (ruler at time of founding of National Police force)

1511 Loyal Service

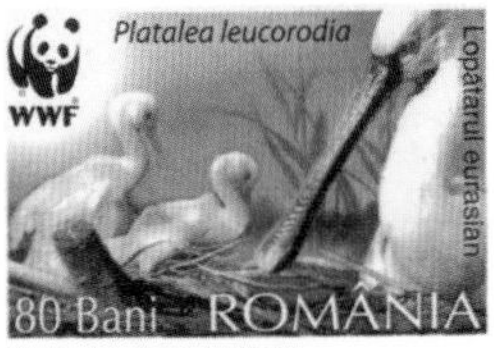

1510 Adult and Chicks

2006 (7 Oct). Tenth Anniv of Romanian Membership of International Police Association. Sheet 95×95 mm. Litho. P 13½.

MS6730 **1509** 8l.70 multicoloured ... 7·25 7·25

(Des M. Vămăşescu. Litho)

2006 (20 Oct). Endangered Species. Eurasian Spoonbill (*Platalea leucorodia*). T **1510** and similar horiz designs. Multicoloured. P 13½.

6731 80b. Type **1510** ... 80 75
6732 80b. Two adults feeding ... 80 75
6733 80b. In flight ... 80 75
6734 80b. Two heads facing right ... 80 75
6731/6734 *Set of 4* ... 2·75 2·75
MS6735 170×120 mm. Nos. 6731/4 ... 2·75 2·75

Nos. 6731/4 were each issued with a *se-tenant* stamp size label showing spoonbills attached at foot.

(Des M. Vămăşescu. Litho)

2006 (30 Oct). National Orders. T **1511** and similar horiz designs. Multicoloured. P 13½.

6736 30b. Type **1511** ... 20 20
6737 80b. Romanian Star ... 65 65
6738 2l.20 For Merit ... 1·90 1·80
6739 2l.50 First Class Sports Merit ... 2·10 2·00
6736/6739 *Set of 4* ... 4·25 4·25

1512 Radu Beligan

1513 Holy Virgin Empress

(Des Simona Bucan. Litho)

2006 (15 Nov). Actors. T **1512** and similar square designs. Multicoloured. P 13½.

6740 40b. Type **1512** ... 35 30
6741 1l. Carmen Stănescu ... 90 85
6742 1l.50 Dina Cocea ... 1·30 1·30
6743 2l.20 Colea Rautu ... 2·10 2·00
6740/6743 *Set of 4* ... 4·25 4·00

2006 (17 Nov). Christmas. Icons. T **1513** and similar square designs. Multicoloured. P 13½.

6744 50b. Type **1513** ... 50 45
6745 50b. Holy Virgin with Baby Jesus on the Throne ... 50 45
6746 50b. Worship of the Magi ... 50 45
6744/6746 *Set of 3* ... 1·40 1·20

1514 "EU"

(Des S. Balezdrov (6747) or S. Târlea (6748). Litho)

2006 (29 Nov). Romania and Bulgaria's Membership of European Union. T **1514** and similar horiz design. Multicoloured. P 13½.

6747 50b. Type **1514** ... 45 40
6748 2l.10 Ballot box and flags ... 1·80 1·70

Stamps of a similar design were issued by Bulgaria.

1515 "AD PERPETUAM REI MEMORIAM"
(For the eternal remembrance)

2006 (30 Nov). Contemporary Art. Works by Ciprian Paleologu. T **1515** and similar horiz design. Multicoloured. P 13½.

6749 30b. Type **1515** 35 30
6750 1l.50 "CUI BONO?" (Whose interest?) .... 1·30 1·30
6751 3l.60 "USQVE AD FINEM" (All the way) .... 3·25 3·25
6749/6751 *Set of 3* .... 4·50 4·25

1516 Obverse of 200 leu Banknote

(Des M. Vămăşescu. Litho)

2006 (1 Dec). New Banknote. T **1516** and similar horiz design. Multicoloured. P 13½.

6752 50b. Type **1516** 45 40
6753 1l.20 Reverse of 200l. banknote .... 1·00 95

1517 Children

(Des M. Vămăşescu. Litho)

2006 (11 Dec). 60th Anniv of UNICEF. P 13½.

6754 **1517** 3l.10 multicoloured .... 2·75 2·50

1518 Sphinx, Bucegi

1519 Altar Rock Cave, Bihorului Mountains

(Des M. Vămăşescu. Litho)

2007 (3 Jan). Romania's Accession to European Union. P 13½.

6755 **1518** 2l.20 multicoloured .... 1·90 1·80

No. 6755 has an attached label showing map of Romania and EU stars.

(Des R. Oltean. Litho)

2007 (19 Jan). Centenary of Publication "Essay on Biospeleological Problems" (study of cave living organisms) by Emil Racovita (Romanian scientific pioneer). T **1519** and similar vert designs. Multicoloured. P 13½.

6756 40b. Type **1519** 35 30
6757 1l.60 Emil Racovita .... 1·30 1·30
6758 7l.20 *Ursus spelaeus* .... 6·25 5·75
6759 8l.70 Microscope and *Typhlocirolana moraguesi* .... 7·25 6·75
6756/6759 *Set of 4* .... 13·50 12·50
MS6760 131×112 mm. Nos. 6756/9 .... 13·50 13·50

1520 Hand and Wire

(Des Simona Bucan. Litho)

2007 (27 Jan). International Holocaust Remembrance Day. P 13½.

6761 **1520** 3l.30 multicoloured .... 2·75 2·50

1521 *Hippocampus hippocampus* (Inscr "Hypocampus hypocampus")

(Des R. Oltean. Litho)

2007 (9 Feb). Black Sea Fauna. T **1521** and similar vert designs. Multicoloured. P 13½.

6762 70b. Type **1521** 65 65
6763 1l.50 *Delphinus delphis* .... 1·50 1·40
6764 3l.10 *Caretta caretta* .... 3·25 3·00
6765 7l.70 *Trigla lucerna* .... 6·75 6·25
6762/6765 *Set of 4* .... 11·00 10·00
MS6766 190×121 mm. Nos. 6762/5 .... 11·00 11·00

1522 Gustave Eiffel (construction engineer)

(Des Penda. Litho)

2007 (23 Feb). Personalities. T **1522** and similar horiz designs. Multicoloured. P 13½.

6767 60b. Type **1522** 55 50
6768 80b. Maria Cutarida (first woman doctor) 80 75
6769 2l.10 Virginia Woolf (writer) .... 2·00 1·90
6770 3l.50 Nicolae Titulescu (politician) .... 3·25 3·00
6767/6770 *Set of 4* .... 6·00 5·50

1523 Decorated Egg, Olt

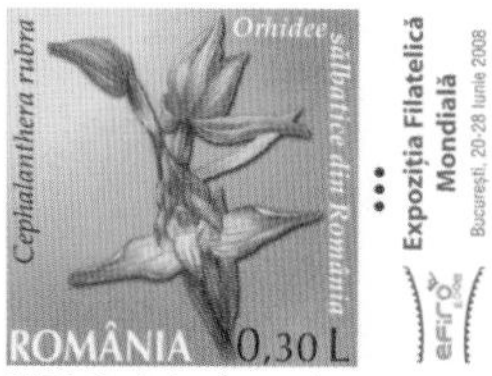

1524 *Cephalanthera rubra*

(Des M. Vămăşescu. Litho)

2007 (9 Mar). Easter. T **1523** and similar square designs. Multicoloured. P 13½.

6771 50b. Type **1523** 40 35
a. Horiz strip of 3. Nos. 6771/3 .... 1·30
6772 50b. The Risen Christ (icon) 40 35
6773 50b. Decorated Egg, Bucovina 40 35
6771/6773 *Set of 3* .... 1·10 95

Nos. 6771/3 were issued in horizontal *se-tenant* strips of three stamps within sheets of nine.

Nos. 6771 and 6773 were perforated in a circle contained in an outer perforated square.

(Des Corina Ardelean. Litho)

2007 (23 Mar). Orchids. T **1524** and similar square designs. Multicoloured. P 13½ (interrupted on right vert side (6774/9)).

6774 30l. Type **1524** 35 30
6775 1l.20 *Epipactis palustris* .... 1·10 1·00
6776 1l.60 *Dactylorhiza maculata* .... 1·50 1·40
6777 2l.50 *Anacamptis pyramidalis* .... 2·20 2·10
6778 2l.70 *Limodorum abortivum* .... 2·50 2·30
6779 6l. *Ophrys scolopax* .... 5·50 5·00
6774/6779 *Set of 6* .... 12·00 11·00
MS6780 148×113 mm. 30b. Type **1524**; 1l.20 *Epipactis palustris*; 1l.60 *Dactylorhiza maculata*; 2l.50 *Anacamptis pyramidalis*; 2l.70 *Limodorum abortivum*; 6l. *Ophrys scolopax* .... 12·00 12·00

Nos. 6774/9 have only three perforation in the centre of each right edge which separate the stamp from a *se-tenant* label inscribed for Efiro 2008 International Stamp Exhibition.

2007 (13 Apr). Pottery (8th issue). Vert designs as T **1455**. Multicoloured. Litho. P 13½.

6781 70b. Brown plate with central rooster (Obaga-Olt) 70 65
6782 1l. Mottled plate inscr "1898" (Vama-Satu Mare) 95 90
6783 2l.10 Cream plate with central soldier (Valea Izea-Maramureş) .... 2·20 2·00
6784 2l.20 Cream bodied plate with overall decoration (Frăgărăş-Braşov) .... 2·30 2·10
6781/6784 *Set of 4* .... 5·50 5·00

1525 *Accipiter nisus* (sparrow hawk)

1526 Scouts

(Des Mihai Vămăşescu. Litho)

2007 (19 Apr). Raptors. T **1525** and similar vert designs. Multicoloured. P 13½.

6785 50b. Type **1525** 55 50
6786 80b. *Circus aeruginosus* (marsh harrier) 80 75
6787 1l.60 *Aquila pomarina* (lesser spotted eagle) .... 1·60 1·50
6788 2l.50 *Buteo buteo* (common buzzard) .... 2·50 2·40
6789 3l.10 *Athene noctua* (little owl) .... 3·25 3·00
6785/6789 *Set of 5* .... 7·75 7·25
MS6790 65×90 mm. 4l.70 *Falco subbuteo* (hobby) (42×52 mm) .... 4·25 4·25

(Des Cătălin Raibuh. Litho)

2007 (3 May). Europa. Centenary of Scouting. Sheet 87×117 mm containing T **1526** and similar vert designs. Multicoloured. P 13½.

6791 2l.10 Type **1526** .... 1·80 1·70
6792 7l.70 Robert Baden-Powell (founder) .... 6·00 5·75

Nos. 6791/2 were issued both in sheets and together, each×2, in sheetlets of four stamps.

1527 Curtea Veche (Principal Court)
(Illustration reduced. Actual size 72×33 mm)

2007 (15 May). Old Bucharest. T **1527** and similar horiz designs. Multicoloured. P 13½.

6792*a* 30b. Type **1527** 25 25
6792*b* 50b. Sturdza Palace 55 50
6792*c* 70b. National Military Circle 70 65
6792*d* 1l.60 National Theatre .... 1·50 1·40
6792*e* 3l.10 I. C. Brătianu Square .... 3·00 2·75
6792*f* 4l.70 Senate Square .... 4·75 4·50
6792*a*/6792*f* *Set of 6* .... 9·75 9·00

(Des Mihai Vămăşescu and Stan Pelteacu. Litho)

2007 (15 May). Old Bucharest. Two sheets containing T **1527** and similar horiz designs. Multicoloured. P 13½.

MS6793 (a) 87×117 mm. 30b. Type **1527**; 50b. Sturdza Palace; 70b. National Military Circle; 1l.60 National Theatre; 3l.10 I. C. Brătianu Square; 4l.70 Senate Square. (b) 131×111 mm. 5l.60 Romanian Athenaeum (52×42 mm) .... 12·00 12·00

2007 (5 June). Pottery (9th issue). Vert designs as T **1455**. Multicoloured. Litho. P 13½.

6794 70b. Cream plate with central spiral design (Vlădeşti-Vâlcea) 70 65
6795 80b. Cream bodied plate with green overall decoration (Viştea-Braşov) 80 75
6796 1l.60 Brown plate with geometric design (Tansa-Iaşi) .... 1·50 1·40
6797 3l.10 Green decorated plate (Româna-Olt) .... 3·00 2·75
6794/6797 *Set of 4* .... 5·50 5·00

Nos. 6794/7, respectively, were each issued in *se-tenant* sheetlets of six stamps with enlarged illustrated margins.

1528 Emblem and Medal

(Des Razvan Popescu. Litho)

2007 (7 June). 60th Anniv of Steaua Sports Club. P 13½.

6798 **1528** 7l.70 multicoloured .... 7·00 6·75

1529 Palace Façade

(Des Mihai Vămăşescu. Litho)

2007 (8 June). 110th Anniv of National Savings Bank Palace. T **1529** and similar horiz design. Multicoloured. P 13½.

6799 4l.70 Type **1529** .... 4·25 4·00
MS6800 145×160 mm. 5l.60 Palace façade .... 5·00 5·00

1530 Altemberger House (Illustration reduced. Actual size 72×33 mm)

(Des Radu Oltean. Litho)

2007 (11 June). Sibiu–European Capital of Culture–2007. Two sheets containing T **1530** and similar horiz designs. Multicoloured. P 13½.

6801 30b. Type **1530** 25 25
6802 50b. Liars' Bridge and Council Tower 55 50
6803 60b. Parochial Evangelical Church 60 60
6804 70b. Grand Square c. 1780 .... 70 65
6805 2l.10 Brukenthal Palace and St. Nepomuk Statue c. 1935 .... 2·00 1·90
6806 5l.60 Panorama c. 1790 (painting) (F. Neuhauser) .... 5·50 5·00
6801/6806 *Set of 6* .... 8·75 8·00
MS6807 (a) 190×160 mm. 30b. As Type **1530**; 50b. As No. 6802; 60b. As No. 6803; 70b. As No. 6804; 2l.10 As No. 6805; 5l.60 As No. 6806. (b) 127×102 mm. 4l.70 Sibiu Fortress c. 1650 (52×42 mm) .... 13·50 13·50

The stamp and margin of No. **MS**6800 form a composite design of Sibiu Fortress.

1530a *Anser erthyropus* (lesser white-fronted goose)

(Des Radu Oltean. Litho)

2007 (12 July). Ducks and Geese. T **1530a** and similar horiz designs. Multicoloured. P 13½.

6808 40b. Type **1530a** ... 40 40
6809 60b. *Branta ruficollis* (red-breasted goose) ... 70 65
6810 1l.60 *Anas acuta* (northern pintail) ... 1·50 1·40
6811 2l.10 *Anser albifrons* (white-fronted goose) ... 2·00 1·90
6812 3l.60 *Netta rufina* (red-crested pochard) ... 3·75 3·50
6813 4l.70 *Anas querquedula* (garganey) ... 4·50 4·25
6808/6813 *Set of 6* ... 11·50 11·00
MS6814 (a) 173×124 mm. 40b. As Type **1528a**; 60b. As No. 6809; 1l.60 As No. 6810; 2l.10 As No. 6811; 3l.60 As No. 6812; 4l.70 As No. 6813. (b) 120×95 mm. 5l.60 *Anas clypeata* (northern shoveler) (52×42 mm) Imperf ... 16·00 16·00

1530b Bisra Local 6 Heller Stamp and Early Carriage (Illustration reduced. Actual size 71×33 mm)

(Des Mircea Dragoteanu. Litho)

2007 (18 July). Stamp Day. Centenary of Bisra Local Post. T **1530b** and similar horiz design. Multicoloured. P 13½.

6815 50b. Type **1530b** ... 45 45
6816 2l.10 Bisra Local 2 Heller Stamp and early postman ... 1·90 2·40

2007 (3–10 Aug). Pottery (10th and 11th issue). Vert designs as T **1455**. Multicoloured. Litho. P 13½.

6817 60b. Fawn plate with all over decoration (Lapus-MaraMureş) ... 70 65
6818 80b. Brown dish with yellow scrafiti designs (Luncavita-Tulcea) ... 80 75
6819 1l.10 Cream dish with star-shaped central decoration (Luncavita-Tulcea) ... 1·10 1·00
6820 1l.40 Brown bodied jar with handle and cream and green decoration (Horezu-Valcea) (10.8) ... 1·40 1·30
6821 1l.60 Cream plate with central green and yellow flowers and border decoration (Radauti-Suceava) ... 1·50 1·40
6822 1l.80 Large green bodied cup with brown and white decoration (Baia Mare-MaraMureş) (10.8) ... 1·80 1·70
6823 2l.90 Cream bodied cup with dark brown orange decoration (Oboga-Olt) (10.8) ... 2·75 2·50
6824 7l.70 Wide bodied cup with brown and white dotted decoration (Baia Mare-MaraMureş) (10.8) ... 7·25 7·00
6817/6824 *Set of 8* ... 16·00 14·50

Nos. 6817/24 were each issued in sheetlets of four stamps with enlarged illustrated right margins.

1530c Father Teoctist

(Des Vlad Vămăşescu. Litho)

2007 (3 Aug). Father Teoctist (Toader Arăpaşu) (Patriarch of Romanian Orthodox Church) Commemoration. P 13½.

6825 **1530c** 80b. multicoloured ... 1·00 95

1530d 1858 5 Parale Stamp (As Type **2**)

1531 Johannes Honterus (1498–1549) (cartographer)

(Des Mihai Vămăşescu and Stan Pelteacu. Litho)

2007 (17 Aug). EFIRO 2008, International Stamp Exhibition, Bucharest (2nd issue). T **1530d** and similar vert designs. Multicoloured. P 13½.

6826 1l.10 Type **1530d** ... 1·10 1·00
6827 2l.10 1858 40 parale stamp (As Type **3**) ... 2·00 1·90
6828 3l.30 1858 80 parale stamp (As No. 10) ... 3·25 3·00
6826/6828 *Set of 3* ... 5·75 5·25
MS6829 120×100 mm 5l.60 Bull's Head emblem ... 5·50 5·50

(Des Radu Oltean. Litho)

2007 (24 Aug). German Personalities in Romania. T **1531** and similar vert designs. Multicoloured. P 13½.

6830 1l.90 Type **1531** ... 1·90 1·80
6831 2l.10 Herman Oberth (1894–1989) (space travel theorist) ... 2·00 1·90
6832 3l.90 Stephan Ludwig Roth (1796–1849) (educationalist) ... 3·75 3·50
6830/6832 *Set of 3* ... 7·00 6·50

1532 Luxembourg House, Sibiu

(Des Octavian Penda. Litho)

2007 (3 Sept). Sibiu Joint European Capital of Culture–2007. T **1532** and similar horiz design. Multicoloured. P 13½.

6833 3l.60 Type **1532** ... 3·50 3·25
MS6834 123×95 mm. 4l.30 Luxembourg House, Sibiu (52×42 mm) ... 4·00 4·00

Stamps of a similar design were issued by Luxembourg.

1533 Obverse and Reverse of 1867 1 ban Coin (Illustration reduced. Actual size 71×36 mm)

(Des Mihai Vămăşescu and Stan Pelteacu. Litho)

2007 (12 Sept). 140th Anniv of Modern Currency. T **1533** and similar multicoloured design. P 13½.

6835 3l.90 Type **1533** ... 3·75 3·50
MS6836 184×108 mm. 5l.60 1870 1 leu silver coin (30×30 mm circular) ... 5·50 5·50

No. 6835 is perforated around the design of the obverse of the 1 ban coin and partially perforated in the centre of the stamp.

The stamp of No. **MS**6836 is perforated in a circle.

1534 Tackle

(Des Razvan Popescu. Litho)

2007 (25 Sept). Rugby World Cup Championship, France. T **1534** and similar horiz design. Multicoloured. P 13½.

6837 1l.80 Type **1534** ... 2·00 1·90
6838 3l.10 Scrum ... 3·50 3·25

1535 *Sputnik* (first man made satellite)

1536 *Birth of Jesus Christ* (icon)

(Des Alec Bartos. Litho)

2007 (4 Oct). 50th Anniv of Space Exploration. T **1535** and horiz design. Multicoloured. P 13½.

6839 3l.10 Type **1535** ... 3·50 3·25
MS6840 85×70 mm. 5l.60 *Sputnik 1* (52×42 mm) ... 6·25 6·25

The stamp and margin of No. **MS**6840 form a composite design of *Sputnik* over the Earth.

2007 (3 Nov). Christmas. P 13½.

6841 **1536** 80b. multicoloured ... 1·00 95

2007 (7 Nov). Pottery (12th issue). Vert designs as T **1455**. Multicoloured. Litho. P 13½.

6842 2l.10 Cream jug with green and brown garlands (Transylvania) ... 2·30 2·20
6843 3l.10 Cream jug with central border and green base (Horezu-Valcea) ... 3·50 3·25
6844 7l.20 Brown cup with blue, green and white decoration (Obarsa-Hunedoara) ... 8·25 7·75
6845 8l.70 Brown cup with white medallion containing flower (Baia Mare-MaraMureş) ... 9·50 9·00
6842/6845 *Set of 4* ... 21·00 20·00

Nos. 6842/5 were each issued in sheetlets of four stamps with enlarged illustrated right margins.

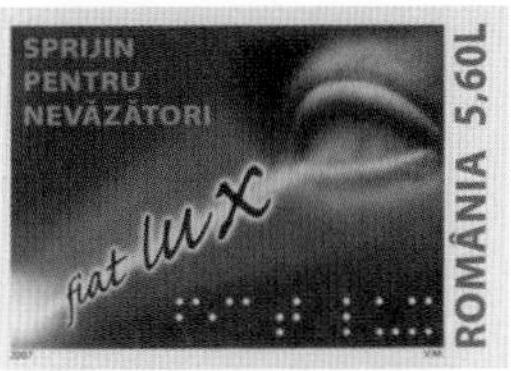

1537 Eye

(Des Vlad Vămăşescu. Litho)

2007 (13 Nov). Support for the Blind. P 13½.

6846 **1537** 5l.60 multicoloured ... 6·25 6·00

1538 *Orsova* (Romania)

2007 (14 Nov). Danube Ports and Ships. T **1538** and similar horiz designs. Multicoloured. P 13½.

6847 1l. Orsova port ... 1·10 1·00
6848 1l.10 Novi Sad port ... 1·20 1·20
MS6849 187×107 mm. 2l.10×2, Type **1538**; *Sirona* (Serbia) ... 5·50 5·50

No. **MS**6847 also contains two stamp size labels, showing arms of Romania and Serbia, which, with the margins, form a composite background design.

Stamps of a similar design were issued by Serbia.

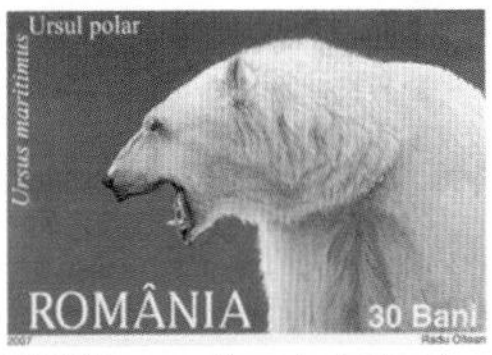

1539 *Ursus maritimus* (polar bear)

(Des Radu Oltean. Litho)

2007 (12 Dec). Polar Fauna. T **1539** and similar multicoloured designs. P 13½.

6850 30b. Type **1539** ... 30 25
6851 50b. *Pagophilus groenlandicus* (harp seal) ... 55 55
6852 1l.90 *Alopex lagopus* (Arctic fox) (vert) ... 2·20 2·00
6853 3l.30 *Aptenodytes forsteri* (emperor penguin) ... 4·25 4·00
6854 3l.60 *Balaenoptera musculus* (blue whale) ... 4·50 4·25
6855 4l.30 *Odobenus rosmarus* (walrus) (vert) ... 5·50 5·25
6850/6855 *Set of 6* ... 16·00 14·50

1540 *Lepiota rhacodes*

(Des Victor Telibasa. Litho)

2008 (18 Jan). Fungi. T **1540** and similar multicoloured designs. P 13½.

6856 1l.20 Type **1540** ... 1·30 1·20
6857 1l.40 *Lactarius deliciosus* ... 1·40 1·40
6858 2l. *Morchella esculenta* ... 2·20 2·00
6859 2l.40 *Paxillus involutus* ... 2·50 2·40
6860 3l. *Gyromitra esculenta* ... 3·25 3·00
6861 4l.50 *Russula emetica* ... 5·00 4·75
6856/6861 *Set of 6* ... 14·00 13·50
MS6862 130×116 mm. Nos. 6856/61 ... 16·00 16·00

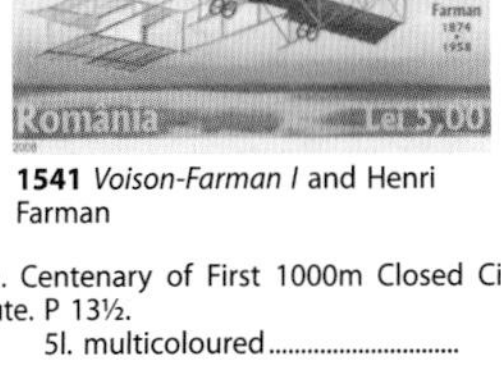

1541 *Voison-Farman I* and Henri Farman

2008 (25 Jan). Centenary of First 1000m Closed Circuit Flight in One Minute. P 13½.

6863 **1541** 5l. multicoloured ... 5·50 5·25

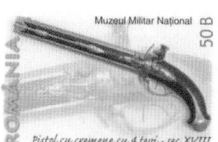

1542 18th-Century European Flint Pistol

(Des Mihai Vămăşescu)

2008 (8 Feb). Pistols from the Collection of National Military Museum. T **1542** and similar horiz designs. Multicoloured. P 13½.

6864	50b. Type **1542**	55	55
6865	1l. 18th-century flint pistol, Liege	1·10	1·10
6866	2l.40 7.65 mm. Mannlicher carbine pistol, 1903	2·50	2·40
6867	5l. 8 mm. Revolver, 1915	5·50	5·25
6864/6867	*Set of 4*	8·75	8·50
MS6868	118×75 mm. Nos. 6864/7	9·50	9·50

1543 *Explorer 1*

(Des Alec Bartos)

2008 (22 Feb). 50th Anniv (2007) of Space Exploration. T **1543** and similar horiz designs. Multicoloured. P 13½.

6869	1l. Type **1543**	1·10	1·10
6870	2l.40 *Sputnik 3*	2·50	2·40
6871	3l.10 *Jupiter AM-13*	3·25	3·00
6869/6871	*Set of 3*	6·25	5·75

1544 Resurrected Christ (iconostasis), Scaune Church, Bucharest

1545 Angel and Emblems

(Des Mihai Vămăşescu)

2008 (12 Mar). Easter. P 13½.

6872	**1544**	1l. multicoloured	1·10	1·10

2008 (21 Mar). Pottery (13th issue). Vert designs as T **1455**. Multicoloured. P 13½.

6873	2l. Brown mug with yellow and lower white decoration (Cosesti, Argeş)	2·20	2·00
6874	2l.40 Cream bodied jug with pictorial decoration (Radauti, Suceava)	2·50	2·40
6875	6l. Brown bodied jug with central decoration (Baia Mare-Maramureş)	6·50	6·00
6876	7l.60 Cream lidded pot with handles (Vladesti, Valcea)	8·25	7·75
6873/6876	*Set of 4*	18·00	16·00

(Des Octavian Penda)

2008 (2 Apr). NATO Summit, Bucharest. T **1545** and similar square designs. Multicoloured. P 13½.

6877	6l. Type **1545**	6·50	6·00
6878	6l. As No. 6877 but with silver emblem	6·50	6·00
6879	6l. As No. 6877 but with gold emblem	6·50	6·00
6877/6879	*Set of 3*	18·00	16·00

1546 *Helarctos malayanus* (sun bear)

1547 Athletics

(Des Radu Oltean)

2008 (21 Apr). Bears. T **1546** and similar multicoloured designs. P 13½.

6880	60b. Type **1546**	70	70
6881	1l.20 *Ursus americanus* (American black bear) (horiz)	1·30	1·20
6882	1l.60 *Ailuropoda melanoleuca* (giant panda) (horiz)	1·90	1·80
6883	3l. *Melursus ursinus* (sloth bear) (horiz)	3·25	3·00
6884	5l. *Tremarctos ornatus* (spectacled bear)	5·50	5·25
6880/6884	*Set of 5*	11·50	11·00
MS6885	77×85 mm. 9l.10 *Ursus arctos* (brown bear) (42×52 mm)	9·75	9·75

(Des Mihai Vămăşescu)

2008 (1 May). Olympic Games, Beijing. Sheet 78×142 mm containing T **1547** and similar horiz designs. Multicoloured. P 13½.

MS6886	1l.×4, Type **1547**; Gymnastics; Swimming; Rowing	5·00	5·00

1548 Map and Outline of Envelope

(Des Constantin Marincea)

2008 (8 May). Europa. The Letter. T **1548** and similar horiz design. Multicoloured. P 13½.

6887	1l.60 Type **1548**	1·90	1·80
6888	8l.10 A 'Priority' envelope and European stars	8·50	8·50
MS6889	122×92 mm. Nos. 6887/8, each×2	22·00	22·00

1549 Fauna

1550 Building, Stars and '€'

(Des Alina Munteanu)

2008 (20 May). Centenary of Grigore Antipa National Natural History Museum. T **1549** and similar vert design. Multicoloured. P 13½.

6890	2l.40 Type **1549**	2·50	2·40
6891	3l. Grigore Antipa (founder)	3·25	3·00

(Des Mihai Vămăşescu)

2008 (26 May). Tenth Anniv of European Central Bank. P 13½.

6892	**1550**	3l.10 multicoloured	3·50	3·25

1551 1859 5p. Stamp (As Type **2**) and Emblems (Illustration reduced. Actual size 71×35 mm)

(Des Mihai Vămăşescu and Stan Pelteacu)

2008 (20 June). EFIRO 2008, International Stamp Exhibition, Bucharest (3rd issue). T **1551** and similar horiz designs showing early stamps and exhibition emblems. Multicoloured. P 13½.

6893	50b. Type **1551**	55	55
6894	1l. 1862 6p. stamp (As No. 24)	1·10	1·10
6895	2l.40 1865 2p. stamp (As Type **5**)	2·50	2·40
6896	3l.10 1891 1½p. stamp (As Type **15**)	3·50	3·25
6897	4l.50 1903 1b. stamp (As No. 464)	5·00	4·75
6898	6l. 1932 6l. stamp (As Type **96**)	6·50	6·00
6893/6898	*Set of 6*	17·00	16·00
MS6899	152×122 mm. 8l.10 Exhibition emblem (30×30 mm)	8·50	8·50
MS6899*a*	192×162 mm. Nos. 6893/8	17·00	17·00

Nos. 6893/9 are partially perforated in the centre of the stamp.
No. **MS**6899 also contains a stamp size label.
The stamp and label of No. **MS**6899 are perforated in a circle.

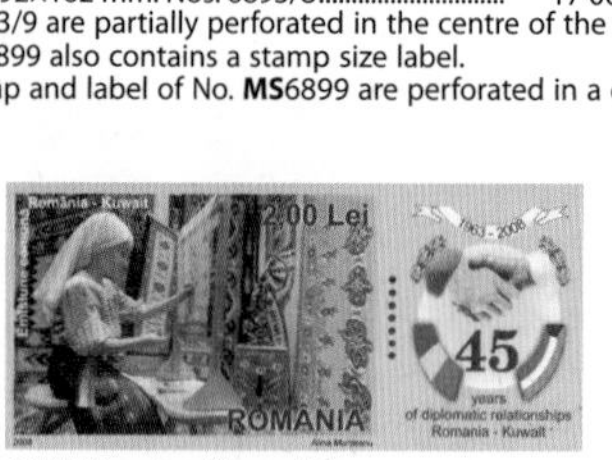

1552 Weaving (Romania)

(Des Alina Munteanu)

2008 (21 June). 45th Anniv of Romania–Kuwait Diplomatic Relations. T **1552** and similar horiz designs. Multicoloured. P 13½.

6900	2l. Type **1552**	2·20	2·00
6901	2l. Model boat builder (Kuwait)	2·20	2·00
MS6902	112×83 mm. 3l.30 Romanian fire appliance	3·50	3·50

Nos. 6900/1 are partially perforated to the right of the image.
Stamps of a similar design were issued by Kuwait.

1553 Scene from *7 Arts* (winning animated film)

(Des Alexandra Irimia)

2008 (22 June). 50th Anniv of Ion Popescu-Gopo's Grand Prix at Film Festival, Tours. T **1553** and similar horiz design. Multicoloured. P 13½.

6903	1l.40 Type **1553**	1·40	1·40
6904	4l.70 Ion Popescu-Gopo and trophy	5·25	5·00
MS6905	100×125 mm. Nos. 6903/4	6·50	6·50

1554 St. Gheorghe Church, Voroneţ Monastery (Romania)

1556 Page from Missal

1555 Făgăraş Castle

(Des Mihai Vămăşescu)

2008 (23 June). UNESCO World Heritages Sites in Romania and Russia. T **1554** and similar square design. Multicoloured. P 13½.

6906	3l. Type **1554**	3·25	3·00
6907	4l.30 St. Dimitrie Church, Vladimir (Russia)	4·50	4·25
MS6908	130×105 mm. Nos. 6906/7	8·50	8·50

Nos. 6906/7 were each issued with a *se-tenant* stamp size label, showing the churches at right.
No. **MS**6908 also contains a stamp size label showing symbols of Romania and Russia.
Stamps of a similar design were issued by Russia.

(Des Radu Oltean)

2008 (24 June). Castles. T **1555** and similar square design. Multicoloured. P 13½.

6909	1l. Type **1555**	1·10	1·10
6910	2l.10 Peles	2·30	2·20
6911	3l. Huniad	3·25	3·00
6912	5l. Bethlen-Cris	5·50	5·25
6909/6912	*Set of 4*	11·00	10·50
MS6913	135×118 mm. Nos. 6909/12	12·00	12·00

(Des Alina Munteanu)

2008 (25 June). 500th Anniv of Printing of *Macarie's Missal* (first book printed in Romania). T **1556** and similar multicoloured design. P 13½.

6914	4l.30 Type **1556**	5·50	5·25
MS6915	97×83 mm. 9l.10 Two pages from missal (52×42 mm)	10·00	10·00

1557 Church of the Three Holy Hierachs

(Des Alina Munteanu)

2008 (26 June). 600th Anniv of Iasi City Documentary Accreditation. T **1557** and similar square designs. P 13½.

6916	1l. Type **1557**	1·10	1·10
6917	1l.60 Metropolitan Cathedral	1·90	1·80
6918	2l.10 Vasile Alecsandri National Theatre	2·30	2·20
6919	3l.10 Museum of Unification	3·50	3·25
6916/6919	*Set of 4*	8·00	7·50
MS6920	133×100 mm. 9l.10 Palace of Culture (42×52 mm)	10·00	10·00
MS6921	182×98 mm. Nos. 6916/19	8·75	8·75

Nos. 6916/19, respectively, were issued in sheetlets of eight stamps each with an illustrated label attached at either right or left, depending on sheet position.

1558 Queen Marie

1559 Moldova

(Des Mihai Vămăşescu)

2008 (15 July). Stamp Day. 70th Death Anniv of Queen Marie of Romania. T **1558** and similar vert design. Multicoloured. P 13½.

6922	1l. Type **1558**	1·10	1·10
6923	3l. Older facing left	3·25	3·00
MS6924	102×68 mm. Nos. 6922/3	4·50	4·50

(Des Octavian Penda)

2008 (4 Sept). Heraldry. T **1559** and similar multicoloured designs showing arms. P 13½.

6925	60b. Type **1559**	70	70
6926	1l. Wallachia	1·10	1·10
6927	3l. Transylvania	3·25	3·00
6928	3l.10 Bucharest	3·50	3·25
6925/6928	*Set of 4*	7·75	7·25
MS6929	126×92 mm. Nos. 6925/8	8·50	8·50
MS6930	119×147 mm. 6l. Seal (42×52 mm)	6·50	6·50

Nos. 6925/8, respectively, were issued in sheetlets of eight stamps surrounding a central stamp size label.

1560 Power Station

(Des Mihai Vămăşescu. Litho)

2008 (21 Oct). Tenth Anniv of Nuclearelectrica. P 13½.

6931	**1560**	2l.10 multicoloured	2·30	2·20

No. 6931 was issued with a *se-tenant* label showing emblem attached at left.

1561 Stylized Airways

1562 The Nativity

(Des Mihai Vămăşescu. Litho)

2008 (28 Oct). 80th Anniv of National Radio Broadcasting Society. P 13½.

6932	**1561**	2l.40 multicoloured	2·50	2·40

No. 6932 was issued both in sheets and also small sheets of two stamps with enlarged illustrated margins.

(Des Mihai Vămăşescu. Litho)

2008 (5 Nov). Christmas. P 13½.

6933	**1562**	1l. multicoloured	1·10	1·10

No. 6933 was issued both in large sheets and also small sheets of eight stamps surrounding a central stamp size label.

1563 *Nymphaea lotus*

(Des Mihai Vămăşescu. Litho)

2008 (8 Nov). Petea Creek Natural Reservation. T **1563** and similar square designs. Multicoloured. P 13½.

6934	1l.40 Type **1563**	1·40	1·40
6935	1l.60 *Scardinius racovitzai*	1·90	1·80
6936	3l.10 *Melanopsis parreyssi*	3·50	3·25
6934/6936	*Set of 3*	6·00	5·75
MS6937	140×100 mm. Nos. 6934/6	6·75	6·75

The stamps and margins of No. **MS**6937 form a composite design.

MACHINE LABELS

Head Post Office, Bucharest

From 2 March 1995 gummed labels in the above design, printed in red by Enschedé were available from Klüssendorf automatic machines. The labels have two elliptical holes at both top and bottom and every fifth stamp is numbered on the back. The value was overprinted at the time of purchase according to the customer's requirements and the labels were available in 1l. steps from 1 to 1700l.

AUSTRO-HUNGARIAN MILITARY POST

German and Austro-Hungarian troops occupied all Romania south-west of the River Sereth after defeating the Romanian armies in September–December 1916. The occupation lasted until November 1918.

100 Bani = 1 Leu

(1)

(2)

3 Charles I of Austria

1917 (1 Nov). T **4/5** of General Issues of Austro-Hungarian Military Post (similar to T **3** above but with pattern in side panels continued in bottom panel) optd with T **1** in red (1/14) or T **2** in black (15/17).

1	**4**	3b. grey	3·50	5·75
2		5b. green	3·50	4·00
3		6b. violet	3·50	4·00
4		10b. orange-brown	60	1·20
5		12b. blue	2·30	4·00
6		15b. bright rose	2·30	4·00
7		20b. red-brown	60	1·20
8		25b. ultramarine	60	1·20
9		30b. slate-green	1·20	1·70
10		40b. olive-bistre	1·20	1·70
		a. Perf 11½	£170	£300
		b. Perf 11½×12½	£170	£300
11		50b. blue-green	1·20	1·70
12		60b. carmine	1·20	1·70
13		80b. blue	60	1·20
14		90b. purple	1·20	2·30
15	**5**	2l. on 2k. carmine/*buff*	1·70	3·00
16		3l. on 3k. green/*blue*	1·70	3·50
17		4l. on 4k. carmine/*green*	2·30	4·00
1/17		*Set of 17*	26·00	42·00

(Recess, value typo)

1918 (1 Mar). Value in black. P 12½.

18	**3**	3b. sepia	60	1·20
19		5b. yellow-green	60	1·20
20		6b. violet	60	1·70
21		10b. chestnut	60	1·70
22		12b. blue	60	1·70
23		15b. rose	60	1·20
24		20b. red-brown	60	1·20
25		25b. ultramarine	60	1·20
26		30b. slate-green	60	1·20
27		40b. olive-bistre	60	1·20
28		50b. green	60	1·20
29		60b. carmine	60	1·20
30		80b. blue	60	1·70
31		90b. purple	60	1·20
32		2l. carmine/*buff*	60	1·70
33		3l. green/*blue*	1·20	4·00
34		4l. carmine/*green*	1·70	4·00
18/34		*Set of 17*	10·50	26·00

Nos. 32/4 have a different pattern in the side panels.

1918. T **8** of General Issues of Austro-Hungarian Military Post (different portrait of Charles I) surch as T **1**.

35	**8**	1b. green	60·00
36		2b. orange	35·00
37		3b. olive-grey	70·00
38		5b. yellow-green	35·00
39		10b. chocolate	£100
40		20b. vermilion	£100
41		25b. blue	41·00
42		30b. bistre	70·00
43		45b. slate-black	75·00
44		50b. green	85·00
45		60b. bright violet	£120
46		80b. rose-pink	£1500
47		90b. brown-purple	£120
35/47		*Set of 13*	£2250

The above issue was put on sale in Vienna a few days before the Armistice but was never in use by the armies.

BULGARIAN OCCUPATION

DOBRUJA DISTRICT, 1916–17

100 Stotinki = 1 Leva

(1)

1916–17. Stamps of Bulgaria of 1915, optd with T **1**. P 11½ (1st., 25st.) or 14 (others).

1	**23**	1st. slate (R.)	25	25
2	**26**	5st. purple-brown and green (R.)	4·75	3·00
3	**27**	10st. sepia and red-brown (B.)	45	35
4	**29**	25st. black and deep blue (B.)	45	35

Many errors of lettering in this overprint are known, also double and inverted overprints.

GERMAN OCCUPATION

1917–1918

Romania entered the war against the Central Powers on 27 August 1916; after early successes her troops were defeated and by January 1917 all Romania S.E. of the River Sereth was in German, Austro-Hungarian or Bulgarian occupation.

100 Bani = 1 Leu
100 Pfennig = 1 Mark

(1)

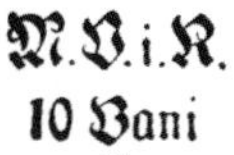

(2)

("M.V.i.R." = Militärverwaltung in Rumänien (Military Administration in Romania))

Contemporary stamps of Germany surcharged.

1917 (1 June). Surch as T **1** (value in black).

1	**24**	15b. on 15pf. slate-violet (R.)	55	1·10
		a. Black surcharge	14·00	17·00
		b. Surch double		
2	**17**	25b. on 20pf. ultramarine	90	1·10
3		40b. on 30pf. black and orange/*buff* (R.)	17·00	29·00
		a. Black surcharge	22·00	28·00
		b. Surch double		

1917 (2 July)–**18**. Surch as T **2**.

4	**17**	10b. on 10pf. rose-carmine	1·20	1·80
5	**24**	15b. on 15pf. slate-violet ('18)	6·25	4·75
6	**17**	25b. on 20pf. blue	3·50	4·50
7		40b. on 30pf. black and orange/*buff*.	1·20	2·20
		a. "40" omitted	90·00	£450

(3)

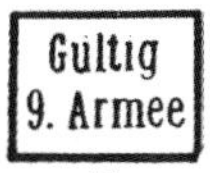

(4)

1918 (1 Mar). Surch as T **3**.

8	**17**	5b. on 5pf. green	70	2·10
9		10b. on 10pf. carmine	70	1·90
10	**24**	15b. on 15pf. slate-violet	20	55
11	**17**	25b. on 20pf. ultramarine	70	1·90
12		40b. on 30pf. black and orange/*buff*.	25	45

1918 (10 Mar). Ninth Army Post. Optd with T **4**.

13	**17**	10pf. carmine	9·75	48·00
14	**24**	15pf. slate-violet	14·00	44·00
15	**17**	20pf. blue	1·30	2·20
16		30pf. black and orange/*buff*	14·00	26·00

POSTAL TAX STAMPS

Stamps of Romania overprinted

(T **1**)

(T **2**)

(T **3**)

1917 (1 June). Large fiscal stamp of Romania (King's portrait, inscr "TIMBRU FISCAL"), optd with Type T **1**, reading upwards.

T1	10b. brown (R.)	55·00	40·00

1917 (25 June). Type T **41** optd with Type T **2**. P 13½, 11½ or 13½×11½.

T2	5b. black (R.)	90	4·50
T3	10b. brown	90	4·50

1917 (10 Aug)–**18**. Type T **41** optd with Type T **3**. P 13½, 11½ or 13½×11½.

T4	5b. black (R.) (1.10.18)	1·80	4·50
	a. Black overprint	60·00	£900
T5	10b. brown	5·25	25·00
T6	10b. purple ('17)	1·10	6·25

1917 (15 Sept). Fiscal type as in No. T **1** in new colour, optd with Type T **3**.

T7	10b. yellow (R.)	3·50	14·00

Nos. T1/7 with overprint in different colours, inverted, double etc. are believed not to be genuine issues.

POSTAGE DUE STAMPS

1918 (1 July). Type D **38** of Romania optd as Type T **3**, in red.

A. Wmkd

D1A	5b. blue/*greenish yellow*	21·00	80·00
D2A	10b. blue/*greenish yellow*	21·00	80·00

Nos. D3A/5A with watermark are forgeries.

B. No wmk

D1B	5b. blue/*greenish yellow*	8·75	13·00
D2B	10b. blue/*greenish yellow*	8·75	13·00
D3B	20b. blue/*greenish yellow*	3·50	3·50
D4B	30b. blue/*greenish yellow*	3·50	3·50
D5B	50b. blue/*greenish yellow*	3·50	3·50

1918 (Sept). POSTAL TAX Type TD **42** of Romania optd as Type T **3**.

D6	10b. red/*greenish*	3·50	13·00

Romanian Post Offices in the Turkish Empire

A. GENERAL ISSUES

40 Paras = 1 Piastre

20PARAS20

(**1**)

1896 (16 March). Stamps of Romania, 1893–99, surch as T **1**.

A. In black

		(a) P 13½		
1	**19**	10pa. on 5b. blue	29·00	29·00
2	**20**	20pa. on 10b. emerald	20·00	20·00
3	**19**	1pi. on 25b. bright mauve	20·00	20·00
		(b) P 11½		
4	**19**	10pa. on 5b. blue	35·00	35·00
5	**20**	20pa. on 10b. emerald	35·00	35·00
6	**19**	1pi. on 25b. bright mauve	33·00	33·00
		(c) Perf compound of 13½ and 11½		
7	**20**	20pa. on 10b. emerald	47·00	47·00
8	**19**	1pi. on 25b. bright mauve	47·00	47·00

B. In violet

		(a) P 13½		
9	**19**	10pa. on 5b. blue	20·00	20·00
10	**20**	20pa. on 10b. emerald	20·00	20·00
11	**19**	1pi. on 25b. bright mauve	20·00	20·00
		(b) P 11½		
12	**19**	10pa. on 5b. blue	21·00	21·00
13	**20**	20pa. on 10b. emerald	21·00	21·00
14	**19**	1pi. on 25b. bright mauve	29·00	29·00
		(c) Perf compound of 13 and 11½		
15	**19**	10pa. on 5b. blue	33·00	33·00
16	**20**	20pa. on 10b. emerald	29·00	29·00
17	**19**	1pi. on 25b. bright mauve	29·00	29·00

The above were used for the Romanian ship post service between Constantza and Constantinople.

B. CONSTANTINOPLE

100 Bani = 7 Leu

(1)

Many forgeries exist of this overprint

1919. Stamps of Romania, optd with T **1**.

		(a) P 13½		
18	**37**	5b. yellow-green	70	1·20
		a. Opt inverted	4·75	
19		10b. carmine	95	1·40
20		15b. red-brown	1·20	1·60
		a. Opt inverted	10·50	
21	**19**	25b. steel-blue (R.)	1·30	2·30
		a. Opt inverted	3·75	
22		40b. grey-brown (R.)		
		(b) P 11½		
23	**37**	10b. carmine	95	1·70
		a. Opt inverted	7·00	
24		15b. red-brown	1·20	2·10
25	**19**	25b. steel-blue (R.)	—	2·30
26		40b. grey-brown (R.)	—	5·25
		(c) Perf compound of 11½ and 13½		
27	**37**	5b. yellow-green	70	1·20
28		10b. carmine	95	1·40
29		15b. red-brown		
30	**19**	25b. steel-blue (R.)	1·30	2·30
31		40b. grey-brown (R.)	4·00	5·75
		a. Opt inverted	28·00	

1919. Optd with T **1**.

		(a) P 13½		
32	T **41**	5b. green	5·75	9·25
		(b) P 13½×11½		
33	T **41**	5b. green	2·00	3·50
		a. Opt inverted	23·00	

This office was only in use for a short time.

Serbia

1866. 40 Para = 1 Grosch
1880. 100 Para = 1 Dinar

The mediaeval kingdom of Serbia became a Turkish province from 1459 to 1804; from 1830 to 1878 Serbia was an autonomous principality, which became completely independent by the Treaty of Berlin on 22 August 1878.

Prince Michael (Obrenovic III)
27 September 1860–28 May (= 10 June) 1868

The dates of issue are according to local computation based on the Julian or Gregorian Calendar in use. In the 19th century the Julian Calendar was twelve days behind the Gregorian Calendar. After 1900 the difference was thirteen days. In Serbia the Gregorian Calendar was introduced 1 February 1919, the 19 January being followed by 1 February.

DATES. The dates given in italic letters relate to the final dates of each printing, not the dates of issue which are not always known.

1 State Arms

2 Prince Michael

(Des M. Djordjevic. Typo State Ptg Wks, Belgrade)

1866. NEWSPAPER. Imperf.

(a) First printing. Thick soft surface-coloured paper (1 May)

N1	1	1p. deep green and lilac-rose	£3250	
N2		2p. greyish green and greyish blue	£3250	

(b) Second printing. Thick soft surface-coloured paper (22 May)

N3	1	1p. yellow-olive and rose	85·00	
		a. Bistre and rose	85·00	
N4		2p. red-brown and lavender (*shades*)	£550	

(c) Third printing. Thin hard surface-coloured paper (14 Nov)

N5	1	1p. green and pale rose	£550	
		a. Deep green and deep rose	£550	
N6		2p. red-brown and grey-blue (*shades*)	£325	
		a. Chocolate and lavender	£650	

(d) Fourth printing. Paper coloured through (14 Dec)

N7	1	1p. deep green/*dull mauve* (*shades*)	85·00	

Nos. N1/7 were each issued in sheets of 12 stamps (4×3) with three continuous vertical lines and eight horizontal lines, each about the width of a stamp, dividing the sheet into sections each containing one stamp. As the clichés forming each plate were taken apart and recomposed during the printings, several settings exist.

Stamps printed by lithography are forgeries.

(Des A. Jovanović. Eng V. Katzler. Typo Austrian State Ptg Wks, Vienna)

1866 (1 July). P 12.

9	2	10p. yellow-orange	£1700	£1000
		a. Orange	£1700	£1000
10		20p. rose	£1100	45·00
		a. Deep rose	£1100	45·00
11		40p. blue	£1200	£190
		a. Deep blue	£1200	£190

(Typo State Ptg Wks, Belgrade)

1866 (29 Oct)–**68**. P 9½.

(a) Pelure paper (29 Oct 1866)

12	2	10p. yellow-orange	£130	£170
		a. Orange	£130	£170
13		20p. rose	£110	22·00
		a. Deep rose	£120	24·00
14		40p. ultramarine	85·00	55·00
		a. Deep ultramarine	90·00	60·00
		b. Imperf between (horiz pair)	£6500	£7500
		c. Bisected (20p.) (on cover)	†	£14000

(b) Wove paper (4–14 Nov 1868)

15	2	20p. rose (12.11.68)	22·00	34·00
		a. Deep rose	26·00	37·00
		b. Rose/*buff*	80·00	
		c. Imperf horiz (vert pair)	£2250	
16		40p. ultramarine (25.1.69)	£350	£400
		a. Deep ultramarine	£400	£450
		b. Bisected (20p.) (on cover)	†	£20000

The clichés used for the Vienna printing were used in recomposed plates for the Belgrade printings.

Dates quoted individually for Nos. 15/16 are those of earliest known use.

No. 14c is known bisected horizontally or vertically from several post offices. No. 16b is known bisected vertically from Karanovac and Požarevac. One example of No. 15 bisected vertically on piece with Kruševac cancellation is also known; its status is uncertain.

(Typo State Ptg Wks, Belgrade)

1867 (11 Mar)–**68**. NEWSPAPER. Wove paper.

(a) P 9½ (11 Mar 1867)

N17	2	1p. olive-green	28·00	£850
N18		2p. yellow-brown	45·00	£850
		a. "ПАРҒ" for "ПАРЕ"	£170	
		b. Deep brown	50·00	£850
		ba. "ПАРҒ" for "ПАРЕ"	£200	
		c. Olive-brown	£130	
		ca. "ПАРҒ" for "ПАРЕ"	£450	

(b) Imperf (14 Nov 1868)

N19	2	1p. green	80·00	
		a. Pale olive-green/buff	£4000	
N20		2p. red-brown	£110	
		a. "ПАРҒ" for "ПАРЕ"	£225	
		b. Bistre/buff	£500	
		ba. "ПАРҒ" for "ПАРЕ"	£1600	

Printed from recomposed plates of the Vienna clichés.

Nos. N18a, N18ba and N18ca occur in position 34 of the sheet of 50. For the November 1868 printing new plates were made with the clichés rearranged, the plate being applied twice to form a sheet of 100 stamps; No. N20a occurs in position 10 of the setting. No. N20*b* comes from a further setting in which the position of No. N20ba is undetermined.

Prince Milan (Obrenovic IV)
18 (= 30) June 1868–22 February (= 6 March) 1882

King Milan I
22 February (= 6 March) 1882–21 February (= 5 March) 1889

3

4

5

The rarer perforations have been faked and should therefore be purchased only from reputable sources.

(Des and eng Carl von Radnitzky. Typo State Ptg Wks, Belgrade)

1869–80. P 12 (varies from 11½-12½).

(a) Group A. Printings of March–28 October 1869 (all values) and 12 May 1870 (10p.). Stamps 2–2½ mm apart; narrow margins. Clear impressions. Medium hard paper

30	3	10p. brown (p 12) (7.69)	£110	17·00
		a. Imperf between (pair)	—	£1100
		b. Perf 9½	£100	13·50
		c. Perf 9½×12	75·00	11·00
		d. Perf 12×9½	£1700	£275
31		15p. orange (p 12) (11.69)	£800	75·00
		b. Perf 9½	£110	50·00
		c. Perf 9½×12	£100	45·00
		d. Perf 12×9½	—	£2250
32		20p. blue (p 12) (7.69)	£550	11·00
		b. Perf 9½	£325	13·50
		c. Perf 9½×12	85·00	4·50
		d. Perf 12×9½	£850	34·00
33		25p. rose (p 12) (11.69)	—	£2250
		b. Perf 9½	£275	34·00
		c. Perf 9½×12	£100	28·00
		d. Perf 12×9½	£190	43·00
34		35p. green (p 12) (11.69)	£130	45·00
		a. Imperf between (pair)	£450	
		b. Perf 9½	£750	£450
		c. Perf 9½×12	6·75	8·00
		d. Perf 12×9½	£1100	£600
		e. Imperf (vert pair)		
35		40p. mauve (p 12) (7.69)	£1500	£450
		a. Imperf between (vert pair)	—	£1000
		b. Perf 9½	£250	8·50
		ba. Bisected on cover (20p.)	†	£1700
		c. Perf 9½×12	80·00	5·50
		ca. Bisected on cover (20p.)	†	£1600
		d. Perf 12×9½	£850	28·00
		da. Bisected on cover (20p.)	†	£3000
36		50p. green (p 9½) (11.69)	13·50	22·00
		c. Perf 9½×12	13·50	22·00

See note below No. 39; the 10p in Group A does not have the crescent.

(b) Group B. Printings of 6 May 1872 (10, 20, 25p.) and 14 June 1873 (20p.). 10p. from new clichés *. Stamps 3–4 mm apart; wider margins. Clear impressions. Medium to thick paper

37	3	10p. cinnamon (p 12)	£180	17·00
		c. Perf 9½×12	£650	£180
		d. Perf 12×9½	£750	£170
		da. Imperf between (pair)		
38		20p. blue (p 12)	£600	4·50
		a. Imperf between (horiz pair)	—	£450
		b. Perf 9½	£275	2·20
		c. Perf 9½×12	£400	11·00
		d. Perf 12×9½	£300	13·50
39		25p. rose (p 12)	4·50	11·00
		a. Imperf between (pair)	£250	
		b. Perf 9½	3·25	9·00
		ba. Imperf between (pair)	£200	
		c. Perf 9½×12	22·00	13·50
		d. Perf 12×9½	6·75	17·00

*The 10p. in Groups B to E was printed from new clichés which show a small "crescent" beneath the Prince's ear.

(c) Group C. Printings of 4 June 1874 (10, 20p.) and 19 May 1875 (20p.). Stamps 3-3½ mm apart; wider margins. Poorer impressions. Thin to medium paper. P 12

40	3	10p. yellow-brown (*medium paper*)	£800	£110
		a. Thin paper	£450	95·00
41		20p. grey-blue (*thin and medium paper*)	£170	4·50
		a. Imperf between (horiz pair)	—	£450
		b. Cobalt (*thin paper*)	£300	34·00

The earliest recorded cancellation of the 10p. is 10 December 1874.

Perforations on this group other than 12 are believed to be fakes.

(d) Group D. Printings of 22 April 1876 (10, 20, 40p.) and 22 August 1877 (10, 20p.). 10 and 20p. stamps 3–3½ mm apart; wider margins. 40p. 2½ mm apart; narrow margins. Poorer impressions. Medium soft paper

42	3	10p. red-brown (p 12)	13·50	7·25
		b. Perf 9½	£100	65·00
		c. Perf 9½×12	£1700	£1000
		d. Perf 12×9½	£1400	£950
43		20p. ultramarine (p 12)	6·75	3·25
		a. Imperf between (pair)	—	£400
		b. Perf 9½	£1400	£200
		c. Perf 9½×12	£1200	£800
		d. Perf 12×9½	£600	£650
44		40p. pale mauve (p 12)	55·00	4·50
		a. Imperf between (pair)	—	£550
		b. Perf 9½	£550	85·00
		c. Perf 9½×12	£1200	£275
		d. Perf 12×9½	£600	£250

The earliest recorded cancellation of the 10p. is 28 December 1875.

(e) Group E. Printings of 29 December 1878 (20p.) and 8 February 1879 (10, 40, 50p.). 10 and 20p. stamps 3–3½ mm apart; wider margins. 40 and 50p. 2½–3 mm apart; narrow margins. Blurred impressions from worn plates. Medium paper. P 12

45	3	10p. orange	3·25	9·00
		a. Imperf between (pair)	£450	
46		20p. grey-blue	2·20	4·00
		a. Imperf between (pair)	£225	
47		40p. bright mauve	3·25	11·00
		a. Imperf between (pair)	£450	
48		50p. bluish green	12·50	85·00
		a. Imperf between (pair)	£325	

The earliest recorded cancellation for the 50p. is 15 October 1879.

1869–79. NEWSPAPER.

(a) Group A. Printing of March–October 1879. Stamps 2 mm apart; narrow margins. Medium paper. P 12

N47	3	1p. yellow	40·00	£450
		a. Perf 9½×12	8·50	£300

(b) Group B. Printings of 6 May 1872 (10p.) and 14 June 1873 (2p.). Stamps 3–4 mm apart; wider margins. Medium to thick paper. Imperf

N51	3	1p. yellow	10·00	28·00
		a. Tête-bêche (pair)		
		b. Perf 12	22·00	£225
N52	4	2p. black (1.7.73)	5·50	28·00

Only one example, an unused horizontal pair, of No. N51a is known.

Strips of No. N51b are found imperforate vertically or horizontally; it is believed they were not issued thus.

No. N52 can be distinguished from No. N53 by the intact "T" (see note below No. N53).

(c) Printing of 29 December 1878 from new clichés. Stamps 2–3 mm apart; narrow margins. Medium paper. Imperf

N53	4	2p. black	2·20	1·10

All clichés of No. N53 have the stem of the "T" of "POSTA" broken. In addition there is a small "crescent" at the back of the head behind the Prince's ear which is not present in clichés of No. N52.

New Currency

(Eng C. Dumont, Paris. Typo Belgrade)

1880 (1 Nov). P 13×13½.

54	5	5p. olive-green	£850	5·50
		a. Blue-green (shades)	2·20	55
		b. Grey-green	4·00	1·10
		c. Deep green	2·20	55
		d. Pale green	1·50	55
55		10p. carmine	3·25	55
		a. Rose-pink	4·50	1·10
56		20p. yellow-orange (*shades*)	1·70	1·10
		a. Cinnamon	6·75	2·75
57		25p. blue	2·75	1·70
		a. Ultramarine	2·20	1·70
58		50p. sepia	2·20	7·25
		a. Slate-purple	£325	6·75
59		1d. lilac	16·00	17·00

IMPERFORATE STAMPS. Stamps from the following issues, with the exception of Nos. 159/63, exist imperforate, but were not regularly issued in this condition.

King Alexander I (Obrenovic V)
22 February (= 6 March) 1889–29 May (= 11 June) 1903

6

7

D 8

(Eng in Berlin. Typo Belgrade)

1890 (3 Mar). P 13×13½.

60	6	5p. green	55	20
61		10p. rose-red	1·90	20
62		15p. reddish lilac	1·70	20
63		20p. orange	1·10	20
64		25p. blue	2·20	55
65		50p. sepia	4·50	4·50
66		1d. lilac	17·00	13·50

Shades exist. The 5, 15 and 20p. are known imperf. The 15p., 20p. and 1d. imperf on thick greyish paper are proofs.

(Eng in Vienna. Typo Belgrade)

1894 (5 Nov)–**1901**.

(a) Granite paper. P 13×13½ (1894–1900)

67	7	5p. green	6·25	20
		a. Perf 11½	11·00	55
68		10p. carmine	8·50	20
		a. Perf 11½	£130	2·20
69		15p. reddish lilac	13·50	35
70		20p. yellow-orange	£100	1·10
		a. Bisected. (10p.) (on cover)	—	£550
71		25p. blue	28·00	55
72		50p. sepia	34·00	1·10
73		1d. deep blue-green	2·20	4·50
74		1d. red-brown/*blue* (1.1.00)	28·00	4·50

(b) Ordinary paper (1896–1902)

A. Perf 13×13½.

75A	7	1p. brown-red (1.3.96)	45	20
76A		5p. green (1.9.98)	5·50	20
		a. Compound perf	22·00	1·70
77A		10p. carmine (20.7.98)	£130	35
		a. Compound perf	£325	13·50
78A		15p. reddish lilac (3.00)	£170	2·20
		a. Compound perf	£275	13·50
80A		25p. blue (9.00)	55·00	1·90
		a. Compound perf	£225	45·00

B. Perf 11½

75B	7	1p. brown-red (1.3.06)	45	20
76B		5p. green (1.9.98)	5·50	20
77B		10p. carmine (20.7.98)	90·00	20
78B		15p. reddish lilac (3.00)	11·00	35
79B		20p. yellow-orange (9.00)	8·50	35
80B		25p. blue (9.00)	8·50	55
		b. Ultramarine (1.8.02)	8·50	55

81B 50p. sepia (12.00) 34·00 5·50
a. *Red-brown* (1.8.02) 22·00 2·75

The compound perf is of 13×13½ and 11½. Other shades exist and all values are known imperf.

(Des D. Milovanovic. Eng in Vienna. Typo Belgrade)

1895–1914. POSTAGE DUE.

(a) Granite paper. P 13×13½ (1.4.95)

D82 D 8 5p. rosy mauve 7·75 1·10
a. Perf 11½ 17·00 4·50
D83 10p. blue 8·50 55
D84 20p. orange-brown 65·00 11·00
D85 30p. green 85 1·10
D86 50p. carmine 85 1·50
a. Error. 5p. carmine £130 £225

(b) Ordinary paper. P 11½ (20.7.98–1904)

D87 D 8 5p. rosy mauve (1904) 80 55
D88 20p. orange-brown 12·50 1·30
a. Tête-bêche (pair) £170 £170
b. *Deep brown* (1904) 8·50 1·10

(c) Laid paper. P 11½ (March 1909)

D89 D 8 5p. rosy mauve 1·10 80
D90 10p. blue 6·75 11·00
D91 20p. deep brown 55 1·10

(d) Thick glazed paper. P 11½ (March 1914)

D92 D 8 5p. rosy mauve 55 2·75
D93 10p. blue 8·50 13·50

10 ПАРА (8) **10 ПАРА** (9)

10

11

1900 (1 Nov). No. 79 but colour changed.

(a) Surch with T **8**

82A 7 10p. on 20p. red 8·50 1·10
a. Compound perf 85·00 7·75
83A 10p. on 20p. red 9·00 1·10
a. Compound perf 80·00 6·75

(b) Surch with T **9**

82B 7 10p. on 20p. red 13·50 1·10
83B 10p. on 20p. red 13·50 1·10
b. "10" 1½ mm. apart £110 9·50

1901 (16 Oct). No. 74 surch as T **8**.

84 7 15p. on 1d. red-brown/*blue* 7·75 2·20

There are four minor types of this surcharge.

(Des D. Milovanovic. Eng A. Scharff. Typo Belgrade)

1901 (1 Jan)–**03**. P 11½.

85 10 5p. green (20.6.01) 1·10 55
a. *Pale yellow-green* 55 35
86 10p. rose-red (12.6.02) 55 35
87 15p. purple (3.03) 55 35
88 20p. orange-yellow (21.2.03) 55 35
89 25p. ultramarine (4.2.03) 55 35
90 50p. yellow-ochre (4.2.03) 1·10 85
91 11 1d. brown (15.1.03) 1·70 2·75
92 3d. deep rose 34·00 13·50
a. *Pink* (6.02) 17·00 22·00
93 5d. deep violet 28·00 14·00
a. *Violet* (6.02) 17·00 22·00
85/93a *Set of* 9 (cheapest) 36·00 44·00

Petar I (Karageorgevic III)
2 (= 15) June 1903–16 August 1921

12 Alexander I

(**13**)

Overprint measures 10×14 mm. on dinar values, 12×15 mm. on para values.

(Des and eng E. Mouchon. Typo Paris)

1903 (25 June). Assassination of King Alexander. Unissued stamps optd in Belgrade as T **13**. Head in black. P 13½.

94 12 1p. dull claret (B.) 1·30 1·70
a. Opt inverted 28·00
95 5p. apple-green (B.) 1·10 55
96 10p. rose 80 55
a. Opt double 28·00
97 15p. drab 80 55
a. Opt double 28·00
98 20p. orange-yellow 1·10 55
99 25p. blue 1·10 55
a. Opt double 28·00
100 50p. blue-grey (R.) 6·75 1·70
101 1d. blue-green 17·00 6·75
102 3d. lilac (Mag.) (p 11½) 4·75 5·00
a. Perf 13½ £170
103 5d. brown (B.) (p 11½) 4·75 5·50
94/103 *Set of* 10 36·00 21·00

The overprint was applied to the 1 and 20p. by lithography and to the dinar values by typography. The other values were overprinted by both methods.

Stamps without overprint come from remainder stocks.

1903 (20 July). T **12** surch with T **13** and new value in carmine, by lithography in Belgrade. P 11½.

104 1p. on 5d. black and brown 3·25 17·00
a. Perf 13½ £1100

1904. T **12** typo in Belgrade from Paris clichés and optd by typography with T **13** (12×15 mm). P 11½.

105 12 5p. apple-green (Violet-blue) (10.7) 1·10 2·20
106 50p. dull grey (Cerise) (21.8) 2·20 11·00
107 1d. blue-green (Bk.) (21.8) 3·25 22·00
105/107 *Set of* 3 6·00 32·00

14 Karageorge and Petar I

15 Karageorge and Insurgents, 1804

(Des D. Jovanović. Eng E. Mouchon. Typo State Ptg Wks, Belgrade, from clichés made in Paris)

1904 (8 Sept). Coronation and Centenary of Karageorgevic Dynasty. P 11½.

108 14 5p. green 1·10 55
109 10p. rose 1·10 55
110 15p. purple 1·10 55
111 25p. blue 2·00 1·10
112 50p. brown 2·20 2·20
113 15 1d. buff 3·25 7·75
114 3d. emerald 4·50 11·00
115 5d. deep violet 5·50 13·50
108/115 *Set of* 8 19·00 33·00

Nos. 108/15 imperforate come from sheets taken from the Printing Works during World War I.

Forgeries of this set are frequently offered.

16 Petar I

17 Petar I

18

(Des and eng G. Tasset. Typo State Ptg Wks, Belgrade, from clichés made in Paris)

1905–11. Centre in black.

(a) Thin paper. P 11½ (1 Jan–23 Mar 1905)

116 16 1p. pale grey 35 10
117 5p. pale green 1·70 20
118 10p. rose-red 4·00 20
119 15p. dull magenta 4·50 20
120 20p. yellow 7·75 35
121 25p. blue 11·00 35
122 30p. grey-green (23.3) 6·75 35
123 50p. deep brown 8·50 80
124 1d. buff 28·00 2·75
125 3d. blue-green 2·75 2·75
126 5d. deep violet 19·00 6·75
116/126 *Set of* 11 85·00 13·50

(b) Thick wove paper. P 12×11½ (Oct 1905 (1p.)–Mar 1906)

127 16 1p. pale grey 35 10
b. Horiz laid paper (1908) 55 10
c. Vert laid paper (1911) 4·50 1·30
128 5p. pale green 1·30 20
b. Horiz laid paper (1907) 3·25 35
c. Vert laid paper (1911) 6·75 1·10
129 10p. rose-red 4·00 20
b. Horiz laid paper (1907) 9·50 20
c. Vert laid paper (1911) 55·00 2·20
130 15p. dull magneta 5·50 35
b. Horiz laid paper (1908) 13·50 35
131 20p. yellow 9·50 35
b. Horiz laid paper (1908) 13·50 55
132 25p. blue 9·50 35
b. Horiz laid paper (1908) 9·50 55
133 30p. grey-green 9·50 35
b. Horiz laid paper (1908) 12·50 55
c. Vert laid paper (1911) 85·00 8·50
134 50p. deep brown 9·50 55
b. Horiz laid paper (1911) 18·00 1·10
135 1d. buff 1·30 55
136 3d. blue-green 1·30 1·30
137 5d. deep violet 5·50 4·00
127/137 *Set of* 11 50·00 7·50

(Des M. Marcovic. Eng P. Anicic. Typo State Ptg Wks, Belgrade)

1911 (29 June–20 Dec). P 12×11½.

146 17 1p. olive-black (Aug) 20 10
147 2p. deep violet (Sept) 20 10
148 5p. yellow-green 45 20
149 10p. carmine 20 10
150 15p. purple (Oct) 45 10
151 20p. yellow (Nov) 45 10
152 25p. blue 65 10
153 30p. blue-green (20.12) 45 35
154 50p. grey-brown (20.12) 80 55
155 1d. orange (20.12) 34·00 65·00
156 3d. lake (20.12) 45·00 £130
157 5d. violet-blue (20.12) 34·00 95·00
146/157 *Set of* 12 £110 £275

See also Nos. 169/77.

(Typo State Ptg Wks, Belgrade)

1911 (1 Dec). Serbian Union of Journalists Fund. Optd with shield surmounted by Crown, in black. P 11½.

158 18 1p. grey 1·10 1·10
159 5p. green 1·10 1·10
160 10p. yellow-orange 1·10 1·10
a. Error. 1p. yellow-orange £1300
161 15p. violet 1·10 1·10
162 20p. yellow 1·10 1·10
a. Error. 50p. yellow £130 £170
163 25p. blue 1·10 1·10
164 30p. slate 11·00 11·00
165 50p. brown 9·00 9·00
166 1d. yellow-brown 9·00 9·00
167 3d. red 9·00 9·00
168 5d. blue-grey 9·00 9·00
158/168 *Set of* 11 48·00 48·00

Nos. 160a and 162a were caused by erroneous clichés in the settings.

All values exist with overprint inverted and with overprint double. Stamps inscribed "TROJ. SABOR" in Cyrillic letters at top are worth about five times the prices quoted.

Nos. 158/68 were originally put on sale without overprint by the Union of Journalists, but had no postal validity. They were subsequently overprinted with the State arms and were valid for postal use on newspapers only between 1 December 1911 and 16 November 1912. Only a few copies of the 30p. to 5d. values were placed on sale at post offices, the remainder being sold by the Union, either cancelled-to-order during the period of their validity or uncancelled after demonetization. The 1 to 25p. could be obtained from the main post office, Belgrade, or from the Postal Depot but were also sold by the Union. Used prices quoted are for cancelled-to-order stamps.

1914 (28 Jan–1 June). Colours changed. P 12×11½.

169 17 5p. pale yellow-green 20 10
170 10p. vermilion 20 10
171 15p. slate-black 20 10
a. Error. Vermilion £1300 †
172 20p. brown 80 45
173 25p. deep blue 20 10
173*a* 30p. bronze 20 45
174 50p. brown-red 65 55
175 1d. slate-green 5·50 11·00
176 3d. yellow (1.6) £225 £1700
177 5d. bluish violet (1.6) 9·00 29·00
169/177 *Set of* 10 £225 £1600

19 King Petar on the Battlefield

(Eng Daussy. Typo State Stamp Printing Works, Niš, from clichés made in Paris)

1915 (15 Oct). P 11½.

178 19 5p. yellow-green 55
179 10p. vermilion 55
179*a* 15p. slate 8·50
179*b* 20p. brown 2·20
179*c* 25p. light blue 17·00
ca. Error. 15p. light blue £500
179*d* 30p. olive 11·00
179*e* 50p. light orange-brown 45·00

No. 179ca was caused by the inclusion of a 15p. cliché in the setting of the 25p. value.

Although Nos. 179*a/e* were issued it is unlikely that they were used for postal purposes, owing to the conquest of Serbia by German, Austro-Hungarian and Bulgarian troops. It is believed, however, that they did do duty as emergency currency. Beware of reprints.

The Serbian army, after a retreat through Albania, recuperated and refitted on Corfu.

POSTES SERBES

After the Serbians reached Corfu they initially used the Greek civilian post office or the French or British field post offices. Later a Serbian civilian post office was established. At first this office used French stamps and the handstamp illustrated above was applied as an origin mark to all mail handled between the Serbian and French offices. The handstamp was usually applied once to each piece of mail and could fall indiscriminately on the stamps or the envelope. The stamps were cancelled with a double-circle postmark inscribed "MINISTARSKA" in cyrillic.

Such genuinely used stamps should be dated between December 1916 and October 1918.

The Serbian postal clerks subsequently applied both the handstamp and the postmark, or the handstamp alone, to quantities of French stamps on request, but these never passed through the post.

On 13 October 1918, following the return of the Serbian government to its homeland, supplies of Serbian stamps were sent to the Corfu office, which closed June 1919.

KINGDOM OF THE SERBS, CROATS AND SLOVENES

On 1 December 1918, Serbia was joined by Montenegro and the Serbo-Croat-speaking portions of the former Austro-Hungarian Monarchy to form the Kingdom of the Serbs, Croats and Slovenes. For the convenience of collectors we list here the issues which continued to be made for Serbia until 1920; the other issues of the Kingdom are listed under Yugoslavia.

20 King Petar I and Prince Alexander

D 21

(Des N. Jeremic. Eng N. Jeremic and Paré. Typo Paris and Belgrade)

1918–20.

I. Paris printing. Clear impression. Medium white paper. P 11 (1.10.18 (Gregorian calendar))

194 20 1p. black 10 10
a. Imperf between (horiz pair) 13·50
195 2p. olive-brown 10 10
a. Imperf between (pair) 13·50
196 5p. apple-green 10 10
197 10p. bright red 10 10
a. Imperf between (horiz pair) 17·00
198 15p. sepia 10 10
199 20p. chestnut 10 10

200 25p. blue 10 10
201 30p. brown-olive 10 10
202 50p. slate-lilac 10 10
a. Imperf between (horiz pair) 17·00
203 1d. purple-brown 1·10 65
204 3d. slate-green 1·70 1·30
205 5d. red-brown 2·75 1·70
194/205 *Set of* 12 5·75 4·00

II. First Belgrade printing Coarse impression. Thick white paper. Rough perf 11½ (9.19)

206 **20** 1p. slate 1·10 35
207 15p. pale red-brown 5·50 2·75
208 20p. purple 5·25 1·30
209 1d. bistre-brown 9·00 2·75
206/209 *Set of* 4 19·00 6·50

III. Second Belgrade printing. Very poor impression. P 11½ (1920)

A. Rough perf. Small holes.

(a) Pelure paper

210A **20** 1p. black 10 10
211A 2p. olive-brown 10 10

(b) Medium to thick paper

212A **20** 5p. yellow-green 10 10
a. Perf 9 85·00 £325
213A 10p. scarlet 10 10
214A 15p. sepia 10 10
215A 20p. chestnut 10 10
216A 20p. deep red-brown 10 10
217A 25p. dull blue 10 10
218A 30p. pale olive-grey 10 10
219A 50p. lilac 10 10
220A 1d. chocolate 55 35
221A 3d. deep blue-green 2·50 1·60
222A 5d. red-brown 4·00 2·20
210A/222A *Set of* 13 7·25 4·75

(c) Medium to thin oily paper

223A **20** 15p. black-brown 1·10 1·10
224A 20p. pale red-brown — 1·10
226A 25p. dull blue — 2·20

B. Clean-cut perf. Large holes

210B **20** 1p. black 10 10
211B 2p. olive-brown 10 10

(b) Medium to thick paper

212B **20** 5p. yellow-green 10 10
213B 10p. scarlet 10 10
214B 15p. sepia 10 10
215B 20p. chesnut 10 10
216B 20p. deep red-brown 10 10
217B 25p. dull blue 10 10
218B 30p. pale olive-gray 10 10
219B 50p. lilac 10 10
220B 1d. chocolate 10 10
221B 3d. deep blue-green 2·75 1·60

(c) Medium to thin oily paper

223B **20** 15p. black brown 2·20 1·10
224B **20** 20p. pale red-brown 1·10 1·10
225B 20p. chesnut 2·20 1·70
226B 25p. dull blue — 1·70

The 15 and 20p are also found pin-perf on thick white paper (*Price* £1.10 *used, each*).

(Des and eng N. Jeremic. Typo in Paris and Belgrade)

1918–19. POSTAGE DUE. P 11½.

(a) Paris printing. Clear impression. Clean-cut perf (1918)

D227 **D 21** 5p. red 55 1·10
D228 10p. yellow-green 55 1·10
D229 20p. olive-brown 55 1·10
D230 30p. deep blue-green 55 1·10
D231 50p. pale chocolate 1·30 2·20

(b) Belgrade printings. Coarse impression. Rough perf (Sept 1919)

D232 **D 21** 5p. red-brown 55 1·10
D233 30p. olive-slate 1·30 1·90
D234 50p. yellow-brown 1·90 2·75
D227/234 *Set of* 8 6·50 11·00

REPUBLIC

100 Paras = 1 Dinar

⁄⁄1 (S **22**) **12** (S **23**)

2003 (3 July)–**04**. No. 2864 surch as Type S **22** and Nos. 2927, 2928 and 2930 surch as Type S **23**. P 13 (S235) or 12½ (others).

S235 1d. on R ultramarine (S **22**) 95 95
S236 12d. on 1p. deep reddish violet and olive-bistre (S **23**) (25.6.04) 1·00 1·00
S236*a* 12d. on 20p. purple and brown-lilac (S **23**) 1·80 1·80
S236*b* 32d. on 5p. deep dull blue and orange (S **23**) (25.6.04) 2·50 2·50
S235/236*b* *Set of* 4 5·50 5·50

S **24** Father Christmas and Reindeer

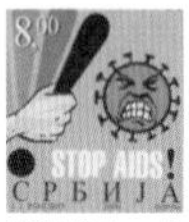

S **25** Bat and Virus as Ball

(Des M. Kalezić. Litho)

2003 (21 Nov). Christmas. Type S **24** and similar vert designs. Multicoloured. P 13½.

S237 10d. Type S **24** 90 90
a. Booklet pane. No. S237×10 9·25
S238 13d.50 Baubles 1·10 1·10
a. Booklet pane. No. S238×10 11·50
S239 26d.20 Snowflakes 1·70 1·70
S237/239 *Set of* 3 3·25 3·25

(Des M. Kalezić. Litho)

2005. AIDS Awareness Campaign. P 13½.

S240 S **25** 8d. multicoloured 55 55

S **26** Children

2006. Red Cross. Type S **26** and similar vert design. Each scarlet-vermilion and blue. P 14.

S241 8d. Type S **26** 55 55
S242 8d. Elderly couple 55 55

S **27**

S **28**

2006. Monasteries. P 13½×14.

S243 S **27** 8d. multicoloured 55 55
S244 S **28** 8d. multicoloured 55 55

S **29** Glass containing Virus

2006. AIDS Awareness Campaign. P 14.

S245 S **29** 8d. multicoloured 55 55

On 3rd of June 2006 Montenegro resigned from the Alliance (Serbia & Montenegro) and Serbia reverted to a single unit.

Currency. 100 Paras = 1 Dinar

30 National Flag

31 Battle Scene (detail) (Paja Jovanović)

2006 (30 June). National Symbols. T **30** and similar multicoloured design. P 13×12½.

246 16d.50 Type **30** 55 55
247 20d. Arms (vert) 65 65

2006 (30 June). Bicentenary of Battle of Misar. P 13½×14.

248 **31** 46d. multicoloured 1·50 1·50

32 Net, Ball and Players

33 Train

2006 (1 Sept). Water Polo Championships, Belgrade. T **32** and similar horiz design. Multicoloured. P 13×12½.

249 **32** 46d. multicoloured 1·50 1·50

2006 (13 Sept). Serbia–2006 Water Polo Champions. Horiz design as T **32**. Multicoloured. P 13×12½.

250 46d. Medal, players and ball 1·50 1·50

(Des M. Kalezić. Litho)

2006 (29 Sept). 38th "Joy in Europe" Meeting. Children's Day. T **33** and similar horiz design. Multicoloured. P 13½×14.

251 46d. Type **33** 1·50 1·50
252 73d. Girl and bird 2·40 2·40

34 Zica Monastery

35 1866 1p. Stamp (As Type **1**)

2006 (7 Oct). P 12½.

253 **34** 8d. multicoloured 25 25

2006 (24 Oct). Stamp Day. 140th Anniv of First Serbian Stamp. P 14×13½.

254 **35** 46d. multicoloured 1·50 1·50

36 Crown

(Des N. Skocajic. Litho)

2006 (30 Oct). Museum Exhibits. Bridal Jewellery. T **36** and similar horiz design. Multicoloured. P 13½×14.

255 16d.50 Type **36** 55 55
a. Horiz pair. Nos. 255 and 257 2·20 2·20
b. Horiz strip. Nos. 255/8 plus label 4·25
256 16d.50 Ring 55 55
a. Horiz pair. Nos. 256 and 258 2·20 2·20
257 46d. Earrings 1·50 1·50
258 46d. Necklace 1·50 1·50
255/258 *Set of* 4 3·75 3·75

Nos. 255 and 257, and 256 and 258, were issued in *se-tenant* pairs, within strips of four stamps surrounding a central stamp size label.

37 Actors and Theatre Façade

38 Wolfgang Amadeus Mozart

(Des M. Kalezić. Litho)

2006 (10 Nov). 50th Anniv of Theatre ATELJE 212. P 14×13½.

259 **37** 46d. multicoloured 1·50 1·50

(Des M. Kalezić. Litho)

2006 (16 Nov). Birth Anniversaries. T **38** and similar vert design. Multicoloured. P 14×13½.

260 46d. Type **38** (composer) (250th) 1·50 1·50
261 46d. Rembrandt Harmenszoon van Rijn (artist) (400th) 1·50 1·50

39 Wine, Apples, Bread and Candle

39a Athletes

(Des N. Skocajic. Litho)

2006 (20 Nov). Christmas. T **39** and similar horiz design. Multicoloured. P 13½×14.

262 16d.50 Type **39** 55 55
263 46d. Candle and decoration 1·50 1·50

(Des M. Kalezić. Litho)

2006 (1 Dec). European Olympic Youth Festival Games, Belgrade. P 14.

263*a* **39a** 8d. multicoloured 25 25

40 Santa Claus and Presents

(Des N. Skocajic. Litho)

2006 (1 Dec). New Year. P 13½×14.

264 **40** 46d. multicoloured 1·50 1·50

41 Children

42 Battle Scene

(Des N. Skocajic. Litho)

2006 (11 Dec). 60th Anniv of UNICEF. P 13½×14.

265 **41** 16d.50 multicoloured 65 65

(Des M. Kalezić. Litho)

2006 (13 Dec). Bicentenary of the Liberation of Belgrade. P 13½×14.

266 **42** 16d.50 multicoloured 65 65

43 Dahlia

44 Western Moravia

(Des N. Skocajic (50p.) or M. Kalezić (others). Litho)

2007 (1 Jan). Flora. T **43** and similar multicoloured designs. P 14×13½ (vert) or 13½×14 (horiz).

267 50p. Type **43** ... 15 15
268 1d. Sunflowers (horiz) ... 15 15
269 5d. Apple tree (horiz) ... 25 25
267/269 *Set of 3* ... 50 50

(Des N. Skocajic (50p.) or M. Kalezić (others). Litho)

2007 (1 Jan). Tourism. T **44** and similar multicoloured designs. P 14×13½ (vert) or 13½×14 (horiz).

270 10d. Type **44** ... 40 40
271 13d. Field and woods, Coc (37×29 mm) ... 55 55
272 33d. Lake and trees, Zlatibov (37×29 mm) ... 1·20 1·20
273 50d. Winter sports centre, Kopaomk (37×29 mm) ... 1·70 1·70
274 100d. National Theatre, Belgrade (29×37 mm) ... 3·50 3·50
270/274 *Set of 5* ... 6·50 6·50

45 Combatants

46 Map and Milutin Milankovic (engineer and geophysicist)

(Des M. Kalezić. Litho)

2007 (22 Jan). European Judo Championships, Belgrade. P 14.

275 **45** 8d. multicoloured ... 25 25

(Des A. Kostic. Litho)

2007 (30 Jan). International Polar Year. P 13½×14.

276 **46** 46d. multicoloured ... 1·60 1·60

47 Petar Dubrinovic

48 Crucifixion (icon)

(Des M. Kalezić. Litho)

2007 (16 Feb). Actors and Actresses. T **47** and similar vert designs. Multicoloured. P 13½×14.

277 16d.50 Type **47** ... 65 65
a. Sheetlet. Nos. 277/84 plus label ... 5·50
278 16d.50 Milka Grgurova Aleksic ... 65 65
279 16d.50 Ljubiša Jovanović ... 65 65
280 16d.50 Rahela Farari ... 65 65
281 16d.50 Miodrag Petrovic Škalja ... 65 65
282 16d.50 Branko Pleša ... 65 65
283 16d.50 Ljuba Tadic ... 65 65
284 16d.50 Danilo Bata Stojkovic ... 65 65
277/284 *Set of 8* ... 4·75 4·75

Nos. 277/84 were issued in *se-tenant* sheetlets of eight stamps surrounding a central illustrated label.

(Des J. J. Vlahovic. Litho)

2007 (1 Mar). Easter. T **48** and similar vert designs. Multicoloured. P 14×13½.

285 20d. Type **48** ... 65 65
286 46d. Crucifixion ... 1·60 1·60

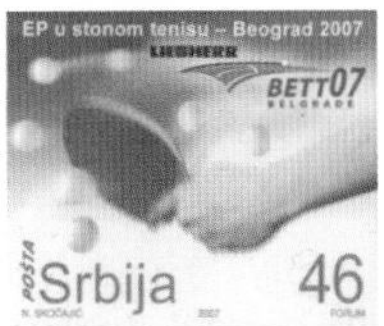
49 Hand, Paddle and Balls

50 Rose

(Des N. Skocajic. Litho)

2007 (23 Mar). European Table Tennis Championship, Belgrade. T **49** and similar horiz design. Multicoloured. P 13½×14.

287 46d. Type **49** ... 1·60 1·60
MS288 99×71 mm. 112d. Emblem, net and player ... 4·00 4·00

The stamp and margin of No. **MS**288 form a composite design.

(Des N. Skocajic. Litho)

2007 (4 Apr). P 13½.

289 **50** 40d. multicoloured ... 1·50 1·50

51 Black Woodpecker

52 City Park, Vrnjacka Banja

(Des M. Kalezić. Litho)

2007 (6 Apr). Endangered Species. Black Woodpecker (*Dryocopus martius*). T **51** and similar vert designs. Multicoloured. P 13½.

290 20d. Type **51** ... 80 80
a. Pair. Nos. 290 and 292 ... 2·40 2·40
a. Horiz strip of 5. Nos. 290/3 plus label ... 4·75
291 20d. Feeding young facing right ... 80 80
a. Pair. Nos. 291 and 293 ... 2·40 2·40
292 40d. Feeding young facing left ... 1·50 1·50
293 40d. Black woodpecker facing right ... 1·50 1·50
290/293 *Set of 4* ... 4·25 4·25

Nos. 290 and 292, and 291 and 293, respectively were issued in horizontal *se-tenant* pairs within strips of four stamps surrounding a central stamp-size label.

(Des M. Kalezić. Litho)

2007 (20 Apr). Nature Protection. T **52** and similar horiz designs. Multicoloured. P 13½×14.

294 40d. Type **52** ... 1·30 1·30
295 46d. Fountain, Pionirski Park, Belgrade ... 1·60 1·60

53 Scouts

54 Emblem and Map

(Des N. Skocajic. Litho)

2007 (3 May). Europa. Centenary of Scouting. T **53** and similar horiz designs. Multicoloured. P 13½×14.

296 20d. Type **53** ... 65 65
297 20d. Milos Popovic (founder of Serbian Scouting) ... 65 65
a. Pair. Nos. 297/8 ... 1·40 1·40
298 20d. Robert Baden-Powell (original founder) ... 65 65
299 46d. Scouts canoeing ... 1·60 1·60
296/299 *Set of 4* ... 3·25 3·25

Nos. 297/8 were issued in vertical and horizontal *se-tenant* pairs within sheetlets of six stamps.

(Des Jaksa Vlahovic. Litho)

2007 (10 May). Serbia's Chairmanship of Council of Europe's Ministers' Committee, May–November 2007. P 13½×14.

300 **54** 20d. multicoloured ... 65 65

55 Amelia Earhart and Lockheed Vega 5b

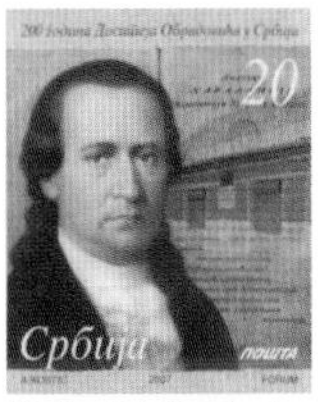
56 Dositej Obradovic (Uros Predic)

(Des Nadezda Skocajic. Litho)

2007 (21 May). 75th Anniv of Amelia Earhart's Transatlantic Flight. P 13½×14.

301 **55** 50d. multicoloured ... 1·60 1·60

(Des Ana Kostic. Litho)

2007 (28 May). Dositej Obradovic (writer, philosopher and linguist) Commemoration. Bicentenary of Return to Serbia. P 14×13½.

302 **56** 20d. multicoloured ... 65 65

57 Jovan Zmaj

58 Prince Stefan Lazarevic (Despot 1402–1427) (fresco) and Arms

(Des Jaksa Vlahovic. Litho)

2007 (1 June). 50th Anniv of Zmaj's Children's Games (youth cultural event). P 13½×14.

303 **57** 20d. multicoloured ... 65 65

(Des Marina Kalezić. Litho)

2007 (11 June). Srbijafila 2007 Philatelic Exhibition. Sheet 95×53 mm containing T **58** and similar horiz design. Multicoloured. P 13½×14.

MS304 20d. Type **58**; 46d. Court at Kalemegdan and seal ... 2·20 2·20

The stamps of No. **MS**304 share a composite background design.

59 Swimmer

60 Eventing

(Des Nadezda Skocajic. Litho)

2007 (20 June). European Olympic Youth Festival, Belgrade. Sheet 95×53 mm containing T **59** and similar horiz design. Multicoloured. P 13½×14.

MS305 46d.×2 Type **59**; Runner ... 3·25 3·25

The stamps and margins of No. **MS**305 form a composite background design.

(Des Ana Kostic. Litho)

2007 (28 June). Equestrian Sports. T **60** and similar horiz designs. Multicoloured. P 13½.

306 20d. Type **60** ... 65 65
a. Pair. Nos. 306 and 308 ... 2·10 2·10
a. Horiz strip of 5. Nos. 306/9 plus label ... 4·25
307 20d. Carriage driving ... 65 65
a. Pair. Nos. 307 and 309 ... 2·10 2·10
308 40d. Dressage ... 1·30 1·30
309 40d. Show jumping ... 1·30 1·30
306/309 *Set of 4* ... 3·50 3·50

Nos. 306 and 308, and 307 and 309, respectively were issued in horizontal *se-tenant* pairs within strips of four stamps surrounding a central stamp-size label.

61 William Thomas Kelvin

62 Peter Lubarda and *Horses' Game* (1960)

(Des Jaksa Vlahovic. Litho)

2007 (10 July). Scientists' Centenaries. T **61** and similar vert designs. Multicoloured. P 14.

310 40d. Type **61** (developed second law of thermodynamics and formulated Kelvin temperature scale) (death centenary) ... 1·30 1·30
311 46d. Giuseppe Occhialini (expert on cosmic radiation) (birth centenary) ... 1·60 1·60
312 46d. Dmitrij Ivanovitch Mendeleev (developed Periodic Table) (death centenary) ... 1·60 1·60
310/312 *Set of 3* ... 4·00 4·00

(Des Marina Kalezić. Litho)

2007 (27 July). Birth Centenary of Peter Lubarda (artist). P 13½×14.

313 **62** 20d. multicoloured ... 65 65

63 Monastery Building

64 *Haliaeetus albicilla* (white-tailed eagle)

(Des Nadezda Skocajic. Litho)

2007 (28 Aug). 600th Anniv of Kalenić Monastery. P 14×13½.

314 **63** 20d. multicoloured ... 65 65

(Des Helga Herger. Photo)

2007 (7 Sept). P 14.

315 **64** 46d. multicoloured ... 1·60 1·60

A stamp of the same design was issued by Austria.

65 Hands

66 Ruins

(Des Jaksa Vlahovic. Litho)

2007 (17 Sept). International Ozone Layer Protection Day. P 14×13½.

316 **65** 20d. multicoloured ... 65 65

(Des Marina Kalezić. Litho)

2007 (21 Sept). UNESCO World Heritage Site. Felix Romuliana, Gamzigrad. T **66** and similar horiz designs. Multicoloured. P 13½×14.

317 46d. Type **66** ... 1·60 1·60
318 46d. Columns surrounding tiled area with bowl ... 1·60 1·60

67 Emblem

68 Children

(Des Jakša Vlahovic. Litho)

2007 (4 Oct). Red Cross. Roma Week. P 13½.
319 **67** 10d. multicoloured 35 35

(Des Ana Kostic. Litho)

2007 (28 Sept). 39th 'Joy in Europe' Meeting. Children's Day. P 13½.
320 **68** 46d. multicoloured .... 1·60 1·60

69 *Sputnik I*

70 Observatory and Medal showing Milan Nedeljkovic

(Des Nadezda Skocajic. Litho)

2007 (4 Oct). 50th Anniv of Space Exploration. P 13½.
321 **69** 46d. multicoloured .... 1·60 1·60

(Des Ana Kostic. Litho)

2007 (15 Oct). 120th Anniv of Astronomical Observatory, Belgrade. 150th Birth Anniv of Milan Nedeljkovic (founder). P 13½.
322 **70** 20d. multicoloured 65 65

71 Erzen Derocco

72 *Rest after Battle* (Djura Jaksic)

(Des Marina Kalezić. Litho)

2007 (24 Oct). Stamp Day. Erzen Derocco (philatelist) Commemoration. P 13½.
323 **71** 46d. multicoloured .... 1·60 1·60

(Des Marina Kalezić. Litho)

2007 (1 Nov). Artists' Anniversaries. T **72** and similar vert designs. Multicoloured. P 13½.
324 20d. Type **72** (175th birth anniv) 65 65
325 46d. *Self Portrait* (Frida Kahlo) (birth centenary) .... 1·60 1·60
326 46d. *Boy at Window* (Uros Predic) (150th birth anniv) .... 1·60 1·60
324/326 *Set of 3* .... 3·50 3·50

73 *The Nativity* (Eremija Profeta)

74 Novi Sad Port

(Des Nadezda Skocajic. Litho)

2007 (9 Nov). Christmas. T **73** and similar horiz design. Multicoloured. P 13½.
327 20d. Type **73** 65 65
328 46d. *The Nativity* ('XVIII century') .... 1·60 1·60

(Des Livia Penda or Marina Kalezić. Litho)

2007 (14 Nov). Danube Ports and Ships. T **74** and similar horiz designs. Multicoloured. P 13½.
329 20d. Type **74** 65 65
330 46d. Orsova port .... 1·60 1·60
MS331 95×53 mm. 40d. *Sirona* (Serbia); 50d. *Orsova* (Romania) .... 3·00 3·00
Stamps of a similar design were issued by Romania.

75 King Milan I Obrenovic and Emperor Meiji of Japan

(Des Nadezda Skocajic. Litho)

2007 (23 Dec). 125th Anniv of Serbia–Japan Bi-lateral Relations. P 13½.
332 **75** 46d. multicoloured .... 1·60 1·60

76 Ladu of Vinca (statue) and Ruins of Neolithic House

77 *Cluny Museum, Paris*

(Des Nadezda Skocajic. Litho)

2008 (28 Jan). Centenary of First Archaeological Dig, Vinca. P 13½.
333 **76** 20d. multicoloured 65 65

(Des Marina Kalezić. Litho)

2008 (4 Feb). Art. Birth Centenary of Peda Milosavljevic. T **77** and similar horiz design. Multicoloured. P 13½.
334 20d. Type **77** 65 65
335 46d. *Notre Dame, Paris* .... 1·60 1·60

78 Swimmer and Emblem

79 Tennis Player

(Des Nadezda Skocajic. Litho)

2008 (18 Feb). Centenary of Swimming Federation (Fina). P 13½.
336 **78** 50d. multicoloured .... 1·70 1·70

(Des Marina Kalezić. Litho)

2008 (7 Mar). Olympic Games, Beijing. T **79** and similar square design. Multicoloured. P 13½.
337 46d. Type **79** .... 1·60 1·60
338 50d. Hurdlers .... 2·00 2·00

80 Christ enclosed (detail) (King Milutin's plastanica (13th–14th century textile))

81 Janko Tipsarevic

(Des Jaksa Vlahovic. Litho)

2008 (21 Mar). Easter. T **80** and similar vert design. Multicoloured. P 13½.
339 20d. Type **80** 65 65
340 46d. Christ enclosed (detail) (15th century icon) .... 1·60 1·60

(Des Marina Kalezić. Litho)

2008 (4 Apr). Olympic Tennis Team. T **81** and similar horiz designs showing players. Multicoloured. P 13½.
341 20d. Type **81** 65 65
342 30d. Nenad Zimonjic 90 90
343 30d. Jelena Jankovic 90 90
344 40d. Ana Ivanovic .... 1·30 1·30
345 46d. Novak Dokovic .... 1·50 1·50
341/345 *Set of 5* .... 4·75 4·75

82 *Cervus elaphus* (red deer)

83 Singer

(Des Marina Kalezić. Litho)

2008 (7 Apr). Fauna. T **82** and similar vert designs. Multicoloured. P 13½.
346 20d. Type **82** 65 65
a. Pair. Nos. 346 and 348 .... 2·40 2·40
347 20d. *Meles meles* (European badger) 65 65
a. Pair. Nos. 347 and 349 .... 2·40 2·40
348 46d. *Felis silvestris* (wildcat) .... 1·60 1·60
349 46d. *Sus scrofa* (wild boar) .... 1·60 1·60
346/349 *Set of 4* .... 4·00 4·00
Nos. 346 and 348, and Nos. 347 and 349, respectively, were issued in horizontal *se-tenant* pairs, separated by an inscribed stamp size label within the sheet.

(Des Ana Kostic)

2008 (11 Apr). Eurovision Song Contest, Belgrade. Sheet 95×53 mm. P 13½.
MS350 **83** 177d. multicoloured .... 5·75 5·75

84 Quill and Envelope

85 Vlasina Plateau

(Des Nadezda Skocajic. Litho)

2008 (5 May). Europa. The Letter. T **84** and similar horiz design. Multicoloured. P 13½.
351 46d. Type **84** .... 1·60 1·60
352 50d. Letter opener .... 2·00 2·00

(Des Marina Kalezic. Litho)

2008 (23 May). European Protection. T **85** and similar horiz design. Multicoloured. P 13½.
353 20d. Type **85** 65 65
354 46d. Djavolija varos (devil's town) .... 1·60 1·60
Nos. 353/4 were each issued with a *se-tenant* stamp size label attached at right.

86 Train and Eiffel Tower

87 Camera and Film

(Des Nadezda Skocajic. Litho)

2008 (9 June). 125th Anniv of Orient Express. T **86** and similar horiz design. Multicoloured. P 13½.
355 20d. Type **86** 65 65
356 50d. Train and mosque .... 1·60 1·60
Nos. 355/6 were each issued with a *se-tenant* stamp size label attached at top.

(Des A. Rostic)

2008 (16 June). 50th Anniv of Television Belgrade. P 13½.
357 **87** 46d. multicoloured .... 1·60 1·60

GERMAN OCCUPATION

From 30 August 1941 Serbia was in theory an independent state, ruled by a Serbian government under General Nedic; in fact it was under German military rule.

The territory comprised most of the pre-1913 Serbia (except for areas around Pirot and Uranje) and a wedge, the Banat, between the Tisza and the old Romanian frontier, extending to just south of Szeged.

PRINTER. All the following issues were printed at the Government Printing Works, Belgrade.

(G **1**)

1941 (5 June). Nos. 414/26 of Yugoslavia (1939 King Peter II issue), optd with Type G **1** on paper with coloured network.
G1 **99** 25p. black .... 45 9·25
G2 50p. orange .... 45 4·75
G3 1d. green .... 45 4·75
G4 1d.50 scarlet .... 45 4·75
G5 2d. carmine-rose .... 45 4·75
G6 3d. red-brown .... 3·25 37·00
G7 4d. bright blue .... 1·90 7·50
G8 5d. blue .... 2·75 19·00
G9 5d.50 dull violet .... 2·75 19·00
G10 6d. deep blue .... 2·75 19·00
G11 8d. chocolate .... 3·75 28·00
G12 12d. violet .... 3·75 28·00
G13 16d. purple .... 5·50 95·00
G14 20d. light blue .... 9·25 £325
G15 30d. pink .... 37·00 £1300
G1/15 *Set of 15* .... 65·00 £1700

GD **2**

GD **3**

(Des S. Grujic. Typo)

1941 (24 June). POSTAGE DUE. Unissued Postage Due stamps optd "SERBIEN" as Types GD **2**/**3**. P 12½.
GD16 GD **2** 0d.50 violet .... 1·90 47·00
GD17 1d. claret .... 1·90 47·00
GD18 2d. deep blue .... 1·90 47·00
GD19 3d. scarlet .... 2·75 70·00
GD20 GD **3** 4d. blue .... 3·75 £170
GD21 5d. orange .... 3·75 £170
GD22 10d. violet .... 6·50 £425
GD23 20d. green .... 16·00 £1100
GD16/23 *Set of 8* .... 35·00 £1900

1941 (19 July). AIR. Nos. 360/7 and 443/4 of Yugoslavia (pictorial air stamps), optd as Type G **1** on paper with coloured network. P 12½, 12½×11½ or 11½×12½.

G16	50p. brown (R.)	9·25	£200
G17	1d. bright green (R.)	9·25	£200
G18	2d. slate-blue (R.)	9·25	£200
G19	2d.50 carmine (Br.)	9·25	£200
G20	5d. violet (R.)	9·25	£200
G21	10d. lake (Br.)	9·25	£200
G22	20d. bluish green (R.)	9·25	£200
G23	30d. bright blue (R.)	9·25	£200
G24	40d. blue-green (R.)	23·00	£750
G25	50d. slate-blue (R.)	33·00	£1300
G16/25 *Set of* 10		£120	£3250

The overprint "SERBIEN" on the above Air Mail set is larger than in Type G **1** and reads diagonally up on Nos. G19, G23 and G25, and down on the remainder: The angle of the letters varies according to the shape of the stamp.

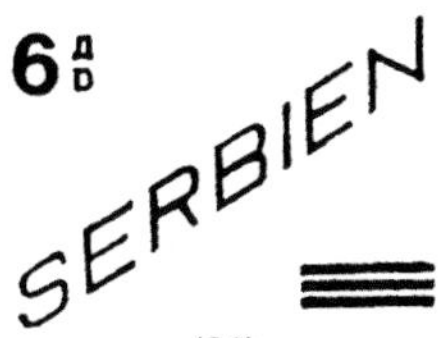

(G **2**)

(G **3**)

1941 (28 July). AIR. As last, without network opt, surch as Type G **2**.

G26	1d. on 10d. lake (Br.)	6·50	£225
G27	3d. on 20d. bluish green (R.)	6·50	£225
G28	6d. on 30d. bright blue (R.)	6·50	£225
G29	8d. on 40d. blue-green (R.)	14·00	£475
G30	12d. on 50d. slate-blue (R.)	23·00	£1000
G26/30 *Set of* 5		50·00	£1900

1941 (1 Sept). Nos. 414/26 of Yugoslavia optd with Type G **3** in black on paper with coloured network.

G31	**99** 25p. black	45	28·00
G32	50p. orange	45	6·50
G33	1d. green	45	6·50
G34	1d.50 scarlet	45	6·50
G35	2d. carmine-rose	45	6·50
G36	3d. red-brown	1·40	24·00
G37	4d. bright blue	1·90	6·50
G38	5d. blue	1·90	12·00
G39	5d.50 dull violet	2·75	24·00
G40	6d. deep blue	2·75	24·00
G41	8d. chocolate	3·75	37·00
G42	12d. violet	5·00	37·00
G43	16d. purple	5·00	£120
G44	20d. light blue	5·00	£375
G45	30d. pink	26·00	£1200
G31/45 *Set of* 15		50·00	£1700

G **4** Smederevo Fortress

G **5** Refugees

(Des S. Grujic. Litho)

1941 (22 Sept). Smederevo Explosion Relief Fund. P 11½×12½.

G46	G **4** 0.50d.+1d. brown	75	1·90
G47	G **5** 1d.+2d. green	75	2·30
G48	1.50d.+3d. purple	1·30	4·25
	a. Perf 12½	10·00	19·00
G49	G **4** 2d.+4d. blue	1·90	5·50
G46/49 *Set of* 4		4·25	12·50

Miniature sheets (149×109-mm.) comprising Nos. G47 and G49, colours changed and with high premiums.

MSG49*a*	1d.+49d. red, 2d.+48d. green P 11½	£130	£550
MSG49*b*	1d.+49d. green, 2d.+48d. red Impf	£130	£550

G **6** Christ and the Virgin Mary

(Des Lj. Cucakovic. Litho)

1941 (5 Dec). Prisoners of War Fund. P 12×11½.

A. With pink burelage

G50A	G **6** 0.50d.+1.50d. brown-red	95	7·50
G51A	1d.+3d. grey-green	95	7·50
G52A	2d.+6d. rosine	95	7·50
G53A	4d.+12d. blue	95	7·50
G50A/53 *Set of* 4		3·50	27·00

B. Without burelage

G50B	G **6** 0.50d.+1.50d. brown-red	3·75	23·00
G51B	1d.+3d. grey-green	3·75	23·00
G52B	2d.+6d. rosine	3·75	23·00
G53B	4d.+12d. blue	3·75	23·00
G50B/53 *Set of* 4		13·50	85·00

The above were each printed in two panes of 25 (5×5) of which twenty have the burelage and the five in the centre (in the form of a cross) are without burelage. In addition four of the stamps with the burelage (positions 7, 9, 17 and 19) bear a large double-lined "C" (resembling an "E"), two normal and two reversed (*Price each value, either state, £26 un, £85 used).*

G **7**

G **8**

(Des S. Grujic. Litho)

1942 (1 Jan). Anti-Masonic Exhibition. Types G **7/8** and similar designs dated "22.X.1941". P 11½×12 (horiz) or 12×11½ (vert).

G54	0.50d.+0.50d. brown	55	4·25
G55	1d.+1d. green	55	4·25
G56	2d.+2d. carmine-lake	95	7·50
G57	4d.+4d. indigo	95	7·50
G54/57 *Set of* 4		2·75	21·00

Designs: Horiz—1d. Hand grasping snake. Vert—4d. Peasant demolishing masonic symbols.

G **9** Kalenić

GD **10**

GD **11**

(Des N. K. Džange. Typo)

1942 (10 Jan)–**43**. Type G **9** and similar designs showing monasteries. P 12×11½ (vert) or 11½×12 (horiz).

G58	0d.50 violet	20	45
G59	1d. scarlet (3.9.42)	20	45
G60	1d.50 brown (3.9.42)	1·70	6·50
G61	1d.50 green (1943)	20	45
G62	2d. purple (12.1.42)	20	45
G63	3d. blue (3.9.42)	1·70	6·50
G64	3d. pink (1943)	20	45
G65	4d. ultramarine	20	45
G66	7d. grey-green	20	45
G67	12d. claret	30	3·25
G68	16d. grey-black (3.9.42)	1·90	3·75
G58/68 *Set of* 11		6·25	21·00

Designs: Vert—0d.50, Lazarica; 1d.50, Ravanica; 12d. Gornjak; 16d. Studenica. Horiz—2d. Manasija; 3d. Ljubostinja; 4d. Sopocani; 7d. Zica.

1942 (10 Jan). POSTAGE DUE. Typo. P 12½.

GD69	GD **10** 1d. claret and green	2·75	9·25
GD70	2d. deep blue and red	2·75	9·25
GD71	3d. scarlet and blue	2·75	14·00
GD72	GD **11** 4d. blue and red	2·75	14·00
GD73	5d. orange and blue	3·75	19·00
GD74	10d. violet and red	3·75	28·00
GD75	20d. green and red	19·00	£110
GD69/75 *Set of* 7		34·00	£180

1942 (24 Mar). As Nos. G50/53, colours changed and without burelage. Thick paper. P 12×11½.

G68*a*	0.50d.+1.50d. brown	2·30	4·75
G68*b*	1d.+3d. blue-green	2·30	4·75
G68*c*	2d.+6d. carmine	2·30	4·75
G68*d*	4d.+12d. ultramarine	2·30	4·75
G68*a*/68*d* *Set of* 4		8·25	17·00

The above were printed in the same sheet formation as Nos. 650/53 except that in place of the five central stamps in the form of a cross there were four blank labels and a centre label which bears the Serbian Arms.

(G **10**)

G **11** Mother and Children

1942 (5 July). AIR. T **99** of Yugoslavia optd with burelage in green and surch as Type G **10**.

G69	2 on 2d.carmine-rose	45	2·30
G70	4 on 4d.bright blue	45	2·30
G71	10 on 12d.violet	45	4·75
G72	14 on 20d.light blue	45	4·75
G73	20 on 30d.pink	1·10	19·00
G69/73 *Set of* 5		2·50	30·00

(Des S. Grujic. Litho)

1942 (13 Sept). War Orphans' Fund. P 11½.

G74	G **11** 2d.+6d. violet	11·00	12·00
G75	4d.+8d. blue	11·00	12·00
G76	7d.+13d. green	11·00	12·00
G77	20d.+40d. lake	11·00	12·00
G74/77 *Set of* 4		40·00	43·00

GO **12**

G **12** Broken Sword

GD **13**

(Des S. Grujic. Typo)

1943 (1 Jan). OFFICIAL. P 12½.

GO78	GO **12** 3d. claret	1·90	2·75

(Des S. Grujic. Litho)

1943 (16 May). War Invalids' Relief Fund. Type G **12** and similar designs. P 12×11½ (vert) or 11½×12 (horiz).

G78	1.50d.+1.50d. chocolate	2·30	3·75
G79	2d.+3d. blue-green	2·30	3·75
G80	3d.+5d. magenta	4·75	5·50
G81	4d.+10d. blue	5·00	6·50
G78/81 *Set of* 4		13·00	18·00

MSG81*a* Two sheets, each 149×110 mm. Thick paper. P 11½. (a) 1d.50+48d.50, 4d.+46d. (b) 2d.+48d., 3d.+47d. £250 £7500

Designs: Horiz—2d. Fallen standard bearer, 3d. Wounded soldier (seated). Vert—4d. Nurse tending soldier.

(Des V. Guljevic. Typo)

1943 (1 July). POSTAGE DUE. P 12½.

GD82	GD **13** 0d.50 black	1·90	7·50
GD83	3d. violet	1·90	7·50
GD84	4d. blue	1·90	7·50
GD85	5d. green	1·90	7·50
GD86	6d. orange	2·75	19·00
GD87	10d. scarlet	3·75	23·00
GD88	20d. ultramarine	9·25	70·00
GD82/88 *Set of* 7		21·00	£130

За пострадале
од англо-америчког
терор. бомбардовања
Ниша — 20-X-1943

G **13** Post Rider

+ 3

(G **14**)

(Des S. Grujic. Litho)

1943 (15 Oct). Postal Centenary. As Type G **13** (dated "15.X.1843—15.X.1943"). P 12½.

G82	3d. red and lilac	1·90	5·50
G83	8d. claret and grey-green	1·90	5·50
G84	9d. green and brown	1·90	5·50
G85	30d. brown and green	1·90	5·50
G86	50d. blue and red-brown	1·90	5·50
G82/86 *Set of* 5		8·50	25·00

Designs: Horiz—8d. Horse wagon; 9d. Railway van; 30d. Postal motor van; 50d Junkers Ju 52/3m mail plane.

The above were issued in special sheets containing each value in a block of four, the 3d. and 8d. at top left and right; the 30d. and 50d. at bottom left and right; and the 9d. in the centre with labels containing a shield on either side with the date "15-X-1843" at left and "15-X-1943" at right (*Price for sheet £55 un, £110 used*).

1943 (11 Dec). Bombing of Nish Relief Fund. "Monasteries" issue of 1942–43 optd with green network and surch with additional value as Type G **14**.

G87	0d.50+2d. violet	45	55·00
G88	1d.+3d. scarlet	45	55·00
G89	1d.50+4d. green	45	55·00
G90	2d.+5d. purple	45	55·00
G91	3d.+7d. pink	45	55·00
G92	4d.+9d. ultramarine	45	55·00
G93	7d.+15d. grey-green	1·20	55·00
G94	12d.+25d. claret	1·20	£250
G95	16d.+33d. grey-black	2·50	£425
G87/95 *Set of* 9		6·75	£950

After the defeat of Germany, Yugoslavia was reconstituted as a Federation with Serbia as a constituent republic. Obligatory tax stamps inscribed "SRBIJA" are listed at the end of Yugoslavia.

AUSTRO-HUNGARIAN MILITARY POST IN SERBIA

The German and Austro-Hungarian offensive against Serbia, which began on 6 October 1915, with Bulgarian co-operation from 14 October, was completely successful; Serbia was in enemy occupation, except for Monastir which was recaptured by French and Serbian troops on 19 November 1916, until after the Allied breakthrough in Macedonia in September 1918.

100 Heller = 1 Krone

SERBIEN

(**1**)

SERBIEN

(**2**)

1916 (6 Mar). T **25** and **26** of Bosnia and Herzegovina (portraits of Emperor Francis Joseph I) optd with T **1**.

1	**25** 1h. olive-green	9·25	23·00
2	2h. turquoise-blue	9·25	23·00

3		3h. lake	9·25	23·00
4		5h. green	1·90	3·75
5		6h. black	9·25	23·00
6		10h. carmine	1·90	3·75
7		12h. sage green	9·25	23·00
8		20h. brown	9·25	23·00
9		25h. ultramarine	9·25	23·00
10		30h. vermilion	9·25	23·00
11	**26**	35h. blackish green	9·25	23·00
12		40h. deep violet	9·25	23·00
13		45h. olive-brown	9·25	23·00
14		50h. Prussian blue	9·25	23·00
15		60h. purple-brown	9·25	23·00
16		72h. deep blue	9·25	23·00
17	**25**	1k. lake-brown/*cream*	23·00	50·00
18		2k. indigo/*blue*	23·00	50·00
19	**26**	3k. carmine/*green*	28·00	60·00
20		5k. indigo-lilac/*greyish*	33·00	75·00
21	**25**	10k. blue/*grey*	65·00	£130
1/21 *Set of 21*			£275	£650

1916 (6 Mar). T **25** and **26** of Bosnia and Herzegovina optd with T **2**.

22	**25**	1h. olive-green	2·75	6·50
23		2h. turquoise-blue	2·75	6·50
24		3h. lake	2·75	6·50
25		5h. green	45	95
26		6h. black	1·90	4·75
27		10h. carmine	45	95
28		12h. sage green	95	2·75
29		20h. brown	95	95
30		25h. ultramarine	95	2·75
31		30h. vermilion	95	1·90
32	**26**	35h. blackish green	95	1·90
33		40h. deep violet	95	1·90
34		45h. olive-brown	95	1·90
35		50h. Prussian blue	95	1·90
36		60h. purple-brown	95	1·90
37		72h. deep blue	95	1·90
38	**25**	1k. lake-brown/*cream*	1·90	2·75
39		2k. indigo/*blue*	1·90	2·75
40	**26**	3k. carmine/*green*	1·90	2·75
41		5k. indigo-lilac/*greyish*	1·90	2·75
42	**25**	10k. blue/*grey*	19·00	37·00
22/42 *Set of 21*			42·00	85·00

Serbia and Montenegro

On 4 February 2003 Yugoslavia became Serbia & Montenegro. See Yugoslavia for previous issues.

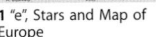

1 "e", Stars and Map of Europe

2 The Descent from the Cross (16th-century icon)

(Des R. Bojanic. Litho)

2003 (3 Apr). Accession to the Council of Europe. T **1** and similar horiz design. Multicoloured. P 14.

1		16d. Type **1**	1·30	1·30
2		28d.70 Smaller "e", stars and map of Europe	2·20	2·20

(Des R. Bojanic. Litho)

2003 (18 Apr). Easter. T **2** and similar vert designs. Multicoloured. P 14.

3		12d. Type **2**	90	90
4		16d. Resurrection (Dimitrije Bacevic)	1·10	1·10
5		26d.20 Mourning Christ (icon, St. Paul's Monastery, Athos) (1616)	2·00	2·00
6		28d.70 Transfiguration of Christ (Giovanni Bellini)	2·20	2·20
3/6 *Set of* 4			5·50	5·50

3 Document and Emblem

4 Pasting up Poster

(Des R. Bojanic. Litho)

2003 (22 Apr). 150th Anniv of First Belgrade Singers' Society. P 13½×14 (with one elliptical hole on each vert side).

7	**3**	16d. multicoloured	3·25	3·25

(Des R. Bojanic. Litho)

2003 (9 May). Europa. Poster Art. T **4** and similar vert design. Multicoloured. P 14.

8		28d.70 Type **4**	2·20	2·20
9		50d. Pasting up poster for Balkan Express	5·50	5·50

5 *Galanthus nivalis*

6 Ilija Stanojevic

(Des M. Kalezić. Litho)

2003 (13 May). Flowers. T **5** and similar horiz designs. Multicoloured. P 14.

10		16d. Type **5**	1·30	1·30
		a. Horiz strip of 4. Nos. 10/13 plus label	7·50	
11		24d. *Erythronium dens canis*	1·80	1·80
12		26d.20 *Hepatica nobilis*	2·00	2·00
13		28d.70 *Anemone runculoides*	2·20	2·20
10/13 *Set of* 4			6·75	6·75

Nos. 10/13 were issued in horizontal *se-tenant* strips of four stamps surrounding a central stamp-size label. Each label showing a different part of a composite design of a valley.

(Des M. Kalezić. Litho)

2003 (20 May). Actors and Actresses. T **6** and similar vert designs. Multicoloured. P 14.

14		16d. Type **6**	1·30	1·30
		a. Sheetlet of 8. Nos. 14/21 plus 8 labels	11·00	
15		16d. Zivana Stokic	1·30	1·30
16		16d. Radomir Plaovic	1·30	1·30
17		16d. Milosav Aleksic	1·30	1·30
18		16d. Dobrivoje Milotinovic	1·30	1·30
19		16d. Lubinka Bobic	1·30	1·30
20		16d. Milivoje Zivanovic	1·30	1·30
21		16d. Zoran Radmilovic	1·30	1·30
14/21 *Set of* 8			9·25	9·25

Nos. 14/21 were issued in *se-tenant* sheetlets of eight stamps, each with a *se-tenant* label showing the actor in character, with an enlarged illustrated margin.

7 Early Car

8 Tree overhanging River

(Des N. Skocajic. Litho)

2003 (3 June). Centenary of First Motor Vehicle in Belgrade. P 13½ (with one elliptical hole on each vert side).

22	**7**	16d. multicoloured	13·50	13·50

(Des M. Kalezić. Litho)

2003 (12 June). Nature Protection. Zasavica Park. T **8** and similar multicoloured design. P 13½ (with one elliptical hole on each vert side (28d.) or each horiz side (50d.)).

23		28d.70 Type **8**	2·00	2·00
24		50d. Boat and river	3·50	3·50

9 Magnifying Glass and Stamp

10 Prince Milan Obrenovic (military reformer)

(Des M. Kalezić. Litho)

2003 (4–8 Aug). Communications. T **9** and similar multicoloured designs. P 14.

25		1d. Type **9**	45	45
26		8d. Parcels in post van	65	65
27		12d. Telephonist (vert)	1·00	1·00
28		16d. Post van (4.8)	1·50	1·50
29		32d. Television screen	3·25	3·25
25/29 *Set of* 5			6·25	6·25

(Des N. Skocajic. Litho)

2003 (27 Aug). 125th Anniv of Belgrade Military Museum. P 13½×14.

30	**10**	16d. multicoloured	1·10	1·10

11 Delfa Ivanic (founder)

12 Serbia State Arms

(Des M. Kalezić. Litho)

2003 (28 Aug). Centenary of Serbian Sisters (humanitarian organization). P 13½ (with one elliptical hole on each horiz side).

31	**11**	16d. multicoloured	1·10	1·10

(Des M. Kalezić. Litho)

2003 (10 Sept). 125th Anniversary of Serbia and Montenegro State. T **12** and similar vert design. Multicoloured. P 13½ (with one elliptical hole on each horiz side).

32		16d. Type **12**	1·10	1·10
33		16d. Montenegro state arms	1·10	1·10

13 Model Rockets

14 Neolithic Carved Figure

(Des N. Skocajic. Litho)

2003 (12 Sept). European Model Rocket Building Championship. P 13½×14.

34	**13**	16d. multicoloured	1·10	1·10

(Des M. Kalezić. Litho)

2003 (17 Sept). Philatelica Danubiana Stamp Exhibition, Belgrade. T **14** and similar vert design. Multicoloured. P 13½×14.

35		16d. Type **14**	1·10	1·10
36		16d. Circular head	1·10	1·10

Nos. 35/6, respectively, were each issued in *se-tenant* sheets of eight stamps surrounding a central label inscribed for Second International Danube Conference on Art and Culture.

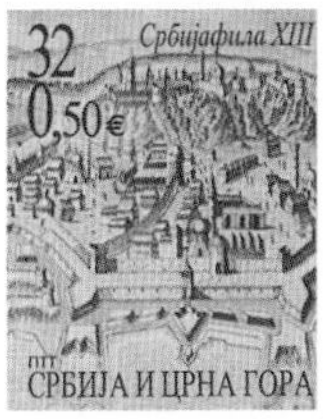

15 17th-century Belgrade

16 Children

2003 (22 Sept). 13th Srbijafila Stamp Exhibition, Belgrade. Sheet 84×57 mm containing T **15** and similar vert design. Multicoloured. Litho. P 13½.

MS37	32d.×2, Type **15**; "Serbia" as woman (sculpture) (Djordje Jovanovic)	9·00	9·00

(Des M. Kalezić. Litho)

2003 (14 Oct). 35th "Joy in Europe" Meeting. Children's Day. T **16** and similar multicoloured design. P 13½.

38		28d.70 Type **16**	2·20	2·20
39		50d. Stylized rabbit (horiz)	3·50	3·50

Nos. 38/9, respectively, were each issued in *se-tenant* sheets of eight stamps surrounding a central label inscribed for Children's Day.

17 Newspaper Vendor

18 Stamp Catalogues

(Des N. Skocajic. Litho)

2003 (16 Oct). 50th Anniv of the Vecernje Novosti Newspaper. P 13½.

40	**17**	32d. multicoloured	2·20	2·20

(Des M. Kalezić. Litho)

2003 (24 Oct). Stamp Day. P 13½.

41	**18**	16d. multicoloured	4·50	4·50

19 Emblem

20 Actors and Theatre Building

(Des N. Skocajic. Litho)

2003 (28 Oct). 50th Anniv of ULUPUDS (Fine and Applied Artists and Designers of Serbia Association). P 13½.

42	**19**	16d. multicoloured	1·10	1·10

(Des M. Kalezić. Litho)

2003 (1 Nov). 50th Anniv of Montenegro National Theatre, Podgorica. P 13½.

43	**20**	50d. multicoloured	2·20	2·20

21 Early City

22 Saint John the Baptist (1645)

(Des N. Skocajic. Litho)

2003 (12 Nov). 850th Anniv of Pancevo City. P 13½.

44	**21**	32d. multicoloured	2·20	2·20

(Des M. Kalezić. Litho)

2003 (26 Nov). Russian Orthodox Museum Exhibits. T **22** and similar vert designs. Multicoloured. P 13½.

45		16d. Type **22**	1·10	1·10
		a. Strip of 4. Nos. 45/8 plus label	7·00	
46		24d. Cross (1602)	1·60	1·60
47		26d.20 Embroidered mitre (15th-century)	1·80	1·80
48		28d.70 Iron work tabernacle (1550)	2·20	2·20
45/48 *Set of* 4			6·00	6·00

Nos. 45/8 were issued in horizontal *se-tenant* strips of four stamps surrounding a central stamp-size label. Each label showing a different museum exhibit.

23 Nativity (Oropos) (1983) **24** Submarine

(Des M. Kalezić. Litho)

2003 (4 Dec). Christmas. Icons. T **23** and similar vert designs. Multicoloured. P 13½.

49	12d. Type **23**	90	90
50	16d. Nativity (Belgrade) (18th-century)	1·10	1·10
51	26d.20 (Panagiota Fourka) (2000)	1·80	1·80
52	28d.70 Wise men bearing gifts (Albreht Durer)	2·20	2·20
49/52	*Set of* 4	5·50	5·50

(Des M. Kalezić. Litho)

2003 (10 Dec). 75th Anniv of Submarine Shipping. P 13½.

53	**24** 32d. multicoloured	2·10	2·10

25 Wilbur and Orville Wright and *Wright Flyer I* **26** Building Façade

(Des M. Kalezić. Litho)

2003 (17 Dec). Centenary of Powered Flight. T **25** and similar horiz design. Multicoloured. P 13½.

54	16d. Type **25**	90	90
55	28d.70 *Wright Flyer I* and horse-drawn carriages	2·10	2·10

(Des M. Kalezić. Litho)

2004 (21 Jan). Centenary of *Politika* Newspaper. T **26** and similar multicoloured design. P 13½.

56	16d. Type **26**	1·10	1·10
57	16d. Typewriter (horiz)	1·10	1·10

27 *Parnassius apollo* **28** Karadorde (Dorde Petrovic) (leader)

(Des M. Kalezić. Litho)

2004 (30 Jan). Endangered Species. Butterflies and Insects. T **27** and similar horiz designs. Multicoloured. P 13½.

58	12d. Type **27**	65	65
	a. Horiz strip of 4. Nos. 58/61 plus label	5·50	
59	16d. *Rosalia alpina*	80	80
60	26d.20 *Aeshna viriridis*	1·80	1·80
61	28d.70 *Saga pedo*	2·10	2·10
58/61	*Set of* 4	4·75	4·75

Nos. 58/61 were issued in horizontal *se-tenant* strips of four stamps surrounding a central stamp-size label.

(Des M. Kalezić. Litho)

2004 (13 Feb). Bicentenary of Serbian Rebellion against Turkey (1st issue). T **28** and similar horiz design. Multicoloured. P 13½×14.

62	16d. Type **28**	1·10	1·10
63	16d. Children and globe	1·10	1·10

See also Nos. 70/3.

29 *Ramonda serbica* **30** Early Greek and Modern Runners

(Des M. Kalezić. Litho)

2004 (14 Feb). Fauna and Flora. T **29** and similar vert designs. Multicoloured. P 14×13½.

64	16d. Type **29**	1·00	1·00
	a. Horiz strip of 4. Nos. 64/7 plus label	6·25	
65	24d. *Ramonda nathaliae*	1·40	1·40
66	26d.20 *Heodes virgaureae*	1·60	1·60
67	28d.70 *Lysandra bellargus*	2·00	2·00
64/67	*Set of* 5	5·50	5·50

Nos. 64/7 were issued in horizontal *se-tenant* strips of four stamps surrounding a central stamp-size label.

(Des R. Bojanic. Litho)

2004 (27 Feb). Olympic Games, Athens (1st issue). T **30** and similar horiz design. Multicoloured. P 13½×14.

68	32d. Type **30**	2·30	2·30
69	56d. Early Greek and modern wrestlers	3·25	3·25

See also Nos. 90/3.

(Des M. Kalezić. Litho)

2004 (1 Mar). Bicentenary of Serbian Rebellion against Turkey (2nd issue). Multicoloured designs as T **28**. P 13½.

70	12d. Freedom fighters	85	85
71	16d. Pistol and flag (vert)	1·00	1·00
72	28d.70 Karadorde (vert)	1·90	1·90
73	32d. Children and globe (vert)	2·10	2·10
70/73	*Set of* 4	5·25	5·25

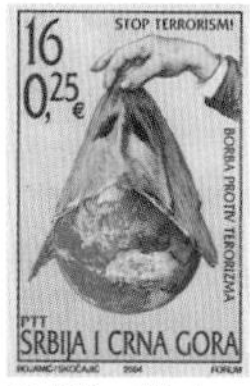

31 Lifting Mask from Globe **32** Crucified Christ and Angels

(Des R. Bojanic and N. Skocajic. Litho)

2004 (12 Mar). Anti-Terrorism Campaign. P 13½×14.

74	**31** 16d. multicoloured	1·00	1·00

(Des N. Skocajic. Litho)

2004 (15 Mar). Easter. T **32** and similar vert design. Multicoloured. P 13½.

75	16d. Type **32**	1·10	1·10
76	28d.70 Risen Christ	2·20	2·20

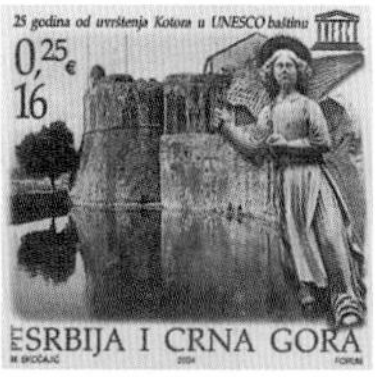

33 Globes and Milutin Milankovic (geophysicist) **34** South (Gurdich) Gate and Beskutcha Family Portal (detail)

(Des N. Skocajic (77) or R. Bojanic (78). Litho)

2004 (22–31 Mar). 125th Birth Anniversaries. T **33** and similar multicoloured design. P 13½×14 (horiz) or 14×13½ (vert).

77	16d. Type **33**	1·00	1·00
78	16d. Albert Einstein (physicist) (vert) (31.3)	1·00	1·00

(Des N. Skocajic. Litho)

2004 (7 Apr). 25th Anniv of Kotor as UNESCO World Heritage Site. P 13½.

79	**34** 16d. multicoloured	1·00	1·00

35 Vasiliji Petrovic (author) **36** Paragliding

(Des M. Kalezić. Litho)

2004 (29 Apr). 250th Anniv of Publication of First History of Montenegro. P 13½.

80	**35** 16d. multicoloured	1·00	1·00

(Des M. Kalezić. Litho)

2004 (5 May). Europa. Holidays. T **36** and similar multicoloured designs. P 14×13½ (vert) or 13½×14 (others).

81	16d. Type **36**	1·30	1·30
82	56d. Sail boat and water-skier in water (horiz)	3·50	3·50
MS83	97×55 mm. 32d. Yacht (35×29 mm); 56d. Rowing boats (35×29 mm)	6·00	6·00

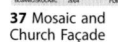

37 Mosaic and Church Façade **38** Michael Pupin

(Des R. Bojanic and N. Skocajic. Litho)

2004 (10 May). Saint Sava's Church, Belgrade. T **37** and similar multicoloured design. P 14×13½ (vert) or 13½×14 (horiz).

84	16d. Type **37**	1·10	1·10
85	28d.70 Church façade and statue (horiz)	2·20	2·20

(Des and eng M. Kalezić. Recess)

2004 (13 May). 150th Birth Anniv of Michael Idvorsky Pupin (Serbian–American physicist). P 13½.

86	**38** 16d. deep reddish lilac	1·00	1·00

39 Emblem **40** River, Ravnjak

(Des N. Skocajic. Litho)

2004 (21 May). Centenary of FIFA (Fédération Internationale de Football Association). P 13½×14.

87	**39** 28d.70 multicoloured	2·30	2·30

(Des M. Kalezić. Litho)

2004 (10 June). Nature Protection. T **40** and similar horiz design. Multicoloured. P 13½×14.

88	32d. Type **40**	2·30	2·30
89	56d. Mountains, Sara	3·50	3·50

41 Early and Modern Runners and Gate of Athene Archgetis **42** Guilielmo Marconi (inventor) and Antenna

(Des R. Bojanic and N. Skocajic. Litho)

2004 (24 June). Olympic Games, Athens (2nd issue). T **41** and similar horiz designs. Multicoloured. P 13½×14.

90	16d. Type **41**	1·20	1·20
91	28d.70 Runners and Parthenon	2·40	2·40
92	32d. Long jumpers and Olympieion	2·50	2·50
93	57d.40 Hurdlers and Temple of Hephaistos	4·00	4·00
90/93	*Set of* 4	9·00	9·00

(Des N. Skocajic. Litho)

2004 (7 Sept). Establishment of First Radio Telegraph Stations in Volujica and Bar. P 13½×14.

94	**42** 16d. multicoloured	1·00	1·00

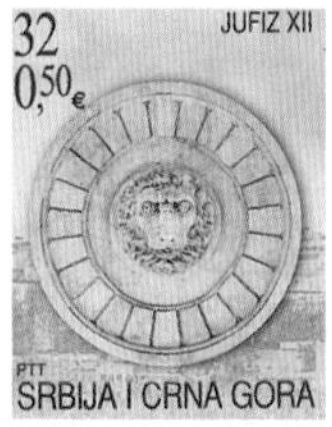

43 Lions Head Medallion **44** Bridge (Angelka Misurovic)

(Des M. Kalezić and N. Skocajic. Litho)

2004 (23 Sept). Jufiz XII, National Philatelic Exhibition, Belgrade. Sheet 88×65 mm containing T **43** and similar vert design. Multicoloured. P 13½.

MS95	32d.×2, Type **43**; Monument	4·25	4·25

(Des M. Kalezić. Litho)

2004 (2 Oct). 35th "Joy in Europe" Meeting. Children's Day. T **44** and similar multicoloured design. P 14.

96	32d. Type **44**	2·50	2·50
97	56d. Houses and church (Karol Sackievicz) (vert)	3·75	3·75

45 Boats **46** Stamp and Magnifier

(Des M. Kalezić. Litho)

2004 (12 Oct). 125th Anniv of Bar (Montenegrin port). P 14.

98	**45** 32d. multicoloured	2·30	2·30

(Des N. Skocajic. Litho)

2004 (22 Oct). Stamp Day. P 14×13½.

99	**46** 16d. multicoloured	1·00	1·00

47 Bank Building Façade **48** Fruit Stand

(Recess and litho)

2004 (28 Oct). 120th Anniv of Serbian National Bank. T **47** and similar vert design. P 13½ (with one elliptical hole on each horiz side).

100 16d. indigo, blue-black and cobalt .... 1·10 1·10
101 32d. multicoloured .... 2·20 2·20

Designs:—16d. Type **47**; 32d. Mr. Djordje Vajfert (Governor of the National Bank of the Kingdom of Serbia, the first Governor of the Kingdom of Serbs, Croats and Slovenes).

(Des M. Kalezić. Litho)

2004 (2 Nov). Museum Exhibits. Silverware. T **48** and similar vert designs. Multicoloured. P 14×13½.

102 16d. Type **48** .... 1·00 1·00
a. Horiz strip of 4. Nos. 102/5 plus label .... 6·50
103 24d. Box .... 1·50 1·50
104 26d.20 Pierced bowl .... 1·70 1·70
105 28d.70 Cup with handles and lid .... 2·10 2·10
102/105 *Set of 4* .... 5·75 5·75

Nos. 102/5 were issued in horizontal *se-tenant* strips of four stamps surrounding a central stamp-size label.

49 Lombardic Palace

50 Mary and Jesus (painting)

(Des M. Kalezić. Litho)

2004 (15 Nov). Architecture. Kotor Palaces. T **49** and similar horiz designs. Multicoloured. P 13½×14.

106 16d. Type **49** .... 1·00 1·00
a. Horiz strip of 4. Nos. 106/9 plus label .... 6·50
107 24d. Pima palace .... 1·50 1·50
108 26d.20 Grgurina palace .... 1·70 1·70
109 28d.70 Bizanti palace .... 2·10 2·10
106/109 *Set of 4* .... 5·75 5·75

Nos. 106/9 were issued in horizontal *se-tenant* strips of four stamps surrounding a central stamp size label.

(Des M. Kalezić. Litho)

2004 (1 Dec). Christmas. T **50** and similar vert design. Multicoloured. P 13½.

110 16d. Type **50** .... 1·00 1·00
111 28d.70 Mary and Jesus (painting) (different) .... 2·30 2·30

51 *Capparis spinosa*

52 Great Egret (*Egretta alba*)

(Des M. Kalezić. Litho)

2005 (30 Jan). Endangered Species. Mammals and Flowers. T **51** and similar horiz designs. Multicoloured. P 13½×14.

112 16d.50 Type **51** .... 1·00 1·00
a. Horiz strip of 4. Nos. 112/15 plus label .... 7·75
113 33d. *Mustela erminea* .... 1·70 1·70
114 41d.50 *Trollius europaeus* .... 2·10 2·10
115 49d.50 *Rupicapra rupicapra* .... 2·75 2·75
112/115 *Set of 4* .... 6·75 6·75

Nos. 112/15 were issued in horizontal *se-tenant* strips of four stamps surrounding a central stamp size label.

(Des M. Kalezić. Litho)

2005 (16 Feb). Birds. T **52** and similar vert designs. Multicoloured. P 14×13½.

116 16d.50 Type **52** .... 1·00 1·00
a. Horiz strip of 4. Nos. 116/19 plus label .... 7·75
117 33d. Black-necked grebe (*Podiceps nigricollis*) .... 1·70 1·70
118 41d.50 Ferruginous duck (*Aythya nyroca*) ... 2·10 2·10
119 49d.50 Black stork (*Ciconia nigra*) .... 2·75 2·75
116/119 *Set of 4* .... 6·75 6·75

Nos. 116/19 were issued in horizontal *se-tenant* strips of four stamps surrounding a central stamp-size label.

53 Bat, Balls and Net

54 18th-century Fresco

(Des N. Skocajic. Litho)

2005 (28 Feb). 50th Anniv of Montenegrin Table Tennis Association. P 13½×14.

120 **53** 16d.50 multicoloured .... 1·00 1·00

(Des N. Skocajic. Litho)

2005 (1 Mar). Easter. T **54** and similar vert design. Multicoloured. P 13½×14.

121 16d.50 Type **54** .... 1·00 1·00
122 28d.70 Crucifixion (carving) (1602) .... 2·30 2·30

55 University Façade, Belgrade

56 Jovan Djordjevic

(Des N. Skocajic. Litho)

2005 (12 Mar). Centenary of First Serbian University. P 13½.

123 **55** 16d.50 multicoloured .... 1·00 1·00

(Des M. Kalezić. Litho)

2005 (25 Mar). Actors and Actresses. T **56** and similar vert designs. Multicoloured. P 14.

124 16d. Type **56** .... 1·10 1·10
a. Sheetlet of 8. Nos. 124/31 plus label 9·00
125 16d. Milan Predic .... 1·10 1·10
126 16d. Milan Grol .... 1·10 1·10
127 16d. Mira Trailovic .... 1·10 1·10
128 16d. Soja Jovanovic .... 1·10 1·10
129 16d. Hugo Klajn .... 1·10 1·10
130 16d. Mata Milosevic .... 1·10 1·10
131 16d. Bojan Stupica .... 1·10 1·10
124/131 *Set of 8* .... 8·00 8·00

Nos. 124/31 were issued in *se-tenant* sheetlets of eight stamps surrounding a central stamp size label, with enlarged illustrated margins.

57 Colonnade (As. No. 1407)

58 "The Little Mermaid"

2005 (31 Mar). 50th Anniv of Europa Stamps. T **57** and similar horiz designs. Multicoloured. Litho. P 13½×14.

132 16d.50 Type **57** .... 1·20 1·20
133 16d.50 Flaming sun (As No. 1425) .... 1·20 1·20
134 16d.50 Europa chain (As No. 1455) .... 1·20 1·20
135 16d.50 Communications (As No. 1514) .... 1·20 1·20
136 41d.50 Europa posthorn (As No. 1553) .... 2·40 2·40
137 41d.50 "Widow and Child" (sculpture, Ivan Mestrovic) (As No. 1604) .... 2·40 2·40
138 41d.50 Bridge (As No. 2138) .... 2·40 2·40
139 41d.50 Combined design (As. No. 132, 134 and 137) .... 2·40 2·40
132/139 *Set of 8* .... 13·00 13·00
MS140 Two sheets, each 90×69 mm. (a) Nos. 132/5; (b) Nos. 136/139 .... 13·00 13·00

(Des M. Kalezić. Litho)

2005 (1 Apr). Birth Bicentenary of Hans Christian Andersen (writer). T **58** and similar vert design. Multicoloured. P 14×13½.

141 41d.50 Type **58** .... 2·10 2·10
142 58d. "Snow Queen" .... 3·25 3·25

59 Bread and Bowl

60 Marko Ivanovic

(Des N. Skocajic. Litho)

2005 (5 May). Europa. Gastronomy. T **59** and similar horiz designs. Multicoloured. P 13½×14.

143 41d.50 Type **59** .... 2·10 2·10
144 73d. Fish .... 4·00 4·00
MS145 93×50 mm. 41d.50 Cake; 73d. Tart .... 6·00 6·00

(Des M. Kalezić. Litho)

2005 (19 May). Boka Kotorska Sea Captains. T **60** and similar horiz designs. Multicoloured. P 14×13½.

146 16d.50 Type **60** .... 1·00 1·00
a. Horiz strip of 4. Nos. 146/9 plus label .... 7·75
147 33d. Petar Zelalic .... 1·70 1·70
148 41d.50 Matija Balovic .... 2·10 2·10
149 49d.50 Ivan Bronza .... 2·75 2·75
146/149 *Set of 4* .... 6·75 6·75

Nos. 146/9 were issued in horizontal *se-tenant* strips of four stamps surrounding a central stamp size label.

61 Crvena Zvezda (Red Star Football Club, Belgrade)

62 Boats and River Bank

(Des J. Vlahovic. Litho)

2005 (23 May). Sports Associations' 60th Anniversaries. T **61** and similar horiz designs. Multicoloured. P 13½×14.

150 16d.50 Type **61** .... 1·10 1·10
151 16d.50 Partizan Football Club, Belgrade ...... 1·10 1·10
MS152 94×53 mm. 16d.50×2, Crvena Zvezda; Partizan .... 2·10 2·10

The stamps and margins of No. **MS**152 form a composite design of knights jousting.

(Des N. Skocajic. Litho)

2005 (6 June). 50th Anniv of Danube Regatta. Sheet 97×49 mm containing T **62** and similar horiz design. Multicoloured. P 13½×14.

MS153 41d.50 Type **62**; 49d.50 Boats, bridge and trees .... 4·75 4·75

The stamps and margins of No. **MS**153 form a composite design of the start of a boat race.

63 Rings surrounding Globe

64 Flowering Tree and Water

(Des N. Skocajic. Litho)

2005 (10 June). International Year of Physics (154) and Centenary of Publication of *Theory of Special Relativity* by Albert Einstein (155). T **63** and similar horiz design. Multicoloured. P 13½×14.

154 41d.50 Type **63** .... 2·10 2·10
155 58d. Albert Einstein .... 3·25 3·25

(Des M. Kalezić. Litho)

2005 (20 June). Nature Protection. Koviljsko Petrovaradinski Rit Special Nature Reserve. T **64** and similar horiz design. Multicoloured. P 13½×14.

156 41d.50 Type **64** .... 2·10 2·10
157 58d. Reeds, shrubs and water .... 3·25 3·25

65 Hands, Net and Ball

66 Ball and Emblem

(Des J. Vlahovic. Litho)

2005 (2 Sept). European Volleyball Championships, Belgrade and Rome. P 13½×14.

158 **65** 16d.50 multicoloured .... 1·30 1·30

(Des A. Kostic. Litho)

2005 (16 Sept). European Basketball Championship (Eurobasket 2005), Belgrade. P 13½×14.

159 **66** 16d.50 multicoloured .... 1·00 1·00

67 Parrot

68 Heart-shaped Graffiti

(Des A. Kostic. Litho)

2005 (21 Sept). 36th "Joy in Europe" Meeting. Children's Day. T **67** and similar multicoloured design. P 13½×14 (vert) or 14×13½ (horiz).

160 41d.50 Type **67** .... 2·10 2·10
161 58d. Figure with raised arms (horiz) .... 3·25 3·25

(Des N. Skocajic. Litho)

2005 (30 Sept). World Youth Day. P 13½×14.

162 **68** 41d.50 multicoloured .... 2·10 2·10

69 Roadway and Stars

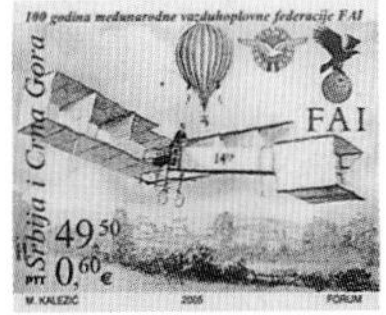

70 Early Airplane and Air Balloon

(Des M. Kalezić. Litho)

2005 (10 Oct). Initiation of Stabilization and Association Agreement with European Union. P 14×13½.

163 **69** 16d.50 multicoloured .... 1·00 1·00

(Des M. Kalezić. Litho)

2005 (14 Oct). Centenary of International Airline Federation. T **70** and similar horiz design. Multicoloured. P 13½×14.

164 49d.50 Type **70** .... 2·50 2·50
165 58d. Glider, parachute and hang glider .. 3·25 3·25

71 Anniversary Emblem

72 Envelope and Aircraft

(Des J. Vlahovic. Litho)

2005 (24 Oct). 60th Anniv of United Nations. P 13½×14.

166 **71** 16d.50 multicoloured .... 1·10 1·10

(Des M. Kalezić. Litho)

2005 (24 Oct). Stamp Day. P 13½×14.

167 **72** 16d.50 multicoloured .... 1·10 1·10

73 Petar I

74 Nicholas I

(Des M. Kalezić. Litho)

2005 (28 Oct). 175th Death Anniv of Vladika Petar I Petrovic (St. Peter Cetinjski (bishop and leader)). P 13½×14.

168 **73** 16d.50 multicoloured .... 1·10 1·10

(Des A. Kostic. Litho)

2005 (28 Oct). Centenary of Montenegro's First Constitution. P 13½×14.

169 **74** 16d.50 multicoloured .... 1·10 1·10

75 Stevan Sremac

76 Sudenica (Djorde Krstic)

(Des N. Skocajic. Litho)

2005 (23 Nov). 150th Birth Anniv of Stevan Sremac (writer). P 13½×14.

170 **75** 16d.50 multicoloured .... 1·10 1·10

(Des M. Kalezić. Litho)

2005 (28 Nov). Paintings of Monasteries. T **76** and similar horiz designs. Multicoloured. P 13½.

171 16d.50 Type **76** .... 1·00 1·00
a. Pair. Nos. 171/2 .... 3·00 3·00
172 33d. Sopocani (Paja Jovanovic) .... 1·70 1·70
173 41d.50 Zica (Djorde Krstic) .... 2·30 2·30
a. Pair. Nos. 173/4 .... 5·25 5·25
174 49d.50 Gracanica (Milan Milanovic) .... 2·75 2·75
171/174 *Set of 4* .... 7·00 7·00

Nos. 171/2 and 173/4 were issued in horizontal *se-tenant* pairs, separated by an illustrated gutter, within the sheet.

77 "Girl with Blue Ribbon" (F. X. Winterhalter)

78 The Nativity

(Des N. Skocajic. Litho)

2005 (9 Dec). Paintings. T **77** and similar vert designs. Multicoloured. P 13½.

175 16d.50 Type **77** .... 1·00 1·00
a. Pair. Nos. 175/6 .... 3·00 3·00
176 33d. "Adoration of the Child" (Andrea Alovidi) .... 1·70 1·70
177 41d.50 "Madonna with the Saints" (Biagio d'Antonio) .... 2·30 2·30
a. Pair. Nos. 177/8 .... 5·25 5·25
178 49d.50 "Remorse" (Vlaho Bukovaa) .... 2·75 2·75
175/178 *Set of 4* .... 7·00 7·00

Nos. 175/6 and 177/8 were issued in horizontal *se-tenant* pairs, separated by an illustrated gutter, within the sheet.

(Des N. Skocajic. Litho)

2005 (12 Dec). Christmas. T **78** and similar vert designs. Multicoloured. P 13½.

179 16d.50 Type **78** .... 1·00 1·00
180 46d. The Nativity (different) .... 2·10 2·10

79 Footprints in Snow

80 Jovan Sterija Popovic (birth bicentenary)

(Des N. Skocajic. Litho)

2005. Tourism. T **79** and similar horiz designs. Multicoloured. P 13½.

181 5d. Type **79** 30 30
182 13d. Frozen lake 85 85
183 16d.50 Snow covered house and trees .... 1·00 1·00
184 33d. Snow covered hills .... 1·70 1·70
181/184 *Set of 4* .... 3·50 3·50

(Des A. Kostic. Litho)

2006 (9 Jan). Writers' Anniversaries. T **80** and similar vert design. Multicoloured. P 13½.

185 33d. Type **80** .... 1·70 1·70
186 46d. Stevan Stojanovic Mokranjac (150th birth anniv) .... 2·10 2·10

81 Ski Jump

82 Easter Egg

(Des A. Kostic. Litho)

2006 (10 Feb). Winter Olympic Games, Turin. T **81** and similar horiz design. Multicoloured. P 13½.

187 53d. Type **81** .... 2·50 2·50
188 73d. Skier .... 3·25 3·25

(Des A. Kostic. Litho)

2006 (1 Mar). Easter. T **82** and similar vert design. Multicoloured. P 13½.

189 16d.50 Type **82** 85 85
190 46d. Basket of eggs .... 2·20 2·20

83 Bridge, Novi Sad

84 *Canis lupus*

(Des N. Skocajic. Litho)

2006 (6 Mar). 150th Anniv of Danube Commission. T **83** and similar horiz designs. Multicoloured. P 13½.

191 16d.50 Type **83** 85 85
a. Pair. Nos. 191 and 193 .... 3·25 3·25
192 16d.50 Castle, Smederevo 85 85
a. Pair. Nos. 192 and 194 .... 3·25 3·25
193 46d. Belgrade from river .... 2·20 2·20
194 46d. Tabula Traiana .... 2·20 2·20
191/194 *Set of 4* .... 5·50 5·50

Nos. 191 and 193, and 192 and 194, respectively, were issued in horizontal *se-tenant* pairs, separated by an illustrated gutter, within the sheet.

(Des N. Skocajic. Litho)

2006 (3 Apr). Fauna. T **84** and similar horiz designs. Multicoloured. P 13½.

195 16d.50 Type **84** 85 85
a. Pair. Nos. 195 and 197 .... 3·25 3·25
196 16d.50 *Otis tarda* 85 85
a. Pair. Nos. 196 and 198 .... 3·25 3·25
197 46d. *Vormela peregusna* .... 2·20 2·20
198 46d. *Ursus arctos* .... 2·20 2·20
195/198 *Set of 4* .... 5·50 5·50

Nos. 195 and 197, and 196 and 198, respectively, were issued in horizontal *se-tenant* pairs, separated by an illustrated gutter, within the sheet.

85 Two Players

86 Eskimo and Penguin on Beach

(Des J. Vlahovic. Litho)

2006 (12 Apr). World Cup Football Championship, Germany. T **85** and similar multicoloured designs. P 13½.

199 33d. Type **85** .... 1·70 1·70
200 33d. Goalkeeper .... 2·20 2·20
MS201 95×55 mm. 46d.×2, Left of stadium (horiz); Right of stadium (horiz) .... 8·75 8·75

The stamps and margins of No. **MS**201 form a composite design.

(Des N. Skocajic. Litho)

2006 (4 May). Europa. Integration. T **86** and similar horiz designs. Multicoloured. P 13½.

202 46d. Type **86** .... 2·20 2·20
203 73d. Lion and lamb .... 3·50 3·50
MS204 95×55 mm. 46d. Women in park; 73d. Couple entering house .... 5·75 5·75

The stamps and margins of No. **MS**204 form a composite design.

87 Nikola Tesla

88 Aqua

(Des M. Kalezić. Litho)

2006 (26 May). 150th Birth Anniv of Nikola Tesla (inventor). T **87** and similar multicoloured designs. P 13½.

205 16d.50 Type **87** 85 85
206 46d. Nikola Tesla and coil .... 2·20 2·20
MS207 124×70 mm. 46d. Nikola Tesla (horiz); 112d. Engine (horiz) .... 7·75 7·75

The stamps and margins of No. **MS**207 form a composite design.

(Des N. Skocajic. Litho)

2006 (7 June). Roses. T **88** and similar horiz designs. Multicoloured. P 13½.

208 16d.50 Type **88** 85 85
a. Pair. Nos. 208 and 210 .... 3·25 3·25
209 16d.50 Vendela 85 85
a. Pair. Nos. 209 and 211 .... 3·25 3·25
210 46d. Sphinx .... 2·20 2·20
211 46d. Red Berlin .... 2·20 2·20
208/211 *Set of 4* .... 5·50 5·50

Nos. 208 and 210, and 209 and 211, respectively, were issued in horizontal *se-tenant* pairs, separated by an illustrated gutter, within the sheet.

89 Belgrade

90 Parkland

(Des N. Skocajic. Litho)

2006. P 13½.

212 **89** 46d. multicoloured .... 2·20 2·20

(Des M. Kalezić. Litho)

2006. Nature Protection. T **90** and similar horiz design. Multicoloured. P 13½×14.

213 46d. Type **90** .... 2·20 2·20
214 58d. Graddski park .... 2·50 2·50

On 3 June 2006 Montenegro declared independence from the Serbia Montenegro Alliance. See separate listings for Montenegro and for Serbia after this date.

Slovenia

Formerly part of Austria-Hungary, in 1918 Slovenia became part of the Kingdom of the Serbs, Croats and Slovenes, later renamed Yugoslavia (q.v.). Issues for Slovenia before general issues were made are listed at the beginning of Yugoslavia.

A. OCCUPATION ISSUES, 1941–45

Germany annexed on 8 July 1941, as the territory of Lower Styria, territory in Slovenia extending south to the Sava, including Maribor, Celje, Kranj and Bled. Stamps of Germany were used.

Italy occupied Ljubljana and a wedge' of Slovenia extending almost to Karlovac; this was annexed to Italy in May 1941 as the province of Lubiana. In September 1943 Italy ended hostilities with the Allies and German forces took over Lubiana, renaming it the Province of Laibach.

ITALIAN OCCUPATION

Yugoslav Currency

PRINTER. The following issues were overprinted by the Merkur Printing Works, Ljubljana.

Co. Ci.

(1)

R.Commissariato
Civile
Territori Sloveni
occupati
LUBIANA

(2)

("Co. Ci"="Commissariato Civile")

1941 (26 Apr). Nos. 330/1 and 414/26 of Yugoslavia, (1935–6 and 1939 King Peter II issues), optd with T **1**.

1	**99**	25p. black	1·40	1·90
2		50p. orange	1·40	1·90
3		1d. green	1·40	1·90
4		1d.50 scarlet	1·40	1·90
5		2d. carmine-rose	1·40	1·90
6		3d. red-brown	1·40	1·90
7		4d. bright blue	1·40	1·90
8		5d. blue	1·40	1·90
9		5d.50 dull violet	1·40	1·90
10		6d. deep blue	1·90	2·30
11		8d. chocolate	2·30	2·75
12	**70**	10d. bright violet	2·30	2·75
13	**99**	12d. violet	4·75	4·25
14	**70**	15d. olive	£375	£400
15	**99**	16d. purple	4·75	4·75
16		20d. light blue	11·00	17·00
17		30d. pink	70·00	80·00
1/17 *Set of* 17			£425	£475

1941 (26 Apr). POSTAGE DUE. Nos. D259/63 II of Yugoslavia optd with T **1**.

D18	**D 56**	50p. violet	1·40	1·90
D19		1d. magenta	1·40	1·90
D20		2d. blue	1·40	1·90
D21		5d. orange	17·00	14·00
D22		10d. chocolate	17·00	14·00
D18/22 *Set of* 5			34·00	30·00

ITALIAN PROVINCE OF LUBIANA

1941 (5 May). Nos. 330 and 414/26 of Yugoslavia optd with T **2**.

23	**99**	25p. black	1·40	95
24		50p. orange	1·40	95
25		1d. green	1·40	95
26		1d.50 scarlet	1·40	95
27		2d. carmine-rose	1·40	95
28		3d. red-brown	1·40	95
29		4d. bright blue	1·40	95
30		5d. blue	1·60	1·10
31		5d.50 dull violet	1·40	95
32		6d. deep blue	1·40	95
33		8d. chocolate	1·40	95
34	**70**	10d. bright violet	3·25	1·90
35	**99**	12d. violet	1·60	1·10
36		16d. purple	3·25	1·90
37		20d. light blue	11·00	9·25
38		30d. pink	£110	85·00
23/38 *Set of* 16			£130	£100

Optd as T **2** but with inscr obliterated by two bars instead of lines of dots

39	**99**	1d.50 scarlet	55·00	95·00

Beware of forgeries.

1941 (5 May). POSTAGE DUE. Nos. D259/63 II of Yugoslavia optd as T **2** but with four lines of dots at top.

D40	**D 56**	50p. violet	95	1·40
D41		1d. magenta	95	1·40
D42		2d. blue	1·90	2·30
D43		5d. orange	55·00	70·00
D44		10d. chocolate	23·00	28·00
D40/44 *Set of* 5			75·00	95·00

1941 (10 May). Anti-Tuberculosis Fund. Nos. 446/9 of Yugoslavia optd as T **2**, but with only three lines of dots at foot.

45	50p. +50p. on 5d. violet	14·00	17·00
46	1d. +1d. on 10d. lake	14·00	17·00
47	1d.50 +1d.50 on 20d. bluish green	14·00	17·00
48	2d. +2d. on 30d. bright blue	14·00	17·00
45/48 *Set of* 4		50·00	60·00

1941 (10 May). AIR. Nos. 360*a*/7*a* and 443/4 of Yugoslavia (pictorial air stamps), optd as T **2** with three or four (No. 57) lines of dots at foot.

49	50p. brown	3·75	4·75
50	1d. bright green	3·75	4·75
51	2d. slate-blue	6·50	7·50
52	2d.50 carmine	6·50	7·50
53	5d. violet	9·25	11·00
54	10d. lake	9·25	11·00
55	20d. bluish green	37·00	37·00
56	30d. bright blue	65·00	75·00
57	40d. blue-green	£225	£250
58	50d. slate-blue	£200	£200
49/58 *Set of* 10		£500	£550

1941 (15 June). Stamps of issue of 5 May surch in addition.

59	**99**	0d.50 on 1d.50 scarlet (26)	95	1·40
60		0d.50 on 1d.50 scarlet (39)	£1400	£1800
61		1d. on 4d. bright blue	95	1·40
59/61 *Set of* 3			£1300	£1600

Beware of forgeries of No. 60.

1941 (20 June). POSTAGE DUE. Nos. D259/61 II of Yugoslavia optd as T **2** but with four lines of dots at top and narrower lettering than on Nos. D40/2.

D62	**D 56**	50p. violet	95	1·90
D63		1d. magenta	1·60	2·75
D64		2d. blue	47·00	55·00
D62/64 *Set of* 3			45·00	55·00

Three sets of stamps overprinted "Alto Commissario per la Provincia di LUBIANA" were prepared but were not put on sale as it was decreed that unoverprinted Italian stamps should be used.

GERMAN OCCUPATION

Italian Currency

PRINTERS. Types 3/8 were overprinted at the Ljudska Printing Works, Ljubljana.

(3)

(4)

1944 (5 Jan–Mar). Stamps of Italy optd with T **3** or **4**.

(a) On Postage stamps Nos. 238, etc. (5 Jan)

65	**4**	5c. brown (B.)	30	2·10
66	**3**	10c. sepia (B.)	30	2·10
67	**4**	15c. blue-green (C.)	30	2·10
68	**3**	20c. carmine (B.)	30	2·10
69	**4**	25c. green (C.)	30	2·10
70	**3**	30c. brown (B.)	30	2·10
71	**4**	35c. blue (Br.)	55	2·10
72	**3**	50c. bright violet (C.)	55	3·50
73	**4**	75c. carmine (B.)	55	5·00
74	**3**	1l. violet (B.)	55	5·00
75	**4**	1l.25 blue (C.)	55	2·50
76	**3**	1l.75 orange-vermilion (B.)	8·00	12·50
77	**4**	2l. brown-lake (B.)	55	5·00
78	**3**	10l. violet (B.)	11·50	60·00
		Surcharged with new value		
79	–	2l.55 on 5c. brown (Bk.)	4·00	12·50
80	**4**	5l. on 25c. green (B.)	4·00	21·00
81		20l. on 20c. carmine (G.)	11·50	70·00
82	**3**	25l. on 2l. brown-lake (G.)	10·50	£140
83	**4**	50l. on 1l.75 orange-vermilion (O.)	42·00	£225
65/83 *Set of* 19			90·00	£500

In No. 79 the overprint inscriptions are at each side of the eagle.

(b) On Air stamps Nos. 270, etc (18 Mar)

84	**4**	25c. grey-green (C.)	6·25	42·00
85	**3**	50c. sepia (C.)	10·50	£140
86	**4**	75c. chestnut (G.)	6·25	42·00
87	**3**	1l. bright violet (C.)	13·00	£140
88	**4**	2l. blue (B.)	6·25	95·00
89	**3**	5l. green (C.)	6·25	£140
90	**4**	10l. carmine-red (G.)	5·25	95·00
84/90 *Set of* 7			48·00	£600

(c) On Air Express stamp No. E370 (18 Mar)

E91	**3**	2l. blue-black (B.)	13·00	95·00

(d) On Express Letter stamp No. E350 (11 Feb)

E92	**3**	1l.25 green (G.)	8·00	25·00

(D 5)

(D 6)

1944 (26 Feb). POSTAGE DUE. Nos. D395, etc. of Italy optd as Type D **5**.

D93	**D 5**	5c. chocolate (Br.)	2·75	75·00
D94	–	10c. blue (B.)	2·75	75·00
D95	**D 5**	20c. bright carmine (C.)	55	£170
D96	–	25c. green (G.)	80	£170
D97	**D 5**	50c. bright violet (V.)	80	£170
D98	–	1l. orange (C.)	80	£170
D99	**D 5**	2l. green (B.)	55	£170
		Surcharged as Type D 6		
D100	**D 6**	30c. on 50c. bright violet (Bk.)	2·75	85·00
D101	–	40c. on 5c. chocolate (B.)	2·75	85·00
D93/101 *Set of* 9			12·50	£300

In Nos. D93/101 values with a hyphen in the type column have the overprint with the alternative language predominating.

(5)

1944 (18 Mar). Red Cross. Express Letter stamps, Nos. E350/1 of Italy surch as T **5**.

102	**5**	1l.25 +50l. green (O.)	37·00	£550
103	–	2l.50 +50l. red-orange (O.)	37·00	£550

(6)

1944 (18 Mar). Homeless Relief Fund. Express Letter stamps, Nos. E350/1 of Italy surch as T **6**.

104	–	1l.25 +50l. green (B.)	34·00	£550
105	**5**	2l.50 +50l. red-orange (G.)	34·00	£550

(7)

(8)

1944 (18 Mar). AIR. Orphans' Fund. Nos. 270 etc. of Italy, surch as T **7**.

106	**7**	25c. +10l. grey-green (B.)	12·50	£425
107	–	50c. +10l. sepia (B.)	12·50	£425
108	**7**	75c. +20l. chestnut (B.)	12·50	£425
109	–	1l. +20l. bright violet (B.)	12·50	£425
110	**7**	2l. +20l. blue (C.)	12·50	£425
111	–	5l. +20l. green (B.)	12·50	£425
106/111 *Set of* 6			70·00	£2250

1944 (18 Mar). AIR. Winter Relief Fund. Nos. 270 etc. of Italy, surch as T **8**.

112	**8**	25c. +10l. grey-green (B.)	12·50	£425
113	–	50c. +10l. sepia (B.)	12·50	£425
114	**8**	75c. +20l. chestnut (B.)	12·50	£425
115	–	1l. +20l. bright violet (B.)	12·50	£425
116	**8**	2l. +20l. blue (Br.)	12·50	£425
117	–	5l. +20l. green (B.)	12·50	£425
112/117 *Set of* 6			70·00	£2250

In Nos. 102/17 the values with a hyphen in the type column have the overprint with the alternative language predominating.

9 Railway Viaduct, Borovnice

10 Church in Novo Mesto

1945. Various landscape designs inscr "PROVINZ LAIBACH" at top as T **9/10**. P 11½×10½ (vert) or 10½×11½ (horiz).

118	5c. black-brown	55	4·25
119	10c. orange	55	4·25
120	20c. lake-brown	55	4·25
121	25c. deep green	55	4·25
122	50c. violet	55	4·25
123	75c. scarlet	55	4·25
124	1l. olive-green	55	4·25
125	1l.25 blue	55	4·25
126	1l.50 grey-green	55	4·25
127	2l. bright blue	80	10·00
128	2l.50 brown	80	10·00
129	3l. bright magenta	1·80	17·00
130	5l. red-brown	2·10	17·00
131	10l. blue-green	4·25	75·00
132	20l. blue	21·00	£225
133	30l. carmine	£120	£950
118/133 *Set of* 16		£140	£1200

Designs: Vert—5c. Stalagmites, Krizna Jama; 1l.25, Kocevje; 1l.50, Borovnice Falls; 3l. Castle, Žužemberg; 30l. View and Tabor Church. Horiz—10c. Zirknitz Lake; 25c. Farm near Ljubljana; 75c. View from Ribnica; 1l. Old Castle, Ljubljana; 2l. Castle, Kostanjevica; 2l.50, Castle, Turjak; 5l. View on River Krka; 10l. Castle, Otocec; 20l. Farm at Dolenjskom.

In 1945, following the defeat of Germany, Yugoslavia was reconstituted as a Federation with Slovenia as a constituent republic.

B. INDEPENDENT STATE

Following the break-up of the Federation, Slovenia, following a referendum, declared its independence on 25 June 1991.

June 1991. 100 Paras = 1 Dinar
October 1991. 100 Stotinas = 1 Tolar
2007. 100 Cents = 1 Euro

Yugoslav stamps were valid for postage in Slovenia until 25 April 1992.

Stamps inscribed "REPUBLIKA SLOVENIJA" were private productions.

PRINTERS. All stamps from No. 134 onwards were printed by Delo Printing Works, Ljubljana, *unless otherwise stated.*

11 Parliament Building

12 Arms

(Des G. Košak. Litho)

1991 (26 June). Declaration of Independence. P 10½.
134 **11** 5d. multicoloured .... 1·00 95

New Currency

100 Stotinas = 1 Tolar

(Des S. Knafelc. Litho)

1991 (26 Dec). P 14.
135 **12** 1t. multicoloured 10 10
136 4t. multicoloured 15 15
137 5t. multicoloured 20 20
138 11t. multicoloured 50 45
135/138 *Set of* 4 .... 85 80

13 Ski Jumping

14 Arms

(Des R. Novak and K. Gatnik. Litho)

1992 (8 Feb). Winter Olympic Games, Albertville. T **13** and similar rhomboid design. Multicoloured. P 14.
139 30t. Type **13** .... 3·00 2·75
a. Horiz pair. Nos. 139/40 .... 7·25 6·75
140 50t. Slalom .... 4·00 3·75

Nos. 139/40 were issued together in horizontal *se-tenant* pairs within sheets of six stamps with decorated and inscribed perforated margins.

(Des S. Knafelc. Litho)

1992 (12 Feb–16 Mar). Multicoloured, background colours given. P 14.
141 **14** 1t. brown (13 Feb) 10 10
142 2t. bright purple (16 Mar) 15 15
143 4t. yellowish green (16 Mar) 20 20
144 5t. scarlet (6 Mar) 25 25
145 6t. orange-yellow 30 30
146 11t. salmon (16 Mar) 40 35
147 15t. new blue (16 Mar) 45 40
148 20t. violet 50 45
149 50t. deep bluish green .... 1·40 1·30
150 100t. grey .... 2·75 2·50
141/150 *Set of* 10 .... 5·75 5·50

Nos. 151/4 are vacant.

15 Opera House

16 Giuseppe Tartini and Violins

(Des B. Fajon. Litho)

1992 (31 Mar). Centenary of Ljubljana Opera House. P 14.
155 **15** 20t. multicoloured .... 1·60 1·50

(Des O. Kogoj. Litho)

1992 (8 Apr). 300th Birth Anniv of Giuseppe Tartini (violinist and composer). P 14.
156 **16** 27t. multicoloured .... 1·60 1·50

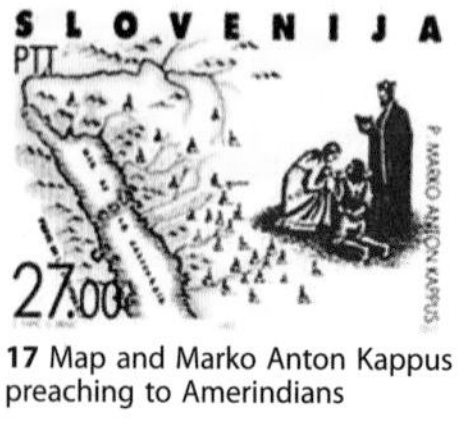

17 Map and Marko Anton Kappus preaching to Amerindians

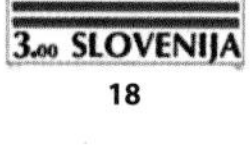

18

(Des Z. Papic and D. Brajič. Litho)

1992 (21 Apr). 500th Anniv of Discovery of America by Columbus. T **17** and similar horiz design. Multicoloured. P 14.
157 27t. Type **17** .... 3·25 3·00
a. Pair. Nos. 157/8 .... 7·75 7·25
158 47t. Map and *Santa Maria* .... 4·25 4·00

Nos. 157/8 were printed together in *se-tenant* pairs within the sheet.

(Des S. Knafelc. Litho)

1992 (8 May). OBLIGATORY TAX. Red Cross. P 14.
159 **18** 3t. black, bright scarlet and ultramarine 85 80
a. Self-adhesive gum 85 80

For compulsory use from 8 to 15 May.

19 Collapsible Chair by Niko Kralj and Map

20 Slomšek

(Des Luks Studio. Litho)

1992 (17 May). 17th World Industrial Design Congress, Ljubljana. P 14.
160 **19** 41t. multicoloured .... 1·00 95

(Des M. Paternoster. Litho)

1992 (29 May). 130th Death Anniv of Anton Slomšek, Bishop of Maribor. P 14.
161 **20** 6t. multicoloured .... 1·00 95

21 Wreckage

22 Rescuing Mountaineer

(Des S. Knafelc. Litho)

1992 (1 June). OBLIGATORY TAX. Solidarity Week.

(a) P 14
162 **21** 3t. orange-brown, black and vermilion 65 60

(b) Self-adhesive. Die-cut
163 **21** 3t. deep brown, black and scarlet 65 60

For compulsory use from 1 to 7 June.

(Des V. Kopac. Litho)

1992 (12 June). 80th Anniv of Alpine Rescue Service. P 14.
164 **22** 41t. multicoloured .... 1·00 95

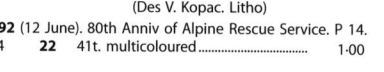

23 River Jousting

24 Linden Leaf and Flowers

(Des Mira Uršič-Šparovec. Litho)

1992 (20 June). 900th Anniv of River Jousting in Ljubljana. P 14.
165 **23** 6t. multicoloured 50 50

(Des M. Licul. Litho)

1992 (25 June). First Anniv of Independence. P 14.
166 **24** 41t. multicoloured .... 1·00 95

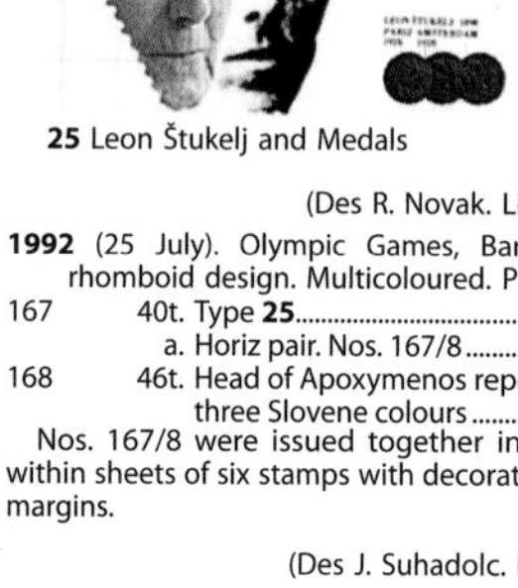

25 Leon Štukelj and Medals

26 Sheepdog

(Des R. Novak. Litho)

1992 (25 July). Olympic Games, Barcelona. T **25** and similar rhomboid design. Multicoloured. P 14.
167 40t. Type **25** .... 1·30 1·20
a. Horiz pair. Nos. 167/8 .... 3·00 2·75
168 46t. Head of Apoxymenos repeated in three Slovene colours .... 1·40 1·30

Nos. 167/8 were issued together in horizontal *se-tenant* pairs within sheets of six stamps with decorated and inscribed perforated margins.

(Des J. Suhadolc. Litho)

1992 (4 Sept). "Psov '92" World Dog-training Championships, Ljubljana. P 14.
169 **26** 40t. multicoloured .... 1·00 95

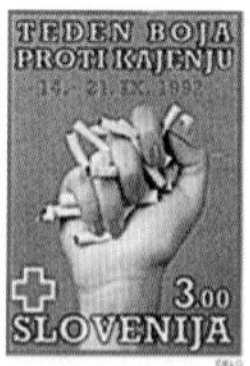

27 Hand crushing Cigarettes

28 Kogoj and scene from *Black Masks* (opera)

1992 (14 Sept). OBLIGATORY TAX. Red Cross. Anti-smoking Week. Litho. P 14.
170 **27** 3t. multicoloured 50 50

For compulsory use from 14 to 21 September.

(Des B. Fajon. Litho)

1992 (30 Sept). Birth Centenary of Marij Kogoj (composer). P 14.
171 **28** 40t. multicoloured .... 1·00 95

29 Langus (self-portrait)

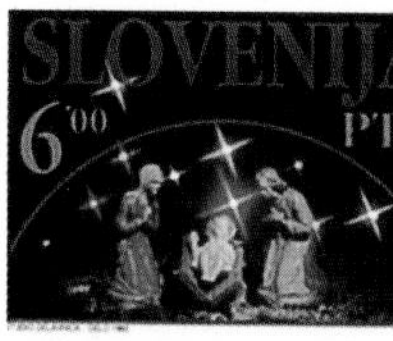

30 Nativity

(Des P. Skalar. Litho)

1992 (30 Oct). Birth Bicentenary of Matevž Langus (painter). P 14.
172 **29** 40t. multicoloured .... 1·00 95

(Des Studio Delavnica (6, 7t.), M. Paternoster (41t.). Litho)

1992 (20 Nov–Dec). Christmas. T **30** and similar multicoloured design. P 14.
173 6t. Type **30** 20 10
174 7t. Type **30** (15 Dec) 50 50
175 41t. "Madonna and Child" (stained-glass window by V. Šorli-Puc in St. Mary's Church, Bovec) (vert) .... 1·00 95
173/175 *Set of* 3 .... 1·50 1·40

31 Potočnik, View of Earth from Space and Satellite

(Des G. Košak. Litho)

1992 (27 Nov). Birth Centenary of Herman Potocnik (space pioneer). P 14.
176 **31** 46t. multicoloured .... 1·00 95

32 Illustration from *Solzice*

(Des M. Vipotnik. Litho)

1993 (22 Jan). Birth Centenary of Prežihov Voranc (writer). P 14.
177 **32** 7t. multicoloured 50 50

33 "Underneath the Birches"

34 Bust of Stefan (J. Savinšek)

(Des M. Vipotnik. Litho)

1993 (22 Jan). 50th Death Anniv of Rihard Jakopic (painter). P 14.
178 **33** 44t. multicoloured .... 1·00 95

(Des J. Suhadolc. Litho)

1993 (22 Jan). Death Centenary of Jožef Stefan (physicist). P 14.
179 **34** 51t. multicoloured .... 1·00 95

35 Honey-cake from Škofja Loka

36 Mountains and Founder Members

(Des M. Licul. Litho)

1993 (18 Feb)–**99**. Slovene Culture. T **35** and similar perf designs. P 14.

180 1t. brown, brown-ochre and deep brown 20 10
181 2t. bronze green and bright green (14.5.93) 20 10
182 5t. olive-grey, brownish grey and dull mauve (14.5.93) 20 10
183 6t. bright green, bottle green and lemon 20 10
184 7t. orange-red, crimson and grey 20 10
185 8t. yellow-green, myrtle green and yellow-olive (25.8.93) 20 10
186 9t. orange-red, purple-brown and grey (25.8.93) 30 15
187 10t. red-brown and brown (14.5.93) 30 15
188 11t. deep blue-green, bright green and olive-yellow (8.7.94) 30 15
189 12t. carmine-lake, reddish orange and grey (8.7.94) 30 15
189*a* 13t. light green, black and deep yellow-green (8.8.97) 30 15
189*b* 14t. orange-red, sepia and greenish slate (8.8.97) 30 15
189*c* 15t. black, drab and brown-lake (23.6.98) 30 15
189*d* 16t. reddish brown, turquoise-blue and pale orange (5.2.99) 30 15
189*e* 17t. chocolate, yellow and light brown (7.5.99) 30 15
189*f* 18t. orange-brown, black and pale blue (17.12.99) 30 15
189*g* 19t. chocolate, yellow and light brown 30 15
190 20t. blackish green and olive-grey (14.5.93) 65 60
191 44t. new blue, deep violet-blue and blue-black .... 1·00 95
192 50t. maroon and deep mauve (14.5.93) .... 1·00 95
193 55t. black, lavender-grey and salmon (22.3.96) 75 70
194 65t. brown-ochre, red-brown and carmine-rose (22.3.96) 95 85
195 70t. greenish grey, reddish brown and blackish green (16.11.95) .... 1·00 95
196 75t. turquoise-green, turquoise-blue and reddish lilac (22.3.96) .... 1·00 95
197 80t. multicoloured (20.3.97) .... 1·30 1·20
197*a* 90t. purple-brown, brown-red and greenish grey (30.5.97) .... 1·40 1·30
198 100t. yellow-brown, Venetian red and light brown (14.5.93) .... 2·20 1·90
198*a* 200t. brown-purple, turquoise-green and ultra-marine (12.11.98) .... 5·00 4·25
198*b* 300t. chestnut and light brown (7.11.94) .... 5·00 4·25
198*c* 400t. bright crimson and yellow-brown (7.11.94) .... 7·00 6·25
198*d* 500t. violet, pale orange and grey (12.11.98) .... 6·50 5·75
180/198*d Set of* 31 .... 35·00 30·00

Designs:—2t. Reed pipes; 5t. Double hay-drying frame; 6t. Shepherd's hut, Velika Planina; 7t. Zither; 8t. Mill on the Mur; 9t. Sledge; 10t. Earthenware double-bass; 11t. Hay basket; 12t. Boy on horse (statuette), Ribnica; 13t. Wind-operated bird-scarer, Prlekija; 14t. Hen-shaped wine jug, Šentjernej; 15t. Blast furnace, Železniki; 16t. Windmill, Stari Gori; 17t. Maize store, Ptujsko polje; 18t. Accordion, Kranjska Gora; 20t. Farmhouse, Prekmurje; 44t. House, Karst; 50t. Wind-propelled pump, Secovlje salt-pans; 55t. Easter eggs, Bela Krajina; 65t. Lamp, Tržič; 70t. Ski; 75t. Wrought iron window lattice; 80t. Palm Sunday bundle, Ljubljana; 90t. Apiary; 100t. Nut cake; 200t. Bootjack in shape of stag beetle; 300t. Straw sculpture; 400t. Wine press.

On the 55 to 75t. values "ptt" is replaced by "POŠTA" and on the 80 and 90t. values by a posthorn.

(Des B. Fajon. Litho)

1993 (27 Feb). Centenary of Alpine Association. P 14.

199 **36** 7t. multicoloured 35 35

37 Čop's Route up Triglav

38 Chainbreaker (1919 stamp design)

(Des E. Berk. Litho)

1993 (27 Feb). Birth Centenary of Jozä Čop (climber and mountain rescuer). P 14.

200 **37** 44t. multicoloured 75 75

(Des G. Košak after I. Vavpotič. Litho)

1993 (19 Mar). 75th Anniv of Slovenian Postal Service. P 14.

201 **38** 7t. multicoloured 20 20

39 "St. Nicholas" (altar painting, Tintoretto)

40 "Table in Pompeii" (Marij Pregelj)

(Des Studio Visio. Litho)

1993 (9 Apr). 500th Anniv of College Chapter of Novo Mesto. T **39** and similar vert design. P 14.

202 7t. Type **39** 10 10
203 44t. Arms .... 1·10 1·10

(Des Z. Papic. Litho)

1993 (29 Apr). Europa. Contemporary Art. T **40** and similar vert design. Multicoloured. P 14.

204 44t. Type **40** .... 2·20 2·20
a. Pair. Nos. 204/5 .... 8·00 8·00
205 159t. "Girl with Toy" (Gabrijel Stupica) .... 5·50 5·50

Nos. 204/5 were issued together in *se-tenant* pairs within sheets of eight stamps.

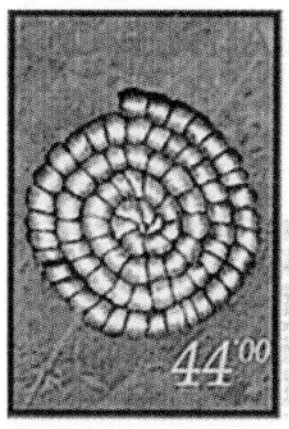

41 *Schwagerina carniolica*

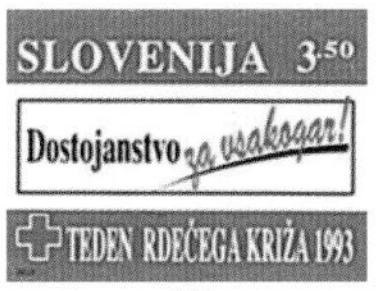

42

(Des Judita Skalar. Litho)

1993 (7 May). Fossils. P 14.

206 **41** 44t. multicoloured .... 1·10 1·10

1993 (8 May). OBLIGATORY TAX. Red Cross. Litho. P 14.

207 **42** 3t.50 black, bright scarlet and new blue 35 35
a. Self-adhesive gum 35 35

For compulsory use from 8 to 14 May.

43 6th-century B.C. Vase

44 Red Cross Rescue Workers

(Des R. Novak. Litho)

1993 (21 May). First Anniv of Admission to United Nations Organization. P 14.

208 **43** 62t. multicoloured .... 1·60 1·60

1993 (1 June). OBLIGATORY TAX. Solidarity Week. Litho. P 14.

209 **44** 3t.50 multicoloured 35 35
a. Self-adhesive gum 35 35

For compulsory use from 1 to 7 June.

45 Basketball, Hurdling and Swimming

46 "Battle of Sisak" (Johann Valvasor)

(Des J. Trobec. Litho)

1993 (8 June). Mediterranean Games, Roussillon (Languedoc), France. P 14.

210 **45** 36t. multicoloured 85 85

(Des D. Brajič. Litho)

1993 (22 June). 400th Anniv of Battle of Sisak. P 14.

211 **46** 49t. multicoloured .... 1·60 1·60

47 *Monolistra spinosissima*

48 Horse and Diagram of Movements

(Des B. Fajon. Litho)

1993 (12 July). Cave Fauna. T **47** and similar vert designs. Multicoloured. P 14.

212 7t. Type **47** 20 20
213 40t. *Aphaenopidius kamnikensis* (insect) .... 1·10 1·10
214 55t. *Proteus anguinus* .... 1·20 1·20
215 65t. *Zospeum spelaeum* (mollusc) .... 1·40 1·40
212/215 *Set of* 4 .... 3·50 3·50

(Des E. Berk and O. Kogoj. Litho)

1993 (30 July). European Dressage Championships, Lipica. P 14.

216 **48** 65t. multicoloured .... 1·60 1·60

49 Boy smoking and Emblem

50 Valvasor Arms

(Des Bregar and Koščak. Litho)

1993 (14 Sept). OBLIGATORY TAX. Red Cross. Anti-smoking Week. P 14.

217 **49** 4t.50 multicoloured 35 35

For compulsory use from 9 to 21 September.

(Des Milena Gregorčič. Litho)

1993 (29 Oct). 300th Anniversaries. T **50** and similar vert design. P 14.

218 9t. black, reddish lilac and gold 20 20
219 65t. black, stone and gold .... 1·40 1·40

Designs:—9t. Type **50** (death anniv of Johann Valvasor (historian)); 65t. Arms of Academia Operosorum.

51 "Slovenian Family at Christmas Crib" (M. Gaspari)

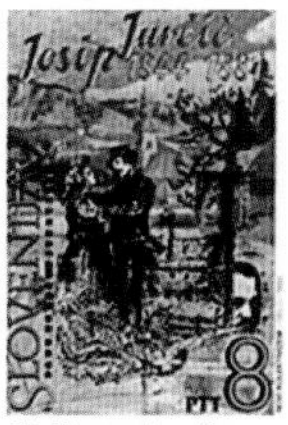

52 Illustration from *The Vagabond*

(Des M. Paternoster. Litho)

1993 (15 Nov). Christmas. T **51** and similar horiz design. Multicoloured. P 14.

220 9t. Type **51** 20 20
221 65t. Dr. Jože Pogačnik (archbishop) (after B. Jakac) and seal .... 1·40 1·40

(Des Novi Kolektivizem. Litho)

1994 (14 Jan). 150th Anniversaries. T **52** and similar vert designs. Multicoloured. P 14.

222 8t. Type **52** (birth anniv of Josip Jurcic (writer)) 10 10
223 9t. Nightingale and bridge over river (birth anniv of Simon Gregorčič, poet) 25 25
224 55t. Book showing Slovenian vowels (birth anniv of Stanislav Škrabec, philologist) .... 1·20 1·20
225 65t. Cover of grammar book (death anniv of Jernej Kopitar, philologist) .... 1·40 1·40
222/225 *Set of* 4 .... 2·75 2·75

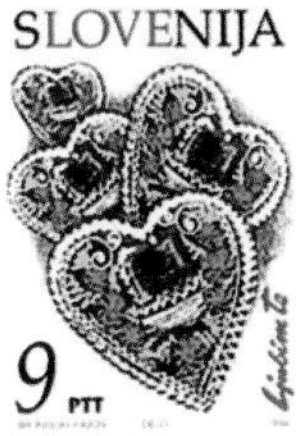

53 Hearts

54 Cross-country Skiing

(Des B. Fajon. Litho)

1994 (25 Jan). Greetings Stamp. P 14.

226 **53** 9t. multicoloured 25 25

(Des Domjan. Litho Cetis)

1994 (4 Feb). Winter Olympic Games, Lillehammer, Norway. T **54** and similar horiz design. Multicoloured. P 14.

227 9t. Type **54** 25 25
a. Pair. Nos. 227/8 .... 2·10 2·10
228 65t. Slalom skiing .... 1·70 1·70

Nos. 227/8 were issued together in *se-tenant* pairs within sheets of six stamps with decorated perforated margins.

55 Ski Jumping

56 Town Names

(Des B. Fajon. Litho)

1994 (11 Mar). 60th Anniv of Ski Jumping Championships, Planica. P 14.

229 **55** 70t. multicoloured .... 1·70 1·70

Issued in sheets of four stamps. Some sheets were overprinted "203 m TONI NIEMINEN" in the margin.

(Des J. Bavčer. Litho)

1994 (25 Mar). 850th Anniv of First Official Record of Ljubljana. P 14.

230 **56** 9t. multicoloured 25 25

57 Janez Puhar and Camera

58 Balloons

(Des B. Kos. Litho)

1994 (22 Apr). Europa. Discoveries and Inventions. T **57** and similar horiz design. Multicoloured. P 14.
231 70t. Type **57** (invention of glass-plate photography) 1·70 1·70
a. Pair. Nos. 231/2 7·75 7·75
232 215t. Moon, natural logarithm diagram and Jurij Vega (mathematician) 5·75 5·75
Nos. 231/2 were issued together in *se-tenant* pairs within sheets of eight stamps.

1994 (8 May). OBLIGATORY TAX. Red Cross. Litho. P 14.
233 **58** 4t.50 multicoloured 35 35
a. Self-adhesive gum 35 35
For compulsory use from 8 to 15 May.

59 *Primula carniolica*

60 Red Cross Worker with Child

(Des D. Košak. Litho)

1994 (20 May). Flowers. T **59** and similar horiz designs. Multicoloured. P 14.
234 9t. Type **59** 25 25
a. Sheetlet. Nos. 234/7 plus 2 labels 4·25
235 44t. *Hladnikia pastinacifolia* 95 95
236 60t. *Daphne blagayana* 1·30 1·30
237 70t. *Campanula zoysii* 1·50 1·50
234/237 *Set of 4* 3·50 3·50
Nos. 234/7 were issued together in *se-tenant* sheetlets of four stamps and two labels showing map of Europe.

1994 (1 June). OBLIGATORY TAX. Solidarity Week. Litho. P 14.
238 **60** 4t.50 multicoloured 35 35
a. Self-adhesive gum 35 35
For compulsory use from 1 to 7 June.

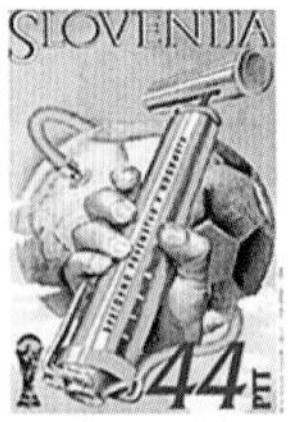

61 Inflating "Globe" Football

62 Globes in Olympic Colours and Flags

(Des Novi Kolektivizem. Litho)

1994 (10 June). World Cup Football Championship, U.S.A. P 14.
239 **61** 44t. multicoloured 95 95

(Des Novi Kolektivizem. Litho)

1994 (10 June). Centenary of International Olympic Committee. P 14.
240 **62** 100t. multicoloured 2·30 2·30

63 Mt. Ojstrica

64 Maks Pleteršnik (compiler) and University of Laibach Professors

(Des E. Berk and M. Lenarcic. Litho)

1994 (1 July). P 14.
241 **63** 12t. multicoloured 60 60

(Des D. Brajič and J. Ošlaj. Litho)

1994 (22 July). Centenary of First Slovenian–German Dictionary. P 14.
242 **64** 70t. multicoloured 1·70 1·70

65 Roman Infantry

66 Post Office

(Des Krea and Gorica. Litho)

1994 (1 Sept). 1600th Anniv of Battle of Frigidus. P 14.
243 **65** 60t. lake, black and deep grey 1·70 1·70

(Des K. Hartman. Litho)

1994 (23 Sept). Centenary of Maribor Post Office. P 14.
244 **66** 70t. multicoloured 1·70 1·70

67 Series "kkStB" Steam Locomotive No. 5722

68 Orchestra Venue and Music

(Des Milena Gregorčič and J. Trpin. Litho)

1994 (24 Sept). Centenary of Ljubljana Railway. P 14.
245 **67** 70t. multicoloured 1·70 1·70

(Des B. Fajon. Litho)

1994 (20 Oct). Bicentenary of Ljubljana Philharmonic Society. T **68** and similar horiz design. Multicoloured. P 14.
246 12t. Type **68** 25 25
247 70t. Ludwig van Beethoven, Johannes Brahms, Antonín Dvorák and Joseph Haydn (composers) and Niccolò Paganini (violinist) 1·50 1·50

69 Christmas Tree, Window and Candles

70 "Madonna and Child" (statue, Loreto Basilica)

(Des Milena Gregorčič (12t.), K. Zelinka Škerlavaj (70t.). Litho)

1994 (18 Nov). Christmas and International Year of the Family. T **69** and similar vert design. P 14.
248 12t. multicoloured 25 25
a. Booklet pane. No. 248×10 2·75
249 70t. cream, black and blue 1·50 1·50
a. Booklet pane. No. 249×10 16·00
Design:—70t. "Children with Christmas Tree" (F. Kralj) and I.Y.F. emblem.
The booklet panes have a narrow perforated margin around their outer edges.

(Des M. Učakar. Litho)

1994 (18 Nov). 700th Anniv of Loreto. P 14.
250 **70** 70t. multicoloured 1·70 1·70

71 Ivan Hribar, Mihajlo Rostohar and Danilo Majaron (founders) and University

72 Postal Emblem

(Des E. Berk. Litho)

1994 (3 Dec). 75th Anniv of Ljubljana University. P 14.
251 **71** 70t. multicoloured 1·70 1·70

(Des Studio Mak. Litho)

1995 (27 Jan). P 14.
252 **72** 13t. multicoloured 60 60

73 Lili Novy (writer, 110th birth)

74 Cats and Hearts (Jure Kos)

(Des Petra Černe (253), J. Suhadolc (254), K. Rodman (255). Litho)

1995 (7 Feb). Anniversaries. T **73** and similar designs. P 14.
253 20t. scarlet, black and greenish grey 60 60
254 70t. greenish yellow, black and gold 1·70 1·70
255 70t. multicoloured 1·70 1·70
253/255 *Set of 3* 3·50 3·50
Designs: Horiz—No. 253, Silhouettes of figures and signature of Anton Tomaž Linhart (dramatist, death bicentenary). Vert—No. 255, Detail of façade of Zadružna Co-operative Bank, Ljubljana (110th birth anniv (1994) of Ivan Vurnik (architect)).

1995 (7 Feb). Greetings Stamp. Litho. P 14.
256 **74** 20t. multicoloured 60 60

75 Allegory

76 Skeleton and Woman

(Des R. Španzel. Litho)

1995 (29 Mar). 50th Anniv of End of Second World War. P 14.
257 **75** 13t. multicoloured 35 35

(Des R. Španzel. Litho)

1995 (29 Mar). Europa. Peace and Freedom. T **76** and similar horiz design. Multicoloured. P 14.
258 60t. Type **76** (50th anniv of liberation of concentration camps) 2·30 2·30
a. Pair. Nos. 258/9 5·00 5·00
259 70t. Woman running free 2·40 2·40
Nos. 258/9 were issued together in *se-tenant* pairs within sheets of eight stamps.

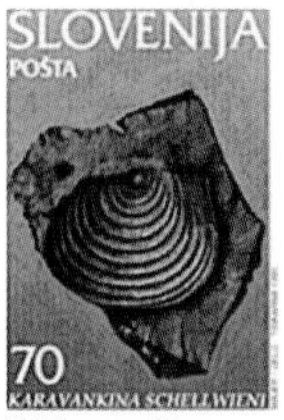

77 *Karavankina schellwieni*

78 Alpine Iris, Triglav National Park and Alpine Poppy

(Des M. Majer. Litho)

1995 (29 Mar). Fossils. P 14.
260 **77** 70t. multicoloured 1·70 1·70

(Des B. Fajon. Litho)

1995 (29 Mar). European Nature Conservation Year. P 14.
261 **78** 70t. multicoloured 1·70 1·70

79 Child painting Red Cross

80 First Aiders tending Casualty

1995 (8 May). OBLIGATORY TAX. Red Cross. Litho. P 14.
262 **79** 6t. multicoloured 35 35
a. Self-adhesive gum 35 35
For compulsory use from 8 to 15 May.

1995 (1 June). OBLIGATORY TAX. Solidarity Week. Litho. P 14.
263 **80** 6t.50 multicoloured 35 35
a. Self-adhesive gum 35 35
For compulsory use from 1 to 7 June.

81 Lesser Kestrel (*Falco naumanni*)

(Des Krea. Litho)

1995 (8 June). Birds. T **81** and similar horiz designs. Multicoloured. P 14.
264 13t. Type **81** 25 25
a. Block of 4. Nos. 264/7 7·25
265 60t. Common roller (*Coracias garrulus*) 1·20 1·20
266 70t. Lesser grey shrike (*Lanius minor*) 1·40 1·40
267 215t. Black-headed bunting (*Emberiza melanocephala*) 4·25 4·25
264/267 *Set of 4* 6·50 6·50
Nos. 264/7 were issued together in *se-tenant* blocks of four stamps within the sheet.

82 Radovljica

(Des Petra Černe. Litho)

1995 (8 June). 500th Anniv of Radovljica. P 14.
268 **82** 44t. multicoloured 95 95

83 Class "KRB 37" Steam Locomotive Podnart

84 Mountain and Presbytery

(Des Milena Gregorčič and J. Trpin. Litho)

1995 (8 June). 125th Anniv of Ljubljana–Jesenice Railway. P 14.
269 **83** 70t. black, carmine-lake and yellow. 1·70 1·70

(Des Krea and Gorica. Litho and thermography Cartor)

1995 (8 June). Centenary of Jakob Aljaz Presbytery, Mount Triglav. P 13½.
270 **84** 100t. deep ultramarine, black and rose-red .... 1·70 1·70

85 Scouts around Campfire

(Des Ančka Gošnik Godec and M. Učakar. Litho)

1995 (26 Sept). Scouting. P 14.
271 **85** 70t. multicoloured .... 1·70 1·70

86 "Death of a Genius"

87 Handshake, Anniversary Emblem and Different Nationalities

(Des M. Vipotnik. Litho)

1995 (26 Sept). Birth Centenary of France Kralj (artist). T **86** and similar horiz design. Multicoloured. P 14.
272 60t. Type **86** .... 1·20 1·20
a. Pair. Nos. 272/3 .... 2·75 2·75
273 70t. "Family of Horses" .... 1·30 1·30
Nos. 272/3 were issued together in *se-tenant* pairs within the sheet.

(Des Krea. Litho)

1995 (26 Sept). 50th Anniversaries of United Nations Organization (274) and Food and Agriculture Organization (275). T **87** and similar vert design. Multicoloured. P 14.
274 70t. Type **87** .... 1·20 1·20
275 70t. Foodstuffs, anniversary emblem and different nationalities .... 1·20 1·20
Nos. 274/5 were issued both in separate sheets and together in *se-tenant* sheetlets of four stamps (*Price for sheetlet*: £5 *un*).

88 "Winter" (Marlenka Stupica)

89 Birds and Heart (Karmen Podgornik)

(Des M. Učakar. Litho)

1995 (16 Nov). Christmas. T **88** and similar vert design showing paintings. Multicoloured. P 14.
276 13t. Type **88** 25 25
a. Booklet pane. No. 276×10 plus 2 labels .... 2·75
277 70t. "Madonna and Child" (Leopold Layer) .... 1·50 1·50
a. Booklet pane. No. 277×10 plus 2 labels .... 16·00

1996 (31 Jan). Greetings Stamp. Litho. P 14.
278 **89** 13t. multicoloured 60 60

90 Swimming

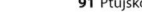

91 Ptujsko Polje

(Des G. Vásárhelyi. Litho)

1996 (31 Jan). The European Pond Turtle (*Emys orbicularis*). T **90** and similar horiz designs. Multicoloured. P 14.
279 13t. Type **90** 35 35
a. Strip of 4. Nos. 279/82 .... 4·00
280 50t. On bank 80 80
281 60t. In water .... 1·20 1·20
282 70t. Pair of turtles climbing up bank .... 1·40 1·40
279/282 *Set of* 4 .... 3·50 3·50
Nos. 279/82 were issued together in *se-tenant* strips of four stamps within the sheet.

(Des Milena Gregorčič. Litho)

1996 (31 Jan). Masked Costumes. T **91** and similar vert design. Multicoloured. P 14.
283 13t. Type **91** 25 25
284 70t. Dravsko Polje .... 1·50 1·50

92 Steam Locomotive *Aussee*

93 Fran Finžgar (writer)

(Des Milena Gregorčič and J. Trpin. Litho)

1996 (31 Jan). 150th Anniv of Slovenian Railways. P 14.
285 **92** 70t. multicoloured .... 1·40 1·40

(Des D. Brajič. Litho)

1996 (18 Apr). Birth Anniversaries. T **93** and similar horiz design. Multicoloured. P 14.
286 13t. Type **93** (125th anniv) 35 35
287 100t. Ita Rina (actress) (89th anniv) .... 2·00 2·00

94 Child feeding Birds and Children of different Nationalities

95 "Vase of Dahlias"

(Des Krea. Litho)

1996 (18 Apr). 50th Anniv of United Nations Children's Fund. P 14.
288 **94** 65t. multicoloured .... 1·20 1·20

(Des Petra Černe. Litho)

1996 (18 Apr). Europa. Famous Women. 70th Death Anniv of Ivana Koblica (painter). T **95** and similar vert design. Multicoloured. P 14.
289 65t. "Children in the Grass" (detail) .... 2·30 2·30
a. Pair. Nos. 289/90 .... 5·00 5·00
290 75t. Type **95** .... 2·40 2·40
Nos. 289/90 were issued together in *se-tenant* pairs within sheets of eight stamps.

96 Pope John Paul II

97 Anniversary Emblem

(Des T. Seifert and J. Suhadolc. Litho)

1996 (18 Apr). Papal Visit. P 14.
291 **96** 75t. multicoloured .... 1·40 1·40
MS292 60×90 mm. **96** 200t. multicoloured .... 3·50 3·50

1996 (8 May). OBLIGATORY TAX. 130th Anniv of Slovenian Red Cross. Litho. P 14.
293 **97** 7t. multicoloured 35 35
a. Self-adhesive gum 35 35
For compulsory use from 8 to 15 May.

98 Clasped Hands

99 Gallenberg Castle

(Des I. Šeme. Litho)

1996 (1 June). OBLIGATORY TAX. Solidarity Week. P 14.
294 **98** 7t. multicoloured 35 35
a. Self-adhesive gum 35 35
For compulsory use from 1 to 7 June.

(Des K. Rodman. Litho)

1996 (6 June). 700th Anniv of Zagorje ob Savi. P 14.
295 **99** 24t. multicoloured 60 60

100 Cyclists

101 Stars over Mountains

(Des Studio Visio. Litho)

1996 (6 June). World Youth Cycling Championships, Novo Mesto. P 14.
296 **100** 55t. multicoloured 95 95

(Des M. Licul. Litho)

1996 (6 June). Fifth Anniv of Independence. P 14.
297 **101** 75t. multicoloured .... 1·70 1·70

102 Chanterelle (*Cantharellus cibarius*)

103 Rowing and Canoeing

(Des Štampfl and Zajec. Litho)

1996 (6 June). Fungi. Sheet 114×80 mm containing T **102** and similar horiz design. Multicoloured. P 14.
MS298 65t. Type **102**; 75t. *Boletus aestivalis* .... 4·00 4·00

(Des B. Fajon. Litho)

1996 (6 June). Centenary of Modern Olympic Games and Olympic Games, Atlanta. T **103** and similar vert design. Multicoloured. P 14.
299 75t. Type **103** .... 1·40 1·40
a. Vert pair or horiz strip .... 3·75 3·75
300 100t. High jumping and hurdling .... 2·10 2·10
Nos. 299/300 were issued together in *se-tenant* sheetlets of six stamps and three different labels. The arrangement gives vertical *se-tenant* pairs and horizontal strips of the two values separated by a label.
The sheetlet exists in two versions, differing in the flag in the bottom margin: either white, red and blue bands (incorrect) or white, blue and red (correct).

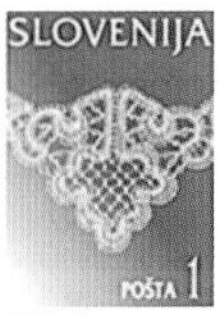
104 Corner

105 "Moscon Family"

1996 (21 June). Traditional Lace Designs from Idria. T **104** and similar vert designs. Litho. Phosphorescent security markings (301/2, 303/4, 305/6, 309/10, 311/12 and 317/18). P 14.
301 1t. olive-brown 25 25
a. Pair. Nos. 301/2 .... 55 55
302 1t. olive-brown 25 25
303 2t. deep rose-red 25 25
a. Pair. Nos. 303/4 .... 55 55
304 2t. deep rose-red 25 25
305 5t. bright new blue 25 25
a. Pair. Nos. 305/6 .... 55 55
306 5t. bright new blue 25 25
307 10t. deep mauve (20.6.97) 25 25
a. Pair. Nos. 307/8 .... 55 55
308 10t. deep mauve (20.6.97) 25 25
309 12t. bright emerald 30 30
a. Pair. Nos. 309/10 .... 65 65
310 12t. bright emerald 30 30
311 13t. rose-vermilion 30 30
a. Pair. Nos. 311/12 .... 65 65
312 13t. rose-vermilion 30 30
313 20t. violet (20.6.97) 35 35
a. Pair. Nos. 313/14 .... 75 75
314 20t. violet (20.6.97) 35 35

315 44t. bright new blue (20.6.97) 80 80
a. Pair. Nos. 315/16 1·70 1·70
316 44t. bright new blue (20.6.97) 80 80
317 50t. bright purple 95 95
a. Pair. Nos. 317/18 2·00 2·00
318 50t. bright purple 95 95
325 100t. chocolate (20.6.97) 1·50 1·50
a. Pair. Nos. 325/6 3·25 3·25
326 100t. chocolate (20.6.97) 1·50 1·50
301/318 *Set of* 20 9·25 9·25

Designs:—No. 302, Corner (different); 303, Rounded collar incorporating scrolls; 304, Pointed collar with scalloped edging; 305, Flowers and leaves forming circular design; 306, Framed rose; 307, Oval with flower in centre; 308, "Q"-shape with trefoil in centre; 309, Flower; 310, Diamond with flower in centre; 311, Square enclosing diamonds containing "flowers"; 312, Square containing circular motifs; 313, Butterfly; 314, Diamond; 315, Square; 316, Circle; 317, Heart-shaped edging; 318, Ornate edging; 325, Leaf; 326, Insect.

Stamps of the same value were issued together in *se-tenant* pairs within their sheets.

Each stamp has phosphorescent security markings consisting of "1996", "Idrijska čipka" or "Idria Lace" on alternate stamps, and a posthorn.

Nos, 303/4 were re-issued with "1997" phosphorescent security markings.

Nos. 307/4, 313/14, 315/16 and 325/6 do not have the phosphorescent markings of the previous issues.

Numbers have been left for additions to this series.

(Des M. Učakar. Litho)

1996 (6 Sept). 130th Death Anniv of Jožef Tominc (painter). P 14.
331 **105** 65t. multicoloured 1·30 1·30

106 Cave

(Des V. Ratkovič. Litho)

1996 (6 Sept). UNESCO World Heritage Sites. Škocjan Cave. P 14.
332 **106** 55t. multicoloured 1·20 1·20

107 Gimbals

108 Heart

(Des Studio Visio. Litho)

1996 (6 Sept). 250th Anniv of Novo Mesto School. P 14.
333 **107** 55t. multicoloured 1·20 1·20

(Des Alenka Sovinc. Litho)

1996 (6 Sept). Centenary of Modern Cardiology. P 14.
334 **108** 12t. bright orange-red, red-brown and cream 60 60

109 Post Office Building, Ljubljana, and Doves carrying Letter

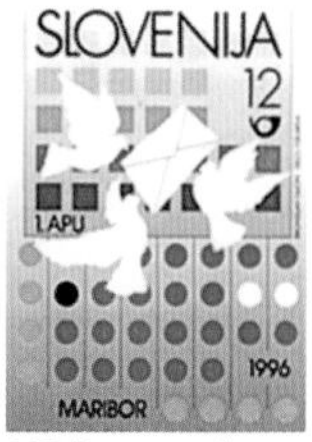

110 Doves carrying Letter and Stylized Letter Sorting

(Des B. Fajon. Litho)

1996 (18 Oct). Centenary of Post and Telecommunications Office. P 14.
335 **109** 100t. multicoloured 1·70 1·70

(Des B. Fajon. Litho)

1996 (20 Oct). Introduction of Automatic Letter Sorting. P 14.
336 **110** 12t. black, rosine and bright orange 60 60

111 Children and Christmas Tree on Sledge

112 Cupids

(Des T. Podgornik and T. Seifert (12t.), T. Seifert (65t.). Litho)

1996 (20 Nov). Christmas. T **111** and similar horiz design. Multicoloured. P 14.
337 12t. Type **111** 25 25
a. Booklet pane. No. 337×10 2·75
338 65t. "Adoration of the Wise Men" (Štefan Šubic) 1·20 1·20
a. Booklet pane. No. 338×10 12·50

The booklet panes have perforated margins around their outer edges.

(Des T. Prekovič. Litho)

1997 (21 Jan). Greetings Stamp. P 14.
339 **112** 15t. multicoloured 35 35

113 Mt. Snežnik

114 "Ta Terjast"

(Des B. Kenda. Litho)

1997 (21 Jan). P 14.
340 **113** 20t. multicoloured 95 95

(Des Milena Gregorčič. Litho)

1997 (21 Jan). Masked Costumes. T **114** and similar vert design. Multicoloured. P 14.
341 20t. Type **114** 35 35
342 80t. "Pust" 1·40 1·40

115 Marbled Trout (*Salmo marmoratus*)

116 The Golden Horns

(Des M. Učakar. Litho)

1997 (27 Mar). Fish. T **115** and similar horiz designs. Multicoloured. P 14.
343 12t. Type **115** 35 35
344 13t. Streber (*Zingel streber*) 60 60
345 80t. Zahrte (*Vimba vimba*) 1·40 1·40
346 90t. European mudminnow (*Umbra krameri*) 1·70 1·70
343/346 *Set of* 4 3·75 3·75
MS347 113×79 mm. As Nos. 343/6 but with inscriptions rearranged and fish enlarged (tails in margin) 4·00 4·00

(Des B. Kenda. Litho)

1997 (27 Mar). Europa. Tales and Legends. P 14.
348 **116** 80t. multicoloured 1·50 1·50

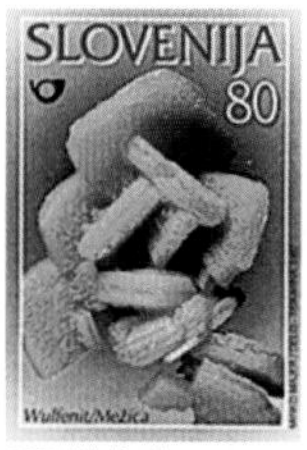

117 Wulfenite

118 Brick

(Des M. Majer. Litho)

1997 (27 Mar). Minerals. P 14.
349 **117** 80t. multicoloured 1·50 1·50

(Des Enigma. Litho)

1997 (8 May). OBLIGATORY TAX. Red Cross. P 14.
350 **118** 7t. multicoloured 35 35
a. Self-adhesive gum 35 35

119 Matija Čop (scholar)

120 Cockerel and Fireman's Helmet

(Des Krea. Litho)

1997 (30 May). Birth Anniversaries. T **119** and similar vert designs. Multicoloured. P 14.
351 13t. Type **119** (bicentenary) 25 25
352 24t. Žiga Zois (naturalist, 250th) 35 35
353 80t. Škof Baraga (missionary, bicentenary) 1·20 1·20
351/353 *Set of* 3 1·60 1·60

(Des B. Fajon. Litho)

1997 (30 May). Fire Service. P 14.
354 **120** 70t. multicoloured 1·20 1·20

121 Series "SŽ" Steam Locomotive

122 Red Cross

(Des Milena Gregorčič and J. Trpin. Litho)

1997 (30 May). 140th Anniv of Ljubljana–Trieste Railway. P 14.
355 **121** 80t. black, lemon and bright scarlet 1·50 1·50

1997 (1 June). OBLIGATORY TAX. Solidarity Week. Litho. P 14.
356 **122** 7t. multicoloured 35 35
a. Self-adhesive gum 35 35

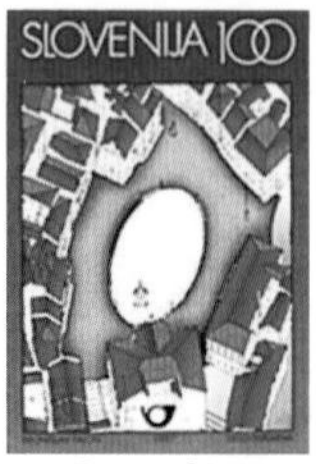

123 Centre of Piran

124 Girl with Dog (Andrejka Cufer)

(Des B. Fajon. Litho)

1997 (6 June). European Summit, Piran. Sheet 134×115 mm containing T **123** and similar vert design. P 14.
MS357 100t. Type **123**; 200t. Arms of participating states 5·25 5·25

1997 (9 Sept). Children's Week. Litho. P 14.
358 **124** 14t. multicoloured 60 60

125 "The Shy Lover"

126 Judo Bout

(Des M. Licul. Litho)

1997 (9 Sept). Birth Centenary of France Gorše (sculptor). T **125** and similar horiz design. Multicoloured. P 14.
359 70t. Type **125** 1·00 1·00
a. Pair. Nos. 359/60 2·30 2·30
360 80t. "The Farmer's Wife" 1·20 1·20

Nos. 359/60 were issued together in *se-tenant* pairs within the sheet.

(Des T. Rojc. Recess and litho)

1997 (9 Sept). European Youth Judo Championships, Ljubljana. P 14.
361 **126** 90t. multicoloured 1·70 1·70

127 Venezia Giulia and Istria 1945 Stamp, Anchor and Rose

128 Children watching Birds

(Des B. Fajon. Litho)

1997 (9 Sept). 50th Anniv of Incorporation of Istria and Slovene Coast into Yugoslavia. P 14.
362 **127** 50t. multicoloured 95 95

(Des A. Cufer. Litho)

1997 (18 Nov). Christmas and New Year. T **128** and similar horiz design. Multicoloured. P 14.
363 14t. Type **128** 25 25
a. Booklet pane. No. 363×5 and No. 364×3 6·00
364 90t. Crib (Liza Hribar), Church of the Blessed Virgin, Krope 1·50 1·50

129 Globe, Golden Vixen and Skier

130 Dove, Envelope and Postal Centre

(Des R. Uran. Litho)

1997 (18 Nov). World Cup Alpine Skiing Championships. P 14.
365 **129** 90t. multicoloured .... 1·70 1·70

(Des B. Fajon. Litho)

1997 (28 Nov). Inauguration of New Postal Centre, Ljubljana. P 14.
366 **130** 30t. multicoloured 60 60

131 Guests and Attendants

(Des Milena Gregorčič. Litho)

1998 (22 Jan). Traditional Pine Brush Wedding. T **131** and similar horiz design. Multicoloured. P 14.
367 20t. Type **131** 35 35
a. Horiz pair. Nos. 367/8 .... 1·70 1·70
368 80t. Priest, accordionist and bride and groom .... 1·20 1·20
Nos. 367/8 were issued together in horizontal *se-tenant* pairs within the sheet, each pair forming a composite design.

132 Figure Skating

(Des M. Učakar. Litho)

1998 (22 Jan). Winter Olympic Games, Nagano, Japan. T **132** and similar horiz design. Multicoloured. P 14.
369 70t. Type **132** .... 1·10 1·10
a. Horiz pair or vert strip .... 2·50 2·50
370 90t. Biathlon .... 1·30 1·30
Nos. 369/70 were issued together in *se-tenant* sheetlets of six stamps and three different labels. The arrangement gives horizontal *se-tenant* pairs and vertical strips of the two values separated by a label.

133 Airplane, Air Traffic Controllers and Flight Paths

134 Lakotnik eating Potato

(Des Krea. Litho)

1998 (22 Jan). 35th Anniv of Eurocontrol Convention (on regional aviation safety co-operation). P 14.
371 **133** 90t. multicoloured .... 1·70 1·70

1998 (25 Mar). Cartoon Characters by Miki Muster. T **134** and similar vert designs. Multicoloured. Litho. P 14.
372 14t. Type **134** 35 35
373 105t. Trdonja (turtle) in sea .... 1·40 1·40
374 118t. Zvitorepec (fox) walking through meadow .... 1·70 1·70
372/374 *Set of* 3 .... 3·00 3·00
MS375 172×100 mm. Nos. 372/4, each×2 .... 7·00 7·00

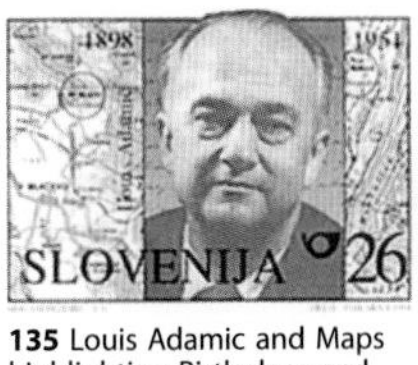

135 Louis Adamic and Maps highlighting Birthplace and American Residence

136 St. George's Festival

(Des M. Pezdirc. Litho)

1998 (25 Mar). Birth Anniversaries. T **135** and similar horiz design. Multicoloured. P 14.
376 26t. Type **135** (writer, centenary) 45 45
377 90t. Altar figure from Zagreb Cathedral and fountain (300th anniv of Francesco Robba (sculptor)) .... 1·30 1·30

(Des B. Fajon. Litho)

1997 (25 Mar). Europa. National Festivals. P 14.
378 **136** 90t. multicoloured .... 1·30 1·30
No. 378 was issued in sheets of eight stamps and one label showing dancers in a circle.

137 Red Cross and Blood Drop

138 Red Cross

(Des Luna. Litho)

1998 (8 May). OBLIGATORY TAX. Red Cross. P 14.
379 **137** 7t. scarlet and black 45 45
a. Self-adhesive gum 45 45
For compulsory use from 8 to 14 May.

(Des Luna. Litho)

1998 (1 June). OBLIGATORY TAX. Solidarity Week. T **138** and similar vert designs. Each rosine and black. P 14.
380 7t. Type **138** 45 45
a. Horiz pair. Nos. 380/1 .... 95 95
b. Self-adhesive gum 45 45
ba. Horiz pair. Nos. 380b/381b 95 95
381 7t. Red cross (value at right) 45 45
b. Self-adhesive gum 45 45
Nos. 380/1 were issued together in horizontal *se-tenant* pairs within the sheet, each pair forming a composite design.
For compulsory use from 1 to 7 June.

139 Mt. Boc

140 Common Juniper (*Juniperus communis*)

(Des Botas Studio. Litho)

1998 (10 June). P 14.
382 **139** 14t. multicoloured 60 60

(Des V. Ravnik and B. Juvanec. Litho)

1998 (10 June). Conifers. Sheet 134×114 mm containing T **140** and similar vert designs. Multicoloured. P 14.
MS383 14t. Type **140**; 15t. Norway spruce (*Picea abies*); 80t. Corsican pine (*Pinus nigra*); 90t. European larch (*Laris decidua*) .... 4·00 4·00

141 Series SŽ06-018 Steam Locomotive

142 Victory Sign

(Des Milena Gregorčič and J. Trpin. Litho)

1998 (10 June). P 14.
384 **141** 80t. multicoloured .... 1·70 1·70

(Des E. Berk and T. Stojko. Litho)

1998 (23 June). 10th Anniv of Committee for Protection of Human Rights. P 14.
385 **142** 15t. multicoloured 60 60

143 Map of Slovenia

(Des M. Licul and J. Zornik. Litho)

1998 (23 June). 150th Anniv of Movement for the Independence of Slovenia. P 14.
386 **143** 80t. multicoloured .... 1·70 1·70

144 St. Bernard of Clairvaux, Sticna Monastery Church and Foundation Document

145 Sound Waves and Cuckoo

(Des A. Cufer. Litho)

1998 (11 Sept). 900th Anniv of Cistercian Order and Centenary of Return of Cistercians to Sticna. P 14.
387 **144** 14t. multicoloured 60 60

(Des Botas Studio. Litho)

1998 (11 Sept). 70th Anniv of Cuckoo Emblem of Radio Ljubljana. P 14.
388 **145** 50t. multicoloured 95 95

146 "The Banker" (watercolour and collage)

147 Hands cradling Sleeping Infant

(Des Novi Kolektivizem. Litho)

1998 (11 Sept). Birth Centenary of August Cernigoj (artist). T **146** and similar vert design. Multicoloured. P 14.
389 70t. Type **146** .... 1·00 1·00
a. Pair. Nos. 389/90 .... 2·30 2·30
390 80t. "El" (sculpture) .... 1·20 1·20
Nos. 39/90 were issued together in *se-tenant* pairs within the sheet.

(Des K. Rodman. Litho)

1998 (11 Sept). 50th Anniv of Universal Declaration of Human Rights. P 14.
391 **147** 100t. multicoloured .... 1·70 1·70

148 Children with Candle (Marjanca Božic)

149 Leon Štukelj

(Des J. Suhadolc. Litho)

1998 (12 Nov). Christmas and New Year. T **148** and similar horiz design. Multicoloured. P 14.
392 15t. Type **148** 25 25
a. Booklet pane. No. 392×10 .... 2·75
b. Booklet pane. Nos. 392×6 and 393×4 .... 7·75
393 90t. "Adoration of the Wise Men" (fresco, St. Nicholas's Church, Mace) .... 1·50 1·50
The booklet panes have perforated margin around the block of stamps.

(Des B. Fajon. Litho)

1998 (12 Nov). Birth Centenary of Leon Štukelj (gymnast). Sheet 135×115 mm containing T **149** and similar multicoloured designs. P 14.
MS394 100t. Type **149**; 100t. Floor exercise; 100t. With Juan Antonio Samaranch (president of International Olympic Committee) (57×40 mm) .. 4·75 4·75

150 Peter Kozler (cartographer)

(Des E. Berk. Litho)

1999 (22 Jan). Anniversaries. T **150** and similar horiz designs. Multicoloured. P 14.
395 14t. Type **150** (125th birth anniv) 25 25
396 15t. Božidar Lavric (surgeon, birth centenary) 35 35
397 70t. General Rudolf Maister (125th birth anniv) .... 1·00 1·00
398 80t. France Prešeren (writer, 150th death anniv) .... 1·30 1·30
395/398 *Set of* 4 .... 2·50 2·50

151 White Horses, Planets and Hearts

(Des D. Brecko. Litho)

1999 (22 Jan). Greetings Stamp. P 14.
399 **151** 15t. multicoloured 60 60

152 Carnival Procession

(Des Milena Gregorčič. Photo)

1999 (22 Jan). Škoromati Carnival. T **152** and similar horiz design. Multicoloured. P 14.

400 20t. Type **152** 35 35
a. Horiz pair. Nos. 400/1 .... 1·80 1·80
401 80t. Horn-blower and procession .... 1·30 1·30

Nos. 400/1 were issued together in horizontal *se-tenant* pairs within the sheet, each pair forming a composite design.

153 Mt. Golica

(Des Studio Botas. Litho)

1999 (23 Mar). P 14.

402 **153** 15t. multicoloured 80 80

154 1919 20v. and 1997 14t. Stamps

(Des A. Cufer and Rubins. Litho)

1999 (23 Mar). 50th Anniv of Slovenian Philatelic Society. P 14.

403 **154** 16t. multicoloured 95 95

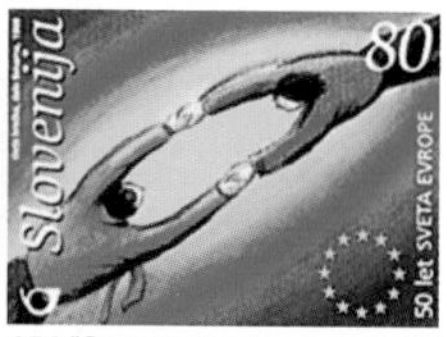

155 Cinnabarite **156** "Co-operation"

(Des M. Učakar and M. Udovc. Litho)

1999 (23 Mar). Minerals. P 14.

404 **155** 80t. multicoloured .... 1·40 1·40

(Des D. Brecko. Litho)

1999 (23 Mar). 50th Anniv of Council of Europe. P 14.

405 **156** 80t. multicoloured .... 1·40 1·40

157 Triglav National Park **158** Figures with Raised Arms

(Des Studio Botas. Litho)

1999 (23 Mar). Europa. Parks and Gardens. P 14.

406 **157** 90t. multicoloured .... 1·50 1·50

1999 (8 May). OBLIGATORY TAX. Red Cross. Litho. P 14.

407 **158** 8d. black and bright scarlet 45 45
a. Self-adhesive gum 45 45

For compulsory use from 8 to 15 May.

159 Early Postman and Moon **160** Slovenian Coldblood

(Des B. Fajon. Litho)

1999 (21 May). 125th Anniv of Universal Postal Union. T **159** and similar vert design. Multicoloured. P 14.

408 30t. Type **159** 45 45
a. Pair. Nos. 408/9 .... 1·90 1·90
409 90t. Astronaut on moon, posthorn and Earth .... 1·30 1·30

Nos. 408/9 were issued together in *se-tenant* pairs within the sheet.

(Des M. Učakar. Litho)

1999 (21 May). Horses. T **160** and similar horiz designs. Multicoloured. P 14.

410 60t. Type **160** 85 85
411 70t. Ljutomer trotting horse .... 1·00 1·00
412 120t. Slovenian warmblood (show jumping) .... 1·60 1·60
413 350t. Lipizzaner .... 4·75 4·75
410/413 *Set of 4* .... 7·50 7·50
MS414 113×80 mm. Nos. 410/13 .... 8·25 8·25

161 Dogs and Handlers

(Des J. Plestenjak. Litho)

1999 (21 May). World Rescue Dogs Championship. P 14.

415 **161** 80t. multicoloured .... 1·30 1·30

162 Children's Toys

(Des M. Kocevar. Litho)

1999 (16 Sept). Year 2000. T **162** and similar horiz designs. Multicoloured. P 14.

416 20t. Type **162** 35 35
a. Block of 4. Nos. 416/19 .... 3·50
417 70t. Forms of communication 85 85
418 80t. Symbols of science and culture .... 1·00 1·00
419 90t. Tree with symbols of education .... 1·10 1·10
416/419 *Set of 4* .... 3·00 3·00

Nos. 416/19 were issued together in *se-tenant* blocks of four stamps within the sheet.

163 "Self-portrait" and "Unravelling the Mysteries of Life"

(Des E. Berk. Litho)

1999 (16 Sept). Birth Centenary of Božidar Jakac (artist). T **163** and similar horiz design. Multicoloured. P 14.

420 70t. Type **163** .... 1·00 1·00
a. Pair. Nos. 420/1 .... 2·20 2·20
421 80t. "Self-portrait" and "Novo Mesto" .... 1·10 1·10

Nos. 420/1 were issued together in *se-tenant* pairs within the sheet.

164 Terglou Locomotive

(Des Milena Gregorčič and J. Trpin. Litho)

1999 (16 Sept). 150th Anniv of Arrival of First Train in Ljubljana. P 14.

422 **164** 80t. multicoloured .... 1·30 1·30

165 Slomšek **166** Family watching Fireworks

(Des A. Cufer and Rubens. Litho)

1999 (16 Sept). Beatification of Bishop Anton Martin Slomšek. P 14.

423 **165** 90t. multicoloured .... 1·60 1·60

1999 (1 Nov). OBLIGATORY TAX. Solidarity Week. Vert designs as T **138**. Each bright orange, black and bright scarlet. Litho. P 14.

424 9t. Red Cross (value at left) 45 45
a. Horiz pair. Nos. 424/5 .... 95 95
b. Self-adhesive gum 45 45
ba. Pair. Nos. 424b/5b 95 95
425 9t. Red Cross (value at right) 45 45
b. Self-adhesive gum 45 45

Nos. 424/5 were issued together in *se-tenant* horizontal pairs within the sheet, each pair forming a composite design of a link in a chain.

For compulsory use from 1 to 7 November.

(Des A. Cufer. Litho)

1999 (18 Nov). Christmas. T **166** and similar vert design. Multicoloured. P 14.

426 17t. Type **166** 50 50
a. Booklet pane. No. 426×10 .... 5·25
b. Booklet pane. No. 426×5 and 428×3, plus two labels .... 4·50
427 18t. Type **166** 55 55
428 80t. Letter "h" illuminated with Nativity scene (Kranj antiphonary) .... 1·30 1·30
429 90t. As No. 428 .... 1·40 1·40
426/429 *Set of 4* .... 3·25 3·25

The booklet panes have a perforated margin around the block of stamps.

167 Teddy Bear and Baby's Bottle

(Des Marjana Šegula. Litho)

2000 (20 Jan). Greetings Stamp. P 14.

430 **167** 34t. multicoloured 85 85

168 Masqueraders

(Des Milena Gregorčič. Litho)

2000 (20 Jan). Pustôvi Carnival Masks. T **168** and similar horiz design. Multicoloured. P 14.

431 34t. Type **168** 45 45
432 80t. Four masqueraders .... 1·20 1·20

169 Sailing Ship and Tone Seliškar (writer) **170** Stage Coach

(Des N. Kolekivizem. Litho)

2000 (20 Jan). Birth Centenaries. T **169** and similar vert design. Multicoloured. P 14.

433 64t. Type **169** .... 1·10 1·10
434 120t. Elvira Kralj (actress) and actors holding masks .... 1·60 1·60

(Des K. Rodman. Litho)

2000 (20 Jan). 500th Anniv of Postal Service in Slovenia. P 14.

435 **170** 500t. multicoloured .... 7·00 7·00

171 Mt. Storžic **172** Muri the Tom Cat

(Des Botas Studio. Litho)

2000 (21 Mar). P 14.

436 **171** 18t. multicoloured 55 55

(Des Suzana Duhovnik. Litho)

2000 (21 Mar). Characters from Children's Books. T **172** and similar vert designs. Multicoloured.

(a) Sheet stamps. P 14

437 20t. Type **172** .... 1·10 1·10
438 20t. Mojca Pokrajculja .... 1·10 1·10
439 20t. Pedenjped .... 1·10 1·10

(b) Self-adhesive booklet stamps. Die-cut wavy edge

440 20t. Type **172** 55 55
441 20t. As No. 438 .... 55 55

442 20t. As No. 439 ... 55 55
437/442 *Set of* 6 ... 4·50 4·50

The booklet also contains nine self-adhesive greetings labels. The individual stamps are peeled directly from the booklet cover and cannot be collected as separate panes.

173 Swallows

(Des Darja Breèko. Litho)

2000 (21 Mar). 55th Anniv Return of Slovene Exiles. P 14.
443 **173** 25t. multicoloured ... 65 65

174 Trilobite

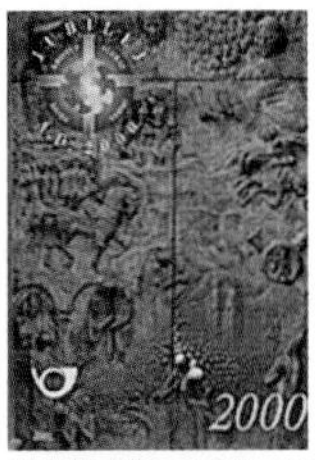

175 Ljubljana Cathedral Doors

(Des M. Učakar. Litho)

2000 (21 Mar). Fossil and Mineral. T **174** and similar horiz design. Multicoloured. P 14.
444 80t. Type **174** ... 1·50 1·50
445 90t. Magnesium-tourmaline ... 1·60 1·60

(Des E. Berk. Litho)

2000 (21 Mar). Holy Year 2000. Sheet 60×90 mm. P 14.
MS446 **175** 2000t. multicoloured ... 33·00 33·00

176 Predjama Castle

177 Apple Blossom Weevil on Flower Bud

(Des Andrejka Èufer. Photo)

2000 (20 Apr). Castles. T **176** and similar vert designs. P 14.
447 1t. olive-brown and bistre ... 10 10
a. Pair. Nos. 447/48 ... 25 25
448 1t. olive-brown and bistre ... 10 10
449 100t. purple-brown and red-brown ... 1·80 1·80
a. Pair. Nos. 449/50 ... 3·75 3·75
450 100t. purple-brown and red-brown ... 1·80 1·80
447/450 *Set of* 4 ... 3·50 3·50

Designs:—No. 448 Velenje Castle; 449 Podsreda Castle; 450 Bled Castle. Stamps of the same value were issued together in *se-tenant* pairs within their sheets.

(Des M. Učakar. Litho)

2000 (20 Apr). The Apple. T **177** and similar vert designs. Multicoloured. P 14.
451 10t. Type **177** ... 10 10
a. Horiz strip of 3. Nos. 451/3 ... 35
452 10t. Apple blossom ... 10 10
453 10t. Apple ... 10 10
451/453 *Set of* 3 ... 25 25

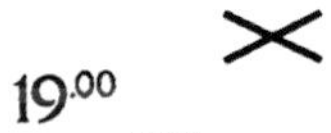

(**178**)

179 Red Cross

2000 (20 Apr). No. 189*e* surch with T **178**.
454 19t. on 17t. chocolate, yellow and light brown ... 40 40

2000 (8 May). OBLIGATORY TAX. Red Cross Week. P 14.
455 **179** 10t. scarlet and black ... 75 75
a. Self-adhesive gum ... 75 75

For compulsory use from 8 to 15 May.

180 Globe and Radio Operator

181 Chicken and Football

(Des P. Skalar. Litho)

2000 (9 May). Third World Radiosport Team Championship and 50th Anniv of Amateur Radio in Slovenia. P 14.
456 **180** 20t. multicoloured ... 55 55

(Des Novi Kolektivizem. Litho)

2000 (9 May). European Football Championship, Belgium and The Netherlands. P 14.
457 **181** 40t. multicoloured ... 1·60 1·60

182 Racing Dinghies

183 "Building Europe"

(Des D. Brajiè. Litho)

2000 (9 May). Olympic Games, Sydney. T **182** and similar horiz design. Multicoloured. P 14.
458 80t. Type **182** ... 2·10 2·10
a. Horiz pair. Nos. 458/9 ... 4·50 4·50
459 90t. Sydney Opera House ... 2·20 2·20

Nos. 458/9 were issued together in horizontal *se-tenant* pairs within sheetlets of six stamps, each pair forming a composite design.

(Des J.-P. Cousin. Litho)

2000 (9 May). Europa. P 14.
460 **183** 90t. multicoloured ... 4·25 4·25

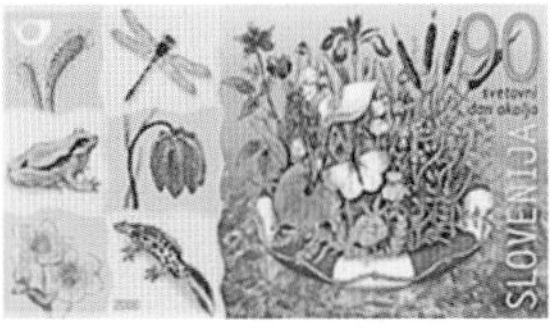

184 Flowers, Frog, Dragonfly and Plants within Life Ring

(Des A. Èufer. Litho)

2000 (9 May). World Environment Day. P 14.
461 **184** 90t. multicoloured ... 22·00 22·00

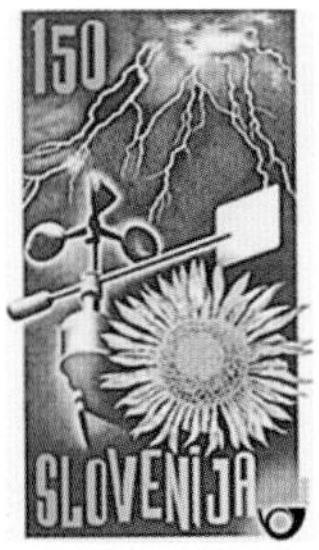

185 Lightning, Weather Vane and Carline Thistle

186 Cherry Blossom

(Des B. Fajon. Litho)

2000 (9 May). World Meteorological Day. 150th Anniv of Meteorological Observation in Slovenia. P 14.
462 **185** 150t. multicoloured ... 22·00 22·00

(Des M. Učakar. Litho)

2000 (23 June). The Cherry. T **186** and similar vert designs. Multicoloured. P 14.
463 5t. Type **186** ... 10 10
a. Horiz strip of 3. Nos. 463/5 ... 35
464 5t. European cherry fruit fly ... 10 10
465 5t. Vigred sweet cherries ... 10 10
463/465 *Set of* 3 ... 25 25

Nos. 463/5 were issued together in *se-tenant* strips of three stamps within the sheet.

187 Ptuj Castle

188 Zelen Grape

(Des A. Cufer. Litho)

2000 (23 June). Castles and Manor Houses (1st series). T **187** and similar vert designs. P 14.
466 A (18t.) deep yellow-brown and orange-yellow ... 65 65
a. Pair. Nos. 466/7 ... 1·40 1·40
467 A (18t.) deep yellow-brown and orange-yellow ... 65 65
468 B (19t.) olive-brown and bright green ... 75 75
a. Pair. Nos. 468/9 ... 1·60 1·60
469 B (19t.) olive-brown and bright green ... 75 75
466/469 *Set of* 4 ... 2·50 2·50

Designs:—No. 466, Type **187**; 467, Otocec Castle; 468, Žužemberk Castle; 469, Turjak Castle.

Nos. 466/7 and 468/9 respectively were issued in *se-tenant* pairs within the sheets.

See also Nos. 520/3 and 646.

(Des A. Sedmak. Litho)

2000 (15 Sept). Wine Grapes. T **188** and similar vert designs. Multicoloured. P 14.
470 20t. Type **188** ... 45 45
471 40t. Ranfol ... 65 65
472 80t. Žametovka ... 1·30 1·30
473 130t. Rumeni plavec ... 2·00 2·00
470/473 *Set of* 4 ... 4·00 4·00
MS474 134×100 mm. Nos. 470/3 ... 4·25 4·25

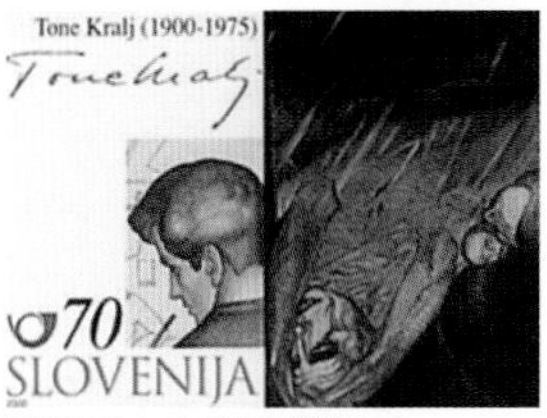

189 "Self-portrait" and "Storm"

(Des E. Berk. Litho)

2000 (15 Sept). Birth Centenary of Tone Kralj (artist). T **189** and similar horiz design. Multicoloured. P 14.
475 70t. Type **189** ... 1·00 1·00
a. Pair. Nos. 475/6 ... 2·30 2·30
476 80t. "Self-portrait" and "Judita" ... 1·20 1·20

Nos. 475/6 were issued together in *se-tenant* pairs within the sheet.

190 Iztok Čop and Luka Špik (coxless pairs)

(Des D. Brajič. Litho)

2000 (16 Oct). Olympic Gold Medal Winners. T **190** and similar horiz designs. Multicoloured. P 14.
477 21t. Type **190** ... 55 55
478 21t. Rajmond Debevec (rifle-shooting) ... 55 55

2000 (1 Nov). OBLIGATORY TAX. Solidarity Week. Vert designs as T **138**. Each grey, black and scarlet. Litho. P 14.
479 10t. Type **191** ... 1·10 1·10
a. Horiz pair. Nos. 479/80 ... 2·30 2·30
b. Self-adhesive gum ... 1·10 1·10
ba. Horiz pair. Nos. 479b/80b ... 2·30 2·30
480 10t. Red Cross (value at right) ... 1·10 1·10
b. Self-adhesive gum ... 1·10 1·10

Nos. 479/80 were issued together in horizontal *se-tenant* pairs, each pair forming a composite design.

For compulsory use from 1 to 7 November.

191 Healthy and Damaged Environments

(Des L. Rubins. Litho)

2000 (21 Nov). New Millennium. EXPO 2000 World's Fair, Hanover, Germany. P 14.
481 **191** 40t. multicoloured ... 55 55

192 Open Book and Tree

193 Children

(Des D. Erdelji. Litho)

2000 (21 Nov). 450th Anniv of First Printed Book in Slovenian Language. P 14.
482 **192** 50t. multicoloured ... 75 75

(Des J. Reichman. Litho)

2000 (21 Nov). Christmas. T **193** and similar horiz design. Multicoloured.

(a) Sheet stamps. Ordinary gum. P 14
483 B (21t.) Type **193** ... 35 35
484 90t. Baby Jesus ... 1·30 1·30

(b) Booklet stamps. Self-adhesive gum. Die-cut wavy edge
485 B (21t.) Type **193** ... 35 35
486 90t. As No. 484 ... 1·30 1·30
483/486 *Set of* 4 ... 3·00 3·00

The booklets also contain two self-adhesive labels.
Nos. 485/6 are peeled directly from the covers and cannot be collected as separate panes.

194 Bucket (Dragotin Kette (poet))

195 Bride and Groom riding Bicycle

(Des Novi Kolektivizem. Litho)

2001 (19 Jan). Birth Anniversaries. T **194** and similar vert designs. Multicoloured. P 14.

487	A	(24t.) Type **194** (125th anniv)	55	55
488		95t. Jar of flowers (Ivan Tavcar (politician and writer)) (150th anniv)	1·50	1·50
489		107t. Cup of coffee (Ivan Cankar (writer)) (125th anniv)	1·60	1·60
487/489 *Set of 3*			3·25	3·25

(Des Marjana Šegula. Litho)

2001 (19 Jan). Wedding Greetings Stamp. P 14.

490	**195**	B (25t.) multicoloured	55	55

196 Colourful Headdresses

(Des Milena Gregorčič. Litho)

2001 (19 Jan). Dobrepolje Folk Masks. T **196** and similar horiz design. Multicoloured. P 14.

491	50t. Type **196**	55	55
492	95t. Procession	1·10	1·10

197 Mt. Jalovec

198 Cowboy Pipec

(Des A. Sedmak. Litho)

2001 (21 Mar). P 14.

493	**197**	B (25t.) multicoloured	85	85

2001 (21 Mar). Cowboy Pipec (cartoon character) by Božo Kos. T **198** and similar horiz design. Multicoloured. Litho.

(a) Sheet stamps. Ordinary gum. P 14

494	B	(25t.) Type **198**	1·10	1·10
495	B	(25t.) Beetroot (Native American boy)	1·10	1·10

(b) Booklet stamps. Self-adhesive gum. Die-cut wavy edge

496	B	(25t.) Type **198**	85	85
497	B	(25t.) As No. 495	85	85
494/497 *Set of 4*			3·50	3·50

Nos. 485/6 are peeled directly from the covers and therefore cannot be collected as separate panes.

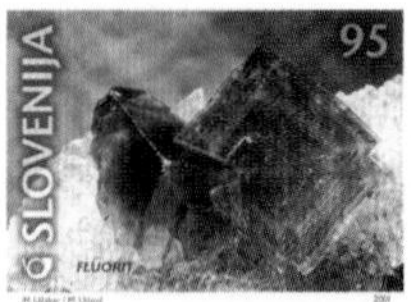

199 Fluorite

(Des M. Učakar. Litho)

2001 (21 Mar). T **199** and similar horiz design. Multicoloured. P 14.

498	95t. Type **199**	1·50	1·50
	a. Horiz pair	3·25	3·25

No. 498 covers any one of two stamps which were issued together in horizontal se-tenant pairs, the position of the pieces of fluorite differing on each stamp. The pair is stated to produce a three-dimensional image without the use of a special viewer.
No. 498 was issued with a *se-tenant* label.

200 Fossilized Starfish

(Des M. Učakar. Litho)

2001 (21 Mar). P 14.

499	**200**	107t. multicoloured	1·60	1·60

201 Stars, Goddess Europa and Bull

202 Soca River and Bridge, Solkan

(Des A. Cufer. Litho)

2001 (21 Mar). Europe Day (9 May). P 14.

500	**201**	221t. multicoloured	2·50	2·50

(Des J. Bavčer. Litho)

2001 (21 Mar). Millenary of Solkan. P 14.

501	**202**	261t. multicoloured	2·75	2·75

203 Dove with Lime Leaf

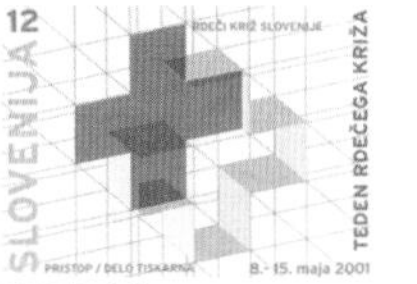

204 Red Cross

(Des M. Licul. Litho)

2001 (24 Apr). 60th Anniv of Liberation Front. P 14.

502	**203**	24t. multicoloured	85	85

2001 (8 May). OBLIGATORY TAX. Red Cross Week. P 14.

503	**204**	12t. bright scarlet and slate	75	75
		a. Self-adhesive gum	75	75

For compulsory use from 8 to 15 May.

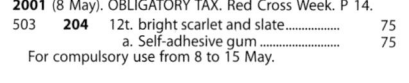

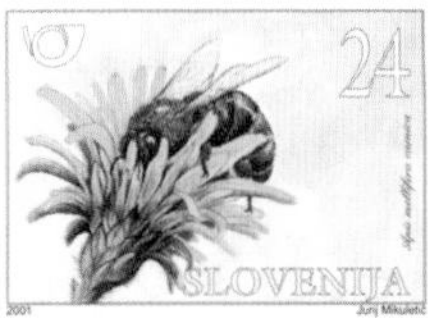

205 Worker Bee gathering Nectar

(Des J. Mikuletic. Litho)

2001 (23 May). The Carniolan Honey Bee (*Apis mellifera carnica*). Sheet 113×80 mm containing T **205** and similar horiz designs. Multicoloured. P 14.

MS504	24t. Type **205**; 48t. Queen bee and drones; 95t. Queen, workers and drones on edge of honeycomb; 170t. Building and swarm	4·25	4·25

206 Flag

(Des B. Fajon. Litho)

2001 (23 May). Tenth Anniv of Independence. P 14.

505	**206**	100t. multicoloured	2·75	2·75

207 Gospodicna Spring, Gorjanci

208 Tramcar No. 5

(Des Agency Kraft & Werk. Litho)

2001 (23 May). Europa. Water Resources. P 14.

506	**207**	107t. multicoloured	2·20	2·20

(Des M. Učakar. Litho)

2001 (23 May). Centenary of Introduction of Trams to Ljubljana. P 14.

507	**208**	113t. multicoloured	2·20	2·20

209 Maxi-Ball and Ljubljana Skyline

210 American and Russian Flags behind Dragon Bridge, Ljubljana

(Des Studio Botas. Litho)

2001 (23 May). Sixth World Maxi-Basketball Championship, Ljubljana. P 14.

508	**209**	261t. multicoloured	3·25	3·25

(Des M. Licul. Litho)

2001 (14 June). First Summit Meeting between Pres. George W. Bush of America and Pres. Vladimir Putin of Russian Federation, Brdo Castle, Kranj. P 14.

509	**210**	107t. multicoloured	1·60	1·60
MS510		60×90 mm. No. 509	1·60	1·60

211 Peach Blossom

212 "Mohorjev koledar" 1920 Calendar Cover

(Des M. Učakar. Litho)

2001 (21 July). Peach Cultivation. T **211** and similar vert designs. Multicoloured. P 14.

511	50t. Type **211**	55	55
	a. Horiz strip of 3. Nos. 511/13	1·80	
512	50t. Green peach aphid	55	55
513	50t. Redhaven peach	55	55
511/513 *Set of 3*		1·50	1·50

Nos. 511/13 were issued together in *se-tenant* strips of three stamps within the sheet.

(Des K. Kopac and M. Paternoster. Litho)

2001 (4 Sept). 150th Anniv of Mohorjeva Družba Publishing House. P 14.

514	**212**	B (31t.) multicoloured	85	85

213 Logarithms, Building and Globe

(Des K. Rodman. Litho)

2001 (21 Sept). Centenary of Jurij Vega Grammar School, Idrija. P 14.

515	**213**	A (26t.) multicoloured	75	75

214 Score and Blaž Arnic

(Des B. Jakac and D. Brajič. Litho)

2001 (21 Sept). Composers. T **214** and similar horz design. Multicoloured. P 14.

516	95t. Type **214**	1·10	1·10
517	107t. Lucijan Marija Škerjanc and score	1·60	1·60

215 Cat

216 Children encircling Globe

(Des M. Dolinar. Litho)

2001 (21 Sept). World Animal Day (4th October). P 14.

518	**215**	107t. multicoloured	1·60	1·60

(Des Agency Kraft & Werk and Urska Golob. Litho)

2001 (21 Sept). United Nations Year of Dialogue among Civilizations. P 14.

519 **216** 107t. multicoloured .... 2·75 2·75

2001 (4 Oct). Castles and Manor Houses (2nd series). Vert designs as T **187**. P 14.

520	C (95t.) lake-brown and vermilion	1·10	1·10
	a. Pair. Nos. 520/1	2·30	2·30
521	C (95t.) lake-brown and vermilion	1·10	1·10
522	D (107t.) deep blue and new blue	1·30	1·30
	a. Pair. Nos. 522/3	2·75	2·75
523	D (107t.) indigo and new blue	1·30	1·30
520/523 *Set of 4*		4·25	4·25

Designs:—No. 520, Dobrovo Manor; 521, Brežice Castle; 522, Olimje Manor; 523, Murska Sobota Manor.

Nos. 520/1 and 522/3 respectively were issued in *se-tenant* pairs within the sheet.

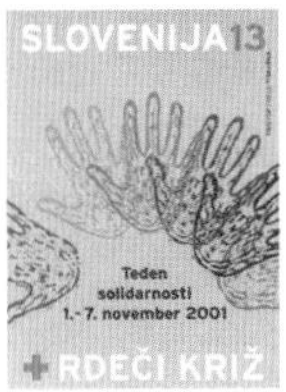

217 Handprints

218 Christmas Tree

(Des Pristop. Litho)

2001 (1 Nov). OBLIGATORY TAX. Solidarity Week. P 14.

524 **217** 13t. multicoloured 75 75

For compulsory use from 1 to 7 November.

(Des Suzana Duhovnik. Litho)

2001 (16 Nov). Christmas. T **218** and similar vert design. Multicoloured.

(a) Sheet stamps. Ordinary gum. P 14

525	B (31t.) Type **218**	35	35
526	D (107t.) Nativity	1·30	1·30

(b) Booklet stamps. Self-adhesive gum. Die-cut 7½

527	B (31t.) Type **218**	35	35
528	D (107t.) As No. 526	1·30	1·30
525/528 *Set of 4*		3·00	3·00

Nos. 527/8 are peeled directly from the covers and cannot therefore be collected as separate panes.

219 Wood Carving

220 Rusa (animal) Mask

(Des Vesna Berk. Litho)

2002 (23 Jan). Greetings Stamp. P 14.

529 **219** B (31t.) multicoloured 55 55

(Des Manica Klenovšek and Milena Gregorčič. Litho)

2002 (23 Jan). Ptuj Folk Masks. T **220** and similar vert design. Multicoloured. P 14.

530	56t. Type **220**	65	65
531	95t. Picek (cockerel) mask	1·00	1·00

221 Jože Plecnik

222 Toboggan

(Des K. Rodman. Litho)

2002 (23 Jan). Birth Anniversaries. T **221** and similar vert design. Multicoloured. P 14.

532	95t. Type **221** (architect) (130th)	1·00	1·00
533	107t. Janko Kersnik (writer and politician) (150th)	1·10	1·10

(Des Manica Klenovšek and Mateja Pocajt. Litho)

2002 (23 Jan). Winter Olympic Games, Salt Lake City. T **222** and similar vert design. Multicoloured. P 14.

534	95t. Type **222**	1·10	1·10
	a. Pair. Nos. 534/5	2·50	2·50
535	107t. Skier	1·30	1·30

Nos. 534/5 were issued in *se-tenant* pairs within sheetlets of six stamps and three labels.

223 Easter Eggs

224 Alpine clematis (*Clematis alpina*) Martuljek Mountains, Triglav National Park

(Des M. Licul. Litho)

2002 (28 Feb). Easter (B) and Palm Sunday (D). T **223** and similar vert design. Multicoloured. P 14.

536	B (31t.) Type **223**	35	35
537	D (107t.) Butarice	1·30	1·30

(Des Z. Simic. Litho)

2002 (21 Mar). Mountains. T **224** and similar horiz design. Multicoloured. P 14.

538	A (30t.) Type **224**	55	55
539	D (107t.) Carniolan lily (*Lilium carniolicum*) and Mt. Spik	1·10	1·10

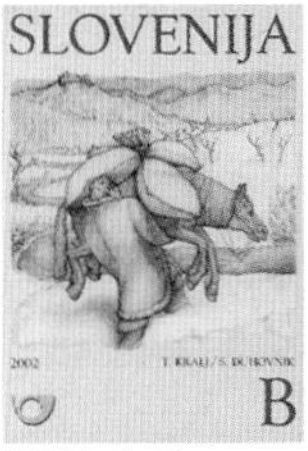

225 Martin Krpan carrying his horse

226 Fossilized Fly

(Des Suzana Duhovinik and T. Kralj. Litho)

2002 (21 Mar). Martin Krpan (character from book by Fran Levstik). T **225** and similar vert designs. Multicoloured.

(a) Sheet stamps. Ordinary gum. P 14

540	B (31t.) Type **225**	1·50	1·50
541	B (31t.) Martin Krpan at forge	1·50	1·50
542	B (31t.) Martin Krpan in Ljubljana	1·50	1·50

(b) Booklet stamps. Self-adhesive gum. Die-cut perf 11

543	B (31t.) As No. 540	1·50	1·50
544	B (31t.) As No. 541	1·50	1·50
545	B (31t.) As No. 542	1·50	1·50
540/545 *Set of 6*		8·00	8·00

(Des M. Učakar and M. Grm. Litho)

2002 (21 Mar). P 14.

546 **226** C (95t.) multicoloured .... 1·80 1·80

227 Monastery and view of Kostanjevica on the Krka

228 Man carrying Heart

(Des Z. Simic. Litho)

2002 (21 Mar). 750th Anniversary of First Written Record of Kostanjevica on the Krka. P 14.

547 **227** D (107t.) multicoloured .... 1·90 1·90

2002 (8 May). OBLIGATORY TAX. Red Cross Week. P 14.

548	**228**	15t. multicoloured	1·20	1·20
		a. Self-adhesive gum	1·20	1·20

For compulsory use from 8 to 15 May.

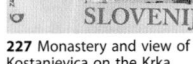

229 Dog Rose (*Rosa canina*)

230 Mouse supporting Elephant

(Des Z. Simic. Litho)

2002 (22 May). Medicinal Plants. T **229** and similar vert designs. Multicoloured. P 14.

549	A (30t.) Type **229**	1·20	1·20
550	B (31t.) Camomile (*Chamomilla recutita*)	1·20	1·20
551	C (95t.) Valerian (*Valeriana officinalis*)	1·40	1·40
549/551 *Set of 3*		3·50	3·50
MS552	60×70 mm. D (107t.) Sweet violet (*Viola odorata*)	1·80	1·80

(Des L. Rubins. Litho)

2002 (22 May). Europa. Circus. P 14.

553 **230** D (107t.) multicoloured .... 22·00 22·00

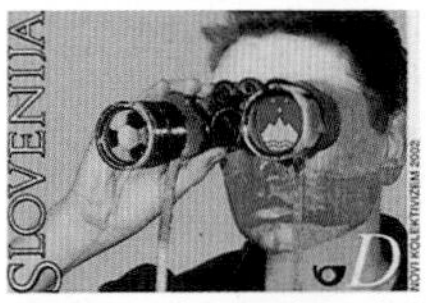

231 Man with Painted Face holding Binoculars

(Des Novi Kolektivizem. Litho)

2002 (22 May). World Cup Football Championships, Japan and South Korea. P 14.

554 **231** D (107t.) multicoloured .... 1·80 1·80

232 Lake Bled enclosed in Map of Central Europe

(Des Studio Botas. Litho)

2002 (22 May). Ninth Central European States Presidential Conference, Bled. Sheet 65×87 mm containing T **232** and similar horiz design. P 14.

MS555 D (107t.) Type **232**; D (107t.) Central Europe map and Brdo Castle (conference venue) .... 3·00 3·00

233 Bilberry Flowers

234 Horse and Competition Emblem

(Des M. Učakar. Litho)

2002 (19 July). The Bilberry (*Vaccinium myrtillus*). T **233** and similar vert designs. Multicoloured. P 14.

556	150t. Type **233**	1·70	1·70
	a. Strip of 3. Nos. 556/8	5·25	
557	150t. Winter moth (pest)	1·70	1·70
558	150t. Bilberry fruit	1·70	1·70
556/558 *Set of 3*		4·50	4·50

Nos. 556/8 were issued in horizontal *se-tenant* strips of three stamps.

(Des M. Licul. Litho)

2002 (19 Sept). 35th Chess Olympiad, Bled. Sheet 70×70 mm containing T **234** and similar horiz design. P 14.

MS559 C (95t.) Type **234**; D (107t.) Fields and emblem .... 3·00 3·00

235 "Kolo" (dance)

(Des Milena Gregorčič. Litho)

2002 (19 Sept). Matija Jama (artist) Commemoration. T **235** and similar horiz design. Multicoloured. P 14.

560	95t. Type **235**	1·60	1·60
561	214t. "Village in Winter"	2·75	2·75

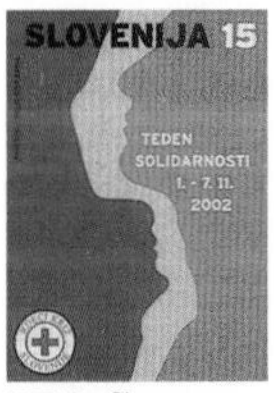

236 Profiles

237 Snowman

(Des Pristop. Litho)

2002 (1 Nov). OBLIGATORY TAX. Solidarity Week. P 14.

562	**236**	15t. multicoloured	1·20	1·20
		a. Self-adhesive gum	1·20	1·20

For compulsory use from 1 to 7 November.

(Des Jelka Reichman. Litho)

2002 (15 Nov). Christmas. T **237** and similar vert design. Multicoloured.

(a) Sheet stamps. Ordinary gum. P 14

563	B (31t.) Type **237**	50	50
564	D (107t.) Girl and house	1·30	1·30

(b) Booklet stamps. Self-adhesive gum. Die-cut perf 7½

565	B (31t.) Type **237**	50	50
566	D (107t.) As No. 564	1·30	1·30
563/566 *Set of 4*		2·75	2·75

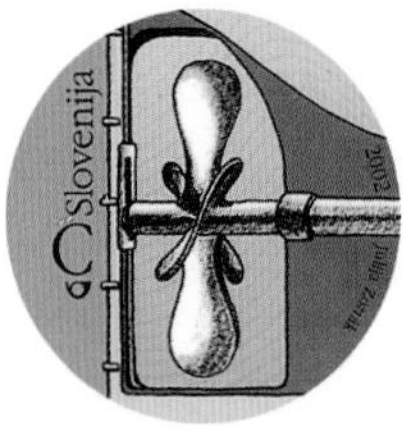

238 Screw Propeller

239 Couple

(Des Julija Zornik. Litho)

2002 (15 Nov). 175th Anniv of Patenting of the Screw Propeller by Josef Ressel. P 14.

567 **238** C (95t.) multicoloured .... 3·00 3·00

No. 567 was perforated in circle contained within an outer perforated square.

(Des Studio Arnold & Varga. Litho)

2003 (21 Jan). National Costumes. Slovene Istria. P 14.

568 **239** A (30t.) multicoloured 95 95

240 Cover of "Observationes Astromice" and Chinese Sextant

(Des Z. Simic. Litho)

2003 (21 Jan). Birth Anniversaries. T **240** and similar horiz design. Multicoloured. P 14.

569 107t. Type **240** (Ferdinand Auguštin Hellerstein, missionary and astronomer) (300th) .... 1·30 1·30

570 221t. Cover of "Flora Exiccata Carniocola" (Alfonz Paulin, botanist and writer) (150th) .... 3·00 3·00

241 Couple on Heart-shaped Balloon

(Des Jelka Reichman. Litho)

2003 (21 Jan). Greetings Stamp. P 11.

571 **241** 180t. multicoloured .... 2·40 2·40

No. 571 was perforated in a heart-shape contained within an outer perforated square and impregnated with the scent of roses which is released when the stamp is rubbed.

242 Three Vixens

243 Avenue of Stalactites

(Des Jelka Reichman. Litho)

2002 (24 Mar). Folk Tales. T **242** and similar multicoloured designs.

(a) Sheet stamps. Ordinary gum. P 14

572 B (31t.) Type **242** 60 60

573 B (31t.) The Golden Bird (vert) 60 60

(b) Booklet stamps. Self-adhesive gum. Die-cut perf 8

574 B (31t.) As No. 571 .... 60 60

575 B (31t.) As No. 572 (vert) 60 60

572/575 *Set of 4* .... 2·20 2·20

(Des Studio Botas. Litho)

2003 (24 Mar). Vilenica Cave, Lokev. P 14.

576 **243** D (107t.) multicoloured .... 1·20 1·20

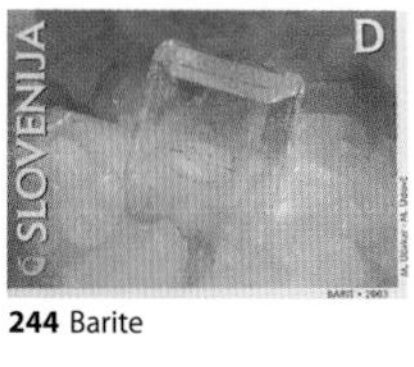

244 Barite

(Des M. Učakar. Litho)

2003 (24 Mar). P 14.

577 **244** D (107t.) multicoloured .... 1·20 1·20

245 Kamen Castle, Begunje

246 Red Droplet

(Des Andrejka Cufer. Litho)

2003 (24 Mar). P 14.

578 **245** 1000t. slate and new blue .... 11·00 11·00

2003 (8 May). OBLIGATORY TAX. Red Cross Week. Litho. P 14.

579 **246** 19t. bright scarlet and slate 85 85

a. Self-adhesive gum 85 85

For compulsory use from 8 to 15 May.

247 Poster, Bucket of Paste and Brush

248 Kresnik (fire spirit)

(Des M. Učakar. Litho)

2003 (22 May). Europa. Poster Art. P 14.

580 **247** D (107t.) multicoloured .... 1·40 1·40

(Des Andrejka Cufer. Litho)

2003 (22 May). Mythology. P 14.

581 **248** 110t. multicoloured .... 1·40 1·40

249 Goddess Europa riding Bull (Zeus)

250 Vilko and Slavko Avsenik

(Des Novi Kolektivizem. Litho)

2003 (22 May). European Water Polo Championships, Kranj and Ljubljana. P 14.

582 **249** 180t. multicoloured .... 2·40 2·40

(Des M. Učakar. Litho)

2003 (22 May). 50th Anniv of Avsenik (music) Ensamble (founded by Slavko Avsenik). Sheet 60×70 mm. P 14.

MS583 **250** 180t. multicoloured .... 2·40 2·40

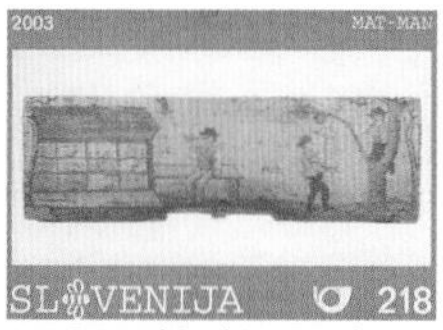

251 Painted Beehive Panel

(Des Mat-Man. Litho)

2003 (22 May). Bee Keeping. P 14.

584 **251** 218t. multicoloured .... 3·00 3·00

252 Letters showing Franking Marks

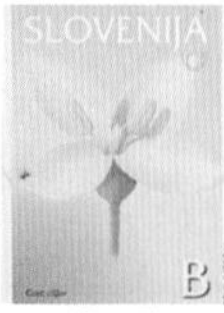

253 Olive Flowers

(Des L. Rubins. Litho)

2003 (18 Sept). Pre-Stamp Postage. P 14.

585 **252** A (30t.) multicoloured 60 60

(Des M. Učakar. Litho)

2002 (18 Sept). The Olive Tree. T **253** and similar vert designs. Multicoloured. P 14.

586 B (31t.) Type **253** 50 50

a. Strip of 3. Nos. 586/8 .... 1·60

587 B (31t.) Olive fruit fly (pest) 50 50

588 B (31t.) Olives 50 50

586/588 *Set of 3* .... 1·40 1·40

Nos. 586/8 were issued in horizontal *se-tenant* strips of three stamps.

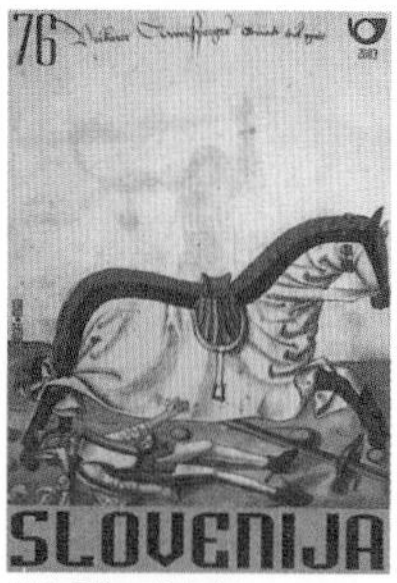

254 Fallen Knight

(Des Mat-Man. Litho)

2003 (18 Sept). Illustrations from Gašper Lamberger's Tournament Book. T **254** and similar vert design. Multicoloured. P 14.

589 76t. Type **254** .... 1·80 1·80

a. Pair. Nos. 589/90 .... 8·00 8·00

590 570t. Gasper Lamberger .... 6·00 6·00

Nos. 589/90 were issued in *se-tenant* pairs forming a composite design of two pages from the book.

255 Black-belted (Krško polje) Pig

256 Emblem

(Des J. Mikuletic. Litho)

2003 (18 Sept). Indigenous Farm Animals. T **255** and similar multicoloured designs. P 14.

591 95t. Type **255** .... 1·10 1·10

592 107t. Solcava sheep .... 1·20 1·20

593 107t. Cica cattle .... 2·40 2·40

591/593 *Set of 3* .... 4·25 4·25

MS594 60×70 mm. 368t. Styrian poultry (vert) .... 4·75 4·75

2003 (1 Nov). OBLIGATORY TAX. Solidarity Week. Litho. P 14.

595 **256** 19t. multicoloured 85 85

a. Self-adhesive gum 85 85

For compulsory use from 1 to 7 November.

257 Automatic Sorting Machine and www.posta.si

258 Post Office Door, Zgormji Otok

(Des M. Učakar. Litho and foil die-stamped Enschedé)

2003 (11 Nov). Mail Sorting and Logistics Centre, Maribor. P 14.

596 **257** 221t. multicoloured .... 2·40 2·40

(Des M. Licul. Litho)

2003 (19 Nov). Cultural Heritage. T **258** and similar vert designs. Multicoloured. P 14.

597 A (38t.) Type **258** 35 35

598 B (44t.) Fishing boat, Piran 50 50

599 C (95t.) Scythe, Ljubno ob Savinji 95 95

600 D (107t.) Horse-collar comb .... 1·20 1·20

597/600 *Set of 4* .... 2·75 2·75

259 Parcel, Flowers, Bell, Bauble and Fir Twig

(Des Z. Simic. Litho)

2003 (19 Nov). Christmas. T **259** and similar horiz design. Multicoloured.

(a) Sheet stamps. P 14

601 B (44t.) Type **259** 85 85

602 D (107t.) The Nativity .... 1·40 1·40

(b) Self-adhesive booklet stamps. Die-cut perf 8

603 B (44t.) No. 601 .... 85 85

604 D (107t.) No. 602 .... 1·40 1·40

601/604 *Set of 4* .... 4·00 4·00

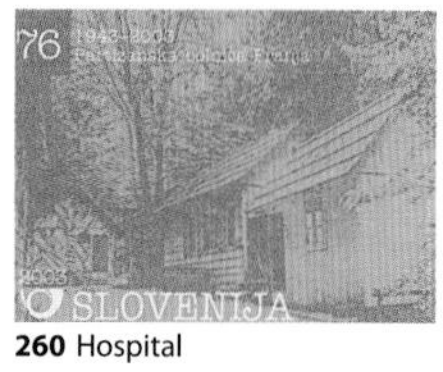

260 Hospital

(Des Studio Arnold+Vuga. Litho)

2003 (19 Nov). 60th Anniv of Franja Partisan Hospital. P 14.

605 **260** 76t. sepia and bronze .... 1·40 1·40

261 Parizar (cart)

262 Couple, Vipava Valley

(Des A. Cufer. Litho)

2003 (19 Nov). P 14.
606 **261** 221t. multicoloured .... 3·50 3·50

(Des Studio Arnold+Vuga. Litho)

2004 (22 Jan). National Costumes. P 14.
607 **262** A (38t.) multicoloured .... 1·00 1·00

263 Soldiers marching through Snow

(Des Studio Botas and J. Petek. Litho)

2004 (22 Jan). 60th Anniv of 14th Division's March to Stajerska. P 14.
608 **263** B (44t.) multicoloured .... 1·00 1·00

264 Edvard Kocbek and Script

(Des S. Duhovnik and M. Smerke. Litho)

2004 (22 Jan). Birth Centenary of Edvard Kocbek (writer and politician). P 14.
609 **264** D (107t.) multicoloured .... 2·00 2·00

265 Two Cats

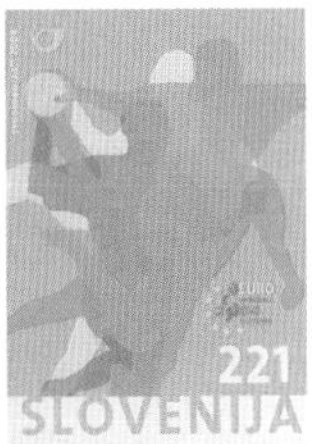

266 Players

(Des Studio Arnold+Vuga and G. Vahen. Litho)

2004 (22 Jan). Greeting Stamp. P 14.
610 **265** 180t. multicoloured .... 3·00 3·00

No. 610 was perforated in a heart-shape contained within an outer perforated square.

(Des Studio Botas. Litho)

2004 (22 Jan). Sixth European Men's Handball Championships, Slovenia. P 14.
611 **266** 221t. multicoloured .... 3·50 3·50

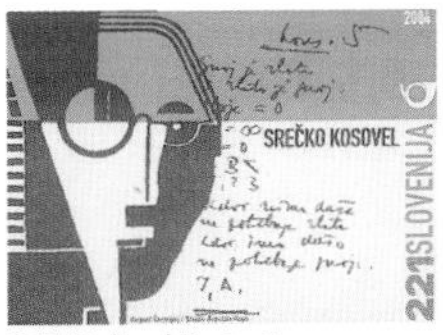

267 Stylized Portrait

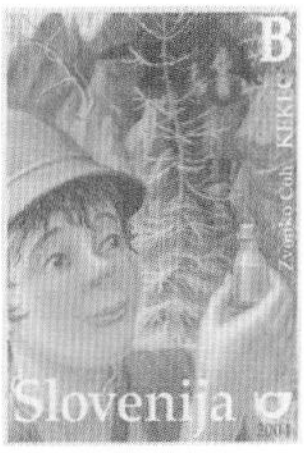

268 Keckec

(Des A. Cernigoi and Studio Arnold+Vuga. Litho)

2004 (22 Jan). Birth Centenary of Srecko Kosovel (writer). P 14.
612 **267** 221t. vermilion and black .... 3·50 3·50

(Des Z. Coh. Litho)

2004 (24 Mar). Keckec (character from children's stories created by Josip Vandot). T **268** and similar vert designs. Multicoloured.

(a) PVA gum. P 14.

613 B (44t.) Type **268** 90 90
614 B (44t.) Pehta 90 90
615 B (44t.) Kosobrin 90 90

(b) Self-adhesive booklet stamps. Die-cut wavy edge

615*a* B (44t.) As Type **268** 90 90
615*b* B (44t.) As No. 614 .... 90 90
615*c* B (44t.) As No. 615 .... 90 90
613/615*c* *Set of* 6 .... 4·75 4·75

Nos. 615*a*/*c* have wavy edges simulating perforations and were issued, each×3, in booklets of nine stamps.

269 Gymnast

(Des MediaArt. Litho)

2004 (24 Mar). European Men's Artistic Gymnastic Championship, Ljubljana. P 14.
616 **269** D (107t.) multicoloured .... 2·10 2·10

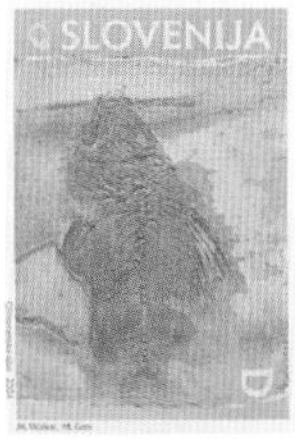

270 Fossilized Fish

(Des M. Učakar. Litho)

2004 (24 Mar). P 14.
617 **270** D (107t.) multicoloured .... 2·10 2·10

271 Bled Castle

272 NATO Emblem

(Des K. Rodman. Litho)

2004 (24 Mar). Bled (town) Millenary. P 14.
618 **271** 218t. multicoloured .... 3·75 3·75

(Des M. Učakar. Litho)

2004 (2 Apr). Slovenia's Accession to North Atlantic Treaty Organization (NATO). P 14.
619 **272** D (107t.) ultramarine and orange-yellow .... 1·90 1·90

273 Stars and New Member's Flags

273a Blood Clot

2004 (1 May). Slovenia's Accession to European Union. Litho. P 14.
620 **273** 95t. multicoloured .... 1·80 1·80

2004 (8 May). OBLIGATORY TAX. Red Cross Week. T **273a** and similar horiz design. Litho. P 14.

620*a* 19t. Type **273a** 35 35
a. Block of 4. Nos. 620*a*/*d* .... 1·50
aa. Self-adhesive gum 35 35
aab. Block of 4. Nos. 620aa/620da .... 1·50
620*b* 19t. Girl 35 35
ba. Self-adhesive gum 35 35
620*c* 19t. Bandaged head 35 35
ca. Self-adhesive gum 35 35
620*d* 19t. Elderly woman 35 35
da. Self-adhesive gum 35 35
620a/620d *Set of* 4 .... 1·30 1·30

Nos. 620*a*/*d* were issued in *se-tenant* blocks of four stamps within the sheet, each block forming a central red cross emblem.

274 Iovrenc Kosir and Birthplace

(Des L. Rubens. Litho)

2004 (21 May). Birth Bicentenary of Iovrenc Kosir (postage stamp pioneer). P 14.
621 **274** B (48t.) multicoloured .... 1·00 1·00

275 Discus

276 Fish with Umbrella

(Des M. Pocajt (mat-man). Litho)

2004 (21 May). Olympic Games, Athens. T **275** and similar horiz design. Multicoloured. P 14.
622 C (95t.) Type **275** .... 1·60 1·60
a. Pair. Nos. 622/3 .... 3·75 3·75
623 D (107t.) Long jump .... 1·80 1·80

Nos. 622/3 were issued in horizontal *se-tenant* pairs within the sheet, each pair forming a composite design.

(Des D. Erdelj. Litho)

2004 (21 May). Europa. Holidays. P 14.
624 **276** D (107t.) multicoloured .... 2·00 2·00

277 Bicycle Chain Wheel

(Des M. Licul. Litho)

2004 (21 May). Puch Bicycles (bicycle manufacture pioneer). P 14.
625 **277** 110t. multicoloured .... 2·00 2·00

278 Miller and Wife (1869)

279 Town House, Trbovlje

(Des Studio Arnold+Vuga and T. Jesenicnik. Litho)

2004 (21 May). Painted Beehive Panels. P 14.
626 **278** 218t. multicoloured .... 3·75 3·75

(Des J. Zornik. Litho)

2004 (3 July). P 14.
627 **279** B (48t.) multicoloured .... 1·00 1·00

280 Posthorn

281 Crni Kal Viaduct

(Des M. Učakar. Litho)

2004 (3 July). Self-adhesive Booklet Stamps. Die-cut perf 12½.
628 **280** B (48t.) new blue and orange-yellow 80 80

(Des S. Radovan and M. Kambic. Litho)

2004 (15 Sept). Completion of Crni Kal Viaduct between Ljubljana and Klanec-Srmin. Sheet 70×60 mm. P 14.
MS629 **281** 95t. multicoloured .... 1·80 1·80

The stamp and margin of No. **MS**629 form a composite design.

282 Pear Flowers

283 Marsh Helleborine (*Epipactis palustris*)

(Des M. Učakar. Litho)

2004 (22 Sept). William Pear (fruit tree). T **282** and similar vert designs. Multicoloured. P 14.
630 A (45t.) Type **282** 85 85
a. Strip of 3. Nos. 630/2 .... 2·75
631 A (45t.) Fruit fly (pest) 85 85
632 A (45t.) Pear 85 85
630/632 *Set of* 3 .... 2·30 2·30

Nos. 630/2 were issued in horizontal *se-tenant* strips of three stamps within the sheet.

(Des J. Zornik. Litho)

2004 (22 Sept). Cultural Heritage. Vert design as T **258**. Multicoloured. P 14.
633 D (107t.) Cupa (fishing boat) .... 2·00 2·00

(Des Z. Simic. Litho)

2004 (22 Sept). Orchids. T **283** and similar horiz design. Multicoloured. P 14.

634 B (52t.) Type **283** ... 1·00 1·00
MS635 70×60 mm D (107t.) Spider orchid (*Ophrys holosericea*) ... 2·00 2·00

284 "750"

(Des Z. Simic. Litho)

2004 (22 Sept). 750th Anniversary of First Documentation of Maribor Town. P 14.

636 **284** C (95t.) multicoloured ... 1·80 1·80

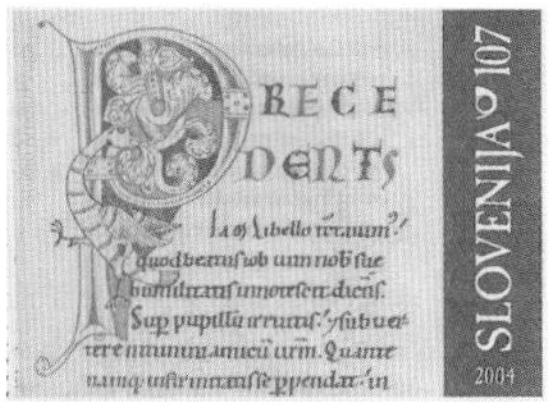

285 Illuminated Writing

(Des Studio Arnold+Vuga. Litho)

2004 (22 Sept). Romanesque Art. T **285** and similar horiz design. Multicoloured. P 14.

637 107t. Type **285** ... 1·90 1·90
a. Pair. Nos. 637/8 ... 4·00 4·00
638 107t. Illuminated writing (different) ... 1·90 1·90

Nos. 637/8 were issued in horizontal *se-tenant* pairs within the sheet.

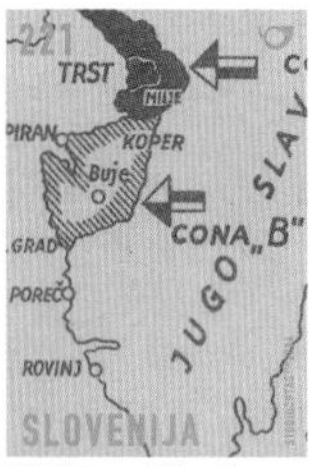

286 Map of Southern Europe

286a Air Drop and Roof

(Des Studio Botas. Litho)

2004 (22 Sept). 50th Anniv of London Memorandum (Italy—Slovenia border demarcation agreement). Sheet 60×70 mm. P 14.

MS639 **286** 221t. multicoloured ... 4·00 4·00

The stamp and margin of No. **MS**639 form a composite design.

2004 (1 Nov). OBLIGATORY TAX. Solidarity Week. T **286a** and similar horiz designs forming burning house. Multicoloured. Litho. P 14.

639*a* 23t. Type **286a** ... 50 50
a. Block of 4. Nos. 639*a/d* ... 2·10
aa. Self-adhesive gum ... 50 50
b. Block of 4. Nos. 639aa/ad ... 2·10
639*b* 23t. Burning roof ... 50 50
ba. Self-adhesive gum ... 50 50
639*c* 23t. Red cross parcels and flower boxes ... 50 50
ca. Self-adhesive gum ... 50 50
639*d* 23t. Damage to lower right of house ... 50 50
da. Self-adhesive gum ... 50 50
639*a*/639*d* *Set of* 4 ... 1·80 1·80

Nos. 639*a/d* were issued in *se-tenant* blocks of four stamps within the sheet, each block forming a composite design of a house. For compulsory use from 1 to 7 November.

287 Children under Umbrella

(Des J. Reichman. Litho)

2004 (18 Nov). Christmas. T **287** and similar vert design. Multicoloured.

(a) Sheet stamps. P 14

640 A (45t.) Type **287** ... 1·00 1·00
641 C (95t.) Jesus enclosed in tree ... 1·80 1·80

(b) Self-adhesive booklet stamps. Die-cut perf 8

642 B (45t.) No. 640 ... 1·00 1·00
643 D (95t.) No. 641 ... 1·80 1·80
640/643 *Set of* 4 ... 5·00 5·00

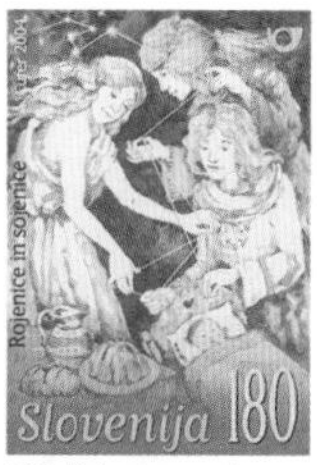

288 Prekmurje Pie Cake

289 Rojenice and Sojenice (Fates)

(Des J. Zomik. Litho)

2004 (18 Nov). Gastronomy. T **288** and similar vert design. Multicoloured. P 14.

644 52t. Type **288** ... 85 85
a. Pair. Nos. 644/5 ... 1·80 1·80
645 52t. Bograc Goulash ... 85 85

Nos. 644/5 were issued in *se-tenant* pairs within the sheet.

(Des A. Cufer. Litho)

2004 (18 Nov). Castles and Manor Houses (3rd series). Vert designs as T **187**. P 14.

646 C (95t.) sepia and bright orange ... 1·80 1·80

Design:–No. 646, Gewerkenegg Castle.

(Des A. Cufer. Litho)

2004 (18 Nov). Mythology. P 14.

647 **289** 180t. multicoloured ... 3·25 3·25

290 Couple, Pohorje and Kobansko

291 Janez Sigmund Valentin Popovic (linguist and scientist) (birth bicentenary)

(Des Studio Arnold+Vuga. Litho)

2005 (21 Jan). National Costumes. P 14.

648 **290** A (45t.) multicoloured ... 1·00 1·00

(Des M. Učakar. Litho)

2005 (21 Jan). Posthorn. Vert design as T **280**. P 14.

649 **280** 83t. new blue and orange-yellow ... 1·50 1·50

(Des M. Klenovsek and M. Pocajt. Litho Czech Post Printing House, Prague)

2005 (21 Jan). Anniversaries. T **291** and similar vert design. Multicoloured. P 11½×12.

650 107t. Type **291** ... 2·00 2·00
651 221t. Janez Trdina (writer) (death centenary) ... 4·00 4·00

292 Cupid

(Des M. Kozjek. Litho)

2005 (21 Jan). Greeting Stamp. P 11.

652 **292** 180t. multicoloured ... 3·25 3·25

No. 652 was perforated in a heart-shape contained within an outer perforated square.

293 Refugees

294 The Grateful Bear

(Des Studio Botas. Litho Czech Post Printing House, Prague)

2005 (18 Mar). 60th Anniv of Return of Slovene Exiles. P 12×11½.

653 **293** A (49t.) multicoloured ... 1·00 1·00

(Des Jelka Reichman. Litho)

2005 (18 Mar). Folk Tales. T **294** and similar vert designs. Multicoloured.

(a) Sheet stamps. Ordinary gum. P 14.

654 A (49t.) Type **294** ... 95 95
655 A (49t.) The Golden Fish ... 95 95

(b) Booklet stamps. Self-adhesive gum. Die-cut perf 8

656 A (49t.) As No. 654 ... 95 95
657 A (49t.) As No. 655 ... 95 95
654/657 *Set of* 4 ... 3·50 3·50

295 Soldiers

(Des M. Kozjek. Litho Czech Post Printing House, Prague)

2005 (18 Mar). 60th Anniv of End of World War II. P 12×11½.

658 **295** B (57t.) multicoloured ... 1·00 1·00

296 Mountain, Waterside, Farmland and Castle

(Des Studio Botas. Litho Czech Post Printing House, Prague)

2005 (18 Mar). Centenary of National Tourist Association. Sheet 69×60 mm. P 11½.

MS659 **296** 100t. multicoloured ... 1·80 1·80

297 Zoisite

298 Stylized Figures

(Des M. Učakar. Litho Czech Post Printing House, Prague)

2005 (18 Mar). P 12×11½.

660 **297** D (107t.) multicoloured ... 1·90 1·90

2005 (8 May). OBLIGATORY TAX. Red Cross Week. Litho. P 14.

661 **298** 25t. bright scarlet and slate ... 1·00 1·00
a. Self-adhesive gum ... 1·00 1·00

299 Sunflower

300 No. 348 (detail), Tweezers and Magnifier

(Des J. Reichman. Litho Austrian State Prg Wks)

2005 (20 May). Greetings Stamp. Self adhesive. Die-cut perf 13.

662 **299** A (49t.) multicoloured ... 1·00 1·00

(Des M. Wraber. Litho)

2005 (20 May). 50th Anniv of Europa Stamps. T **300** and similar horiz designs showing previous Europa stamps. Multicoloured.

(a) Sheet stamps. Enschedé. P 14×13½

663 60t. Type **300** ... 1·20 1·20
664 60t. No. 406 (detail) ... 1·20 1·20
665 60t. No. 553 (detail) ... 1·20 1·20
666 60t. No. 232 (detail) ... 1·20 1·20
663/666 *Set of* 4 ... 4·25 4·25

(b) Miniature sheet. Austrian State Ptg Wks. P 14×14½

MS667 135×85 mm. Nos. 663/6 ... 4·25 4·25

301 Puch Motorbike (1910)

302 Potica (rolled cakes)

(Des J. P. Grom. Litho Czech Post Printing House, Prague)

2005 (20 May). Janez Puh (Johann Puch) (cycle pioneer) Commemoration. P 11½.

668 **301** 98t. multicoloured ... 1·80 1·80

(Des M. Učakar. Litho Czech Post Printing House, Prague)

2005 (20 May). Europa. Gastronomy. P 12×11½.

669 **302** D (107t.) multicoloured ... 2·00 2·00

303 Horse-drawn Post Van and Early Post Box **304** Vesna

(Des L. Rubins. Litho Czech Post Printing House, Prague)

2005 (20 May). Postal Museum Exhibits. P 11½.
670 **303** 107t. multicoloured ..... 2·00 2·00

(Des A. Cufer. Litho Czech Post Printing House, Prague)

2005 (20 May). Mythology. P 11½×12.
671 **304** 180t. multicoloured ..... 3·25 3·25

305 Shepherd shooting Eagle **306** Institute Building and Bishop Anton Jeglic (founder)

(Des Studio Arnold+Vuga and T. Jesenicnik. Litho Czech Post Printing House, Prague)

2005 (20 May). Painted Beehive Panels. P 12×11½.
672 **305** 221t. multicoloured ..... 4·00 4·00

(Des Studio Arnold+Vuga. Litho Czech Post Printing House, Prague)

2005 (20 May). Centenary of St. Stanislav's Institute (educational and cultural institution). P 12×11½.
673 **306** 221t. multicoloured ..... 4·00 4·00

307 Apricot Flowers **308** Posavec Hound

(Des M. Učakar. Litho Czech Post Printing House, Prague)

2005 (5 July). Apricot. T **307** and similar vert designs. Multicoloured. P 12×11½.
674 D (107t.) Type **307** ..... 1·80 1·80
a. Strip of 3. Nos. 674/6 ..... 5·75
675 D (107t.) Fruit ..... 1·80 1·80
676 D (107t.) Pest ..... 1·80 1·80
674/676 *Set of 3* ..... 4·75 4·75
Nos. 674/6 were issued in horizontal *se-tenant* strips of three stamps within the sheet.

(Des J. Mikuletic. Litho Czech Post Printing House, Prague)

2005 (23 Sept). Dogs. T **308** and similar multicoloured designs. P 11½ (**MS**680) or 12×11½ (others).
677 A (49t.) Type **308** ..... 1·00 1·00
678 B (57t.) Istrian rough-coated hound ..... 1·40 1·40
679 C (95t.) Slovenian mountain hound ..... 2·00 2·00
677/679 *Set of 3* ..... 4·00 4·00
MS680 60×70 mm. D (107t.) Istrian smooth-coated hound (28×41 mm) ..... 2·10 2·10

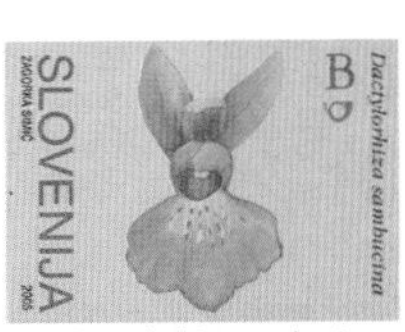

309 *Dactylorhiza sambucina*

(Des Z. Simic. Litho Czech Post Printing House, Prague)

2005 (23 Sept). Orchids. T **309** and similar horiz design. Multicoloured. P 11½ (**MS**682) or 12×11½ (681).
681 B (57t.) Type **309** ..... 1·10 1·10
MS682 70×60 mm. D (107t.) *Platanthera biflora* ..... 2·10 2·10

310 Priest, Skeleton and Bishop

(Des Villa Creativa. Litho and embossed)

2005 (23 Sept). Art. Dance of Death (fresco by Janez of Kastav). T **310** and similar horiz design. Multicoloured. P 14.
683 107t. Type **310** ..... 2·00 2·00
a. Horiz pair. Nos. 683/4 ..... 4·25 4·25
684 107t. Two skeletons and cardinal ..... 2·00 2·00
Nos. 683/4 were issued in horizontal *se-tenant* pairs within the sheet, each pair forming a composite design.

310a Houses

2005 (1 Nov). OBLIGATORY TAX. Solidarity Week. T **310a** and similar vert design. Multicoloured. Litho. P 14.
684*a* 25c. Type **310a** 55 55
a. Pair. Nos. 684*a*/*b* ..... 1·20 1·20
aa. Self-adhesive gum 55 55
ab. Pair. Nos. 684aa/ba ..... 1·20 1·00
684*b* 25c. Flood water 55 55
ba. Self-adhesive gum 55 55
Nos. 684*a*/*b* were issued in horizontal *se-tenant* pairs within the sheet.
For compulsory use from 1 to 7 November.

311 Child at Window

(Des J. Reichman. Litho Czech Post Printing House, Prague (684/5))

2005 (18 Nov). Christmas. T **311** and similar horiz design. Multicoloured.

(a) Sheet stamps. P 12×11½
685 A (49t.) Type **311** 85 85
686 C (95t.) Children carrying candles ..... 1·70 1·70

(b) Self-adhesive booklet stamps. Die-cut perf 8
687 A (49t.) As No. 685 ..... 85 85
688 C (95t.) As No. 686 ..... 1·70 1·70
685/688 *Set of 4* ..... 4·50 4·50

312 Prleška Gibanica and Ajdov Krapec (cakes) **313** Umbrella and Jigsaw

(Des M. Učakar. Litho Czech Post Printing House, Prague)

2005 (18 Nov). Gastronomy. T **312** and similar horiz design. Multicoloured. P 12×11½.
689 52t. Type **312** ..... 2·00 2·00
a. Horiz pair. Nos. 689/90 ..... 4·25 4·25
690 52t. Tunka (barrel), bread and meat ..... 2·00 2·00
Nos. 689/90 were issued in horizontal *se-tenant* pairs within the sheet.

(Des B. Kos. Litho Czech Post Printing House, Prague)

2005 (18 Nov). Slovenia's Chairmanship of Organization for Security and Co-operation in Europe (OSCE). P 11½×12.
691 **313** 107t. multicoloured ..... 1·40 1·40

2005. Vert designs as Nos. 197a, 536/7, 597/600, 627 and 633. Size 25×36 mm. Purple-brown, brown-red and greenish grey (197a) or multicoloured (others). P 11½×12.
691*a* B (31t.) Type **223** (536) ..... 1·00 1·00
691*b* A (38t.) Type **258** (597) ..... 1·10 1·10
691*c* B (44t.) Fishing boat, Piran (598) ..... 1·20 1·20
691*d* B (48t.) Type **279** (627) ..... 1·30 1·30
691*e* 90t. Apiary (197a) ..... 1·70 1·70
691*f* C (95t.) Scythe, Ljubno ob Savinji (599) ..... 2·00 2·00
691*g* D (107t.) Butarice (537) ..... 2·20 2·20
691*h* D (107t.) Horse collar comb (600) ..... 2·20 2·20
691*i* D (107t.) Cupa (fishing boat) (633) ..... 2·20 2·20
691*a*/691*i* *Set of 9* ..... 13·50 13·50

2005. Vert designs as Nos. 447/50 and 520. Size 26×36 mm. P 11½×12.
691*j* 1t. olive-brown and bistre 20 20
691*k* 1t. olive-brown and bistre 20 20
691*l* C (95t.) lake-brown and vermilion ..... 1·70 1·70
691*m* 100t. purple-brown and red-brown ..... 2·00 2·00
691*n* 100t. purple-brown and red-brown ..... 2·00 2·00
691*j*/691*n* *Set of 5* ..... 5·50 5·50
Designs: 1t. Predjama Castle (447); 1t. Velenje Castle (448); C (95t.) Dobrovo Manor (520); 100t. Podsreda Castle (449); 100t. Bled Castle (450).

2005. Vert designs as Nos. 463/5, 511/13 and 630/2. Size 21×25 mm. P 11½×12.
691*o* 5t. Type **186** (463) 20 20
691*p* 5t. European cherry fruit fly (464) 20 20
691*q* 5t. Vigred sweet cherries (465) 20 20
691*r* 10t. Type **177** (451) 45 45
691*s* 10t. Apple blossom (452) 45 45
691*t* 10t. Apple (453) 45 45
691*u* A (49t.) Type **258** (630) ..... 1·10 1·10
691*v* A (49t.) Fruit fly (631) ..... 1·10 1·10
691*w* A (49t.) Pear (632) ..... 1·10 1·10
691*x* 50t. Type **211** (511) ..... 1·10 1·10
691*y* 50t. Green peach aphid (512) ..... 1·10 1·10
691*z* 50t. Redhaven peach (513) ..... 1·10 1·10
691*za* B (57t.) Type **253** (586) ..... 1·20 1·20
691*zb* B (57t.) Olive fruit fly (587) ..... 1·20 1·20
691*zc* B (57t.) Olives (588) ..... 1·20 1·20
691*zd* 150t. Type **233** (556) ..... 2·75 2·75
691*ze* 150t. Winter moth (557) ..... 2·75 2·75
691*zf* 150t. Bilberry fruit (558) ..... 2·75 2·75
691*o*/691*zf* *Set of 18* ..... 18·00 18·00

314 Couple, Carinthia **315** Anton Trstenjak

(Des Studio Arnold+Vuga. Litho)

2006 (20 Jan). National Costumes. P 14.
692 **314** A (49t.) multicoloured ..... 1·00 1·00

(Des D. Arrigler and J. Grom. Litho)

2006 (20 Jan). Birth Centenary of Anton Trstenjak (theologian and anthropologist). P 14.
693 **315** B (57t.) multicoloured ..... 1·00 1·00

316 Couple **317** Skier

(Des Poanta and S. Černe. Litho)

2006 (20 Jan). Greetings Stamp. P 11.
694 **316** B (57t.) multicoloured ..... 1·00 1·00
No. 694 was perforated in a heart shape contained in an outer perforated square.

(Des Manica Klenovsek and Mateja Pocajt. Litho Oriental Press, Bahrain)

2006 (20 Jan). Winter Olympics, Turin. T **317** and similar vert design. Multicoloured. P 11.
695 95t. Type **317** ..... 1·70 1·70
696 107t. Snowboarder ..... 1·80 1·80

318 The Cocks, Ponikeve

(Des Milena Gregorčič. Litho)

2006 (20 Jan). Folk Masks. P 14.
697 **318** 420t. multicoloured ..... 7·25 7·25

319 Twinkle Sleepyhead **320** *Erannis ankeraria*

(Des Studio Arnold+Vuga and G. Vahen. Litho)

2006 (24 Mar). Children's Book Characters. T **319** and similar vert design. Multicoloured.

(a) Ordinary gum. P 14
698 A (49t.) Type **319** ..... 1·00 1·00
699 A (49t.) Spotty the ball ..... 1·00 1·00

(b) Self-adhesive booklet stamps. Die-cut perf 7
700 A (49t.) As Type **319** ..... 1·00 1·00
701 A (49t.) As No. 699 ..... 1·00 1·00
698/701 *Set of 4* ..... 3·50 3·50

(Des Julija Zornik. Litho)

2006 (24 Mar). Butterflies. T **320** and similar horiz design. Multicoloured. P 14.
702 D (107t.) Type **320** ..... 1·10 1·10
MS703 71×60 mm. D (107t.) *Erebia calcaria* ..... 1·90 1·90

321 Pericnik Waterfall

322 Fossil Shell

(Des Studio Botas and B. Burger. Litho)

2006 (24 Mar). P 14.

704	**321**	D (107t.) multicoloured	1·90	1·90

(Des Maja Licul. Litho)

2006 (24 Mar). P 14.

705	**322**	D (107t.) multicoloured	1·90	1·90

323 Nurses

2006 (8 May). OBLIGATORY TAX. Red Cross Week. 140th Anniv of Slovenia Red Cross. Litho. P 14.

706	**323**	25t. multicoloured	1·00	1·00

324 Bouquet

325 Competitor

(Des J. Reichman. Litho)

2006 (19 May). Greetings Stamp. Self-adhesive. Die-cut perf 9.

707	**324**	C (95t.) multicoloured	1·60	1·60

(Des Poanta and S. Rakover. Litho)

2006 (19 May). Junior World White Water Slalom Kayak Competition, Solkan. P 14.

708	**325**	C (95t.) multicoloured	1·60	1·60

326 Cats (Sara Popovic)

327 Svarog

2006 (19 May). Europa. Integration. Winning Design in Children's Painting Competition. Litho. P 14.

709	**326**	C (95t.) multicoloured	1·90	1·90

(Des Andrejka Cufer. Litho)

2006 (19 May). Mythology. P 14.

710	**327**	D (107t.) multicoloured	1·90	1·90

328 Couple

(Des Studio Arnold+Vuga. Litho)

2006 (19 May). Painted Beehive Panels. P 14.

711	**328**	D (107t.) multicoloured	1·90	1·90

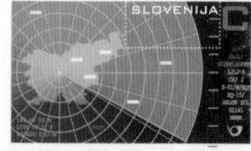

329 Radar Screen

2006 (25 June). 15th Anniv of Independence, Stamp Issuing and Slovenia Air Traffic Control and Air Navigation Services. Sheet 90×60 mm. P 13½×14.

MS712	**329**	C (95t.) multicoloured	1·70	1·70

330 Plant

331 Rack Wagon

(Des Julija Zornik. Litho)

2006 (22 Sept). Salvinia natans. T **330** and similar vert design. Multicoloured. P 14.

713	A (49t.) Type **330**	1·10	1·10
MS714	60×70 mm. D (107t.) Plant (different)	1·90	1·90

2006 (22 Sept). Transport. P 14.

715	**331**	D (107t.) multicoloured	1·90	1·90

332 Ceiling

332a Fire-fighters

(Des M. Kozjek and T. Lauko. Litho)

2006 (22 Sept). 17th-century Painted Ceiling. Celje Mansion. Sheet 114×85 mm containing T **332** and similar horiz designs showing parts of the ceiling. Multicoloured. P 14.

MS716	D (107t.)×4, Type **332**; Top right; Bottom left; Bottom right	7·50	7·50

The stamps and margin of No. **MS**716 form a composite design of the ceiling and frescoes.

2006 (9 Oct). OBLIGATORY TAX. Litho. P 14.

716*a*	**332a**	25t. multicoloured	1·00	1·00

For compulsory use from 9 to 14 October.

332b Hands enclosing Globe

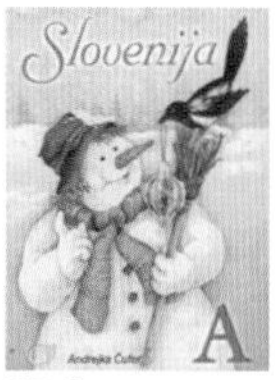

333 Snowman

2006 (1 Nov). OBLIGATORY TAX. Solidarity Week. Litho. P 14.

716*b*	**332b**	25t. multicoloured	1·00	1·00

For compulsory use from 1 to 7 November.

(Des Andrejka Cufer. Litho)

2006 (17 Nov). Christmas. T **333** and similar vert designs. Multicoloured.

(a) Sheet stamps. Ordinary gum. P 14

717	A (49t.) Type **333**	1·00	1·00
718	C (95t.) Carollers	1·80	1·80

(b) Booklet stamps. Self-adhesive gum. Die-cut perf 8

719	A (49t.) As No. 717	1·00	1·00
720	C (95t.) As No. 718	1·80	1·80
717/720	*Set of* 4	5·00	5·00

Nos. 719/20 were each issued in booklets of ten stamps.

334 Soldiers

335 Father Asic

(Des Maja Licul. Litho)

2006 (17 Nov). Partisan Signallers and Couriers. P 14.

721	**334**	C (95t.) multicoloured	1·70	1·70

(Des M. Ciglic. Litho)

2006 (17 Nov). Birth Centenary of Father Simon Asic (herbalist). Sheet 71×61 mm. P 14.

MS722	**335**	D (107t.) multicoloured	1·90	1·90

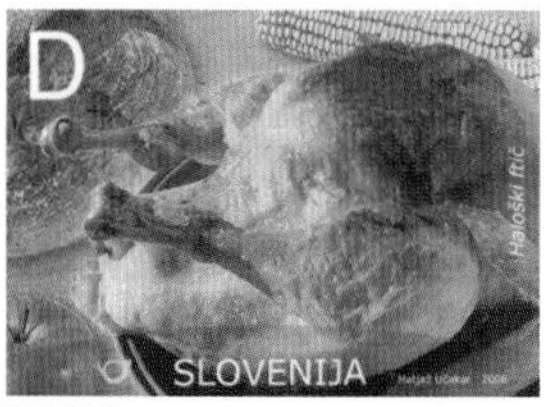

336 Turkey

337 Persimmon Flower

(Des Matjaž Učakar. Litho)

2006 (17 Nov). Gastronomy. T **336** and similar horiz design. Multicoloured. P 14.

723	D (107t.) Type **336**	1·80	1·80
	a. Pair. Nos. 723/4	3·75	3·75
724	D (107t.) Yeast cake	1·80	1·80

Nos. 723/4 were issued in *se-tenant* pairs within the sheet.

(Des M. Učakar. Litho Czech Post Printing House, Prague)

2006 (17 Nov). Persimmon. T **337** and similar vert designs. Multicoloured. P 12×11½.

725	D (107t.) Type **337**	1·80	1·80
	a. Strip of 3. Nos. 725/6	5·75	
726	D (107t.) Fruit	1·80	1·80
727	D (107t.) Pest	1·80	1·80
725/727	*Set of* 3	4·75	4·75

Nos. 725/6 were issued in horizontal *se-tenant* strips of three stamps within the sheet.

Currency Change

2007. 100 Cents = 1 Euro

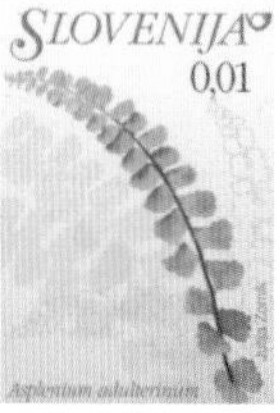

338 *Asplenium adulterinum*

339 Coins

(Des Julija Zornik. Litho)

2007 (1 Jan). Flora. T **338** and similar vert designs. Multicoloured. P 11½×12.

728	1c. Type **338**	20	20
729	2c. *Moebringia tommasinii*	20	20
730	5c. *Himantoglossum adriaticum*	20	20
731	10c. *Pulsatilis grandis*	45	45
732	20c. *Primula carniolica*	85	85
733	25c. *Galdiolus palustis*	85	85
734	35c. *Ceratium dinaricum*	1·10	1·10
735	48c. *Adenophora liliifolia*	1·30	1·30
736	A (49c.) *Campanula zoysii*	1·30	1·30
737	50c. *Aqualegia bertolonii*	1·30	1·30
738	B (57c.) *Cypripedium calceolus*	1·60	1·60
739	75c. *Liparis loeslii*	1·80	1·80
740	92c. *Scilla litardierei*	2·20	2·20
741	C (95c.) *Serratula lycopifolia*	2·75	2·75
742	100c. *Eryngium alpinum*	3·00	3·00
743	D (107c.) *Genista bolopetala*	3·25	3·25
744	200c. *Rhododendron luteum*	6·50	6·50
728/744	*Set of* 17	26·00	26·00

(Des Maja Licul. Litho)

2007 (1 Jan). Introduction of the Euro. Sheet 100×50 mm. P 13½×13 (with one elliptical hole on each vert side).

MS745	**339**	100c. multicoloured	4·25	4·25

340 Couple, Smlednik

(Des Studio Arnold+Vuga. Litho)

2007 (24 Jan). National Costumes. P 14.

746	**340**	20c. multicoloured	1·00	1·00

341 Newly Weds

(Des M. Kozjek. Litho)

2007 (24 Jan). Greetings Stamp. P 11.

747	**341**	24c. multicoloured	1·00	1·00

No. 747 was perforated in a heart shape contained in an outer perforated square.

342 **Vasja Pirc**

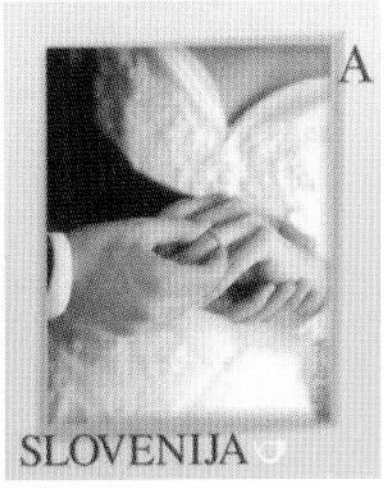

343 Bride and Groom

(Des G. Arch. Litho)

2007 (24 Jan). Birth Centenary of Vasja Pirc (chess grand master). P 11.
748 **342** 48c. multicoloured .... 2·00 2·00

(Des Julija Zornik. Litho Enschedé)

2007 (24 Jan). Personal Stamps. T **343** and similar multicoloured designs. Self-adhesive. Die-cut perf 12.
749 A (49c.) Type **343** 90 90
750 A (49c.) Stork carrying babies (horiz) 90 90
751 A (49c.) Postman 90 90
752 A (49c.) Parcel (horiz) 90 90
749/752 *Set of* 4 .... 3·25 3·25
Nos. 749/52 were for personalization by the addition of a photograph or logo.

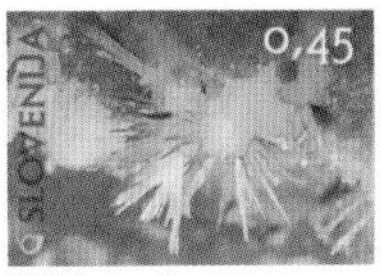

344 Aragonite

345 Mangart Mountain and Creeping Avens

(Des Matjaž Učakar. Litho)

2007 (23 Mar). P 12×11½.
753 **344** 45c. multicoloured .... 1·90 1·90

(Des Poanta. Litho)

2007 (23 Mar). Tourism. P 12×11½.
754 **345** 45c. multicoloured .... 1·90 1·90

346 Eurasian Red Squirrel

347 Animals as Scouts

(Des Jurij Mikuletic. Litho)

2007 (23 Mar). Endangered Species. Eurasian Red Squirrel (*Sciurus vulgaris*). T **346** and similar horiz designs. Multicoloured. P 13×13½.
755 48c. Type **346** .... 2·00 2·00
a. Block of 4. Nos. 755/8 .... 8·25
756 48c. Eating .... 2·00 2·00
757 48c. Two squirrels .... 2·00 2·00
758 48c. Mother and babies .... 2·00 2·00
755/758 *Set of* 4 .... 7·25 7·25
Nos. 755/8 were issued in *se-tenant* blocks of four stamps within the sheet.

(Des Matjaž Učakar. Litho)

2007 (23 Mar). Europa. Centenary of Scouting. P 13×13½.
759 **347** 50c. multicoloured .... 2·10 2·10

348 Stylized Elderly Person and Child

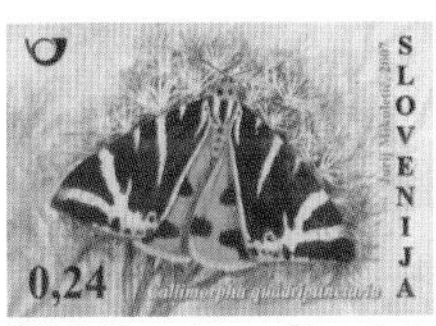

349 *Callimorpha quadripunctaria* (tiger moth)

2007 (8 May). OBLIGATORY TAX. Red Cross Week. Generations. T **348** and similar vert designs showing elderly person and child. Litho. P 14.
760 10c. Type **348** 45 45
a. Block of 4. Nos. 760/3 .... 1·90
761 10c. Walking contained in triangle 45 45
762 10c. On see-saw 45 45
763 10c. Listening using headphones 45 45
760/763 *Set of* 4 .... 1·60 1·60
Nos. 760/3 were issued in *se-tenant* blocks of four stamps within the sheet.
For compulsory use from 8 to 15 May.

(Des Jurij Mikuletic. Litho Oriental Press Bahrain)

2007 (25 May). Butterfly and Moth. T **349** and similar multicoloured design. P 14½.
764 24c. Type **349** .... 1·00 1·00
MS765 61×71 mm. 45c. *Colias myrmidone* (Danube clouded yellow) (vert) .... 1·90 1·90

350 Perkmandeljc, Taus, Catež (elves)

351 Windmill and Stars

(Des Andrejka Cufer. Litho Oriental Press Bahrain)

2007 (25 May). Mythology. P 14½×14.
766 **350** 45c. multicoloured .... 1·90 1·90

(Des Matjaž Učakar. Litho Post Office Ptg Wks, Prague)

2007 (25 May). 50th Anniv of Treaty of Rome. P 11½×12.
767 **351** 45c. multicoloured .... 1·90 1·90

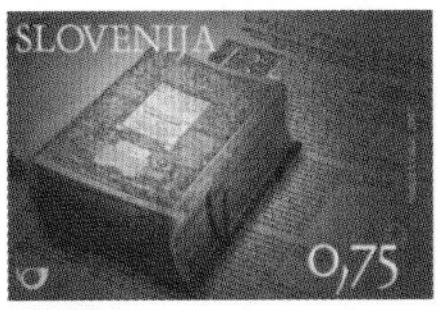

352 Bible

(Des Matjaž Učakar. Litho Oriental Press Bahrain)

2007 (25 May). Year of the Bible. Sheet 61×71 mm. P 14.
MS768 **352** 75c. multicoloured .... 3·00 3·00

353 Buggy

354 Bridge, Moon, Sun and Church

(Des Jurij Mikuletic. Litho Oriental Press Bahrain)

2007 (25 May). Transport. P 14.
769 **353** 92c. multicoloured .... 3·75 3·75

(Des Božo Cos. Litho)

2007 (22 June). Lent. P 14.
770 **354** €1 multicoloured .... 4·25 4·25

355 *Nuphar luteum*

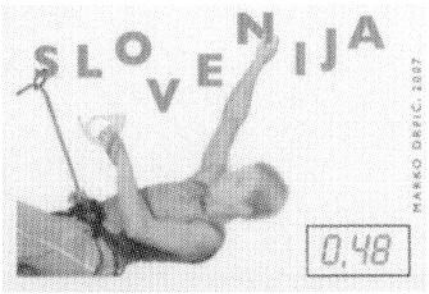

356 Climber

(Des Tjasa Stempihar. Litho Oriental Press, Bahrain)

2007 (26 Sept). Flowering Aquatic Plants. T **355** and similar multicoloured designs. P 14.
771 20c. Type **355** 85 85
772 24c. *Hydrocharis morsus-ranae* .... 1·10 1·10
773 40c. *Nyphoides peltata* .... 2·00 2·00
771/773 *Set of* 3 .... 3·50 3·50
MS774 60×70 mm. 45c. *Nymphaea alba* (horiz) .... 1·90 1·90

(Des Marko Drpic. Litho)

2007 (26 Sept). Sport. Rock Climbing. P 14.
775 **356** 48c. multicoloured .... 2·00 2·00

357 Ceiling Fresco, Church of St. Nicholas (Giulio Quaglio)

358 Fire Fighters

(Des Masa Kozjek. Litho)

2007 (26 Sept). Art.
776 **357** 92c. multicoloured .... 3·75 3·75

2007 (8 Oct). OBLIGATORY TAX. P 14.
777 **358** 11c. multicoloured .... 1·00 1·00
No. 777 was for use during the week 8—13th October.

358a Circles and Figures

359 Car passing through Checkpoint

2007 (1 Nov). OBLIGATORY TAX. Solidarity Week. T **358a** and similar horiz designs. Multicoloured. Litho. P 14.
777*a* 10c. Type **358a** 45 45
a. Block of 4. Nos. 777*a*/*d* .... 1·90
777*b* 10c. As Type **358a** but central circle blue 45 45
777*c* 10c. As Type **358a** but central circle green 45 45
777*d* 10c. As Type **358a** but central circle orange 45 45
777*a*/777*d* *Set of* 4 .... 1·60 1·60
Nos. 777*a*/*d* were issued in *se-tenant* blocks of four stamps within the sheet.

(Des Matjaž Učakar. Litho)

2007 (23 Nov). Slovenia's Entry into Schengen Zone (European Union area without border controls). P 14.
778 **359** 45c. multicoloured .... 1·90 1·90

360 Stajerska Sour Soup and Pohorski Pisker (stew)

(Des Meta Wraber. Litho)

2007 (23 Nov). Gastronomy. T **360** and similar horiz design. Multicoloured. P 14.
779 45c. Type **360** .... 1·80 1·80
a. Pair. Nos. 779/80 .... 3·75 3·75
780 45c. Pohorje omelet .... 1·80 1·80
Nos. 779/80 were issued in horizontal *se-tenant* pairs within the sheet.

361 Symbols of Good Luck

362 Sledge

(Des Matjaž Učakar. Litho)

2007 (23 Nov). New Year. P 14.
781 **361** A (49c.) multicoloured .... 1·00 1·00

(Des Julija Zornik, Matjaž Učakar and Božo Kos. Litho)

2007 (23 Nov). Personal Stamps. T **362** and similar multicoloured designs. Self-adhesive gum. Die-cut perf 12.
782 A (49c.) Type **362** 90 90
783 A (49c.) Nativity (vert) 90 90
784 C (95c.) Postman delivering deluxe telegram (vert) .... 1·90 1·90
785 C (95c.) Running shoe (Hitra Posta express mail) .... 1·90 1·90
782/785 *Set of* 4 .... 5·00 5·00
Nos. 782/5 could be personalised by the addition of a photograph or logo.

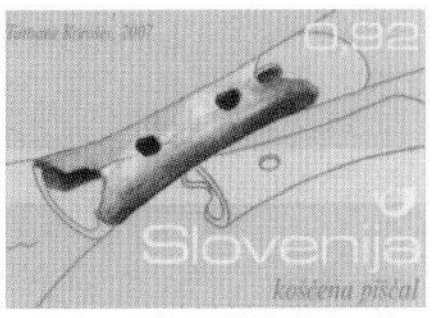

363 Bone Flute, Divje Babe Cave

364 The Nativity (Christmas crib made by Janez Kosnik)

(Des Tamara Korošec. Litho)

2007 (23 Nov). Archaeological Finds. Sheet 72×62 mm. P 14.
MS786 **363** 92c. multicoloured .... 3·75 3·75

(Des Matjaž Učakar. Litho)

2007 (23 Nov). Christmas. P 14.
787 **364** C (92c.) multicoloured .... 1·60 1·60

365 Map of Slovenia and EU Members Flags

366 Couple, Scavnica and Pesnica

(Des Matjaž Učakar. Litho)

2008 (1 Jan). Slovenia's Presidency of European Union. Sheet 70×60 mm. P 14.
788 **365** €2.38 multicoloured .... 10·50 10·50

(Des Studio Arnold+Vuga. Litho)

2008 (29 Jan). National Costumes. P 14.
789 **366** 20c. multicoloured .... 1·00 1·00

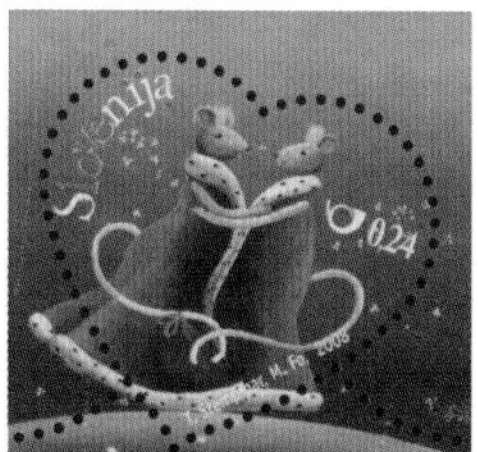

367 Mouse Couple

(Des Tjasa Stempihar and Mojca Fo. Litho)

2008 (29 Jan). Greetings Stamp. P 14.
790 **367** 24c. multicoloured .... 1·10 1·10
No. 791 was perforated in a heart shape contained in an outer perforated square.

368 Primoz Trubar and Frontispiece

(Des Matjaž Učakar. Litho)

2008 (29 Jan). 500th Birth Anniv of Primoz Trubar (author of the first Slovenian book). P 14.
791 **368** 48c. multicoloured .... 2·10 2·10

369 Black and White Masks, Vrbica

(Des Milena Gregorčič. Litho)

2008 (29 Jan). Folk Masks. P 14.
792 **369** €1.75 multicoloured .... 7·75 7·75

370 *Paeonia officinalis*

371 Julius Kugy and Trenta Valley

(Des Tjasa Stempihar and Branko Vres. Litho)

2008 (28 Mar). Flora. T **370** and similar multicoloured designs. P 14.
793 20c. Type **370** .... 1·00 1·00
794 24c. *Pulsatilla Montana* .... 1·20 1·20
795 40c. *Iris illyrica* .... 2·00 2·00
793/795 *Set of* 3 .... 3·75 3·75
MS796 60×70 mm. 45c. *Gentiana tergestina* (horiz) . 2·00 2·00

(Des Masa Kozjek and Matjaž Smalc. Litho)

2008 (28 Mar). 150th Birth Anniv of Julius Kugy (mountaineer and writer). P 14.
797 **371** 45c. multicoloured .... 2·00 2·00

372 Boy

373 Academy of Sciences and Arts Building and Rajko Nahtigal

(Des Studio Kvadrat. Litho)

2008 (8 May). OBLIGATORY TAX. Red Cross Week. T **372** and similar vert design. Multicoloured. P 14.
798 10c. Type **372** 50 50
a. Pair. Nos. 798/9 .... 1·10 1·10
799 10c. Girl 50 50
Nos. 798/9 were for compulsory use between 8th and 15th May.
Nos. 798/9 were issued in horizontal *se-tenant* pairs within the sheet, each pair forming a composite design.

(Des Studio Arnoldvuga)

2008 (29 May). 70th Anniv of Academy of Science and Arts. 50th Death Anniv of Rajko Nahtigal (linguist). P 14.
800 **373** 40c. multicoloured .... 1·80 1·80

374 Temple and Stylized Athletes (wrestling)

375 Mokos (goddess of life)

(Des Matjaž Učakar. Litho)

2008 (29 May). Olympic Games, Beijing. T **374** and similar horiz design. Multicoloured. P 14.
801 40c. Type **374** .... 1·70 1·70
a. Pair. Nos. 801/2 .... 3·75 3·75
802 45c. Pagoda and stylized athlete (sailing) 1·80 1·80
Nos. 801/2 were issued in *se-tenant* pairs within the sheet.

(Des Andrejka Cufer. Litho)

2008 (29 May). Mythology. P 14.
803 **375** 45c. multicoloured .... 2·00 2·00

376 Winged Mail

(Des Matjaž Učakar. Litho)

2008 (29 May). Europa. The Letter. T **376** and similar horiz design. Multicoloured.
804 45c. Type **376** .... 2·00 2·00
805 92c. Mail van and envelopes as figures .... 4·00 4·00

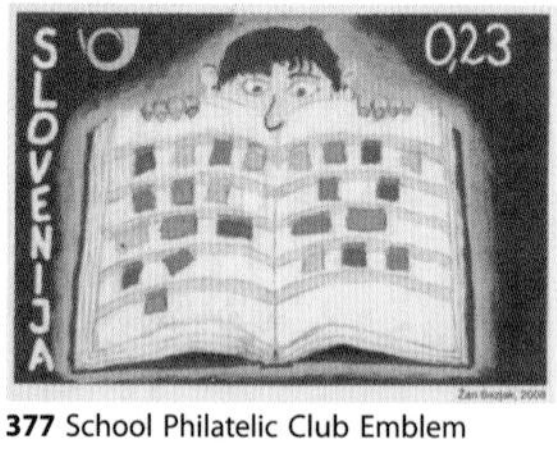

377 School Philatelic Club Emblem

(Des Zan Bezjak. Litho)

2008 (29 Sept). Stamp Day. P 11½×12.
806 **377** 23c. multicoloured .... 1·00 1·00

378 *Rana latastei* (Italian agile frog)

(Des Jurij Mikuletic. Litho)

2008 (29 Sept). Fauna. T **378** and similar horiz designs. Multicoloured. P 14.
807 23c. Type **378** .... 1·20 1·20
808 27c. *Bombina bombina* (fire-bellied toad) 1·40 1·40
809 40c. *Triturus carnifex* (Italian crested newt) .... 2·10 2·10
807/809 *Set of* 3 .... 4·25 4·25
MS810 70×60 mm. 45c. *Elaphe quatuorlineata* (Four-lined snake) .... 2·20 2·20

379 Alojzij Sustar

(Des Gorazd Učakar. Litho)

2008 (29 Sept). Alojzij Sustar (Archbishop of Ljubljana) Commemoration. P 14.
811 **379** 45c. multicoloured .... 2·20 2·20

380 Stucco, Gruber Palace

(Des Tjasa Stempihar. Litho)

2008 (29 Sept). Rococo Decoration. P 11½×12.
812 **380** 92c. multicoloured .... 4·50 4·50

381 Cargo Sledge

(Des Jurij Mikuletic. Litho)

2008 (29 Sept). P 14.
813 **381** 92c. multicoloured .... 4·50 4·50

382 Boy and Flute

(Des Gorazd Učakar. Litho Enschedé)

2008 (29 Sept). 80th Anniv of Radio and 50th Anniv of Television in Slovenia. Sheet 70×60 mm. P 13½×14½ (with one elliptical hole on each vert side).
MS814 **382** 92c. multicoloured .... 4·50 4·50

383 Children as Firefighters

384 Primož Kozmus

(Des Matjaž Učakar and S. Veber. Litho)

2008 (6 Oct). OBLIGATORY TAX. P 14.
815 **383** 12c. multicoloured .... 1·00 1·00
No. 815 was for use during the week 6—11th October.

(Des Tjasa Stempihar. Litho)

2008 (14 Oct). Primož Kozmus—2008 Olympic Gold Medal Wiiner for Hammer Thro. P 14.
816 **384** 45c. multicoloured .... 2·10 2·10

385 Figures holding Jigsaw Puzzle Pieces

(Des Studio Kavdrat)

2008 (1 Nov). OBLIGATORY TAX. Red Cross Solidarity Week. P 14.
817 **385** 12c. multicoloured .... 1·00 1·00

STAMP BOOKLETS

The following checklist covers, in simplified form, booklets issued by Slovenia. It is intended that it should be used in conjunction with the main listings and details of stamps and panes listed there are not repeated.

Prices are for complete booklets

Booklet No.	*Date*	*Contents and Cover Price*	*Price*
SB1	18.11.94	Christmas (T **69**) 1 pane, No. 248a (120t.)	3·00
SB2	18.11 94	International Year of the Family 1 pane, No. 249a (700t.)	17·00
SB3	16.11.95	Christmas (T **88**) 1 pane, No. 276a (130t.)	3·00
SB4	6.11.95	Christmas 1 pane, No. 277a (700t.)	17·00
SB5	20.11.96	Christmas (T **111**) 1 pane, No. 337a (120t.)	3·00
SB6	20.11.96	Christmas 1 pane, No. 338a (650t.)	13·00
SB7	18.11.97	Christmas 1 pane, No. 363a (340t.)	6·25
SB8	12.11.98	Christmas 1 pane, No. 392a (150t.)	3·00
SB9	12.11.98	Christmas 1 pane, No. 392b (450t.)	8·00
SB10	18.11.99	Christmas 1 pane, No. 426a (170t.)	5·50
SB11	18.11.99	Christmas 1 pane, No. 426b (325t.)	4·75
SB12	21.3.00	Characters from Children's Books Nos. 440/2, each×3 plus 9 labels. (180t.)	5·25
SB13	21.11.00	Christmas No. 485×10 (210t.)	3·75
SB14	21.11.00	Christmas No. 485×6 and No. 486×4 (486t.)	7·50
SB15	21.3.01	Cowboy Pipec Nos. 496/7, each×4 (200t.)	7·00
SB16	16.11.01	Christmas No. 527×12 (372t.)	4·25
SB17	16.11.01	Christmas No. 527/8, each×6 (828t.)	10·00
SB18	21.3.02	Martin Krpan (T **225**) No. 543/5, each×3 (279t.)	13·50
SB19	15.11.02	Christmas (T **237**) No. 565×12 (372t.)	6·00
SB20	15.11.02	Christmas Nos. 565/6, each×6 (828t.)	11·00
SB21	21.3.03	Folk Tales (T **242**) Nos. 574/5, each×4 (248t.)	4·75
SB22	19.11.03	Christmas. Self adhesive No. 603×12 (528t.)	10·00
SB23	19.11.03	Christmas. Self adhesive No. 604×12 (1284t.)	17·00
SB23*a*	24.3.04	Keckec. Self adhesive 1 pane, Nos. 615a/c, each×3 (396t.)	8·50
SB24	3.7.04	Posthorn Pane. No. 628×8 (384t.)	6·50
SB25	18.11.04	Christmas. Self adhesive No. 642×12 (540t.)	12·00
SB26	18.11.04	Christmas. Self adhesive No. 643×12 (1140t.)	22·00
SB27	18.3.05	Folk Tales. Self adhesive Nos. 656/7, each×4 (392t.)	7·50
SB28	18.11.05	Christmas. Self adhesive No. 686×12 (576t.)	10·00
SB29	18.11.05	Christmas. Self adhesive No. 688×12 (576t.)	20·00
SB30	24.3.06	Children's Book Characters. Self adhesive Nos. 700/1, each×4 (392t.)	8·00
SB31	17.11.06	Christmas. Self adhesive No. 719×10	10·00
SB32	17.11.06	Christmas. Self adhesive No. 720×10	18·00

Where the same design, or subject, appears more than once in a set only the first number is given. Scenes and buildings are listed under the town or geographical area in which they are situated. Portraits are listed under surnames only. In cases of difficulty part of the inscription has been used to identify the stamp.

Trieste

A Free Territory of Trieste was created by the Treaty of Paris, 10 February 1947. It consisted of two zones: Zone A, including the city of Trieste and a coastal strip to the west, administered by a joint British and United States Military Government; and Zone B, including the villages of Koper, Pirran and Novigrad to the south of Trieste, administered by a Yugoslav Military Government.

ZONE A

ALLIED MILITARY GOVERNMENT

100 Centesimi = 1 Lira

From 1945 to 1947 the stamps of Venezia Giulia (Italian stamps overprinted "A.M.G. V.G.") were used in this area.

Stamps of Italy overprinted

(1) (2) (3)

1947 (1 Oct)–**48**. Stamps of 1945–48 (T **192/7**) variously optd as T **1** to **3**.

1	**1**	25c. greenish blue	20	10
2		50c. violet	20	10
3		1l. green	20	10
4		2l. purple-brown	20	10
5		3l. scarlet	20	10
6		4l. vermilion	20	10
7		5l. dull blue	20	10
8		6l. bluish violet	20	10
9		8l. blue-green (1.3.48)	2·10	1·80
10		10l. grey	20	10
11		10l. vermilion (1.3.48)	7·75	20
12		15l. pale blue	50	10
13		20l. purple	2·50	10
14	**2**	25l. deep green	3·75	2·10
15	**1**	30l. bright blue (1.3.48)	£190	3·25
16	**2**	50l. brown-purple	3·75	2·10
17	**3**	100l. carmine	26·00	14·50
1/17 *Set of* 17			£225	23·00

(3a) (P 4)

1947 (1 Oct)–**48**. AIR. Air stamps of 1945–48 optd with T **3** (1l. to 50l.) or T **3a** (others).

18	**198**	1l. greenish slate	30	20
19	**199**	2l. dull ultramarine	30	20
20		5l. deep green	2·40	1·60
21	**198**	10l. carmine-red	2·50	1·60
22	**199**	25l. yellow-brown	8·25	2·50
23	**198**	50l. reddish violet	33·00	3·75
24	**204**	100l. deep bluish green (1.3.48)	80·00	3·50
25		300l. magneta (1.3.48)	11·50	12·50
26		500l. dull ultramarine (1.3.48)	16·00	14·50
27		1000l. purple-brown (24.9.48)	£160	£140
18/27 *Set of* 10			£275	£160

1947 (1 Oct)–**48**. EXPRESS LETTER. Nos. E681/3 and E685 optd with T **3**.

E28	E **201**	15l. lake	20	20
E29	E **200**	25l. red-orange (1.3.48)	37·00	5·25
E30		30l. violet	65	65
E31	E **201**	60l. carmine (1.3.48)	26·00	10·50
E28/31 *Set of* 4			55·00	15·00

1947 (1 Oct)–**48**. PARCEL POST. Contemporary Parcel Post stamps optd with Type P **4** on each half of the stamp.

			Un pair	*Used pair*	*Used half*
P32	P **201**	1l. yellow-brown	50	20	20
P33		2l. turquoise-blue	65	25	20
P34		3l. red-orange	75	30	20
P35		4l. grey	1·00	80	20
P36		5l. brt purple (1.3.48)	2·10	1·50	30
P37		10l. violet	4·25	3·00	50
P38		20l. brown-purple	6·25	4·25	65
P39		50l. vermilion	10·50	8·25	75
P40		100l. blue	12·50	10·50	1·30
P41		200l. deep green (1.3.48)	£425	£450	6·25
P42		300l. deep claret	£225	£250	5·25
P43		500l. deep brown (1.3.48)	£130	£160	2·10
P32/43 *Set of* 12			£750	£800	16·00

The left-hand portion is affixed to the packet-card, the right-hand portion to the receipt. Prices in the first column are for unused complete pairs, in the second column for used pairs (usually cancelled-to-order) and in the third column for the left half used.

1947 (1 Oct)–**49**. CONCESSIONAL LETTER POST. Optd with T **1**. W **191**. P 14.

CL44	–	1l. brown (No. CL649)	20	10
CL45	CL **201**	8l. rose-red (29.10.47)	7·75	1·60
CL46	CL **220**	15l. violet (30.7.49)	42·00	4·75
CL44/46 *Set of* 3			45·00	5·75

1947 (1 Oct). POSTAGE DUE. Optd with T **1**. W **191**. P 14.

D44	D **192**	1l. orange	65	40
D45		5l. violet	4·50	30
		a. No wmk	£3250	£130
D46		10l. blue	10·50	1·00
D47		20l. carmine	23·00	1·60
D44/47 *Set of* 4			35·00	3·00

1947 (1 Oct)–**49**. POSTAGE DUE. Optd with T **1**.

D48	D **201**	1l. red-orange (15.4.49)	40	75
D49		2l. blue-green	40	20
D50		3l. carmine (24.1.49)	75	1·30
D51		4l. sepia (24.1.49)	7·25	8·25
D52		5l. violet (15.4.49)	85·00	12·50
D53		6l. ultramarine (2-4.1.49)	23·00	22·00
D54		8l. mauve (24.1.49)	50·00	60·00
D55		10l. blue (15.4.49)	£120	12·50
D56		12l. brown (24.1.49)	18·00	19·00
D57		20l. bright purple (15.4.49)	16·00	3·75
D58		50l. turquoise-green	2·10	50
D48/58 *Set of* 11			£300	£130

1947 (19 Nov). AIR. 50th Anniv of Radio. Nos. 688/93 optd with T **2**.

59	**202**	6l. bluish violet	1·60	1·80
60	**203**	10l. deep carmine-red	1·60	1·80
61	–	20l. reddish orange	7·75	2·50
62	**202**	25l. turquoise-blue	1·80	2·10
63	**203**	35l. deep dull blue	2·10	2·50
64	–	50l. bright purple	7·75	2·50
59/64 *Set of* 6			20·00	12·00

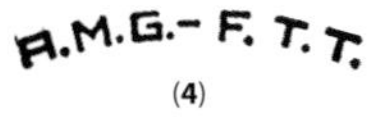

(4)

1948 (1 July). Centenary of 1848 Revolution. Nos. 706/17 optd with T **4**.

65		3l. sepia	25	20
66		4l. bright purple	25	20
67		5l. blue	25	20
68		6l. green	25	20
69		8l. chocolate	25	20
70		10l. rose-red	35	20
71		12l. grey-green	50	1·00
72		15l. black	20·00	7·25
73		20l. carmine	21·00	7·25
74		30l. blue	2·50	1·60
75		50l. violet	12·50	16·00
76		100l. slate-blue	42·00	37·00
65/76 *Set of* 12			90·00	65·00

(5) (5a)

1948 (8 Sept). Trieste Philatelic Congress.

(a) POSTAGE Nos. 661, 663 and 667, optd with T **5**

77	**192**	8l. blue-green (R.)	20	20
78	**193**	10l. vermilion (R.)	20	20
79	**194**	30l. bright blue (R.)	2·10	2·10

(b) AIR. Nos. 674, 676 and 678 optd with T **5a**

80	**198**	10l. carmine	30	30
81	**199**	25l. brown	75	75
82	**198**	50l. violet	75	75
77/82 *Set of* 6			3·75	3·75

1948 (24 Sept). EXPRESS LETTER. Centenary of 1848 Revolution. No. E718 optd with T **4**.

E83	E **209**	35l. violet	8·25	5·25

1948 (15 Oct). Bassano Bridge. No. 718 optd with T **4**.

84	**209**	15l. deep blue-green (R.)	1·30	1·20

(6) (7) (8)

1948 (15 Nov). Donizetti. No. 719 optd with T **6**.

85	**210**	15l. sepia (G.)	8·25	1·30

1949 (2 May). 25th Biennial Art Exhibition, Venice. Nos. 721/4 optd with T **3a**.

86		5l. brown-red and flesh	1·30	1·00
87		15l. green and cream	8·25	9·00
88		20l. red-brown and buff	6·25	1·30
89		50l. blue and lemon	12·50	7·25
86/89 *Set of* 4			25·00	17·00

1949 (2 May). 27th Milan Fair. No. 720 optd with T **4**.

90	**211**	20l. sepia (R.)	9·50	2·40

1949 (2 May). 75th Anniv of Founding of Universal Postal Union. No. 725 optd with T **4**.

91	**213**	50l. ultramarine (R.)	4·25	3·75

1949 (30 May). Centenary of Roman Republic. No. 726 optd with T **4**.

92	**214**	100l. brown (R.)	80·00	80·00

1949 (8 June). First Trieste Free Election. No. 732 optd as T **7** (smaller).

93	**218**	20l. lake (G.)	4·25	2·10

1949 (15 June). European Recovery Plan. Nos. 727/9 optd with T **3a**.

94	**215**	5l. blue-green	10·50	5·50
		a. Opt inverted	£1600	
95		15l. violet	10·50	12·50
96		20l. brown	10·50	8·25
94/96 *Set of* 3			28·00	24·00

1949 (8 July). Second World Health Congress, Rome. No. 733 optd with T **3a**.

97	**219**	20l. violet (R.)	12·50	4·25

1949 (16 July). Honouring Giuseppe Mazzini (revolutionary). No. 730 optd with T **6**.

98	**216**	20l. grey-black (R.)	9·50	3·25

1949 (16 July). Bicentenary of Birth of Vittorio Alfieri (poet). No. 731 optd with T **6**.

99	**217**	20l. sepia (R.)	9·50	3·25

1949 (27 Aug). 400th Anniv of Completion of Palladio's Basilica at Vicenza. No. 734 optd with T **3a**.

100	**220**	20l. violet	18·00	11·50

1949 (27 Aug). 500th Anniv of Birth of Lorenzo de Medici ("The Magnificent"). No. 735 optd with T **6**.

101	**221**	20l. violet-blue	9·50	3·25

1949 (10 Sept). Thirteenth Bari Fair. No. 736 optd with T **4**.

102	**222**	20l. scarlet (G.)	9·50	3·25

1949 (21 Oct)–**50**. Stamps of 1945–48 optd with T **7**.

103	**195**	1l. green (28.12.49)	20	20
104	–	2l. purple-brown (No. 656) (28.12.49)	20	20
105	**194**	3l. scarlet (21.10.49)	20	20
106	**193**	5l. dull blue (5.11.49)	20	20
107	**195**	6l. bluish violet (28.12.49)	20	20
108	**192**	8l. blue-green (28.12.49)	21·00	7·25
109	**193**	10l. vermilion (7.11.49)	20	20
110	**195**	15l. pale blue (28.11.49)	1·70	50
111	**194**	20l. purple (21.10.49)	1·30	50
112	**196**	25l. deep green (25.2.50)	26·00	3·25
113		50l. brown-purple (19.1.50)	37·00	1·60
114	**197**	100l. carmine (23.11.49)	£120	10·50
103/114 *Set of* 12			£190	22·00

1949 (7 Nov)–**52**. AIR. Air stamps of 1945–46 and 1948 optd with T **7**.

115	**198**	10l. carmine (28.12.49)	20	10
116	**199**	25l. brown (23.1.50)	20	10
117	**198**	50l. violet (5.12.49)	20	10
118	**204**	100l. blue-green (7.11.49)	1·00	10
119		300l. magenta (25.11.50)	10·50	6·25
120		500l. blue (25.11.50)	12·50	9·50
121		1000l. brown-purple (18.2.52)	27·00	21·00
115/121 *Set of* 7			46·00	33·00

1949 (7 Nov)–**52**. CONCESSIONAL LETTER POST. Nos. CL734/5 optd with T **7**.

CL122	CL **220**	15l. violet	1·60	20
CL123		20l. reddish violet (4.2.52)	7·75	20

1949 (7 Nov)–**52**. POSTAGE DUE. Nos. D690/703 optd with T **7**.

D122	D **201**	1l. red-orange (22.11.49)	20	10
D123		2l. blue-green (28.12.49)	20	10
D124		3l. carmine (28.12.49)	20	10
D125		5l. violet (7.11.49)	75	10
D126		6l. ultramarine (7.11.49)	30	10
D127		8l. mauve (16.5.50)	30	10
D128		10l. blue (16.5.50)	50	10
D129		12l. brown (7.11.49)	1·30	10
D130		20l. bright purple (16.5.50)	3·25	20
D131		25l. brown-red (28.12.49)	4·00	1·80
D132		50l. turquoise-green (7.11.49)	3·25	1·00
D133		100l. brown-orange (25.11.50)	10·50	75
D134		500l. reddish purple and blue (11.2.52)	65·00	18·00
D122/134 *Set of* 13			80·00	20·00

1949 (7 Nov). 150th Anniv of Volta's Discovery of the Electric Cell. Nos. 737/8 optd with T **7**.

135	**223**	20l. carmine-red	3·25	3·25
136	**224**	50l. blue	12·50	12·50

1949 (7 Nov). Rebuilding of Holy Trinity Bridge, Florence. No. 739 optd with T **7**.

137	**225**	20l. green	4·25	2·10

1949 (7 Nov). Bimillenary of Death of Catullus (poet). No. 740 optd with T **7**.

138	**226**	20l. blue	3·25	2·10

1949 (22 Nov)–**54**. PARCEL POST. Contemporary Parcel Post stamps optd on each half of the stamp as T **7** but smaller.

			Un pair	*Used pair*	*Used half*
P139	P **201**	1l. yellow-brn (7.10.50)	1·00	1·30	20
P140		2l. turquoise-bl (1.8.51)	30	10	10
P141		3l. red-orange (1.8.51)	30	10	10
P142		4l. grey (1.8.51)	30	10	10
P143		5l. bright purple	30	10	10
P144		10l. violet	1·30	30	20
P145		20l. brown-purple	1·30	30	20
P146		30l. reddish pur (6.3.52)	75	30	20
P147		50l. vermilion (10.3.50)	1·00	30	20
P148		100l. blue (9.11.50)	3·25	2·50	50
P149		200l. deep green	26·00	31·00	65
P150		300l. deep claret (9.1.50)	80·00	95·00	65
P151		500l. dp brown (25.12.50)	49·00	60·00	95
P152	P **298**	1000l. ultram (12.8.54)	£180	£180	6·25
P139/152 *Set of* 14			£300	£325	9·25

See note below No. P43.

1949 (28 Dec). Bicentenary of Birth of Domenico Cimarosa (composer). No. 741 optd with T **7**.

153	**227**	20l. slate-violet (R.)	4·75	2·10
		a. Opt double	£1000	

1950 (12 Apr). 28th Milan Fair. No. 742 optd as T **7** (smaller).

154	**228**	20l. brown (R.)	4·25	1·80

1950 (29 Apr). 32nd International Automobile Exhibition, Turin. No. 743 optd as T **7** (smaller).

155	**229**	20l. grey-violet (R.)	1·60	1·40

1950 (22 May). Fifth General Conference of U.N.E.S.C.O. Nos. 744/5 optd as T **7** (smaller).

156	–	20l. grey-green (R.)	2·50	1·00
157	**230**	55l. blue (R.)	10·50	9·50

1950 (29 May). Holy Year. Nos. 746/7 optd with T **7**.

158	**231**	20l. violet	3·25	1·00
159		55l. blue	12·50	10·50

1950 (10 June). Honouring Gaudenzio Ferrari (painter). No. 748 optd as T **7** (smaller).

160	**232**	20l. grey-green (R.)	2·50	2·10

1950 (15 July). International Radio Conference. Nos. 749/50 optd as T 7 (smaller).
161 **233** 20l. violet (R.) 6·25 4·75
162 55l. blue (R.) 18·00 19·00

1950 (22 July). Bicentenary of Death of Ludovico Muratori (historian). No. 751 optd with T **7**.
163 **234** 20l. brown 4·75 2·10

1950 (29 July). 900th Anniv of Death of Guido D'Arezzo. No. 752 optd "AMG/FTT" in two lines.
164 **235** 20l. green (R.) 4·75 2·10

1950 (21 Aug). 14th Levant Fair, Bari. No. 753 optd as T **7** (smaller).
165 **236** 20l. red-brown 2·50 2·10

1950 (27 Aug). Second Trieste Fair. Nos. 664/5 optd with T **8**.
166 **195** 15l. pale blue 2·10 2·30
167 **194** 20l. purple 2·50 85
a. Opt inverted £130 £190

1950 (11 Sept). Wool Industry Pioneers. No. 754 optd "AMG/FTT" in two lines.
168 **237** 20l. deep blue (R.) 1·60 1·30

1950 (16 Sept). European Tobacco Conference, Rome. Nos. 755/7 optd with T **7**.
169 **238** 5l. green and magenta 1·00 95
170 – 20l. green and brown 2·20 2·00
171 – 55l. brown and bright blue 23·00 22·00
169/171 *Set of 3* 24·00 22·00

1950 (16 Sept). Bicentenary of Academy of Fine Arts. No. 758 optd with T **7**.
172 **239** 20l. red-brown and brown 3·25 1·60

1950 (16 Sept). Centenary of Birth of Augusto Righi. No. 759 optd with T **7**.
173 **240** 20l. black and buff 4·75 1·60

1950 (27 Sept)–**52**. EXPRESS LETTER. Nos. E684/5 optd with T **7**.
E174 E **200** 50l. bright purple (4.2.52) 4·75 1·30
E175 E **201** 60l. carmine 7·75 1·60

1950 (20 Oct). Stamps of 1950 (Nos. 760/78) optd as T **7**, but smaller. (Nos. 176/92 12½ mm. long. Nos. 193/4 10½ mm.).
176 50c. violet-blue 20 10
177 1l. blackish violet 20 10
178 2l. black-brown 20 10
179 5l. black 20 10
180 6l. purple-brown 20 10
181 10l. green 50 20
182 12l. turquoise-green 75 30
183 15l. slate-blue 1·00 20
184 20l. bright violet 75 10
185 25l. orange-brown 2·10 20
186 30l. bright purple 65 50
187 35l. carmine 1·30 1·00
188 40l. brown 1·00 30
189 50l. violet 20 10
190 55l. blue 20 20
191 60l. scarlet 5·25 4·25
192 65l. blue-green 20 20
193 100l. chestnut 3·75 20
194 200l. yellow-brown 2·10 2·50
176/194 *Set of 19* 19·00 9·75

1951 (27 Mar). Centenary of First Tuscan Stamp. Nos. 779/80 optd as T **7** (smaller).
195 **242** 20l. scarlet and bright purple 2·75 2·50
196 55l. blue and ultramarine 37·00 33·00

1951 (2 Apr). 33rd International Automobile Exhibition, Turin. No. 781 optd as T **7** (smaller).
197 **243** 20l. blue-green 1·70 1·80

1951 (11 Apr). Consecration of Hall of Peace, Rome. No. 782 optd as T **7** (smaller).
198 **244** 20l. bright violet 2·10 1·80

1951 (12 Apr). 29th Milan Fair. Nos. 783/4 optd with T **7** (20l.) or smaller (55l.).
199 **245** 20l. yellow-brown 2·50 2·30
200 **246** 55l. blue 2·10 2·50

1951 (26 Apr). Tenth International Textiles Exhibition, Turin. No. 785 optd as T **7** (smaller).
201 **247** 20l. violet 2·10 1·80

1951 (5 May). Fifth Centenary of Birth of Columbus. No. 786 optd with T **7**.
202 **248** 20l. turquoise-green 2·75 2·75

1951 (18 May). Int. Gymnastic Festival, Florence. Nos. 787/9 optd with T **7**.
203 **249** 5l. scarlet and sepia 7·25 12·50
204 10l. scarlet and turquoise-green 7·25 12·50
205 15l. scarlet and ultramarine 7·25 12·50
203/205 *Set of 3* 20·00 34·00

1951 (18 June). Restoration of Montecassino Abbey. Nos. 790/1 optd as T **7** (smaller).
206 **250** 20l. violet 85 75
207 – 55l. blue 1·90 1·80

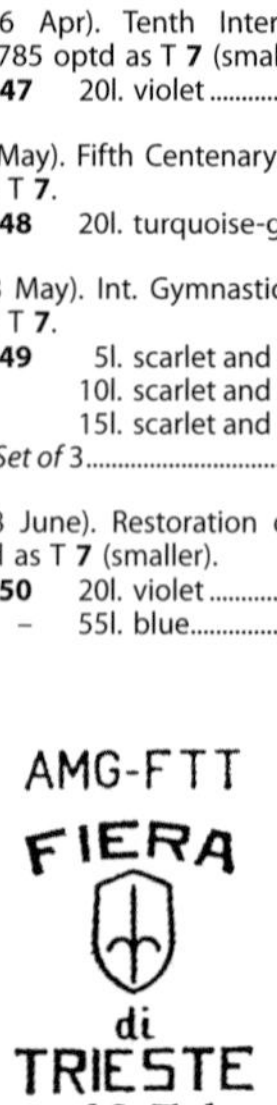

(**9**)

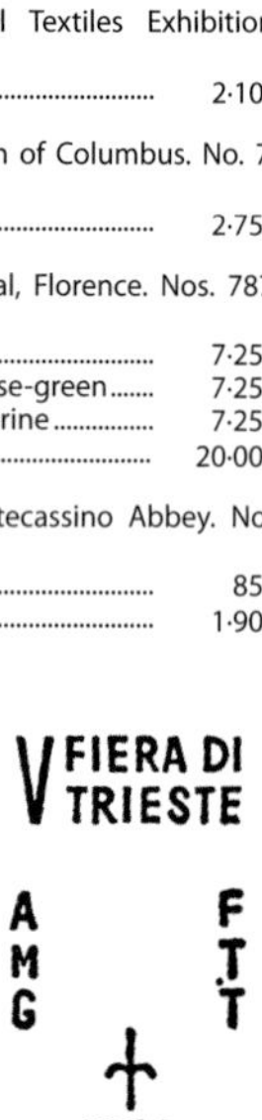

(**10**)

1951 (24 June). Third Trieste Fair. Nos. 764, 768 and 774 optd with T **9**.
208 6l. purple-brown 50 40
209 20l. bright violet 75 65
210 55l. blue 1·00 95
208/210 *Set of 3* 2·00 1·80

1951 (23 July). 500th Anniv of Birth of Perugino (painter). No. 792 optd "AMG/FTT" in two lines.
211 **251** 20l. red-brown and sepia 1·00 95

1951 (23 July). Triennial Art Exhibition, Milan. Nos. 793/4 optd "AMG/FTT" (in two lines, 20l.) or with T **7** (55l.).
212 **252** 20l. black and grey-green (R.) 1·00 1·20
213 – 55l. pink and blue (R.) 2·10 2·30

1951 (23 Aug). World Cycling Championship. No. 795 optd as T **7** (smaller).
214 **253** 25l. grey-black (R.) 5·25 1·60

1951 (8 Sept). Fifteenth Levant Fair, Bari. No. 796 optd as T **7** (smaller).
215 **254** 25l. bright blue 1·20 1·00

1951 (15 Sept). Centenary of Birth of F. P. Michetti. No. 797 optd with T **7**.
216 **255** 25l. deep brown (R.) 1·20 1·00

1951 (11 Oct). Sardinian Stamp Centenary. Nos. 798/800 optd "AMG FTT" in blue.
217 **256** 10l. black and sepia 65 75
218 – 25l. blue-green and carmine 75 50
219 – 60l. orange-red and blue 1·00 1·20
217/219 *Set of 3* 2·20 2·20

1951 (31 Oct). Industrial Census. No. 801 optd "AMG FTT".
220 **257** 10l. green 75 65

1951 (31 Oct). National Census. No. 802 optd "AMG FTT".
221 **258** 25l. violet-black 85 75

1951 (21 Nov). Forestry Festival. Nos. 806/7 optd as T **7** (smaller).
222 **260** 10l. deep green and olive-green 85 75
223 – 25l. deep green 1·00 85

1951 (23 Nov). Verdi. Nos. 803/5 optd "AMG FTT".
224 – 10l. blue-green and purple 75 65
225 **259** 25l. sepia and reddish brown 85 75
226 – 60l. deep blue and blue-green 1·50 1·40
224/226 *Set of 3* 2·75 2·50

1952 (28 Jan). Bellini. No. 808 optd "AMG FTT".
227 **261** 25l. grey-black 1·00 75

1952 (1 Feb). Caserta Palace. No. 809 optd as T **7** (smaller).
228 **262** 25l. bistre and deep green 1·00 75

1952 (26 Mar). Sports Stamps Exhibition. No. 810 optd as T **7** (smaller).
229 **263** 25l. brown and grey-black 90 75

1952 (12 Apr). 30th Milan Fair. No. 811 optd as T **7** (smaller).
230 **264** 60l. bright blue (B.) 1·70 2·30

1952. Leonardo da Vinci. Nos. 812/14 optd as T **7** but smaller, in gold (60l.) or black.
231 **265** 25l. orange (17 Apr) 20 20
232 **266** 60l. ultramarine (31 Dec) 1·30 1·00
233 **265** 80l. brown-red (31 Dec) 2·10 1·00
231/233 *Set of 3* 3·25 2·00

1952 (7 June). Overseas Fair, Naples. No. 817 optd as T **7** (smaller).
234 **268** 25l. bright blue 80 55

1952 (14 June). Modena and Parma Stamp Centenaries. Nos. 815/16 optd "AMG FTT" in two vertical lines.
235 **267** 25l. black and red-brown 65 55
236 60l. indigo and blue 80 65

1952 (14 June). Art Exhibition, Venice. No. 818 optd "AMG/FTT".
237 **269** 25l. black and cream 90 80

1952 (19 June). Thirteenth Padua Fair. No. 819 optd "AMG/FTT" in two lines, in red.
238 **270** 25l. red and slate-blue 80 55

1952 (28 June). 4th Trieste Fair. No. 820 optd "AMG/FTT" in two lines.
239 **271** 25l. green, red and brown 80 55

1952 (6 Sept). Sixteenth Levant Fair. No. 821 optd as T **7** (smaller).
240 **272** 25l. deep green 80 55

1952 (20 Sept). Savonarola. No. 822 optd as T **7** (smaller), in gold.
241 **273** 25l. bluish violet 80 55

1952 (1 Oct). Private Aeronautics Conference. No. 823 optd as T **7** (smaller).
242 **274** 60l. blue and ultramarine (B.) 1·70 2·20

1952 (4 Oct). Alpine Troops Exhibition. No. 824 optd "AMG FTT".
243 **275** 25l. grey-black 1·00 65

1952 (3 Nov). Armed Forces Day. No. 825 optd as T **7** (smaller), and Nos. 826/7 optd "AMG FTT" in two vertical lines.
244 **276** 10l. myrtle-green 20 10
245 **277** 25l. black-brown and grey-brown 55 35
246 – 60l. black and pale blue 80 1·00
244/246 *Set of 3* 1·40 1·30

1952 (21 Nov). Ethiopia Mission. No. 828 optd as T **7** (smaller).
247 **278** 25l. brown and orange-brown 1·10 55

1952 (6 Dec). Centenary of Birth of Gemito (sculptor). No. 829 optd as T **7** but smaller.
248 **279** 25l. red-brown 1·00 55

1952 (6 Dec). Centenary of Birth of Mancini (painter). No. 830 optd as T **7** but smaller.
249 **280** 25l. blackish green 1·00 55

1953 (5 Jan). Centenary of Martyrdom of Belfiore. No. 831 optd "AMG FTT".
250 **281** 25l. deep blue and black (B.) 1·00 55

1953 (21 Feb). Antonello Exhibition, Messina. No. 832 optd as T **7** (smaller).
251 **282** 25l. brown-red 90 55

1953 (24 Apr). 20th "Mille Miglia" Car Race. No. 833 optd as T **7** (smaller).
252 **283** 25l. bright violet 90 55

1953 (30 Apr). Creation of Orders of Meritorious Labour. No. 834 optd as T **7** (smaller).
253 **284** 25l. bright violet 90 55

1953 (30 May). Third Centenary of Birth of Corelli (composer). No. 835 optd as T **7** (smaller).
254 **285** 25l. brown 90 55

1953 (16 June)–**54**. Stamps of 1953–54 (Nos. 836/44) optd as T **7** (smaller).
255 **286** 5l. slate 20 10
256 10l. orange-red 20 10
257 12l. deep bluish green 20 10
258 13l. bright reddish purple (1.2.54) 20 10
259 20l. sepia 30 15
260 25l. reddish violet 35 20
261 35l. carmine-red 45 45
262 60l. blue 55 55
263 80l. orange-brown 65 65
255/263 *Set of 9* 2·75 2·20

1953 (27 June). Seventh Centenary of Death of St. Clare. No. 847 optd as T **7** (smaller).
264 **287** 25l. brown-red and deep brown 1·10 80

1953 (27 June). Fifth Trieste Fair. Nos. 765, 769 and 775 optd with T **10**.
265 10l. green (R.) 35 45
266 25l. orange-brown (G.) 55 45
267 60l. scarlet (G.) 55 70
265/267 *Set of 3* 1·30 1·40

1953 (8 July). CONCESSIONAL PARCEL POST. Nos. CP848/51 optd as T **7** (smaller).

			Un pair	*Used left*	*Used right*
CP268	CP **288**	40l. brown-orange	8·50	1·70	2·20
CP269		50l. blue	8·50	1·70	2·20
CP270		75l. sepia	8·50	1·70	2·20
CP271		110l. lilac-rose	8·50	1·70	2·20
CP268/CP271 *Set of 4*			31·00	6·00	8·00

Prices for used pairs are same as for unused.

1953 (11 July). Mountains Festival No. 848 optd as T **7** (smaller).
272 **288** 25l. blue-green 1·10 80

1953 (16 July). International Agriculture Exhibition, Rome Nos. 849/50 optd as T **7** (smaller).
273 **289** 25l. sepia 55 45
274 60l. blue 65 65

1953 (6 Aug). Fourth Anniv of Atlantic Pact. Nos. 851/2 optd "AMG FTT".
275 **290** 25l. deep turquoise and yellow-orange 1·10 80
276 60l. violet-blue and mauve 2·75 3·25

1953 (13 Aug). Fifth Centenary of Birth of Signorelli (painter). No. 853 optd as T **7** (smaller).
277 **291** 25l. grey-green and sepia 1·00 80

1953 (5 Sept). Sixth International Microbiological Congress. No. 854 optd as T **7** (smaller).
278 **292** 25l. sepia and greenish black 1·00 80

1954 (26 Jan). Tourist Series. Nos. 855/60 optd as T **7** (smaller).
279 10l. red-brown and sepia 20 20
280 12l. black and greenish blue 25 25
281 20l. reddish brown and brown-orange 30 20
282 25l. deep blue-green and pale blue 30 15
283 35l. brown and buff 40 60
284 60l. deep blue and turquoise-green 55 70
279/284 *Set of 6* 1·80 1·90

1954 (11 Feb). 25th Anniv of Lateran Treaty. Nos. 861/2 optd as T **7** (smaller).
285 **254** 25l. sepia and bistre-brown 45 35
286 60l. blue and bright blue 65 80

1954 (25 Feb). Introduction of Television in Italy. Nos. 863/4 optd "AMG/FTT" in two lines.
287 **295** 25l. bluish violet 45 35
288 60l. deep turquoise-green 65 80

1954 (20 Mar). Encouragement to Taxpayers. No. 865 optd as T **7** (smaller).
289 **296** 25l. reddish violet 1·10 55

1954 (24 Apr). First Experimental Helicopter Mail Flight, Milan–Turin. No. 866 optd "AMG FTT".
290 **297** 25l. blackish green 65 55

1954 (1 June). Tenth Anniv of Resistance Movement. No. 867 optd as T **7** but smaller.
291 **298** 25l. grey-black and orange-brown 65 55

1954 (18 June). Sixth Trieste Fair. Nos. 282 and 284 of Trieste additionally optd "FIERA DI/TRIESTE/1954".
292 25l. deep blue-green and pale blue 65 55
293 60l. deep blue and turquoise-green 80 65

1954 (19 June). Centenary of Birth of Catalani (composer). No. 868 optd "AMG FTT".
294 **299** 25l. deep grey-green 65 55

1954 (8 July). Seventh Centenary of Birth of Marco Polo. Nos. 869/70 optd as T **7** but smaller.
295 **300** 25l. brown 45 35
296 60l. slate-green 65 80

1954 (6 Sept). 60th Anniv of Italian Touring Club. No. 871 optd as T **7** (smaller).
297 **301** 25l. deep green and scarlet 80 65

1954 (30 Oct). International Police Congress, Rome. Nos. 872/3 optd as T **7** (smaller).
298 **302** 25l. carmine-red 45 35
299 60l. bright blue 55 45

The use of stamps of the Allied Military Government ceased on 15 November 1954.

ZONE B

YUGOSLAV MILITARY GOVERNMENT

For Italian stamps surcharged "1.V. 1945 TRIESTE/TRST", new value and star, see Venezia Giulia.

Stamps of Yugoslavia overprinted (unless otherwise indicated)

PRINTERS. The "STT VUJA" overprints on Yugoslav stamps were printed in Belgrade and the stamps without overprints were printed by the "Ljuska" Printing Works, Ljubljana.

Italian Currency

B 1

B 2

(Des Sakside. Litho)

1948 (1 May). Labour Day. P 10½×11½.

A. Inscr in Slovene: "I. MAJ 1948 V STO"

B. Inscr in Italian: "I. MAGGIO 1948 NEL TLT".

C. Inscr in Croat: "I. SVIBANJ 1948 U STT".

B1 **B 1** 100l. carmine-red and stone (A) 5·50 2·75
a. Strip of 3. Nos. B1/3 50·00
B2 100l. carmine-red and stone (B) 5·50 2·75
B3 100l. carmine-red and stone (C) 5·50 2·75
B1/3 *Set of* 3 15·00 7·50

Nos. B1/3 were issued together in *se-tenant* strips of three stamps within the sheet.

1948 (23 May). Red Cross. No. 545 surch "VUJA/S.T.T." and new value, in blue.
B3*a* **131** 2l. on 50p. brown and red 45·00 45·00

1948 (23 May). POSTAGE DUE. Red Cross. No. D546 surch "VUJA STT" and new value, in red.
BD4 2l. on 50p. green and red £325 £325

(Des M. Strenar. Typo)

1948 (17 Oct). AIR. Economic Exhibition, Capodistria. P 12½×11½.
B4 **B 2** 25l. grey 1·10 1·10
B5 50l. orange 1·10 1·10

B **3** Clasped Hands, Hammer and Sickle

B **4** Fishermen and Flying Boat

B **5** Man with Donkey

B **6** Mediterranean Gull over Chimneys

(Des M. Strenar. Litho)

1949 (1 May). Labour Day. P 11½×12½.
B6 **B 3** 10l. blackish green 1·10 1·10

(Des M. Strenar (100l.), R. Krošelj (others). Litho)

1949 (1 June). AIR. P 11½.
B7 **B 4** 1l. turquoise 55 35
B8 **B 5** 2l. red-brown 55 35
B9 **B 4** 5l. blue 55 35
B10 **B 5** 10l. violet 2·75 2·20
B11 **B 4** 25l. yellow-brown 7·75 5·50
B12 **B 5** 50l. grey-green 7·75 5·50
B13 **B 6** 100l. purple-brown 14·50 10·00
B7/13 *Set of* 7 31·00 22·00

Yugoslav Currency

STT VUJA (B **7**)

STT VUJA (B **8**)

DIN 30 (B **9**)

1949 (15 Aug–20 Sept). Nos. 502/3, 505, 508/9, 511 and 514/17 optd with Type B **7** (2d. and 4d.) or as B **8** (others).
B14 **119** 0d.50 olive-grey (R.) 55 45
B15 1d. blue-green (R.) 55 45
a. Opt inverted £200 60·00
B16 **120** 2d. scarlet (B.) 55 45
B17 **121** 3d. vermilion (B.) 55 45
B18 **120** 4d. blue (R.) (20.9) 1·10 45
B19 **121** 5d. blue (R.) 1·10 45
B20 – 9d. magenta (B.) (20.9) 7·75 1·10
B21 – 12d. ultramarine (R.) 7·75 5·50
a. Opt inverted £225 £170
B22 **119** 16d. light blue (R.) (20.9) 11·00 6·75
B23 – 20d. vermilion (B.) 22·00 9·00
B14/23 *Set of* 10 48·00 23·00

The space between the lines of overprint in Type B **8** varies. It is 1¼ mm. on No. B20, 2½ mm. on Nos. B14/15 and B21/3 and 4 mm. on Nos. B17 and B19.

1949 (8 Sept). 75th Anniv of Universal Postal Union. As Nos. 612/13 on paper with network in colour of stamp, optd "VUJA-STT" in red.
B24 5d. blue 11·00 11·00
B25 12d. brown 11·00 11·00

1949 (15 Sept). POSTAGE DUE. Nos. D527/31 optd with Type B **8**.
BD26 **D 126** 50p. deep orange (B.) 1·10 55
BD27 1d. orange (B.) 1·10 55
BD28 2d. blue (R.) 1·10 55
BD29 3d. green (R.) 2·20 55
BD30 5d. violet (R.) 5·50 2·20
BD26/30 *Set of* 5 10·00 4·00

1949 (5 Nov). AIR. Nos. B7/13 optd "DIN" (B26/9) or surch as Type B **9** (others).
B26 **B 4** 1d. turquoise 55 35
B27 **B 5** 2d. red-brown (Br.) 55 35
B28 **B 4** 5d. blue (B.) 55 35
B29 **B 5** 10d. violet (V.) 55 35
B30 **B 4** 15d. on 25l. yellow-brown (Br.) 22·00 13·50
B31 **B 5** 20d. on 50l. grey-green (G.) 6·75 4·50
B32 **B 6** 30d. on 100l. purple-brown 7·75 5·50
B26/32 *Set of* 7 35·00 22·00

1950 (21 Jan). Centenary of Yugoslav Railways. Nos. 631/33*a* all on paper with network in colour of stamp, optd "VUJA-STT" in red.

(a) POSTAGE
B33 2d. green 4·50 1·10
B34 3d. carmine 4·50 1·10
B35 5d. blue 4·50 3·25
B36 10d. orange 20·00 11·00
a. Opt inverted £800
B33/B36 *Set of* 4 30·00 15·00

(b) AIR. No. **MS**633b with similar opt, in red

A. P 11½×12½
MSB36A*a* 10d. purple £275 £225
b. Opt inverted £850
c. Opt double £850

B. Imperf
MSB36B*a* 10d. purple £275 £225
b. Opt inverted £850
c. Opt double £850

This sheet has an engine-turned background which is not present on the Yugoslav sheet.

B **10** Girl on Donkey

B **11** Workers

BD **12** European Anchovy

(Des M. Strenar. Photo)

1950 (7 Apr)–**51**. Type B **10** and similar animal designs. P 12½.
B37 50p. greenish slate 55 55
B38 1d. lake 55 55
B38*a* 1d. orange-brown (1.3.51) 1·70 55
B39 2d. blue 55 55
B39*a* 2d. light blue (1.3.51) 1·70 55
B40 3d. red-brown 55 55
B40*a* 3d. brown-red (1.3.51) 2·20 55
B41 5d. turquoise-green 4·50 55
B42 10d. brown 4·50 55
B43 15d. bluish violet 28·00 11·00
B44 20d. blackish green 11·00 5·50
B37/44 *Set of* 11 50·00 19·00

Designs:—1d. Cockerel; 2d. Geese; 3d. Bees on honeycomb; 5d. Oxen; 10d. Turkey; 15d. Kids; 20d. Silkworms on mulberry leaves.

1950 (1 May). May Day. P 12½.
B45 **B 11** 3d. violet 80 65
B46 10d. carmine 1·50 1·30

1950 (3 July). Red Cross. No. 616 optd "VUJA/STT".
B47 **160** 50p. brown and red 2·20 1·70

1950 (3 July). POSTAGE DUE. Red Cross. No. D617 optd "VUJA/STT".
BD48 50p. bright purple and red 2·20 1·70

(Des R. Krošelj. Photo)

1950 (1 Nov). POSTAGE DUE. Fish. Type BD **12** and similar design. P 12½.
BD49 – 50p. orange-brown 5·50 1·10
BD50 – 1d. grey-green 5·50 2·20
BD51 **BD 12** 2d. greenish blue 5·50 2·20
BD52 3d. deep blue 5·50 2·20
BD53 5d. reddish purple 28·00 9·00
BD49/53 *Set of* 5 45·00 15·00

Design:—50p., 1d. Two meagres.

B **12** Worker

B **13** P. P. Vergerio, Jr.

(Des B. Jakac. Photo)

1951 (1 May). May Day. P 12½.
B48 **B 12** 3d. red 1·10 55
B49 10d. olive 1·70 1·10

1951 (7 Oct). Red Cross. No. 702 optd "STT/VUJA".
B49*a* **191** 0d.50 ultramarine and red £275 £275

1951 (30 Oct). POSTAGE DUE. Red Cross. No. D703 optd "STT/VUJA".
BD54 0d.50 emerald and red £275 £275

(Des R. Krošelj. Litho)

1951 (21 Oct). Festival of Italian Culture. P 12½.
B50 **B 13** 5d. blue 1·10 1·10
B51 10d. claret 1·10 1·10
B52 20d. blackish brown 1·10 1·10
B50/52 *Set of* 3 3·00 3·00

STT VUJA

(B **14**)

1951. Cultural Anniversaries. As Nos. 698/9 but colours changed and optd with Type B **14**.
B53 10d. brown-orange (B.) (4 Nov) 1·30 1·10
B54 12d. slate-black (R.) (29 Nov) 1·30 1·10

B **14a** Koper Square

B **15** Cyclists

(Des A. Jovanovic. Photo)

1952 (4 Feb). AIR. 75th Anniv of Universal Postal Union. Type B **14a** and similar designs. P 12½.
B54*a* 5d. yellow-brown 17·00 17·00
B54*b* 15d. blue 11·00 11·00
B54*c* 25d. myrtle-green 11·00 11·00
B54*a/c* *Set of* 3 35·00 35·00

Designs: Vert—15d. Lighthouse, Piran. Horiz—25d. Hotel, Portorož.

(Des J. Trpin. Photo)

1952 (26 Mar). Physical Culture Propaganda. Type B **15** and similar horiz designs. P 12½.
B55 5d. yellow-brown 95 45
B56 10d. green (Footballers) 95 45
B57 15d. carmine (Rowing Four) 95 45
B58 28d. deep ultramarine (Yachting) 2·20 1·70
B59 50d. lake (Netball-players) 8·00 5·25
B60 100d. deep slate-blue (Diver) 21·00 12·50
B55/60 *Set of* 6 31·00 19·00

1952 (25 May). 60th Birth Anniv of Marshal Tito. As Nos. 727/9 but additionally inscr "STT VUJA".
B61 **196** 15d. deep brown 3·25 1·70
B62 **197** 28d. brown-lake 3·25 2·75
B63 – 50d. deep green 6·75 4·00
B61/63 *Set of* 3 12·00 7·50

1952 (22 June). Children's Week. As No. 730 but colour changed and optd "STT VUJA" reading upwards.
B64 **198** 15d. carmine-pink (B.) 2·20 1·10

STT
VUJNA
(B **16**)

1952 (26 July). Fifteenth Olympic Games, Helsinki. As Nos. 731/6 but colours changed and optd with Type B **16**, in red.
B65 5d. chocolate/*flesh* (Sal.) 2·20 55
B66 10d. deep green/*cream* (G.) 2·20 55
B67 15d. violet/*mauve* (B.) 2·20 55
B68 28d. chocolate/*buff* (Br.) 2·20 2·20
B69 50d. brown/*yellow* (O.) 19·00 13·50
B70 100d. ultramarine/*pink* (V.) 45·00 39·00
B65/70 *Set of* 6 65·00 50·00

1952 (13 Sept). Navy Day. Nos. 737/9 optd "STT/VUJNA", in red.
B71 15d. brown-purple 2·75 2·20
B72 28d. deep brown 3·25 2·20
B73 50d. greenish black 5·00 2·75
B71/73 *Set of* 3 10·00 6·50

1952 (15 Oct). POSTAGE DUE. Nos. D724/31 optd "STT/ VUJNA".
BD74 **D 126** 1d. chocolate (B.) 55 35
BD75 2d. emerald-green (R.) 55 35
BD76 5d. blue (R.) 55 35
BD77 10d. scarlet (B.) 55 35
BD78 20d. reddish violet (R.) 55 35
BD79 30d. orange (B.) 55 35
BD80 50d. ultramarine. (R.) 55 35
BD81 100d. reddish purple (B.) 19·00 11·00
BD74/81 *Set of* 8 21·00 12·00

1952 (26 Oct). Red Cross. No. 740 optd "STT VUJNA" reading upwards, in red.
B74 **201** 50p. red, grey and black 1·70 1·10

1952 (26 Oct). POSTAGE DUE. Red Cross. No. D741 optd "STT VUJNA" reading upwards, in red.
BD82 **D 202** 50p. red and olive-grey 1·70 1·10

1952 (4 Nov). Sixth Yugoslav Communist Party Congress. Nos. 741/4 optd "VUJNA STT".
B75 **202** 15d. lake-brown (R.) 1·30 90
B76 15d. turquoise (R.) 1·30 90
B77 15d. chocolate (R.) 1·30 90
B78 15d. deep violet-blue (R.) 1·30 90
B75/78 *Set of* 4 4·75 3·25

B **17** European Anchovy and Starfish

(Des R. Krošelj. Photo)

1952 (29 Nov). Philatelic Exhibition, Koper. P 11½.
B78*a* B **17** 15d. red-brown 5·50 5·50
MSB78*b* 48×70 mm. B **17** 50d. blue-green. Imperf (sold at 85d.) 80·00 80·00

1953 (3 Feb). Tenth Death Anniv of Tesla (inventor). As Nos. 745/6 but colours changed and optd as Type B **16**.
B79 **203** 15d. scarlet (B.) 55 55
B80 30d. violet-blue (R.) 2·20 2·20

1953 (23 Feb–13 Mar). Stamps of Yugoslavia, some with colours changed, optd "STT/VUJNA" without serifs.
(a) As Nos. 705/14. Recess (13 March)
B81 1d. grey 13·50 10·00
B82 3d. scarlet (R.) 55 45
B83 10d. green (G.) 55 45
B84 30d. blue (B.) 5·50 3·25
B85 50d. turquoise (B.) 11·00 5·50
(b) As Nos. 718/23. Litho (25 Feb)
B86 2d. carmine-red (P.) 55 45
B87 5d. orange (Br.) 55 45
B88 15d. scarlet (R.) 1·10 1·00
B81/88 *Set of* 8 30·00 19·00
For overprint with serifs see Nos. B105/7.

1953 (21 Apr). United Nations Commemoration. Nos. 747/9 optd "STT VUJNA".
B89 15d. bronze-green (R.) 30 20
B90 30d. deep blue (R.) 55 35
B91 50d. brown-lake (B.) 1·50 1·30
B89/91 *Set of* 3 2·10 1·70

1953 (2 June). Adriatic Car and Motor-cycle Rally. As Nos. 750/3 but colours changed and additionally inscr "STT/VUJNA".
B92 15d. brown and yellow 55 35
B93 30d. bronze-green and pale emerald 55 35
B94 50d. deep magenta and salmon 55 35
B95 70d. deep blue and light blue 4·00 2·75
B92/95 *Set of* 4 5·00 3·50

1953 (18 July). As No. 754 (Marshal Tito), but colour changed, optd "STT/VUJNA".
B96 **206** 50d. deep grey-green (R.) 5·50 5·50

1953 (31 July). 38th Esperanto Congress, Zagreb. As Nos. 755/6 but colours changed, optd "STT/VUJNA", in red.
(a) POSTAGE
B97 **207** 15d. dull green and deep turquoise 2·75 2·75
(b) AIR
B98 **207** 300d. green and violet £400 £400

1953 (5 Sept). Tenth Anniv of Liberation of Istria and Slovene Coast. As No. 759, but colour changed, optd "STT/VUJNA".
B99 **209** 15d. blue (R.) 5·50 5·50

1953 (3 Oct). Death Centenary of Radicevic (poet). As No. 760 but colour changed, optd "STT/VUJNA".
B100 **210** 15d. black (R.) 2·20 1·70

1953 (25 Oct). Red Cross. As No. 761 but colour changed and optd "STT/VUJNA".
B101 **211** 2d. scarlet and bistre (B.) 1·70 1·10

1953 (25 Oct). POSTAGE DUE. Red Cross. As No. D762 but colour changed and optd "STT/VUJNA".
BD102 2d. scarlet and bright purple (B.) 1·70 1·10

1953 (29 Nov). 10th Anniv of First Republican Legislative Assembly. As Nos. 762/4 but colours changed and optd "STT/VUJNA", in the colour of the stamp.
B102 15d. slate-violet 1·60 1·10
B103 30d. lake 1·60 1·10
B104 50d. deep turquoise-green 1·60 1·10
B102/104 *Set of* 3 4·25 3·00

STT
VUJNA
(B **18**)

1954 (5 Mar). As Nos. 719, 721 and 723, but optd with Type B **18** (serifed capitals).
B105 5d. orange (V.) 1·30 55
B106 10d. green (R.) 1·10 55
B107 15d. scarlet (G.) 1·50 55
B105/107 *Set of* 3 3·50 1·50

1954 (16 Apr–9 Oct). AIR. As Nos. 675/83c but colours changed and optd "STT VUJNA".
B108 1d. deep lilac 1·10 55
B109 2d. blue-green (G.) 1·10 55
B110 3d. claret (Br.) 1·10 55
B111 5d. deep brown 1·10 55
B112 10d. turquoise 1·10 55
B113 20d. brown (Br.) 1·10 55
B114 30d. blue 1·10 55
B115 50d. olive-black 1·10 80
B116 100d. scarlet (R.) 3·25 2·20
B117 200d. blackish violet (V.) 6·75 4·50
B118 500d. orange (Br.) (9 Oct) 39·00 28·00
B108/118 *Set of* 11 50·00 35·00

1954 (30 June). Animal designs as Nos. 765/76 but colours changed and optd "STT VUJNA", in red.
B119 2d. slate, buff and Venetian red 1·10 55
B120 5d. slate, buff and bluish grey 1·10 55
B121 10d. brown and green 1·10 55
B122 15d. brown and deep turquoise-blue 1·10 55
B123 17d. sepia and black-brown 1·10 55
B124 25d. yellow, grey-blue and brown-ochre 1·10 55
B125 30d. sepia and violet-grey 1·10 55
B126 35d. slate-black and reddish purple 1·10 1·10
B127 50d. chocolate and yellow-green 2·20 1·70
B128 65d. slate-black and orange-brown 6·75 4·50
B129 70d. orange-brown and blue 17·00 9·00
B130 100d. black and pale blue 45·00 36·00
B119/130 *Set of* 12 70·00 50·00

1954 (8 Oct). 150th Anniv of Serbian Insurrection. As Nos. 778/781, but colours changed and optd "STT VUJNA" in one line (15, 50d.) or two lines (others).
B131 15d. red, blue, fawn and lake 1·10 80
B132 30d. brn-lake, flesh, turq-grn & bl (G.) 1·10 80
B133 50d. red, buff, red-brown & sepia (G.) 1·10 80
B134 70d. black-brown, turquoise-green, pale brown & deep blue-grn (R.) 2·20 1·70
B131/134 *Set of* 4 5·00 3·75

The use of stamps of the Yugoslav Military Government ceased on 25 October 1954.

On 26 October 1954, under a Four-Power Agreement, Zone A, except for three villages south of Trieste; was to be ruled by Italy, and Zone B, with the three villages, by Yugoslavia.

A final agreement between Italy and Yugoslavia, on the incorporation of these areas in the two countries, was signed at Ancona on 10 November 1975.

United Nations

KOSOVO

UNITED NATIONS INTERIM ADMINISTRATION MISSION

The following stamps were issued by the United Nations Interim Administration Mission (U.N.M.I.K.) and the Post & Telecommunications of Kosovo for postal purposes in Kosovo. They were for local use only for the first two months with international use commencing May 2000.

K **1** Orpheus (mosaic, 5–6th century, Podujeve)

K **2** Bird

(Des Sh. Nimani. Litho State Ptg Wks, Paris)

2000 (14 Mar). Artefacts. Type K **1** and similar vert designs. Multicoloured. P 13½ (30pf.) or 13½×13 (others).
K1 20pf. Type K **1** 50 50
K2 30pf. "Dardanian idol", 3500 B.C. 95 95
K3 50pf. Obverse and reverse of 4th-century B.C. silver coin, Damastion 1·50 1·50
K4 1m. Mother Teresa (statue, Prizren) 2·40 2·40
K5 2m. Map of Kosovo showing various sites 4·25 4·25
K1/K5 *Set of* 5 8·75 8·75

(Des M. Naser (20pf.), Y. Buginca (30pf.), X. Deda (50pf.), B. Palokaj (1m.), D. Duman and B. Beha (2m.). Litho)

2001 (12 Nov). Art. Type K **2** and similar multicoloured designs. P 14.
K6 20pf. Type K **2** 50 50
K7 30pf. Musician 95 95
K8 50pf. Butterfly and pear (horiz) 1·50 1·50
K9 1m. Children and stars 2·40 2·40
K10 2m. Handprints surrounding globe 4·25 4·25
K6/K10 *Set of* 5 8·75 8·75
Nos. K6/10 have the face values shown in deutsche marks and euros.

Venezia Giulia and Istria

100 Centesimi = 1 Italian Lira

A. YUGOSLAV OCCUPATION

Yugoslav partisans, who had occupied much of the Istrian peninsula in 1943–44, attacked the cities of Venezia Giulia in the last days of the war. They entered Trieste on 30 April 1945 and on 2 May the German garrison surrendered to the New Zealand Division.

The following provisional issues were made by the Yugoslavs.

ISSUE FOR TRIESTE

1.V.1945
TRIESTE +
★ L.2
TRST
(**1**)

1945 (15 June). Stamps of the Italian Social Republic, 1944–45, surch as T **1**.
(a) W **8** of Italy (Crown)
1 **14** +1l. on 30c. brown (Drummer) £550 £650
2 **12** 2+2l. on 25c. green (R.) (San Lorenzo) 20 80
3 **14** 10+10l. on 30c. brown 34·00 55·00
(b) Without wmk
4 – 20c.+1l. on 5c. brown (R.) (St. Ciriaco's Church) 20 80
5 **13** +1l. on 25c. green (B.) (San Lorenzo) 20 80
6 **14** +1l. on 30c. brown 20 80
7 **15** +1l. on 50c. violet (Fascist allegory) 20 80
8 – +1l. on 1l. violet (Montecassino Abbey) 20 80
9 – +2l. on 1l.25 blue (R.) (St. Mary of Grace, Milan) 20 80
10 – +2l. on 3l. green (R.) (St. Mary of Grace, Milan) 20 80
11 – 5+5l. on 1l. violet (R.) 55 80
12 **14** 10+10l. on 30c. brown (R.) 20 80
13 – 20+20l. on 5c. brown (B.) 9·00 11·00
2/13 *Set of* 12 41·00 65·00
A 1l. sepia and 1l. lilac-rose depicting San Giusto Cathedral, Trieste, were prepared but not issued.

ISSUE FOR ISTRIA

In June 1945 various stamps of Italy were overprinted "ISTRA" and further surcharged for use in Istria and Pola (now Pula) but they were not issued. However, four of these were further surcharged and issued on 1 July.

ISTRA
L. 6.—
(**2**)

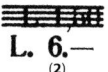

1945 (1 July). Stamp of Italy (No. 14) or Italian Social Republic (others) surch as T **2**.
14 **99** 4l. on 2l. on 1l. violet (249) (Julius Caesar) 1·10 1·10
15 **14** 6l. on 1,50l. on 75c. carmine (105) 4·50 9·00
16 – 10l. on 0,10l. on 5c. brown (106) 29·00 22·00
17 **103** 20l. on 1l. on 50c. violet (59) (Victor Emmanuel III) 5·50 9·50
14/17 *Set of* 4 36·00 37·00

ISSUE FOR FIUME (Rijeka)

(**3**)

1945 (26 July). Stamps of Italian Social Republic, 1944–45, surch as T **3**.
(a) W **8** of Italy (Crown)
18 **12** 2l. on 25c. green 1·10 80
19 **14** 16l. on 75c. carmine 9·00 17·00
(b) Without wmk
20 – 4l. on 1l. violet 1·10 80
21 – 5l. on 10c. brown 1·10 80
22 – 6l. on 10c. brown 1·10 80
23 **13** 10l. on 25c. green 1·10 80
24 **14** 16l. on 75c. red £190 £275
(c) On Express Letter stamp (Palermo Cathedral)
25 E **16** 20l. on 1l.25 green 3·25 6·25
18/25 *Set of* 8 £190 £275
On No. 25 the surcharge is much larger to conform with the horizontal format of the design.

On 9 June 1945 an agreement was signed in Belgrade under which Trieste and the roads and railways from there to Austria via Gorizia, Caporetto and Tarvisio, as well as Pola, should be under the control of the Supreme Allied Commander. The remainder of Venezia Giulia would be under Yugoslav control. The agreement formally came into effect on 12 June but the lines of demarcation were settled by an agreement signed by Lt.-Gen. Morgan and Gen. Jovanovic on 20 June.

B. ALLIED MILITARY GOVERNMENT

The area under British and United States control included Trieste, Pola, Gorizia and the Isonzo valley.

A.M.G.
V.G.
(**4**)

A.M.G.
V. G.
(**5**)

(="Allied Military Government Venezia Giulia")

1945 (22 Sept)–**47**. Stamps of Italy optd with T **4** or **5** (100l.).
(a) Imperial series
26 **100** 10c. sepia (No. 241) 20 55
27 10c. sepia (No. 633) (25.9.45) 20 55
28 **99** 20c. carmine (No. 243) (9.12.46) 20 35
29 20c. carmine (No. 634) (25.9.45) 20 1·10
30 20c. carmine. (No. 640) 55 45
31 **101** 60c. orange-vermilion (No. 636) (25.9.45) 20 55
32 **103** 60c. green (No. 641) 20 45
33 **99** 1l. violet (No. 642) 55 20
34 **101** 2l. brown-lake (No. 644) 55 20

35	**98**	5l. carmine (No. 645) (16.10.45)	80	45
36	**101**	10l. violet (No. 646)	90	45
37	**99**	20l. yellow-grn (No. 257) (10.7.46)	2·20	2·75
26/37 *Set of* 12			6·00	7·25
		(b) Stamps of 1945–48 (Nos. 649, etc.)		
38	**194**	25c. greenish blue (8.1.47)	20	55
39	–	2l. purple-brown (17.7.47)	55	45
40	**194**	3l. scarlet (8.1.47)	55	35
41		4l. vermilion (2.1.47)	55	35
42	**195**	6l. bluish violet (17.7.47)	1·90	1·30
43	**194**	20l. purple (23.7.47)	55·00	2·20
44	**196**	25l. deep green (10.7.46)	5·50	5·50
45		50l. brown-purple (10.7.46)	5·50	8·50
46	**197**	100l. carmine (13.9.46)	25·00	45·00
38/46 *Set of* 9			85·00	60·00

1945–47. AIR. Air stamps of Italy optd with T **4** (50c.) or **5** (others).

47	**110**	50c. sepia (22.9.45)	20	35
48	**198**	1l. slate (23.7.47)	55	1·10
49	**199**	2l. blue (16.1.47)	55	1·10
50		5l. deep green (23.1.47)	3·25	2·75
51	**198**	10l. carmine (23.1.47)	3·25	2·75
52	**199**	25l. blue (13.9.46)	3·25	2·75
53		25l. brown (23.7.47)	22·00	31·00
54	**198**	50l. deep green (13.9.46)	5·50	9·00
47/54 *Set of* 8			35·00	46·00

1946 (13 Sept). EXPRESS LETTER. Nos. E680 and E683 of Italy optd with T **5**.

E55	E **201**	10l. blue	5·50	3·25
E56	E **200**	30l. violet	11·00	17·00

C. YUGOSLAV MILITARY GOVERNMENT

The area under Yugoslav control included Fiume (Rijeka), all the Istrian peninsula except Pola (Pula), and former Italian territory to the N.E. of Trieste, including Postumia (Postojna).

6 Grapes

7 Roman Amphitheatre, Pula, and Istrian Fishing Vessel

8 Blue-finned Tuna

(Des M. Oražem. Photo Ljudska Ptg Wks, Ljubljana)

1945 (15 Aug–24 Dec). T **6/8** and similar designs. P 10½×11½.

57	**6**	0.25l. slate-green	55	1·50
58	–	0.50l. lake-brown	65	80
59	–	1l. scarlet (13.12)	35	65
60	–	1.50l. deep olive (24.12)	55	1·50
61	–	2l. deep blue-green	35	45
62	**7**	4l. light blue (24.12)	35	45
63	–	5l. slate (13.12)	35	45
64	–	10l. brown	1·50	1·30
65	**8**	20l. purple (13.12)	10·00	7·25
66	–	30l. bright magenta (24.12)	7·25	6·75
57/66 *Set of* 10			20·00	19·00

Designs: As T **6**—0.50l. Donkey and view; 1l. Rebuilding damaged homes; 1.50l. Olive-branch; 2l. Duino Castle, nr. Trieste. As T **7**—5l. Birthplace of Vladimir Gortan at Piran; 10l. Ploughing. As T **8**—30l. Viaduct over the Solkan.

See also Nos. 74/83 and 98/101.

(D **9**)

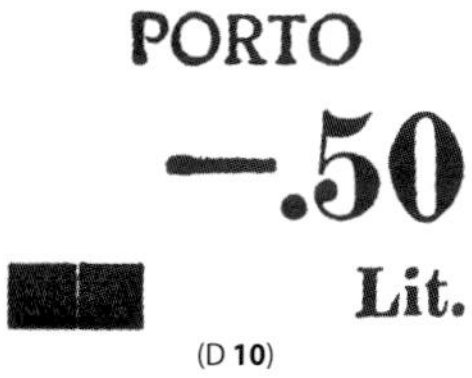

(D **10**)

1945–46. POSTAGE DUE. Stamps as last surch with value expressed in "Lit", by Tipografia Commerciale, Rijeka.

	(a) As Type D **9** (31.12.45)		
D67	1l. on 0.25l. slate-green	17·00	2·75
D68	4l. on 0.50l. lake-brown	1·90	1·10
D69	8l. on 0.50l. lake-brown	1·90	1·10
D70	10l. on 0.50l. lake-brown	11·00	3·25
D71	20l. on 0.50l. lake-brown	12·50	5·50
	(b) Surch as Type D **10** (22.2.46)		
D72	0.50l. on 20l. purple	1·10	1·50
	a. Straight top to "5" instead of curved	28·00	39·00
D73	2l. on 30l. bright magenta	2·50	3·25
	a. Curved bottom to "2" instead of straight	6·75	8·50
D67/73 *Set of* 7		43·00	17·00

(Photo Tipografija, Zagreb)

1946 (11 Feb–7 Mar). P 12 and some colours changed.

74	**6**	0.25l. grey-green (26.2)	80	55
75	–	0.50l. red-brown (18.2)	45	55
76	–	1l. green (26.2)	45	55
77	–	1.50l. deep olive (26.2)	45	55
78	–	2l. deep blue-green	45	55
79	**7**	4l. scarlet (18.2)	45	55
80	–	5l. black	45	55
81	–	10l. brown (26.2)	45	55
82	**8**	20l. blue (7.3)	4·50	1·10
83	–	30l. bright magenta (7.3)	4·00	1·10
74/83 *Set of* 10			11·00	6·00

See also Nos. 98/101.

(D **11**)

(D **12**)

1946 (25 Mar–11 May). POSTAGE DUE. Nos. 76 and 83 surch as Types D **11/12**, by Narodna Stamparija, Rijeka. Value expressed in "Lira".

D84	1l. on 1l. green	65	55
D85	2l. on 1l. green	65	55
D86	4l. on 1l. green	90	55
D87	10l. on 30l. bright magenta (11.5)	7·25	3·25
D88	20l. on 30l. bright magenta (11.5)	11·00	6·25
D89	30l. on 30l. bright magenta (11.5)	11·00	6·25
D84/89 *Set of* 6		28·00	16·00

(D **13**)

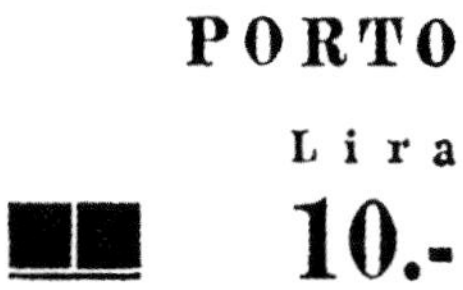

(D **14**)

1946 (7 Sept). POSTAGE DUE. Nos. 74 and 82 surch as Types D **13/14**, respectively, by Tipografia Commerciale, Rijeka.

D90	**6**	1l. on 0.25l. grey-green	1·10	80
		a. Thin "1"	60·00	36·00
D91		2l. on 0.25l. grey-green	1·90	1·10
		a. Thin "2"	36·00	31·00
D92		4l. on 0.25l. grey-green	1·10	80
		a. Thin "4"	36·00	31·00
D93	**8**	10l. on 20l. blue	6·25	2·75
		a. Thin "10"	36·00	36·00
D94		20l. on 20l. blue	12·50	6·75
		a. Thin "20"	45·00	45·00
D95		30l. on 20l. blue	14·50	7·75
		a. Thin "30"	£325	£200
D90/95 *Set of* 6			34·00	18·00

In Nos. D90a/95a the figures of value are of various sizes but all are thinner with either very small serifs or none; the variety occurs on positions 94, 95, 99 and 100.

1946 (15 Nov). Nos. 82/3 surch with new value and three bars over old value, by Urania, Rijeka.

96	1 on 20l. blue	1·70	1·70
97	2 on 30l. bright magenta	1·70	1·70

(Photo State Ptg Wks, Belgrade)

1946 (30 Nov). P 11½ and new values.

98	–	1l. yellow-green (as 76)	90	90
99	–	2l. deep blue-green (as 78)	1·00	1·00
100	–	3l. rose-carmine (as 2l.)	4·00	2·50
101	**7**	6l. ultramarine	9·00	6·75
98/101 *Set of* 4			13·50	10·00

(**15**)

(D **16**)

1947 (8 Feb). Nos. 514 and O540 of Yugoslavia, but colours changed, optd with T **15**, in Belgrade.

102	1l. on 9d. pink	45	55
103	1.50l. on 0.50d. blue	45	55
104	2l. on 9d. pink	45	55
105	3l. on 0.50d. blue	45	55
106	5l. on 9d. pink	55	65
107	6l. on 0.50d. blue	45	55
108	10l. on 9d. pink	55	65
109	15l. on 0.50d. blue	80	90
110	35l. on 9d. pink	80	1·10
111	50l. on 0.50d. blue	1·10	1·20
102/111 *Set of* 10		5·50	6·50

1947 (8 Feb). POSTAGE DUE. No. D528 of Yugoslavia, but colour changed, surch as Type D **16**, in Belgrade.

D112	1l. on 1d. blue-green	45	65
D113	2l. on 1d. blue-green	45	65
D114	6l. on 1d. blue-green	45	65
D115	10l. on 1d. blue-green	45	65
D116	30l. on 1d. blue-green	65	90
D112/116 *Set of* 5		2·20	3·25

By the Treaty of Paris, 10 February 1947, all former Italian territory in Venezia Giulia and Istria was included in Yugoslavia, except Gorizia and the area to be comprised in the Free Territory of Trieste (q.v.).

VENEZIA GIULIA. Stamps of Austria and Italy overprinted "Venezia Giulia" in 1918–19 are listed in both Part 2 (*Austria & Hungary*) and Part 8 (*Italy & Switzerland*) of this catalogue, under Austrian Territories Acquired by Italy.

Yugoslavia

The Pact of Corfu, 20 July 1917, signed by Serbian, Croatian, Slovene and Montenegrin representatives, declared that their peoples should form a single nation, to be ruled by the Serbian dynasty. On the break-up of the Austro-Hungarian empire in October 1918, the South Slav provinces of the empire entered into a state union, with a national council. At the request of this council Prince Regent Alexander proclaimed the union of this state with Serbia and Montenegro on 1 December 1918, as the Kingdom of the Serbs, Croats and Slovenes.

In 1918–20 separate issues of stamps were made in Bosnia and Herzegovina, Croatia, Slovenia and Serbia. For the issues of Serbia, 1918–20, see under that country.

Kingdom of the Serbs, Croats and Slovenes

King Petar I

1 December 1918–16 August 1921

(His Son, Prince Alexander, acted as Regent)

I. ISSUES FOR BOSNIA AND HERZEGOVINA

100 Heller = 1 Kruna

In the following issues many stamps exist with overprint inverted, double, etc, or overprinted in wrong colours, and there are also many typographical errors and varieties.

Stamps of Bosinia and Herzegovina overprinted at the State Printing Works, Sarajevo.

DRZAVA S.H.S.
1918 1918
Bosna i Hercegovina

(1)

ДРЖАВА СХС
1918 1918
■ 80 x ■
Носна и Херцеговина

(2)

DRZAVA
S. H. S.
1918 1918
■ 4 K ■
Bosna I Hercenovina

(3)

1918 (Nov–Dec). Stamps of 1910, as T **20/21**, optd or surch as T **1/3**.

1	**1**	3h. olive-yellow	50	1·00
2	**2**	5h. deep green (R.)	50	50
3	**1**	10h. carmine	50	50
4		20h. sepia (R.)	50	50
5		25h. deep blue (R.)	50	50
6	**2**	30h. green	50	50
7		40h. orange	50	50
8		45h. red	50	50
9		50h. purple-brown	75	1·00
10	**1**	60h. on 50h. purple-brown	50	50
11	**2**	80h. on 6h. brown	50	50
12	**1**	90h. on 35h. deep green	50	50
13	**3**	2k. myrtle-green	50	50
14	**2**	3k. on 3h. olive-yellow	2·50	3·75
15	**3**	4k. on 1k. lake	5·25	6·25
16	**2**	10k. on 2h. violet	7·75	9·00
1/16 *Set of* 16			20·00	24·00

DRŽAVA S. H. S.
BOSNA I
HERCEGOVINA

ДРЖАВА С.Х.С.
БОСНА И
ХЕРЦЕГОВИНА

HELERA

(D 4)

хелера

(D 5)

1918 (Dec). Newspaper Express stamps. Type N **35**, optd with Types D **4/5**. P 12½.

17	D **5**	2h. vermilion	7·75	7·75
		a. Perf 11½×12½	65·00	65·00
		b. Optd Type D **4**	£160	£180
18	D **4**	5h. olive-green	4·25	4·25
		a. Optd Type D **5**	65·00	65·00

These were issued for use as ordinary postage stamps.

1918 (20 Dec). POSTAGE DUE. As Type D **35** of Bosnia optd with Types D **4** or D **5**.

D19	D **5**	2h. carmine	10	10
D20	D **4**	4h. carmine	75	80
D21	D **5**	5h. carmine	10	10
D22	D **4**	6h. carmine	1·20	1·20
D23	D **5**	10h. carmine	10	10
D24	D **4**	15h. carmine	9·00	9·50
D25	D **5**	20h. carmine	10	10
D26	D **4**	25h. carmine	75	80
D27	D **5**	30h. carmine	75	80
D28	D **4**	40h. carmine	20	20
D29	D **5**	50h. carmine	1·60	1·70
D30	D **4**	1k. blue (R.)	75	80
D31	D **5**	3k. blue (R.)	50	55
D19/31 *Set of* 13			14·50	15·00

DRŽAVA
S. H. S.

ДРЖАВА
С. Х. С.

Bosna
Hercegovina

(4)

Босна и
Херцеговина

(5)

1918 (Dec). Bosnian War Invalids' Fund stamps optd with T **5** (No. 21) or T **4** (others).

19	**31**	5h. (+2h.) green (391)	£225	£250
		a. Optd T **5**	£475	£500
20	**32**	10h. (+2h.) claret (392)	£140	£150
21		10h. (+2h.) blue-green (434)	1·00	1·10
		a. Optd T **4**	70·00	75·00
22	**31**	15h. (+2h.) red-brown (435)	2·50	2·75
		a. Optd T **5**	65·00	75·00
19/22 *Set of* 4			£325	£375

■ 5 ■

(6)

1918 (Dec). Newspaper stamps surch as T **6**. Imperf.

23	N **27**	3 on 2h. ultramarine	50	55
24		5 on 6h. mauve	50	55

Most of these were used for ordinary postage purposes.

1919 (Feb). As Nos. N383/6 of Bosnia but P 11½.

25	N **27**	2h. ultramarine	50	55
26		6h. mauve	2·50	3·25
27		10h. carmine	1·00	1·70
28		20h. green	50	55
25/28 *Set of* 4			4·00	5·50

The above were issued for use as ordinary postage stamps.

КРАЉЕВСТВО
С. Х. С

KRALJEVSTVO
S. H. S.
■ 50 h ■

(7) "Kingdom—Serbs, Croats, Slovenes" (8)

1919 (Mar). Various stamps optd or surch as T **7/8**.

29	**25**	3h. lake (**7**)	50	1·10
30		5h. green (**8**)	50	55
31		10 on 6h. black (**8**)	50	55
32	**26**	20 on 35h. blackish green (**7**)	50	55
33	**25**	25h. ultramarine (**8**)	50	55
34		30h. vermilion (**7**)	50	55
35	**26**	45h. olive-brown (**7**)	50	55
36	**33**	45 on 80h. orange-brown (p 12½) (**7**)	50	55
		a. Perf 11½	1·80	2·20
37	**26**	50h. Prussian blue (**8**)	£100	£130
38		50 on 72h. deep blue (**8**)	50	55
39		60h. purple-brown (**7**)	50	55
40	**33**	80h. orange-brown (p 12½) (**8**)	50	55
		a. Perf 11½	6·25	2·75
41		90h. deep purple (p 12½) (**7**)	50	55
		a. Perf 11½	4·75	3·25
42	**6**	2k. myrtle-green (p 12½) (**8**)	50	55
		a. Perf 9½	4·25	2·75
		b. Perf 10½, 12½ and compound	10·50	11·00
43	**26**	3k. carmine/*green* (**7**)	50	80
44	**34**	4k. carmine/*green* (**8**)	2·10	2·75
45	**26**	5k. indigo-lilac/*greyish* (**7**)	2·10	3·25
46	**34**	10k. violet/*grey* (**8**)	4·25	5·50
29/46 *Set of* 18			£100	£140

On No. 36 the old value is cancelled by a rectangular block instead of bars; there are no bars in the overprint on the 80h., 90h., 4k. and 10k.; the 2k. is overprinted "KRALJEVSTVO S. H. S." only.

КРАЉЕВСТВО
Срба, Хрвата и Словенаца
■ 10x + 10x ■

(9)

KRALJEVSTVO
Srba, Hrvata i Slovenaca
■ 20 h + 10 h ■

(10)

КРАЉЕВСТВО
Срба, Хрвата и
Словенаца
45 x + 15 x
■ ■

(11)

1919 (Mar). War Victims' Fund. As T **4/5** of Bosnia, surch with T **9/11**.

47	10x.+10x. on 40h. orange	1·60	2·75
48	20h.+10h. on 20h. sepia	75	2·50
49	45x.+15x. on 1k. lake	6·25	9·00
47/49 *Set of* 3		7·75	13·00

KRALJEVSTVO
SRBA, HRVATA
I SLOVENACA
PORTO
■ 20h ■

(D 12)

КРАЉЕВСТВО
СРБА, ХРВАТА
И СЛОВЕНАЦА
ПОРТО
■ 5 x ■

(D 13)

1919 (May). POSTAGE DUE. T **2** of Bosnia (Eagle) surch as Types D **12** or D **13**. P 12½.

D50	D **13**	2h. on 35h. deep blue and black	75	1·10
D51		5h. on 45h. greenish blue and black	1·30	1·70
D52	D **12**	10h. on 10h. red	10	10
D53	D **13**	15h. on 40h. orange and black	50	65
D54	D **12**	20h. on 5h. green	10	15
D55	D **13**	25h. on 20h. pink and black	50	80
D56	D **12**	30h. on 30h. bistre and black	50	80
D57	D **13**	1k. on 50h. red-lilac	20	80
D58		3k. on 25h. blue	65	80
D50/58 *Set of* 9			4·25	6·25

КРАЉЕВСТВО
СРБА, ХРВАТА
И СЛОВЕНАЦА
■ 40 ■
40 хелера 40

(D 14)

KRALJEVSTVO
SRBA HRVATA
SLOVENACA
■ 50 ■
50 helera 50

(D 15)

1919 (May). POSTAGE DUE. Type D **4** of Bosnia surch as Types D **14** (40h.) or D **15** (others).

D59	40h. on 6h. black, red and yellow	10	10
D60	50h. on 8h. black, red and yellow	10	10
D61	200h. black, red and green	10·50	9·50
D62	4k. on 7h. black, red and yellow	50	80
	a. Narrow tall "4"	10·50	17·00
D59/62 *Set of* 4		10·00	9·50

1919 (13 Nov). Newspaper stamps. Type N **27**, surch as T **6** but with circular instead of square cancellation marks. Imperf.

50	2 on 6h. mauve	£200	£225
51	2 on 10h. carmine	50·00	55·00
52	2 on 20h. green	10·50	11·00
50/52 *Set of* 3		£225	£250

The above were issued for use as ordinary postage stamps.

Beware of forgeries.

II. ISSUES FOR CROATIA

100 Filir (Heller) = 1 Kruna (Krone)

The provisional issues on Hungarian stamps were sold in Yugoslavian "heller" and "krone" currency, but as this is not expressed on the stamps (except for Nos. 69/73) we have retained the Hungarian descriptions to facilitate reference to the original stamps.

Nos. 53/D92 are the stamps officially overprinted and placed on sale at post offices. Because of a shortage of some denominations, permission was given for the printers to accept unoverprinted Hungarian stamps in private possession and either exchange them for overprinted stamps of an equivalent value, from which come many errors, test printings etc., or to overprint them for later collection. Thus many stamps not listed exist overprinted from the original plates, and those that are listed also exist with the "wrong" overprint.

The original overprinting plates had been destroyed by mid-February 1919 but because of continuing demand, mainly from collectors and dealers, new plates were made and the printers continued to overprint any Hungarian stamps presented to them. Forgeries also exist.

Overprints signify "Croatia, Serbs, Croats, Slovenes".

HRVATSKA
SHS

(12)

SHS
HRVATSKA

(13)

1918 (18 Nov–Dec). Various stamps of Hungary overprinted.

(a) "Turul" Type, W **11**, with T **12**, in blue

53	**7**	6f. olive (3.12)	1·00	2·20
54		50f. carmine/*blue*	1·60	2·75

(b) Harvesters Types, with T **13**, in blue

55	**18**	2f. yellow-brown	50	55
56		3f. dull claret	50	55
57		5f. green	50	55
58		6f. greenish blue	50	55
59		10f. rose-red (3.12)	10·50	11·00
60	**17**	15f. violet	£100	£170
61	**18**	15f. violet	50	55
62		20f. grey-brown (28.11)	50	55
63		25f. blue (19.11)	50	55
64		35f. brown (19.11)	50	55
65		40f. olive-green	50	1·10

Type **17** has white figures of value, type **18** coloured.

(**14**)

(**15**)

(c) Parliament Type, with T **14** (filir values) or **15** (others), in blue

66	**19**	50f. dull purple (20.11)	50	55
67		75f. turquoise-blue (20.11)	50	55
68		80f. yellow-green (20.11)	50	55
69		1k. lake (29.11)	50	55
70		2k. bistre-brown (29.11)	50	55
71		3k. grey and dull violet (29.11)	50	55
72		5k. pale brown and brown (29.11)	3·25	4·00
73		10k. magenta and chocolate (29.11)	16·00	19·00
53/73 *Set of* 21			£130	£200

The 1, 5 and 10k. have the value expressed as "KRUNA" and the 2 and 3k. as "KRUNE".

(**16**)

(**17**)

(d) Charles and Zita Types, with T **16** and **17** respectively

74	**27**	10f. rose (B.) (Dec)	50	55
75		20f. deep brown	50	55
76		25f. blue (R.) (Dec)	50	1·10
77	**28**	40f. olive-green (B.) (19.11)	50	55
74/77 *Set of* 4			1·80	2·50

(**18**)

(**19**)

(e) War Charity stamps of 1916–17, optd with T **18** or **19** (40f.), in blue (Nov)

78	**20**	10+2f. carmine	50	65
79	**21**	15+2f. dull violet	50	55
80	**22**	40+2f. lake	50	55

(f) Coronation stamps, with T **17**, in blue

81	**23**	10f. magenta	£100	£170
82	**24**	15f. red	£100	£170

(N **20**)

(E **20**)

(D **20**)

(g) Newspaper stamp W **11**, with Type N **20**

N83	N **9**	(2f.) orange (No. N136) (23.11)	50	55

(h) Express Letter stamp, with Type E **20**

E84	E **18**	2f. olive and red (No. E245) (B.) (29.11)	50	55

1918 (18 Nov–Dec). POSTAGE DUE. Postage Due stamps of Hungary optd with Type D **20**, in blue. W **11** (sideways) P 15.

D85	D **9**	1f. red and green	37·00	50·00
D86		2f. red and green	1·80	1·90
D87		10f. red and green	1·30	1·30
D88		12f. red and green	£100	£120
D89		15f. red and green	1·00	1·10
D90		20f. red and green	1·00	1·10
D91		30f. red and green	2·50	2·75
D92		50f. black and green	42·00	55·00
D85/92 *Set of* 8			£170	£200

20 "Freedom of Croatia"

(Des R. Valić and R. Sabljak. Litho State Ptg Wks, Zagreb)

1918 (29 Nov). P 11½.

83	**20**	10h. lake	3·25	3·25
84		20h. violet	3·25	3·25
85		25h. blue	6·75	9·00
86		45h. greenish slate	65·00	75·00
83/86 *Set of* 4			70·00	80·00

21 Angel of Peace

22 Sailor with Standard and Falcon

23 Falcon ("Liberty")

24

N **25**

(Des L. Crnčić-Viran (**21**), O. Antonini (**22**), A. Koželj (**23**). Litho State Ptg Works, Zagreb)

1919 (15 Jan).

A. P 11½

87A	**21**	2f. brown	10	55
88A		3f. mauve	10	65
89A		5f. green	10	10
90A	**22**	10f. red	10	10
91A		20f. brown	10	10
92A		25f. blue	10	10
93A		45f. olive-green	20	20
94A	**23**	1k. carmine	30	35
95A	**24**	3k. purple-brown	1·00	1·30
96A		5k. brown	1·60	1·10
87A/96A *Set of* 10			3·25	4·00

B. P 12½

87B	**21**	2f. brown	3·75	3·75
88B		3f. mauve	3·75	3·75
89B		5f. green	18·00	18·00
90B	**22**	10f. red	3·75	3·75
91B		20f. brown	3·75	3·75

(Litho State Ptg Works, Zagreb)

1919 (15 Jan). NEWSPAPER. Imperf.

N97	N **25**	2h. orange-yellow	20	1·70

III. ISSUES FOR SLOVENIA

1919. 100 Vinar (Heller) = 1 Krona (Krone)

1920. 100 Paras = 1 Dinar

25

Chainbreakers

26

27 "Yugoslavia" with Three Falcons

28 Angel of Peace

29 King Petar I

Lithographed — Typographed

3v., 5v. and 15v.

Chain short

Chain touches bottom label

10v.

Large figures

Small figures

20v.

Mountain faint or absent

Mountain clearly outlined

25v.

Wavy line reaches margin

Wavy line stops short

30v.

Figures near top label

Figures farther from top

40v.

Wide figures

Narrow figures

(Des I. Vavpotič. Litho I. Blaznik, Ljubljana)

1919 (3 Jan)–**20**. Clear impressions. P 11½.

97	**25**	3v. deep violet (12.2.19)	30	20
		a. Grey-violet	30	20
		b. Bright violet	30	20
98		5v. green (15.1.19)	30	20
		a. Yellow-green	30	20
		b. Emerald	30	20
		c. Blue-green	40	20
		d. Porous laid pinhole paper (*emer*)	21·00	11·00
99		10v. deep carmine	50	20
		a. Carmine	50	20
		b. Red	50	20
		c. Scarlet	50	20
100		15v. dull blue (20.9.19)	30	20
		a. Ultramarine	1·00	55
		b. Porous laid pinhole paper (*shades*)	30	35
101	**26**	20v. chocolate (*shades*)	85	20
		a. Purple-brown	2·10	55
		b. Sepia (shades)	1·00	35
		c. Grey-brown	3·25	1·40
102		25v. blue (*shades*) (15.2.19)	40	20
		a. Deep blue	95	20
103		30v. lilac-rose (4.10.19)	40	20
		a. Carmine-lake (shades)	1·60	90
		b. Porous laid pinhole paper (*shades*)	85	85
104		40v. ochre (26.2.19)	40	20
		a. Yellow-brown	45	20
		b. Orange-buff	2·00	90
97/104 *Set of* 8			3·00	1·40

There is a much wider range of shades of the 15v. and 30v. on the porous paper.

Redrawn without shading in value tablets
Background of flesh-coloured wavy lines
Chalk-surfaced paper (15.5.20).

105	**29**	15k. green (*shades*)	16·00	20·00
106		20k. purple (*shades*)	3·25	4·00

The 3, 5, 10, 20v. and 15 and 20k. exist on thin, rough white paper; all values except the 3v., 15 and 20k. exist on smooth white paper.

(Typo Govt Ptg Works, Ljubljana)

1919 (Apr)–**20**. Coarser Impressions.

(a) Zigzag roulette

Smooth white or cream paper

107	**25**	5v. yellow-green	20	10
		a. Zigzag roul×perf 11½		
108		10v. carmine (*shades*)	20	10
		a. Zigzag roul×perf 11½	37·00	
		b. Red (shades)	20	10
		ba. Zigzag roul×perf 11½	36·00	39·00
109		15v. grey-blue	40	20
		a. Zigzag roul×perf 11½		
110	**26**	20v. brown	85	20
		a. Zigzag roul×perf 11½	42·00	39·00
		b. Zigzag×straight roul	75	55
		c. Sepia	75	20
		ca. Zigzag roul×perf 11½		
		cb. Zigzag×straight roul	75	20
111		30v. carmine	40	20
		a. Zigzag roul×perf 11½		
		b. Zigzag×straight roul	4·25	45
		c. Pale carmine	75	20
		ca. Zigzag×straight roul	8·25	4·00
112	**27**	50v. green (8.9.19)	40	10
		a. Zigzag roul×perf 11½	23·00	20·00
		b. Deep green	70	20

113		60v. slate-purple (23.4.19)	1·30	50
		a. Zigzag roul×perf 11½	65·00	
		b. Violet	1·90	50
114	**28**	1k. red (19.4.19)	1·80	55
		a. Zigzag roul×perf 11½		
		b. Orange-scarlet	1·80	50
		c. Pale vermilion	2·00	55
115		2k. dull blue (19.4.19)	11·50	4·00
107/115 *Set of 9*			15·00	5·50

(b) P 11½. Smooth white or cream paper

116	**25**	10v. red	65	10
117		15v. grey-blue	2·10	10
118	**26**	20v. brown	1·00	20
119		30v. carmine	75	10
120	**28**	2k. ultramarine	90	20
116/120 *Set of 5*			4·75	65

Care has to be taken in distinguishing these from the Vienna printings, Nos. 129, etc.

(c) P 11½. Thin, hard transparent paper

121	**26**	20v. brown	1·00	35
122	**27**	50v. green	50	10
		a. Deep green	85	20
123		60v. indigo-lilac	1·30	40
		a. Slate-violet	2·10	55
124	**28**	1k. scarlet	85	30
125		2k. deep blue	2·00	1·00
126	**29**	5k. carmine-lake (22.4.19)	85	30
121/126 *Set of 6*			8·50	3·00

The 20 and 30v. values with zigzag roulette were printed in sheets of 200 (20×10). In the 20v. the tenth vertical row was zigzag×straight roulette on the right and the eleventh vertical row was zigzag×straight roulette on the left. In the 30v. the first two and last three vertical rows were zigzag×straight roulette.

(Typo from same plates A. Reisser, Vienna)

1919–20. Coarse impressions. P 11½.

(a) Thicker white paper, 5v. usually with small pinholes

127	**25**	3v. grey-violet	20	10
128		5v. pale emerald	40	10
		a. Deep emerald	40	10
129		10v. bright scarlet	65	15
130		15v. blue	65	10
		a. Perf 11	2·10	1·10
		b. Greenish blue	4·25	1·70
		ba. Perf 11	2·00	95
131	**26**	20v. brown	95	20
		a. Yellow-brown	1·60	20
		b. Red-brown	2·30	1·10
132		25v. violet-blue	1·00	10
		a. Deep blue	1·00	10
		b. Grey-blue	1·00	10
133		30v. carmine	1·20	10
134		40v. orange	2·00	10
		a. Yellow-orange	70	10
		b. Yellow-brown	95	10
135	**27**	60v. grey-lilac	1·20	60
		a. Mauve	2·10	60
136	**28**	1k. scarlet	95	35
		a. Pale orange-scarlet	2·00	1·00
137		2k. indigo-blue	1·00	20
		a. Blue	2·10	60
		b. Perf 11. *Blue*	12·50	5·50
138	**29**	5k. brown-red	4·25	1·70
		a. Brown-rose	2·00	35
		b. Carton paper. *Brown-rose*		
		c. Rose	21·00	5·00
		d. Perf 11. *Brown-red*	65·00	14·50
139		10k. deep ultramarine (1.4.20)	4·75	1·10
		a. Pale ultramarine	4·75	1·10
		b. Do. Carton paper	40·00	13·50

(b) Grey paper

140	**25**	3v. bright violet	20	10
		a. Perf 11	8·25	3·25
		b. Plum	20	10
		ba. Perf 11	7·75	2·75
141		5v. emerald	8·25	3·25
142		10v. bright scarlet	12·50	9·00
143		15v. blue	13·00	10·00
		a. Perf 11	8·00	9·00
144	**26**	20v. brown	95	20
		a. Reddish brown	95	20
145		25v. violet-blue	1·40	20
		a. Grey-blue	1·40	20
		b. Do. Carton paper	21·00	13·50
146		30v. scarlet	1·20	40
		a. Carmine	1·30	40
147		40v. orange	1·30	40
		a. Yellow-orange	1·20	40
148	**27**	50v. olive-green	5·50	2·75
		a. Perf 11	16·00	8·25
149	**28**	1k. orange-scarlet	2·50	1·50
149*a*	**29**	5k. red	1·20	20
149*b*		10k. deep ultramarine	8·00	3·25

D **30**

D **31**

In the Ljubljana printing the letters of the inscription are larger and thicker than in the Vienna printing. The figures of value also differ greatly in size.

(Des I. Vavpotič. Litho I. Blaznik, Ljubljana, later A. Reisser, Vienna)

1919. POSTAGE DUE. P 11½.

(a) Ljubljana printing (18 Mar)

D150	D **30**	5v. carmine	10	10
		a. Deep scarlet	10	10
D151		10v. carmine	10	10
		a. Deep scarlet	10	10
D152		20v. carmine	10	10
		a. Deep scarlet	10	10
D153		50v. carmine	20	10
		a. Deep scarlet	40	20
D154	D **31**	1k. blue	30	30
D155		5k. blue	75	30
D156		10k. blue	1·70	90
D150/156 *Set of 7*			3·00	1·70

The vinar values exist on smooth and rough paper; the krone values are on thick greyish paper.

D **32**

D **33**

(b) Vienna printing (10 Dec)

D157	D **32**	5v. scarlet	10	10
		a. Deep scarlet	2·50	10
		b. Red	20	10
D158		10v. scarlet	10	10
		a. Deep scarlet	7·25	10
		b. Red	20	10
D159		20v. scarlet	20	10
		a. Deep scarlet	4·50	10
		b. Red	20	10
D160		50v. scarlet	30	15
		a. Deep scarlet	7·25	20
		b. Red	30	20
D161	D **33**	1k. indigo	90	55
		a. Dull blue	75	55
D162		5k. indigo	3·00	1·10
		a. Dull blue	2·10	55
D163		10k. indigo	8·25	4·50
		a. Dull blue	5·25	3·25
D157/163*a* *Set of 7 (cheapest)*			8·00	4·25

The above are all on smooth white paper.

N **30** Cherub with Newspapers

(Des I. Vavpotič. Litho I. Blaznik, Ljubljana, later A. Reisser, Vienna)

1919. NEWSPAPER. Imperf.

(a) Ljubljana printing (15 May)

In the Ljubljana printing the 2h. has thick "2" with pronounced ball; in the 4h. the foot of the "4" is to right of the value label; in the 6h. the final curve of the "6" is parallel to the top curve; in the 10h. the "1" is thin and the "0" bulges to the right.

N150	N **30**	2v. grey	10	15
N151		4v. grey	20	55
N152		6v. grey	4·75	5·50
N153		10v. grey	10	20
N154		30v. grey	10	55
N150/154 *Set of 5*			4·75	6·25

The above are on thin rough white paper but the 2 and 4v. also exist on porous paper.

(a) Vienna printing (15 Nov)

The Vienna printing shows a thin "2" with small ball; the foot of the "4" is above the centre of the value label; in the "6" the final curve bends downwards; and the "10" is thicker and in the centre of the label. There are also differences in the impression.

A. Blue

N155A	N **30**	2v.	90	95
N156A		4v.	90	95
N157A		6v.	50·00	65·00
N158A		10v.	90	95
N155A/158A *Set of 4*			47·00	60·00

B. Grey

N155B	N **30**	2v.	10	10
N156B		4v.	10	10
N157B		6v.	5·75	6·75
N158B		10v.	10	10
N155B/158B *Set of 4*			5·50	6·25

The 2, 4 and 10v. exist in both colours on smooth, white paper and in shades of blue only on thick, grey paper. All four values exist in shades of blue and the 2v. and 6v. also in grey on rough yellowish paper.

31 Chainbreaker

32 "Yugoslavia" with Three Falcons

33 King Petar I

34 King Petar I

(Des I. Vavpotič. 5p. to 1d. typo. 2d. to 10d. litho Ljubljana)

1920 (9 June–Oct). New currency.

(a) Zigzag roulette

150	**31**	5p. olive (24.6)	50	10
151		10p. green (23.9)	20	10
152		15p. brown (16.6)	20	10
153		20p. carmine (9.10)	1·00	55
154		25p. chocolate (24.6)	1·00	10
155	**32**	40p. violet (9.10)	20	20
156		45p. yellow (29.9)	20	20
157		50p. blue (11.9)	20	10
158		60p. red-brown (13.7)	20	10
159	**33**	1d. chocolate (7.7)	20	10

(b) P 11½. With burelé background (except 4d.)

160	**34**	2d. lilac (*flesh*) (18.6)	20	10
161	**33**	4d. greenish slate (typo) (7.7)	85	45
162	**34**	6d. olive (*flesh*) (9.6)	50	1·30
		a. Without designer's name (2nd ptg)	85	3·25
163		10d. red-brown (*grey*) (21.6)	85	1·10
150/163 *Set of 14*			5·75	4·25

(D **35**)

(D **36**)

1920 (5 July). POSTAGE DUE. T **25**/**26** surch respectively as Types D **35**/**6**.

(a) Litho at Ljubljana. P 11½

D164	**25**	5p. on 15v. dull blue	10	10
D165		10p. on 15v. dull blue	1·60	1·60
D166		20p. on 15v. dull blue	20	10
D167		50p. on 15v. dull blue	10	10
D168	**26**	1d. on 30v. lilac-rose	30	20
D169		3d. on 30v. lilac-rose	50	20
D170		8d. on 30v. lilac-rose	4·25	1·10

(b) Typo at Ljubljana. Zigzag roulette

D171	**25**	5p. on 15v. grey-blue	2·10	55
D172		10p. on 15v. grey-blue	7·25	2·75
D173		20p. on 15v. grey-blue	1·80	55
D174		50p. on 15v. grey-blue	3·25	55
D175	**26**	1d. on 30v. carmine	2·10	55
		a. Zigzag×straight roul	2·50	1·20
D176		3d. on 30v. carmine	3·25	1·10
		a. Zigzag×straight roul	8·25	1·80
D177		8d. on 30v. carmine	37·00	10·00
		a. Zigzag×straight roul	42·00	13·50
D164/177 *Set of 14*			55·00	18·00

(c) Typo in Vienna. P 11½

A. Thick white paper

D178A	**25**	5p. on 15v.	37·00	13·50
D179A		10p. on 15v.	£200	£275
D180A		20p. on 15v.	27·00	9·00
D181A		50p. on 15v.	7·75	11·00
D178A/181A *Set of 4*			£250	£275

B. Grey paper

D178B	**25**	5p. on 15v.	10·50	2·20
D179B		10p. on 15v.	37·00	17·00
D180B		20p. on 15v.	11·50	5·50
D181B		50p. on 15v.	8·25	5·50
D178B/181B *Set of 4*			60·00	27·00

Nos. D178A/81A are in greenish blue and Nos. D178B/81B in pale blue.

The sheet of 100 (10×10) of the "para" values contains 3 horizontal rows of 5p., 1 row of 10p., 3 of 20p. and 3 of 50p. In the "dinar" values the sheet contains 5 vertical rows of 1d., 3 of 3d. and 2 of 8d.

(N **35**)

(N **36**)

1920 (2 Sept). NEWSPAPER. Surch as Type N **35** (2 to 6p.) or N **36** (others).

(a) Surch on No. N150

N164	N **30**	2p. on 2v. grey	75	1·30
N165		4p. on 2v. grey	75	1·30
N166		6p. on 2v. grey	1·00	1·30
N167		10p. on 2v. grey	1·30	1·70
N168		30p. on 2v. grey	1·30	1·70

(b) Surch on No. N155A

N169	N **30**	2p. on 2v. blue	10	55
N170		4p. on 2v. blue	10	55
N171		6p. on 2v. blue	10	55
N172		10p. on 2v. blue	30	80
N173		30p. on 2v. blue	50	1·10
N164/173 *Set of* 10			5·50	9·75

The sheet of 100 (10 rows of 10) comprises 3 horizontal rows of 2p., 3 of 4p., 2 of 6p. and one each of 10 and 30p., with a horizontal line of perforation (11½) dividing each value. Thus the 2, 4, 6 and 30p. may be found with one horizontal side perf 11½, while the 10p. has both horizontal sides perf.

(34a)

1920 (Sept–Oct). Issue for Plebiscite in Carinthia. No. N150/1 surch as T **34a**, in deep red, in Ljubljana.

163*a*	N **30**	5p. on 4v. grey	10	35
163*b*		15p. on 4v. grey	10	35
163*c*		25p. on 4v. grey	20	80
163*d*		45p. on 2v. grey	20	1·70
163*e*		50p. on 2v. grey	30	1·90
163*f*		2din. on 2v. grey	2·50	8·50
163*a/f Set of* 6			3·00	12·00

The type of surcharge differs for each value.

The three lowest value surcharges were applied to the sheets of 100 in one setting: 5p. on the first four horiz rows (40 stamps), 15p. on rows 5–7 (30 stamps) and 25p. on rows 8–10 (30 stamps). The sheets of 2v. stamps were divided in half and the higher value surcharges applied in two settings of 50—setting 1: Nos. 1–15, 45p., Nos. 16–45, 50p., Nos. 46–50, 2d.; setting 2: Nos. 1–40, 2d., Nos. 41–50, 45p.

These were sold throughout Slovenia at three times face value to provide funds to help Carinthians outside their province to travel and vote. The result of the plebiscite was a vote for Carinthia to remain part of Austria.

IV. GENERAL ISSUES FOR THE WHOLE KINGDOM

100 Paras = 1 Dinar

35 King Alexander when Prince

36 King Petar I

(Recess American Bank Note Co.)

1921 (16 Jan). P 12.

164	**35**	2p. sepia	10	10
165		5p. green	10	10
166		10p. carmine	10	10
167		15p. purple	10	10
168		20p. black	10	10
169		25p. indigo	10	10
170		50p. olive-green	10	10
171		60p. vermilion	20	10
172		75p. violet	10	10
173	**36**	1d. orange	50	10
174		2d. olive-brown	75	10
175		4d. blue-green	1·60	10
176		5d. carmine	5·25	10
177		10d. red-brown	16·00	55
164/177 *Set of* 14			23·00	1·70

Imperforate remainders of Nos. 164/77 were distributed during 1975.

See also Nos. 189/93.

37 Kosovo Maiden, 1389

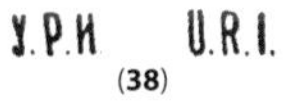

(**38**)

(Recess American Bank Note Co.)

1921 (30 Jan). Disabled Soldiers' Fund. T **37** and similar horiz designs. P 12.

178	10+10p. carmine	10	10
179	15+15p. chocolate	10	10
180	25+25p. light blue	10	10
178/180 *Set of* 3		25	25

Designs:—15p. Wounded Soldier typifying Retreat through Albania, 1915; 25p. Symbol of National Unity.

No. 178 with opt T **38** is a charity label which had no franking value.

Imperforate remainders of Nos. 178/80 were distributed during 1975.

D **39** King Alexander I when Prince

(Des M. Peroš. Typo Belgrade)

1921 (9 Apr). POSTAGE DUE. Postage stamps prepared for use but not issued, surch as in Type D **39**. P 11½.

D182	10 on 5p. bright green (R.)	30	10
D183	30 on 5p. bright green	50	10

King Alexander

16 August 1921–3 October 1929

D **40**

D **41**

(Des M. Peroš. Die eng D. Wagner. Typo)

1921 (22 Nov). POSTAGE DUE. Printed in Belgrade. Size 22½×28½ mm. P 11½ (rough).

D184	D **40**	10p. rose-carmine	10	10
D185		30p. yellowish green	50	10
D186		50p. violet	50	10
D187		1d. reddish brown	75	10
D188		2d. blue	1·00	10
D189	D **41**	5d. orange	5·25	10
D190		10d. maroon	16·00	55
		a. Error. 10p. maroon	£450	£500
D191		25d. rose	90·00	2·20
D192		50d. deep blue-green	80·00	2·50
D184/192 *Set of* 9			£170	5·25

No. D190a is an error caused by the accidental inclusion of a cliché of the 10p. in the plate of the 10d.

See also Nos. D195/203.

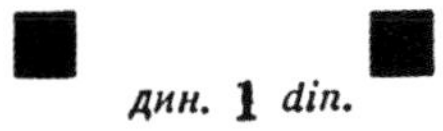

(**40**)

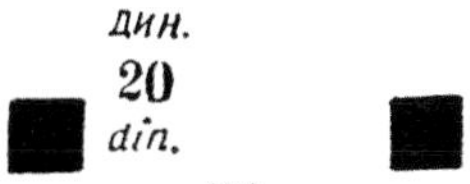

(**41**)

1922 (1 July)–**24**. As T **37**, surch as T **40** or **41**.

181	**40**	1d. on 10p. carmine (11.22)	10	10
182		1d. on 25p. light blue (Br.)	10	10
183	**41**	1d. on 15p. chocolate (5.24)	10	10
184		3d. on 15p. chocolate (B.) (6.11.23)	3·25	1·70
185		3d. on 15p. chocolate (G.) (6.11.23)	65	10
186		8d. on 15p. chocolate (G.)	3·75	20
		a. Error "9d." for "8d." (pos. 11)	£425	
		b. Surch double		
187		20d. on 15p. chocolate	21·00	1·10
		a. Straight foot on "2" (pos. 8, 66, 75)	50·00	5·50
188		30d. on 15p. chocolate (B.)	33·00	2·20
181/188 *Set of* 8			55·00	5·00

1923 (23 Jan). T **35** (redrawn). "KRALJEVINA" for "KRAL JEVSTVO" at foot. P 12.

189	1d. red-brown	5·25	20
190	5d. carmine	10·50	20
191	8d. purple	21·00	35
192	20d. green	50·00	1·10
193	30d. orange	£180	3·75
189/193 *Set of* 5		£250	5·00

1923 (July)–**31**. POSTAGE DUE. Printed in Belgrade. New plates made in Vienna. Differences in figures of value. Size 21½×28 mm. P 10½ (clean cut).

D195	D **41**	10p. rose-red	10	10
		a. Perf 9 (1926–28)	16·00	7·75
		b. Perf 11½ (1931)	1·30	35
D196		30p. yellow-green	85	55
D197		50p. violet	10	10
		a. Perf 9 (1926–28)	1·60	10
		b. Perf 11½ (1931)	£100	13·50
D198		1d. brown	50	10
		a. Perf 9 (1926–28)	2·50	30
		b. Perf 11½ (1931)	5·25	35
D199		2d. blue	1·30	10
		a. Perf 9 (1926–28)	6·25	10
		b. Perf 11½ (1931)	26·00	55
D200		5d. pale orange	4·25	10
		a. Perf 9 (1926–28)	13·50	10
		b. Perf 11½ (1931)	80·00	35
D201		10d. maroon	27·00	20
		a. Perf 9 (1926–28)	31·00	20
D202		25d. pink	£170	1·70
D203		50d. deep green	£130	1·70
D195/203 *Set of* 9			£300	4·25

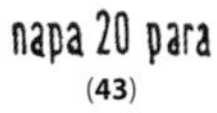

(**43**)

44 King Alexander

(**45**)

1924. Nos. 171 and 191 surch as T **43**.

195	**35**	20p. on 60p. vermilion (18.2)	75	10
196		5d. on 8d. purple (5.3)	23·00	1·00

(Recess De La Rue & Co.)

1924 (1 July). T **44**. Head in oval. P 14.

197	20p. black	10	10
198	50p. brown	10	10
199	1d. scarlet	10	10
200	2d. myrtle-green	50	10
201	3d. ultramarine	50	10
202	5d. brown	3·75	10
	As T **44**, but head in square panel. P 14.		
203	10d. violet	31·00	10
204	15d. olive-green	21·00	20
205	20d. orange	21·00	20
206	30d. green	16·00	1·50
197/206 *Set of* 10		85·00	2·30

1925 (5 June). T **44** surch as T **45**.

207	25p. on 3d. ultramarine	50	10
208	50p. on 3d. ultramarine	50	10

46 King Alexander

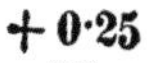

(**47**)

(**48**)

(D **49**)

(Des and eng D. Wagner. Typo in Belgrade from plates made in Austria)

1926 (25 Jan)–**27**. P 12½.

209	**46**	25p. green	10	10
210		50p. sepia	10	10
211		1d. scarlet	50	10
212		2d. black (10.3.26)	50	10
213		3d. dull blue (10.3.26)	75	10
214		4d. vermilion (10.3.26)	1·30	10
215		5d. violet (10.3.26)	2·10	10
216		8d. grey-brown (10.3.26)	10·50	10
217		10d. olive (10.3.26)	5·25	10
218		15d. brown (2.3.27)	31·00	10
219		20d. violet (2.3.27)	42·00	35
220		30d. orange (2.3.27)	£160	55
209/220 *Set of* 12			£225	1·70

1926 (1 Nov). Danube Flood Fund. Surch as T **47**, in carmine.

221	**46**	25p. +0.25 green	10	10
222		50p. +0.50 sepia	10	10
223		1d. +0.50 scarlet	10	10
224		2d. +0.50 black	50	10
225		3d. +0.50 dull blue	50	10
226		4d. +0.50 vermilion	75	10
227		5d. +0.50 violet	1·30	10
228		8d. +0.50 grey-brown	2·50	55
229		10d. +1.—, olive	5·25	10
230		15d. +1.—, brown	16·00	1·10
231		20d. +1.—, violet	21·00	80
232		30d. +1.—, orange	60·00	4·50
221/232 *Set of* 12			95·00	7·00

1928 (2 May). POSTAGE DUE. Nos. D202/3 surch with Type D **49**.

D233	D **41**	10 on 25d. pink	8·25	55
D234		10 on 50d. deep green	8·25	55

1928 (July). Charity stamps of 1926 with opt T **48** obliterating T **47**.

233	**46**	1d. scarlet	50	20
234		2d. black	1·60	20
235		3d. dull blue	2·50	45
236		4d. vermilion	6·25	65
237		5d. violet	5·25	20
238		8d. grey-brown	21·00	1·10
239		10d. olive	42·00	20
240		15d. brown	£250	3·25
241		20d. violet	£160	3·25
242		30d. orange	£350	13·50
233/242 *Set of* 10			£750	21·00

Earliest known date of cancellation is 27 July 1928.

PRINTERS. All stamps of Yugoslavia from 1929 to 1947 (No. D546) were printed at the Government Printing Works, Belgrade, *unless otherwise stated.*

Kingdom of Yugoslavia

King Alexander

3 October 1929–9 October 1934

The name of the Kingdom was changed to Yugoslavia on 3 October 1929.

49 Duvno Cathedral

50 Kings Tomislav and Alexander I

(Des M. Peroš. Eng D. Wagner. Typo)

1929 (1 Nov). Millenary of Croatian Kingdom (1925). T **49** (and similar type) and **50**. P 12½ or 11½×12 (No. 244).

243	50p. +50p. olive-green	50	20
244	1d. +50p. carmine	1·60	55
245	3d. +1d. blue (King Tomislav)	4·25	1·50
243/245 *Set of* 3		5·75	2·00

52 Dobropolje

53 Serbian War Memorial, Paris

(Des and eng D. Wagner. Typo)

1931 (1 Apr). Serbian War Memorial (Paris) Fund. T **52** (and similar type) and **53**. P 12½ or 11½ (No. 247).

246	50p. +50p. blue-green	10	10
247	1d. +50p. scarlet	10	10
248	3d. +1d. deep ultramarine	20	20
246/248 *Set of* 3		35	35

Design:—3d. Kajmakčalan.

55 King Alexander

D **56**

(Des P. Stojičević. Eng D. Wagner. Typo)

1931–33. P 12½.

		A. With engraver's name (1.9.31)		
249A	**55**	25p. black	30	10
250A		50p. green	30	10
251A		1d. scarlet	30	10
252A		3d. dull blue	16·00	10
253A		4d. orange-vermilion	7·75	10
254A		5d. violet	7·75	10
255A		10d. deep olive	26·00	10
256A		15d. brown	26·00	10
257A		20d. purple	50·00	10
258A		30d. bright magenta	27·00	65
249A/258A *Set of* 10			£150	1·40
		B. Without name (1932–33)		
249B	**55**	25p. black	10	10
		a. Thin paper ('32)	30	35
250B		50p. green	10	10
		a. Thin paper ('32)	30	35
251B		1d. scarlet	65	10
252B		3d. dull blue	2·50	10
253B		4d. orange-vermilion	9·00	10
254B		5d. violet	10·50	20
255B		10d. deep olive	42·00	20
256B		15d. brown	50·00	35
257B		20d. purple	70·00	35
258B		30d. bright magenta	80·00	35
249B/258B *Set of* 10			£250	1·80

1931–40. POSTAGE DUE. Typo. P 12½.

		A. With engraver's name (1.9.31)		
D259A	D **56**	50p. violet	3·75	35
D260A		1d. magenta	7·75	35
D261A		2d. blue	21·00	35
D262A		5d. orange	4·75	35
D263A		10d. chocolate	27·00	2·00
D259A/263A *Set of* 5			60·00	3·00
		B. Without name (1932–40)		
D259B	D **56**	50p. violet	10	10
D260B		1d. magenta	10	10
D261B		2d. blue	10	10
D262B		5d. orange	10	10
D263B		10d. chocolate	50	20
D259B/263B *Set of* 5			80	55

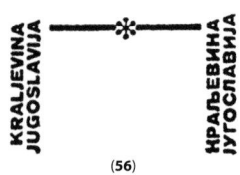

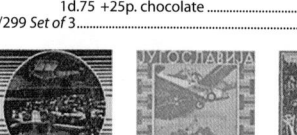

(**56**)

1931 (1 Nov). Nos. 243/45 variously optd as T **56**.

259	50p. +50p. olive-green	10	10
260	1d. +50p. carmine	10	10
261	3d. +1d. blue	75	90
259/261 *Set of* 3		85	1·00

The 50p. is overprinted with the Cyrillic version (as at the right of Type **56**) only and the 3d. with the roman version only; in both cases one word appears on the left of the stamp and one word on the right.

1932 (1 Apr)–**34**. T **55** but with names of designer and engraver (Stojičević and Wagner) in Cyrillic characters. P 12½.

262	75p. deep green	75	10
263	1d.50 rose	1·90	10
	a. Thin paper (1932)	8·25	55
263*b*	1d.75 lake (18.8.34)	3·25	45
263*c*	3d.50 bright blue (18.8.34)	4·25	45
262/263*c* *Set of* 4		9·25	1·00

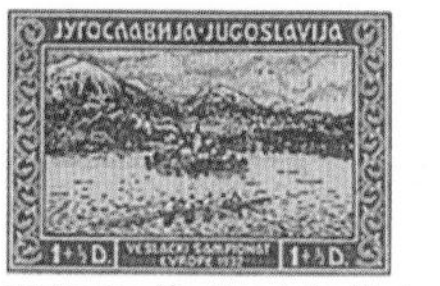

57 Rowing "four" on Lake Bled

58 Rowing "pair" on river, and Zagreb Cathedral

(Des V. Tutović. Typo)

1932 (2 Sept). European Rowing Championship. T **57**, **58** and similar types. Colour of shaded background in brackets. P 11½.

264	75p. +50p. deep green (*blue*)	85	1·30
265	1d. +½d. scarlet (*blue*)	85	1·30
266	1½d. +½d. carmine (*green*)	1·50	1·90
267	3d. +1d. deep blue (*blue*)	2·50	3·25
268	4d. +1d. orange (*blue*)	10·50	22·00
269	5d. +1d. violet (*lilac*)	10·50	17·00
264/269 *Set of* 6		24·00	42·00

Designs: Horiz—75p. Single-sculler on Danube at Smederevo; 1½d. Rowing "eight" on Danube at Belgrade; 3d. Rowing "pair" at Split harbour. Vert—5d. Prince Peter.

59

60 Crown Prince Petar in "Sokol" Uniform

1933 (25 May). Eleventh International PEN Club Congress, Dubrovnik. Typo. P 12½.

270	**59**	50p. +25p. black	10·50	13·50
271		75p. +25p. yellow-green	10·50	13·50
272		1d.50 +50p. rose	10·50	13·50
273		3d. +1d. ultramarine	10·50	13·50
274		4d. +1d. blue-green	10·50	13·50
275		5d. +1d. orange-yellow	10·50	13·50
270/275 *Set of* 6			55·00	75·00

Nos. 271/2 have the same imprint below the design as Nos. 262/3.

The commemorative inscription at foot of Nos. 271, 273 and 275 is in Cyrillic characters.

(Des S. Grujić. Typo)

1933 (28 June). "Sokol" Meeting, Ljubljana. P 12½.

276	**60**	75p. +25p. green	50	35
277		1½d. +½d. scarlet	50	35

(**61**)

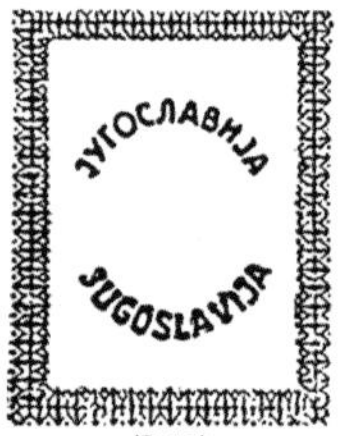

(D **62**)

1933 (5 Sept). Optd as T **61** (without bars). P 12½.

278	**46**	25p. green	10	10
279		50p. sepia	10	10
280		1d. scarlet	1·00	10
281		2d. black	1·60	10
282		3d. dull blue	5·25	10
283		4d. vermilion	2·50	10
284		5d. violet	5·25	10
285		8d. grey-brown	16·00	1·90
286		10d. olive	31·00	20
287		15d. brown	50·00	2·50
288		20d. violet	75·00	1·10
289		30d. orange	70·00	1·10
278/289 *Set of* 12			£225	6·75

Most of the above exist with overprint inverted, double or both.

1933 (5 Sept). Charity stamps of 1926 (Nos. 221/3) optd with T **61**.

290	25p. +0.25 green	1·30	20
291	50p. +0.50 sepia	1·30	20
292	1d. +0.50 scarlet	3·75	65
290/292 *Set of* 3		5·75	95

All values exist with overprint double (*price £25 each un*).

1933 (5 Sept). POSTAGE DUE. Postage Due stamps of 1923–31 optd with Type D **62**. P 10½.

D293	D **41**	50p. violet (G.)	75	10
		a. Perf 9	20	10
D294		1d. brown (B.)	5·25	1·90
		a. Perf 9	30	10
		b. Perf 11½	30	10
D295		2d. blue (V.)	2·50	1·70
		a. Perf 9	65	10
		b. Perf 11½	65	10
D296		5d. orange (B.)	2·10	1·10
		a. Perf 9	3·75	10
		b. Perf 11½	2·10	10
D297		10d. chocolate (B.)	10·50	35
		a. Perf 9	10·50	10
D293/297 *Set of* 5 (*cheapest*)			12·50	45

OBLIGATORY TAX STAMPS. These were for compulsory use on inland mail during certain periods of the year for the benefit of the Red Cross and later for other organizations. In default of their use the appropriate special Postage Due stamps were applied and the tax collected from the recipient. Special postage due stamps were not issued after 1963.

Until 1976 their issue was arranged by the Federal Post Office; from 1976 the issue of tax stamps was the responsibility of the individual republics and autonomous regions.

62

D **63**

(Types **62** and D **63** des D. Kovalenko. Typo)

1933 (17 Sept). OBLIGATORY TAX. Red Cross. Cross in red. P 12½.

293	**62**	50p. red and blue	30	20

This stamp was issued for the benefit of the Red Cross Society during the third weeks of September from 1933–35 and in 1937 and 1939. Although other Red Cross stamps were issued in 1936 and 1938, examples of No. 293 are known postally used in these years as well.

1933 (17 Sept). POSTAGE DUE. Red Cross. Cross in red. P 12½.

D298	D **63**	50p. red and green	85	35
		a. Perf 11½	26·00	11·00

63 Osprey over R. Bosna

64 Athlete and Falcon (from sculpture by Kršinić)

(Des P. Šain. Typo)

1934 (1 June). 20th Anniv of "Sokol" Games, Sarajevo. P 12½.

294	**63**	75p. +25p. emerald-green	10·50	12·50
295		1d.50 +50p. scarlet	16·00	13·50
296		1d.75 +25p. chocolate	26·00	13·50
294/296 *Set of* 3			47·00	36·00

(Des from sculpture by Kršinić. Typo)

1934 (1 June). 60th Anniv of Croat "Sokol" Games, Zagreb. P 12½.

297	**64**	75p. +25p. blue-green	5·25	4·50
298		1d.50 +50p. scarlet	5·25	6·75
299		1d.75 +25p. chocolate	12·50	17·00
297/299 *Set of* 3			21·00	25·00

65 Dubrovnik

66 Lake Bled

67 Waterfall at Jajce

68 Oplenac

69 Mostar Bridge

70 King Petar II

(Des J. Trpin (50p.), J. Omahen and D. Serajnik (1d.), M. Peroš (2d.), R. Gorjup (3d.), D. Andrejević-Kun (10d.). Typo)

1934 (15 June). AIR. P 12½.

300	**65**	50p. blackish purple	10	20
301	**66**	1d. green	20	20
302	**67**	2d. scarlet	75	55
303	**68**	3d. ultramarine	2·30	80
304	**69**	10d. orange	5·25	5·25
300/304 *Set of* 5			7·75	6·25

King Petar II

9 October 1934–29 November 1945

1934 (17 Oct). King Alexander Mourning. Black margins. P 12½. (a) Without, (b) with engraver's name.

305	**55**	25p. black (a)	10	10
306		50p. green (a)	10	10
307		75p. deep green (b)	10	10
308		1d. scarlet (a)	10	10
309		1d.50 rose (b)	10	10
310		1d.75 lake (b)	10	10
311		3d. dull blue (a)	10	10
312		3d.50 ultramarine (b)	50	10
313		4d. orange-vermilion (a)	50	10
314		5d. violet (a)	1·30	10
315		10d. deep olive (a)	3·75	10
316		15d. brown (a)	7·75	35
317		20d. purple (a)	16·00	35
318		30d. bright magenta (a)	10·50	55
305/318 *Set of* 14			37·00	2·10

1935 (1 Jan). AIR. King Alexander Mourning Issue. Black margins. P 12½.

319	**68**	3d. ultramarine	6·25	5·50

(Des S. Grujić. Typo)

1935 (6 Sept)–**36**. (a) "DIN" in Roman. (b) "DIN" in Cyrillic. P 13×12½.

320	**70**	25p. blackish brown (b) (18.11.35)	10	10
		a. Thick paper	5·25	2·75
321		50p. bright orange (a)	10	10
		a. Thick paper	5·25	2·75
322		75p. green (b)	20	10
323		1d. red-brown (a) (18.11.35)	20	10
324		1d.50 bright rose (b)	30	10
325		1d.75 carmine (a)	50	10
325*a*		2d. deep claret (a) (1.8.36)	30	10
326		3d. brown-orange (b) (18.11.35)	30	10
327		3d.50 ultramarine (a)	75	10
328		4d. yellow-green (b) (18.11.35)	2·50	10
329		4d. steel-blue (b) (1.8.36)	50	10
330		10d. bright violet (a) (18.11.35)	2·50	10
331		15d. deep brown (b) (18.11.35)	2·75	10
332		20d. light blue (a) (18.11.35)	10·50	35
333		30d. carmine-pink (b) (18.11.35)	5·25	35
320/333 *Set of* 15			24·00	1·80

71 King Alexander

72

73 Queen Marie

(Des S. Grujić and M. Marković. Typo)

1935 (9 Oct). First Anniv of King Alexander's Assassination. Nos. 334/5, P 12½×11½; 336/8, P 11½.

334	**71**	75p. emerald-green	50	55
335		1d.50 scarlet	50	55
336		1d.75 brown	75	1·10
337		3d.50 ultramarine	4·25	4·50
338		7d.50 carmine	2·50	2·75
334/338 *Set of* 5			7·75	8·50

(Des V. Filakovac. Litho)

1935 (25 Dec). Winter Relief Fund. P 12½×11½.

339	**72**	1d.50 +1d. deep and pale brown	3·25	1·70
340		3d.50 +1d.50 bright blue and blue	5·25	4·00

(Des Emilija Ognjanova. Litho)

1936 (3 May). Child Welfare. P 12½×11½.

341	**73**	75p. +25p. turquoise-green	50	55
342		1d.50 +50p. rose	50	55
343		1d.75 +75p. brown	3·25	3·25
344		3d.50 +1d. blue	4·25	4·50
341/344 *Set of* 4			7·75	8·00

74 Tesla

75 Prince Paul

76 Dr. Vladan Djordjevic (founder)

(Des V. Filakovac. Litho)

1936 (28 May). 80th Birthday of Dr. Nikola Tesla (physicist). P 12½×11½.

345	**74**	75p. brown and yellow-green	40	35
346		1d.75 slate and dull blue	65	40

(Des S. Grujić. Typo)

1936 (20 Sept). Red Cross. Cross in scarlet. P 12½.

347	**75**	75p. +50p. emerald-green	40	45
348		1d.50 +50p. carmine-pink	40	45

(Des S. Grujić. Typo)

1936 (20 Sept). OBLIGATORY TAX. Jubilee of Serbian Red Cross. Cross in scarlet. P 12½.

349	**76**	50p. olive-brown	50	35

77 Princes Tomislav and Andrej

78 Oplenac

(Nos. 350/5 des Emilija Ognjanova and S. Grujić. Litho)

1937 (1 May). Child Welfare. T **77** and similar type. P 11½×12½ (25p., 75p.) or 12½×11½.

350	**77**	25p. +25p. brown-lake	30	35
351	–	75p. +75p. blue-green	50	55
352	–	1d.50 +1d. scarlet-vermilion	85	90
353	**77**	2d. +1d. bright magenta	1·60	1·70
350/353 *Set of* 4			3·00	3·25

Design:—25p., 75p. Horiz portrait (27×22½ mm.).

1937 (1 July). Little Entente. P 12½×11½.

354	**78**	3d. blue-green	2·50	80
		a. Perf 12½	31·00	39·00
355		4d. deep blue	2·50	1·70

79 Macedonian Costume

80 St. Naum Convent, Lake Ohrid

83 Arms of Yugoslavia, Greece, Romania and Turkey

(Des Emilija Ognjanova and S. Grujić. Litho)

1937 (12 Sept). First Yugoslav Philatelic Exhibition, Belgrade (ZEFIB). Sheet (109×150 mm.) comprising T **79** and similar designs showing girls in national costumes. P 14.

MS356 1d. green (T **79**); 1d.50, purple (Bosnia); 2d. scarlet (Slovenia); 4d. blue (Croatia) 13·50 13·50

Sold at the Exhibition P.O. at 15d.

(Des S. Grujić. Litho)

1937 (12 Sept). AIR. As T **80** (various views). P 12½.

360	**80**	50p. brown	10	10
		a. Perf 12½×11½	15	15
361	–	1d. bright green	15	10
		a. Perf 12½×11½	20	15
362	–	2d. slate-blue	20	15
		a. Perf 11½×12½	20	15
363	–	2d.50 carmine	30	20
		a. Perf 11½×12½	30	20
364	**80**	5d. violet	50	35
		a. Perf 12½×11½	50	20
365	–	10d. lake	1·80	35
		a. Perf 12½×11½	1·30	35
366	–	20d. bluish green	2·00	2·00
		a. Perf 11½×12½	10·50	13·50
367	–	30d. bright blue	2·50	2·50
		a. Perf 11½×12½	37·00	45·00
360/367 *Set of* 8			6·75	5·25

Views: Vert—1d., 10d. Rab Harbour. Horiz—2d., 20d. Sarajevo; 2d.50, 30d. Ljubljana.

This issue was reprinted in 1941 during the German occupation and overprinted "SERBIEN". The reprints are on thinner paper and in slightly different shades.

See also Nos. 443/4.

(Des S. Grujić. Litho)

1937 (29 Oct). Balkan Entente. P 11, 11½, 12½ or compounds.

368	**83**	3d. emerald	2·50	55
369		4d. bright blue	3·25	1·30

84

85

86 Searchlight Display and Parachute Tower

(Des Emilija Ognjanova. Litho)

1938 (1 May). Child Welfare. P 12½×11½ (T **84**) or 11½×12½ (T **85**).

370	**84**	50p. +50p. chocolate	30	20
371	**85**	1d. +1d. blue-green	50	45
372	**84**	1d.50 +1d.50 scarlet	1·30	1·10
373	**85**	2d. +2d. magenta	3·25	2·75
370/373 *Set of* 4			4·75	4·00

(Des S. Grujić. Litho)

1938 (28 May). International Aeronautical Exhibition, Belgrade, and Yugoslav Air Club Fund. P 11½×12½.

374	**86**	1d. +50p. blue-green	1·00	1·10
375		1d.50 +1d. scarlet	1·60	1·70
		a. Perf 11½	21·00	25·00
376		2d. +1d. magenta	3·25	3·25
		a. Perf 11½	37·00	45·00
377		3d. +1d.50 bright blue	5·25	5·50
374/377 *Set of* 4			10·00	10·50

87 Entrance to Demir Kapija Cliff

88 King Alexander

(Des L. Čučaković. Litho)

1938 (1 Aug). Railway Employees' Hospital Fund. As T **87/8** (various designs inscr "ZA BOLNICU U DEMIR KAPIJI" in Cyrillic or Roman). P 12½×11½ (Nos. 378/9) or 11½×12½.

378	1d. +1d. blue-green	1·00	55
379	1d.50 +1d.50 scarlet	1·80	80
380	2d. +2d. magenta	4·50	4·50
381	3d. +3d. bright blue	4·75	4·50
378/381 *Set of* 4		11·00	9·25

Designs: Horiz—1d.50, Demir Kapija Hospital. Vert—2d. Runner carrying torch.

The longer inscription on these stamps reads "Memorial to the heroic King Alexander, the Uniter".

89 Breasting the Tape

90 Hurdling

(Des S. Grujić. Litho)

1938 (11 Sept). 9th Balkan Games. As T **89/90** (inscr "IX BALKANSKE IGRE 1938" in Cyrillic or Roman). P 11½×12½ (vert) or 12½×11½ (horiz).

382	50p. +50p. brown-orange	3·25	3·25
383	1d. +1d. blue-green	3·25	3·25
384	1d.50 +1d.50 magenta	3·25	3·25
385	2d. +2d. bright blue	6·25	6·75
382/385 *Set of* 4		14·50	15·00

Designs: Horiz—1d.50, Pole vaulting. Vert—2d. Putting the shot.

91 Maiden of Kosovo (after P. Jovanović)

SALVATE
PARVULOS

(**92** = "Save the Children")

1938 (18 Sept)–**40**. OBLIGATORY TAX. Red Cross. Litho. P 12½.

386	**91**	50p. red, green, yellow and blue	50	35
386*a*		50p. red and slate-blue (15.9.40)	75	55

1938 (1 Oct). Child Welfare. Optd as T **92** (1d., 2d.), or smaller opt (5¾×2½ mm., others). P 12½.

387	**84**	50p. +50p. chocolate	1·00	80
		a. Pair, one without opt	£200	
388	**85**	1d. +1d. blue-green	1·00	1·10
389	**84**	1d.50 +1d.50 scarlet	1·60	1·70
390	**85**	2d. +2d. magenta	3·25	3·25
387/390 *Set of* 4			6·25	6·25

93 Mail Carrier

94 Meal-time

(Des S. Grujić. Litho)

1939 (15 Mar). Postal Centenary and Railway Benevolent Association Fund. As T **93** (inscr "1839 1939"). P 11½×12.

391	50p. +50p. yellow-orange and brown	75	80
392	1d. +1d. blue-green and black	75	80
393	1d.50 +1d.50 carmine and lake	4·25	2·75
394	2d. +2d. purple and violet	4·25	4·00
395	4d. +4d. blue and dull blue	5·25	5·50
391/395 *Set of* 5		13·50	12·50

Designs:—50p. Mounted postmen; 1d.50, Steam mail train; 2d. Mail coach; 4d. Lockheed 10 Electra mail plane.

(Des S. Grujić. Litho)

1939 (1 May). Child Welfare. Designs inscr as T **94**, in Cyrillic or Roman. P 12½.

396	1d. +1d. blue-green and myrtle	1·30	1·30
397	1d.50 +1d.50 salmon and brown	5·25	4·50
	a. Perf 11½	£180	£225
398	2d. +2d. magenta and brown	3·75	4·00
399	4d. +4d. light blue and blue	3·75	4·25
396/399 *Set of* 4		12·50	12·50

Designs: Horiz—2d. Young carpenter. Vert—1d.50, Children playing on sands; 4d. Children whispering.

95 Miloš Obilic

96 Motor Cycle and Sidecar

(Des S. Grujić. Litho)

1939 (28 June). 550th Anniv of Battle of Kosovo. T **95** and similar vert design. P 11½.

400	1d. +1d. turquoise-green and blackish olive (Prince Lazar)	4·25	2·20
401	1d.50 +1d.50 carmine-red and dp carmine	4·25	2·20

(Des M. Marković. Litho)

1939 (3 Sept). First International Motor Races, Belgrade. As T **96** (inscr "I. MEĐUNARODNE AUTO I MOTO TRKE U BEOGRADU 3–IX–1939"). P 12×11½ (vert) or 11½×12 (others).

402	50p. +50p. orange and brown	1·30	1·10
403	1d. +1d. turquoise-green and black	2·50	2·20
404	1d.50 +1d.50 carmine and lake	3·75	3·25
405	2d. +2d. bright blue and indigo	6·25	5·50
402/405 *Set of* 4		12·50	11·00

Designs: Vert—1d.50, Motor Cycle. Horiz—1d., 2d. Racing Cars.

97 *Jadran* (cadet barquentine)

98 Unknown Warrior's Tomb, Avala

(Eng K. Seizinger. Recess)

1939 (6 Sept). King Petar's Birthday and Adriatic Guard Fund. T **97** and similar horiz designs. P 11½×12.

406	50p. +50p. dull vermilion	1·00	1·10
407	1d. +50p. deep bluish green	2·10	2·20
408	1d.50 +1d. carmine	3·25	3·25
409	2d. +1d.50 deep blue	5·25	5·50
406/409 *Set of 4*		10·50	11·00

Designs:—1d. *King Alexander* (liner); 1d.50, *Triglav* (freighter); 2d. *Dubrovnik* (destroyer).

(Des S. Grujić. Litho)

1939 (9 Oct). 5th Anniv of King Alexander's Death. War Invalids' Fund. P 12½.

410	**98**	1d. +50p. blue-green	2·50	2·20
411		1d.50 +1d. scarlet	2·50	2·20
412		2d. +1d.50 purple	3·25	3·25
413		3d. +2d. blue	6·25	5·50
410/413 *Set of 4*			13·00	12·00

99 King Petar II

100 Postman delivering Letters

(Des S. Grujić. Die eng R. Stojanović. Typo)

1939–40. P 12½.

414	**99**	25p. black (1940)	30	10
415		50p. orange (2.40)	30	10
416		1d. green (11.12.39)	30	10
417		1d.50 scarlet (9.10.39)	30	10
418		2d. carmine-rose (1940)	30	10
419		3d. red-brown (11.12.39)	50	10
420		4d. bright blue (9.10.39)	50	10
420*a*		5d. blue (1.11.40)	50	20
420*b*		5d.50 dull violet (1.11.40)	1·30	20
421		6d. deep blue (9.10.39)	2·50	20
422		8d. chocolate (9.10.39)	3·25	20
423		12d. violet (9.10.39)	4·75	20
424		16d. purple (9.10.39)	6·25	35
425		20d. light blue (2.40)	6·25	35
426		30d. pink (2.40)	14·50	80
414/426 *Set of 15*			38·00	3·00

(Des V. Andrejević-Kun. Litho)

1940 (1 Jan). Belgrade Postal Employees' Fund. As T **100** (various designs inscr "ZA DOM P.T.T. ZVAN. I SLUZ" in Cyrillic or Roman). P 12½.

427	50p. +50p. orange and brown	1·40	1·70
428	1d. +1d. turquoise-green and black	1·40	1·70
429	1d.50 +1d.50 scarlet and red-brown	2·50	3·25
430	2d. +2d. magenta and purple	3·25	3·25
431	4d. +4d. blue and grey	10·50	9·00
427/431 *Set of 5*		17·00	17·00

Designs: Vert—1d. Postman collecting letters; 4d. Telegraph linesman. Horiz—1d.50, Mail van; 2d. Loading mail train.

101 Arrival of Thorval

102 Winter Games

(Des S. Benković, Lavrenčić and Price. Typo)

1940 (1 Mar). Zagreb Postal Employees' Fund. T **101** and other designs inscr "ZA DOM P.T.T. CINOV. U ZAGREBU". P 11½×12 (horiz) or 12×11½ (vert).

432	50p. +50p. orange-brown	75	80
433	1d. +1d. green	75	80
434	1d.50 +1d.50 scarlet	1·30	80
435	2d. +2d. carmine-rose	3·25	3·25
436	4d. +2d. blue	3·75	4·00
432/436 *Set of 5*		8·75	8·75

Designs: 25½×35½ mm—1d. King Tomislav enthroned; 1d.50, Death of Matija Gubec. 37×27 mm—2d. Radic Brothers. 34×25 mm—4d. Divisional map of Yugoslavia.

(Des Mladena Josić. Litho)

1940 (1 May). Child Welfare. T **102** and smaller type (20×26 mm.), inscr "ZA NASU DECU" in Cyrillic or Roman. P 11½ (T **102**) or 12½ (1d. and 2d.).

437	50p. +50p. yellow-orange and orange-red	50	55
438	1d. +1d. blue-green and olive-green	50	55
439	1d.50 +1d.50 scarlet and brown	1·60	1·10
440	2d. +2d. magenta and violet	2·75	2·20
437/440 *Set of 4*		4·75	4·00

Designs:—1d.50, as T **102**; 1d., 2d. Children at seaside (Summer games).

103 Arms of Yugoslavia, Greece, Romania and Turkey

104 Zagreb Cathedral and Junkers Ju 86

(Des S. Grujić. Typo)

1940 (27 May). Balkan Entente. T **103**, inscr "JUGOSLAVIJA" alternately in Cyrillic (C.) or Roman (R.) at the top of designs throughout the sheet, and "ENTENTE BALKANIQUE" at the bottom of every stamp. P 12½.

441C	3d. bright blue	2·10	65
442C	4d. deep blue	2·10	65
441R	3d. bright blue	2·10	65
442R	4d. deep blue	2·10	65

(Des S. Grujić. Litho)

1940 (15 Aug). AIR. T **104** and similar horiz design. P 12½.

443	40d. blue-green	6·75	2·75
444	50d. slate-blue	9·00	5·00

Design:—50d. Suspension Bridge at Belgrade and Fokker F.VIIa/3m.

The note below No. 367 concerning reprints also applies here.

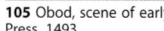

105 Obod, scene of early Press, 1493

2+2

(**106**)

(Des S. Grujić. Litho)

1940 (29 Sept). 500th Anniv of Invention of Printing Press by Johannes Gutenberg. P 12½.

445	**105**	5d.50 slate-green and dull blue-green	4·75	4·50

1940 (23 Dec). Anti-Tuberculosis Fund, Nos. 364/7 variously surch as T **106**, in red. P 12½×11½ (vert) or 11½×12½ (horiz).

446	50p.+50p. on 5d. violet	30	35
	a. Surch inverted	65·00	80·00
447	1d.+1d. on 10d. lake	50	55
	a. Surch inverted	70·00	85·00
	b. Perf 12½	31·00	34·00
448	1d.50+1d.50 on 20d. bluish green	2·10	1·90
449	2d.+2d. on 30d. bright blue	2·30	2·50
	a. Perf 12½	60·00	95·00
446/449 *Set of 4*		4·75	4·75

107 St. Peter's Cemetery, Ljubljana

108 National Costumes

(Des S. Grujić (1d.50), M. Marković (others). Litho)

1941 (1 Jan). Ljubljana War Veterans' Fund. Various designs as T **107/8**. P 12½.

450	50p. +50p. yellow-green	50	55
451	1d. +1d. brown-lake	50	55
452	1d.50 +1d.50 blue-green	1·60	1·70
453	2d. +2d. lilac and blue	2·50	2·75
450/453 *Set of 4*		4·50	5·00

Designs: Horiz—2d. War Memorial, Brezje. Vert—1d.50, Memorial Chapel, Kajmakčalan.

109 Kamenita Gate, Zagreb

(Des O. Antonini. Eng K. Seizinger. Recess)

1941. T **109** and similar vert design. P 11½.

(a) For 2nd Croatian Philatelic Exhibition, Zagreb (16 March)

454	1d.50 +1d.50 chocolate	1·60	1·70
	a. Perf 9½ at right	26·00	28·00
	b. With engraver's initial "S"	37·00	39·00
455	4d. +3d. blue-black	1·60	1·70
	a. Perf 9½ at right	26·00	28·00

(b) For 1st Philatelic Exhibition, Slav Brod (13 April)

456	1d.50 +1d.50 blue-black	23·00	28·00
	a. Perf 9½ at right	65·00	85·00
	b. With engraver's initial "S"	£300	£325
457	4d. +3d. chocolate	23·00	28·00
	a. Perf 9½ at right	65·00	85·00

Design:—4d. Old Cathedral, Zagreb.

The above were printed in sheets of 16 with nine *se-tenant* labels.

The engraver's initial is found near the second lower window of the left-hand building and occurs on stamp No. 6.

WARTIME OCCUPATION ISSUES

Yugoslavia was invaded by German, Italian, Hungarian and Bulgarian troops on 6 April 1941. The Yugoslav forces capitulated on 17 April, and the country was divided up as follows:—

1. Germany on 8 July 1941 annexed, as the province of Lower Styria, territory in Slovenia extending south to the Sava, including Maribor, Celje, Kranj and Bled.

2. Italy occupied Sušak and the basin of the Kupa (the Fiume and Kupa Zone, for which stamps were issued (see at end of Yugoslavia)); on 3 May 1941 she annexed this area. She also occupied Ljubljana and a wedge of Slovenia extending almost to Karlovac (stamps were also issued for this occupied area (see under Slovenia) until it was also annexed on 3 May); on 18 May 1941, Italy's Zara (now Zadar) enclave was enlarged to include Benkovac, Šibenik and Trogir, and became the province of Dalmatia; as a naval base she acquired the area around the Gulf of Kotor, including Kotor and Hercegnovi; also annexed were the islands of Korcula, Krk, Mljet and Šolta.

3. Hungary acquired, by decree of 27 December 1941, all Yugoslav territory north of the Drava and west of the Tisza, including Subotica, Novi Sad and Sombor.

4. Albania was given, on 29 June 1941, a large area including Ulcinj on the coast and the inland towns of Pec, Dakovica, Priština, Prizren and Kicevo. The area was officially annexed on 12 September 1942.

5. Bulgaria, in April 1941, occupied Yugoslav Macedonia as far as a line running south and east of Bela Palanka, Lescovac and Gnjilane; this included Pirot, Skopje, Prilep, Bitola and Ohrid.

The stamps used in transferred areas were those of the countries which acquired them apart from those that were specially issued.

The remainder of Yugoslavia was divided into three states:—

Croatia, proclaimed independent on 10 April 1941: a kingdom in theory, but ruled by the Poglavnik, or leader, Ante Pavelic. From 7 July 1941 this comprised Bosnia and Herzegovina, the Dalmatian coast from Crikvenica to Cavtat inclusive (except for the Zara enclave) and all territory south of the Drava and as far west as Varaždin, including Zagreb, the capital. In September 1943 Šibenik was taken over from the Italians. The stamps are listed under Croatia.

Montenegro was made an Italian Governorship on 3 October 1941. It consisted of the Montenegro of 1913, with additions west of Novi Pazar, but without the Pec and Dakovica areas. The stamps are listed under Montenegro.

Serbia: in theory an independent state, ruled by a Serbian government under General Nedic from 30 August 1941; in fact under German military rule. It comprised most of the pre-1913 Serbia (except for areas round Pirot and Vranje), and a wedge of territory, the Banat, between the Tisza and the old Romanian frontier, extending to just south of Szeged. The stamps are listed under Serbia.

In September 1943 the King of Italy and Marshal Badoglio ended hostilities with the Allies, and German forces took over Montenegro, Italian Slovenia (renamed Province of Laibach) and the Italian areas round Zara and Kotor. They made issues of stamps for these areas (see under Montenegro, Slovenia and German Occupation of Dalmatia (at end of Yugoslavia) respectively).

On 8 September 1944, Bulgaria signed an armistice and Macedonia was occupied by German troops and declared its independence, which lasted till German troops left on 13 November. Stamps were issued (see under Macedonia).

ISSUES OF THE YUGOSLAV GOVERNMENT IN EXILE

The following three issues were made by the Yugoslav government in exile in London, for the use of the Yugoslav Merchant Navy working with the Allies.

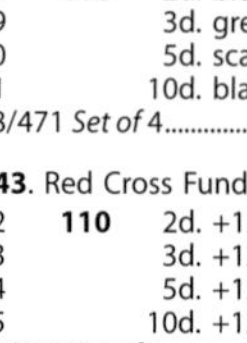

110 King Petar II

CRVENI KRST
+ 12.50

(**111**)

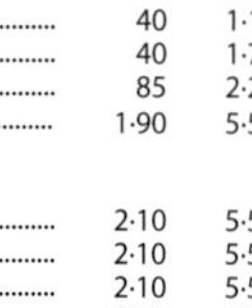

112 V. Vodnik (poet)

(Typo Waterlow & Sons)

1943 (27 Mar). Second Anniv of Overthrow of Regency Govt and of King Petar's Assumption of Power. P 12½×13.

468	**110**	2d. blue	40	1·10
469		3d. grey	40	1·10
470		5d. scarlet	40	1·70
471		10d. black	85	2·20
468/471 *Set of 4*			1·90	5·50

1943. Red Cross Fund. Surch with T **111**.

472	**110**	2d. +12d.50 blue (Verm.)	2·10	5·50
473		3d. +12d.50 grey (Verm.)	2·10	5·50
474		5d. +12d.50 scarlet (Bk.)	2·10	5·50
475		10d. +12d.50 black (Verm.)	2·10	5·50
472/475 *Set of 4*			7·50	20·00

(Recess Waterlow & Sons)

1943 (1 Dec). 25th Anniv of Formation of Yugoslavia. T **112** and similar vert designs. P 12½×13.

476	1d. black and vermilion	50	
477	2d. black and green	85	
478	3d. black and royal blue	85	
479	4d. agate and deep violet	1·60	
480	5d. agate and maroon	1·60	
481	10d. sepia and reddish brown	5·25	
476/481 *Set of 6*		9·50	
MS481*a* 127×185 mm. Nos. 476/81		75·00	

Designs:—2d. Petar Njegoš (poet); 3d. Ljudevit Gaj (writer); 4d. Vuk Karadžić (poet); 5d. Bishop Josip Strosmajer (politician); 10d. Djordje Petrovic (Karageorge).

DEMOCRATIC FEDERATION OF YUGOSLAVIA

The partisans under Marshal Tito seized power throughout Yugoslavia after the defeat of Germany. Yugoslavia, in theory still a monarchy, became a Democratic Federation.

Owing to the general shortage of stamps occupation issues were overprinted at various places and widely used. These were partly made necessary because of the different currencies in use.

(a) Regional Issues

Bosnia and Herzegovina

Currency: Croatian Kunas

(R 1)

1945 (28 Apr). Mostar issue. Stamps of Croatia surch as Type R **1**.

		(a) Pictorial stamps of 1941–43		
R1		10k. on 25b. brown-red	1·00	1·00
R2		10k. on 50b. myrtle-green (R.)	1·00	1·00
R3		10k. on 2k. claret	1·00	1·00
R4		10k. on 3k.50 purple-brown (78)	1·00	1·00
R5		40k. on 1k. blue-green (R.)	1·00	1·00
R6		50k. on 4k. ultramarine (R.)	5·25	5·25
R7		50k. on 5k. greenish blue (R.)	26·00	26·00
R8		50k. on 6k. brown-olive	5·25	5·25
R9		50k. on 7k. orange-red	£100	£100
R10		50k. on 8k. red-brown	£130	£130
R11		50k. on 10k. brown-violet (R.)	1·00	1·00
		(b) Famous Croats issue of 1943		
R12		30k. on 1k. blue (R.)	1·00	1·00
R13		30k. on 3k.50 carmine	1·00	1·00
		(c) Boskovic issue of 1943		
R14	**28**	30k. on 3k.50 brown-lake	1·00	1·00
R15		30k. on 12k.50 brown-purple	2·50	2·50
		(d) War Victims Charity Tax stamps of 1944		
R16	**34**	20k. on 1k. blue-green (R.)	1·00	1·00
R17	**35**	20k. on 2k. claret	1·00	1·00
R18		20k. on 5k. blackish green (R.)	1·00	1·00
R19		20k. on 10k. blue (R.)	1·00	1·00
R20		20k. on 20k. brown	1·00	1·00
R1/20 *Set of* 20			£250	£250

On 7 July 1945 eight pictorial stamps and the five war victims charity stamps of Croatia were overprinted in three lines and arms and surcharged in dinars and placed on sale in Sarajevo. The issue was cancelled by the Belgrade postal authorities and the stamps were withdrawn after three days (*Price per set of* 13: £500 *un*).

Croatia

Currency: Kunas

(R 2)

1945 (1–21 Mar). Split issue. Stamps of Croatia, 1941–43, surch as Type R **2**.

R21	10k. on 25b. brown-red	50	50
R22	10k. on 50b. myrtle-green (R.)	50	50
R23	10k. on 75b. olive-green (R.)	50	50
R24	10k. on 1k. blue-green (R.)	50	50
R25	20k. on 2k. claret	50	50
R26	20k. on 3k. brown-lake	50	50
R27	20k. on 3k.50 purple-brown (78)	50	50
R28	20k. on 4k. ultramarine (R.)	50	50
R29	20k. on 5k. greenish blue (R.)	50	50
R30	20k. on 6k. brown-olive (R.)	16·00	16·00
R31	30k. on 7k. orange-red (G.)	50	50
R32	30k. on 8k. red-brown (G.)	19·00	19·00
R33	30k. on 10k. brown-violet (G.)	50	50
R34	30k. on 12k.50 black (79) (R.)	50	50
R35	40k. on 20k. brown (R.)	50	50
R36	40k. on 30k. purple-brown (R.)	50	50
R37	50k. on 50k. blackish green (R.)	50	50
R21/37 *Set of* 17		38·00	38·00

1945 (20 June). Zagreb issue. Stamps of Croatia, 1941–43, surch as Type R **3**.

R38	20k. on 5k. greenish blue (R.)	30	30
R39	40k. on 1k. blue-green (R.)	30	30
R40	60k. on 3k.50 purple-brown (78) (R.)	30	30
R41	80k. on 2k. claret	30	30
R42	160k. on 50b. myrtle-green (R.)	30	30
R43	200k. on 12k.50 black (79) (R.)	30	30
R44	400k. on 25b. brown-red	30	30
R38/44 *Set of* 7		1·90	1·90

(R 3)

1945 (20 June). Zagreb issue. POSTAGE DUE. Croatian Postage Due stamps of 1943–44 (litho), surch similarly to Type R **3**, in red.

RD45	D **15**	40k. on 50b. grey-brown and light blue	30	30
RD46		60k. on 1k. grey-brown and light blue	30	30
RD47		80k. on 2k. grey-brown and light blue	30	30
RD48		100k. on 5k. grey-brown and light blue	30	30
RD49		200k. on 6k. grey-brown and light blue	30	30
RD45/49 *Set of* 5			1·40	1·40

Montenegro

Currency: Italian Lire

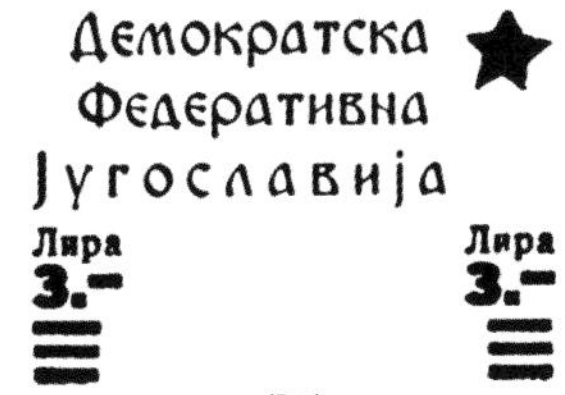

(R 4)

1945 (1 Mar). Cetinje issue. Stamps of Italian Occupation surch as Type R **4**.

	(a) National Poem issue of 1943		
R50	1l. on 10c. olive-green (R.)	2·10	2·10
R51	2l. on 25c. green (R.)	1·00	1·00
R52	3l. on 50c. rose-magenta (B.)	1·00	1·00
R53	5l. on 1l.25 blue (R.)	1·00	1·00
R54	10l. on 15c. brown (R.)	2·10	2·10
R55	15l. on 20c. brown-orange (R.)	2·10	2·10
R56	20l. on 2l. blue-green (R.)	2·10	2·10
	(b) Air stamps of 1943, for use as ordinary postage stamps		
R57	3l. on 50c. brown (R.)	5·25	5·25
R58	6l. on 1l. ultramarine (R.)	5·25	5·25
R59	10l. on 2l. rose-carmine (B.)	5·25	5·25
R60	20l. on 5l. green (R.)	5·25	5·25
R50/60 *Set of* 11		29·00	29·00

1945 (1 Mar). Cetinje issue. POSTAGE DUE. National Poem issue of Italian Occupation surch as Type R **4**, with "PORTO" in addition.

RD61	10l. on 5c. violet (R.)	£325	£325
RD62	20l. on 5l. carmine/*buff* (Bl.)	£160	£160

Serbia

Currency: Hungarian Filler

1944 (20 Oct). Senta issue. Various stamps of Hungary optd with a large Star. in red and "8.X.1944" and "Yugoslavia" in Cyrillic characters, in black.

R63	1f. greenish grey (732)	8·25	8·25
R64	2f. orange-red (733)	8·25	8·25
R65	3f. ultramarine (734)	8·25	8·25
R66	4f. brown (735)	8·25	8·25
R67	5f. vermilion (736)	8·25	8·25
R68	8f. grey-green (738)	8·25	8·25
R69	10f. brown (739)	£190	£190
R70	24f. brown-lake (702)	£325	£325
R71	24f. purple (743)	10·50	10·50
R72	30f. carmine (745)	£190	£190
R63/72 *Set of* 10		£700	£700

1944 (20 Oct). Senta issue. POSTAGE DUE. No. D684B of Hungary optd as above and surch in addition.

RD73	D **115**	10f. on 2f. carmine-brown	50·00	50·00

Senta, in the Banat, was incorporated in Hungary from 1941 to 1944.

Other postage and postage due stamps of Hungary with this overprint were prepared but not issued.

Slovenia

Currencies: Italian (Ljubljana)

German (Maribor)

Hungarian (Murska Sobota)

(R 5)

(R 6)

1945 (7 June). Ljubljana issue. Pictorial stamps of German Occupation, 1945, optd as Type R **5**, in black.

R74	5c. black-brown	30	30
R75	10c. orange	30	30
R76	20c. lake-brown	30	30
R77	25c. deep green	30	30
R78	50c. violet	30	30
R79	75c. scarlet	30	30
R80	1l. olive-green	30	30
	a. Red opt	21·00	21·00
R81	1l.25 blue	30	30
R82	1l.50 grey-green	30	30
R83	2l. bright blue	30	30
R84	2l.50 brown	30	30
R85	3l. bright magenta	50	50
R86	5l. red-brown	75	75
R87	10l. blue-green	50	50
R88	20l. blue	4·25	4·25
R89	30l. carmine	26·00	26·00
R74/89 *Set of* 16		32·00	32·00

1945 (15 June). Maribor issue. Hitler stamps of Germany, 1941–44, optd as Type R **6**, in black.

R90	**173**	1pf. deep grey	5·25	5·25
R91		3pf. yellow-brown	50	50
R92		4pf. slate-blue	4·25	4·25
R93		5pf. dull yellowish green	3·25	3·25
R94		6pf. reddish violet	50	50
R95		8pf. bright orange-red	75	75
		a. Opt double	75·00	
R96		10pf. brown (775)	3·25	3·25
R97		12pf. scarlet-vermilion (776)	35	35
R98		15pf. lake	6·25	6·25
R99		20pf. blue	4·00	4·00
R100		24pf. orange-brown	4·25	4·25
R101		25pf. ultramarine	10·50	10·50
R102		30pf. olive-green	1·00	1·00
R103		40pf. deep magenta	1·00	1·00
R104	**225**	42pf. emerald-green	1·00	1·00
R105	**173**	50pf. bottle green	3·75	3·75
R106		60pf. purple-brown	1·00	1·00
R107		80pf. deep blue	2·50	2·50
		a. Opt double	85·00	
R90/107 *Set of* 18			48·00	48·00

1945 (22 June). Murska Sobota issue. Various stamps of Hungary optd as Type R **6**, in black.

R108	1f. greenish grey (732)	6·25	6·25
R109	4f. brown (735)	50	50
R110	5f. vermilion (736)	6·25	6·25
R111	10f. brown (739)	50	50
R112	18f. grey-black (741)	50	50
R113	20f. red-brown (742)	50	50
R114	30f. carmine (744)	50	50
R115	30f. carmine-red (782)	50	50
R116	50f. blue (783)	10·50	10·50
R117	70f. orange-brown (784)	10·50	10·50
R118	80f. brown (747)	50·00	50·00
R119	1p. green (748)	7·75	7·75
R108/119 *Set of* 12		85·00	85·00

The issues for Rijeka and Trieste are listed under Venezia Giulia.

(b) General Issues

Currency Revaluation

100 Paras = 1 (Occupation) Dinar

(113)

(D 114)

1944 (14 Dec)–**45**. Monasteries. Nos. 64/6 of German Occupation of Serbia, surch as T **113**.

	(a) With blue network background		
482	3d. +2d. pink (G.) (16.12.44)	20	20
483	7d. +3d. grey-green (R.) (14.12.44)	20	20
	(b) Without network (24.1.45)		
484	3d. +2d. pink (G.)	20	20
485	4d. +21d. ultramarine (Bk.)	20	20
486	7d. +3d. grey-green (R.)	20	20
482/486 *Set of* 5		90	90

1944 (25 Dec). POSTAGE DUE. Postage Due stamps of Serbia (Arms and Numeral type), optd "Demokratska/Federativna/Jugoslavija" in Cyrillic characters, as Type D **114**. P 12½.

D487	10d. scarlet	1·60	75
D488	20d. ultramarine	1·60	75

It is not known if Nos. 482/D488 were in use outside Serbia.

D **115**

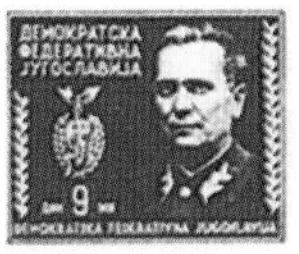

114 Marshal Tito

115 Chapel at Prohor Pcinjski

(Des D. Andrejević-Kun. Litho)

1945 (13 Feb–Mar). POSTAGE DUE. Numerals in black. P 12½.

D489	D **115**	2d. brown-purple (26.2)	40	10
D490		3d. bright reddish violet (26.2)	40	10
D491		5d. yellow-green (1.3)	40	10
D492		7d. Indian red (1.3)	40	10
D493		10d. magenta	40	10
D494		20d. blue	40	10
D495		30d. blue-green (3.3)	1·00	40
D496		40d. rose-red (3.3)	1·00	50
D489/496 *Set of* 8			4·00	1·40

See also Nos. D497/501.

(Des D. Andrejević-Kun. Litho)

1945 (21 Feb–4 Apr). P 12½.

487	**114**	5d. deep bluish green (4.3)	10	10
488		10d. deep carmine (21.2)	10	10
489		25d. reddish violet (30.3)	20	15
490		30d. royal blue (4.4)	25	15
487/490 *Set of* 4			60	45

Currency Revaluation

1 Dinar = 20 (Occupation) Dinars

1945 (19 May–19 Sept). P 12½.

491	**114**	25p. blue-green (19.9)	30	10
492		50p. deep green (14.6)	30	10
493		1d. red (4.9)	3·25	40

494		2d. carmine (15.5)	30	10
495		4d. deep blue (19.6)	40	10
496		6d. reddish violet (1.6)	50	10
497		9d. orange-brown (4.9)	1·00	20
498		20d. yellow-orange (19.9)	4·75	2·10
491/498 *Set of* 8			9·75	3·00

1945 (28 June–July). Numerals in colour. P 12½.

D497	D **115**	1d. blue-green	30	10
D498		1d.50 blue	30	10
D499		2d. rose-red (4.7)	1·00	10
D500		3d. brown-purple (4.7)	1·00	10
D501		4d. bright reddish violet (12.7)	1·60	20
D497/501 *Set of* 5			3·75	55

(Des V. Andrejević-Kun. Typo)

1945 (2 Aug). 1st Anniv of Anti-fascist Chamber of Deputies, Macedonia. P 11½.

499	**115**	2d. scarlet	5·25	2·50

116 Partisans

117 Child

(Des. D. Andrejević- Kun. Typo)

1945 (15 Sept). Red Cross Fund. P 11½.

500	**116**	1d. +4d. ultramarine	1·30	1·00
501	**117**	2d. +6d. scarlet	1·30	1·00

119 Partisans

120 Marshal Tito

121 Jajce

(Des D. Mihajlović (T **119**), I. Marković (1d.50, etc.), V. Andrejević-Kun (T **120**), S. Stral (T **121**), A. Andrejević (2d.50, etc.). Typo)

1945–47. T **119/21** and similar designs. Various papers. P 12½.

502	**119**	0d.50 olive-brown (30.10.45)	30	10
503		1d. bright blue-green (25.10.45)	30	10
504	–	1d.50 chestnut (30.10.45)	30	10
505	**120**	2d. scarlet-vermilion (8.10.45)	30	10
506	–	2d.50 orange-red (20.1.47)	85	10
507	**121**	3d. lake-brown (30.10.45)	4·75	10
508		3d. scarlet (8.1.47)	1·30	10
509	**120**	4d. blue (8.10.45)	85	10
510	**121**	5d. deep green (25.10.45)	2·75	10
511		5d. blue (8.1.47)	3·75	10
512	–	6d. black (25.10.45)	1·30	10
513	–	8d. bright orange (20.1.47)	2·10	10
514	–	9d. purple (18.10.45)	1·00	10
515	–	12d. ultramarine (18.10.45)	2·30	10
516	**119**	16d. greenish blue (3.11.45)	2·30	10
517	–	20d. orange-red (3.11.45)	4·25	50
502/517 *Set of* 16			26·00	1·80

Designs: Vert—1d.50, 12, 20d. Riflemen. Horiz—2d.50, 6, 8, 9d. Girl with flag.

The above may be found on surfaced, ordinary and thin paper. There are many shades.

122 Russian and Yugoslav Flags

124 "Industry and Agriculture"

(Des M. Zlamalik. Litho Tipografija, Zagreb)

1945 (20 Oct). First Anniv of Liberation of Belgrade. P 11½.

518	**122**	2d. +5d. brown, red, blue and buff	2·10	2·10

(Des D. Andrejević-Kun, after drawings by J. Trpin and D. Mihajlović. Photo Tipografija, Zagreb)

1945 (29 Nov). Meeting of the Constituent Assembly. Inscr in Cyrillic at top and Roman characters at bottom (A) or vice versa (B). P 12.

519	**124**	2d. brown-lake (A)	4·25	4·25
		a. Horiz pair. Types A and B	8·75	8·75
519*b*		2d. brown-lake (B)	4·25	4·25
520		4d. blue (A)	4·25	4·25
		a. Horiz pair. Types A and B	8·75	8·75
520*b*		4d. blue (B)	4·25	4·25
521		6d. slate-green (A)	4·25	4·25
		a. Horiz pair. Types A and B	8·75	8·75
521*b*		6d. slate-green (B)	4·25	4·25
522		9d. orange-red (A)	4·25	4·25
		a. Horiz pair. Types A and B	8·75	8·75
522*b*		9d. orange-red (B)	4·25	4·25
523		16d. bright blue (A)	4·25	4·25
		a. Horiz pair. Types A and B	8·75	8·75
523*b*		16d. bright blue (B)	4·25	4·25
524		20d. brown (A)	4·25	4·25
		a. Horiz pair. Types A and B	8·75	8·75
524*b*		20d. brown (B)	4·25	4·25
519/524*b* *Set of* 12			46·00	46·00

The stamps contained in one half of the sheet have Cyrillic characters at the top and Roman at the bottom. In the other half the inscriptions are reversed. There are thus horizontal pairs with both combinations of lettering in the middle of each sheet.

Miniature sheet (150×110 mm). P 11 Inscr in Cyrillic at left and Roman characters at right (A) or vice versa (B).

MS524*c*	Nos. 522 and 524 (A)	31·00	31·00
MS524*d*	Nos. 522*b* and 524*b* (B)	31·00	31·00

FEDERAL PEOPLE'S REPUBLIC

On 29 November 1945, a Constituent Assembly proclaimed the Federal People's Republic of Yugoslavia.

(**125**)

D **126**

126

1946 (1 Apr). Girl with flag (as Nos. 512 and 514, but colours changed), surch as T **125**.

525	2d.50 on 6d. vermilion	1·00	30
	a. Surch omitted	£1300	£1000
526	8d. on 9d. orange	1·30	30
	a. Surch omitted	£500	£475

(Des S. Grujić. Typo)

1946 (3 May)–**47**. POSTAGE DUE. P 12½.

D527	D **126**	50p. deep orange (1.1.47)	20	10
D528		1d. orange	20	10
D529		2d. blue	20	10
D530		3d. green	20	10
D531		5d. violet	20	10
D532		7d. red	1·80	10
D533		10d. pink (1.1.47)	2·10	30
D534		20d. lake (1.1.47)	5·25	75
D527/534 *Set of* 8			9·25	1·50

See also Nos. D724/31 and D1029/33.

(Des F. Radočaj. Typo)

1946 (9 May). First Anniv of Victory over Fascism. Star in red. P 12½.

527	**126**	1d.50 orange-yellow	1·00	75
528		2d.50 carmine	2·10	1·00
529		5d. blue	7·25	2·10
527/529 *Set of* 3			9·25	3·50

127 Symbols of Communications

128 Railway Construction

129 Svetozar Marković

(Des S. Garić. Litho)

1946 (10 May). Postal Congress. P 12½.

530	**127**	1d.50 +1d. emerald	5·25	4·25
531		2d.50 +1d.50 carmine	5·25	4·25
532		5d. +2d. blue	5·25	4·25
533		8d. +3d.50 brown	5·25	4·25
530/533 *Set of* 4			19·00	15·00

1946 (1 Aug). Volunteer Workers' Railway Reconstruction Fund. Litho. Toned background. P 12½.

534	**128**	50p. +50p. brown, blue and red	3·75	2·10
535		1d.50 +1d. green, blue and red	3·75	2·10
536		2d.50 +2d. lilac, blue and red	3·75	2·10
537		5d. +3d. blue-grey, blue and red	3·75	2·10
534/537 *Set of* 4			13·50	7·50

(Des S. Grujić. Litho)

1946 (22 Sept). Birth Centenary of S. Marković (socialist writer). Toned background. P 12½.

538	**129**	1d.50 blue-green	1·70	50
539		2d.50 purple	1·70	75

O **130**

(Des M. Zlamalik. Typo)

1946 (1 Nov). OFFICIAL. P 12½.

O540	O **130**	0d.50 orange	20	10
O541		1d. blue-green	20	10
O542		1d.50 olive-green	35	10
O543		2d.50 scarlet	35	10
O544		4d. yellow-brown	1·10	10
O545		5d. deep blue	1·70	10
O546		8d. chocolate	3·25	20
O547		12d. violet	4·00	30
O540/547 *Set of* 8			10·00	1·00

130 Theatre in Sofia

130a Sigismund Monument, Warsaw

(Des S. Dokić and M. Zlamalik. Litho)

1946 (8 Dec). Slav Congress. As T **130a** (various designs). P 11½.

540	½d. brown and buff	3·25	3·00
541	1d. green and pale green	3·25	3·00
542	1½d. rose and pale rose	3·25	3·00
543	2½d. brown-orange and buff	3·25	3·00
544	5d. blue and pale blue	3·25	3·00
540/544 *Set of* 5		14·50	13·50

Designs: Vert—2½d. Victory Monument, Belgrade; 5d. Kremlin Tower, Moscow. Horiz—1d. Charles Bridge and Hradcany, Prague.

131 Roofless Houses

132 Ilyushin Il-4 DB-3 Bomber over Kalimegdan Terrace, Belgrade

(Des Emilija Ognjanova. Litho)

1947 (1 Jan). OBLIGATORY TAX. Red Cross. Cross in red. P 12½.

545	**131**	50p. brown	35	10

1947 (1 Jan). POSTAGE DUE. Red Cross. As No. 545, but inscr "PORTO". Colour changed.

D546	50p. green and red	65	30

PRINTER. From 1947 all stamps of Yugoslavia were printed at the Institute for the Production of Bank Notes, Belgrade, later The Mint, *unless otherwise stated.*

(Des S. Grujić. Typo)

1947 (21 Apr). AIR. T **132** and similar design. Inscr in Cyrillic at top and Roman characters at bottom (A) or vice versa (B). P 11½.

546	50p. yellow-olive and reddish brown (A)	20	20
	a. Horiz pair. Types A and B	45	45
546*b*	50p. yellow-olive and reddish brown (B)	20	20
547	1d. yellow-olive and carmine (A)	30	20
	a. Horiz pair. Types A and B	65	45
547*b*	1d. yellow-olive and carmine (B)	30	20
548	2d. new blue and black (A)	45	20
	a. Horiz pair. Types A and B	95	45
548*b*	2d. new blue and black (B)	45	20
549	5d. drab and green (A)	55	30
	a. Horiz pair. Types A and B	1·20	65
549*b*	5d. drab and green (B)	55	30
550	10d. bistre and sepia (A)	65	40
	a. Horiz pair. Types A and B	1·40	85
550*b*	10d. bistre and sepia (B)	65	40
551	20d. yellow-olive and ultramarine (A)	1·30	1·00
	a. Horiz pair. Types A and B	2·75	2·10
551*b*	20d. yellow-olive and ultramarine (B)	1·30	1·00
546/551*b* *Set of* 12		6·25	4·25

Designs:—50p., 2, 10d. Type **132**; 1, 5, 20d. Ilyushin Il-4 DB-3 over Dubrovnik.

The note below No. 524 also applies here.

133 *Wreath of Mountains*

134 Petar Njegoš (author)

(Des Emil Vicić. Typo)

1947 (8 June). Centenary of Publication of *Wreath of Mountains.* P 12½.

552	**133**	1½d. black and green	75	60
553	**134**	2d.50 carmine and drab	75	60
554	**133**	5d. black and blue	75	60
552/554 *Set of* 3			2·00	1·60

135 Girl Athlete, Star and Flags

136 Parade of Athletes

(Des A. Štukelj. Litho Rožankovsky, Zagreb)

1947 (15 June). Federal Sports Meeting. T **135** (and similar design inscr "DAN FISKULTURNIKA 1947") and T **136**. P 11.

555	1d.50 brown	1·50	70
556	2d.50 scarlet	1·50	70
557	4d. blue	1·60	75
555/557 *Set of* 3		4·25	1·90

Design: Vert—1d.50, Composite portrait of Physical Training Groups.

137 Gymnast

138 Star and Map of Julian Province

(Des J. Trpin. Photo "Ljudska" Ptg Wks, Ljubljana)

1947 (5 Sept). Balkan Games. P 11½.

558	**137**	1d.50 +0.50 green	3·50	3·25
559		2d.50 +0.50 carmine	3·50	3·25
560		4d. +0.50 blue	3·50	3·25
558/560 *Set of* 3			9·50	8·75

(Des E. Vicić. Typo)

1947 (16 Sept). Annexation of Julian Province to Yugoslavia. P 12½.

561	**138**	2d.50 carmine and blue	65	60
562		5d. brown and green	65	60

139 Railway Construction

(Des A. Jovanović. Litho)

1947 (25 Sept). Juvenile Labour Organizations' Relief Fund. P 11½.

563	**139**	1d. +0.50 orange	95	85
564		1d.50 +1d. green	95	85
565		2d.50 +1d.50 carmine	95	85
566		5d. +2d. blue	95	85
563/566 *Set of* 4			3·50	3·00

140 Music Book and Fiddle

141 Vuk Karadžić (poet)

(Des V. Andrejević- Kun. Litho)

1947 (27 Sept). Centenary of Serbian Literature. P 11½ or 12½ (2d.50).

567	**140**	1d.50 green	65	60
568	**141**	2d.50 vermilion	65	60
569	**140**	5d. violet-blue	65	60
567/569 *Set of* 3			1·80	1·60

142 "B.C.G. Vaccine Defeating Tuberculosis"

143 "Illness and Recovery"

144 "Fight against Tuberculosis"

(Des E. Vicić. Litho)

1948 (1 Apr). Anti-Tuberculosis Fund. P 12½.

570	**142**	1d.50 +1d. blue-green and red	75	70
571	**143**	2d.50 +2d. grey-green and red	75	70
572	**144**	5d. +3d. blue and red	75	70
570/572 *Set of* 3			2·00	1·90

145 Map of Yugoslavia and Symbols of Industry and Agriculture

146 Flag-bearers

(Des I. Režek. Litho)

1948 (8 Apr). International Fair, Zagreb. P 12½.

573	**145**	1d.50 green, blue and red	2·00	1·40
574		2d.50 purple, blue and red	2·00	1·40
575		5d. indigo, blue and red	2·00	1·40
573/575 *Set of* 3			5·50	3·75

(Des M. Zlamalik. Litho)

1948 (21 July–3 Aug). Fifth Yugoslav Communist Party Congress, Belgrade. P 12½.

576	**146**	2d. green and deep green (3.8)	65	35
577		3d. claret and lake	25·00	21·00
		a. Perf 11½	1·70	1·60
		b. Perf 12½×11½	1·00	60
578		10d. ultramarine and blue	22·00	21·00
		a. Perf 11½	1·00	60
576/578 *Set of* 3			2·40	1·40

147 Djura Danicic

148 *Krajina* (former royal yacht) passing under Danube Railway Bridge

(Des I. Režek. Photo "Ognjen Prica", Zagreb)

1948 (28 July). 80th Anniv of Yugoslav Academy. As T **147** (portraits). P 11.

579	**147**	1d.50 +0.50 blackish green	75	70
580	–	2d.50 +1d. lake	75	70
581	–	4d. +2d. blue	75	70
579/581 *Set of* 3			2·00	1·90

Portraits:—2d.50, Franjo Racki; 4d. Bishop Josip Strosmajer (inscr "Strossmayer").

(Des S. Grujić. Litho)

1948 (30 July). Danube Conference. P 12½.

582	**148**	2d. yellow-green	3·75	3·50
583		3d. lake	3·75	3·50
584		5d. blue	3·75	3·50
585		10d. brown	3·75	3·50
582/585 *Set of* 4			13·50	12·50

149 Lovrenz Košir

150 Košir and his Birthplace

(Des S. Grujić (15d.), J. Trpin (others))

1948 (21 Aug). 80th Death Anniv of Košir ("ideological creator of first postage stamp").

(a) POSTAGE. Litho. P 12½

586	**149**	3d. reddish purple	65	35
587		5d. blue	65	35
588		10d. orange	65	35
589		12d. grey-green	65	35

(b) AIR. Recess. P 11½

590	**150**	15d. magenta	1·30	1·10
586/590 *Set of* 5			3·50	2·30

No. 590 was issued *se-tenant* with a label bearing an inscription in both Serbo-Croat and French.

151 Putting the Shot

152

153 Arms of Montenegro

(Des S. Grujić. Eng T. Krnjajić. Recess)

1948 (10 Sept). Projected Balkan Games. T **151** and similar vert designs inscr "BALKANSKO SREDNJE EVROPSKE IGRE U ATLETICI, 1948". P 12½.

591		2d. +1d. dull green	75	70
592		3d. +1d. scarlet (Girl hurdler)	75	70
593		5d. +2d. deep blue (Pole vaulting)	1·80	1·20
591/593 *Set of* 3			3·00	2·40

(Des E. Vicić. Litho Govt Ptg Wks, Belgrade)

1948 (1 Oct). OBLIGATORY TAX. Red Cross. Cross in red. P 12½.

594	**152**	50p. rose-red and dark blue	35	20

1948 (1 Oct). POSTAGE DUE. Red Cross. As No. 594, but inscr "PORTO" in red. Colour changed.

D595		50p. rose-red and dark green	55	20

(Des S. Grujić. Eng T. Krnjajić and B. Kocmut. Recess)

1948 (29 Nov). Fifth Anniv of Republic. Various vert designs showing Arms as T **153**. P 12×11½ (10d.), 12½ (others).

595		3d. grey-blue (Serbia)	70	65
596		3d. red (Croatia)	70	65
597		3d. orange (Slovenia)	70	65
598		3d. green (Bosnia and Herzegovina)	70	65
599		3d. magenta (Macedonia)	70	65
600		3d. black (Type **153**)	70	65
601		10d. claret (Yugoslavia) (24½×34½ mm.)	1·70	1·60
595/601 *Set of* 7			5·25	5·00

154 Prešeren

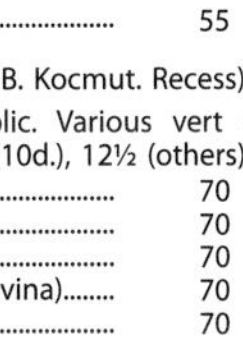

155 Ski Jump, Planica

(Des B. Jakac. Photo "Ljudska" Ptg Wks, Ljubljana)

1949 (8 Feb). Death Centenary of France Prešeren (author). P 12×11½.

602	**154**	3d. dark blue	55	20
603		5d. brown-orange	55	30
604		10d. sepia	2·75	1·00
602/604 *Set of* 3			3·50	1·40

(Des O. Antonini (10d.), J. Trpin (12d.). Eng S. Grujić. Recess)

1949 (20 Mar). Ski Jumping Competition, Planica. T **155** and similar vert design. P 12½×11½.

605		10d. bright crimson	1·10	85
606		12d. indigo (Ski jumper)	2·20	95

156 Soldiers

AVIONSKA POŠTA

(157)

(Des S. Grujić. Recess)

1949 (2–25 Aug). Fifth Anniv of Liberation of Macedonia. T **156** and similar vert types inscr "1944–1949 H.P.", etc. P 12½.

(a) POSTAGE (2 Aug)

607	**156**	3d. carmine	90	85
608	–	5d. grey-blue	1·10	1·00
608*a*	–	12d. red-brown	3·50	3·25

(b) AIR. Optd with T **157** (25 Aug)

609	**156**	3d. carmine (B.)	10·00	9·25
610	–	5d. grey-blue (R.)	10·00	9·25
610*a*	–	12d. red-brown (B.)	10·00	9·25
607/610*a* *Set of* 6			32·00	30·00

Designs:—5d. Industrial and agricultural workers; 12d. Arms and flags of Yugoslavia and Macedonia.

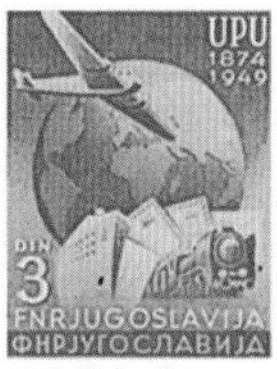

158 Globe, Letters and Forms of Transport

3
=

(159)

3
=

160 Nurse and Child

(Des A. Jovanović (5d.), S. Grujić (others). Recess)

1949 (8 Sept). 75th Anniv of Universal Postal Union. T **158** and similar design. P 12½.

611	**158**	3d. scarlet	4·00	3·75
612	–	5d. blue	80	75
613	**158**	12d. brown	80	75
611/613 *Set of* 3			5·00	4·75

Design: Horiz—5d. Airplane, train and mail coach.

1949 (4–12 Oct). Nos. O546/7 surch with T **159** for postal use.

614	O **130**	3d. on 8d. chocolate (12.10)	1·30	50
		a. Surch inverted	45·00	45·00
615		3d. on 12d. violet	1·30	50
		a. Surch inverted	45·00	45·00

(Des A. Jovanović. Litho)

1949 (5 Nov). OBLIGATORY TAX. Red Cross. P 12½.

616	**160**	50p. brown and red	35	20

1949 (5 Nov). POSTAGE DUE. Red Cross. As No. 616, but inscr "PORTO".

D617		50p. bright purple and red	80	30

ФНР ЈУГОСЛАВИЈА
≡ д3
FNR JUGOSLAVIJA

(161)

F
N d10
R ═
JUGOSLAVIJA

(162)

1949–50. Nos. 513 and 517 surch with T **161/2**.

617		3d. on 8d. orange (2.1.50)	1·10	20
		a. Surch inverted	40·00	40·00
618		10d. on 20d. vermilion (19.12.49)	1·20	20
		a. Surch inverted	40·00	40·00

Ф Н Р

FNR JUGOSLAVIJA

(163)

F N R

(164)

F
N
R
JUGOSLAVIJA

(165)

1949 (8 Dec)–**50**. Various designs, as T **119/121** optd with T **163/5**. Nos. 621, 623, 625 and 627 as 1945–47 issue, but colours changed. P 12½.

619	**165**	0d.50 olive-grey (502)	55	10
620		1d. blue-green (503)	55	10
621		1d. yellow-orange (as 503) (1.50)	1·10	20
622	**163**	2d. scarlet (505)	55	10
623		2d. blue-green (as 505) (1.50)	1·10	20
624	**164**	3d. vermilion (508)	55	10
625		3d. magenta (as 508) (1.50)	1·70	30
		a. Perf 12½×11½	1·10	20
626		5d. blue (511)	55	20
627		5d. light blue (as 511) (1.50)	1·70	30
		a. Perf 12½×11½	1·10	20
628	**165**	12d. ultramarine (515)	55	10
629		16d. light blue (516)	1·50	75
630		20d. vermilion (517)	1·10	30
619/630 *Set of* 12			10·50	2·50

166 Steam Locomotive of 1849

167 Surveying

(Des S. Grujić. Photo)

1949 (15 Dec). Railway Centenary. T **166** and similar horiz designs inscr "1849–1949" showing 1949 locomotives. P 12½.

631		2d. green	2·75	2·50
632		3d. carmine (Steam)	2·75	2·50
633		5d. blue (Diesel)	2·75	2·50
633*a*		10d. orange (Electric)	50·00	31·00
631/633*a* *Set of* 4			50·00	35·00

Miniature sheet (49×70 mm.). As No. 633*a* but colour changed.

A. P 11½×12½

MS633A*b* 10d. bright purple ... £225 £140

B. Imperf

MS633B*b* 10d. bright purple ... £225 £140

(Des P. Gavranić (2d.), S. Grujić (3d.), A. Jovanović (5d.). Photo)

1950 (16 Jan). Completion of Belgrade–Zagreb Road. T **167** and similar horiz designs. P 12½.

634		2d. blue-green	95	70
635		3d. claret	95	70
636		5d. blue	1·50	1·20
634/636 *Set of* 3			3·00	2·30

Designs:—3d. Map, road and car; 5d. Youth, road and flag.

ФНР ЈУГОСЛАВИЈА

FNR JUGOSLAVIJA

(D **168**)

168 Marshal Tito

169 A Child Eating

1950 (26 Jan). POSTAGE DUE. Nos. D498 and D500/1 optd with Type D **168**.

D637	D **115**	1d.50 blue	55	10
		a. Opt inverted	35·00	35·00
D638		3d. lilac-brown	55	10
		a. Opt inverted	35·00	35·00
D639		4d. violet	55	20
D637/639 *Set of* 3			1·50	35

(Des and eng T. Krnjajić. Recess)

1950 (30 Apr). May Day. P 12½.

637	**168**	3d. scarlet	2·75	1·00
638		5d. blue	2·75	1·00
639		10d. brown	36·00	26·00
640		12d. black	2·75	2·75
637/640 *Set of* 4			40·00	28·00

(Des S. Grujić. Litho)

1950 (1 June). Child Welfare. P 12½.

641	**169**	3d. vermilion	2·20	65

170 Launching Model Glider

171 Chessboard and Bishop

172 Girl Harvester

(Des P. Gavranić, J. Trpin and S. Grujić. Recess)

1950 (2 July). Third Aeronautical Meeting. T **170** and similar vert types inscr "VAZDUHOPLOVNI SLET 1950". P 12½.

642		2d. green	4·50	4·25
643		3d. brown-red (Glider in flight)	4·50	4·25
644		5d. violet (Parachutists landing)	4·50	4·25
645		10d. purple-brown (Woman pilot)	4·50	4·25
646		20d. ultramarine (Glider on water)	35·00	35·00
642/646 *Set of* 5			48·00	47·00

(Des J. Trpin (5, 10d.). O. Antonini (others). Photo Courvoisier)

1950 (20 Aug). Ninth Chess Olympiad, Dubrovnik. T **171** and similar vert designs. P 11½.

647		2d. purple-brown	1·30	1·00
648		3d. bistre, blackish brown and drab	1·30	1·00
649		5d. new blue, lemon and myrtle green	2·75	1·00
650		10d. yellow, deep reddish purple and new blue	2·75	2·50
651		20d. yellow and blue	60·00	29·00
647/651 *Set of* 5			60·00	31·00

Designs:—3d. Rook and flags; 5d. Globe and chessboard showing 1924 Capablanca v Lasker game; 10d. Chequered globe, map and players; 20d. Knight and flags.

(Des P. Gravanic. Eng T. Krnjajić. Recess)

1950 (1 Sept)–**51**. T **172** and similar vert designs. P 12½.

652		50p. sepia (26.1.51)	20	10
653		1d. blue-green (9.50)	20	10
654		2d. orange	20	10
655		3d. carmine	20	10
656		5d. ultramarine (9.50)	1·70	10
657		7d. grey	1·70	10
658		10d. chocolate	1·70	10
659		12d. purple-brown (26.1.51)	5·50	10
660		16d. blue (6.2.51)	4·50	30
661		20d. olive-green (16.2.51)	4·50	40
662		30d. brown-lake (1951)	11·00	75
662*a*		50d. violet (10.51)	50·00	31·00
652/662*a* *Set of* 12			75·00	30·00

Designs:—50p. Metallurgy; 1d. Electrical supply engineer; 3d. Man and woman with wheelbarrow; 5d. Fishing; 7d. Miners; 10d. Picking Apples; 12d. Lumbering; 16d. Picking sunflowers; 20d. Woman and farm animals; 30d. Girl printer; 50d. Dockers unloading cargo.

See also Nos. 705/23*a*.

173 Steam Locomotive and Map

174 Girl in National Costume

D **175** Map

(Des J. Trpin. Photo)

1950 (23 Sept). Zagreb Exhibition. P 12½.

663	**173**	3d. lake	2·20	50

(Des O. Antonini. Litho)

1950 (1 Oct). OBLIGATORY TAX. Red Cross. P 12½.

664	**174**	50p. blackish green and red	35	20

(Des F. Bis. Litho)

1950 (1 Oct). POSTAGE DUE. Red Cross. P 12½.

D665	D **175**	50p. brown and red	55	30

175 Galleon

176 Patriots of 1941

(Des O. Antonini, P. Gavranić and J. Trpin. Recess)

1950 (29 Nov). Navy Day. T **175** and similar horiz designs inscr "DAN MORNARICE 1950" in Roman (2, 5, 12d.) or Cyrillic (3, 10, 20d.). P 12½.

665		2d. reddish purple	55	20
666		3d. chestnut	55	20
667		5d. blue-green	55	20
668		10d. light blue	55	20
669		12d. deep blue	2·20	65
670		20d. maroon	25·00	3·75
665/670 *Set of* 6			26·00	4·75

Designs:—3d. Partisan patrol boat; 5d. Freighter discharging cargo; 10d. *Zagreb* (freighter) and globe; 12d. Yachts; 20d. Sailor, gun and *Golesnica* (torpedo boat).

(Des B. Kocmut. Recess)

1951 (27 Mar). Tenth Anniv of Revolt against Pact with Axis. P 12½.

671	**176**	3d. brown-red and scarlet	10·00	4·75

177 Franc Stane-Rozman

178 Children Painting

(Des B. Jakac. Photo "Ljudska" Ptg Wks, Ljubljana)

1951 (27 Apr). Tenth Anniv of Partisan Rising in Slovenia. T **177** and similar horiz design inscr "SLOVENIJE 1941–1951". P 12½.

672		3d. red-brown	65	50
673		5d. deep blue (Boy courier)	1·30	85

(Des S. Grujić. Photo)

1951 (3 June). International Children's Day. P 12½.

674	**178**	3d. scarlet	2·20	30

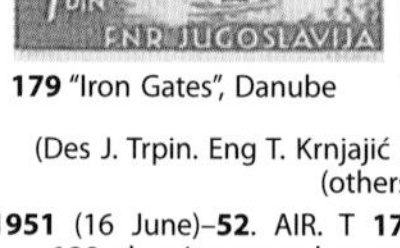

179 "Iron Gates", Danube

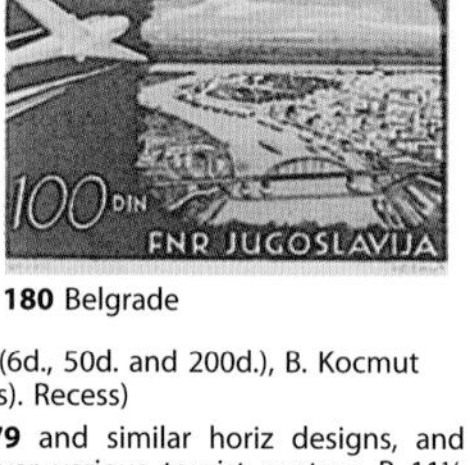

180 Belgrade

(Des J. Trpin. Eng T. Krnjajić (6d., 50d. and 200d.), B. Kocmut (others). Recess)

1951 (16 June)–**52**. AIR. T **179** and similar horiz designs, and **180** showing aeroplane over various tourist centres. P 11½ (T **180**), 12½ (others).

675	**179**	1d. brown-orange	20	10
676	–	2d. blue-green	20	10
677	–	3d. scarlet	55	10
677*a*	–	5d. yellow-brown (21.2.52)	55	10
678	–	6d. ultramarine	5·50	5·25
679	–	10d. brown	55	10
680	–	20d. grey-green	1·10	10
681	–	30d. claret	2·75	10
682	–	50d. violet	4·00	10
683	**180**	100d. grey-blue	80·00	11·50
683*a*	–	100d. green (7.12.51)	2·20	20
683*b*	–	200d. carmine (20.3.52)	3·25	30
683*c*	**180**	500d. violet-blue (21.2.52)	11·00	50
675/683*c* *Set of* 13			£100	17·00

Designs: Horiz—2d., 5d. Plitvice Cascades; 3d., 100d. (No. 683*a*), Mountain Village, Gozd Martuljak; 6d., 200d. Old Bridge, Mostar; 10d. Ohrid, 20d. Kotor Bay; 30d. Dubrovnik; 50d. Bled.

ZEFIZ
1951

(**180a**)

181 Živorad Jovanović

182 Armed Insurgents

1951 (16 June). AIR. Zagreb Philatelic Exhibition. As No. 678, but colour changed. Optd with T **180a**, in red.

684		6d. (+10d.) green	11·00	4·75

Miniature sheet (70×70 mm.). As No. 683 but colour changed. Imperf.

MS633A*b* 10d. bright purple ... £225 £140

(Des M. Zlamalik (3d.), F. Bis (5d.). Photo)

1951 (7 July). Tenth Anniv of Serbian Insurrection. P 12½.

685	**181**	3d. red-brown	80	65
686	**182**	5d. blue	1·50	1·20

183 Mt. Kopaonik, Serbia

184 Sava Kovacevic

(Des S. Grujić. Photo)

1951 (7–13 July). AIR. International Mountaineering Association Meeting, Bled. T **183** and similar vert designs inscr "UIAA-1951". P 12½.

687		3d. magenta (7 July)	3·25	3·00
688		5d. blue (13 July)	3·25	3·00
689		20d. blue-green (13 July)	95·00	65·00
687/689 *Set of* 3			90·00	65·00

Designs: Vert—5d. Mt. Triglav, Slovenia; 20d.—Mt. Kalnik, Croatia.

(Des S. Garić (3d.), M. Lehner (5d.). Photo)

1951 (13 July). Tenth Anniv of Montenegrin Insurrection. T **184** and horiz design as T **182**, but inscr "1941/13 VII/1951". P 12½.

690		3d. carmine	1·10	65
691		5d. light blue (Partisan and Mountains)	2·50	1·50

185 Marko Orešković (statue)

186 Simo Solaja

(Des F. Bis. Photo)

1951 (27 July). Tenth Anniv of Croatian Insurrection. T **185** and similar vert type inscr "USTANAK U HRVATSKOJ". P 12½.

692		3d. claret	1·10	65
693		5d. deep blue-green	1·70	1·20

Design:—5d. "Transport of a Wounded Man" (sculpture, A. Augustinčić).

(Des M. Lechner (3d.), O. Antonini (5d.). Photo)

1951 (27 July). Tenth Anniv of Insurrection in Bosnia and Herzegovina. T **186** and vert type inscr "USTANAK U BOSNI I HERCEGOVINI". P 12½.

694		3d. brown-red	1·10	65
695		5d. blue (Group of Insurgents)	1·70	1·20

187 Parachutists Landing

I SVETSKO TAKMIČENJE
PADOBRANACA 1951

(**188**)

189 Primož Trubar (writer)

(Des S. Grujić. Recess)

1951 (16 Aug). AIR. First World Parachute Jumping Championships, Bled. P 12½.

(a) T **187**

696	**187**	6d. lake	5·50	2·50

(b) As No. 682, but colour changed. Optd with T **188** in red

697	–	50d. light blue	90·00	50·00

(Des P. Gavranić. Eng T. Krnjajić. Recess)

1951 (9 Sept). Cultural Anniversaries. T **189** and similar vert designs. P 12½.

698		10d. blue-black	5·75	5·25
699		12d. Indian red	5·75	5·25
700		20d. deep lilac	18·00	17·00
698/700 *Set of* 3			27·00	25·00

Designs:—10d. Type **189** (400th anniv of first book in Slovenian language); 12d. Marko Marulić (Croatian writer, 500th birth anniv (1950)); 20d. Tsar Stepan Dušan (600th anniv (1949) of *Tsar Dušan's Book of Laws*).

190 National Products

191 Hoisting the Flag

(Des S. Grujić. Typo)

1951 (15 Sept). Zagreb International Fair. P 12×11½.
701 **190** 3d. yellow, red and blue .... 3·25 1·60

(Des Z. Prica. Litho)

1951 (7 Oct). OBLIGATORY TAX. Red Cross. P 12½.
702 **191** 0d.50 ultramarine and red 35 20

1951 (7 Oct). POSTAGE DUE. Red Cross. As T **191**, but inscr "PORTO".
D703 0d.50 emerald and red 55 30

192 Mirce Acev

193 P. P. Njegoš

(Des M. Lechner. Photo)

1951 (11 Oct). Tenth Anniv of Macedonian Insurrection. T **192** and horiz design as T **182** but inscr "1941/11. X/1951". P 12½.
703 **192** 3d. magenta .... 1·10 85
704 – 5d. violet-blue .... 2·20 1·60
Design:—5d. War Victims' Monument, Skopje.

1951 (12 Nov)–**55**. As No. 652/62*a* but colours changed and new values. P 12½.

(a) Recess
705 1d. grey (29.1.52) 20 10
706 2d. carmine (25.4.52) 55 10
707 5d. orange (1.4.52) .... 2·20 10
708 10d. green (25.4.52) .... 11·00 20
709 15d. scarlet (3.3.52) .... 55·00 30
710 20d. dull purple (26.12.51) .... 5·50 10
711 25d. bistre-brown (21.6.52) .... 34·00 1·80
a. Redrawn. Imprint below design (1955?) .... 22·00 10
712 30d. blue (20.12.51) .... 2·75 10
a. Perf 12½×11½ .... 45·00 1·60
713 35d. red-brown (3.52) .... 4·00 20
714 50d. turquoise (shades) (12.11.51) .... 2·75 10
715 75d. violet (12.12.52) .... 5·50 20
a. Perf 11½ .... 34·00 2·50
716 100d. sepia (8.52) .... 11·00 20
705/716 *Set of* 12 (*cheapest*) .... £110 1·60

(b) Litho
717 1d. grey (10.2.53) .... 1·10 10
718 2d. carmine-red (10.2.53) .... 2·75 10
719 5d. orange (10.2.53) .... 8·50 10
720 8d. grey-blue (5.6.52) .... 5·50 20
721 10d. green (10.2.53) .... 11·00 10
722 12d. purple-brown (10.2.53) .... 50·00 30
723 15d. scarlet (10.2.53) .... 22·00 10
723*a* 17d. maroon (28.2.55) .... 5·50 20
717/723*a Set of* 8 .... 95·00 1·10
Designs:—8d. Miners; 15d. Picking sunflowers; 17d. Woman and farm animals; 25d. T **172**; 35d. Man and woman with wheel-barrow; 75d. Lumbering; 100d. Metallurgy.
Other values as before.

1951 (15 Nov)–**52**. POSTAGE DUE. As Nos. D528 etc., but colours changed.
D724 D **126** 1d. chocolate (6.52) 55 10
D725 2d. emerald-green 55 10
D726 5d. blue 80 10
D727 10d. scarlet .... 2·75 10
D728 20d. reddish violet .... 2·75 10
D729 30d. orange (4.52) .... 5·50 10
D730 50d. ultramarine .... 22·00 50
D731 100d. reddish purple (4.52) .... 80·00 2·50
D724/731 *Set of* 8 .... £100 3·25
See also Nos. D1029/33.

(Des P. Gavranić. Eng T. Krnjajić. Recess)

1951 (29 Nov). Death Centenary of Petar Njegoš (poet). P 12½.
724 **193** 15d. deep claret .... 4·50 1·00

194 Soldier and Badge

195 Marshal Tito

(Des M. Zlamalik (15d.), photo. Des S. Grujić (150d.), recess)

1951 (29 Nov–Dec). Army Day. P 12½.

(a) POSTAGE
725 **194** 15d. carmine-red (29. Nov) 65 10

(b) AIR. Inscr "AVIONSKA POSTA"
726 **195** 150d. blue (22 Dec) .... 13·50 10·50

196 Marshal Tito

197 Marshal Tito

(Des B. Jakac. Photo Courvoisier)

1952 (25 May). 60th Birthday of Marshal Tito. T **196** and similar vert design and **197**. P 11½.
727 **196** 15d. deep brown .... 1·10 1·00
728 **197** 28d. brown-lake .... 2·00 1·80
729 – 50d. deep green .... 55·00 40·00
727/729 *Set of* 3 .... 50·00 39·00

198

199 Gymnastics

(Des S. Nikolić. Litho)

1952 (1 June). Children's Week. P 12½.
730 **198** 15d. carmine-red .... 8·50 3·75

(Des P. Gavranić. Recess)

1952 (10 July). 15th Olympic Games, Helsinki. T **199** and similar vert designs. On paper with vert burelage in colours shown in brackets. P 12½.
731 5d. chocolate/*buff* (Br.) .... 1·10 25
732 10d. brown/*yellow* (O.) .... 1·70 25
733 15d. ultramarine/*pink* (V.) .... 1·70 50
734 28d. chocolate/*flesh* (Salmon) .... 4·00 1·00
735 50d. deep green/*cream* (G.) .... 6·75 5·75
736 100d. brown/*mauve* (B.) .... 65·00 36·00
731/736 *Set of* 6 .... 70·00 39·00
Designs:—10d. Running; 15d. Swimming;, 28d. Boxing; 50d. Basketball; 100d. Football.

200 "Fishing-boat" (from relief by Kršinić)

200a Belgrade (XVI Cent)

(Des O. Antonini. Recess)

1952 (10 Sept). Navy Day. T **200** and vert views inscr "1952". P 12½.
737 15d. brown-purple .... 1·10 1·00
738 28d. deep brown .... 2·20 2·10
739 50d. greenish black .... 25·00 19·00
737/739 *Set of* 3 .... 25·00 20·00
Designs:—15d. Split, Dalmatia; 50d. Sveti Stefan, Montenegro.

(Eng T. Krnjajić. Recess)

1952 (14 Sept). Philatelic Exhibition, Belgrade. P 11½×12.
739*a* **200a** 15d. purple .... 13·50 13·50
No. 739*a* was only sold at the Exhibition, at 35d. (face value+20d. entrance fee).

201

D **202**

202 Workers in Procession (from fresco by Slavko Pengov)

(Des P. Dabović. Litho)

1952 (5 Oct). OBLIGATORY TAX. Red Cross. P 12½.
740 **201** 50p. red, grey and black 35 20

(Des P. Dabović. Litho)

1952 (5 Oct). POSTAGE DUE. Red Cross. P 12½.
D741 D **202** 50p. red and olive-grey 65 30

(Des S. Grujić. Recess)

1952 (2 Nov). Sixth Yugoslav Communist Party Congress. P 12½.
741 **202** 15d. lake-brown .... 1·70 1·60
742 15d. turquoise .... 1·70 1·60
743 15d. chocolate .... 1·70 1·60
744 15d. deep violet-blue .... 1·70 1·60
741/744 *Set of* 4 .... 6·00 5·75

203 Nikola Tesla

204 Fresco, Sopocani Monastery

205

(Des P. Dabović. Eng T. Krnjajić (15d.), R. Stojanović (30d.). Recess)

1953 (7 Jan). Tenth Death Anniv of Tesla (inventor). P 12½.
745 **203** 15d. lake .... 1·10 20
746 30d. deep violet-blue .... 4·50 85

(Des R. Debenjak and M. Sedej. Photo "Ljudska" Ptg Wks, Ljubljana)

1953 (24 Mar). United Nations Commemoration. T **204** and similar vert designs. P 11½.
747 15d. bronze-green .... 1·10 85
748 30d. deep blue .... 2·20 85
749 50d. brown-lake .... 25·00 5·75
747/749 *Set of* 3 .... 25·00 6·75
Designs:—30d. Fresco, Church of St. Panteleimon, Nerezim, Skopje; 50d. Fresco, St. Dimitri Church, Pec.

(Des J. Trpin. Photo "Ljudska" Ptg Wks, Ljubljana)

1953 (10 May). Adriatic Car and Motor Cycle Rally. T **205** and similar horiz designs. P 12½.
750 15d. deep magenta and salmon 55 30
751 30d. deep blue and light blue 90 30
752 50d. brown and yellow .... 1·70 50
753 70d. bronze-green and pale emerald .... 43·00 6·25
750/753 *Set of* 4 .... 42·00 6·50
Designs:—30d. Motor cyclist and coastline; 50d. Racing car and flags; 70d. Saloon car descending mountain roadway.

206 Marshal Tito

207

208 "Insurrection" (Borko Lazevski)

(Des T. Krnjajić and P. Mladenović (after sculpture by A. Augustinčić); eng T. Krnjajić. Recess)

1953 (28 June). Marshal Tito Commemoration. P 12½.
754 **206** 50d. deep reddish violet .... 17·00 10·50

(Des P. Matković, eng S. Babić)

1953 (July). 38th Esperanto Congress, Zagreb. Design recess, star typo (15d.); recess (300d.). P 12½.

(a) POSTAGE (25 July)
755 **207** 15d. dull green and black .... 4·00 3·25

(b) AIR Inscr "AVIONSKA POSTA" (31 July)
756 **207** 300d. green and blue £250 £225

(Des P. Mladenović. Recess and photo)

1953 (2 Aug). 50th Anniv of Macedonian Insurrection. T **208** and vert portrait inscr "1903 1953". P 12½.
757 15d. brown-purple 90 85
758 30d. deep grey-green .... 4·75 4·25
Portrait:—30d. Nikola Karev (revolutionary).

209

210 B. Radicevic

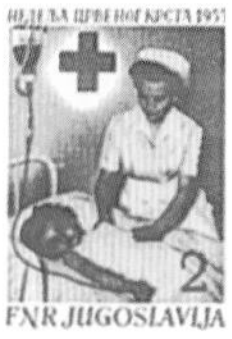
211 Blood-transfusion

(Des J. Trpin. Litho)

1953 (6 Sept). Tenth Anniv of Liberation of Istria and Slovene Coast. P 12½.
759 **209** 15d. blue-green .... £225 75·00

(Des P. Gavranić. Eng B. Kocmut. Recess)

1953 (1 Oct). Death Centenary of Branko Radicevic (poet). P 12½.
760 **210** 15d. slate-purple .... 6·75 2·50

(Des T. Krnjajić. Litho)

1953 (25 Oct). OBLIGATORY TAX. Red Cross. P 12½.
761 **211** 2d. scarlet and bright purple 55 20

1953 (25 Oct). POSTAGE DUE. Red Cross. As No. 761 but colour changed and inscr "PORTO".
D762 2d. scarlet and bistre .... 1·10 50

212 Jajce

213 European Souslik (*Citellus citellus*)

(Des M. Zlamalik. Eng B. Kocmut (30d.), T. Krnjajić (others). Recess)

1953 (29 Nov). 10th Anniv of First Republican Legislative Assembly. T **212** and similar vert designs inscr "1943–1953". P 12½.

762	15d. deep bluish green	1·20	1·00
763	30d. carmine	1·70	1·60
764	50d. sepia	11·50	10·50
762/764 *Set of 3*		13·00	12·00

Designs:—30d. Assembly building; 50d. Marshal Tito addressing assembly.

(Des M. Zlamalik. Photo Courvoisier)

1954 (30 June). Animal designs as T **213**. P 11½.

765	2d. slate, buff and bluish green	35	20
766	5d. brown, buff and slate-green	60	20
767	10d. brown and grey-black	1·20	20
768	15d. brown and deep grey-blue	1·40	20
769	17d. sepia and deep dull purple	2·30	20
770	25d. yellow, grey-blue and violet	3·50	50
771	30d. sepia and chalky blue	4·00	50
772	35d. slate-black and brown	4·75	75
773	50d. chocolate and bronze-green	15·00	2·50
774	65d. state-black and brownish lake	26·00	13·50
775	70d. orange-brown and turquoise-green	23·00	13·50
776	100d. black and bright blue	95·00	42·00
765/776 *Set of 12*		£160	65·00

Designs: Horiz—5d. Lynx (*Lynx lynx*); 10d. Red deer (*Cervus elaphus montanus*); 15d. Brown bear (*Ursus arctos bosniensis*); 17d. Chamois (*Rupicapra rupicapra*); 25d. Eastern white pelican (*Pelecanus onocrotalus*). Vert—30d. Lammergeier (*Gypaëtus barbatus aureus*); 35d. *Procerus gigas* (ground beetle); 50d. *Callimenus pancici* (cricket); 65d. Black Dalmatian lizard (*Lacerta melisellensis*); 70d. Blind cave-dwelling salamander (*Proteus anguineus*); 100d. Brown trout (*Salmo trutta*).

See also Nos. 956/64 and 1047/55.

214 Ljubljana (XVII Cent)

215 Cannon, 1804

(Des T. Krnjajić after engr by I. Valvazor. Recess)

1954 (29 July). Philatelic Exhibition, Ljubljana ("JUFIZ II"). P 11½×12.

777	**214**	15d. indigo, brown and green	14·00	12·50

No. 777 was only sold at the Exhibition, at 35d., (face value+20d. entrance fee).

(Des M. Milunović (15d.), D. Andrejević-Kun (others). Eng T. Krnjajić (15d., 50d.), B. Kocmut (30d., 70d.). Design recess, background litho)

1954 (3 Oct). 150th Anniv of Serbian Insurrection. T **215** and similar horiz designs inscr "1804 1954". Multicoloured. P 12½.

778	15d. Serbian flag, 1804	1·20	30
779	30d. Type **215**	1·70	75
780	50d. Seal of insurgents' council	5·75	3·25
781	70d. Karageorge	44·00	27·00
778/781 *Set of 4*		47·00	28·00

215a

216

1954 (4 Oct). Children's Week. Litho. P 12½.

781*a*	**215a**	2d. brown-red	1·70	85

This was not officially issued as an obligatory tax stamp but it was on sale at post offices.

(Des M. Josić. Litho)

1954 (1 Nov). OBLIGATORY TAX. Red Cross. P 12½.

782	**216**	2d. scarlet and grey-green	60	40

1954 (1 Nov). POSTAGE DUE. Red Cross. As No. 782 but colour changed and inscr "PORTO".

D783	2d. scarlet and lilac	1·00	40

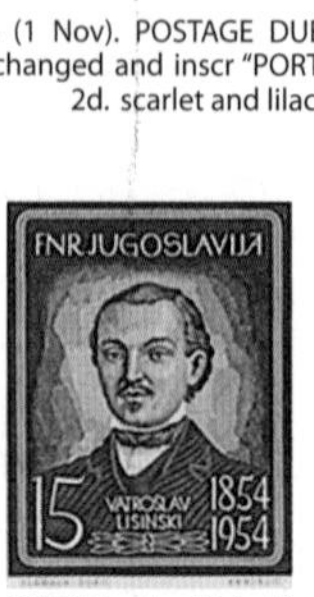

217 Vatroslav Lisinski (composer)

218 *A Midsummer Night's Dream* (Shakespeare)

(Des M. Zlamalik and S. Grujić. Eng T. Krnjajić (15d.), B. Kocmut (30d., 50d.), S. Babić (70d., 100d.). Recess)

1954 (25 Dec). Cultural Anniversaries. T **217** and similar vert portraits. P 12½.

783	15d. slate-green	3·00	2·50
784	30d. chocolate	3·00	2·50
785	50d. deep claret	3·00	2·50
786	70d. deep blue	8·75	7·75
787	100d. deep violet	29·00	21·00
783/787 *Set of 5*		42·00	33·00

Portraits:—15d. Type **217** (death centenary); 30d. Andrija Kačić-Miošić (writer, 250th birth anniv); 50d. Jurij Vega (mathematician, birth bicentenary); 70d. Jovan Jovanović- Zmaj (poet, 50th death anniv); 100d. Filip Višnjic (poet and musician, 120th death anniv).

See also Nos. 975/80.

(Des B. Lazarević. Litho)

1955 (6 June). Dubrovnik Festival. T **218** and similar design inscr "DUBROVACKI FESTIVAL 1955". P 12½.

788	15d. brownish lake and pink	1·20	50
789	30d. blue and pale blue	4·75	2·50

Design: Vert—15d. *Robinja* (Hanibal Lučić).

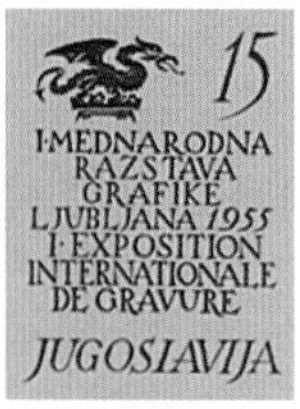

219

220

(Des B. Jakac. Eng T. Krnjajić. Recess)

1955 (3 July). First International Exhibition of Engraving, Ljubljana. P 12½.

790	**219**	15d. brown and deep bluish green/*stone*	8·75	5·25

(Des B. Kršić. Eng B. Kocmut. Recess)

1955 (23 Aug). Second World Congress of the Deaf and Dumb. P 12½.

791	**220**	15d. brown-carmine	3·00	65

221 Hop (*Humulus lupulus*)

222 Laughing Girl

223 Peace Monument, U.N. Building, New York (A. Augustinčić).

(Des M. Zlamalik. Photo Courvoisier)

1955 (24 Sept). Various vert floral designs as T **221**. P 11½.

792	5d. green, brown & dp turquoise-grn	25	10
793	10d. maroon, green and brown-orange	25	10
794	15d. blue, green, maroon & bistre-brn	25	10
795	17d. yellow-green, green & red-brown	25	10
796	25d. yellow, grey, green and ultramarine	35	15
797	30d. purple, green, blackish violet and grey-black	70	30
798	50d. scarlet, green, slate-grn and dp brn	3·50	2·10
799	70d. yellow, green and chocolate	5·75	3·75
800	100d. orange, yellow, blue-green and grey	30·00	19·00
792/800 *Set of 9*		37·00	23·00

Flowers:—10d. Tobacco (*Nicotiana tabacum*); 15d. Opium poppy (*Papaver somniferum*); 17d. Small-leaved lime (*Tilla cordata*); 25d. False chamomile (*Matricaria chamomilla*); 30d. Sage (*Salvia officinalis*); 50d. Dog rose (*Rosa canina*); 70d. Great yellow gentian (*Gentiana lutea*); 100d. Yellow pheasant's-eye (*Adonis vernalis*).

(Des B. Lazarević. Litho)

1955 (2 Oct). OBLIGATORY TAX. Children's Week. P 12½.

801	**222**	2d. brown-red and cream	60	30

1955 (2 Oct). POSTAGE DUE. Children's Week. As No. 801 but colours changed and inscr "PORTO".

D802	2d. deep yellow-green and pale green	80	30

(Des S. Nikolić. Litho)

1955 (24 Oct). Tenth Anniv of United Nations. P 12½.

802	**223**	30d. blue-black and pale blue	1·20	1·00

224 Red Cross Nurse

225 Woman and Dove

226 St. Donat's Church, Zadar

(Des S. Nikolić. Litho)

1955 (31 Oct). OBLIGATORY TAX. Red Cross. P 12½.

803	**224**	2d. blue-black, grey and red	35	20

1955 (31 Oct). POSTAGE DUE. Red Cross. As No. 803 but colours changed and inscr "PORTO".

D804	2d. deep brown, pale chocolate and red	1·20	30

(Des B. Lazarević. Eng S. Babić. Recess)

1955 (29 Nov). Tenth Anniv of Republic. P 12½.

804	**225**	15d. deep violet	1·20	75

(Des R. Debenjak. Photo "Ljudska" Ptg Wks, Ljubljana)

1956 (24 Mar). Yugoslav Art. T **226** and similar designs. P 11½.

805	5d. indigo	60	20
806	10d. blackish green	60	20
807	15d. deep bistre-brown	60	20
808	20d. lake-brown	60	20
809	25d. blackish sepia	60	20
810	30d. deep claret	60	20
811	35d. olive-green	1·70	50
812	40d. lake-brown	3·00	75
813	50d. deep bistre-brown	3·50	1·00
814	70d. deep green	11·50	10·50
815	100d. deep brown-purple	41·00	26·00
816	200d. blue	£100	42·00
805/816 *Set of 12*		£150	75·00

Designs: Vert—10d. Bas-relief of Croat King, Diocletian Palace, Split; 15d. Church portal, Studenic, Serbia; 20d. Master Radovan's portal, Trogir Cathedral; 25d. Fresco, Sopocani, Serbia; 30d. Monument, Radimlje, Herzegovina; 50d. Detail from Božidarevic Triptych, Dubrovnik; 70d. Carved figure, Belec Church, Croatia; 100d. Self-portrait of Rikard Jakopic; 200d. Peace Monument by A. Augustinčić, New York. Horiz—35d. Heads from Cathedral cornice, Šibenik, Dalmatia; 40d. Frieze; Kotor Cathedral, Montenegro.

227 Zagreb through the Centuries

228 Houses ruined by Avalanche

(Des P. Gavranić. Eng S. Babić. Recess)

1956 (20 Apr–20 May). Yugoslav International Philatelic Exhibition, Zagreb ("JUFIZ III"). P 11½.

(a) POSTAGE (20 Apr)

817	**227**	15d. deep brown, yellow-brown and black	1·20	20
		a. Booklet pane. No. 817×4	13·00	

(b) AIR. Inscr "AVIONSKA POŠTA" (20 May)

818	**227**	30d. deep violet-blue, orange-red and black	4·75	1·80

The booklet pane has an imperforate margin around the block.

(Des B. Lazarević. Litho)

1956 (6 May). OBLIGATORY TAX. Red Cross. P 12½.

819	**228**	2d. sepia, grey-brown and red	45	30

1956 (6 May). POSTAGE DUE. Red Cross. As No. 819 but colours changed and inscr "PORTO".

D820	2d. deep bluish green, turq-grn & red	80	30

229 "Technical Education"

230 Induction Motor

(Des Ide and M. Ćirić. Litho)

1956 (15 June). AIR. Tenth Anniv of Technical Education. P 12×11½.

820	**229**	30d. black and carmine	2·00	1·80

(Des B. Lazarević and B. Stanojčić. Photo "Ljudska" Ptg Wks, Ljubljana)

1956 (10 July). Birth Centenary of Nikola Tesla (inventor). T **230** and similar vert designs. P 11½×12½.

821	10d. deep olive	60	30
822	15d. lake-brown	60	30
	a. Perf 12½	17·00	13·50
823	30d. blue	3·00	1·60
	a. Perf 12½	17·00	13·50
824	50d. deep dull purple	7·50	3·75
821/824 *Set of 4*		10·50	5·25

Designs:—15d. Transformer; 30d. "Telekomanda" (invented by Tesla); 50d. Portrait of Tesla.

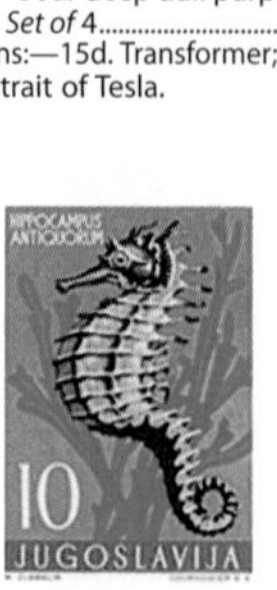

231 Short-snouted Seahorse (*Hippocampus antiquorum*)

232

(Des M. Zlamalik. Photo Courvoisier)

1956 (10 Sept). Adriatic Sea Creatures. T **231** and similar designs. P 11½.

825	10d. ochre, slate-purple and emerald	60	30
826	15d. black, rose and bright blue	60	30
827	20d. multicoloured	60	30
828	25d. multicoloured	1·20	30
829	30d. multicoloured	1·20	30
830	35d. magenta, yellow and turquoise-blue	2·30	75
831	50d. scarlet, lemon and deep blue	5·75	3·25
832	70d. multicoloured	11·50	5·25
833	100d. multicoloured	47·00	26·00
825/833 *Set of 9*		65·00	33·00

Designs: Horiz—15d. Common paper nautilus (*Argonauta argo*); 20d. Rock lobster (*Palinurus vulgaris*); 25d. Rainbow wrasse (*Coris julis*); 30d. Painted comber (*Serranus scriba*); 35d. Red mullet (*Mullus surmuletus*); 50d. Red scorpionfish (*Scorpaena scrofa*); 70d. Cuckoo wrasse (*Labrus bimaculatus*); 100d. John Dory (*Zeus pungio*).

(Des P. Dabović. Litho)

1956 (30 Sept). OBLIGATORY TAX. Children's Week. P 12½.

834	**232**	2d. bronze-green and pale green	60	30

1956 (30 Sept). POSTAGE DUE. Children's Week. As No. 834 but colours changed and inscr "PORTO".

D835	2d. chocolate and pale chocolate	80	30

233 Running

234

(Des Ide and M. Ćirić. Litho)

1956 (24 Oct). Olympic Games. T **233** and similar horiz designs. P 12½.

835	10d. ochre and brown-carmine	1·20	50
836	15d. ochre and deep blue	1·20	50
837	20d. ochre and ultramarine	2·30	1·00
838	30d. ochre and deep dull green	2·30	1·00
839	35d. ochre and sepia	2·30	1·00
840	50d. ochre and dull green	2·30	1·00
841	70d. ochre and maroon	£120	29·00
842	100d. ochre and brown-red	£120	29·00
835/842 *Set of 8*		£225	55·00

Designs:—15d. Canoeing; 20d. Skiing; 30d. Swimming; 35d. Football; 50d. Water polo; 70d. Table tennis; 100d. Shooting.

(Des Ide and M. Ćirić. Litho)

1957 (5 May). OBLIGATORY TAX. Red Cross. P 12½.

843	**234**	2d. red, black and pale blue	45	30

1957 (5 May). POSTAGE DUE. Red Cross. As No. 843 but colours changed and inscr "PORTO".

D844	2d. red, black and pale grey	80	30

235 Common Centaury (*Erythraea centaurium*)

236 Factory in Worker's Hand

(Des M. Zlamalik. Photo Courvoisier)

1957 (25 May). Flowers. T **235** and similar vert designs. Multicoloured. P 11½.

844	10d. Type **235**	10	10
845	15d. Deadly nightshade (*Atropa belladonna*)	15	10
846	20d. Autumn saffron (*Colchicum autumnale*)	25	10
847	25d. Marsh mallow (*Althaea officinalis*)	25	10
848	30d. Common valerian (*Valeriana officinalis*)	35	20
849	35d. Woolly foxglove (*Digitalis lanata*)	80	20
850	50d. Male fern (*Dryopteris filix mas*)	1·70	65
851	70d. Green-winged orchid (*Orchis mario*)	3·00	1·60
852	100d. Pyrethrum	20·00	9·00
844/852 *Set of 9*		24·00	11·00

(Des M. Stančić. Eng T. Krnjajić. Recess)

1957 (25 June). First Congress of Workers' Councils, Belgrade. P 12½.

853	**236**	15d. crimson-lake	60	30
854		30d. deep violet-blue	1·70	1·00

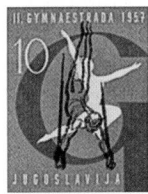

237 Gymnasts

239 Musician and Dancers of Slovenia

(Des F. Bis. Photo "Ljudska" Ptg Wks, Ljubljana)

1957 (1 July). Second Gymnastics Festival, Zagreb. T **237** and similar designs inscr "II GYMNAESTRADA 1957". P 12½.

855	10d. olive-green and black	35	20
856	15d. red-brown and black	35	20
857	30d. greenish blue and black	1·20	20
858	50d. brown and black	5·25	1·60
855/858 *Set of 4*		6·50	2·00

(Des Z. Sertić. Typo)

1957 (25 Sept). Yugoslav Costumes (1st series). T **239** and similar designs. P 12½.

860	10d. red, blue, deep brown and light brown	25	10
861	15d. red, black, deep brown and light brown	35	10
862	30d. red, deep brown, blue-green and light brown	45	20
863	50d. deep brown, blue-green and light brown	60	30
864	70d. black, deep brown and light brown	80	50
865	100d. red, deep brown, blue-green and light brown	11·50	4·50
860/865 *Set of 6*		12·50	5·25

Designs: Horiz—10d. Montenegrin musician, man and woman; 15d. Macedonian dancers; 30d. Croatian shepherdess and shepherd boys. Vert—50d. Serbian peasants; 70d. Bosnian villagers.

240 Children

241 Revolutionaries

(Des P. Dabović from plaque by A. Augustinčić. Litho)

1957 (30 Sept). OBLIGATORY TAX. Children's Week. P 12½.

866	**240**	2d. grey-black and pale brown-red	45	30

1957 (30 Sept). POSTAGE DUE. Children's Week. As No. 866 but colours changed and inscr "PORTO".

D867	**240**	2d. bistre-brown and light blue	80	20

(Des B. Lazevski. Eng B. Kocmut. Recess, background litho)

1957 (7 Nov). 40th Anniv of Russian Revolution. P 11½×12½.

867	**241**	15d. scarlet and ochre	95	65
		a. Perf 12½		

242 Simon Gregorcic (poet)

243 Steel Plant, Sisak

(Des B. Jakac. Eng T. Krnjajić (15d., 30d., 70d.), B. Kocmut (50d.), S. Babić (100d.). Recess)

1957 (3 Dec). Cultural Anniversaries. T **242** and similar vert portraits. P 12½.

868	15d. brownish black	60	30
869	30d. indigo	60	30
870	50d. red-brown	1·20	50
871	70d. blackish violet	9·25	6·25
872	100d. bronze-green	14·00	10·50
868/872 *Set of 5*		23·00	16·00

Portraits:—15d. Type **242** (50th death anniv (1956)); 30d. Anton Linhart (dramatist, birth bicentenary (1956)); 50d. Oton Kučera (physicist, birth centenary); 70d. Stevan Mokranjac (composer, birth centenary (1956)); 100d. Jovan Popović (writer, death centenary (1956)).

(Des R. Debenjak (873/*a*), T. Krnjajić (874, 876), B. Kocmut (875/*a*). Typo)

1958 (24 Mar)–**61**. Coil stamps. T **243** and similar vert designs. P 12½×imperf.

873	10d. deep green	21·00	7·75
873*a*	10d. chocolate (17.4.61)	8·75	1·30
874	15d. deep orange-red	21·00	7·75
875	15d. deep green (12.6.59)	9·25	1·60
875*a*	15d. bright emerald (18.5.61)	17·00	5·25
876	20d. light red (1.4.59)	9·25	1·60
873/876 *Set of 6*		80·00	23·00

Designs:—15d. (874), 20d. Jablanica Dam; 15d. (875/*a*) Ljubljana—Zagreb motor road.

See also Nos. 891/911, 983/99 and 1194/1204.

244

245 Fresco of Sopocani Monastery

(Des M. Stančić. Photo "Ljudska" Ptg Wks, Ljubljana)

1958 (22 Apr). Seventh Yugoslav Communist Party Congress. P 12½.

877	**244**	15d. brown-purple	1·20	20

(Des R. Stević. Photo)

1958 (4 May). OBLIGATORY TAX. Red Cross. P 12½.

878	**245**	2d. multicoloured	60	30

1958 (4 May). POSTAGE DUE. Red Cross. As No. 878 but additionally inscr "PORTO".

D879	2d. multicoloured	1·20	50

246 Mallard (*Anas platyrhvncha*)

247 Pigeon

(Des M. Zlamalik. Photo Courvoisier)

1958 (25 May). Yugoslav Game Birds. Birds as T **246** in natural colours. Background colours given below. P 11½.

879	10d. brown	10	10
880	15d. magenta	15	10
881	20d. indigo	35	15
882	25d. green	60	20
883	30d. blue-green	80	25
884	35d. bistre	1·70	30
885	50d. purple	4·00	2·10
886	70d. blue	7·00	3·25
887	100d. orange-brown	30·00	21·00
879/887 *Set of 9*		40·00	25·00

Designs: Horiz—15d. Capercaillie (*Tetrao urogallus*); 20d. Ring-necked pheasant (*Phasianus colchicus*); 30d. Water rail (*Rallus aquaticus*); 70d. Woodcock (*Scolopax rusticola*). Vert—25d. Common coot (*Fulica atra*); 35d. Great bustard (*Otis tarda*); 50d. Rock partridge (*Alectoris graeca*); 100d. Common crane (*Grus grus*).

(Des R. Stević. Eng T. Krnjajić. Recess)

1958 (14 June). Opening of Postal Museum, Belgrade. P 12½.

888	**247**	15d. blue-black	1·20	20

248 Battle Flag

249 Pomet (hero of Držic's comedy *Dundo Maroje*) and Ancient Fountain at Dubrovnik

(Des D. Andrejević-Kun. Eng S. Babić. Recess)

1958 (1 July). 15th Anniv of Battle of Sutjeska River. P 12½.

889	**248**	15d. brown-lake	70	40

(Des after lino-cut by B. Kršić. Litho)

1958 (10 Aug). 450th Anniv of Birth of Marin Držic (writer). P 12½.

890	**249**	15d. bistre-brown and black	2·30	20

(Des T. Krnjajić (896, 905), R. Debenjak (others). Eng B. Kocmut, S. Babić and T. Krnjajić. Recess)

1958 (25 Sept)–**59**. Various pictorial designs as T **243**. P 12½.

891	2d. yellow-olive	10	10
892	5d. Venetian red	25	10
893	8d. reddish purple (30.5.59)	25	10
894	10d. bluish green	35	10
895	10d. grey-green (1.7.59)	45	10
896	15d. deep orange-red	60	10
897	15d. deep green (30.5.59)	60	10
898	17d. reddish purple	60	10
899	20d. deep orange-red (1.4.59)	60	10
900	25d. greenish grey	60	10
901	30d. indigo	60	10
902	35d. carmine-red	60	10
903	40d. carmine	60	10
904	40d. blue (11.6.59)	8·25	10
905	50d. blue	60	10
906	55d. carmine (30.5.59)	9·25	10
907	70d. orange-red	1·70	10
908	80d. orange-red (8.6.59)	21·00	10
909	100d. myrtle-green	9·25	10
910	200d. red-brown	4·00	10
911	500d. greenish blue	9·25	10
891/911 *Set of 21*		65·00	1·90

Designs: Vert—2d. Oil derricks; 5d. Shipbuilding; 8d., 17d. Timber industry, cable railway; 10d. (2), T **243**; 15d. (896), 20d. Jablanica Dam; 15d. (897), 25d. Ljubljana-Zagreb motor-road; 30d. "Litostroj" turbine factory, Ljubljana; 35d. Coke plant, Lukavac. Horiz—40d. (2), Hotel, Titograd; 50d., 55d. Skopje; 70d., 80d. Sarajevo railway station and obelisk; 100d. Bridge, Ljubljana; 200d. Theatre, Zagreb; 500d. Parliament House, Belgrade.

250 Children at Play

D **251** Child with Toy

(Des A. Milenković. Litho)

1958 (5 Oct). OBLIGATORY TAX. Children's Week. P 12½.

912	**250**	2d. black, olive and yellow	35	20

(Des B. Lazarević. Litho)

1958 (5 Oct). POSTAGE DUE. Children's Week. P 12½.

D913	D **251**	2d. black and blue	80	30

251 Ship with Oceanographic Equipment

252 "Human Rights"

(Des B. Kršić. Eng T. Krnjajić (15d.), S. Babić (300d.). Recess)

1958 (24 Oct). International Geophysical Year. T **251** and a similar vert design inscr "MGG-AGI 1957–58". P 12½.

(a) POSTAGE

913	15d. brown-purple	60	30

(b) AIR. Inscr "AVIONSKA POSTA"

914	300d. deep blue	10·50	4·00

Design:—300d. Moon, and earth with orbital tracks of artificial satellites.

(Des R. Stević. Eng T. Krnjajić. Recess)

1958 (10 Dec). Tenth Anniv of Declaration of Human Rights. P 12½.

915	**252**	30d. deep bluish green	1·30	1·00

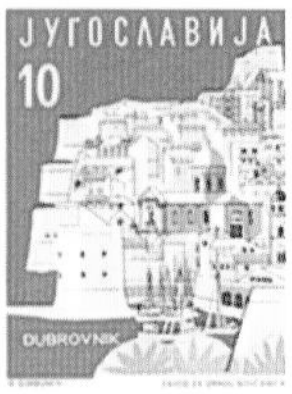

253 Old City, Dubrovnik

254 Communist Party, Emblem and Red Flags

(Des D. Gorbunov. Litho)

1959 (16 Feb). Tourist Publicity (1st series). Views as T **253**. P 12½.

916	10d. yellow-olive and rose-red	10	10
917	10d. violet-blue and emerald	10	10
918	15d. reddish violet and turquoise-blue	10	10
919	15d. blue-green and blue	10	10
920	20d. emerald-green and bistre-brown	15	10
921	20d. green and turquoise-blue	15	10
922	30d. reddish violet and yellow-orange	1·20	10
923	30d. sage-green and grey-blue	1·20	10
924	70d. grey-black and turquoise-blue	6·50	4·25
916/924 *Set of 9*		8·75	4·50

Designs: Vert—No. 916, T **253**; 917, Bled; 918, Postojna grottoes; 919, Ohrid; 920, Plitvice Lakes; 921, Opatija; 922, Split; 923, Sveti Stefan; 924, Belgrade.

See also Nos. 1033/41 and 1080/5.

(Des D. Andrejević-Kun. Typo)

1959 (20 Apr). 40th Anniv of Yugoslav Communist Party. P 12½.

925	**254**	20d. multicoloured	1·70	20

255 "Family Assistance"

256 Dubrovnik (XV Cent)

(Des B. Spremo and A. Milenković. Litho)

1959 (3 May). OBLIGATORY TAX. Red Cross. P 12½.

926	**255**	2d. deep violet-blue and red	45	20

1959 (3 May). POSTAGE DUE. Red Cross. As No. 926 but colour changed and inscr "PORTO".

D927	2d. yellow-orange and red	80	30

(Des and eng T. Krnjajić. Recess)

1959 (24 May). Philatelic Exhibition, Dubrovnik ("JUFIZ IV"). P 11½×12.

927	**256**	20d. deep bronze-green, yellow-green and greenish blue	10·50	4·75

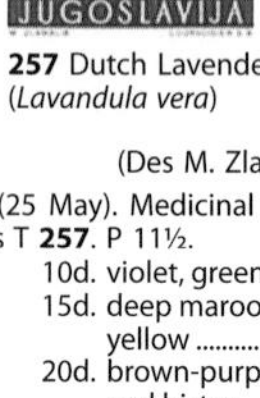

257 Dutch Lavender (*Lavandula vera*)

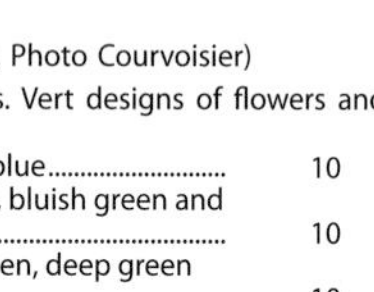

258 Tug-of-War

(Des M. Zlamalik. Photo Courvoisier)

1959 (25 May). Medicinal Plants. Vert designs of flowers and fruit as T **257**. P 11½.

928	10d. violet, green and blue	10	10
929	15d. deep maroon, red, bluish green and yellow	10	10
930	20d. brown-purple, green, deep green and bistre	10	10
931	25d. deep lilac, bluish green and light olive	20	10
932	30d. green, deep blue and pink	35	15
933	35d. ultramarine, green and yellow-brown	60	30
934	50d. yellow, deep green and purple-brown	3·00	50
935	70d. red, green, yellow and ochre	3·50	1·30
936	100d. grey, yellow-green, dp grn & brn	16·00	7·75
928/936 *Set of 9*		22·00	9·25

Designs:—15d. Alder blackthorn (*Rhamnus frangula*); 20d. Scopolia (*Scopolia carniolica*); 25d. Monkshood (*Aconitum napellus*); 30d. Bilberry (*Vaccinium myrtillus*); 35d. Common juniper (*Juniperus communis*); 50d. Cowslip (*Primula veris*); 70d. Pomegranate (*Punica granatum*); 100d. Thorn-apple (*Datura stramonium*).

See also Nos. 1000/8 and 1074/9.

(Des B. Spremo, A. Milenković. Litho)

1959 (26 June). "Partisan" Physical Culture Festival, Belgrade. T **258** and similar designs inscr "1959". P 12½.

937	10d. blue-black and ochre	10	10
938	15d. violet-blue and sepia	10	10
939	20d. reddish violet and olive-brown	10	10
940	35d. maroon and grey	25	10
941	40d. bluish violet and grey	35	10
942	55d. deep grey-green and olive-brown	70	10
943	80d. olive-green and slate	1·20	65
944	100d. reddish violet and ochre	8·75	4·50
937/944 *Set of 8*		10·50	5·25

Designs: Horiz—15d. High jumping and running: 20d. Gymnastics; 35d. Female exercises with hoops; 40d. Sailors' exercises; 55d. Handball and basketball; 80d. Swimming and diving. Vert—100d. "Partisan" Association insignia.

259 Fair Emblem

260

(Des F. Bis. Litho)

1959 (5 Sept). Zagreb International Fair. P 12½.

945	**259**	20d. black and blue	3·00	1·60

(Des B. Kršić. Litho)

1959 (5 Oct). OBLIGATORY TAX. Children's Week. P 12½.

946	**260**	2d. slate and orange-yellow	45	20

1959 (5 Oct). POSTAGE DUE. Children's Week. Design similar to T **260** but additionally inscr "PORTO". P 12½.

D947	2d. brown-purple and orange-yellow	60	20

Design:—2d. Tree, cockerel and ears of wheat.

261 Athletes

262 "Reconstruction" (sculpture by L. Dolinar)

(Des B. Spremo and A. Milenković. Litho)

1960 (25 Apr). Olympic Games. Vert designs as T **261**. P 12½.

947	15d. yellow, buff and slate-violet	60	50
948	20d. drab, lavender and grey-blue	60	50
949	30d. light blue, stone and ultramarine	60	50
950	35d. grey, brown and purple	60	50
951	40d. drab, light green and bronze-green	60	50
952	55d. grey-blue, drab and deep bluish green	60	50
953	80d. ochre, grey and carmine	10·50	5·25
954	100d. ochre, drab and violet	10·50	5·25
947/954 *Set of 8*		22·00	12·00

Designs:—20d. Swimming; 30d. Skiing; 35d. Graeco-Roman wrestling; 40d. Cycling; 55d. Yachting; 80d. Equestrian; 100d. Fencing.

(Des B. Lazarević. Litho)

1960 (8 May). OBLIGATORY TAX. Red Cross. Cross in red. P 12½.

955	**262**	2d. indigo	45	20

1960 (8 May). POSTAGE DUE. Red Cross. As No. 955 but additionally inscr "PORTO" and colour changed.

D956	**262**	2d. dull purple and red	70	30

(Des M. Zlamalik. Photo Courvoisier)

1960 (25 May). Horiz designs as T **213**. Animals in natural colours; background colours below. P 11½.

956	15d. indigo	25	20
957	20d. bronze-green	35	30
958	25d. deep bluish green	45	40
959	30d. blackish green	60	50
960	35d. chocolate	70	65
961	40d. brown-lake	80	75
962	55d. bright blue	1·50	1·40
963	80d. blue-violet	1·70	1·60
964	100d. red	4·75	4·25
956/964 *Set of 9*		10·00	9·00

Designs:—15d. West European hedgehog (*Erinaceus europaeus*); 20d. Eurasian red squirrel (*Sciurus vulgaris*); 25d. Pine marten (*Martes martes*); 30d. Brown hare (*Lepus europaeus*); 35d. Red fox (*Vulpes vulpes*); 40d. Eurasian badger (*Meles meles*); 55d. Wolf (*Canis lupus*); 80d. Roe deer (*Capreolus capreolus*); 100d. Wild boar (*sus scrofa*).

263 Lenin

264 Accelerator

(Des T. Krnjajić. Recess)

1960 (22 June). 90th Birth Anniv of Lenin. P 12½.

965	**263**	20d. grey-green and deep green	25	10

(Des M. Rodiči. Eng S. Babić (15d.), B. Kocmut (20d.), T. Krnjajić (40d.). Recess)

1960 (23 Aug). Nuclear Energy Exhibition, Belgrade. T **264** and similar vert designs. P 12½.

966	15d. bluish green	11·50	10·50
967	20d. brown-purple	11·50	10·50
968	40d. violet-blue	11·50	10·50
966/968 *Set of 3*		31·00	28·00

Designs:—20d. Neutron generator; 40d. Nuclear reactor.

265 Young Girl

266 Serbian National Theatre, Novi Sad (Centenary)

(Des A. Huter. Litho)

1960 (2 Oct). OBLIGATORY TAX. Children's Week. P 12½.

969	**265**	2d. red	35	20

1960 (2 Oct). POSTAGE DUE. Children's Week. Design similar to T **265** but additionally inscr "PORTO".

D970	2d. slate-blue (Young boy)	45	20

(Des B. Spremo and A. Milenković (40d.), M. Vujačić (others). Eng V. Cvetković (15d., 40d.), S. Babić (20d.), B. Kocmut (55d.), T. Krnjajić (80d.). Recess)

1960 (24 Oct). Anniversaries. T **266** and similar vert designs. P 12½.

970	15d. black	70	65
971	20d. sepia	80	75
972	40d. blue-black	1·00	95
973	55d. brown-purple	1·20	1·00
974	80d. deep green	1·40	1·30
970/974 *Set of 5*		4·50	4·25

Designs:—20d. Detail of "Illyrian Renaissance" (V. Bukovac) (centenary of Croat National Theatre, Zagreb); 40d. Edvard Rusijan and Blériot XI airplane (50th anniv of first flight in Yugoslavia); 55d. Symbolic hand holding fruit (15th anniv of Republic); 80d. Symbol of nuclear energy (15th anniv of United Nations).

(Des M. Zlamalik. Eng T. Krnjajić (15, 20, 100d.), V. Cvetković (40, 80d.), S. Babić (55d.). Recess)

1960 (24 Dec). Portraits as T **217**. P 12½.

975	15d. deep green	60	40
976	20d. chestnut	60	40
977	40d. olive-brown	60	40
978	55d. crimson	60	40
979	80d. deep ultramarine	60	40
980	100d. greenish blue	60	40
975/980 *Set of 6*		3·25	2·20

Portraits:—15d. Ivan Cankar (writer); 20d. Silvije Kranjcevic (poet); 40d. Paja Jovanović (painter); 55d. Djura Jakšic (writer); 80d. Mihajlo Pupin (physicist); 100d. Rudjer Boškovic (astronomer).

268 "Blood Transfusion"

269 "Atomic Energy"

(Des B. Kršić. Litho)

1961 (7 May). OBLIGATORY TAX. Red Cross. P 12½.

981	**268**	2d. red, yellow, orange and deep brown	45	20
		a. Imperf	20·00	20·00

1961 (7 May). POSTAGE DUE. Red Cross. As No. 981 but additionally inscr "PORTO" and colours changed. P 12½.

D982	2d. red, yellow, orange and deep green	60	20
	a. Imperf	23·00	23·00

(Des B. Lazarević. Recess and litho)

1961 (15 May). International Nuclear Electronic Conference, Belgrade. P 12½.

982	**269**	25d. blue, red, carmine and grey	1·20	20

1961–65. As Nos. 891/911, new colours and values. P 12½.

983	5d. orange (23.5.61)	30	10
984	8d. slate-violet (29.6.61)	25	10
985	10d. chocolate (13.7.61)	25	10
986	15d. bright emerald (29.6.61)	35	10
987	20d. deep violet-blue (12.12.61)	80	10
987*a*	20d. bright emerald (10.9.65)	45	10
988	25d. vermilion (17.5.61)	30	10
989	30d. brown (29.6.61)	8·75	10
989*a*	30d. vermilion (10.9.65)	80	10

990	40d. maroon (22.1.62)	25	10
991	50d. blue (17.8.61)	2·30	10
992	65d. bluish green (22.8.61)	25	10
993	100d. yellow-olive (12.12.61)	3·50	10
994	150d. carmine-red (22.1.62)	1·20	10
995	200d. slate-blue (22.1.62)	80	10
996	300d. olive-green (22.1.62)	2·20	10
997	500d. deep violet (23.10.61)	1·40	10
998	1000d. sepia (16.10.61)	3·00	10
999	2000d. brown-purple (16.10.61)	8·75	50
983/999 *Set of* 19		32·00	2·10

Designs: Vert—5d. Shipbuilding; 8d. Timber industry, cable railway; 10d. T **243**; 15d. Ljubljana-Zagreb motor road; 20d. Jablanica Dam; 25d. Cable industry; 30d. "Litostroj" turbine factory, Ljubljana; 40d. Coke plant, Lukavac; 50d. Iron foundry, Zenica; 65d. Furnace, Sovojno; 100d. Oil derricks. Horiz—150d. Hotel, Titograd; 260d. Skopje; 300d. Sarajevo railway station and obelisk; 500d. Bridge, Ljubljana; 1000d. Theatre, Zagreb; 2000d. Parliament House, Belgrade.

For stamps as above but with values expressed "0.05" etc., see Nos. 1194/1204.

(Des M. Zlamalik. Photo Courvoisier)

1961 (25 May). Medicinal Plants. Vert designs as T **257** inscr "1941–1961". Multicoloured. P 11½.

1000	10d. Yellow foxglove (*Digitalis ambigua*)	45	20
1001	15d. Marjoram (*Origanum majorana*)	45	20
1002	20d. Hyssop (*Hyssopus officinalis*)	45	20
1003	25d. Hawthorn (*Crataegus monogyna*)	45	20
1004	40d. Hollyhock (*Althaea rosea*)	45	20
1005	50d. Soapwort (*Saponaria officinalis*)	45	20
1006	60d. Clary (*Salvia sclarea*)	45	20
1007	80d. Blackthorn (*Prunus spinosa*)	90	20
1008	100d. Pot marigold (*Calendula officinalis*)	13·00	6·75
1000/1008 *Set of* 9		15·00	7·50

271 Stevan Filipovic (statue by V. Bakic)

272

(Des M. Zlamalik. Photo Courvoisier)

1961 (3 July). 20th Anniv of Yugoslav Insurrection. T **271** and similar vert designs inscr "1941–1961". P 12½.

1009	15d. red-brown, rose-red and gold	25	10
1010	20d. greenish yellow, sepia and gold	25	10
1011	25d. grey-green, bluish green and gold	25	10
1012	60d. reddish violet, violet-blue and gold	25	10
1013	100d. indigo, deep blue and gold	35	20
1009/1013 *Set of* 5		1·20	55
MS1013*a* 64×82 mm. 500d. indigo, deep blue and gold. Imperf		£170	£170

Designs:—20d. Insurrection Monument, Bosansko Grahovo (relief by S. Stojanović); 25d. Executed Inhabitants Monument, Kragujevac (by A. Gržetić); 60d. Nova Gradiška Victory Monument (by A. Augustinčić); 100d., 500d. Marshal Tito (Revolution Monument, Titovo Užice, statue by F. Kršinić).

(Des B. Jakac (T **272**), D. Gorbunov (others). Litho (No. 1014), recess and litho (1016), recess (others))

1961 (1 Sept). Non-Aligned Countries Conference, Belgrade. T **272** and another horiz design inscr "BEOGRADSKA KONFERENCIJA". P 11½.

(a) POSTAGE

1014	**272**	25d. sepia	10	10
1015	–	50d. deep bluish green	25	10
MS1015*a* 72×65 mm. 1000d. brown-purple (T **272**) Imperf			23·00	23·00

(b) AIR. Airplane incorporated in design

1016	**272**	250d. blackish purple	1·30	75
1017	–	500d. deep blue	2·50	1·60

Design:—50, 500d. National Assembly Building, Belgrade.

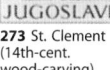

273 St. Clement (14th-cent. wood-carving)

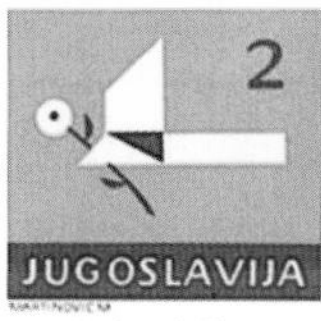

274 Bird with Flower in Beak

(Des B. Spremo and A. Milenković. Eng V. Cvetković. Recess)

1961 (10 Sept). Twelfth International Congress of Byzantine Studies, Ohrid. P 12½.

1018	**273**	25d. deep brown and olive	3·75	85

(Des M. Martinović. Litho)

1961 (1 Oct). OBLIGATORY TAX. Children's Week. P 12½.

1019	**274**	2d. orange and violet	35	20

1961 (1 Oct). POSTAGE DUE. Children's Week. As No. 1019 but colours changed and inscr "PORTO".

D1020	2d. light yellow-green and sepia	45	20

(Des Z. Serlić. Litho)

1961 (28 Nov). Yugoslav Costumes (2nd series). Designs as T **239** inscr "1941–1961". P 12½.

1020	15d. red, black, sepia and light brown	25	10
1021	25d. black, red-brown and light brown	25	10
1022	30d. sepia, brown-red and light brown	25	10
1023	50d. red, black, sepia and light brown	25	10
1024	65d. red, yellow, light brown and sepia	50	15
1025	100d. brown-red, sepia, deep bluish green and light brown	2·30	1·00
1020/1025 *Set of* 6		3·50	1·40

Designs: Horiz—Costumes of: 15d. Serbia; 25d. Montenegro; 30d. Bosnia and Herzegovina; 50d. Macedonia; 65d. Croatia; 100d. Slovenia.

275 Luka Vukalović (revolutionary leader)

276 Hands holding Flower and Rifle

(Des B. Lazarević. Eng V. Cvetković. Recess)

1961 (15 Dec). Centenary of Herzegovina Insurrection. P 12½.

1026	**275**	25d. black	25	10

(Des B. Spremo and A. Milenković. Eng S. Babić. Recess)

1961 (22 Dec). 20th Anniv of Yugoslav Partisan Army. P 12½.

1027	**276**	25d. violet-blue and red	25	10

277 Dimitur and Konstantin Miladinov

(Des B. Lazarević. Litho)

1961 (25 Dec). Centenary of Publication of Macedonian National Songs by Miladinov Brothers. P 12½.

1028	**277**	25d. brown-purple and buff	25	10

1962 (5 Mar). POSTAGE DUE. As Nos. D727/31 but litho.

D1029	D **126**	10d. vermilion	4·75	20
D1030		20d. reddish violet	4·75	20
D1031		30d. yellow-orange	10·00	20
D1032		50d. ultramarine	47·00	1·00
D1033		100d. claret	29·00	1·60
D1029/1033 *Set of* 5			85·00	3·00

278 "Mother's Play" (after F. Kršinić)

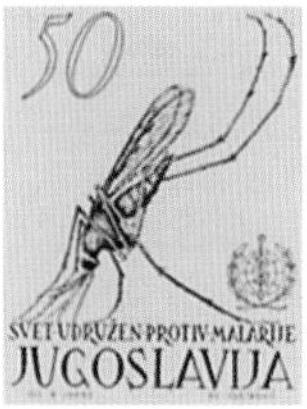

279 Mosquito

(Des B. Jakac. Eng T. Krnjajić. Recess)

1962 (7 Apr). 15th Anniv of United Nations Children's Fund. P 12½.

1029	**278**	50d. black/*pale drab*	25	10

(Des B. Jakac. Eng V. Cvetković. Recess)

1962 (7 Apr). Malaria Eradication. P 12½.

1030	**279**	50d. black/*pale blue*	25	10

280 Goddess Isis (from temple at Kalabscha)

281 Bandages and Symbols

(Des B. Jakac. Eng T. Krnjajić (25d.), S. Babić (50d.). Recess)

1962 (10 Apr). 15th Anniv of United Nations Educational, Scientific and Cultural Organization. Save Nubian Monuments. T **280** and similar vert design. P 12½.

1031	25d. blackish green/*stone*	10	10
1032	50d. brown/*pale drab*	25	10

Design:—50d. Rameses II (from temple, Abu Simbel).

(Des D. Gorbunov. Litho)

1962 (24 Apr). Tourist Publicity (2nd series). Vert designs similar to T **253** inscr "1941–1961". P 12½.

1033	15d. olive-brown and blue	35	10
1034	15d. olive-bistre and turquoise	35	10
1035	25d. red-brown and blue	35	10
1036	25d. blue and light blue	35	10
1037	30d. greenish blue and yellow-brown	35	10
1038	30d. blue and slate-purple	45	10
1039	50d. greenish blue and olive-bistre	1·20	10
1040	50d. blue and bistre	1·20	10
1041	100d. blue-grey and black-green	10·50	4·25
1033/1041 *Set of* 9		13·50	4·50

Designs: Views of—No. 1033, Portorož; 1034, Jajce; 1035, Zadar; 1036, Popova Šapka; 1037, Hvar; 1038, Kotor Bay; 1039, Djerdap; 1040, Rab; 1041, Zagreb.

(Des B. Kršić. Litho)

1962 (30 Apr). OBLIGATORY TAX. Red Cross. P 12½.

1042	**281**	5d. red, brown-red and grey	35	20

1962 (30 Apr). POSTAGE DUE. Red Cross. As No. 1042 but colours changed and inscr "PORTO".

D1043	5d. red, brown-purple and blue	45	20

282 Marshal Tito (after sculpture by A. Augustinčić)

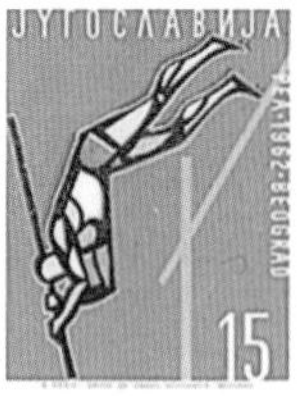

283 Pole Vaulting

(Des B. Lazarević. Eng T. Krnjajić (T **282**), S. Babić (others). Recess)

1962 (25 May). 70th Birthday of Marshal Tito. T **282** and similar vert design inscr "1892 1962". P 12½.

1043	**282**	25d. bluish green	10	10
1044	–	50d. deep brown	35	10
1045	**282**	100d. deep blue	1·20	20
1046	–	200d. deep bluish green and brown	2·30	1·00
1043/1046 *Set of* 4			3·50	1·30
MS1046*a* 76×104 mm. Nos. 1043/6. Imperf (sold at 400d.)			47·00	47·00

Design:—50d., 200d. As T **282** but profile view of bust.

(Des M. Zlamalik. Photo Courvoisier)

1962 (8 June). Amphibians and Reptiles. Horiz designs as T **213**. P 11½.

1047	15d. brown, orange-red and green	60	40
1048	20d. blue-black, yellow and reddish violet	60	40
1049	25d. multicoloured	60	40
1050	30d. deep brown, yellow-green and dull ultramarine	60	40
1051	50d. agate, yellow and brown-red	60	40
1052	65d. black, yellow-ochre and blue-green	60	40
1053	100d. bright green, lake-brown and black	1·60	1·50
1054	150d. scarlet, black and brown	2·40	2·20
1055	200d. black, drab and carmine	13·50	7·50
1047/1055 *Set of* 9		19·00	12·00

Designs:—15d. Crested newt (*Triturus cristatus*); 20d. Spotted salamander (*Salamandra maculosa*); 25d. Yellow-bellied toad (*Bombinator pachypus*); 30d. Marsh frog (*Rana ridibunda*); 50d. European pond turtle (*Emys orbicularis*); 65d. Wall lizard (*Lacerta serpa*); 100d. Green lizard (*Lacerta viridis*); 150d. Leopard snake (*Coluber leopardinus*); 200d. Adder (*Vipera berus*).

(Des B. Kršić. Litho)

1962 (10 July–Sept). Seventh European Athletic Championships, Belgrade. T **283** and similar designs. P 12½.

1056	15d. black and light greenish blue	45	20
1057	25d. black and reddish purple	45	20
1058	30d. black and emerald-green	45	20
1059	50d. black and rose-red	45	20
1060	65d. black and bright blue	45	20
1061	100d. black and blue-green	1·00	20
1062	150d. black and orange	4·25	40
1063	200d. black and light red-brown	10·50	80
1056/1063 *Set of* 8		16·00	2·20
MS1063*a* 57×71 mm. 600d. black and bright bluish violet. Imperf (12.9)		17·00	17·00

Designs: Horiz—25d. Throwing the discus; 50d. Throwing the javelin; 100d. Start of sprint; 200d. High jumping. Vert— 30d. Running; 65d. Putting the shot; 150d. Hurdling; 600d. Army Stadium, Belgrade.

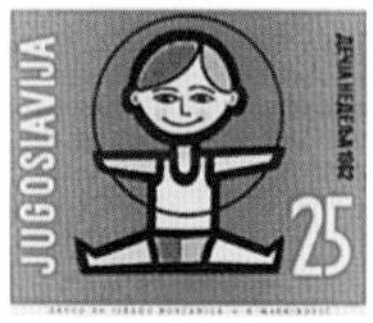

284 "Physical Culture"

285 "Bathing the Newborn Child" (Decani Monastery)

(Des N. Masniković. Recess and litho)

1962 (1 Oct). Children's Week. P 12½.

1064	**284**	25d. black and red	25	10

(Des D. Kažić and S. Fileki. Photo Courvoisier)

1962 (28 Nov). Yugoslav Art. Designs as T **285**. Multicoloured. P 12½.

1065	25d. Situla of Vace (detail from bronze vessel) (horiz)	25	25
1066	30d. Golden Mask of Trebenište (5th-cent, burial mask) (horiz)	25	25
1067	50d. The God Kairos (Trogir Monastery)	25	25
1068	65d. Pigeons of Nerezi (detail from series of frescoes, "The Visitation", Nerezi Church, Skopje)	25	25
1069	100d. Type **285**	40	40
1070	150d. Icon of Ohrid (detail from 14th-cent icon, "The Annunciation") (horiz)	1·60	85
1065/1070 *Set of* 6		2·75	2·00

See also Nos. 1098/1103.

HAVE YOU READ THE NOTES AT THE BEGINNING OF THIS CATALOGUE?
These often provide answers to the enquiries we receive

286 Ear of Wheat and Parched Earth

287 Andrija Mohorovicic (meteorologist)

(Des B. Jakac. Eng V. Cvetković. Recess)

1963 (21 Apr). Freedom from Hunger. P 12½.
1071 **286** 50d. black-purple/*stone* 25 10

(Des B. Jakac. Eng T. Krnjajić. Recess)

1963 (23 Apr). World Meteorological Day. P 12½.
1072 **287** 50d. deep ultramarine/*pale grey* 25 10

288 Centenary Emblem

289 Partisans in File

(Des N. Milošević. Litho)

1963 (5 May). OBLIGATORY TAX. Red Cross Centenary and Red Cross Week. P 12½.
1073 **288** 5d. red, grey and yellow-ochre 45 20

1963 (5 May). POSTAGE DUE. Red Cross Centenary and Red Cross Week. As No. 1073, but colours changed and inscr "PORTO".
D1074 5d. red, dull purple and light orange 70 30

(Des M. Zlamalik and N. Masniković. Photo Courvoisier)

1963 (25 May). Medicinal Plants. Vert designs as T **257**. P 11½.
1074 15d. black, green and dull yellowish green 35 30
1075 25d. multicoloured 35 30
1076 30d. multicoloured 35 30
1077 50d. multicoloured 35 30
1078 65d. multicoloured 75 65
1079 100d. drab, bright green and slate-black .... 4·00 2·75
1074/1079 *Set of 6* .... 5·50 4·25

Designs:—15d. Lily of the valley (*Convallaria majalis*); 25d. Iris; 30d. Bistort (*Polygonum bistorta*); 50d. Henbane (*Hyoscyamus niger*); 65d. Perforate St. John's wort (*Hypericum perforatum*); 100d. Caraway (*Carum carvi*).

(Des D. Gorbunov. Litho)

1963 (6 June). Tourist Publicity (3rd series). Vert designs similar to T **253** inscr "1963". Multicoloured. P 12½.
1080 15d. Pula 10 10
1081 25d. Vrnjacka Banja 10 10
1082 30d. Crikvenica 10 10
1083 50d. Korcula 25 10
1084 65d. Durmitor 25 15
1085 100d. Ljubljana .... 2·10 65
1080/1085 *Set of 6* .... 2·50 1·10

(Des T. Krnjajić. 25d. litho, after painting by B. Šotra; others recess and litho after wood-carvings by D. Andrejević-Kun)

1963 (3 July). 20th Anniv of Battle of Sutjeska River. T **289** and similar designs. P 12½.
1086 15d. deep bluish green and pale drab 10 10
1087 25d. deep slate-green 10 10
1088 50d. violet and pale brown 20 10
1086/1088 *Set of 3* 35 25

Designs: Vert—25d. Sutjeska Gorge. Horiz—50d. Partisans in battle.

See also No. 1125.

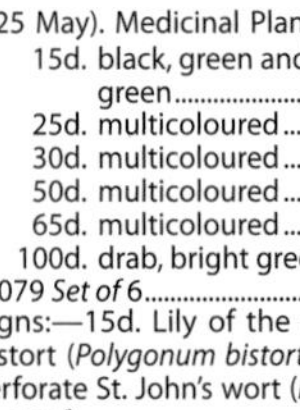

290 Gymnast on "Horse"

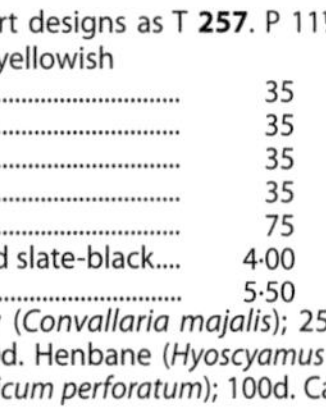

291 "Mother"

(Des N. Masniković. Litho)

1963 (6 July). Fifth European Cup Gymnastic Championships. T **290** and similar vert designs. P 12½.
1089 25d. olive-green and black 60 20
1090 50d. light blue and black .... 1·20 35
1091 100d. olive-brown and black .... 1·70 50
1089/1091 *Set of 3* .... 3·25 95

Designs:—Gymnast: 50d. on parallel bars; 100d. Exercising with rings.

(Des B. Jakac. Eng S. Babić (25d., 65d.), T. Krnjajić (50d.), V. Cvetković (100d.). Recess)

1963 (28 Sept). Sculptures by Ivan Meštrović. T **291** and similar vert designs. P 12½.
1092 25d. bistre-brown/*pale cinnamon* 10 10
1093 50d. deep olive/*pale olive-green* 25 10
1094 65d. black-green/*pale bluish green* 80 30
1095 100d. black/*pale grey* .... 1·20 65
1092/1095 *Set of 4* .... 2·10 1·00

Sculptures:—50d. "Reminiscence" (nude female figure); 65d. "Kraljević Marko" (head); 100d. "Indian on horseback".

292 Children with Toys

293 Soldier and Emblem

(Des B. Lazarević, after drawing by M. Musović. Litho)

1963 (5 Oct). Children's Week. P 12½.
1096 **292** 25d. multicoloured 45 20

(Des and eng T. Krnjajić after drawing by D. Andrejević-Kun. Recess and litho)

1963 (28 Nov). 20th Anniv of Yugoslav Democratic Federation. P 12½.
1097 **293** 25d. red, yellow-olive and pale olive-drab 25 10

(Des D. Kažić (25d., 30d., 65d.), S. Fileki (others). Photo Courvoisier)

1963 (28 Nov). Yugoslav Art. Various designs as T **285** inscr "1963". Multicoloured. P 11½.
1098 25d. "Man", relief on Radimlje tombstone (13th-15th cents) 25 10
1099 30d. Detail of relief on door of Split Cathedral (Andrija Buvina) (13th cent) (horiz) 25 10
1100 50d. Detail of fresco in Beram Church (15th cent) (horiz) 25 10
1101 65d. Archangel Michael, from plaque in Dominican Monastery, Dubrovnik (15th cent) 25 10
1102 100d. Figure of man on Baroque fountain by Francesco Robba, Ljubljana (18th cent) 25 10
1103 150d. Archbishop Eufraise—detail of mosaic in Porec Basilica (6th cent) .... 1·10 70
1098/1103 *Set of 6* .... 2·10 1·10

294 Dositej Obradovic (writer)

295 Parachute

(Des B. Jakac. Eng S. Babić (25d., 30d., 100d.), T. Krnjajić (50d.), V. Cvetković (65d.). Recess)

1963 (10 Dec). Cultural Celebrities. T **294** and similar vert portraits. P 12½.
1104 25d. black/*pale buff* 25 10
1105 30d. black/*pale blue* 25 10
1106 50d. black/*pale cream* 25 10
1107 65d. black/*pale lavender* .... 1·00 10
1108 100d. black/*pale pink* .... 1·30 65
1104/1108 Set o1 5 .... 2·75 95

Portraits:—30d. Vuk Karadžić (language reformer); 50d. Franc Miklošić (philologist); 65d. Ljudevit Gaj (writer); 100d. Petar Njegoš (poet).

See also Nos. 1174/9.

(Des B. Kršić. Litho)

1964 (27 Apr). OBLIGATORY TAX. 20th Anniv of Yugoslav Red Cross and Red Cross Week. P 12½.
1109 **295** 5d. red, crimson and blue 35 20

296 Peacock (*Vanessa io*)

297 Fireman saving Child

(Des B. Spremo and A. Milenković. Photo Courvoisier)

1964 (25 May). Butterflies and Moths. T **296** and similar vert designs. Multicoloured. P 11½.
1110 25d. Type **296** 45 40
1111 30d. Camberwell beauty (*Vanessa antiopa*) 45 40
1112 40d. Oleander hawk moth (*Daphnis nerii*) 45 40
1113 50d. Apollo (*Parnassius apollo*) 45 40
1114 150d. Viennese emperor moth (*Saturnia pyri*) .... 4·75 4·25
1115 200d. Swallowtail (*Papilio machaon*) .... 4·75 4·25
1110/1115 *Set of 6* .... 10·00 9·00

(Des S. Fileki. Litho)

1964 (14 June). Centenary of Voluntary Fire Brigade. P 12½.
1116 **297** 25d. deep sepia and red 25 10

298 Running

299 "Reconstruction"

(Des N. Masniković. Litho)

1964 (1 July). Olympic Games, Tokyo. T **298** and similar horiz designs. P 12½.
1117 25d. greenish yellow, black and grey 35 20
1118 30d. violet, black and grey 35 20
1119 40d. light green, black and grey 35 20
1120 50d. red, pink, black and grey 35 20
1121 150d. yellow-ochre, buff, black & grey .... 5·50 1·20
1122 200d. light blue, black and grey .... 5·50 1·20
1117/1122 *Set of 6* .... 11·00 3·00

Designs:—30d. Boxing; 40d. Rowing; 50d. Basketball; 150d. Football; 200d. Water polo.

(Des B. Kršić. Eng Cvetković (25d.), T. Krnjajić (50d.). Recess)

1964 (26 July). First Anniv of Skopje Earthquake. T **299** and similar vert design. P 12½.
1123 25d. brown 25 10
1124 50d. blue 25 10

Design:—50d. "International Aid" (U.N. flag over town).

1964 (27 July). 20th Anniv of Occupation of Vis Island. As T **289** but inscr "VIS 1944–1964". P 12½.
1125 25d. lake and pale grey 25 10

300 Costumes of Kosovó-Metohija (Serbia)

301 Friedrich Engels

(Des Z. Sertić. Litho)

1964 (5 Aug). Yugoslav Costumes (3rd series). Designs as T **300** inscr with name of province. Multicoloured. P 12½.
1126 25d. Type **300** 60 55
1127 30d. Slovenia 60 55
1128 40d. Bosnia and Herzegovina 60 55
1129 50d. Hrvatska (Croatia) 60 55
1130 150d. Macedonia .... 3·00 2·50
1131 200d. Crna Gora (Montenegro) .... 3·00 2·50
1126/1131 *Set of 6* .... 7·50 6·50

(Des B. Lazarević. Eng T. Krnjajić (25d.), V. Cvetković (50d.). Recess)

1964 (28 Sept). Centenary of "First International". T **301** and similar vert design. P 11½.
1132 25d. black/*pale cream* 25 10
1133 50d. black/*pale lilac* (Karl Marx) 25 10

302 Children on Scooter

303 "Victor" (after Ivan Meštrovic)

(Des B. Lazarević (after A. Smailović). Litho)

1964 (4 Oct). Children's Week. P 12½.
1134 **302** 25d. grey-green, black and red 25 10

(Des B. Lazarević. Eng T. Krnjajić. Recess and litho)

1964 (20 Oct). 20th Anniv of Liberation of Belgrade. P 12×11½.
1135 **303** 25d. black and yellow-olive/*pale pink* 25 10

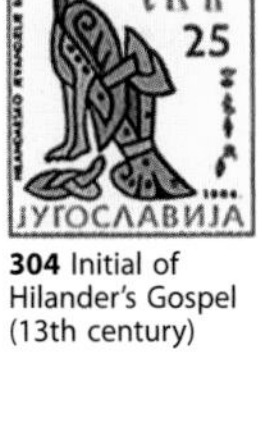

304 Initial of Hilander's Gospel (13th century)

305 "Hand of Equality"

(Des D. Kažić and S. Fileki. Photo)

1964 (29 Nov). Yugoslav Art. T **304** and similar designs inscr "1964". Multicoloured. P 12×11½ (200d.), or 11½×12 (others).

1136 25d. Type **304** 25 10
1137 30d. Initial of Miroslav's gospel (12th cent) 25 10
1138 40d. Detail from Cetinje octateuch (15th cent) 25 10
1139 50d. Miniature from Trogir's gospel (13th cent) 25 10
1140 150d. Miniature from Hrvoe's missal (15th cent) 40 10
1141 200d. Miniature from Herman Priory, Bistrica (14th cent) (horiz) 80 40
1136/1141 *Set of* 6 .... 2·00 80

(Des M. Stančić. Photo)

1964 (7 Dec). 8th Yugoslav Communist League Congress. T **305** and similar vert designs. Multicoloured. P 12.

1142 25d. Type **305** 10 10
1143 50d. Dove and factory ("Peace and Socialism") 25 10
1144 100d. Industrial plant ("Socialism") 45 20
1142/1144 *Set of* 3 .... 70 35

306 Player

307 Children around Red Cross

(Des T. Krnjajić. Litho)

1965 (15 Apr). World Table Tennis Championships, Ljubljana. T **306** and similar vert design. P 12½.

1145 50d. brown, turquoise, grey and red .... 4·75 4·25
1146 150d. violet, blue, grey and red .... 4·75 4·25

Design:—150d. As T **306** but design arranged in reverse.

(Des A. Dimitrijević. Litho)

1965 (20 Apr). OBLIGATORY TAX. Red Cross Week. P 12½.

1147 **307** 5d. red and bistre-brown 25 10

308 Titograd

309 Young Partisan (after D. Andrejević-Kun)

(Des A. Milenković. Eng V. Cvetković (25d., 40d.), S. Babić (30d., 200d.), T. Krnjajić (50d., 100d.). Recess)

1965 (8 May). 20th Anniv of Liberation. Yugoslav Capitals. T **308** and similar vert designs inscr "15.V.1945–1965". P 12½.

1148 25d. reddish purple 25 10
1149 30d. deep red-brown (Skopje) 25 10
1150 40d. blackish violet (Sarajevo) 25 10
1151 50d. blackish green (Ljubljana) 70 65
1152 150d. deep reddish violet (Zagreb) 70 65
1153 200d. indigo (Belgrade) 95 85
1148/1153 *Set of* 6 .... 2·75 2·20

(Des B. Lazarević. Recess and litho)

1965 (10 May). "Twenty Years of Freedom" Pioneer Games. P 12½.

1154 **309** 25d. black and bistre-brown/*pale buff* 25 10

310 T.V. Tower, Avala (Belgrade)

311 Yarrow (*Achillea clypeolata*)

(Des B. Lazarević. Eng V. Cvetković. Recess)

1965 (17 May). I.T.U. Centenary. P 11½.

1155 **310** 50d. indigo 25 10

1965 (20 May). Inauguration of Djerdap Hydro-Electric Project. Nos. 3271/2 and **MS**3273 of Romania.

1156 25d. (30b.) deep green and light grey 25 10
1157 50d. (55b.) lake-red and light grey 60 20
MS1157*a* 103×80 mm. 80b., 1l.20, 100d., 150d. multicoloured (sold at 500d. or 4l.) .... 5·75 5·75

Nos. 1156/7 and the miniature sheet were issued simultaneously in Romania and are listed again here for convenience.

(Des B. Spremo and A. Milenković. Photo Courvoisier)

1965 (25 May). Medicinal Plants. T **311** and similar vert designs. Multicoloured. P 11½.

1158 25d. Type **311** 45 40
1159 30d. Rosemary (*Rosmarinus officinalis*) 45 40
1160 40d. Elecampane (*Inula helenium*) 45 40
1161 50d. Deadly nightshade (*Atropa belladonna*) 45 40
1162 150d. Peppermint (*Mentha piperita*) 45 40
1163 200d. Rusty foxglove (*Digitalis ferriginea*) .... 3·00 2·50
1158/1163 *Set of* 6 .... 4·75 4·00

312 I.C.Y. Emblem

(Des B. Lazarević. Recess and litho)

1965 (26 June). International Co-operation Year. P 12½.

1164 **312** 50d. deep violet-blue, indigo and light blue 25 10

No. 1164 exists in two types of the engraved handclasp and wreath—(a) matt, smooth printing; (b) shiny rough printing on blackish violet-blue (*same prices either type*).

313 Šibenik

314 Cat

(**315**)

(Des D. Gorbunov. Litho)

1965 (6 July). Tourist Publicity (4th series). T **313** and similar vert designs. Multicoloured. P 12½.

1165 25d. Rogaška Slatina 60 50
1166 30d. Type **313** 60 50
1167 40d. Prespa Lake 60 50
1168 50d. Prizren 60 50
1169 150d. Skadar Lake .... 1·70 1·60
1170 200d. Sarajevo .... 3·00 2·50
1165/1170 *Set of* 6 .... 6·50 5·50

(Des B. Lazarević (after D. Grubić). Litho)

1965 (3 Oct). Children's Week. P 12½.

1171 **314** 30d. lake and light yellow 35 10

1965 (Nov). Nos. 984 and 988 surch as T **315**, in red.

1172 5d. on 8d. slate-violet (1.11) 45 10
1173 50d. on 25d. vermilion (12.11) 70 10

(Des B. Jakac. Eng S. Babić (30d., 500d.), T. Krnjajić (60d., 85d.), V. Cvetković (50d., 200d.). Recess)

1965 (28 Nov). Cultural Celebrities. Portraits as T **294** but with dates at top left and right. P 12½.

1174 30d. brown-red/*pale pink* 35 30
1175 50d. slate-blue/*pale blue* 35 30
1176 60d. sepia/*pale yellow-brown* 35 30
1177 85d. indigo/*pale blue* 35 30
1178 200d. blackish olive/*pale yellow-olive* 35 30
1179 500d. maroon/*pale purple* 60 50
1174/1179 *Set of* 6 .... 2·10 1·80

Portraits:—30d. Branislav Nušić (author and dramatist); 50d. Antun Matoš (poet); 60d. Ivan Mažuranić (author); 85d. Fran Levstik (writer); 200d. Josif Pančić (botanist); 500d. Dimitrije Tucović (politician).

Currency Revaluation

100 Paras = 1 (new) Dinar = 100 (old) Dinars

316 Marshal Tito

317 Long Jumping (Balkan Games, Sarajevo)

(Des B. Jakac (after engraving by T. Krnjajić). Litho)

1966 (5 Jan). P 12½.

1180 **316** 20p. blue-green 25 10
1181 30p. carmine 25 10

(Des J. Trpin. Eng S. Babić (30p., 1d.), C. Cvetković (50p., 5d.), T. Krnjajić (3d.). Recess)

1966 (1 Mar). Sports Events. T **317** and similar horiz designs. P 12½.

1182 30p. crimson 25 10
1183 50p. deep reddish violet 25 10
1184 1d. deep bluish green 25 10
1185 3d. lake-brown .... 1·60 1·40
1186 5d. deep blue .... 1·60 1·40
1182/1186 *Set of* 5 .... 3·50 2·75

Designs and events:—50p. Ice hockey and 3d. Ice hockey sticks and puck (World Ice Hockey Championships, Jesenice, Ljubljana and Zagreb); 1d. Rowing and 5d. Oars (World Rowing Championships, Bled).

318 "T", 15th-cent Psalter

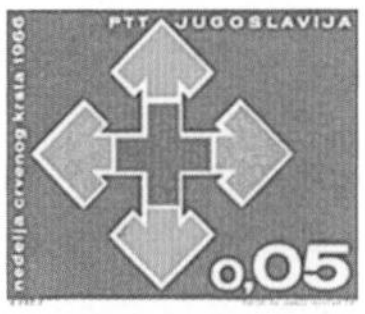

319 Red Cross Emblem

(Des D. Kažić and S. Fileki. Photo Courvoisier)

1966 (25 Apr). Yugoslav Art. T **318** and similar vert designs inscr "1965" and incorporating manuscript initials. Multicoloured. P 12×12½.

1187 30p. Type **318** 10 10
1188 50p. "V", 14th-cent Divos gospel 10 10
1189 60p. "R", 12th-cent Libri moralium of Gregory I 10 10
1190 85p. "P", 12th-cent Miroslav gospel 10 10
1191 2d. "B", 13th-cent Radomir gospel 25 10
1192 5d. "F", 11th-cent passional 60 50
1187/1192 *Set of* 6 .... 1·10 90

(Des B. Kršić. Litho)

1966 (28 Apr–June). OBLIGATORY TAX. Red Cross Week. P 12½.

1193 **319** 5p. multicoloured 25 10

1966 (28 Apr–June). As Nos. 983 etc., but values expressed "0.05" etc., colours changed and new values.

1194 5p. brown-orange (10.6) 40 30
1195 10p. brown (8.6) 40 30
1196 15p. deep violet-blue (10.6) 40 30
1197 20p. bright emerald 65 30
1198 30p. vermilion .... 1·00 30
1199 40p. maroon (8.6) 40 30
1200 50p. blue (8.6) 50 30
1201 60p. lake-brown (12.5) 50 30
1202 65p. bluish green (12.5) 75 30
1203 85p. plum (12.5) .... 1·20 30
1204 1d. yellow-olive (18.6) .... 1·70 30
1194/1204 *Set of* 11 .... 7·00 3·00

New values:—60p. as No. 988; 85p. as No. 984.

320 Beam Aerial on Globe

321 Stag Beetle (*Lucanus cervis*)

(Des B. Lazarević. Eng V. Cvetković. Recess)

1966 (23 May). International Amateur Radio Union Regional Conference, Opatija. P 12½.

1205 **320** 85p. deep ultramarine .... 1·90 85

(Des J. Bernik and S. Fileki. Photo Courvoisier)

1966 (25 May). Insects. T **321** and similar vert designs. Multicoloured. P 12×12½.

1206 30p. Type **321** 35 20
1207 50p. Rose chafer (*Potosia aeruginosa*) 35 20
1208 60p. *Meloe violaceus* (oil beetle) 35 20
1209 85p. Seven-spotted ladybird (*Coccinella septempunctata*) 35 20
1210 2d. Alpine longhorn beetle (*Rosalia alpina*) 35 20
1211 5d. Great diving beetle (*Dytiscus marginalis*) 60 30
1206/1211 *Set of* 6 .... 2·10 1·20

322 Serbian 1 para Stamp of 1866

323 Rebels on Shield

(Des B. Spremo and A. Milenković. Recess and litho)

1966 (25 June). Serbian Stamp Centenary. T **322** and similar vert designs. P 12½.

1212 30p. bronze-green, red-brn and yell-brn. 25 10
1213 50p. red-brown, bistre-brown and yellow-ochre 25 10
1214 60p. orange and olive-green 25 10
1215 85p. red and royal blue 25 10
1216 2d. blue, blackish green and grey-green 60 30
1212/1216 *Set of* 5 .... 1·40 65
MS1217 62½×73½ mm. 10d. multicoloured. Imperf .... 2·30 2·30

Designs: Serbian stamps of 1866—50p.—2p.; 60p.—10p.; 85p.—20p.; 2d.—40p.; 10d.—1p.

(Des S. Fileki, after R. Stojadinović. Recess and litho)

1966 (2 July). 25th Anniv of Yugoslav Insurrection. P 12½.

1218 **323** 20p. red-brown, gold and light grey-green 10 10
1219 30p. magenta, gold and light buff 10 10
1220 85p. greenish blue, gold and light stone 10 10
1221 2d. bluish violet, gold and pale blue 15 15
1218/1221 *Set of* 4 .... 40 40

324 Josip Strossmayer and Franjo Racki (founders)

325 Old Bridge, Mostar

(Des A. Milenković. Eng S. Babić. Recess and litho)

1966 (15 July). Centenary of Yugoslav Academy, Zagreb. P 12½.

1222 **324** 30p. black, stone and drab 25 10

(Des B. Spremo and A. Milenković. Eng S. Babić. Recess)

1966 (24 Sept). 400th Anniv of Old Bridge, Mostar. P 12½.

1223 **325** 30p. claret .... 3·75 1·20

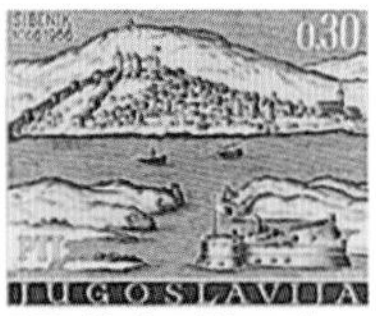

325a Medieval View of Šibenik

326 "The Girl in Pigtails"

(Des B. Lazarević. Eng T. Krnjajić. Recess)

1966 (24 Sept). 900th Anniv of Šibenik. P 12½.

1224 **325a** 30p. maroon 25 10

(Des B. Lazarević, after drawing by S. Skoric. Litho)

1966 (2 Oct). Children's Week. P 12½.

1225 **326** 30p. multicoloured .... 1·80 1·60

327 U.N.E.S.C.O. Emblem

328 Stylized Winter Landscape

(Des A. Milenković. Litho)

1966 (4 Nov). 20th Anniv of United Nations Educational, Scientific and Cultural Organization. P 12½.

1226 **327** 85p. ultramarine 25 10

(Des B. Spremo and A. Milenković. Litho)

1966 (25 Nov). Christmas. T **328** and similar vert designs. P 12½.

1227 15p. yellow and deep blue 45 20
1228 20p. yellow and reddish violet 45 20
1229 30p. yellow and myrtle-green 45 20
1227/1229 *Set of 3* .... 1·20 55

Designs:—20p. Father Christmas; 30p. Stylized Christmas tree.

See also Nos. 1236/8.

329 Dinar of Durad I Balšic

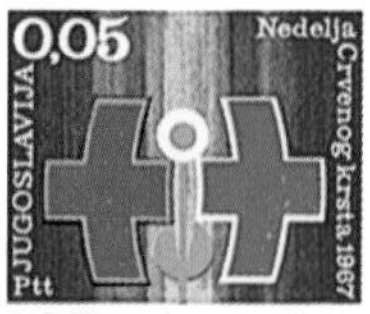

330 Flower between Red Crosses

(Des D. Kažić and S. Fileki. Photo Courvoisier)

1966 (28 Nov). Yugoslav Art. T **329** and similar horiz designs showing coins. Coins bronze-green, silver and black with date, description and "PTT" also in black. Background colours given. P 12½.

1230 30p. red 10 10
1231 50p. bright blue 10 10
1232 60p. reddish purple 10 10
1233 85p. chalky blue 10 10
1234 2d. yellow-bistre 25 10
1235 5d. blue-green 60 20
1230/1235 *Set of 6* .... 1·10 65

Medieval coins: Dinars of—50p. King Stefan Tomaševic; 60p. Djurad Brankovic; 85p. Ljubljana; 2d. Split; 5d. Tsar Stefan Dušan.

1966 (23 Dec). New Year. As Nos. 1227/9 but colours changed and photo.

1236 15p. gold, light blue and deep blue 25 15
1237 20p. gold, scarlet and pink 25 15
1238 30p. gold, myrtle-green and light green.. 25 15
1236/1238 *Set of 3* 70 40

(Des B. Kršić. Litho)

1967 (28 Apr). OBLIGATORY TAX. Red Cross Week. P 12½.

1239 **330** 5p. red, yellow-green and deep violet-blue 25 10

331 Arnica (*Arnica montana*)

332 President Tito

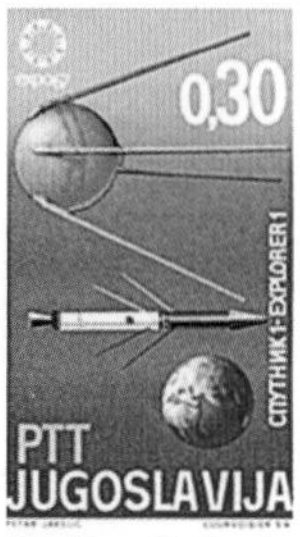

333 "Sputnik 1" and "Explorer 1"

(Des B. Spremo and A. Milenković. Photo Courvoisier)

1967 (25 May). Medicinal Plants. T **331** and similar vert designs. Multicoloured. P 11½.

1240 30p. Type **331** 25 10
1241 50p. Common flax (*Linum usitatissimum*). 25 10
1242 85p. Oleander (*Nerium oleander*) 25 10
1243 1d.20 Gentian (*Gentiana cruciata*) 25 10
1244 3d. Laurel (*Laurus nobilis*) 35 10
1245 5d. African rue (*Peganum harmala*) .... 1·20 85
1240/1245 *Set of 6* .... 2·30 1·20

(Des B. Jakac. Eng V. Cvetković. Recess)

1967 (25 May). President Tito's 75th Birthday. Glazed paper. P 12½.

1246 **332** 5p. orange-red 10 10
1247 10p. purple-brown 10 10
1248 15p. slate-violet 10 10
1249 20p. green 10 10
1250 30p. red 10 10
1251 40p. black 10 10
1252 50p. turquoise 10 10
1253 60p. reddish lilac 15 10
1254 85p. steel-blue 20 10
1255 1d. claret 25 10
1246/1255 *Set of 10* .... 1·20 90

Nos. 1246/55 were each issued in sheets of 15 (5×3) with dates and olive branch at top and bottom.

PHOSPHOR BANDS. These are similar to those used on British issues. On Nos. 1466/83 they are somewhat difficult to see, due to the highly glazed paper, but can be detected by the naked eye when held at a certain angle to the light.

(Des B. Jakac. Eng T. Krnjajić (2d. to 20d.), V. Cvetković (5p. to 1d.50). Recess (coil stamps photo))

1967 (25 May)–**72**. Definitive issue. Plain thinner paper. P 12½.

(a) Size 20×27 mm

1256 **332** 5p. red-orange (1.11.67) 25 10
1257 10p. deep red-brown (16.11.67) 25 10
1258 15p. deep slate-violet (23.11.67) 25 10
a. Two phosphor bands (25.10.71) 70 50
1259 20p. deep green (18.7.67) 25 10
a. Coil. P 12½×imperf (glazed paper) (15.2.68) 35 10
1260 20p. deep ultramarine (10.7.68) .... 1·70 10
1261 25p. claret (10.9.68) 25 10
1262 30p. vermilion (25.5.67) 60 10
a. Coil. P 12½×imperf (glazed paper) (15.2.68) 35 10
1263 30p. myrtle-green (10.7.68) 35 10
1264 40p. black (22.8.67) 20 10
1265 50p. deep turquoise (7.6.67) .... 2·30 10
1266 50p. vermilion (10.7.68) .... 1·20 10
a. Coil. P 12½×imperf (glazed paper) (15.8.69) 35 10
1267 60p. plum (1.9.67) 20 10
1268 70p. blackish brown (10.9.68) 45 10
1269 75p. slate-green (10.7.68) 60 10
1270 80p. olive-brown (10.9.68) .... 3·00 10
1270*a* 80p. vermilion (18.9.72) 60 10
1271 85p. deep steel-blue (15.7.67) 35 10
1272 90p. olive-brown (16.10.67) 35 10
1273 1d. brown-lake (5.10.67) 25 10
1274 1d.20 deep chalky blue (17.1.68) 70 10
1274*a* 1d.20 slate-green (18.9.72) 70 10
1275 1d.25 blue (10.7.68) 45 10
1276 1d.50 slate-green (17.1.68) 60 10

(b) Size 20×30 mm.

1277 **332** 2d. sepia (4.3.68) .... 3·00 10
1278 2d.50 deep bluish green (10.9.68) .... 1·70 10
1279 5d. purple (4.3.68) .... 1·20 20
1280 10d. slate-purple (4.3.68) .... 3·00 50
1281 20d. blackish green (10.6.68) .... 2·75 30
1256/281 *Set of 28* (*cheapest*) .... 24·00 3·25

Nos. 1256/76 were issued in full sheets of 100.

Apart from the deeper shades the reissue can easily be distinguished by the portrait which is clearly visible from the back of the stamp.

(Des P. Jakelić. Photo Courvoisier)

1967 (26 June). World Fair, Montreal. Space Achievements. T **333** and similar vert designs. Multicoloured. P 11½.

1282 30p. Type **333** 10 10
1283 50p. "Tiros", "Telstar" and "Molnya" 10 10
1284 85p. "Luna 9" and lunar orbiter 10 10
1285 1d.20 "Mariner 4" and "Venus 3" 10 10
1286 3d. "Vostok 1" and Gemini-Agena space vehicle 45 20
1287 5d. Leonov in space .... 4·00 3·75
1282/1287 *Set of 6* .... 4·25 4·00

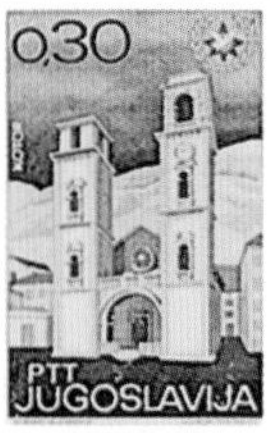

334 St. Tripun's Church, Kotor

335 Bobwhite (*Perdix perdix*)

(Des B. Spremo and A. Milenković. Eng V. Cvetković (30p., 5d.), S. Babić (50p., 3d.), T. Krnjajić (85p., 1d.20). Recess)

1967 (17 July). International Tourist Year. T **334** and similar vert designs. P 12×11½.

1288 30p. yellow-olive and slate-blue 10 10
1289 50p. deep reddish violet and light brown 10 10
1290 85p. reddish purple and deep blue 10 10
1291 1d.20 yellow-brown and maroon 20 10
1292 3d. blackish olive and red-brown 25 10
1293 5d. light brown and olive-brown .... 2·50 50
1288/1293 *Set of 6* .... 3·00 90

Designs:—50p. Town Hall, Maribor; 85p. Trogir Cathedral; 1d.20, Fortress gate, Niš; 3d. Bridge, Višegrad; 5d. Ancient bath, Skopje.

(Des B. Spremo and A. Milenković. Photo German Bank Note Ptg Co., Leipzig)

1967 (22 Sept). International Hunting and Fishing Exhibition and Fair, Novi Sad. T **335** and similar vert designs. Multicoloured. P 13½×14.

1294 30p. Type **335** 50 30
1295 50p. Northern pike (*Esox lucius*) 50 30
1296 1d.20 Red deer stag (*Cervus elaphus*) 70 45
1297 5d. Peregrine falcon (*Falco peregrinus*).... 2·00 1·20
1294/1297 *Set of 4* .... 3·25 2·00

336 Congress Emblem

337 Old Theatre Building

(Des A. Milenković. Recess and litho)

1967 (25 Sept). International Astronautical Federation Congress, Belgrade. P 12½.

1298 **336** 85p. gold, light blue and deep blue.. 25 10

(Des B. Spremo and A. Milenković. Eng V. Cvetković. Recess)

1967 (29 Sept). Centenary of Slovene National Theatre, Ljubljana. P 12½.

1299 **337** 30p. blackish brown and blackish green 25 10

338 "Winter Landscape" (A. Becirovic)

339 "Lenin" (from bust by Ivan Meštrovic)

(Des A. Milenković (after child's prize-winning drawing). Litho)

1967 (2 Oct). Children's Week. P 12½.

1300 **338** 30p. multicoloured 70 10

(Des B. Jakac. Eng S. Babić. Recess)

1967 (7 Nov). 50th Anniv of October Revolution. P 12½.

1301 **339** 30p. blackish violet 10 10
1302 85p. deep olive-brown 25 10
MS1303 58×77 mm. **339** 10d. lake. Imperf .... 9·50 9·50

340 Four-leaved Clover

342 Ski Jumping

341 "The Young Sultana" (Vlaho Bukovac)

(Des B. Spremo and A. Milenković. Photo German Bank Note Ptg Co., Leipzig)

1967 (15 Nov). New Year. T **340** and similar vert designs, inscribed "1968". P 14.

1304 20p. gold, blue and bright green 10 10
1305 30p. gold, violet and yellow 10 10
1306 50p. gold, carmine-red and lilac 10 10
1304/1306 *Set of 3* 25 25

Designs:—30p. Sweep with ladder; 50p. Horseshoe and flower.
See also Nos. 1347/9.

(Des A. Milenković. Eng S. Babić (85p., 2d.), T. Krnjajić (1d.), V. Cvetković (3d., 5d.). (Recess and litho)

1967 (28 Nov). Yugoslav Paintings. T **341** and similar designs. Multicoloured. P 11½.

1307 85p. "The Watchtower" (Djura Jakšić) (vert) 1·90 40
1308 1d. Type **341** 1·90 40
1309 2d. "At Home" (Josip Petkovšek) 1·90 40
1310 3d. "The Cock-fight" (Paja Jovanović) 1·90 40
1311 5d. "Summer" (Ivana Kobilca) (vert) 6·50 3·00
1307/1311 *Set of 5* 12·50 4·25

See also Nos. 1337/41.

(Des M. Rodiči. Recess)

1968 (5 Feb). Winter Olympic Games, Grenoble. T **342** and similar vert designs. P 12½.

1312 50p. deep plum and indigo 45 15
1313 1d. blackish olive and brown 45 15
1314 2d. lake and black 95 45
1315 5d. deep blue and blackish olive 6·50 2·75
1312/1315 *Set of 4* 7·50 3·25

Designs:—1d. Figure skating (pairs); 2d. Downhill skiing; 5d. Ice hockey.

343 "The Madonna and Child" (St. George's Church, Prizren)

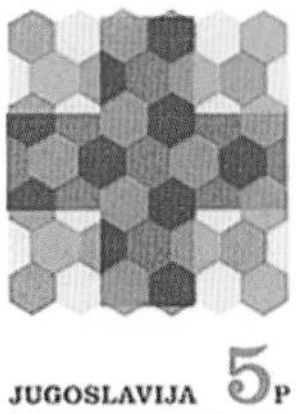

344 Honeycomb on Red Cross

(Des A. Milenković. Photo State Ptg Wks, Vienna)

1968 (20 Apr). Medieval Icons. T **343** and similar vert designs. Multicoloured. P 13½.

1316 50p. Type **343** 10 10
1317 1d. "The Annunciation" (Ohrid Museum) 15 10
1318 1d.50 "St. Sava and St. Simeon" (Belgrade Museum) 20 10
1319 2d. "The Descent" (Ohrid Museum) 30 15
1320 3d. "The Crucifixion" (St. Clement's Church, Ohrid) 45 40
1321 5d. "The Madonna and Child" (Gospe od zvonika Church, Split) 75 60
1316/1321 *Set of 6* 1·80 1·30

(Des B. Kršić. Litho)

1968 (30 Apr). OBLIGATORY TAX. Red Cross Week. P 12.

1322 **344** 5p. multicoloured 25 10

345 Bullfinch (*Pyrrhula pyrrhula*)

346 Running (Women's 800 Metres)

(Des B. Spremo and A. Milenković. Photo Courvoisier)

1968 (25 May). Song Birds. T **345** and similar vert designs. Multicoloured. P 11½.

1323 50p. Type **345** 45 40
1324 1d. Goldfinch (*Carduelis carduelis*) 45 40
1325 1d.50 Chaffinch (*Fringilla coelebs*) 45 40
1326 2d. Greenfinch (*Chloris chloris*) 45 40
1327 3d. Red crossbill (*Loxia curvirostra*) 45 40
1328 5d. Hawfinch (*Coccothraustes coccothraustes*) 5·50 3·00
1323/1328 *Set of 6* 7·00 4·50

(Des M. Rodiči. Eng V. Cvetković (50p., 1d., 3d.), T. Krnjajić (others). Recess and litho)

1968 (28 June). Olympic Games, Mexico. T **346** and similar vert designs. P 12½.

1329 50p. deep maroon and olive-brown/*pale cream* 45 40
1330 1d. blackish olive & turq-bl/*pale grn* 45 40
1331 1d.50 sepia and steel-blue/*pale flesh* 45 40
1332 2d. slate-green and bistre-brown/*pale cream* 1·90 40
1333 3d. indigo and deep violet/*pale blue* 1·90 40
1334 5d. deep slate-purple and blackish green/*pale mauve* 21·00 5·00
1329/1334 *Set of 6* 24·00 6·25

Designs:—1d. Basketball; 1d.50, Gymnastics; 2d. Sculling; 3d. Water polo; 5d. Wrestling.

347 Rebel Cannon

348 "Mother and Children" (fresco in Hrastovlje Church, Slovenia)

(Des A. Milenković. Photo)

1968 (2 Aug). 65th Anniv of Ilinden Uprising. P 12½.

1335 **347** 50p. chestnut and gold 25 10

(Des A. Milenković. Litho)

1968 (9 Sept). 25th Anniv of Partisan Occupation of Istria and Slovenian Littoral. P 12½.

1336 **348** 50p. multicoloured 25 10

349 "Lake of Klanško" (Marko Pernhart)

(Des A. Milenković. Recess and photo Austrian State Ptg Wks, Vienna)

1968 (3 Oct). Yugoslav Paintings. 19th-century Landscapes. T **349** and similar horiz designs. Multicoloured. P 14×13½.

1337 1d. Type **349** 20 10
1338 1d.50 "Bavarian Landscape" (Milan Popovic) 20 10
1339 2d. "Gateway, Zadar" (Ferdo Quiquerez) 20 10
1340 3d. "Triglav from Bohinj" (Anton Karinger) 35 25
1341 5d. "Studenica Monastery" (Djordje Krstic) 2·00 80
1337/1341 *Set of 5* 2·75 1·20

350 A. Šantić

351 "Promenade" (Marina Čudov)

(Des A. Milenković. Eng V. Cvetković. Recess)

1968 (5 Oct). Birth Centenary of Aleksa Šantić (poet). P 12½.

1342 **350** 50p. deep blue 25 10

(Des A. Milenković (after child's prize-winning sketch). Litho)

1968 (6 Oct). Children's Week. P 12½.

1343 **351** 50p. multicoloured 25 10

352 Karl Marx (after sculpture by N. Mitric)

353 Aztec Emblem and Olympic Rings

(Des A. Milenković. Eng T. Krnjajić. Recess)

1968 (11 Oct). 150th Birth Anniv of Karl Marx. P 12½.

1344 **352** 50p. brown-lake 25 10

(Des A. Milenković. Litho)

1968 (12 Oct). OBLIGATORY TAX. Olympic Games Fund. P 12½.

1345 **353** 10p. multicoloured 25 10

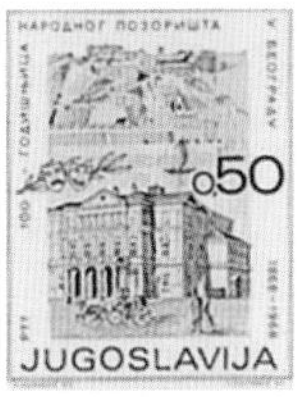

354 Old Theatre and View of Kalemegdan

355 Hasan Brkic

(Des A. Milenković. Eng V. Cvetković. Recess)

1968 (22 Nov). Centenary of Serbian National Theatre, Belgrade. P 12½.

1346 **354** 50p. bistre-brown and deep bluish green 25 10

(Des B. Spremo and A. Milenković. Photo German Banknote Ptg Co., Leipzig)

1968 (25 Nov). New Year. Designs as Nos. 1304/6, but colours changed and inscribed "1969". P 14.

1347 20p. gold, new blue and lilac 35 15
1348 30p. gold, violet and green 35 15
1349 50p. gold, cerise and lemon 35 15
1347/1349 *Set of 3* 95 40

(Des B. Jakac. Eng V. Cvetković (50p., 2d.50), T. Krnjajić (75p., 1d. 25), D. Andrić (2d., 5d.). Recess)

1968 (28 Nov). Yugoslav National Heroes. T **355** and similar vert portraits. P 12½.

1350 50p. blackish violet 20 10
1351 75p. black 20 10
1352 1d.25 red-brown 20 10
1353 2d. indigo 20 10
1354 2d.50 blackish green 30 15
1355 5d. brown-lake 1·40 80
1350/1355 *Set of 6* 2·20 1·20
MS1356 Two sheets each 156×108 mm. (a) 2× Nos. 1350/2 (b) 2×1353/5. Pair 28·00 28·00

Portraits:—75p. Ivan Milutinovic; 1d.25, Rade Koncar; 2d. Kuzman Josifovski; 2d.50, Tone Tomšic; 5d. Moša Pijade.

356 "Family" (sculpture by J. Soldatovic) and Human Rights Emblem

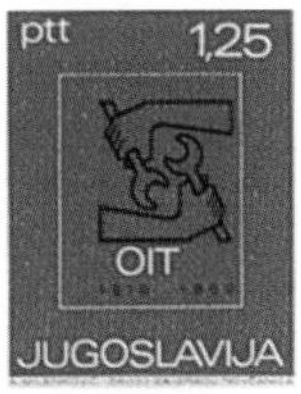

357 I.L.O. Emblem

(Des A. Milenković. Eng V. Cvetković. Recess)

1968 (10 Dec). Human Rights Year. P 12½.

1357 **356** 1d.25 deep blue 30 15

(Des A. Milenković. Recess and litho)

1969 (27 Jan). 50th Anniv of International Labour Organization. P 12½.

1358 **357** 1d.25 black and red 30 15

358 Dove on Hammer and Sickle Emblem

359 "St. Nikita" (Manasija Monastery)

(Des A. Milenković. Eng B. Andrić (50p.), T. Krnjajić (75p.), V. Cvetković (1d. 25). Recess (10d.) or recess and litho)

1969 (11 Mar). 50th Anniv of Yugoslav Communist Party. T **358** and similar vert designs. P 12½.

1359 50p. red and black 10 10
1360 75p. black and light ochre 10 10
1361 1d.25 black and red 15 10
1359/1361 *Set of 3* 30 25
MS1362 118×140 mm. Nos. 1359 (4), 1360 (2), 1361 (2) and 10d. chocolate 7·50 7·50

Designs:—75p. "Tito" and star (wall graffiti); 1d.25, Five-pointed crystal formation; 10d. President Tito.

(Des A. Milenković. Photo State Ptg Wks, Vienna)

1969 (7 Apr). Medieval Frescoes in Yugoslav Monasteries. T **359** and similar vert designs. Multicoloured. P 13½.

1363 50p. Type **359** 20 10
1364 75p. "Jesus and the Apostles" (Sopocani) 20 10
1365 1d.25 "The Crucifixion" (Studenica) 20 10
1366 2d. "Cana Wedding Feast" (Kalenic) 20 10
1367 3d. "Angel guarding Tomb" (Mileševa) 35 10
1368 5d. "Mourning over Christ" (Nerezi) 2·75 70
1363/1368 *Set of 6* 3·50 1·10

360 Roman Memorial and View of Ptuj

361 Vasil Glavinov

(Des B. Jakac. Eng D. Andrić. Recess)

1969 (23 Apr). 1900th Anniversary of Ptuj (Poetovio) (Slovene town). P 11½.

1369 **360** 50p. purple-brown 20 10

(Des A. Milenković. Eng V. Cvetković. Recess)

1969 (8 May). Birth Centenary of Vasil Glavinov (Macedonian revolutionary). P 12½.

1370 **361** 50p. reddish purple and lake-brown 20 10

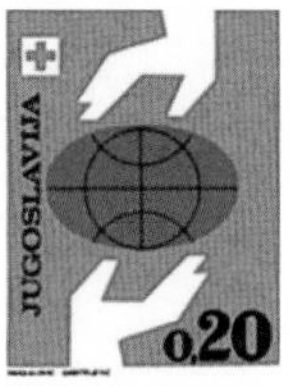

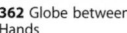

362 Globe between Hands

363 Thin-leafed Peony (*Paeonia tenuifolia*)

(Des A. Daskalović and A. Dimitrijević. Litho State Ptg Wks, Budapest)

1969 (18 May). OBLIGATORY TAX. Red Cross Week. P 12.
1371 **362** 20p. black, carmine and orange-red. 20 10

(Des B. Spremo and A. Milenković. Photo Courvoisier)

1969 (25 May). Flowers. T **363** and similar vert designs. Multicoloured. P 11½.
1372 50p. Type **363** 20 10
1373 75p. Coltsfoot (*Tussilago farfara*) 20 10
1374 1d.25 Primrose (*Primula acaulis*) 20 10
1375 2d. Hellebore (*Helleborus odorus*) 20 10
1376 2d.50 Sweet violet (*Viola odorata*) 20 10
1377 5d. Pasque flower (*Anemone pulsatilla*) 3·25 3·25
1372/1377 *Set of 6* 3·75 3·50

364 "Eber" (V. Ivankovic)

(Des A. Milenković. Photo Courvoisier)

1969 (10 July). Dubrovnik Summer Festival. Sailing Ships. T **364** and similar horiz designs. Multicoloured. P 11½.
1378 50p. Type **364** 20 10
1379 1d.25 "Tare in Storm" (Franasovic) 20 10
1380 1d.50 "Brigantine Sela" (V. Ivankovic) 25 10
1381 2d.50 "16th-Century Dubrovnik Galleon" 35 20
1382 3d.25 "Frigate Madre Mimbelli" (A. Roux) 60 35
1383 5d. "Shipwreck" (16th-century icon) 1·40 1·10
1378/1383 *Set of 6* 2·75 1·80

365 Games' Emblem

366 Bosnian Mountain Horse

(Des A. Milenković. Eng V. Cvetković. Recess)

1969 (9 Aug). 9th World Deaf and Dumb Games, Belgrade. P 12½.
1384 **365** 1d.25 deep slate-lilac and lake 20 10

(Des A. Milenković. Photo Courvoisier)

1969 (26 Sept). 50th Anniversary of Veterinary Faculty, Zagreb. T **366** and similar horiz designs, showing horses. Multicoloured. P 11½.
1385 75p. Type **366** 30 15
1386 1d.25 Lipizzaner 30 15
1387 3d.25 Ljutomer trotter 35 15
1388 5d. Yugoslav half-breed 3·75 1·00
1385/1388 *Set of 4* 4·25 1·30

367 Children and Chicks

368 Arms of Belgrade

(Des A. Milenković from drawing by schoolgirl, Tanje Vucajnik. Litho)

1969 (5 Oct). Children's Week. P 12½.
1389 **367** 50p. multicoloured 20 10

(Des A. Milenković. Litho or litho and embossed (**MS**1396))

1969–70. 25th Anniversary of Yugoslav Liberation. T **368** and similar vert designs, showing Arms of Regional Capitals. Multicoloured. P 12½.
1390 50p. Type **368** (20.10.69) 20 10
1391 50p. Skopje (13.11.69) 20 10
1392 50p. Titograd (Podgorica) (19.12.69) 20 10
1393 50p. Sarajevo (6.4.70) 20 10
1394 50p. Zagreb (8.5.70) 20 10
1395 50p. Ljubljana (9.5.70) 20 10
1390/1395 *Set of 6* 1·10 55
MS1396 89×106 mm. Nos. 1390/5 and 12d. gold, red and black (Yugoslav Arms) with two stamp-size labels. Size of individual designs reduced to 21½×27½ mm. (15.5.70) 16·00 16·00

369 Dr. Josip Smodlaka

370 Torch, Globe and Olympic Rings

(Des A. Milenković. Eng D. Andrić. Recess)

1969 (9 Nov). Birth Centenary of Dr. Josip Smodlaka (politician). P 12½.
1397 **369** 50p. deep blue 20 10

(Des A. Milenković. Litho Italian Institute of Graphic Art, Bergamo)

1969 (24 Nov). OBLIGATORY TAX. Olympic Games Fund. P 11.
1398 **370** 10p. multicoloured 45 15
a. Imperf between (horiz pair)

371 "Gipsy Girl" (Nikola Martinoski)

372 University Building

(Des A. Milenković. Recess and photo Austrian State Ptg Wks, Vienna)

1969 (28 Nov). Yugoslav Nude Paintings. T **371** and similar multicoloured designs. P 13½.
1399 50p. Type **371** 20 10
1400 1d.25 "Girl in Red Armchair" (Sava Šumanovic) 20 10
1401 1d.50 "Girl Brushing Hair" (Marin Tartaglia) 20 10
1402 2d.50 "Olympia" (Miroslav Kraljevic) (horiz) 45 30
1403 3d.25 "The Bather" (Jovan Bijelic) 75 40
1404 5d. "Woman on a Couch" (Matej Sternen) (horiz) 1·90 1·50
1399/1404 *Set of 6* 3·25 2·30

(Des B. Jakac. Eng D. Andrić. Recess)

1969 (9 Dec). 50th Anniversary of Ljubljana University. P 11½.
1405 **372** 50p. blackish green 20 10

373 University Seal

374 Colonnade

(Des A. Milenković. Recess and liiho)

1969 (17 Dec). 300th Anniversary of Zagreb University. P 12½.
1406 **373** 50p. gold, maroon and blue 20 10

(Des L. Gasbarra, G. Belli and A. Milenković. Photo Courvoisier)

1969 (20 Dec). Europa. P 11½.
1407 **374** 1d.25 red-brown, yellow-brown and grey-green 1·60 1·60
1408 3d.25 blue, grey and bright purple 6·25 6·25

375 Jovan Cvijic (geographer)

376 "Punishment of Dirka" (4th-cent mosaic)

(Des A. Milenković. Eng D. Andrić (50p., 1d.50, 2d.50), V. Cvetković (others). Recess)

1970 (16 Feb). Famous Yugoslavs. T **375** and similar vert portraits. P 12½.
1409 50p. brown-purple 10 10
1410 1d.25 black 10 10
1411 1d.50 purple 15 10
1412 2d.50 blackish olive 15 10
1413 3d.25 purple-brown 25 10
1414 5d. deep ultramarine 30 25
1409/1414 *Set of 6* 95 70
Designs:—1d.25, Dr. Andrija Štampar (hygienist); 1d.50, Joakim Krcovski (author); 2d.50, Marko Miljanov (soldier); 3d.25, Vasa Pelagic (socialist revolutionary); 5d. Oton Župancic (poet).

(Des A. Milenković. Photo Austrian State Ptg Wks, Vienna)

1970 (16 Mar). Mosaics. T **376** and similar multicoloured designs. P 13½.
1415 50p. Type **376** 30 15
1416 1d.25 "Cerberus" (5th-cent) (horiz) 30 15
1417 1d.50 "Angel of Annunciation" (6th-cent) 30 15
1418 2d.50 "Hunters" (4th-cent) 30 15
1419 3d.25 "Bull beside Cherries" (5th- cent) (horiz) 60 15
1420 5d. "Virgin and Child Enthroned" (6th-cent) 1·60 1·20
1415/1420 *Set of 6* 3·00 1·80

377 Lenin (after sculpture by S. Stojanović)

378 Trying for Goal

(Des A. Milenković. Eng D. Andrić (50p.), V. Cvetković (1d.25). Recess)

1970 (22 Apr). Birth Centenary of Lenin. T **377** and similar vert design. P 12½.
1421 50p. brown-lake 20 10
1422 1d.25 slate-blue 20 10
Design:—1d.25, Same sculpture, seen from right.

(Des A. Milenković. Eng V. Cvetković. Recess)

1970 (25 Apr). 6th World Basketball Championships. P 12½.
1423 **378** 1d.25 crimson 20 10

379 Red Cross Trefoil

380 "Flaming Sun"

(Des A. Milenković. Litho German Bank Note Ptg Co, Leipzig)

1970 (27 Apr). OBLIGATORY TAX. Red Cross Week. P 13.
1424 **379** 20p. multicoloured 20 10

(Des L. le Brocquy and A. Milenković. Photo Courvoisier)

1970 (4 May). Europa. P 11½.
1425 **380** 1d.25 deep blue, pale turquoise and greenish blue 20 10
1426 3d.25 deep brown, pale violet and bright purple 50 40

381 Istrian Short-haired Hound

382 Olympic Flag

(Des A. Milenković. Photo Courvoisier)

1970 (25 May). Yugoslav Dogs. T **381** and similar horiz designs. Multicoloured. P 11½.
1427 50p. Type **381** 10 10
1428 1d.25 Yugoslav tricolour hound 10 10
1429 1d.50 Istrian hard-haired hound 10 10
1430 2d.50 Balkan hound 10 10
1431 3d.25 Dalmatian 10 10
1432 5d. Shara mountain dog 3·00 2·30
1427/1432 *Set of 6* 3·25 2·50

(Des A. Milenković. Litho German Bank Note Ptg Co, Leipzig)

1970 (10 June). OBLIGATORY TAX. Olympic Games Fund. P 13.
1433 **382** 10p. multicoloured 20 10

383 Telegraph Key

384 "Bird in Meadow" (Lidija Dobronjovska)

(Des A. Milenković. Litho)

1970 (20 June). Centenary of Montenegro Telegraph Service. P 12½.
1434 **383** 50p. gold, black and lake-brown 20 10

(Des A. Milenković. Litho)

1970 (5 Oct). Children's Week. P 12½.
1435 **384** 50p. multicoloured 20 10

385 "Gymnast" (Championships emblem)

386 "Hand Holding Dove" (Makoto)

(Des A. Milenković after emblem by F. Popek. Recess)

1970 (22 Oct). 17th World Gymnastics Championships, Ljubljana. P 12½.
1436 **385** 1d.25 deep blue and bright purple...... 20 10

(Des A. Milenković. Eng V. Cvetković. Recess and litho)

1970 (24 Oct). 25th Anniversary of United Nations. P 11½.
1437 **386** 1d.25 multicoloured.................................. 20 10

387 "The Ascension" (Teodor Kracun)

388 Rusty-leaved Alpenrose

(Des A. Milenković. Recess and photo Austrian State Ptg Wks, Vienna)

1970 (28 Nov). Yugoslav Paintings. Baroque Period. T **387** and similar vert designs. Multicoloured. P 13½.
1438 50p. Type **387**.. 20 10
1439 75p. "Abraham's Sacrifice" (Federiko Benkovic)... 20 10
1440 1d.25 "The Holy Family" (Francišek Jelovšek)... 20 10
1441 2d.50 "Jacob's Dream" (Hristofor Žefarovic) 20 10
1442 3d.25 "Baptism of Christ" (Serbian village artist).. 30 10
1443 5d.75 "Coronation of the Virgin" (Tripo Kokolja).. 80 60
1438/1443 *Set of* 6.. 1·70 1·00

(Des A. Milenković. Photo Courvoisier)

1970 (14 Dec). Nature Conservation Year. T **388** and similar horiz design. Multicoloured. P 11½.
1444 1d.25 Type **388**.. 1·70 1·20
1445 3d.25 Larnmergeier (*Gypaëtus barbatus*).... 16·00 7·75

389 Frano Supilo

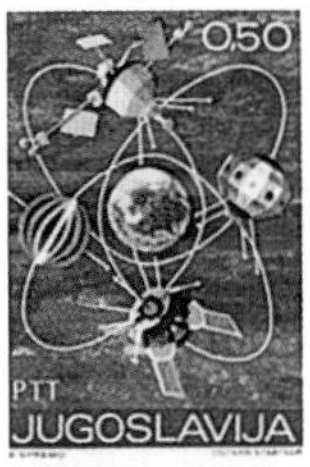

390 Different Nations' Satellites ("International Co-operation")

(Des A. Milenković. Eng D. Andrić. Recess and litho)

1971 (25 Jan). Birth Centenary of Frano Supilo (politician). P 12½.
1446 **389** 50p. sepia and pale buff 20 10

(Des B. Spremo. Photo Austrian State Ptg Wks, Vienna)

1971 (8 Feb). Space Exploration. T **390** and similar multicoloured designs. P 13½.
1447 50p. Type **390**.. 20 10
1448 75p. Telecommunications satellite............ 20 10
1449 1d.25 Unmanned Moon flights 20 10
1450 2d.50 Exploration of Mars and Venus (horiz).. 55 25
1451 3d.25 Space-station (horiz) 70 50
1452 5d.75 Astronauts on the Moon (horiz)......... 1·70 1·30
1447/1452 *Set of* 6.. 3·25 2·10

391 "Proclamation of the Commune" (A. Daudenarde after A. Lamy)

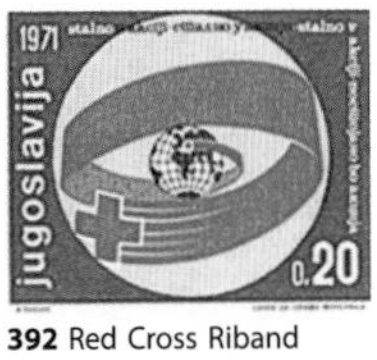

392 Red Cross Riband

(Des A. Milenković. Eng D. Andrić. Recess and litho)

1971 (18 Mar). Centenary of the Paris Commune. P 11½.
1453 **391** 1d.25 sepia and orange-brown............ 20 10

(Des A. Svedica. Litho)

1971 (26 Apr). OBLIGATORY TAX. Red Cross Week. P 12½.
1454 **392** 20p. multicoloured................................... 20 10

393 Europa Chain

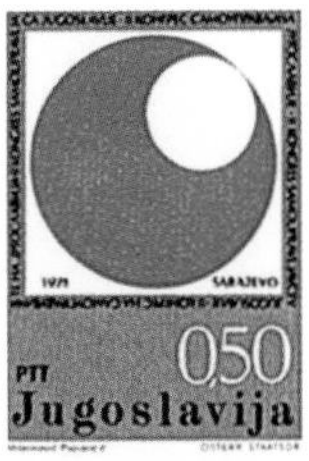

394 Congress Emblem (A. Pajvancic)

(Des H. Haffdason, adapted A. Milenković. Photo Courvoisier)

1971 (4 May). Europa. P 11½.
1455 **393** 1d.50 multicoloured................................ 20 15
1456 4d. pale salmon, deep purple and bright purple.................................... 65 55

(Des A. Milenković. Photo Austrian State Ptg Wks, Vienna)

1971 (5 May). 20th Anniversary of Yugoslav "Self-Managers" Movement (50p.), and Second Congress (1d.25). T **394** and similar vert design. P 13½.
1457 50p. red, black and gold 75 55
1458 1d.25 red, black and gold.................................. 1·90 1·40
Design:—1d.25, "Self-Managers" emblem (designed by M. Miodragovic).

395 Common Mallow (*Malva silvestris*)

396 Olympic "Spiral" and Rings

397 Krk, Dalmatia

(Des A. Milenković. Photo Courvoisier)

1971 (25 May). Flowers. T **395** and similar vert designs. Multicoloured. P 11½.
1459 50p. Type **395**.. 30 15
1460 1d.50 Buckthorn (*Rhamnus catharica*) 30 15
1461 2d. White water-lily (*Nymphaea alba*) 30 15
1462 2d.50 Common poppy (*Papaver rhoeas*)..... 40 15
1463 4d. Chicory (*Cichorium intybus*) 85 60
1464 6d. Chinese lantern (*Physalis alkekengi*).. 4·50 3·25
1459/1464 *Set of* 6.. 6·00 4·00

(Des A. Milenković. Litho)

1971 (15 June). OBLIGATORY TAX. Olympic Games Fund. P 12½.
1465 **396** 10p. black, purple and greenish blue.. 20 10

(Des A. Milenković. Eng V. Cvetković (5, 35, 50, 60p., 1d.20), Andrić (10p.), A. D. (20, 30, 75p.), D. Matić (40p., 1d., 1d.20 to 2d.50). Recess)

1971 (21 June)–**73**. T **397** and similar vert views. With imprint at foot. Glazed, chalk-surfaced paper (C) or ordinary paper (O). P 13½.
1466 5p. red-orange (25.4.73) (O)........................ 20 10
1467 10p. reddish-brown (25.1.72) (C)................ 20 10
ao. Ordinary paper.. 20 10
1468 20p. blackish lilac (25.12.72) (O)................ 20 10
1469 30p. myrtle-green (C) 60 10
ao. Ordinary paper.. 2·00 40
1470 30p. olive-brown (1.11.72) (O)..................... 20 10
1471 35p. brown-red (15.5.73) (O)........................ 20 10
1472 40p. blackish olive (1.11.72) (O) 20 10
1473 50p. vermilion (C)... 1·00 15
1474 50p. deep green (8.7.72) (O)......................... 20 10
1475 60p. plum (13.11.72) (O) 20 10
1476 75p. blackish green (C).................................. 50 10
1477 80p. vermilion (18.10.72) (O)....................... 1·20 15
1478 1d. crimson (6.7.71) (C)................................ 2·50 30
ao. Ordinary paper.. 1·50 25
1479 1d.20 slate-green (18.10.72) (O)................... 1·50 15
1480 1d.25 steel-blue (3.10.71) (C)........................ 70 15
1481 1d.50 deep violet-blue (25.12.72) (O)........... 30 10
1482 2d. greenish blue (12.7.72) (O)................... 65 10
1483 2d.50 slate-violet (26.3.73) (O)...................... 65 10
1466/1483 *Set of* 18 (*cheapest*).. 9·25 1·90
Designs:—5p. Kruševo, Macedonia; 10p. Gradacac; 20p., 75p. Bohinj, Slovenia; 35p. Omiš, Dalmatia; 40p. Pec; 50p. Kruševac, Serbia; 60p. Logarska valley; 80p. Piran; 1d. Bitola, Macedonia; 1d.20, Pocitelj; 1d.25, 1d.50, Herceg Novi; 2d. Novi Sad; 2d.50, Rijeka Crnojevica, Montenegro.
Issues on chalk-surfaced paper have matt, almost invisible, gum; those on ordinary paper have either shiny or matt gum, some values existing with both.
Except for No. 1469ao, which has no bands, all the above exist with or without phosphor bands, similar to those used on British issues. They are very difficult to detect with the naked eye and for this reason are not listed.
For designs as above but printed in litho, see Nos. 1641/75.

398 "Prince Lazar Hrebeljanovic" (from fresco, Lazarica Church)

399 "Satyr"

(Des A. Milenković. Photo Austrian State Ptg Wks, Vienna)

1971 (28 June). 600th Anniversary of City of Kruševac. P 13½.
1487 **398** 50p. multicoloured.................................. 20 10

(Des A. Milenković. Photo Austrian State Ptg Wks, Vienna)

1971 (20 Sept). Archaeological Discoveries. T **399** and similar vert designs, showing bronze objects. Multicoloured. P 13½.
1488 50p. Head of Emperor Constantine........... 10 10
1489 1d.50 "Boy with Fish" (statuette) 10 10
1490 2d. "Hercules" (statuette) 10 10
1491 2d.50 Type **399**... 10 10
1492 4d. "Goddess Aphrodite" (head)................ 30 15
1493 6d. "Citizen of Emona" (statue).................. 65 45
1488/1493 *Set of* 6.. 1·20 90

400 Children in Balloon

401 "Old Man at Ljubljana" (Matevž Langus)

(Des A. Milenković from drawing by schoolgirl, Durdica Zatezalo. Litho German Bank Note Ptg Co, Leipzig)

1971 (4 Oct). Children's Week and 25th Anniv of United Nations Children's Fund. P 13.
1494 **400** 50p. multicoloured................................ 20 10

(Des A. Milenković. Recess and photo Austrian State Ptg Wks, Vienna)

1971 (27 Nov). Yugoslav Paintings. Portraits. T **401** and similar vert designs. Multicoloured. P 13½.
1495 50p. "Girl in Serbian Costume" (Katarina Ivanovic) 10 10
1496 1d.50 "Ivanišević the Merchant" (Anastas Bocaric)... 10 10
1497 2d. "Anne Krešić" (Vjekoslav Karas).......... 10 10
1498 2d.50 "Pavla Jagodica" (Konstantin Danil).. 20 10
1499 4d. "Louise Pasjakove" (Mihael Stroj)....... 30 15
1500 6d. Type **401** .... 1·00 80
1495/1500 *Set of* 6.. 1·60 1·20

402 "Postal Codes"

403 Dame Gruev

(Des A. Milenković. Photo German Bank Note Ptg Co, Leipzig)

1971 (15 Dec). Introduction of Postal Codes. P 13½×14.
1501 **402** 50p. multicoloured................................ 20 10

(Des A. Milenković. Eng V. Cvetković. Recess)

1971 (22 Dec). Birth Centenary of Dame Gruev (Macedonian revolutionary). P 12½.
1502 **403** 50p. indigo.. 20 15

404 Speed Skating

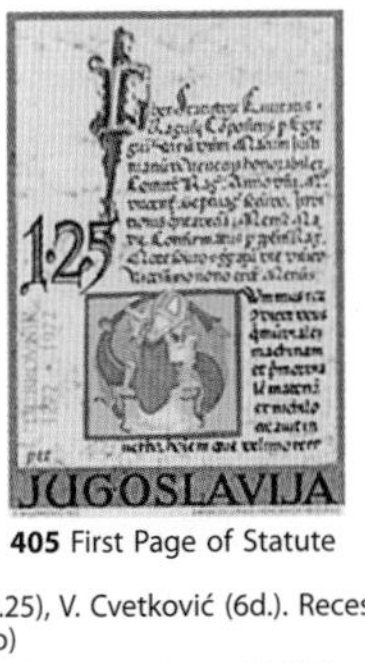

405 First Page of Statute

(Des A. Milenković. Eng D. Matić (1d.25), V. Cvetković (6d.). Recess and litho)

1972 (3 Feb). Winter Olympic Games, Sapporo, Japan. T **404** and similar horiz design. Multicoloured. P 11½.
1503 1d.25 Type **404**... 60 45
1504 6d. Skiing .... 2·50 1·90

(Des A. Milenković. Recess and litho)

1972 (15 Mar). 700th Anniversary of Dubrovnik Law Statutes. P 13.
1505 **405** 1d.25 multicoloured 20 10

406 Ski Jump, Planica

407 Water Polo

(Des A. Milenković. Eng D. Matić. Recess and litho)

1972 (21 Mar). First World Ski Jumping Championships, Planica. P 11½.
1506 **406** 1d.25 multicoloured 20 10

(Des P. Jakelić. Litho)

1972 (17 Apr). Olympic Games, Munich. T **407** and similar vert designs. Multicoloured. P 12½.
1507 50p. Type **407** 10 10
1508 1d.25 Basketball 10 10
1509 2d.50 Swimming 15 10
1510 3d.25 Boxing 30 10
1511 5d. Running 50 15
1512 6d.50 Sailing .... 1·00 65
1507/1512 *Set of 6* .... 1·90 1·10

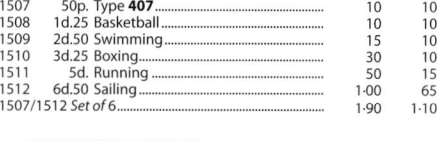

408 Red Cross and Hemispheres

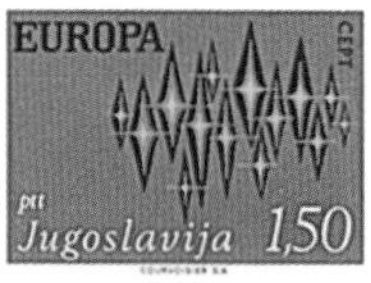
409 "Communications"

(Des A. Milenković. Litho German Bank Note Ptg Co, Leipzig)

1972 (27 Apr). OBLIGATORY TAX. Red Cross Week. P 13.
1513 **408** 20p. multicoloured 20 10

(Des P. Huovinen, adapted A. Milenković. Photo Courvoisier)

1972 (3 May). Europa. P 11½.
1514 **409** 1d.50 multicoloured 50 40
1515 5d. multicoloured .... 1·00 80

410 Wallcreeper (*Tichodroma muraria*)

411 President Tito

(Des A. Milenković. Photo Courvoisier)

1972 (8 May). Birds. Vert designs as T **410**. Multicoloured. P 11½.
1516 50p. Type **410** 30 15
1517 1d.25 Little bustard (*Otis tetrax*) 30 15
1518 2d.50 Chough (*Pyrrhocorax pyrrhocorax*) 35 15
1519 3d.25 White spoonbill (*Platalea leucorodia*) 90 15
1520 5d. Eagle owl (*Bubo bubo*) .... 1·60 60
1521 6d.50 Rock ptarmigan (*Lagopus mutus*) .... 3·75 2·30
1516/1521 *Set of 6* .... 6·50 3·25

(Des B. Jakac and A. Milenković. Litho)

1972 (25 May). President Tito's 80th Birthday. P 12½.
1522 **411** 50p. purple-brown and pale buff 20 10
1523 1d.25 indigo and pale grey 50 20
MS1524 61×76 mm. **411** 10d. blackish brown and pale drab. Imperf .... 3·00 3·00

Two stamps and a miniature sheet showing a full-face portrait of President Tito, designed by A. Milenković, and printed in recess or recess and litho, were prepared, but were withdrawn and destroyed before issue, being replaced by the listed stamps.

412 Communications Tower, Olympic Rings and 1972 Games' Emblems

413 Locomotive No. 1 *King of Serbia*, 1882

(Des A. Milenković. Litho German Bank Note Ptg Co, Leipzig)

1972 (1 June). OBLIGATORY TAX. Olympic Games Fund. P 13.
1525 **412** 10p. multicoloured 20 10

(Des A. Milenković. Photo Courvoisier)

1972 (12 June). 50th Anniversary of International Railway Union. T **413** and similar horiz design. Multicoloured. P 11½.
1526 1d.50 Type **413** 30 10
1527 5d. Modern "Bo-Bo" electric locomotive .... 1·00 55

414 Glider in Flight

415 Pawn

(Des A. Milenković. Litho)

1972 (8 July). 13th World Gliding Championships, Vršac. P 12½.
1528 **414** 2d. black, slate-blue and gold 20 15

(Des A. Milenković. Photo Courvoisier)

1972 (18 Sept). 20th Chess Olympiad, Skopje. T **415** and similar vert design. P 11½.
1529 1d.50 drab, deep reddish violet & mar 30 10
1530 6d. black, new blue and Prussian blue .... 1·60 1·00
Design:—6d. Chessboard, king and queen.

416 "Child on Horse" (B. Zlatec)

417 G. Delcev

(Des A. Milenković (after child's prize-winning drawing). Litho)

1972 (2 Oct). Children's Week. P 12½.
1531 **416** 80p. multicoloured 20 10

(Des A. Milenković. Litho)

1972 (16 Oct). Birth Centenary of Goce Delcev (Macedonian revolutionary). P 13×13½.
1532 **417** 80p. black and olive-yellow 20 10

418 Father Martic (sculpture, Ivan Meštrovic)

419 National Library

(Des A. Milenković. Litho)

1972 (3 Nov). 150th Birth Anniv of Father Grge Martic (politician). P 12½.
1533 **418** 80p. black, olive-yellow and orange-vermilion 20 10

(Des A. Milenković. Eng V. Cvetković. Recess)

1972 (25 Nov). 140th Anniv and Re-opening of National Library, Belgrade. P 11½.
1534 **419** 50p. chocolate 20 10

420 "Fruit Dish and Broken Majolica Vase" (Miloš Tenkovic)

(Des A. Milenković. Recess and photo Austrian State Ptg Wks, Vienna)

1972 (28 Nov). Yugoslav Art. Still Life. T **420** and similar multicoloured designs. P 13½.
1535 50p. Type **420** 10 10
1536 1d.25 "Mandoline and Book" (Jožef Petkovšec) (vert) 10 10
1537 2d.50 "Basket with Grapes" (Katarina Ivanovic) 20 10
1538 3d.25 "Water-melon" (Konstantin Danil) 30 15
1539 5d. "In a Stable" (Nikola Mašic) (vert) 50 20
1540 6d.50 "Scrap-books" (Celestin Medovic) 75 65
1535/1540 *Set of 6* .... 1·80 1·20

421 Battle of Stubica

(Des A. Milenković. Photo Courvoisier)

1973 (29 Jan). 500th Anniv of Slovenian Peasant Risings and 400th Anniv of Croatian-Slovenian Rebellion. T **421** and similar horiz design. Multicoloured. P 11½.
1541 2d. Type **421** 30 10
1542 6d. Battle of Krško .... 1·00 75

422 R. Domanović

423 Škofja Loka

(Des A. Milenković. Litho)

1973 (3 Feb). Birth Centenary of Radoje Domanović (Serbian satirist). P 12½.
1543 **422** 80p. sepia and light drab 40 10

(Des A. Milenković. Photo)

1973 (15 Feb). Millenary of Škofja Loka. P 11½.
1544 **423** 80p. light brown and pale buff 30 10

424 "Novi Sad" (Petar Demetrovic)

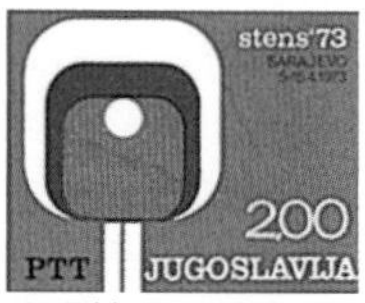
425 Table Tennis Bat and Ball

(Des A. Milenković. Recess and photo Austrian State Ptg Wks, Vienna)

1973 (15 Mar). Old Engravings of Yugoslav Towns. T **424** and similar horiz designs. Each black and gold. P 13½.
1545 50p. Type **424** 10 10
1546 1d.25 "Zagreb" (Josef Szeman) 10 10
1547 2d.50 "Kotor" (Pierre Montier) 15 10
1548 3d.25 "Belgrade" (Mancini) 15 10
1549 5d. "Split" (Louis Cassas) 30 15
1550 6d.50 "Kranj" (Matthäus Merian) 65 50
1545/1550 *Set of 6* .... 1·30 95

(Des A. Milenković. Litho German Bank Note Ptg Co, Leipzig)

1973 (5 Apr). 32nd World Table Tennis Championships, Sarajevo. P 13.
1551 **425** 2d. multicoloured 35 10

426 Red Cross Emblem

427 Europa "Posthorn"

(Des A. Milenković. Litho)

1973 (24 Apr). OBLIGATORY TAX. Red Cross Week. P 13×13½.
1552 **426** 20p. multicoloured 20 10

(Des L. F. Anisdahl. Photo Courvoisier)

1973 (30 Apr). Europa. P 11½.
1553 **427** 2d. bright lilac, turquoise-green and Prussian blue 35 30
1554 5d.50 salmon, apple-green and bright purple .... 1·50 1·30

428 Birthwort (*Aristolochia clematatis*)

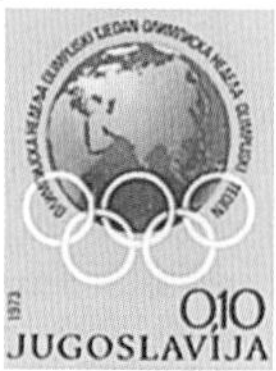
429 Globe and Olympic Rings

(Des A. Milenković. Photo Courvoisier)

1973 (25 May). Medicinal Plants. T **428** and similar vert designs. Multicoloured. P 11½.
1555 80p. Type **428** 20 10
1556 2d. Globe thistle (*Echinops ritro*) 20 10
1557 3d. Olive (*Olea europaea*) 30 10
1558 4d. *Corydalis cava* 50 10
1559 5d. Mistletoe (*Viscum album*) 75 50
1560 6d. Comfrey (*Symphytum officinale*) .... 2·30 2·00
1555/1560 *Set of 6* .... 3·75 2·50

(Des A. Milenković. Litho German Bank Note Ptg Co, Leipzig)

1973 (1 June). OBLIGATORY TAX. Olympic Games Fund. P 13.
1561 **429** 10p. multicoloured 20 10

430 A. Janša and Bee

431 Aquatic Symbol

(Des B. Jakac. Eng D. Andrić. Recess)

1973 (25 Aug). Death Bicentenary of Anton Janša (apiculturist). P 12½.

1562	**430**	80p. black	40	10

(Des A. Milenković. Litho German Bank Note Ptg Co, Leipzig)

1973 (1 Sept). First World Aquatic Championships, Belgrade. P 13.

1563	**431**	2d. multicoloured	30	10

432 "Children on Boat" (Ivan Vukovic)

433 Posthorn

(Des A. Milenković. Litho)

1973 (1 Oct). Children's Week. P 12½.

1564	**432**	80p. multicoloured	1·60	1·00

(Photo Harrison)

1973 (5 Oct)–**77**. Coil stamps. Two phosphor bands. P 15×14.

1565	**433**	30p. red-brown	20	10
1565*a*		50p. grey-blue	20	10
1566		80p. rosine (26.3.74)	20	10
1566*a*		1d. dull green (28.7.77)	20	10
1567		1d.20 red (27.12.74)	20	10
1567*a*		1d.50 vermilion (28.7.77)	20	10
1565/1567*a* *Set of* 6			1·10	55

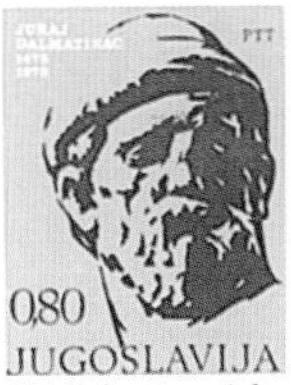

434 Dalmatinac (after sculpture by Ivan Meštrovic)

435 "Self-portrait"

(Des A. Milenković. Litho)

1973 (8 Oct). 500th Death Anniv of Juraj Dalmatinac (sculptor and architect). P 12½.

1568	**434**	80p. bronze-green and pale grey	25	10

(Des A. Milenković. Recess and litho)

1973 (12 Oct). Birth Centenary of Nadežda Petrović (painter). P 11½.

1569	**435**	2d. multicoloured	30	20

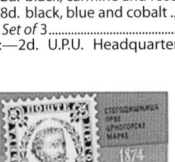

436 "The Plaster Head" (Marko Celebonovic)

(Des A. Milenković. Photo Austrian State Ptg Wks, Vienna)

1973 (20 Oct). Yugoslav Art. Interiors. T **436** and similar horiz designs. Multicoloured. P 13½.

1570	80p. Type **436**	10	10
1571	2d. "St. Duja Church" (Emanuel Vidovic)	10	10
1572	3d. "Slovenian Housewife" (Marino Tartaglia)	10	10
1573	4d. "Dedicated to Karas" (Miljenko Stančić)	15	10
1574	5d. "My Studio" (Milan Konjović)	25	20
1575	6d. "Tavern in Stara Loka" (France Slana)	65	50
1570/1575 *Set of* 6		1·20	1·00

437 Dragojlo Dudic

438 "M" for "Metrication"

(Des A. Milenković. Eng D. Matić (Nos. 1576, 1579), N. Hrvanovic (No. 1581), D. Andrić (others). Recess)

1973 (28 Nov). National Heroes. T **437** and similar vert designs. P 12½.

(a) Each blue-black

1576		80p. Type **437**	10	10
		a. Sheet of 8. Nos. 1576/83	1·30	
1577		80p. Strahil Pindžur	10	10
1578		80p. Boris Kidic	10	10
1579		80p. Radoje Dakić	10	10

(b) Each maroon

1580		2d. Josip Mažar-Šoša	20	20
1581		2d. Žarko Zrenjanin	20	20
1582		2d. Emin Duraku	20	20
1583		2d. Ivan Lola Ribar	20	20
1576/1583 *Set of* 8			1·10	1·10

Nos. 1576/83 were issued together in *se-tenant* sheets of eight stamps.

(Des A. Milenković. Litho)

1974 (10 Jan). Centenary of Introduction of Metric System in Yugoslavia. P 13½×13.

1584	**438**	80p. multicoloured	25	10

439 Skater

440 Satjeska Monument

(Des A. Milenković, from sketch by B. Stranic. Litho)

1974 (29 Jan). European Figure Skating Championships, Zagreb. P 13×13½.

1585	**439**	2d. multicoloured	60	30

(Des A. Milenković. Eng N. Hrvanovic (3d., 50d.) D. Matić (4d.50, 20d.), V. Cvetković (5d.), D. Andrić (10d.). Recess)

1974 (30 Jan–29 May). T **440** and similar designs showing monuments. P 12½.

1586	3d. grey-green (29.5)	95	20
1587	4d.50 brown-lake (29.5)	1·40	20
1588	5d. bluish violet (29.5)	1·40	20
	a. Perf 13½	8·75	50
1589	10d. slate-green (5.2)	2·30	30
1590	20d. deep dull purple	2·50	30
1591	50d. deep chalky blue	5·75	1·30
1586/1591 *Set of* 6		13·00	2·30

Monuments: Vert—3d. Ljubljana; 4d.50, Kozara; 5d. Belcišta. Horiz—20d. Podgaric; 50d. Kragujevac.

Nos. 1588/9 were reissued on matt, almost invisible gum.

For designs as above but printed in litho, see Nos. 1825/8.

441 Mailcoach

(Des A. Milenković. Eng V. Cvetković (80p.), D. Matić (2d.), D. Andrić (8d.). Recess and litho)

1974 (25 Feb). Centenary of Universal Postal Union. T **441** and similar horiz designs. P 11½.

1592	80p. black, yellow-ochre and buff	10	10
1593	2d. black, carmine and rose	10	10
1594	8d. black, blue and cobalt	65	55
1592/1594 *Set of* 3		75	70

Designs:—2d. U.P.U. Headquarters Building; 8d. Boeing 707 jetliner.

442 Montenegrin 25n. Stamp of 1874

443 President Tito

(Des A. Milenković. Recess and litho)

1974 (11 Mar). Montenegro Stamp Centenary. T **442** and similar horiz design. P 13½×13.

1595	80p. bistre, gold and pale sage-green	25	10
1596	6d. maroon, gold and claret	45	40

Designs:—80p. Montenegrin 2n. stamp of 1874.

(Des B. Jakac. Litho)

1974 (26 Mar)–**81**. P 13.

1597	**443**	50p. dull green (9.4.74)	10	10
		a. Perf 13½×12½ (1981)	70	10
		p. Two phosphor bands	25	10
1598		80p. light red (1.4.74)	25	10
		p. Two phosphor bands	25	10
1599		1d.20 grey-green (16.4.74)	25	10
		p. Two phosphor bands	35	10
1600		2d. grey-blue	30	10
		a. Perf 13½×12½ (1981)	60	10
		p. Two phosphor bands	30	10
1597/1600 *Set of* 4			80	35

Nos. 1597/9 exist with both shiny and matt, almost invisible, gum.

444 Lenin

445 Red Cross Emblems

(Des A. Milenković, from sculpture by N. Glid. Litho)

1974 (20 Apr). 50th Death Anniv of Lenin. P 13×13½.

1601	**444**	2d. black and silver	30	10

(Des A. Milenković. Litho)

1974 (25 Apr). OBLIGATORY TAX. Red Cross Week. P 13½×13.

1602	**445**	20p. multicoloured	25	10

446 "Dwarf" (Lepenski settlement, c 4950 B.C.)

447 Great Tit

(Des A. Milenković. Photo Courvoisier)

1974 (29 Apr). Europa. Sculptures. T **446** and similar horiz design. Multicoloured. P 11½.

1603	2d. Type **446**	35	30
1604	6d. "Widow and Child" (Ivan Meštrovic)	1·30	1·30

(Des A. Milenković. Photo Courvoiser)

1974 (25 May). Youth Day. T **447** and similar vert designs. Multicoloured. P 11½.

1605	80p. Type **447**	25	10
1606	2d. Roses	65	20
1607	6d. Cabbage White (butterfly)	1·60	1·20
1605/1607 *Set of* 3		2·30	1·40

448 Congress Poster

449 Olympic Rings and Stadium

(Des A. Milenković, from poster by M. Nedeljkovic. Litho)

1974 (27 May). Tenth Yugoslav League of Communists' Congress, Belgrade. P 11½.

1608	**448**	80p. multicoloured	10	10
1609		2d. multicoloured	25	10
1610		6d. multicoloured	60	40
1608/1610 *Set of* 3			85	55

(Des A. Milenković. Litho)

1974 (1 June). OBLIGATORY TAX. Olympic Games Fund. P 13½×13.

1611	**449**	10p. multicoloured	25	10

450 Dish Aerial, Ivanjica

451 World Cup

(Des A. Milenković. Eng N. Hrvanovic (80p.), D. Matić (6d.). Recess)

1974 (7 June). Inauguration of Satellite Communications Station, Ivanjica. T **450** and similar vert design. P 13×13½.

1612	80p. deep violet-blue	25	10
1613	6d. slate-lilac	1·00	65

Design:—6d. "Intelsat 4" in orbit.

(Des A. Milenković. Litho German Bank Note Ptg Co, Leipzig)

1974 (13 June). World Cup Football Championship, West Germany. P 13.

1614	**451**	4d.50 multicoloured	1·10	70

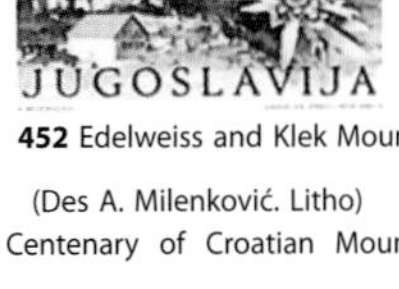

452 Edelweiss and Klek Mountain

(Des A. Milenković. Litho)

1974 (15 June). Centenary of Croatian Mountaineers' Society. P 13½×13.

1615	**452**	2d. multicoloured	30	10

453 "Children's Dance" (Jano Knjazovic)

(Des A. Milenković. Photo Courvoisier)

1974 (9 Sept). Paintings. T **453** and similar multicoloured designs. P 11½.

1616 80p. Type **453** ... 25 10
1617 2d. "Crucified Rooster" (Ivan Generalic) (vert) ... 25 10
1618 5d. "Laundresses" (Ivan Lackovic) (vert).. 50 35
1619 8d. "Dance" (Janko Brasic) ... 1·30 1·10
1616/1619 *Set of* 4 ... 2·10 1·50

454 "Rooster and Flower" (Kaca Milinojšin)

455 Interior of Library

(Des A. Milenković. Litho)

1974 (1 Oct). Children's Week and Sixth "Joy of Europe" Meeting, Belgrade Children's Paintings. T **454** and similar multicoloured designs. P 13.

1620 1d.20 Type **454** ... 10 10
1621 3d.20 "Girl and Boy" (Eva Medrzecka) (vert) ... 25 10
1622 5d. "Cat and Kitten" (Jelena Anastasijevic) ... 60 30
1620/1622 *Set of* 3 ... 85 45

(Des B. Jakac. Eng V. Cvetković. Recess)

1974 (21 Oct). Bicentenary of National and University Library. P 13.

1623 **455** 1d.20 black ... 25 10

456 "White Peonies" (Petar Dobrovic)

457 Title Page of Volume 1

(Des A. Milenković. Photo Courvoisier)

1974 (28 Nov). Floral Paintings. T **456** and similar vert designs. Multicoloured. P 11½.

1624 80p. Type **456** ... 10 10
1625 2d. "Carnations" (Vilko Gecan) ... 10 10
1626 3d. "Flowers" (Milan Konjović) ... 10 10
1627 4d. "White Vase" (Sava Šumanovic) ... 25 15
1628 5d. "Branching Larkspurs" (Stane Kregar) ... 45 20
1629 8d. "Roses" (Petar Lubarda) ... 1·00 50
1624/1629 *Set of* 6 ... 1·80 1·00

(Des A. Milenković. Litho)

1975 (8 Jan). 150th Anniv of "Matica Srpska" Annals. P 13.

1630 **457** 1d.20 blk, brn-ol & pale yell-grn ... 25 10
a. Perf 12½ ... 35·00 35·00

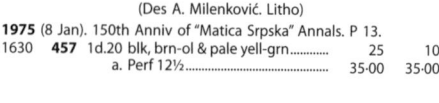

458 Dove and Map of Europe

459 Gold-plated Bronze Ear-ring (14th-15th-century), Ališici, Bosnia

(Des A. Milenković. Litho)

1975 (30 Jan). Second European Security and Co-operation Conference, Belgrade. P 11½.

1631 **458** 3d.20 multicoloured ... 45 20
1632 8d. multicoloured ... 1·50 80

(Des A. Milenković. Photo Enschedé)

1975 (25 Feb). Archaeological Discoveries. T **459** and similar horiz designs. Multicoloured. P 14×12½.

1633 1d.20 Type **459** ... 10 10
1634 2d.10 Silver bracelet (19th-century), Kosovo ... 10 10
1635 3d.20 Gold-plated silver buckle (18th-century), Bitola ... 15 10
1636 5d. Gold-plated ring (14th-century), Novi Sad ... 25 10
1637 6d. Silver necklace (17th-century), Kosovo ... 55 30
1638 8d. Gold-plated, bronze bracelet (18th-century), Bitola ... 65 55
1633/1638 *Set of* 6 ... 1·60 1·10

460 "Svetozar Marković" (sculpture by S. Bodnarov)

461 "Fettered" (sculpture by F. Kršinić)

(Des A. Milenković. Eng D. Matić. Recess)

1975 (26 Feb). Death Centenary of Svetozar Marković (writer and statesman). P 13.

1639 **460** 1d.20 blue-black ... 40 10

(Des A. Milenković. Photo Harrison)

1975 (8 Mar). International Women's Year. P 14½×14.

1640 **461** 3d.20 deep greyish brn & gold ... 25 20

(Des D. Lučić (6, 38d.), D. Čudov (5, 10d., 16d.50, 26d.), R. Bojanić (70d.), A. Milenković (others). Litho)

1975 (20 Mar)–**85**. As Nos. 1466/83 (some designs changed), and new values, but litho. 20p. with printer's imprint, others without. Ordinary paper. P 13½.

1641 5p. red-orange (17.6.80) ... 60 20
a. Perf 13½×12½ (1981) ... 1·70 75
1642 10p. red-brown (17.6.80) ... 60 30
a. Perf 13½×12½ (1981) ... 80 30
1643 20p. reddish lilac (1.11.78) ... 1·20 50
a. Perf 13½×12½ (1981) ... 1·20 50
1644 25p. claret (15.8.76) ... 1·70 20
1645 30p. brown-olive (17.6.80) ... 60 20
a. Perf 13½×12½ (1981) ... 1·20 50
1646 35p. brown-red (17.6.80) ... 1·20 75
a. Perf 13½×12½ (1981) ... 1·70 1·00
1647 40p. blackish olive (1978) ... 60 20
a. Perf 13½×12½ (17.6.80) ... 80 20
1650 60p. deep reddish purple (1980) ... 60 20
a. Perf 13½×12½ (9.4.84) ... 80 50
1652 75p. purple (24.11.76) ... 1·20 20
1656 1d. slate-lilac (20.3.75) ... 25 10
1657 1d. dull yellowish green (15.9.76) ... 60 10
a. Perf 13½×12½ (1981) ... 60 20
1660 1d.50 red (20.8.76) ... 1·70 20
a. Perf 13½×12½ ... 35·00 31·00
1661 2d.10 deep dull green (20.3.75) ... 25 10
1662 2d.50 dull vermilion (p 13½×12½) (23.6.80) ... 1·20 30
a. Perf 13½ (1981) ... 1·20 20
1663 2d.50 slate-blue (9.3.81) ... 25 10
a. Perf 13½×12½ ... 35 10
ab. Chalky paper ... 1·20
1664 3d. greenish slate (15.11.82) ... 35 10
a. Perf 13½×12½ ... 35 10
1665 3d.20 Prussian blue (20.3.75) ... 25 10
1666 3d.40 dull green (24.6.77) ... 1·20 20
a. Perf 13½×12½ (1981) ... 1·70 30
1667 3d.50 orange-red (9.3.81) ... 25 10
a. Chalky paper ... 85
b. Perf 13½×12½ ... 40 40
ba. Chalky paper ... 4·75
1668 4d. dull vermilion (15.11.82) ... 35 10
a. Perf 13½×12½ ... 35 10
1669 4d.90 slate-blue (26.5.76) ... 4·00 20
1670 5d. bright blue-green (24.8.83) ... 60 20
a. Chalky paper ... 1·70
b. Perf 13½×12½ ... 60 20
ba. Chalky paper ... 1·70
1671 5d.60 grey-olive (9.3.81) ... 25 10
a. Perf 13½×12½ ... 60 10
1672 6d. chestnut (6.10.84) ... 60 10
a. Chalky paper ... 1·70
b. Perf 13½×12½ ... 1·20 30
ba. Chalky paper ... 1·70
1673 6d.10 bronze green (23.12.82) ... 1·20 50
a. Perf 13½×12½ ... 60 20
1674 8d. greenish slate (9.3.81) ... 35 10
a. Perf 13½×12½ ... 80 10
1675 8d.80 bluish grey (11.10.82) ... 1·70 75
a. Perf 13½×12½ ... 60 20
1676 10d. deep magenta (2.9.83) ... 60 10
a. Perf 13½×12½ ... 1·20 20
1677 16d.50 steel blue (8.6.83) ... 35 10
a. Perf 13½×12½ ... 4·75 4·25
1678 26d. grey-blue (9.7.84) ... 35 10
a. Perf 13½×12½ ... 70 20
1679 38d. bright magenta (9.7.84) ... 60 10
a. Perf 13½×12½ ... 2·30 30
1680 70d. ultramarine (1.7.85) ... 80 65
a. Perf 13½×12½ ... 1·70 75
1641/1680 *Set of* 32 (*cheapest*) ... 22·00 5·75

Designs:—5p. Kruševo, Macedonia; 10p. Gradacac; 20p. Bohinj, Slovenia; 25p. Budva; 30p. Type **397**; 35p. Omiš, Dalmatia; 40p. Pec; 60p. Logarska valley; 75p. Rijeka; 1d. (both), Ohrid; 1d.50, Bihac; 2d.10, 6d.10, Hvar; 2d.50 (both), Kragujevac; 3d., 3d.20, Skofja Loka; 3d.40, Vranje; 3d.50, Vršac; 4d. Pocitelj; 4d.90, Perast; 5d. Osijek, 5d.60, Travnik; 6d. Kikinda; 8d. Dubrovnik; 8d.80, Herceg Novi; 10d. Sarajevo; 16d.50, Ohrid (different); 26d. Korcula. 38d. Maribor, 70d. Zagreb.

Nos. 1656, 1661 and 1665 exist both with and without phosphor bands.

462 Red Cross and Hands

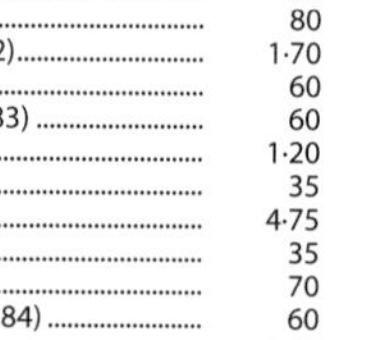

463 "Still Life with Eggs" (Moša Pijade)

(Des A. Milenković. Litho)

1975 (23 Apr). OBLIGATORY TAX. Red Cross Week. P 13.

1681 **462** 20p. multicoloured ... 25 10

(Des A. Milenković. Photo Courvoisier)

1975 (28 Apr). Europa. Paintings. T **463** and similar horiz design. Multicoloured. P 11½.

1682 3d.20 Type **463** ... 25 20
1683 8d. "Three Graces" (Ivan Radovic) ... 70 65

464 "Liberation Monument" (Džamonja)

465 Garland Flower (*Daphne cneorum*)

(Des A. Milenković. Litho)

1975 (9 May). 30th Anniv of Liberation. P 13.

1684 **464** 3d.20 multicoloured ... 25 10

(Des B. Spremo. Photo Harrison)

1975 (24 May). National Youth Day. Flowers. T **465** and similar vert designs. Multicoloured. P 14×14½.

1685 1d.20 Type **465** ... 10 10
1686 2d.10 Touch-me-not balsam (*Impatiens nolitangere*) ... 10 10
1687 3d.20 Rose-mallow (*Malva alcea*) ... 10 10
1688 5d. Dusky cranesbill (*Geranium phaeum*) ... 25 15
1689 6d. Crocus (*Crocus bannaticus*) ... 35 20
1690 8d. Rosebay willowherb (*Epilobium angustifolium*) ... 1·40 1·30
1685/1690 *Set of* 6 ... 2·10 1·80

466 Games Emblem

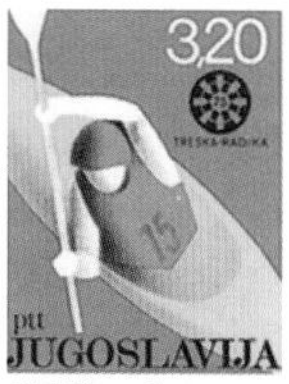

467 Canoeing

(Des A. Milenković. Litho)

1975 (2 June). OBLIGATORY TAX. Olympic Games Fund. P 13½×13.

1691 **466** 10p. multicoloured ... 25 10

(Des A. Milenković. Litho German Bank Note Ptg Co, Leipzig)

1975 (20 June). World Canoeing Championships, Macedonia. P 13.

1692 **467** 3d.20 multicoloured ... 25 10

468 "Herzegovinian Insurgents in Ambush"

469 "Skopje Earthquake"

(Des A. Milenković. Photo Harrison)

1975 (9 July). Centenary of Bosnian-Herzegovinian Uprising. P 13½×14.

1693 **468** 1d.20 multicoloured ... 25 10

(Des D. Andrić. Litho)

1975 (15 July). OBLIGATORY TAX. Solidarity Week. P 13.

1694 **469** 30p. black, greenish grey and deep blue ... 25 10

No. 1694 was re-issued in 1976, 1977 and 1978.

See also Nos. 1885 and 1933.

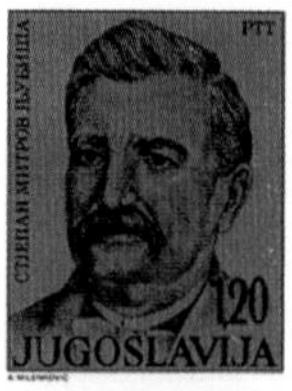

470 Stjepan Mitrov Ljubiša

471 "Young Lion" (A. Savic)

(Des A. Milenković. Litho German Bank Note Ptg Co, Leipzig)

1975 (16 Sept). Writers. T **470** and similar vert designs. P 13×13½.

1695 1d.20 black and brown-rose ... 10 10
1696 2d.10 black and dull blue-green ... 10 10
1697 3d.20 black and olive-bistre ... 10 10
1698 5d. black and pale orange ... 15 10
1699 6d. black and dull yellowish green ... 25 10
1700 8d. black and light blue ... 60 40
1695/1700 *Set of* 6 ... 1·20 80

Designs:—2d.10, Ivan Prijatelj; 3d.20, Jakov Ignjatovic; 5d. Dragojla Jarnevic; 6d. Svetozar Corivic; 8d. Ivana Brlic-Mažuranic.

(Des A. Milenković. Litho German Bank Note Ptg Co, Leipzig)

1975 (1 Oct). Children's Week and Seventh "Joy of Europe" meeting, Belgrade Children's Paintings T **471** and similar horiz design. Multicoloured. P 13.

1701 3d.20 Type **471** ... 35 10
1702 6d. "Baby in Pram" ... 1·30 55

472 Peace Dove within "EUROPA"

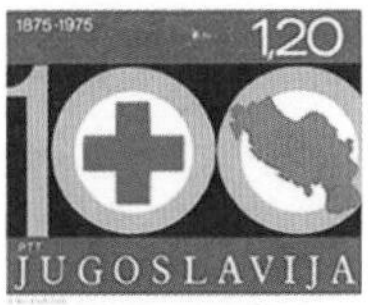
473 Red Cross and Map within "100"

(Des A. Milenković. Litho)

1975 (10 Oct). European Security and Co-operation Conference, Helsinki. P 13.

1703 **472** 3d.20 multicoloured 15 10
1704 8d. multicoloured 65 40

(Des A. Milenković. Litho German Bank Note Ptg Co, Leipzig)

1975 (1 Nov). Centenary of Red Cross. T **473** and similar horiz design. Multicoloured. P 13.

1705 1d.20 Type **473** 15 10
1706 8d. Red Cross and people 60 30

474 "Folk Kitchen" (Djordje Andrejević-Kun)

475 Diocletian's Palace, Split (3rd-century)

(Des A. Milenković. Photo Harrison)

1975 (28 Nov). Republic Day. Paintings. T **474** and similar multicoloured designs. P 14.

1707 1d.20 Type **474** 10 10
1708 2d.10 "On the Doorstep" (Vinko Grdan) 10 10
1709 3d.20 "Drunken Coach-load" (Marijan Detoni) (horiz) 10 10
1710 5d. "Luncheon" (Tone Kralj) (horiz) 20 10
1711 6d. "Waterwheel" (Lazar Licenoski) 35 10
1712 8d. "Justice" (Krsto Hegedušic) 65 50
1707/1712 *Set of* 6 1·40 90

(Des A. Milenković and D. Lučić. Eng. N. Hrvanovic (1d.20.), V. Cvetković (3d.20, 8d.). Recess)

1975 (10 Dec). European Architectural Heritage Year. T **475** and similar designs. P 13.

1713 1d.20 chocolate 10 10
1714 3d.20 blue-black 10 10
1715 8d. agate 65 40
1713/1715 *Set of* 3 75 55

Designs: Vert—3d.20, House in Ohrid (19th century). Horiz—8d. Gracanica Monastery, Kosovo (14th century).

476 Ski Jumping

477 Red Flag

(Des D. Lučić. Eng D. Andrić (3d.20.), D. Matić (8d.). Recess)

1976 (4 Feb). Winter Olympic Games, Innsbruck. T **476** and similar horiz design. P 13.

1716 3d.20 blue-black 25 10
1717 8d. carmine 80 50

Design:—8d. Figure skating.

(Des A. Milenković. Litho)

1976 (14 Feb). Centenary of "Red Flag" Insurrection (workers demonstrations), Kragujevac, Serbia. P 13.

1718 **477** 1d.20 multicoloured 25 10

478 Svetozar Miletic

479 Bora Stankovic

(Des A. Milenković. Litho German Bank Note Ptg Co, Leipzig)

1976 (23 Feb). 150th Birth Anniv of Svetozar Miletic (politician). P 13.

1719 **478** 1d.20 deep grey-green and pale grey-green 25 10

(Des A. Milenković. Litho German Bank Note Pig Co, Leipzig)

1976 (31 Mar). Birth Centenary of Bora Stankovic (writer). P 13.

1720 **479** 1d.20 maroon, brown-olive and olive-yellow 25 10

480 "King Matthias" (sculpture, J. Pogorelec)

481 Ivan Cankar

(Des A. Milenković. Photo Courvoisier)

1976 (26 Apr). Europa. Handicrafts. T **480** and similar horiz design. Multicoloured. P 11½.

1721 3d.20 Type **480** 25 10
1722 8d. Base of a beaker 45 40

(Des D. Lučić. Litho German Bank Note Pig Co, Leipzig)

1976 (8 May). Birth Centenary of Ivan Cankar (Slovenian writer). P 13.

1723 **481** 1d.20 brown-purple, cinnamon and flesh 25 10

482 Stylized Figure

483 Train crossing Viaduct

1976 (8 May). OBLIGATORY TAX. Red Cross Week. Litho. P 12½.

1724 **482** 20p. multicoloured 1·20 75

(Des A. Milenković. Eng D. Andrić (3d.20.), D. Matić (8d.). Recess)

1976 (15 May). Inauguration of Belgrade–Bar Railway. T **483** and similar horiz design. P 13.

1725 3d.20 brown-lake 35 20
1726 8d. deep blue 1·00 50

Design:—8d. Train crossing bridge.

484 Emperor Dragonfly (*Anax imperator*)

485 Vladimir Nazor

(Des B. Spremo. Litho Enschedé)

1976 (25 May). Youth Day. Freshwater Fauna. T **484** and similar horiz designs. Multicoloured. P 13½.

1727 1d.20 Type **484** 35 30
1728 2d.10 River snail (*Viviparus viviparus*) 35 30
1729 3d.20 Rudd (*Scardinius erythrophtalmus*) 35 30
1730 5d. Common frog (*Rana esculenta*) 1·20 1·00
1731 6d. Ferruginous duck (*Aythya nyroca*) 1·20 1·00
1732 8d. Muskrat (*Ondatra zibethica*) 3·50 3·25
1727/1732 *Set of* 6 6·25 5·50

(Des A. Milenković. Litho German Bank Note Ptg Co, Leipzig)

1976 (29 May). Birth Centenary of Vladimir Nazor (writer). P 13.

1733 **485** 1d.20 slate-blue and pale lilac 25 15

486 "Battle of Vucji Dol" (from "Eagle" journal, 1876)

(Des A. Milenković. Litho)

1976 (16 June). Centenary of Montenegrin Liberation Wars. P 13.

1734 **486** 1d.20 olive-brown, pale greenish yellow and gold 25 15

487 Jug, Aleksandrovac, Serbia

488 Nikola Tesla Monument and Niagara Falls

(Des A. Milenković. Photo Enschedé)

1976 (22 June). Ancient Pottery. T **487** and similar horiz designs. Multicoloured. P 14×12½.

1735 1d.20 Type **487** 10 10
1736 2d.10 Pitcher, Ptuj, Slovenia 10 10
1737 3d.20 Coffee-pot, Višnjica, Sarajevo 10 10
1738 5d. Pitcher, Backi Breg, Vojvodina 20 10
1739 6d. Goblet, Vraneštica, Macedonia 30 15
1740 8d. Jug, Prizren, Kosovo 75 40
1735/1740 *Set of* 6 1·40 85

(Des. A. Milenković. Eng V. Cvetković. Recess)

1976 (10 July). 120th Birth Anniv of Nikola Tesla (scientist). P 13.

1741 **488** 5d. indigo and grey green 60 40

489 Long Jumping

490 Stadium and Olympic Rings

(Des D. Lučić. Eng D. Andrić (1d.20.), N. Hrvanovic (3d.20.), D. Matić (5d.), V. Cvetković (8d.). Recess)

1976 (17 July). Olympic Games, Montreal. T **489** and similar horiz designs. P 13.

1742 1d.20 brown-purple 25 10
1743 3d.20 bottle-green 25 10
1744 5d. deep brown 25 10
1745 8d. blue-black 1·80 1·20
1742/1745 *Set of* 4 2·30 1·40

Designs:—3d.20, Handball; 5d. Shooting; 8d. Rowing.

1976 (26 July). OBLIGATORY TAX. Olympic Games Fund. Litho. P 13½.

1746 **490** 10p. chalky blue 25 10

491 Globe

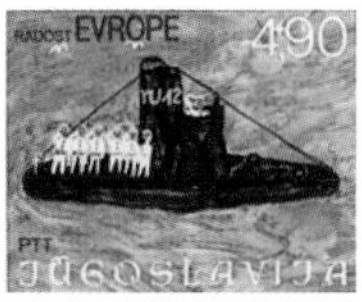
492 "Navy Day" (Nikola Mitar)

(Des A. Milenković. Litho)

1976 (16 Aug). Fifth Non-aligned Nations' Summit Conference, Columbo. P 13.

1747 **491** 4d.90 multicoloured 35 10

(Des A. Milenković. Litho German Bank Note Ptg Co, Leipzig)

1976 (2 Oct). Children's Week and 8th "Joy of Europe" meeting, Belgrade. Children's Paintings. T **492** and similar horiz design., Multicoloured. P 13.

1748 4d.90 Type **492** 30 10
1749 8d. "Children's Train" (Wiggo Gulbrandsen) 75 50

493 "Battle of Montenegrins" (Djura Jakšić)

1,00

(**494**)

495 Nenadovic (after Uroš Kneževic)

(Des A. Milenković. Photo Enschedé)

1976 (27 Nov). Paintings showing Historical Events. T **493** and similar multicoloured designs. P 13½×12½.

1750 1d.20 Type **493** 10 10
1751 2d.10 "Nikola Subic Zrinjski at Siget" (Oton Ivekovic) 10 10
1752 3d.20 "Herzegovian Fugitives" (Uroš Predic) (horiz) 15 10
1753 5d. "Uprising of Razlovci" (Borko Lazeski) (horiz) 25 10
1754 6d. "Enthroning of the Slovenian Duke Gosposvetsko Field" (Anton Gojmir Kos) (horiz) 45 20
1755 8d. "Breach of the Solun Front" (Veljko Stanojevic) (horiz) 1·20 1·00
1750/1755 *Set of* 6 2·00 1·40

1976 (8 Dec). No. 1203 surch with T **494** in red.

1756 1d. on plum 85p. 60 20

(Des A. Milenković. Litho German Bank Note Ptg Co, Leipzig)

1977 (4 Feb). Birth Bicentenary of Prota Mateja Nenadovic (soldier and diplomat). P 13½×14.

1757 **495** 4d.90 multicoloured 35 20

496 Rajko Žinzifov

497 Phlox (*Phlox paniculata*)

(Des A. Milenković. Litho German Bank Note Ptg Co, Leipzig)

1977 (10 Feb). Death Centenary, of Rajko Žinzifov (writer). P 13×13½.

1758 **496** 1d.50 bistre-brown, ochre and light brown 25 10

(Des A. Milenković. Litho Enschedé)

1977 (8 Mar). Flowers. T **497** and similar vert designs. Multicoloured. P 13½.

1759 1d.50 Type **497** ... 10 10
1760 3d.40 Tiger lily (*Lilium tigrinum*) ... 15 10
1761 4d.90 Bleeding heart (*Dicentra spectabilis*) ... 25 10
1762 6d. Zinnia (*Zinnia elegans*) ... 35 10
1763 8d. French marigold (*Tagetes parula nana*) ... 45 20
1764 10d. Geranium (*Pelargonium zonale*) ... 1·50 1·00
1759/1764 *Set of* 6 ... 2·50 1·40

498 Institute Building

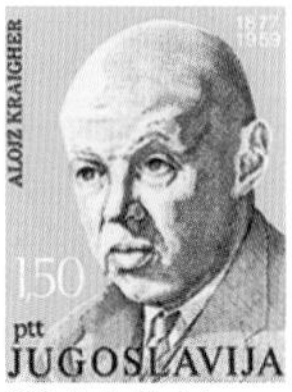

499 Alojz Kraigher

(Des D. Lučić. Eng V. Cvetković. Recess)

1977 (4 Apr). 150th Anniv of Croatian Music Institute. P 13.

1765 **498** 4d.90 sepia and blue-black ... 35 20

(Des A. Milenković. Litho)

1977 (11 Apr). Birth Centenary of Alojz Kraigher (author). P 13.

1766 **499** 1d.50 agate and pale bistre ... 25 10

500 "Kotor Bay" (Milo Milunovic)

501 Figure and Emblems

(Des A. Milenković. Photo Courvoisier)

1977 (4 May). Europa. Landscapes. T **500** and similar horiz design. Multicoloured. P 11½.

1767 4d.90 Type **500** ... 25 10
1768 10d. "Zagorje in November" (Ljubo Babić) ... 60 50

1977 (7 May). OBLIGATORY TAX. Red Cross Week. Litho. P 13×13½.

1769 **501** 20p. deep carmine and chocolate ... 3·50 1·00
1770 50p. deep carmine and deep brownish olive ... 3·00 85
1771 1d. deep carmine and Prussian blue ... 2·30 50
1769/1771 *Set of* 3 ... 8·00 2·10

The 20p. was for use in Serbia and Kosovo, 50p. in Bosnia and Herzegovina and Vojvodina, 1d. in the rest of Yugoslavia.

502 "President Tito" (Omer Mujadžic)

503 Alpine Scene

(Des A. Milenković. Photo Courvoisier)

1977 (25 May). 85th Birthday of President Tito. P 11½.

1772 **502** 1d.50 sepia, pale olive-sepia and gold ... 25 10
1773 4d.90 sepia, salmon-pink & gold ... 35 20
1774 8d. sepia, yellow-olive and gold ... 70 50
1772/1774 *Set of* 3 ... 1·20 70

(Des A. Milenković. Litho German Bank Note Ptg Co, Leipzig)

1977 (6 June). International Environment Protection Day. T **503** and similar vert design. Multicoloured. P 13.

1775 4d.90 Type **503** ... 35 10
1776 10d. Plitvice waterfall and red-breasted flycatcher ... 80 50

504 Petar Kocic

505 Dove and Map of Europe

(Des A. Milenković. Litho)

1977 (15 June). Birth Centenary of Petar Kocic (writer). P 13.

1777 **504** 1d.50 maroon & pale grey-green ... 25 10

(Des A Milenković. Litho)

1977 (15 June). European Security and Co-operation Conference, Belgrade. P 13.

1778 **505** 4d.90 multicoloured ... 35 20
1779 10d. multicoloured ... 1·90 1·70

506 Tree

507 "Bather" (Mrak Franci)

1977 (14 Sept). OBLIGATORY TAX. Anti-tuberculosis Week. Litho. P 13½.

1780 **506** 50p. multicoloured ... 17·00 17·00
1781 1d. multicoloured ... 1·20 1·00

(Des A. Milenković. Litho German Bank Note Ptg Co, Leipzig)

1977 (3 Oct). Children's Week and 9th "Joy of Europe" meeting, Belgrade. Children's Paintings. T **507** and similar horiz design. Multicoloured. P 13.

1782 4d.90 Type **507** ... 35 10
1783 10d. "One Fruit into Pail—the other into Mouth" (Tanja Ilinskaja) ... 80 55

508 Congress Building, Belgrade

509 Exhibition Emblem

(Des A. Milenković. Litho)

1977 (4 Oct). European Security and Co-operation Conference, Belgrade. P 13.

1784 **508** 4d.90 deep grey-blue, new blue and gold ... 35 20
1785 10d. deep claret, bright rose-red and gold ... 2·20 2·00

(Des A. Milenković. Litho)

1977 (20 Oct). Balkanphila 6 Stamp Exhibition, Belgrade. P 13.

1786 **509** 4d.90 multicoloured ... 25 10

510 Double Flute

511 Ivan Vavpotič

(Des D. Lučić. Eng D. Matić (1d.50, 4d.90, 8d.), N. Hrvanovic (3d.40, 6d., 10d.). Recess)

1977 (25 Oct). Musical Instruments in Ethnographical Museum, Belgrade. T **510** and similar horiz designs. P 13.

1787 1d.50 chestnut and yellow-brown ... 10 10
1788 3d.40 red-brown and deep blue-green ... 10 10
1789 4d.90 yellow and sepia ... 15 10
1790 6d. red-brown and deep ultramarine ... 25 10
1791 8d. sepia and orange-brown ... 35 20
1792 10d. bistre and myrtle-green ... 80 65
1787/1792 *Set of* 6 ... 1·60 1·10

Designs:—3d.40, Tambura (string instrument); 4d.90, Gusle (string instrument); 6d. Lijerica (string instrument); 8d, Bagpipe; 10d. Pan's flute.

(Des A. Milenković. Photo Enschedé)

1977 (26 Nov). Self-portraits. T **511** and similar vert designs. Multicoloured. P 13½×12½.

1793 1d.50 Type **511** ... 10 10
1794 3d.40 Mihailo Vukotic ... 15 10
1795 4d.90 Kosta Hakman ... 20 10
1796 6d. Miroslav Kraljevic ... 25 15
1797 8d. Nikola Martinovski ... 35 20
1798 10d. Milena Pavlovic-Barili ... 75 65
1793/1798 *Set of* 6 ... 2·75 1·20

512 Globe and Olympic Rings

513 "Ceremony of Testaccio" (miniature from Officium Virginis)

1977 (17 Dec). OBLIGATORY TAX. Olympic Games Fund. Litho. P 13.

1799 **512** 10p. lemon, light greenish blue and dull ultramarine ... 25 10

(Des A. Milenković. Photo German Bank Note Ptg Co, Leipzig)

1978 (14 Jan). 400th Death Anniv of Julije Klovic (Croat miniaturist). T **513** and similar horiz design. Multicoloured. P 14.

1800 4d.90 Type **513** ... 20 10
1801 10d. Portrait of Klovic (El Greco) ... 50 35

514 Pre-stamp Letter (Bavanište–Kubin)

515 Battle of Pirot

(Des D. Lučić. Photo Enschedé)

1978 (28 Jan). Post Office Museum Exhibits. T **514** and similar vert designs. Multicoloured. P 12½×14.

1802 1d.50 Type **514** ... 10 10
1803 3d.40 19th century mail box ... 10 10
1804 4d.90 Ericsson induction table telephone ... 15 10
1805 10d. Morse's first electro-magnetic telegraph set ... 45 40
1802/1805 *Set of* 4 ... 70 65

(Des A. Milenković. Litho)

1978 (20 Feb). Centenary of Serbo-Turkish War. P 13.

1806 **515** 1d.50 multicoloured ... 2·50 2·20

516 S-49A Trainer, 1949

517 Golubac

(Des D. Lučić. Litho)

1978 (24 Apr). Aeronautical Day. T **516** and similar horiz designs. P 13.

1807 1d.50 flesh, brown and salmon ... 10 10
1808 3d.40 pale blue, black and slate-blue ... 20 10
1809 4d.90 black and pale red-brown ... 30 10
1810 10d. pale yellow, deep brown and grey-olive ... 85 65
1807/1810 *Set of* 4 ... 1·30 85

Designs:—3d.40, Soko Galeb 3 jet trainer; 4d.90, UTVA 75 elementary trainer; 10d. Jurom Orao jet fighter.

(Des A. Milenković. Photo Courvoisier)

1978 (3 May). Europa. T **517** and similar horiz design. Multicoloured. P 11½.

1811 4d.90 Type **517** ... 25 20
1812 10d. St. Naum Monastery ... 1·20 1·10

518 Boxing Glove on Globe

519 Symbols of Red Crescent, Red Cross and Red Lion

(Des D. Lučić. Litho)

1978 (5 May). Second World Amateur Boxing Championship, Belgrade. P 13½.

1813 **518** 4d.90 red-brown, new blue and indigo ... 35 10

1978 (7 May). OBLIGATORY TAX. Red Cross Week. No. 1814 surcharged. Litho. P 13½×13.

1814 **519** 20p. on 1d. new blue and vermilion ... 75 35
1815 1d. new blue and vermilion ... 35 20

520 Honey Bee (*Apis mellifica*)

521 Filip Filipovic and Radovan Dragovic

(Des A. Milenković. Photo Courvoisier)

1978 (25 May). Bees. T **520** and similar vert designs. Multicoloured. P 11½.

1816 1d.50 Type **520** ... 10 10
1817 3d.40 *Halictus scabiosae* (mining bee) ... 25 15
1818 4d.90 Blue carpenter bee (*Xylocopa violacea*) ... 50 20
1819 10d. Buff-tailed bumble bee (*Bombus terrestris*) ... 1·40 1·20
1816/1819 *Set of* 4 ... 2·00 1·50

1978 (19 June). Birth Centenaries of F. Filipovic and R. Dragovic (socialist movement leaders). P 13½.

1820 **521** 1d.50 deep olive and deep rose-lilac ... 25 10

522 President Tito (poster)

0,35
(523)

524 Conference Emblem over Belgrade

(Des A. Milenković after M. Žarković and M. Trebotić. Litho)

1978 (20 June). 11th Communist League Congress. T **522** and similar vert design. Multicoloured. P 13½.

1821 2d. Type **522** ... 25 10
1822 4d.90 Hammer and sickle (poster) ... 50 35
MS1823 70×93 mm. 15d. As No. 1821. Imperf ... 3·25 3·00

1978–82. As Nos. 1588/91 but litho. P 12½.

1825 5d. slate-violet (1978) ... 2·50 55
1826 10d. slate-green (1981) ... 2·50 55
1827 20d. deep rose-lilac (1981) ... 5·00 80
1828 50d. chalky blue (15.2.82) ... 3·75 1·70
1825/1828 *Set of 4* ... 12·50 3·25

1978 (17 July–13 Nov). Various stamps surch as T **523**.

1829 – 35p. on 10p. deep brown (No. 1467ao) (13.11) ... 1·50 30
1830 **332** 60p. on 85p. deep steel-blue (No. 1271) (13.11) ... 1·50 30
1831 **443** 80p. on 1d.20 grey-green (No. 1599) (13.11) ... 1·50 30
1832 – 2d. on 1d. dull yellowish green (No. 1657) (Br.) ... 6·50 20
1833 – 3d.40 on 2d.10 deep dull green (No. 1661) (Br.) (1.8) ... 60 20
1829/1833 *Set of 5* ... 10·50 1·20

(Des D. Lučić. Photo German Bank Note Ptg Co, Leipzig)

1978 (25 July). Conference of Foreign Ministers of Non-aligned Countries. P 13½×14.

1834 **524** 4d.90 new blue and pale blue ... 25 10

525 Championship Emblem

526 North Face, Mount Triglav

(Des D. Lučić. Litho German Bank Note Ptg Co, Leipzig)

1978 (10 Aug). 14th Kayak and Canoe "Still Water" World Championship, Belgrade. P 13.

1835 **525** 4d.90 blue-black, dull ultramarine and light blue ... 25 10

(Des D. Lučić. Photo German Bank Note Ptg Co, Leipzig)

1978 (26 Aug). Bicentenary of First Ascent of Mount Triglav. P 13½×14.

1836 **526** 2d. multicoloured ... 25 10

527 Hand holding Flame

528 Black Lake, Durmitor

(Des A. Daskalović. Litho)

1978 (14 Sept). OBLIGATORY TAX. Anti-tuberculosis Week. P 13.

1837 **527** 1d. multicoloured ... 1·00 55

(Des A. Milenković. Photo German Bank Note Ptg Co, Leipzig)

1978 (20 Sept). Protection of the Environment. T **528** and similar horiz design. Multicoloured. P 14×13½.

1838 4d.90 Type **528** ... 25 10
1839 10d. River Tara ... 75 55

529 Olympic Rings on Map of World

530 Star Map

1978 (Sept). OBLIGATORY TAX. Olympic Games Fund. Litho. P 13.

1840 **529** 30p. multicoloured ... 50 20

(Des D. Lučić. Litho German Bank Note Ptg Co, Leipzig)

1978 (30 Sept). 29th International Astronautical Federation Congress, Dubrovnik. P 13×12½.

1841 **530** 4d.90 multicoloured ... 25 10

531 "People in Forest" (Ivana Balen)

532 Seal

(Des A. Milenković. Litho German Bank Note Ptg Co, Leipzig)

1978 (2 Oct). Children's Week and Tenth "Joy of Europe" Meeting, Belgrade. T **531** and similar horiz design. Multicoloured. P 13.

1842 4d.90 Type **531** ... 25 10
1843 10d. "Family round a Pond" (Vincent Christel) ... 70 50

(Des A. Milenković. Litho)

1978 (5 Oct). Centenary of Kresna Uprising. P 13.

1844 **532** 2d. black, deep brown and gold ... 25 10

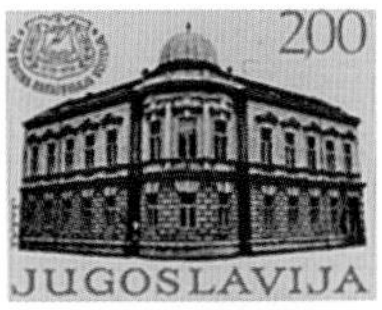

533 Old College Building

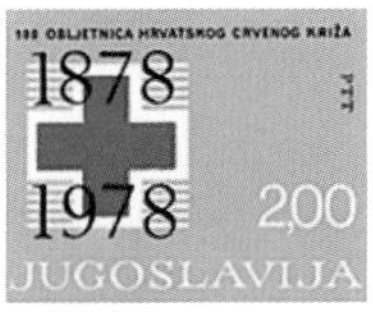

534 Red Cross

(Des A. Milenković. Litho)

1978 (16 Oct). Bicentenary of Teachers' Training College, Sombor. P 13.

1845 **533** 2d. deep brown, olive-yellow and gold ... 25 10

(Des F. Bis. Litho)

1978 (21 Oct). Centenary of Croatian Red Cross. P 13.

1846 **534** 2d. scarlet-vermilion, pale turquoise-blue and black ... 25 10

535 Metallic Sculpture "XXII" (Dušan Džamonja)

536 "Crossing the Neretva" (Ismet Mujezinovic)

(Des V. Cvetković. Litho German Bank Note Ptg Co, Leipzig)

1978 (4 Nov). Modern Sculpture. T **535** and similar designs. P 13.

1847 2d. brownish black, pale buff and silver ... 10 10
1848 3d.40 deep blue, pale brownish grey and silver ... 20 10
1849 4d.90 grey olive, stone and silver ... 20 10
1850 10d. sepia, buff and silver ... 80 55
1847/1850 *Set of 4* ... 1·20 75

Designs: Vert—3d.40, "Circulation in Space I" (Vojin Bakic); 4d.90, "Tectonic Octopod" (Olga Jevric). Horiz—10d. "The Tree of Life" (Drago Tršar).

(Des A. Milenković. Litho)

1978 (10 Nov). 35th Anniv of Battle of Neretva. P 13.

1851 **536** 2d. multicoloured ... 25 10

537 "People from the Seine" (Marijan Detoni)

538 Eurasian Red Squirrel

(Des A. Milenković. Photo German Bank Note Ptg Co, Leipzig)

1978 (28 Nov). Republic Day. Graphic Art. T **537** and similar vert designs. P 14×13½.

1852 2d. black, stone and gold ... 10 10
1853 3d.40 black, pale grey and gold ... 10 10
1854 4d.90 black, pale yellow and gold ... 25 10
1855 6d. black, pale flesh and gold ... 35 20
1856 10d. black, flesh and gold ... 1·00 90
1852/1856 *Set of 5* ... 1·60 1·30

Designs:—3d.40, "Labourers" (Maksim Sedej): 4d.90, "Felling of Trees" (Daniel Ozmo); 6d. "At a Meal" (Pivo Karamatijevic); 10d. "They are not afraid even at a most loathsome crime" (Djordje Andrejevic Kun).

(Des A. Milenković. Litho German Bank Note Ptg Co, Leipzig)

1978 (11 Dec). New Year. T **538** and similar vert designs. Multicoloured. P 13×12½.

1857 1d.50 Type **538** ... 25 10
1858 1d.50 Larch ... 25 10
1859 2d. Red deer (*bright blue background*) ... 25 10
a. Dull blue background. Booklets ... 25 10
b. Booklet pane. Nos. 1859a×4 and 1860a×4 ... 2·10
1860 2d. Sycamore (*bright blue background*) ... 25 10
a. *Dull blue background.* Booklets ... 25 10
1861 3d.40 Rock partridge (*deep salmon-pink background*) ... 50 20
a. *Bright yellow-olive background.* Booklets ... 50 20
b. Booklet pane. Nos. 1861a×2, 1862a×2, 1863a×2 and 1864a×2 ... 4·75
1862 3d.40 Alder (*deep salmon-pink background*) ... 50 20
a. *Bright yellow-olive background.* Booklets ... 50 20
1863 4d.90 Capercaillie (*apple green background*) ... 60 20
a. *Deep yellow-ochre background.* Booklets ... 60 20
1864 4d.90 Oak (*apple green background*) ... 60 20
a. *Deep yellow-ochre background.* Booklets ... 60 20
1857/1864 *Set of 8* ... 3·00 1·10

Nos. 1857/64 were issued in small sheets of 25 stamps of each value, containing various combinations of the two designs. Row 1: aaabb; Row 2: aabbb; Row 3: ababa; Row 4: bbbaa; Row 5: bbaaa.

539 Masthead

540 Flags

(Des D. Lučić. Litho)

1979 (25 Jan). 75th Anniv of *Politika* Newspaper. P 13.

1865 **539** 2d. black and gold ... 25 10

(Des A. Milenković. Litho)

1979 (15 Feb). 10th Anniv of Self-Managers' Meetings, Kragujevac. P 13.

1866 **540** 2d. multicoloured ... 25 10

541 Games Mascot

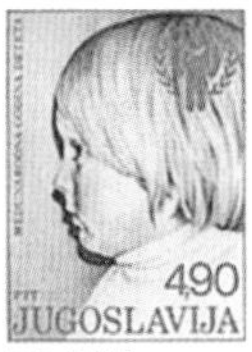

542 Child

(Des A. Milenković. Litho)

1979 (1 Mar). OBLIGATORY TAX. Mediterranean Games Fund. P 13.

1867 **541** 1d. ultramarine and violet-blue ... 35 20

See also No. 1886.

(Des A. Milenković. Photo State Ptg Wks, Vienna)

1979 (1 Mar). International Year of the Child. P 11½×12.

1868 **542** 4d.90 dull violet-blue and gold ... 55 35

543 Sabre, Mace and Enamluk (box holding Koranic texts)

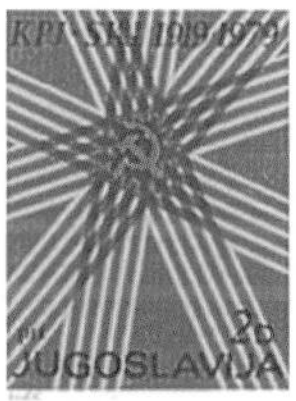

544 Hammer and Sickle on Star

(Des D. Lučić. Litho German Bank Note Ptg Co, Leipzig)

1979 (26 Mar). Ancient Weapons from Belgrade Ethnographic Museum. T **543** and similar horiz designs. Multicoloured. P 14.

1869 2d. Type **543** ... 10 10
1870 3d.40 Pistol and ammunition stick ... 10 10
1871 4d.90 Carbine and powder-horn ... 25 10
1872 10d. Rifle and cartridge-pouch ... 75 65
1869/1872 *Set of 4* ... 1·10 85

(Des D. Lučić. Litho)

1979 (20 Apr). 60th Anniv of Yugoslav Communist Party and League of Communist Youth. P 13.

1873 **544** 2d. multicoloured ... 10 10
1874 4d.90 multicoloured ... 25 10

545 University

546 "Panorama of Belgrade" (Carl Goebel)

(Des A. Milenković. Litho)

1979 (24 Apr). 30th Anniv of Cyril and Methodius University, Skopje. P 13.

1875 **545** 2d. brown, stone and salmon ... 25 10

(Des A. Milenković. Photo Courvoisier)

1979 (30 Apr). Europa. T **546** and similar horiz design. Multicoloured. P 11½.
1876 4d.90 Type **546** ... 60 55
1877 10d. Postilion and view of Ljubljana (after Jan van der Heyden) ... 75 65

547 Stylized Bird

548 Alpine Snow-thistle (*Cicerbita alpina*)

(Des A. Daskalović. Litho)

1979 (6 May). OBLIGATORY TAX. Red Cross Week. P 13½.
1878 **547** 1d. light greenish blue, deep blue and vermilion ... 25 10

(Des A. Milenković. Photo German Bank Note Ptg Co, Leipzig)

1979 (25 May). Alpine Flowers. T **548** and similar vert designs. Multicoloured. P 13½×14.
1879 2d. Type **548** ... 10 10
1880 3d.40 *Anemone narcissiflora* ... 10 10
1881 4d.90 Milk-vetch (*Astragalus sempervirens*) ... 25 10
1882 10d. Alpine clover (*Trifolium alpinum*) ... 1·10 1·00
1879/1882 *Set of 4* ... 1·40 1·20

549 Milutin Milankovic (after Paja Jovanović)

550 Kosta Abraševic

(Des A. Milenković. Photo)

1979 (28 May). Birth Centenary of Milutin Milankovic (scientist). P 13½.
1883 **549** 4d.90 multicoloured ... 35 10

(Des D. Lučić. Litho)

1979 (29 May). Birth Centenary of Kosta Abraševic (poet). P 13½.
1884 **550** 2d. grey, salmon and black ... 25 10

1979 (1 June). OBLIGATORY TAX. Solidarity Week. As T **469** but date changed to "1.-7.VI". Litho. P 13.
1885 **469** 30p. black, bluish grey and deep blue ... 50 30
See also Nos. 1933 and 2218/19.

1979 (1 Aug). OBLIGATORY TAX. Mediterranean Games Fund. As No. 1867 but colour changed. P 13.
1886 **541** 1d. green-blue and deep green-blue ... 25 10

551 Rowing Crew

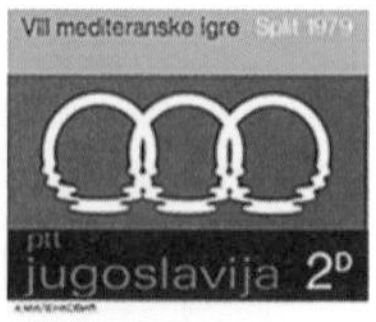

552 Games Emblem

(Des D. Lučić. Litho)

1979 (28 Aug). 9th World Rowing Championship, Bled. P 13.
1887 **551** 4d.90 multicoloured ... 50 10

(Des A. Milenković. Litho)

1979 (10 Sept). Eighth Mediterranean Games. T **552** and similar horiz designs. Multicoloured. P 13½.
1888 2d. Type **552** ... 10 10
1889 4d.90 Mascot and emblem ... 20 10
1890 10d. Map and flags of participating countries ... 55 35
1888/1890 *Set of 3* ... 75 50

553 Girl playing Hopscotch

554 Arms of Zagreb, 1499

(Des A. Daskalović. Litho)

1979 (14 Sept). OBLIGATORY TAX. Anti-tuberculosis Week. P 13½.
1891 **553** 1d. multicoloured ... 50 20

(Des A. Milenković. Litho)

1979 (14 Sept). 450th Anniv of Postal Service in Zagreb. P 12½.
1892 **554** 2d. black, grey and carmine ... 25 10

555 Lake Palic

556 Emblems

(Des A. Milenković. Photo German Bank Note Ptg Co, Leipzig)

1979 (20 Sept). Protection of the Environment. T **555** and similar horiz design. Multicoloured. P 14×13½.
1893 4d.90 Type **555** ... 25 10
1894 10d. Lake in Prokletije range ... 60 55

(Des A. Milenković. Recess and photo State Ptg Wks, Vienna)

1979 (1 Oct). Meeting of International Bank for Reconstruction and Development and of International Monetary Fund. P 13½.
1895 **556** 4d.90 multicoloured ... 25 10
1896 10d. multicoloured ... 60 45

557 Street in Winter (Mirjana Marković)

558 Mihailo Pupin

(Des A. Milenković. Litho)

1979 (2 Oct). 11th "Joy of Europe" Meeting, Belgrade. T **557** and similar horiz design showing children's drawings. Multicoloured. P 13½.
1897 4d.90 Type **557** ... 30 10
1898 10d. House and garden (Jacques An) ... 75 65

(Des D. Sandić. Litho German Bank Note Ptg Co, Leipzig)

1979 (9 Oct). 125th Birth Anniv of Mihailo Pupin (scientist). P 13.
1899 **558** 4d.90 brown, blue and deep blue ... 30 10

559 Olympic Rings

560 Marko Cepenkov

1979 (15 Oct). OBLIGATORY TAX. Olympic Games Fund. Litho. P 14.
1900 **559** 30p. light carmine and blue ... 25 10

(Des D. Sandić. Litho)

1979 (15 Nov). 150th Birth Anniv of Marko Cepenkov (author and folklorist). P 13.
1901 **560** 2d. reddish brown, sage green and deep olive ... 25 10

561 Priština University

562 Lion on Column (Trogir Cathedral)

(Des A. Milenković. Litho)

1979 (17 Nov). Tenth Anniv of Priština University. P 13.
1902 **561** 2d. multicoloured ... 25 10

(Des A. Milenković. Photo State Ptg Wks, Vienna)

1979 (29 Nov). Romanesque Sculpture. T **562** and similar vert designs. Multicoloured. P 13½.
1903 2d. Type **562** ... 10 10
1904 3d.40 Apostle (detail of choir stall, Split Cathedral) ... 20 10
1905 4d.90 Window (Church of the Ascension, Decani) ... 25 10
1906 6d. Detail of Buvina door (Split Cathedral) ... 35 10
1907 10d. Virgin and child (West door, Church of the Virgin, Studenica) ... 55 45
1903/1907 *Set of 5* ... 1·30 75

563 Sarajevo University

564 Djakovic and Hecimovic

(Des D. Lučić. Litho)

1979 (1 Dec). 30th Anniv of Sarajevo University. P 13.
1908 **563** 2d. black, pale red-brown and pale grey ... 25 10

(Des A. Milenković. Litho)

1979 (10 Dec). 50th Death Anniv of Djuro Djakovic and Nikola Hecimovic (leaders of socialist movement). P 13.
1909 **564** 2d. multicoloured ... 25 10

565 Paddle-steamer *Srbija*

566 Milton Manaki

(Des D. Lučić. Litho)

1979 (14 Dec). Danube Conference. T **565** and similar horiz design. Multicoloured. P 13.
1910 4d.90 Paddle-steamer *Deligrad* ... 75 65
1911 10d. Type **565** ... 1·60 1·40

(Des D. Sandić. Litho)

1980 (21 Jan). Birth Centenary of Milton Manaki (first Balkan film maker). P 13.
1912 **566** 2d. dull claret, pale yellow and yellow-brown ... 25 10

567 Edvard Kardelj

PLOČE 1980 KARDELJEVO

(568)

569 Speed Skating

(Des D. Lučić. Litho)

1980 (26 Jan). 70th Birth Anniv of Edvard Kardelj (politician). P 13½.
1913 **567** 2d. multicoloured ... 25 10

1980 (2 Feb). Change of Name of Ploce to Kardeljevo. No. 1913 optd with T **568**, in red.
1914 **567** 2d. multicoloured ... 25 10

(Des M. Rakic. Litho)

1980 (13 Feb). Winter Olympics, Lake Placid. T **569** and similar horiz design. Multicoloured. P 13½×13.
1915 4d.90 Type **569** ... 35 20
1916 10d. Skiing ... 2·20 2·00

570 Belgrade University

571 Fencing

1980 (27 Feb). 75th Anniv of Belgrade University. P 13½.
1917 **570** 2d. multicoloured ... 25 10

(Des D. Lučić. Litho)

1980 (21 Apr). Olympic Games, Moscow. T **571** and similar horiz designs. Multicoloured. P 13×13½.
1918 2d. Type **571** ... 10 10
1919 3d.40 Cycling ... 20 10
1920 4d.90 Hockey ... 25 15
1921 10d. Archery ... 75 65
1918/1921 *Set of 4* ... 1·20 90

572 Pres. Tito (relief by Antun Augustincic)

573 Pres. Tito

(Des A. Milenković. Photo Courvoisier)

1980 (28 Apr). Europa. T **572** and similar horiz design. Multicoloured. P 11½.
1922 4d.90 Type **572** ... 30 30
1923 13d. Portrait of Tito by Djordje Prudnikov ... 1·60 1·40

(Des A. Milenković. Litho)

1980 (4 May). Death of President Tito. T **573** and similar vert design showing portraits of Tito by Božidar Jakac. P 13½.
1924 2d.50 slate-purple ... 35 10
a. Perf 10½ ... 50 30
1925 4d.90 slate-black ... 1·00 1·00
Nos. 1924/5 were each issued in sheets of eight stamps and one central inscribed label.
Both comb and line perforated versions of the 2d.50, perf 13½, exist.

574 Sculpture by S. Kovacevic

575 Sava Kovacevic

(Des A. Daskalović. Litho)

1980 (4 May). OBLIGATORY TAX. Red Cross Week. P 13½.
1926 **574** 1d. multicoloured 50 20

(Des D. Sandić. Litho)

1980 (12 May). 75th Birth Anniv of Sava Kovacevic (partisan). P 13½.
1927 **575** 2d.50 yellow-brown, reddish orange and yellow 25 10

576 Estafette and Letter from Youth of Belgrade, 1945

577 Flying Gurnard (*Dactylopterus volitans*)

(Des A. Milenković. Litho)

1980 (14 May). 35th Anniv of First Tito's Estafette (youth celebration of Tito's birthday). P 13½.
1928 **576** 2d. multicoloured 25 10

(Des A. Milenković. Photo Courvoisier)

1980 (24 May). Adriatic Sea Fauna. T **577** and similar horiz designs. Multicoloured. P 11½.
1929 2d. Type **557** 20 10
1930 3d.40 Turtle (*Caretta caretta*) 30 15
1931 4d.90 Little tern (*Sterna albifrons*) 45 20
1932 10d. Common dolphin (*Delphinus delphis*) .... 2·20 2·00
1929/1932 *Set of* 4 .... 2·75 2·20

1980 (1 June). OBLIGATORY TAX. Solidarity Week. As No. 1885. Litho. P 13½.
1933 **469** 1d. black, bluish grey and deep blue 50 35
No. 1933 was re-issued in 1981, 1982, 1983 and 1984.

2,50
(**579**)

578 Decius Trajan (249-51)

(Des D. Lučić. Photo German Bank Note Ptg Co, Leipzig)

1980 (10 June). Roman Emperors on Coins. T **578** and similar vert designs. Multicoloured. P 14.
1934 2d. Type **578** 10 10
1935 3d.40 Aurelian (270-75) 20 10
1936 4d.90 Probus (276-82) 35 10
1937 10d. Diocletian (284-305) 75 45
1934/1937 *Set of* 4 .... 1·30 70

1980 (17 June–Oct). Nos. 1660 and 1652 surch as T **579**.
1938 2d.50 on 1d.50 red 60 10
1939 5d. on 75p. purple (15.10) .... 2·20 20
See also Nos. 1992/3.

580 Lipica Horses

581 Tito

(Des B. Jakac. Litho)

1980 (25 June). 400th Anniv of Lipica Stud Farm. P 13½.
1940 **580** 2d.50 black 25 10

(Des D. Lučić. Litho)

1980 (27 June). 30th Anniv of Self-management Law. P 13½.
1941 **581** 2d.50 carmine and vermilion 25 10

582 Novi Sad University

583 Mljet

(Des D. Lučić. Litho)

1980 (28 June). 20th Anniv of Novi Sad University. P 13½.
1942 **582** 2d.50 deep blue-green 25 10

(Des D. Čudov. Photo German Bank Note Ptg Co, Leipzig)

1980 (5 Sept). Protection of the Environment. T **583** and similar horiz design showing national parks. Multicoloured. P 14.
1943 4d.90 Type **583** 35 15
1944 13d. Galicica, Ohrid 80 55

584 Pyrrhotine

585 Lake

(Des D. Lučić. Litho)

1980 (10 Sept). Crystals. T **584** and similar vert designs. Multicoloured. P 13½.
1945 2d.50 Type **584** 10 10
1946 3d.40 Dolomite 20 10
1947 4d.90 Sphalerite 30 20
1948 13d. Wulfenite 75 65
1945/1948 *Set of* 4 .... 1·20 95

1980 (14 Sept). OBLIGATORY TAX. Anti-tuberculosis Week. Litho. P 13½.
1949 **585** 1d. multicoloured 35 10

586 Kotor

587 "Children with Balloons" (Gabrijela Radojevic)

(Des A. Milenković. Litho)

1980 (23 Sept). 21st Session of U.N.E.S.C.O. General Conference, Belgrade. P 13×13½.
1950 **586** 4d.90 grey-bl, gold & dp ultram 35 10

(Des A. Milenković. Litho German Bank Note Ptg Co, Leipzig)

1980 (2 Oct). 12th "Joy of Europe" Meeting, Belgrade. T **587** and similar horiz design showing children's drawings. Multicoloured. P 13½×13.
1951 4d.90 Type **587** 30 15
1952 13d. Face (Renata Pisarcikova) 80 55

588 Olympic Flag and Globe

589 Dove and Madrid

(Litho German Bank Note Ptg Co, Leipzig)

1980 (20 Oct). OBLIGATORY TAX. Olympic Games Fund. P 14.
1953 **588** 50p. multicoloured 25 10

(Des A. Milenković. Eng D. Matić. Recess and litho)

1980 (11 Nov). European Security and Co-operation Conference, Madrid. P 13½.
1954 **589** 4d.90 deep turquoise-green and deep dull green 25 10
1955 13d. bistre and blackish brown 65 55

590 Flag of Bosnia and Herzegovina Socialist Republic

591 "Complaint" (Miloš Vuškovic)

(Des A. Milenković. Litho)

1980 (28 Nov). Flags of Yugoslav Socialist Republics and of Federal Republic. T **590** and similar horiz designs. P 12½.
1956 2d.50 multicoloured 20 10
1957 2d.50 multicoloured 20 10
1958 2d.50 multicoloured 20 10
1959 2d.50 multicoloured 20 10
1960 2d.50 multicoloured 20 10
1961 2d.50 vermilion, gold and brownish grey 20 10
1962 2d.50 multicoloured 20 10
1963 2d.50 multicoloured 20 10
1956/1963 *Set of* 8 .... 1·40 70

Designs:—No. 1956, Type **590**; 1957, Montenegro; 1958, Croatia; 1959, Yugoslavia (inscr in Roman alphabet); 1960, Yugoslavia (inscr in Cyrillic alphabet); 1961, Macedonia; 1962, Slovenia; 1963, Serbia.
Nos. 1956/9 were issued together in sheetlets of 16, each design occurring in a block of four; Nos. 1960/3 were similarly arranged. A *se-tenant* block of four different designs was available from the centre of each sheet (*Price for* se-tenant *block of* 4; 85p. *un*).

(Des A. Milenković. Litho)

1980 (16 Dec). Paintings. T **591** and similar multicoloured designs. P 13½.
1964 2d.50 "Woman in a Straw Hat" (Stojan Aralica) (horiz) 10 10
1965 3d.40 "Atelier No. 1" (Gabrijel Stupica) (horiz) 10 10
1966 4d.90 "To the Glory of Sutjeska Fighters" (detail, Ismet Mujezinovic) (horiz) 15 10
1967 8d. "Serenity" (Marino Tartaglia) 25 10
1968 13d. Type **591** .... 1·20 1·10
1964/1968 *Set of* 5 .... 1·60 1·40

592 Sports Complex, Novi Sad

593 Ivan Ribar

(Des D. Lučić. Litho)

1980 (20 Dec). OBLIGATORY TAX. World Table Tennis Championships, Novi Sad. P 13½.
1969 **592** 1d. deep blue-green, yellow and new blue 25 10

(Des D. Lučić. Litho)

1981 (21 Jan). Birth Centenary of Ivan Ribar (politician). P 13½.
1970 **593** 2d.50 black and carmine 25 10

594 "Cementuša" Hand Bomb

595 Virgin of Eleousa Monastery

(Des D. Lučić. Litho)

1981 (16 Feb). Partisan Arms in Belgrade Military Museum. T **594** and similar horiz designs. P 13½.
1971 3d.50 black and Venetian red 10 10
1972 5d.60 black and deep green 20 10
1973 8d. black and yellow-brown 25 15
1974 13d. black and purple 75 65
1971/1974 *Set of* 4 .... 1·20 90
Designs:—5d.60, "Partizanka" rifle; 8d. Cannon; 13d. Tank.

(Des D. Čudov. Litho)

1981 (3 Mar). 900th Anniv of Virgin of Eleousa Monastery,. Veljusa, Macedonia. P 13½.
1975 **595** 3d.50 grey, red-brown and Prussian blue .... 1·00 90

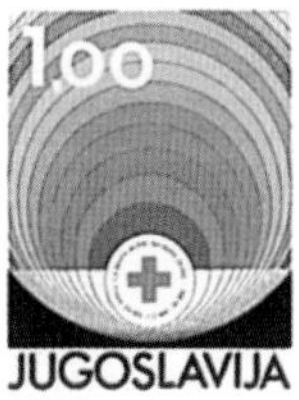

596 Table Tennis

597 "Lamp"

(Des D. Lučić. Litho)

1981 (14 Apr). SPENS '81 World Table Tennis Championships, Novi Sad. P 13½.
1976 **596** 8d. multicoloured 45 20

1981 (4 May). OBLIGATORY TAX. Red Cross Week. Litho. P 13½×13.
1977 **597** 1d. multicoloured 25 10

598 "Herzegovinan Wedding" (detail)

599 Tucovic and Dimitrije Tucovic Square

(Des A. Milenković. Photo Courvoisier)

1981 (5 May). Europa. T **598** and similar horiz design showing paintings by Nikola Arsenovic. Multicoloured. P 11½.
1978 8d. Type **598** 50 20
1979 13d. "Witnesses at a Wedding" 60 40

(Des D. Lučić. Litho)

1981 (13 May). Birth Centenary of Dimitrije Tucovic (socialist leader and editor). P 13½×13.
1980 **599** 3d.50 dp violet-blue & carmine 25 10

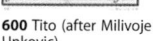

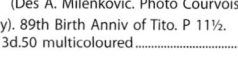

600 Tito (after Milivoje Unkovic)

601 Sunflower (*Helianthus annuus*)

(Des A. Milenković. Photo Courvoisier)

1981 (25 May). 89th Birth Anniv of Tito. P 11½.
1981 **600** 3d.50 multicoloured 50 20

(Des A. Milenković. Photo Courvoisier)

1981 (28 May). Cultivated Plants. T **601** and similar vert designs. Multicoloured. P 11½.
1982 3d.50 Type **601** 15 10
1983 5d.60 Hop (*Humulus lupulus*) 20 10
1984 8d. Corn (*Zea mays*) 35 20
1985 13d. Wheat (*Triticum vulgare*) 70 55
1982/1985 *Set of* 4 .... 1·30 85

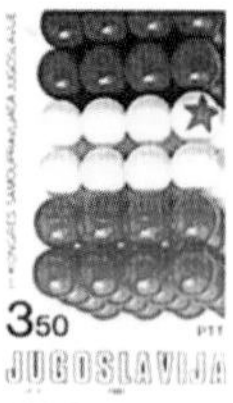

602 Congress Emblem

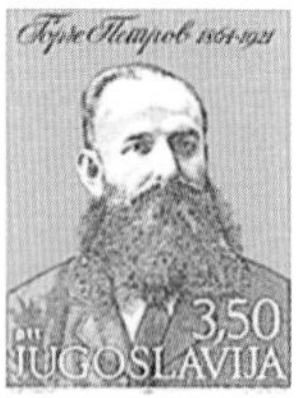

603 Djordje Petrov

(Des D. Lučić. Litho)

1981 (16 June). Third Congress of Self-managers. P 13½.
1986 **602** 3d.50 multicoloured 25 10

(Des A. Milenković. Litho)

1981 (22 June). 60th Death Anniv of Djordje Petrov (politician). P 13½.
1987 **603** 3d.50 black and ochre 25 10

604 Star

605 Apple and Target

(Des D. Lučić. Litho)

1981 (4 July). 40th Anniv of Yugoslav Insurrection. T **604** and similar horiz design. P 12½.
1988 **604** 3d.50 yellow and orange-red 25 10
1989 8d. red-orange and bright scarlet 45 20
MS1990 60×83 mm. 30d. purple-brown, gold and silver. Imperf .... 1·90 1·90
Design:—30d. Lenin Monument and star of Order.

(Des V. Radonjić. Litho)

1981 (15 Aug). OBLIGATORY TAX. Spet '81 European Shooting Championships, Titograd. P 13½.
1991 **605** 1d. deep blue, scarlet and reddish orange .... 9·00 9·00
No. 1991 was for use in Montenegro.

1981 (18 Aug–Oct). Nos. 1666 and 1669 surch as T **579**.
1992 3d.50 on 3d.40 dull green (9.10) 60 20
a. Perf 13½×12½ .... 1·90 35
1993 5d. on 4d.90 slate-blue .... 1·20 20
a. Perf 13½×12½ .... 1·90 55

606 Varaždin (18th-century illustration)

607 Parliament Building, Belgrade

(Des D. Lučić. Litho)

1981 (20 Aug). 800th Anniv of Varaždin. P 13½.
1994 **606** 3d.50 yellow and deep ultramarine 25 10

(Des D. Lučić. Litho)

1981 (1 Sept). 20th Anniv of First Non-aligned Countries Conference, Belgrade. P 13×13½.
1995 **607** 8d. deep blue and scarlet 25 10

608 "Flower"

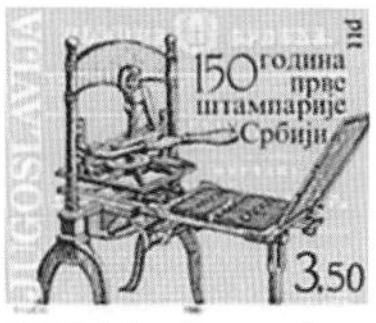

609 Printing Press and Serbian Newspaper

(Des A. Daskalović. Litho)

1981 (14 Sept). OBLIGATORY TAX. Anti-tuberculosis Week. P 13×13½.
1996 **608** 1d. bright carmine, lemon and turquoise-blue 25 10

(Des D. Lučić. Litho)

1981 (15 Sept). 150th Anniv of First Serbian Printing House. P 13½.
1997 **609** 3d.50 pink and deep blue 25 10

610 Fran Levstik

611 "Village Scene" (Sašo Arsovski)

(Des D. Lučić. Litho)

1981 (28 Sept). 150th Birth Anniv of Fran Levstik (writer). P 12×11½.
1998 **610** 3d.50 grey and brown-red 25 10

(Des D. Čudov. Litho)

1981 (2 Oct). 13th "Joy of Europe" Meeting, Belgrade. T **611** and similar vert design showing children's drawings. Multicoloured. P 13×13½.
1999 8d. Type **611** 25 10
2000 13d. "Skiers" (Aino Jokinen) 55 45

612 Tug *Karlovac* pushing Barges

613 Postal Savings Bank Emblem

(Des D. Lučić. Litho)

1981 (28 Oct). 125th Anniv of Danube Commission. T **612** and similar horiz design. Multicoloured. P 13½×13.
2001 8d. Type **612** 35 35
2002 13d. Paddle-steamer towed by railway locomotive on Sip Canal 85 80

(Des D. Lučić. Litho)

1981 (31 Oct). 60th Anniv of Postal Savings Bank. P 11½×12.
2003 **613** 3d.50 deep carmine-red and orange-yellow 25 10

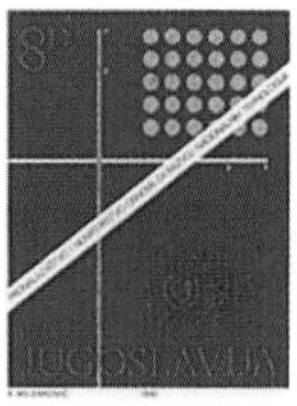

614 Emblem

615 Forsythia and Rugovo Ravine

(Des A. Milenković. Litho)

1981 (4 Nov). World Intellectual Property Organization Conference. P 13½.
2004 **614** 8d. deep carmine and gold 35 20

(Des D. Lučić. Litho)

1981 (14 Nov). Protection of Nature. T **615** and similar horiz design. Multicoloured. P 13½.
2005 8d. Type **615** 35 20
2006 13d. Lynx and Prokletije .... 1·10 1·00

616 August Šenoa

617 "Still Life with Fish" (Jovan Bijelic)

(Des A. Milenković. Litho)

1981 (12 Dec). Death Centenary of August Šenoa (writer). P 11½×12.
2007 **616** 3d.50 dp dull purple & yell-brn 25 10

(Des A. Milenković. Photo State Ptg Wks, Vienna)

1981 (29 Dec). Paintings of Animals. T **617** and similar horiz designs. Multicoloured. P 13½.
2008 3d.50 Type **617** 25 10
2009 5d.60 "Raven" (Milo Milunovic) 25 10
2010 8d. "Bird on Blue Background" (Marko Celebonovic) 25 10
2011 10d. "Horses" (Petar Lubarda) 45 20
2012 13d. "Sheep" (Nikola Mašic) 85 80
2008/2012 *Set of* 5 .... 1·80 1·20

618 Moša Pijade (politician)

619 Mastheads

(Des A. Milenković. Litho)

1982 (14 Jan). 40th Anniv of Foca Regulations. P 13½.
2013 **618** 3d.50 deep grey-blue and pale reddish lilac 25 10

(Des D. Lučić. Litho)

1982 (19 Feb). 60th Anniv of *Borba* (newspaper).
2014 **619** 3d.50 black and orange-vermilion 25 10

620 Cetinje

621 Visin's Ship *Splendido*

(Des D. Lučić. Litho)

1982 (10 Mar). 500th Anniv of City of Cetinje. P 13½.
2015 **620** 3d.50 pale red-brown and grey-black 25 10

(Des A. Milenković. Photo Courvoisier)

1982 (5 May). Europa. T **621** and similar horiz design. Multicoloured. P 11½.
2016 8d. Capt. Ivo Visin (first Yugoslav to sail round world) and naval chart 35 20
2017 15d. Type **621** 60 55

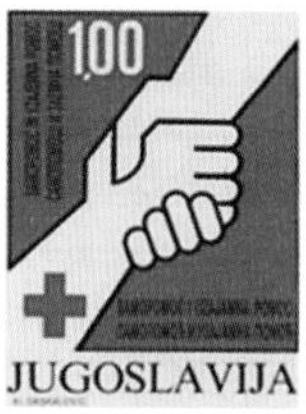

622 Clasped Hands

623 Ball placed for Kick-off

(Des A. Daskalović. Litho)

1982 (8 May). OBLIGATORY TAX. Red Cross Week. P 13½.
2018 **622** 1d. black and bright scarlet 25 10

(Des D. Lučić. Photo Courvoisier)

1982 (14 May). World Cup Football Championship, Spain. Sheet 97×84 mm containing T **623** and similar horiz designs. Multicoloured. P 11½.
MS2019 3d.50, Type **623**; 5d.60, Ball placed for corner kick; 8d. Ball in top of net; 15d. Player carrying ball under arm .... 2·50 2·50

624 House Sparrow (*Passer domesticus*) (male)

625 Tito (after Dragan Došen)

(Des A. Milenković. Litho)

1982 (24 May). Birds. T **624** and similar horiz designs. Multicoloured. P 13½.
2020 3d.50 Type **624** 25 10
2021 5d.60 House sparrow (female) 30 20
2022 8d. Spanish sparrow (female) 50 45
2023 15d. Tree sparrow (*Passer montanus*) (male) .... 1·70 1·60
2020/2023 *Set of* 4 .... 2·50 2·10
The 8d. is wrongly inscribed "Passer montanus".

(Des A. Milenković. Photo Courvoisier)

1982 (25 May). 90th Birth Anniv of Tito. Granite paper. P 11½.
2024 **625** 3d.50 multicoloured 25 10

626 Poster (Dobrilo Nikolic)

627 Jakšić (self-portrait)

(Des D. Lučić. Litho)

1982 (26 June). 12th Communist League Congress, Belgrade. P 13½.
2025 **626** 3d.50 cinnamon, salmon and scarlet... 25 10
2026 8d. olive-grey, brownish grey and scarlet ... 35 20
MS2027 70×95 mm. **626** 10d. dull orange and scarlet; 20d. bluish grey, olive-grey and scarlet..... 1·60 1·40

(Des A. Milenković. Litho Forum, Novi Sad)

1982 (27 July). 150th Birth Anniv of Dura Jakšić (writer and painter). P 14.
2028 **627** 3d.50 multicoloured ... 25 10

628 Kayaks

629 Ivan Zajc

(Des D. Lučić. Litho)

1982 (30 July). Sports Championships. T **628** and similar horiz designs. P 13½.
2029 8d. pale blue and dull blue... 75 35
2030 8d. pale green and bronze green... 75 35
2031 8d. pale rose and carmine-lake ... 75 35
2029/2031 *Set of* 3... 2·00 95
Designs and events:—No. 2029, Type **628** (17th World Kayak and Canoe Still Water Championships, Belgrade); 2030, Weightlifting (36th World Weightlifting Championships, Ljubljana); 2031, Gymnastics (Sixth World Gymnastics Cup, Zagreb).

(Des A. Milenković. Litho)

1982 (3 Aug). 150th Birth Anniv of Ivan Zajc (composer). P 13½.
2032 **629** 4d. pale orange and brown... 25 10

630 Breguet 19 and Potez 25 Biplanes

(Des D. Lučić. Litho)

1982 (1 Sept). 40th Anniv of Air Force, Anti-aircraft Defence and Navy. T **630** and similar horiz designs. P 13½.
2033 4d. olive-black and blue... 25 10
2034 6d.10 multicoloured... 30 10
2035 8d.80 black and grey-green... 45 20
2036 15d. multicoloured... 75 65
2033/2036 *Set of* 4... 1·60 95
Designs:—6d.10, Soko G-4 Super Galeb jet trainer; 8d.80, National Liberation Army armed tug; 15d. *Rade Koncar* (missile gunboat).

631 Tara National Park and Pine Cones

(Des D. Lučić. Litho)

1982 (3 Sept). Nature Protection. T **631** and similar horiz design. Multicoloured. P 13½.
2037 8d.80 Type **631**... 50 20
2038 15d. Kornati National Park and Mediterranean monk seal ... 85 80

632 Dr. Robert Koch

(Des A. Daskalović. Litho)

1982 (14 Sept). OBLIGATORY TAX. Anti-tuberculosis Week. P 13½.
2039 **632** 1d. orange, black and bright rose-red... 35 15

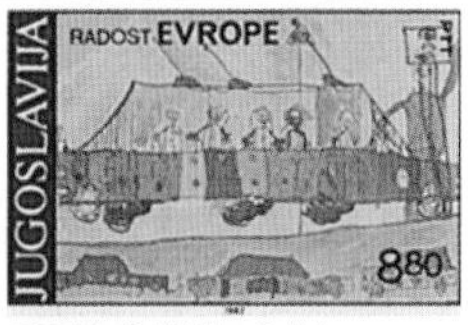

633 "Traffic" (Tibo Božo)

(Des C. Čudov. Litho)

1982 (2 Oct). 14th "Joy of Europe" Meeting, Belgrade. T **633** and similar horiz design showing children's drawings. Multicoloured. P 13½.
2040 8d.80 Type **633**... 35 20
2041 15d. "In the Bath" (Heiko Jäkel)... 75 65

634 Small Onofrio Fountain, Dubrovnik

635 Herceg Novi (from old engraving)

(Des D. Čudov. Litho)

1982 (23 Oct). 16th World Federation of Travel Agents' Associations Congress, Dubrovnik. P 13½.
2042 **634** 8d.80 multicoloured... 25 15

(Des A. Milenković. Litho)

1982 (28 Oct). 600th Anniv of Herceg Novi. P 13½.
2043 **635** 4d. multicoloured... 65 55

636 Bridge, Miljacka

637 Bihac

(Des A. Milenković. Litho)

1982 (20 Nov). Winter Olympic Games, Sarajevo. T **636** and similar horiz designs, each grey-black, azure and deep greenish blue. P 12½.
2044 4d. Type **636**... 25 20
2045 6d.10 Mosque tower and cable cars, Sarajevo... 35 25
2046 8d.80 Evangelical Church, Sarajevo... 65 55
2047 15d. Old street, Sarajevo... 1·70 1·50
2044/2047 *Set of* 4... 2·75 2·30

(Des D. Lučić. Litho)

1982 (26 Nov). 40th Anniv of Avnoj-a (anti-fascist council) Session, Bihac. P 13½.
2048 **637** 4d. red-brown and pale orange... 25 10

638 "Prophet on Golden Background" (Jože Ciuha)

639 Predic (self-portrait)

0,50
(**640**)

(Des A. Milenković. Litho)

1982 (27 Nov). Modern Art. T **638** and similar multicoloured designs. P 13½.
2049 4d. Type **638**... 25 10
2050 6d.10 "Journey to the West" (Andrej Jemec)... 25 10
2051 8d.80 "Black Comb with Red Band" (Riko Debenjak)... 25 10
2052 10d. "Manuscript" (Janez Bernik) (horiz)... 25 10
2053 15d. "Display Case" (Adriana Maraž) (horiz) 90 80
2049/2053 *Set of* 5... 1·70 1·10

(Des D. Lučić. Litho)

1982 (7 Dec). 125th Birth Anniv of Uros Predic (painter). P 13½.
2054 **639** 4d. orange and deep brown-ochre. 25 10

1982 (23 Dec). No. 1663 surch with T **640** in blue.
2055 50p. on 2d.50 slate-blue... 1·00 25
a. Perf 13½×12½ ... 2·00 35
See also No. 2057.

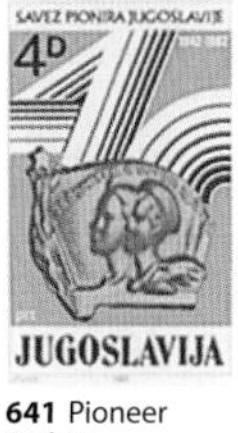

641 Pioneer Badge

0,60
(**642**)

1,00
(**643**)

(Des D. Čudov. Litho)

1982 (27 Dec). 40th Anniv of Pioneer League. P 11½×12.
2056 **641** 4d. chocolate, silver and carmine.... 25 10

1983 (11 Jan–Feb). Nos. 1663/a, 1667 and 1667b surch as T **640** (30p.), **642** (60p., 2d.) or with T **643** (1d.).
2057 30p. on 2d.50 slate-blue (R.)... 1·30 20
a. Perf 13½×12½ ... 65 20
2058 60p. on 2d.50 slate-blue (p 13½×12½) (28.2)... 25 20
a. Perf 13½... 80 20
2059 1d. on 3d.50 orange-red (p 13½) (12.1)... 1·10 20
a. Perf 13½×12½ ... 25 20
2060 2d. on 2d.50 slate-blue (p 13½×12½) (Mag.)... 2·75 20
2057/2060 *Set of* 4 (*cheapest*)... 3·50 70

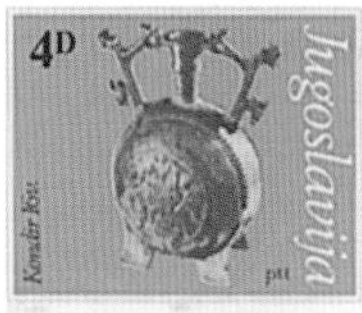

644 Lead Pitcher (16th century)

645 Jalovec Mountain Peak and Edelweiss

(Des D. Čudov. Litho)

1983 (19 Feb). Museum Exhibits. T **644** and similar horiz designs. P 13½.
2061 4d. black, bistre and silver... 25 10
2062 6d.10 black, orange-brown and silver... 25 10
2063 8d.80 gold, maroon and light grey... 25 10
2064 15d. gold, maroon and grey... 55 45
2061/2064 *Set of* 4... 1·20 70
Designs:—6d.10, Silver plated tin jar (18th century); 8d.80, Silver-gilt dish (16th century); 15d. Bronze mortar (15th century).

(Des. A. Milenković. Litho)

1983 (26 Feb). 90th Anniv of Slovenian Mountaineering Society. P 13½.
2065 **645** 4d. blue, light blue and deep blue.. 25 10

646 Ericsson Wall Telephone and War Ministry, Belgrade

647 I.M.O. Emblem and Freighters

(Des D. Lučić. Litho)

1983 (15 Mar). Centenary of Telephone in Serbia. P 13½.
2066 **646** 3d. yellow-brown and new blue ... 25 10

(Des A. Milenković. Litho Forum, Novi Sad)

1983 (17 Mar). 25th Anniv of International Maritime Organization. P 14.
2067 **647** 8d.80 multicoloured... 25 10

648 Field Mushroom (*Agaricus campestris*)

649 Series "401" Steam Locomotive

(Des A. Milenković. Litho Forum, Novi Sad)

1983 (21 Mar). Edible Mushrooms. T **648** and similar horiz designs. Multicoloured. P 14.
2068 4d. Type **648**... 40 35
2069 6d.10 Commom morel (*Morchella vulgaris*) 40 35
2070 8d.80 Cep (*Boletus edulis*)... 40 35
2071 15d. Chanterelle (*Cantharellus cibarius*).... 1·10 90
2068/2071 *Set of* 4... 2·10 1·80

(Des D. Lučić. Litho)

1983 (5 Apr). 110th Anniv of Rijeka Railway. T **649** and similar horiz design, each olive-grey and brown-rose. P 13½.
2072 4d. Type **649**... 35 30
2073 23d.70 on 8d.80 Series "442" electric locomotive (Br.) ... 70 55
No. 2073 was not issued unsurcharged.

650 Monument, Landovica

651 Nobel Prize Medal and Manuscript of *Travnik Chronicle* by Andrić

(Des A. Milenković. Litho)

1983 (10 Apr). 40th Death Annivs of Boro Vukmirivic and Ramiz Sadiku (revolutionaries). P 13½.
2074 **650** 4d. slate-purple and slate-violet 30 10

(Des A. Milenković. Photo Courvoisier)

1983 (5 May). Europa. T **651** and similar horiz design. Multicoloured. Granite paper. P 11½.
2075 8d.80 Type **651**... 30 15
2076 20d. Ivo Andrić (author and Nobel Prize winner) and bridge over the Drina ... 55 45

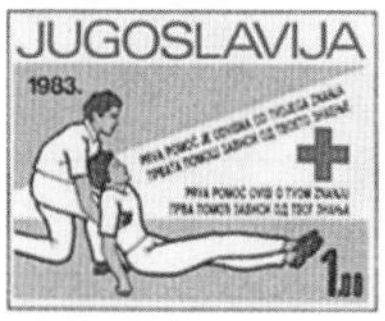
652 First Aid

653 Combine Harvester

1983 (8 May). OBLIGATORY TAX. Red Cross Week. Litho. P 13½.
2077 **652** 1d. reddish brown, orange-brown and rosine ... 30 10
2078 2d. reddish brown, orange-brown and rosine ... 30 10
No. 2078 was for use in Croatia and Slovenia, No. 2077 in the rest of Yugoslavia.

(Des D. Lučić. Litho Forum, Novi Sad)

1983 (13 May). 50th International Agricultural Fair, Novi Sad. P 14.
2079 **653** 4d. apple green and purple ... 30 10

654 "Assault" (Pivo Karamatijevic)

655 Tito (after Božidar Jakac) and Parliament Building

(Des D. Čudov. Litho)

1983 (14 May). 40th Anniv of Battle of Sutjeska. P 12½.
2080 **654** 3d. brown-rose and brown ... 30 10

(Des A. Milenković. Litho)

1983 (25 May). 30th Anniv of Tito's Election to Presidency. P 13½.
2081 **655** 4d. reddish brown and slate-green. 30 10
a. Perf 12½ ... 1·80 1·30
b. Perf 13×12½ ... 1·40 1·10

656 Delahaye Postbus, 1903

657 Statue by V. Bakic, Valjevo

(Des D. Lučić. Litho)

1983 (27 May). 80th Anniv of Postbus Service in Montenegro. T **656** and similar horiz design, each blue-black and orange-brown. P 13½.
2082 4d. Type **656** ... 30 10
2083 16d.50 Road used by first postbus ... 55 35

(Des D. Čudov. Litho)

1983 (1 June). Monuments. T **657** and similar horiz design. P 12½.
2084 100d. orange and greenish blue ... 4·25 55
a. Perf 13½ ... 2·20 55
2085 200d. orange and green ... 3·75 1·30
a. Perf 13½ ... 6·25 1·30
Design:—200d. Triumphal arch, Titograd.

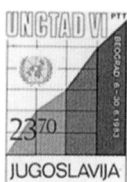

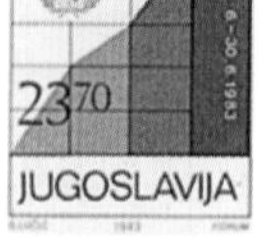
658 Graph

659 Pazin (after engraving by Valvasor)

(Des D. Lučić. Litho Forum, Novi Sad)

1983 (6 June). Sixth United Nations Conference for Trade and Development Session, Belgrade. P 14.
2086 **658** 23d.70 multicoloured ... 1·00 40

(Des D. Čudov. Litho)

1983 (7 June). Millenary of Pazin. P 12½.
2087 **659** 4d. red-brown and deep grey-green ... 30 10

660 Skopje

661 "The Victor"

(Des D. Čudov. Litho)

1983 (26 July). 20th Anniv of Skopje Earthquake. P 12½.
2088 **660** 23d.70 crimson ... 70 30
a. Perf 13½ (24.4.84) ... 1·00 85

(Des D. Lučić. Litho)

1983 (15 Aug). Birth Centenary of Ivan Meštrovic (sculptor). P 12½.
2089 **661** 6d. deep brown, chestnut and turquoise-blue ... 30 10

662 Gentian and Kupaonik National Park

663 Apple

(Des D. Lučić. Litho)

1983 (10 Sept). Nature Protection. T **662** and similar horiz design. Multicoloured. P 13½.
2090 16d.50 Type **662** ... 55 45
2091 23d.70 Chamois and Sutjeska National Park 1·10 90

1983 (14 Sept). OBLIGATORY TAX. Anti-tuberculosis Week. Litho. P 13½.
2092 **663** 1d. orange-vermilion, black and deep turquoise ... 30 10
2093 2d. orange-vermilion, black and deep turquoise ... 30 10

664 "Newly Weds" (Vesna Paunkovid)

665 School and Seal

(Des D. Čudov. Litho Forum, Novi Sad)

1983 (3 Oct). 15th "Joy of Europe" Meeting, Belgrade. T **664** and similar vert design showing children's drawings. P 14.
2094 16d.50 lemon, black and vermilion ... 30 20
2095 23d.70 multicoloured ... 70 55
Design:—23d.70, "Andres and his Mother" (Marta Lopez-Ibor).

(Des D. Čudov. Litho)

1983 (7 Oct). 150th Anniv of Kragujevac Grammar School. P 12½.
2096 **665** 5d. orange-brown and deep blue ... 30 10

666 Monument by Antun Augustincic

667 Skier and Games Emblem

(Des D. Čudov. Litho)

1983 (17 Oct). Centenary of Timocka Buna Uprising. P 13½.
2097 **666** 5d. new blue and magenta ... 30 10

(Des A. Milenković. Litho)

1983 (20 Oct). OBLIGATORY TAX. Winter Olympic Games, Sarajevo. P 12½.
2098 **667** 2d. greenish blue and deep greenish blue ... 30 10
No. 2098 was issued both in sheets of 25 and in sheets of 9.

668 Zmaj and *Neven* Periodical

669 Ski Jump, Malo Polje, Mt. Igman

(Des D. Lučić. Litho)

1983 (24 Nov). 150th Birth Anniv of Jovan Jovanović Zmaj (poet and editor). P 12½.
2099 **668** 5d. Venetian red and deep bluish green ... 30 10

(Des A. Milenković. Litho (50d.), recess (others))

1983 (25 Nov). Winter Olympic Games, Sarajevo (First issue). T **669** and similar designs. P 13½.
2100 4d. blue-black, deep green and olive-sepia ... 20 10
2101 4d. deep blue, dull blue and olive-sepia 20 10
2102 16d.50 blackish lilac, choc & ol-sep ... 60 20
2103 16d.50 slate-green, dull bl & olive-sep ... 60 20
2104 23d.70 red-brown, brown-ol & ol-sep ... 90 55
2105 23d.70 black, blackish green & ol-sep ... 90 55
2100/2105 *Set of* 6 ... 3·00 1·50
MS2106 60×74 mm. 50d. dull ultramarine and magenta. Imperf ... 2·40 2·40
Designs: As T **669**—No. 2101, Women's slalom run, Mt. Jahorina; 2102, Bob-sleigh and luge run, Mt. Trebevic; 2103, Men's alpine downhill ski run, Mt. Bjelašnica; 2104, Olympic Hall (for ice hockey and figure skating), Zetra; 2105, Speed skating rink, Zetra. 26×33 mm—50d. Games emblem.

670 "The Peasant Wedding" (Brueghel the Younger)

671 Jajce

(Des A. Milenković. Litho Forum, Novi Sad)

1983 (26 Nov). Paintings. T **670** and similar vert designs. Multicoloured. P 14.
2107 4d. Type **670** ... 30 10
2108 16d.50 "Susanna and the Elders" (Master of "The Prodigal Son") ... 40 20
2109 16d.50 "Allegory of Wisdom and Strength" (Paolo Veronese) ... 40 20
2110 23d.70 "Virgin Mary from Salamanca" (Robert Campin) ... 1·00 55
2111 23d.70 "St. Anne with the Madonna. and Jesus" (Albrecht Dürer) ... 1·00 55
2107/2111 *Set of* 5 ... 2·75 1·40

(Des D. Čudov (5d.), A. Milenković (30d.). Litho)

1983 (28 Nov). 40th Anniv of Second Avnoj-a (anti-fascist council) Session, Jajce. P 12½.
2112 **671** 5d. Venetian red and grey-blue ... 30 10
MS2113 59×74 mm. 30d. Venetian red, greenish grey and gold (Tito). Imperf ... 1·70 1·70

672 Drawing by Hasukic Sabina

673 Koco Racin

(Des A. Milenković. Litho)

1983 (10 Dec). World Communications Year. P 13½.
2114 **672** 23d.70 multicoloured ... 50 25

(Des D. Čudov. Litho)

1983 (22 Dec). 75th Birth Anniv of Koco Racin (writer). P 13½.
2115 **673** 5d. deep dull blue and red-brown .. 30 10

674 First Issue of *Politika*

675 Veljko Petrović

(Des R. Pešic. Litho)

1984 (25 Jan). 80th Anniv of *Politika* (daily newspaper). P 12½.
2116 **674** 5d. black and scarlet-vermilion ... 30 10

(Des D. Lučić. Litho)

1984 (4 Feb). Birth Centenary of Veljko Petrović (writer). P 13½.
2117 **675** 5d. brown, orange and slate ... 30 10

676 Giant Slalom

677 Marija Bursac

(Des A. Milenković. Litho)

1984 (8 Feb). Winter Olympic Games, Sarajevo (Second issue). T **676** and similar designs. P 13½.
2118 4d. multicoloured ... 30 20
2119 4d. multicoloured ... 30 20
2120 5d. multicoloured ... 30 20
2121 5d. multicoloured ... 30 20
2122 16d.50 multicoloured ... 40 20
2123 16d.50 multicoloured ... 40 20
2124 23d.70 multicoloured ... 70 35
2125 23d.70 multicoloured ... 70 35
2118/2125 *Set of* 8 ... 3·00 1·70
MS2126 Two sheets, each 60×74 mm. Imperf (a) 50d. bright blue, magenta and silver; (b) 100d. deep magenta, gold and bright blue ... 7·00 7·00
Designs: As T **676**—No. 2119, Biathlon; 2120, Slalom: 2121, Bobsleigh; 2122, Speed skating; 2123, Ice hockey; 2124, Ski jumping; 2125, Downhill skiing. 26×33 mm—50d. Olympic flame; 100d. Flame and map of Yugoslavia.

(Des D. Lučić. Litho Forum, Novi Sad)

1984 (8 Mar). Women's Day. National Heroines. T **677** and similar horiz designs, each grey, dull ultramarine and black. P 14.
2127 5d. Type **677** ... 30 10
a. Sheetlet. Nos. 2127/34 plus label ... 2·50
2128 5d. Jelena Cetkovic ... 30 10
2129 5d. Nada Dimic ... 30 10
2130 5d. Elpida Karamandi ... 30 10
2131 5d. Toncka Cec Olga ... 30 10

2132 5d. Spasenija Babovic Cana 30 10
2133 5d. Jovanka Radivojevic Kica 30 10
2134 5d. Sonja Marinkovic 30 10
2127/2134 *Set of 8* .... 2·20 70

Nos. 2127/34 were issued together in *se-tenant* sheetlets of eight stamps and one central label depicting Order of National Hero.

678 Bond and Banknote

679 Belgrade Central Station and Steam Mail Train, 1884

(Des D. Čudov. Litho)

1984 (12 Mar). 40th Anniv of Slovenian Monetary Institute. P 12½.
2135 **678** 5d. deep turquoise-blue and crimson 30 10

(Des D. Lučić. Litho)

1984 (9 Apr). Centenary of Serbian Railway. P 13½.
2136 **679** 5d. lake-brown and blackish brown 70 20

680 Jure Franko and Silver Medal

681 Bridge

(Des A. Milenković. Litho)

1984 (28 Apr). First Yugoslav Winter Olympics Medal. P 13½.
2137 **680** 23d.70 multicoloured .... 1·40 1·10

No. 2137 was issued in sheetlets of eight stamps and one central label depicting Olympics silver medal.

(Des J. Larrivière. Litho Forum, Novi Sad)

1984 (30 Apr). Europa. 25th Anniv of European Post and Telecommunications Conference. P 14.
2138 **681** 23d.70 multicoloured 40 35
2139 50d. multicoloured .... 1·10 90

No. 2138 has the country name in roman script, No. 2139 in cyrillic script.

682 Globe as Jigsaw Pieces

683 Basketball

(Des A. Daskalović. Litho)

1984 (7 May). OBLIGATORY TAX. Red Cross Week. P 13½.
2140 **682** 1d. multicoloured 15 10
2141 2d. multicoloured 30 20
2142 4d. multicoloured 40 35
2143 5d. multicoloured 85 65
2140/2143 *Set of 4* .... 1·50 1·20

The 1d. was for use in Bosnia and Herzegovina, Macedonia and Serbia, the 2d. in Montenegro, Slovenia, Vojvodina and Kosovo and all values in Croatia.

(Des A. Milenković. Litho Forum, Novi Sad)

1984 (14 May). Olympic Games, Los Angeles. T **683** and similar horiz designs. Multicoloured. P 14.
2144 5d. Type **683** 30 10
2145 16d.50 Diving 40 20
2146 23d.70 Equestrian .... 1·00 80
2147 50d. Running .... 3·50 2·75
2144/2147 *Set of 4* .... 4·75 3·50

Nos. 2144/7 were each issued in sheetlets of eight stamps and one central label depicting the Olympic emblem.

684 Tito (after Boždar Jakac)

685 "Skopje Earthquake"

(Des D. Lučić. Litho)

1984 (25 May). 40th Anniv of Failure of German Attack on National Liberation Movement's Headquarters at Drvar. P 13½.
2148 **684** 5d. orange-brown and chestnut 30 10

1984 (1 June). OBLIGATORY TAX. Solidarity Week. Self-adhesive. Imperf.
2149 **685** 1d.50 metallic blue and vermilion .... 1·00 55

The stamps were separated by rotary knife so that individual stamps could be removed from the backing paper.

No. 2149 was used in Croatia in addition to No. 1933, to give an overall rate of 2d.50.

686 Mt. Biokovo Natural Park and *Centaurea gloriosa*

687 Great Black-backed Gull (*Larus marinus*)

(Des C. Lučić. Litho)

1984 (11 June). Nature Protection. T **686** and similar horiz design. Multicoloured. P 13½.
2150 26d. Type **686** 70 55
2151 40d. Pekel Cave and *Anophthalmus schmidti* (longhorn beetle) .... 1·10 90

(Des A. Milenković. Litho Forum, Novi Sad)

1984 (28 June). Birds. T **687** and similar horiz designs. Multicoloured. P 14.
2152 4d. Type **687** 70 45
2153 5d. Black-headed gull (*Larus ridibundus*) 70 45
2154 16d.50 Herring gull (*Larus argentatus*) 70 45
2155 40d. Common tern (*Sterna hirundo*) .... 4·50 2·00
2152/2155 *Set of 4* .... 6·00 3·00

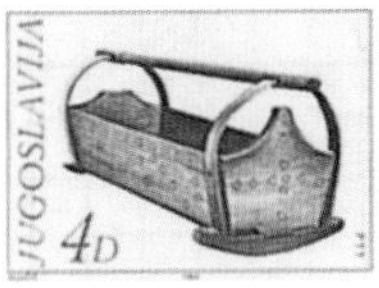

688 Cradle from Bihac, Bosnia and Herzegovina

689 Red Cross and Leaves

(Des D. Lučić. Litho)

1984 (1 Sept). Museum Exhibits. Cradles. T **688** and similar horiz designs. P 12½.
2156 4d. bronze green 15 10
2157 5d. brown-purple and claret 30 20
2158 26d. light brown and orange-brown 70 55
2159 40d. ochre and dull orange .... 1·10 90
2156/2159 *Set of 4* .... 2·00 1·60

Designs: Cradles from—5d. Montenegro; 26d. Macedonia; 40d. Rasina, Serbia.

1984 (13 Sept). OBLIGATORY TAX. Anti-tuberculosis Week. Litho. P 13½.
2160 **689** 1d. multicoloured 30 10
2161 2d. multicoloured 30 10
2162 2d.50 multicoloured 30 10
2163 4d. multicoloured 30 20
2164 5d. multicoloured 40 35
2160/2164 *Set of 5* .... 1·40 75

The 1d. was for use in Bosnia and Herzegovina and Macedonia, 2d. in Montenegro, Serbia, Slovenia and Kosovo, 2d.50 in Vojvodina, 2, 4 and 5d. in Croatia.

690 Olive Tree, Mirovica

691 National Costume (Erika Sarcevic)

(Des D. Čudov. Litho)

1984 (15 Sept). P 13½.
2165 **690** 5d. multicoloured 30 10

(Des D. Čudov. Litho Forum, Novi Sad)

1984 (2 Oct). 16th "Joy of Europe" Meeting, Belgrade. T **691** and similar vert design showing children's paintings. Multicoloured. P 14.
2166 26d. Type **691** 55 45
2167 40d. Girl pushing bear in buggy (Eva Gug) .... 1·50 1·20

692 Virovitica (17th-century engraving)

693 Map and Radio Waves

(Des C. Lučić. Litho)

1984 (4 Oct). 750th Anniv of Virovitica. P 13½.
2168 **692** 5d. dull orange and black 30 10

(Des D. Lučić. Litho)

1984 (10 Oct). 80th Anniv of Radio-Telegraphic Service in Montenegro. P 13½.
2169 **693** 6d. greenish blue and apple green 30 10

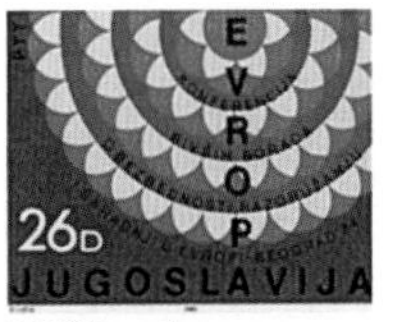

694 "Flower"

695 City Arms and "40"

(Des D. Lučić. Litho)

1984 (18 Oct). Veterans' Conference on Security, Disarmament and Co-operation in Europe, Belgrade. P 13½.
2170 **694** 26d. bright rose, black and violet .... 1·50 1·20
2171 40d. light green, black and new blue .... 2·10 1·70

Nos. 2170/1 were each printed in sheetlets of eight stamps and one central label bearing an extract from Tito's Helsinki speech.

(Des D. Lučić. Litho)

1984 (20 Oct). 40th Anniv of Liberation of Belgrade. P 13½.
2172 **695** 6d. deep rose-red, silver and deep blue 30 10

696 Milojevic and Music Score

697 Issues of 1944 and 1984

(Des D. Lučić. Litho)

1984 (27 Oct). Birth Centenary of Miloje Milojevic (composer). P 13½.
2173 **696** 6d. slate-lilac and green 30 10

(Des D. Čudov. Litho)

1984 (29 Oct). 40th Anniv of Nova Makedonija (newspaper). P 13½.
2174 **697** 6d. royal blue and orange-red 30 10

698 Boxing

699 "Madame Tatichek" (Ferdinand Waldmüller)

(Des D. Lučić. Litho)

1984 (14 Nov). Yugoslav Olympic Games Medal Winners. T **698** and similar horiz designs, each deep ultramarine and vermilion. P 13½.
2175 26d. Type **698** 40 35
a. Sheetlet. Nos. 2175/82 plus label .... 3·50
2176 26d. Wrestling 40 35
2177 26d. Canoeing 40 35
2178 26d. Handball 40 35
2179 26d. Football 40 35
2180 26d. Basketball 40 35
2181 26d. Water polo 40 35
2182 26d. Rowing 40 35
2175/2182 *Set of 8* .... 3·00 2·50

Nos. 2175/82 were issued together in *se-tenant* sheetlets of eight stamps and one central label showing Olympic medal.

(Des D. Čudov. Litho Forum, Novi Sad)

1984 (15 Nov). Paintings. T **699** and similar multicoloured designs. P 14.
2183 6d. Type **699** 30 20
2184 26d. "The Bathers" (Pierre-Auguste Renoir) 40 35
2185 26d. "At the Window" (Henri Matisse) 40 35
2186 38d. "The Tahitians" (Paul Gauguin) (horiz) 70 55
2187 40d. "The Ballerinas" (Edgar Degas) (horiz) 85 65
2183/2187 *Set of 5* .... 2·40 1·90

═ 2-D

(**700**)

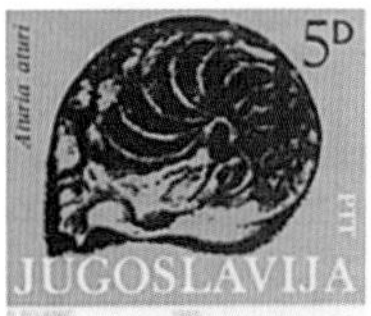

701 *Aturia aturi* (cephalopod)

1984 (26 Nov–Dec). Nos. 1675/a, 1668/a and 2088a surch as T **700**.
2188 2d. on 8d.80 bluish grey (p 13½×12½) (17.12) .... 2·75 2·20
a. Perf 13½ 70 20
2189 6d. on 4d. dull vermilion (Lake.) (p 13½×12½) 70 20
a. Perf 13½ .... 1·00 55

2190 20d. on 23d.70 crimson (p 13½) (17.12)....... 70 35
2188/2190 *Set of 3*.. 1·40 70

(Des R. Bojanić. Litho)

1985 (4 Feb). Museum Exhibits. Fossils. T **701** and similar horiz designs. P 12½.
2191 5d. maroon and light blue.......................... 15 10
2192 6d. reddish brown and orange-brown... 30 20
2193 33d. reddish brown and olive-yellow........ 70 55
2194 60d. reddish brown and pale orange......... 1·50 1·20
2191/2194 *Set of 4*... 2·40 1·80
Designs:—6d. *Pachyophis woodwardi* (snake); 33d. Hoefer's butterflyfish (*Chaetodon hoeferi*); 60d. Skull of Neanderthal man.

702 Hopovo Church

703 Three Herons in Flight

(Des D. Čudov. Litho)

1985 (20 Feb). 40th Anniv of Organized Protection of Yugoslav Cultural Monuments. P 12½.
2195 **702** 6d. lake, greenish yellow and yellow-olive...................................... 40 20

(Des D. Klun. Litho)

1985 (15 Mar). 50th Anniv of Planica Ski-jump. P 13½.
2196 **703** 6d. multicoloured.................................. 6·00 2·00

704 Lammergeier and Douglas DC-10 Jetliner over Mountains

705 Osprey (*Pandion haliaetus*)

(Des D. Čudov. Litho)

1985 (16 Mar)–**88**. AIR. T **704** and similar horiz design. Multicoloured. Fluorescent security markings. P 12½.
2197 500d. Type **704**.. 6·25 2·20
a. Perf 13½ (1987)....................................... 3·00 1·10
2198 1000d. Red-rumped swallow and airplane at airport.. 10·50 4·50
a. Perf 13½ (20.1.88)................................. 4·25 2·00
The fluorescent markings consist of "SFRJ" in roman and cyrillic characters repeated sideways over the whole stamp.

Nos. 2199/2201 are vacant.

(Des D. Čudov. Litho Forum, Novi Sad)

1985 (30 Mar). Nature Protection. Birds. T **705** and similar vert design. Multicoloured. P 14.
2202 42d. Type **705**.. 2·10 1·10
2203 60d. Hoopoe (*Upupa epops*)......................... 4·25 1·70

706 Three Herons in Flight

707 St. Methodius (detail, "Seven Slav Saints", St. Naum's Church, Ohrid)

(Des D. Klun and D. Čudov. Litho Forum; Novi Sad)

1985 (1 Apr). OBLIGATORY TAX. 50th Anniv of Planica Ski-jump. P 14.
2204 **706** 2d. ultramarine and greenish blue.. 30 10

(Des D. Čudov. Litho)

1985 (6 Apr). 1100th Death Anniv of Saint Methodius, Archbishop of Moravia. P 11½×12.
2205 **707** 10d. multicoloured.................................. 2·10 1·10

708 Handshake

709 Flute, Darabukka and Josip Slavenski (composer)

(Des O. Kogoj. Litho)

1985 (16 Apr). Tenth Anniv of Osimo Agreements between Yugoslavia and Italy. P 12½.
2206 **708** 6d. light new blue and deep ultramarine... 30 10

(Des D. Čudov. Litho Forum, Novi Sad)

1985 (29 Apr). Europa. T **709** and similar horiz design. Multicoloured. P 14.
2207 60d. Type **709**.. 85 65
2208 80d. Score of *Balkanophonia* (Slavenski).. 85 65

710 Red Cross and Faces

711 Vujic (after Dimitrije Auramovic)

(Des A. Daskalović. Litho)

1985 (8 May). OBLIGATORY TAX. Red Cross Week. P 13½.
2209 **710** 1d. violet and scarlet-vermilion........ 20 10
2210 2d. violet and scarlet-vermilion........ 20 10
2211 3d. violet and scarlet-vermilion........ 20 10
2212 4d. violet and scarlet-vermilion........ 20 10
2209/2212 *Set of 4*.. 70 35
1d. was for use in Bosnia and Herzegovina, 3d. in Vojvodina, 2, 3 and 4d. in Croatia, 2d. in rest of Yugoslavia.

(Des C. Čudov. Litho)

1985 (8 May). 150th Anniv of Joakim Vujic Theatre, Kragujevac. P 12.
2213 **711** 10d. multicoloured.................................. 30 10

712 Order of Liberty

713 Franjo Kluz and Rudi Cajavec (pilots) and Potez 25 Biplane

(Des C. Čudov. Litho)

1985 (9 May). 40th Anniv of V. E. (Victory in Europe) Day. T **712** and similar horiz design. Multicoloured. P 13½.
2214 10d. Type **712**.. 30 10
2215 10d. Order of National Liberation.............. 30 10

(Des R. Bojanić and V. Cvetković. Litho)

1985 (21 May). Air Force Day. P 12½.
2216 **713** 10d. ultramarine, maroon and chestnut.. 40 20

714 Tito (after Božidar Jakac)

715 Red Cross and "Skopje Earthquake"

(Des D. Čudov. Litho)

1985 (25 May). 93rd Birth Anniv of Tito. P 13½.
2217 **714** 10d. multicoloured.................................. 70 35

(Litho Mint, Belgrade (2218/19), Orbis, Zagreb (2220))

1985 (1 June). OBLIGATORY TAX. Solidarity Week.

(a) As Nos. 1885 and 1933. Litho. P 13½.
2218 **469** 2d.50 black, bluish grey and deep blue... 70 55
2219 3d. black, bluish grey and deep blue... 85 55

(b) Type **715**. Litho. Rouletted
2220 **715** 3d. metallic grey-blue and scarlet-vermilion.. 2·10 1·70
2218/2220 *Set of 3*.. 3·25 2·50
No. 2218 was for use in Montenegro, No. 2220 in Croatia and No. 2219 in the other regions of Yugoslavia.
See also Nos. 2315/16, 2460, 2532, 2636 and 2716.

716 Villa, Map of islands and Arms

717 U.N. Emblem and Rainbow

(Des D. Čudov. Litho)

1985 (12 June). Centenary of Tourism in Cres-Lošinj Region. P 13½.
2221 **716** 10d. multicoloured.................................. 1·10 90

(Des D. Čudov. Litho)

1985 (26 June). 40th Anniv of United Nations Organization. P 12½.
2222 **717** 70d. multicoloured.................................. 70 35

718 Regatta Emblem

719 Aerial View of Yacht

(Des D. Čudov. Litho Forum, Novi Sad)

1985 (29 June). 30th Anniv of International European Danubian Regatta. T **718** and similar horiz design. P 14.
2223 **718** 70d. multicoloured.................................. 70 55
MS2224 95×79 mm. 100d. silver, greenish blue and deep blue (regatta course) (34×28 mm).................. 2·20 2·20
No. 2223 was issued in sheetlets of eight stamps and one central label bearing 30th anniversary emblem.

(Des R. Bojanić. Litho Forum, Novi Sad)

1985 (1 July). Nautical Tourism. T **1719** and similar vert designs. Multicoloured. P 14.
2225 8d. Type **719**.. 40 35
2226 10d. Windsurfing... 70 55
2227 50d. Yacht in sunset...................................... 1·40 1·10
2228 70d. Yacht and coastline.............................. 4·25 3·25
2225/2228 *Set of 4*... 6·00 4·75

720 Model Airplane

721 Emblem and Text

(Des R. Bojanić. Litho)

1985 (10 Aug). World Free Flight Aeromodels Championships, Litho. P 12½.
2229 **720** 70d. multicoloured.................................. 1·00 80

(Des I. Jakic. Litho)

1985 (12 Aug). OBLIGATORY TAX. 20th European Shooting Championships, Osijek. P 12.
2230 **721** 3d. turquoise-blue.................................. 40 20
No. 2230 was for use in Croatia.

722 Boy with Football

723 *Corallina officinalis* and Seahorses

(Des A. Daskalović. Litho)

1985 (14 Sept). OBLIGATORY TAX. Anti-Tuberculosis Week. P 13½.
2231 **722** 2d. black, yellow-orange and vermilion.. 15 10
2232 3d. black, yellow-orange and vermilion.. 15 10
2233 4d. black, yellow-orange and vermilion.. 20 10
2234 5d. on 2d. black, yellow-orange and vermilion.................................. 55 45
2231/2234 *Set of 4*... 95 70
2d. was for use in Bosnia and Herzegovina, Montenegro, Slovenia and Kosovo, 3d. in Macedonia and Vojvodina, 5d. in Serbia and 2, 3 and 4d. in Croatia.

(Des R. Bojanić. Litho Forum, Novi Sad)

1985 (20 Sept). Marine Flora. T **723** and similar horiz designs. Multicoloured. P 14.
2235 8d. Type **723**.. 15 10
2236 10d. *Desmarestia viridis*............................... 30 20
2237 50d. Bladder wrack seaweed (*Fucus vesiculosus*)... 40 35
2238 70d. *Padina pavonia*....................................... 2·50 2·00
2235/2238 *Set of 4*... 3·00 2·40

724 Federation Emblem

725 Selling Vegetables from Cart (Brarika Lukic)

(Des D. Čudov. Litho)

1985 (21 Sept). 73rd International Stomatologists Federation Congress, Belgrade. P 12×11½.
2239 **724** 70d. multicoloured.................................. 70 55

(Des D. Čudov. Litho Forum, Novi Sad)

1985 (2 Oct). 17th "Joy of Europe" Meeting, Belgrade. T **725** and similar horiz design showing children's paintings. Multicoloured. P 14.
2240 50d. Type **725**.. 70 55
2241 70d. "Children playing" (Suzanne Straathof)... 2·10 1·70

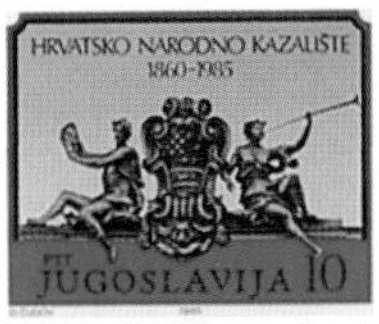

726 Detail of Theatre Facade

727 Miladin Popovic

(Des D. Čudov. Litho)

1985 (23 Nov). 125th Anniv of Croatian National Theatre, Zagreb. P 12½.
2242 **726** 10d. multicoloured ... 40 35

(Des D. Čudov. Litho)

1985 (26 Nov). 75th Birth Anniv and 40th Death Anniv of Miladin Popovic (Communist Party worker). P 11½×12.
2243 **727** 10d. red-brown and reddish orange. 30 10

728 State Arms

729 "Royal Procession" (Iromie Wijewardena)

(Des D. Čudov. Litho)

1985 (28 Nov). 40th Anniv of Federal Republic. P 13½.
2244 **728** 10d. multicoloured ... 30 10
MS2245 62×75 mm. **728** 100d. multicoloured (15×25 mm). Imperf ... 1·70 1·70

(Des D. Čudov. Litho Forum, Novi Sad)

1985 (2 Dec). Paintings. T **729** and similar multicoloured designs. P 14.
2246 8d. Type **729** ... 20 10
2247 10d. "Return from Hunting" (Mama Cangare) ... 30 20
2248 50d. "Drum of Coca" (Agnes Ovando Sanz de Franck) ... 50 35
2249 50d. "The Cock" (Mariano Rodriguez) (vert) ... 50 35
2250 70d. "Three Women" (Quamrul Hassan) (vert) ... 2·40 1·90
2246/2250 *Set of* 5 ... 3·50 2·50

1 D
(730)

731 Zagreb Exhibition Hall

1985 (4–25 Dec). Nos. 1641/a, 1644, 1646/a, 1671/a, 1672, 1672b, 1677, 1678/a and 1679a surch as T **730** in brown.
2251 1d. on 25p. claret (25.12) ... 1·40 10
2252 2d. on 5p. red-orange (p 13½) (18.12) ... 70 10
a. Perf 13½×12½ ... 70 10
2253 3d. on 35p. brown-red (p 13½) (25.12) ... 40 10
a. Perf 13½×12½ ... 40 10
2254 4d. on 5d.60 grey-olive (p 13½) (25.12) ... 40 10
a. Perf 13½×12½ ... 1·40 65
2255 8d. on 6d. chestnut (p 13½) ... 40 10
a. Perf 13½×12½ ... 40 10
2256 20d. on 26d. grey-blue (p 13½×12½) ... 40 20
a. Perf 13½ ... 12·00 5·50
2257 50d. on 16d.50 steel blue (25.12) ... 1·40 35
2258 70d. on 38d. bright magenta ... 1·70 55
2251/2258 *Set of* 8 ... 6·00 1·40

(Des D. Čudov. Litho Forum, Novi Sad)

1985 (6 Dec). P 14.
2259 **731** 100d. reddish violet and orange-yellow ... 85 35

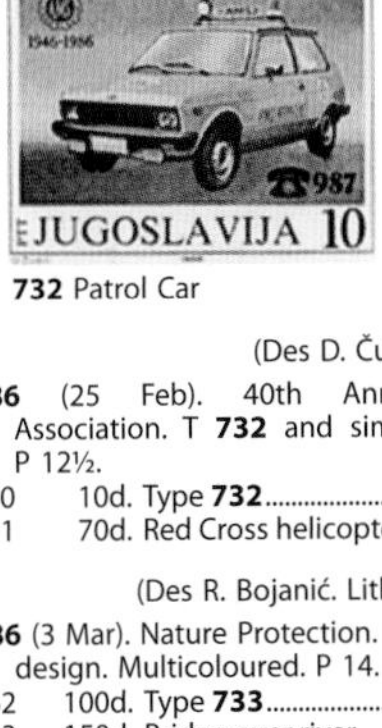

732 Patrol Car

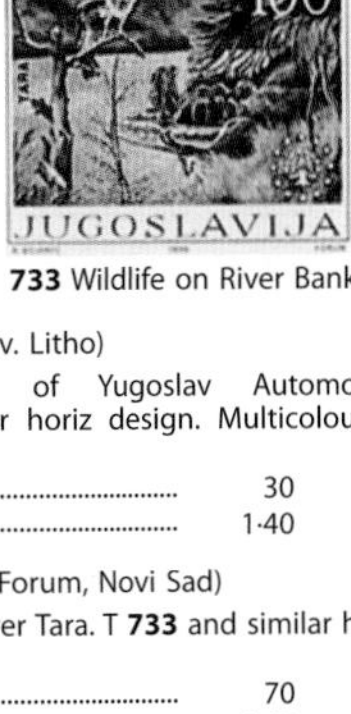

733 Wildlife on River Bank

(Des D. Čudov. Litho)

1986 (25 Feb). 40th Anniv of Yugoslav Automobile Association. T **732** and similar horiz design. Multicoloured. P 12½.
2260 10d. Type **732** ... 30 10
2261 70d. Red Cross helicopter ... 1·40 1·10

(Des R. Bojanić. Litho Forum, Novi Sad)

1986 (3 Mar). Nature Protection. River Tara. T **733** and similar horiz design. Multicoloured. P 14.
2262 100d. Type **733** ... 70 55
2263 150d. Bridge over river ... 1·40 1·10

734 Church of the Virgin

735 Postman on Motor Cycle

(Des D. Čudov. Litho)

1986 (15 Mar). 800th Anniv of Studenica Monastery. P 13½.
2264 **734** 10d. brown-red, deep bluish green and deep turquoise ... 1·00 55

(Des R. Bojanić (20, 30, 50, 60, 800, 10000, 20000d.), Marina Kalezić-Krajinović (106d. (both), 140d.), D. Čudov (others). Litho Forum, Novi Sad (100d.), Mint, Belgrade (others))

1986 (17 Mar)–**89**. Postal Services. T **735** and similar designs. P 14 (100d.) or 13½ (others).
2265 20d. bright magenta ... 70 20
a. Perf 12½×13½ ... 70 20
2266 30d. red-brown (26.7.86) ... 40 20
a. Perf 13½×12½ ... 1·40 20
2267 40d. scarlet-vermilion (17.7.86) ... 70 20
a. Perf 12½×13½ ... 70 20
2268 50d. bright violet (4.6.86) ... 70 20
a. Perf 12½×13½ ... 70 20
2269 60d. yellow-green (25.5.87) ... 70 20
2270 93d. ultramarine (16.12.87) ... 70 20
2271 100d. deep reddish purple (12.6.86) ... 1·40 20
2272 106d. rose-carmine (10.12.87) ... 70 20
2272*a* 106d. chestnut (22.1.88) ... 70 20
2273 120d. turquoise-green (11.8.88) ... 30 10
2274 140d. bright rose-red (11.8.88) ... 30 10
2275 170d. blue-green (17.11.88) ... 70 20
2276 200d. turquoise-blue (4.6.86) ... 1·50 55
a. Perf 12½×13½ ... 10·50 2·75
b. Perf 12½ (8.9.89) ... 3·50 2·20
2277 220d. chestnut (6.12.88) ... 70 20
2278 300d. rose-red (11.5.89) ... 70 20
2279 500d. deep blue and dull orange (11.4.88) ... 2·75 55
2279*a* 500d. blue and bistre-yellow (23.6.88) ... 70 55
ab. Perf 12½ (1.11.89) ... 30 20
2280 800d. ultramarine (20.7.89) ... 30 20
a. Perf 12½ (8.12.89) ... 30 20
2281 1000d. violet and blue-green (21.7.88) ... 1·00 65
a. Perf 12½ (6.10.89) ... 30 20
2282 2000d. turquoise and yellow-orange (20.7.89) ... 40 20
a. Perf 12½ ... 40 20
2283 5000d. ultramarine and brown-red (20.1.89) ... 1·40 55
a. Perf 12½ ... 1·40 55
2284 10000d. bright reddish violet and bright orange (28.11.89) ... 1·00 20
a. Perf 12½ ... 30 20
2285 20000d. chestnut and yellow-green (8.12.89) ... 1·00 80
a. Perf 12½ ... 30 20
2265/2285 *Set of* 23 (cheapest) ... 15·00 5·00

Designs: As T **735**. Horiz—20, 800d. Type **735**; 40d. Forklift truck; 50, 20000d. Electric train; 200d. Freighter. Vert—30, 10000d. Postman giving letters to man; 60d. Posting letters; 93d. Envelope and leaflet; 106d. (2272), Woman working at computer and woman filling envelopes; 106 (2272*a*), 140d. Woman working at computer; 120d. Woman with Valentine card; 170, 300d. Flower and post box; 220d. Mail coach and cover; 500d. (both), Postal sorter; 1000d. Woman using public telephone; 2000d. Telephone card, tokens and handset; 5000d. Posthorn, globe and bird with stamp. 20×18 mm—100d. Postman and van.

A wide variety of fluorescent and non-fluorescent papers exist.

See also Nos. 2587/98.

736 Player and Ball in Goal

737 St. Clement and Model of Ohrid (fresco, Church of St. Spas)

(Des R. Bojanić. Litho Forum, Novi Sad)

1986 (5 Apr). World Cup Football Championship, Mexico. T **736** and similar horiz design. Multicoloured. P 14.
2286 70d. Type **736** ... 1·10 90
2287 150d. Players and ball in goal ... 1·40 1·10

Nos. 2286/7 were each printed in sheetlets of eight stamps and one central label depicting a cactus and footballs.

(Des D. Čudov. Litho)

1986 (12 Apr). 1100th Anniv of Arrival of St. Clement of Ohrid in Macedonia. P 12½.
2288 **737** 10d. multicoloured ... 8·25 6·75

5,00
(738)

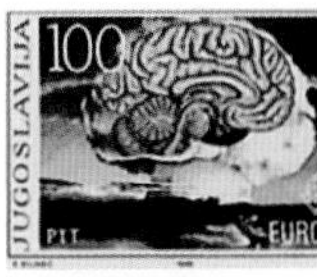

739 Human Brain as Nuclear Cloud

740 Judo

1986 (16 Apr). No. 1674 surch with T **738** in brown.
2289 5d. on 8d. greenish slate ... 70 20
a. Perf 13½×12½ ... 1·40 1·10

(Des R. Bojanić. Litho Forum, Novi Sad)

1986 (28 Apr). Europa. T **739** and similar horiz design. Multicoloured. P 14.
2290 100d. Type **739** ... 70 55
2291 200d. Injured deer on road ... 2·10 1·10

(Des C. Čudov. Litho)

1986 (7 May). European Men's Judo Championships, Belgrade. P 12½.
2292 **740** 70d. brown, cerise and deep ultramarine ... 85 55

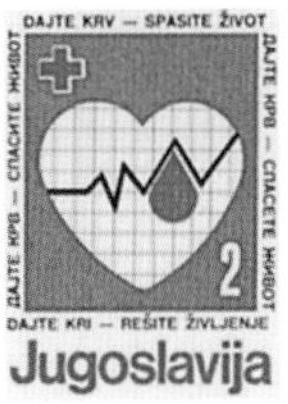

741 Graph and Blood Drop within Heart

742 Costume of Slovenia

743 Yachts

1986 (8 May). OBLIGATORY TAX. Red Cross Week. Litho. P 13½.
2293 **741** 2d. black, greenish blue and scarlet-vermilion ... 15 10
2294 3d. black, greenish blue and scarlet-vermilion ... 15 10
2295 4d. black, greenish blue and scarlet-vermilion ... 30 20
2296 5d. black, greenish blue and scarlet-vermilion ... 30 20
2297 11d. black, greenish blue and scarlet-vermilion ... 30 20
2298 20d. black, greenish blue and scarlet-vermilion ... 1·00 80
2293/2298 *Set of* 6 ... 2·00 1·40

2d. was for use in Macedonia and Slovenia, 5d. in Serbia, Vojvodina and Kosovo, 2, 3 and 4d. in Croatia and 11 and 20d. in Bosnia and Herzegovina.

(Des R. Bojanić. Litho)

1986 (22 May). Yugoslav Costumes. Booklet stamps. T **742** and similar vert designs. Multicoloured. P 12×13.
2299 50d. Type **742** ... 70 55
a. Booklet pane. Nos. 2299/2306 ... 5·75
2300 50d. Vojvodina (woman with red apron) ... 70 55
2301 50d. Croatia (man in embroidered trousers) ... 70 55
2302 50d. Macedonia (woman hand spinning) ... 70 55
2303 50d. Serbia (woman in bolero) ... 70 55
2304 50d. Montenegro (man with rifle) ... 70 55
2305 50d. Kosovo (woman carrying basket) ... 70 55
2306 50d. Bosnia and Herzegovina (man carrying bag on back) ... 70 55
2299/2306 *Set of* 8 ... 5·00 4·00

(Des R. Bojanić. Litho Forum, Novi Sad)

1986 (23 May). "Flying Dutchman" Class European Yachting Championships, Mošcenicka Draga. T **743** and similar vert designs. Multicoloured. P 14.
2307 50d. Type **743** ... 40 20
2308 80d. Yachts (different) ... 70 55
MS2309 66×85 mm. 100d. Yachts (different). Imperf ... 5·50 5·50

Nos. 2307/8 were each issued in sheetlets of eight stamps and one central label showing championships emblem and yacht.

744 Tito (after Safet Zec)

745 Peacock Moth (*Eudia pavonia*)

(Des D. Čudov. Litho)

1986 (24 May). 94th Birth Anniv of Tito. P 12½.
2310 **744** 10d. multicoloured ... 30 10

(Des R. Bojanić. Litho Forum, Novi Sad)

1986 (26 May). Butterflies and Moths. T **745** and similar horiz designs. Multicoloured. P 14.
2311 10d. Type **745** ... 40 35
2312 20d. Peacock (*Inachis io*) ... 70 55
2313 50d. Apollo (*Parnassius apollo*) ... 1·40 1·10
2314 100d. Purple emperor (*Apatura iris*) ... 2·75 2·20
2311/2314 *Set of* 4 ... 4·75 3·75

746 "Skopje Earthquake"

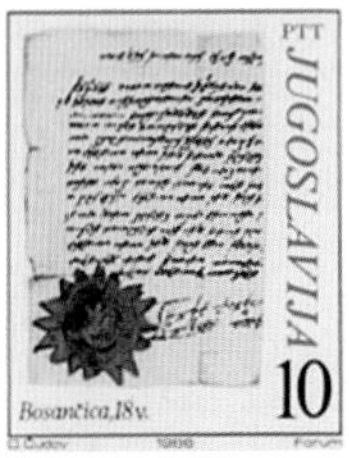

747 Bosancica MS

1986 (1 June). OBLIGATORY TAX. Solidarity Week.

(a) As No. 2220. Litho. Rouletted

2315 **715** 10d. metallic grey-blue and vermilion .... 1·40 80
a. Perf 11 .... 70 50

(b) As Type **715** but inscr "Solidarity Week" in four languages. Litho. P 10

2316 10d. metallic grey-blue and vermilion .... 1·40 80
a. Rouletted .... 1·40 80
b. Perf 11 .... 1·40 80

(c) Type **746**. Litho. P 10

2317 **746** 10d. rose-lilac and vermilion .... 1·40 80

No. 2315 was for use in Croatia, No. 2317 in Macedonia, No. 2316 in the rest of Yugoslavia.

No. 2318 is vacant.

(Des D. Čudov. Litho Forum, Novi Sad)

1986 (12 June). Museum Exhibits. Ancient Manuscripts. T **747** and similar vert designs. Multicoloured. P 14.

2319 10d. Type **747** 15 10
2320 20d. Leontije's Gospel 30 20
2321 50d. Astrological writing, Mesopotamia 70 55
2322 100d. Hagada (ritual book), Spain .... 1·10 90
2319/2322 *Set of 4* .... 2·00 1·60

748 Congress Poster (Branislav Dobanovacki)

749 Trubar and Title Page of *Abecedari*

(Des D. Čudov. Litho)

1986 (25 June). 13th Communist League Congress, Belgrade. T **748** and similar horiz designs, showing parts of Congress advertising poster. P 12½.

2323 10d. black and orange-red 30 10
2324 20d. black and orange-red 30 10
MS2325 60×75 mm. 100d. black and orange-vermilion. Imperf .... 1·40 1·40

(Des R. Bojanić. Litho)

1986 (28 June). 400th Death Anniv of Primož Trubar (founder of Slovenian literary language and religious reformer). P 12½.

2326 **749** 20d. multicoloured .... 1·00 55

750 Emblem

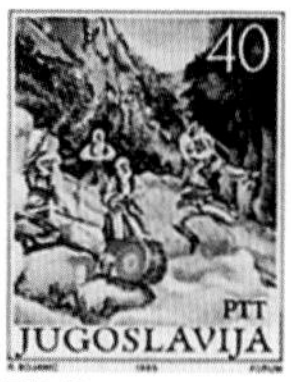

751 Dancers

(Des D. Čudov. Litho Forum, Novi Sad)

1986 (28 July). 125th Anniv of Serbian National Theatre, Novi Sad. P 14.

2327 **750** 40d. multicoloured 30 10

(Des R. Bojanić. Litho Forum, Novi Sad)

1986 (10 Sept). Rugovo Dance. P 14.

2328 **751** 40d. multicoloured 30 10

753 Crosses forming Earth and Sky

754 Volleyball

(Des Bachrach and B. Kristofic. Litho)

1986 (14 Sept). OBLIGATORY TAX. Anti-Tuberculosis Week. P 10½.

2330 **753** 2d. multicoloured 30 10
2331 5d. multicoloured 30 10
2332 6d. multicoloured 30 10
2333 7d. multicoloured 30 10
2334 8d. multicoloured 30 10
2335 10d. multicoloured 30 10
a. Perf 13½ .... 1·40 1·10
2336 11d. multicoloured 40 35
2337 14d. multicoloured 40 35
2338 20d. multicoloured 40 35
a. Perf 13½ .... 1·40 1·10
2330/2338 *Set of 9* .... 2·75 1·50

(Des D. Čudov. Litho)

1986 (22 Sept). Universiade '87 University Games, Zagreb. T **754** and similar vert designs featuring Zagi (games mascot). Multicoloured. P 13½.

2339 30d. Type **754** 40 35
2340 40d. Canoeing 55 45
2341 100d. Gymnastic .... 1·00 80
2342 150d. Fencing .... 1·40 1·10
2339/2342 *Set of 4* .... 3·00 2·40

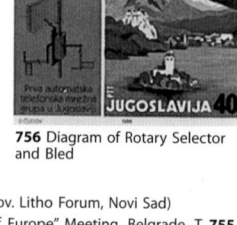

755 Bird and Child running on Globe (Tanja Faletic)

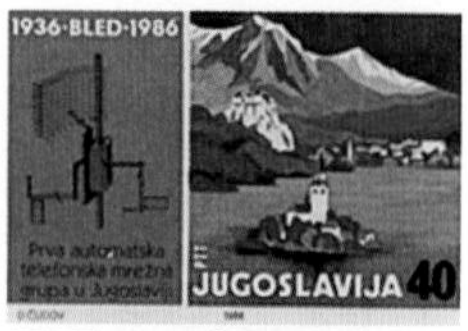

756 Diagram of Rotary Selector and Bled

(Des D. Čudov. Litho Forum, Novi Sad)

1986 (2 Oct). 18th "Joy of Europe" Meeting, Belgrade. T **755** and similar vert designs showing children's paintings. Multicoloured. P 14.

2343 100d. Type **755** .... 1·00 80
2344 150d. City of the Future (Johanna Kraus) .... 1·40 1·10

(Des D. Čudov. Litho)

1986 (4 Oct). 50th Anniv of Automatic Telephone Exchange Network. P 13½.

2345 **756** 40d. multicoloured 30 10

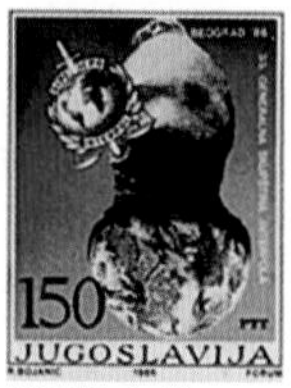

757 Criminal in Stocking Mask

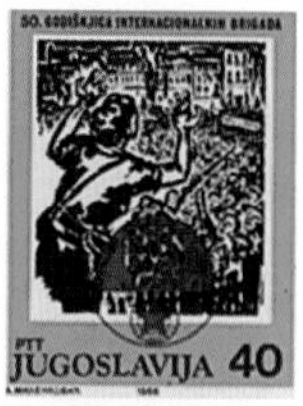

758 Brigade Member addressing Crowd (after Djordje Andrejević-Kun)

(Des R. Bojanić. Litho Forum, Novi Sad)

1986 (6 Oct). 55th Interpol General Assembly Session, Belgrade. P 14.

2346 **757** 150d. multicoloured 70 55

(Des A. Milenković. Litho)

1986 (21 Oct). 50th Anniv of Formation of International Brigades in Spain. P 13½.

2347 **758** 40d. deep lake-brown, gold and yellow-orange 30 10

759 Academy

760 People riding on Doves (Branislav Barnak)

(Des D. Čudov. Litho)

1986 (1 Nov). Centenary of Serbian Academy of Arts and Sciences. P 13½.

2348 **759** 40d. multicoloured 30 10

(Des D. Čudov. Litho)

1986 (20 Nov). International Peace Year. P 13½.

2349 **760** 150d. multicoloured 85 65

761 "Portrait" (Bernard Buffet)

762 European Otter (*Lutra lutra*)

(Des D. Čudov. Litho Forum, Novi Sad)

1986 (10 Dec). Paintings in Museum of Contemporary Arts, Skopje. T **761** and similar multicoloured designs. P 14.

2350 30d. "Still Life" (František Muzika) (horiz) 15 10
2351 40d. "Disturbance" (detail, Rafael Canogar) (horiz) 30 20
2352 100d. Type **761** 70 55
2353 100d. "IOL" (Victor Vasarely) 70 55
2354 150d. "Woman's Head" (Pablo Picasso) .... 1·10 90
2350/2354 *Set of 5* .... 2·75 2·10

(Des R. Bojanić. Litho Forum, Novi Sad)

1987 (22 Jan). Protected Animals. T **762** and similar vert designs. Multicoloured. P 14.

2355 30d. Type **762** .... 1·10 90
a. Horiz strip. Nos. 2355/8 plus label .... 4·75
2356 40d. Argali (*Ovis musimon*) .... 1·10 90
2357 100d. Red deer (*Cervus elaphus*) .... 1·10 90
2358 150d. Brown bear (*Ursus arctos*) .... 1·10 90
2355/2358 *Set of 4* .... 4·00 3·25

Nos. 2355/8 were issued together in horizontal *se-tenant* strips of four stamps and central stamp-size label showing a mountain landscape.

763 Boškovic, Brera Observatory and Solar Eclipse

764 Mountains, Woodland and Animal Feeder

(Des D. Čudov. Litho Forum, Novi Sad)

1987 (13 Feb). Death Bicentenary of Ruder Boškovic (astronomer). P 14.

2359 **763** 150d. multicoloured 85 55

(Des R. Bojanić. Litho Forum, Novi Sad)

1987 (9 Mar). Nature Protection. Triglav National Park. T **764** and similar vert design. Multicoloured. P 14.

2360 150d. Type **764** .... 1·70 1·30
2361 400d. Mountains, woodland and glacial lake .... 2·50 2·00

765 Potez 29-4 Biplane

766 Mateja Svet

(Des R. Bojanić. Litho Forum, Novi Sad)

1987 (20 Mar). 60th Anniv of Civil Aviation in Yugoslavia. T **765** and similar horiz design. Multicoloured. P 14.

2362 150d. Type **765** .... 1·00 80
2363 400d. Douglas DC-10 jetliner .... 2·10 1·70

Nos. 2362 and 2363 were each issued in sheetlets of eight stamps and one central label showing routes map or close-up of airplane engine respectively.

(Des R. Bojanić. Litho Forum, Novi Sad)

1987 (20 Mar). Yugoslav Medals at World Alpine Skiing Championships, Crans Montana. P 14.

2364 **766** 200d. multicoloured .... 4·25 3·25

No. 2364 was issued in sheetlets of eight stamps and one central label showing Svet's medals.

767 Kole Nedelkovski

768 Gusle and Battle Flags of Vucji Do and Grahovo

(Des D. Čudov. Litho)

1987 (2 Apr). 75th Birth Anniv of Kole Nedelkovski (poet and revolutionary). P 13½.

2365 **767** 40d. multicoloured 30 10

(Des D. Čudov. Litho)

1987 (16 Apr). 125th Anniv of Montenegrin Wars of Liberation. P 13½.

2366 **768** 40d. multicoloured 30 10

769 "Founding the Party at Cebine, 1937" (Anton Gojmir Kos)

770 Tito Bridge, Krk (Ilija Stojadinovic)

(Des D. Čudov. Litho Forum, Novi Sad)

1987 (18 Apr). 50th Anniv of Slovenian Communist Party. P 14.

2367 **769** 40d. multicoloured 30 10

(Des D. Čudov. Litho Forum, Novi Sad)

1987 (30 Apr). Europa. Architecture. T **770** and similar horiz designs. Multicoloured. P 14.

2368 200d. Type **770** .... 1·00 80
2369 400d. Bridges over River Ljubljanica (Joze Plecnik) .... 1·40 1·10

771 Children of Different Races in Flower

772 Almond (*Amygdalus communis*)

(Des J. Reichman. Litho)

1987 (8 May). OBLIGATORY TAX. Red Cross Week. P 10.

2370	**771**	2d. multicoloured		40	35
		a. Perf 11		55	40
2371		4d. multicoloured		40	35
2372		5d. multicoloured		40	35
		a. Perf 11		55	40
2373		6d. multicoloured		40	35
2374		7d. multicoloured		40	35
		a. Perf 11		55	40
2375		8d. multicoloured		40	35
2376		10d. multicoloured		40	35
2377		11d. multicoloured		40	35
2378		12d. multicoloured		40	35
2379		14d. multicoloured		40	35
2380		17d. multicoloured		40	35
		a. Perf 11		55	40
2381		20d. multicoloured		40	35
		a. Magenta omitted			
2370/2381 *Set of 12*				4·25	3·75

Nos. 2370/81 were used in the republics as follows: Bosnia and Herzegovina 11, 14, 17, 20d.; Croatia 5, 6, 7, 8d.; Kosovo and Montenegro 2d.; Macedonia 4, 8, 12d.; Serbia 5, 10, 20d.; Slovenia and Vojvodina 10, 20d.

Perforate and imperforate sheetlets containing Type **771** with country name in gold (instead of black) were sold in Macedonia.

(Des R. Bojanić. Litho Forum, Novi Sad)

1987 (15 May). Fruit. T **772** and similar horiz designs. Multicoloured. P 14.

2382	60d. Type **772**	30	20
2383	150d. Pear (*Pirus communis*)	1·00	80
2384	200d. Apple (*Malus domestica*)	1·40	1·10
2385	400d. Plum (*Prunus domestica*)	2·20	1·80
2382/2385 *Set of 4*		4·50	3·50

773 Tito (after Moša Pijade)

774 "Skopje Earthquake"

(Des D. Čudov. Litho Forum, Novi Sad)

1987 (25 May). 95th Birth Anniv of Josip Broz Tito. P 14.

2386	**773**	60d. multicoloured	40	35

1987 (1 June). OBLIGATORY TAX. Solidarity Week. Litho. P 10.

2387	**774**	30d. multicoloured	70	35

No. 2387 was issued in sheets of 70 stamps and two inscribed labels.

775 Bust of Karadžic (Petar Ubavkic), Tršic (birthplace) and Vienna

776 Mail Coach in Zrenjanin

(Des D. Čudov. Litho Forum, Novi Sad)

1987 (10 June). Birth Bicentenary of Vuk Stefanovic Karadžic (linguist and historian). T **775** and similar horiz design. Multicoloured. P 14.

2388	60d. Type **775**	30	10
2389	200d. Serbian alphabet and Karadžic (portrait by Uroš Kneževic)	70	55

(Des R. Bojanić. Litho)

1987 (22 June). 250th Anniv of Postal Service in Zrenjanin. P 13½.

2390	**776**	60d. multicoloured	30	10

777 Emblem and Mascot

778 Hurdling

(Des D. Čudov. Litho)

1987 (8 July). OBLIGATORY TAX. Universiade '87 University Games, Zagreb. P 11½×12.

2391	**777**	20d. ultramarine and deep turquoise-green	70	35

No. 2391 was for use in Croatia.

(Des R. Bojanić. Litho)

1987 (8 July). Universiade '87 University Games, Zagreb. T **778** and similar vert designs. Multicoloured. P 13½.

2392	60d. Type **778**	40	35
2393	150d. Basketball	70	55
2394	200d. Gymnastics	1·00	80
2395	400d. Swimming	2·10	1·70
2392/2395 *Set of 4*		3·75	3·00

Nos. 2392/5 were each issued in sheetlets of eight stamps and one central label showing the games emblem and a relevant pictogram.

779 Canadair CL-215 Amphibian spraying Forest Fire

780 Monument, Anindol Park

(Des R. Bojanić. Litho Forum, Novi Sad)

1987 (20 July). Fire Fighting. T **779** and similar horiz design. Multicoloured. P 14.

2396	60d. Type **779**	30	20
2397	200d. Fire-fighting tug	65	20

Nos. 2396/7 were each issued in sheetlets of eight stamps and one central label depicting animals fleeing from forest fire.

(Des R. Bojanić. Litho)

1987 (1 Aug). 50th Anniv of Croatian Communist Party. P 13½.

2398	**780**	60d. multicoloured	30	10

781 School and Foundation Document

782 Crosses and Children's Heads

(Des D. Čudov. Litho)

1987 (10 Sept). 150th Anniv of Šabac High School. P 13½.

2399	**781**	80d. reddish brown, yellow-orange and deep ultramarine	30	10

(Des N. Pešev-Kokan. Litho)

1987 (14 Sept). OBLIGATORY TAX. Anti-Tuberculosis Week. P 10.

2400	**782**	2d. multicoloured	30	10
2401		4d. multicoloured	30	10
2402		6d. multicoloured	30	10
2403		8d. multicoloured	30	10
2404		10d. multicoloured	30	10
2405		12d. multicoloured	30	10
2406		14d. multicoloured	30	10
2407		20d. multicoloured	30	10
2408		25d. multicoloured	30	10
2409		40d. multicoloured	30	10
2400/2409 *Set of 10*			2·75	90

Nos. 2400/9 were each issued in sheets of 70 stamps and two inscribed labels.

Nos. 2400/9 were used in the republics as follows: Bosnia and Herzegovina 14, 25d.; Croatia 6, 8d.; Kosovo and Montenegro 2d.; Macedonia 4, 8, 12d.; Serbia 10, 20d.; Slovenia and Vojvodina 40d.

783 Emblem, Map and Flowers

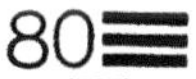

(784)

(Des D. Čudov. Litho Forum, Novi Sad)

1987 (19 Sept). Balkanfila XI Balkans Stamp Exhibition, Novi Sad. T **783** and similar multicoloured design. P 14.

2410	250d. Type **783**	70	55
MS2411	60×75 mm. 400d. Novi Sad behind Petrovaradin Fortress (22×32 mm). Imperf	2·10	2·10

1987 (22 Sept). No. 2269 surch with T **784**.

2412	80d. on 60d. yellow-green	70	20

785 Children playing amongst Trees (Bedic Aranka)

786 SPRAM Emblem

(Des D. Čudov. Litho Forum, Novi Sad)

1987 (2 Oct). 19th "Joy of Europe" Meeting. T **785** and similar vert design. Multicoloured. P 14.

2413	250d. Type **785**	1·10	90
2414	400d. Child and scarecrow in orchard (Ingeborg Schäffer)	1·40	1·10

1987 (5 Oct). OBLIGATORY TAX. Model Airplane Championships, Belgrade. P 14.

2415	**786**	20d. blue	30	10

No. 2415 was for use in Serbia.

787 Arslanagica Bridge, Trebinje

788 Tug in Lock on Dunav–Tisa Canal

(Des D. Čudov. Litho Forum, Novi Sad)

1987 (15 Oct). Bridges. T **787** and similar horiz design. Multicoloured. P 14½.

2416	80d. Type **787**	40	35
2417	250d. Terzija bridge, Djakovica	70	55

(Des R. Bojanić. Litho)

1987 (20 Oct). 600th Anniv of Titov Vrbas. P 13½.

2418	**788**	80d. multicoloured	30	10

789 Eclipse, First Telescope and Old Observatory Building

790 "St. Luke the Evangelist" (Raphael)

(Des D. Čudov. Litho Forum, Novi Sad)

1987 (21 Nov). Centenary of Astronomical and Meteorological Observatory, Belgrade. P 14.

2419	**789**	80d. multicoloured	30	10

(Des D. Čudov. Litho Forum, Novi Sad)

1987 (28 Nov). Paintings in Mimara Museum, Zagreb. T **790** and similar vert designs. Multicoloured. P 14.

2420	80d. Type **790**	30	20
2421	200d. "Infanta Maria Theresa" (Diego Velázquez)	70	55
2422	250d. "Nikolaus Rubens" (Peter Paul Rubens)	75	60
2423	400d. "Louise Laure Sennegon" (Camille Corot)	1·80	1·50
2420/2423 *Set of 4*		3·25	2·50

791 Bull Fighting (Grmec)

792 Codex and Novi Vinodol

(Des R. Bojanić. Litho Forum, Novi Sad)

1987 (10 Dec). Museum Exhibits. Folk Games. T **791** and similar vert designs. Multicoloured. P 14.

2424	80d. Type **791**	30	20
2425	200d. Sword used in Ljuvicevo Horse Games	70	55
2426	250d. Crown worn at Moresca Games (Korcula)	75	60
2427	400d. Sinj Iron Ring	2·50	2·00
2424/2427 *Set of 4*		3·75	3·00

(Des D. Čudov. Litho Forum, Novi Sad)

1988 (6 Jan). 700th Anniv of Vinodol Law Codex. P 14.

2428	**792**	100d. multicoloured	30	10

793 Skier

794 Cub

(Des R. Bojanić. Litho Forum, Novi Sad)

1988 (30 Jan). 25th Anniv of Golden Fox Women's Skiing Competition, Maribor. P 14.

2429	**793**	350d. multicoloured	30	10

No. 2429 was issued in sheetlets of eight stamps and one central label depicting games emblem and fox.

(Des R. Bojanić. Litho Forum, Novi Sad)

1988 (1 Feb). Protected Wildlife. The Brown Bear (*Ursus arctos*). T **794** and similar horiz designs. Multicoloured. P 14.

2430	70d. Type **794**	3·00	2·20
2431	80d. Bears among branches	3·00	2·20
2432	200d. Adult bear	3·25	2·20
2433	350d. Adult stalking prey	10·00	6·75
2430/2433 *Set of 4*		18·00	12·00

795 Skier

796 Map of Europe

(Des R. Bojanić. Litho Forum, Novi Sad)

1988 (23 Feb). Winter Olympic Games, Calgary. T **795** and similar vert design. P 14.

2434 350d. Type **795** .... 1·40 1·10
2435 1200d. Ice hockey .... 2·10 1·70

Nos. 2434/5 were each issued in sheetlets of eight stamps and one central label bearing a games motif.

(Des D. Čudov. Litho Forum, Novi Sad)

1988 (24 Feb). Balkan Countries' Foreign Affairs Ministers Meeting, Belgrade. Sheet 60×75 mm. Imperf.

MS2436 **796** 1500d. multicoloured .... 3·00 3·00

797 Basketball

798 White Carnations

(Des R. Bojanić. Litho Forum, Novi Sad)

1988 (21 Mar). Olympic Games, Seoul. T **797** and similar vert designs. Multicoloured. P 14.

2437 106d. Type **797** 70 55
2438 450d. High jumping 90 75
2439 500d. Gymnastics .... 1·00 80
2440 1200d. Boxing .... 2·40 2·00
2437/2440 *Set of 4* .... 4·50 3·75
MS2441 62×77 mm. 1500d. Korean landscape. Imperf .... 3·50 3·50

Nos. 2437/40 were each issued in sheetlets of eight stamps and one central label, depicting the Games mascot in the appropriate sport.

(Des Z. A. Popovski. Litho)

1988 (Mar). OBLIGATORY TAX. Anti-Cancer Campaign. T **798** and similar vert designs. Muticoloured. P 10.

2442 4d. Type **798** 30 10
2443 8d. Red flowers 30 10
2444 12d. Red roses 30 10
2442/2444 *Set of 3* 80 25

Nos. 2442/4 were for use in Macedonia.

799 "INTELSAT V-A", Globe and Dish Aerials, Ivanjica

800 Anniversary Emblem

(Des D. Čudov. Litho Forum, Novi Sad)

1988 (30 Apr). Europa. Transport and Communications. T **799** and similar horiz design. Multicoloured. P 13½×14.

2445 450d. Type **799** 70 55
2446 1200d. Woman using mobile telephone and methods of transport .... 1·40 1·10

1988 (8 May). OBLIGATORY TAX. 125th Anniv of Red Cross. P 10.

2447 **800** 4d. deep violet-blue, bright scarlet and brownish grey 40 20
2448 8d. deep violet-blue, bright scarlet and brownish grey 40 20
2449 10d. deep violet-blue, bright scarlet and brownish grey 40 20
2450 12d. deep violet-blue, bright scarlet and brownish grey 40 20
2451 20d. deep violet-blue, bright scarlet and brownish grey 40 20
2452 30d. deep violet-blue, bright scarlet and brownish grey 40 20
2453 50d. deep violet-blue, bright scarlet and brownish grey 40 20
2447/2453 *Set of 7* .... 2·50 1·30

Nos. 2447/53 were used in the republics as follows: Bosnia and Herzegovina 30d.; Croatia, Slovenia and Vojvodina 50d.; Kosovo and Montenegro 10d.; Macedonia 4, 8, 12d.; Serbia 10, 20d.

801 Great Top Shell (*Gibbula magus*)

802 Tito

(Des R. Bojanić. Litho Forum, Novi Sad)

1988 (14 May). Molluscs. T **801** and similar horiz designs. Multicoloured. P 14.

2454 106d. Type **801** 70 55
2455 550d. St. James's scallop (*Pecten jacobaeus*) .... 1·10 90
2456 600d. Giant tun (*Tonna galea*) .... 1·40 1·10
2457 1000d. *Argonauta cygnus* (wrongly inscr "argo") .... 1·70 1·30
2454/2457 *Set of 4* .... 4·50 3·50

(Des D. Čudov. Litho Forum, Novi Sad)

1988 (25 May). 60th Anniv of Trial of Josip Broz Tito. P 14.

2458 **802** 106d. chestnut and black 30 10

No. 2458 was issued with *se-tenant* half stamp-size label bearing Tito's statement at the trial.

803 "Skopje Earthquake"

50

(**804**)

1988 (1 June). OBLIGATORY TAX. Solidarity Week.

(a) Type **803**. Litho. P 10

2459 **803** 50d. slate, yellow-ochre and bright scarlet 70 20

(b) As No. 2220 but value changed. Litho. P 11

2460 **715** 50d. metallic grey-blue and scarlet-vermilion 70 20

(c) No. 2387 surch with T **804** in silver

2461 **774** 50d. on 30d. multicoloured 70 20
2459/2461 *Set of 3* .... 1·90 55

No. 2460 was for use in Croatia, No. 2461 in Macedonia and No. 2459 in the other regions of Yugoslavia.

A 50d. sheetlet containing "Skopje Earthquake" design was sold in Macedonia.

805 First Lyceum Building

806 Krleža

(Des D. Čudov. Litho)

1988 (14 June). 150th Anniv of Belgrade University. P 13½.

2462 **805** 106d. multicoloured 30 10

(Des D. Čudov. Litho)

1988 (16 June). OBLIGATORY TAX. Culture Fund. 95th Birth Anniv of Miroslav Krleža (writer). P 13½.

2463 **806** 30d. deep brown and reddish orange 30 10

No. 2463 was for use in Croatia.

≡ 120

(**807**)

808 *Phelypaea boissieri*

1988 (24 June). Nos. 2270 and 2272*a* surch as T **807**.

2464 120d. on 93d. ultramarine 30 10
2465 140d. on 106d. chestnut 30 10

(Des R. Bojanić. Litho Forum, Novi Sad)

1988 (2 July). Nature Protection. Macedonian Plants. T **808** and similar vert design. Multicoloured. P 14.

2466 600d. Type **808** .... 1·10 90
2467 1000d. *Campanula formanekiana* .... 1·40 1·10

809 Globe and Flags

810 Shipping on the Danube

(Des D. Čudov. Litho)

1988 (14 July). Centenary of Esperanto (invented language). P 13½.

2468 **809** 600d. dull violet-blue and deep yellow-green .... 1·40 80

No. 2468 was issued in sheets of eight stamps and one central label showing Ludwig Zamenhof (inventor).

(Des R. Bojanić (1000d.), D. Čudov (2000d.). Litho Forum, Novi Sad)

1988 (18 Aug). 40th Anniv of Danube Conference. T **810** and similar horiz design. Multicoloured. P 14.

2469 1000d. Type **810** 85 65
MS2470 84×68 mm. 2000d. Map of Danube. Imperf .... 5·50 5·50

811 Globe as Ball in Basket

812 Horses Racing

(Des R. Bojanić. Litho Forum, Novi Sad)

1988 (20 Aug). 13th European Junior Basketball Championship, Titov Vrbas and Srbobran. P 14.

2471 **811** 600d. multicoloured 70 55

(Des R. Bojanić. Litho Forum, Novi Sad)

1988 (27 Aug). 125th Anniv of Belgrade Horse Races. T **812** and similar horiz designs. Multicoloured. P 14.

2472 140d. Type **812** 40 35
2473 600d. Show jumping .... 1·00 80
2474 1000d. Trotting race .... 1·40 1·10
2472/2474 *Set of 3* .... 2·50 2·00

813 Douglas DC-10 Jetliner and Globe

814 Museum and Bosnian Bellflower

(Des D. Čudov. Litho)

1988 (5 Sept). AIR. P 13½.

2475 **813** 2000d. multicoloured .... 1·70 65

(Des Marina Kalezić-Krajinović. Litho)

1988 (10 Sept). Centenary of Bosnia and Herzegovina Museum, Sarajevo. P 13½.

2476 **814** 140d. multicoloured 30 10

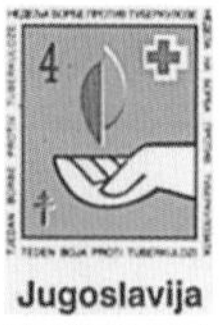

815 Flame and Hand

1988

▮ 12

(**816**)

1988 (14 Sept). OBLIGATORY TAX. Anti-Tuberculosis Week.

(a) P 10

2477 **815** 4d. multicoloured 30 20
2478 8d. multicoloured 30 20
2479 12d. multicoloured 30 20
2480 20d. multicoloured 30 20
2481 50d. multicoloured 30 20
2482 70d. multicoloured 30 20
2477/2482 *Set of 6* .... 1·60 1·10

(b) No. 2039 surch with T **816** in metallic greenish slate

2483 **632** 12d. on 1d. orange, black and bright rose-red .... 7·75 7·75

Nos. 2477/83 were used in the republics as follows: Bosnia and Herzegovina 70d.; Croatia, Montenegro, Slovenia and Vojvodina No. 2483; Macedonia 4 to 20d.; Kosovo and Serbia 50d.

Perforate and imperforate sheetlets containing Nos. 2477/82 but with country name in gold (instead of blue) were on sale in Macedonia.

817 Arm and Crab's Claw (anti-cancer)

818 "Daughter of the Artist" (Petar Ranosovic)

(Des J. Vlahovic. Litho Forum, Novi Sad)

1988 (24 Sept). Health Campaigns. T **817** and similar horiz design. Multicoloured. P 14.

2484 140d. Type **817** 30 10
2485 1000d. Screaming mouth in splash of blood (anti-AIDS) .... 1·10 90

(Des D. Čudov. Litho Forum, Novi Sad)

1988 (1 Oct). 20th "Joy of Europe" Meeting. T **818** and similar vert design. Multicoloured. P 14.

2486 1000d. Type **818** .... 1·10 90
2487 1100d. "Girl with Straw Hat" (Pierre-Auguste Renoir) .... 1·40 1·10

819 1701 Arms and Present Emblem

820 Galicnik Wedding

(Des D. Čudov. Litho Forum, Novi Sad)

1988 (13 Oct). 50th Anniv of Slovenian Academy of Arts and Sciences. P 14.
2488 **819** 200d. multicoloured 30 10

(Des R. Bojanić. Litho Forum, Novi Sad)

1988 (18 Oct). Museum Exhibits. Traditional Crafts and Customs. T **820** and similar multicoloured designs. P 14.
2489 200d. Type **820** 30 20
2490 1000d. Weapons from Bay of Kotor ..... 1·00 85
2491 1000d. Vojvodina embroidery (horiz) ..... 1·00 85
2492 1100d. Masks from Ptuj (horiz) ..... 1·10 90
2489/2492 *Set of 4* ..... 3·00 2·50

821 Title Page of *Gorski Vijenac* and Petar II (after J. Böss)

822 "Girl with Lyre"

(Des D. Čudov. Litho Forum, Novi Sad)

1988 (1 Nov). 175th Birth Anniv of Prince-Bishop Petar II of Montenegro. T **821** and similar horiz designs. Multicoloured. P 14.
2493 200d. Type **821** 40 35
2494 1000d. Njegoš Mausoleum at Lovcen and Petar II in bishop's robes (after Josip Tominc) ..... 1·00 80

(Des D. Čudov. Litho Forum, Novi Sad)

1988 (28 Nov). Ancient Greek Terracotta Figures from Josip Broz Tito Memorial Centre, Belgrade. T **822** and similar vert designs. Multicoloured. P 14.
2495 200d. Type **822** 30 20
2496 1000d. "Girl on a Stone" 85 65
2497 1000d. "Eros and Psyche" 85 65
2498 1100d. "Girl by Stele" ..... 1·00 85
2495/2498 *Set of 4* ..... 2·75 2·10

823 Krsmanovic House, Belgrade

170
(**824**)

(Des Marina Kalezić-Krajinović. Litho Forum, Novi Sad)

1988 (1 Dec). 70th Anniv of Yugoslavian State. P 14.
2499 **823** 200d. multicoloured 30 10

1988 (15 Dec). Nos. 2273/4 surch as T **824**.
2500 170d. on 120d. turquoise-green (21 Dec) ..... 1·40 35
2501 220d. on 140d. bright rose-red ..... 1·40 35

825 Pistol shooting

826 Gudulic and Dubrovnik

(Des Marina Kalezić-Krajinović. Litho Forum, Novi Sad)

1988 (31 Dec). Yugoslavian Medals at Seoul Olympic Games. T **825** and similar horiz designs. Multicoloured. P 14.
2502 500d. Type **825** (2 gold, 1 bronze) 55 45
a. Sheetlet. Nos. 2502/9 plus label ..... 4·75
2503 500d. Handball (bronze) 55 45
2504 500d. Table tennis (silver and bronze) 55 45
2505 500d. Wrestling (silver) 55 45
2506 500d. Rowing (bronze) 55 45
2507 500d. Basketball (2 silver) 55 45
2508 500d. Water polo (gold) 55 45
2509 500d. Boxing (bronze) 55 45
2502/2509 *Set of 8* ..... 4·00 3·25
Nos. 2502/9 were issued together in *se-tenant* sheetlets of eight stamps and one central label showing gold, silver and bronze medals.

(Des D. Čudov. Litho)

1989 (7 Jan). 400th Birth Anniv of Ivan Gundulic (poet). P 13½.
2510 **826** 220d. multicoloured 70 45

827 Mallards (*Anas platyrhynchos*)

827a Emblem

(Des R. Bojanić. Litho Forum, Novi Sad)

1989 (23 Feb). Wild Ducks. T **827** and similar horiz designs. Multicoloured. P 14.
2511 300d. Type **827** ..... 1·30 90
a. Horiz strip. Nos. 2511/14 plus label ..... 9·00
2512 2100d. Green-winged teal (*Anas crecca*) ..... 2·50 1·40
2513 2200d. Pintail (*Anas acuta*) ..... 2·50 1·40
2514 2200d. Common shoveler (*Anas clypeata*) ..... 2·50 1·40
2511/2514 *Set of 4* ..... 8·00 4·50
Nos. 2511/14 were issued together in horizontal *se-tenant* strips of four stamps and a central label, bearing the World Wildlife Fund emblem.

(Des N. Pešev-Kokan (2514*a*). Litho)

1989 (1 Mar). OBLIGATORY TAX. Anti-Cancer Week. P 10.

(a) Type **827a**
2514*a* **827a** 110d. multicoloured 40 20

(b) Similar vert design inscr "YIJGOSLAVIJA MAKEDONIJA" and surch in silver with year date
2514*b* – 110d. on 20d. black, rose-red and gold 40 20
Design:—No. 2514*b*, Sword emblem with blade doubling as Aesculapius rod enclosing crab against background of "flower".
Nos. 2514*a*/*b* were for use in Macedonia. A folder containing imperforate and perforate souvenir sheets as No. 2514*a* but with face value in silver (instead of red) was also on sale.

828 Valvasor and Wagensperg Castle

829 *Bulbocodium vernum*

(Des D. Čudov. Litho)

1989 (10 Mar). 300th Anniv of Publication of *The Glory of the Duchy of Kranjska* by Johann Weickhard Valvasor. P 13½.
2515 **828** 300d. multicoloured 30 10

(Des Marina Kalezić-Krajinović. Litho Forum, Novi Sad)

1989 (20 Mar). Flowers. T **829** and similar multicoloured designs. P 14.
2516 300d. Type **829** 95 75
2517 2100d. White water-lily (*Nymphaea alba*) ..... 1·40 90
2518 2200d. *Fritillaria degeniana* (vert) ..... 1·50 90
2519 3000d. *Orchis simia* (vert) ..... 1·70 1·00
2516/2519 *Set of 4* ..... 5·00 3·25

830 Envelopes and Dish Aerial

100
(**831**)

(Des D. Čudov. Litho)

1989 (22 Mar–July). AIR. T **830** and similar horiz design. P 13½.
2520 10000d. ultramarine, bright magenta and orange-yellow ..... 2·10 1·00
2521 20000d. reddish orange, deep violet and deep carmine (19 July) ..... 1·40 90
Design:—20000d. Europe on globe and satellite.
Paper variations exist for both values.

1989 (6 Apr). No. 1657/*a* surch with T **831**.
2522 100d. on 1d. dull yellowish green (p 13½) ..... 1·40 20
a. Perf 13½×12½ ..... 1·40 20

832 Competitor

833 Girl looking through Magic Cube

(Des Marina Kalezić-Krajinović. Litho Forum, Novi Sad)

1989 (26 Apr). Sixth World Air Gun Championships, Sarajevo. P 14.
2523 **832** 3000d. multicoloured 85 65

(Des R. Bojanić. Litho Forum, Novi Sad)

1989 (29 Apr). Europa. Children's Games and Toys. T **833** and similar horiz design. Multicoloured. P 14.
2524 3000d. Type **833** ..... 1·40 1·10
2525 6000d. Boy playing with marbles and paper boats ..... 1·80 1·40

834 Anniversary Emblem

835 Josip Broz Tito

1989 (8 May). OBLIGATORY TAX. 125th Anniv (1988) of International Red Cross. P 10.
2526 **834** 20d. deep violet-blue, silver and rose-red 30 20
2527 80d. deep violet-blue, silver and rose-red 30 20
2528 150d. deep violet-blue, silver and rose-red 30 20
2529 160d. deep violet-blue, silver and rose-red 30 20
2526/2529 *Set of 4* ..... 1·10 70
A folder containing imperforate and perforate souvenir sheets containing the four values, but with year date and value in white (instead of silver), was on sale in Macedonia.

(Des Marina Kalezić-Krajinović. Litho Forum, Novi Sad)

1989 (25 May). 70th Anniv of Yugoslav Communist Party. P 14.
2530 **835** 300d. brown, black and gold 30 10

836 "Skopje Earthquake"

837 Pole Vaulting

1989 (1 June). OBLIGATORY TAX. Solidarity Week.

(a) Type **836**. Litho. P 10
2531 **836** 250d. silver and rosine ..... 1·00 55

(b) As T **715**. Litho. Rouletted
2532 **715** 400d. metallic cobalt and rose-red ..... 1·80 65
No. 2532 was for use in Croatia and No. 2531 in the rest of Yugoslavia.
A folder containing imperforate and perforate souvenir sheets containing an enlarged version of No. 2531 was on sale in Macedonia.

(Des Marina Kalezić-Krajinović. Litho)

1989 (1 June). 15th European Trophy Athletic Clubs Championship, Belgrade. P 13½.
2533 **837** 4000d. multicoloured ..... 1·40 1·10
No. 2533 was issued in sheets of eight stamps and one central label bearing the names and home towns of participating clubs together with their national flags.

838 Racers

839 Ancient Greek Galleys

(Des R. Bojanić. Litho Forum, Novi Sad)

1989 (9 June). Motor Cycle Grand Prix, Rijeka. T **838** and similar horiz designs. Multicoloured. P 13½×14.
2534 500d. Type **838** 30 20
2535 4000d. Racers (different) 70 55
a. "PTT" omitted (pos 8) ..... 14·00 14·00
MS2536 85×65 mm. 6000d. Race participants numbers 18 and 6 (53×34 mm). P 14 ..... 2·50 2·50
Nos. 2534/5 were each issued in sheetlets of eight stamps and one central label showing racers.

(Des R. Bojanić. Litho Unicover Corporation, Cheyenne, U.S.A.)

1989 (10 June). Sailing Ships. Booklet stamps. T **839** and similar horiz designs. Multicoloured. P 13½.
2537 1000d. Type **839** 55 35
a. Booklet pane. Nos. 2537/**MS**2543 ..... 3·50
2538 1000d. Roman warships 55 35
2539 1000d. 13th-century Crusader nefs 55 35
2540 1000d. 16th-century Dubrovnik navas 55 35
2541 1000d. 17th-century French warships 55 35
2542 1000d. 18th-century ships of the line 55 35
2537/2542 *Set of 6* ..... 3·00 1·90
MS2543 115×85 mm. 3000d. Engraving of Dubrovnik (74×32 mm) ..... 1·10 1·10

HAVE YOU READ THE NOTES AT THE BEGINNING OF THIS CATALOGUE?
These often provide answers to the enquiries we receive

840 Flags of Netherlands, Italy, U.S.S.R. and Spain and Ball

841 "Battle of Kosovo" (lithograph, Adam Stefanovic)

(Des D. Čudov. Litho Forum, Novi Sad)

1989 (20 June). 26th European Men's Basketball Championship, Zagreb. T **840** and similar horiz design. Multicoloured. P 14.

2544	2000d. Type **840** (Group A)	30	10
2545	2000d. Flags of France, Yugoslavia, Greece and Bulgaria and ball (Group B)	30	10

Nos. 2544/5 were each issued in sheetlets of eight stamps and one central label showing a motif and inscription in Serbo-Croat or English respectively.

(Des R. Bojanić. Litho Forum, Novi Sad)

1989 (28 June). 600th Anniv of Battle of Kosovo. P 14.

2546	**841** 500d. multicoloured	30	10

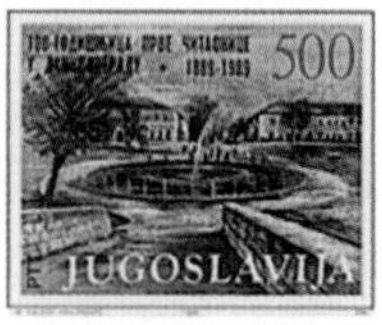

842 Danilovgrad

700

(843)

(Des Marina Kalezić-Krajinović. Litho)

1989 (15 July). Centenary of First Reading Room at Danilovgrad. P 13½.

2547	**842** 500d. multicoloured	30	10

1989 (19 July). No. 2277 surch with T **843**.

2548	700d. on 220d. chestnut	1·40	20

400

(844)

845 Stone Tablet, Detail of Charter and Mule Train

1989 (10–23 Aug). Nos. 2266 and 2275 surch as T **844**.

2549	400d. on 30d. red-brown (23 Aug)	1·40	20
2550	700d. on 170d. blue-green	1·40	20

(Des D. Čudov. Litho Forum, Novi Sad)

1989 (29 Aug). 800th Anniv of Kulin Ban Charter (granting free trade to Dubrovnik). P 14.

2551	**845** 500d. multicoloured	30	10

846 Emblem

847 Rowers on Bled Lake

(Des D. Čudov. Litho)

1989 (1 Sept). OBLIGATORY TAX. Construction of Youth House, Bihac. P 13½.

2552	**846** 400d. new blue and rose-red	30	10
	a. Perf 12½	30	10

(Des Marina Kalezić-Krajinović. Litho)

1989 (2 Sept). World Rowing Championship, Bled. P 13½.

2553	**847** 10000d. multicoloured	85	65

848 Houses of Parliament, London

849 Belgrade and Cairo

(Des R. Bojanić. Litho Forum, Novi Sad)

1989 (4 Sept). Centenary of Interparliamentary Union. T **848** and similar horiz design. P 13½×14.

2554	10000d. Type **848**	70	55
2555	10000d. Notre Dame Cathedral, Paris	70	55

Nos. 2554/5 were each issued in sheetlets of eight stamps and one central label showing a motif and inscription in Serbo-Croat plus English or French respectively.

(Des D. Čudov (20000d.), R. Bojanić (others). Litho Forum, Novi Sad)

1989 (4 Sept). Ninth Heads of Non-aligned Countries Conference, Belgrade. T **849** and similar horiz designs showing previous host cities. Multicoloured. P 14.

2556	10000d. Type **849**	70	55
2557	10000d. Lusaka and Algiers	70	55
2558	10000d. Colombo and Havana	70	55
2559	10000d. New Delhi and Harare	70	55
2556/2559 *Set of 4*		2·50	2·00
MS2560	64×85 mm. 20000d. View of Belgrade and maps showing member states in 1961 and 1989	2·20	2·20

850 Jažinac Lake, Brezovica, and *Paeonia officinalis*

851 Crosses as Basket of Flowers

(Des Marina Kalezić-Krajinović. Litho Forum, Novi Sad)

1989 (11 Sept). Nature Protection. Kosovo. T **850** and similar horiz designs. Multicoloured. P 14.

2561	8000d. Type **850**	70	55
2562	10000d. Miruša Canyon and *Paeonia corallina*	85	65

1989 (14 Sept). OBLIGATORY TAX. Anti-tuberculosis Week. P 10.

2563	**851** 20d. bright scarlet and black	30	20
2564	200d. bright scarlet and black	30	20
2565	250d. bright scarlet and black	30	20
2566	400d. bright scarlet and black	30	20
2567	650d. bright scarlet and black	30	20
	a. Redrawn. Perf 11	1·00	80
2563/2567 *Set of 5*		1·40	90

No. 2567a differs from Type **851** in having more vertical background lines and smaller figures.

852 "Child with Lamb" (Jovan Popovic)

853 Men fighting

(Des D. Čudov. Litho Forum, Novi Sad)

1989 (2 Oct). 21st "Joy of Europe" Meeting. T **852** and similar vert design. Multicoloured. P 14.

2568	10000d. Type **852**	85	65
2569	10000d. "Girl feeding Dog" (Aelbert Cuyp)	85	65

(Des Marina Kalezić-Krajinović. Litho)

1989 (20 Oct). 300th Anniv of Karpoš Insurrection. P 13½.

2570	**853** 1200d. multicoloured	30	10

854 Cancelled 100d. Stamp, Quill and Seal

855 Packsaddle Maker

(Des R. Bojanić. Litho Forum, Novi Sad)

1989 (31 Oct). Stamp Day. P 14.

2571	**854** 1200d. multicoloured	30	10

(Des R. Bojanić. Litho Forum, Novi Sad)

1989 (2 Nov). Museum Exhibits. Traditional Crafts. T **855** and similar horiz designs. Multicoloured. P 14.

2572	1200d. Type **855**	30	10
2573	14000d. Cooper	1·00	80
2574	15000d. Wine maker	1·40	1·10
2575	30000d. Weaver	2·20	1·80
2572/2575 *Set of 4*		4·50	3·50

856 Aerospatiale/Aeritalia ATR 42 Airliner, Arrows and Map

856a Emblem

(Des R. Čudov. Litho)

1989 (8 Nov). AIR. P 13½.

2576	**856** 50000d. greenish blue and reddish orange	1·70	1·30

(Des D. Čudov. Litho)

1989 (Nov). OBLIGATORY TAX. 29th Chess Olympiad, Novi Sad. P 12½.

2577	**856a** 600d. black and new blue	40	20

See also No. 2660.

857 "Apostle Matthias"

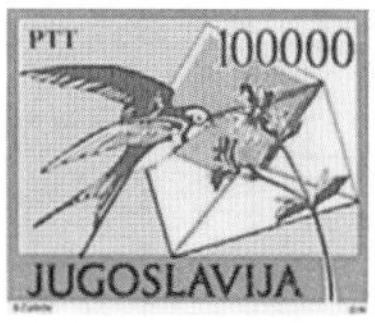

858 Barn Swallow, Envelope and Flower

(Des D. Čudov. Litho Forum, Novi Sad)

1989 (28 Nov). Frescoes by Iohannes de Kastua from Holy Trinity Church, Hrastovlje, Slovenia. T **857** and similar multicoloured designs. P 14.

2578	2100d. Type **857**	30	10
2579	21000d. "St. Barbara"	70	55
2580	30000d. "Creation of the Universe, the Fourth Day" (horiz)	1·40	1·10
2581	50000d. "Creation of the Universe, the Fifth Day" (horiz)	2·10	1·70
2578/2581 *Set of 4*		4·00	3·00

(Des D. Čudov. Litho)

1989 (4 Dec). P 13½.

2582	**858** 100000d. deep blue-green and bright orange	2·10	1·50

700

(859)

860 Colour Spectrum entering Star

1989 (13 Dec). No. 1680 surch with T **859**.

2583	700d. on 70d. ultramarine	70	20

(Des D. Čudov (100000d.), J. Vlahovic (others). Litho Forum, Novi Sad)

1990 (20 Jan). 14th Extraordinary Congress of League of Communists of Yugoslavia, Belgrade. T **860** and similar designs. P 14.

2584	10000d. multicoloured	40	35
2585	50000d. multicoloured	1·00	80
MS2586	66×86 mm. 100000d. red, dull ultramarine and silver. Imperf	2·20	2·20

Designs: Horiz—50000d. Hammer and sickle on computer screen. Vert—100000d. Congress poster (Ivan Dorogi).

Currency Reform

10000 (old) Dinars = 1 (new) Dinar

(Des R. Bojanić (10, 30p., 1d.), D. Čudov (others). Litho)

1990 (24 Jan)–**92**. Postal Services. Designs as T **735** but in revised currency. P 12½.

2587	10p. bluish violet and bright green (9.2.90)	30	10
	a. Perf 13½	70	20
2588	20p. bright crimson and yellow-orange (9.2.90)	30	10
	a. Perf 13½	70	20
2589	30p. yellowish green and reddish orange	30	10
	a. Perf 13½	30	20
2590	40p. blue-green and bright purple	30	10
	a. Perf 13½	30	20
2591	50p. blue-green and reddish violet (29.1.90)	40	10
	a. Perf 13½ (29.1.90)	40	20
2592	60p. bright mauve and orange-vermilion (6.2.90)	40	10
	a. Perf 13½	40	35
2593	1d. turquoise-blue and bright purple (24.5.90)	70	20
	a. Perf 13½	2·75	1·70
2594	2d. new blue and bright crimson (14.2.90)	1·40	20
	a. Perf 13½ (14.2.90)	1·40	35
2595	3d. blue and orange-red (22.2.90)	1·40	35
	a. Perf 13½	3·75	2·50
2596	5d. ultramarine and greenish blue (31.1.90)	1·40	55
	a. Perf 13½	1·80	1·30
2597	10d. dull violet-blue and vermilion (12.6.90)	2·75	1·70
2598	20d. brown-lake and yellow-orange (p 13½) (27.1.92)	70	35
2587/2598 *Set of 12*		9·25	3·50

Designs: Vert—10p. Man posting letters; 20p. Postal sorter; 30p. Postman giving letters to man; 40p., 20d. Woman telephoning; 50p. Posthorn, globe and bird; 60p. Telephone card, tokens and handset; 3d. Post-box; 5d. Airplane, letters and map; 10d. Barn swallow, flower and envelope. Horiz—1d. Electric train; 2d. Freighter.

A range of different papers was used for this issue.

Nos. 2599/2604 are vacant.

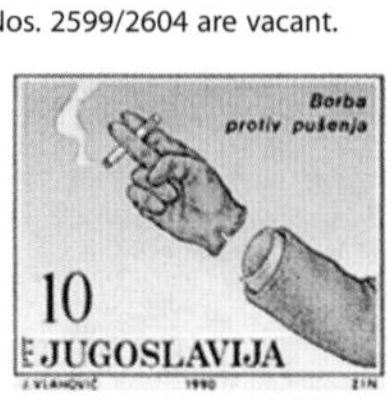

861 Gloved Hand holding Lighted Cigarette

862 Northern Pike (*Esox lucius*)

(Des J. Vlahovic. Litho)

1990 (31 Jan). Anti-smoking Campaign. P 13½.
2605 **861** 10d. multicoloured .... 1·80 1·10

(Des R. Bojanić. Litho Forum, Novi Sad)

1990 (15 Feb). Endangered Fishes. T **862** and similar horiz designs. Multicoloured. P 14.
2606 1d. Type **862** .... 1·20 90
a. Strip. Nos. 2606/9 plus label .... 8·00
2607 5d. Wels (*Silurus glanis*) .... 1·60 1·10
2608 10d. Burbot (*Lota lota*) .... 2·10 1·30
2609 15d. Eurasian perch (*Perca fluviatilis*) .... 2·75 1·60
2606/2609 *Set of 4* .... 7·00 4·50
Nos. 2606/9 were issued together in *se-tenant* horizontal strips of four stamps and a central label showing a fish leaping out of water.

862a Pink Flowers

863 Žabljak Fortress, Printed Page from 1494 and Arms

(Des Ž. Popovski. Litho)

1990 (1 Mar). OBLIGATORY TAX. Anti-cancer Week. T **862a** and similar vert design. P 10.
2610 30p. Type **862a** 40 10
a. Pair. Nos. 2610/11 .... 85 25
2611 30p. Yellow flowers 40 10
Nos. 2610/11 were issued together in *se-tenant* pairs within the sheet.
Folders containing imperforate and perforate souvenir sheets consisting of Nos. 2610/11 but with frames in silver (instead of gold) plus two labels were also on sale.

(Des D. Čudov. Litho Forum, Novi Sad)

1990 (9 Mar). 500th Anniv of Enthronement of Djuradj Crnojevic of Montenegro. P 14.
2612 **863** 50p. multicoloured .... 1·80 1·50

864 Telegraphist and V.D.U.

865 Footballers

(Des Marina Kalezić-Krajinović. Litho Forum, Novi Sad)

1990 (23 Mar). 125th Anniv of International Telecommunications Union. P 14.
2613 **864** 6d.50 multicoloured .... 1·40 1·10

(Des R. Bojanić. Litho Forum, Novi Sad)

1990 (16 Apr). World Cup Football Championship, Italy. T **865** and similar vert design showing footballers. P 14.
2614 6d.50 multicoloured .... 2·10 1·70
2615 10d. multicoloured .... 2·50 2·00
Nos. 2614/15 were each issued in sheetlets of eight stamps and one label showing a footballer and the championship mascot.

866 Skopje Posts and Telecommunications Centre

(Des D. Čudov. Litho Forum, Novi Sad)

1990 (23 Apr). Europa. Post Office Buildings. T **866** and similar horiz design. Multicoloured. P 14.
2616 6d.50 Type **866** .... 2·10 1·70
2617 10d. Belgrade Telephone Exchange .... 2·50 2·00

867 Chicago Water Tower and Carnation

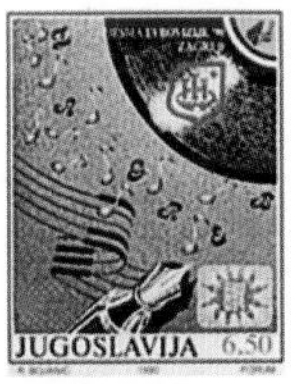

868 Record, Notes and Pen

(Des Marina Kalezić-Krajinović. Litho)

1990 (30 Apr). Centenary of Labour Day. P 13½.
2618 **867** 6d.50 multicoloured .... 1·50 1·20

(Des R. Bojanić. Litho Forum, Novi Sad)

1990 (5 May). Eurovision Song Contest, Zagreb. T **868** and similar vert design. Multicoloured. P 14.
2619 6d.50 Type **868** .... 1·70 1·30
2620 10d. Conductor and score of *Te Deum* by Marc-Antoine Charpentier (theme tune of contest) .... 2·10 1·70
Nos. 2619/20 were each issued in sheets of eight stamps and one label showing various motifs.

869 Cross and Leaves

870 Large Yellow Flowers

(Des A. Daskalović (2624/6). Litho)

1990 (8 May). OBLIGATORY TAX. Red Cross Week.

(a) P 13½
2621 **869** 10p. vermilion and deep green 30 20
2622 20p. vermilion and deep green 30 20
a. Perf 12½ 30 20
2623 30p. vermilion and deep green (p 12½) 30 20
2621/2623 *Set of 3* 80 55

(b) 45th Anniv of Macedonian Red Cross. Flower paintings by Živko Popovski. T **870** and similar vert designs. Multicoloured. P 10
2624 20p. Type **870** 30 20
a. Block. Nos. 2624/6 plus label 95
2625 20p. Arrangement of small yellow flowers 30 20
2626 20p. Anniversary emblem 30 20
2624/2626 *Set of 3* 80 55
Nos. 2624/6 were issued together in *se-tenant* blocks of three stamps and one inscribed label.
Folders containing imperforate and perforate souvenir sheets consisting of a block as No. 2624a but with frames in silver (instead of gold) were on sale in Macedonia.
See also Nos. 2633/4.

871 Server

0,50

(872)

(Des R. Bojanić. Litho Forum, Novi Sad)

1990 (15 May). Yugoslav Open Tennis Championship, Umag. T **871** and similar vert design. Multicoloured. P 14.
2627 6d.50 Type **871** .... 2·10 1·70
2628 10d. Receiver .... 2·40 1·90
Nos. 2627/8 were each issued in sheets of eight stamps and one label showing emblems.

1990 (24 May). No. 2280 surch with T **872**.
2629 **735** 50p. on 800d. ultramarine 70 20
a. Perf 12½ 70 20

873 Tito (bronze, Antun Augustincic)

874 "Tatar Post Riders" (Carl Goebel)

(Des D. Čudov. Litho Forum, Novi Sad)

1990 (25 May). 98th Birth Anniv of Josip Broz Tito. P 13½×14.
2630 **873** 50p. multicoloured 40 35

(Des D. Čudov. Litho Forum, Novi Sad)

1990 (25 May). 150th Anniv of Public Postal Service in Serbia. P 14.
2631 **874** 50p. multicoloured .... 3·50 1·90

875 "Skopje Earthquake"

876 "Skopje Earthquake"

(Des D. Andrić (2638))

1996 (1 June). OBLIGATORY TAX. Solidarity Week. Litho.

(a) For use in Macedonia. T **875** and vert designs as T **870**. P 10
2632 **875** 20p. olive-brown, silver and rose-carmine .... 1·00 55
a. Block. Nos. 2632/4 plus label .... 1·70
2633 – 20p. multicoloured 30 10
2634 – 20p. multicoloured 30 10
Designs:—No. 2633, Mauve flowers; 2634, Red and yellow flowers.
Nos. 2632/4 were issued together in *se-tenant* blocks of three stamps and one inscribed label within the sheet.

Folders containing imperforate and perforate souvenir sheets consisting of a block as No. 2632a but with frames in gold (instead of silver) were also on sale.

(b) For use in Serbia. P 12½
2635 **876** 20p. chalky blue and bright scarlet 70 55

(c) For use in Croatia. P 11
2636 **715** 30p. metallic grey-blue and vermilion 55 35
a. Roulетted 55 35
2632/2636 *Set of 5* .... 3·00 1·80
See also No. 2711.

877 Fantail

878 Idrija Town

(Des Marina Kalezić-Krajinović. Litho Forum, Novi Sad)

1990 (8 June). Pigeons. T **877** and similar multicoloured designs. P 14.
2637 50p. Type **877** 85 65
2638 5d. Serbian high flier .... 1·40 1·10
2639 6d.50 Carrier pigeon (vert) .... 1·70 1·30
2640 10d. Pouter (vert) .... 4·25 3·25
2637/2640 *Set of 4* .... 7·50 5·75

(Des D. Čudov. Litho Forum, Novi Sad)

1990 (22 June). 500th Anniversaries of Idrija Town (2641) and Mercury Mine (2642). T **878** and similar vert design. Multicoloured. P 14.
2641 50p. Type **878** 30 10
2642 6d.50 Mine .... 1·50 1·20

879 Newspaper Offices, Museum and Mastheads

0,50

(880)

(Des Marina Kalezić-Krajinović. Litho)

1990 (23 June). 50th Anniv of *Vjesnik* (newspaper). P 13½.
2643 **879** 60p. multicoloured .... 1·10 90

1990 (7 Aug–18 Sept). Nos. 2588/a and 2589/a surch as T **880**.
2644 50p. on 20p. bright crimson and yellow-orange (18 Sept) 70 20
a. Perf 13½ .... 5·50 3·25
2645 1d. on 30p. yellowish green and reddish orange 70 20
a. Perf 13½ .... 5·50 4·00

881 Runners leaving Blocks

881a Emblem

(Des R. Bojanić. Litho Forum, Novi Sad)

1990 (27 Aug). European Athletics Championships, Split. T **881** and similar horiz designs. Multicoloured. P 13½×14.
2646 1d. Type **881** .... 1·00 80
2647 6d.50 Runners' feet .... 1·40 1·10
MS2648 85×65 mm. 10d. Runners and their reflections (52×34 mm). P 14×13½ .... 3·50 3·50

(Des B. Ljubicic. Litho Forum, Novi Sad)

1990 (Aug). OBLIGATORY TAX. European Athletics Championships, Split. P 14.
2649 **881a** 50p. ultramarine and rose-red 40 20
No. 2649 was for use in Croatia.

882 Nurse and Sun

883 Flower in Vase and Birds

(Des N. Pešev-Kokan (2653). Litho)

1990 (14 Sept). OBLIGATORY TAX. Anti-tuberculosis Week. P 10.
2650 **882** 20p. lemon, royal blue and bright scarlet 30 10
2651 25p. lemon, royal blue and bright scarlet 30 10

2652 50p. lemon, royal blue and bright scarlet ... 40 20
2653 **883** 50p. bistre-brown, bright scarlet and brownish grey ... 40 20
2650/2653 *Set of 4* ... 1·30 55

No. 2653 was for use in Macedonia and Nos. 2650/2 in the rest of Yugoslavia.

Imperforate and perforate souvenir sheets containing an enlarged version of No. 2653 were also on sale in Macedonia.

884 "Pec Patriachate" (Dimitrije Čudov)

(885)

(886)

(Des D. Čudov. Litho Forum, Novi Sad)

1990 (20 Sept). 300th Anniv of Great Migration of Serbs. T **884** and similar horiz design. Multicoloured. P 14.

2654 1d. Type **884** ... 30 10
2655 6d.50 "Migration of Serbs" (Paja Jovanović) ... 1·40 1·10

(Surch Forum, Novi Sad (2656) or The Mint, Belgrade (2657))

1990 (2 Oct). Nos. 2590/a surch with T **885/6**.

2656 **885** 2d. on 40p. blue-green and bright purple (p 12½) ... 1·40 55
a. Perf 13½ ... 3·50 2·75
2657 **886** 2d. on 40p. blue-green and bright purple (p 13½) ... 2·10 1·10

887 "Little Sisters" (Ivana Kobilca)

888 Chess Pieces

(Des D. Čudov. Litho Forum, Novi Sad)

1990 (2 Oct). 22nd "Joy of Europe" Meeting. T **887** and similar multicoloured design. P 14.

2658 6d.50 Type **887** ... 1·80 1·50
2659 10d. "Willem III of Orange as a Child" (Adriaen Hanneman) (vert) ... 2·40 1·90

(Des D. Čudov. Litho)

1990 (Oct). OBLIGATORY TAX. 29th Chess Olympiad, Novi Sad. As No. 2577 but value in reformed currency. P 12½.

2660 **856a** 1d. black and new blue ... 40 20

(Des R. Bojanić. Photo Courvoisier)

1990 (18 Oct). 29th Chess Olympiad, Novi Sad. T **888** and similar vert designs. Multicoloured. Granite paper. P 11½.

2661 1d. Type **888** ... 35 20
a. Sheetlet. Nos. 2661/4 ... 7·00
2662 5d. Rook, bishop, knight and chessboard ... 1·70 1·40
2663 6d.50 Knights, queen, king, pawn and chessboard ... 2·00 1·60
2664 10d. Chess pieces and symbols ... 2·75 2·20
2661/2664 *Set of 4* ... 6·00 4·75
MS2665 84×97 mm. As Nos. 2661/4 but with emblem in gold (instead of silver). Imperf ... 12·50 12·50

Nos. 2661/4 were issued together in *se-tenant* sheetlets of four stamps.

888a Dubrovnik

889 "St. Vlaho and Ragusa" (detail of triptych. Nikola Božidarevic) and Penny Black

(Des D. Čudov. Litho)

1990 (21 Oct). OBLIGATORY TAX. European Judo Championships, Dubrovnik. P 12½.

2666 **888a** 1d. bright violet and greenish blue ... 40 20

No. 2666 was for use in Croatia.

(Des D. Čudov. Litho Forum, Novi Sad)

1990 (31 Oct). Stamp Day. P 14.

2667 **889** 2d. multicoloured ... 1·00 65

890 Vransko Lake

891 "King Milutin" and Monastery of Our Lady, Ljeviška

(Des R. Bojanić. Litho Forum, Novi Sad)

1990 (16 Nov). Nature Protection. T **890** and similar horiz design. Multicoloured. P 14.

2668 6d.50 Type **890** ... 1·80 1·50
2669 10d. Griffon vulture (*Gyps fulvus*) ... 2·40 1·90

(Des D. Čudov. Litho Forum, Novi Sad)

1990 (28 Nov). Monastery Frescoes. T **891** and similar horiz designs. Multicoloured. P 14.

2670 2d. Type **891** ... 70 55
2671 5d. "St. Sava" and Mileševa Monastery ... 1·40 1·10
2672 6d.50 "St. Elias" and Moraca Monastery ... 1·70 1·30
2673 10d. "Jesus Christ" and Sopocani Monastery ... 2·10 1·70
2670/2673 *Set of 4* ... 5·25 4·25

892 Milanovic and Kringa (birthplace)

893 "Arrival of Mary in the Temple"

(Des D. Čudov. Litho)

1990 (20 Dec). Birth Centenary of Dr. Božo Milanovic (politician). P 13½.

2674 **892** 2d. multicoloured ... 40 35

(Des R. Bojanić. Litho Forum, Novi Sad)

1990 (24 Dec). Museum Exhibits. Icon Screens of St. Jovan Bigorski Monastery, Bistra. T **893** and similar multicoloured designs. P 14.

2675 2d. Type **893** ... 70 55
2676 5d. "Nativity" ... 1·10 90
2677 6d.50 "Flight into Egypt" (horiz) ... 1·40 1·10
2678 10d. "Entry into Jerusalem" (horiz) ... 1·70 1·30
2675/2678 *Set of 4* ... 4·50 3·50

894 Lapwing (*Vanellus vanellus*)

895 *Crocus kosaninii*

(Des R. Bojanić. Litho Forum, Novi Sad)

1991 (31 Jan). Protected Birds. T **894** and similar vert designs. Multicoloured. P 14.

2679 2d. Type **894** ... 35 30
a. Horiz strip. Nos. 2679/82 plus label ... 4·75
2680 5d. Woodchat shrike (*Lanius senator*) ... 95 75
2681 6d.50 Common crane (*Grus grus*) ... 1·30 1·00
2682 10d. Goosander (*Mergus merganser*) ... 1·90 1·50
2679/2682 *Set of 4* ... 4·00 3·25

Nos. 2679/82 were issued together in horizontal *se-tenant* strips of four stamps and one central label showing a lake.

(Des D. Čudov. Litho Forum, Novi Sad)

1991 (20 Feb). Crocuses. T **895** and similar vert designs. Multicoloured. P 14.

2683 2d. Type **895** ... 70 55
2684 6d. *Crocus scardicus* ... 85 65
2685 7d.50 *Crocus rujanensis* ... 1·00 80
2686 15d. *Crocus adamii* ... 3·00 2·50
2683/2686 *Set of 4* ... 5·00 4·00

895a Hands and Flower

895b Emblem

(Des R. Bojanić (2687). Litho)

1991 (1 Mar). OBLIGATORY TAX. Anti-cancer Week.

(a) For use in republics other than Macedonia. P 12½

2687 **895a** 1d. new blue and red-orange ... 40 20

(b) For use in Macedonia. T **895b** and similar vert designs. P 10

2688 1d.20 multicoloured ... 40 20
a. Block of 4. Nos. 2688/91 ... 1·70
2689 1d.20 Butterfly ... 40 20
2690 1d.20 Sunbathers on rocky beach ... 40 20
2691 1d.20 Street in town ... 40 20
2687/2691 *Set of 5* ... 1·80 90

Nos. 2688/91 were issued together in *se-tenant* blocks of four stamps within the sheet. The block also exists in imperforate and perforate souvenir sheets.

896 Bishop Josip Strossmayer (founder) (after Vlaho Bukovac)

897 Mozart (after P. Lorenzoni)

(Des D. Čudov. Litho Forum, Novi Sad)

1991 (4 Mar). 125th Anniv of Yugoslav Academy of Arts and Sciences. P 14.

2692 **896** 2d. multicoloured ... 1·40 65

(Des D. Čudov. Litho Forum, Novi Sad)

1991 (20 Mar). Death Bicentenary of Wolfgang Amadeus Mozart (composer). P 14.

2693 **897** 7d.50 multicoloured ... 1·70 1·30

898 Edvard Rusjan (Slovenian pioneer) and Blériot XI

899 Route of Climb and Cesen

(Des R. Bojanić. Litho Forum, Novi Sad)

1991 (1 Apr). Centenary of First Heavier-than-Air Flight by Lilienthal. T **898** and similar horiz design. Multicoloured. P 14.

2694 7d.50 Type **898** ... 1·70 1·30
2695 15d. Otto Lilienthal and Lilienthal biplane glider ... 2·10 1·70

Nos. 2694/5 were each issued in sheets of eight stamps and one label showing men flying.

(Des D. Čudov. Litho Forum, Novi Sad)

1991 (24 Apr). First Anniv of Tomo Cesen's Ascent of South Face of Lhotse Peak. P 14.

2696 **899** 7d.50 multicoloured ... 1·70 1·30

900 Satellite and Earth

(Des R. Bojanić. Litho Forum, Novi Sad)

1991 (6 May). Europa. Europe in Space. T **900** and similar horiz design. Multicoloured. P 13×14.

2697 7d.50 Type **900** ... 1·70 1·30
2698 15d. Dish aerial reflecting rays from satellite to telephone ... 2·75 2·20

901 Figures

902 Red Cross and Rays

(Des A. Daskalović; litho Forum, Novi Sad (2699/2701). Des Z. Popovski (2704/2706). Litho)

1991 (6 May). OBLIGATORY TAX. Red Cross Week.

(a) For use in Bosnia and Herzegovina (60p.), Montenegro and Slovenia (1d.20), Serbia (2d.50). P 14

2699 **901** 60p. multicoloured ... 15 10
2700 1d.20 multicoloured ... 30 20
2701 2d.50 multicoloured ... 55 45

(b) For use in Croatia. Design with motif as in T **901** but differently inscribed. Size 29×24 mm. P 11

2702 1d.70 multicoloured ... 30 20

(c) For use in Macedonia. T **902** and similar vert designs. Multicoloured. P 10

2703 1d.70 Type **902** ... 30 20
a. Block of 4. Nos. 2703/6 ... 1·30
2704 1d.70 Pink flowers ... 30 20
2705 1d.70 Children on globe ... 30 20
2706 1d.70 Yellow flowers ... 30 20
2699/2706 *Set of 8* ... 2·30 1·60

Nos. 2703/6 were issued together in *se-tenant* blocks of four within the sheet. The block also exists in imperforate and perforate souvenir sheets.

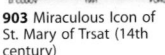

903 Miraculous Icon of St. Mary of Trsat (14th century)

904 Danube River Steamer

(Des D. Čudov. Litho Forum, Novi Sad)

1991 (10 May). 700th Anniv of Franciscan Monastery, Rijeka. P 14.
2707 **903** 3d.50 multicoloured ..... 1·30 65

(Des R. Bojanić. Litho Forum, Novi Sad)

1991 (15 May). Community of Danubian Regions Conference, Belgrade. T **904** and similar multicoloured designs. P 14.
2708 7d.50 Type **904** ..... 1·40 1·10
2709 15d. Steamer on river at sunset ..... 2·10 1·70
MS2710 85×65 mm. 20d. Map of Danube (54×34 mm) ..... 9·75 9·75

Nos. 2708/9 were each issued in sheets of eight stamps and one label showing a river scene.

905 Woman with Horse

906 "Karavanke Pass" (17th-century engraving, Johann Valvasor)

(Des D. Andrić (2711), N. Pešev-Kokan (2712/15). Litho)

1991 (1 June). OBLIGATORY TAX. Solidarity Week.

(a) For use in areas other than Macedonia and Croatia. As T **876** but dated "1991". P 12½
2711 **876** 2d. grey-green and orange 40 35

(b) For use in Macedonia. T **905** and similar vert designs. Each reddish brown, bright scarlet and gold. P 10
2712 2d. "Skopje Earthquake" 40 35
a. Block of 4. Nos. 2712/15 ..... 1·70
2713 2d. Type **905** 40 35
2714 2d. Woman and tree 40 35
2715 2d. Woman holding cockerel 40 35

(c) For use in Croatia. As T **715** but size 20×30 mm. P 11
2716 **715** 2d.20 metallic grey-blue and rosine 65 45
2711/2716 *Set of* 6 ..... 2·40 2·00

Nos. 2712/15 were issued together in blocks of four stamps within the sheet.

(Des D. Čudov. Litho Forum, Novi Sad)

1991 (1 June). Opening of Karavanke Road Tunnel. T **906** and similar horiz design. Multicoloured. P 14.
2717 4d.50 Type **906** ..... 1·00 80
2718 11d. Tunnel entrance ..... 1·40 1·10

907 Balls and Baskets

907a Exhibitor carrying Painting

(Des R. Bojanić. Litho Forum, Novi Sad)

1991 (15 June). Centenary of Basketball. T **907** and similar horiz design. Multicoloured. P 14.
2719 11d. Type **907** ..... 1·70 1·30
2720 15d. Aerial view of baskets ..... 2·20 1·80

Nos. 2719/20 were each issued in sheets of eight stamps and one label showing a basket and player.

(Des D. Čudov. Litho)

1991 (July). OBLIGATORY TAX. Cetinje Biennale. P 12½.
2721 **907a** 2d. brown-red and chalky blue 40 20

No. 2721 was for use in Montenegro.

908 Order of the Partisan Star

909 Ujevic

(Des D. Čudov. Litho Forum, Novi Sad)

1991 (4 July). 50th Anniversaries of Yugoslav Insurrection and of National Army. T **908** and similar vert design. Multicoloured. P 14.
2722 4d.50 Type **908** 55 45
2723 11d. Order for Bravery ..... 1·10 90

(Des Marina Kalezić-Krajinović. Litho)

1991 (5 July). Birth Centenary of Tin Ujevic (writer). P 13½.
2724 **909** 4d.50 multicoloured ..... 1·00 55

910 Score and Gallus

911 Savudrija, 1818

(Des D. Čudov. Litho)

1991 (18 July). 400th Death Anniv of Jacobus Gallus (composer). P 13½.
2725 **910** 11d. multicoloured ..... 1·10 90

(Des R. Bojanić. Litho Unicover Corporation, Cheyenne, U.S.A.)

1991 (25 July). Lighthouses of the Adriatic and the Danube. Booklet stamps. T **911** and similar horiz designs. Multicoloured. P 13½.
2726 10d. Type **911** ..... 1·40 1·10
a. Booklet pane. Nos. 2726/37 ..... 18·00
2727 10d. Sveti Ivan na Pucini, 1853 ..... 1·40 1·10
2728 10d. Porer, 1833 ..... 1·40 1·10
2729 10d. Stoncica, 1865 ..... 1·40 1·10
2730 10d. Olipa, 1842 ..... 1·40 1·10
2731 10d. Glavat, 1884 ..... 1·40 1·10
2732 10d. Veli Rat, 1849 ..... 1·40 1·10
2733 10d. Vir, 1881 ..... 1·40 1·10
2734 10d. Tajerske Sestrice, 1876 ..... 1·40 1·10
2735 10d. Ražanj, 1875 ..... 1·40 1·10
2736 10d. Djerdap, Danube ..... 1·40 1·10
2737 10d. Tamiš, Danube ..... 1·40 1·10
2726/2737 *Set of* 12 ..... 15·00 12·00

912 "Sremski Karlovci School" (Ljubica Sokic)

(Des R. Bojanić. Litho Forum, Novi Sad)

1991 (12 Sept). Bicentenary of Sremski Karlovci High School. P 14.
2738 **912** 4d.50 multicoloured 70 35

913 Girl

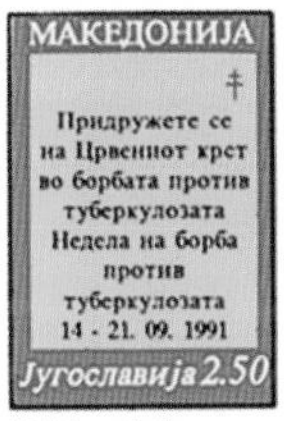

914 Inscription

(Des A. Daskalović (2739/40). Litho)

1991 (14 Sept). OBLIGATORY TAX. Anti-tuberculosis Week.

(a) For use in Serbia, Montenegro and Bosnia and Herzegovina. P 12½
2739 **913** 1d.20 blue, rosine and pale lemon 20 10
2740 2d.50 blue, rosine and pale lemon 30 20

(b) For use in Macedonia. T **914** and similar vert designs. P 10
2741 2d.50 black, greenish yellow and magenta 30 20
a. Block of 4. Nos. 2741/4 ..... 1·30
2742 2d.50 multicoloured 30 20
2743 2d.50 multicoloured 30 20
2744 2d.50 black, greenish yellow and magenta 30 20
2739/2744 *Set of* 6 ..... 1·50 1·00

Designs:—No. 2742, Doctor and patient; 2743, Children on path; 2744, Girls with birds and flowers.

Nos. 2741/4 were issued together in *se-tenant* blocks of four stamps within the sheet. The block also exists in imperforate and perforate souvenir sheets.

915 Mayfly (*Palingenia longicauda*)

916 Town Hall (stained glass)

(Des R. Bojanić. Litho Forum, Novi Sad)

1991 (24 Sept). Nature Protection. T **915** and similar horiz design. Multicoloured. P 14.
2745 11d. Type **915** ..... 1·50 1·20
2746 15d. Pygmy cormorants (*Phalacrocorax pygmaeus*) ..... 2·00 1·60

(Des D. Čudov. Litho Forum, Novi Sad)

1991 (28 Sept). 600th Anniv of Subotica. P 14.
2747 **916** 4d.50 multicoloured 70 55

917 Honey Bees and Congress Emblem

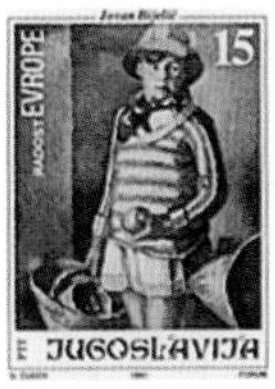

918 "Little Dubravka" (Jovan Bijelic)

(Des R. Bojanić. Litho Forum, Novi Sad)

1991 (28 Sept). Apimondia 33rd International Bee Keeping Congress, Split. P 14.
2748 **917** 11d. multicoloured ..... 1·70 1·20

(Des D. Čudov. Litho Forum, Novi Sad)

1991 (2 Oct). 23rd "Joy of Europe" Meeting. T **918** and similar vert design. Multicoloured. P 14.
2749 15d. Type **918** ..... 1·10 90
2750 30d. "Little Girl with a Cat" (Mary Cassatt) ..... 1·70 1·30

919 Statue of Prince Mihael Obrenovic and Serbian 1866 1p. Newspaper Stamp

919a Protecting Refugee

(Des D. Čudov. Litho Forum, Novi Sad)

1991 (31 Oct). Stamp Day. P 14.
2751 **919** 4d.50 multicoloured ..... 1·00 80

(Des D. Čudov. Litho Forum, Novi Sad)

1991 (1 Nov). OBLIGATORY TAX. Serbian Refugee Fund. P 14.
2752 **919a** 2d. magenta and ultramarine 45 20

920 Battle of Vucji Flag and Medal for Military Valour

921 Angel carrying Sun (Andrija Raicevic) (17th century)

(Des R. Bojanić. Litho Forum, Novi Sad)

1991 (28 Nov). Cetinje Museum Exhibits. Montenegrin Flags and Medals. T **920** and similar vert designs. Multicoloured. P 14.
2753 20d. Type **920** 45 35
2754 30d. Battle of Grahovo flag and medal 70 55
2755 40d. State flag and Medal for Bravery ..... 1·00 80
2756 50d. Court flag and Petrović dynasty commemorative medal ..... 1·70 1·30
2753/2756 *Set of* 4 ..... 3·50 2·75

(Des D. Čudov. Litho Forum, Novi Sad)

1991 (12 Dec). Illustrations from Ancient Manuscripts. T **921** and similar vert designs. Multicoloured. P 14.
2757 20d. Type **921** 45 35
2758 30d. "April" (Celnica Gospel) (14th century) 70 55
2759 40d. "Annunciation" (Trogir Evangeliarum) (13th century) ..... 1·00 80
2760 50d. Mary Magdalene in initial V (Miroslav Gospel) (12th century) ..... 1·70 1·30
2757/2760 *Set of* 4 ..... 3·50 2·75

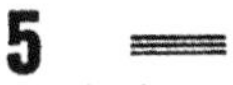

(922)

923 Delcev

1991 (12–17 Dec). Nos. 2592 and 2587 surch as T **922**.
2761 5d. on 60p. bright mauve and orange-vermilion (17 Dec) ... 70 20
2762 10d. on 10p. bluish violet and bright green ... 70 35
a. Perf 13½ ... 1·70 65
On No. 2762 the figures are thinner.

(Des Marina Kalezić-Krajinović. Litho)

1992 (29 Jan). 120th Birth Anniv of Goce Delcev (Macedonian revolutionary). P 13½.
2763 **923** 5d. multicoloured ... 3·25 2·50

924 Trophies and Club Emblem

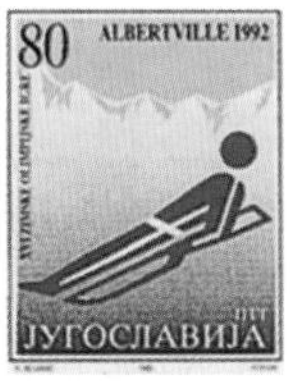

925 Luge

(Des R. Bojanić. Litho Forum, Novi Sad)

1992 (31 Jan). Victories of Red Star Club, Belgrade, in European and World Football Championships. P 14.
2764 **924** 17d. multicoloured ... 3·50 2·75
No. 2764 was issued in sheetlets of eight stamps and one label showing the club emblem and ball.

(Des R. Bojanić. Litho Forum, Novi Sad)

1992 (8 Feb). Winter Olympic Games, Albertville, France. T **925** and similar vert design. Multicoloured. P 14.
2765 80d. Type **925** ... 2·30 1·80
2766 100d. Acrobatic skiing ... 2·75 2·20
Nos. 2765/6 were each issued in sheetlets of eight stamps and one label showing world map, Olympic rings and motif as on the stamp.

926 European Hare (*Lepus europaeus*)

927 "Mary feeding Jesus" (fresco, Pec Patriarchate)

(Des Marina Kalezić-Krajinović. Litho Forum, Novi Sad)

1992 (10 Mar). Protected Animals. T **926** and similar vert designs. Multicoloured. P 14.
2767 50d. Type **926** ... 1·40 1·10
a. Horiz strip. Nos. 2767/70 plus label... 7·50
2768 60d. Siberian flying squirrels (*Pteromys volans*) ... 1·60 1·20
2769 80d. Forest dormouse (*Dryomys nitedula*) 1·90 1·50
2770 100d. Common hamsters (*Cricetus cricetus*) ... 2·30 1·80
2767/2770 *Set of 4* ... 6·50 5·00
Nos. 2767/70 were issued together in horizontal *se-tenant* strips of four stamps and one central label showing a landscape.

(Des D. Čudov. Litho Forum, Novi Sad)

1992 (14 Mar). United Nations Children's Fund Breastfeeding Campaign. P 14.
2771 **927** 80d. multicoloured ... 1·70 1·30

928 Skier

929 Fountain, Belgrade

(Des Marina Kalezić-Krajinović. Litho Forum, Novi Sad)

1992 (25 Mar). Centenary of Skiing in Montenegro. P 14.
2772 **928** 8d. multicoloured ... 5·50 4·25

(Des D. Čudov. Litho)

1992 (25 Mar–May). T **929** and similar vert design. P 13½.
2773 50d. violet and lilac ... 70 55
2774 100d. deep dull green and sage green (6 May) ... 45 20
Design:—100d. Fisherman Fountain, Kalemegdan Fortress, Belgrade.
See also Nos. 2825/32 and 2889/90.

Nos. 2775/82 are vacant.

930 *Titanic*

931 La Barqueta Bridge and Seville (engraving)

(Des R. Bojanić. Litho Forum, Novi Sad)

1992 (14 Apr). 80th Anniv of Sinking of Liner *Titanic*. P 14.
2783 **930** 150d. multicoloured ... 1·60 1·10

(Des D. Čudov. Litho Forum, Novi Sad)

1992 (20 Apr). Expo '92 World's Fair, Seville. P 14.
2784 **931** 150d. multicoloured ... 1·60 1·10

From 27 April 1992, following the secession of the other republics, the Federation of Yugoslavia consisted of the Republics of Montenegro and Serbia and the two autonomous provinces of Kosovo and Vojvodina.

932 Christopher Columbus

(Des R. Bojanić. Litho Forum, Novi Sad)

1992 (5 May). Europa. 500th Anniv of Discovery of America by Columbus. T **932** and similar horiz designs. Multicoloured. P 14.
2785 300d. Type **932** ... 4·50 3·50
2786 500d. Columbus's fleet ... 5·25 4·25
MS2787 85×65 mm. 1200d. "Lisbon Harbour" (engraving) (52×34 mm) ... 14·50 14·50

934 Water Polo

935 Players' Legs

(Des Marina Kalezić-Krajinović. Litho Forum, Novi Sad)

1992 (20 May). Olympic Games, Barcelona. T **934** and similar vert designs. Multicoloured. P 14.
2791 500d. Type **934** ... 1·40 1·10
2792 500d. Shooting ... 1·40 1·10
2793 500d. Tennis ... 1·40 1·10
2794 500d. Handball ... 1·40 1·10
2791/2794 *Set of 4* ... 5·00 4·00
Nos. 2791/4 were each issued in sheets of eight stamps and one label showing different Barcelona landmarks.

(Des Marina Kalezić-Krajinović. Litho)

1992 (1 June). European Football Championship, Sweden. T **935** and similar horiz design. Multicoloured. P 13½.
2795 1000d. Type **935** ... 2·50 2·00
2796 1000d. Players ... 2·50 2·00
Nos. 2795/6 were each issued in sheets of eight stamps and one label showing emblems of national team and Union of European Football Associations.

936 Red Tabby

937 JDŽ 162, 1880

(Des Marina Kalezić-Krajinović. Litho Forum, Novi Sad)

1992 (25 June). Domestic Cats. T **936** and similar horiz designs. Multicoloured. P 14.
2797 1000d. Type **936** ... 2·50 2·00
2798 1000d. White Persian ... 2·50 2·00
2799 1000d. Blue and white British shorthair ... 2·50 2·00
2800 1000d. Red-point colourpoint longhair ... 2·50 2·00
2797/2800 *Set of 4* ... 9·00 7·25

(Des R. Bojanić. Litho Forum, Novi Sad)

1992 (3 July). Steam Railway Locomotives. Booklet stamps. T **937** and similar horiz designs. Multicoloured. P 14.
2801 1000d. Type **937** ... 3·25 2·50
a. Booklet pane. Nos. 2801/6 ... 21·00
2802 1000d. JDŽ 151, 1885 ... 3·25 2·50
2803 1000d. JDŽ 73, 1913 ... 3·25 2·50
2804 1000d. JDŽ 83, 1929 ... 3·25 2·50
2805 1000d. JDŽ 16, 1936 ... 3·25 2·50
2806 1000d. Private train of Prince Nicolas, 1909 3·25 2·50
2801/2806 *Set of 6* ... 18·00 13·50

Currency Reform

10 (old) Dinars = 1 (new) Diner

**
5
(**938**)

939 Fischer (champion, 1972–75)

1992 (6 Aug–9 Nov). Various stamps surch as T **938**.
2807 2d. on 30p. yellowish green and reddish orange (No. 2589) (26.10.92) .. 2·75 55
2808 5d. on 20p. bright crimson and yellow-orange (2588) (12.9.92) ... 2·75 55
2809 5d. on 40p. blue-green and bright purple (2590a) (26.10.92) ... 2·75 55
2810 10d. on 50p. blue-green and reddish violet (2591) (17.9.92) ... 2·75 55
2811 10d. on 5d. ultramarine and greenish blue (2596a) (29.10.92) ... 2·75 55
2812 20d. on 1d. turquoise-blue and bright purple (2593a) ... 4·25 1·10
2813 20d. on 5d. deep blue, turquoise-green & bistre-yellow (as No. 2596) (p 13½) (9.11.92) ... 2·75 55
2814 50d. on 2d. new blue and bright crimson (2594a) ... 2·75 55
2815 100d. on 3d. blue and orange-red (2595a). 5·75 1·10
2807/2815 *Set of 9* ... 26·00 5·50
No. 2813 was not issued without surcharge.
Nos. 2811/15 have a single star obliterating the old value.

(Des R. Bojanić. Litho Forum, Novi Sad)

1992 (14 Sept). Unofficial Chess Re-match between Former World Champions Robert Fischer and Boris Spassky. T **939** and similar horiz design. Multicoloured. P 14.
2816 500d. Type **939** ... 2·75 2·10
2817 500d. Spassky (1969–72) ... 2·75 2·10
Nos. 2816/17 were each issued in sheets of eight stamps and one label showing chessmen.

940 Old Telephone and Buildings in Novi Sad, Subotica and Zrenjanin

941 "Ballerina" (Edgar Degas)

(Des R. Bojanić. Litho Forum, Novi Sad)

1992 (1 Oct). Centenary of Telephone Service in Vojvodina. P 14.
2818 **940** 10d. multicoloured ... 2·20 1·70

(Des D. Čudov. Litho Forum, Novi Sad)

1992 (2 Oct). 24th "Joy of Europe" Meeting. Paintings. T **941** and similar vert design. Multicoloured. P 14.
2819 500d. Type **941** ... 2·20 1·70
2820 500d. Youth (V. Kneževic) ... 2·20 1·70

942 Montenegro 1874 25n. Stamp and Musician

943 Capercaillie (*Tetrao urogallus*), Durmitor Mountains

(Des D. Čudov. Litho Forum, Novi Sad)

1992 (31 Oct). Stamp Day. P 14.
2821 **942** 50d. multicoloured ... 1·70 1·30

(Des Marina Kalezić-Krajinović. Litho)

1992 (14 Nov). Nature Protection. T **943** and similar vert design. Multicoloured. P 13½.
2822 500d. Type **943** ... 5·75 4·50
2823 500d. Eastern white pelican (*Pelecanus onocrotalus*), Skadar Sea ... 5·75 4·50

944 Book and Emblem

945 Brvnara Summer Pasture Hut, Zlatibor

(Des D. Čudov. Litho Forum, Novi Sad)

1992 (20 Nov). Centenary of Serbian Literary Association. P 14.
2824 **944** 100d. multicoloured ... 1·40 1·10

(Des Marina Kalezić-Krajinović (500d.), D. Čudov (others). Litho)

1992 (24 Nov)–**93**. Vert designs as T **929**. P 12½ (3000d.) or 13½ (others).
2825 5d. brown and yellow-olive ... 1·40 20
2826 50d. blue and azure (15.12.92) ... 70 20
2827 100d. brown-lilac and pale pink (22.12.92) ... 70 20
2828 300d. brown and chestnut (3.12.92) ... 70 20
2829 500d. brown-olive and flesh (14.1.93) .. 1·40 20
2830 3000d. red-orange (23.4.93) ... 70 20
2831 5000d. purple and yellow (18.3.93) ... 70 20
2832 500000d. reddish violet and new blue (10.8.93) ... 85 35
2825/2832 *Set of 8* ... 6·50 1·60
Designs:—5d. 14th-century relief; 50d. As No. 2774; 100d. Type **929**; 300d. Fountain, Kalemegdan Fortress, Belgrade; 500d. Fountain, Sremski Korlovci; 3000d. Fountain, Studenica; 5000d. Fountain, Oplenac; 500000d. Thermal baths, Vrnjacka Banja.

(Des R. Bojanić. Litho Forum, Novi Sad)

1992 (12 Dec). Museum Exhibits. Traditional Houses. T **945** and similar horiz designs. Multicoloured. P 14.

2833 500d. Type **945** ... 1·40 1·10
2834 500d. House, Morava ... 1·40 1·10
2835 500d. House, Metohija ... 1·40 1·10
2836 500d. Farmhouse, Vojvodina ... 1·40 1·10
2833/2836 *Set of 4* ... 5·00 4·00

946 Sun over Able-bodied and Disabled People

947 St. Simeon Nemanja with Model of Church of the Blessed Virgin, Studenica (mosaic, Oplenac)

(Des Marina Kalezić-Krajinović. Litho Forum, Novi Sad)

1992 (6 Dec). OBLIGATORY TAX. Disabled Persons' Week. P 14.

2837 **946** 13d. lemon and new blue ... 45 20

(Des D. Čudov. Litho Forum, Novi Sad)

1992 (15 Dec). Mosaics and Icons. T **947** and similar multicoloured designs. P 14.

2838 500d. Type **947** ... 1·40 1·10
2839 500d. Prince Lazarević with model of Ravanica Monastery (mosaic, Oplenac) ... 1·40 1·10
2840 500d. St. Petka (icon) and St. Petka's Church, Belgrade (horiz) ... 1·40 1·10
2841 500d. St. Vasilije Ostronoski (icon) and Monastery, Montenegro (horiz) ... 1·40 1·10
2838/2841 *Set of 4* ... 5·00 4·00

948 Blériot XI Monoplane

949 Detail of Fresco, Sirmium

(Des R. Bojanić. Litho Forum, Novi Sad)

1992 (24 Dec). 80th Anniv of Aviation in Yugoslavia. P 14.

2842 **948** 500d. multicoloured ... 1·90 1·50

(Des D. Čudov. Litho)

1993 (28 Jan). 1700th Anniv of Formation of the Tetrarchy (Diocletian's reform of government of Roman Empire). P 13½.

2843 **949** 1500d. multicoloured ... 1·70 1·30

950 Museum and Medal

1500

(**951**)

(Des R. Bojanić. Litho Forum, Novi Sad)

1993 (12 Feb). Centenary of Cetinje State Museum. P 13½×14.

2844 **950** 2500d. multicoloured ... 1·70 1·30

1993 (1 Mar). OBLIGATORY TAX. Anti-cancer Week. No. 2687 surch with T **951**.

2844*a* **895a** 1500d. on 1d. new blue and red-orange ... 1·70 1·30

952 Common Sturgeon (*Acipenser sturio*)

953 Charter and 1868 10p. Coin

(Des Marina Kalezić-Krajinović. Litho)

1993 (20 Mar). Marine Animals. T **952** and similar horiz designs. Multicoloured. P 13½.

2845 10000d. Type **952** ... 2·20 1·70
a. Horiz strip. Nos. 2845/8 plus label ... 9·00
2846 10000d. Red scorpionfish (*Scorpaena scrofa*) ... 2·20 1·70
2847 10000d. Swordfish (*Xiphias gladius*) ... 2·20 1·70
2848 10000d. Bottle-nosed dolphin (*Tursiops truncatus*) ... 2·20 1·70
2845/2848 *Set of 4* ... 8·00 6·25

Nos. 2845/8 were issued together in horizontal *se-tenant* strips of four stamps and one central label showing sea anemones within the sheet.

(Des R. Bojanić. Litho)

1993 (30 Mar). 125th Anniv of Reintroduction of Serbian Coins (2849) and 120th Anniv of the Dinar (2850). T **953** and similar vert design. Multicoloured. P 13½.

2849 10000d. Type **953** ... 2·20 1·70
2850 10000d. 5d. banknote and 1879 5d. coin ... 2·20 1·70

Nos. 2849/50 were each issued in sheets of eight stamps and one label showing the Serbian National Bank or the Mint respectively.

954 Miloš Crnjanski (writer)

955 Bird and Girl holding Flowers (M. Markovski)

(Des Marina Kalezić-Krajinović. Litho Forum, Novi Sad)

1993 (1 Apr). Anniversaries. T **954** and similar vert designs. Multicoloured. P 14.

2851 40000d. Type **954** (birth centenary) ... 2·30 1·80
2852 40000d. Nikola Tesla (physicist, 50th death anniv) ... 2·30 1·80
2853 40000d. Mihailo Petrović (mathematician, 50th death anniv) ... 2·30 1·80
2854 40000d. Aleksa Šantic (poet, 125th birth anniv) ... 2·30 1·80
2851/2854 *Set of 4* ... 8·25 6·50

1993 (5 Apr). Children for Peace. T **955** and similar vert design. Multicoloured. Litho. P 13½.

2855 50000d. Type **955** ... 2·40 1·90
2856 50000d. Birds flying above children (J. Rugovac) ... 2·40 1·90

956 Illuminated Letter from Miroslav Gospel

957 "Nude with Mirror" (M. Milunovic)

958

(Des D. Čudov. Litho)

1993 (5 Apr). No value expressed. P 13½.

2857 **956** A vermilion ... 2·75 55
a. Perf 12½ ... 5·75 55

No. 2857 exists with imprint dates 1993 and 1996 and No. 2857a with imprint dates 1993, 1996 and 1997.

The original 1993 issue was sold at 3000d.

(Des D. Čudov. Litho)

1993 (5 May). Europa. Contemporary Art. T **957** and similar vert designs. Multicoloured. P 13½.

2858 95000d. Type **957** ... 4·25 3·25
2859 95000d. "Composition" (Milena Barili) ... 4·25 3·25

(Des A. Daskalović. Litho)

1993 (8 May). OBLIGATORY TAX. Red Cross Week. P 13½ (350d.) or 12½ (1000d.).

2860 **958** 350d. black and rose-red ... 45 20
2861 1000d. black and rose-red ... 70 35

No. 2860 was for use in Montenegro and No. 2861 in Serbia.

959 Map of Europe and Envelopes

R **960** Hands holding Envelope

(Des D. Čudov. Litho)

1993 (10–28 June). T **959** and similar vert design. P 13½.

2862 500000d. silver and steel blue ... 70 20
2863 100000d. ultramarine and carmine-red (28.6) ... 1·40 55

Designs:—100000d. Airplane.

(Des R. Bojanić. Litho)

1993 (28 June). REGISTERED. No value expressed. P 12½.

R2864 R **960** R ultramarine ... 55 15

No. R2864 exists with imprint dates 1993 and 1997. The 1993 issue was sold at 11000d.

NEW INFORMATION

The editor is always interested to correspond with people who have new information that will improve or correct the catalogue

961 Sutorina

962 Marguerites and Roses

(Des R. Bojanić. Litho)

1993 (9 July). Fortresses. Booklet stamps. T **961** and similar horiz designs. Multicoloured. P 13½.

2865 900000d. Type **961** ... 1·70 1·30
a. Booklet pane. Nos. 2865/70 ... 10·50
2866 900000d. Kalemegdan, Belgrade ... 1·70 1·30
2867 900000d. Medun ... 1·70 1·30
2868 900000d. Petrovaradin ... 1·70 1·30
2869 900000d. Bar ... 1·70 1·30
2870 900000d. Golubac ... 1·70 1·30
2865/2870 *Set of 6* ... 9·25 7·00

(Des Marina Kalezić-Krajinović. Litho Forum, Novi Sad)

1993 (10 July). Flower Arrangements. T **962** and similar vert designs. Multicoloured. P 14.

2871 1000000d. Type **962** ... 2·20 1·70
2872 1000000d. Roses and gerbera ... 2·20 1·70
2873 1000000d. Roses and lilies ... 2·20 1·70
2874 1000000d. Rose, carnations and stephanotis ... 2·20 1·70
2871/2874 *Set of 4* ... 8·00 6·00

963 Generating Plant, Street Lamp and Town

964 Jays (*Garrulus glandarius*)

(Des D. Čudov. Litho)

1993 (28 July). Centenary of Electrification of Serbia. P 13½.

2875 **963** 2500000d. multicoloured ... 1·20 90

(Des Marina Kalezić-Krajinović. Litho)

1993 (20 Sept). Nature Protection. Fruška Highlands. T **964** and similar horiz design. Multicoloured. P 13½.

2876 300,000,000d. Type **964** ... 10·50 7·75
2877 300,000,000d. Golden oriole (*Oriolus oriolus*) ... 10·50 7·75

Currency Reform

1000000 (old) Dinars = 1 (new) Dinar

10

(**965**)

966 River Freighters

1993 (18 Oct–Nov). Various stamps surch as T **965**.

2878 10d. on 100000d. ultramarine and carmine-red (No. 2863) (p 12½) ... 1·50 35
2879 50d. on 5d. brown and yellow-olive (No. 2825) ... 1·50 35
2880 100d. on 5000d. purple and yellow (No. 2831) ... 1·50 35
2881 500d. on 50d. blue and azure (No. 2826) ... 1·50 35
2882 1000d. on 3000d. red-orange (No. 2830) (p 13½) ... 1·50 35
2883 10000d. on 300d. brown and chestnut (No. 2828) ... 1·50 35
2884 50000d. on 5d. stone, brown and yellow-olive (as No. 2825) (9 Nov) ... 1·50 35
2878/2884 *Set of 7* ... 9·50 2·20

On No. 2882 the old value is cancelled with a different emblem; on No. 2883 the new value is sideways and in a smaller font.

No. 2884 was not issued unsurcharged.

(Des R. Bojanić. Litho Forum, Novi Sad)

1993 (20 Oct). The Danube, "River of Co-operation". T **966** and similar horiz design. Multicoloured. P 14.

2885 15000d. Type **966** ... 2·30 1·70
2886 15000d. Passenger ferry ... 2·30 1·70
MS2887 87×57 mm. 20000d. Course of River Danube on map (34×29 mm) ... 4·50 4·50

967 Jagodina Cancellation and Market

968 "Boy with Cat" (Sava Šumanovic)

(Des D. Čudov. Litho)

1993 (30 Oct). Stamp Day. 150th Anniv of Jagodina Postal Service. P 13½.
2888 **967** 12000d. multicoloured .... 2·00 1·50

(Des D. Čudov (10000d.), Marina Kalezić-Krajinović (100000d.). Litho)

1993 (9 Nov–Dec). Thermal Baths. Vert designs as T **929**. P 13½.
2889 10000d. greenish blue and violet .... 1·50 20
2890 100000d. brown and brown-red (6 Dec) .... 1·50 20
Designs:—10000d. As No. 2832; 100000d. Bukovicka Banja.

(Des D. Čudov. Litho)

1993 (26 Nov). 25th "Joy of Europe" Meeting. T **968** and similar vert design. Multicoloured. P 13½.
2891 2000000d. Type **968** .... 2·30 1·70
2892 2000000d. "Circus Rider" (Georges Rouault) .... 2·30 1·70

969 "Madonna and Child" (from Bogorodica Ljeviška)

970 Summer Pasture Hut, Savardak

(Des D. Čudov. Litho)

1993 (15 Dec). Icons. T **969** and similar vert designs. Multicoloured. P 13½.
2893 400,000,000d. Type **969** .... 1·50 1·10
2894 400,000,000d. "Christ entering Jerusalem" (from Oplenac) .... 1·50 1·10
2895 400,000,000d. "Birth of Christ" (from Studenica) .... 1·50 1·10
2896 400,000,000d. "The Annunciation" (from Mileševa) .... 1·50 1·10
2893/2896 *Set of* 4 .... 5·50 4·00

Currency Reform

1,000,000,000 (old) Dinars = 1 (new) Dinar

(Des R. Bojanić. Litho)

1993 (31 Dec). Museum Exhibits. Traditional Buildings. T **970** and similar multicoloured designs. P 13½.
2897 50d. Type **970** .... 1·50 1·10
2898 50d. "Crmnicka" house, Bar .... 1·50 1·10
2899 50d. Watchtower, Cardak (vert) .... 1·50 1·10
2900 50d. Coast house, Primoršten (vert) .... 1·50 1·10
2897/2900 *Set of* 4 .... 5·50 4·00

971 Illuminated Page

972 Egyptian Vultures (*Neophron percnopterus*)

(Des D. Čudov. Litho)

1994 (17 Jan). 500th Anniv of Printing of Oktoukh (book). T **971** and similar vert design. Multicoloured. P 13½.
2901 10000d. Type **971** .... 1·20 90
2902 10000d. Illustration of church and saints .... 1·20 90

Currency Reform

13,000,000 (old) Dinars = 1 new Dinar

(Des Marina Kalezić-Krajinović. Litho)

1994 (7 Feb). Birds. T **972** and similar horiz designs. Multicoloured. P 13½.
2903 80p. Type **972** .... 3·25 2·50
a. Strip. Nos. 2903/6 plus label .... 13·50
2904 80p. Saker falcons (*Falco cherrug*) .... 3·25 2·50
2905 80p. Long-legged buzzards (*Buteo rufinus*) .... 3·25 2·50
2906 80p. Lesser kestrels (*Falco naumanni*) .... 3·25 2·50
2903/2906 *Set of* 4 .... 11·50 9·00
Nos. 2903/6 were issued together in horizontal *se-tenant* strips of four stamps and one central label, the vertical row of labels within the sheet forming a composite design of a bird in a forest.

973 Mimosa

974 Illumination from Miroslav Gospel and Museum

(Des Marina Kalezić-Krajinović. Litho)

1994 (28 Feb). International Mimosa Festival, Herceg Novi. P 13½.
2907 **973** 80p. multicoloured .... 2·30 1·70

(Des D. Čudov (2908), R. Bojanić (2909). Litho)

1994 (19 Mar). 150th Anniv of National Museum (2908) and 125th Anniv of National Theatre (2909), Belgrade. T **974** and similar horiz design. Multicoloured. P 13½.
2908 80p. Type **974** .... 2·30 1·70
2909 80p. Prince Miloš Obrenovic and theatre .... 2·30 1·70

975 Speed Skating

976 Caudron C-61 and Route Map

(Des Marina Kalezić-Krajinović. Litho)

1994 (11 Apr). Winter Olympic Games, Lillehammer, Norway. T **975** and similar vert designs. Multicoloured. P 13½.
2910 60p. Type **975** .... 1·70 1·20
a. Strip of 3. Nos. 2910/12 .... 5·25
2911 60p. Olympic rings and flame .... 1·70 1·20
2912 60p. Skiing .... 1·70 1·20
2910/2912 *Set of* 3 .... 4·50 3·25
Nos. 2910/12 were issued together in horizontal *se-tenant* strips of three stamps within the sheet.

(Des R. Bojanić. Litho)

1994 (5 May). Europa. 71st Anniv of First Paris–Belgrade–Bucharest–Istanbul Regular Night Flight. T **976** and similar horiz design. Multicoloured. P 13½.
2913 60p. Type **976** .... 3·00 2·20
2914 1d.80 Caudron C-61, Belgrade and route map .... 3·75 2·75
Nos. 2913/14 were each issued in sheets of eight stamps and one label showing aircraft and route map.

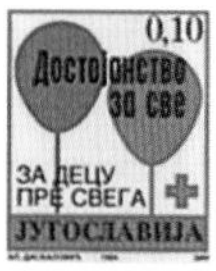
977 Balloons

978 "The Burning of St. Sava"

(Des A. Daskalović. Litho)

1994 (8 May). OBLIGATORY TAX. Red Cross Week. P 13½.
2915 **977** 10p. red, black and new blue 75 55

(Des D. Čudov. Litho Forum, Novi Sad)

1994 (10 May). 400th Anniv of Burning of St. Sava's Relics. P 14.
2916 **978** 60p. multicoloured .... 3·00 2·20
No. 2916 was issued in sheets of eight stamps and one label showing an icon of St. Sava.

979 Jubilant Players

980 Basset Hound

(Des Marina Kalezić-Krajinović. Litho)

1994 (10 June). World Cup Football Championship, U.S.A. T **979** and similar horiz design. Multicoloured. P 13½.
2917 60p. Type **979** .... 2·30 1·70
2918 1d. Goalkeeper and players on ground .... 2·30 1·70
Nos. 2917/18 were each issued in sheets of eight stamps and one label.

(Des Marina Kalezić-Krajinović. Litho)

1994 (8 July). Dogs. T **980** and similar vert designs. Multicoloured. P 13½.
2919 60p. Type **980** .... 2·30 1·70
2920 60p. Maltese terrier .... 2·30 1·70
2921 60p. Welsh terrier .... 2·30 1·70
2922 1d. Husky .... 2·30 1·70
2919/2922 *Set of* 4 .... 8·25 6·00

0,10 нд
(**981**)

982 Bell and Globe

1994 (15 July). Nos. 2889/90 surch as T **981**.
2923 10p. on 100000d. brown and brown-red 75 55
2924 50p. on 10000d. greenish blue and violet .... 1·50 80

(Des B. Likic. Litho)

1994 (20 July). Assembly of Eastern Orthodox Nations. P 13½.
2925 **982** 60p. multicoloured .... 2·30 1·70

983 River Valley

984 Moraca

(Des R. Bojanić. Litho)

1994 (28 July). Protection of Environment in Montenegro. P 13½.
2926 **983** 50p. multicoloured .... 2·30 1·70

(Des D. Čudov. Litho)

1994 (15 Aug)–**98**. Churches. T **984** and similar vert designs. P 12½ (5 to 20d.) or 13½ (others).
2927 1p. deep reddish violet and olive-bistre .... 2·30 20
a. Perf 12½ (12.97) .... 2·30 20
2928 5p. deep dull blue and dull orange .... 2·30 20
a. Perf 12½ (5.98) .... 2·30 20
2929 10p. slate-green and crimson (10.11.94) 90 20
2930 20p. black and rose-carmine .... 30·00 20
2931 20p. purple and brown-lilac (10.9.94) .... 1·50 20
a. Perf 12½ (5.98) .... 3·00 20
2932 50p. deep claret and deep reddish violet (10.11.94) 90 20
a. Perf 12½ 90 20
2933 1d. Indian red and dull blue .... 2·30 55
a. Perf 12½ (6.97) .... 2·30 55
2935 5d. bright reddish violet and greenish blue (29.2.96) .... 3·00 1·70
2936 10d. brown-lake and pale orange (29.2.96) .... 6·00 3·25
2938 20d. deep turquoise-blue and new blue (29.2.96) .... 12·00 6·75
2927/2938 *Set of* 10 .... 55·00 12·00
Designs:—5p. Gracanica; 10p. Ostrog Monastery; 20p. (2930/1) Lazarica; 50p. Studenica; 1d. Sopocani; 5d. Ljeviška; 10d. Zica Monastery; 20d. Decani Monastery.
No. 2932 was issued with "1997" imprint date in October 1997.
Nos. 2934, 2937 and 2939 are vacant.

985 St. Arsenius and Sremski

986 Syringe

(Des D. Čudov. Litho)

1994 (10 Sept). Bicentenary of St. Arsenius Seminary, Sremski Karlovci. P 13½.
2940 **985** 50p. multicoloured .... 1·50 1·10

1994 (14 Sept). OBLIGATORY TAX. Anti-tuberculosis Week. P 13½.
2941 **986** 10p. black, greenish yellow and carmine-red 75 55

987 River Bojana

988 Painting by U. Kneževic

(Des Marina Kalezić-Krajinović. Litho)

1994 (20 Sept). Nature Protection. T **987** and similar horiz design. Multicoloured. P 13½.
2942 1d. Type **987** .... 4·50 3·00
2943 1d.50 Lake Biograd .... 5·00 3·25
Nos. 2942/3 were each issued in sheets of eight stamps and one label.

(Des D. Čudov. Litho Forum; Novi Sad)

1994 (5 Oct). 26th "Joy of Europe" Meeting. P 14.
2944 **988** 1d. multicoloured .... 3·25 2·20
No. 2944 was issued in sheets of eight stamps and one label.

989 *Revenge* (English galleon)

990 Aerospatiale ATR 42 Mail Plane, Mail Coach and Letter

(Des R. Bojanić. Litho)

1994 (27 Oct). Ships in Bottles. Booklet stamps. T **989** and similar vert designs. Multicoloured. P 13½.

2945 50p. Type **989** 1·50 1·10
a. Booklet pane. Nos. 2945/50 9·25
2946 50p. 17th-century yacht 1·50 1·10
2947 50p. *Santa Maria* (Columbus's flagship) 1·50 1·10
2948 50p. 15th-century nau 1·50 1·10
2949 50p. *Mayflower* (Pilgrim Fathers' ship) 1·50 1·10
2950 50p. 14th-century caravel 1·50 1·10
2945/2950 *Set of 6* 8·00 6·00

(Des D. Čudov. Litho)

1994 (31 Oct). Stamp Day. P 13½.
2951 **990** 50p. multicoloured 6·00 4·50

991 Tombstone

992 "Madonna and Child" (T. Cešljar)

(Des R. Bojanić. Litho)

1994 (25 Nov). Museum Exhibits. Illustrated Tombstones. T **991** and similar vert designs. Multicoloured. P 13½.

2952 50p. Type **991** 1·40 1·00
2953 50p. Double stone and railing 1·40 1·00
2954 50p. Two stones 1·40 1·00
2955 50p. Cemetery 1·40 1·00
2952/2955 *Set of 4* 5·00 3·50

(Des D. Čudov. Litho)

1994 (15 Dec). Paintings. T **992** and similar vert designs. Multicoloured. P 13½.

2956 60p. Type **992** 1·50 1·10
2957 60p. "Adoration of the Three Wise Men" (N. Neškovic) 1·50 1·10
2958 60p. "The Annunciation" (D. Bacevic) 1·50 1·10
2959 60p. "St. John baptizing Christ" (T. Kracun) 1·50 1·10
2956/2959 *Set of 4* 5·50 4·00

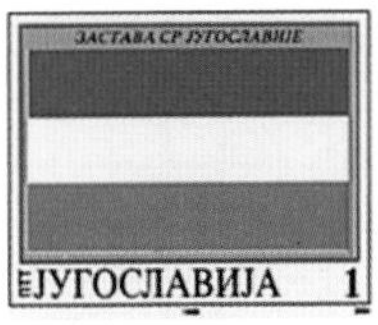
993 National Flag

994 Wilhelm Steinitz (1886–94)

1995 (26 Jan). T **993** and similar horiz design. Multicoloured. Litho. P 13½.

2960 1d. Type **993** 2·30 1·70
2961 1d. National arms 2·30 1·70

(Des R. Bojanić (2962/3, 2965, 2967), Marina Kalezić (others). Litho)

1995 (28 Feb). Chess (First series). T **994** and similar horiz designs showing chessmen or World Champions. Multicoloured. P 13½.

2962 60p. Type **994** 1·80 1·30
a. Sheetlet. Nos. 2962/9 plus label 15·00
2963 60p. Pieces 1·80 1·30
2964 60p. Emanuel Lasker (1894–1921) 1·80 1·30
2965 60p. Black knight 1·80 1·30
2966 60p. Pawns, king and knight 1·80 1·30
2967 60p. José Raúl Capablanca (1921–27) 1·80 1·30
2968 60p. Rook, bishop, queen and pawns 1·80 1·30
2969 60p. Aleksandr Alekhine (1927–35 and 1937–46) 1·80 1·30
2962/2969 *Set of 8* 13·00 9·25

Nos. 2962/9 were issued together in *se-tenant* sheetlets of eight stamps and one central label showing an emblematic design of the king.

See also Nos. 2988/95 and 3021/9.

995 Emblem

996 Fire Salamander (*Salamandra salamandra*)

(Des R. Bojanić. Litho)

1995 (4 Mar). 50th Anniv of Red Star Sports Club, Belgrade. P 13½.

2970 **995** 60p. scarlet-vermilion, ultramarine and gold 2·50 1·90

No. 2970 was issued in sheets of eight stamps and one label.

(Des Marina Kalezić. Litho)

1995 (23 Mar). Amphibians. T **996** and similar horiz designs. Multicoloured. P 13½.

2971 60p. Type **996** 2·00 1·50
a. Horiz strip. Nos. 2971/4 plus label 8·25
2972 60p. Alpine newt (*Triturus alpestris*) 2·00 1·50
2973 60p. Stream frog (*Rana graeca*) 2·00 1·50
2974 60p. Eastern spadefoot (*Pelobates syriacus balcanicus*) 2·00 1·50
2971/2974 *Set of 4* 7·25 5·50

Nos. 2971/4 were issued together in horizontal *se-tenant* strips of four stamps and one central label, the vertical row of labels within the sheet forming a composite design of a landscape.

997 Sportsman and Emblem

998 Eagle over Mountainside

(Des R. Bojanić. Litho)

1995 (20 Apr). 75th Anniv of Radnicki Sports Club, Belgrade. P 13½.

2975 **997** 60p. multicoloured 2·30 1·70

(Des R. Bojanić. Litho)

1995 (6 May). Europa. Peace and Freedom. T **998** and similar multicoloured design. P 13½.

2976 60p. Type **998** 4·50 2·75
2977 1d.90 Child on tricycle and elderly couple on park bench (horiz) 4·50 2·75

Nos. 2976/7 were each issued in sheets of eight stamps and one label.

999 Globes

1000 Dove with Black Bird in Beak

(Des A. Daskalović. Litho)

1995 (8 May). OBLIGATORY TAX. Red Cross Week. P 13½.

2978 **999** 10p. greenish yellow, indigo and vermilion 75 55

(Des D. Čudov. Litho)

1995 (9 May). 50th Anniv of End of Second World War. P 13½.

2979 **1000** 60p. multicoloured 2·30 1·70

1001 Station Concourse and Train

1002 Leaves and Flowers

(Des Marina Kalezić. Litho)

1995 (28 May). Opening of Vukov Monument Underground Railway Station, Belgrade. P 13½.

2980 **1001** 60p. multicoloured 3·00 2·20

(Des Marina Kalezić. Litho)

1995 (12 June). The Whitlow-grass (*Draba bertiscea*). T **1002** and similar horiz designs. Multicoloured. P 13½.

2981 60p. Type **1002** 2·30 1·70
a. Horiz strip. Nos. 2981/4 plus label 9·50
2982 60p. Clumps of leaves and flowers 2·30 1·70
2983 60p. Plant growing on mountainside 2·30 1·70
2984 60p. Plant and tree branch 2·30 1·70
2981/2984 *Set of 4* 8·25 6·00

Nos. 2981/4 were issued together in horizontal *se-tenant* strips of four stamps and one central label, the vertical row of labels within the sheet forming a composite design of a mountainside.

1003 Shore Lark (*Eremophila alpestris*), Rtanj

(Des Marina Kalezić. Litho)

1995 (10 July). Nature Protection. T **1003** and similar horiz design. Multicoloured. P 13½.

2985 60p. Type **1003** 3·00 2·20
2986 1d.90 Blasius's horseshoe bat (*Rhinolophus blasii*), Lazareva Reka Canyon 3·75 2·75

Nos. 2985/6 were each issued in sheets of eight stamps and one label showing a mountainous landscape.

1004 "Slovakian Village Gathering" (Zuzka Medvedóvá)

1005 Wilhelm Röntgen (discoverer of X-rays)

(Des D. Čudov. Litho Forum, Novi Sad)

1995 (3 Aug). P 14.

2987 **1004** 60p. multicoloured 1·80 1·30

(Des Marina Kalezić (2994/5), R. Bojanić (others). Litho)

1995 (1 Sept). Chess (Second series). Horiz designs as T **994** showing chessmen or World Champions. Multicoloured. P 13½.

2988 60p. Max Euwe (1935–37) 1·20 90
a. Sheetlet. Nos. 2988/95 plus label 9·75
2989 60p. Pawn, chessboard and pieces 1·20 90
2990 60p. Mikhail Botvinnik (1948–57, 1958–60 and 1961–63) 1·20 90
2991 60p. Queen, chessboard and pieces 1·20 90
2992 60p. Board, white bishop and knight 1·20 90
2993 60p. Vasily Smyslov (1957–58) 1·20 90
2994 60p. Rook, knight, queen and board 1·20 90
2995 60p. Mikhail Tal (1960–61) 1·20 90
2988/2995 *Set of 8* 8·75 6·50

Nos. 2988/95 were issued together in *se-tenant* sheetlets of eight stamps and one central label showing chessmen and board.

(Des A. Daskalović. Litho)

1995 (9 Sept). OBLIGATORY TAX. Anti-tuberculosis Week. P 13½.

2996 **1005** 10p. red and deep dull blue 75 55

1006 Player on Globe

1007 Church

(Des R. Bojanić. Litho)

1995 (10 Sept). Centenary of Volleyball. P 13½.

2997 **1006** 90p. multicoloured 1·80 1·30

(Des Marina Kalezić. Litho)

1995 (20 Sept). 800th Anniv of St. Luke's Church, Kotor. P 13½.

2998 **1007** 80p. multicoloured 1·80 1·30

1008 Coronation of King Petar II

1009 Club Emblem

(Des R. Bojanić. Litho)

1995 (3 Oct). Centenary of Motion Pictures. T **1008** and similar horiz design. Each reddish brown and salmon. P 13½.

2999 1d.10 Type **1008** 2·00 1·50
3000 2d.20 Auguste and Louis Lumière (cine camera pioneers) 3·00 1·70

(Des R. Bojanić. Litho)

1995 (4 Oct). 50th Anniv of Partizan Army Sports Club. P 13½.

3001 **1009** 80p. multicoloured 1·80 1·30

No. 3001 was issued in sheets of eight stamps and one label.

1010 "Flower Seller" (Miloš Tenkovic)

1011 Golden Gate Bridge, San Francisco

(Des D. Čudov. Litho)

1995 (5 Oct). 27th "Joy of Europe" Meeting. T **1010** and similar vert design. Multicoloured. P 13½.

3002 1d.10 Type **1010** 2·00 1·50
3003 2d.20 "Child at Table" (Pierre Bonnard) 3·00 1·70

Nos. 3002/3 were each issued in sheets of eight stamps and one label.

(Des D. Čudov. Litho)

1995 (24 Oct). 50th Anniv of United Nations Organization. P 13½.

3004 **1011** 1d.10 multicoloured 1·80 1·30

San Francisco was where the Charter was signed.

1012 Post Office, Seal and Letter

1013 Montenegro 1898 10n. and Serbia 1866 40p. Stamps

(Des D. Čudov. Litho)

1995 (31 Oct). Stamp Day. P 13½.
3005 **1012** 1d.10 multicoloured 1·80 1·30

(Des D. Čudov. Litho Forum, Novi Sad)

1995 (13 Dec). Jufiz VIII National Stamp Exhibition, Budva. Sheet 71×95 mm. P 14.
MS3006 **1013** 2d.50, multicoloured 3·25 3·25

1014 Saric No. 1

1015 "Birth of Christ" (D. Milojevic)

(Des R. Bojanić. Litho)

1995 (26 Dec). Museum Exhibits. Aircraft. T **1014** and similar horiz designs. Multicoloured. P 13½.

3007	1d.10 Type **1014**	75	55
3008	1d.10 Douglas DC-3	75	55
3009	2d.20 Fizir FN biplane	1·50	1·10
3010	2d.20 Sud Aviation Caravelle jetliner	1·50	1·10
3007/3010	*Set of 4*	4·00	3·00

(Des D. Čudov. Litho)

1995 (26 Dec). Paintings. T **1015** and similar multicoloured designs. P 13½.

3011	1d.10 Type **1015**	75	55
3012	1d.10 "Flight into Egypt" (Z. Halupova) (horiz)	75	55
3013	2d.20 "Sunday" (M. Rašic)	1·50	1·10
3014	2d.20 "Traditional Christmas Festival" (J. Brašic) (horiz)	1·50	1·10
3011/3014	*Set of 4*	4·00	3·00

1016 Battle Scene

1017 Painting

(Des D. Čudov. Litho)

1996 (6 Jan). 70th Anniv of Battle of Mojkovac. P 13½.
3015 **1016** 1d.10 multicoloured 75 55

(Des D. Čudov. Litho)

1996 (22 Jan). Birth Centenary of Sava Šumanovic (painter). P 13½.
3016 **1017** 1d.10 multicoloured 75 55

1018 *Pyrgomorphela serbica*

1019 Discus Throwers

(Des Marina Kalezić. Litho)

1996 (15 Feb). Protected Insects. T **1018** and similar horiz designs. Multicoloured. P 13½.

3017	1d.10 Type **1018**	75	55
	a. Horiz strip. Nos. 3017/20 plus label	4·75	
3018	1d.10 Red wood ant (*Formica rufa*)	75	55
3019	2d.20 Searcher (*Calosoma sycophanta*)	1·50	1·10
3020	2d.20 Owl-fly (*Ascalaphus macaronius*)	1·50	1·10
3017/3020	*Set of 4*	4·00	3·00

Nos. 3017/20 were issued together in horizontal *se-tenant* strips of four stamps and one central label.

(Des R. Bojanić (3021, 3026, 3028/9), Marina Kalezić (others). Litho)

1996 (15 Mar). Chess (Third series). Horiz designs as T **994** showing chessmen and timepieces or World Champions. Multicoloured. P 13½.

3021	1d.50 Tigran Vartanovich Petrosyan (1963–69)	75	55
	a. Sheetlet of 9. Nos. 3021/9	7·00	
3022	1d.50 Queen, knight and portable sundial	75	55
3023	1d.50 Boris Vasilevich Spassky (1969–72)	75	55
3024	1d.50 Competition clock, chessboard and pieces	75	55
3025	1d.50 Garry Kimovich Kasparov (1985–93)	75	55
3026	1d.50 Chessboard, pieces and hourglass	75	55
3027	1d.50 Robert Fischer (1972–75)	75	55
3028	1d.50 Chess pieces, clocks and chessboard	75	55
3029	1d.50 Anatoly Yevgenievich Karpov (1975–85 and 1993–)	75	55
3021/3029	*Set of 9*	6·00	4·50

Nos. 3021/9 were issued together in *se-tenant* sheetlets of nine stamps.

(Des R. Bojanić. Litho)

1996 (30 Mar). Centenary of Modern Olympic Games. T **1019** and similar horiz design. Multicoloured. P 13½.

3030	1d.50 Type **1019**	1·10	80
3031	2d.50 Ancient Greek and modern athletes	2·00	1·50

1020 Athletics

1021 Postman, Railway Mail Van and Arms of Royal Serbian Post

(Des R. Bojanić. Litho)

1996 (12 Apr). Olympic Games, Atlanta. T **1020** and similar horiz designs. Multicoloured. P 13½.

3032	1d.50 Type **1020**	2·30	1·70
3033	1d.50 Basketball	2·30	1·70
3034	1d.50 Handball	2·30	1·70
3035	1d.50 Shooting	2·30	1·70
3036	1d.50 Volleyball	2·30	1·70
3037	1d.50 Water polo	2·30	1·70
3032/3037	*Set of 6*	12·50	9·25
MS3038	107×60 mm. 5d. Tara (house from *Gone with the Wind*)	3·25	3·25

Nos. 3032/7 were each issued in sheets of eight stamps and one label.

(Des D. Čudov. Litho)

1996 (30 Apr). Stamp Day. P 13½.
3039 **1021** 1d.50 multicoloured 90 65

1022 Isidora Sekulic

1023 Dr. Vladan Djordjevic (founder)

(Des Marina Kalezić. Litho)

1996 (7 May). Europa. Famous Women Writers. T **1022** and similar vert design. Multicoloured. P 13½.

3040	2d.50 Type **1022**	3·00	2·20
3041	5d. Desanka Maksimović	4·00	3·00

Nos. 3040/1 were each issued in sheets of eight stamps and one label.

(Des Marina Kalezić. Litho)

1996 (8 May). 120th Anniv of Serbian Red Cross. P 13½.
3042 **1023** 1d.50 multicoloured 90 65

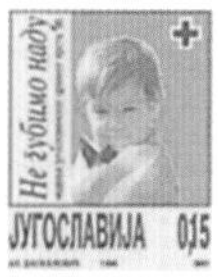

1024 Child and Cross

1025 Columns, Caryatid and Diagrams of Proportion

(Des A. Daskalović. Litho)

1996 (8 May). OBLIGATORY TAX. Red Cross Week. P 12½.
3043 **1024** 15p. blue, ochre and scarlet 60 45

(Des R. Bojanić. Litho)

1996 (1 June). 150th Anniv of Architecture Education in Serbia. P 13½.
3044 **1025** 1d.50 pale blue, deep dull blue and greenish blue 90 65

1026 White Spoonbill (*Platalea leucorodia*)

1027 Prince Petar I Petrović (Battle of Martinici)

(Des Marina Kalezić. Litho)

1996 (28 June). Nature Protection. T **1026** and similar horiz design. Multicoloured. P 13½.

3045	2d.50 Type **1026**	1·50	1·10
3046	5d. Glossy ibis (*Plegadis falcinellus*)	3·00	2·20

Nos. 3045/6 were each issued in sheets of eight stamps and one label.

(Des D. Čudov. Litho)

1996 (22 July). Battle Bicentenaries. T **1027** and similar multicoloured design. P 13½.

3047	1d.50 Type **1027**	75	55
3048	2d.50 "Prince's Guard" (Théodore Valerio) (Battle of Kruse) (vert)	1·50	1·10

1028 Waiting for the Off

1029 Palm Cockatoo (*Probosciger aterrimus*)

(Des R. Bojanić. Litho)

1996 (31 Aug). Ljubicevo Race Meeting. T **1028** and similar horiz design. Multicoloured. P 13½.

3049	1d.50 Type **1028**	75	55
3050	2d.50 Horses racing	1·50	1·10

(Des Marina Kalezić. Litho)

1996 (5 Sept). 60th Anniv of Belgrade Zoo. T **1029** and similar horiz designs. Multicoloured. P 13½.

3051	1d.50 Type **1029**	75	55
	a. Horiz strip. Nos. 3051/4 plus label	4·75	
3052	1d.50 Common zebra (*Equus burchelli*)	75	55
3053	2d.50 Maroon-breasted crowned pigeon (*Goura scheepmakeri*)	1·50	1·10
3054	2d.50 Tiger (*Pantheris tigris*)	1·50	1·10
3051/3054	*Set of 4*	4·00	3·00

Nos. 3051/4 were issued together in horizontal *se-tenant* strips of four stamps and one central label.

1030 Landscape on Leaf

1031 Fantasy Scene

(Des A. Daskalović. Litho)

1996 (Sept). OBLIGATORY TAX. Anti-tuberculosis Week. P 12½.
3055 **1030** 20p. multicoloured 60 45

(Des D. Čudov. Litho)

1996 (2 Oct). 28th "Joy of Europe" Meeting. T **1031** and similar horiz design. Multicoloured. P 13½.

3056	1d.50 Type **1031**	75	55
3057	2d.50 Toucan	1·50	1·10

Nos. 3056/7 were each issued in sheets of eight stamps and one label.

1032 Basketball (silver)

1033 Coins, Banknotes and Credit Card

(Des R. Bojanić. Litho)

1996 (17 Oct). Olympic Games Medal Winners. T **1032** and similar horiz designs. Multicoloured. P 13½.

3058	2d.50 Type **1032**	1·80	1·30
3059	2d.50 Small-bore rifle shooting (gold)	1·80	1·30
3060	2d.50 Air-rifle shooting (bronze)	1·80	1·30
3061	2d.50 Volleyball (bronze)	1·80	1·30
3058/3061	*Set of 4*	6·50	4·75

Nos. 3058/61 were each issued in sheets of eight stamps and one label.

(Des R. Bojanić. Litho)

1996 (31 Oct). 75th Anniv of Post Office Savings Bank. P 13½.
3062 **1033** 1d.50 multicoloured 1·10 80

1034 Footballer

1035 Mother and Child (statuette)

(Des R. Bojanić. Litho)

1996 (8 Nov). Centenary of Football in Serbia. P 13½.
3063 **1034** 1d.50 multicoloured 1·10 80

(Des D. Čudov. Litho)

1996 (25 Nov). Museum Exhibits. Archaeological Finds. T **1035** and similar vert designs. Multicoloured. P 13½.

3064	1d.50 Type **1035**	1·10	80
3065	1d.50 Tombstone depicting Genius, god of autumn (Komani, nr. Pljevlja)	1·10	80

3066 2d.50 Marble head of woman (from Podgorica) 1·50 1·10
3067 2d.50 Statuette of red-headed goddess 1·50 1·10
3064/3067 *Set of* 4 4·75 3·50

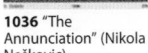

1036 "The Annunciation" (Nikola Neškovic)

1037 Putnik in Dress Uniform

(Des D. Čudov. Litho)

1996 (10 Dec). Icons from Serbian Orthodox Church Museum, Belgrade. T **1036** and similar vert designs. Multicoloured. P 13½.
3068 1d.50 Type **1036** 1·10 80
3069 1d.50 "Madonna and Child" 1·10 80
3070 2d.50 "Nativity" 1·50 1·10
3071 2d.50 "Entry of Christ into Jerusalem" (Stanoje Popovic) 1·50 1·10
3068/3071 *Set of* 4 4·75 3·50

(Des Marina Kalezić. Litho)

1997 (24 Jan). 150th Birth Anniv of Radomir Putnik (army Commander in Chief). P 13½.
3072 **1037** 1d.50 multicoloured 90 65

1038 Film Frames

1039 Great Spotted Woodpecker (*Dendrocopos major*)

(Des R. Bojanić. Litho)

1997 (31 Jan). 25th International Film Festival, Belgrade. P 13½.
3073 **1038** 1d.50 multicoloured 90 65
No. 3073 was issued in sheets of eight stamps and one label.

(Des Marina Kalezić. Litho)

1997 (21 Feb). Woodland Birds. T **1039** and similar vert designs. Multicoloured. P 13½.
3074 1d.50 Type **1039** 90 65
a. Horiz strip. Nos. 3074/77 plus label 5·00
3075 1d.50 Crested tit (*Parus cristatus*) 90 65
3076 2d.50 Nutcracker (*Nucifraga caryocatactes*) 1·40 1·00
3077 2d.50 European robin (*Erithacus rubecula*) 1·40 1·00
3074/3077 *Set of* 4 4·25 3·00
Nos. 3074/7 were issued together in horizontal *se-tenant* strips of four stamps and one central label.

1040 Christ and King Dragutin holding Model of Church (fresco)

1041 St. Petar

(Des Marina Kalezić. Litho)

1997 (17 Mar). 700th Anniv of St. Ahilije's Church, Arilje. P 13½.
3078 **1040** 1d.50 multicoloured 1·50 1·10

(Des R. Bojanić. Litho)

1997 (3 Apr). 250th Birth Anniv of Prince-Bishop Petar I of Montenegro (St. Petar of Cetinje). P 13½.
3079 **1041** 1d.50 multicoloured 1·50 1·10

1042 Belgrade and Emblem

1043 Ambulance, 1876, and Association Building

(Des R. Bojanić. Litho)

1997 (19 Apr). Tenth Belgrade Marathon. P 13½.
3080 **1042** 2d.50 multicoloured 2·00 1·50
No. 3080 was issued in sheets of eight stamps and one label.

(Des Marina Kalezić. Litho)

1997 (22 Apr). 125th Anniv of Serbian Medical Association. P 13½.
3081 **1043** 2d.50 multicoloured 2·00 1·50

1044 Loading Air Mail at Night

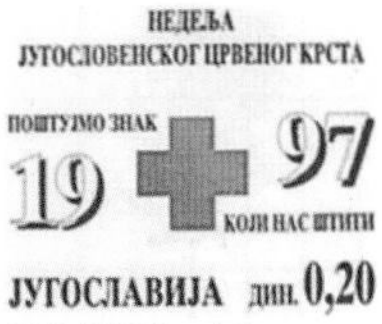

1045 "1997" and Cross

(Des R. Bojanić. Litho)

1997 (3 May). Stamp Day. P 13½.
3082 **1044** 2d.50 multicoloured 2·00 1·50

1997 (8 May). OBLIGATORY TAX. Red Cross Week. Litho. P 13½.
3083 **1045** 20p. scarlet and chalky blue 60 45

1046 Belgrade

1047 Baš Celik shackled before King

(Des R. Bojanić. Litho)

1997 (8 May). Tennis Championships in Yugoslavia. T **1046** and similar vert designs showing player and town arms. Multicoloured. P 13½.
3084 2d.50 Type **1046** 2·00 1·50
3085 2d.50 Budva 2·00 1·50
3086 2d.50 Novi Sad 2·00 1·50
3084/3086 *Set of* 3 5·50 4·00
Nos. 3084/6 were each issued in sheets of eight stamps and one label.

(Des R. Bojanić. Litho Courvoisier)

1997 (30 May). Europa. Myths and Legends. T **1047** and similar horiz design. Multicoloured. P 11½.
3087 2d.50 Type **1047** 2·00 1·50
3088 6d. Prince on horseback fighting chained Baš Celik 3·00 2·30
Nos. 3087/8 were each issued in sheetlets of eight stamps and one central label.

1048 *Cerambyx cerdo* (longhorn beetle)

1049 Prince Bishop Peter Njegoš, Village and Printing Press

(Des Marina Kalezić. Litho)

1997 (5 June). Nature Protection. T **1048** and similar horiz design. Multicoloured. P 11½.
3089 2d.50 Type **1048** 1·60 1·20
3090 6d. Pedunculate oak (*Quercus robur*) 3·00 2·30

(Des Marina Kalezić. Litho)

1997 (7 June). 150th Anniv of Publication of *Gorski Vijenc*. P 13½.
3091 **1049** 2d.50 multicoloured 1·60 1·20

1050 Stanislav Binicki

1051 *Pelargonium grandiflorum*

(Des R. Bojanić. Litho)

1997 (25 June). 125th Birth Anniv of Stanislav Binicki (composer). P 13½.
3092 **1050** 2d.50 multicoloured 1·60 1·20

(Des Marina Kalezić. Litho)

1997 (10 Sept). Flowers. T **1051** and similar vert designs. Multicoloured. P 13½.
3093 1d.50 Type **1051** 80 60
a. Horiz strip of 4 plus label 5·00
3094 1d.50 Hydrangea x macrophy 80 60
3095 2d.50 African violet (Saintpaulia ionantha) 1·60 1·20
3096 2d.50 *Oncidium varicosum* 1·60 1·20
3093/3096 *Set of* 4 4·25 3·25

Nos. 3093/6 were issued together in horizontal *se-tenant* strips of four stamps and one central label, the vertical row of labels forming a composite design of flowers.

1052 Statue by Dragomir Arambašic before Cvijeta Zuzoric Art Gallery (venue)

1053 Dr. Milutin Rankovic

(Des R. Bojanić. Litho Forum, Novi Sad)

1997 (11 Sept). Jufiz IX National Stamp Exhibition, Belgrade. Sheet 96×75 mm. P 14.
MS3097 **1052** 5d. multicoloured 4·00 4·00

(Des R. Bojanić. Litho Forum, Novi Sad)

1997 (14 Sept). OBLIGATORY TAX. Anti-tuberculosis Week. P 14.
3098 **1053** 20p. red-brown, yellow-ochre and bright scarlet 60 45

1054 Society Emblem

1055 Collage (Milan Ugrišic)

(Des Marina Kalezić. Litho Forum, Novi Sad)

1997 (24 Sept). Centenary of Serbian Chemical Association. P 14.
3099 **1054** 2d.50 multicoloured 1·60 1·20

(Des D. Čudov. Litho Forum, Novi Sad)

1997 (2 Oct). No value expressed. As No. 2857 but 18×20 mm. P 14.
3100 **956** A vermilion 1·60 25
No. 3100 exists with "1997" and "1999" imprint dates.

(Des R. Bojanić. Litho Forum, Novi Sad)

1997 (2 Oct). 29th "Joy of Europe" Meeting. T **1055** and similar vert design. Multicoloured. P 14.
3101 2d.50 Type **1055** 1·60 1·20
3102 5d. Collage (Stanislava Antic) 3·00 2·30

1056 "May Assembly, Sremski Karlovci, 1848" (Pavle Simic)

(Des Marina Kalezić. Litho Forum, Novi Sad)

1997 (10 Oct). 150th Anniv of Matica Srpska Art Gallery. P 14.
3103 **1056** 2d.50 multicoloured 1·60 1·20

1057 Helmet from Srem (4th century)

1058 "Christ Pantocrator"

(Des R. Bojanić. Litho Forum, Novi Sad)

1997 (12 Nov). Museum Exhibits. Archaeological Finds in Vojvodina Museum. T **1057** and similar vert designs. Multicoloured. P 14.
3104 1d.50 Type **1057** 80 60
3105 1d.50 Two-headed terracotta figure from Srem 80 60
3106 2d.50 Teracotta figure from Backa 1·60 1·20
3107 2d.50 "Madonna and Child" (relief from Srem, 12th century) 1·60 1·20
3104/3107 *Set of* 4 4·25 3·25

(Des R. Bojanić. Photo Courvoisier)

1997 (2 Dec). Icons from Chelandari Serbian Monastery, Mount Athos. T **1058** and similar vert designs. Multicoloured. Granite paper. P 11½.
3108 1d.50 Type **1058** 80 60
3109 1d.50 "Madonna and Child" 80 60
3110 2d.50 "Madonna and Child" (different) 1·60 1·20
3111 2d.50 "Three-handed Madonna with Child" 1·60 1·20
3108/3111 *Set of* 4 4·25 3·25

1059 Savina

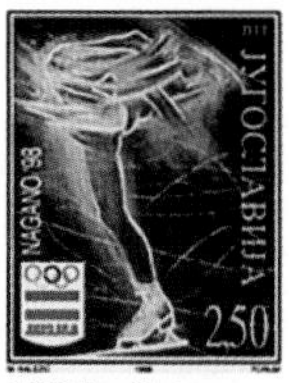

1060 Ice Skater

(Des Marina Kalezić. Litho)

1998 (20 Jan). Monasteries in Montenegro. T **1059** and similar vert design. Multicoloured. P 13½.

3112 1d.50 Type **1059** ... 95 70
3113 2d.50 Donji Brceli ... 1·60 1·20

(Des Marina Kalezić. Litho Forum, Novi Sad)

1998 (6 Feb). Winter Olympic Games, Nagano, Japan. T **1060** and similar vert designs. Multicoloured. P 14.

3114 2d.50 Type **1060** ... 1·60 1·20
3115 6d. Skier ... 3·50 2·50

1061 Mare and Foal

(Des R. Bojanić. Photo Courvoisier)

1998 (26 Feb). Horses. T **1061** and similar horiz designs. Multicoloured. P 12.

3116 1d.50 Type **1061** ... 1·60 1·20
a. Horiz strip. Nos. 3116/19 plus label... 8·00
3117 1d.50 Stallion ... 1·60 1·20
3118 2d.50 Head of grey ... 2·30 1·70
3119 2d.50 Racehorse ... 2·30 1·70
3116/3119 *Set of 4* ... 7·00 5·25

Nos. 3116/19 were issued together in horizontal *se-tenant* strips of four stamps and one central label.

1062 Women and Flowers

1063 Glider and Emblems

(Des Marina Kalezić. Litho Forum, Novi Sad)

1998 (7 Mar). International Women's Day. P 14.

3120 **1062** 2d.50 multicoloured ... 1·60 1·20

(Des R. Bojanić. Litho)

1998 (24 Apr). 50th Anniv of Yugoslav Aeronautics Association. P 13½.

3121 **1063** 2d.50 multicoloured ... 1·60 1·20

1064 "The Adornment of the Bride" (Paja Jovanović)

1065 Metropolitan Mihailo Jovanović

(Des R. Bojanić. Photo Courvoisier)

1998 (4 May). Europa. National Festivals. T **1064** and similar horiz design. Multicoloured. P 11½.

3122 6d. Type **1064** ... 4·75 3·50
3123 9d. "The Prince-Bishop celebrates Victory" (Pero Pocek) ... 4·75 3·50

Nos. 3122/3 were each issued in sheets of eight stamps and one label.

(Des R. Bojanić. Litho Forum, Novi Sad)

1998 (8 May). OBLIGATORY TAX. Red Cross Week. P 14.

3124 **1065** 20p. multicoloured ... 60 45

1066 Player evading Tackle

(Des R. Bojanić. Photo)

1998 (15 May). World Cup Football Championship, France. T **1066** and similar vert design. Multicoloured. P 13½.

3125 6d. Type **1066** ... 2·75 2·10
3126 9d. Goalkeeper and players ... 4·25 3·25

Nos. 3125/6 were each issued in sheets of eight stamps and one label.

1067 Map of Europe

(Des R. Bojanić. Litho Forum, Novi Sad)

1998 (19 May). 50th Anniv of Danube Commission. Sheet 88×65 mm. P 14×13½.

MS3127 **1067** 9d. multicoloured ... 6·25 6·00

1068 *Hieracium blecicii*

1069 Djura Jakšić (poet and painter)

(Des Marina Kalezić. Litho Forum, Novi Sad)

1998 (17 June). Nature Protection. T **1068** and similar multicoloured design. P 14.

3128 6d. Type **1068** ... 2·00 1·50
3129 9d. Oceanic sunfish (*Mola mola*) ... 2·75 2·00

(Des Marina Kalezić. Photo Courvoisier)

1998 (30 June). Anniversaries. T **1069** and similar vert designs. Each reddish brown, black and yellow-ochre. Granite paper. P 11½×12.

3130 1d.50 Type **1069** (120th death anniv) ... 60 45
a. Sheetlet. Nos. 3130/7 plus label ... 5·00
3131 1d.50 Nadežda Petrović (painter, 125th birth anniv) ... 60 45
3132 1d.50 Radoje Domanović (satirist, 125th birth anniv) ... 60 45
3133 1d.50 Vasilije Mokranjac (composer, 75th birth anniv) ... 60 45
3134 1d.50 Sreten Stojanović (sculptor, birth centenary) ... 60 45
3135 1d.50 Milan Konjović (painter, birth centenary) ... 60 45
3136 1d.50 Desanka Maksimović (writer, birth centenary) ... 60 45
3137 1d.50 Ivan Tabaković (painter, birth centenary) ... 60 45
3130/3137 *Set of 8* ... 4·25 3·25

Nos. 3030/7 were issued together in *se-tenant* sheetlets of eight stamps and one label.

1070 Trophy

1071 Pine Marten (*Martes martes*)

1998 (21 Aug). Victory of Yugoslavia in World Basketball Championship, Athens. Sheet 80×98 mm. Litho. P 13½.

MS3138 **1070** 10d. multicoloured ... 9·25 9·25

(Des Marina Kalezić. Litho)

1998 (2 Sept). 50th Anniv of Serbian Nature Protection Institute. T **1071** and similar vert designs. P 13½.

3139 2d. Type **1071** ... 1·20 95
a. Horiz strip. Nos. 3139/42 plus label... 7·25
3140 2d. Demoiselle crane (*Anthropoides virgo*) ... 1·20 95
3141 5d. Lynx (*Lynx lynx*) ... 2·30 1·70
3142 5d. Red crossbill (*Loxia curvirostra*) ... 2·30 1·70
3139/3142 *Set of 4* ... 6·25 4·75

Nos. 3139/42 were issued together in horizontal *se-tenant* strips of four stamps and one central label, the vertical row of labels forming a composite design.

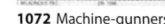

1072 Machine-gunners

1073 "50 Years" on Stamp

(Des I. Miladinović. Eng D. Matić (3143), A. Dimitrijević (3144). Recess)

1998 (15 Sept). 80th Anniv of Thessalonica Front. T **1072** and similar horiz design. P 13½.

3143 5d. greenish slate and red-brown ... 2·75 2·10
3144 5d. dull chocolate and olive-sepia ... 2·75 2·10

Design:—No. 3144, Field gun.

(Des R. Bojanić. Recess)

1998 (28 Sept). Stamp Day. 50th Anniv of Serbian Philatelic Society. P 13½.

3145 **1073** 6d. steel blue ... 2·20 1·60

1074 "Sea Life" (Bojan Dakić)

1075 Steam Locomotive, 1847

(Des M. Kalezić. Litho Forum, Novi Sad)

1998 (2 Oct). 30th "Joy of Europe" Meeting. T **1074** and similar horiz design. Multicoloured. P 13½.

3146 6d. Type **1074** ... 2·30 1·70
3147 9d. "Sea Life" (collage by Ana Rockov) ... 3·00 2·30

(Des R. Bojanić. Litho Forum, Novi Sad)

1998 (3 Nov). Locomotives. Booklet stamps. T **1075** and similar horiz designs. Multicoloured. P 14.

3148 2d.50 Type **1075** ... 2·30 1·70
a. Booklet pane. Nos. 3148/53 ... 14·50
3149 2d.50 Steam locomotive, 1900 ... 2·30 1·70
3150 2d.50 Steam locomotive,1920 ... 2·30 1·70
3151 2d.50 Steam locomotive, 1930 ... 2·30 1·70
3152 2d.50 Diesel locomotive "Kennedy" ... 2·30 1·70
3153 2d.50 High speed train, 1990 ... 2·30 1·70
3148/3152 *Set of 6* ...

1076 *Pjerino* (brig), 1883

(Des R. Bojanić. Photo Courvoisier)

1998 (21 Nov). Museum Exhibits. Ship Paintings by Vasilije Ivankovic. T **1076** and similar horiz designs. Multicoloured. Granite paper. P 12.

3154 2d. Type **1076** ... 80 60
3155 2d. *Vera Cruz* (steamer), 1873 ... 80 60
3156 5d. *Vizin-Florio* (full-rigged ship) ... 2·30 1·70
3157 5d. *Draghetto* (barque), 1865 ... 2·30 1·70
3154/3157 *Set of 4* ... 5·50 4·25

1077 Hilandar Monastery

(Des R. Bojanić. Litho Forum, Novi Sad)

1998 (9 Dec). 800th Anniv of Hilandar Monastery. Paintings by Milutin Dedic. T **1077** and similar horiz designs. Multicoloured. P 14.

3158 2d. Type **1077** ... 80 60
3159 2d. Monastery façade ... 80 60
3160 5d. Hills behind Monastery buildings ... 2·30 1·70
3161 5d. Aerial view of Monastery ... 2·30 1·70
3158/3161 *Set of 4* ... 5·50 4·25

1078 Flags around Envelope on Map

1079 Volleyball

(Des R. Bojanić. Litho Forum, Novi Sad)

1998 (17 Dec). South-East European Postal Ministers Congress. P 14.

3162 **1078** 5d. multicoloured ... 4·75 3·50

(Des Marina Kalezić. Litho)

1998 (19 Dec). Yugoslavia, Silver Medal Winners in World Volleyball Championship, Japan. Sheet 70×78 mm. P 13½.

MS3163 **1079** 10d. multicoloured ... 60·00 60·00

1080 Postal Messenger arriving in Belgrade

1081 Visoki Decani Monastery

(Des R. Bojanić. Eng B. Dimitrijević (3164), D. Matić (3165). Recess)

1998 (21 Dec). 75th Anniv of Post and Telecommunications Museum. T **1080** and similar vert design. P 13½.
3164 5d. olive-brown and slate-green ... 1·60 1·20
3165 5d. scarlet-vermilion and lake-brown ... 1·60 1·20

(Des R. Bojanić. Litho Forum, Novi Sad)

1999 (14 Jan). Serbian Monasteries. Paintings by Milutin Dedic. T **1081** and similar vert design. Multicoloured. P 14.
3166 2d. Type **1081** ... 95 70
3167 5d. Gracanica Monastery ... 2·50 1·90

1082 Woolly Pig

1083 Scouts making Campfire and Emblem

(Des Marina Kalezić. Litho)

1999 (5 Feb). Animals. T **1082** and similar horiz designs. Multicoloured. P 13½.
3168 2d. Type **1082** ... 80 60
a. Horiz strip. Nos. 3168/71 plus label... 5·75
3169 2d. Cattle ... 80 60
3170 6d. Balkan goat ... 2·00 1·50
3171 6d. Hungarian sheep ... 2·00 1·50
3168/3171 *Set of 4* ... 5·00 3·75
Nos. 3168/71 were issued together in horizontal *se-tenant* strips of four stamps and one central label within the sheet.

(Des Marina Kalezić. Litho)

1999 (24 Feb). Scouts. P 13½.
3172 **1083** 6d. multicoloured ... 3·00 2·30

1084 Emblem, Goddess Justitia and Globe

1085 Target

(Des Marina Kalezić. Photo)

1999 (19 Mar). 70th Anniv of Bar Association. P 13½.
3173 **1084** 6d. chestnut and buff ... 2·20 1·60

(Des R. Bojanić. Litho)

1999 (27 Mar–7 Apr). No value expressed. P 12½.
3174 A black ... 4·75 3·50
3175 A black and bright scarlet (7.4.99) ... 4·75 3·50
Design:—No. 3175, Target with heart at centre.

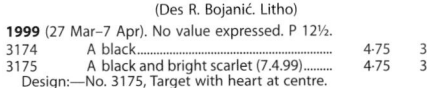

1086 Emblem and Player

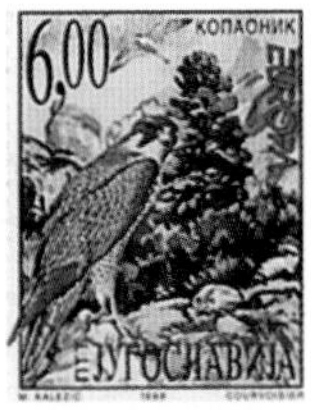

1087 Kopaonik National Park

(Des Marina Kalezić. Litho)

1999 (9 Apr). World Table Tennis Championships, Belgrade. T **1086** and similar horiz design. Multicoloured. P 13½.
3176 6d. Type **1086** ... 3·00 2·30
3177 6d. Player facing left ... 3·00 2·30

(Des Marina Kalezić. Photo Courvoisier)

1999 (5 May). Europa. Parks and Gardens. T **1087** and similar vert design. Multicoloured. Granite paper. P 12.
3178 6d. Type **1087** ... 4·75 3·50
3179 15d. Lovcen National Park ... 7·75 5·75

1088 Red Cross Volunteers

1089 Emblem, Cobweb and Spade

(Des R. Bojanić. Litho Forum, Novi Sad)

1999 (8 May). OBLIGATORY TAX. Red Cross Week. P 14.
3180 **1088** 1d. multicoloured ... 60 45

(Des R. Bojanić. Photo Courvoisier)

1999 (13 May). Nature Protection. T **1089** and similar vert design. Multicoloured. Granite paper. P 12.
3181 6d. Type **1089** ... 4·00 3·00
3182 15d. Thumb squeezing water droplet from Earth ... 4·25 3·25
Nos. 3181/2 were each issued in sheets of eight stamps and one label.

1090 Destroying Angel (*Amanita virosa*)

1091 Stjepan Mitrov Ljubiša (author)

(Des R. Bojanić. Photo Courvoisier)

1999 (18 June). Fungi. T **1090** and similar vert designs. Multicoloured. Granite paper. P 12.
3183 6d. Type **1090** ... 2·30 1·70
a. Horiz strip. Nos. 3183/6 plus label ... 9·50
3184 6d. False blusher (*Amanita pantherina*) .. 2·30 1·70
3185 6d. Clustered woodlover (*Hypholoma fasciculare*) ... 2·30 1·70
3186 6d. *Ramaria pallida* ... 2·30 1·70
3183/3186 *Set of 4* ... 8·25 6·00
Nos. 3183/6 were issued together in horizontal *se-tenant* strips of four stamps and one central label.

(Des Marina Kalezić. Litho)

1999 (30 June). Personalities. T **1091** and similar vert designs. Each red-brown, pale yellow and black. P 13½.
3187 2d. Type **1091** ... 60 45
a. Sheetlet of 8. Nos. 3187/94 plus label ... 5·00
3188 2d. Marko Miljanov (author) ... 60 45
3189 2d. Pero Pocek (painter) ... 60 45
3190 2d. Risto Stijovic (sculptor) ... 60 45
3191 2d. Milo Milunovic (painter) ... 60 45
3192 2d. Petar Lubarda (painter) ... 60 45
3193 2d. Vuko Radovic (painter) ... 60 45
3194 2d. Mihailo Lalic (author) ... 60 45
3187/3194 *Set of 8* ... 4·25 3·25
Nos. 3187/94 were issued together in *se-tenant* sheetlets of eight stamps and one central label.

1092 Thistle

1093 World Map and Emblem

(Des Marina Kalezić. Litho Forum, Novi Sad)

1999 (14 Sept). OBLIGATORY TAX. Anti-tuberculosis Week. P 14.
3195 **1092** 1d. multicoloured ... 1·10 80

(Des R. Bojanić. Litho)

1999 (15 Sept). 125th Anniv of Universal Postal Union. T **1093** and similar horiz design. Multicoloured. P 13½.
3196 6d. Type **1093** ... 1·60 1·20
3197 12d. Envelopes encircling globe ... 3·00 2·30

1094 Lion (Luka Minic)

1095 Frédéric Chopin and Music Score

(Des Marina Kalezić. Litho Forum, Novi Sad)

1999 (1 Oct). 31st "Joy in Europe" Meeting. Winning Designs in Children's Painting Competition. T **1094** and similar multicoloured design. P 14.
3198 6d. Type **1094** ... 1·60 1·20
3199 15d. Girl with doll (Andreas Kaparis) (vert) ... 4·00 3·00

(Des Marina Kalezić. Litho)

1999 (15 Oct). 150th Death Anniv of Frédéric Chopin (composer). P 13½.
3200 **1095** 10d. multicoloured ... 3·50 2·50

1096 Mastheads

1097 Murino Bridge

(Des Marina Kalezić. Litho)

1999 (18 Oct). Stamp Day. 50th Anniv of *Philatelist* (magazine). P 13½.
3201 **1096** 10d. multicoloured ... 2·30 1·70

(Des Marina Kalezić and R. Bojanić. Litho Forum, Novi Sad)

1999 (29 Oct). Bombed Bridges. T **1097** and similar horiz designs. Multicoloured. P 14.
3202 2d. Type **1097** ... 80 60
3203 2d. Varadinski Most ... 80 60
3204 2d. Ostružnica ... 80 60
3205 6d. Bistrica ... 1·60 1·20
3206 6d. Grdelica ... 1·60 1·20
3207 6d. Željezev Most ... 1·60 1·20
3202/3207 *Set of 6* ... 6·50 4·75

1098 Fragments of Roman Altars, Sremska Mitrovica and Jupiter (statue), Šabac

1099 Fireman dousing Flames

(Des R. Bojanić. Litho Forum, Novi Sad)

1999 (19 Nov). Year 2000. Booklet stamps. T **1098** and similar horiz designs. Multicoloured. P 14.
3208 6d. Type **1098** ... 1·60 1·20
a. Booklet pane. Nos. 3208/**MS**3214 ... 9·75
3209 6d. Mosaic depicting Emperor Trajan with army leaders, Sirmium, lamp and lead mirror ... 1·60 1·20
3210 6d. Mosaic of Dionysus and painting of Belgrade ... 1·60 1·20
3211 6d. Haghia Sophia, mosaic and bust of Emperor Constantin ... 1·60 1·20
3212 6d. Gold artefacts, pot and lamp ... 1·60 1·20
3213 6d. St. Peter's Church and title page of Temnic ... 1·60 1·20
3208/3213 *Set of 6* ... 8·75 6·50
MS3214 138×88 mm. 15d. Birth and crucifixion of Christ, ships and scenes of everyday life (104×54 mm) ... 2·30 2·30

(Des Marina Kalezić and R. Bojanić. Litho Forum, Novi Sad)

1999 (27 Nov). Bombed Buildings. T **1099** and similar horiz designs. Multicoloured. P 14.
3215 2d. Type **1099** ... 80 60
3216 2d. Oil refinery ... 80 60
3217 2d. Dish aerials ... 80 60
3218 6d. Hospital ... 1·60 1·20
3219 6d. Radio and television station ... 1·60 1·20
3220 6d. Television tower, Mt. Avala ... 1·60 1·20
3215/3220 *Set of 6* ... 6·50 4·75

1100 Saints

(Des R. Bojanić. Litho Forum, Novi Sad)

1999 (23 Dec). 500th Anniv of Poganovo Monastery Frescoes. T **1100** and similar horiz designs. Multicoloured. P 14.
3221 6d. Type **1100** ... 1·20 95
3222 6d. Four saints with long beards ... 1·20 95
3223 6d. Four saints, one holding a scroll and one an open book ... 1·20 95
3224 6d. Four saints, three holding scrolls and one with a stick ... 1·20 95
3221/3224 *Set of 4* ... 4·25 3·50

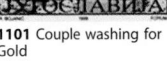

1101 Couple washing for Gold

1102 Krushedol Monastery

(Des R. Bojanić. Litho Forum, Novi Sad)

1999 (30 Dec). Museum Exhibits. Gold Washing on the River Pek. T **1101** and similar vert designs. Multicoloured. P 14.
3225 6d. Type **1101** ... 1·20 95
3226 6d. Man and two youths panning for gold ... 1·20 95

3227 6d. Women digging gravel panning for gold 1·20 95
3228 6d. Man holding spade and pan with two boys 1·20 95
3225/3228 *Set of* 4 4·25 3·50

(Des R. Bojanić. Litho)

2000 (13 Jan). Monasteries. T **1102** and similar horiz design. Multicoloured. P 13½.
3229 10d. Type **1102** 2·30 1·70
3230 10d. Rakovac Monastery 2·30 1·70

1103 Building and Emblem

1104 Large Tortoiseshell (*Nymphalis antiopa*)

(Des R. Bojanić. Litho)

2000 (21 Jan). 50th Anniv of National Archives. P 13½.
3231 **1103** 10d. deep lilac and bright turquoise-blue 35·00 35·00

(Des R. Bojanić. Litho Forum, Novi Sad)

2000 (25 Feb). Butterflies. T **1104** and similar vert designs. Multicoloured. P 14.
3232 10d. Type **1104** 4·00 3·00
a. Horiz strip of 4. Nos. 3232/5 plus label 17·00
3233 10d. Southern festoon (*Parnalius polyxena*) 4·00 3·00
3234 10d. Poplar admiral (*Limenitis populi*) 4·00 3·00
3235 10d. Marbled white (*Melanargia galathea*) 4·00 3·00
3232/3235 *Set of* 4 14·50 11·00
Nos. 3232/5 were issued together in horizontal *se-tenant* strips of four stamps and one central label within the sheet.

1105 Grey Partridges (*Perdix perdix*)

1106 General Staff Building, Belgrade

(Des R. Bojanić. Photo Courvoisier)

2000 (14 Mar). Endangered Species. Partridges. T **1105** and similar horiz designs. Multicoloured. P 12.
3236 10d. Type **1105** 4·00 3·00
a. Horiz strip of 4. Nos. 3236/9 plus label 17·00
3237 10d. Grey partridge (different) 4·00 3·00
3238 10d. Rock partridge (*Alectoris graeca*) on nest 4·00 3·00
3239 10d. Two rock partridges 4·00 3·00
3236/3239 *Set of* 4 14·50 11·00
Nos. 3236/9 were issued together in horizontal *se-tenant* strips of four stamps and one central label within the sheet.

(Des R. Bojanić. Recess)

2000 (24 Mar). Bombed Buildings. T **1106** and similar horiz design. P 13½.
3240 10d. deep blue 4·00 3·00
3241 20d. lake-brown 4·25 3·25
Designs:—No. 3241, Air Force and Air Defence Command, Zemun.

1107 Exhibition Medal

1108 Tree and World Map

(Des Marina Kalezić. Litho)

2000 (2 May). Jufiz X National Stamp Exhibition, Belgrade. Sheet 68×75 mm. P 13½.
MS3242 **1107** 15d. multicoloured 75·00 75·00

(Des R. Bojanić. Photo Courvoisier)

2000 (4 May). Environment Protection. T **1108** and similar multicoloured design. P 12.
3243 30d. Type **1108** 3·00 2·30
3244 30d. Birds in nest 3·00 2·30
Nos. 3243/4 were each issued in sheets of eight stamps and one label.

1109 "2000" and View of Bethlehem

1110 Players chasing Ball

(Des R. Bojanić. Photo Courvoisier)

2000 (9 May). Europa. T **1109** and similar vert design. Multicoloured. P 12.
3245 30d. Type **1109** 6·25 4·75
3246 30d. "2000" and astronaut on Moon 6·25 4·75

(Des R. Bojanić. Litho Forum, Novi Sad)

2000 (30 May). European Football Championship, Belgium and The Netherlands. T **1110** and similar vert design. Multicoloured. P 14.
3247 30d. Type **1110** 4·75 3·50
3248 30d. Players heading ball 4·75 3·50

1111 Post Office Building, Post Van, Post Box, Letter, Envelope and Quill

1112 Map of Australia and Kangaroo

(Des R. Bojanić. Litho Forum, Novi Sad)

2000 (7 June). 160th Anniv of Postal Service in Serbia. P 14.
3249 **1111** 10d. multicoloured 3·00 2·30

(Des R. Bojanić. Litho Forum, Novi Sad)

2000 (28 June). Olympic Games, Sydney. T **1112** and similar vert designs showing map of Australia and animal or bird. Multicoloured. P 13½.
3250 6d. Type **1112** 80 60
3251 12d. Emu 1·20 95
3252 24d. Koala 2·30 1·70
3253 30d. Cockatoo 3·00 2·30
3250/3253 *Set of* 4 6·50 5·00

1113 Airship LZ-127 "Graf Zeppelin" (1928) and Cover

1114 Goats

(Des Marina Kalezić. Litho)

2000 (26 Sept). Stamp Day. Centenary of First Zeppelin Flight. P 13½.
3254 **1113** 10d. multicoloured 7·00 5·25

(Des Marina Kalezić. Litho)

2000 (2 Oct). 32nd "Joy in Europe" Meeting. Winning Designs in Children's Painting Competition. T **1114** and similar multicoloured design. P 13½.
3255 30d. Type **1114** 2·50 1·90
3256 40d. Storks (vert) 3·00 2·30

1115 Hand holding Pen

1116 Bee on Flower

(Des R. Bojanić. Litho)

2000 (5 Oct). UNESCO World Teachers' Day. P 13½.
3257 **1115** 10d. multicoloured 30·00 30·00

(Des Marina Kalezić. Litho)

2000 (6 Oct). 13th Apislavia (Slavonic bee-keeping association) Congress. P 13½.
3258 **1116** 10d. multicoloured 7·75 7·75

1117 Water Polo (bronze)

1118 Sailing Ships

(Des R. Bojanić. Litho)

2000 (23 Oct). Yugoslav Medals at Olympic Games. T **1117** and similar multicoloured designs. P 14.
3259 20d. Type **1117** 2·30 1·70
3260 20d. Air pistol (silver) 2·30 1·70
MS3261 70×83 mm. 30d. Volleyball (gold) (34×46 mm) 30·00 30·00

(Des R. Bojanić. Litho Forum, Novi Sad)

2000 (2 Nov). New Millennium. Booklet stamps. T **1118** and similar horiz designs. Multicoloured. P 14.
3262 12d. Type **1118** 95 70
a. Booklet pane. Nos. 3261/**MS**3267 6·00
3263 12d. Parchment production 95 70
3264 12d. Man and instruments (first accurate maps and optical instruments) 95 70
3264 12d. G. and R. Stephenson's Rocket (1829) and *Clermont* (first commercial paddle-steamer)
3266 12d. Nikola Tesla (Yugoslav scientist), telegraph and telephone 95 70
3267 12d. Futuristic settlement, astronaut and satellite 95 70
3262/3267 *Set of* 6 5·25 3·75
MS3268 138×86 mm. 40d. Horses on river bank, ship in full sail and ice-bound ship (104×54 mm) 3·75 3·75

1119 Christ bathing (fresco, Monastery, Pec)

1120 Waistcoat (Jagodina)

(Des R. Bojanić. Litho Forum, Novi Sad)

2000 (7 Nov). No value expressed. P 14.
3269 **1119** A multicoloured 5·50 60

(Des Marina Kalezić. Litho Forum, Novi Sad)

2000 (7 Dec). Museum Exhibits. 19th-century Serbian Costumes. T **1120** and similar vert designs. Multicoloured. P 13½.
3270 6d. Type **1120** 45 35
3271 12d. Dress (Metohija) 80 60
3272 24d. Blouse (Pec) 1·60 1·20
3273 30d. Waistcoat (Kupres) 1·90 1·40
3270/3273 *Set of* 4 4·25 3·25

1121 Mary and Jesus (icon, Piva Monastery)

1122 Map of Europe and Emblem

(Des R. Bojanić. Litho Forum, Novi Sad)

2000 (12 Dec). Art. Icons and Frescoes of Montenegro. T **1121** and similar vert designs. Multicoloured. P 14.
3274 6d. Type **1121** 45 35
3275 12d. Nativity (fresco, Holy Cross Church) 80 60
3276 24d. St. Luke painting an icon (fresco, Moraca Monastery) 1·60 1·20
3277 30d. Mary and Jesus, St. John and St. Stephen (fresco, Mary of the Ascension Church, Moraca) 1·90 1·40
3274/3277 *Set of* 4 4·25 3·25

(Des Marina Kalezić and R. Bojanić. Litho Forum, Novi Sad)

2000 (29 Dec). Yugoslavia's Resumption of Membership of the Organization for Security and Co-operation in Europe (3278) and the United Nations (3279). T **1122** and similar multicoloured design. P 14.
3278 6d. Type **1122** 80 60
3279 12d. Emblem (vert) 95 70

1123 Vatoped Monastery

1124 Association Building

(Des R. Bojanić. Litho)

2001 (14 Jan). Monasteries on Mount Athos. T **1123** and similar horiz design. Multicoloured. P 13½.
3280 10d. Type **1123** 80 60
3281 27d. Esfigmen monastery 2·30 1·70

(Des R. Bojanić. Litho Forum, Novi Sad)

2001 (16 Feb). 175th Anniv of "Matice Srpske" (Serbian literary association). P 14.
3282 **1124** 15d. multicoloured 1·60 1·20

1125 Lions

1126 Vera Mencikova

(Des Marina Kalezić. Litho Forum, Novi Sad)

2001 (26 Feb). 50th Anniv of Zoo Palic, Subotica. Endangered Species. T **1125** and similar vert designs. Multicoloured. P 14.

3283 6d. Type **1125** (*Panthera leo*) (inscr "Felis leo") 60 45
a. Horiz strip. Nos. 3283/6 plus label 5·75
3284 12d. Polar bear and cub (*Ursus maritimus*) 1·20 95
3285 24d. Japanese macaques (*Macaca fuscata*) 1·60 1·20
3286 30d. Humboldt penguins (*Spheniscus humboldti*) 2·00 1·50
3283/3286 *Set of 4* 4·75 3·75

Nos. 3283/6 were issued in horizontal *se-tenant* strips of four stamps with a central stamp-sized label.

(Des Marina Kalezić (3287/90) R. Bojanić (others). Litho)

2001 (18 Mar). Women World Chess Champions. T **1126** and similar vert designs. Multicoloured. P 13½.

3287 10d. Type **1126** 60 45
a. Sheetlet. Nos. 3287/94 plus label 5·00
3288 10d. Lyudmila Vladimirovna Rudenko 60 45
3289 10d. Elizaveta Ivanova Bykova 60 45
3290 10d. Olga Nikelaevna Rubtsova 60 45
3291 10d. Nona Terentievna Gaprindashvili 60 45
3292 10d. Maia Grigorevna Chiburdanidze 60 45
3293 10d. Zsusza Polgar 60 45
3294 10d. Jun Xie 60 45
3287/3294 *Set of 8* 4·25 3·25

Nos. 3287/94 were issued together in *se-tenant* sheetlets of eight stamps with a central label.

1127 Stevan Stojanović Mokranjac (portrait, Uroš Predic)

1128 Rose-of-Sharon (*Hibiscus syriacus*)

(Des R. Bojanić. Litho Forum, Novi Sad)

2001 (19 Mar). Personalities. T **1127** and similar vert design. Multicoloured. P 14.

3295 50d. Type **1127** (composer) 3·50 2·50
3296 100d. Nikola Tesla (inventor) 6·75 5·00

(Des Marina Kalezić. Photo Courvoisier)

2001 (13 Apr). Flora. T **1128** and similar horiz designs. Multicoloured. P 12.

3297 6d. Type **1128** 45 35
a. Horiz strip. Nos. 3297/300 plus label 5·00
3298 12d. Oleander (*Nerium oleander*) 80 60
3299 24d. Chilean bellflower (*Lapageria rosea*) 1·40 1·00
3300 30d. Rowan (*Sorbus aucuparia*) 2·00 1·50
3297/3300 *Set of 4* 4·25 3·00

Nos. 3297/3300 were issued together in horizontal strips of four stamps with a central stamp-sized label.

1129 River Vratna, Eastern Serbia

1130 Mountains, Emblem and Climbers

(Des R. Bojanić. Photo Courvoisier)

2001 (4 May). Europa. Water Resources. T **1129** and similar vert design. Multicoloured. P 12.

3301 30d. Type **1129** 4·00 3·00
3302 45d. Jerme Gorge, Dimitrovgrad 4·25 3·25

(Des R. Bojanić. Litho)

2001 (8 June). Centenary of Serbian Mountaineering Association. P 13½.

3303 **1130** 15d. multicoloured 1·90 1·40

1131 Lake Ludaško and Heron

1132 Illuminated Letter

(Des Marina Kalezić. Photo Courvoisier)

2001 (13 June). Nature Protection. Lakes. T **1131** and similar horiz design. Multicoloured. P 12.

3304 30d. Type **1131** 2·30 1·70
3305 45d. Lake and stork in flight, Carska Bara Special Nature Reserve 3·00 2·30

(Des R. Bojanić. Litho)

2001 (2 July). No value expressed. P 13.

3306 **1132** E multicoloured 2·30 1·70

Numbers have been left for additions to this series.

1133 Players and Ball

(Des R. Bojanić. Litho Forum, Novi Sad)

2001 (5 July). European Water Polo Champions. Sheet 86×67 mm. P 14.

MS3307 **1133** 30d. multicoloured 9·25 9·25

1134 Seated Figure

1135 Sun and Emblems

(Des Marina Kalezić and R. Bojanić. Litho Forum, Novi Sad)

2001 (8 Sept). 50th Anniv of Serbian Stamps. SRBIJAFILA O2 National Stamp Exhibition. Sheet 97×85 mm. P 13½×14.

MS3308 **1134** 30d. multicoloured 4·00 4·00

(Des R. Bojanić. Litho Forum, Novi Sad)

2001 (19 Sept). Energy Conservation. Solar Power. P 13½.

3309 **1135** 15d. multicoloured 1·60 1·20

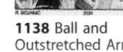

1136 Hands holding Bridge

1137 "The Child" (Marko Celbonović)

(Des R. Bojanić. Litho Forum, Novi Sad)

2001 (20 Sept). Danube Commission. Cleaning the Danube. T **1136** and similar horiz design. Multicoloured. P 13½.

3310 30d. Type **1136** 3·00 2·30
3311 45d. Hand, clock and ship 4·00 3·00

(Des M. Kalezić. Litho)

2001 (2 Oct). 33rd "Joy in Europe" Meeting. Children's Day. T **1137** and similar vert design showing paintings. Multicoloured. P 13½.

3312 30d. Type **1137** 3·00 2·30
3313 45d. "Girl in Orchard" (Beta Vukanovic) 4·00 3·00

1138 Ball and Outstretched Arms

1139 Stamps and Society Emblem

(Des R. Bojanić. Litho)

2001 (11 Oct). Yugoslavia, European Basketball (No. 3314) and Volleyball (3315) Champions. T **1138** and similar vert design. Multicoloured. P 13½.

3314 30d. Type **1138** 23·00 23·00
3315 30d. Players, ball and net 23·00 23·00

(Des M. Kalezić. Litho)

2001 (24 Oct). Stamp Day. 75th Anniv of Fédération Internationale de Philatélie (the International Philatelic Federation or FIP). P 13½.

3316 **1139** 15d. multicoloured 2·30 1·70

1140 Antimonite

1141 School Building

(Des R. Bojanić. Litho)

2001 (2 Nov). Museum Exhibits. Minerals. T **1140** and similar horiz designs. Multicoloured. P 13½.

3317 7d. Type **1140** 45 35
a. Horiz strip. Nos. 3317/20 plus label 4·50
3318 14d. Calcite 80 60
3319 26d.20 Quartz 1·40 1·00
3320 28d.70 Calcite and Galenite 1·60 1·20
3317/3320 *Set of 4* 3·75 2·75

Nos. 3317/20 were issued together in horizontal *se-tenant* strips of four stamps with a central label, the labels forming a composite design of a cave within the sheet.

(Des M. Kalezić. Litho)

2001 (18 Nov). Centenary of Tanasije Pejanovic Secondary School, Pljevlja. P 13½.

3321 **1141** 15d. multicoloured 3·00 2·30

1142 Telephone Box and Man using "Candlestick" Telephone

1143 The Nativity (14th-century fresco)

(Des R. Bojanić. Litho)

2001 (20 Nov). Centenary of First Serbian Telephone Box. P 13½.

3322 **1142** 15d. multicoloured 2·30 1·70

(Des R. Bojanić. Litho Forum Novi Sad)

2001 (1 Dec). Christmas. T **1143** and similar vert designs showing paintings of the Nativity. Multicoloured. P 14.

3323 7d. Type **1143** 80 60
3324 14d. Nativity, Lesnovo Monastery 1·60 1·20
3325 26d.20 Nativity (different) 1·90 1·40
3326 28d.70 Nativity, Sveta Trojica 2·00 1·50
3323/3326 *Set of 4* 5·75 4·25

1144 Players

1145 Skier

(Des M. Kalezić. Litho)

2002 (5 Jan). Junior World Ice Hockey Championship, Czech Republic. P 13½.

3327 **1144** 14d. multicoloured 14·00 10·50

(Des M. Kalezić. Litho)

2002 (25 Jan). Winter Olympic Games, Salt Lake City. T **1145** and similar multicoloured design. P 13½.

3328 28d.70 Type **1145** 16·00 11·50
3329 50d. Bobsleigh (vert) 19·00 14·00

1146 Jovan Karamata

1147 Stonechat (*Saxicola torquata*)

(Des R. Bojanić. Litho)

2002 (1 Feb). Birth Centenary of Jovan Karamata (mathematician). P 13.

3330 **1146** 14d. multicoloured 16·00 11·50

(Des M. Kalezić. Litho)

2002 (22 Feb). Songbirds. T **1147** and similar vert designs. Multicoloured. P 13½.

3331 7d. Type **1147** 2·30 1·70
a. Strip of 4. Nos. 3331/4 plus label 23·00
3332 14d. Whinchat (*Saxicola rubetra*) 4·00 3·00
3333 26d.20 Blue tit (*Parus caeruleus*) 7·75 5·75
3334 28d.70 Song thrush (*Turdus philomelos*) 7·75 5·75
3331/3334 *Set of 4* 20·00 14·50

Nos. 3331/4 were issued in horizontal *se-tenant* strips of four stamps surrounding a central stamp-size label. Each label showing a different part of a composite design of songbirds and musical notes.

1148 Crucified Christ (1208) **1149** Woman wearing Blouse and Skirt with Sash (Bunjevac)

(Des R. Bojanić. Litho Forum Novi Sad)

2002 (7 Mar). Easter. T **1148** and similar vert designs. Multicoloured. P 13½×14.

3335 7d. Type **1148** .... 2·30 1·70
3336 14d. Christ surrounded by angels (1300) .... 4·00 3·00
3337 26d.20 Resurrection (1540) .... 7·75 5·75
3338 28d.70 Churches and acorn (painting) (1980) .... 7·75 5·75
3335/3338 *Set of 4* .... 20·00 14·50

(Des R. Bojanić. Litho)

2002 (29 Mar). National Costumes. T **1149** and similar vert design. Multicoloured. P 13½.

3339 7d. Type **1149** .... 3·00 2·30
3340 28d.70 Woman wearing dress and bonnet carrying scarf (Bunjevac) .... 4·00 3·00

1150 Zarko Tomic-Sremac **1151** Roach (*Rutilus rutilus*)

(Des R. Bojanić. Litho)

2002 (15 Apr). Zarko Tomic-Sremac (folk hero) Commemoration. P 13½.

3341 **1150** 14d. multicoloured .... 17·00 13·00

(Des R. Bojanić. Litho)

2002 (23 Apr). Fish. T **1151** and similar horiz designs. Multicoloured. P 13½.

3342 7d. Type **1151** .... 2·30 1·70
a. Strip of 4. Nos. 3342/5 plus 1 label ... 23·00
3343 14d. Sterlet (*Acipenser ruthenus*) .... 4·00 3·00
3344 26d.20 Beluga (*Huso huso*) .... 7·75 5·75
3345 28d.70 Zander (*Stizostedion lucioperca*) .... 7·75 5·75
3342/3345 *Set of 4* .... 20·00 14·50

Nos. 3342/5 were issued in horizontal *se-tenant* strips of four stamps surrounding a central stamp-size label. Each label showing a different part of a composite design of a lake and wading birds.

1152 Trapeze Artistes **1153** Potez 29 Bi-plane

(Des R. Bojanić. Litho Forum Novi Sad)

2002 (30 May). Europa. Circus. T **1152** and similar horiz design. Multicoloured. P 13½.

3346 28d.70 Type **1152** .... 7·75 5·75
3347 50d. Tigers .... 9·25 7·00
MS3348 85×74 mm. 45d. Circus ring (47×35 mm) .. 80·00 80·00

(Des R. Bojanić. Litho)

2002 (17 June). 75th Anniv of Civil Aviation. T **1153** and similar horiz design. P 13½ (with one elliptical hole on each vert side).

3349 7d. Type **1153** .... 20·00 15·00
3350 28d.70 Boeing 737 .... 26·00 20·00

Nos. 3349/50, respectively, were each issued with a stamp-size label showing an outline of the aircraft shown.

1154 Valley, Tara National Park **1155** Windmill, Melenci

(Des M. Kalezić. Litho)

2002 (28 June). Nature Protection. National Parks. T **1154** and similar horiz design. Multicoloured. P 13½ (with one elliptical hole on each vert side).

3351 28d.70 Type **1154** .... 4·75 3·50
3352 50d. Flower and hills, Golija .... 8·50 6·50

(Des M. Kalezić. Litho)

2002 (14 Sept). Mills. T **1155** and similar vert design. Multicoloured. P 13½ (with one elliptical hole on each horiz side).

3353 7d. Type **1155** .... 6·25 4·75
3354 28d.70 Watermill, Ljuberadja .... 7·75 5·75

1156 City Museum, Niksic **1157** Hand and Globe

(Des R. Bojanić. Litho Forum Novi Sad)

2002 (18 Sept). 125th Anniv of Liberation of Niksic. P 13½.

3355 **1156** 14d. multicoloured .... 31·00 10·50

(Des R. Bojanić. Litho Forum Novi Sad)

2002 (20 Sept). Yugoslavia—World Basketball Champions, Indianapolis (2002). Sheet 84×73 mm. P 13½.

MS3356 **1157** 30d. multicoloured .... 17·00 17·00

1158 Buildings, Belgrade

(Litho Forum Novi Sad)

2002 (23 Sept). Jufiz XI, Yugoslav Philatelic Exhibition, Belgrade. Sheet 84×65 mm. P 13½.

MS3357 **1158** 30d. multicoloured .... 14·00 14·00

1159 Houseboat (Jana Misurovic) **1160** John the Baptist and Monastery

(Des M. Kalezić. Litho Forum Novi Sad)

2002 (2 Oct). 34th "Joy in Europe" Meeting. Children's Day. T **1159** and similar vert design. P 13½.

3358 28d.70 Type **1159** .... 4·75 3·50
3359 50d. Bird (Manja Pavicevic) .... 8·50 6·50

(Des N. Skocajic. Litho Forum Novi Sad)

2002 (10 Oct). 750th Anniv of Maraca Monastery. P 13½.

3360 **1160** 16d. multicoloured .... 19·00 14·00

0,50

(**1161**) **1162** World Map and Mercury

2002 (17 Oct). No. 2928 surch as T **1161**. P 12½.

3361 50p. on 5p. deep dull blue and dull orange .... 4·00 3·00

(Des N. Skocajic. Litho Forum Novi Sad)

2002 (24 Oct). Stamp Day. 50th Anniv of ifsda (International Federation of Stamp Dealers Association). P 13½.

3362 **1162** 16d. multicoloured .... 11·50 8·75

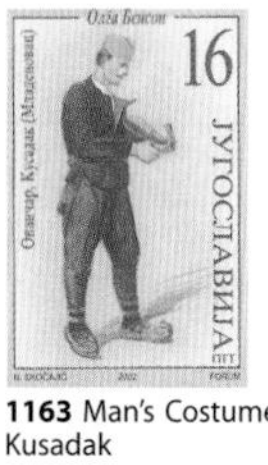

10

1163 Man's Costume, Kusadak (**1164**)

(Des N. Skocajic. Litho Forum Novi Sad)

2002 (8 Nov). Museum Exhibits. Serbian Folk Costumes. T **1163** and similar vert designs. Multicoloured. P 13½.

3363 16d. Type **1163** .... 1·60 1·20
a. Strip of 4. Nos. 3363/6 plus 1 label ... 10·00
3364 24d. Woman's costume, Komodraz .... 2·50 1·90
3365 26d.20 Man's costume, Novo Selo .... 2·75 2·10
3366 28d.70 Woman and child, Kumodraz .... 3·00 2·30
3363/3366 *Set of 4* .... 8·75 6·75

Nos. 3363/6 were issued in horizontal *se-tenant* strips of four stamps surrounding a central stamp-size label. Each label showing a different part of a composite design of costumes.

2002 (28 Nov). No. 2889 surch as T **1164**. P 13½.

3367 10d. on 10000d. greenish blue and violet ... 9·25 7·00

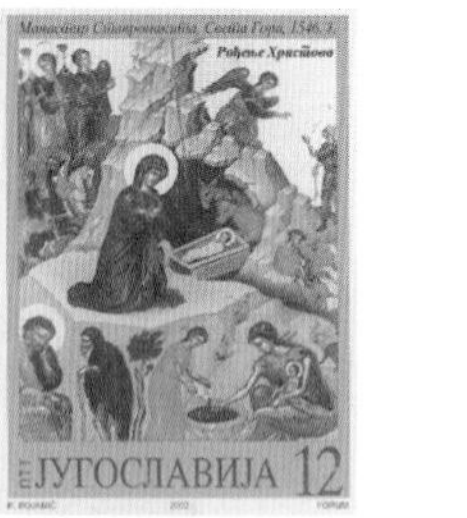

12

1165 The Nativity (1546) (**1166**)

(Des R. Bojanić. Litho Forum Novi Sad)

2002 (2 Dec). Christmas. Art. T **1165** and similar vert designs. Multicoloured. P 13½.

3368 12d. Type **1165** .... 1·60 1·20
3369 16d. Nativity (1618) .... 2·30 1·70
3370 26d.20 Nativity (15th-century) .... 4·00 3·00
3371 28d.70 Nativity (Sandro Botticelli) .... 4·25 3·25
3368/3371 *Set of 4* .... 11·00 8·25

2002 (19 Dec). No. 2927 surch as T **1166**. P 12½.

3372 12d. on 1p. deep reddish violet and olive-bistre .... 8·50 6·50

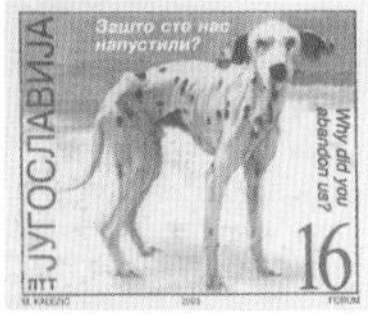

1167 Emaciated Dog

(Des M. Kalezić. Litho Forum Novi Sad)

2003 (31 Jan). Prevention of Abandoned Dogs Campaign. T **1167** and similar horiz designs. Multicoloured. P 13½×14.

3373 16d. Type **1167** .... 2·30 1·70
a. Strip of 4. Nos. 3373/6 plus 1 label. 14·00
3374 24d. Caged dog .... 3·00 2·30
3375 26d.20 Two dogs .... 4·00 3·00
3376 28d.70 Puppy .... 4·25 3·25
3373/3376 *Set of 4* .... 12·00 9·25

Nos. 3373/6 were issued in horizontal *se-tenant* strips of four stamps surrounding a central stamp-size label. Each label showing a different part of a composite design of dogs.

On 4 February 2003 Yugoslavia became Serbia & Montenegro. See Serbia & Montenegro for subsequent issues.

STAMP BOOKLETS

The following checklist covers, in simplified form, booklets issued by Yugoslavia. It is intended that it should be used in conjunction with the main listings and details of stamps and panes listed there are not repeated.

Prices are for complete booklets

Booklet No.	*Date*	*Contents and Cover Price*	*Price*
SB1	20.4.56	"JUFIZ III" Stamp Exhibition (T **227**) 1 pane, No. 817a (sold at exhibition for 75d.)	13·50
SB2	11.12.78	New Year 1 pane, No. 1859b;1 pane, No. 1861b (49d.20)	7·00
SB3	22.5.86	Yugoslav Costumes 1 pane, No. 2299a (400d.)	6·00
SB4	10.6.89	Sailing Ships 1 pane, No. 2537a (9000d.)	3·75
SB5	25.7.91	Lighthouses 1 pane, No. 2726a (120d.)	19·00
SB6	3.7.92	Steam Railway Locomotives 1 pane, No. 2801a (6000d.)	22·00
SB7	9.7.93	Fortresses 1 pane, No. 2865a (5400000d.)	11·00
SB8	27.10.94	Ships in Bottles 1 pane, No. 2945a (3d.)	9·50
SB9	3.11.98	Locomotives 1 pane, No. 3148a (15d.)	15·00
SB10	19.11.99	Year 2000 1 pane, No. 3208a (51d.)	10·00
SB11	2.11.00	New Millennium 1 pane, No. 3262a (112d.)	6·25

OBLIGATORY TAX STAMPS FOR SERBIA

The following obligatory tax stamps were for use in Serbia only. Except for the Children's Week issues they are all inscribed "SRBIJA".

S **1** Child S **2** Children S **3** Hands and Flower

1990 (1 Oct). Children's Week. Litho. P 12½.
S1 **S 1** 30p. scarlet 40 10

1991 (7 Oct). Children's Week. Litho. P 13½.
S2 **S 2** 3d. indigo 55 20

(Des R. Bojanić. Litho Forum, Novi Sad)

1992 (1 Mar). Anti-cancer Week. P 13½×14.
S3 **S 3** 3d. bluish violet and reddish orange 55 10

1993 (1 Mar). Anti-cancer Week. No. S3 surch.
S4 **S 3** 1500d. on 3d. bluish violet and reddish orange .... 2·10 1·10

S 4 Mother and Child

S 5 Hands and Flower

S 6

(Des Marina Kalezić-Krajinović. Litho)

1993. Serbian Refugee Fund. P 13½.
S5 **S 4** 42d. yellow-olive and pale greenish yellow 40 10
S6 75d. deep violet-blue and light blue 40 15
S7 150d. reddish violet and pale reddish lilac 70 20
S5/7 *Set of* 3 .... 1·40 40

(Des R. Bojanić. Litho)

1994 (1 Mar). Anti-cancer Week. P 13½.
S8 **S 5** 12p. bluish violet 55 20
See also No. S11.

(Des D. Čudov. Litho)

1994. P 13½.
S9 **S 6** 6p. deep claret 40 10

S 7 Museum

(Des R. Bojanić. Litho)

1994. 150th Anniv of National Museum, Belgrade. P 13½.
S10 **S 7** 5p. turquoise-blue 40 10

(Des R. Bojanić. Litho)

1995 (1 Mar). Anti-cancer Week. P 13½.
S11 **S 5** 6p. deep magenta 40 10

ITALIAN OCCUPATION OF FIUME AND KUPA ZONE

Yugoslav Currency

PRINTER. Types **1/4** were overprinted by Lloyd, Rijeka.

ZONA
OCCUPATA
FIUMANO
K U P A
(1)

O.N.M.I.
(2)

1941 (16 May). Nos. 414 etc of Yugoslavia (1939 King Petar II issue) optd with T **1**.
1 **99** 25p. black .... 5·25 3·25
2 50p. orange .... 2·50 1·60
3 1d. green .... 2·50 1·60
4 1d.50 scarlet .... 2·50 1·60
5 3d. red-brown .... 3·25 2·10
6 4d. bright blue .... 6·25 4·25
7 5d. blue .... 12·50 7·75
8 5d.50 dull violet .... 12·50 7·75
9 6d. deep blue .... 47·00 26·00
10 8d. chocolate .... 33·00 18·00
11 12d. violet £800 £450
12 16d. purple £225 £120
13 20d. light blue £2000 £1300
14 30d. pink £11000 £9000
In addition the sheets were continuously overprinted "ZOFK" (Zona Occupata Fiumano Kupa) between the horizontal rows.

1941 (16 May). Maternity and Child Welfare Fund. Nos. 2/4 further optd with T **2** (=Opera Nazionale Maternita e Infanzia).
15 **99** 50p. orange .... 5·25 6·25
16 1d. green .... 5·25 6·25
17 1d.50 scarlet .... 5·25 6·25
15/17 *Set of* 3 .... 14·00 17·00

(3)

(4)

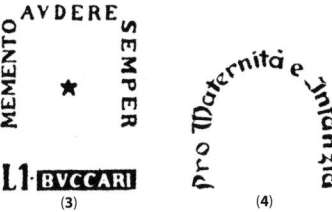

1941 (17 May). Italian Naval Exploit at Buccari (Bakar), 1918. No. 415 of Yugoslavia surch with T **3**.
18 **99** 1l. on 50p. orange (Bk.) .... 31·00 37·00
In addition the sheets were continuously overprinted "MAS" (Memento Audere Semper) between the horizontal rows.

1942 (2 June). Maternity and Child Welfare Fund. Nos. 15/17 further optd with T **4**.
19 **99** 50p. orange (R.) .... 12·50 16·00
20 1d. green (V.) .... 12·50 16·00
21 1d.50 scarlet (B.) .... 12·50 16·00
19/21 *Set of* 3 .... 34·00 43·00
Nos. 1/21 were valid until 26 May 1942.

Italian stamps came into use after the area was annexed on 3 May 1941. This area was reoccupied in 1945 by the Yugoslavs and the stamps issued then are listed under Venezia Giulia.

GERMAN OCCUPATION OF DALMATIA

The areas in Dalmatia under Italian control were occupied by the Germans after the armistice of 8 September 1943 between the Kingdom of Italy and the Allies.

ZARA (Zadar)

Italian Currency

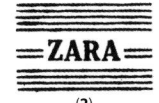

Deutsche
Besetzung
Zara
(1)

=ZARA=
(2)

1943 (9 Oct). Imperial series of Italy, 1929–42, optd with T **1**.
1 **98** 5c. brown .... 47·00 £150
2 **100** 10c. sepia .... 4·00 12·00
3 **101** 15c. blue-green .... 6·75 21·00
4 **99** 20c. carmine .... 4·00 14·50
5 **102** 25c. green .... 4·00 14·50
6 **103** 30c. brown .... 4·00 14·50
7 **101** 35c. blue £275 £500
8 **102** 75c. carmine .... 13·00 34·00
9 **99** 1l. violet .... 4·25 14·50
10 **102** 1l.25 blue .... 5·75 21·00
11 **100** 1l.75 orange-vermilion .... 18·00 55·00
12 **101** 2l. brown-lake .... 42·00 85·00
13 **98** 2l.55 grey-green £225 £550
14 3l.70 bright violet £1400 £2250
15 5l. carmine .... 34·00 85·00
16 **101** 10l. violet £950 £1700
17 **99** 20l. yellow-green £11000 £16000
18 **100** 25l. blue-black £24000 £34000
19 **103** 50l. deep violet £19000 £21000

1943 (9 Oct). War Propaganda stamps of Italy (Nos. 571/4 optd with T **1**, on stamp and on attached label.
20 **103** 50c. bright violet (Navy) .... 10·50 25·00
21 50c. bright violet (Army) .... 10·50 25·00
22 50c. bright violet (Air Force) .... 10·50 25·00
23 50c. bright violet (Militia) .... 10·50 25·00
20/23 *Set of* 4 .... 38·00 90·00

1943 (9 Oct). EXPRESS LETTER. Nos. E350/1 of Italy optd as T **1**, but larger.
E24 **E 132** 1l.25 green .... 10·50 30·00
E25 2l.50 red-orange .... 80·00 £140

1943 (9 Oct). AIR. Nos. 270/7 of Italy optd with T **1**, larger on 2l.
26 **111** 25c. grey-green .... 6·25 20·00
27 **110** 50c. sepia .... 5·25 19·00
28 **112** 75c. chestnut £275 £500
29 **111** 80c. orange-vermilion .... 26·00 70·00
30 **112** 1l. bright violet .... 8·00 20·00
31 **113** 2l. blue .... 18·00 42·00
32 **110** 5l. green £5500 £7500
33 10l. carmine-red £16000 £24000

1943 (9 Oct). AIR EXPRESS. No. E370 of Italy optd as T **1**, but larger.
E34 **E 133** 2l. blue-black .... 19·00 42·00

1943 (9 Oct). POSTAGE DUE. Italian Postage Due stamps of 1934 optd as T **1**, sideways.
D35 **D 141** 5c. chocolate .... 21·00 85·00
D36 10c. blue .... 21·00 85·00
D37 20c. bright carmine .... 19·00 85·00
D38 25c. green £550 £1000
D39 30c. orange-vermilion .... 20·00 85·00
D40 40c. sepia .... 20·00 85·00
D41 50c. bright violet .... 20·00 85·00
D42 60c. slate-blue £550 £1000
D43 **D 142** 1l. orange £475 £1000
D44 2l. green £650 £1000
D45 5l. bright violet £475 £950
D35/45 *Set of* 11 .... £2500 £5000

1943 (4 Nov). Imperial series of Italy, 1929–42, optd with T **2**.
46 **103** 50c. bright violet .... 4·25 17·00
47 **102** 75c. carmine .... 5·25 20·00
48 1l.25 blue .... 40·00 £140
46/48 *Set of* 3 .... 45·00 £160

1943 (4 Nov). War Propaganda stamps of Italy (Nos. 563/70), optd with T **2**, on stamp and attached label.
49 **102** 25c. green (Navy) .... 9·00 25·00
50 25c. green (Army) .... 9·00 25·00
51 25c. green (Air Force) .... 9·00 25·00
52 25c. green (Militia) .... 9·00 25·00
53 **103** 30c. brown (Navy) .... 9·00 22·00
54 30c. brown (Army) .... 9·00 22·00
55 30c. brown (Air Force) .... 9·00 22·00
56 30c. brown (Militia) .... 9·00 22·00
49/56 *Set of* 8 .... 65·00 £170

1943 (4 Nov). EXPRESS LETTER. Nos. E350/1 of Italy, optd with T **2**, twice.
E57 **E 132** 1l.25 green .... 10·50 34·00
E58 2l.50 red-orange .... 80·00 £225

BRAC

The following issue for the island of Brac, south of Split, was authorised by the Head of the Army Fieldpost, with the approval of the Commander of the Panzer Army.

Croatian Currency

1944 (May). Island Welfare Fund. King Petar II stamps of Yugoslavia, 1939, and a Postage Due stamp, optd "BRAC" and value in kuna, No. 6 also optd "FRANCO", by Jadran Printing Works, Dubrovnik.
1 **99** 2+2k. on 25p. black (R.) £200 £500
2 4+4k. on 50p. orange £180 £550
3 8+8k. on 2d. carmine-rose £200 £500
4 16+16k. on 25p. black (R.) £180 £550
5 32+32k. on 2d. carmine-rose £180 £500
6 **D 56** 50+50k. on 1d. magenta (D260l.) £180 £500
1/6 *Set of* 6 .... £1000 £2750
Similar charity issues were prepared for the islands of Hvar and Korcula, but these were not issued.

GULF OF KOTOR

Italian and German Currency

This part of Dalmatia, annexed by Italy in 1941, was occupied by the Germans after the armistice of 8 September 1943 between the Kingdom of Italy and the Allies. Since 1945 it has been part of the Federated Republic of Montenegro.

Deutsche
Militär-
verwaltung
Kotor
LIT. 4.-
(1)

0,10 R.M.
Boka
Kotorska
(2)

1944 (10 Feb). Imperial series of Italy, 1929, surch as T **1**, by State Printing Works, Cetinje.
1 **100** 0.50 LIT. on 10c. sepia (R.) .... 37·00 65·00
2 **102** 1 LIT. on 25c. green (R.) .... 85·00 £150
3 **103** 1.50 LIT. on 50c. bright violet (R.) .... 37·00 65·00
4 3 LIT. on 30c. brown (R.) .... 37·00 65·00
5 **99** 4 LIT. on 20c. carmine .... 37·00 65·00
6 10 LIT. on 20c. carmine .... 37·00 65·00
1/6 *Set of* 6 .... £250 £425

1944 (16 Sept). Nos. 419/20 of Yugoslavia (1939 King Petar II issue) surch as T **2**, by State Printing Works, Cetinje.
7 **99** 0,10 R.M. on 3d. red-brown .... 4·75 5·00
8 0,15 R.M. on 3d. red-brown .... 4·75 5·00
9 0,25 R.M. on 4d. bright blue .... 5·25 10·00
10 0,50 R.M. on 4d. bright blue .... 9·00 15·00
7/10 *Set of* 4 .... 21·00 32·00

Pictorial designs inscribed "BOKA KOTORSKA" were printed in Vienna but were not issued.
Stamps similar to Nos. 1/6 were prepared for use in Podgorica but were not issued.